The New Grove Dictionary of

American Music

Volume Three

The New Grove Dictionary of American Music

Volume Three
L-Q

Edited by
H. Wiley Hitchcock
and
Stanley Sadie

Editorial Coordinator
Susan Feder

MACMILLAN PRESS LIMITED, LONDON
GROVE'S DICTIONARIES OF MUSIC INC., NEW YORK, NY

The New Grove Dictionary of American Music
edited by H. Wiley Hitchcock and Stanley Sadie, in four volumes, 1986

First published 1986 by the Macmillan Press Limited, London.
In the United States of America and Canada, the Macmillan Press has appointed
Grove's Dictionaries of Music Inc., New York, NY, as sole distributor.

Parts of this dictionary were first published in
The New Grove Dictionary of Music and Musicians ®
edited by Stanley Sadie, in twenty volumes, 1980
© Macmillan Publishers Limited 1980

and

The New Grove Dictionary of Musical Instruments
edited by Stanley Sadie, in three volumes, 1984
© Macmillan Press Limited 1984

Library of Congress Cataloging in Publication Data

The New Grove dictionary of American music.
Includes bibliographies
1. Music—United States—Dictionaries.
2. Music—United States—Bio-bibliography.
I. Hitchcock, H. Wiley (Hugh Wiley), 1923–
II. Sadie, Stanley
ML101.U6N48 1986 781.773'03'21 86-404
ISBN 0-943818-36-2 (set)

British Library Cataloguing in Publication Data

The New Grove dictionary of American music.
1. Music—United States—Dictionaries
I. Hitchcock, H. Wiley II. Sadie, Stanley
781.773'03'21 ML100
ISBN 0-333-37879-2

Typeset by Edwards Brothers Inc., Ann Arbor, MI, USA
Music examples processed by Halstan & Co. Ltd, Amersham, England

Printed and bound in Hong Kong

Contents

Editors

H. Wiley Hitchcock

Stanley Sadie

Editorial Coordinator

Susan Feder

Principal Advisers

Edward A. Berlin
Horace Clarence Boyer
William Brooks
Raoul Camus
Richard Crawford
Vernon Gotwals
George N. Heller
Cynthia Adams Hoover
Michael Hovland
Bill C. Malone
Paula Morgan
Helen Myers
Pauline Norton
Carol J. Oja
Paul Oliver
William Osborne
J. Bradford Robinson
John Rockwell
Deane L. Root
Patrick J. Smith
Susan Thiemann Sommer
Eileen Southern
Judith Tick

General Abbreviations

A	alto, contralto [voice]
a	alto [instrument]
AA	Associate of the Arts
AB	Bachelor of Arts
ABC	American Broadcasting Company
ABI	Alexander Broude, Inc.
ACA	American Composers Alliance
acc.	accompaniment, accompanied (by)
AD	anno Domini (Lat.: in the year of our Lord)
addl	additional
addn	addition
ad lib	ad libitum (Lat.: at pleasure)
AK	Alaska
AL	Alabama
Alb.	Alberta (Canada)
a.m.	ante meridiem (Lat.: before noon)
amp	amplified
AMS	American Musicological Society
anon.	anonymous(ly)
appx	appendix
AR	Arkansas
arr.	arrangement, arranged (by/for)
ARSC	Association for Recorded Sound Collections
AS	American Samoa
ASCAP	American Society of Composers, Authors and Publishers
attrib.	attribution, attributed (to)
Aug	August
aut.	autumn
AZ	Arizona

B	bass [voice]
B	Brainard catalogue [of G. Tartini's works]
b	bass [instrument]
b	born
BA	Bachelor of Arts
Bar	baritone [voice]
bar	baritone [instrument]
BBC	British Broadcasting Corporation
BC	British Columbia (Canada)
BC	before Christ
bc	basso continuo
BEd	Bachelor of Education
BFA	Bachelor of Fine Arts
BLitt	Bachelor of Letters; Bachelor of Literature
BM	Bachelor of Music
BME; BMEd	Bachelor of Music Education
BMI	Broadcast Music, Inc.
BMus	Bachelor of Music
bn	bassoon
Bros.	Brothers
BS	Bachelor of Science
BSM	Bachelor of Sacred Music
BWV	Bach-Werke-Verzeichnis [Schmieder, catalogue of J. S. Bach's works]

c	circa (Lat.: about)
¢	cent(s)
CA	California
cb	contrabass [instrument]
CBC	Canadian Broadcasting Corporation
CBE	Commander of the Order of the British Empire
cbn	contrabassoon
CBS	Columbia Broadcasting System; CBS, Inc.
cel	celesta
cf	confer (Lat.: compare)
CFE	Composers Facsimile Edition
chap.	chapter
Chin.	Chinese
chit	chitarrone
Cie	Compagnie (Fr.: Company)
cimb	cimbalom
cl	clarinet
clvd	clavichord
CM	Northern Mariana Islands (US Trust Territory of the Pacific Islands)
cm	centimeter(s)
CNRS	Centre National de la Recherche Scientifique (France)
CO	Colorado

Co. Company; County
col. column
coll. collection, collected (by)
collab. (in) collaboration (with)
comp. compiler, compiled (by)
conc. concerto
cond. conductor, conducted (by)
cont continuo
Corp. Corporation
CPE Composer/Performer Edition
c.p.s. cycle(s) per second
cptr computer
CRI Composers Recordings, Inc.
CT Connecticut
Ct countertenor
CUNY City University of New York
Cz Czech

D Deutsch catalogue [of F. Schubert's works]; Dounias catalogue [of G. Tartini's works]
d died
d. denarius, denarii (Lat.: penny, pence [sterling])
DA Doctor of Arts
Dan. Danish
db double bass
DBE Dame Commander of the Order of the British Empire
DC District of Columbia
DE Delaware
Dec December
ded. dedication, dedicated (to)
Dept Department
DFA Doctor of Fine Arts
dir. director, directed (by)
diss. dissertation
DLitt Doctor of Letters; Doctor of Literature
DM Doctor of Music
DMA Doctor of Musical Arts
DME; DMEd Doctor of Music Education
DMus Doctor of Music
DMusEd Doctor of Music Education
DPhil Doctor of Philosophy
Dr. Doctor
DSc Doctor of Science; Doctor of Historical Sciences
DSM Doctor of Sacred Music

ed. editor, edited (by)
EdD Doctor of Education
edn edition
EdS Education Specialist
e.g. exempli gratia (Lat.: for example)
elec electric, electronic
EMI Electrical and Musical Industries
Eng. English
eng hn english horn
ens ensemble
EP extended-play (record)
esp. especially
etc. et cetera (Lat.: and so on)
ex., exx. example, examples

f following (page)
f forte
f. folio
facs. facsimile
fasc. fascicle
Feb February
ff following (pages)
ff fortissimo
ff. folios
fff fortississimo
fig. figure [illustration]
FL Florida
fl flute
fl floruit (Lat.: he/she flourished)
fp fortepiano
Fr. French
frag. fragment

GA Georgia
Ger. German
Gk. Greek
glock glockenspiel
GU Guam
gui guitar

H Hoboken catalogue [of J. Haydn's works]
Heb. Hebrew
HI Hawaii
HMV His Master's Voice
hn horn
Hon. Honorary
hpd harpsichord
Hung. Hungarian
Hz Hertz [cycle(s) per second]

IA Iowa
ibid. ibidem (Lat.: in the same place)
ID Idaho
i.e. id est (Lat.: that is)
IFMC International Folk Music Council
IL Illinois
IN Indiana
Inc. Incorporated
inc. incomplete
incl. includes, including
inst instrument, instrumental
IRCAM Institut de Recherche et de Coordination Acoustique/Musique (France)
ISAM Institute for Studies in American Music
ISCM International Society for Contemporary Music
It. Italian

Jan January
Jap. Japanese
Jb Jahrbuch (Ger.: yearbook)
JD Doctor of Jurisprudence
Jg. Jahrgang (Ger.: year of publication, volume)
Jr. Junior

K	Köchel catalogue [of W. A. Mozart's works; number following a / is from the 6th edn]
kbd	keyboard
KBE	Knight of the Order of the British Empire
kHz	kilohertz [1000 cycles per second]
km	kilometer(s)
KS	Kansas
KY	Kentucky
L	Longo catalogue [of D. Scarlatti's works]
£	libra, librae (Lat.: pound, pounds [sterling])
LA	Louisiana
Lat.	Latin
lb	libra (Lat.: pound [weight])
lib.	libretto
LLB	Bachelor of Laws
LLD	Doctor of Laws
LP	long-play (record)
Ltd.	Limited
M.	Monsieur
MA	Massachusetts; Master of Arts
MALS	Master of Arts in Library Science
Man.	Manitoba (Canada)
mand	mandolin
mar	marimba
MAT	Master of Arts and Teaching
MB	Bachelor of Music
MD	Maryland; Doctor of Medicine
ME	Maine
MEd	Master of Education
Mez	mezzo-soprano
mf	mezzo-forte
MFA	Master of Fine Arts
MGM	Metro-Goldwyn-Mayer
MI	Michigan
mic	microphone
MIT	Massachusetts Institute of Technology
MLA	Music Library Association
MLitt	Master of Letters; Master of Literature
Mlle.	Mademoiselle
MLS	Master of Library Science
MM	Master of Music
M.M.	Metronom Maelzel (Ger.: Maelzel's metronome) [tempo indication showing number of notes of a given value per minute]
mm	millimeter(s)
MMA	Master of Musical Arts
MME	Master of Music Education
Mme.	Madame
MMEd	Master of Music Education
MMT	Master of Music in Teaching
MMus	Master of Music
MN	Minnesota
MO	Missouri
mod	modulator
movt	movement
mp	mezzo-piano
MPhil	Master of Philosophy
MS	Mississippi; manuscript; Master of Science(s)
Msgr.	Monsignor
MSLS	Master of Science in Library and Information Science
MSM	Master of Sacred Music
MSS	manuscripts
MT	Montana
MusB; MusBac	Bachelor of Music
MusD; MusDoc	Doctor of Music
MusM	Master of Music
nar	narrator
NB	New Brunswick (Canada)
NBC	National Broadcasting Company
NC	North Carolina
ND	North Dakota
n.d.	no date (of publication)
NE	Nebraska
NEA	National Endowment for the Arts
NEH	National Endowment for the Humanities
Nfld	Newfoundland (Canada)
NH	New Hampshire
NJ	New Jersey
NM	New Mexico
no.	number
Nor.	Norwegian
Nov	November
n.p.	no place (of publication)
n.pub.	no publisher
nr	near
NS	Nova Scotia (Canada)
NV	Nevada
NWT	North West Territories (Canada)
NY	New York (state)
ob	oboe
obbl	obbligato
Oct	October
OH	Ohio
OK	Oklahoma
Ont.	Ontario (Canada)
op.	opus (Lat.: work)
op. cit.	opere citato (Lat.: in the work cited)
opp.	opera (Lat.: works)
opt.	optional
OR	Oregon
orch	orchestra, orchestral
orchd	orchestrated (by)
org	organ
orig.	original(ly)
ORTF	Office de Radiodiffusion-Télévision Française (France)
OUP	Oxford University Press
ov.	overture
P	Pincherle catalogue [of A. Vivaldi's works]
p	piano
p.	page
PA	Pennsylvania

p.a.	per annum (Lat.: by the year, annually)
PBS	Public Broadcasting System
PEI	Prince Edward Island (Canada)
perc	percussion
perf.	performance, performed (by)
pf	piano(forte)
pfmr	performer
PhB	Bachelor of Philosophy
PhD	Doctor of Philosophy
PhDEd	Doctor of Philosophy in Education
pic	piccolo
pl.	plate; plural
p.m.	post meridiem (Lat.: after noon)
PO	Philharmonic Orchestra
Pol.	Polish
pop.	population
Port.	Portuguese
posth.	posthumous(ly)
POW	prisoner of war
pp	pianissimo
pp.	pages
ppp	pianississimo
PR	Puerto Rico
pr.	printed
prol.	prologue
Ps.	Psalm
pseud.	pseudonym
Pss.	Psalms
pt.	part
ptbk	partbook
pubd	published (by)
pubn	publication
Que.	Quebec (Canada)
qnt	quintet
qt	quartet
R	(editorial) revision [in signature]
R	Ryom catalogue [of A. Vivaldi's works]
R	photographic reprint
r	recto
RAI	Radio Audizioni Italiane (Italy)
RCA	Radio Corporation of America; RCA Corporation
rec	recorder
rec.	recorded
recit	recitative
red.	reduction, reduced (for)
repr.	reprinted
Rev.	Reverend
rev.	revision, revised (by)
RI	Rhode Island
RILM	Répertoire International de Littérature Musicale
RISM	Répertoire International des Sources Musicales (Germany)
RKO	Radio-Keith-Orpheum
RO	Radio Orchestra
Rom.	Romanian
r.p.m.	revolution(s) per minute
Rt Hon.	Right Honourable
Russ.	Russian
S	soprano [voice]
S.	San, Santa
$	dollar(s)
s	soprano [instrument]
s.	solidus, solidi (Lat.: shilling, shillings [sterling])
Sask.	Saskatchewan (Canada)
sax	saxophone
SC	South Carolina
SD	South Dakota
Sept	September
ser.	series
sf, *sfz*	sforzando, sforzato
sing.	singular
SO	Symphony Orchestra
Sp.	Spanish
spr.	spring
sq.	square
Sr.	Senior
SSR	Soviet Socialist Republic
St.	Saint
STB	Bachelor of Sacred Theology
str	string(s)
sum.	summer
SUNY	State University of New York
suppl.	supplement, supplementary
Swed.	Swedish
sym.	symphony, symphonic
synth	synthesizer, synthesized
T	tenor [voice]
t	tenor [instrument]
ThM	Master of Theology
timp	timpani
TN	Tennessee
tpt	trumpet
Tr	treble [voice]
tr	treble [instrument]
trad.	traditional
trans.	translation, translated (by)
transcr.	transcription, transcribed (by/for)
trbn	trombone
TT	Trust Territory
TX	Texas
U.	University
UCLA	University of California, Los Angeles
UHF	ultra-high frequency
UK	United Kingdom of Great Britain and Northern Ireland
unacc.	unaccompanied
unattrib.	unattributed
UNESCO	United Nations Educational, Scientific and Cultural Organization
unorchd	unorchestrated
unperf.	unperformed
unpubd	unpublished
UP	University Press
US	United States [adjective]
USA	United States of America
USO	United Service Organizations

USSR	Union of Soviet Socialist Republics
UT	Utah
v	voice
v	verso
v.	verse
VA	Virginia
va	viola
vc	(violon)cello
VHF	very high frequency
VI	Virgin Islands
vib	vibraphone
viz.	videlicet (Lat.: namely)
vle	violone
vn	violin
vol.	volume
vs	vocal score, piano-vocal score
VT	Vermont
vv	voices
vv.	verses
WA	Washington
WI	Wisconsin
win.	winter
WoO	Werk(e) ohne Opuszahl (Ger.: work(s) without opus number)
WPA	Works Progress Administration
WQ	Wotquenne catalogue [of C. P. E. Bach's works]
WV	West Virginia
ww	woodwind
WY	Wyoming
xyl	xylophone
YT	Yukon Territory (Canada)

Discographical Abbreviations

The abbreviations used in this dictionary for the names of record labels are listed below. In recording-lists the label on which each recording was originally issued is cited, and no attempt is made here to indicate the affiliations of labels to companies. The names of a number of record labels consist of series of capital letters; although these may be abbreviated forms of company names they are not generally listed here as they constitute the full names of the labels concerned.

AAFS	Archive of American Folksong (Library of Congress)
Ari.	Arista
Asy.	Asylum
Atl.	Atlantic
BN	Blue Note
Bruns.	Brunswick
Cad.	Cadence
Can.	Canyon
Cap.	Capitol
Cas.	Casablanca
Col.	Columbia
Com.	Commodore
Conc.	Concord
Cont.	Contemporary
Cot.	Cotillion
Elek.	Elektra
Fan.	Fantasy
FW	Folkways
Gal.	Galaxy
Hick.	Hickory
Hor.	Horizon
IH	Indian House
Imp.	Impulse
Imper.	Imperial
Isl.	Island
Lml.	Limelight
Mer.	Mercury
Mlst.	Milestone
NW	New World
OK	Okeh
Para.	Paramount
Per.	Perfect
Phi.	Philips
Pol.	Polydor
Prst.	Prestige
Rep.	Reprise
Riv.	Riverside
Roul.	Roulette
Tak.	Takoma
TL	Time-Life
UA	United Artists
Van.	Vanguard
Vic.	Victor
Voc.	Vocalion
WB	Warner Bros.

Bibliographical Abbreviations

The bibliographical abbreviations used in this dictionary are listed below. Full bibliographical information is not normally supplied for nonmusical sources (national biographical dictionaries) or if it may be found elsewhere in this dictionary (in the lists following the articles "Dictionaries," "Histories," and "Periodicals") or in *The New Grove Dictionary of Music and Musicians* (in the lists that form parts of the articles "Dictionaries and encyclopedias of music," "Editions, historical," and "Periodicals"). The serial numbers of entries in the two articles "Periodicals" are given here in brackets; an asterisk denotes the appearance of an item in the article in this dictionary. The typographical conventions used throughout the dictionary are followed here: broadly, italic type is used for periodicals and reference works, and roman type for anthologies, series, etc. (titles of individual volumes are italicized).

ACAB — *American Composers Alliance Bulletin* [*US557]
AcM — *Acta musicologica* (1928/9–) [Intl 5]
AMw — *Archiv für Musikwissenschaft* (1918/19–) [Germany 552]
AMZ — *Allgemeine musikalische Zeitung* (1798/9–1882) [Germany 32, 154, 170]
AMz — *Allgemeine Musik-Zeitung* (1874–1943) [Germany 203]
Anderson 2 — E. R. Anderson: *Contemporary American Composers: a Biographical Dictionary* (Boston, 2/1982)
AnM — *Anuario musical* (1946–) [Spain 91]
AnMc — *Analecta musicologica* (some vols. in series Studien zur italienisch-deutschen Musikgeschichte), Veröffentlichungen der Musikabteilung des Deutschen historischen Instituts in Rom (Cologne, Germany, 1963–)
AnnM — *Annales musicologiques* (1953–) [France 638]
Baker 5(–7) — *Baker's Biographical Dictionary of Musicians*, rev. N. Slonimsky (New York, 5/1958/*R*1965, 6/1978, 7/1984; suppls., 1965, 1971)
BAMS — *Bulletin of the American Musicological Society* [*US550]
BMB — Biblioteca musica bononiensis (Bologna, Italy, 1959–)
BMw — *Beiträge zur Musikwissenschaft* [Germany 1013]
BPiM — *The Black Perspective in Music* [*US941]
BWQ — *Brass and Woodwind Quarterly* [*US811]
CBY — *Current Biography Yearbook* (New York, 1940–)
CEKM — Corpus of Early Keyboard Music (Rome, 1963–)
CMc — *Current Musicology* [*US800]
CMM — Corpus mensurabilis musicae (Rome, 1947–)
DAB — *Dictionary of American Biography* (New York, 1928–36; 7 suppls., 1944–81)
DBL — *Dansk biografisk leksikon* (Copenhagen, 1887–1905, 2/1933–)
DBY — *Down Beat Yearbook* [*US709]
DJbM — *Deutsches Jahrbuch der Musikwissenschaft* (1957–) [Germany 980]
DNB — *Dictionary of National Biography* (London, 1885–1901, suppls.)
EDM — Das Erbe deutscher Musik (Berlin and elsewhere, 1935–)
EitnerQ — R. Eitner: *Biographisch-bibliographisches Quellen-Lexikon* (Leipzig, Germany, 1900–04, rev. 2/1959–60)
EM — *Ethnomusicology* [*US692]
ES — F. D'Amico: *Enciclopedia dello spettacolo* (Rome and Florence, 1954–62; suppl., 1966)
EwenD — D. Ewen: *American Composers: a Biographical Dictionary* (New York, 1982)
FAM — *Fontes artis musicae* (1954–) [Intl 16]
FétisB (FétisBS) — F.-J. Fétis: *Biographie universelle des musiciens* (Brussels, 2/1860–65/*R*1972; suppl., 1878–80/*R*1972)
Grove 1(–5) — G. Grove, ed.: *A Dictionary of Music and Musicians* (London, 1878–90; 2/1904–10 ed. J. A. Fuller Maitland, 3/1927–8 and 4/1940 ed. H. C. Colles, 5/1954 ed. E. Blom with suppl. 1961, all as *Grove's Dictionary of Music and Musicians*)
Grove 6 — S. Sadie, ed.: *The New Grove Dictionary of Music and Musicians* (London, 1980)
GroveAS — W. S. Pratt, ed.: *Grove's Dictionary of Music and Musicians: American Supplement* (New York, 1920, 2/1928, many reprs.)

GroveI S. Sadie, ed.: *The New Grove Dictionary of Musical Instruments* (London, 1984)

GSJ *The Galpin Society Journal* (1948–) [Great Britain 415]

HiFi *High Fidelity* [*US681]

HiFi/MusAm *High Fidelity/Musical America* [*US681]

HMYB *Hinrichsen's Musical Year Book* (1944–61) [Great Britain 381]

IAJRCJ *International Association of Jazz Record Collectors Journal* [*Intl 10]

IMSCR *International Musicological Society Congress Report* (1930–)

IRASM *International Review of the Aesthetics and Sociology of Music* (1970–) [Intl 32]

ISAMm Institute for Studies in American Music, monograph [see entry on the institute]

ITO *In Theory Only* [*US974]

JAMIS *Journal of the American Musical Instrument Society* [*US983]

JAMS *Journal of the American Musicological Society* [*US633]

JbMP *Jahrbuch der Musikbibliothek Peters* (1895–1941) [Germany 336]

JEFDSS *The Journal of the English Folk Dance and Song Society* (1932–64) [Great Britain 341]

JEMF Quarterly *J[ohn] E[dwards] M[emorial] F[oundation] Quarterly* [*US802]

JFSS *The Journal of the Folk-song Society* (1899–1904; 1927–31) [Great Britain 183]

JIFMC *Journal of the International Folk Music Council* (1949–68) [Intl 10]

JMT *Journal of Music Theory* [*US716]

JRBM *Journal of Renaissance and Baroque Music* [*US609]

JRME *Journal of Research in Music Education* [*US693]

JVdGSA *Journal of the Viola da Gamba Society of America* [*US791]

LaMusicaD G. M. Gatti and A. Basso: *La musica: dizionario* (Turin, Italy, 1968–71)

MB Musica britannica (London, 1951–)

MD *Musica disciplina* [*US609]

MEJ *Music Educators Journal* [*US435]

Mf *Die Musikforschung* (1948–) [Germany 839]

MGG F. Blume, ed.: *Die Musik in Geschichte und Gegenwart* (Kassel, Germany, and Basle, Switzerland, 1949–68; suppl., 1973–9)

MJ *Music Journal* [*US592]

ML *Music and Letters* (1920–) [Great Britain 280]

MM *Modern Music* [*US493]

MMR *The Monthly Musical Record* (1871–1960) [Great Britain 75]

MO *Musical Opinion* (1877/8–) [Great Britain 90]

MQ *The Musical Quarterly* [*US451]

MR *The Music Review* (1940–) [Great Britain 376]

MSD Musicological Studies and Documents (Rome, 1951–)

MT *The Musical Times* (1844/5–) [Great Britain 33]

MTNAP *Music Teachers National Association: Proceedings* [*US119, 370]

MusAm *Musical America* [*US302, 681]

NAW E. T. James, J. W. James, and P. S. Boyer, eds.: *Notable American Women* (Cambridge, MA, 1971; suppl., 1980)

NOHM *The New Oxford History of Music*, ed. E. Wellesz, J. A. Westrup, and G. Abraham (London, 1954–)

NRMI *Nuova rivista musicale italiana* (1967–) [Italy 282]

NZM *Neue Zeitschrift für Musik* (1834–) [Germany 75, 1088] [retitled 1920, see *ZfM*]

ÖMz *Österreichische Musikzeitschrift* (1946–) [Austria 233]

PAMS *Papers of the American Musicological Society* [*US553]

PASUC *Proceedings of the American Society of University Composers* [*US809]

PMA *Proceedings of the Musical Association* (1874/5–) [Great Britain 80] [retitled 1944, see *PRMA*]

PMFC Polyphonic Music of the Fourteenth Century, ed. L. Schrade and F. Ll. Harrison (Monaco, 1956–)

PNM *Perspectives of New Music* [*US771]

PRMA *Proceedings of the Royal Musical Association* [see *PMA*]

RaM *La rassegna musicale* (1928–72) [Italy 197, 272]

RBM *Revue belge de musicologie* (1946–) [Belgium 126]

RdM *Revue de musicologie* (1917–) [France 462]

ReM *La revue musicale* (1920–) [France 475]

RiemannL 12 *Riemann Musik Lexikon*, rev. W. Gurlitt (Mainz, Germany, 12/1959–75)

RISM *Répertoire international des sources musicales* (Munich, Duisburg, and Kassel, Germany, 1971–)

RN *Renaissance News* [*US609]

RRAM Recent Researches in American Music (Madison, WI, 1977–)

SH *Slovenská hudba* (1957–71) [Czechoslovakia 192]

SIMG *Sammelbände der Internationalen Musik-Gesellschaft* (1899/1900–1913/14) [Intl 2]

SM *Studia musicologica Academiae scientiarum hungaricae* (1961–) [Hungary 89]

SMA *Studies in Music* (1967–) [Australia 20]

SMz *Schweizerische Musikzeitung/Revue musicale suisse* (1861–) [Switzerland 4]

SouthernB E. Southern: *Biographical Dictionary of Afro-American and African Musicians* (Westport, CT, 1982)

Thompson 1(–10) O. Thompson: *The International Cyclopedia of Music and Musicians* (New York, 1939, 2/1943 and 3/1944 ed. O. Thompson and G. W. Harris, 4/1946–8/1958 ed. N. Slonimsky, 9/1964 ed. R. Sabin, 10/1974 ed. B. Bohle)

VintonD J. Vinton, ed.: *Dictionary of Contemporary Music* (New York, 1974)

VMw *Vierteljahrsschrift für Musikwissenschaft* (1885–94) [Germany 282]

YIFMC *Yearbook of the International Folk Music Council* [*Intl 11]

ZfM *Zeitschrift für Musik* [see *NZM*]

ZIMG *Zeitschrift der Internationalen Musik-Gesellschaft* (1899/1900–1913/14) [Intl 3]

Library Abbreviations

The abbreviations used in this dictionary for the names of libraries are those established by the Catalog Publication Division of the Library of Congress and published in *Symbols of American Libraries* (Washington, DC, rev. 12/1980). Only those abbreviations that appear in the dictionary (where they are always printed in italic type) are listed here.

A-Ar	Alabama Department of Archives and History, Montgomery, AL
AB	Birmingham Public and Jefferson County Free Library, Birmingham, AL
ABH	Samford University, Birmingham, AL
AkU	University of Alaska, Fairbanks, AK
ArU	University of Arkansas, Fayetteville, AR
ATrT	Troy State University, Troy, AL
AU	University of Alabama, University, AL
AzTeS	Arizona State University, Tempe, AZ
AzTP	Arizona Historical Society, Tucson, AZ
AzU	University of Arizona, Tucson, AZ
CBGTU	Graduate Theological Union, Berkeley, CA
CBbWD	Walt Disney Productions, Burbank, CA
CCC	Honnold Library, Claremont, CA
CHi	California Historical Society, San Francisco, CA
CL	Los Angeles Public Library, Los Angeles, CA
CLAS	Arnold Schoenberg Institute, University of Southern California, Los Angeles, CA
CLobS	California State University, Long Beach, Long Beach, CA
CLS	California State University, Los Angeles, Los Angeles, CA
CLSU-Music	University of Southern California, Music Library, Los Angeles, CA
CLU-MUS	University of California, Los Angeles, Music Library, Los Angeles, CA
CO	Oakland Public Library, Oakland, CA
CoD	Denver Public Library, Denver, CO
CoHi	Colorado State Historical Society, Denver, CO
COMC	Mills College, Oakland, CA
COMus	Oakland Museum, Oakland, CA
CoU	University of Colorado, Boulder, CO
CSd	San Diego Public Library, San Diego, CA
CSf	San Francisco Public Library, San Francisco, CA
CSfCP	Society of California Pioneers, San Francisco, CA
CSfSt	San Francisco State University, San Francisco, CA
CSmH	Henry E. Huntington Library, San Marino, CA
CSt-H	Stanford University, Hoover Institution on War, Revolution, and Peace, Stanford, CA
Ct	Connecticut State Library, Hartford, CT
CtHi	Connecticut Historical Society, Hartford, CT
CtHT	Trinity College, Hartford, CT
CtHT-W	Trinity College, Watkinson Library, Hartford, CT
CtNhHi	New Haven Colony Historical Society, New Haven, CT
CtW	Wesleyan University, Middletown, CT
CtWeharU	University of Hartford, West Hartford, CT
CtY	Yale University, New Haven, CT
CtY-Mus	Yale University, School of Music, New Haven, CT
CU-MUSI	University of California, Berkeley, Music Library, Berkeley, CA
CU-Riv	University of California, Riverside, Main Library, Riverside, CA
CU-S	University of California, San Diego, Main Library, La Jolla, CA
CU-SB	University of California, Santa Barbara, Main Library, Santa Barbara, CA
DCU	Catholic University of America, Washington, DC
DeHi	Historical Society of Delaware, Wilmington, DE
DeU	University of Delaware, Newark, DE
DeWint-M	Henry Frances DuPont Winterthur Museum, Joseph Downs Manuscript and Microfilm Collection, Winterthur, DE
DFo	Folger Shakespeare Library, Washington, DC
DHU	Howard University, Washington, DC
DLC	United States Library of Congress, Washington, DC
DMaM	United States Marine Corps Museum, Washington, DC
DNA	United States National Archives and Records Service, National Archives Library, Washington, DC
DNC	Washington Cathedral, Washington, DC
DOAS	Organization of American States, Washington, DC
DSI	Smithsonian Institution, Washington, DC
FMU	University of Miami, Coral Gables, FL
FTaSU	Florida State University, Tallahassee, FL

GAHi	Atlanta Historical Society, Atlanta, GA
G-Ar	Georgia State Department of Archives and History, Atlanta, GA
GASU	Georgia State University, Atlanta, GA
GAU	Atlanta University, Atlanta, GA
GEU	Emory University, Atlanta, GA
GEU-T	Emory University, Candler School of Theology, Atlanta, GA
GU	University of Georgia, Athens, GA
H-Ar	Public Archives, Honolulu, HI
HHB	Bernice P. Bishop Museum, Honolulu, HI
HHMC	Hawaiian Mission Children's Society, Honolulu, HI
HU	University of Hawaii, Honolulu, HI
IaDm	Des Moines Public Library, Des Moines, IA
IaHi	State Historical Society of Iowa, Iowa City, IA
IaU	University of Iowa, Iowa City, IA
IBloHi	McLean County Historical Society, Bloomington, IL
IBloW	Illinois Wesleyan University, Bloomington, IL
IC	Chicago Public Library, Chicago, IL
ICarbS	Southern Illinois University, Carbondale, IL
ICD	De Paul University, Chicago, IL
ICHi	Chicago Historical Society, Chicago, IL
ICIU	University of Illinois, Chicago Circle, Chicago, IL
ICN	Newberry Library, Chicago, IL
ICU	University of Chicago, Chicago, IL
IdCaC	College of Idaho, Caldwell, ID
IE	Evanston Public Library, Evanston, IL
IEdS	Southern Illinois University, Edwardsville Campus, Edwardsville, IL
IEN	Northwestern University, Evanston, IL
IEWT	National Women's Christian Temperance Union, Evanston, IL
IHi	Illinois State Historical Library, Springfield, IL
InGo	Goshen College, Goshen, IN
InHi	Indiana Historical Society, Indianapolis, IN
InI	Indianapolis–Marion County Public Library, Indianapolis, IN
InMuB	Ball State University, Muncie, IN
InNd	University of Notre Dame, Notre Dame, IN
INS	Illinois State University, Normal, IL
InU	Indiana University, Bloomington, IN
IU-Mu	University of Illinois, Music Library, Urbana, IL
IWW	Wheaton College, Wheaton, IL
KHi	Kansas State Historical Society, Topeka, KS
KNnB	Bethel College, North Newton, KS
KU	University of Kansas, Lawrence, KS
KU-S	University of Kansas, Kenneth Spencer Research Library, Lawrence, KS
KWiU	Wichita State University, Wichita, KS
KyBB	Berea College, Berea, KY
KyBgW	Western Kentucky University, Bowling Green, KY
KyBgW-K	Western Kentucky University, Kentucky Library, Bowling Green, KY
KyLo	Louisville Free Public Library, Louisville, KY
KyLoF	Filson Club, Louisville, KY
KyLoS	Southern Baptist Theological Seminary, Louisville, KY
KyLoU	University of Louisville, Louisville, KY
KyLoU-Ar	University of Louisville, University Archives and Records Center, Louisville, KY
KyU	University of Kentucky, Lexington, KY
LLafS	University of Southwestern Louisiana, Lafayette, LA
L-M	Louisiana State Museum, New Orleans, LA
LN	New Orleans Public Library, New Orleans, LA
LNB	New Orleans Baptist Theological Seminary, New Orleans, LA
LNT	Tulane University, New Orleans, LA
LU	Louisiana State University, Baton Rouge, LA
MB	Boston Public Library and Eastern Massachusetts Regional Public Library System, Boston, MA
MBAt	Boston Athenaeum, Boston, MA
MBBS	Bostonian Society, Boston, MA
MBCM	New England Conservatory of Music, Boston, MA
MBG	Isabella Stewart Gardner Museum, Boston, MA
MBHM	Harvard Musical Association, Boston, MA
MBU	Boston University, Boston, MA
MBU-T	Boston University, School of Theology, Boston, MA
MCM	Massachusetts Institute of Technology, Cambridge, MA
MCR-S	Radcliffe College, Schlesinger Library on the History of Women in America, Cambridge, MA
MdBE	Enoch Pratt Free Library, Baltimore, MD
MdBJ	Johns Hopkins University, Baltimore, MD
MdBMC	Morgan State College, Baltimore, MD
MdBP	Enoch Pratt Free Library, George Peabody Branch, Baltimore, MD
MdBPC	Peabody Conservatory of Music, Baltimore, MD
MdHi	Maryland Historical Society, Baltimore, MD
MdU	University of Maryland, College Park, MD
Me	Maine State Library, Augusta, ME
MeHi	Maine Historical Society, Portland, ME
MeP	Portland Public Library, Portland, ME
MeU	University of Maine, Orono, ME
MH	Harvard University, Cambridge, MA
MH-AH	Harvard University, Andover-Harvard Theological Library, Cambridge, MA
MH-BA	Harvard University, Graduate School of Business Administration, Boston, MA
MH-Ed	Harvard University, Graduate School of Education, Cambridge, MA
MH-H	Harvard University, Houghton Library, Cambridge, MA
MHi	Massachusetts Historical Society, Boston, MA
MH-Mu	Harvard University, Music Library, Cambridge, MA
MH-P	Harvard University, Peabody Museum, Cambridge, MA
MiD	Detroit Public Library, Detroit, MI
MiDbEI	Edison Institute, Henry Ford Museum, and Greenfield Village Library, Dearborn, MI
MiDW	Wayne State University, Detroit, MI
MiGrC	Calvin College and Seminary, Grand Rapids, MI
MiKW	Western Michigan University, Kalamazoo, MI
MiU-C	University of Michigan, William L. Clements Library, Ann Arbor, MI
MiU-H	University of Michigan, Michigan Historical Collection, Ann Arbor, MI
MMeT	Tufts University, Medford, MA
MMHi	Milton Historical Society, Milton, MA
MnCS	St. John's University, Collegeville, MN
MNe	Newburyport Public Library, Newburyport, MA
MnHi	Minnesota Historical Society, St. Paul, MN
MnM	Minneapolis Public Library, Minneapolis, MN
MnNHi	Norwegian-American Historical Association, c/o St. Olaf College, Northfield, MN
MnNS	St. Olaf College, Northfield, MN
MNS	Smith College, Northampton, MA
MnU	University of Minnesota, Minneapolis, MN
MnU-IA	University of Minnesota, Immigration History Research Center, St. Paul, MN
MnU-SW	University of Minnesota, Social Welfare History Archives Center, St. Paul, MN

MoHi	Missouri State Historical Society, Columbia, MO
MoK	Kansas City Public Library, Kansas City, MO
MoKB	Bar Library Association of Kansas City, Kansas City, MO
MoKU	University of Missouri at Kansas City, Kansas City, MO
MoKU-Mus	University of Missouri at Kansas City, Music Conservatory, Kansas City, MO
MoS	St. Louis Public Library, St. Louis, MO
MoSHi	Missouri Historical Society, St. Louis, MO
MoSW	Washington University, St. Louis, MO
MoU	University of Missouri, Columbia, MO
MPB	Berkshire Athenaeum, Pittsfield, MA
MSaE	Essex Institute, Salem, MA
Ms-Ar	Mississippi Department of Archives and History, Jackson, MS
MsHaW	William Carey College, Hattiesburg, MS
MsJMC	Millsaps College, Jackson, MS
MStuO	Old Sturbridge Village Library, Sturbridge, MA
MU	University of Massachusetts, Amherst, MA
MWA	American Antiquarian Society, Worcester, MA
MWalB	Brandeis University, Waltham, MA
MWelC	Wellesley College, Wellesley, MA
MWiW	Williams College, Williamstown, MA

NB	Brooklyn Public Library, Brooklyn, NY
NBC	Brooklyn College, City University of New York, Brooklyn, NY
NbHi	Nebraska State Historical Society, Lincoln, NE
NbL	Lincoln City Libraries, Lincoln, NE
NbRcW	Willa Cather Pioneer Memorial, Red Cloud, NE
NbU	University of Nebraska, Lincoln, NE
NBuU-AR	State University of New York, Buffalo, Archives, Buffalo, NY
NBuU-Mu	State University of New York, Buffalo, Music Library, Buffalo, NY
NbWi	Dvoracek Memorial Library, Wilber, NE
Nc-Ar	North Carolina State Department of Archives and History, Raleigh, NC
NcBoA	Appalachian State University, Boone, NC
NcD	Duke University, Durham, NC
NcGU	University of North Carolina, Greensboro, Greensboro, NC
NcU	University of North Carolina, Chapel Hill, NC
NcWsMM	Moravian Music Foundation, Inc., Winston-Salem, NC
NdU	University of North Dakota, Grand Forks, ND
Nh	New Hampshire State Library, Concord, NH
NhD	Dartmouth College, Hanover, NH
NhHi	New Hampshire Historical Society, Concord, NH
NHi	New-York Historical Society, New York, NY
NhM	Manchester City Library, Manchester, NH
NhU	University of New Hampshire, Durham, NH
NIC	Cornell University, Ithaca, NY
NIHi	DeWitt Historical Society of Tompkins County, Ithaca, NY
NjHi	New Jersey Historical Society, Newark, NJ
NjMD	Drew University, Madison, NJ
NjP	Princeton University, Princeton, NJ
NjR	Rutgers, the State University of New Jersey, New Brunswick, NJ
NmLvH	New Mexico Highlands University, Las Vegas, NM
NN	New York Public Library, New York, NY
NNAL	American Academy of Arts and Letters, New York, NY
NNC	Columbia University, New York, NY
NNCU-G	City University of New York, Graduate Center, New York, NY
NNH	Hispanic Society of America, New York, NY
NNJu	Juilliard School of Music, New York, NY
NNL	Herbert H. Lehman College, City University of New York, New York, NY
NN-L	New York Public Library, Research Library for the Performing Arts at Lincoln Center, New York, NY
NNLBI	Leo Baeck Institute, New York, NY
NNMMA	Museum of Modern Art, New York, NY
NNPM	Pierpont Morgan Library, New York, NY
NNR	City College, City University of New York, New York, NY
NN-Sc	New York Public Library, Schomburg Collection, New York, NY
NNU	New York University, New York, NY
NNUT	Union Theological Seminary, New York, NY
NNYI	Yivo Institute for Jewish Research, New York, NY
NPotU	State University of New York, College at Potsdam, Potsdam, NY
NPurU	State University of New York, College at Purchase, Purchase, NY
NPV	Vassar College, Poughkeepsie, NY
NRU-Mus	University of Rochester, Eastman School of Music, Rochester, NY
NSbSU	State University of New York, Stony Brook, Stony Brook, NY
NSyU	Syracuse University, Syracuse, NY
NvHi	Nevada State Historical Society, Reno, NV

OBerB	Baldwin-Wallace College, Berea, OH
OBgU	Bowling Green State University, Bowling Green, OH
OC	Public Library of Cincinnati and Hamilton County, Cincinnati, OH
OCH	Hebrew Union College–Jewish Institute of Religion, Cincinnati, OH
OCHP	Cincinnati Historical Society, Cincinnati, OH
OCl	Cleveland Public Library, Cleveland, OH
OClCIM	Cleveland Institute of Music, Cleveland, OH
OClU	Cleveland State University, Cleveland, OH
OClWHi	Western Reserve Historical Society, Cleveland, OH
OClW-S	Case Western Reserve University, Sears Library, Cleveland, OH
OCU-Mu	University of Cincinnati, College Conservatory of Music, Cincinnati, OH
ODW	Ohio Wesleyan University, Delaware, OH
OHi	Ohio Historical Society, Columbus, OH
OkU	University of Oklahoma, Norman, OK
OOC	Oberlin College Conservatory of Music, Oberlin, OH
OOxM	Miami University, Oxford, OH
OrCs	Oregon State University, Corvallis, OR
OrHi	Oregon Historical Society, Portland, OR
OrP	Library Association of Portland (Public Library for Portland and Multnomah County), Portland, OR
OrU	University of Oregon, Eugene, OR
OSW	Wittenberg University, Springfield, OH
OU	Ohio State University, Columbus, OH
OYU	Youngstown State University, Youngstown, OH

P	Pennsylvania State Library, Harrisburg, PA
PBMCA	Archives of the Moravian Church, Bethlehem, PA
PHarH	Pennsylvania Historical and Museum Commission, Harrisburg, PA
PHi	Historical Society of Pennsylvania, Philadelphia, PA
PLatS	St. Vincent College and Archabbey, Latrobe, PA
PP	Free Library of Philadelphia, Philadelphia, PA
PPAmP	American Philosophical Society, Philadelphia, PA
PPCI	Curtis Institute of Music, Philadelphia, PA
PPi	Carnegie Library of Pittsburgh, Pittsburgh, PA

PPiHi	Historical Society of Western Pennsylvania, Pittsburgh, PA
PPiPT	Pittsburgh Theological Seminary, Pittsburgh, PA
PPiU	University of Pittsburgh, Pittsburgh, PA
PPL	Library Company of Philadelphia, Philadelphia, PA
PPPCity	Philadelphia City Institute Branch Free Library, Philadelphia, PA [collection no longer available]
PPT	Temple University, Philadelphia, PA
PrU	University of Puerto Rico, Rio Piedras, PR
PSt	Pennsylvania State University, University Park, PA
PU	University of Pennsylvania, Philadelphia, PA
PU-Music	University of Pennsylvania, School of Music, Philadelphia, PA
RHi	Rhode Island Historical Society, Providence, RI
RP	Providence Public Library, Providence, RI
RPB	Brown University, Providence, RI
RPB-JH	Brown University, John Hay Library of Rare Books and Special Collections, Providence, RI
ScHi	South Carolina Historical Society, Charleston, SC
ScSpC	Converse College, Spartanburg, SC
ScU	University of South Carolina, Columbia, SC
SdU	University of South Dakota, Vermillion, SD
TMM	Memphis State University, Memphis, TN
TNC	Country Music Foundation Library and Media Center, Nashville, TN
TNJ	Joint University Libraries, Nashville, TN
TNSB	Southern Baptist Convention Historical Commission, Nashville, TN
TU	University of Tennessee, Knoxville, TN
TxAm	Amarillo Public Library, Amarillo, TX
TxDa	Dallas Public Library, Dallas, TX
TxDaM	Southern Methodist University, Dallas, TX
TxDN	North Texas State University, Denton, TX
TxFS	Southwestern Baptist Theological Seminary, Fort Worth, TX
TxHR	Rice University, Houston, TX
TxLT	Texas Tech University, Lubbock, TX
TxSa	San Antonio Public Library, San Antonio, TX
TxU	University of Texas, Austin, TX
TxWB	Baylor University, Waco, TX
UCS	Southern Utah State College, Cedar City, UT
UHi	Utah State Historical Society, Salt Lake City, UT
Uk	British Library, London, England
UPB	Brigham Young University, Provo, UT
USIC	Church of Jesus Christ of Latter-day Saints, Historian's Office, Salt Lake City, UT
UU	University of Utah, Salt Lake City, UT
ViFGM	George Mason University, Fairfax, VA
ViHal	Hampton Institute, Hampton, VA
ViHi	Virginia Historical Society, Richmond, VA
ViR	Richmond Public Library, Richmond, VA
ViSwC	Sweet Briar College, Sweet Briar, VA
ViU	University of Virginia, Charlottesville, VA
ViU-Mu	University of Virginia, Music Library, Charlottesville, VA
ViWC	Colonial Williamsburg, Inc., Williamsburg, VA
VtHi	Vermont Historical Society, Montpelier, VT
VtMiM	Middlebury College, Middlebury, VT.
VtU	University of Vermont and State Agricultural College, Burlington, VT
WaPS	Washington State University, Pullman, WA
WaS	Seattle Public Library, Seattle, WA
WaU	University of Washington, Seattle, WA
WBaraC	Circus World Museum, Baraboo, WI
WHi	State Historical Society of Wisconsin, Madison, WI
WKenOS	Old Songs Library, Kenosha, WI
WM	Milwaukee Public Library, Milwaukee, WI
WMUW	University of Wisconsin-Milwaukee, Milwaukee, WI
WU	University of Wisconsin, Madison, WI
WvU	West Virginia University, Morgantown, WV
Wy-Ar	Wyoming State Archives and Historical Department, Cheyenne, WY
WyU	University of Wyoming, Laramie, WY

Volume Three

L–Q

A Note on the Use of the Dictionary

This note is intended as a short guide to the basic procedures and organization of the dictionary. A fuller account will be found in the Introduction, vol. 1, pp. xi–xvii.

Alphabetization of headings is based on the principle that words are read continuously, ignoring spaces, hyphens, accents, parenthesized and bracketed matter, etc., up to the first comma; the same principle applies thereafter. "Mc" and "Mac" are alphabetized as "Mac," "St." as "Saint."

Cross-references are shown in small capitals, with a large capital at the beginning of the first word of the entry referred to. Thus "The UNIVERSITY OF CALIFORNIA established a campus at Berkeley in 1868" means that the entry referred to is not "**University of California**" but "**California, University of.**"

Abbreviations used in the dictionary are listed on pp. vii–xviii, in the order General (beginning on p. vii), Discographical (p. xii), Bibliographical (p. xiii), and Library (p. xv).

Work-lists are normally arranged chronologically (within section, where divided), in order of year of composition or first publication (in the latter case dates are given in parentheses). Italicized abbreviations (such as *DLC* and *NN-L*) stand for libraries holding sources and are explained on pp. xv–xviii.

Recording-lists are arranged chronologically (within section, where divided), in order of date of recording for jazz musicians and date of issue for others (dates respectively precede and follow issue information). Abbreviations standing for record labels are explained on p. xii.

Bibliographies are arranged chronologically (within section, where divided), in order of year of first publication, and alphabetically by author within years. Abbreviations standing for periodicals and reference works are explained on pp. xiii–xiv.

L

La Barbara [née Lotz; Subotnick], **Joan** (*b* Philadelphia, PA, 8 June 1947). Composer and vocal performer. She studied voice with Helen Boatwright at Syracuse University and composition at New York University (BS 1970), and received additional vocal training from Curtin at the Berkshire Music Center and from Marion Szekely Freschl at the Juilliard School. In 1973 she helped found the New Wilderness Preservation Band, a cooperative improvisational group that presented a two-year series of performances in New York with poets and writers; during the 1970s she was a vocalist with both Reich's and Glass's ensembles and performed in world premières of works by Cage, Lucier, Ashley, Subotnick, and others. La Barbara has toured extensively in the USA and in Europe, presenting concerts of her works and workshops in extended vocal techniques. In 1981 she was appointed to teach composition and singing at the California Institute of the Arts, Valencia. She has received grants from the New York State Council on the Arts (1975, 1978) and the NEA (1979, 1980); in 1979 she served as a composer-in-residence in West Berlin under the sponsorship of the Deutscher Akademischer Austauschdienst. She has received commissions from Joan Tower, Radio Bremen and RIAS Radio, Berlin, and the Los Angeles Olympic Arts Festival. Active as a writer and critic of new music, she became a contributing editor of *High Fidelity/Musical America* in 1977. She is married to the composer MORTON SUBOTNICK.

La Barbara has been an influential figure in experimental music since the early 1970s, when she developed a repertory of extended vocal techniques, including multiphonics and circular breathing; some of these techniques, such as throat clicks and a high flutter, are recognized as her own "signature" effects. Most of her compositions are designed for her specialized vocal skills. Early solo works like *Voice Piece: One-note Internal Resonance Investigation* (1974) are rigorous explorations – for performer and listener alike – of vocal production. More often, however, she incorporates the vocal material into more elaborately textured ensemble and tape pieces.

WORKS

(all voices amplified)

Large ens: Chandra, v(v), male vv, chamber orch, 1978, rev. 1983; The Solar Wind III, 1v, chamber orch, 1984

Amp v(v), inst: Thunder, 1v, 6 timp, elec, 1975; Ides of March I–VIII, 1v, insts, 1975–7; An Exaltation of Larks, 1v, elec, 1976; Chords and Gongs, 1v, cimb, gongs, 1976; Loisaida, 1v, kalimba, cimb, steel drum, 1977; Silent Scroll, 1v, fl, cl/db, perc, gong, zoomoozophone, 1982; Vlissingen Harbor,

Joan La Barbara, 1984

1v, fl + pic, cl, tpt, harp, pf + cel, vc, perc, 1982; The Solar Wind I, 1 or 2 solo vv, 8 insts, tape, perc, 1983, II, 16 solo vv, 2 perc, fl, elec kbd, 1983

Amp v(v): Hear what I Feel, 1v, 1974; Performance Piece, 1v, 1974, rev. 1979; Voice Piece: One-note Internal Resonance Investigation, 1v, 1974; Circular Song, 1v, 1975; Vocal Extensions, 1v, live elec, 1975; Les oiseaux qui chantent dans ma tête, 1v, 1976; Space Testing, acoustic v, 1976; Cathing, 1v, tape, 1977; Twelvesong, 1v, tape, 1977; Klee Alee, 1v, tape, 1979; Shadowsong, 1v, tape, 1979; Twelve for Five in Eight, 5 or more vv, 1979; Erin, 1v, tape, 1980; October Music: Star Showers and Extraterrestrials, 1v, tape, 1980; Winds of the Canyon, 1v, tape, 1982; Berliner Träume (Berlin Dreaming), 1v, 16-track tape, 1983; After "Obervogelsang," 1v, tape, 1984; Time(d) Trials and Unscheduled Events, 8 solo vv, tape, 1984; Loose Tongues, 8 solo vv, tape, 1985

Tape: The Executioner's Bracelet, 1979; Quatre petites bêtes, 1979; Responsive Resonance with Feathers, pf, tape, 1979; Autumn Signal, 1982

Other: Hunters, video, 1975; Vermont II, video, 1975; Cyclone, amp v, tape, light-panning activating device, 1976, rev. as sound installation, 16-track tape, 1979; She is Always Alone, video, 1979; As lightning comes, in flashes, 2–6 amp vv, dancers, video, 1982; 3 Space Trio/A Lament for the Wizard, video, 1982, collab. E. Emshwiller

BIBLIOGRAPHY

T. Johnson: "Research & Development," *Village Voice* (27 Jan 1975)
J. Rockwell: "Joan La Barbara Sings Own Works," *New York Times* (19 Jan 1975)
W. Zimmermann: "Joan La Barbara," *Desert Plants: Conversations with 23 American Musicians* (Vancouver, 1976), 149
P. Frank: "New American Music on Records," *New York Arts Journal*, ii/1 (1977), 27
D. Sofer: "Joan La Barbara: Voice is the Original Instrument," *Synapse*, i/6 (1977), 22
R. Palmer: "Joan La Barbara Sings a 'Collage'," *New York Times* (21 Feb 1978)
K. Jensen: "Joan La Barbara," *Contact*, no.22 (1981), 21

LINDA SANDERS

Labunski, Felix [Łabuński, Feliks Roderyk] (*b* Ksawerynów, Poland, 27 Dec 1892; *d* Cincinnati, OH, 28 April 1979). Composer and teacher, brother of Wiktor Labunski. He studied with Lucjan Marczewski and Witold Maliszewski at the Warsaw Conservatory (1922–4) and with Paul Dukas and Boulanger (composition) and Georges Migot (musicology) at the Ecole Normale de Musique, Paris (1924–34). In 1927 he helped to found the Association of Young Polish Composers in Paris. He was director of classical music for Polish radio in Warsaw from 1934 until 1936, when he moved to the USA (he took American citizenship in 1941). In 1940–41 he was professor of counterpoint and composition at Marymount College in Tarrytown, New York, and in 1945 he joined the faculty of the Cincinnati College of Music. He appeared as a pianist, mostly in his own compositions, and was active as a music critic. His music is fundamentally Romantic, with traits assimilated from the Paris school.

WORKS

(only those composed in the USA)

Orch: Suite, str, 1938; Variations, 1947; Sym., D, 1954; Elegy, 1955; Xaveriana, fantasy, 2 pf, orch, 1956; Symphonic Dialogues, 1961; Canto di aspirazione (1963); Polish Renaissance Suite (1967); Salut à Paris, ballet suite (1968); Music, pf, orch (1968); Primavera, 1974; several other works

Ballet: God's Man, 1937

Vocal: Song without Words, S, str (1946); There is no Death, cantata, chorus, orch, 1950; Images of Youth, cantata, 1956; other choral works and songs

Inst: 3 Bagatelles, brass qt, 1955; Divertimento, fl, ob, cl, bn (1956); Diptych, ob, pf (1958); Str Qt no.2 (1962); Intrada festiva, brass choir (1968); additional chamber works; pf and org pieces

Principal publishers: Polskie Wydawnictwo Muzyczne, World Library

BIBLIOGRAPHY

EwenD
L. Erhardt: "Felix Roderyk Łabuński w Ameryce," *Ruch muzyczny*, v/9 (1961), 5

BOGUSŁAW SCHÄFFER/R

Labunski [Łabuński], **Wiktor** (*b* St. Petersburg [now Leningrad], Russia, 14 April 1895; *d* Kansas City, MO, 26 Jan 1974). Pianist, composer, and teacher of Polish origin, brother of Felix Labunski. He studied piano and theory at the St. Petersburg Conservatory and conducting in Poland. After directing the piano department of the Kraków Conservatory (1919–28) he came to the USA, where he made his début as a pianist at Carnegie Hall in 1928. He taught at the Nashville Conservatory (1928–31) and was professor and director at the Memphis College of Music (1931–7). In 1937 he joined the piano faculty of the Kansas City Conservatory, of which he was director from 1941 until his retirement 30 years later. Well known for his lecture-recitals, he had a repertory of more than 1500 works. His own compositions are in a conventional style.

WORKS

(only those composed in the USA)

Pf Concertino, 1932; Sym., g, 1936; Pf Conc., C, 1937; Variations on a Theme of Paganini, pf, 1943; Variations, pf, orch, 1945; Conc., 2 pf, orch, 1951; many other pf pieces; songs

Principal publisher: Polskie Wydawnictwo Muzyczne

BIBLIOGRAPHY

W. Waliszewska: "O Wiktorze Łabunskim," *Ruch muzyczny*, xii/23 (1968), 18
"Wiktor Labunski, 78, Conservatory Dean," *New York Times* (27 Jan 1974)
J. R. Belanger: *Wiktor Labunski: Polish-American Musician in Kansas City, 1937–1974* (diss., Columbia U., 1982)

BOGUSŁAW SCHÄFFER/R

Lachmund, Carl V(alentine) (*b* Booneville, MO, 27 March 1857; *d* Yonkers, NY, 20 Feb 1928). Pianist, teacher, composer, and conductor. He was educated in the USA and then attended the Cologne Conservatory, where he studied with Stephen Heller, graduating in 1875. From 1881 to 1884 he was a pupil of Liszt in Weimar. He made a number of concert tours in the USA, most notably with August Wilhelmj in 1880 and Marianne Brandt in 1887. He settled in Minneapolis in the mid-1880s and in New York in 1891, where he established the Lachmund Conservatory in 1905. In 1896 he became conductor of the Women's String Orchestra of New York, a post he held for the next ten years. Lachmund's compositions are chiefly unpublished; they include two concert overtures, the "Italian" Suite for orchestra, chamber works, and piano music. He wrote a book about his experiences as a pupil of Liszt (published in German translation as *Mein Leben mit Liszt*, 1970).

CAROL NEULS-BATES

Lacy, Steve [Lackritz, Steven Norman] (*b* New York, 23 July 1934). Jazz soprano saxophonist and composer. He was inspired by Sidney Bechet to take up the soprano saxophone and to play dixieland jazz with older musicians, including Rex Stewart, who in 1953 renamed him "Lacy." Then, in a stylistic leap, he joined a quartet led by Cecil Taylor, who was beginning to embrace free jazz (1955–7). After playing with Thelonious Monk in 1960 Lacy co-led with Roswell Rudd a quartet dedicated exclusively to the performance of Monk's music (1961–4). He then played free jazz with Don Cherry, Carla Bley, Enrico Rava, and others, eventually moving to Rome in 1967 and finally to Paris in 1970. During these years he gradually established a quintet with Irene Aebi (voice and strings), Steven Potts (saxophones), Kent Carter (double bass), and Oliver Johnson (drums), to perform his own avant-garde pieces, which combine elements of formal composition with jazz improvisation and poetry. Since 1972 he has also given many solo performances on soprano saxophone.

RECORDINGS
(selective list)

As leader: *Soprano Sax* (1957, Prst. 7125); *The Straight Horn of Steve Lacy* (1960, Candid 8007); *Epistrophy* (1969, BYG 529.126); *Solo* (1972, Emanem 301); *The Way* (1979, hat Hut 2R03); *Songs* (1981, hat Art 1985–6)

As sideman: C. Taylor: *Jazz Advance* (1956, Transition 19); T. Monk: *Big Band and Quartet in Concert* (1963, Col. CS8964); C. Bley: *Jazz Realities* (1966, Fontana 881010); Musica Elettronica Viva: *United Patchwork* (1977, Horo 15–16)

BIBLIOGRAPHY

I. Gitler: "Steve Lacy," *Down Beat*, xxviii/5 (1961), 15

M. Harrison: "Steve Lacy," *Jazz Monthly*, xii/1 (1966), 7

L. Jeske: "Prolific Steve Lacy and his Poly-free Bag," *Down Beat*, xlvii/5 (1980), 20

B. Case: "Steve Lacy," *The Wire*, no.1 (1982), 6

H. Lindenmaier: *25 Years of Fish Horn Recording: the Steve Lacy Discography, 1954/79* (Freiburg, Germany, 1982)

C. Preiss: *The Steve Lacy Festival Handbook* (New York, *c*1982)

BARRY KERNFELD

Laderman, Ezra (*b* Brooklyn, NY, 29 June 1924). Composer. He attended the High School of Music and Art, New York, where he was the soloist in the first performance of his Piano Concerto (1939), given with the school orchestra. During World War II he served in the US Army and composed the *Leipzig Symphony*, which was performed in Wiesbaden in 1945. On returning to New York he studied composition with Stefan Wolpe (1946–9), who introduced him to atonal and dodecaphonic music, and at Brooklyn College, CUNY, with Miriam Gideon (BA 1949). In 1952 he received an MA from Columbia University, where he was a pupil of Otto Luening and Douglas Moore. Luening encouraged him to free himself from the more rigid aspects of atonality and to develop the long lyrical line which would become characteristic of his compositions. Having supported himself on commissions for several film and television scores, Laderman began teaching in 1960–61 at Sarah Lawrence College, where he returned in 1965–6. From 1971 to 1982 he was composer-in-residence and professor at SUNY, Binghamton. He has served in various administrative positions, including chairman of the NEA's composer-librettist program (1972), president of the American Music Center (1973–6), and director of the music program of the NEA (1979–82). Among his honors are three Guggenheim fellowships (1955, 1958, 1964), the Rome Prize (1963), and residencies at the Bennington Composers Conference (summers of 1967 and 1968) and the American Academy in Rome (1982–3).

Ezra Laderman, 1982

Laderman was one of the first of a number of composers who, in the 1970s, sought new ways of maintaining a lyrical style within a contemporary idiom. He has a genuine melodic gift, but two other characteristics of his style are particularly striking. One is the ease with which he combines tonal material with atonal or aleatory material, as in *Priorities*, for jazz ensemble, rock band, and string quartet, and the slow movement of the Piano Concerto no.1, which opens with a tonal lyric theme that is later combined in counterpoint with 12-tone material. The second characteristic is the unusual formal structures of his music, many of which arise from transformations of unexpected ideas into musical shapes; in *Double Helix* the oboe and flute repeatedly return at the same time to the tonic pitch and then move away in independent melodic and harmonic lines, thus duplicating musically the shape of DNA.

Some of Laderman's most interesting experiments appear in his string quartets. In the Fourth Quartet each instrument has its own dynamic range, "gesture" (first violin is Romantic; second violin, neoclassical; viola, expressionistic; cello, neobaroque), tempo, sound, "attitude" ("quixotic," "cool yet satiric," "dramatic and destructive," and "compassionate"), harmonic language, and meter. The voices gradually move from total independence through a series of conciliatory duets to an exultant, but short-lived, unification. The Fifth Quartet comprises three large movements: a dance suite, a sonata, and a set of variations in which a "row" based on tone colors (pizzicato, *col legno*, glissando, etc.) is used, at one point against a lyric tonal line. Laderman reused the theme of the variations, in which he again effortlessly combines tonal with atonal implications, in the second movement of his Violin Concerto. The Seventh Quartet, in one movement, begins with five separate ideas that are elaborated to suggest a combined development and recapitulation; the coda suddenly reveals a tonal melody, dirgelike and deeply moving, and the composition is transformed from an abstraction to a personal and overtly programmatic statement.

WORKS

DRAMATIC

Jacob and the Indians (opera, 3, E. Kinoy, after S. V. Benét), 1954; Woodstock, NY, 24 July 1957

Duet for Flute and Dancer (J. Erdman), 1956

Goodbye to the Clowns (opera, 1, Kinoy), 1956

Dance Quartet (Erdman), fl, cl, vc, dancer, 1957

The Hunting of the Snark (opera-cantata, 1, L. Carroll), 1958; New York, 25 March 1961, staged New York, 13 April 1978

Sarah (opera, 1, C. Roskam), 1959; CBS television, 29 Nov 1959

Machinal (incidental music, S. Treadwell), 1960; New York, 7 April 1960

Esther (dance score, Erdman), nar, ob, str orch, 1960

Song of Songs (dance score, Old Testament, choreographed A. Sokolow), S, pf, 1960

Solos and Chorale (dance score, Erdman), 4 mixed vv, 1960

Dominique (musical comedy, 2, J. Darion, after Kinoy), 1962

Air Raid (opera, 1, A. MacLeish), 1965
Shadows among us (opera, 2, N. Rosten), 1967
And David Wept (opera-cantata, 1, Darion), 1970; CBS television, 11 April 1971, staged New York, 31 May 1980
The Lincoln Mask (incidental music, V. J. Longhi), 1972; New York, 30 Oct 1972
The Questions of Abraham (opera-cantata, 1, Darion), 1973; CBS television, 30 Sept 1973
Galileo Galilei (opera, 3, Darion), 1978 [based on The Trials of Galileo]; Binghamton, NY, 3 Feb 1979
Film scores: The Charter, 1958; The Invisible Atom, 1958; The Black Fox, 1962; The Question Tree, 1962; Odyssey, 1964; The Eleanor Roosevelt Story, 1965; Magic Prison, 1966 [see also ORCHESTRAL]; The Meaning of Modern Art, 1967; Confrontation, 1968; Image of Love, 1968; The Bible as Literature, 1972; Burden of Mystery, 1972
Television scores: Herschel, 1959; The Invisible City, 1961; The Voice of the Desert, 1962; Eltanin, ?1963; Grand Canyon, 1964; The Forgotten Peninsula, 1967; Our Endangered Wildlife, 1967; California the Most, 1968; Before Cortez, 1970; In the Fall of 1844, 1971; Cave People of the Philippines, 1972; Lamp unto my Feet, 1978

ORCHESTRAL

Piano Concerto, 1939; New York, June 1939
Leipzig Symphony, 1945; Wiesbaden, Germany, May 1945
Concerto, bn, str, 1948
Concerto (Chai ivri), vn, chamber orch, 1951, rev. 1960; CBS television, 10 Nov 1963
Organization no. 1, 1952
Sinfonia, 1956; New York, 1956
Piano Concerto, 1957
Identity, 1959
Stanzas, 21 solo insts, 1959
Symphony no. 1, 1964; Rome, 2 July 1964
Magic Prison (Dickinson, Higginson, arr. MacLeish), 2 nar, orch, 1967 [based on the film score]; New York, 12 June 1967
Concerto for Orchestra (Satire), 1968; Minneapolis, 24 Oct 1968
Flute Concerto (Celestial Bodies), fl, strings, 1968; Milwaukee, 1968
Priorities, jazz band, rock band, str qt, 1969; Binghamton, NY, 1969
Symphony no. 2 "Luther," 1969
Symphony no. 3 "Jerusalem," 1973; Jerusalem, 7 Nov 1976
Viola Concerto, va, chamber orch, 1977; St. Paul, 13 April 1978
Violin Concerto, 1978; Philadelphia, 11 Dec 1980
Piano Concerto no. 1, 1978; Washington, DC, 12 May 1979
Symphony no. 4, 1980; Los Angeles, 22 Oct 1981
Summer Solstice, 1980; Philadelphia, 5 Aug 1980
Concerto, str qt, orch, 1981; Pittsburgh, 6 Feb 1981
Symphony no. 5 "Isaiah," S, orch, 1982; Washington, DC, 15 March 1983
Concerto, fl, bn, orch, 1982; Philadelphia, 27 Jan 1983
Sonore, 1983; Denver, 10 Nov 1983
Symphony no. 6, 1983; Houston, 28 Sept 1985
Symphony no. 7, 1984
Cello Concerto, 1984

VOCAL

The Eagle Stirred (Roskam), oratorio, solo vv, chorus, orch, 1961; Songs for Eve (MacLeish), S, pf, 1966; The Trials of Galileo (Darion), oratorio, solo vv, chorus, orch, 1967; Songs from Michelangelo, Bar, pf, 1968; From the Psalms, S, pf, 1970; Thrive upon the Rock (Rosten), chorus, pf, 1973; A Handful of Souls (Darion), cantata, solo vv, chorus, org, 1975
Columbus (N. Kazantsakis), cantata, B-Bar, orch, 1975; Worship (Rosten), S, T, pf, 1976; Song of Songs, chamber cantata, S, fl, cl, vn, vc, pf, 1977 [based on the dance work]; A Mass for Cain (Darion), oratorio, solo vv, chorus, orch, 1983

CHAMBER

Prelude in the Form of a Passacaglia, pf, late 1940s; Vc Sonata, 1948; Prelude, org, 1950; Fl Sonata, 1951; Pf Qnt, 1951; Pf Sonata no. 1, 1952; Str Qt, 1953; Theme and Variations, vn, pf, 1954; Ww Qnt, 1954; Duo, vn, vc, 1955; Music for Winds, Str & Hpd, 1955; Pf Sonata no. 2, 1955; Pf Trio, 1955, rev. 1959; Serenade, cl, 1956; 3 Pieces, cl, vc, pf, 1956; 3 Pieces, pf, 1956; Vn Sonata, 1956
Fl Sonata, 1957; Partita, vc, 1957, choreographed J. Erdman as Fearful Symmetry, 1959; Theme, Variations & Finale, 4 wind, 4 str, 1957; Wind Octet, 1957; Cl Sonata, 1958; Portraits, vn, 1959; Sextet, wind qnt, db, 1959; Str Qt no. 1, 1959; Ob Qt, 1960; Str Qt no. 2, 1962; Duo, vn, vc, 1963; Str Qt no. 3, 1966; A Single Voice, ob, str qt, 1967; Double Helix, fl, ob, str qt, 1968; Nonette, pf, str, wind, brass, 1968; Duo, vn, pf, 1970; 5 Trios and Fantasy, ww qnt, 1972
Partita (Meditations on Isaiah), vc, 1972; Elegy, va, 1973; Momenti, pf, 1974; Str Qt no. 4, 1974; Conc. (Echoes in Anticipation), ob, 7 insts, 1975; 25 Preludes for Org in Different Forms, 1975; Other Voices, va, tape, 1976; Str Qt no. 5, 1976; Cadence, 2 fl, 9 str, 1978; Str Qt no. 6, 1980; Partita, vn, 1982; Remembrances, vn, cl, vc, pf, 1982; Double Str Qt, 1983; Str Qt no. 7, 1983; Duo, vc, pf, 1984; Str Qt no. 8, 1985

Principal publishers: Oxford UP, G. Schirmer

BIBLIOGRAPHY

EwenD
S. Fleming: "Musician of the Month: Ezra Laderman," *HiFi/MusAm*, xxx/3 (1980), 4

PHILIP FRIEDHEIM

Lady Day. *See* HOLIDAY, BILLIE.

LaFaro, Scott (*b* Newark, NJ, 3 April 1936; *d* Geneva, NY, 6 July 1961). Jazz double bass player. He started playing the clarinet at the age of 14; later, in high school, he took up the tenor saxophone, and finally studied double bass in Ithaca and Syracuse. In 1955–6 he traveled with Buddy Morrow's band to Los Angeles, where he began his jazz career in Chet Baker's combo (1956–7). After moving to New York in 1959 he joined a trio led by the pianist Bill Evans (with the drummer Paul Motian), where he remained until his early death in an automobile accident. His recordings with Evans and Ornette Coleman (1960–61) set the standard for a new generation of jazz bass players who varied their accompaniments by mixing traditional timekeeping bass lines with far-ranging countermelodies in free rhythm.

RECORDINGS
(*selective list*)

As sideman: B. Evans: *Portrait in Jazz* (1959, Riv. 315); G. Schuller: *Jazz Abstractions* (1960, Atl. 1365); O. Coleman: *Free Jazz* (1960; Atl. 1364), *Ornette* (1961, Atl. 1378); B. Evans: *Explorations* (1961, Riv. 351), *Sunday at the Village Vanguard* (1961, Riv. 376), *Waltz for Debby* (1961, Riv. 399)

BIBLIOGRAPHY

M. Williams: "Introducing Scott LaFaro," *Jazz Review*, iii/7 (1960), 16
"A Light Gone Out," *Down Beat*, xxviii/17 (1961), 13

BARRY KERNFELD

La Forge, Frank (*b* Rockford, IL, 22 Oct 1879; *d* New York, 5 May 1953). Pianist, accompanist, teacher, and composer. Having taken piano lessons as a child with his sister, he went to Chicago at the age of 17 to study for four years with Harrison Wild, and spent the next four years in Vienna working primarily with Theodor Leschetizky, but with Josef Labor and Karel Navrátil as well. While in Vienna he gave a recital devoted entirely to the works of MacDowell. He moved to Berlin, established himself as a piano teacher, soloist, and accompanist, and, after touring Europe with Sembrich, was brought to the USA by Gadski. He became probably the most admired of recital accompanists and was much in demand by such artists as Schumann-Heink, Clément, Matzenauer, and Alda; by memorizing all his music, he was able to watch the singer at all times. He accompanied many singers in recordings and also recorded a series of accompaniments for studio use. His songs were very popular in their day and some were usually included in the programs that he accompanied; the most successful were *I came with a song*, *To a Messenger* (a favorite of Sembrich), *Like a Rosebud*, *Before the Crucifix*, *Song of the Open*, *When your dear hands*, and an arrangement of Ponce's *Estrellita*. He also published several volumes of practical editions of selections from the vocal repertory, and a number of pieces for piano (he invariably won praise for the solos he performed during song recitals – which was the custom of the time). Though he had originally established himself as a piano teacher, after World War I La Forge was sought out more as a teacher of singing and a coach; among his best-known pupils were Tibbett and Crooks. He died while playing the piano at a dinner given by the Musicians' Club of New York, of which he was president.

PHILIP LIESON MILLER

La Hache [Lahache], **Theodore (Felix) von** [De la Hache, Theodore] (*b* Dresden, Germany, March 1822/3; *d* New Orleans, LA, 21 Nov 1869). Composer. He was a pupil of Karl Gottlieb Reissiger in Dresden before immigrating to the USA in 1842. He established himself in New Orleans as a piano teacher and concert organizer. In 1850 he became organist at St. Theresa of Avila and began to write a large quantity of church music, including masses, anthems, and hymns. He was also a prolific writer of parlor piano pieces and sentimental songs; during the 1860s these reflected the patriotic fervor of the Confederate cause. After the Civil War La Hache suffered lead poisoning and was forced to curtail his teaching and performing activities; he then became a piano merchant and sheet music publisher. While his parlor music lost popularity, editions of his masses continued to be published into the early 20th century.

BIBLIOGRAPHY

W. C. Fields: *The Life and Works of Theodore von La Hache* (diss., U. of Iowa, 1973)

FRANK HOOGERWERF

Lahee, Henry Charles (*b* London, England, 2 July 1856; *d* Hingham, MA, 11 April 1953). Writer on music. After service in the British merchant marine (1871–9), he settled in Boston around 1883, where from 1891 to 1899 he was secretary of the New England Conservatory. In 1899 he established his own musical agency, from which he retired in 1951. He was the author of a number of popular historical and biographical surveys, among them several on American music; his *Annals of Music in America* includes a chronological listing of performances of important works.

WRITINGS

Famous Singers of To-day and Yesterday (Boston, 1898/*R* 1978, rev. 2/1936)
Famous Violinists of To-day and Yesterday (Boston, 1899/*R* 1977, rev. 2/1925)
Famous Pianists of To-day and Yesterday (Boston, 1901, rev. 2/1913)
Grand Opera in America (Boston, 1902/*R* 1973)
The Organ and its Masters (Boston, 1903/*R* 1976, rev. 2/1927)
The Grand Opera Singers of Today (Boston, 1912, rev. 2/1922)
Annals of Music in America (Boston, 1922/*R* 1969)
The Orchestra: a Brief Outline of its Development in Europe and America (Boston, 1925)

PAULA MORGAN

Lahmer, Reuel (*b* Maple, Ont., 27 March 1912). Composer and choirmaster. He took the BM at Westminster Choir College and did graduate work at Columbia University and Cornell University; his composition teachers were Bingham and Harris. He has taught at Cornell (1940–41), Carroll College, Waukesha, Wisconsin (1946–8), and Colorado College as head of theory and composition (1948–51); he was composer-in-residence at the American College, Leysin, Switzerland (1967–71), and Franklin College, Lugano, Switzerland (from 1971). In addition, he has served as music director of various churches and was conductor of the Pittsburgh Madrigal Singers, as well as of other choruses and choral festivals in the USA and Europe. He has appeared as an organ, harpsichord, and American folksong recitalist in several countries. His compositions are traditional in style and often based on American folk melodies or similar patterns. Festivals devoted entirely to his music were given in Rome (1959) and on Budapest radio (1966).

WORKS

(selective list)

Choral: Choral Suite, 8vv, 2 pf, 1946; Folk Fun, unison vv, fl, cl, 2 pf, 1947; Folk Fantasy, unison vv, orch, 1948; Paul Bunyan, nar, chorus, orch, 1948; The Campbells are Coming, chorus, band, 1948; Civil War Suite, chorus, 2 pf, 1956; Sing the Sweet Land, chorus, pf, wind, 1957; Glory to God, chorus, org, brass, 1960; The Passing, S, female vv, pf, 1962; Synthesis, 1973; many other pieces

Orch: Prelude and Fugal Fantasy, ww, str, 1945; Sym. Piece no. 1, 1946; Theme with Variations, str, 1946; 4 Chorale Preludes, 1948; Conc. grosso, str trio, str, 1949; Sym. Piece no. 2, 1954; Sym. for 9, 1963

Solo vocal: Song Universal, Mez, str qt, 1939; God be Merciful, S, ob/vn, va, vc, 1949; Folk Song Cycle, 1v, pf, 1950; The Way, song cycle, T, lute, viols, 1968; In the Beginning was the Word, T, vn, pf, 1970; many songs

Inst: Passacaglia and Fugue, cl, pf 4 hands, 1949; Suite on American Folk Hymns, vn, 1949; Variations on a Folk Hymn, cl, 1949; pieces for org, pf, band

Edn: *Western Pennsylvania Hymn Tune Collection* (Pittsburgh, 1957)

PEGGY GLANVILLE-HICKS/BARBARA H. RENTON

Laine, Frankie [LoVecchio, Frank Paul] (*b* Chicago, IL, 30 March 1913). Popular singer. The son of Sicilian immigrants, he received his musical training in a Catholic church choir in Chicago. He began his career as a nightclub entertainer at the age of 15 and later performed on radio programs. He modified his manner of singing from that of the contemporary crooners to a style modeled on Louis Armstrong and reminiscent of jazz singing. With his adoption of an Afro-American sound and its rhythmic liberties, pitch inflections, and jazz phrasings, Laine acquired a distinctive manner that included a host of exaggerated facial contractions and body gestures. He finally achieved recognition in Hollywood in 1946 while performing with Hoagy Carmichael, and his first recording contract (with Mercury) soon followed. His most popular recordings include *That's my desire* (1947), *Shine* (1948), *Mule Train* (1949), *That lucky old sun* (1949), *Jezebel* (1951), *High Noon* (1952), *I believe* (1953), and *Moonlight Gambler* (1957). Laine has also written several lyrics and songs, such as *We'll be together again*, *Deuces Wild*, *Horses and Women*, and *What could be sweeter*.

BIBLIOGRAPHY

"Laine, Frankie," *CBY 1956*

MICHAEL J. BUDDS

Laine, Papa Jack [George Vital] (*b* New Orleans, LA, 21 Sept 1873; *d* New Orleans, 1 June 1966). Drummer, alto horn player, and bandleader. He formed his Reliance Band in New Orleans during the 1890s, and continued to lead it for over 40 years. It was principally a marching band, and through its ranks passed many young white musicians who subsequently achieved success, including the Brunies brothers, Tom Brown, Sharkey Bonano, and various members of the Original Dixieland Jazz Band. The success of his first band led Laine to form other similar groups, and at one time he was the music director of five Reliance Bands. He also led smaller dance bands. None of his bands made recordings.

The repertory of the Laine band often included numbers that had jazz associations, but the bands themselves did not specialize in improvisation. Thus the title given to Laine, "the father of white jazz," is misleading; it was bestowed more for Laine's role as an employer and benefactor of jazz musicians than for his musical contributions. His son Alfred (1895–1957) was a well-known trumpeter in New Orleans.

BIBLIOGRAPHY

E. Souchon: "The End of an Era," *Second Line*, xvii (1966), 79

JOHN CHILTON

Lake, Mayhew [Meyhew; Mike] **(Lester)** (*b* Southville, MA, 25 Oct 1879; *d* Palisade, NJ, 16 March 1955). Composer, conductor, editor, arranger, and teacher. He studied at the New England Conservatory, and by the age of 16 was playing violin with professional symphony orchestras in Boston. From 1896 to 1910 he conducted various theater orchestras, including that of the Teatro Payret in Havana, then one of the largest theaters in the western hemisphere. He moved to New York, where he wrote arrangements for Herbert, Sousa, Edwin Franko Goldman, Grainger, Hadley, and Cohan. In 1913 he became editor-in-chief of band and orchestral music for Carl Fischer, a position he held for 35 years; his textbook, *The American Band Arranger*, was published by Fischer in 1920. He was a member of the faculty at the Ernest Williams School of Music, at Columbia University, and at New York University, where he taught orchestration. He conducted his Symphony in Gold, a symphonic band, for NBC radio. He wrote more than 3000 arrangements and compositions, some of which were published under the pseudonym Lester Brockton; examples of his arrangements are held in manuscript at the American Bandmasters Association Research Center at the University of Maryland. The Heritage of the March series of recordings (compiled by ROBERT HOE, JR.), subseries 79, includes a sample of his work. Lake also wrote an autobiography, *Great Guys: Laughs and Gripes of Fifty Years of Show-music Business* (1983).

WORKS

Selective list. All works for band unless otherwise stated; many also arranged for orch.

The Joker (1912); American Trumpeter (1914); Le siffleur coquet (1914); Lakesonian (1915); The Booster (1915); Crimson (1916); Evolution of Dixie (1916); Good Old Pals (1916); Hail, Hail the Gang's All Here (1916); Slidus Trombonus (1916); Gen. Pershing's Carry-on (1917); In a Bird Store (1917); Old Timer's Waltz (1917); Evolution of Yankee Doodle (1919); Londonderry Air (1923); American Spirit (1924); Forward March (1929)

Parade of the Gendarmes (1929); The Pilgrim (1929); Parade of Jack and Jill (1930); Ernest Williams Band School March (1932); Caprice (1934); Democracy (1934); Hungarian Fantasy (1934); Valse Caprice (1934); Yankee Rhythm (1934); Nutty Noodles (1935); Opera in the Barnyard (1935); Pleasant Recollections (1935); The Roosters Lay Eggs in Kansas (1936); Yea, Drummer (1936); Assembly Selection (1937); Coming Home (1937)

Robin Hood Fantasy (1939); Naida, cornet, band (1940); Golden Century Ov. (1941); Little Red Riding Hood (1944); In the Land of Shangri-La (1946); Kreutzer in Waukegan (1950); All Out for America (1951); Sweetheart, 3 tpt, 3 trbn, band (1982); many arrs., incl. works by Bizet, Grieg, Herbert, Massenet, Meyerbeer, Tchaikovsky, Wagner

Principal publishers: C. Fischer

RAOUL CAMUS, LEONARD B. SMITH (work-list)

Lake, Oliver (Eugene) (*b* Marianna, AR, 14 Sept 1942). Jazz saxophonist and composer. He began playing drums as a boy in St. Louis, but took up the alto saxophone at the age of 18 and later also learned flute. After studies at Lincoln University (BA 1968) he taught in public schools, played in rhythm-and-blues bands, and led the Black Artists Group (BAG), an organization similar to the Association for the Advancement of Creative Musicians in Chicago. From 1972 to 1974 he was in Paris with a BAG quintet. Since moving to New York in 1974 he has performed avant-garde jazz and classical music: he co-founded the World Saxophone Quartet in 1976; he led a trio with the guitarist Michael Gregory Jackson and the drummer Pheeroan ak Laff; he staged the *Life Dance of Is* (1977), a theatrical piece for which he wrote both music and poetry; and he has given solo concerts. He also presented a program of compositions for string quartet at Carnegie Hall (*c*1979). As leader of a commercially successful quintet, Jump Up (formed in 1981), he has added a new and startling dimension to his music: the group provides a reggae foundation that supports his characteristically screaming, chromatic, blues-drenched saxophone melodies. With Jump Up he plays alto, tenor, and soprano saxophones, and also sings.

RECORDINGS

(selective list)

As leader: *Holding Together* (1976, Black Saint 0009); *Life Dance of Is* (1978, Arista Novus 3003); *Prophet* (1980, Black Saint 0044); *Clevont Fitzhubert* (1981, Black Saint 0054); *Jump Up* (1982, Gramavision 8106); *Plug It* (1982, Gramavision 1206)

As co-leader: with J. Bowie: *In Concert* (1976, Sackville 2010); with J. Hemphill: *Buster Bee* (1978, Sackville 3018); *Steppin' with the World Saxophone Quartet* (1978, Black Saint 0027)

BIBLIOGRAPHY

D. Jackson: "Profile: Julius Hemphill, Oliver Lake," *Down Beat*, xlii/12 (1975), 32

C. J. Safane: "The World Saxophone Quartet," *Down Beat*, xlvi/16 (1979), 26

B. McRae: "Oliver Lake and Joe McPhee," *Jazz Journal International*, xxxiii/2 (1980), 25

B. Milkowski: "Oliver Lake: Sax in the Hip Pocket," *Down Beat*, l/5 (1983), 22

BARRY KERNFELD

Lakota [Teton]. American Plains Indian group belonging to the SIOUX.

Lamb, Joseph F(rancis) (*b* Montclair, NJ, 6 Dec 1877; *d* Brooklyn, NY, 3 Sept 1960). Ragtime composer. A protégé of Scott Joplin, he remained unidentified for decades because he was assumed to be a black midwesterner like Joplin and James Scott, with whom he shares honors as one of the three outstanding piano ragtime composers. His first published rag, *Sensation*, appeared in 1909 with an endorsement from Joplin. From then until 1919 he produced 12 rags on which his high reputation is based. Because Lamb spent his adult life working in the textile trade in Brooklyn, he became romanticized as a recluse amid the commercialism of Tin Pan Alley. After being rediscovered by Blesh and Janis in 1949 he resumed composing rags, occasionally performed his works in public, and recorded for the first time in 1959. An anthology of his works was published in 1964.

According to Lamb's own account he consciously composed in two distinct styles: the "light rags" (e.g., *Champagne* and *Bohemia*), making use of tuneful lines and transparent textures and culminating in the commercial idiom of the cakewalk and two-step; and the "heavy rags" (*American Beauty* and *The Ragtime Nightingale*), which abound in complex syncopations, dense textures, and virtuoso passages. In these latter works he synthesized the styles of Joplin and Scott with some of his own identifying traits: a diversity of texture (as in the opening period of *Excelsior*), diatonic and chromatic (rather than pentatonic) melodies, and chromatic harmony – including a predilection for the diminished 7th chord with an upper-neighbor appoggiatura. He made considerable use of sequential writing, creating a sense of development very uncommon to ragtime, and concentrated on an eight-bar period, in contrast to Joplin's emphasis on four-bar phrases and Scott's tendency towards two-bar phrases and an

Joseph F. Lamb, c1910

AAB structure. This last trait led to Lamb's most remarkable structural accomplishment: the complete elision of the four-bar caesura, exemplified in the opening strains of *American Beauty* and *Top Liner*.

Contrary to legend, Lamb did in fact seek a career in Tin Pan Alley, and published several songs and miscellaneous pieces. He continued to write into the 1920s; some of his pieces in the novelty style influenced his later rags. Lamb refined the piano rag into a very intimate composition, of which the prime example is his posthumously published *Alaskan Rag*, considered by many to be the supreme lyric and melodic achievement in the piano ragtime literature.

WORKS

(all printed works published in New York)

Edition: *Ragtime Treasures: Piano Solos by Joseph F. Lamb* (New York, 1964) [L]

Pf rags: Sensation (1908); Ethiopia Rag (1909); Excelsior Rag (1909); Champagne Rag (1910); American Beauty Rag (1913); Cleopatra Rag (1915); Contentment Rag (1915); The Ragtime Nightingale (1915); Reindeer (1915); Patricia Rag (1916); Top Liner Rag (1916); Bohemia Rag (1919); Alabama Rag, Arctic Sunset, Bird Brain Rag, Blue Grass Rag, Chimes of Dixie, Cottontail Rag, Firefly Rag, Good and Plenty Rag, Hot Cinders, The Old Home Rag, Ragtime Bobolink, Thorough Bred Rag, Toad Stool Rag, L; Alaskan Rag, in R. Blesh and H. Janis: *They All Played Ragtime* (New York, 3/1966); 10 others, unpubd

Other pf: Celestine Waltzes (1905); The Lilliputian's Bazaar (1905); Florentine Waltzes (1906); 11 others, unpubd

Songs: Dear Blue Eyes (L. Wood) (1908); If love is a dream let me never awake (Wood) (1908); I'm jealous of you (H. Moore) (1908); In the shade of the maple by the gate (R. Dingman) (1908); The Lost Letter (M. A. Cawthorpe) (1908); Love's Ebb Tide (S. A. White) (1908); Three leaves of shamrock on a watermelon vine (Moore) (1908); Twilight Dreams (C. E. Wellinger) (1908); Gee kid but I like you (Lamb) (1909); The homestead where the Swanee River flows (Lamb) (1909); Love in Absence (M. A. O'Reilly) (1909); I love you just the same (Lamb) (1910); My Fairy Iceberg Queen (M. Wood) (1910); Playmates (W. Wilander) (1910); I'll follow the crowd to Coney (G. Satterlee) (1913); I want to be a birdman (Satterlee) (1913); 27 others, unpubd

Principal publisher: J. Stark

BIBLIOGRAPHY

R. Blesh and H. Janis: *They All Played Ragtime* (New York, 1950, rev. 4/1971)

M. Montgomery: "A Visit with Joe Lamb," *Jazz Report* (Dec 1957)

R. Cassidy: "Joseph Lamb: Last of the Ragtime Composers," *Jazz Report*, i (Jan–Aug 1961); repr. in *Jazz Monthly*, vii (1961), no.8, p.4; no.10, p.11; no.11, p.9; no.12, p.15

M. Montgomery: "Joseph F. Lamb: a Ragtime Paradox, 1887–1960," *Second Line*, xii/3–4 (1961), 17

T. J. Tichenor: "The World of Joseph Lamb: an Exploration," *Jazz Report*, i (Jan–Aug 1961); repr. in *Jazz Monthly*, vii (1961), no.8, p.7; no.10, p.15; no.11, p.10; no.12, p.16

M. F. Den: *Joseph F. Lamb, a Ragtime Composer Recalled* (thesis, Brooklyn College, CUNY, 1975)

J. R. Scotti: *Joe Lamb: a Study of Ragtime's Paradox* (diss., U. of Cincinnati, 1977) [with list of works]

——: "The Musical Legacy of Joe Lamb," *Ragtime: its History, Composers, and Music*, ed. J. E. Hasse (New York, 1985)

JOSEPH R. SCOTTI

Lambert, Louis. Name of the composer of *When Johnny comes marching home* (1863), assumed to be the pseudonym of PATRICK S. GILMORE.

Lambord, Benjamin (*b* Portland, ME, 10 June 1879; *d* Lake Hopatcong, NJ, 7 June 1915). Organist, conductor, and composer. He had piano lessons with Arthur Whiting in Boston, then from 1897 studied with MacDowell and Cornelius Rybner at Columbia University. From 1905 to 1906 he traveled and studied in Europe, and in 1910 he studied with Paul Vidal in Paris. He served as organist at St. Luke's Cathedral, Portland, at the Fordham Reformed, Christ Presbyterian, and West End Presbyterian churches in New York, and at the Rye Presbyterian Church, Rye, New York. In 1912 he set up and became conductor of the Lambord Choral Society (from 1914 the Modern Music Society) to promote works by contemporary (especially American) composers. He was a staunch supporter of Wagner and Richard Strauss; about 1905 he presented six concerts of works by Strauss, and he organized a Wagner centennial celebration in New York in 1913. He was well regarded as a composer for his harmonic ingenuity and contrapuntal skills, but he produced only a small repertory of works, including songs, choral works, orchestral music, and piano pieces. Examples of his finest writing are found in *Clytie* op.10 no.2 for voice and orchestra and *Verses from Omar* op.11 for chorus and orchestra.

BIBLIOGRAPHY

GroveAS

A. Farwell and W. D. Darby: *Music in America*, The Art of Music, iv (New York, 1915), 420

Obituary, *New York Times* (9 June 1915)

C. Saerchinger: "A Tribute to the Memory of Benjamin Lambord," *MusAm*, xxii/7 (1915), 36

JOHN GILLESPIE

La Montaine, John (*b* Chicago, IL, 17 March 1920). Composer. He studied composition with Rogers and Hanson at the Eastman School (BM 1942), with Wagenaar at the Juilliard School, and with Boulanger at the American Conservatory in Fontainebleau, near Paris. Subsequently he was pianist with the NBC SO under Toscanini (1950–54) and taught at the Eastman School (1964–5). He has received numerous awards and commissions, including two Guggenheim Fellowships, a Pulitzer Prize (1959, for the Piano Concerto, a commission from the Ford Foundation), and an award from the American Academy of Arts and Letters (1962). A growing interest in the sounds of nature has led him to include them in several pieces, such as *Birds of Paradise*, the *Mass of*

Nature, *Wilderness Journal*, and *De rebus naturae*, the last a result of a three-week sojourn in Africa gathering bird and animal sounds. His works are predominantly lyrical and reflect a wide range of influences, including medieval music, serialism, folksong, and jazz.

WORKS

Dramatic: Spreading the News (opera), op.27, 1957; Novellis, novellis (Christmas pageant opera, La Montaine, after medieval Eng.), op.31, 1960; The Shephardes Playe (Christmas pageant opera, La Montaine, after medieval Eng.), op.38, 1967; Erode the Great (Christmas pageant opera, La Montaine, after medieval Eng.), op.40, 1969; Be Glad then America (opera, La Montaine), op.43, 1974

Orch: Canons, op.10a; Ode, ob, orch, op.11, 1957; Sonnets, op.12a, 1957; Colloquy, str, op.21; Passacaglia and Fugue, str, op.21a; Sym. no.1, op.28, 1957; Pf. Conc., op.9, 1958–9; Ov.: from Sea to Shining Sea, op.30, 1960; A Summer's Day, op.32; Canticle, op.33; Birds of Paradise, pf, orch, op.34, 1964; Incantation, jazz band, op.39; Ov.: an Early American Sampler (Be Glad then America), op.43a, 1974; Fl Conc., op.48; 2 Scenes from the Song of Solomon, fl, orch/pf, op.49; Conc. for Str Orch, op.51, 1981; Sym. Variations, pf, orch, op.50, 1982

Vocal: Songs of the Rose of Sharon (Bible), 7 songs, S, orch, op.6, 1948, arr. S, pf; Cantata: Sanctuary, Bar, chorus, org, op.17; Wonder Tidings (Christmas carols), chorus, org, harp, perc, op.23, 1957; Fragments from the Song of Songs (Bible), S, orch, op.29, 1959; Te Deum, nar, chorus, wind orch, perc, op.35, 1964; Mass of Nature, nar, chorus, orch, op.37, 1966; Wilderness Journal (Thoreau), Bar, org, orch, op.41, 1972; The Nine Lessons of Christmas (various texts), nar, solo vv, chorus, harp, perc, op.44, 1975; The Lessons of Advent, chorus/double chorus, solo vv, nar, tpt, drums, handbells, harp, ob, gui, org, op.52, 1983; The Marshes of Glynn, B, chorus, orch, op.53, 1984; other works for SATB; many songs

Chamber: Str Qt, op.16, 1957; Ww Qt, op.24a; Sonata, pf 4 hands, op.25; Conversations, cl/fl/trbn/vn/va/mar, pf, op.42; 12 Studies, 2 fl, op.46, 1979; Canonic Variations, fl, cl, op.47, 1980; other chamber works; many pf pieces

Principal publishers: Broude, C. Fischer, Fredonia

BIBLIOGRAPHY

EwenD

W. THOMAS MARROCCO/R

Lancers. A social dance popular in the second half of the 19th century, the most common variant of the QUADRILLE.

Landau, Jon(athan) (*b* Brooklyn, NY, 14 May 1947). Rock critic, record producer, and manager. While a student at Brandeis University (BA in history, 1969) he contributed regularly to *Crawdaddy!* magazine in New York and to *Rolling Stone* in San Francisco, and produced recordings by the MC5 and Livingston Taylor. In 1971 he became recordings editor of *Rolling Stone*, and also wrote film criticism. In 1974 he described Bruce Springsteen as "rock and roll future" in the *Real Paper*, and six months later helped produce Springsteen's *Born to Run* album. He also produced Jackson Browne's album *The Pretender* (1976). After a protracted legal battle with Springsteen's former manager and producer, Mike Appel, he became Springsteen's full-time manager and producer in 1978, having abandoned criticism the previous year. Landau's criticism is not the work of a polished stylist, but he achieved considerable influence through his knowledge of rock's roots, his penchant for technical explanation (as opposed to literary and metaphysical effusions), and his "auteur" theory of rock, adapted from the film criticism of Andrew Sarris. As the overseer of Springsteen's career he helped facilitate his ascendancy as a rock star. A collection of Landau's writings, *It's Too Late to Stop Now*, was published in 1972.

JOHN ROCKWELL

Landauer, Erich. *See* LEINSDORF, ERICH.

Landon, H(oward) C(handler) Robbins (*b* Boston, MA, 6 March 1926). Musicologist. After studying at Swarthmore College (1943–5) and Boston University (BM 1947), he worked as a music critic for American papers in England, France, the Netherlands, and Austria (1947–9). In 1949 he founded the Haydn Society, which planned a complete edition of Haydn's works. He has also held appointments at Queens College, New York (1969), and the University of California, Davis (1970).

Landon started publishing material on Haydn and critical editions of his music in the late 1940s. This culminated in his book *The Symphonies of Joseph Haydn* (1955; suppl., 1961), which discusses new chronologies and new texts, and places the works in the broad context of 18th-century music and of Haydn's output as a whole; it is a major landmark in Haydn studies. Landon drew fresh attention to other Haydn works, notably the masses and operas, stimulating performances and provoking a reappraisal of Haydn as a dramatic composer. More recently, he has written a massive five-volume biography, *Haydn: Chronicle and Works* (1976–80). He has also contributed to Mozart scholarship and has done much work on the sources of Austrian 18th-century music in general. He has been a prolific writer of articles, liner notes, and reviews, and has broadcast and appeared on television.

PAULA MORGAN

Landowska, Wanda (*b* Warsaw, Poland, 5 July 1879; *d* Lakeville, CT, 16 Aug 1959). Keyboard player. She was a champion of 17th- and 18th-century music and the leading figure in the 20th-century revival of the harpsichord. Having played the piano from the age of four, she first studied with Jan Kleczyński and then, at the Warsaw Conservatory, Alexander Michałowski, both Chopin specialists; in 1896 she studied composition under Heinrich Urban in Berlin, but was, in her own words, "refractory to rules." She moved to Paris in 1900, married Henry Lew (an authority on Hebrew folklore, killed in an automobile accident in 1919), and with his help threw herself energetically into research on every aspect of 17th- and 18th-century music and its interpretation. She played Bach concertos (on the piano) at the Schola Cantorum, with which she was associated for the next decade, but became increasingly convinced that only the harpsichord was really appropriate to this period. She first played the harpsichord in public in 1903 and subsequently made concert tours in Europe (including Russia, where Tolstoy was much interested in her playing and in her ideas), at the same time assiduously writing what she herself later recognized as "belligerent" articles to overcome the resistance widely shown towards the harpsichord, largely on account of the feeble tone of the available instruments. In 1909 she published her book *Musique ancienne* (7/1921), and three years later at the Breslau Bach Festival triumphantly introduced a large two-manual harpsichord built to her own specification by Pleyel.

Immediately after World War I (during which she was detained in Berlin as a civil prisoner), Landowska played a harpsichord continuo in the *St. Matthew Passion* – for the first time in this century – in Basle. She settled in Paris, where she taught at the Sorbonne and the Ecole Normale; nearby she established her own school, the Ecole de Musique Ancienne, in 1925. With four Pleyel harpsichords, she made her first visit to the USA in 1923, appearing with the Philadelphia Orchestra under Stokowski and making her first phonograph recordings (she had made some piano rolls in 1905); she also toured extensively in other countries. When the Germans approached Paris in 1940 Landowska had to abandon the school, her library of over 10,000 volumes, and her valuable collection of instruments; she left for the USA, where she eventually settled. She toured the country widely, performing and teaching, and found a new home in Lakeville, Connecticut.

Decorated by both the French and Polish governments, Landowska was also held in the highest esteem by the entire musical world. Concertos were written for her by Falla and Poulenc (*Concert champêtre*), and many of her pupils (among them Lucille Wallace, Ralph Kirkpatrick, and Rafael Puyana) later became eminent harpsichordists. She exercised an even wider influence through her numerous writings and recordings, the finest of which included Bach's *Das wohltemperirte Clavier* (recorded when she was 70), Goldberg Variations, Inventions, and Chromatic Fantasia and Fugue, as well as several Scarlatti sonatas and Handel suites. She developed modern harpsichord technique, particularly in matters of fingering, and laid emphasis on good touch and on the acquisition of a true legato and of variety of articulation. Her own playing was characterized by its vigor and sparkling vitality, and she always gave spirit precedence over letter. The registrations in her recordings appear over-colored according to later taste, but they resulted partly from the nature of the instrument she used and, like the vehemence of many of her writings, seemed necessary at the time to counter objections to the "bloodlessness" of the harpsichord. An extensive selection of her writings is to be found in *Landowska on Music* (1964), edited by her disciple Denise Restout.

BIBLIOGRAPHY

N. Dufourcq: *Le clavecin* (Paris, 1948), chap.9
R. Gelatt: *Music-makers* (New York, 1953), 254
B. Gavoty and R. Hauert: *Wanda Landowska* (Geneva, 1957)
R. Subin: "And so I am going on . . .," *American Record Guide*, xxvi (1959), 239 [with discography by I. Kipnis]
T. Bainbridge: "Wanda Landowska and her Repertoire: a Note," *Early Music*, iii (1975), 39
R. Dyson: "Bend the Finger at All Three Joints: a First-hand Record of Landowska's Teaching Methods," *Early Music*, iii (1975), 240
H. Schott: "Wanda Landowska," *Early Music*, vii (1979), 467

LIONEL SALTER/R

Landry, Richard [Dickie] (*b* Cecilia, LA, 16 Nov 1938). Saxophonist and composer. He received the BME from the University of Southwestern Louisiana in 1962 and studied instrumental performance technique with Arthur Lora in the early 1960s. He was well known for his work as saxophonist with the Philip Glass Ensemble from 1968 until 1981, during which time he appeared in all of the ensemble's recordings, including the highly acclaimed *Einstein on the Beach* (1979). In the early 1970s he began pursuing his own solo career and gave recitals throughout Europe and the USA. In 1973 he developed a new electronic performance process – quadraphonic delay – that enables him to perform with four mirror images or echoes of himself. This technique is best demonstrated in his solo album *15 Saxophones*. His strictly improvisational compositions combine the various styles and idioms of jazz, classical, and contemporary music. Landry was also one of the early pioneers of video art; his videotapes, showing him in performance, often with close-up images of his hands or mouth, have been exhibited in museums and galleries throughout the USA and Europe.

RECORDINGS

4 Cuts Placed In (Chatham Square 10, 1972); *Solos* (Chatham Square 17, 1972); *15 Saxophones* (Northern Lights 87003, 1976)

VIDEOTAPES
(distributed by Castelli-Sonnabend)

1, 2, 3, 4 (1969); Sax I (1970); Sax II (1972); Quadraphonic Delay Suite (1973); Divided Alto (1974); Six of Hearts (1974); Terri Split (1974); Two Holes (1974)

BIBLIOGRAPHY

T. Johnson: "Music on Videotape," *Village Voice* (14 Nov 1974), 62
E. Ward: "Avant-garde Sound finds a Home," *Austin American-Statesman* (15 March 1983), 3

CHARLES PASSY

Lane [Levy], **Burton** (*b* New York, 2 Feb 1912). Songwriter. At the age of 15 he was engaged as pianist by Remick music publishers, serving an apprenticeship that prepared him for a career of songwriting in revues, movies, and musical plays. On the recommendation of George Gershwin he studied music with Simon Bucharoff. His earliest compositions were songs for revues, including *Three's A Crowd* (1930), *The Third Little Show* (1931), the *Earl Carroll Vanities* (1931), and *New Americana* (1932). From 1933 to 1954 he lived in California, where he wrote songs for approximately 40 film scores, including "How about you?" (*Babes on Broadway*, 1941) and "Too late now" (*Royal Wedding*, 1951). During this period he returned to work on Broadway on three occasions, providing scores for *Hold on to Your Hats* (1940, E. Y. Harburg), *Laffing Room Only* (1944, Lane), and *Finian's Rainbow* (1947, Harburg), in the last of which his sense of melodic grace ("Something sort of grandish") and harmonic invention ("Old Devil Moon") found its most consistent outlet. Lane's meticulous craftsmanship remains evident in his only two subsequent Broadway theater scores, *On a Clear Day you Can See Forever* (1965) and *Carmelina* (1979), both collaborations with lyricist Alan Jay Lerner, and the animated musical film *Heidi's Song* (1982, S. Cahn).

BIBLIOGRAPHY

A. Wilder: *American Popular Song: The Great Innovators, 1900–1950* (New York, 1972)
W. Craig: *Sweet and Lowdown* (Metuchen, NJ, 1978)
S. Green: *The World of Musical Comedy* (New York, 1960, rev. and enlarged 4/1980)

LARRY STEMPEL

Lane, Eastwood (*b* Brewerton, NY, 22 May 1879; *d* Central Square, NY, 22 Jan 1951). Composer. His ambition in late adolescence was to become a virtuoso pianist. In 1898 he enrolled in the *belles lettres* program of the Fine Arts School at Syracuse University, but he left after three and a half years without completing a degree. Supported by a modest inheritance, he spent the next eight years reading voraciously, practicing, listening to music, and composing. In 1910 he was asked by Alexander Russell, a former classmate from Syracuse, to become assistant director of the Wanamaker Concerts in New York, a position he held for 23 years.

Lane considered himself a musical amateur and his composing a hobby; he cared little for the mechanics or theory of music. Self-taught, he learned to play the piano using the Ampico (a type of player piano) as a kinesthetic aid, and did not learn to read music until late in his career. Because music notation was a painfully slow process for him he composed entirely in his mind, perfecting a work before committing it to paper. Lane believed that all music is program music, and his works, which are in a light, descriptive vein, attempt to establish a mood or convey an image rather than tell a story. His favored medium was the piano, although he also wrote some songs; the titles of his works reveal his love of nature and interest in American subjects. Lane's compositions are miniatures characterized by simplicity, lack of sophistication, intuitive craftsmanship, engaging melodies, and spontaneity. Moderately well known during his lifetime, they are almost completely forgotten today. Lane was married to Modena Scovill, professor of composition at New York University.

WORKS

Pf: In Sleepy Hollow, 4 tone pictures (1913); 5 American Dances (1919); Adirondack Sketches (1922); Mongoliana, suite (1922); Eastern Seas, suite (1925), incl. Sea Burial, orchd F. Grofé; Persimmon Pucker (1926), orchd Grofé; Sold Down the River, ballet suite (1928); Pantomines (*c*1933); Fourth of July (1935), orchd Grofé; Here are Ladies, 5 pieces (1944); Colonial Suite; 4 other pubd pieces, 1 arr., other works

3 songs, 1v, pf; partsongs

Principal publishers: J. Fischer, Robbins

BIBLIOGRAPHY

J. T. Howard: "Eastwood Lane," *Contemporary American Composers* (New York, 1925), 23

N. P. Gentieu: "Eastwood Lane," *Journal of Jazz Studies*, iii/2 (1976), 58

KATHERINE K. PRESTON

Lane, Louis (*b* Eagle Pass, TX, 25 Dec 1923). Conductor. He studied composition with Kent Kennan at the University of Texas (BMus 1943), with Bernard Rogers at the Eastman School (MMus 1947), and with Martinů at the Berkshire Music Center (1946), where he later studied opera with Sarah Caldwell (1950). Since winning the Cleveland Orchestra's competition for apprentice conductors in 1947 and serving as its associate conductor (1956–73), he has held positions with the Akron (Ohio) SO (from 1959), the Dallas SO (1973–8), and the Atlanta SO (from 1977); he has also appeared as guest conductor with major orchestras throughout the USA and in the USSR, Poland, Finland, South Africa, Uruguay, Mexico, and Canada (where he made his international début in 1960 with Glenn Gould at the Vancouver International Festival). In 1969 he joined the faculty of the University of Akron. Lane is known for his solid craftsmanship, straightforward interpretations of the standard repertory, and vital interest in new music. His recordings with the Cleveland Orchestra include several of contemporary American music.

JAMES WIERZBICKI

Lang, B(enjamin) J(ohnson) (*b* Salem, MA, 28 Dec 1837; *d* Boston, MA, 4 April 1909). Pianist, conductor, organist, teacher, and composer. After early studies with his father, Benjamin Lang, and Francis G. Hill in Boston, he became organist and choirmaster of a Boston church at the age of 15. He went to Europe in 1855 to study composition in Berlin and piano with Alfred Jaëll and Liszt. He made his first public appearance in Boston immediately after his return in 1858, and from the early 1860s was prominent as a pianist. His fame rested particularly on his abilities as an ensemble performer and accompanist, and he performed regularly with the Mendelssohn Quintette Club. He was also active as a soloist and promoted many new works, including Tchaikovsky's First Concerto and Brahms's Second, which he played with the Boston SO (he had been the conductor at the world première of the Tchaikovsky concerto in Hans von Bülow's Boston concert in 1875); in two "Bach Concerto Concerts," in December 1898 and January 1899, he played on an Erard harpsichord imported from Paris.

Lang was active as an organist all his life, and held posts at South Congregational Church for 20 years, at Old South, and at King's Chapel; he had a reputation as a magnificent improviser. He played an important part in the planning of the organ in Boston's Music Hall, and he performed in the inaugural concerts for the instrument in 1863. From 1859 to 1895 he was the organist of the Handel and Haydn Society and assistant to its director, Carl Zerrahn; he served briefly as director (1895–7) on Zerrahn's retirement.

An ardent Wagnerian, Lang visited Wagner in July 1871 and offered his assistance in publicizing the Bayreuth Festival in America. In 1876 he was an honored guest at the first performance of the *Ring* in Bayreuth.

Lang devoted much time to teaching. Arthur Foote began piano and organ lessons with him in 1874, and Lang also taught Ethelbert Nevin, W. F. Apthorp, and his daughter Margaret Ruthven Lang. He was imaginative in the invention of exercises not found in published methods and promoted "the principle of sensible relaxation at a time when few teachers . . . had awakened to the importance of this" (Foote).

Lang's career as a conductor was of signal importance in Boston's musical life. He was a solid orchestral conductor and unsurpassed as a choral director, in which area he was Boston's principal exponent for four decades. He made his début in Boston on 3 May 1862 with the local première of Mendelssohn's *Die erste Walpurgisnacht*. On New Year's Day 1863 he shared the honors with Zerrahn in a concert to celebrate the Emancipation Proclamation. His major contribution as a choral conductor came from his work with the Apollo Club and the Cecilia Society, both of which he formed and led for several years. The Apollo Club, a men's singing society, was founded in 1868. The Cecilia Society was a mixed chorus, established in 1874 as a choral adjunct of the Harvard Musical Association and reorganized independently in 1876; Lang was conductor until 1907. The early repertory of both choirs consisted mostly of German works, some of which were given their first Boston (or even first American) performances under Lang. From about 1880 he began to introduce much more American music, including works composed especially for the singers, such as Dudley Buck's *The Nun of Nidaros*, George E. Whiting's *March of the Monks of Bangor*, and Chadwick's *The Viking's Last Voyage*.

Lang's many connections with singers and instrumentalists in Boston and his remarkable abilities as an organizer made possible two of his most elaborate contributions to Boston's musical life: the first complete performances there of Berlioz's *La damnation de Faust* (1880, with George Henschel as Mephistopheles and Lillian Bailey Henschel as Gretchen) and *Parsifal* in concert form (1891); for both of these he individually contracted singers and instrumentalists, and gathered an audience by private subscription. He was also an innovator in other aspects of concert presentation: for example, he experimented with the use of heavy paper for programs so they would not rustle in the hands of the audience, and had the texts of vocal compositions printed in the program in such a way as to avoid page turns at particularly quiet passages.

Lang composed, though he published little; even with the ensembles he conducted, he rarely performed his own music. Yet he produced an oratorio, *David*, as well as symphonies, overtures, piano pieces, church music, and songs. It was Foote's opinion that "The only thing in his musical career to regret is his steady refusal to bring his compositions before the public; there is no doubt that a genuine loss to American composition was the result." Yale awarded him an honorary MA in 1903. Lang's family papers, correspondence, and diaries, together with some scrapbooks of programs from 1861 to 1906, are in the Boston Public Library.

BIBLIOGRAPHY

T. Ryan: *Recollections of an Old Musician* (New York, 1899/*R* 1979), 84f
A. Foote: "A Near View of Mr. Lang," *Boston Evening Transcript* (1 May 1909)
W. F. Apthorp: "Thirty Years of the Symphony Orchestra," *Boston Evening Transcript* (30 Sept 1911)
G. Henschel: *Musings and Memories of a Musician* (New York, 1919/*R* 1979), 268ff
L. C. Elson: *The History of American Music* (New York, 1904, enlarged by A. Elson 3/1925/*R* 1971)
A. Foote: *An Autobiography* (Norwood, MA, 1946/*R* 1979)
M. Gregor-Dellin and D. Mack, eds.: *Cosima Wagner: die Tagebücher 1869–1877*, i (Munich and Zurich, 1976; Eng. trans. as *Cosima Wagner's Diaries*, New York, 1978)

STEVEN LEDBETTER

Lang, Eddie [Massaro, Salvatore] (*b* Philadelphia, PA, 25 Oct 1902; *d* New York, 26 March 1933). Jazz guitarist. He studied violin formally for 11 years and learned guitar from his father, a guitarist and instrument maker. He formed a successful and long-lived partnership with the jazz violinist Joe Venuti, his former schoolmate in Philadelphia, and performed with him in the early 1920s in Atlantic City. By 1924, when he recorded with the Mound City Blue Blowers, he had moved to New York. There he performed and recorded frequently with, among others, Red Nichols, Jean Goldkette, Frank Trumbauer, the Dorsey brothers, Paul Whiteman, and above all Venuti, with whom he made a series of duet recordings in 1926–8, including the noteworthy *Stringing the Blues*, their recomposition of *Tiger Rag*. After playing with Whiteman in 1929–30 he became Bing Crosby's accompanist. Lang was the first well-known solo jazz guitarist and, from the mid-1920s, was widely influential. His career coincided with the development of recording techniques suited to the acoustic guitar, which partly through his influence supplanted the banjo as a jazz instrument. He was highly regarded for his single-string solos and his accompaniments, which usually interspersed chords and single-string lines in the middle register. Although some contemporary black guitarists were better soloists, Lang's accompaniments resulted in interesting textures (but with rather undirected lines at times); he was a good rhythm guitarist with a fine technique and attained a consistently high level of performance.

RECORDINGS
(selective list)

As leader: Eddie's Twister (1927, OK 40807)
Duos with J. Venuti: Stringing the Blues (1926, Col. 914D); Doin' Things/Goin' Places (1927, OK 40825)
As sideman: L. Johnson: A Handful of Riffs (1929, OK 8695); L. Armstrong: Knockin' a Jug (1929, OK 8703); L. Johnson: Guitar Blues/Blue Guitar (1929, OK 8711)

BIBLIOGRAPHY

N. Shapiro and N. Hentoff, eds.: *Hear me Talkin' to ya* (New York, 1955), 246
R. Hadlock: *Jazz Masters of the Twenties* (New York, 1965, 2/1974), 239
A. McCarthy: *Jazz on Record* (London, 1968), 174
——: *Big Band Jazz* (London, 1974), 172

JAMES DAPOGNY/R

Lang, Margaret Ruthven (*b* Boston, MA, 27 Nov 1867; *d* Boston, 30 May 1972). Composer. She studied piano and composition with her father, Benjamin Johnson Lang, and wrote her first works at the age of 12. She learned violin with Louis Schmidt

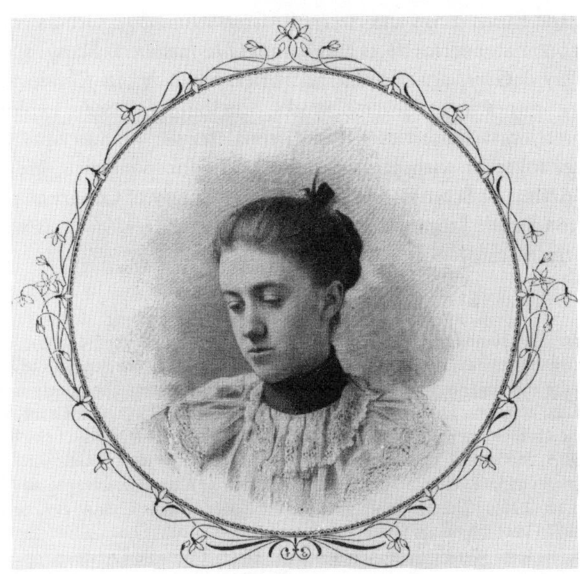

Margaret Ruthven Lang, from "Century Magazine" (March 1898)

in Boston, continuing with Franz Drechsler and Ludwig Abel in Munich (1886–7), where she also studied counterpoint and fugue with Victor Gluth. On her return to Boston she worked on orchestration with Chadwick and MacDowell. Her father continued to act as her mentor: Lang submitted for publication only those works that pleased him and, as conductor of the Cecilia and Apollo Clubs, he was regularly able to include his daughter's works in his programs.

The first works by Lang to receive a public performance were five songs included in a Boston recital by Myron W. Whitney on 14 December 1887, which received favorable reviews from local critics. Her song *Ojalá* was performed at a concert of representative American works given at the Trocadéro during the Paris Exposition of 1889; this established her reputation and the same song was repeated at the inauguration of the Lincoln Concert Hall in Washington, DC, on 26 March 1890. The soprano Mrs. Gerrit Smith gave the first of many all-Lang concerts in New York two years later. Many leading singers performed Lang's songs, including Schumann-Heink, who favored *An Irish Love Song* as an encore.

Lang was the first woman in the USA to have a work played by a major orchestra. On 7 April 1893 the Boston SO under Arthur Nikisch gave the première of her *Dramatic Overture* op. 12. The same year her overture *Witichis* op. 10 received three performances at the World's Columbian Exposition, Chicago, conducted by Theodore Thomas and Max Bendix. Other orchestral works were given by leading orchestras, and the *Ballade* op. 36 received its première on 14 March 1901 at the Women in Music Grand Concert given by the Baltimore SO. *Wind* op. 53 was commissioned by Victor Harris for his St. Cecilia Chorus of New York, and was regularly included in the group's programs. Lang's last published work, the *Elegy* op. 58 for piano, appeared in 1917, after which she ceased to compose. She remained interested in new music, however, and continued to attend concerts of the Boston SO, which gave a concert in honor of her 100th birthday.

Unlike her contemporaries, Lang made use of a restrained harmonic vocabulary with judicious use of dissonance. A number of her works draw on Scottish and Irish folk elements (for example, the Burns songs and *An Irish Mother's Lullaby*). Others contain onomatopoetic effects and humor (*The Jumblies*). Many, such as *Day is Gone*, are strophic and brief; the *Nonsense Rhymes* are witty miniatures. Several works, including *Wind*, explore impressionist sonorities within a tonal frame. Manuscripts by Lang, together with printed music and correspondence, are in the Arthur P. Schmidt Collection at the Library of Congress; the Boston Public Library has four scrapbooks (1887–1967), as well as printed music.

WORKS

(selective list; all printed works published in Boston)

Choral: The Jumblies (E. Lear), B, male chorus 4vv, 2 pf, op.5 (1890); The Wild Huntsman, 1v, 4vv, orch, lost; Te Deum, 4vv, org, op.34 (1899); Praise the Lord, o my soul, S, A, T, B, male chorus 4vv; The Lonely Rose (P. B. Marston), cantata, S, female chorus 4vv, pf, op.43 (1906); Grant, we beseech thee, merciful Lord, 4vv, org, op.51 (1912); The Night of the Star (D. A. McCarthy), cantata, 4vv, orch, op.52 (1913); Wind (J. Galsworthy), female chorus 8vv, op.53 (1913); In praesepio (R. L. Gales), 4vv, org ad lib, op.56 (1916); The Heavenly Noël (Gales), Mez, female chorus 4vv, orch, op.57 (1916); 8 others

Orch, all lost: Witichis, ov., op.10, perf. 1893; Dramatic Overture, op.12, perf. 1893; Sappho's Prayer to Aphrodite, Mez, orch, perf. 1895; Armida, S, orch, op.24, perf. 1896; Phoebus' Denunciation of the Furies at the Delphian Shrine, B, orch; Totila, ov., op.23; Ballade, d, op.36, perf. 1901; The Princess Far Away (E. Rostand), incidental music, perf. 1906

Chamber: Evening Chimes, vn, pf, op.29, perf. 1898; 2 others

Piano: Petit roman, op.18 (1894); Rhapsody, op.21 (1895); Meditation, op.26 (1897); Springtime, op.30 (1899); Revery, op.31 (1899); A Spring Idyll, op.33 (1899); The Spirit of the Old House: Elegy, op.58 (1917)

Songs, for 1v, pf, unless otherwise stated: Ghosts (R. Munkittrick) (1889); Ojalá (G. Eliot) (1889); Lament (S. Galler), op.6 no.3 (1891); The Grief of Love (J. A. Symonds), op.19 no.2 (1894); An Irish Love Song, op.22 (1895); An Irish Mother's Lullaby (M. E. Blake), with vn obbl, op.34 (1900); The Hills of Skye (W. McLennan), op.37 no.3 (1901); Day is Gone (J. V. Cheney), op.40 no.2 (1904); Nonsense Rhymes and Pictures (E. Lear), op.42 (1905); More Nonsense Rhymes and Pictures (Lear), op.43 (1907); Spring, op.47 (1909); *c*140 others

Principal publisher: Schmidt

BIBLIOGRAPHY

T. F. Ryan: *Recollections of an Old Musician* (New York, 1899/*R*1979), 85

E. Syford: "Margaret Ruthven Lang," *New England Magazine*, xlvi (March 1912), 22

Obituary, *Boston Globe* (31 May 1972)

C. Ammer: *Unsung: a History of Women in American Music* (Westport, CT, 1980), 86

ADRIENNE FRIED BLOCK

Lang, Paul Henry [Láng, Pál] (*b* Budapest, Hungary, 28 Aug 1901). Musicologist. He graduated from the Budapest Academy of Music (1922). In 1924 he began the study of musicology and comparative literature at the University of Heidelberg. He continued his work at the Sorbonne, receiving a degree in literature in 1928; while in Paris he was also assistant to Henry Prunières at the *Revue musicale*. Lang began his teaching career in the USA at Vassar (1930–31) and Wells College (1931–3). At Cornell he was awarded the PhD with a dissertation on French literature and philology in 1934, the year he became an American citizen. In 1933 he joined the faculty of Columbia University, where he was for many years professor of musicology (1939–69).

Lang took an active and influential part in American musical life. His monumental *Music in Western Civilization* (1941) is one of the outstanding 20th-century contributions to cultural history and probably his major achievement. He is also the author of *George Frideric Handel* (1966) and has published numerous articles. As editor of the *Musical Quarterly* (1945–73) he continued the development of this journal with literary and scholarly contributions, and he opened its pages to contemporary music. He was also chief music critic of the *New York Herald Tribune*, 1954–63. He was one of the founders of the American Musicological Society (1934) and served as president of the International Musicological Society (1955–8). He is also a fellow of the American Academy of Arts and Sciences.

CARLETON SPRAGUE SMITH/PAULA MORGAN

Lange, Charles. Pseudonym of CHARLES BALMER.

Lange, Hans (*b* Istanbul, Turkey, 17 Feb 1884; *d* Albuquerque, NM, 13 Aug 1960). Conductor and violinist of German descent. He studied violin at the Prague Conservatory with Otakar Ševčik (diploma 1902) and in 1903 he made his début with the Berlin PO. From 1905 to 1920 he was concertmaster of the Frankfurt Opera, among other posts. He came to the USA in 1923 and was engaged first as a violinist and then as assistant concertmaster and assistant conductor of the New York PO, relinquishing his violin position in 1931. His programs with the New York PO included works by contemporary English composers and Americans such as Luening, McBride, Bernard Rogers, and Ruggles. In 1936 he was appointed associate conductor of the Chicago SO, where he remained for 11 years; from 1946 to 1949 he directed the Friends of Music Orchestra in Toledo. In 1951 he became conductor of the Albuquerque SO and held that post until his retirement in 1958. In addition to conducting a number of other organizations throughout his career, Lange organized two string quartets and a chamber series, and made several recordings.

ROBERT SKINNER

Langer, Susanne K(atherina) (*b* New York, 20 Dec 1895; *d* Old Lyme, CT, 17 July 1985). Philosopher. After studying philosophy at Radcliffe College (PhD 1926), she taught at various institutions between 1927 and 1954, when she was appointed professor at Connecticut College; she was a research scholar there until her retirement in 1962. Between 1940 and 1960 her publications centered on a philosophy of art derived from a theory of musical meaning which in turn exemplified a general philosophy of mind. According to *Philosophy in a New Key* (1942, 3/1957), all the modes of understanding characteristic of mankind are forms of symbolic transformation: that is, we understand any phenomenon by constructing an object analogous to it or referring to it. The structural principles embodied in these constructed objects are amenable to logical analysis. Langer used music as a paradigm of a system of symbols whose elements are presentational rather than discursive, have meaning but do not assert anything. Her later works, *Feeling and Form* (1953) and *Problems of Art* (1957), generalize this account into a theory of all the fine arts.

F. E. SPARSHOTT/PAULA MORGAN

Lanier, Sidney (Clopton) (*b* Macon, GA, 3 Feb 1842; *d* Lynn, NC, 7 Sept 1881). Poet, writer on music, flutist, and composer. He was descended from a family of musicians associated with the English court in the late 16th and early 17th centuries. He became proficient on many instruments as a child, later proclaiming himself self-taught in most musical matters. He graduated from Oglethorpe University in 1860 and served in the Confederate Army during the Civil War. He then spent several years in family business ventures, but in 1873 resolved to devote his time and energy entirely to literary and musical pursuits.

As a writer Lanier is best known for his sensitive poetry, some of which (notably *The Ballad of Trees and the Master* and *Evening Song*) was set to music by Chadwick, Hadley, and others, but he also produced several books and scholarly essays on music, a translation of Wagner's *Das Rheingold*, and a libretto for Buck's cantata *The Centennial Meditation of Columbus* (1876), and gave lectures on music and literature at Johns Hopkins University. He was highly regarded as a flutist, known particularly for his facile technique and an unusual skill in sight-reading. His compositions for the flute, as well as those for other instruments, are generated more by idiomatic qualities than by a mature grasp of musical composition. He was appointed solo flutist with the Peabody Orchestra in Baltimore, which provided him with recognition as a professional musician at a time when most orchestras were dominated by performers from abroad. His work with the orchestra, coupled with brief visits to New York, introduced him to the repertory and the progressive musical thought of the late 19th century.

Lanier became an ardent admirer of Richard Wagner and put forth views similar to Wagner's own on the interrelation of art, science, and religion. Much of his work dealt with a systematic study of the relation between poetry and music: he developed a technique of describing poetic meter through musical notation, and compared the phonetic structure of poetry with the timbre of music. His views have generated considerable debate between those extolling his systematic approach to a complex problem and those criticizing his efforts as ill-founded and essentially naive. His principal publications on the subject were *The Science of English Verse* (1880), an important study of English prosody, *The English Novel* (1883), and *Music and Poetry* (1899). A collection of his writings (*The Centennial Edition of the Works of Sidney Lanier*), edited by C. R. Anderson, was published in 1945.

WORKS

Inst (for solo fl unless otherwise stated): Sacred Memories, perf. 1868; Bird Song, 1872; Condilicatezza, 1872; Heimweh Polka, 1872; Song of the Lost Spirit, 1872; Danse des moucherons (Gnat Symphony), fl, pf, op. 1, 1873; Fieldlarks and Blackbirds, 1873; Wind Song, 1874; Wald-Einsamkeit; The Widow Sings the Child to Sleep (Orphan's Cradle Song), fl, pf; Old Sister Phebe, fl, vn; Die Wacht am Rhein, pf; sketches; arrs. for 3 fl/fl, pf of works by Verdi, Donizetti, others

Songs (for 1v, pf unless otherwise stated): The Song of Elaine (A. Tennyson), *c*1862; The Song of Love and Death (Tennyson), 1862; Little Ella (Lanier) (Montgomery, AL, 1866); Break, break, break (Tennyson), *c*1871; Flow down, cold rivulet (Tennyson), *c*1871; Love that hath us in the net (Tennyson) (New Orleans, 1884); The Cuckoo Song, 4vv; My life is like a summer rose (H. Wilde), lost

MSS in *MdBJ*

BIBLIOGRAPHY

E. Mims: *Sidney Lanier* (Boston, 1905)

T. E. Dewey: *Poetry in Song* (Kansas City, 1907)

J. W. Wayland: *Sidney Lanier at Rockingham Springs* (New York, 1912/*R*1971)

E. D. Lamar: *Sidney Lanier: Musician, Poet, Soldier* (Macon, GA, 1922)

H. C. Thorpe: "Sidney Lanier: a Poet for Musicians," *MQ*, xi (1925), 373

E. Mims: "Lanier, Sidney," *DAB*

A. H. Starke: *Sidney Lanier: a Biographical and Critical Study* (Chapel Hill, 1933)

——: "Sidney Lanier as a Musician," *MQ*, xx (1934), 384; repr. in *Music in Georgia*, ed. F. Hoogerwerf (New York, 1983)

L. Lorenz: *The Life of Sidney Lanier* (New York, 1935)

J. W. Hendren: "Time and Stress in English Verse with special reference to Lanier's Theory of Rhythm," *Rice Institute Pamphlet*, xlvi/2 (1959) [complete issue]

J. S. Edwards: "Sidney Lanier: Musical Pioneer," *Georgia Review*, xxii (1968), 473; repr. in *Music in Georgia*, ed. F. Hoogerwerf (New York, 1983)

M. H. Frank: *Music in American Literary History: a Survey of the Significance of Music in the Writings of Eight American Literary Figures* (diss., New York U., 1968)

R. Higgins: *Sidney Lanier, Musician* (diss., Peabody Conservatory, 1969)

J. De Bellis: *Sidney Lanier* (New York, 1972)

J. S. Gabin: *A Living Minstrelsy: the Poetry and Music of Sidney Lanier* (diss., U. of North Carolina, 1977)

J. De Bellis: *Sidney Lanier, Henry Timrod, and Paul Hamilton Hayne* (Boston, 1978)

M. A. Hovland: *Musical Settings of American Poetry: a Bibliography* (Westport, CT, in preparation) [incl. list of settings]

DOUGLAS A. LEE

Lansky, Paul (*b* New York, 18 June 1944). Composer. He studied at Queens College, CUNY, with Perle and Weisgall (BA 1966) and with Babbitt, Cone, and Kim at Princeton University (PhD 1969), where he was appointed to the faculty in 1969. He played horn in the Dorian Wind Quintet (1965–6) and became associate editor of *Perspectives of New Music* in 1972. He has received a League of Composers-ISCM electronic music award (1975), awards from the American Academy and Institute of Arts and Letters (1977) and the Koussevitzky Foundation (1981), and an NEA grant (1981).

In his dissertation (*Affine Music*, 1969) Lansky developed a theoretically systematized statement of Perle's 12-tone tonality; this system's pitch and chord derivations and their embedded relationships are the basis for Lansky's compositions, which display firm tonal relationships within each section and in global structures, as well as sensitivity to the functions of timbre and timbral mixtures. He has written for conventional instruments and voice but also uses computer-generated sounds, including manipulation of voice and text (as in the Campion fantasies).

WORKS

Inst: Modal Fantasy, pf, 1969; Str Qt, 1972–7; Crossworks, pf, fl, cl, vn, vc, 1974–5; As If, str trio, cptr, 1982; other chamber and tape works

Cptr: Mild und leise, 1973–4; Artifice (on Ferdinand's Reflections), 1975–6; 6 Fantasies on a Poem by Thomas Campion, 1978–9; Folk Images, 1980–81; As it Grew Dark, 1981–3

Principal publisher: Boelke-Bomart

RICHARD SWIFT

Lanza, Alcides (*b* Rosario, Argentina, 2 June 1929). Argentinian composer. He studied in Buenos Aires at the Torcuato di Tella Institute with Ginastera, Messiaen, Copland, Maderna, and Malipiero (1963–4), and in New York at the Columbia-Princeton Electronic Music Center with Ussachevsky (1965). He was awarded a Guggenheim Fellowship in 1965, and lived in the USA until 1971, composing and teaching electronic music at the Columbia-Princeton Electronic Music Center (1966–70) and lecturing on music appreciation. In 1971 he joined the music faculty of McGill University, Montreal, Canada. He has been active in promoting performances of contemporary music in many cities of North and South America, is director of the Composer's Group for International Performance, and music director of the Composers/Performers Group, based in New York. His major preoccupation has been with electronic music, especially its composition, recording, and notation. *Eidesis II*, first performed at the Berkshire Music Center in 1967, is described in Lanza's words as "masses of sound in motion, with an enormous charge of sensuality." Other important works from Lanza's years in the USA are *Plectros II* (1966), *Strobo I* (1967), *Ekphonesis II–III* (1968–9), and *Penetrations II–V* (1969–70). Since his youth he has traveled extensively in the Americas as a pianist and conductor.

BIBLIOGRAPHY
Compositores de América/Composers of the Americas, ed. Pan American Union, xvii (Washington, DC, 1971)

SUSANA SALGADO/R

Lanza, Mario [Cocozza, Alfred Arnold] (*b* Philadelphia, PA, 31 Jan 1921; *d* Rome, Italy, 7 Oct 1959). Tenor. He first studied singing while working as a piano mover in Philadelphia, and in 1942 was awarded a summer scholarship at the Berkshire Music Center. Shortly afterwards he entered the Special Services of the armed forces and sang regularly for military radio shows during World War II. After his discharge he made a series of concert appearances, including a performance at the Hollywood Bowl in 1946. His first film role in *That Midnight Kiss* (1949) brought him immediate national recognition and fame. He subsequently made six further films, including *The Great Caruso* and *The Toast of New Orleans*, in which he sang his greatest hit, *Be my Love*. Although he possessed a voice of great power and range, Lanza sang in only one opera, Puccini's *Madama Butterfly*, with the New Orleans Opera (1948). He was idolized as a romantic figure with a marvelous voice who chose films over opera. In the early 1950s he presented his own radio show. At this time his problems with obesity became increasingly severe, and they may have contributed to his early death at the age of 38.

JEAN W. THOMAS

Laotian-American music. *See* ASIAN-AMERICAN MUSIC, §6(i)(a).

Lap dulcimer. *See* APPALACHIAN DULCIMER.

Laredo (y Unzueta), Jaime (Eduardo) (*b* Cochabamba, Bolivia, 7 June 1941). Violinist and conductor. His family moved to the USA when he was seven to enable him to further his musical training; he was taught by Antonio de Grassi and Frank Houser in San Francisco, Josef Gingold in Cleveland, and Ivan Galamian at the Curtis Institute. After making his professional début with the San Francisco SO at the age of 11, he toured Latin America on a number of occasions. In 1959 he became the youngest winner of the Queen Elisabeth Competition in Brussels; in the same year he appeared with the orchestras of Boston, Philadelphia, and Cleveland, and made his Carnegie Hall début on 19 October. He has since performed throughout the USA and Europe. A frequent visitor to the Marlboro Festival, he has recorded Beethoven's Triple Concerto with Rudolf Serkin, Leslie Parnas, and the Marlboro Festival Orchestra, a recording which well represents his style. He also recorded the Bach violin sonatas with Glenn Gould. In 1974 Laredo became artistic director of the chamber music program at the 92nd Street "Y," New York. Two years later he formed a trio with the pianist Joseph Kalichstein and the cellist Sharon Robinson (*b* Houston, TX, 2 Dec 1949), his second wife (he was formerly married to the pianist Ruth Meckler Laredo). He has also been a member of the Chamber Music Society of Lincoln Center. In 1977 he became associated with the Scottish Chamber Orchestra, with which he has appeared frequently as soloist and conductor, notably on tours of the USA in 1981 and 1983. He joined the faculty of the St. Louis Conservatory in 1983.

Laredo is an aristocratic and predominantly lyrical performer; he is not as demonstrative as other Galamian pupils, but his clean intonation and meticulous phrasing make him valuable as an ensemble player. He owns a 1717 violin by Stradivari known as the "ex-Gariel." His honors include the New York City Handel Medallion (1960) and a series of Bolivian airmail stamps which bear his portrait and the notes A, D, and C (la-re-do).

BIBLIOGRAPHY
"Laredo (Y Unzueta), Jaime," *CBY 1967*
B. Schwarz: *Great Masters of the Violin* (New York, 1983)

RICHARD BERNAS/R

Laredo, [née Meckler], **Ruth** (*b* Detroit, MI, 20 Nov 1937). Pianist. She studied at the Curtis Institute under Rudolf Serkin, gaining the BM in 1960; in that year she married the violinist Jaime Laredo, from whom she was divorced in 1976. She made her orchestral début with Stokowski and the American SO at Carnegie Hall in 1962 and has since appeared with many of the major orchestras in the USA and toured widely as a soloist; she has played much of the chamber music repertory and has participated regularly in the Mostly Mozart, Marlboro, Aspen, Caramoor, and Spoleto festivals. She is particularly known for her recordings of the complete solo piano works of Rachmaninoff (on which she published an article in *Keynote*, vii/2, 1983, p.6) and the complete piano sonatas and preludes of Scriabin, which helped to revive interest in that composer in the USA. She has held teaching positions at SUNY, Binghamton (1972–3), Kent State University (1969–71), and the Yale School of Music (1977–9).

ELLEN HIGHSTEIN

LaRocca, Nick [Dominic]. Jazz cornetist who cofounded and led the ORIGINAL DIXIELAND JAZZ BAND.

Larsen [Reece], **Libby** [Elizabeth] **(Brown)** (*b* Wilmington, DE, 24 Dec 1950). Composer. She studied composition with Argento, Stokes, and Paul Fetler at the University of Minnesota, where she received the BA (1971), MM (1975), and PhD (1978) in theory and composition. In 1973, with Stephen Paulus, she founded the Minnesota Composers Forum in Minneapolis, thereafter serving as one of the organization's managing composers. In 1983, again with Paulus, she was appointed one of the Minnesota Orchestra's composers-in-residence. She was awarded a composition grant from the Minnesota State Arts Board in 1977 and a National Opera Institute fellowship in 1980. Her music draws on a wide variety of stylistic models, including American popular music. The lyric passages prominent in her works for solo instruments and voices are typically spiced with atonal digressions; the closely packed blocks of pitches characteristic of her orchestral works are generally rooted in clearly defined and often repeated harmonic patterns.

WORKS

Stage: The Words upon the Windowpane (opera, 1, Yeats), 1978, Minneapolis, 1978; The Silver Fox (children's opera, 1, J. Olive), 1979, St. Paul, MN, 1979; Tumbledown Dick (opera, 2, V. Sutton), 1980, St. Paul, 1980; Clair de lune (opera, 3, P. Hampl), 1984, Little Rock, AR, 1985

Inst: Theme and Deviations, harp, 1972; Tom Twist (W. A. Butler), nar, mime, orch, 1975; Weaver's Song and Jig, str band, chamber orch, 1978; Bronze Veils, trbn, perc, 1979; 3 Cartoons, orch, 1979; Ulloa's Ring, fl, pf, 1980; Scudding, vc, 1980; Triage, harp, 1981; Aubade, fl, 1982; Pinions, vn, chamber orch, 1982; Ov., Parachute Dancing, orch, 1984; Sym. no. 1 "Water Music," New York, 30 Jan 1985; *c*5 other inst works

Vocal: Lacrimosa Christe (various poets), solo vv, chorus, orch, 1974; Saints without Tears (P. McGinley), S, fl, bn, 1976; 3 Rilke Songs, S, harp, fl, gui, 1977; Eurydice (H. D.), S, str qt, 1978; Dance Set, SATB, cl, vc, perc, pf, 1980; In a Winter Garden (Hampl), S, T, SATB, chamber orch, 1982;

A Creeley Collection (R. Creeley), T, SATB, fl, perc, 1984; a few other solo and choral works

Principal publisher: E. C. Schirmer

JAMES WIERZBICKI

LaRue, (Adrian) Jan (Pieters) (*b* Kisaran, Sumatra, Indonesia, 31 July 1918). Musicologist. He attended Harvard (BS 1940) and began graduate work at Princeton (MFA 1942), then returned to Harvard for additional studies (PhD 1952). After teaching at Wellesley College (1942–3, 1946–57) he joined the faculty of New York University in 1957.

LaRue has done research in both ethnomusicology and historical musicology. He has studied the native vocal and instrumental music of Okinawa and wrote his dissertation on this subject. Among his more recent interests are late 18th-century music, style analysis, and tools of research, including watermark analysis, study of publishers' catalogues, and computer applications in musicology. He has sought to combine and relate these interests through such projects as computer-aided preparation of thematic catalogues and use of the computer for problems of analysis. His examinations of 18th-century publishers' catalogues have furnished information concerning dating of publications, musical tastes, and the speed with which music prints were disseminated throughout Europe. *Guidelines for Style Analysis* (1970) provides both a methodology and a system of analytical symbols for the student. LaRue's professional activities have included a period as president of the American Musicological Society (1966–8); he was co-editor of the Deutsch 80th-birthday Festschrift, the Reese Festschrift, and the eighth International Musicological Society congress report.

PAULA MORGAN

LaSalle Quartet. String quartet. It was formed in 1949 by students from the Juilliard School. The first violinist, Walter Levin (*b* Berlin, Germany, 6 Dec 1924), studied under Galamian at Juilliard; the second violinist, Henry Meyer (*b* Dresden, Germany, 29 June 1923), studied at the Prague Music Academy, in Paris with George Enescu and Rene Benedetti, and with Galamian at Juilliard; the violist, Peter Kamnitzer (*b* Berlin, 27 Nov 1922), studied at the Manhattan and Juilliard schools; the cellist, Lee Fiser (*b* Portland, OR, 26 April 1947), who joined the quartet in 1975 (replacing Jack Kirstein, a member from 1955), studied at the Cleveland Institute and was a member of the Cincinnati SO up to 1975. The ensemble was quartet-in-residence at Colorado College (1949–53), and then at the Cincinnati College-Conservatory of Music, where all four members became professors (in October 1982 they gave a concert in Alice Tully Hall to celebrate the 30th year of their residency). The quartet made its European début in 1954 and has toured extensively in the USA and abroad. It performs works of all periods but is best known for its performances and recordings of Schoenberg, Berg, and Webern, and the late quartets of Beethoven. Among the many composers who have written music for the quartet are Hans Erich Apostel, Herbert Brün, Earle Brown, Henri Pousseur, Wolf Rosenberg, Kagel, Ligeti, Penderecki, and Lutosławski. In 1958 the quartet acquired a matched set of Amati instruments: two violins by Nicolo (1648 and 1682), a viola by Antonio and Girolamo (1619), and a cello by Nicolo (1670). Although the LaSalle Quartet is associated mainly with 20th-century music, its playing of it is not archetypally "modern." Rather it is compounded of tonal richness (with pronounced vibrato), broad tempos, and, at all times, linear clarity. In its famous performances and recordings of the works of the Second Viennese School, the quartet is able to project the essence of the music's "modernity" while at the same time exposing its roots in 19th-century Romanticism.

HERBERT GLASS

Lateef, Yusef [Evans, William] (*b* Chattanooga, TN, 9 Oct 1920). Jazz tenor saxophonist and composer. He began playing music while in high school in Detroit, and gained experience with Roy Eldridge, Dizzy Gillespie, and others before forming his own bands in Detroit in the 1950s. After moving to New York in 1959 he began to gain recognition for his use of Asian and Middle Eastern rhythms and instruments in his groups; he was also noted for his sturdy, full sound on tenor saxophone and tasteful solos on flute. In the early 1960s he played in the bands of Charles Mingus, Cannonball Adderley, and several others; since then he has led his own groups, recording prolifically and occasionally performing on the oboe with remarkable success. Lateef is also a noted painter and writer, and has spent much of his time teaching in recent years. He has written a number of sonatas and other works for flute and piano or chamber groups.

RECORDINGS

(selective list)

The Dreamer (1959, Savoy 12139); *Eastern Sounds* (1961, Moodsville 22); *Club Date* (1964, Imp. 9310); *Psychicemotus* (1965, Imp. 92); *The Golden Flute* (1966, Imp. 9125); *Yusef Lateef* (*c*1968, Cadet 816); *In a Temple Garden* (1979, CTI 7088)

BIBLIOGRAPHY

SouthernB

L. Feather: *The Pleasures of Jazz* (New York, 1976/*R*1977)

L. Lyons: "Life Begins at 60," *Down Beat*, xlv/6 (1978), 17

A. Groves: "Consistent Craftsman," *Jazz Journal International*, xxxiii/9 (1980), 14

LEE JESKE

Lateiner, Jacob (*b* Havana, Cuba, 31 May 1928). Pianist. From 1934 to 1940 he studied in Havana with Jascha Fischermann, and in 1940 he went to the Curtis Institute, where he studied piano with Isabelle Vengerova and chamber music with Primrose and Piatigorsky; he also studied composition with Felix Greissle and, in 1950, with Schoenberg. He made his début in 1945 with the Philadelphia Orchestra under Ormandy, as winner of the Philadelphia Youth Competition. In 1947 he was engaged by Koussevitzky for the Berkshire Music Festival and he made his New York recital début the following year. By this time he had already made many appearances in the USA and had toured Australia. After service in the US Army he continued his career, and from 1954 he played throughout the USA and made a number of appearances in Europe. Lateiner has been associated particularly with Beethoven (on whom he has taught courses and lectured) and with contemporary American music. He commissioned Elliott Carter's Piano Concerto under a Ford Foundation Fellowship for performing artists; in 1967 he gave its première with the Boston SO under Leinsdorf, and he later recorded it. In 1968 he gave the first performance of Sessions's Third Piano Sonata. He frequently played and recorded chamber music with Heifetz and Piatigorsky. From 1963 to 1970 he taught at the Mannes College, and in 1966 he joined the faculty of the Juilliard School. He has served on many international piano competition juries.

RONALD KINLOCH ANDERSON/R

Latin American music. The rhythms and instrumentation of Latin American folk music have exercised a far-reaching influence on some genres of American popular music and have also found their way into concert music. *See* especially HISPANIC-AMERICAN MUSIC, §3, LATIN JAZZ, and SALSA; *see also* AFRO-CUBAN JAZZ.

Latin jazz. A term applied to jazz in which elements of Latin American music, chiefly its dance rhythms, are particularly prominent. It utilizes duple subdivisions of the beat, in striking contrast to the triple subdivisions prevalent in jazz that swings. But unlike ragtime and jazz-rock, which also have a duple subdivision, Latin jazz rhythms are built from strings or multiples of a basic durational unit, grouped unequally so that the accents fall irregularly in a one- or two-bar pattern. The habanera (or danza) rhythm (ex. 1) is the simplest and commonest of these

Ex.1 Habanera rhythm

groupings. The rhythmic ostinato may be played by members of a conventional rhythm section (piano, guitar, double bass, and drums), or by Latin American instruments, particularly Afro-Cuban or Brazilian percussion such as the *conga* drum, bongos, claves, cowbells, and *cuíca*; the bass line often oscillates between the roots and fifths of chords.

Latin American elements are found in early jazz and related musics. Isolated instances of habanera rhythm, which also formed the basis of the tango, occur in left-hand figurations in published piano rags (Neil Moret's *Cubanola (Cuban Danza)*, 1902; Scott Joplin's and Louis Chauvin's *Heliotrope Bouquet*, 1907; Joe Jordan's *Tango: Two Step*, 1913; and Artie Matthews's *Pastime Rag no.5*, 1918), as well as in the second section of W. C. Handy's famous *St. Louis Blues* (1914). These rhythmic patterns were probably carried over into the earliest jazz, though the lack of recordings from this era makes it difficult to establish the sequence of development. By 1923, at all events, Latin ostinatos were already part of Jelly Roll Morton's style: in his recordings of *New Orleans Joys* (also known as *New Orleans Blues*; 1923) and portions of *Mamamita* (1924), he maintains a habanera rhythm in his left hand. Calling it "the Spanish tinge," Morton claimed that this rhythmic element was essential to jazz.

During the 1930s new Latin dances entered the mainstream of American popular music through bandleaders such as Don Azpiazú (who popularized the rumba) and Xavier Cugat. They occasionally found their way into jazz, as in Duke Ellington's recordings of two compositions by his Puerto Rican trombonist Juan Tizol: *Caravan* (1937) and *Conga Brava* (1940). In the 1940s Cuban instruments and instrumentalists became firmly linked to jazz through a reciprocal process. In New York in the early part of the decade the bandleader Machito formed the Afro-Cubans, in which big-band instrumentation and arranging techniques were combined with Cuban percussion and musical structures; from 1948 to the 1960s he engaged famous jazzmen, including Brew Moore, Charlie Parker, Flip Phillips, Howard McGhee, Cannonball Adderley, Cecil Payne, and Johnny Griffin, as soloists. In 1947 Dizzy Gillespie established his Afro-Cuban jazz orchestra, which included the conga drummer Chano Pozo, and in the same year Stan Kenton introduced the Brazilian guitarist Laurindo Almeida and the bongo drummer Jack Costanzo into his jazz orchestra.

During the 1950s another generation of Latin dances became popular in the USA: the mambo, the merengue, and the cha cha cha were quickly incorporated into the repertories of big bands that played jazz for dancing. In small bop groups Latin tunes regularly supplemented the normal fare of swing standards, ballads, and blues; examples include Parker's *My Little Suede Shoes* (1951) and Bud Powell's *Un poco loco* (1951). Latin elements became so integral to the bop style that by the late 1950s their presence was no longer remarkable; but some bop musicians laid particular emphasis on Latin sounds, among them George Shearing, Cal Tjader, Sonny Rollins (composer of and improviser on calypso tunes), Horace Silver, and Herbie Mann.

The 1960s witnessed the emergence of strong Brazilian influences on jazz. The energetic samba and the quiet bossa nova reached a wide audience through the recordings of Stan Getz, the guitarist Charlie Byrd, the singer Astrud Gilberto, and the composer Antonio Carlos Jobim. Cuban elements continued to be prevalent, both through bop and in the music of the percussionists Mongo Santamaria and Willie Bobo, whose bands combined popular songs, Cuban vamps, and impassioned hard-bop improvisations. In the late 1960s the percussionist Airto Moreira initiated a second period of Brazilian influence by introducing Brazilian rhythms and dozens of native instruments into jazz-rock groups in the USA. He recorded with Miles Davis (whose many improvisations on Spanish flamenco music are perhaps related to Latin jazz); during the early 1970s he was the first of a series of Brazilian percussionists in the group Weather Report, and he was in Chick Corea's first Return to Forever group, as was his wife, the Brazilian singer Flora Purim.

Other facets of Latin jazz developed within free jazz, a music that encourages experimentation with various ethnic styles. During the 1970s Gato Barbieri made many recordings in which Argentinian rhythmic vamps are combined with his wildly energetic tenor saxophone playing. The Art Ensemble of Chicago recorded a playful distortion of reggae music, *Ja* (1978), and the free-jazz saxophonist Oliver Lake founded Jump Up, a commercial reggae group, in 1981. Two musicians embody the continued influence of Latin music on jazz in the 1980s: the Brazilian percussion and berimbau player Nana Vasconcelos has been a member of Pat Metheny's jazz-rock groups and of the free-jazz trio Codona, with Don Cherry and Collin Walcott; the alto saxophonist Paquito D'Rivera leads small bop combos in performances of Afro-Cuban jazz. *See also* AFRO-CUBAN JAZZ.

BIBLIOGRAPHY

J.-E. Berendt: *Das Jazzbuch: Entwicklung und Bedeutung der Jazzmusik* (Frankfurt am Main, Germany, 1953; Eng. trans. as *The New Jazz Book: a History and Guide*, New York, 1962, rev. and enlarged as *The Jazz Book: from New Orleans to Jazz Rock and Beyond*, 1982)

M. Williams: "Jelly Roll Morton," *Jazz*, ed. N. Hentoff and A. J. McCarthy (New York, 1959/*R*1974), 59

J. S. Roberts: "Latin Persuasions: a Brief Overview of a Vital Musical Genre," *Down Beat*, xliv/8 (1977), 13

——: *The Latin Tinge* (New York, 1979)

E. A. Berlin: *Ragtime: a Musical and Cultural History* (Berkeley, CA, 1980/*R*1984 with addenda), 115

BARRY KERNFELD

Latter-day Saints, music of the Church of the. *See* CHURCH OF JESUS CHRIST OF LATTER-DAY SAINTS, MUSIC OF THE.

Latvian-American music. The music of the Latvian community in the USA is discussed as part of the Baltic tradition; *see* EUROPEAN-AMERICAN MUSIC, §III, 3.

Lauper, Cyndi (*b* New York, 20 June 1953). Rock singer and songwriter. She became involved in folk and rock music in New York as a teenager, and in the late 1970s sang in a band called Blue Angel, which recorded a critically admired but popularly ignored album in 1980. Her first solo album, *She's So Unusual* (Portrait BFR38930, 1983), contained five hit singles and sold four million copies. Lauper has a powerful rock voice, a stylistically wide-ranging musicality, a songwriter's gift and a facility for selecting and adapting songs by others; she also has a dizzy, endearing personality.

BIBLIOGRAPHY

K. Loder: "Dream Girl," *Rolling Stone* (24 May 1984), 13
K. K. Willis, Jr.: *Cyndi Lauper* (New York, 1984)

JOHN ROCKWELL

Laurendeau, Louis-Philippe (*b* St. Hyacinthe, Que., 1861; *d* Montreal, Que., 13 Feb 1916). Canadian composer and arranger. Early in his career he was director of music at the military school of Saint-Jean in Quebec. He moved to New York to join the firm of Carl Fischer, where he was staff composer and arranger for 30 years, maintaining this association even after his return to Canada. His *Practical Band Arranger*, published by Fischer in 1911, was for many years the standard text on the subject. Laurendeau wrote more than 400 compositions, including galops, waltzes, serenades, and polkas; of his original works, only the nautical medleys *Before the Mast* and *Our Jackies* are well known, but many of his arrangements remain popular. Some of his works appeared under the pseudonyms G. H. Reeves (which has led to his being confused with the march composer and bandmaster David Wallis Reeves) and Paul Laurent. A number of his compositions are recorded in the Heritage of the March series (compiled by ROBERT HOE, JR.), subseries 23, 33, S, W, II, and HHHH.

WORKS

(most works published in versions for band, orch, and theater or chamber orch)

*c*85 marches, incl. Advance Guard, Alexandria, Athletic Club, Brocktonian, The Chairman, The Clubman, Conqueror, Flag of Truce, Golconda, Lance and Shield, Mount Royal, Oregonia, Semper vivax, White Feather; *c*25 waltzes, incl. Dark Eyes, Florencita Waltz, Mariposa, Sparkling Waves; *c*20 ovs., incl. Bouquet, Fairy Tale, Golden Wand, Little Corporal, Seminole Ov.; *c*15 galops, incl. Charger, Make Way, Stampede; *c*15 polkas, incl. Elegance Polka, Mimi, The Sparrow; *c*15 schottisches, incl. Florence, Light Heart, Pretty Pauline; *c*10 quadrilles, incl. Flora Quadrille, Hyacinthe, Starlight; *c*200 other works; many arrs.

Principal publishers: Church, Coleman, Cundy, C. Fischer, Gay

RAOUL CAMUS

Laurens, A. M. Pseudonym of CHARLES LLOYD BARNHOUSE.

Laurent, Paul. Pseudonym of LOUIS-PHILIPPE LAURENDEAU.

Lavallée, Calixa (*b* Ste. Théodosie de Verchères [now Calixa-Lavallée], Que., 28 Dec 1842; *d* Boston, MA, 21 Jan 1891). Canadian composer and pianist. Lavallée received his early musical training in St. Hyacinthe and Montreal. Having become proficient on the piano, the violin, and the cornet, he worked as a traveling theater musician from about 1857. In 1861–2 Lavallée was enrolled as a bandsman in a northern regiment during the American Civil War. There followed years as a traveling musician and teacher in Montreal, California, New Orleans, and Lowell, Massachusetts, until he was appointed conductor and artistic director of the New York Grand Opera House (more minstrel-show theater than opera house) in about 1870. After the closing of the theater in 1872, Lavallée returned for a time to Montreal, where friends raised money to enable him to complete his education at the Paris Conservatoire (1873–5). His teachers included Bazin, Boieldieu *fils*, and Marmontel.

On returning to Canada Lavallée set up a studio (an embryonic conservatory) with Frantz and Rosita Jehin-Prume and became choirmaster at a Montreal church. In 1880 he wrote *O Canada* for the Fête Nationale des Canadiens-français; the song has become the national anthem of Canada. Shortly thereafter Lavallée once again moved to the USA, where he became music director of the Roman Catholic cathedral in Boston and a teacher at the Petersilea Conservatory there. In the early 1880s he accompanied the Hungarian soprano Etelka Gerster on an American concert tour. His *opéra comique The Widow* was performed in several American cities in 1882, and many of his works were published, including *Tiq*, a melodrama on "the Indian question" and its solution by the US government. He was active in the Music Teachers' National Association, organizing some of the first all-American concerts from 1884. He became the MTNA's president in 1886 and represented the USA at the London conference of the National Society of Professional Musicians in 1888.

Nearly all of Lavallée's unpublished music is lost, and since the published works were those written for the broad public it is easy to get the impression that Lavallée catered to popular taste. All accounts indicate, however, that he was a serious musician, at home in the classics as much as in the operetta music of his day. The piano piece *Le papillon* enjoyed popularity in Europe as well as North America for many decades. Lavallée's greatest talent lay in melodic invention. He is regarded as the first native Canadian creative composer.

WORKS

Stage: Lou-Lou (comic opera, 3), lost; The Widow (opéra comique, F. H. Nelson), Springfield, IL, 1882, vs (Boston, 1882); Tiq, or Settled at Last (melodramatic musical satire, 2, W. F. Sage, P. Hawley), vs (Boston, 1883)

Orch and choral: Tu es Petrus, offertorium (Boston, 1883); 3 ovs., band (Boston, 1885–8): Bridal Rose, Golden Fleece, King of Diamonds; 4 unpubd orch works, lost, incl. Sym. ded. City of Boston; 3 unpubd choral works, lost

Other works: Le papillon, étude de concert, op. 18 (Paris, *c*1875); Grande fantaisie, op.75, Meditation, both cornet, pf (New York, *c*1880); O Canada (A. B. Routhier; Eng. version, R. S. Weir) (Quebec, 1880); Andalouse, bolero, lv, pf, op.38 (Boston, 1886); 6 other pubd pf pieces; 5 chamber works, lost; many other pf pieces and songs, some lost

Principal publishers: Boucher; Cundy; Eveillard & Jacquot; C. Fischer; Lavigne; Russell; White, Smith, & Co.

BIBLIOGRAPHY

D. J. Logan: "Canadian Creative Composers," *Canadian Magazine*, xli (1913), 489
S. Salter: "Early Encouragements to American Composers," *MQ*, xviii (1932), 76
E. Lapierre: *Calixa Lavallée* (Montreal, 1936/*R*1966)
H. Kallmann and others, eds.: "Lavallée, Calixa," " 'O Canada'," *Encyclopedia of Music in Canada* (Toronto, 1981)

HELMUT KALLMANN

La Violette, Wesley (*b* St. James, MN, 4 Jan 1894; *d* Escondido, CA, 29 July 1978). Composer and educator. He was brought up in Spokane, Washington, and graduated in 1917 from the Northwestern University School of Music. After serving with the US Army in France during World War I, he attended the Chicago Musical College (DMus 1925), where he was eventually appointed dean. From 1933 to 1940 he taught at De Paul University, Chicago, and also served as director of De Paul University

Press, established for the publication of American music. During this period he was president of the Chicago section of the ISCM and was active in organizing the first Yaddo Festival. Subsequently he settled in southern California and taught both privately and at the Los Angeles Conservatory; he also lectured on philosophy, religion, and the arts. La Violette is the author of *Music and its Makers* (1938) and wrote several books on religious mysticism, one of which, *The Crown of Wisdom* (1949), was nominated for the Nobel Prize in literature. Frequently atonal and often contrapuntal, La Violette's music is nevertheless conservative and straightforward, with broad lines and marked rhythms. Most of his vocal settings are of his own texts.

WORKS

Dramatic: Shylock (opera, La Violette, after Shakespeare), 1929; Schubertiana (ballet), 1935; The Enlightened One (opera, La Violette), 1935

Orch: Penetrella, str, 1928; Osiris, orch, 1929; 4 concs., vn, 1929, pf, 1937, vn, 1938, str qt, 1939; 3 syms., 1936, 1939, 1952; Music from the High Sierras, orch, 1941; other works

Inst: 3 str qts, 1926, 1933, 1936; Pf Qnt, 1927; 4 sonatas, 2 vn, 1931, vn, 1934, vn, 1937, fl, 1941; Qnt, fl, str qt, 1943; other works

Other: 6 songs; 4 choruses

MSS in *DLC, ICD*

Principal publishers: De Paul UP, Delkas

BIBLIOGRAPHY

C. R. Reis: *American Composers of Today* (New York, 1930, rev. and enlarged 4/1947/*R*1977 as *Composers in America: Biographical Sketches*)

B. Kremenliev: "Wesley La Violette," *Music of the West*, vii/9 (1952), 9

F. Kelley: "Prez among Doctors," *Metronome*, lxxii/9 (1956), 24

MICHAEL MECKNA

Law, Andrew (*b* Milford, CT, 21 March 1749; *d* Cheshire, CT, 13 July 1821). Singing teacher and tunebook compiler. He is reported as playing and teaching violin and flute in Connecticut as early as 1770, but there is no other evidence that he ever performed on either instrument. By 1772 he had established a singing-school at Rhode Island College (Brown University) in Providence, where he graduated in 1775; that year a Connecticut newspaper referred to him as "Mr. Andrew Law, Singing Master." He studied theology and obtained a license to preach in Congregational churches in 1776; in 1787 he was ordained as a minister in both the Congregational and Presbyterian churches. By 1778, however, he was involved in a musical career that made him perhaps the most widely traveled American-born musician of his age, and certainly the most prolific compiler.

At first Law remained at the family home in Cheshire teaching singing-schools and compiling tunebooks, which were printed by his brother William. The first work he edited, *Select Harmony* (Cheshire, 1779, 2/1782), was also the first American sacred tunebook to combine music by English and American psalmodists in roughly equal proportion. In 1783 he began to travel widely both in New England and elsewhere, teaching from his tunebooks and engaging others to do the same; he established schools in Philadelphia, Boston, New York, and Charleston, and doubtless in connection with these activities he published *The Rudiments of Music* (Cheshire, 1783, 4/1793). Between 1789 and 1792 he sought to extend his influence into the countryside, conducting schools in Alexandria (Virginia) and Baltimore, and supervising a staff of young New England singing masters who taught from his books in rural Maryland, Virginia, and the Carolinas. The collapse of that enterprise brought him back to Connecticut where, in 1793, he declared a preference for European music and organized his publications into a comprehensive vocal method, *The Art of Singing* (Cheshire, 1794, 4/1810). Law worked to promote his method and his reform ideology in New England (to 1798) and Philadelphia (1798–1802). In 1803 he devised a staffless shape-notation and issued tunebooks using it; he worked towards its acceptance mostly from Philadelphia, where he lived from 1806 until 1813, and where in 1807 he published *The Harmonic Companion* (4/1819). After 1813 he resumed his travels and continued to teach and publish until his death. His later works include *Essays on Music* (Philadelphia, 1814; Hartford, 1821).

A contentious, self-righteous Calvinist, Law received little financial benefit from the ascendancy of his reform views, partly because in his shape-note tunebooks he stubbornly refused to employ a staff, which limited their sale. He was influential as a compiler, however, especially in his earlier years. He was the first to print compositions by many psalmodists from Connecticut and Massachusetts, including Oliver Brownson, Alexander Gillet, Oliver King, and Abraham Wood. He was also the first American compiler to print pieces from Martin Madan's *Lock Hospital Collection* (London, 1769), a work whose Methodist style won wide popularity among American reformers of the 1790s and later.

The Andrew Law Papers, a large collection including letters, business documents, memoranda, and musical manuscripts, is owned by the William L. Clements Library, University of Michigan, Ann Arbor.

See also PSALMODY, §4, SHAPE-NOTE HYMNODY, §2, and SINGING-SCHOOL.

BIBLIOGRAPHY

F. J. Metcalf: "Law, Andrew," *DAB*

I. Lowens: *Music and Musicians in Early America* (New York, 1964), 58

R. Crawford: *Andrew Law, American Psalmodist* (Evanston, IL, 1968/*R*1981)

C. Hamm: "The Ecstatic and the Didactic: a Pattern in American Music," *Current Thought in Musicology*, ed. J. W. Grubbs (Austin, TX, 1976), 44

RICHARD CRAWFORD

Lawrence, Dorothea Dix (*b* New York, 22 Sept 1899; *d* Plainfield, NJ, 23 May 1979). Soprano and folklorist. She studied singing in New York with Cesare Stunai, Henry Russell, and Katherine Opdycke, and made her début in 1929, as Gounod's Marguerite, with the Quebec Opera Company, Montreal. During the 1930s, while continuing to sing opera in New York, Philadelphia, and elsewhere (her roles included Aida, Tosca, and Carmen), she became interested in American folk music and folklore and began collecting songs, particularly from residents of the Pine Barrens of New Jersey and the Zuni Indians of New Mexico. Her recital programs (from 1937) ranged from Hopkinson and Billings to MacDowell, Farwell, and Gershwin (often performed from manuscript); she also sang American Indian songs in original languages and folk songs from all over the USA. A frequent performer on radio, she was the soloist on 12 October 1940 for the first radio broadcast from the USA to Admiral Byrd's Antarctic expedition; the program consisted exclusively of American music.

In 1945 Lawrence produced a "Folklore Music Map of the United States," which was widely distributed in American schools and formed the basis of her subsequent lecture-recitals. The songs, whose incipits appeared on the map, were later published in her book *Folklore Songs of the United States* (1959). From 1952 to 1954 she toured Europe, giving over 250 recitals and lectures on American music and presenting papers on Zuni music at conferences in England and Austria. She continued to give her "Musically Mapping America" talks throughout the USA and Mexico until her retirement in 1970. Lawrence was made a fellow of the Royal Anthropological Society, Great Britain (1952), and in 1958 was the founder of a folklore society bearing her name. Although she was praised for her rich tone and dramatic presence as a singer, her chief contribution was in the collection and international dissemination of American music, both cultivated and vernacular. Her papers form the Dorothea Dix Lawrence Collection at the Library of Congress.

SUSAN FEDER

Lawrence, Gertrude [Klasen, Gertrud Alexandra Dagmar Lawrence] (*b* London, England, 4 July 1898; *d* New York, 6 Sept 1952). British actress, singer, and dancer. Her New York début in the London show *André Charlot's Revue* (1924) brought her immediately to the attention of leading American songwriters; her first successful song was *You were meant for me* by Noble Sissle and Eubie Blake. George and Ira Gershwin wrote the musicals *Oh, Kay!* (1926, including the song "Someone to watch over me") and *Treasure Girl* (1928) for her. During the Depression, Lawrence performed mostly spoken drama in both England and the USA, notably *Private Lives* (1930) with Noel Coward, but she resumed her position as a leading Broadway musical actress when she appeared in Weill's *Lady in the Dark* (1941), which was written for her and included the sultry song "The Saga of Jenny." In 1950 she suggested to Richard Rodgers and Oscar Hammerstein II a musical adaptation of the film *Anna and the King of Siam*; the work that resulted, *The King and I* (1951), marked the climax of her career.

Lawrence was a most distinguished, fervent, inexhaustible, and sophisticated actress in American musical theater for three decades. Atkinson described her as "a unique phenomenon – a superb performer in any medium, exuberant, supple, and animated, a formidable craftsman in the arts of the stage." According to Rodgers, despite a narrow vocal range and "an unfortunate tendency to sing flat . . . Gertrude had a distinctive quality all her own," and a "style and feel for music [which] would compensate for her faulty pitch." Lawrence made at least 13 recordings and wrote an autobiography, *A Star Danced* (1945).

BIBLIOGRAPHY

R. Aldrich: *Gertrude Lawrence as Mrs. A* (New York, 1954)
B. Atkinson: *Broadway* (New York, 1970)
R. Rodgers: *Musical Stages* (New York, 1975), 270ff

DEANE L. ROOT

Lawrence, Lucile (*b* New Orleans, LA, 7 Feb 1907). Harpist. She studied privately with Salzedo, beginning at the age of 11. She was first harpist with the Salzedo Harp Ensemble, founded the Lawrence Harp Quintet, and has appeared as a soloist with leading orchestras and chamber groups. In 1925 she toured Australia and New Zealand and has since toured the USA and Canada. She was a member of the faculty of the Curtis Institute from 1927 until 1930, when she left to found the harp department at the Philadelphia Musical Academy. She has also taught at the Mannes College from 1945, at the Manhattan School from 1967, and at Boston University and the Berkshire Music Center, beginning, respectively, in 1966 and 1968. She has published methods, transcriptions, and editions for harp and has edited and recorded contemporary compositions. Active in musical organizations, she is a past president of the American Harp Society. Lawrence is a noted interpreter of the works of Salzedo. Her sensitive performances are characterized by technical brilliance, a sweet sound, and great control and finesse in the use of tone color.

MARTHA WOODWARD

Lawrence, Marjorie (Florence) (*b* Dean's Marsh, nr Melbourne, Australia, 17 Feb 1909; *d* Little Rock, AR, 13 Jan 1979). Soprano. After winning a local contest, on the advice of John Brownlee she went to Paris, studying with Cécile Gilly, and making her opera début at Monte Carlo in 1932, as Elisabeth in *Tannhäuser*. In 1933 she first appeared at the Paris Opéra (Ortrud in *Lohengrin*, 25 February), returning until 1936 as Brünnhilde, Salomé (Massenet's *Hérodiade*), Rachel (Halévy's *La juive*), Aida, Donna Anna, Brunehild (Ernest Reyer's *Sigurd*), Brangäne (*Tristan*), and Valentine (Meyerbeer's *Les Huguenots*). On 21 December 1935 she made her Metropolitan Opera début as the *Walküre* Brünnhilde, appearing there for six seasons, mostly in the Wagnerian repertory but also as the heroines of Gluck's *Alceste*, Strauss's *Salome*, and Massenet's *Thaïs*. Although she had polio in 1941, she was able in 1943 to resume her career in a limited way, in specially staged performances during which she was always seated; later she appeared in concerts. She retired to Harmony Hills, a ranch in Hot Springs near Little Rock, in 1952; this has become the site of a summer music school. Lawrence possessed a large, vibrant, and expressive voice of mezzo-soprano quality. Her not always secure singing gave pleasure because of its physical impact and distinctive sound. She was a naturalized American.

BIBLIOGRAPHY

M. Lawrence: *Interrupted Melody: the Story of my Life* (New York, 1949)
B. MacKenzie and F. MacKenzie: *Singers of Australia* (Melbourne, 1967), 155
J. Rockwell: Obituary, *New York Times* (15 Jan 1979)

MAX DE SCHAUENSEE

Lawrence [Cohen], **Robert** (*b* New York, 18 March 1912; *d* New York, 9 Aug 1981). Conductor and music critic. He studied at Columbia University (MA 1934) and the Institute of Musical Art, and was a critic for the *New York Herald Tribune* from 1939 to 1943. During World War II he served with the US Army in Italy; in 1944 he conducted opera performances at Rome's Teatro Quirino, and in 1944 and 1945 conducted at the Rome Opera, working with such artists as Tagliavini, Gigli, and Maria Caniglia. He led the Phoenix SO from 1949 to 1952, then went to Turkey where he was conductor of the Ankara So from 1957 to 1958. In 1959 and 1960 he led the American Opera Society in complete performances of Berlioz's *Les troyens* at Carnegie Hall when the scheduled conductor, Sir Thomas Beecham, was indisposed. In 1961 he founded the Friends of French Opera, which presented a number of neglected works, especially those of Jules Massenet. In the early 1970s he was director of Opera Atlanta, then head of the opera department at the Peabody Conservatory. For more than 40 years his radio commentaries were heard during the intermissions of Metropolitan Opera broadcasts. His published writings include *The World of Opera* (with Mary Ellis Peltz, 1958) and *A Rage for Opera* (1971).

CHARLES JAHANT

Lawrence, Vera Brodsky (*b* Norfolk, VA, 1 July 1909). Pianist, editor, and music historian. She studied at the Juilliard School (1928–32) with Josef and Rosina Lhévinne (piano) and Rubin Goldmark and Bernard Wagenaar (theory). A concert pianist from 1930 to 1965, she was a performing member of the music staff of CBS, 1939–46. From 1967 to 1970 she was administrator of publications for the Contemporary Music Project, and compiled and edited the CMP Library of some 500 works and its three-volume catalogue (1967, 1969). Three notable facsimile publications have been edited by her: *The Piano Works of Louis Moreau Gottschalk* (1969), *The Wa-Wan Press, 1901–11* (1970, the complete run of Farwell's Wa-Wan Press), and *The Collected Works of Scott Joplin* (1971, rev. 2/1983). Her *Music for Patriots, Politicians, and Presidents* (1975), a study of the interaction of music and politics in the USA during the 18th and 19th centuries, won an ASCAP Deems Taylor award in 1976. In 1975 she acted as artistic consultant for the Houston Grand Opera production of Joplin's *Treemonisha*, and she served as music adviser and consultant to the NEA, 1977–80. Lawrence has held grants from the Rockefeller Foundation (1970, 1971), a Guggenheim Fellowship (1976), and two grants from the NEH (1978–80, 1980–84).

H. WILEY HITCHCOCK

Laws, Hubert (*b* Houston, TX, 10 Nov 1939). Flutist. He began his career in Texas playing with the Jazz Crusaders, at the same time studying and performing classical music in Houston. His clear, full sound and pure intonation made him widely popular in both the jazz and classical fields, although most of his solo work has been in a jazz context. He is one of the few jazz musicians to concentrate solely on the flute, an instrument he helped popularize in the 1960s and 1970s with his many jazz recordings for Atlantic and CTI; during this period he was a member of the Metropolitan Opera Orchestra and also played with the New York PO. In the 1980s he participated in several concerts with the classical flutist Jean-Pierre Rampal, while continuing to record jazz in a largely commercial vein.

RECORDINGS
(selective list)

The Laws of Jazz (1964, Atl. 1432); *Crying Song* (1970, CTI 1002); *Afro Classic* (1971, CTI 6006); *Morning Star* (1972, CTI 6022); *At Carnegie Hall* (1973, CTI 6025); *How to Beat the High Cost of Living* (1980, Col. JS36741)

BIBLIOGRAPHY

SouthernB

J. Schaffer: "In Review," *Down Beat*, xl/16 (1973), 13

C. Berg: "Pied Piper of Houston," *Down Beat*, xliv/10 (1977), 15

LEE JESKE

Lawson, Warner (*b* Hartford, CT, 3 Aug 1903; *d* Washington, DC, 3 June 1971). Conductor and music educator. He was taught piano from the age of five by his father, the concert pianist Raymond Lawson (*b* Shelbyville, KY, 23 March 1875; *d* Hartford, CT, Feb 1959), and received his education at Fisk University (BA 1926) and Yale University (BM 1929). In 1929 and 1930 he studied in Berlin with Artur Schnabel. He was a member of the faculty of Fisk University from 1930 to 1934, and then moved to Boston where he conducted a WPA chorus; he received an MA from Harvard in 1936. After serving as choirmaster at North Carolina Agricultural and Technical State University, Greensboro (1936–42), he was appointed dean of the music school at Howard University, Washington, DC, where he remained until his death. Under his direction the Howard University chorus began to appear regularly with the National SO, and in 1960 went on a European tour under the sponsorship of the US State Department. Lawson was awarded honorary doctorates by the Hartt School of Music (1954) and Temple University (1966).

BIBLIOGRAPHY

SouthernB

DOMINIQUE-RENÉ DE LERMA

Lawton, Dorothy (*b* Sheffield, England, 31 July 1874; *d* Bournemouth, England, 19 Feb 1960). English music librarian. She was brought as a child to the USA, where she studied piano with Stojowski and theory with Eduard Hermann. She taught and lectured in New York until 1920, when she joined the staff of the New York Public Library to organize and direct the newly established circulating music library. Despite her lack of formal training as a librarian, she did the task with distinction until 1945. In 1930 she organized a similar department for the American Library in Paris. She worked to attract private funds to improve the New York collection of scores, parts, and sound recordings, and helped to establish the library's section on dance, as well as a course in music librarianship at the New York College of Music. In 1946 she returned to England, where she helped to organize the Central Music Library in London. She retired in 1950.

RAMONA H. MATTHEWS

Layton, Billy Jim (*b* Corsicana, TX, 14 Nov 1924). Composer. His early musical experience was in school bands and dance orchestras, playing saxophone and clarinet and writing arrangements; this involvement with jazz and other popular music was fundamental to his musical thought. After a period of service in the Air Force during World War II he attended the New England Conservatory and studied composition under Francis Judd Cooke and Carl McKinley. After graduating (BMus 1948) he continued his composition studies with Quincy Porter at Yale University (MMus 1950), and then proceeded to Harvard to study musicology under Gombosi and composition under Piston. Layton was awarded the Rome Prize in composition in 1954 and spent three years at the American Academy in Rome. On returning to Harvard in 1957 he completed a dissertation under Pirrotta on medieval settings of the Mass Ordinary. He then remained at Harvard as assistant professor until 1966, when he was appointed professor of music and the first chairman of the music department at SUNY, Stony Brook. As chairman until 1972 he had a major role in its development.

Layton may be regarded as a progressive conservative in the tradition of Busoni's "Junge Klassizität." In a polemical essay of 1965 ("The New Liberalism," *PNM*, iii/2, 1965, p.137), he attacked the radical purists of constructivism on the one hand and the apostles of chance music on the other. He favored instead a centrist "new liberalism," which he defined as "a new, rich, meaningful, varied, understandable and vital music which maintains contact with the great cultural tradition of humanism in the West." This fairly describes his own music. The seven compositions he wrote within a 12-year period are marked by meticulous craftsmanship, timbral sensitivity, and structural resourcefulness. Animated by his early experience of jazz and popular music and his later musicological studies, Layton integrates a wide variety of techniques including metrical modulation and multiple ostinatos, free atonality and harmonic serialism, cantus firmus and isorhythm, jazz improvisation and blues chord changes, and passages of indeterminate notation imbedded in a determinate context. His structures range from a single continuous process to highly complex arrangements of disjunct images that encompass both absolute stasis and intense activity.

WORKS

5 Studies, vn, pf, op.1, 1952; An American Portrait, sym. ov., op.2, 1953; 3 Dylan Thomas Poems, chorus, brass sextet, op.3, 1954–6; Str Qt, op.4, 1956; 3 Studies, pf, op.5, 1957; Divertimento, cl, bn, trbn, hpd, perc, vn, vc, op.6, 1958–60; Dance Fantasy, orch, op.7, 1964

Principal publisher: G. Schirmer

BIBLIOGRAPHY

W. Mellers: *Music in a New Found Land* (New York, 1964), 230

R. Browne: "Billy Jim Layton: Dance Fantasy," *PNM*, iv/1 (1965), 161

AUSTIN CLARKSON

Layton Walker, Sarah (Jane). *See* CAHIER, MME. CHARLES.

Lazarof, Henri (*b* Sofia, Bulgaria, 12 April 1932). Composer. He graduated from the Sofia Academy in 1948 and then studied at the New Conservatory in Jerusalem (1949–52), with Petrassi at the Accademia di S. Cecilia, Rome (1955–7), and at Brandeis University (1957–9, MFA 1959). In 1962 he joined the faculty of UCLA, where he was appointed professor of composition. His music is highly individual, atonal in harmony, and, in some works, freely serial.

WORKS

(selective list)

Orch: Pf Conc., 1956; Piccola serenata, 1959; Va Conc., 1959–60; Conc., pf, 20 insts, 1960–61; Odes, 1962–3; Structures sonores, 1966; Mutazione, 1967; Vc Conc., 1968; Textures, pf, 5 ens, 1970; Konkordia, str, 1971; Spectrum, tpt, orch, tape, 1972–3; Fl Conc., 1973; Ritratto, 1974; Chamber Conc. no.3, 1974; Volo, va, 2 str ens, 1975; Chamber Sym., 1976; Conc. for Orch, 1977; Sym., 1978; Mirrors, Mirrors . . ., ballet, 1980; Sinfonietta, 1981

Choral: Cantata, nar, chorus, inst ens, 1958; The First Day, chorus, ww qnt/unacc. chorus, 1959; Canti, 1971

Chamber: 3 str qts, 1956, 1961–2, 1980; Inventions, va, pf, 1962; Tempi concertati, vn, va, 7 insts, 1964; Rhapsody, vn, pf, 1966, orchd 1969; Espaces, 2 fl, 2 cl, 2 va, 2 vc, 2 pf, 1966; Cadence: I, vc, 1969, III, vn, 2 perc, 1970, IV, pf, 1970; Continuum, str trio, 1970; Duo, vc, pf, 1973; Adieu, cl, pf, 1974; Fanfare, 6 tpt, 1980; Trio, wind, 1981; many other kbd and chamber pieces

With tape: Quantetti, pf, 3 pf on tape, 1963; Cadence II, va, tape, 1969; Partita, brass qnt, tape, 1971; Cadence: V, fl, tape, 1972, VI, tuba, tape, 1973; Concertazioni, tpt, 6 insts, tape, 1973

Principal publishers: Associated, Bote & Bock, Israeli, Merion, Presser

W. THOMAS MARROCCO

Lazzari, Virgilio (*b* Assisi, Italy, 20 April 1887; *d* Castel Gandolfo, Italy, 4 Oct 1953). Bass. He began his career with the Vitale Operetta Company (1908–11), then studied with Antonio Cotogni in Rome, where he made his operatic début in 1914. After appearing in South America, he made his North American début in St. Louis as Ramfis (*Aida*, 1916). He then settled in the USA and became an American citizen. He sang regularly with the Chicago Opera from 1918 to 1933; that year he joined the Metropolitan Opera and remained with it until 1940, and again from 1943 to 1951, taking more than 22 roles. From 1934 to 1939 he appeared regularly at the Salzburg Festival. His most famous role was that of the blind king, Archibaldo, in Montemezzi's *L'amore dei tre re*, which he first sang in 1916 in Mexico City and as late as 1953 in Genoa. Although not blessed with a great voice (he was in any case more a light *basso cantante* than a deep-voiced bass like Ezio Pinza or Tancredi Pasero), Lazzari was generally considered one of the best singing-actors in his particular repertory.

HAROLD ROSENTHAL/R

Leadbelly [Ledbetter, Huddie] (*b* Mooringsport, LA, 21 Jan 1885; *d* New York, 6 Dec 1949). Songster, blues singer, and guitarist. By the age of 15 he was well known in the Caddo Lake region of Louisiana as a musician. He learned to play the 12-string guitar early in the 1900s and accompanied Blind Lemon Jefferson in the streets and bars of Dallas. In 1918 he was sentenced for murder in Texas; reprieved in 1925, he was again sentenced in 1930 for intent to murder, in Angola, Louisiana. There he was discovered in 1933 by the folklorist John A. Lomax, who recorded him for the Library of Congress and secured his

Leadbelly (right) with Bunk Johnson, c1940

parole. Leadbelly went to New York with Lomax the following year, and from 1935 to 1940 was extensively recorded for the Library of Congress. These recordings, which are remarkable for their variety, included a beautiful version of Jefferson's *Match Box Blues*, played with a knife on the guitar strings, and the haunting *If it wasn't for Dicky* (both 1935, Elek. 301). Among his earliest commercial recordings, made for the American Recording Company, were the powerful *Honey I'm all out and down* (1935, Melotone 3327) and the ballad *Becky Deem, she was a gamblin' gal* (1935, ARC 6-04-55); although dramatically performed, they were anachronistic to black audiences and did not sell well.

In New York Leadbelly found a welcome audience among jazz supporters, who viewed him as the last of the blues singers, and he had a moderate success as a performer in nightclubs and on college campuses. His *Good Morning Blues* (1940, Bluebird 8791), with a spoken introduction defining blues, was his most admired song. In his last years he made a very large number of recordings for specialist folk labels, including several with the virtuoso harmonica player Sonny Terry, such as *On a Monday* (1943, Asch 343-3). During his "Last Session" in 1948 he recorded a free-ranging reminiscence with many traditional and work songs, including *I ain't goin' down to the well no more* (1948, FW 241). Shortly before his death he performed in Paris.

Leadbelly was the most prolific of all songsters, with a repertory of perhaps 500 songs. A notable custodian of the black song tradition, his work is distinguished for its wide range and variety, his full-throated singing with rough vibrato, and his accomplished, highly rhythmic playing of the 12-string guitar. These features are abundantly evident on an early version of his best-known song, *Goodnight Irene* (1943, Asch 343-2). Among many other songs *Rock Island Line* (1949, Playboy 119), recorded shortly before his death, became virtually an anthem of the skiffle craze in England, resulting in a temporary devaluation of his reputation as a musician. In 1975 Leadbelly's life was made the subject of a Hollywood film, *Leadbelly*; the singing was provided by HiTide Harris.

BIBLIOGRAPHY

SouthernB

L. Cohn: Liner notes, *Leadbelly: the Library of Congress Recordings* (1935–40, Elek. 301/2)

J. A. Lomax and A. Lomax, eds.: *Negro Folk Songs as Sung by Leadbelly* (New York, 1936)

M. Jones and A. McCarthy: *A Tribute to Huddie Ledbetter* (London, 1946)

M. Asch and A. Lomax, eds.: *The Leadbelly Songbook* (New York, 1962)

J. Lester and P. Seeger: *The 12-string Guitar as played by Leadbelly* (New York, 1965)

E. Lambert: "Leadbelly's Last Sessions," *Jazz Monthly*, no.171 (1969), 11

P. Oliver: *The Story of the Blues* (London, 1969)

PAUL OLIVER

League of Composers. An organization founded in 1923 in New York by members of the INTERNATIONAL COMPOSERS' GUILD in order to promote the composition and performance of contemporary music. Before it merged with the INTERNATIONAL SOCIETY FOR CONTEMPORARY MUSIC in 1954, the league had commissioned 110 works by outstanding American and European composers (including Copland, Bartók, and Barber), sponsored American stage premières of Stravinsky's *The Rite of Spring*, *Oedipus rex*, and *The Wedding*, and mounted some of the first radio broadcasts of contemporary music sponsored by the PAN AMERICAN ASSOCIATION OF COMPOSERS. It also gave concerts and receptions honoring Schoenberg, Hindemith, Milhaud, and other composers who had recently immigrated to the USA. Its quarterly *Modern Music* (1924–46/*R*1966), which contained critical reviews of new works and articles by leading composers, did much to increase awareness and appreciation of contemporary music. The executive chairmen were CLAIRE R. REIS (1923–48) and Copland (1948–50). Since the League's merger with the ISCM, there have been more premières of music by Schoenberg, Berg, Webern, and Stravinsky, as well as Americans such as Copland, Schuman, Cowell, Thompson, Moore, Cage, Druckman, and Shapey. The combined League-ISCM, which has headquarters in New York, presents an annual concert series there. In 1976 it helped organize the World Music Days, held in Boston. The organization also sponsors international competitions and an annual National Composers Competition (1977–).

BIBLIOGRAPHY

C. R. Reis: *Composers, Conductors and Critics* (New York, 1955/*R*1974)

M. Meckna: "Copland, Sessions, and *Modern Music*: the Rise of the Composer-critic in America," *American Music*, iii (1985), 198

RITA H. MEAD

League of Women Composers. *See* INTERNATIONAL LEAGUE OF WOMEN COMPOSERS.

Lear [née Shulman], **Evelyn** (*b* Brooklyn, NY, 8 Jan 1926). Soprano. She studied piano and horn (playing in the orchestra at the Berkshire Music Center under Bernstein), before entering the Juilliard School, where she studied singing, making her New York recital début in 1955. After further study in Berlin, she joined the Berlin Städtische Oper; in 1961 she created the title role in Giselher Klebe's *Alkmene* at the Deutsche Oper, Berlin (where she has since performed regularly), and in 1963 she created Jeanne in Werner Egk's *Die Verlobung in San Domingo* at the opening celebrations of the rebuilt National Theater, Munich. Her Metropolitan Opera début was as Lavinia in the first performance of Marvin David Levy's *Mourning Becomes Electra* (17 March 1967), during the first Lincoln Center season. Since her first performance as Berg's Lulu (in concert) in Vienna in May 1960 she has been closely associated with the role, recording it under Karl Böhm. Her repertory includes both Cherubino and the Countess, Fiordiligi, Pamina, Handel's Cleopatra, Mimì, Verdi's Desdemona, Tchaikovsky's Tatyana, and Oktavian; from 1972 she began to undertake heavier roles, including Tosca and the Marschallin. She created Irina Arkadina in Pasatieri's *The Seagull* (1974), and Magda in Robert Ward's *Minutes to Midnight* (1982). She is a distinguished recitalist, singing in seven languages. Her voice, though not large, is of distinctively warm and affecting quality and is well produced and projected apart from occasional upper-register strain; her performances are marked by an intelligent treatment of the text and an appealing stage presence. She married the baritone Thomas Stewart in 1955.

BIBLIOGRAPHY

"Lear, Evelyn," *CBY 1973*

HAROLD ROSENTHAL/R

Leavitt, Donald (Lee) (*b* Annapolis, MD, 2 Sept 1929; *d* Lanham, MD, 28 Nov 1985). Music librarian. He graduated from American University (BA 1951) and undertook graduate studies in musicology at Indiana University (1951–6). In 1956 he began a long association with the Library of Congress, first as reference librarian in the folksong archive (1956–62), then as head of the recorded sound division (1962–72), and then as assistant chief of the music division (1972–8); in 1978 he was appointed chief. He was head of the International Association of Sound Archives (1969–74) and president of the record libraries commission of the International Association of Music Libraries (1974–6); he was also active in the Music Library Association and the Association for Recorded Sound Collections. He wrote numerous journal articles and reviews, and from 1956 to 1963 he was a music critic for the *Washington Star*.

PAULA MORGAN

Leavitt, Joshua (*b* Heath, MA, 8 Sept 1794; *d* New York, 16 Jan 1873). Tunebook compiler. A graduate of Yale (1814), he was ordained in 1825 and three years later settled in New York, where he became editor of various religious and abolitionist journals. In 1830 he founded *The Evangelist*, a leading organ of the new style of revivalism espoused by Charles G. Finney, and by October that year had begun printing revival hymns with tunes in issues of the journal. These hymns were published separately in two volumes as *The Christian Lyre* (New York, 1831); a *Supplement to the Christian Lyre*, containing traditional psalm tunes, was issued the same year and a *Companion to the Christian Lyre*, consisting only of texts, in 1833 (both again in New York). *The Christian Lyre* was enormously influential and controversial; it reached 26 editions by 1842 and was the most imitated revival collection before the Civil War. According to the preface of the first volume, Leavitt possessed "no musical skill beyond that of ordinary plain singers," and selected his pieces solely on the basis of their "known popularity and good influence." His chief innovations were to print full texts and tunes (melody and bass line only) together in a pocket-size format, and to include numerous lively secular melodies, folk spirituals, and camp-meeting hymns with choruses. Leavitt's papers, including correspondence, are in the Library of Congress. (*See also* HYMNODY, §2(i).)

BIBLIOGRAPHY

F. W. Coburn: "Leavitt, Joshua," *DAB*

C. G. Cole, Jr.: *The Social Ideas of the Northern Evangelists* (New York, 1954), 39

P. G. Hammond: *Music in Urban Revivalism in the Northern United States, 1800–1835* (diss., Southern Baptist Theological Seminary, 1974)

PAUL C. ECHOLS

Leblanc. Firm of instrument makers and distributors. It was formed in France in 1904 when the Leblanc family of woodwind instrument makers acquired the firm of Noblet (founded 1750). The French firm, G. Leblanc et Cie, established an international reputation, particularly for clarinets. In 1946 Léon Leblanc (*b* La Couture Boussey, France, 24 Nov 1900), anxious to expand his business, formed a distributing company in the USA with Vito Pascucci (*b* Kenosha, WI, 12 Oct 1922) as president. Known as the G. Leblanc Corporation, it has remained a privately held affiliate of the French firm. Its factory in Kenosha at first only acclimatized and remanufactured the French clarinets, but later began making its own brass and woodwind instruments, notably a range of Vito student clarinets. The corporation acquired the Frank Holton Band Instrument Manufacturing Company (1964), the Woodwind Mouthpiece Company (1968), and the Martin Band Instrument Company (1971). It is also the American agent for the French firms of Courtois (brass instruments) and Vandoren (woodwind mouthpieces, reeds, and accessories) as well as the Japanese firm of Yanagisawa (saxophones), but it is known primarily for distributing the French-made Leblanc instruments, which comprise oboes, flutes, and a notable range of clarinets (normally built of African blackwood, with nickel-silver mounts and keys).

Ledbetter, Huddie. *See* LEADBELLY.

Lederman (Daniel), Minna (*b* New York, 3 March 1898). Editor and writer on music and dance. She had professional training in music, dance, and drama before graduating in 1917 from Barnard College. In 1923 she was a founding member of the League of Composers, and the following year she helped launch its *Review* (renamed *Modern Music* in 1925), the first American journal to manifest an interest in contemporary composers. As the sole editor (1924–46) she developed the journal's distinctive literary style and was responsible for bringing into its pages the writings of such rising young composers as Blitzstein, Bowles, Cage, Carter, Copland, Sessions, and Thomson, thereby nurturing an entire generation of composer-critics. Equally important were the articles by scholars, critics, and European composers including Bartók, Berg, and Schoenberg. For over two decades *Modern Music* was a lively force in the international music world, chronicling developments in concert music, jazz, musical theater, film, radio, and dance in the USA, Europe, and Latin America. In 1974 Lederman established the archives of *Modern Music* in the Library of Congress, and she has written about the journal and her experience as editor in *The Life and Death of a Small Magazine* (1983). She wrote on criticism and dance for *Modern Music*, edited the anthology *Stravinsky in the Theatre* (1947, rev. 2/1949/*R*1975), and has contributed to *American Mercury*, *Saturday Review of Literature*, *The Nation*, and other periodicals.

R. ALLEN LOTT

Leduc, Alphonse. Pseudonym of CHARLES BALMER.

Lee, Brenda [Tarpley, Brenda Mae] (*b* Lithonia, GA, 11 Dec 1944). Popular singer. At the age of five she won a local talent contest in Georgia; at seven, she was appearing regularly on the radio program "Starmakers' Revue" and as a guest on "TV Ranch," both in Atlanta. Red Foley heard her perform and engaged her for his "Ozark Jubilee Show" (1956). Foley's manager, Dub Albritten, then organized concerts for her with Foley and arranged for her to sing on television programs hosted by Steve Allen, Ed Sullivan, Red Skelton, Bob Hope, and Danny Thomas. She signed a recording contract with Decca in 1956 and had her first hit with *One step at a time* (1957). By 1969, 48 of Lee's singles and 15 of her albums had reached the popular chart. In the late 1950s and early 1960s she was one of the leading popular singers in the USA and Europe, with an eclectic repertory that ranged from rock (*Dynamite* 1957; *Sweet Nothin's*, 1959; *Rockin' around the Christmas tree*, 1960) to ballads (*I'm sorry*, 1960; *As usual*, 1963). In the 1970s Lee returned to her country-music heritage, a change of direction exemplified by the album *Memphis Portrait* (1970) and the hit single *The Cowgirl and the Dandy* (1980). Known as "Little Miss Dynamite," Lee has a powerful voice that is as renowned for its volume as for its melodic qualities. She has been equally successful in hard-edged rock, country-music, and easy-listening genres.

DON CUSIC

Lee, Dai-Keong (*b* Honolulu, HI, 2 Sept 1915). Composer. After premedical studies at the University of Hawaii (1933–6), he decided on a career in music and went to New York, where he was a pupil of Sessions and of Jacobi at the Juilliard Graduate School (1938–41); he also studied with Copland at the Berkshire Music Center (1941) and with Luening at Columbia University (MA 1951). Lee has been awarded two Guggenheim fellowships (1945, 1951) and has received commissions from the Institute of Musical Art (1940) and the League of Composers (1947). His works have been performed by major orchestras throughout the USA, under such conductors as Reiner, Stokowski, and William Steinberg, and several of them have been recorded, including the *Prelude and Hula*, the *Polynesian Suite*, and the Symphony no. 1.

Lee writes in a variety of styles. His Polynesian background is reflected in the use of percussion instruments such as the Tahitian wood block, the use of the Polynesian tetratonic scale in *Prelude and Hula* and *Hawaiian Festival Overture*, the quotation of Hawaiian chants in *Mele olili*, and the borrowing of native dance styles (Tahitian dance, hula) in the *Polynesian Suite*, written to celebrate Hawaii's statehood in 1959. Other less exotically tinged works, such as the Symphony no. 1, a neoclassical work begun during study with Copland, are modal but freely dissonant. Throughout his career, Lee has been interested in music for the stage; in 1951 he wrote *Open the Gates*, an opera based on the life of Mary Magdalene, commissioned and produced by the Blackfriars Theater Guild of New York, and he has since produced a number of short operas in the tradition of Weill, such as *Ballad of Kitty the Barkeep*. Among his best-known stage works is the incidental music for *Teahouse of the August Moon*, first performed at the Martin Beck Theater on 15 October 1953.

WORKS

Stage: Open the Gates (opera, R. Payne), 1951; Waltzing Matilda (ballet), 1951; Phineas and the Nightingale (opera, R. Healy), 1952, withdrawn; Teahouse of the August Moon (incidental music, J. Patrick), 1953, arr. orch suite, 1954; Speakeasy (Healy), 1957, withdrawn; 2 Knickerbocker Tales (operas, 1, Healy, Lee), 1957; Noa Noa (musical play), 1972; Ballad of Kitty the Barkeep (opera, Healy, Lee), 1979 [based on Speakeasy]; Jenny Lind (musical play, after P. T. Barnum: Recollections), 1981 [based on Phineas and the Nightingale]; other early works, withdrawn

Orch: Prelude and Hula, 1939; Hawaiian Festival Ov., 1940; Golden Gate Ov., 1941; Introduction and Scherzo, str orch, 1941; Sym. no. 1, 1941–2, rev. 1946; Pacific Prayer, 1943, rev. 1968 as Canticle of the Pacific (Lotus sutra), chorus, orch; Vn Conc., 1947, rev. 1955; Sym. no. 2, 1952; Polynesian Suite, 1958; Mele olili (Joyful Songs) (ancient Hawaiian chants), solo vv, chorus, orch, 1960; Conc. grosso, str orch, 1985; other works, withdrawn

Other works: chamber pieces, incl. Pf Sonatina, ?1943, Introduction and Allegro, vc, pf, 1947, Incantation and Dance, vn, pf, 1948; film scores; songs

Principal publisher: Belwin-Mills

BIBLIOGRAPHY

EwenD

ALLAN B. HO

Lee, Dixie. Stage name of MOLLY O'DAY.

Lee, Peggy [Egstrom, Norma Dolores] (*b* Jamestown, ND, 26 May 1920). Popular singer, songwriter, and actress. She began singing in a church choir, then on the radio, and from 1936 toured with dance bands. Her first hit was *Why don't you do right?* (1942) with Benny Goodman's band. In 1943 she married the guitarist Dave Barbour, with whom she wrote the song *Mañana* (1947), and in 1944 she left the swing bands and began a career on her own. She had a successful film début in a remake of *The Jazz Singer* (1953), and portrayed an alcoholic blues singer in *Pete Kelly's Blues* (1955). Lee's voice is small, with a compass of little more than an octave and a half; her distinction lies in her characterization of songs, achieved through vocal color and inflection with careful attention to the subtleties of language, to musical arrangements, and to stage manner and presentation. Although she was primarily a singer in the swing style, unlike many of her colleagues she did little improvisation. She has written or collaborated on more than 500 songs.

BIBLIOGRAPHY

"Lee, Peggy," *CBY 1963*
H. Pleasants: *The Great American Popular Singers* (New York, 1974)

HENRY PLEASANTS

Lee & Walker. Firm of music publishers. It was established in Philadelphia in 1848 by George W. Lee (*d* 1875) and Julius Walker (*d* 1857), and in 1856 absorbed the business of George Willig (both men had worked as clerks in Willig's music store). The firm published early editions of such patriotic songs as *Dixie* (1860) and *Columbia, the Gem of the Ocean* (1861), as well as popular songs and dance tunes, including the *Lincoln Quick Step* (1860), the *Home Run Quick Step* (1861), and several songs by Septimus Winner. After the death of Lee the firm's catalogue was purchased by Ditson; its name was continued by Lee's son Julius Lee, Jr., in partnership with J. F. Morrison.

BARBARA TURCHIN

Leedy. Firm of drum makers. It was established in Indianapolis in 1900 by Ulysses G. Leedy and Samuel L. Cooley as Leedy & Cooley, and made "everything for the band and orchestra drummer." Leedy (*b* Fostoria, OH, 1867; *d* Indianapolis, IN, 7 Jan 1931), a professional musician and amateur drum maker, became sole owner in 1903, changing the firm's name to Leedy Manufacturing Co. He expanded the firm's production to include over 900 items, among them orchestral bells, vibraphones, and numerous sound-effect instruments to accompany silent movies. Most important were the timpani designed by the factory superintendent CECIL H. STRUPE and patented in 1923. In addition to design improvements these had their copper bowls formed in a hydraulic press rather than hammered over wooden molds, and they became the model for the first English pedal timpani. Leedy was purchased by the firm of C. G. Conn in 1927 and its production was combined with that of Ludwig & Ludwig, which was acquired by Conn in 1930. In 1955 the Leedy portion of the Leedy–Ludwig division was sold to the Slingerland Drum Co.; production of Leedy instruments ceased in 1958.

EDMUND A. BOWLES

Leedy, Douglas (*b* Portland, OR, 3 March 1938). Composer. He studied music at Pomona College (Claremont, California) and composition at the University of California, Berkeley (MA 1962); he was Crofts Fellow at the Berkshire Music Center, 1958. From 1960 to 1965 he played French horn in the Oakland SO and San Francisco Opera and Ballet orchestras, and in 1965–6 traveled to Poland on a joint US-Polish government grant to investigate contemporary Polish music. He designed the electronic music studio at the University of California, Los Angeles, where he taught and conducted two ensembles, 1967–70; subsequently he also taught at Reed College, the University of Southern California, and the Centro Simon Bolivar, Caracas, Venezuela, but in 1980 he turned to other activities. He has written a number of articles on alternative tunings and edited volume 1 of *Chansons* *from Petrucci in Original Notation and in Transcription* (1983); in 1984 he became music director of the Portland Baroque Orchestra, and he also served as coordinator of the Portland Handel Festival, 1985. His own music is concerned with rhythm and line, even in such mobile-form pieces as *Exhibition Music* and *Quaderno rossiniano*. Among the influences apparent in his works are plainchant, Dufay, Stravinsky, Sibelius, Carnatic music, and early Western music. In the 1970s Leedy, following Partch and Harrison, abandoned equal-temperament; in this he was also influenced by Young and Riley (fellow students at Berkeley) and especially by a year of study with the singer K. V. Narayanaswamy in Madras, 1979–80. Leedy has described himself as "a strictly West Coast, empirical, non-academic musician."

WORKS

Perspectives, hn, 1964; Qnt 1964, cl, bn, tpt, db, org, 1964; Antifonia, 2 tpt, 2 trbn, 1965; Exhibition Music, 4 or more insts/vv, 1965; Octet: Quaderno rossiniano, 7 insts, perc, 1965; Str Qt, 1965–75; Usable Music I for Very Small Insts with Holes, 1966; Usable Music II, chamber ens, 1966; Entropical Paradise: 6 Sonic Environments, elec, 1969; 88 is Great, pf 18 hands, 1969; Gloria, S, vv, orch, 1970

Sebastian (chamber opera, Leedy, after J. S. Bach documents), 1971–4; Hpd Book, pt 1, 1974; Canti: Music for Db and Chamber Ens, 1975; Symphoniae sacrae (Bible), S, va da gamba, hpd, 1976; Sur la couche de miettes, 2 hpd, ens, 1981; Hpd Book, pt 3, 1982; 4 Hymns (Rigveda), chorus, gamelan, 1982–3; 5 Org Chorales, 1983; Music for Meantone Org, 1984–; a few other works

CHARLES SHERE

Lees, Benjamin (*b* Harbin, China, 8 Jan 1924). Composer of Russian parentage. When very young, Lees moved with his parents to the USA and took American citizenship through their naturalization. He was educated in California. After military service (1942–5), he studied at the University of Southern California (1945–8) under Halsey Stevens (composition), Ernst Kanitz, and Ingolf Dahl. Impressed by his compositions, Antheil undertook to teach him, and after some four years' study recognition came with a Fromm Foundation Award in 1953. In 1954 Lees received a Guggenheim Fellowship allowing him to work in Europe. His aim was to remain uninfluenced by the turbulent American scene and to create his own style. He worked away from the academic centers where many American composers had studied, living at Longpont-sur-Orge, France (1954–5 and 1957–61), Vienna (1955–6), and Helsinki (1956–7). He returned to the USA in 1961 with many mature and impressive works, thereafter dividing his time between composition and teaching, at the Peabody Conservatory (1962–4, 1966–8) and in New York at Queens College (1964–6), the Manhattan School (1972–4), and the Juilliard School (1976–7). He has fulfilled many commissions, among them the String Quartet no. 3 (for the Tokyo String Quartet) and the Concerto for Brass Choir and Orchestra (for the Dallas SO), and has had many works played by major American symphony orchestras. Several of his orchestral and chamber works have been recorded. In 1981 he received an award from the NEA.

Lees's music is basically traditional in approach; his musical development, comparatively free from the influence of avant-garde fashions and schools, has been steady and consistent. From an early interest in the bittersweet melodic style of Prokofiev and the bizarre and surrealist aspects of Bartók's music, he progressed naturally under the unconventional guidance of Antheil. He extended the tonal system with semitonal inflections, both harmonic and melodic, around not only the 3rd, but also the root, 5th, and octave of the major and minor chords. Rhythmically his music is active, with frequent changes of time signature and shifts of accent present even in his early works, particularly the award-winning String Quartet no. 1 and Sonata for two pianos, and his masterly Second Quartet. Having refined his style, he embarked on a series of large-scale works in which his secure command of orchestral technique and form is everywhere apparent. The Second Symphony with its recurring motifs and slow-movement finale (also a feature of the Third Symphony) is particularly notable. Of comparable stature are the Concerto for Orchestra (influenced by Bartók's), the virtuoso Violin Concerto, and the cantata–oratorio *Visions of Poets*. The ironic musical juxtapositions found occasionally in these earlier works dominate the Third Symphony and the bizarre *Medea of Corinth*. In the 1970s Lees concentrated on orchestral and chamber music, returning to writing songs at the end of the decade and to concertos with groups of soloists (as in the earlier Concerto for String Quartet and Orchestra) in the early 1980s.

WORKS

VOCAL AND CHORAL

Operas: The Oracle (1, Lees), 1956; The Gilded Cage (3, A. Reid), 1970–72, withdrawn

Other works: Songs of the Night (J. R. Nickson), S, pf, 1952; 3 Songs (Nickson, Blake), A, pf, 1959; Cyprian Songs (Nickson), Bar, pf, 1960; Visions of Poets (Whitman), S, T, chorus, orch, 1961; Medea of Corinth (R. Jeffers), S, Mez, Bar, B, wind qnt, timp, 1970; The Trumpet of the Swan (E. B. White), nar, orch, 1972; Staves (Nickson), S, pf, 1979; Omen (Nickson), S, pf, 1980; Paumanok (Whitman), Mez, pf, 1980

ORCHESTRAL

Profile, 1952; Declamations, str, pf, 1953; 4 syms., 1953, 1958, 1968, 1985; 2 pf concs., 1955, 1966; Divertimento-burlesca, 1957; Interlude, str, 1957; Vn Conc., 1958; Conc. for Orch, 1959; Concertante breve, 1959; Prologue, Capriccio and Epilogue, 1959; Ob Conc., 1963; Conc. for Str Qt and Orch, 1964; Spectrum, 1964; Conc., chamber orch, 1966; Fanfare for a Centennial, brass, perc, 1966; Silhouettes, 1967; Etudes, pf, orch, 1974; Labyrinths, band, 1975; Passacaglia, 1975; Conc. for Ww Qnt and Orch, 1976; Variations, pf, orch, 1976; Scarlatti Portfolio, ballet, chamber orch, 1978; Mobiles, 1980; Double Conc., vc, pf, orch, 1982; Conc. for Brass Choir and Orch, 1983; Portrait of Rodin, 1984

CHAMBER AND INSTRUMENTAL

Hn Sonata, 1951; 3 str qts, 1952, 1955, 1980–81; Evocation, fl, 1953; 2 vn sonatas, 1953, 1973; Movement da camera, fl, cl, pf, vc, 1954; 3 Variables, ob, cl, bn, hn, pf, 1955; Invenzione, vn, 1965; Duo, fl, cl, 1967; Study no. 1, vc, 1969; Collage, wind qnt, perc, str qt, 1973; Soliloquy Music for King Lear, fl, 1975; Dialogue, vc, pf, 1977; Vc Sonata, 1981; Pf Trio, 1983

Pf: 4 sonatas, 1949, 1950, 1956 (Sonata breve), 1963; Sonata, 2 pf, 1951; Toccata, 1953; Fantasia, 1954; 10 Pieces, 1954; 6 Ornamental Etudes, 1957; Kaleidoscopes, 1959; Epigrams, 1960, withdrawn; 3 Preludes, 1962; Odyssey, 1970; Fantasy Variations, 1984

Principal publisher: Boosey & Hawkes

BIBLIOGRAPHY

EwenD

D. Cooke: "The Music of Benjamin Lees," *Tempo*, no. 51 (1959), 20

——: "The Recent Music of Benjamin Lees," *Tempo*, no. 64 (1963), 11

——: "Benjamin Lees's Visions of Poets," *Tempo*, no. 68 (1964), 25

N. O'Loughlin: "Benjamin Lees's String Quartet Concerto," *Tempo*, no. 82 (1967), 21

——: "Two Works by Benjamin Lees," *Tempo*, no. 93 (1970), 19

N. Slonimsky: "Benjamin Lees in Excelsis," *Tempo*, no. 113 (1975), 14

NIALL O'LOUGHLIN

Leginska [Liggins], **Ethel** (*b* Hull, England, 13 April 1886; *d* Los Angeles, CA, 26 Feb 1970). Pianist, composer, and conductor. She early showed prodigious ability as a pianist; thanks to the patronage of a Hull shipping magnate and his wife, she was able to study at the Hoch Conservatory in Frankfurt, with Theodor Leschetizky in Vienna for three years, and in Berlin.

She adopted the name Leginska early in her professional career, and became widely known as the "Paderewski of woman pianists." She made her official début in London at the age of 16 and then gave concert tours in Europe before coming to the USA in 1913, where she achieved her greatest success in the 1916–17 season. A great favorite with the public, she was noted for her demanding programs and her innovations, such as playing an entire Chopin program without an intermission. In 1914 Leginska began to compose, studying formally with Bloch in 1918. Her output is relatively small and dates chiefly from the period of her lessons with Bloch and the 1920s; it includes songs, piano and chamber music, symphonic poems, a fantasy for piano and orchestra, and two operas. It is to her credit that Leginska was able to secure performances of her larger works at a time when women's compositions were rarely heard in public.

Because of nervous disorders, in 1926 Leginska retired as a pianist to concentrate on composition and conducting. After studying conducting with Goossens and Robert Heger during 1923, she established herself as one of the first female conductors, directing major orchestras in Munich, Paris, London, and Berlin in 1924. Her American conducting début took place on 9 January 1925 with the New York SO, and was followed by a triumphant performance at the Hollywood Bowl in August of that year. She conducted the Boston PO in 1926–7, the Boston Woman's SO in 1926–30, and the Woman's SO of Chicago in 1927–9. In 1930–31 she conducted at leading European opera houses. Notable performances included Beethoven's Ninth Symphony in Havana in 1933 and Dallas in 1934, and the première of her one-act opera *Gale* in 1935 by the Chicago City Opera, which she directed. After 1935 the novelty of Leginska's activities as a conductor faded, and in 1940 she moved to Los Angeles, where she taught piano into the 1950s. (*See also* WOMEN IN MUSIC, §3.)

BIBLIOGRAPHY

C. Neuls-Bates: "Leginska, Ethel," *NAW*

CAROL NEULS-BATES

Lehmann, Lilli (*b* Würzburg, Germany, 24 Nov 1848; *d* Berlin, Germany, 17 May 1929). German soprano. After making her operatic début in Prague (20 October 1865), she sang with great success in Danzig, Leipzig, Vienna, and London, and took part in the first complete performance of *Der Ring* at Bayreuth (1876). She was engaged permanently by the Royal Opera, Berlin, in 1870, but in 1885 broke her contract there and made her début at the Metropolitan Opera on 25 November as Carmen. During her first season at the Metropolitan, she also sang Brünnhilde (*Die Walküre*), Bertha (*Le prophète*), Marguerite, Irene (*Rienzi*), and Venus (*Tannhäuser*), adding Rachel (in Halévy's *La juive*), Meyerbeer's Valentine (*Les Huguenots*) and Selika (*L'africaine*), Norma, Aida, and Leonora (*Il trovatore*) to her repertory during the next six years. She took part in the first American performances of Karl Goldmark's *Die Königin von Saba* (2 December 1885) and *Merlin* (3 January 1887), *Tristan und Isolde* (1 December 1886), *Siegfried* (9 November 1887), and *Götterdämmerung* (25 January 1888), as well as the first complete *Ring* cycle given in the USA (March 1889). Her previous long experience in Germany gave her performances of these roles an authenticity and authority that were enormously influential in New York, where she was generally much admired.

In 1891 Lehmann went back to Berlin, but returned to New York to perform with the Damrosch Opera Company (1897) and appeared for one last season (her seventh) with the Metropolitan (1898–9). She made a final concert tour of the USA in 1901–2 before retiring. A successful teacher, she had many famous pupils including Olive Fremstad and Geraldine Farrar. Lehmann published among other works a manual on singing, *Meine Gesangskunst* (1902, 3/1922; Eng. trans., 1902, as *How to Sing*, enlarged 3/1924/*R*1972), and edited arias and songs for Peters. In 1888 she married the tenor Paul Kalisch, with whom she occasionally performed.

BIBLIOGRAPHY

L. Lehmann: *Mein Weg* (Leipzig, 1913, 2/1920; Eng. trans., 1914/*R*1977, as *My Path through Life*, rev. and enlarged 3/1924, repr. 1949)
W. J. Henderson: *The Art of Singing* (New York, 1938), 359
H. Pleasants: "Lilli Lehmann," *The Great Singers* (New York, 1966), 233

ELIZABETH FORBES

Lehmann, Lotte (*b* Perleberg, Germany, 27 Feb 1888; *d* Santa Barbara, CA, 26 Aug 1976). Soprano. She studied singing in Berlin with Mathilde Mallinger, Wagner's original Eva, and began her career in 1910 with the Hamburg Opera. She sang at Drury Lane, London, in 1914, and moved to Vienna two years later. Widely recognized after the end of World War I as one of the most eminent lyric-dramatic sopranos of her time, she retained her links with Vienna until the Anschluss; distaste for the Nazi regime drove her from Austria in 1938. She began her American career with a season at the Chicago Lyric Opera, making her début, as Wagner's Sieglinde, on 28 October 1930. Her Metropolitan début, in the same role, was on 11 January 1934, after which she sang regularly with the company until 1945. Her roles included Wagner's Elisabeth, Eva, and Elsa, as well as Tosca and the Marschallin (*Der Rosenkavalier*). During her stage career she performed in every major opera house in Europe and the USA. Her final operatic performance, as the Marschallin, was in October 1946 in San Francisco.

Lehmann also had an immensely successful career as a recitalist, appearing in concert for six years after her retirement from the Metropolitan; her lieder recitals won her a following no less devoted than her operatic public. Her final New York concert (Town Hall, 16 February 1951) was marked by emotional scenes. She sang once again in public, on 7 August 1951, at Santa Barbara, where she had settled in 1934. (She had become an American citizen during World War II.) After her retirement Lehmann remained busy writing and painting; she taught at the Music Academy of the West, Santa Barbara, and gave public master classes in lieder singing and operatic performance. She published verses and a novel as well as autobiographical writings and studies in interpretation. In 1962 she returned to the Metropolitan to direct a production of *Der Rosenkavalier*.

Though Prussian by birth, Lehmann came to represent to the world the traditional Viennese qualities of charm, breeding, and warm-heartedness. Along with her rich vocal gift went a rare theatrical power, though it was sometimes thought that the vivid personality expressed by her voice affected the purity and technical control of her singing. The best of her many records, made between 1917 and 1946, convey a vivid impression of her voice and urgently dramatic style.

WRITINGS

Midway in my Song (New York, 1938)
Five Operas and Richard Strauss (New York, 1964)
Eighteen Song Cycles (New York, 1971)

BIBLIOGRAPHY

L. Lehmann: *More than Singing* (New York, 1945)
——: *My Many Lives* (New York, 1948)

R. Gelatt: "Lotte Lehmann," *Music-makers* (New York, 1953), 121
P. L. Miller: "Lotte Lehmann," *Record News*, iv (1960), 391, 440; v (1960), 20, 45 [with discography]
R. Celletti: "Lehmann, Lotte," *Le grandi voci* (Rome, 1964) [with opera discography by R. Vegeto]
B. W. Wessling: *Lotte Lehmann . . . mehr als eine Sängerin* (Salzburg, 1969)
"Lehmann, Lotte," *CBY 1970*
M. de Schauensee: "The Maestro's Singers: Lotte Lehmann," *The Maestro*, iii/1–2 (1971), 14 [with discography by H. P. Court]
L. Rasponi: "Lotte Lehmann," *The Last Prima Donnas* (New York, 1982), 477

DESMOND SHAWE-TAYLOR/R

Lehrer, Tom [Thomas] **(Andrew)** (*b* New York, 9 April 1928). Songwriter and performer. He began piano lessons at the age of eight, and started writing and performing songs while a student of mathematics at Harvard University. He built up a cult following in Boston performing songs about current events and American social problems, and in 1953 began producing his own recordings and performing professionally in nightclubs on the East and West coasts. He made tours of Britain, Australia, and New Zealand in 1959–60, then retired from performing to return to studying and teaching mathematics; he taught first at the Massachusetts Institute of Technology (1962–71) and then at Cowell College, University of California, Santa Cruz, where he also lectured on the history of American musical comedy. He continued, however, to write songs – for the NBC television show "That Was the Week that Was" (1964–5) and for "The Electric Company" series made by the Children's Television Workshop for public television (1970–71). 27 of his songs were assembled in a revue, *Tomfoolery*, performed in Britain (1980) and the USA (1981).

Lehrer began to write songs at the time of the folksong revival, but unlike most songs of social commentary of that era his lyrics were often bitingly irreverent and even gruesome: *The Old Dope Peddler*, to the tune of *The Old Lamp Lighter*, caricatures certain sentimental songs; *The Hunting Song* is about sportsmen shooting each other; *We will all go together when we go* offers the prospect of total annihilation because of the proliferation of nuclear armaments; and *The Vatican Rag* satirizes church ritual. Other songs are brilliant parodies. Lehrer's conversational, sardonic tone of delivery has inspired a generation of musical comedians.

WORKS

Collections: *The Tom Lehrer Song Book* (New York, 1954) [L1]
Tom Lehrer's Second Song Book (New York, 1968) [L2]
Too Many Songs by Tom Lehrer (New York, 1981) [L3]

Selective list. Unless otherwise stated, dates are those of copyright for all published works; for unpublished works dates are those of first recording.

Alma, 1965; Be prepared, 1953, L1, L3; Bright College Days, 1953, L3; A Christmas Carol, 1954, L1, L3; Clementine, 1959; The Elements, 1959, L2, L3; Fight fiercely, Harvard!, 1953, L1, L3; The Folk Song Army, 1965, L2, L3; George Murphy, 1965; The Hunting Song, 1953, L1, L3; I got it from Agnes, 1953, L3; I hold your hand in mine, 1953, L1, L3; In old Mexico, 1959, L3; The Irish Ballad, 1952, L1, L3; It makes a fellow proud to be a soldier, 1959; I wanna go back to Dixie, 1953, L1, L3; Lobachevsky, recorded 1953, L3; L–Y, 1972, L3

The Masochism Tango, 1958, L2, L3; M. L. F. Lullaby, 1964, L2, L3; My Home Town, 1953, L1, L3; National Brotherhood Week, 1964, L2, L3; New Math, 1965, L3; Oedipus Rex, 1959; The Old Dope Peddler, 1953, L1, L3; Poisoning Pigeons in the Park, 1953, L2, L3; Pollution, 1965, L2, L3; Send the Marines, 1965, L2, L3; She's my girl, 1959, L3; Silent E, 1971, L3; Smut, 1965, L2, L3; So long, Mom (A Song for World War III), 1965, L2, L3; The Vatican Rag, 1965, L2, L3; Wernher von Braun, 1965, L2, L3; We will all go together when we go, 1958, L2, L3; Whatever became of Hubert?, recorded 1965, L2; When you are old and gray, 1953, L1, L3; Who's next?, 1965, L2, L3; The Wiener Schnitzel Waltz, 1953, L1, L3; The Wild West is where I want to be, 1953, L1, L3

BIBLIOGRAPHY

"Lehrer, Tom," *CBY 1982*
J. Bernstein: "Out of my Mind: Tom Lehrer Having Fun," *American Scholar*, liii (1984), 295

DEANE L. ROOT

Leiber and Stoller. Team of songwriters and producers. Lyricist Jerry Leiber (*b* Baltimore, MD, 25 April 1933) and composer Mike Stoller (*b* New York, 13 March 1933) began working with rhythm-and-blues singers and vocal groups while still in their teens; their first important hit, in 1953, was *Hound Dog*, recorded by Big Mama Thornton (later recorded by Presley). From 1957 to 1961 they were under contract to Atlantic Records, during which time they wrote and produced a series of comedy and novelty songs for the COASTERS, including *Riot in Cell Block no.9* (1954), *Yakety yak* (no.1, 1958), and *Charlie Brown* (no.2, 1959), that were marked by a wit unprecedented in rock-and-roll songwriting. For the Drifters they wrote and produced songs like *There goes my baby* (no.2, 1959) that used strings or Latin percussion to suggest a symphonic sound; they also worked with Ben E. King, LaVerne Baker, Ruth Brown, and Presley, for whom they wrote songs and film scores (including *Jailhouse Rock*, 1957). They formed Trio Music, which was located in the Brill Building in New York, and with which the songwriting team of Jeff Barry and Ellie Greenwich was associated. In 1969 they wrote and produced Peggy Lee's hit *Is that all there is?* (no.11), one of many later songs that aspired to a mordant sophistication reminiscent of Brecht and Weill. Leiber and Stoller helped define the fusion of rhythm-and-blues and pop that came to be known as pop-soul.

BIBLIOGRAPHY

W. Bolcom: Liner notes, *Other Songs by Leiber & Stoller* (Nonesuch H71346, 1978)

STEPHEN HOLDEN

Leich, Roland (Jacobi) (*b* Evansville, IN, 6 March 1911). Composer and teacher. He studied at the Gunn School of Music, Chicago, the Curtis Institute (BM 1934), Dartmouth College (BA 1935), and the Eastman School (MM 1942). His composition teachers were Borowski, Sowerby, Scalero, and Bernard Rogers; he also studied privately in Vienna for a brief period in 1933–4 with Webern. He taught at Dartmouth (1935–41) and after serving in the US Army during World War II was principal cellist of the Army's GI SO until it disbanded in March 1946. In that year he was appointed to the music faculty of Carnegie Institute of Technology (later Carnegie-Mellon University), where he taught theory and composition. He was director of the student chorus (1953–66) and served as acting head of the music department for two years shortly before his retirement in 1976. Leich has taken a keen interest in the musical life of Pittsburgh: he was accompanist and associate director of the Mendelssohn Choir (1952–68) and, from 1964, has served as program annotator for the Pittsburgh Chamber Music Society. He was twice a recipient of the Joseph H. Bearns Prize, in 1933 for *Housman Songs* and in 1937 for the String Quartet; he also received the Lauber Award (1933), and was a resident of the MacDowell Colony in 1947. Leich's songs are his most notable achievement. Clear, singable melodies abound in all his works, and although he uses a wide variety of harmonies and contrapuntal textures, his music is basically tonal and in balanced, often traditional, forms.

WORKS

Orch: Rondo, 1942; Concert Piece, ob, str, 1952; Prelude and Fugue, 1954
Songs, 1v, pf, unless otherwise stated: Housman Songs, 1932; 5 songs (Housman),

1939–78; 40 songs (Milne), 1940; 47 songs (Dickinson), 1940–65; 17 songs (S. H. Hay), 1956–84; Midsummer, 1976 (Hay), Mez, str, 1976; Seasonal Haiku (D. Goodfellow), Mez, pf/str qt, 1981; over 50 others

Choral: O Light Invisible (T. S. Eliot), cantata, SATB, orch, 1950; 2 Madrigals (Eliot), SATB, cl, 1956; The Town of Pittsburgh (H. H. Brackenridge), cantata, Bar, SATB, orch, 1958; Christmas the Year One A. D. (S. H. Hay), SATB, str, 1964; Fantasia on Hark the Herald Angels Sing, SATB, brass, timp, str, 1965; The Oxen (Hardy), SAB, orch, 1981; over 45 other works incl. Americana settings, 5 hymn tunes, folk melody arrs., hymn arrs.

Inst: 7 chorale preludes, org, 1931; Variations for Str Qt on a Theme by J. A. P. Schulz, 1932; Variations on a Theme by Schumann, pf, 1932; Str Qt, 1936; Aria and Tarantella, vc, pf, 1941; Fl Sonata, 1953; For Alice, pf, 1959; A Musical Christmas Wreath, ww qnt, harp, 1980; miscellaneous pf pieces, 1928–38

MSS in *PP*, *PPi*

Principal publishers: G. Schirmer, Shawnee, Westminster

BIBLIOGRAPHY

F. Dorian: "Current Chronicle," *MQ*, xlii (1956), 396

A. Petit: "Chorus of Centuries," *Pittsburgh Press* (28 July 1957), 3

J. Ball: "Praise of City Offered in Special Text," *Pittsburgh Press* (26 Nov 1958), 9

WILLIAM CRITSER

Leichtentritt, Hugo (*b* Pleschen, Posen [now Pleszow, Poznań, Poland], 1 Jan 1874; *d* Cambridge, MA, 13 Nov 1951). German musicologist, music critic, and composer. At the age of 15 he came to the USA where he studied liberal arts at Harvard University (BA 1894) and music with John Knowles Paine; he continued his musical studies in Paris (1894–5) and at the Hochschule für Musik in Berlin (1895–8). Subsequently he studied music history, philosophy, aesthetics, classical and modern literature, and art at Berlin University under Oscar Fleischer and Max Friedlaender (1898–1901), receiving the doctorate there in 1901 with a dissertation on Reinhard Keiser's operas. He taught in Berlin until 1933, then settled in the USA at the invitation of Harvard University, where he was a lecturer in music until his retirement in 1940; thereafter he lectured at Radcliffe College and New York University (1940–44).

Leichtentritt hoped to re-establish himself in the USA as a respected musicologist, writer on music, and (especially) composer, and the failure of his music to gain acceptance greatly disappointed him. As a writer on music his hopes were only partly realized, and as a musicologist he suffered for his strong opinions and characteristic directness of expression. He was an extremely thorough and painstaking scholar. For his monumental *Geschichte der Motette* (1908) he analyzed over 600 motets in score. Two works represent the culmination of his writings and the synthesis of his thought: *Music, History, and Ideas* (1938) and *Music of the Western Nations* (1956). He also published *Serge Koussevitzky, the Boston Symphony Orchestra and the New American Music* (1946). After his death his personal library was purchased by the University of Utah, and his manuscripts and personal papers were deposited in the Library of Congress.

BIBLIOGRAPHY

C. E. Selby: *A Catalogue of Books and Music Acquired from the Library of Dr. Hugo Leichtentritt by the University of Utah Library* (Salt Lake City, 1954)

N. Slonimsky: "Hugo Leichtentritt (1874–1951)," *Music of the Western Nations* (Cambridge, MA, 1956)

J. E. Seiach: *Leichtentritt's "History of the Motet": a Study and Translation (Chapters 7–15)* (diss., U. of Utah, 1958)

RODNEY H. MILL/R

Leidzén, Erik W(illiam) G(ustav) (*b* Stockholm, Sweden, 25 March 1894; *d* New York, 20 Dec 1962). Composer, arranger, conductor, and educator. He studied at the Royal Conservatory in Stockholm, immigrated to the USA in 1915, and assumed leadership of the Salvation Army New England Staff Band. He moved to New York, where he became music director of the Salvation Army's Centennial Memorial Temple, and wrote hundreds of vocal and instrumental compositions for the Army. He made orchestral transcriptions and wrote original works for the Goldman Band, many of which were published by Carl Fischer and Charles Colin. He was head of the theory department at the Ernest Williams School of Music for eight years, director of the Swedish Glee Club of Brooklyn and the Arma Company band, and a teacher at the National Music Camp, Interlochen, Michigan. Between 1951 and 1962 he taught at the Salvation Army's Star Lake Musicamp. In 1954 he conducted the US Air Force Orchestra in the première of his Irish Symphony. His published writings include *An Invitation to Band Arranging* (1950).

WORKS

Band, orch: 2 syms., incl. Irish Sym., 1939; 9 suites, incl. Suite in C, str, 1939; 11 ovs., incl. Holiday Ov., 1939; 7 chorale preludes, incl. Doxology, 1946; 8 rhapsodies, incl. 2 Swedish rhapsodies, 1950, 1952; Concertino, trbn, band, 1952; Sinfonietta, brass band, 1955; None Other Name, 1958; 33 works, solo inst, band; 63 sacred works, brass; 65 marches; *c*85 transcrs. of works by Bach, Bartók, Berlioz, Dvořák, Glière, Mussorgsky, Rimsky-Korsakov, Wagner, others

Inst: Wind septet, 1914; 2 suites, pf, 1915; 9 programmatic pieces, pf, 1916–40; Str Qt, 1920; Petite suite suédoise, vn, pf, 1922; Variations on a Theme of Chopin, 2 pf, 1932

Vocal: 114 works, chorus; 64 solo songs; 21 hymns, carols

Principal publishers: Associated, Belwin-Mills, Colin, C. Fischer, Salvation Army, G. Schirmer

BIBLIOGRAPHY

L. Fossey: *This Man Leidzén* (London, 1966)

R. W. Holz: *A History of the Hymn Tune Meditation and Related Forms in Salvation Army Instrumental Music in Great Britain and North America, 1880–1980* (diss., U. of Connecticut, 1981)

RAOUL CAMUS, RONALD W. HOLZ (work-list)

Leigh, Mitch [Mitchnick, Irwin] (*b* Brooklyn, NY, 30 Jan 1928). Composer and conductor. After studying music with Hindemith at Yale, he started a career as a jazz musician. In 1954 he began writing music for television and radio commercials, and in 1957 founded Music Makers Inc. to produce them. He composed the incidental music for a revival of G. B. Shaw's *Too True to be Good* (1963) and the Broadway play *Never Live over a Pretzel Factory* (1964), and achieved international success with the musical play *Man of La Mancha* (J. Darion, after Cervantes; 1965). Its successors, *Chu Chem* (lyrics by J. Haines and J. Wohl; 1966), *Cry for us All* (W. Alfred and P. Robinson; 1970), *Odyssey* (E. Segal; 1974), *Home Sweet Homer* (1976), and *Saravá* (N. R. Nash; 1978), had less success. Leigh was also the composer, conductor, and co-producer of the film *Once in Paris* (1978). Leigh is at home in a range of styles, which he has put to effective dramatic use in his treatment of varied subjects.

BIBLIOGRAPHY

S. Green: *The World of Musical Comedy* (New York, 1960, rev. and enlarged 4/1980)

ANDREW LAMB

Leinsdorf [Landauer], **Erich** (*b* Vienna, Austria, 4 Feb 1912). Conductor. He began serious piano studies at the age of eight; from the age of 11 he studied piano with Paul Emerich, and later had cello lessons with Emerich's sister; he also studied theory and composition with Paul Pisk. In the summer of 1930 he attended a master class in conducting at the Salzburg Mozarteum;

he then studied briefly at Vienna University and for two years (1931–3) at the State Academy of Music there. On his graduation he made his conducting début in the Musikvereinsaal. His early experience included a stint as a singing coach (1931–4), and he was rehearsal pianist for Webern's Singverein der Sozialdemokratischen Kunststelle. A quick learner, a fluent pianist, and gifted with an exceptional memory, he became Bruno Walter's assistant at Salzburg in 1934. In 1937, on Lotte Lehmann's recommendation to Bodanzky, he went to the Metropolitan Opera as assistant conductor. He made his début with *Die Walküre* on 21 January 1938, impressing with his energy and technical assurance. He conducted more Wagner and Strauss's *Elektra*, and, despite opposition from Melchior (who disliked his insistence on rehearsals) and Flagstad (who wanted to establish Edwin McArthur in the house), he was put in charge of the German wing after Bodanzky's death in November 1939. He became an American citizen in 1942.

In 1943 Leinsdorf succeeded Rodzinski as music director of the Cleveland Orchestra, but during his army service (1944) Cleveland made other plans. He again worked at the Metropolitan, took guest engagements (among them with the Cleveland Orchestra), and was conductor of the Rochester PO (1947–55). In 1956 he became music director of the New York City Opera, but in spite of his energetic attempts to enliven its repertory and style of performance, the appointment was not well received. In 1957 he returned to the Metropolitan as conductor and music consultant. In 1962 he succeeded Munch as music director of the Boston SO. He expanded the repertory and restored some of the technical finesse that had been lost in previous years. After some genuine excitement at the beginning (as Munch's personal and musical polar opposite, he had advantages as well as problems) it became evident that the arrangement was not a success, a situation it took the participants longer to admit than to observe. In 1969 he left Boston and began once more to travel. Except for conducting some Wagner at the Metropolitan, he has been more active in concert than in opera. From 1977 to 1980 he was principal conductor of the Berlin Radio SO. His honors include a fellowship in the American Academy of Arts and Sciences and honorary degrees from several colleges and universities in the USA. In 1979 he became a member of the National Council on the Arts.

Leinsdorf is curious and informed about many matters in and out of music, and articulate to the point of virtuosity in his adopted as well as his mother tongue. He has written his autobiography (1976) and the book *The Composer's Advocate: a Radical Orthodoxy for Musicians* (1981). Of quick intelligence, he has a remarkable capacity for recovering from difficult professional reverses. Because the restraint he has learned to apply to his nervous, restless temperament is strong, he is often an inhibited performer. An impression of tightness, of insufficient breathing space, is reinforced by a rhythmic weakness that leads him to rush the approach to the bar-line. Words, particularly German, inspire him, and some of his most memorable achievements have been with Schumann's *Szenen aus Goethe's "Faust,"* the earlier versions of *Fidelio* and Strauss's *Ariadne auf Naxos* (unfamiliar *ur*-versions being a special interest of his), and Brahms's *Ein deutsches Requiem*.

BIBLIOGRAPHY

H. Stoddard: "Erich Leinsdorf," *Symphony Conductors of the U.S.A.* (New York, 1957), 258

A. Blyth: "Erich Leinsdorf Talks," *Gramophone*, x/vii (1969–70), 740

E. Leinsdorf: *Cadenza: a Musical Career* (Boston, 1976)

J. Badal: "An Interview with Erich Leinsdorf," *Fanfare*, viii/1 (1984), 123

MICHAEL STEINBERG/R

Leisner, David (*b* Los Angeles, CA, 22 Dec 1953). Guitarist and composer. He studied at Wesleyan University (BA 1976); his principal teachers were John Duarte, David Starobin, and Angelo Gilardino (guitar), John Kirkpatrick and Karen Tuttle (interpretation), and Richard Winslow (composition). He won second prize at the Toronto International Guitar Competition (1975) and a silver medal at the International Guitar Competition of Geneva (1981). His New York début was in December 1979 at Merkin Hall, where he performed works by Bach, Johann Kaspar Mertz, Ives, Britten, and himself. He has taught guitar at Amherst College (1976–8) and, beginning in 1980, at the New England Conservatory. In addition to his deeply felt musicianship, he is noted for his fluent and secure technique and his championing of contemporary American guitar works, including some by Glass, Thomson, and Rorem. He has composed a String Quartet (1981), as well as works for solo guitar and duos for guitar with violin, cello, or voice (1982–4).

Erich Leinsdorf, 1970

BIBLIOGRAPHY

J. Wager-Schneider: "A Conversation with David Leisner," *Soundboard*, viii/2 (1981), 71

THOMAS F. HECK

Lemare, Edwin (Henry) (*b* Ventnor, Isle of Wight, England, 9 Sept 1865; *d* Hollywood, CA, 24 Sept 1934). Organist and composer. He received initial training under his father, a choirmaster and organist, and spent three years at the Royal Academy of Music, where he later became professor (in 1892). His reputation as a performer was established through the 100 recitals (two a day for several months) he played at the Invention Exhibition of 1882 on an instrument built by Bindley and Foster to demonstrate their new tubular-pneumatic action. Success led immediately to his employment by competing builders and as many as four programs per day on various instruments. In 1886 he began playing weekly programs in the Park Hall, Cardiff, while serving as organist and choirmaster at Sheffield Parish Church. In London he became organist of Holy Trinity Church, Sloane Street (in 1892) and of St. Margaret's, Westminster (1897), where a new Walker instrument was built for him.

A 100-recital tour of the USA and Canada during 1900–1 led to his engagement as organist of the Carnegie Institute, Pittsburgh (1902–5). He was one of the most brilliant and successful players of his day (tours took him across the Atlantic several dozen times, the Pacific four times) and a gifted extemporizer. His numerous recitals at the San Francisco Exposition of 1915 led to his employment as municipal organist in San Francisco in 1917, and further appointments in Portland, Maine, and Chattanooga until 1929. He also dedicated the gargantuan instrument in the Ocean Grove (New Jersey) Auditorium. He made 24 player rolls for the Aeolian Company and 96 for Welte.

Lemare's compositions include about 200 works for the organ, solo songs, anthems, settings of liturgical texts, and an Easter cantata. The *Andantino in D♭* became so popular that Lemare recast it in waltz form (with lyrics by Neil Moret) as *Moonlight and Roses*. He also made between 600 and 800 transcriptions (including many of Wagner's works), firmly believing that these would save the instrument from the confines of ecclesiastical music. His principal publishers were Novello, Schott, and G. Schirmer.

BIBLIOGRAPHY

E. H. Lemare: *Organs I have Met: the Autobiography of Edwin H. Lemare, 1866–1934, together with Reminiscences by his Wife and Friends* (Los Angeles, 1956) [incl. list of works]

WILLIAM OSBORNE

Lennon, John (Ono) [Winston] (*b* Liverpool, England, 9 Oct 1940; *d* New York, 8 Dec 1980). English rock-and-roll singer, songwriter, guitarist, and pianist. A member of the BEATLES from its formation in 1957 (as the Quarrymen), Lennon, with Paul McCartney, was primarily responsible for the unprecedented international influence the group exercised over popular music from 1962. In 1969 he married the Japanese conceptual artist Yoko Ono (whose name he incorporated into his own, and with whom he had been collaborating since 1966); after the Beatles disbanded in 1970 he worked almost exclusively in, and oriented his work towards, the USA. After a long battle with the Immigration and Naturalization Service, which had sought to deport him as a subversive, he was granted permanent residency in 1975 (see Wiener, 1984). He then began a five-year period of seclusion from public life; when he emerged in 1980, with new music, he was shot dead by a Beatles fan.

Lennon's progress as a solo artist was itself a sort of tragedy. From his first experimental albums with Ono in 1968 to *Rock 'n' Roll*, made in 1975, his music was marked by a confusion of motives: he simultaneously worked to retain his power as a pop star who could speak directly to millions of people, to realize himself as an avant-garde artist whose ideas were so profound as to be accessible only to an élite, and to change the world as the tribune of a mass political movement. Thus from one album to the next, and sometimes simultaneously, he communicated solipsism, generosity, rage, compassion, pomposity, intelligence, stupidity, desperation, and despair, and, at his best, an irreducible sense of struggle.

John Lennon and Yoko Ono, November 1980

Lennon's only successful synthesis of these opposed impulses came in 1970 with *John Lennon/Plastic Ono Band*, on which he presented himself as isolated and alienated but nevertheless linked with the world. As if for the first time, he confronted his troubled family past, his status as a mythic figure within popular culture, and structures of ideological domination both political and aesthetic. Such thematic concerns sparked his most interesting and adventurous music. As a singer he summoned up the most passionate and controlled voice of his career on *God*. In instrumentation he worked as if he were reinventing the rock-and-roll style; supplementing his own guitar and piano with Klaus Voorman's bass guitar and Ringo Starr's drums, he produced a rough-edged, primitive, sometimes violent sound, which demolished conventional pop rhythms and melodies. Presaging the style employed by punk groups such as the Sex Pistols in the mid-1970s, it was perhaps the most radical music any pop musician had offered an expectant audience, and compared with the first solo albums by McCartney and George Harrison, both of which reached no. 1, it did not sell well, rising only to no. 6. In the fiercely competitive milieu of mass-market pop, Lennon pulled back in 1970 with *Imagine*, a strong but far more ordinary recording, and was rewarded with a place at the top of the charts. At the same time, however, he was striking out in other directions. With Ono he staged a series of bizarre "Bed-Ins for Peace" and made experimental films. With various left-wing musicians and promoters, he issued an artistically and commercially disastrous collection of banal protest songs (*Some Time in New York City*, no.48, 1972), and made plans for a national tour to voice opposition to President Richard Nixon. Like the projected "Toronto Peace Festival," which was to have been staged in 1970 before a non-paying audience of a million and to have involved the participation of beings from other planets, this scheme was abandoned.

Musically Lennon retreated further into a bland pop style with *Mind Games* (no.9, 1973), *Walls and Bridges* (no.1, 1974), and *Rock 'n' Roll*. The last was a collection of mostly stiff renderings of classic 1950s rock songs (such albums were a pop commonplace at the time); Lennon's need to reveal himself to his enormous audience as a challenging individual, and at the same time to be unquestioningly accepted, had finally led to his having nothing to say. As a craftsman he could still create chart successes, but as a pop artist, who defines what is new, or an avant-garde artist, who defines what will be, he had virtually ceased to function. So he withdrew.

When he returned in 1980 with *Double Fantasy*, a collaboration with Ono, it was clear that he had found no new direction. The music was flat and the theme of the album – a celebration of family life – sentimental. But the singing was vibrant and vital, full of conviction and playfulness, and it pointed to a real artistic future. Lennon's entire solo career was an attempt to escape the group identity of the Beatles and to define himself, within a public context, as an individual with his own music. Just at the time when he finally seemed ready to pursue that goal his career came to an abrupt end.

RECORDINGS

Selective list, only those made in the USA; recorded for Apple unless otherwise stated.

As soloist: Instant Karma (1818, 1970); *John Lennon/Plastic Ono Band* (3372, 1970), incl. God; Do the Oz (1835, 1971); *Imagine* (3379, 1971); *Mind Games* (3414, 1973); *Walls and Bridges* (3416, 1974); *Rock 'n' Roll* (3419, 1975); *Shaved Fish* (3421, 1975), incl. Instant Karma, We all shine on

With Y. Ono: *Unfinished Music no.1: Two Virgins* (5001, 1968); *Unfinished Music no.2: Life with the Lions* (Zapple 3357, 1969); *Wedding Album* (3361, 1969); *Live Peace in Toronto* (3362, 1970), incl. Cold Turkey, Give peace a chance; *Some Time in New York City* (3392, 1972); *Double Fantasy* (Geffen 2001, 1980); *Milk and Honey* (Polygram 8171601, 1984)

BIBLIOGRAPHY

"Lennon, John," *CBY 1965*

J. Wenner: *Lennon Remembers* (San Francisco, 1971)

R. Christgau: "Living without the Beatles," *Any Old Way You Choose It: Rock and Other Pop Music, 1967–1973* (Baltimore, 1973), 229

B. Ballister: "Who and What Killed the Toronto Pop Festival?," *The Rolling Stone Rock 'n' Roll Reader*, ed. B. Fong-Torres (New York, 1974), 571–611

J. Cocks: "The Last Day in the Life," *Time*, cxvi/25 (22 Dec 1980), 18

G. Marcus: "John Lennon," *New West*, vi/1 (Jan 1981), 128

D. Sheff and G. Golson: *The Playboy Interviews with John Lennon and Yoko Ono* (New York, 1981)

J. Cott and C. Doudna, eds.: *The Ballad of John & Yoko* (Garden City, NY, 1982)

M. Pang and H. Edwards: *Loving John* (New York, 1983)

J. Wiener: *Come Together: John Lennon in his Time* (New York, 1984)

R. Coleman: *Lennon* (New York, 1985)

GREIL MARCUS

Lenox Quartet. String quartet, founded at the Berkshire Music Center, Lenox, Massachusetts, in 1958. Its original members were Peter Marsh (first violin, 1958–80), Theodora Mantz (second violin, 1958–80), Scott Nickrenz (viola, 1958–61), and Donald McCall (cello, 1958–77). Marsh was succeeded by Paul Kantor; Delmar Pettys alternated with Mantz as second violinist during the years 1965–77, and Warwick Lister held this position from 1978. Other violists have been Paul Hersh (1962–74), Toby Appel (1975–77), Patricia McCarty (1978–80), and Darrell Barnes (1980–). Einar Holm (1978–) succeeded McCall as cellist. The ensemble, which was first sponsored by the Fromm Foundation, has appeared at many major festivals including, in the USA, those at Aspen, Ravinia Park (Chicago), and Lincoln Center (New York). The Lenox Quartet has made a specialization of performing 20th-century works; it gave the premières of Luciano Berio's *Sincronie* and Ezra Sims's String Quartet no.3, both in 1965, and of John Cooper's *Ratalis* in 1983. The group has held residencies at Grinnell (Iowa) College; SUNY, Binghamton; and Ithaca (New York) College.

NADIA TURBIDE

Lenox String Quartet. String quartet, active from 1922 to 1928. Its members were SANDOR HARMATI (first violinist), Wolfe Wolfinsohn (second, and later first, violinist), Edwin Edeler (second violinist), Nicholas Moldovan (violist, succeeded by Herbert Borodkin), and Emmeran Stoeber (cellist). The group presented many works by prominent American composers of the time, including Daniel Gregory Mason, David Stanley Smith, Rosario Scalero, and Frederick Jacobi. The quartet was unrelated to the Lenox Quartet.

NADIA TURBIDE

Lentz, Daniel K(irkland) (*b* Latrobe, PA, 10 March 1942). Composer. He studied music and philosophy at St. Vincent College (BA 1962), music history and composition at Ohio University (MA 1965), and composition with Arthur Berger, Alvin Lucier, and Harold Shapero at Brandeis University (1965–7) and with Sessions and Rochberg at the Berkshire Music Center (1966). He has been visiting lecturer at the University of California, Santa Barbara (1968–70), and at Antioch College in Yellow Springs, Ohio (1973). His honors include a Gaudeamus award (1972), grants from the Howard Foundation (1974), the NEA (1973, 1975, 1977, 1979), and the Deutscher Akademischer Austauschdienst (1979), and various commissions. Many of Lentz's early works are theater pieces imbued with black humor, involving performers, tape and lighting systems, and props; notable among them is *A Piano: Piece*, in which the pianist acts as a surgeon (complete with a stethoscope and hospital smock) while a concert grand piano "gives birth" to a baby grand (a toy piano placed beforehand inside the concert grand). During this period Lentz organized a performing group, the California Time Machine; its members included the sculptor and performance artist Wolfgang Stoerchle and the composer Harold Budd, both of whom later toured with him as a trio. Lentz's mature works are lyrical and consonant; they often involve rich polyphony, reminiscent of the Renaissance, which is created through the use of an echo delay system. Principal among these is *Missa umbrarum*, in which the singers rub and strike the rims of wine glasses, producing pitches which rise during the course of the music as the performers sip wine from the glasses. During the late 1970s Lentz turned more to the recording studio as a context in which to create music, though he continues to perform live and to direct his own ensemble, LENTZ, formed in Los Angeles in the mid-1980s.

WORKS

Theater and mixed-media pieces: A Piano: Piece, 1965; Ecumenical Council, 1965; Gospel Meeting, 1965; Paul and Judy Meet the Time Tunnel, 1966; Paul and Judy Meet Startrek, 1966; Hi-yo Paint, 1968; Air Meal Spatial Delivery, conceptual piece, 1969; Work of Crow, 1970

Pfmrs, echo delay: Canon and Fugue (Canon and Fugle), 1971; King Speech Songs, 1972; You can't see the forest . . . Music, 1972; Missa umbrarum, 1973; Song(s) of the Sirens (Les sirènes), 1973; 3 Pretty Madrigals, 1976; Dancing on the Sun, 1980; Music by Candlelight (Love and Death), 1980; Uitoto, 1980; Is it Love, 1984; Bacchus, 1985

Vocal: I, a Double Conc. (Senescence sonorum), amp body sounds, chorus, orch, 1970; Fermentation Notebooks: 1 Kissing Song, 2 Rising Song, 3 Drinking Song, 28–48 unacc. vv, no.3 with wine glasses, 1972; O-Ke-Wa (North American Eclipse), 12 solo vv, bells, rasps, drums, 1974; Sun Tropes, 7 solo vv, recs, kalimbas, 1975; Composition in Contrary and Parallel Motion, 16 solo vv, perc, 4 kbd, 1977; The Elysian Nymph, 8 solo vv, 8 mar, 1978; Wolf is Dead, vv, perc, 1979, rev. 6 solo vv, 8 kbd, 1982; Wail Song, 1v, 5 solo vv, 8 kbd, 1983; On the Leopard Altar (Aztec Altar), 1v, 2 kbd, 1983; 9 other works, 1965–76

Inst: Pf Piece for Little Kids with Big Hands, 1962; 3 Episodes from Exodus, org, perc, 1962; 3 Haiku in 4 Movts, str qt, 1963; 8 Dialectics 8, 18 insts, 1964; Fünke (Rhapsody), fl, vib, drums, db, pf, 1964; Sermon: Saying Something with Music, str qt, elec, 1966; The Last Concert, in 3: Love and Conception, Birth and Death, Fate and Death, pf, elec, 1968; Pastime, str inst, elec, 1969; 10 Minus 30 Minutes, str orch, 1970; Point Conception, 9 pf, 1981; Lascaux (Chumash Tombs), wine glasses, 1984

Tape: Montage Shift, 1963; No Exit, 1963; Eleison, 1965; Medeighnia's, 1965

Principal publisher: Soundings, Source

BIBLIOGRAPHY

D. Cope: *New Directions in Music* (Dubuque, IA, 1971, 3/1981), 65
D. Lentz: "Music Lib," *Soundings*, nos.3–4 (1972), 24
G. Eister: "Dan'l Lentz: Words and Music," *Soundings*, no.10 (1976)
I. D. Marshall: "Ny musik i Californien," *Nutida Musik*, xx/1 (1976), 5
J. Diliberto: "Daniel Lentz," *Down Beat*, lii/6 (1985), 38

PETER GARLAND

Lenya [Lenja], **Lotte** [Blamauer, Karoline Wilhelmine] (*b* Vienna, Austria, 18 Oct 1898; *d* New York, 27 Nov 1981). Singing actress. She studied dance in Zurich (1914–20) before going to Berlin, where she turned to the spoken theater. Her professional collaboration with KURT WEILL began shortly after their marriage in 1926, when she appeared in his and Brecht's *Mahagonny* at Baden-Baden (1927). With her creation of Jenny in *Die Dreigroschenoper* (Berlin, 1928; later translated by Marc Blitzstein as *The Threepenny Opera*) and the subsequent recordings and film (directed by G. W. Pabst), she established an international reputation. While continuing a notable career as an actress, she created three further roles in works by Weill, singing Anna in the choral ballet *Die sieben Todsünden* in Paris (1933), Miriam in *The Eternal Road* (1937), and the Duchess in *The Firebrand of Florence* (1945) in New York, where the couple had settled in 1935.

Soon after Weill's death in 1950, Lenya began to devote much of her time to the revival of some of his most important works from the German years and recreated Jenny in the long-running New York production of *The Threepenny Opera* (see illustration). Her live and recorded performances won for her and for Weill a new or renewed reputation in many lands, and established as "classical" a performing style whose characteristics of timbre and tessitura were markedly different from those of her Berlin years. But what had survived from those years, and most remarkably developed and matured, was that combination of dramatic insight and musical instinct, of intelligence, wit, coolness, and passion, which arose from a strictly inimitable and seemingly monogamous relationship with the music itself. Although her tastes in both popular and classical music were broad, as a performer she confined herself almost entirely to the songs of her husband, and to the one extended work he composed especially for her, *Die sieben Todsünden*; this was enough to establish her as one of the outstanding *diseuses* of the time.

BIBLIOGRAPHY

"Lenya, Lotte," *CBY 1959*
C. Osborne: "Berlin in the Twenties: Conversations with Otto Klemperer and Lotte Lenya," *London Magazine*, i/2 (1961), 43
H. Marx, ed.: *Weill-Lenya* (New York, 1976)

DAVID DREW

Leonard, Eddie [Toney, Lemuel Gordon] (*b* Richmond, VA, 1875; *d* New York, 29 July 1941). Minstrel and vaudeville performer and composer. He served in the army from 1895 to 1898. He also attempted to become a professional baseball player in Baltimore, and it is said that he became a minstrel after George Primrose saw him entertaining the other players in the clubhouse, having failed to make the team. He then went to work for Primrose and West's Minstrels, where he changed his name and soon became a star performer. He played in vaudeville until that form declined in the late 1920s, then occasionally appeared in nightclubs; he also performed in a number of Broadway shows. Leonard wrote many of his own songs, including his first hit *Just because she made them Goo-goo Eyes*, *Roll dem Boly Boly Eyes*, *I Lost my Mandy*, and his most famous song, *Ida, Sweet as Apple Cider* (1903). Leonard's 40-year career gave him a reputation as one of the greatest minstrels of his day. He had a natural talent for song and dance, and his style significantly influenced later performers such as Al Jolson and Eddie Cantor.

Lotte Lenya as Jenny in the 1954 New York production of Kurt Weill's "The Threepenny Opera": painting (1954) by Saul Bolasni in the National Portrait Gallery, Smithsonian Institution

BIBLIOGRAPHY

E. Leonard: *What a Life: I'm Telling you* (New York, 1935)

Obituary, *New York Times* (30 July 1941)

ROBERT B. WINANS

Leonhard, Charles (*b* Anadarko, OK, 8 Dec 1915). Music educator. He obtained a BM in public school music in 1937 and another in piano in 1938 at the University of Oklahoma and an MA at Columbia University Teachers College (1941). He was an assistant professor of music education at Teachers College (1946–51) and took the EdD there (1949). In 1951 he joined the faculty of the University of Illinois, where he was chairman of the graduate committee for music education. *Foundations and Principles of Music Education* (1959, 2/1972), which he wrote with Robert W. House, has long been an important text in music teacher education. He also edited a basic series for elementary and junior high school music classes, *Discovering Music Together* (1966–70), and the series *Contemporary Perspectives in Music Education* (1970–73). He has written extensively on the philosophy of music education, music aesthetics, program development, and musicianship.

GEORGE N. HELLER

Leppard, Raymond (John) (*b* London, England, 11 Aug 1927). Conductor, harpsichordist, and editor. He studied at the University of Cambridge (1948–52) and made his London début as a conductor in 1952; he soon became known particularly for his lively interpretations, mainly with the English Chamber Orchestra, of 17th- and 18th-century music. He made his Covent Garden début in 1959 in Handel's *Samson*. From 1973 to 1980 he was principal conductor of the BBC Northern SO in Manchester. He made his American début as a guest conductor of the New York PO in 1969 and thereafter conducted many of the leading American orchestras, including the Boston SO, Chicago SO, Detroit SO, and Pittsburgh SO. In 1976 he settled in the USA, becoming an American citizen in 1983. His first opera performances in the USA were in Santa Fe in 1974; he has since conducted at the San Francisco Opera, New York City Opera, and Metropolitan Opera. In 1984 he became principal guest conductor of the St. Louis SO.

Leppard is particularly known for his appealing versions of early Italian operas, which he has conducted at Glyndebourne (Monteverdi's *L'incoronazione di Poppea*, 1962), Santa Fe (Cavalli's *Egisto*, 1974), and elsewhere, though their free approach to the texts has not passed without criticism. Several of his editions have been published, and he has made some recordings based on the Glyndebourne performances. His conducting is characterized by his light, dance-like rhythms, his polished phrasing, and his keen sense of color. Among his recordings are many of music by Bach, Handel, and French composers (he conducted Rameau's *Dardanus* at the Paris Opéra in 1981), and Thomson's *The Mother of us all* with the Santa Fe Opera.

BIBLIOGRAPHY

A. Blyth: "Raymond Leppard Talks to Alan Blyth," *The Gramophone*, xlix (1971–2), 614

R. S. Clark: "Raymond Leppard," *Stereo Review*, xxxii/2 (1974), 76

S. Fleming: "Raymond Leppard," *HiFi/MusAm*, xxviii/9 (1978), 6

M. Mayer: "Changing His Spots," *Opera News*, xliii/21 (1979), 14

"Leppard, Raymond (John)," *CBY 1980*

J. L. Holmes: "Leppard, Raymond," *Conductors on Record* (Westport, CT, 1982), 389

D. J. Soria: "Raymond Leppard," *HiFi/MusAm*, xxxii/8 (1982), 6

STANLEY SADIE

Lerdahl, Fred [Alfred] **(Whitford)** (*b* Madison, WI, 10 March 1943). Composer and theorist. He studied at Lawrence University (BM 1965) and Princeton (MFA 1968), where his teachers included Kim, Cone, and Babbitt. On a Fulbright scholarship in 1968–9 he attended the Freiburg Hochschule für Musik, where he was a pupil of Wolfgang Fortner. He has received many other awards, among them the Koussevitzky Composition Prize (1966), a National Institute of Arts and Letters Award (1971), and a Guggenheim Fellowship (1974–5); in 1981–2 he was composer-in-residence at IRCAM in Paris. He has had works commissioned by, among others, the Fromm Foundation with the Berkshire Music Center (*Chords*, 1974), the Koussevitzky Music Foundation with the Chamber Music Society of Lincoln Center (*Eros*, 1975), the Orpheus Trio (*Etudes*, 1977), the Juilliard Quartet with the Joslyn Art Museum (String Quartet no. 1, 1978), and the Pro Arte Quartet (String Quartet no.2, 1980–82). Lerdahl has taught at the University of California, Berkeley (1969–71), Harvard University (1970–9), and Columbia University (1979–85); from 1985 he was on the faculty of the University of Michigan.

Lerdahl's early music, post-Schoenbergian in style, is well exemplified by *Wake* (1968), which draws on *Finnegans Wake*. Lines and phrases from Joyce are assembled so as to echo the novel's major themes and structure. Instrumentation, melodic design, rhythm, and texture are used to reflect and elaborate the text, and thus interpret Joyce's power to transmit abstract sound through language. With *Chords* (1974, rev. 1983) and *Eros* (1975) a new stage in Lerdahl's musical syntax began. Tonal elements were incorporated into his musical language, redefining musical procedures in a highly original and expressive way. At the same time, his treatment of form became more strict. *Eros* consists of 21 continuous variations, each 20 measures long. The text, "Coitus," from *Lustra* (1915) by Ezra Pound, serves as a point of departure: it is intoned in its entirety only once, in the first variation, and is thereafter varied along with the music. The passionate utterance of the singer contrasts with the classical variation technique utilized throughout. A rigorous underlying structure governs the unfolding of all melodic, rhythmic, and harmonic details. The work as a whole may be viewed as three increasingly climactic cycles of seven variations each.

From the variation technique of *Eros* spring Lerdahl's most ambitious works, the First and Second String Quartets (1978, 1980–82). Although they were written as independent works, the Second is a sequel to the First. Written in "expanding variation" form each variation is half as long again as the preceding one; thus the initial variation lasts seconds, the final one six minutes. The Second Quartet continues this variation procedure with its two parts, nine and thirteen minutes in length. The First Quartet is inward, given to sudden changes and silences; the Second is outwardly intense and full of sweep.

Lerdahl has also been productive as a theorist. Since 1974 he and the linguist Ray Jackendoff have developed in a series of articles an innovative theory of tonal music that is based on generative linguistics and cognitive science; their monograph, *A Generative Theory of Tonal Music*, appeared in 1983. Lerdahl has continued to explore areas of musical cognition, and has pursued interests in computer-assisted composition and timbre. His work in theory, in addition to having independent value, serves as a foundation for his own creative activity as a composer.

WORKS

Pf Fantasy, 1964; Str Trio, 1965–6; Wake (Joyce), Mez, vn, va, vc, harp, perc ens, 1968; Chromorhythmos, orch, 1972; Aftermath (Lerdahl), cantata, S, Mez, Bar, chamber ens, 1973; Chords, orch, 1974, rev. 1983; Eros: Variations (Pound: Coitus), Mez, a fl, va, harp, pf, elec gui, elec db, perc, 1975; 6 Etudes, fl, va, harp, 1977; 2 str qts, 1978, 1980–82; Waltzes, vn, va, vc, db, 1981; Beyond the Realm of Bird (Dickinson), S, chamber orch, 1981–4; Episodes and Refrains, wind qnt, 1982

Principal publishers: ACA, Mobart

NOEL B. ZAHLER

Lerner, Alan Jay (*b* New York, 31 Aug 1918). Lyricist and librettist. He studied at the Institute of Musical Art, New York, and at Harvard University (BS 1940), where he contributed to student shows. After graduation he worked as a scriptwriter for radio. In 1942 he met the composer FREDERICK LOEWE, with whom he wrote a remarkable series of musicals, including *Brigadoon* (1947), *Paint your Wagon* (1951), *My Fair Lady* (1956), and *Camelot* (1960). Lerner also collaborated with Weill on *Love Life* (1948), with Burton Lane on *On a Clear Day you Can See Forever* (1965) and *Carmelina* (1979), with Previn on *Coco* (1969), with Leonard Bernstein on *1600 Pennsylvania Avenue* (1976), and with Strouse on *Dance a Little Closer* (1983). Although none of these works enjoyed the success of his shows with Loewe, Lerner's lyrics, among the most elegantly literate of his time, are of the highest quality. His superior dialogue flows smoothly and evolves into warm, witty songs; in *My Fair Lady* both lyrics and dialogue are so thoroughly Shavian that it is difficult to tell which are Shaw's and which Lerner's. His librettos, however, frequently betray a lack of theatrical tension. Lerner wrote an autobiographical account of the making of *My Fair Lady*, *Camelot*, and the film *Gigi*, entitled *The Street where I Live* (1978). Lerner and Loewe were recipients of a Kennedy Center Award in 1985.

For illustration *see* LOEWE, FREDERICK.

WORKS

Edition: *The Lerner and Loewe Songbook*, ed. A. Sirmay (New York, 1962)

STAGE

Unless otherwise indicated, Lerner wrote both librettos and lyrics, music is by F. Loewe, and dates are those of first New York performance.

Life of the Party (lyrics E. Crooker), Detroit, 8 Oct 1942
What's Up (lib. with A. Pierson), 11 Nov 1943
The Day before Spring, 22 Nov 1945
Brigadoon, 13 March 1947 [incl. The Heather on the Hill; Come to me, bend to me; Almost like being in love; I'll go home with bonnie Jean], film, 1954
Love Life, music by K. Weill, 7 Oct 1948 [incl. Here I'll Stay, Green-up Time]
Paint your Wagon, 12 Nov 1951 [incl. I talk to the trees], film, 1969
My Fair Lady (after G. B. Shaw: Pygmalion), 15 March 1956 [incl. The rain in Spain; I could have danced all night; On the street where you live; Get me to the church on time; I've grown accustomed to her face], film, 1964
Camelot (after T. H. White: The Once and Future King), 3 Dec 1960 [incl. Camelot, If ever I would leave you], film, 1967
On a Clear Day you Can See Forever, music by B. Lane, 17 Oct 1965 [incl. On a clear day you can see forever]
Coco, music by A. Previn, 18 Dec 1969
1600 Pennsylvania Avenue, music by L. Bernstein, 4 May 1976
Carmelina (lib. with J. Stein), music by Lane, 8 April 1979
Dance a Little Closer, music by C. Strouse, 11 May 1983

FILMS

An American in Paris (screenplay), music by G. Gershwin, 1951
Royal Wedding, music by Lane, 1951
Gigi (after Colette), music by Loewe, 1958 [incl. Thank heaven for little girls; I remember it well; Gigi; The night they invented champagne]; adapted for stage, New York, 13 Nov 1973
The Little Prince (after A. de Saint-Exupéry: Le petit prince), music by Loewe, 1974

BIBLIOGRAPHY

"Lerner, Alan Jay [and] Loewe, Frederick," *CBY 1958*
A. J. Lerner: *The Street where I Live* (New York, 1978)

GERALD BORDMAN

Leslie, Herbert. Pseudonym of CHARLES L. JOHNSON.

Lessard, John (Ayres) (*b* San Francisco, CA, 3 July 1920). Composer. He began piano lessons at the age of five and trumpet at nine and two years later joined the San Francisco Civic SO. He studied piano and theory with Elsie Belenky and also worked briefly with Cowell. From 1937 to 1940 he was a pupil of Boulanger, Georges Dandelot, Alfred Cortot, and Ernst Lévy at the Ecole Normale de Musique, Paris. The following year he continued his studies with Boulanger at the Longy School of Music, Cambridge, Massachusetts. He has received two Guggenheim fellowships (1946, 1953) and awards from the Alice M. Ditson Fund (1946) and the American Academy of Arts and Letters (1952). In 1962 he was appointed to teach at SUNY, Stony Brook. He is also an accomplished pianist and conductor.

Lessard's compositions, eloquent and dramatic, are neo-classical in style; he also employs serial techniques though is not dependent on any rigid system. The Piano Sonata, presented in 1941, won him high critical praise from Virgil Thomson and wide public recognition. In the early postwar years he was fortunate to have peformances of several of his orchestral works led by Barzin, Bernstein, and Thor Johnson (in New York and elsewhere). During the period 1949–64 Lessard concentrated on songs for voice and piano, composing over 35 settings. *Movements*, a series of works begun in 1976, explores the interaction of the trumpet with other instruments.

WORKS

Orch: Vn Conc., 1942; Box Hill, ov., 1946; Cantilena, ob, str, 1947; Little Concert, 1947; Conc. for Wind Insts, 1949; Conc., (fl, cl)/(2 ob, hn), bn, str, 1952; Serenade, str, 1953; Don Quixote and the Sheep, Bar, B, orch, 1955; Serenade, 1957; Suite, 1959; Sinfonietta concertante, 1961; Harp Conc., 1963; Pastimes and an Alleluia, 1974

Vocal: over 35 songs, 1v, pf, incl. Ariel (Shakespeare), 1941, Orpheus (Shakespeare), 1943, Full Fathom Five (Shakespeare), 1948, When as in Silks my Julia Goes (Herrick), 1951, Rose-cheekt Laura (Campion), 1960; 2 Madrigals, SSATB, 1955; 12 Songs from Mother Goose, 1v, str trio, 1964; Stars, Hill, Valley, S, pf, 1983

Chamber: Wind Octet, 1952; Vc Sonata, 1956; Trios of Consanguinity, fl, va, vc, 1957; Trio in sei parti, pf trio, 1966; Quodlibets I–III, 2 tpt, trbn, 1967; Fragments from the Cantos of Ezra Pound, cantata, Bar, chamber ens, 1969; Wind Qnt no. 2, 1970; Brass Qnt, 1971; Movements I–VIII, tpt, other inst(s), 1976–9; Concert Duo, va, gui, 1981; Divertimento, gui, 1981; Music nos. 1–3, gui, perc, 1983; Concert Duo, 2 gui, 1984; other duets, trios, qnts

Kbd: Pf Sonata, 1940; Mask, pf, 1946; Little Concert, pf, 1947; Toccata in 4 Movts, hpd, 1951; Threads of Sound Recalled, pf, 1980; other pf and hpd works

Principal publishers: ACA, Joshua

BARBARA A. PETERSEN

Lev, Ray (*b* Rostov-na-Donu, Russia, 8 May 1912; *d* New York, 20 May 1968). Pianist. Her family immigrated to the USA when she was a year old. She began to study piano at the age of 13 with Walter Ruel Cowles, and later she was a pupil of Rebecca Davidson and Gaston Déthier. Having won the American Matthay Association Prize in 1930, she went to study in London with Matthay. She made her concert début in 1931 at the Eastbourne (Sussex) Festival and her recital début the following summer at Wigmore Hall. She returned to the USA in 1933, performing for her American début the Tchaikovsky Piano Concerto no. 1 with the National Orchestral Association. Between 1934 and 1938 she toured extensively throughout Europe and North America, and she continued to give recitals and concerts with major American orchestras until shortly before her death. She was a champion of contemporary American music and introduced many works by neglected or lesser-known composers such as Riegger, William Mayer, and Roy Travis. Her numerous recordings included both solo and chamber works, chiefly of the 19th-century repertory.

BIBLIOGRAPHY

G. Kehler: *The Piano in Concert*, i (Metuchen, NJ, 1982), 736

CECIL B. ARNOLD

Levant, Oscar (*b* Pittsburgh, PA, 27 Dec 1906; *d* Beverly Hills, CA, 14 Aug 1972). Pianist, composer, and writer. After training with local teachers in Pittsburgh he moved to New York, where he studied with the pianist Zygmunt Stojowski; later he briefly studied composition with Schoenberg. He was active as a pianist with jazz bands and as a composer of popular songs, but achieved prominence as a sympathetic interpreter of Gershwin's music. His works for the Broadway stage brought his talents to the attention of Hollywood, and after moving to the West Coast he wrote the scores for several films (including *Street Girl* and *Tanned Legs*) and also appeared in some (including *Dance of Life* and *An American in Paris*). Among his compositions are a piano concerto, which he played with the NBC SO in 1942, a *Nocturne* for orchestra (1937), two string quartets, and many popular songs. His writings include three books of autobiographical reminiscences, *A Smattering of Ignorance* (1940), *The Memoirs of an Amnesiac* (1965), and *The Unimportance of Being Oscar* (1968), which are caustic in content and conversational in tone.

GEORGE GELLES/R

Levarie, Siegmund (*b* Vienna, Austria, 24 July 1914). Musicologist, teacher, and conductor. He took a diploma in conducting at the New Vienna Conservatory (1935) and was trained as a musicologist at the University of Vienna (PhD 1938). Moving to the USA, he joined the faculty of the University of Chicago, where he taught from 1938 to 1952. There he organized (in 1938) a collegium musicum, one of the first in the USA, and directed the group in performances of early music. He was dean of the Chicago Musical College (1952–4), then accepted appointment as professor at Brooklyn College, CUNY; he served as chairman of the music department (1954–62) and taught there, as well as at the Graduate School, CUNY, until his retirement in 1984. In addition to his academic duties he was executive director of the Fromm Music Foundation (1952–6) and directed the Brooklyn Community SO (1954–8); he has been a participant in the Metropolitan Opera radio quiz program during every season since 1957.

Levarie's interests are broad and his research has crossed disciplinary lines, drawing on the fields of education, philosophy, and physics. Besides many articles and reviews (in four languages), his most important writings are *Mozart's "Le Nozze di Figaro": a Critical Analysis* (1952/*R*1977), *Guillaume de Machaut* (1954/*R*1969), and two books with Ernst Lévy, *Tone: a Study in Musical Acoustics* (1968, rev. 2/1980) and *Musical Morphology: a Discourse and a Dictionary* (1983).

PAULA MORGAN, H. WILEY HITCHCOCK

Leventritt, Edgar M(ilton) (*b* San Francisco, CA, 18 Oct 1873; *d* New York, 31 May 1939). Patron. After graduating from the University of California in 1894, he studied law in New York, was admitted to the bar in 1896, and practiced briefly in San Francisco before returning to New York. He was a devoted amateur pianist, a member of the Bohemian Club, and a patron of music. His support made possible the founding of the Perolé String Quartet in 1925. By the terms of his will, the Edgar M. Leventritt Foundation was established to oversee an annual competition for young musicians (*see* AWARDS, §2). It began in 1940 and has launched many notable careers, including those of the pianists Browning, Cliburn, Istomin, and Weissenberg, and of the violinists Perlman and Zukerman.

MICHAEL FLEMING

Levine, James (*b* Cincinnati, OH, 23 June 1943). Conductor and pianist. He was able to pick out tunes on the piano at the age of two and began formal study two years later; he gave his first recital when he was six and performed Mendelssohn's Piano Concerto no.2 with the Cincinnati SO at the age of ten. His first conducting experience was at the Marlboro Music Festival (1956), leading the brief choruses in Mozart's *Così fan tutte*. In 1961 he entered the Juilliard School, where he studied piano with Rosina Lhévinne and conducting with Jean Morel; later he also studied with Rudolf Serkin (piano) and Alfred Wallenstein, Max Rudolf, and Fausto Cleva (conducting). During his third year at Juilliard, Levine was selected as a participant in the American Conductors Project in Baltimore; there he met George Szell, who in 1964 invited him to become assistant conductor of the Cleveland Orchestra. Levine stayed in Cleveland for six years, during which he founded and directed the University Circle Orchestra, was chairman of the department of orchestral training at the Cleveland Institute, and conducted and taught at the Aspen Music School and Festival (1966–70) as well as at Meadow Brook, the summer home of the Detroit SO.

James Levine

In 1970 Levine was engaged by the San Francisco Opera for several performances of *Tosca* (début, 22 November). He made his Metropolitan début leading the same work (5 June 1971); in 1973 he became the company's principal conductor, a post renamed music director in 1975 (and, as a result of his increasingly administrative role, artistic director in 1986). Also in 1973 Levine became director of the Ravinia Festival and the Cincinnati May

Festival; he relinquished the latter post in 1978. He made his British opera début in 1970 (*Aida*, Welsh National Opera) and his German début in 1975 (*Otello*, Hamburg State Opera). Although he devotes most of his time to the Metropolitan he appears regularly at the Salzburg Festival in Austria (orchestral début 1975, opera début 1976) and annually at Bayreuth, where he made his début leading the centennial production of *Parsifal* in 1982.

Levine has become one of the most influential operatic conductors in the USA and has an increasing international reputation. His position at the Metropolitan enables him to exercise considerable control over the careers of its singers, and his personal taste in repertory to a large extent sets policy for the rest of the country. His enthusiasms encompass the complete operas of Mozart and Verdi; he has led notable productions (by Jean Pierre Ponnelle) of *Idomeneo* in Salzburg and New York, as well as revivals of Verdi's *Ernani* and *Macbeth*. Less traditional repertory at the Metropolitan has included Ravel's *L'enfant et les sortilèges*, Stravinsky's *Oedipus rex*, Weill's *Mahagonny*, Berg's *Lulu*, and Riccardo Zandonai's *Francesca da Rimini*. Although the Metropolitan under Levine has generally eschewed contemporary works, it commissioned operas from Druckman and Corigliano as part of its centenary celebration (1983). Levine has also popularized the company through his appearances on television, principally during intermission features of "Live from the Met" broadcasts, and through conducting film versions of Ponnelle's opera productions, including Mozart's *La clemenza di Tito* and *Die Zauberflöte*. While Levine remains especially admired for his Mozart and Verdi, he has also become an accomplished Wagnerian, as evidenced by his performances of *Parsifal* in Bayreuth and New York.

As an orchestral conductor, Levine has appeared with the Chicago SO, the London SO, and the Philadelphia Orchestra, with which he has begun recording a Mahler symphony cycle. He has also recorded a Brahms symphony cycle with the Chicago SO and orchestral music by Mozart with the Vienna PO. (Surprisingly, he is less active in the recording studio as an opera conductor.) His performances of Mahler's symphonic music have been noted for their emotional discipline and structurally clear outlook, though his tendency to revel in bold, brassy sounds can be coarsening. An excellent pianist, he continues to perform sporadically, principally in chamber music and song recitals.

BIBLIOGRAPHY

J. Levine: ". . .Which Brings me to *Otello*," *Opera News*, xxxvii/6 (1972), 28
R. C. Marsh: "Musician of the Month: James Levine," *HiFi/MusAm*, xxiv/3 (1974), 10
"Levine, James," *CBY 1975*
L. Harris: "Festive Spirit," *Records and Recording*, xx/5 (1977), 16
P. Hart: "James Levine," *Conductors: a New Generation* (New York, 1979), 221
B. Jacobson: "James Levine on Verdi and Mozart," *Conductors on Conducting* (Frenchtown, NJ, 1979), 29
R. Jacobson: "Men of the Met: Working Visionary," *Opera News*, xlv/3 (1980), 13
H. Matheopoulos: "James Levine: the Met's Maestro," *Maestro: Encounters with Conductors of Today* (London, 1982), 278
M. Walsh: "Maestro of the Met," *Time*, cxxi (17 Jan 1983), 52
P. J. Smith: *A Year at the Met* (New York, 1983)
W. Crutchfield: "James Levine: New Era at the Met," *New York Times Magazine* (22 Sept 1985), 23

MICHAEL WALSH

Levine, Julius (*b* New York, 23 Dec 1921). Double bass player. He attended Brooklyn College, CUNY, and the Juilliard School, where his teacher was Frederic Zimmerman; he has also been highly influenced by Pablo Casals and Alexander Schneider. Levine played in the orchestra of the Casals Festival at Perpignan (1951) and Prades (1953), and served for 20 years as principal bass player in the Casals Festival, Puerto Rico. From 1960 he participated in the Marlboro (Vermont) Music Festival; he has also performed with numerous chamber music ensembles. Levine has held a number of teaching positions at American universities. From 1980 he taught at Mannes College, and he became director of chamber music at SUNY, Stony Brook, in 1982. His musical philosophy, influenced by Casals, includes the belief that music is a reflection of life; the energy used to create sound becomes the principal agent of musical expression.

BIBLIOGRAPHY

D. Rosenberg and B. Rosenberg: *The Music Makers* (New York, 1979), 263

MARGARET DOUTT

Levitzki, Mischa [Levitsky, Misha] (*b* Kremenchug, Ukraine, 25 May 1898; *d* Avon-by-the-Sea, NJ, 2 Jan 1941). Pianist and composer. He studied piano with Alexander Michalowski in Warsaw (1905–6) and made his concert début in Antwerp in 1906 before coming to New York with his parents, both naturalized American citizens. Shortly after his arrival, he came to the attention of Walter Damrosch and received a scholarship to the Institute of Musical Art, where he was a pupil of Stojowski (1907–11). He also studied with Ernő Dohnányi at the Berlin Hochschule für Musik, where in 1915 he won the Mendelssohn Prize. In 1912 he toured extensively in Europe. His American début was on 17 October 1916 at Aeolian Hall, New York; later he toured frequently in the USA and the Orient. Although best known for his virtuoso performances of the Romantic literature, Levitzki preferred the Classical repertory, particularly the works of Mozart. His own compositions include several waltzes and other ingratiating pieces for piano, and a cadenza for the first movement of Beethoven's Piano Concerto no.3.

BIBLIOGRAPHY

H. Brower: *Piano Mastery*, 2nd ser. (New York, 1917), 224
Obituary, *MusAm*, lxi/1 (1941), 32
E. Blom: "Levitsky, Misha," *Grove 5*
G. Kehler: *The Piano in Concert*, i (Metuchen, NJ, 1982), 738

MINA F. MILLER

Levy, Edward (Irving) (*b* Brooklyn, NY, 2 May 1929). Composer. He studied at City College, New York (BA 1957), Princeton University (MFA 1960) with Babbitt, and Columbia University Teachers College (EdD 1967); he also studied privately with Wolpe and Shapey. Levy taught at C. W. Post College, Long Island University, from 1961 to 1967, when he became professor of music at Yeshiva University. He is a Danforth Foundation associate.

Levy's musical style draws on models provided by the music of Wolpe and Babbitt and his experiences with jazz improvisation. Although several compositions use triadic tonality (Variations on a Theme by Brahms and *Concatenations*), most of his music is generated by means of serial procedures. *Movement* uses an ordered 12-tone set that is presented in surface details as subsets or as derived sets; stable chord structures, derived from ordered elements of sets, supply progressions against which its melodic contours may range. The thematic materials, improvisatory in character, are progressively modified. Levy has written many articles on the perception of musical structures and the teaching of analytical skills, published mainly in the *Music Educators Journal* and *College Music Symposium*.

WORKS

Duo, vn, vc, 1950; 2 Songs (Lorca), Mez, pf, 1951; Cl Sonata, 1956; Str Trio, 1959; Trio, cl, vn, pf, 1961; Images (Rothenberg), S, pf, 1961; Qnt, fl, a sax, vib, va, db, 1967; Variations on a Theme by Brahms, fl, cl, hn, 1979; Concatenations, 2 fl, cl, vc, 1980; Movt, brass qnt, 1980; other chamber and pf pieces; works for chorus, chamber orch

RICHARD SWIFT

Lévy, Ernst (*b* Basle, Switzerland, 18 Nov 1895; *d* Morges, Switzerland, 19 April 1981). Swiss composer and pianist. He studied in Basle and Paris; among his teachers were Hans Huber, Raoul Pugno, and Egon Petri. From 1917 to 1921 he directed the piano master class at the Basle Conservatory. Between the wars, he lived in Paris, where in 1928 he founded the Choeur Philharmonique; with this organization he gave first performances in Paris of Brahms's *Ein Deutsches Requiem* and Liszt's *Christus*. Between 1941 and 1966 he was active in the USA, giving piano recitals and teaching at the New England Conservatory (1941–5), Bennington College (to 1949), the University of Chicago (to 1954), the Massachusetts Institute of Technology (to 1959), and Brooklyn College, CUNY (until his retirement, in 1966). He spent the last 15 years of his life in his native Switzerland.

Lévy's style as a composer is highly individual and not identifiable with any school. He believed in the principle of tonality as a harmonic force naturally given by the structure of tone. To him composing meant uncovering and unfolding new specific tonal fields. A man of wide culture, he contributed to the revival of the Pythagorean tradition through lectures and writings. His piano recordings, particularly of the last Beethoven sonatas and the Lizst sonata, have become collectors' items.

WORKS

(American period only)

Vocal: Cantatas nos.1–4, 1945, 1948, 1950, 1966; many songs; motets, a cappella choruses, other choral works

Inst: Syms. nos.10–14, 1944, 1949, 1951, 1955, 1962; orch suites nos.2–4, 1951, 1957, 1959; many chamber works, incl. Str Qt no.3, 1958, str trios nos.1–2, 1953, 1960, other trios, duos for pf and 1 inst; many other works, incl. pf, clvd, harp, org pieces

MSS in Basle, Bibliothèque Universitaire

WRITINGS

with S. Levarie: *Tone: a Study in Musical Acoustics* (Kent, OH, 1968, rev. 2/1980)

Des rapports entre la musique et la société suivi de réflexions (Neuchâtel, Switzerland, 1979)

with S. Levarie: *Musical Morphology: a Discourse and a Dictionary* (Kent, OH, 1983)

A Theory of Harmony (Albany, NY, 1985)

SIEGMUND LEVARIE

Levy, Jules (*b* London, England, 24 April 1838; *d* Chicago, IL, 28 Nov 1903). English cornetist. By the age of nine he was appearing as a theater and opera house extra. It is thought that, since his parents continually lacked the funds to purchase him an instrument, he developed his early technique on a mouthpiece. He was engaged at the Princess Theatre in London for the 1860–61 season, where his performance one evening between acts literally stopped the show. He then became a member of the Royal Opera House orchestra. In Paris in 1864 he was engaged by Pape Bateman for a tour of the USA, where he made his début in Boston in 1865. He continued his career as a freelance soloist in the USA and England, and even made an extended visit to Russia. The latter part of Levy's life was spent largely in America; he was one of the first performers to make recordings with the Edison Company and was later affiliated with the band instrument firm of C. G. Conn. Levy's technical abilities were perhaps unequaled, and he is supposed to have developed different embouchures to reduce fatigue. He was frequently billed as the world's greatest cornetist, a description appropriate to his vanity and sense of showmanship.

BIBLIOGRAPHY

H. W. Schwartz: *Bands of America* (New York, 1957)

G. D. Bridges: *Pioneers in Brass* (Detroit, 1965)

R. E. SHELDON

Levy, Kenneth J(ay) (*b* New York, 26 Feb 1927). Musicologist. He studied at Queens College, New York (BA 1947), and at Princeton (MFA 1949, PhD 1955). He taught at Princeton (1952–4) and at Brandeis University (1954–66), then returned to Princeton as a professor. His interests include Gregorian, Byzantine, and Old Slavonic liturgical chant, medieval polyphony, and the 16th-century French chanson. In his chanson research he has concentrated on the composers and secular forms of the later 16th century, and has drawn on social and political background for a comprehensive view. More recently he has worked on liturgical chant, making comparative studies of Byzantine and Western chant, including the Old Roman, Ambrosian, Beneventan, and Ravennate repertories, and has drawn tentative conclusions regarding the relationships of certain Western chants to Byzantine models and between modal patterns and performing practices common to East and West. He approached the problem of transcription of Slavonic *kondakarion* notation by proposing "counterpart transcriptions," which relate Slavonic melodic formulae to those occurring in transcribable Byzantine melodies.

Levy has achieved considerable success as a teacher of undergraduates; his *Music: a Listener's Introduction* (1983) is intended both for classroom use and for the general music lover.

PAULA MORGAN

Levy, Lester (Stern) (*b* Philadelphia, PA, 22 Oct 1896). Collector of and writer on American popular music. He received a degree in economics from Johns Hopkins University (BA 1918), then for 40 years was a manufacturer of men's hats. In his own time he assembled a collection of around 30,000 pieces of American sheet music from the late 18th century onwards; perhaps the most important private collection of its kind in the USA, it includes songs for political campaigns and presidential inaugurations, humorous songs, and items in many different popular styles. Levy's material, now held by the Eisenhower Library at Johns Hopkins University, has been used by publishers, students, and musicologists (*see* LIBRARIES AND COLLECTIONS, §3, Maryland). Levy was a founding member of the Sonneck Society in 1974, and he has lectured widely on the history and sociology of popular music.

WRITINGS

Grace Notes in American History: Popular Sheet Music from 1820 to 1900 (Norman, OK, 1967)

Flashes of Merriment: a Century of Humorous Songs in America, 1805–1905 (Norman, 1971)

Give me Yesterday: America in Song, 1890–1920 (Norman, 1975)

Picture the Songs: Lithographs from the Sheet Music of 19th-century America (Baltimore, 1976)

PAULA MORGAN

Levy, Marvin David (*b* Passaic, NJ, 2 Aug 1932). Composer. He studied under Philip James at New York University, under Luening at Columbia University, and in Europe. His music, which is essentially theatrical, is atonal and flexible in its treatment of rhythm. *Mourning Becomes Electra* is one of the few operas by an American to have been commissioned for the Metropolitan Opera, where it remained in the repertory for several seasons. He was awarded two Guggenheim Fellowships (1960, 1964) and two Rome Prizes (1962, 1965).

WORKS

Operas: Sotoba Komachi (1, S. H. Brock, after noh play), New York, 1957; The Tower (5 scenes, T. Brewster), Santa Fe, 1957; Escorial (1, L. Abel, trans. M. de Ghelderode), New York, 1958; Mourning Becomes Electra (3, after E. O'Neill), New York, 17 March 1967; The Balcony (after J. Genet), 1978

Orch: Caramoor Festival Ov., 1959; Sym., 1960; Kyros, dance poem, chamber orch, 1961; Pf Conc., 1970; Sonata strofico, chamber orch, 1970; Trialogues, 1972; In memoriam W. H. Auden, 1974; Canto de los Marranos, S, orch, 1977; A Winter's Tale (D. Thomas), A, orch

Vocal: Echoes (Hopkins), S, ens, 1956; For the Time Being (Auden), 1959; Christmas oratorio, 1959; One Person, cantata (E. Wylie), A, orch, 1962; Sacred Service, 1964 [for Park Avenue Synagogue, New York]; Masada, oratorio, nar, T, chorus, orch, 1973; Since Nine O'Clock, lv, orch; songs and choruses

Chamber: Str Qt, 1955; Rhapsody, vn, cl, harp, 1956; Chassidic Suite, hn, pf, 1956

Incidental music to The Recruiting Officer (G. Farquhar), 1955; film scores

BIBLIOGRAPHY

P. G. Davis: "And we Quote . . . Marvin David Levy," *HiFi/MusAm*, xvii/3 (1967), 20

R. Ericson: "As 'Mourning' becomes an Opera," *New York Times* (12 March 1967), §II, p.19

Opera News, xxxi/23 (1967) [contains several articles on *Mourning Becomes Electra*]

Lewenthal, Raymond (*b* San Antonio, TX, 29 Aug 1926). Pianist. He studied with Samaroff at the Juilliard School, then with Cortot, and spent a year teaching in Rio de Janeiro. His career has been marked by special concern for neglected composers of the early 19th century, among them Hummel, Dušek, Adolf Henselt, Sigismond Thalberg, and, notably, Alkan (he has edited an Alkan collection). He has recorded etudés and parts of the symphony for piano by Alkan, the solo version of the *Hexameron* by Liszt and others, and concertos by Henselt and Rubinstein. He is an articulate spokesman on behalf of his chosen repertory. At his recitals, he achieves atmosphere by means of low lights, high temperatures, and quasi-period costume. His performances tend to be marked more by generalized flair than by specific pianistic skills of the first order.

MICHAEL STEINBERG

Lewin, David (Benjamin) (*b* New York, 2 July 1933). Composer and theorist. He studied piano, harmony, and composition with Steuermann (1945–50), mathematics at Harvard University (BA 1954), and theory and composition at Princeton Unversity with Sessions, Babbitt, Cone, and Kim (MFA 1958). He returned to Harvard on a junior fellowship (1958–61), and in 1959 became one of the first to be invited to work on the composition of computer music at the Bell Laboratories (in Murray Hill, New Jersey). He has taught at the University of California, Berkeley (1961–7), SUNY, Stony Brook (1967–80), and Yale University (1979–85), and was appointed professor at Harvard University in 1985. He is a member of the ACA and is on the board of directors of the American Brahms Society. He received a Guggenheim Fellowship (1983–4) for research on "generalized musical intervals and transformations."

Lewin is regarded as one of the country's foremost theorists. From 1981 to 1984 he served on the executive board of the Society for Music Theory and then was appointed president for the period 1985–8. Over 40 of his theoretical studies have been published, chiefly in *Journal of Music Theory* and *Perspectives of New Music*. Most are detailed studies of single works, ranging from Jean-Philippe Rameau's *Traité de l'harmonie* to Wagner's *Parsifal* and Schoenberg's *Moses und Aron*. They are often based on mathematical procedures and contain sophisticated mathematical analogies for dealing with generalized principles of pitch relations. Lewin's own compositions are written for a variety of instrumental forces and display the same painstaking attention to detail that marks his writings.

WORKS

4 Short Pieces, str qt, 1956, rev. 1969; Va Sonata, 1957–8; Essay on a Subject by Webern, chamber orch, 1958; Classical Variations on a Theme by Schoenberg, vc, pf, 1960; 2 Studies, cptr, 1961; Fantasia, org, 1962; 5 Characteristic Pieces, 2 pf, 1964; Fantasy-Adagio, vn, orch, 1963–6; Quartet Piece, str qt, 1969; Ww Trio, 1969; Computer Music, cptr, 1970–71; Just a Minute, Roger, pf, 1978; Fanfare, b cl, vc, pf, 1980; For Piano, 1982; a few songs and other short vn and pf pieces

NOEL B. ZAHLER

Lewis, Daniel (*b* Flagstaff, AZ, 10 May 1925). Conductor. As a youth he studied violin, composition, and orchestration. During World War II he was stationed in Hawaii, where he became concertmaster of the Honolulu SO, first violinist of the resident US Navy string quartet, and conductor of various naval ensembles. Later he attended San Diego State College (BM 1949) and Claremont Graduate School (MA 1950). After working at the San Diego SO as assistant conductor, 1954–6, and associate conductor and concertmaster, 1956–9, he received a Fulbright Scholarship to study conducting with Eugen Jochum at the Munich Hochschule; he also attended Herbert von Karajan's conducting seminar in Salzburg. Lewis has been affiliated with many orchestras and festivals in southern California, and has conducted at the Aspen and Alaska summer music festivals. As music director of the Pasadena (California) SO (1972–83) he brought the orchestra unprecedented critical acclaim and awards for adventurous programming of contemporary music; he also revived seldom-heard orchestral works by C. P. E. Bach, Cherubini, Arthur Foote, MacDowell, and others. While anything but a flamboyant, glamor-seeking musician and satisfied with his regional success, he has been guest conductor of prominent American orchestras including the Los Angeles PO, Los Angeles Chamber Orchestra, the Atlanta SO, the Minnesota Orchestra, and the Louisville Orchestra. He has taught at California State University, Fullerton, and since 1970 at the University of Southern California, where he is chairman of the conducting studies department.

BIBLIOGRAPHY

D. Perlmutter: "Daniel Lewis: Conducting his own Career," *Los Angeles Herald Examiner* (11 Oct 1981), §E, p.9

PETER MOSE

Lewis [Zeno], **George (Louis Francis)** (i) (*b* New Orleans, LA, 13 July 1900; *d* New Orleans, 31 Dec 1968). Jazz clarinetist. He played clarinet from the age of 16 and began his professional career shortly thereafter with Buddy Petit, Kid Ory, Kid Rena, and other New Orleans groups. In 1923 he joined the Eureka Brass Band, and in the same year began to lead his own groups. He made his first recording in 1942 with Bunk Johnson and worked with him intermittently until 1946. From 1952 he often performed outside Louisiana, making a tour of Japan and several of Europe. Lewis was a leading figure in the New Orleans revival. When playing in a traditional New Orleans setting he showed a limited technique that could disguise his debt to popular clarinetists of the 1930s (he was often mistakenly regarded as an unspoiled example of his local idiom). Nevertheless, the sincerity of his performances of simple pieces was widely appreciated, and he acquired many imitators (mostly outside the USA).

RECORDINGS
(selective list)

As leader: Deep Bayou Blues (1943, Climax 101); Burgundy Street Blues (1944, American Music 531); *George Lewis Jam Session* (1950, Pax 6001); *George Lewis and his New Orleans Stompers*, i–ii (1955, BN 7027–8)

As sideman: B. Johnson: Down by the Riverside/Panama (1942, Jazz Man 8)

BIBLIOGRAPHY

SouthernB

D. Mangurian: "George Lewis: a Portrait of the New Orleans Clarinetist," *Down Beat*, xxx/24 (1963), 18

J. Stuart [D. Tate]: *Call him George* (London, 1961)

M. Williams: *Jazz Masters of New Orleans* (New York, 1967), 233

E. Lambert: "William Russell's New Orleans Recordings," *Jazz Monthly*, no. 183 (1970), 3

T. Bethell: *George Lewis: a Jazzman from New Orleans* (Berkeley, CA, 1977)

J. R. TAYLOR/R

Lewis, George (ii) (*b* Chicago, IL, 14 July 1952). Composer and trombonist. He was trained originally as a jazz trombonist and studied with Dean Hey; later, while an undergraduate at Yale University (BA 1974), he became active in the Association for the Advancement of Creative Musicians (AACM), a Chicago-based group devoted to exploring possibilities in contemporary jazz. Lewis studied theory with Muhal Richard Abrams, the founder of AACM, and worked closely with other members including Anthony Braxton and Roscoe Mitchell. During this period he emerged as a leading figure of the jazz avant garde, especially after the release of his *Solo Trombone Record* (Sackville 3012, 1977).

Although Lewis has been associated mainly with jazz artists and has released recordings with Douglas Ewart and Anthony Braxton, he refuses to be categorized as a jazz musician. His compositions have been influenced by free improvisation, live contemporary art music, and electronic and computer music. Some of the earlier works, including the *Shadowgraph* series nos. 1–3 (1975, 1976, 1978), are scored for the standard jazz big band and combine improvisation with notated parts. Later compositions, often more loosely notated, are to be performed by an unspecified number of instrumentalists playing for an unspecified time. Lewis has incorporated electronics into some of his works, combining different live sounds with tapes of musical and extra-musical sounds, and has frequently collaborated with the synthesizer soloist Richard Teitelbaum. His later music draws on the experiments of David Behrman; in works such as *Audio Tick* (1983) computers are linked to digital synthesizers and programmed to respond to live sounds produced by instrumentalists. From 1980 to 1982, Lewis served as music director of the Kitchen, an avant-garde cultural center in New York.

WORKS

Shadowgraph no. 1, 4 tpt, 4 trbn, 5 sax, pf, db, perc, 1975; Untitled Dream Sequence, trbn, 1975; Blues, 2 kbd, 2 wind, 1976; Shadowgraph no. 2, 1v, 4 tpt, 4 trbn, 5 sax, pf, db, perc, bn, 1976; Tone Burst, trbn, tape, 1976; Chicago Slow Dance, any inst(s), tape, 1977; Monads, any inst(s), 1977; Shadowgraph no. 5, any inst(s), 1977; Triple Slow Mix, tuba, 2 insts, 1977; Homage to Charles Parker, a sax, elec kbd, synth, perc, elec, 1978; Imaginary Suite, any inst(s), 1978

Shadowgraph no. 3, 4 tpt, 4 trbn, 5 sax, pf, db, perc, 1978; Shadowgraph no. 4, any inst(s), 1978; Tone Bow, trbn, elec, 1978; Chamber Music for Humans and Non-humans, any inst(s), interactive cptr, 1979–84; A Friend, tape, 1 inst, 1980; Second Woodstock Fragment, pf, 1980; Carthera, trbn, pf, 1981; Audio Tick, 3 insts, interactive cptr, 1983; Tick, 3 insts, 1983; Rainbow Family, any inst(s), interactive cptr, 1984; other solo inst and ens works

BIBLIOGRAPHY

J. Rockwell: "A New Music Director Comes to the Avant-garde Kitchen," *New York Times* (1 Sept 1980)

CHARLES PASSY

Lewis, Henry (*b* Los Angeles, CA, 16 Oct 1932). Conductor. As a boy, Lewis studied piano and double bass, and at 16 became a double bass player in the Los Angeles PO. In 1956 he was conductor of the 7th US Army SO in Stuttgart. After his return, he founded the Los Angeles Chamber Orchestra, then became assistant conductor of the Los Angeles PO, making his professional début with that orchestra in 1963. In 1968 he became music director of the New Jersey SO, a post he held until 1976. He conducted at La Scala in 1965, and at the Metropolitan Opera in 1972, and in 1982 appeared for the first time at the Paris Opéra. He has been a guest conductor with most major American orchestras, including those in Boston, Chicago, Cleveland, and New York, and has appeared extensively in Europe. His recordings include a number made with the mezzo-soprano Marilyn Horne (to whom he was married), notably of the music of Rossini. He holds honorary doctorates from several colleges and universities.

Although Lewis works with singers and in opera with special sympathy, he is also active in other fields. By temperament thoughtful rather than fiery, his broadly paced Metropolitan Opera performances of *La bohème* and *Carmen* were notable for what they revealed in orchestral detail. In New Jersey, with an organization designed to serve a region rather than one particular city, he strikingly broadened the orchestra's repertory, audience, and scope of operations.

BIBLIOGRAPHY

SouthernB

"Lewis, Henry," *CBY 1973*

MICHAEL STEINBERG/R

Lewis, Jerry Lee (*b* Ferriday, LA, 29 Sept 1935). Rockabilly and country-music singer and pianist. He grew up in Ferriday with his cousins, Mickey Gilley, who became a successful country-music singer in the mid-1970s, and Jimmy Swaggart, later a television evangelist. His earliest musical influences were Al Jolson, Gene Autry, Jimmie Rodgers, and the blues performers who played at Haney's Big House, a black nightclub in Ferriday. In 1949, after playing piano for six years in a style strongly influenced by the gospel musicians of the church that he attended, Lewis made his public début at the opening of an automobile showroom in Ferriday. The following year he enrolled in a Bible school in Waxahachie, Texas, but was expelled for playing hymns in boogie-woogie style during services. He returned to Ferriday, working (at first as a drummer) with local bands there and across the Mississippi River in Natchez, Mississippi.

By the time he made his first recording (*Crazy Arms*) for the Sun firm of Memphis in 1956, Lewis had already evolved his

Jerry Lee Lewis, c1957

unique, "pumping" piano style, which relied heavily on glissandos and rolling bass lines. In 1957 *Whole lotta shakin' goin' on* became one of the first recordings ever to reach the top of the pop, country, and rhythm-and-blues charts simultaneously. He repeated the feat later that year with *Great balls of fire*, and was widely hailed as the most likely challenger to Elvis Presley as the "king" of rock-and-roll. The following year, however, his career suffered a severe setback when, during a tour of England, it was revealed that his traveling companion was his third wife, his 13-year-old third cousin Myra Gale Brown; heavily censured by the British press, Lewis canceled the tour and returned to the USA, where he found an informal boycott of his music in operation: disc jockeys would no longer play his records, and Sun would no longer promote them.

For most of the next decade Lewis was forced to make his living touring; he adopted an uninhibited performing style that earned him the nickname "the Killer" but gained him virtually no recording successes. In 1963 he left Sun for Smash and Mercury, but he achieved little with the new company until 1968, when with the help of his producer Jerry Kennedy he decided to stop recording rock-and-roll and turn to country-and-western music. His first recording in the new style, *Another place, another time*, rose to no.4 on the country chart. His first country song to reach no. 1 was *To make love sweeter for you* (1968); it was followed by the album *Together*, made with his sister Linda Gail Lewis, and further hit singles, most notably *There must be more to love than this* (no.1, 1970) and *Would you take another chance on me* (no.1, 1971). In 1972 Lewis returned to the rock-and-roll idiom, mixing it with country music, in *Chantilly Lace* (no. 1); he pursued and emphasized this hybrid style in two albums made in 1973 – *The Session*, based on a studio session with British rock musicians Rory Gallagher, Alvin Lee, and Peter Frampton, and *Southern Roots*, in which he was accompanied by southern soul and rockabilly stars. By the end of the decade he had achieved more than 30 successes, mostly in the mixed rock and country style.

As his new-found success solidified, Lewis's personal life became increasingly unhappy. Both his sons and two of his wives were killed in accidents, and Lewis was arrested many times for offences related to drinking, drug-taking, and possession of weapons, as well as for evasion of income tax. In 1978, his career again at a low ebb, Lewis signed a contract with Elektra Records, and he was enjoying renewed commercial success until he became seriously ill in 1981; though he returned to touring by the end of that year, his performances lacked energy and commitment. Except for a guest appearance with Carl Perkins on an album by Johnny Cash (*Survivors*, 1982), Lewis has made no more recordings.

RECORDINGS

(selective list)

Singles: Crazy Arms (Sun 259, 1956); Whole lotta shakin' goin' on (Sun 267, 1957); Great balls of fire (Sun 281, 1957); Another place, another time (Smash 2146, 1968); What's made Milwaukee famous (Smash 2164, 1968); She still comes around (Smash 2186, 1968); To make love sweeter for you (Smash 2202, 1968); There must be more to love than this (Mer. 73099, 1970); Would you take another chance on me (Mer. 73248, 1971); Chantilly Lace (Mer. 73273, 1972); Middle-age Crazy (Mer. 35044, 1977)

Albums: *Together* (Smash 67126, 1969), with L. G. Lewis; *The Session* (Mer. 2803, 1973); *Southern Roots* (Mer. 1690, 1973); *Jerry Lee Lewis Keeps Rockin'* (Mer. 5010, 1978); *Jerry Lee Lewis* (Elek. 6E184, 1979); *Killer Country* (Elek. 291, 1980)

BIBLIOGRAPHY

J. Grissim: "Whole Lotta Shakin' at the DJ Hop," *Country Music: the White Man's Blues* (New York, 1970), 271

P. Guralnick: "Jerry Lee Lewis: Hang up my Rock 'n' Roll Shoes," *Feel like Going Home* (New York, 1971), 146

N. Tosches: "Loud Covenants," *Country: the Biggest Music in America* (New York, 1977), 57

C. Escott and M. Hawkins: *Sun Records: the Brief History of the Legendary Record Label* (New York, 1980)

R. Cain: *Whole Lotta Shakin' Goin' on* (New York, 1981)

R. Palmer: *Jerry Lee Lewis Rocks* (New York, 1981)

N. Tosches: *Hellfire: the Jerry Lee Lewis Story* (New York, 1982)

H. Davis, C. Escott, and M. Hawkins: "Jerry Lee Lewis, the Killer: November 1956–August 1963," *The Sun Years* (British Sun 102, 1983) [liner notes]

JOHN MORTHLAND

Lewis, John (Aaron) (*b* LaGrange, IL, 3 May 1920). Jazz pianist and composer. He grew up in Albuquerque, New Mexico, where he began studying the piano at the age of seven. His musical studies continued at the University of New Mexico. While in the US Army during World War II he met the drummer Kenny Clarke, an early developer of the bop style. After the war Clarke introduced Lewis to the trumpeter Dizzy Gillespie, another bop pioneer, and in 1946 they both joined Gillespie's bop-style big band in New York. There Lewis developed his skills as a composer and arranger, both by writing for Gillespie's band and by studying at the Manhattan School of Music. These studies, which led to a master's degree in 1953, were interrupted in 1948 when the band made a concert tour of Europe. After returning to the USA Lewis worked for Lester Young, Charlie Parker, Miles Davis, Gillespie, Illinois Jacquet, and Ella Fitzgerald. In 1951–2 he served as pianist with the Milt Jackson Quartet, recording on four separate occasions. By the end of 1952 this group was renamed the MODERN JAZZ QUARTET, with Lewis as its music director. For the next two decades Lewis's musical activity centered on the MJQ, for which he wrote many pieces. Lewis also served from 1958 to 1982 as music director of the annual Monterey Jazz Festival, was head of faculty at the summer jazz clinics in Lenox, Massachusetts, during the late 1950s, and founded Orchestra USA, which performed and recorded third-stream compositions (1962–5). After the MJQ disbanded temporarily in 1974 he held teaching positions at the City College of New York and at Harvard University. By the early 1980s he was performing with the reunited MJQ and with a sextet, the John Lewis Group.

Lewis is among the most conservative of bop pianists. His improvised melodies, played with a delicate touch, are usually simple and quiet; the accompaniments are correspondingly light, with Lewis's left hand often just grazing the keys to produce a barely audible sound. His method of accompanying soloists is similarly understated: rather than comping – punctuating the melody with irregularly placed chords – he often plays simple counter-melodies in octaves which combine with the solo and bass parts to form a polyphonic texture. Occasionally Lewis plays in a manner resembling the stride styles of James P. Johnson and Fats Waller, all the while retaining his light touch.

Many of Lewis's solos have a degree of motivic unity which is rare in jazz. For example, in *Bluesology* (1956) each chorus of his solo builds on the previous one by establishing a link from the end of one chorus to the beginning of the next. His 64-bar solo in *Between the Devil and the Deep Blue Sea* (1957) derives almost entirely from its first two bars, which in turn derive from the first four notes of the theme (ex. 1). As the solo progresses Lewis subjects its opening motif to inversion (bar 9), chromatic alteration (bars 47 and 57), and a variety of other alterations in pitch and shape (bars 25–6, 41), which nevertheless retain their links with the basic figure.

Ex.1 From *Between the Devil and the Deep Blue Sea*, on *The Modern Jazz Quartet* (1957, Atl. 1265), transcr. T. Owens

Lewis is similarly conservative as a composer, for his music draws heavily on harmonic and melodic practices found in 18th-century European compositions. Since the 1950s he has written a number of third-stream works combining European compositional techniques and jazz improvisation. Most of these were written for the MJQ, or for the quartet with instrumental ensembles of various sizes. Among his best pieces for the MJQ are *Django* (1960), the ballet suite *The Comedy* (1962), and especially the four pieces *Versailles* (1956), *Three Windows* (1957), *Vendome* (1960), and *Concorde* (1963), all of which combine fugal imitation and nonimitative polyphonic jazz in highly effective ways.

WORKS
(selective list)

Bluesology, 1956; Versailles, 1956; Three Windows, 1957; Exposure, 1959–60; Sketch for Double String Quartet, 1959–60; Django, 1960; Vendome, 1960; England's Carol, 1960; Original Sin, 1961; The Comedy, 1962; Concorde, 1963; Three Little Feelings, 1963; In Memoriam, 1973; Mirjana of My Heart and Soul, 1975

Principal publisher: MJQ Music
For selective list of recordings *see* MODERN JAZZ QUARTET.

BIBLIOGRAPHY

J. E. Berendt: "John Lewis: König des Cool Jazz," *Melos*, xxii/12 (1955), 348
S. Pease: "John Lewis Piano Style," *Down Beat*, xxiii/3 (1956), 46
N. Hentoff: "John Lewis," *Down Beat*, xxiv/4 (1957), 15
J. Lewis: "The Golden Age: Time Future," *Esquire*, li/1 (1959), 112
N. Hentoff: *John Lewis* (New York, 1960)
F. Thorne: "An Afternoon with John Lewis," *Jazz Review*, iii/3 (1960), 6
G. Schuller: "John Lewis on the Modern Jazz Beachhead," *High Fidelity*, x/10 (1960), 54
N. Hentoff: "John Lewis: Success with Integrity," *International Musician*, lix/6 (1961), 16
"Lewis, John (Aaron)," *CBY 1962*
M. Williams: "John Lewis and the Modern Jazz Quartet," *Evergreen Review*, vi/23 (1962), 112; repr. in *The Jazz Tradition*, ed. M. Williams (New York, 1970, rev. 2/1983)
T. Owens: *Improvisation Techniques of the Modern Jazz Quartet* (thesis, UCLA, 1965)
M. Williams: "John Lewis," *International Musician*, lxx/1 (1972), 9
N. Koyama and others: "John Lewis and MJQ Discography," *Swing Journal*, xxviii/3 (1974), 266
R. J. Gleason: *Celebrating the Duke* (New York, 1975), 109ff
T. Owens: "The Fugal Pieces of the Modern Jazz Quartet," *Journal of Jazz Studies*, iv (1976), 25
L. Feather: "Piano Giants of Jazz: John Lewis," *Contemporary Keyboard*, iii/7 (1977), 55
B. Korall: "John Lewis: Pianist-Composer-Leader-Teacher," *International Musician*, lxxv/7 (1977), 8
C. J. Stuessy: *The Confluence of Jazz and Classical Music from 1950 to 1970* (diss., U. of Rochester, 1978), 348ff, 402ff
L. Feather: "MJQ: the Quartet that Wouldn't Die," *Los Angeles Times Calendar* (27 March 1983), 68
I. Gitler: "The Return of the Modern Jazz Quartet," *Jazz Times* (March 1983), 10

THOMAS OWENS

Lewis, Meade (Anderson) "Lux" (*b* Chicago, IL, 4 Sept 1905; *d* Minneapolis, MN, 7 June 1964). Jazz pianist. Influenced by Fats Waller and the Chicago blues pianist Jimmy Yancey, he played in Chicago bars and clubs before recording his celebrated masterpiece *Honky Tonk Train Blues* (1927), which was not issued until 18 months later. Rediscovered by the entrepreneur John Hammond in late 1935, he again recorded this work and issued a number of other pieces in boogie-woogie style over the next few years, most notably the influential *Yancey Special*, *Bear Cat Crawl*, *Tell your Story*, and *Bass on Top*. His technical ability, energetic cross-rhythms, and remarkable invention made him one of the most important figures of the boogie-woogie craze of the late 1930s. In 1939 he formed a short-lived trio with two other important pianists of this school, Albert Ammons and Pete Johnson, but he soon returned to working alone in New York and California nightclubs. He also performed with such jazz musicians as Sidney Bechet, and was occasionally recorded playing the celesta and harpsichord. He grew increasingly dissatisfied with being identified exclusively as a blues and boogie-woogie player, and his later playing was often rushed and perfunctory.

RECORDINGS
(selective list)

Honky Tonk Train Blues (1927, Para. 12896); Honky Tonk Train Blues (1935, Para. R-2187); Yancey Special (1936, Decca 819); with A. Ammons and P. Johnson: Boogie Woogie Prayer, pts i–ii (1938, Voc. 4606); Bear Cat Crawl (1938, Voc. 4608); The Blues, pts i–iv (1939, BN 8–9); Bass on Top (1940, BN 16); Tell your Story (1940, BN 15); Self-Portrait, hpd (1941, BN 19)

BIBLIOGRAPHY

SouthernB
W. Russell: "Boogie Woogie," *Jazzmen*, ed. F. Ramsey, Jr., and C. E. Smith (New York, 1939), 183

M. Harrison: "Boogie Woogie," *Jazz*, ed. N. Hentoff and A. J. McCarthy (New York, 1959), 105–37
W. Russell: "Three Boogie Woogie Pianists," *The Art of Jazz*, ed. M. Williams (New York, 1959), 104

MARTIN WILLIAMS/R

Lewis, Mel (*b* 1929). Jazz drummer and bandleader, who with Thad Jones formed the Thad Jones–Mel Lewis Orchestra in December 1965. *See* JONES family, (2) Thad.

Lewis, Robert Hall (*b* Portland, OR, 22 April 1926). Composer. He studied with Rogers and Hanson at the Eastman School (BM 1949, MM 1951, PhD 1964), with Nadia Boulanger and Eugène Bigot in Paris (1952–3), and with Hans Erich Apostel, Ernst Krenek, and Karl Schiske in Vienna (1955–7). In 1954 he attended Monteux's conducting school. Lewis has taught at Goucher College and the Peabody Conservatory from 1958 and, from 1969 to 1980, at Johns Hopkins University, where he became professor in 1972. He has performed professionally on the trumpet and has appeared as a conductor in the USA and abroad. Among his awards are a Kosciuszko Foundation Chopin Award (1951), two Fulbright Scholarships (1955–7), two Guggenheim Fellowships (1966, 1980), an NEA grant (1976), and an award from the American Academy and Institute of Arts and Letters (1976).

Lewis composes mostly chamber and orchestral music. His earlier compositions are concerned with linear developmental processes using serial methods, but the ordered growth and evolution apparent in his music of the 1960s and 1970s reflect a change in style. Beyond his basic predilection for inventive textures, unusual timbres, complex rhythms, fluent polyphony, and rich harmony in a freely atonal context, Lewis has sought new modes of expression in works since the early 1970s. These include spatial effects (*Moto, Due madrigali*), quotations (*Atto, Kantaten*), taped sounds (whale songs in *Nuances II*), passages in different tempos played simultaneously (*Osservazioni II, Moto*), and limited use of aleatory techniques. All of these elements are controlled by a strong intellect and by technical skills of the highest order. Many of his works have been recorded.

WORKS

ORCHESTRAL

Poem, str, 1949; Concert Ov., 1951; Sinfonia, Expression for Orch, 1955; Prelude and Finale, 1959; Designs, 1963; Sym. no. 1, 1964; Music for 12 Players, 1965; 3 Pieces, 1965, rev. 1966; Conc. for Chamber Orch, 1967, rev. 1972; Sym. no. 2, 1971; Intermezzi, 1972; Nuances II, 1975; Osservazioni II, wind, kbd, harp, perc, 1978; Moto, 1980; Atto, str, 1981; Sym. no. 3, 1982–5; Conc., str, 4 tpt, harp, pf, 1984; Destini, str, wind, 1985

INSTRUMENTAL

3 str qts, 1956, 1962, 1981; 5 Movts, pf, 1960; Toccata, vn, perc, 1963; Music for Brass Qnt, 1966; Trio, cl, vn, pf, 1966; Monophonies I–IX, solo wind, 1966–77; Tangents, double brass qt, 1968; Sonata, vn, 1968; Divertimento, 6 insts, 1969; Inflections I, db, 1969, II, pf trio, 1970; Serenades I, pf, 1970, II, fl + pic, vc, pf, 1976, III, brass qnt, 1982; Fantasiemusik I, vc, pf, 1973, II, cl, pf, 1978, III, sax, pf, perc, 1984; Combinazioni I, cl, vn, vc, pf, 1974, II, 8 perc, pf, 1974, III (J. Rubin), nar, ob + eng hn, perc, 1977, IV, vc, pf, 1977, V, 4 va, 1982

Nuances I, vn, pf, 1974; Osservazioni I, fls, pf, perc, 1975; Duetto da camera, vn, pf, 1977; Facets, vc, pf, 1978; A due I, fl + pic + a fl, harp, 1981, II, ob + eng hn, perc, 1981, III, bn, harp, 1985; Qnt, wind, 1983; Archi, pf, 1984

VOCAL

Acquainted with the Night (Frost), S, chamber orch, 1951; 5 Songs (R. Felmayer), S, cl, hn, vc, pf, 1957; 2 madrigali (G. Ungaretti), chorus, 1972; 3 Prayers of Jane Austen, small chorus, pf, perc, 1977; Kantaten (anon.), chorus, pf, 1980; Monophony X (anon.), S, 1983

Principal publishers: Doblinger, Presser, Seesaw

BIBLIOGRAPHY

L. Gonzalez: *The Symphonies of Robert Hall Lewis* (diss., Peabody Conservatory, 1979)

SAM DI BONAVENTURA

Lewis, Smiley [Lemons, Overton Amos] (*b* Union, LA, 5 July 1920; *d* New Orleans, LA, 7 Oct 1966). Rhythm-and-blues singer, songwriter, and guitarist. Though he began recording in 1947, he achieved hit songs only in the 1950s when he worked with the band of the record producer Dave Bartholomew. Two of these songs reached the Top Ten on the rhythm-and-blues charts, *I hear you knockin'* (Imp. 5356, 1955; no. 2) and *The bells are ringing* (Imp. 5372, 1955; no. 10), yet his recording of the latter was overwhelmed by the success of Gale Storm's pop cover version, and another of his songs, *One night of sin*, became a hit only when Elvis Presley recorded it (in an expurgated version) in 1958. Lewis's deep, booming voice was more like that of a blues "shouter" than a rhythm-and-blues or rock singer, and the style of his songs owed more to traditional forms than did those of most New Orleans rockers. Although he is recognized in retrospect as a key transitional figure in modern New Orleans rhythm-and-blues, Lewis's recording career was sporadic and brought him little success.

BIBLIOGRAPHY

J. Broven: *Walking to New Orleans: the Story of New Orleans Rhythm & Blues* (Bexhill-on-Sea, England, 1974)

JOHN MORTHLAND

Lewis, Ted [Friedman, Theodore Leopold] (*b* Circleville, OH, 6 June 1892; *d* New York, 25 Aug 1971). Bandleader, clarinetist, and entertainer. After early experience in tent shows and on the vaudeville circuit he settled in New York, first playing with Earl Fuller's band, then forming his own group in 1917. This had a successful engagement at Rector's and within two years began recording for Columbia and appearing in various revues: the *Greenwich Village Follies* (1919 and 1921), *Ziegfeld's Midnight Frolics* (1919), and the *Ted Lewis Frolics* (1923). In the early 1930s Lewis recorded with such first-rate jazz musicians as Muggsy Spanier, Georg Brunis, Frank Teschemacher, Jimmy Dorsey, Benny Goodman, and Fats Waller. He continued to lead groups of various sizes through the mid-1960s, working most often at hotels, resorts, and nightclubs. Lewis's approach changed little over the years. At the end of his career he still appeared with battered top hat and cane performing old vaudeville routines, delivering songs he had popularized years before (*When my baby smiles at me, Me and My Shadow*) in his characteristic patter style (more spoken than sung), playing his old Albert-system clarinet, and asking his favorite, time-worn question, "Is everybody happy?"

BIBLIOGRAPHY

B. Rust: *The Dance Bands* (New Rochelle, NY, 1972)
L. Walker: *The Wonderful Era of the Great Dance Bands* (Garden City, NY, 1972)

MARK TUCKER

Lewis, William. Firm of violin dealers and publishers. It was founded in Chicago in 1874 by William Lewis (1838–1902), and in 1888 its name became William Lewis & Son when Frederick C. Lewis (1874–1940) joined the company. It compiled an outstanding collection of old violins, violas, cellos, and bows, primarily through purchases in Europe. The first of its illustrated catalogues, which have become collectors' items, was published in 1906. It also had a good repair department, employing such violinmakers as the Carl Beckers (Sr. and Jr.), Hans Weisshaar, Zenon Petesh, and Fritz and Gunther Reuter. In 1935 on Frederick Lewis's retirement, Reuben A. Olson, an employee of the firm from 1899, became manager and then in 1940 president. In 1937, with the purchase of the business of ERNEST N. DORING, the company began publishing the magazine *Violins and Violinists*, and later Doring's books and also *Bows for Stringed Instruments* (1959) by Joseph Roda. In 1951 the company was purchased by the Chicago Musical Instrument Co., which gradually phased out the work with old violins, retaining the firm only as a student-instrument wholesaler. The RAO violin strings and accessories (named after Olson) are still manufactured.

PHILIP J. KASS

Lewis and Clark College. Private liberal-arts college founded (as Albany College) in Albany, Oregon, in 1867. It moved to Portland, Oregon, in 1942. *See* PORTLAND (ii).

Lewisohn, Adolph (*b* Hamburg, Germany, 27 May 1849; *d* Saranac Lake, NY, 17 Aug 1938). Philanthropist. He came to the USA in 1867, and became president of the firm that bears his name and head of many mining companies scattered throughout the country. He was an enthusiastic amateur singer, and in 1914 donated the finances to build Lewisohn Stadium, a gift to City College, New York. He established summer concerts at the stadium in 1918, and in 1932 set up a chamber music foundation at Hunter College, New York. His generosity has been the means of bringing music to thousands of people in the New York area. He also made a number of large gifts to other charitable and educational institutions.

WILLIAM McCLELLAN

Lhévinne, Josef (*b* Orel, nr Moscow, Russia, 13 Dec 1874; *d* New York, 2 Dec 1944). Russian pianist. He studied piano with Vasily Safonov at the Moscow Conservatory (1885–91), graduating with the gold medal. He then began giving concerts abroad, but was recalled to Russia for military service. In 1898 he married Rosina Bessie, also a pianist. After teaching in Tiflis (1900–02) and at the Moscow Conservatory (1902–6), Lhévinne returned to his concert career, while living principally in Berlin. He made his American début in New York on 27 January 1906 with Safonov and the Russian SO, and made six concert tours of the USA before the outbreak of World War I, when the Lhévinnes were interned in Berlin because they were Russian. This experience played a large part in their decision to move to New York after the war. In 1924 Lhévinne and his wife joined the staff of the new Juilliard Graduate School (later the Juilliard School). His pupils included Adele Marcus, Sascha Gorodnitzki, Brooks Smith, and Homer Samuels.

Lhévinne's few phonograph recordings clearly reflect the prodigious technique that was one of the most famous of his day. But the success of his playing lay in his ability to combine this technique with a sure control of tone and phrasing. His playing of Chopin was noted for its firm lines within rubato, and he performed even the most exhibitionist 19th-century works with a compelling musicianship. He was shy and almost without competitive impulse, and in his later years would have made fewer appearances than he did but for his wife's virtual management of his career. He wrote *Basic Principles in Pianoforte Playing* (1924/*R*1972).

BIBLIOGRAPHY

G. Sherman: "Josef Lhévinne," *Recorded Sound*, no.44 (1971), 784 [with discography by H. L. Anderson]

F. C. Campbell: "Lhévinne, Josef," *DAB*

R. R. Gerig: *Famous Pianists and their Technique* (Washington and New York, 1974), 300

R. K. Wallace: *A Century of Music-making: the Lives of Josef and Rosina Lhevinne* (Bloomington, IN, 1976)

JERROLD NORTHROP MOORE/R

Lhévinne [née Bessie], **Rosina** (*b* Kiev, Ukraine, 29 March 1880; *d* Glendale, CA, 9 Nov 1976). Pianist and teacher. She began piano studies at the age of seven and in 1889 entered the Imperial Conservatory in Moscow as a pupil of Remesov, later studying with Vasily Safonov; among her fellow students were Rachmaninoff and Scriabin. There she also met Josef Lhévinne, whom she married in 1898 a week after graduating from the conservatory with a gold medal, the youngest woman ever to win that award. In 1906 the Lhévinnes came to the USA, then in 1908 moved to Berlin, where they were interned during World War I, an experience that helped to decide them to settle permanently in New York. During these years Rosina gave a few solo recitals and played two-piano concerts with her husband but devoted most of her time to supervising Josef's career and to teaching. She joined the faculty of the Juilliard Graduate School in 1924 and remained there until shortly before her death; she came to be regarded as one of the great teachers of the time, and among her many famous pupils were Van Cliburn, John Browning, Arthur Gold, James Levine, and Misha Dichter. As a teacher Madame Lhévinne emphasized the beauty of tone, long line, and spontaneity of expression that characterized the late 19th-century school of Russian pianism. She returned to solo playing after Josef's death, performing the Chopin E minor Piano Concerto with the New York PO when she was 81.

Josef and Rosina Lhévinne

BIBLIOGRAPHY
"Lhevinne, Rosina," *CBY 1961*
R. K. Wallace: *A Century of Music-making: the Lives of Josef and Rosina Lhevinne* (Bloomington, IN, 1976)

ELLEN HIGHSTEIN

Liberace, (Walter) [Wladziu Valentino] (*b* West Allis, WI, 16 May 1919). Pianist. He studied with Florence Kelly and by the age of 14 was playing in an ice cream parlor. He made his début at the age of 17 at the Society of Musical Arts, Milwaukee, and appeared as soloist with the Chicago SO on 15 January 1940 playing Liszt's Second Piano Concerto. He went to New York in 1940 and performed in nightclubs, at first adopting the pseudonym Walter Busterkeys, but later using only the name Liberace. He toured with United Service Organizations camp shows and in 1956 made a series of television programs which were shown weekly throughout the USA and Canada. By the mid-1950s Liberace's recordings had become best-sellers and his concerts in Carnegie Hall and Madison Square Garden were given before capacity audiences. He created a glamorous stage persona and wore gorgeous outfits that glittered in the cunningly planned stage light (always including candles in one or more candelabra on the piano); a more serious side to his image was his championship of the virtues of family, religion, and patriotism. His programs included orchestrated arrangements of classical and popular works designed to show his elaborate keyboard technique, as well as his own compositions, such as *Rhapsody by Candlelight* and *Boogie-woogie Variations*. He also appeared in films (e.g., *Sincerely yours* and *The Loved Ones*).

BIBLIOGRAPHY
"Liberace," *International Musician*, i/10 (1952), 24
"Liberace, (Wladziu Valentino)," *CBY 1954*
Liberace: *Liberace: an Autobiography* (New York, 1973)
——: *The Things I Love*, ed. T. Palmer (New York, 1976)
J. R. Gaines: "Liberace," *People*, xviii (4 Oct 1982), 57
E. Rothstein: "Liberace, the King of Kitsch," *New Republic*, cxci (2 July 1984), 25

MARTHA WOODWARD

Liberace, 1969

Liberati, Alessandro (*b* Frascati, Italy, 7 July/24 Aug 1847; *d* New York, 6 Nov 1927). Cornetist, bandmaster, and composer. He began studying cornet with his father when he was 12, and first performed in public at the age of 14. In 1864 he joined the Papal Army, in which he was a cornetist, and in 1866 Garibaldi's army, in which he was chief bugler and cornet soloist. He came to the USA in 1872, but left for Canada to lead the Governor General's Foot Guards Band in Ottawa. He returned to the USA in 1876 and became director of the Michigan National Guard's Light Guard Band in Detroit. In 1879 he joined Gilmore's band, and soon alternated as cornet soloist with Jules Levy. He then left Gilmore to appear as soloist with Dodworth's New York band and Baldwin's Band of Boston. He also led the band of the 71st Regiment in New York, and from 1889 to 1890 toured the USA and Canada with his own ensemble, Liberati's Grand Military Band, which remained active for 20 years. His band concerts included one-act abridgments of grand operas, and in 1907 he formed the Liberati Grand Opera Company, which by 1915 consisted of a 65-piece band, a chorus, and ten soloists. In 1919, at the age of 72, he became bandmaster of the Dodge Brothers Concert Band in Detroit, and continued to play cornet. In 1923 he moved to New York to teach. As a cornetist Liberati was noted for his sight-reading facility, rapid tonguing, and ability to play octave leaps. His compositions, which were once quite popular, have now disappeared from the repertory. The Heritage of the March series (compiled by ROBERT HOE, JR.), subseries 75, includes a sample of his work.

BIBLIOGRAPHY
G. D. Bridges: *Pioneers in Brass* (Detroit, 1965), 60
H. L. Clarke: "Famous Cornetists of the Past: Alessandro Liberati," *Jacobs' Orchestra Monthly*, xxii/9 (1931), 6

RAOUL CAMUS

Libraries and collections. This article surveys repositories of music and music literature in the USA. For a fuller discussion of other kinds of repository *see* INSTRUMENTS, COLLECTIONS OF, and SOUND AND FILM ARCHIVES; for a discussion of the methodology of using such musical resources and the research tools available for that purpose *see* BIBLIOGRAPHIES.

1. History and funding. 2. Classification and cataloguing systems. 3. List.

1. HISTORY AND FUNDING. Music collections are amassed by private individuals and by various kinds of institution, including private libraries, supported by members and/or donors; privately supported historical societies and archives; private universities and colleges, which are geared to the needs of their own students, faculty, and graduates, and are funded principally through tuition fees; public universities and colleges, supported chiefly (and sometimes irregularly) by state government appropriations and therefore responsible to a broader educational community; public libraries, supported directly and entirely by city taxes or by a mixture of public and private support, and responsible to a broad public sector with or without academic concerns; music information centers, national in scope and international in service and variously supported; and national libraries, supported by federal taxes and nominally responsible to the legislature but in fact answerable to all its constituents. Some music collections are independent, self-sufficient libraries, while others are branches or departments of general collections, sharing administrative support and services with them, whether they are separately housed or not. An academic library typically places the general,

actively circulating music collection in the same building as the music faculty and classrooms, and preserves the rare materials in the treasure room of the general campus library. If the music collection is integrated within the general library, the rare materials are similarly segregated. The descriptions of the collections in the list that follows (§3 below) are designed to show these variations.

In the 19th century, American libraries (unlike those in Europe) were generally established by institutions committed to the principle of mass education. Music libraries were founded in the same spirit, many under the influence of the comprehensive music periodical *Dwight's Journal of Music* (1852–81) and the theories of the pioneer music educator Lowell Mason. Of the three major historical collections of music in existence before 1900, two were established in the public libraries of New York and Boston, and the third in the Newberry Library in Chicago, a private library that was open to the public.

During the first half of the 20th century public library collections expanded thanks to subventions from the Carnegie endowments (*see* CARNEGIE, ANDREW). The extensive and unexpected growth of college and university collections in the 1960s was the result of government policy in two areas: a brief but massive effort to improve libraries through direct grants for materials, equipment, and buildings, and the changes in the taxation of individual incomes that made gifts to nonprofit institutions financially attractive. A burst of vigor in the publishing industry, which began after World War II, partly as the result of new production techniques, quickly fattened the catalogues of music publishers, and libraries, working with increased budgets, were able to take advantage of the flow of new materials. Particularly fortunate during these years were the libraries of the state universities of California and North Carolina. The 1970s brought reversals of the favorable tax policies and consequently tighter budgets, and in the early 1980s at least two conservatory libraries, those of the Curtis Institute of Music and the New England Conservatory, sold some of their treasures at auction in order to raise necessary funds. Libraries that could afford to buy, notably the Pierpont Morgan Library and the library of the University of Texas, Austin, became major music collectors for the first time during this period.

The advent of computer technology has made possible the creation of massive national data bases, particularly online union catalogues (see below), and has hastened the onset of regional and national library consortia and networks. Although cooperative acquisitioning is still an elusive goal, funds have been shifted into joint cataloguing efforts, which is consistent with the principle of American libraries that their catalogues of holdings be accessible to readers as well as representative of what is available.

2. CLASSIFICATION AND CATALOGUING SYSTEMS. Libraries classify and arrange their collections by content according to one of several systems. The scheme developed and instituted by Oscar G. T. Sonneck in 1902 at the Library of Congress is now the most widely used. It was taken up by many other libraries, particularly after World War II, when the Library of Congress increased the distribution of its printed cards listing music materials. Although in some classes its characteristics were specific to the collection in the Library of Congress, the system was adopted by many new libraries, as well as by established institutions, which reclassified their collections to reduce future cataloguing costs. The result of these efforts has produced a somewhat standard practice nationwide, contributing to ease of access by scholars and students as they carry out research in various libraries. The Dewey decimal classification, still in use especially in

Library of Congress

the smaller public libraries, did not distinguish music from music literature until its 16th edition (1958), by which time many libraries had abandoned it or long since created detailed adaptations. A highly respected, multifaceted scheme devised in 1938 by George Sherman Dickinson for the music scores of Vassar College was soon adapted by Columbia University; it is not widely used, however, in spite of its provision for alternative forms of classification to suit libraries of differing purposes. Some research libraries established before 1900, such as the Boston Public Library, instituted "fixed location" systems rather than classified ones (i.e., each new acquisition was given the next in a series of shelfmarks, which identified its location uniquely); such libraries generally tended to adopt the Library of Congress system after a certain date without reclassifying retrospectively. Others, however, including the New York Public Library, devised broadly classified schemes of their own, and have tended to maintain them.

The descriptive cataloguing of music differs from that of other printed matter, largely owing to two long-established practices among music publishers. It is commonly the case that the true title of a work is not that printed on the title page of a publication of it (if indeed there is a title page); moreover different editions or issues of a single work may each carry its own version of the work's title. It is necessary therefore to establish a standard title so that all forms of a work may be identified and collocated. Secondly, manifestations of the same work for different performing forces, or in different presentations (e.g., full score, vocal score, parts), must be clearly described and distinguished for the convenience of the user. Once Sonneck had recognized the peculiar characteristics of musical documents, music cataloguing in the USA evolved as a series of compromises within the context of general American cataloguing codes, designed to accommodate and deal adequately with the special requirements of music.

Soon after the formation of the Music Library Association in 1931, committees were appointed to prepare codes for cataloguing music and sound recordings. Preliminary versions were issued in 1941–2, and a full code was issued jointly with the American Library Association in 1958. These have been superseded by two editions of an Anglo-American code, in 1967 and 1978 respectively, the second of which reflects the development of machine-readable cataloguing. The changes made in this code were so pervasive that the Library of Congress closed its current catalogue in January 1981; many other libraries followed suit, beginning new catalogues on cards, or in data bases, or both. The Library of Congress continues to distribute printed cards, and also distributes computer tapes standardized in the Machine Readable Cataloging (MARC) format to those libraries (and systems) equipped to receive them, notably the online union catalogues of the three major networks – the Online Computer Library Center (OCLC), the Research Libraries Information Network (RLIN), and the Western (formerly Washington) Library Network (WLN).

3. LIST. The following list of repositories with important music holdings is arranged alphabetically by state (or territory), city, and the name of the institution or private collector. Sigla assigned to individual institutions by the Library of Congress in its publication *Symbols of American Libraries* (rev. 12/1980) are given where applicable. (In general, sigla apply to the library system of the institution as a whole, but in some cases the library has requested separate sigla for some or all of its subdivisions; these are provided where they are known to exist.) Each separately housed library within a single institution is designated by an asterisk. In addition to the general bibliography on American libraries at the end of this article, selective bibliographies are provided for most of the libraries cited. References to *CMc*, no. 17 (1974), pertain to D. Seaton's article "Important Library Holdings at Forty-one North American Universities," which contains individual descriptions of some of these repositories by different contributors. Manuscripts listed in the bibliographies are assumed to be at the library or collection under which they are cited. For some entries the period of coverage is given in brackets. For fuller information concerning the organizations, universities, and private collectors cited in this list, see the individual articles on these subjects elsewhere in this dictionary.

ALABAMA

Important local music history repositories include the Birmingham and Jefferson County Free Library (*AB*), the State of Alabama Department of Archives and History (*A-Ar*) in Montgomery, and the University of Alabama (*AU*) in University. Paul V. Yoder's band music collection is at Troy State University (*ATrT*), and the School of Music Library of Samford University (*ABH*) in Birmingham holds the Edward Simon Lorenz Collection of hymnals and scrapbooks.

ALASKA

Native and local music sources are preserved in the Elmer E. Rasmuson Library and the University Archives of the University of Alaska (*AkU*) in Fairbanks, the Sheldon Museum in Haines, and the Alaska Historical Library and Museum (*AkHi*) in Juneau.

ARIZONA

Important collections of American Indian music, in addition to those mentioned below, are located in the Heard Museum in Phoenix and the Arizona State Museum in Tucson. Materials of local musical interest can be found at the Arizona Historical Society (*AzTP*) in Tucson.

TEMPE. Arizona State University (*AzTeS*). Established in 1952, the *Music Library has been in the present music building since 1971 and holds about 30,000 titles (books and scores) and 12,700 sound recordings. Notable among its holdings are the Wayne King Collection of Popular Music, with over 5600 MS orchestrations, charts, and parts of popular music used since the early 1930s, as well as sound recordings and more than 100 films; the Casals International Cello Library, supported by the Arizona Cello Society; the International Percussion Reference Library, founded by Mervin Britton in the 1940s and transferred in 1970 to the Music Library, where it now contains over 2400 items – scores, instructional materials, and recordings – available for short loan by mail (a catalogue, revised biannually, is available); 5300 sheet music items, chiefly songs popular in America from the 1920s through the 1940s; and 200 American hymnals published since 1836. The university music department maintains the *Southwest Tape Archive, consisting mostly of recordings from American Indian communities in Arizona and some Spanish-American materials. In the music building is the *Laura Boulton collection of about 350 ethnic instruments, 1000 hours of taped recordings of traditional music from many parts of the world, and a large amount of ethnomusicological material presented after her death in 1980.

TUCSON. University of Arizona (*AzU*). Founded in 1959, the *Music Collection (in the music building) now numbers some 66,000 volumes and 21,000 recordings and is known chiefly as the repository for the National Flute Association, the International Trombone Association, and the National Opera Association. The library also has rich holdings of sheet music, of which about 20,000 instrumental and vocal items are catalogued. The Historical American Collection of over 9000 items published between about 1850 and 1950 (mostly 1920s and 1930s) and the Grant L. Hill collection of mostly 20th-century items have finding aids. Also notable is the Louis Belden jazz collection of some 13,000 early 78 r.p.m. discs. Other repositories of music at the university include the Southwest Collection (in the *University Library's Special Collections), containing about four linear meters of published music and recordings by Arizona composers, cowboy songs and folksongs, and Mexican-American and American Indian music; the *Center for Creative Photography, which has a collection of photographs by the composer Ernest Bloch; and the *Southwestern Folklore Center, containing Arizona field recordings from the 1940s through the 1960s.

ARKANSAS

FAYETTEVILLE. University of Arkansas (*ArU*). The *David W. Mullins Library, founded in 1972, is notable for the Vance and Mary Celestia Parler Randolph collections of research materials on Arkansas folklore (MSS, typescripts, transcriptions, and tape recordings, 1946–65) and the musical estates of the black composers Florence Price and William Grant Still, the latter consisting of 88 MS scores and sketches, and soon to include his papers.

S. A. Sizer: *A Guide to Selected Manuscript Collections in the University of Arkansas Library* (Fayetteville, AR, 1976)

CALIFORNIA

Among the repositories of early local music sources other than those listed below are the Los Angeles Music Center Archives, the Oakland Museum (*COMus*), the Pioneer Museum in Stockton, and the Art and Music Section and California Room of the San Diego Public Library (*CSd*). Corinne Swall's personal collection in Kentfield and the Society of California Pioneers (*CSfCP*) in San Francisco specialize in early Californiana. Also notable are the Walt Disney Archives (*CBbWD*) in Burbank, which has early film collections; the Miles Kreuger Collection at the Institute of the American Musical in Los Angeles; the Darius Milhaud holdings at Mills College (*COMC*) in Oakland; the San Francisco Conservatory, which has materials relating to Ernest Bloch; and the Kirsten Flagstad Memorial Collection at the California Historical Society (*CHi*) in San Francisco.

W. Rubsamen: "Unusual Music Holdings of Libraries on the West Coast," *Notes*, x (1952–3), 546; H. W. Azhderian: *Reference Works in Music and Literature in Five Libraries of Los Angeles County* (Los Angeles, 1953); S. M. Fry, ed.: *Directory and Index of Special Music Collections in Southern California Libraries and in the Libraries of the Campuses of the University of California* (n.p., 1970, rev. D. L. Hixon 2/1976 as *A Directory of Special Music Collections in Southern California Libraries and in the Libraries of the University of California and the California State Universities and Colleges*); M. L. Crouch: "An Annotated Bibliography and Commentary concerning Mission Music of Alta California from 1769 to 1834," *CMc*, no.22 (1976), 88

BERKELEY. University of California (*CU*). Although Charles Seeger saw to it as early as 1912 that the General Library purchased European collected editions, the real impetus for a separate and expanded *Music Library (*CU-MUSI*) began when Manfred Bukofzer joined the faculty in 1941. The library was formally established in 1947 and moved to its present quarters in 1958. Its reference collections expanded rapidly through a university grant and in the 1950s through the acquisition of the private libraries of Alfred Einstein (about 3000 items related to Italian madrigals as well as his Mozart studies) and Bukofzer himself. Vincent Duckles, librarian 1947–81, and Harriet Nicewonger, reference librarian 1947–70, guided the collections through their formative years and established the repository as one of the first large academic research libraries. Holdings now number about 115,000 volumes, 5000 MSS, 27,000 discs, and 4500 microforms.

The first major purchase, some 5000 18th- and 19th-century opera vocal scores from the music publisher Harris D. H. Connick in 1950, was strengthened three years later with the acquisition of the Sigmund Romberg Collection (4500 volumes of 18th- to early 20th-century operas) and in 1965 by about 327 full scores and some 300 librettos of operas, chiefly 18th-century French, from the collection of Alfred Cortot. Other operatic materials include 25 MS volumes of mid-18th-century English opera arias and ensembles, a 900-volume collection of operas from the 17th to the 20th centuries performed in Sicily, the Taddei collection of about 4400 Italian opera librettos, and 45 unpublished letters of Nicolò Jommelli.

The library has acquired an important representative body of rare sources dating from the 11th century (including the Wolffheim Antiphoner), treatises, 159 partbooks of the 16th and 17th centuries acquired in 1956 (from the Italian dealer Aldo Olschki), 1967, and 1970 (from Cortot's library), English and French keyboard music of the 17th–18th centuries, some Beethoven sketches, and a first edition of Schoenberg's *Gurrelieder* (1912) with corrections in the composer's hand. A major MS source of the 18th-century Paduan violin school of Tartini, which was purchased in 1958, includes some 990 MSS containing works by 82 composers. Extended buying trips in 1963 and 1969 reaped chiefly early 19th-century music and literature, early instrumental methods, and works on opera and music theory.

Special collections include the A. P. Berggreen Collection (all editions of the composer's works as well as Danish folksong material), the William Buck collection of Scots bagpipe music, the Alice Lawson Aber collection of early 19th-century harp music, Franz Liszt materials (some 900 volumes of early editions and literature), and materials relating to Bloch, Denny, Elkus, Felciano, Hertz, Imbrie, Charles Seeger, Oscar Weil, and many other California musicians. The library's recorded music collection includes the WPA Federal Music Project Archive of about 100 acetate discs of California folk music from field expeditions, as well as large (formerly private) collections of 78 r.p.m. recordings. The Archive of California Folk Music collected by Sidney Robertson Cowell in the early 1940s is also located here.

Other collections of music at Berkeley are found in the *Bancroft Library (*CU-BANC*), which has programs, publications, and miscellaneous MSS documenting early San Francisco concert life; the *Graduate Theological Union Library (*CBGTU*); and the *Lowie Museum of Anthropology (*CU-ANTH*), containing California Indian music represented on wire recordings, 3500 cylinders with magnetic tape copies, and film.

The library publishes the newsletter *Cum notis variorum* (1976–). V. Duckles and M. Elmer: *Thematic Catalog of a Manuscript Collection of Eighteenth-century Italian Instrumental Music in the University of California, Berkeley Music Library* (Berkeley and Los Angeles, 1963); F. Traficante: "Dispersal of the Cortot Collection: 290 Treatises in Lexington," *Notes*, xxvi (1969–70), 713; A. Curtis: "Musique classique française à Berkeley," *RdM*, lvi (1970), 123 [includes inventory of 11-volume MS collection copied by De la Barre]; *CMc*, no. 17 (1974), 33; V. Duckles: "The University of California (Berkeley) Music Library," *Notes*, xxxvi (1979–80), 7; J. Emerson and S. Fry: *Combined Catalog of the Opera Collections in the Music*

Libraries at the University of California at Berkeley and the University of California, Los Angeles (Boston, 1982)

CLAREMONT. Claremont Colleges (*CCC*). The *Honnold Library, founded in its present organizational and physical structure in 1952, is supported by various libraries of the Claremont Colleges, each of which also retains parts of its original collections separately. In 1957 the library received the collection of the teacher and pianist Robert G. McCutchan, consisting of 650 18th- and 19th-century American tunebooks and works on hymnology (described by C. E. Lindsley in *Notes*, xxix, 1972–3, p.671), as well as his articles, correspondence, and lecture notes (catalogued in 1954). Also here are the collections assembled by the composer John Laurence Seymour, containing 600 volumes of scores, librettos, and works about opera as well as published editions of his own works, and 300 vocal scores used and annotated by the contralto Ernestine Schumann-Heink.

The *Claremont Graduate School Library holds the personal papers of the pianist Lee Pattison and materials of the WPA Federal Music Project in New York, including concert programs, correspondence, and reports (chiefly 1936–7).

LONG BEACH. California State University (*CLobS*). Music MSS are housed in the Special Collections Department of the *University Library (founded 1949), as is the Oral History of the Arts in Southern California Archive, consisting of MSS, personal effects, correspondence, and interviews (chiefly taped) with about 100 composers, performers, and musicologists. Materials (from 1939 onwards) relating to musicologists can also be found in the Southern California Chapter of the American Musicological Society Archive. Particularly rich are the collections of the composers Gerald Strang and Dane Rudhyar, and the Wesley Kuhnle Archive on Historic Tunings and Temperaments.

The *Music Library was established in 1970 in what is now known as the Media, Fine Arts and Humanities Department. It has a collection of some 25,000 volumes and 10,000 discs, including complete scores for film or stage by Richard Addinsell, Miklós Rózsa, and Gruenberg, and songs by Kern, Berlin, Cole Porter, George Gershwin, Richard Rodgers, and many others acquired from the MGM Music Library (of which a complete inventory is available).

C. G. Raynor, "The Wesley Kuhnle Repository at California State University, Long Beach," *Notes*, xxxiii (1976–7), 16

LOS ANGELES. Arnold Schoenberg Institute Archive: see Los Angeles, University of Southern California.

——: John Edwards Memorial Foundation: see North Carolina, Chapel Hill, University of North Carolina.

——: Los Angeles Public Library (*CL*). A separate Art and Music Department was established when the library opened a new building in 1914, and the music collection now comprises over 47,000 scores, 25,000 works about music, and 33,000 sound recordings. A special group of about 1000 Spanish and South American songs supplements strong holdings in opera, song anthologies, musical comedy, and jazz. In 1934 William Andrews Clark, Jr. (the son of the US senator), bequeathed about 750 orchestral scores and parts; 1000 more were later purchased from the collector Earl Wilson, and in 1981 the library received a gift of $75,000 from the Chevron corporation to refurbish and extend the collection. These works, including operatic arias, light operas, and oratorios, enjoy frequent circulation to about 90 performing groups in ten Southern California communities. The library also received in 1981 Vojmer Attl's collection of about 800 opera and symphonic harp parts. American music is highlighted by 100,000 items of popular sheet music dating from 1841 to the present, popular songbooks, 3000 items relating to the WPA programs, music MSS of California composers, and local concert scrapbooks (from 1894).

A catalogue of the collection of orchestral scores and parts was issued in 1977, and a proposed supplement will include items purchased with the Chevron gift.

——: University of California (*CLU*). Initiated in 1942 by the transfer to the university of about 8000 scores and parts of orchestral and choral music copied by participants in the WPA Federal Music Project, what is now the Walter H. Rubsamen Music Library (*CLU-MUS*) became a branch library in 1955 and moved into the newly built music building, *Schoenberg Hall, the following year. The collection has grown to about 80,000 volumes, 28,000 recordings, and 3900 microfilm reels and cards. Strongly represented, by scores and recordings, are California composers, such as Antheil, Chihara, Henry Leland Clarke, Dillon, Roy Harris, Korngold, Lazarof, McPhee, Edward B. Powell, Frances Marion Ralston, Joseph Rumshinsky (Yiddish theater music), Helen Louise Shaffer, John Vincent, and Erich Zeisl, and, in the area of film, William Lava, Mancini, Shelley Manne, Alex North, Edward Ward, Lee Zahler, and Eugene Zador; there are also materials of the musicologists Boris Kremenliev and Mantle Hood. Among the special archives are the Ernst Toch Archive (inventoried in UCLA theses by C. A. Johnson, 1973; B. J. Davis, 1974; and P. B. Brown, 1975), the Rudolf Friml Library of Music (containing 200 holographs), and the Alfred Newman Collections (of film-music recordings).

Earlier music is also well represented. Of particular interest is the 117-volume set of 1215 librettos printed in Venice and Padua for operas performed there between 1635 and 1769. Supplementing these are late 18th-century English, German, and French librettos, as well as 1150 *comédies-vaudevilles* performed in Paris at the Théâtre de Vaudeville and the Théâtre de Gymnase, 1792–1855, and materials relating to the Paris Opéra. Recent acquisitions of theater music include scores by the English composers Samuel Arnold, Thomas Linley, William Shield, and Stephen Storace. The library also owns early printed editions of French motets and operas, MS copies of Lully's *Isis* and *Thésée*, Dutch psalters and secular songbooks of the 17th and 18th centuries, and folksongs and dances of the British Isles. Notable instrumental collections include an early 17th-century Italian keyboard MS (described by R. Hudson in *JAMS*, xxvi, 1973, p.345) and 174 printed compositions (catalogued by M. S. Cole in *Notes*, xxix, 1972–3, p.215), chiefly chamber works by Pleyel. Recently the library has begun to acquire a comprehensive collection of theoretical treatises of the 16th–20th centuries. Acquisitions of contemporary material are rich in guitar music and Japanese works, the latter through the generosity of Paul Chihara.

Among the music collections in the Department of Special Collections of the *University Research Library (*CLU-URL*) are significant holdings of early American hymns, folksongs, and broadside ballads. George Pullen Jackson's collection of religious folksongs and hymns and Royal B. Stanton's collection of hymnals were supplemented in 1966 by the acquisition of MS hymns composed or copied by the Massachusetts musician and bookbinder Joseph C. Stone (described by W. Salloch, *Catalogue 237*, 1966). A collection of 1800 broadside ballads of 1770–1865 includes 500 American items, and dance manuals and histories of the 17th–19th centuries are also well represented. More recent

Americana include the MS music and other memorabilia of Lionel Barrymore, film scores and sketches in the Stanley Kramer collection, scrapbooks of the singer Jeanette MacDonald, and personal papers of the dancer Ruth St. Denis, including music for her ballets. Among materials from the WPA Federal Theatre Project are three volumes of ballad and folksong transcriptions. A collection of popular sheet music published in California numbers about 7200 items. The Theater Arts Research Library holds a collection of thematic cue sheets for use by motion picture companies.

The nucleus of the *Archive of Popular American Music (located in Kinsey Hall), containing about 500,000 items of sheet music, song folios, band arrangements, and recordings, is the Meredith Willson Archive of Popular American Sheet Music. It had been the stock of Stanley Ring's Hollywood music store – some 250,000 items of sheet music published 1830–1960, 30,000 78 r.p.m. discs, and 250 cylinders (descriptive report by B. Thomas, 1976) – which the composer purchased and presented to the university in 1965. It has been augmented by the collections of Hal Levy, the Music Mart, Thomas Radcliff, and Harry Warren, consisting of 20th-century sheet music, song folios, and commercial orchestrations, and most recently by the W. Lloyd Keepers collection of sheet music published since the early 19th century.

The *William Andrews Clark Memorial Library (*CLU-C*) was bequeathed to the university in 1934 as a memorial to Senator Clark by his son, a musical amateur and supporter of the Los Angeles PO. It specializes in English life and thought between 1640 and 1750 and is rich in original editions of dramatic works in many forms (librettos, full scores, and "favourite songs" from English and Italian operas, masques, ballad operas, and other music-theater works, 1728–1810); composers represented in original editions include Blow, Carey, Handel, Henry Lawes, Leveridge, Morley, Purcell, Ravenscroft, Pietro Reggio, J.-J. Rousseau, and Vanbrugh. About 40 collections of quarto sheets represent English and Scottish songs of the 17th and 18th centuries. MSS include contemporary copies of dance tunes, chamber music (fancies, solo motets, and continuo songs), Cecilian odes, Campra's ballet *L'Europe galante*, and Italian vocal music. Supporting these collections are Baroque treatises on aesthetics and theory, psalms, hymns, and sermons. The younger Clark presented letters of Haydn, Mendelssohn, Liszt, Wagner, Berlioz, Gounod, and Saint-Saëns, two essays by Gounod, and MSS of minor compositions by Grieg and Mendelssohn. Also here are his papers relating to the founding of the Los Angeles PO and his father's correspondence with musicians.

The Institute of Ethnomusicology Archive (in Schoenberg Hall) specializes in oriental music and contains, in addition to Colin McPhee's Balinese materials (acquired in 1974), a large number of Indian, Southeast Asian, African, Balkan, and Latin American instruments. Recently the holdings of American Indian materials have been expanded through the acquisition of field recordings made by Charlotte Heth of Cherokee Indian music. Other materials include some 8000 commercial sound recordings, 7000 field recordings, slides, photographs, reprints from nonmusic sources, and videotapes. Printed ethnomusicological materials are generally to be found in the Rubsamen Music Library, except for reprints, dissertations, and an 800-volume collection of music and prose in Oriental languages.

The *Center for the Study of Comparative Folklore and Mythology Research Collection (founded in 1961) houses materials connected with several research projects initiated under private auspices. The musical holdings are chiefly the work of D. K. Wilgus and consist of collections of commercial discs representing music of the world, particularly Afro- and Anglo-American music; the Archive of California and Western Folklore, strong in Irish, Spanish, and Portuguese music, as well as folksongs of California and Arkansas (2000 tapes in all); the Western Kentucky Folklore Archive, containing 150 tapes and incorporating the Josiah H. Combs collection (mostly MSS) of songs and rhymes, augmented by B. A. Botkin's materials, collected in the 1920s and indexed in Wilgus's edition of Combs's *Folksongs of the Southern United States* (1967); and the Reverend Andrew Jenkins Collection, documenting the life of the folk composer and teacher.

In the Oral History Archives (in the *Powell Library) transcripts of interviews with the harpsichordist Alice Ehlers, the critics and musicologists Lawrence Morton, Charles Seeger, Nicolas Slonimsky, and Peter Yates, and the widows of Ernst Toch and Erich Zeisl supplement those in the Music Library.

The music library publishes the journal *Full Score* (1984–). *List of the Letters and MSS of Musicians in the William Andrews Clark Memorial Library*, ed. WPA, Historical Records Survey, California (Los Angeles, 1940); *Catalog of the Music Library*, ed. UCLA Library (Los Angeles, 1947); D. K. Wilgus: "The Western Kentucky Folklore Archive," *Folklore and Folk Music Archivist*, i/4 (1958), 3; P. J. Revitt: *The George Pullen Jackson Collection of Southern Hymnody (a Bibliography)*, UCLA Library Occasional Papers, no. 13 (Los Angeles, 1964); F. Freedman: *A Bibliography of Baroque Materials in the UCLA Music Library* (Los Angeles, 1966); N. Pirrotta: "Early Venetian Libretti at Los Angeles," *Essays in Honor of Dragan Plamenac on his 70th Birthday* (Pittsburgh, 1969), 233; *CMc*, no. 17 (1974), 36; B. Barclay and M. S. Cole: "The Toch and Zeisl Archives at UCLA: Samples of Southern California Activity to Preserve the Heritage of its Emigré Composers," *Notes*, xxxv (1978–9), 556; "The Ethnomusicology Archive," *UCLA Librarian*, xxxii (1979), 58; J. Emerson and S. Fry: *Combined Catalog of the Opera Collections in the Music Libraries at the University of California at Berkeley and the University of California, Los Angeles* (Boston, 1982)

——. University of Southern California, Arnold Schoenberg Institute Archive (*CLAS*). This collection was first assembled in 1974 at the John F. Kennedy Memorial Library at California State University in Los Angeles under the auspices of a consortium, which included in addition to California State the University of California, Los Angeles, the California Institute of the Arts, and the University of Southern California; the Schoenberg Institute was given its own building at the University of Southern California in 1976. Holdings include the musical and literary MSS of Arnold Schoenberg, published music by Schoenberg (complete) and others (1500 items), and other printed materials associated with the composer, as well as memorabilia. Supplementary materials have been presented by the conductor Fritz Stiedry and his wife, Mrs. Adolf Koldofsky, Lawrence Morton, Paul A. Pisk, Gerald Strang, Leonard Stein, and H. H. Stuckenschmidt. Clara Steuermann (archivist 1975–82) presented the library with the collection of her late husband, the pianist Edward Steuermann.

The *Arnold Schoenberg Institute Bulletin* (1975–6) was superseded by the *Journal of the Arnold Schoenberg Institute* in 1976. J. Rufer: *The Works of Arnold Schoenberg* (New York, 1963); J. Meggett and R. Moritz: "The Schoenberg Legacy," *Notes*, xxxi (1974–5), 30; C. Steuermann: "From the Archives: Procedures, Materials, and Acknowledgments," *Journal of the Arnold Schoenberg Institute*, i (1976–7), 49

OAKLAND. Oakland Public Library (*CO*). Although the library was established in 1868, the nucleus of the music collection was formed in 1914 by two gifts: 375 anthems in multiple copies from O. M. Vesper and a substantial collection of organ music from Mrs. C. T. M. Parker. The library continued to grow chiefly through gifts of sacred music, and in 1948 it inaugurated one of the country's earliest circulating record collections under the direction of its music librarian, Edward Colby. Now a standard public library collection of about 15,000 volumes and 10,000 recordings, the library continues to circulate its large collection of about 30,000 items of choral octavo music to church choirs. It holds a sheet-music collection of 14 bound volumes (1830–90) and 10,000 separate items (1890–).

Sacred and Secular Music List, including the Vesper, Hughes and Dow Gifts, ed. Oakland Public Library (Oakland, CA, 1937); R. Colvig: "The Oakland Public Library: Art, Music and Recreation," *Cum notis variorum*, no.39 (1980), 5

PALO ALTO. Stanford University (*CSt*). The Memorial Library of Music in the *Cecil H. Green Library (the main university library) was presented by Mr. and Mrs. George Keating in 1950 and continues to amass autograph MSS and autographed copies of first editions from as early as the late 17th century, but especially those of living composers. In 1953 the number of autograph MSS it owned was second only to that of the Library of Congress. Items of particular distinction are Purcell's *Te Deum* and *Jubilate*, vocal works by Blow and Handel, Alessandro Scarlatti's oratorio *La sposa dei sacri cantici*, a Bach keyboard suite, Schubert's overture to *Rosamunde*, Schumann's vocal duets op.43, Mendelssohn's Sinfonia no.9, the score of Mascagni's *Cavalleria rusticana* dated 1890 and submitted by the composer to a contest sponsored by the Milan publisher Sonzogno, Stravinsky's *Danses concertantes*, and Martinů's sketches for his String Sextet. Holographs of American composers include major works by Berlin (*White Christmas*), Cowell, Crist, Herbert, Hermann Lohn, and Thomson. The library has recently acquired published works and about 100 MSS from Dane Rudhyar. Music materials in the library's Bender Room include the Chester Barker collection of vocal scores of operettas and musical comedies.

Founded in 1948, the *Music Library (*CSt-Mus*, in the Braun Music Center) of about 84,000 items is particularly strong in 18th-century theoretical works and 19th-century chamber music, opera, and materials related to performance practice. In 1983 the Lully Archive was established as a repository for microfilms of primary sources of the composer's works; in 1984 the archive acquired four contemporary MSS. The *Hoover Institution (*CSt-H*) library, founded in 1919, has over a million items, among which are notable materials relating to music and politics (including political songs in totalitarian countries) and songbooks with and without music, especially of the American, English, German, and Polish armies in the two world wars.

Separately housed, the *Archive of Recorded Sound includes well over 150,000 items in many recorded forms documenting all aspects of culture in the 20th century. There are especially strong collections of performances by Kirsten Flagstad, and Hollywood Bowl and Stanford University Music Department concerts, the last including taped performances of early music by Putnam Aldrich and George Houle. Related materials include record catalogues (e.g., a complete file of the Bettini Phonograph Library), periodicals about records and the recording industry, programs, and biographical information regarding performers.

N. Almond and H. H. Fisher, eds.: *Special Collections in the Hoover Library on War, Revolution and Peace* (Stanford, CA, 1940); N. van Patten: *Catalog of the Memorial Library of Music* (Stanford, CA, 1950); *Catalog of the Western Language Collections* (Boston, 1970; suppls., 1972, 1977) [Hoover Institution]; *CMc*, no.17 (1974), 32; M. Bahmann: "The Stanford University Music Library," *Cum notis variorum*, no.36 (1979), 3

RIVERSIDE. University of California (*CU-Riv*). The music collection here, established in 1963, is divided between the *Music Library (16,000 scores and 10,000 discs) and the *University Library (about 12,000 books, 2500 discs, and Special Collections). The Music Library is rich in dramatic music, chiefly from the library of Peter Claas (1300 first and early editions acquired from the conductor Willy Salomon), but also from the Marcella Craft Collection of opera scores, some with stage directions by Anton Fuchs (the artistic director at Bayreuth under Wagner). It has much Danish music (including the complete published works of Niels Gade), research materials in organology, nearly all available music for the carillon, and some 2000 orchestral scores and parts from the WPA Southern California Music Project.

In Special Collections is the Oswald Jonas Memorial Collection, which includes the Heinrich Schenker Archive. The first segment, purchased in 1976, contained in addition to four Brahms MSS 500 first and early editions by Handel (3), Haydn (8), Mozart (13), Beethoven (66), Mendelssohn (42), Schubert (81), Schumann (90), Chopin (74), and Brahms (136); in 1978 the library received Schenker's correspondence and MS notebooks, including a 4000-page diary (1896–1935) (a checklist of the collection is available). A gift presented in 1980 of the MSS and materials of Harry James (who studied the Cahuilla and Hopi Indians) and some 4000 sound recordings stimulated the formation of the Harry and Grace James Collection and Recorded Sound Archive, which now numbers about 10,000 recorded items, including extensive but scattered holdings of phonograph catalogues of Columbia (1936–52), Decca (1942–8), and Victor (1921–51).

S. M. Fry: "A Progress Report on a Special Collection of Bell and Carillon Literature," *Bulletin of the Guild of Carillonneurs in North America*, xxi (1970), 19; *CMc*, no.17 (1974), 39; J. D. Kunselman: "University of California, Riverside: the Oswald Jonas Memorial Collection," *CMc*, no.28 (1979), 7

SAN FRANCISCO. Bay Area Music Archives. The Archives were founded in 1977 to preserve books, magazines, recordings, posters, clippings, and other memorabilia relating to popular music in San Francisco beginning in the early 1960s. About 7000 recordings, the bulk of the present collection, were acquired from the estate of the *San Francisco Chronicle* correspondent John Wasserman.

G. Fullington: "The Bay Area Music Archives," *Cum notis variorum*, no.41 (1980), 6

——. San Francisco Public Library (*CSf*). All the materials owned by the library were destroyed in the 1906 earthquake. When the present building opened in 1917, a separate Music Section was established in the Art and Music Department. The documentation of local music and musical life here is prodigious: over 90 scrapbooks compiled for 1849–1956 are supplemented by files on topics, organizations, individuals, and performing ensembles (especially rock groups). A reference collection of sheet music in 250 bound volumes containing 8500 songs issued between 1800 and the 1950s is supplemented by 979 songs of the Gold Rush era (*c*1849) and 20 volumes of mostly 19th-century songs published in or about San Francisco and elsewhere in the West. (A similar collection of 6000 items is in the San Francisco History Room.) Among the 25,000 scores is a reference collection of 65 works by California composers in MS scores and parts copied for the WPA Federal Music Project, and circulating orchestral sets. There are also 15,000 books, 400 periodical subscriptions, and 7500 recordings.

Music materials in the *Archives of the Performing Arts (located in the War Memorial Opera House) document through film and prints the history of San Francisco theaters; they include a sheet music collection of 10,000 items intended to be useful chiefly through their illustrated covers, more than 3500 recordings, and some 100 taped interviews.

M. Ashe: "San Francisco Public Library Art and Music Department," *Cum notis variorum*, no.31 (1979), 3

——. San Francisco State University (*CSfSt*). From 1945 until his death in 1968 Frank V. de Bellis amassed a library of books and music illustrating Italian culture; he donated all except about 200 incunabula in 1963 to the trustees of the California State Colleges, who agreed to house the collection in the *J. Paul Leonard Library at San Francisco State. De Bellis's interest was originally in pre-electric disc and cylinder recordings, of which he collected some 20,000, including nearly the entire output of Pathé and Fonotipia and a large quantity of Edison cylinders and shellac discs, all documenting the styles of Italian singers of the first quarter of the 20th century. He also gathered some 3000 electric recordings for his radio program "Music of the Italian Masters" (still aired weekly), including a rare example of a recording of Monteverdi's *Orfeo* (Musiche Italiane Antiche, 1935).

In 1952 De Bellis began to acquire his collection of 5000 early editions and 500 MSS of Italian music and arrange for performances of these works in the San Francisco area. The earliest MSS include part of an Italian choirbook (*c*1380) and an antiphoner of 1497 with modified gothic script. The 16th century is represented by a folio requiem mass, a printed *Cantorinus* (1513), and a number of secular partbooks printed by Gardano and others, including collections of works by Du Pont (1551), Luzzaschi (1576), Palestrina (1596, 1601, 1619), and Alessandro Striggio (1585), among others, in addition to anthologies; Rinuccini's librettos for *Dafne* (1594) and *Arianna* (1608) are present in first editions. 17th-century partbooks contain madrigals, motets, and psalms by such composers as Felice Anerio, Gesualdo, Giovanni del Turco, and d'India. There are also MS songbooks with pieces by Luigi Rossi and G. M. Bononcini, among others, and a Milanese lute MS dated 1615.

The collection is particularly strong in works of the 18th century, including a holograph MS by Alessandro Scarlatti of his oratorio *Cain, overo Il primo omicidio* of 1707 and MS instrumental music from *c*1750 once owned by the flutist Filippo Ruge. Notable first editions include Benedetto Marcello's *Estro poetico-armonico* (1724–6) and full scores of operas by such composers as Paisiello, Cimarosa, Piccinni, and Cherubini. Among the many compositions for solo voice are cantatas by Porpora, Giovanni Bononcini, and Alessandro Scarlatti; works by castrato singers are represented by Girolamo Crescentini's vocal music and methods. 100 Italian works for chamber orchestra in contemporary parts occur in MSS and in editions published by Sieber, Pleyel, Le Duc, and Offenbach in Paris, Roger and Le Cène in Amsterdam, and Walsh, Johnson, and Cocks in London. There are also numerous printed works for smaller chamber combinations, notably the collected quintets of Boccherini, contemporary editions of string music (Piani, etc.), and first editions of Clementi's keyboard works.

About 1000 books on music, chiefly theoretical works published before 1600, contain treatises by Aaron, Zarlino, and Galilei, as well as a dissertation (2/1597) by Diruta on keyboard playing and the earliest source on the African origin of the bassoon (by T. Albonesi, 1539). There are also definitive works on instruments (such as Filippo Bonanni's, 1722), others containing engravings of early instruments, and 17th- and 18th-century books relating chiefly to figured bass and contrapuntal techniques. De Bellis also acquired a number of autograph letters and 18th- and 19th-century contemporary portraits of composers and performers. Acquisitions are currently supported by both private funds and state subsidy.

The Creative Arts Library, founded in 1948, contains some 25,000 music volumes (two-thirds of which are scores) and about 15,000 recordings.

A card catalogue of the De Bellis collection is in progress. *The Frank V. de Bellis Collection in the Library of San Francisco State College* (San Francisco, 1964, 2/1967); J. LaRue and M. W. Cobin: "The Ruge-Seignelay Catalogue: an Exercise in Automated Entries," *Elektronische Datenverarbeitung in der Musikwissenschaft*, ed. H. Heckmann (Regensburg, Germany, 1967), 41

SAN MARINO. Henry E. Huntington Library and Art Gallery (*CSmH*). From 1910 to his death in 1927 Henry Huntington amassed a collection, strong in English and American history and literature, of some 175,000 volumes, about 5500 of which relate to music. Most are English and American items of the 16th to 18th centuries and derive principally from three music collections (described in *Grove 2*, ii, pp.707, 700, and 704, respectively): the Bridgewater House Library, founded during the reign of Queen Elizabeth I by Thomas Egerton and rich in Renaissance and 17th-century materials (purchased in its entirety in 1917); the Britwell Court Library, founded by W. H. Miller and noted for its English madrigals, American broadsides, and early songbooks in fine editions (purchased at Sotheby's, 1916–27); and the library of Henry Huth, containing liturgies, psalm books, MS and printed madrigals, and popular songs and theater music, including about 500 early 18th-century broadside songs (purchased 1911–20).

Copies of about 90% of all the musical items published in England between 1500 and 1640 are in the Huntington collections. About 900 of these are English madrigals, lute songs, and instrumental works; there are also Dutch Reformed, English, French, German, and Italian psalm books and English theoretical works as well as Italian ones known in England at the time. The only complete set of five partbooks of Thomas Whythorne's *Songes, for Three, Fower and Five Voyces* (1571) is found here. Music of the later 17th century is represented by a large collection of Playford's songbooks, numerous vocal works by Henry and William Lawes, a rare copy of *Tripla concordia* (1677), instrumental methods by Christopher Simpson and Thomas Mace, rare publications of the printer John Forbes of Aberdeen, Scotland, early broadside melodies, and the historic *A Short Direction for the Performance of Cathedrall Service* (1661), edited by Edward Lowe, who had been authorized by Charles II to restore the Anglican liturgical service.

The greatest quantity of music here is of 18th-century origin. The Huth Collection (see above) is augmented by 40 ballad operas, the John Larpent Collection of 18th- and 19th-century English and Italian MS plays and librettos (catalogued by D. MacMillan, 1939), the J. P. Kemble–Duke of Devonshire Collection of about 4000 printed English plays and 40 volumes of playbills, a large collection of mid-18th-century British magazine music, and a number of French operettas and musical comedies. American music of the same period is represented by hymnals, anthems, and other sacred music (including the German psalm books of the Ephrata Cloister), a number of heated debates published in the early 1700s over the "rote *v.* note" controversy in psalmody, and two MS librettos of Francis Hopkinson's *The Temple of Minerva* (1781), as well as 106 musical items relating to George Washington in the Walter Updike Lewisson Collection and other items of patriotic sheet music.

Early American music and 19th-century American sheet music relating to Virginia and other southeastern states are found in the Robert Alonzo Brock Collection. Included are songs and songsters relating to the War of 1812, the Whig Convention of 1840, the Civil War, and the influence of Harriet Beecher Stowe; very early Afro-American and minstrel songs; ballads by Henry Russell, J. H. Hewitt, and Stephen Foster; music of the London, New York, and Philadelphia stages; and hymnals.

Of the 129 musical incunabula, about two-thirds are theoretical works without notation. 18 early liturgical MSS are supplemented by a 14th-century theological miscellany (Gwysaney 19914, acquired in 1959). A fine MS collection of Italian madrigals copied for Thomas Egerton contains one by John Coprario, whose *Rules How to Compose*, dated 1610, is also present in MS. Two notable autograph MSS in the library are a collection of *airs* by J.-J. Rousseau and 28 anthems, 1775–1803, by Charles Wesley; most of the library's few other autograph MSS stem from the 19th century, notably three by Gounod, Liszt's Rákóczy March, and Mendelssohn's *Lieder ohne Worte*, op. 19*b*. Of the remaining 200 musical MSS, most are copies of popular 19th-century songs, 84 of them by Thomas Moore.

Although the music collections are largely static, additions during the last decade include some 300 engraved English broadside songs and a large collection of 19th- and early 20th-century American sheet music. Since music constitutes only a small portion of this library, which holds about 500,000 books and 5,000,000 MSS in all, visiting scholars should not expect to find the usual musical reference works here.

The *Huntington Library Bulletin*, published irregularly 1931–7, was superseded by the *Huntington Library Quarterly* in 1937. E. N. Backus: "The Music Resources of the Huntington Library," *Notes*, 1st ser., no. 14 (1942), 27; E. N. Backus: *Catalogue of Music in the Huntington Library Printed before 1801* (San Marino, CA, 1949)

SAN RAFAEL. Dominican College, American Music Research Center (*CSrD*). Founded in 1968, the center preserves and disseminates information about American music and fosters performances of this repertory. The Archbishop Alemany Library there specializes in music of the 18th and 19th centuries, but also houses presentation copies of works by 20th-century composers, such as Lou Harrison, Rorem, Sibyl Schneller, Jon Sutton, Still, and Thomson. There are about 150 psalm books and tunebooks, 1726–1920, in original and facsimile or microfilm editions; comic operas and works written and/or performed in the USA; and a collection of California mission music, including microfilms of music and photographic slides of instruments used in the missions.

M. D. Ray: "The American Music Research Center," *Cum notis variorum*, no. 37 (1979), 5

SANTA BARBARA. University of California (*CU-SB*). The *Arts Library has grown rapidly since its inception in 1968 and now numbers some 40,000 volumes and 16,000 sound recordings. The Goethe and Music Collection illustrates the poet's influence through more than 200 books, plays, pamphlets, and scores (including first editions of songs by Schubert, Beethoven, and C. F. Zelter). The library holds the complete works of its faculty composers, Edward Applebaum, John Biggs, Emma Lou Diemer, Peter Racine Fricker, Roger Chapman, Douglas Green, Stanley Krebs, and Thea Musgrave, and microfilm copies of mission music. It also maintains an archive of recorded sound of about 20,000 items based on the collections of Anthony Boucher (emphasizing the "Golden Age" of opera, 1900–50) and Joseph P. Strohl (Eastern European labels and artists, supplemented by more than 500 items recorded by both Imperial and Soviet Russian performers and substantial selections by Scandinavian and Dutch artists).

The Lotte Lehmann collection (in the Department of Special Collections of the *University Library) contains the singer's personal and business papers, including correspondence with Bruno Walter and Toscanini, photographs, memorabilia of her life in Vienna, Salzburg, and Santa Barbara, films, tapes (including master classes, of which a typescript catalogue exists), and radio and television transcripts.

S. Sonnet: *Printed Catalogs of the Archive of Sound Recordings Collection of the Arts Library, University of California, Santa Barbara* (Santa Barbara, CA, 1974); *CMc*, no. 17 (1974), 40; W. Summers: "Music of the California Missions: an Inventory and Discussion of Selected Printed Music Books Used in Hispanic California, 1769–1836," *Soundings: Collections of the University Library*, ix (1977), 13 [*CU-SB* and the Mission Santa Barbara Archive Library]

STANFORD. Stanford University: see Palo Alto.

COLORADO

Major local music history repositories include the Colorado State Historical Society at the Colorado Heritage Center (*CoHi*) in Denver, both the Western History and the Fine Arts and Recreation departments in the Denver Public Library (*CoD*), the Pioneer Museum and Historical Society in Florence, and the Municipal Museum in Greeley.

BOULDER. University of Colorado (*CoU*). The *Music Library (in the music building) is notable chiefly for its American materials. The printed music includes hymnals, glees, choruses, tutors, and songbooks, principally from the late 19th and early 20th centuries and in the English traditions (inventoried in 1973). The recorded music falls into two groups: country and folk. Joe Buzzard, Jr., presented 48 tapes containing 800 hillbilly songs (with about 2000 variants) sung by some 100 performers (e.g., Gene Autry, Eva Davis, Uncle Dave Macon), recorded commercially and in the field between 1923 and 1932. The Ben Gray Lumpkin Folksong Collection consists of about 1500 items, mostly vocal tunes, recorded in the 1950s and 1960s; the repertory is largely Anglo-American and includes children's songs, broadsides, and 19th-century popular and vaudeville tunes, in addition to ethnic music, chiefly of Spanish origin. The library also houses the archives of the College Music Society.

The Western Historical Collections in the *Norlin Library (the main university library) include materials on local and regional music since the 1860s.

The library publishes the newsletter *Jots & Titles* (1976–). *CMc*, no. 17 (1974), 43; G. A. Culwell: *The English Language Songs in the Ben Gray Lumpkin Collection of Colorado Folklore* (diss., U. of Colorado, 1976); E. Arquimbau and J. A. Brennan: *A Guide to Manuscript Collections* (Boulder, CO, 1977) [Western Historical Collections]

CONNECTICUT

Major historical collections other than those listed below can be found at the Connecticut Historical Society (*CtHi*) and in the History and Genealogy Department and the State Archive at the Connecticut State Library (*Ct*), both in Hartford, and in the Hartt College of Music library and the University Archives at the University of Hartford (*CtWeharU*) in West Hartford. The Warrington, Paine, and Pratt hymnology collections, formerly at the Hartford Seminary Foundation, are now for the most part dispersed (see Georgia, Atlanta, Emory University).

HARTFORD. Trinity College (*CtHT*). The *Watkinson Library has amassed a strong collection of 18th- and 19th-century American music. Among the MSS are 25 songbooks and copybooks, including one owned by the violinist Micah Hawkins dated 1824. Musical compositions, a study of Connecticut music history, and personal correspondence, scrapbooks, programs, and photographs of the Hartford organist Nathan Henry Allen are also found here. 20th-century American popular music is well documented in the Edward Abbé Niles Collection by about 200 letters of Berlin, Gershwin, Handy, various publishers, and others, as well as by editions of blues compositions and other popular sheet music. There are 24,000 additional items of sheet music from the 18th century through the 1940s and extended runs of several 19th-century American music journals.

Billings to Joplin: Popular Music in 19th-century America (Hartford, 1980) [exhibition catalogue]; M. F. Sax: *Music in the Watkinson Library* (Hartford, 1981)

MIDDLETOWN. Wesleyan University (*CtW*). The Special Collections and Archives Department of the *Olin Library contain a number of musical collections associated with the university's history, as well as MSS, music, programs, and other materials related to the Continental Vocalists, an ensemble that toured widely between 1854 and 1885 (described by P. Bruce in a typescript paper, 1978). The *Music Library in the Center for the Arts houses the World Music Archives, which is particularly strong in recordings of American Indian music, especially of Navajo ceremonies.

NEW HAVEN. New Haven Colony Historical Society (*CtNhHi*). The New Haven Music Collection comprises about 6500 items of music written or published in New Haven 1798–1976 and is supplemented by programs and clippings. It also holds the papers of the music educator Benjamin Jepson and the music critic H. Earle Johnson and is particularly noted for the papers and tunebooks (MS and printed) by or used by the 18th-century composer Daniel Read (letters discussed and inventoried by I. Lowens in *Notes*, ix, 1952–3, p.233).

——. Yale University (*CtY*). A separate music library was created in 1917 when Sprague Hall was built to house the School of Music. At that time, most of the 10,000 items from the Lowell Mason Library, which had been given to the university's theological department in 1873, were transferred to the new library, where they occupied about two-thirds of the shelves. The music library was considerably enlarged in 1956 through a gift in honor of a 1934 alumnus for whom the library was then named. The *John Herrick Jackson Music Library (*CtY-Mus*) now numbers 110,000 volumes and 16,000 recordings, of which about 16,000 items (MSS and early prints) can be found in a department of special collections.

A MS catalogue of the Mason Library compiled by J. S. Smith (1874–7) reveals that only parts of the collections have been classified and absorbed into the music library proper. These include about 250 MSS, early imprints, and the works of Mason himself and the organist and pedagogue Johann Christian Heinrich Rinck, from whose son Mason had bought the bulk of the collection in 1852. Rinck's library is rich in contemporary MS copies acquired from sources close to the composers. Notable among these are 33 recently authenticated early chorale preludes by Bach, the Lowell Mason Codex (no.5056 in Smith's catalogue), one of the most important sources of keyboard music of the late 17th and early 18th centuries and a unique source for works by Dietrich Buxtehude, Alessandro Poglietti, J. M. Radeck, and N. A. Strungk (discussion and inventory by F. W. Riedel in *Quellenkundliche Beiträge*, 1960, p.99), and two small MS volumes of 16th-century German texts (discussed by H. M. Hewitt in *Germanic Review*, xxi, 1946, pp.9–47). Most of Mason's original collection reflects his own professional interests – hymnals, other sacred vocal music, and methods published 1750–1850, mainly in the USA.

The library continues to specialize in music of the 18th century and now owns the holograph MS of J. S. Bach's *Clavier-Büchlein* for Wilhelm Friedemann Bach (Albrecht, *Census*, 49; facs., 1959/*R*1979) and a number of early printed editions of C. P. E. Bach and Clementi. Outstanding among the many vocal works are about 20 operas by Lully in 18th-century Ballard editions and MS scores of operas by Hasse and J. F. Agricola.

Other notable collections include a comprehensive group of theoretical treatises amassed through systematic purchase, and the Filmer Collection of about a dozen printed works and 40 MSS deposited in 1946 (catalogued by R. Ford in *Notes*, xxxiv, 1977–8, p.814), which contain English madrigals, motets, lute songs, solo works for lute and harpsichord, consort pieces, and solo anthems by such composers as Dering, William Lawes, Thomas Lupo, John Wilson, Jenkins, and Purcell. The library also owns the archive of the musicologist Dragan Plamenac (5250 volumes, of which 436 are printed and MS works dating from between 1546 and 1800); Ellsworth Grumman's collection of first and early editions of Beethoven piano sonatas; a collection of about 150 MSS and 25 editions (1810–40) purchased in 1972 from the descendants of the Italian violinist, composer, and theorist Francesco Galeazzi, which contains scenes from operas by Rossini, Mercadante, and others and some chamber music; and a substantial collection of Gilbert and Sullivan materials.

Miscellaneous MSS of particular interest include several medieval illuminated MSS; the 16th-century Wickhambrook Lute MS (described in D. E. R. Stephens's thesis for Yale University, 1959); vocal works by Alessandro Scarlatti and Salieri; sketches by Beethoven and Berg; autograph MSS by Clementi, Chopin, Schubert, Schumann, Mendelssohn, and Brahms; and autograph full scores by Sibelius, C. V. Stanford, and S. Coleridge-Taylor.

Beginning in 1955 with the acquisition of the complete MSS and papers of Charles Ives (catalogued by J. Kirkpatrick, 1960/*R*1973), the library has become an important repository of American music. The Archive of American Music (founded in 1972) now contains more than 150 linear meters of MS music, correspondence, and papers of Ives himself and such other composers as Lowell Mason, Gustave Stoeckel, Horatio Parker (described by W. C. Rorick in *FAM*, xxvi, 1979, p.298), his pupil David Stanley Smith, Henry Gilbert, J. Rosamond Johnson, Carl Ruggles, Thomas de Hartmann, Percy Grainger, Richard Donovan, Leo Ornstein (inventory by V. Perlis in *Notes*, xxxi, 1974–5, p.735), Virgil Thomson, Quincy Porter, Duke Ellington, Kurt Weill, Armin Loos, Lehman Engel, and Seymour Shifrin. The library is now the American branch of the Hindemith archives in Frankfurt am Main, Germany, and holds nine of the composer's holograph MSS and some sketches. The Love Family Papers comprise about 1500 letters concerning the activities of the Kneisel Quartet between 1890 and 1925, and other 20th-century MSS include holographs of works by Bax, Berg, Dello Joio, and Durey, as well as 112 items of 20th-century harpsichord music (chiefly MS scores with his own annotations) presented by Ralph Kirkpatrick.

Soon after Yale received the Ives papers, Vivian Perlis conceived the idea of interviewing the composer's friends, family, musical and business associates, and music critics; the tapes and transcripts of some 60 interviews are now housed in the music library. Similar projects concerning Hindemith and Duke Ellington are under way, as is a project now numbering some 100 interviews with piano technicians, dealers, performers, the employees of the Steinway piano manufacturing firm, and the Steinway family. Perlis has also collected copies of tapes from other oral history projects, including materials from WQXR (New York), KPFK (Los Angeles), and WYBC (New Haven).

The *Sterling Memorial Library (the main university library) has a number of important musical items in its collections, especially American songbooks, folksongs, and the carol collection of Edward Bliss Reed, who was secretary of the Carol Society in New Haven, 1923–40, during which time volumes of carols of various nationalities were issued annually. About 50 musical items (printed and MS) relate to Charles Lindbergh's 1927 Atlantic flight.

The nucleus of the Historical Sound Recordings collection (in the Sterling Library), inaugurated in 1960 and now numbering some 100,000 items, was formed by the rare-book dealer and record collector Laurence C. Witten II, who acquired from George T. Keating in California a comprehensive collection of rare 19th- and early 20th-century vocal recordings representative of the various schools of singing and offered it, together with portions of his own collections (annually), to the university. Since then other notable collections have been acquired: from H. William Fitelson private recordings of the Theatre Guild radio productions (*c*1930–1950); from Warren H. Lowenhaupt a large number of central European recordings, including complete issues of some series, performances by Toscanini and Josef Hofmann, and early phonograph equipment; from Lucius H. Balbour his father's collections of late acoustic and early electric recordings; and from the widow of George J. Openhym European recordings (1935–50) and the piano music of the S. J. Capes collection. The archive is rich in performances given by late 19th- and early 20th-century European composers, and has extended its scope to include jazz and ethnic music on 78 r.p.m. discs. Supporting materials such as record company catalogues, programs, and photographs are also collected extensively.

Among the musical items in the general holdings of the *Beinecke Rare Book and Manuscript Library (*CtY-BR*) are a Cistercian gradual of *c*1300, medieval antiphoners and graduals, many late medieval MS leaves, and the late 15th-century Burgundian chansonnier acquired in 1939 and known by the name of its donor, Paul Mellon (facs., 1979). The William A. Speck Collection (in the German Literature collection) includes autographs and early editions of songs and other music based on or inspired by Goethe's poetry and prose, or otherwise related to his life.

Most notable is the James Marshall and Marie-Louise Osborn Collection, chiefly of 17th- and 18th-century English verse, but containing important musical MSS from the 16th to the 20th centuries. Particularly important are the Braye Lutebook of *c*1560 and autograph scores by Alessandro Scarlatti, Britten, Dohnányi, Holst, Vaughan Williams, and Mahler (*Das klagende Lied* and the first two symphonies, the performance rights of which Mrs. Osborn assigned to the New Haven SO). Also here are about 900 letters, notebooks, and MSS of the English historian Charles Burney, as well as letters to him from Haydn and others. Late 18th-century Italian operas are represented in Lady Emma Hamilton's collection of MS vocal scores, and a significant collection of Wagner correspondence was bequeathed by Charles J. Rosenbloom.

Early Americana are best represented by five editions of the Bay Psalm Book (1640–1758), as well as other 18th-century sacred collections. American Indian and Mormon hymnals are found in the Western Americana Collection. The James Weldon Johnson Collection contains not only the composer's personal papers, but also editions, recordings (about 1200), and 62 autograph scores of music by black composers.

With a large gift from Robert Barlow in early 1954 of sheet music, vocal scores, recordings, and books, the Beinecke established the Literature of the American Musical Theatre collection, which aims to include copies of all musical comedies produced on the American stage and the collected works of stage composers in any media (excluding the operettas of Offenbach, Johann Strauss, and Sullivan, for whom special collections exist elsewhere). Access is through the Historical Sound Recordings collection (see above), which now holds all the recorded works. Included are the MSS, papers, and printed music of Cole Porter, Harold Rome, E. Y. Harburg, and Albert Seldon, a large portion of the published works of Irving Berlin, and significant materials relating to Noble Sissle and Eubie Blake. About 30,000 items of sheet music from 1890 onwards are uncatalogued but indexed, and about 20 boxes of programs are arranged by title. Programs and other materials relating to musical theater, variety shows, circuses, and movies are found in the separately maintained J. R. Crawford Theatre Collection.

In addition to archival materials of the Yale band and other early American bands, the *Yale Band Library contains MS scores and parts (some holograph) by the Italian-American band conductor and opera impresario Giuseppe Creatore from the early 1900s and MS scores by Carl Ruggles prepared for the University of Miami Band in the 1930s. Almost all of Percy Grainger's published band music is also here, much of it with MS performance annotations by the composer.

R. Barlow: "A University Approach to the American Musical Theatre," *Notes*, xii (1954–5), 25; B. Shephard, Jr.: "Yale's Music Library Revised," *Notes*, xiii (1955–6), 421; H. C. Fall: *A Critical Bibliographical Study of the Rinck Collection* (thesis, Yale U., 1958); J. N. Moore: "The Historical Sound Recordings Program at Yale University," *Notes*, xix (1961–2), 283; J. N. Moore: "The Capes–Openhym Collection of Piano Recordings," *Yale University Library Gazette*, xl (1965), 104; R. E. Kimball: "The Cole Porter Collection at Yale," *Yale University Library Gazette*, xliv (1969), 8; D. Boito: "MS Music in the James Marshall and Marie-Louise Osborn Collection," *Notes*, xxvii (1970–71), 237 [annotated list]; E. J. O'Meara: "The Lowell Mason Library," *Notes*, xxviii (1971–2), 197; V. Perlis: "Ives and Oral History," *Notes*, xxviii (1971–2), 629; K. Berger: "The Yale Collection of Historical Sound Recordings," *Journal* [Association for Recorded Sound Collections], vi/1 (1974), 13; *CMc*, no.17 (1974), 66; H. W. Liebert: "The Charles J. Rosenbloom Bequest," *Yale University Library Gazette*, xlix (1975), 309–46; R. L. Brown: *Music, Printed and Manuscript, in the James Johnson Memorial Collection of Negro Arts and Letters* (New York, 1982); W. Crutchfield: "Grooves of Academe," *Opera News*, xlviii/2 (1983), 26 [Historical Sound Recordings collection]

DELAWARE

Early local musical activities are documented in the Historical Society of Delaware (*DeHi*) in Wilmington and in the Henry Francis DuPont Winterthur Museum (*DeWint*) in Winterthur.

NEWARK. University of Delaware (*DeU*). The *Folklore Archive of the Folklore and Ethnic Art Center (supervised by the English professor Robert Bethke) documents with audio and videotape recordings and slides the traditional music of Delaware and its neighboring states, particularly that of the Eastern shore communities. Genres include black music, bluegrass, and vocal and instrumental music of Latin American, Nanticoke Indian, and other ethnic groups.

The center publishes *Delaware Folk Heritage* (1978–).

DISTRICT OF COLUMBIA

Materials relating to the US Marine Band and John Philip Sousa are found in the band's library at the Marine Barracks and at the United States Marine Corps Museum (*DMaM*), and items concerning the US Navy Band can be found at the Naval Historical Center and at the band's library in the Navy Yard. Important research materials on a wide range of subjects are scattered through the various divisional collections of the National Archives Library (*DNA*) and the Smithsonian Institution (*DSI*).

WASHINGTON. District of Columbia Public Library, Martin Luther King Memorial Library (*DWP*). The Music and Recreation Division, established in 1934, holds some 50,000 volumes and 20,000 discs. Extensive holdings of works by and about black musicians are found here (scores and discs) and in the Black Studies Division. The library also holds materials relating to Hans Kindler, founding conductor of the National SO, including 6500 sets of orchestral parts.

E. Z. Posell: "First Eighteen Months of the Music Division in the Public Library of the District of Columbia," *ALA Bulletin*, xxx (1936), 628; V. E. Lowens, "The Public Library Music Division: a Glimpse of Past, Present, Future," *FAM*, xvi (1969), 129

——. Folger Shakespeare Library (*DFo*). The music holdings of the Folger collection (opened to the public in 1932 and administered by the trustees of Amherst College) nearly doubled in 1937 with the acquisition of the Sir Leicester Harmsworth Collection of early music books; it has remained fairly stable since then. The combined collections include copies of about half of all known Elizabethan printed music, as well as MSS and historical and theoretical works from the same period. Notable among the MSS are autographs by John Dowland (lute songs and dances) and Robert Jones; John Playford's own copy of the songs in *The Tempest*, set by John Wilson; and two collections (English madrigals, liturgical music). Rare printed items include a unique copy of Morley's *First Booke of Ayres* (1600) and copies of early books by John Day (1565), John Cosyn (1585), Byrd (1589), East (1604), and Leighton (1614). The library has a large MS collection of operas based on Shakespeare plays as well as incidental music and individual song settings, with major works in the hands of N. A. Zingarelli and J. L. Hatton.

Catalog of Printed Books of the Folger Shakespeare Library (Boston, 1970; suppl., 1976) [incl. MSS]

——. Howard University (*DHU*). The *Fine Arts Library maintains a research collection documenting the activities of Blacks in the arts. In addition to sound recordings of jazz, the general collection contains published American art music and about 300 MS and holograph compositions by black composers of the 1920s–40s, notably Hall Johnson and J. Rosamond Johnson.

The *Moorland–Spingarn Research Center Library takes its name from the Jesse E. Moorland Collection of Negro Life and History and the Arthur B. Spingarn Collection of Negro Authors, the latter consisting of some 2000 items of sheet music. Composers extensively represented in both are James A. Bland, James T. Brymn, Harry T. Burleigh, Samuel Coleridge-Taylor, Will Marion Cook, R. Nathaniel Dett, Duke Ellington, W. C. Handy, J. Rosamond Johnson, Samuel Lucas Milady, Maceo Pinkard, Florence B. Price, Christopher Smith, and William Grant Still. Several other smaller collections document the works of black musicians, notably the songwriter Andy Razaf and the educator Isabele Taliafero Spiller. Scattered in various collections of the Channing Pollock Theatre Collection (in the *Founders Library) are items of sheet music and materials regarding musical theater, notably the diaries, correspondence, scrapbooks, and promptbooks of the actor William Warren II associated with the Boston Museum, which was a theater in the 1880s.

K. L. Jefferson: *The Glenn Carrington Collection: a Guide to the Books, Manuscripts, Music and Recordings* (Washington, DC, 1977)

——. Library of Congress (*DLC*). In 1982 the total music holdings in three of the four divisions in the Library of Congress containing music (the fourth being the US Copyright Office) numbered something more than 10 million items, including sound recordings. About 55,000 items are added annually through copyright deposit, gift, purchase, transfer, and exchange. A provision of the US copyright law requires that all registered works be deposited in the Copyright Office for possible addition to the library's collections, which accounts to a large extent for the rapid growth of the collections and gives special significance to the holdings of present-day publications.

The Music Division is a service and custodial division in the Research Services Department of the library, and as such its first responsibility of service is to the US Congress, then to the various agencies of the Federal government, and finally to the public concerned with music in all its manifestations. Its services and resources (of material and personnel) are available to other libraries, scholars, students, teachers, professional societies, industry, and the public at large.

The first books on music, which included treatises by Burney and Geminiani, were probably received in 1815 as part of the purchase of Thomas Jefferson's personal library (Jefferson's considerable library of scores, however, remained in Charlottesville at the University of Virginia). Nearly 200,000 pieces of music were amassed during the 19th century, principally through copyright deposit, and the division was established officially in 1897 under the direction of Walter Rose Whittlesey.

The director from 1902 to 1917 was the redoubtable Oscar G. T. Sonneck, who displayed extraordinary skill and energy in developing and organizing the collection and bringing it to international prominence. Two of Sonneck's most important accomplishments were made early in his administration. He had all the books on music transferred from the general collections to the Music Division, and in so doing required greater subject expertise from the staff, who had previously been responsible only for music formats (i.e., scores). Indeed, the Music Division is unique among all the specialized divisions of the Library of Congress in combining materials in nearly all kinds of formats: books, scores, periodicals, photographs, and MSS. Sonneck also devised a classification system, which, revised and amplified by his successors, has been adopted by many other libraries. He charted the archive's direction for international growth, but gave primacy to Americana. His work was continued and extended by Carl Engel (1922–34), Oliver Strunk (1934–7), Harold Spivacke (1937–72), Edward N. Waters (1972–6), and Donald L. Leavitt (1976–85).

The division is one of the richest in existence, and in certain broad fields, such as opera, chamber music, American music, and music of the 20th century, it is unrivaled. Its collections of music and books on music printed before 1800 are extensive; the holdings of autograph scores and letters of master composers, particularly those of the 20th century, are without peer. The breadth and variety of these holdings make them significant documents, not only of musical history but of American social and political history as well.

One of the conspicuous features of the collection is the juxtaposition on the shelves of all kinds of music. With the exception of certain special categories, MSS that are not holographs are in general placed alongside music imprints; thus, an 18th-century copyist's set of parts for a concerto by C. P. E. Bach lies next to a printed score, or the MS lead sheet of a popular song next to the printed edition. Among the MSS are many representing works that have never been published. At the sales of the Cummings, Weckerlin, Prieger, and Landau collections, the division secured enviable acquisitions that greatly increased its holdings of early primary sources and research materials.

The following musical autographs in the division's collections are representative of the most valuable single holdings: Bach's cantatas nos.9 and 10; Barber's *Knoxville: Summer of 1915*; Bartók's Concerto for Orchestra and String Quartet no.5; Beethoven's Piano Sonata in E major op. 109 and the Presto of his String Quartet op. 130; Berg's Violin Concerto and *Wozzeck*; Bernstein's *West Side Story*; Brahms's Variations and Fugue on a Theme by Handel, Sextet no. 1, Piano Quintet, Horn Trio, Third Symphony, and Violin Concerto; Britten's *Peter Grimes*; Ernest Chausson's *Poème*; Copland's *Appalachian Spring* and Third Symphony; Debussy's *Nocturnes*; Gershwin's *Porgy and Bess*; Hindemith's *Hérodiade*; E. W. Korngold's *Die tote Stadt*; Leoncavallo's *Pagliacci*; Liszt's *Festpolonaise* and *Soirées de Vienne*; Prokofiev's String Quartet no. 1; Rachmaninoff's Rhapsody on a Theme of Paganini, Fourth Piano Concerto, Third Symphony, and Symphonic Dances; Ravel's *Chansons madécasses*; Schoenberg's *Verklärte Nacht*, *Pierrot lunaire*, *A Survivor from Warsaw*, and string quartets; Schumann's First Symphony; Stravinsky's *Apollon musagète*, *Le baiser de la fée*, Mass, and *Oedipus rex*; and Webern's String Quartet op.28.

Among the vast array of sources that are owned by the library, the following are representative for quality, rarity, and importance: the 12th-century treatise by Johannes Afflighemensis, *De musica*, the Laborde Chansonnier, many very early imprints such as Petrucci's *Harmonice musices odhecaton C* of 1504 and Josquin Desprez's *Liber primus missarum* of 1516, collections of sacred works by Mouton, Gombert, Palestrina, and Victoria and of madrigals by Marenzio and Gibbons, early operas by Peri and Marco da Gagliano, and other works of great historical importance by Beaujoyeux, Caroso, and Caccini.

Theoretical writers such as the following are profusely represented in contemporary editions: Aaron, Adlung, Martin Agricola, Banchieri, Bonaventura da Brescia, Burney, Cerone, Fux, Gaffurius, Galilei, Glarean, Hawkins, Kircher, Marpurg, Martini, Mattheson, Mersenne, Morley, Michael Praetorius, Printz, Rameau, J.-J. Rousseau, Tinctoris, and Zarlino. Special collections of autograph music MSS, sketches, correspondence, personal papers, scrapbooks, and photographs not only by and about the collectors but also by and about other composers, musicians, and dancers include those of Antheil, Harold Bauer, Bloch, Elizabeth Sprague Coolidge, the Damrosch family, Delibes, Agnes DeMille, Diaghilev, Vernon Duke, Geraldine Farrar, Irving Fine, George and Ira Gershwin, Leopold Godowsky, Oscar Hammerstein II, Heifetz, Victor Herbert, Korngold, Koussevitzky, Kreisler, Loeffler, Paul Löwenburg (Viennese waltz music, especially of the Lanner and Strauss families), Edward and Marian MacDowell, Rachmaninoff, Richard Rodgers, Romberg, Harry Rosenthall (Liszt autograph MSS and letters), Schoenberg, Charles and Ruth Crawford Seeger, Slonimsky, Sonneck, W. T. Upton (American art songs), and Alexander Zemlinsky.

Of great national importance are the first printing of *The Star-Spangled Banner* (as a broadside), the first edition with music, and a holograph copy of the Francis Scott Key poem. The accumulation of American music imprints from the earliest years of the nation's history onwards is looked upon as a primary responsibility; the sheet-music and songster collections contain American popular songs and dances as well as art songs and instrumental works. In addition, the division houses the archives of the journal *Modern Music* and the publications of the Music Critics Association, the Sonneck Society, and the publishing company of Arthur P. Schmidt, who was noted for his support of American composers.

Incorporated in the division's holdings are compositions and other materials generated by a number of foundations and activities resulting from private philanthropy. These enable the Library of Congress not only to exert an influence in the world of music rarely associated with libraries in this country, but also to acquire autograph scores. Important among these projects for their commissions and for the performances that sometimes go with them are the Elizabeth Sprague Coolidge Foundation (*see* COOLIDGE, ELIZABETH SPRAGUE); the Serge Koussevitzky Music Foundation in the Library of Congress (*see* KOUSSEVITZKY FOUNDATIONS); the McKim Fund, established through a bequest of Leonora Jackson McKim in 1970 and devoted to the commissioning and performance of new works by American composers (MSS received include those of works by Kupferman, Laderman, Rorem, and Siegmeister) and performance of works for violin and piano; and the Kindler Foundation (*see* AWARDS). In order to bring concerts in the Coolidge Auditorium to a larger audience than the hall itself can accommodate, the Katie and Walter Louchheim Fund was established in 1968 to subsidize recording services and broadcasting. In recent years all of these endowments have joined the Coolidge Foundation in sponsoring periodic chamber music festivals.

Financial contributions from the following sources support acquisitions, performances, lectures, and research: the William and Adeline Croft Fund, the Louis Charles Elson Memorial Fund, the Heineman Foundation, the Irving and Mae Jurow Fund, the Charles Martin Loeffler Foundation, the Nicholas Longworth Foundation, the Norman P. Scala Memorial Fund, and the Sonneck Memorial Fund.

The Music Division owns and maintains a large number of valuable musical instruments, many of which were acquired and are being maintained and heard in performances through bequests. Among the most important are the Dayton C. Miller Flute Collection (which includes literature and music relating to the flute) and the Gertrude Clarke Whittall Foundation (Stradivari instruments and Tourte bows).

The *Archive of Folk Culture (formerly the Archive of Folk Song) has been devoted since 1928 to assembling a national collection of folk music and folklore. Once part of the Music Division, it is now administratively linked to the newly formed American Folklife Center; the recordings are actually housed in the Motion Picture, Broadcasting, and Recorded Sound Division (see below), but scholarly access is gained through the archive. It acts as a coordinator, disseminating information on the subject area and publishing lists and bibliographies. The rapidly growing holdings, which are international in scope but concentrate on materials relating to the folk culture of the USA, include more than 350,000 instantaneous recorded items (i.e., those not for commercial use, such as field recordings) and 100,000 MS pages. The collection is particularly strong in recordings from the Appalachians, the Deep South, the Ozark area, Texas, California, Wisconsin, Michigan, Ohio, New York, and Maine, but many other areas have solid representation. Its holdings in the area of American Indian music and lore are extensive; in particular, it owns the nearly 4000 cylinders of the Frances Densmore-Smithsonian Institution collection (transferred in 1948). The recorded and MS materials assembled by scholars associated with the early development of the archive, Robert W. Gordon and John and Alan Lomax, form the core of its rich and varied holdings in Anglo-American and Afro-American folk music.

The custody and service of the audio materials in the Library of Congress (save those especially maintained and distributed by the Division for the Blind and Physically Handicapped) are the responsibility of the *Motion Picture, Broadcasting, and Recorded Sound Division (the latter formerly the Recorded Sound Section of the Music Division). The section was established officially in 1965, although the library acquired its first sound recording in 1906. Significant gifts from the American record industry have come to the division since 1924, and a 1972 amendment to the US copyright law has extended obligatory deposit to registered published recordings as well as to books and scores.

In the development of the recorded sound collections relating to music, emphasis has been given to the areas of special strength noted in the Music Division's holdings. Thus, Americana receive special attention, as do operas, chamber music, and folk music in performances by their creators. Among the artists represented by complete or near-complete recorded repertories (both published and unpublished) are Olimpia Boronat, Caruso, Farrar, McCormack, Sigrid Onegin, Ponselle, and Rachmaninoff. The total recorded sound collection numbers about 1,300,000 items, with an estimated 7,000,000 titles. The first part of *The Rigler and Deutsch Record Index* (1985), the first of several steps to gain bibliographic control of the audio collection, gives direct access to the 100,000-odd 78 r.p.m. disc recordings in collections. The listing will eventually include LPs, 45s, and all other media.

About 30% of the music in the Library of Congress is in the Copyright Office, which contains unpublished copyrighted music (chiefly film and popular music) from 1929 to the present and a variety of music editions and recordings. Access is by computerized finding aids and published catalogues of copyright entries; copyright searches may be commissioned for a fee.

The activities of the Music Division are described in its journal *Impromptu* (1982–). For a fuller discussion of the publication history of the Library of Congress catalogues cited in this bibliography, *see* BIBLIOGRAPHIES. *Catalogue of Title Entries*, later *Catalogue of Copyright Entries* (Washington, DC, 1891–); *A Catalog of Books . . . to July 31, 1942* (Ann Arbor, MI, 1942–6/*R*1967; suppl., 1948/*R*1967); *Check-list of Recorded Songs in the English Language in the Archive of American Folk Song, to July, 1940* (Washington, DC, 1942); *Cumulative Catalog of Library of Congress Printed Cards* (Washington, DC, 1947–55); *Library of Congress Author Catalog . . . 1948–1952* (Ann Arbor, MI, 1953); *Library of Congress Catalog Books: Subjects* (Ann Arbor, MI, 1955–); *The National Union Catalog: a Cumulative Author List* (Ann Arbor, MI, 1958–69; suppl., 1961); *The National Union Catalog: Music and Phonorecords* (Ann Arbor, MI, later Washington, DC, 1958–); *The National Union Catalog, Pre-1956 Imprints* (London, 1968–80; suppls., 1980–81); *Library of Congress and National Union Catalog Author Lists, 1942–1962: a Master Cumulation*, ed. Gale Research Company (Detroit, 1969–71); D. L. Leavitt: "Recorded Sound in the Library of Congress," *Library Trends*, xxi/1 (1972), 53; *Shelflist of the Library of Congress* (Ann Arbor, MI, 1979) [in microform; microfiche nos. 1511–729 cover the catalogued collections in the Music Division]; A. Melville: *Special Collections in the Library of Congress: a Selective Guide* (Washington, DC, 1980); P. T. Bartis: *A History of the Archive of Folk Song at the Library of Congress: the First Fifty Years* (diss., U. of Pennsylvania, 1982); *The Rigler and Deutsch Record Index – a National Union Catalog of Sound Recordings* (Syracuse, NY, 1985) [pt i: 78 r.p.m. recordings in ARSC holdings; in microform]

——. Washington Cathedral Library (*DNC*). This small library of rare materials contains two notable collections of sacred music: the personal library of the organist, composer, and student of plainchant Charles Winfred Douglas, consisting of about 1000 hymnals and books on hymnology, and the George C. Stebbins Memorial Collection of gospel materials collected by the singing evangelist, containing about 1200 hymnals and tunebooks which include his own compositions and working notebooks and reflect in particular the work of the Moody and Sankey movement.

L. Ellinwood and A. W. Douglas: "The Douglas Collection in the Washington Cathedral Library," *To Praise God: the Life and Work of Charles Winfred Douglas*, Hymn Society of America Papers, xxiii (New York, 1958), 38–72

FLORIDA

In addition to the libraries mentioned below, the Bok Singing Tower in Lake Wales is important for its collection of carillon music.

CORAL GABLES. University of Miami (*FMU*). Books on music are found in the *Otto G. Richter Library (the main university library), and about 33,000 recorded items, particularly jazz and Latin American, American Indian, and Yiddish music, are housed in the *Handleman Institute of Recorded Sound. The adjoining *Albert Pick Music Library, which is strong in contemporary Jewish art and folk music, holds MS copies of works by Ruggles and Beeson with the composers' corrections. Materials owned by the band department, including the personal papers, MSS, and published scores of the bandmaster, composer, and publisher Henry Fillmore and MS compositions and arrangements of the bandleader Arthur Pryor, are housed in the *Fillmore Museum (band department).

GAINESVILLE. University of Florida (*FU*). Of special interest here in the Division of Special Resources (in the *general library) is the (Sara Yancey) Belknap Collection of the Performing Arts (formerly the Dance, Music, and Theatre Archives, renamed in 1973 for its founder and first curator), which collects programs, playbills, scripts, scrapbooks, production information, and photographs (some 10,000 items) related to the performing arts. Special holdings include the Green Collection of American Sheet Music (mostly from musical theater) and the Ringling Museum Theatre Collection of playbills (150,000), programs, scripts, and scrapbooks. Systematic efforts are also made to collect information on performing arts groups in colleges and universities throughout the USA.

The Rare Books and Manuscripts Department of the same library is the repository for the American Liszt Society Archives and holds the papers of Zora Neale Hurston, some of which concern her activities with the Federal Negro Theater project and presentations of black folklore and folk music in the 1930s. The University Archives contain the papers of the Florida Bandmasters' Association (70 boxes, 1920 onwards) and the Florida

Composers' League. The *Music Library (in the music building) has a good collection of early 20th-century American songbooks and hymnals.

L. Correll: "The Belknap Collection of the Performing Arts," *Performing Arts Resources*, i (1974), 56

MIAMI. University of Miami: see Coral Gables

TALLAHASSEE. Florida State University (*FTaSU*). The *Warren D. Allen Music Library, established in 1946, was moved with the music department to a new building in 1979 and now numbers some 45,000 volumes. The personal library of the critic Olin Downes (whose papers are at the University of Georgia in Athens, see below) was purchased in 1956 and is now in the Special Collections Department of the *Robert Manning Strozier Library; included are a MS of Sibelius's *Jokamies* and scores and MSS of Dohnányi and Floyd.

E. S. Opperman: *Annals of the School of Music* (Tallahassee, FL, n.d.); M. R. Swingle: *A History of the Florida State University School of Music* (Tallahassee, FL, n.d. [?1974])

GEORGIA

Local music history repositories in addition to those listed below include the Atlanta Historical Society (*GAHi*), the Georgia State Department of Archives and History (*G-Ar*), and the Georgia Folklore Archives at Georgia State University (*GASU*), all in Atlanta; and the Institute for Music in Georgia at Agnes Scott College (*GDS*) in Decatur.

ATHENS. University of Georgia (*GU*). The music holdings here are found in several departments of the main university library, the *Ilah Dunlap Little Library (Rare Books and Manuscripts, Music Reference Library, Music Recordings Archive, Electromedia Department, the Georgia Room, and the general stacks), numbering some 50,000 volumes and 15,000 tapes in all. The nucleus of the present collections was acquired in 1948 through the purchase of the library (about 1200 books, periodicals, and scores) of the Viennese musicologist Guido Adler; his personal papers, consisting of 74 boxes of clippings, writings, and correspondence, some with American colleagues or on American subjects (inventoried by E. R. Reilly in 1975), were purchased three years later. The papers of the critic Olin Downes were purchased in 1966 (see also Florida, Tallahassee); they include about 50,000 clippings, memorabilia, and letters, many to and from such composers as Bloch, Stravinsky, and Varèse, in addition to musicologists, performers, and other critics. There are Prokofiev letters both in the Downes collection and in the Serge Prokofiev Collection (61 items). American music is also found in the Lucy Bates collection of dance items, 1711–1969; the Katherine Cowen DeBaillou papers, containing correspondence relating to 20th-century American music (especially of Paul Bowles); the Carol Robinson collection, which includes a MS score by Antheil; and 50 MSS of the Boston composer and teacher Arthur Mansfield Curry. Of special interest to folklorists are some 10,000 volumes from the library of the German scholar and bibliographer Archer Taylor and field recordings (about 300 tapes) of sacred and secular music collected in southern Georgia and the Sea Islands during the 1960s and 1970s.

J. Réti-Forbes: "The Olin Downes Papers," *Georgia Review*, xxi (1967), 165; M. G. Means: *A Catalogue of Printed Books and Music in the Guido Adler Collection* (thesis, U. of Georgia, 1968)

ATLANTA. Atlanta University (*GAU*). Two important collections of black music have been amassed in the *Trevor Arnett Library (the main university library): the papers of the pianist Maud Cuney Hare, which include music MSS, sheet music, minstrel songs, photographs, programs, and biographies of musicians, and the Countee Cullen Memorial Collection, founded in 1942 by Harold Jackman, a New York teacher and patron, to illustrate the black contribution in the performing arts in the 20th century. Cullen's own papers include his songs, typescripts of his translation of Virgil Thomson's *Medea* choruses, and his play with music, *The Third Fourth of July*. There are items relating to W. C. Handy, the Handy Brothers music company, and the W. C. Handy Foundation for the Blind; Langston Hughes (three cantatas); the anthropologist Eslanda Goode Robeson (letters concerning concert tours in the 1930s with her husband, Paul Robeson); and the violinist and composer Clarence Cameron White. Other materials include items by or about Marian Anderson, H. T. Burleigh, Roland Hayes, Bill "Bojangles" Robinson, P. D. Schuyler, and Arthur B. Spingarn, among others.

Guide to the Manuscripts and Archives in the Negro Collection (Atlanta, 1971)

——. Emory University (*GEU*). The *Robert W. Woodruff Library was established with the founding of the university in 1915, but music was not added to the curriculum until 1927 and musical materials still form only a small part of the general collections. The Special Collections Department, however, includes an important collection of Confederate sheet music and the papers, MSS, and published music of the playwright, songwriter, and journalist John Hill Hewitt (documented by F. W. Hoogerwerf). The papers of James Osgood Andrew Clark include stories about Negro spirituals and musical editions of these songs collected by his wife, Ella Anderson Clark. Musical items can also be found in the papers of two literary figures: Joel Chandler Harris (MacDowell's MS sketch for *Of Br'er Rabbit*) and Margaret Mitchell (materials relating to Harold Rome's musical adaption of her *Gone with the Wind*). Also housed here are the papers of John Wesley, the founder of Methodism, and his family, with numerous remarks concerning music and their musical activities.

In 1975 the Woodruff Library purchased the Warrington–Pratt–Soule Collection of Hymnology from the Case Memorial Library of the Hartford Seminary Foundation. Now known as the Hartford Collection, it includes about 8800 items: 16th-century psalters, 19th-century American shape-note tunebooks, more recent denominational and other hymnbooks, gospel songbooks, and sacred and secular songsters. This and the Wesleyana Collection of 2700 hymnals and books on hymnology are located in the *Pitts Theology Library (*GEU-T*) at the Candler School of Theology.

J. Warrington: *Short Titles of Books Relating to or Illustrating the History and Practice of Psalmody in the United States: 1620–1820* (Philadelphia, 1898/*R*1971); I. Lowens: "The Warrington Collection: a Research Adventure at Case Memorial Library," *Bulletin* [Hartford Seminary Foundation], xii (1952), 29, repr. in *Music and Musicians in Early America* (New York, 1964), 272; "Warrington–Pratt–Soule Collection Sold," *The Hymn*, xxviii (1977), 24; F. W. Hoogerwerf: "Confederate Sheet Music at the Robert W. Woodruff Library," *Notes*, xxxiv (1977–8), 7

HAWAII

Major collections of native music can be found in the Bernice P. Bishop Museum (*HHB*), the Hawaii State Archives (*H-Ar*), the Hawaiian Mission Children's Society Library (*HHMC*), and the University of Hawaii (*HU*), all in Honolulu.

IDAHO

Local music history sources can be found in the Terteling Library and the Folklore Archive, both at the College of Idaho

(*IdCaC*) in Caldwell, and in the Musical Heritage Studies department at Ricks College (*IdRR*) in Rexburg.

ILLINOIS

Specialized holdings other than those mentioned below include the local history materials at the McLean County Historical Society (*IBloHi*) and Illinois Wesleyan University (*IBloW*) in Bloomington; the Paderewski holdings in the Polish Museum and the settlement music materials in the Jane Addams Hull House at the University of Illinois (*ICIU*), both in Chicago; the temperance song collection in the National Women's Christian Temperance Union (*IEWT*) in Evanston; the collection of chamber music and orchestral scores and parts (chiefly European) copied under the auspices of the WPA Illinois Music Project and housed at the public library (*IC*) in Chicago (formerly at the Newberry Library); the extensive WPA research materials in the Illinois State Historical Library (*IHi*) in Springfield; a large collection of early cylinders and discs at the Seven Acres Museum in Union; and the gospel music holdings of the Billy Graham Center at Wheaton College (*IWW*) in Wheaton.

CARBONDALE. Southern Illinois University (*ICarbS*). The music collection in the *Delyte W. Morris Library (the main university library) contains about 20,000 volumes. Special collections include correspondence, pictures, programs, music, and librettos formerly owned by the singer Marjorie Lawrence and 28 boxes of materials relating to the dancer Katherine Mary Dunham, including orchestral arrangements used by her company.

The *Department of Anthropology houses the Project in Ethnomusicology, which has collected about 300 tapes of world music; it is particularly strong in Indo-Chinese, Afro-American, and midwestern music, the last recorded by the folk-music historian David McIntosh. The collection also includes about 100 musical instruments.

CHICAGO. Chicago Historical Society (*ICHi*). The library's holdings document Chicago's rich cultural history. There are about 7500 items of sheet music printed in Chicago from 1807 onwards, including a comprehensive group of those published by G. F. Root. Among the many organizational archives housed here are the 27 volumes of German songs sung by the Germania Club (?1869–87), the papers of the Nordamerikanischer Sängerbund, materials relating to the Chicago Mendelssohn Club (1894–1943), and the Musicians Club of Women (formerly the Amateur Musical Club); there are also important musical references in the archives of the Jewish community centers of Chicago during the first half of this century. Orchestral materials include the papers of the Chicago SO manager Henry E. Voegeli, especially his correspondence with the orchestra's conductor, Frederick Stock, and 25 scrapbooks containing programs of concerts conducted by Theodore Thomas. Opera is well documented by the correspondence and clippings (1872–1942) of Julia Gerstenberg, the archival records of William David Saltiel (manager of the Chicago City Opera Company, 1929–53), and three boxes of materials (1883–1962) collected by Richard Longley Kilmer towards a history of opera in Chicago. Two important sources span a broad chronological range of Chicago's musical history: six volumes of notes and clippings (1847–91) compiled by the critic George P. Upton and 53 volumes of journals (1879–1921) kept by the Chicago patron Frances Macbeth Glessner. The society collects and systematically arranges concert and opera programs; recordings are omitted save for five music-box discs from the 1890s.

D. J. Epstein: *Music Publishing in Chicago before 1871: the Firm of Root & Cady, 1858–1871* (Detroit, 1969); R. L. Brubaker: *Making Music Chicago Style* (Chicago, 1985)

——. Chicago Public Library (*IC*). By an agreement with the Newberry Library (see below) in 1895, this library began to collect standard musical works and, later, recordings. A separate music section was established in 1914 to contain scores, and in 1949 a full-fledged Music Department was created in the Fine Arts Division (in the *Cultural Center Building) to hold books, scores, and recordings, which now number about 26,000, 40,000, and 44,000 items respectively. The current acquisition policy emphasizes graduate research materials.

Chicago's musical history is amply documented through newspaper clippings (1873–), first performance indexes (1933–), bio-bibliographical information on Illinois composers, and programs of the Chicago SO (1955–) and opera companies (1910–). An index is being prepared to the periodical *Musical Leader* for 1900–67, an extensive run of which is here. Some 10,000 items of sheet music are housed in the Plitt Theatre Music Collection (800 boxes of MSS, letters, programs, photographs, financial records, and music publishers' catalogues for the period 1920–50, now in storage) and the "Old Pop" Lyrics and Songs collection (1830s to the 1970s).

The Special Collections Division (also in the Cultural Center Building) contains sheet music, a few items related to musical theater before the Chicago fire of 1871, and the World's Columbian Exposition Collection, containing an official scrapbook, programs, and a book on the musical instruments. Music and recordings relating to Afro-Americans, as well as a WPA report on black musicians in Illinois to 1939, are found in the Vivian G. Harsh Collection of Afro-American History and Literature in the *Woodson Regional Library.

Music: Catalog of the Collection of Instrumental and Vocal Scores in the Chicago Public Library (Chicago, 1923; suppl., 1926); *Books about Music* (Chicago, 1940); *Treasures of the Chicago Public Library* (Chicago, 1977); *One Hundred Important Additions to the Civil War and American History Research Collection: an Exhibition of Acquisitions 1974–1978* (Chicago, 1978)

——. Newberry Library (*ICN*). Founded in 1887 and located in the present building since 1893, the Newberry is a privately supported research library with a music collection of some 200,000 items, half of which are sheet music. It is particularly strong in materials of the European Renaissance and Baroque and in Americana to 1918.

In 1889 the library purchased some 751 items from the Florentine collector Count Pio Resse, including the rare first edition folio score and libretto of Peri's opera *Euridice*. As a result of the efforts of the Chicago music critics George P. Upton (who donated his own collection in 1920) and Felix Borowski, the library received many private collections during subsequent decades; these included materials from the Beethoven Society of Chicago (1890), Julius Fuchs (1891), Otto Lob (1892), Theodore Thomas (personal papers, scrapbooks, and scores, including the autograph of Wagner's *Grosser Festmarsch*), the music publisher H. P. Main (3000 English and American hymnals and gospel songs, 1906), Mme. T. Le Carpenthier-Morphy (1911), W. J. Wolffheim (17th- and 18th-century scores, 1929), Frederick Stock (papers covering his years as conductor of the Chicago SO, 1904–42, and many of his own compositions), the theorist Bernhard Ziehn, and the ethnomusicologist Yuri Arbatsky. In 1966 the library purchased 315 items from the library of Alfred Cortot, among which were early Lutheran and Catholic hymnology sources, theoretical treatises (including a fine copy of Mersenne's *Harmonie universelle*, 1636–7), and mid-18th century pamphlets relating to the *Querelle des Bouffons*. From the opera singer Claire Dux (*d* 1967) came two of the library's four Mozart autographs.

The collection is particularly strong in medieval and Renaissance treatises, with works such as a 12th-century MS of Boethius's *De musica*, a 15th-century MS containing works by Marchetto da Padova and Jehan des Murs, an *Ars perfecta in musica* ascribed to Philippe de Vitry, and major works of Gaffurius, Zarlino, Martin Agricola, Glarean, and Michael Praetorius. It is also strong in Renaissance and Baroque music, notably early Mexican and Lutheran choirbooks (described by E. A. Schleifer in *Notes*, xxx, 1973–4, p.231), over 100 sacred and secular partbooks (including Arcadelt's four-part madrigals and Florentine partsongs prepared for King Henry VIII of England), and lute music (by Vincenzo Capirola, Francesco da Milano, Luis de Milán, Bermudo, Fuenllana, and Nicolas Vallet, and two Petrucci editions). The 18th and 19th centuries are represented primarily by treatises, since the library for many years collected only full scores even though many early chamber works were issued only in parts. A small number of MSS by master composers has been acquired and about 1000 full scores and 3500 vocal scores of operas. A strong Americana collection includes several 18th-century printings (with music) of the Bay Psalm Book, the major tunebooks of William Billings and Andrew Law, and 20th-century items, particularly those that document musical life in Chicago, such as the personal papers, MSS, and annotated scores of Theodore Thomas, Frederick Stock, Bernhard Ziehn, Frederick G. Gleason, John Alden Carpenter, Rudolf Ganz, Eric De Lamarter, and the singer Janet Fairbank (1903–1947; collection discussed by E. Borroff in *College Music Symposium*, xvi, 1966, p.105). The J. Francis Driscoll collection of about 83,000 items of American sheet music (acquired in 1967) is particularly rich in black minstrelsy and songs of Boston and New England.

D. W. Krummel: "The Newberry Library, Chicago," *FAM*, xvi (1969), 119; S. Floyd, Jr.: "Black Music in the Driscoll Collection," *BPiM*, ii (1974), 158; D. W. Krummel: *Bibliographical Inventory to the Early Music in the Newberry Library, Chicago, Illinois* (Boston, 1977); R. Charteris: "Some Manuscript Discoveries of Henry Purcell and his Contemporaries in the Newberry Library," *Notes*, xxxvii (1980–81), 7; B. E. Wilson: *The Newberry Library Catalog of Early American Printed Sheet Music* (Boston, 1983)

——. University of Chicago (*ICU*). The *Joseph Regenstein Library has sought to acquire MSS and first editions to complement those in the Newberry Library, particularly music of the 18th and 19th centuries. Important among the 20th-century materials are ten letters (1946–7) of Schoenberg, 27 (1923–62) of Krenek, and 115 (1939–51) of Artur Schnabel in the John U. and Elinor Castle Nef collection; MS compositions by Ralph Shapey, Donald Martino, Jean Martinon, and Easley Blackwood; and the Fromm Music Foundation collection of microfilm copies of 396 compositions submitted by 266 American composers. The library's Chicago Jazz Archive was established in 1976.

H. Lenneberg and L. Libin: "Unknown Handel Sources in Chicago," *JAMS*, xxii (1969), 85 [*ICU* 437]; *Music in the University of Chicago Library Selected for an Exhibition at the Joseph Regenstein Library July–October 1972* (Chicago, 1972); *CMc*, no.17 (1974), 41

EDWARDSVILLE. Southern Illinois University (*IEdS*). In the 1960s, the *Lovejoy Library acquired quantities of music from three noted sources: the Essex Institute in Salem, Massachusetts (about 700 hymnals and tunebooks and about 10,000 items of sheet music, chiefly from the 1830s and 1840s); the St. Louis radio station KMOX (30,000 items of sheet music and about 15,000 items of original and stock arrangements, 1910–60); and the estate of the violinist and collector Carl Tollefsen (about 4000 items of string chamber music, including Schumann's holograph of an early version of *Ich grolle nicht*, first editions, musical instruments, autographed photographs, and signatures). The KMOX collection is augmented by some 15,000 stock band charts (1920–60) for the dance and theater orchestras in St. Louis of Ben Rader and Russ David.

L. McKee: *Guide to Research Collections: Lovejoy Library, Southern Illinois University at Edwardsville* (Edwardsville, IL, 1971)

EVANSTON. Northwestern University (*IEN*). Established as a separate library in 1945, the *Music Library now numbers some 70,000 volumes and specializes in 20th-century MSS and editions. The complete holograph MSS of K. B. Jirák are found here. All the MSS collected and catalogued by Cage for his book *Notations* (1969), as well as the related correspondence, are on deposit. Comprehensive publishers' collections include the Ricordi Collection of some 700 printed items (chiefly of the 19th century) and about 800 letters written by and to the firm and the microfilm archive of the published music issued by the Summy Birchard Co. and a number of related companies (the Clayton F. Summy Co., C. C. Birchard & Co., McLaughlin & Reilly, the Chart Music Publishing House, and the Arthur P. Schmidt Co.). About 310 letters received by Eric Oldberg, a former president of the Chicago SO Association, include those from Fritz Reiner, George Szell, Bruno Walter (102), and Artur Schnabel; there are also some 200 letters to the double bass player and composer Domenico Dragonetti. From Hans Moldenhauer the library acquired a core collection of works by 19th- and 20th-century composers, mostly English but some Italian, and from Fritz Reiner his library of music scores, literature, and memorabilia, and some of his correspondence. The library of Boris Goldovsky has been acquired, but not yet transferred. 300,000 cards generated from a WPA project in the 1930s to index music periodicals in the Newberry Library are now here. The *University Library holds the field notes and research correspondence of the ethnomusicologist Melville Herskovitz in its Africana Collection.

The library publishes a newsletter, *NU Quarter Notes* (formerly *1810 Overture*; 1976–). A. Tischler: *Karel Bohuslav Jirák: a Catalog of his Works* (Detroit, 1975)

NORMAL. Illinois State University (*INS*). The *Milner Library (the main university library) owns the archive of the Anglo-American organist and theorist George K. Jackson, which includes autograph MSS of 49 of his compositions and pedagogical materials, acquired from William Salloch. Most important is a comprehensive collection of some 100,000 circus items, among which are circus band scores from the collections of Sverre O. Braathen and Charles H. Tinney, Braathen's collection of essays on the historical development of the circus band (*c*1940), and catalogues of band music and musical instruments.

[*Salloch*] *Catalogue 301* (Ossining, NY, 1973) [summarized in *Notes*, xxxii (1975–6), 743]; R. Sokan: *A Descriptive and Bibliographic Catalog of the Circus and Related Arts Collection* (Bloomington, IL, 1976)

URBANA. University of Illinois at Urbana-Champaign (*IU*). The *Music Library (*IU-Mu*), founded in 1944 and located in the music building, has various collections that comprehensively support a wide variety of music programs. Included are the stock of some 500,000 items acquired in 1974 from the Hunleth Music Store in St. Louis (chiefly American imprints from 1900) and a performance library consisting of multiple copies or parts of about

200,000 items. Special collections include the library of the pianist Rafael Joseffy containing some 200 MSS and 2000 editions of 19th-century piano music with his annotations; Joseph Szigeti's collection of editions and MSS (chiefly violin music); the collection assembled by the music dealer Harry Dichter, originally containing 3300 items of American sheet music, 1830–76, and now much expanded with more recent materials acquired from Millie Emory (450 imprints published by Von Tilzer), the collectors Richard B. Harwell (see also below) and Lester Levy, and the American Antiquarian Society; more than 800 first and early editions of music by European masters, collected by the entomologist Gottfried Fraenkel; and the personal papers, recordings, and copies of MSS compositions of Harry Partch. The library supports the university's Musicological Archive for Renaissance Manuscript Studies through microfilm collections of music manuscripts dating from 1400 to 1550.

The special collections in the Rare Book Room (*IU-R*) of the *University Library are also rich in American music, with a collection of over 800 items in 15 volumes printed in Chicago before the 1871 fire, and Confederate imprints, including R. B. Harwell's sheet-music collection. Also here are a late 15th-century MS book of chants and Lamentations for the Office, English items printed before 1700, a contemporary copy of Gluck's *Alceste*, and an autograph score of Stravinsky's *Mavra*. The John Philip Sousa collection of more than 3000 instrumentations and sets of parts is administered by the University Band Department.

Musical Library Owned by Rafael Joseffy (New York, *c*1935) [sale catalogue]; J. Allen: "The Music Library at the University of Illinois," *Notes: Supplement for Members*, nos.6–7 (1949), 3; R. B. Harwell: *More Confederate Imprints* (Richmond, VA, 1957), i, 225; D. J. Epstein: *Music Publishing in Chicago before 1871: the Firm of Root & Cady, 1858–1871* (Detroit, 1969); C. Hamm and H. Kellman: "The Musicological Archive for Renaissance Manuscript Studies," *FAM*, xvi (1969), 148; *CMc*, no.17 (1974), 44; "Recent Acquisitions," *Notes*, xxxi (1974–5), 282

INDIANA

In addition to the libraries cited below, general local music history materials are found at the Indiana Historical Society (*InHi*) and the Indianapolis–Marion County Public Library (*InI*) in Indianapolis and at the Marshall County Historical Society (*InPlyHi*) in Plymouth. The University of Notre Dame (*InNd*) near South Bend now owns much of the William Bacon Stevens Library of liturgical materials, formerly in Philadelphia. Sam DeVincent, a collector in Fort Wayne, has an extensive archive of sheet music.

BLOOMINGTON. Indiana University (*InU*). The *School of Music Library holds about 450,000 items, including material acquired in support of the Latin American and Black Music centers established in 1960 and 1968 respectively. Holdings of opera scores are comprehensive, and substantial additions from the estate of the collector Bernardo Mendel have been recently acquired. Willi Apel's collection of materials related to early keyboard and violin music are here, and there are about 150 reels of taped rehearsals and performances of the conductors Fritz Busch and Leopold Stokowski.

Most of the rare musical items acquired since 1960 are housed in the *Lilly Library. These include Handel scores and related material from the collections of William C. Smith and Gerald Coke, annotated scores of Fritz Busch, a collection of first edition opera scores and librettos purchased and donated from Mendel's library, and Saul Starr's collection (from Mendel's estate) of more than 100,000 items of vocal and instrumental American sheet music from 1750 onwards (described in an unpublished guide). Mendel also donated his collection of Latin Americana, including four 16th-century Guatemalan MSS of music by Spanish and Flemish composers. The library owns a copy of Juan Navarro's *Liber in quo quatuor passiones Christi Domini continentur* (1604), believed to be the oldest example of printed music composed in the Americas. The Ege, Poole, and Ricketts MS collections, chiefly of medieval and Renaissance materials of a general nature, contain several liturgical works. Musical MSS and correspondence of Hoagy Carmichael are also housed here.

Research notes, MSS, and recorded interviews with composers once held in the Black Music Center are now housed in the *Afro-American Arts Institute. The *Folklore Archives contain materials (chiefly songs and interviews) gathered by students since 1950 and organized by ethnic or religious group. The better-known *Archives of Traditional Music, which was founded at Columbia University by George Herzog in 1936 and transferred to Bloomington in 1948, contains sound recordings (commercial and field recordings) of 350,000 songs and other items from many parts of the world. The collection is particularly strong in African, Latin American, Asian, and American Indian music. The recordings include 7000 wax cylinders, 35,000 discs, 100 wire spools, and 20,000 original tape rolls.

The library publishes a newsletter, *Annotations* (1978–) and the Archives published the journal *Folklore and Folk Music Archivist* (1958–68) and now publishes *Resound* (1982–). J. A. Orrego-Salas, ed.: *Music from Latin America available at Indiana University: Scores, Tapes, and Records* (Bloomington, IN, 1964, 2/1971); *American Patriotic Songs* (Bloomington, IN, 1968) [exhibition catalogue]; P. M. Peek: *Catalog of Afroamerican Music and Oral Data Holdings* (Bloomington, IN, 1970); D. R. de Lerma: *The Fritz Busch Collection*, Lilly Library Publication, xv (Bloomington, IN, 1972); J. O. Falconer: "Music in the Lilly Library: Handel, Opera, and Latin Americana," *Notes*, xxix (1972–3), 5; *An Exhibition Honoring the Seventy-Fifth Birthday of Hoagland Howard Carmichael* (Bloomington, IN, 1974); *CMc*, no.17 (1974), 20; *A Catalog of Phonorecordings of Music and Oral Data Held by the Archives of Traditional Music* (Boston, 1975); M. M. Fling: *A Catalog of Dissertations, Theses, and Documents Submitted by Indiana University Graduate Students in the School of Music and Held in its Music Library* (Bloomington, IN, 3/1976); R. M. Stone and F. J. Gillis: *African Music and Oral Data: a Catalog of Field Recordings, 1901–1975* (Bloomington, IN, 1976); K. Talalay: *Women in American Music: a Checklist of Secondary and Unpublished Materials by and about Women in American Music, Housed at the Indiana University School of Music Library* (Bloomington, IN, 1977); D. S. Lee: *Native North American Music and Oral Data: a Catalogue of Sound Recordings, 1893–1976* (Bloomington, IN, 1979); M. B. Graf: *A Catalog of Indiana Music and Folklore Held by the Archives of Traditional Music, Indiana University* (Bloomington, IN, 1981)

GOSHEN. Goshen College (*InGo*). The J. D. Hartzler collection of about 2750 volumes of early American church and instructional music is accessible through the *Mennonite Historical Library (*InGoM*), which contains hymnals, singing-school books, and dissertations related to the Anabaptist and Mennonite traditions throughout the world. The archives of the Mennonite Church deposited here also include musical items.

N. P. Springer: "The Mennonite Historical Library at Goshen College," *Mennonite Quarterly Review*, xxv (1951), 307; A. T. Luper: *A Partial Check List of Printed Collections of Church Music with American Imprint in the Private Library of Mr. J. D. Hartzler, Wellman, Iowa* (Iowa City, IA, 1961); G. E. Fouts: *Music Instruction in America to around 1830 Suggested by the Hartzler Collection of Early Protestant American Tune Books* (diss., U. of Iowa, 1968); N. P. Springer and A. J. Klassen: *Mennonite Bibliography, 1631–1961*, ii (Scottsdale, PA, 1977), 285 [hymnals]

MUNCIE. Ball State University (*InMuB*). Of particular interest in the *Bracken Library (the main university library) are archival materials relating to the C. G. Conn instrument manufacturing and Buescher Saxophone companies, both of Elkhart, Indiana, and to the concert saxophonist Cecil Leeson, the Chicago SO horn player Max Pottag, and the International Horn Society.

IOWA

In addition to the university library described below, major repositories of local music history include the Iowa Historical Museum in Des Moines, the State Historical Society (*IaHi*) in Iowa City, and the Museum of Repertoire Americana in Mount Pleasant. Luther College (*IaDL*) in Decorah holds the collection of 50,000 items of sheet music assembled by Frederick Wolhowe in Minot, North Dakota.

IOWA CITY. University of Iowa (*IaU*). The *Rita Benton Music Library, named after the well-known music librarian, has leaves of Gregorian chant (the earliest from a 13th-century English gradual) and a few 16th- and 17th-century treatises. Its greatest strength lies in printed 18th- and 19th-century keyboard works, chamber music, and treatises. After Benton's death in 1980, the library received her personal collection of about 100 compositions written or published by Pleyel. The Special Collections of the *Main Library of the university hold the Edwin Ford Piper collection of ballads, folksongs, and other musical materials relating to local and midwestern history, particularly the Chautauqua movement; notable among these are the papers of the psychologist of music Carl E. Seashore. The *University Bands hold over 3800 published scores and parts and 130 MS scores of works composed or arranged for or performed by the Edwin Franko Goldman Band.

H. D. Peterson: *Syllabus of the Ballad Collection of Edwin Ford Piper* (thesis, U. of Iowa, 1934); A. T. Luper: *An Exhibit of Music and Materials on Music: Early and Rare* (Iowa City, IA, 1953); F. K. Gable: *An Annotated Catalog of Rare Musical Items in the Libraries of the University* (Iowa City, IA, 1963); H. Oster: "The Edwin Ford Piper Collection of Folksongs," *Books at Iowa*, no.1 (1964), 28; R. Benton: "The Music Library at the University of Iowa," *FAM*, xvi (1969), 124; R. A. McCown: "Records of the Redpath Chautauqua," *Books at Iowa*, no.23 (1973), 8; G. S. Rowley: *An Annotated Catalog of Rare Musical Items in the Libraries of the University of Iowa: Additions 1963–1972* (Iowa City, IA, 1973); *CMc*, no.17 (1974), 46; M. D. Welch: "The Goldman Band Library," pt i, *Journal of Band Research*, xix/2 (1984), 26

KANSAS

In addition to the university library described below, the Kansas State Historical Society (*KHi*) and the Shawnee County Historical Society, both in Topeka, document local music history. The Mennonite Library and Archives at Bethel College (*KNnB*) in North Newton holds important hymnals.

LAWRENCE. University of Kansas (*KU*). The Henry M. Katzman collection of MSS and early editions of music by George Gershwin, Irving Berlin, Jerome Kern, and others, used in radio programs in 1933–4 that featured Gershwin presenting his music, is found in the *Kenneth Spencer Research Library (*KU-S*). Also here are several MS music books of the early 19th century and the papers of the vaudeville performer Roger Imhof, including his songs and lyrics.

The Archives of Recorded Sound was established in 1982, following the acquisition of major collections from two professors and radio hosts, James Seaver (opera) and Dick Wright (jazz). The archive has continued to specialize in these two areas with the addition of collections of rare opera recordings (the Robert and Eva Platzman Collection of recordings from Germany and Scandinavia and selected examples of American recordings assembled by the singer Warren Wooldridge) and the jazz collections of Howard D. Rittmaster and Red Nichols. Other notable holdings are author Paul Bierley's collection of rare discs of John Philip Sousa's band, including a unique test pressing made in 1902, and tapes of all the performances given at the International Carnival for Experimental Music in London in 1972. The archive contains about 66,000 items. Finding aids have been prepared by the donors and the staff for several of the collections, but the collection as a whole is not yet catalogued.

D. Freuh: *The Henry M. Katzman Collection: Gershwin Materials* (MS, 1972); *CMc*, no.17 (1974), 48; R. Camus: *Some Thoughts on Early American Band Music* (MS, 1978)

KENTUCKY

Important sources of local music history are located, in addition to the libraries cited below, at Berea College (*KyBB*) in Berea, mostly in the Appalachian Center; Western Kentucky University (*KyBgW*) in Bowling Green, mostly in the Kentucky Library and the Folk-lore and Folk-life Archive; the Filson Club (*KyLoF*) in Louisville; and the Louisville Free Public Library (*KyLo*), which is famous for its audio-visual program.

LEXINGTON. University of Kentucky (*KyU*). Housed in the Department of Special Collections of the *Margaret I. King Library is part of the library of Alfred Cortot, purchased in 1967 (chiefly early theory treatises). MS songbooks and correspondence from the 19th-century Shaker community in Pleasant Hill, Kentucky, are on deposit.

F. Traficante: "Dispersal of the Cortot Collection: 290 Treatises at Lexington," *Notes*, xxvi (1969–70), 713; F. Traficante: "The Alfred Cortot Collection at the University of Kentucky Libraries," *University of Kentucky Library Notes*, i (spring 1970) [complete issue]

LOUISVILLE. University of Louisville (*KyLoU*). Special collections in the *Dwight Anderson Memorial Music Library include MSS by Kentucky composers and early Kentucky imprints; an archive devoted to the correspondence, original compositions, and works edited by the pianist Isidore Philipp under the aegis of the American Liszt Society; and folksongs, field recordings, and correspondence of the "Traipsin' Woman," Jean Thomas. The papers of the Louisville Orchestra and its predecessors (1866 onwards), including scores and recordings from the LOUISVILLE ORCHESTRA COMMISSIONING PROJECT in the 1950s by Antheil, Elliott Carter, Copland, Lou Harrison, Hovhaness, Krenek, Lees, Piston, Riegger, Rorem, Schuman, Sessions, Halsey Stevens, Toch, Chou Wen-chung, and others are divided between this library and the *University Archives and Records Center (*KyLoU-Ar*).

M. Korda: "University of Louisville," *Notes: Supplement for Members*, no.25 (1957), 21; "The ALS Isidore Philipp Archives and Memorial Library," *Journal of the American Liszt Society*, i (1977), 27

——. Southern Baptist Theological Seminary (*KyLoS*). The Music Library (located in the *main library) contains all facets of church music, including organ compositions, tunebooks, and hymnals from 1770 to 1940 (notably the Converse Hymnal Collection), gospel songbooks, and some 30,000 items of sacred music from 1880 onwards, comprising anthems and the Janet T. Ingersoll Gospel Music Collection.

LOUISIANA

In addition to the libraries listed below, the Historic New Orleans Collection, the Louisiana State Museum (*L-M*), the New Orleans Public Library (*LN*), and the private collection of Al Rose all document the musical history of New Orleans. The Center for Acadian and Creole Folklore at the University of Southwestern Louisiana (*LLafS*) in Lafayette maintains an extensive sound archive.

BATON ROUGE. Louisiana State University (*LU*). Housed in the *Troy H. Middleton Library (the main university library) are books about music and a number of special collections, including the library of the St. Louis Philharmonic Society (*c*1832–1838), librettos published in Louisiana, 1850–70, sheet music, and songbooks. The library's Department of Archives and Manuscripts (*LU-Ar*) is rich in music and personal papers of French émigré and native musicians of the 19th century, musical items in the papers of other families, sheet music, scrapbooks, programs, and broadsides. The *School of Music maintains a small collection of scores and recordings.

NEW ORLEANS. New Orleans Baptist Theological Seminary (*LNB*). The *Martin Music Library contains the Edmond D. Keith Collection of about 3000 items of Baptist and gospel hymnody and the Ernest O. Sellers–William P. Martin Hymnal Collection of some 400 items.

A. H. Daniel: *The Sellers–Martin Hymnal Collection: a Source for the History of Gospel Hymnody* (thesis, New Orleans Baptist Theological Seminary, 1970)

——. Tulane University (*LNT*). The Maxwell Music Library, founded in 1909 at the H. Sophie Newcomb Memorial College, moved with the music department to the Tulane campus in 1919 and was later named for Professor Leon Ryder Maxwell; it was relocated in the *Howard–Tilton Memorial Library in 1980. The collection has some 30,000 items of American sheet music, 1830–1940, and an additional 80 bound volumes. The Special Collections here richly document New Orleans concert life of both European and American origin in the second half of the 19th century; notable are the Gottschalk memorabilia. The sheet-music collection consists chiefly of New Orleans imprints. Diverse materials relating to the history of New Orleans jazz have been collected since 1958 and housed in the William Ransom Hogan Jazz Archive (in Special Collections); these include discs, cylinders, piano rolls, tapes (783 reels of music and 1466 of interviews), motion pictures, videotapes, sheet music, scrapbooks, correspondence, photographs, record catalogues, journals, and books.

R. B. Allen: "The Archive of New Orleans Jazz," *Yearbook for Inter-American Music Research*, iii (1967), 141; R. Crawford: *Music in the Street* (New Orleans, 1983) [catalogue of an exhibition of items from Hogan Jazz Archive and Historic New Orleans Collection]; *Catalog of the William Ransom Hogan Jazz Archive* (Boston, 1984)

MAINE

Major repositories of local music sources include the Maine State Library (*Me*) in Augusta, the University of Maine (*MeU*) in Orono, the Maine Historical Society (*MeHi*) in Portland, and the Portland Public Library (*MeP*).

MARYLAND

In addition to the archives listed below, the Enoch Pratt Free Library (*MdBE*) provides public library music services to Baltimore, partly through collections formerly owned by the Peabody Institute: MSS of early faculty members of the Peabody Conservatory (see Baltimore, Johns Hopkins University below), including works by Asger Hamerik, Theodor Hemberger, John Itzel, and Gustav Strube, are held jointly with the conservatory and preserved in the George Peabody Department of the Pratt Library. The Morris A. Soper Library of Morgan State College (*MdBMC*), also in Baltimore, has acquired Dominique-René de Lerma's collection of books, scores, recordings, letters, and MSS relating to black music.

BALTIMORE. Johns Hopkins University (*MdBJ*). The *Milton S. Eisenhower Library (the main university library) contains a collection donated by Lester Levy of about 30,000 items of American sheet music from the years 1793 to 1929, sorted into collections by topic or composer, including part of his extensive material relating to *The Star-Spangled Banner* (the other part is in the Maryland Historical Society). Levy's books *Grace Notes in American History* (1967), *Flashes of Merriment* (1971), *Give me Yesterday* (1976), and *Picture the Songs* (1976) are based on the music in his collections. The *John Work Garrett Library holds two notable archival collections: documents relating to the Tuesday Club of Annapolis, *c*1740–1770, including MS secular music (with scoring indicated), and the papers (among which are 50 music MSS) of the poet and flutist Sidney Lanier. Sheet music includes the Peabody Collection of 4000 items (chiefly songs, *c*1830–80), transferred from the Peabody Institute.

The *Peabody Conservatory (*MdBP*), affiliated with the university since 1977, opened in 1868 as part of the Peabody Institute; in 1966 the library of the institute merged with the Enoch Pratt Free Library (see Maryland introduction above) but the conservatory library remained independent. Of interest are the libraries of Virgil Thomson (about 600 volumes) and the physicist Otto Ortmann, letters of Beethoven, Bloch, Falla, Grieg, Landowska, Liszt, and Messager, and musical MSS by Beethoven and Efrem Zimbalist.

L. S. Levy: *Some pre-1801 Imprints in the Lester S. Levy Collection of American Sheet Music: a Thematic Catalogue and Subject Index* (MS, n.d.); R. Higgins: *Sidney Lanier, Musician* (thesis, Peabody Conservatory, 1969); G. Ostrove: "Conservatory Libraries in the United States," *FAM*, xvi (1969), 136; R. E. Robinson: *A History of the Peabody Conservatory of Music* (thesis, Indiana U., 1969); L. S. Levy: "Recollections of a Sheet Music Collector," *Notes*, xxxii (1975–6), 491; *Guide to the Lester S. Levy Collection of Sheet Music*, ed. Milton S. Eisenhower Library (Baltimore, 1984)

——. Margery Lowens collection. The music critic and historian Irving Lowens amassed an important collection of early American sacred music, from which about 1000 tunebooks were transferred to the Moravian Music Foundation in Winston-Salem, North Carolina, in 1956. Remaining, at the time of Lowens's death, were about 150 musical commonplace books (mostly sacred and many connected with Pennsylvania Germans, copied *c*1750–1850) and from the pre-Civil War period letters, singing-school lectures, songsters, tunebooks, and periodicals; further items were donated to the Moravian Music Foundation and the songster collection was moved to the American Antiquarian Society in Worcester, Massachusetts. Holdings also include a comprehensive collection of the music of Edward MacDowell (50 letters, holograph sketches, the complete works, and some early recordings); about 2000 letters of American composers, performers, and critics since 1850; and about 100 musical MSS of American composers, including unpublished songs by Jerome Kern and the personal papers (10,000 items) and photograph collection of the Chicago music critic W. L. Hubbard. Of considerable interest is a unique collection of some 7500 printed musical ephemera, including trade cards, postcards, postage stamps, and programs. Lowens's working library is particularly rich in music histories documenting various American localities.

——. Maryland Historical Society (*MdHi*). The extensive collection of Maryland sheet music began with a large gift from the Peabody Institute librarian Louis H. Dielman in the 1930s, chiefly of Baltimore imprints. Lester Levy divided his collection of editions of *The Star-Spangled Banner* between this library and Johns Hopkins University. Among the important archives of early musical organizations are those of the Maryland Diocese of the Protestant Episcopal Church in the 18th and early 19th centuries and the Charles M. Stieff Piano Co. (1873–1909).

W. T. Upton: "18th Century American Imprints in the Society's Dielman Collection of Music," *Maryland Historical Magazine*, xxxv (1940), 374; P. W. Filby: "Music in the Maryland Historical Society," *Notes*, xxxii (1975–6), 503

COLLEGE PARK. University of Maryland (*MdU*). The Music Library (in the *Hornbake Library) holds three notable collections: J. M. Coopersmith's working library, rich in Handel materials; the Alfred Wallenstein Collection, consisting of the performance library of radio station WOR, New York, from the 1920s through the early 1950s (28,000 titles ranging from sheet music to orchestral parts); and the International Piano Archives at Maryland (formerly the International Piano Library of New York City), containing scores, tapes, phonodiscs, piano rolls, cylinders, record catalogues, and MSS.

The Special Collections in Music at the Hornbake Library has become the repository for the archives of several musical organizations: the American Bandmasters Association (1929–), the Music Educators National Conference (1907–), and the Music Library Association (1931–). It also holds the organizational papers of the College Band Directors National Association, the Music Industries Council, the National School Band, Orchestra and Vocal Association, and others. Consequently, a number of research centers have been established: the American Bandmasters Association Research Center, which includes materials relating to the Banda Mexicana, the ensemble Symphony in Gold for Brass and Percussion, and the bands of Herbert L. Clarke, Patrick Conway, Patrick S. Gilmore, Edwin Franko Goldman, Arthur Pryor, Sousa, and others; the Music Educators National Conference Historical Center, which has collected the papers of the music educator Clifford V. Buttelman, Frances Elliott Clark, Lowell and Luther Whiting Mason, C. M. Tremaine, and others, as well as publishers' files of graded materials; the International Clarinet Society Research Center, which includes Burnet C. Tuthill's library of some 2000 MSS and printed editions of clarinet music; and the National Association of College Wind and Percussion Instructors Research Center.

Also of note are the Maryland sheet-music collection (including Bromo-Seltzer editions) in the Archives and Manuscripts Department of the *McKeldin Library; the André Kostelanetz collection of original works and arrangements from the 1930s through the 1970s in the *Department of Music; and the *Maryland Folklore Archive in the Department of English, which contains recordings of local traditional songs and instrumental music.

CMc, no. 17 (1974), 49; *Catalog of the International Clarinet Society Score Collection*, ed. International Clarinet Society (College Park, MD, 1983); *Catalog of the Reproducing Piano Rolls in the International Piano Archives at Maryland* (College Park, MD, 1983); *Microfiche Catalog of the Disc Recordings* (College Park, MD, 1983)

PIKESVILLE. Lester S. Levy collection. Levy's library contains about 150 American songsters from *c*1790 through the 1880s and about 300 broadsides, mostly from the Civil War period. Much of his collection has been transferred to Johns Hopkins University and the Maryland Historical Society in Baltimore.

MASSACHUSETTS

There are a number of important music archives in Massachusetts other than the libraries described below. Colonial music sources are among the holdings of the Massachusetts Historical Society (*MHi*) in Boston and the Stoughton Historical Society, which also houses the archives of several music societies dating back to the federal period; interesting materials are also held by the Bostonian Society (*MBBS*) and the Isabella Stewart Gardner Museum (*MBG*), both in Boston. A large collection of Shaker music is still owned by the Shaker community at Hancock near Pittsfield. Significant academic music holdings are found at Brandeis University (*MWalB*) in Waltham, the Massachusetts Institute of Technology (*MCM*) in Cambridge, and Wellesley College (*MWelC*). The music programs at the Berkshire Athenaeum (*MPB*) in Pittsfield and at the Newburyport Public Library (*MNe*) have both been curtailed, the latter because of a fire in 1977.

BOSTON. Boston Athenaeum (*MBAt*). In addition to materials relating to the early history of music in Boston, this proprietary library is noted for its sheet music, hymnals, and songsters with Confederate imprints (about 600 items); a similar number of items reflect the library's interest in Boston imprints and illustrated covers. The A. H. Nichols and M. H. N. Shurcliff collection of campanology, particularly items related to the Bell-Ringers Guild of Boston, 1854–1952, is also found here.

Catalogue of the Library of the Boston Athenaeum 1807–71 (Boston, 1874–82); M. L. Crandall: *Confederate Imprints: a Check List Based Principally on the Collection of the Boston Athenaeum*, ii (Boston, 1955)

——. Boston Public Library (*MB*). In 1859 the library's principal early benefactor, Joshua Bates, commissioned A. W. Thayer to purchase the 400-volume library of the Viennese army officer Joseph Koudelka (1773–1850), consisting mainly of historical and theoretical works of the 15th and 16th centuries. This archive and 100 volumes from Thayer's own library became the nucleus of the Music Department's research collections. In 1894 the library received its most noted collection, some 6400 volumes of chiefly European music, amassed by the collector Allen A. Brown (1835–1916). Other collections in the Music Department acquired from well-known musicians include autograph works by John Barnett; scrapbooks from Arthur Foote; MS compositions, letters, scrapbooks, and Latin Americana from Nicolas Slonimsky; organ music of Florence Rich King; and the Serge Koussevitzky Archive, containing annotated scores, books, MSS, and memorabilia (a typescript inventory exists). There are holographs by minor 19th-century German composers, and by A. W. Bach, Samuel Wesley, Franck, Tosti, Samuel Coleridge-Taylor (*Hiawatha's Wedding Feast*), and the Boston organist and composer George E. Whiting, and collections of works by Mabel Wheeler Daniels and Gardner Read. Also preserved are autograph fragments of works by Mozart, Schubert, Shostakovich, and Virgil Thomson. The library is noted for its scrapbooks on Boston musical events and special topics, compiled chiefly by the staff and by Brown.

In the 1970s the library acquired several important collections, some of which are preserved in the Rare Books and Manuscripts Department: incidental music performed in London at the Haymarket (from 1888) and Her Majesty's (1897–1916) theaters, including several autograph scores of Coleridge-Taylor, and works of Edward German, Bantock, Adolf Schmid, Raymond Roze, George Henschel, and Mascagni; the library of the Boston Handel and Haydn Society (founded in 1815), which includes material from the earlier Massachusetts and Old Colony musical societies, the libraries of Gottlieb Graupner and George K. Jackson (rich in early annotated performing editions of Handel and Haydn), and holographs of a few commissioned works by New England composers, notably Randall Thompson (partial inventory by J.

Sheveloff, 1972); 14 holograph MS compositions of Walter Piston; MSS and printed editions of music and arrangements by Victor Young; and the Gorokhoff Collection of Russian choral music. Also in the Rare Books and Manuscripts Department are the B. J. Lang family papers, which include scrapbooks (1887–1967) of the composer Margaret Ruthven Lang, the papers of the journal editor J. S. Dwight, and two volumes of records of the Federal Street Theatre, Boston, from the 1790s.

Although it is not yet open to the public, a Sound Archive was formed in the 1960s when the Music Department removed its 78 r.p.m. recordings, augmented by a large gift from the RCA and Columbia companies, to a warehouse in Charlestown and retained a curator for the collection. Now returned to the main building as a separate department, the collection of some 125,000 titles (225,000 items), equally divided between 78 and $33\frac{1}{3}$ r.p.m. discs, consists chiefly of the complete (or nearly complete) outputs of major American recording companies and smaller New England firms. Special collections include recordings from the estates of Walter Piston and Serge Koussevitzky, and Boston oral-history tapes.

Catalogue de livres de musique rares . . . de feu M. de Koudelka (Berlin, Germany, 1859); *Catalogue of the Allen A. Brown Collection* (Boston, 1910–16); L. K. Wilkin: *U.S. Secular Songsters, pre-1851, to be Found in the Boston Public Library* (MS, 1953); J. Sheveloff: *Rare Old Music and Books on Music in Boston* (MS, 1972) [partial inventory of Handel and Haydn Society]; *Dictionary Catalogue of the Music Collection* (Boston, 1972; suppl., 1977)

——. Boston University (*MBU*). The Byzantine research materials of the musicologist Egon Wellesz were recently added to the general music collections in the *Mugar Memorial Library (the main university library). On the death of the conductor Arthur Fiedler in 1979, a room in Special Collections was given over to his 1000 orchestral scores, 2200 opera and miniature scores, papers, letters, and extensive collection of sound recordings. The archives of the Boston SO have been established here; they include programs (1881–), holograph MSS of commissioned works, tapes made from broadcast performances, and a miscellaneous collection of 18th- and 19th-century MS operas. Also in this department are archives of the Paris Conservatoire (1796 to the early 20th century) and a Liszt collection of books, pamphlets, first editions, some MSS, and memorabilia. In the Twentieth Century Archive are research materials pertaining to Rudolf Bing, Alexander Brailowsky, Cab Calloway, Samuel Chotzinoff, Sylvia Dee, Mischa Elman, Ella Fitzgerald, Martyn Green, George R. Marek, Vaughn Monroe, Anthony Newley, Henry Pleasants, H. C. Robbins Landon, Harold Schonberg, Artie Shaw, Albert Spalding, Risë Stevens, Joseph Szigeti, and Rosalyn Tureck.

The hymnology collection in the *School of Theology Library (*MBU-T*) numbers some 5000 items, chiefly early Methodist and other Protestant music, including volumes from the collections of the hymnologists Frank J. Metcalf and Charles Sumner Nutter.

CMc, no.17 (1974), 7

——. Harvard Musical Association (*MBHM*). The association was formed in 1837, and sporadic purchases and gifts through the years, frequently reported in *Dwight's Journal of Music* (1852–81), form an 18th- and 19th-century repertory of some 10,000 volumes. The collection has letters of Liszt, Mendelssohn, Berlioz, Schumann, and Verdi; 18th- and early 19th-century imprints and MSS from the publisher Gottlieb Graupner; material on the piano manufacturers Chickering & Sons; and autograph MSS of the Boston composers Frederick S. Converse and Arthur Foote and of more recent works commissioned by the association.

The *Library of the Harvard Musical Association Bulletin* was published irregularly from 1934 to 1959. *Catalogue of the Library* (Boston, 1857); C. R. Nutter: *History of the Harvard Musical Association, 1837–1962* (Boston, 1968)

——. New England Conservatory (*MBCM*). In 1870 the private library of the conservatory's founder and director, Eben Tourjée, became the nucleus of a small collection. Earlier Americana in what is now the *Harriet M. Spaulding Library include 18th-century books on singing, psalmody, and glees, and letters and memorabilia of Boston musicians. The library holds a fairly extensive collection of autograph MS scores and parts by the "Boston classicists" (e.g., Edward Ballantine, Amy Marcy Beach, Frederick S. Converse, George W. Chadwick, and Arthur Foote). 19 MS works for the saxophone commissioned between 1901 and 1914 by Elise Coolidge Hall, including holographs by Charles M. Loeffler, André Caplet, and Debussy, are on deposit; other holographs are found in a collection of 100 songs with texts by Norma Farber set by the 20th-century composers Theodore Chanler, David Diamond, Normand Lockwood, Daniel Pinkham, Jr., and Arthur Shepherd. The John A. Preston Collection of 19th-century letters (including some by Beethoven, Berlioz, Liszt, Mendelssohn, Schumann, and Wagner) is complemented by the extensive correspondence of the organist and conductor Wallace Goodrich (1895–1953), Isabelle Tompson Moore (1890–1955, with her teacher Edward MacDowell and Ethelbert Nevin), and the Baerman Society (1909–68, in Gunther Schuller's collection). The Napier Lothian Theater Orchestra Collection is noted for its orchestrations of about 100 works by Josef, Eduard, and the younger Johann Strauss.

The record collection was named the *Isabelle Firestone Audio Library in the 1970s when the library acquired 1600 MS instrumental and vocal arrangements, recordings, and kinescopes of the "Voice of Firestone" radio and television broadcasts, sponsored by the Firestone Tire and Rubber Co. from 1928 to 1958. Also of note are early jazz recordings and the Vaughn Monroe Collection of orchestrations and recordings.

CAMBRIDGE. Harvard University (*MH*). The university began its music collection around 1870 in support of its first chair in music, and in 1898 the music department formed its own collection. The two were amalgamated to form the *Eda Kuhn Loeb Music Library (*MH-Mu*) in 1956, and at that time the critic Richard Aldrich presented his collection, of which more than 100 items were books printed before 1800.

Among other early items in the library is a series of 224 volumes of MS librettos for more than 1500 Italian sacred and secular dramatic works. John M. Ward's collection of ethnomusicological materials has been deposited in the Charles Seeger Room. The Isham Library, established in Memorial Church in 1936 and originally comprising early keyboard music, was moved to the Music Library in the 1970s and now collects microforms of all music and musical literature before 1800.

The *Houghton Library (*MH-H*) is rich in important MSS, many of which are autographs. The earliest are three late 11th-century Marian sequences copied at the end of the 13th century in northern France, a 14th-century stichērarion in Middle Byzantine notation, and fragments of a 14th-century motet and a Credo. Music by John Dunstable is found both in an anonymous MS *Speculum exemplorum* of 1481 and in examples copied by Gaffurius in the autograph second book of his *Practica musicae*, dated 1480.

The 17th century is represented by autograph compositions for lyra viol by William Lawes. 18th-century MS holdings are extensive and include autographs of J. S. and J. C. F. Bach, Thomas Arne, Durante, G. B. Martini, Haydn, and J.-J. Rousseau. MSS include a collection of 70 French and Italian violin sonatas copied in 1721 and copies of works by Boccherini and Samuel Arnold. Popular British ballads of the late 18th and early 19th centuries are contained in several MS anthologies compiled by Thomas Moore and others. Major 19th-century composers represented by autographs are Beethoven, Bellini, Brahms, Cherubini, Debussy, Elgar, Franz, Liszt, Mahler, Mendelssohn, Puccini, Reger, Rossini, Anton Rubinstein, Schubert, Schumann, Verdi, and Wagner. In 1970 the library purchased an important collection of Italian materials, including 58 MSS from Rossini's *Péchés de vieillesse*. There is a collection of printed music by 19th- and 20th-century Russian composers, with autographs and letters (described by M. Velimirović in *Notes*, xvii, 1959–60, p.539). Autograph MSS of the same period include works of Berg, Arthur Berger, Fauré, Holst, Leon Kirchner, Daniel Pinkham, Jr., John Knowles Paine, Walter Piston, Satie, Roger Sessions, Sibelius, Johann Strauss, Randall Thompson (most of his works, on deposit), Varèse (sketches), and Webern. Recently acquired from Hans Moldenhauer's collection are substantial numbers of works by Paul Pisk, Alexander Zemlinsky, and others.

An extensive collection of autograph letters begins with ten by the 16th-century theorist Girolamo Mei, and includes some by Handel, Beethoven, Brahms (to Wagner), Verdi, and Puccini. From the papers of the conductor Wilhelm Gericke there are letters from Brahms, Bruckner, Dohnányi, Dvořák, and Mahler. Also notable are those of Jenny Lind, Alban and Helene Berg, Koussevitzky, Alma Mahler, Nathan Milstein, Schoenberg, Sessions, Stokowski, and Webern to Louis Krasner (on deposit), and of the American musicians Frederick S. Converse, George Gershwin, Edward Burlingame Hill, Paine, Piston, and Randall Thompson. There are a collection of 1500 songsters (78 pre-1821) and a sheet music collection of some 185,000 items.

The Theatre Collection is a department of the Houghton Library now located in the adjoining *Nathan M. Pusey Library. It is noted for its MSS, prints, scrapbooks, playbills, programs, reviews, promptbooks, librettos, and portraits relating to stage productions of opera and other forms of musical theater. Letters by early 19th-century singers and 18th- and 19th-century opera composers in six volumes collected by John Benjamin Heath (dated 1865) have been selectively described and translated by Hans Nathan (*Notes*, v, 1947–8, p.461). The Edwin Vose collection includes 12,000 items of sheet music and 3000 recordings mostly from American musical comedies from the 1920s to the 1950s.

Many of the university's other libraries contain music materials. The *Widener Memorial Library holds materials related to the folklore studies of A. B. Lord, the Milman Parry Collection of Oral Literature (which includes examples of Afro-American preaching and early blues), and the J. A. Notopoulos Collection of traditional music from Yugoslavia, Greece, Africa, and Iran. The *Andover–Harvard Theological Library (*MH-AH*) at the Harvard Divinity School has a large collection of 19th-century American Unitarian Universalist hymnology, and the *Monroe C. Gutman Library (*MH-Ed*) of the Graduate School of Education has a collection of music textbooks (1870–1936) arranged chronologically. In the *Baker Library (*MH-BA*) of the Graduate School of Business Administration are the personal papers (1870–1919) of Henry Lee Higginson, founder of the Boston SO. The *Arthur and Elizabeth Schlesinger Library on the History of Women in America (at Radcliffe College) holds the personal papers of the composer Mabel Wheeler Daniels (including holograph music MSS and extensive correspondence) and the singer Vera Curtis (1879–1962). The *Peabody Museum of Archaeology and Ethnology (*MH-P*) has important musical materials and artifacts of American Plains and northwestern tribal Indians.

In preparation are a catalogue of the music MSS in the Houghton Library by B. M. Wolff, *Card Catalog of the Harvard Music Library: Books and Scores Dictionary Catalog*, and *Books and Scores Shelf List* [microfiche listing of Loeb and Isham libraries and selected other holdings]. R. Aldrich: *A Catalogue of Books Relating to Music in the Library of Richard Aldrich* (New York, 1931); W. Apel: "The Collection of Photographic Reproductions at the Isham Memorial Library," *JRBM*, i (1946), 68, 144, 235; W. Van Lennep: "The Harvard Theatre Collection," *Harvard Library Bulletin*, vi (1952), 281; A. B. Lord, ed.: *Serbo-Croatian Heroic Songs*, i (Cambridge, MA, 1953) [partial catalogue of the Parry Collection]; N. Pirrotta: "The Eda Kuhn Loeb Music Library," *Harvard Library Bulletin*, xii (1958), 410; C. Wright: "Report from Cambridge: Rare Music Manuscripts at Harvard," *CMc*, no.10 (1970), 25; D. E. Bynum: "Child's Legacy Enlarged: Oral Literary Studies at Harvard since 1856," *Harvard Library Bulletin*, xx (1974), 237–67 [materials in the Widener Library]; *CMc*, no.17 (1974), 19; D. Wood: *Music in Harvard Libraries: a Catalogue of Early Printed Music and Books on Music in the Houghton [and] Loeb* (Cambridge, MA, 1980); R. G. Dennis: "Note: an Exhibition of Music Manuscripts at the Houghton Library to Honor the B[oston] SO," *Harvard Library Bulletin*, xxxi (1983), 88

MEDFORD. Tufts University (*MMeT*). The Nils Yngve Wessell Library owns the collection of the music historian Frédéric L. Ritter, which was purchased by Albert Metcalf and presented in 1897. A catalogue prepared shortly thereafter reveals holdings of about 1500 books and 500 scores, rich in treatises of the 16th to 18th centuries and 19th-century opera. The family library of Asa Alford Tufts includes songbooks and sheet music published in 19th-century Boston. In 1982 the library received over 200 tapes and several hundred scores from the estate of the composer Roslyn Brogue Henning, whose own works were divided between Tufts and Harvard University.

Catalogue of the Music Library of the Late Frédéric Louis Ritter (n.d. [?1890s]); H. A. Hersey: *A History of Music in Tufts College* (Medford, MA, 1947)

NORTHAMPTON. Forbes Library (*MNF*). Opened in 1894, this public library was, in its formative years, under the direction of the noted librarian Charles B. Cutter. The sheet-music collection (in the Art and Music Department) of some 3000 items of 18th- and 19th-century Anglo-American vocal music is well indexed, and there are about 160 tunebooks, songbooks, and hymnals of the same period, chiefly in the Elbridge Kingsley collection; both groups of materials include many Northampton imprints. There is a special collection relating to Jenny Lind's residency in Northampton in 1852.

L. E. Wikander: *Disposed to Learn: the First Seventy-five Years of the Forbes Library* (Northampton, MA, 1972)

——. Smith College (*MNS*). The *Werner Josten Library acquired early musical treatises from the libraries of the Boston critic Philip Hale and Alfred Einstein, as well as MS transcriptions of 15th- and 16th-century Italian vocal compositions (chiefly madrigals) and 16th- and 17th-century instrumental music, some of which were published in the Smith College Music Archives series (1935–78). The music collection of Henry S. Drinker and Sophie Drinker was deposited in 1965; Sophie Drinker's 16 volumes of women's history materials (1933–48) are separately housed, however, in the Sophia Smith Collection of the *Women's History Archive (*MNS-S*, in the Nielson Library), which also has letters of Geraldine Farrar.

R. D. Welch: "Some Treasures in the Library of the Department of Music," *Smith Alumnae Quarterly*, xxii (1931), 138

SALEM. Essex Institute (*MSaE*). The *James Duncan Phillips Library has a small but distinguished collection of Americana, including tunebooks, vocal and instrumental partbooks, and early music and dancing instruction books in printed and MS copies. Later MSS and publications are restricted to Essex County musicians, such as Arthur Foote, Patrick S. Gilmore, the Hutchinson family, and Henry K. Oliver; the music MSS dating from 1785 to 1860 have been inventoried and indexed. (Most of the uncatalogued music referred to by H. E. Johnson in *Notes*, v, 1947–8, p. 169, was sold in 1971; see Illinois, Edwardsville, Southern Illinois University.)

The library publishes the quarterly *Historical Collections* (1859–).

STURBRIDGE. Old Sturbridge Village (*MStu*). The music collection in the *Research Library supports village programs presenting reconstructions of life in rural New England from 1790 to 1840. At least half the music collection (prints and MSS) originates from this period and is strong in popular songs, folksongs, broadsides, hymnals, tunebooks, and letters with musical references; the 600 items of sheet music in the collection were for the most part published or used in New England before 1850.

WILLIAMSTOWN. Williams College (*MWiW*). Although the music department retains its own collection in the *Bernhard Music Center, a larger number of books and scores is found at the *Sawyer Library (the main library), where Cole Porter's collection of scores has been incorporated; also of interest are 50 printed and MS volumes of Shaker music, 1836–64. Located in *Stetson Hall are two other music collections: the Chapin Library of the college's rare materials, containing some 350 items of musical significance from the 12th to the 20th centuries, and the legacy of the bandleader Paul Whiteman, consisting of some 3500 original works and arrangements (1920–50), recordings of them issued on various labels, and related research materials, including 2000 items of sheet music, 1890–1940. Whiteman's library has been augmented by collections from George Eberle, George Royal, and Stanley Stearns.

J. Nin-Culmell and M. L. Richmond: *Four Hundred Years of Music: an Exhibit* (Williamstown, MA, 1950) [catalogue of an exhibition of items from the Chapin Library]; I. Shainman: "The Whiteman Collection at Williams College," *Notes*, xiv (1956–7), 189; H. E. Cook: *Shaker Music: a Manifestation of American Folk Culture* (Lewisburg, PA, 1973), 292; C. Johnson: *Paul Whiteman: a Chronology* (Williamstown, MA, 1976)

WORCESTER. American Antiquarian Society (*MWA*). Founded by the publisher Isaiah Thomas in 1812 as the first national historical society in the USA, the library has amassed near-complete collections of published works on American history and culture to 1876; regarding music, special emphasis is given to acquiring and cataloguing works printed before 1821. The collection of early sacred American tunebooks is the largest in the country, and there are many hymnals from the period 1821–80. There are also extensive collections of instrumental instruction books issued before 1820, early vocal tutors, music periodicals (especially those before 1853), programs, and music catalogues, and of broadside ballads, including patriotic and popular songs purchased in 1814. The MS collections include diaries, musical copybooks, papers, correspondence, and accounts of various early music teachers, publishers, and rural and military amateur musicians; similar materials relating to the composer Timothy Swan and the hymnologist Frank J. Metcalf are also present.

W. C. Ford: "The Isaiah Thomas Collection of Ballads," *Proceedings* [American Antiquarian Society], xxxiii (1924), 34–112; L. K. Wilkin: *U.S. Secular Songsters, pre-1851, to be Found in the American Antiquarian Society* (MS, n.d. [1950s]); *Dictionary Catalog of American Books Pertaining to the 17th through 19th Centuries*, ed. American Antiquarian Society (Westport, CT, 1971) [excludes music printed 1821–76 and all sheet music]; I. Lowens: *A Bibliography of Songsters Printed in America before 1821* (Worcester, MA, 1976)

MICHIGAN

In addition to the libraries cited below, regional and local music is preserved at Kimball House in Battle Creek and at Western Michigan University (*MiKW*) in Kalamazoo. Wayne State University (*MiDW*) has specialized in music associated with the labor movement, Greenfield Village (*MiDbEI*) in Dearborn preserves the artifacts and archives associated with the collecting program of Henry Ford, and Bly Corning in Flint owns the sheet music assembled for Thomas A. Edison (see Ann Arbor, University of Michigan, below).

ANN ARBOR. University of Michigan (*MiU*). The *Music Library was established in 1941 to provide specialized services to the recently incorporated School of Music. The university's dispersed music holdings were consolidated here in 1964, and the library now contains over 62,000 volumes. Its research resources were greatly strengthened in 1954 with the purchase of the collection of the Belgian musicologist J.-A. Stellfeld; of the some 10,000 items about 1600 are pre-1800 imprints or MSS, and the collection is rich in 18th-century opera and music by the sons of J. S. Bach. Collections more recently acquired include papers related to the Handel studies of the musicologist J. M. Coopersmith, presented by his widow in 1977; the big-band jazz MS compositions and arrangements for radio and early television by Glenn Osser; the Albert Luconi collection of woodwind ensemble music; and a collection of music and some papers by 400 women composers assembled by and including those of Ethel Smyth (containing about 2000 scores published in Europe 1780–1960, of which there are about 100 each by Cécile Chaminade, Loïsa Puget, Augusta Holmès, and Liza Lehmann). The library's recorded music collection supports a strong program in ethnomusicology.

Separately maintained in the School of Music are the Eva Jessye Afro-American Music Collection of music editions and memorabilia related to Eubie Blake, Arthur Cunningham, W. L. Dawson, Jessye herself, and W. G. Still; David E. Mattern's large collection of music education materials (a separate catalogue is in the Music Library); and extensive materials (especially audiovisual items) relating to Japanese and Indonesian music.

In the *Harlan Hatcher Graduate Library are a group of papyri, including one of five known with musical notation (Greek text, 2nd century AD). Also found here are Shaker MS music books (1840–80), letters to the conductor Frederick Stock, and letters from Roberto Gerhard, Elliott Carter, Riegger, and others regarding commissions by the Stanley Quartet. Schoenberg's family has donated letters to the composer from Alfred Wallenstein, Artur Schnabel, Wilhelm Furtwängler, and others.

The holdings of early Americana and the building that houses them were presented to the university in 1922 by William L. Clements, for whom the *library was named (*MiU-C*). The music collection, now numbering some 35,000 items, embraces American printed music and books about music up to 1900. A large collection of early sacred and secular MS and printed tunebooks includes 20 shape-note volumes. To complement the 25 tunebooks and other publications of Andrew Law, the library purchased about 1200 documents of the composer and his brother William. There is a collection of music in honor of Lafayette (including a volume of some 29 printed and MS songs of 1824–5). Books include 45 songbooks and 83 discourses on early American church music. 35,000 items of sheet music, chiefly from the collection of Bly Corning, are being catalogued.

L. E. Cuyler and others: "The University of Michigan's Purchase of the Stellfeld Music Library," *Notes*, xii (1954–5), 41; R. Crawford and H. W. Hitchcock: *The Papers of Andrew Law* (Ann Arbor, MI, 1961); M. C. Blanding: *A Catalogue of the Eva Jessye Afro-American Music Collection* (thesis, U. of Michigan, 1974); *CMc*, no.17 (1974), 50; P. Daub and J. Tsou: *Musical Rarities: an Exhibit . . . Nov. 4–7, 1982* (MS, 1982)

DETROIT. Detroit Public Library (*MiD*). Musical life in Detroit is richly documented through notable collections in the Music and Performing Arts Department: the E. Azalia Hackley Memorial Collection documenting black achievements in music, drama, and dance; the Michigan Collection of autograph works by Michigan composers; early American hymnals and songbooks; and MS arrangements by the bandleader Jimmy Clark. There is much popular American sheet music both in the Hackley collection and in the Burton Historical Collection (elsewhere in the library), where are also found the letters of Thomas Hastings to his brother, dating from 1817–52 (discussed by M. Teal in *Notes*, xxxv, 1978–9, p.303).

K. Myers: *The Music and Drama Department of the Detroit Public Library* (Detroit, 1957); *Catalog of the E. Azalia Hackley Collection of Music, Dance and Drama* (Boston, 1979)

MINNESOTA

In addition to the libraries cited below, the American Swedish Institute in Minneapolis contains materials pertaining to immigrants, the Chatfield Brass Band Free Music Lending Library maintains an extensive collection, and the Hill Monastic Manuscripts Library at St. Johns University (*MnCS*) in Collegeville preserves a large microfilm collection of medieval and later liturgical sources (cited in P. Jeffery, *Notes*, xxxv, 1978–9, p.7).

MINNEAPOLIS. Minneapolis Public Library and Information Center (*MnU*). The music library (in the Art, Music, and Films Department) has become the largest public music collection (about 100,000 editions) in the Midwest and one of the largest in the country. It is particularly strong in chamber music and orchestral scores. Uncatalogued are a file of 19th- and 20th-century sheet music and extensive additions to the collections of band, orchestral, and vocal music (especially 19th-century music for solo voice and solo piano). Beginning in 1940 the library pioneered the circulation of sound recordings to patrons.

G. Wilson: "Minneapolis Public Library," *Notes: Supplement for Members*, no.25 (1957), 20

——. University of Minnesota (*MnU*). The Music Library (in the *Walter Library) contains the Donald N. Ferguson Collection, which includes, in addition to the musicologist's papers and early compositions, about 340 volumes of early treatises and liturgical books and several hundred opera scores of the 18th and 19th centuries, many in first editions. Items of American origin include early tunebooks and hymnals in European languages used by the early settlers; music, collections, periodicals, and method books, 1864–1940; and the Kenneth Berger Band Library of books and early periodicals on wind and brass instruments, military music, and band music in general. A strong collection of Latin American music was recently augmented by a gift from Ricordi Americana of music by Argentinian composers.

Music can also be found in the university's *Immigration History Research Center (*MnU-IA*), the *Collection of Minnesota Ethnic Music in the music department (field recordings, MSS, transcriptions, and published music for the accordion), and the *Social Welfare History Archives Center (*MnU-SW*), which holds the papers and music from such noted settlement houses as Hull House in Chicago, the Cleveland Music School Settlement, and the Henry Street Settlement Music School in New York.

A Selected Catalog of Music and Books on Music, European and American, ed. University of Minnesota Department of Music (Minneapolis, 1954)

NORTHFIELD. St. Olaf College (*MnNS*). The Christiansen Hall of Music library was named for the music educator and conductor F. Melius Christiansen, who as editor of the St. Olaf Choir Series issued 128 works (1919–32), all of which are here. MSS of his published works are in the college library. The *Rolvaag Memorial Library (formerly the Norwegian-American Historical Association, *MnNHi*) contains works by Christiansen and other Norwegian-American composers (chiefly Lutheran sacred choral music) and related materials.

ST. PAUL. Minnesota Historical Society (*MnHi*). Music is found in several departments. In the *Division of Archives and Manuscripts are the papers of various Scandinavian musical organizations, local WPA projects, and the Folk Arts Foundation of America, 1943–65, including the musical studies of Frances Densmore, some concerning the Dakota, Ojibwe, and other Minnesota Indians. In addition to items of local musical interest, there are letters to Emil Oberhoffer (first conductor of the Minneapolis SO) from Percy Grainger, Marian MacDowell, Frederick Stock, and others.

In the *main building of the historical society are the Special Libraries, which contain photographs, oral-history tapes, and recordings of Minnesota musicians, and the Reference Library, which houses American Indian, French-Canadian, Scandinavian, and English-language songbooks, tunebooks, and sheet music.

J. T. Dunn: "A Century of Song: Popular Music in Minnesota," *Minnesota History*, xliv (1974), 122

MISSISSIPPI

Apart from the holdings of the University of Mississippi, of note are the collections of the composer Clarence Dickinson at William Carey College (*MsHaW*) in Hattiesburg and of the Broadway musical conductor Lehman Engel at Millsaps College (*MsJMC*) in Jackson. Regional materials can be found at the Mississippi Department of Archives and History (*Ms-Ar*) in Jackson and at Mississippi State University (*MsSM*) in Mississippi State.

UNIVERSITY. University of Mississippi (*MsU*). In the Archives and Special Collections department of the *John Davis Williams Library are the papers (1911–45) of the poet Henry Bellamann, which include his correspondence with Charles Ives, Isidore Philipp, and other musicians. Here also is the collection of the Pennsylvania folklorist Kenneth S. Goldstein, consisting of journals, 3000 books, and 4500 recordings of Anglo-American folk music and lore.

MISSOURI

In addition to the libraries cited below, the public libraries of Kansas City (*MoK*) and St. Louis (*MoS*) contain some local history materials. Other regional interests have been reflected in the holdings of the State Historical Society (*MoHi*) and the University of Missouri (*MoU*), both in Columbia. State Fair Community College in Sedalia is developing a program for preserving the music of Scott Joplin and his associates. The Harry S. Truman Library (*MoIt*) in Independence reflects the musical tastes of the former president. Religious music resources include the Vatican film collection in the Pius XII Memorial Library at St. Louis University (*MoSU*), the Charles Haddon Spurgeon hymnology collection at William Jewell College (*MoLiWJ*) in Liberty, and the music in the Concordia Historical Institute (*MoSCH*) in St. Louis, which reflects in particular the hymnody of the Missouri Synod of the Lutheran Church.

KANSAS CITY. University of Missouri (*MoKU*). In 1982 the Conservatory Library was transferred to the *General Library, where it is maintained as a separate department, and rare materials were incorporated into the special collections. In the same year the library also received the Virgil Thomson Collection, containing copies of all his published music and sound recordings, portraits, articles by and about him, concert programs from 1928 onwards, selected memorabilia, and copies of his correspondence. Other Americana here include about 60,000 items of sheet music (including imprints of various midwestern publishers and composers), tunebooks and hymnals from the library of Isaac Baker Woodbury, holographs and other MSS of Amy Marcy Beach, music by composers resident at the MacDowell Colony 1920–50, and the Warner Brothers Orchestral Library of 13,000 scores and parts for silent-film accompaniment. The Institute for Studies in American Music here established special finding aids and sponsored workshops and festivals.

ST. LOUIS. Missouri State Historical Society (*MoSHi*). The library acquires music and related materials (programs, contracts, account books, correspondence, diaries) associated with St. Louis or Missouri. Major holdings of sheet music with St. Louis and midwestern imprints are indexed in detail, as are programs and playbills of musical organizations. Numerous personal and organizational papers include programs, clippings, bound volumes of sheet music, and correspondence from the collection of the musicologist Ernst C. Krohn, whose principal legacy is at Washington University (see below).

——. Washington University (*MoSW*). Ernst C. Krohn (see also above) had an important influence on the *Gaylord Music Library, which began in 1966 to acquire his musicological library containing more than 400 Festschriften as well as research files, 52,000 items of sheet music, and extensive music ephemera with an emphasis on midwestern Americana. More recently it acquired an outstanding collection of full scores of 18th- and 19th-century vocal music in first and early editions. The George C. Krick Collection contains 21 bound volumes of music for classical guitar.

E. C. Krohn: "On Classifying Sheet Music," *Notes*, xxvi (1969–70), 473; M. D. Fleming: "Report from Washington University: the Music Library," *CMc*, no.19 (1975), 20; G. R. Keck: *Pre-1875 Sheet Music in the Ernst C. Krohn Special Collection* (thesis, Iowa City, IA, 1982)

MONTANA

Various materials associated with the state are preserved in the Montana Historical Society (*MtHi*) in Helena.

NEBRASKA

Music of the state is reflected in the miscellaneous holdings of the Nebraska State Historical Society (*NbHi*) and the University of Nebraska (*NbU*), both in Lincoln. The former includes papers of the music educator Hazel Gertrude Kinscella (1893–1960); the latter preserves the folklore library from the 1930s of Benjamin A. Botkin. The papers of the violinist Carl-Frederic Steckelberg (including MS studies for violin) and the pianist Ouida Steckelberg are also in Lincoln, at the Lincoln City Libraries (*NbL*). The musical interests of the author Willa Cather are reflected at the Willa Cather Historical Center (*NbRcW*) in Red Cloud, and musical works by Czech immigrants are preserved at the Dvoracek Memorial Library (*NbWi*) in Wilber.

NEVADA

Musical documents associated with the state are preserved at the Nevada Historical Society (*NvHi*) in Reno.

NEW HAMPSHIRE

In addition to the music collections at Dartmouth College, important materials include the collections of MSS, printed music, and correspondence of Amy Marcy Beach at the New Hampshire State Library (*Nh*) in Concord and the University of New Hampshire (*NhU*) in Durham; the local music materials in the New Hampshire Historical Society (*NhHi*) in Concord, Manchester City Library (*NhM*), and the Manchester Historic Association; and Shaker music, 1890–1920, at Shaker Village in Canterbury.

HANOVER. Dartmouth College (*NhD*). The Special Collections in the *Baker Memorial Library (the main library) have strengths in all periods of American music. From the 18th and early 19th centuries there are printed and MS tunebooks (sacred and secular) and 470 volumes, including many other tunebooks, from the presses of Isaiah Thomas, presented to the library in 1819; from the middle and later part of the 19th century there are music and documentary materials relating to the Hutchinson (1843–92) and Baker (1845–66) families. The library holds the papers and personal archive of the critic James G. Huneker, including his correspondence with Walter Damrosch, Leopold Godowsky, Mary Garden, Victor Herbert, and others; the Roger H. Burrill collection of sheet music (1790–1960) containing about 14,000 items; and the MSS and published works commissioned by the college for its summer program Congregation of the Arts, 1963–9 (tapes of these works are in the tape archive of the *Hopkins Center).

The Isaiah Thomas Donation (Hanover, NH, 1949); R. H. Burrill: "The Dartmouth Collection of American Popular Songs," *Dartmouth College Library Bulletin*, no.14 (1974), 73; W. B. Tilghman: "Music in Special Collections," *Dartmouth College Library Bulletin*, no.15 (1974), 18

NEW JERSEY

In addition to the libraries described below, a large collection of Methodist music, including the Creamer Hymnology Collection, is at Drew University (*NjMD*) in Madison, and local music history sources are found at the New Jersey Historical Society (*NjHi*) in Newark.

NEWARK. Rutgers, State University of New Jersey, Institute of Jazz Studies (*NjNIJS*). Founded by the jazz historian Marshall Stearns and transferred to Rutgers in 1967, this archival collection of written and recorded jazz and related materials has since doubled to encompass some 50,000 recordings in all formats, sheet music and arrangements, correspondence, oral-history interviews, promotional materials, catalogues, and research files. On permanent loan from the University of Wisconsin, Milwaukee, is the John Dale Owen Collection of 12,000 recordings from 1917 to the 1950s, rich in transcriptions of radio broadcasts.

The institute published the *Journal of Jazz Studies* (1973–9), which continues as the *Annual Review of Jazz Studies* (1982–). *A Computerized Catalog of the Recorded Sound Collection of the Rutgers Institute of Jazz Studies* (Newark, 1980–) [cumulated microfiche register and indexes]

NEW BRUNSWICK. Rutgers, State University of New Jersey (*NjR*). In the *Archibald Stevens Alexander Library is a collection of 18th-century prints and MSS (the latter chiefly anthems) by Handel, purchased about 1950 by Alfred Mann. Part of Curt Sachs's library is here, including his early treatises and research materials in organology and ethnomusicology. Hymnals, tutors, journals, and about 5000 pieces of 19th-century sheet music constitute the significant holdings in American music.

H. F. Smith: *Guide to the Manuscript Collection of Rutgers University Library* (New Brunswick, NJ, 1964); M. Picker: "Handeliana in the Rutgers University Library," *Journal of the Rutgers University Library*, xxix (1965), 1; O. S. Coad: "Songs America Used to Sing," *Journal of the Rutgers University Library*, xxxi (1968), 33; *CMc*, no. 17 (1974), 30; D. A. Sinclair: *A Guide to Manuscripts, Diaries and Journals in the Special Collections Department* (New Brunswick, NJ, 1979)

PRINCETON. Princeton Theological Seminary (*NjPT*). Housed in the *Robert E. Speer Library is the hymnology collection of Louis F. Benson (1855–1930), one of the largest in the country; it is especially strong in music of the Reformed and Presbyterian churches, although important holdings in gospel, Sunday-school, and children's music abound.

K. Gapp: "The Theological Seminary Library," *Princeton University Library Chronicle*, xxv (1963–4), 10

——. Princeton University (*NjP*). Important holdings, rich in medieval and Renaissance music and later autograph MSS, are spread among several collections. The Music Collection (in the *Harvey S. Firestone Memorial Library) was established in 1935. Divided between this repository and some of the collections administered by the Department of Rare Books and Special Collections are early editions of works by Palestrina, Wilbye, Purcell, Bach, Handel, Haydn, Mozart, and Brahms. The special collections include the Robert Garrett Collection (including 13th-century English psalters, an important group of English motets from *c*1300, early 15th-century fragments of Latin treatises, and 15th- and 16th-century Byzantine, Armenian, Slavic, French, Italian, and Spanish liturgical books); the Greenville Kane Collection (early European psalters, 14th- and 15th-century German and Italian choirbooks, and a 13th-century English copy of a treatise by Boethius); the Princeton Collection (including a 12th-century French *missale plenum* with Aquitanian neumes, a 13th-century English troper, and German, Spanish, and northern Italian MSS up to the 17th century); and the James S. Hall Handel Collection (nearly all the published 18th-century editions of Handel's works and important contemporary MSS).

The Theatre Collection has the Tams–Witmark Collection of scores and parts, promptbooks, and stage managers' guides for musical comedies, 1895–1915, and the Robert B. Sour Collection of Music of the Theatre, containing 12,000 songs. In the Western Americana Collection is a comprehensive group of Mormon hymnals, and the Manuscripts Collection holds important individual autograph scores by Antheil, Hindemith, and Stravinsky as well as many by Roger Sessions. The Scheide Photographic Archive of Bach Manuscripts is also in the main part of the library.

On deposit in a separate wing is the distinguished private collection of William H. Scheide, which consists of medieval liturgical MSS (including a 9th- or early 10th-century evangeliary with ekphonetic notation, an 11th-century French antiphoner, an early 14th-century antiphoner, a Rhenish psalter of the same period, and a 15th-century English gradual); musical incunabula (including the earliest known example of Gerson's *Collectorium super Magnificat*, 1473; Niger's *Grammatica brevis*, 1480; and a *Missale romanum*, *c*1482); and autograph MSS by Bach, Mozart, Beethoven, Schubert, and Wagner (*Das Rheingold*).

Finding List for the Music Library, 1908 (Princeton, NJ, 1909); M. R. Bryan and P. Morgan: "Library Notes: Music Exhibition," *Princeton University Library Chronicle*, xxviii (1966–7), 106; M. R. Bryan: "Portrait of a Bibliophile, XVII: the Scheide Library," *Book Collector*, xxi (1972), 489; J. M. Knapp: "The Hall Handel Collection," *Princeton University Library Chronicle*, xxxvi (1974–5), 3; *CMc*, no. 17 (1974), 27

——. Westminster Choir College. In the *Talbott Library is a choral archive of some 3000 titles in 250,000 multiple copies, which is augmented by a sample file of 20,000 titles. Included are the former rental library of Tams–Witmark (including full conductor's scores of works by members of the Second New England School) and Stokowski's collection of 200 marked miniature and full scores.

NEW MEXICO

Native and local music is found, in addition to the university library below, in the Museum of International Folk Art and in the Wheelwright Museum of the American Indian, both in Santa Fe.

ALBUQUERQUE. University of New Mexico (*NmU*). Of principal interest in the *Fine Arts Library are American and Hispanic materials of the Southwest. In the Manuel Areu Collection are MSS, printed scores, lyrics, and dramatic prose of zarzuelas performed in New Mexico and Arizona, 1850–1920. The Archive of Southwestern Music preserves field recordings and videotapes of Indian, Spanish, Anglo-American, black, and Mexican cultures.

D. L. Roberts: "The Archive of Southwestern Music," *Folklore and Folk Music Archivist*, ix (win. 1966–7), 47; N. Sublette, ed.: *A Discography of Hispanic Music in the Fine Arts Library* (Albuquerque, 1973)

NEW YORK

General repositories in the city of New York other than those listed below include the music libraries at New York University (*NNU*) and the Brooklyn Public Library (*NB*). Ethnic music can be found at the Hispanic Society of America (*NNH*), which preserves important early materials; the Leo Baeck Institute (*NNLBI*), which specializes in Judaica; the Yivo Institute for Jewish Research (*NNYI*), devoted to Jewish and Yiddish matters and noted for its theatrical collections; and the Museum of the American Indian–Heye Foundation. The Shubert Archive documents a major Broadway theatrical institution, important broadcast scripts and recordings are housed at the Museum of Broadcasting, and early film materials (including cue sheets and scores) can be found at the Museum of Modern Art (*NNMoMA*). The American Society of Composers, Authors and Publishers (ASCAP) has important source materials at its headquarters. Major private collectors in New York City include Rudolf and Lillian Kallir, Jacob Lateiner, and Robert Owen Lehman. Collectors of popular music (sheet music and recordings) include David Jasen in ragtime, Morris Young for American popular music in general, and Daniel B. ("Banjo Dan") McCall. Among the private collections of recordings, the cylinders of Allen Koenigsberg are important.

Elsewhere in New York State, the DeWitt Historical Society (*NIHi*) in Ithaca is a major repository for local music history materials. The academic music libraries at SUNY, Potsdam (*NPotU*), Stony Brook (*NSbSU*), and Purchase (*NPurU*) are notable, the last of these for the Oliver Daniel collection of 20th-century materials, and the Frances R. Conole Archive at the

Binghamton campus (*NBiSU*) is devoted primarily to vocal recordings. Robert Hoe, Jr., in Poughkeepsie assembled an outstanding collection of band music, and the collectors Frank and Anne Warner in Old Brookville specialize in folk-music materials.

BUFFALO. Buffalo and Erie County Public Library (*NBu*). Formed by merger in 1954, the library includes the former Grosvenor Library collection of popular Americana, with a large and distinguished collection of sheet music, bound volumes of 18th- and 19th-century songs and piano pieces, songbooks, hymnals, and broadsides. In the Rare Book Room are holographs by the 20th-century composers David Diamond, Lukas Foss, Alexei Haieff, Darius Milhaud, Ned Rorem, Leo Smit, and others.

"Transportation in American Popular Songs: a Bibliography of Items in the Grosvenor Library," *Grosvenor Library Bulletin*, xxvii (1945), 61-106; M. M. Mott: "Sports and Recreations in American Popular Songs," *Notes*, vi (1948–9), 379-418, vii (1949–50), 522-61, ix (1951–2), 33

——. State University of New York at Buffalo (*NBuU*). The *Music Library (*NBuU-Mu*, in Baird Hall) opened in 1970 and has continued to expand rapidly, serving as custodian of the MS music, correspondence, and scrapbooks relating to the avant-garde composers associated with the Center for the Creative and Performing Arts established at the university by Lukas Foss in 1963. Rare items include about a dozen MS copies of Lully operas and librettos, MSS and early prints of works by G. C. M. Clari and Ferdinando Paer, and early editions of 18th-century operas and chamber music. Also here are research materials including oral-history interviews with, and the papers of, American music librarians. A separate ethnomusicological sound recording collection is maintained as the *Archive of Folklore, Traditional Music and Oral History (*NBuU-AR*, in Clemens Hall).

C. J. Bradley: *The Genesis of American Music Librarianship, 1902–1942* (diss., Florida State U., 1978)

ITHACA. Cornell University (*NIC*). Otto Kinkeldey, the renowned musicologist and librarian of the university 1930–46, was responsible for the early growth of the music collection (housed in the *Music Library), which is particularly strong in 18th- and early 19th-century opera full scores (chiefly French), and the music of 20th-century composers. In the early 1950s Donald J. Grout assembled on microfilm a comprehensive collection (since expanded) of music and theoretical works printed in Italy from 1500 to 1527. In 1970 Vaughan Williams's widow donated microfilm copies of his MSS, as well as printed proof copies, published scores with his annotations, and correspondence. American music is well represented in a large collection of vocal sheet music published before 1920.

The Rare Books Department of the *Olin Library houses autograph scores and letters of some 70 composers, including items by Mozart, Beethoven, and Gounod, and letters of Beethoven, Mendelssohn, and Wagner. The Lavoisier Collection includes the personal library of Madame Lavoisier, an amateur musician, as well as piano music and operas of Mozart and Rossini. The Harris Hymnal Collection has a wide sampling of 18th- and 19th-century German, English, and American Protestant hymnals.

S. L. Gilman: "German Hymnals in the Harris Hymnal Collection: a Short-title Checklist," *Cornell Library Journal*, x (1970), 40; D. Robbins: "Eighteenth-century Editions of Handel at Cornell," *Cornell University Library Bulletin*, clxxxvi (1973), 1; *CMc*, no. 17 (1974), 16

——. Ithaca College (*NIIC*). Radio music is well represented in the *college library, both in the Gustave Haenschen collection of 50,000 radio-orchestra scores and parts and in the Donald Vořhees collection of scripts and music used in the "Bell Telephone Hour" broadcasts, 1940–50. The papers and recordings of the Metropolitan Opera soprano Roberta Peters are also here.

NEW YORK. American Composers Alliance. Founded in 1938 under the direction of Aaron Copland and other leading composers, the organization maintains a library of some 4000 scores and performance parts by its composer members (usually nearly all a member's MSS unless they are held by a publisher). Copies are available to the public through the catalogues of the Composers Facsimile Edition (known as the American Composers Edition from 1972).

The organization published a *Bulletin* in 1938 and from 1952 to 1965.

——. American Music Center. The Center was formed in 1940 by six composers in order to assemble scores and recordings of contemporary American music and to promote its performance. In 1962 it was designated by the National Music Council as the official US Information Center for American music and, as such, it makes available inexpensive musical reproductions and maintains biographical files on about 1200 composers. By arrangement with the New York Public Library, its holdings are listed in the catalogue of the Library and Museum of the Performing Arts, to where a composer's works are transferred 25 years after his or her death.

Activities of the center are reported in a quarterly *Newsletter* (originally *Music Today*, 1958–). J. Browning: "The American Music Center," *FAM*, xvi (1969), 144; *AMC Library Catalog* (New York, 1975–) [circulating library]; J. G. Finell: *Catalog of Choral and Vocal Works* (New York, 1975); K. M. Famera: *Catalog of the American Music Center Library*, ii: *Chamber Music* (New York, 1978); *National Endowment for the Arts Composer/Librettist Program Collection at the American Music Center*, ed. American Music Center (New York, 1979)

——. Broadcast Music, Inc. (BMI). Carl Haverlin, president of BMI 1947–63, assembled nearly complete sets of first editions of works by Beethoven, Chopin, and Wagner (among others), as well as letters, autographs, and MSS of many other composers and musicians (particularly Americans of the 20th century). In an effort to document all aspects of American history from colonial times to the present, part of the collection was exhibited widely during the US Bicentennial (brochure, 1976). The library now also includes jazz and popular music, MSS, and rare editions.

——. Brooklyn College, City University of New York (*NBC*). The *Institute for Studies in American Music has a small collection acquired from various sources: about 2500 pieces of sheet music (including 700 from the early 20th-century American Yiddish theater); a special collection of works by and about Henry Cowell; the library of the pianist Alfred de Voto (including works by early 20th-century American composers); and bio-bibliographical files on 20th-century American composers. The *Walter Gerboth Music Library is particularly strong in musical Festschriften and holds copies of unpublished English translations of various treatises (produced under a project formerly known as the AMS/MLA Translations Center). The Manuscripts and Special Collections department of the *Brooklyn College Library has Edward B. Wisely's recorded collection of musical theater and vaudeville (1875–1940) in the USA, Great Britain, and Ireland.

The institute publishes a biannual *Newsletter* (1971–).

——. City College, City University of New York (*NNR*). The *Music Library holds the personal library of one of its faculty members, Mark Brunswick, which includes four holograph MSS

(1923–6, partly photocopies) by Roger Sessions and copies of MSS of his own works. Brunswick's papers, including correspondence related to the Placement Committee for German & Austrian Musicians (1938–45) and 23 holograph MSS (1919–70), are housed in the *City College Archives.

——. Columbia University (*NNC*). The Music Library (in *Dodge Hall) is strong in opera scores and first and early editions (chiefly from the Bass Collection) of the late 18th and early 19th centuries. The library has Erich Hertzmann's large film collection of Beethoven materials and the personal libraries of Edward MacDowell and Anton Seidl; the Judah A. Joffe record collection documents early recording techniques through the acoustic era. In the same building is the Center for Studies in Ethnomusicology, which includes, in addition to the Laura Boulton Collection of Traditional and Liturgical Music (more than 10,000 field recordings), many musical materials relating to all geographic and language groups, in photographs, films, and written documents collected by faculty members and students.

In the Rare Book and Manuscript Libraries of *Butler Memorial Library (the main university library) are the papers of Edward MacDowell, Daniel Gregory Mason, Nicolai Berezowsky, and Douglas S. Moore, and many autograph letters of composers and performers of the 18th to 20th centuries, including Jacques Barzun's assemblage of correspondence and material (the Hector Berlioz Collections) and the Anton Seidl Collection of Musical Autographs, which relates to his activities as a conductor. Other collections include Eda Rothstein Rappaport's holographs and the Isidore Witmark Collection of MS scores and letters to American publishers from song composers.

An important collection of early liturgical MSS assembled by George A. Plimpton ranges from a 10th-century neumed German lectionary to an 18th-century collection of Greek hymns that includes a large group of antiphoners. The largest single collection (some 30,000 items) was assembled by Arthur Billings Hunt and purchased through a gift by Alfred C. Berol; it is chiefly noted for its early American sheet music. The library's autograph scores include works by 19th- and 20th-century composers (among them Brahms, Bruckner, Richard Strauss, Babbitt, Copland, Holst, and MacDowell). In 1943 Béla Bartók gave the library MSS of his Romanian, Turkish, and Serbo-Croatian folk material.

The Oral History Collection in Butler Library contains transcriptions of oral-history interviews with musicians and critics, and others that have resulted from special projects (e.g., on early jazz and the music of various immigrant groups). The Columbiana Collection in the *Low Library includes the scores of musical comedies written by Richard Rodgers as a student.

Catalog of the Isidore Witmark Collection of Autographed Books and Musical Scores in the Columbia University Libraries (New York, 1942); A. B. Hunt: *The Hunt Library of Music* (Pound Ridge, NY, 1946); *CMc*, no.17 (1974), 12; J. Lord-Wood: *Musical Americana in the Hunt–Berol Collection at the Columbia University Libraries* (thesis, Columbia U., 1975); E. B. Mason and L. M. Starr, eds.: *The Oral History Collection of Columbia University* (New York, 1979)

——. James J. Fuld collection. This private collection contains first and rare editions of classical and popular music (including works by Bach, Haydn, Mozart, and Beethoven), opera librettos, autograph MSS from 1750 onwards (works by Bach, Handel, Mozart, Beethoven, Mussorgsky, and American composers including Joplin), and musical ephemera. Many of the printed editions provided material for Fuld's books, *American Popular Music (Reference Book), 1875–1950* (1955; suppl., 1956), *The Book of World-Famous Music* (1966, rev. 2/1971), and *The Book of World-Famous Libretti* (1984). Areas of strength include early and Confederate patriotic songs, especially *The Star-Spangled Banner*, *Yankee Doodle*, and *Hail Columbia!*, 18th-century American secular music MSS, works by black composers, music and cue sheets for silent films, autographed letters and documents, and first editions of nearly all the songs by Irving Berlin, George Gershwin, Jerome Kern, Cole Porter, and Richard Rodgers.

J. J. Fuld: "Surrounded by One's Friends," *Notes*, xxxii (1975–6), 479; J. J. Fuld: "A Collection of Music Autographs," *Manuscripts*, xxxii (1980), 13; J. J. Fuld: "Music Posters: the Need for an Inventory," *Notes*, xxxvii (1980–81), 520

——. Juilliard School (*NNJu*). The Institute of Musical Art, founded in 1905 by Frank Damrosch, established a music library in 1906; the institute merged with the Juilliard Graduate School in 1926. The *Lila Acheson Wallace Library includes a few holograph scores, letters, the papers of the critic Ernest Newman (1868–1959), a number of MSS by Ysaÿe, and a special collection of early editions of Liszt's piano music.

CMc, no.17 (1974), 22

——. Metropolitan Opera Association Archives. In addition to papers, pictorial material, scrapbooks, and financial records, the archive (established in 1958) has bound programs from 1881 onwards with MS corrections regarding casts entered by the stage manager; indexed both by title and performer, these supersede the published lists in the Seltsam annals.

W. H. Seltsam: *Metropolitan Opera Annals* (New York, 1947; suppls., 1957, 1968, 1978); M. E. Peltz: "The Metropolitan Opera Archives," *American Archivist*, xxx (1967), 471

——. New-York Historical Society (*NHi*). Founded in 1804, the society is noted for its collections of historical materials relating not only to the city and state of New York but to the entire country. The music holdings are rich in sheet music (especially Confederate imprints and Spanish-American War music; the collections of Bella C. Landauer, held at the society, have been reproduced in her books *My City, 'Tis of Thee: New York City on Sheet Music Covers*, *Striking the Right Note in Advertising*, and *Some Terpsichorean Ephemera*, published 1951–3), tunebooks and hymnals, MSS, and papers, including an extensive collection of Emma Thursby materials and the diaries of G. T. Strong, 1837–75.

The society's *Quarterly Bulletin* (1917–) contains articles based on the collections.
A. J. Breton: *A Guide to the Manuscript Collections of the New-York Historical Society* (Westport, CT, 1972)

——. New York Public Library (*NN*). The nucleus of the Music Division of the *Library and Museum of the Performing Arts (*NN-L*) at Lincoln Center is a collection of music, books on music, and autographs assembled by H. F. Albrecht in Europe between 1845 and 1858 and purchased by the Philadelphia financier Joseph Drexel, who by 1871 had also acquired the libraries of R. La Roche and E. F. Rimbault. Drexel issued a catalogue in 1869 of the musical writings and compiled MS catalogues of the music and autographs. The 6000 items in the collection were bequeathed to the Lenox Library (opened to the public in 1870) in 1888; these included incunabula, theoretical works (especially Italian of the 15th–18th centuries), the only known copy of *Parthenia in-violata* (*c*1624–5), and, especially, English MSS for the virginal (one Gibbons autograph), instrumental consorts, and voice (the Sambrooke MS, Drexel 4302).

The library of John Jacob Astor (about 4000 music items) and the Lenox Library, with support from the Tilden Foundation, were opened to the public in 1877 and 1887 respectively. The

Music Division of the Reference Department was established in 1911 when the new building opened at 42nd Street; it was moved to Lincoln Center in 1965 with the theater and dance collections to form the Library and Museum of the Performing Arts.

The library's special collections hold a number of incunabula, including items by Boethius, Aristides Quintilianus, and Gaffurius; 16th-century publications by J. F. Agricola, Galilei, Fuenllana, Lassus, and Beaujoyeux; and important 17th-century imprints (other than the Drexel items mentioned above), including works by Lassus, Schadaeus, Besard, and Vallet, as well as many theoretical works. Early and rare editions of Beethoven's works were received from the Beethoven Association when it dissolved in 1940.

A few autograph MSS had been acquired by the time the library opened in 1911, including works by Beethoven, Haydn, and Mozart. By 1915, holograph compositions by Mercadante, Paganini, Liszt, and Glinka had been added, and in 1932 a gift in memory of Lizzie Bliss and Christian A. Herter containing MSS by Bach, Handel, Haydn, Mozart, Schubert, and Schumann was received. In 1950 the pianist Angela Diller presented the autographs of Stravinsky's *Symphony of Psalms* and *Capriccio*. Seven Brahms autographs were bequeathed by Paul Wittgenstein, as well as piano music for the left hand he had commissioned from Ravel, Prokofiev, and others. There are Liszt MSS and documents in the Carl Lachmund collection and elsewhere (notably the autograph and revised copy of *Réminiscences de Don Juan*), and a Duke Ellington autograph. An unusual set of MSS, acquired in 1970 and known as the Chirk Castle partbooks (after their Welsh place of origin), contains 65 pre-Restoration Anglican services and anthems that survived the English Civil War in their original bindings. In 1975 CBS presented about 200,000 pieces of MS music from its library (founded in 1929), which contained hundreds of commissioned compositions and arrangements for musical broadcasts, including holographs of Antheil, Copland, Gould, Milhaud, Giannini, Deems Taylor, and Alec Wilder; the Music Division retained these as well as pre-1962 popular song sheets (85,000) and cue sheets, while the remainder of the collection was absorbed into the circulating division (see below).

A substantial number of autograph letters was received in the Drexel collection, in the Bliss–Herter gift, and in a donation of Howard van Sinderen in 1929, which also contained the papers of the pianist William Mason; numerous others (as well as photographs and MS fragments) were received in the estate of the pianist Alexander Lambert. The Hufstaders presented some correspondence and photographs of well-known musicians in 1965, and five years later the library purchased a collection of about 700 unpublished letters of Mendelssohn and the correspondence of Giuditta Pasta (containing letters from Bellini, Donizetti, Rossini, Liszt, Malibran, and others). From the estate of Ernst F. Oster it received a large collection of Schenker's writings in MS, and from that of Bruno Walter his correspondence with Mahler and others and a number of Mahler MSS.

The Americana Collection grew out of a memorial to the composer and conductor Henry Hadley. In addition to MSS of Ruggles, Varèse, and Harris, it contains many MSS of Gottschalk, his diaries and letters, and holographs acquired in 1983 from a direct descendant, Lily Glover. The personal papers (with a number of music MSS) of Elliott Carter are on deposit (exhibition catalogue, 1973). The archive of the League of Composers, containing many letters and other documents, was presented in 1966 by Claire R. Reis, and musical scores by American composers of works performed at the monthly meetings of the Composers' Forum became the property of the Americana Collection. There are 350,000 titles of American sheet music, and the collection is known for its special indexes (e.g., instrumental music published in the USA 1830–70).

The Toscanini Memorial Archives, established in 1964, consists chiefly of microfilms of autograph MSS of major composers and a few first and early editions.

The Music Division has been responsible for a number of publications. In the 1930s and 1940s, editions issued of works in its collections included the Ozalid Print Series of early American sacred and secular music, a number of early symphonies, concertos, and chamber works, and 16th- and 17th-century consort music.

The circulating music collection (established in 1920 at the library branch on East 58th Street and now at Lincoln Center) received the library of the American Orchestral Society in 1929 and the CBS orchestral library in 1975. The Billy Rose Theatre Collection contains personal papers, promptbooks, costume and scenery designs, scrapbooks, and programs relating to musical theater and related arts (circus, vaudeville, minstrel shows, etc.). The Dance Collection has extensive holdings of works about dance music of all periods.

In 1935 Columbia Records donated a large collection of materials to the New York Public Library, forming the nucleus of an archive that grew rapidly from other corporate and private gifts. After the collection was moved to Lincoln Center, a gift from the Rodgers and Hammerstein Foundation enabled the library to purchase equipment and provide a partial catalogue. With a grant from the Avalon Foundation, the library established an archival taping and preservation laboratory which has pioneered tape-transfer techniques. Through other grant funds, it acquired the Jan Holcman Collection of Historic Piano Recordings and a large number of Flagstad tapes (including her Metropolitan Opera début) from the collector A. F. R. Lawrence. Notable gifts of recordings include 9000 rare operatic and vocal recordings from G. Lauder Greenway, including 120 wax cylinders of live Metropolitan performances recorded by Lionel Mapleson, for which special transfer techniques had to be devised. The radio station WNEW presented 20,000 of the popular and jazz singles it had acquired before 1967 (with a catalogue). The library, now known as the Rodgers and Hammerstein Archives of Recorded Sound, also acquires and preserves supplemental printed materials documenting the recording history of the USA, England, France, Germany, and Italy.

Several special collections at the *main library on 42nd Street include notable music items: the Arents Tobacco Collection and the Arents Collection of Books in Parts; the Berg Collection of English and American Literature; the Spencer Collection of works representative of the development of book arts; and the Manuscripts and Archives Division in certain collections, even though most of the musical resources were transferred to Lincoln Center in 1965.

The *Schomburg Center for Research in Black Culture (*NN-Sc*) has, in addition to about 2000 items of music, books about music, and recordings, a number of archival collections relating to about 20 composers and musicians, containing programs, clippings, and photographs.

The library publishes a quarterly *Bulletin* (1897–). H. Botstiber: "Musicalia in der New York Public Library," *SIMG*, iv (1902–3), 738; *Dictionary Catalog*, vi (Boston, 1962; suppls., 1967, 1972), 4784–813 [Schomburg Center]; *Dictionary*

Catalog of the Music Collection, ed. New York Public Library (Boston, 1964; cumulative suppl., 1973 [1964–71]; suppl., 1976 [1974]; annual suppls., 1976–, as *Bibliographic Guide to Music*); *Dictionary Catalog of the Manuscript Division*, ii (Boston, 1967), 601; S. P. Williams: *Guide to the Research Collections of the New York Public Library* (Chicago, 1975); S. Sommer and R. Koprowski: "The Toscanini Memorial Archives at the New York Public Library," *College Music Symposium*, xvii/2 (1977), 103; P. L. Miller and F. C. Campbell: "How the Music Division of the New York Public Library Grew – a Memoir," *Notes*, xxxv (1978–9), 537, xxxvi (1979–80), 65, xxxviii (1981–2), 121; *Dictionary Catalog of the Rodgers and Hammerstein Archives of Recorded Sound* (Boston, 1981)

——. Pierpont Morgan Library (*NNPM*). This important, privately endowed library was founded in 1924; in 1971 it owned about 20 printed books on music, an equal number of printed scores, and about 300 music MSS. Important items in the original collection are a 13th-century Provençal chansonnier, an early 15th-century MS with four chansons of Machaut, the unique complete copy of an anthology *Motetti e canzoni* (1521, possibly published by Antico; part of the Toovey Collection, acquired in 1899), autograph MSS of short vocal works by J.-J. Rousseau, Haydn, N. A. Zingarelli, Nicola Vaccai, and Rossini, and autograph scores of Beethoven (Violin Sonata op.96), Gounod, and Frederick S. Converse (*The Pipe of Desire* and Symphony no.6). There is also a collection of letters, which includes a document signed by Palestrina, Mozart's two earliest surviving letters (both 13 December 1769), and important groups of correspondence by Mendelssohn and Wagner.

In 1949 the collector Reginald Allen presented the first of many gifts from his collection of the works of Gilbert and Sullivan. In 1962 the library received a group of books and MSS collected by the financier Dannie N. Heineman. Important among these are fragments and parts of works by Bach, Haydn, Mozart, Mendelssohn, and Wagner; sketches of works by Beethoven and Richard Strauss; and complete autograph MSS of works by Mozart, Schubert, Schumann, Chopin, Brahms, Strauss, and Wagner. There are also two Wagner imprints heavily annotated by the composer (the proof of the full score of *Die Meistersinger von Nürnberg* and his own copy of the 1853 edition of *Der Ring des Nibelungen*) and a small but distinctive group of letters, notably from Haydn, Beethoven, Mozart, and Rossini.

Mrs. Janos Scholz has presented several important autograph MSS from the library of Ernest Schelling, including works by Chopin and Schumann. Beginning in 1968, gifts from the distinguished private collection of Robert Owen Lehman were received annually until the whole was eventually deposited; of particular interest among them is a large group of French autograph MSS formerly owned by Alfred Cortot, including works by Fauré, Massenet, Saint-Saëns, Franck, and Arthur Honegger. Four autographs of Chausson and others by Berlioz, Gounod, Hahn, d'Indy, Koechlin, Milhaud, Offenbach, Ropartz, and Florent Schmitt supplement the Cortot items. There are autograph full scores of works by the younger Johann Strauss, Moscheles, and Paderewski. An album of musical autographs collected from 1842 to 1856 by the Paris Opéra oboist Gustave Vogt includes 63 short pieces (inventoried by B. Friedland in *Notes*, xxxi, 1974–5, p.262). Recent gifts include autographs of nine Berg songs, several Webern MSS, and a previously unknown self-portrait by Schoenberg; acquired at auction were autograph MSS of Debussy's *Pelléas et Mélisande* and Schumann songs (op.79).

A large gift of some 90 autograph MSS of great distinction was received in 1968 from the estate of Mary Flagler Cary, and in 1969 the trust established in her name gave 60 more. The earliest of the Cary archive MSS is a neumed 13th-century German gradual; among the other items are autograph or holograph scores of Bach's Cantata no.112, Beethoven's Piano Trio op.70 no.1, Schubert's *Winterreise* and *Schwanengesang*, Cherubini's Sonata for two organs, Brahms's Sonata for two pianos op.34*b*, Liszt's *Glanes de Woronince* and three versions of *Am Grabe Richard Wagners*, and Strauss's *Don Juan* and *Tod und Verklärung*, as well as works by Mozart, Weber, Chopin, Ponchielli, and Mahler. Also in the collection are Beethoven sketches, the autograph voice part and annotated engraver's copy of Schumann's *Frauenliebe und -leben*, and part of Berlioz's *Mémoires*. 19th- and 20th-century Italians represented by autograph works include Bellini, Giordano, Mascagni, Mercadante, Puccini, Rossini, and Spontini; also present are minor compositions in the hand of Cimarosa, Verdi, and others, as well as a collection of bel canto cadenzas for some 30 operas, as sung by Barbara Marchisio and her sister Carlotta. There is also an autograph MS of Louis Spohr's *Violin-Schule*. To supplement the works by French composers, the Cary trustees later acquired autograph full scores of two operas by Offenbach (*Les contes d'Hoffmann* and *La permission de dix heures*), Gounod's *Mireille*, Lecocq's *Le petit duc*, and Massenet's *Manon*, as well as autographs of works by Debussy and Fauré (Pavane, op.50).

Most interesting among the few 20th-century works is Diaghilev's copy of a full score of Stravinsky's *Firebird*, containing many revisions in the hand of the composer and various conductors who directed the work, as well as MS and printed orchestral parts; there are also the first drafts of parts of Schoenberg's *Moses und Aron* and *Gurrelieder*.

By far the largest part of the Cary collection is the 3000 autograph letters of composers and musicians collected by her father, Harry Harkness Flagler, many of which are addressed to the Flaglers and the Carys. A large number of letters (and some scores) originally owned by the Leipzig publishers C. F. Peters were confiscated in World War II, then released to Walter Hinrichsen, who brought them to the USA. Other letters were acquired from Alfred Cortot and the English music critic Joseph Bennett. The earliest is from Nicolas Gombert (1547); from the 19th century are letters of Berlioz (33), Schumann (10), Wagner (25), Wolf (11), Richard Strauss (22), Chabrier (34), Verdi (31), Julius Benedict (22), Sullivan (34), and George Grove (22); 20th-century composers are represented by Schoenberg (43), Berg (69), and Webern (14). Other musical documents include a group relating to the Vienna Court Orchestra, 1781–1810, and contemporary portraits, notably of Brahms, Mendelssohn, and Schubert.

E. N. Waters: "The Music Collection of the Heineman Foundation," *Notes*, vii (1949–50), 181–216 [incl. facsimiles of unpublished MSS]; *Books and Manuscripts from the Heineman Collection*, ed. Pierpont Morgan Library (New York, 1963) [catalogue]; *The Mary Flagler Cary Music Collection* (New York, 1970); O. Albrecht: "Musical Treasures in the Morgan Library," *Notes*, xxviii (1971–2), 643 [supplements the 1970 catalogue]; E. A. Bowles: "A Checklist of Musical Instruments in Fifteenth-century Illuminated Manuscripts at the Pierpont Morgan Library," *Notes*, xxx (1973–4), 759; R. Allen and G. R. D'Luny: *Sir Arthur Sullivan: Composer and Personage*, ed. Pierpont Morgan Library (New York, 1975) [exhibition catalogue]; *The Dannie and Hettie Heineman Collection* (New York, 1978); J. R. Turner: *Nineteenth-century Autograph Music MSS in the Pierpont Morgan Music Library* (New York, 1982)

——. Union Theological Seminary (*NNUT*). Music comprises a small but significant portion of the holdings here, beginning with the hymnology collection of Frederick M. Byrd presented in 1888. The Hymn Society of America Collection of some 1800 books and pamphlets was deposited in 1925. Today there are about 2000 hymnals including those in the Missionary Research Library, books on hymnology in the Henry Day Collection, theses and dissertations from the Seminary's School of Sacred Music (1930–73), and some secular music.

Alphabetical Arrangement of Main Entries from the Shelf List (Boston, 1960); *The Shelf List of the Union Theological Seminary Library in New York City, in Classification Order* (Boston, 1960)

POUGHKEEPSIE. Vassar College (*NPV*). In the *George Sherman Dickinson Music Library is a special collection of materials (including MSS) by women composers and modest collections of other MSS, mainly of former faculty members but also including 18th-century works and letters. Notable private collections acquired include chamber music parts from Edward Dannreuther (a pupil of F. L. Ritter, the first music teacher at the college), the Kate Chittenden Library of Pianoforte Music, the library of the Venezuelan musician Teresa Carreño, and MSS of the violinist and composer Boris Koutzen (1901–66).

A catalogue of the library's holdings is available on microfilm. C. J. Bradley and J. B. Coover: "Vassar's Music Library: the First Hundred Years," *Notes*, xxxv (1978–9), 819–46

ROCHESTER. University of Rochester, Eastman School of Music (*NRU-Mus*). The *Sibley Music Library was established within the main library of the university in 1904 and moved to the new Eastman School in 1921. The first important purchase was the archive of the French music critic and pedagogue Arthur Pougin in 1923, which contained some 3000 items related to French theater and opera from the 17th to the 19th centuries. Oscar G. T. Sonneck's personal library, including materials for the preparation of the Library of Congress classification scheme for music, was also acquired in these early years. The 11th-century Reichenau MS and the 12th-century Admont-Rochester MS 494 were acquired in 1929 and 1936 respectively; these contain treatises by Hermannus Contractus, William of Bernon, Wilhelm of Hirsau, Grutolf of Michelsberg, Aribo (*De musica*), and Guido of Arezzo (*Micrologus*). A MS collection illustrating musical notation from the 10th century to the 16th, amassed by Oskar Fleischer and purchased in 1935, has 35 volumes of music and treatises. The library has continued to collect theoretical works of all periods, and has incunabula by Niger and Keinspeck.

During the early 1930s some 16th-century partbooks were acquired, including unique copies of Italian madrigals and early editions of works by Palestrina, Josquin Desprez, Morales, Pietro Vinci, and Lassus. The Leo S. Olschki Collection of 17th-century sacred partbooks was purchased in 1940. Autograph scores include trio sonatas by Purcell, fragments of works by Haydn, Mozart, and Beethoven, songs by Schubert and Brahms, piano arrangements by Liszt of Weber overtures, and major works by Debussy, Fauré, Saint-Saëns, and Krenek.

During the 1950s, collections of Italian songs, ballets and comic operas of late 18th-century London and Paris, as well as nearly 1000 operas (mostly French, 1880–1930), were acquired. Howard Hanson presented 23 of his holograph MSS in 1949 and others later. The library also owns holographs of numerous American works acquired through the Festivals of American Music (1930–71) and the American Composers' Concert Series (1925–54). In recent decades the library has purchased the music of two entire catalogues issued in 1965 and 1977 by the publisher and dealer Dan Fog in Copenhagen, containing works of Carl Nielsen and Franz Kuhlau. In the sheet music collections are some 75,000 items from the 1790s to the 1940s (mostly pre-1900), and 25,000 more in 600 bound volumes, as well as the Fanny and Julius Israel collection of European and American illustrated editions.

The separately housed *Ensemble Library contains the legacies of several theater orchestras, resulting in a collection of 8000 works for orchestra (scores and parts), 2000 for theater orchestra (including film scores), 3200 works for other ensembles (including jazz), and 1400 works for chorus.

A *Library Bulletin* has been published since 1946. *Catalogue of the Sibley Musical Library* (Rochester, 1906; suppl., 1909 [1906–9]; L. S. Olschki: "Une nouvelle collection de musique du xviie siècle contenant plusieurs ouvrages uniques et inconnus des bibliographes," *La bibliofilia*, xl (1938), 1; B. Duncan: "The Sibley Music Library," *Library Bulletin*, i (1946), 26; *CMc*, no.17 (1974), 60; R. Watanabe: "The Sibley Music Library of the Eastman School of Music, University of Rochester," *Notes*, xxxiii (1976–7), 783 [cites most of her earlier articles in the *Library Bulletin* on specific collections]; *Sibley Music Library Catalog of Sound Recordings* (Boston, 1977)

SYRACUSE. Syracuse University (*NSyU*). The George Arents Research Library (in the *Bird Library) contains the Liechtenstein microfilm collection of MS parts of 17th-century central European sacred vocal and instrumental compositions, a 19th-century collection of Italian librettos, and MS music and papers of Ernst Bacon, George Barati, William H. Berwald, Arna Bontemps (including correspondence with Pearl Bailey and William Grant Still), Louis Gruenberg (journals), Bernard Rogers, Miklós Rózsa, Leo Sowerby, and Franz Waxman. Louis Krasner deposited here his personal library of printed chamber music, which includes first editions of works by Beethoven and Mozart and a proof copy with MS corrections of Berg's Violin Concerto.

The *Diane and Arthur Belfer Audio Library and Archive is the only such collection to be housed in a building especially constructed (in 1982) for the purpose, and it specializes in restoration through use of laser and fiber-optic technology. The archive was formed in 1963 when the university acquired the collection of Joseph and Max Bell who had owned a record store in New York. It has strong holdings of Edison cylinders (a catalogue is in preparation) and Hispanic music of the 1950s on 45 r.p.m. discs (25,000–30,000). Special collections include acetate discs of film music by Rózsa and Waxman.

A. S. Garlington, Jr.: *Sources for the Study of Nineteenth Century Italian Opera in the Syracuse University Libraries: an Annotated Libretto List* (Syracuse, 1976); C. A. Otto: *Seventeenth-century Music from Kroměříž, Czechoslovakia: a Catalog of the Liechtenstein Music Collection on Microfilm at Syracuse University* (Syracuse, 1977); *The Rigler and Deutsch Record Index: a National Union Catalog of Sound Recordings* (Syracuse, 1985) [pt 1: 78 r.p.m. recordings in Association for Recorded Sound Collections holdings; in microform]

NORTH CAROLINA

In addition to the libraries cited below, extensive local music history holdings are found in the W. L. Eury Collection at Appalachian State University (*NcBoA*) in Boone, at Duke University (*NcD*) in Durham, and at the North Carolina State Department of Archives and History (*Nc-Ar*) in Raleigh.

CHAPEL HILL. University of North Carolina (*NcU*). Founded in 1932, the *Music Library (in Hill Hall) is the largest in the southeastern USA, with about 80,000 volumes. It is particularly strong in Renaissance music, including representative early prints and many microfilms, and in works relating to William S. Newman's studies of the sonata (particularly his three-volume *History of the Sonata Idea*, 1959–69, rev. 3/1983). Newman has gradually been transferring his collection of first and early editions of keyboard sonatas from the 17th to the 20th centuries, one of the largest of its kind, to the Music Library. In 1982 the library purchased more than 4000 Italian librettos from the same period. Also here are the Early American Music Collection (about 5000 items, chiefly sheet music and other imprints) and the extensive

American Religious Tunebook Collection of original and microfilm editions, including the Dan Yoder and the Annabel Morris Buchanan collections. The Religious Tunebook Collection is especially strong in German-American, 19th-century shape-note, and 20th-century gospel tunebooks.

The MSS of Annabel Buchanan, a composer and folklorist, are in the Southern Historical Collection in the *Louis Round Wilson Library. The Wilson Library will by 1987 house the Southern Documentary Recording and Film Collection, the largest university collection of published recordings of the traditional music of North America, the British Isles, and the Caribbean, with emphasis on the music of the southern USA. It also includes field recordings and films made by faculty members and students of the university and the recently acquired collection of the John Edwards Memorial Foundation of Los Angeles, containing 28,000 78 r.p.m. and 45 r.p.m. disc recordings and an extensive collection of song folios, sheet music, and materials relating to folk and traditional music issued on commercial labels in the period 1920–50 (including Cajun music, blues, black and white gospel, and, in particular, Anglo-American string-band and country music).

The John Edwards Memorial Foundation issues the *JEMF Quarterly* (1965–, originally a newsletter) and several series (the Reprint Series and Special Series, both chiefly discographical, and Sound Documents, which contains musical recordings with booklets). E. W. Earle: "Collectors and Collections: the John Edwards Memorial Foundation, Inc.," *Western Folklore*, xxiii (1964), 111; E. W. Earle: "The John Edwards Memorial Foundation," *Western Folklore*, xxx (1971), 177; *CMc*, no.17 (1974), 54; B. B. Boggs and D. W. Patterson, eds.: *An Index of Selected Folk Recordings* (Chapel Hill, 1984) [microfiche set and guide to Folk Music Archives]

——. William S. Newman collection: see University of North Carolina.

GREENSBORO. University of North Carolina at Greensboro (*NcGU*). The Department of Special Collections at the *Walter Clinton Jackson Library is noted for its MSS of North Carolina composers and others acquired through the "restful music" prizes established by E. B. Benjamin. Also here is the personal library of the cellist Luigi Silva, including his unfinished study on the history of the cello, and MS copies of many American works for the instrument.

H. W. Eichhorn and T. W. Mathis: *North Carolina Composers, as Represented in the Holograph Collection of the Library of the Woman's College of the University of North Carolina* (Greensboro, NC, 1945); B. B. Cassell and C. H. Karnes III: *Cello Music Collections in the Jackson Library*, i (Greensboro, NC, 1978) [Silva Collection]

WINSTON-SALEM. Moravian Music Foundation (*NcWsMM*). The purpose of the foundation when it was created in 1956, largely through the efforts of Donald M. McCorkle, was to preserve and encourage the study of Moravian music in Germany and the USA, but its scope now extends to Protestant hymnody and European music of the 18th and 19th centuries, particularly orchestral and chamber works. The Moravian Music Archives of sacred vocal and secular instrumental music (mainly in MS) used in the Moravian communities of North Carolina contains the Salem Congregation Collection (parts for arias and anthems, *c*1760–1830), the Johannes Herbst Collection (arias, anthems, and larger choral works, chiefly in score, *c*1760–1810), the Collegium Musicum Salem Collection (orchestral and chamber works by 18th- and 19th-century European composers, nearly half in MS), the Salem Band Collection (partbooks containing 18th-century German chorales and American Civil War music), and miscellaneous copybooks and documents. Other collections of the foundation are the Irving Lowens Musical Americana Collection (over 2000 volumes, chiefly tunebooks), the Richard A. Kurth Collection of compositions and arrangements, and the Peter Memorial Library, containing reference works, miscellaneous 18th- and 19th-century editions, and MSS. The foundation now administers the collections of the Moravian Archives in Bethlehem, Pennsylvania (see below).

Many Moravian works have been published in modern editions, and a half-yearly *Bulletin* is issued (1956–). D. M. McCorkle: "The Moravian Contribution to American Music," *Notes*, xiii (1955–6), 597; D. M. McCorkle: *Moravian Music in Salem: a German-American Heritage* (diss., Indiana U., 1958); M. Gombosi: *Catalog of the Johannes Herbst Collection* (Chapel Hill, 1970); J. S. Ingram: "Repertory and Resources of the Salem Collegium Musicum, 1780–1790," *FAM*, xxvi (1979), 267; F. Cumnock: *Catalog of the Salem Congregation Collection* (Chapel Hill, 1980)

NORTH DAKOTA

Local music history sources can be found at the University of North Dakota (*NdU*) in Grand Forks.

OHIO

Among the academic libraries in Ohio other than those listed below, Bowling Green State University (*OBgU*) specializes in popular culture, and Wittenberg University (*OSW*) in Springfield has important Lutheran hymnals, including the materials of the Hymn Society of America. Case Western Reserve University (*OClW-S*) in Cleveland, the Cleveland Institute (*OClCIM*), Ohio University (*OAU*) in Athens, and Miami University (*OOxM*) in Oxford all claim major music collections. The Organ Historical Society maintains an archival collection through Ohio Wesleyan University (*ODW*) in Delaware.

BEREA. Baldwin-Wallace College (*OBerB*). The general music collections here are divided between the *Ritter Library (works about music, the Methodist Historical Collection including 250 19th-century hymnals, and the Harry E. Ridenour Folksong Collection) and the *Fern Patterson Jones Memorial Music Library (scores and recordings).

The *Riemenschneider Bach Institute was founded in 1969 to promote the collections in its library (located in Merner-Pfeiffer Hall), which include the Emilie and Karl Riemenschneider Memorial Bach Collection, presented to the college in 1950, containing MSS and early editions of Bach's works; the Emmy Martin Collection of first editions from the 17th to the 20th centuries (notably of Beethoven); and the Hans T. David Collection of Renaissance and Baroque materials, acquired in 1970.

The Riemenschneider Bach Institute publishes the quarterly journal, *Bach* (1970–). A. Riemenschneider: "Bach Library at Berea, Ohio," *Notes*, 1st ser., no.8 (1940), 39; S. W. Kenney: *Catalog of the Emilie and Karl Riemenschneider Memorial Bach Library* (New York, 1960; suppls., 1970–)

BOWLING GREEN. Bowling Green State University (*OBgU*). The *Popular Culture Library and Audio Center was founded in 1967 as the recordings center in a new library building; it has expanded to become a major resource for the study of popular culture in the USA. To begin with it acquired its materials chiefly from flea markets and radio stations that were discarding old recordings, but later, as its reputation grew, it attracted gifts from major donors: 1000 rhythm-and-blues 45 r.p.m. discs (1954–9) collected by the sociology professor David Stupple of Ypsilanti, Michigan; several thousand early jazz and rhythm-and-blues recordings from the Cleveland disc jockey William Randle; and the entire collection of rare jazz 78 r.p.m. discs (1925–45) of Alfred K. Pearson of Gardner, Massachusetts. The holdings now number 100,000 $33\frac{1}{3}$ r.p.m. discs, 145,000 45 r.p.m. discs,

45,000 78 r.p.m. discs, and 800 cylinders, with supporting collections of 14,000 items of sheet music, 500 song folios, 1250 reference works (chiefly discographies), journals, dealers' catalogues and auction lists, record release notices, and pictorial materials.

The Center for the Study of Popular Culture publishes the journal *Popular Music and Society* (1971/2–). W. R. Schurk: "A Description of the Sound Recordings Archives at Bowling Green State University," *Journal* [Association for Recorded Sound Collections], xiv/3 (1982), 5; B. L. Cooper and W. R. Schurk: "Huntin' for Discs with Wild Bill: William R. Schurk, Sound Archivist," *Journal* [Association for Recorded Sound Collections], xiv/3 (1982), 9 [interview]

CINCINNATI. Cincinnati Historical Society (*OCHP*). Formerly the Historical and Philosophical Society of Ohio, the society collects genealogies, scrapbooks, published and unpublished writings, sheet music, posters, and other materials related to people and organizations in Cincinnati, southwestern Ohio, and the entire Ohio River Valley. Among the Lucien Wulsin family papers are 60 meters of documents, photographs, and correspondence, 1865–1964, of the Baldwin Piano Co.

——. Hebrew Union College (*OCH*). The nucleus of the music holdings (about 12,000 volumes) in the *Klau Library of the Jewish Institute of Religion is the Eduard Birnbaum Collection, which is particularly strong in cantorial music of the 19th century; it includes a thematic catalogue of European music, 1700–1910, held in the library. An important MS compilation (1791) of the Berlin cantor Aaron Baer contains 447 compositions arranged in a cycle for the year's 53 Sabbath services. In the Yiddish theater collection are European and American materials (1000 music MSS and 3100 publicity items) of the period 1900–30 and "penny" songs, 1890–1910. In addition to personal papers and other MS materials of Jewish musical figures, the American Jewish Archives holds a number of unpublished studies relating to Jewish music in the USA.

E. Werner: "Manuscripts of Jewish Music in the Edward Birnbaum Collection," *Hebrew Union College Annual*, xviii (1944), 420; *Dictionary Catalog of the Klau Library, Cincinnati*, ed. Hebrew Union College (Boston, 1964); *Manuscript Catalog* (Boston, 1971; suppl., 1979)

——. Public Library of Cincinnati and Hamilton County (*OC*). Among the holdings of the Art and Music Department are 29,000 sheet music titles primarily of the period 1910–40, with a separate collection of Cincinnati imprints. The Delta Omicron Composer's Library of 1500 items supplements MSS and printed editions of works by 20th-century Cincinnati composers. There are some 900 indexed volumes of programs of more than 36 symphony orchestras. Within the Inland Rivers Library of the Rare Books and Special Collections Department are typescript texts, posters, and photographs of showboat productions and recordings of calliope and other riverboat music.

T. Kolmschlag: "Cincinnati Public Library," *Notes*, 1st ser., no.8 (1940), 6; Mrs. E. G. Mead: *Catalog of Composer's Library* (Cincinnati, 1977)

——. University of Cincinnati (*OCU*). The Cincinnati Conservatory of Music (founded in 1867) and the College of Music (1878) merged in 1955 to form the College-Conservatory of Music, which became part of the university in 1962. Their library holdings were combined in 1967 and housed in the *Gorno Memorial Music Library (*OCU-Mu*, in the Corbett Center for the Performing Arts). The collections include 19th-century singing-school books, about 3000 items from the library of Everett Helm (early editions of 18th- and 19th-century scores, particularly French, 1750–1850) complemented by the Wurlitzer Collection of rare chamber music of the same period, and the Anatole Chujoy Memorial Dance Collection. Composers' MSS include nine holographs of Edward Burlingame Hill, 75 of Albino Gorno, and sketches and scores by the film composer Leigh Harline, beginning with those he wrote for some of Walt Disney's short animated films in the 1930s.

CLEVELAND. Cleveland Public Library (*OCl*). The Fine Arts Department is noted for its services (indexes, music appreciation courses, concerts) as well as its collection of orchestral parts, partly prepared by the WPA Federal Music Project and used for concerts sponsored by the city. The John G. White Department of Folklore, Orientalia, and Chess contains large holdings of folksongs, ballads, lyrics, and unpublished field recordings of American, Canadian (especially lumberjack), French, Provençal, Spanish, and Italian folksongs.

Catalog of Folklore, Folklife and Folk Songs (Boston, 1964, 2/1978)

——. Western Reserve Historical Society (*OClWHi*). The archive contains the nation's principal collection of Shaker materials, estimated at 90% of all published items (including 16 music editions, books, and pamphlets) and 507 music MSS. There are items of sheet music, songbooks, and tunebooks with midwestern imprints from the mid-19th century, and a complete run of *Brainard's Musical World* (1864–95).

K. Pike: *A Guide to the Manuscripts and Archives of the Western Reserve Historical Society* (Cleveland, 1972); H. E. Cook: *Shaker Music: a Manifestation of American Folk Culture* (Lewisburg, PA, 1973), 252–85, 299; *A Guide to Shaker Manuscripts in the Library of the Western Reserve Historical Society* (Cleveland, 1974)

COLUMBUS. Ohio Historical Society (*OHi*). Among the archival collections here are the papers of Dan Emmett (including song and instrumental MSS and published editions and correspondence) and the music of Pearl R. Nye, an Akron canal-boat captain who wrote and collected canal songs of the period 1870–1937.

——. Ohio State University (*OU*). In addition to supporting various doctoral programs in music, the Music Library has a collection of popular and gospel songs and vocal and instrumental arrangements, the latter mostly in MSS, compiled at radio station WENR, Chicago, by ABC.

B. Ellis: *An Evaluation of the Popular Music Holdings in the Music Library, Ohio State University* (MS, 1977)

OBERLIN. Oberlin College Conservatory of Music (*OOC*). The conservatory and the college maintained separate music libraries until 1964, when both collections were moved into the new conservatory building. Important holdings of the *Mary M. Vial Library (also referred to as the Conservatory Library) include a late 16th-century antiphoner and the holograph of Stravinsky's *Threni* (in Special Collections at the *Seeley G. Mudd Learning Center, as is the Mr. and Mrs. C. W. Best Collection of Autographs, bequeathed in 1948 and containing letters of European and American musicians). The private libraries of the music educator Karl Gehrkens, the clarinetist Gustave Langenus (containing clarinet methods, including the original MS of his own), and the French organ scholar Félix Raugel are also in the Conservatory Library.

Mr. and Mrs. C. W. Best Collection of Autographs (Oberlin, OH, 1967); W. F. Warch: *Our First 100 Years: a Brief History of the Oberlin College Conservatory* (Oberlin, OH, 1967); E. B. Chamberlain: *The Music of Oberlin . . . in Tribute to the Centennial . . . 1867–1967* (Oberlin, OH, 1968)

OKLAHOMA

NORMAN. University of Oklahoma (*OkU*). The Western History Collections in the *Division of Manuscripts includes music and papers of Oklahoma musicians, scripts for the Wichita Mountain Easter Pageants, 1935–47, and recordings of speeches and songs in Indian languages made for the Tulsa Indian Exposition, 1938.

OREGON

Early pioneer music is found at the Aurora County Historical Society in Aurora, the Horner Museum at Oregon State University (*OrCS*) in Corvallis, and the Oregon Historical Society (*OrHi*) in Portland.

EUGENE. University of Oregon (*OrU*). Within the general collections of the *Library are about 20,000 items of sheet music and music by Oregon composers. The Department of Special Collections has music holdings that include 1100 stock arrangements by the dance-band musician Henry J. Beau and 1500 scores and arrangements from the trumpeter and composer Axel Stordahl; personal papers (1909–34) of the folklorist Robert Winslow Gordon, who founded the Archive of American Folk Song in the Library of Congress; papers and performance materials from the band of Red Nichols; and music MSS of the film composer George Steiner (1900–67). The *Randall V. Mills Memorial Archive of Northwest Folklore (in the English Department) holds 200 taped field recordings of Oregon folksongs.

E. F. Soule: "Tutta la forza imaginevole," *Call Number* [University of Oregon Library], xxviii (1967), 4 [sheet music]; M. F. Schmitt: *Catalogue of Manuscripts in the University of Oregon Library* (Eugene, OR, 1971; microfiche suppls.); E. F. Soule and C. G. Olson: *Contemporary Oregon Composers: a List of Works* (MS, 1976)

PENNSYLVANIA

In addition to the libraries described below, the American Philosophical Society (*PPAmP*) in Philadelphia has important scientific holdings on various musical topics, among them American Indian field recording collections. The Pittsburgh Theological Seminary (*PPiPT*) holds the tunebook collections and research files of the hymnologist James Warrington. Pennsylvania State University (*PSt*) in University Park, Temple University (*PPT*) in Philadelphia, the Historical Society of Western Pennsylvania (*PPiHi*) in Pittsburgh, and the Pennsylvania Historical Museum (*PHarH*) and State Library (*P*), both in Harrisburg, have historical collections. The Wimmer Music Collection of St. Vincent College and Archabbey (*PLatS*) in Latrobe reflects the rich musical life of a 19th-century Benedictine community, and Old Economy Village in Ambridge includes early material of the Harmony Society (1805–1906).

BETHLEHEM. Moravian Archives (*PBMCA*; closed – inquiries to the Moravian Music Foundation in Winston-Salem, NC). The archives date from the organization of the Moravian Church in Bethlehem in 1741 and include, in addition to many hymnals and other choral music of the Moravian Church (the earliest from 1545), important special collections of church music from Bethlehem, Lancaster, Lititz, and Nazareth, Pennsylvania, and from Dover, Ohio. They also contain instrumental music of the philharmonic societies of Bethlehem and Lititz.

A catalogue of the sacred music collections of the Bethlehem, Dover (Ohio), Lancaster, Lititz, and Nazareth congregations by R. F. Steelman is in preparation. R. A. Grider: *Historical Notes on Music in Bethlehem* (Philadelphia, 1873) [MS copy in the archives has annotations and illustrations]; A. G. Rau and H. T. David: *Catalogue of Music by American Moravians, 1742–1842* (Bethlehem, PA, 1938/*R*1970) [superseded by various card catalogues]; K. G. Hamilton: "The Resources of the Moravian Church Archives," *Pennsylvania History*, xxvii (1960), 263; R. D. Claypool: "Archival Collections of the Moravian Music Foundation and Some Notes on the Philharmonic Society of Bethlehem," *FAM*, xxiii (1976), 177

PHILADELPHIA. Curtis Institute of Music (*PPCI*). Mary Louise Curtis Bok, who founded the institute in 1924, was a benefactor of the *Library until her death in 1970. In 1931 she purchased from the heirs of Mary Banks Burrell a collection of Wagneriana, which has now been dispersed. The most notable autograph MSS among her many gifts were sold at auction in 1982, as was the Ileborgh organ tablature of 1448. The library has a number of important collections of music for various instruments amassed by former faculty members; these include 18th- and 19th-century printed music and books from the pianist Charles Jarvis, music for double bass from Anton Torello, harp music from Carlos Salzedo (including holograph MSS of his works and arrangements), flute music from William Kincaid, and 1500 heavily marked orchestral scores and parts from Leopold Stokowski. There are also holograph MSS of composers associated with the institute, such as Antheil, Barber, and Menotti.

G. Mapes: *Music Manuscripts in the Anton Torello Bequest* (MS)

——. Free Library of Philadelphia (*PP*). The first planned purchase of music was in 1897, five years after the founding of the Free Library, and a separate Music Department was created in 1927. The Musical Fund Society (established 1820) has supported the library through gifts and deposits. The collections are strong in Americana, with special emphasis on the music of Philadelphia from colonial times, with imprints, MSS, and memorabilia of Benjamin Carr, Rayner Taylor, Alexander Reinagle, Frank Johnson, W. W. Gilchrist, Charles Jarvis, Charles Zeuner, Samuel Laciar, Domenico Brescia, and Frances McCollin. Other important Americana include 190,000 items of sheet music (about 1000 in the Edwin I. Keffer Collection of pre-1850 imprints); similar materials from Harry Dichter, Theodore Presser, and the collectors Edith A. Wright and Josephine A. McDevitt; songbooks, broadsides, psalms, and hymns; American music periodicals dating from the early 19th century; and diaries, correspondence, and pictures relating to Gottschalk. Among the library's historical recordings are the Harvey Husten Jazz Library and early 78 r.p.m. discs donated by the RCA Victor Company.

The Drinker Library of Choral Music, established in 1938 in the office of the Association of American Colleges in New York and supported by the Carnegie Corporation until 1943, was moved to the Westminster Choir College in Princeton, New Jersey, then deposited at the Free Library in 1957. Supported by independent funds, it is a subscription lending library of 16th- to 20th-century choral works, particularly strong in German choruses as translated by Henry S. Drinker. It is complemented by the American Choral Foundation library (also in the Free Library), which has many contemporary works.

The Edwin A. Fleisher Collection of Orchestral Music grew from Fleisher's donation of 4000 compositions in 1929 to about 14,000 works in scores and parts (and many others on microfilm) for orchestra, band, and other large ensembles. Primarily a research collection, it lends to performing organizations under certain circumstances. Acquisitions include 2000 scores and parts (particularly music by American composers copied under a WPA project), the Philadelphia Composers Forum Library, André Kostelanetz's arrangements for his Chesterfield and "Ethyl Hour" broadcasts, and the Max Schmidt music library.

B. B. Larrabee: "The Music Department of the Free Library of Philadelphia," *Library Trends*, viii (1960), 574; *The Drinker Library of Choral Music and the*

American Choral Foundation Library of the Free Library of Philadelphia: Catalog (Philadelphia, 1971); *The Edwin A. Fleisher Collection of Orchestral Music in the Free Library of Philadelphia: a Cumulative Catalog, 1929–1977* (Boston, 1979); A. Milner: "The Fleisher Collection at Philadelphia," *Wilson Library Bulletin*, liv (1980), 305

——. Historical Society of Pennsylvania (*PHi*). Founded in 1824 and on its present site since 1883, the library has a few European autograph MSS but is noted chiefly for its American music of the colonial and federal periods. Its collections are divided between the Library (which holds the printed works, including music) and the Manuscripts Department. Many of the society's works printed before 1820 are made available at the Library Company of Philadelphia (see below) and accessible through its catalogues, and some of that library's MSS (e.g., 45 holographs of vocal and instrumental scores by Fry) are, similarly, accessible here. Among the major MS collections are musical scores and letters of many 18th- to early 20th-century American musicians; smaller collections of music and references to music can be found in the American Negro Historical Society Papers, the Hopkinson family archives, the papers of the Musical Fund Society (from 1820), the Ringgold Brass Band Papers (1870–80), and the papers of Septimus Winner.

H. L. Carson: *A History of the Historical Society of Pennsylvania* (Philadelphia, 1940); *Guide to the Manuscript Collections* (Philadelphia, 1949) [under revision]; N. B. Wainwright: *One Hundred and Fifty Years of Collecting by the Historical Society of Pennsylvania* (Philadelphia, 1974)

——. Library Company of Philadelphia (*PPL*). Founded in 1731, this library has specialized in American history, Pennsylvania imprints, and books on printing, and contains sheet music and musical broadsides. There are items from two 19th-century music libraries: theoretical works from the collection of the pioneer musicologist Albert G. Emerick and musical works used by James Rush for his studies of the human voice.

W. T. Upton: *The Musical Works of William Henry Fry in the Collections of the Library Company of Philadelphia* (Philadelphia, 1946); E. Wolf II: *American Song Sheets, Slip Ballads and Poetical Broadsides, 1850–1870* (Philadelphia, 1963)

——. University of Pennsylvania (*PU*). The Otto E. Albrecht Music Library (*PU-Music*), now in the *Van Pelt Library, was named in 1970 for the music curator of the university libraries from 1937 to 1969, who had amassed some 1800 items of early printed music and MSS. The strength of this collection, established in 1953, lies in music of the 18th and early 19th centuries. French and English operas (notably those from the library of Pierce Butler and his wife, the English actress Fanny Kemble), librettos, and instrumental music are represented by first and early editions. Notable collections in the Rare Books Department of the Van Pelt Library are the library of Francis Hopkinson, which includes three MS volumes (the earliest dated 1759; a fourth is in the Library of Congress) containing songs and music for the harpsichord, a MS partbook of psalms by Farnaby (possibly holograph), and 18th-century editions of Italian and German concertos; letters and papers (1800–40) of the Boston music journalist John Rowe Parker; some 25 cartons of letters and journals of Alma Mahler Werfel, with letters from Mahler, Berg, Webern, and Schoenberg; and the Marian Anderson Archives of vocal scores, correspondence, and memorabilia. The Yarnall Library of Theology of St. Clement's Church, containing musical liturgies, is on deposit here. Other distinguished items include a 14th-century volume of poems containing works by Machaut and others, many unpublished 15th- and 16th-century treatises, and several first editions of works by Haydn.

The *Folklore Archives contains recordings of Afro-American, Anglo-American, Greek-American, and Irish-American music from eastern Pennsylvania, Virginia, West Virginia, and Newfoundland, collected through a WPA project and by the folklorists Samuel Bayard, Kenneth Goldstein, and Ralph Rinzler. Also here are the papers of the folklorist MacEdward Leach and transcriptions and tapes amassed by him in Jamaica.

N. P. Zacour and R. Hirsch: *Catalog of the Manuscripts in the Libraries of the University of Pennsylvania to 1800* (Philadelphia, 1965; suppls. in *Library Chronicle of the University of Pennsylvania*, xxxv–xxxvii, 1969–71); C. Richards: *An Eighteenth-century Music Collection* (thesis, U. of Pennsylvania, 1968) [Hopkinson library]; A. Klarmann and R. Hirsch: "A Note on the Alma Mahler Werfel Collection," *Library Chronicle of the University of Pennsylvania*, xxxv (1969), 33; O. E. Albrecht: *A Check-list of Music and Books about Music Printed before 1801 in the Libraries of the University of Pennsylvania* (Philadelphia, 1979); J. L. White: "Biographical and Historical Background of the Yarnall Library of Theology," *Library Chronicle of the University of Pennsylvania*, xliii (1979), 134; N. M. Westlake and O. E. Albrecht: *Marian Anderson: a Catalog of the Collection at the University of Pennsylvania Library* (Philadelphia, 1981)

PITTSBURGH. Carnegie Library of Pittsburgh (*PPi*). When this public library opened in 1895, the nucleus of the music holdings in the Music and Art Division was the library of Karl Merz, founder of the Conservatory of Music at what was then the University of Wooster. Most of the music MSS in the present collection relate to musical life in Pittsburgh: the sketches for Emil Paur's symphony *In der Natur*, the draft of Gardner Read's *Pennsylvania*, and MSS of works by Dallapiccola, Ross Lee Finney, Isadore Freed, Ginastera, Villa-Lobos, and others, commissioned for the Pittsburgh ISCM Festival (1952) and the Pittsburgh Bicentennial (1958). There are autograph letters from Saint-Saëns, Victor Herbert, Ives, Varèse, Walter Damrosch, and others, and documents relating to the early 19th-century singing-school conductor William Evens. The library of the Pittsburgh organist and scholar Charles N. Boyd, which includes material on Pittsburgh music, was purchased in 1938.

Catalog of the Karl Merz Music Library (Pittsburgh, 1892); M. Emich: *Catalog of Music Books and Scores Published before 1801 Located in Carnegie Library of Pittsburgh* (thesis, Western Reserve U. School of Library Science, 1952); T. M. Finney: *A Union Catalogue of Music and Books on Music Printed before 1801 in Pittsburgh Libraries* (Pittsburgh, 1959, 2/1963; suppl., 1964); I. Millen: "Andrew Carnegie's Music Library," *Notes*, xxii (1965–6), 681

——. University of Pittsburgh (*PPiU*). The *Theodore M. Finney Music Library (*PPiU-SF*), organized in 1966, includes the private collection of Finney (chairman of the music department, 1936–68). It is rich in early editions of 17th- and 18th-century music and English and early American popular ballads and hymnbooks; it also holds extensive collections of papers and holographs by the Pittsburgh composers Adolph M. Foerster and Ethelbert Nevin, as well as 800 scores, facsimiles, presentation copies, and recordings of symphonic works presented by the conductor William Steinberg.

In the Special Collections Department of the *Hillman Library (the main library) is Finney's MS collection, which includes in addition to 1500 works of the 19th-century composer Fidelis Zitterbart about 25 folios of monophonic chant fragments from the 11th to 15th centuries (the earliest in St. Gall notation) and a Haydn holograph. The Curtis and Merriman collections contain numerous scrapbooks relating to Pittsburgh and New York theaters from the Civil War to the present.

The Foster Hall Collection in the *Stephen Foster Memorial was established by J. K. Lilly in Indianapolis in 1930 and presented to the University in 1937. It is the most extensive collection of Foster materials, numbering some 10,000 items (holographs and other MSS, correspondence, papers, memorabilia, etc.). First and early editions are represented in *Foster Hall Reproductions of the Songs, Compositions and Arrangements by Stephen Collins Foster* (1933).

F. Hodges, Jr.: "A Pittsburgh Composer and his Memorial," *Western Pennsylvania Historical Magazine*, xxi (1938) [description of the library, p.23]; T. M. Finney: *A Union Catalogue of Music and Books on Music Printed before 1801 in Pittsburgh Libraries* (Pittsburgh, 1959, 2/1963; suppl., 1964); S. P. Kniseley: *Catalogue of the Manuscripts and Printed Music of Adolph M. Foerster in the Music Library, University of Pittsburgh* (Pittsburgh, 1960); N. A. Bowman: *Comprehensive Index to the Merriman Scrapbook Collection on Pittsburgh and New York Theatre* (Pittsburgh, 1966); *CMc*, no.17 (1974), 59; R. F. Schmalz: "The Zitterbart Collection, a Legacy Unevaluated," *College Music Symposium*, xix/2 (1979), 77

PUERTO RICO

In addition to the libraries mentioned below, the Conservatorio de Música (Puerto Rico Conservatory) in San Juan contains Puerto Rican and Latin American music, and the Museo Pablo Casals (Pablo Casals Museum) in Old San Juan houses documents and memorabilia of Casals donated by his widow.

C. Dower: "Libraries and Music Collections in the Caribbean Islands," *Notes*, xxxiv (1977–8), 27; D. Thompson: "Music Research in Puerto Rico," *College Music Symposium*, xx/1 (1983), 81

RÍO PIEDRAS. Universidad de Puerto Rico (*PrU*). The *Biblioteca de Música (Music Library) was established in 1953 and is now in the Agustín Stahl Building with the music department. It contains more than 40,000 items of various kinds (books, scores, recordings, periodicals, and microforms), some of them important sources for Puerto Rican, Caribbean, and Latin American music. A special collection of some 30 bound and indexed albums of local newspaper clippings and printed programs collected by the historian and folklorist Monserrate Deliz covers musical activity in Puerto Rico during the first half of the 20th century. A file of newspaper clippings, concert programs, and materials relating to music in Puerto Rico in more recent decades is maintained, and the library possesses scores (MS and photocopies) by a number of contemporary Puerto Rican composers.

The Colección Puertorriqueña (Puerto Rico Collection), established in 1940, is housed in the *José M. Lázaro Memorial Library (the main university library). It includes books on Caribbean music, essays on musical instruction by Puerto Rican authors, information on Puerto Rican folklore, folk music, and festivals, and printed music by Puerto Rican composers. The Biblioteca Regional del Caribe (Caribbean Regional Library) was established in Puerto Rico as a trusteeship in 1965, and has been housed since 1975 as an autonomous unit in the Lázaro Library. Based on a collection inherited from the Caribbean Commission (1946–60) and its successor, the Caribbean Organization (1961–5), it has books and periodicals on Caribbean folklore (including folk music) and publishes *Current Caribbean Bibliography*.

The *library of the Seminario de Estudios Hispánicos Federico de Onís (Federico de Onís Hispanic Studies Seminary) in the Faculty of Humanities contains books, periodicals, and other publications relating to or printed in Spain and Hispanic America, including folklore, music, and zarzuela librettos.

SAN JUAN. Archivo General de Puerto Rico (Puerto Rico General Archive). The original library, the Archivo General del Estado, was destroyed by fire in 1926 but reopened in 1955; it has been at its present location since 1973. The Music Division houses more than 5000 MSS (the earliest dated 1859), in addition to sketchbooks and early editions by Puerto Rican composers. Important collections include those of the composer Alfredo Romero (about 400 works by him and Braulio Dueño Colón), Antonio Otero (works by R. Retana and José Ignacio Quintón, who is also represented in other collections), the composer Braulio Dueño Colón (donated by his daughter in 1973 and containing about 200 MSS of his works), Herminio Brau (donated in 1974 and containing about 700 MSS, first editions, and items of rare sheet music, 1880–1930), and Juan F. Acosta (150 MSS of his *danzas*), as well as the Colección Villavicencio (MSS of Simón Madera). Among the other composers represented are Rafael Balseiro Dávila, Fernando Callejo Ferrer, Domingo Delgado, Monsita Ferrer Otero, Juan Morel Campos, Heraclio Ramos, Juan Rios Ovalle, Luis R. Miranda, Angel Mislán, Arturo Pasarell, and Jaime Pericás.

A complete list of MSS is at the Inter-American Institute of Indiana University, Bloomington. T. Mathews: "Documentación sobre Puerto Rico en la Biblioteca del Congreso," *Historia*, vi/2 (1966), 89–142

——. Ateneo Puertorriqueño. Founded in 1876, the organization sponsors contests for artists, writers, and composers and houses the winning music MSS. Island composers represented include José Aguilló y Prats, Rafael Balseiro Dávila, Monsita Ferrer Otero, Juan Morel Campos, Manuel Gregorio Tavárez, Jack Delano, and Héctor Campos-Parsi.

——. Instituto de Cultura Puertorriqueña (Institute of Puerto Rican Culture). In the institute's library is a small collection of 16th-century Spanish choirbooks, three of them printed. The *Casa del Libro, a separate subsidiary of the institute, has a small but valuable collection, including processionals of 1494 and *c*1500, a Spanish MS choirbook of 1556, the only copy in the western hemisphere of Guillermo de Podio's theoretical treatise *Ars musicorum* (1495), and a neumed Ethiopian MS.

R. Stevenson: *Spanish Music in the Age of Columbus* (The Hague, 1960), 73ff; R. Stevenson: "Caribbean Music History: a Selective Annotated Bibliography with Musical Supplement," *Inter-American Music Review*, iv (1981–2), 36

RHODE ISLAND

In addition to Brown University, the Rhode Island Historical Society (*RHi*) in Providence and the Providence Public Library (*RP*) document regional musical activities.

PROVIDENCE. Brown University (*RPB*). The *John Hay Library (*RPB-JH*) has several collections containing music. The C. Fiske Harris Collection of American Poetry and Plays, given to the library in 1884, has been considerably enlarged through the acquisition of parts of the libraries of Harry T. Burleigh, Jerome Kern, and Ewen McColl. There are many music imprints of 1820–60, including dramatic music, songbooks, broadsides, and materials relating to music publishing in Boston (particularly the Graupner firm), and songsters from 1779 onwards. The sheet music collection, which was developed chiefly through the efforts of one of its former curators, S. Foster Damon, consists of about 150,000 vocal works, 100,000 instrumental items, 300 bound volumes, 100,000 folio orchestrations, and 100,000 miscellaneous items from which several subject collections have been culled. The Hamilton C. MacDougall Collection of about 3000 hymnals and psalters is noted for its early 18th-century Moravian and Shaker works, and sheet music of the Civil War period can be found in the McLellan Lincoln Collection.

American music printed before 1801 is collected and indexed by the *John Carter Brown Library (*RPJCB*), which is strong in early music of the Americas; it owns a 1604 publication of Juan Navarro. It also holds a 12th-century MS gradual from Ottobeuren for Benedictine use.

The *Annmary Brown Memorial Library collects incunabula, including theoretical treatises on music and liturgical works. The *John D. Rockefeller, Jr., Library (the main university library) contains the collection that supports the music curriculum and is strong in ethnomusicological materials. The formation of a *music library is in progress.

L. C. Wroth: *The First Century of the John Carter Brown Library: a History and Guide to the Collection* (Providence, 1946); S. F. Damon: "The Harris Collection of Sheet Music," *Books at Brown*, xiii (May 1951), 1; A. Banks: "They're not Writing Songs like that Anymore," *Brown Alumni Monthly* (March 1973), 24 [sheet music]; *Dictionary Catalog of the Harris Collection of American Poetry and Plays* (Boston, 1974; suppl., 1977) [partial listing]; *Music in Colonial America* (1975) [exhibition catalogue]

SOUTH CAROLINA

Important local music history materials can be found in the South Carolina Historical Society (*ScHi*) in Charleston, at the University of South Carolina (*ScU*) in Columbia, and at Converse College (*ScSpC*) in Spartanburg.

SOUTH DAKOTA

VERMILLION. University of South Dakota (*SdU*). Founded in 1966 by Arne B. Larson, the *Shrine to Music Museum and Library, which contains his collection of some 1800 instruments, holds the Golden Age of Bands collection (175 meters of band and dance-band arrangements, including MS parts used in the Midwest around 1900 by bands of central European origin), supplemented by photographs and recordings. The sheet-music collection numbers some 20,000 items from 1880 onwards, including the stock of several music stores in the region. In the Oral History Center (in the *W. H. Over Museum) are tapes of music recorded in the northern Great Plains, including that of the American Indians of South Dakota, and oral documentation of the construction and use of musical instruments.

A. P. Larson, ed.: *Catalog of the Collections* (Vermillion, SD, 1980–) [instrument collections]

TENNESSEE

In addition to the libraries cited below, the Southern Baptist Convention Historical Commission (*TNSB*) has sacred music sources and the Vanderbilt University Library (*TNJ*) has materials from the Peabody Conservatory; both are in Nashville. Local music documents can be found in the Southern Music Archive at Memphis State University (*TMM*), and Harry Godwin (also in Memphis) has an important collection of early jazz and blues.

KNOXVILLE. University of Tennessee (*TU*). The *Music Library (in the Music Building) holds the personal library (1600 scores) of the pianist and St. Louis teacher Gottfried Galston (1879–1950). Galston's MSS and memorabilia, together with those of Ferruccio Busoni, form the Galston–Busoni Archive in the Special Collections Department of the *James D. Hoskins Library, which also contains shape-note tunebooks, minstrel songbooks, and sheet music with Tennessee imprints.

P. S. Bayne: *The Gottfried Galston Music Collection and the Galston–Busoni Archive* (Knoxville, 1978)

NASHVILLE. Country Music Foundation (*TNC*). The *Library and Media Center of the foundation is a research facility for the study of country music and related genres, and as such collects books, periodicals (including ephemeral fan magazines), audio and video recordings, manufacturers' catalogues, correspondence (including letters of Jimmie Rodgers, 1897–1933), memorabilia, programs, and posters relating to bluegrass, country music, and gospel. The Roy Acuff collection has been inventoried.

The foundation publishes the *Journal of Country Music*, begun in 1970 as a newsletter.

——. Fisk University (*TNF*). In Special Collections of the *University Library is the George Gershwin Memorial Collection, the composer's personal library. It was presented by Carl Van Vechten in 1944 along with his own scrapbooks containing letters from Mary Garden, Stravinsky, Adelina Patti, Saint-Saëns, and others. The library also has papers and music of the Jubilee Singers, Countee P. Cullen, W. C. Handy, James Weldon Johnson, Scott Joplin, and others.

Selected Items from the George Gershwin Memorial Collection, ed. Fisk University Library (Nashville, 1947) [exhibition catalogue]

——. Tennessee State Library and Archives (*T*). Music and papers concerning music in Nashville, the state of Tennessee, and the South are found in a number of collections here. Of primary interest is the sheet music collection of the violinist Kenneth Daniel Rose (1888–1960), some 10,000 items in addition to his papers and the MS of his unpublished three-volume study *Pioneer Nashville: its Songs and Tunes, 1780–1860*.

K. D. Rose: "The Story of a Music Collection," *Tennessee Historical Quarterly*, xv (1956), 356

TEXAS

Important libraries other than those listed below are at Rice University (*TxHR*) in Houston and Texas Tech University (*TxLT*) in Lubbock, both of which have early regional materials in their general collections. A branch of the San Antonio Public Library (*TxSa*) specializes in early circus music.

AUSTIN. University of Texas (*TxU*). Music holdings in the *Harry Ransom Humanities Research Center (*TxU-Hu*) have grown rapidly in size and value, especially in autograph music MSS and letters of French composers (notably Debussy, Fauré, Ravel, Dukas, and Roussel), of which this library is now the largest American repository. The first major acquisitions (in 1958) were 10,000 volumes from the violinist and collector Edwin Bachmann, of which 600 are first and early editions of works by major composers, and a few autograph letters and MSS. In 1969 H. P. Kraus donated a collection of 4000 librettos from the early 17th century to the 20th.

The earliest MS is an 11th-century treatise, *Epistola Hieronimi ad Dardanum de generibus musicorum*. Although there are a few 14th-century chant MSS and four Spanish provincial MSS from the 15th and 16th centuries, the bulk of the sacred music consists of later Catholic and Calvinist psalms and hymns in the vernacular, chiefly purchased in 1980 from the library of Alfred Cortot (see Oliphant and Zigal, short-title list). Other early MSS include a 17th-century compilation by John Gostling, containing anthems by Purcell and others (facs., 1977), and an Italian trumpet tablature of *c*1620. Later music MSS and letters of interest, in addition to the French works cited above, are those of David Guion, Paul Bowles, and Ezra Pound and, in the Edith Sitwell Collection, the holograph of William Walton's *Façade*.

The center's collections are strong in popular materials, housed mainly in the Hoblitzelle Theatre Arts Library. There are about 10,000 minstrel items (1830–1940), 75,000 items of vaudeville music, 15,000 pieces of sheet music, playbills, biographical and photograph files, and the Joe E. Ward Collection of materials on American circuses, 1850–1950. In 1981 the library acquired the papers and jazz collection of Ross Russell, the founder of Dial Records.

Incorporated in the large general collection of the *Performance Library (in the music department) is chamber music from the library of Adolfo Betti, one of the violinists of the Flonzaley Quartet. The *Barker Texas History Center holds, in addition to organizational archives of Texas music associations, the personal papers and music MSS of numerous composers associated with Texas (e.g., Paul A. Pisk) and scholars (e.g., the folklorist John A. Lomax). Its holdings of recordings made by local companies (including black gospel and blues from the 1930s and 1940s) document commercial music in Texas. Established in 1957, the *Center for Intercultural Studies in Folklore and Ethnomusicology contains taped field recordings, especially of black, Anglo-American, and Mexican songs and fiddle tunes, from the South and Southwest.

D. J. Grout: "Music Collections in the Library of the University of Texas," *Library Chronicle* [University of Texas], i (1944), 10; D. B. Jones: *The Adolfo Betti Music Collection at the University of Texas* (thesis, U. of Texas, 1956); C. V. Kielman: *The University of Texas Archives* (Austin, 1967); *CMc*, no.17 (1974), 61; J. T. Escalante: "The Latin American Sound Recordings Collection at the University of Texas at Austin," *Newsletter* [Music Online Computer Library Center Users Group], no.6 (1979), 7; D. Oliphant and T. Zigal, eds.: "Perspectives on Music," *Library Chronicle*, new ser., nos.25–6 (1984) [special issue]

DALLAS. Dallas Public Library (*TxDa*). Local materials in the Fine Arts Division include indexed programs of the Dallas SO and the Dallas Opera, as well as 200 artists' renderings of sets and costumes. The division has commissioned and collected MSS of works by Milhaud, Schuller, Ginastera, and others. In the Manuscript Archives Collection are works of composers born or resident in Texas (a list is available from the library) and the papers of the music educator Marion Flagg and the critic John Rosenfield. The William E. Hill Theater Collection contains several hundred thousand items, including memorabilia related to vaudeville, minstrel shows, the circus, and popular concerts.

L. Grove: *Dallas Public Library: The First Seventy-five Years* (Dallas, 1977)

——. Southern Methodist University (*TxDaM*). In the *Music Library (in the Owen Fine Arts Center) are MSS from German settlements in southern Texas, sheet music, local concert programs, and historical recordings, especially of jazz. The *Fondren Library holds Ferde Grofé's collection of MSS and orchestrations, a complete set of Schirmer's Galaxy Library, and the E. B. Marks Printed Concert Music Collection. The *Bridwell Library of the Perkins School of Theology (*TxDaM-P*) has a large collection of United Methodist Church hymnals and their antecedents from 1737, as well as papers related to the preparation of the 1935 and 1964 hymnals. The *Oral History Collection in the DeGolyer Institute for American Studies contains interviews with various popular musicians.

D. H. Turner and others: *Special Collections in the Libraries at Southern Methodist University* (Dallas, 1973); *Oral History Collection on the Performing Arts*, ed. DeGolyer Institute for American Studies (Dallas, 1978)

DENTON. North Texas State University (*TxDN*). The *Music Library contains about 80,000 volumes and is particularly strong in music of the 20th century. It has acquired two important contemporary collections: 33 MSS by Schoenberg and his letters of 1909–49 to Hans Nachod, and material relating to Duke Ellington. Other contemporary music includes the holographs in the North Texas Composers Archives; the papers, musical MSS, and tapes of Don Gillis; and thousands of sheet-music items and orchestrations from radio stations WFAA in Dallas and WBAP in Fort Worth. Among the earlier research materials are the libraries of two musicologists, the medieval specialist Lloyd Hibberd (including many 18th-century French and English stage works) and the Renaissance specialist Helen Hewitt, who was music librarian, 1940–65.

Special bibliographies compiled by students are on file. A. H. Heyer: *A Bibliography of Contemporary Music in the Music Library, North Texas State College, March, 1955* (Denton, TX, 1955); A. H. Heyer: *North Texas State University Music Library: its History* (MS, 1969); J. A. Kimmey: *The Arnold Schoenberg–Hans Nachod Collection at North Texas State University* (Detroit, 1979)

FORT WORTH. Southwestern Baptist Theological Seminary (*TxFS*). The *Music Library (in the School of Church Music) contains perhaps the largest single collection of Baptist music (hymnals, gospel songbooks, and tunebooks, 1780–1940, in English and in other languages) and maintains a choral octavo collection of some 27,000 items.

S. Thompson: "A Library of, and for, Music," *Pioneer*, xxiv (1961), 10

WACO. Baylor University (*TxWB*). Noted among the special collections in the *Crouch Music Library is the Frances G. Spencer Collection of American Printed Music, which was presented in 1965 and contains about 27,000 pieces of sheet music (strongest in theater, film, and black music), songsters, and light opera scores from the late 18th century to the 1950s. It is complemented by the Travis Johnson Collection of early American songbooks. There are also large holdings of sacred and wind-ensemble music, musical MSS and papers of the composer David Guion, and, in the J. W. Jennings Collection, medieval MSS and early printed music. The *Armstrong Browning Library (*TxWB-B*) contains musical settings of poetry by Robert and Elizabeth Barrett Browning.

Master's theses, including J. Minniear's *Annotated Catalog of the Rare Music Collection in the Baylor University Library* (Baylor U., 1963) and supplements to it by other students, serve as unpublished finding aids. S. K. C. East: *Browning Music: a Descriptive Catalog of the Music . . . in the Armstrong Browning Library, 1972* (Waco, TX, 1973); S. McCullogh: *David Guion and the Guion Collection* (thesis, Baylor U., 1975)

UTAH

In addition to the libraries mentioned below, Southern Utah State College (*UCS*) in Cedar City is among the recipients of the opera and theater-music benefactions of John Laurence Seymour; Utah State Historical Society (*UHi*) in Salt Lake City has biographical materials on local musicians; and extensive holdings of Mormon musical materials, including the papers of musicians in the Tabernacle Choir, can be found in the library and archives of the Church of Jesus Christ of Latter-Day Saints (*USlC*), also in Salt Lake City.

PROVO. Brigham Young University (*UPB*). A large quantity of MS and published orchestral music for stage and radio can be found in the *Harold B. Lee Library in the collections of Josef Bonime, Percy Faith, Republic Pictures, Capitol Records, and the Radio-Keith-Orpheum (RKO) vaudeville circuit (a typescript description of which was prepared by its donor, Willard Gleeson). Sheet music is found mainly in the Harry F. Bruning collection of bound volumes. Supplementing her collection of early instruments (in the *Music Department) are the papers of Lotta van Buren (1877–1960), which relate to her restoration of and performance on these instruments. The William Primrose Viola Library, comprising his papers, music, MSS, and discs, was founded in 1977 as a resource collection to be expanded. Research materials in Mormonism include a virtually complete collection of Mormon hymnals from 1835. Field recordings of the music of the Ute Indian Reservation can be found here and in the *Folklore Archives of the Department of English.

H. M. Knight: *Brigham Young University Library Centennial History: 1875–1975* (Provo, UT, 1976); D. Day: "Brigham Young University: William Primrose Viola Library," *CMc*, no.28 (1979), 9

SALT LAKE CITY. University of Utah (*UU*). In the *Marriott Library are the papers and library of the musicologist Hugo Leichtentritt, the papers and MS compositions of Arthur Shepherd and Leroy J. Robertson, and published music by 79 other Utah composers.

C. E. Selby: "A Catalogue of Books and Music Acquired from the Library of Dr. Hugo Leichtentritt," *Bulletin* [University of Utah], xlv/10 (1954) [complete issue]

VERMONT

Besides those at Middlebury College, miscellaneous local music materials can be found at the University of Vermont (*VtU*) in Burlington and the Vermont Historical Society (*VtHi*) in Montpelier.

MIDDLEBURY. Middlebury College (*VtMiM*). Scores and discs are separately housed in the *Christian A. Johnson Memorial Music Library. In the *Egbert Starr Library are books about music and, notably, the Helen Hartness Flanders Ballad Collection, which is separately maintained. The 3500 musical field recordings on wax cylinders, discs, and tapes consist of ballads, songs, fiddle tunes, and commentary recorded (chiefly by Flanders) in Vermont from the 1930s to the early 1950s, with supporting printed, MS, and photographic materials. The collection has recently been supplemented by the papers of Flanders's collaborator, Margaret Olney (who was curator, 1941–60), and the folksinger Margaret MacArthur.

H. H. Flanders, ed.: *Ancient Ballads Traditionally Sung in New England* (Philadelphia, 1960–65); D. Cockrell: "The Helen Hartness Flanders Ballad Collection, Middlebury College," *Notes*, xxxix (1982–3), 31; J. P. Quinn: *An Index to the Field Recordings in the Flanders Ballad Collection at Middlebury College, Middlebury, Vermont* (Middlebury, VT, 1983)

VIRGINIA

The 18th-century musical culture of tidelands Virginia is well documented, mostly through an extensive transcript and copying program, at Colonial Williamsburg (*ViWC*). In addition to the music holdings at the libraries described below, Confederate music can be found in the Richmond Public Library (*ViR*) and early black sources at the Hampton Institute (*ViHal*). An important Mennonite hymnal collection is at the Menno Simons Historical Library (*ViHarEM*) in Harrisonburg. The Keith C. Clark hymnology collection, formerly in Houghton, New York, is now at CBN University in Virginia Beach (affiliated with the Christian Broadcasting Network). Sweet Briar College (*ViSwC*) has the library of Sigrid Onegin, and George Mason University (*ViFGM*) in Fairfax holds the archives of the WPA Federal Theater Project.

CHARLOTTESVILLE. University of Virginia (*ViU*). The *Alderman Library (the main university library) houses the Monticello Music Collection of MS and printed music of the period 1723–90 associated with the family of Thomas Jefferson, partly from his own library. Included are MS copies of contemporary nursery songs, made by his descendants, and a rare copy of Hopkinson's songs. Other 18th-century materials are the Alexander MacKay-Smith collection of European chamber music and instrumental tutors and the Mather Collection of nine editions of the Bay Psalm Book (1698–1773). There is a collection of 19th-century sheet music, and extensive but disparate collections of 20th-century materials include the library and research notes of the composer and historian of Russian music Alfred Swan; MSS, published music, correspondence, and recordings of the composer and pianist John Powell; and personal papers of Randall Thompson, including MSS and printed copies of *The Testament of Freedom*. Extensive folksong materials, chiefly acquired through the WPA Federal Music Project (1932–41), are found both here and in the *Virginia Folklore Society Archives in the Department of Anthropology.

B. A. Rosenberg: *The Folksongs of Virginia: a Checklist of the WPA Holdings* (Charlottesville, VA, 1969); H. L. Cripe: *Thomas Jefferson and Music* (Charlottesville, VA, 1974); C. Taylor: *A Catalog of the John Powell Collection Housed in the Rare Book Division* (thesis, U. of Virginia, 1975); L. T. McRae: *Computer Catalog of 19th-century American Imprint Sheet Music* (Charlottesville, VA, 1977); M. Velimirović: "The Swan Music Collection," *Chapter & Verse* [University of Virginia Library], v/5 (1977), 20

IVY. William A. Little collection. Little's collection of German materials contains some music (18th-century choral and organ MSS and printed editions, and MSS by the 20th-century composer Max Drischner) and related materials, notably diaries and family albums, including one with an entry by Constanze Mozart.

RICHMOND. Virginia Historical Society (*ViHi*). Music and references to it are found among a vast quantity of family papers and in a small collection of 19th-century popular sheet music, printed mostly in the Confederate states.

The society publishes a quarterly, *Virginia Magazine of History and Biography* (1893–).

WASHINGTON

In addition to the libraries described below, local music sources can be found in the Seattle Public Library (*WaS*).

SEATTLE. University of Washington (*WAU*). The Hazel Gertrude Kinscella Collection of Americana in the *Music Library contains a large number of early tunebooks and a number of items related to Edward and Marian MacDowell; it is supplemented by a sheet-music collection of 10,000 items. Erich Offenbacher's extensive holdings of Mozart's vocal music on disc was donated to the library in 1978, augmenting the Melvin Harris collection of early recordings of wind music and a large recorded ethnomusicological collection, part of which is housed in the *Archives of Ethnic Music and Dance at the School of Music and Center for Asian Arts. The Music Library also owns 128 letters, 1867–1912, of Jules Massenet; ten others, of Béla Bartók, dated 1941–3, are housed in the School of Music Archives in the *Suzzallo Library.

CMc, no.17 (1974), 62

SPOKANE. Moldenhauer Archives. The pianist and musicologist Hans Moldenhauer has amassed one of the largest private collections in the world of holograph MSS, letters, and documents. It is particularly rich in materials of the 20th century, although autographs of other periods also abound. The Anton Webern Archive (a separate subdivision) is the largest repository of the composer's works and associated documents, and the music of Schoenberg and Berg is especially well represented. Since 1971 Moldenhauer has sold parts of the collection to Northwestern University in Evanston (chiefly MSS of Italian and English composers; see Illinois above), the Bayerische Staatsbibliothek, Munich (MSS of the composers Richard Strauss and Max Reger), the Stadtbibliothek, Vienna (MSS of 18th- and 19th-century Viennese composers), Washington State University in Pullman (the estate of the conductor Hans Rosbaud), and Harvard University (the Americana portion of the collection; see Massachusetts, Cambridge, Harvard University).

A catalogue of the collection is in preparation. H. Moldenhauer: "From my Autograph Collection: C. Ph. E. Bach–Dittersdorf–Mozart," *Kongressbericht: Wien, Mozartjahr 1956*, ed. E. Schenk (Graz, Austria, and Cologne, Germany, 1958), 412; P. Nettl: "Hans Moldenhauer, Pionier der Musikwissenschaft: seine Sammlung in Spokane," *Festschrift Alfred Orel zum 70. Geburtstag* (Wiesbaden, Germany, and Vienna, 1960), 133; H. Moldenhauer: "A Webern Archive in America," *Anton von Webern: Perspectives* (Seattle, 1966), 117–66 [catalogue of the holdings]; "Die Wiener Stadtbibliothek erwarb Musikautographen aus der Moldenhauer-Sammlung," *ÖMz*, xxxvi (1981), 160

WEST VIRGINIA

Regional music history sources have been collected at West Virginia University (*WvU*) in Morgantown.

WISCONSIN

In addition to the libraries mentioned below, circus music is found at the Circus World Museum (*WBaraC*) in Baraboo, and works for barbershop quartet have been collected by the Old Songs Library at Harmony Hall (*WKenOS*) in Kenosha. The Milwaukee Public Library (*WM*) has a diversified collection of local historical materials serving local needs.

MADISON. State Historical Society of Wisconsin (*WHi*). MSS in the Archives Division include 99 boxes of personal papers and music, including MS scores of the composer Marc Blitzstein; 53 holograph orchestrations by Nelson Riddle of songs with lyrics by Ira Gershwin, each signed by them and Ella Fitzgerald; 40 boxes of papers (1935–69), MS sketches, and scores by the composer Ernest Gold; 1000 MS scores and parts (some of them arrangements) by the bandleader Skitch Henderson; 464 boxes of archival papers (1923–60) and 3200 disc recordings of NBC; and 186 boxes of rental scores, stage managers' guides, and scripts of musical comedies and operas (1790–1925) from the Tams–Witmark Music Library.

S. L. Sundell: *An Index to Selected Music in the State Historical Society of Wisconsin* (MS, 1977)

——. University of Wisconsin (*WU*). The Charles H. Mills Music Library (in the *Memorial Library) has about 10,000 items of Tams–Witmark materials similar to those in the State Historical Society (see above), as well as the Leo Kissel Collection of 907 theater orchestrations of European and American music performed in Milwaukee theaters from 1881. The holdings also include a holograph score of John Knowles Paine's symphonic poem *The Tempest* and the published music from his library, and the papers of Helene Stratman–Thomas Blotz, which include notes and field recordings of Wisconsin folk music of German, Polish, French-Canadian, Cornish, Scandinavian, and American Indian origin collected in the 1940s.

MILWAUKEE. University of Wisconsin, Milwaukee (*WMUW*). The music collection in the *Golda Meir Library is beginning to acquire music of the ethnic groups of the region. It has received the Archive of the American Arriaga Society, concerned with the works of Juan de Arriaga (1806–26), and the papers of the pianist Nellie Hobbs Smythe (*d* 1940), which include her observations on musical life in Wisconsin, Minnesota, and Chicago. The John Dale Owen Collection of recordings of early jazz is now on deposit at the Institute of Jazz Studies at Rutgers, in New Jersey (see New Jersey, Newark, Rutgers).

WYOMING

In addition to the university library below, the Wyoming State Archives (*Wy-Ar*) in Cheyenne has collected documents relating to the history of music in the state.

LARAMIE. University of Wyoming (*WyU*). The *Archive Collections of Film Music were established here in 1968; they include a remarkable number of works for radio, television, and film, and, by extension, big-band music of the 1930s and 1940s, as represented by the works of Les Brown, Bob Crosby, Carmen Dragon, Eddy Duchin, Harry James, Hal Kemp, Nathan Van Cleave, and Hugo Winterhalter. The film-music scores range from symphonic works for "epics" to simpler scoring for animations; most are complete with timing cues. Representative composers are Maurice Jarre (*Doctor Zhivago* and *Lawrence of Arabia*), Adolph Deutsch (musical adaptions for film versions of the musicals *Oklahoma!* and *Annie Get your Gun*), and Eugene Zador (*Quo vadis*, *Ben Hur*, and *El Cid*, among others).

CMc, no. 17 (1974), 64; E. J. Lewis: *The Archive Collections of Film Music at the University of Wyoming: a Descriptive Guide for Scholars* (MS, 1976)

BIBLIOGRAPHY

Class M, Music: Class ML, Literature of Music; Class MT, Musical Instruction; Adopted December 1902, as in Force April 1904, ed. Subject Cataloging Division, Library of Congress (Washington, DC, 1904, rev. 2/1917, rev. 3/1978)

G. S. Dickinson: *Classification of Musical Compositions: a Decimal-symbol System* (Poughkeepsie, NY, 1938); repr. in C. J. Bradley: *The Dickinson Classification: a Cataloguing and Classification Manual for Music* (Carlisle, PA, 1968), 1–43

O. E. Deutsch: "Music Bibliography and Catalogues," *The Library*, 4th ser., xxiii (1943), 151

"Notes for Notes," *Notes*, 2nd ser. (1943/4–) [reports new acquisitions and locations]

O. E. Albrecht: *A Census of Autograph Music Manuscripts of European Composers in American Libraries* (Philadelphia, 1953)

Code for Cataloging Music and Phonorecords, ed. Music Library Association (Chicago, 1958)

I. Cazeaux: "Cataloging and Classification," *Manual of Music Librarianship*, ed. C. J. Bradley (Ann Arbor, MI, 1966), 30

C. S. Spalding, ed.: *Anglo-American Cataloging Rules* (Chicago, 1967, rev. P. W. Winkler and M. Gorman 2/1978)

Music Cataloging Bulletin [Music Library Association] (1970–) [reports changes in classification, cataloguing rules, and subject headings]

D. Seaton: "Important Library Holdings at Forty-one North American Universities," *CMc*, no. 17 (1974), 7–68

C. J. Bradley: *The Genesis of American Music Librarianship, 1902–1942* (diss., Florida State U., 1978); Appx B, "Chronology of the Establishment of Music Collections in American Libraries," rev. as *Music Collections in American Libraries: a Chronology* (Detroit, 1981)

Symbols of American Libraries, ed. Catalog Publication Division, Library of Congress (Washington, DC, rev. 12/1980)

D. W. Krummel and others: *Resources of American Music History: a Directory of Source Materials from Colonial Times to World War II* (Urbana, IL, 1981)

C. Lindahl: "United States," *Directory of Music Research Libraries*, ed. R. Benton, RISM, C/i (Kassel, Germany, and New York, 2/1983), 47–282

MARY WALLACE DAVIDSON, D. W. KRUMMEL
(with DONALD THOMPSON, Puerto Rico)

Library of Congress. National public archive founded in 1800 and supported by congressional funding. Its music holdings are dispersed among three of its divisions: the Music Division, the Motion Picture, Broadcasting, and Recorded Sound Division, and the Copyright Office. *See* LIBRARIES AND COLLECTIONS, §§1, 2, 3; SOUND AND FILM ARCHIVES, §1; and WASHINGTON.

Lichtenwanger, William (John) (*b* Asheville, NC, 28 Feb 1915). Music librarian. He attended the University of Michigan (BM 1937, MM 1940) and did further graduate work at Indiana University. He was music librarian at the University of Michigan (1937–40), then joined the staff of the Library of Congress, where he served as head of the music reference section (1960–74).

Lichtenwanger's principal interests as a librarian were music reference problems and services, and musical lexicography. He was general editor of the "Bibliography of Asiatic Musics" published in *Notes* (1947–51) and of one volume of *Church Music and Musical Life in 18th-century Pennsylvania* (1947), contributed to *Collier's Encyclopedia* (1947–51), and has also written for the *Dictionary of American Biography* (1958–73) and *Notable American Women, 1607–1950* (1971). In 1960–63 he was editor of *Notes*, the journal of the Music Library Association. As co-compiler (with Laura Gilliam) of the checklist of instruments in the Dayton C. Miller Collection (1961) Lichtenwanger was responsible for providing a guide to the large collection of flutes housed in the Library of Congress; he was also chairman of the committee of the Music Library Association that compiled *A Survey of Musical Instruments Collections in the United States and Canada* (1974). With Carolyn Lichtenwanger he edited Wayne D. Shirley's analytical index to *Modern Music* (1976), and he edited and annotated *Oscar Sonneck and American Music* (1983), a collection of essays by and about Sonneck. In the early 1980s much of Lichtenwanger's time went to the preparation of a catalogue of the works of Cowell (published in 1986).

PAULA MORGAN

Lieberson, Goddard (*b* Hanley, Staffordshire, England, 5 April 1911; *d* New York, 29 May 1977). Recording executive and composer. Brought to the USA in childhood, he grew up in Seattle. After studying composition with George Frederick McKay at the University of Washington and Bernard Rogers at the Eastman School, he worked as a teacher and critic in Rochester. In 1936 he went to New York, where he continued to write criticism (sometimes under the pseudonym "John Sebastian") and composed; he was one of the founders in 1938 of the American Composers Alliance. He joined the classical music (Masterworks) department of Columbia Records in 1939, becoming the company's president as well as a vice-president and director of CBS (of which Columbia Records was a division) in 1956. Lieberson brought the sensibilities of a creative musician to a position of great power and influence that has more commonly been filled by people trained in the law, finance, or marketing. In 1940 he supervised the first recordings of Berg's Violin Concerto and Schoenberg's *Pierrot lunaire* (conducted by the composer). During his directorship Columbia issued important series of recordings of modern American music and works by black composers, and between 1947 and 1976 recorded 69 Broadway musicals; Lieberson also inaugurated the company's activities in the areas of the spoken word and documentary recording.

Lieberson's compositions, most of which were written in the 1930s, include incidental music for *Alice in Wonderland* and the ballet *Yellow Poodle*, several orchestral pieces (among them a symphony), a string quartet, and other chamber, choral, and piano works. His novel *Three for Bedroom C* (1947) was made into a film, and a collection of his essays was published privately in 1957. The composer Peter Lieberson is his son. The Lieberson Fellowships, granted to young composers by the American Academy and Institute of Arts and Letters, were established in his memory in 1978.

BIBLIOGRAPHY

C. Reis: *Composers in America: Biographical Sketches* (New York, 3/1938 of *American Composers*, rev. and enlarged 4/1947/*R*1977)

"Lieberson, Goddard," *CBY 1976*

LEONARD BURKAT

Lieberson, Peter (*b* New York, 25 Oct 1946). Composer, son of the recording executive and composer Goddard Lieberson. After early piano lessons he abandoned music until his college years, when he returned to the piano and worked as a production engineer for WNCN-FM, New York. After completing a degree in English literature at New York University (1972) he began theory work through the Juilliard Extension Divison. He studied informally with Babbitt for several years, later formally with Wuorinen and Sollberger at Columbia University, where he received an MA in composition in 1974. A performance of his *Variations* for solo flute by the Group for Contemporary Music (1972) led to commissions and performances from, among others, Speculum Musicae, the Berkshire Music Center, Boulez and the New York PO, and Tashi. In 1972 Lieberson was an assistant to Leonard Bernstein and assistant producer of the Young People's Concerts for CBS; he also founded and conducted two contemporary music groups, the Composer's Ensemble and New Structures Ensemble. He was awarded the Rapoport Prize in 1972, the Ives scholarship of the National Institute of Arts and Letters in 1973, and the Goddard Lieberson Fellowship in 1984.

Lieberson devoted the years 1976–81 to the study of Tibetan Buddhism, attending a seminary in Boulder, Colorado, and founding a meditation program in Boston. In 1981 he began doctoral studies in composition at Brandeis University with Martino and Boykan. He had already begun his Piano Concerto, commissioned by the Boston SO for its centennial and written for Peter Serkin, who played the première under Ozawa on 22 April 1983. It is a large, romantically virtuoso score in three connected movements, conceived as a reflection of the Buddhist concepts of "Earth," "Man," and "Heaven." The most overt musical influences are of Stravinsky and the syncopations of popular song, though the piece employs a 12-tone set (dominated by major 2nds) and its derivations in a gradual expansion from dense, rhythmically active textures in "Earth" to the airy, widespread, shimmering colors of "Heaven." As a result of the work's success the Boston SO commissioned Lieberson to write a symphony.

WORKS

Variations, fl, 1971; Motetti di Eugenio Montali, S, A, cl, b cl, harp, pf, 1971–2; Double Entendre (Shelley, Swift), S, fl, cl, va, 1972; Conc., 4 inst groups, 1972–3; Conc., vc, 12 insts, 1974; Pf Fantasy, 1975; Accordance, a fl, b cl, vib/glock, harp, pf, va, db, 1975–7; Tashi Qt, cl, vn, vc, pf, 1978–9; Pf Conc., 1980–83; 3 Songs (Penick), S, chamber orch, 1982; Lalita (Chamber Variations), fl + pic, ob, cl + b cl, hn, perc, vn, va, vc, db, pf, 1984

Principal publisher: G. Schirmer

BIBLIOGRAPHY

R. Dyer: "Peter Lieberson: a Composer who makes Music Talk," *Boston Globe* (17 April 1983), A2

STEVEN LEDBETTER

Liebling, Emil (*b* Pless [now Pszczyna, Poland], 12 April 1851; *d* Chicago, IL, 20 Jan 1914). German pianist, composer, writer, and teacher. He was the brother of George (Lothar) Liebling (1865–1946), who was also a musician. He studied piano with Heinrich Ehrlich and Theodore Kullak in Berlin, with Joseph Dachs in Vienna, and with Liszt in Weimar. He also studied composition with Heinrich Dorn in Berlin. From 1872 to 1874 he taught in Chicago, and from 1874 to 1876 at the Kullak Academy in Berlin. After returning to Chicago, he became established as a noted performer, teacher, and critic. He wrote many salon works for piano, including *Florence Waltz*, *Feu follet*, *Album-blatt*, Two Romances, *Cradle Song*, Canzonetta, *Menuetto scherzoso*,

Mazurka de concert, and *Spring Song*. He collaborated with W. S. B. Mathews in *A Pronouncing and Defining Dictionary of Music* (1896), edited and wrote pedagogical works on piano playing, and was one of the editors of *The American History and Encyclopedia of Music* (1908).

BIBLIOGRAPHY

H. C. Schonberg: *The Great Pianists* (New York, 1963)

JOSEPH REZITS

Liebling, Estelle (*b* New York, 21 April 1880; *d* New York, 25 Sept 1970). Soprano and teacher. Trained in Paris by Mathilde Marchesi and in Berlin by Selma Nicklass-Kempner, she made her début at the Dresden Royal Opera in the title role of Donizetti's *Lucia di Lammermoor* at the age of 18. She then sang with the Stuttgart Opera, at the Opéra-Comique, and at the Metropolitan Opera (1903–4). In addition to appearing with a number of orchestras in the USA and Europe, she toured with Sousa's band, giving over 1600 concerts. After her 50th birthday she turned her energies to teaching and was on the faculty of the Curtis Institute from 1936 to 1938. Thereafter she settled in New York, where her students included Beverly Sills. She wrote an influential book on singing technique, *The Estelle Liebling Coloratura Digest* (1943).

KAREN MONSON

Lieurance, Thurlow (Weed) (*b* Oskaloosa, IA, 21 March 1878; *d* Boulder, CO, 9 Oct 1963). Composer. He studied cornet and played in various bands around Neosho Falls, Kansas. His first compositions range from marches for band (lost) to the oratorio *Queen Esther* (1897). He served as a bandmaster during the Spanish-American War, then studied harmony and arranging at Cincinnati College of Music for a short period. After two seasons in the Castle Square Opera Company chorus Lieurance returned to Kansas in about 1901 as a piano and singing teacher. In 1903 he visited the Crow Reservation in Montana and thereby began a life-long fascination with the music and customs of American Indians. He made many attempts to obtain a position with the US government for the purpose of collecting Indian music but his offers were consistently declined, though he may have worked as a collector with the Wanamaker expedition of 1908. His first field recordings date from 1911; the results of this and subsequent trips comprise a large and important collection of Indian music now in the Archive of Folk Culture at the Library of Congress. Between 1917 and 1926 he led a touring group on the Chautauqua circuit which presented his arrangements of Indian melodies. After appointment as a faculty member of the Municipal University of Wichita he continued to devote most of his energies to studying Indian culture and was one of several composers who attempted to develop an indigenous American music based on Indian materials. One of his large-scale compositions, *Minisa*, won a Presser award; the majority of his works are songs and piano pieces, many of which he arranged for other forces. His best-known work, the song *By the Waters of Minnetonka* (also known as *Moon Deer*), has enjoyed widespread and enduring popularity.

WORKS

(printed works published in Philadelphia unless otherwise stated)

Stage: Drama of the Yellowstone, lost

Orch: Minisa, 1930; Sym. Sketches – Paris, France, 1931; Trails Southwest, 1932; The Conquistador, 1934; Colonial Exposition Sketches, lost; Medicine Dance; Water Moon Maiden

Choral: Queen Esther, oratorio, vv, pf, 1897; [11] Indian Love Songs (E. D. Proctor, A. Fletcher, Lieurance), SSA (1925); [10] Indian Songs (L. Wolf, C. Roos, Proctor, E. Guiwits, F. Densmore, J. M. Cavanass, Lieurance), SATB (1934); 11 partsongs; many arrs.

Songs, all 1v, pf: 5 Songs (W. Felter) (Kansas City, MO, 1907); 9 Indian Songs (Proctor, Felter, K. Jones, Lieurance) (1913); By the Waters of Minnetonka (Moon Deer) (Cavanass) (1917); Songs of the North American Indian (Cavanass, Fletcher, Lieurance) (1920); Songs from the Yellowstone (Lieurance) (1920–21); 8 Songs from Green Timber (Roos) (1921); Forgotten Trails (Roos), 4 songs (1923); 3 Songs, each in his own Tongue (W. H. Carruth) (1925); 6 Songs from Stray Birds (R. Tagore) (1937); From the Land in the Sky (Lieurance), 3 songs (1941); Singing Children of the Sun (Cavanass, Fletcher, Wolf, Jones, Guiwits, Roos, Lieurance), 16 songs (1943) [incl. 8 repr. from previous collections]

Chamber: over 200 salon pieces for various combinations of 1v, fl, vn, pf, 1904–55, incl. solo pf works; many arrs.

MSS in *KWiU*

Principal publisher: Presser

BIBLIOGRAPHY

Anon. [?T. W. Lieurance]: "Legend of a Famous Lieurance Song," *The Etude*, xxxix (1921), 94

——: "From Broadway to the Pueblos," *The Etude*, xli (1923), 231

——: "Thurlow Lieurance (An Authentic Biography)," *The Etude*, xli (1923), 232

H. G. Kinscella: "Lieurance Traces American Indian Music to Oriental Origins," *MusAm*, xxxvii/24 (1923), 3

E. Reinbach: *Music and Musicians in Kansas* (Topeka, KS, 1930)

J. S. Owen: "Kansas Folks Worth Knowing," *Kansas Teacher and Western School Journal*, xl/2 (1940)

DOUGLAS A. LEE

Ligon, Willie Joe (*b* Troy, AL, 11 Sept 1942). Gospel singer. While still in high school in Los Angeles in 1959 he helped organize a male quartet, the Mighty Clouds of Joy. The original members were Ligon (lead), Elmore Franklin, Johnny Martin, and Richard Wallace; Paul Beasley joined in 1980. The group negotiated a recording contract with Peacock Records and by 1962 was one of the leading male gospel quartets. They began performing in the "hard" gospel style, singing very loudly and rhythmically at the extremes of their vocal range, but were one of the first groups to embrace the softer, contemporary gospel style. At the same time they employed a backup group of two guitarists, an organist, and a drummer, though later recordings include full orchestral accompaniment. The group performs many traditional gospel songs, but in the 1970s they added "message" songs to their repertory – songs with lyrics that permit them to be interpreted as either sacred or secular, for example, *You've got a friend*. This made the group popular with a multiracial and secular audience. They have appeared with such artists as Earth, Wind and Fire, the Rolling Stones, James Brown, Gladys Knight and the Pips, and Smokey Robinson, and have performed in major concert halls throughout the country as well as on television. Ligon possesses a unique voice, with a gritty timbre, that is capable of displaying many different colors and emotions; his range encompasses several octaves. His solo lead has earned two Grammy awards for the group.

BIBLIOGRAPHY

A. A. Burgess: "Can Gospel Rock? No! James Cleveland, Yes! Mighty Clouds," *Jet Magazine*, 1/6 (1976), 23

M. Warrick and others: *The Program of Gospel Music* (New York, 1977)

HORACE CLARENCE BOYER

Lili'uokalani [Kamaka'eha Paki, Lydia] (*b* Honolulu, HI, 2 Sept 1838; *d* Honolulu, 11 Nov 1917). Composer. She was queen of Hawaii from 1891 to 1893, but was deposed by American interests. She was the most gifted of a musical family, and began her musical training at the age of four at the Chiefs' Children's School. She was an accomplished pianist, choir director, and organist, and the first native Hawaiian to be musically literate. Her first published song was *Nani nā pua* (1869), and her most famous composition, *Aloha 'oe* (1878). Her other compositions include *Ku'u pua i paoakalani*, *Queen's Jubilee*, *Ho'oheno Song*, and *He mele lahui Hawaii* (the Hawaiian national anthem). Through her compositions and her transcriptions of traditional Hawaiian chants she was instrumental in synthesizing ancient Hawaiian and Western musical traditions.

BIBLIOGRAPHY

G. S. Kanahele, ed.: *Hawaiian Music and Musicians: an Illustrated History* (Honolulu, 1979)

SAMUEL S. BRYLAWSKI

Limelighters. Folk group. It was formed in 1959 and became one of the most popular and successful groups of the folk-music revival. The members were Lou Gottlieb (*b* Los Angeles, CA, 1923), double bass player; baritone Alex Hassilev (*b* Paris, France, 11 July 1932), who also played banjo; and tenor and guitarist Glenn Yarbrough (*b* Milwaukee, WI, 12 Jan 1930). The group achieved distinction with their skillful arrangements, tight choral harmonies, and polished delivery; their sophisticated and humorous prefatory patter appealed greatly to well-educated nightclub and college audiences. Their repertory consisted of updated versions of traditional American folk music, songs of European origin, and contemporary material of a topical or satirical nature; they issued several successful albums, including *The Slightly Fabulous Limelighters* and *Tonite in Person* (both 1961). After the group broke up in the mid-1960s Yarbrough followed a successful solo career and Hassilev worked as an actor and record producer.

BIBLIOGRAPHY

"The Faculty," *Time*, lxxvii (16 June 1961), 56

E. Linn: "Eggheads with a Big Beat," *Saturday Evening Post*, no.234 (16 Dec 1961), 32

O. Brand: *The Ballad Mongers* (New York, 1962)

K. Baggelaar and D. Milton: "The Limelighters," *Folk Music: More than a Song* (New York, 1976), 228

CRAIG A. LOCKARD

Lincoln, Harry B(arnard) (*b* Fergus Falls, MN, 6 March 1922). Musicologist. He graduated from Macalester College in 1946 and Northwestern University (PhD 1951). Since 1951 he has been on the faculty of SUNY, Binghamton. He has edited and written about Italian secular music of the 16th and early 17th centuries and was responsible for the volume *Seventeenth-century Keyboard Music in the Chigi Manuscripts of the Vatican Library* (CEKM, xxxii, 1968). His edition of the madrigal collection *L'amorosa Ero* (1968) makes available in a practical modern transcription a group of pieces by some of the major madrigal composers of the late 16th century; since all of these pieces use the same text and mode, they provide an interesting comparison of the ways in which different composers approached text setting in madrigals. Lincoln is also one of the principal exponents of the application of computer technology to musical research, particularly thematic indexing; he edited the anthology *The Computer and Music* (1970).

PAULA MORGAN

Lincoln Center for the Performing Arts. Arts complex in New York comprising Avery Fisher Hall, the Metropolitan Opera, the New York State Theater, the Library and Museum of the Performing Arts, and other facilities. *See* NEW YORK, §3; *see also* LIBRARIES AND COLLECTIONS, §3, New York, New York Public Library.

Lind, Jenny [Johanna Maria; Mme. Goldschmidt] (*b* Stockholm, Sweden, 6 Oct 1820; *d* Wynds Point, Herefordshire, England, 2 Nov 1887). Swedish soprano. Having attended the Royal Swedish Opera School from the age of ten, Lind began her career in 1838 when she sang Agathe in *Der Freischütz* with its

Jenny Lind portrayed in the title roles of Donizetti's "La fille du régiment" (left) and Bellini's "Norma": from a broadside (1850) greeting her arrival in New York

main opera company. After a short stay in Paris in 1841 for lessons with Manuel García, she returned to the stage and by the mid-1840s had become one of the most famous coloraturas of the day. She sang in Paris, Germany, Denmark, and Vienna before making her long-delayed and sensational English début in 1847 as Alice in Meyerbeer's *Robert le diable*. Partly to avoid celebrity, Lind turned increasingly to concert and oratorio singing; she gave her last operatic performance in London on 10 May 1849.

In January 1850 Lind signed a contract with P. T. Barnum for an American tour with the baritone Giovanni Belletti and the conductor, pianist, and composer Julius Benedict. She was to receive at least $1000 and all her expenses for each concert; although she would not appear in opera, she would be allowed to select her own concert repertory and be free to perform for charities. When it later became clear that the proceeds would exceed Barnum's expectations, a new contract was drafted which gave her in addition a portion of the profits. Barnum mounted a masterly publicity campaign, and a crowd of more than 30,000 greeted Lind when she arrived on 1 September 1850 in New York (for illustration *see* BARNUM, P. T.; for further illustration *see* NEW YORK, fig.1). Public opinion of Lind was enhanced when she donated her share of the receipts for the first two concerts (nearly $15,000) to charity. Her subsequent appearances in Boston and Philadelphia were equally well received and profitable. The tour she began on 25 November ranged south to Havana and west to St. Louis, and included Baltimore and Washington.

A month after the start of a new season of concerts beginning on 7 May 1851, Lind broke with Barnum. Benedict returned to England, and Otto Goldschmidt, a young German pianist who had accompanied Lind in England, became the music director of a new troupe which gave a number of concerts in Boston and other northeastern cities in June and July. A round of farewell appearances in the Midwest and New England followed, but a series of concerts planned for New York was canceled in late December when Lind learned of her mother's death. Goldschmidt and Lind were married in Boston on 5 February 1852 and spent the next three months in seclusion in Northampton, Massachusetts. In May Mme. Goldschmidt (as she now called herself) gave three farewell concerts in New York. She and her husband then left for Europe, where they settled first in Dresden and then in England. She remained musically active into the 1880s, and in 1883, the year of her last public performance, became professor of singing at the Royal College of Music, London.

Jenny Lind's position in American culture was unique among 19th-century musicians. Nicknamed "the Swedish nightingale," she was held in esteem as much for her contributions to charity as for the quality of her voice and her musicianship, and in the popular mind she became something of a symbol of purity and virtue. At the same time, Barnum's astute management gave her name immense commercial value, not only in the world of entertainment, but in manufacturing as well, where she became associated with products ranging from pianos and sewing machines to cigars; her concert tour was arguably the most successful in American history and marked the beginning of modern promotional and managerial methods. In this sense, Lind's greatest impact was on America's music industry rather than on American music itself.

BIBLIOGRAPHY

C. G. Rosenberg: *Jenny Lind in America* (New York, 1851)
J. M. C. Maude: *The Life of Jenny Lind* (London, 1926/*R*1979)
R. Aldrich: "Jenny Lind and Barnum," *Musical Discourse from the New York Times* (London, 1928/*R*1971), 218
E. Wagenknecht: *Jenny Lind* (Boston, 1931/*R*1980)
G. D. Schultz: *Jenny Lind, the Swedish Nightingale* (Philadelphia, 1962)
E. C. Wagenknecht: *Seven Daughters of the Theater* (Norman, OK, 1964), 3–49
H. Pleasants: *The Great Singers* (New York, 1966), 197
W. P. Ware and T. C. Lockard, Jr.: *P. T. Barnum Presents Jenny Lind* (Baton Rouge, LA, 1980)

WILLIAM BROOKS

Lindsay, (Nicholas) Vachel (*b* Springfield, IL, 10 Nov 1879; *d* Springfield, 5 Dec 1931). Poet. He made his work known in public recitations throughout the USA between 1915 and 1920, having attracted much attention with *General William Booth Enters into Heaven and other Poems* (1913) and *The Congo and other Poems* (1914). In several of his poems Lindsay provided performance directions, such as "bass drum beaten loudly," "sweet flute music," "tambourines to the foreground" (in *General William Booth*); "a deep rolling bass," "solemnly chanted," "shrilly and with a heavily accented meter," "in a rather high key" (in *The Congo*); and "to be repeated three times, very softly and slowly," "here the audience roars with the leader" (in *Daniel*). Sometimes he also referred to well-known hymns or popular songs in his poems, for instance *The Blood of the Lamb* in *General William Booth*; *Hark, Ten Thousand Harps and Voices* in *The Congo*; *Dixie* and *Alexander's Ragtime Band* in *Daniel*; and *East Side, West Side* in *John L. Sullivan*.

Although Lindsay himself was dissatisfied with musical settings of his work ("No musical notation ever invented can express the same musical scheme as the 26 letters of the alphabet"), his powerful musical imagery, folk heroism, and fascination with Afro-American subjects attracted many composers, including Arthur Bergh (*The Congo*), Charles Ives (*General William Booth Enters into Heaven*), Louis Gruenberg (*The Daniel Jazz*), and Sidney Homer (*General William Booth*). Later generations of composers have drawn on him particularly for choral settings. Notable among these are Elie Siegmeister's *Abraham Lincoln Walks at Midnight*, Gail Kubik's *In Praise of Johnny Appleseed*, and Douglas Moore's *Simon Legree*. Other composers who have set Lindsay poems include Norman Dello Joio, Roy Harris, and George McKay.

BIBLIOGRAPHY

C. McGlinchee: "American Literature in American Music," *MQ*, xxxi (1945), 101
C. S. Lenhart: *Musical Influence on American Poetry* (Athens, GA, 1956)
K. S. Diehl: *Hymns and Tunes: an Index* (New York, 1966)
J. T. Flanagan, ed.: *Profile of Vachel Lindsay* (Columbus, OH, 1970)
R. C. Friedberg: *American Art Song and American Poetry* (Metuchen, NJ, 1981)
M. A. Hovland: *Musical Settings of American Poetry: a Bibliography* (in preparation) [incl. list of settings]

DONALD JENNI

Lindy [lindy hop]. A lively and often acrobatic social dance that originated in the Savoy and other Harlem ballrooms and private clubs during the 1920s. It became increasingly athletic and achieved greater popularity in the late 1930s and 1940s when it was performed to the music of the swing bands; during this period the dance was also called the "jitterbug." The exhibitionist nature of the dance was characterized by "breakaway" sections, in which the dancers improvised their own steps; it was also known for its "air" steps (athletic stunts and movements performed in the air) and the "geechie walk" (a strutting step performed with a shimmy). Examples of compositions that were suitable for lindy dancing include *Stomping at the Savoy*, by Benny Goodman, Edgar

Sampson, and Chick Webb (performed by Chick Webb's Savoy Orchestra on a recording of 1934), *Sing, Sing, Sing* by Louis Prima (recorded by Benny Goodman and his orchestra in 1937), and Count Basie's *One O'clock Jump* (1937) and *Jumpin' at the Woodside* (1938). In the 1950s, the lindy served as the basis for some of the dances associated with rock-and-roll.

BIBLIOGRAPHY

M. Stearns and J. Stearns: *Jazz Dance: the Story of American Vernacular Dance* (New York, 1968)

L. F. Emery: *Black Dance in the United States from 1619 to 1970* (Palo Alto, CA, 1970)

PAULINE NORTON

Lining out. The practice whereby a minister, elder, or precentor reads or chants each line, or pair of lines, of a hymn (or metrical psalm) before the same text is sung by the congregation; he does not necessarily anticipate the same melodic phrase that the congregation will sing. The custom is confined to Anglo-Saxon Protestant churches and is found only in association with the OLD WAY OF SINGING (see N. Temperley: "The Old Way of Singing: its Origins and Development," *JAMS*, xxxiv, 1981, p.512).

Linn, Robert (*b* San Francisco, CA, 11 Aug 1925). Composer. He studied with Milhaud at Mills College, 1947–9, and with Sessions, Stevens, and Dahl at the University of Southern California, Los Angeles (MM 1951), where he later became a faculty member (1958) and chairman of the department of music theory and composition (from 1973). He has received grants and commissions from the Louisville Orchestra, the Huntington Hartford Foundation, the American Guild of Organists, and others, and has been a fellow at the MacDowell Colony. His Fantasia for cello and string orchestra (1975–6) was given its première by Nathaniel Rosen and the Los Angeles Chamber Orchestra; in 1981 his music was included in two important concerts devoted to works by Los Angeles composers.

Linn's style is characterized by long, lyric melodies, sonorous, consonant, and nontriadic harmonies, and a use of clear cadences. He often works freely with traditional forms, employing them as elastic frames of reference. The diversity of his works, both in size and instrumentation, demonstrates Linn's dexterity. In particular *Hexameron* (1963) exemplifies his sense of classical balance and deft application of contemporary tone color.

WORKS

Dramatic: The Story Tellers of the Canterbury Tales (film score, Chaucer), 1952; Pied Piper of Hamlin (oratorio, R. Browning), 1968

Orch: Ov. for Sym. Orch, 1952; Sym. in 1 Movt, 1956, rev. 1961; Hexameron, pf, orch, 1963 [reconstruction of Liszt orchestration: Hexaméron, variations on a theme by Bellini]; Sinfonia, str orch, 1967, rev. 1972; Concertino, ob, hn, perc, str orch, 1972; Fantasia, vc, str orch, 1975–6; Concertino, ww qnt, str orch, 1981–2; 2 other works

Large ens: 4 Pieces for Concert Band, 1954; March of the Olympians, band, 1959; Conc. grosso, tpt, hn, trbn, band, 1961; Elevations, ww orch, 1964; Propagula, ww orch, 1970; Conc., fl, ww orch, 1980; Partita, ww ens, 1980; Conc., pf, ww orch, 1984

Inst: Cl Sonata, 1949; 5 Pieces, fl, cl, 1950; Str Qt no.1, 1951; Qt, 4 sax, 1953; 2 pf sonatas, 1955, 1964; Qt, 4 hn, 1957; Duo, cl, vc, 1959; Prelude and Dance, 4 sax, 1960; Brass Qnt, 1963; Ww Qnt, 1963; Dithyramb, 8 vc, 1965; Concertino, vn, wind octet, 1965; Duo, vc, pf, 1971; Fanfares, 3 cl, 1972; 5 Preludes, pf, 1973; Vino, vn, pf, 1975; Twelve, chamber ens, 1976–7; Saxifrage Blue, bar sax, pf, 1977; Trompe l'oeil, b trbn, pf, 1978; Diversions, 6 bn, 1979; Trombosis, 12 trbn, 1979; Serenade, fl, cl, vc, gui, 1982; 3 Pieces for fl, a sax, gui, 1983; many other works

Vocal: 3 Madrigals, 1951; 5 Children's Songs, 1954; An Anthem of Wisdom (Bible), SATB, orch, 1958; 3 German Folk Songs, male chorus, 1959; John Burns of Gettysburg (B. Harte), nar, SATB, pf, 1976; Home from the Sea (R. L. Stevenson), solo vv, SATB, pf, 1976; Songs of William Blake, SATB, 1981

Principal publishers: Lawson-Gould, C. Fischer, Avant Music, Mills Music, Pro Art, Shawnee, Walt Disney

DAVID COPE

Lipan. APACHE Indian group of the Southwest.

Lipkin, Seymour (*b* Detroit, MI, 14 May 1927). Pianist and conductor. He received his musical training at the Curtis Institute, where he was a piano pupil of David Saperton (1938–41), and Rudolf Serkin and Mieczysław Horszowski (1941–7). Essentially self-taught as a conductor, he worked with Koussevitzky at the Berkshire Music Center for three summers (1946, 1948, and 1949) and served as apprentice conductor to Szell with the Cleveland Orchestra (1947–8). He made his conducting début with the Cleveland Little SO in 1948, the same year in which he won the Rachmaninoff Piano Competition. As a pianist, he made his New York début as soloist with the New York PO under Munch (1949) and subsequently performed with most of the major American orchestras. He taught conducting at the Berkshire Music Center, 1951–64, and in 1959 received a Ford Foundation award. He held conducting posts with the New York City Opera in 1958, the New York PO in 1959, the Huntington SO (renamed the Long Island SO in 1975 and the Long Island PO in 1979) from 1963 to 1979, and the Joffrey Ballet from 1966 to 1979; he has appeared as guest conductor with other leading orchestras. After more than two decades of concert activities limited to conducting, Lipkin resumed his career as a concert pianist with a recital in New York (28 February 1981) which clearly confirmed his achievement in that field. He has taught piano at the Curtis Institute (from 1969) and the Manhattan School (from 1972).

BIBLIOGRAPHY

G. Kehler: *The Piano in Concert*, i (Metuchen, NJ, 1982), 753

MINA F. MILLER

Lipman, Samuel (*b* Los Gatos, CA, 7 June 1934). Essayist, pianist, and music critic. He studied piano with Lev Shorr, Alexander Libermann, and Rosina Lhévinne, attended San Francisco State College (BA 1956), and did graduate work in political science at the University of California, Berkeley (MA 1958); he then taught political science at Berkeley (1957–8). He was appointed to the faculty of the Aspen Music School in 1971 and to that of the Waterloo Music Festival, New Jersey, in 1976; he was named artistic director of the festival in 1985. He became music critic of *Commentary* in 1976, publisher of the *New Criterion* in 1982, and in the same year was appointed to the National Council on the Arts. He won the Deems Taylor Award in 1977 and 1980 for criticism and again in 1980 for his collection of essays *Music after Modernism* (1979). His other writings include *The House of Music: Art in an Era of Institutions* (1982). As a pianist, he has appeared in the USA and abroad; he gave the first New York performance of Elliott Carter's Piano Concerto in 1975.

Lipman's critical writings are uncompromisingly rigorous, demanding of composer, performer, and management alike the highest standard of artistic excellence. He deals both with the works themselves and with the philosophical meaning of music, and comments with acerbity on the place of serious music in a media-oriented, middlebrow culture. Lipman is closely allied with the group of neo-conservative thinkers that includes Norman Podhoretz and Hilton Kramer.

PATRICK J. SMITH

Lippincott, Joan (*b* East Orange, NJ, 25 Dec 1935). Organist. Her early piano and organ studies were with William Jancovius. She studied organ with Alexander McCurdy at Westminster Choir College in Princeton (BM 1957, MM 1961) and at the Curtis Institute (diploma 1960), and piano with Vladimir Sokoloff, also at Curtis. She did graduate study at the School of Sacred Music of Union Theological Seminary. She joined the organ faculty of Westminster Choir College in 1960, where she became head of the organ department in 1967. Lippincott has given recitals widely in the USA and abroad (including many American premières), has recorded, and has conducted many summer organ institutes and European study trips. She has had an extensive career as a recitalist and is much admired for her solid technique and her energetic teaching.

VERNON GOTWALS

Lippman, Edward A(rthur) (*b* New York, 24 May 1920). Musicologist. He studied at the City College of New York (BS), New York University (MA), and Columbia University (PhD 1951). Since 1954 he has been on the faculty at Columbia, where in 1969 he was appointed professor of music. Lippman is one of the leading American writers on the philosophy and aesthetics of music. *Musical Thought in Ancient Greece* (1964) is an important exposition of Greek philosophies of music and one of the few compilations of this size and scope in English. In *A Humanistic Philosophy of Music* (1977), Lippman views music in society from the perspective of the historical musicologist and argues his case for music as a humanistic discipline. He has also written on the ideas of 19th-century Romanticism, particularly the music and writings of Schumann.

PAULA MORGAN

Lipscomb, Mance (*b* Navasota, TX, 9 April 1895; *d* Navasota, 30 Jan 1976). Songster and guitarist. Before being recorded at the age of 66 he was a farm laborer and sharecropper in Navasota. He had acquired an extensive reputation in Texas for his effortless playing of dances, such as *Buck Dance* (1961, Rep. 2012) and *Sugar babe, it's all over now* (1960, Arhoolie 1001), and for his singing of old ballads like *Ella Speed*. From 1960 he was a popular performer at concerts and festivals, still playing fluently until forced by ill-health to retire in 1973. In 1971 he was the subject of a film, *A Well-spent Life*. Because of his previous isolation Lipscomb represented the songster tradition in its purest form. His recording of *Freddie* (1960, Arhoolie 1001) is the only collected version of this ballad; he often drew on his earliest recollections, as in *Take me Back* (1964, Arhoolie 1026) or *Captain Captain* (1961, Rep. 2012), a memory of his life as a field hand on a Brazos River plantation. Like all songsters, however, he was catholic in his tastes, and could easily follow these pieces with a popular song like *Shine on harvest moon* or a spiritual like *Motherless Children* (both 1964, Arhoolie 1026). As a guitarist he must be numbered among the most gifted in the black folk idiom; his style perhaps reflects the proximity of Mexican guitarists in Texas, as suggested by *Spanish Flang Dang* (1964, Arhoolie 1023).

BIBLIOGRAPHY

SouthernB
M. McCormick: Liner notes, *Mance Lipscomb: Texas Sharecropper and Songster* (Arhoolie 1001, 1960)
P. Oliver: *Conversation with the Blues* (London, 1965)
P. Welding: Liner notes, *Mance Lipscomb, Vol. 4* (Arhoolie 1033, 1967)

PAUL OLIVER

List [Fleissig], **Emanuel** (*b* Vienna, Austria, 22 March 1886; *d* Vienna, 21 June 1967). Bass. He was a chorister at the Theater an der Wien, then toured Europe as a member of a comic vocal quartet. After immigrating to the USA he appeared in burlesque, vaudeville, and minstrel shows, and then studied with Josiah Zuro. He returned to Vienna in 1920 and made his operatic début at the Volksoper in 1922 as Gounod's Mephistopheles. The next year he went to the Berlin Städtische Oper, and from 1925 to 1933 was a member of the Staatsoper. In 1933 he made his début at the Metropolitan Opera as the Landgrave in Wagner's *Tannhäuser*, and performed there until 1950; his roles included Wagner's Hunding, King Marke, Fafner, Pogner, and Hagen, Sarastro in *Die Zauberflöte*, Baron Ochs in Strauss's *Der Rosenkavalier*, and Rocco in Beethoven's *Fidelio*. During this time he also sang at San Francisco, Chicago, and in Argentina at Buenos Aires, and continued to perform in Europe – at Covent Garden (1934–6), Salzburg (1931–5), and at Bayreuth (1933). Forced by the Nazis to leave Germany, he did not appear there again until 1950, when he returned to Berlin. List had a deep, rich bass which, with his imposing presence, admirably fitted him for the Wagner villains he so tellingly portrayed.

HAROLD ROSENTHAL/R

List, Eugene (*b* Philadelphia, PA, 6 July 1918; *d* New York, 1 March 1985). Pianist. Brought up in Los Angeles, he made his début with the Los Angeles PO at the age of 12. The following year he returned to Philadelphia and won a scholarship to study with Samaroff. At 16 he won a Philadelphia Orchestra competition, and as his prize gave with the orchestra the American première of Shostakovich's First Concerto; he played it again during the next season with the New York PO, with which, under Mitropoulos, he presented the American première of Chávez's Piano Concerto in 1942. He then spent four years in the army, entertained American troops abroad, and gave a notable concert in Potsdam in 1945 at the meeting of Truman, Churchill, and Stalin. From 1946 he toured with his wife, the violinist CARROLL GLENN; in 1952 they were the soloists in Paris for the first performance of Manuel Rosenthal's *Aesopi convivium*, under the composer's direction. A spirited performer, List was an enthusiastic champion of music outside the standard repertory: he played works by Viotti, Domenico Puccini, MacDowell, and, particularly, music by Gottschalk; he played an important part in restoring Gottschalk's music to the repertory, resurrecting a number of pieces that were thought to be lost and commissioning arrangements of several others. He was also involved in discovering Liszt's Duo Sonata for violin and piano (see A. Walker: "Liszt's Duo Sonata," *MT*, cxvi, 1975, p.620). From 1964 to 1975 he taught at the Eastman School, and then joined the faculty of New York University.

BIBLIOGRAPHY

[J. F. Cooper]: "Concert in Berlin," *The Etude*, lxiii (1945), 543
R. Heylbut: "Preparation for Potsdam," *The Etude*, lxiv (1946), 305
N. Bachus: "Eugene List: a Musical Experience," *Clavier*, xviii/5 (1979), 10

S. Isacoff: "Eugene List," *Virtuoso*, ii/4 (1981), 2
H. C. Schonberg: Obituary, *New York Times* (2 March 1985)

GEORGE GELLES/R

List, Garrett (*b* Phoenix, AZ, 10 Sept 1943). Composer and trombonist. He attended California State University, Long Beach, where he studied with Bertram McGarrity, and the Juilliard School (BM 1968, MM 1969); he also studied privately with Hall Overton. As a performer of new music and an organizer of concerts of contemporary music he participated in the first performances of works by European composers such as Berio and Maderna and a wide range of Americans from Cage and his associates in the avant garde to Coleman, Braxton, and other jazz musicians. He was an original member of The Ensemble, the performing group for the "New and Newer Music" series at Lincoln Center, New York, and served as co-conductor with Dennis Russell Davies during the 1973–4 season. He was also music director of the Kitchen from 1975 to 1977. From 1971 he was associated with Musica Elettronica Viva, a group devoted to live electronic music and improvisation, and through it he came into contact with Holland, Berger, and Moses. He has received commissions from the St. Paul Chamber Symphony for conventionally conceived compositions, and with Bayard Lancaster and others he founded in 1977 the A-1 Band to perform and record his jazz-fusion works. In 1975 List accompanied the Creative Associates of SUNY, Buffalo, on a tour of Eastern Europe; his compositions are widely performed in the USA and in Europe. In 1980 he took up a teaching position at the Liège Conservatory, Belgium.

In his music List combines elements of jazz with ethnic idioms and more conservative aspects of contemporary art music. Because of his closeness to jazz and other popular forms, he has been notably successful in making a "music of the people." In such works of the 1970s as *Standard Existence*, which includes a setting of a passage of Studs Terkel's *Working*, List's use of music to make a political statement is apparent.

WORKS

Large ens: Orch Etudes, 12 pieces, 1972–9; 9 Sets of 7, chamber orch, 1975; Songs, chamber orch, 1975; I am Electric, jazz band, 1976; The Girls (S. Terkel), nar, small orch, 1977; Escape Story (E. Friedman), soloists, orch, 1979; Fear and Understanding, jazz band, 1981

Inst: 2 Wind Studies, 9–16 wind, 1971; Songs, 7–12 insts, 1972; Your own Self, any inst(s), 1972; Elegy: to the People of Chile, any inst(s), 1973; Requiem for Helen Lopez, pf, 4–6 insts, 1981; Flesh and Steel, pf, gui(s), inst(s), 1982; Baudelaire, inst(s), 1983; Hôtel des étrangers, 5–21 insts [incl. 1v], 1983; pieces for solo trbn

Vocal: American Images (found texts), cantata, 1v, inst(s), 1972; Standard Existence (S. Terkel, J. Apple, List), 1v, inst(s), 1977; over 30 songs, incl. Now and How (G. List), 1972, Fly Hollywood (E. Friedman), 1v, chamber ens, 1974, Fire and Ice (Frost), 1979, My Mother's Belly (B. Cendrars, trans. A. Levitt), 1979, You are more Beautiful than the Sky and the Sea (B. Cendrars, trans. A. Levitt), 1979

Other: The Man Ray Cycles, 4 film scores, 1983; Time and Desire, dance score, tape, trbn, 1984–5

Principal publisher: Serious Music

BIBLIOGRAPHY

W. Zimmermann: "Garrett List," *Desert Plants: Conversations with 23 American Musicians* (Vancouver, BC, 1976), 287

JOAN LA BARBARA

Listemann, Bernhard (*b* Schlotheim, Germany, 28 Aug 1841; *d* Chicago, IL, 11 Feb 1917). Violinist and conductor. He studied with Ferdinand David, Joseph Joachim, and Henry Vieuxtemps, and for nine years was court *Kammervirtuos* in Rudolstadt. He came to New York in October 1867 and made his début in Steinway Hall the following month. He made his Boston début in 1868 playing Joachim's Hungarian Concerto at a Harvard Musical Association concert, and for the next two years he lived and worked in Boston. From 1871 to 1874 he was Theodore Thomas's concertmaster in New York, but he returned to Boston to resume his career as a solo and chamber music player and conductor. He organized and led the Boston Philharmonic Club and Orchestra, and for a while played with the Mendelssohn Quintette Club.

Listemann was appointed concertmaster of the Boston SO on its formation in 1881, and during his four-year tenure played with the orchestra as a soloist 24 times. He continued his independent career in Boston as head of the Listemann Club, the Listemann String Quartet, and the Bernhard Listemann Company, and from 1893 taught at the Chicago College of Music. Listemann was joined in many of his activities by his brother, Fritz (1839–1909), a violinist, and by his sons, Paul (1871–1950), a violinist, and Franz (1873–1930), a cellist. His *Modern Method of Violin Playing* was published in 1869. According to the obituary in *The Violinist*, "There was no limit to his technical ability, and his interpretation of the most difficult selections had a precision and beauty of rendering which was marvelous."

BIBLIOGRAPHY

J. S. Dwight: "The History of Music in Boston," *The Memorial History of Boston*, ed. J. Winsor, iv (Boston, 1881), 415–64
M. A. D. Howe: *The Boston Symphony Orchestra: an Historical Sketch* (Boston, 1914, rev. and enlarged 2/1931/*R*1978)
Obituary, *The Violinist*, xxi (1917), 99

LEONARD BURKAT

Lithuanian-American music. The music of the Lithuanian community in the USA is discussed as part of the Baltic tradition; *see* EUROPEAN-AMERICAN MUSIC, §III, 3.

Litti, Oscar. Pseudonym of LOUIS MOREAU GOTTSCHALK.

Little, William (*fl* Philadelphia, PA, 1798–1805). Music printer and tunebook compiler. In 1801, in collaboration with William Smith, he published in Philadelphia *The Easy Instructor, or A New Method of Teaching Sacred Harmony*. This volume employed a notation based on fasola solmization – the first shape-note system to gain acceptance. Little apparently filed the title of the book to receive copyright protection in 1798, but no edition published in that year has been traced. The music in *The Easy Instructor* is almost entirely American (100 of 105 pieces); Little himself contributed four works to the volume, while Smith is represented by one. Smith (who is assumed by Kaufman to be the man of that name *b* Hopewell, NJ, 1761; *d* 1808) brought out a second volume of the book on his own (Hopewell, NJ, 1803, 2/1806), but neither compiler was associated with any of the subsequent issues of *The Easy Instructor*. By 1831 it had reached 35 editions, sold several thousand copies, and become influential throughout the country.

See also NOTATION, §1, and SHAPE-NOTE HYMNODY, §2.

BIBLIOGRAPHY

I. Lowens and A. P. Britton: "*The Easy Instructor* (1798–1831): a History and Bibliography of the First Shape-note Tune-book," *Music and Musicians in Early America* (New York, 1964), 115, 292
C. H. Kaufman: *Music in New Jersey, 1655–1860: a Study of Musical Activity and Musicians in New Jersey from its First Settlement to the Civil War* (diss., New York U., 1974)

Little Anthony [Gourdine, Anthony] (*b* Brooklyn, NY, 10 Jan 1940). Soul singer. In 1955 he became lead singer of the Duponts, and then formed the Chesters with Ernie (Ernest, Jr.) Wright (*b* Brooklyn, NY, 24 Aug 1941) and Clarence Collins (*b* Brooklyn, NY, 17 March 1941). In 1958 they regrouped as the Imperials, and were dubbed Little Anthony and the Imperials by the disc jockey Alan Freed in reference to the small stature of their lead singer. The other members of the group during its heyday were Tracy Lord (later replaced by Sam Strain) and Gloucester Rogers. All the members were singers; they used backup instrumentalists. Their first hit single, *Tears on my pillow*, reached no.4 in 1958, and the group continued with some success until 1960. Gourdine then attempted a solo career for a few years, but again reestablished the group in 1964, making a strong comeback with songs such as *Goin' out of my head* (no.6, 1964), *Hurt so bad* (no.10, 1965), and *Take me back* (no.11, 1965).

The Imperials never again attained Top Ten status, but continued recording steadily into the 1970s, breaking up and reforming occasionally but enjoying successful engagements in nostalgia-oriented venues. Gourdine has also had some success as a film and television actor. Their style was derived from doo-wop but soon took on the coloration of the soul-music fashions of the 1960s; their songs were marked by Gourdine's teasing, impassioned tenor (with piercing falsetto extensions) and imploring, gospel-inflected phrasing.

RECORDINGS

(selective list; all recorded with the Imperials)

Tears on my pillow (End 1027, 1958); Shimmy, shimmy, ko-ko-bop (End 1060, 1959); Goin' out of my head (DCP 1119, 1964); Hurt so bad (DCP 1128, 1965); Take me back (DCP 1136, 1965); I'm falling in love with you (Arco 4635, 1974)

JOHN ROCKWELL

Little apple. Social dance popular in the late 1930s and early 1940s using the same steps as the big apple but performed by individual couples rather than a large group; *see* BIG APPLE.

Little-Augustithis [née Little], **Vera (Pearl)** (*b* Memphis, TN, 10 Dec 1927). Mezzo-soprano. She studied at Talladega College, Alabama, then traveled to Paris on a Fulbright scholarship. In 1958 she made her stage début as Carmen in Berlin, where she has been engaged at the Deutsche Oper from 1963, holding the title of *Kammersängerin*. She has appeared at La Scala and also extensively in Germany, including Hamburg and Munich, and in Vienna. Her repertory of 35 roles includes Monteverdi's Ottavia, Wagner's Erda, Saint-Saëns's Dalilah, Strauss's Klytemnestra and Gaea, and numerous Verdi roles. She has also taken part in many contemporary operas, singing Pythia in the first stage performance of Milhaud's *Orestia* (1963), Baba the Turk (Stravinsky's *The Rake's Progress*), Jocasta (Stravinsky's *Oedipus Rex*), Circe and Melantho (Dallapiccola's *Ulisse*), Begonia in the première of Hans Werner Henze's *Der junge Lord* (Berlin, 1965), and Beroe in the première of Henze's *The Bassarids* (Salzburg, 1966). Her warm, vibrant mezzo-soprano encompasses with equal facility the music and styles of composers as diverse as Wagner, Verdi, Strauss, and Stravinsky.

ELIZABETH FORBES

Little Feat. Rock group. It was formed in 1969 by the guitarist Lowell George (*b* Texas, 1945; *d* Arlington, VA, 29 June 1979) and the keyboard player Bill (William) Payne (*b* Waco, TX, 12 March 1949); the other founding members were the bass guitarist Roy Estrada and drummer Richard Hayward. A multi-instrumentalist and former member of the Mothers of Invention, George was the group's leader and principal songwriter. Payne, a classically trained pianist, also wrote songs, and the contrast between his penchant for chromatic harmonies and complex rhythms and George's ornate, blues-influenced singing and precise slide-guitar playing was a feature of Little Feat's style; for example, the song *Strawberry Flats* from their first album set an idiosyncratic chord progression against a country arrangement. On their first two albums they encompassed blues, country music, and basic rock, but George's lyrics were distinctive for their absurd humor (one of his more serious and least characteristic songs, *Willin'*, has been covered by a number of country-rock performers). After the commercial failure of Little Feat's second album, *Sailin' Shoes* (1972), Estrada was replaced by Kenny Gradney (*b* New Orleans, LA), and the group was augmented by the guitarist Paul Barrere (*b* Burbank, CA, 3 July 1948) and the conga drummer Sam Clayton. *Dixie Chicken* (1973), probably their finest album, blended New Orleans funk (recalling the Meters), twin lead-guitar lines (reminiscent of the Allman Brothers), and hints of *mariachi* and gospel music; one song, *The Fan*, in a driving 7/4, is an early example of the group's experiments with jazz-rock.

Little Feat made successful tours and developed a large following, especially in the East and South; but there was continual tension within the group, and its members, particularly Payne, were in demand as session musicians. Gradually Payne and Barrere began writing and singing the greater part of Little Feat's material. *The Last Record Album* (1975) and *Time Loves a Hero* (1977) moved closer to jazz-rock and show less of George's direct influence. However, the double concert album *Waiting for Columbus*, which became Little Feat's only gold record, was a showcase for George's songs and performances. In 1979, after years of work, George completed a solo album, *Thanks, I'll Eat it Here.* He announced that Little Feat had broken up and went on tour with his own group; he died after a performance in Washington, DC. The remaining members completed the album *Down on the Farm* (1979) and then disbanded. Payne and Hayward continued to work as sidemen in studios and on tours, and Barrere toured and recorded with his own group. *Hoy-hoy!*, released in 1981, was a collection of out-takes, excerpts from concert performances, and demonstration tapes.

Throughout a turbulent career Little Feat was more influential than popular; its style mixed funk, blues, rock, jazz, and tinges of classical music, and showed a flair for verbal and musical surrealism. The group claimed many of the popular-music styles of the American South – New Orleans funk, Texas blues, Georgia boogie, and Memphis soul – and added its own clever, self-conscious twists.

RECORDINGS

(selective list; all recorded for Warner Bros.)

Little Feat (1890, 1971); *Sailin' Shoes* (2600, 1972); *Dixie Chicken* (2688, 1973); *Feats don't Fail me Now* (2784, 1974); *The Last Record Album* (2884, 1975); *Time Loves a Hero* (3015, 1977); *Waiting for Columbus* (3140, 1978); *Down on the Farm* (3345, 1979); *Hoy-hoy!* (3538, 1981)

JON PARELES

Little Richard [Penniman, Richard] (*b* Macon, GA, 25 Dec 1935). Rhythm-and-blues and rock-and-roll singer, songwriter, and pianist. One of 12 children, he grew up in a devout Seventh

Day Adventist family and played piano and sang in a local church. Rejected by his father when he was 13, he went to live with a white couple, Ann and Johnny Johnson, who ran a nightclub in Macon, where he gained his first professional experience. In 1951 his successful audition at a contest in Atlanta led to a recording contract with RCA Victor. During the next two years he made recordings with a small group in the jump-blues style of the period. In 1952 he moved to Houston, where he recorded more jump blues, for Don Robey's Peacock label, with the Deuces of Rhythm, the Tempo Toppers and, in 1955, the Johnny Otis orchestra, but he had no success.

Little Richard, early 1960s

After his return to Macon a meeting with the rhythm-and-blues singer Lloyd Price led to his submitting a demonstration tape of his song *Tutti Frutti* to Specialty Records of Los Angeles, whose owner Art Rupe teamed him with producer Bumps Blackwell and a band of leading New Orleans session musicians. *Tutti Frutti* was an immediate success (no. 17, 1956). It was the first of many recordings in a new style, in which the songs were performed at extraordinarily fast tempos (few of them lasting more than two minutes). Little Richard's vocal style ranged from a squeal to a piercing shriek, punctuated by breathless panting, moaning, and semiyodeling; the lyrics, usually nonsensical to begin with, were mostly unintelligible. Though session pianists were reportedly sometimes used, he most often accompanied himself, playing in a pounding, boogie-woogie style, with emphasis on the upbeat; saxophone solos were added, usually by Lee Allen or Red Tyler. During the 1950s Little Richard recorded about 36 songs for the Specialty label, six of which, besides *Tutti Frutti*, became top sellers: *Long tall Sally* (no.6) and *Rip it up* (no. 17) in 1956; *Lucille* (no.21), *Jenny, Jenny* (no.10), and *Keep a knockin'* (no.8) in 1957; and *Good golly, Miss Molly* (no. 10) in 1958. These recordings, all produced by Blackwell, were some of the wildest and noisiest in the history of rock-and-roll; they virtually defined the genre and had a lasting influence on later musicians, including Paul McCartney and Creedence Clearwater Revival. In live performances Little Richard's appearance matched his music: he sported an outrageous pompadour hairstyle, capes decorated with glass, rhinestones, and sequins, and heavy make-up. During this period he also appeared in three rock-and-roll films: *Don't Knock the Rock* and *The Girl Can't Help it* (1956), and *Mister Rock 'n' Roll* (1957).

In 1957 Little Richard renounced his musical career for the Church, following a mystical experience during a journey home from a tour of Australia. He enrolled immediately at Oakwood College in Huntsville, Alabama, where he received the BA; he was then ordained as a minister in the Seventh Day Adventist Church. Between tent-show revival meetings and Bible study, he recorded one gospel album for Mercury, with arrangements by Quincy Jones. It failed to find an audience among either gospel or rock fans, and in 1964, inspired by the Beatles, he returned to rock-and-roll, but recordings on a variety of labels did nothing to restore his popularity.

By the late 1960s Little Richard had become a regular performer in Las Vegas, on the psychedelic-ballroom circuit, and on late-night television talk shows, billing himself as "the bronze Liberace." In the early 1970s he recorded three albums for Reprise, but only *The Rill Thing*, in a style that fused rock and soul, hinted at the power of his earlier work. By the beginning of the 1980s he had returned to the Church.

RECORDINGS

(selective list; recorded for Specialty unless otherwise stated)

Singles: Tutti Frutti (561, 1956); Long tall Sally (572, 1956); Rip it up (579, 1956); Lucille (598, 1957); Jenny, Jenny (606, 1957); Keep a knockin' (611, 1957); Good golly, Miss Molly (624, 1958); Freedom Blues (Rep. 0907, 1970)

Albums: *Little Richard* (2103, 1958); *The Fabulous Little Richard* (2104, 1959); *Well alright* (2136, 1959); *It's Real* (Mer. 60656, 1961); *The Rill Thing* (Rep. 6406, 1970)

BIBLIOGRAPHY

SouthernB ("Penniman, Richard")

L. Winner: "Little Richard," *The Rolling Stone Illustrated History of Rock & Roll*, ed. J. Miller (New York, 1976, rev. 2/1980), 48

D. Dalton: "Little Richard," *The Rolling Stone Interviews: Talking with the Legends of Rock & Roll* (New York, 1981), 88

C. White: *The Life and Times of Little Richard* (New York, 1984)

JOHN MORTHLAND

Little Rock. Capital city of Arkansas (pop. 158,461; metropolitan area 393,774). It is near the center of the state, and its musical life has been shaped by disparate influences: the Anglo-American folk music of the Ozark Mountains, the blues traditions of Memphis and the Mississippi River delta, and the European concert tradition espoused by mid-19th-century German settlers and their descendants. In 1821 a Mr. Fries gave a concert in the Arkansas Hotel; by 1832 monthly concerts were held at the Little Rock Presbyterian Church; and in 1836 a Mr. Wagner offered piano lessons in students' homes or on his own "first-rate German piano." The Ashley Slave Band's first known performance was in 1836; it became famous beyond Arkansas for its appearances at dances, steamboat arrivals, and other events. The ensemble consisted of as many as seven self-taught slave musicians who played string and brass instruments, and it remained in existence until shortly after the Civil War, when most of its members died in a steamboat accident. In 1840 Colonel Sandford Faulkner (1806–74), a local planter, wrote the musical sketch *The Arkansas Traveler*, which achieved national popularity with its utilization of a mountain fiddle tune and comic dialogue.

Mass migration towards Texas and California in the 1840s, the Civil War in the 1860s, and the expansion of railroads in the 1880s brought Little Rock increased population and more wide-ranging contacts. A guide to the city published in 1890 lists five musical instrument dealers and 14 music teachers serving a population of about 25,000. German influence was reflected in the city's beer gardens, annual Mai-Fest, newspapers (including *Staats Zeitung*), and many musical and social clubs. Men's clubs included the Maennerchor (founded in 1882) and Gesang and Zither (1890). Among women's clubs were the Aesthetic Club (1883) and Musical Coterie (1893), both of which continue as members of state and national federations, sponsoring performances by their own members and visiting artists. In 1982 the Arkansas Federation of Music Clubs, with 31 member organizations, presented 17 recitals by winners of national auditions for young musicians.

Although hymn and gospel singing contests are an Arkansas tradition, choral organizations in Little Rock have tended to be short-lived. Among these was the Arkansas State Opera, which produced Gian Carlo Menotti's *Amahl and the Night Visitors* in 1960 and Engelbert Humperdinck's *Hänsel und Gretel* in 1961. The Arkansas Opera Theatre, directed by Ann Chotard from its founding in 1973, has produced two full-length stage works each year and ventured into operetta, children's opera, and sacred works; its 1984–5 productions included *Die Entführung aus dem Serail*, *La bohème*, *Iolanthe*, and the world première of Libby Larsen's *Clair de lune*. Two Arkansas resort areas are used as centers for opera study and production during the summer; these are the Inspiration Point Fine Arts Colony in Eureka Springs, founded in 1950 by Henry Hobart, and Harmony Hills, the ranch in Hot Springs which became the site of a music school when the soprano Marjorie Lawrence retired to the area in 1952.

Amateur orchestras had been formed in Little Rock by 1906. The Little Rock SO, organized in 1933 by its conductor Laurence Powell, disbanded when he left the city in 1939. It was succeeded the following year by the Arkansas State SO, conducted by David R. Robertson. The Arkansas SO, founded in 1966, by the mid-1980s consisted of 85 professional musicians; it gives 12 subscription concerts and three "pops" concerts a year, and several chamber groups are drawn from its membership. Its permanent conductors have been Francis McBeth (1970–73), Kurt Klippstatter (1973–80), and Robert Henderson (from 1981). Chamber music in Little Rock dates back to at least the 1880s, when a traveling reporter for *Harper's Monthly Magazine* noted the high quality of a string ensemble he heard there. The Chamber Music Society of Little Rock was formed in 1954 and presents four concerts a year, from 1960 including internationally known artists.

The city's earliest performance venues included the Little Rock Theatre (seating 400; converted from a coffee house in 1839), an ornate Grand Opera House (completed in 1873), and the Capital Theater (seating 1400). The outdoor Forest Park Theater opened in 1904 and the Majestic Theater opened the following year. All of these played host to touring musical productions and vaudeville shows and had been demolished by 1940. Later the city's facilities included the Joseph Taylor Robinson Memorial Auditorium (seating 2655; built in 1939, remodeled in 1972), the Fine Arts Auditorium at the University of Arkansas (seating 719; built in 1965), the Arkansas Arts Center in MacArthur Park (seating 389; built in 1962), and the T. H. Barton Coliseum (seating 10,000), a former rodeo arena used for rock and pop concerts.

Music degrees are offered by the University of Arkansas at Little Rock, Philander Smith College, and Shorter College in North Little Rock. The Arkansas Arts Center in Little Rock houses the John D. Reid collection of early American jazz. The composers William Grant Still and Florence Bea Price both grew up in Little Rock.

BIBLIOGRAPHY

Guide to the City of Little Rock (Little Rock, 1890)
Arkansas Guide (New York, 1939) [Federal Writers' Project pubn]
W. Moffatt: "Cultural and Recreational Activities in Pioneer Arkansas," *Arkansas Historical Quarterly*, xiii (1954), 372
D. A. Stokes: "The First Theatrical Season in Arkansas: Little Rock, 1838–39," *Arkansas Historical Quarterly*, xxiii (1964), 166
W. G. Still: "My Arkansas Boyhood," *Arkansas Historical Quarterly*, xxvi (1967), 285
M. D. Hudgins: " 'Arkansas Traveler': Multi-parented Wayfarer," *Arkansas Historical Quarterly*, xxx (1971), 146

DAVID WRIGHT

Little Walter [Jacobs, Marion Walter] (*b* Alexandria, LA, 1 May 1930; *d* Chicago, IL, 15 Feb 1968). Blues harmonica player and singer. Born into extreme poverty, he began to earn a living playing harmonica at the age of eight. A decade later he was a street musician in Chicago, where he recorded *Ora Nelle Blues* (1947, Ora Nelle 711) in the style of Sonny Boy Williamson (ii). He soon developed his own technique of amplified harmonica playing, making use of pronounced vibrato or "warble," as on *Mean Old World* (1952, Checker 764). He had an undistinguished singing voice and expressed himself most effectively through the harmonica, especially in slow numbers such as *Blue Lights*, with Robert Lockwood on guitar (1954, Checker 799), which made use of heavy amplification and overblowing. Little Walter's best performances were in support of other blues artists, as in his "country" flavored accompaniment to Leroy Foster on *Rollin' and Tumblin'* (1950, Parkway 501), and above all the sessions with Muddy Waters that produced *Long Distance Call* (1951, Chess 1452) and *All Night Long* (1952, Chess 1509). Many younger urban blues musicians were influenced by his playing, and he had acquired a strong following in Europe long before he toured there in the 1960s.

Little Walter, 1964

BIBLIOGRAPHY

SouthernB ["Jacobs, Marion ('Little') Walter"]

W. Lindemann and B. Iglauer: "Little Walter and Louis Myers," *Living Blues*, vi (1971), 17
M. Rowe: *Chicago Breakdown* (London, 1973)
S. Harris: *Blues Who's Who* (New Rochelle, NY, 1979)

PAUL OLIVER

Little Willie John [Woods, William J.] (*b* Camden, AK, 15 Nov 1937; *d* Walla Walla, WA, 26 May 1968). Rhythm-and-blues singer. Brought up in Detroit, he began singing in his very early teens with big bands led by Count Basie, Paul Williams, and Duke Ellington. As early as 1953 he made recordings for such labels as Prize, Savoy, and Rama. John signed a contract with King Records in 1955, and, working with the producer Henry Glover, immediately made two hits, *All around the world* and *Need your love so bad*. In 1956 he wrote (with Eddie Cooley) and recorded *Fever*, a phenomenal success both for himself and later for Peggy Lee (her version (1958) rose higher on the charts, but his sold more records). From 1955 to 1961 John recorded 14 hit singles for King which sold more than 7,000,000 copies. These songs were essentially in one of two styles: an almost crooning blues-ballad type, influenced by Nat "King" Cole and others, and a softly swinging jump style, influenced by James Brown and Wynonie Harris. As his record sales declined, beginning in 1962, John began to drink heavily, and he killed a railroad worker in a barroom brawl; he was sent to the Washington State Penitentiary, where he died of pneumonia in 1968.

RECORDINGS

(selective list; all recorded for King)

All around the world (4818, 1956); Fever (4935, 1956); Need your love so bad (4841, 1956); Talk to me, talk to me (5108, 1958); Leave my kitten alone (5219, 1959); Let them talk (5274, 1959); Heartbreak (5356, 1960); Sleep (5428, 1960); Take my love (5516, 1961)

DAVE MARSH

Livingston, Fud [Joseph Anthony] (*b* Charleston, SC, 10 April 1906; *d* New York, 25 March 1957). Jazz tenor saxophonist, clarinetist, and arranger-composer. He began working as a performer and arranger with influential New York jazz groups such as Ben Pollack's band and the California Ramblers. His many recordings of the late 1920s show him to have been a leader of the white jazz avant garde, an influential arranger, and an instrumentalist in the style of his contemporary PeeWee Russell. The 1927 recordings of his compositions *Humpty Dumpty* and *Feelin' no Pain* show, respectively, an advanced harmonic style for that time and an incisive concept of "hot" small-band jazz. Livingston arranged scores for Paul Whiteman (1930–33), Benny Goodman (1934), and Jimmy Dorsey (1935–7); he then turned primarily to commercial music and music publishing.

RECORDINGS

(selective list)

As sideman: B. Pollack: 'Deed I do (1926, Vic. 20408); R. Nichols: Riverboat Shuffle/Eccentric (1927, Bruns. 3627); M. Mole: Imagination/Feelin' no Pain (1927, OK 40890); F. Trumbauer: Humpty Dumpty (1927, OK 40926); B. Goodman: Room 1411 (1928, Bruns. 4013); M. Mole: Crazy Rhythm (1928, OK 41098)

JAMES DAPOGNY/R

Lloyd, David (*b* Minneapolis, MN, 29 Feb 1920). Tenor. He studied at the Minneapolis College of Music (BA 1941), then, on the advice of Mitropoulos, attended the Curtis Institute, where he studied with Bonelli; he returned to the latter in 1946 after serving in the US Navy. He made his début with the New York City Opera in 1950 and was long associated with that company. He also sang with the New England Opera Theater, the Boston Opera Group, the Washington Opera, the New Orleans Opera, the St. Paul Civic Opera, and the Montreal Opera Guild. Abroad he appeared at Glyndebourne and at the first Athens Festival in 1955. In 1974 he was appointed director of the Lake George Opera Festival. His voice was well suited to the works of Mozart (notably Idomeneus in *Idomeneo* and Belmonte in *Die Entführung aus dem Serail*), Rossini (Ramiro in *La Cenerentola*), and Richard Strauss (Flamand in *Capriccio*), and he was one of the most active lyric tenors of his time; he was often cast in operas sung in English. Among his other roles were Rodolfo in *La bohème*, Jacquino in *Fidelio*, Gonzalve in Ravel's *L'heure espagnole*, and Andres in Berg's *Wozzeck*. He appeared with the Boston SO in Liszt's *Faust-Symphonie*, and with the Philadelphia Orchestra in Rachmaninoff's *The Bells*; in the early 1960s he gave a number of solo recitals in New York. He joined the faculty of the University of Illinois, Urbana, in 1971.

CHARLES JAHANT

Lloyd, Norman (*b* Pottsville, PA, 8 Nov 1909; *d* Greenwich, CT, 30 July 1980). Music educator and composer. He studied at New York University (BS 1932, MS 1936), and then joined the music faculty of Sarah Lawrence College, Bronxville, New York, where he remained for ten years. There and during summers spent at Bennington College in the 1930s he developed relationships with several established choreographers, among them Hanya Holm, Doris Humphrey, Martha Graham, and José Limón, for whom he composed and conducted scores. From 1946 to 1949 he was director of education at the Juilliard School, where with the collaboration of some of the choreographers he had known at Bennington he set up a dance department. With William Schuman he designed the Literature and Materials of Music system of teaching theory at Juilliard, a method which focused on class discussion and the study of actual musical scores rather than textbooks, employed only composers as theory teachers, and integrated the traditionally separate areas of harmony and counterpoint into a single study. In 1963 Lloyd left Juilliard to become dean of the Oberlin College Conservatory, and two years later he joined the Rockefeller Foundation as director of arts programming; after his retirement in 1972 he continued to act as a private consultant for various foundations and educational institutions.

Lloyd's published compositions include a Piano Sonata (1958) and other works for piano, and several pieces for band and for chorus; much of his music, however, notably the many dance and film scores, remains unpublished. His collections of folksong arrangements, including *The Fireside Book of Favorite American Songs* (1947) and *The Fireside Book of Love Songs* (1954), and the popular *Golden Encyclopedia of Music* (1968) have become standard works in their areas.

ELLEN HIGHSTEIN

Lloyd Webber, Andrew (*b* London, England, 22 March 1948). English composer. His father was a conductor and director of the London College of Music and his mother was a piano teacher, so he received a solid education in classical music. However, he has been highly successful in transferring modern musical idioms, especially those deriving from rock, to the stage; *Jesus Christ Superstar* (1971) was in fact a best-selling rock album before it evolved into a stage show, and one of its most popular songs, "I don't know how to love him," also became a hit record. Three more of Lloyd Webber's shows have been successfully produced on Broadway: *Joseph and the Amazing Technicolor Dreamcoat* (1977), *Evita* (1979, including the song "Don't cry for me, Argentina"), and *Cats* (1982). Tim Rice was lyricist for all but the last-named, which is based on T. S. Eliot's poems in *Old Possum's Book of Practical Cats*. Lloyd Webber's Requiem, a work written in a similar vein to that of his stage shows, was given its première in St. Thomas's Church, New York, in February 1985.

GERALD BORDMAN

Lockwood, Annea [Anna] **(Ferguson)** (*b* Christchurch, New Zealand, 29 July 1939). New Zealand composer and instrument builder. After attending Canterbury University, New Zealand (BMus 1961), she studied piano with E. Kendall Taylor and composition with Peter R. Fricker at the Royal College of Music, London (diplomas, 1963). She also studied composition at the Ferienkurs für Neue Musik, Darmstadt (1961–2), with Gottfried Michael Koenig at the Staatliche Hochschule für Musik, Cologne, the Electronic Music Center, Bilthoven, the Netherlands (1963–4), and Electronic Music Studios, Putney, London (1970). From 1969 to 1972 she studied psychoacoustics at Southampton University's Institute of Sound and Vibration Research. In 1973 Lockwood joined the faculty of Hunter College, CUNY, and subsequently taught composition and electronic music as a visiting professor at numerous American universities, including Queens College, CUNY. She has given lectures on and performed her works in England, Scotland, New Zealand, Australia, France, West Germany, and Sweden. In 1983 she joined the faculty of Vassar College. Her honors include Arts Council of Great Britain awards (1970, 1972, 1973), Gulbenkian Foundation grants (1972, 1973), a Creative Artists Public Service grant (1977), and an NEA fellowship (1979–80).

Lockwood's early works, including the Violin Concerto (1962) and the chamber cantatas *A Abélard, Héloise* (1963) and *Aspekte einer Parabel* (1964), are atonal. Her work as an instrument builder began with *Glass Concert* for two performers and an environment of glass objects (which has come to be known by the same name) that serves as both scenery and instruments; the performers move about in it striking, rubbing, shaking, and even snapping the various pieces. Later Lockwood turned her attention increasingly to environmental installations and applications of taped sound. Her work about 1970 included a variety of treatments of old, mainly upright, pianos under the collective title *Piano Transplants*. They were prepared, burned, "drowned" in a shallow lake, or installed in an outdoor "piano garden"; the instruments were subjected in these ways to the activity of the four elements, and careful documentation on tape was made regularly of their rapid decay and transformation.

In the USA Lockwood has composed mainly electronic and performance pieces, including *Tiger Balm* (1970), *Malaman* (1974, for the Merce Cunningham Dance Company), *Spirit Catchers* (1974), *Conversations with the Ancestors* (1979), and *Delta Run* (1981, for the New Music America Festival, Chicago, 1982). In the 1970s Lockwood also began to explore documentary forms, mixed media, and environmental sound: in *The River Archive* (1973–) sounds of rivers such as the Ganges and Hudson are recorded, and in *World Rhythms* (1975) widely spaced strokes on a single gong resonate in response to natural sounds played back from ten tape tracks. These works demonstrate the holistic and meditation techniques Lockwood learned from studying non-Western music and in her activities in avant-garde theater and performance; they have been performed during the 1980s at festivals and galleries and in concerts in the USA, Europe, and Australasia.

WORKS

Orch: Vn Conc., 1962

Vocal: Serenade no.1 (Sappho, Anakreon), S, fl, 1962; A Abélard, Héloise (Heloise), chamber cantata, Mez, 10 insts, 1963; Aspekte einer Parabel (Kafka), Bar, 10 insts, 1964; Serenade no.2 (St. Joan Perse), S, orch, tape, 1965; Humming, mixed chorus, 1972; Malaman, 1v/4 solo vv, 1974

Elec and mixed media: Glass Concert, 2 pfmrs, amp glass insts, 1966; Shone, mixed media, 1966; Sound Hat, Sound Umbrella, sound sculptures, 1969; Piano Transplants, sound sculptures, 1970; Tiger Balm, tape, 1970; Windhover, tape, 1972; Glide, wine glasses, 1973; Cloud Music, tape, 1973; Deep Dream Dive, db, elec, 1973; The River Archive: Play the Ganges Backwards One More Time, Sam, mixed-media installation, 1973–4, Sound Map of the Hudson River, tape installation, 1982; Spirit Catchers, 4 amp vv, 1974; World Rhythms, 10-track tape, gong, 1975; Spirit Songs Unfolding, tape, slides, 1977; Woman Murder, tape, 1977; Conversations with the Ancestors, mixed-media installation, 1979; Delta Run, tape, slides, 1981

Principal publishers: Morrow, G. Schirmer, Source

ELIZABETH WOOD, HUGH DAVIES

Lockwood, Lewis (Henry) (*b* New York, 16 Dec 1930). Musicologist. He graduated from Queens College, New York (BA 1952), and Princeton University (MFA 1955, PhD 1960). He joined the faculty at Princeton in 1958 and was professor from 1968 until 1980, when he was appointed professor at Harvard. He was editor of the *Journal of the American Musicological Society* (1963–6) and acted as consulting editor in the USA for *The New Grove*. Lockwood's principal areas of research are Renaissance music and Beethoven studies. In *The Counter-Reformation and the Masses of Vincenzo Ruffo* (1970), he discusses the musical reforms that followed the Council of Trent and the role of Ruffo in their implementation. He has also examined the problems of *musica ficta*, as well as musical activities at the court of Ercole I d'Este at Ferrara; his studies of the latter culminated in the book *Music in Renaissance Ferrara* (1984). In 1985 Lockwood was elected president of the American Musicological Society.

A leading Beethoven scholar, Lockwood is concerned with the use of sketches and autograph scores in textual criticism. His research into the sources of the Cello Sonata op.69 and the unfinished piano concerto of 1815 indicate no clear line of development from sketch through working score to fair copy, but rather a complexinterrelationship between these sources.

PAULA MORGAN

Lockwood, Normand (*b* New York, 19 March 1906). Composer. As a youth he studied piano and composition at the University of Michigan, where his father Samuel and uncle Albert headed the violin and piano departments, respectively. He continued his studies with Respighi in Rome (1924–5), with Boulanger in Paris (1925–8), and as a fellow of the American Academy in Rome (1929–32). He then taught at various American institutions: Oberlin Conservatory (1932–43), Columbia University and the School of Sacred Music, Union Theological Seminary (1945–53), Trinity University, San Antonio (1953–5), and, briefly, Yale University, Westminster Choir College, and the universities of Oregon and Hawaii. He was professor of composition and composer-in-residence at the University of Denver from 1961 until he retired as Professor Emeritus in 1975. Among the many honors he has received are the Swift Prize of the Chicago SO for *A Year's Chronicle* (1934), two successive Guggenheim Fellowships (1943–5), a commission from the Alice M. Ditson fund for *The Scarecrow* (1945), awards from the National Institute of Arts and Letters (1947) and the Colorado Council on the Arts and Humanities (1971), and the Marjorie Peabody Waite Award (1981).

Lockwood is a prolific composer. His music is usually logical and concise, unified by such devices as germinal chords, repeated rhythmic and melodic fragments, and quoted tunes; it is nonetheless accessible and at times romantic. Lockwood has been especially original and expressive in his numerous vocal works, and has shown a particular interest in setting American poetry.

WORKS

OPERAS

The Scarecrow (chamber opera, 3, D. Lockwood, after P. McKaye), 1945; Early Dawn (3, R. Porter), 1961; The Wizards of Balizar (children's opera, 2, Porter), 1962; The Hanging Judge (3, Porter), 1964 [orig. entitled The Inevitable Hour]; Requiem for a Rich Young Man (1, D. Sutherland), 1964

VOCAL

(choral)

Out of the Cradle endlessly Rocking (Whitman), 1938; The Birth of Moses, SSA, fl, pf, 1947; Elegy for a Hero (Whitman), 1951; The Closing Doxology (Ps. cl), chorus, sym. wind band, perc, 1952; Prairie (Sandburg), chorus, orch, 1952; Magnificat, S, chorus, orch, 1954; Children of God (C. C. Cooper), oratorio, 1956; Light out of Darkness, oratorio, 1957; Land of Promise (Porter), oratorio, 1960; Choreographic Cantata, 1968

For the Time Being (Auden), oratorio, 1971; Life Triumphant, chorus, fl, brass, 1976; Mass for Children and Orch, 1976; Donne's Last Sermon, chorus, org, 1978; Thought of him I love (Whitman), children's vv, orch, 1982; A Child's Christmas in Wales (D. Thomas), children's vv, pf, 1984; *c*60 other sacred and secular works, incl. cantatas, oratorios

(solo vocal)

Prelude to Western Star (S. V. Benét), B, pf, 1948; Psalm xxiii, S, org, 1955; The Dialogue of Abraham and Isaac (Sutherland), T, pf, 1965; Fallen is Babylon the Great! Hallelujah! (Revelations), Mez, pf, 1967; To Margarita Debayle (R. Dario), S, pf, 1978; 4 Songs: a Cycle (Whitman), S, vn, org, 1979, arr. S, pf; Psalms xvii, cxiv, Mez, org, 1985; *c*25 others

INSTRUMENTAL

Orch: A Year's Chronicle, 1934; Sym., 1934; 2 concs., org, brass, 1951, 1978; Ob Conc., 1968; Org Conc., chamber orch, 1973; Pf Conc., 1974; Panegyric, str, hn, 1979; Sym., large orch, 1979; Conc., 2 harp, orch, 1981; Prayers and Fanfares, brass, str, perc, 1982; other works

Chamber: 7 str qts, 1933–50; Trio, fl, va, harp, 1940; Cl Qnt, 1959; Processional Voluntary, org, 1962; Sonata-Fantasia, accordion, 1964; Fantasia, pf, 1971; Fl Sonata, 1971; Festive Service, org, 1976; Valley Suite, vn, pf, 1976; 8 Org Preludes, 1980; Tripartito, fl, gui, 1980; 3 Chorale Voluntaries, tpt, org, 1982; Pf Trio, 1985; many others incl. kbd works

Principal publishers: ACA, Associated, Augsburg, Broude, Kjos, Peters, G. Schirmer, Shawnee, Waterloo (Canada), Wilshorn

BIBLIOGRAPHY

EwenD

G. Lynn: "Normand Lockwood and Choral Music," *ACAB*, vi/4 (1957), 3

J. McDowell: "A Note on Some Facets of Normand Lockwood's Music," *ACAB*, vi/4 (1957), 7

T. M. Davis: *A Study of Stylistic Characteristics in Selected Major Choral Works of Normand Lockwood* (diss., U. of Missouri, 1980)

SUSAN L. PORTER

Loder, George (*b* Bath, England, *c*1816; *d* Adelaide, Australia, 15 July 1868). English conductor and composer. He was a member of a prominent musical family in Bath, where his father, George Loder, was a flutist. He immigrated to the USA and settled in Baltimore in 1836; he first appeared in New York as a composer and conductor of stage productions during the 1839–40 season. He was a founding member in 1842 of the New York Philharmonic Symphony Society, and played the double bass in the orchestra for five seasons; he conducted the American première of Beethoven's Ninth Symphony on 20 May 1846, and remained on the roster of Philharmonic conductors for seven seasons. In 1844 he became principal of the New York Vocal Institute, for which he compiled *The New York Glee Book* (1843), including in it many of his own partsongs; he later published *The Philadelphia and New York Glee Book* (1857). In 1856 he went to Australia, with Anna Bishop, to conduct William Saurin Lyster's opera company. Four years later he was in London, where he published two comic operettas, *Pets of the Parterre* and *The Old House at Home*, which were produced at the Lyceum (1861–2). In 1863 he returned to Australia for another visit, conducting that year in Melbourne the first Australian performance of *Les Huguenots*. He died there after a long illness.

BIBLIOGRAPHY

L. Middleton: "Loder, George," *DNB*

G. C. D. Odell: *Annals of the New York Stage*, iv (New York, 1928/*R*1970); v (New York, 1931/*R*1970)

W. A. Orchard: *Music in Australia* (Melbourne, 1952), 147

H. Shanet: *Philharmonic: a History of New York's Orchestra* (Garden City, NY, 1975)

ROBERT STEVENSON

Lodge, (Thomas) Henry (*b* Providence, RI, 9 Feb 1884; *d* West Palm Beach, FL, 16 Feb 1933). Popular pianist and composer. He began composing in his teens and had at least three pieces published in 1904 (two songs and a march); between 1904 and 1918 he issued some 17 rags and ragtime blues. Having moved to New York, he played piano in theater and dance orchestras and was engaged for solo cabaret appearances. In the 1920s, while playing in dance orchestras in New York and West Palm Beach, Florida, he also wrote background music for films, spending part of 1930 in Hollywood writing film music.

Lodge is best remembered for his rags, and especially for *Temptation Rag* (1909). One of the most successful works in the genre, it was recorded more than any other rag in the years preceding 1920. Lodge's earlier rags were sophisticated danceable pieces which lent themselves well to orchestral treatment, but his later ragtime blues were more somber and increasingly adventurous in harmony and structure. More than any other rag composer, Lodge explored and developed the use of minor tonalities. Among his more than 100 published works are pieces of all types, including songs, waltzes, and various pieces of instrumental dance music. His biggest song hit was *That Red Head Gal* (1922).

WORKS

(selective list; all printed works published in New York)

Pf rags: Temptation Rag (1909); Red Pepper: Spicy Rag (1909); Oh! You Turkey: a Rag Trot (1914); Geraldine: Valse Hesitation (1915); Silver Fox: a Raggy Fox Trot (1915); Baltimore Blues (1917); The Bounding Buck: a Rag Dance (1918)

Song: That Red Head Gal (G. Van, J. Schenck) (1922)

BIBLIOGRAPHY

D. A. Jasen: *Recorded Ragtime 1897–1958* (Hamden, CT, 1973)

D. Zimmerman: "The Henry Lodge Story," *Rag Times*, ix/5 (1976), 1

D. A. Jasen and T. J. Tichenor: *Rags and Ragtime: a Musical History* (New York, 1978)

RICHARD ZIMMERMAN

Loeffler, Charles [Karl] **Martin** (*b* Schöneberg, nr Berlin, Germany, or Mulhouse, Alsace, France, 30 Jan 1861; *d* Medfield, MA, 19 May 1935). Composer and violinist. He claimed Alsatian birth; his parents, however, were natives of Berlin, and the records of the Hochschule für Musik give one of their residences, Schöneberg, as the composer's birthplace. The later political difficulties endured by his father, including imprisonment (to which Loeffler attributed his father's death), made the son so hostile towards Germany that he adopted French manners, tastes, and style. He had his first violin lessons in the late 1860s from a German member of the Russian Imperial Orchestra. By the age of 13 he had decided to become a professional violinist, and from 1874 to 1877 studied violin with Joseph Joachim and Eduard Rappoldi and theory with Friedrich Kiel and Woldemar Bargiel at the Hochschule für Musik in Berlin. He continued his musical studies in Paris, taking private lessons in violin from Lambert Joseph Massart and in composition from Ernest Guiraud. He was a member of J. E. Pasdeloup's orchestra for a season, then played in the private orchestra of Paul de Derwies (1879–81).

After the death of Derwies in June 1881 Loeffler came to the USA. Although he returned several times to Europe (he studied violin with Hubert Léonard in Paris in 1884), he decided to settle in the country he found "quick to reward genuine musical merit and to reward it far more generously than Europe," and became an American citizen in 1887. During the 1881–2 season he played in Leopold Damrosch's orchestra in New York. In May 1882 he participated in Theodore Thomas's New York Festival and the following summer in his "Highway" tour. In the autumn of 1882 Loeffler joined the Boston SO as second concertmaster, a position he held for 21 years, and he became a favorite soloist with the Boston public. He was a proponent of contemporary music and played the American premières of works by such composers as Max Bruch, Saint-Saëns, and Edouard Lalo. Loeffler's brother Erich played the cello in the Boston SO. Loeffler was also a popular composer. The first of his works to receive a public performance was one movement of the String Quartet in A minor, played by the Adamowski Quartette in Philadelphia in 1889. The Boston SO gave the première of his first orchestral work, *Les veillées de l'Ukraine*, in 1891.

1. Charles Martin Loeffler: painting (1903) by John Singer Sargent in the Isabella Stewart Gardner Museum, Boston

Loeffler retired from the orchestra at the end of the 1902–3 season. After spending a year (1904–5) in Paris he settled in Medfield, Massachusetts, where he shared his time between his working farm, his thoroughbred horses, and his musical activities. He taught violin and coached chamber ensembles, and founded the female American String Quartette in 1908. For a time he directed a boys' choir in Gregorian chant, and in 1909 visited the Benedictine Monastery at Maria Laach, Germany, where he studied chant practice. He remained active in the musical life of Boston, retaining unofficial ties with the Boston SO; he was a member of the board of directors of the Boston Opera Company, and served as an adviser on various competition juries. Loeffler also had interests in New York, serving as an adviser on the foundation of the Juilliard Graduate School (1924).

Loeffler's major occupation was composition. He was a skilled and careful, even fastidious, composer, who was severely self-critical; he repeatedly revised his compositions and withheld most of them from publication. His music was, nevertheless, often performed. Early in his career he was considered "avant garde," primarily for his use of programmatic forms and advanced harmonies. He was also known as a symbolist and was frequently designated "decadent" for the bizarre and sinister moods that colored many of his early works (for example *La mort de Tintagiles*, *Rapsodies* (fig.2), and *Quatre poèmes*). Loeffler espoused no particular school of composition: his technique was based on a Germanic foundation, but his style was most strongly influenced by French composers; he also borrowed heavily from Russian music, especially in early compositions such as the String Sextet, the Quintet, and *Les veillées de l'Ukraine*. His music displays fluid rhythmic and melodic writing, a marked ingenuity of orchestration, and sensitivity to harmonic color.

Loeffler supported American musical activity and admired many native composers. With the exception of some works that incorporated jazz elements (for example, the Partita for violin and piano), however, he did not attempt to write in an American style. He drew from a variety of literary inspirations, including Virgil, St. Francis, Gogol, Whitman, Poe, Yeats, Maeterlinck, and Verlaine. His musical interests, equally eclectic, ranged from Gregorian chant (used notably in *Canticum fratris solis* and Music for Four Stringed Instruments) to national musics (the *Divertissement espagnol* and the Five Irish Fantasies draw respectively on Spanish and Irish themes).

A man of aristocratic bearing and cosmopolitan culture, Loeffler was extremely well read (especially in French literature) and was esteemed as an intellectual as well as an artist. John S. Sargent, who painted his portrait, was among his friends. Among the many honors Loeffler received as a composer were membership in the National Institute of Arts and Letters (1908), which later awarded him a Gold Medal (1920), an honorary doctorate from Yale (1926), and election to the American Academy of Arts and Letters (1931). He was also named an Officer de l'Académie des Beaux Arts (1906) and a Chevalier of the Légion d'honneur (1919).

WORKS

Catalogue: E. Knight: *Charles Martin Loeffler: Catalog of Works* (MS, 1985, *DLC*)

STAGE

Ouverture pour le T. C. Minstrel Entertainment (incidental music), 2 vn, pf, Boston, ?1906, *DLC*

2. *Autograph score of the opening of "La cornemuse" from "Rapsodies," 1898 (DLC)*

The Passion of Hilarion (opera, 1 act and 2 tableaux, W. Sharp), 1912–13 (Boston, 1936)

Les amants jaloux (opera, Loeffler), 1918, *DLC* (sketches)

The Peony Lantern (opera, Loeffler, after Okakura-Kakuzo), *c*1919, *DLC* (sketches)

The Countess Cathleen (incidental music, W. B. Yeats), 1924, Concord, MA, 8 May, 1924, lost

The Reveller (incidental music, D. Sargent), 1925, Boston, 22 Dec 1925, vs (New York, 1926)

ORCHESTRAL

Les veillées de l'Ukraine, vn, orch, 1890, Boston, 20 Nov 1891, *DLC*; arr. vn, pf, *c*1891, *DLC*; rev. 1899; 1st movt separately rev. as Rapsodie russe, vn, pf, 2nd movt separately rev. as Une nuit de Mai, vn, orch, *DLC*

Morceau fantastique (Fantastic Concerto), vc, orch, 1893, Boston, 2 Feb 1894, *DLC* (inc.)

Divertissement, a, vn, orch, op.1, 1894, Boston, 4 Jan 1895, *DLC*, *MBG*; arr. vn, pf

La mort de Tintagiles, 2 va d'amore, orch, op.6, 1897, Boston, 7 Jan 1898, *DLC*; rev. 1 va d'amore, orch, 1900 (New York, 1905)

Divertissement espagnol, sax, orch, 1900, Boston, 29 Jan 1901, *MBCM*

Poem (La bonne chanson; Avant que tu ne t'en ailles), 1901, Boston, 11 April 1902, *DLC*; rev. 1915 (New York, 1923)

La villanelle du diable, op.9, 1901, Boston, 11 April 1902 (New York, 1905) [rev. of no.3 of Rapsodies, see "Songs"]

A Pagan Poem, op.14, 1906, Boston, 29 Oct 1907 (New York, 1909) [rev. of Poème païen, see "Chamber"]

Hora mystica, orch, male chorus, 1915, Norfolk, CT, 6 June 1916, *DLC*

Poème: scène dramatique, vc, orch, lost [arr. of work for vc, pf, see "Chamber"]

Memories of my Childhood (Life in a Russian Village), 1924, Evanston, IL, 30 May 1924 (New York, 1925)

Evocation, orch, female chorus, 1930, Cleveland, 5 Feb 1931 (Boston, 1932)

Untitled work, str orch, org, *DLC* (unfinished)

SOLO VOCAL WITH ORCHESTRA

Five Irish Fantasies, 1920, Boston, 10 March 1922 (New York, 1935)

Canticum fratris solis, 1925, Washington, DC, 28 Oct 1925 (Washington, DC, 1929); arr. female chorus 3vv, 1925

La cloche fêlée, Sérénade, *DLC* [arrs. of nos.1 and 4 of Quatre poèmes, see "Songs"]

CHAMBER, INSTRUMENTAL

Danse bizarre, vn, 1881, *DLC*

Berceuse, vn, pf, by 1884 (Paris, n.d. [1884])

Violin Sonata, 1886, lost

String Quartet, a, 1889, *DLC*

Les veillées de l'Ukraine, vn, pf, *c*1891, *DLC* [arr. of work for vn, orch, see "Orchestral"]

String Sextet, *c*1891, *DLC*; 2nd movt rev. as Le passeur d'eau, 1900

Quintet (Lyrisches Kammermusikstück; Eine Frühlingsmusik), 3 vn, va, vc, 1894 (New York, 1938)

Requiem, vn, by 1894 *DLC* (inc.)

Divertissement, vn, pf, *c*1895, *CtY*, *DLC* [arr. of work for vn, orch, see "Orchestral"]

Octet, 2 cl, harp, 2 vn, va, vc, db, *c*1896, *DLC*

Le passeur d'eau, str sextet, 1900, *DLC* [rev. of 2nd movt of String Sextet, *c*1891]

Deux rapsodies, ob, va, pf, 1901 (New York, 1905) [rev. of L'étang, La cornemuse, from Rapsodies, see "Songs"]

Poème païen (Poème antique), 2 fl, ob, cl, eng hn, 3 tpt, 2 hn, va, db, pf, 1902, *DLC*; version for 3 tpt, 2 pf, 1902, lost

Ballade carnavalesque, fl, ob, sax, bn, pf, 1902, *DLC*, *MBCM*

Airs tziganes, vn, pf, *DLC*, *CtY*

Barcarolle, vn, pf, *DLC*

Capriccio russe, vn, pf, *DLC*

Grave, vn, pf, *DLC*

Norske land, va d'amore, pf, *CtY*; rev. as Eery Moonlight, vn/va d'amore, pf, *DLC*, *CtY*; rev. as Norske saga, db, pf, 1929, *CtY*, *MB*

Romance russe, vn, pf, *DLC* (inc.)

Spring Danse (Danse norvégienne), vn, pf, *DLC*

Tarantella, vn, pf, *DLC*

Poème: scène dramatique (Poème espagnole; Conte espagnole), vc, pf, 1916, *DLC*; arr. vc, orch

Music for Four Stringed Instruments, str qt, 1917–19 (New York, 1923)

Historiettes, str qt, harp, 1922, *DLC*

Paraphrase on Two Western Cowboy Songs (The Lone Prairie), sax, va d'amore, pf, *DLC* (unfinished)
Cynthia, vn, pf, 1926, *CtY*
Partita, vn, pf, 1930 (New York, 1937)
Allegretto, vn, pf, *DLC*
Divigations sur des airs tziganes (Repülj fecske'm), vn, pf, *DLC* (sketches)
Joe Bibb (Joe Bibb: the Clown), vn, pf, *DLC* (sketch)
Mescolanza "Olla Podrida," va d'amore, pf, *CtY*
Une nuit de Mai, vn, pf, *DLC* (unfinished) [rev. of 2nd movt of Les veillées de l'Ukraine, see "Orchestral"]
Rapsodie russe, vn, pf, *DLC* [rev. of 1st movt of Les veillées de l'Ukraine, see "Orchestral"]
Rêverie-barcarolle, vn, pf, *DLC*
Rondo, vn, pf, *DLC* (sketch)
III, vn, pf, *DLC* (unfinished) [rev. of 4th movt of Les veillées de l'Ukraine, see "Orchestral"]
Zapateado, vn, pf, *CtY* (sketch)

CHORAL

L'archet (C. Cros), S, female chorus 4vv, va d'amore, pf, op.26, *c*1900, *DLC*
The Sermon on the Mount, female chorus 4vv, 2 va d'amore, va da gamba, harp, org, *DLC* (unfinished)
Ps. cxxxvii (By the rivers of Babylon), female chorus 4vv, 2 fl, vc, harp, org, op.3, *c*1901 (New York, 1907); version with pf acc. (New York, 1907)
For One who Fell in Battle (T. W. Parsons), 8vv, 1906 (New York, 1911); rev. 1911 as Ode for One who Fell in Battle (New York, 1911)
Poème mystique (G. Kahn), boys' chorus, chorus, 4 hn, 2 ob, harp, org, 1907, *DLC* (sketches)
Ave maris stella, S, boys' chorus, str orch, pf, org, *DLC*
Drei Marienlieder (Angelus Domini), 8vv, 1919–20, *DLC*
Beat! Beat! Drums! (Drum Taps) (W. Whitman), unison male vv, pf, 1917 (Boston, 1932); version with wind, brass, perc acc. (Boston, 1932); version with pf, 4 tpt, fifes, perc, *DLC*
Canticum fratris solis, female chorus 3vv, 1925, *DLC* [arr. of work for 1v, orch, see "Orchestral"]
Prière (R. Dévigne), 4vv, pf, 1926, *DLC* [also version for 1v, pf, see "Songs"]

SONGS

Edition: *C. M. Loeffler: Selected Songs with Chamber Accompaniment*, ed. E. Knight, RRAM (in preparation) [K]

(all for 1v, pf, unless otherwise stated)

Busslied, *DLC*
Marie (A. de Musset), *DLC*
Madrigal (P. Bourget), *DLC*
Les hirondelles (A. d'Hotelier), *DLC*
Rêverie, *DLC*
La chanson des ingénues (P. Verlaine), 1v, va, pf, *c*1893, *DLC*; K
Harmonie du soir (C. P. Baudelaire), 1v, va/va d'amore, pf, *c*1893, *DLC*; K
La lune blanche (Verlaine), 1v, va, pf, *c*1893, *MBG*; K
Rêverie en sourdine (Verlaine), 1v, va, pf, *c*1893, *MBG*; K
Le rossignol (Verlaine), 1v, va, pf, *c*1893, *DLC*, *MBG*; K
Quatre poèmes, op.5 (New York, 1904): La cloche fêlée (Baudelaire), Dansons la gigue! (Verlaine), Le son du cor s'afflige vers les bois (Paysage triste) (Verlaine), Sérénade (Verlaine), 1v, va, pf, *c*1893 [nos.1 and 4 rev. with orch acc.]; K
Rapsodies (M. Rollinat), 1v, cl, va, pf, 1898: L'étang, La cornemuse, La villanelle du diable, *DLC* [nos.1 and 2 arr. ob, va, pf]; K
Quatre mélodies (G. Kahn), op.10, 1899 (New York, 1903): Timbres oubliés, Adieu pour jamais, Les soirs d'automne, Les paons
Bolero triste (Kahn), (1v, pf)/(1v, vn, pf), 1900, Moldenhauer Archives, Spokane, WA, *DLC*; K
Le flambeau vivant (Baudelaire), *c*1902, lost
A une femme (Verlaine), (1v, pf)/(1v, vn, pf), 1904, *DLC*; K
Four Poems, op.15, 1905 (New York, 1906): Sudden Light (D. G. Rossetti), A Dream Within a Dream (E. A. Poe), To Helen (Poe), Sonnet (G. C. Lodge)
Der Kehraus (J. F. von Eichendorff), 1906, *CtY*
Vereinsamt (F. Nietzsche), 1906, *CtY*
The Wind among the Reeds (W. B. Yeats), 1906–7 (New York, 1908): The Hosting of the Sidhe, The Host of the Air; rev. in Five Irish Fantasies, 1920
Je te vis (Hommage) (Kahn), 1908, *DLC*
Ton souvenir est comme un livre bien-aimé (A. Samain), by 1911, *DLC*
Hymne (Hymne d'église; Hymne à Dieu; Prière) (Dévigne), S, str qnt, org, pf, 1919, *DLC*
Five Irish Fantasies, 1920 (New York, 1934): The Hosting of the Sidhe, The Host of the Air (Yeats) [revs. of The Wind among the Reeds, 1906–7], The Fiddler of Dooney (Yeats), The Ballad of the Foxhunter (Yeats), Caitilin ni Uallachain (W. Heffernan)
Vieille chanson d'amour (15th century), 1925, *DLC*
Prière (Dévigne), 1926 (Boston, 1936), *DLC* [also version for 4vv, pf, see "Choral"]
Vassar College Song, *DLC*
Girl and Boy Guides Prayer Hymn, *DLC* (sketches)

OTHER WORKS

Jazz band, all in *DLC*: Suite, 1v, dance orch, 1927, unfinished, incl. Creole Blues (De 'tit zozos), Tango-drag, 1926; Intermezzo (Clowns), 1928; Todavia estes a tiempo, 1932; By-an'-by, sketch
Pedagogical: Violin Studies for the Development of the Left Hand, 1920 (New York, 1936); Violin Exercises, *CtY*
*c*50 arrs., most for vn/va d'amore/other str inst, pf, of works by other composers, 4 pubd, MSS in *CtY, DLC*
Cadenzas, all in *DLC*: Saint-Saëns: Vn Conc. op.1, 1893, Morceau de concert, op.62, 1894; Brahms: Vn Conc. op.77, 1897; Paganini: Vn Conc. op.6

Principal publishers: G. Schirmer, Boston Music Co., C. C. Birchard

BIBLIOGRAPHY

EwenD
ThompsonI
O. Downes: "Originality in Composer's Art means Sophistication," *MusAm*, xi/23 (1910), 3
"Music of Charles Martin Loeffler," *Christian Science Monitor* (29 Jan 1910)
L. Gilman: "The Music of Loeffler," *North American Review*, cxciii (1911), 47
C. Engel: "Charles Martin Loeffler," *MQ*, xi (1925), 311
A. H. Meyer: "Loeffler at Seventy finds all Music Good," *MusAm*, li/2 (1931), 5
C. Engel: "Views and Reviews," *MQ*, xxi (1935), 368
E. B. Hill: "Charles Martin Loeffler," *MM*, xiii (1935–6), 26
W. Damrosch: *Charles Martin Loeffler* (New York, 1936)
"From the Correspondence of Charles Martin Loeffler," *A Birthday Offering to C[arl] E[ngel]*, ed. G. Reese (New York, 1943)
H. Colvin: *Charles Martin Loeffler: his Life and Works* (diss., U. of Rochester, 1957)
A. Dowd: *A Descriptive Catalog of the Loeffler Collection of the Library of Congress Music Division* (MS, 1959, *DCU*)
R. P. Locke: "Charles Martin Loeffler: Composer at Court," *Fenway Court: Isabella Stewart Gardner Museum* [annual report] (1974), 30
E. L. Henry: *Impressionism in the Arts and its Influence on Selected Works of Charles Martin Loeffler and Charles Tomlinson Griffes* (diss., U. of Cincinnati, 1976)
P. Cohen: "The Saxophone Music of Charles Martin Loeffler," *Saxophone Symposium*, vi/4 (1981), 10
E. Knight: "Mr. Loeffler, Mrs. Gardner, and the Viola d'amore," *Newsletter* [Viola d'amore Society of America], v/1 (1981), 4
——: "Chamber Music Including Viola by Charles Martin Loeffler," *Newsletter* [American Viola Society], xxi/1 (1981), 10
——: "The Evolution of Loeffler's 'Music for Four Stringed Instruments'," *American Music*, ii/3 (1984), 66
——: "Charles Martin Loeffler and George Gershwin: a Forgotten Friendship," *American Music*, iii (1985), 452
J. Hansen: "Charles Martin Loeffler and the Eberle Viola d'amore," *Fenway Court* (1985), 41

ELLEN KNIGHT

Loesser, Arthur (*b* New York, 26 Aug 1894; *d* Cleveland, OH, 4 Jan 1969). Pianist and writer on music, half-brother of Frank Loesser. He studied at City College of New York, Columbia University, and the Institute of Musical Art, New York. He made his début as a pianist in Berlin in 1913 and in New York in 1916, and thereafter toured the USA, Australia, and the Far East. Loesser joined the piano faculty of the Cleveland Institute in 1926; he was head of the piano department there from 1953 until his death. He also wrote program notes for the Cleveland Orchestra (1927–42) and was music critic of the *Cleveland Press* (1939–56). During World War II Loesser was an intelligence officer with the US Army; after the war he was posted to Japan, where he performed with the Japan SO (1946) and lectured (in Japanese). He was the author of *Humor in American Song* (1943) and *Men, Women and Pianos: a Social History* (1954).

PAULA MORGAN

Loesser, Frank (Henry) (*b* New York, 29 June 1910; *d* New York, 26 July 1969). Composer, lyricist, and librettist. Although his father Henry and half-brother Arthur were both pianists, he refused piano lessons and was largely self-taught in music. He took a series of jobs, working in journalism and as a pianist in nightclubs, during which time he began to write satirical lyrics and sketches for vaudeville. His first published song was *In Love with a Memory of you* (1931), written with his friend William Schuman. In 1936 he moved to Hollywood, having been awarded a contract by Universal Pictures as a result of his lyrics for the revue *The Illustrators' Show*. Between 1938 and 1945 he wrote lyrics for 20 musical films and those of individual songs for nearly 40 others; among his more successful contributions were the words for Hoagy Carmichael's *Two Sleepy People* (1938), Styne's *I don't want to walk without you* (1942), Joseph Lilley's *Jingle, jangle, jingle* (1942), Jimmy McHugh's *"Murder," he says* (1943), and Arthur Schwartz's *They're either too young or too old* (1943). He began to compose his own music during World War II when, as a member of the Army Air Forces, he wrote songs for army shows; he achieved great success with *Praise the Lord and pass the ammunition* (1942) and *Rodger Young* (1945). His film score for *Hans Christian Andersen* (1952) contains many distinctive songs.

Loesser is best known, however, for his Broadway shows, beginning in 1948 with *Where's Charley?* (based on the Victorian farce *Charley's Aunt*), which ran for two years. *Guys and Dolls* (1950) was even more popular, its success deriving in part from Loesser's witty lyrics and the remarkable cohesion and varied pacing of the score. Loesser also wrote the libretto for his next show, *The Most Happy Fella* (1956); it is his most ambitious work, a quasi-opera (he referred to it as an "extended musical comedy"), with less than 15 minutes of pure spoken dialogue. The libretto is a bold adaptation, by Loesser himself, of a drama of the 1920s concerning the romance between an old Italian farmer and a young waitress; Loesser exploited the cultural mixture of the plot by writing songs in traditional Broadway styles for the American characters ("Big 'D' " and "Standing on the corner" became hits) and music tinged with Neapolitan melody and bel canto for the Italians. *Greenwillow* (1960), an unusual, bucolic musical, was a commercial failure, though it gained a body of devotees and is still highly regarded by some, but *How to Succeed in Business without Really Trying* (1961) won a Pulitzer Prize and ran for a total of 1416 performances. Loesser's last work, *Pleasures and Palaces* (1965), was the only one to fail to reach Broadway.

Loesser's music and lyrics were unrivaled among his contemporaries. No other songwriter so successfully caught the flavor of colloquial speech, not only in his rhymes but in his often witty melodies. His effective employment of such traditional forms as waltzes and college hymns was matched by the inventive use of freer, newer forms and fresh harmonies; known for his daring, he tried never to repeat the style or tone of an earlier work. He was also a generous colleague and played a large part in promoting the careers of Richard Adler, Jerry Ross, and Meredith Willson.

WORKS
(selective list)

STAGE

All lyrics and, unless otherwise indicated, all librettos by Loesser; dates are those of first New York performance.

Where's Charley? (G. Abbott), 11 Oct 1948 [incl. My darling, my darling; Once in love with Amy]; film, 1952

Guys and Dolls (A. Burrows, J. Swerling, after D. Runyon), 24 Nov 1950 [incl. Adelaide's Lament; A bushel and a peck; Guys and Dolls; If I were a bell; I've never been in love before; Sit down, you're rockin' the boat]; film, 1955

The Most Happy Fella (after S. Howard: They Knew what they Wanted), 3 May 1956 [incl. Big "D"; Somebody somewhere; Standing on the corner]

Greenwillow (lib. with L. Samuels), 8 March 1960 [incl. The Music of Home]

How to Succeed in Business without Really Trying (Burrows, J. Weinstock, W. Gilbert), 14 Oct 1961 [incl. Brotherhood of Man; I believe in you]; film, 1966

Pleasures and Palaces (lib. with S. Spewack), Detroit, 1965

FILMS

The Perils of Pauline, 1947 [incl. I wish I didn't love you so; Poppa, don't preach to me]; Variety Girl, 1947; Neptune's Daughter, 1949 [incl. Baby, it's cold outside]; Red, Hot and Blue, 1949; Let's Dance, 1950; Hans Christian Andersen, 1952 [incl. Anywhere I wander; No two people; Thumbelina; The Ugly Duckling]

SONGS

Most associated with films. All lyrics and, unless otherwise indicated, all music by Loesser; other composers listed in parentheses.

In Love with a Memory of you (W. Schuman), 1931; Says my Heart (B. Lane), in Cocoanut Grove, 1938; Small Fry (H. Carmichael), in Sing you Sinners, 1938; Two Sleepy People (Carmichael), in Thanks for the Memory, 1938; Blue Nightfall (Lane), in St. Louis Blues, 1939; The Boys in the Back Room (F. Hollander), in Destry Rides Again, 1939; The Lady's in Love with you (Lane), in Some Like it Hot, 1939; Dolores (L. Alter), in Las Vegas Nights, 1941; Kiss the Boys Goodbye (V. Schertzinger), in Kiss the Boys Goodbye, 1941

Can't get out of this mood (J. McHugh), in Seven Days Leave, 1942; I don't want to walk without you (Styne), in Sweater Girl, 1942; Jingle, jangle, jingle (J. Lilley), in The Forest Rangers, 1942; Praise the Lord and pass the ammunition, 1942; Let's Get Lost, "Murder," he says (McHugh), in Happy Go Lucky, 1943; They're either too young or too old (A. Schwartz), in Thank Your Lucky Stars, 1943; Spring will be a little late this year, in Christmas Holiday, 1944; Rodger Young, 1945; On a Slow Boat to China, 1948

BIBLIOGRAPHY

A. Loesser: "My Brother Frank," *Notes*, vii (1949–50), 217 [incl. list of songs]
S. Green: *The World of Musical Comedy* (New York, 1960, rev. 4/1980)
D. Ewen: *Great Men of American Popular Song* (Englewood Cliffs, NJ, 1970)
M. A. Mann: *The Musicals of Frank Loesser* (diss., CUNY, 1974)
Frank Loesser Remembered (New York, 1977) [incl. list of pubd songs]

GERALD BORDMAN, STEVEN LEDBETTER

Loewe, Frederick (*b* Berlin, Germany, 10 June 1901). Composer. His father, Edmund Loewe, was a well-known tenor in operetta. Loewe studied piano with Ferruccio Busoni and Eugen d'Albert and composition with E. N. von Rezniček, and began to write songs while in his teens. (Information about Loewe's early years is cloudy and contradictory; printed sources disagree even about his date of birth.) He immigrated to the USA in 1924, and supported himself with a variety of jobs, musical and otherwise, before breaking into the professional theater. Two of his songs – both of them waltzes – were placed in Broadway productions of the mid-1930s: "Love tiptoed through my heart," in the play *Petticoat Fever* (1935), and "A waltz was born in Vienna," interpolated in the revue *The Illustrators' Show* (1936). The first of Loewe's shows to be produced were *Great Lady* (1938), composed in the outmoded Viennese operetta style, and *Salute to Spring* (1937), some of the songs from which were reused in *Life of the Party* (1942). Alan Jay Lerner, who rewrote the play

Frederick Loewe (left) with Alan Jay Lerner

of this last shortly before the opening, has been the lyricist and playwright for all of Loewe's subsequent works. The first Broadway shows they wrote together were *What's Up* (1943), a brief-lived musical comedy, and, two years later, *The Day before Spring*. These early works contain elements from operetta as well as popular songs modeled on those of the swing era, many of which contain far more adventurous harmonic writing than Loewe ever used again. This uneasy mixture of divergent styles was resolved in *Brigadoon* (1947) which established the team's reputation. Like the musical plays of Rodgers and Hammerstein, which *Brigadoon* resembles, here too there is a synthesis of elements from the American musical – its quicker pacing and more credible book – with aspects of European operetta: the prominence of the chorus, the inclusion of ballet, the use of trained voices for the romantic and more serious roles, a plot set in the past in an exotic locale (18th-century Scotland), and a musical idiom owing little to contemporary popular song (though "Almost like being in love," cast in the *AABA* format typical of Tin Pan Alley songs, has become a favorite of popular singers). *Paint your Wagon* (1951) is the only one of Lerner and Loewe's mature shows to be set in the USA – during the California gold strikes of the 1850s. The highlights of the score are the strong, driving numbers sung by secondary male characters or the chorus: "Where'm I goin'?" and "They call the wind Maria."

The most successful of the musicals Lerner and Loewe wrote together has been *My Fair Lady* (1956, adapted from G. B. Shaw's *Pygmalion*). Music and plot are closely integrated as, for example, in the changes in the character of Eliza, which are paralleled by the types of song she is given: a cozy cockney number, "Wouldn't it be loverly?"; "Just you wait," where she seethes with indignation over her insensitive treatment by the bullying Henry Higgins; and finally "Without you," in which she adopts Higgins's own impeccably pronounced upper-class disdain. To accommodate the untrained singing voice of the leading actor, Rex Harrison, Loewe set all of his songs except the last (the main section of "I've grown accustomed to her face") in fast, sputtering rhythms; Harrison performed them in a sort of speech-song in which the notated pitches were not always sung. *My Fair Lady* broke the box-office record of its day by running for 2717 performances. The film *Gigi* (1958, adapted from the novella by Colette) is similar to *My Fair Lady* in its turn-of-the-century milieu and in having a leading character (Louis Jourdan) who is also no singer and talk-sings his numbers. Many of the songs were written in a gentle, relaxed style for the veteran performer Maurice Chevalier ("Thank heaven for little girls," "I'm glad I'm not young anymore"). *Gigi* won several Academy awards, including that for best motion picture of the year. The last of Lerner and Loewe's wholly original stage shows was *Camelot* (1960, based on T. H. White's *The Once and Future King*, a retelling of the Arthurian legends). White's novel was possibly too long and unwieldy to be put into tractable dramatic shape, and *Camelot* was extensively rewritten even after its Broadway opening, with musical numbers excised to reduce the playing time and to bring the story into better focus. As in *My Fair Lady*, the leading male role was taken by an actor of limited singing ability, and the authors created for Richard Burton a form of melodrama for his two extensive solo spots at the end of each act, in which he recited his verses over orchestral accompaniment. After *Camelot* Loewe seemingly retired, although he and Lerner collaborated again in the film *The Little Prince* (1974), as well as writing new songs for a stage version of *Gigi* in the preceding year.

Other than the now-forgotten pop songs of Loewe's earliest shows, his music bears few marks that distinguish it as coming from a composer living in the USA in the postwar years, and there is an undeniable old-fashioned operetta element in the vehicles he and Lerner have chosen to write. The style of his music differs with the demands of each play, managing to be sufficiently Scottish-sounding for *Brigadoon* or akin to lower-class music-hall song for Eliza's boozing father without ever resorting to quotations or parodies. It is thus difficult to pinpoint strong compositional features of Loewe's music, aside from its being well-written for the voice and suited to the dramatic requirements of the script. Unlike that of the earlier generation of Broadway composers – Kern, Gershwin, and Porter – there is little about Loewe's music that stamps it indelibly as his, and this self-abnegating approach – where the style of writing depends less upon the composer's individual imprint than upon the needs of the period and the play – is one bequeathed to a younger generation of theater writers.

WORKS

Edition: *The Lerner and Loewe Songbook*, ed. A. Sirmay (New York, 1962)

STAGE

Unless otherwise indicated, all librettos and lyrics are by A. J. Lerner and all dates are those of first New York performance; selections published in vocal score.

Salute to Spring (E. Crooker), St. Louis, 12 July 1937

Great Lady (Crooker, L. Brentano; Crooker), orchd H. Spialek, 1 Dec 1938

Life of the Party (Lerner; Crooker), orchd Spialek, R. R. Bennett, T. Royal, Detroit, 8 Oct 1942

What's Up (Lerner, A. Pierson; Lerner), orchd V. Cleave, 11 Nov 1943

The Day before Spring, orchd H. Byrns, 22 Nov 1945

Brigadoon, orchd Royal, 13 March 1947 [incl. Brigadoon; The Heather on the Hill; Come to me, bend to me; Almost like being in love], film, 1954

Paint your Wagon, orchd Royal, 12 Nov 1951 [incl. Where 'm I goin'?; I talk to the trees; They call the wind Maria; I still see Elisa; Another Autumn; Wand'rin' star], film, 1969 [incl. 5 new songs (Lerner), music by A. Previn]

My Fair Lady (after G. B. Shaw: Pygmalion), orchd Bennett, P. Lang, 15 March 1956 [incl. Wouldn't it be loverly; With a little bit of luck; Just you wait; The rain in Spain; I could have danced all night; On the street where you live;

Get me to the church on time; Without you; I've grown accustomed to her face], film, 1964

Camelot (after T. H. White: The Once and Future King), orchd Bennett, Lang, 3 Dec 1960 [incl. Camelot; What do the simple folk do?; If ever I would leave you], film, 1967

FILMS

Gigi (Lerner, after Colette), orchd C. Salinger, 1958 [incl. Thank heaven for little girls; Waltz at Maxim's; I remember it well; I'm glad I'm not young anymore; Gigi]; adapted for stage, 13 Nov 1973 [incl. 5 new songs]

The Little Prince (Lerner, after A. de Saint-Exupéry: Le petit prince), orchd A. Morley, 1974 [incl. Be happy; I'm on your side]

SONGS
(selective list)

Love tiptoed through my heart (I. Alexander), in M. Reed: Petticoat Fever, New York, 4 March 1935; A waltz was born in Vienna (Crooker), in The Illustrators' Show (revue), New York, 22 Jan 1936

Principal publisher: Chappell

BIBLIOGRAPHY

S. Green: *The World of Musical Comedy* (New York, 1960, rev. and enlarged 4/1980)
C. Palmer: "A Cosmopolitan of Music: Frederick Loewe," *Crescendo International*, xii/12 (1974), 23
G. Bordman: *American Musical Theatre: a Chronicle* (New York, 1978)
A. J. Lerner: *The Street where I Live* (New York, 1978)

WILLIAM W. DEGUIRE

Lofton, Cripple Clarence (*b* Kingsport, TN, 28 March 1887; *d* Chicago, IL, 9 Jan 1957). Blues pianist and singer. He was born with a club foot, and may have earned his living as a musician from an early age. In 1917 he moved to Chicago, where he became celebrated as a "rent-party" pianist; from 1938 he entertained audiences in his own saloon, the Big Apple, on State Street. In spite of his deformity he is remembered as a dynamic performer, dancing, whistling, singing, and tapping rhythms while he played piano. His earliest recordings included *Brown Skin Girls* (1935, Melotone 6-11-66) and *Strut that Thing* (1935, Voc. 02951), which, with his own characteristically gritty singing, is a vigorous example of boogie-woogie and barrelhouse style. He also accompanied a few singers, notably Red Nelson, whose *Streamline Train* (1936, Decca 7171) contains a rolling version of the *Cow Cow Blues* with strong "walking" bass figures in the piano. Lofton enjoyed brief attention during the boogie-woogie craze of the 1940s, when he made further notable recordings, including *House Rent Struggle* (1943, Riv. 1037) and *Policy Blues* (1943, Session 10-014). Ill-health hindered his playing later in life, and in his final years he worked as a garage cleaner.

BIBLIOGRAPHY

SouthernB
W. Russell: "Boogie Woogie," *Jazzmen*, ed. F. Ramsey and C. E. Smith (New York, 1939), 196ff
B. Hall and R. Noblett: "A Handful of Keys: the Apochryphal Clarence Lofton," *Blues Unlimited*, no.113 (1975), 14

PAUL OLIVER

Logan, Joshua (Lockwood) (*b* Texarkana, TX, 5 Oct 1908). Theatrical director and librettist. He studied at Princeton University and with Konstantin Stanislavsky in Moscow, and was one of the founding members of the University Players. He directed his first Broadway show in 1935 but did not turn his attention to musicals until 1938, when he staged and also assisted Lorenz Hart with the libretto of Rodgers's *I Married an Angel*. He directed Weill's *Knickerbocker Holiday* (1938), Arthur Schwartz's *Stars in your Eyes* (1939), and Rodgers's *Higher and Higher* (1940), where again he collaborated with Hart on the libretto, and *By Jupiter* (1942). Later productions in which he was involved as a librettist included *South Pacific* (1949, with Hammerstein), *Wish you Were Here* (1952, with Arthur Kober), and *Fanny* (1954, with S. N. Behrman). Logan also directed the film versions of *South Pacific* (1958), *Camelot* (1967), and *Paint your Wagon* (1969). His strength as a director was in imparting a sense of movement on stage, but he was occasionally criticized for underscoring comic and romantic moments.

BIBLIOGRAPHY

"Logan, Joshua (Lockwood)," *CBY 1949*
J. Logan: *Josh: my Up and Down, In and Out Life* (New York, 1976)
——: *Movie Stars, Real People and Me* (New York, 1978)

GERALD BORDMAN

Logan, Wendell (Morris) (*b* Thomson, GA, 24 Nov 1940). Composer and educator. He studied at Florida Agricultural & Mechanical University, Tallahassee (BS 1962), with Bottje at Southern Illinois University, Carbondale (MMus 1964), and with Hervig at the University of Iowa (PhD 1968). In his youth he was influenced by the music of James Brown, Fats Domino, and other popular music entertainers; while in college, he played trumpet and arranged music for jazz ensembles and marching and concert bands. He taught at Florida Agricultural & Mechanical University (1962–3, 1969–70), Ball State University, Muncie, Indiana (1967–9), where he organized the New Music Ensemble, and Western Illinois University, Macomb (1970–73), before joining the faculty of the Oberlin College Conservatory in 1973. He has received grants from the NEA (1973, 1980), the Martha Baird Rockefeller Fund (1979), and the A. H. Powers Fund. His compositions vary in style from those based on jazz idioms to those using electronic techniques. He is the author of a *Primer for Keyboard Improvisation in the Jazz/Rock Idiom* (1980).

WORKS

Orch: Concert Music, 1963; Polyphony I, 1968; Orbits, band, 1982; *c*80 original pieces and arrs. for various jazz ens

Vocal: 3 Fragments (K. Patchen), S, cl, pf, perc, 1969; Songs of our Time, SATB, chamber ens, 1969; From Hell to Breakfast, S, Bar, nar, 2 actors, 2 dancers, jazz ens, tape, 1973–4; Malcolm, Malcolm, SATB, tape, 1974; Ice and Fire (M. Evans), song cycle, S, Bar, pf, 1975; Hughes Set (L. Hughes), TTB, perc, 1978; Dream Boogie (Hughes), 1v, pf, 1979; Requiem for Charles "Yardbird" Parker, S, T, a sax, t sax, chorus, orch, 1981; Sling Along (J. W. Johnson), 1v, 1982; Noah Built the Ark (musical play), nar, chorus, brass, pf, db, drums, elec, 1983; Prayer, nar, chorus, pf, db, drums, 1983

Chamber: Ww Qnt, 1963; Stanzas for 3 Players, fl, vc, pf, 1966; Proportions for 9 Players and Cond, fl, cl, tpt, vn, vc, pf, perc, 1968; Evocation, harmonica, tape, 1972; Memories Of, chamber orch, 1972, rev. 1979; Song of the Witchdoktor, fl, vn, pf, perc, 1976; 3 Pieces, vn, elec pf, 1977; Duo Exchanges, cl, perc, 1978; The Eye of the Sparrow, fl, t sax, tpt, pf, drums, 1978; 5 Pieces, pf, 1978; Outside Ornette's Head, tpt, gui, vib, drums, 1979; To Mingus, gui, vib, 1979

BIBLIOGRAPHY

SouthernB
A. Tischler: *Fifteen Black American Composers: a Bibliography of their Works* (Detroit, 1981)

DORIS EVANS McGINTY

Lomax, Alan (*b* Austin, TX, 15 Jan 1915). Folksong scholar. He studied at Harvard University (1932–3), the University of Texas (BA 1936), and Columbia University. In 1937 he began working under his father, John A. Lomax, in the Archive of American Folksong at the Library of Congress. He has produced numerous educational radio programs on folk music and has recorded and studied folksong in Great Britain, Haiti, Italy, Spain, the USA, and elsewhere. In 1963 he became director of the cantometrics project at Columbia University, an international study of the folksong in its cultural matrix.

Lomax's principal interests include recording and describing folksongs and studying the role of the performer; as a writer he has discussed the behavioral aspect of song performance and the place of folksong in society. He has published biographies of Jelly Roll Morton and a black American preacher and folksinger (*The Rainbow Sign*), providing valuable insight into Afro-American life and culture in the American South. Among the editions and collections he has published are several books of American folksongs and ballads, and one of songs sung by Huddie Ledbetter ("Leadbelly").

WRITINGS

with S. R. Cowell: *American Folk Song and Folk Lore: a Regional Bibliography* (New York, 1942/*R*1972)
Mister Jelly Roll: the Fortunes of Jelly Roll Morton (New York, 1950, rev. 2/1973)
Harriett and her Harmonium (London, 1955)
The Rainbow Sign (New York, 1959)
Folk Song Style and Culture (Washington, DC, 1968)
Cantometrics: a Handbook and Training Method (Berkeley, CA, 1976)
Index of World Song (New York, 1977)

DARIUS L. THIEME/R

Lombardo, Guy [Gaetano] **(Alberto)** (*b* London, Ont., 19 June 1902; *d* Houston, TX, 5 Nov 1977). Bandleader. He organized his first group around 1917 in London, Ontario. By 1923 they had begun to play in the USA, and a year later made their first recordings for Gennett as Guy Lombardo and his Royal Canadians. After a successful engagement at the Granada Cafe, Chicago (1927–8), the group went to New York and in 1929 began a record-breaking engagement of more than 33 years at the Roosevelt Grill. From this time on Lombardo and his band prospered: their records sold well; they appeared on radio, in films, and on television; and they toured extensively, always playing in major hotels, ballrooms, and nightclubs. For years CBS broadcast the band's New Year's Eve performances nationwide from the Roosevelt Grill (later from the Waldorf-Astoria).

Lombardo's band was among the most popular and long-lived dance orchestras in 20-century American musical life. His music was always pleasant and accessible as Lombardo aimed for, and reached, the broadest possible audience. The fairly stable membership of his band over the years assured continuity of style and performance. This was partly due to the participation of family members: Lebert (trumpet), Victor (clarinet and saxophone), singer Rose Marie, and especially Carmen (*b* London, Ont., 16 July 1903; *d* Miami, FL, 17 April 1971), who composed for the band, sang, played the saxophone, and served as music director. The band's emphasis on melody, its perfectly gauged tempos, its "sweet" sound (from the saxophone section's heavy vibrato, the rippling two-piano accompaniment, and the unobtrusive rhythm section), its carefully crafted arrangements (many by Dewey Bergman), and its choice of popular material all added up to a formula that continued to please audiences – particularly dancers – year after year, despite changes in musical style and the demise of many similar ensembles.

BIBLIOGRAPHY

B. Herndon: *The Sweetest Music this Side of Heaven* (New York, 1964)
J. R. Failows: "Louis Armstrong and Guy Lombardo," *Jazz*, v/9 (1966), 16
G. Simon: *The Big Bands* (New York, 1967, rev. 4/1981), 99
L. Walker: *The Wonderful Era of the Great Dance Bands* (Garden City, NY, 1972)
G. Lees: "Guy Lombardo: the Melody Lingers On," *HiFi/MusAm*, xxiv/4 (1974), 24
"Lombardo, Guy (Albert)," *CBY 1975*
G. Lombardo and J. Altshul: *Auld acquaintance* (New York, 1975)
B. F. Cline: *The Lombardo Story* (Don Mills, Ont., 1979)
S. Richman: *Guy: the Life and Times of Guy Lombardo* (New York, 1980)

MARK TUCKER

London, Edwin (*b* Philadelphia, PA, 16 March 1929). Composer. He attended the Oberlin College Conservatory, where he majored in french horn (BM 1952), and the University of Iowa (PhD in composition, 1961). He was a pupil of Schuller at the Manhattan School of Music in 1956 and studied composition with, among others, Luigi Dallapiccola and Darius Milhaud. He also studied conducting with Izler Solomon. From 1960 to 1968 he taught at Smith College, Northampton, Massachusetts. Following a year as visiting professor at the University of California, San Diego (1972–3), he joined the faculty of the University of Illinois, where he taught theory and composition for 10 years and founded and directed the Ineluctable Modality, a choral ensemble that presented much experimental new music. From 1978 he was chairman of the music department of Cleveland State University, and he founded and is leader of the Cleveland Chamber Orchestra. London has received awards from the Guggenheim Foundation (1969), the NEA (1973, 1974, 1979), and the International Society for New Music Performance (1980); he won a grant from the Hamburg Opera Contemporary Festival and has several times been a resident of the MacDowell Colony. From 1974 to 1981 he served as an administrator for the American Society of University Composers.

London's style is wide-ranging and at times lyrical, and juxtaposes intense drama with humor. Yet he manages to avoid the melodramatic effects characteristic of many composers with such a wide stylistic compass. His control of pitch and rhythm owe much to a theatrical sense of timing.

WORKS

(selective list)

Dramatic: Santa Claus (mime opera, E. E. Cummings), solo vv, dancer, chorus, chamber ens, 1960; Portraits of 3 Ladies (W. R. Benét, S. V. Benét), nar, Mez, chamber ens, mixed-media effects, 1967; The Iron Hand (after Melville: The Martyr), oratorio, 1975 [incl. material from The Death of Lincoln]; The Death of Lincoln (opera, Justice), 1976; Metaphysical Vegas (musical, London), solo vv, dancers, insts, 1981

Vocal: 3 Settings of Psalm xxiii, solo vv, SSAA, TTBB, SATB, 1961; 4 Proverbs, S, female vv, 2 tpt, bn, 1968; Psalm of These Days I–V (Bible), various vocal ens, insts, 1976–80

Inst: Trio, fl, cl, pf, 1956; Ww Qnt, 1958; Sonatina, va, pf, 1962; Brass Qnt, 1965; other works, incl. several large ens and several tape pieces

Principal publishers: European-American Music, Gun-Mar, MJQ, New Valley Music, Peters

DAVID COPE

London [Burnstein, Burnson], **George** (*b* Montreal, Que., 5 May 1919; *d* Armonk, NY, 24 March 1985). Bass-baritone. His parents took him at an early age to Los Angeles, where he later enrolled at City College, studying with Richard Lert, Hugo Strelitzer, and Nathan Stewart. In 1941 he made his début, as George Burnson, in a concert performance of Albert Coates's *Gainsborough's Duchess* in Los Angeles (20 April), then sang Dr. Grenville in *La traviata* at the Hollywood Bowl (5 August); two years later he appeared with the San Francisco Opera. In 1946 he went to New York, where he continued his vocal studies with Enrico Rosati and Paola Novikova and sang in the world première of Hindemith's Requiem, this time as George London. He toured throughout the USA and Europe in 1947 as a member of the Bel Canto Trio, with Frances Yeend and Mario Lanza. He began his international operatic career at the Vienna Staatsoper as Amonasro (3 September 1949). Engagements followed at Glyndebourne, Bayreuth, La Scala, and the Bolshoi, where he was the first American to sing Boris Godunov (1960), a role he later recorded in Moscow; in time he made guest appearances in most of the important opera houses in Europe and North and South America. His long collaboration with Wieland Wagner culminated in his singing Wotan in the complete *Ring* cycle in Cologne in 1962–4. He sang many times at the Metropolitan, making his first and last appearances as Amonasro (13 November 1951, 10 March 1966); he also took the part of Mandryka in the Metropolitan première of *Arabella* (1955) and the title role in Menotti's *Le dernier sauvage* (in English, 1964). His other notable roles included Don Giovanni and the Count, Gounod's Mephistopheles, Escamillo, the multiple villains in *Les contes d'Hoffmann*, Wagner's Dutchman, and Scarpia in *Tosca*. At the height of his career London's performances were distinguished by a rare dramatic individuality and vocal power.

London abandoned his opera career in 1967 for medical reasons and turned instead to arts administration, serving in Washington, DC, at the Kennedy Center (1968–71), the National Opera Institute (executive director, 1971–7), and the Opera Society of Washington (general director, 1975–7). He was also active as a director, staging the first complete English-language *Ring* in the USA (Seattle, 1975), a production that forswore Wieland Wagner's modernism in favor of storybook realism.

BIBLIOGRAPHY

"London, George," *CBY 1953*

J. Wechsberg: "The Vocal Mission," *New Yorker*, xxxiii (26 Oct 1957), 49

R. Celletti: "London, George," *Le grandi voci* (Rome, 1964) [with opera discography by R. Vegeto and C. Williams]

T. Page: Obituary, *New York Times* (26 March 1985)

T. Stewart: "George London," *Opera News*, i/1 (1985), 32

MARTIN BERNHEIMER/R

Long, Edgar. Pseudonym of WALLINGFORD RIEGGER.

Longfellow, Henry Wadsworth (*b* Portland, ME, 27 Feb 1807; *d* Cambridge, MA, 24 March 1882). Poet. After private schooling in Portland, where he also studied piano and flute and attended singing-school, he completed his formal education at Bowdoin College, Brunswick, Maine. It is possible that his family owned the first piano known in Portland, perhaps in Maine. He spent a year studying general literature at Harvard University, learning French and Italian. At the age of 18 he was appointed to a new chair of modern languages at Bowdoin, which he assumed in 1830, having spent the intervening years traveling and studying in France, Spain, Italy, and Germany. After another visit to Europe, especially in Germany and Scandinavia, he settled in Cambridge in 1936 assuming a position at Harvard College, where he remained until 1954. He made further visits to Europe in 1842 and 1868–9.

Longfellow was probably the most frequently set American poet of the 19th century. There are over 1200 settings of his texts, by over 650 composers; many of them, primarily settings for solo voice and keyboard, were composed before 1890 and published in England. The text that has been most often set is "Stars of the Summer Night" from *The Spanish Student* (1843). Choral settings include Rutland Boughton's *The Skeleton in Armour*, Dudley Buck's *Scenes from the Golden Legend* and *Paul Revere's Ride* (the latter for male chorus), and Elgar's *Spanish Serenade*.

Generally considered Longfellow's most enduring poem, *Hiawatha* (1855), on American-Indian themes and written in trochaic dimeters, has appealed to many composers, notably Samuel Coleridge-Taylor, whose cantata *Hiawatha's Wedding Feast* was particularly well received in England and the USA. It has also inspired several orchestral works, including symphonic poems by Louis Coerne, Delius, and Goldmark.

BIBLIOGRAPHY

G. T. Edwards: *Music and Musicians of Maine* (Portland, ME, 1928)

A. W. Kelley: *Music and Literature in the American Romantic Movement: a Study of the Knowledge of, Use of, and Ideas relating to the Art of Music in Emerson, Hawthorne, Longfellow, Poe, Thoreau, Lowell, Whitman, and Lanier* (diss., U. of North Carolina, 1929)

C. McGlinchee: "American Literature in American Music," *MQ*, xxxi (1945), 101

C. S. Lenhart: *Musical Influence on American Poetry* (Athens, GA, 1956)

A. Newton: *Longfellow: his Life and Work* (Boston, 1962)

H. E. Johnson: *Operas on American Subjects* (New York, 1964)

A. S. Arnell and R. Volz: "Longfellow and Music," *Henry Wadsworth Longfellow Reconsidered: a Symposium*, ed. J. S. Mathews (Hartford, 1970)

H. E. Johnson: "Musical Interests of certain American Literary and Political Figures," *JRME*, xix (1971), 272

R. S. Silverman: "Longfellow, Liszt, and Sullivan," *MR*, xxxvi (1975), 254

R. C. Friedberg: *American Art Song and American Poetry*, i: *America Comes of Age* (Metuchen, NJ, 1981)

M. Hovland: *Musical Settings of American Poetry: a Bibliography* (in preparation) [incl. list of settings]

MIRIAM W. BARNDT-WEBB

Longy, (Gustave-)Georges(-Léopold) (*b* Abbeville, France, ?28 Aug 1868; *d* Moreuil, France, 29 March 1930). Oboist, conductor, educator, and composer. He studied oboe at the Paris Conservatoire with Georges Gillet, and in 1886 was awarded a *premier prix*. He played with various Paris orchestras, and from 1898 to 1925 was first oboist of the Boston SO, during which time he played as soloist seven times. In 1900 he founded the Longy Club to give concerts of chamber music, principally for wind instruments and often by American composers. In 1916 he opened the Longy School of Music, which he directed for many years with the assistance of his daughter, Renée Longy-Miquelle.

He held several conducting appointments in Boston, including the Boston Orchestral Club (1899–1913), the MacDowell Club (1915–25), and the Cecilia Society chorus. From 1919 to 1921 he led the Boston Musical Association, which specialized in contemporary works. A dispute with Koussevitzky during the latter's first season as conductor of the Boston SO led to Longy's resignation as first oboe, and he returned to his native region of France.

When Longy died, invitations to a grand memorial concert in Boston were issued by a committee including, ironically, Koussevitzky. Longy's compositions have never been catalogued, but two works he is known to have written during his Boston years are a *Divertissement* for orchestra on folk tunes from Normandy and Picardy, and a *Rapsodie* for solo saxophone with an ensemble of two clarinets, bassoon, double bass, harp, and timpani. Loeffler's *Deux rapsodies* for oboe, viola, and piano (1905) were written for Longy and dedicated to him. There is a large amount of archival material on Longy in the Boston Public Library.

BIBLIOGRAPHY

P. Hale: "Georges Longy: his Beneficent Activity as Oboist and Conductor in Boston's Musical Life," *Boston Herald* (26 April 1925)

M. Smith: *Koussevitzky* (New York, 1947)

H. E. Johnson: *Symphony Hall, Boston* (Boston, 1950/*R*1979)

LEONARD BURKAT

Loomis, Clarence (*b* Sioux City, SD, 13 Dec 1889; *d* Aptos, CA, 3 July 1965). Composer. As a child he studied piano and music theory with T. C. Tjaden. He attended Dakota Wesleyan University, Mitchell, South Dakota (BM 1912), and the American Conservatory in Chicago (MA, DMA), where he was a pupil in piano with Heniot Lévy and in composition with Adolph Weidig, and won gold medals in both departments. In 1914 he joined the theory and composition faculty of the conservatory, remaining there until 1929. While on leave in Vienna in 1918–19 he studied piano with Godowsky and composition with Franz Schreker. Loomis subsequently taught at Chicago Musical College (1929–30), Arthur Jordan Conservatory, Indianapolis (1930–36), New Mexico Highlands University, Las Vegas (1945–55), and Jamestown (North Dakota) College (1955–6).

Loomis composed in a tonal, chromatic idiom. Chiefly interested in opera, he sought consciously to subordinate the music to the text, which led him to eschew virtuosity in both vocal and instrumental parts. His operas make use of American material, notably poems of Poe and melodies by Stephen Foster. *Yolanda of Cyprus*, the best-known of his operas, was performed 22 times in four cities and in 1926 received the David Bispham Memorial Medal of the Opera Society of Chicago.

WORKS

Dramatic: Yolanda of Cyprus (opera, 4, C. Y. Rice), 1919–26; The Flapper and the Quarterback (comic ballet), Kyoto, Japan, 1928; Susanna don't You Cry (theater piece), perf. 1931; A Night in Avignon (opera, 1), perf. 1932; The White Cloud (opera), perf. 1935; The Fall of the House of Usher (opera, 6 scenes, after Poe), perf. 1941; Revival (opera, 1), perf. 1943; The Captive Woman (opera), perf. 1953

Inst: Gargoyles, orch (1936); Gaelic Suite, str (1953); 3 str qts (1953, 1963, 1965); Fantasy, pf, orch (1954); Macbeth, orch (1954); The Passion Play, chorus, orch (1955); pf suites; org works

Choral: Dream Fantasy (1930); Abaldo Sea (1953); Song of the White Earth (1956); America the Eleventh (1957); Erin (1958)

Song cycles

MSS in *NmLvH*

Principal publishers: C. Fischer, Clayton F. Summy

BIBLIOGRAPHY

E. E. Hipsher: *American Opera and its Composers* (Philadelphia, 1927/*R*1978), 263

J. T. Howard: *Our Contemporary Composers: American Music in the Twentieth Century* (New York, 1941/*R*1975), 70

——: *Our American Music: Three Hundred Years of It* (New York, rev. 3/1946/*R*1954), 437

SEVERINE NEFF

Loomis, Harvey Worthington (*b* Brooklyn, NY, 5 Feb 1865; *d* Boston, MA, 25 Dec 1930). Composer. A pupil of Dvořák at the National Conservatory, New York, he composed over 500 works, but only a few were published before 1900. Some based on American Indian melodies, such as *Lyrics of the Red Man* op.76 (1903–4), were printed by the Wa-Wan Press. He appears to have been most successful in composing stage music, including the one-act opera *The Traitor Mandolin*, first performed in 1898, the dramatic recitation *The Song of the Pear Tree* (1913), the melodrama *Sandalphon* (1896), which he described as "musical symbolism," and two burlesque operas, *The Maid of Athens* and *The Burglar's Bride*. He also composed a cantata for children, *Fairy Hill* (1895), a violin sonata, and many piano pieces of a descriptive nature. Most of his manuscripts are in the Library of Congress.

BIBLIOGRAPHY

R. Hughes: *Contemporary American Composers* (Boston, 1900)

V. B. Lawrence, ed.: *The Wa-Wan Press, 1901–1911* (New York, 1970)

W. THOMAS MARROCCO

Loos, Armin [Mathias Jacob Friedrich] (*b* Darmstadt, Germany, 20 Feb 1904; *d* New Britain, CT, 23 March 1971). Composer. His father, a banker, intended him for a career in banking and finance, and with this aim he studied law at the University of Dresden and continued studies at the universities of Berlin and Geneva and at the Ecole Supérieure de Commerce in Neuchâtel, Switzerland. In Dresden he also studied piano and at one time composition with Paul Buettner. He came to the USA in 1928 and settled in New York. In 1938 he was awarded second prize in a choral competition sponsored by the WPA for *Elegy*, the only one of his works Loos heard performed publicly. In 1940 Loos became an American citizen and moved to New Britain to manage a small family business, composing at night and on weekends in almost total obscurity. He wrote both 12-tone and tonal music, in a style influenced by Bartók and Busoni. The Armin Loos Memorial Fund, established to promote his music, has led to performances by the Berkshire Music Center Orchestra (under Gunther Schuller) and the Guild of Composers, New York.

WORKS

Orch: Sym., in memoriam Ferruccio Busoni, 1940; Sym., str, 1940; Pastoral and Perpetuum mobile, 1941; Sym., in Canon Form, 1941; Percepts, chamber orch, 1968; Aquarius 70, str, 1970; Lento: Prelude to Easter, 1970; 7 other works, 1929–48

Vocal: Te Deum, SSAATTBB, 1934; Elegy, SATB, 1937; Missa spiritorum, SATB, orch, 1948; Psalm cxx, SATTB, orch, 1963; Psalm cxx, SSATB (3 va, 2 vc ad lib), 1963; 9 songs, 1929–62

Chamber: 4 str qts, 1933–63; Ww Qnt, 1964; 2 vn sonatas, 1968, 1970–71; 35 pf pieces, 1918–64; 5 transcrs. for kbd, 1933–70; 11 other works for various ens

MSS in *CtY-Mus*

Principal publishers: Association for the Promotion of New Music, Mobart

VIVIAN PERLIS

Lopatnikoff [Lopatnikov], **Nikolai** [Nikolay] **(Lvovich)** (*b* Reval [now Tallinn], Estonia, 16 March 1903; *d* Pittsburgh, PA, 7 Oct 1976). Composer and pianist. He studied piano with B. Sakharov and theory with Alexander Zhitomirsky at the St. Petersburg Conservatory (until 1917), theory with Erik Furuhjelm at the Helsinki Conservatory (1918–20), civil engineering at the Technische Hochschule, Karlsruhe (1921–7), and took private composition lessons with Toch. Among his earliest works was the Piano Concerto no.1 (1921), of which the first performance was given by Hans Bruch in Cologne in 1925; the Second Concerto was given its première in 1930 and received many performances throughout Europe thereafter, including one at the 1932 ISCM Festival. Another work that received high praise was the Symphony no.1 of 1928; performed by major orchestras both in Europe and the USA, it was taken on tour by the Philadelphia Orchestra in 1930. During these years Lopatnikoff enjoyed success as a soloist and recitalist, often in performances of his own works. He lived in Berlin (1929–33) and London (1933–9) before coming to the USA, of which he became a citizen in 1944. He held appointments as head of theory and composition at Hartt College, Hartford, Connecticut, and the Westchester Conservatory, White Plains, New York (1939–45), and as professor of composition at Carnegie Institute of Technology (later Carnegie-Mellon University, 1945–69).

Lopatnikoff's move to New York resulted in part from an association with Koussevitzky. In 1927 Copland heard his Two Pieces for mechanical piano and brought them to Koussevitzky's attention. The conductor commissioned an orchestration of one of the pieces, played the resulting Scherzo in 1928, and offered a publication contract. There began a stormy but fruitful relationship between the two men which continued to the end of Koussevitzky's life; Koussevitzky conducted the Boston SO in the premières of Lopatnikoff's Second Symphony (in 1939), Violin Concerto (1942), and Concertino for Orchestra (1945), which had been commissioned by the Koussevitzky Foundation. Lopatnikoff once said that he considered himself influenced at first by Borodin and Mussorgsky and later by Stravinsky and Hindemith, but it is mainly in the later works that the early influences may be discerned; his early experiments in rhythm and dissonance recall Stravinsky's of the same period. Prominent features of his work include linearity, motivic development, and a lightly held, floating tonality. His slow movements show at once his capacity for linear working and the emotional Russian quality of his work. But, above all, he had a considerable talent for structural equipoise. His honors included two Guggenheim Fellowships (1945, 1953), a grant and citation from the National Institute of Arts and Letters, of which he was elected a member in 1963, and an NEA grant (1975) for *Melting Pot*, commissioned by the Indianapolis Ballet. From 1929 to 1937 he contributed several articles to *Modern Music*.

WORKS

(for juvenilia, details of first performances and publication, etc., see Critser)

STAGE

Danton (opera, 3, G. Büchner), op.20, 1930–32, orch suite, op.21, 1933, concert excerpts, A, Bar, orch, 1965, Pittsburgh, 25 March 1967

Melting Pot (ballet, 6 scenes), 1975, Indianapolis, 26 March 1976

ORCHESTRAL

Prelude to a Drama, op.3, 1920; 2 pf concs., op.5, 1921, op.15, 1930; Introduction and Scherzo, op.10, 1927; 4 syms., op.12, 1928, op.24, 1938–9, withdrawn, op.35, 1953–4, op.46, 1970–71; Short Ov., op.14, 1932; 2 Russian Nocturnes, op.25, 1939; Vn Conc., op.26, 1941; Sinfonietta, op.27, 1942; Opus sinfonicum, op.28, 1942; Concertino, op.30, 1944

2 Pf Conc., op.33, 1950–51; Divertimento, op.34, 1951; Variazioni concertanti, op.38, 1958; Music for Orch, op.39, 1958; Festival Ov., op.40, 1960; Conc. for Wind, op.41, 1963; Conc. for Orch, op.43, 1964; Partita concertante, chamber orch, op.45, 1966

CHAMBER AND INSTRUMENTAL

Pf Trio, 1918; 3 str qts, op.4, 1920, op.6a, 1928, op.36, 1955; Duo, vn, vc, op.8, 1927; Sonata, vn, pf, perc, op.9, 1927; Vc Sonata, op.11, 1929; Arabesque, vc/bn, pf, 1931; 3 Pieces, vn, pf, op.17, 1931; Elegietta, vc, pf, 1934; Pf Trio, op.23, 1935; Arietta, vn, pf, 1942; Variations and Epilogue, vc, pf, op.31, 1946, arr. vc, orch, op.31a, 1973; Vn Sonata no.2, op.32, 1948; Fantasia concertante, vn, pf, op.42, 1962; Divertimento da camera, chamber ens, op.44, 1965

Pf: 4 Small Pieces, op.1, 1920; Prelude and Fugue, op.2, 1920; Sonatina, op.7, 1926; 2 Pieces, mechanical pf, 1927; 2 Danses ironiques, op.13, 1928; Gavotte, 1929; 5 Contrasts, op.16, 1930; Dialogues, op.18, 1932; Variations, op.22, 1933; Arabesque, 2 pf, 1941; Sonata, E, op.29, 1943; Dance Piece, 1955; Intervals, op.37, 1957

CHORAL

Time is Infinite Movement (Tolstoy), canon, 3vv, 1946; Vocalise in modo russo, 4vv, 1952

MSS in *DLC*; Edwin A. Fleisher Collection, *PP*; *PPi*

Principal publishers: Associated, Edition Russe, E. B. Marks, MCA, Schott

BIBLIOGRAPHY

EwenD; *VintonD*

F. Dorian: "Symphony no.3," *MQ*, xli (1955), 367

L. Trimble: "Variazioni Concertanti," *The Nation*, clxxxvii (6 Dec 1958), 435

——: "Nikolai Lopatnikoff: Symphony No. 3, Op. 35," *Notes*, xvi (1958–9), 475

Compositores de América/Composers of the Americas, ed. Pan American Union, xii (Washington, DC, 1966)

V. Thomson: *American Music since 1910* (New York, 1971)

W. Critser: "The Compositions of Nikolai Lopatnikoff: a Catalogue" [Pittsburgh, PA, 1979, unpubd]

LESTER TRIMBLE (work-list with WILLIAM CRITSER)

Los Angeles. City in California (pop. 2,966,850, ranked third largest in the USA; metropolitan area 7,477,503). It was founded in 1781 by settlers who were chiefly of Spanish, African, and Mexican Indian descent, and incorporated in 1850.

1. Early settlers. 2. Opera and concert life, 1850–1900. 3. Development of a local musical culture. 4. The modern era: (i) Orchestras (ii) Vocal and chamber music (iii) Concert halls (iv) Sacred music (v) Education and libraries (vi) Publishing (vii) Film music (viii) Jazz and popular music.

1. EARLY SETTLERS. The early history of religious music in Los Angeles is the history of the San Gabriel Mission, which was founded in 1771. The Beñeme and Jeniguechi Indians gathered there each day, and sang an *alabado* (praise song) at dusk and dawn and a *bendito* (grace) before each meal. In 1776 Pedro Font, a Franciscan from Mexico, visited the mission and led a mass that he accompanied on his psaltery; until 1834 the singing of the mass was always accompanied by instruments (such as flutes, violins, and trumpets) that local Indians had been taught to play by missionaries. (*See also* CALIFORNIA MISSION MUSIC.)

The first account in English of music played by Indians at San Gabriel was written by Harrison G. Rogers of Missouri. He described a "band of musick that played for 2 hours" in 1826 as "consisting of two small violins, one bass violin, a trumpet and a triangle. . . . They made tolerable good music, the most in imitation of whites that I ever heard." Alfred Robinson (1807–95) of Boston described church music at San Gabriel in 1829 as "well selected," and noted that the Indians' voices accorded harmoniously with the flutes and violins that accompanied them; after the service the musicians played waltzes and marches. In 1844 Ignacio Coronel opened a school north of Arcadia Street where he was assisted by his daughter Soledad, a harpist. As late as the mid-1850s the harp remained the favorite instrument of the local aristocracy. By this time musical performances were being described in a newly established local newspaper. *La Estrella de Los Angeles*, a weekly, bilingual publication, noted in 1852 that a "competent band" had played the overture to José Zorrilla's drama *Don Juan Tenorio*. Musical events were given fuller treatment in two newspapers in Spanish, *El clamor público* (published from 1855 to 1859) and *La crónica* (from 1872).

In 1855 Blas Raho (1806–62), a Lazarite from southern Italy, arrived in Los Angeles to become parish priest of Our Lady of the Angels Church (fig. 1, p. 108); a skilled musician, he paid for a new organ and sought to organize a choir for services. In 1856 six Sisters of Charity, including three from Spain, arrived in the city and in 1857–8 trained a choir at their girls' school. At the school's graduation ceremonies in 1858 the choir sang a program (printed in *El clamor público* on 3 July) that included *Gaude Virgo* and *Ave sanctissima*, the vernacular hymn *Dios te salve*, W. W. Wallace's *It is better far to speak softly*, W. E. Hickson's *O come, come away*, and *The Star-spangled Banner*.

2. Opera and concert life, 1850–1900. Visiting musical attractions in the late 1850s included an army band from Fort Tejon and minstrel troupes. The California Minstrels, a group with six members including Lew Rattler and Henry Hallett, visited Los Angeles in 1856; it returned to play for three nights at Jesús Domínguez's ranch and at the Nichols salon (1858), Stearns Hall (1859), and the Temple Theater (1865). Frank Hussey's Minstrels and the Metropolitan Minstrels played at the Temple in 1861. During the rest of the 1860s about 33 minstrel performances were given. On 21 and 23 November 1865 the Gerardo López del Castillo Spanish Company from Mexico City performed one act of Verdi's *Attila* at the Temple Theater between acts of *La trenza de sus cabellos* by Tomás Rodríguez Rubí.

In the 1870s a number of sizable concert halls were constructed that could accommodate larger opera and concert performances. Merced Theater (capacity 400) opened on 30 December 1870 with a "grand vocal and instrumental concert" at which the 21st Wilmington Army Band performed. Turnverein Hall, a large hall in a two-story building on Spring Street, opened on 22 September 1872 and was the site of theatrical performances from 1874 and concerts from the following year. In April 1875 the English pianist Arabella Goddard (1836–1922) gave two concerts there, having brought her own Steinway grand piano from San Francisco. She was assisted by two local musicians, the singing teacher Franzini Marra and A. H. Havell.

Teresa Carreño and her husband, the violinist Emile Sauret, gave four Turnverein concerts in June and July 1875; Sauret also played duos with the guitarist Miguel S. Arévalo (*b* Guadalajara, Mexico, 5 July 1843; *d* Los Angeles, 29 June 1900). Arévalo had studied in Mexico, taught for two years in San Francisco, and moved to Los Angeles in 1871, where he became music director of the newly formed Los Angeles Musical Association. For three decades he was a leading concert performer, composer, and teacher, as well as a founder of *La crónica*. He helped the area's Mexican culture withstand the pressure of German and Anglo-American musical influences that resulted from waves of immigration in the 1880s.

The completion in 1876 of the Southern Pacific railway link with San Francisco and in 1881 of a link eastward made Los Angeles virtually an obligatory stop for all concert artists touring the West. The violinist August Wilhelmj visited the city in 1880, as did the Tyrolean Alpine Singers, the Fabbri-Müller opera company (which performed scenes from Bellini's *Norma*, Weber's *Der Freischütz*, and Donizetti's *Linda di Chamounix* in costume), the Mendelssohn Quintette Club of Boston in 1881, and the San Francisco Comic Opera Company in 1882.

Ozro W. Childs's Grand Opera House, an elegant auditorium built in a horseshoe configuration with wide aisles, unobstructed views, and 500 seats, opened on 27 May 1884 with a house orchestra led by Peter Engels and including two violins, double bass, flute, clarinet, cornet, trombone, and percussion. These musicians settled in Los Angeles having established their reputations elsewhere, a trend that has continued. In 1885 Emma Abbott brought her English Opera Company to the Grand Opera House and performed Donizetti's *Lucia di Lammermoor*, Gounod's *Faust* (into which she interpolated *Nearer my God to thee* and *Asleep in Jesus*), Friedrich Flotow's *Martha*, Ambroise Thomas' *Mignon*, and Verdi's *La traviata* and *Il trovatore*. The company returned in 1886–7 with Donizetti's *Lucrezia Borgia*, Bellini's *La sonnambula*, and Luigi and Federico Ricci's *Crispino e la Comare*. In 1887 large crowds heard Theodore Thomas and Gustav Heinrichs conduct the National Opera Company in *Faust*, Delibes' *Lakmé*, Nicolai's *The Merry Wives of Windsor*, Verdi's *Aida*, Wagner's *Lohengrin* and *Der fliegende Holländer*, Anton Rubinstein's *Nero*, and Delibes' ballet *Coppélia* at the newly opened Hazard's Pavilion. This building, also known as the Academy of Music when

1. Our Lady of the Angels Church, Los Angeles, 1857; the city's oldest church, it was dedicated in 1822 and after 1860 became known as Our Lady Queen of Angels or Plaza Church

first opened, seated 4000 (razed after Alfred Hertz conducted *Parsifal* there in 1905); it would not have been large enough to accommodate the crowd that heard Patti sing the role of Semiramide (Rossini) at Mott Hall in 1887, which was "the largest audience in both numbers and money receipts" that had ever gathered in Los Angeles.

Among the more successful performances at the Grand Opera House were those of a troupe led by Emma Nevada (1885) and of the Típica Orchestra from Mexico City (1886), led by Encarnación García, who played a 99-string *salterio*. In the late 1880s other troupes performed works by Gilbert and Sullivan and Viennese operettas. In 1887 the *Los Angeles Times* advertised performances by the Bijou Opera, Carleton Opera, Hazard's American Opera, and Pike Opera companies; by I. W. Baird's Mammoth and Billy Emerson's Minstrels; and by Zerega's Royal Spanish Troubadours. A Hispano-Mexicano Opera Company performed zarzuelas by Asenjo Barbieri and Gaztambide at Armory Hall in 1888.

In the next decade the number of touring opera companies visiting Los Angeles increased; the city heard more operas in the 1890s than it would in the 1980s. Emma Juch gave performances at the Grand Opera House in 1890 (including the local première of Rossini's *Guillaume Tell*); later that year Abbott appeared at the Los Angeles Theater in Verdi's *Ernani*, Gounod's *Roméo et Juliette*, and Donizetti's *Anna Bolena*. On 19 November 1891 the Columbia Opera Company gave the first performance in Los Angeles of Mascagni's *Cavalleria rusticana*. Juch sang eight operas in 1892; the same year the Arcaraz Spanish Grand Opera Company performed works by Bizet, Suppé (*Boccaccio* and *Donna Juanita*), Ruperto Chapí (*La tempestad*), and Federico Chueca (*La gran via*) at the Grand Opera House, and the Alessandro Salvini Co. performed Mascagni's *L'amico Fritz* (18 November) before it was heard in New York. The first American performance of Puccini's *La bohème* was given by the Del Conte Italian Opera Company on 14 October 1897 at the Los Angeles Theater.

Among those peformers who visited Los Angeles in the 1890s were Gilmore (1891), Sousa (with the US Marine Band in 1892, and with his own ensemble in 1896), Adele Aus der Ohe (1890), Musin (1892), Ysaÿe (1895), Paderewski (1896), Moriz Rosenthal (1898), and Emil von Sauer (1899).

After 1875 Blacks played an important part in the history of Los Angeles. Biddy Mason arrived in 1851 and three years later was a founding member of the African Methodist Episcopal Church; by the time of her death in 1891 she had amassed a sizable fortune. Touring black groups enjoyed great success in her lifetime. In 1876 the Jubilee Singers from Fisk University sang *Massa's in de cold, cold ground*, *Listen to the mocking bird*, *Rock my soul in the bosom of Abraham*, and *Wasn't that a broad river* (with Mason joining in the choruses) at Turnverein Hall, which was filled to capacity. All-black minstrel groups that performed in the city included the Original Georgia Minstrels (Merced Theater, 1876), the New Orleans Minstrels and Brass Band (Turnverein, 1881), Callender's Minstrels (Turnverein, 1882), Richard and Pringle's Georgia Minstrels (Los Angeles Theater, 1889, and the Grand Opera House, 1891–3), Lew Johnson's Refined Minstrels (Grand Opera House, 1890), and Cleveland's Colored Minstrels (Grand Opera House, 1890). Such well-known performers as William Kersands and Sam Lucas toured frequently with these troupes. The Fisk Jubilee Singers continued to visit Los Angeles until 1890, when they performed at Illinois Hall. Their concerts included songs by Foster and were attended by a racially mixed public. Flora Batson appeared at the Los Angeles Theater in 1889 and returned to the city for three concerts sponsored by the Methodist church the following year. In February 1890 the Hyers Sisters staged *Out of Bondage*, a musical theater piece written for them, at Los Angeles Theater.

3. Development of a local musical culture. On 10 March 1892 Paul Colberg, the founder of a local conservatory, sponsored a concert of his own compositions at Turner Hall; this was the first performance devoted entirely to the works of a Los Angeles resident. Colberg soon left the city, however, convinced that no national reputation could accrue to one of its inhabitants. Preston Ware Orem (1865–1938), a composer, pianist, and organist who lived in the city from 1889 to 1897, left for the same reason. In 1895 Carlyle Petersilea, a pianist and teacher from Boston, gave a recital at the Young Men's Christian Association auditorium. The following year he played all Beethoven's piano sonatas in a series of 11 recitals, the first time such a cycle had been given west of the Rocky Mountains, and a feat not to be repeated in Los Angeles until 1946.

The first amateur musical association in Los Angeles, the Ellis Club, was formed in 1888; the following year a women's club, the Treble Clef (later the Lyric Club) was organized. The number of such organizations had grown to 17 by 1922. During roughly the same period the number of private teachers advertising in city directories also rose dramatically: from five in 1881–2 to 808 in 1916. In 1883 Emily J. Valentine founded the Los Angeles Conservatory of Music (from 1892 the Los Angeles Conservatory of Music and Art) and with the aid of her daughter directed it until her death in 1910; she bequeathed it to Adeltha Valentine Carter and Earl B. Valentine. (The conservatory moved many times during the next half-century before merging in 1961 with the Chouinard Art Institute to form the California Institute of the Arts, at Valencia, about 56 km north of Los Angeles.) In 1880 the University of Southern California was founded (see §4(v) below).

In the 1880s and 1890s a number of institutions of higher learning offered specialized musical instruction, including St. Vincent's College (later Los Angeles College) and Ellis College; both retained Emilie Lassaugue as a teacher until 1884, when she left amid some controversy to establish her own musical college in Nadeau Block. In 1888 Occidental College engaged Asbury Kent, who also taught at McPherrin Academy, as a piano and singing teacher. The teaching of music in Los Angeles public schools began in 1885. In 1893 Juliet Powell Rice was elected "principal of music" to teach singing in elementary schools; three years later she joined the faculty of the State Normal School. Gertrude E. Parsons was supervisor of music in the Los Angeles public schools from 1897 to 1900, and returned as assistant supervisor after 1904. Kathryn Emilie Stone, elected supervisor in 1900, published an *Outline for Music Appreciation for Elementary Schools* (1916), one of the first music appreciation texts intended to be used in conjunction with phonograph recordings. In 1910 Jennie Jones became supervisor of an elementary-school orchestra program; by the 1913–14 school year there were 77 elementary-school orchestras, and ten years later 122 elementary and 27 high-school ensembles with a total of 2800 players.

Churches have played an important role in Los Angeles's musical life. St. Vibiana's Cathedral was consecrated on 30 April 1876; this was modeled on San Miguel del Puerto in Barcelona and seated 1600. During the last quarter of the 19th century

2. *Wilshire Boulevard (formerly B'nai B'rith) Temple*

orchestral masses were led from the organ by such German immigrants as August J. Stamm and A. G. Gardner. Among Protestant churches the more notable included First Presbyterian (formed 1855), where congregational singing was accompanied first by H. D. Barrows playing flute, then by Almira Russell Hancock, who played an organ sent from San Francisco. First Congregational (formed 1868) received a Bergstrom two-manual organ from San Francisco that was acclaimed as the best in Los Angeles when dedicated on 26 November 1883. The first three-manual organ in the city was one from St. Louis built by Kilgen and dedicated on 2 July 1887 at First Baptist. In 1896 Wilhelm Middelschulte dedicated at First Congregational an instrument with 2000 speaking pipes.

In 1895 Murray M. Harris, born in Illinois in 1866 and in California since 1883, established "the only complete Organ Factory in the West." In 1903 he announced a $67,000 contract to build an organ for Kansas City Convention Hall (never installed) that was first to be exhibited at the Louisiana Purchase Exhibition in St. Louis (1904). The project's spiraling costs ruined him and led him to cede his assets to the Los Angeles Art Organ Company; under this company's marque the "world's largest organ," with 140 stops, was played at the exhibition by Alexandre Guilmant. The first church with a vested boys' choir was St. Paul's Episcopal, where Alfred J. F. McKiernan was precentor from 1886 to 1889. He was assisted at St. Paul's School by M. L. Laxton, a school teacher from London. Mamie Perry (1862–1949), a native of the city who had studied opera in Milan, was particularly sought after to sing in various churches in Los Angeles after giving her début at Turnverein Hall on 18 February 1882. The most widely performed and published composer of church solos, anthems, and cantatas was Frederick Stevenson (*b* Newark-on-Trent, England, 16 Sept 1845; *d* Los Angeles, 25 Oct 1925); he moved to the city from Denver in 1894 to conduct at St. John's Episcopal Church and Temple B'nai B'rith.

B'nai B'rith (from 13 December 1933 the Wilshire Boulevard Temple; fig.2) was a center of musical activity as early as 1869, when the temple's building fund sponsored three concerts that included an eight-hand piano arrangement of the overture to Hérold's *Zampa* led by Van Gulpen (or Gulpin), a local piano teacher. From 1862 to 1886 services were led by Abraham Wolf Edelman, an Orthodox rabbi from Warsaw. Later a more liberal ritual was instituted; during the tenure (1899–1919) of Rabbi Sigmund Hecht, from Hungary, the congregation not only employed a gentile mixed choir and organist but more than once welcomed "Christian worship." Congregation Sinai, a Conservative organization founded in B'nai B'rith hall in 1906, began with a cantor named Katz; from its inception Sinai allowed organ playing, although at first it had no choir.

Charles Edmund Day (*b* Port Jackson, NY, 1 July 1846; *d* Los Angeles, 4 Nov 1902), a chorus leader, arrived in Los Angeles in 1877 and was active in church and community musical affairs for the next quarter-century. A pupil of Zerrahn in Boston and of G. F. Root in Chicago, he soon organized a three-day Jubilee Festival, held in a tent on Spring Street (4–6 June 1878). The programs included excerpts from Handel's *Messiah* and *Judas Maccabaeus*, Haydn's *Creation*, and Rossini's *Mosè in Egitto*, and the overtures to Verdi's *Nabucco* and Offenbach's *La Grande-Duchesse de Gérolstein*; it ended with the Anvil Chorus from Verdi's *Il trovatore*, with real anvils and cannon.

4. The modern era.

(i) Orchestras. The Los Angeles Philharmonic Society was formed in June 1878 and revitalized in 1888. The orchestra gave four concerts during the 1888–9 season under the direction of Adolph Willhartitz (*b* Prague, 6 June 1836; *d* Los Angeles, 12 Jan 1915); the programs included Beethoven's Fifth Symphony, Mozart's Concerto for two pianos, Haydn's *Creation*, Mendelssohn's *Lobgesang*, two tone poems by the local composer Franz Nebelung,

and works by Brahms and Wagner. Theater musicians made up most of the 35-piece orchestra when August J. Stamm opened a four-concert season on 9 January 1893 at the Grand Opera House.

In 1898 Harley Hamilton (*b* Oneida, NY, 18 March 1861; *d* Los Angeles, 14 May 1933), the concertmaster of Stamm's orchestra, formed the Los Angeles SO, which he conducted until 1913. He followed the example set by Willhartitz and Stamm when, during the orchestra's early years, he drew its string players from local theater ensembles, but he also drew on the Seventh Regiment Band, which he conducted in 1898. Unlike his predecessors in Los Angeles, Hamilton was an apt program builder. In his first season, when he had only 33 players, he performed Beethoven's First Symphony; when the orchestra had nearly doubled in size in 1900 he conducted Tchaikovsky's *Pathétique*. He championed the works of several local composers, including Morton Freeman Mason (*b* Natick, MA, 12 Sept 1859; *d* Pasadena, CA, 26 Dec 1927), who played bassoon in the Los Angeles SO until 1907 (he conducted his Two Lyric Pieces, Novelette, Grand Polonaise, Symphonic Overture, and Overture in F minor); Charles Edward Pemberton, the orchestra's oboist in 1904–5, then a member of its violin section (his *Rêverie* for strings); Henry Schoenefeld (*Suite caractéristique* on Indian themes); and Stevenson (*Queen Mab*). He also performed works by other Americans, including Chadwick, MacDowell, Shapleigh, Arthur Foote, and Frederick Zech. Later, Hamilton's programs became more ambitious; in 1912 he led the orchestra in a program that included Glazunov's *Carnaval*, Tchaikovsky's *Romeo and Juliet*, Rachmaninoff's Second Symphony, and Harold Bauer performing Beethoven's "Emperor" Concerto. In addition to leading the Los Angeles SO he conducted the Women's Orchestra of Los Angeles for 20 seasons beginning in 1893.

From 1913 to 1920 the Los Angeles SO played under Adolph Tandler (*b* Vienna, 2 Nov 1875; *d* Los Angeles, 30 Sept 1953), who conducted the Los Angeles premières of 52 compositions. A graduate of the Konservatorium in Vienna and founder of the Tandler Quartet (brought to Los Angeles in 1909), he was the first conductor in the western USA to perform Beethoven's Ninth Symphony, and also introduced Berlioz's *Harold in Italy*, Scriabin's *Le poème de l'extase*, Sibelius's First Symphony, Ernest Bloch's setting of Psalm cxxxvii, Samuel Coleridge-Taylor's *Danse nègre*, and Frederick Delius's *On Hearing the First Cuckoo in Spring* to local audiences. He took a special interest in works that were once popular but have since fallen into obscurity (Victor Herbert's *Irish Rhapsody*, Rosseter G. Cole's *Pioneer Overture*), in compositions by women composers (Amy Marcy Beach's *Gaelic Symphony*, Mana-Zucca's Piano Concerto, and Fannie Charles Dillon's *Celebration of Victory*), and in the music of such composers from the eastern USA as Chadwick, MacDowell, and Horatio Parker. He performed works by many local composers, including Dillon, Mason (Overture in C), Pemberton (*The Light that Failed*, Festival Overture), Stevenson (Character Pieces from the *Rubaiyat*), Diggle (*Fairy Suite*), Albert J. Adams (Viola Concerto), Homer Grunn (*Marche héroïque* for piano and orchestra), Frank Colby (Festival March), and Jaroslaw de Zielinski (*Marche héroïque*); in 1917 he conducted the world première of Cadman's *Thunderbird Suite*. Tandler conducted at least four of his own compositions: *The Sustained C*, *In Memoriam A. C. Bilicke*, *California Sketches*, and the Symphony in A minor.

After performing in Trinity Auditorium through the 1916–17 season the Los Angeles SO moved for its last three seasons to The Auditorium (known as Clune's between 1915 and 1919). This auditorium, seating 2600, was inaugurated in 1906 and was then the largest reinforced concrete building in California; it also had the first theater balcony in Los Angeles built without supporting columns. It became known as Philharmonic Auditorium in 1920 when the Los Angeles PO began performing there.

Founded in 1919 and financed until 1934 by William Andrews Clark, Jr., the Los Angeles PO was intended to be "as fine an orchestral institution as has existed in America." Clark was unable to engage Rachmaninoff as its first conductor, and instead chose, on Alfred Hertz's recommendation, Walter Henry Rothwell (*b* London, England, 22 Sept 1872; *d* Santa Monica, CA, 12 March 1927), formerly the conductor of the St. Paul Symphony. He was followed by Georg Schnéevoigt (1927–9), Artur Rodzinski (1929–33), and Otto Klemperer (1933–9). Clark subsidized the orchestra generously but left it no bequest; on his death in 1934 the Southern California Symphony Association intervened and continued Klemperer's contract.

Between 1943 and 1956 the orchestra was led by Alfred Wallenstein, one of the first American-born music directors of a major orchestra. His tenure was especially noteworthy for performances of such large choral works as Beethoven's *Missa solemnis* and for his successful association with the choral director Roger Wagner. The chorale bearing Wagner's name was formed in Los Angeles in 1946, from which time it participated in all concerts by the Los Angeles PO involving chorus. Wallenstein's successor, Eduard van Beinum, accepted the music directorship on condition that he be allowed to continue as director of the Amsterdam Concertgebouw. The high point of his tenure in Los Angeles was a performance of Beethoven's Ninth Symphony before an audience of 6600 in Shrine Auditorium in 1958. Stricken by a heart attack in 1959, he was succeeded, after Solti refused the appointment, by Zubin Mehta, who was music director and conductor from 1962 to 1978. Carlo Maria Giulini led the orchestra from 1978 to 1983; his term was marked by a successful series of eight performances of Verdi's *Falstaff* in 1982. Michael Tilson Thomas and Simon Rattle served as principal guest conductors until 1985, when André Previn's appointment as music director became effective.

On 11 July 1922 members of the Los Angeles PO, conducted by Alfred Hertz, gave the opening concert in the first ten-week summer season of "Symphonies under the Stars" at Hollywood Bowl. The Bowl – a 60-acre canyon possessing great natural acoustical advantages – had been sold to the Theater Arts Alliance in 1919 for $47,500; after improvements, it was assigned by deed by the Community Park and Art Association to Los Angeles County in 1924 for $1,500,000 (thereafter escaping taxes). It was operated under the management of the Hollywood Bowl Association in 1924–32 and 1945–51, and from 1951 to 1966 in cooperation with the Southern California Symphony Association; it fluctuated widely in public appeal up to 1969, when Ernest Fleischmann became artistic director. The largest attendances on record include 24,000 for Ernestine Schumann-Heink on 27 July 1928 and 26,410 for Lily Pons on 7 August 1936. Many prominent conductors have appeared there, including Hertz (who was known as "father of the bowl"), Albert Coates, José Iturbi, Otto Klemperer, Pierre Monteux, Eugene Ormandy, Artur Rodzinski, William Steinberg, Leopold Stokowski, and Bruno Walter. Arturo Toscanini was the only famous conductor of the time never to appear there. Among the pianists who played there were Iturbi, Vladimir Horowitz, and Artur Rubinstein, as well as Sergei Rachmaninoff (in 1942); Jascha Heifetz holds the record among instrumentalists for drawing the largest crowds. 15,000 people were present in 1928 when Percy Grainger was married in the bowl, on which occasion he conducted a performance of a work of his own. On 23 August 1964 the Beatles drew an audience of 17,200; like numbers attended their return appearances in 1965. In 1967 came Count Basie, Cannonball Adderley's Quintet, Jimi Hendrix, the Lovin' Spoonful, the Mamas and the Papas, and Mariachi Los Camperos. To revive audiences for classical music, Fleischmann inaugurated spectaculars and mini-marathons; a wide range of popular artists and classical concerts were given in the 1985 season.

The Japanese PO of Los Angeles, formed in 1961 with 31 members, had 100 players by 1975, most of whom were professional musicians of Japanese descent. Led by Akira Kikukawa, it is the only Japanese symphony orchestra outside Japan and until 1975 was the only important ethnic symphony orchestra in the USA. It has performed, and in some cases given the American premières of, music by such composers as Michio Miyagi and Yasushi Akutagawa.

Los Angeles's other orchestras include the Los Angeles Chamber Symphony, led by Neville Marriner from 1969, then by Gerard Schwarz (1978–85); and more than 20 community orchestras, including the Glendale SO (formed 1923 and led by Carmen Dragon from 1963 until his death in 1984), and well-known ensembles in Long Beach and Pasadena.

(ii) Vocal and chamber music. Los Angeles has long supported choral music. The Roger Wagner Chorale was founded by Wagner in 1946. Out of it grew the Los Angeles Master Chorale, founded by Wagner in 1965, which during the next two decades was the only professional resident chorus in the country giving its own series of concerts; its programs included sacred works and operas performed in concert versions. Numerous attempts to form locally based opera companies, however, have not prospered in the face of visiting companies. The Chicago Opera made in 1913 the first of several visits, the San Francisco Opera visited annually from 1937 to 1969, and the New York City Opera made visits from 1967 to 1982.

The first of an annual series of chamber music concerts was presented by the Coleman Chamber Music Association in 1904. Other chamber music programs are sponsored by the Monday Evening Concerts in the Art Museum, the Music Guild, and the Los Angeles Chamber Music Association. The Los Angeles chapter of the National Association for American Composers and Conductors sponsored concerts by its members between 1955 and 1975; these were chronicled in the chapter's publication, *The Composer and Conductor*. After the organization changed its name to the National Association of Composers, USA, in 1975, the chapter's activities were reported in the bulletin *Composer/USA*. The International Congress on Women in Music, founded at Los Angeles in 1982, held area meetings (1982–5) which were recorded in the *Congress Newsletter* which began in 1983.

(iii) Concert halls. Los Angeles did not acquire adequate concert venues until relatively late in its history. Shrine Auditorium, a massive structure built in 1927, was only partly satisfactory for opera and ballet performances. In the 1960s, however, a group of citizens led by Dorothy Buffum Chandler oversaw the financing and construction of the Music Center, a complex of three auditoriums in central Los Angeles. The Dorothy Chandler Pavilion (capacity 3200) is used chiefly for symphonic and operatic performances, the Mark Taper Forum (753) for chamber music concerts, and the Ahmanson Theater (2100) for drama, light opera, and musical comedy.

Other important halls include the Leo S. Bing Center (602) at the Los Angeles County Museum of Art, the site from 1965 of a series of Bing Concerts, and of Monday Evening Concerts that emphasize contemporary music; the Wilshire-Ebell Theater, used for chamber music performances; and the Embassy Theater (formerly Trinity Auditorium), where the Los Angeles Chamber Symphony began performing in 1984. There are also several auditoriums connected with academic institutions: Royce Hall (seating 1892 when built in 1939, slightly fewer after remodeling in 1984) and Schoenberg Hall (528) at UCLA; Ingalls Audito-

3. Hollywood Bowl, 1960

rium (2000) at East Los Angeles College; Bovard Hall (1600) at the University of Southern California; and Thorne Hall (960) at Occidental College. Shubert Theater (1824) is the city's principal venue for musical theater. (For venues of rock concerts, see §4 (viii) below.)

(iv) Sacred music. Several churches and synagogues in Los Angeles have been important centers of musical activity. First Congregational's annual Bach festival was started in 1924 by John Smallman (*b* Leamington Spa, England, 8 Jan 1886; *d* Los Angeles, 19 Dec 1937). A former pupil of Emil Mollenhauer in Boston, Smallman settled in Los Angeles in 1918, directed music at First Congregational from 1921, founded the first *a cappella* choir in southern California in 1923, and conducted the Los Angeles Oratorio Society in the local premières of Elgar's *Dream of Gerontius*, Horatio Parker's *Hora novissima*, and works by Cadman, Hadley, and Deems Taylor. In 1932 a Skinner organ with four manuals was installed; in 1969 this was enlarged to 4323 pipes and Schlicker provided the church with a gallery organ of 6866 pipes. Lloyd Holzgraf became the church's organist in 1959, and began an annual recital series in 1969.

In 1928 the Church of the Blessed Sacrament acquired a Casavant organ with four manuals and 58 ranks, and engaged Richard Keyes Biggs (*b* Glendale, OH, 16 Sept 1886; *d* Los Angeles, 17 Dec 1962) as its organist. Biggs played and recorded prolifically, composed many masses (of which 15 are published), and presented a series of organ recitals at which such local virtuosos as Clarence Mader, W. Brownell Martin, and David Craighead performed. A Wangerin organ with four manuals and 3420 pipes was dedicated at St. Vibiana's Cathedral in 1929; Roger Wagner began two decades as organist and choirmaster at St. Joseph's in 1944. Paul Salamunovich, who succeeded Biggs as director of the Blessed Sacrament Men's Choir, is music director at St. Basil's (1985); other prominent music directors have included Jonathan Wattenbarger at St. Paul the Apostle and James Vail at St. Alban's.

With more than 100 synagogues and a Jewish population exceeding half a million, Los Angeles is an important center of Jewish musical traditions. At Wilshire Boulevard Temple, the largest Reform congregation on the West Coast, Charles Feldman is the music director and Anita Priest the organist (1985). The area's best-known cantors include Meir Finkelstein at Temple Sinai and Binyamin Glickman at Beth Jacob in Beverly Hills.

(v) Education and libraries. In 1882 a branch of the San Jose Normal School was formally opened in Los Angeles; this became independent (renamed the Los Angeles Normal School) in 1887. It moved in 1914, and in 1919 (when student enrollment was 2300) it became the southern branch of the state university system (*see* CALIFORNIA, UNIVERSITY OF), being empowered to grant its own degrees in 1924 and assuming its present name, the University of California at Los Angeles (UCLA), in 1927; it moved to its present campus in 1929.

Vocal instruction was introduced at the school in 1883, and the prospectus of 1884–5 states that to qualify for public school teaching "each student receives two lessons per week in musical theory and practice." Emily J. Valentine taught from 1883 to 1885 and was succeeded by R. L. Kent from 1885 to 1893; he was in turn replaced by Juliet P. Rice, music supervisor in the Los Angeles municipal schools from 1890. She wrote the first detailed "Outline of Course of Music Study," and organized two choral groups, the Philharmonic Society (1894) and the Normal School Glee Club (1897), both of which she conducted until she resigned in 1898 to become public-school music supervisor in Santa Barbara. William Mead, a local flutist, directed the school orchestra (founded in 1897).

In 1911 a music department was formally established; it included three teachers and was directed by Jennie Goodwin, formerly public-school music supervisor in Des Moines, Iowa, and a teacher at Drake University; she was succeeded in 1914 by Frances A. Wright. In 1915 the department became a school of music with five faculty members. The school became the department of music of the new southern branch of the University of California in 1919. In 1921 William J. Kraft, formerly of Teachers College, Columbia University, became the school's first male instructor on his appointment as theory and composition teacher. The following year Squire Coop, who had been a choral director in Salt Lake City, joined the faculty and in 1923 became its chairman; the concert pianist George S. McManus, who joined the faculty in 1929, succeeded Coop as chairman for three years. From 1930 to 1939 Alexander Schreiner was UCLA organist and played three recitals weekly on the Harvey Mudd Skinner organ in Royce Hall. In this hall *Baal Hamon*, a tone poem for orchestra, chorus, soloists, and organ by Theodore Stearns, a chairman of the department, was given its première in 1935. Stearns was succeeded by Leroy Allen, formerly of Los Angeles City College, who was also active as conductor of the Reserve Officers' Training Corps and Bruin bands. The musicologists Robert U. Nelson and Walter H. Rubsamen joined the UCLA music faculty in 1938; the following year McManus returned to the university to succeed Schreiner as its organist (he remained until 1942) and a music major was first made available. The MA degree was authorized in 1940, and the PhD was first conferred in 1949.

In 1947–8 12 faculty members were appointed, including Boris A. Kremenliev, Guy Maier, and Feri Roth. Roger Wagner, who had taught in Raymond Moremen's stead in 1949–50, returned in 1954 as a choral director and remained at UCLA until 1981. In 1951–2 John Vincent engaged four wind players from the Los Angeles PO as instrumental instructors.

Clarence Sawhill left the University of Southern California in 1952 to begin a quarter-century as director of the UCLA bands. Mantle Hood, who began teaching at the university in 1954, founded the Institute of Ethnomusicology in 1961; this was absorbed by UCLA's music department on his retirement in 1973. Among those who have taught at the university are the composers Schoenberg (1936–44), Lukas Foss (1953–62), Carlos Chávez (1960), Roy Harris (1961–73), Nicolas Slonimsky (1964–7), and Paul Chihara (1966–73), and the violinist Jascha Heifetz (1959–61). In the mid-1980s the music department had about 225 undergraduate and 110 graduate students, 80 instructors, and offered the BA, MA, MFA, and PhD degrees in musicology, ethnomusicology, music education, composition, and performance practice.

The UNIVERSITY OF SOUTHERN CALIFORNIA (USC), a private institution, was founded in 1880. Musical instruction was offered beginning with the 1883–4 school year, when 248 students were enrolled in the university conservatory. The music program's first directors were Mrs. C. S. Nellis (1883–7), Lucy H. Stagg (1887–95), and Frederick Albert Bacon (1895–8). Walter Fischer Skeele (*b* Hartford, CT, 26 Sept 1865; *d* Los Angeles, 18 April 1935), an organist, then assumed leadership of the school, until 1933. In its early years USC maintained an agricultural branch in Ontario, California, where from 1887 to 1896 the music director was William Ludwig Piutti. A graduate of Stuttgart Conservatory who had studied with Liszt, Wilhelm Speidel, and Joachim Raff, he played three- and four-hour solo recitals in Los Angeles, where he taught privately at other schools until he assumed a deanship in San Jose in 1896. In the mid-1980s the music department had about 375 undergraduate and 225 graduate students, 60 full-time and 55 part-time instructors, and offered BA, BM, MA, MM, MMEd, DMA, and PhD degrees in performance, music education, choral music, church music, theory, composition, music history, conducting, and musicology. Among those who have taught at the university are Primrose and Piatigorsky (both 1961–5) and, after he left UCLA, Heifetz.

In addition to UCLA and USC there are strong composition programs at the CALIFORNIA INSTITUTE OF THE ARTS (which absorbed the Los Angeles Conservatory of Music established in 1883), where Subotnick and Mel Powell both joined the faculty in 1969; and at CALIFORNIA STATE UNIVERSITY, Northridge, where the faculty includes Daniel Kessner and Aurelio de la Vega.

In 1974 USC and UCLA joined with other educational institutions in the Los Angeles area to establish the Arnold Schoenberg Institute, a repository of the composer's manuscripts and memorabilia. The library of UCLA includes rare early Venetian opera librettos, the Meredith Willson Library of American popular music, and film scores; that of USC contains a collection of Russian operas, 18th-century *opéras comiques*, and film and television music. The Los Angeles Public Library (established in 1913) holds the George Dobinson collection of 19th-century Los Angeles theater programs and issues of early local newspapers. Other libraries in the area with important local music history material include the Henry E. Huntington Library in San Marino (which holds the scrapbooks of Lynden Ellsworth Behymer, documenting the history of symphonic and operatic performances in Los Angeles from 1898 to 1947); the William A. Clark Memorial Library; the Walt Disney Archives in Burbank; the Los Angeles Music Center Archives; the Pasadena Public Library; the library of the Academy of Motion Picture Arts and Sciences in Beverly Hills; and the libraries of the California State University branches in Los Angeles, Long Beach, and Northridge. (*See also* LIBRARIES AND COLLECTIONS, §3.)

(vi) Publishing. Between 1885 and 1945 there were 29 music publishers in Los Angeles. Of these W. A. Quincke & Co. was active for the longest period; the firm was established in 1906 and was in operation at least until 1929. West Coast Publishing Co., which specialized in shape-note gospel music, was active until at least 1924. Other local music publishers and printers during this period were Southern California Music Publishing Co., Falconer & Loveland Music Printers, Frank E. Garbett, Freed & Powers, Saunders Publications, Boris Morris Music Co., Wright Music Co., and Harry G. Neville. In the mid-1980s the city's leading music publishers included Belmont Music Publishers, Criterion Music Corp., and Warner Bros. Music.

Musical activities in Los Angeles between 1911 and 1948 were described in the *Pacific Coast Musician*, a periodical founded and edited by Frank Colby (*b* Milwaukee, WI, 1 Sept 1867; *d* Los Angeles, 15 Feb 1940), an organist, conductor, and composer. *Music of the West*, a monthly issued in Pasadena from 1945 to 1969, also focused on local musical events. The *Journal of the Arnold Schoenberg Institute* (1976–), edited by Leonard Stein, and the *Inter-American Music Review* (1978–), edited by Robert Stevenson, which specializes in the history of American music before 1800, both publish two or three issues a year.

(vii) Film music. The temperate southern California climate attracted the first film companies to Los Angeles in 1913; instrumentalists were needed to play background music for silent films, and such composers as Henry Hadley and Joseph Carl Breil soon became involved in the film industry. The advent of sound films in 1927 created a far greater demand for composers and performers; Malotte settled in the city that year, founded a school for theater organists, and wrote and conducted film scores for Walt Disney. Each motion-picture studio employed an orchestra of symphonic proportions, providing a vast pool of musical talent that helped make Los Angeles a center for radio, television, and the recording industry. The best-known composers of film scores in Hollywood included Korngold, Rózsa, Steiner, Still, Tiomkin, Waxman, Elmer Bernstein, and Alfred Newman. (*See also* FILM MUSIC.)

(viii) Jazz and popular music. Among the most influential jazz musicians in Los Angeles was Stan Kenton, who initiated several progressive-jazz ensembles that performed throughout the USA. Other jazz musicians who achieved prominence in Los Angeles include Shelly Manne, Les McCann, and Shorty Rogers. Howard Rumsey's series of Concerts by the Sea made the Lighthouse in Hermosa Beach one of the most popular jazz clubs in southern California.

The leading exponent of modern black gospel music, James L. Cleveland, settled in Los Angeles in 1962. He formed the Southern California Community Choir in 1968, and in 1971 became pastor of the Cornerstone Institutional Baptist Church.

Los Angeles has long been an important center for rock music. Two of the best-known groups of the 1960s, the Doors and Frank Zappa's Mothers of Invention, began their careers in the area. In the 1970s and early 1980s such bands as Van Halen, Tom Petty and the Heartbreakers, X, Black Flag, Oingo Boingo, Quiet Riot, and Dream Syndicate were based in or near the city. Concerts are held in the many local rock clubs as well as such larger venues as the Greek Theater, the Beverly Theater, the Universal Amphitheater, and the Hollywood Palladium, or the Country Club in nearby Reseda, Perkins Palace in Pasadena, the Forum in Inglewood, the Pacific Amphitheater in Costa Mesa, and Irvine Meadows in Irvine. Several recording companies in Los Angeles specialize in rock, especially the music of local groups; the best-known labels include Posh Boy, Bomp, I. R. S./Fawlty Products, Unicorn, Rhino, and Frontier.

See also ASIAN-AMERICAN MUSIC.

BIBLIOGRAPHY

A. Robinson: *Life in California* (New York, 1846)

Thompson and West's History of Los Angeles County, California, with Illustrations (Oakland, CA, 1880)

An Illustrated History of Los Angeles County, California (Chicago, 1889)

J. M. Guinn: *Historical and Biographical Record of Southern California* (Chicago, 1902)

J. N. McCorkle: "A History of Southern California Journalism," *Annual Publications, Historical Society of Southern California*, x/1–2 (1915–16), 24

H. Newmark: *Sixty Years in Southern California* (New York, 1916)

J. Dupuy: "Looking Backwards on Musical Los Angeles," *Pacific Coast Musician*, viii (1919), no.7, p.6; no.8, p.17; no.9, p.25; no.10, p.17; no.11, p.21; no.12, p.27

W. F. Gates: "Symphony History in Los Angeles," *Pacific Coast Musician*, xi/12 (1922), 36

——: *Who's Who in Music in California* (Los Angeles, 1920, suppl. 1922)

C. L. Bagley: "History of Band and Orchestra in Los Angeles," *Overture*, iv/16 (1925), 14
Z. Engelhardt: *San Fernando Rey: the Mission of the Valley* (Chicago, 1927)
——: *San Gabriel Mission and the Beginnings of Los Angeles* (San Gabriel, CA, 1927)
F. Colby: "Music in Los Angeles," *Pacific Coast Musician Year Book* (1927–8)
——: "Fiftieth Anniversary of the Southern California Music Company," *Pacific Coast Musician*, xix/16 (1930), 7
C. E. Smith: *The Philharmonic Orchestra of Los Angeles: the First Decade* (Los Angeles, 1930)
J. M. Fredricks: *California Composers: Biographical Notes* (San Francisco, 1934)
I. M. Jones: *Hollywood Bowl* (New York, 1936)
S. B. Dakin: *A Scotch Paisano: Hugo Reid's Life in California, 1832–1852, Derived from his Correspondence* (Berkeley, CA, 1939)
G. Caldwell: "The Library's Service," *Music and Dance in California*, ed. J. Rodríguez (Hollywood, CA, 1940), 282
F. Colby: "The Woman's Contribution," *Music and Dance in California*, ed. J. Rodríguez (Hollywood, 1940), 276
J. K. Wallace: "The Musicians' Union," *Music and Dance in California*, ed. J. Rodríguez (Hollywood, 1940), 71
S. W. Earnest: *An Historical Study of the Growth of the Theatre in Southern California* (diss., U. of Southern California, 1947)
G. Caldwell: "Free for the Asking," *Music and Dance in California and the West*, ed. R. D. Saunders (Hollywood, 1948), 74
H. Swan: *Music in the Southwest* (San Marino, CA, 1952/*R*1977) [review by R. Stevenson in *Inter-American Music Review*, iv/2 (1982), 85]
H. W. Splitter: "Music in Los Angeles," *Historical Society of Southern California Quarterly*, xxxviii/4 (1956), 307–44
A. A. Nordskog: *Earliest Musical History of Hollywood Bowl* (Los Angeles, 1957)
F. H. Baxter: *A History of Music Education in the Los Angeles Public Schools* (diss., U. of Southern California, 1960)
J. O. Northcutt: *Symphony: the Story of the Los Angeles Philharmonic Orchestra* (Los Angeles, 1963)
B. L. Karson: *Music Criticism in Los Angeles 1895–1919* (diss., U. of Southern California, 1964)
"Musical Memories of Los Angeles," *Pavilion* [Journal of the Southern California Symphony Association], i/1 (1964), 29
H. A. Sutherland: "Requiem for the Los Angeles Philharmonic Auditorium," *Southern California Quarterly*, xlvii/3 (1965), 303
R. G. Heidsiek: *Music of the Luiseño Indians of Southern California* (diss., UCLA, 1966)
N. E. Wilson: *A History of Opera and Associated Educational Activities in Los Angeles* (diss., Indiana U., 1967)
G. G. Koopal: *Miracle of Music: the History of the Hollywood Bowl* (Los Angeles, 1972)
D. B. Nunis, Jr., ed.: *Los Angeles and its Environs in the Twentieth Century: a Bibliography of a Metropolis* (Los Angeles, 1973)
J. Sanders: "Los Angeles Grand Opera Association: the Formative Years, 1924–1926," *Southern California Quarterly*, lv/3 (1973), 261–302
S. H. Sobel: *A Compendium of Music at Blessed Sacrament Church* (Los Angeles, 1975)
R. Stevenson: "Roy Harris at UCLA: Neglected Documentation," *Inter-American Music Review*, ii/1 (1979), 59
D. L. Smith: *Murray M. Harris and Organ Building in Los Angeles: 1894–1913* (diss., U. of Rochester, 1980)
C. B. Parker: *John Vincent (1902–1977), an Alabama Composer's Odyssey* (diss., UCLA, 1981)
R. Stevenson: "Carlos Chávez's Los Angeles Connection," *Inter-American Music Review*, iii/2 (1981), 133
——: "John Cage on his 70th Birthday: West Coast Background," *Inter-American Music Review*, v/1 (1982), 3
——: "William Andrews Clark Jr., Founder of the Los Angeles Philharmonic Orchestra," *Inter-American Music Review*, iv/2 (1982), 65
——: "Carreño's 1875 California Appearances," *Inter-American Music Review*, v/2 (1983), 9

ROBERT STEVENSON

Losey, Frank Hoyt (*b* Rochester, NY, 18 March 1872; *d* Erie, PA, 3 May 1931). Composer, arranger, and teacher. He began studying cornet, violin, and piano at the age of 15, and after several years taught brass instruments at the Mansfield (Pennsylvania) Conservatory of Music. Because of a lip injury he changed from cornet to trombone and euphonium. From 1902 to 1908 he composed and arranged for the publisher Carl Fischer, then became editor for the Vandersloot Music Company; in 1914 he founded Losey's Military Band School in Erie. Losey made more than 2500 arrangements for band and orchestra; aside from those made for Fischer and Vandersloot, some were made for the Edison Phonograph Company, others for Henry Ford's personal orchestra. He also wrote more than 400 original compositions, of which the *Gloria* march is the best-known; the *Stabat mater* and *Lenoir* marches and *Ida and Dottie* polka are still played. A number of his works are recorded in the Heritage of the March series (compiled by ROBERT HOE, JR.), subseries 5, F, K, Y, and AAA.

WORKS

(for band unless otherwise indicated)

*c*130 marches, two-steps, incl. Admiral Farragut, Colonel Quay's March, Excelsis, Gloria, Lenoir, Muttering Fritz, Old Ironsides, Sons of Liberty, Stabat mater; *c*35 mazurkas, polkas, waltzes, galops, other dances, incl. Ida and Dottie, Ocean Queen, Shooting Stars; 9 ovs., incl. Grand National, Impromptu; *c*20 serenades, caprices, romances, incl. Old Black Joe, cornet solo, Tanglefoot Rag, Woodland Whispers, cornet, trbn; *c*200 other pieces; *c*2500 arrs., band, orch

Principal publishers: Church, Coleman, C. Fischer, Seitz, Vandersloot

BIBLIOGRAPHY

R. Hoe, Jr., ed.: "Brief Biographies of Famous March Composers," *Journal of Band Research*, xvii/2 (1982), 52

RAOUL CAMUS

Loud. Family of piano makers. Thomas Loud (i) (*b c*1762; *d* New York, 2 Jan 1833) was active in London in the early 19th century. In 1802 he was granted a British patent for an upright piano just under two meters high, with diagonal stringing. He immigrated to New York about 1816, and was building overstrung "piccolo" upright pianos by 1830. He may have been connected with the firm of Loud & Brothers of Philadelphia, but the exact relationship remains unclear.

In 1812 the Philadelphia *Aurora* announced the dissolution of a partnership between Thomas Loud Evenden, Sr. (Thomas Loud (ii)), and the cabinet maker Joshua Baker. A square piano of about 1810 (now owned by the Austrian pianist Jörg Demus), marked "New Patent. Thomas Loud from Clementi & Compy," may be the work of Thomas Loud (i) or (ii), if indeed they are distinct. Thomas Loud (i) was survived by a widow, Harriet; from 1814 a Harriet Evenden is listed in Philadelphia directories with a Thomas Loud Evenden, Jr. A piano of about 1815 marked "Tho. L. Evenden & Son, from London" (in the Metropolitan Museum of Art, New York) is the only known instrument bearing the Evenden name, which was dropped in 1817 when Thomas Loud (ii) went into business with his brother John. Their piano of about 1818–22 marked "Thomas & John Loud" is in the Smithsonian Institution.

Around 1825 Philologus Loud joined the partnership, now known as Loud & Brothers; Joseph Edward Loud entered in 1828, when the firm expanded to new quarters on Chesnut Street, Philadelphia. By this time the family firm was among the most prolific in the USA, producing about 600 pianos annually at retail prices of $180 to $1200 and exporting instruments to the West Indies and South America. In 1832 the firm exhibited two distinctive square pianos at the Franklin Institute, Philadelphia, one of them triple strung for greater brilliance, the other better suited to vocal accompaniment – evidence that musical function was considered in tonal design. In 1830 the Louds advertised a metal frame, which they did not patent until 1835. In this year the firm was renamed Loud & Co. Their other six patents between 1827 and 1865 include a transposing action (1842) and swell device (1865); their upright piano dated as early as 1831 (in the Metropolitan Museum) is equipped with pedal-operated swell shutters and a curiously shifted action. Other family members in the piano business included Thomas C., William H., and Joseph R. Loud. Joseph R.'s career paralleled the firm's decline: in 1855 he was listed as a piano maker, in 1860 as a tuner, and in 1862 as a plumber.

BIBLIOGRAPHY

D. Spillane: *History of the American Pianoforte* (New York, 1890/*R*1969)

R. E. M. Harding: *The Piano-forte: its History Traced to the Great Exhibition of 1851* (Cambridge, England, 1933, rev. 2/1978)

K. G. Grafing: *Alpheus Babcock: American Pianoforte Maker* (diss., U. of Missouri, 1972)

W. E. Mann: *Piano Making in Philadelphia before 1825* (diss., U. of Iowa, 1977)

L. Libin: *American Musical Instruments in the Metropolitan Museum of Art* (New York, 1981) [unpubd catalogue]

MARGARET CRANMER, LAURENCE LIBIN

Louisiana State University. State-supported university (founded 1860) with a school of music at Baton Rouge. The university introduced music instruction in 1915, and from 1922 offered a BM degree. By the 1980s the department had become the largest music school in the state, with about 240 undergraduates studying music history, theory, composition, education, and performance in the schools of music, education, and arts and sciences; there were also 80 graduate students in music education and music history (MM, MMEd, MA, and PhD degrees), and performance and composition (DMA). The Troy H. Middleton Library and the music library have record and tape collections as well as over 22,000 books on music and scores, and the archives and manuscripts division has important musical and American documents (*see also* LIBRARIES AND COLLECTIONS, §3). In 1945 the university initiated an annual festival of contemporary music.

JOHN H. BARON

Loudermilk. The name of two brothers, Ira (1924–65) and Charlie (*b* 1927), who performed as a country-music duo, assuming the name Louvin in 1947; *see* LOUVIN BROTHERS.

Louisiana Hayride. Country-music radio program presented by the BAILES BROTHERS on station KWKH in Shreveport, Louisiana, from 1948; *see also* BARN DANCE.

Louisville. The largest city in Kentucky (pop. 298,451; metropolitan area 906,152). Music has played a significant role in Louisville from the time of its settlement on Corn Island (1778), when settlers danced to the fiddle tunes played by Cato Watts (a slave on George Rogers Clark's founding expedition), to the present resurgence of interest in the arts. In the 1840s a number of singing societies were established by German immigrants who settled in Louisville. Some of these groups, including the Liederkranz Society and the Louisville Sozialer Maennerchor (now the Social Male Chorus), built concert halls, for example the Weisiger and Mozart halls, where such renowned artists as Jenny Lind and Gottschalk appeared. Music-publishing firms, some of which also sold musical merchandise, flourished in the mid- and late 19th century; the most important of these between 1840 and 1890 were William Cumming Peters, Henry J. Peters, David P. Faulds, Tripp & Cragg, and G. W. Brainard. The site of many musical performances in the last decades of the century was Macauley's Theatre, which opened in 1873 and was the best known of the city's halls at the time; it was demolished in 1925. The Speed Music Room, on the property of the pianist and philanthropist Hattie Bishop (Mrs. James Breckinridge) Speed, served from 1914 to 1952 as a studio and concert hall for performances of local musicians and visiting artists, and an endowed concert series at the J. B. Speed Art Museum now continues this tradition.

Of the many attempts to create a permanent symphony orchestra and affiliated chorus, the Louisville Philharmonic Society, founded in 1866 by Louis Hast (1823–90), was the earliest; the Louisville Civic SO organized 50 years later by Morris Simon evolved into the present Young Men's Hebrew Association orchestra. The Louisville Orchestra (known as the Louisville Philharmonic Society, 1942–77) was founded in 1937 by the Louisville Civic Arts Association, which engaged Robert Whitney as its first conductor. With Whitney's support, the mayor, Charles P. Farnsley, initiated the Louisville Orchestra Commissioning project in 1948 to fund new works that would be performed at each of the orchestra's subscription concerts. The project was partly financed in the early years by the Greater Louisville Fund for the Arts (established in 1949); further grants received from the Rockefeller Foundation in 1953 and 1955 provided for the formation of the orchestra's own recording label, First Edition Records, on which the commissioned works were issued. Whitney was succeeded by Jorge Mester (1967), Akiro Endo (1980), and Lawrence Leighton Smith (1983).

The orchestra continues to receive financial support from the Greater Louisville Fund, which also supports 12 other organizations, including the Louisville Bach Society (founded in 1964 by Melvin and Margaret Dickinson) and the Louisville–Jefferson County Youth Orchestra. The Louisville Orchestra, the Kentucky Opera (directed from 1981 by Thomas Smillie, who succeeded Moritz von Bomhard), and the Louisville Ballet are among the city's musical organizations that perform in the new Kentucky Center for the Arts (opened 1983), which has two halls, the 2400-seat Robert S. Whitney Hall and the 620-seat Moritz von Bomhard Theater.

The University of Louisville School of Music was established with the help of the Juilliard Foundation in 1932 after the demise of the Louisville Conservatory of Music (founded in 1915). The first dean of the school, Jacques Jolas, was succeeded in 1935 by Dwight Anderson, a distinguished pianist and teacher who helped found the Chamber Music Society (1938) and the Kentucky Opera Association (1952). Claude Marion Almand (1915–57) came to Louisville in 1941 to teach at the Southern Baptist Theological Seminary and at the university; he received two commissions from the Louisville Orchestra, which resulted in *John Gilbert: a Steamboat Overture* (1948) and the Concerto for Piano and Orchestra (1949). The composer and jazz pianist Nelson Keyes (*b* 1928) holds the position of composer-in-residence at the university. The school's recital hall, which was built in 1980 and has been acclaimed for its acoustics, has a tracker-action organ with 38 stops and 64 ranks built by Steiner-Reck; it is among the largest organs with mechanical action in the USA. The music department offers the BM and BME degrees, an MA in historical musicology, and an MM in history and literature, music education, performance, and theory and composition. In 1977 the Isidore Philipp Archive and Memorial Library was established at the university under the aegis of the American Liszt Society (*see* LIBRARIES AND COLLECTIONS, §3).

Music degrees are also offered by the School of Church Music at the Southern Baptist Theological Seminary (founded 1944); the Louisville Academy of Music (1954) is a private, nonprofit preparatory music school. Louisville was one of the first cities in the USA to have included music as part of the curriculum of its public schools (1853). A Youth Performing Arts School was completed in 1979.

Louisville has been the home of the composers Will S. Hays, Granville English, and Karl Kroeger (all of whom were born there) and of George Perle and Phillip Rhodes. Clifford Shaw (1911–76), who wrote popular music and works for the concert stage, joined the staff of the radio station WAVE in 1933 and eventually became the music director of the radio station and its television counterpart, WAVE-TV.

An annual bluegrass music festival initiated by the city in 1977 (renamed the Kentucky Fried Chicken Bluegrass Festival in 1981, when the national fast-food chain became its sponsor) is the largest event of its kind in the USA.

BIBLIOGRAPHY

J. S. Johnston: *Memorial History of Louisville from its First Settlement to the Year 1896* (Chicago and New York, 1896)

P. Hart: "Louisville Orchestra," *Orpheus in the New World: the Symphony Orchestra as an American Cultural Institution* (New York, 1973), 192

M. G. Money: *A History of the Louisville Conservatory of Music and Music at the University of Louisville: 1907–1935* (diss., U. of Louisville, 1976)

C. C. Birkhead: *The History of the Orchestra in Louisville* (diss., U. of Louisville, 1977)

E. Barret: "Louisville, 1853," *Essays on the Music of J. S. Bach and other Divers Subjects*, ed. R. L. Weaver (Louisville, 1981), 255

J. Belfy: *The Louisville Orchestra New Music Project: an American Experiment in the Patronage of International Contemporary Music* (Louisville, 1983) [incl. selected letters of the composers]

MARION KORDA

Louisville Orchestra Commissioning Project. A program initiated in 1948 by the mayor of Louisville, Charles P. Farnsley, and developed with the support and leadership of Robert Whitney, conductor of the Louisville Orchestra. Using resources from the Greater Louisville Fund for the Arts, the orchestra embarked on an extensive project to commission from renowned composers new works for an ensemble of about 50 players; one work was to be presented at each of the orchestra's regular subscription concerts. The intention was to focus attention on the composers and their music rather than the performers. The project drew considerable national interest in 1950 when the orchestra performed some of the commissioned works at Carnegie Hall in New York; included on the program were Claude Almand's *John Gilbert: a Steamboat Overture* (1948), Schuman's ballet *Judith* (1949, with Martha Graham in the title role), David Diamond's *Timon of Athens* (1949), Martinů's *Intermezzo* (1950), Thomson's *Wheat Field at Noon* (1948), and Persichetti's Serenade no.5 (1950). With grants from the Rockefeller Foundation amounting to $500,000 between 1953 and 1955, the project was able to continue until 1960; the Rockefeller funds also provided for the formation of the orchestra's own recording label, First Edition Records, which issued about 100 of the commissioned works (several early recordings of commissioned works had been made by Columbia and Mercury). Approximately 120 works for small orchestra were commissioned, in addition to several operas and 21 works by student composers.

The following is a list of works commissioned by the Louisville Orchestra as part of the Commissioning Project, 1948–60 (with some later additions). Manuscripts and scores are located in *KyLoU* (in the Dwight Anderson Memorial Music Library) and *KyLoU-Ar*.

C. Almand, Piano Concerto, *John Gilbert: a Steamboat Overture*; G. Antheil, *The Wish* (opera); E. Bacon, *Enchanted Isle*; H. Badings, Symphony no.7; C. Baker, *The Glass Bead Game*; D. Baker, *Le chat qui pêche*; P. Ben Haim, *To the Chief Musician*; R. R. Bennett, Variations; N. V. Bentzon, *Pezzi sinfonici*; A. Berger, *Polyphony*; W. Bergsma, *A Carol on 12th Night*; B. Blacher, *Studie im Pianissimo*; A. Bliss, *Discourse*; F. Borowski, *The Mirror*; C. Bricken, *Daniel Boone*; R. Caamaño, Magnificat; E. Carter, Variations; M. Castelnuovo-Tedesco, *Much Ado about Nothing*; C. Chávez, Symphony no.4

Chou Wen-chung, *And the Fallen Petals*; A. Copland, Orchestral Variations; H. Cowell, *Ongaku*, Symphony no.11; P. Creston, *Invocation and Dance*; I. Dahl, *The Tower of St. Barbara*; L. Dallapiccola, *Variazioni*; N. Dello Joio, *The Triumph of St. Joan*; R. Dennis, "Pennsylvania Station" from *The Open Window*; D. Diamond, *Timon of Athens*; K. Egge, Symphony no.3; G. von Einem, *Meditations*; H. Elwell, Concert Suite; I. Fine, *Serious Song*; L. Foss, *A Parable of Death*; A. Ginastera, *Pampeana no.3*; P. Glanville-Hicks, *The Transposed Heads* (opera); R. Goeb, Concertino no.2; C. Guarnieri, *Suite IV centenário*

A. Haieff, Ballet in E; R. Harris, *Kentucky Spring*, Piano Concerto no.2; L. Harrison, *4 Strict Songs*; E. Helm, Piano Concerto no.2; P. Hindemith, Sinfonietta in E; A. Honegger, *Suite archaïque*; A. Hovhaness, Concerto no.7; J. Ibert, *Louisville-concert*; A. Jolivet, *Suite transocéane*; U. Kay, Serenade; N. Keyes, *Bridges*; P. J. Korn, *Variations on a Tune from The Beggar's Opera*; E. Krenek, *11 Transparencies*; G. Kubik, Symphony no.2; M. Kupferman, Symphony no.4; B. Lees, Symphony no.2; A. Letelier, *Suite Aculeo*; R. Liebermann, *Die Schule der Frauen* (opera); N. Lopatnikoff, *Music for Orchestra*

O. Luening, *Kentucky Concerto* [orig. title *Louisville Concerto*], Rhapsodic Variations (collab. V. Ussachevsky); R. McKuen, *The City*; C. McPhee, Symphony no.2; G. F. Malipiero, Piano Concerto, *Fantasie di ogni giorno*; B. Martinů, *3 estampes*, Intermezzo; P. Mennin, Symphony no.6; D. Milhaud, *Kentuckiana*, arr. 2 pf, *Ouverture méditerranéenne*; R. Mohaupt, *Double Trouble* (opera); J. P. Moncayo García, *Cumbres*; H. Morris, Passacaglia, Adagio, and Finale; R. Muczynski, Piano Concerto no.1; P. Müller-Zürich, Cello Concerto; N. Nabokov, *The Holy Devil* (opera), *Symboli chrestiani*; P. Nordoff, *Lost Summer*, *Winter Symphony*

J. Orrego-Salas, Serenata concertante; G. Perle, Rhapsody, Symphony no.2; V. Persichetti, Serenade no.5, Symphony for Strings; W. Piston, Serenata; Q. Porter, Concerto concertante; K. Rathaus, Louisville Prelude; G. Read, *Toccata giocosa*; B. Reichel, *Suite symphonique*; W. Riegger, Variations, pf, orch, Variations, vn, orch; V. Rieti, *Introduzione e gioco delle ore*; J. Rodrigo, *4 madrigales amatorios*; B. Rogers, *Dance Scenes*; N. Rorem, *Design for Orchestra*; H. Rosenberg, Concerto no.3; E. Rubbra, *Improvisation* op.89; R. L. Sanders, Little Symphony no.2

H. Sauguet, *Les 3 lys*; P. Schickele, *The Fantastic Garden*; W. Schuman, *Judith* (ballet); T. Scott, Fanfare and Cantilena; R. Sessions, *Idyll of Theocritus*; H. Shapero, Credo; L. Sowerby, *All on a Summer's Day*; H. Stevens, *Sinfonia breve*, *Triskelion*; C. Surinach, *Feria mágica*, *Sinfonietta flamenca*; T. Svoboda, *Ex libris*; H. Swanson, Concerto for Orchestra; A. Tansman, Capriccio; A. Tcherepnin, Suite; V. Thomson, *Five Songs from William Blake*, *Wheat Field at Noon*; E. Toch, *Notturno*

V. Ussachevsky, Rhapsodic Variations (collab. O. Luening); D. Van Vactor, Fantasia, Chaconne and Allegro; H. Villa-Lobos, *Dawn in a Tropical Forest*, *Erosão (Origem do rio Amazonas)*; J. Vincent, Symphony in D; B. Wagenaar, Concert Overture; S. Walden, "Circus" from *The Open Window*; R. Ward, *Euphony*; B. Weber, Prelude and Passacaglia

BIBLIOGRAPHY

J. Belfy: *The Louisville Orchestra New Music Project: an American Experiment in the Patronage of International Contemporary Music* (Louisville, 1983) [incl. selected letters of the composers]

MARION KORDA

Louvin Brothers. Country-music duo. Its members were Ira Loudermilk (*b* Rainsville, AL, 21 April 1924; *d* nr Jefferson City, MO, 20 June 1965), who played mandolin, and his brother Charlie Loudermilk (*b* Rainsville, AL, 7 July 1927), a guitarist. They won a talent contest in Chattanooga, Tennessee, in 1943 and as a result presented their own daily radio show on WDEF there. They later performed on radio stations in Knoxville (where they took the name Louvin in 1947), Memphis, and Wheeling, West Virginia, and joined the "Grand Ole Opry" in 1955. Fred

Rose helped them to obtain a recording contract with MGM in 1949 and another, two years later, with Capitol, for which they recorded more than 100 singles and 20 albums. In the early years of their career the Louvins' guitar and mandolin instrumentation, vocal harmony, and repertory were strongly influenced by earlier duos, such as the Blue Sky Boys, the Monroe Brothers, and the Delmore Brothers. They first gained recognition as gospel singers, but after 1955, when they recorded their most successful song, *When I stop dreaming*, they performed secular country songs almost exclusively. Probably the greatest traditional country duo in history, they were known for their close, high harmony and their penchant for exchanging lines during the course of a song. Many of their songs are still performed regularly by such singers as Emmylou Harris and, particularly, bluegrass musicians.

The duo ceased its activities in 1963 so that the brothers could pursue solo careers. Ira often sang with his wife Florence (known professionally as Anne Young); they were killed in an automobile accident. Charlie's career continued into the 1980s; he remained with the "Opry" and recorded successfully for Capitol and, after 1973, for United Artists.

RECORDINGS

(selective list; all recorded for Capitol)

When I stop dreaming (3177, 1955); I don't believe you've met my baby (3300, 1956); Hoping that you're hoping (3413, 1956); You're running wild (3532, 1956); My baby's gone (4055, 1958); *The Family who Prays* (T1061, 1959)

BIBLIOGRAPHY

D. Rhodes: "Looking back on the Louvin Brothers," *Pickin'*, iii/2 (1976), 4

B. Garbutt: "The Louvin Brothers," *Goldmine*, no.58 (1981), 25

S. L. Geno: "Charlie and Ira – the Louvin Brothers," *Bluegrass Unlimited*, xvii/9 (1983), 12

BILL C. MALONE/R

Love. Rock group. Formed in Los Angeles in 1965, its original members were Arthur Lee (*b* Memphis, TN, *c*1944), singer and guitarist; Bryan MacLean (*b* Los Angeles, CA, *c*1947), singer and guitarist; John Echols (*b* Memphis, *c*1945), lead guitarist; Ken Forssi (*b* Cleveland, OH, *c*1943), bass guitarist; Don Conka, drummer; and Alban "Snoopy" Pfisterer (*b* Switzerland, *c*1947), drummer. After the group had recorded three albums, Lee re-formed it with Jay Donellan, guitarist (later replaced by Gary Rowles), Frank Fayad, bass guitarist, George Suranovitch, drummer (replaced by Michael Stuart), and Tjay Cantrelli, saxophonist. The group's first album, *Love* (1966), combined folk-rock in the style of the Byrds and blues that recall the Rolling Stones; one of its songs, *My Little Red Book* (by Bacharach and David), was a minor hit, and it also contained an original blues number, *Signed D.C.* The album *Da capo* (1967) included an extended jazz-rock improvisation, *Revelation*, which was innovative, if somewhat unaccomplished. The group's finest album, *Forever Changes* (1968), was in a psychedelic style in which hallucinatory lyrics were backed by string and brass arrangements.

Influenced by current trends, Lee exploited Donellan's country-rock and psychedelic guitar styles in the new group. After *Four Sail* (1969), a set of smooth pop songs, Love went on to experiment with novelty tunes, long instrumental solos, and funk rhythms on their uneven double album *Out Here* (1969). *False Start* (1970) explores a vocal style that owes more to black music and blues rhythms, while *Reel to Real* (1974), for which Lee gathered a large group of musicians, shows a lighter rhythm-and-blues style. Lee pursued a number of solo projects and re-formed Love on several occasions through the early 1980s, but these efforts were less successful.

RECORDINGS

(selective list; recorded for Elektra unless otherwise stated)

Love (74001, 1966); *Da capo* (74005, 1967), incl. Seven and Seven is; *Forever Changes* (74013, 1968), incl. The Red Telephone, You Set the Scene; *Four Sail* (74049, 1969); *Out Here* (Blue Thumb 9000, 1969); *False Start* (Blue Thumb 8822, 1970), incl. The Everlasting First, Stand Out; *Reel to Real* (RSO 4804, 1974)

JOHN PICCARELLA

Love Center Choir. Gospel group organized by Walter Hawkins; *see* HAWKINS, EDWIN R. and GOSPEL MUSIC, §II, 2(iii)(c).

Loveless, Wendell Phillips (*b* Wheaton, IL, 2 Feb 1892). Radio evangelist and gospel songwriter. He studied singing in Chicago and in 1914 was chosen as a member of the Musical Company of Nine. He toured the USA with this group for six seasons, gaining experience in vocal and dramatic performance, and as a pianist and master of ceremonies, all of which he later used in the Christian ministry. In 1926 he joined the staff of the Moody Bible Institute in Chicago, and under its aegis established the first "radio ministry" on WMBI, which he directed until 1947. He was later pastor of churches in Wheaton, Illinois, Boca Raton, Florida, and Honolulu. He wrote a manual on gospel broadcasting and many gospel songs and choruses, most of which were published in his five volumes of *Radio Songs and Choruses of the Gospel* (1935–46); his best-known chorus is *Every day with Jesus is sweeter than the day before* (1936). Loveless's works often make use of chromatic melodic movement, a complex harmonic structure, and romantic texts.

See also GOSPEL MUSIC, §I, 1(v) and ex.3.

BIBLIOGRAPHY

P. Kerr: "Wendell P. Loveless," *Music in Evangelism and Stories of Famous Christian Songs* (Glendale, CA, 1939, 3/1950)

D. P. Hustad: *Dictionary-handbook to Hymns for the Living Church* (Carol Stream, IL, 1978)

HARRY ESKEW

Love of Life Orchestra. Art-rock performing group, formed in 1977 by PETER GORDON and David Van Tieghem.

Lovin' Spoonful. Folk-rock vocal quartet. Formed in New York in 1965, its members were John Sebastian (*b* New York, 17 March 1944), singer, guitarist, and autoharp and harmonica player; Zal Yanovsky (*b* Toronto, Ont., 19 Dec 1944), singer and lead guitarist; Steve Boone (*b* Camp Lejeune, nr Jacksonville, NC, 23 Sept 1943), bass guitarist; and Joe Butler (*b* New York, 19 Jan 1943), drummer. Their first single recording, *Do you believe in magic?* (1965), reached no.9 on the pop chart, and their later successes included three hits in 1966 (*Daydream*, no.2; *Did you ever have to make up your mind?*, no.2; and *Summer in the City*, no.1) and the soundtracks to Woody Allen's *What's Up, Tiger Lily?* and Francis Ford Coppola's *You're a Big Boy Now.* The Lovin' Spoonful's style blended the noisy passion of rock with the affable sincerity of urban folk music, a contrast exemplified by Sebastian's soft voice and the raucous guitar playing of Yanovsky. Most of their work is gentle and good-humored, at times evoking the sound of a jug band. After the group disbanded in 1968, Sebastian pursued a successful solo career.

RECORDINGS

(selective list; all recorded for Kama Sutra)

Do you Believe in Magic? (8050, 1965), incl. Do you believe in magic?, Did you ever have to make up your mind?; *Daydream* (8051, 1966), incl. Daydream;

Hums of the Lovin' Spoonful (8054, 1966), incl. Summer in the City; *What's Up, Tiger Lily?* (8053, 1966); *You're a Big Boy Now* (8058, 1967); *Revelation: Revolution '69* (8073, 1968)

KEN TUCKER

Lowell, Amy (*b* Brookline, MA, 9 Feb 1874; *d* Brookline, 12 May 1925). Poet. She produced over 650 poems from 1912 to her death, as well as several volumes of critical essays, a biography of John Keats, and a translation of Rostand's *Weeping Pierrot and Laughing Pierrot* for a musical adaptation by Jean Hubert. As a member of the prominent Massachusetts family, she was active in the cultural life of Boston and maintained close personal and professional relationships with such composers as Charles Martin Loeffler, Carl Engel, and Edward Burlingame Hill.

Engel and Hill introduced Lowell in 1908 to the music of such modern French composers as Debussy, Fauré, and Ravel. This led her to the Symbolist poets and their school of *vers libre*, with its unrhymed lines and fluctuating rhythms. The other significant influence on her poetry was the Imagist group of poets, led by Ezra Pound, discovered on a trip to London in 1913. The compression, free rhythm, and visual nature of Imagist poetry were naturally suited to capture the sounds and colors of new musical idioms such as jazz and the compositions of Stravinsky. (Her poem "Stravinsky's Three Pieces, Grotesques, for String Quartet" of 1916 is one example of a verbal representation of a musical composition.) That she saw the interdependence of art forms is evident in the musical terminology she employed both in her critical theory – as, for example, in her article "Some Musical Analogies in Modern Poetry" (*MQ*, vi, 1920, p. 127) – and in her poems. She contributed the concept of "polyphonic prose" to the new poetics, a technique which employed a mixture of prose and poetry with irregular meter and incidental rhyme. Musical themes and imagery play an important part in over 30 of her poems; she used the ballad form intermittently throughout her career.

Many songwriters have been attracted to Lowell's texts because of their brevity and concrete subject matter. Engel set five of her poems to music during her lifetime. Other composers include Virgil Thomson, Camille Zeckwer, and Alexander Steinert in the 1920s and, later, Celius Dougherty. At least two of her poems have been used in choral settings by James Case, and Edward Burlingame Hill's choral symphonic work *Lilacs, Poem for Orchestra (after Amy Lowell)* was based on her poem of the same title.

BIBLIOGRAPHY

J. G. Fletcher: "Miss Lowell's Discovery: Polyphonic Prose," *Poetry*, vi (1915), 32

C. Aiken: "The Technique of Polyphonic Prose," *Scepticisms: Notes on Contemporary Poetry* (New York, 1919), 115, 251

S. F. Damon: *Amy Lowell: a Chronicle* (New York, 1935/*R*1966)

W. C. Bedford: "A Musical Apprentice: Amy Lowell to Carl Engel," *MQ*, lviii (1972), 519

J. Gould: *The World of Amy Lowell and the Imagist Movement* (New York, 1975)

M. A. Hovland: *Musical Settings of American Poetry: a Bibliography* (in preparation) [incl. list of settings]

MARILYN FRITZ SHARDLOW

Lowell, James Russell (*b* Cambridge, MA, 22 Feb 1819; *d* Cambridge, 12 Aug 1891). Poet. He studied law at Harvard University, after which he devoted several years to writing and editing works opposed to slavery. From 1855 to 1875 he was Smith Professor of Modern Languages at Harvard, succeeding Longfellow; during this time he edited the *Atlantic Monthly* and the *North American Review*. In later life he served as ambassador to Spain (1877–80) and England (1880–85). His extensive writings include several volumes of poetry, critical essays, and speeches, and the popular *Biglow Papers*.

Taken as a whole, the more than 80 published musical settings of Lowell's poetry do not present a very representative or flattering picture of his considerable achievements as a writer. Many of the poems most often set, such as *The Fountain* and "O moonlight deep and tender," are from his earlier works, which tend to be sentimental, romantic, and insubstantial. Less popular with composers were those poems showing Lowell as a moralist, satirist, and social critic. Though compared with Holmes he was not a noted hymn writer, several of Lowell's poems were set as hymns, including *A Christmas Carol*, *Longing*, and *The Fatherland*. Excerpts from his poems have also been adapted for use as hymns, most notably "Once to every man and nation" from *The Present Crisis*. One of the few anti-slavery poems to have been set is the vigorous *Stanzas on Freedom*. The humorous and satiric in Lowell's poetry is represented in two settings from the *Biglow Papers*, "The Courtin' " and "Jonathan and John." Among the composers who have set Lowell's poems are Ernst Bacon, Cecil Burleigh, Daniel Pinkham, Jr., Arthur Shepherd, and Robert Ward.

Lowell frequently used music as a subject and image in his prose and verse. In particular, he treated the organ in such poems as *L'Envoi, to the Muse*, *A Legend of Brittany*, and *The Vision of Sir Launfal*. In a more humorous vein, Lowell helped Francis Child revise his comic operetta *Il pesceballo* with music supposedly composed by "Maestro Rosibelli-Donimozarti."

BIBLIOGRAPHY

J. Julian, ed.: *A Dictionary of Hymnology* (New York, 1892, 2/1907/*R*1957)

H. A. Clarke: "The Relations of Music to Poetry in American Poets," *Music*, vi (1894), 163

H. T. Henry: "Music in Lowell's Prose and Verse," *MQ*, x (1924), 546

A. W. Kelley: *Music and Literature in the American Romantic Movement: a Study of the Knowledge of, Use of, and Ideas relating to the Art of Music in Emerson, Hawthorne, Longfellow, Poe, Thoreau, Lowell, Whitman, and Lanier* (diss., U. of North Carolina, 1929)

C. McGlinchee: "American Literature in American Music," *MQ*, xxxi (1945), 101

M. A. D. Howe: " 'Il Pesceballo': the Fishball Operetta of Francis James Child," *New England Quarterly*, xxiii (1950), 187

C. S. Lenhart: *Musical Influence on American Poetry* (Athens, GA, 1956)

K. S. Diehl: *Hymns and Tunes: an Index* (New York, 1966)

H. E. Johnson: "Musical Interests of Certain American Literary and Political Figures," *JRME*, xix (1971), 272

E. Wagenknecht: *James Russell Lowell: Portrait of a Many-sided Man* (New York, 1971)

M. A. Hovland: *Musical Settings of American Poetry: a Bibliography* (in preparation) [incl. list of settings]

MICHAEL HOVLAND

Lowens, Irving (*b* New York, 19 Aug 1916; *d* Baltimore, MD, 14 Nov 1983). Musicologist, critic, and librarian. He attended Columbia University (BS 1939) and the University of Maryland (MA 1957, PhD 1965). He contributed music criticism to the *Washington Star* from 1953, and was its chief music critic from 1961 to 1978. He was assistant head of the reference section of the music division of the Library of Congress (1961–6), served as president of the Music Library Association (1965–6), the Music Critics Association (1971–5), and the Sonneck Society (1975–81), vice-president of the Inter-American Music Critics Association (1973–83), and was on the board of the American Musicological Society (1964–5) and the Inter-American Music and Arts Foundation (1977–83). From 1977 to 1983 Lowens was on the faculty of the Peabody Conservatory, during which time he also held administrative posts (1978–81). He wrote *Music and Musicians of Early America* (1964) and compiled the *Bibliography of Songsters Printed in America before 1821* (1976). As a critic, Lowens sought to improve both the standards of criticism and the working conditions of critics in the USA; he was also instrumental in the establishing of the Kennedy Center Friedheim Awards for composition. *Music in America and American Music* (1978), a pair of essays, includes a selective list of his published work in the years 1942–77. Lowens composed a number of orchestral works, songs, and choruses and edited 18th- and early 19th-century American choral music. His extensive library included distinguished collections of songsters (now at the American Antiquarian Society, Worcester, Massachusetts) and tunebooks (now at the Moravian Music Foundation, Winston-Salem, North Carolina).

WRITINGS

Music and Musicians in Early America (New York, 1964)
The Elson Lectures on the History and Art of Music (New York, 1968)
Bibliography of Songsters Printed in America before 1821 (Worcester, MA, 1976)
Music in America and American Music, ISAMm, viii (Brooklyn, NY, 1978)
Haydn in America, Bibliographies in American Music, v (Detroit, 1979) [incl. O. Albrecht: "Haydn Autographs in the United States"]
with R. Crawford and A. P. Britton: *A Bibliography of Tune Books Printed in America before 1811* (in preparation)

BIBLIOGRAPHY

Obituaries: *Proceedings of the American Antiquarian Society*, xciv (1984), 40; *Sonneck Society Newsletter*, x (spr. 1984), 1

PATRICK J. SMITH

Lowenthal, Jerome (Nathaniel) (*b* Philadelphia, PA, 11 Feb 1932). Pianist. He received his early piano training from Joseph Schwartz and later studied with Samaroff at the Philadelphia Conservatory (1947–50). He attended the University of Pennsylvania and at the same time studied piano privately with William Kapell (1950–53). He was a pupil of Edward Steuermann at the Juilliard School (MS 1957) and of Alfred Cortot at the Ecole Normale de Musique, Paris (*licence de concert* 1958). He took prizes in major competitions including the Busoni (1957), Darmstadt (1957), and Queen Elisabeth of Belgium (1960) before making his professional début, with the New York PO under Josef Krips (1963; he had appeared with the Philadelphia Orchestra 18 years previously). He has played in North and South America, Japan, Southeast Asia, and the USSR, and in 1964 he toured 14 European and Middle Eastern countries with the Pittsburgh SO. He has given first performances of works by Rorem and Rochberg, but his reputation has been attained largely through performances and recordings of the 19th-century repertory.

BIBLIOGRAPHY

G. Kehler: *The Piano in Concert*, i (Metuchen, NJ, 1982), 775

CECIL B. ARNOLD

Lower Creek. American Indian group of Creek origin now known as the SEMINOLE.

Lowinsky, Edward E(lias) (*b* Stuttgart, Germany, 12 Jan 1908; *d* Chicago, IL, 11 Oct 1985). Musicologist. He studied at the Hochschule für Musik in Stuttgart (1923–8) and the University of Heidelberg (PhD 1933). After coming to the USA in 1940, Lowinsky taught at Black Mountain College (1942–7), Queens College, New York (1947–56), and the University of California, Berkeley (1956–61). In 1961 he was appointed Ferdinand Schevill Distinguished Service Professor at the University of Chicago. From 1964 to 1977 he was general editor of the series Monuments of Renaissance Music, published by the University of Chicago Press. In 1971 he organized and presided over the highly successful international Josquin festival-conference; he was general editor of the conference proceedings.

One of the major figures of postwar musicology, Lowinsky had already made a distinguished contribution to scholarship in 1937 with his PhD dissertation on Lassus's Antwerp motet book. His next major work, *Secret Chromatic Art in the Netherlands Motet* (1946/*R*1967), caused a controversy that stimulated much debate about problems of *musica ficta*. His work as an editor (including his edition of *The Medici Codex of 1518*, 1968) and his studies of Renaissance theoretical sources and individual musical manuscripts led him to formulate demanding criteria for modern editions. His numerous writings include provocative and challenging articles on the relationship between music and the history of ideas.

HOWARD MAYER BROWN/PAULA MORGAN

Lowry, Robert (*b* Philadelphia, PA, 12 March 1826; *d* Plainfield, NJ, 25 Nov 1899). Writer of Sunday-school and gospel hymns, and hymnbook compiler. For over 40 years he was pastor of several Baptist churches in New York, Pennsylvania, and New Jersey, and from 1869 to 1875 he was Professor of Belles Lettres at the University of Lewisburg (now Bucknell University). In 1868 he succeeded William Bradbury as editor of Sunday-school music at Biglow & Main, where he compiled a number of popular collections of hymns, often collaborating with William Doane.

Lowry was one of the first writers of gospel songs to supply both his own words and music – a practice which later became a distinguishing feature of the gospel-song movement. When setting the texts of other poets, he often wrote a refrain from the last line of the existing poem or added a chorus of his own. His tunes for *I need Thee every hour* (1872) and Fanny Crosby's *All the way my Savior leads me* (1875), and his own hymn *Low in the grave He lay* (1875) have become a part of standard hymnody. His *Shall we gather at the river?* (1865) and *Where is my wandering boy tonight?* (1877) have become the religious counterparts of Stephen Foster's secular songs as far as fame and usage are concerned.

BIBLIOGRAPHY

W. Cathcart, ed.: *The Baptist Encyclopedia* (Philadelphia, 1881)
J. Julian, ed.: *A Dictionary of Hymnology* (New York, 1892, 2/1907/*R*1957)
J. H. Hall: *Biography of Gospel Song and Hymn Writers* (New York, 1914/*R*1971).
J. F. Zellner III: "Robert Lowry: Early American Hymn Writer," *The Hymn*, xxvi (1975), 117; xxvii (1976), 15
M. R. Wilhoit: *A Guide to the Principal Authors and Composers of Gospel Song in the Nineteenth Century* (diss., Southern Baptist Theological Seminary, 1982)

MEL R. WILHOIT

Luboshutz, Lea (*b* Odessa, Ukraine, 12 Feb 1885; *d* Philadelphia, PA, 18 March 1965). Violinist. She graduated with a gold medal from the Moscow Conservatory (diploma 1903) and then studied with Eugène Ysaÿe in Belgium (1905–6). With her brother Pierre, a pianist, and her sister Anna, a cellist, she formed a trio. She immigrated to the USA in 1924 (she was later naturalized) and performed with leading orchestras; in 1941 she gave the world première of Lopatnikoff's Violin Concerto, op.26. She appeared in joint recitals with Josef Hofmann and with her brother Pierre and her son, the pianist Boris Goldovsky, and from 1927 to 1945 taught at the Curtis Institute. Her playing was admired for its strength and vitality.

BIBLIOGRAPHY

G. Saleski: *Famous Musicians of a Wandering Race* (New York, 1927)

——: *Famous Musicians of Jewish Origin* (New York, 1949), 369

NADIA TURBIDE

Luboshutz, Pierre (*b* Odessa, Ukraine, 22 June 1891; *d* Rockport, ME, 17 April 1971). Pianist. He graduated from the Moscow Conservatory in 1912 and the same year made his début as a soloist with the Koussevitzky Orchestra in Moscow. Later he was a pupil of Edouard Risler in Paris. With his sisters Lea (a violinist) and Anna (a cellist), he formed a trio. He immigrated to the USA in 1926 and was an accompanist for Gregor Piatigorsky, Paul Kochansky, and others. After he married the pianist Genia Nemenoff in 1931, the two appeared as the Luboshutz-Nemenoff Duo, introducing new works by Martinů, Giannini, Arrieu, and Koutzen; they have recorded some of his two-piano arrangements as well as original works. From 1962 to 1968 they taught at Michigan State University, East Lansing.

BIBLIOGRAPHY

G. Saleski: *Famous Musicians of a Wandering Race* (New York, 1927)

——: *Famous Musicians of Jewish Origin* (New York, 1949), 647

NADIA TURBIDE

Luca, Sergiu (*b* Bucharest, Romania, 4 April 1943). Violinist and teacher. He began his musical studies at the age of four, and the following year entered the Bucharest Conservatory. In 1950 he moved with his parents to Israel, and two years later made his solo début with the Haifa SO. He studied with Max Rostal, briefly in London and then, from 1958, at the Berne Conservatory. At Isaac Stern's suggestion Luca came to the USA in 1961 and enrolled at the Curtis Institute, where his mentor was Galamian. He was a finalist in the 1965 Leventritt Competition, and the same year he won the Philadelphia Orchestra Youth Auditions and the Sibelius Competition, which led to his American début that year with the Philadelphia Orchestra under Ormandy, playing Sibelius's Concerto. He became an American citizen in 1966. In 1971 he founded the Chamber Music Northwest Festival in Portland, Oregon, and directed it until 1980, when he was appointed professor of violin at the University of Illinois. In 1983 he took the posts of professor of violin and violinist-in-residence at the Shepherd School of Music, Rice University, Houston, and became music director of the Texas Chamber Orchestra.

Luca has performed throughout the USA as well as in Europe and Japan, both as a soloist and as a recitalist. Since 1973 he has increasingly devoted his energies to stylistically authentic readings of Baroque music: he received wide critical attention for his recording of the complete unaccompanied violin works of Bach, the first to be made with an original instrument and a Baroque bow. He has also worked with Bilson performing the complete violin and keyboard sonatas of Mozart. Luca is also well known for his performances of contemporary works, notably Bolcom's Violin Sonata and David Liptak's Sonata for unaccompanied violin, of which he is the dedicatee. Among his other recordings is the complete music for violin and piano of Bartók. He owns a Stradivari violin (the "d'Egdille" or "Wirth") of 1712 and a Sanctus Seraphin of 1733 with original fittings.

GEORGE GELLES/SORAB MODI

Lucas, Sam [Milady, Samuel] (*b* Washington, OH, 7 Aug 1840; *d* New York, 9 Jan 1916). Minstrel performer. He began to play the guitar in 1859 while working as a barber in Cincinnati, then served in the Union Army during the Civil War, studied at Wilberforce University, and taught in New Orleans before joining Lew Johnson's Plantation Minstrels in 1871. He toured with Callender's Original Georgia Minstrels from 1873, and joined the Hyers Sisters in 1876 for their productions of musical shows, leaving them to tour with Sprague's Georgia Minstrels. In 1878 he became the first black actor to play the title role in *Uncle Tom's Cabin*. He organized his own troupe, the Hub Concert Company, in Boston in 1882, though he still worked with other groups. He toured with Haverly's Genuine Colored Minstrels in the early 1880s, performed in the Callender Consolidated Minstrel Festival in New York in 1883, and appeared in the Bergen Star Concerts. He was joined by his wife in Sam T. Jack's *The Creole Show*, which opened in Haverhill, Massachusetts, on 4 August 1890, and subsequently moved to Boston, Chicago, and New York. He also appeared in John W. Vogel's *Darkest America*, John Isham's *Octoroons*, and Bob Cole and Billy Johnson's *A Trip to Coontown*, which toured for four years (from 1898). In the 1890s Lucas toured the USA with his wife in a vaudeville act, "Mr. and Mrs. Sam Lucas." He played leading roles in *Rufus Rastus* by Ernest Hogan and Joe Jordan (1905–6) and in two shows by J. Rosamond Johnson, *The Shoo-fly Regiment* (1907–8) and *The Red Moon* (1909–10). Lucas retired in 1912, but appeared in a film version of *Uncle Tom's Cabin* one year before his death.

BIBLIOGRAPHY

SouthernB

M. C. Hare: *Negro Musicians and their Music* (Washington, DC, 1936/*R*1974)

E. Southern: *The Music of Black Americans* (New York, 1971, rev. 2/1983)

——: "The Origin and Development of the Black Musical Theater," *Black Music Research Journal* (1981–2), 1

DOMINIQUE-RENÉ DE LERMA

Lucier, Alvin (Augustus, Jr.) (*b* Nashua, NH, 14 May 1931). Composer. He was educated at Yale (BA 1954) and Brandeis (MFA 1960) universities, where his teachers included Berger, Irving Fine, and Shapero; he also studied privately with Quincy Porter and was a pupil of Copland and Foss at the Berkshire Music Center (1958, 1959). After two years in Rome on a Fulbright fellowship, he joined the Brandeis faculty in 1963 as director of the choral union; later he was head of the electronic music studio. From 1969 he has taught at Wesleyan University, where he became chairman of the world music department in 1979. Lucier, who abandoned the conventional idiom of his early works in favor of the experimental approach associated with John Cage, was a co-founder, with Ashley, Behrman, and Mumma, of the Sonic Arts Union, an influential electronic music performance ensemble. He also toured extensively on his own, both in the USA and in Europe. He has received commissions from the Merce Cunningham and Viola Farber dance companies (he was associated with the latter as music director, 1972–7), Radio Bremen, the Fort Worth Museum of Art, and the New Music Ensemble, Providence; his awards include grants from the Rockefeller Foundation, New York State Council on the Arts, and the NEA (1977, 1981). Active as a writer, he has contributed articles to *Electronic Music Review*, *Arts in Society*, *Musical Quarterly*, and other journals, and with Douglas Simon edited *Chambers* (1981), a collection of his music and interviews.

In the mid-1960s Lucier began to explore sonic environments,

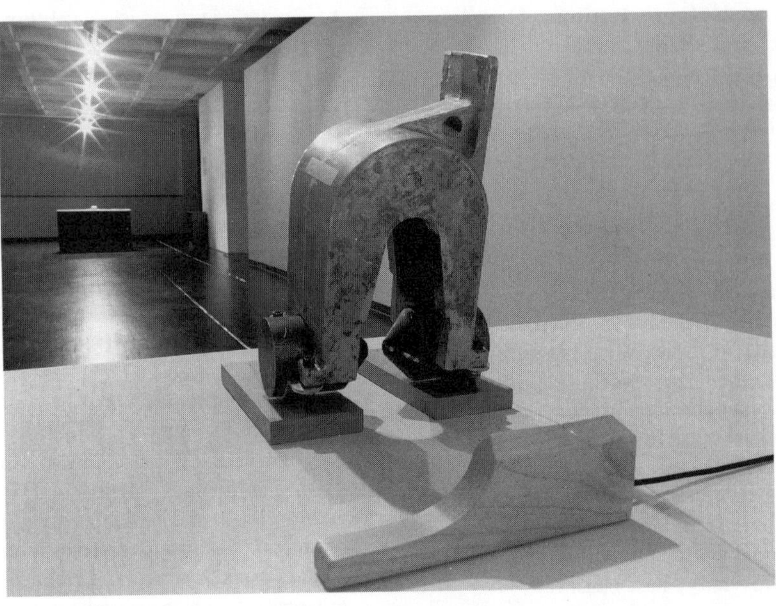

Alvin Lucier's "Music on a Long Thin Wire," 1977 (Arnolfini Gallery, Bristol, England)

particularly sounds that "would never – in ordinary circumstances – reach our ears." With performers, electronics, instruments, and found objects, he devises open-ended processes that are specifically adapted to the acoustical phenomena he chooses to investigate or reveal. Some works exploit unusual sound sources such as brain waves (*Music for Solo Performer*) or radio frequency emissions in the ionosphere (*Sferics*), while others focus on acoustic behavior, chiefly the resonant properties of architectural spaces. In *Vespers*, performers take the acoustical measure of a room by means of echo-location devices, seeking to orient themselves in the manner of bats and dolphins. In *Music on a Long Thin Wire*, the player activates a simple system – a vibrating wire with resonant chamber (see illustration) – which then plays itself, producing a multiplicity of subtle pitches, timbres, and rhythmic patterns. *I am Sitting in a Room* uses a processed tape loop to effect the drastic transformation of a spoken text in accordance with the room's resonant frequencies. Lucier has explored the directionality of sound (*Directions of Sounds from the Bridge*), produced exact visual equivalents of sound by means of vibrating surfaces and solids (*The Queen of the South*), and designed solar-powered sound installations. Particularly in live performance, the investigative element in Lucier's work assumes the aspect of drama. The implicit theatricality of inanimate objects assuming life through (invisible) sound forces, or the revelation of the acoustic potential of sources as remote as the ionosphere or as drolly commonplace as a chest of drawers (*Job's Coffin*), lends an air of piquant mystery to Lucier's best work.

WORKS

Orch: Conc., tpt, chamber orch, 1959; Music, bn, str, 1959; Fragments for Str, 1961; (Hartford) Memory Space, orch, 1970

Chamber: Sonata da camera, brass, perc, 1956; Festival Music, 5 wind, 1960; Composition for Pianist & Mother, 1964; 2 pf works, 1955, 1962; 2 pieces for S, 1958, 1963

Elec: 35 works, incl. Music for Solo Pfmr, amp brain waves, elec, perc, 1965; North American Time Capsule, vv, vocoder, tape, 1967; Vespers, pfmrs, echo-location devices, 1967; Whistlers, elec, 1967; Chambers, pfmrs, resonant environments, 1968; Hymn, amp pfmrs, 1970; I am Sitting in a Room, speaker, tape, 1970; The Duke of York, v(v), synth, 1971; The Queen of the South, pfmrs, resonant environment, live video, 1972; Still and Moving Lines of Silence in Families of Hyperbolas, vv, insts, dancers, perc, 1973–4, rev. S, insts, oscillators, 1982–4; The Fires in the Minds of the Dancers, 4-track playback environment, 1974; Bird and Person Dyning, pfmr, elec, 1975; Music on a Long Thin Wire, audio oscillators, elec monochord, 1977; Directions of Sounds from the Bridge, 1 str, oscillator, lights, 1978; Ghosts, pfmr, light, oscillator, loudspeakers, 1978; Job's Coffin, amp chest of drawers, 1979; Solar Sounder I, solar elec music system, 1979; Music for Pure Waves, perc, acoustic pendulums, oscillator, 1980; Reflections of Sounds from the Wall, elec, 1981; Sferics, tape, 1981; Crossings, small orch, oscillator, 1982–4; Intervals, vv, sound-sensitive lights, 1983; Seesaw, sound installation, 1983; Spinner, sound installation, 1984; Serenade, 13 insts, oscillators, 1985

Other: incidental music for 4 plays, 1958–69; 2 film scores, 1967–9; music for television, 1967–70

Principal publishers: Berandol, CPE, Criss-Cross Art Communications

BIBLIOGRAPHY

G. Mumma: "Alvin Lucier's Music for Solo Performer (1965)," *Source*, no.2 (1968), 68

M. Nyman: *Experimental Music: Cage and Beyond* (New York, 1974), 286

J. Rockwell: "Sound's the Thing in Work by Lucier," *New York Times* (23 Feb 1975)

T. Johnson: "New Music," *HiFi/MusAm*, xxv/5 (1975), 13

S. Marshall: "Alvin Lucier's Music of Signs in Space," *Studio International*, cxcii (1976), 285

W. Zimmermann: *Desert Plants: Conversations with 23 American Musicians* (Vancouver, BC, 1976), 137

D. Reck: *Music of the Whole Earth* (New York, 1977), 518

A. Sondheim: "Alvin Lucier," *Parachute*, xii (1978) [repr. in *Ear*, iv/8–9 (1978–9)]

J. Rockwell: "New Music: Festival in Chicago," *New York Times* (7 July 1982)

T. DeLio: *Circumscribing the Open Universe: Essays on Cage, Feldman, Wolff, Ashley and Lucier* (Washington, DC, 1984)

LINDA SANDERS

Luders, Gustav (Carl) (*b* Bremen, Germany, 13 Dec 1865; *d* New York, 24 Jan 1913). Composer. He studied in Germany and in 1888 went to Milwaukee, where he conducted popular orchestras and led a light opera company. From 1889 he was an arranger for a branch of Witmark and directed theater orchestras in Chicago. He wrote at least 13 operettas, musical comedies, and musical plays, many of which were performed in Chicago before they appeared on Broadway. His chief lyricist was Frank Pixley. Their most successful work was *The Prince of Pilsen* (1903), which was performed in Boston, New York, St. Louis, and London and revived until at least 1957; it includes the songs "The Tale of the Seashell," "The Message of the Violet," and "The Heidelberg Stein Song," which retains prominence in the college glee-club repertory. Other successful works by Luders include *The Burgomaster* (1900), *Woodland* (1904), and *The Sho-gun* (1904).

Luders's style reveals a familiarity with both Viennese operetta and the music of Arthur Sullivan. His works have an abundance of graceful waltzes and humorous or sentimental love songs, with sophisticated melodies, simple but varied rhythms and phrases, and a wider harmonic vocabulary than most stage musicals of the time.

WORKS

All are operettas or musical plays, and unless otherwise indicated dates are those of first New York performance.

Little Robinson Crusoe (H. B. Smith), Chicago, 1899; The Burgomaster (F. Pixley), 31 Dec 1900 [incl. The Tale of the Kangaroo]; King Dodo (Pixley), 12 May 1902 [incl. The Tale of the Bumble Bee]; The Prince of Pilsen (Pixley), 17 March 1903 [incl. The Heidelberg Stein Song, The Message of the Violet, The Tale of the Seashell]; Mam'selle Napoleon (J. W. Herbert), 8 Dec 1903; The Sho-gun (G. Ade), 10 Oct 1904; Woodland (Pixley), 21 Nov 1904 [incl. The Tale of the Turtle Dove, The Message of Spring]; The Grand Mogul (Pixley), 25 March 1907; Marcelle (Pixley), 1 Oct 1908; The Fair Co-ed (Ade), 1 Feb 1909; The Old Town (Ade), 10 Jan 1910; The Gypsy (Pixley), 14 Nov 1912; Somewhere Else (A. Hopwood), 20 Jan 1913

Principal publisher: Witmark

BIBLIOGRAPHY

J. W. McSpadden: *Light Opera and Musical Comedy* (New York, 1936)
S. Spaeth: *A History of Popular Music in America* (New York, 1948)
D. Ewen: *Popular American Composers* (New York, 1962; suppl. 1972)

DEANE L. ROOT

Ludwig. Firm of percussion instrument makers. William F. Ludwig, Sr. (*b* Nenderoth, Germany, 15 July 1879; *d* Chicago, IL, 14 June 1973), went to Chicago as a boy, and in 1909 founded Ludwig & Ludwig with his brother Theobald (1888–1917); their first product was a pedal for trap drums. Having played hand-tuned kettledrums in the Pittsburgh SO, Ludwig decided to build his own pedal timpani. With his brother-in-law, the engineer Robert C. Danly, he designed a model, patented in 1913, with a hydraulic pump and an expandable rubber tube that pressed a hoop against the membrane from inside the kettle. An improved model that had flexible tuning cables operated by a pedal with a self-locking device was patented in 1920. The "Natural Way Balanced Action" timpani, patented in 1923, made use of a compression spring for tension balance to hold the pedal in place. The firm expanded and made quantities of trap-drum sets and sound-effects instruments for the flourishing silent-film industry. However, the arrival of talking pictures and the Depression resulted in declining sales, and in 1930 the company merged with C. G. Conn. Its production was combined with that of the LEEDY drum division and moved to Elkhart, Indiana, with Ludwig as its manager. During this period he introduced the first lightweight, chromatic bell-lyra for marching bands (see illustration). In 1936 he resigned to set up the W. F. L. Drum Co. in Chicago, and over the next 20 years produced several new models of timpani and a variety of percussion instruments. In 1955 he purchased the Ludwig portion of Conn's percussion business, which became the Ludwig Drum Co. The Musser Marimba Co. (a manufacturer of vibraphones, marimbas, xylophones, bells, and chimes) and its two subsidiaries were acquired in 1966; Ludwig Industries was subsequently organized as a parent company over all the divisions. William F. Ludwig, Jr., became president in 1972, and in 1982 the firm was acquired by Selmer.

EDMUND A. BOWLES

Luening, Otto (Clarence) (*b* Milwaukee, WI, 15 June 1900). Composer, teacher, conductor, and flutist. His mother was an amateur singer and his father a conductor, pianist, and noted teacher who studied at the Leipzig Conservatory, and who supervised his son's musical education without trying to influence his first idiosyncratic compositions of 1906. In 1912 the family moved to Munich, where Luening studied theory at the Staatliche Hochschule für Musik with Anton Beer-Walbrunn (1915–17) and made his début as a flutist (1916). When the USA entered World War I he moved to Switzerland; he studied in Zurich at the conservatory and at the university (1919–20), and also privately with Philipp Jarnach and Ferruccio Busoni, who both deeply influenced Luening's conception of music and his teaching methods. While in Zurich he played flute in the Tonhalle Orchestra and at the Municipal Opera, and for a season was an actor and stage manager with James Joyce's English Players Company. He made his début as composer-conductor in 1917.

In 1920 Luening came to Chicago, where he studied with Wilhelm Middelschulte. His musical life ranged from conducting the American Grand Opera Company in performances of operas in English (including Cadman's *Shanewis*) to playing Baroque

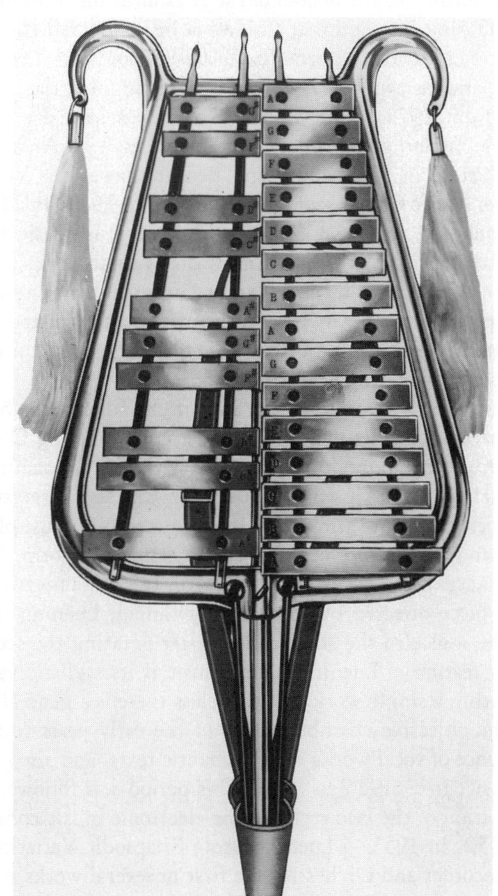

Bell-lyra by the Ludwig Drum Co.

and contemporary chamber music and teaching music theory; and from providing music for silent films to arranging gospel hymns by Homer Rodeheaver for export to Japan. From 1925 to 1928 Luening was at the Eastman School as executive director of the opera department and conductor of the Rochester American Opera Company (and later of its offshoot, the American Opera Company). Then, after a year in Cologne (1928–9), he lived in New York, where he conducted musical comedy, opera, and symphony concerts over radio station WOR, until he was awarded two Guggenheim fellowships (1930–31, 1931–2; he was awarded a third in 1974), which enabled him to write the text and music of his opera *Evangeline*. In 1932 Luening began teaching at the University of Arizona, where he reorganized the theory and composition department, and in 1934 he was appointed chairman of the music department at Bennington (Vermont) College, remaining until 1944.

Under the WPA program Luening conducted and played extensively in Vermont, New York, and elsewhere. In 1936 he was associate conductor, under Hans Lange, of the New York Philharmonic Symphony Chamber Orchestra, which gave a series in New York (for the benefit of Bennington College) of lesser-known old and new music. The series ran for two years. On leaving Bennington in 1944 Luening was appointed director of opera productions at Columbia University, where he developed a graduate seminar for composers, and professor at Barnard College. He retired from Barnard in 1964 but continued to teach at Columbia until 1968, when he became professor emeritus and music chairman of the School of the Arts until his retirement in 1970. During his tenure at Columbia he conducted the world premières of Menotti's opera *The Medium*, Thomson's *The Mother of us all*, and his own opera, *Evangeline*. He taught at the Juilliard School from 1971 to 1973. In 1975 he was named a Hadley Fellow at Bennington College, and together with Alan Carter he was active in Middlebury and Bennington at the Vermont Chamber Music Composers' Conferences from 1941. In addition to co-founding the ACA (1938), the American Music Center (1939), and CRI (1954), Luening was at various times a board member or presiding officer of most US organizations engaged in the promotion of American music. He was a trustee of the American Academy in Rome from 1953 to 1970 and was composer-in-residence there in 1958, 1961, and 1965.

Luening's early works written in Zurich, notably the Sextet, the Sonatina for flute and piano, and the First String Quartet, are highly contrapuntal, often tonal, with overt atonality and polytonality and incipient serialism; he was also interested in "acoustical harmony" (involving the recognition and use of overtones), and the concept of timbre as an element of form. At the performance in Rochester of *Sister Beatrice* (1926), a multi-media theater piece directed by Rouben Mamoulian, Luening improvised the music to the stage action, later notating the score. A striking feature of Luening's later music is its stylistic variety, even within a single work. Nevertheless there is a general trend from the objective chamber music of the early years to a preponderance of vocal works with Romantic texts, and also orchestral music, from 1925 to 1952. This period was followed by a combination of the two styles in the electronic music composed after 1952. In 1953–4 Luening wrote Rhapsodic Variations for Tape Recorder and Orchestra, the first of several works done in collaboration with Ussachevsky (for illustration *see* USSACHEVSKY, VLADIMIR) and one of the first works of this genre, and they subsequently established an electronic music center at Columbia University (later named the Columbia-Princeton Electronic Music Center). In the late 1960s he returned to his interest in chamber music, using simpler but still individualistic materials and structures. Throughout these works, as in Busoni's music, the juxtaposition of styles is an essential forming principle. This catholic thinking has been evident in Luening's teaching, and among his many pupils are composers of widely different stylistic inclinations; they include Carlos, Chou Wen-chung, Davidovsky, Dodge, Kander, Laderman, Shifrin, and Wuorinen.

Otto Luening, 1980

Among Luening's honors are an award from the National Institute of Arts and Letters (1946), to which he was elected in 1952, the ACA Laurel Leaf (1970), two NEA grants (1974, 1977), the Brandeis Creative Arts Award (1981), the American Eagle Award from the National Music Council (1985), the first ACA Laurel Wreath Award (1985), several honorary degrees, and various commissions. His writings include articles on electronic music, the books *Music Materials and the Public Library* (1949), *Electronic Tape Music, 1952: the First Compositions* (with Ussachevsky, 1977), and an autobiography, *The Odyssey of an American Composer* (1980).

WORKS

STAGE

Sister Beatrice (incidental music, Maeterlinck), 1926; Rochester, 15 Jan 1926

Evangeline (opera, Luening, after Longfellow), 1930–32, rev. 1947–8; New York, 5 May 1948, cond. Luening

Blood Wedding (incidental music, Lorca), 1940; Bennington, VT, 1 Dec 1940

See also "Electronic"

ORCHESTRAL

Concertino, fl, chamber orch, 1923; Philadelphia, 1935, Luening, cond. I. Freed

Music for Orchestra, 1923; New York, 26 May 1978, American Composers Orch, cond. Schuller

Symphonic Fantasia I, 1924; Rochester, 25 Nov 1925, cond. Hanson

Serenade, 3 hn, str orch, 1927; Rochester, 12 Jan 1928, Rochester PO, cond. Goossens
Two Symphonic Interludes, 1935; New York, 11 April 1936, New York PO, cond. Lange
Prelude to a Hymn Tune by William Billings, chamber orch, 1937; New York, 1 Feb 1937, cond. Luening
Suite, str orch, 1937; Saratoga Springs, NY, 12 Sept 1937, New York PO, cond. F. C. Adler
Symphonic Fantasia II, 1939–49; New York, 13 Oct 1957, New York PO, cond. D. Broekman
Pilgrim's Hymn, chamber orch, 1946; Saratoga Springs, NY, 14 Sept 1946, cond. Luening
Prelude, chamber orch, 1946; Saratoga Springs, NY, 14 Sept 1946, cond. Luening
Legend, ob, str orch, 1951; New York, WNYC radio, 1 July 1951, R. Bloom, cond. P. Wolfe
Kentucky Concerto [orig. entitled Louisville Concerto]: Louisville, Lexington, Kentucky Rondo, 1951; Louisville, 5 March 1951, cond. Luening
Wisconsin Suite: of Childhood Tunes Remembered, 1954; New York, 28 March 1954, cond. D. Broekman
Serenade, fl, str orch, 1956; New York, 19 Oct 1956, A. Handy, cond. D. Broekman
Lyric Scene, fl, str orch, 1958; Arlington, VA, 25 Oct 1964
Fantasia, str qt, orch, 1959; New York, 18 April 1959, cond. Shanet
Broekman Fantasia, str orch, 1966; Munich, radio broadcast, 1979, cond. Serebrier
Symphonic Fantasia III, 1969–82; New York, 26 Jan 1982, cond. Serebrier
Symphonic Fantasia IV, 1969–82; New York, 14 May 1984, cond. L. Slatkin
Sonority Forms no.1, 1973; North Bennington, VT, 14 Oct 1973, cond. Luening
Wisconsin Symphony, 1975; Milwaukee, 3 Jan 1976, cond. Schermerhorn
Symphonic Interlude no.3, 1975; Lenox, MA, 13 Aug 1980, cond. Schuller
Short Symphony, chamber orch, 1979; Milwaukee, 28 Feb 1982, cond. Foss
Symphonic Fantasia V, 1979–85
Potawatomi Legends, chamber orch, 1980; Parkside, WI, 13 April 1980, cond. Luening
Sonority Forms II, 1983; Bennington, VT, 4 June 1983, cond. Luening
Symphonic Fantasia VI, 1985
Symphonic Interlude no.4, 1985

ELECTRONIC

Fantasy in Space, tape, 1952; New York, 28 Oct 1952
Invention in 12 Notes, tape, 1952; New York, 28 Oct 1952
Low Speed, tape, 1952; New York, 28 Oct 1952
Theatre Piece no.2 (J. Limón), ballet, lv, insts, tape, 1956; New York, 20 April 1956
Dynamophonic Suite, 1958
Gargoyles, vn, tape, 1960
A Day in the Country, vn, tape, 1961
A Study in Synthesized Sounds, 1961
Sonority Canon, 1962
Synthesis, orch, tape, 1962; Erie, PA, 22 Oct 1963
Moonflight, tape, 1968
In the Beginning, 1970
Variations on "Fugue and Chorale Fantasy," org, elec doubles, 1973

(collab. Ussachevsky)

Incantation, 1953
Rhapsodic Variations, orch, tape, 1953–4; Louisville, KY, 20 March 1954, Louisville Orch, cond. R. Whitney
A Poem in Cycles and Bells, orch, tape, 1954; Los Angeles, 18 Nov 1954, Los Angeles PO, cond. Wallenstein
Of Identity, ballet, 1954; New York, 9 Feb 1955, American Mime Theater
Carlsbad Caverns, television score, 1955
King Lear (Shakespeare), incidental music, 3 versions, tape, 1956
Back to Methuselah (Shaw), incidental music, 1960
Concerted Piece, orch, tape, 1960; New York, 10 March 1960, New York PO, cond. Bernstein
Incredible Voyage, television score, 1968, collab. Shields, Smiley

(collab. H. El- Dabh)

Diffusion of Bells, 1962–5
Electronic Fanfare, 1962–5

CHAMBER

Piece, str qt, 1914; Gavotte, vc, pf, 1917; Minuet, vc, pf, 1917; Vn Sonata no.1, 1917; Sextet, fl, cl, hn, vn, va, vc, 1918; Variations on Christus der ist mein Leben, 4 hn, 1918; Fl Sonatina, 1919; Fugue, str qt, 1919; Str Qt no.1, 1919–20; Pf Trio, 1921; Variations on "Yankee Doodle," pic, pf, 1922; Vn Sonata no.2, 1922; Str Qt no.2, 1923; Legend, vn, pf, 1923–4; Sonata, vc, 1924; Str Qt no.3, 1928; Fantasia brevis, fl, pf, 1929
Short Fantasy, vn, hn, 1930; Mañana, vn, pf, 1933; Fantasia brevis, cl, pf, 1936; Fantasia brevis, vn, va, vc, 1936; Short Ballad, 2 cl, str, 1937; Short Sonata no.1, fl, pf/hpd, 1937; Variations on a Theme Song for a Silent Movie, eng hn, pf, 1937; Fuguing Tune, fl, ob, cl, hn, bn, 1938; Short Fantasy, vn, pf, 1938; The Bass with the Delicate Air, fl, ob, cl, bn, 1940; Variations on Bach's Chorale Prelude "Liebster Jesu wir sind hier," vc, pf, 1942
Andante and Variations (Vn Sonata no.3), 1943–51; Suite, vn, va, vc, 1944–66; Suite, vc/va, pf, 1946; Suite no.1, fl, 1947; Easy March, rec, fl, ob, pf, 1950; Suite, db, pf, 1950; 3 Nocturnes, ob, pf, 1951; Sonata, bn/vc, pf, 1952; Trio, fl, vn, pf, 1952; Suite no.2, fl, 1953; Trbn Sonata, 1953; Sonata Composed in 2 Dayturns, vc, 1958; Sonata, db, 1958; Sonata, va, 1958; Sonata no.1, vn, 1958; Song, Poem and Dance, fl, str qt, 1958; 3 Fantasias, gui, 1960; Suite no.3, fl, 1961
Sonority Canon, 2–37 fl, 1962; 3 Duets, 2 fl, 1962; Trio, fl, vc, pf, 1962; Duo, vn, va, 1963; Elegy, vn, 1963; March for Diverse High and Low Insts, 1963; Suite for Diverse High and Low Insts, 1963; Suite no.4, fl, 1963; Entrance and Exit Music, 3 tpt, 3 trbn, cymbals, 1964; Fanfare for a Festive Occasion, 3 hn, 3 tpt, 3 trbn, timp, bells, 1965; Fantasia, vc, 1966; Trio for 3 Flutists, 1966; 2 Pieces (Short Sonata no.3), fl, pf, 1966; 14 Easy Duets, 2 rec, 1967; Meditation, vn, 1968; Sonata no.2, vn, 1968; Suite no.5, fl, 1969
Trio, tpt, hn, trbn, 1969; Introduction and Allegro, tpt, pf, 1970; Sonata no.3, vn, 1970; Easy Suite, str, 1971; 8 Tone Poems, 2 va, 1971; Short Sonata no.2, fl, pf, 1971; Elegy for the Lonesome Ones, 2 cl, str, 1974; Mexican Serenades, db, wind, perc, 1974; Prelude and Fugue, fl, cl, bn, 1974; Short Suite (4 Cartoons), str trio/(fl, cl, bn), 1974; Suite, 2 fl, pf, vc ad lib, 1976; Triadic Canons, 2 vn, fl, 1976; Potawatomi Legends no.2: Fantasias on Indian Motives, fl, 1979
10 Canons, 2 fl, 1979; Fantasia, vn, vc, pf, 1981; Fantasia, cl, 1982; Fantasia, vn, 1982; Serenade, vn, vc, pf, 1983; Fantasia and Dance in memoriam Max Pollikoff, vn, 1984; Opera Fantasia, vn, pf, 1985; Serenade and Dialogue, fl, pf, 1985; 3 Canons, 2 fl, 1985; Duo, fl, va, 1985

KEYBOARD

(pf solo unless otherwise stated)

Little Miniature Pieces, 1906; Theme with Variations, 1907; Pf Piece, 1913; Waltz, 1913; Fantasie Stücke, 1915; 4 Short Pf Pieces, 1915; Org Piece, 1916; Fugue, 1917; Gavotte, 1917; One Step, 1917; Pf Piece, 1917; Thema con variazione, 1917; Choral Vorspiel zu "Christus der ist mein Leben," org, 1918; Fuga a 3 voci, 1918; Slumbersong, 1918; Music for Piano: a Contrapuntal Study, 1921; Coal Scuttle Blues, 1922, version for 2 pf, 1943, collab. E. Bacon; Choral Fantasy, org, 1922; 2 Bagatelles, 1924; Hymn to Bacchus, 1926; Dance Sonata, 1928
8 Pieces, 1928; Intermezzo III, 1928; 6 Short and Easy Pieces, 1928; Fantasia, org, 1929; 3 Pieces: Birds, Swans, Stars, 1932–3; 5 Intermezzi, 1932–6; Fantasia no.2, 1933; Phantasy, 1935; Waltz, 1935; 6 Preludes, 1935–51; Andante, 1936; 8 Preludes, 1936; 2 Inventions, 1938; 6 Inventions, 1938–9; Fuga a 3 voci no.2, 1939; Short Sonata no.1, 1940; Variations, hpd/pf, 1940; Canonical Study, 1941; Canons, hpd/pf, 1941; Easy Canons, 1941; Fantasia, hpd/pf, 1942; Canon in the Octave, 1945
10 Pieces for 5 Fingers, 1946; Sonata in memoriam Ferruccio Busoni, 1955; Gay Picture, 1957; Short Sonatas nos.2–3, 1958; The Bells of Bellagio, pf 4/6 hands, 1967; Rondo, accordion, 1967; Short Sonata no.4, 1967; Fugue, org, 1971; Short Sonatas nos.5–7, 1979; Sonority Forms I, 1982–3; Sonority Forms II: the Right Hand Path, pf right hand, 1984; Tango, 1985

SONGS

(all for S, pf, unless otherwise stated)

An den Traume (Cornelius), 1915; Der Eichwald (Lenan), 1915; Septembermorgen (Mörike), 1915; Wir wandeln alle den Weg (Bodenstadt), 1915; 2 Songs (Ger. sacred), 1916–17; In Weihnachtszeiten (Hesse), 1917; Mysterium (Frey), 1917; Requiescat (Wilde), 1917; Frühling (Hesse), 1918; Wie sind die Tage (Hesse), 1918; Transcience (Naidu), 1922; Gliding o'er All (Whitman), 1927; A Roman's Chamber (Shelley), 1928; Auguries of Innocence (Blake), 1928; Infant Joy (Blake), 1928; Locations and Times (Whitman), 1928
To Morning (Blake), 1928; Visored (Whitman), 1928; Wake the serpent not (Shelley), 1928; Young Love (Blake), 1928; A Farm Picture (Whitman), 1929; For like a chariot's wheel (anon.), 1929; Goodnight (Shelley), 1929; Here the frailest leaves of me (Whitman), 1929; I faint, I perish (Shelley), 1929; The Dawn (anon.), 1930; At the Last (Whitman), 1936; Forever Lost (Taggard),

1936; Only themselves understand themselves (Whitman), 1936; Swing, swing and swoon (Taggard), 1936

9 Songs to Emily Dickinson Texts, 1942–51; Love's Secret (Blake), 1949; Divine Image (Blake), 1949; She walks in beauty (Byron), 1951; The harp the monarch minstrel swept (Byron), 1951; 6 Proverbs, A, pf, 1973; The Little Vagabond (Blake), 1980; Silent, Silent Night (Blake), 1980; Ah! Sunflower (Blake), 1984; The Lily (Blake), 1984

OTHER VOCAL

Trio, S, Mez, A, 1914; Cum spiritu sancto, SATB, 1917; 3 Swiss Folksongs, SATB, 1917; 3 Songs: At Christmastime (Hesse), Noon Silence (Sharpe), Venilia (Sharpe), S, pf, 1917–22, arr. S, orch, 1927; Vater unser in Himmelreich, SATB, 1918; Enigma Canon [after Bach], SSAATB, 1922; The Soundless Song (Luening), S, fl, cl, str qt, pf, dancers, lights, 1923; Trio, S, fl, vn, 1924; If that High World (Byron), SSA, 1927; Sun of the Sleepless (Byron), SSA, 1927

Songs of Experience (Blake), B-Bar, pf, 1928; Behold the Tabernacle of God, S, SATB, pf/org, 1931; Anthem, SATB, org, 1932; When in the languor of evening (Gibbon), S, chorus, str qt/ww qt, pf, 1932; Hast never come to thee, S, fl, 1936; Suite, S, fl, 1936; Christ is Arisen, SSAATB, pf/org, str, fl ad lib, cl ad lib, bn ad lib, 1940; Ich denke Dein, SSAA, 1942; Alleluia, SATB, 1944; Pilgrim's Hymn (Moss), SA, pf/orch, 1946

The Maidens of Shang-ti, SSA, 1949; Vocalise, SSAA, 1949; The Tiger's Ghost (Swenson), TTBB, 1951; Lines from a Song for Occupations (Whitman), SATB, 1964; Psalm cxlvi, SATB, 1970; No Jerusalem but this (Menashe), cantata, solo vv, mixed chorus, 15 insts, 1982; Lines from The First Book of Urizen and Vala, or a Dream of 9 Nights (Blake), solo vv, chorus, 1983; Laughing Song (Blake), T, Bar, Bar/Ct, 1984

MSS in *NN-L*

BIBLIOGRAPHY

EwenD

E. Carter: "Late Winter, New York, 1937," *MM*, xiv (1936–7), 154 [on Prelude to a Hymn Tune by William Billings]

A. Copland: "Scores and Records," *MM*, xv (1937–8), 180 [on Two Symphonic Interludes]

B. Rogers: "Rochester Twenty Years After," *MM*, xxii (1944–5), 262 [on Second Quartet]

V. Thomson: "Luening's 'Evangeline'," *New York Herald Tribune* (16 May 1948), §V, p.5

J. Beeson: "Otto Luening," *ACAB*, iii/3 (1953), 2

Composers of the Americas/Compositores de América, ed. Pan American Union, vii (Washington, DC, 1961)

V. Thomson: *American Music since 1910* (New York, 1970)

C. Wuorinen: "Conversation with Otto Luening," *PNM*, x/1 (1971), 200

H. Russcol: *The Liberation of Sound* (Englewood Cliffs, NJ, 1972/*R*1985)

E. Schwartz: *Electronic Music* (New York, 1973)

L. R. Wyatt: *The Mid-twentieth-century Orchestral Variation, 1953–1963: an Analysis and Comparison of Selected Works by Major Composers* (diss., U. of Rochester, 1974) [incl. a discussion of the Rhapsodic Variations]

V. A. Kellogg: *A New Repertoire: Works for Solo Violin and Tape* (diss., Eastman School, 1975) [incl. a discussion of *Gargoyles*]

O. Luening: *The Odyssey of an American Composer* (New York, 1980) [autobiography]

D. W. Moore: "Composers Recordings: at the Quarter-century Mark, Carter Harmon and Otto Luening Talk about CRI's Past, Present, and Future," *American Record Guide*, xliii/4 (1980), 6

J. Rockwell: "An Influential Musician at 80," *New York Times* (15 June 1980), 27

R. Moog: "The Columbia-Princeton Electronic Music Center: Thirty Years of Explorations in Sound," *Contemporary Keyboard*, vii/5 (1981), 22

W. J. Richards: *An Analysis of Three Works by Luening, Rochberg, and Wolff as Representative of Unaccompanied Solo Violin Literature Composed 1970–79* (diss., U. of Northern Colorado, 1983) [on Vn Sonata no.3]

J. Chute: "Hey Fred! Otto's Really Made It!," *Milwaukee Journal* (27 May 1984) [interview]

J. Krutz: "Otto Luening: an 85-year Investment in American Music," *The Sinfonian*, xxxv/1 (1985), 10

B. Wentz: "Otto Luening at 85: an Interview," *HiFi/MusAm*, xxxv/11 (1985), 24

LESTER TRIMBLE

Luke the Drifter. Name under which HANK WILLIAMS sometimes recorded.

Lummi. American Indian group of the northwest coast; *see* SALISH.

Lummis, Charles Fletcher (*b* Lynn, MA, 1 March 1859; *d* Los Angeles, CA, 25 Nov 1928). Ethnomusicologist. He studied Latin, Greek, and Hebrew with his father and attended Harvard University (1877–80), but left without graduating. After spending three years in and around Cleveland, he began the cross-country walk to California which was to kindle his interest in the cultures of the American Indians and Mexican Americans. In 1893 he published 15 New Mexican folksongs in *Land of Poco tiempo*, then began recording folksongs and American Indian music on as many as 400 wax cylinders, 200 of which have survived and are now in the Southwest Museum, Los Angeles, which Lummis founded in 1907; the museum also houses Lummis's large collection of Indian artifacts. He also founded the (California) Landmarks Club (1895) and the Sequoia Club (1902), which fought for the rights of Indians, and was city editor for the *Los Angeles Daily Times* (1885–7) and editor of *Land of Sunshine* (1894–1901) and *Out West* (1902–9). His writings include 16 novels, poetry, and numerous descriptive articles dealing with his travels in the Southwest; with Arthur Farwell he published *Spanish Songs of Old California* (1923, repr. 1929) containing 20 of his recorded songs. The edition is remarkable for the accuracy of its transcriptions.

BIBLIOGRAPHY

M. Newmark: "Charles Fletcher Lummis," *Historical Society of Southern California Quarterly*, xxxii/1 (1950), 44

E. R. Bingham: *Charles F. Lummis: Editor of the Southwest* (San Marino, CA, 1955)

M. Simmons: *Two Southwesterners: Charles Lummis and Amando Chaves* (Cerillos, NM, 1968)

D. Gordon: *Charles F. Lummis: Crusader in Corduroy* (Los Angeles, 1972)

T. L. Fiske and K. Lummis: *Charles F. Lummis: the Man and his West* (Norman, OK, 1975)

R. E. Fleming: *Charles F. Lummis* (Boise, ID, 1981)

WILLIAM SUMMERS

Lunceford, Jimmie [Jimmy; James Melvin] (*b* Fulton, MO, 6 June 1902; *d* Seaside, OR, 12 July 1947). Jazz bandleader. He learned several instruments as a child in Denver, where he played in George Morrison's band. After studying music at Fisk University (BMus 1926), and at the City College, New York, he taught music at Manassa High School, Memphis. Here, in 1927, he organized a student jazz band, the Chickasaw Syncopators. The group began a professional career in 1929 and issued its first recordings in 1930. After playing for several years in Cleveland and Buffalo, the band began an important engagement at the Cotton Club, Harlem, in 1934. Two "hot" recordings of that year, *Jazznocracy* and *White Heat*, with arrangements by Will Hudson, immediately attracted attention, and by 1935 the group, then called Jimmie Lunceford's Orchestra, had achieved a national reputation as an outstanding black swing band (see illustration).

Unlike many big bands of the 1930s, Lunceford's group was noted less for its soloists than for its ensemble work, particularly its distinctive two-beat swing at medium tempo. This and its practiced showmanship were widely imitated by other groups, but they seldom achieved the polish and good humor that marked so many of Lunceford's performances. The band drew its early style partly from Alphonso Trent and from the Casa Loma Orchestra, as is most apparent in the crude, insistent riff patterns in the "hot" recordings of 1934. A certain experimental vein is also

Jimmie Lunceford (foreground) with his orchestra at Shea's Buffalo Theater, 1935: (on podium, front row, left to right) Sy Oliver, Paul Webster, Eddie Thompkins (trumpets), Eddie Wilcox (piano), Willie Smith, LaForest Dent, Joe Thomas, Earl Carruthers (saxophones); (at rear, left to right) Russell Bowles, Eddie Durham, Elmer Crumbley (trombones), Jimmy Crawford (drums), Al Norris (guitar), and Moses Allen (double bass)

unmistakable in these years, for instance in Willie Smith's curious recasting of Ellington's *Mood Indigo* (1934). Soon after, however, there emerged a distinctive "Lunceford style," largely the result of the highly imaginative arrangements of the group's trumpeter, Sy Oliver. The varied interplay of soloists and brass and reed sections in Oliver's best work, such as *For Dancers Only* (1937) and *Margie* (1938), set high standards for dance-band arrangers of the time and proved extremely fruitful for postwar big-band styles. Perhaps even more remarkable was his fusion of novelty effects and bizarre contrasts into coherent musical argument, as in his famous *Organ Grinder's Swing* of 1936, which uses wood-blocks, celesta, and slap-tongued saxophones. These arrangements, however complex, left ample scope for the group's soloists, the most important of whom were Joe Thomas (tenor saxophone), Trummy Young (trombone), Eddie Durham (guitar; he also played trombone), and the alto saxophonist Willie Smith, who also trained and led Lunceford's outstanding reed section from the group's inception in 1929.

After Oliver's departure in 1939 and Smith's in 1942, the group's style became somewhat unfocused, despite some excellent arrangements by Tadd Dameron (1941–2) and George Duvivier (1945–7). The band continued for a year after Lunceford's death under the joint direction of Eddie Wilcox and Joe Thomas, and for several years after that under Wilcox alone. Later attempts to revive the band's sound and Oliver's arrangements with other musicians have been unsuccessful.

RECORDINGS
(selective list)

White Heat (1934, Vic. 24586); Jazznocracy (1934, Vic. 24522); Mood Indigo (1934, Decca 131); Rhythm is our Business (1934, Decca 369); Organ Grinder's Swing (1936, Decca 908); For Dancers Only (1937, Decca 1340); Margie (1938, Decca 1617); Lunceford Special (1939, Voc./OK 5326); What's your Story, Mornin' Glory? (1940, Col. 33510); Yard Dog Mazurka (1941, Decca 4032)

BIBLIOGRAPHY

SouthernB
W. Russo: "Jimmy Lunceford," *Jazz Panorama*, ed. M. Williams (New York, 1962/*R*1979), 132
F. Driggs: "Sy Oliver," *Sounds and Fury*, i (1965), 49
E. Edwards and others, eds.: *The Jimmie Lunceford Band* (Whittier, CA, 1965) [discography]
S. Dance: "Willie Smith," *The World of Swing* (New York, 1974), 93
A. McCarthy: *Big Band Jazz* (London, 1974), 47ff
B. Hall and others: "Jimmy Lunceford Broadcasts, Transcriptions and Filmtracks," *Micrography*, no.42 (1976), 14
M. Harrison: *A Jazz Retrospect* (Newton Abbot, England, 1976), 76ff

J. BRADFORD ROBINSON

Lundberg, Robert (*b* Berkeley, CA, 25 June 1948). Lute maker. He began to make musical instruments as a hobby, using craft skills developed through his work as a model maker and racing-car designer. In 1971 he began an apprenticeship with Paul Schuback, a violin maker trained in Mirecourt, France, and in 1973 became journeyman in the workshop of the Dutch lute maker Jacob van de Geest at Vevey, Switzerland. During these years Lundberg photographed, measured, and studied the lutes and viols in major European collections. By the mid-1970s he had established his own workshop in Portland, Oregon, and gained a reputation as an important maker of lutes and related instruments based on historical models. Lundberg has also restored historical instruments for museums and collectors. He has lectured frequently on lute construction, in particular at Erlangen, Germany, where he began teaching on a regular basis in 1978.

HOWARD SCHOTT

Lunetta, Stanley (*b* Sacramento, CA, 5 June 1937). Composer. He received a BA from Sacramento State College and an MA from the University of California, Davis, where his teachers in composition were Larry Austin, Jerome Rosen, and Richard Swift. Other teachers included Stockhausen, Tudor, and Cage. He was a founder of the New Music Ensemble (1963) and was an editor of *Source: Music of the Avant Garde* from 1971 until it ceased publication in 1977. He resides in Sacramento, where he is active as a percussionist, teacher, and composer.

Lunetta's music, which frequently includes slide projections, dancers, theater, electronics, and set-sculptures, is highly inventive, exhibiting at times a biting wit or offering keen social commentary; much of it displays a theatrical flare and Lunetta's interest in percussion. Since 1967 his creative energies have been increasingly devoted to constructing special electronic devices for use in his compositions. In 1970 he built *Moosack Machine*, the first of a series of self-playing sound sculptures based on electronic sound-sources and equipped with digital sequencers and memories. The sculptures emphasize everyday and scrap materials and are often festooned with electronic circuitry and wiring. *Sound Hat* is activated when the wearer removes his "hat"; most of the other machines are activated by changes in the environment (light, temperature, wind). *Cosmic Cube* is a self-playing synthesizer that can also be operated by a performer.

WORKS

Stage: Twomanshow, environmental theater piece, 1968; The Unseen Force, orch, chamber ens, perc, elec, sound sculptures, nar, dancers, 1976

Large ens: Many Things, orch, 1966

Mixed media, inst: PFFT, perc trio, 1965; Pf Music, 1966; A Piece for Bandoneon and Str, 1966; Free Music, 1967; Ta-Ta, chorus, mailing tubes, 1967; The Wringer, 1967; Funkart, mixers, lights, audio-visual equipment, 1967; Hulk, 1967; Spider Song, collab. L. Austin, 1968; Mr. Machine, fl, elec, 1969; A Day in the Life of the Moosack Machines, 1972; other works, 1965–70

BIBLIOGRAPHY

S. Lunetta: "Moosack Machine," *Source*, no.8 (1970), 46 [incl. recording]

——: "Moosack Machines: Sound Hat, De Daddle Dee," *Source*, no.11 (1972), 40

DAVID COPE, HUGH DAVIES

Lunsford, Bascom Lamar (*b* Mars Hill, NC, 21 March 1882; *d* Asheville, NC, 4 Sept 1973). Folk-music collector and performer. He played the fiddle and sang as a child, but had no formal musical training. His first job, as a traveling fruit-tree salesman in the mountain areas of the Carolinas, Georgia, and Tennessee, brought him into contact with the Appalachian folk-music tradition. He learned folklore methodology and observed professional standards of collection; in order to preserve the culture he organized the Mountain Dance and Folk Festival in Asheville, North Carolina, in 1928, which has taken place annually since then. Lunsford was also involved in the establishment of several other folk festivals, and in 1949 was invited to represent the USA at the first International Folk Music Festival in Venice, Italy. He recorded for the Library of Congress his own collection of over 300 folksongs, tales, and other items, and made numerous commercial recordings. He also traveled widely to lecture on and perform traditional music. His compositions include the extremely popular *Mountain Dew* (1920).

BIBLIOGRAPHY

H. H. Martin: "Minstrel Man of the Appalachians," *Saturday Evening Post* (22 May 1948), 31

L. Jones: "The Minstrel of the Appalachians," *JEMF Quarterly*, ix (1973), 2 [incl. discography]

B. Finger: "Bascom Lamar Lunsford: the Limits of a Folk Hero," *Southern Exposure*, ii/1 (1974), 27

L. Jones: "Minstrel of the Appalachians," *North Carolina Folklore Journal*, xxv/1 (1977), 1

——: *Minstrel of the Appalachians: the Story of Bascom Lamar Lunceford* (Boone, NC, 1984)

LOYAL JONES

Luther, Frank [Crow, Francis Luther] (*b* nr Hutchinson, KS, 5 Aug 1905). Country-music singer and songwriter. He came from a rural background, which gave him a love of folksongs. After formal training in singing and piano he began a career as a concert singer, but this was curtailed by a throat ailment. In the late 1920s he moved to New York, where he began a long songwriting and singing partnership with CARSON J. ROBISON. As Bud and Joe Billings, the pair recorded many hits, including *Birmingham Jail*, *The Utah Trail*, and *When it's springtime in the Rockies* (all 1929); as songwriters, one of their most successful compositions was *Barnacle Bill the Sailor* (1928). Luther soon developed an ability to mimic a variety of singing styles, which made him even more attractive to recording companies; he recorded under dozens of pseudonyms for many different labels, and his output eventually reached some 3000 sides. After parting from Robison in 1932, Luther began working with his wife, Zora Layman, and performed on a successful radio show on NBC, "Hillbilly Heart-throbs" (later "Heart Throbs of the Hills"). In 1936 he had unexpected success with an album of Mother Goose songs on Decca, and he therefore devoted most of his later career to making recordings for children. He became an expert in music education and in 1942 wrote *Americans and their Songs*. In later years he became an executive with Decca, but continued to record children's songs and stories, as well as albums of songs by Stephen Foster and Civil War songs.

RECORDINGS
(selective list)

As soloist: The Old Spinning Wheel (Melotone 12929, 1934); When they cut down the old pine tree (Decca 5009, 1934); You better let that liar alone (Decca 5050, 1934)

With C. J. Robison: Birmingham Jail (Vic. 40031, 1929); The Utah Trail (Vic. 40040, 1929); When it's springtime in the Rockies (Vic. 40088, 1929)

With Z. Layman: Seven years with the wrong man (Brunswick 6908, 1934)

BIBLIOGRAPHY

G. F. Vaughn: "Ray Whitley's Tribute to Frank Luther," *JEMF Quarterly*, xiii (1977), 17

CHARLES K. WOLFE

Lutheran Church, music of the.

1. Up to the mid-20th century. 2. Later developments.

1. UP TO THE MID-20TH CENTURY. A number of independent settlements of Lutherans on the East Coast existed in the 17th century, but these were essentially foreign churches, supported and staffed by the home country. A significant increase in the immigration of Lutherans occurred under British rule in the 18th century. Many settled in Pennsylvania, where Henry Melchior Muhlenberg (1711–87), "the patriarch of the Lutheran Church in America," rose to a position of influence and leadership. He was ordained in Leipzig on 24 August 1739, in a ceremony at which J. S. Bach may have acted as musical director. Muhlenberg was himself a noted organist, and Gotthilf August Francke, the director of the Pietist missionary enterprises in Halle, commissioned him to minister in America. Muhlenberg found that organs were a rarity here and that hymn singing was either appalling or nonexistent. His love of music provided the inspiration for the first German hymnbook produced in America, the *Erbauliche Lieder-Sammlung* (Germantown, PA, 1786), which drew largely

on the Pietistic *Neues geistreiches Gesangbuch* of Freylinghausen. The influence of Pietism in these pioneer days was such that little music other than hymn singing flourished.

In the mid-19th century there was a new influx of immigrants from different areas of Germany, each of which had its own hymnal. In their desire to be doctrinally orthodox they turned away from much in these hymnals and rediscovered the rugged hymns of the 16th century. They abandoned the later isometric forms of the melodies in favor of the original rhythmic forms as they found them in Friedrich Layriz's chorale books, *Kern des deutschen Kirchengesang* (Nördlingen, 1844–55). These volumes, and his liturgical settings for Loehe's *Agenda* (Nördlingen, 1853), helped to make Layriz influential in forming the musical ideals of Lutheranism in the USA. As in Germany, the recovery of early Lutheran hymnody led to a rediscovery of classic Lutheran composers and their music.

After World War I the effects of the *Orgelbewegung* in Germany began to reach the USA as American organists and builders returned from study abroad, and the colleges and universities of all Lutheran bodies soon began to offer degrees with majors in church music, some also offering graduate study. As a result there arose a new generation of church musicians who not only adopted the great tradition of the "golden age" of Lutheran church music, notably in choral singing, but also made important contributions in composition, designs for organ building, and performance. The renaissance of choral music owed much to the efforts of F. Melius Christiansen, composer and conductor at St. Olaf Lutheran College, Northfield, Minnesota. In 1944 Theodore Hoelty-Nickel founded the Valparaiso University Church Music Seminar, which became an annual event and which has provided information and inspiration to Lutheran composers and musicians in the USA. Other pioneers included Carl P. Pfatteicher and, especially, Walter E. Buszin, both organists who exerted great influence through their writings, lectures, recitals, and performing editions.

2. LATER DEVELOPMENTS. Consideration of current Lutheran worship music should take into account the contributions of the three major bodies in the denomination: the American Lutheran Church (ALC), the Lutheran Church in America (LCA), and the Lutheran Church–Missouri Synod (LCMS). Numerous initiatives aimed at pan-Lutheran cooperation in matters of liturgy and hymnody have been undertaken from the late 1950s. For example, the ALC and the LCA cooperated in the publication of the *Service Book and Hymnal* (1958) and on 8 September 1982 voted to form a new Lutheran Church, also including the Association of Evangelical Lutheran Churches.

When the LCMS wished to update its own worship resource, the *Lutheran Hymnal* (1941), it sought the collaboration of the other groups. This led to the establishment of the *Inter-Lutheran Commission on Worship*, made up of clergy, liturgical scholars, and musicians from all three bodies. An early result of this collaboration was the *Worship Supplement* (1969), followed by ten pamphlets called *Contemporary Worship* (1969–76) intended as preparation for the *Lutheran Book of Worship* (1978). As well as 569 hymns both traditional and contemporary, this volume contains three settings of the Choral Eucharist, by Richard Hillert, Ronald Nelson, and Gerhardt Cartford, the last-named revising Regina Fryxell's setting in the 1958 hymnal. The liturgical section also contains choral settings for Morning and Evening Prayer as well as for Compline. For theological reasons the LCMS did not adopt this book, and in 1982 it produced its own version, *Lutheran Worship*, which, even so, includes two Eucharist settings, as well as other features, from the *Lutheran Book of Worship*. Both books bear witness to the painstaking efforts of all who participated in their production. One of their outstanding features is the attempt to have congregational participation in the chanting of the Psalter, achieved through the use of very simple formulae and an easy-to-follow system of pointing. Another most valuable contribution to hymnody is the *Hymnal Companion to the Lutheran Book of Worship* (1981), edited by Marilyn Kay Stulken, a large volume containing a number of historical essays on hymnody and valuable information on the texts and tunes of the hymns in the 1978 book.

In recent years the publication agencies of the three bodies, Augsburg Publishing House, Minneapolis (ALC), Concordia Publishing House, St. Louis (LCMS), and Fortress Press, Philadelphia (LCA), have published works by a number of gifted Lutheran composers, among them Jan Bender, Thomas Beck, Paul Bunjes, Richard Hillert, Paul Manz, Daniel Moe, Ronald Nelson, Leland Sateren, Carl Schalk, Ralph Schultz, and Richard Wienhorst. Outstanding among Lutheran organists are Timothy Albrecht, Heinrich Fleischer, Philip Gehring, Will Headlee, Richard Heschke, Frederick Jackisch, Paul Manz, Karl Moyer, and Walter Pelz. They are not only involved with their parochial duties as directors of music but are also in demand for recitals, workshops, master classes, and hymn festivals. This has resulted in parish music, both choral and organ, of the highest quality. Paul Bunjes has been among notable scholars to collaborate with organ builders in working out Baroque specifications for organs in Lutheran and other churches. Parochial schools are a part of the tradition of the ALC and, especially, the LCMS, and some groups also maintain high schools in the larger metropolitan areas. The benefits deriving from such integrated musical education can be seen in the parishes where such programs are pursued. Excellent choral traditions are maintained at all of the Lutheran educational institutions; among the outstanding choral groups are the St. Olaf Choir, Augustana College Choir, the various Concordia College choirs, and those of Gettysburg College and Valparaiso University.

In addition to the long-established seminars of church music at Valparaiso University, practically all Lutheran colleges have annual church music workshops intended as continuing education for the professional musician, as well as training for the volunteer. Some, like Concordia College, River Forest, Illinois, have also established annual lectures in church music. A recent development in music education is the formation of Lutheran Music Programs, Inc., with headquarters at Lincoln, Nebraska. One program, which operates a "Sounds of Summer" camp on the campuses of various Lutheran colleges and universities, provides training for talented young singers and instrumentalists in a context of Christian worship and also seeks to foster broader-based support for music in the church.

Practically all of the Lutheran bodies have established worship-and-music commissions made up of knowledgeable clergy and professional musicians. These function not only at the national but also at the synodical (diocesan) or district level and act as resource agencies for those working in the parishes. Some of them also publish regular newsletters with reviews of new organ, vocal, and choral music, and articles of interest to the parish musician.

Lutheranism was affected, in some places deeply, by the flood of folk and pop music and jazz that inundated churches of all denominations during the 1960s and 1970s. The pendulum has, however, swung back, and Lutheran worship music has absorbed what was best in these idioms, as evidenced in the jazz masses and vespers regularly heard at St. Peter's Lutheran Church in midtown New York. Such works coexist with music of the great Lutheran heritage, well represented by the regular performances of Bach cantatas directed by Frederick Grimes at Sunday Vespers at the Lutheran Church of the Holy Trinity, also in New York.

Recent developments display a forward-looking ecumenical thrust, and dialogues with the Catholic and Episcopal church authorities, while mainly concerned with theological issues, also recognize the important role that music plays in liturgy and worship in the life of the church. It is no exaggeration to state that the Lutheran Church–which has frequently been called the *ecclesia cantans* (the "singing church"), a designation attributed to Luther himself – has assumed a position of musical leadership among the Christian churches in the USA today.

BIBLIOGRAPHY

F. Lochner: *Der Hauptgottesdienst der Evangelisch-Lutherischen Kirche* (St. Louis, 1895)
G. C. A. Kaeppel: *Die Orgel im Gottesdienst* (St. Louis, 1932)
T. Hoelty-Nickel, ed.: *The Musical Heritage of the Lutheran Church* (Valparaiso, IN, and St. Louis, 1944–70) [proceedings of Valparaiso U. seminars on church music]
W. E. Buszin: "Luther on Music," *MQ*, xxxii (1946), 80
W. J. Hinke: "Lutheran and Reformed Church Hymnody in Early Pennsylvania," *Church Music and Musical Life in Pennsylvania*, ed. Pennsylvania Society of the Colonial Dames of America, iii/2 (Philadelphia, 1947), 259–300
L. D. Reed: *The Lutheran Liturgy* (Philadelphia, 1947, rev. 2/1959)
P. Nettl: *Luther and Music* (Philadelphia, 1948)
C. Halter: *Practice of Church Music* (St. Louis, 1955)
T. Hoelty-Nickel: "Luther and Music," *Luther and Culture*, Martin Luther Lectures, iv (Decorah, IA, 1960), 143–211
E. C. Wolf: *Lutheran Church Music in America during the Eighteenth and Early Nineteenth Centuries* (diss., U. of Illinois, 1960)
G. M. Cartford: *Music in the Norwegian Lutheran Church: a Study of its Development and its Transfer to America 1825–1917* (diss., U. of Minnesota, 1961)
C. Halter: *God and Man in Music* (St. Louis, 1963)
P. Bunjes: *The Formulary Tones Annotated* (St. Louis, 1965)
W. E. Buszin: "Music of the Lutheran Church," *The Encyclopaedia of the Lutheran Church*, iii (Minneapolis, 1965), 1676
——: "Criteria of Church Music in the 17th and 18th Centuries," *Festschrift Theodore Hoelty-Nickel: a Collection of Essays on Church Music* (Valparaiso, IN, 1967), 13
J. Riedel, ed.: *Cantors at the Crossroads: Essays on Church Music in Honor of Walter E. Buszin* (St. Louis, 1967)
H. Lindemann: *The New Mood in Lutheran Worship* (Minneapolis, 1971)
C. Halter and C. Schalk, eds.: *A Handbook of Church Music* (St. Louis, 1978)
C. Schalk: *Key Words in Church Music* (St. Louis, 1978)
R. A. Leaver and A. Bond: "Luther, Martin," *Grove 6*
M. K. Stulken, ed.: *The Hymnal Companion to the Lutheran Book of Worship* (Philadelphia, 1981)
M. P. Bangert: *Edward Rechlin: Organist and Musician of the Church* (diss., U. of Minnesota, 1984)

ROBIN A. LEAVER, ANN BOND (1)
M. ALFRED BICHSEL (2)

Lutkin, Peter Christian (*b* Thompsonville, WI, 27 March 1858; *d* Evanston, IL, 27 Dec 1931). Music educator, organist, conductor, and composer. He was a chorister at the Episcopal Cathedral in Chicago and taught piano at Northwestern University in Evanston (1879–81) before studying with Joachim Raff, Woldemar Bargiel, and Karl August Haupt in Berlin, and Moritz Moszkowski in Paris (1881–4). On returning to Chicago he served as organist of St. Clement's (1884–91) and St. James's (1891–7). His main achievement was the founding and development of the Northwestern University School of Music, of which he was the first dean (1895–1928); he established the Chicago North Shore Festival (1909–30), and served as its choral conductor. He was a founder of the American Guild of Organists (1896) and received an honorary MusD from Syracuse University (1900). Lutkin's compositions consist mostly of church music. His writings include *Music in the Church* (1910), *Hymn-Singing and Hymn-Playing* (1930), and a *History of Music in Northwestern University* (unpublished manuscript, in the music library at Northwestern University).

BIBLIOGRAPHY

GroveAS [incl. list of works]
R. G. Cole: "Lutkin, Peter Christian," *DAB*

BRUCE CARR

Luvisi, Lee (*b* Louisville, KY, 12 Dec 1937). Pianist. He attended the Curtis Institute (1952–7), where he was a pupil of Serkin and Horszowski. On his graduation he was named to the Curtis faculty, becoming the youngest teacher in Curtis's history up to that time. His Carnegie Hall début took place in November 1957, and the following year he returned there as soloist with the New York PO under Bernstein. He left Curtis in 1962 and in 1963 became artist-in-residence at the School of Music of the University of Louisville, where he was later appointed head of the piano department. He has maintained an active and respected career as a soloist and chamber musician and has performed at the Mostly Mozart, the Marlboro, and the Aspen festivals; after a period as a guest artist with the Chamber Music Society of Lincoln Center (for illustration *see* CHAMBER MUSIC SOCIETY OF LINCOLN CENTER), he became an artist-member of that ensemble in 1983. Luvisi's musical style is consistent with his unspectacular yet substantial career. A superb chamber performer, who is able to play with considerable power, he is more interested in penetrating a work's substance than in dazzling an audience with his technique.

JAMES CHUTE

Lybbert, Donald (*b* Cresco, IA, 19 Feb 1923; *d* New York, 26 July 1981). Composer and teacher. He studied at the University of Iowa with Wagenaar (BM 1946), at Columbia University with Carter and Luening (MA 1950), and at Fontainebleau near Paris with Boulanger. During World War II he served as an officer in the US Navy. He was a teaching fellow at the Juilliard School (1947–8), and from 1954 to 1980 taught at Hunter College, CUNY. While some works are in part serial, his basic style is freely atonal with an emphasis on audible formal structure. He wrote (with F. Davis) *The Essentials of Counterpoint* (1969).

WORKS
(selective list)

2 operas: Monica, 1952; The Scarlet Letter, 1965
Introduction and Toccata, brass, pf, 1956; Chamber Sonata, va, hn, pf, 1958; Concert Ov., orch, 1958; Austro terris inflente, 3 motets, 1961; Sonata brevis, pf, 1962; Praeludium, brass, perc, 1963; Lines for the Fallen, S, 2 ¼-tone-tuned pf; Zap, choruses, 4 ens, rock group, 1970; Conc., pf, tape, n.d.; Octagon (after J. Joyce: Ulysses), S, ens, 1975; 2 other pf sonatas, song cycles
Principal publisher: Peters

OLIVER DANIEL

Lyceum. *See* CHAUTAUQUA AND LYCEUM.

Lymon, Frankie (*b* New York, 30 Sept 1942; *d* New York, 28 Feb 1968). Singer and songwriter. In 1954 he joined a vocal group from Harlem called the Teenagers, the other members of which were Sherman Garnes (*b* New York, 8 June 1940; *d* 1978), bass; Joe Negroni (*b* New York, 9 Sept 1940; *d* New York, 1977), baritone; Herman Santiago (*b* New York, 18 Feb 1941), first tenor; and Jimmy Merchant (*b* New York, 10 Feb 1940), second tenor. With Lymon's strong boy soprano as the leading voice, the group made its first successful recording with *Why do fools fall in love?*, which reached no.6 on the pop chart in 1956, and was followed by further hits in the same year. At the age of 14 Lymon became one of the first teenage rock-and-roll idols; the group's rise to fame was rapid, and they were nominated for several awards. They sang "I'm not a juvenile delinquent" and "Baby baby" in the film *Rock, Rock, Rock*, which also starred Alan Freed. Freed was one of the first disc jockeys to play the Teenagers' recordings on his radio programs, and he engaged them to play at the concerts that he organized in New York. Lymon left the Teenagers in 1957 and embarked on a career as a soloist. After making a hit with a version of standard *Goody, goody* and appearing in the film *Mr. Rock and Roll* (1957), he achieved little further success, in part because his voice had broken to an unremarkable tenor, but also because of his addiction to heroin, which led to poverty and his early death. Although it was Lymon's only major songwriting success, *Why do fools fall in love?* has become something of a standard, and has been recorded by many singers, including Joni Mitchell (1980) and Diana Ross (1981).

BIBLIOGRAPHY

SouthernB

Lynes, Frank (*b* Cambridge, MA, 16 May 1858; *d* Bristol, NH, 24 June 1913). Organist and composer. He studied first at the New England Conservatory and then piano and organ with Benjamin J. Lang and harmony with John Knowles Paine. He attended the Leipzig Conservatory (1883–5), where he was a pupil of Salomon Jadassohn and then returned to Boston. There he remained for the rest of his career, serving as organist of the First Parish Church, Cambridge (1888–90), and the Church of the Disciples, Boston (from about 1891 until his death), and teaching piano privately. As a pedagogue Lynes insisted that his pupils acquire a sound musical intelligence as well as dexterity at the keyboard. He composed for the piano (sets of programmatic miniatures and didactic studies) and organ, and wrote songs (at least 19 sets), partsongs, and anthems, as well as liturgical music. Most of his works were published by Arthur P. Schmidt.

BIBLIOGRAPHY

O. Downes: *Frank Lynes* (Boston, 1914)

WILLIAM OSBORNE

Lynn, Frank. Pseudonym of JOSEPH SCHILLINGER.

Lynn [née Webb], **Loretta** (*b* Butcher Hollow, nr Van Lear, KY, 14 April 1935). Country-music singer, songwriter, and guitarist. She was born into an impoverished coal-mining family in eastern Kentucky. At the age of 13 she married Oliver V. "Mooney" Lynn and moved to Bellingham, Washington, where she sang on radio and in clubs. She made her first recording, *Honky Tonk Girl*, for the Zero label in 1960. The following year, represented by the Wilburn Brothers' talent agency, she signed a contract with Decca. She received invaluable national exposure on the "Grand Ole Opry," where she made her first guest appearance in 1960, and on the Wilburn Brothers' nationally syndicated television show. In 1962 she became a regular cast member of the "Opry"; in the 1970s and 1980s she had particular success performing with Conway Twitty. She became internationally known through her best-selling autobiography, *Coal Miner's Daughter* (1976), and the film based on it (1980). Although both Kitty Wells and Patsy Cline had been successful, no female country singer before Lynn had gained such national recognition. Her refreshing style, honesty, and open charm have made her a popular guest on national television shows. Many of the lyrics she has written, such as *Don't come home a-drinkin'* (1966), *Fist City* (1968), *Coal Miner's Daughter* (1970), and *You're looking at country* (1971), support the accepted view of her as sincere and ingenuous.

Loretta Lynn, c1981

RECORDINGS
(selective list)

Honky Tonk Girl (Zero 1011, 1960); Success (Decca 31384, 1962); Don't come home a-drinkin' (Decca 32045, 1966); Fist City (Decca 32264, 1968); Woman of the World (Leave my world alone) (Decca 32439, 1969); Coal Miner's Daughter (Decca 32749, 1970); One's on the way (Decca 32900, 1971); You're looking at country (Decca 32851, 1971); Trouble in Paradise (MCA 40283, 1974); Feelin's (MCA 40420, 1975); Somebody somewhere (don't know what he's missin' tonight) (MCA 40607, 1976)

With C. Twitty: Louisiana Woman, Mississippi Man (MCA 40079, 1973); As soon as I hang up the phone (MCA 40251, 1974); The Letter (MCA 40572, 1976)

BIBLIOGRAPHY

"Lynn, Loretta," *CBY 1973*

D. A. Horstman: "Loretta Lynn," *Stars of Country Music*, ed. B. C. Malone and J. McCulloh (Urbana, IL, 1975), 309

L. Lynn and G. Vecsey: *Loretta Lynn: Coal Miner's Daughter* (Chicago, 1976) [autobiography]

BILL C. MALONE

Lynyrd Skynyrd. Rock group. Its members were Ronnie Van Zant, singer, Gary Rossington, guitarist, Allen Collins, guitarist, Ed King, guitarist (replaced in 1974 by Stephen Gaines),

Billy Powell, keyboard player, Leon Wilkeson, bass guitarist, and Bob Burns, drummer (replaced in 1975 by Artimus Pyle). Formed in Jacksonville, Florida, in 1966, the group adapted its name from that of the members' high school gym teacher, Leonard Skinner. After playing locally for several years, the group toured with The Who in 1973 and began to record for MCA. In 1974 its single *Sweet Home Alabama*, an answer to two negative songs by Neil Young, *Alabama* and *Southern Man*, reached the Top Ten. Subsequent hit songs were a studio recording of *Free Bird* (1974), *Saturday Night Special* (1975), and a concert version of *Free Bird* (1976). By 1976 Lynyrd Skynyrd had become a leading American concert attraction; its characteristic sound was based on a driving beat that underpinned intricate counterpoint between three lead guitars and the deep, powerful voice of Ronnie Van Zant. It played typical hard-edged southern rock, though it was influenced as much by British bands as by the Allman Brothers Band; in concert performances and on recordings it created a quintessential sleazy barroom atmosphere. On 22 October 1977, the group's chartered plane crashed outside Gillsburg, Mississippi, killing Van Zant, Gaines, and four other members. After a final hit single, *What's your name?* (recorded before the accident), the rest of the group disbanded in 1978; two years later some former members reunited as the Rossington–Collins Band.

RECORDINGS

(selective list; all recorded for MCA)

Pronounced Leh-nerd Skinnerd (363, 1973); *Second Helping* (413, 1974), incl. Free Bird, Sweet Home Alabama; Saturday Night Special (40416, 1975); Free Bird (40665, 1976) [concert version]; *One More for the Road* (2–6001, 1976); *Street Survivors* (3029, 1977); What's your name? (40819, 1978)

BIBLIOGRAPHY

"Rotgut Life: Lynyrd Skynyrd," *Time*, cviii (18 Oct 1967), 70

T. Dupree: "Lynyrd Skynyrd in Sweet Home Atlanta," *Rolling Stone*, no.172 (24 Oct 1974), 14

D. Marsh: "Skynyrd's Recorded Legacy," *Rolling Stone*, no.267 (15 June 1978), 13

GARY THEROUX

Lyon, James (*b* Newark, NJ, 1 July 1735; *d* Machias, ME, 12 Oct 1794). Composer and tunebook compiler. He graduated from the College of New Jersey (Princeton) on 26 September 1759; on the occasion, an ode set to music by him was performed. In 1760 he taught a singing-school in Philadelphia, and before the end of 1761 he brought out his tunebook *Urania, or A Choice Collection of Psalm-Tunes, Anthems, and Hymns* (Philadelphia, 1761/*R*1974). In May of that year an anthem by him was sung at the University of Pennsylvania's public commencement ceremony in Philadelphia. He was granted an MA degree by Princeton in September 1762, and shortly afterwards was licensed to preach by the Presbyterian Synod of New Brunswick, New Jersey. He devoted the rest of his life to the Church, moving to Nova Scotia in 1764 and accepting in 1772 a pastorate in Machias, Maine, which he held until his death (though he left briefly in 1773–4 and again in 1783–5). An active patriot during the War of Independence, he was chairman of the Machias Committee of Safety and Correspondence; he even proposed in a letter to George Washington that as a former resident of Nova Scotia who had explored much of its territory, he lead an expedition to wrest it from British occupation. His continued involvement with music into the 1770s is documented in the diary of Philip Vickers Fithian, who met Lyon, "that great master of Music," in Cohansey, New Jersey, in April 1774. "He sung at my request," wrote Fithian, "with his usual softness and accuracy. He is about publishing a new Book of Tunes which are to be chiefly of his own Composition." Lyon's "new book" was never published, but new compositions by him occasionally appeared in American tunebooks of the 1770s and 1780s, indicating that he kept in contact with active musicians.

Only about a dozen of Lyon's compositions appeared in print, yet by compiling *Urania* he earned a place of importance in American psalmody. *Urania* is an American musical landmark: far larger than any earlier American tunebook, it was also the first to contain English fuging-tunes and anthems and the first to identify native compositions. It was drawn primarily from British sources and was the earliest American work to include music by Tuckey; it also contained the first printed compositions of Lyon and Hopkinson. *Urania* was reprinted at least five times and served as a source for a generation of American compilers.

See also PSALMODY, §2.

BIBLIOGRAPHY

O. G. T. Sonneck: *Francis Hopkinson, the First American Poet-composer (1737–1791) and James Lyon, Patriot, Preacher, Psalmodist (1735–1794): Two Studies in Early American Music* (Washington, DC, 1905/*R*1967)

F. J. Metcalf: *American Writers and Compilers of Sacred Music* (New York, 1925/*R*1967)

F. W. Coburn: "Lyon, James," *DAB*

R. Crawford: Preface to repr. (1974) of J. Lyon: *Urania* (Philadelphia, 1761)

K. Silverman: *A Cultural History of the American Revolution* (New York, 1976), 42

RICHARD CRAWFORD

Lyon & Healy. Firm of instrument manufacturers and music dealers. Founded in 1864 in Chicago by George Washburn Lyon and Patrick Joseph Healy as a Midwest outlet for the publications of the Boston company of Oliver Ditson, the firm rapidly expanded to include retail distribution of music from all publishers and musical instruments of all types, some of which were manufactured by the firm itself. Under Healy's direction (Lyon retired in 1889) the store became widely known in Chicago and throughout the USA for its broad range of merchandise and advanced advertising and selling methods. It was one of the first businesses in the USA to appraise instruments. From about 1890 the firm used the marque "George Washburn" for its better fretted instruments, including guitars, mandolins, mandolas, banjos, zithers, and ukuleles. In about 1928 the trade name and activities other than piano and harp manufacture were acquired by the Tonk Bros. Co., which continued to sell instruments under the name into the 1930s. Tonk Bros. was acquired by C. G. Conn in 1947. In 1979 Lyon & Healy closed all its retail music stores, and the name of the firm was changed to Lyon & Healy Harps.

As an instrument manufacturer, the firm is best known for the Lyon & Healy harp, first placed on the market in 1889. Healy was interested in developing a harp that would be better suited to the rigors of the American climate than the available European models, and his engineers, basing their instruments on Erard's pedal harp, succeeded in producing a harp notable for its strength, reliability of pitch, and freedom from unwanted vibration. When Wurlitzer, the firm's major competitor, stopped producing harps before World War II, Lyon & Healy remained the sole large-scale harp builder in the USA. Other contributions to American harp manufacture made by Lyon & Healy include innovations in the style of the instrument, notably the modern, ungilded Salzedo model of 1935, and the development of a small, pedal-less instrument after medieval models (the Troubador, 1962) intended, according to the firm, for "beginners and hobbyists."

ANNETTE FERN (with JAY SCOTT ODELL)

Lyons, James (*b* Peabody, MA, 24 Nov 1925; *d* New York, 13 Nov 1973). Critic and writer on music. He graduated from Boston University in 1947 and later studied psychology at New York University (MA 1964). He was assistant editor of *Musical America* (1953–5) and, from 1957 until his death, editor and publisher of the *American Record Guide*. In addition to writing articles and reviews on a wide variety of topics for the New York *Herald Tribune*, *High Fidelity*, and *Stereo Review*, he wrote *Modern Music* (with John Tasker Howard, 1957), a revision of Howard's *This Modern Music* (1942).

PAULA MORGAN

Lyric Opera of Chicago. Opera company founded by CAROL FOX as the Lyric Theatre in 1954. *See* CHICAGO (i), §2.

M

Ma, Yo-Yo (*b* Paris, France, 7 Oct 1955). Cellist. He began studying cello at the age of four, playing a scaled-down instrument, and made his début when he was five. After his family moved to the USA, he studied with Leonard Rose in the preparatory division of the Juilliard School (1964–71), and made his first appearance in New York when he was 15; he came to international attention when Leonard Bernstein presented him on television in a fund-raising program for the Kennedy Center. He studied humanities at Harvard University between 1972 and 1976 and continued his musical pursuits in the summers, principally at the Marlboro Music Festival. His full-time career began in 1976 and in 1978 he won the Avery Fisher Prize. He has performed with major orchestras around the world, including the New York PO, the Chicago SO, the Berlin PO, the London SO, and the Israel PO, under Karajan, Mehta, Previn, Maazel, and Ozawa, among others. His tours also include solo recitals, and chamber performances with such artists as Leonard Rose, Pinchas Zukerman, Yehudi Menuhin, and Emanuel Ax, with whom he has recorded Beethoven's cello sonatas. His repertory ranges from the suites of Bach to concertos by Saint-Saëns, Lalo, Kabalevsky, and Shostakovich. Ma owes his popularity not only to a comprehensive command of his instrument and elegant musicianship, nor his responsiveness as a superb chamber music player, but also to the warmth and sensitivity he projects in all his music-making.

BIBLIOGRAPHY

"Ma, Yo Yo," *CBY 1982*

RICHARD DYER

Maazel, Lorin (Varencove) (*b* Neuilly, nr Paris, France, 6 March 1930). Conductor and violinist. He came to the USA at the age of two and was brought up in Los Angeles and Pittsburgh, studying violin and piano from the age of five and being coached in conducting by Vladimir Bakaleinikoff. On 13 July 1938 he made his début as a conductor, in Los Angeles with the visiting University of Idaho Orchestra; his début as a violinist was the same year. When he was nine he conducted at the New York World's Fair (1939), and from 1941 gave complete concerts with major American orchestras, including an appearance with the NBC SO that earned Toscanini's commendation. He concentrated on violin and gave a recital in 1945 at Pittsburgh; in the same year he became the leader of the Fine Arts Quartet of Pittsburgh. He then entered the University of Pittsburgh to study languages, mathematics, and philosophy, and joined the Pittsburgh SO as a violinist in 1948, becoming its apprentice conductor (1949–51). In 1951 he went to Italy on a Fulbright scholarship for research into Baroque music, and on 23 December 1953 he made his adult début in Catania; this was followed by performances elsewhere in Italy and in Austria and Germany. He made his London début in 1960 in a BBC SO concert, when his performance of Mahler was acclaimed for its coherence, scrupulous articulation, and expressive power. The same year he became the first American to conduct at the Bayreuth Festival (in *Lohengrin*, returning to conduct the *Ring* in 1968 and 1969).

In 1962 Maazel again appeared in New York, with L'Orchestre National de France, and he made his Metropolitan Opera début later that year with *Don Giovanni*. He began touring widely as a guest conductor, visiting the USSR and Japan in 1963. At Rome in 1965 he both produced and conducted Tchaikovsky's *Eugene Onegin*, and that year took the double post of artistic director at the Deutsche Oper, Berlin, and music director of the Berlin Radio SO. Until 1971 he remained at the Deutsche Oper, where he conducted the première of Dallapiccola's *Ulisse* (1968) in addition to the standard repertory, and was admired for his forceful, secure musical direction. His appointment with the Berlin Radio SO continued until 1975; he also led the (then New) Philharmonia Orchestra, London, as associate principal conductor (1971–2) and principal guest conductor (1976–82).

From 1972 to 1982 Maazel was music director of the Cleveland Orchestra in succession to Szell. He widened the repertory, giving the world premières of works by Druckman, Gould, Donald Harris, Martirano, and Wuorinen (among others), several of which were commissioned for the orchestra, and the American premières of 11 works, including Berio's *Coro*. In 1974 he brought staged opera into the Cleveland season. His approach to the organization and performance of opera is described in an interview in *Opera News* (xl/5, 1975, p. 18). With the Cleveland Orchestra he toured Australia, the Far East, Latin America, and Europe, and he made more than 30 recordings. During his tenure at Cleveland he continued to make guest appearances elsewhere, notably with the Vienna PO, with which he has recorded, among other works, all the symphonies of Sibelius and Tchaikovsky.

Lorin Maazel: caricature by Olga Koussevitzky (private collection)

His long affiliation with the Vienna PO led to his appointment as conductor of its New Year's Day concerts from 1980. In 1982 he became artistic director and general manager of the Vienna Staatsoper, the first American to hold these dual responsibilities, but the association was an unhappy one, and he broke his contract in 1984. He became music adviser to the Pittsburgh SO later that year.

Maazel has maintained his activity as a violinist, giving concerts and making records as a soloist-conductor in Mozart with the English Chamber Orchestra. He has also been active as a conductor-commentator on television, and recorded in six languages the narration for his recording with L'Orchestre National of *Peter and the Wolf.* He has received many honors, including an honorary MusD from the University of Pittsburgh and the Commander's Cross of the Order of Merit of West Germany; he has also been made an Officier de la Légion d'honneur. His second marriage, in 1969, was to the pianist Israela Margalit, who has often appeared as soloist at his concerts.

BIBLIOGRAPHY

"Maazel, Lorin," *CBY 1965*

A. Blyth: "Lorin Maazel Talks," *Gramophone*, xlviii (1970–71), 1449

I. Geleng: *Lorin Maazel: Monographie eines Musikers* (Berlin, 1971) [with discography]

C. Nott: "The Vanishing Breed," *Records and Recording*, xx/7 (1977), 24

H. Matheopoulos: "Lorin Maazel: Master Technician," *Maestro: Encounters with Conductors of Today* (London, 1982)

R. Gelatt: "Lorin Maazel," *Ovation*, v/ii (1984), 15

ARTHUR JACOBS/DENNIS K. McINTIRE

McAllester, David (Park) (*b* Everett, MA, 6 Aug 1916). Ethnomusicologist. He studied anthropology at Harvard University (BA 1934) and Columbia University (PhD 1939). In 1947 he joined the faculty of the anthropology department at Wesleyan University, where he became professor of anthropology and music in 1972. McAllester's research interests are American Indian ethnography and religious arts, on which he has written several books; as a performer he specializes in American songs.

WRITINGS

Peyote Music (New York, 1949)

Enemy Way Music (Cambridge, MA, 1954)

The Myth and Prayers of the Great Star Chant (Santa Fe, 1956)

ed.: *Readings in Ethnomusicology* (New York, 1971)

ed. with C. Frisbie: *Navajo Blessingway Singer: the Autobiography of Frank Mitchell, 1881–1967* (Tucson, 1978)

with S. McAllester: *Hogans: Navajo Houses and House Songs* (Middletown, CT, 1980)

PAULA MORGAN

McBeth, W(illiam) Francis (*b* Lubbock, TX, 9 March 1933). Composer, conductor, and music educator. He attended Hardin Simmons University (BM 1954, DMus 1971), the University of Texas (MM 1957), and the Eastman School, and studied with Hanson, Kennan, Clifton Williams, and Bernard Rogers. In 1957 he joined the faculty of Ouachita University in Arkadelphia, Arkansas, as resident composer and chairman of the theory and composition department. Until 1973 he was conductor of the Arkansas SO in Little Rock, and he has appeared as a guest conductor of orchestras in the USA, Canada, Europe, and Japan. His compositions, published by Southern Music Company of San Antonio, include works for band, chorus, chamber ensemble, and orchestra; his Third Symphony won the Hanson Prize in 1963. McBeth's published writings include *Effective Performance of Band Music* (1972) and *New Theories of Theory* (1979).

WORKS

(selective list)

BAND

Orfadh, 1952; Divertimento, 1953; Suite no.2, 1962; Chant and Jubilo, 1963; Narrative, 1963; Mosaic, 1964; Reflections Past, 1965; Joyant Narrative, 1966; Battaglia, 1967; Cantique and Faranade, 1967; Masque, 1968; Drammatico, 1969; Divergents, 1970; The Seventh Seal, 1972; Festive Centennial, 1974; To be Fed by Ravens, 1975; Capriccio Concertant, 1976; Canto, 1977; Kaddish, 1977; Caccia, 1980; Cavata, 1981; Feast of Trumpets, 1982; Grace Praeludium, 1982; Flourishes, 1983; Praises, 1983; Beowulf, 1984; 8 field fanfares

ORCHESTRAL

4 syms., 1955, 1957, 1963, 1970; Pastorale, ww, str, 1956; Suite on a Biblical Event, 1956; Ov., 1959; Quanah, 1960; Pastorale and Allegro, 1961; Allegro Agitato, 1962; Grace, Praeludium and Response, 1975; The Badlands, 1976; Kaddish, 1977

CHAMBER AND INSTRUMENTAL

Three Pieces, pf, 1958; Scherzo, pf, 1961; Five Projections, pf, 1962; Canticle, 11 ww, perc, 1969; Four Frescoes, 5 brass insts, 1973

VOCAL

Gloria (McBeth), mixed vv, 1958; And Isaiah Prophesied (Bible), mixed vv, 2 tpt, 2 hn, 2 trbn, tuba, 1959; Lamentation and Gloria of David (McBeth), 1959; Young Thought (McBeth), 1960; The Snow Leopard (McBeth), 1961; Come Wandering Shepherds (G. Costeley), mixed vv, 1963; Billy in the Darbies (Melville), mixed vv, 1971; Eulogies from the Bard of the Great Falls (C. M. Russell), mixed vv, 1976; Tenebrae (Bible), mixed vv, 1983

Principal publishers: Broadman, C. Fischer, Southern

RAOUL CAMUS

McBride, Robert (Guyn) (*b* Tucson, AZ, 20 Feb 1911). Composer and instrumentalist. At a very early age he learned, mostly by himself, to play the clarinet, oboe, saxophone, and piano, performing locally in jazz bands and school music groups. He studied composition with Luening at the University of Arizona (BM 1933, MM 1935), where he later taught (1957–76). He also taught at Bennington College (1935–46) and in various summer music programs. He has appeared in public as an oboe and clarinet soloist, and on New Music Quarterly Recordings. In 1941 he toured South America as a member of the League of Composers Woodwind Quintet. During the years 1945–7 he was a composer and arranger for Triumph Films in New York, producing scores for *Farewell to Yesterday*, *The Man with My Face*, and others. In 1952, on commission by F. Campbell-Watson, he reorchestrated Gershwin's *Second Rhapsody*. Among the honors he has received are a Guggenheim Fellowship, commissions from the League of Composers and the New York City Ballet, and awards from the American Academy of Arts and Letters, the Composers Press, and the University of Arizona. The titles and musical idioms of his works reflect his interest and involvement in jazz and theatrical music.

WORKS

Ballets: Show Piece (E. Hawkins), 1937; Punch and the Judy (M. Graham), 1941; Furlough Music, pf, 1945; Jazz Sym., 1954; Brooms of Mexico (A. Gordon), 1970

Orch: Fugato on a Well Known Theme, 1935; Mexican Rhapsody, 1935; Prelude to a Tragedy, 1935; Workout, chamber orch, 1936; Swing Stuff, cl, orch, 1940; Stuff in G, 1942; Strawberry Jam (Homemade), 1943; Sherlock Holmes Suite, band, 1945–6; Conc. for Doubles, cl, b cl, a sax, orch, 1947; Variety Day, vn conc., 1948; Hollywood Suite, band, *c*1950; Panorama of Mexico, 1960; Hill-country Sym., wind orch, 1962; Country Music Fantasy, wind orch, 1963; Sym. Melody, 1968; Folksong Fantasy, 1973; Light Fantastic, 1976–7; Sportmusic, band, 1976–7; film scores, incl. Farewell to Yesterday, The Man with My Face; various short pieces for orch, inst with orch, band

Chamber: Depression Sonata, vn, pf, 1934; Workout, ob, pf, 1936; Qnt, pf, str, 1937; Pumpkin-Eater's Little Fugue, str orch, 1955; 5 Winds Blowing, wind qnt, 1957; String Foursome, str qt, 1957; Variations on Various Popularisms, eng hn, cl, bn, 1965; 1776 Ov., pf 4 hands, 1975; other short inst and kbd pieces

Vocal: Sir Patrick Spence (anon.), male vv, 1932; Hot Stuff (We Hope) (McBride), TTBB, cl, pf, 1938; The Golden Sequence (11th-century anon.), SATB, org, 1974; Improvisation (McBride), TrTrAA, 1976; songs

MSS in ACA, New York

Principal publishers: Associated, C. Fischer, Gornston (Sam Fox), Peters

BIBLIOGRAPHY

EwenD

N. McKelvey: "Practical Music Maker: Robert McBride," *ACAB*, viii/1 (1958), 7

STEVEN E. GILBERT

McCandless, Paul (*b* 1947). Oboist, co-founder of the jazz chamber ensemble OREGON.

McClain, Ernest G(lenn) (*b* Canton, OH, 6 Aug 1918). Educator and scholar. He studied at Oberlin College (BMus 1940), Northwestern University (MMus 1946), and Columbia University (EdD 1959). Originally a clarinetist and band director at Denison University (1946–7) and the University of Hawaii (1947–50), he taught at Brooklyn College, CUNY, from 1950 until his retirement in 1981. He has developed effective techniques for using the monochord in the teaching of tuning systems. McClain's interest in acoustical theory led him increasingly to historical studies in the origins of mathematical harmonics and the influence of music on the philosophy, literature, and religions of ancient civilizations. In articles and his books, *The Myth of Invariance: the Origin of the Gods, Mathematics, and Music from the Ṛg-Veda to Plato* (1976), *The Pythagorean Plato: Prelude to the Song Itself* (1978/*R*1984), and *Meditations through the Quran: Tonal Images in an Oral Culture* (1981), he has offered original explanations of the musical allegories that dominate Plato's political theory, and, applying Platonic methods to the mathematical elements of the Hindu Ṛg-Veda, the Bible, the Muslim Quran, and other religious texts, he has uncovered a continuous tradition of invariant musical factors in mythic imagery.

SIEGMUND LEVARIE

McClellan, William (M(onson)) (*b* Groton, MA, 7 Jan 1934). Music librarian. He studied music history at Colorado College (BA 1956, MA 1961) and library science at the University of Michigan (MA 1959). He taught and served as music librarian at the University of Colorado from 1959 to 1965, when he became music librarian and professor of library administration at the University of Illinois. McClellan was president of the Music Library Association, 1971–3, and editor of *Notes*, the journal of the Music Library Association, 1977–82. His professional interests have included the formulation of guidelines for the development of academic music libraries.

PAULA MORGAN

McConathy, Osbourne (*b* Pitts Point, KY, 15 Jan 1875; *d* Pattenberg, NJ, 2 April 1947). Music educator. While a music supervisor in Louisville (1893–1903) he studied public school music, harmony, conducting, and horn. He was supervisor of music in Chelsea, Massachusetts (1904–13), where he developed a course of study in music appreciation, music theory, and applied music for high school students in 1905, and in class violin instruction in 1911. He was on the music faculty of Northwestern University from 1913 to 1925, concurrently holding positions in Illinois high schools. From 1908 to 1947 he was associated with the American Institute of Normal Methods, serving from 1925 to 1947 as director of both the Eastern and Western sessions; during that period he was also executive music editor for Silver, Burdett & Co. McConathy was co-author of the *Mason School Music Course* (1898–9) and the *Progressive Music Series* (1914–25), and was chief editor of the *Music Hour* (1927–38) and *New Music Horizons* (1944–7). He was also active as a composer, music editor, and writer on music education.

BIBLIOGRAPHY

C. V. Buttelman: "Osbourne McConathy," *MEJ*, xxxiii/5 (1947), 15

Obituary, *New York Times* (3 April 1947)

M. C. Platt: *Osbourne McConathy, American Music Educator* (diss., U. of Michigan, 1971)

——: "Osbourne McConathy: American Music Educator," *JRME*, xxi/2 (1973), 169

GEORGE N. HELLER

McCorkle, Donald M(acomber) (*b* Cleveland, OH, 20 Feb 1929; *d* Vancouver, BC, 6 Feb 1978). Musicologist. He attended Brown University, Bradley University (BMus 1951), and Indiana University (MA 1953, PhD 1958). In Winston-Salem, North Carolina, he taught at Salem College (1954–64) and did important work as director of the Moravian Music Foundation (1956–64); he was professor of musicology at the University of Maryland from 1964 to 1972, when he joined the University of British Columbia, as head of the department of music (1972–5) and as professor of musicology (from 1972). McCorkle was interested in 18th- and 19th-century historical musicology; he studied and edited the music of the colonial German tradition in the USA, particularly the musical culture of the Moravian settlers of North Carolina which was the subject of his dissertation. In 1964 he began work on a thematic catalogue of Brahms's works and a descriptive catalogue of the autographs. He was editor of *College Music Symposium* in 1961–2 and 1970.

PAULA MORGAN

McCormack, John (*b* Athlone, Ireland, 14 June 1884; *d* Dublin, Ireland, 16 Sept 1945). Tenor. He began his studies in Dublin as a member of the Roman Catholic Cathedral choir under Vincent O'Brien, and in 1905 went to Milan to take further lessons with Vincenzo Sabatini. He made his stage début at Savona, near Genoa, the following year under the assumed name of Giovanni Foli, after which he returned to England and sang with much success in the 1907–8 season at Covent Garden, first as Turiddù in *Cavalleria rusticana*, then as the Duke of Mantua (*Rigoletto*) and Don Ottavio; he continued to perform there regularly until 1914. He made both his New York début (with Oscar Hammerstein's Manhattan Opera, 10 November 1909) and his Metropolitan Opera début (29 November 1910) as Alfredo in *La traviata*; between 1910 and 1918 he performed with the Metropolitan for five seasons and intermittently with the Boston and Chicago companies. By his own admission a poor actor, he eventually abandoned the stage altogether and devoted himself to recitals.

Enormously popular as a concert artist, McCormack was a remarkable interpreter, not only of Handel, Mozart, and the Italian classics, but also of German lieder. The preponderance in his programs of sentimental and popular ballads alienated many musical people as much as it pleased the wider public, but whatever the song, he never debased his style. Having become an American citizen in 1918, he returned to live in Ireland in 1928, and for another decade continued to give concerts, especially in the British Isles. His numerous recordings made from 1910 on (earlier issues are immature) enjoyed a success that still persists in the form of LP reissues; these show the singular sweetness of his tone and the perfection of his style and technique in his prime, and many of his later recordings of lieder and Irish folksongs illustrate other aspects of his versatile art. In 1984 the postal services of both the USA and Ireland issued commemorative stamps in his honor.

BIBLIOGRAPHY

J. McCormack: *John McCormack: his Own Life Story*, transcr. P. V. R. Key (Boston, 1918/*R*1973)

L. A. G. Strong: *John McCormack* (London, 1941/*R*1949)

L. McCormack: *I Hear you Calling me* (Milwaukee, 1949/*R*1976) [with discography by P. F. Roden]

L. F. X. MacDermott Roe: *John McCormack: the Complete Discography* (London, 1956, 2/1972)

R. Foxall: *John McCormack* (Staten Island, NY, 1964)

J. B. Richards: "McCormack, John," *Le grandi voci*, ed. R. Celletti (Rome, 1964) [with discography by J. B. Richards and J. P. Kenyon]

G. T. Ledbetter: *The Great Irish Tenor* (New York, 1978)

B. Fawcett-Johnston: "John Count McCormack," *Record Collector*, xxix (1984), 5, 77 [with discography]

DESMOND SHAWE-TAYLOR/R

McCracken, James (Eugene) (*b* Gary, IN, 16 Dec 1926). Tenor. He attended Columbia University and augmented his income by singing with the chorus at the Roxy Theatre and in several Broadway shows. His principal teacher was Wellington Ezekiel, who coached him for his professional début as Rodolfo in *La bohème* at the Central City Opera, Colorado, in 1952. He made his début at the Metropolitan Opera a year later (21 November 1953) as Parpignol in the same opera and took many other *comprimario* roles for several seasons before leaving for Europe in 1957 to gain wider experience. He was subsequently engaged by the Bonn Opera to sing Max (in Weber's *Der Freischütz*), Radames (*Aida*), and Canio (*Pagliacci*).

The turning-point in McCracken's career was an engagement with the Washington Opera in 1960 as Othello, which became, and remained, his most celebrated role in Europe (Zurich and Vienna in 1960, Covent Garden in 1964) and in the USA. He performed the same role in his remarkably successful return to the Metropolitan in 1963, the first time it had ever been sung there by a native American. Remaining with the company for the next 15 years, he sang in five notable new productions in the 1970s – *Aida*, *Carmen*, *Otello* (the second of two new productions of the opera in which he has performed), Meyerbeer's *Le prophète*, and *Tannhäuser*. As John of Leiden in *Le prophète*, he adopted the controversial device of using head tones to portray the character's visions. The following season, having for a long time resisted Wagnerian roles, he earned lavish praise for his first Tannhäuser.

McCracken broke with the Metropolitan – for the second time – at the end of the 1977–8 season over the casting of a televised production of *Otello* scheduled for the following year; he returned after an absence of five seasons on the occasion of the company's centennial celebrations in October 1983 and for performances of *Aida* in 1984–5. He has sung in most of the world's leading houses and is a mainstay of the Boston company. Besides those already mentioned, his roles include Florestan (*Fidelio*), Bizet's Don José, Verdi's Manrico (*Il trovatore*) and Don Alvaro (*La forza del destino*), Puccini's Calaf (*Turandot*), Strauss's Bacchus (*Ariadne auf Naxos*), and Saint-Saëns' Samson.

A powerful and convincing actor, despite his ample physique, McCracken has an emotional intensity and a dark-timbred tenor of exceptional fervor. As a concert performer, he has sung with leading orchestras throughout the USA and Europe; in recitals he is sometimes joined by his wife, the mezzo-soprano SANDRA WARFIELD, whom he married in 1954 and with whom he collaborated on his autobiography. His recordings include an award-winning Othello and Schoenberg's *Gurrelieder*. He contributed an article, "Economics of Singing," to *Opera News* in 1965 (xxx/4, p.8).

BIBLIOGRAPHY

"McCracken, James," *CBY 1963*

A. Williamson: "James McCracken," *Opera*, xviii (1967), 7

J. McCracken and S. Warfield: *A Star in the Family*, ed. R. Daley (New York, 1971)

S. Wadsworth: "Finding Tannhäuser," *Opera News*, xlii/11 (1978), 14

J. Hines: "James McCracken," *Great Singers on Great Singing* (Garden City, NY, 1982), 156

B. Paolucci: "America's Heroic Tenor: James McCracken," *Ovation*, vi/8 (1985), 15

MARTIN BERNHEIMER/DOUGLAS A. MACKINNON

McCurdy, Alexander (*b* Eureka, CA, 18 Aug 1905; *d* Philadelphia, PA, 1 June 1983). Organist. A pupil of Farnam (1924–7), he made his début in Town Hall, New York, in 1926 and graduated from the Curtis Institute in 1934. His career was closely tied to three institutions: from 1927 to 1971 he was organist and choirmaster at Second (later combined with First) Presbyterian Church, Philadelphia, from 1935 to 1972 he was head of the organ department at the Curtis Institute, and from 1940 to 1965 he held the same post at Westminster Choir College, Princeton. Thus by performing and teaching he influenced many young recitalists and church musicians. His wife, Flora Greenwood, a harpist whom he married in 1932, often joined him in recitals. To a splendid innate musical ability he added the attention to rhythm, accuracy, and colorful registration that had been the special marks of Farnam's playing. He published articles in *The American Organist* and *The Etude*, of which he was organ editor from 1946 to 1957.

BIBLIOGRAPHY

J. Weaver: "Alexander McCurdy, 1905–1983," *American Organist*, xvii/9 (1983), 32

VERNON GOTWALS

McCurdy, John H. Pseudonym of WALLINGFORD RIEGGER.

McCurry, John Gordon (*b* Hart Co., GA, 26 April 1821; *d* Bio, Hart Co., 4 Dec 1886). Composer and tunebook compiler. He compiled *The Social Harp* (Philadelphia, 1855/*R*1973), containing 222 pieces in four-shape notation, most of which are three-part camp-meeting songs, though some dozen are essentially secular songs; 49 are attributed to McCurry and at least half the songs in the book were newly arranged by McCurry and his associates. In his "Rudiments of Music," published with the collection, McCurry presented instructions on writing harmony that provide insight into the thinking of the singing-school teacher. Although *The Social Harp* was never as popular outside northeast Georgia as B. F. White's and E. J. King's *The Sacred Harp* and faded from use even there towards the end of the 19th century, an annual Social Harp all-day singing was instituted at the University of Georgia in 1973.

BIBLIOGRAPHY

J. W. Baker: *History of Hart County* (n.p., 1933/*R*1970)
G. P. Jackson: *White Spirituals in the Southern Uplands* (Chapel Hill, 1933/*R*1965), 74
D. W. Patterson: Liner notes, *The Social Harp* (Rounder 0094, 1978)

JOHN F. GARST

McDaniel, Barry (*b* Lyndon, KS, 18 Oct 1930). Baritone. He studied at the Juilliard School and at the Stuttgart Hochschule für Musik, and made his recital début at Stuttgart in 1953. After short periods with the opera companies in Mainz, Stuttgart, and Karlsruhe, he joined the Deutsche Oper, West Berlin, in 1962, and has appeared as a guest at the Vienna Staatsoper, the Bavarian Staatsoper, and the Metropolitan Opera. His mellifluous voice has been heard to particular advantage in Mozart, as Pelléas, and in Strauss (the Barber in *Die schweigsame Frau* and Olivier in *Capriccio* are among his best parts). He is noted for his performances in 20th-century operas: he created the Secretary in Henze's *Der junge Lord* at Berlin in 1965, and won praise for his witty performance as the Husband in Poulenc's *Les mamelles de Tirésias* at the Munich Festival in 1974. He has given recitals in New York and in all the major European capitals; his interpretations of *Die schöne Müllerin* and *Winterreise* are ranked high for his sense of line and for his understanding and projection of the texts, and he is a noted Bach singer. Richard Rodney Bennett composed his *Tenebrae* for him.

ALAN BLYTH

McDaniel, Elias. *See* BO DIDDLEY.

McDermott, Vincent (*b* Atlantic City, NJ, 5 Sept 1933). Composer. He attended the University of Pennsylvania (BFA in composition, 1959; PhD in music history and theory, 1966) and the University of California, Berkeley (MA in music history, 1961); his teachers in composition included Rochberg, Milhaud, and Stockhausen. In 1966–7 he was a faculty member at the Hampton Institute in Virginia; from 1967 to 1977 he taught at the Wisconsin Conservatory of Music, Milwaukee, where he became dean and director, and from 1977 he taught at Lewis and Clark College, Portland, Oregon, where he is professor of music. McDermott has a deep interest in Asian music and philosophy: he studied the tablā at the Ali Akbar Khan College, Oakland, in 1973, and has accompanied the sitarist Ira Das Gupta in performance. He was also twice a student of Javanese gamelan at the Akademi Seni Karawitan Indonesia in Surakarta (1971, 1978); at Lewis and Clark College he directs the resident gamelan. He has written articles for *Ethnomusicology*, *Journal of Aesthetics and Art Criticism*, and *Asterisk, a Journal of New Music*. His awards include a Fulbright fellowship (1978) and a grant from the Oregon Arts Commission (1979).

McDermott combines in his music a pragmatic eclecticism with a strong lyric impulse, drawing on his training in Western music and Eastern traditions; a number of his works are for gamelan.

WORKS

Stage: The King of Bali (opera), singers, puppets, gamelan, 1984–

Orch: Siftings upon Siftings, 1976

Inst: Three for Five, fl, a sax, vib, pf, tabla/bongos, cymbal, 1970; Komal Usha-Rudra Nisha, sitar, fl, gui, db, 1972; Time Let Me Plan and Be Golden in the Mercy of his Means, gui, hpd, 1973; Dreams, Listen, va, pf, 1974; Solonese Conc., pf, Bar, 10 insts, 1979; Kagoklaras (A Different Song), prepared pf, gamelan, 1981; The Bells of Tajilor, gamelan, 1984

1 inst: 5 Bagatelles, pf, 1967; Who, if I Cried, Would Hear Me among the Angelic Orders, vc, 1973; Magic Grounds, pf, 1975; Smoke of Burning Cloves, sax/mar/cl/va, 1978

Tape/mixed media: He Who Ascends by Ecstasy into Contemplation of Sublime Things Sleeps and Sees a Dream, pf, tape, 1972; Pictures at an Exhibition, tape, slides, 1975; Orpheus, tape, video, 1975; Rain of Hollow Reeds, tape, 1977; A Perpetual Dream, 1v, tape, 1 or 2 dancers, 1978; Execution – What! What? What, theater piece, 1980

Vocal: Mixes (Cantata no. 1) (McDermott, Tagore, Tibetan Book of the Dead), vv, vn, perc, 1971; Thou Restless, Ungathered (Cantata no. 2) (Mother Goose, Burns, Pound), S, cl, tape, 1973; Swift Wind (Cantata no. 3) (Aeschylus, Blake, Hopkins, Whitman), high v, db, 1974; Slayer of Time, Ancient of Days (Cantata no. 4) (Rigveda, Bhagavadgita, Tagore), solo vv, chorus, eng hn, gui, perc, 1977; Laudamus, vv, 1980; The Book of the Lover, the Beloved, and the Alone, vv, 1 or more insts, 1980; Tagore Songs, S, gui, 1981; The Dark Laments of Ariadne and of Attis – 2 Songs after Catullus, S, narrator, va, tape, 1984

DOUGLAS LEEDY

McDonald, Harl (*b* nr Boulder, CO, 27 July 1899; *d* Princeton, NJ, 30 March 1955). Composer, pianist, conductor, and teacher. He studied with Vernon Spencer, Ernest Douglas, and Yaraslav de Zielinsky, and received the BMus at the University of Southern California (1921). Thereafter he studied in Liepzig, at the conservatory and the university (diploma 1922). Returning to the USA in 1923, he toured as a piano soloist and accompanist. He taught at the Philadelphia Musical Academy (1924–6) and at the University of Pennsylvania (1926–46), where he was successively lecturer, assistant professor, professor, and director. In addition, he was general manager of the Philadelphia Orchestra (1939–55) and conducted research in acoustics and sound measurement for the Rockefeller Foundation (1930–33), publishing with O. H. Schenck *New Methods of Measuring Sound* (1935), for which he was elected to the scientific fraternity Sigma Xi. His compositional style ranges from the impressionist to the objective, employing by turns traditional tonality, contemporary dance rhythms, various ethnic traits, extremely dissonant harmonies, and harsh tone-colors.

WORKS

(selective list)

Orch: 4 syms., "The Santa Fe Trail," 1932, "The Rhumba," 1934, "Lamentations of Fu Hsuan," S, chorus, orch, 1935, "Festival of the Workers," 1937;

3 Poems on Aramaic Themes, 1935; Conc., 2 pf, orch, 1936; 2 Nocturnes "San Juan Capistrano," 1938; The Legend of the Arkansas Traveler, 1939; Chameleon Variations, 1940; From Childhood, harp, orch, 1940; Bataan, 1943; Saga of the Mississippi, 1943; My Country at War, sym. suite, 1943; Vn Conc., 1943; Song of the Nations, S, orch, 1945; Ov. for Children, 1950

Choral: The Breadth and Extent of Man's Empire, 1938; Songs of Conquest, 1938; Lament for the Stolen, female vv, orch, 1939; Dirge for Two Veterans (Whitman), female vv, orch, 1940; Wind in the Palm Trees, female vv, str, 1940; God Give us Men, vv, orch, 1950; many other pieces

Other works: 2 pf trios, 1931, 1932; Fantasy, str qt, 1932; Str Qt on Negro Themes, 1933; many pf pieces

Principal publisher: G. Schirmer

BIBLIOGRAPHY

EwenD

M. Goss: *Modern Music-makers* (New York, 1952), 303

BARBARA H. RENTON

MacDonald, Jeanette (*b* Philadelphia, PA, 18 June ?1901; *d* Houston, TX, 14 Jan 1965). Soprano. She began her stage career in 1917 as a chorus girl at the Capitol Theater, New York. She played some minor parts in Broadway musicals during the 1920s and had her first starring role in *Yes, Yes, Yvette* (1927). She is best known for her performances in film musicals in operetta style; she first appeared opposite Maurice Chevalier, and then with Nelson Eddy in such films as *Naughty Marietta* (1935), *Rose-Marie* (1936), *Sweethearts* (1938), and *New Moon* (1940). Although her voice lacked flexibility and warmth, MacDonald projected an image of charm and beauty appropriate to the romantic heroines she portrayed. She left film work in 1942 in order to make concert tours, radio appearances, and recordings. She also began a brief career in opera in 1943, when she appeared with Ezio Pinza in Gounod's *Roméo et Juliette* in Montreal; her only other role was as Marguerite in *Faust* with the Chicago Civic Opera and Cincinnati Summer Opera the following year. MacDonald was married to the actor and composer Gene Raymond, whose songs she performed on her concert programs.

BIBLIOGRAPHY

P. Castanza: *The Films of Jeanette MacDonald and Nelson Eddy* (Secaucus, NJ, 1978)

J. Harvey: "MacDonald, Jeanette," *NAW*

JEAN W. THOMAS

McDonald, Susann (*b* Rock Island, IL, 26 May 1935). Harpist and teacher. After training in Chicago and New York, she studied from the age of 15 in Paris, at first privately with Henriette Renié, then with Lily Laskine at the Conservatoire, where she gained a *premier prix* in 1955. She won second prize at the first Israel International Harp Contest in 1959. Technically impeccable, she has played as a soloist in Europe, Australia, Japan, Israel, and South America, as well as in the USA and Canada. She has recorded much of the more neglected harp repertory, and has given the first performances of many works composed for her, including Joseph Wagner's Fantasy Sonata, LaSalle Spier's Sonata, and Camil Van Hulse's Suite, all for solo harp. An excellent teacher, she directed the harp departments at several universities before succeeding Marcel Grandjany at the Juilliard School in 1975; since 1981 she has also been chairman of the harp department at Indiana University. Her publications include five volumes of her own graded recital pieces for the harp and numerous editions and transcriptions, including six sonatas by Rosetti and many volumes of sacred and Spanish music. She currently serves as secretary of the World Harp Congress.

ANN GRIFFITHS/R

MacDowell [McDowell], **Edward (Alexander)** (*b* New York, 18 Dec 1860; *d* New York, 23 Jan 1908). Composer, pianist, and teacher. He was the best-known American composer before the 20th century and one of the first to receive international recognition.

1. Life: (i) 1860–88: Childhood and the years abroad. (ii) 1888–96: Years in Boston. (iii) 1896–1908: Years in New York. 2. Works.

1. Life.

(i) 1860–88: Childhood and the years abroad. His mother's ancestors were English settlers who immigrated to Connecticut before the Revolutionary War, and his father's family were Quakers of Scottish and Irish extraction who immigrated from Belfast to New York in 1812. At the time of Edward's birth, his father owned a milk delivery business near the house at 220 Clinton Street where Edward was born. Edward was the third son of Thomas and Frances Knapp McDowell (the family changed its name to MacDowell after Edward did so in the late 1870s). The artistically and musically talented boy began piano lessons at the age of eight with Juan Buitrago, a Colombian violinist who received room and board from the McDowells in exchange for the lessons. The young Venezuelan pianist Teresa Carreño, a friend of Buitrago, also gave him much encouragement and occasional lessons. At the age of about ten, Edward left public school and enrolled in the Charlier Institute, where he remained until January 1875. For some time he had been studying with Pablo Desvernine, a Cuban pianist who had been trained in Paris and who advocated further musical studies there for the boy. In April 1876 Edward, his mother, and Buitrago moved to Paris, where Edward studied piano privately with Antoine-François Marmontel, attended Augustin Savard's theory classes at the Conservatoire, and spent much time composing. (His artistic talents were recognized by the prominent painter Carolus Duran, who offered him three years' free art instruction, but Marmontel convinced him to decline the offer and continue in music.) On 8 February 1877 Edward was officially admitted to the Conservatoire, where he attended Marmontel's piano class and studied solfège with Marmontel's son Antonin. On 31 October 1877 he won a scholarship and admission as a regular piano student.

After hearing Nikolay Rubinstein perform Tchaikovsky's Piano Concerto in B♭ minor at the Paris Exposition on 9 September 1878, MacDowell withdrew from the Conservatoire to continue his piano study in Germany. A month with Siegmund Lebert at the Stuttgart Conservatory, however, was little improvement over Paris, and the violinist Emile Sauret, a family friend, recommended that Edward go to Wiesbaden to study piano with Carl Heymann and theory and composition with Louis Ehlert. He worked privately with Ehlert until May 1879 when he entered the Hoch Conservatory in Frankfurt am Main; there he was finally able to study with Heymann, and he also studied advanced composition with the conservatory's director Joachim Raff and counterpoint and fugue with Franz Böhme. MacDowell's first concert appearance at the conservatory was on the occasion of a visit on 9 June 1879 by Franz Liszt, in whose honor the students presented a recital of his compositions. This included a two-piano transcription of "Lamento e trionfo" from the symphonic poem *Tasso*, played by MacDowell and Theodor Müller of Dresden; Liszt also heard MacDowell play twice in May of the following year.

At the end of July 1880 MacDowell left the conservatory and began to take private piano pupils of his own. In August, after much hesitation on both sides, he accepted Marian Griswold

Nevins, an American sent him by Raff. (Nevins had come to the conservatory to study with Clara Schumann but refused to accept the pre-condition of study with Schumann's daughters.) During the autumn and winter of 1880 MacDowell continued private study of piano and composition with Heymann and Raff and supplemented his teaching income by accompanying singers and appearing with orchestras. Early in 1881, when Heymann was forced to resign his teaching position because of poor health, he recommended MacDowell as his successor. Although he failed to get that appointment, MacDowell was soon hired as "first teacher of pianoforte" at the Darmstadt Conservatory, where he taught from March 1881 to March 1882, resigning because the position left him insufficient time to compose.

MacDowell began the *Erste moderne Suite* op. 10 for piano while attending Raff's class at the Frankfurt conservatory, but the piece was not completed until 1881. On Raff's suggestion, he sent the work to Liszt, who recommended it for performance at the 9–12 July 1882 meeting in Zurich of the Allgemeiner Deutscher Musikverein. When MacDowell visited Liszt at Weimar in June 1882 and played his First Piano Concerto (with Eugen d'Albert playing the orchestral accompaniment on a second piano), he received further strong encouragement.

Raff's death late in June 1882 affected MacDowell so deeply that he had much trouble preparing for his forthcoming Zurich appearance. He did not even attempt to memorize his composition, thinking it unworthy of such an expenditure of time. However, the tremendous success of that occasion made him realize for the first time that composition was his true métier. In 1883 he turned for advice to his friend and former teacher, Teresa Carreño, who wrote to him encouragingly about his compositions and introduced his music to the USA, playing the Andantino and Allegretto from the *Erste moderne Suite* on 4 August 1883 in the Saratoga (New York) Town Hall and the entire *Zweite moderne Suite* op. 14 in both Chicago and Detroit early in 1884. Both suites had been published in 1883 by Breitkopf & Härtel on Liszt's recommendation, a considerable honor for the 22-year-old MacDowell. By the end of 1884 Breitkopf & Härtel and three other German firms had published ten of his works, including a two-piano version of the First Piano Concerto (dedicated to Liszt).

1. Edward MacDowell, c1905

On 9 July 1884 MacDowell secretly married Marian Nevins in a civil ceremony in New York, twelve days before a second ceremony at her family home in Waterford, Connecticut. The couple settled in Frankfurt where MacDowell taught piano and composed. By this time his music was played frequently both in the USA and Europe, but these performances did not materially increase the couple's meagre income. In June 1885 MacDowell went to London to compete for an appointment as Edinburgh examiner for the Royal Academy of Music; he was unsuccessful, due partly to his age, his nationality, and his known association with Liszt. That autumn the MacDowells moved to Wiesbaden where Edward devoted himself entirely to composition. The next three years saw the completion of 30 solo piano pieces, 8 piano duets, 12 songs, 3 partsongs, the Second Piano Concerto, three orchestral tone poems, and the *Romanze* for cello and orchestra. During these years, he was both challenged and stimulated by his friendship with another young American composer, George Templeton Strong, Jr., who was living in Wiesbaden. Both men had numerous American visitors, among them the musicians George Chadwick, Arthur Foote, and Benjamin Johnson Lang, whose eloquence convinced MacDowell to return to America in the autumn of 1888.

(ii) 1888–96: Years in Boston. Soon after settling in Boston, MacDowell realized the need for sacrificing composition to piano playing, although practice and performance appealed to him even less than they had years before. With little time to prepare he made his American début as composer-pianist at a Kneisel Quartet concert in Chickering Hall, Boston, on 19 November 1888, playing three movements from his *Erste moderne Suite* and assisting in Goldmark's Piano Quintet in B♭. His performance fell far short of complete success, but he fared somewhat better at his next public appearance, an Apollo Club concert under Lang's direction on 10 December at the Boston Music Hall; in addition to playing a group of solo piano pieces, he accompanied Strong's *Die verlassne Mühle*.

On Lang's recommendation Wilhelm Gericke invited MacDowell late in 1888 to perform his new Second Piano Concerto with the Boston SO in the spring of 1889. Lang had also recommended the work to Theodore Thomas, who proposed a specific date, 5 March, and asked MacDowell to play the solo piano part. The première of the concerto thus took place in Chickering Hall, New York, at an orchestral concert under Thomas's direction, more than a month before the Boston concert on 12 April. The conductor Frank Van der Stucken also invited MacDowell to play the concerto in a concert of American music at the Paris Exposition Universelle on 12 July, an invitation the composer accepted. The concert was repeated in Washington, DC, the following 26 March under the auspices of the National Conservatory, but MacDowell refused to participate because of a growing aversion to "all-American" concerts, so his symphonic poem *Lancelot und Elaine* was substituted.

MacDowell's successes continued. On 10 and 11 January 1890 *Lancelot und Elaine* op.25 was played by the Boston SO under Nikisch. The First Orchestral Suite op.42 was first performed – over the composer's objections – at a Worcester (Massachusetts) Festival concert under Carl Zerrahn's direction on 24 September 1891. The Boston PO, conducted by Bernhard Listemann, gave the first performance of *Die Sarazenen* and *Die schöne Aldâ* op.30 on 5 November 1891 at the Tremont Theatre, Boston, the day before MacDowell's first full-length piano recital in Boston. On 12 January 1892, Nikisch and the Boston SO played the First Orchestral Suite at a concert in New York, and the suite was also played in Louisville on 18 January and in Chicago on 19 March by Theodore Thomas and the newly formed Chicago Orchestra. Nikisch and the Boston SO performed *Hamlet* and *Ophelia* op.22 on 27 and 28 January 1893 before sold-out houses (Paderewski was performing his own piano concerto on the same program). MacDowell played his Second Piano Concerto with the New York PO under Anton Seidl on 14–15 December 1894 in Carnegie Hall to great critical acclaim, and on 23 January 1896 he played the First Piano Concerto with the Boston SO led by Emil Paur at the Metropolitan Opera House in a program that also included the first performance of his Second ("Indian") Orchestral Suite op.48 and later proved to be the zenith of his performing career; the reviews were laudatory in the extreme and the success of the evening changed the whole course of his life.

The Boston years were productive and financially rewarding for MacDowell: he acquired many piano and composition pupils, among them Henry F. Gilbert and Ethelbert Nevin; he gave many concerts; and he composed with an intensity that marked the period as the most fruitful of his life. Between 1888 and 1896 he composed the *Sonata tragica* op.45, the *Sonata eroica* op.50, 24 studies, and the *Woodland Sketches* op.51 for piano, as well as 16 songs, five partsongs, and the two orchestral suites. He also edited 31 keyboard works by other composers (sometimes going beyond mere editing to compose new material) and reworked some of Strong's music while preparing it for publication in the USA. By the mid-1890s he was recognized as a leading figure in American musical life, as composer, performer, and teacher.

(iii) 1896–1908: Years in New York. In May 1896 the trustees of Columbia University, calling MacDowell "the greatest musical genius America has produced," offered him an appointment as Columbia's first professor of music. He accepted, and that autumn he plunged into teaching with enthusiasm, devoting almost all his time and energy to the arduous task of establishing a new department of music. He carried the burden of the department and its extra-curricular activities alone until the autumn of 1898 when Leonard B. McWhood, a former student, was appointed as his assistant; in 1899 Gustav Hinrichs joined the faculty as conductor of the student orchestra and chorus.

In addition to teaching, MacDowell conducted (in 1896–8) the Mendelssohn Glee Club, a prominent men's chorus (for which he composed 13 partsongs and edited 11 choral works by other composers), taught piano privately, and gave concerts during most of the winter vacations between semesters. Serious composition had to be relegated to summers, but even so, the New York years saw the creation of some of his best piano music – the *Sea Pieces* op.55, the Third ("Norse") Sonata op.57, the Fourth ("Keltic") Sonata op.59, *Fireside Tales* op.61, and *New England Idyls* op.62 – as well as *College Songs* for male voices, partsongs for female voices, and 12 solo songs. All these works were published by 1902, with major revisions of four other piano works (opp.10, 28, 31, and 38). MacDowell published six additional piano pieces and four of the partsongs for male voices under the pseudonym Edgar Thorn (also Thorne), whose royalties went to a former nurse of his wife. From 1899 to 1900 he also served as president of the newly formed Society of American Musicians and Composers (a successor to the Manuscript Society of New York), which he vainly attempted to build into a national organization.

During his sabbatical year (1902–3), MacDowell toured the USA and Canada as a pianist; he completed the season on 14 May 1903 with a performance in London of his Second Piano Concerto at a Philharmonic Society concert in Queen's Hall. When he returned to New York in the autumn of 1903 after a vacation in Switzerland (where he spent some time with his old friend Strong), he found that Columbia's new president, Nicholas Murray Butler (who had succeeded MacDowell's mentor Seth Low shortly before MacDowell had gone on sabbatical), had realigned courses in the department of music with those in Columbia's Teachers College. The personalities of Butler and MacDowell had clashed before, and their antagonism escalated as the term progressed. Early in 1904, MacDowell told Butler of his intention to resign at the end of the academic year; in the interim their disagreements over the newly established division of fine arts, among other things, were aired in the local press (see Howard, 1931, Moore, 1957, and M. M. Lowens, 1971), and the public conflict became a source of much embarrassment to both the university administration and MacDowell.

After leaving Columbia in mid-1904, MacDowell continued to live in New York, teaching piano privately and working on behalf of the National Academy of Arts and Letters (elected 1898), the American Academy of Arts and Letters (of which he was one of the seven founders in 1904), and the American Academy in Rome. During the winter of 1903–4 (possibly in March) he had been injured in a street accident in which he was run over by a hansom cab. By December 1904 he was showing definite signs of mental illness, and by the following autumn he regressed to a childlike state, with intermittent rational periods. His remaining winters were spent in New York, and summers at the MacDowells' home in Peterborough, New Hampshire. During one lucid period MacDowell conceived the idea of transforming the Peterborough property into an artists' colony, and his wife arranged for two persons to work there during the summer of 1907. The Mendelssohn Glee Club and the newly formed MacDowell Association of New York helped to raise money to provide for MacDowell's welfare during his last three years. After his death from paresis (general paralytica) and a funeral ceremony in St. George's Episcopal Church in New York, at which the Mendelssohn Glee Club sang and the American SO conducted by Sam Franko performed, MacDowell's body was transported to Peterborough for interment.

2. WORKS. MacDowell was a Romantic by temperament, and his musical imagination was largely roused by nature, literature (especially poetry), and other extramusical stimuli. He often used literary quotations as suggestive mottoes in purely instrumental works, and some of his early orchestral works (*Lancelot und Elaine*, for instance) were far more programmatically conceived than the composer chose to admit in later years. In his songs the words took primacy over the music, so that eventually his difficulty in finding acceptable texts led him to write his own.

2. *Autograph MS of the opening of "From Uncle Remus," the seventh of the "Woodland Sketches" op.51, 1896 (DLC)*

MacDowell was no innovator, and his creativity was limited by the traditions and conventions of his essentially Teutonic training. Not surprisingly his music is largely derivative: one can easily trace in it influences of Raff (the two modern suites), Liszt (the two piano concertos, *Hamlet*, and *Lamia*), and Wagner (certain numbers within opp. 17, 19, 28, 32, and 38). His mature work (especially opp. 51, 61, and 62) is most akin to that of Grieg, with whom he shared a Scottish ancestry and an intense interest in Celtic and Nordic legends. Like Grieg, MacDowell was essentially a miniaturist; his most successful (and most numerous) works are the smaller lyric and characteristic pieces for piano, such as "To a Wild Rose" and "From Uncle Remus" (fig. 2) from the *Woodland Sketches*, but he also composed such virtuoso pieces as the *Etude de concert*, and "Elfentanz" and "Märzwind" from *Zwölf Virtuosen-Etüden*.

Much of MacDowell's music is characterized by dense textures, chromatic harmony, enharmonic modulation, and dramatic dynamic contrasts (especially in the four piano sonatas, and "In Mid-ocean" from *Sea Pieces*). He employed all the expanded harmonic and tonal resources of his day, notably in his free handling of nonharmonic passing tones and appoggiaturas, which he at times employed as unifying devices. Other compositions, such as the "Song" from *Sea Pieces*, are much lighter in texture, more diatonic than chromatic in both melody and harmony, and hold much more melodic interest.

The melodies, which usually lie in the upper voice and are occasionally doubled at the octave in the lowest voice, show a preference for stepwise motion (except when approaching a final tone). In his larger works he usually employed sonata form but with variants in the recapitulation, such as reversal of themes or omission of one theme; in general he preferred ternary forms. Of his rhythmic style, perhaps the most striking feature is his frequent use of the "Scotch snap."

It is ironic that in his day MacDowell should have been widely regarded as "the great American composer," since it is hard to find anything distinctively American about his music. Indeed he never aspired to write nationalist music; his ambition was to be a fine composer, and he simply happened to be American. He developed an explicit aversion to concerts consisting only of American works and finally refused to allow his music to be performed at these increasingly popular events, insisting that music ought to be presented on its own merits and not on account of its composer's nationality.

It was not because his compatriots were less well trained or less gifted than he that MacDowell attained his position as the foremost American composer of his time, but rather due to Liszt's quick recognition of his talents, to Teresa Carreño's championing of his piano music, and to the success of his own recitals. After his return to the USA in 1888, his rapidly growing reputation as a teacher and performer left him little time for composition, and he eventually concentrated on piano pieces and songs (for which there was then a great commercial demand) instead of orchestral music, which had been of particular interest to him earlier in his career.

MacDowell's leading position in American music remained unchallenged for many years, but in the late 1930s his reputation began to decline; only occasional performances of the Second Piano Concerto, the *Indian Suite*, and a few of the smaller genre pieces for piano managed to retain a tenuous hold in the American repertory. From the late 1970s, however, attributable at least in part to many recordings and renewed critical interest, more of his music has been performed, most notably the First Piano Concerto and the four piano sonatas, the four works which MacDowell believed to be the compositions that might bring him any lasting fame.

MacDowell was an inveterate revisionist: he constantly reworked compositions even after they had been published (as in the case of the various revisions and publications of the *Erste moderne Suite*). Study of his manuscripts is complicated as they are widely scattered throughout the world, due chiefly to his widow's dispersal of separate holograph pages to friends and admirers.

See also MACDOWELL COLONY; ORCHESTRAL MUSIC, §2; PIANO MUSIC, §2.

WORKS

Editions: *In Passing Moods: Album of Selected Pianoforte Compositions by Edward MacDowell* (Boston and New York, 1906; repr. 1916) [1906]

Stimmungsbilder: Ausgewählte Klavier-Stücke von Edward MacDowell (Boston and New York, 1908) [1908]

Six Selected Songs by Edward MacDowell: High Voice (Boston and New York, 1912) [1912^{1}]

Six Selected Songs by Edward MacDowell: Low Voice (Boston and New York, 1912) [1912^{2}]

MacDowell: Ausgewählte Klavierstücke, ed. W. Weismann (Leipzig, 1960) [W]

Music by MacDowell for Piano Solo, ed. G. Anson (New York, 1962) [A]

Edward MacDowell: Songs (Opp. 40, 47, 56, 58, 60), with introduction by H. W. Hitchcock, Earlier American Music, vii (New York, 1972) [Hi]

Edward MacDowell: Piano Pieces (Opp. 51, 55, 61, 62), with introduction by H. W. Hitchcock, Earlier American Music, viii (New York, 1972) [Hii]

Opp. 1–7 published under pseudonym Edgar Thorn(e). Earliest published editions preferred in this list; for further details see Sonneck (1917). Major collections of MSS, published music, letters, and memorabilia are in *DLC*, *NNC*, *NN-L*, the MacDowell Colony, and private collection of M. M. Lowens; see also Lowens (1971).

op.

ORCHESTRAL

15 Piano Concerto no. 1, a, 1882, 2 pf (Leipzig, Brussels, and New York, 1884), orch score (Leipzig and New York, 1911); movts 2 and 3, New York, 30 March 1885, complete, Boston, 3 April 1888

22 Hamlet, Ophelia, sym. poems, 1884–5 (Breslau and New York, 1885), pf 4 hands (Breslau and New York, 1885); Ophelia, New York, 4 Nov 1886, complete, Wiesbaden, Germany, 26 Dec 1886

23 Piano Concerto no. 2, d, 1884–6, 2 pf (Leipzig and Brussels, 1890), orch score (Leipzig and New York, 1907); New York, 5 March 1889

25 Lancelot und Elaine, sym. poem after Tennyson, 1886 (Breslau and New York, 1888), pf 4 hands (Breslau and New York, 1888); Boston, 10 Jan 1890

29 Lamia, sym. poem after Keats, 1887 (Boston, Leipzig, and New York, 1908), pf 4 hands (Boston, Leipzig, and New York, 1908); ?Boston, 23 Oct 1908

30 Die Sarazenen, Die schöne Aldâ, 2 frags. after The Song of Roland, 1886–90 (Leipzig and New York, 1891), pf 4 hands (Leipzig and New York, 1891); Boston, 5 Nov 1891

35 Romanze, vc, orch, 1887 (Breslau and New York, 1888), vc, pf (Breslau and New York, 1888); Darmstadt 1887–8

42 Suite, a, 1888–91 (Boston and Leipzig, 1891), pf 4 hands (Boston and Leipzig, 1883), no. 3 added 1893 (Boston, 1893): 1 In einem verwünschten Walde (In a Haunted Forest), 2 Sommer-Idylle (Summer Idyll), 3 Im Oktober (In October), 4 Gesang der Hirtin (The Shepherdess's Song), arr. pf (1906; 1908), 5 Waldgeister (Forest Spirits); Worcester, MA, 24 Sept 1891, complete, Boston, 25 Oct 1895

48 Suite no. 2 "Indian," e, 1891–5 (Leipzig and New York, 1897): 1 Legend, 2 Love Song, 3 In War-time, 4 Dirge, 5 Village Festival; New York, 23 Jan 1896

PIANO

(for 2 hands unless otherwise stated)

Improvisations: Rêverie, 1876, MS op. 1, *DLC*

8 chansons fugitives, 1876, MS op. 2, *DLC*

Petits morceaux, 1876, MS op. 3, *DLC*

3 petits morceaux, 1876, MS op. 4, *DLC*, *NN-L* [as op. 5]: 1 Prélude, 2 Mélodie, 3 La chasse

Suite de 5 morceaux, 1876: 1 Barcarolle, MS op.5, *DLC*; 2 La petite glaneuse, 3 Dans la nuit, 4 Le réveille matin, 5 Cauchemar, lost

10 Erste moderne Suite, e, 1880–81 (Leipzig, 1883), rev. 1904–5 (Leipzig and New York, 1906): 1 Praeludium, rev. 1904 (Leipzig and New York, 1904), 2 Presto, 3 Andantino und Allegretto, 4 Intermezzo, 5 Rhapsodie, 6 Fuge; Zurich, 11 July 1882

13 Prélude et fugue, d, 1881 (Leipzig, 1883); ?Chicago, 2 May 1885

14 Zweite moderne Suite, a, 1882 (Leipzig, 1883): 1 Praeludium, 2 Fugato, 3 Rhapsodie, 4 Scherzino, 5 Marsch, 6 Phantasie-Tanz; ?Chicago, 8 March 1884

16 Serenade, 1882 (Leipzig, 1883)

17 Zwei Fantasiestücke, 1883 (Breslau and New York, 1884): 1 Erzählung, 2 Hexentanz; ?Chicago, 2 May 1885

18 Zwei Stücke, 1884 (Breslau and New York, 1884): 1 Barcarolle, 2 Humoreske

19 Wald Idyllen, 1884 (Leipzig, 1884): 1 Waldesstille, 2 Spiel der Nymphen, 3 Träumerei, 4 Driaden-Tanz

20 Drei Poesien, 4 hands, 1885 (Breslau and New York, 1886): 1 Nachts am Meere, 2 Erzählung aus der Ritterzeit, 3 Ballade

21 Mondbilder nach H. C. Andersen's Bilderbuch ohne Bilder, 4 hands, 1885 (Breslau and New York, 1886): 1 Das Hindumädchen, 2 Storchgeschichte, 3 In Tyrol, 4 Der Schwan, 5 Bärenbesuch

24 Vier Stücke, 1886 (Breslau and New York, 1887): 1 Humoreske, 2 Marsch, 3 Wiegenlied, 4 Czardas; no.1 ed. in A

28 Idyllen: Sechs kleine Stücke, 1887 (Breslau and New York, 1887), rev. as Six Idyls after Goethe, 1901 (Boston and New York, 1901): 1 Ich ging im Walde (In the Woods), 2 Unter des grünen blühender Kraft (Siesta), 3 Füllest wieder Busch und Thal (To the Moonlight), 4 Leichte silberwolken Schweben (Silver Clouds), 5 Bei dem Glanz der Abendröthe (Flute Idyl), 6 Ein Blumenglöckchen (The Bluebell); nos.1 and 3 ed. in A

31 Sechs Gedichte nach Heinrich Heine, 1887 (Breslau and New York, 1887), rev. as Six Poems after Heine, 1901 (Boston and New York, 1901): 1 Wir sassen am Fischerhause (From a Fisherman's Hut), 2 Fern an schottischer Felsenküste (Scotch Poem), 3 Mein Kind, wir waren Kinder (From Long Ago), 4 Wir führen allein im dunkeln (The Postwaggon), 5 König ist der Hirtenknabe (The Shepherd Boy), 6 Der Tod, das ist die kühle Nacht (Monologue); no.2 (1906), ed. in A

32 Vier kleine Poesien, 1887 (Leipzig and New York, 1888): 1 Der Adler (The Eagle) [after Tennyson], 2 Das Bächlein (The Brook) [after Bulwer-Lytton], 3 Mondschein (Moonshine) [after D. G. Rossetti], 4 Winter [after Shelley]; nos.1 and 3 ed. in A

36 Etude de concert, 1887 (Boston, 1889); ?Chicago, 15 Feb 1888

37 Les orientales: 3 morceaux [after Hugo], 1887–8 (Boston and Leipzig, 1889): 1 Clair de lune, 2 Dans le hamac, 3 Danse andalouse; no.3 (1908), ed. in W

38 Marionetten, 1888 (Breslau and New York, 1888); rev. as Marionettes, 1901 (Boston and New York, 1901) [nos.1 and 8 added 1901]: 1 Prologue, 2 Soubrette, 3 Liebhaber (Lover), 4 Bube (Villain), 5 Liebhaberin (Lady-love), 6 Clown, 7 Hexe (Witch), 8 Epilogue; nos.1 and 8 (1908), nos.2, 4, and 6 ed. in A

39 12 Etüden, 1889–90 (Boston and Leipzig, 1890): 1 Jagdlied (Hunting Song), 2 Alla tarantella, 3 Romanze (Romance), 4 Arabeske (Arabesque), 5 Waldfahrt (In the Forest), 6 Gnomentanz (Dance of the Gnomes), 7 Idylle (Idyl), 8 Schattentanz (Shadow Dance), 9 Intermezzo, 10 Melodie (Melody), 11 Scherzino, 12 Ungarisch (Hungarian); nos.2 and 10 (1906; 1908), nos.2 and 12 ed. in A

45 Sonata tragica, g, 1891–2 (Leipzig and New York, 1893); movt 3, Boston, 18 March 1892, complete, Boston, 27 March 1893

46 Zwölf Virtuosen-Etüden, 1893–4 (Leipzig and New York, 1894): 1 Novelette, 2 Moto perpetuo, 3 Wilde Jagd, 4 Improvisation, 5 Elfentanz, 6 Valse triste, 7 Burleske, 8 Bluette, 9 Träumerei, 10 Märzwind, 11 Impromptu, 12 Polonaise; nos.1, 4, and 10 ed. in A

49 Air et rigaudon, ?1894 (Boston, 1894); Rigaudon ed. in A

50 Sonata eroica, g, 1894–5 (Leipzig and New York, 1895); New York, 28 Feb 1895

51 Woodland Sketches, 1896 (New York, 1896): 1 To a Wild Rose, 2 Will o' the Wisp, 3 At an Old Trysting-Place, 4 In Autumn, 5 From an Indian Lodge, 6 To a Water-lily, 7 From Uncle Remus [after J. C. Harris], 8 A Deserted Farm, 9 By a Meadow Brook, 10 Told at Sunset; nos.5 and 8 (1906), no.8 (1908), no.1 transcr. 1v, pf (1912[1], 1912[2]), nos.1, 4, and 7–9 ed. in W, nos.1, 5–7 ed. in A, nos.1–10 in Hii

1 Amourette, 1896 (New York, 1896); (1906)

2 In Lilting Rhythm, 1896 (New York, 1897)

55 Sea Pieces, 1896–8 (New York, 1898): 1 To the Sea, 2 From a Wandering Iceberg, 3 A.D. MDCXX, 4 Starlight, 5 Song, 6 From the Depths, 7 Nautilus, 8 In Mid-Ocean; no.5, as Sea Song (1906), no.5 (1908), nos.3 and 5 ed. in W, nos.2, 4, and 5 ed. in A, nos.1–8 in Hii

4 Forgotten Fairy Tales, 1897 (New York, 1897): 1 Sung Outside the Prince's Door, 2 Of a Tailor and a Bear, 3 Beauty in the Rose-garden, 4 From Dwarfland; no.1 ed. in A

7 Six Fancies, 1898 (New York, 1898): 1 A Tin Soldier's Love, 2 To a Humming Bird, 3 Summer Song, 4 Across Fields, 5 Bluette, 6 An Elfin Round; no.2 (1906), no.1 ed. in A

57 Sonata no.3 ["Norse"], d, 1898–9 (Boston, Leipzig, and New York, 1900)

59 Sonata no.4 "Keltic," e, 1900 (Boston, Leipzig, and New York, 1901); ?Wilkes Barre, PA, 11 Feb 1901

61 Fireside Tales, 1901–2 (Boston, Leipzig, and New York, 1902): 1 An Old Love Story, 2 Of Br'er Rabbit [after J. C. Harris], 3 From a German Forest, 4 Of Salamanders, 5 A Haunted House, 6 By Smouldering Embers; no.6 (1906), no.1 (1908), nos.1, 4, and 6 ed. in W, no.2 ed. in A, nos.1–6 in Hii

62 New England Idyls, 1901–2 (Boston, Leipzig, and New York, 1902): 1 An Old Garden, 2 Mid-summer, 3 Mid-winter, 4 With Sweet Lavender, 5 In Deep Woods, 6 Indian Idyl, 7 To an Old White Pine, 8 From Puritan Days, 9 From a Log Cabin, 10 The Joy of Autumn; no.9 (1908), nos.1, 4, 6, 8, and 9 ed. in W, nos.7 and 9 ed. in A, nos.1–10 in Hii

SONGS

(all for 1v, pf)

– Der Fichtenbaum (H. Heine), *NNC*

– Lieber Schatz (W. Osterwald), *NNC*

– O mistress mine (Shakespeare), ?1884, *DLC*

11 Drei Lieder, 1881 (Leipzig, 1883): 1 Mein Liebchen (unknown), 2 Du liebst mich nicht (Heine), 3 Oben wo die Sterne (Heine)

12 Zwei Lieder, 1880–81 (Leipzig, 1883): 1 Nachtlied (E. Geibel), 2 Das Rosenband (Klopstock); Nachtlied orchd 1880, *DLC*

26 From an Old Garden (M. Deland), 1886–7 (New York, 1887): 1 The Pansy, 2 The Myrtle, 3 The Clover, 4 The Yellow Daisy, 5 The Bluebell, 6 The Mignonette

33 Drei Lieder, 1887–8 (Breslau and New York, 1889): 1 Bitte (A Request) (J. C. Glücklich, trans. MacDowell), 2 Geistliches Wiegenlied (Cradle Hymn) (Lat. anon.), 3 Idylle (Idyll) (Goethe, trans. MacDowell); nos.2 and 3 rev. ?1894, no.2 with Eng. text by S. T. Coleridge (New York, 1894)

34/2 If I had but two little wings, ?1887, MS lost [photocopies, MacDowell Colony and private collection of Lowens]

34 Two Songs (R. Burns), 1887 (Boston, 1889): 1 Menie, 2 My Jean; no.1 (1912[1]), no.2 (1912[2])

40 Six Love Songs (W. H. Gardner), 1890 (Boston, Leipzig, and New York, 1890): 1 Sweet blue-eyed maid, 2 Sweetheart, tell me, 3 Thy beaming eyes, 4 For sweet love's sake, 5 O lovely rose, 6 I ask but this; no.3 (1912[1], 1912[2]), nos.1–6 in Hi

47 Eight Songs, 1893 (Leipzig and New York, 1893): 1 The robin sings in the apple-tree (MacDowell), 2 Midsummer Lullaby (after Goethe), 3 Folksong (W. D. Howells), 4 Confidence (MacDowell), 5 The west-wind croons in the cedar-trees (MacDowell), 6 In the Woods (after Goethe), 7 The Sea (Howells), 8 Through the Meadow (Howells); nos.1–8 in Hi

9 Two Old Songs, 1894 (New York, 1894): 1 Deserted (R. Burns), 2 Slumber Song (MacDowell); no.1 (1912[1], 1912[2])

56 Four Songs (MacDowell), 1898 (New York, 1898): 1 Long ago, 2 The swan bent low to the lily, 3 A maid sings light, 4 As the gloaming shadows creep; no.2 (1912[2]), no.3 (1912[1]), nos.1–4 in Hi

58 Three Songs (MacDowell), 1899 (Boston, Leipzig, and New York, 1899): 1 Constancy (New England A. D. 1899), 2 Sunrise, 3 Merry Maiden Spring; nos.1–3 in Hi

60 Three Songs (MacDowell), 1901 (Boston, Leipzig, and New York, 1902): 1 Tyrant Love, 2 Fair Springtide, 3 To the Golden Rod; no.2 (1912[1]), no.3 (1912[2]), nos.1–3 in Hi

CHORUSES

(with pf acc. unless otherwise stated)

27 Drei Lieder für vierstimmigen Männerchor, unacc., 1887 (Boston and Leipzig, 1890): 1 Oben wo die Sterne glühen (In the starry sky above us) (Heine, trans. MacDowell), 2 Schweizerlied (Springtime) (Goethe, trans. MacDowell), 3 Der Fischerknabe (The Fisherboy) (Schiller, trans. MacDowell)

41 [2 partsongs], 4-part male chorus, 1890 (Boston, Leipzig, and New York, 1890): 1 Cradle Song (MacDowell, after P. Cornelius), 2 Dance of Gnomes (MacDowell)
43 Two Northern Songs (MacDowell), 4-part mixed chorus, 1890–91 (Boston, Leipzig, and New York, 1891): 1 The Brook, 2 Slumber Song
44 Barcarole (F. von Bodenstedt, trans. MacDowell), 8-part mixed chorus, pf 4 hands, 1890 (Boston and Leipzig, 1892)
3 [2 partsongs], 4-part male chorus (New York, 1897): 1 Love and Time (M. Farley), 1896, 2 The Rose and the Gardener (A. Dobson), 1897
52 [3 partsongs], 4-part male chorus, 1896–7 (New York, 1897): 1 Hush, hush! (T. Moore), 2 From the Sea (MacDowell), 3 The Crusaders (MacDowell)
53 [2 partsongs] (R. Burns), 4-part male chorus, 1897 (New York, 1897): 1 Bonnie Ann, 2 The Collier Lassie
54 [2 partsongs] (MacDowell), 4-part male chorus (New York, 1898): 1 A Ballad of Charles the Bold, 1897, 2 Midsummer Clouds, 1887
5 The Witch (MacDowell), 4-part male chorus, 1897 (New York, 1898)
– Two Songs from the Thirteenth Century (trans. MacDowell), 4-part male chorus, 1897 (New York, 1897): 1 Winter wraps his grimmest spell (after N. von Reuenthal), 2 As the gloaming shadows creep (after Frauenlob)
6 War Song (MacDowell), 4-part male chorus, 1898 (New York, 1898)
– College Songs for Male Voices, 1900–1 (Boston and New York, 1901): 1 Columbia's Sons (E. Keppler), unison male vv; 2 We love thee well, Manhattanland (MacDowell), 3 Columbia! O alma mater (MacDowell), 4 Sturdy and Strong (MacDowell), 5 O wise old alma mater (MacDowell), 6 At Parting (MacDowell), unacc. 4-part male chorus
– Two College Songs (MacDowell), 4-part female chorus, ?1901–2 (Boston and New York, 1907): 1 Alma mater, 2 At Parting [rev. of College Songs for Male Voices, nos.3 and 6]
– Summer Wind (R. Hovey), 4-part female chorus, ?1902 (Boston and New York, 1902)

OTHER WORKS

– Suite, vn, pf, ?1877, *DLC*
– Cadenza for Mozart: Conc., d, 1st movt, K466, pf, ?1882, *DLC*
– Technical Exercises, Pt 1, pf, 1893–4 (Leipzig and New York, 1894)
– Technical Exercises, Pt 2, pf, 1893–5 (Leipzig and New York, 1895)

EDITIONS, ARRANGEMENTS

Orch: J. Raff: Romeo und Juliet Ov., Macbeth Ov., 1890–91 (Boston, 1891) [also arr. 2 pf]

Pf: kbd pieces by J. S. Bach [6], 1890 (Boston and Leipzig, 1890); H. Huber, Handel-Lavignac, M. van Westerhout, 1894 (New York, 1894); Glinka-Balakirev, F. Liszt, M. Moszkowski [2], G. Pierné [2], H. Reinhold, N. V. Stcherbatcheff, J. Ten-Brink, Van Westerhout, N. A. Rimsky-Korsakov, G. Martucci, P. Geisler, T. Dubois, C. Cui, 1894–5 (New York, 1895); Liszt, Geisler [2], Alkan-MacDowell, P. Lacombe, F. Couperin, Pierné, 1896 (New York, 1896); G. B. Grazioli, 1899 (Boston, Leipzig, and New York, 1900); J. B. Loeillet, J.-P. Rameau [2], J. Mattheson, Couperin, C. F. Graun, 1899–1900 (Boston, Leipzig, and New York, 1900); Couperin, 1900 (Boston, Leipzig, and New York, 1900); Loeillet, 1902 (Boston, Leipzig, and New York, 1902)

4-part male chorus: partsongs by S. Moniuszko, A. P. Borodin, N. A. Sokolov, M. Filke, G. Ingraham, C. Beines, Rimsky-Korsakov, F. von Holstein, 1897 (New York, 1897); Sokolov, J. V. von Wöss, M. Arnold, 1897–8 (New York, 1898)

Principal publishers: Breitkopf & Härtel, Hainauer, Jung, Kahnt, Schmidt

WRITINGS

Verses ([1903]; rev. Boston, 1908)

W. J. Baltzell, ed.: *Critical and Historical Essays: Lectures Delivered at Columbia University* (Boston, 1912/*R*1969 with introduction by I. Lowens)

BIBLIOGRAPHY

EwenD

R. Hughes: "Music in America: Edward Alexander MacDowell," *Godey's Magazine*, cxxxi (1895), 80; rev. and enlarged in R. Hughes: "The Innovators," *Contemporary American Composers* (Boston, 1900), 34

H. T. Finck: "An American Composer: Edward A. MacDowell," *Century Magazine*, liii (1897), 449

"Edward MacDowell: a Biographical Sketch," *MT*, xliv (1904), 221

H. T. Finck: "Creative Americans: Edward MacDowell, Musician and Composer," *Outlook*, lxxxiv (1906), 983

L. Gilman: *Edward MacDowell* (London, 1906; rev. and enlarged 2/1909/*R*1969 as *Edward MacDowell: a Study*, with introduction by M. L. Morgan)

H. F. Gilbert: "Personal Recollections of Edward MacDowell," *New Music Review*, xi (1912), 494

O. G. Sonneck: "MacDowell *versus* MacDowell," *MTNAP*, vi (1912), 96; repr. in *Suum Cuique* (New York, 1916), 87

T. P. Currier: "Edward MacDowell as I Knew Him," *MQ*, i (1915), 17–51; some portions repr. in Currier: "Some MacDowell Anecdotes," *Music Student*, vii (1915), 259

G. T. Strong: "MacDowell as I Knew Him," *Music Student*, vii (1915), 233; viii (1915–16), 5, 29, 51, 81, 127, 151, 189, 223, 274, 276, 298, 300, cccxxiii, cccxxiv

O. G. Sonneck: *Catalogue of First Editions of Edward MacDowell (1861–1908)* (Washington, DC, 1917/*R*1971)

W. H. Humiston: *MacDowell* (New York, 1921)

J. Huneker: "An American Composer: the Passing of Edward MacDowell," *Unicorns* (New York, 1921), 6

J. F. Porte: *Edward MacDowell: a Great American Tone Poet, his Life and Music* (New York, 1922/*R*1978)

L. B. McWhood: "Edward MacDowell at Columbia University," *MTNAP*, xviii (1924), 71

U. Sinclair: "Memories of Edward MacDowell," *Sackbut*, vi (1925), 127; repr. as "MacDowell," *American Mercury*, vii (1926), 50

H. Garland: *Companions on the Trail: a Literary Chronicle* (New York, 1931)

J. T. Howard: "Edward MacDowell," *Our American Music* (New York, 1931, rev. 3/1946/*R*1954 with suppl. by J. Lyons, rev. 4/1965)

J. Erskine: "MacDowell, Edward Alexander," *DAB*

[R. S. Angell, compiler]: *Catalogue of an Exhibition Illustrating the Life and Work of Edward MacDowell, 1861–1908* (New York, 1938)

B. Lien: *An Analytical Study of Selected Piano Works by Edward MacDowell* (thesis, Eastman School, 1940)

M. Milinowski: *Teresa Carreño "by the Grace of God"* (New Haven, CT, 1940/*R*1977)

J. Erskine: "MacDowell at Columbia: Some Recollections," *MQ*, xxviii (1942), 395

——: "Edward MacDowell," *My Life in Music* (New York, 1950), 10

M. MacDowell: *Random Notes on Edward MacDowell and his Music* (Boston, 1950)

N. L. Eagle: *The Pianoforte Sonatas of Edward A. MacDowell: a Style-critical Study* (thesis, U. of North Carolina, 1952)

D. Moore: "The Department of Music," *A History of the Faculty of Philosophy: Columbia University*, ed. J. Barzun (New York, 1957), 270

I. Lowens: "Edward MacDowell," *HiFi/Stereo Review*, xix/6 (1967), 61

M. M. Lowens: *The New York Years of Edward MacDowell* (diss., U. of Michigan, 1971)

D. R. Mumper: *The Four Piano Sonatas of Edward MacDowell* (diss., Indiana U., 1971)

A. T. Schwab: "Edward MacDowell's Birthdate: a Correction," *MQ*, lxi (1975), 233

V. Malham: *Eighteen Part Songs for Male Chorus of Edward MacDowell: a Study and Performing Edition* (diss., U. of Laval, Quebec, 1977)

S. Summerville: "The Songs of Edward MacDowell," *NATS Bulletin*, xxxv/4 (1979), 36

F. P. Brancaleone: *The Short Piano Works of Edward MacDowell* (diss., CUNY, 1982)

I. Lowens: "Edward MacDowell: Inveterate Tinkerer, Near Master," *HiFi*, xxxii/11 (1982), 74

C. B. Kefferstan: *The Piano Concertos of Edward MacDowell* (diss., U. of Cincinnati, 1984)

MARGERY MORGAN LOWENS

McDowell, John Herbert (*b* Washington, DC, 21 Dec 1926; *d* Scarsdale, NY, 3 Sept 1985). Composer and choreographer. He studied English literature at Colgate University (BA 1948), and music at Columbia University (MA 1957), where his teachers included Luening and Beeson, and with Goeb, among others, at the Bennington Conference. McDowell has taught at a number of universities and festivals, including the New School for Social Research, Hunter College, CUNY, the Pratt Institute, and the American Dance Festival. He also served as music director of the Gulbenkian Dance School (now the International Course for Professional Choreographers and Composers) held at the University of Surrey, England (1976–82); of dance companies directed by Paul Taylor, James Waring, Cliff Keuter, Dorothy Vislocky,

Gus Solomons, Elaine Summer, and others; and of various festivals. In the 1960s he was associated with the Judson Dance Theater, a group of avant-garde choreographers in New York, and he has served on the board of directors of the Theater for the New City. He was editor of the ACA *Bulletin* in 1957–8.

McDowell was a prolific composer with some 400 works to his credit. His principal interests from the late 1950s were music for dance and theater, and experimental music; he wrote dance scores for many American and European dance companies, among them the Netherlands Dance Theater, London Contemporary Dance Theater, and the Manhattan Festival Ballet Company. His theater works often involve large groups of performers in unusual contexts; *Tumescent lingam* (1971), for example, requires 101 people, an infant, and a dog, and also employs a variety of visual effects. In a number of works he calls for both untrained and professional musicians, and often for audience participation. McDowell's music includes a wide range of styles and idioms, from contrapuntal textures reminiscent of Bach to the collage techniques first explored by Ives. He began composing tape music in 1952 and was among the first American composers to work in the medium. His work is characterized by the juxtaposition of sharply differing styles, in which texture becomes a principal structural determinant.

WORKS

Operas: Oklahoma Danger Remark (1, A. Williams, J. Waring), 1965; A Dog's Love (M. Smith), 1971

Theater pieces: False Leg Mescolanza, 1969; Tumescent lingam, ob, chorus, tape, 101 pfmrs, dog, infant, visual effects, 1971; With Waterfalls and Dancing on the Table, 1972; *c*60 other theater works for diverse inst ens, many incl. tape

Dance scores: over 140, incl. Tentative Changes, va, 1953; Arena, chamber orch, 1958; Poet's Vaudeville, S, chamber orch, 1963; Fantastic Gardens, collab. others, 1964; Candide, chamber orch, 1968; Dark Psalters, org, str, perc, 1968; Screenplay, orch, 1968; Still Life, chamber orch, 1971; 3rd of July, 1972; A Christmas Story, orch, 1974; numerous dance pieces for tape

Orch: Four 6s and a 9, vn, bn, tpt, vc, orch, 1960; The Parlor Trick with Ferns, concertinos for vn, bn, vc, orch, 1960; Dance concertante no.3, 1961; Insects and Heros, 1961; From Sea to Shining Sea, 1965; Phantom of the Opera, 1967; Practical Magic, 1977; Rondo, 1980

Chamber: Suite, hpd 4 hands, 1954; Modulamen, hpd, str qt, 1960; Homage to Billy Sunday, db, wind qnt, 1961; Comes the Revolution, vc, pf, tape, 1969; A Few Minutes . . . in Memory of Joan Kilpatrick, fl, vn, pf, 1979

Vocal: Vocalise, 7 S, 1954; The Harbinger of Health, S, pf, 1955; Disenchanted Songs, Bar, pf, 1955; Good News from Heaven, Christmas cantata, solo vv, chamber orch, 1956; Missa brevis no.2, T, chamber orch, 1957; Canticle of Expectation, men's chorus, org, perc, 1962; Lyra Davidica, Easter anthem, S, chorus, congregation, org, harp, gong, orch, 1966; God has Gone up with a Shout, vv, brass, harp, org, 1974; other choral works, songs

Other orch and chamber works, numerous tape pieces, processional pieces

LANCE W. BRUNNER

MacDowell Colony. A working retreat for composers, writers, and artists in Peterborough, New Hampshire. The colony consists of three residence halls, a library, a dining and recreation center, and 29 separate studios scattered over more than 400 acres of woodlands and meadows. Founded in 1907 and built around the summer home of Edward MacDowell, it was managed until 1946 by his widow and former pupil, the pianist Marian Nevins MacDowell (1857–1956), who helped support the colony by performing her husband's music throughout the USA. Pageants were given there (1910, 1919), as were music festivals (from 1911). Composer-colonists have included Amy Marcy Beach, Leonard Bernstein, Charles Wakefield Cadman, Copland, Dello Joio, Del Tredici, Foss, Harris, Hoiby, Gail Kubik, Edgar S. Kelley, Douglas S. Moore, Gardner Read, Rorem, Talma, Virgil Thomson, and Ernst Toch. The MacDowell Medal has been

Music room in the Stillcrest residence at the MacDowell Colony

awarded yearly since 1960 by the colony to a distinguished composer, writer, or artist. The composers so honored have been Copland (1961), Varèse (1965), Sessions (1968), Schuman (1971), Piston (1974), Thomson (1977), Barber (1980), and Carter (1983).

BIBLIOGRAPHY

P. Fillmore: "A Great Composer's House of Dreams," *Delineator*, lxxix (1912), 476

E. A. Robinson: "The Peterborough Idea," *North American Review*, cciv (1916), 448

M. Wisehart: "I've Done the Best I Could, and That's Victory," *American Magazine*, c (1925), 18, 222

M. MacDowell: "MacDowell's 'Peterborough Idea,' " *MQ*, xviii (1932), 33

"*Life* Visits the MacDowell Colony," *Life*, xxv (23 Aug 1948), 107

R. W. Brown: "Mrs. MacDowell and her Colony," *Atlantic Monthly*, clxxxiv/1 (1949), 42

M. MacDowell: *The First Twenty Years of the Colony* (Peterborough, NH, 1951)

H. Kubly: "The Care and Feeding of Artists," *Horizon*, v/4 (1963), 26

C. Carmer: "Marian MacDowell: Woman with a Possible Dream," *Yankee*, xxxvi (1972), 86, 156

L. Hillyer: "And the Dream Goes On," *Yankee*, xxxvi (1972), 88

A. T. Schwab: "MacDowell, Marian Griswold Nevins," *NAW*

The MacDowell Colony: a History of its Development and Architecture (Peterborough, NH, 1981)

ARNOLD T. SCHWAB

Macedonian-American music. The music of Macedonian immigrants to the USA is discussed as part of traditions shared with Bulgarian and Yugoslav peoples in the USA; *see* EUROPEAN-AMERICAN MUSIC, §§III, 4, 12 (iii).

Macero, Teo [Attilio Joseph] (*b* Glens Falls, NY, 30 Oct 1925). Composer. He attended the Juilliard School (1949–53, BS and MS), where he was a pupil of Brant. After teaching for several years he became in 1957 a producer for Columbia Records, remaining until 1975, when he became president of Teo Productions, a recording company. As a producer he has specialized in jazz recordings. He was awarded two Guggenheim fellowships (1953–4, 1958) and an NEA grant (1974) for composition and has received commissions from the New York PO, Buffalo SO, Kansas City SO, and the Juilliard School. Especially prolific as a composer of jazz, he has recorded several hundred of his more than one thousand original jazz works. His other interests include ballet and films for television and screen; he has written numerous dance scores for the Pennsylvania Ballet, Joffrey Ballet, London Ballet, and other companies, as well as over 80 scores for documentary films. He received Emmy awards for his music for *The Body Human* series (1977–) and the *Lifeline* series (1979). Macero's innovations in writing for films and television, particularly his use of microtones and original orchestral devices, have been influential in bridging the gap between standard or avant-garde and more popular styles of film scoring. As a performer he appears both as a saxophonist and as conductor of various ensembles.

WORKS

Stage: several operas, incl. The Heart (B. Ulanov), 1970, The Share (R. Capra), 1978, Twelve Years a Slave (B. Winder) [in progress]; over 80 ballets, incl. Ride the Culture Loop (Anna Sokolow Ballet), 1970, Mr. B. (Joffrey Ballet), 1983, Jamboree (Joffrey), 1984

Large ens: Paths, Fusions, 1956; C, a sax, vn, va, orch, 1957; Polaris, 1960; Torsion in Space, orch, 1961; Time Plus Seven, chamber orch, 1963; Pressure, orch, 1964; One and Three Quarters, chamber orch, 1968; Paths, chamber orch, 1971; Le grand spectacle, ov., large orch, 1975; Timeless Viewpoint, str orch, 1980; Virgo Clusters – M87, chamber orch, 1981; The Jupiter Effect, a sax, chamber orch, 1983, rev. a sax, chamber orch, 1984; many other works

Inst: Wi, pf, 1973; Adieu mon amour, vc, tape, 1974; Pagoda Sunset, vn, pf, 1974; Violent Non Violent, 2 pf, a sax, 1974; Rounds, 2 perc, pf, 1976; Butter & a Big Horn, tuba, tape, 1977; Goodbye Mr. Good Bass, chamber ens, 1979; A Jazz Presence, nar, jazz ens, 1980; Theme for the Uncommon Man, brass, perc, 1981; numerous other works

Film scores: The Body Human (television, 1977–); Lifeline (television, 1979); Omni (television, 1982); several feature films, incl. AKA Cassius Clay, End of the Road, Jack Johnson; over 50 documentaries, incl. The Miracle Months, Frank Lloyd Wright, Eugene O'Neill

Principal publishers: Davimar, BMI

DAVID COPE

McFerrin, Robert (*b* Marianna, AR, 19 March 1921). Baritone. He studied at Fisk University, Nashville, at the Chicago Musical College with George Graham (BM 1948), and at the Kathryn Turney Long School in New York. After appearing in 1949 in Weill's *Lost in the Stars*, in William Grant Still's *Troubled Island* at the New York City Opera, and as Amonasro in *Aida* with Mary Cardwell Dawson's National Negro Opera Company, he joined the New England Opera Company in 1950; during his time with that company he created roles in Marc Connelly's play *The Green Pastures* (New York, 1951; music by Hall Johnson) and *My Darlin' Aida* (1952), a version of Verdi's opera with a new libretto set in the Confederacy. He won the Metropolitan Opera Auditions of the Air in 1953 and later joined the Metropolitan company (he was the first male Black to do so), making his début on 27 January 1955 as Amonasro; his other roles were Valentin in *Faust* and Rigoletto. After a period in Naples at the Teatro S. Carlo, he was chosen to sing the role of Porgy (who was played by Sidney Poitier) in the soundtrack of the film of Gershwin's *Porgy and Bess* (1959); he also sang on a later recording. He toured internationally as a recitalist, presenting arias from opera and oratorio, art songs, and spirituals. He was also active as a teacher, at the Sibelius Academy in Helsinki (1959), the Nelson School of Fine Arts, British Columbia (1961), and Roosevelt University (1976).

BIBLIOGRAPHY

SouthernB

P. Turner: *Afro-American Singers* (Minneapolis, 1977)

DOMINIQUE-RENÉ DE LERMA

McGee, Sam (1894–1975). Country-music guitarist and banjoist. With his brother Kirk, he played in the Dixieliners, a string band led by ARTHUR SMITH, and made recordings with UNCLE DAVE MACON.

McGhee, Brownie [Walter Brown] (*b* 1915). Blues guitarist who performed in partnership with SONNY TERRY.

McGill, Josephine (*b* Louisville, KY, 20 Oct 1877; *d* Louisville, 24 Feb 1919). Composer and folksong collector. She had no formal training as a composer. At the suggestion of May Stone of the Hindman Settlement School in Knott County (Kentucky), she spent the summer of 1914 in Knott and Letcher counties transcribing folksongs and tracing their origins to English and Scottish ballads. By her own description the people of the area called her "the strange woman huntin' song-ballets." She published *Folk-songs of the Kentucky Mountains* (1917, repr. 1922, 1926, 1937), in which 13 of the 20 songs are traced to precursors in Child's *English and Scottish Popular Ballads* (1882–98). At a time when many American composers turned to folk music as the source of a distinctive voice, McGill's activities contributed to the search for an American national music. Among her own compositions are the songs *Duna, when I was a little lad* (1914),

Less than Clouds, and *O Sleep*. She also wrote articles for the *Musical Quarterly* (1917, 1918). (*See also* WILLIAMS, WILLIAM CARLOS.)

BIBLIOGRAPHY

O. A. Rothbert: "Josephine McGill – Pioneer in the Kentucky Ballad Field," *History Quarterly of the Filson Club*, v/3 (Louisville, 1928), 28

BARBARA L. TISCHLER

McGlaughlin, William (*b* Philadelphia, PA, 3 Oct 1943). Conductor and trombonist. After study at Temple University (BM 1967, MM 1969) he was associate principal trombonist with the Pittsburgh SO, then assistant principal trombonist with the Philadelphia Orchestra. In Pittsburgh in 1973 he founded and conducted the Pittsburgh Symphony Players and the Pittsburgh Camerata; in 1975 he was named assistant conductor of the Pittsburgh Chamber Orchestra. His reputation grew with his subsequent affiliation with the St. Paul Chamber Orchestra, under the auspices of the Exxon/Arts Endowment Conductors Program (1975–8). In 1980 he was appointed music director and presenter of the National Public Radio program "St. Paul Sunday Morning." He became music director of the Eugene (Oregon) SO in 1981; while maintaining that position, in 1983 he was named music director of the Tucson SO. McGlaughlin rapidly gained acclaim for his bold programming and his concerns for improving the quality of both orchestras. He has a strong commitment to contemporary music and has given the premières of works by Larsen, Oliveros, Paulus, Elliott Schwartz, Svoboda, and others.

KAREN MONSON

McGranahan, James (*b* nr Adamsville, PA, 4 July 1840; *d* Kinsman, OH, 7 July 1907). Composer of Sunday-school and gospel hymns, and hymnbook compiler. He studied with G. J. Webb, Zerrahn, F. W. Root, and George Macfarren, and in 1875 became a teacher and director of the National Normal Institute founded by G. F. Root, where he taught for three summers. In 1877 he joined the evangelist Daniel Whittle as music director. He compiled numerous song collections for use in their revival meetings, often composing the tunes while Whittle supplied the texts. McGranahan was a pioneer in the use of men's voices for revival services, and he issued a number of collections of works arranged for male chorus. In 1877 he became an editor, with Sankey and Stebbins, of the already successful series *Gospel Hymns and Sacred Songs*, collaborating with them on volumes 3 to 6 (Cincinnati, 1878–91); the series (printed together as *Gospel Hymns nos. 1–6 Complete*, 1894/*R*1973) eventually became the "bible" of gospel hymnody. The most successful of McGranahan's more than 150 tunes, including those for the hymns *Hallelujah for the cross* (1882), *I know whom I have believed* (1883), *Christ receiveth sinful men* (1883), *Showers of blessing* (1883), *I will sing of my Redeemer* (1887), and *The banner of the cross* (1887), were printed in these collections. Often employing compound rhythms and varied harmonies, his tunes reflect a growing sophistication in early gospel hymnody. (*See also* GOSPEL MUSIC, §I, 1, ex. 1.)

BIBLIOGRAPHY

J. H. Hall: *Biography of Gospel Song and Hymn Writers* (New York, 1914/*R*1971)

M. R. Wilhoit: *A Guide to the Principal Authors and Composers of Gospel Song in the Nineteenth Century* (diss., Southern Baptist Theological Seminary, 1982)

MEL R. WILHOIT

McGraw, Hugh (Winford) (*b* Heard County, GA, 20 Feb 1931). Shape-note hymnodist, singer, and administrator. In 1953 he attended his first Sacred Harp singing (*see* SHAPE-NOTE HYMNODY, §2) and soon began to study singing with his second cousin, "Uncle Bud" McGraw. He was elected to the board of directors of the Sacred Harp Publishing Company and later became its executive secretary. His experience as a businessman helped put the company on a sound financial footing, and assure the distribution of songbooks. He taught and promoted Sacred Harp singing, chiefly in Georgia and Alabama, and wrote many hymns that became part of the shape-note repertory, including *Living Hope*. He performed at Expo 67 in Montreal, and at the Festival of American Folklife organized by the Smithsonian Institution in 1970, 1976 and 1982, when he was also awarded a National Heritage Fellowship by the NEA.

BIBLIOGRAPHY

E. B. Cobb, Jr.: *The Sacred Harp: a Tradition and its Music* (Athens, GA, 1978)

DANIEL SHEEHY

McGuire, John (Howard) (*b* Artesia, nr Los Angeles, CA, 27 June 1942). Composer. His first composition studies were in Los Angeles, with Robert Gross at Occidental College (BA, 1964) and Dahl at the University of Southern California (1963). He continued his studies in Berkeley with Kohn (1964) and then with Shifrin (1964–6) at the University of California (MA 1970). He received three Hertz scholarships in the period 1965–8 which enabled him to study in Germany, with Krzysztof Penderecki at the Folkwang Hochschule, Essen (1966–7), and with Karlheinz Stockhausen at Darmstadt (summers of 1967 and 1968). His String Trio won the Nicolo de Lorenzo prize at Berkeley in 1965 and he won first prize in the International Gaudeamus Composers' Composition for *Decay* in 1971; he has since had works commissioned by Radio Bremen (1978) and West German Radio (1974, 1979, 1981, 1983). In 1970 he settled in Cologne; he is married to the soprano, Beth Griffiths.

McGuire's music (since 1969) is in the "pulse music" tradition of Reich and Glass, but more complex. Instead of using a series of repeating modules, it is completely through-composed; for example, the 22-minute work *Frieze* (1969–74) is some 90 pages long. His works are energetic and virtuosic, with sudden shifts of harmony and tempo. The multiple layers have complex melodic and rhythmic interconnections which, at their best, encourage the listener to approach the music from a number of different aural planes.

WORKS

Str Trio, 1965; Decay, 8 hn, 1967–70; Frieze, 4 pf, 1969–74; Pulse Music I, tape, 1975–6; Pulse Music II, 4 pf, chamber orch, 1975–7; 48 Variations for 2 pf, 1976–80; Pulse Music III, tape, 1978; Music for 2 pf, 4 hn, cymbals, 1981; Cadence Music, orch, 1981–4; other chamber works

Principal publishers: Brietkopf & Härtel, Feedback

BIBLIOGRAPHY

EwenD

G. Gronemeyer: "Ohne Zentrum und Akzente, neue Musik in Köln: der amerikanische Meister John McGuire," *Kölner Stadt-Anzeiger* (14 Jan 1981)

W. Zimmermann: *Desert Plants: Conversations with 23 American Musicians* (Vancouver, 1976)

STEPHEN MONTAGUE

Machito [Grillo, Frank Raul] (*b* Havana, Cuba, 16 Feb 1912; *d* London, England, 15 April 1984). Bandleader, singer, and maraca player. Although he was a professional musician when he arrived in the USA in 1937, his musical maturity and influence date from 1940. In that year, after working in the New York area and recording with several local dance bands, Machito formed the first of his groups known as the Afro-Cubans. The following year he was joined by his brother-in-law, the big-band trumpeter and saxophonist Mario Bauza, who engaged black arrangers to give jazz voicings to the Cuban melodies of Machito's band. As a result the Afro-Cubans became one of the most influential forces in the music later to be called salsa. By the mid-1940s the Afro-Cubans had played in concert with Stan Kenton's big band, and from 1940 recorded or played with most of the leading bop musicians – including Charlie Parker and Dizzy Gillespie – giving rise to a fusion style known as AFRO-CUBAN JAZZ or "cubop." Machito's preeminence continued during the mambo era of the 1950s and 1960s, when his group was one of three big bands playing regularly at the New York dance hall Palladium. In the early 1980s he still appeared regularly in New York, in both salsa and jazz-oriented clubs and concerts.

BIBLIOGRAPHY

J. S. Roberts: *The Latin Tinge* (New York, 1979)
"Machito," *CBY 1983*
Obituary, *New York Times* (17 April 1984)

JOHN STORM ROBERTS

Machlis, Joseph (*b* Riga, Latvia, 11 Aug 1906). Writer on music. Having come to America at an early age, he studied at City College, New York (BA 1927), and the Institute of Musical Art, where he received a teacher's diploma; he also gained a degree in English literature from Columbia University (MA 1938). He joined the music faculty of Queens College, CUNY, in 1938. Machlis is the author of two widely used introductory texts, *The Enjoyment of Music* (1955, rev. 4/1977) and *Introduction to Contemporary Music* (1961). For younger readers he wrote *American Composers of our Time* (1963) and *Getting to know Music* (1966). He has made translations of opera librettos from the standard repertory for the NBC Opera Company and other groups, and has written several novels, under his own name and the pseudonym George Selcamm.

PAULA MORGAN

Machover, Tod (*b* New York, 24 Nov 1953). Composer, cellist, and conductor. He studied composition at the Juilliard School (BM 1975, MM 1977), the University of California, Santa Cruz (1971–3), and Columbia University (1973–4), and computer music at the Massachusetts Institute of Technology and Stanford University. His principal teachers were Dallapiccola (1973), Sessions (1973–5), and Elliott Carter (1975–8). He was principal cellist of the National Opera of Canada, Toronto (1975–6), and a guest composer at IRCAM, Paris (1978–9), where he was director of musical research from 1980 to 1984. In 1985 he was appointed to the faculty of the Massachusetts Institute of Technology. He has received numerous awards, including the Gershwin Prize (1975), the Charles Ives Fellowship from the National Institute of Arts and Letters (1976), NEA grants (1981, 1982, 1983), and awards from the Koussevitzky Foundation (1983) and the French Ministry of Culture (1984). He has had works commissioned by IRCAM (1979), the Gulbenkian Foundation (1980), the Tokyo String Quartet (1981), the Venice Biennale (1982), the French Commande d'Etat (1983), and New World Records (1984).

Machover has composed both acoustic and electronic music. In the latter a primary interest has been the use of computers and their performance capabilities (*Fusione Fugace*, 1981). His electronic tape works using live performers (*Soft Morning, City!*, 1980, *Electric Etudes*, 1983) attempt a partial fusion of the acoustic and electronic sound worlds. He has consistently drawn inspiration from the human voice. His music is lyrical, even when atonal, with a strong tendency towards dramatic, evolving forms.

WORKS

Vocal and inst: Sun, pf, 1975; Fresh Spring (Spenser), Bar, 10 insts, 1977; Ye Gentle Birds (Spenser), S, Mez, 2 fl, ob, hn, bn, cbn, 1977; Yoku Mireba, fl, vc, pf, 1977; With Dadaji in Paradise, vc, 1977–8, rev. 1983; Conc. for Amp Gui and Chamber Ens, 1978; 2 songs (R. Moss), S, fl, cl, harp, va, db, 1978; Light, 15 insts, 1979; Str Qt no.1, 1981; Winter Variations, 9 insts, 1981; Chansons d'amour, pf, 1982; Desires, large orch, 1983–4; Hidden Sparks, vn, 1984

Elec: Deplacements, gui, tape, 1979; Soft Morning, City! (Joyce: Finnegans Wake), S, db, cptr tape, 1980; Fusione Fugace, 4-track tape/cptr, 1981; Elec Etudes, vc, tape, elec, 1983; Spectres Parisiens, fl, hn, vc, synth, 18 insts, cptr, 1983–4

Principal publisher: Ricordi

BIBLIOGRAPHY

P. de Lara: "Un nouveau mode de composer," *Dialectiques* (1980), win., 55
F. Lewis: "Boulez, Computers and Music," *New York Times* (7 Jan 1980)
S. McBride: "IRCAM in Paris: where Composers Go to Play with Sound," *Christian Science Monitor* (11 Feb 1982), §B, p.2
D. Jameux: "Qui cherche trouve: un colloque international à l'IRCAM," *Art Press*, no.69 (1983), 38
J. Peyser: "American Technology Thrives in Paris," *New York Times* (6 May 1984), §II, p.25 [interview]

STEPHEN MONTAGUE

McHugh, Jimmy [James] **(Francis)** (*b* Boston, MA, 10 July 1894; *d* Beverly Hills, CA, 23 May 1969). Songwriter, pianist, and music publisher. He learned piano from his mother, and in 1915 became a rehearsal pianist for the Boston Opera. From 1916 he was a song-plugger in Boston for Irving Berlin Music and from 1921 in New York for the F. A. Mills Co., of which he later became a partner. In the 1920s he wrote several popular songs, including *When my sugar walks down the street* (1924), and revues for the Cotton Club in Harlem. In 1928 he began a long association with the lyricist Dorothy Fields; their all-black revue *The Blackbirds of 1928* included the song "I can't give you anything but love," which was an early success for dancer Bill "Bojangles" Robinson. Fields and McHugh were among the most successful songwriters in Hollywood in the 1930s, writing for such films as *Love in the Rough* (1930), *Cuban Love Song* (1931), *Flying High* (1931), and *Hooray for Love* (1935). McHugh made a return to Broadway with *The Streets of Paris* (1939), and wrote several popular songs with the lyricist Harold Adamson, some of them for films, including *Comin' in on a wing and a prayer*, *A lovely way to spend an evening*, and *I couldn't sleep a wink last night* (all 1943), and *It's a most unusual day* (1948).

McHugh received an honorary doctorate in music from Los Angeles City College in 1941. He led a dance band in the 1950s, performing his songs on tours in the USA and Europe and on television, and in 1959 founded his own music publishing company with Pete Rugolo. In 1970 an annual composition award was established in his memory at the University of Southern California.

McHugh was one of the best and most prolific of Hollywood composers, contributing to some 45 films. He was equally fluent in writing simple, elegant, or vocally demanding melodies, and made use of a wide range, extended or irregular phrase lengths to suit the lyrics, and unusual harmonies. Wilder considered his songs among the best of mid-20th-century American popular music for their attention to "the fine points of song writing and the things that create surprises instead of simply good but uninspired writing."

WORKS

(selective list)

STAGE

Unless otherwise stated, all are revues, and all dates are those of first New York performance.

The Blackbirds of 1928 (D. Fields), 9 May 1928 [incl. I can't give you anything but love, Diga diga doo]

Hello Daddy (H. and D. Fields), 26 Dec 1928 [incl. In a great big way]

International Revue (D. Fields), 25 Feb 1930 [incl. On the sunny side of the street, Exactly like you]

The Vanderbilt Revue (D. Fields, E. Y. Harburg, K. Nicholson), 5 Nov 1930 [incl. Blue Again]

Rhapsody in Black (D. Fields), 4 May 1931 [incl. I'm feelin' blue]

Shoot the Works (D. Fields), 21 July 1931 [incl. How's your uncle?]

The Streets of Paris (A. Dubin), 19 June 1939 [incl. South American Way]

Keep Off the Grass (musical, H. Dietz, Dubin), 23 May 1940

As the Girls Go (musical, H. Adamson), 13 Nov 1948 [incl. As the girls go, I got lucky in the rain, You say the nicest things]

FILMS

Love in the Rough, 1930 [incl. Go home and tell your mother, One More Waltz]; Cuban Love Song, 1931 [incl. Cuban Love Song]; Flying High, 1931; Hooray for Love, 1935; Top of the Town, 1937 [incl. Where are you?]; You're the One, 1941; Happy Go Lucky, 1943 [incl. Let's Get Lost, "Murder," he says]; Higher and Higher, 1943 [incl. A lovely way to spend an evening, I couldn't sleep a wink last night]; Bring on the Girls, 1945; If you Knew Susie, 1948

SONGS

(most associated with films; lyrics by D. Fields unless otherwise indicated)

When my sugar walks down the street (I. Mills, G. Austin), 1924; I can't believe that you're in love with me (C. Gaskill), 1926; Don't Blame me, in Dinner at Eight, 1933; Lost in a Fog, in Have a Heart, 1934; Every Little Moment, 1935; I feel a song comin' on, I'm in the mood for love, in Every Night at Eight, 1935; I'm shooting high (T. Koehler), in King of Burlesque, 1935; Lovely to Look at, in Roberta, 1935

It's great to be in love again, 1936; Say it over and over again (F. Loesser), in Buck Benny Rides Again, 1940; Comin' in on a wing and a prayer (H. Adamson), 1943; It's a most unusual day (Adamson), in A Date with Judy, 1948; Dream, dream, dream (M. Parish), 1954; Too Young to go Steady (Adamson), 1955

BIBLIOGRAPHY

D. Ewen: *Popular American Composers* (New York, 1962; suppl. 1972)

A. Wilder: *American Popular Song: the Great Innovators, 1900–1950* (New York, 1972)

DEANE L. ROOT

McIntosh, Rigdon McCoy (*b* Maury Co., TN, 3 April 1836; *d* Atlanta, GA, 2 July 1899). Composer and arranger of Sunday-school and gospel hymns, and hymnbook compiler. He received his musical training from L. C. and A. B. Everett, and was associated with them for several years as a composer and editor and as a teacher of singing-schools and normal music schools in the Southeast. In the 1860s he became an editor for the publishing house of the Methodist Episcopal Church, South, in Nashville, a position he held for some 30 years. He became head of the music department of Vanderbilt University in 1875, and two years later accepted a similar position at Emory College, Oxford, Georgia. He left college teaching in 1895 to devote himself to his publishing business, the R. M. McIntosh Publishing Company, in Atlanta. He published more than 15 collections for church, Sunday-school, and singing-school use, including *Tabor* (1866), *Light and Life* (1881), *New Life* (1881), *Prayer and Praise* (with A. G. Haygood, 1885), *Christian Hymns* (with E. G. Sewell, 1889), *Words of Truth* (with H. R. Christie, 1892), *McIntosh's Class and Chorus* (1893), and *Gospel Grace* (1895). McIntosh is best known as the arranger of the camp-meeting tune *Promised Land*, which he changed to a major key to fit the gospel hymn style. Although few of his tunes remain in use today, the popular *Broadman Hymnal* (1940) contains his settings of the texts "Gathering home," "The kingdom is coming," and "Tell it again."

See also SHAPE-NOTE HYMNODY, §4.

BIBLIOGRAPHY

W. J. Reynolds: *Companion to Baptist Hymnal* (Nashville, 1976)

HARRY ESKEW

Mack, Edward (*b* Stuttgart, Germany, 24 Aug 1826; *d* Philadelphia, PA, 7 Jan 1882). Composer. He was brought to the USA when he was five years old and early received musical training. By the age of 18 he was apparently blind, since he then entered Philadelphia's Institute for the Blind. After a short period in New London, Connecticut, he returned to Philadelphia, where he may have become involved in music education and filled a post as an organist, in addition to his activities as a composer. Mack wrote a large number of simple, stylized dance pieces for the piano; his marches, such as *General Grant's Grand March* (*c*1868) and a series (published in 1875) to commemorate the Centennial Exposition in Philadelphia in 1876, were particularly popular. He also compiled instruction books for the piano, reed organ, and violin.

WORKS

Edition: *Royal Folio of Music: a Collection of Standard American Compositions for the Pianoforte*, ed. E. R. Parkhurst (London, n.d.) [P]

(selective list; all for pf and published in Philadelphia)

General McClellan's Grand March (1861); Dirge (for President Lincoln) (1865); President Lincoln's Funeral March (1865); General Grant's Grand March (*c*1868), P; General Meade's Funeral March (*c*1872); Charles Sumner's Funeral March (*c*1874); Agricultural March (1875); Centennial March (1875); Horticultural March (1875); Machinery March (1875); Memorial March (1875); General Winfield S. Hancock's Cincinnati Grand March (*c*1880); The Chick Waltz, P; Purity, P

DALE COCKRELL

Mackay [Mackey]. Family of merchants. During the first half of the 19th century members of the family gave financial backing to various Boston instrument makers, including Alpheus Babcock, Thomas Appleton, and Jonas Chickering. Their most active member was John Mackay (*d* at sea, 1841), a mariner and merchant, who is credited with a patent (first issued 14 August 1822, reissued 23 April 1839) for fitting metal into leather-covered piano hammers to produce a fuller tone.

Mackay supported the builders Babcock, Appleton, and William Goodrich at 6 Milk Street, Boston, from the dissolution of the partnership of Hayts, Babcock & Appleton in 1815 until 1820. By 1823 Mackay's nephew George D. Mackay (*d* at sea, 15 Dec 1824) had set up a piano factory at 7 Parkman's Market with Babcock as his superintendent. An inventory of the factory, made by Babcock and Appleton on 24 January 1825, lists nine workbenches, nine finished and nine unfinished square pianos, and one unfinished grand piano, as well as tools and supplies. Another inventory, dating from 17 October 1825, indicates that the factory was financed by John Mackay's mother, Ruth Mackay (*b* 1743; *d* Weston, MA, 10 April 1833), who continued to support her son's business with Babcock until 1829. During this time pianos produced by Babcock, marked "Babcock for G. D. Mackay" or "Babcock for R. Mackay," included the earliest square pianos to have one-piece cast-iron frames.

From 1830 until his death John Mackay was in business with Jonas CHICKERING in premises on Washington Street, Boston;

Mackay's son William H. Mackay was also involved in the firm, but sold the family's interest to Jonas Chickering in 1842, after his father's death. The Mackays continued their association with Babcock, who worked for Chickering & Mackays and in 1839 assigned to the firm his patent (no. 1389) on piano actions. In all his associations with keyboard makers, John Mackay provided capital and business expertise, found new buyers in North and South America, and imported exotic woods and other raw materials.

BIBLIOGRAPHY

"Biographical Memoir of William Goodrich, Organ Builder," *New-England Magazine*, vi (1834), 25

R. G. Parker: *A Tribute to the Life and Character of Jonas Chickering by one who Knew him Well* (Boston, 1854)

C. M. Ayars: *Contributions to the Art of Music by the Music Industries of Boston 1640 to 1936* (New York, 1937), 106ff

K. G. Grafing: *Alpheus Babcock: American Pianoforte Maker (1785–1842), his Life, Instruments, and Patents* (diss., U. of Missouri, Kansas City, 1972)

CYNTHIA ADAMS HOOVER

McKay, George Frederick (*b* Harrington, WA, 11 June 1899; *d* Stateline, NV, 4 Oct 1970). Composer and educator. He studied at the Eastman School with Christian Sinding and Selim Palmgren and was the school's first composition graduate (BM 1923). He joined the faculty of the University of Washington, Seattle, in 1927, became full professor in 1943, and remained there until his retirement in 1968. He served as visiting professor at the universities of Southern California, Michigan, and Oregon. Described as a folklorist, McKay was interested in portraying the spirit of the American West by evoking in his music what he called a "folk feeling," using American folk idioms and incorporating folk melodies, through paraphrase or direct quotation. He won a number of prizes, including an award from the American Guild of Organists in 1939 and the Harvey Gaul Prize in 1961, and wrote many works on commission. He is the author of *Creative Orchestration* (1963).

See also EMERSON, RALPH WALDO.

WORKS

(– date of first performance)*

Orch: 4 sinfoniettas, 1925–42; Fantasy on a Western Folksong, *1933; From a Mountain Town (Sinfonietta), 1934; To a Liberator (A Lincoln Tribute), 1939–40; Vn Conc., 1940; Prairie Portrait, *1941; Vc Conc., 1942; Music of the Americas, programmatic suites (1947–50); Evocation Sym., 1951; Song over the Great Plains, *1954; 6 Pieces on Winter Moods and Patterns, 1961; 2 Sym. Miniatures; at least 4 other orch works; many pieces for student ens

Chamber, inst: Org Sonata no. 1, 1930; Wind Qnt, 1930; Pf Trio, 1931; American Street Scenes, cl, bn, trbn, sax, pf, 1935; Trbn Sonata (1951); Suite, b insts (1958); Suite on 16th-century Hymns, org (1960); Suite, harp, fl, 1960; Sonatina expressiva, brass qnt (1966); Andante mistico, 8 vc, pf (1968); 4 str qts; *c*25 org pieces; *c*20 pf pieces

Chorus: Pioneers (Whitman), SATB, orch (1942); Lincoln Lyrics (E. Markham), cantata (1949); *c*40 partsongs, suites, rhapsodies, many for student ens

5 works for band, incl. 2 suites; piece for brass ens

MSS in *DLC*, *WaU*, Moldenhauer Archives, Spokane, WA

Principal publishers: Barnhouse, Birchard, Fischer, Presser

BIBLIOGRAPHY

EwenD

"George Frederick McKay," *The Instrumentalist*, viii/2 (1953), 36

M. T. Coolen: *Creative Melodist: the Life and Orchestral Works of George Frederick McKay (1899–1970)* (thesis, U. of Washington, 1972) [incl. list of works]

KATHERINE K. PRESTON

McKenna, Dave [David J.] (*b* Woonsocket, RI, 30 May 1930). Jazz pianist. He took piano lessons as a child, but learned to play jazz chiefly from listening to the radio and recordings. At the age of 12 he began to play with pickup groups at weddings and other occasions, and at 15 joined the musicians' union. By 1947 he was performing in and around Boston with a group led by the saxophonist Henry "Boots" Mussulli. In 1949 he joined Charlie Ventura's band, then played with Woody Herman (1950–51) before serving two years in the US Army. He rejoined Ventura's band in 1953 for 18 months, but thereafter worked mostly with smaller groups, playing with Gene Krupa, Stan Getz, Zoot Sims, Al Cohn, Bobby Hackett, and others. In 1967 he moved from New York to South Yarmouth on Cape Cod, Massachusetts, and since around 1970 has worked regularly as a solo player in piano bars, chiefly in Boston and on the Cape.

McKenna combines enormous rhythmic drive with melodic inventiveness and a profound strain of lyricism; while playing a wide range of tunes, he especially favors Tin Pan Alley standards. He treats ballads lovingly, drawing on his command of the rich harmonic idiom of the progressive jazz of the 1940s and 1950s, and paying close attention to details of sound. At faster tempos he seems to ride along on the energy of his powerful left hand, which may play one-note lines, strummed chords or, more rarely, stride figures. At its best, his music maintains the coherence and conviction that mastery of a classic style can confer, but without sacrificing vitality and excitement.

RECORDINGS

(selective list)

As soloist: *Solo Piano* (1955, ABC-Para. 104); *Solo Piano* (1973, Chiaroscuro 119); *Giant Strides* (1979, Conc. 99); *Left Handed Complement* (1979, Conc. 123); *A Celebration of Hoagy Carmichael* (1983, Conc. 227)

Duos: with J. Venuti: *Alone at the Palace* (1977, Chiaroscuro 160); with D. Johnson: *Spider's Blues* (1980, Conc. 135)

As leader: *Piano Scene* (1958, Epic 3558); *No Bass Hit* (1979, Conc. 97); *The Dave McKenna Trio Plays the Music of Harry Warren* (1981, Conc. 174)

As sideman: Z. Sims: *Down Home* (1960, Bethlehem 6051); B. Wilber: *New Clarinet in Town* (1960, Classic Jazz 8); S. Hamilton: *Tenorshoes* (1979, Conc. 127)

BIBLIOGRAPHY

B. Doerschuk: "Dave McKenna Carrying on the Jazz Piano Tradition," *Contemporary Keyboard*, vi/10 (1980), 20

W. Balliett: *Jelly Roll, Jabbo, and Fats: 19 Portraits in Jazz* (New York, 1983), 153

RICHARD CRAWFORD

McKim, Lucy. *See* GARRISON, LUCY MCKIM.

McKinley, William Thomas (*b* New Kensington, PA, 9 Dec 1938). Composer. He was educated at Carnegie-Mellon University, Pittsburgh (BA 1960), and received an MM degree from Yale University, where his teachers included Schuller, Powell, Wyner, and Moss. He was a member of the faculty of the University of Chicago, 1969–73, and has taught composition and jazz at the New England Conservatory, Boston (from 1973), and at the Berkshire Music Center. He is also active as a jazz pianist. He has received many commissions from Richard Stoltzman, the clarinetist, and has won awards from the Koussevitzky Foundation, the Fromm Foundation (1976), the NEA (1981), the American Academy of Arts and Letters (1983), and the Guggenheim Foundation (1985). He was commissioned by the Chamber Music Society of Lincoln Center to write a viola sonata for its 1985–6 series. During the 1970s his style was post-Schoenbergian expressionist; for example, the Clarinet Concerto (1977) was inspired by Schoenberg's monodrama, *Erwartung*. In more recent works such as *Symphony for Thirteen* (1983) he has achieved a new euphony and a simpler and more accessible manner. McKinley has written several hundred jazz tunes, and undoubtedly jazz has contributed most to the improvisatory impulse evident in his earlier as well as his later art music.

WORKS

Large ens: Triple Conc., pf, db, drums, 1971; Pf Conc., 1975; Conc., cl, 1977; Concertino, orch, 1977; 4 syms., 1979, 1980, 1983, 1985; Conc., orch, 1980; The Mountain, tone poem, 1982; Sym. for 13, 1983; Poem of Light, pf, chamber orch, 1983; Scarlet, big band, 1983; many other works, incl. other cl conc., 2 va concs., 1 vc conc., 1 cl, vn conc.

Inst: For One, cl, 1971; August Sym., fl, cl, vn, vc, pf, 1982–3; Paintings VII, chamber ens, 1982; Duo concertante, cl, pf, 1983; 2 Entratas, cl, 1983; 2 Nocturnes, cl, vc, 1983; Trio appassionata, cl, va, pf, 1983; Double Conc., db, b cl, chamber ens, 1984; Duo, fl, pf, 1984; Romances, vn, cl, pf, 1984; Summer Dances, conc., vn, chamber ens, 1984; numerous other chamber works, incl. 6 str qts, over 30 pf pieces, other solo inst works

Vocal: Deliverance Amen (M. M. McKinley), oratorio, SATB, chamber ens, org, 1982–3; several other choral works; songs

McKinney, Baylus Benjamin (*b* Heflin, LA, 22 July 1886; *d* Bryson City, NC, 7 Sept 1952). Writer and editor of gospel hymns, and church music administrator. He studied at Mt. Lebanon (Louisiana) Academy, Louisiana College, and the Southwestern Baptist Theological Seminary, where he taught from 1919 to 1932. He was also music editor for the Dallas publisher Robert H. Coleman from 1918 to 1935, and many of his gospel songs were first published in Coleman's songbooks and hymnals. He served as assistant pastor of the Travis Avenue Baptist Church, Fort Worth (1931–5), then in 1935 became music editor for the Baptist Sunday School Board, Nashville, where he edited the popular *Broadman Hymnal* (1940). In 1941 he became secretary of the newly formed Church Music Department of the Sunday School Board. McKinney wrote the words and music of about 150 gospel hymns and composed settings for about 115 texts by others. More than a dozen of his hymns are in the *Baptist Hymnal* (1975), including *Have faith in God* and the tune for *Wherever he leads I'll go*. The Southern Baptist denominational program of church music, which McKinney initiated, has developed into the largest sponsored by any church body in the USA.

BIBLIOGRAPHY

P. R. Powell: *A Biographical and Bibliographical Study of Baylus Benjamin McKinney (1886–1952)* (thesis, New Orleans Baptist Theological Seminary, 1973)

W. J. Reynolds and A. C. Faircloth: *The Songs of B. B. McKinney* (Nashville, 1974)

W. J. Reynolds: *Companion to Baptist Hymnal* (Nashville, 1976)

T. C. Terry: *B. B. McKinney: a Shaping Force in Southern Protestant Music* (diss., North Texas State U., 1981)

HARRY ESKEW

McKinney's Cotton Pickers. Jazz ensemble. It was formed in Springfield, Ohio, from the Synco Jazz Band, a group organized by the drummer William McKinney shortly after World War I. In 1923 McKinney decided to conduct the band himself, and consequently engaged the drummer Cuba Austin as the band's percussionist. At the behest of their agent the band became known as McKinney's Cotton Pickers. With their musical versatility and inspired showmanship they blended comedy routines and light music with jazz numbers arranged by their trumpeter, John Nesbitt. From 1927, when DON REDMAN became music director and principal arranger, the band developed its own distinctive style, which highlighted the precision of the saxophones and brass and emphasized the buoyancy of the rhythm section.

The band's first recordings in July 1928 helped establish the group nationally, and brought widespread praise for the brilliance of Redman's arrangements and the solo improvisations of Prince Robinson on reed instruments. The Cotton Pickers' golden era took place during their long residence at the Graystone Ballroom in Detroit (beginning in 1927), where they gained a reputation equal to that of the two other leading black bands of that era, those of Duke Ellington and Fletcher Henderson. Claude Jones, who at various times played trombone in all three groups, later claimed that McKinney's Cotton Pickers was the best of the three. Bright-sounding ensembles, good intonation, and effective soloists were the band's principal strengths; these assets, combined with the appealing singing of the saxophonist George Thomas, the banjoist Dave Wilborn, and the multi-instrumentalist Don Redman, made the Cotton Pickers popular with dancers, listeners, and other musicians.

In 1931 the band suffered a serious setback when Redman left to form his own big band, taking some key sidemen with him. The Cotton Pickers reformed, and even found superior replacements in the new members Joe Smith, Benny Carter, and Rex Stewart; but they never regained their former popularity. Internal dissension caused many personnel changes during the mid-1930s, and by 1936 almost all the original members had left. McKinney continued to lead the band until the early 1940s, hiring various musicians to direct while he concentrated on administration. Unfortunately the group made no recordings after September 1931.

RECORDINGS
(selective list)

Crying and Sighing (1928, Vic. 38000); Peggy (1929, Vic. 38133); I'll Make Fun for You (1930, Vic. 38142); If I Could Be with you One Hour Tonight (1930, Vic. 38118); Do You Believe in Love at Sight? (1931, Vic. 22811)

BIBLIOGRAPHY

B. Howard: "Old Cotton Pickers could Outrock Modern Jazz Orchestras," *Down Beat*, ix/11 (1942), 8

T. Grove and M. Grove: "McKinney's Cotton Pickers," *Record Changer* (Nov 1951), 3

G. Blonston: "Stompin' at the Pontch," *Detroit Free Press* (11 Feb 1973)

J. Chilton: *McKinney's Music* (London, 1978)

N. Gentieu: "Don Redman's Masterpiece," *IAJRCJ*, xiv/1 (1981), 8

JOHN CHILTON

McKuen, Rod (Marvin) (*b* Oakland, CA, 29 April 1933). Composer, poet, and singer. He ran away from home at the age of 11 and traveled for a few years working at odd jobs. By the time he was 17 he had settled back in Oakland and ran a popular radio show, "Rendezvous with Rod," on which he read his own poems and sang his own songs. After serving for two years in the US Army he began a career as a performer and appeared in several films and on television. In 1959 he went to New York, where he worked as a singer and continued to write songs. During a stay in Paris (1963–4) he was influenced by such artists as Jacques Brel and began to develop his singing style after the French *chansonniers*. McKuen has written more than 1000 songs, many of which have become best-sellers in recordings by the Limelighters, the Kingston Trio, Glenn Yarbrough, Jimmie Rodgers, and Petula Clark. His music for films includes *The Prime of Miss Jean Brodie* (1968) and *A Boy Named Charlie Brown* (1970), both of which were nominated for Academy awards. McKuen is also a prolific composer of concert works; as well as a "gothic musical," *The Black Eagle* (1976), and several ballets, he has produced four symphonies, seven concertos, and a number of piano pieces. Although critics have generally found his works undistinguished, his performances have been well received and he is acknowledged an effective showman.

WORKS
(selective list)

STAGE
(all ballets unless otherwise indicated)

The Black Eagle (musical, 2, McKuen), op.47, 1976; Americana RFD, 1979; Seven Elizabethan Dances, 1979; The Minotaur (Man to Himself), 1980; Volga Song, 1980; The Man who Tracked the Stars, 1980; 15 other ballets, 1976–84

ORCHESTRAL

The Zodiac, suite, str, ww, op.4; Sym. no.1 "All Men Love Something," op.7; Conc., 4 hpd, orch, op.20; 3 Ovs., ondes martenot, orch, op.23, 1969; Gui Conc. "Someday we'll See Spain Together," op.33, 1970; Adagio, harp, str, op.17, 1971; Pf Conc. "The Cathedrals of England," op.27, 1972; The Plains of my Country, sym. suite, op.38, 1972; Ballad of Distances, sym. suite, op.40, 1973; The City, suite, nar, orch, op.42, 1973; I Hear America Singing, suite, S, nar, orch, op.43, 1973; Sym. no.3 "A Piece of the Continent, a Part of the Main," op.45, 1975; Vc Conc., op.41, 1976; Balloon Conc., orch, op.46, 1976; Sym. no.4 "Birch Trees," op.53

FILM SCORES

Joanna, 1968; The Prime of Miss Jean Brodie, 1968; A Boy Named Charlie Brown, 1970; Come to your Senses, 1971; Scandalous John, 1971; The Borrowers, 1973; Emily, 1975; The Unknown War, 1979; The Living End, 1983; Death Rides this Trail, 1984

PIANO

Riders in the Distance, variations, op.32; 4 Trios and 4 Qts, op.48; 6 sonatas

SONGS
(all lyrics by McKuen)

Ally Ally Oxen Free; The Beautiful Strangers; Everybody's rich but us; I'll catch the sun; Jean; Kaleidoscope; Love's been good to me; A Man Alone; One by One; Rusting in the Rain; So Many Others; Three; The world I used to know

Principal publishers: Artemus, Chappell, Intersong, Marks, Stanyan

BIBLIOGRAPHY

D. Ewen: *Popular American Composers* (New York, 1962; suppl. 1972)
"McKuen, Rod," *CBY 1970*
N. Deiter: "Interview: Rod McKuen," *The Advocate* (8 Sept 1976), 19
R. McKuen: *Finding my Father: One Man's Search for Identity* (Los Angeles, 1976) [autobiography]

ROBERT SKINNER

MacLaine, Shirley [Beatty, Shirley MacLean] (*b* Richmond, VA, 24 April 1934). Actress and singer. She was a chorus girl in the Rodgers and Hammerstein Broadway musical *Me and Juliet* in 1953, and also in the Bissell–Abbott musical *The Pajama Game* the following year, when her performance as a replacement for the show's injured leading dancer was much acclaimed and subsequently led to a long and varied film career. Although she has sung and danced in several film musicals, including *Artists and Models* (1956), *Can-can* (1960), *What a way to Go* (1964), and *Sweet Charity* (1968), most of her films are not musicals, and it is for these that she has been nominated for four Academy awards, winning one in 1984. MacLaine has also pursued a successful career as a television entertainer and as a performer in her own stage revues, in which she shows a characteristic exuberance and comedic flair. She is the author of several books, three of which are autobiographical: *"Don't Fall off the Mountain"* (1970), *You Can Get There From Here* (1975), and *Out on a Limb* (1983).

BIBLIOGRAPHY

P. Erens: *Films of Shirley MacLaine* (South Brunswick, NJ, 1977)
"MacLaine, Shirley," *CBY 1978*

ROBERT SKINNER

McLaughlin, John (*b* Yorkshire, England, 4 Jan 1942). Jazz-rock guitarist and bandleader. He is essentially self-taught on his instrument, and was early influenced by the recordings of Django Reinhardt. In the 1960s he was active in London, where he played with such rock musicians as Jack Bruce, Mick Jagger, and Eric Clapton. He immigrated to the USA in 1968, joining Tony William's group Lifetime and participating in Miles Davis's recordings *In a Silent Way* and *Bitches Brew*. In 1971 he formed his own group, the MAHAVISHNU ORCHESTRA, which was influential in blending jazz with rock and Indian music. McLaughlin then formed an acoustic group, Shakti, consisting of violin, tablā, mṛdaṅga, ghaṭa, and hollow-bodied guitar. During the early 1980s he appeared in duos and trios playing hollow-bodied guitars with Larry Coryell, Al DiMeola, Christian Escoude, and the Spanish flamenco guitarist Paco de Lucia.

Notable for his considerable technical proficiency, McLaughlin is probably the most influential jazz guitarist since Wes Montgomery. His improvised solos usually contain far less of the pronounced syncopation and relaxed swing common to jazz, and instead are more typical of rock; others are built of long passages of 16th notes with interludes of held notes which are distorted in waveform and expressively "bent" in pitch. McLaughlin's improvisation does not share the bouncy, twisting and turning conception that characterized the guitar tradition of Charlie Christian and Kenny Burrell, and his work is also devoid of the gentle lyricism of Jim Hall. He prefers instead the hard, metallic and cutting tone obtained by rock guitarists, which he frequently alters by means of the wah-wah pedal and phase shifter. His choice of notes is reminiscent of the modal approaches of the jazz saxophonist John Coltrane (both McLaughlin and Coltrane studied Indian music).

In the early 1970s McLaughlin employed a specially built electric guitar with two necks, one having six and the other 12 strings. Later, for the group Shakti, he designed another guitar-like instrument based on the Indian vīṇā and formed much like an autoharp, having a scalloped fingerboard and resonating strings.

RECORDINGS
(selective list)

As leader: *My Goal's Beyond* (1970, Douglas 9); *The Inner Mounting Flame* (1971, Col. KC31067); *Birds of Fire* (1972, Col. KC31996); *Apocalypse* (1974, Col. KC32957); *Shakti* (1975, Col. KC34162)

As sideman: M. Davis: *In a Silent Way* (1969, Col. CS9875), *Bitches Brew* (1969, Col. GP26); T. Williams: *Emergency* (1969, Pol. 25-3001); M. Davis: *A Tribute to Jack Johnson* (1970, Col. KC30455); T. Williams: *Turn it Over* (1970, Pol. 24-4021); L. Coryell: *Spaces* (1970, Van. 6558)

BIBLIOGRAPHY

M. Delorme and A. Tercinet: "Discographie de John McLaughlin," *Jazz hot*, no.269 (1971), 14
J. E. Berendt: "Mahavishnu John McLaughlin," *Jazz Forum*, no.27 (1974), 43
C. Berg: "John McLaughlin: Evolution of a Master," *Down Beat*, xlv/12 (1978), 14
D. Menn and C. Stern: "John McLaughlin: After Mahavishnu and Shakti, a Return to Electric Guitar," *Guitar Player*, xii/8 (1978), 40
S. Rosen: "John McLaughlin," *The Guitar Player Book* (New York, 1978), 148

MARK C. GRIDLEY

McLean, Barton (Keith) (*b* Poughkeepsie, NY, 8 April 1938). Composer and performer. He was educated at SUNY, Potsdam (BS 1960), the Eastman School (MM 1965), where he was a pupil of Cowell, and at Indiana University, Bloomington (DMA 1972). He taught music theory and double bass at SUNY, Potsdam, from 1960 to 1966. In 1969 he joined the music faculty at Indiana University, South Bend, where he became head of the theory and composition department and director of the electronic music center. From 1976 to 1983 he directed the electronic music center and taught at the University of Texas, Austin. McLean has received a number of awards, including fellowships to the

MacDowell Colony and an NEA media-arts grant (1978). He has served the American Society of University Composers in several executive or administrative capacities and has contributed articles and reviews on contemporary music to *Perspectives of New Music* and other journals. He began to compose in the early 1960s; since 1973 he has turned to electronic techniques (both *musique concrète* and synthesized sound) and limited aleatoric procedures, and has evolved new concepts of notation. With his wife, the composer Priscilla McLean, he performs as the McLean Mix, presenting their music in the USA and elsewhere; in these concerts he plays the piano or synthesizer. The McLeans' artistic goals are precise control, a certain sonic quality, and disciplined virtuosity in the interdependent domains of composition and performance.

WORKS

Large ens: Divertimento for Cl Choir, 1962; Rondo, band, 1962; Scherzo, orch, 1962; Legend no.1, band, 1962, no.2, wind, perc, 1966, rev. 1970; Ov., Pardon my Ambition, 1966; Suite, str, 1966; Farewell to H, orch, 1967, rev. as The Purging of Hindemith, 1975; Metamorphosis, orch, 1972

Inst: Pastorale, ob, cl, pf, 1962; Fantasia, pf, 1967; Pf Trio, 1968, rev. 1974; Brass Qnt, 1970; Ixtlan, 2 pf, 1982; Ritual of Dawn, 6 insts, 1982; Pathways, wind, 1983

Elec: Genesis, tape, 1973; Dimensions I – VIII, 1 inst, tape, 1973–82; Spirals, 2-/4-track tape, 1973; The Sorcerer Revisited, 2-track tape, 1975, rev. 1977; Identity I, installation, 1977; Song of the Nahuatl, 2-/4-/8-track tape, 1977; Heavy Music for 4 Crowbars, elec, 1979; The Electric Sinfonia, 2-track tape, 1982; Etunytude, 2-track tape, 1982; The Last 10 Minutes, 4-track tape, 1982

Vocal: Agnus Dei, female vv, 1961; Trilogy (P. McLean), cantata, T, SATB, str qt, ww qt, perc, pf, 1968; 3 Songs (Sandburg), 1970; Mysteries from the Ancient Nahuatl (Nahuatl poems, trans. D. Brinton), chorus, solo vv, nar, 15 insts, 4-track tape, 1978 [incorporates Song of the Nahuatl, 1977; abridged version as Excerpts from Mysteries from the Ancient Nahuatl, 1980]

Principal publishers: A. Broude, Dorn, Galaxy, Shawnee

BIBLIOGRAPHY

D. Ernst: "Composer Profile," *Polyphony*, iv/2 (1978), 40
——: "The Electronic Music of Barton and Priscilla McLean," *Polyphony*, iv/3 (1978), 40
R. L. Caravan: "McLean's *Dimensions III* and *IV*," *Saxophone Symposium*, v/4 (1980), 6

BARBARA A. PETERSEN

McLean, Jackie [John Lenwood] (*b* New York, 17 May 1932). Jazz alto saxophonist. He was influenced by Charlie Parker, and played alto saxophone with some of the leading bands of the 1950s, including Charles Mingus's group and Art Blakey's Jazz Messengers (1956–8); he also recorded with Miles Davis. In the 1960s he made several recordings for Blue Note, displaying a raw, urgent style that was grounded in bop but greatly affected by the free jazz movement of the time. His playing has continued to develop and to exert a wide influence on alto saxophonists, but since 1968 he has spent most of his time teaching Afro-American music at Hartt College at the University of Hartford. During the summers he often tours (sometimes with his son Rene, a tenor saxophonist), and occasionally teaches in Europe. McLean is the subject of a short documentary film, *Jackie McLean on Mars* (1982), where he is seen teaching, playing, and discussing his views on life and music.

RECORDINGS
(*selective list*)

As leader: *New Soil* (1959, BN 4013); *Capuchin Swing* (1960, BN 4038); *Bluesnik* (1961, BN 84067); *Destination Out* (1963, BN 84165); *'Bout Soul* (1967, BN 84284); *The Meeting* (1973, SteepleChase 1006)

As co-leader with J. Jenkins: *Alto Madness* (1957, Prst. 7114)

BIBLIOGRAPHY

SouthernB
A. B. Spellman: *Black Music: Four Lives* (New York, 1966)
R. Wilbraham: *Jackie McLean: a Discography with Biography* (London, 1968)
V. Wilmer: *Jazz People* (Indianapolis, 1970, 2/1977)
H. Nolan: "The Connection between Today and Yesterday," *Down Beat*, xlii/7 (1975), 11
R. Brown: "Ah! Unh! Mr. Funk," *Down Beat*, xlvi/16 (1979), 22

LEE JESKE

McLean [née Taylor], **Priscilla (Anne)** (*b* Fitchburg, MA, 27 May 1942). Composer and performer. She attended the State College at Fitchburg (BEd 1963), the University of Lowell (BME 1965), and Indiana University (MM 1969). Among her composition teachers were Hugo Norden, Richard Kent, Bernhard Heiden, and Thomas Beversdorf. She has taught at Indiana University, Kokomo (1971–3), and at St. Mary's College, Notre Dame (1973–6); in 1985 she was visiting professor at the University of Hawaii. From 1976 to 1980 she produced the American Society of Composers "Radiofest" series. Among her many awards are grants from the NEA and the Martha Baird Rockefeller Fund for Music. Since 1974 she has performed with her husband, Barton McLean, as the McLean Mix, presenting concerts of their own music in which she sings and plays the piano, synthesizer, percussion, and native wooden flutes.

In her works, McLean combines animal- or man-made sounds with synthesized music according to an "imago-abstract" concept. Her compositions, unquestionably dramatic, are neither busy nor fussy, and are unencumbered by complex electronics. The sonic tension and large-scale coherence in her recorded compositions have been widely acclaimed. McLean has contributed articles to *Musical America*, *Perspectives of New Music*, and other journals.

WORKS

Large ens: Holiday for Youth, concert band, 1964–5; Variations and Mosaics on a Theme of Stravinsky, orch, 1967–9, rev. 1975; Messages, double chorus, 4 solo vv, chamber ens, elec, 1972–4

Chamber: Interplanes, 2 pf, 1970; Spectra I, perc ens, synth, 1971; Spectra II, perc ens, prepared pf, 1972; Ah-Syn!, autoharp, synth, 1974, rev. 1976; Beneath the Horizon I, 4 tubas, tape [whale sounds], 1977–8; Beneath the Horizon II, tuba, tape [whale sounds], 1978, rev. as III, 1979; Fantasies for Adults and Other Children (Cummings), S, amp pf, 1978–9; Inner Universe (8 tone poems), amp pf, tape, slides, 1979–82; Elan! A Dance to All Things Rising from the Earth, fl, pf, perc, vn, vc, 1980–82; other vocal and chamber pieces

Tape: Night Images, 2-track, 1973; Dance of Dawn, 4-track, 1974; Invisible Chariots, 4-track, 1975–7

Principal publishers: ACA, Continuo Music (ABI)

BIBLIOGRAPHY

D. Ernst: "The Electronic Music of Barton and Priscilla McLean," *Polyphony*, iv/3 (1978), 40

BARBARA A. PETERSEN

Mac Low, Jackson (*b* Chicago, IL, 12 Sept 1922). Performance artist, composer, and poet. After early training in piano, violin, and harmony at the Chicago Musical College (1927–32) and the Northwestern University School of Music (1932–6), he studied philosophy at the University of Chicago (1939–43, AA 1941) and, later, Greek with Vera Lachmann at Brooklyn College, CUNY (BA 1958); he also studied piano with Shirley Gabis (1943–4), Grete Sultan (1953–5), and Franz Kamin (1976–9), composition with Erich Katz (1948–9), and experimental music with Cage (1957–60). In 1954 he began using aleatory procedures to compose poetry, plays, music, and performance works.

He is best known for his "simultaneities," performances in which visual, musical, and verbal elements are blended according to precise instructions; the performers move at will through the text-sound scores, layering words, speech-sounds, and pitched material in a complex, freely flowing fabric of sound. His scores often take the form of crossword puzzles and include methods for translating letters to pitch classes. Mac Low has written many books, including several volumes of poetry. His compositions have been published independently and in such collections as La Monte Young's *An Anthology* (1963, 2/1970) and Cage's *Notations* (1969). On Mac Low's 60th birthday an eight-hour concert of his works was performed in his honor by Cage, Simone Forti, Malcolm Goldstein, Kenneth King, Steve Paxton, Carolee Schneeman, the S. E. M. Ensemble, Bernadette Mayer, Ned Sublette, and Young, many of whom were influenced by his "multilevel approach to language, sound, and action."

WORKS

Selective list; all texts by Mac Low; for unspecified forces unless otherwise stated.

A Vocabulary for Carl Fernbach-Flarsheim (1968); A Vocabulary for Sharon Belle Matlin (1974); A Vocabulary for Vera Regina Lachmann (1974); A Vocabulary for Peter Innisfree Moore (1975); Guru-Guru Gatha (1975); 1st Milarepa Gatha (1976); 1st Sharon Belle Matlin Vocabulary Crossword Gatha (1976); Homage to Leona Bleiweiss (1976, 2/1978); The WBAI Vocabulary Gatha (1977, rev. 1979); A Notated Vocabulary for Eve Rosenthal (1978); A Vocabulary Gatha for Pete Rose (1978); Musicwords (for Phill Niblock) (1978)

A Vocabulary Gatha for Anne Tardos (1980); Dream Meditation (1980, rev. 1982); A Vocabulary Gatha for Malcolm Goldstein (1981); Dialog unter Dichtern/Dialog among Poets (1982); 1st Happy Birthday, Anne, Vocabulary Gatha (1982); Milarepa Qt, 4 like insts (1982); Pauline Meditation (1982); 2nd Happy Birthday, Anne, Vocabulary Gatha (1982); Unstructured Meditative Improvisation for Vocalists and Instrumentalists on the Word "Nucleus" (1982); The Summer Solstice Vocabulary Gatha (1983); Thanks/Danke (1983); 2 Heterophonies: from "Hereford Bosons 1 & 2" (1984); Phonemicon from "Hereford Bosons 1" (1984)

Principal publishers: Mac Low, Membrane, Printed Editions, Something Else, Station Hill

JOAN LA BARBARA

McNabb, Michael (Don) (*b* Salinas, CA, 5 July 1952). Composer and saxophonist. He studied composition with Jolas at the Paris Conservatoire in 1975, and with Leland Smith and Chowning at Stanford University (BA composition 1974, MA 1975, DMA 1980). In 1981 he became visiting composer at the Center for Computer Research in Music and Acoustics at Stanford. His awards include two from the Festival international des musiques experimentales, Bourge, France (1978, 1982), a League of Composers-ISCM award, for *Dreamsong*, in 1978, and a grant from the NEA (1982). After some early works for conventional forces, McNabb has composed almost exclusively for the computer, sometimes using voices or acoustic instruments as material to be synthesized, as in *Dreamsong*, for taped soprano and computer. *Mars Suite* (1979), for computer, was composed for the NASA film *Mars in 3D*. His recording *Michael McNabb: Computer Music* was the first produced entirely by digital processing methods.

WORKS

Solstice, orch, 1975; Having Lost my Sons (J. Wright), speaker, ens, 1976; Laughing Buddha, perc ens, 1976; Dreamsong, taped S, cptr, 1978; Mars Suite, cptr, 1979 [from film score Mars in 3D]; Love in the Asylum, cptr, 1981

STEPHEN RUPPENTHAL

MacNeil, Cornell (*b* Minneapolis, MN, 24 Sept 1922). Baritone. While working as a machinist, he performed in radio plays and sang minor roles on Broadway before winning a scholarship to the Hartt College of Music in Hartford, where he studied with Friedrich Schorr. He made his operatic début in March 1950 when Menotti chose him to sing the role of Sorel in the première of *The Consul* in Philadelphia. After appearing with a number of small American opera companies, he was engaged by the New York City Opera to sing Tonio (*Pagliacci*, 4 April 1953) and other roles in the Italian repertory. Guest appearances included his débuts at San Francisco (1955), Chicago (1957), and Mexico City (1957). His reputation was firmly established internationally in 1959, when he made his débuts at La Scala (as Don Carlo in *Ernani*, 5 March), and at the Metropolitan Opera (as Rigoletto, 21 March), in both cases substituting for indisposed singers. In 1960 he opened the Metropolitan season in the title role of the company's first production of Verdi's *Nabucco*, and has since sung there such roles as Amonasro (*Aida*), Barnaba (*La Gioconda*), Wagner's Dutchman, and Guy de Monfort (in Verdi's *Les vêpres siciliennes*). He has also sung with much success at Covent Garden (where he made his début as Macbeth in 1964), the Vienna Staatsoper, the Paris Opéra, and in other European houses.

MacNeil is a true Verdi baritone, gifted with a magnificent top register (though not always well knit to the middle); the high tessitura of Di Luna (*Il trovatore*), for example, is presented with a technical control that few contemporary singers can rival. He has been praised more for his pure and even legato than for his dramatic involvement, and it might be said that his many recordings present a better view of his art than his stage appearances.

BIBLIOGRAPHY

H. E. Phillips: "Backstage with Boccanegra," *Opera News*, xxxiii/7 (1968), 26
E. C. Mordden: "Big Mac," *Opera News*, xxxix/19 (1975), 16
"MacNeil, Cornell," *CBY 1976*
J. Hines: "Cornell MacNeil," *Great Singers on Great Singing* (Garden City, NY, 1982), 144

RICHARD BERNAS/R

Macon, Uncle Dave [David Harrison] (*b* Smart Station, TN, 7 Oct 1870; *d* Murfreesboro, TN, 22 March 1952). Country-music singer, banjoist, and comedian. He grew up in Nashville, where he became acquainted with vaudeville and circus performers who stayed at his father's hotel. He became a farmer and from 1900 to 1920 operated the Macon Midway Mule and Wagon Transportation Company. When competition from trucks put him out of business, he began playing banjo professionally. In 1923 he toured for Loew's Theaters with the fiddler and guitarist Sid Harkreader as part of a vaudeville show, and in 1924 made his first recordings for Aeolian; among the earliest releases were *Chewing Gum*, his most popular comedy song, and *Keep my skillet good and greasy*. In 1925 he made his first appearance on the "WSM Barn Dance" (renamed the "Grand Ole Opry" in 1927); he was the show's first vocal star, its most popular performer well into the 1940s, and a regular cast member until 1952. For his "Opry" appearances he was often backed by a string band, the Fruit Jar Drinkers; for sacred songs he renamed the group the Dixie Sacred Singers. During the 1930s Macon continued to record for several labels, often with Kirk and Sam McGee and his son Dorris Macon (1910–82; see illustration, p. 156); during this period he was known as the "Dixie Dewdrop." He appeared in the film *Grand Ole Opry* (1940).

Macon's style was a valuable link between that of 19th-century folk and popular music and 20th-century country music. Much of his repertory as well as his banjo-playing technique was derived

Uncle Dave Macon (seated right), with a group including Kirk McGee (fiddle), Sam McGee (banjo), Humphrey Bate (harmonica), Dorris Macon (guitar), and Alcyone Bate Beasley (ukulele)

from minstrel and vaudeville sources. He often accompanied his performances with clog-dance steps and high kicks, and shouted encouragement to his fellow performers. He was renowned for his irrepressible good humor and a large repertory of jokes as well as for doing visual tricks with his banjo. Macon was elected to the Country Music Hall of Fame in 1966.

RECORDINGS

(selective list)

Keep my skillet good and greasy (Voc. 14848, 1924); Chewing Gum/I'm going away to leave you (Voc. 14847, 1924); The Bible's true/He won the heart of my Sarah Jane (Voc. 14322, 1926); We are up against it now/I ain't got long to stay (Voc. 15447, 1926); The Cross-eyed Butcher and the Cackling Hen (Voc. 14353, 1926); From Earth to Heaven [with Sam McGee, guitar] (Brunswick 329, 1928); Wreck of the Tennessee Gravy Train [with Sam McGee, banjo and guitar] (OK 45507, 1930); Just one way to the pearly gates [with Delmore Brothers] (Bluebird 5296, 1935); Country Ham and Red Gravy (Bluebird 7951, 1938)

BIBLIOGRAPHY

R. Rinzler and N. Cohen: *Uncle Dave Macon: a Bio-discography*, John Edwards Memorial Foundation Special Series, iii (Los Angeles, 1970)
C. K. Wolfe: *The Grand Ole Opry: the Early Years, 1925–35* (London, 1975)
C. K. Wolfe: "Uncle Dave Macon," *Stars of Country Music*, ed. B. C. Malone and J. McCulloh (Urbana, IL, 1975), 40

BILL C. MALONE

McPartland [née Turner], **(Margaret) Marian** (*b* Slough, England, 20 March 1920). Jazz pianist. She left the Guildhall School of Music, London, to join a four-piano vaudeville act, and later performed for British and American troops during World War II. In Belgium in 1944 she met the cornetist Jimmy McPartland, whom she married and with whom she moved to the USA in 1946. Gradually overcoming the inborn resistance of American jazz musicians to her nationality and sex, she established her own trio, which first played in New York at the Embers Club (1950) and later at the Hickory House (1952–64). Known for her elegant modern style and remarkable technique, she has appeared at the major jazz venues, acted as host and producer of a nationally syndicated radio series, "Jazz Piano," and established her own record company, Halcyon. Since 1955 she has spent much time introducing jazz to schoolchildren. In the early 1980s she returned to classical music, performing Grieg's Piano Concerto throughout the country. Among her best-known compositions are *In the Days of our Love*, *Twilight World*, *So Many Things*, *With You in my Mind*, and *Ambiance*.

RECORDINGS

(selective list)

As leader: *Jazz at the Hickory House* (1952–3, Savoy 8032); *With You in Mind* (1957, Cap. T895), incl. With You in my Mind; *At the London House* (1958, Argo 640), incl. So Many Things; *Ambiance* (1970, Halcyon 703); *Marian McPartland Plays the Music of Alec Wilder* (1973, Halcyon 109); *From this Moment on* (1978, Conc. 86), incl. Ambiance; *At the Festival* (1979, Conc. 118), incl. In the Days of our Love
Duo with G. Shearing: *Alone Together* (1981, Conc. 171)

BIBLIOGRAPHY

W. Balliett: *Alec Wilder and his Friends* (Boston, 1974)
"McPartland, Marian," *CBY 1976*
L. Feather: "Marian McPartland," *Contemporary Keyboard*, iii/12 (1977), 63
J. Waz: "Marian McPartland: a Fine Romance," *Jazz Forum*, no.52 (1978), 34
L. Lyons: *The Great Jazz Pianists* (New York, 1983), 167

KAREN MONSON

McPhee, Colin (Carhart) (*b* Montreal, Que., 15 March 1900; *d* Los Angeles, CA, 7 Jan 1964). Composer, ethnomusicologist, and writer. He studied composition and piano at Peabody Conservatory with Harold Randolph and Gustav Strube (1918–21), then returned to Toronto for piano studies with Arthur Friedheim. In 1920 he gave the première of his Piano Concerto no.1 with the Peabody Orchestra and in 1924 performed his Piano Concerto no.2 with the Toronto New SO. From 1924 to 1926 he studied in Paris with Paul Le Flem and Isidore Philipp and then went to New York, where for five years he was an active participant in new-music societies and concerts. A decisive event in McPhee's career occurred in the late 1920s, when he first heard newly released recordings of the Balinese gamelan. He was inspired to travel to Bali in 1931 and remained there, with only a few interruptions, until late 1938. His pathbreaking research on Balinese music documented a decade when the island was still relatively free from outside influences and culminated in the writing of *Music in Bali* (1966), which remains the principal treatise on the island's music. McPhee studied thriving musical traditions, as well as those on the wane, by traveling around the island to work with a variety of orchestras and by turning his native-style house in Sayan into a gathering place for local musicians. He founded several ensembles, including a *gamelan semar pegulingan* and a *gamelan angklung*, to revive dying repertories. While in Bali he associated with a group of Western anthropologists and artists that included Gregory Bateson, Jane Belo, Claire Holt, Margaret Mead, and Walter Spies.

McPhee combined the roles of composer and scholar in his approach to Balinese music. He transcribed dozens of gamelan works for two pianos, solo piano, and flute and piano (a number of which he recorded with Britten and Barrère in 1941), and in 1936 he wrote *Tabuh-tabuhan*, his first major orchestral work to incorporate Balinese materials. It was first performed in the same year by Carlos Chávez and the Orquesta Sinfónica de México. After McPhee returned to New York early in 1939, he faced great difficulty in reestablishing and supporting himself. During the 1940s he worked for the Office of War Information (1945–7) and turned principally to prose as his creative medium. He wrote articles about Bali and reviews of scores and recordings for *Modern Music*, *Musical Quarterly*, and *Harper's*, and poetically captured the atmosphere of his stay in *A House in Bali* (1946). During this time he made a few unsatisfying attempts at musical composition, including incidental music for plays by Tennessee Williams and Eugene O'Neill and *Four Iroquois Dances* for orchestra. These works, together with most of his early music, were either destroyed or renounced by him. After *Tabuh-tabuhan* finally received its first American performance in 1953 (conducted by Stokowski), McPhee began to compose again. He received commissions from the Koussevitzky Foundation, the Louisville Orchestra, the United Nations, the Contemporary Music Society, Robert Boudreau's American Wind Symphony, and BMI. Other honors included a National Institute of Arts and Letters Award (1954) and Guggenheim and Bollingen fellowships. He joined the faculty at UCLA in 1960.

The hallmark of McPhee's musical style is an acute sensitivity to individual timbres coupled with a predilection for textures of multi-layered rhythms. These traits are present in his few surviving early pieces, especially the Concerto for Piano and Wind Octet (1928), a neoclassical work characterized by frequent explosive sound conjunctions, and they also continue in the compositions McPhee wrote after he left Bali. No experimentalist, McPhee stayed within traditional forms and tonal harmonies even after his imagination was fired by the gamelan. He delighted in making large, dramatic gestures and wrote principally for orchestra and piano. In *Tabuh-tabuhan*, his best-known composition, McPhee used a standard symphony orchestra and a "nuclear gamelan" of Western instruments (two pianos, celesta, xylophone, marimba, and glockenspiel) and two Balinese gongs. Much of the musical material in this and his later works, such as the Symphony no.2 and the Nocturne for Chamber Orchestra, was drawn from the many transcriptions he made in Bali – all of which sensitively transfer note-for-note the gamelan's intricate melodic interweavings to Western instruments.

WORKS

(all unpublished unless otherwise stated)

DRAMATIC

The Emperor Jones (incidental music, O'Neill), 1940, lost; Westport, CT, 5 Aug 1940

Battle of Angels (incidental music, Williams), 1940, lost; Boston, 1940

Film scores: Mechanical Principles, 1931, lost; H_2O, 1931, lost; Air Skills, 1957; Blue Vanguard, 1957; In our Hands, ?1957

Radio score: Broken Arrow, 1948, lost; CBS, 22 May 1948

ORCHESTRAL

Piano Concerto no.1 "La mort d'Arthur," 1920, lost; Baltimore, 26 May 1920

Piano Concerto no.2, 1923, lost; Toronto, 15 Jan 1924

Symphony no.1, 1930, lost

Tabuh-tabuhan, 2 pf, orch, 1936, pubd; Mexico City, 4 Sept 1936, cond. Chávez

Four Iroquois Dances, orch, 1944, pubd

Transitions, orch, 1954; Vancouver, 20 March 1955

Symphony no.2 "Pastorale," 1957; Louisville, 15 Jan 1958

Nocturne, chamber orch, 1958, pubd; New York, 3 Dec 1958

Concerto, wind, 1960, pubd; Pittsburgh, July 1960

Symphony no.3, 1960, inc.

CHORAL

Sea Shanty Suite (trad.), Bar, male vv, 2 pf, timp, 1929, pubd; New York, 13 March 1929

From the Revelation of St. John the Divine, male vv, 3 tpt, 2 pf, timp, 1936, lost; New York, 27 March 1936

OTHER WORKS

*c*40 transcrs. gamelan music, 2 pf and solo pf, 1931–62, incl. Balinese Ceremonial Music, 2 pf, 1934, 1938, pubd

2 transcrs. gamelan music, fl, pf, 1935–6

[Suite of Balinese transcrs.], 3 pf, cel, xyl, glock, vc, db; New York, 13 Jan 1947

Chamber: 4 Pf Sketches, op.1, 1916, pubd; 3 Moods, pf, 1924, lost; Pastorale and Rondino, 2 fl, cl, tpt, pf, ?1925, lost; Sarabande, pf, ?1925, lost; Invention, pf, 1926, pubd; Conc., pf, 8 wind, 1928, arr. 2 pf, 1957, pubd; Kinesis, pf, 1930, pubd; pf arrs. of works by Britten and Buxtehude; *c*25 juvenile pf works, lost

Songs: Arm, Canadians (V. Wyldes), 1v, pf, 1917, pubd; C'est la bergère Nanette, Cradle song, Petit chaperon rouge, Theris, all S, pf, ?1928, lost

MSS in *CLU-MUS*, *NN-L*

Principal publishers: Associated, Kalmus, Peters, G. Schirmer

WRITINGS

A House in Bali (New York, 1946/*R*1981)

A Club of Small Men (New York, 1948)

Maghi, musici e attori a Bali, trans. F. Cadeo (Milan, 1951)

Music in Bali (New Haven, CT, 1966/*R*1976)

BIBLIOGRAPHY

C. Reis: *American Composers of Today* (New York, 1930, rev. and enlarged 4/1947/*R*1977 as *Composers in America: Biographical Sketches*)

W. Riegger: "Adolph Weiss and Colin McPhee," *American Composers on American Music*, ed. H. Cowell (Stanford, CA, 1933/*R*1962), 36

H. Cowell, "Current Chronicle," *MQ*, xxxiv (1948), 410

C. Sigmon: "Colin McPhee," *ACAB*, xii/1 (1964), 15

C. J. Oja: "Colin McPhee: a Composer who Fell in Love with Bali," *New York Times* (7 Nov 1982), §H, p.19

R. Mueller: *Imitation and Stylization in the Balinese Music of Colin McPhee* (diss., U. of Chicago, 1983)

C. J. Oja: "Colin McPhee: a Composer Turned Explorer," *Tempo*, no.148 (1984), 2

D. Young: "Colin McPhee's Music: (1) From West to East," *Tempo*, no.150 (1984), 11

C. J. Oja: *Colin McPhee (1900–1964): a Composer in Two Worlds* (diss., CUNY, 1985)

CAROL J. OJA

McRae, Carmen (*b* New York, 8 April 1922). Jazz singer. She studied piano privately in her early years and began her career as a singer with Benny Carter's orchestra (1946). After singing with the Count Basie and Mercer Ellington bands in the late 1940s she worked at Minton's Playhouse in Harlem as an intermission singer and pianist. While there, she listened to and absorbed the sounds of bop, and came under the influence of Sarah Vaughan. She began to attract the attention of musicians in 1953 with her recordings for the Stardust and Venus labels. In the following year she won *Down Beat* magazine's new singer award and signed a recording contract with Decca, which issued her superb renditions of *Yardbird Suite*, *You Took Advantage of Me*, and *Suppertime* in 1955. Since then she has been an active performer at jazz clubs, concerts, and festivals.

McRae is among the most important female jazz vocalists in the group of singers that was directly influenced by bop. She has an immediately recognizable, "smoky" timbre, and performs popular ballads and jazz numbers with bop phrasing and inflections. She is especially inventive as a scat singer and has an instinctive feeling for rhythm. McRae is also a thoroughly competent jazz pianist in the bop style.

RECORDINGS

(selective list)

Suppertime, Yardbird Suite, on *By Special Request* (1955, Decca 8173); You Took Advantage of Me (1955, Decca ED2281); Little Things Mean a Lot, Exactly Like You, on *After Glow* (1957, Decca 8583); Love is a Simple Thing, Falling in Love with You, on *Something to Swing About* (1959, Kapp 1169); *Great American Songbook* (1971, Atl. 2-904); *As Time Goes By* (1973, Catalyst 7904); *You're Lookin at Me* (1983, Conc. 235)

BIBLIOGRAPHY

B. Gardner: "On the Threshold: Singer's Singer Carmen McRae," *Down Beat*, xxix/24 (1962), 19
R. J. Gleason: *Celebrating the Duke* (Boston, 1975), 118
L. Lyons: *The 101 Best Jazz Albums* (New York, 1980)
"Carmen McRae," *Swing Journal*, xxxv/2 (1981), 192
A. Taylor: *Notes and Tones: Musician to Musician Interviews* (New York, 1982)
"McRae, Carmen," *CBY 1983*

ED BEMIS

McReynolds Brothers. Country-music duo; *see* JIM AND JESSE.

McTell, Blind Willie (*b* Thomson, GA, *c*1898; *d* Milledgeville, GA, 19 Aug 1959). Blues singer, songster, and guitarist. Blind from birth, he was trained at schools for the blind in Georgia, New York, and Michigan. Most of his life was spent in Atlanta, though he traveled as far as Mexico in order to perform. His first recording, made in Atlanta, included *Mama 'tain't long fo' day* (1927, Vic. 21124), which revealed his effortless "bottleneck" slide style on the 12-string guitar. *Atlanta Strut* (1929, Col. 14657) is a ragtime dance theme with imitative, impressionistic guitar breaks and spoken narrative. There followed a long series of recordings with extremely varied instrumental accompaniments which established McTell as the most versatile of the "Piedmont" school; his voice was more "white" than that of many Georgia blues singers, but nevertheless ideally suited to the blues, as on *Death Cell Blues* (1933, Voc. 02577) with its excellent lyrics. In 1940 McTell was recorded for the Library of Congress in a session that showed the great breadth of his repertory, including the ballads *Chainey* and *Delia* (1940, Storyville 186). This songster aspect of his work was also evident when, 16 years later, he made his last recordings, which included the ribald *Beedle um bum* and a final version of his celebrated guitar rag *Kill it Kid* (both 1956, Bluesville 1040).

BIBLIOGRAPHY

D. Evans: "Blind Willie McTell," *Atlanta Blues* (John Edwards Memorial Foundation 106, 1979) [liner notes]

PAUL OLIVER

Macurdy, John (*b* Detroit, MI, 18 March 1929). Bass. After study at the Wayne State University Engineering College, he served as a radar-electronics instructor in the Air Force. Turning to music, he trained with Avery Crew and Boris Goldovsky, and in the latter's opera workshops at the Berkshire Music Center, Oglebay (West Virginia), and Pittsburgh. After appearances with companies in New Orleans and Santa Fe, he joined the New York City Opera in 1959 and moved to the Metropolitan Opera in 1962 (début as Samuele in *Un ballo in maschera*). He has appeared there annually since then, graduating in time to such assignments as King Marke, Hagen, Sarastro, and Gounod's Mephistopheles; he sang Ezra Mannon at the première of Marvin David Levy's *Mourning Becomes Electra* in 1967. In addition to engagements with most leading orchestras and opera companies in the USA (including the San Francisco Opera and the Lyric Opera of Chicago), he has appeared at Aix-en-Provence (Arkel, 1972), in Paris (Arkel, 1973), and at La Scala (Pizarro, 1974), as well as with Scottish Opera and in Geneva, Orange, Arles, Marseilles, Strasbourg, and Bonn. Although Macurdy may sometimes seem temperamentally bland, his singing is notable for its breadth of range and dynamics as well as evenness and warmth.

MARTIN BERNHEIMER/R

Maddox Brothers and Rose. Country-music group. The Maddox family left Alabama in 1933 as part of the great Okie migration during the Depression, and settled in the San Joaquin Valley in California. The children, Cal, Henry, Fred, Don, and Rose (*b* Boaz, AL, 15 Aug 1925), formed a group in which the first three brothers played respectively guitar and harmonica, mandolin, and double bass, Don was the comedian, and Rose the singer. They persuaded the producer of a regular country show on radio station KTRB in Modesto to allow them to appear, and for several years they played in honky tonks and at rodeos. In 1939 they began a year's engagement on a radio show that was syndicated throughout the West, but two of the brothers were drafted into the army, and it was not until 1946 that the Maddox Brothers and Rose resumed their performing activities. They then began a ten-year recording career during which they worked for three companies, Decca, Columbia, and 4-Star. Woody Guthrie's *Philadelphia Lawyer* was their most successful song, and they also had hits with the high-spirited and raucous *Momma says it's naughty* (1949) and *Old Black Choo Choo* (1952). By the time the group broke up in 1956 it had attracted a nationwide following through appearances on the "Louisiana Hayride" on station KWKH, Shreveport, and recordings and tours; its early experimentation with electric guitars and boogie-woogie rhythms helped to pave the way for rockabilly and rock-and-roll.

Rose Maddox continued to have chart successes as a soloist throughout the 1960s; they included *Gambler's Love* (1959), *Sing a little song of heartache* (1962), and *Down to the river* (1963), all recorded for Capitol. She also recorded with Buck Owens and, in bluegrass and traditional styles, with Bill Monroe, Don Reno, Red Smiley, and Donna Stoneman. By the late 1970s her style had become even more traditional, and she was recording for small specialist labels, such as Takoma and Arhoolie.

BIBLIOGRAPHY

K. Olesen: Liner notes, *Maddox Brothers and Rose* (Arhoolie 5016-17, 1976)

CHARLES K. WOLFE

Maddy, Joseph E(dgar) (*b* Wellington, KS, 14 Oct 1891; *d* Traverse City, MI, 18 April 1966). Music educator. He studied at Bethany College, Lindsborg, Kansas (1906–7), and the Wichita College of Music (1907–8), and then played viola in the Minneapolis SO from 1909 to 1914. He was director of the College of Music, Wichita Falls, Texas (1915–17), and taught wind instruments at the Metropolitan School of Music, Chicago

(1917–18), before working in the public schools of Rochester, New York (1918–20), and Richmond, Indiana (1920–24). After leaving Richmond he was supervisor of music in the Ann Arbor public schools and professor of music education at the University of Michigan until 1927. Under the auspices of the Music Supervisors National Conference, he organized the National High School Orchestra in 1926, which led to the founding of the National Music Camp at Interlochen, Michigan, with Thaddeus P. Giddings in 1928. (The camp was called the National High School Orchestra Camp until 1931.) In 1931 Maddy began radio instruction in music from the University of Michigan and from 1935 to 1939 broadcast instrumental music instruction on NBC. He was co-author, with W. Otto Miessner and Giddings, of many songbooks, instrumental music methods, and textbooks on instrumental music education. He was president of the Music Educators National Conference, 1936–8, and was a charter member of the Association for Education by Radio.

BIBLIOGRAPHY

N. L. Browning: *Joe Maddy of Interlochen* (Chicago, 1963)
Obituary, *New York Times* (19 April 1966)

GEORGE N. HELLER

Madeira [née Browning], **Jean** (*b* Centralia, IL, 14 Nov 1918; *d* Providence, RI, 10 July 1972). Contralto. She studied at the Juilliard School and, under her maiden name, made her début at the Chautauqua Opera in 1943 as Nancy in Flotow's *Martha*. In June 1947 she married the conductor Francis Madeira, and later that summer was chosen by Menotti to alternate with Marie Powers in the European tour of *The Medium*. She joined the Metropolitan Opera, making her début in 1948 as the First Norn (*Götterdämmerung*). From 1955 she sang mostly in Europe: she appeared as Clytemnestra (in Strauss's *Elektra*), one of her greatest roles, at Salzburg (1956), as Carmen at Aix-en-Provence (1957), and as Erda at Covent Garden, Bayreuth, and Munich. She created Circe in Dallapiccola's *Ulisse* in Berlin in 1968, and continued to sing until 1971. She had a rich, dark voice, and was a compelling figure on the stage.

BIBLIOGRAPHY

"Madeira, Jean (Browning)," *CBY 1963*

HAROLD ROSENTHAL

Mader, Clarence (Victor) (*b* Easton, PA, 23 Jan 1904; *d* Los Angeles, CA, 7 July 1971). Organist. The son of a minister, he became organist of St. Peter's Reformed Church in Easton at the age of 11. Charles Davis was his first teacher. After his family moved to California in 1920, he played at Holliston Avenue Methodist Church in Pasadena and studied with Homer Grunn. In 1926–7 he was a pupil of Lynnwood Farnam in New York. From 1929 to 1966 he served as organist and choirmaster of Immanuel Presbyterian Church in Los Angeles. He was also head of the Occidental College organ department (1955–68). Mader was active as a recitalist and much interested in the affairs of the American Guild of Organists. His compositions, which span his whole career, include an organ concerto. It is as a teacher of organists, however, that his name endures; he inspired devotion in his students, among whom were David Craighead, Thomas Murray, Orpha Ochse, and Ladd Thomas. His wife, Ruth Goodrich Mader, was also an active organist. The Clarence V. Mader Archive is in the UCLA Music Library; a catalogue was published in 1980.

VERNON GOTWALS

Madonna [Ciccone, Madonna Louise] (*b* Rochester, MI, 16 Aug 1959). Rock singer and songwriter, and film actress. She studied dance as a child and, for five semesters, at the University of Michigan. After moving to New York in the late 1970s, she studied and danced with Alvin Ailey and Pearl Lang, acted in underground films, and played with several rock groups. She lived for some time in Paris, toured with the disco singer Patrick Hernandez, then returned to New York, where she continued her musical career. Having begun to write her own songs, she signed a contract in 1982 with Sire Records and recorded a dance single, *Everybody*, with an accompanying promotional videotape. Her first album, *Madonna*, was issued in 1983; more than a million copies were sold, and two songs, *Borderline* and *Lucky Star*, became hit singles. In late 1984 the album *Like a Virgin* achieved even greater commercial success, as did single recordings of its title song and of *Material Girl*. In 1985 she won critical and popular acclaim for her portrayal of the title role in Susan Seidelman's film *Desperately Seeking Susan*; she also had a hit single with *Crazy for you* from the soundtrack of a film called *Vision Quest*, in which she did not appear. Madonna has a thin, forceful pop soprano and a knack for clever, catchy dance songs and arrangements. Her ability to capitalize on the mid-1980s fashion for pop music linked with provocative videos of considerable flair and originality has brought her wide recognition.

RECORDINGS
(selective list)

Everybody (Sire 29841, 1982); *Madonna* (Sire 23867, 1983); *Like a Virgin* (Sire 25157, 1984); Crazy for you (Geffen 29051, 1985)

BIBLIOGRAPHY

M. McKenzie: *Madonna: Lucky Star* (Chicago, 1985)
J. Skow: "Madonna Rocks the Land," *Time*, cxxv (27 May 1985), 74
D. Worrell: "Now: Madonna on Madonna," *Time*, cxxv (27 May 1985), 78 [interview]

JOHN ROCKWELL

Maeder, James G(aspard) (*b* Dublin, Ireland, *c*1809; *d* 28 May 1876). Pianist, composer, and teacher. By 1830 he was in London as singing coach to Joseph Wood. He toured the USA with Joseph and Mary Anne Wood in 1833–4 and then settled in Boston where, on 6 December 1834, he married Clara Fisher, a celebrated actress. The Maeders travelled extensively, but lived principally in New Orleans (1835–6), Providence (1838–9), Boston (1841–6), Albany (1849–51), and New York (1852–64). In these cities Maeder accompanied and coached singers, led theater orchestras, and composed and arranged music. After 1860 Maeder and his wife performed infrequently, devoting themselves primarily to teaching. His "grand fairy opera," *The Peri*, first performed in Boston on 10 February 1844, was based on an episode from Washington Irving's *Life of Columbus*; its scope and locale distinguish it from the ordinary extravaganzas of the period. And John Brougham's *Po-ca-hon-tas* (1855), with music "dislocated and re-set" by Maeder, was a landmark in the history of music theater. The scores of both these works have been lost.

BIBLIOGRAPHY

W. W. Clapp: *A Record of the Boston Stage* (Boston, 1853/*R*1968)
H. P. Phelps: *Players of a Century* (Albany, NY, 1890)
C. F. Maeder: *Autobiography* (New York, 1897/*R*1970)
G. C. D. Odell: *Annals of the New York Stage*, iii–xv (New York, 1928–49/*R*1970)

WILLIAM BROOKS

Maganini, Quinto (*b* Fairfield, CA, 30 Nov 1897; *d* Greenwich, CT, 10 March 1974). Composer, conductor, and flutist. He studied privately with Emilio Puyans, Georges Barrère, and Domenico Brescia, and at the American Conservatory at Fontainebleau with Boulanger (1926–7), also playing in the San Francisco SO (1917–19) and the New York SO (1919–28). Subsequently he worked as a conductor, in 1930 with the New York Sinfonietta, then from 1932 with his Maganini Chamber SO, with which he toured, and (1939–70) the Norwalk (Connecticut) SO. He wrote an opera *Tennessee's Partner* (given in 1942), many orchestral works, chamber pieces, and arrangements.

GUSTAVE REESE/R

Magnes [née Shapiro], **Frances** (*b* Cleveland, OH, 27 April 1919). Violinist. She comes from a long line of professional violinists, one of whom was a court musician to Czar Nicholas II. She began lessons at the age of six, first with her grandfather, then Herman Rosen, a former student of Auer. At 14 she made her début with the Cleveland Orchestra under Rodzinski, and continued her studies in New York with Persinger and Adolf Busch. Invited to become a member of the Busch Chamber Players, she toured the USA with that group in 1945–6 and recorded Bach's Concerto for two violins with Busch. In 1946 she made her recital début in New York at Carnegie Hall to critical acclaim, followed by appearances in England, France, and Israel in 1949. She was heard in Canada, South America, and Europe as well as the USA with major orchestras under conductors including Bernstein, Boult, Monteux, Mitropoulos, Jenkins, and others. Under Busch's influence she acquired a broad command of the classical tradition, but she also maintained a lively interest in contemporary music; among works first performed by (and dedicated to) her were Wolpe's Violin Sonata (1949) and Serly's Sonata for violin solo (in 1950), both of which she recorded, as well as the Violin Concerto no.2 by Ernő Dohnányi (14 February 1952, with the New York PO). Beginning in the 1960s many of her musical activities were centered around her home in Westchester County, New York; she was concertmaster of the Westchester SO under Jenkins in 1963–4, led the Baroque Chamber Orchestra of Scarsdale (1966–80), and taught. In May 1981 she appeared at Carnegie Hall in a revival of the Dohnányi concerto. Magnes plays with authority and vigor, commanding technique, and warm musical temperament.

BORIS SCHWARZ

Mahavishnu Orchestra. Jazz-fusion group. It was formed in summer 1971 by the guitarist JOHN MCLAUGHLIN; Mahavishnu was the spiritual name bestowed on McLaughlin by his guru. The group made its début in New York as a quintet with Jerry Goodman (violin), Jan Hammer (keyboards), Rick Laird (electric bass guitar), and Billy Cobham (drums). Their music incorporated various elements: the biting electronic sound, sustained high volume, and dance rhythms of hard rock; the virtuoso improvisation and complex meters of jazz; and spiritual, mantra-like ostinatos, borrowed from Indian religious traditions. A second, 11-piece group was formed in May 1974, brass, reeds, and strings being added to a central core whose members were, with the exception of the violinist Jean-Luc Ponty, weaker than before. Ponty left over a dispute about royalties in spring 1975, McLaughlin dismissed the additional players the following July, and the group completed its concert and recording commitments as a quartet. McLaughlin formed a new Mahavishnu Orchestra with Cobham in 1984.

RECORDINGS

(*selective list*)

The Inner Mounting Flame (1971, Col. KC31067); *Birds of Fire* (1972, Col. KC31996); *Apocalypse* (1974, Col. KC32957); *Mahavishnu* (1984, WB 25190)

BIBLIOGRAPHY

B. Korall: "My Goal's Beyond," *Melody Maker*, xlviii (17 Feb 1973), 13

J. P. Schaffer: "An Innermost Vision," *Down Beat*, xl/8 (1973), 11

C. Welch: "Music of the Gods," *Melody Maker*, xlviii (23 June 1973), 13

L. Cauffiel: "Mahavishnu Demystifies: McLaughlin Fires Orchestra," *Rolling Stone*, no.204 (15 Jan 1976), 14

BARRY KERNFELD

Mahler, David (*b* Plainfield, NJ, 13 Aug 1944). Composer. After studies at Concordia College (River Forest, Illinois; BA 1967), he taught and worked as a choir director in the Midwest for several years. His principal training in composition was at the California Institute of the Arts (MFA 1972) with James Tenney and Harold Budd. From 1975 to 1982 he was music director at And/Or, an alternative arts performance center in Seattle, where he produced many concerts, taught workshops in electronic music, and edited anthologies of music by local composers. He has received two NEA grants (1978, 1979). Mahler's interest in country-and-western, jazz, and gospel music is reflected in his compositions, which are often disarmingly simple and bridge the gap between popular and serious music. Works such as *Illinois Sleep* (1974) employ minimalist techniques in an extended format while other pieces, such as *King of Angels* (1978), based on an Elvis Presley song, are witty and concise.

WORKS

Wind Peace, tape, 1972; The Wonderful One-part Invention, org, 1974; Aviva, tape, 1974; Early Winters, 2 pf, 1974; Illinois Sleep, org, 1974; Winter Man, 5 tpt, 1975; A Rose Blooming for Charles Ives, pf, 1976; King of Angels, tape, 1978; Only Music can Save me Now, pf, 1978

Fantastic Slides for Thurman Munson, vn, vc, 1979; Independent Orders and Mystic Unions Abound, unspecified insts, 1980; Walt Disney, pf, toy pf, trbn, chorus of whistlers, 1981; Speech with Interpreter, tape, 1981; Singing in the Style of the Voice of the Poet, tape, 1982; Ty Cobb, pf, 1982; other works

Principal publishers: Soundings, Wind-up

INGRAM D. MARSHALL

Mahler, Fritz (*b* Vienna, Austria, 16 July 1901; *d* Winston-Salem, NC, 18 June 1973). Conductor and composer. A second cousin of Gustav Mahler, he studied conducting with Leopold Reichwein and musicology with Guido Adler at the University of Vienna (1920–24); during this time he also studied composition privately with Schoenberg and Berg. He was assistant conductor of the Vienna Volksoper (from 1921) and conducted summer orchestras in Bad Hall (1924–6). After further experience in Mannheim, Dresden, and Berlin, he became a conductor with the Danish Broadcasting Company in Copenhagen (1931–35). He immigrated to the USA in 1936 (becoming an American citizen in 1939), and made his New York début with the CBS SO on 18 August that year. He subsequently conducted the National Youth Administration Orchestra (1940–42), the Erie (Pennsylvania) PO (1947–53), and the Hartford SO (1953–64), with which he made several recordings. He taught conducting at the Juilliard Summer School from 1938 to 1953, during which time he was also director of its opera department. Throughout his career Mahler was guest conductor of many orchestras, including the Boston SO, and he conducted opera in Philadelphia and at La Scala; in the 1960s he toured Europe, South America, and Asia. He was known particularly for his interpretations of the music of Bruckner and Gustav Mahler. His own compositions include a symphonic poem, chamber music, and songs. He contributed frequently to musical periodicals and wrote a brief analysis of Berg's *Wozzeck* (1957).

GENE BIRINGER

Maidu. American Indians. They occupied the northern Sierra Nevada mountains and Sacramento Valley in north-central California (*see* INDIANS, AMERICAN, fig. 1). The Maidu comprised three main divisions: the mountain Maidu, the Nisenan (southern, or valley, Maidu), and the Konkow (northwestern, or foothills, Maidu). Their music, like that of other California Indians, was principally vocal, and singing was bound to religion and practical functions rather than viewed as an art form or as entertainment. Each ceremony had appropriate songs, and the percussion instruments used as rhythmic accompaniment tended to be linked with particular personages or functions.

The Maidu shared the Kuksu religion with their neighbors to the west (the POMO) and to the north (the WINTUN). In the Kuksu cult, disguised dancers and singers impersonated mythic deities. Among the Maidu Kuksu ceremonials followed an annual cycle beginning in the late autumn with an important ritual known as the Hesi Dance. Songs of the Hesi Dance cycle normally consisted of very short texts that were repeated a variable number of times. Their lyrics were often obscure, incorporating cryptic or archaic language that would make complete sense only to the initiated.

These simple, litany-type melodies were sung by a soloist or unison chorus and accompanied by the beat of a slit-drum (*kilemi*) made from a huge log. The log was hollowed out and placed over a trench in the rear of a large, semisubterranean assembly chamber in which Kuksu rituals were held. It produced a deep, booming sound when stomped upon by a dancer or beaten with a heavy club. Membrane-covered drums were unknown. The Hesi Dance may also have involved a form of ensemble music in which whistles made from the leg-bone of a crane or other large bird were played. Several dancers, each with a whistle of different pitch, played them in concert, using the set as a rudimentary panpipe (Densmore, 1958, p. 14f). The female puberty ritual (*wulu*) was another important ceremony with specific songs and dances; it lasted ten days, during which time the pubescent girl carried a deer-hoof rattle. This instrument was symbolically identified with her, just as the cocoon rattle was linked to the medicine man and the slit-drum to the Hesi Dance. Instruments and songs were generally more important for what they represented spiritually than for their musical function.

Maidu music and ceremonies were influenced by those of their neighbors to the south, the YOKUTS. Like them, the Maidu sang Hand Game songs and performed vocal music connected with the Annual Mourning Ceremony and various forms of shamanism; they also played the same instruments in similar ways. Maidu songs were short and repetitive, but they lacked the formal device of paired phrases that has been noted among the Yokuts, and the melodic compass of the songs was more narrow, generally a major 6th or less. As elsewhere in central California, the singing style was smooth and relaxed.

Most songs of the Hesi cycle are in duple meter; other genres are in triple or changing meter. Slow tempos (M.M. 55–65) predominated in the ceremonial songs; pentatonic scales are common, but many songs use only four pitches. Like the Yokuts the Maidu population was severely reduced by disease and their way of life destroyed by miners and other settlers during the Gold Rush of the 1850s. The survival of their music is documented in recordings made between 1965 and 1974 by Coyote Man. There are, however, considerable disparities between this contemporary evidence and earlier ethnographic accounts that attempted to describe Maidu traditions. Until more archival research is conducted their music will remain poorly comprehended and difficult for modern listeners to appreciate.

See also INDIANS, AMERICAN, esp. §I, 4(ii)(c).

DISCOGRAPHY

Songs of the California Indians, i: *Concow, Nisenan, Mountain Maidu* (Pacific Western Traders, 1975)

BIBLIOGRAPHY

A. L. Kroeber: *Handbook of the Indians of California*, Bureau of American Ethnology Bulletin, no. 78 (Washington, DC, 1925)

F. Densmore: *Music of the Maidu Indians of California* (Los Angeles, 1958)

W. Wallace: "Music and Musical Instruments," *Handbook of the North American Indians*, viii, ed. R. F. Heizer (Washington, DC, 1978)

RICHARD KEELING

Maier, Guy (*b* Buffalo, NY, 15 Aug 1892; *d* Santa Monica, CA, 24 Sept 1956). Pianist and teacher. He studied at the New England Conservatory, graduating in 1913, and with Schnabel in Berlin (1913–14). After making his American début in Boston in 1914, he formed a duo-piano team with LEE PATTISON in 1916; the two performed together regularly from 1919 to 1931, and a number of American composers, including John Alden Carpenter, Edward Burlingame Hill, and Leo Sowerby, dedicated works to them. Beginning in 1920, Maier promoted concerts for young people in which he not only performed (mostly descriptive pieces of the late 19th- and earlier 20th-century) but also talked about the music and told stories; later he used slides in a series of "Musical Journeys." Maier also wrote textbooks on piano playing, held special classes for teachers, and served as a contributing editor of *The Etude* from 1935 until shortly before his death. He taught at the University of Michigan (1924–31), the Juilliard School (1935–42), and UCLA (1946–56).

R. ALLEN LOTT

Mailman, Martin (*b* New York, 30 June 1932). Composer. He studied with Wayne Barlow, Rogers, and Hanson at the Eastman School (BM 1954, MM 1955, PhD 1960). Under the auspices of the Ford Foundation Young Composers Project he acted as composer-in-residence in the Jacksonville, Florida, high schools during 1959–61. He taught at the Brevard (North Carolina) Music Center (1960–61), West Virginia University (1963), and East Carolina College (1961–6) before being appointed professor of composition at North Texas State University. In 1954 he received an Edward Benjamin award for *Autumn Landscape*; Four Songs for Soprano won first prize in the 1966 Birmingham Arts Festival, and the Sinfonietta was awarded first prize in the Walla Walla SO anniversary competition in 1967. Mailman has been very active in the Contemporary Music Workshop (1959–72) and the Faculty for Comprehensive Musicianship workshops. His style follows in the lyric tradition of the American neoclassicists. Although not innovative, he achieves structural clarity and a satisfying balance between harmonic and contrapuntal functions.

WORKS

Opera: The Hunted (1, Mailman, after D. Friedkin, M. Fine), 1959

Orch: Autumn Landscape, 1954; Suite in 3 Movts, 1961; Sinfonietta, 1964; Generations 2, 3 str orch, perc, 1969; 3 syms., 1969, 1979, 1983; Vn Conc., 1982; other works

Band: 4 Miniatures, 1960; Geometrics I–V, 1961–76; Concertino, tpt, band, 1963; Liturgical Music, 1964; In memoriam Frankie Newton, 1970; Shouts, Hymns, and Praises, 1972; Decorations: Music for a Celebration, 1974; Exaltations, 1981; other works

Inst: Promenade, brass, perc, 1953; Str Qt, 1962; 4 Divisions, perc ens, 1966; Variations on a Short Theme, pf, 1966; Partita no.4, 9 pfmrs, 1967; In memoriam Silvio Scionti, pf, 1974; Wind Across the Nations, 1v, fl, gui, pf, perc, 1975; Clastics I–III, various insts, 1977–80; other chamber and pf works

Vocal: West Wind (Shelley), S, pf, 1956; 3 Madrigals (Shakespeare), chorus, 1960; 4 Songs, S, pf, 1962; Leaves of Grass (Whitman), nar, chorus, band, 1963; Shakespearean Serenade, chorus, 4 insts, 1968; Requiem, Requiem (R. Sale), solo vv, chorus, orch, 1970; Generations 3: Messengers (Mailman), 1v, children's choruses, band, 1977; Secular Hours (Mailman), chorus, 1982; other choral works

Other: incidental music, music for television

Principal publishers: Belwin-Mills, Boosey & Hawkes

DAVID COPE

Main, Hubert P(latt) (*b* Ridgefield, CT, 17 Aug 1839; *d* Newark, NJ, 7 Oct 1925). Composer, arranger, and editor of gospel songs. His father, Sylvester Main (1817–73), was a Methodist singing-school teacher, who from 1854 worked in New York assisting William Bradbury and Isaac Woodbury in compiling their Sunday-school collections. Hubert, musically trained by his father, began helping with editorial work in 1855. In 1864 he moved to Cincinnati to work as a musical arranger for the gospel song composer and publisher Philip Phillips, serving as assistant editor of the official Methodist *Hymn and Tune Book* (1866). The following year he formally joined Bradbury's publishing house in New York, and when the firm was reorganized after Bradbury's death (1868) as a partnership between Lucius H. Biglow and Sylvester Main, Hubert became its chief music editor; he retired from this post in 1922. During his time with BIGLOW & MAIN he edited, harmonized, and arranged music by virtually all the contemporary prominent gospel songwriters. He also composed about 1000 tunes for Sunday-school and gospel songs, of which the best-known are "We Shall Meet By and By" (for John Atkinson's text "We shall meet beyond the river") and "Ellesdie" (sung to Henry F. Lyte's "Jesus, I my cross have taken"). Main was a widely respected authority on American hymns and tunes. He amassed a library of over 4000 volumes of music, mostly tunebooks, the bulk of which he sold to the Newberry Library, Chicago, in 1891.

BIBLIOGRAPHY

T. Brown and H. Butterworth: *The Story of the Hymns and Tunes* (New York, 1906)

J. H. Hall: *Biography of Gospel Song and Hymn Writers* (New York, 1914/*R*1971), 141

G. C. Stebbins: *Reminiscences and Gospel Hymn Stories* (New York, 1924/*R*1971), 294

R. G. McCutchan: *Our Hymnody* (New York, 2/1937), 297

PAUL C. ECHOLS

Mainstream jazz. A term coined in the 1950s by the writer on jazz Stanley Dance to describe the work of contemporary musicians working in the swing idiom of the 1930s and 1940s. However, it is now more widely used of any jazz improvised on chord sequences in the essentially solo style developed by Louis Armstrong and others in the late 1920s. Some writers have broadened it further to apply to jazz-rock and other fusion styles, but most would exclude the free or aleatory jazz of the avant garde, rock-based jazz, and dixieland and other traditional forms. *See also* JAZZ, §V, 9.

JAMES LINCOLN COLLIER

Majeske, Daniel (Harold) (*b* Detroit, MI, 17 Sept 1932). Violinist. Having studied violin from the age of four, he made his recital début when he was 13 and three years later appeared as a soloist with the Detroit SO. He won a four-year scholarship to the Curtis Institute, where he studied with Ivan Galamian. Having joined the Cleveland Orchestra in 1955, he was made concertmaster in 1969, a post he still holds; he is also the first violinist of the Cleveland Orchestra String Quartet, which was founded in 1971, and has made many appearances as a soloist. Since 1965 Majeske has been on the faculty of the Cleveland Music School Settlement as both teacher of violin and performance coach, and he gives frequent master classes in Cleveland and elsewhere. In 1976 he recorded Paganini's 24 Caprices op.1 for solo violin; the same year he served as concertmaster of the Casals Festival Orchestra in Puerto Rico. He owns the "Marquis de Riviera" Stradivari violin, which dates from 1718. His playing is notable for its smoothness of line, and he is scrupulous in his musicianship.

ROBERT FINN

Makah. American Indian group of Cape Flattery, Washington state; *see* NOOTKA.

Makeba, Miriam (*b* Prospect, nr Johannesburg, South Africa, 4 March 1932). Folk and popular singer. As a child she learned traditional African tribal music and jazz-influenced popular music. She spent several years as a band singer and actress and first attracted attention when she sang the leading role in the African opera *King Kong* in London in 1959. She then came to the USA, where she achieved a national reputation performing in New York nightclubs and on television, introducing contemporary African music to enthusiastic American audiences. Her concerts and albums demonstrated eclectic taste, including West Indian and Israeli folk music as well as Broadway show tunes. She became best known, however, for her interpretations of such traditional and modern songs of the Xhosa and Zulu peoples as the robust *Click Song*, where her strong, dynamic singing recreated the material in a powerful, sophisticated, Western, urban idiom. She was also capable of sensitive interpretation in such gentle songs as the Indonesian lullaby *Suliram*, and she performed anti-Apartheid protest songs in her campaign against the South African regime. Among her many albums *The Best of Miriam Makeba* (1968) demonstrates her varied talents to good effect. Makeba married the American black activist Stokeley Carmichael, with whom she moved to Guinea; since that time she has performed mostly in Africa and Europe.

BIBLIOGRAPHY

SouthernB

M. Bracker: "Xhosa Songstress," *New York Times Magazine*, cix (28 Feb 1960), 32

"Good to my Ear," *Time*, lxxv (1 Feb 1960), 52

G. Hoefer: "Caught in the Act," *Down Beat*, xxvii/2 (1960), 41

"With a Touch of Zulu," *Newsweek*, lv (25 Jan 1960), 84

"Makeba, Miriam," *CBY 1965*

M. Makeba: *The World of African Song* (Chicago, 1971)

S. Gayle: "Makeba at 50," *Essence*, xiii/3 (1982), 62

CRAIG A. LOCKARD

Malas, Spiro (*b* Baltimore, MD, 28 Jan 1935). Bass-baritone. He studied singing with Elsa Baklor and was coached by Ivor Chichagov. After making both his stage début (at the Baltimore Opera in 1959) and his first appearance with the New York City

Opera (5 October 1961) in *comprimario* roles in Puccini's *Gianni Schicchi*, he came to the attention of Richard Bonynge and was asked to tour Australia with the Sutherland/Williamson International Grand Opera Company in 1965. For his Covent Garden début the following year he played Sulpice in Donizetti's *La fille du régiment*, the same role he sang in his first performance at the Metropolitan Opera on 8 October 1983. In his first season at the Lyric Opera of Chicago he sang Rossini's Assur (*Semiramide*) and Dr. Bartolo (1971). A leading bass-baritone of the City Opera, he has appeared there as General Boom in *The Grand Duchess of Malfi*, Falstaff in both the Verdi opera and Nicolai's *Die lustigen Weiber von Windsor*, Mozart's Figaro and Leporello, and Frank in Johann Strauss's *Die Fledermaus*. He has performed with major companies in Rome, Naples, Salzburg, Vienna, and Florence, and has appeared in several television productions and with many leading symphony orchestras; in recital he is occasionally joined by his wife, the soprano Marlene Kleinman. Most of his recordings have been made in conjunction with Sutherland and Bonynge. Malas's voice is not large, but it has a natural beauty that overcomes the lack of impact. The lowest tones tend to be lost in large houses, but he compensates for this by his well-thought-out characterizations. He is currently a member of the faculty of the Peabody Conservatory.

BIBLIOGRAPHY

Q. Eaton: "Spiro Malas," *Opera News*, xxxiv/26 (1970), 12

RICHARD LeSUEUR

Malcolm, Alexander (*b* ?Edinburgh, Scotland, 25 Dec 1685; *d* Queen Anne County, MD, 15 June 1763). Scottish theorist and teacher. His father was a minister in Edinburgh (1681–7) so he is likely to have spent his childhood there. As a young man, Malcolm devoted much time to teaching mathematics and related disciplines and to compiling various treatises, read both in Europe and America; three such treatises were published, in 1718, 1730 and 1731. It was his *Treatise of Musick: Speculative, Practical and Historical* (Edinburgh, 1721, 1775/*R*1969), however, which established his musical reputation. Relying on the writings of Descartes, Kircher, Mersenne, and others, Malcolm's object was to "gather together in one system what lay scattered in several treatises." Hawkins considered it "one of the most valuable treatises on the subject of theoretical and practical music to be found in any of the modern languages."

By 1734 Malcolm had immigrated with his two sons to New York where, as master of the grammar school, he advertised, in the *New York Gazette*, his concern for public education. From 1740 he was in Marblehead, Massachusetts, as rector of St. Michael's Church. Because of ill-health and insufficient income, Malcolm decided to seek a warmer climate and in 1749 accepted the rectorship offered him at St. Anne's Parish Church, Annapolis, Maryland. Several weeks later he joined the Tuesday Club, an organization founded in 1745, whose purpose as expressed in the minutes of its meetings was to "meet, converse, laugh, drink, differ, argue, pun, sing, dance, and fiddle together." Malcolm was not a composer, but was often asked to play his violin and flute. In 1754 he was appointed rector of St. Paul's Parish Church in Queen Anne County, Maryland, and later he was also appointed master of the Free School there. He was forced to resign that position in 1759 because of his disputes with the school board about what was to be taught in the school, and about his inability to attract a sufficient number of students.

BIBLIOGRAPHY

M. Lloyd, Jr.: "Alexander Malcolm, Writer on Mathematics and Music," *Scottish Notes and Queries*, 3rd ser., vi (1928), 234
M. Maurer: "Alexander Malcolm in America," *ML*, xxxiii (1952), 226
R. Stone: *An Evaluative Study of Alexander Malcolm's "Treatise of Music": Speculative, Practical and Historical* (diss., Catholic U., 1974)
J. R. Heintze: "Alexander Malcolm: Musician, Clergyman, and Schoolmaster," *Maryland Historical Magazine*, lxxiii (1978), 226

JAMES R. HEINTZE

Malecite [Maliseet]. American Indian tribe of the WABANAKI confederacy.

Malfitano, Catherine (*b* New York, 18 April 1948). Soprano. Her father, Joseph Malfitano, is a violinist in the Metropolitan Opera Orchestra. She was trained at the Manhattan School (BA 1971). After making her professional début at the Central City Opera in 1972 as Verdi's Nannetta, she sang Rosina (*Il barbiere di Siviglia*) with the Minnesota Opera Company during the 1972–3 season. From 1973 to 1979 she sang regularly with the New York City Opera. She made her European début as Mozart's Susanna at the 1974 Holland Festival, her Metropolitan Opera début as Gretel in 1979, and her Vienna Staatsoper début as Violetta in 1982. She has performed with most of the major American opera companies, and sang the leading roles in the premières of Conrad Susa's *Transformations* (1973), Floyd's *Bilby's Doll* (1976), and Pasatieri's *Washington Square* (1976). She is also a notable Mozart performer, and appeared as Servilia in *La clemenza di Tito* for the Unitel film of the opera, conducted by James Levine (having sung the same role for her Salzburg début in 1976). In 1984 she made her début with the New York PO. Malfitano has a pure, rich voice remarkable for its ease of phrasing, which makes her especially suited to such roles as Violetta, and Puccini's Liù and Mimì.

MICHAEL WALSH

Malibran [née García], **Maria (Felicia)** (*b* Paris, France, 24 March 1808; *d* Manchester, England, 23 Sept 1836). Spanish mezzo-soprano. She was the elder daughter of Manuel García, with whom she studied singing from the age of 15, and sister of Manuel García and Pauline Viardot (both of whom became outstanding teachers). Malibran made her début in London on 7 June 1825 as Rosina in *Il barbiere di Siviglia*. Five months later she traveled with her father's opera company to New York, where she participated in several operas by Rossini, Mozart's *Don Giovanni*, and a number of other works at the Park Theatre. Unquestionably the finest singer that Americans had yet heard, she electrified audiences with her fresh voice, pure tones, and flexible execution of ornaments; not a little of her popularity was owing as well to her admirable figure, convincing dramatic gesticulations, and ability to project strong emotions.

On 23 March 1826 she married Eugène Malibran, a French merchant, in order to free herself from her despotic father. After García and his company left the country, she remained in New York and appeared in a number of English operas, including Thomas Arne's *Love in a Village* and Horn's and Braham's *The Devil's Bridge* at the Bowery Theatre. She also became a soloist at Grace Church, sang in Adrien Boieldieu's *Jean de Paris* (1827), and gave concerts in and around New York, in which she presented operatic arias, Irish airs, and improvisations. After her husband went bankrupt, Malibran made a last appearance in New York on 28 October 1827 and then sailed for Europe, where for the remainder of her brief life she sang to great acclaim in Paris, Milan, Rome, Naples, Bologna, and London. She married the violinist Charles-Auguste de Bériot in 1936, but died half a year later from an illness that resulted from injuries she had sustained in a riding accident.

BIBLIOGRAPHY

I. Nathan: *Memoirs of Madame Malibran de Bériot* (London, 1836)
Countess M. Merlin: *Madame Malibran* (Brussels, 1838)
——: *Memoirs of Madame Malibran* (London, 1840)
H. Pleasants: "Maria Malibran," *The Great Singers* (New York, 1966), 146
H. Bushnell: *Maria Malibran: a Biography of the Singer* (University Park, PA, 1979)

NICHOLAS E. TAWA

Malkin, Joseph (*b* Propoisk, nr Odessa, Ukraine, 24 Sept 1879; *d* New York, 1 Sept 1969). Cellist. After early training in Odessa, he entered the Paris Conservatoire in 1895, winning the *premier prix* in 1898. Following a tour of France and Germany, he was first cellist with the Berlin Philharmonic under Arthur Nikisch (1902–8). He made his American début on 28 November 1909 at the Manhattan Opera House, playing one of Saint-Saëns' concertos, then toured the USA as a member of the Brussels Quartet. From 1914 to 1919 he was first cellist with the Boston SO, and from 1919 to 1922 with the Chicago SO. He then formed the Malkin Trio with his brothers Jacques (*b* Slobodka, nr Odessa, 16 Dec 1875; *d* New York, 8 Dec 1964), violin, and Manfred (*b* Odessa, 11 Aug 1884; *d* New York, 8 Jan 1966), piano. Malkin also toured with the soprano Geraldine Farrar. In 1933 he founded the Malkin Conservatory of Music in Boston and was its director until it closed in 1943. He then returned to orchestral work, playing with the New York PO until 1949. In 1961 Malkin received the first Piatigorsky Award from the Violoncello Society of New York. He published several arrangements and studies for cello.

GENE BIRINGER

Mallard. The name under which the Magic Band of CAPTAIN BEEFHEART made recordings independently in the 1970s.

Mallet, Francis (*d* Boston, MA, 3 Aug 1834). Organist, singer, publisher, and composer. He was probably of French origin, and may have immigrated to the USA from London. He lived in Boston from 1793 to 1813, in New York in 1819 and 1820, and again in Boston from 1827 to 1832. (The Francis D. Mallet listed in Boston directories from 1818 to 1825 and in New York from 1829 to 1832 as a dancing teacher is not the same man.) His first public concert appearances in the USA were in Philadelphia and Newport, Rhode Island, in 1793. In the same year he settled in Boston, where he served as church organist and sang and played in concerts. His reputation as a performer rested mainly on his singing of oratorios, especially *Messiah*. In 1801, with Gottlieb Graupner and Filippo Trajetta, he established the first conservatory of music in the USA. The "Conservatorio" or "musical academy" in Rowe's Lane operated only from 1801 to 1802; during this time Graupner and Mallet were publishing partners, issuing some 20 items. From 1803 to 1807 Mallet published music independently and was a distributor in Boston for the Philadelphia publishers Carr and Schetky; he also sold American and English pianos from his "musical repository" on Devonshire Street (1805–7).

Mallet's few known compositions are settings of sentimental or patriotic texts: *Rule New England* (1802), *The Negroe's Humanity* (1802), *The Pride of our Plain* (1802), and *The Serenade* (*c*1820). While not a distinguished performer and of little importance as a composer, his contributions to musical instruction, performance, and publishing in Boston are significant; he was one of the few professional musicians who sustained the musical life of the city in the late 18th century and the early 19th. His daughter Sarah, a pianist and singer, was active in Salem, Massachusetts; the two performed Kočwara's *The Battle of Prague* together at a concert in 1805.

BIBLIOGRAPHY

H. Brooks: *Olden-time Music: a Compilation from Newspapers and Books* (Boston, 1888)
O. G. T. Sonneck: *Early Concert-life in America (1731–1800)* (Leipzig, 1907/*R*1978)
C. M. Ayars: *Contributions to the Art of Music in America by the Music Industries of Boston, 1640 to 1936* (New York, 1937/*R*1969)
H. E. Johnson: *Musical Interludes in Boston, 1795–1830* (New York, 1943)
R. J. Wolfe: *Secular Music in America, 1801–1825: a Bibliography* (New York, 1964)
——: *Early American Music Engraving and Printing* (Urbana, IL, 1980)

ANNE DHU SHAPIRO

Malm, William P(aul) (*b* La Grange, IL, 6 March 1928). Ethnomusicologist. He studied composition at Northwestern University (BM 1949, MM 1950) and began his teaching career at the University of Illinois in 1950. After serving as an instructor at the US Naval School of Music (1951–3), he resumed graduate studies at UCLA (PhD 1959), where he also taught (1958–60). Since 1960 he has been on the faculty at the University of Michigan, where he was appointed professor of music in 1966.

Malm specializes in Asian ethnomusicology, particularly music for the dance and Japanese music. His monograph *Japanese Music and Musical Instruments* (1959) is the first scholarly and comprehensive survey of its subject in English; *Nagauta: the Heart of Kabuki Music* (1963), which grew out of his doctoral dissertation, is one of the first detailed English-language studies of a particular genre of Japanese music. Other studies include *The Special Characteristics of Gagaku* (1971) and, with J. Brandon and D. Shively, *Studies in Kabuki* (1977). He is the author of a general survey of Asian music, *Music Cultures of the Pacific, the Near East and Asia* (1967, 2/1977).

PAULA MORGAN

Malotte, Albert Hay (*b* Philadelphia, PA, 19 May 1895; *d* Hollywood, CA, 16 Nov 1964). Composer, lyricist, and organist. The son of a choirmaster, he was a boy chorister and studied piano and organ at an early age. He continued his training in Europe, working as a theater organist for motion-picture houses, and studied composition with Georges Jacob in Paris. After returning to the USA he moved to Hollywood, where he opened a school in 1927 to train theater organists. However, the introduction of sound into films forced him to close his school the following year. He joined Walt Disney's studio as a composer in April 1935 and later became music director. He composed the scores for 15 of Disney's animated films during the 1930s, including five of the *Silly Symphonies* series and *Ferdinand the Bull* (1938). Though film soundtracks and songs comprise the major part of his output, he also wrote two ballets (*Little Red Riding Hood*, *Carnival of Venice*) and sacred music works for solo voices and for chorus; he is best known for his setting of The Lord's Prayer (1935). His manuscript scores are held at the Library of

Congress and his papers at the Enoch Pratt Free Library, Baltimore.

PAUL C. ECHOLS

Mamas and the Papas. Folk-pop vocal group. Its members were John Phillips (*b* Parris Island, nr Port Royal, SC, 30 Aug 1935), singer and guitarist; Dennis Doherty (*b* Halifax, NS, 29 Nov 1941), singer; (Holly) Michelle Phillips (née Gilliam) (*b* Long Beach, CA, 6 April 1944); and Cass Elliot (*b* Baltimore, MD, 19 Sept 1943; *d* London, England, 29 July 1974), singer. The group was formed in New York in 1965, and began recording for the Dunhill label the following year. Its first two albums, *If you Can Believe your Eyes and Ears* and *The Mamas and the Papas* (both from 1966), each sold more than one million copies and contained several songs that became successful singles. The Mamas and the Papas' music was an intricate, richly harmonized brand of psychedelic folk-pop, which was sophisticated for its time. Their material, most of which was written by John Phillips (whose *San Francisco*, recorded in 1967 by Scott Mackenzie, became the anthem of the San Francisco "flower people"), consisted of utopian, faintly melancholy songs, such as *California Dreamin'* and *Monday, Monday*, with flowing melodies and light, jaunty rhythms; their close folk harmonies were modeled after those of Peter, Paul and Mary but were considerably richer. The elaborate productions (by Lou Adler) on their albums prepared the way for the opulent recording style of such groups as Fleetwood Mac in the 1970s. The Mamas and the Papas helped to organize, and performed at, the Monterey (California) Pop Festival in 1967; they disbanded the following year. Phillips re-formed the group briefly in 1970, then again in 1982 with his daughter Mackenzie Phillips, Doherty, and Elaine "Spanky" McFarlane.

RECORDINGS

(selective list; all recorded for Dunhill)

If you Can Believe your Eyes and Ears (50006, 1966), incl. California Dreamin', Monday, Monday; *The Mamas and the Papas* (50010, 1966), incl. Dancing in the street, Words of Love; *Deliver* (50014, 1967); *A Gathering of Flowers* (50073, 1970)

STEPHEN HOLDEN

Mambo. A social dance created and popularized in the USA by the Cuban dance-band leader Perez Prado in the late 1940s. The mambo is derived from Caribbean dance forms and jazz. The two partners stand facing each other with knees bent and perform kicks, shimmies, and hip undulations; the dance step rests on beat four. Music for the mambo is written in 4/4 and is characterized by the rhythmic pattern shown in ex. 1; an occasional vocalized "ugh!" became a hallmark of the Prado band.

Ex.1 A typical mambo rhythm

BIBLIOGRAPHY

P. Buckman: *Let's Dance: Social, Ballroom & Folk Dancing* (New York, 1978)

J. S. Roberts: *The Latin Tinge: the Impact of Latin American Music on the United States* (New York, 1979), 123

PAULINE NORTON

Mamlok, Ursula (*b* Berlin, Germany, 1 Feb 1928). Composer and teacher. She studied piano and composition as a child in Berlin; when her family moved to Ecuador for a year she continued her studies there. After immigrating to the USA in 1941, she finished her schooling in New York, where she has since lived. She became an American citizen in 1945. At the Mannes College (1942–6) she was a pupil of Szell, and at the Manhattan School of Music (BM and MM 1958) she studied with Giannini; she also received private instruction from Wolpe, Sessions, Steuermann, and Shapey. She has taught at New York University (1967–76), Kingsborough Community College (1972–5), and the Manhattan School (from 1976). Her awards include two NEA grants (1974, 1981) and recording grants from the Martha Baird Rockefeller Fund for Music and the American Academy and Institute of Arts and Letters (both 1981). She has received a number of commissions, including two from Sigma Alpha Iota.

Mamlok has always shown an affinity for chamber music and piano works, and has written many teaching pieces in these media. As a young composer she was greatly influenced by Schoenberg and his circle. The difficult and uncompromising String Quartet (1962) in particular invites comparison with the works of Carter. Elegantly crafted, her music has considerable nuance and delicacy as well as dramatic intensity. In her own words, she has consolidated "old and new techniques which best serve to express the work at hand." Mamlok's music has been performed by major soloists and chamber ensembles in the USA, South America, and Europe. Perhaps most frequently presented have been her String Quartet, Woodwind Quintet, and the later *Panta Rhei* and *When Summer Sang*. The last was chosen to represent the USA at the 1984 International Rostrum of Composers.

WORKS

Orch: Conc., str, 1950; Grasshoppers (6 Humoresques), 1956; 4 German Songs, medium v, str orch, 1957; Ob Conc., 1976

Chamber: Ww Qnt, 1955; Sonatina, 2 cl, 1957; Variations, fl, 1961; Composition, vc, 1962; Designs, vn, pf, 1962; Str Qt, 1962; Stray Birds, S, fl, vc, 1963; Concert Piece for 4, fl, ob, va, perc, 1964; Sculpture I, pf, 1964; Capriccios, ob, pf, 1967; Haiku Settings, S, fl, 1967; Polyphony, cl, 1968; Sintra, a fl, vc, 1969; Variations and Interludes, perc qt, 1971; Polyphony II, eng hn, 1972; Sextet, fl + pic, cl, b cl, vn, db, pf, 1978; Festive Sounds, ww qnt, 1978; When Summer Sang, fl, cl, vn, vc, pf, 1980; Panta Rhei (Time in Flux), vn, vc, pf, 1981; Str Qnt, 1981; Fantasie Variations, vc, 1982; From my Garden, no.1, vn + crotales, 1983, no.2, ob, hn, pf/hpd, crotales, no.3, va + crotales, 1984; other works for solo inst or small ens

Other: songs; 2 choruses; Sonar Trajectory, tape, 1967; teaching pieces

Principal publishers: ACA, C. F. Peters

BARBARA A. PETERSEN

Mana Zucca [Zuckermann, Augusta; Zuckermann, Gussie] (*b* New York, 25 Dec 1885; *d* Miami, FL, 8 March 1981). Composer and pianist. She changed her name to Mana Zucca in her teens and became a protégée of the pianist and teacher Alexander Lambert; according to her unpublished memoirs she performed with major orchestras in New York before the age of ten (although this and other claims in her memoirs have not been verified). In 1902 she played an arrangement of Liszt's 14th Hungarian Rhapsody with Frank Damrosch as part of his concert series for young people at Carnegie Hall. About 1907 she went to Europe, where she met several prominent musicians and gave successful concert tours with the Spanish violinist Juan Manon. Her lively descriptions of Teresa Carreño, Ferruccio Busoni, Leopold Godowsky, and the composition teacher Max Vogrich were published in American music magazines. She also performed as a singer, notably in Franz Lehár's *Der Graf von Luxemburg* in London (1919). After her marriage in 1921, and especially after 1941, Mana Zucca's musical activities were concentrated in her home town of Miami.

On her return to the USA, Mana Zucca began to publish her compositions after 1915. Her privately issued catalogue of published works lists approximately 390 titles (all undated), though she claimed to have published around 1100 works and to have written 1000 more. Included in the catalogue are the operas *Hypatia* and *Queue of Ki-Lu* (both *c*1920), the Piano Concerto op.49 (1919) and Violin Concerto op.224 (1955), 172 songs, 3 choral works, over 20 chamber works, and numerous educational pieces. She was a gifted melodist. Many of her songs were performed by leading singers in the 1920s and 1930s: Gadski favored the *Kinder-Lieder*; Galli-Curci often sang *Le petit papillon*; and the most famous, *I Love Life* (1923), was performed by Tibbett, John Charles Thomas, and Nelson Eddy. *Honey Lamb*, *There's Joy in My Heart*, *Time and Time Again*, and *The Big Brown Bear* were also well known. Many of her songs with Yiddish texts, among them *Rachem* (1919) and *Nichevo* (1921), were dramatic set-pieces. Mana Zucca's more serious ambitions as a composer met limited yet noteworthy recognition: the Cincinnati SO performed *Novelette* and *Fugato humoresque* in 1917; the New York PO also played the latter piece in 1917; Mana Zucca herself gave the first performance of her Piano Concerto on 20 August 1919 with the Los Angeles SO; and in 1955 the American SO gave the première of the Violin Concerto. Her manuscripts and papers are at the University of Miami; her principal publishers are Boston Music, Congress Music, and G. Schirmer.

BIBLIOGRAPHY

"Mana Zucca, Humorist," *Musical Courier*, lxxv/3 (1917), 42
H. Brower: "American Women Pianists: their Views and Achievements," *MusAm*, xxviii/26 (1918), 18
M. Stanley: "Mana Zucca tells why Rachem was written," *MusAm*, xxxi/4 (1919), 19
J. T. Howard: *Our American Music* (New York, 1931, rev. 4/1965)

JUDITH TICK

Mancini, Henry (*b* Cleveland, OH, 16 April 1924). Arranger, composer, conductor, and pianist. He learned flute and piano as a child, and later studied with the theater conductor and arranger Max Adkins in Pittsburgh. In 1942 he enrolled at the Juilliard Graduate School, but his studies were interrupted by military service. After the war he worked as a pianist and arranger for the Tex Beneke Orchestra and studied privately in Los Angeles with Krenek, Castelnuovo-Tedesco, and Sendrey. He began composing for films in 1952, when he became a staff composer for Universal; by the time his contract was terminated in 1958 he had contributed to more than 100 films. He continued to devote much time to composing for films and television, and established a longstanding collaboration with the director Blake Edwards. Many of his scores have proved highly popular, and Mancini frequently rewrites soundtrack material for issue on albums, some of which (e.g., *The Thorn Birds*, recorded with Jean-Pierre Rampal) have become best-sellers. He also enjoys a successful career as a guest pianist and conductor of "pops" orchestras.

Starting in the late 1950s, Mancini made innovative and sophisticated use of jazz idioms, especially cool jazz – as in his scores for the television series *Peter Gunn* and the film series *The Pink Panther* (in which he also demonstrated his great wit). At the same time he composed many memorable songs, notably for *Breakfast at Tiffany's* ("Moon River"), *The Days of Wine and Roses*, and *Charade* (all with lyrics by Johnny Mercer). These themes, used with effective restraint in the films, exemplify his lucid, refined melodic style. But some of his most ambitious and unusual music has been composed for films that failed commercially (e.g., *The Molly Maguires*, *The Night Visitor*, and *The White Dawn*). Mancini is skilled in writing for small ensembles as well as orchestral forces, and in his less fully scored works produces some novel instrumental colors. He is able to move from a light, popular idiom to a heavier, dramatic style to accommodate the demands of a particular film. He has written a practical guide to orchestration, *Sounds and Scores* (1962).

WORKS
(selective list)

Collection: *Henry Mancini Songbook*, ed. M. Okun (n.p., 1981)

Film scores: more than 70, contributions to more than 100, incl. The Glenn Miller Story (as arranger), 1953; Touch of Evil, 1958; Breakfast at Tiffany's, 1961; The Days of Wine and Roses, 1962; Experiment in Terror, 1962; Hatari, 1962; Charade, 1963; The Pink Panther, 1964; Two for the Road, 1967; The Molly Maguires, 1970; The Night Visitor, 1971; Sometimes a Great Notion, 1971; Oklahoma Crude, 1973; The White Dawn, 1974; The Silver Streak, 1977; 10, 1979; S.O.B., 1981; Victor/Victoria, 1982

Television music: Peter Gunn, 1958; Mr. Lucky, 1960; The Thorn Birds, 1983

Orch: Beaver Valley, '37, suite, 1978

BIBLIOGRAPHY

"Mancini, Henry," *CBY 1964*
T. Thomas: *Music for the Movies* (South Brunswick, NJ, 1973)
P. Cook: "The Sound Track," *Films in Review*, xxvi/7 (1975), 426
P. Baretta: "Henry Mancini: Music with a Sense of Drama," *Songwriter Magazine*, ii/6 (1977), 24
C. Berg: "Henry Mancini: Sounds in the Dark," *Down Beat*, xlv/20 (1978), 14, 36, 44
T. Thomas: *Film Score: the View from the Podium* (South Brunswick, NJ, 1979)
P. Lehman and W. Luhr: *Blake Edwards* (Athens, OH, 1981)

MARTIN MARKS

Mandac, Evelyn (*b* Malaybalay, Mindanao, 16 Aug 1945). Filipina soprano. She moved with her family to Manila when she was two. She studied singing at the University of the Philippines under Lourdes Razon and Aurelio Estanislao. In 1964 she moved to the USA, where a Rockefeller grant enabled her to train at Oberlin College Conservatory and later at the Juilliard School. Her professional début was in 1968 in Mobile, Alabama (a concert performance of Orff's *Carmina burana*, a work she later recorded with the Boston SO under Ozawa). She has specialized in lyric roles in Washington, DC (where she made her opera début as Mimì in 1969), San Francisco (where she was Inez in the 1972 revival of Meyerbeer's *L'africaine*), Geneva, Rome, Amsterdam, Glyndebourne, and Salzburg. Her Metropolitan Opera début was on 19 December 1975 as Lauretta in *Gianni Schicchi*, and she returned as Humperdinck's Gretel. She sang Mélisande at Santa Fe in 1977, and Lisa in *The Queen of Spades* for American television, opposite the Countess of Jennie Tourel, with whom she had studied at Juilliard; she participated in the American premières of Berio's *Passaggio* and Bennett's *The Mines of Sulphur* (Jenny), and also in the world premières of Pasatieri's *Black Widow* (Berta) and *Ines de Castro* (Ines). She has frequently sung Mahler and Bach in concerts, and in 1969 toured with the Juilliard Quartet as soloist in Schoenberg's Quartet no.2. A singer of considerable refinement and charm, she is especially well cast in Mozart's soubrette roles.

MARTIN BERNHEIMER/R

Mandelbaum, (Mayer) Joel (*b* New York, 12 Oct 1932). Composer. He was educated at the universities of Harvard (BA 1953), Brandeis (MFA 1955), and Indiana (PhD 1961) and also studied at the Berkshire Music Center and the Berlin Hochschule für Musik. His teachers in composition included Boris Blacher, Luigi Dallapiccola, Irving Fine, Walter Piston, and Harold Shapero. Since 1961 he has taught at Queens College, CUNY, where he is director of the Aaron Copland School of Music. He was awarded a Fulbright scholarship in 1957 and in 1968 was a fellow at the MacDowell Colony. In the late 1950s Mandelbaum became interested in microtonal music and the theory and practice of microtonal tunings. His dissertation, *Multiple Division of the Octave and the Tonal Resources of 19-tone Temperament* (1961), extends the work of the 17th-century mathematician Christiaan Huygens and of the physicist Adriaan Fokker (1887–1972) and generalizes principles of 19- and 31-tone tunings, exploring their compositional possibilities. Mandelbaum, who was to some extent inspired by Partch, believes that microtonality will permit an infinite expansion of tonality and thus offers the tonally oriented contemporary composer an inexhaustible resource. His own music is greatly influenced by traditional tonality, his textures and rhythms often being reminiscent of Brahms and Mozart; through the use of microtonal tunings, however, his tonal language is constantly evolving. In *Sinfonia concertante* (1962) the violinist must tune a particular pitch to "the 11th partial of F, which is the quarter-tone between B and B♭." Such instructions are common in his music. More recently performances of his works have been aided by the use of the Scalatron, an instrument equipped with a color-coordinated keyboard that can be rearranged into divisions of the octave up to, and including, 31 tones. He has contributed several articles on microtonality to *Perspectives of New Music* and other journals.

WORKS

Stage: The Man in the Man-made Moon (opera, 1, J. Mandelbaum), 1955; The four Chaplains (opera, 1, M. R. Mandelbaum), 1956; The Dybbuk (opera, 4, J. Mandelbaum, after S. Ansky), 1971, rev. 1978; several musicals and light operas, incl. As You Dislike it (L. Fichandler), 1983; incidental music for 3 plays

Orch: Convocation Ov., 1951; Pf Conc., 1953; Sursum corda, 1960; Sinfonia concertante, ob, hn, vn, vc, small orch, 1962; Memorial, str orch, 1965; Tpt Conc., 1970

Inst: Moderato, vc, pf, 1949; Fl Sonata, 1950; Wind Qnt, 1957; 2 str qts, 1959, 1979; Moderato, 2 pf, 1965; Xenophony no.1, 3 hn, trbn, 1966; Romance, str trio, 1973; Fanfare, brass, 1974; Allegro agitato, 2 pf, 1979; 3 Tonal Studies, large chamber ens, 1979; Xenophony no.2, vn, vc, db, ww qnt, org, 1979; Ob Sonata, 1981; Cl Sonata, 1983; several other works

Kbd: 2 Short Pieces, 1950; Pf Sonata, 1958; 9 Preludes in 19-tone Temperament, for 2 Specially Tuned Pf, 1961; 10 Studies for Fokker Org Based on the Conora Suler, 1964; 4 Miniatures in 31-tone Temperament, Archiphone/Scalatron, 1979; other pf works

Vocal: Mass, male vv, org, 1954; Psalms clxxx and cxxi, vv, pf/insts, 1960; 3 Choruses to Pastoral Texts (A. Macleish), vv, cl, b cl, 1967; Psalm cxxvi, vv, org/4 insts, 1979; A Lady Thinks she's Thirty, chorus, 1983; Light and Shade (S. Fox), S, ob, pf, 1983; 6 other choruses; 3 works for 2–4 solo vv, incl. 10 Settings (Yeats), 1964; 14 works for solo voice, incl. 3 Dream Songs (J. Woolfe), S, (2 vn, org)/pf, 1973, Rainbows of Darkness (L. Eliasoph), Mez, pf, 1973

2 film scores

Principal publishers: Fanning Verlag (Germany), Diapason (Netherlands), Harold Branch

NOEL B. ZAHLER

Mandolin. A plucked string instrument. Mandolin players and makers in the USA have gradually forsaken the 18th-century Neapolitan form of the instrument, though they retain its double courses and tuning (*g–d′–a′–e″*). American makers have adopted three shapes for the mandolin body: teardrop-shaped, with flat backs and tops and an oval soundhole (e.g., Martin's "A" style, introduced in 1914); pear-shaped, with carved tops and backs and either oval soundholes or f-holes like a violin's (e.g., the prototypes of Orville H. Gibson, developed in the 1880s and standardized *c*1904–9); and an elaborate version of the pear-shaped type, with the upper left side voluted and two angular projections ("points") on the right, and whorls of unequal size and opposing direction at the top of the peghead (created by Gibson *c*1900 and designated by him "Artist" or "F" styles, now known as "Florentine" style). The instrument is made in many sizes, but Gibson's style "A," about 25 cm across the widest part of the body and 34 cm in length from the bottom to the 12th fret, may be regarded as typical of contemporary American mandolins. The addition of f-holes to the Gibson F-5 in 1922 improved the instrument's capacity to project. Gibson employees invented and patented the vertically adjustable bridge and the neck truss rod in the early 1920s; these devices enabled players to change the height of the strings as well as the angle and curvature of the neck. Mandolins are usually played with a plectrum or flat pick, often featuring tremolo effects on one or two strings; American playing, in folk and especially bluegrass music, is also characterized by chordal accompaniments.

Mandolins were brought to the USA by Italian immigrants as early as the late colonial period, but were limited to infrequent, small public concerts and private use in the ghettos until the last 20 years of the 19th century. Ironically, it was the Figaro Spanish Students – an internationally known ensemble of string players brought to the USA in 1880 by the English impresario Henry Abbey – who initially generated interest in mandolin-like instruments in the USA and paved the way for the appreciation of the Neapolitan mandolin. The group played solo passages on *bandurrias*, misconstrued by some as the "Spanish mandolin"; its repertory was primarily drawn from Spanish instrumental and dance music and arrangements of well-known sonatas and overtures. Imitative ensembles, also calling themselves Spanish Students, were soon formed by Italian violinists such as Carlo Curti; they toured throughout the USA until 1885, further popularizing the mandolin. Its popularity was at its peak between about 1895 and the outbreak of World War I. People learned to play the mandolin for their individual enjoyment, and later many joined with one another and with guitar accompanists to form small, informal groups. Instrument manufacturers such as Lyon & Healy in Chicago responded to the new market and produced thousands of instruments; the Gibson Mandolin-Guitar Company promoted its mandolins and guitars under the slogan "The Music Pals of the Nation."

The musically more sophisticated players joined banjo and zither clubs, the zither eventually displacing some of the original instruments. Independent mandolin clubs were formed in northeastern cities and on college campuses, and subsequently in the Midwest and in communities of all sizes. Manufacturers began to produce consorts of mandolins, including mandolas, mandocellos, mandobasses, and unusually large guitars; mandolin, or plectral, orchestras proliferated, and a few of them have survived. Repertories were as varied as the players' interests and reflected contemporary musical fashions: rags, jigs, and marches; parlor, salon, and light classical music; and arrangements of the classics.

Specialty periodicals were founded, the most significant of which were *The Cadenza* (1894–1924) and *The Crescendo* (1908–33). These monthly periodicals, followed by the fortnightly *Fretted Instrument News* (1937–57), were published by the American Guild of Banjoists, Mandolinists, and Guitarists (founded in 1902). The Fretted Instrument Guild of America, founded in Chicago in 1957, issues *FIGA* (previously titled *FIGA News*, then *FIGA Review*).

The popularity of the mandolin began to wane just before

World War I as interest moved towards "Hawaiian" music and the ukulele, and the developing jazz, which incorporated the banjo-mandolin (a transitional form that led to the widespread use of the tenor banjo in the 1920s). During World War I, however, Gibson produced special, low-cost Army-Navy mandolins for servicemen. The exuberance of the subsequent "jazz age" generally excluded the sorts of music suited to the delicate tonal charms of the mandolin.

Though the mandolin fell into general disuse, it was slowly assimilated into white folk culture in the 1920s and then incorporated into stringbands and hillbilly bands during the 1930s. Fraternal duets, such as Charlie and Bill Monroe and the Blue Sky Boys, brought the mandolin to prominence in the Southeast. With the development of BLUEGRASS MUSIC in the late 1940s the mandolin increasingly appeared in acoustic ensembles including fiddle, five-string banjo, various types of guitar, and double bass.

Among the most accomplished mandolin players active in the USA were Valentine Abt (*d* 1923), a composer and the first recognized American concert virtuoso; Giuseppe Pettine (1876–1966), a composer and teacher who was a prolific author of instructional manuals and did much to popularize the mandolin among the musically literate in the USA; Pettine's pupil William Place, Jr. (1889–1959); and Walter K. Bauer (*b* 1899), a teacher, conductor, and composer who originated the plectrophonic system of orchestration. BILL MONROE, considered the father of bluegrass music, brought the mandolin new recognition. Other notable bluegrass mandolinists include Jesse McReynolds (*b* 1929), innovator of a cross-picking technique (patterned after Earl Scruggs's right-hand fingering of the five-string banjo), and Bobby Osborne (*b* 1931), who evolved a fluent, iteratively embellished approach to melody and improvisation. The new directions in acoustic music of the 1980s have been spearheaded by DAVID GRISMAN, whose groups feature the instrument in a fusion of jazz, classical, and bluegrass styles that he calls "dawg" music; Grisman also publishes *Mandolin World News* (1976–).

BIBLIOGRAPHY

P. J. Bone: *The Guitar and Mandolin: Biographies of Celebrated Players and Composers* (London, 1914, rev. and enlarged 2/1954/*R*1972)

L. A. Loar: "Fretted Instruments: their Origin, Development, and Marketing," *Music Trade Review*, lxxxiii/28 (1929), 65

M. Longworth: *Martin Guitars: a History* (Cedar Knolls, NJ, 1975, rev. 2/1980)

S. Hambly: *Mandolins in the United States since 1880: an Industrial and Sociocultural History of Form* (diss., U. of Pennsylvania, 1977)

——: "Mandolin Bibliography," *Mandolin World News*, v (1980), no. 1, p. 20; no. 2, p. 15

H. Rasof: *The Folk, Country, and Bluegrass Musician's Catalogue* (New York, 1982)

R. C. Hartman: *Guitars and Mandolins in America* (Hoffman Estates, IL, 1984)

SCOTT HAMBLY

Mangione, Chuck [Charles Frank] (*b* Rochester, NY, 29 Nov 1940). Jazz trumpeter and bandleader. He studied music at the Eastman School (BA 1963) and first gained notice as a trumpeter with such bandleaders as Woody Herman (1965), Maynard Ferguson (1965), and Art Blakey (1965–7), playing in the style of Miles Davis and Clifford Brown. In the 1970s he attracted a large following with performances of catchy original melodies – particularly *Feels So Good* and *Land of Make Believe* – using little improvisation and only elementary accompaniments; his album *Feels So Good* sold more than two million copies, making his name a byword for jazz in the popular imagination. Equally successful was his film score for *Children of Sanchez* (1978; the album sold about 673,000 copies), which combined a jazz flavor with soft tone colors, uncomplicated melodies, and Latin American rhythms. In addition to his pretty tunes, Mangione's greatest contributions were to make jazz palatable to a large nonjazz audience, and to popularize the flugelhorn as a jazz instrument to a greater extent.

RECORDINGS

(selective list)

As leader or co-leader: *The Jazz Brothers* (1960, Riv. 335); *The Chuck Mangione Quartet* (1972, Mer. SRM1-631), incl. Land of Make Believe; *Bellavia* (1975, A&M 4557); *Feels So Good* (1977, A&M 4658); *Children of Sanchez* (1978, A&M 6700)

As sideman: A. Blakey: *Buttercorn Lady* (1966, Lml. 86034)

BIBLIOGRAPHY

L. Underwood: "Chuck Mangione: an Open Feeling, a Sound of Love," *Down Beat*, xlii/9 (1975), 11

G. Brown: "Thou Shalt Always Have a Good Time and Groove with the Music: the Chuck Mangione Story," *Black Music and Jazz Review*, i/12 (1978), 12

"Mangione, Chuck," *CBY 1980*

MARK C. GRIDLEY

Manhattans. Soul vocal group. Its members have included George "Smitty" Smith (*b* Macon, GA; *d* 1970), lead tenor, replaced in 1970 by Gerald Alston (*b* 8 Nov 1942); Edward "Sonny" Bivins (*b* ?New Jersey, 15 Jan 1942), tenor; Kenneth Kelley (*b* New Jersey, 9 Jan 1943), second tenor; Richard Taylor (*b* ?New Jersey), who left the group in 1977; and Winfred "Blue" Lovett (*b* New York, 16 Nov 1943), bass. In 1961 Bivins and Taylor, who had met in Germany while they were serving in the Army, joined three others in New York to form the Dulcets, which produced a single rhythm-and-blues hit, *Pork Chops*, before disbanding in 1962. They next joined Smith, Kelley, and Lovett in Jersey City, New Jersey, to form the Manhattans. In 1964 the group won third prize in an Apollo Theater contest and were signed to the Carnival label; their first pop hit was *I wanna be your everything* (1965), written by Lovett. Later hits, most of which were written by Lovett, Bivins, or Taylor, included *Follow your Heart* (1966), *Baby I Need you* (1966), and *I Call it Love* (1967). In 1968 the group signed a new recording contract and enjoyed only minor successes for several years; after signing a contract with Columbia in 1972, however, they enjoyed a new series of hits, including *There's no me without you* (1973), *You'd Better Believe it* (1973), *Don't Take your Love* (1975), *Kiss and Say Goodbye* (no. 1, 1976), and *Shining Star* (1980). They continued to tour and record into the mid-1980s.

The Manhattans' style evolved from doo-wop harmonizing into a brand of smooth soul ballad singing that resisted the shifting fashions of pop music and the growing emphasis on rhythm in black disco and funk. Their music is based on high tenor and falsetto harmonies and on Lovett's earnest narrative recitations. While never at the very top of their field in either renown or commercial success, the group has sustained a career of unusual longevity and consistency.

RECORDINGS

(selective list; recorded for Columbia unless otherwise stated)

I wanna be your everything (Carnival 507, 1965); Baby I Need you (Carnival 514, 1966); Follow your Heart (Carnival 512, 1966); I Call it Love (Carnival 533, 1967); If my Heart could Speak (Deluxe 122, 1970); There's no me without you (PC32444, 1973); You'd Better Believe it (45927, 1973); Don't Take your Love (10045, 1975); Kiss and Say Goodbye (10310, 1976); *The Manhattans* (PC33820, 1976); *It Feels So Good* (PC34450, 1977); Shining Star (11222, 1980); *Too Hot to Stop it* (FC39277, 1985)

JOHN ROCKWELL

Manhattan School of Music. Conservatory in New York City founded by the philanthropist Janet D. Schenck in 1917; *see* NEW YORK, §12.

Manhattan String Quartet. String quartet formed in 1970 by Eric Lewis, John McLeod, Andrew Berdahl, and Judith Glyde (who married Lewis in 1970); all the players studied at the Manhattan School, where Lewis was a pupil of Rachmael Weinstock, who had led a quartet of the same name in the 1930s. (The other members of this earlier quartet, which made its début at Town Hall, New York, in 1932, were Harris Danziger, violin, Julius Shaier, viola, and Oliver Edel, cello (for illustration *see* CHAMBER MUSIC, fig.2).) McLeod was replaced in 1972 by Mahlon Darlington, who was followed by Roy Lewis (*b* 1950) in 1975; Berdahl was succeeded by Rosemary Glyde in 1975, then by John Dexter in 1980. The quartet made its début in San Francisco in 1971; its participation in the Young Artists Program in Binghamton, New York, led to residencies at Cornell University (1971–2), Grinnell College (1972–5), the Manhattan School (1976–7), and Music Mountain, Falls Village, Connecticut (from 1981). The ensemble also teaches at Interlochen (Michigan) and at the Mexican Instituto Nacional de Bellas Artes, and has toured Central and South America, Europe, and the USSR. Known for its interest in new music, the group has had works written for it by Howard Boatwright, Ludmilla Ulehla, Benjamin Johnston, Gregory Kosteck, and Alice Parker, among others.

ELLEN HIGHSTEIN

Manilow, Barry (*b* New York, 17 June 1946). Popular singer, songwriter, and arranger. He began his career as a composer and arranger of off-Broadway musicals and television commercials. His first hit, *Mandy*, was released in 1974; it was followed by numerous recordings of soaring, sentimental ballads, which made him commercially the most successful male pop singer of the late 1970s (between 1975 and 1981 16 of his singles reached the Top Ten on the pop chart). He exploited an appealing, well-trained baritone voice to create a style that blended the formal sentimentality of Italian-American singers of the 1950s and 1960s with a more neutral emotional approach that owed something to other forms of contemporary pop. In 1984 Manilow recorded *2:00 AM: Paradise Café*, an album of his own compositions in a jazz-flavored style.

RECORDINGS

(selective list; recorded for Arista unless otherwise stated)

Mandy (Bell 45613, 1974); Could it be magic (0126, 1975); I write the songs (0157, 1975); Tryin' to get the feeling again (0172, 1976); Weekend in New England (0212, 1976); Looks like we made it (0244, 1977); Can't smile without you (0305, 1978); Copacabana (0339, 1978); Ships (0464, 1979); Somewhere in the night (0382, 1979); I made it through the rain (0566, 1980); *2:00 AM: Paradise Café* (88254, 1984)

STEPHEN HOLDEN

Mann, Alfred (*b* Hamburg, Germany, 28 April 1917). Musicologist. He studied at the Milan Conservatory and the Berlin Hochschule für Musik, where he taught in 1937, before returning to Milan as an instructor at the Scuola Musicale (1938). He was on the faculty of the Curtis Institute (1939–42), where he received a diploma, and he also gained degrees at Columbia University (MA 1950, PhD 1955); he became professor of music at Rutgers University in 1947. Mann was appointed director of publications of the American Choral Foundation in 1961 and has been active in musical performance. He specializes in the history of music theory, particularly the writings of J. J. Fux. His translation of part of *Gradus ad Parnassum*, as *Steps to Parnassus: the Study of Counterpoint* (1943, rev. 2/1963), is preceded by a discussion of the concepts of counterpoint and attitudes towards it up to Fux's time, as well as an appraisal of the influence of Fux's work. In *The Study of Fugue* (1965) he gives a brief historical outline of methods of teaching fugue, and presents extracts from works by Fux, Marpurg, Albrechtsberger, and Martini that deal with the study of the technique.

PAULA MORGAN/R

Mann, Elias (*b* Canton, MA, 8 May 1750; *d* Northampton, MA, 12 May 1825). Composer and singing master. A carpenter by trade, he was a celebrated teacher, who taught in almost all the principal towns in Massachusetts. In 1786, when living in or near Worcester, he contributed tunes to Isaiah Thomas's *The Worcester Collection*, and he served as Thomas's musical adviser for subsequent editions of that work (1792, 1794). In 1795 Mann moved to Northampton, where he married Asceneth Wright, sister of Daniel Wright who in 1797 became the first Northampton resident to print music from movable type. Mann was Northampton's leading musician until his departure in about 1802; he was engaged at the town's expense to teach singing (1795–6, 1798–9); he directed a choir that sang special music at an ordination in Chesterfield (1796); and he brought out *The Northampton Collection* (1797, 2/1802), a sacred tunebook in which his own compositions were intermixed with pieces by other American and European psalmodists. After leaving Northampton he lived briefly in Roxbury (1803), but by 1805 he had moved to Boston, where he was one of 11 founding members of the Massachusetts Musical Society (organized 20 June 1807, dissolved 5 July 1810), a group dedicated to the reform of sacred music and a forerunner of the Boston Handel and Haydn Society (founded 1815). Mann's *Massachusetts Collection of Sacred Harmony* (Boston, 1807) emphasized European music, and made a point of omitting "those wild fugues, and rapid confused movements, which have so long been the disgrace of congregational psalmody." Mann may also have helped to compile *LXXX Psalm and Hymn Tunes* (Boston, 1810) for Boston's Brattle Street Church. Besides his activities in sacred music, he composed and published four secular songs, of which the best-known, *The Grasshopper*, appeared in print at least four times between 1790 and 1817.

BIBLIOGRAPHY

C. C. Perkins and J. S. Dwight: *History of the Handel and Haydn Society, of Boston, Massachusetts*, i (Boston, 1883–93/R1977), 31

F. J. Metcalf: *American Writers and Compilers of Sacred Music* (New York, 1925/R1967)

K. D. Kroeger: *The Worcester Collection of Sacred Harmony and Sacred Music in America, 1786–1803* (diss., Brown U., 1976), 66, 84, 90

P. R. Osterhout: *Music in Northampton, Massachusetts, to 1820* (diss., U. of Michigan, 1978), 289

RICHARD CRAWFORD

Mann, Robert (Nathaniel) (*b* Portland, OR, 19 July 1920). Violinist and composer. He began violin lessons at the age of nine and later studied with Edouard Déthier, a chamber music enthusiast, at the Juilliard Graduate School; other teachers included Adolfo Betti, Felix Salmond, and Hans Letz (ensemble playing), Wagenaar and Wolpe (composition), and Edgar Schenkman (conducting). He won the Naumburg Competition in 1941 and gave his New York début recital later that year. In 1946, after serving in the US Army, he joined the faculty of the Juilliard School;

two years later he was a founding member of the JUILLIARD STRING QUARTET, of which he has remained first violinist through many changes in the other chairs. He has also performed in the Lyric Trio, a group consisting of Mann, his wife Lucy Rowan as narrator, and a pianist (at different times Harriet Wingreen, Leonid Hambro, and Brooks Smith). In 1980 he formed the Mann Duo with his son, the violinist Nicholas Mann (*b* 1957). As a soloist he has given noteworthy performances including a Beethoven sonata cycle (in 1980, with Ax) at the Library of Congress and in New York. He appears from time to time as a conductor in contemporary works, and has performed and lectured at the Aspen Music Festival. In 1971 he became president of the Naumburg Foundation; work with the NEA culminated in his chairing a new chamber music panel for that body in 1980. Mann's compositions include orchestral and chamber works (among the latter are many pieces for violin, piano, and narrator written for the Lyric Trio), and choral pieces, songs, and cadenzas.

In his playing and teaching Mann strives towards what he has called "the original, vulnerable state of the newborn," a principle he traces to his Reichian analysis (including sessions with Wilhelm Reich himself) during the late 1940s and early 1950s. He is coach to many younger ensembles, including the Concord, Tokyo, American, LaSalle, Emerson, and New World quartets. Ensemble playing is, to him, an intimate experience; he has noted (and deplored) a virtuoso mentality behind the renewed interest in chamber music during the 1970s and 1980s. Nevertheless, by his performing, teaching, and organizational work, he has been extremely influential in fostering that interest.

BIBLIOGRAPHY

S. Fleming: "Musician of the Month: Robert Mann," *HiFi/MusAm*, xxx/6 (1980), 6

J. Peyser: "Robert Mann's Life in Chamber Music," *New York Times* (6 July 1980), section 2, p.13

B. Schwarz: *Great Masters of the Violin* (New York, 1983)

DAVID WRIGHT

Manne, Shelly [Sheldon] (*b* New York, 11 June 1920; *d* Los Angeles, CA, 26 Sept 1984). Jazz drummer. He began as a saxophonist and changed to drums at the age of 18. He played on Coleman Hawkins's famous recording of *The Man I Love* (1943) and Dizzy Gillespie's first bop sessions (1945). In 1946 he began a productive association with Stan Kenton which lasted until 1952. After moving to Los Angeles Manne became a central figure in the carefully arranged, cool derivative of bop known as West Coast jazz. He was the leader of a remarkably stable series of jazz combos from 1956, co-leader with Barney Kessel and Ray Brown of the Poll-Winners (1957–60, 1975), and a member of André Previn's trio; with Previn he recorded instrumental versions of songs from *My Fair Lady* (1956), first in Previn's trendsetting series of jazz interpretations of material from Broadway musicals. From 1960 to 1974 he ran a jazz club, Shelly's Manne-Hole, and in 1974 he was a founding member of the L. A. Four. Manne was a traditional swinging drummer who was opposed to technical displays; his sensitivity to percussive pitches allowed him to develop a restrained, "melodic" approach to drumming.

RECORDINGS

(selective list)

As leader or co-leader: *The Three* (1954, Cont. 2516); *My Fair Lady* (1956, Cont. 3527); with B. Kessel and R. Brown: *The Poll-Winners* (1957, Cont. 3535); *At the Black Hawk*, pts. i–iv (1959, Cont. 3577-80); *2-3-4* (1962, Imp. 20); *Outside* (1969, Cont. 7624); *French Concert* (1977, Gal. 5101)

As sideman: C. Hawkins: The Man I Love (1943, Signature 9001); D. Gillespie: Blue 'n Boogie (1945, Guild 1001); S. Kenton: Artistry in Percussion (1946, Cap. 289), Shelly Manne (1950, Cap. 28008); A Previn: *Pal Joey* (1957, Cont. 3543); L. A. Four: *The L. A. Four Scores* (1974, Conc. 8)

BIBLIOGRAPHY

L. Feather: "Shelly: the Whole Manne," *Down Beat*, xxxvii/25 (1970), 16

S. Traill: "The Shelly Manne Story," *Jazz Journal International*, xxxii/8 (1979), 21

D. Levine: "Shelly Manne," *Modern Drummer*, v/7 (1981), 10

BARRY KERNFELD

Mannello, Angelo (*b* Morcone, Italy, 11 Sept 1858; *d* New York, 4 July 1922). Mandolin maker. Son of a carpenter, he was apprenticed to a Neapolitan woodworker before immigrating in 1885 to New York, where he opened a prosperous workshop. By 1887, when he married Filomena Buccini, he was employing helpers from his native village. Before 1900 his workshop occupied several quarters in "Little Italy," and by 1903 he was operating a manufactory in the Bronx, where up to 75 workers, including family members, produced mandolins, guitars, and banjos; many of these were sold wholesale to C. Bruno & Sons (a major New York musical instrument distributor) for retailing under Bruno's name. Around 1917 Mannello founded the Società Morconese, a fellowship that later became a lodge of the Sons of Italy. In 1918 his factory was destroyed by arson and business declined thereafter.

Mannello was highly regarded for his mandolins, which are of ordinary proportions but ornately inlaid with expensive materials. They gained awards at the World's Columbian Exposition (Chicago, 1893), Tennessee Centennial Exposition (Memphis, 1897), Exposition Universelle Internationale (Paris, 1900), San Francisco Midwinter International Exposition (1900), Pan American Exposition (Buffalo, 1901), and Louisiana Purchase Exposition (St. Louis, 1904). He supplied instruments for professional bands and was represented in Chicago by the sales agent Cesare Valisi. He presented a fine mandolin to the soprano Adelina Patti. Of Mannello's seven children, three sons worked in the shop but none was adequately trained to carry on the business, which failed in the Depression. Two of his mandolins were presented by his descendants to the Metropolitan Museum of Art, New York.

BIBLIOGRAPHY

L. Libin: *American Musical Instruments in the Metropolitan Museum of Art* (New York, 1985)

LAURENCE LIBIN

Mannes, David (*b* New York, 16 Feb 1866; *d* New York, 25 April 1959). Music educator, violinist, and conductor. He studied violin in New York with August Zeiss and C. R. Nicolai, in Berlin with Heinrich de Ahna and Carl Halíř, and in Brussels with Ysaÿe. After several years as a freelance player in theater orchestras in New York, he was invited by Walter Damrosch in 1895 to join the New York Symphony Society, of which he subsequently became concertmaster (1903–12). His lifelong concern with the provision of music education for the young, the underprivileged, and the informed amateur inspired in 1894 the foundation of the Music School Settlement (later the Third Street Music School Settlement at East 3rd Street), one of the first schools of its kind in the USA, and the Music School Settlement for Colored Children in Harlem (1912). He also founded and conducted a series of free concerts at the Metropolitan Museum of Art (1918–47).

In 1916 Mannes and his wife, Clara Mannes (née Damrosch)

(*b* Breslau, Germany [now Wrocław, Poland], 12 Dec 1869; *d* New York, 16 March 1948), founded the David Mannes Music School (from 1953 the Mannes College of Music) in New York. Several notable European composers were engaged as teachers of theory and composition, including Ernest Bloch (1917–19), Rosario Scalero (1919–28), and Hans Weisse (1931–9). The last-named had been a student of Heinrich Schenker and, as a result of his appointment, the school became the first American educational institution to offer instruction in Schenkerian analysis; in 1933 it sponsored the publication of Schenker's *Five Graphic Analyses* for use in Weisse's classes.

Clara Mannes, who had studied piano with her father Leopold Damrosch and in Berlin with Ferruccio Busoni, taught privately in New York and also coached chamber music ensembles at the Mannes School. She gave recitals throughout the USA with her husband, often performing in cities where no such concerts had ever been presented.

BIBLIOGRAPHY

A. W. K[ramer]: "David Mannes, who Directs Musical Destinies of 800 East-side Children, Urges them to Shun Musical Careers," *MusAm*, xv/19 (1912), 3

G. Saenger: "David Mannes: the Romance of an American Musical Career," *Musical Observer*, viii (1913), 693

D. Mannes: *Music is my Faith* (New York, 1938/*R*1978)

M. Mannes: *Out of my Time* (Garden City, NY, 1971)

G. Martin: *The Damrosch Dynasty: America's First Family of Music* (Boston, 1983)

B. Schwarz: *Great Masters of the Violin* (New York, 1983), 501

CHANNAN WILLNER

Mannes, Leopold Damrosch (*b* New York, 26 Dec 1899; *d* Martha's Vineyard, MA, 11 Aug 1964). Music educator, pianist, and composer. The son of David and Clara Mannes, he studied piano with Elizabeth Quaile, Guy Maier, Berthe Bert, and Alfred Cortot, and composition with Johannes Schreyer, Goetschius, and Scalero. He made his début as a pianist on 29 October 1922 in a performance at Aeolian Hall, New York, of Saint-Saëns's *Le carnaval des animaux*. From 1927 to 1931 and from 1946 to 1948 he taught theory and composition at the Mannes School, of which he was director (1940–48), co-director (1948–52), and president (1950–64). Under his leadership the school's curriculum became the first in the USA to incorporate Heinrich Schenker's approach to music analysis.

Mannes won a Pulitzer scholarship for composition in 1925 for his orchestral Suite and a Guggenheim fellowship for his String Quartet in C Minor (1927). Apart from a Suite for two pianos (1925), however, his compositions were mostly small-scale pieces for piano or organ, works for vocal ensembles, and solo songs. In 1948 he formed the Mannes Trio with the violinist Vittorio Brero and the cellist Luigi Silva. After two seasons Brero was replaced by Bronislav Gimpel, and the group became known as the Mannes-Gimpel-Silva Trio. Gimpel withdrew in 1955, after which Mannes ceased to perform in public.

Mannes was also a scientist with a strong interest in photography; with Leopold Godowsky he conducted experiments that led to the invention of the Kodachrome Color Process (1935).

BIBLIOGRAPHY

M. Mannes: *Out of my Time* (Garden City, NY, 1971)

G. Martin: *The Damrosch Dynasty: America's First Family of Music* (Boston, 1983)

CHANNAN WILLNER

Mannes College of Music. A conservatory in New York founded as the David Mannes Music School by David and Clara Damrosch Mannes in 1916; *see* NEW YORK, §12.

Manning, Kathleen Lockhart (*b* Hollywood, CA, 24 Oct 1890; *d* Los Angeles, CA, 20 March 1951). Composer and singer. She studied composition in Paris with Moritz Moszkowski in 1908 and then toured France and England between 1909 and 1914, spending the 1911–12 season as a singer with the Hammerstein Opera Company in London. She performed briefly in the USA in 1926 and joined ASCAP in 1932. As a composer, Manning specialized in vocal compositions, for which she usually wrote her own texts, and was influenced by the orientalisms used by impressionist composers. This is most apparent in *Nang-ping* and *Pagoda Bells* (from *Chinese Impressions*). Several of her song cycles evoke the cities and countries of their titles, and one of these, *In the Luxembourg Gardens* (from the *Sketches of Paris*), was so popular that she arranged it for women's choir.

WORKS

Operas: Operetta in Mozartian Style; Mr. Wu (L. J. Milu), 1925–6; For the Soul of Rafael

Inst: 4 sym. poems; Pf Conc.; Str Qt; Playtime, pf, 1924; Sundown Tales, pf, 1924; 3 Dance Impressions, pf; In the Summer, pf

Songs: Water Lily, 1923; Japanese Ghost Songs, 1924; Sketches of Paris, 1925; Sketches of London, 1929; Chinese Impressions, 6 songs, 1931; 5 Fragments, 1931; Vignettes, 25 songs, 1933; Sketches of New York, 1936; 4 Songs of Bilitis; Shoes

Principal publishers: Boosey & Hawkes, Composers' Music Corporation, C. Fischer, G. Schirmer

BARBARA L. TISCHLER

Mantia, Simone (*b* nr Palermo, Sicily, 6 Feb 1873; *d* Flushing, NY, 25 June 1951). Euphonium player, trombonist, and conductor. He came to the USA at an early age, and while still in his teens played professionally as a trombonist in orchestras and as a euphonium player in bands. He studied with Joseph Raffayolo, a euphonium soloist in Patrick Gilmore's band, and later in the Sousa Band; when Raffayolo died in 1896 Mantia was asked to take his place. He played under Sousa for seven years, acquiring a reputation equal to that of Herbert L. Clarke and Arthur Pryor. When Pryor left Sousa in 1903 to form his own band, Mantia joined him as soloist and assistant conductor; he appeared with the band for 20 years, playing and conducting during its summer seasons. In 1909 he joined the Metropolitan Opera in New York as first trombonist. He played with the Metropolitan's orchestra for 35 years, for the last ten of which he was also personnel manager. From 1921 to 1925 he conducted his own orchestra at Asbury Park, New Jersey. He played briefly with the Victor Herbert Orchestra and the New York PO, and made a number of early recordings. He appeared as a soloist at the age of 67 during the New York World's Fair, and continued to play in Paul Lavalle's Band of America until after he was 75. He normally used a five-valve, two-bell euphonium on which he played difficult cornet and trombone solos. He was noted for his exceptional range, sonorous tone, and dazzling technique. Mantia wrote a number of solos for trombone and euphonium, and is best remembered for his *Priscilla Waltz* and variations on *Believe me if all those endearing young charms*. He also wrote a widely used trombone method.

BIBLIOGRAPHY

G. D. Bridges: *Pioneers in Brass* (Detroit, 1965), 96

RAOUL CAMUS

Mapleson, James Henry (*b* London, England, 4 May 1830; *d* London, 14 Nov 1901). English impresario. He studied at the Royal Academy of Music in London and opened a musical agency

Fate Marable (piano) and his riverboat band, c1920, with Johnny St. Cyr (banjo), Louis Armstrong (cornet), and Baby Dodds (drums)

in 1856. He began his career as an operatic impresario at the Lyceum in 1861, and until 1889 presented seasons at several London theaters. In 1878 his company offered simultaneous seasons in London and New York, and the American group toured in the East and Midwest. Its success brought Mapleson a three-year contract with the Academy of Music in New York, where from 1879 to 1883 he presented opera in an unprecedentedly glamorous style. The company also went on tour, to Detroit, Cleveland, Buffalo, Pittsburgh, Indianapolis, Chicago, and St. Louis, and gave an annual opera festival in Cincinnati.

When Henry Abbey opened the Metropolitan Opera in New York in 1883, he and Mapleson battled for singers and patrons. Mapleson abandoned his New York season early, barely managing to survive an ambitious tour that ranged west to San Francisco. In 1884–5 the "opera war" drained Mapleson's resources further; the 1885–6 season and tour were a fiasco, with Mapleson being hounded by sheriffs and lawyers from San Francisco to London. His American career was effectively ended, although he returned briefly to the Academy of Music in 1896. Mapleson was a flamboyant and resourceful promoter who sought to popularize opera through tours and festivals; his downfall came when he challenged the social and financial élite behind the Metropolitan.

BIBLIOGRAPHY

J. H. Mapleson: *The Mapleson Memoirs* (London, 1888); ed. H. Rosenthal (London, 1966)

J. F. Cone: *First Rival of the Metropolitan Opera* (New York, 1983)

WILLIAM BROOKS

Marable, Fate (*b* Paducah, KY, 2 Dec 1890; *d* St. Louis, MO, 16 Jan 1947). Jazz pianist and bandleader. Beginning in 1907 he played piano and calliope aboard the Mississippi steamer *J.S.* A decade later he formed his own riverboat band, and although it was based in St. Louis he made a point of recruiting his key musicians in New Orleans. He continued to lead bands until the early 1940s when illness restricted his activities.

Marable spent most of his working life leading, or playing in, bands aboard Mississippi steamers. So many of his sidemen later achieved fame that his band became known as "the floating conservatoire"; Louis Armstrong, Henry "Red" Allen, Baby Dodds, and Jimmy Blanton were all former members of Marable's band. Despite Marable's reputation among fellow musicians, his band recorded only two titles: *Frankie and Johnny* and *Pianoflage* (1924); neither of these recordings captured exceptional performances.

BIBLIOGRAPHY

P. Vandervoort, II: "The King of Riverboat Jazz," *Jazz Journal*, xxiii/8 (1970), 12

W. Dobie: "Remembering Fate Marable," *Storyville*, no.38 (1971–2), 44

JOHN CHILTON

March. A basic walking step and the generic term for a variety of music that could be used to accompany this step in parades and in dance. American march music of the 19th century was influenced most strongly by the quickstep, a march genre which had developed from the musical accompaniment to the military cadenced step of the late 18th century. Music for the cadenced step (faster than the ceremonial march that preceded it) had a marked beat in either simple or compound duple meter and varied rhythmic patterns often borrowed from popular dances. March composition in the USA can be traced through three distinct styles. The first, most common in the late 18th and early 19th centuries, was a modified form (somewhat faster) of the old ceremonial or grand march, a slow piece in 4/4 with a chordal, homorhythmic texture and a fanfare melody (ex.1). The second form of the march appeared in the 1830s, most commonly in compositions bearing the name "quickstep." This music was characterized by a faster tempo, lilting eight-bar phrases, and a light chordal accompaniment, usually with oscillating or drum-bass figures (ex.2). Composers often arranged well-known melodies, particularly excerpts from Italian operas, for this type of march. Grand marches and polonaises were used for the opening processionals of 19th-century balls; quicksteps commonly accompanied the quadrilles and cotillions. Late 19th-century compo-

Ex.1 James Hewitt: *Governor Tomkins New Grand March* (*c*1808)

Ex.2 Claudio S. Grafulla: *Livingston Guards Quick Step* (1838)

sitions labeled as marches were moderately fast with a heavier, more marked rhythmic accent, greater melodic and rhythmic independence from the bass (demonstrated by the appearance of counter-melodies), and a lyrical melody presented within the context of a richer harmonic texture (ex.3).

Ex.3 R. Fassett: *Brook's Triumphant March* (1894)

The trio, a contrasting section usually more lyrical than the opening, emerged in the mid-1830s in the quickstep, producing an *ABA* form. It evolved from the paired relationship of the grand march and quickstep and the alternation of brass sonorities with those of the fifes and drums in parade music. In the late 19th century "trio" came to refer to the last strain of the march and the immediately preceding "break" strain. The latter, an elaboration of the earlier drum interlude or short passage introducing the contrasting section of the mid-19th-century quickstep, is characteristically nonmelodic, highly rhythmic, and percussive, with forte dynamics and antiphonal interplay between the treble and bass. The practice of alternating the break strain and the trio melody two or three times to conclude with a climactic rendering of the trio melody was established by Sousa in his marches *The Thunderer* (1889), *King Cotton* (1895), and *The Stars and Stripes Forever* (1896); the form of these marches, five to seven strains long, became standard in the 20th-century American march.

Music for the polka and galop, which was characterized by duple meters and marked rhythms, was commonly used for marching as well, giving rise to the march genres known as the "polka quickstep" (or "military polka") and the "double quick march" (about 140 beats to the minute). Polka quicksteps borrowed the rhythm and meter of the polka but intensified the accent on the downbeat; examples include James Couenhoven's *National Guards Polka Quick Step* (1851) and Edward Clapham's *The American Army Polka* (1864). The double quick march used music for the galop such as William Dressler's *The Massachusetts Volunteer Galop Quick Step* (1862). In the 1890s the two-step march, typified by Sousa's *The Washington Post* (1889), was used to accompany both social dancing and parade marching.

Late 19th-century march composition is marked by the influence of the concert hall and musical theater and the emergence of the march composer as a musical personality in his own right. The bravura march was a showpiece composition for piano, intended for domestic or concert performance. Besides Sousa, composers of this period who wrote marches include Jean Missud, Charles Barnhouse, Victor Herbert, and George Chadwick. The circus march and marches for the concert hall have become the most commonly composed types in the 20th century. The circus march is noted for its extremely fast tempo and its lyrical trio melodies (*see* CIRCUS MUSIC).

BIBLIOGRAPHY

D. Hazeltine, Jr.: *Instructor in Martial Musick* (Exeter, NH, 1810)
D. D. Emmett: *Bruce and Emmett Fife and Drum Instructor* (New York, 1862)
W. D. Allen: *Our Marching Civilization* (Stanford, CA, 1943/*R*1978)
R. F. Goldman: "Band Music in America," *One Hundred Years of Music in America*, ed. P. H. Lang (New York, 1961)
R. Camus: *Military Music of the American Revolution* (Chapel Hill, NC, 1976)
——: "On the Cadence of the March," *Journal of Band Research*, xvi/2 (1981), 13
P. Norton: *March Music in Nineteenth-century America* (diss., U. of Michigan, 1983)

For further bibliography, *see* BANDS, DANCE, MILITARY MUSIC.

PAULINE NORTON

Marco, Guy Anthony (*b* New York, 4 Oct 1927). Musicologist and librarian. He attended DePaul University and the American Conservatory of Music, Chicago (BM 1951), and received advanced training at the University of Chicago, in music (MA 1952, PhD 1956) and library science (MA 1955). He began his career as librarian and instructor at the Chicago Musical College (1953–4), then worked for Chicago City Junior College as both librarian and instructor in music and humanities (1954–60). As dean of the Kent State University library school (1960–77), he developed programs for music librarians. He served as chief of the General Reference and Bibliography Division, Library of Congress (1977–8) and as director of the library school, San Jose (California) State University (1981–3); he is internationally active as a consultant on library planning. He has written many articles on librarianship and reviews of about 100 books, as well as articles on 17th and 18th century music and on opera. With Palisca he translated and edited part three of Gioseffo Zarlino's *Le istitutioni harmoniche* (1968/*R*1976); he also wrote *Information on Music: a Handbook of Reference Sources in European Languages* (vols.i–iii, 1975–84) and *Opera: a Research and Information Guide* (1984).

SIEGMUND LEVARIE

Marcus, Adele (*b* Kansas City, MO, ?1909). Pianist and teacher. After early training in music in Los Angeles, at the age of 15 she entered the Juilliard Graduate School, where she studied under Josef Lhévinne for four years before making her New York début, as a winner of the Naumburg Prize, in 1929; later she studied in Berlin with Schnabel. She taught at Juilliard for seven years as Lhévinne's assistant before joining the faculty there in 1954; among her outstanding pupils are Anievas, Gutierrez, Janis, and Tedd Joselson. Marcus has performed both in recitals and as a soloist with orchestras throughout the USA and in Canada, Europe, and Israel; she has also given master classes and lectures at the Aspen Music Festival, Temple University, the University of Maryland at College Park, and elsewhere. In 1980 she established her own summer piano festival in Norway.

ELLEN HIGHSTEIN

Marcus, Greil (*b* San Francisco, CA, 19 June 1945). Rock critic. He attended the University of California, Berkeley (BA and MA in American studies), and taught there, 1971–2. An early contributor to *Rolling Stone*, he acted as its recordings editor in 1969–70, and has written regularly or been a rock-music columnist for other magazines including the *Village Voice*, *Creem*, *New West* (renamed *California*), and *Artforum*. He has also written literary columns for *Rolling Stone* and *New West* and a television column for *City*, and has served as a board member for the National Book Critics Circle. Best known as the author of *Mystery Train: Images of America in Rock 'n' Roll Music* (1975, 2/1982), he has also edited two anthologies, *Rock and Roll will Stand* (1969) and *Stranded: Rock and Roll for a Desert Island* (1979).

Marcus's writings have won him unparalleled respect both inside and outside the rock community. He is the most influential writer among American intellectuals to have emerged from the ranks of rock critics. His work combines a scholarly knowledge of rock with a more wideranging erudition and intellectual curiosity; his prose style is clear and lively. Underlying his aesthetic concerns is a commitment to moral and political issues that lends his best writing an almost bardic quality.

JOHN ROCKWELL

Marcuse, Sibyl (*b* Frankfurt am Main, Germany, 13 Feb 1911). Musicologist. Of Swiss and English parentage, she was educated at several European universities. From 1932 to 1935 she lived in China. Following the outbreak of World War II, she immigrated to the USA, where she was naturalized in 1945. She studied at a school for piano technicians in New York and for several summers served as an apprentice to the harpsichord maker John Challis. In 1950 she established herself as a harpsichord and piano technician in New York. Although an autodidact in musicology, she soon gained a reputation as an organologist of encyclopedic knowledge. From 1953 to 1960 she served as curator of the Yale University Collection of Musical Instruments. After retiring, Marcuse published two comprehensive and complementary reference books: *Musical Instruments, a Comprehensive Dictionary* (1964, rev. 2/1975) defines and describes individual instruments, while *A Survey of Musical Instruments* (1975) is a historical survey that deals with instruments by groups, according to the standard Hornbostel–Sachs classification scheme. In recognition of her scholarly contributions Marcuse received the Curt Sachs Award of the American Musical Instrument Society in 1984.

HOWARD SCHOTT

Marek, George R(ichard) (*b* Vienna, Austria, 13 July 1902). Writer on music. He studied at the University of Vienna from 1918 to 1920, when he immigrated to the USA. Beginning his career as an advertising executive, he became a vice-president of RCA in 1950. From 1941 to 1957 he was music editor of *Good Housekeeping*; he has been a regular panel member of the Metropolitan Opera Quiz. Marek has written a number of popular biographies of composers and books on opera.

WRITINGS

Puccini: a Biography (New York, 1951)
ed.: *The World Treasury of Grand Opera* (New York, 1957/*R*1971)
Opera as Theater (New York, 1962/*R*1977)
Richard Strauss: the Life of a Non-hero (New York, 1967)
Beethoven: Biography of a Genius (New York, 1969)
Gentle Genius: the Story of Felix Mendelssohn (New York, 1972)
Toscanini (New York, 1975)
with A. Smith: *Chopin* (New York, 1978)
Cosima Wagner (New York, 1981)

PAULA MORGAN

Mares, Paul. Jazz trumpeter, co-founder and leader of the NEW ORLEANS RHYTHM KINGS.

Maretzek, Max (*b* Brünn [now Brno, Czechoslovakia], 28 June 1821; *d* New York, 14 May 1897). Conductor, impresario, and composer. From 1840 he was active as a conductor and composer in central Europe. In 1842 he was invited to Paris, and two years later became chorus master at Covent Garden. In 1848 Edward Fry invited him to conduct Italian opera at Astor Place Opera House in New York; Fry's company opened in Philadelphia, where Maretzek first appeared on 5 October. Fry retired after one season, and in March 1849 Maretzek began a career as impresario. From then until 1878 he conducted and managed companies in New York (principally at the Academy of Music), and toured the USA, Cuba, and Mexico. His seasons were enlivened by frequent struggles between himself, Bernard Ullman, and the Strakosch brothers to employ various opera stars, as well as by competition for sponsors, experiments in producing extravaganza, and various ticket-pricing schemes. He managed to engage excellent singers, and conducted the American premières of, among other works, Verdi's *La traviata* (1856) and *Don Carlos* (1877). His managerial policies helped to establish continuing popular support for opera in New York. In 1878 Maretzek retired from management, though he continued to conduct and teach. His contributions were honored in a testimonial concert at the Metropolitan Opera House on 12 February 1889. He composed ballets and operas, including *Sleepy Hollow, or The Headless Horseman* (1879), and his two volumes of reminiscences provide an entertaining account of musical America in the mid-19th century.

See also NEW YORK, §4.

BIBLIOGRAPHY

M. Maretzek: *Crotchets and Quavers* (New York, 1855/*R*1968 in *Revelations of an Opera Manager in 19th Century America*)
——: *Sharps and Flats* (New York, 1890/*R*1968 in *Revelations of an Opera Manager in 19th Century America*)
W. Rieck: "Max Maretzek: Impresario, Conductor and Composer," *Musical Courier*, lxxxiv (22 June 1922), 6

WILLIAM BROOKS

Mariana Islands. An archipelago of volcanic islands of Micronesia; the principal island, GUAM, is a territory of the USA.

Mario [Tillotson], **Queena** (*b* Akron, OH, 21 Aug 1896; *d* New York, 28 May 1951). Soprano. Her father had been a drummer boy in the Civil War. After moving to Plainfield, New Jersey, in 1906, the family lost everything in the economic crisis a year later. Her mother died when Queena was 13. In order to earn money for singing lessons, she moved to New York and wrote women's columns (under the names Queena Tillotson and Florence Bryan) for the *Evening Telegram*, the *Evening World*, and *The Sun*. She studied first with Oscar Saenger and later with Marcella Sembrich; she was twice turned down in auditions for the Metropolitan Opera, but with the help of Caruso was engaged by the San Carlo Opera Company, with which she made her début in *Les contes d'Hoffmann* on 4 September 1918. After two seasons with that company and another two with the Scotti Grand Opera Company, Mario made her début at the Metropolitan in the role of Micaela (Thanksgiving Day, 1922). For the next 17 seasons she sang there a wide variety of lyric and coloratura parts, enjoying her greatest success as Engelbert Humperdinck's Gretel, a role she also performed in the first complete opera broadcast live from the Metropolitan stage (Christmas Day, 1931) and at her farewell performance with the company (26 December 1938). She sang for several seasons (1923–4, 1929–30, 1932) with the San Francisco Opera, notably as the Child in the American première of Ravel's *L'enfant et les sortilèges* (19 September 1930). As a recitalist, Mario was especially admired for her sensitivity to word inflections and for the silvery tone of her voice. In her later years she devoted herself to teaching, succeeding Sembrich at the Curtis Institute in 1931. She opened her own studio in New York three years later, joined the faculty of the Juilliard School in 1942, and instituted a summer opera school in a converted Connecticut barn; her pupils included Rose Bampton and Helen Jepson. She was the author of three mystery novels.

BIBLIOGRAPHY

"Christmas Memories for Queena Mario," *Opera News*, x/8 (1945), 28

PHILIP LIESON MILLER

Marklove, John Gale (*b* England, 1827; *d* Utica, NY, 1891). Organ builder. He studied at the University of Oxford, immigrated to the USA around 1852, and entered the organ-building firm of Alvinza Andrews in Utica in 1853. In 1857 or 1858 he began his own firm, which built a number of notable instruments; most of these were in central New York, some were as far west as Minnesota and South Dakota, and one, a fairly large organ, was built for St. John's Church, Montgomery, Alabama. The three-manual organ at Christ Church, Utica (1883), may have been one of Marklove's larger instruments. After his death the firm was continued by his son Clifford, in partnership with Clarence E. Morey and Al Barnes, and soon became known as Morey & Barnes; the company continued under Morey from 1897 to 1935.

BIBLIOGRAPHY

R. J. Reich: "John G. Marklove," *The Tracker*, ii/2 (1957), 3

BARBARA OWEN

Marks, Alan (*b* Chicago, IL, 14 May 1949). Pianist. After moving to St. Louis as a child, Marks studied piano with Shirley Parnas Adams. He won a prize at Interlochen in 1965 and a year later gave his first recital in St. Louis. In 1967 he enrolled at the Juilliard School (BM 1971), where he studied with Irwin Freundlich. In 1970 he won a piano competition sponsored by the Concert Artists Guild, which led to his New York début on 6 January 1971. Marks then toured various American cities as a solo recitalist, and joined the violinist Daniel Heifetz in a series of recitals in prisons, hospitals, and schools (1971–2); during this time he continued his studies with Leon Fleisher at the Peabody Conservatory. He has made tours of the USA, Europe (début London, 1979), and Japan, and has also been active as a chamber musician, appearing at the Marlboro and Sante Fe festivals. Marks possesses an almost flawless technique and approaches both classical and contemporary works with sensitive musicianship: he gave the belated premières of Chávez's Seven Pieces (1975) and *Caprichos* (1976), and has recorded works by Chávez, Boulez, Sessions, and Rochberg. He taught at the 92nd Street "Y" in New York (1972–80) and at the Lincoln Center Institute (1979–81).

GENE BIRINGER

Marks, Edward B(ennett) (*b* Troy, NY, 28 Nov 1865; *d* Mineola, NY, 17 Dec 1945). Music publisher. In 1894 he and Joseph Stern established the music publishing firm of Joseph W. Stern & Company. In 1920 Marks purchased Stern's interest and renamed the firm the Edward B. Marks Music Company; in 1932 it became the Edward B. Marks Music Corporation. The firm was a leading publisher of American and Latin American popular music. One of its earliest successes was *The Little Lost Child* (1894), written by Marks and Stern, which sold more than a million copies and was the first song to be introduced to singing audiences through illustrated slides. The firm also issued *Sweet Rosie O'Grady* (1896), *Take back your gold* (1897), *Under the bamboo tree* (1902), *Malagueña* (1928), *The Peanut Vendor* (1931), and *Paper Doll* (1942). During the 1930s Marks began to publish much serious music; its composers include Beglarian, Bolcom, Chatman, Davidovsky, Dello Joio, Robert Jager, Moevs, Alfred Reed, Sessions, Hale Smith, Thorne, Gilbert Trythall, and Ward-Steinman. In 1967 Marks purchased the catalogue of the George M. Cohan Music Publishing Co. and began publishing all Cohan's songs. Marks is also the agent in the USA and Canada for parts of the catalogues of the Polish firm Polskie Wydawnictwo Muzyczne and Josef Weinberger of England. After Marks's death his son Herbert Edward Marks served as president of the firm until 1971; in 1973 Belwin-Mills took over the distribution of its publications.

Marks wrote two books: *They All Sang: from Tony Pastor to Rudy Vallée* (1934) concerns the popular music industry and includes information on the early history of his firm, and *They All had Glamour: from the Swedish Nightingale to the Naked Lady* (1944/*R* 1972) deals with opera singers, musical theater, and popular music of the 19th century.

BIBLIOGRAPHY

H. I. Brock: "Tin Pan Alley is Always in Tune," *New York Times Magazine* (13 Feb 1944), 14, 23

" 'Little Lost Child' to 'Paper Doll': 50 Years of Hits for House of Hits," *Newsweek*, xxiii (21 Feb 1944), 70

"Marks, Edward Bennett," *The National Cyclopedia of American Biography*, xxxiv (New York, 1948/*R* 1967), 176

R. ALLEN LOTT

Marlboro Music Festival. International festival of chamber music founded in Marlboro, Vermont, in 1950. Its founders Rudolf Serkin (artistic director), Adolf and Hermann Busch, and Marcel and Louis Moyse conceived it as a workshop in which approximately 85 professional musicians would study and perform chamber music for eight weeks. The basic tenet of the festival was that there be no students or teachers, only participants. Pablo

Casals, Alexander Schneider, Felix Galimir, and Mieczysław Horszowski are among the renowned concert artists who participated regularly. Public performances are now given weekly in Persons Auditorium (capacity 650) at Marlboro College in Vermont during a five-week summer season. The festival has reached a wide audience through its recording series, the many taped performances it makes available to broadcasting stations, and through Music from Marlboro, a touring program created in 1965 to extend the summer activities into the autumn and spring. Music from Marlboro annually engages about 25 musicians from the summer program to perform throughout the USA. The ensembles, which vary in size, often combine veteran performers with less experienced players, consistent with the ideals of the festival. Among the musicians who have toured with Music from Marlboro (over 150 by the mid-1980s) are the pianists Ruth Laredo, Lee Luvisi, André-Michel Schub, and Peter Serkin; the violinists James Buswell, Ani Kavafian, and Jaime Laredo; and the cellists Nathaniel Rosen and Leslie Parnas.

JAMES CHUTE

Marlowe [Sapira], **Sylvia** (*b* New York, 26 Sept 1908; *d* New York, 10 Dec 1981). Harpsichordist. She studied piano and organ while attending high school and university, then continued her musical education at the Ecole Normale in Paris, where she took further instruction on these instruments and studied composition with Nadia Boulanger. It was there that she first heard and was impressed by Wanda Landowska, but she did not study with her until years later. On returning to the USA, Marlowe received a national music award to perform Bach's *Das wohltemperirte Clavier* on the piano in a series of radio broadcasts. Gradually she gave up the piano in favor of the harpsichord. For some years she specialized in radio performances, in which she presented not only the standard repertory of Renaissance and Baroque works, but contemporary music as well, including jazz. From the late 1940s she increased the number of her recitals, engagements with orchestras, and recordings, and made concert tours in North and South America, Europe, and the Far East; she was also a member of the Harpsichord Quartet, during the 1950s. Marlowe's repertory was extensive, and her sensitive playing was distinguished by a highly developed sense of style. In 1957 she founded the Harpsichord Music Society, which aims at fostering the creation of a contemporary repertory for the instrument, and commissioned works from Carter, Haieff, Hovhaness, Rieti, Rorem, and Henri Sauguet. She was appointed to the faculty of the Mannes College in 1948. In addition to her editions of works by Couperin, she published the article "A 'Dead' Instrument" (*MJ*, xx/1, 1962, p.70).

BIBLIOGRAPHY

"Sylvia Marlowe," *New Yorker*, lvii (11 Jan 1982), 27

K. Cooper: "Sylvia Marlowe: Wit, Warmth, and Wisdom," *HiFi/MusAm*, xxxii/6 (1982), 55 [with discography]

HOWARD SCHOTT/R

Marriner, Sir Neville (*b* Lincoln, England, 15 April 1924). English conductor and violinist. He studied at the Royal College of Music, London, and for a year at the Paris Conservatoire. He then taught at Eton College (1947–8), played in the Martin String Quartet (1946–53), and joined Thurston Dart in forming the Jacobean Ensemble, specializing in 17th- and 18th-century music. He also taught violin at the Royal College of Music (1949–59), formed the Virtuoso String Trio (in 1950), and played in the Philharmonia Orchestra (London) and the London SO (1956–68). In 1959, after studying conducting with Pierre Monteux, he formed the Academy of St. Martin-in-the-Fields, which has won a number of international recording awards. In 1969 he also became music director of the Los Angeles Chamber Orchestra, with which he toured Britain in 1974; he was associated with several other orchestras during the 1970s and in 1977 became artistic director of the Detroit SO's Meadow Brook Music Festival (Rochester, Michigan). In 1979 he was appointed music director of the Minnesota Orchestra, and in 1980 he became principal conductor of the Süddeutscher RO, Stuttgart. Marriner has made well over 100 recordings and has won a number of awards, among them the Mozart Gemeinde prize (three times), the Edison Award (five times), and the Grand Prix du Disque. He was made a CBE in 1979 and knighted in 1985.

BIBLIOGRAPHY

"Neville Marriner Talks to Alan Blyth," *Gramophone*, lii (1974), 661

M. Oliver: "From Director to Conductor," *Gramophone*, lvi (1978), 441

C. W. Van Ausdall: "Neville Marriner," *Stereo Review*, xli/5 (1978), 92

"Marriner, Neville," *CBY 1978*

D. R. Martin: "Neville Marriner," *Fugue*, iii (1979), July–Aug, 20

A. Keener: "Neville Marriner," *Gramophone*, lix (1982), 1359

D. Rosenberg and B. Rosenberg: "Neville Marriner," *The Music Makers* (New York, 1979), 171

NOËL GOODWIN/RUTH B. HILTON

Marrocco, W(illiam) Thomas (*b* West New York, NJ, 5 Dec 1909). Musicologist. He trained as a violinist at the Royal Conservatory of Music, Naples, and performed for several years with the Roth String Quartet before attending the Eastman School (BM 1934, MM 1940) and UCLA (PhD 1952). He taught at Elmira College (1936–9), Iowa University (1945–6), and the University of Kansas (1946–9), and in 1950 became professor of music at UCLA. Marrocco specializes in the music of 14th-century Italy; he has edited the entire body of Italian secular music of the Ars Nova for L'Oiseau-Lyre and has published separate editions of Italian cacce and the works of Jacopo da Bologna. Also interested in early American music, he edited *Music in America* (with H. Gleason, 1964), which was one of the first such anthologies of US music.

PAULA MORGAN

Marsalis, Wynton (*b* New Orleans, LA, 18 Oct 1961). Trumpeter. The son of the jazz pianist Ellis Marsalis, he received training in classical music, and performed with the New Orleans PO when he was 14. While studying at the Juilliard School, in 1980 Marsalis joined Art Blakey and the Jazz Messengers, a hard-bop group long recognized as a springboard for young jazz trumpeters. Critical accolades were immediate and effusive, and Marsalis was hailed as one of the finest jazz soloists of recent times, his dazzling technique being balanced by emotional depth and improvisational ability. Marsalis spent the summer of 1981 touring with Herbie Hancock while planning to record his first album as leader, *Wynton Marsalis*. In early 1982 he left Blakey to form his own band with his older brother, Branford Marsalis, on tenor saxophone. In 1983 Marsalis's second jazz album appeared, along with a recording of trumpet concertos by Haydn, Hummel, and Leopold Mozart; unprecedentedly, both albums won Grammy awards in their respective categories in 1984.

RECORDINGS

As leader: *Wynton Marsalis* (1981, Col. FC37574); *Think of One* (1982, Col. FC38641); *Black Codes (from the Underground)* (1985, Col. FC40009)

As sideman with A. Blakey: *Recorded Live at Bubba's* (1980, Who's Who in Jazz 21019); *Straight Ahead* (1981, Conc. 168); *Keystone 3* (1982, Conc. 196)

BIBLIOGRAPHY

A. J. Liska: "Wynton and Branford Marsalis: a Common Understanding," *Down Beat*, xlix/12 (1982), 14
M. Seidel: "Profile: Wynton Marsalis," *Down Beat*, xlix/12 (1982), 52
L. Jeske: "Who is Wynton Marsalis?," *Jazz*, iii (May–June 1983), 4
C. Murray: "Wynton Marsalis," *The Wire*, no. 1 (1982), 28
H. I. West: "Wynton Marsalis: Blowing his own Horn, Speaking his own Mind," *Jazz Times*, vi (July 1983), 10
"Marsalis, Wynton," *CBY 1984*
J. Pareles: "Jazz Swings Back to Tradition," *New York Times Magazine* (17 June 1984), 22

LEE JESKE

Marsh, Dave (*b* Pontiac, MI, 1 March 1950). Rock critic. Shortly after leaving Wayne State University, Detroit, in 1969, he became unofficial editor of the collectively organized *Creem* magazine. In 1973 he moved to the East Coast. For short periods he was rock critic for *Newsday*, a newspaper on Long Island, and music editor of the *Real Paper* in Boston; from 1975 to 1977 he was recordings editor of *Rolling Stone*, for which he wrote a column, 1976–9. Marsh's biography *Born to Run: the Bruce Springsteen Story* (1979) inaugurated a series of books that have become the principal focus of his career. He has edited several anthologies, including one of his own writings, *Fortunate Son* (1985), and in 1983 he founded a muckraking newsletter, *Rock & Roll Confidential*. Until 1984 he was a columnist for *The Record*.

Marsh is probably the best-known critic among the general rock audience. He helped define the irreverent, slangy style of *Creem*. Later he grew disillusioned with the pretensions of the so-called psychedelic and collegiate soft- and folk-rock movements and became a champion of black music and direct, no-nonsense, mid-American working-class rock, with Springsteen as its quintessential exponent. In the early 1980s left-wing populist politics became increasingly evident in his writing. Impatient with anything he disagrees with, Marsh makes up in passionate commitment what he sometimes lacks in tolerance and intellectual refinement.

WRITINGS

Born to Run: the Bruce Springsteen Story (New York, 1979)
ed., with J. Swenson: *The Rolling Stone Record Guide* (New York, 1979, 2/1983)
ed., with K. Stein: *The Book of Rock Lists* (New York, 1981)
Elvis (New York, 1982)
Before I get Old: the Story of the Who (New York, 1983)
Fortunate Son (New York, 1985)

JOHN ROCKWELL

Marsh, Robert C(harles) (*b* Columbus, OH, 5 Aug 1924). Music critic. He studied journalism (BS 1945) and philosophy (MA 1946) at Northwestern University, and music and philosophy at Cornell University, the University of Chicago, Harvard University, Oxford University, and Trinity College, Cambridge. Among his teachers were Paul Hindemith and Thurston Dart. He taught at various colleges from 1947 to 1968. Meanwhile, in 1956 he became music critic for the Chicago *Sun-Times* and since then has written approximately 200 articles each year for that newspaper; his other publications include *Toscanini and the Art of Orchestral Performance* (1956, rev. 2/1962) and *The Cleveland Orchestra* (1967), and he is preparing the first comprehensive history of opera in Chicago. He has also written articles for numerous philosophical journals. He shared the Peabody Award for music broadcasting in 1976 and in 1983 won a Deems Taylor Award for music criticism. Marsh is one of the most important music critics in the Midwest, by virtue of his association for so many years with the musical center of the area.

PATRICK J. SMITH

Marshall, Ingram D(ouglass) (*b* Mount Vernon, NY, 10 May 1942). Composer. After graduating from Lake Forest (Illinois) College (BA 1964), he studied with Lang (musicology) and Ussachevsky (electronic music) at Columbia University (1964–6) and with Subotnick at both the School of the Arts, New York University (1969–70), and the California Institute of the Arts, Valencia (MFA 1971), where he also studied traditional Indonesian music with K. R. T. Wasitodipura. Until 1974 he taught at the California Institute of the Arts (his associates included Tenney, Serge Tcherepnin, Palestine, and Budd). In 1975 he went to Stockholm on a Fulbright scholarship, where he was guest composer with Fylkingen; he has also won two NEA grants (1979, 1981) and a Rockefeller Foundation grant (1982). He received commissions from the San Francisco Contemporary Music Players, the Oakland SO, and the Fromm Foundation, among others. Marshall has contributed music criticism to *New West*, the *Berkeley Barb*, and other publications, and articles to *Numus West* and *Soundings*.

Marshall's travels to Java and Bali (1971), Scandinavia, and elsewhere have influenced his music significantly. His imagery incorporates "on-location" elements – footsteps, distant voices, altered concrete sounds – and local atmosphere, as in *The Fragility Cycles* (1976), with its bleak textures evocative of Scandinavia. *Fillmore* (1978) even includes slides and narration to describe a walk the composer took in the California hills. Though his performances – in which he combines composed music, improvisation on the *gambuh* (a Balinese flute), singing, and live electronics – suggest his affinity with other performing artists who emerged in the 1970s, Marshall's concern with not only expressive narration but also his philosophical relationship to past music (as in *Non confundar*, with its contrapuntal basis) is distinctive. *Spiritus* (1981) and others of his conventionally notated works use rhythmic-cell techniques that recall the early music of John Adams but also reflect the influence of Sibelius and Javanese gamelan music.

WORKS

(selective list)

Transmogrification (W. Blake), tape, 1966; 3 Buchla Studies, synth, 1968–9; The East is Red, variations, tape, 1971–2; Cortez (D. McCaig), text-sound piece, tape, 1973; Ricebowlthundersock, prepared pf, perc, elec, 1973; Augmented Triad Ascending, pf, 2 mar, vib, glock, 1974; The Emperor's Birthday, text-sound piece, tape, 1974; Weather Report, tape, 1974; Tourist Songs, I–II, tape, 1975; Vibrosuperball, 4 amp perc, 1975

Ikon: Ayiasma (G. Ekelöf), text-sound piece, tape, reciter, live elec, 1976; The Fragility Cycles, 1v, gambuh, live elec, tape, 1976 [incl. part of Tourist Songs]; Non confundar, str sextet, a fl, cl, elec, 1977, rev. 1978; Sung (G. Ekelöf), text-sound piece, tape, reciter, live elec, 1977; Landscape Parts (Fields/bands) (Ekelöf, Tranströmer), 1v, gambuhs, tape, live elec, 1978; Fillmore, gambuh, tape, slides, live elec, 1978

Addendum: in aeternum, cl, fl, str sextet, 1979; Landscape Parts II, va, fl, cl, perc, pf, 1v, live elec, 1979; Gradual Requiem, synth, mand, pf, 1v, gambuh, tape, live elec, 1980; Magnificat Strophes, Synclavier, 1981; Spiritus, 6 str, 4 fl, hpd, vib, 1981, rev. str orch, 1983; Fog Tropes, 6 brass, tape, live elec, 1982; Woodstone, gamelan, 1982; Alcatraz, kbds, tape, slides, elec, 1983–4, collab. J. Bengston; Str Qt: Voces resonae, 1984 [with live elec]

CHARLES SHERE

Marshall, Robert L(ewis) (*b* New York, 12 Oct 1939). Musicologist. He graduated from Columbia University (BA 1960), then studied at Princeton (PhD 1968). In 1966 he was appointed to the faculty of the University of Chicago and was chairman of the department of music, 1972–5. Marshall's special interest is 18th-century music, particularly the works of J. S. Bach. He is also interested in the history of German church music to 1750, Lutheran chorale settings, and 17th-century keyboard music. His dissertation *The Compositional Process of J. S. Bach*, for which he was awarded the Otto Kinkeldey prize of the American Musicological Society, is the first detailed study of the autograph scores of Bach's vocal works and the first systematic attempt to find in them evidence of Bach's working methods. He also edited *Studies in Renaissance and Baroque Music in Honor of Arthur Mendel* (1974).

PAULA MORGAN

Martens, Frederick Herman (*b* New York, 6 July 1874; *d* Mountain Lakes, NJ, 18 Dec 1932). Librettist and writer on music. He was educated by tutors and studied music privately in New York. He wrote texts for a number of operettas, cantatas, and songs, and was also active as a translator, providing English versions of the librettos of such operas as Falla's *La vida breve* (1925), Spontini's *La vestale* (1925), and Krenek's *Jonny spielt auf* (1928). From 1907, however, his main occupation was the writing of books and essays, chiefly on opera and string playing, though he also wrote a monograph on the futurist composer Leo Ornstein, with whom in 1930 he shared first prize in a national anthem competition. He contributed articles to *Musical Quarterly*, *Musical America*, and *Monthly Musical Record*, among other publications.

WRITINGS

Leo Ornstein: the Man, his Ideas, his Work (New York, 1918/*R* 1975)
Violin Mastery (New York, 1919)
The Art of the Prima Donna and Concert Singer (New York, 1923/*R* 1977)
String Mastery (New York, 1923)
The Book of the Opera and the Ballet and History of the Opera (New York, 1925/*R* 1984)
A Thousand and One Nights of Opera (New York, 1926/*R* 1978)

PAULA MORGAN

Martha and the Vandellas. Rhythm-and-blues vocal group. Martha Reeves (*b* Detroit, MI, 18 July 1941) worked as a secretary for the Motown Record Corporation; she came to the attention of Berry Gordy, Jr., the company's president, when she formed a backing group (with Rosalind Ashford and Annette Sterling) that sang on Marvin Gaye's *Stubborn Kind of Fellow* (1962). Taking the name Martha and the Vandellas, the group began to record on their own account, and their second single, *Come and get these memories* (1963), reached no. 30 on the pop chart; this was followed by *Heat Wave* a few months afterwards. Reeves's aggressive, flamboyant style and the sympathetic writing and production of the Holland-Dozier-Holland team helped the Vandellas avoid being categorized simply as a girl group; in fact they recorded some of the toughest music produced by Motown, including *Dancing in the street* (1964), a good example of the obsessive, sophisticated offbeat typical of the Motown sound. A succession of infectious hit singles followed, culminating with the delightful *Jimmy Mack* (1967); the group made no further hit recordings and disbanded in 1972, after which Reeves pursued a solo career with slight success.

RECORDINGS

(selective list; all recorded for Gordy)

Come and get these memories (7014, 1963); *Heat Wave* (907, 1963); Quicksand (7025, 1963); *Dance Party* (915, 1964); Dancing in the street (7033, 1964); Nowhere to run (7039, 1965); I'm ready for love (7056, 1966); Jimmy Mack (7058, 1967); *Live* (925, 1967)

BIBLIOGRAPHY

SouthernB ("Reeves, Martha")
J. Futrell and others: *The Illustrated Encyclopedia of Black Music*, ed. R. Bonds (New York, 1982), 75
J. Miller and J. McEwen: "Motown," *The Rolling Stone Illustrated History of Rock & Roll*, ed. J. Miller (New York, 1976, rev. 2/1980), 227

JOSEPH McEWEN

Martin, C. F. Firm of guitar manufacturers. It was founded in New York by Christian Friedrich Martin (*b* Markneukirchen, Germany, 31 Jan 1796; *d* Nazareth, PA, 15 Feb 1873). Martin and his father, Johann Georg Martin, were members of the cabinet makers' guild in Markneukirchen, and were described as guitar makers during a legal dispute. Martin is mentioned as having made guitars since before 1826 and as having been foreman in the factory of the Viennese maker of guitars and violins, Johann Georg Stauffer. In autumn 1833 Martin immigrated to the USA, setting up a shop and workshop at 196 Hudson Street, New York. A fellow guitar maker from Markneukirchen, Heinrich Schatz, bought land near Nazareth, Pennsylvania, in 1835, and by 1837 was making guitars and selling them through Martin's New York shop, some guitars bearing the label "Martin and Schatz." In 1839 Martin moved to the Nazareth area and sold his New York agency to Ludecus & Wolter. Towards the end of this period, Martin also had an association with Charles Bruno, founder of the musical merchandise house C. Bruno & Son, some guitars being labelled "Martin and Bruno." By 1850 Martin had a New York sales outlet at 385 Broadway, and some guitars of this period are labeled "Martin and Coupa." In about 1850 the Martin factory was enlarged and in 1859 was moved to Main and North Street, Nazareth. (For illustration of an early Martin guitar *see* GUITAR, fig. 1.)

In 1867 the founder and his son, Christian Frederick, Jr. (1825–88), formed a partnership with the founder's nephew C. F. Hartmann under the name C. F. Martin & Co.; in 1921 the company was incorporated. A new workshop and factory were built in 1963 close to the original family home. Until 1982, when C. Hugh Bloom became president, the business was headed by further members of the Martin family: Frank Henry (1866–1948), Christian Frederick III (*b* 1894), and Frank Herbert (*b* 1933); Christian Frederick IV (*b* 1955) has remained involved in the company.

Martin's earliest guitars were influenced by the German maker Stauffer, but as the 19th century progressed the Martin brand came to be associated with more distinctive instruments. One of the best and most popular is the Dreadnought (introduced in 1931), a large, flat-top acoustic guitar with a distinctive wide-waisted shape that has been much copied by other makers. Martin guitars are given model numbers based on a complex system of coding that can indicate size, shape, and other design features.

The firm has also, at various times, produced electric guitars, carved-top guitars, mandolins, ukuleles, and tiples, but the principal part of their production is devoted to flat-top guitars, in which they are unequalled. Since 1970 guitars based on Martin designs have been built in Japan and marketed under the name Sigma.

BIBLIOGRAPHY

M. Longworth: *Martin Guitars: a History* (Cedar Knolls, NJ, 1975, 2/1980)

JAY SCOTT ODELL, TONY BACON

Martin, David Irwin, (Sr.) (*b* Asheville, NC, *c*1880; *d* New York, 28 Aug 1923). Music educator. After teaching violin for four years in New York, he served as head of the newly established Music School Settlement for Colored (1911–14); allied with the school's educational program was a series of concerts, presented at Carnegie Hall, which included such black American musicians as Marian Anderson, Roland Hayes, Henry T. Burleigh, and various chamber and orchestral ensembles in performances of music by Will Marion Cook, Samuel Coleridge-Taylor, Burleigh, Dett, and others. In 1919 he founded (with Helen Elise Smith) the Martin-Smith School of Music, which absorbed the Music School Settlement; its most accomplished pupils were Martin's own children, Gertrude and Eugene Mars (violinists), and David (cellist).

BIBLIOGRAPHY

SouthernB
R. Abdul: *Blacks in Classical Music* (New York, 1977)

DOMINIQUE-RENÉ DE LERMA

Martin, Dean [Crocetti, Dino Paul] (*b* Steubenville, OH, 7/17 June 1917). Popular singer and actor. He worked at various occupations, including boxer, steelworker, and croupier, before taking up a singing career, first in his hometown and then in Cleveland. By 1946 he was firmly established, having performed in New York and Atlantic City, New Jersey. That year he joined forces with the comedian Jerry Lewis: their partnership was enormously popular in nightclubs and on television shows, and they made 16 films between 1949 and 1956, when their association ended. Martin produced several best-selling recordings, often of Italian love songs such as *That's amore* (1953), *Return to me* (1958), and *Everybody loves somebody* (1964). From 1965 until the early 1970s his music-variety television show commanded a national audience. His singing style was greatly influenced by Bing Crosby; he had a resonant baritone voice and a charming, relaxed delivery.

BIBLIOGRAPHY

"Martin, Dean," *CBY 1964*
A. Marx: *Everybody Loves Somebody Sometime (Especially Himself): the Story of Dean Martin and Jerry Lewis* (New York, 1974)

MICHAEL J. BUDDS

Martin, (Thomas) Grady (*b* nr Lewisburg, TN, 17 Jan 1929). Country-music and pop guitarist, arranger, and fiddler. As a boy he learned traditional fiddle tunes and styles and at 15 he played for the first time as a professional with Big Jeff Bess and his Nashville radio band. This led to engagements with performers such as the Bailes Brothers, Uncle Dave Macon, and the champion fiddler Curly Fox, who all appeared on the "Grand Ole Opry" radio program. While with Fox, Martin switched to electric guitar, and he then worked with other pioneers of that instrument in the Nashville area, including Mose Rager, Zeke Turner, Hank Garland, and Jabbo Arrington; influenced by jazz guitarists, Garland and his circle had begun to explore the possibilities of playing the electric guitar in finger-picking styles and using it both as a solo instrument and as a replacement for the older country-music background of fiddle, mandolin, piano, or banjo. After he played on Red Foley's *Chattanoogie Shoe Shine Boy* (no. 1, 1949), Martin was engaged to work as a session musician with many of the singers who came to Nashville to record, including Little Jimmy Dickens, Marty Robbins, Patsy Cline, Lefty Frizzell, Johnny Cash, Jim Reeves, and Elvis Presley. Martin formed his own pop-jazz group, called the Slewfoot Five, which recorded extensively for Decca; in 1954 he and Garland recorded an album called *Dance-o-rama*, which included flashing improvisations, such as *Pork Chop Stomp* and *Wooly Boogie*. In 1960 Martin attracted national attention when he accidentally created the "fuzz" effect by using a faulty amplifier on Marty Robbins's hit *Don't Worry*. He also worked with popular artists such as Bing Crosby, Al Hirt, Perry Como, Henry Mancini, and Burl Ives. Martin's character and career were embodied in the character played by Slim Pickens in Willie Nelson's film *Honeysuckle Rose* (1980), for which Martin played the soundtrack; he also appeared in Nelson's road show in the early 1980s and on many of his albums.

Like many studio musicians, Martin became proficient in several styles, but he preferred a flat-picked style, and often built solos around a single-string technique that featured long melodic lines accented by blues phrases and occasional dissonance. Next to Chet Atkins, Martin was the most influential post-war Nashville electric guitarist, and a prime architect of the NASHVILLE SOUND. In 1983 the Nashville Music Association awarded him its first Master Tribute Award for studio musicians.

CHARLES K. WOLFE

Martin, Janis (*b* Sacramento, CA, 1939). Mezzo-soprano, later soprano. She sang minor roles at the San Francisco Opera for two seasons, then won the 1962 Metropolitan Opera Auditions. By 1965 she was singing such roles as Marina (*Boris Godunov*), Venus (*Tannhäuser*), and Meg Page (*Falstaff*) with the San Francisco company. In 1968 she sang the Composer (*Ariadne auf Naxos*) in Munich and Fricka at Bayreuth. Engaged for a year at Nuremberg, she added Hansel and Oktavian to her repertory. In the early 1970s she began to sing soprano roles, appearing as Tosca, Eva, Sieglinde, and Kundry in leading European houses, and at San Diego and Chicago. She made her London début at Covent Garden in 1973 as Marie (*Wozzeck*), a role she repeated a year later at the Metropolitan. Her repertory also includes Brangäne, Senta, Elisabeth (*Tannhäuser*), Ortrud, Adriano (*Rienzi*), Yaroslavna (*Prince Igor*), Ariadne, Judith (*Duke Bluebeard's Castle*), and the Woman in Schoenberg's *Erwartung*, which she sang at La Scala in 1980. The rich middle register characteristic of the mezzo-soprano voice was not lost when she became a dramatic soprano.

ELIZABETH FORBES

Martin, Mary (Virginia) (*b* Weatherford, TX, 1 Dec 1913). Actress, singer, and dancer. Her mother was a violinist. Martin taught social and stage dance, sang on radio and in films, and achieved fame in 1938 performing "My heart belongs to daddy" in Cole Porter's *Leave it to me*, a song with which she remained associated throughout her career. She performed in Broadway musicals, beginning with Weill's *One Touch of Venus* (1943, including the song "That's him"). Richard Rodgers and Oscar Hammerstein II wrote *South Pacific* (1949) for her and the bass Ezio Pinza; Rodgers recalled (in his autobiography, *Musical Stages*, 1975) that Martin, concerned about their unequal voices, was promised no duets: moreover, "her songs were colloquial, direct, sunny and youthful, whereas his were sophisticated, romantic, even philosophical" in lyrics and music. She later suggested adapting the film *The Trapp Family Singers*, which Rodgers and Hammerstein accomplished as their final work together, *The Sound of Music* (1959). Rodgers praised Martin's extraordinary diligence in vocal preparation and interpretation of his songs.

Martin continued to star in Broadway shows, including *I Do! I Do!* (1966), in films, and in children's musicals for television, most notably versions of the stage musical *Peter Pan* in the 1950s.

One of the best-loved American musical performers, she created several vibrant roles with her clear soprano and her warmth, vigor, control, and agility. She wrote an autobiography, *My Heart Belongs* (1976), and made many recordings.

DEANE L. ROOT

Martin, Riccardo [Whitefield, Hugh] (*b* Hopkinsville, KY, 18 Nov 1874; *d* New York, 11 Aug 1952). Tenor and composer. He studied singing in France, with Franklin Cannone in Milan, and with Vincenzo Lombardi in Florence (*c*1908), and composition at Columbia University with MacDowell. He made his opera début as Faust (Nantes, France, October 1904) under the name Richard Martin; when he sang in Italy the next year (in the title role of Umberto Giordano's *Andrea Chenier* in Verona on 4 November), he was called Riccardo. He made his American début in New Orleans as Canio (*Pagliacci*) in 1906, and after singing Don José (*Carmen*) and other roles on tour with the San Carlo Opera Company (1906–7), he appeared for the first time at the Metropolitan Opera as Faust in Arrigo Boito's *Mefistofele* in 1907; he remained with the company until 1915, specializing in the great Italian lyric roles (including Pinkerton, Cavaradossi, and Rodolfo), but also creating Quintus in Horatio Parker's *Mona* (1912) and Christian in Walter Damrosch's *Cyrano* (1913). During the same period he sang Pinkerton at Covent Garden (1910) and appeared with the Boston Grand Opera Company (1910–11, 1912–13). He returned to the Metropolitan in 1917–18, then sang Radames (*Aida*), Nicias (in Massenet's *Thaïs*), and Don José with the Chicago Opera (1920–23). Among his performances as recitalist and soloist were an appearance with the St. Paul SO and joint recitals with Rudolf Ganz. Martin retired in the late 1920s.

Throughout his career, Martin suffered from comparisons with Caruso, whose repertory he largely shared; his voice was a *spinto* tenor of great beauty (though it lacked individuality), and he had a fine stage presence. He made a number of recordings, one of the best of which is the Siciliana from *Cavalleria rusticana*. His compositions include several songs, an orchestral work (*Une nuit à l'oasis*), and a ballet.

BIBLIOGRAPHY

O. Thompson: *The American Singer* (New York, 1937/*R*1969), 279

M. de Schauensee: "A Tribute to Riccardo Martin," *Opera News*, xvii/6 (1952), 12

RICHARD LeSUEUR

Martin, Roberta (*b* Helena, AR, 12 Feb 1907; *d* Chicago, IL, 18 Jan 1969). Gospel singer, pianist, and composer. She began piano lessons at an early age with the intention of becoming a concert pianist. After her family moved to Chicago when she was a teenager she sang in Thomas A. Dorsey's newly formed gospel choir at the Ebenezer Baptist Church, and shortly afterwards became its pianist. With the composer Theodore R. Frye, an associate of Dorsey, she organized in 1933 the Martin-Frye Quartet; its original members were Willie Webb, Narsalus McKissick, Eugene Smith, and Robert Anderson, and Martin served as accompanist. By 1935 the group had become known as the Roberta Martin Singers. Although they occasionally performed routine jubilee or "shout" songs, their performance style was generally refined and controlled. Martin's style of accompaniment was characterized by middle-register chords punctuated rhythmically in the bass.

Martin wrote her first gospel song, *Try Jesus, he satisfies*, in 1943. The most popular of her approximately 100 works are *God is Still on the Throne* (1959), *Let it Be* (1962), and *Just Jesus and Me* (1966). Her songs are characterized by a sophisticated use of melody in the verse section and exotic harmonies in the chorus. She published her music through her own company, the Roberta Martin Studio of Music, which was established in Chicago in 1939. Martin was honored in a series of lectures and recitals at the Smithsonian Institution in February 1981.

BIBLIOGRAPHY

SouthernB

H. C. Boyer: *The Gospel Song: a Historical and Analytical Study* (thesis, Eastman School of Music, 1964)

T. Heilbut: *The Gospel Sound: Good News and Bad Times* (New York, 1971/*R*1975)

I. V. Jackson: *Afro-American Gospel Music and its Social Setting with Special Attention to Roberta Martin* (diss., Wesleyan U., 1974)

——: *Afro-American Religious Music: a Bibliography and Catalogue of Gospel Music* (Westport, CT, 1979)

HORACE CLARENCE BOYER

Martin, Sallie (*b* Pittfield, GA, 20 Nov 1896). Gospel singer. She did not begin singing until 1932, when she joined Thomas A. Dorsey's gospel group at the Ebenezer Baptist Church in Chicago. It was a year before Dorsey assigned her a solo, however, partly because of the dark color of her voice, but also on account of her tendency to croak at the beginning of a phrase and to mispronounce words. Dorsey also considered her manner to be curt and abrasive: from the beginning there was an adversarial relationship between the two, although they continued to work together into the early 1980s. In 1932 Martin joined Dorsey in the organization of the National Convention of Gospel Choirs and Choruses, with which she remained closely involved until 1940. She then opened the Martin and Morris Music Company with Kenneth Morris in Chicago, a publishing company she co-directed until 1975. In 1940 Martin formed the Sallie Martin Singers, with whom she toured throughout the USA and Europe. She was an active supporter of Martin Luther King and represented him at the ceremony marking the Independence of Nigeria in 1960. Her visit to Africa inspired her to make financial contributions to the Nigerian health program, and as a result a building in Isslu-uka was named in her honor. She still performs occasionally, but is best known for her recording with Alex Bradford of *He'll wash you whiter than snow* (1955).

BIBLIOGRAPHY

SouthernB

I. V. Jackson: *Afro-American Religious Music: a Bibliography and Catalogue of Gospel Music* (Westport, CT, 1979)

HORACE CLARENCE BOYER

Martin, Thomas Philipp (*b* Vienna, Austria, 28 May 1909; *d* New York, 14 May 1984). Translator of librettos and opera conductor. He graduated from the Vienna Conservatory and conducted at the Vienna Volksoper. After touring with the Salzburg International Opera Guild, 1937–8, he settled in the USA and conducted opera in St. Louis, Cincinnati, and Chicago, and also in Havana, Cuba, and San Juan, Puerto Rico. In 1941 Martin and his wife, Ruth, submitted an English translation of Mozart's *Die Zauberflöte* to the Metropolitan Opera. This was the first of over 50 opera translations, including the major Mozart operas and many works of Verdi, Puccini, Rossini, Donizetti, and Lortzing, on which they collaborated. In 1981 the Martins received a medal of honor from the Austrian government for their work. Martin was for over 40 years a staff conductor with both the

Metropolitan and New York City operas and also conducted for the Lake George Opera, the Bel Canto Opera, the Liederkranz Foundation, and the Reimann Opera Studio, New York University.

ELIZABETH A. WRIGHT

Martinelli, Giovanni (*b* Montagnana, Italy, 22 Oct 1885; *d* New York, 2 Feb 1969). Tenor. He studied singing in Milan, where he made his début in Rossini's *Stabat mater* and then sang in the title role of Verdi's *Ernani* in December 1910. After further appearances in Italy, notably at Rome in *La fanciulla del West* under Toscanini, he was engaged for Covent Garden, where he sang in more than 90 performances of 15 operas. At Puccini's insistence, Martinelli sang in the first performance of *La fanciulla del West* at La Scala (December 1912). His début at the Metropolitan Opera in *La bohème* on 20 November 1913 initiated a career with the company that lasted without interruption for 30 years, with a few still later appearances in 1945 and 1946. During this long period he sang in about 1000 performances of 36 operas, both in the New York house and on tour. His appearances outside the USA became rare, but he was as firm a favorite in Chicago and San Francisco as in New York.

Over the years Martinelli developed an unimpeachable technique and scrupulous style, and in New York he became, after the death of Caruso, the leading exponent of dramatic and heroic roles, especially Verdi's Manrico (*Il trovatore*), Radamès (*Aida*), Don Alvaro (*La forza del destino*), and Don Carlos, Canio (*Pagliacci*), Gounod's Faust, Don José (*Carmen*), Saint-Saëns' Samson, and Eléazar (in Halévy's *La juive*; see illustration); he was also successful in such lyrical roles as Rodolfo (*La traviata*) and Puccini's Pinkerton and Cavaradossi. The clarion ring of his upper register, the distinctness and purity of his declamation, and the sustained legato phrasing made possible by remarkable breath control were the outstanding features of his mature style. He retained his vocal powers to an advanced age, singing his last *Otello* in Philadelphia in 1947, and making his final stage appearance in Seattle, as the Emperor in three performances of *Turandot* in 1967. His recordings, especially those made by the Victor company between 1914 and 1939, well display his splendid tone and style. He continued to make semi-private recordings of rare items from his repertory until a few months before his death.

Giovanni Martinelli as Eléazar in Halévy's "La juive"

BIBLIOGRAPHY

J. B. Richards and J. A. Gibson: "Giovanni Martinelli," *Record Collector*, v (1950), 173 [with discography]

C. Williams: "The 'Private Off the Air' Recordings of Giovanni Martinelli," *Record Collector*, x (1955–6), 241 [with discography of Edison recordings]

D. Aylward: "Martinelli on LP Records," *Recorded Sound*, no. 1 (1962), 239

L. Luconi: "Il divo," *Opera News*, xxviii/2 (1963), 23

C. Williams: "Martinelli, Giovanni," *Le grandi voci*, ed. R. Celletti (Rome, 1964) [with discography]

J. C. Adams: "Giovanni Martinelli and the Joy of Singing," *II° congresso internazionale di studi verdiani: Verona 1969*, ed. M. Medici (Parma, 1971), 593

R. R. Wile: "The First Martinelli Recordings: a Selection from . . . the Edison National Historic Site," *Journal* [Association of Recorded Sound Collections], iii/2–3 (1971), 25 [incl. correspondence]

R. Bebb: "The Art of Giovanni Martinelli," *Recorded Sound*, no. 53 (1974), 247

W. J. Collins: "Giovanni Martinelli," *Record Collector*, xxv (1979–80), 149, 221 [with discography]

RICHARD CAPELL/DESMOND SHAWE-TAYLOR/R

Martinez, Narciso (*b* Matamoros, Mexico, 29 Oct 1911). Accordionist. He taught himself to play the diatonic accordion in the style of folk music prevalent in Mexico and Texas known as *música norteña*, and made his first commercial recording in 1935 (Bluebird 2910). His style differs markedly from that of other early *norteño* accordionists, whose playing is closer to the German tradition: instead of relying heavily on the left-hand bass elements of the instrument for accompaniment, he emphasized the right-hand melody buttons, and left the accompaniment to the *bajo sexto*, a double-course, 12-string guitar played by his partner Santiago Almeida. He developed a staccato articulation that was especially pronounced in his polkas, which have traditionally been the most characteristic genre of *música norteña*. He was awarded a National Heritage Fellowship by the NEA, and continues to perform in south Texas, where he has lived the greater part of his life. Examples of his playing are heard in the Texas-Mexican Border Music series of recordings (issued by Folklyric Records). Martinez influenced many other accordionists; he is sometimes known by the nickname "El huracán del valle."

BIBLIOGRAPHY

C. Strachwitz: Liner notes, *El Huracán del Valle: his First Recordings, 1936–1937* (Folklyric 9017, 1977)

M. Peña: "The Emergence of *Conjunto* Music, 1935–1955," *"And Other Neighborly Names": Social Process and Cultural Image in Texas Folklore*, ed. R. Bauman and R. D. Abrahams (Austin, 1981), 280

J. Reyna: "Notes on *Tejano* Music," *Aztlan: International Journal of Chicano Studies*, xiii (1982), 81

M. Peña: "From *Ranchero* to *Jaitón*: Ethnicity and Class in Texas-Mexican Music," *EM*, xxix (1985), 29

——: *The Texas-Mexican Conjunto: History of a Working-Class Music* (Austin, 1985)

MANUEL PEÑA

Martinez, Odaline de la (*b* Matanzas, Cuba, 31 Oct 1949). Conductor and composer. She immigrated to the USA in 1961 and became an American citizen in 1971. After attending Tulane University (BFA 1972), she studied composition with Paul Patterson at the Royal Academy of Music, London (1972–6), and with Reginald Smith Brindle (1975–7) at the University of Surrey (MM 1977). She has been the recipient of numerous awards, including a Marshall Scholarship (1972–5), a Watson Fellowship (1975–6), a Danforth Fellowship (1975–80), and a Guggenheim

Fellowship (1980–81). From 1972 Martinez has resided in London. She is best known in Europe as the conductor of Lontano, a professional chamber ensemble she helped found in 1976 to perform and record contemporary music; the group is based in London but tours widely. In 1982 she founded the Contemporary Chamber Orchestra, of which she is principal conductor. Martinez's own works are eclectic, influenced by George Crumb, by electronic music, and by her Latin-American heritage. Much of her music possesses a simple and direct "minimalist" quality. The opera *Sister Aimee* (1978–83), based on the life of the American evangelist Aimee Semple McPherson, makes use of a host of styles and techniques, including gospel music and aleatory procedures.

WORKS

Inst: Little Piece, fl, 1975; Phasing, chamber orch, 1975; Eos, org, 1976; A Moment's Madness, fl, pf, 1977; Improvisations, vn, 1977; Colour Studies, pf, 1978; Litanies, fls, harp, str trio, 1981; Asonancias, vn, 1982; Suite, eng hn, vc, 1982; Str Qt, 1984–5

Vocal: 5 Imagist Songs (D. H. Lawrence, W. C. Williams, R. Aldington, H. D.), S, cl, pf, 1974; After Sylvia (S. Plath), S, pf, 1976; Absalom (2 Samuel xviii.33), Ct, T, T, Bar, B, 1977; Psalmos, chorus, brass qnt, timp, org, 1977; Sister Aimee (opera, J. Whiting), 1978–83; 2 American Madrigals (E. Dickinson), unacc. chorus, 1979; Canciones (F. García Lorca), S, perc, pf, 1983; Cantos de amor, S, pf, str trio, 1985

Elec: Hallucination, tape, 1975; Visions and Dreams, tape, 1977–8; Lamento, S, A, T, B (all amp), tape, 1978; 3 Studies, perc, elec, 1980

MSS in AMC, British Music Information Centre

BIBLIOGRAPHY

O. Maxwell: "Odaline de la Martinez," *Music and Musicians* (1983), Oct, 10
H. Cole: "First Lady of the Proms," *The Guardian* (London, 17 Aug 1984)
A. Burn: "Odaline de la Martinez," *MT*, cxxvi (1985), 401

STEPHEN MONTAGUE

Martino, Donald (James) (*b* Plainfield, NJ, 16 May 1931). Composer. He attended Syracuse (BM 1952) and Princeton (MFA 1954) universities and studied composition with Bacon, Sessions, and Babbitt; on a Fulbright scholarship (1954–6) he studied with Dallapiccola in Florence. Martino taught at the Third Street Settlement in New York (1956–7), Princeton University (1957–9), and Yale University (1959–69), and from 1969 to 1981 was chairman of the composition department at the New England Conservatory; he also taught at Harvard University in 1971. After serving as Irving Fine Professor of Music at Brandeis University from 1980 to 1983, he joined the faculty of Harvard in 1983. He has spent several summers lecturing on contemporary music at the Berkshire Music Center. In 1978 he founded a publishing company, Dantalian, Inc., for the promotion of his own music. Martino's honors include awards from BMI, the National Institute of Arts and Letters, and the NEA, a Brandeis University Creative Arts Award (1964), three Guggenheim fellowships (1967–8, 1973–4, 1982–3), the Classical Critics Citation (1976), a grant from the Massachusetts Arts Council (1982), and commissions from such organizations as the Boston SO, the Koussevitzky Foundation, and the Coolidge Foundation. A Naumburg Award in 1973 resulted in the composition of *Notturno*, for which he won a Pulitzer Prize in 1974. In 1981 he became a member of the Institute of the American Academy and Institute of Arts and Letters.

Martino's imagination and craftsmanship are evident both in his ensemble and in his solo works. The latter contain numerous specific and original notations for fingerings, bowings, attacks, releases, etc., to ensure that all sounds are produced in as integral and precise a manner as that in which they were conceived; yet the many *espressivo* and tempo indications allow the performer considerable flexibility within a rigorous framework. Martino not only employs the attributes unique to a particular instrument but seems to enlarge them: it is as if a new instrument has been invented, and by the end of a work the listener's preconceptions and experience of the instrument and of music itself may be radically transformed and enriched.

Moreover, the various instrumental sonorities that Martino specifies are closely correlated to the projection of musical structures. Register, dynamics, and specific modes of tone production are used to mark structurally significant pitch sets. For example, in the first section of his work for solo cello, *Parisonatina al'dodecafonia* (1964), each mode of performance (harmonics, *presso il ponticello*, pizzicato, *sul tasto*, and *col legno battuto*) is associated with a particular 12-tone pitch-class set, thus articulating the polyphonic implications of the music. Two distinct sets are presented in harmonics (each in a separate octave – *c'* to *b'* and *d''* to *c♯'''*); another is presented pizzicato (notated with square note heads) and in the octave *F* to *e*; another (in the octave *C* to *B*) is presented *sul tasto* and *col legno battuto* and completed with the only accented note in the passage (*E*) before the coda-motto; and another is presented in *modo ordinario* (in the octave *a♭* to *g'*). The entire passage may also be interpreted in terms of its note-to-note pitch structure, which consists of six presentations of different hexachords from the "polyphonically" projected sets discussed above.

Martino's ensemble pieces are characterized by interplays between densely textured blocks of sound and solo passages; elegantly contoured lines reminiscent of cadenzas emerge out of the denser patches only to be subsumed within the next polyphonic block. The solos in the Concerto for Wind Quintet (1964), especially the one for clarinet (Martino is an accomplished clarinetist), and the woodwind tunes in *Notturno* (1973) are memorable in this regard. In form, much of his music can be described as rondo-like. Individual sections contain harmonic progressions (often aggregate-forming partitionings of linear 12-tone sets) which are derived from the set that opens the work. In ex. 1, from *Notturno*, a segment immediately following a vibraphone solo presents six set forms, one in each instrument. Segments of the set forms are variously partitioned, forming six vertical aggregates. The latter three aggregates are each partitioned into six dyads (each instrument presenting one dyad), and the same interval class is presented in each instrument during the unfolding of aggregates four, five, and six.

The order of the set is often most clearly presented in the solo passages, whereas constituent "set-motif members" may be more freely distributed among various instruments in the densely textured sections. A polyphonic effect is also created in the solo works, not only those for solo cello but those for violin and piano as well. In the opening of the Fantasy-variations (1962) and *Pianississimo* (1970), the "simultaneously progressing total-set forms" are delineated by registral stratification and differentiated dynamics and articulation; in subsequent passages, set forms are presented consecutively in relatively homogeneous contexts.

In works since the mid-1970s Martino has been concerned with the projection of longer-range linear connections between pitches. He has extended the technique of presenting structurally significant sets as timbrally and/or registrally connected non-consecutive pitches within a single instrumental line. In conceiving means to connect nonconsecutive pitches over long musical spans, Martino has been able to articulate clear "outer-voice

Ex.1 *Notturno*, bars 31–8

structures" in his recent works. Such structures are conceptually related to Schenker's notion of the "outer-voice structure" (*Ausensatz*) in tonal music (see Rothstein, 1980).

Martino's music has been aptly described as expressive, dense, lucid, dramatic, and romantic. But it is his ability to conjure up a world of palpable musical presences and conceptions, which persevere in intensity from the beginning to the end of one piece and from one piece to another, that seems most remarkable.

WORKS

(all published unless otherwise stated)

ORCHESTRAL

Sinfonia, 1953, withdrawn, unpubd
Contemplations, 1956; Lenox, MA, 13 Aug 1964
Piano Concerto, 1965; New Haven, CT, 1 March 1966
Mosaic for Grand Orchestra, 1967; Chicago, May 1967
Cello Concerto, 1972; Cincinnati, OH, 16 Oct 1979
Ritorno, 1976; Plainfield, NJ, 12 Dec 1976; arr. band, 1977
Triple Concerto, cl, b cl, cb cl, 1977; New York, 18 Dec 1978
Divertisements for Youth Orchestra, 1981; Groton, MA, 8 May 1982

CHAMBER

Str Qt no.1, withdrawn, unpubd; Cl Sonata, 1950–51; Str Qt no.2, 1952, withdrawn, unpubd; Suite of Variations on Medieval Melodies, vc, 1952, rev. 1954; A Set, cl, 1954, rev. 1974; Harmonica Piece, 1954; Quodlibets, fl, 1954; Str Qt no.3, 1954, withdrawn, unpubd; 7 canoni enigmatici, canons with resolutions for 2 va, 2 vc/2 bn, 1955, str qt, 1962, 2 cl, a cl/basset hn, b cl, 1966 [may be combined with version of 1955]; Str Trio, 1955, withdrawn, unpubd; Qt, cl, str trio, 1957; Fantasy, pf, 1958; Trio, cl, vn, pf, 1959

5 frammenti, ob, db, 1961; Fantasy-variations, vn, 1962; Conc., wind qnt, 1964; Parisonatina al'dodecafonia, vc, 1964; B, A, B, B, IT, T, cl with extensions, 1966; Strata, b cl, 1966; Notturno, pic + fl + a fl, cl + b cl, vn + va, vc, pf, perc, 1973; Pianississimo, pf sonata, 1970; Impromptu for Roger, pf, 1977; Fantasies and Impromptus, pf, 1980; Quodlibets II, fl, 1980, Suite in Old Form (Parody Suite), pf, 1982, unpubd; Str Qt [no.4], 1983; Canzone e tarantella sul nome Petrassi, cl, vc, 1984

VOCAL

Separate Songs: All day I hear the noise of waters (J. Joyce), The half-moon westers low, my love (A. E. Housman), high v, pf, 1951; From the Bad Child's Book of Beasts (H. Belloc), high v, pf, 1952; Portraits: a Secular Cantata (E. St. V. Millay, W. Whitman, E. E. Cummings), Mez, B, chorus, orch, 1954, Anyone lived in a pretty how town, arr. SATB, pf 4 hands, opt. perc; 3 Songs (Joyce): Alone, Tutto e sciolto, A Memory of the Players in a Mirror at Midnight, B/S, pf, 1955; 2 Rilke Songs: Die Laute, Aus einem Sturmnacht VIII, Mez, pf, 1961; 7 Pious Pieces (R. Herrick), chorus, opt. pf/org, 1972; Paradiso Choruses (Dante), solo vv, chorus, orch, tape, 1974

OTHER WORKS

Augenmusik, a Mixed Mediocritique, actress/danseuse/uninhibited female percussionist, tape, 1972
Film scores: The White Rooster, *c*1950, The Lonely Crime, 1958, both unpubd
Many popular songs and jazz arrs., all unpubd

Principal publishers: Ione, Dantalian

BIBLIOGRAPHY

EwenD
H. Weinberg: "Donald Martino: 'Trio,'" *PNM*, ii/1 (1963), 82
B. Fennelly: "Donald Martino: 'Parisonatina al'dodecafonia,'" *PNM*, viii/1 (1969), 133
W. Rothstein: "Linear Structure in the Twelve-tone System: an Analysis of Donald Martino's 'Pianississimo,'" *JMT*, xiv/2 (1980), 129–65
J. Chute: "Publish or Perish," *HiFi/MusAm*, xxxii/1 (1982), 18

ELAINE BARKIN, MARTIN BRODY

Martino [Azzara], **Pat** (*b* Philadelphia, PA, 25 Aug 1944). Jazz guitarist. He played professionally from the age of 15 with the saxophonists Willis Jackson and Red Holloway and in many organists' combos, particularly that of Jimmy Smith. He joined John Handy's group briefly in 1966, attracting critical attention; since then he has led his own groups and taught privately. Although not particularly influential, Martino has a high reputation as a sophisticated and intelligent guitarist with excellent technique and taste. He often improvises lines in octaves in the manner of Wes Montgomery (an important early influence) and, like his contemporaries John McLaughlin and Pat Metheny, uses the electric 12-string guitar. In the 1970s he showed an interest in the music of Stockhausen and Elliott Carter. With T. Baruso he wrote a guitar method, *Linear Expressions* (1983).

RECORDINGS
(selective list)

El Hombre (1967, Prst. 7513); *East* (1968, Prst. 7562); *The Visit* (1972, Cobblestone 9015); *Consciousness* (1974, Muse 5039)

BIBLIOGRAPHY

K. Hazen: "Lightning Bug in Eclectic Jar," *Down Beat*, xlii/16 (1975), 16
V. Trigger: "Pat Martino," *The Guitar Player Book* (New York, 1978), 140

MARK C. GRIDLEY

Martinů, Bohuslav (Jan) (*b* Polička [now in Czechoslovakia], 8 Dec 1890; *d* Liestal, Switzerland, 28 Aug 1959). Czech composer. He studied violin from the age of seven and gave his first recital in 1905. He had composed numerous chamber works by 1906, when he entered the Prague Conservatory as a violin student; his interest in theater and in literature led him to neglect his studies there, and he was expelled in June 1910. He worked as a music teacher in Polička, played violin in the Czech PO (1918–23; during these years he also studied composition for a time with Josef Suk at the conservatory), and in the summer of 1923 settled in Paris, where he took composition lessons from Albert Roussel, and where he remained for the next 17 years. The String Quintet (1927) brought him the Coolidge Prize in 1932, by which time his music was being heard in North America where Koussevitzky added *La bagarre* (1926) to the repertory of the Boston SO.

Blacklisted by the Nazis, Martinů left Paris on 10 June 1940; he arrived in New York on 31 March 1941. Adjusting to life in the New World was difficult, as Martinů spoke no English. However, a commission from Koussevitzky led to the composition of the Symphony no.1, and with it he regained his confidence and embarked on a project to write a symphony each year; between 1942 and 1946 he produced five symphonies as well as numerous concertos and chamber pieces. He lived in Middlebury (Vermont), Darien (Connecticut), and Jamaica (New York), but with the end of hostilities in Europe he planned to return to Prague to take up a position as professor at the conservatory. The communist regime of 1947–8 made his return impossible, and instead he accepted a summer teaching post at the Berkshire Music Center, a commitment he was unable to fulfill as the result of a serious accident which troubled his health for several years. In 1948–51 he taught at Princeton University, where he composed several chamber works, including the *Sinfonia concertante* (1949) and the Piano Trio no.2, both of which were influenced by Haydn. He also wrote the television operas *Čim člověk žije* ("What men live by") and *Ženitba* ("The marriage"), but the climax of his American stay was the *Fantaisies symphoniques*, commissioned by Charles Munch for the 75th anniversary of the Boston SO and first performed in Boston on 12 January 1955. There were many other important and successful performances of Martinů's works during his years in the USA; especially well received were the premières of the *Concerto grosso* (Boston, 15 November 1941), the Symphony no.1 (Boston, 13 November 1942), the Symphony no.2 (Cleveland, 28 October 1943), the Concerto for Two Pianos (Philadelphia, 3 November 1943), and the Violin Concerto (Boston, 1 December 1943). After spending 1953–5 in Nice, Martinů returned to the USA in 1955 to teach at the Curtis Institute; that same year he was elected to the National Institute of Arts and Letters. In 1956 he left to accept a professorship at the American Academy in Rome.

Martinů composed rapidly, rarely revised his work, and repressed nothing; as a result the quality of his output is uneven. A gifted and professional craftsman, he wrote with the same readiness for any medium and in any genre. He was not a great innovator, he founded no school, and he kept his working methods to himself. Despite his long residence abroad he remained profoundly Czech. He used Czech folk music pervasively in his songs and cantatas, and it shaped his melodic and rhythmic invention in general. After Czech folklore it was the music of Debussy that most colored Martinů's work: like Debussy he possessed a keen sensitivity to timbre, and he often extended the orchestra with a piano, an accordion, or wordless voices. Although he never lost his feeling for tone-color, Martinu rejected impressionism for jazz and ragtime with his move to Paris in 1923. He made contact with Les Six and Stravinsky, associated with the surrealists, and experimented with various styles. From this welter of influences there began to emerge an individual style founded on melodic spontaneity, rhythmic flexibility, and the 18th-century toccata elements that contribute much to the drive and energy of his music. During the 1930s he rediscovered his Czech nationalism, but the most pressing influence at this time was the political tension that led to World War II. In North America his style grew more mellow and simple: he came to stress lyrical qualities and to perfect the techniques that had occupied him since 1930. The achieving of unity from continuously developing cells became his favored formal process, and it appeared at its richest in the *Fantaisies symphoniques* and the Piano Concerto no.4 ("Incantations," 1955–6). Nearly everything he composed after 1953 has a particularly strong Czech flavor, reflecting the nostalgia he felt for his homeland.

Though Martinů shared the exile of Hindemith and Bartók, it is perhaps with Prokofiev that he can best be compared. Both composers had nationalist backgrounds, both found academic training irksome, both joined the neoclassical movement in Paris, and both retrieved their nationalism in the years before World War II. But where Prokofiev effected his return, Martinů remained a refugee, ever seeking and achieving new modes of expression.

WORKS
(only those composed in 1941–52)

DRAMATIC

Uškrcovač [The strangler] (ballet, R. Fitzgerald), 1948; New London, CT, 1948
Čim člověk žije [What men live by] (television opera, Martinů, after Tolstoy), 1952; New York, 1953
Ženitba [The marriage] (television opera, Martinů, after Gogol), 1952; New York, 1953

OTHER WORKS

Orch: Conc. da camera, vn, pf, perc, str, 1941; 6 syms., no.1, 1942, no.2, 1943, no.3, 1944, no.4, 1945, no.5, 1946, Fantaisies symphoniques (no.6), 1951–3; Památník Lidicím [Memorial to Lidice], 1943; Double Pf Conc., 1943; Vn Conc., 1943; Vc Conc. no.2, 1944–5; Thunderbolt P-17, 1945; Toccata e due canzoni, 1946; Conc. da camera [arr. Str Qt no.7], 1947; Pf Conc. no.3, 1948; Sinfonia concertante, ob, bn, vn, vc, chamber orch, 1949; Double Vn Conc. no.2, 1950; Intermezzo, 1950; Sinfonietta "La jolla," pf, orch, 1950; Rhapsodie, va, orch, 1952

Chamber: 2 vc sonatas, 1941 1952; Madrigalová sonata, fl, vn, pf, 1942; Pf Qt, 1942; Variace na thema Rossiniho, vc, pf, 1942; 5 Madrigal Stanzas, vn, pf, 1943; Fantasie, theremin, ob, str qt, pf, 1944; Pf Qnt no.2, 1944; Trio, fl, vc, pf, 1944; Vn Sonata no.3, 1944; Česká rapsódie, vn, pf, 1945; Fl Sonata, 1945; Str Qt no.6, 1946; Qt, ob, pf trio, 1947; Str Qt no.7 (Conc. da camera), 1947; 3 madrigaly, vn, va, 1947; Mazurka-nokturno, ob, 2 vn, vc, 1949; Duets, vn, va, 1950; Pf Trio no.2, 1950; Pf Trio no.3, 1951; Serenade, 2 cl, str trio, 1951; Stowe Pastorals, 5 rec, cl, 2 vn, vc, 1951

Pf: Dumka, 1941; Mazurka, 1941; Etudy a polky, 1945; Les bouquinistes du quai Malaquais, 1948; The Fifth Day of the Fifth Moon, 1948; Barcarolle, 1949; Morceau facile, 1949; 3 české tance, 2 pf, 1949; Improvisace, 1951

Choral: 5 český madrigalů, unacc. chorus, 1948; 3 Choruses (trad.), unacc. female chorus, 1952; 3 trojhlasé písně posvátné, female chorus, vn, 1952
Solo vocal: Nový špalíček (Moravian trad.), 1v, pf, 1942; Pisničky na jednu stránku [Songs on one page] (Moravian trad.), 1v, pf, 1943; Pisničky na dva stránky [Songs on two pages] (Moravian trad.), 1v, pf, 1944

Principal publishers: Associated, Boosey & Hawkes, Ceský hudebný fond, Eschig, Heugel, Leduc, Schott, Universal

BIBLIOGRAPHY

P. O. Ferroud: *A Great Musician Today: Martinů* (London, 1937)
M. Šafránek: *Bohuslav Martinů: the Man and his Music* (London, 1946)
——: *Bohuslav Martinů: his Life and Works* (London, 1962)
R. Pečman: *Stage Works of Martinů* (Prague, 1967)
J. Mihule: *Martinů* (Prague, 1972)
B. Large: *Martinů* (London, 1975) [incl. detailed list of works]

BRIAN LARGE/R

Martirano, Salvatore (*b* Yonkers, NY, 12 Jan 1927). Composer. He studied with Elwell at the Oberlin College Conservatory (1947–51), with Bernard Rogers at the Eastman School (1952), and with Dallapiccola in Florence (1952–4). From 1956 to 1959 he was in Rome as a Fellow of the American Academy, and in 1960 he received a Guggenheim Fellowship and an award from the American Academy of Arts and Letters. At this time he had works commissioned by the Koussevitzky and Fromm foundations. He joined the faculty of the University of Illinois at Urbana in 1963. From 1968, Martirano concentrated on developing hybrid sound systems consisting of analog modules driven by digital circuits; these culminated in the Sal-Mar Construction, completed in 1971. Like its predecessors, the Malmstadt-Enke Blues and the Mar-Vil Construction, this instrument permits simultaneous creation and performance of improvisatory compositions. In 1983 Martirano received a grant from IRCAM to complete a program for computer-aided composition to simulate algorithms utilized in the Sal-Mar Construction.

Until the late 1950s Martirano followed dodecaphonic principles in his compositions, a style represented by the Mass for double chorus (1952–5). By 1958 he had begun to incorporate elements of jazz and popular music, as in the choral work *O, O, O, O, that Shakespeherian Rag*. At the University of Illinois he became one of the first to work with computers in composition. His first computer-generated piece, *123-456* (1964), was followed by the computer-aided work *Underworld* (1964–5). This led to the political and theatrical mixed-media work *L.'s G. A.* (Lincoln's Gettysburg Address), which was Martirano's most popular work of the 1960s and which received many performances during the 1960s and 1970s, including one in 1969 at the Electric Circus, New York, a forum for rock music with psychedelic lighting.

Martirano's compositions of the 1970s and 1980s are characterized by the use of a wide variety of styles and media. The electronic tape works *Fifty One* (1978) and *In memoriam Luigi Dallapiccola* (1978) were developed using the Sal-Mar Construction; *Fantasy* (1980) employs the techniques of *musique concrète*. Unlike many of his works after *Underworld*, *Stuck on Stella* (1979) for piano and *Thrown*, a sextet for wind and percussion (1984), use standard notation.

WORKS

Stage: The Cherry Orchard (incidental music, Chekhov), 1949; Richard III (incidental music, Shakespeare), 1950; The Magic Stone (chamber opera, after Boccaccio), 1951
Vocal: Mass, double chorus, 1952–5; Chansons innocentes (Cummings), S, pf, 1957; O, O, O, O, that Shakespeherian Rag (T. S. Eliot), chorus, ens, 1958; Ballad (popular songs, 1930–50), amp 1v, ens, 1965
Inst: Wind Sextet, 1949; Prelude, orch, 1950; Variations, fl, pf, 1950; Str Qt, 1951; Piece, orch, 1952; Vn Sonata, 1952; Contrasto, orch, 1954; Cocktail Music, pf, 1962; Octet, fl, a cl, b cl, mar, cel, vn, vc, db, 1963; Selections, a fl, b cl, vn, vc, 1969; Stuck on Stella, pf, 1979; Thrown, 5 wind, perc, 1984; Sampler, amp vn, live elec, 1985; short pf pieces; other inst works
Tape and cptr: 3 Elec Dances, tape, 1963; 123-456, cptr, tape, 1964; Buffet, tape, 1965; Sal-Mar Construction I–VII, 4-track tape, 1971–5; Shop Talk, tape, 1974; Fast Forward, 2-track tape, 1977; Fifty One, 4-track tape, 1978; In memoriam Luigi Dallapiccola, 2-track tape, 1978; She Spoke, nar, 2-track tape, 1979; Fantasy, vn, 4-track tape, 1980; other tape works
Mixed-media: Underworld (S. Martirano), 4 actors, t sax, perc, 2 db, 2-track tape, cptr, 1964–5, arr. video, 1982; L.'s G. A. (Lincoln), pfmrs, helium bomb, 2-track tape, film, 1967–8; Action Analysis (Martirano), 12 pfmrs, bunny, controller, 1968; The Proposal, tape, slides, 1968; Omaggio à Sally Rand, video, 1982; Look at the Back of my Head for Awhile, video, 1985; L.'s G. A. Update, video, 1985
Juvenilia and student works, educational pieces

Principal publishers: Lingua Press, MCA, G. Schirmer, Schott

BIBLIOGRAPHY

VintonD
D. Hamilton: "Some Newer Figures in America," *HiFi/MusAm*, xviii/9 (1968), 57
"Another Instrument has Appeared Quietly," *Arts Reporting Service*, xv (1971), 2
R. Reynolds: *Mind Models* (New York, 1975), 196, 211
M. Behm: "Stuck on Stella," *PNM*, xx (1981–2), 605 [review]
R. Pellegrino: *The Electronic Arts of Sound and Light* (New York, 1983), 25, 95

GILBERT CHASE, JEAN GEIL

Marvelettes. Pop vocal group. Its members were Gladys Horton, Wanda Young, Katherine Anderson, Juanita Cowart, and Georgeanna Dobbins, who were all born in 1944; they attended high school in Inkster, Michigan, where their performance in a talent contest attracted attention and led to a contract with Motown Records. Their first single, *Please Mr. Postman* (1961), written by Dobbins, was the most successful recording on the Motown label up to that date. Dobbins and Cowart soon left the group, which continued as a trio. The Marvelettes worked with a greater variety of writers and producers than most Motown groups. Since both Horton and Young sang lead parts (Horton's voice was hoarse and full-blooded, Young's more silky), the group lacked a recognizable star. This may have contributed to the decline of the Marvelettes' career, but it enabled them to bring out the best in a remarkably wide range of songs, from the girlish charm of *Beechwood 4-5789* (1962) and the thumping intensity of *Too many fish in the sea* (1964) to the slinky sophistication of their collaborations with Smokey Robinson, including *Don't mess with Bill* (1966) and *The Hunter gets Captured by the Game* (1967). The trio disbanded in the late 1960s, though groups using the same name continued to perform and tour.

BIBLIOGRAPHY

SouthernB
A. Fuchs: "My Guy," *Girl Groups: the Story of a Sound*, ed. A. Betrock (New York, 1982), 64

KEN EMERSON

Marvin, Frederick (*b* Los Angeles, CA, 11 June 1923). Pianist and musicologist. He studied with Maurice Zam (1935–9) and Milan Blanchet (1940–41, 1945–8) in Los Angeles, with Rudolf Serkin at the Curtis Institute (1939–40), and with Claudio Arrau (1950–54). In 1938 he made his professional début, and ten years later (21 November 1948) he gave his first New York recital, for which he won the Carnegie Hall award for the outstanding début of the season. He has toured throughout the USA, Central America, India, and Europe, where he lived from 1954 to 1958. Marvin's repertory is extensive, and he is known for his provocative programs; in addition to resurrecting lesser-known works by Liszt, Adolf Henselt, Ignaz Moscheles, Ludwig Berger, and Jan Ladislav Dussek, whose complete piano sonatas he is recording for the Genesis label, he has given the premières of such 20th-century works as Antheil's Sonatas nos. 4–5. He taught at several institutions before accepting a position as professor and artist-in-residence at Syracuse University in 1968.

As a musicologist, Marvin has worked to revive interest in the Spanish composer Antonio Soler (1729–83). He has unearthed some 700 of Soler's manuscripts including more than 200 keyboard sonatas, 65 of which he has edited for publication (along with several vocal works) and 28 of which he has recorded. He has contributed articles on Soler to *Clavier*, the *Music Journal*, and the *Piano Quarterly*, and his system of numbering the works (*Marvin Verzeichnis*) has been adopted in various sources. In recognition of his work Marvin was decorated by the Spanish government. Other honors include a Fulbright fellowship, the Beethoven Medal, and an award from the French government.

BIBLIOGRAPHY

G. Kehler: *The Piano in Concert*, ii (Metuchen, NJ, 1982)

ALLAN B. HO

Masi, Francesco (*d* Washington, DC, 1853). Italian organist, music teacher, publisher, and composer. The earliest documentary evidence of his activity in the USA is an advertisement in the *Columbian Centinel* (28 November 1807), where he describes himself as "Music Master of the Italian Band, teacher Piano Forte, Clarionet, Violoncello, Violin, French Horn, Trumpet, Flute, French Guitar, &c. Produces certificates from Church of St. Peter in Rome." He gave an organ concert at Boylston Hall, Boston, in December 1814. After about 1826 he probably abandoned his career in music for one as a jeweller and silversmith, but in his wide-ranging activities he was a typical early 19th-century immigrant musician. He composed and published several instrumental pieces, including marches and waltzes, a piano sonata, *The Battles of Lake Champlain and Plattsburg* (1815; for illustration *see* BATTLE MUSIC), songs, and a mass for three-part chorus and organ (MS in *ICN*). His brother Vincent Masi, active briefly as a dancing master in Boston and Washington, DC, issued a set of 12 dances for flute and piano entitled *The Cotillion Party's Assistant and Ladies' Musical Companion*, which are now lost. Masi probably published only his own compositions. His music engraving is elegant, and the title page of his piano sonata is among "the most handsome of the War of 1812 illustrations" (Wolfe, 1980). Judging from the plate numbers found on two of his extant publications, many of Masi's earlier publications are lost.

BIBLIOGRAPHY

C. M. Ayars: *Contributions to the Art of Music in America by the Music Industries of Boston, 1640–1936* (New York, 1937)
H. E. Johnson: *Musical Interludes in Boston, 1795–1830* (New York, 1943)
R. J. Wolfe: *Secular Music in America, 1801–1825: a Bibliography* (New York, 1964)
——: *Early American Music Engraving and Printing* (Urbana, IL, 1980)

ANNE DHU SHAPIRO

Maslanka, David (Henry) (*b* New Bedford, MA, 30 Aug 1943). Composer. After attending the New England Conservatory (1959–61), he studied composition with Joseph Wood and clarinet with George Waln at Oberlin College Conservatory (BM 1965) and conducting with Gerhardt Wimberger at the Salzburg Mozarteum (1963–4); at Michigan State University (1965–70, MM, PhD), he studied clarinet with Elsa Ludwig, composition with H. Owen Reed, and theory with Paul Harder. He has taught at the Geneseo College of SUNY (1970–74), Sarah Lawrence College (1974–80), New York University (1980–81), and CUNY, Lehman College (from 1981). Maslanka's awards for composition include four MacDowell Colony fellowships and grants from the NEA (1974, 1975) and the Martha Baird Rockefeller Fund for Music (1978). Among his many commissions are those from SUNY for his chamber opera *Death and the Maiden* (1974); the Clarinet and Friends Series for Three Pieces for clarinet and piano (1974); and the Northwestern University Wind Ensemble for *A Child's Garden of Dreams* (1981). His music is characterized by Romantic gestures and tonal language, remaining clear in structure and purpose.

WORKS

Death and the Maiden (chamber opera, R. Bradbury, J. Wiles), 1974

Orch: Sym., 1970; Fragments, ballet, 1971; Conc., pf, wind, perc, 1974–6; 5 Songs, S, Bar, chamber orch, 1975–6; Intermezzo, chamber orch, 1979; A Child's Garden of Dreams, Book I, sym. wind ens, 1981, Book II, orch, 1982

Chamber: Str Qt, 1968; Trio, vn, cl, pf, 1971; Duo, fl, pf, 1972; Trio no.2, va, cl, pf, 1973; 3 Pieces, cl, pf, 1974–5; Pray for Tender Voices in the Darkness, harp, pf, 1974; Variations on Lost Love, mar, 1977; Orpheus, 2 bn, mar, 1977; Vc Songs, vc, pf, 1978; Pf Song, 1978; Music for Dr. Who, bn, pf, 1979; 4th Piece, cl, pf, 1979; My Lady White, mar, 1980; Heaven to Clear when Day did Close, t sax, str qt, 1981; Meditation on "Dr. Affectionate" by Günter Grass, gui, 1981; Arcadia, 4 vc, 1982; Arcadia II: conc., mar, perc ens, 1982

Vocal: Anne Sexton Songs, S, pf, 1975; Hills of May (R. Graves), S, str qt, 1978; numerous arrs. medieval and Renaissance music for women's voices, unacc. and with insts; 2 works for women's chorus, 3 pieces for mixed chorus

PAUL PHILLIPS

Mason. Family of musicians, music publishers, and instrument builders. Members of the family were important in American musical life throughout most of the 19th century and the early 20th; no other family, indeed, contributed so much to American music during this period.

(1) **Lowell Mason (i)** (*b* Medfield, MA, 8 Jan 1792; *d* Orange, NJ, 11 Aug 1872). Music educator, composer, anthologist, and conductor. He was the foremost pioneer in the introduction of music instruction to American public schools and in the establishment of teacher training in music education. He led a reform movement in American church music based on European models and spread his ideals through numerous widely accepted collections of sacred music (*see* HYMNODY, §§2(ii), 3(ii)). Mason's hymn tunes dominated 19th-century American hymnals and still occupy a substantial place in most American collections of church song.

1. LIFE. Mason's parents, Johnson and Caty Mason, sang in their church choir for over 30 years; his father played the bass viol. When he was about 13 Mason attended his first singing-school, and was taught by Amos Albee, compiler of *The Norfolk Collection of Sacred Harmony* (1805); he also studied in Dedham, Massachusetts, with Oliver Shaw. He learned to play numerous musical instruments. By the age of 16 he directed the choir of the Medfield church and two years later led the Medfield band.

In 1812 Mason went to Savannah, Georgia, where he worked in a dry-goods store, becoming a partner in the firm (then known as Stebbins & Mason) by 1817. After the death of his partner in about 1819 he became a clerk at the Planter's Bank. He was a leader in the Independent Presbyterian Church, superintendent of the Sunday School from 1815 to 1827, and a founder and active member of the Savannah Missionary Society established in 1818. In 1817 the German-born Frederick L. Abel settled in

Savannah, providing Mason with a new opportunity to study harmony and composition; under Abel's direction he began composing hymn tunes and anthems. From 1813 to as late as 1824 Mason taught in singing-schools. In 1815 he was appointed "principal of the singers" and in 1820 organist of the Independent Presbyterian Church, where he remained until shortly before leaving the city in 1827.

While studying with Abel, Mason compiled a collection of hymn tunes based on the Englishman William Gardiner's *Sacred Melodies*, consisting of hymns set to tunes arranged from Mozart, Haydn, and other European composers. In 1822 this collection, *The Boston Handel and Haydn Society Collection of Church Music*, was published by the society in Boston. It appeared without Mason's name, for he did not wish to be known as a professional musician; later however, after its noteworthy success, his name appeared on the title-page as editor. The success of his tunebook and his growing reputation as a choirmaster and spokesman for reform in church music led to invitations to move to Boston. In 1827 he accepted an invitation to supervise the music of three Boston Congregational churches. In 1831 he became choirmaster of Lyman Beecher's Bowdoin Street Church; during his 14 years of leadership there the choir of about 70 gained a national reputation. From 1844 to his retirement in 1851 Mason was organist and choirmaster of the Central Church, where the choir of about 100 maintained his reputation for excellence.

Lowell Mason: engraving, inscribed in the lower left-hand corner "F. Moras Phil."

From 1827 to 1832 Mason was president and music director of the Boston Handel and Haydn Society, which achieved a renewed vitality under his leadership. His retirement from the society's presidency was partly due to his interest in teaching vocal music to children. In 1829 he had compiled what he believed to be the first Sunday-school collection with music, the *Juvenile Psalmist*, followed in 1830–31 by the *Juvenile Lyre*, a school music collection. In 1832–3 he taught a children's vocal music class at Bowdoin Street Church and gave children's concerts. From 1832 he taught music in private schools. The Boston Academy of Music was established in 1833, with Mason as its guiding spirit and George James Webb as an associate; its purpose was to promote music education among the masses and bring about higher standards of church music. In 1834 the *Manual of the Boston Academy of Music*, an edited translation of G. F. Kuebler's *Anleitung zum Gesang-Unterrichte in Schulen* (1826), appeared under Mason's name; the *Manual* was used extensively by music teachers. Mason claimed that it was based on Pestalozzian principles (but recent research has questioned this). Beginning in summer 1834 Mason and others taught classes for music teachers under the auspices of the academy. Through the efforts of the academy, music was taught on an experimental basis in four Boston public schools in 1837. Mason taught at one school on a volunteer basis, and his success led to the regular inclusion of music in the curriculum of Boston public schools from 1838, the first time in the USA that music achieved a comparable status with other subjects. From 1838 to 1845 Mason was superintendent of music in the Boston schools, where he continued to teach until 1851 (*see* EDUCATION IN MUSIC, §I, 2). For a decade beginning in 1845 he was a staff member of the teachers' institutes of the Massachusetts State Board of Education and was involved in state-sponsored teacher training. He was also active in musical conventions and normal institutes, through which he trained or influenced a large proportion of the public school music teachers of his day, assuring dominance for his ideas in the music education movement in the USA after his time.

Mason's first journey to Europe in 1837 included visits to England, Germany, Switzerland, and France. He visited numerous European musicians and educators, purchased much music, and observed the teaching of music in schools. He made a second and longer visit from December 1851 until April 1853, when he spent time in the British Isles lecturing on congregational singing and the Pestalozzian method of teaching; he reported on this visit in his *Musical Letters from Abroad*.

After his return from Europe Mason made New York his business headquarters and a large estate in nearby Orange, New Jersey, his home. His later years were in large measure occupied with numerous publications, including books, tunebooks, compositions, and articles. In 1855 he was awarded an honorary doctorate in music by New York University, the second such degree given by an American institution. Mason's library of 10,300 items is now in the Yale University music library.

2. WORKS. It is not possible to compile a complete list of Mason's works since many of them were published without attribution (see H. L. Mason, 1941, 1944). The majority of his known compositions are sacred vocal works, which he published in the numerous collections he compiled, sometimes with collaborators. Mason's influence on American music was marked. In establishing a more sophisticated means of music education, he replaced the indigenous fuging-tunes and anthems of the 18th-century singing-schools with hymn tunes and anthems arranged from European music, or original compositions based on "correct" harmonies. These include the arrangements "Azmon" ("O for a thousand tongues to sing"), "Dennis" ("Blest be the tie that binds"), "Hamburg" ("When I survey the wondrous cross"), and "Antioch" ("Joy to the world, the Lord is come"), of which the last-named is an ingenious arrangement of themes from Handel's *Messiah*, and the original tunes "Hebron" ("The heavens declare thy glory, Lord"), "Olivet" ("My faith looks up to thee"), "Boylston" ("A charge to keep I have"), "Rockingham" ("Jesus, thou joy of loving hearts"), "Laban" ("My soul, be on thy guard"),

and "Bethany" ("Nearer, my God, to thee"). In keeping with his view of music for worship, Mason's tunes are simple and chaste; their diatonic melodies have a logical phrase structure that strikes a suitable balance between repetition and contrast. Harmonies are also simple, often using only the tonic, subdominant, and dominant chords. Although "Rockingham" is a folk-like pentatonic melody, Mason opposed the secular idiom of revivalism as represented in Joshua Leavitt's *The Christian Lyre* (1830); he and Thomas Hastings sought to counteract its influence in their joint compilation, *Spiritual Songs for Social Worship* (1831–2). Nevertheless, some of their tunes reflect the secular style that was to become associated with Sunday-school hymnody and gospel hymnody. Mason's "Work Song" ("Work for the night is coming") and "Harwell" ("Hark, ten thousand harps and voices"), for example, incorporate such traits as repeated dotted eighth- and 16th-notes, and bar-long repeated notes in the tenor and bass voices – both prominent characteristics of late 19th-century popular hymnody.

WORKS

Selective list, not including works published individually or without attribution, or occasional works; for a fuller list, see Rich and Pemberton. Unless otherwise indicated, items before 1850 were published in Boston, those from 1850 in New York.

CHURCH MUSIC COLLECTIONS

The Boston Handel and Haydn Society Collection of Church Music (1822/*R*1973); Select Chants, Doxologies &c. Adapted to the Use of the Protestant Episcopal Church in the United States of America (1824); Choral Harmony (1828); Church Psalmody (with D. Greene) (1831); Spiritual Songs for Social Worship (with T. Hastings) (Utica, NY, 1831–2, 2/1833); The Choir, or Union Collection of Church Music (1832); Lyra sacra (1832); Manual of Christian Psalmody (with Greene) (1832); Sacred Melodies (with G. J. Webb) (1833)

The Boston Collection of Anthems, Choruses, &c. (1834); Sentences, or Short Anthems, Hymn Tunes and Chants (1834); Union Hymns (with Greene, R. Babcock, Jr.) (1834); The Boston Academy's Collection of Church Music (1835); The Sacred Harp, or Eclectic Harmony (with Timothy Mason) (Cincinnati and Boston, 1835); Select Pieces of Sacred Music (1835); The Boston Academy's Collection of Choruses (1836); Occasional Psalm and Hymn Tunes, Selected and Original (1836); Selections for the Choir of the Boston Academy of Music, i (1836)

The Boston Anthem Book (Boston and New York, 1839); The Modern Psalmist (1839); Carmina sacra (Boston and New York, 1841); The Harp (with Timothy Mason) (Cincinnati, 1841); The Sacred Harp (with T. B. Mason) (1841–50); Book of Chants (Boston and New York, 1842); Chapel Hymns (1842); Sacred Songs for Family and Social Worship (with Hastings) (New York, 1842); Musical Service of the Protestant Episcopal Church (1843); Songs of Asaph (1843); Songs of Chenaniah, no. 1 (1844); The Psaltery (with Webb) (Boston and New York, 1845)

The Boston Chorus Book (Boston and New York, 1846); The Cherokee Singing Book (with G. Guess) (1846); The Choralist (1847); The Congregational Tune-book (with Webb) (Boston and New York, 1848); The National Psalmist (with Webb) (1848); 59 Select Psalm and Hymn Tunes (1848); Cantica laudis, or The American Book of Church Music (with Webb) (1850); The Hymnist (Boston, 1850); The New Carmina sacra, or Boston Collection of Church Music (Boston and New York, 1850); Mason's Hand-book of Psalmody (London and New York, 1852)

The Hallelujah (Boston and New York, 1854); The Sabbath Hymn and Tune Book (with E. A. Park, A. Phelps) (New York and Hartford, CT, 1859); The People's Tune Book (1860); The New Sabbath Hymn and Tune Book (with Park, Phelps) (Boston, 1866); The Temple Choir (with W. B. Bradbury, T. F. Seward) (1867); Carmina sacra Enlarged (Boston, 1869); Congregational Church Music (with J. Goss, W. H. Havergal, others) (London, 1869); The Coronation (with Seward, C. G. Allen) (New York and Chicago, 1872)

SECULAR (OR SECULAR AND SACRED) COLLECTIONS

The Odeon (with Webb) (1837); The Boston Glee Book (1838/*R*1977); The Lyrist (with Webb) (1838); The Gentlemen's Glee Book (1841); 21 Madrigals, Glees and Part Songs (with Webb) (1843); The Vocalist (with Webb) (1844); The Glee Hive (with Webb) (1851, rev. 2/1853); School Songs and Hymns (1854); The Singing School (New York and Boston, 1854); The New Odeon (with Webb) (1855); The Young Men's Singing Book (with G. F. Root) (1855); Mason's Normal Singer (1856); Asaph, or The Choir Book (with W. Mason) (1861)

CHILDREN'S COLLECTIONS AND MUSICAL EXERCISES

Juvenile Psalmist (1829); Juvenile Lyre (with E. Ives, Jr.) (1831); Sabbath School Songs (1833); The Sabbath School Harp (1836); The Juvenile Singing School (with Webb) (1837); The Juvenile Songster (Boston and London, 1837–8); Juvenile Music (1839); Little Songs for Little Singers (1840); The Boston School Song Book (1841); Vocal Exercises and Solfeggios (1842); The American Sabbath School Singing Book (Philadelphia, 1843); The Primary School Song Book (with Webb) (1846)

The Song-book of the School-room (with Webb) (Boston and New York, 1847); Large Musical Exercises (Boston and New York, 1851); A Complete Course of Elementary Instruction, Vocal Exercises and Solfeggios, in G. F. Root: The Academy Vocalist (Boston and New York, 1852); Mason's Mammoth Exercises (1856); The Song-garden (New York and Boston, 1864)

MUSIC PERIODICALS

The Musical Library (with Webb), monthly (July 1835–June 1836); *The Seraph*, monthly (Aug 1838–July 1840); *Periodical Psalmody* (April 1842); *The Hymnist: a Collection of Sacred Music, Original and Selected* (with W. Mason), 2 issues (1849)

Principal publishers: Ditson, Mason Brothers, Wilkins & Carter

WRITINGS

Address on Church Music (Boston, 1826/*R*1965–6)
Manual of the Boston Academy of Music (Boston, 1834)
Musical Exercises for Singing Schools (Boston and New York, 1838)
An Address on Church Music, delivered July 8, 1851, in Boston (Boston, 1851)
Musical Letters from Abroad (Boston and New York, 1853/*R*1967)
Musical Notation in a Nutshell (New York and Boston, 1854)
Guide to Musical Notation (New York, 1855)
How Shall I Teach? (New York and Boston, 1860)
Music and its Notation (Boston, 1860)
A Glance at Pestalozzianism (New York, 1863)
The Elements of Music and its Notation (Boston, 1869)
with T. F. Seward: *The Pestalozzian Music Teacher* (New York, 1871)

BIBLIOGRAPHY

T. F. Seward: *The Educational Work of Dr. Lowell Mason* (n.p., 1879)
A. W. Thayer: "Lowell Mason," *Dwight's Journal of Music*, xxxix (1879–80), 186, 195
W. Mason: *Memories of a Musical Life* (New York, 1901)
F. J. Metcalf: *American Writers and Compilers of Sacred Music* (New York, 1925/*R*1967)
H. L. Mason: *Lowell Mason: an Appreciation of his Life and Work* (New York, 1941)
——: *Hymn Tunes of Lowell Mason: a Bibliography* (Cambridge, MA, 1944/*R*1976)
M. F. LaFar: "Lowell Mason's Varied Activities in Savannah," *Georgia Historical Quarterly*, xxviii (1944), 113
A. L. Rich: *Lowell Mason* (Chapel Hill, 1946)
H. E. Ellis: "Lowell Mason and the *Manual of the Boston Academy of Music*," *JRME*, iii (1955), 3
V. Higginson: "Notes on Lowell Mason's Hymn Tunes," *The Hymn*, xviii (1967), 37
C. A. Pemberton: *Lowell Mason: his Life and Work* (diss., U. of Minnesota, 1971; pubd Ann Arbor, MI, 1985)
E. J. O'Meara: "The Lowell Mason Library," *Notes*, xxviii (1971–2), 197
J. K. Ogasapian: "Lowell Mason as a Church Musician," *Journal of Church Music*, xxi/7 (1979), 6

(2) Daniel Gregory Mason (i) (*b* 1820; *d* 1869). Music publisher, son of (1) Lowell Mason (i). He founded the firm Mason Brothers in 1853 with his brother (3) Lowell Mason (ii); they were later joined by a third brother, Timothy, who had been associated with the T. Mason and G. Lane publishing house. They were well known as publishers of religious music and had begun publishing independently as early as 1840 (*The Harmonist* by T. Mason and G. Lane). The firm moved from New York to Boston and published hymnals such as Woodbury's *The Jubilee*, *The Key Note*, and *The Shawm*. Many of the Mason Brothers' publications are printed with shape-notes. The business continued until the death of Lowell Mason (ii).

(3) **Lowell Mason (ii)** (*b* 1823; *d* 1885). Music publisher, son of (1) Lowell Mason (i). See (2) Daniel Gregory Mason (i).

(4) **Mason, William** (*b* Boston, 24 Jan 1829; *d* New York, 14 July 1908). Pianist, teacher, and composer, son of (1) Lowell Mason (i). He studied with his father and with Henry Schmidt before making his début at the Boston Academy of Music on 7 March 1846. In 1849 he was sent to Europe, where he studied in Leipzig with Ignaz Moscheles, Moritz Hauptmann, and E. F. Richter, in Prague with Alexander Dreyschock, and in Weimar with Liszt (1853 and 1854). His *Memories of a Musical Life* are valuable for an anecdotal account of Liszt's Weimar circle. While in Europe he traveled and performed in many countries, playing in London in 1853 with the Harmonic Union and enjoying the prestige accorded a virtuoso protégé of Liszt. He returned to the USA in July 1854.

Mason was possibly the first pianist to give concerts in the USA without assisting artists, but he disliked touring and settled in New York to teach. He wrote several important teaching manuals for the piano and propounded a pulling-finger motion known in the USA as "the Mason touch." During his lifetime he was regarded as "the dean of American piano teachers." In 1855, with Theodore Thomas and others, he established the Mason and Thomas Chamber Music Soirées, which for 13 years introduced Romantic works to American audiences (for illustration *see* CHAMBER MUSIC, fig. 1). His compositions include over 50 virtuoso piano pieces which, though conservative in style, are notable for their high quality. In 1872 he received the DMus from Yale College.

WORKS

INSTRUMENTAL

Over 50 pf works, incl. Amitié pour amitié, op.4 (Boston, 1854); Badinage, pf 4 hands, op.27 (New York, 1869); Capriccio fantastico, op.50 (New York, 1897)

Serenata, pf, vc, op.39a (New York, 1882)

COLLECTIONS

(some including choruses by Mason)

The Social Glee Book (with S. A. Bancroft) (Boston, 1847); Fireside Harmony (Boston, 1848); The Melodist (with G. J. Webb) (New York, 1850); Asaph, or The Choir Book (with L. Mason (i)) (New York, 1861)

PEDAGOGICAL WORKS

with E. S. Hoadley: A Method for the Piano-forte (New York, 1867)

——: A System for Beginners (Boston, 1871)

A System of Technical Exercises for the Piano-forte (Boston, 1878)

Touch and Technique, op.44 (Philadelphia, 1889)

WRITINGS

with W. S. B. Mathews: *A Primer of Music* (Cincinnati, 1894)

EDITIONS

C. M. von Weber: Complete Works for the Pianoforte (New York, 1893)

Two and Three Part Inventions of J. S. Bach (New York, 1894)

BIBLIOGRAPHY

F. O. Jones, ed.: *A Handbook of American Music and Musicians* (Canaseraga, NY, 1886/R1971), 92f

E. M. Bowman: "A Glimpse into Dr. Mason's Studio," *The Pianist*, i (1895), 23 [with list of works]

W. Mason: *Memories of a Musical Life* (New York, 1901)

F. H. Martens: "Mason, William," *DAB*

K. G. Graber: *The Life and Works of William Mason* (diss., U. of Iowa, 1976)

(5) **Henry Mason** (*b* 1831; *d* 1890). Instrument builder, son of (1) Lowell Mason (i). *See* MASON & HAMLIN.

(6) **Daniel Gregory Mason (ii)** (*b* Brookline, MA, 20 Nov 1873; *d* Greenwich, CT, 4 Dec 1953). Composer, writer on music, and teacher, son of (5) Henry Mason. He studied at Harvard (1891–5) and continued his composition training under Chadwick and Goetschius. In 1894 he composed his op. 1, but he soon turned temporarily to the career of a writer on music, and in 1902 published his first book, *From Grieg to Brahms*. His long association with Columbia University began in 1905 with his appointment as lecturer in music; he later became assistant professor (1910) and MacDowell Professor (1929), serving as head of the music department until 1940 and retiring in 1942. From 1907 he concentrated increasingly on composition, and in 1913 he went to Paris for further studies with Vincent d'Indy, who influenced him strongly without erasing his affinity with Brahms. He received honorary doctorates from Tufts College (1929), Oberlin College (1931), and the Eastman School (1932); he was a member of the National Institute of Arts and Letters (elected 1938); and he gained publication prizes from the Society for the Publication of American Music and the Juilliard Foundation.

In style and outlook Mason was staunchly conservative. His models were the great Austro-German masters and, though he admired César Franck and d'Indy, he had little sympathy with the French impressionists and totally opposed 20th-century modernism. He is often regarded as one of the "Boston classicists" and he considered himself a "musical humanist." He fought for the recognition of American music and tried occasionally to color his scores with indigenous material; later he became convinced that "for better or for worse American music is necessarily eclectic and cosmopolitan, and that the kind of distinctiveness to be looked for in it is individual rather than national" (letter to J. T. Howard, 1930).

Mason was a meticulous technician and a perpetual reviser. His writing for instruments is idiomatic and his textures are opulent, at times Brahmsian, though his orchestration reveals occasional touches of French coloring. Randall Thompson remarked that "A certain sinister and foreboding pessimism, a dour and bitter irony in Mason's music has not been fully appreciated. His exuberant *Chanticleer*, so widely played, refutes the characterization but the paradox is all to his credit." Of his symphonies, the last, subtitled "A Lincoln Symphony," tries to capture the personality of the great emancipator. The movements have the titles "The Candidate from Springfield," "Massa Linkum," "Old Abe's Yarns," and "1865 – marcia funebre," and the music is evocative of time and place though only one popular tune of the 1860s, *Quaboug Quickstep*, is used. Mason, however, preferred his "music without program." For all his musical intelligence and sensitive idealism he was unable to develop a strong creative profile, and his ingrained conservatism alienated him from the mainstream of American music. His best music is to be found in the chamber works.

Mason's books, particularly his analyses of chamber music by Beethoven and Brahms, are written with elegance and insight. He was a pioneer in the sphere of music appreciation and could "explain" music to the layman without condescension. *Artistic Ideals*, which he considered his best book, contains his credo as a creative artist. Other essays are polemical and controversial: in *The Dilemma of American Music* he referred to American composers as "polyglot parrots" and urged them to find their own voice through elastic eclecticism; and in *Tune in, America*, subtitled "a study of our coming musical independence," he criticized Toscanini and other "imported" conductors for neglecting American music. Yet he himself received the strongest encouragement from such "imported" musicians as Gabrilowitsch and Bruno Walter. His autobiographical *Music in my Time* paints a vivid picture of musical and intellectual life in New York and New England.

WORKS

(selective list)

Orch: Sym. no.1, c, op.11, 1913–14; Prelude and Fugue, pf, orch, op.12, 1914; Chanticleer, festival ov., 1926; Sym. no.2, A, op.30, 1928–9; Suite after English Folksongs, op.32, 1933–4; Sym. no.3 "A Lincoln Symphony," op.35, 1935–6; Prelude and Fugue, c, str, op.37, 1939; incidental music, transcrs.

Vocal: 4 Songs, 1v, pf, op.4, 1906; 6 Love Songs, 1v, pf, op.15, 1914–15, arr. S, orch, 1935; Russians, song cycle, 1v, pf, op.18, 1915–17, arr. Bar, orch, 1915–17; Songs of the Countryside, chorus, orch, op.23, 1923; 5 Songs of Love and Life, 1v, pf, op.36, 1895–1922; 3 (Nautical) Songs, 1v, pf, op.38, 1941; 2 Songs, Bar, pf, op.41, 1946–7; Soldiers, song cycle, Bar, pf, op.42, 1948–9; *c*50 songs without op. nos.; unacc. choral pieces, opp.25, 29

Chamber: Sonata, vn, pf, op.5, 1907–8; Pf Qt, op.7, 1909–11; Pastorale, vn, cl/va, pf, op.8, 1909–12; 3 Pieces, fl, harp, str qt, op.13, 1911–12; Sonata, cl/vn, pf, op.14, 1912–15; Intermezzo, str qt, op.17, 1916; Str Qt on Negro Themes, op.19, 1918–19; Variations on a Theme of John Powell, str qt, 1924–5; Divertimento, wind qnt, op.26b, 1926; Fanny Blair, folksong fantasy, str qt, op.28, 1927; Serenade, str qt, op.31, 1931; Sentimental Sketches, op.34, pf trio; Variations on a Quiet Theme, str qt, op.40, 1939

Kbd: Birthday Waltzes, pf, op.1, 1894; Yankee Doodle, pf, op.6, *c*1911; Passacaglia and Fugue, org, op.10, 1912; 2 Choral Preludes on Lowell Mason's Tunes, org, op.39, 1941; other pf pieces, opp.2, 3, 9, 16, 21, 33

MSS in *NNC*

Principal publishers: American Music Edition, Birchard, J. Fischer, G. Schirmer, Society for the Publication of American Music, Universal

WRITINGS

From Grieg to Brahms (New York, 1902, rev. 2/1927/*R*1971)
Beethoven and his Forerunners (New York, 1904, 2/1930)
The Romantic Composers (New York, 1906)
with T. W. Surette: *The Appreciation of Music* (New York, 1907)
The Orchestral Instruments (New York, 1908)
A Guide to Music (New York, 1909)
A Neglected Sense in Piano Playing (New York, 1912)
with M. L. Mason: *Great Modern Composers* (New York, 1916, 2/1968)
Contemporary Composers (New York, 1918)
Short Studies of Great Masterpieces (New York, 1918)
Music as a Humanity (New York, 1920)
From Song to Symphony (New York, 1924)
Artistic Ideals (New York, 1925)
The Dilemma of American Music and Other Essays (New York, 1928)
Tune in, America (New York, 1931/*R*1969)
The Chamber Music of Brahms (New York, 1933/*R*1970)
Music in my Time, and Other Reminiscences (New York, 1938)
The Quartets of Beethoven (New York, 1947)

BIBLIOGRAPHY

EwenD
O. Downes: "An American Composer," *MQ*, iv (1918), 35
R. Thompson: "The Contemporary Scene in American Music," *MQ*, xviii (1932), 13
B. C. Tuthill: "Daniel Gregory Mason," *MQ*, xxxiv (1948), 46
M. J. Klein: *The Contribution of D. G. Mason to American Music* (diss., Catholic U. of America, 1957)
R. B. Lewis: *The Life and Music of Daniel Gregory Mason* (diss., U. of Rochester, 1959)
H. E. Johnson: "Mason, Daniel Gregory," *DAB*

HARRY ESKEW (1), W. THOMAS MARROCCO, MARK JACOBS (2), WILLIAM E. BOSWELL (4), BORIS SCHWARZ (6)

Mason, Edith (Barnes) (*b* St. Louis, MO, 22 March 1893; *d* San Diego, CA, 26 Nov 1973). Soprano. She studied in Cincinnati, and in Paris with Enrico Bertran and Edmond Clément, making her début in Marseilles in 1911. She sang with the Boston Grand Opera Company, with which she first appeared as Nedda (*Pagliacci*) in January 1912, in Montreal (1912) and Nice (1914), and with the Century Company, New York (1914–15), before making her Metropolitan Opera début (on 20 November 1915) as Strauss's Sophie; she performed at the Metropolitan until 1917, and again in the 1935–6 season. She was heard in Paris at the Lyrique-Vaudeville (1919–20) and later at the Opéra and Opéra-Comique, and also at La Scala as Mimì under Toscanini (1923) and at Salzburg as Nannetta (*Falstaff*) (1935). A long, important career at Chicago, where she was first engaged by Mary Garden, began in 1921; she was the first Chicago Sophie (1925), and Snow Maiden in Rimsky-Korsakov's opera, and also the principal interpreter there of Gilda, Gounod's Marguerite and Boito's Margherita. She also played Massenet's Thaïs, Elsa (*Lohengrin*), Fiora (in Italo Montemezzi's *L'amore dei tre re*), and, notably, Butterfly. Her stage appearances were marked by the natural beauty and easy production of her voice, her meticulous attention to the musical text, and the graceful restraint of her acting. She retired in 1939, after playing Desdemona to Martinelli and Tibbett, but on 28 November 1941 made a single reappearance in Chicago as Mimì. She was twice married to the conductor Giorgio Polacco.

BIBLIOGRAPHY

O. Thompson: *The American Singer* (New York, 1937/*R*1969), 351
A. E. Knight: "Edith Mason," *Record Collector*, x (1955–6), 77 [with discography]

RICHARD D. FLETCHER

Mason, Luther Whiting (*b* Turner, nr Lewiston, ME, 2 or 3 April 1818; *d* Buckfield, nr Auburn, ME, 14 July 1896). Music educator and editor of school songbooks. He was a pupil of Lowell Mason at the Boston Academy of Music (he is purported to have been a distant relative of Mason). His early career was as a leader of singing classes and church choirs. In 1853 he went to Louisville as a music teacher in the public schools, where he gained recognition for his pioneering efforts at instructing the primary grades. He moved to Cincinnati in 1856, again attracting favorable attention as a teacher of the youngest children. In 1864 he was called to Boston and set up a plan for primary schools whereby general classroom teachers taught their pupils singing under his supervision. This plan was widely emulated.

In 1880 Mason was invited to go to Japan, where he spent two years setting up a national training program for school music teachers. He imported Western instruments, taught Western notation and harmony to the imperial court musicians, and retuned their ancient instruments to the Western scale. School music in Japan became known as "Mason song" because of the widespread use of his songbooks, which contained Western songs in translation and other East/West hybrids. The Japanese government awarded him high honors.

Mason traveled extensively in Europe, where his work was respected and published. He was best known in the USA for the immensely successful National Music Course, a series of school music textbooks, charts, and guides. In its original form it comprised three student books (the *First, Second, and Third Music Readers*, 1870, rev. 2/1885), a teacher's guide (*The National Music Teacher*, 1870), and three sets of charts. This was the first graded series of school music books and charts to be widely used in the USA. Based on the work of the German pedagogue Christian Heinrich Hohmann, Mason's method was to teach young children to sing by rote, and then introduce musical elements in song, principally translations of German folksongs. *Mason's Hymn and Tune Book* and *The Mason School Music Course* were published in 1882 and 1898 respectively.

BIBLIOGRAPHY
F. H. Martens: "Mason, Luther Whiting," *DAB*
O. McConathy: *Luther Whiting Mason and his Contribution to Music in the Schools of Three Continents* (MS, 1942, *MdU*)
K. Hartley: *A Study of the Life and Works of Luther Whiting Mason* (diss., Florida State U., 1960)
E. May: *The Influence of the Meiji Period on Japanese Children's Music* (Berkeley, CA, 1963)
B. Hall: *The Luther Whiting Mason–Osbourne McConathy Collection* (thesis, U. of Maryland, 1983)
——: "Luther Whiting Mason's European Song Books," *Notes*, xli (1984–5), 482

BONLYN HALL

Mason, Marilyn (May) (*b* Alva, OK, 29 June 1925). Organist. She studied at Oklahoma State University, with Palmer Christian at the University of Michigan, and at Union Theological Seminary, New York (DSM 1954); she also worked with Nadia Boulanger and Maurice Duruflé, and studied Schoenberg's Variations on a Recitative op.40 with the composer in 1950. In 1946 she joined the faculty of the University of Michigan, where she became chairman of the organ department in 1962 and professor in 1965. She has also taught for brief periods at Columbia University, at Union Seminary, and in Parana, Brazil. Mason has toured throughout the USA and Canada, in Europe, Africa, Australia, and South America, and has played with the Philadelphia and Detroit orchestras. She has recorded music by Satie, Sessions, and Thomson as well as Schoenberg's Variations, has edited organ pieces, published articles, and commissioned works by Albright, Cowell, Krenek, Sowerby, Wyton, Ross Lee Finney, and Ulysses Kay, among others. As her record suggests, Mason has a tireless personality and is a brilliant technician and a superb musician.

BIBLIOGRAPHY
J. S. Hettrick: "An Interview with Marilyn Mason," *American Organist*, xvii/8 (1983), 30

VERNON GOTWALS

Mason, Mark. Pseudonym of SEPTIMUS WINNER.

Mason, Redfern (James) (*b* Manchester, England, 12 May 1867; *d* Yuba City, CA, 16 April 1941). Music critic. Educated at the Mechanics Institute, Manchester, he studied music privately. He wrote his first article for the Birmingham *Daily Gazette* in April 1894, and remained with the newspaper until the death of his first wife, Linda Clare Martin Mason, in 1896; she had been a pupil of Clara Schumann. In May 1900 he immigrated to the USA, settling in Rochester, New York. Shortly thereafter he joined the *Post-Express* as music editor; he remained in that post until 1912, when he moved to California, soon becoming music critic for the San Francisco *Examiner*, succeeding Thomas Nunan. From February 1918 to October 1919 he took a leave from the newspaper to manage Isadora Duncan's dance troupe, then became field secretary of the Knights of Columbus in Paris. On 25 November 1934 Mason was fired from the *Examiner* for union activities and was replaced by Alexander Fried. Mason ran unsuccessfully for mayor of San Francisco (1935), was music critic for the Boston *Evening Transcript* (1937), then retired to Mill Valley, California. Mason's critical acumen reflected his scholarly interests in literature, history, and languages, and he wrote with articulate grace. He was profoundly sympathetic to social issues, particularly the disastrous effects of the Depression. He wrote two books about Ireland and a one-act comedy, *The Girl who Knows*, which was performed in San Francisco in 1931; his memoirs remain unpublished. Mason's papers are held by the Bancroft Library, University of California, Berkeley, and the Archives of the San Francisco Public Library.

JOHN A. EMERSON

Mason & Hamlin. Firm of piano and reed organ makers. It was founded in Boston in 1854 by Henry Mason (1831–90), son of the composer Lowell Mason, and Emmons Hamlin (1821–85). Hamlin had previously been employed by the George A. Prince melodeon factory as superintendent of tuning, in which capacity he had developed the art of voicing free reeds to produce imitative effects. The firm's first instruments were of the traditional melodeon type; it soon began making larger models with a greater variety of stops, and in 1861 changed the name of this product to "cabinet organ" (sometimes referred to as "flat top" melodeon). By 1867, when it was awarded a first prize at the Universal Exhibition in Paris, the firm was producing about a quarter of the reed organs manufactured in the USA. In the 1890s the models for these ranged from the tiny "Baby" organ (introduced 1881), popular for Sunday schools and summer cottages, to the two-manual-and-pedal "Church" organ, complete with a superstructure of dummy organ pipes. At about the turn of the century the firm produced a few pipe organs.

Henry Mason retired as president of the firm in 1869; he was succeeded by Lowell Mason, Jr. (1823–85), who remained until his death. Subsequent presidents included Henry Mason's sons Edward Palmer Mason and Henry Lowell Mason (1864–1957). The latter entered the firm in 1888 and became president in 1915; he also wrote several books on music, including a history of the cabinet organ, published in 1901.

In 1883 Mason & Hamlin began making pianos. Like Brinsmead they developed a machine-screw threaded into a flange on the frame instead of using the usual wrest plank and tuning-pins, in order to eradicate loose pins. This costly process was discontinued in 1905. Richard Gertz, who joined the firm in 1895, developed the "tension resonator" and the "duplex scale." The tension resonator, patented in 1900, consists of radial arms of rigid steel joined under the soundboard and fixed to the inner rim of grands and the frame of uprights. It safeguards the vital $\frac{1}{8}''$ per foot crown that the soundboard needs for full resonance, and can, if necessary, be adjusted to restore this curvature. The duplex scale is a system of stringing that provides sympathetic resonance to enrich the treble of the piano. From about the turn of the century to the 1920s Mason & Hamlin was one of the important American piano makers, producing a relatively small number of high quality grands and uprights. An unusual feature of the firm's grand pianos is that their spines are angled slightly to the left to permit a larger soundboard. In 1911 the reed organ business was sold to the Aeolian Co., but no further reed organs were built. The piano business passed to other companies and in 1932 the Boston plant was moved to East Rochester, New York. The firm subsequently became part of the Aeolian American Corporation in East Rochester, but it has continued to make pianos under its own name.

For illustration *see* REED ORGAN.

BIBLIOGRAPHY
H. Greeley, L. Case, and others: *The Great Industries of the United States* (Hartford, Chicago, and Cincinnati, 1872), 109
A. Dolge: *Pianos and their Makers*, i (Covina, CA, 1911/*R*1972)
R. F. Gellerman: *The American Reed Organ* (Vestal, NY, 1973)

MARGARET CRANMER, BARBARA OWEN

Masselos, William (*b* Niagara Falls, NY, 11 Aug 1920). Pianist. He studied at the Juilliard School, where his principal teacher was Carl Friedberg, and also worked for a time with David Saperton. He made his début in New York in 1939 and quickly became known for his sympathies with contemporary music. He gave the first performance (on 17 February 1949) of Ives's First Piano Sonata (the work was finished ten years before Masselos was born), and of Copland's Piano Fantasy in 1957, both of which he has recorded. In 1960 he gave the première of Carlos Chávez's *Invención*. Through a Ford Foundation grant he commissioned a piano concerto from Ben Weber, and played it in 1961. Satie interests him particularly, and he also plays Schumann and Brahms with rare penetration. A strong technician, Masselos is one of the most individual and interesting figures among American performers. He has experimented with changing the customary concert format, particularly by playing programs of unusual length and diversity. He has taught at several music schools, colleges, and universities including the Catholic University of America (from 1976) and the Juilliard School (from 1977). His honors include the Elizabeth Sprague Coolidge Memorial Medal, the Harriet Cohen International Prize, the Award of Merit of the National Association for American Composers and Conductors, and a doctorate from Hamilton College.

MICHAEL STEINBERG/R

Mastersounds. Jazz group formed in the mid-1950s by WES MONTGOMERY and his brothers.

Mata, Eduardo (*b* Mexico City, Mexico, 5 Sept 1942). Mexican conductor and composer. He studied with Chávez and Orbón at the Mexican National Conservatory (1960–63). In 1964 he received a Koussevitzky Fellowship which enabled him to study at the Berkshire Music Center with Rudolf, Leinsdorf, and Schuller. He has served as music director of the Guadalajara SO (1964–6), the University of Mexico PO (1966–75), the Phoenix SO (1974–7), the National SO of Mexico (1976–7), and the Dallas SO (from 1977). He has also been music director of the Festival of Puebla and of the Mexican Festival Casals (1976). Mata has appeared widely as a guest conductor with leading orchestras in Europe and the USA and has recorded extensively for RCA. In 1975 he was awarded the Sourasky Prize, one of Mexico's highest arts awards. As a composer he was most active up to 1967.

WORKS

Orch: 3 syms., no.1 "Classical," 1962, no.2 "Romantic," 1963, no.3, hn obbl, wind, 1966; Debora, ballet suite, 1965; Improvisations no.2, str, 2 pf, 1965

Inst: Trio to Vaughan Williams, cl, snare drum, vc, 1957; Pf Sonata, 1960; Twelfth Night (incidental music, Shakespeare), 8 rec, va, gui, 1961; La venganza del pescador, suite, 8 insts, 1964; Improvisations, cl, pf, 1961; Improvisations no.1, str qt, pf 4 hands, 1964; Improvisations no.3, vn, pf, 1965; Vc Sonata, 1966

Other: Aires [on 16th-century themes], Mez, 8 insts, 1964; Los huesos secos, ballet, tape, 1967

Principal publishers: Ediciones Mexicanas de Música, Peer-Southern

BIBLIOGRAPHY

J. Ardoin: "A Shake-up at the Symphony," *HiFi/MusAm*, xxix/4 (1979), 32

"Letters," *HiFi/MusAm*, xxix/9 (1979), 2

A. Hughes: "Mexican, in New York, Conducts Mozart Mostly," *New York Times* (1 Aug 1980), §III, p.14

JUAN A. ORREGO-SALAS

Mathews, Max V(ernon) (*b* Columbus, NE, 13 Nov 1926). Computer scientist and composer. He studied electrical engineering at the California Institute of Technology (BS 1950), and at the Massachusetts Institute of Technology (MS 1952, DSc 1954). In 1955 he began working at the Bell Telephone Laboratories in Murray Hill, New Jersey, where he developed the MUSIC programs, the first computer sound-synthesis languages, with which the composer can modify and generate sound material, simulating such devices as oscillators, filters, and modulators. The MUSIC4 and MUSIC5 languages became the basis for virtually all further developments in the field. At Mathews's invitation, James Tenney, Jean-Claude Risset, and other composers went to Bell Laboratories to use his early sound-synthesis programs. In 1968 Mathews turned his attention to problems of the real-time control of synthetic sounds and with his colleagues at the laboratories developed in 1970 the GROOVE (Generated Real-time Operations on Voltage-controlled Equipment) system. GROOVE allowed the composer to develop or modify a set of instructions interactively, by using a console that was interfaced both with the computer and the electronic devices; these modifications could be recorded by the computer for editing and playback. Mathews also developed a number of electronic violins, and the "Sequential Drum," an input device for controlling synthetic sounds. In addition to his work at Bell Laboratories, Mathews has been instrumental in the establishment and development of a number of other centers for computer-music research and composition, including that of Stanford University, and IRCAM in Paris. His writings include many articles and a book, *The Technology of Computer Music* (1969).

For further information on his pioneering work in computer music, *see* COMPUTERS AND MUSIC, §3.

WORKS

(all for computer)

May Carol II, 1960; Numerology, 1960; The Second Law, 1961; Masquerades, 1963; Slider, 1965; International Lullaby, 1966, collab. O. Fujimura; Swansong, 1966

BIBLIOGRAPHY

C. Roads: "Interview with Max Mathews," *Computer Music Journal*, iv/4 (1980), 15

P. Manning: "Computer," §§3 and 4, *Grove I*

NEIL B. ROLNICK

Mathews, W(illiam) S(mythe) B(abcock) (*b* ?London, NH, 8 May 1837; *d* Denver, CO, 1 April 1912). Teacher, editor, and writer on music. He was basically self-taught in music, his formal education consisting of study with local teachers in New Hampshire, piano lessons with Lucien H. Southard of Boston in the early 1850s, and lessons with William Mason in Binghamton, New York, during the summers of 1871 to 1873. Mason's teaching became the basis of Mathews's own pedagogical approaches, and the two later collaborated on textbooks and piano methods. At the age of 15 Mathews was already teaching music at the Appleton Academy in Mount Vernon, New Hampshire; he taught at the Wesleyan Female Institute in Macon, Georgia (*c*1860–61), before taking posts in North Carolina, West Virginia, Alabama, and Illinois. In 1867 he settled in the Chicago area, where he was organist at the Centenary Methodist Episcopal Church (until 1893), and taught piano, organ, piano pedagogy, and general music at various schools, including the Chicago Musical College (1886–94) and the American Conservatory (1889–97). Mathews played an important role in the development of normal institute training for piano teachers, and began his own yearly institutes in Chicago in 1895. He was instrumental in organizing the American College of Musicians, a teacher certification program sponsored by the Music Teachers National Association, and in 1892 he pioneered a system of correspondence study for pianists called the Music Extension Society. In addition to publishing many piano methods and annotated collections of piano music, he wrote books on understanding music, American music, music history, and great composers. He contributed numerous articles and monthly columns to music periodicals, including *Dwight's Journal of Music* (1859–80) and *The Etude* (1884–1911), and was the music critic for three Chicago newspapers at various times from 1878 to 1886. Among the journals of which he was editor were the *Musical Independent* (1868–71), the *Journal of School Music* (1908–9), and *Music* (1892–1902), which he founded himself. In about 1910 he became chief editorial consultant for the newly created Arts Publication Society. Four volumes of his papers are in the Newberry Library, Chicago.

WRITINGS

An Outline of Musical Form (Boston, 1868)
How to Understand Music (Philadelphia, 1888/*R*1971)
ed.: *A Hundred Years of Music in America* (Chicago, 1889/*R*1970)
Studies in Phrasing (Philadelphia, 1889–90)
Primer of Musical Forms (Boston and New York, 1890)
A Popular History of the Art of Music (Philadelphia, 1891)
Standard Graded Course of Studies for the Pianoforte (Philadelphia, 1892–4)
with W. Mason: *A Primer of Music* (Cincinnati, 1894)
ed.: *Mathews' Graded Materials* (Cincinnati, *c*1894–5)
with E. Liebling: *Pronouncing and Defining Dictionary of Music* (Cincinnati, 1896)
Music, its Ideals and Methods (Philadelphia, 1897/*R*1972)
The Masters and their Music (Philadelphia, 1898/*R*1971)
The Great in Music (Chicago, 1900–02)
Teacher's Manual of Mason's Pianoforte Technics (Chicago, 1901)

BIBLIOGRAPHY

F. H. Martens: "Mathews, William Smythe Babcock," *DAB*
"W. S. B. Mathews," *Brainard's Musical World*, xvi (1879), 18
Obituary, *Rocky Mountain News* (2 April 1912)
A. M. Larsen: "William Smythe Babcock Mathews, American Music Scrivener," *American Music Teacher*, xxv/2 (1975), 15
K. Graber: *The Life and Works of William Mason* (diss., U. of Iowa, 1976)
R. W. Groves: *The Life and Works of W. S. B. Mathews* (diss., U. of Iowa, 1981)
J. W. Clarke: *Prof. W. S. B. Mathews (1837–1912): Self-made Musician of the Gilded Age (Illinois)* (diss., U. of Minnesota, 1983)

ROBERT W. GROVES

Mathis, Johnny [John Royce] (*b* San Francisco, CA, 30 Sept 1935). Popular singer. He was trained as a singer and performed in a jazz sextet while a student at San Francisco State University. He won a recording contract with Columbia Records and engagements at prestigious New York clubs in the summer of 1955 after an audition in a San Francisco nightclub. He formed a smooth style of ballad singing that was tinged with Afro-American nuances, and achieved great success despite the ascendancy at the time of rock-and-roll as the dominating form of popular musical expression. Mathis excelled in the performance of sentimental love songs in the Tin Pan Alley tradition, such as *Wonderful, Wonderful* (1956), *Chances are* (1957), *The Twelfth of Never* (1957), and *Misty* (1959). Mathis remains a popular nightclub artist and has enjoyed considerable chart success, particularly in Britain. Two duets, one with Deniece Williams (*Too much, too little, too late*, 1978), and one with Dionne Warwick (*Friends in Love*, 1982) are among his best-known recordings.

BIBLIOGRAPHY

SouthernB
"Mathis, Johnny," *CBY 1965*

MICHAEL J. BUDDS

Mattfeld, Julius (*b* New York, 8 Aug 1893; *d* New York, 31 July 1968). Librarian, musicologist, and organist. After studying at the German Conservatory in New York, he worked at the New York Public Library (1910–26), where he was appointed acting chief of the Music Division in 1923; he left to become music librarian at NBC and then held a similar position at CBS (1929–59). As an organist, he held positions at Fordham Lutheran Church, New York (1915–32), and was official organist of the New York World's Fair (1939–40); for several years he had a Sunday morning organ program on CBS radio. With Varèse, Mattfeld was a founder of the International Composers Guild in 1921. He is the author of *The Folk Music of the Western Hemisphere* (1925), *A Hundred Years of Grand Opera in New York, 1825–1925* (1927), *Variety Music Cavalcade, 1620–1950* (1952), and *A Handbook of American Operatic Premieres, 1731–1962* (1963).

PAULA MORGAN

Mattfeld, Victor H(enry) (*b* Bunceton, MO, 1 Sept 1917). Teacher, organist, and editor. He studied at Concordia College in River Forest, Illinois, the University of Chicago (BA 1942), the American Conservatory (BMus 1944, MMus 1946), and Yale University (PhD 1960); he also studied conducting with Nikolai Malko. His first teaching appointment was in organ and theory at the American Conservatory (1945–7), followed by posts in music history at Yale (1952–5) and as assistant professor at the Massachusetts Institute of Technology from 1957 to 1966. From 1967 until his retirement in 1983 he was first associate professor and later professor at the College of Staten Island, CUNY.

As organist Mattfeld was associated with several churches in Chicago, New York, New Jersey, and New England (1938–63), and at the Massachusetts Institute of Technology (MIT) (1958–66). He was music director of Musica Sacra in Cambridge, Massachusetts (1961–5), and of the Camerata at the Boston Museum of Fine Arts (1962–5). In his capacity as editor-in-chief of E. C. Schirmer (1956–68) he was responsible for editions of several choral works. Among his awards are grants from MIT (1964) and the American Philosophical Society (1965). His writings include *Georg Rhaw's Publications for Vespers* (1966) and articles in *The New Grove*.

Mattfeld's wife Jacquelyn (*b* Baltimore, MD, 5 Oct 1925) studied at Goucher College (BA 1948) and Yale University (PhD 1959) and has held administrative posts at academic institutions in the Boston area including Radcliffe College (around 1960) and MIT (1963–5), at Sarah Lawrence College (1965–71), and at Brown University (from 1971), where she has also served as professor of music. Her musicological studies are devoted mainly to cantus firmus practices of Josquin, the subject of her dissertation.

SORAB MODI

Matthews, Artie (*b* Braidwood, IL, 15 Nov 1888; *d* Cincinnati, OH, 25 Oct 1958). Ragtime composer and music educator. He grew up in Springfield, Illinois, where he learned ragtime from two local pianists, Banty Morgan and Art Dillingham, and played professionally in the tenderloin district. After moving to St. Louis about 1908 he studied piano, organ, and theory, and composed and arranged for local theaters. He also transcribed rags by other composers for the music publisher John Stark, who issued Matthews's five *Pastime* rags. Jelly Roll Morton, who visited St. Louis at this time, recalled Matthews as "the best musician in town." In 1915 Matthews took a position as church organist in

Chicago and shortly thereafter one at the Berea Church in Cincinnati, where he settled at the end of World War I. There he earned a degree at the Metropolitan College of Music and Dramatic Arts (1918) and, with his wife Anna, founded in 1921 the Cosmopolitan School of Music, a classical conservatory for the black community, where he taught until his death.

Matthews's elegant *Pastime* rags were his greatest contribution to the literature. These dramatic, innovative, highly pianistic pieces display the stylistic features of black ragtime pianists who performed in vaudeville: they abound in breaks, "walking" bass patterns, stop-time, chromatic runs, triplets, tango rhythms, and, in no.4, dissonant tone clusters. These pieces form part of the second generation of St. Louis ragtime which, like most of the better ragtime of the 1920s, was becoming increasingly virtuoso, reflecting both the physically demanding dances of the time and the emergence of jazz. Matthews notated two other masterworks of late St. Louis ragtime, Robert Hampton's *Cataract Rag* and Charles Thompson's *Lily Rag* (both 1914) and arranged the first piece to be copyrighted with the word "blues" in its title, *Baby Seals Blues* (1912). His most successful composition, *Weary Blues* (1915), became a jazz standard.

WORKS

(selective list; unless otherwise stated, all printed works published in St. Louis)

Pf: Pastime Rag, no.1 (1913); Pastime Rag, no.2 (1913); Weary Blues (1915); Pastime Rag, no.3 (1916); Pastime Rag, no.5 (1918); Pastime Rag, no.4 (1920)

Pf arrs.: Baby Seals Blues (1912); Lily Rag (music by C. Thompson) (1914); Cataract Rag (music by R. Hampton) (1914); Jinx Rag (music by L. P. Gibson) (1915)

Songs: Give me dear just one more chance (F. H. Hayes) (1908); Everybody makes love to someone (P. Franzi) (New York, 1912); Lucky Dan, my gamblin' man (Hunter) (1913); Princess Prance (C. A. Hunter) (1913); Everything he does just pleases me (A. Matthews) (1916)

BIBLIOGRAPHY

W. P. Dabney: *Cincinnati's Colored Citizens* (Cincinnati, 1926)

R. Blesh and H. Janis: *They All Played Ragtime* (New York, 1950, rev. 4/1971)

D. A. Jasen and T. J. Tichenor: *Rags and Ragtime: a Musical History* (New York, 1978)

TREBOR JAY TICHENOR

Matzenauer, Margaret(e) (*b* Temesvár [now Timişoara, Romania], 1 June 1881; *d* Van Nuys, CA, 19 May 1963). Contralto. Born of German parents who were musicians, she learned to play the piano as a child and had already appeared in opera before studying in Graz with Georgine von Januschowsky-Neuendorff and in Berlin with Antonia Mielke and Franz Emerich. She made her début in Strasbourg as Puck in *Oberon* on 15 September 1901 and sang more than 15 roles in her first season there. She made guest appearances with many companies (including those of Covent Garden and Bayreuth) before her American début at the Metropolitan Opera as Amneris under Toscanini (13 November 1911). During her 19 seasons at the Metropolitan, she took part in a great number of new productions and revivals, notably *Fidelio*, *Samson et Dalila* and *Le prophète* (both with Caruso), and *Jenůfa*. Enthusiastically praised for her acting, Matzenauer had a photographic memory (she performed Kundry on 24 hours' notice having never sung the part before), and her musicianship was exceptional. Although her voice was a sumptuous contralto, she was often listed as a soprano and her repertory was vast. In a single season in the 1920s, she sang Isolde, Brünnhilde, Delilah, Azucena, and Amneris, and although her ventures into the soprano repertory took their toll on her voice, it retained its contralto richness. As a concert artist she is especially remembered for her performances of *Das Lied von der Erde* under Willem Mengelberg, the American première of *Oedipus rex* under Koussevitzky, and many Bach works under Bodanzky. After leaving the Metropolitan she continued to give concerts and recitals, appeared occasionally in opera, and was active as a teacher. She is known to have made 85 recordings. Her second husband was the tenor Ferrari-Fontana.

BIBLIOGRAPHY

P. L. Miller: "Margaret Matzenauer," *Record Collector*, xxiii (1976–7), 5 [with discography]

PHILIP LIESON MILLER

Mauceri, John (*b* New York, 12 Sept 1945). Conductor. He studied at Yale University (BA 1967, MPhil 1972), where he became an associate professor in 1968, and attended the Berkshire Music Center in 1971. He conducted the Yale SO (1968–74), and gave the European première of Bernstein's Mass (Vienna, 1973) and the first performance of the original version of Ives's *Three Places in New England* (1974). His début with a professional orchestra took place in 1973 with the Los Angeles PO; his operatic début, also in 1973, was conducting Menotti's *The Saint of Bleecker Street* at the Wolf Trap Festival. He has since developed a fine reputation as an opera conductor in the USA (at the Metropolitan, the New York City Opera, the Santa Fe Opera, and the San Francisco Opera, where he conducted the première of Imbrie's *Angle of Repose* in 1976) and abroad (notably in London and Italy). As an orchestral conductor he has appeared with the National SO, the San Francisco SO, and the orchestras of Cleveland and Philadelphia; he has also made guest appearances with the Orchestre National de France, the Israel PO, and the London SO, among others. Mauceri has taken a keen interest in music theater and served as music director for Hal Prince's production of Bernstein's *Candide* (1974). With Roger Stevens he produced a revival of the Rodgers and Hart musical comedy *On your Toes* (1982), for which he won a Tony Award. In 1979 he was appointed music director of orchestras at the Kennedy Center, where he became consultant for music theater in 1981; he also served as music director of the Washington Opera from 1980 to 1982. He conducted the American and European premières of Bernstein's *A Quiet Place* (Washington, DC, and La Scala, Milan) in 1984, and in that year was appointed music director of the American SO.

SORAB MODI

Ma'wo [mawu, mawuwí]. Musical bow of the Indians of California, including the Yokuts (*ma'wo*), Maidu (*mawu*, *mawuwí*), Pomo, Karok, Miwok, Yurok, and Diegueño. Musical bows were also found among the Tlingit of Alaska. Apart from the Apache fiddle (*see* KÍZH KÍZH DÍHÍ) it was the only native chordophone of the USA. Various forms existed, ranging from the hunting bow used as a musical instrument by the Yurok to specially-made bows consisting of a thin strip of wood with a string or sinew stretched between the two ends. More elaborate versions, with a central bridge, were used by the Maidu and the Tlingit; the bows of the Yokuts had a tuning peg. The length varied from 90 cm to 2 meters.

The method of playing was similar for all types. The bow was held in the left hand with most of the instrument projecting over the player's left shoulder. The wooden part of the lower end, or sometimes the string, was held between the teeth or in front of the open mouth; the string was either plucked with the fingers of the right hand, or struck lightly with the fingernails, or a twig, or a bone. Different notes could be produced by varying the size and shape of the mouth cavity, which was used as a resonating chamber.

The instrument was barely audible and was commonly played for one's own entertainment, as a restful diversion. The Yokuts also played it in mourning for a deceased friend or relative; among the Maidu it was a shaman's instrument.

BIBLIOGRAPHY

H. Besseler and M. Schneider, eds.: *Amerika*, Musikgeschichte in Bildern, i/2 (Leipzig, Germany, 1968; Eng. trans., 1973 as *Music of the Americas: an Illustrated Music Anthology of the Eskimo and American Indian Peoples*), 70

W. Wallace: "Music and Musical Instruments," *Handbook of North American Indians*, viii: *California*, ed. R. F. Heizer (Washington, DC, 1978), 642

MARY RIEMER-WELLER

Má'xe onéhavo'e (Cheyenne: "bass drum"). Large double-headed bass drum of the Cheyenne Indians of the northern Plains.

The "big drum" (a name commonly used to distinguish the bass drum from the smaller hand-held frame drum) is found over a wide area of the USA, from the western Great Lakes to the northern and southern Plains. It may be of recent origin, influenced by the European bass drum or snare drum. It is generally broad and shallow, about 60 cm in diameter and 20 to 23 cm deep. The Cheyenne now commonly use a European bass drum, the calfskin or plastic heads of which may be replaced with deerhide (as among the Flathead of Montana) or buffalo skin (as among the SIOUX Indians for use in their Sun Dance). Drums made by the OJIBWE of the western Great Lakes have painted heads (for the Dream Dance) and are elaborately decorated with cloth and beadwork; they are suspended from four stakes driven into the ground.

The bass drum is usually played by at least four men who sit, kneel, or stand round the instrument and sing while playing it; each holds a padded beater in his right hand. The drum is used both for sacred and secular occasions; with the rise of pan-Indianism it has become the central instrument of the intertribal powwow.

MARY RIEMER-WELLER

Maxfield, Richard (Vance) (*b* Seattle, WA, 2 Feb 1927; *d* Los Angeles, CA, 27 June 1969). Composer. He studied with Sessions at the University of California, Berkeley, and with Babbitt at Princeton University (MFA 1955). His other teachers included Krenek, Copland (at the Berkshire Music Center, 1953), Dallapiccola (on a Fulbright scholarship in Italy, 1955–7), and Cage, whom he ultimately succeeded as teacher of the composition and performance class at the New School for Social Research in New York, 1959–61; during this time he also worked as a freelance technician and audio engineer. Maxfield is acknowledged as the first teacher of electronic music techniques in the USA. He founded and was briefly director of the electronic music studio at San Francisco State College (1966–7). In his contribution to La Monte Young's *An Anthology of Chance Operations* (1963) he established an aesthetic of electronic composition as an independent art form, in which he viewed the tape medium as similar to a poem being read: "We become both the audience and interpreter, face to face with the poet's own writing without intermediary."

Maxfield's *Five Movements* for orchestra won the Gershwin Prize in 1959, but his main contribution was as a composer of electronic music. He was one of the first in the USA to compose for acoustic instruments with tape. *Night Music* (1960), for tape, contains supersonic and infrasonic frequencies which are modulated to produce sounds; this has since become a classic technique of electronic composition. In *Clarinet Music* (1961) he prescribed unconventional playing techniques and in the prerecorded portions of *Dromenon* (1961) made use of unequally tempered tuning. He frequently composed more than one tape realization for performances of pieces including tape and live performers, to avoid rigidity. At the time of his death (by suicide) Maxfield had been working as a freelance composer and engineer in Southern California; his major works, including *Night Music*, *Amazing Grace*, and *Piano Concert for David Tudor*, were not recognized for their technical and musical innovations for over a decade afterwards.

WORKS

Inst: Suite, orch, 1945; 3 pf sonatas, 1947–50; Sonata no.2, cl, pf, 1951; Str Trio, 1951; Sym., str orch, 1951; Structures, 10 wind, 1954; Composition, vn, pf, 1955; Composition, cl, pf, 1956; Variations, str qt, 1956; 5 Movements, orch, 1959

Inst with tape: Peripateia, sax, vn, tape, 1960; Perspectives, vn, tape, 1960; Clarinet Music, 5 cl, 5 tapes, 1961; Dromenon, dance, lighting, fl, sax, pf, vib, vn, db, tape, 1961; Perspectives II for La Monte Young, vn, unspecified str, tape, 1961; Piano Concert for David Tudor, pf, tape, 1961; Toy Sym., fl, vn, toys, wooden boxes, ceramic vase, tape, 1962; Wind, sax, tape, 1962

Tape: A Swarm of Butterflies Encountered on the Ocean, 1958; Cough Music, 1959; Cunamble; Pastoral Sym., 1959; White Noise Piece, 1959; Amazing Grace, 1960; Fermentation, 1960; Night Music, 1960; Dishes, 1961; Radio, 1961; Steam, 1961; Bacchanale, 1963; Bhagavad Gita Sym., 1963; Garden Music, 1963; Elec Sym., 1964; Bacchanale II, 1966; Dream, 1967; Venus Impulses, 1967

Opera: Stacked Deck (D. Higgins), vv, tape, 1960–61

Tapes in the La Monte Young archives of the Dia Art Foundation, New York

BIBLIOGRAPHY

L. Young, ed.: *An Anthology of Chance Operations* (New York, 1963, rev. 2/1970)

E. Schwartz and B. Childs, eds.: *Contemporary Composers on Contemporary Music* (New York, 1967), 850

H. Davies: *Répertoire international des musiques électroacoustiques/International Electronic Music Catalog* (Cambridge, MA, 1968) [incl. list of works]

STEPHEN RUPPENTHAL

May, Brother Joe (*b* Macon, MS, 1912; *d* Thomasville, GA, 1972). Gospel singer. He began singing in a church quartet in his home town. In the early 1940s he moved to East St. Louis, Illinois, where he met the gospel singer Willie Mae Ford Smith. He traveled with her for a few years and learned her technique of engaging a congregation, before obtaining a recording contract with Specialty Records. His first recording, Thomas A. Dorsey's *Search me Lord* (1959), sold over 500,000 copies, and as a result May achieved widespread popularity. He subsequently toured and recorded with the Sallie Martin Singers, James Alexander and the Pilgrim Travelers, and Sister Wynona Carr. His solo recordings included such hits as *Willing to run* (1964), *I'm gonna live the life I sing about* (1964), *What is this?* (1964), and *Eternal in heaven* (1970). May had a raspy but flexible tenor voice, and was often compared with Mahalia Jackson for his mixture of lyrical and yet percussive phrasing. He was known throughout his career as the "Thunderbolt of the Middle West," a title bestowed on him by Smith. May's daughter Annette and son Charles are gospel singers associated with James Cleveland.

BIBLIOGRAPHY

H. C. Boyer: "An Overview: Gospel Music Comes Of Age," *Black World*, xxiii (1973), 42, 79

T. Heilbut: *The Gospel Sound: Good News and Bad Times* (New York, 1971/*R*1975)

HORACE CLARENCE BOYER

Mayer, T. Pseudonym of CHARLES BALMER.

Mayer, William (Robert) (*b* New York, 18 Nov 1925). Composer. He studied at Yale University, principally with Richard Donovan and Herbert Baumgartner, and received the BA degree in 1949. In the same year he spent the summer at the Juilliard School studying composition with Sessions. From 1949 to 1952 he worked with Salzer at the Mannes College and in 1960 studied conducting with Solomon at the Aspen Music School. He has won various awards, including a Guggenheim Fellowship (1966), a Ford Foundation recording grant (1969), and an NEA composition fellowship (1977). He has also received commissions from the Chautauqua Institution (*Overture for an American*, 1958), the New York Choral Society (*Spring Came on Forever*, 1975), and the Minnesota Opera Company (*A Death in the Family*, 1982, cited as the outstanding new American opera or musical theater work of 1983 by the National Institute for Musical Theater). Active in professional organizations, he has been associated with CRI since 1972 (chairman, 1977–81) and has served as secretary and treasurer for the MacDowell Colony; in 1980 he acted as secretary to the National Music Council. Mayer is a prolific composer with an extensive list of large works. His style is characterized by a contrasting of transparent textures with humorous, highly rhythmic and densely scored passages. Bartók, Stravinsky, Barber, and the show tunes of Jerome Kern have been the major influences on his development as a composer. Several of his works have been recorded, notably *Octagon* by Masselos with the Minnesota SO.

WORKS

Stage: One Christmas Long Ago (opera, Mayer), 1962; Snow Queen (ballet), 1963; A Death in the Family (opera, Mayer, after J. Agee), 1982

Orch: Hello World!, 1956; Andante for Str, 1956; Concert Piece, tpt, str orch, 1956; Ov. for an American, 1958; 2 Pastels, 1959; Scenes from the Snow Queen, suite, 1966; Octagon, pf, orch, 1971; Inner and Outer Strings, str qt, str orch, 1982

Inst: Essay for Brass and Winds, ww qnt, brass qnt, 1954; Pf Sonata, 1959; Brass Qnt, 1965; 8 Miniatures (Mayer, D. Parker, A. Noyes, E. Aleinikoff), high v, 7 insts, 1967; Messages, fl, vn, va, vc, perc, 1973; Dream's End, ob, cl, hn, vn, vc, pf, 1976; other pf and chamber pieces

Vocal: Eve of St. Agnes (Keats), solo vv, chorus, orch, 1967; Letters Home (American and Vietnamese soldiers), chorus, orch, 1968; Lines on Light (S. Coleridge, D. Thomas), female vv, pf, 1971; Spring Came on Forever (Bible, V. Lindsay, J. Stephens), solo vv, chorus, orch, 1975; Enter Ariel (S. Teasdale, H. Crane, L. Hughes, Cummings), song cycle, S, cl, pf, 1980; Passage (J. Aubrey, C. Sandburg, Shelley, Mayer, E. Aleinikoff), song cycle, Mez, fl, harp, 1981; other choruses and songs

Principal publishers: Belwin-Mills, Boosey & Hawkes, C. Fischer, Galaxy, Lawson-Gould, Presser

BIBLIOGRAPHY

EwenD

DAVID COPE

Mayes, Samuel (Houston) (*b* St. Louis, MO, 11 Aug 1917). Cellist. His formal music education was at the Curtis Institute with Felix Salmond (1929–37). He joined the Philadelphia Orchestra in 1936, becoming principal cellist three years later. At Koussevitzky's invitation he became principal cellist of the Boston SO (1948–64) and then returned to his former position in Philadelphia (1964–73). He played in the Los Angeles PO during the 1974–5 season. A frequent soloist, he gave the American première of Kabalevsky's First Cello Concerto op.49 with the Hartford SO (28 October 1953), repeating the performance with the Boston SO three days later. His recordings include Prokofiev's Symphony-Concerto with the Boston SO and Strauss's *Don Quixote* with the Philadelphia Orchestra. He has taught at the New England Conservatory, Boston University, and, from 1975, the University of Michigan.

THOR ECKERT, JR.

May Festival. An annual music festival, held since 1873 in Cincinnati (*see* CINCINNATI, §2); *see also* FESTIVALS.

Mayfield, Curtis (*b* Chicago, IL, 3 June 1942). Rhythm-and-blues and soul singer, songwriter, and guitarist. He began singing in the choir of his grandmother's Travelling Soul Spiritualistic Church, where he met Jerry Butler. In his early teens Mayfield formed a vocal group, the Roosters, with Arthur and Richard Brooks and Sam Gooden. With the addition of Butler, the group became the Impressions in 1956, and made its first recording, *For your precious love*, in 1958. After this became a hit, Butler, the lead singer, left to embark on a solo career; Mayfield joined him as guitarist and songwriter, and wrote for him *He will break your heart*, which Butler made a hit in 1960. In 1961 Mayfield rejoined the Impressions, who had meanwhile enlisted Fred Cash, and they immediately had a hit with *Gypsy Woman*, the first of a lengthy series of romantic songs with fantasy lyrics and sophisticated arrangements worked out by Mayfield and Johnny Pate. In 1964 Mayfield unveiled a new, more significant songwriting style, best characterized as secular gospel music, with *I'm so proud* and *Keep on pushing*; instead of adapting the musical ecstasies of the Pentecostal church to popular music, he borrowed the lyrical imagery of gospel and turned it to romantic or socio-political purpose. Musically the Impressions remained one of the smoothest, most emotionally restrained soul groups – perhaps necessarily, given Mayfield's thin tenor lead voice.

Mayfield left the Impressions in 1970 and recorded a variety of solo albums, which maintained essentially the same writing and singing style but relied more on his guitar playing and explored some of the lighter possibilities of the expanded black popular style pioneered by Norman Whitfield and Sly Stone. His greatest success came with the soundtrack to the film *Superfly* (1972), which produced two Top Ten singles, *Freddie's dead* and *Superfly*, both with militantly moralistic lyrics dealing with the evils of drugs. During the 1970s Mayfield was also active as a producer, working with such singers as Aretha Franklin, Gladys Knight, and Mavis Staples. He has continued to record and perform.

RECORDINGS
(selective list)

As soloist: *Curtis* (Curtom 8005, 1970); *Roots* (Curtom 8009, 1971); *Superfly* (Curtom 8014, 1972), incl. Freddie's dead, Superfly; Future shock (Curtom 1987, 1973); *Honesty* (Boardwalk NB33256-1, 1982)

With the Impressions: For your precious love (Abner 1013, 1958); Gypsy Woman (ABC 10241, 1961); I'm so proud (ABC 10544, 1964); Keep on pushing (ABC 9554, 1964)

DAVE MARSH

Maynor [Mainor], **Dorothy (Leigh)** (*b* Norfolk, VA, 3 Sept 1910). Soprano. She first sang in choirs and choruses, making a European tour with the famous chorus of the Hampton Institute, where she received her high school and college education (BS 1933). She later attended the Westminster Choir College in Princeton, and studied in New York with William Klamroth and John Alan Haughton. During the 1939 Berkshire Festival at Tanglewood, she sang for Koussevitzky and was subsequently offered recording engagements with the Boston SO under his direction. Her fame spread, and she made her formal New York début at Town Hall on 19 November 1939. National and international tours followed, during which she appeared as a soloist with many of the principal orchestras in the USA and abroad. She founded the Harlem School of the Arts in 1963, which she directed until 1979 and where she also taught. Maynor had a soaring, bell-like soprano capable of exquisite musical effects, supported by a sincere and ardent temperament. She sang many operatic arias (and recorded Leonore in *Fidelio* under Toscanini), but never appeared in opera.

BIBLIOGRAPHY

SouthernB

G. Diedrichs: "A Respect for Talent: the Harlem School of the Arts," *Opera News*, xxxix/4 (1974), 39

MAX DE SCHAUENSEE/R

Mazurka. A folk dance of Polish origin that appeared in the USA as a social round dance in the middle of the 19th century (*see* DANCE, §II, 1). Performed in a moderate 3/4, the mazurka is governed by accents on the third beat (sometimes the second) and dotted note values (ex. 1). The step pattern, complete in one

Ex.1 Frank M. Davis: *Twilight Hour Mazurka* (1871)

measure, includes a slide, step close, and hop. Regarded as an elaborate version of the waltz, the mazurka never gained popularity with dancing-masters, who felt that its tempo was "rather too slow." In the polka mazurka, polka steps were alternated with those of the mazurka.

BIBLIOGRAPHY

E. Howe: *Howe's Complete Ball-room Handbook* (Philadelphia, 1858)

E. B. Reilly: *The Amateur's Vademecum: a Practical Treatise on the Art of Dancing* (Philadelphia, 1870)

A. Dodworth: *Dancing and its Relations to Education and Social Life* (New York, 1885, 3/1900)

For further bibliography *see* DANCE.

PAULINE NORTON

Mazzola, John (William) (*b* Bayonne, NJ, 20 Jan 1928). Music administrator and lawyer. He attended Tufts University (BA 1949) and continued his studies at Fordham University, where he received an LLB in 1952; he practiced law in New York from 1952 to 1964. He held a staff position at the Lincoln Center for the Performing Arts from 1962 and then became successively general manager (1969–70), managing director (1970–77), and president (from 1977). He has managed operations at the center on a sound financial basis, combining successful fund raising with audience development and cost-efficient procedures. Mazzola has also acted as a consultant for many foreign and domestic performing arts centers, and has served on the boards of the Maurice Ravel Academy in France, the Chopin Foundation of the United States, and the Van Cliburn International Piano Competition, among others.

WILLIAM McCLELLAN

Mc. Names beginning with "Mc" are alphabetized as "Mac."

MCA Music. Firm of music publishers. Founded in 1965 as a division of MCA Inc., it is based in New York and represents Music Corporation of America, Inc., Leeds Music Corp. (founded in 1939 and acquired by MCA Inc. in 1964), Duchess Music Corp., Pickwick Music, Northern Music Co., Champion Music Corp., Hawaii Music Co., Williamson Music, Inc., Spanks Music Corp., and Flanks Music Corp. The MCA catalogue contains over 50,000 compositions, and numerous popular songs are added weekly. The firm handles a wide range of music by modern Russian symphonists, and publishes works by contemporary American composers, including Warren Benson, Brant, Colgrass, Ulysses Kay, William Kraft, Siegmeister, Starer, and Subotnick. MCA also publishes educational music for band, orchestra, chorus, and instrumental groups. In 1973 MCA Music formed a joint venture with the Mills Music division of Belwin-Mills.

W. THOMAS MARROCCO, MARK JACOBS/R

MC5. Rock group. Its members were Wayne Kramer (*b* Detroit, MI, 30 April 1948), guitarist and singer; Fred Smith, guitarist and singer; Rob Tyner, singer; Michael Davis, bass guitarist; and Dennis Thompson, drummer. Formed in the Detroit suburb of Lincoln Park about 1965, the group took as its name the acronym of "Motor City Five." After moving into Detroit, the MC5 became involved with the bohemian arts community. With the poet and propagandist John Sinclair (leader of the White Panthers, a radical political party) as its chief rhetorician and manager, the group developed a loud, fast style and a sound that relied on thick-textured, massive arrangements. The MC5's music incorporated elements of 1950s rock-and-roll and rhythm-and-blues, electronic distortion as practiced by The Who and the Yardbirds, and free jazz, while its lyrics celebrated free love, drugs, and the revolution in youth culture; its stage performances borrowed devices and techniques from the Living Theatre and other avant-garde troupes. Having built a substantial local following, the MC5 acquired a national audience after its performance during the Democratic Party's national convention in Chicago in 1968 (Norman Mailer described the group as "a cross between Sun Ra and 'the Flight of the Bumblebee' "). The group signed a contract with Elektra and in 1969 released its first album, *Kick out the Jams*, a recording of a concert. Elektra dropped the MC5 as a result of difficulties with record retailers, who alleged that the album's lyrics were obscene; the group was then taken up by Atlantic Records, for which it recorded two albums, the first produced by the former critic Jon Landau. After moving to England in 1972 the MC5 disbanded for financial reasons and because of problems arising from drug addiction. Several of the members then pursued solo careers or formed other groups.

The MC5's chief importance lies in its having laid the conceptual and musical groundwork for the punk rock of the late 1970s, primarily through its influence on the New York Dolls.

RECORDINGS

(selective list)

Kick out the Jams (Elek. 45648, 1969); *Back in the U.S.A.* (Atl. 8247, 1970); *High Time* (Atl. 8285, 1971)

BIBLIOGRAPHY

N. Mailer: *Miami and the Siege of Chicago* (Boston, 1969)

DAVE MARSH

Mdewkanton. American Plains Indian group belonging to the Santee division of the SIOUX.

Meacham. Family of wind instrument and piano makers. John Meacham, Jr. (*b* Enfield, CT, 2 May 1785; *d* Albany, NY, 8 Dec 1844), and Horace Meacham (*b* Enfield, CT, 19 July 1789; *d* ?Albany, NY, ?1861) were brothers, and were among the first American wind instrument makers. They may have served an apprenticeship with George Catlin. The only Meacham instruments known to have been made in Hartford are a boxwood "straight" model two-key oboe with ivory mounts, the earliest known American oboe, and a handsome four-key bassoon, which is one of the earliest American bassoons (for illustrations, see Eliason, 1979–80). In either 1810 or 1811 John moved to Albany, and was soon followed by Horace; in 1814 they bought a store and workshop for $7000. They used a number of different stamps, of which three are clearly from the period 1811–27: Meacham, J. Meacham, and J. & H. Meacham. When Sylvanus Pond (later of Firth, Hall & Pond) was taken on as a partner the firm became known as Meacham & Pond (1828–32), and after his departure as Meacham & Co. (1833–*c*1850). The Meachams eventually began also to make pianos, apparently under the influence of Horace's son Roswell. It is doubtful if any instruments were made after about 1850, although Roswell maintained a "music and military store" until about 1860. Of the 31 surviving Meacham instruments (see Young, 1982), most are boxwood flutes and clarinets, but in addition to the oboe and bassoon mentioned above, there is a four-key bassoon (stamped "Meacham/Albany"), a drum, a piccolo, and a copper keyed bugle. Another interesting Meacham instrument is the four-key flute once owned by the philosopher Henry David Thoreau (now in the Antiquarian Society at Concord, Massachusetts), who carved his name and the date 1845 on the instrument.

BIBLIOGRAPHY

R. E. Eliason: "Oboes, Bassoons, and Bass Clarinets, made by Hartford, Connecticut, Makers before 1815," *GSJ*, xxx (1977), 43

——: "The Meachams, Musical Instrument Makers of Hartford and Albany," *JAMIS*, v-vi (1979–80), 54

P. T. Young: *2500 Historical Woodwind Instruments: an Inventory of the Major Collections* (New York, 1982)

PHILLIP T. YOUNG

Mead (Green), Olive (*b* Cambridge, MA, 22 Nov 1874; *d* Cambridge, 27 Feb 1946). Violinist. She came from a family of musicians, and began piano lessons when she was still very young; at the age of seven she switched to violin, studying with Eichberg and later becoming a protégée of Kneisel's. Her solo début in 1895 was at Steinert Hall, Boston. In 1897 she visited Europe with Kneisel and met Brahms shortly before his death. Her début with the Boston SO, the first of 14 appearances with them, was on 28 January 1898 under Emil Paur; she then toured widely, playing with many leading orchestras, and made her London début in 1900. In 1902 she formed the Olive Mead Quartet with Bertha Bucklin, Gladys North, and Lillian Littlehales. (The personnel remained constant except for changes of second violinist.) One of the finest chamber ensembles of its time, the quartet was much praised for its tone quality, rhythmic verve, and vitality, and was compared favorably with the Kneisel Quartet. In 1907 Mead conducted the orchestra of the Women's Philharmonic Society of New York and later became the first woman to teach strings at the Institute of Musical Art (1911–12). As a soloist Mead was praised for her rich tone, technical brilliance, and fine interpretations. She continued to give solo and quartet performances until her retirement around 1917.

BIBLIOGRAPHY

E. L.: "A Chat with Olive Mead," *MusAm*, v/25 (1907), 11

Obituary, *New York Times* (1 March 1946)

ADRIENNE FRIED BLOCK

Meader, George (*b* Minneapolis, MN, 6 July 1888; *d* Hollywood, CA, 19 Dec 1963). Tenor. Meader sang as a boy in Minneapolis, Chicago, and New York. While studying law at the University of Minnesota, he joined the glee club and studied singing with Anna Schoen-René, whom he accompanied to Germany after graduating. He later studied with Pauline Viardot in Paris and appeared in recitals before making his début in Leipzig in 1911 as the Steersman in *Der fliegende Holländer*. A year later he joined the Stuttgart Opera, where he sang Scaramuccio in the world première of *Ariadne auf Naxos* (25 October 1912). Willem Mengelberg chose him to sing in *Das Lied von der Erde* in Amsterdam in 1913. In 1919 he returned to the USA, where he gave recitals before making his début at the Metropolitan Opera as Victorin in Korngold's *Die tote Stadt* (19 November 1921). In his years with the company he was especially admired as David (*Die Meistersinger*), Mime, Vašek (*The Bartered Bride*), and Ferrando in the company's first production of *Così fan tutte*. In 1931 he left the opera to sing in Jerome Kern's highly successful *The Cat and the Fiddle* and other light operas and musicals on Broadway. He later went to Hollywood, where he taught singing and took character parts in several films. Meader's lyric voice was limited in power but of an ingratiating quality, and he used it with consummate art. Because of his slight build, he was best suited to character roles, and his portrayals of many of them were considered to be among the greatest of his time. He was also admired as a lieder singer and for his interpretation of the Evangelists in the Bach Passions.

PHILIP LIESON MILLER

Meat Loaf [Aday, Marvin Lee] (*b* Dallas, TX, 27 Sept 1947). Rock singer. After moving from Dallas to California in 1966, he first worked as a professional musician in a group called at different times Popcorn Blizzard and Meat Loaf Soul (Meat Loaf was a name given to him in high school). During the early 1970s he took prominent roles in several rock musicals, including *Hair* and the *Rocky Horror Show*. In 1975 he appeared in *More than you Deserve*, a show by Jim Steinman, who wrote the material for Meat Loaf's first album, *Bat out of Hell* (1977). Produced by Todd Rundgren, this was an extravagant blend of orchestral music, hard, driving rock, and the melodrama of horror films; the lyrics verged on parody of the traditional concerns of teenagers – sex, alcohol, music, and fast cars. *Bat out of Hell* eventually sold several million copies and stayed on the album chart for over four years; it also yielded three hit singles – *Two out of three ain't bad* (no.11, 1978), *Paradise by the Dashboard Light* (no.39, 1978), and *You took the words right out of my mouth* (no.39, 1979). It proved difficult for Meat Loaf to repeat the success of this first album, and the recording of his next was severely delayed owing to problems with his voice. He had been working with Steinman on an album called *Bad for Good*, which Steinman eventually released as his own. Meat Loaf's *Dead Ringer* reached no.1 on the chart in 1981, and its title song, a duet with Cher, became a hit single. In 1983 he released *Midnight at the Lost and Found*,

Meat Loaf

which was slightly more muted and restrained than his earlier work, but *Bad Attitude* (1985) contained a number of songs of the same epic nature as *Bat Out of Hell*. *Modern Girl*, for example, captures (and criticizes) the traditional values of family life with uncanny accuracy; it has a broad, emotive melody, supported by lush production and punctuated by almost operatic outbursts in the chorus.

ANTHONY MARKS

Meet the Composer. Sponsoring organization. It promotes the music of living American composers, encourages the commissioning and recording of new works, and seeks to develop audiences. It was formed in 1974, under the auspices of the American Music Center, with a grant from the New York State Council on the Arts; John Duffy (*b* 1929), a composer of music for the theater and films, was appointed its director and continued as president and director when the organization became independent of the American Music Center in 1978. Meet the Composer focuses its support on composers who are ineligible for traditional sources of funds, and it encourages composers to exchange ideas with their audiences by sponsoring concerts at which they perform, conduct, or discuss their works. Approximately 50% of the organization's resources are devoted to classical music, 30% to jazz, and 15% to dance; folk and ethnic music and music for the theater and films have also been represented. Between 1974 and 1984 Meet the Composer gave $2.3 million to 4081 organizations sponsoring 7801 composers; with support from more than 45 foundations, corporations, individuals, and government agencies, its annual budget has increased from $66,000 in 1974 to $1.6 million in 1985.

In 1982, with grants from the Exxon Corporation, the Rockefeller Foundation, and the National Endowment for the Arts, Meet the Composer established the Orchestra Residencies Program to promote the performance of orchestral music by American composers and the creation of endowed chairs for composers with American orchestras. A composer selected under the program is expected to organize concerts of new music, review scores and tapes of new works, assist the host orchestra's music director, and write a work to be performed and recorded (for Nonesuch Records) by the orchestra. Six pairs of orchestras and composers were chosen to inaugurate the program: the San Francisco SO and John Adams; the New York PO and Jacob Druckman; the St. Louis SO and Joseph Schwantner; the Pittsburgh SO and John Harbison; the Los Angeles PO and William Kraft; and the Dallas SO and Robert Xavier Rodriguez. The Minnesota Orchestra, with Libby Larsen and Stephen Paulus, joined the program in 1983, as did the orchestras of Indianapolis (with Christopher Rouse), Houston (Tobias Picker), Atlanta (Alvin Singleton), and Seattle (Stephen Albert) in 1985. In 1984 Scott Lindroth was the first recipient of the Charles H. Revson Foundation Composer-in-residence Fellowship, sponsored and administered by Meet the Composer, with the New York PO; the first ASCAP/Meet the Composer commissions were awarded to Kevin Hanlon, Howard McCreary, and Horace Silver.

Meet the Composer has been associated with many radio broadcasts, and with a series of documentaries for television, entitled "Soundings," devoted to individual composers. The organization offers technical assistance to composers and sponsors, and has published a handbook, *Commissioning Music* (1984), for composers and prospective patrons.

BIBLIOGRAPHY

J. Duffy: "Put a Composer in Your Life," *Arts Chronicle* (Sept 1980), 9
M. Carrington: "Bringing 'em Back Alive," *American Arts*, xii/6 (1981), 1
——: "6 Orchestras Adopt a Composer," *Symphony Magazine*, xxxiv/1 (1983), 24
M. Colgrass: "Meet the Composer," *Music Magazine*, vii/1 (1984), 38
J. Rockwell: " 'Horizons' Gives a Hearing to Living Composers," *New York Times* (27 May 1984), §II, p.7

EMILY GOOD

Meetz, Raymond [?Richard] (*fl c*1806–1836). Pianist, teacher, publisher, and composer, probably of French origin. He was one of the musicians in New York in the early 19th century who dabbled in several musical activities in order to earn a living. He appeared as pianist, taught (advertising himself as a pupil of Mozart), sold pianos, and sold and published music. Meetz was primarily the New York agent for the Philadelphia music publisher George E. Blake, though he did publish a few titles under his own name; two of his works for piano, *General LaFayette's Grand March and Quick Step* (1824) and *General Montgomery's Dead March* (?1818), bear a Philadelphia imprint. He was probably related to the pianist Cesarine Meetz and the pianist and singer JULIUS METZ.

BIBLIOGRAPHY

R. J. Wolfe: *Secular Music in America, 1801–1825: a Bibliography* (New York, 1964)
B. Wolverton: *Keyboard Music and Musicians in the Colonies and United States of America before 1830* (diss., Indiana U., 1966)
R. J. Wolfe: *Early American Music Engraving and Printing* (Urbana, IL, 1980)

RICHARD JACKSON

Mehta, Mehli (*b* Bombay, India, 25 Sept 1908). Violinist and conductor. He studied at the University of Bombay and at Trinity College of Music, London. He founded the Bombay SO in 1935 and served as its concertmaster for ten years before becoming its conductor. In 1940 he formed the Bombay String Quartet, which he led for 15 years. Encouraged by Efrem Zimbalist, he studied for a time with Galamian at the Juilliard School, then served as assistant concertmaster of the Hallé Orchestra in Manchester, England, under Barbirolli (1955–9). He returned to America in 1959, at which time he joined the Curtis String Quartet in Philadelphia, performing with them throughout the USA for five years. In Los Angeles, where he settled in 1964, he founded the American Youth SO (1964) and served on the faculty of UCLA (1964–76), directing the orchestra department and conducting the symphony and chamber orchestras. The conductor Zubin Mehta is his son.

KAREN MONSON

Mehta, Zubin (*b* Bombay, India, 29 April 1936). Conductor, son of Mehli Mehta. He learned piano and violin as a child and developed an ambition to conduct. He was persuaded to study medicine, which he abandoned at 18 to enter the Vienna Academy, where he studied with Hans Swarowsky and played the double bass in the orchestra. After forming student orchestras to conduct, he entered the first international conductors' competition organized by the Royal Liverpool PO in 1958 and won the major prize (reserved for British and Commonwealth entrants) of a year as musical assistant in Liverpool.

When this expired Mehta left Britain and quickly made a favorable impression as a guest conductor with the Vienna PO, and in Montreal and Los Angeles substituting for other conductors. His spectacular success led to his appointment to the Montreal SO (1960–67), and to the Los Angeles PO, as associate conductor in 1960, and music director in 1962. He was then the youngest to hold such an appointment with a leading orchestra in the USA, and the first in North America to share a joint appointment with two major orchestras. At Los Angeles he transformed an undistinguished orchestra into a superior ensemble within a few years, spreading his own and the orchestra's reputation by some outstanding recordings.

Mehta first conducted opera at Montreal in 1964 (*Tosca*), made his début at the Metropolitan Opera in 1965 (*Aida*), and at Covent Garden in 1977 (*Otello*), having first appeared in London at a Royal PO concert in 1961. At that time he began to make regular guest appearances with the Berlin PO and Vienna PO, at the Salzburg Festival (from 1962), and with the Israel PO, of which he became chief musical adviser in 1969. He led the Israel PO on numerous tours to Europe, North and South America, and Australia, and was named music director for life in 1981. From 1970 to 1978 he was also music director of the Hollywood Bowl Summer Festival. He succeeded Boulez as music director of the New York PO from the 1978–9 season, and has made recordings with the orchestra of works by Berlioz, Brahms, and Stravinsky, as well as Barber and John Corigliano, Jr. In 1984 he gave a series of concerts in India as part of a Far Eastern tour.

Mehta's performances generally favor romantic warmth of expression and voluptuous sonority, combined with bold attack and rhythmic vigor and reinforced by boundless self-confidence. An awareness of his audience is often reflected in platform gestures indicative not so much of the musical content as of the desired response of the audience to it. He has received Padma bhushan (Order of the Lotus), the Indian government's highest cultural award, and in 1976 was appointed Commendatore by the Italian government.

BIBLIOGRAPHY

Anon: "Gypsy Boy," *Time*, xci (19 Jan 1968), 76
"Mehta, Zubin," *CBY 1969*
R. Yockey and M. Bookspan: *Zubin: the Zubin Mehta Story* (New York, 1978)
P. Hart: "Zubin Mehta," *Conductors: a New Generation* (New York, 1979), 127–63
H. Matheopoulos: "Zubin Mehta: the Meteor with Good 'Sitzfleisch'," *Maestro: Encounters with Conductors of Today* (London, 1982), 335

NOËL GOODWIN

Meier, Gustav (*b* Wettinger, Switzerland, 13 Aug 1929). Conductor. He attended the Zurich Conservatory, 1944–8 and 1951–3, studying under Paul Müller, and the Accademia Chigiana in Siena in 1952 and 1953. After spending two years as conductor of the Imperial Court Orchestra in Addis Ababa, Ethiopia, he was appointed assistant conductor of the Zurich Opera, where he worked from 1956 to 1958. Meanwhile, in 1957, he had spent the first of two summers at the Berkshire Music Center, studying under Eleazar de Carvalho; in 1958 he moved permanently to the USA. In addition to guest engagements with a number of American and European orchestras and opera companies, Meier was conductor of the New Haven Chorale (1960–73) and professor of conducting at Yale University (1961–73). After teaching at the Eastman School (1973–6), he joined the faculty of the University of Michigan in 1976, where he is director of orchestras and opera production and conductor of the symphony orchestra. He was appointed music director of the Greater Bridgeport (Connecticut) SO in 1971 and of the Lansing (Michigan) SO in 1979. Some of his most distinguished work has been with contemporary music, in which his ability to render lucidly the textures of such music as Elliott Carter's mature works has been especially valuable.

BERNARD JACOBSON

Meignen, Leopold (*b* France, 1793; *d* Philadelphia, PA, 4 June 1873). Publisher, composer, conductor, and teacher. He was a bandmaster in Napoleon's army before immigrating to the USA, where he settled in Philadelphia. He was a founder of the music publishing firm of Fiot and Meignen with which he remained active from 1835 to 1855. He conducted the première of William Henry Fry's *Leonora* on 4 June 1845, and in 1846 succeeded Charles Hupfeld as conductor of the Musical Fund Society's orchestra, which he led until 1857. In this capacity he conducted

Zubin Mehta

the first Philadelphia performances of Beethoven's second and third symphonies, as well as those of the overtures to Weber's *Oberon* and Mendelssohn's *A Midsummer Night's Dream*. He also led the orchestra of the Handel and Haydn Society in the 1850s. He wrote a *Grand Military Symphony*, and the words and music of a sacred cantata, *The Deluge* (1856), which was performed by the Harmonia Sacred Music Society.

Meignen was joint author (with William W. Keys) of *The Music Reader, or the Practice and Principles of the Art, especially Adapted to Vocal Music* (1865), and compiler (with John Winebrenner) of *The Seraphina, or Christian Library of Church Music*. He produced *The Art of Singing* (1860), and also published transcriptions for the guitar. But perhaps his chief importance was as the teacher of the Philadelphia composers Fry, Michael Cross, Charles Jarvis, and Septimus Winner.

BIBLIOGRAPHY

Obituary, *Philadelphia Bulletin* (5 June 1873); repr. in *Dwight's Journal of Music*, xxxiii (1873), 43

OTTO E. ALBRECHT

Meineke [Meinecke, Meincke], **Christopher** [Charles, Christian, Karl] (*b* Germany, 1782; *d* Baltimore, MD, 6 Nov 1850). Pianist, organist, and composer. He was probably a son of the organist and composer Karl Meineke of Oldenburg, with whom he is sometimes confused. In 1800 he came to Baltimore, where he was organist at St. Paul's Episcopal Church. He became active in the Handelian Society in 1803, and later in the Anacreontic Society (founded 1822). He was in Vienna from 1817 to 1819, where he met Beethoven and heard him improvise; Beethoven is said to have praised a concerto by Meineke.

Meineke wrote a great quantity of songs and piano pieces, a few of which were published by 1810, though most date from the 1820s after his return from Vienna. His piano music exhibits imagination and flair, and is often demanding for the performer. His growth in style and virtuosity may be seen in two sets of variations on Mozart's "Das klinget so herrlich" (from *Die Zauberflöte*), one contained in the medley *Pot pourri* (n.d. [1807–9]) and the other issued, under the title *Away with Melancholy*, in the 1830s. He also wrote church music, including a Te Deum (1821), of which a performance at St. Paul's Church was reviewed in *The Euterpeiad* (2 March 1822) as "appealing to a higher class of musicians than are every where found in our country." His *Music for the Church* (1844), written for the St. Paul's choir, contains 62 psalm and hymn tunes.

WORKS

Published in Baltimore, n.d., unless otherwise indicated; estimated dates of publication are given in brackets.

VOCAL

Sacred: Te Deum, 4vv ([1821]); Praise to thee great Creator, solo v, chorus ([1830s]); Music for the Church (1844) [62 psalm and hymn tunes]

Songs, lv, pf: The Gentle Maid (E. C. Pinkney) (1826); Love lurks upon my lady's lips (Meineke) (1827); The Trumpet (Mrs. Hemans) (1827); I remember, I remember (T. Hood) (1828); Not love thee (Meineke) (1828); My Highland Mary (Lady Norton) (1829); Summers gone (Norton) (1832); The Bird at Sea (Hemans) (1834); I go sweet friends (Hemans) (1836); When the early stars are peeping (F. Wilson) (1843); *c*35 others

PIANO

Variations: Nos galen, or New Year's Night ([1824]); Araby's Daughter [after Kiallmark] (1826); The Hunter's Chorus [after C. M. von Weber: Der Freischütz] (1826); Au clair de la lune ([1827]), ed. in RRAM, ii (1977); Brignal Banks (1827); My Heart and Lute (1827); I left thee where I found thee love [after C. H. Gilfert] (1828); Non più andrai [after Mozart: Le nozze di Figaro] (1828); Le petit tambour (1828); Malbrouk ([1829]); Away with Melancholy [after Mozart: Das klinget so herrlich, from Die Zauberflöte] ([1830s]); The Voice of Grace, or The Coronach (1843); 16 other sets

Waltzes: Antwerp Waltz ([1825–33]); The Emperor Nicholas' Waltz ([1826–31]); The Rose ([1826–31]); The Nightingale ([*c*1828]); The Cambridge Waltz ([1830s]); The Harlem Waltz (1843); 4 others

Marches: Rail Road March (1828); Grand National March . . . General Andrew Jackson (1829); Baltimore City Guard's March ([1830s]); Funeral March . . . Lafayette ([1834]); Grand Turkish March ([?1835]); President Taylor's Inauguration March (1849); *c*10 others

*c*12 others, incl. Pot pourri ([1807–9]); Divertimento (1825), ed. in RRAM, ii (1977)

PEDAGOGICAL

A New Instruction for the Piano Forte (1823, 3/1840); Exercises for the Piano Forte (Philadelphia, 1828)

BIBLIOGRAPHY

L. Keefer: *Baltimore's Music* (Baltimore, 1962)

R. J. Wolfe: *Secular Music in America, 1801–1825: a Bibliography* (New York, 1964)

B. A. Wolverton: *Keyboard Music and Musicians in the Colonies and United States of America before 1830* (diss., Indiana U., 1966)

J. BUNKER CLARK

Melba, Dame **Nellie** [Mitchell, Helen Porter] (*b* Richmond, nr Melbourne, Australia, 19 May 1861; *d* Sydney, Australia, 23 Feb 1931). Soprano. Melba had already received a great deal of musical training (especially in piano) before 1886, the year she left Australia for further study as a singer in Europe. She worked with Mathilde Marchesi in Paris for a year and by 1894 had established herself in Brussels, Paris, London, St. Petersburg, and Italy as the most accomplished and renowned soprano of her time. Her association with the Metropolitan Opera lasted, with interruptions, from her début as Donizetti's Lucia (4 December 1893) to 1910. There and with such other American companies as the Damrosch Opera, Hammerstein's Manhattan Opera, and the Chicago Grand Opera she became renowned for her portrayals of Gilda, Gounod's Juliet and Marguerite, Massenet's Manon, and Micaela. Melba undertook numerous international concert tours and sang at Covent Garden in nearly every season from 1888 to World War I. Her trill, staccato singing, and scales (both diatonic and chromatic) were as precise as if played on a keyboard, and in smoothness and steadiness of tone, in spontaneity of emission and virtually flawless intonation, perhaps no singer of this century has equalled her. Her popularity was enormous. She made some 150 recordings between 1904 and 1926, and her name became commercially valuable (peach melba and melba toast were both named after her). She was created Dame of the British Empire in 1918. In 1926 she retired from the stage and became president of the Melba Memorial Conservatorium in Melbourne.

BIBLIOGRAPHY

A. G. Murphy: *Melba: a Biography* (London, 1909/*R*1977) [with chapters by Melba]

N. Melba: *Melodies and Memories* (New York, 1926/*R*1971)

P. Colson: *Melba: an Unconventional Biography* (London, 1932)

H. H. Harvey and G. Whelan: "Nellie Melba," *Record Collector*, iv (1949), 203 [with discography]; rev. by W. Hogarth in *Record Collector*, xxvii (1982), 67

J. Wechsberg: *Red Plush and Black Velvet: the Story of Melba and her Times* (Boston, 1961)

G. W. Hutton: *Melba* (New York, 1962)

J. B. Richards: "Melba, Nellie," *Le grandi voci*, ed. R. Celletti (Rome, 1964) [with discography]

H. Pleasants: "Nellie Melba," *The Great Singers* (New York, 1966), 270

B. and F. MacKenzie: "Nellie Melba," *Singers of Australia* (Melbourne, 1967), 35

J. A. Hetherington: *Melba: a Biography* (New York, 1968)

M. Casey: *Melba Revisited* (Melbourne, 1975)
W. R. Moran, ed.: *Nellie Melba: a Contemporary Review* (Westport, CT, 1984) [with bibliography and discography]

DESMOND SHAWE-TAYLOR/R

Melchior, Lauritz [Hommel, Lebrecht] (*b* Copenhagen, Denmark, 20 March 1890; *d* Santa Monica, CA, 18 March 1973). Tenor. He studied at the Royal Opera School, Copenhagen, and sang various baritone roles until his studies with Vilhelm Herold revealed him as a tenor. After a second début in 1918, he studied Wagner roles with eminent teachers, and sang them in Bayreuth and at Covent Garden from 1924 to 1939. His Metropolitan début on 17 February 1926, as Tannhäuser, and subsequent appearances during that and the next season in *Die Walküre*, *Siegfried*, and *Parsifal* were not wholly successful; his great New York period began only with his return, after a season's absence and a period of further study (with Egon Pollak at the Hamburg Opera), to complete his Wagner repertory with Tristan, Lohengrin, and the *Götterdämmerung* Siegfried in 1929 and 1930. He remained at the Metropolitan until disagreements with the Bing regime prompted him to leave in 1950. During those years he also appeared in Europe and Buenos Aires, and latterly in Broadway shows, films, concerts, and radio performances. He became an American citizen in 1947.

Melchior sang each of the heaviest Wagner roles more than 100 times, and Tristan more than 200 times – figures suggestive of the stamina that made him the only Wagner tenor of his time who could still sound fresh in the last acts of *Tristan* and *Götterdämmerung*. He retained a baritonal warmth without constriction in his top notes. These virtues, coupled with a vivid and expressive enunciation of the text, induced his admirers to overlook his dramatic limitations and even some musical defects, especially vagueness in matters of rhythm. The heroic scale of his singing, in person and on his many recordings, has made it clear that he was the outstanding *Heldentenor* of the century.

BIBLIOGRAPHY

E. B. Mortensen and J. Zachs: "A Lauritz Melchior Discography," *Record News*, iii (1959), 433; iv (1959), 12
H. Hansen: *Lauritz Melchior: a Discography* (Copenhagen, 1965, 2/1972)
C. L. Osborne: "Melchior as Tristan," *HiFi/MusAm*, xxvi/10 (1976), 91

DESMOND SHAWE-TAYLOR/R

Melodeon. A term extensively used in the USA during the first half of the 19th century to designate a small REED ORGAN with a single keyboard and one or two sets of reeds.

Melodrama. A type of drama, or a section of a drama, in which spoken words alternate with, or are accompanied by, passages of music that heighten their dramatic effect; the term is also applied to the technique of setting words in this manner. Popular throughout the 19th century in American theater, melodrama is also found in 20th-century art music.

1. European background. 2. To 1850. 3. 1850–1900. 4. The 20th century.

1. EUROPEAN BACKGROUND. Jean-Jacques Rousseau's *Pygmalion* (subtitled "scène lyrique" and first performed in 1770), with musical interludes by Horace Coignet, was, according to its author, the first drama in which the spoken word was "announced and prepared by the musical phrase." The genre found sporadic imitators in Germany in the 18th century (Georg Benda, C. G. Neefe, J. R. Reichardt and Mozart), and gained widespread popularity in post-Revolutionary France, where, as an entertainment enjoyed mostly by the lower classes, it grew out of the traditions of pantomime, opéra-comique, and domestic drama. Its characteristic French form was a five-act drama; short passages of music, often borrowed and unattributed, were used at the entries and exits of performers to underline dramatic moods and to provide color and background for mimed action at climactic moments.

2. TO 1850. The first melodrama to be presented in the USA was probably *Ariadne Abandoned by Theseus in the Isle of Naxos* by the immigrant French composer Victor Pelissier. This was advertised in New York in 1797 as a drama in which "between the different passages spoken by the actors will be full orchestral Music expressive of each situation and passion." The work is lost, but Pelissier's melodramatic style can be seen in his setting of William Collins's *Ode on the Passions* for speaker and piano (1812) and his incidental music to William Dunlap's *The Voice of Nature* (1803).

The first melodrama to achieve lasting success in the USA was Thomas Holcroft's *A Tale of Mystery*, a translation of Guilbert de Pixèrécourt's *Coeline, ou L'enfant mystère*, performed in New York and Philadelphia in 1802. While the play was imported from England, new music was composed by James Hewitt, and songs interpolated by Pelissier. Hewitt's music is no longer extant – a fate shared by most American scores of instrumental music for melodrama; although interpolated songs generally appeared in print, the instrumental accompaniment remained in manuscript. Published instructions in texts and manuscript additions to prompt books and cue-sheets, however, often reveal quite explicit directions as to how the music should be performed. In *A Tale of Mystery*, one direction reads: "MUSIC loud and discordant at the moment the eye of MONTANO catches the figure of Romaldi; at which Montano starts with terror and indignation. He then assumes the eye and attitude of menace which Romaldi returns. The music ceases." The music was played during the dialogue, marking a departure from the practice of Rousseau and Pelissier, who used music in alternation with speech.

The only extant American instrumental music for melodrama before 1850 is that for James Nelson Barker's *The Indian Princess* with music by John Bray. The vocal score, published separately from the libretto in 1808 (for illustration *see* OPERA, fig. 1), gives some idea of the conventions of early melodrama (ex. 1). Because the work is a hybrid – opera with passages of melodrama – instrumental sections constitute only a portion of the music (18 of 32 numbers); the remainder, as in English comic opera of the

Ex.1 John Bray: *The Indian Princess* (1808)

PRINCESS: My father, dost thou love thy daughter? Listen to her voice; look upon her tears: they ask for mercy to the captive. Is thy child dear to thee, my father? Thy child will die with the white man.

(Plaintive music. She bows her head to his feet. Powhatan, after some deliberation, looking on his daughter with tenderness, presents her with a string of white wampum . . .)

period, consists of songs, choruses, and glees (there are no recitatives). Even in pure melodrama of this period there were likely to be opening choruses or dances for each act and interpolated songs and marches.

Most popular melodramas before 1850 came from England or from France via England, though many of them were doubtless provided with new music by American composers: among these were *The Bridal Ring*, and Dibdin's *Lady of the Lake* (1811) and *Valentine and Orson*, all with music by Pelissier. Works by American authors were also performed, but were less popular; they included, besides *Ariadne* and *The Indian Princess*, *The Rose of Arragon, or the Vigil of St. Mark* (1822) by S. B. H. Judah with music by Rayner Taylor, and *Trial without Jury, or The Magpie and the Maid* (1815) by J. H. Payne with music by Bray. A few interpolated songs from these survive, but they show nothing of the special qualities of melodrama. (Wolfe lists the songs associated with some of the American melodramas.)

3. 1850–1900. After about 1850 melodrama was produced in the East in theaters that catered to the urban lower middle class, but in the West and South its audience was drawn from a broader spectrum of society. It is from this period that the stereotype of melodrama as a play of good versus evil, with daring last-minute rescues and escapes and spectacular scenic effects, has been formed. The few extant scores for such works indicate that the music (usually up to 30 or 40 short instrumental numbers) was composed, not improvised or borrowed, employed full theater orchestra, and was carefully coordinated with lighting and scenery to achieve maximum dramatic effect. *Under the Palms* (1864), an adaptation of Tennyson's poem *Enoch Arden*, had music probably by Thomas Baker, a musician trained in England who came to New York as the concertmaster for Jullien's concerts and stayed to work in the theaters. In Act 1 the music, in conjunction with calcium lighting and a sliding set, is used to underline the emotional scene in which Enoch's wife Annie, when he has been absent for 13 years, is tempted to remarry and sees him in a vision. The scene is performed mostly without dialogue; the music has to portray several changes of mood and much use is made of such devices as the tremolo and the diminished 7th chord. A legacy of PANTOMIME that is frequently employed to heighten a particular dramatic effect is "hurry music," a short instrumental tune to accompany hurried action or convey emotional agitation (ex.2).

Ex.2 *Monte Cristo* (*c*1873), Act 1 scene i

There is evidence of the occasional use in "straight" dramas of the 19th century of the technique of melodrama, often in conjunction with interpolated songs and dances. For example, George Aitken's dramatization of *Uncle Tom's Cabin* (1852) made use of melodramatic hurry music.

Late 19th-century melodrama was a direct precursor of the silent film: *Monte Cristo*, an adaptation by Charles Fechter of the novel by Alexandre Dumas the elder, was filmed in 1913 with James O'Neill, who had played the Count more than 4000 times since 1883, in the title role; *The Birth of a Nation* (1915) had been produced as a melodrama under the title *The Clansman* in 1906; and E. S. Kelley's *Ben Hur* (1899) appeared as a film in 1925. Musical techniques developed for melodrama had to be extended to form continuous accompaniment for early silent films, but many of the same conventions were utilized (*see* FILM MUSIC, §1).

4. THE 20TH CENTURY. During the 19th century melodrama became less popular in the theater but more widely used in concert music. Such European examples as Beethoven's incidental music to *Die Ruinen von Athen* (1811) and *König Stephan* (1811), Humperdinck's *Königskinder* (1897), and Richard Strauss's *Enoch Arden* (1897) were followed in the USA from about 1895 to 1915 by nontheatrical melodramas for voice and piano, often to texts by H. W. Longfellow, E. A. Poe, and W. B. Yeats. J. M. Wootton, H. W. Loomis, Stanley Hawley, Max Heinrich, Arthur Bergh, Lawrence Gilman, and H. F. Gilbert all contributed works of this kind. They are continuous and through-composed, often starting with an introduction in tempo followed by held chords or tremolos underlying the recitation; expression marks are in English, for example "tensely, with passionate melancholy" (Gilman: *The Curlew*, 1904). Unlike contemporaneous works by Berg and Schoenberg written in Sprechstimme, pitches are almost never, and rhythms rather seldom, indicated; in Bergh's setting of Poe's *The Raven* (1909), for example, rhythmic values are indicated only for some of the lines rhyming with "nevermore" (ex.3). The singer David Bispham, to whom Bergh's work is

Ex.3 Arthur Bergh: *The Raven* (1909)

dedicated, writes of "acting out" the character in recitals (*A Quaker Singer's Recollections*, 1921/*R*1977); he frequently included melodrama in his recitals after about 1900, and mentions Rossetter G. Cole's setting of Longfellow's *King Robert of Sicily* (*c*1906) for voice and orchestra as the most satisfactory.

From about the mid-20th century melodrama has been employed by many American composers, often in connection with patriotic works and Americana, for example Blitzstein's *The Airborne* (1944–6), Copland's *Lincoln Portrait* (1942) and *Preamble for a Solemn*

Ex.4 Copland: *Lincoln Portrait* (1942)

Occasion (1949), Siegmeister's *I See a Land* (*c*1962) and *I Have a Dream* (1967); in works for children, including Siegmeister's *Dick Whittington and his Cat* (1966) and Kubik's *Gerald McBoing-Boing* (1950); and for settings of mythological and biblical texts, such as Foss's *Fragments of Archilochos* (1965), Starer's *Joseph and his Brothers* (1966), and Burrill Phillips's *The Return of Odysseus* (1956). In contrast to earlier melodrama, the narration in many of these works is not meant to be dramatic; in *Lincoln Portrait* Copland cautions the narrator against "undue emphasis in the delivery of Lincoln's words . . . They are meant to be read simply and directly without a trace of exaggerated sentiment." The text in both Copland's works is reserved for the final third of the piece, and the accompanying music serves to punctuate rather than reflect emotions (see ex.4, where a triadic motif predominates regardless of the meaning of the text). The emphasis of melodrama has shifted in the later 20th century away from the exaggerated sentiment of the 19th-century form (which is reflected in the common usage of the word "melodramatic") back to the narrower interpretation of the term articulated by Rousseau – that of music that announces and prepares for the spoken phrase. In recognition of this change, composers have for the most part shed the title "melodrama" and have called their works "recitations" or "narrations."

BIBLIOGRAPHY

C. Durang: "The Philadelphia Stage," *Philadelphia Sunday Dispatch* (1854, 1856, 1860) [series of articles; compiled by T. Westcott as *History of the Philadelphia Stage, between the Years 1749 and 1855*, 1868, *PU*; similar compilations as *The Philadelphia Stage* in *PPL*, *History of the Philadelphia Stage* in *PHi*]

J. F. Mason: *The Melodrama in France from the Revolution to the Beginning of Romantic Drama, 1790–1830* (Baltimore, 1912)

W. S. Dye: *A Study of Melodrama in England from 1800–1840* (diss., U. of Pennsylvania, 1919)

G. C. D. Odell: *Annals of the New York Stage* (New York, 1927–49/*R*1970)

G. H. Leverton: *The Production of Later 19th Century Drama* (New York, 1936)

H. W. Hitchcock: "An Early American Melodrama: The Indian Princess," *Notes*, xii (1954–5), 375

R. J. Wolfe: *Secular Music in America, 1801–1825: a Bibliography* (New York, 1964)

F. Rahill: *The World of Melodrama* (University Park, PA, 1967)

D. Grimsted: *Melodrama Unveiled: American Theater and Culture, 1800–1850* (Chicago, 1968)

J. L. Fell: "Dissolve by Gaslight: Antecedents to the Motion Picture in 19th Century Melodrama," *Film Quarterly*, xxiii (1970), 22

S. Trussler: "A Chronology of Early Melodrama," *Theatre Quarterly*, i/4 (1971), 19, 93

J. S. Smith: *Melodrama* (London, 1973)

E. F. Bergainnier: "Melodrama as Formula," *Journal of Popular Culture*, viii (1975), 726

E. F. Kravitt: "The Joining of Words and Music in Late Romantic Melodrama," *MQ*, lxii (1976), 571

M. Matlaw: "English and American Dramatizations of The Count of Monte Cristo," *Nineteenth Century Theatre Research*, vii (1979), 39

A. D. Shapiro: "Action Music in American Pantomime and Melodrama, 1730–1913," *American Music*, ii (1984), 49

ANNE DHU SHAPIRO

Melton, James (*b* Moultrie, GA, 2 Jan 1904; *d* New York, 21 April 1961). Tenor. He studied with Enrico Rosati. After singing popular music in radio broadcasts and making two musical films, he made his stage début in 1938 as Pinkerton with the Cincinnati Opera. In 1942 he made his début at the Metropolitan Opera as Tamino under Bruno Walter; he remained there until 1950, singing such lyric roles as Alfredo, Wilhelm Meister (in Ambroise Thomas' *Mignon*), and Pinkerton. He also appeared with the San Carlo Opera Company (1938–9) and the Chicago Opera (1938–42). He was also popular as a recitalist, and later made several television appearances. A handsome man and a confident stage presence, Melton had a voice of great beauty but limited power. His recording of excerpts from *Madama Butterfly* with Albanese is justly admired.

BIBLIOGRAPHY

"The New Tamino: James Melton," *Opera News*, vii/8 (1942), 10

RICHARD LESUEUR

Melville, Herman (*b* New York, 1 Aug 1819; *d* New York, 28 Sept 1891). Novelist, short-story writer, and poet. As a seaman he was steeped in sea ballads, songs, and shanties, and his novels, particularly *Mardi*, include many songs which he either wrote himself, borrowed directly, or adapted. Among the songs set to music are, from *Mardi*, "Departed the Pride, and the Glory of Mardi" and "Her Bower is not of the Vine" by Robert Helps; and from *Moby Dick* Ernst Bacon's *The Sermon (Jonah's Song)* and Leonard Kastle's *Three Whale Songs from Moby Dick*.

Melville's often highly cadenced prose is well suited for musical treatment; most settings have been drawn from *Moby Dick*, among them Marshall Bialosky's "There is a Wisdom that is Woe," Jeffrey Hall's *Two Settings from Ahab*, and John McCabe's *Aspects of Whiteness*. Roger Reynolds's *Blind Men* is based on a collection of fragments from *Journal up the Straits*. One Melville novel in particular, *Typee*, has been of interest to ethnomusicologists for its detailed descriptions of Polynesian instruments and music.

Although best known for his fiction, Melville produced a considerable amount of poetry throughout his life. Most of the poems set to music have themes of war, such as *Shiloh: a Requiem*, *The Portent*, *Under the Ground*, and *The Night-march*. David Diamond and William Flanagan have set several each, the latter in his cycle *Time's Long Ago!*. The few operatic adaptations are mostly derived from *Billy Budd*, notably that by Benjamin Britten; others have been made from the novels *Bartleby the Scrivener* and *Moby Dick*, and the short stories *The Bell-Tower* and *Benito Cereno*. Almost all the Melville musical settings were written after 1940. One of the most recent is George Rochberg's opera *The Confidence Man*.

BIBLIOGRAPHY

C. McGlinchee: "American Literature in American Music," *MQ*, xxxi (1945), 101

H. R. Stevens: "Melville's Music," *Musicology*, ii (1949), 405

D. Battenfeld: "The Source for the Hymn in *Moby Dick*," *American Literature*, xxvii (1955), 393

J. LaRue: "Melville and Musicology," *EM*, iv (1960), 64

A. D. Cannon: "Melville's Use of Sea Ballads and Songs," *Western Folklore*, xxiii (1964), 1

W. Aschaffenburg: "Random Notes on 'Bartleby'," *Opera Journal*, ii (1969), 5

H. E. Johnson: "Musical Interests of Certain American Literary and Political Figures," *JRME*, xix (1971), 272

R. J. Schwendinger: "The Language of the Sea: Relationships Between the Language of Herman Melville and Sea Shanties of the 19th Century," *Southern Folklore Quarterly*, xxxvii (1973), 53

J. Fougerousse: *Billy Budd from Novel to Opera: a Comparative Study of Herman Melville's 'Billy Budd, Sailor' and Benjamin Britten's Opera, 'Billy Budd'* (diss., U. of Innsbruck, 1975)

L. M. Freibert: "A Checklist of Musical Compositions Inspired by Herman Melville's Works," *Extracts*, xxiii (1975), 3

M. J. Clark: "Blending Cadences: Rhythm and Structure in *Moby Dick*," *Studies in the Novel*, viii (1976), 158

M. A. Hovland: *Musical Settings of American Poetry: a Bibliography* (in preparation) [incl. list of settings]

MICHAEL HOVLAND

Melvin, Harold, and the Blue Notes. Harold Melvin (*b* 24 May 1941) formed the Blue Notes, a doo-wop (later soul) group, in Philadelphia in 1956 with John Atkins, Lawrence Brown, and Bernard Wilson; Lloyd Parks later joined the group. After establishing itself locally the quartet began to take lucrative supper-club engagements in the resorts of Nevada and Florida. It made its first recordings in 1956 but had little success until 1970 when Teddy Pendergrass (*b* 19 May 1950) replaced John Atkins as lead singer. Pendergrass, formerly a drummer, had a baritone voice, which he exploited in a deeply emotional soul-music style, enhanced by a seductive stage presence that attracted large audiences. The songwriting and producing team Gamble and Huff signed Harold Melvin and the Blue Notes to Philadelphia International Records, and they recorded a series of hit songs, beginning with two that became gold records – *If you don't know me by now* (no.3, 1972), after which Parks was replaced by Jerry Cummings, and *The love I lost* (no.7, 1973). Melvin was the group's nominal leader on its recordings, but Pendergrass was the lead singer and the most prominent member of the group; Pendergrass's dissatisfaction with this arrangement led to his leaving the Blue Notes in 1976. He pursued a successful career as a soloist (making hit recordings, including *Close the door*, 1978, and *Two hearts* with Stephanie Mills, 1981) but this was interrupted when he suffered permanent injury in an automobile accident in 1982; he resumed recording in 1984 with the album *Love Language*. Although the Blue Notes continued to perform and record, the popularity of the group quickly faded after Pendergrass's departure; Melvin made a solo album, *The Trip is Over* (ABC 1093), in 1978.

RECORDINGS

(*selective list; recorded for Philadelphia International unless otherwise stated*)

I Miss You (31468, 1972), incl. If you don't know me by now; *Black and Blue* (32407, 1973), incl. The love I lost; *To be True* (33148, 1975), incl. Bad Luck; *Wake up Everybody* (33808, 1975); *Collector's Item* (34232, 1976); *Now is the Time* (ABC 1041, 1977); *The Blue Album* (Source 3197, 1980); *All Things Happen in Time* (MCA 5261, 1981)

GARY THEROUX

Memphis. City in Tennessee (pop. 646,356, ranked 14th largest in the USA; metropolitan area 913,472). In the southwest corner of the state, on the Mississippi River, it was founded in 1820 and incorporated in 1826. It has been influential as a center of popular music in the 20th century.

1. Art music. 2. Folk and popular music.

1. ART MUSIC. Because Memphis was for some time a rough frontier town, art music was slow to play an important role in the cultural life of the city. Once steamboat travel to St. Louis and New Orleans had been established in the 1850s, however, and rail connections to the West had been completed, Memphis began to acquire both wealth and culture, with cotton and timber making fortunes for many. In 1851 Jenny Lind appeared in a well-attended concert, which was enthusiastically received, and from 1857 traveling opera companies played at the newly opened New Memphis Theatre (capacity 1000). Nevertheless, only a few concerts were in the cultivated tradition, and most evening entertainment consisted of vaudeville and minstrel shows.

Although Memphis was occupied by Union forces in June 1862 after a decisive river battle, the city suffered little during the Civil War. The Greenlaw Opera House (capacity 1600), built in 1866 at a cost of $220,000, was the site of operatic performances and concerts by such groups as the Mozart Musical Society and the Theodore Thomas Orchestra; it was destroyed by fire in 1884. In spite of plagues in 1873 and 1878 that reduced the population to 33,000 through death and flight, Memphis had 102,000 inhabitants at the turn of the century and was the second largest city in the South after New Orleans. Marching and concert bands were popular. The Memphis-born musician William Saxby was typical of local bandleaders who performed cultivated music (never ragtime) in open-air concerts.

The Beethoven Club, a women's sponsoring organization founded in 1888, has remained active and has presented such leading artists as Ernestine Schumann-Heink and Josef Lhévinne as well as the New York SO. It was also responsible for a local symphony orchestra founded in 1909 and the first of several ensembles known as the Memphis SO; it had 30 members and was disbanded in the 1920s. The second Memphis SO was formed by the clarinetist and composer Burnet C. Tuthill, who served as its conductor from 1947 to 1958. In 1952 Vincent de Frank founded the Memphis Sinfonietta, later renamed the Memphis SO, which he conducted until 1984, when Alan Balter succeeded him as music director. In 1958 the orchestra moved to Ellis Auditorium, which had been extensively remodeled from the original edifice built in the early 1900s; it has two halls, seating 2400 and 3600. In 1966 the orchestra began sponsoring an excellent youth ensemble of 70 players.

Opera has been important in Memphis since the 1950s, when the Metropolitan Opera began to include the city on the itinerary of its annual tours; the Memphis Opera Theatre was formed in 1956 and gives two operas each season. The Memphis Open Air Theatre presents lavish productions of musicals and operettas in Overton Park.

Higher education in music is offered at Memphis State University (which began in 1912 as West Tennessee State Normal School and evolved into Memphis State University in 1957) and at Southwestern University (which moved to Memphis in 1925). Memphis State offers undergraduate degrees, an MA, MM, and DMA in various subjects, and a PhD in both musicology and ethnomusicology; it also has a strong program in regional music, an orchestra, opera company, and string quartet in residence. The Memphis College of Music was incorporated into Southwestern University in 1943, largely through the efforts of Tuthill, who was director of the college at the time.

2. FOLK AND POPULAR MUSIC. As the only large city in the area, Memphis attracted both black and white musicians from the northern Mississippi Delta region and provided a context in which rural styles could confront and sometimes evolve into urban ones. Blacks have always made up 30–50% of the city's population and, despite racial restrictions, have had considerable influence and independence in its musical history.

In the 19th century thousands of people, both black and white, participated in outdoor revival camp meetings, where hymn singing was an integral part of the proceedings. Immigrant communities in the 1840s and 1850s helped to popularize such European dances as the polka; the Irish, who in 1860 temporarily outnumbered the black population, introduced fiddle music and jigs to the city and enthusiastically supported the theatrical shows presented on the steamboats.

Against a background of race riots between the Blacks and the Irish, the black population increased dramatically, reaching 15,000 by 1865; many had taken refuge in the Union-occupied city during the war. Thomas Bethune (Blind Tom), a famous black pianist who was reputed to be able to imitate any sound vocally and to reproduce difficult piano pieces after one hearing, was especially popular in the 1870s. Mardi Gras parades were held from 1872 to 1878, but were abandoned with the yellow fever epidemic; they were revived in the 20th century as the Cotton Club Carnival.

By the 1890s Memphis's famous Beale Street, in the black section of the city, was lined with saloons patronized not only by Blacks but, on special "Whites-only" occasions, by Whites as well. Blacks from the surrounding rural areas came to the city to play on Beale Street and at white gambling houses, medicine shows, parties, and occasionally Sunday suppers. It was on Beale Street around 1909 that the black bandleader W. C. Handy was inspired to write and perform his sophisticated urban blues songs exemplified by *St. Louis Blues* and *Beale Street Blues* (see illustration). A blues-influenced composition entitled *Mr. Crump* not only helped E. H. "Boss" Crump to a long and controversial political career but gave Handy his start: the song was published as *Memphis Blues* and became enormously popular.

Sheet-music cover of "Beale Street Blues" by W. C. Handy, published by Handy Brothers Music Co. in New York in 1917

After World War I, black musicians often formed jug bands, which ranged from the rural style of Frank Stokes to the urban, medicine-show style of Jim Jackson. The groups were recorded frequently in the late 1920s (*see* BLUES, esp. §3). After World War II the area around Memphis (Helena, Arkansas, and the northern Delta) was crowded with blues musicians developing a new urban style. They performed and also worked as disc jockeys on the Memphis radio station WDIA, which was the first station in the USA to adopt an all-black format (in 1949), and recorded at the studio of Sam Phillips from 1950 to 1954. Phillips was a white man who loved black music. He worked with musicians such as Bobby "Blue" Bland, Junior Parker, and Howlin' Wolf, helping them to develop their styles before they moved on to Chicago and elsewhere, and sent some of their recordings to Chess Records in Chicago; he released others on his own label, Sun Records.

The gradual exodus of these musicians from Memphis prompted Phillips to look for others, including Whites. In 1954 he found Elvis Presley, who had spent his teenage years in Memphis and had graduated from high school there in 1953. Presley had ambition, good looks, and a love of black music, while Phillips had experience and the intuition to recognize the value in the amalgam of southern musical traditions that Presley created. Although Presley left Memphis in 1956 to sign a contract with RCA, his success inspired Jerry Lee Lewis and others to record with Sun Records, creating with Phillips the style known as "rockabilly."

In the 1960s two other black styles became popular in Memphis. Led by such performers as Rufus Thomas and his daughter Carla and the white musicians Donald "Duck" Dunn and Steve Cropper (an arranger and guitarist), Memphis musicians drew on a blend of urban and rural musical traditions and created many hits in soul music; these included Wilson Pickett's *In the Midnight Hour* and Sam and Dave's *Soul Man*. The celebrated soul singer Aretha Franklin worked with Memphis musicians and often recorded in nearby Muscle Shoals, Alabama. In the late 1960s Isaac Hayes, who was born near Memphis, was one of the pioneers of a new style that led to funk, examples of which include Arthur Conley's *Funky Street* and Sam and Dave's *I thank you*, both recorded in 1968. Once again key musicians left Memphis for Los Angeles, and the city's recording industry declined. Memphis has continued, however, to nurture musicians, among them the singer Al Green and the black band Con-Funk-Shun. The Memphis Blues Festival was organized in 1966 to help fund a blues archive in the city; renamed Memphis in May in 1977, the festival, held annually, now covers blues, country-and-western, rock, and other kinds of popular music program.

BIBLIOGRAPHY

J. Young, ed.: *Standard History of Memphis* (Knoxville, 1912)
G. Lee: *Beale Street: Where the Blues Began* (New York, 1934/*R*1969)
K. Myracle: *Music in Memphis, 1880–1900* (thesis, Memphis State U., 1975)
J. Miller, ed.: "The Sound of Memphis," *The Rolling Stone Illustrated History of Rock & Roll* (New York, 1976, rev. 2/1980)
K. Plunkett: *A Pictorial History of Memphis* (Norfolk, VA, 1976)
R. Palmer: *A Tale of Two Cities: Memphis Rock and New Orleans Roll*, ISAMm, xii (Brooklyn, NY, 1979)
M. McKee and F. Chisenhall: *Beale Black and Blue* (Baton Rouge, LA, 1981)
C. Ornelas-Struve and F. Coulter: *Memphis: 1800–1900* (Memphis, 1982)

STEPHEN E. YOUNG

Memphis Minnie [Douglas, Minnie; Douglas, Lizzie] (*b* Algiers, LA, 3 June 1896; *d* Memphis, TN, 6 Aug 1973). Blues singer and guitarist. At the age of eight she went to Memphis, where, as Kid Douglas, she earned her living as a street musician. In 1928 she moved to Chicago, and with her first husband, the Mississippi blues guitarist and mandolin player Joe McCoy, began a highly popular series of blues recordings. After their divorce in 1935 she recorded with Black Bob (piano) and her second husband Casey Bill Weldon (guitar), with whom she made the rousing *Joe Louis Strut* (1935, Voc. 3046). Her third husband, Ernest "Lil Son" Lawler, also a blues guitarist, supported her on *Me and my Chauffeur Blues* (1941, OK 06288). For nearly 30 years her "Blue Monday" parties in Chicago were celebrated among blues singers. In 1957 she returned to Memphis and five years later had a stroke which ended her singing career. Memphis Minnie enjoyed unequaled stature among women country-blues singers. Her performances were greatly admired by male blues artists, and she was the only significant female blues instrumentalist, playing the guitar with the forceful, swinging rhythm characteristic of many Memphis-based musicians. Her voice was strong, with breadth in the middle range, and her guitar playing well phrased, as for example on her best-selling *Bumble Bee* (1930, Voc. 1476). Many of her blues were topical or autobiographical, as in *Memphis Minnie-Jitis Blues* (1930, Voc. 1588), referring to her illness. Among her finest recordings were the guitar duets with McCoy, including the exceptional *Let's Go to Town* (1931, Voc. 1660).

BIBLIOGRAPHY

S. Harris: "Douglas, Lizzie," *Blues Who's Who* (New Rochelle, NY, 1979)

PAUL OLIVER

Menasce, Jacques de (*b* Bad Ischl, Austria, 19 Aug 1905; *d* Gstaad, Switzerland, 28 Jan 1960). Composer and pianist. He graduated from the Schotten-Gymnasium in Vienna in 1924. His first piano teacher was Emil Friedberger, and at the age of 14 he began work with Emil von Sauer. After some years of travel he went to the Vienna Music Academy to study piano and composition; later he was a composition pupil of Pisk and Berg. From 1932 he appeared widely in Europe and the USA as a pianist, notably in performances of his own and other modern chamber music. His activities were centered in New York from the 1940s; he became an American citizen, and he took part in the work of the League of Composers and other organizations promoting new music. His music is not easy to classify: structurally it bears some relation to impressionism, while its somberness and its vivid, crisp chromaticism recall late Bartók.

WORKS
(selective list)

Ballets: The Fate of my People, dancer, pf, 1945; Status quo, 1947
Orch: 2 pf concs., 1935, 1939; Divertimento on a Children's Song, pf, str, 1940
Vocal: Le chemin d'écume, song cycle, S, orch, 1940; 3 Romantic Songs, 1943; 2 Poems (H. Wolfe), 1v, pf, 1944; choruses
Inst: Vn Sonata, 1940; Hebrew Melodies, vn, pf; Va Sonata, 1955
Pf: Variations, 1933; Visionen, 1934; 3 sonatinas, 1934, 1942, 1945; Toccata, 1935; 2 sonatas, 1936, 1947; Improvisations on a Chorale Theme, 1937; 5 Fingerprints, 1943; Perpetuum mobile, 1944; Pour une princesse, 1947; Romantic Suite, 1950

PEGGY GLANVILLE-HICKS/R

MENC. *See* MUSIC EDUCATORS NATIONAL CONFERENCE.

Mendel, Arthur (*b* Boston, MA, 6 June 1905; *d* Newark, NJ, 14 Oct 1979). Musicologist. From Harvard University (BA 1925) he went to Paris, where he studied with Nadia Boulanger (1925–7). He was music critic of *The Nation* (1930–33), literary editor for G. Schirmer (1930–38), editor of the American Musicological Society's journal (1940–43), and editor for Associated Music Publishers (1941–7); he was also an active translator. From 1936 to 1953 he conducted the Cantata Singers, one of the first groups in the USA to give authentic performances of Baroque music. He taught at the Dalcroze School of Music and the Diller-Quaile School in New York (1938–50), serving as president of the former (1947–50).

In the late 1940s Mendel gained recognition as a musicologist. He was appointed professor of music at Princeton Unversity (1952), where he was department chairman (1952–67), and held the Henry Putnam University Professorship from 1969 until his retirement in 1973. He was a member of the editorial boards of the Neue Bach-Ausgabe and the new Josquin edition. Mendel published studies on the history of musical pitch and the rhythmic structure of Renaissance and Baroque music. His editions and studies of Bach's life and works, most notably the documentary biography *The Bach Reader* (1945, with Hans T. David), and his practical and critical editions of the *St. John Passion* (1951, 1974), brought him recognition as the foremost American Bach scholar of his generation. In his later years he investigated the music of

Josquin and possible applications of computer technology to musicological problems. A Festschrift in his honor, *Studies in Renaissance and Baroque Music*, was published in 1974 (edited by Robert L. Marshall).

ROBERT L. MARSHALL/R

Mendelssohn Quintette Club. Chamber ensemble organized in Boston in 1849. It grew out of informal chamber music sessions at the home of the Boston businessman John Bigelow, and the first concert was given in Boston on 14 December 1849 by August Fries (first violin), Francis Riha (second violin), Edward Lehmann (viola, flute), Thomas Ryan (viola, clarinet), and Wulf Fries (cello). Ryan managed the Club and remained active with it throughout its existence, though the other personnel changed often – over 30 musicians (many of them orchestral players and teachers in Boston) were associated with it at one time or another; for a period (1876–80) a double bass was added to the ensemble, but for the most part the instrumentation remained unchanged. The group gave subscription concerts in the Boston and Providence areas each season, and made its first tour outside New England – to Baltimore, Philadelphia, and Washington – in 1859. Following a three-week trial tour of the Midwest in 1861–2, it made a long tour in 1862–3, and during the following decade traveled throughout the East, Midwest, and South. The members served as resident musicians at the National College of Music, Boston, in 1872–3. In 1881 they traveled to California, then to Australia, New Zealand, and Honolulu, and on their return toured the USA and Canada. The touring party usually included vocal and instrumental soloists besides the regular members. The Club disbanded in 1895. Contemporary reviewers noted the group's fine professional playing and praised the quality of its programs, which included the Classical repertory, contemporary American and European works, and adaptations of popular operatic and traditional melodies.

BIBLIOGRAPHY

T. Ryan: *Recollections of an Old Musician* (New York, 1899/*R*1979)

S. Franko: *Chords and Dischords* (New York, 1938)

J. Mattfeld: "Doubling on the Clarinet and Viola: the Story of Thomas Ryan and the Mendelssohn Quintette Club," *Symphony*, vi (Oct 1952), 8

R. Phelps: "The Mendelssohn Quintet Club: a Milestone in American Music Education," *JRME*, viii (1960), 39

JEFFREY R. REHBACH

Mendoza, Lydia (*b* Houston, TX, 31 May 1916). Singer, songwriter, and guitarist. She studied guitar at an early age and began performing at the age of ten. In 1927 and 1928 she performed throughout the lower Rio Grande valley with her family's ensemble, El Cuarteto Carta Blanca; in 1928 she recorded ten sides for Okeh Records. Her family moved to Detroit in 1928, returned to Texas in 1930, and performed at the Plaza del Zacate in San Antonio until 1934. At this time she began performing as a soloist and became well known locally through appearances on radio; during the next six years she made nearly 200 recordings for Bluebird Records and toured the American Southwest extensively. Her career was interrupted in 1940, but she resumed touring and recording in 1947. Her compositions and recordings are mainly in the ranchera, corrido, tango, and habanera forms. In 1982 she received a National Heritage Fellowship from the NEA. Examples of her work are included in the series of recordings *Una historia de la música de la frontera: Texas-Mexican Border Music*, subseries 15–17, issued by Folklyric Records.

BIBLIOGRAPHY

L. Mendoza: "The Lark of the Border," *Ethnic Recordings in America: a Neglected Heritage*, ed. J. Griffith (Washington, DC, 1982), 119

DANIEL SHEEHY

Mennin [Mennini], **Peter** (*b* Erie, PA, 17 May 1923; *d* New York, 17 June 1983). Composer and educator, brother of Louis Mennini. He studied briefly at Oberlin College Conservatory under Normand Lockwood before joining the US armed forces (1942). After military service he attended the Eastman School, where he studied with Hanson and Rogers (BM and MM 1945, PhD 1947). On graduating he was appointed to the composition faculty of the Juilliard School. He remained there until 1958, when he was named director of the Peabody Conservatory. In 1962 he became president of the Juilliard School, a position he held until his death. Throughout his time at the Juilliard School Mennin emphasized the value of performance skills and was also responsible for the establishment of its Theater Center (1968), American Opera Center (1970), and Contemporary Music Festival. A major accomplishment was his introduction in 1972 of a permanent program for conductors.

Peter Mennin, 1974

Although Mennin is often grouped with the traditional school of American symphonists, his music is more international than that of many of his colleagues. While its aggressive energy and syncopated rhythmic drive suggest American roots, its abstract, linear emphasis and lofty tone indicate an affinity with such northern European symphonists as Edmund Rubbra, Vagn Holmboe, and even Allan Pettersson. From the beginning Mennin concentrated almost exclusively on serious works in large forms. He exhibited a natural gift for flowing counterpoint as early as the 1940s, and acknowledged the influence of Renaissance polyphony on his development as a composer. The grandeur and vigor, as well as the robust bass lines found in early compositions such as the Symphonies nos.3, 4, and 5 suggest the influence of Vaughan Williams's Fourth Symphony. Mennin's succeeding works revealed a consistent evolution towards greater astringency and compression, culminating in the Symphony no.8 (1973) which almost abandons a linear framework altogether in its exploration of terse coloristic gestures. Symphony no.9 (1981), however, returns to a more characteristic language. Except for the *Cantata de virtute* (1969), his one major excursion into programmatic music, his means of expression was purely abstract. Perhaps the most distinctive quality of his music is its nervous energy, abating only for periods of grave reflection. Some have charged that this singleminded severity has resulted in too narrow an expressive palette, while others feel that the eloquence and power of each work compensate for any lack of breadth.

Mennin's music is performed widely, and much has been recorded. He received commissions from America's leading organizations including the Coolidge Foundation in the Library of Congress and the Cleveland Orchestra, National SO, and New York PO. Among his many awards were the Bearns Prize and the first Gershwin Memorial Award, both given in 1945 for his Symphony no.2, an award from the National Institute of Arts and Letters (1946), two Guggenheim Fellowships (1949, 1957), and a Naumburg Award (1952). He served on the boards of many organizatons, including the Composers Forum, the Koussevitzky Foundation, ASCAP, the National Institute of Arts and Letters (to which he was elected in 1965), and the State Department Advisory Committee on the Arts.

WORKS

ORCHESTRAL

Symphony no.1, 1941, Rochester, 1941, withdrawn
Symphony no.2, 1944, Rochester, 27 March 1945
Symphony no.3, 1946, New York, 27 Feb 1947
Symphony no.4 "The Cycle" (Mennin), SATB, orch, 1948, New York, 18 March 1949
Symphony no.5, 1950, Dallas, 2 April 1950
Symphony no.6, 1953, Louisville, 18 Nov 1953
Symphony no.7 "Variation-Symphony," 1963, Cleveland, 23 Jan 1964
Symphony no.8, 1973, New York, 21 Nov 1974
Symphony no.9, 1981, Washington, DC, 10 March 1981
Fl Concertino, str, perc, 1944; Folk Ov., 1945; Sinfonia, chamber orch, 1946; Fantasia, str, 1947; Canzona, band, 1951; Concertato "Moby Dick," 1952; Vc Conc., 1956; Pf Conc., 1958; Canto, 1963; Sinfonia, 1971, withdrawn; Fl Conc., 1983

VOCAL

4 Songs (Dickinson), S, pf, 1941, withdrawn; Alleluia, SATB, 1941; 4 Chinese Poems (Kiang Kang-Ku, trans. W. Bynner): A Song of the Palace, Crossing the Han River, In the Quiet Night, The Gold Threaded Robe, SATB, 1948; 2 Choruses: Bought Hair (Martial), Tumbling Locks (Cummings), SSA, pf, 1949
The Christmas Story, S, T, SATB, brass qt, timp, str, 1949; Cantata de virtute: Pied Piper of Hamelin (Browning, liturgical), nar, T, B, SSAATTBB, children's chorus, orch, 1969; Voices (Thoreau, Melville, Whitman, Dickinson), 1v, pf, harp, hpd, perc, 1975; Reflections of Emily (Dickinson), boys' chorus, harp, pf, perc, 1978

INSTRUMENTAL

Org Sonata, 1941, withdrawn; Str Qt no.1, 1941, withdrawn; 5 Pieces, pf, 1949; Str Qt no.2, 1951; Sonata concertante, vn, pf, 1959; Pf Sonata, 1963

Principal publishers: C. Fischer, G. Schirmer

BIBLIOGRAPHY

EwenD
W. Hendl: "Music of Peter Mennin," *Juilliard Review*, i/2 (1954), 18
"Mennin, Peter," *CBY 1964*
M. Mayer: "Peter Mennin of Juilliard," *New York Times* (28 Sept 1969), 17 [abridged in *ASCAP Today*, iii/2 (1969), 10]
P. Snook: "Mennin's Symphony No.6," *Fanfare*, i/6 (1978), 125
W. Simmons: "Mennin: Symphony No.7; Concerto for Piano and Orchestra," *Fanfare*, iii/1 (1979), 223
D. Owens: "Composer Peter Mennin: an Interview," *Christian Science Monitor* (29, 30 July 1981)
Obituary, *New York Times* (18 June 1983)

WALTER G. SIMMONS

Mennini, Louis (Alfred) (*b* Erie, PA, 18 Nov 1920). Composer and educator, brother of Peter Mennin. He began piano lessons as a child and studied music at the Oberlin College Conservatory (1939–42). After serving in the US Army Air Force (1942–5) he studied composition at the Eastman School with Rogers and Hanson (BM 1947, MM 1948). He taught for a year at the University of Texas, Austin, before returning to Eastman as professor of composition and orchestration (1949–65); he received the doctorate in composition in 1961. He served as dean of the School of Music at the North Carolina School of the Arts (1965–71), and, from 1973 to his retirement in 1983, was chairman of the music department of Mercyhurst College, Erie. His many awards and commissions include a grant from the National Institute of Arts and Letters (1949), two commissions from the Koussevitzky Foundation (one for *The Rope*), and an NEA grant (1979) to compose another opera.

Mennini's first notable compositions, Andante (1947) and Allegro energico and Arioso (both 1948), written while he was still a student, demonstrate what were to become the most distinctive elements of his mature style: a somewhat conservative harmonic idiom, an expert command of contrapuntal texture, strong rhythmic drive, and a lyrical, flowing melodic line. Later large-scale works, particularly the two symphonies *Da Chiesa* (1960) and *Da Festa* (1963), show his great skill as an orchestrator.

WORKS

Operas: The Well (L. Mennini), Rochester, NY, 1951; The Rope (chamber opera, 1, Mennini, after E. O'Neill), Lenox, MA, 1955
Orch: Overtura breve, 1949; Cantilena, 1950; Canzona, chamber orch, 1950; Credo, 1955; Sym. no.1 "Da Chiesa," 1960; Sym. no.2 "Da Festa," 1963; Tenebrae, 1963; Conc. grosso, 1975
Str: Andante, 1947; Allegro energico, 1948; Arioso, 1948
Chamber: Vn Sonata, 1947; Vc Sonatina, 1952; Str Qt, 1961; numerous pf works

Principal publisher: Boosey & Hawkes

BIBLIOGRAPHY

EwenD
J. S. Harrison: "What it Takes to Write Opera," *New York Herald-Tribune* (7 Aug 1955), IV, 5
H. Taubman: "Music: Premiere of 'Rope' at Lenox," *New York Times* (9 Aug 1955), 29

PAUL C. ECHOLS

Mennonite music. *See* AMISH AND MENNONITE MUSIC.

Menotti, Gian Carlo (*b* Cadegliano, Italy, 7 July 1911). Composer of Italian birth.

1. Up to 1950. 2. 1951–72. 3. From 1973. 4. Style.

1. UP TO 1950. The sixth of ten children, he was born in a country town on Lake Lugano. His father was a prosperous businessman and his mother a talented amateur musician. He had already written two operas when he entered the Milan Conservatory at the age of 13. In 1928 he began studies with Scalero at the Curtis Institute, where a close friendship with his fellow student Samuel Barber began. The two spent several summers in Europe attending opera performances in Vienna and in Italy. It was in Vienna, having received his diploma with honors from

Gian Carlo Menotti (right) with Samuel Barber, c1949

the Curtis Institute in 1933, that Menotti began the libretto for a one-act *opera buffa*, *Amelia al ballo*. He completed the orchestration on his return to the USA in 1935; the opera received its première in an English translation by George Mead as *Amelia Goes to the Ball*. A few days later it was performed in New York with such success that the Metropolitan Opera accepted it for the following season.

The success of *Amelia* brought Menotti a commission from NBC for a radio opera. Using the *opera buffa* tradition of set numbers, Menotti wrote his first libretto in English, *The Old Maid and the Thief*. His next opera, *The Island God*, was poorly received. Menotti remained in the USA but retained his Italian citizenship. During World War II he wrote the Piano Concerto in F and a dramatic ballet, *Sebastian*, set in 17th-century Venice.

A commission by the Alice M. Ditson Fund led to the very successful opera *The Medium*, a tragedy in two acts for five singers, a dance-mime role, and a chamber orchestra of 14 players. The melodramatic story is the "tragedy of a person caught between two worlds, the world of reality which she cannot comprehend, and the supernatural world in which she cannot believe." The work is theatrically effective and the music, often quite dissonant, conveys an eerie, morbid atmosphere. Typical of the Italian operatic tradition, *The Medium* has memorable melodies such as the folklike "O, black swan." The opera had a run of 211 performances during 1947–8 at the Ethel Barrymore Theatre on Broadway. As a curtain-raiser for these performances of *The Medium* (and a striking contrast), Menotti wrote a light one-act comedy, *The Telephone*, subtitled *L'amour à trois*. The State Department organized a European tour of these works in 1955. In 1951 Menotti directed a successful film version of *The Medium*.

Menotti's versatile dramatic skills, as director, librettist, and composer, brought him a contract from Metro-Goldwyn-Mayer to write film scripts. Although his scripts were never filmed, one contained the seeds of his first full-length opera, *The Consul*, considered by many to be his greatest work. It uses the verismo of Puccini's day to treat a contemporary situation: the impossibility of obtaining a visa to leave a police state. Music and stage techniques combine to communicate strongly and directly. The New York première at the Ethel Barrymore Theatre on 15 March 1950 was a great success and performances continued there for about eight months. The work received the Pulitzer Prize and the Drama Critics' Circle Award. It has been translated into 12 languages and has been performed in over 20 countries. With *The Consul* and his next two operas, Menotti seemed at the height of his powers and of public acclaim.

2. 1951–72. *Amahl and the Night Visitors*, commissioned by NBC, was the first opera written expressly for television. In writing it, Menotti was influenced by *The Adoration of the Magi* of Hieronymus Bosch. The work was first televised on Christmas eve 1951 and has been broadcast annually. The roles, particularly the main part for boy soprano, are skillfully conceived so that they can be performed by amateurs. The charm and clear diatonicism of the work have helped to make it one of the most frequently performed operas of the 20th century. Menotti's next opera, *The Saint of Bleecker Street*, is a full-length piece in the broad and serious style of *The Consul*. It is an effective drama set in contemporary New York and concerned with the conflict of the physical and spiritual worlds. Again a contemporary plot is set in a Puccinian manner. The opera received the Drama Critics' Circle Award for the best play, the New York Music Critics' Circle Award for the best opera, and the Pulitzer Prize in music for 1955.

Choral music was an important element in *Amahl* and *The Saint of Bleecker Street*; it is basic to the "madrigal fable" *The Unicorn, the Gorgon and the Manticore*. Commissioned by the Elizabeth Sprague Coolidge Foundation, it is one of Menotti's most charming works. The model was the late Renaissance madrigal comedy (such as Vecchi's *L'amfiparnaso*), and the work consists of an introduction, 12 madrigals (some *a cappella*), and six instrumental interludes. At about the same time Menotti wrote the text for Barber's opera *Vanessa*.

Menotti's next opera, *Maria Golovin*, was again commissioned by NBC. It was performed in New York in November of 1958, but with little success, and later broadcast by NBC. From 1958 much of Menotti's time was taken up by the Spoleto Festival of Two Worlds, which he founded and directed. Thomas Schippers became music director of this major summer festival in 1967, but Menotti continued as president of the organization. However, new works began to appear again in 1963: *Labyrinth*, written for NBC television, exploits the possibilities of special camera techniques. A cantata *The Death of the Bishop of Brindisi* (concerning the Children's Crusade of 1212) was commissioned by the Cincinnati May Festival; and *Le dernier sauvage* was written for the Paris Opéra. The première of the latter work in fact occurred at the Opéra-Comique, and it was later given a lavish production at the Metropolitan Opera in New York.

A CBS commission for the 1964 Bath Festival was fulfilled by a church opera in one act, *Martin's Lie*, which was broadcast in the USA in the following year. Other works of this period include *Canti della lontananza*, a cycle of seven songs on Menotti's own texts written for Elisabeth Schwarzkopf; *Help, Help, the Globolinks!*, a 70-minute "opera in one act for children and those who like children" commissioned by the Hamburg Staatsoper;

and an opera commissioned by the New York City Opera, *The Most Important Man*. A drama without music, *The Leper*, was first performed in Tallahassee, Florida, on 22 April 1970.

3. FROM 1973. In 1973 Menotti and Barber sold their home, called Capricorn (Mt. Kisco, New York), where they had lived since 1943. Menotti, with his adopted son Chip, moved to Scotland and bought a spacious country home of 1789 called Yester House. In 1977 he expanded his Spoleto Festival to Charleston, South Carolina (the other of its Two Worlds). In spite of the organizational, managerial, and operational claims on his time, which include directing plays as well as operas, he still maintains an active creative career. As an elaborate farewell vehicle for Beverly Sills he wrote the opera *La loca* which tells the story of the daughter of Isabella and Ferdinand of Spain. He has also written nonoperatic works, such as the Symphony no. 1 "The Halcyon" which he has said represents "the most sincere and optimistic days of my youth, when the horizon [was] unclouded." For soloists, chorus, and orchestra he wrote *Missa O pulchritudo*, a Mass to beauty which replaces the Credo with a setting of a poem by St. Augustine. His most recent operas have been directed toward children, both as subjects and as performers: *The Egg* (a companion piece to *Martin's Lie* for a Washington Cathedral performance, 1976), *The Trial of the Gypsy*, *Chip and his Dog*, *A Bride from Pluto*, and *The Boy who Grew too Fast*. In 1984 Menotti was awarded a Kennedy Center Honor for lifetime achievement in the arts.

4. STYLE. Menotti cares about his audience and about the human voice. He has written: "There is a certain indolence towards the use of the voice today, a tendency to treat the voice instrumentally, as if composers feared that its texture is too expressive, too *human*" (1964). Like Puccini he is sensitive to new musical techniques that will serve his dramatic purpose: a high, sustained dissonant chord in *The Consul* as Magda turns on the gas stove to commit suicide; the 12-tone music used to parody contemporary civilization (and indirectly the avant-garde composer) in Act 2 of *Le dernier sauvage*; or electronic tape music to represent the invaders from outer space in *Help, Help, the Globolinks!* Also like Puccini he gives first place to the human voice and the effective theatrical moment. Menotti's melodies are tonal, sometimes with a modal flavor, and often easily remembered. Sequence and repetition are common, but aria-like passages tend to be brief so as not to interrupt the dramatic flow. The continuous, recitative-like passages set the text with naturalness and clarity. His harmony is tonal, sometimes using parallel chords over a clear and simple tonal basis. Many of his more commanding musical gestures, such as the opening of *The Medium*, reflect his avowed fondness for Mussorgsky. His orchestration tends to be light and open and he writes particularly well for small instrumental ensembles. His rhythms, even when metrical irregularities are used, are natural and easily grasped by performer and listener.

Critical appraisal of Menotti's works has ranged from sincere appreciation (Sargeant) to bitter denunciation (Kerman). His techniques are traditional and conservative, and while some have faulted his style as sentimental or even dull, his best works can be powerful (*The Consul*) or charming (The Scarlattian Piano Concerto, or *Amahl and the Night Visitors*). The best summary of his achievement is by Hitchcock: "Menotti combined the theatrical sense of a popular playwright and a Pucciniesque musical vocabulary with an Italianate love of liquid language and a humane interest in characters as real human beings; the result was opera more accessible than anyone else's at the time."

WORKS

(all texts by Menotti unless otherwise stated)

OPERAS, BALLETS, CANTATAS

Amelia al ballo (opera buffa, 1), 1936; Philadelphia, 1 April 1937, cond. Reiner
The Old Maid and the Thief (radio opera, 1), 1939; NBC, 22 April 1939; stage, Philadelphia, 11 Feb 1941, cond. A. Erede
The Island God (opera, 1), 1942; New York, Metropolitan, 20 Feb 1942, cond. E. Panizza
Sebastian (ballet, 1), 1944; New York, 31 Oct 1944
The Medium (tragedy, 2), 1945; New York, 8 May 1946, cond. Luening
The Telephone (opera buffa, 1), 1946; New York, 18 Feb 1947, cond. L. Barzin
Errand into the Maze (ballet), 1947; New York, 2 Feb 1947
The Consul (musical drama, 3), 1949; Philadelphia, 1 March 1950, cond. L. Engel
Amahl and the Night Visitors (television opera, 1), 1951; NBC-TV, 24 Dec 1951; stage, Bloomington, 21 Feb 1952, cond. Schippers
The Saint of Bleecker Street (opera, 3), 1954; New York, 27 Dec 1954, cond. Schippers
The Unicorn, the Gorgon and the Manticore, or The Three Sundays of a Poet (madrigal ballet or madrigal fable), chorus, 10 dancers, 9 insts, 1956; Washington, DC, 21 Oct 1956, cond. P. Callaway
Maria Golovin (music drama, 3), 1958; Brussels, 20 Aug 1958, cond. H. Adler
Labyrinth (television opera, 1), 1963; NBC-TV, 3 March 1963
The Death of the Bishop of Brindisi (cantata), S, B, children's chorus, chorus, orch, 1963; Cincinnati, 18 May 1963, cond. M. Rudolf
Le dernier sauvage (opéra-bouffe, 3), 1963; Paris, Opéra-Comique, 21 Oct 1963, cond. S. Baudo
Martin's Lie (children's church opera, 1), 1964; Bristol, England, 3 June 1964, cond. L. Leonard
Help, Help, the Globolinks! (opera, 1), 1968; Hamburg, Staatsoper, 21 Dec 1968, cond. M. Kuntzsch
The Most Important Man (opera), 1971; New York, 12 March 1971, cond. C. Keene
Tamu-Tamu (opera, 2), 1973; Chicago, 5 Sept 1973, cond. Keene
The Egg (children's church opera), 1976; Washington, DC, 17 June 1976, cond. Callaway
The Hero (comic opera), 1976; Philadelphia, 1 June 1976
Landscapes and Remembrances (cantata), 1976; Milwaukee, 14 May 1976
The Trial of the Gypsy (children's opera), tr vv, pf, 1978; New York, 24 May 1978, cond. T. Shook
Chip and his Dog (children's opera), tr vv, pf, drum, 1979; Guelph, Canada, 5 May 1979
La loca (opera, 3), 1979; San Diego, 3 June 1979, cond. C. Simmons
A Bride from Pluto (children's opera), 1982; New York, 14 April 1982, cond. L. R. Muti
The Boy who Grew too Fast (children's opera), 1982; Wilmington, DE, 24 Sept 1982, cond. E. Swensson
Muero porque no muero (cantata, St. Teresa of Avila), S, chorus, orch, 1982; Washington, DC, 15 Oct 1982, M. Martin, cond. R Ricks

ORCHESTRAL

Piano Concerto, F, 1945; Boston, Nov 1945, R. Burgin, cond. R. Firkušný
Sebastian, suite from the ballet, 1945; New York, Aug 1945
Apocalypse, 1951; movts 1–2, Pittsburgh, 19 Oct 1951; perf. complete, Philadelphia, 18 Jan 1952, cond. V. de Sabata
Violin Concerto, a, 1952; Philadelphia, 5 Dec 1952, E. Zimbalist, cond. Ormandy
Triplo Concerto a tre, 9 soloists forming 3 trios (pf, harp, perc; ob, cl, bn; vn, va, vc), orch, 1970; New York, 6 Oct 1970, cond. Stokowski
Symphony no. 1 "The Halcyon," 1976; Saratoga, NY, 4 Aug 1976, cond. Ormandy
Doublebass Concerto, 1983; New York, 20 Oct 1983, J. VanDemark, cond. Mehta

MISCELLANEOUS

Variations on a Theme of Schumann, pf, 1931
Pastorale and Dance, pf, str orch, 1934
Six Compositions for Carillon, 1934
Four Pieces, str qt, 1936

Trio for a House-warming Party, pf, vc, fl, 1936
Poemetti per Maria Rosa, 12 pieces for children, pf, 1937
The Hero (R. Horan), 1v, pf, 1952
Ricercare and Toccata on a Theme from The Old Maid and the Thief, pf, 1953
Canti della lontananza, cycle of 7 songs, S, pf, 1967; New York, 18 March 1967, E. Schwarzkopf
Suite, 2 vc, pf, 1973; New York, 20 May 1973, G. Piatigorsky, L. Parnas, C. Wadsworth
Fantasia, vc, orch, 1976; Turin, Italy, RAI broadcast, 16 Jan 1976
Cantilena scherzo, harp, str qt, 1977; New York, 15 March 1977
Miracles, 1979; Fort Worth, TX, 22 April 1979
Missa O pulchritudo, S, A, T, B, chorus, orch; Spoleto, Italy, sum. 1979
Four Songs, T, pf, 1981; New York, 21 Oct 1981
Notturno, 1v, harp, str qnt, 1982
Moans, Groans, Cries and Sighs, motet, unacc. chorus

Principal publishers: G. Schirmer, Ricordi

WRITINGS

A Hand of Bridge [lib. for opera by Barber] (New York, 1960)
Introductions and Goodbyes [lib. for opera by Foss] (New York, 1961)
Vanessa [lib. for opera by Barber] (New York, 1964)
The Leper [play]; Tallahassee, FL, 22 April 1970

BIBLIOGRAPHY

EwenD
J. Kerman: *Opera as Drama* (New York, 1956)
W. Sargeant: "Orlando in Mount Kisco," *New Yorker*, xxxix (4 May 1963), 49–89
R. Tricoire: *Gian Carlo Menotti: l'homme et son oeuvre* (Paris, 1966)
D. Ewen: "Gian Carlo Menotti," *The World of Twentieth-century Music* (Englewood Cliffs, NJ, 1968), 481ff
H. W. Hitchcock: *Music in the United States: a Historical Introduction* (Englewood Cliffs, NJ, 1969, rev. 2/1974), 211f
L. Grieb: *The Operas of Gian Carlo Menotti, 1937–1972: a Selective Bibliography* (Metuchen, NJ, 1974)
J. Gruen: *Menotti: a Biography* (New York, 1978)
"Menotti, Gian Carlo," *CBY 1979*
J. Ardoin: "A Welcome Gift," *Opera News*, xlv/20 (1981), 9, 16
——: *The Stages of Menotti* (Garden City, NY, 1985)

BRUCE ARCHIBALD

Menudo. Puerto Rican pop-rock vocal group. Formed in 1977 by Edgardo Diaz, it originally comprised three of his cousins and the sons of a neighboring family. It sang slickly professional pop-rock music in Spanish. Menudo was a group with a gimmick: no member was allowed to remain in the group after the age of 15; the result has been a steady turnover in personnel but no loss of popularity in the Spanish market. The group's first album in English, *Reaching Out* (RCA ARL1-4993, 1984), failed, however, to generate similar enthusiasm among non-Latin teenagers.

JOHN ROCKWELL

Menuhin, Sir **Yehudi** (*b* New York, 22 April 1916). Violinist. He had his first lessons in San Francisco from Sigmund Anker a few months after his fourth birthday and continued his studies with Persinger, progressing so rapidly that he made his first public appearance with the San Francisco SO on 29 February 1924. His first professional appearances, in recitals in San Francisco (30 March 1925) and New York (17 January 1926), met with considerable success but were surpassed by his sensational début in Paris (6 February 1927). After several months of study there with George Enescu, he returned to New York and became a world celebrity overnight when he played the Beethoven Concerto under Fritz Busch. Tours throughout the USA and Europe followed (débuts in Berlin, 1928, and London, 10 November 1929), as did his first recordings, in 1928. Further periods of study with Enescu (whose musical personality has been a lasting influence on Menuhin) and Adolf Busch alternated with many

Yehudi Menuhin

enormously successful concert appearances. The dominant characteristics of Menuhin's playing during this period, apart from his remarkable technical ability, were the maturity and depth of his musical understanding, and his spontaneity and freshness. These qualities enabled the 12-year-old boy to play works of the stature of the Beethoven Concerto and Bach's Chaconne with absolute conviction, and Mozart's concertos with a completeness of identification that has seldom been equalled. One of the notable events of his youth was the performance and phonograph recording, in 1932, of Elgar's Violin Concerto conducted by the composer, then aged 75.

Menuhin has rarely been absent for any length of time from the international concert platform. During World War II he gave over 500 concerts for American and Allied troops in many theaters of war. He was the first artist to appear in the reopened Paris Opéra immediately after the German occupation, and the first Jewish artist to play with the Berlin PO under Furtwängler after the overthrow of the Nazi regime (an action for which he was much criticized, especially among Jewish communities, but which he defended with courage and conviction). On his reappearances under more normal conditions, it was noted that his playing, while it had maintained many of its old qualities and added a further nobility and depth, had at times lost something in spontaneity and technical reliability. Menuhin has indeed made no secret of the fact that he has gone through periods during which he has had to rethink the whole basis of his approach to violin technique.

In 1959 Menuhin settled in London. He has directed several European music festivals, and has given many concerts playing with and conducting his own chamber orchestra, founded in 1958, during tours throughout the world. He has also conducted many of the leading symphony orchestras in Europe and America, and encouraged and collaborated in the performance of Indian music in Western culture. In 1962 he started a boarding school for musically talented children at Stoke d'Abernon, Surrey.

Menuhin has achieved a remarkable position as a world citizen with diverse interests apart from music. As a violinist the purity of style and depth of interpretive power that he displays in his finest performances place them in the highest category. He has edited Bartók's Sonata for solo violin (1947), one of the many works written for him; Walton's Sonata for violin and piano (1950), written for him and his brother-in-law Louis Kentner; and Mendelssohn's early Concerto in D minor (1952). Among his many honors and awards from governments, seats of learning, and musical and nonmusical organizations, he received the Nehru Award for International Understanding and an honorary knighthood from Queen Elizabeth II (1965); after being made an honorary British citizen in 1985, he formally became Sir Yehudi.

Menuhin's sisters, Hephzibah (*b* San Francisco, 20 May 1920; *d* London, 1 Jan 1981) and Yaltah (*b* San Francisco, 7 Oct 1922), have also become widely known as musicians. Hephzibah studied piano in San Francisco and with Marcel Ciampi in Paris, where in 1934 she made her début with her brother, thus starting a partnership in sonata recitals that continued until her death. She also made many appearances as a soloist throughout the world but particularly in Australia, where she lived for some years. Yaltah also studied piano with Ciampi, and additionally in Rome and New York (under Carl Friedberg). She has appeared in many countries as a soloist and has collaborated in chamber music with a number of distinguished colleagues. Menuhin's son, Jeremy (*b* San Francisco, 2 Nov 1951), studied piano in Paris, Vienna, and Italy, and made his début at the Gstaad Festival in 1965. He has often played as a soloist under his father's baton and independently in Europe and America.

WRITINGS

Six Lessons with Yehudi Menuhin (London, 1971)
Theme and Variations (London, 1972)
Violin: Six Lessons with Yehudi Menuhin (London, 1975)
with W. Primrose: *Violin and Viola* (London, 1975)
Sir Edward Elgar, my Musical Grandfather (London, 1976)
My Favourite Music Stories (London, 1977)
Unfinished Journey (London, 1977) [autobiography]
with C. W. Davis: *The Music of Man* (London, 1980)

BIBLIOGRAPHY

R. Magidoff: *Yehudi Menuhin, the Story of the Man and the Music* (Garden City, NY, 1955, 2/1973) [with discography]
N. Wymer: *Yehudi Menuhin* (London, 1961)
J. Hartnack: *Grosse Geiger unserer Zeit* (Munich, 1967), 223ff
E. Fenby: *Menuhin's House of Music* (London, 1969)
R. Daniels: *Conversations with Menuhin* (London, 1979)
B. Schwarz: *Great Masters of the Violin* (New York, 1983), 520
M. Menuhin: *The Menuhin Saga* (London, 1984)

RONALD KINLOCH ANDERSON/R

Mercer, Johnny [John Herndon] (*b* Savannah, GA, 18 Nov 1909; *d* Los Angeles, CA, 25 June 1976). Lyricist and composer. He went to New York with an acting troupe from Savannah in 1927, and performed several small theater roles while writing lyrics in his spare time. His first successful song was *Lazybones* (1933), and subsequently he contributed the lyrics to over 100 other successful popular, film, and theater songs. Mercer's lyrics cover an enormous range of styles; his particular gift was for incorporating southern vernacular speech and images of country settings into a more cultivated urban genre. These rural images are conveyed in such songs as *Mister Meadowlark* (1940), *Skylark* (1942), *Blues in the Night* (1941), *In the cool, cool, cool of the evening* (1951), and *Moon River* (1961). His talents, however, also embraced the whimsical, for example *Hooray for Hollywood* (1938) and *Jeepers creepers* (1938); the sophisticated, as in *Too marvelous for words* (1937); and the gentle, such as *Dearly Beloved* (1942) and *My Shining Hour* (1943). Mercer sang with the Paul Whiteman, Benny Goodman, and Bob Crosby bands and presented radio programs. He founded Capitol Records in 1942 with Glen Wallichs and Buddy DeSylva, and established the Songwriters' Hall of Fame in 1968 with Howard Richmond and Abe Olman. He wrote lyrics for Broadway musicals, such as *St. Louis Woman* (1946), *Li'l Abner* (1956), and *Saratoga* (1959), and wrote both words and music to many songs, including *I'm an old cowhand* (1936) and *Something's gotta give* (1955), as well as for the musical *Top Banana* (1951).

WORKS

(selective list; names of composers given in parentheses)

FILMS

Ready, Willing and Able (R. Whiting), 1937 [incl. Too marvelous for words]; Going Places (H. Warren), 1938 [incl. Jeepers creepers]; Hollywood Hotel (Whiting), 1938 [incl. Hooray for Hollywood]; Blues in the Night (H. Arlen), 1941 [incl. Blues in the Night]; The Fleet's In (V. Schertzinger), 1942 [incl. Tangerine, Arthur Murray taught me dancing in a hurry]; Star Spangled Rhythm (Arlen), 1942 [incl. That old black magic]; You were Never Lovelier (J. Kern), 1942 [incl. You were never lovelier, Dearly Beloved, I'm old fashioned]

The Sky's the Limit (Arlen), 1943 [incl. One for my baby, My Shining Hour]; Here Come the Waves (Arlen), 1944 [incl. Ac-cent-tchu-ate the positive]; The Harvey Girls (Warren), 1946 [incl. On the Atchison, Topeka and the Santa Fe]; Here Comes the Groom (H. Carmichael), 1951 [incl. In the cool, cool, cool of the evening]; Daddy Long Legs (Mercer), 1955 [incl. Something's gotta give]

STAGE

St. Louis Woman (Arlen), 1946 [incl. Come rain or come shine]
Texas, Li'l Darlin' (R. E. Dolan), 1949
Top Banana (Mercer), 1 Nov 1951; film, 1954
Li'l Abner (G. de Paul), 15 Nov 1956 [incl. Namely you]; film, 1959
Saratoga (Arlen), 1959
Foxy (Dolan), 1964 [incl. Talk to me, baby]

SONGS

Out of breath and scared to death of you (E. Miller), in Garrick Gaieties (revue), 1930; Lazybones (Carmichael), 1933; Pardon my southern accent (M. Malneck), 1934; Goody Goody (Malneck), 1936; I'm an old cowhand (Mercer), in Rhythm on the Range (film), 1936; And the angels sing (Z. Elman), 1939; Fools rush in (R. Bloom), 1940; Mister Meadowlark (W. Donaldson), 1940; Skylark (Carmichael), 1942; The Strip Polka (Mercer), 1942; GI Jive (Mercer), 1944; Dream (Mercer), 1945; Laura (D. Raksin), 1945; I wanna be around (Mercer), 1959

Moon River (H. Mancini), in Breakfast at Tiffany's (film), 1961; The Days of Wine and Roses (Mancini), in The Days of Wine and Roses (film), 1962; Charade (Mancini), in Charade (film), 1963; Barefoot in the Park (N. Hefti), in Barefoot in the Park (film), 1967

BIBLIOGRAPHY

"Johnny Mercer: the Bard from Savannah," *ASCAP Today*, v/2 (1971), 6
R. Bach and G. Mercer: *Our Huckleberry Friend: the Life, Times and Lyrics of Johnny Mercer* (Secaucus, NJ, 1982)

SAMUEL S. BRYLAWSKI

Mercer, Mabel (*b* Burton-on-Trent, England, 3 Feb 1900; *d* Pittsfield, MA, 20 April 1984). Popular singer. She was the daughter of a black American, who died before she was born, and a white English music-hall singer and actress. At the age of 14 she formed a family act with her mother and two cousins. During World War I she joined a black touring show called Coloured Society, later becoming its conductor and music director, and after the war she went to Europe and toured as a dancer and singer. She spent several years in Paris at Bricktop's cabaret, where she introduced the practice (later customary in nightclubs) of singing from a seated position. From this time onwards she was something of a cult figure, greatly admired not only by her audiences but by other singers in every field. In 1938 Mercer went to New York (she became an American citizen in 1952). She was engaged first at Le Ruban Bleu, then at Tony's on 52nd Street; she also sang at the Byline and at the St. Regis Hotel. Her voice, originally soprano, became more limited in range as she grew older. She was always more a diseuse than a singer, and her ability to convey the emotional sense of a song influenced many other performers, notably Frank Sinatra, Billie Holiday, Peggy Lee, and Tony Bennett. Composers such as Cole Porter, Bart Howard, Cy Coleman, and Alec Wilder were also inspired by her interpretive skills; many of their songs were made popular by other singers who had fallen under the influence of Mercer's performances.

BIBLIOGRAPHY

"Mercer, Mabel," *CBY 1973*

HENRY PLEASANTS

Merengue. A moderately fast ballroom dance. It originated as a folk and social dance in the Dominican Republic and became popular in the USA in the mid-1950s, particularly through the music of the bandleader Angel Viloria. A couple dance, it is characterized by a lame-legged step on each second beat and undulating hip movements. The central rhythmic figure (ex. 1)

Ex.1 A typical merengue rhythm

in the musical accompaniment is played on the *tambora* (a double-headed drum) or on equivalent percussion instruments. Viloria's *Macario y Felipo* and *A lo oscuro* (both recorded on Ansonia 2078) are examples of merengue dance-songs.

BIBLIOGRAPHY

A. Butler and J. Butler: "The Merengue," *Dance Magazine*, xxix/3 (1955), 52
H. Morales and H. Adler: *Latin American Rhythm Instruments* (Melville, NY, 1966)
J. S. Roberts: *The Latin Tinge* (New York, 1979)

BARRY KERNFELD

Merman [Zimmermann], **Ethel (Agnes)** (*b* Astoria, NY, 16 Jan 1908; *d* New York, 15 Feb 1984). Actress and singer. She worked briefly in nightclubs and vaudeville before obtaining a role in Gershwin's *Girl Crazy* (1930), where her powerful performance of the songs "I got rhythm" and "Sam and Delilah" stopped the show. She then appeared in *George White's Scandals of 1931* and *Take a Chance* (1932), and consolidated her reputation in Cole Porter's *Anything Goes* (1934, with "Blow, Gabriel, Blow," "I get a kick out of you," and "You're the top"). She had further successes in Porter's *Red, Hot and Blue* (1936), *Du Barry was a Lady* (1939), and *Panama Hattie* (1940), but her greatest triumph was in Berlin's *Annie Get your Gun* (1946), where as Annie Oakley (see illustration) she confirmed her position as the leading musical comedy star of her generation; the song *There's no business like show business* from this show became one of her most famous songs and a theme song of Broadway. Berlin also wrote *Call me Madam* (1950) for her. Merman's last major new role was in Styne's *Gypsy* (1959), which she, and many critics, considered her finest part. She returned to Broadway in 1966 for a revival of *Annie Get your Gun* and in 1970 for *Hello, Dolly!*. Between 1930 and 1954 she also appeared in numerous films, but they did not achieve the level of success of her live performances.

Ethel Merman as Annie Oakley, the role she created in 1946 in Irving Berlin's "Annie Get your Gun": painting (1971) by Rosemarie Sloat in the National Portrait Gallery, Smithsonian Institution

Merman had one of the longest careers as a leading star on Broadway. She changed the nature of the role of the musical comedy heroine, which before had been to project a studied coyness and innocence; Merman, with her unique brassy delivery and her marked New York City accent, conveyed toughness and worldliness. Her voice was often described as big, but her true asset was her ability to project and enunciate the lyrics of her songs. She wrote two memoirs, *Who Could Ask for Anything More?* (1955) and *Merman: an Autobiography* (1978).

BIBLIOGRAPHY

"Merman, Ethel," *CBY 1955*
Obituary, *New York Times* (16 Feb 1984)

GERALD BORDMAN

Merola, Gaetano (*b* Naples, Italy, 4 Jan 1881; *d* San Francisco, CA, 30 Aug 1953). Conductor and impresario. Son of a violinist, he graduated from the Naples Conservatory in 1898 and the following year secured a post as assistant conductor at the Metropolitan Opera in New York. After touring with Henry Savage's opera company, he became associated with Oscar Hammerstein's two companies (the Manhattan Opera, 1906–10, and the London Opera, 1910–12), and conducted the San Carlo Opera in San Francisco between 1918 and 1922. A year later he founded the San Francisco Opera, and as its first general director conducted the inaugural performance, *La bohème*, on 26 September at the

Civic Auditorium. In the 30 years he held the position, the San Francisco Opera became one of America's leading opera companies. Merola filled most of the principal roles with singers from the Metropolitan, and he worked almost entirely within the confines of the standard French, Italian, and German repertory. Nevertheless, he introduced San Francisco to Wagner's *Ring* (1935), gave the American première of Ravel's *L'enfant et les sortilèges* (1931), and presented such comparative rarities from the contemporary repertory as Franco Vittadini's *Anima allegra* (1925), Umberto Giordano's *La cena delle beffe* (1927), and Henri Rabaud's *Mârouf* (1931). From 1924 to 1931 he was also the general director of the Los Angeles Grand Opera Association. Merola died of a heart attack while conducting at the Stern Grove Festival.

BIBLIOGRAPHY

W. Zakariasen: "Fior d'Italia," *Opera News*, xxxvii/4 (1972), 16
A. Bloomfield: *The San Francisco Opera: 1922–1978* (Sausalito, CA, 1978)
C. Bishop: *The San Carlo Opera Company, 1913–1955* (Santa Monica, CA, 1978)

ALLAN ULRICH

Merriam, Alan P(arkhurst) (*b* Missoula, MT, 1 Nov 1923; *d* nr Warsaw, Poland, 14 March 1980). Ethnomusicologist. He studied at the University of Montana (BA 1947) and Northwestern University (MM 1948, PhD 1951), then taught anthropology at Northwestern (1953–4, 1956–62) and at the University of Wisconsin (1954–6). In 1962 he became professor of anthropology at Indiana University, where he was chairman of the department from 1966 to 1969. In the spring of 1976 he was senior scholar in anthropology at Sydney University. He died in an air crash.

Merriam conducted field research among the Flathead Indians in the USA (1950, 1958) and among the tribes of Zaïre (1951–2, 1959–60, 1973). His approach to ethnomusicology as the study of music in culture is reflected in *The Anthropology of Music*, which stresses the importance of cultural and social factors in any discussion of the process of musical creation within a culture, its musical aesthetics, and the training of its performers (*see also* ETHNOMUSICOLOGY, §3). The principles of this book are applied in *Ethnomusicology of the Flathead Indians*, one of the most exhaustive studies of an individual musical culture. In addition to his numerous articles concerning the arts and cultures of African and American Indian tribes, he wrote *A Bibliography of Jazz* (with R. Benford).

WRITINGS

with R. Benford: *A Bibliography of Jazz* (Philadelphia, 1954/*R*1970)
A Prologue to the Study of African Arts (Yellow Springs, OH, 1962)
The Anthropology of Music (Evanston, IL, 1964)
with F. Gillis: *Ethnomusicology and Folk Music: an International Bibliography of Dissertations and Theses* (Middletown, CT, 1966)
Ethnomusicology of the Flathead Indians (Chicago, 1967)
African Music on LP: an Annotated Discography (Evanston, IL, 1970)
The Arts and Humanities in African Studies (Bloomington, IN, 1972)
An African World: the Basongye Village of Lupupa Ngye (Bloomington, IN, 1974)
Culture History of the Basongye (Bloomington, IN, 1975)

PAULA MORGAN

Merrill, Nathaniel (*b* Newton, MA, 8 Feb 1927). Opera director. He was a pupil of Boris Goldovsky at the New England Conservatory of Music, and also gained experience in Europe with Carl Ebert, Herbert Graf, Günther Rennert, and Friedrich Schramm. He made his début in Boston in 1952, when he directed the American première of Lully's *Amadis*. In 1955 he joined the Metropolitan Opera, and remained as resident stage director for two decades; he took charge of more than a dozen new productions, many of them in collaboration with the designer Robert O'Hearn. He also served the Opéra du Rhin, Strasbourg, in the same capacity, and has directed operas in Vancouver and for the open-air Arena in Verona. He excels in the deployment of large forces on stage, as in Verdi's *Aida*, Wagner's *Die Meistersinger von Nürnberg*, and Berlioz's *Les troyens*, all of which he staged at the Metropolitan.

BIBLIOGRAPHY

N. Merrill: "The Making of a Director," *Opera News*, xxxii/16 (1968), 8

FRANK MERKLING

Merrill, Robert (*b* Brooklyn, NY, 4 June 1917). Baritone. He was trained first by his mother, Lillian Miller Merrill, a concert singer, then by Samuel Margolis in New York. Although he occasionally appeared in Europe and South America, he preferred to base his career at the Metropolitan Opera, where he sang all the major baritone roles of the Italian and French repertories. In vocal endowment, technical security, and longevity, he was unequalled among baritones of his generation at the Metropolitan. He made his début there as Germont in *La traviata* on 15 December 1945 and celebrated his 500th performance on 5 March 1973, still singing with undiminished vigor; he remained on the company's roster through the 1974–5 season. Also as Germont, he made his European début at La Fenice, Venice, in 1961. Merrill's career has extended to radio, television, and film (*Aaron Slick from Punkin Crick*, 1952), and he has appeared frequently in recital, sometimes accompanied by his wife, Marion Machno, and with every important orchestra in the USA. Among his recordings are many complete operas, including *La traviata* and *Un ballo in maschera* under Toscanini, musical comedies (e.g., *Show Boat* and *Carousel*), and works from the concert repertory (notably, his joint recital with Richard Tucker at Carnegie Hall, 1973). In his 1975 London concert début, Merrill won praise for the generosity, if not the subtlety, of his singing; for all the natural beauty and healthy resonance of his voice, he has never been highly regarded as an imaginative interpreter or a compelling actor. He has received a number of awards, including New York's highly prized Handel Medallion (1970), and has published, in addition to his autobiographical works, a novel, *The Divas* (1978).

BIBLIOGRAPHY

L. Riemens: "Merrill, Robert," *Le grandi voci*, ed. R. Celletti (Rome, 1964) [with discography by S. Smolian]
R. Merrill and S. Dody: *Once More from the Beginning* (New York, 1965)
H. Rosenthal: "Robert Merrill," *Great Singers of Today* (London, 1966), 113
H. E. Phillips: "Merrill's Milestone," *Opera News*, xxxv/11 (1971), 14
R. Merrill and R. Saffron: *Between Acts* (New York, 1977)

PETER G. DAVIS/R

Merriman, Nan [Katherine-Ann] (*b* Pittsburgh, PA, 28 April 1920). Mezzo-soprano. She studied in Los Angeles with Alexia Bassian and began her career singing background music for Hollywood films. In 1940 she toured the USA with Laurence Olivier and Vivien Leigh in *Romeo and Juliet*, singing music by Palestrina and Purcell during scene changes. She made her operatic début in 1942 at the Cincinnati Summer Opera as La Cieca in *La Gioconda*. The following year she won a singing competition which resulted in a 15-minute NBC broadcast; Toscanini heard it and engaged her for his broadcasts and recordings of Gluck's *Orfeo*, *Falstaff* (Meg), *Rigoletto* (Maddelena), and *Otello* (Emilia).

She sang Mozart's Dorabella at Aix-en-Provence (1953, 1955, 1959), La Piccola Scala (1955–6), and Glyndebourne (1956), and she took part in Karajan's recording. She played Baba the Turk in the British première of *The Rake's Progress* (Edinburgh Festival, 1953), and Laura in Alexander Dargomïzhsky's *The Stone Guest* at La Piccola Scala (1958). Merriman undertook many recitals and orchestral concerts, but decided to retire in 1965 while her appealingly vibrant mezzo-soprano was still at the height of its powers.

HAROLD ROSENTHAL/R

Merritt, A(rthur) Tillman (*b* Calhoun, MO, 15 Feb 1902). Musicologist. He graduated from the University of Missouri (BA 1924, BFA 1926), then obtained the MA at Harvard (1927). After studying in Paris with Nadia Boulanger and Paul Dukas, he taught at Trinity College, Hartford, Connecticut (1930–32). In 1932 he became professor of music at Harvard, where he twice served as chairman of the department (1942–52, 1968–72). On his retirement in 1972 he became curator of the Isham Memorial Library at Harvard.

Merritt specializes in the music of the Renaissance, particularly the 16th-century chanson. He has co-edited the complete secular works of Janequin (1965–71) and edited several volumes of motets (1962–4) originally published by Attaingnant. His widely used textbook on counterpoint, *Sixteenth-century Polyphony: a Basis for the Study of Counterpoint* (1939), includes a thorough discussion of 16th-century contrapuntal practice and offers a pedagogical alternative to the traditional species approach.

PAULA MORGAN

Merz, Karl (*b* Bensheim, Germany, 10 Sept 1836; *d* Wooster, OH, 30 Jan 1890). Music educator and composer. He received musical instruction from his father, a schoolteacher, and from F. J. Kunkel, and then taught briefly in a Catholic school in Appenheim. In 1854 he immigrated to the USA, settling in Philadelphia, where he worked in a music store and theaters, and then as organist of the Sixth Presbyterian Church. Subsequently he held several teaching posts in Pennsylvania and Virginia before joining the faculty of Oxford (Ohio) Female College in 1861. In 1882 he organized and became head of the music program at Wooster College, a position he filled with distinction until his death.

Merz was an early and influential popularizer of musical culture in America. From 1871 he served as associate editor and from 1873 to 1890 as editor-in-chief of *Brainard's Musical World*, the house organ of the Cleveland firm S. Brainard and Sons; to this journal he contributed numerous articles and editorials, and some music. He also wrote *Musical Hints for the Million* (1875), two piano methods and a reed organ method, and *Elements of Harmony and Musical Composition* (1881). As a composer he left works in several genres; among those compositions particularly noted in contemporary journals were the Piano Sonata op.50 and the operettas *Runaway Flirt* (1868), *Last Will and Testament* (1877), and *Katie Dean* (1880). His choral works include *Great and Marvellous are thy Works* (published in 1867) and a mass. A number of his lectures and essays were published on his death by his sons as *Music and Culture* (1890).

BIBLIOGRAPHY

GroveAS

W. S. B. Mathews, ed.: *A Hundred Years of Music in America* (Chicago, 1889/*R*1970), 399

M. T. Macmillan: "The Wisdom of a Great Teacher, Karl Merz," *The Etude*, xlviii (1930), 399

M. H. Osburn: *Ohio Composers and Musical Authors* (Columbus, OH, 1942), 136

J. HEYWOOD ALEXANDER

Mescalero. APACHE Indian group of the Southwest.

Messiter, Arthur H(enry) (*b* Frome, England, 12 April 1834; *d* New York, 2 July 1916). Organist. He was trained privately in music and immigrated to New York in 1863, where he sang briefly as a volunteer tenor under Henry S. Cutler at Trinity Church. During the next three years he was active as an organist in Philadelphia at several different churches; in 1866 he returned to New York to become organist of Trinity Church, serving in that capacity with unusual distinction until 1897. He and his predecessor, Cutler, were pioneers who had a formative influence on church music in a period of transition; their aim was to introduce the innovations of the Oxford Movement by celebrating choral services of musical gravity and consistency, sung by well-trained, vested male choirs. In 1870 Messiter began using an orchestra to accompany his services; the orchestra played at the front of the nave, about 100 meters from the choir in the rear gallery, with separate organs supporting each component. Messiter compiled three books of service music and was editor of an eight-volume *Literature of Music* (1900); he also wrote *A History of Church Music at Trinity Church, New York* (1906/*R*1970). Today he is recalled mainly for the hymn tune "Marion" (1883), to which are sung most often Edward H. Plumptre's words beginning "Rejoice, ye pure in heart!"

WILLIAM OSBORNE

Mester, Jorge (*b* Mexico City, Mexico, 10 April 1935). Conductor. As a student at the Juilliard School, he concentrated on conducting, principally with Morel; he also worked with Bernstein (Berkshire Music Center, 1955) and Albert Wolff. He made his début in 1955 with the Orquesta Sinfónica Nacional de México and has since conducted most major orchestras and several opera companies in the USA, as well as the BBC SO and the Royal PO in London, and worked with leading dance companies. He won the Naumburg Award for conducting in 1968. He has been music director of the Louisville Orchestra (1967–79), the Aspen Music Festival (from 1970), and the Casals Festival in Puerto Rico (from 1980), and between 1971 and 1974 he was music adviser and principal conductor of the Kansas City PO. In 1984 he became music director of the Pasadena (California) SO. During his first period on the faculty of the Juilliard School (1957–67) he conducted the American premières of Hindemith's *Long Christmas Dinner*, Henze's *Elegy for Young Lovers* and Cavalli's *L'Ormindo*; he resumed teaching there in 1980 and became chairman of conducting studies.

Mester's association with the Louisville Orchestra resulted in nearly 200 premières and made him one of the most recorded conductors of his generation: Blacher, Cowell, Crumb, Dallapiccola, Ginastera, Koechlin, Penderecki, Petrassi, Schuller, Schuman, and Shostakovich are among the composers whose works he has been the first to record; he has also made first recordings of music as unusual and interesting as *Dante* by Granados, Bruch's Symphony no.2, and (with Charles Treger) Joachim's Hungarian Concerto. More an intuitive than an intellectual musician, Mester has nonetheless conducted brilliantly works as difficult as Sessions's *Trial of Lucullus*, and though the projection of color and temperament is his particular strength, he has also given notably effective performances of Haydn and Mozart.

MICHAEL STEINBERG/R

Metcalf, Frank J(ohnson) (*b* Ashland, MA, 4 April 1865; *d* Washington, DC, 25 Feb 1945). Bibliographer and writer on music. He was educated at Boston University (BA 1886), and, after a period as a schoolteacher, in 1893 became a correspondence clerk responsible for war records. An avid collector, he amassed some 6000 religious works and 2000 American tunebooks and hymnals. He published three valuable books, *American Psalmody, or Titles of Books Containing Tunes Printed in America from 1721 to 1820* (1917/*R*1968), *American Writers and Compilers of Sacred Music* (1925), and *Stories of Hymn Tunes* (1928); he also wrote a number of articles. His writings have been superseded, but in their time they broke fresh ground.

BIBLIOGRAPHY

R. Crawford: Review of *American Psalmody*, *Notes*, xxvi (1969–70), 42

ROBERT STEVENSON

Meters. Rhythm-and-blues group. It was formed in New Orleans in 1967 by keyboard player Art Neville (*b* New Orleans, LA, 1937), guitarist Leo Nocentelli (*b* New Orleans), drummer Joseph "Zigaboo" Modeliste (*b* New Orleans), and bass guitarist George Porter (*b* New Orleans); all the members of the group also sang. The Meters began their career as a purely instrumental dance band, achieving most popularity in their native New Orleans; they were also engaged as the house band at the recording studio of producer Allen Toussaint. They recorded hit songs on the Josie label such as *Sophisticated Cissy* (pop no.34, soul no.7, 1969), *Cissy Strut* (pop no.23, soul no.4, 1969), *Look-ka py py* (soul no.11, 1969), and *Chicken Strut* (soul no.11, 1970). Their style reduced the syncopated rhythms of New Orleans music to the bare essentials, underlined by thumping bass lines and elaborated on guitar and hissing cymbals. When they changed recording companies in the 1970s, signing a contract with Warner Bros., they began to place more emphasis on vocal sound and adopted a pop style intended to have a wider appeal; but they made few significant recordings between then and the time they disbanded in 1977. During most of the decade they continued to work for Toussaint and played on albums recorded by Dr. John, Robert Palmer, Jess Roden, Labelle, King Biscuit Boy, and Paul McCartney. Their music was a formative influence on white funk groups such as Little Feat and on several Jamaican reggae musicians who later became popular in the USA.

RECORDINGS

(selective list)

Sophisticated Cissy (Josie 1001, 1969); Cissy Strut (Josie 1005, 1969); Look-ka py py (Josie 1015, 1969); Chicken Strut (Josie 1018, 1970); *Cabbage Alley* (Rep. 2076, 1972); *Rejuvenation* (Rep. 2200, 1974); *Cissy Strut* (Isl. 9250, 1975); Be my lady (WB 8434, 1977)

BIBLIOGRAPHY

J. Broven: *Walking to New Orleans: the Story of New Orleans Rhythm & Blues* (Bexhill-on-Sea, England, 1974), 207

JOHN MORTHLAND

Metheny, Pat(rick Bruce) (*b* Lee's Summit, MO, 12 Aug 1954). Jazz-rock guitarist. While still a teenager he was discovered by the vibraphonist Gary Burton, who engaged him for his quartet. In the early 1970s he taught at the University of Miami and the Berklee College of Music in Boston. Since the mid-1970s he has played and toured widely with his own groups.

Metheny is a highly proficient player of both the standard and 12-string electric guitars, playing quick passages with ease and making tasteful use of electronic sound-delay devices for "slap-back echo." His approach is more lyrical than that of his contemporaries John McLaughlin and Larry Coryell, and unlike many guitarists with his dexterity he seems to strive for simplicity in his improvisations. He cites the guitar styles of Jim Hall and Wes Montgomery as his favorites. The excellent sales of his album *The Pat Metheny Group* (1978) gained him, during the late 1970s and early 1980s, a larger and wider audience than that attained by all but the most successful jazz musicians. He also wrote the music for the film *Twice in a Lifetime* (1985). In the early 1980s he incorporated the tunes and improvisational attack of the saxophonist Ornette Coleman into his playing (as well as using some of Coleman's former sidemen), which clearly distinguishes his style from that of the guitarists of this period who were influenced by McLaughlin.

RECORDINGS

(selective list)

As leader: *Bright Size Life* (1975, ECM 1073), incl. Unity Valley, Missouri Uncompromised, Midwestern Night's Dream; *Watercolors* (1977, ECM 1097), incl. River Quay; *The Pat Metheny Group* (1978, ECM 1114), incl. April Joy; *80/81* (1980, ECM 1180–81)

As sideman: G. Burton: *Ring* (1974, ECM 1051), *Passengers* (1976, ECM 1092)

BIBLIOGRAPHY

F. Bourque and N. Tesser: "Pat Metheny: Musings on Neo-Fusion," *Down Beat*, xlvi/6 (1979), 12

D. Forte: "Pat Metheny," *Guitar Player*, xv/12 (1981), 90

MARK C. GRIDLEY

Methodist Church, music of the. Methodist music in the USA, which consists principally of a tradition of spirited hymn singing, has been affected by two aspects of the church's history: the fragmentation of the denomination into various branches and their reunification, which resulted in the publication of numerous official hymnbooks; and the leading role played by Methodists in the 19th-century revival and Sunday-school movements, which fostered a strong element of populism in the church's music.

1. Introduction. 2. Early hymnals. 3. Popular hymnody. 4. Authorized hymnals: (i) Methodist Episcopal Church (ii) Methodist Protestant Church (iii) The unified church. 5. Performing practice and other musical activities.

1. INTRODUCTION. The first Methodist society or congregation in America was probably that established by the Irishman Robert Strawbridge in northern Maryland in 1764. Philip Embury formed a society, now the John Street Methodist Church, in New York in 1766, and others were shortly set up in the principal eastern cities, such as Old St. George's Church in Philadelphia. John Wesley first sent preachers to America in 1769, and in 1771 Francis Asbury arrived in Philadelphia, from where he began to work to spread Methodism. Early American Methodists were dependent on the Episcopal Church for the administration of the sacraments, an unsatisfactory arrangement, especially for converts in far-flung regions; Wesley therefore authorized a conference in Baltimore in 1784, at which his representative Thomas Coke ordained Asbury, and the two proceeded with the ordination of preachers. This action and decisions taken at the conference led to the founding of the Methodist Episcopal Church, the first officially constituted Methodist church in the world. Its services, organization, and rules of faith were laid down by Wesley himself.

Among the preachers present at the first conference was Richard Allen, who in 1787 led Blacks out of the white church into the Free African Society, which by 1794 became a new denomination, the African Methodist Episcopal Church (*see* AFRO-AMERICAN MUSIC, §1). The 19th century saw further schisms, which resulted in the establishment of many separate bodies of Methodists: the most important were the Methodist Protestant Church (1830), the Methodist Episcopal Church, South (1846), and the Methodist Church (1867, consisting of the Northern and Western conferences of the Methodist Protestant Church). All the congregations of the Protestant denomination were reunited in 1877 and the entire Methodist communion in the USA came together in 1939. The United Methodist Church (the official title of the church in the USA) was formed in 1968 when two independent bodies, the United Brethren in Christ and the Evangelical Association, both originally active among German-speaking Pennsylvanians, became part of the church.

2. EARLY HYMNALS. John Wesley's first hymnbook for Methodists, *A Collection of Psalms and Hymns* (1737), was a sophisticated, enticingly singable collection of fine texts set to tunes from various sources (art music, popular melodies, German chorales, and metrical psalms). Although popular in England, this book was hardly suited to early American congregations, whose members were often illiterate and musically unlearned; a version of it prepared specially by Wesley for the American church was an austere collection containing more psalms than hymns and clearly designed to protect the function of the hymnbook as a vehicle for the teaching of doctrine. *A Pocket Hymn Book* (1781), a collection without music compiled by the Englishman Robert Spence and consisting of Wesleyan hymns and hymns that the Wesleys considered worthless, was printed in America in 1786 and quickly overtook the official book in popularity. The 1786 edition included 27 hymns added by the American bishops, and an edition of 1793 was enlarged to contain 300 hymns; some tunes were named and several related tunebooks were published, one by Andrew Law. It was Spence's book, with what Wesley called its "grevious doggerel," that became the core of American Methodist hymnody until well into the 19th century; it set the pattern, which long continued, of conflict between Wesley's high theological and aesthetic standards of texts and melodies and the needs of American congregations. Throughout the 19th century the authorized Methodist hymnals only reluctantly accommodated popular sacred song, maintaining instead a firm adherence to traditional European and English hymnody.

3. POPULAR HYMNODY. The revival movements that swept through Presbyterian, Baptist, and Methodist churches from 1800 onwards were carried forward by camp meetings (*see* SPIRITUAL, §I, 2; *see also* GOSPEL MUSIC, §I, 1, and HYMNODY). Methodist music, preaching, and free style of worship were ideally suited to the camp meeting, which, particularly in rural areas, helped Methodism to spread quickly in the 19th century. Revival hymnody had memorable, engaging, rhythmically vital melodies, frequently based on modal scales; the simple, semi-improvised texts often incorporated "wandering" choruses (i.e., lines that were transferred at will from one hymn to another), and call-and-response performance was common. The publication of music for Methodist camp meetings began slowly but swelled to enormous quantities. It included Thomas G. Hinde's *The Pilgrim Songster* (1810), used for many years at camp meetings in Kentucky and Tennessee, Moses L. Scudder's *The Wesleyan Psalmist* (1842), which was unusual in that it contained music (melodies, and a few two- and three-part arrangements), and Marshall W. Taylor's *A Collection of Revival Hymns and Plantation Melodies* (1883), which again included music. Methodists also made an important contribution to a number of the landmark collections of the period, such as John Wyeth's *Repository of Sacred Music, Part Second* (2/1820) and William Walker's *Southern Harmony* (1835).

The setting up of permanent Methodist camp-meeting sites, such as Ocean Grove, New Jersey, and Round Lake, New York, the popularity of revival services in local churches, prayer meetings, and above all the rise of the Sunday-school movement (*see* GOSPEL MUSIC, §I, 1(ii)) signaled a change in unofficial Methodist music. So-called "social" hymnbooks sought, in the words of Stephen Parks in the preface to his *Methodist Social Hymn Book* (1856), to reconcile "the stern and elevated taste" of official hymnody with "the light and irreverent style of singing" of the camp meeting; popular books included *The Wesleyan Sacred Harp* (1855), *The Chorus* (1858), and *Sacred Melodies for Social Worship* (1859). By the mid-century Methodist Sunday schools were flourishing; the simple music and texts, many with choruses, in the Sunday-school songbooks of Joseph Hillman, George F. Root, William B. Bradbury, Robert Lowry, and William G. Fischer were instrumental in setting Methodist taste in hymnody for the next century. A prominent Methodist composer of Sunday-school hymns was Phebe Palmer Knapp, who wrote the music to numerous texts, many by her friend Mary D. James.

The ubiquitous gospel song of the later 19th century and the 20th grew out of the camp-meeting and Sunday-school movements. Important in the establishing of gospel music in the Methodist church was *The Revivalist* (*c*1868, 7/1872), compiled by Joseph Hillman chiefly from works by Methodists, including William McDonald, John W. Dadmun, and Fischer. Ira D. Sankey and Fanny Crosby, the most prominent writers of gospel songs, were both Methodists; the almost total absence of their enormously popular hymns from authorized hymnals until well into the 20th century amply illustrates the split between official and unofficial singing in the Methodist church. Semiofficial recognition of the vast corpus of popular hymnody was achieved in the publication by the Methodist Episcopal Church, South, of *The Cokesbury Hymnal* (1923), which though intended for general worship consisted mainly of gospel hymns. A "companion," *Best Revival Songs*, was published in 1924, and the revised edition of the original hymnal in 1938 as *The Cokesbury Worship Hymnal*; the latter remains popular, combining many of the gospel hymns from the earlier edition with a number of mainstream Protestant hymns.

4. AUTHORIZED HYMNALS.

(i) Methodist Episcopal Church. The principal hymnbook of the original Methodist denomination in the 19th century was *A Collection of Hymns . . . Principally from the Collection of . . . John Wesley* (1821, rev. and enlarged 2/1832 and 3/1836), which despite its title was a revision of Spence's *A Pocket Hymn Book* (1802 edn) and its supplement (1808). Simultaneously *The Methodist Harmonist* (1821, rev. and enlarged 2/1833 and 3/1837) was published, the tunes in which were cross-referred to the texts in *A Collection of Hymns*. The revised editions of both books contained supplementary hymns, but the character of the contents remained unaffected by the rise of popular hymnody. When revivalism was at its height the Northern conference brought out a further revision, *Hymns for the Use of the Methodist Episcopal Church* (1849), which though it was one of the most complete

and faithful presentations of Wesleyan hymns published in the USA proved more useful as a devotional collection than as a hymnal; an official tunebook was issued in 1857 and several unauthorized ones followed, including the *Tune Book* (1866) of the gospel singer Philip Phillips. A more wide-ranging choice of hymns, including Sunday-school and gospel songs, and hymns translated from Greek, Latin, and German, appeared in the *Hymnal for the Methodist Episcopal Church* (1878); tunes harmonized in four parts were included (two or three texts were placed with each), and the book also contained an order of worship (the first American hymnal to do so) and a collection of psalm chants.

The first sect to secede from the Episcopal branch of Methodism, the African Methodist Episcopal Church, used Allen's *Collection of Spiritual Songs and Hymns* (1801), the first hymnbook compiled by a Black; it contained 54 hymns, increased to 64 in a revision of the same year, without tunes. The Southern conference of the Methodist Episcopal Church, meeting in 1846 after declaring its independence, appointed a commission to prepare its own hymnal; *A Collection of Hymns for Public, Social and Domestic Worship* (1847) contained no fewer than 1047 hymns (600 by the Wesleys, 150 by Isaac Watts), yet in a short time a supplement of 503 hymns, *Songs of Zion* (1851, rev. and enlarged 1873), was issued; this included some camp-meeting and social hymns, in response to popular demand, and became so successful that within 30 years it was effectively the standard hymnbook. The first edition of *A Collection of Hymns* to be published with music came out in 1874, though the privately issued *Wesleyan Hymn and Tune Book* (1859) had long served as the church's tunebook. Revisions of the 1847 collection and its supplement were published in 1881 (*The New Hymn Book*) and 1889 (*Hymn Book of the Methodist Episcopal Church, South*); the latter was a fine book in which traditional Methodist hymns (294 by the Wesleys) were combined with popular camp-meeting and gospel songs.

The work of the Northern and Southern branches of the church among German settlers led to the publication by the former of *Deutsches Gesang- und Melodienbuch der Bischöflichen Methodisten-Kirche* (1880) and by the latter of *Deutsches Gesangbuch der Südlichen Bischöflichen Methodistenkirche* (1900); in 1910 both churches settled on a version of the Northern book containing 780 hymns.

(ii) Methodist Protestant Church. When Methodist Protestants broke away from the parent church in 1830 they adopted a book already in common use, *A Compilation of Hymns, Adapted to Public and Social Divine Worship* (1828). The new church soon felt a need for its own hymnal, however, and produced one of the finest Methodist hymnals published to that date, *Hymn Book of the Methodist Protestant Church* (1837), which formed the basis of most later books and introduced the innovation of citing authors' names. A revision (1859) prepared by the Eastern and Southern conferences, included 73 spiritual songs, which it was hoped would keep Methodists from using revival songbooks; this edition listed a dozen tunebooks as sources for the melodies for the hymns. The Methodist Church, formed in 1867 from the Northern and Western conferences, prepared *The Voice of Praise* (1872) for its use, made up not only of hymns from the 1837 collection but of items from manuscript sources and journals. On the reunification of the church in 1877 a new book combining existing sources was authorized; published in 1882 as *The Tribute of Praise and Methodist Protestant Hymn Book*, it was the first Methodist Protestant book to have texts and tunes printed together. More important was *The Methodist Protestant Church Hymnal* (1901), which was issued only in a music version; its layout (one hymn to a page with texts interlined with musical staves) and some of the hymns in it were borrowed from contemporary hymnals of other denominations. Besides its eclectic selection of hymns (only 69 by the Wesleys, together with gospel and spiritual songs), the book contained a lengthy section of scripture readings and ritual.

(iii) The unified church. The meetings that began in 1874 between the separated branches of Methodism with the aim of unifying the church included a "committee on hymn book," which in 1886 suggested that a "pan-Methodistic hymnal" be prepared. *The Methodist Hymnal* was published in 1905 (the Methodist Protestant Church played no part in its production); the editors concluded the preface with the earnest hope that the hymnal might "supplant those unauthorized publications which often teach what Methodism does not hold, and which, by excluding the nobler music of the earlier and later days, prevent the growth of true musical taste." 717 hymns, holding fast to the traditional center of Methodist hymnody, were printed, one stanza of each text being interlined with a four-part harmonization of the tune. Musically the book achieved a new high standard under the editorship of Peter C. Lutkin and Karl P. Harington, each of whom contributed 34 tunes. The book remained in use for 30 years until a hymnal acceptable to all three principal branches of the church was published shortly before the official reunification: *The Methodist Hymnal* (1935) saw a reduction in the number of hymns by the Wesleys (61) and other 18th-century writers; a few gospel songs were included and a serious and commendable attempt was made to include 20th-century hymns. For the first time in a Methodist hymnal the texts were totally interlined with the staves of music. In 1960 a revision of the 1935 hymnal was authorized and it was published in 1964 (later editions were called *The Book of Hymns*); it contains 552 hymns, 11 chants, 48 items of service music, and two complete communion services. The eclecticism of the contents mirrors the pluralism of the church itself: they include black spirituals, an American Indian hymn, Chinese hymns, camp-meeting hymns, folk hymns, Latin, Greek, and German hymns, metrical psalms, French carols, plainchant, and contemporary tunes and texts; a surprising number of well-known tunes appear in newly harmonized versions. A supplement published in 1982 sought further to represent the diversity of congregational song in the church by including selections from the hymnody of the United Brethren in Christ, old and new gospel hymns, and items from the repertories of ethnic minority groups; an attempt was also made to eliminate discriminatory language.

Other official and semiofficial books designed to cater to specific groups within the church were published in the late 1970s and early 1980s: *Songs of Zion* (1981) represents the black religious tradition; *Celebremos* (1979–83) is a two-part collection of choruses and hymns for Hispanic Methodists (who already had their own Spanish version of the hymnal, 1973, with a number of texts and tunes by Hispanics); and *Hymns from the Four Winds* (1983) consists of 125 hymns and psalms for Asian-American Methodists. Of the American Indian tribes in the Oklahoma Indian Missionary Conference of the United Methodist Church only the Cherokee have a written language and hymnal; the important body of Methodist hymnody among the Indians is mostly preserved only in oral tradition. The existence of these varied sources of Methodist hymnody led in 1984 to the commissioning of a new hymnal under the editorship of Carlton P. Young.

Beginning in 1980 the United Methodist Church has expended much effort in the recovery of psalm singing. A new translation of the psalter has been prepared, and experiments in styles of chanting have been made; *Psalms for Singing* (1984) is a collection of 26 of the psalms set to newly composed chants.

5. PERFORMING PRACTICE AND OTHER MUSICAL ACTIVITIES. The first American Methodists met in humble rooms; their music consisted of unaccompanied singing of hymns learned by rote. The church held to these ways longer than most other denominations because of its close association with settlers on the frontier and with the camp meeting. But as urbanization progressed in the 19th century more and more congregations met in larger church buildings; after 1862 reed organs were commonly used and many churches had a quartet choir. During the first quarter of the 20th century pipe organs were installed in the wealthier churches and large choirs flourished; by the 1940s many churches had more than one choir.

In 1956 at the instigation of some leading Methodist musicians – Austin Lovelace, J. Edward Moyer, William Rice, Cecil Lapo, and Walter Towner – the National Fellowship of Methodist Musicians (NaFOMM) was formed. Among its important activities were the publication of *Music Ministry*, a monthly church music magazine, and the setting up of a church music department in the Abingdon Press (both projects had been discontinued by the late 1970s); NaFOMM played an important role in the editing of the 1964 hymnal. In 1969 the name of the organization was changed to the Fellowship of United Methodist Musicians (FUMM), and in 1979 bodies dedicated to the cultivation of worship and other arts joined it to form the Fellowship of United Methodists in Worship, Music, and Other Arts (FUMWMOA).

Many Methodist colleges have undergraduate programs in church music; these have played an important role in raising standards of music in Methodist churches. The Methodist seminary of Emory College, Oxford, Georgia, and Garrett-Evangelical Theological Seminary, Evanston, Illinois, offer extensive courses in church music to both musicians and theological students. In 1959 the Perkins School of Theology at Southern Methodist University, Dallas, established a graduate program in sacred music leading to the master's degree.

BIBLIOGRAPHY

N. D. Gould: *Church Music in America, Comprising its History and its Peculiarities at Different Periods, with Cursory Remarks on its Legitimate Use and its Abuse* (Boston, 1853)

C. S. Nutter and W. F. Tillett, eds.: *The Hymns and Hymn Writers of the Church* (New York, 1911)

C. F. Price: *The Music and Hymnody of The Methodist Hymnal* (Cincinnati, 1911)

H. Bett: *The Hymns of Methodism* (London, 1913, rev. 3/1945)

L. F. Benson: *The English Hymn* (New York, 1915/*R*1962)

F. J. Metcalf: *American Writers and Compilers of Sacred Music* (New York, 1925/*R*1967)

R. G. McCutchan, E. H. Hughes, J. M. Walker, and others: *Worship in Music* (Cincinnati, 1929)

J. M. Walker: *Better Music in our Churches* (Cincinnati, 1932)

R. G. McCutchan: "The Deluge of New Hymnals," *MTNAP*, xxviii (1933), 23

M. C. Powell: *Guiding the Experience of Worship* (Cincinnati, 1935)

R. G. McCutchan: *Our Hymnody: a Manual of the Methodist Hymnal* (New York and Cincinnati, 1937, 2/1942)

B. F. Crawford: *Theological Trends in Methodist Hymnody* (Carnegie, PA, 1939)

L. A. Pfautsch: *A Curriculum of Church Music for a Theological Seminary: a Historical Justification and a Formulation* (thesis, Union Theological Seminary, 1948)

R. Stevenson: *Patterns of Protestant Church Music* (Durham, 1953)

D. E. Hill: *A Study of Tastes in American Church Music as Reflected in the Music of the Methodist Episcopal Church to 1900* (diss., U. of Illinois, 1963)

R. Stevenson: *Protestant Church Music in America* (New York, 1966)

F. D. Gealy, A. C. Lovelace, and C. R. Young: *Companion to the Hymnal: a Handbook to the 1964 Methodist Hymnal* (Nashville, 1970)

F. A. Norwood: *The Story of American Methodism* (Nashville, 1974)

B. E. Bailey: "The Lined-hymn Tradition in Black Mississippi Churches," *BPiM*, vi (1978), 3

G. F. Lockwood: *Recent Developments in U.S. Hispanic and Latin American Protestant Church Music* (thesis, School of Theology, Claremont, CA, 1981)

T. D. Bilhartz: *Francis Asbury's America: an Album of Early American Methodism* (Grand Rapids, MI, 1984)

ROGER DESCHNER

Metropolitan Opera House. The most important New York opera house, built in 1883; a new house opened at Lincoln Center for the Performing Arts in 1966. *See* NEW YORK, §3.

Metz, Julius (*fl* New York, 1819–58). Composer, teacher, singer, and pianist, probably of French origin. He appeared in public concerts in New York from 1819 to about 1834 as a singer and pianist, and was a pianist for the first and second seasons of the New York Philharmonic Symphony Society in 1842–4. His compositions for piano, some of which are in the Library of Congress, were published between the 1820s and the 1850s, and include some half dozen sets of fine and technically demanding variations. He also wrote polkas, waltzes, cotillions, and other dance music, and a few songs, some with chorus. He may have been related to RAYMOND MEETZ, another pianist, teacher, and composer active in New York.

WORKS

Selective list. All were published in New York, n.d., unless otherwise indicated; estimated dates of publication are given in brackets.

Pf: Spanish Waltz, variations ([1818–21]); Clermont Waltz, variations ([1820]); Petit pot pourri ([1821–3]), ed. in RRAM, ii (1977); The Vesper Hymn (Russian Air), variations ([1822]); The Frankfort Waltz ([1823–6]); A Schliefer ([1823–6]); The Temple to Friendship (Spanish Air) (n.p., n.d. [1823–6]); West Point March (1825); Alliance, waltz ([1835]); Tyrolean Waltz, variations ([1835]); Soffri amore, divertimento [after Rossini: L'italiana in Algeri] (Boston, n.d. [1830s])

Songs: The Primrose ([1818–26]); Have a care mon ami (J. H. Payne) ([1833]); Be kind to each other, song and chorus (1856)

Principal publishers: Dubois & Stodart, Geib

BIBLIOGRAPHY

R. J. Wolfe: *Secular Music in America, 1801–1825: a Bibliography* (New York, 1964)

B. A. Wolverton: *Keyboard Music and Musicians in the Colonies and United States of America before 1830* (diss., Indiana U., 1966)

H. Shanet: *Philharmonic: a History of New York's Orchestra* (Garden City, NY, 1975)

J. BUNKER CLARK

Metz, Theodore August (*b* Hanover, Germany, 14 March 1848; *d* New York, 12 Jan 1936). Composer and vaudeville and minstrel-show musician. He began his musical career as a bandmaster during the Franco-Prussian War. After coming to the USA (1879) he worked as a violinist first in saloons, then with theater and minstrel-show orchestras. He was orchestra leader for the McIntyre and Heath Minstrels when he composed *A Hot Time in the Old Town Tonight* (1886, repr. in *Favorite Songs of the Nineties*, ed. R. A. Fremont, 1973), the work for which he is remembered. Originally cast as a march for minstrel street parades, the piece generated little interest; a decade later, with added lyrics in black dialect, it was a hit on the musical stage. Its fame became international in 1898 when, during the Spanish-American War, it was used as a rallying song by Theodore Roosevelt's "Rough Riders" while charging up San Juan Hill; it consequently became known as a patriotic war song and – relieved of its ethnic connotations – is still heard today at political rallies.

None of Metz's other music achieved popularity. He maintained that he had composed *Ta-ra-ra Boom-de-ay!* (published in 1891 with Henry J. Sayers listed as composer) but, when challenged, admitted he had no "legal" claim to the song. He also asserted that Monroe Rosenfeld's *With all her faults I love her still* was stolen from him, but never pressed his claim. His most ambitious work, *Poketa*, an operetta on an Indian subject written in collaboration with Rosenfeld, was apparently neither produced nor published.

BIBLIOGRAPHY

I. Goldberg: *Tin Pan Alley: a Chronicle of the American Popular Music Racket* (New York, 1930/*R*1961 as *Tin Pan Alley: a Chronicle of American Popular Music*)

EDWARD A. BERLIN

Metzger, Alfred (*b* Landau, Germany, 5 May 1875; *d* San Francisco, CA, 29 June 1943). Publisher, editor, and critic. He studied music while attending preparatory schools in Germany, and came to the USA in 1889. After beginning his journalistic career in Santa Cruz, California, in 1893, he moved to San Francisco in 1898 and worked for various newspapers there as music critic until 1903. On 15 March 1903 he took over *La bohémienne*, a monthly music newsletter with only 125 subscribers, and renamed it the *Musical Review*. By November 1906 its circulation had risen to over 6000, and on 5 October 1907 it became a weekly under the masthead of the *Pacific Coast Musical Review*. Metzger was its indefatigable publisher, editor, principal writer, and business manager until the journal collapsed in November 1933 as a result of the Depression. In April 1935 Metzger replaced Ernst Bacon as music editor of the San Francisco *Argonaut* and remained until July 1940, when he was succeeded by William Tenison Deane.

The *Pacific Coast Musical Review* was aimed principally at professional and amateur musicians and music lovers in the San Francisco Bay area, and it maintained a conservative and stern editorial tone. It contained articles on prominent musical personalities, local talent, and current musical activities, accompanied by many photographs. Metzger vigorously supported many local causes through its pages, for example, Hertz and the reorganization of the San Francisco SO, the establishment of the California State Music Teachers' Association, the performance of opera, and the encouragement of local talent. On the other hand he protested vehemently against state licensing of music teachers, detested ragtime music, and dismissed the works of Schoenberg on the grounds that they were beyond audiences' judgment. The *Review* is now the primary documentary source for the history of music in San Francisco during its period. Metzger also edited the *Musical Blue Book of California: Season of 1924/25* (1924).

BIBLIOGRAPHY

An Anthology of Music Criticism, History of Music in San Francisco, vii (San Francisco, 1942/*R*1972), 235

JOHN A. EMERSON

Mexican-American music. *See* HISPANIC-AMERICAN MUSIC, §2 (i).

Meyer, Conrad (*b* Marburg, Germany; *d* Philadelphia, PA, 1881). Piano maker. He immigrated to the USA and settled in Baltimore in 1819, subsequently working for the piano maker Joseph Hisky. In 1829 he settled in Philadelphia where he started his own firm, and in 1833 exhibited one piano with "shifting or transposing action" and a square piano with an iron frame at the Franklin Institute. He later claimed that this square was made in 1832 and was unique in the USA for its single cast-iron frame. He did not patent it, and was in fact preceded by Alpheus Babcock, who patented a similar frame in 1825. But Meyer was often credited with this clever design, which permitted greater string tension and consequently a more resonant tone. Spillane (1890) wrote that Meyer made excellent pianos and that on Meyer's death the firm passed to his sons. The firm continued into at least the 1890s.

BIBLIOGRAPHY

D. Spillane: *History of the American Pianoforte* (New York, 1890/*R*1969)

The Crosby Brown Collection of Musical Instruments of all Nations: Catalogue of Keyboard Instruments (New York, 1903)

MARGARET CRANMER

Meyer, Ferdinand. Pseudonym of ARTHUR FOOTE.

Meyer, Leonard B(unce) (*b* New York, 12 Jan 1918). Musicologist and writer on aesthetics. He studied philosophy and music at Columbia University (MA in music, 1948) and the history of culture at the University of Chicago (PhD 1954). In 1946 he became a member of the department of music at the University of Chicago (professor, 1961–75) and in 1975 was appointed professor of music and the humanities at the University of Pennsylvania. He is best known for the theory of musical meaning expounded in *Emotion and Meaning in Music* (1956), which develops in psychological terms a dynamic view of musical significance, derived from Heinrich Schenker. He interprets musical forms and styles as historically evolving systems of expectations; the confirmations and frustrations of these expectations give rise to patterns of tensions aroused, sustained, and finally resolved, which musicians experience primarily as musical order and laymen primarily as a source of affect. Meyer's theory thus contrives a fusion of formal and expressive properties, which other aestheticians find it necessary to contrast. In *Music, the Arts, and Ideas* (1967) he reformulates his theory in terms of the mathematical theory of information and predicts a situation in which radically divergent musical arts, derived from different world-views, will co-exist without mingling in a pluralistic civilization. His book *Explaining Music* (1973) explores the principles of structure in tonal music, and its relation to criticism.

See also THEORY, §5(iii).

BIBLIOGRAPHY

R. S. Cox: *The Aesthetics of Leonard Meyer: Musical Formalism in the Twentieth Century* (diss., Ohio State U., 1983)

F. E. SPARSHOTT/R

Meyerowitz, Jan (*b* Breslau [now Wrocław, Poland], 23 April 1913). Composer of German birth. He studied at the Hochschule für Musik, Berlin, with Walther Gmeindl and Alexander Zemlinsky; in 1933 he left Germany and went to Rome, where he was a pupil of Respighi and Casella in composition and Bernardino Molinari in conducting at the Accademia di S. Cecilia. In 1946 he married the French singer Marguerite Fricker and immigrated to the USA; he became a citizen in 1951. A strong believer in the role of music in education, he held teaching positions at the opera department of the Berkshire Music Center (1948–51) and at Brooklyn (1954–61) and City (1962–80) colleges, CUNY. He has lectured frequently for German radio services and wrote a monograph on Schoenberg (1967). He has also appeared as a pianist and conductor, mainly in Italy. His awards include two Guggenheim fellowships, in 1956 and 1958, and an NEA grant (1977).

As a composer, Meyerowitz has adhered to tonality and attempted to build his own style on Classic-Romantic traditions. Occasionally his music betrays the influences of Schoenberg and Berg. Meyerowitz himself considers Italian neoclassicism the principal influence on his formative years, while the lyric expressionism of his operas testifies to 19th-century ideals (Meyerbeer, Verdi, Ponchielli). Without abandoning the European substance of his style, he has utilized typically American idioms in his operas on American topics. *The Barrier*, on a libretto by Langston Hughes dealing with the racial problems in the South, was performed on Broadway (1950) and revived by the Teatro San Carlo, Naples (1971).

WORKS

(only those composed after 1946)

Operas: Simoon (P. Stephens, after Strindberg), 1948; The Barrier (2, L. Hughes), 1950; Eastward in Eden (5 scenes, D. Gardner), 1951, renamed Emily Dickinson; Bad Boys in School (Meyerowitz, after J. Nestroy), 1953; Esther (3, L. Hughes), 1957; Port Town (1, L. Hughes), 1960; Godfather Death (3, P. Stephens), 1961; Winterballade (3, after G. Hauptmann), 1967

Vocal: The Glory around his Head (L. Hughes), B, chorus, orch, 1955; The Five Foolish Virgins (L. Hughes), chorus, orch, 1956; Stabat Mater, chorus, orch, 1957; Hebrew Service, T, Mez, chorus, org, 1962; I rabbini (Talmud), solo vv, chorus, orch, 1962; Missa Rachel plorans, S, T, chorus, org ad lib, 1962; other works, incl. 3 cantatas, 1954–6; choruses; songs and song cycles, incl. 6 Songs (A. von Platen), 1976

Orch/band: 3 Comments on War, band, 1957; Silesian Sym., orch, 1957; Esther Midrash, sym., orch, 1957; Flemish Ov., orch, 1959; Ob Conc., 1962; Fl Conc., 1963; 6 Pieces, orch, 1967; Sinfonia brevissima, orch, 1968; 7 Pieces, orch, 1974; 4 Romantic Pieces, band, 1978; other works

Inst: Homage to Hieronymus Bosch, 2 pf, 1945; Vc Sonata, 1946; Trio, fl, vc, pf, 1946; Ww Qnt, 1954; Str Qt, 1955; Pf Sonata, 1958; Vn Sonata, 1960; Fl Sonata, 1961; other works

Principal publishers: Associated, Broude

SIEGMUND LEVARIE

Mezzrow, Mezz [Mesirow, Milton] (*b* Chicago, IL, 9 Nov 1899; *d* Paris, France, 5 Aug 1972). Jazz clarinetist. In the early 1920s he played occasionally with the Austin High School Gang in Chicago. Later he worked as a freelance musician in New York, where in the 1930s he organized many recording sessions and founded one of the earliest interracial jazz bands (1937). During the early 1950s he moved to France and worked as an entrepreneur, organizing all-star touring bands.

The success that Mezzrow achieved with *Really the Blues*, the lurid story of his life, has placed undue importance on his clarinet playing, which was marred by a shrill tone, trivial ideas, and a limited sense of rhythm and harmony. His greatest contribution to jazz was doubtless the many worthwhile recording sessions he organized, particularly those with Sidney Bechet and the previously neglected trumpeter Tommy Ladnier. Mezzrow rarely played clarinet in public during the last years of his life, but often promulgated his candid evaluations of jazz performances; he remained a staunch devotee of black music in general and of Louis Armstrong's work in particular.

For illustration *see* BECHET, SIDNEY.

BIBLIOGRAPHY

M. Mezzrow and B. Wolfe: *Really the Blues* (New York, 1946)
H. Panassié: *Quand Mezzrow enregistre* (Paris, 1952)
——: "Mezz," *Bulletin du Hot Club de France* (Nov 1969), 3
R. Peronnet: "Swinging with Mezz," *Bulletin du Hot Club de France* (March 1970), 29

JOHN CHILTON

Miami. City in Florida (pop. 346,865; metropolitan area 1,625,781). A diffused urban area made up of a string of population centers, it is the musical center of the state, both in number and variety of performing groups. Although Florida is a southern state, it is culturally closer to the northeastern USA and to the Caribbean area than to the Deep South. In its art music it is an outpost of New York, while in its popular and folk music it is for the most part Latin American. Until the late 19th century it was a small town, isolated except by water travel. During the first decade of the 20th century, Flagler's coastal railroad connected Miami with the rest of the East Coast, and the town began to grow. Within 20 years, Miami was famous as a beach resort and as a refuge from winter cold.

1. Art music. 2. Popular and folk music.

1. ART MUSIC. There is a wealth of professional, semiprofessional, and amateur music-making in Miami, and a great emphasis on community involvement and performance. The 1983 edition of the *Florida Cultural Directory* lists 49 organizations in the greater Miami area involved with the performance, teaching, or promotion of art music and dance. There are four main academic institutions which have performing ensembles and departments of music: Barry College (founded 1940), Florida International University (1972), Miami-Dade Community College (1960), and the University of Miami (1925; *see also* LIBRARIES AND COLLECTIONS, §3, Florida, Coral Gables).

The city's regional professional symphony orchestra, the Florida PO, was founded in 1965 as the Greater Miami SO, changed its name in 1977, and disbanded in 1982; other full orchestras are the Miami Beach SO (1953) and the Washington Federal Senior Citizens Orchestra (1973). There are two chamber orchestras, the Greater Miami Chamber Orchestra and the Mann Chamber Music Ensemble. There are also three youth orchestras and several organizations devoted to the works of particular composers, for example the Chopin Foundation and the Pro Mozart Society. Opera companies include the Opera Guild of Greater Miami (founded 1941), the Florida Opera Repertory, and the Miami Civic Opera. There are two main choral groups, one of which, the Choral Cubana, shows the growing influence of the Latin community in Miami. There are also organizations which specialize in light classics, such as the Coral Gables Family Pop Concerts. Dance ensembles range in style from classical ballet to jazz-ballet and dance theater. The University of Miami has a separate dance department.

2. POPULAR AND FOLK MUSIC. Latin jazz is the most important form of popular music in Miami, with groups from the various islands and regions of the circum-Caribbean playing their countries' particular styles, for example Cuban salsa, Haitian *compas*, Jamaican reggae, Trinidadian calypso, Dominican merengue, and Colombian *currulao*. Bands change and exchange membership frequently; this fluidity, as well as the high rate of new composition, contributes to a dynamic, creative environment similar to that of jazz performers in Kansas City and Chicago earlier in the 20th century.

There are several festivals of folk and popular music in Miami: the Big Orange Festival, founded in 1980 and held every February, is primarily jazz-oriented; the Eighth Street Festival (1978; March) highlights Cuban music and the culture of Miami's "Little Havana" area; and Hispanic Heritage Week (1973; October) focuses on Latin arts of all kinds. Less evident to the public are the continuing folk traditions of many of these same Latin groups, as well as those of other ethnic groups including Mexican migrant workers, Afro-Americans, the Seminole and Miccosukee Indians (whose reservations are close to Miami), and the Jewish community. Afro-Caribbean cult religions such as Cuban *santeria* and Haitian *vodun* now have many adherents in Miami, their rituals involving drum music and songs to summon the "saints." In late July the Miccosukee Tribe of Indians of Florida holds an outdoor music festival on its lands along the Tamiami Trail just west of Miami. The sizable community of Afro-Americans in Miami continues its traditions of spirituals and gospel music. And, within the large population of Jews who have retired to Miami Beach, groups have formed to continue singing Yiddish folksongs learned as children in neighborhoods thousands of miles from Miami.

BIBLIOGRAPHY

Florida: a Guide to the Southernmost State (New York, 1939)

R. Smith: *Culture in Florida* (Tallahassee, 1963)

Florida Cultural Directory: a Guide to Florida's Cultural, Scientific and Historic Resources (Tallahassee, 1983)

M. L. Braz: *A History of the Greater Miami Opera, 1941–1983* (diss., Florida State U., 1984)

DORIS J. DYEN

Miami, Joe. Pseudonym of LOUIS W. BALLARD.

Michael, David Moritz (*b* Keinhausen, nr Erfurt, Germany, 21 Oct 1751; *d* Neuwied, Germany, 26 Feb 1827). German Moravian musician and composer. He was educated at the Erfurt Gymnasium, then in the mid-1770s joined the Hessian troops at Ülzen and Hameln as a musician. In 1781 he became a member of the Moravian Church, working at Barby and Niesky, Saxony, in clerical and teaching posts. He was sent to the USA in 1795 to teach at the Moravian boys' school in Nazareth, Pennsylvania, where he enlivened the music by instituting a weekly (later biweekly) series of concerts, the contents of which are recorded in *Verzeichniss derer Musicalien welche in Concert sind gemacht worden, Nazareth den 14t Octbr 1796 zum 30 Janry 1845* (in *PBMCA*). In 1804 he became superintendent of the unmarried brethren in Nazareth, and from 1808 occupied that post in the larger community of Bethlehem. In 1815 he retired from active church service and returned to Germany, where he settled in Neuwied.

Michael is reputed to have been the most versatile musician in the American Moravian communities. A fine violinist and clarinetist, he is also said to have been able to play two horns simultaneously. In 1811 he led the Bethlehem collegium musicum in the earliest known American performance of Haydn's *Creation*, and he participated in many other performances of symphonic, choral, and chamber music in Nazareth and Bethlehem during his 20-year residence. Michael's compositions consist of 14 woodwind *Parthien* and two "Water-music" suites (mostly for two clarinets, two horns, and two bassoons), 18 anthems for chorus or solo voice and instruments, and a setting of Psalm ciii for soloists, chorus, and orchestra. Most of his manuscripts are preserved in the Archives of the Moravian Church in Bethlehem, and a few in the Moravian Foundation at Winston-Salem, North Carolina. Michael's style may be characterized as pragmatically Classical. While he emphasized rhythmic and textural clarity and balance, he did not attempt to compose technically demanding or artistically imposing works.

See also MORAVIAN CHURCH, MUSIC OF THE.

BIBLIOGRAPHY

A. G. Rau and H. T. David: *A Catalogue of Music by American Moravians, 1742–1842* (Bethlehem, PA, 1938/*R*1970), 98

K. Kroeger: "David Moritz Michael's Psalm 103: an Early American Sacred Cantata," *Moravian Music Foundation Bulletin*, xxi/2 (1976), 10

B. J. Strauss: *A Register of Music Performed in Concert, Nazareth, Pennsylvania, from 1796–1845* (thesis, U. of Arizona, 1976)

D. A. Roberts: *The Sacred Vocal Music of David Moritz Michael: an American Moravian Composer* (diss., U. of Kentucky, 1978)

K. A. Hahn: *The Wind Ensemble Music of David Moritz Michael* (thesis, U. of Missouri, 1979)

KARL KROEGER

Michalsky, Donal (*b* Pasadena, CA, 13 July 1928; *d* Newport Beach, CA, 31 Dec 1975). Composer. He attended the University of Southern California, Los Angeles, where he studied music theory with Halsey Stevens and orchestration with Ingolf Dahl (PhD 1965). As a Fulbright scholar in Germany (1958) he was a pupil of Wolfgang Fortner in Freiberg. From 1960 until his death he was professor of composition at California State University, Fullerton. During these years he received many ASCAP awards. Michalsky's music is characterized by lyric lines, effective use of counterpoint, and generally conservative harmonies and phrasing. His forms paraphrase traditional models.

WORKS

(all unpubd)

Der arme Heinrich (opera), inc., lost

Large ens: Concertino, trbn, band, 1953; Little Sym., band, 1959; Wheels of Time (Sym. no. 1), chorus, orch, 1967; Sinfonia concertante (Sym. no.2), cl, pf, orch, 1969; Sym. no.3, orch, 1975; other band works

Chamber: Qnt, 2 tpt, 2 cl, pf, 1951; Divertimento, 2 cl, b cl, 1952; 6 Pieces, chamber orch, 1956; Sonata, 2 pf, 1957; Partita, ob d'amore, str trio, str, 1958; Vc Sonata, 1958; Morning Music, chamber ens, 1959; Sonata concertante, pf, 1961; Trio Concertino, fl, ob, hn, 1961; Variations, cl, pf, 1962; Fantasia alla marcia, brass qt, 1963; Partita piccola, fl, pf, 1964; Allegretto, cl, str, 1964; Song Suite, pf, 1970; Cantata memoriam, high v, 12 insts, 1971; 3 × 4, sax qt, 1972; songs

DAVID COPE

Michigan, University of. State-supported university established in Ann Arbor in 1817. The Ann Arbor School of Music, founded in 1880 and from 1892 called the University School of Music, was at first administered by the University Musical Society and directed by Calvin B. Cady; it became an integral part of the university in 1940. In the 1980s the school had about 850 students and a faculty of 110; the National Music Camp at Interlochen, Michigan (founded 1928; affiliated with the university from 1941), enrolls about 200 college-level students each summer. Among the degrees offered by the school are the BM, BA, MM, and MA in music; the DMA in composition, performance, and conducting; and the PhD in musicology, theory, and music education. The school has a wide range of facilities, including the Stearns Collection of Musical Instruments (established 1899), the Charles Baird Carillon (1935), an electronic studio (1965), and a Javanese gamelan (1966). The resident Stanley Quartet (founded in 1949 and named for Albert A. Stanley) has commissioned works from many American composers. The university's orchestra and chamber choir have toured successfully abroad as well as in the USA, as has its symphony band (notably a tour of the USSR in 1961, under the sponsorship of the US State Department); its marching band is one of the most famous in the USA. The music library contains the Stellfeld Collection (rich in 18th-century opera), the Eva Jessye Afro-American Music Collection, and much American sheet music; the Clements Library includes many musical items in its collection of early Americana, notably the papers of Andrew Law (*see* LIBRARIES AND COLLECTIONS, §3). In 1951 the NATIONAL ASSOCIATION OF COLLEGE WIND AND PERCUSSION INSTRUCTORS was founded at the university.

In 1894 the University Musical Society founded the annual Ann Arbor May Festival, in which important composers, international soloists, the University Choral Union, and such leading orchestras as the Boston Festival Orchestra conducted by Emil Mollenhauer, the Chicago SO under Frederick Stock, the Philadelphia Orchestra under Stokowski, Ormandy, and Muti, and the Pittsburgh SO have performed.

BIBLIOGRAPHY

"The University Musical Society and the School of Music," *The University of Michigan: an Encyclopedic Survey* (Ann Arbor, MI, 1953), iii, 1121

L. Cuyler, G. Sutherland, and H. David: "The University of Michigan's Purchase of the Stellfeld Music Library," *Notes*, xii (1954–5), 41

S. L. Schrader: *A History of the University Musical Society . . . 1879–1892* (diss., U. of Michigan, 1968)

100 Years of Music at Michigan 1880–1980 (Ann Arbor, MI, 1979)

The University Musical Society of the University of Michigan Celebrates 100 Years, 1879–1979 (Ann Arbor, MI, 1980)

BRUCE CARR, RITA H. MEAD

Michigan State University. State-supported university (founded 1855) in East Lansing. Its department of music, in the college of arts and letters, was established in 1927, though the university was offering music instruction by 1896. By the mid-1980s it had 350 undergraduate and 150 graduate students, and 60 instructors. BA, BM, MA, MM, DMA, and PhD degrees are offered in performance, theory, composition, music education, piano technology, and musicology, and the university was the first in the USA to introduce a music therapy program. A national symposium of new music for wind instruments is held annually at the university.

WILLIAM McCLELLAN

Micmac. Indian tribe of the WABANAKI confederacy.

Microtonal tunings. *See* TUNING SYSTEMS.

Midler, Bette (*b* Paterson, NJ, 1 Dec 1945). Singer, actress, and comedian. She studied drama in Honolulu before moving to New York, where she sang in clubs, performed in off-Broadway shows, and spent three years as a member of the cast of *Fiddler on the Roof*. In 1970 she devised a cabaret show which she performed with great success at the Continental Baths, a "gay" men's club. Her stage persona, "the Divine Miss M," was a synthesis of several elements of show business, embracing Sophie Tucker's off-color humor, Ethel Merman's brassy theatrical shout, Barbra Streisand's dramatic histrionics, and Janis Joplin's rock-and-roll earthiness. Her repertory of swing, blues, rock-and-roll, and vaudeville material was equally eclectic. She began to appear on television in 1972 and her first album, *The Divine Miss M*, gained a gold record the following year. She made successful nationwide tours in 1973 and 1975, but her later recordings failed commercially. In 1979 she starred in the film *The Rose* (loosely based on the life of Janis Joplin), which earned her an Academy Award nomination; the title song secured a platinum record. Although her singing was technically unreliable, her wide-ranging talents and emotional volatility made Midler one of the most exceptional entertainers to emerge from the cabaret revival in New York in the early 1970s; her sophisticated stage personality is inadequately captured on her recordings.

Bette Midler in the film "The Rose" (1979)

BIBLIOGRAPHY

"Midler, Bette," *CBY 1973*

STEPHEN HOLDEN

Miessner, W(illiam) Otto (*b* Huntingburg, IN, 26 May 1880; *d* Connersville, IN, 27 May 1967). Music educator. He completed a diploma course at the Cincinnati College of Music (1900), where he studied public school music and conducting. He then taught in Indiana public schools for ten years, organizing a high school band in Connersville in 1907, which was one of the first in the USA. In 1909 he traveled to Berlin to study with Alexander Heinemann, Max Reger, Engelbert Humperdinck, and Edgar Stillman Kelley. After teaching in Oak Park, Illinois (1910–14), he became chairman of the music department at the Wisconsin State Teachers College in Milwaukee (1914–22), serving concurrently on the faculty of the American Institute of Normal Methods (1911–24); he later became chairman of the music education department at the University of Kansas (1936–45), where he initiated graduate study in music education. Miessner was president of the Music Supervisors National Conference (1923–4) and a member of the editorial staff of Silver, Burdett & Co., 1911–54. From 1918 to 1928 he headed a piano company which manufactured instruments specifically for school use. He also wrote several books and articles on music education and a number of teaching methods.

BIBLIOGRAPHY

J. W. Beattie: "Meet Mister Miessner," *MEJ*, xlii/3 (1956), 24

S. D. Miller: *W. Otto Miessner and His Contributions to Music in American Schools*, (diss., U. of Michigan, 1962)
Obituary, *MEJ*, liv/1 (1967), 110
S. D. Miller: "Visionary of What Might be: the Story of W. Otto Miessner," *Bulletin of Historical Research in Music Education*, ii/2 (1981), 21

GEORGE N. HELLER

Migenes-Johnson, Julia (*b* New York, ?1945). Soprano. Of Puerto Rican, Irish, and Greek descent, she appeared as a small child in a production of Puccini's *Madama Butterfly*. While she was attending the High School of Music and Art in New York she was selected by Bernstein to perform in a televised concert version of Copland's *The Second Hurricane*. After graduating she sang in Broadway productions of *West Side Story* and *Fiddler on the Roof* and with the New York City Opera in Menotti's *The Saint of Bleecker Street*, and also appeared with regional opera companies. In the early 1970s Migenes-Johnson went to Europe. In Vienna she took further singing lessons and became a popular performer with the Vienna Volksoper and in Cologne studied with Gisela Ultmann, who exerted an important influence on her vocal technique and dramatic style. While in Germany she often appeared on television and won several awards. She made her American operatic début in 1978 as Musetta in Puccini's *La bohème* with the San Francisco Opera; her first appearance with the Metropolitan Opera was the following year as Jenny in Weill's *The Rise and Fall of the City of Mahagonny*. In 1984 she gained the attention of a wide public with her performance of the title role in Francesco Rosi's cinematic version of Bizet's *Carmen*. Her most successful stage role has been as Berg's Lulu in the Metropolitan Opera production of 1985, for which both her singing and acting were highly praised.

BIBLIOGRAPHY

F. Gannon: "Carmen Chameleon: a Profile of Julia Migenes-Johnson," *Saturday Review*, xii/4 (1985), 59

KATHLEEN HAEFLIGER

Mighty Clouds of Joy. Male gospel quartet formed in 1959 by WILLIE JOE LIGON and others.

Mignon, Charlotte. *See* CRABTREE, LOTTA.

Mikhashoff [Mychasiw; MacKay], **Yvar Emilian** (*b* Troy, NY, 8 March 1941). Pianist and composer. He was educated at the Eastman School, the Juilliard School, the University of Houston, and the University of Texas, Austin (DMA 1973). His teachers have included Armand Basile, Adele Marcus, and Beveridge Webster. In 1968 he received a Fulbright scholarship to study composition with Nadia Boulanger in France, and he has also won two New York State research fellowships (1974, 1978) and an American-Scandinavian Foundation grant (1982). In 1973 he joined the faculty of SUNY, Buffalo, where he is an associate professor.

Mikhashoff commands an extensive repertory of contemporary piano music, much of which he has recorded, and tours widely in the USA and in Europe, where he has established a reputation as an advocate of 19th- and 20th-century American music. For the 1982 Holland Festival Mikhashoff produced "Revolution and Revelation," a series of nine programs offering a survey of American music from the colonial era to the present. And for the Almeida International Festival of Contemporary Music and Performance (London, June 1985) he organized "At the Tomb of Charles Ives," 20 programs "in celebration of American experimental music, 1905–1985." He has commissioned piano works from American composers including Brant, Cage, Foss, and Hiller and from Per Nørgård, Sylvano Bussotti, and other prominent Europeans. To commemorate the sesquicentennial of the city of Buffalo in 1982 he commissioned 15 composers to write piano works, and in 1983 he asked 100 composers from 30 countries to contribute to a collection of tangos. His own music has been most influenced by Debussy, but from 1974 it has also reflected folk music, especially that of central Europe and the American Indians. He has made many chamber-music transcriptions of works by Copland, Georges Auric, Thomson, Krenek, and Nancarrow.

WORKS
(selective list)

Vocal: Canciones de Lorca, S, pf, 1967; Nocturne (G. Trakl), 1v, str qt, harp, 1969, rev. 1973; Traceries (W. C. Williams), 1v, fl, 1970; In Memoriam Igor Stravinsky (Marcus Aurelius), 1v, fl, cl, vc, 1971; 4 Figures of a Drowned Maiden (Shakespeare, Rimbaud, Blok, Rilke), S, speaker, chamber ens, 1972; Long Eyes of Earth, pf, 1975, rev. 1981; Improvisations on the Last Words of Chief Seattle, speaker, perc, mime-dancer, syllabist, 1976

Inst: Dances for Davia I, fl, pf, 1958, II, fl, pf, 1979; Conc. no. 1, pf, wind, perc, 1965; Conc., va, orch, 1969; Nocturne, vc, pf, 1977; HWALC, tape [whale songs], vc, 1978; I Chose a Hyacinth, pf, 1979; Small Knocking Woods, pf, 1979; Light from a Distant Garden, str qt, 1983; Grand Bowery Tango, fl, ens, 1985; Night Dances, str trio, 1985

Principal publishers: Boosey & Hawkes, Southern

BIBLIOGRAPHY

D. Gillespie: "The Holland Festival: Revolution and Revelation," *HiFi/MusAm*, xxxii/12 (1982), 37
H. Trotter: "Debuts and Reappearances: Buffalo," *HiFi/MusAm*, xxxiii/7 (1983), 22

DON C. GILLESPIE

Milanov [Kunc Milanov Ilić], **Zinka** (*b* Zagreb [now in Yugoslavia], 17 May 1906). Yugoslav soprano. She used her maiden name, Kunc, until her first marriage, in 1937, to Pedrag Milanov, a Yugoslav actor. After studying at the Zagreb Academy of Music, and with Milka Ternina, Maria Kostrenčić, and Fernando Carpi, she made her operatic début as Verdi's Leonora at Ljubljana in 1927. From 1928 to 1935 she was the leading soprano at the Zagreb Opera, where she gave more than 350 performances in such roles as Sieglinde, the Marschallin, Rachel (Meyerbeer's *La juive*), and Minnie (Puccini's *La fanciulla del West*), all sung in Serbo-Croat. After appearances in Prague and at the 1937 Salzburg Festival, she began her long association with the Metropolitan Opera on 17 December 1937 as Leonora. Appearing every season (except for 1941–2 and 1947–50) until her farewell performance as Madeleine de Coigny (in Umberto Giordano's *Andrea Chenier*) on 13 April 1966, she gave 424 performances in 14 works – notably as the principal Verdi and Puccini heroines, but also as Norma, Donna Anna in Bruno Walter's revival of *Don Giovanni* (1941), and in the title role of *La Gioconda*. She also appeared in Buenos Aires, San Francisco, and Chicago, but her European performances after 1939 were few. In 1977 she joined the faculty of the Curtis Institute.

Milanov's voice was one of translucent beauty as well as great power, and she was able to spin out the most exquisite *pianissimo* phrases with little or no apparent effort. Even at the peak of her career, however, she was not a perfect vocalist, and an impeccable performance on one evening could be followed by an erratic one on the next. A certain unsteadiness of tone, noticeable in some of her recordings, at times marred her performances, while in the theater, uncertainties of pitch were not unknown. In the

1940s and 1950s, however, she had few equals in Verdi roles, as her recording of *Il trovatore* demonstrates. She was a handsome and even stately figure on the stage, relying mostly on her voice to achieve dramatic effects; by postwar standards her acting was old-fashioned.

BIBLIOGRAPHY

L. Riemens: "Milanov, Zinka," *Le grandi voci*, ed. R. Celletti (Rome, 1964) [with opera discography by S. Smolian]

H. Rosenthal: "Zinka Milanov," *Great Singers of Today* (London, 1966), 114

E. K. Einstein: "Zinka Milanov Discography," *Grand Baton*, v/2 (1968), 7

R. Jacobson: "The Most Beautiful Voice in the World," *Opera News*, xli/22 (1977), 11

L. Rasponi: "The Great Dramatics," *The Last Prima Donnas* (New York, 1982), 216

HAROLD ROSENTHAL/R

Milburn, Ellsworth (*b* Greensburg, PA, 6 Feb 1938). Composer. He attended UCLA (1959–62), where he studied with Travis and Lazarof, and was a pupil of Milhaud at Mills College (1966–8); his other teachers included Scott Huston and Paul Cooper. From 1970 to 1975 he taught at the Cincinnati College-Conservatory; he then joined the faculty of Rice University, Houston. His honors include the Crothers Fellowship, Merritt Prize, Morse Fellowship, and an NEA grant. Characteristic of Milburn's dramatic style are thinly veiled, soloistic textures and *subito* dynamic interruptions. He also contrasts pointillism with more lyric phrases, and subtle timbral nuances often shade otherwise conventionally conceived motifs and passages. His forms flow in a stream-of-consciousness manner rather than strictly paraphrasing traditional models.

WORKS

5 Inventions, 2 fl, 1965; Massacre of the Innocents (Auden), chorus, 1965; Conc., pf, chamber orch, 1967; Str Trio, 1968; Soli nos. 1–4, chamber ens, 1968–72; Str Qnt, 1969; 2 Love Songs (E. St. V. Millay), high v, 1970; Voussoirs, orch, 1970; Lament, harp, 1972; Vn Sonata, 1972; Gesualdo (opera), 1973; Spiritus mundi, high v, 5 insts, 1974

DAVID COPE

Miley, Bubber [James Wesley] (*b* Aiken, SC, ?19 ?Jan 1903; *d* New York, ?24 May 1932). Jazz trumpeter. He moved to New York at the age of six, and studied trombone before learning cornet. He was active professionally from 1920 with Willie Gant, Mamie Smith, and others, and in 1923 joined Elmer Snowden's Washingtonians, who soon afterwards came under the leadership of Duke Ellington. Miley remained with Ellington until early 1929, and then worked with Noble Sissle (touring to Paris in 1929), Zutty Singleton, and others. In the last months of his life he led his own orchestra.

Miley's melodic and rhythmic styles were influenced by King Oliver and the trumpeter Johnny Dunn. But he is noted for having begun the practice of using a "wah-wah" tone modifier on an already muted trumpet, thus combining two techniques employed separately by Oliver. His "growl" effect was adopted by Sidney de Paris, Cootie Williams, Ray Nance, and many other jazz trumpeters, and formed an important element of Ellington's style. He was the most impressive of the early Ellington soloists, and collaborated on or strongly influenced many of Ellington's early compositions; the better sections of *Black and Tan Fantasy*, *East St. Louis Toodle-oo*, and *Doin' the Voom-voom* are thought to be Miley's work.

RECORDINGS

(selective list; all with Duke Ellington)

Choo-Choo (1924, Blu-Disc T-1002); Animal Crackers (1926, Gennet 3342); East St. Louis Toodle-oo (1926, Voc. 1064); Immigration Blues (1926, Voc. 1077); Black and Tan Fantasy (1927, Bruns. 3526); Creole Love Call (1927, Vic. 21137); Jubilee Stomp (1928, Vic. 21580); The Mooche (1928, Bruns. 4122)

BIBLIOGRAPHY

SouthernB

R. Dodge: "Harpsichords and Jazz Trumpets," *Frontiers of Jazz*, ed. R. de Toledano (New York, 1947), 13

G. Schuller: *Early Jazz: its Roots and Musical Development* (New York, 1968), 320

E. K. Ellington: *Music is my Mistress* (Garden City, NY, 1973/*R*1976), 106

J. R. TAYLOR

Milhaud, Darius (*b* Aix-en-Provence, France, 4 Sept 1892; *d* Geneva, Switzerland, 22 June 1974). French composer. He entered the Paris Conservatoire in 1905 as a violinist but soon began to concentrate on composing and had early successes with theater music (*Protée*, 1913–19; *La brebis égarée*, 1910–15; *Les choëphores*, 1915). His first taste of the Americas was in 1916, when he went to Rio de Janeiro as secretary to Paul Claudel, who had been appointed French minister to Brazil. Milhaud spent almost two years there, and his absorption of its atmosphere and music is reflected in the ballet *L'homme et son désir* (1918) and two sets of dances for piano, *Saudades do Brasil* (1920–21).

Back in Paris in 1918, Milhaud was soon involved in the circle of writers, artists, and composers around Jean Cocteau and was named one of the unofficial group of composers called Les Six. On a visit to London in 1920 he first heard American jazz, and was immediately attracted to that and other American popular music. During a tour of the USA in 1922, he had firsthand experience of authentic black jazz in Harlem. Ragtime and jazz are obviously in the background of such works as *Trois rag caprices* (1922), for piano, and the ballet *La création du monde* (1923), generally conceded to be one of Milhaud's masterpieces.

Despite his extensive travels in the 1920s and 1930s, Milhaud produced a huge number of compositions of all kinds. In 1940 the fall of France to Nazi Germany led Milhaud, who was Jewish, to emigrate; he came with his wife Madeleine and son Daniel to the USA. Offered positions in the East, he chose instead, for reasons of health (he suffered from rheumatoid arthritis and was eventually confined to a wheelchair) and perhaps of temperament, to accept a teaching post at Mills College, Oakland, California, where he remained on the full-time faculty until 1947. In 1949 he was also among the founders of the Aspen Music Festival, where he taught regularly during summers, and during those years was composer-in-residence at the Music Academy of the West, Santa Barbara, California, and at the Berkshire Music Center (1948). Even after his postwar repatriation he continued to return to the USA every other year to teach at Mills College and elsewhere until he retired permanently in 1971.

Ever prolific, Milhaud produced many works during his American years. Few reveal specific musical influences of the USA, although a number are related in subject matter to the American scene. The Tenth String Quartet (1940) was written for the Coolidge Festival, Library of Congress; in 1941 Milhaud himself was soloist in the première of his Second Piano Concerto with the Chicago SO. He received commissions from the Koussevitzky Foundation, the New York PO, the Cleveland Orchestra, and the League of Composers–ISCM; the titles of a number of orchestral works bear witness to still others: *Aspen Serenade* (1957), *Music for Boston* (1965), *Music for Indiana* (1966), *Music for New Orleans* (1966), *Music for San Francisco* (1971). This last, a unique concerto for orchestra with audience participation including clapping, stamping, and humming, was written on commission from the San Francisco SO's Summer Youth Workshop and reveals an undiminished flexibility of approach to contemporary circumstances. Similarly, with *Meurtre d'un grand chef d'état* (1963), given its première by the Oakland SO within a week of the assassination of President Kennedy, he responded with immediacy to a calamitous American event.

Milhaud's influence on music in the USA was primarily as a teacher of composers. Among his many American pupils were William Bolcom, Dave and Howard Brubeck, Pauline Oliveros, Steve Reich, Leland Smith, William O. Smith, and Morton Subotnick.

WORKS

(only those composed from 1940)

DRAMATIC

Bolivar (opera, 3, M. Milhaud, J. Supervielle), op.236, 1943; Paris, Opéra, 1950

David (opera, 5, Lunel), op.320, 1952; Jerusalem, 1954

Fiesta (opera, 1, Vian), op.370, 1958; Berlin, Staatsoper, 1958

La mère coupable (opera, 3, M. Milhaud, after Beaumarchais), op.412, 1964; Geneva, 1965

Saint Louis, roi de France (opera-oratorio, 2 parts, Claudel, M. Doublier), op.434, 1970; Radio Audizioni Italiane, 1972

Ballets: Moïse (Opus americanum no.2), op.219, 1940; Jeux de printemps, op.243, 1944; Les cloches (after Poe), op.259, 1945; 'Adame Miroir (Genet), op.283, 1948; La cueillette des citrons, op.298, 1949–50; Vendanges (Rothschild), op.317, 1952; La rose des vents (Vidalie), op.367, 1957; La branche des oiseaux (Chamson), op.374, 1958–9

Incidental music: Un petit ange de rien du tout (Puget), op.215, 1940; L'annonce faite à Marie (Claudel), op.231, 1942; Lidoire (Courteline), op.264, 1946; Shéhérazade (Supervielle), op.285, 1948; Le conte d'hiver (Shakespeare), op.306, 1950; Christophe Colomb (Claudel) [new incidental music for stage play with only 1 reference to opera of 1930], op.318, 1952; Saül (Gide), op.334, 1954; Protée (Claudel), op.341, 1955; Juanito (Humblot), op.349, 1955; Mother Courage (Brecht), op.379, 1959; Judith (Giraudoux), op.392, 1961; Jérusalem à Carpentras (Lunel), op.419, 1966; Tobie et Sarah (Claudel), 1968

Film scores: The Private Affairs of Bel Ami (dir. Lewin, after Maupassant), op.272, 1946; Dreams that Money can Buy, Man Ray sequence only, op.273, 1947; Gauguin (dir. Resnais), op.299, 1950; La vie commence demain (dir. N. Vedres), op.304, 1950; Ils étaient tous des volontaires, op.336, 1954; Celle qui n'était plus (Histoire d'une folle) (dir. Gerard, Colpi), op.364, 1957; Péron et Evita, op.372, 1958; Burma Road, op.375, 1959

Radio scores, unpubd: Le grand testament (N. Franck), op.282, 1948; La fin du monde (Cendrars), op.297, 1949; Le repos du septième jour (Claudel), op.301, 1950; Samaël (Spire), op.321, 1953; Le dibbouk (Anski), op.329, 1953; Etude poétique (C. Roy), op.333, 1954

Miscellanea: Vézelay, la colline éternelle (son et lumière, M. Druon), op.423, 1967

ORCHESTRAL

Indicatif et marche pour les bons d'armement, op.212, 1940; Introduction et allegro [after Couperin: La sultane], op.220, 1940; Mills Fanfare, str, op.224, 1941; Pf Conc. no.2, op.225, 1941; 2 Pf Conc., op.228, 1941; Cl Conc., op.230, 1941; Suite in 3 Parts, vn/reed org, orch, op.234, 1942; Fanfare de la liberté, op.235, 1942; Sym. no.2, op.247, 1944; Vc Conc. no.2, op.255, 1945; 2 marches, op.260, 1945–6; Vn Conc. no.2, op.263, 1946; 7 danses sur des airs palestiniens, op.267, 1946–7; Pf Conc. no.3, op.270, 1946; Conc., mar, vib, orch, op.278, 1947

Suite concertante, pf, orch, op.278a [after op.278], 1952; Sym. no.4, op.281, 1947; Kentuckiana, op.287, 1948, arr. 2 pf; Pf Conc. no.4, op.295, 1949; Suite, 2 pf, orch, op.300, 1950; Concertino d'automne, 2 pf, 8 insts, op.309, 1950; Concertino d'été, va, chamber orch, op.311, 1950; Sym. no.5, op.322, 1953; Harp Conc., op.323, 1953; Concertino d'hiver, trbn, str, op.327, 1953; Suite campagnarde, op.329, 1953; Ouverture méditerranéenne, op.330, 1953; Suite cisalpine, vc, orch, op.332, 1954; Va Conc. no.2, op.340, 1954–5; Pensée amicale, str, op.342, 1955

Sym. no.6, op.343, 1955; Sym. no.7, op.344, 1955; Pf Conc. no.5, op.346, 1955; Les charmes de la vie (Hommage à Watteau), op.360, 1957; Aspen Serenade, op.361, 1957; Sym. no.8 "Rhodanienne," op.362, 1957; Symphoniette, str, op.363, 1957; Ob Conc., op.365, 1957; Vn Conc. no.3 (Concert royal), op.373, 1958; Sym. no.9, op.380, 1959; Sym. no.10, op.382, 1960; Sym. no.11 "Romantique," op.384, 1960; Les funérailles de Phocion (Hommage à Poussin), op.385, 1960; Aubade, op.387, 1960; Sym. no.12 "Rurale," op.390, 1961; Conc., 2 pf, 4 perc, op.394, 1961; Ouverture philharmonique, op.397, 1962

A Frenchman in New York, op.399, 1962; Meurtre d'un grand chef d'état, op.405, 1963; Ode pour les morts des guerres, op.406, 1963; Hpd Conc., op.407, 1964; Music for Boston, op.414, 1965; Music for Prague, op.415, 1965; Elégie pour Pierre, va, perc, op.416, 1965; Music for Indiana, op.418, 1966; Music for Lisbon, op.420, 1966; Music for New Orleans, op.422, 1966; Promenade concert, op.424, 1967; Musique pour l'univers claudélien, op.427, 1968; Music for Graz, op.429, 1968-9; Suite, G, op.431, 1969; Music for Ars Nova, op.432, 1969; Music for San Francisco, op.436, 1971; Ode pour Jérusalem, op.440, 1972

Brass band: Suite française, op.248, 1944, also for orch, addl movts for ballet, op.254, 1945; West Point Suite, op.313, 1951; Fanfare, 4 hn, 3 tpt, 3 trbn, tuba, op.396, 1962; Fanfare, 2 tpt, trbn, op.400, 1962; Musique de théâtre [after incidental music Saül], op.334b, 1954–70

Also orchestrations of pf works

CHORAL

Cantate de la guerre (Claudel), unacc., op.213, 1940; Borechou schema Israël, 1v, chorus, org, op.239, 1944; Prière pour les morts, 1v, chorus ad lib, org, op.250, 1945; Sym. no.3 (Te Deum), chorus, orch, op.271, 1946; Service sacré, Bar, reciter, chorus, orch/org, op.279, 1947; L'choh dodi, 1v, chorus, org, op.290, 1948; Naissance de Vénus (Supervielle), cantata, unacc., op.292, 1949; Barba Garibo (trad., Lunel), chorus, orch, op.298, 1949–50; Cantate des proverbes, female vv, harp, ob, vc, op.310, 1950

Les miracles de la foi (Bible), cantata, T, chorus, orch, op.314, 1951; Le château de feu (Cassou), cantata, chorus, orch, op.338, 1954; Trois psaumes de David, unacc., op.339, 1954; Deux poèmes de Louise de Vilmorin, chorus/vocal qt, op.347, 1955; Le mariage de la feuille et du cliché (Gerard), solo vv, chorus, orch, tape, op.357, 1956; La tragédie humaine (d'Aubigné), chorus, orch, op.369, 1958; Huit poèmes de Jorge Guillen, unacc., op.371, 1958; Cantate de la croix de charité (Masson), solo vv, chorus, children's vv, orch, op.381, 1959–60; Cantate sur des textes de Chaucer, chorus, orch, op.386, 1960

Cantate de l'initiation (Bar Mitzvah Israël), chorus, orch, op.388, 1960; Traversée (Verlaine), unacc., op.393, 1961; Invocation à l'ange Raphaël (Claudel), female vv (2 groups), op.395, 1962; Caroles (Charles d'Orléans), cantata, 4 solo groups, chorus, op.402, 1963

Pacem in terris (Pope John XXIII), choral sym., Bar, chorus, orch, op.404, 1963; Cantate de Job, 1v, chorus, org, op.413, 1965; Promesse de Dieu (Bible), unacc., op.438, 1971–2; Les momies d'Egypte (Regnard), choral comedy, unacc., op.439, 1972; Ani maamin, un chant perdu et retrouvé (Elie Wiesel), cantata, S, 4 reciters, chorus, orch, op.441, 1972

SOLO VOCAL

Couronne de gloire (Gabirol, Lunel), 1v, pf/(str qt, fl, tpt), op.211, 1940; 4 chansons de Ronsard, 1v, pf/orch, op.223, 1940; 5 prières, 1v, org, op.231c, 1942; Caïn et Abel, reciter, orch, op.241, 1944; Le jeu de Robin et de Marion (Adam de la Halle), 1v, 5 insts, 1948; Fontaines et sources (Jammes), 1v, pf/orch, op.352, 1956

Suite de quatrains (Jammes), reciter, 8 insts, op.398, 1962; Suite de sonnets (du Bellay, Jodelle, de Magny, Jamin), cantata, vocal qt, 6 insts, op.401, 1963; Adieu (Rimbaud), cantata, 1v, fl, va, harp, op.410, 1964; Adam (Cocteau), S, 2 T, 2 Bar, op.411, 1964; Hommage à Comenius (Comenius), cantata, S, Bar, orch, op.421, 1966; Cantate de psaumes (trans. Claudel), Bar, orch, op.425, 1967

SONGS

Rêves, op.233, 1942; Le voyage d'été (Paliard), op.216, 1946; Chants de misère (Paliard), op.265, 1946; 6 sonnets composés au secret (Cassou), op.266, 1946; 3 poèmes (Supervielle), op.276, 1947; Petites légendes (Carême), op.319, 1952; Tristesse (Jammes), op.355, 1956

Numerous single songs

CHAMBER

Str qts: no.10, op.218, 1940; no.11, op.232, 1942; no.12, op.252, 1945; no.13, op.268, 1946; nos.14–15, op.291 [playable separately or together as octet], 1948–9; no.16, op.303, 1950; no.17, op.307, 1950; no.18, op.308, 1950

Other works: Sonatine à 3, str trio, op.221b, 1940; Str Trio, op.274, 1947; L'apothéose de Molière, suite, hpd, fl, ob, cl, bn, str, op.286, 1948; Les rêves de Jacob, dance suite, ob, str trio, db, op.294, 1949; Divertissement [after film score Gauguin], wind qnt, op.299b, 1958; Qnt no.1, pf qnt, op.312; Qnt no.2, str qt, db, op.316, 1952; Qnt no.3, va, str qt, op.325, 1953; Qnt no.4, vc, str qt, op.350, 1956; Str Sextet, 2 vn, 2 va, 2 vc, op.368, 1958; Concert de chambre, pf, wind qnt, str qnt, op.389, 1961; Str Septet,

2 vn, 2 va, 2 vc, db, op.408, 1964; Pf Qt, op.417, 1966; Pf Trio, op.428, 1968; Stanford Serenade, chamber orch, op.430, 1969; Hommage à Igor Stravinsky, str qt, op.435, 1971

INSTRUMENTAL

Sonatina, 2 vn, op.221, 1940; Sonatina, vn, va, op.226, 1941; 4 visages, va, pf, op.238, 1943; Va Sonata no.1, op.240, 1944; Va Sonata no.2, op.244, 1944; Elégie, va, pf, op.251, 1945; Danses de Jacaremirim, vn, pf, op.256, 1945; Sonata, vn, hpd, op.257, 1945; Duo, 2 vn, op.258, 1945; Farandoleurs, vn, pf, op.262, 1946; Sonatina, vn, vc, op.324, 1953; Sonatina, ob, pf, op.337, 1954; Duo concertante, cl, pf, op.351, 1956; Ségoviana, gui, op.366, 1957; Vc Sonata, op.377, 1959; Va Sonatina, op.378, 1959; Sonatina pastorale, vn, op.383, 1960; Sonata, harp, op.437, 1971

KEYBOARD

Pf: 4 esquisses, op.227, 1941, arr. orch/wind qnt; La libertadora, pf/2 pf, op.236, 1943; La muse menagère, op.245, 1945; Une journée, op.269, 1946; L'enfant aimé, op.289, 1948; Sonata no.2, op.293, 1949; Candélabre à sept branches, op.315, 1951; Hymne de glorification, op.331, 1953–4; La couronne de Marguerite, op.353, 1956, orchd; Sonatina, op.354, 1956; Le globetrotter, op.358, 1956, orchd

2 pf: Songes, op.237, 1943; Le bal martiniquais, op.249, 1944, orchd; Carnaval à la Nouvelle-Orléans, op.275, 1947; 6 danses en 3 mouvements, op.433, 1969–70

4 pf: Paris, op.284, 1948, orchd

Org: Pastorale, op.229, 1941; 9 Preludes, op.231b [after incidental music L'annonce faite à Marie, op.231], 1942; Petite suite, op.348, 1955

CHILDREN'S WORKS

Sornettes (Mistral), 2vv, op.214, 1940; Cours de solfège, 1v, pf, op.217, 1940; Touches noires, touches blanches, pf, op.222, 1941; Accueil amical, pf, op.326, 1944–7; Service pour la veille du sabbat, vv, org, op.345, 1955

BIBLIOGRAPHY

P. Collaer: *Darius Milhaud* (Antwerp and Paris, 1948)
G. Beck: *Darius Milhaud* (Paris, 1949)
"Milhaud, Darius," *CBY 1961*
J. Roy: *Darius Milhaud* (Paris, 1968)
R. Crichton: Obituary, *MT*, cxv (1974), 684
M. J. Rupert: *The Piano Music of Darius Milhaud: a Survey* (diss., Indiana U., 1974)
C. Palmer: *Milhaud* (London, 1976)
W. Bolcom: "Reminiscences of Darius Milhaud," *Musical Newsletter*, vii (1977), 3
P. Collaer: *Darius Milhaud* (Geneva and Paris, 1982) [incl. complete catalogue of works, editions, discography, writings, and translations]

H. WILEY HITCHCOCK,
CHRISTOPHER PALMER (work-list)

Military music. Instrumental music associated with the ceremonies, functions, and duties of military organizations; *see also* BANDS.

1. Definitions and functions. 2. The field music. 3. Camp duties. 4. The band of music.

1. DEFINITIONS AND FUNCTIONS. By the 17th century, when settlers brought European culture to America, military music served several functions, some practical and others ceremonial; these included strengthening the morale of soldiers, conveying signals and commands, and providing accompaniment for ceremonial, social, and recreational activities. The armed forces of the American colonies preserved a distinction, which existed in Europe, between two types of musical unit, the "field music" and the "band of music." The field music consisted of the several company musicians of a battalion or regiment. An American infantry regiment, for example, usually had eight line companies, and a field music usually consisted of two musicians from each company, or up to as many as 16 drummers and fifers (see fig. 1). When assembled, the field music was under the command of a drum or fife major, who was part of the military headquarters staff. Its principal function was to sound the "camp duties," a system of signals and commands that regulated each day's military activities. The band of music, on the other hand, had a ceremonial purpose. It was composed of professional musicians, often civilians, and was a separate unit under the control of a music master or bandmaster. Its members were frequently "double-handed," or capable of playing a number of different string and wind instruments.

1. *Field music: Federal fife and drum corps of the Civil War*

2. *The US Army Band (1980) under Colonel Eugene W. Allen, with the Herald Trumpets (on raised level at rear)*

2. THE FIELD MUSIC. The colonial field music evolved from English models. Each infantry company included one or two drummers and fifers, and each troop of horse had a trumpeter. Irish and Scottish settlers sometimes used bagpipes instead of fifes, and bugles were later used by light infantry and detached parties of mounted men. Black soldiers, who were required to serve but in many colonies forbidden to bear arms, were often musicians. Field musicians, who held the rank of corporal, were usually given rudimentary musical training by the battalion's drum or fife major. In addition to their musical responsibilities, they were required to do duty as soldiers. Drummers, for example, were expected to remain with their companies in battle, giving drum signals as required, and usually marching immediately behind the advancing line; they also attended to the wounded after battle, and were responsible for carrying out punishments. Because of their importance as signalmen, military musicians were usually dressed differently from other soldiers. This enabled their commanders to locate them quickly in the smoke and confusion of battle.

At various times the field music consisted of fifes, trumpets, bugles, and drums. The early fife was a one-piece, wooden, transverse flute about 60 cm long; it had six finger-holes and was pitched in D. In the late 18th century C and B♭ fifes became standard, but most military music continued to be written in the keys of G and D. The trumpet, which was made of brass or silver, had two rings to which a banner could be attached. Early trumpets were in D, but by the Civil War the regulation trumpet was in F; its range for military purposes was from the third to the ninth or tenth partial. The bugle horn, a short, curved, wide-bore horn, was used in the late 18th century by light infantry and dismounted units to differentiate them from the line infantry. In the early 19th century the conical tubing was lengthened and coiled, resulting in an instrument pitched in C or B♭. The bugle, or field trumpet, gradually replaced the fife and drum, and by the end of the 19th century was the principal military signaling instrument; at this time it was pitched in G with a tuning-slide to alter the pitch to F when the instrument was used in a band.

During the colonial and Revolutionary periods the military drum was a snare or side drum between 37.5 and 45 cm in height and diameter. It had a wooden shell, and two gut cords stretched across its bottom membrane; when not in use it was suspended from the shoulder by means of a plaited cord, or drag rope. The bass drum did not become part of the American field music until the early 19th century. Kettledrums were rarely included in the field music, but mounted regimental bands could use timpani instead of snare and bass drums.

By the 20th century the military field music had been rendered obsolete by technological advances. Some vestiges of earlier practices remain, however; for example, the US Army Band's Herald Trumpets (fig.2) open ceremonies and announce the arrival of the president and other dignitaries. Many traditions of the field music are carried on by historical societies that maintain modern fife and drum units. There are about 2500 of these in the USA, many in New England; they often perform in Revolutionary uniforms.

3. CAMP DUTIES. Military life was regulated by a system of musical signals and commands, the camp duties, which in the infantry were given first by drums, then by fifes and drums. (Mounted units, which were few in number, had their own system of trumpet calls.) During the colonial period British signals were used; in the Revolutionary era the basis for American practice was Friedrich von Steuben's *Regulations for the Order and Discipline of the Troops of the United States* (1779). This ordered nine "beats" of the drum into use: "The General," "The Assembly," "The March," "The Reveilly," "The Troop," "The Retreat," "The Tattoo," "To Arms," and "The Parley." Also included were 12 signals that were not regulated by the clock, or that did not apply to the whole army. (For a full explanation of these and other calls, see Camus, 1976.) As the *Regulations* contained no music, the Continental Army's musicians depended to a large extent on British practices and on the teachings of the army's inspector of music, JOHN HIWELL, and regimental drum majors. The drum beats alone were sufficient to give signals and com-

mands; fife melodies were eventually added for interest, however, and by the last third of the 18th century these became standard. In ex.1 the "Drummer's Call" is combined with a fife melody found in a manuscript of Giles Gibbs (1777).

In the early 19th century the first printed drum manuals appeared; in these, as in early manuals, drum beats were not notated conventionally, but rather described. David Hazeltine, in his *Instructor in Martial Music* (1810), describes the "Drummer's Call" as "A ten and a stroke, a flam and a stroke, and one flam, twice over; then a ten and a stroke, then a flam and a stroke, five times over; then one flam." Comparison with contemporary British and American works shows that his ten-stroke roll more often consisted of seven or nine strokes, and by the time of the Civil War it had become an eleven-stroke roll.

The fife and drum were used to sound camp duties until well after the Civil War. The orderly drummer would beat the "Drummer's Call" to assemble the company drummers and fifers for one of the day's routines, such as reveille, troop, retreat, or tattoo. By the end of the 19th century, when the bugle had supplanted the fife and drum, a new set of signals was developed. Army manuals of 1957 list 20 calls and four ceremonial compositions, but except for *Taps*, which is still played at funerals, these have fallen into disuse.

4. THE BAND OF MUSIC. The instrumentation of the band of music, and of the military band that succeeded it in the late 19th century and the 20th, was larger and more diverse than that of the field music. Besides post, ship, and divisional bands, each branch of the armed services (the army, navy, marines, air force, and coastguard) has a special band, and the army, navy, and air force also have academy bands. The oldest of the special bands is the US Marine Band, which has been in continuous operation since 1798. Every military band is required to function as a concert as well as a marching band, and to provide small jazz, rock, and popular groups for social occasions. The special bands, which may have as many as 165 members, frequently have one or more marching units, several small groups, a chorus, and a chamber orchestra, as well as the full symphonic band (see fig.2).

BIBLIOGRAPHY

[F. von Steuben:] *Regulations for the Order and Discipline of the Troops of the United States* (Philadelphia, PA, 1779/*R*1966)

A. Meyers: *Ten Years in the Ranks, U.S. Army* (New York, 1914/*R*1979)

Field Music (Washington, DC, 1940) [US War Department pubn TM 20-250]

W. C. White: *A History of Military Music in America* (New York, 1944/*R*1975) [see also R. F. Camus: "A Re-evaluation of the American Band Tradition," *Journal of Band Research*, vii/1 (1970), 5]

The Band (Washington, DC, 1946) [US War Department pubn FM 12-50]

The Marching Band (Washington, DC, 1957) [US Department of the Army pubn FM 12-50]

A. T. Luper, ed.: "Civil War Music," *Civil War History*, iv/3 (1958) [complete issue]

H. H. Hall: *A Johnny Reb Band from Salem* (Raleigh, 1963/*R*1980)

S. V. Anderson: *American Music during the War for Independence, 1775–1783* (diss., U. of Michigan, 1965)

K. A. Bernard: *Lincoln and the Music of the Civil War* (Caldwell, ID, 1966)

F. A. Lord and A. Wise: *Bands and Drummer Boys of the Civil War* (New York, 1966/*R*1979)

T. E. Warner: *An Annotated Bibliography of Woodwind Instruction Books 1600–1830* (Detroit, 1967)

F. Fennell: "The Civil War: its Music and its Sounds," *Journal of Band Research*, iv/2 (1968), 36; v/1 (1968), 8; v/2 (1969), 4; vi/1 (1969), 46

R. F. Camus: *The Military Band in the United States Army Prior to 1834* (diss., New York U., 1969)

K. W. Carpenter: *A History of the United States Marine Band* (diss., U. of Iowa, 1970)

D. C. McCormick: *A History of the United States Army Band to 1946* (diss., Northwestern U., 1970)

K. E. Olson: *Yankee Bands of the Civil War* (diss., U. of Minnesota, 1971)

S. G. Patrick: *A History of the Regimental Bands of Minnesota during the Civil War* (diss., U. of North Dakota, 1972)

W. A. Bufkin: *Union Bands of the Civil War (1862–65): Instrumentation and Score Analysis* (diss., Louisiana State U., 1973)

P. J. LeClair: *The Band Music in the Francis Scala Collection: Music Played by the Marine Band at the Time of the Civil War* (diss., Catholic U. of America, 1973)

R. F. Camus: *Military Music of the American Revolution* (Chapel Hill, 1976)

G. C. Caba: *United States Military Drums 1845–1865: a Pictorial Survey* (Harrisburg, PA, 1977)

K. E. Olson: *Music and Musket: Bands and Bandsmen of the American Civil War* (Westport, CT, 1981)

C. A. Hoover: "Ceremonial and Military Music," "Epilogue to Secular Music in Early Massachusetts," *Music in Colonial Massachusetts, 1630–1820*, ed. B. Lambert, ii (Boston, 1985)

For further bibliography *see* BANDS.

RAOUL CAMUS

Millard, Harrison (*b* Boston, MA, 27 Nov 1830; *d* Boston, 10 Sept 1895). Tenor and composer. He sang as an alto in the Handel and Haydn Society chorus in Boston as early as 1845, then studied music in Italy from 1851 to 1854. He made a concert tour of the British Isles with the soprano Catherine Hayes in 1854 before returning to Boston, where he taught singing and appeared as a tenor soloist. John Sullivan Dwight, the respected contemporary music critic, found his voice weak and his interpretations ineloquent. In 1856 Millard went to teach and sing in New York.

Millard served in the army during the Civil War, and was severely wounded at Chickamauga in 1863; he returned to New York to become a clerk with the US Customs Service. He composed about 350 songs, some of which manifest Italian characteristics, while others attempt to reconcile European and popular American styles; he also arranged or adapted many songs from French, German, and Italian. Several of his songs were well received, including *Viva l'America* (1859), *Under the Daisies* (1865), *Waiting* (1867), *Longing* (1870), *When the Tide Comes In* (1875), and *Baby Mine* (1878). He also wrote anthems, four services, four Te Deum settings, a Grand Mass, and an opera to an Italian libretto, *Deborah*.

BIBLIOGRAPHY

F. O. Jones, ed.: *A Handbook of American Music and Musicians* (Canaseraga, NY, 1886/*R*1971)

W. T. Upton: *Art-song in America* (Boston, 1930)

S. Spaeth: *A History of Popular Music in America* (New York, 1948)

H. E. Johnson: *Hallelujah, Amen!* (Boston, 1965)

NICHOLAS E. TAWA

Millay, Edna St. Vincent (*b* Rockland, ME, 22 Feb 1892; *d* Austerlitz, NY, 19 Oct 1950). Poet and playwright. She studied piano in her youth and composed the text and music of the baccalaureate hymn for her graduation from Vassar College in 1917. By this time she had already been acclaimed for her first mature poem, *Renascence* (1912), also the title of her first published collection (1917). These works clearly revealed her gift for sweeping, lyric verse, her preference for romantic subject matter (the trials of love, the beauty of nature, life's transience), and her choice of traditional poetic forms and rhyme schemes. Later collections – *The Harp-weaver and other Poems* (1923), *The Buck in the Snow* (1928), and *Wine from These Grapes* (1934) – were tempered by greater contemplation and emotional control but still treated similar subjects and feelings. It was in the collection *A Few Figs from Thistles* (1920) that her work reflected a certain disillusionment characteristic of many writers after World War I.

Millay collaborated with Deems Taylor on *The King's Henchman* (1927) for the Metropolitan Opera. Her play *Aria da Capo* (1921) has also been set as an opera, by Robert Baksa. There are over 100 settings of her poems, those from *Fatal Interview* (1931) predominating. Composers include Leonard Bernstein, Arthur Farwell, Arthur Bliss, William Schuman, Vincent Persichetti, Ernst Bacon, and, writing extended song cycles, Harrison Kerr, Elinor Warren, and Ellis Kohs.

BIBLIOGRAPHY

C. McGlinchee: "American Literature in American Music," *MQ*, xxxi (1945), 101

K. S. Diehl: *Hymns and Tunes: an Index* (New York, 1966)

J. Gould: *The Poet and her Book: a Biography of Edna St. Vincent Millay* (New York, 1969)

R. Zeschin: "Ladies of the Libretto," *Opera News*, xxxvi/17 (1972), 26

M. A. Hovland: *Musical Settings of American Poetry: a Bibliography* (in preparation) [incl. list of settings]

KATHLEEN HAEFLIGER

Miller, Dayton C(larence) (*b* Strongsville, OH, 13 March 1866; *d* Cleveland, OH, 22 Feb 1941). Acoustician. He studied at Princeton (DSc 1890) and held appointments there before becoming head of the physics department at the Case School of Applied Science, Cleveland. He was an accomplished flutist, and wrote extensively about the instrument, provided a catalogue of literature on the flute, and gathered an important collection of flutes (now in the Library of Congress). His most important contribution as an acoustician was the development in 1909 of the "phonodeik," which incorporated a diaphragm of thin glass closing the end of a receiving horn; this allowed him to analyze waveforms of various instruments – by means of a thin wire attached to the center of the diaphragm, which passed over a spindle pulley, the rotation of the spindle (due to movement of the diaphragm) was recorded by light reflected from a mirror affixed to the spindle. He also carried out experiments on organ pipes and trumpets having walls of different thicknesses, and produced results suggesting that desirable physical qualities for the containing walls of an instrument, for the maximum fullness of the partials, were softness, thinness, flexibility, and high density. He became an expert on engineering acoustics and was responsible for the design of many concert halls. His 32-element harmonic synthesizer won him a medal from the Franklin Institute.

Miller's *The Science of Musical Sounds* (1916) incorporates the results of his charting of instrument waveforms; his *Anecdotal History of the Science of Sound* (1935), if it leaves something to be desired as an historical work, is the first broad history of acoustical studies.

JAMES F. BELL, R. W. B. STEPHENS

Miller, (Alton) Glenn (*b* Clarinda, IA, 1 March 1904; *d* between London and Paris, ?15 Dec 1944). Bandleader and trombonist. He grew up in Fort Morgan, Colorado, where he studied music. He played with the locally popular Boyd Senter Orchestra in 1921, attended the University of Colorado briefly, and in 1924 joined Ben Pollack's band on the West Coast. After moving to New York with Pollack in 1928 he performed freelance for several years, working at times with Red Nichols, Smith Ballew, and the Dorsey brothers, both as arranger and trombonist.

In 1934 Miller helped organize an orchestra for Ray Noble which later became popular through its radio broadcasts. By the mid-1930s he was well-known in dance-band circles, and in 1937 organized an orchestra of his own. Although it made a few recordings for Decca, it failed to interest the public, and Miller disbanded it. In 1938 he organized a second group; again public interest was slow to develop, and the band's recordings did not sell well. Eventually, in March 1939, the group was chosen to play the summer season at the prestigious Glen Island Casino in a suburb of New York, which led to another important engagement, at Meadowbrook, in New Jersey, in spring of the same year. Both places offered frequent radio broadcasts, and by midsummer the Miller orchestra had developed a nationwide following. In autumn 1939 it began a series of radio broadcasts for Chesterfield cigarettes, which increased its already great popularity. Thereafter the band was in constant demand for recording sessions, and appeared in two films, *Sun Valley Serenade* (1941) and *Orchestra Wives* (1942; see illustration, p.232).

In October 1942, as a patriotic gesture, Miller disbanded his group and joined the US Army Air Force with the rank of captain. He assembled a high-quality dance band to play for the troops, which in 1944 moved its base to England. On 15 December Miller set off by airplane in bad weather for Paris to arrange for his band's appearance there, but the airplane never arrived, and no trace of it was found. Miller was mourned internationally and attained the status of a war hero. His recordings remain popular in the USA and also in England, and at times various Glenn Miller orchestras, under several leaders, have been formed to play his music.

Miller led one of the most popular and best-remembered dance bands of the swing era. In his lifetime he was seen as an intense, ambitious perfectionist, and his success was built on the precise playing of carefully crafted arrangements, rather than propulsive swing or fine jazz solo improvisation (his only important jazz soloists were the cornetist Bobby Hackett and the tenor saxophonist Tex Beneke). He was particularly noted for the device of doubling a melody on saxophone with a clarinet an octave higher. His arrangements were seamless and rich. Paradoxically, however, although he had many hits with sentimental ballads performed by such singers as Ray Eberle and Marion Hutton, it was his swinging riff tunes, for example *In the Mood* and *Tuxedo Junction*, which became most famous.

RECORDINGS

(selective list)

Moonlight Serenade (1939, Bluebird 10214-B); Little Brown Jug (1939, Bluebird 10286-A); In the Mood (1939, Bluebird 10416-A); My Prayer (1939, Bluebird 10404-B); Tuxedo Junction (1940, Bluebird 10612-A); Pennsylvania

Glenn Miller (far left) in the film "Orchestra Wives" (1942), with musicians including (seated foreground, left to right) the saxophonists Tex Beneke, Ernie Caceres, and Skip Martin

6-5000 (1940, Bluebird 10754-A); Chattanooga Choo Choo (1941, Bluebird 11230-B); A String of Pearls (1941, Bluebird 11382-B); Kalamazoo (1942, Vic. 27934-A)

BIBLIOGRAPHY

S. F. Bedwell: *A Glenn Miller Discography and Biography* (London, 1955, 2/1956)
J. Flower: *Moonlight Serenade: a Bio-discography of the Glenn Miller Civilian Band* (New Rochelle, NY, 1972)
G. Simon: *Glenn Miller and his Orchestra* (New York, 1974)
J. Green: *Glenn Miller and the Age of Swing* (London, 1976)

JAMES LINCOLN COLLIER

Miller, Mitch(ell William) (*b* Rochester, NY, 4 July 1911). Oboist, conductor, and record producer. He first earned distinction as an oboist, studying at the Eastman School and playing with the Syracuse SO and the Rochester PO. In the early 1930s he settled in New York, where he joined the CBS SO in 1936 and worked as a freelance for the next decade (Alec Wilder's woodwind quintets and oboe concerto from around this time were written with Miller in mind). In the late 1940s he began artist-and-repertory work for Keynote and Mercury, then moved to Columbia records in 1950; within a few years his eye for talent and ear for potentially successful songs had made Columbia the nation's top-selling record company. He produced recordings for a number of popular singers, including Doris Day, Rosemary Clooney, Jo Stafford, Frankie Laine, Johnnie Ray, and Johnny Mathis. In the late 1950s and early 1960s he popularized a form of participatory home music-making known as "Sing Along with Mitch," first through a series of record albums and later in a television show. After the "Sing Along" vogue passed, Miller turned increasingly to guest conducting with various symphony orchestras.

BIBLIOGRAPHY

R. Rice: "The Fractured Oboist," *New Yorker*, xxix (6 June 1953), 43
"Miller, Mitch(ell William)," *CBY 1956*
M. Miller: "They Like to Sing Along," *MJ*, xix/3 (1961), 14

MARK TUCKER

Miller, Philip Lieson (*b* Woodland, NY, 23 April 1906). Music librarian and writer on music. He studied piano and music theory at the Manhattan School (1923–7) and singing at the Institute of Musical Art (1927–9). Beginning in 1927, he was associated with the Music Division of the New York Public Library, first as a reference assistant (1927–45) and later as assistant chief (1946–59) and chief (1959–66); during his tenure the division was transferred to Lincoln Center and the Rodgers and Hammerstein Archives of Recorded Sound and the Toscanini Memorial Archives were established. He has served as president of both the Music Library Association (1963–4) and the Association for Recorded Sound Collections (1966–8). Miller has written many reviews and articles, chiefly on recordings and the recording industry, for such journals as *American Record Guide*, *High Fidelity*, *Saturday Review*, *Notes* (the journal of the Music Library Association), and *Musical Quarterly*, and has published two books, *Vocal Music* (1955) and *The Ring of Words: an Anthology of Song Texts* (1963).

PAULA MORGAN

Miller, Robert (*b* New York, 5 Dec 1930; *d* Bronxville, NY, 30 Nov 1981). Pianist. He studied piano with Mathilde McKinney and Abbey Simon, attended Princeton University (BA 1952), then entered the US Army. On his discharge in 1954, he enrolled at Columbia University Law School but furthered his musical career during the summers of 1955–7 by serving as choral accompanist and, in 1958, as the first pianist to hold the Fromm Foundation fellowship at the Berkshire Music Center. He made his Carnegie Recital Hall début in 1957. While continuing his profession as a lawyer, in 1964 he performed for the first time with the organizations with which he subsequently became closely identified: the Group for Contemporary Music and the Composers' Conference. He also taught piano at Princeton in the 1960s. His exceptional skills, as a soloist and ensemble player, in the knowing performance of the most demanding contemporary music led to the creation of works for him by, among many, Babbitt, Crumb, Davidovsky, Harbison, Wolpe, and Wuorinen, and to his giving the first performances of hundreds of works; he capped a career of performing, recording, and teaching with a series of three solo recitals of American works in New York during the season of 1974–5 (when he was already suffering from the cancer that was to take his life), and a recital of American works at the Berlin Festival of 1976.

BIBLIOGRAPHY

Obituary, *New York Times* (1 Dec 1981)

MILTON BABBITT

Miller, Roger (Dean) (*b* Fort Worth, TX, 2 Jan 1936). Country-music singer, songwriter, and instrumentalist. As a child in Erick, Oklahoma, he learned to play the guitar. He left school after the eighth grade and while working at odd jobs learned to play drums and fiddle. He served in the army in Korea, playing all three instruments in a country-music band that entertained the troops. After his discharge he moved to Nashville, where he performed as a backup musician for Minnie Pearl, Faron Young, and Ray Price. In 1958 he had his first success as a songwriter when recordings of three of his songs became hits: *Invitation to the Blues* for Price, *Half a Mind* for Ernest Tubb, and *Billy Bayou* for Jim Reeves. In 1960 he signed a contract with RCA and began to record his own songs; *When two worlds collide*, written with Bill Anderson, was his first release to reach the Top Ten. In 1964 he moved to the Smash label, and such songs as *Dang me*, *Chug-a-lug*, and *King of the Road*, which employed pop instrumentation, established him as one of the most successful singers and songwriters of the decade. Miller received 11 Grammy awards, five of them in one year (1964) – a number unequaled until 1983 – and gold records for four of his albums. He made film and television appearances and for a short time from 1966 presented his own program on NBC. In 1985 he received a Tony award for his songs in *Big River*, a Broadway musical based on Mark Twain's *Huckleberry Finn*.

Miller's enormous popular appeal was rooted in an engaging personality, a distinctive vocal style sometimes compared to scat singing (though he used his voice to imitate the twang of the electric guitar rather than wind instruments, as in jazz), and a smooth, urbanized image that disguised his rural origins. His witty, poignant songs were successful on both the country and popular charts.

RECORDINGS

(selective list; recorded for Smash unless otherwise stated)

When two worlds collide (RCA 7878, 1961); Chug-a-lug (1926, 1964); Dang me (1881, 1964); King of the Road (1965, 1965); *Roger Miller, the Third Time Around* (67068, 1965); *The Return of Roger Miller* (67061, 1965); Walkin' in the sunshine (2081, 1967); Little Green Apples (2148, 1968); *Dear Folks, Sorry I haven't Written Lately* (Col. 32449, 1973); I believe in sunshine (Col. 4-45948, 1973); Our Love (Col. 10052, 1974); Everyone gets crazy now and then (Elek. 47192, 1981)

BIBLIOGRAPHY

B. C. Malone: *Country Music U.S.A.: a Fifty-year History* (Austin, 1968, 2/1985)

DON CUSIC

Miller, Steve (*b* Milwaukee, WI, 5 Oct 1943). Pop-rock composer, guitarist, and bandleader. As a teenager in Wisconsin, he formed a group, the members of which included the singer and guitarist Boz Scaggs and Ben Sidran. His interest in the blues led to an informal apprenticeship on Chicago's South Side, where he made contact with other young, white bluesmen. In 1966 he moved to San Francisco, where he formed the Steve Miller Blues Band ("Blues" disappeared from its name in the late 1960s). After successful appearances with Chuck Berry at the Fillmore Auditorium and at the Monterey Pop Festival in 1967, the group signed a recording contract with Capitol and made three critically acclaimed blues-rock albums in 1968 and 1969. A hiatus occurred in its activities during the next few years, in part because Miller suffered a serious accident and illness.

In 1973 he released *The Joker*, the first in a series of smoothly crafted, deft, and eclectic pop-rock albums that gained him considerable commercial success. He moved to an Oregon farm in 1978, where he built his own recording studio and courted a public anonymity foreign to most rock stars of his popularity. His return to recording in 1981 showed that his commercial appeal was undimmed.

RECORDINGS

(selective list; all recorded for Capitol)

Children of the Future (2920, 1968); *Sailor* (2984, 1968); *Brave New World* (184, 1969); *The Joker* (11235, 1973); *Fly Like an Eagle* (11497, 1976); *Book of Dreams* (11630, 1977); *Circle of Love* (12121, 1981); *Abracadabra* (12216, 1982)

JOHN ROCKWELL

Miller & Beacham. Firm of music publishers. It was established in Baltimore in 1853 by William C. Miller (*b* Baltimore, MD, 1826; *d* Baltimore, 30 March 1894) and Joseph R. Beacham, who took over the business of Frederick D. Benteen, a piano dealer who had also published music since 1839. From 1865 to 1872 the company operated under the name of W. C. Miller; in 1873 it was taken over by Ditson. Among the pieces published by the firm was the earliest edition (1861) of *Maryland! My Maryland.*

BARBARA TURCHIN

Miller Music. Firm of music publishers. It was founded in New York in about 1930 by William H. Woodin (1868–1934), a financier and later Secretary of the Treasury whose chief hobby was music, and the composer Charles Miller. The two men had been introduced by Jerome Kern who, with Miller, worked for the music publisher Harms. The Miller catalogue consists of popular songs such as *Whispering*, *More than you know*, *The Whiffenpoof Song*, *Be my love*, *If I give my heart to you*, and *Love is a many splendored thing*, as well as Hawaiian popular songs. In 1939 Miller became part of the Big 3 Music Corporation, which came under the ownership of United Artists in 1973.

FRANCES BARULICH

Milligan, Harold Vincent (*b* Astoria, OR, 31 Oct 1888; *d* New York, 12 April 1951). Organist, composer, and writer on music. His early years were spent in Oregon, Washington, and Idaho; from the age of 12 he was organist in churches where his father was minister. He moved to New York in 1907 to study with William Crane Carl, organist of the Old First Presbyterian Church, and at the Guilmant Organ School. His teachers included T. Tertius Noble, Clement R. Gale, and Arthur E. Johnstone. Milligan spent a year as organist at the First Presbyterian Church of Orange, New Jersey, five years at Rutgers Presbyterian Church in New York, and two years at Plymouth Church in Brooklyn, New York. In 1915 he became organist at the Fifth Avenue Baptist Church (later the Riverside Church), New York, a position he held until his retirement in 1940. He was president of the National Association of Organists (1929–32) and national secretary of the American Guild of Organists (1926–51).

Milligan collected and edited four volumes of previously undiscovered 18th-century American songs, chiefly by Francis Hopkinson. He also published four songs with lyrics by Benjamin Franklin and wrote the first biography of Stephen C. Foster (1920). For many years he was music critic for *The Diapason* and the *New Music Review*, and he also wrote for the *Woman's Home Companion*. He lectured on opera at Columbia University, and was associate director of the Metropolitan Opera radio broadcasts. He wrote *Stories of Famous Operas* (1950, rev. 2/1955) and edited (with Geraldine Souvaine) *The Opera Quiz Book* (1948). He composed two operettas for children, *The Outlaws of Etiquette* (1914) and *The Laughabet* (1918), as well as incidental music for plays, numerous songs, secular and sacred choral works, and organ pieces.

BIBLIOGRAPHY

"Contemporary American Musicians: Harold Vincent Milligan," *MusAm*, xxxiv/20 (1921), 19

Obituaries, *MusAm*, lxxi/8 (1951), 26; *The Diapason*, xlii/6 (1951), 1

MARY A. WISCHUSEN

Mills, Charles (Borromeo) (*b* Asheville, NC, 8 Jan 1914; *d* New York, 7 March 1982). Composer. He was musically self-taught, and at the age of 17 earned his living by playing saxophone, clarinet, and flute in jazz bands. In 1933 he went to New York to begin composition studies with Max Garfield; he subsequently studied with Copland, Sessions, and Harris. For eight years he was radio critic of *Modern Music* and was head of the composition department of the Manhattan School in 1954–5; throughout his career, however, he concentrated on composition. He wrote in traditional forms such as fugue, sonata, and concerto, and composed many works for recorder (he was an accomplished recorder player). His music shows the influence of the spirituals and folksongs heard during his childhood in the Carolinas, and the jazz of the dance orchestras in which he played as a young man. He was a convert to Roman Catholicism in 1944, and this experience is evident in the spirit of reverence and contemplation found in subsequent works. Among the awards Mills received is a Guggenheim Fellowship (1952).

WORKS

Orch: Sym. no.1, e, 1940; Sym. no.2, C, 1942; Sym. no.3, d, 1946; Pf Conc., 1948; Theme and Variations, 1951; Toccata, 1951; Prelude and Fugue, 1952; Prologue and Dithyramb, str, 1954; Concertino, ob, str, 1957; Sym. no.4 "Crazy Horse," 1958; Serenade, wind, str, 1960; In a Mule Drawn Wagon, str, 1969; Sym. Ode, str, 1976; Sym. no.5, str, 1980; Sym. no.6, 1981

Vocal: The Dark Night (Bible), female vv, str, 1946; The Constant Lover (J. Suckling), male vv, 1952; Why so pale and wan fond lover? (Suckling), male vv, 1952; The True Beauty, 5 solo vv, 1953; The Ascension (Bible), cantata, SATB, 1954; 12 choral works, 1958, incl. Ballad of Trees and the Master (S. Lanier), O Christ, Redeemer (Mills), The First Thanksgiving (W. Bradford: Of Plymouth Plantation), settings of Pss. viii, cxxi, cxxx; numerous songs, S, pf

Chamber: 5 str qts, 1939, 1942, 1943, 1952, 1958; 6 vn sonatas, 1940, 1942, 1948, 1970, 1974, 1977; Chamber Conc., 10 insts, 1942; Ob Sonata, 1943; The 4th Joyful Mystery, 2 vn, pf, 1946; Serenade, fl, hn, pf, 1946; Eng Hn Sonata, 1946; Conc. sereno, 8 ww, 1948; Suite, 2 fl, 1951; Duo fantasie, vc, pf, 1953; Sonata fantasia, ww qnt, 1958; Brass Qnt, 1962; Piece, fl, rec, str trio, 1963; Sonata, t rec, pf, 1964; Prelude and Allegro, vn, pf, 1966; Sonata da chiesa, t rec, hpd, 1972; The 5 Moons of Uranus, t rec, pf, 1972; Duo eclogue, t rec, org, 1974; numerous other works for solo vn, fl, cl, ob, rec, org

Kbd: 2 pf sonatas, 1941, 1942; 5 pf sonatines, 1942–5; Toccata, hpd, 1956; many others

Other works: John Brown, ballet, 1945; Divine Dances of the Apocalypse, ballet, 1960; 4 film scores, incl. On the Bowery, 1956; 3 jazz ens works

Principal publisher: ACA

BIBLIOGRAPHY

EwenD

BARBARA H. RENTON/R

Mills, Kerry [Frederick Allen] (*b* Philadelphia, PA, 1 Feb 1869; *d* Hawthorne, CA, 5 Dec 1948). Popular-music composer and publisher. He started his professional career as a violinist and taught that instrument during the 1892–3 semester at the University School of Music, a private conservatory (not affiliated with the University of Michigan) in Ann Arbor, Michigan. Under the name Kerry Mills he published his composition *Rufus on Parade* (1895), a cakewalk march which became associated with early ragtime. Encouraged by the success of this work he moved to New York, where he opened his own publishing house, F. A. Mills, specializing in ragtime songs and instrumental pieces. His own ragtime cakewalks were particularly successful, especially *At a Georgia Camp Meeting* (1897), which was considered preeminent in its genre and, through performances by the Sousa band and others, attained wide renown in both the USA and Europe; his *Whistling Rufus* (1899) was also published in Germany as *Rufus das Pfeifgeigerl*. Of his nonragtime pieces *Meet Me in St. Louis, Louis* was a notable success in 1904, the year of the Louisiana Purchase Exposition in St. Louis, and was revived in 1944 when Judy Garland appeared in the film of the same title. Under his real name Mills composed religious songs (such as *Wonderful Is Jesus*, 1908), which were issued by other publishers, but these received little notice.

BIBLIOGRAPHY

E. A. Berlin: *Ragtime: a Musical and Cultural History* (Berkeley, CA, 1980/*R*1984 with addenda)

EDWARD A. BERLIN

Mills, Sebastian Bach (*b* Cirencester, England, 13 March 1839; *d* Wiesbaden, Germany, 21 Dec 1898). English pianist, teacher, and composer. He was taught by his father, an organist, and Cipriani Potter in London, then in 1847 was sent to the Leipzig Conservatory, where he studied with Ignaz Moscheles, Louis Plaidy, Julius Rietz, and Moritz Hauptmann, and came under the influence of Liszt's circle. He maintained German ties throughout his life, making successful concert tours in Germany in 1859, 1867, and 1878.

In 1855 Mills was serving as organist of the Roman Catholic Cathedral in Sheffield, but shortly afterwards came to New York; he settled there but never became an American citizen. After an initially discouraging reception, he met Carl Bergmann, who arranged for and conducted his début with the New York Philharmonic Society in the American première of Schumann's concerto (26 March 1859). He became a highly successful piano teacher in New York, where his pupils included Rivé-King and Bartlett. He appeared as a soloist with the Philharmonic in every season from 1859 to 1877. During this time he gave the American premières of several concertos, including those of Chopin (no. 2, 1861), Ferdinand Hiller (1863), Liszt (no. 1, 1867), and Mozart (no. 25, 1865). Jones describes his playing style as full of bravura but lacking in grace, though he notes that it later mellowed. An album of Mills's popular piano solos was printed as late as 1913.

BIBLIOGRAPHY

F. O. Jones, ed.: *A Handbook of American Music and Musicians* (Canaseraga, NY, 1886/*R*1971)

"Mills, Sebastian Bach," *Cyclopedia of Music and Musicians*, ed. J. D. Champlin and W. F. Apthorp (New York, 1888–90) [autobiographical article]

H. E. Krehbiel: *The Philharmonic Society of New York: a Memorial* (New York, 1892/*R*1979)

BRUCE CARR

Sherrill Milnes as Rodrigo in Verdi's "Don Carlos"

Mills Brothers. Popular vocal group. Its principal members were the three brothers Herbert Mills (*b* Piqua, OH, 2 April 1912), Harry Mills (*b* Piqua, 19 Aug 1913; *d* Los Angeles, CA, 28 June 1982), and Donald Mills (*b* Piqua, 29 April 1915). A fourth brother, John Mills, Jr. (*d* Bellefontaine, OH, 1935), played guitar and sang bass in the group until his death, after which his place was taken by his father John Mills, Sr. (*b* Bellefonte, PA, 11 Feb 1882; *d* Bellefontaine, 9 Dec 1967). The group began singing in small-town vaudeville and tent shows, then in the late 1920s were featured for ten months on radio station WLW in Cincinnati. By 1930 they were in New York performing in theaters, clubs, and on radio, and soon began recording for Brunswick and appearing in films. During the 1930s and 1940s they had many hit songs; *Paper Doll* (1943) was their biggest success, selling some six million copies. John Mills, Sr., retired in 1957, but Herbert, Harry, and Donald continued to perform together throughout the 1970s.

The Mills Brothers were one of the first vocal groups to achieve great commercial success, and among the earliest black musicians to attract a nationwide following. Early in their career they sang accompanied only by guitar. Later they were backed by orchestras and big bands, but their trademark remained a smooth and mellow three- or four-part harmony, closer to white popular music traditions than to Afro-American singing styles.

BIBLIOGRAPHY

SouthernB

D. Ewen: *All the Years of American Popular Music* (Englewood Cliffs, NJ, 1977)

MARK TUCKER

Mills College. Private college in Oakland, California, with a music program from 1894; *see* SAN FRANCISCO, §II, 7.

Milnes, Sherrill (Eustace) (*b* Downers Grove, IL, 10 Jan 1935). Baritone. After studies at Drake University with Andrew White and at Northwestern University under Hermanus Baer, he made his début with the Margaret Hillis Choir in Chicago. He also sang in the chorus of the Santa Fe Opera, augmenting ensemble duties with occasional appearances in small roles. His first important engagement was as Masetto in *Don Giovanni* with Goldovsky's touring Boston opera company in 1960. In 1961 he sang Gérard (*Andrea Chenier*) for Ponselle's Baltimore Civic Opera. He made his New York City Opera début as Valentin in *Faust*, the role that took him to the Metropolitan Opera with Caballé for his début on 22 December 1965. Since then he has appeared with extraordinary success in Mexico City, Santiago, Buenos Aires, San Francisco, and Chicago, and in the principal European opera houses; he has also become one of the most prolific recording artists of his time. His repertory includes all the leading Verdi baritone roles, and Escamillo, Tonio, Don Giovanni, and Barnaba (*La Gioconda*); in 1967 he created Adam Brant in Marvin David Levy's *Mourning Becomes Electra* at the Metropolitan. Milnes's brilliant top voice, general fervor, and extraordinary command of legato have occasioned credible comparisons with such predecessors as Lawrence Tibbett, Leonard Warren, and Robert Merrill. He married the soprano Nancy Stokes.

BIBLIOGRAPHY

"Milnes, Sherrill," *CBY 1970*

S. Milnes: "A Role in Hand," *Opera News*, xxxvi/2 (1971), 12

W. Sargeant: "Sherrill Milnes," *New Yorker*, lii (29 March 1976), 36

J. Spong: *The First Forty-Five* (West Des Moines, IA, 1978)

T. Lanier: "Sherrill Milnes," *Opera*, xxxi/6 (1980), 538

J. Hines: "Sherrill Milnes," *Great Singers on Great Singing* (Garden City, NY, 1982), 173

D. J. Soria: "Sherrill Milnes," *HiFi/MusAm*, xxxv/3 (1985), 6

MARTIN BERNHEIMER/R

Milstein, Nathan (Mironovich) (*b* Odessa, Ukraine, 31 Dec 1904). Violinist. At the age of seven he began to study with Pyotr Stolyarsky and remained with him until 1914. (At the final student concert that spring, he shared the stage with five-year-old David Oistrakh.) He later studied with Auer at the St. Petersburg Conservatory. In 1917 he returned to Odessa where he made his official début in 1920. For the next five years he enjoyed growing success in Russia. He often appeared in joint recitals with Vladimir Horowitz, when his accompanist was Vladimir's sister, Regina. Notable was his performance of the Glazunov concerto under the composer's baton in Petrograd in 1923. Milstein and Vladimir Horowitz left the USSR on a concert tour in December 1925 and decided to remain abroad. Occasionally they were joined for trio concerts by Piatigorsky, also a recent émigré. In 1926 Milstein went to Brussels, where he received artistic advice from Ysaÿe. He made his American début with the Philadelphia Orchestra on 28 October 1929 and settled in the USA, becoming an American citizen in 1942. After World War II, Milstein reestablished his European reputation. Among his honors is that of Officier de la Légion d'honneur (1969) and the Austrian Cross of Honor (1969).

Milstein is, perhaps, the least "Russian" among Russian violinists because his violinistic instincts are so controlled by intellect. He began his career as a virtuoso and matured into a most individual interpreter. His fiery temperament is firmly disciplined, his line classically pure. His tone, though not large, has great carrying power; he changes his bowing frequently to produce power through sweep rather than by pressure. His intonation is incomparably true because his vibrato never becomes too wide or cloying. His interpretations of the great concertos are full of nobility and reveal a stimulating mind. It is clear when he plays his own *Paganiniana* (1954), his cadenza to Beethoven's Violin Concerto, or his transcription for solo violin (1981) of Liszt's *Mephisto Waltz* no.1 that he can be a dazzling technician. He ranks among the foremost violinists of his generation. In recent years Milstein has offered summer master classes in Switzerland; he also taught a master class at the Juilliard School in 1973–4.

BIBLIOGRAPHY

B. Gavoty: *Nathan Milstein* (Geneva, 1956) [with discography]

P. Kogan: *Vmeste s muzykantam* [Together with musicians] (Moscow, 1964)

J. Hartnack: *Grosse Geiger unserer Zeit* (Gütersloh, Germany, 1968)

J. Creighton: *Discopaedia of the Violin, 1889–1971* (Toronto, 1974)

E. Kerner: "Nathan Milstein: Brahmin with Violin," *HiFi/MusAm*, xxvii/11 (1977), 84

B. Schwarz: *Great Masters of the Violin* (New York, 1983)

BORIS SCHWARZ

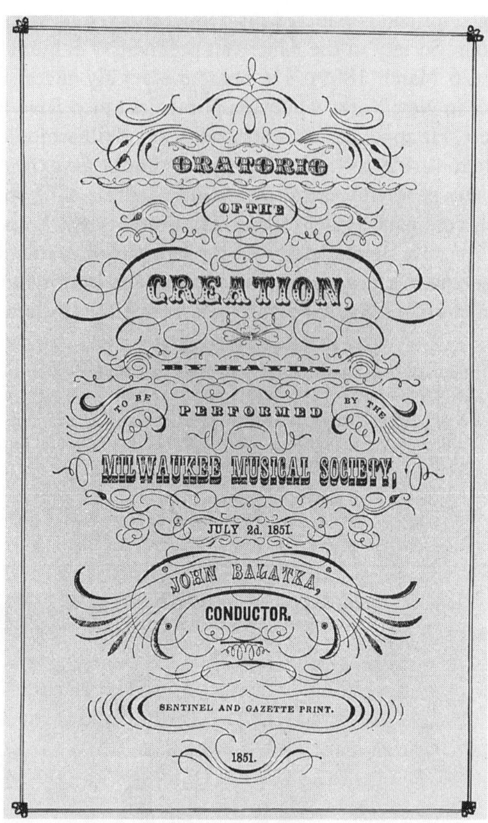

Announcement of Milwaukee Musical Society's performance of Haydn's "The Creation" on 2 July 1851, the first complete oratorio presented in Milwaukee; it took place in the Methodist Church and was conducted by Hans ("John") Balatka with an orchestra of 30 and a chorus of 100

Milwaukee. The largest city in Wisconsin (pop. 636,212; metropolitan area 1,397,143). The village of Milwaukee was founded in 1839, 21 years after the arrival of the first settlers; it was incorporated as a city in 1846. Informal musical groups that played for parades and provided accompaniments for dances are known to have existed during the earliest years of the city's history, but the first documented musical organization was the short-lived Milwaukee Beethoven Society, founded in 1843 "for the purpose of advancing the science of instrumental and vocal music." The society's first concert, consisting of excerpts from operas by Rossini, Bellini, and Weber and from Haydn's *The Creation*, was performed by a 35-member vocal ensemble directed by L. T. Zander at the county court house. Two German singing societies, established in 1847 and 1849 and both called the German Male Quartette, merged with a string quartet in 1850 to form the Milwaukee Musical Society, which in 1851 gave the first complete oratorio in Milwaukee, performing *The Creation* under the first director Hans Balatka (referred to as "John" in the announcement; see illustration).

During the next half-century Milwaukee developed into the most important musical center in the upper Midwest, becoming known as the "German Athens on Lake Michigan" because of the rich cultural life fostered there, particularly by the German immigrant population. Balatka directed several singing societies, beginning in 1855 with the Nord-West Sängerbund, and these groups were successful in competitions held in Cleveland, Detroit, and other cities in the Midwest. Milwaukee itself hosted numerous singing-society conventions between 1855 and 1920. The most important of the 49 musical organizations (mostly choral groups) that existed at the turn of the century were the Milwaukee Liedertafel (founded 1858), the Arion Musical Club and Cecilian Choir (1876), and the Milwaukee Liederkranz (1878). As a result of its strong choral tradition, Milwaukee became a center of the Cecilian movement, which sought to restore chant and Renaissance polyphony in the rites of the Roman Catholic Church. John Singenberger, who immigrated from Regensburg, Germany, in 1873 and studied with the founder of that movement, Franz Witt, became a teacher at a Catholic normal school in St. Francis, a Milwaukee suburb, where he conducted performances of masses and motets by Palestrina, Hassler, and Victoria.

Regular references in *Dwight's Journal of Music* are evidence of the city's importance as an opera center. The Milwaukee Musical Society, which relied almost entirely on local talent, staged productions of opera, including works by Mozart, Flotow, and Donizetti; the first complete opera it mounted was Lortzing's *Zar und Zimmermann* (April 1853). The German composer Eduard Sobolewski arrived in the city in 1859 and in October presented the world première of his opera *Mohega, die Blume des Waldes*, on an American-Indian theme. The American première of Wagner's Prelude to *Parsifal* was given in Milwaukee in 1882.

In addition to choral and operatic performances, regular weekly concerts of symphonic and chamber music were heard in the second half of the 19th century, performed by both local groups and visiting organizations. These included American premières of works by Mendelssohn (*An die Künstler*, 1859), Beethoven (Triple Concerto, 1864), and Brahms (the *Liebeslieder* waltzes, 1875, and *Nänie*, 1883). Notable among the performing ensembles were Severence and William's Band (founded 1850), Christopher Bach's Orchestra (1855), Zeitze's Orchestra (1857), John Koehler's Bay View Orchestra (1862), the Heine family string quartet (1875), and Clauder's Orchestra (1878). Christopher Bach (1835–1927), a composer of 350 works (including three comic operas) and a musical presence of considerable importance to Milwaukee for more than 30 years, introduced a wide assortment of operatic and symphonic music to the city.

By 1870 there were over a dozen private music teachers and 14 music publishers and retail stores in Milwaukee. Its 1500-seat Music Hall, inaugurated in 1864 and renamed the Academy of Music in 1872, was acoustically excellent and reputed to be the finest auditorium between Philadelphia and the West Coast. Such virtuoso instrumentalists as Ole Bull, Henry Vieuxtemps, Henryk Wieniawski, Sigismond Thalberg, Anton Rubinstein, and Rafael Joseffy, and the singers Jenny Lind, Adelina Patti, and Carl Formes were frequent visitors to the city; they appeared at the academy and at Nunnemacher's Grand Opera House (capacity 855), which opened in 1871 and was destroyed by fire in 1893, and at the Pabst Theater (capacity 1820), which was inaugurated in 1893.

The Orion Musical Club began supporting annual appearances of the Theodore Thomas Orchestra in 1884 and, later, the Chicago SO; it continued to present other groups and individual artists until the 1950s. Printed programs from as early as 1892 refer to a local symphony orchestra, and there were at least three attempts before 1936 to found a philharmonic society. Carl Eppert conducted a Milwaukee Civic Orchestra (1921–6), a Wisconsin Symphony existed in 1933–5, and Julius Ehrlich directed a Milwaukee Sinfonietta in 1941. After World War II civic interest in the establishment of a professional symphony orchestra was revived. The Milwaukee Pops Orchestra was founded in 1954, but it was not until 1958 that a permanent professional symphonic ensemble, the Milwaukee SO, was established. The first music director was Harry John Brown; under his successors, Kenneth Schermerhorn and Lukas Foss, it has become one of the leading orchestras in the USA. In 1985 the Czech conductor Zdeněk Mócal was named music director (his appointment to take effect the following year) and JoAnn Falleta became associate conductor. Performances are given at Uihlein Hall (capacity 2331) in the Milwaukee County Performing Arts Center, built in 1969. A symphony chorus under the direction of Margaret Hawkins is affiliated with the orchestra, and a summer series of orchestral concerts (Music under the Stars) was initiated in 1969.

The Polish and Slovenian populations of Milwaukee have been particularly active musically. After World War I the city became the home of the only Polish opera company in the USA; the group presented, in addition to works in the standard repertory, the American première of *Halka* by Stanisław Moniuszko. Other significant performing ensembles that have remained active are the Florentine Opera Company (founded 1933 by John Anello, Sr.), a professional company that draws on members of the Milwaukee SO for its productions; the Skylight Opera (started in 1960), another professional company; the Bach Chamber Orchestra and Choir (1969); the Bel Canto Chorus (1945) and the Milwaukee Choristers (both amateur ensembles); and the Milwaukee Ballet.

The first school devoted to the study of music was William A. Ehlman's Milwaukee College of Music (1874–80). Others included the Milwaukee Musical School, founded by Franz Heusler in 1875; the Conservatory of Music (1878–91), founded by William and August Mickler and later renamed the Wisconsin Conservatory of Music; and John C. Fillmore's Milwaukee School of Music (1884–95). In 1888 Eugene Luening (1852–1945), father of the composer Otto Luening (both were born in the city), established the Luening Conservatory, which merged with the Wisconsin College of Music in 1899. This school then merged with the Wisconsin Conservatory to form the Wisconsin College-Conservatory of Music, changing its name back to the Wisconsin Conservatory of Music in 1968.

The School of Fine Arts of the University of Wisconsin, Milwaukee, was founded in 1962 and offers, in addition to an undergraduate program, an MM in various subjects and an MFA in composition and chamber music (*see also* LIBRARIES AND COLLECTIONS, §3). The internationally acclaimed Fine Arts Quartet was appointed quartet-in-residence in 1963, and in 1983 the Institute of Chamber Music was inaugurated. Undergraduate music instruction is also provided by Alverno College and Cardinal Stritch College.

Accounts of popular and folk music are quite sketchy, but the folksingers Mailton Lobell (*b* 1854) and Dan Tanner (*b* 1865) are frequently mentioned, and Milwaukee became well known for its mandolin orchestras. Christopher Bach wrote numerous polkas, marches, quicksteps, and galops, but the best-known composers of popular music were Charles K. Harris, whose songs *Hello, Central, give me heaven* and *After the ball* were exceptionally successful (the latter selling more than a million copies), and Nora Bayes, who with her husband wrote *Shine on, harvest moon* and *Take me out to the ball game*. The Milwaukee area is also remembered as the birthplace of Woody Herman and Liberace.

BIBLIOGRAPHY

R. A. Koss: *Milwaukee* (Milwaukee, 1871) [in Ger.]

H. L. Conard, ed.: *History of Milwaukee from its First Settlement to the Year 1895* (Chicago, 1895)

O. Burkhardt: *Der Musikverein von Milwaukee: 1850–1900, eine Chronik* (Milwaukee, 1900)

J. G. Gregory: *History of Milwaukee, Wisconsin* (Chicago and Milwaukee, 1931)

J. J. Schlicher: "Hans Balatka and the Milwaukee Musical Society," *Wisconsin Magazine of History*, xxvii (1943–4), 40

——: "The Milwaukee Musical Society in Time of Stress," *Wisconsin Magazine of History*, xxvii (1943–4), 178

T. Schleiss: *Opera in Milwaukee: 1850–1900* (thesis, U. of Wisconsin, 1974)

A. A. Suppan: *A Climate of Creativity* (Milwaukee, 1979)

A. B. Reagan: *Art Music in Milwaukee in the Late Nineteenth Century, 1850–1900* (diss., U. of Wisconsin, 1980)

FRANKLIN S. MILLER

Mimaroğlu, İlhan (Kemaleddin) (*b* Istanbul, Turkey, 11 March 1926). Turkish composer and record producer. While studying law at Ankara University, he played clarinet and developed a career as a music critic and author. In 1955 he traveled on a Rockefeller Foundation fellowship to New York, where he studied musicology and composition at Columbia University (MA 1966) under Paul Henry Lang, Douglas Stewart Moore, and Vladimir Ussachevsky; he also worked privately with Varèse. Throughout the 1960s he was associated with the Columbia-Princeton Electronic Music Center, where he realized many of his works. He also worked in the studios of the Groupe de Recherches Musicales, Paris (1968), which commissioned the composition *La ruche*. In 1970–71 he taught at Columbia University Teachers College, and in 1971–2 he received a Guggenheim Fellowship. Mimaroğlu is best known for his electronic music, which is often based on concrete or instrumental sources; some of the early concrete pieces such as *Agony* and *Bowery Bum* were recorded commercially and brought him recognition as one of the originators of electronic music. During the 1970s he increasingly used instruments that were prerecorded and then electronically processed. Mimaroğlu likens his work to that of a film director: the composer transmits his ideas to the performer in a variety of ways ranging from conventional notation to verbal instructions; the performance is recorded; and the work takes its final shape in the electronic studio. Beginning with *Sing me a Song of Songmy* (1971) his music has shown a growing commitment to left wing politics. His work as a record producer for Atlantic records (from 1969) and for Finnadar records, which he founded in 1972, has brought much new music to light; many of his own compositions have been recorded.

WORKS

(selective list)

TAPE

Intermezzo, 1964; Le tombeau d'Edgar Poe (Mallarmé), 1964; Visual Studies, incl. no.3 "Bowery Bum" [after J. Dubuffet], no.4 "Agony" [after A. Gorky], no.5 "White Cockatoo" [after J. Pollack], 1964–6; Anacolutha, 1965; Pf Music for Pfmr and Composer, 1966–7; 12 Preludes, 1966–7; La ruche, 1968; Wings of the Delirious Demon, 1969; Hyperbole, 1971; Interlude II (Daglarca, Nha-Khe), 1971

Provocations, 1971; Sing me a Song of Songmy (Daglarca, Kierkegaard, Nha-Khe, others), 1971; Tract (Mimaroğlu, J. B. Clement, N. Hikmet, others), 1972–4; Coucou Bazar (incidental music, J. Dubuffet), 1973; To Kill a Sunrise (Mimaroğlu, Guevara, others), 1974; Session (Mimaroğlu, K. Marx), 1975; The Offering [after Bach], 1977; Mao Sketches (Mao Tse-Tung), 1978; The Last Allegro non troppo in Oberammergau, 1984

OTHER WORKS

Parodie sérieuse, str qt, 1947; Cl Conc., 1950; 4 Pieces, cl, pf, 1952; 3 Pieces, pf, 1952; Metropolis, orch, 1955; Pièces sentimentales, pf, 1957; Pièces futiles, cl, vc, 1958; Bagatelles, pf, 1959; Epicedium, Mez, ens, 1961; Trio, vn, cl, pf, 1961; 2 × e. e. (Cummings), 4 solo vv, 1963; Conjectus I, 3 insts, 1964; Music, 4 bn, vc, 1964; Pf Sonata, 1964; Str Qt no.2, 1964; Trenodia, pf, 1965; Conjectus II, 2 or more pf, 1966; September Moon, orch, 1967

Str Qt no.3 "Elocutio contorta," 1968; Music plus One, vn, tape, 1970; Cristal de Bohème, perc ens, 1971; Ulrike my Hope, pf, 1977; Rosa, pf, 1978; Str Qt no.4 "Like there's Tomorrow" (N. Hikmet), str qt, S obbl, 1978; Sleepsong for Sleepers, cl, pf, tape, 1980; Still Life 1980, vc, tape, 1980; Songs of Darkness, str orch, 1982; Immolation Scene (S. Ertan, Heine), 1v, tape, 1983; Valses ignobles et sentencieuses, pf, 1984; Van (minimalist-parody of Beethoven, Mimaroğlu), 1984

Principal publishers: Cherry Lane, Cotillion, MCA, Seesaw, Walden

BIBLIOGRAPHY

D. Ernst: *The Evolution of Electronic Music* (New York, 1977)

INGRAM D. MARSHALL

Mingus, Charles (*b* Nogales, AZ, 22 April 1922; *d* Cuernavaca, Mexico, 5 Jan 1979). Jazz double bass player, pianist, composer, and bandleader.

1. LIFE. Mingus grew up in the Watts area of Los Angeles. He first attempted to learn trombone and cello, but after being frustrated by poor teachers he took up double bass in high school, studying with Red Callender and a former bassist with the New York PO, Herman Rheinschagen. He also studied composition with Lloyd Reese, writing *What Love* in 1939 and *Half-mast Inhibitions* in 1940–41 (both were recorded in the 1960s). He played with Kid Ory in Barney Bigard's ensemble (1942), and toured as bassist in the big bands of Louis Armstrong (*c*1943) and Lionel Hampton (1947–8). In his first recordings as a bassist he accompanied jazz musicians and rhythm-and-blues singers, and as "Baron Mingus" led diverse ensembles. He gained national attention in Red Norvo's trio (with Tal Farlow) in 1950–51. Thereafter he settled in New York, where in the early 1950s he worked with Billy Taylor, Duke Ellington, Stan Getz, Art Tatum, and Bud Powell. Some of his performances during this period, including the famous Massey Hall concert in Toronto with Charlie Parker and Dizzy Gillespie and several of his early Jazz Workshop sessions, are preserved on recordings issued by Mingus's own company, Debut Records (1952–5).

Charles Mingus

In the mid-1950s Mingus's activities as a composer became increasingly important. Along with Teo Macero, Teddy Charles, and other experimenters, he contributed written works to a Jazz Composer's Workshop in 1953–5. Realizing that musical notation was inadequate for his approach to composition, he founded a new workshop in 1955 in which he transmitted the details of his works by dictating lines to each player. Over the years this four- to 11-piece group included such musicians as Jimmy Knepper, Booker Ervin, John Handy, Eric Dolphy, Roland Kirk, Jaki Byard, and Mingus's lasting associate, the drummer Dannie Richmond.

The early 1960s saw the birth of Mingus's most complex musical creations – his compositions *The Black Saint and the Sinner Lady* and *Meditations on Integration*, and his many performances with Dolphy. In the same years he endeavored, unsuccessfully, to free himself from economic dependence on the white commercial jazz scene. In 1960 he arranged some concerts in competition with the Newport Jazz Festival; from these came the Jazz Artists Guild, a short-lived organization intended to provide jazzmen with means for promoting their own businesses. He presented a disastrous rehearsal–concert at New York's Town

Hall in 1962, and was unable to find a publisher for his remarkable autobiography, *Beneath the Underdog*; his second recording company, the Charles Mingus label, issued only a few titles in 1964–5 before collapsing. By then Mingus was in dire financial straits and suffering from deep-seated psychological problems. Rarely performing, he essentially withdrew from public life from 1966 to 1969; Tom Reichman's film *Mingus* (1968) documented his sad eviction from a New York apartment.

Financial pressures forced Mingus to resume his career in June 1969; his enthusiasm was rekindled in 1971 by the granting of a Guggenheim fellowship in composition and the publication of his autobiography. During his remaining years he wrote big-band music and two suites for films and collaborated on an LP with Joni Mitchell. He traveled extensively with his workshop until 1977, when he fell seriously ill; he supervised his last recording session (January 1978) from a wheelchair.

2. MUSIC. Mingus's accomplishments surpass in historic and stylistic breadth those of any other major figure in jazz. As a double bass player he commanded an awesome technique and was thoroughly conversant with all styles of jazz extant during his lifetime. He developed a new "conversational" approach to his instrument in his dialogues with Dolphy (*What Love*, 1960; *Epitaph*, 1962), and also a "pianistic" approach that simultaneously combined the bass line, inner harmonies, and improvised counter-melodies (*Stormy Weather*, 1960). Other fine examples of his double bass solos may be found on *Cryin' Blues*, *Tensions* (both 1959), *Mood Indigo* (1963), *Orange was the Color of her Dress*, *Sophisticated Lady*, *I Got it Bad*, *Meditations on Integration* (all 1964), and *New Fables* (1968).

Mingus's bop works are a coherent blend of New Orleans jazz, blues, and black gospel music; he also made use of material from pieces by Duke Ellington. In almost every composition he modified conventional blues and popular-song forms by adding rhythmic contrasts: double-, half-, or stop-time passages, shifting tempos or meters, and "walking," "shuffle," "two-beat," or Latin patterns. (*Fables of Faubus*, 1959, and *The Black Saint and the Sinner Lady*, 1963, summarize these procedures.) He frequently changed textures, and had a particular preference for dense sonorities generated by low-pitched instruments (double bass, trombone, baritone saxophone, tuba), striking dissonances (most obvious in his reharmonization of the melody of *Ladybird*, 1955), collective improvisation (*Wednesday Night Prayer Meeting*), and overlapping riffs. These traits are all present in the 12-bar blues *Hora decubitus*, the first four bars of which are given in ex. 1. The numbers to the left of the example refer to the entries of instruments in successive choruses (2–7), reading from bottom to top; the "walking" patterns on the double bass are varied, but the other parts remain constant. Mingus's rhythmic and textural devices often anticipated features associated with free jazz, just as his use of pedal points and oscillating chords (*Love Chant*, 1955; *Ysabel's Table Dance*, 1957) anticipated Miles Davis's influential compositions of the late 1950s. The theatrical side of his art emerged in humorous or biting vocal pieces such as *Eat that Chicken* (1961) and *Freedom* (1962).

Ex.1 Bars 1–4 of *Hora decubitus*, from *Mingus, Mingus, Mingus, Mingus, Mingus* (1963, Imp. 54), transcr. B. Kernfeld

In the Jazz Workshop Mingus was not especially concerned with creating perfect, polished performances. Instead he experimented, continually revising a central core of compositions. The results were chains of related pieces. Some were obviously linked by title and substance: *My Jelly Roll Soul* (1959), *Jelly Roll* (1959); *Fables of Faubus* (1959), *Original Faubus Fables* (1960), *Fables of Faubus* (1964), *New Fables* (1968); *Song with Orange* (1959), *Orange was the Color of her Dress* (1963, 1964). Retitling disguised others: *Haitian Fight Song* (1955), *II B. S.* (1963); *E's Flat, Ah's Flat Too* (1959), *Hora decubitus* (1963); *Goodbye Pork Pie Hat* (1959), *Theme for Lester Young* (1963); and the *Meditation* pieces (1964, 1965, 1968), initially entitled *Praying with Eric* because of Dolphy's death (1964). Others shared themes but included substantial sections of new material: *Pithecanthropus erectus* (1956), *Epitaph* (1962), *Opus 3* (1973); *Nourogg* (1957), *Open Letter to Duke* (1959), *Don't Come Back* (1962), *I X Love* (1963); *Wednesday Night Prayer Meeting* (1959), *Better Get it in your Soul* (1959), *Slop* (1959). Among these evolving works the two series *Fables* and *Meditations* demonstrate Mingus's greatest achievement; he obliterated the standard distinctions between improvisation and composition and brought the spontaneity of improvised jazz to complex structures.

Although Mingus continued to notate big-band music and compositions containing sections of art music, his finest works were dictated. He used the piano in rehearsals to outline structures, assign individual lines, and set limitations on improvised sections. In nightclubs he directed from the bass, playing while shouting instructions. In 1961–2 he engaged other double bass players and performed as the workshop's pianist. He frequently stopped in mid-tune to correct mistakes and to upbraid inattentive audiences; his several explosive confrontations with the public brought him considerable notoriety. Nevertheless in his performances he generally managed to convey his lofty musical standards and a sense of jazz history.

For further illustration *see* PARKER, CHARLIE.

RECORDINGS
(selective list)

AS LEADER

Charles Mingus Quintet (1955, Debut 139), incl. Ladybird, Haitian Fight Song, Love Chant; *Pithecanthropus erectus* (1956, Atl. 1237); *The Clown* (1957, Atl. 1260), incl. Reincarnation of a Lovebird; *Tijuana Moods* (1957, RCA LSP2533), incl. Ysabel's Table Dance; *A Modern Jazz Symposium of Music and Poetry* (1957, Bethlehem 6026), incl. Nourogg; *Blues and Roots* (1959, Atl. 1305), incl. E's Flat, Ah's Flat Too, My Jelly Roll Soul, Tensions, Cryin' Blues, Wednesday Night Prayer Meeting; *Mingus Ah Um* (1959, Col. CL1370), incl. Better Get it in your Soul, Fables of Faubus, Jelly Roll, Open Letter to Duke, Goodbye Pork Pie Hat; *Mingus Dynasty* (1959, Col. CL1440), incl. Song with Orange, Slop

Pre-Bird (1960, Mer. 20627), incl. Half-mast Inhibitions; *Presents Charles Mingus* (1960, Candid 8005), incl. Original Faubus Fables, What Love; *Mingus!* (1960, Candid 8021), incl. Stormy Weather; *Oh Yeah* (1961, Atl. 1377), incl. Ecclusiastics, Oh Lord, Don't Let Them Drop that Atomic Bomb on Me, Eat that Chicken; *Tonight at Noon* (1961, Atl. 1416), incl. Peggy's Blue Skylight; *Town Hall Concert* (1962, UA 15024), incl. Epitaph, Freedom; *The Black Saint and the Sinner Lady* (1963, Imp. 35); *Mingus Plays Piano* (1963, Imp. 60), incl. Orange was the Color of her Dress; *Mingus, Mingus, Mingus, Mingus, Mingus* (1963, Imp. 54), incl. II B. S., Mood Indigo, Theme for Lester Young, Hora decubitus, I X Love

Town Hall Concert (1964, Charles Mingus 005), incl. Praying with Eric; *The Great Concert of Charles Mingus* (1964, America 003–5), incl. Orange was the Color of her Dress, Fables of Faubus, Sophisticated Lady; *Mingus at Monterey* (1964, Charles Mingus 001-002), incl. I Got it Bad, Orange was the Color of her Dress, Meditations on Integration; *Charles Mingus* (1965, Charles Mingus 0013-0014), incl. Meditation on Inner Space; *Right Now* (1968, Fan. 86017), incl. New Fables, Meditation for a Pair of Wire Cutters; *Mingus Moves* (1973, Atl. 1653), incl. Opus 3; *Cumbia and Jazz Fusion* (1976–7, Atl. 8801); *Three or Four Shades of Blues* (1977, Atl. 1700)

AS SIDEMAN

L. Hampton: Mingus Fingers (1947, Decca 24428); R. Norvo: Godchild (1951, Discovery 167); Quintet of the Year: Hot House (1953, Debut 4)

BIBLIOGRAPHY

N. Hentoff: "Charlie Mingus: Cafe Bohemia, New York," *Down Beat*, xxiii/1 (1956), 8

I. Gitler: "Mingus Speaks, and Bluntly," *Down Beat*, xxvii/15 (1960), 29

G. Lees: "Newport: the Trouble," *Down Beat*, xxvii/17 (1960), 20

B. Coss: *Charles Mingus: a List of Compositions Licensed by B.M.I.* (New York, 1961)

N. Hentoff: *The Jazz Life* (New York, 1961/*R*1975)

T. White: "Mingus at Town Hall," *Jazz*, i/3 (1963), 13

J. Berendt: "Mingus and the Shadow of Duke Ellington," *Jazz*, iv/4 (1965), 17

I. Goldberg: *Jazz Masters of the Fifties* (New York, 1965/*R*1980)

D. Locke: "Jazz Paradox," *Jazz Monthly*, xi/9 (1965), 23

W. Balliett: *Ecstasy at the Onion* (New York, 1971), 263

C. Mingus: *Beneath the Underdog*, ed. N. King (New York, 1971)

E. Jost: *Free Jazz* (Graz, Austria, 1974/*R*1981)

J. Litweiler: "There's a Mingus Among Us," *Down Beat*, xlii/4 (1975), 12

G. Giddins: "Three or Four Shades of Mingus," *Village Voice* (3 July 1978), 53

B. Primack: "The Gospel According to Mingus: Disciples Carry the Tune," *Down Beat*, xlv/20 (1978), 12

B. Sidran: "Charles Mingus Finds a New Voice," *Rolling Stone* (28 Dec 1978–11 Jan 1979), 33

L. Feather: "Joni Mitchell Makes Mingus Sing," *Down Beat*, xlvi/15 (1979), 16

D. Morgenstern: "Charles Mingus 1922–1979," *Radio Free Jazz* (Feb 1979), 14

B. Priestley: *Mingus: a Critical Biography* (London, 1982)

H. L. Lindenmaier and H. J. Salewski: *The Man who Never Sleeps: the Charles Mingus Discography 1945–1978* (Freiburg, Germany, 1983)

BARRY KERNFELD

Miniconjou. American Plains Indian group belonging to the Teton subgroup of the SIOUX.

Minimalism. A term applied from the early 1970s to various compositional practices, current from the early 1960s, the features of which (harmonic stasis, the use of rhythmic patterns, and repetition) have as their underlying impulse the radical reduction of compositional materials. Minimalist music was created in its purest and most rigorous form between the early 1960s and mid-1970s in San Francisco and, principally, New York. It has an affinity with minimalist art, and indeed was first performed in such untraditional settings as lofts and art galleries, where the work of visual artists like Sol LeWitt, Donald Judd, and Richard Serra was produced and exhibited. The term "minimalism" became a convenient rubric for a type of music that seemed to have a great deal in common with the artistic environment in which it was heard; the label has been repudiated by many composers, however, who feel that it belittles their achievements and obscures their individuality.

The best-known composers of minimalist music are La Monte Young, Terry Riley, Steve Reich, and Philip Glass, whose backgrounds have many similarities. All were born in the mid-1930s, were educated in universities and conservatories when serialism was the dominant musical style, and found academic music intellectually oppressive and emotionally irrelevant. All were drawn to other art forms, such as dance, theater, and jazz (for its directness and the way of life associated with it), and all performed their own music as soloists or leaders of ensembles. Finally, all displayed an interest in the physical properties of sound, and in the music and ideas of Africa and Asia. The four knew and to some extent influenced one another: Young and Riley worked together as students on the West Coast and later in New York; it was also on the West Coast that Reich came into contact with Riley, and through him with Young's work. By the mid-1960s Young, Riley, and Reich were all in New York, to which Glass returned from Paris in 1967. The city, with its large community of performers, visual artists, dancers, and writers, proved a fertile environment for their musical experiments.

Despite their similar backgrounds, the four struck out on different paths. Young, considered by many to be the principal exponent of the minimalist genre because of his influential, uncompromising ideas about sound, wrote works concerned almost exclusively with the properties of harmony and temperament, which he considers a function of time. His *Trio for Strings* (1958), with its extended, monodynamic tones and absence of rhythm, prepared the way for minimalist music. Although Riley was inspired by Young's devotion to harmonic purity, he found especially fruitful their shared experimentation with variations over a drone. *In C*, his seminal working-out of these early ideas, introduced the element of pulse and the repetition of tiny motivic cells in a single harmony. This work, the first performance of which at the San Francisco Tape Music Center in 1964 lasted more than one and a half hours, marks a crucial point in the minimalist repertory. Reich was intrigued not only by the possibilities of pulse (almost to the exclusion of harmonic change), but also by the gradually shifting relationships that occur when material is played out of phase with itself (that is, played by several instruments, voices, or tape tracks at slightly different speeds). His first experiments with phasing (e.g., *Come Out*, 1966) were achieved with tape loops, but he soon turned to performers to accomplish the same effect. His works of this period, which he regards as ending with *Drumming* (1971), display a persistent preoccupation with what he called "music as gradual process." Glass's distinctive and equally stringent approach creates rhythmic change by the addition and subtraction of subcells of a musical phrase: a characteristically loud, fast, intense motif is first established by repetition before fragments of it begin to be repeated or omitted while the fundamental pace remains unchanged. *1 + 1* (1968), a work for a soloist performing on an amplified tabletop, is an early example of a style that became more and more dynamic as it began to involve an ensemble of players, and to include cyclic and polyrhythmic processes; Glass considers *Music in 12 Parts* (1971–4) to be the work that

1
2
3
Piano I
Piano II
4
5
6

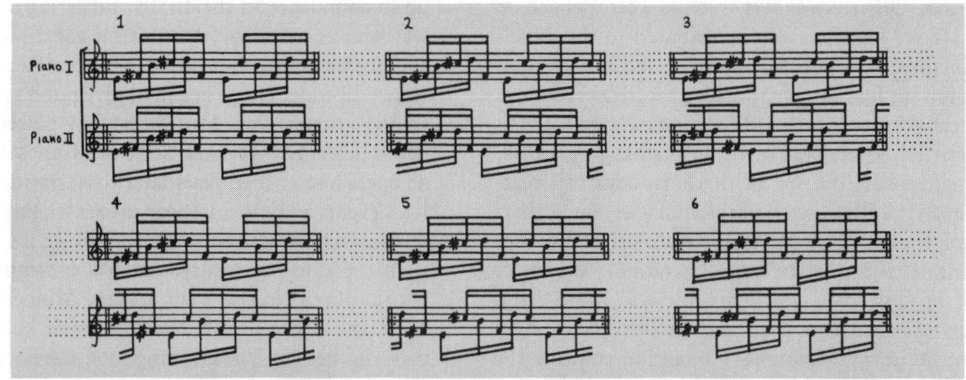

(a)

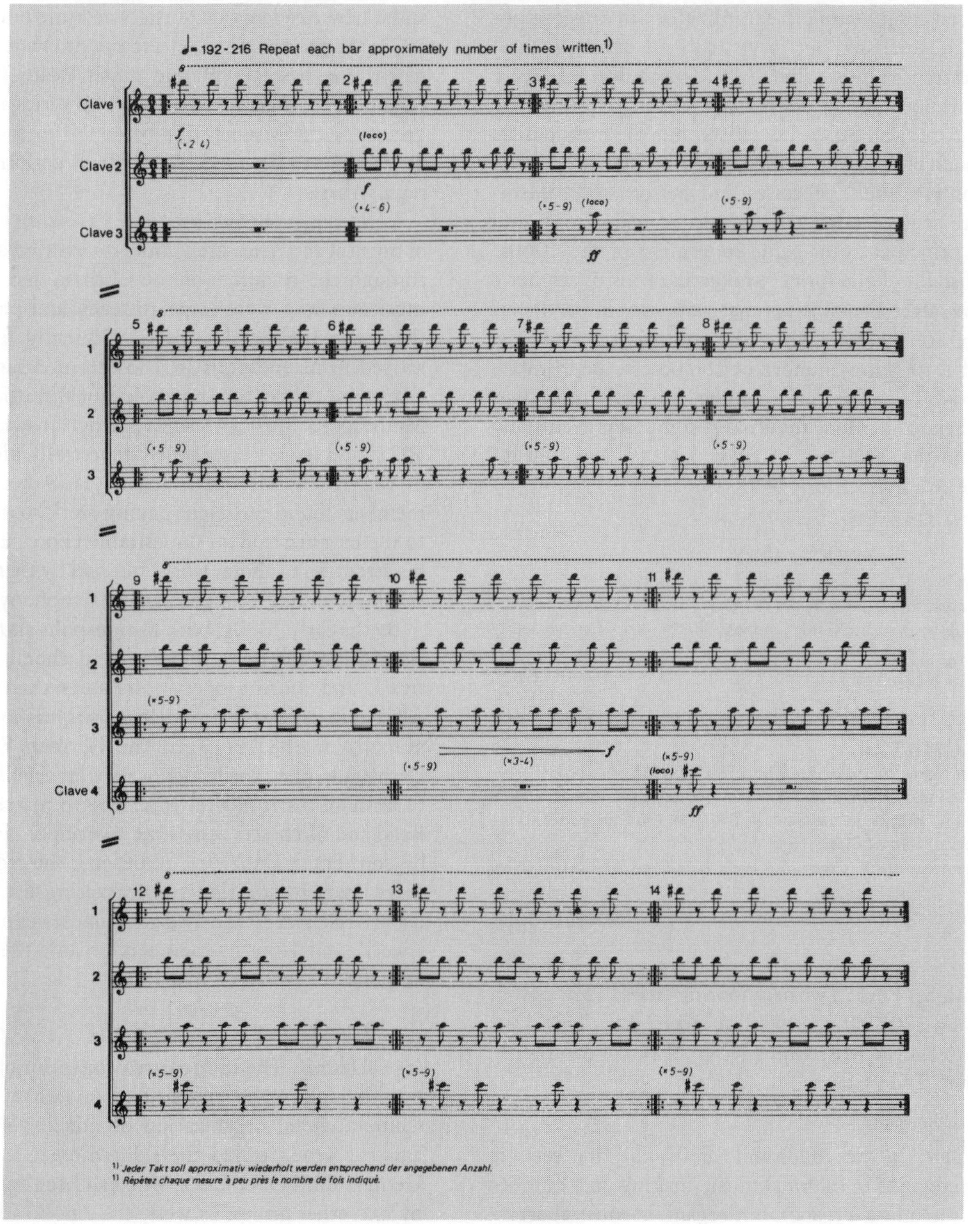

♩= 192-216 Repeat each bar approximately number of times written.1)
Clave 1
Clave 2
Clave 3
Clave 4
(loco)
1) Jeder Takt soll approximativ wiederholt werden entsprechend der angegebenen Anzahl.
1) Répétez chaque mesure à peu près le nombre de fois indiqué.

(b)

1. Two examples of repetitive scores by Steve Reich: (a) the opening of "Piano Phase," 1967, with dotted lines indicating an unspecified number of repetitions during which the second piano part accelerates to achieve a new synchronization with the first, as shown in the next notated bar, and (b) the opening of "Music for Pieces of Wood," 1973 (London, 1980), in which an approximate number of repetitions is specified for each bar sums up this period. Other composers, such as Terry Jennings, Jon Gibson, and Tom Johnson, also contributed to the development of minimalism and pursued highly individual compositional paths. Johnson, for example, pursued the idea of reduced compositional means to an extreme in *The Four-note Opera* (1972).

Ceaseless repetition of material with an unchanging pulse, elongation of single tones, phasing of rhythms, additive treatment of small motivic cells, use of simple tonal or modal harmonies, and exploitation of single timbres are all techniques employed by minimalist composers (see illustration). Whatever the technique or process, it is clearly audible and works itself out very gradually. The extreme stasis and microscopic changes of minimalist music draw the listener's attention towards the fundamental level of sound itself. Its narrowness of musical means and lack of notated complexity place minimalism in direct opposition not only to serialism, but to virtually all developmental principles of Western art music after 1600. This radical departure occurred in an atmosphere of aesthetic pioneering fostered by Cage and other American experimentalists, but the minimalists differed from much of the avant garde in their insistence on strict control over compositional processes and performance. Minimalism therefore evolved outside the academic mainstream and apart from the principal avant-garde movement of the 1960s, incurring the disdain of the former and accusations of aesthetic fascism from the latter. But the popular response, in particular to the works of Reich and Glass, was enthusiastic from the beginning, and a growing number of composers, performers, performance artists, dancers, and popular and rock musicians were drawn to the music. Many minimalist composers eventually moved away from the style, but its rigor, vitality, and concentration continue to inform music of all kinds.

See also EXPERIMENTAL MUSIC, §3.

BIBLIOGRAPHY

M. Nyman: *Experimental Music: Cage and Beyond* (New York, 1974)
S. Reich: *Writings about Music* (New York, 1974)
D. Bither: "Philip Glass: an Avant-Garde Composer for the '80s," *Horizon*, xxiii/3 (1980), 38
M. Nyman: "Against Intellectual Complexity in Music," *October*, no.13 (1980), 81
P. Gena: "Freedom in Experimental Music: the New York Revolution," *TriQuarterly*, no.52 (1981), 223
P. Griffiths: *Modern Music: the Avant-garde since 1945* (New York, 1981)
T. Johnson: "The Original Minimalists," *Village Voice*, xxvii (27 July 1982), 69
M. Walsh: "The Heart is Back in the Game," *Time*, cxx (20 Sept 1982), 60
W. Mertens: *American Minimal Music* (New York, 1983)
J. Rockwell: *All American Music: Composition in the Late Twentieth Century* (New York, 1983)

RUTH DREIER

Minneapolis and St. Paul. Two neighboring cities in Minnesota (pop. 370,951 and 270,230; metropolitan area 2,113,533). Facing each other across the Mississippi River, they are commonly referred to as the "Twin Cities."

1. 19th century. 2. 20th century.

1. 19TH CENTURY. In the 1820s and 1830s, the first settlers at Fort Snelling engaged in informal music-making on a number of instruments (including a piano), but organized musical activities did not take place until the middle of the century. Occasional concerts were given by visiting artists, such as the Hutchinson family of singers (in 1855) and the Norwegian violinist Ole Bull, who gave recitals in St. Paul and nearby Stillwater with the 13-year-old soprano Adelina Patti (1856). Singing-schools also sprang up in abundance in the 1850s, initiating a choral tradition that was later enriched by the musical contributions of the German and Scandinavian immigrants; the St. Paul Liederkranz (a German male-voice choir) began to give public concerts in the 1870s. In 1863 the St. Paul Musical Society played the first symphony heard in the five-year-old state of Minnesota, and the city built an opera house three years later to accommodate the burgeoning local events and the European artists who were heading westward on lucrative American tours.

In the spirit of rivalry that has continued to generate competition between the Twin Cities, Minneapolis inaugurated in 1867 the Pence Opera House, which boasted the only grand piano in the city. The building soon was not able to accommodate the growing number of instrumental and choral organizations, and a new Academy of Music was built only four years later, in 1871. At the opening concert the St. Paul Musical Society presented the first symphonic music heard in Minneapolis. The cultural exchange between the two cities is continued by such groups as the Minneapolis-based Minnesota Orchestra and the St. Paul Chamber Orchestra, which perform in both cities on a regular basis.

With expanded facilities and a growing population, the range of musical activities grew more diversified after 1870, especially through the resources of the German and Austrian immigrant musicians who were eager to teach and perform. Chief among these was Ludwig Harmsen, originally from Hamburg, who arrived in Minneapolis in 1865 from Atlanta, Georgia. As the city's first conductor and professional musician, he led both the Minneapolis Musical Society, which made its début on 6 June 1872, and its successor, the Orchestral Union, which flourished in the 1870s but disbanded in 1879 because its professional members found sufficient paying work to make their free service to the organization an undesirable chore. Harmsen then shifted his attention to choral work, but had by then created the impetus for the founding of a permanent symphony orchestra.

By the early 1880s, both Minneapolis and St. Paul had become flourishing commercial cities, and choral societies, music festivals, and touring opera companies thrived in the affluence. Always in competition with its slightly older neighbor, Minneapolis in 1881 engaged the German Frank Danz, born in Darmstadt, then the leader of the Fort Snelling regimental band, to form an instrumental ensemble to match the Great Western Band and Orchestra across the river in St. Paul; Danz persuaded his son, Frank Danz, Jr., to become the orchestra's director two years later. In addition to contracting for social occasions, the Danz Orchestra established a regular series of concerts, held twice a week, and 16 of its members became the nucleus of the Minneapolis SO, founded in 1903.

2. 20TH CENTURY.

(i) Orchestras. The immediate progenitor of the Minneapolis SO was the informally constituted orchestra of the Philharmonic Club, a choral organization of mixed voices derived from an amateur group called the Filharmonix; it was directed by the German Emil Oberhoffer, who had been engaged as choral leader by two other groups as well, the Apollo Club and the Schubert Club (see below). Oberhoffer worked to secure an endowment for a permanent orchestra, and his efforts were realized on 5 November 1903, when the 60-member Minneapolis SO played its first concert. Similar efforts to found a permanent ensemble had been made in St. Paul, where the enterprising but contro-

The interior of Orchestra Hall, Minneapolis, on the occasion of a gala performance of Scandinavian music by the Minnesota Orchestra, choirs, and Scandinavian and American guest performers, conducted by Neville Marriner (11 September 1982)

versial Anna Eugenie Schoen-René, founder of the University of Minnesota Choral Union, had already secured financial backing for an orchestra that she had hoped to launch under the name of the Northwest SO. She immediately withdrew her efforts, but her belief that a symphony orchestra in the area would have regional potential was affirmed 65 years later, when the Minneapolis SO, by that time an internationally renowned ensemble, changed its name to the Minnesota Orchestra in recognition of its association with both cities and the entire state.

In 1905 the Minneapolis SO began to give concerts in the new Minneapolis Auditorium (later called the Lyceum), which became the site of the orchestra's first permanent home in 1974 when Orchestra Hall was built. The first tours were made in 1906, and the orchestra made its New York début in 1912. A subscription series was held in St. Paul from 1914 to 1931 and continued until 1974 at the Northrop Auditorium (capacity 4832) on the campus of the University of Minnesota, near the border between the two cities and accessible from both. A St. Paul series was reinstated in 1970 upon the opening of I. A. O'Shaughnessy Auditorium (capacity 1800) at the College of St. Catherine. The similarly sized Ordway Music Theatre became the orchestra's permanent home in St. Paul in January 1985.

Oberhoffer was succeeded by the Belgian Henri Verbrugghen (1923–31), the young Eugene Ormandy (1931–6), under whose leadership the orchestra acquired an international reputation, and Dimitri Mitropoulos (1937–49), who vastly enlarged the repertory, risking his reputation and his popularity by championing the works of Schoenberg, Berg (including the American première of his Violin Concerto), Krenek (who was resident in St. Paul at Hamline University, 1942–7), and Shostakovich; he also conducted the world première of Hindemith's Symphony in E♭ (1941). The orchestra toured and recorded extensively under Ormandy and Mitropoulos.

The taste for new music initiated by Mitropoulos was expanded by the orchestra's subsequent conductors: Antal Dorati (1949–60), who introduced works by Bartók; the Polish-born Stanisław Skrowaczewski (1960–79), who directed the American premières of Penderecki's *St. Luke Passion* (1967) and other works, and who earned for the orchestra several ASCAP awards; and Neville Marriner (1979–86), under whose direction a plan to enlarge the orchestra to 100 members by 1987 was initiated. In 1985 Edo de Waart was named to succeed Marriner as music director. Orchestra Hall (capacity 2543), designed by Cyril M. Harris and known for its outstanding acoustics (see illustration), is also used for recitals, a jazz series, concerts of popular music, and, from 1980, for the month-long Sommerfest, an annual festival under the artistic direction of Leonard Slatkin.

The 34-member St. Paul Chamber Orchestra, founded in 1959, was in 1985 the only full-time professional chamber orchestra in the USA. Its first conductor, Leopold Sipe, was succeeded in 1972 by Dennis Russell Davies, whose imaginative programs contained music from both early and 20th-century repertories. Nearly half the works performed have been contemporary (chiefly American), and the orchestra has engaged various composers, including Elliott Carter and Hans Werner Henze, for short-term residencies. Pinchas Zukerman was appointed music director in 1980 and often presides over the orchestra as both leader and performer. He has sought out works for chamber orchestra from the Romantic period, while otherwise emphasizing the Baroque and Classical; the pianist and composer Marc Neikrug has been appointed special consultant for contemporary programs. The Minnesota Orchestra and St. Paul Chamber Orchestra have both commissioned many new works, the former from Dominick Argento, Stephen Paulus and Libby Larsen (the last two of whom shared the position of composer-in-residence at the Minnesota Orchestra, 1983–6), and the latter from Henze and William Bolcom.

(ii) Opera. Apart from the annual spring visits of the Metropolitan Opera (1945–86), local opera production has been dominated by two companies: the tradition-oriented St. Paul Opera, founded during the Depression as an incentive to local musical theater, and the Minnesota Opera, which began in 1962 as the Center Opera under the auspices of the Walker Art Center. On the demise of the St. Paul Opera in 1973, the Minnesota Opera (as it was known from 1964) expanded its repertory but continued a policy of performing only in English through the 1984–5 season. The company's productions were mounted in the Tyrone Guthrie Theater and the Orpheum in Minneapolis and the O'Shaughnessy Auditorium in St. Paul until the opening in 1985 of the Ordway Music Theatre in St. Paul. There the company presented the world première of Argento's *Casanova's Homecoming* (April 1985), which had been specially commissioned for the new house. It has mounted the works of a number of American composers, including Conrad Susa, John Gessner, Eric Stokes, and Paul and Martha Boesing. The company's name reflects statewide ambitions. The low-budget Opera St. Paul, founded in 1981, is equally dedicated to encouraging young American singers.

(iii) Other musical activities. The performances presented by the principal tenants of St. Paul's Ordway Music Theatre (the St. Paul Chamber Orchestra, the Minnesota Opera, and the Schubert Club) are supplemented by musical events similar to those given in Minneapolis at Orchestra Hall. The emphasis at Northrop Auditorium has, however, shifted to dance events, although it also hosted the visits of the Metropolitan Opera and presents other large-scale musical events. Chamber music is sponsored by such organizations as the Walker Art Center (especially for new music), the Minneapolis Institute of Arts, the Bakken Library, and the Schubert Club; various groups are drawn from the Minnesota SO, the St. Paul Chamber Orchestra, the Minneapolis Chamber Symphony, the Minneapolis Civic Orchestra, and various suburban and student ensembles.

The most enduring sponsoring organization in the Twin Cities area is the Schubert Club of St. Paul, which was organized in 1882 and is one of the few societies of its kind in the USA that has not only survived but expanded since World War II. Its main programs include recitals by international performers, a chamber music series, sponsorship of recordings (especially on instruments from its distinguished collection at the Landmark Center), a scholarship program, and films, often in collaboration with other local organizations; its museum of keyboard instruments, which opened in 1980, houses a spinet harpsichord of 1542 by the Italian maker Annibale d'Rossi, the earliest keyboard instrument by a known maker in the USA. The club's counterpart in Minneapolis is the Thursday Musical (founded as the Lorelei Club in 1892), which promotes musicians resident in the area through concerts and offers scholarships to young artists.

The Minnesota Composers Forum, launched in April 1973 under the joint leadership of the composers Libby Larsen and Stephen Paulus, has provided opportunities for new music to be heard in Minnesota through reading sessions, public concerts (some in collaboration with the St. Paul Chamber Orchestra), and radio broadcasts. There are more than 260 members, and some 70 works have resulted from its commissioning program, which is partly subsidized by private individuals and corporations. Other musical organizations include Plymouth Congregational Church, which began sponsoring concerts in the cities' pioneer days; its current activities include commissioning new works and presenting local premières, notably of Handel's oratorios and music by Benjamin Britten and Aaron Copland.

The University of Minnesota, Minneapolis (founded 1851), has been an important center of musical activity since 1919, and renowned visitors to the campus have included Rachmaninoff and Stravinsky. In addition to events at the Northrop Auditorium, the school of music (founded 1903) and its opera workshop present music programs at various campus venues. The school offers a variety of undergraduate and graduate degree programs in music, including a PhD program in historical musicology, theory, composition, and music education. Music degrees are also offered at Augsburg College in Minneapolis, Hamline University and Bethel College in St. Paul, and other local schools. The music library of the Minneapolis Public Library is one of the largest collections in the country (*see* LIBRARIES AND COLLECTIONS, §3).

BIBLIOGRAPHY

J. K. Sherman: *Music and Maestros* (Minneapolis, 1952)
G. Seltzer: *The Professional Symphony Orchestra* (Metuchen, NJ, 1975)
B. Flanagan: *Ovation* (Minneapolis, 1977)
J. T. Dunn: *Saint Paul's Schubert Club* (St. Paul, 1983)
B. S. Lamb: *Thursday Musical in the Musical Life of Minneapolis (Minnesota)* (diss., U. of Minnesota, 1983)

MARY ANN FELDMAN

Minnelli, Liza (*b* Los Angeles, CA, 12 March 1946). Actress and singer. She is the daughter of singer Judy Garland and film director Vincente Minnelli. She achieved early success on Broadway, becoming the youngest actress to win a Tony Award for her performance in Kander's *Flora, the Red Menace* in 1965. She received the same honor for her one-woman show *Liza* (1974) and for her role in Kander's *The Act* (1977), and was acclaimed in two further musicals by Kander, *Chicago* (1975) and *The Rink* (1984). Her performances in the films *The Sterile Cuckoo* (1969) and *Cabaret* (1972) also won her awards; other films in which she has played leading roles include *New York, New York* (1977) and *Arthur* (1981). She has been successful on television with her own show, "Liza with a Z" (1972), and in 1980 appeared with Goldie Hawn in "Goldie and Liza Together." Minnelli served as narrator for Martha Graham's ballet *The Owl and the Pussycat* in the Metropolitan Opera House in 1978 and 1980, and in 1979 became the first performer to sell out Carnegie Hall for a series of solo concerts. She is best-known for her robust, impassioned singing style, and has issued a number of record albums.

BIBLIOGRAPHY

"Minnelli, Liza," *CBY 1970*

HARRY SUMRALL

Minnesota, University of. Institute of higher education founded in Minneapolis in 1851. Its school of music was founded in

1903. *See* MINNEAPOLIS AND ST. PAUL, §2 (iii); *see also* LIBRARIES AND COLLECTIONS, §3.

Minnesota Opera. Professional opera company founded in 1962 as the Center Opera in Minneapolis; *see* MINNEAPOLIS AND ST. PAUL, §2 (ii).

Minnesota Orchestra. Professional orchestra founded in 1903 as the Minneapolis SO; *see* MINNEAPOLIS AND ST. PAUL, §2 (i).

Minstrelsy. A type of popular entertainment, principally of the 19th century, which consisted of the theatrical presentation of ostensible elements of black life in song, dance, and speech; at first performed by Whites impersonating Blacks, minstrelsy only later was participated in by Blacks. Minstrelsy took the theatrical productions of the Englishman Charles Mathews as one point of departure. Black music and dialect greatly attracted Mathews during his visit to the USA in 1822 and he incorporated the latter element in his skits, sketches, stump speeches, and songs. Before Mathews, Charles Dibdin had used black material in his musical extravaganzas, which began in 1768 and were still popular well into the first decade of the 19th century. Southern plantation and frontier songs, black tunes patterned on English musical models, banjo tunes and playing styles, English plays and operas with black subjects and plots, British dance types and tunes, and direct observation of Blacks constituted other sources and models for early minstrelsy.

By the end of the 1820s there had evolved, from the convergence of the various lines of interest in the Black, an indigenous and novel American, or blackface, minstrelsy. The performances of George Washington Dixon and of THOMAS DARTMOUTH ("Daddy") RICE represented the incipient stages of the form. The performer blackened his face with burnt cork and wore costumes that represented, to the white audience, the typical Black: the uncouth, naive, devil-may-care southern plantation slave (Jim Crow) in his tattered clothing, or the ludicrous urban dandy (Zip Coon or Dandy Jim) complete with blue coat and tails. These two exaggerated stereotypes persisted in minstrelsy for several decades. Rice developed the minstrel show, or "Ethiopian opera," expanding the use of black dialect plantation songs, virtuoso dancing, banjo and fiddle music, and crude humor, and providing the whole with a greater degree of organization. Nevertheless its function continued to be primarily that of an entr'acte in the theater or in the circus ring.

The classic age of blackface minstrelsy (*c*1840–70) was heralded in the late 1830s, when a modicum of dramatic continuity was introduced and performers began to join together to form duos (most frequently a banjoist and a dancer), trios, and finally quartets. The instruments they used were the banjo, tambourine, violin, BONES, and sometimes accordion, all except the last associated with the southern plantation Black. At least one musician in the group doubled as a dancer. The Virginia Minstrels presented the first entire show of this new type at the Bowery Amphitheatre in New York on 6 February 1843; this performance was given as part of a circus but the group was soon appearing alone (see illustration). The Virginia Minstrels consisted of DAN

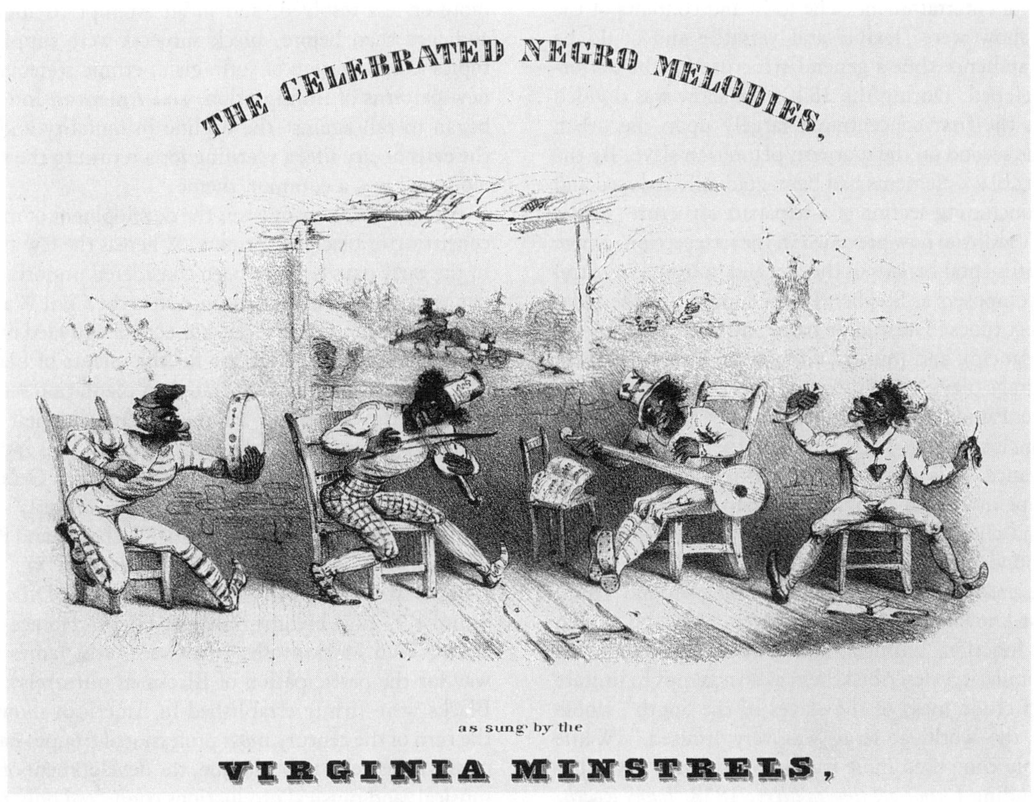

The Virginia Minstrels, Dan Emmett (center, fiddle), Dick Pelham (tambourine), Billy Whitlock (banjo), and Frank Brower (bones): from the title page of a song collection published in Boston in 1843

EMMETT, who played the fiddle, Billy Whitlock (banjo), Frank Brower (bones), and Dick Pelham (tambourine). Emmett had established his reputation as a banjo player and singer in the circus ring and was a versatile, practical musician who enjoyed a long and productive life on the minstrel stage, first as a performer, then as both performer and composer of a large number of the finest examples of classic minstrel music. Emmett's most popular contribution to minstrelsy was *I wish I was in Dixie's land* (copyright 1860), better known as *Dixie*, the melody and text of which eventually transcended boundaries of region, nation, and genre. The Virginia Minstrels met with spectacular success in cities of the eastern USA in the spring of 1843 and in concerts during a brief tour of the British Isles that summer. Although the original group disbanded in July 1843, Emmett reestablished it on his return to the USA, replacing Pelham and Whitlock, who had chosen to remain permanently in England.

The Virginia Minstrels provided the prototype for the instrumentation and stage action of the many troupes that were formed in the 1840s, such as the Ethiopian Serenaders, the Virginia Serenaders, Christy's Minstrels, Buckley's New Orleans Serenaders, the Kentucky Minstrels, White's Minstrels, and the Kitchen Minstrels. The members of the troupe arranged themselves in a semicircle with bones and tambourine players at either end as focuses of attention. One of these players would serve as master of ceremonies, a role later assumed by an interlocutor at the center of the band.

While minstrelsy frequently retained its connections with the theater and circus as an entr'acte, these associations became increasingly attenuated as the minstrel show grew in scope and changed in content; more and more it stood by itself as a fully developed form of entertainment. The form and contents of the early minstrel show were flexible and versatile and could be adapted to the audience, but a general structure for the performance was developed. During the 1840s the show was divided into two parts: the first concentrated largely upon the urban black dandy, the second on the southern plantation slave. By the 1850s, however, black elements had been gradually reduced and moved to the concluding section of a tripartite structure. Music of the "genteel" tradition now prevailed in the first section, where popular and sentimental ballads of the day and polished minstrel songs by such composers as Stephen Foster supplanted the older and cruder dialect tunes. The middle part consisted of the "olio," a potpourri of dancing and musical virtuosity, with parodies of Italian operas, stage plays, and visiting European singing groups such as the Rainer Family. In the third section the WALK-AROUND, at once the conclusion and high point of the show, took on primary importance. This was an ensemble finale in which members of the troupe in various combinations participated in song, instrumental and choral music, and dance. Although examples of the walk-around performed by a solo dancer exist from the late 1840s, the ensemble finale dates from only around 1858. *Dixie* is the best-known example of this genre, although it soon lost its original function. Emmett, whose walk-arounds enjoyed an enormous popularity, described them as an attempt to imitate "the habits and crude ideas of the slaves of the South" whose "knowledge of the world at large was very limited." While Emmett probably composed more walk-arounds than any other individual (including *I ain't got time to tarry*, 1858; *Jonny Roach*, 1859; *Wide Awake*, 1860; *Ober in Jarsey*, 1863; and *Old Times Rocks*, 1865), other important contributions to the genre were made by Sam Lucas (*Hannah boil dat cabbage down*, 1878) and Ned Straight (*Old Times Roxy*, 1880).

Shows from this classic age of blackface minstrelsy were immensely popular, especially in the Northeast. Bryant's Minstrels and Christy's Minstrels were the outstanding examples of successful troupes, though other companies that remained popular throughout the 1850s were the Harmoneon Troupe, White's Minstrels, the Buckeye Minstrels, the Ethiopian Serenaders, Wood's Minstrels, Buckley's New Orleans Serenaders, Campbell's Minstrels, the Sable Harmonists, Ordway's Aeolians, and Sanford's Opera Troupe.

The inclusion of music from the "genteel" tradition and the varied fare of the olio began a movement away from the primitive quality of early minstrelsy towards a more sophisticated and standardized variety show. However, from 1857 to 1866 Bryant's Minstrels, led by DAN BRYANT, temporarily slowed this trend with their productions of a rejuvenated minstrel show; full of the vitality characteristic of the 1840s, their performances were unqualified financial successes even during the Civil War. But their classic type of minstrelsy gradually fell from fashion, to be replaced by a show with a wider variety of styles. By 1870 many of the smaller troupes had been driven out of business by such companies as Leavitt's Gigantean Minstrels and Cleveland's Colossals (gigantism in any field greatly impressed many Americans at the time). While men had always played wenches' roles in the classic minstrel show and continued as female impersonators, women minstrels now began to appear; some minstrel troupes, in fact, consisted only of women, thus serving as prototypes of the later "girlie" shows. Some troupes abandoned the burnt cork makeup and performed in whiteface. There was also a change in the contents of the show. With the issue of slavery more or less resolved, and in an attempt to appeal to a wider audience than before, black subjects were supplanted by such topics as satirization of suffragists, ethnic stereotypes reflecting new patterns of immigration, and American Indians. Minstrels began to rail against the decline in morality and warn against the evils of city life; a yearning for a return to the simpler, "good old days" was a common theme.

An important change was the development of minstrel troupes consisting of black performers. Whereas the few that had existed in the early days had not been considered important, black companies attained true significance after the Civil War. Often under the management of Whites, but occasionally led by Blacks, these troupes provided a showcase for the talents of black musicians. Black troupes often concentrated on plantation scenes and incorporated Afro-American religious music in their shows. Those that were successful in achieving extended runs included Brooker and Clayton's Georgia Minstrels, the Original Georgia Minstrels, Callender's Original Georgia Minstrels, Haverly's Colored Minstrels, Sprague's Georgia Minstrels, Richard's and Pringle's Georgia Minstrels, the Kersands Minstrels, and W. S. Cleveland's Colored Minstrels. Billy Kersands, Thomas Dilward ("Japanese Tommy"), Bob Height, Charles Hicks, Horace Weston, Sam Lucas, Tom Mackintosh, Jim Grace, and James Bland led the way for the participation of Blacks in minstrelsy, and by 1890 Blacks were firmly established in American show business. By the turn of the century most professional troupes had turned from classic minstrelsy to burlesque, the development of the Broadway musical, and musical productions connected only tenuously with the minstrel show. Nevertheless, among amateur performers and producers, minstrelsy continued as a popular form of American entertainment until the early 1950s.

Many of the tunes in the early minstrel show derived from British dance types; others seem to share a common Afro-American heritage, with an insistence on irregular rhythmic accentuations achieved through phrasing, rests, textures, ornamentation, and metrical shifts. The main emphasis in much minstrel music is a rhythmic, rather than a melodic or harmonic, one. While the rhythmic element is often highly complicated, the melodies tend to be based on brief motifs that are varied only slightly upon repetition. Melodies constructed on pentatonic or anhemitonic figures and triadic formulas, and lying within a relatively narrow compass, are commonly found. Many give no hint of any sort of harmonic progression. Diatonicism prevails in the accompaniments of later tunes, interrupted briefly on occasion by a diminished seventh or secondary dominant chord preceding a cadence. Common to many of the songs is a verse-and-refrain design. Initially a soloist sang the verse, and was joined in unison by the entire troupe for the refrain; before long, however, it became more common for the troupe to sing the refrain in four-part harmony – a particular characteristic of the minstrel songs.

Many striking similarities exist between the traditional oral music of the southern Appalachians and early minstrel songs, but it has not yet been determined which (if either) provided the original inspiration for the other. It is certain, however, that the animated rhythmic element of the banjo tunes composed for minstrel shows between 1840 and 1890 greatly influenced American popular music.

Important collections of documents concerning minstrelsy are in the Harvard Theatre Collection, the New York Public Library at Lincoln Center, Brown University (Harris Collection), and the State Library of Ohio in Columbus.

See also DANCE, §II, 3; POPULAR MUSIC, §II, 3, and fig.1; MUSICAL THEATER, §II, 1.

BIBLIOGRAPHY

C. Wittke: *Tambo and Bones: a History of the American Minstrel Stage* (Durham, 1930)

C. Rourke: *American Humor* (New York, 1930/*R*1953)

——: *Roots of American Culture* (New York, 1942), 262ff

H. Nathan: *Dan Emmett and the Rise of Early Negro Minstrelsy* (Norman, OK, 1962/*R*1977)

N. I. Huggins: *Harlem Renaissance* (New York, 1971)

R. C. Toll: *Blacking Up: the Minstrel Show in Nineteenth-century America* (New York, 1974)

G. F. Rehin: "Harlequin Jim Crow: Continuity and Convergence in Blackface Clowning," *Journal of Popular Culture*, ix (1975), 682

——: "The Darker Image: American Negro Minstrelsy through the Historian's Lens," *Journal of American Studies*, ix (1975), 365

R. B. Winans: "The Folk, the Stage, and the Five-string Banjo in the Nineteenth Century," *Journal of American Folklore*, lxxxix (1976), 407–37

——: "Early Minstrel Show Music, 1843–1852," *Musical Theatre in America: Greenvale, NY, 1981*, ed. G. Loney (Westport, CT, 1984), 71

CLAYTON W. HENDERSON

Miracles. Rhythm-and-blues and soul vocal group formed in the mid-1950s by SMOKEY ROBINSON.

Miranda, Carmen [Miranda da Cunha, Maria do Carmo] (*b* Marco de Canaveses, nr Lisbon, Portugal, 9 Feb 1909; *d* Beverly Hills, CA, 5 Aug 1955). Singer and actress. She grew up in Rio de Janeiro, and had established herself as a popular entertainer with a reputation throughout South America by the time she appeared on Broadway in 1939. Known as "the Brazilian Bombshell," she captivated American audiences with her extravagant presentation of South American novelty songs and Tin Pan Alley imitations. Her samba-related dance movements, syncopated and staccato singing style, and outlandishly theatrical mode of dress were highly distinctive. From her initial successes in the revue *The Streets of Paris* (1939) and the film *Down Argentine Way* (1940) until her death, Miranda performed extensively in nightclubs, theaters, on television, and in motion picture musicals, making altogether 19 films and 154 recordings. Her film appearances were typically secondary roles capitalizing on her exotic qualities, and were usually played with a sense of self-parody. The height of her popularity – the 1940s – coincided with a great craze in the USA for Latin-American culture.

BIBLIOGRAPHY

"Miranda, Carmen," *CBY 1941*

J. Queiróz Júnior: *Carmen Miranda: vida, glória, amor e morte* (Rio de Janeiro, 1956)

D. Nasser: *A vida trepidante de Carmem Mirando* (Rio de Janeiro, 1966)

A. Cardoso Júnior: *Carmen Miranda: a cantora do Brasil* (São Paulo, 1978)

J. S. Roberts: *The Latin Tinge: the Impact of Latin American Music on the United States* (New York, 1979)

MICHAEL J. BUDDS

Mischakoff, Mischa (*b* Proskurov, Ukraine, 16 April 1896; *d* Petoskey, MI, 1 Feb 1981). Violinist. He studied with S. Korguyev at the St. Petersburg Conservatory and made his début in Berlin in 1912. After various teaching and orchestral posts he settled in the USA in 1921. There he chose the career of an orchestral player: he was concertmaster in 1924–7 with the New York SO (when Damrosch was conductor), 1927–30 with the Philadelphia Orchestra (under Stokowski), 1930–37 with the Chicago SO (under Stock), 1937–52 with the NBC SO in New York (under Toscanini), and 1952–68 with the Detroit SO (under Paray and Ehrling). In 1968–9 he was the guest concertmaster of the Baltimore SO. For 40 summers (1925–65) he served as concertmaster and soloist of the Chautauqua SO. Mischakoff was on the faculty of the Juilliard School (1941–52) and, from 1952, of Wayne State University in Detroit; he was also frequently a guest professor. For many years he led the Mischakoff String Quartet.

Mischakoff's style was ideally suited to his career. His tone was strong yet beautiful, and his rhythm robust. Untroubled by nerves, he conveyed his rock-like assurance to the orchestra, yet was always sensitive to the conductor's wishes. His experienced advice was highly prized, especially by Toscanini. In spite of his years of orchestral playing, Mischakoff never lost the refinement necessary for solo and chamber music. A connoisseur of fine instruments, he owned at one time two Stradivari violins known as the "Booth" and the "General Kyd," as well as a Guarneri "del Gesù." Later he played the "Adam" Stradivari.

BIBLIOGRAPHY

Obituary, *New York Times* (3 Feb 1981)

BORIS SCHWARZ

Mission music, California. *See* CALIFORNIA MISSION MUSIC.

Missourians. Dance band led by CAB CALLOWAY from 1928 to 1948.

Missud, Jean (Marie) (*b* Villefranche, nr Nice, France, 25 April 1852; *d* Marblehead, MA, 17 July 1941). Bandmaster, composer, and music publisher. At 13 he entered the conservatory in Nice, and at 17 enlisted in the US navy, in which he was a clarinetist and with which he came to the USA. He settled in Massachusetts in 1870, and played with groups in and around

Boston, including Harry Brown's Brigade Band. In 1878 he formed the Salem (Massachusetts) Cadet Band, which provided the music for the Second Corps of Cadets, Massachusetts National Guard, during the next 40 years, and for Boston's Ancient and Honorable Artillery Company on its tours of the USA, Canada, and England. He also performed at 50 annual commencement ceremonies at Tufts College, Medford, Massachusetts. In the late 1880s he began his own music publishing company, which continued until 1912. He wrote polkas, galops, waltzes, and more than 60 marches, but only his clarinet solo *Magnolia Serenade* remains in the repertory; some of his works are recorded in the Heritage of the March series (compiled by ROBERT HOE, JR.). His personal papers and manuscripts, and memorabilia relating to the Salem Cadet Band, are held at the Essex Institute in Salem.

RAOUL CAMUS

Mr. B. *See* ECKSTINE, BILLY.

Mitchell, Howard (*b* Lyons, NE, 11 March 1911). Conductor and cellist. As a child he studied piano and trumpet in Sioux City, Iowa, his family's home, before moving to Baltimore, where he took up cello at the Peabody Conservatory. He then went to the Curtis Institute as a pupil of Felix Salmond (1930–35), and while still a student he was engaged as principal cellist of the National SO of Washington, DC. He held this position from 1933 until 1944, when he was appointed assistant conductor to Hans Kindler; in 1948 he became associate conductor, succeeding Kindler as principal conductor in 1949. He gave the premières of Paul Creston's fourth and fifth symphonies (1952, 1956), Quincy Porter's *New England Episodes* (1958), and Villa-Lobos's Symphony no. 12 (1958). He resigned from the National SO in 1969, becoming music director emeritus, and was appointed principal conductor of the SODRE SO (the orchestra of the Uruguayan national broadcasting service) in Montevideo. Repeatedly honored for his services to American music, he received the Ditson Award of Columbia University, a citation of merit from the National Association for American Composers and Conductors, and an award for distinguished services from the National Music Council. Conservative in his musical tastes and competent as a conductor, he brought the National SO to the verge of becoming a first-rate orchestra before leaving it for his work in Uruguay.

BIBLIOGRAPHY

H. Stoddard: "Howard Mitchell," *Symphony Conductors of the U. S. A.* (New York, 1957), 119

GEORGE GELLES/R

Mitchell, Joni [Anderson, Roberta Joan] (*b* McLeod [now Fort Macleod], Alb., 1 Nov 1943). Pop singer and songwriter. She grew up in Saskatoon, Canada, where she took piano lessons, and according to some sources taught herself to play guitar from an instruction book by Pete Seeger (though others state that she learned guitar only after she took up ukulele at the age of 20). She studied commercial art for a year at the Alberta College of Art in Calgary, where she began singing folksongs. In the early 1960s she started to perform around Toronto, and she married Chuck Mitchell, a folksinger; the couple separated after moving to Detroit. Critical acclaim there and in New York led to Mitchell's signing a recording contract with Reprise. Her early songs were recorded by Tom Rush (*The Circle Game*) and Judy Collins (*Both sides now*, a hit in 1968), among others. Her own albums, on which she usually accompanied herself on acoustic guitar or dulcimer, at first attracted a small but devoted following. *Clouds* (1969), including Mitchell's own version of *Both sides now*, won a Grammy Award as the best folk performance of 1970.

By the end of the 1960s Mitchell had moved to the Laurel Canyon area of Los Angeles, with which many of her songs are closely associated. Crosby, Stills, Nash and Young made a hit with her song *Woodstock*, and her own album *Ladies of the Canyon* (1970), which included *Big Yellow Taxi*, a humorous, ecological protest song, and *For Free*, the first of her songs to deal with her own fame (a subject that runs through much of her later work), was her first album to gain a gold record. *Blue* (1971), on which James Taylor played guitar, began a phase in which her songs became progressively more meditative and personal, and her folk style began to move towards a cabaret approach. *For the Roses* (1972) was distinguished by a new willingness to mix a pop backing with her folk guitar; one of the songs, *You turn me on I'm a radio*, in an atypical country style, became a hit single. On *Court and Spark* (1974) Mitchell turned decisively towards a pop style; she was backed on the album and during the tour that followed its release (recorded on *Miles of Aisles*, 1974) by the saxophonist Tom Scott and members of his pop-jazz group the L. A. Express. *Help me* and *Free man in Paris* were hit singles, and *Court and Spark* became her best-selling LP recording.

From that point Mitchell began a period of experimentation. On *The Hissing of Summer Lawns* (1975) she used synthesizers and Burundian drumming, along with more conventional rock backing, while her poetic lines grew even longer. *Hejira* (1976), an album of songs about travel on which her singing was set in counterpoint against improvisatory bass guitar lines played by Jaco Pastorius, garnered both laudatory and adverse critical reviews; *Don Juan's Reckless Daughter* (1977), which included a long orchestral piece that was intended to be played while listeners read a narrative on the album's cover, was widely dismissed as self-indulgent. Mitchell's next phase led her to a jazz style. She collaborated with Charles Mingus in 1978, writing lyrics for his tunes and completing the album *Mingus* (after his death) with earnest tributes of her own. At this point she was trying to learn to sing jazz, but her distinctive vocal style, in which each note has its own timbre, was not light enough to adjust to jazz phrasing. *Shadows and Light* (1980), recorded in concert with a band

Joni Mitchell, c1979

that included Pastorius, the guitarist Pat Metheny, and the keyboard player Lyle Mays, was also an unsuccessful experiment. On *Wild Things Run Fast* (1982) Mitchell simplified her diction and shortened her melodic lines; the backing hinted at the jazz style of her previous releases, but the songwriting showed a return to the directness of pop music. The album yielded a hit single, a version of the Leiber and Stoller song *Baby I don't care*. In 1982 Mitchell married Larry Klein, the bass guitarist on the album.

An important influence on pop songwriting in the late 1960s and early 1970s, Mitchell's early work consisted largely of confessional love-songs, characterized by tremulous singing accompanied by strummed guitar in "open" tunings and rudimentary piano figuration, often arpeggios. Her later work, in which she addressed larger issues and expanded her musical vocabulary to include more pop and jazz elements, is both more personal and more experimental, but it often overreaches itself.

For further illustration *see* CROSBY, STILLS AND NASH.

RECORDINGS

(selective list)

Joni Mitchell (Rep. 6293, 1968); *Clouds* (Rep. 6341, 1969); *Ladies of the Canyon* (Rep. 6376, 1970); *Blue* (Rep. 2038, 1971); *For the Roses* (Asy. 5057, 1972); *Court and Spark* (Elek. 1001, 1974); *Miles of Aisles* (Asy. 202, 1974); *The Hissing of Summer Lawns* (Asy. 1051, 1975); *Hejira* (Asy. 1087, 1976); *Don Juan's Reckless Daughter* (Asy. 701, 1977); *Mingus* (Asy. 505, 1979); *Shadows and Light* (Asy. 704, 1980); *Wild Things Run Fast* (Geffen 2019, 1982); *Dog Eat Dog* (Geffen 24074, 1985)

BIBLIOGRAPHY

S. G. Lydon: "In her House, Love," *New York Times* (20 April 1969), §II, p.19
L. LeBlanc: "Joni Takes a Break," *Rolling Stone*, no.77 (1971), 28
Malka: "Face to Face," *Maclean's*, lxxxvii/6 (1974), 28
"Rock 'n' Roll's Leading Lady," *Time*, civ (16 Dec 1974), 63
L. Fleischer: *Joni Mitchell* (New York, 1976)
"Mitchell, Joni," *CBY 1976*

JON PARELES

Mitchell, Leona (*b* Enid, OK, 13 Oct 1949). Soprano. She began her career singing in the choir of her father's church. Unable to read music, she learned an aria from *Aida* by rote and won a full scholarship to Oklahoma City University (BA 1971). While a student there, she performed in Isaac Van Grove's *The Story of Ruth*; she had never before seen an opera. In 1971, she won first place in the Merola Opera Program, sponsored by the San Francisco Opera, whose general director, Kurt Herbert Adler, guided her career. She made her professional début as Micaela (Bizet's *Carmen*) at the San Francisco Spring Opera Theater in 1972. The following year, after obtaining a grant from Opera America, she moved to Los Angeles to study with Ernest St. John Metz, who has continued to be her vocal coach.

Mitchell's Metropolitan Opera début, also as Micaela, took place in December 1975; the same year, she sang Bess on Maazel's recording of Gershwin's opera. At the Metropolitan she has also sung Pamina (*Die Zauberflöte*), the Prioress (Poulenc's *Dialogues des carmélites*), Puccini's Butterfly and Musetta, and Verdi's Leonora (*La forza del destino*) and Elvira (*Ernani*). She made her European operatic début at the Geneva Opera (1976), singing Liù (*Turandot*), a role she repeated in 1980 at Covent Garden and the Paris Opéra. Her voice has been described as a cross between Price's husky chest tones and Freni's radiant upper register. Although Mitchell's early career was as a lyric soprano, in the early 1980s she was moving into the *spinto* repertory.

BIBLIOGRAPHY

SouthernB
S. Wadsworth: "Here to Sing: Soprano on the rise: Leona Mitchell comes into her own with no less than five roles at the Met this season," *Opera News*, xliii/14 (1979), 10
H. Waleson: "A Lyric Soprano Ventures into Heavier Fare," *New York Times* (20 March 1983), §2, p.23

MICHAEL WALSH

Mitchell, Nellie Brown. *See* BROWN, NELLIE E.

Mitchell, Roscoe. Jazz musician and founding member of the ART ENSEMBLE OF CHICAGO.

Mitchell, William (*b* Billquay, Durham, England, 1798; *d* New York, 12 May 1856). Actor and theater manager. He acted in Newcastle upon Tyne before making his London début at the Strand Theatre; his New York début was at the National Theatre on 29 August 1836. In December 1839 he became manager of the Olympic Theatre in New York. He reduced prices, assembled a gifted and loyal company, and each night offered three or four short farces intermixed with songs, dances, and novelties. Musical burlesques were an important part of the Olympic's program, and operatic travesties included *The Roof Scambler* (Bellini's *La sonnambula*), *The Bohea-Man's Girl* (Balfe's *The Bohemian Girl*), *Fried Shots* (Weber's *Der Freischütz*), and *Buy-it-Dear, 'Tis Made of Cashmere* (Catel's *Les bayadères*). Mitchell also presented "straight" opera in English adaptations: for a time M. R. Lacy's *Cinderella*, based on Rossini's *La Cenerentola*, ran concurrently with a burlesque on the same work. With its mixed bills, topical parodies, and extensive use of music, the Olympic was a significant precursor of variety and musical comedy. During the 1846–7 season Mitchell fell seriously ill, and appeared only infrequently thereafter; pressed hard by William Burton, whose new theater (opened 10 July 1848) emulated his innovations, Mitchell closed the Olympic on 9 March 1850 and retired.

BIBLIOGRAPHY

Obituary, *New York Herald* (13 May 1856)
E. F. Edgett: "Mitchell, William," *DAB*
G. C. D. Odell: *Annals of the New York Stage*, iv–v (New York, 1928–31/*R*1970)

WILLIAM BROOKS

Mitchell, William J(ohn) (*b* New York, 21 Nov 1906; *d* Binghamton, NY, 17 Aug 1971). Musicologist. He studied in New York at the Institute for Musical Art and at Columbia University (BA 1930, MA 1938). After two years in Vienna (1930–32) he returned to join the Columbia faculty (1932–67), and chaired the department of music, 1962–7. He also lectured at Mannes College (1957–68) and at SUNY, Binghamton. He was president of the American Musicological Society, 1965–6.

Mitchell's main area of interest was music theory; he devised the curriculum in this subject as an academic discipline at Columbia University and wrote a number of works on the theory and historical practice of harmony and musical structure including *Elementary Harmony* (1939, 3/1965) and an edition and translation (1949) of C. P. E. Bach's *Versuch über die wahre Art das Clavier zu spielen*. Previously he had edited and translated E. Herriot's *La vie de Beethoven* (1935). He was co-editor of the first three volumes of *Music Forum* (1967–73).

PAULA MORGAN

Mitropoulos, Dimitri (*b* Athens, Greece, 1 March 1896; *d* Milan, Italy, 2 Nov 1960). Conductor, pianist, and composer. His studies at the Athens Odeion Conservatory under Ludwig von Wassenhoven (piano) and Armand Marsick (harmony) brought him a gold medal for piano playing in 1918, and two years later the production at the conservatory of his opera based on Maurice Maeterlinck's *Soeur Béatrice*. He went to Brussels for composition studies with Paul Gilson (1920–21), and was accepted for Busoni's piano master class at the Berlin Hochschule für Musik, which he attended in 1921–4 while working as vocal coach at the Staatsoper. Returning to Athens in 1924 he began to conduct the conservatory orchestra and in 1930 to teach composition. His work in raising orchestral standards and widening the repertory brought him more than local attention; in 1930 he was engaged to conduct the Berlin PO, which led to tours as a pianist and conductor in Europe and the USSR. In 1936 he was engaged by Koussevitzky as guest conductor for the Boston SO, making his American début on 21 January in Providence, Rhode Island, and first appearing in Boston three days later; thereafter he settled in the USA, taking American citizenship in 1946.

Dimitri Mitropoulos, c1948

Mitropoulos succeeded Ormandy in 1937 as conductor of the Minneapolis SO, remaining for 12 years, then shared the direction of the New York PO with Stokowski for a few weeks in 1949 before Stokowski resigned and Mitropoulos became sole conductor until 1958 (when he resigned and was succeeded by Bernstein). During these years he much improved the Minneapolis SO standards; devoted much care and effort to enriching the American concert repertory with works by Berg, Krenek, Schoenberg, and others at a time when they were considered avant garde; received the medal of the American Mahler Society in 1940 for his promotion of Mahler's music; and gave concert performances of such operas as Strauss's *Elektra*, Schoenberg's *Erwartung*, Berg's *Wozzeck*, and Busoni's *Arlecchino* when they were seldom seen on the stage. In 1950 he appeared with the New York PO at the Roxy Theatre for two weeks, giving four performances daily between showings of a feature film, a successful experiment later repeated. With the same orchestra he conducted at the 1951 and 1955 Edinburgh Festivals, and in 1955 in London (where he was a rare visitor). Mitropoulos seldom worked in the opera house until his début at the Metropolitan Opera in 1954 with Strauss's *Salome*. He returned each season until his death, and gave the première there of Barber's *Vanessa* (15 January 1958), which he introduced to Europe at the Salzburg Festival the same year. He also appeared at other European opera centers, including Florence (at the Maggio Musicale) and La Scala, Milan. An ascetic by temperament, he was an unorthodox conductor, preferring no baton and no score (but having a total command of the music's detail), using jerky and imprecise gestures which were sometimes found to vary an interpretation between rehearsal and performance. He obtained performances of an impassioned intensity that at times put severe strain on the structure of Classical and Romantic works. His Edinburgh performances of the Fourth Symphonies of Beethoven and Vaughan Williams were described (in *The Times*, London) as "hateful" and "revelatory" respectively, but it was also well said of him (in *The Observer*) that when it came to more problematic music, he was "not one of those who pass by on the other side." He died after a heart attack while rehearsing Mahler's Third Symphony with the orchestra of La Scala. An international conductors' competition bearing his name was established in New York in 1961. His compositions, besides *Soeur Béatrice*, include a symphonic poem *La mise au tombeau de Christ* (1916), a Concerto grosso (1929), a Piano Sonata (1919), and *Fête crétoise* (1928), orchestrated by Nikos Skalkottas, a song cycle *Hedonica* (1927; poems by Constantine Cavafy), incidental music for plays, other piano and chamber music, and orchestrations of organ works by Bach.

BIBLIOGRAPHY

D. Brook: *International Gallery of Conductors* (London, 1951), 121ff
R. Gelatt: "Dimitri Mitropoulos," *Music-makers* (New York, 1953), 34
"The Conductor Speaks," *Opera News*, xix/9 (1955), 8
W. S. Meadmore: "Dimitri Mitropoulos," *Gramophone*, xxxiii (1955–6), 344
D. Mitropoulos: "What I Believe," *Hi-Fi Music at Home*, iii/2 (1956), 24
H. Stoddard: *Symphony Conductors of the U. S. A.* (New York, 1957), 126ff
H. Levinger: "Dimitri Mitropoulos, 1896–1960," *MusAm*, lxxx/13 (1960), 22
R. Cumming: "The Legend of Mitropoulos," *MJ*, xix/4 (1961), 20
H. C. Schonberg: *The Great Conductors* (New York, 1967)
D. Wooldridge: *Conductor's World* (New York, 1970)
Dimitri Mitropoulos [and] Katy Katsoyanis: a Correspondence, 1930–1960 (New York, 1973)

NOËL GOODWIN

Mizelle, (Dary) John (*b* Stillwater, OK, 14 June 1940). Composer. He studied trombone at California State University, Sacramento (BA 1965), and composition at the University of California, Davis (MA 1967), and the University of California, San Diego (PhD 1973), where his teachers included Gaburo, Oliveros, Reynolds, and Stockhausen. He has taught at the University of South Florida, Tampa (1973–5), and Oberlin College Conservatory (1975–9); in 1979–80 he was technical director of the Sonavera Studio of Sonic Arts in Hawthorne, New York. Mizelle specializes in the use of live electronics, digital as well as analog, with various instruments (ranging from trombone to shakuhachi) often played by himself, and/or voices. His works, which are austere in character and often employ minimalist processes and improvisation, show the influence of Eastern music. A number have been recorded, notably *Primavera-heterophony*, *Polyphonies I* (performed by Mizelle), and various compositions for percussion and electronics.

WORKS

Green and Red, vn, hn, bn, cl, hpd, 1966; Straight Ahead, vn, fl, tpt, trbn, perc, tape, 1966; Radial Energy I, unspecified insts, 1967; Mass (anon.), chorus, elec, 1968; Polyphonies I, II, III, elec, shakuhachi, dancer, actress,

1975; Transforms, pf, 1975–81; Soundscape, perc ens, 1976; Quanta & Hymn to Matter (P. Teilhard de Chardin), orch, chorus, 1977; Polytempus I, tpt, tape, 1978; Primavera-heterophony, vc choir, 1978; Samadhi, cptr tape, 1978; Quanta II & Hymn of the Word (Rg-Veda), 2 choruses, 1979; Polytempus II, mar, tape, 1980

Principal publishers: Composer Performer Edition, Lingua, Mizelle

INGRAM D. MARSHALL

MJQ. *See* MODERN JAZZ QUARTET.

MLA. *See* MUSIC LIBRARY ASSOCIATION.

Mobart Music Publications. Firm of music publishers founded as a sister company to BOELKE-BOMART.

Moby Grape. Rock group. Formed in San Francisco in 1966, its members were Skip Spence (*b* Windsor, Ont., 18 April 1946), singer and guitarist (formerly of the group Jefferson Airplane), Peter Lewis (*b* Los Angeles, CA, 15 July 1945), singer and guitarist, Jerry Miller (*b* Tacoma, WA, 10 July 1943), singer and guitarist, Bob Mosley (*b* Paradise Valley, CA, 4 Dec 1942), singer and bass guitarist, and Don Stevenson (*b* Seattle, WA, 15 Oct 1942), singer and drummer. Their first album, *Moby Grape*, produced by their manager, David Rubinson, was released simultaneously with five singles in 1967; containing songs by all five members of the group (all of whom also sang on the album), it distilled a concise, dense style from country music, rhythm-and-blues, and rock-and-roll, supported by layered pop harmonies, and featuring multiple lead guitars. It was one of the strongest and most stylistically unified American rock albums of the 1960s. The much less successful *Wow!* (1968) included novelty effects and contained a "bonus" disc carrying a blues instrumental *Grape Jam*, played by the group, Al Kooper, and Michael Bloomfield. Spence left Moby Grape in 1968 to record *Oar*, an album of acoustic country blues and electric psychedelic rock, on which he played all the instruments. The group released *Moby Grape '69*, which had a country-music flavor, and, when Mosley left, the remaining trio recorded the even softer *Truly Fine Citizen* (1970). All the original members reunited briefly in 1971 to record *20 Granite Creek*.

RECORDINGS

(selective list; recorded for Columbia unless otherwise stated)

Moby Grape (9498, 1967); *Wow!* (9613, 1968); *Moby Grape '69* (9696, 1969); *Truly Fine Citizen* (9912, 1970); *20 Granite Creek* (Rep. 6460, 1971)

JOHN PICCARELLA

Mockridge, Cyril (John) (*b* London, England, 6 Aug 1896; *d* Honolulu, HI, 18 Jan 1979). Composer. He studied at the Royal Academy of Music in London and, after war service, settled in the USA in 1922. He worked on Broadway as a rehearsal pianist and vaudeville accompanist and made piano arrangements for musicals by Rodgers and Hart. In 1932 he joined the Fox Film Corporation as a rehearsal pianist and arranger, but later began to compose and direct. He was one of the mainstays of the 20th Century-Fox music department until he began to work as a freelance in 1960, contributing music to more than 200 films; many scores were composed in collaboration with David Buttolph, Hugo Friedhofer, Alfred Newman, or David Raksin. Among his own most notable scores are those for *The Ox-bow Incident* and *Nightmare Alley*. He also wrote the theme music for the television series "Laramie" and scored numerous comedy and dramatic programs.

WORKS

(selective list; all film scores)

The Ox-bow Incident, 1943; The Eve of St. Mark, 1944; Captain Eddie, 1945; Colonel Effingham's Raid, 1945; The Late George Apley, 1947; Miracle on 34th Street, 1947; Nightmare Alley, 1947; I was a Male War Bride, 1949; American Guerrilla in the Philippines, 1950; Dreamboat, 1952; Woman's World, 1954; Many Rivers to Cross, 1955; Desk Set, 1957; Will Success Spoil Rock Hunter?, 1957; Rally 'Round the Flag, Boys!, 1958; The Man who Shot Liberty Valance, 1962; Donovan's Reef, 1963

CHRISTOPHER PALMER/FRED STEINER

Modal jazz. A style of jazz developed in the late 1950s in which modal scales (or their general characteristics) dictate the melodic and harmonic content. Modal jazz rarely adheres strictly to the classical modes (Dorian, Phrygian, etc.), but it creates their flavor, or in some cases that of other nondiatonic scales, such as those of Spanish or Indian music. Modal improvisation has attracted musicians partly because it is relatively undemanding by comparison with that based on chord progressions. It allows the development of a motif over a long period because it is free of frequent harmonic interruption in the form of chord changes. As a result modal jazz can more easily create an unhurried and meditative feeling than can improvisation based on chord progressions. Most performances are based on a two-chord sequence, usually derived from one of the "minor" modes; numerous groups in the 1960s and 1970s recorded entire albums in which the harmonic basis consisted of nothing more than simple, repeating patterns, and in fact the absence of frequent chord changes alone is sometimes regarded as defining modal jazz.

The first widely known jazz improvisation based on modes is Miles Davis's *Milestones* on the album of the same name (1958); it has the form *AABBA*, in which *A* uses a Dorian mode on G, and *B* an Aeolian mode on A. (Although Davis adheres closely to the notes of the mode in his improvisation, his saxophonists, Cannonball Adderley and John Coltrane, explore more freely, referring more to the chords that form the accompaniment: Gm^7/C in the *A* section and Dm^7/E in the *B* section; ex. 1.) This was

Ex.1 Modal bases of *Milestones* on M. Davis: *Milestones* (1958, Col. PC9428)

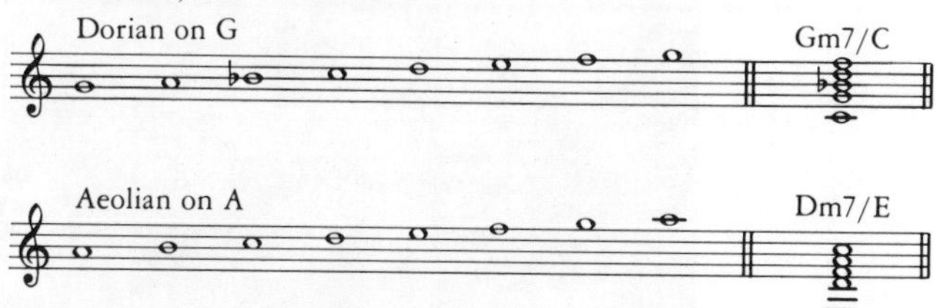

followed in 1959 by Davis's collaboration with the pianist Bill Evans on the album *Kind of Blue*, in which they developed ideas that had appeared in Evans's *Peace Piece* (on *Peace Piece and Other Pieces*, 1958) and Davis's *Sketches of Spain* (1959–60). *Flamenco Sketches* (often mistakenly identified as *All Blues*) on *Kind of Blue* is not based on an existing theme but it consists solely of improvisations on a scheme of five modes. Another piece on the album, *So What*, the melody of which is stated by pizzicato bass, has a 32-bar, *AABA* structure; the solo improvisations in the *A* section are in D Dorian (over a Dm^7 harmony), while in the *B* section the mode is simply shifted up a half-step (over an E♭m^7 harmony; ex. 2, p. 252). The form and modal bases of *So What* were followed by John Coltrane in his *Impressions* on the album of the same name (1961–3). Another pioneering modal improvisation is Da-

Ex.2 Modal bases of *So What* on M. Davis: *Kind of Blue* (1959, Col. PC8163)

vis's trumpet solo in *Solea* on *Sketches of Spain*, which rests on an ostinato bass figure and a drum pattern. Popularization of modal techniques in jazz was substantially aided by the enthusiastic reception that greeted John Coltrane's version (1960) of *My Favorite Things* by Rodgers and Hammerstein, in which his improvisations did not follow the tune's chord progressions; the pianist McCoy Tyner accompanied Coltrane with a two-bar, two-chord pattern, which he repeated at length in E minor and then in E major. This became a much imitated technique (as did the accompaniment voicings used by Bill Evans and McCoy Tyner on various recordings). During the 1960s Davis concentrated more on chord progressions, but he eventually adopted improvisational techniques based almost exclusively on modes when he began to combine jazz and funk, beginning with his influential albums *In a Silent Way* and *Bitches Brew* (both recorded in 1969). The group's harmonies are usually founded on a repeating bass figure, but the improvisations often imply more changes of harmony that are played because the soloists (using an approach pioneered by John Coltrane) conceptually juxtapose distantly related chords. Davis and many other bandleaders continued to use these techniques into the 1980s. Besides those already mentioned, influential figures in the development of modal jazz include Pharoah Sanders, Don Ellis, and Don Cherry.

Modal jazz and free jazz are in some cases difficult to distinguish largely because the lack of a predetermined harmonic structure in modal jazz may be easily confused with the avoidance of a tonal center in free jazz; moreover, free jazz sometimes acquires a modal orientation in the course of improvisation. Coltrane's *Ascension* (1965), for example, has sometimes been classified as free jazz because it resembles Ornette Coleman's *Free Jazz* (1960), but it is, in fact, based on four modes.

See also JAZZ, §VI, 2.

BIBLIOGRAPHY

E. Jost: *Free Jazz* (Graz, Austria, 1974), chap. 1
J. Pressing: "Towards an Understanding of Scales in Jazz," *Jazzforschung*, ix (1977), 25
M. Gridley: *Jazz Styles: History and Analysis* (Englewood Cliffs, NJ, 1978, rev. 2/1985), 217, 287, 384, 418

MARK C. GRIDLEY

Modern jazz. A term used collectively of the jazz styles developed between the early 1940s and the 1960s; it covers mainly bop and its offshoots. *See* JAZZ, §V.

Modern Jazz Quartet (MJQ). Jazz ensemble. Its original members – MILT JACKSON (vibraphone), JOHN LEWIS (piano and director), Ray Brown (double bass), and Kenny Clarke (drums) – first performed together in 1946 in Dizzy Gillespie's big band. In 1951–2 these four players made recordings under the name of the Milt Jackson Quartet. By 1952, when the first recordings under the name Modern Jazz Quartet were issued, Percy Heath had replaced Brown as bassist. The group began performing regularly in concert halls and nightclubs from 1954. In the following year Clarke was replaced by Connie Kay, thus establishing the group's present membership. By virtue of their recordings and international concert tours the MJQ soon acquired a reputation as a superior jazz ensemble. Beginning in the early 1960s the group disbanded during the summer months, enabling Lewis to pursue his activities as a composer and teacher, and the other members to perform in different jazz contexts. In 1974, primarily because of Jackson's desire to perform full-time as a

The Modern Jazz Quartet, 1965, with John Lewis (piano), Percy Heath (bass), Connie Kay (drums), and Milt Jackson (vibraphone)

leader, the MJQ broke up. For several years its members pursued separate careers, reuniting occasionally for short concert tours, but in the early 1980s they resumed playing together for several months each year.

The MJQ plays in a restrained, conservative bop style that is sometimes referred to as cool jazz. In its best moments it has a finely honed ensemble sound, owing in part to the longstanding association of the four excellent players and in part to Lewis's compositions, which include some of the most carefully organized works in jazz history. The main soloist is Jackson, whose exuberant and rhythmically complex solos contrast effectively with Lewis's restrained and deceptively simple manner of playing. By frequently accompanying Jackson with subsidiary countermelodies rather than the usual chordal punctuations of bop, Lewis creates a distinctive contrapuntal texture seldom heard in other bop performances.

Throughout its long career the MJQ has also performed and recorded much third-stream music, combining techniques of European art music and jazz improvisation. These works, written by Lewis, Gunther Schuller, André Hodeir, and others, are uneven in quality, some suffering from disparities between the composed and improvised sections, others from pretentiousness. Among the best are Lewis's *England's Carol* and his fugal pieces *Versailles*, *Concorde*, *Vendome*, and *Three Windows*.

RECORDINGS

(selective list)

As the Milt Jackson Quartet: Softly as in a Morning Sunrise/True Blues (1952, Hi-Lo 1412)

As the Modern Jazz Quartet: *Fontessa* (1956, Atl. 1231), incl. Versailles; *The Modern Jazz Quartet* (1957, Atl. 1265); *One Never Knows* (1957, Atl. 1284), incl. Three Windows; *Third Stream Music* (1957, Atl. 1345); *The Modern Jazz Quartet and Orchestra* (1960, Atl. 1359), incl. England's Carol; *European Concert* (1960, Atl. 1385/6), incl. Vendome; *The Comedy* (1962, Atl. 1390); *A Quartet is a Quartet is a Quartet* (1963, Atl. 1420), incl. Concorde; *Blues at Carnegie Hall* (1966, Atl. 1468); *The Last Concert* (1974, Atl. 2-909)

BIBLIOGRAPHY

N. Hentoff: "Jazz Reviews: Modern Jazz Quartet," *Down Beat*, xx/22 (1953), 16

——: "The Modern Jazz Quartet," *High Fidelity*, v/3 (1955), 36

M. Harrison: "Looking Back at the Modern Jazz Quartet," *Jazz Monthly*, v/4 (1958); repr. in *The Art of Jazz*, ed. M. Williams (New York, 1959), 219

M. Williams: "Closing Chorus for the MJQ," *Saturday Review*, xlv (14 July 1962), 34

G. Marne: "The Modern Jazz Quartet," *International Musician*, lxii/1 (1964), 8

M. Williams: "Early MJQ: an Appreciation," *Kulchur*, iv (spr. 1964), 94

T. Owens: *Improvisation Techniques of the Modern Jazz Quartet* (thesis, UCLA, 1965)

N. Koyama and others: "John Lewis and MJQ Discography," *Swing Journal*, xxviii/3 (1974), 266

C. Mitchell: "Modern Jazz Quartet Calls it Quits," *Down Beat*, xli/15 (1974), 9

T. Owens: "The Fugal Pieces of the Modern Jazz Quartet," *Journal of Jazz Studies*, iv/1 (1976), 25

L. Feather: "MJQ: the Quartet that Wouldn't Die," *Los Angeles Times Calendar* (27 March 1983), 68

I. Gitler: "The Return of the Modern Jazz Quartet," *Jazz Times* (March 1983), 10

THOMAS OWENS

Modern Lovers. Rock group led by JONATHAN RICHMAN.

Moennig. Family of instrument makers and dealers. William Heinrich Moennig (*b* Markneukirchen, Saxony, Germany, 29 June 1883; *d* Philadelphia, PA, 1962) trained as a violin maker with an uncle in Budapest before going to work with his brother-in-law Julius Guetter in Philadelphia at the beginning of the 20th century. In 1909 he established his own firm, which has been carried on by his descendants as William Moennig & Son. In 1925 he sponsored the immigration of his nephew, (William) Hans Moennig (*b* Markneukirchen, 14 Dec 1903), who had worked for the German firm of Heckel as a bassoon maker and repairer. After a brief period working for the flute maker William S. Haynes in Boston, Hans established his own business in Philadelphia, where he was a highly regarded maker, dealer, and repairer of wind instruments; it was disbanded in 1983.

William Heinrich's son, William Herrman Moennig, Jr. (*b* Philadelphia, 21 July 1905), became a pupil of his father, who then sent him to study in Markneukirchen and Mittenwald; he qualified as a master violin maker under the auspices of the German Guild. After World War II William Moennig, Jr., built up a business with a fine reputation among musicians and teachers throughout the USA for fair dealing in old instruments. He is one of the leading experts on fine old violins and was the first American member of the International Society of Violin and Bow Makers. His son William Harry Moennig III (*b* Philadelphia, 28 Aug 1930) is an excellent craftsman. He trained with Amédée Dieudonné in Mirecourt, France, and at the violin making school in Mittenwald with Leo Aschauer, before studying repairing in Philadelphia. In 1975 he took over the running of the business from his father. Also active in the firm is William Harry's son William Raymond Moennig IV (*b* Philadelphia, 10 April 1957), who received his training from his father and grandfather.

CHARLES BEARE

Moevs, Robert (Walter) (*b* La Crosse, WI, 2 Dec 1920). Composer. He gave his first piano recital in La Crosse in 1929 and has remained active as a concert and ensemble pianist. After studying music at Harvard University (BA 1942), he entered the US Air Force and served as a pilot, and later as an officer in the Allied Control Commission in Romania (until 1947). He resumed his musical studies at the Paris Conservatoire (1947–51) and then returned to Harvard (MA 1952); his principal teachers were Piston at Harvard and Boulanger in Paris. For the next three years he was at the American Academy in Rome as a Rome Prize Fellow. Moevs is a masterly and rigorous teacher; he has served on the faculty at Harvard University (1955–63) and at Rutgers, the State University of New Jersey (from 1964), where he has been chairman of the music department. He was composer-in-residence at the American Academy in Rome in 1960–61 and a Guggenheim Fellow in 1963–4. Awards made to him include one from the National Institute of Arts and Sciences (1956) and several from ASCAP. In Italy in 1978 he received the Stockhausen International Prize in Composition for Concerto grosso for piano, percussion, and orchestra, recorded on the CRI label.

Moevs's broad compositional structures are logical and balanced, with an extremely impassioned content; he writes skillfully for orchestra and in particular for percussion. While Beethoven and Stravinsky seemed the spiritual sources of his music in the 1950s, later works present the same passion and control in what Moevs labels "the new international contemporary style, still called the 'avant-garde.' "

WORKS

INSTRUMENTAL

Orch: Endymion, ballet, 1948; Introduction and Fugue, 1949; Ov., 1950; 14 Variations, 1952; 3 Sym. Pieces, 1955; Conc. grosso, pf, perc, orch, 1960–68; In festivitate, wind, perc, 1962; Main-travelled Roads (Sym. Piece no.4),

1973; Prometheus: Music for Small Orch I, 1980; Pandora: Music for Small Orch II, 1983; Sym. Piece no.5, 1984

Chamber: Pf Sonatina, 1947; Pf Sonata, 1950; Spring, 4 vn, tpt, 1950; Pan, fl, 1951; Fantasia sopra uno motivo, pf, 1951; Duo, ob, eng hn, 1953; Vn Sonata, 1956; Str Qt, 1957; Variazioni sopra una melodia, va, vc, 1961; Musica da camera, 9 insts, 1965; Fanfara canonica, 6 tpt, 1966; Piece for Synket, 1969; Heptachronon, vc, 1969; B-A-C-H Es ist genug, org, 1970; Paths and Ways, dancer, sax, 1970; Phoenix, pf, 1971; Musica da camera II, 9 insts, 1972; Ludi praeteriti: Games of the Past, 2 pf, 1976; Una collana musicale, pf, 1977; Crystals, fl, 1979; Postlude, org, 1980; Pf Trio, 1980; 3 Pieces, vn, pf, 1982

VOCAL

Choral: Great nations of this earth (Moevs), women's chorus, 1942; The Bacchantes (after Euripides), 1947; Cantata sacra (Easter liturgy), Bar, men's chorus, fl, 4 trbn, timp, 1952; Attis (Catullus), S, T, chorus, perc, orch, 1958–63; Et nunc, reges, female chorus, fl, cl, b cl, 1963; Et occidentem illustra (Dante, etc), chorus, orch, 1964; Ave Maria, 1966; Alleluia for Michaelmas, congregation, org, 1967; A Brief Mass, chorus, org, vib, gui, db, 1968; The Aulos Player (D'Annunzio), S, 2 choruses, 2 org, 1975

Songs: Youthful Song (Moevs), 3 songs, 1940–51; Villanelle (Desportes), 1950; Time, Mez, pf, 1969; Epigram (Moirous), 1v, pf, 1978

Several early works, withdrawn

MSS in *DLC*

Principal publishers: Belwin-Mills, Eschig, Harvard UP, Piedmont, Presser, Ricordi, E. C. Schirmer

BIBLIOGRAPHY

EwenD

B. Archibald: "Composers of Importance Today: Robert Moevs," *Musical Newsletter*, ii/1 (1971), 19

BRUCE ARCHIBALD

Moffo, Anna (*b* Wayne, PA, 27 June 1932). Soprano. She studied at the Curtis Institute with Eufemia Giannini-Gregory and in Rome with Luigi Ricci and Mercedes Llopart, making her début in 1955 at the Teatro Sperimentale, Spoleto, as Donizetti's Norina. For Italian television she played Butterfly (1956), and subsequently Nannetta, Amina, Lucia, and Marie (*La fille du régiment*). In 1956 she sang Zerlina at Aix-en-Provence, and after many appearances throughout Italy, made her American début the following year as Mimì at the Chicago Lyric Opera. She joined the Metropolitan Opera in 1959, making her début there as Violetta; her more than 25 roles with the company during the 1960s and early 1970s included Pamina, Norina, Gilda, Luisa Miller, the four heroines of *Les contes d'Hoffmann*, Juliet, Gounod's Marguerite, Massenet's Manon, Mélisande, and the title role in *La Périchole*. She sang in all the leading opera houses of Europe, and appeared widely in concert. Notable among her recordings are a selection of Verdi arias, *Hänsel und Gretel*, and Canteloube's *Chants d'Auvergne*, all of which won awards. A lyric soprano of warm, full, radiant tone, she was capable of undertaking coloratura parts. As Violetta, a role in which she was internationally acclaimed, notably on film and record, and as a guest artist in Felsenstein's production at the Komische Oper, Berlin, the range and versatility of her voice and her charming stage presence were put to particularly good use. Unfortunately her musical and dramatic talent was exploited, and she appeared in the theater and on record in unsuitable roles. This led to a vocal breakdown in 1974–5, but in 1976 she made a fresh start.

BIBLIOGRAPHY

"Moffo, Anna," *CBY 1961*

J. Hines: "Anna Moffo," *Great Singers on Great Singing* (Garden City, NY, 1982), 182

HAROLD ROSENTHAL/R

Mohaupt, Richard (*b* Breslau [now Wrocław, Poland], 14 Sept 1904; *d* Reichenau, Austria, 3 July 1957). German composer. After studying at Breslau University, he worked as a vocal coach and opera conductor, toured as pianist and conductor (1931–2), and spent several years in Berlin as composer and pianist for a film company. Conflicts with the Nazi regime led to his immigration to New York (1939), where he taught and composed most of his serious works, including *Stadtpfeifermusik*, based on Dürer's mural. He received several commissions, among them one from the Louisville Orchestra for his opera *Double Trouble* (first performed 4 Dec 1954), and was highly successful as a composer of works for children, films, and broadcasting. In 1955 he moved to Austria. His music shows great technical facility combined with the simplicity developed in his popular music. Among his most interesting works are those for the stage, most of them comic. Mohaupt is almost certainly the pseudonymous "Fugitivus," author of the article "Inside Germany," published in *Modern Music* (xvi/4, 1939, p.203), which describes the debasement of German culture and his own experience under the Nazi regime.

WORKS

(selective list)

Operas: Die Bremer Stadtmusikanten, 1944; Double Trouble (Zwillingskomödie) (after Plautus), 1954

Ballets: Lysistrata, dance-comedy, solo vv, chorus, orch, 1941, rev. as Der Weiberstreik von Athen, orch, 1955; Max und Moritz, dance-burlesque, 1945; The Legend of the Charlatan, mimodrama, 1949

Orch: Stadtpfeifermusik, 1939, rev. wind, 1953; Sym. "Rhythmus und Variationen," 1940; Conc. for Orch, 1942; Vn Conc., 1945; Lysistrata, choreographic episodes, 1946; Max und Moritz [after ballet], nar, orch, 1946; Banchetto musicale, 12 insts, orch, 1955; Offenbachiana, 1955

Vocal: Trilogy (Euripides, Sappho, Aristophanes), A, orch, 1951; Das goldene Byzanz, dramatic cantata, chorus, ens, 1954; Bucolica, 4 solo vv, chorus, orch, 1955; lieder, children's songs

Chamber and pf pieces, music for the cinema and broadcasting, arrs.

Principal publishers: Associated, Universal

BIBLIOGRAPHY

R. Bilke: "Richard Mohaupt," *Musica*, iv (1950), 324

JOSEPH CLARK/RUTH B. HILTON

Mohawk. Indian tribe of the IROQUOIS confederacy.

Mojave. American Indian tribe, northernmost of a group of related tribes that live along the Colorado River (*see* INDIANS, AMERICAN, fig.1). Like the Quechan, located downriver, the Mojave were traditionally leaders in trade and war who traveled hundreds of miles in every direction to attack, trade, or visit. Singing is an important part of social interaction between tribes; as a result Mojave musical traditions have spread throughout much of Arizona and southern California. The influence is evident in the many songs of other tribes that are attributed to the Mojave, and many American Indian communities in Arizona and California still invite Mojave singers to lead the singing in various social gatherings.

Mojave music is principally vocal; singing plays an important role in all traditional Mojave ceremonial events, including healing ceremonies, funerals and memorials, preparations for war and victory celebrations, and social dances. In the Mojave tradition dreams are believed to be the basis of everything in life, including music. All new songs are received through dreams, and old ones, which are heard frequently, must be dreamed about before a person has the right to sing them.

The Colorado River tribes, including the Mojave, developed to an extreme degree a highly distinctive mode of singing, which has become known as the Yuman musical style. Its traits include:

a relatively relaxed vocal style, with no strong accents or pulsations; alternating two-unit and three-unit rhythmic figures; use of the rise – a phrase imitating the main motive on a higher tonal level; and the organization of songs into long cycles, each containing from 100 to 200 songs. The songs in each of these have closely related melodies and text forms. Each cycle is based on a myth: "all the cycles have their songs strung on a thread of myth, of which the singer is conscious, although practically nothing of the story appears in the brief, stylistically chosen, and distorted words of the songs" (Kroeber, 1925, p.755).

A cycle may take many nights to perform. Songs are sung solo or, more often, by a group in unison following a lead singer. Some cycles use a rattle accompaniment, others a basket beaten with a stick, and a few have no accompaniment. The singing of many cycles is supplemented by dancing, the most common style of which involves two lines of dancers who face each other and move alternately forwards and backwards in silence. There are dozens of different cycles, including the Akaka (raven), Yelak (goose), Ahta (cane), Kapeta (turtle), Hacha, Nyohaiva, and Tumanpa.

Trading of song cycles among tribes is common. Besides their own the Mojave sing cycles that they attribute to the Chemehuevi, the Kamia, and the Quechan.

See also INDIANS, AMERICAN, esp. §I, 4(ii)(c).

BIBLIOGRAPHY

A. L. Kroeber: "A Preliminary Sketch of the Mohave Indians," *American Anthropologist*, iv (1902), 276

——: *Handbook of the Indians of California*, Bureau of American Ethnology Bulletin, no.78 (Washington, DC, 1925)

G. Herzog: "The Yuman Musical Style," *Journal of American Folklore*, xli (1928), 183

F. Densmore: *Yuman and Yaqui Music* (Washington, DC, 1932/*R*1972)

G. Devereux: "Dream Learning and Individual Ritual Differences in Mohave Shamanism," *American Anthropologist*, lix (1957), 1036

K. M. Steward: "Mojave Indian Shamanism," *Masterkey*, xliv (1970), 15

LEANNE HINTON

Moldenhauer, Hans (*b* Mainz, Germany, 13 Dec 1906). Musicologist. He graduated from the Musikhochschule in Mainz. After immigrating to America in 1938, he studied at Whitworth College, Spokane (BA 1945), and the Chicago Musical College of Roosevelt University (DFA 1951). In 1942 he founded the Spokane Conservatory and became its president in 1946. He also taught at the University of Washington from 1961 to 1964 and has lectured at colleges and universities throughout Europe and America. Moldenhauer is the founder and director of the Moldenhauer Archive, which contains autograph musical manuscripts, letters, and documents. Parts of the archive are located in Spokane, Washington, and parts are housed at Northwestern University; the Americana was acquired by Harvard University in 1984. An important section of this collection is the Webern Archive; Moldenhauer's long-standing interest in the composer is reflected in this compilation of manuscripts and memorabilia and in his many articles about Webern. Moldenhauer has published a number of music manuscripts from the archive, including some of the sketches, in facsimile or practical editions.

WRITINGS

The Death of Anton Webern: a Drama in Documents (New York, 1961)

ed. with D. Irvine: *Anton von Webern: Perspectives: 1st Webern Festival, Seattle 1962* (Seattle, 1966) [catalogue of the Webern Archive]

with R. Moldenhauer: *Anton von Webern: a Chronicle of his Life and Work* (New York, 1979)

PAULA MORGAN

Mole, Miff [Irving Milfred] (*b* Roosevelt, NY, 11 March 1898; *d* New York, 29 April 1961). Jazz trombonist. He played violin, alto horn, and piano before learning trombone. Based in New York, he made hundreds of recordings with many groups, the most influential being those with the Original Memphis Five and with Red Nichols's innovative groups in the 1920s. In these years he fashioned the first distinctive and influential jazz trombone style, free from the glissandos and rudimentary bass-line paraphrases of "tailgate" playing and characterized by precise execution, wide leaps and short rhythmic values. This style was already formed by the time he recorded his own composition *Slippin' Around* with Nichols (1927). In 1929 he joined the NBC radio orchestra, where he remained for most of the 1930s. After playing briefly with Paul Whiteman (1938–40) and Benny Goodman (1943) he returned to small-group jazz, sometimes with Muggsy Spanier. Illness prevented him from playing in the mid-1950s, but he continued to work sporadically until his death.

For illustration *see* GOODMAN, BENNY.

RECORDINGS

(selective list)

As leader: Shim-me-sha-wabble (1928, OK 41445); Crazy rhythm (1928, OK 41098); I've got a Feeling I'm Falling (1929, OK 41232)

As co-leader with R. Nichols: Davenport Blues (1927, Vic. 20778); Slippin' Around (1927, Vic. 21397)

As sideman: E. Condon: A Good Man is Hard to Find, pts i–iv (1940, Com. 1504–5)

BIBLIOGRAPHY

J. L. Anderson: "Evolution of Jazz," *Down Beat*, xvii/20 (1950), 11

N. Shapiro and N. Hentoff, eds.: *Hear me talkin' to ya* (New York, 1955), 244

M. Harrison: *A Jazz Retrospect* (Newton Abbot, England 1976), 157

JAMES DAPOGNY/R

Mollenhauer, Edward (*b* Erfurt, Germany, 12 April 1827; *d* Owatoma, MN, 7 May 1914). Composer. He began his career as a violinist in Germany before going to London to play in Jullien's orchestra. After the orchestra made a tour of the USA in 1853, Mollenhauer and his brother Friedrich stayed in New York as teachers. Edward appeared as a soloist with the New York PO and composed symphonies, concertos, and solo works for the violin; he also composed several light operas, including *The Corsican Bride* (1863) and *Manhattan Beach, or Love Among the Breakers* (1878). He was conductor of the orchestra at Daly's Theatre, and on occasion arranged and augmented the scores of the musical productions there.

RICHARD C. LYNCH

Mollenhauer, Emil (*b* Brooklyn, NY, 4 Aug 1855; *d* New York, 10 Dec 1927). Violinist and conductor. He was the son of the violinist Friedrich Mollenhauer, who had come to the USA with Jullien's orchestra in 1853. He learned violin as a child and made his début in Niblo's Garden, New York, on 8 February 1864. By the time he was 14 he was playing in Booth's Theatre and at the age of 17 joined the Theodore Thomas Orchestra; he also played with the New York Symphony Society, for which he served as piano accompanist for guest singers.

In 1883 he went to Boston, where he played in the orchestra of the Bijou Theatre before joining the Boston SO the following year. In 1889 he and trombonist George W. Stewart resigned to form the BOSTON FESTIVAL ORCHESTRA; Stewart became manager and Mollenhauer was concertmaster for three seasons, after which he became conductor, remaining in that post for 22 years. Stewart had also begun to manage the Germania Band (from

1904 the Boston Band), and in 1889 he appointed Mollenhauer conductor. Mollenhauer also organized and led the Boston Municipal Band and directed the People's Symphony Orchestra. In 1894 he became a choral conductor when he deputized for Carl Zerrahn at a performance by the Salem Oratorio Society. This led to other choral engagements, and in 1898 he succeeded B. J. Lang as conductor of the Handel and Haydn Society, which he reorganized and revitalized after a period of musical decline. He took over the directorship of the Apollo Club after Lang's retirement in 1901, and also led choral societies in Brookline, Lynn, Salem, and Newburyport.

Mollenhauer's musical talents and learning were indisputable, and he inspired admiration in the musicians he trained; his lack of social graces and interests other than music, however, meant that he often came into conflict with his colleagues and superiors.

BIBLIOGRAPHY

W. F. Bradbury and C. Guild: *History of the Handel and Haydn Society of Boston, Massachusetts*, ii (Cambridge, MA, and Boston, 1911–34/*R*1977–9)

H. Woelber: "Famous Bandmasters: Emil Mollenhauer," *International Musician*, xxx/6 (1932), 12

H. E. Johnson: *Hallelujah, Amen!* (Boston, 1965/*R*1981)

STEVEN LEDBETTER

Möller. Firm of organ builders. It was founded as M. P. Möller at Warren, Pennsylvania, in 1875 by Mathias Peter Möller (*b* Bornholm, Denmark, 1854; *d* Hagerstown, MD, 1937). After training as a mechanic Möller immigrated to the USA in 1872 and worked for Derrick & Felgemaker, organ builders, of Erie, Pennsylvania; while there he introduced an improved wind-chest. In 1880 he moved his business to Hagerstown, where it has remained, becoming the largest manufacturer of pipe organs in the USA. During the 1930s Richard Whitelegg, a noted voicer, was Möller's tonal director. On Möller's death, his son, M. P. Möller, Jr. (1902–61), became president of the firm. Control has stayed with the founder's family: his son-in-law W. Riley Daniels became president in 1961, his grandson Kevin Mackenzie Möller in 1978, and another grandson, Peter Möller Daniels, in 1984.

The first Möller organs had mechanical action, but Möller soon developed a reliable pneumatic action which was used until electropneumatic action was adopted about 1918. Although Möller was responsible for some of the largest organ installations in the USA, the firm is also known for its pioneering work in the development of small self-contained organs, sold originally under the name of "Möller Artiste" but now known as "Series 70" after revision along more classic lines. Important installations include those in St. George's Church, New York (1958), the Cathedral of Mary Our Queen, Baltimore (1959), the National Shrine of the Immaculate Conception, Washington, DC (1965), Heinz Chapel at the University of Pittsburgh (1970), Orchestra Hall, Chicago (1981), National City Christian Church, Washington, DC (1981), and West End United Methodist Church, Nashville (1983).

BIBLIOGRAPHY

W. H. Barnes: *The Contemporary American Organ* (Glen Rock, NJ, 8/1964)

O. Ochse: *The History of the Organ in the United States* (Bloomington, IN, 1975)

BARBARA OWEN

Moller, John Christopher [Möller, Johann Christoph] (*b* Germany, 1755; *d* New York, 21 Sept 1803). Composer, organist, concert manager, and music publisher. After about a decade in London, where his major works were published (*c*1775–1785), he moved to the USA. He was prominent in the musical life of Philadelphia (October 1790–November 1795) as organist of Zion Lutheran Church and co-manager (with Reinagle) of the City Concerts (1790–93), performing as a pianist, harpsichordist, and violist. In New York he was organist of Trinity Episcopal Church and concert manager at fashionable summer pleasure gardens. Moller's and Capron's press (established in March 1793) was among the earliest in the USA for the exclusive printing of music. Moller subsequently issued alone over 40 publications in New York and Philadelphia. In addition to the major works (six quartets, 12 sonatas, and other pieces) published in London, he composed a cantata, *Dank und Gebet* (1794), and several keyboard pieces issued in Philadelphia, including a Sinfonia (1793; the Sinfonia is edited by W. T. Marrocco and H. Gleason in *Music in America*, 1964, and two piano pieces are in RRAM, i, 1977). Moller's manuscripts are held mainly by the British Library, London, the New York Public Library at Lincoln Center, and the Library of Congress. Moller is buried in Trinity Churchyard, New York.

BIBLIOGRAPHY

O. G. T. Sonneck: *Early Concert-life in America (1731–1800)* (Leipzig, 1907/*R*1978)

E. C. Wolf: *Lutheran Church Music in America during the Eighteenth and Early Nineteenth Centuries* (diss., U. of Illinois, 1960) [incl. text and music of *Dank und Gebet*]

R. D. Stetzel: *John Christopher Moller (1755–1803) and his Role in Early American Music* (diss., U. of Iowa, 1965) [incl. complete list of works with incipits, and several complete compositions]

E. C. Wolf: "Music in Old Zion, Philadelphia, 1750–1850," *MQ*, lviii (1972), 622–52

R. J. Wolfe: *Early American Music Engraving and Printing* (Urbana, IL, 1980)

RONALD D. STETZEL

Monk, Meredith (*b* Lima, Peru, 20 Nov 1943). Composer and singer. She was born in Peru while her mother – a pop and show singer known professionally as Audrey Marsh – was on tour; she grew up in New York and Connecticut, and in 1964 graduated from Sarah Lawrence College, Bronxville, New York, with a BA in performing arts. From the beginning of her career Monk's interests have included solo singing, film making (she made her first film in 1966), choreography, and directing; her first theater piece, *Juice*, was given its première at the Guggenheim Museum, New York, in 1969. During the 1970s she became one of the most popular members of the "downtown" avant-garde and, more recently, one of the most highly regarded creators of music-theater anywhere. In 1978 she founded the Meredith Monk Vocal Ensemble, a chamber group that performs with her in the USA and in Europe (see illustration).

Monk's compositions depend on extended vocal techniques – including, with conventionally sung notes over a four-octave range, a variety of insistent, wistful, fey, or humorous cries (always wordless); at times Monk sounds as if she might be singing ethnic music from a culture she invented herself. Her solo pieces, some with repetitive piano accompaniments derived both from minimalism and from popular music, are built from simple, often modal melodies and melodic cells, repeated with constant small variations and alternated with other material to form additive structures reminiscent of birdsong. The ensemble pieces such as *Dolmen Music* (1979) are more tentative: the added voices are muted, at least compared with Monk's solo singing, and the variety they introduce is accommodated at the expense of continuity. Nevertheless these pieces enjoy tremendous pop-

Meredith Monk Vocal Ensemble: (left to right) Meredith Monk, Paul Langland, Bob Een, Naaz Hosseini, Julius Eastman, and Andrea Goodman

ularity. Monk's most highly developed works are powerfully affecting theater pieces such as *Quarry* (1976), in which music, film, dance, acting, and scraps of text are combined to create the assured flow produced in conventional opera by music alone. However, *The Games* (1983), a view of reconstruction after a nuclear holocaust, relies more heavily on its unusually dissonant and varied score.

WORKS

SOLO VOCAL

16 Millimeter Earrings, 1v, gui, 1966; Candy Bullets and Moon, 1v, elec org, elec db, perc, 1967, collab. D. Preston; Blueprint: Overload/Blueprint 2, 1v, tape, live elec, 1967; A Raw Recital, 1v, elec org, 1970; Our Lady of the Late, 1v, wine glass, 1972–3, arr. 1v, wine glass, perc, 1974; Songs from the Hill, 1976–7; View no.2, 1v, synth, 1982

VOCAL ENSEMBLE

Tablet, 4 solo vv, 2 s rec, pf 4 hands, 1977; Dolmen Music, 6 solo vv, vc, perc, 1979; Tokyo Cha-cha, 6 solo vv, 2 elec org, 1983; 2 Men Walking, 3 solo vv, elec org, 1983; Book of Days, 5 solo vv, chorus, elec org, 1985

THEATER PIECES

Juice, theater cantata, 85 solo vv, 85 jew's harps, 2 vn, 1969; Needle-brain Lloyd and the Systems Kid, 150 solo vv, elec org, fl, gui, 1970; Plainsong for Bill's Bojo (incidental music, W. Dunas), elec org, 1971; Vessel (opera epic), 75 solo vv, elec org, accordion, 2 dulcimers, 1971; Paris, 2 solo vv, pf, 1972; Education of the Girlchild (opera), 6 solo vv, elec org, pf, 1972–3; Chacon, 25 vv, pf, perc, 1974; Quarry (opera), 38 solo vv, 2 harmoniums, 2 s rec, tape, 1976; Venice/Milan, 15 solo vv, pf 4 hands, 1976; The Plateau Series, 5 solo vv, tape, 1977; Recent Ruins, 12 vv, vc, 1979; Specimen Days (opera), 14 solo vv, 2 pf, 2 elec org, 1981; View no.1, 1v, pf, synth, 1981, collab. Ping Chong; The Games, 16 solo vv, synth, elec kbds, bagpipes, Flemish bagpipes, Chinese hn, Rauschpfeife, 1983, collab. Ping Chong; Turtle Dreams (cabaret), 4 solo vv, 2 elec org, 1983

OTHER WORKS

View no. 1, video score, 1v, pf, synth, 1981, collab. Ping Chong; Engine Steps, tape collage, 1983

BIBLIOGRAPHY

L. K. Telberg: "Meredith Monk – Renaissance Woman," *MJ*, xxxvii/6 (1979), 6

M. Monk: "Notes on the Voice," *Terpsichore in Sneakers*, ed. S. Banes (Boston, 1980)

K. Bernard: "Some Observations on Recent Ruins," *Theater* [Yale School of Drama], xiii/2 (1982), 88 [on *Specimen Days*]

G. Sandow: "Invisible Theater: the Music of Meredith Monk," *The Musical Woman: an International Perspective, 1983*, ed. J. L. Zaimont (Westport, CT, 1984), 147

J. Pareles: "Meredith Monk, Two Decades Later," *New York Times* (17 May 1985)

"Monk, Meredith," *CBY 1985*

GREGORY SANDOW

Monk, Thelonious (Sphere) [Thelious Junior] (*b* Rocky Mount, NC, 10 Oct 1917; *d* Weehawken, NJ, 17 Feb 1982). Jazz pianist and composer. Although he remained long misunderstood and little known, both his playing and his compositions had a formative influence on modern jazz.

1. Life. 2. Compositions. 3. Piano style.

1. Life. When Monk was four his family moved to New York, which was his home until he retired. In the early 1940s he worked as a sideman in jazz groups and became house pianist at Minton's Playhouse in South Harlem. Here he encouraged the young jazz pianist Bud Powell (who achieved success far earlier than Monk himself) and was first recorded in 1941 in Minton's house quartet, when the guitarist Charlie Christian was making a guest appearance. In these and similar performances with visiting musicians, such as Don Byas, Roy Eldridge, and Helen Humes, Monk helped to formulate the emerging bop style.

In 1944 Monk made his first known visit to a recording studio, as a member of the Coleman Hawkins Quartet; in the same year his well-known tune *'Round about Midnight* was recorded by Cootie Williams, who collaborated with him in its composition. By this time Monk was playing at the Spotlite Club on 52nd Street with the Dizzy Gillespie Orchestra. Three years later, in 1947, Monk made the first recordings under his own name in a sextet session for Blue Note, which included his compositions *Humph* and *Thelonious*. This and five other recordings issued by Blue Note between 1947 and 1952, including such masterpieces as *Evidence*, *Criss Cross*, and a bizarre arrangement of *Carolina Moon*, are regarded as the first characteristic works of Monk's output, along with the recordings he made as a sideman for Charlie Parker in 1950, which included *Bloomdido* and *My Melancholy Baby*.

Thelonious Monk in the 1940s

In 1952 Monk acquired a contract from Prestige Records, where he remained for three years. Although this was perhaps the leanest period in his career in terms of live performances, he recorded such notable works as the remarkable *Little Rootie Tootie* (dedicated to his son), a daring version of Jerome Kern's *Smoke Gets in your Eyes*, and perhaps his finest solo performance, *Bags' Groove*, in a memorable session with the Miles Davis All Stars on Christmas Eve 1954. Two months earlier he had recorded an album with the tenor saxophonist Sonny Rollins, and in June 1954 he made his first solo album in Paris for Swing Records. This album offers great insight into the audacity of Monk's music, his version of *Eronel* in particular being outstanding for its considerable pianistic demands.

In 1955 Prestige, dissatisfied with the low sales of Monk's recordings, sold his contract to Riverside Records. Monk remained with Riverside until 1961. His first two recording sessions were conceived with the intent of introducing his music to a wider audience, and were given a lukewarm reception by the critics. Between these two dates Monk also recorded his highly complex piece *Gallop's Gallop* with Gigi Gryce for Signal Records (1955) and made an album with Art Blakey for Atlantic (1957). This latter recording and his three subsequent Riverside albums (*Brilliant Corners*, *Thelonious Himself*, and a septet album with John Coltrane) were masterpieces, and Monk became the most acclaimed and controversial jazz improviser of the late 1950s almost overnight.

Monk's professional career now took a dramatic turn for the better, and in 1957 he began appearing regularly with Coltrane, Wilbur Ware, and Shadow Wilson at the Five Spot Club in New York. During the next few years his group included such noteworthy musicians as Johnny Griffin, Roy Haynes, and the tenor saxophonist Charlie Rouse, his lifelong associate. He began to tour the USA regularly and also to appear in Europe. Perhaps his most memorable performance of this period was in 1959 at Town Hall, New York, where he appeared with an orchestra playing his compositions in skillful arrangements by Hall Overton. He also continued to issue albums for Riverside.

In 1962 Monk's popularity was such that he was put under contract by Columbia records. He was also made the subject of a cover story by *Time* (1964), an honor bestowed on only three other jazz musicians. He made several overseas tours, including visits to Mexico and Japan. Around 1970 he disbanded his group and joined the Giants of Jazz together with Dizzy Gillespie, Kai Winding, Sonny Stitt, Al McKibbon, and Art Blakey. In November 1971 he made solo and trio recordings for Black Lion Records in London which some critics felt heralded a new era in his development, but shortly afterwards he suddenly retired from public view. He made three final performances with an orchestra at Carnegie Hall, and appeared with a quartet at the Newport Jazz Festival in 1975 and 1976, but otherwise spent his final years in seclusion in Weehawken, New Jersey, at the home of the Baroness Pannonica de Koenigswarter, his lifelong friend and patron.

2. Compositions. Monk's compositions fall into three periods: those recorded for Blue Note in the 1940s, his works in the 1950s for Riverside and Signal, and a few tunes written after 1960 for Columbia. Most critics consider those of his first two periods the most significant. Of the first-period works *'Round about Midnight* is his most popular, both with the public and with musicians. *Evidence*, *Misterioso*, and particularly *Criss Cross* are considered his masterpieces in purely instrumental terms; quite different from each other, they are united by vigorous, angular melodies of a strongly pianistic character. The first eight bars of *Criss Cross*, for example, consist of two contrasting motifs and demonstrate Monk's highly personal use of rhythmic displacement (ex. 1). Each piece of this period reveals fresh facets of his thinking:

Ex.1 *Criss Cross* (1951, BN 1590)

Eronel demonstrates his affection for bop, and *Hornin' In* his fascination with the whole-tone scale, which allowed him to suspend the work's tonality for bars at a time (ex.2). Another aspect of Monk's first-period pieces is his reworking of standard

Ex.2 *Hornin' In* (1952, BN 1603)

tunes, such as *Smoke Gets in your Eyes* and *Carolina Moon*, in which he dramatically alters and develops familiar material in an unorthodox and entirely characteristic fashion.

In his second period Monk produced many carefree popular pieces such as *Jackie-ing*, but also substantial works, including *Pannonica*, the highly dissonant *Crepuscule with Nellie*, and *Gallop's Gallop*, a tour de force of "wrong" notes which unexpectedly interrupt the conventional harmonies. His most important composition of the 1950s, and perhaps the most unorthodox work of his career, was *Brilliant Corners*, whose melody skirts the whole-tone, chromatic, and Lydian scales and is furthest removed from his Afro-American roots.

3. PIANO STYLE. It is as a performer that Monk was most misunderstood. He did not always exhibit the customary right-hand dexterity of most jazz pianists and, more importantly, his fellow jazz musicians quite often disagreed with his choice of notes. But his style, based on the Harlem stride tradition, had many strengths: a highly distinctive timbre, an ability to provide uncanny rhythmic surprises, and a wide variety of articulation. More importantly, Monk invented and developed ideas rather than merely embroidering chord changes. Some of his performances, such as *I Should Care* (1957), show a fresh use of rubato quite different from that of other jazz or lounge pianists. Monk also favored "crushed" notes and clusters which "evaporated" to leave a few key pitches. But his most important contribution as a pianist was his remarkable ability to improvise a coherent musical argument with a logic and structure comparable to the best of his notated compositions. Brilliant examples can be found in his solos and accompaniments on the Blue Note recordings of *Misterioso* and especially *Bags' Groove*, both with Milt Jackson. Although several young musicians of the 1970s and 1980s have borrowed and reinterpreted Monk's melodies for their own improvisations, most jazz pianists seem incapable or unwilling to pursue the introverted, quirky, yet meticulous thought processes that inspired Monk's greatest solos.

For further illustration *see* PARKER, CHARLIE.

RECORDINGS

(selective list)

AS LEADER

Humph/Misterioso (1947–8, BN 560); Evonce (1947, BN 547); Suburban Eyes/Thelonious (1947, BN 542); Ruby, my Dear/Evidence (1947–8, BN 549); 'Round about Midnight (1947, BN 543); Criss Cross/Eronel (1951, BN 1590); Carolina Moon/Hornin' In (1952, BN 1603); Little Rootie Tootie (1954, Prst. 850); Smoke Gets in your Eyes (1954, Prst. 180); *Thelonious Monk* (1954, Swing 33342), incl. Eronel; *Brilliant Corners* (1956, Riv. 226), incl. Pannonica; *Thelonious Himself* (1957, Riv. 235), incl. I Should Care, 'Round Midnight

Monk's Music (1957, Riv. 242), incl. Crepuscule with Nellie, Ruby, my Dear; *Thelonious Monk with John Coltrane* (1957, Jazzland S9/JL46); *The Thelonious Monk Orchestra at Town Hall* (1959, Riv. 300), incl. Crepuscule with Nellie; *5 by Monk by 5* (1959, Riv. 305), incl. Jackie-ing; *Solo Monk* (1964, Col. CS9149), incl. I Should Care, Ruby, my Dear; *Straight, No Chaser* (1966–7, Col. CS9451); *Something in Blue* (1971, Black Lion 152), incl. Nice Work if You Can Get It; *The Man I Love* (1971, Black Lion 197)

AS SIDEMAN

C. Christian: Swing to Bop, on *The Harlem Jazz Scene* (1941, Esoteric 4); C. Hawkins: Drifting on a Reed/Flyin' Hawk (1944, Joe Davis 8250); C. Parker: Bloomdido/My Melancholy Baby (1950, Mer./Clef 11058); S. Rollins: *Sonny Rollins Quintet* (1954, Prst. 190); M. Davis: Bags' Groove (1954, Prst. 196), Bemsha Swing/The Man I Love (1954, Prst. 200); G. Gryce: Gallop's Gallop, on *Gigi Gryce Quartet* (1955, Signal 1021); A. Blakey: *Art Blakey's Jazz Messengers and Thelonious Monk* (1957, Atl. 1278); Giants of Jazz: *The Giants of Jazz* (1972, Atl. 2-905)

BIBLIOGRAPHY

O. Keepnews: "Thelonious Monk," *Record Changer*, ii/4 (1948), 5

L. Malson: *Les maîtres du jazz* (Paris, 1952, rev. 2/1972)

G. Schuller: "Thelonious Monk," *Jazz Review*, i/1 (1958), 22; iii/6 (1960), 26; repr. in *Jazz Panorama*, ed. M. Williams (New York, 1962/*R*1979)

M. Harrison: "Thelonious Monk," *Just Jazz Three*, ed. S. Traill (London, 1959), 14

M. James: "Thelonious Monk," *Ten Jazzmen* (London, 1960)

N. Hentoff: "The Private World of Thelonious Monk," *Esquire*, liii/4 (1960), 133

——: *Thelonious Monk* (New York, 1961)

——: *The Jazz Life* (New York, 1961/*R*1975)

A. Hodeir: *Toward Jazz* (New York, 1962/*R*1976)

"Loneliest Monk," *Time*, lxxxiii (28 Feb 1964), 84

"Monk, Thelonious (Sphere)," *CBY 1964*

J. Goldberg: *Jazz Masters of the Fifties* (New York, 1965/*R*1980)

J. G. Jepsen: *A Discography of Thelonious Monk/Bud Powell* (Copenhagen, *c*1969)

J. Langford: "Monk's Horns," *Jazz Journal*, xxiii/11 (1970), 2

M. Williams: *The Jazz Tradition* (New York, 1970, rev. 2/1983)

M. Harrison: *A Jazz Retrospect* (Newton Abbot, England, 1976), 28

M. Ruppli: "Discographie de Thelonious Monk," *Jazz hot*, no.331 (1976), 22

J. Réda: *L'improviste* (Paris, 1980), 128

L. Bijl and F. Conté: *Monk on Record: a Discography of Thelonious Monk* (Amsterdam, 1982)

RAN BLAKE

Monkees. Pop group. Its members were Davey Jones (singer), Mike Nesmith (guitarist and singer), Peter Tork (bass guitarist and singer), and Mickey Dolenz (drummer and singer). The group was formed in 1966 as American television's calculated answer to the Beatles. Nesmith and Tork were aspiring musicians, but Jones and Dolenz openly stated that they were hired primarily as actors to take part in a television series about a pop group. Nevertheless, they had pleasant voices and their first album (*The Monkees*, 1966) received a gold record and yielded three hit singles: *Last train to Clarksville* (no.1, 1966), *I'm a believer* (no.1, 1966), and *Steppin' stone* (no.20, 1966). Although it was revealed that session musicians had been employed to make this recording, the Monkees proved in worldwide tours and further recordings (such as *A Little bit me, a little bit you*, no.2, 1967, and *Daydream believer*, no.1, 1967) that they were competent musicians. Tork left the group in 1968, and they continued as a trio until Nesmith left two years later to pursue what proved to be a successful solo career as a country singer and songwriter. After a period of inactivity, Dolenz and Jones revived the group in 1975 with Tommy Boyce and Bobby Hart, the songwriters responsible for many of the Monkees' most successful songs.

RECORDINGS

(selective list; all recorded for Colgens)

Last Train to Clarksville (1001, 1966); I'm a believer (1002, 1966); A little bit me, a little bit you (1004, 1967); Pleasant Valley Sunday (1007, 1967); Daydream believer (1012, 1967); Valleri (1019, 1968)

BIBLIOGRAPHY

R. W. Lewis: "When Four Nice Boys Go Ape!," *Saturday Evening Post*, ccxl/2 (1967), 74

B. Dawbarn: "The Monkees," *Melody Maker*, xlii (11 March 1967), pp.i–iv

BARRY KERNFELD

Mono, western. American Indian group of California. Their music bore a resemblance to that of the YOKUTS.

Monod, Jacques-Louis (*b* Asnières, nr Paris, France, 25 Feb 1927). French conductor, composer, and pianist. He entered the Paris Conservatoire below the official age of nine, taking courses in various disciplines. In 1944 he attended Messiaen's seminars, then went on to study theory, composition, and analysis with René Leibowitz (1944–50). He came to the USA with Leibowitz in 1951, and studied at the Juilliard School (composition with Wagenaar) and Columbia University (conducting with Rudolf Thomas). At Juilliard he was also a teaching assistant to Richard Franko Goldman, in whose class he prepared and directed the first all-Webern concert ever given, on 8 May 1951. Later he studied with Boris Blacher and Josef Rufer in Berlin. Monod made his piano début in a concert conducted by Leibowitz in Paris in 1949 to celebrate Schoenberg's 75th birthday. He was subsequently active as a pianist, in many song recitals with the American soprano Bethany Beardslee (then his wife), and as a conductor. He played or conducted the premières of Schoenberg's Songs op.48, Webern's Songs opp.17 and 25, the two versions of Berg's *Schliesse mir die Augen beide*, and Babbitt's *Widow's Lament* and *Du* (written for him and Beardslee). Between 1960 and 1966 he gave the first European performances of several American works, and he has made the first recordings of much 20th-century music.

Monod's compositions (published by Boelke-Bomart, of which he was chief editor from 1952 until 1982) include many settings of texts by Eluard, Valéry, Renard, and René Char, chamber and solo works, two chamber cantatas, and works for orchestra. He has taught at the New England Conservatory, Princeton, Harvard, and Columbia universities, and Hunter and Queens colleges, CUNY.

MICHAEL STEINBERG

Monosoff [Pancaldo], **Sonya** (*b* Cleveland, OH, 11 June 1927). Violinist. After training at the Juilliard School, where her instrumental teacher was Persinger and her chamber music coaches were Salmond and Hans Letz, she became a founding member of the New York Pro Musica under Noah Greenberg. In 1963 she founded and directed the Baroque Players of New York, later called the Chamber Players. An advocate of Baroque and Classical music played on original instruments, she has increasingly devoted her energies to playing and lecturing on early music. She has recorded sonatas by Bach, Biber, Corelli, and Geminiani, and, with fortepiano, several Mozart sonatas; the Corelli recording in particular demonstrates her command of Baroque ornamentation. A former Fellow of the Radcliffe Institute and a research associate of the Smithsonian Institution, she was appointed associate professor at Cornell University in 1972 and full professor in 1974. In 1979 she was artist-in-residence at Wellesley College. She plays with Malcolm Bilson (fortepiano) and John Hsu (cello) in the Amadé Trio; founded in 1974, the group has toured extensively throughout the USA and Europe.

GEORGE GELLES

Monroe, Bill [William Smith] (*b* nr Rosine, KY, 13 Sept 1911). Country-music singer, songwriter, and mandolin player. He learned music from his uncle Pen (Pemberton) Vandiver, a fiddler with whom he lived for several years, and from other local musicians. In 1929 he moved to Chicago where, with two older brothers, he joined an exhibition square-dance team sponsored by radio station WLS (1932). From 1934 to 1938 he and his brother Charlie Monroe were professional hillbilly radio singers, gaining national popularity through broadcasts, appearances in the Southeast, and recordings. In 1938 Bill Monroe formed the Blue Grass Boys; the group joined the "Grand Ole Opry" in 1939 and made numerous lastingly popular recordings. Monroe's compositions include instrumental works and religious and secular songs. He plays the mandolin and sings in a distinctive high tenor voice. During the 1940s he developed an innovative ensemble style based on earlier string-band music of the Southeast; the sound was copied during the late 1940s and by the mid-1950s had become known as BLUEGRASS MUSIC. In the 1960s Monroe was a central figure in the establishment of bluegrass festivals and in 1970 he was elected to the Country Music Hall of Fame. He was among the first artists to be awarded the NEA's National Heritage Fellowship in recognition of his contribution to American culture (1981).

RECORDINGS

(selective list)

Mule Skinner Blues (Bluebird 8568, 1940); Kentucky Waltz (Col. 20013, 1946); Blue Moon of Kentucky (Col. 20370, 1947); Along about daybreak (Col. 20595, 1948); Memories of you/Blue Grass Ramble (Decca 46266, 1950); On the old Kentucky shore (Decca 46298, 1951); Memories of Mother and Dad (Decca 28878, 1953); Cheyenne (Decca 29406, 1955); Gotta travel on (Decca 30809, 1959); *Mr. Blue Grass* (Decca 4080, 1961); *I'll Meet you in Church Sunday Morning* (Decca 4537, 1964); *Original Bluegrass Sound* (Harmony 7338, 1965); *Bean Blossom* (MCA 2-8002, 1973)

BIBLIOGRAPHY

R. Rinzler: "Bill Monroe: the Daddy of Blue Grass Music," *Sing Out*, xiii/1 (1963), 5

J. Rooney: *Bossmen: Bill Monroe & Muddy Waters* (New York, 1971)

N. V. Rosenberg: *Bill Monroe and his Blue Grass Boys: an Illustrated Discography* (Nashville, 1974)

R. Rinzler: "Bill Monroe," *Stars of Country Music*, ed. B. C. Malone and J. McCulloh (Urbana, IL, 1975), 202

P. Guralnick: "Bill Monroe: Hard-workingman Blues," *Country Music*, ix/9 (1981), 8

NEIL V. ROSENBERG/R

Monroe, Vaughn (Wilton) (*b* Akron, OH, 7 Oct 1912; *d* Stuart, FL, 21 May 1973). Bandleader and singer. He began to play the trumpet as a boy and at the age of 11 won the Wisconsin State trumpet-playing contest. He studied engineering, but left college in 1932 to play first in Austin Wylie's band and then in Larry Funk's orchestra. In 1936 bandleader Jack Marshard engaged him to lead one of his society bands in the Boston area, during which time he was able to study at the New England Conservatory of Music. In 1939 Monroe decided to form his own band and gradually altered his musical style to appeal to a wider audience. With his good looks, he had considerable personal appeal as a showman; although his singing was nasal and frequently off-key, he became widely popular and was soon nationally known. He issued several hit records in the 1940s and 1950s, such as *There! I've said it again* (1945), *Ballerina* (1947), *Riders in the Sky* (1949), and *Mule Train* (1949), and also wrote a number of songs, including *Racing with the Moon*, the theme song for his own "Camel Caravan" radio show. By the late 1940s he was the leading American dance-band leader. In the 1950s he had further successes with novelty numbers such as *The Battle of New Orleans* and *Black Denim Trousers*, but his popularity waned as rock-and-roll became established; nevertheless he remained active, performing in nightclubs and on cruise ships, until shortly before his death.

BIBLIOGRAPHY

"Monroe, Vaughn (Wilton)," *CBY 1942*

B. Davidson: "Voice with Muscles," *Colliers*, cxxiv (20 Aug 1949), 30

IAN WHITCOMB

Montague, Stephen (Rowley) (*b* Syracuse, NY, 10 March 1943). Composer and pianist. He attended St. Petersburg (Florida) Junior College and Florida State University (BM 1965, MM in theory, 1967); his principal teachers were his father Richard Montague, John Boda, and Carlisle Floyd. After teaching at Butler University, Indianapolis (1967–9), he resumed study at Ohio State University with Marshall Barnes, Behrman, Brün, and Wolf Rosenberg (DMA in composition, 1972). In 1972 he received a Fulbright scholarship to study in Warsaw, where he worked in the electronic studio of Polish Radio for 16 months. In 1974 he moved to England. After a year as composer-in-residence with the Strider Dance Company in London (1974–5) he worked as a freelance composer and pianist. His music has been performed and broadcast in many countries, and he has done much to promote his own work and that of other contemporary composers, both as a pianist and, from 1980, as a founding member and concert director of the Electro-Acoustic Music Association of Great Britain. He has contributed articles to *Contact*, *Classical Music*, and other periodicals.

Montague's early compositions were influenced by the music of Floyd, and he remained outside most of the avant-garde movements of the 1950s and early 1960s. His mature style incorporates later trends such as minimalist techniques. *Strummin'* (1975, rev. 1981) pays homage to Cowell by using the older composer's techniques for playing inside the piano, though to a much more obviously romantic effect. The harmonic and rhythmic features of *Paramell V* (1981) demonstrate Montague's affinities with the repetitive music of such composers as Riley and Reich, though its shape is closer to the 19th-century tradition. Montague's output includes works for tape collage and *musique concrète* (*Slow Dance on a Burial Ground*, 1982–3), and works specifying audience participation (listeners are requested to hum a B♭ throughout *Paramell III*). One of Montague's most successful large works is the ballet *Median* (commissioned by the Sadler's Wells Royal Ballet), which, drawing on his orchestral compositions *From the White Edge of Phrygia* and *Prologue*, combines all the elements of his mature style.

WORKS

Stage: Largo con moto (dance music, E. Karczag), tape, 1975; Criseyde (Chaucer), S, ocarina, slide, tape, 1976; Into the Sun (ballet, T. Gilbert), perc, tape, 1977; Footfalls (dance, M. Duprès), tape, 1979; I, Giselle (dance/theater piece, J. Lansley, F. Early), insts, tape, 1980; Splitter (dance music, Duprès), tape, 1981; Gravity is Proving most Difficult (dance music, S. MacLennan), cl/b cl, elec, tape, dancer, 1984; Median (ballet, J. Jackson), orch, 1984 [arr. of Prologue, orch, and From the White Edge of Phrygia, orch]; The Montague Stomp (dance music, Jackson), 1984

Orch: Argalus, youth orch, 1968; Voussoirs, large orch, tape, 1972; Sound Round, orch, tape delay, 1973; Varshavian Spring (S. Montague), chorus, chamber orch, 1973, rev. 1980; At the White Edge of Phrygia, chamber orch, 1983; From the White Edge of Phrygia, orch, 1984; Prologue, orch, 1984

Chamber and inst: Quiet Washes, 3 trbn, 3 pf, 1974 [also version for trbn, pf, tape]; Paramell I, trbn, pf, 1977; Paramell II: Entity, 5 perc, prepared pf, 1977, rev. 1981; Paramell III, pf, audience drone, 1981; Paramell V, 2 pf, 1981; Paramell Va, pf, 1981; Paramell VI, fl, cl, vc, pf, 1981; 6 others

Elec: The Eyes of Ambush, 1–5 insts, vv, tape delay, 1973; Inundations I, 3 amp pf, tape, 1975; Strummin', pf, light, tape, 1975, rev. 1981; Inundations II: Willow, S, pf, tape, 1976; Sotto voce, graphic score, chorus, elec, 1976; Passim, pf, perc, tape, live elec, 1977; Quintet, soloist, 4-track tape, 1978; Paramell IV, tuba, b trbn, tape, 1979; Mouth of Anger, b cl, pf, perc, tape, elec, 1981, rev. 1983; Scythia, tape, 1981; Slow Dance on a Burial Ground, tape, 1982–3; Tigida Pipa (Montague), 4 amp vv, perc, tape, 1983; Tongues of Fire, pf, tape, live elec, 1983; *c*10 others

3 Iberian Sketches (F. García Lorca), S, pf, 1970

MSS in American Music Center, British Music Information Centre

Principal publishers: Edition Modern (Munich), Presser, United Music Publishers (London)

BIBLIOGRAPHY

K. Potter: "A Romantic Minimalist," *Classical Music* (London, 6 Nov 1982), 14

O. Maxwell: "Rhythm Crazy," *Time Out* (London, 18 Feb 1983), 56

KEITH POTTER

Monterey Jazz Festival. Annual jazz festival founded in 1958 near Monterey, California. It was initiated by the disc jockey Jimmy Lyons, who has remained its general manager. Held for three days in September at the Monterey County Fairgrounds (capacity 7000), about 1.6 km from the city, the festival has since its inception used its profits for music and education programs, particularly for young people. It sponsors the annual California High School Jazz Competition, whose winners perform in its Sunday afternoon show with artists that have appeared at the festival. The stature of the musicians who have appeared, such as Dizzy Gillespie, Louis Armstrong, Gerry Mulligan, Dave Brubeck, and Thelonious Monk, as well as the natural beauty and climate of the area, have contributed to the increasing popularity of the event.

SARA VELEZ

Monteux, Claude (*b* Brookline, MA, 15 Oct 1920). Conductor and flutist, son of Pierre Monteux. He first studied flute with Georges Laurent and he made his solo début with an orchestra at the age of 20. In 1946 he joined the Kansas City PO and three years later began his conducting career with the itinerant Ballets Russes. He has been a guest conductor of the London SO, and of orchestras in Germany, France, the Netherlands, and Scandinavia. From 1953 to 1956 he was conductor of the Columbus (Ohio) Orchestra and from 1959 to 1975 he was music director of the Hudson Valley PO in Poughkeepsie, New York; both orchestras grew considerably during his tenure. He has given master classes for conductors with the Canadian National Youth Orchestra and has directed the conducting department of the Peabody Conservatory. As a flutist he is admired for his clean technique and charm of manner. He and his father collaborated as soloist and conductor in some recordings. He was a member of the Harpsichord Quartet (1947–54).

GEORGE GELLES/R

Monteux, Pierre (*b* Paris, France, 4 April 1875; *d* Hancock, ME, 1 July 1964). Conductor, father of Claude Monteux. He studied violin at the Paris Conservatoire and became assistant conductor of the Concerts Colonne in 1894. In 1911, as well as founding the Concerts Berlioz, he was appointed conductor of Diaghilev's Ballets Russes; he first came to the USA on tour with them in 1916–17. In the summer of 1917 he conducted the New York Civic Orchestra, and then became conductor in charge of the French repertory at the Metropolitan Opera (1917–19). While there he conducted the American premières of Rimsky-Korsakov's *The Golden Cockerel* and Henry F. Gilbert's *The Dance in Place Congo*. In 1919 he moved to the Boston SO, where he introduced numerous contemporary works, despite opposition by an audience and orchestra accustomed to the German repertory. Although many of the new compositions were French (Debussy, Chausson, Milhaud, and others), he also included works by British, Italian, and, in particular, American composers (e.g., Foote, Gilbert, Chadwick, Loeffler, Griffes, Frank B. Converse, and Skilton). He remained in Boston until Koussevitzky replaced him in 1924, when he returned to Europe (for illustration *see* BOSTON (i), fig.2).

Monteux appeared as guest conductor of the Philadelphia Orchestra during the 1927–8 season, and in 1934 was invited by Otto Klemperer to conduct the Los Angeles PO for five weeks. He returned to the USA in 1936 as conductor of the San Francisco SO (until 1952) and became an American citizen in 1942. During his tenure in San Francisco he raised the standard of the orchestra to an international level. In 1954 he was guest conductor of the San Francisco Opera. After leaving California he continued to conduct in Europe and the USA, and during the 1950s appeared frequently with the Boston SO, notably on its first European tours (1952 and 1956). He made many recordings which were highly praised, though he once said that he hated all of them because of the lack of spontaneity in the technique of recording. He preferred live concerts and remained active to an advanced age, accepting his final appointment in 1961 as chief conductor of the London SO, on a contract for 25 years.

Monteux was never an ostentatious conductor, preparing his orchestra in often arduous rehearsal and then using small but decisive gestures to obtain playing of fine texture, careful detail, and powerful effect, retaining to the last his extraordinary grasp of musical structure and a faultless ear for sound quality. Always interested in the development of young talent, he founded the Ecole Monteux in Paris in 1932 for the coaching of conductors, and later continued this work at his American home at Hancock, Maine; his pupils in the USA included Neville Marriner and André Previn. Monteux was awarded two honorary doctorates, from the University of California and Mills College, and was the recipient of a fellowship from Stanford University.

BIBLIOGRAPHY

H. Stoddard: "Pierre Monteux," *Symphony Conductors of the U.S.A.* (New York, 1957), 266

L. W. Armsby: *We Shall Have Music* (San Francisco, 1960)

M. Rayment: "Pierre Monteux," *Audio & Record Review*, ii/5 (1963), 20 [with discography by F. F. Clough and G. J. Cuming]

D. Monteux: *It's all in the Music* (New York and Toronto, 1965) [with discography by E. Kunzel]

D. Schneider: *The San Francisco Symphony: Music, Maestros, and Musicians* (Novato, CA, 1983)

MARTIN COOPER/KATHERINE K. PRESTON

Montgomery, Little Brother [Eurreal Wilford] (*b* Kentwood, LA, 18 April 1906; *d* Chicago, IL, 6 Sept 1985). Blues and jazz pianist and singer. He was the son of a honky-tonk owner, and heard many blues singers and pianists as a child; he began to play piano himself at the age of five. He was performing for a living by the time he was 11 and, possessing a remarkable aural memory, was able to recall and re-create the piano styles of the numerous musicians he heard and worked with. Besides blues he played ragtime, jazz, and novelty pieces and, after working in many locations in Mississippi and Louisiana, sat in with Sam Morgan's Jazz Band in New Orleans. He performed with touring jazz groups, playing in Nebraska with Clarence Desdune's Joyland Revelers, and arrived in Chicago in 1928. *Vicksburg Blues* (1930, Para. 13006), his first recording, was a version of *The Forty-fours* (already recorded by Roosevelt Sykes), and showed his mastery of bass figures and subtle right-hand work. *Frisco Hiball Blues* (1931, Voc. 02706) was played with characteristic lightness of touch. In October 1936 Montgomery recorded 18 titles at a single sitting, an unprecedented feat made more remarkable by the exceptional quality of the result. *Something keeps a-worryin' me* (1936, Bluebird 6658) is an example of his high-pitched, whinnying singing style and has a piano accompaniment that bears comparison with the work of Earl Hines. *Farish Street Jive* (1936, Bluebird 6894), on the other hand, has strong ragtime and boogie-woogie strains. In spite of his fame in blues circles, Montgomery made few recordings; later issues included a rolling version (on which he also sang) of Charles Davenport's *Cow Cow Blues* (*c*1954, Ebony 1000) and Cooney Vaughn's previously unrecorded *Trembling Blues* (1960, "77" LA 12/21). A consistent, sensitive musician and an individual singer, Montgomery represents the contemplative, artistically well-structured, and impeccably performed aspects of the blues.

BIBLIOGRAPHY

SouthernB

P. Oliver: *Conversation with the Blues* (New York, 1965)

K. Gert zur Heide: *Deep South Piano: the Story of Little Brother Montgomery* (London, 1970)

PAUL OLIVER

Montgomery, Merle (*b* Davidson, OK, 15 May 1904). Administrator and educator. She attended the University of Oklahoma (BFA 1924) and later studied in France privately and at the American Conservatory in Fontainebleau (diploma 1933), with Philipp (piano) and Boulanger (composition). She received both the MM (1938) and PhD (1948) in music theory from the Eastman School, Rochester. She was head of the music department at Southwestern Institute (now Southwestern Oklahoma State University), Weatherford, 1938–41, was for two years Oklahoma state supervisor for the WPA, and served as an instructor at the Eastman School, 1943–5. She then began a career in publishing in New York, acting as national educational representative and later vice president of Carl Fischer and as staff member and consultant for Oxford University Press. During this time she edited music and books on music, produced numerous radio programs of American music and films for educational television, and taught at the Westchester Conservatory and Turtle Bay Music School. From 1971 to 1975 Montgomery was president of the National Federation of Music Clubs; thenceforth she devoted most of her energies to this organization, the National Music Council, Mu Phi Epsilon, and other local, national, and international music organizations. While serving as president of the National Music Council (1975–9), she oversaw the development of the "Parade of American Music" programs for the US Bicentennial; as chairman she gave lectures in all 50 states and presided over symposia and workshops throughout the world, promoting American music. She has also been active as a composer, mostly of songs and piano music; some of her works have been published under the pseudonym Aline Campbell. Montgomery has been recognized by several civic organizations in her native state, honored by the Sioux Indians of South Dakota in a naming ceremony, and presented with a citation by the New York State Music Teachers' Association.

BARBARA A. PETERSEN

Montgomery, Wes [John Leslie] (*b* Indianapolis, IN, 6 March 1923; *d* Indianapolis, 15 June 1968). Jazz guitarist. He began to teach himself guitar about 1943 and soon played in local bands. He toured and recorded with Lionel Hampton from 1948 until the beginning of 1950, playing brief solos on live broadcasts and also recording with the tenor saxophonist Gene Morris and with one of Hampton's vocalists, Sonny Parker. Returning to Indianapolis, he worked in obscurity until joining a group with his brothers Monk (double bass) and Buddy (piano and vibraphone). He recorded his first extended solos in several groups with his brothers from 1955 to 1959. In the latter year he organized his own trio with organ and drums; their first recording, *The Wes Montgomery Trio*, initiated a series of albums for Riverside. These represent Montgomery at his peak, accompanied by the finest rhythm sections available, including Tommy Flanagan, Hank Jones, Ron Carter, Albert Heath, and Louis Hayes. These recordings brought him belated recognition, and he soon began to dominate the *Down Beat* and *Playboy* jazz polls.

In 1960 Montgomery moved to the San Francisco Bay area, where he continued to perform with his brothers, though he also appeared with John Coltrane in 1961–2. After returning to Indianapolis in 1962 he resumed touring in March 1963, now with his trio. In 1964 he began recording for Verve Records with background arrangements for string orchestras and large jazz bands. Though unrepresentative of his talents, these recordings considerably broadened his audience; his rendition of *Goin' out of my Head* (1965) won a Grammy Award. His album *A Day in the Life*, recorded for the A&M label, was the best-selling jazz LP of 1967. In live performances, however, Montgomery continued to appear in small groups, notably with the Wynton Kelly Trio and in a quintet that included his brothers. He died unexpectedly at the height of his career.

Critics generally consider Montgomery the most important and influential jazz guitarist after Charlie Christian. Like Christian, whose recorded solos he memorized in his youth, Montgomery invented perfectly shaped phrases with tremendous rhythmic drive. But he also took advantage of recent developments in jazz harmony and melody, as well as improvements in the construction of electric guitars, to create a unique style. He used his thumb instead of a plectrum, achieving a soft attack and freeing his fingers for the playing of octaves and chordal passages, and for various kinds of strumming. His mastery of these techniques created a sensation among younger guitarists, and the playing of octaves, in particular, became a trademark of the Montgomery style.

Montgomery tended to build his solos from melodies in single notes to octave passages and finally to chords. He had a highly original melodic imagination and, at his best, constantly produced refreshing ideas that broke off unexpectedly. Even when he paraphrased a melody he managed to invest it with rhythmic excitement; ex. 1 shows a melody of quarter-notes used as the starting-point of a long line of triplet eighth-notes spanning more than three octaves in which interesting ambiguities of phrasing (bracketed) are created. Montgomery's playing abounded in subtle embellishments, deep blues sentiment, and a highly expressive use of portamento, tremolo, and other effects. In his sincere, unsensational way, he expanded the resources of jazz guitar, and his influence has been acknowledged by many later guitarists, including George Benson and Pat Martino.

Ex. 1

(a) Opening of T. Dameron: *If you could see me now*

(b) Montgomery's improvisation on the opening of *If you could see me now* (1965, Verve 22513), transcr. L. Porter

RECORDINGS

(selective list)

As leader: *Finger Pickin'* (1957, Pacific Jazz 301); *Montgomeryland* (1958–9, Pacific Jazz 5), incl. Far Wes'; *The Wes Montgomery Trio* (1959, Riv. 310); *The Incredible Jazz Guitar of Wes Montgomery* (1960, Riv. 320); *Movin' Along* (1960, Riv. 342); *So Much Guitar!* (1961, Riv. 382); *Full House* (1962, Riv. 434); *Goin' out of my Head* (1965, Verve 68642); *A Day in the Life* (1967, A&M 3001)

As sideman or co-leader: L. Hampton: Adam Blew his Hat/Brant Inn Boogie (1948, Alamac 2419); Montgomery Brothers: Love for Sale, on *Almost Forgotten* (1955, Col. FC38509), *The Montgomery Brothers and Five Others* (1957, World Pacific 1240); The Mastersounds: *Kismet* (1958, World Pacific 1243); M. Jackson: *Bags Meets Wes* (1961, Riv. 407); W. Kelly: *Smokin' at the Half Note* (1965, Verve 68633)

BIBLIOGRAPHY

L. Garson and J. Stewart: *Wes Montgomery Jazz Guitar Method* (New York, 1968)

B. Quinn: "The Thumb's Up, or What the View is Like from the Top," *Down Beat*, xxxv/13 (1968), 17

R. J. Gleason: "Wes Montgomery, 1925–1968: a Rare, Unpublished Interview," *Guitar Player*, vii/5 (1973), 22; repr. in *Jazz Guitarists: Collected Interviews from Guitar Player Magazine* (Saratoga, CA, 1978), 75

S. Khan: *The Wes Montgomery Guitar Folio* (New York, 1978)

"Wes Montgomery," *Swing Journal*, xxxii/8 (1978), 314 [discography]

D. Wild: "Wes and Trane: an Unrecorded Sextet," *Disc'ribe*, no. 1 (1980), 3

LEWIS PORTER

Moody, Dwight L(yman) (*b* Northfield, MA, 5 Feb 1837; *d* Northfield, 22 Dec 1899). Evangelist and popularizer of gospel hymnody. He moved to Chicago in 1856, and after several years in Sunday-school and evangelistic work, resigned from business to become an independent city missionary. In 1866 he became president of the Chicago YMCA, for which he erected the first Association building in the country. At a YMCA convention in Indianapolis in 1870 he met the singer Ira D. Sankey and invited him to become his musical associate; in June 1873 the two men went to England to conduct evangelistic services, remaining there until August 1875. Music was highly regarded by Moody for its mass appeal; other singers with whom he worked were Philip Phillips, Philip P. Bliss, George C. Stebbins, James McGranahan, Charles M. Alexander, and Daniel B. Towner. Towner became head of the music department of the Moody Bible Institute in Chicago, a school which exerted a significant influence on gospel hymnody by training evangelistic singers and composers. Through his use of music and his encouragement of evangelistic singer–composers, Moody fostered the growth of gospel hymnody more than any other evangelist.

For illustration *see* GOSPEL MUSIC, fig. 1*a*.

BIBLIOGRAPHY

L. A. Weigle: "Moody, Dwight Lyman," *DAB*

R. Stevenson: "Ira D. Sankey and the Growth of 'Gospel Hymnody'," *Patterns of Protestant Church Music* (Durham, 1953), 151

A. G. Debus: "The Recordings of Moody and Sankey," *Hobbies*, lxi/3 (1956), 33

J. C. Pollock: *Moody* (New York, 1963)
J. F. Findlay, Jr.: *Dwight L. Moody: American Evangelist, 1837–1899* (Chicago, 1969)

HARRY ESKEW

Moog, Robert A(rthur) (*b* New York, 23 May 1934). Designer of electronic instruments. His name is primarily associated with a range of synthesizers manufactured by the R. A. Moog Co., which he founded in New York in 1954; early on the name "Moog" was even used, loosely, to mean any type of synthesizer. He financed his studies at Queens College, CUNY, and later at Columbia University by building and marketing theremins, producing five models by 1962. In 1957 he moved to Ithaca, New York, where he gained a doctorate in engineering physics at Cornell University in 1965. At nearby Trumansburg in the spring and summer of 1964 he began to develop his first synthesizer modules in collaboration with the composer Herbert Deutsch; they were demonstrated that autumn at the Audio Engineering Society convention in New York. At the end of 1964 Moog's company marketed the first commercial modular synthesizer. Between 1966 and 1969 he sponsored the Independent Electronic Music Center at the R. A. Moog Co., which published the *Electronic Music Review* (1967–8; it contains several of his articles) and ran an open-access electronic music studio.

In 1970, faced with competition from newer synthesizer companies, Moog worked with James Scott, William Hemsath, and Chad Hunt to develop the Minimoog, an innovative, fully portable monophonic instrument which became especially popular in rock music. In 1971 the company became Moog Music and moved to Buffalo, New York. Since then it has developed over a dozen synthesizers, most of which have been discontinued; the last to which Moog made some design contribution was the Micromoog (marketed 1973–5). When Moog Music became a division of Norlin Industries in 1973, Moog was involved mainly in promotional and managerial duties. At the end of 1977 he left Norlin and in the following year started a new company, Big Briar, in Leicester, North Carolina, manufacturing a range of devices (with keyboards, theremin-type fingerboards, or touch-sensitive plates) for precision control of analog and digital synthesizers. From 1975 Moog has contributed a regular monthly column on synthesizers to *Contemporary Keyboard* (now *Keyboard*). As a pioneer and figurehead of the development of the synthesizer, he has become much sought after as a lecturer and has also appeared at trade fairs, festivals, conferences, and competitions (such as the Ars Electronica in Linz, Austria); he has also endorsed newer developments, including the Fairlight C(omputer) M(usical) I(nstrument). In 1984 Moog was engaged as a consultant by Kurzweil Music Systems (manufacturer of the Kurzweil 250 digital keyboard synthesizer) of Boston, where he became Chief Scientist.

Moog has also developed circuitry for a wide range of applications: guitar amplifiers, effects boxes, mixers, multi-track tape recorders, and variable-speed controllers for tape recorders. He has worked closely with both classical and rock musicians, designing and equipping complete electronic music studios, and developing custom-built synthesizer systems for Walter Carlos (*see* CARLOS, WENDY) and the rock keyboard player Keith Emerson, and for the electronic music studio at SUNY, Albany. He has created specialized electronic instruments and systems for a number of composers, among which are the dancer-responsive antennae used to activate tape recorders in *Variations V* (1965) by John Cage with the Merce Cunningham Dance Company, and three microtonal instruments, including a four-octave 43-note electronic keyboard instrument for Donald Erb's *Reconnaissance* (1967).

See also ELECTROACOUSTIC MUSIC, §4.

Robert A. Moog with three synthesizers designed by him: a Moog Modular System Series 900, c1964 (rear), the Minimoog Model D, c1970 (foreground right), and the Moog Sonic Six, c1970

BIBLIOGRAPHY

D. Crombie: "The Moog Story," *Sound International*, no.6 (1978), 66

T. Rhea: "The Moog Synthesizer," *Contemporary Keyboard*, vii/3 (1981), 58

J. Lee: "Interview: Robert Moog," *Polyphony*, vii/4 (1982)

H. Davies: "Moog," and "Moog, Robert A(rthur)," *Grove I*

HUGH DAVIES

Moore, A. David (*b* Hanover, NH, 8 Feb 1946). Organ builder. After graduating from the University of Vermont, he was apprenticed to C. B. Fisk and made two study trips to Europe. He began his own business in North Pomfret, Vermont, completing his first organ, a small one-manual instrument, in 1972. His later work includes large two-manual organs for Grace Church, Washington, DC (1981), St. James's Church, Woodstock, Vermont (1985), and a number of restorations. His organs are strongly influenced by French classical design. All the parts for his instruments, including the pipes, are made in his workshop, and locally grown woods, particularly butternut, are used extensively.

BIBLIOGRAPHY

L. Waters: "An Interview with A. David Moore," *American Organist*, xvii (1983), 58

BARBARA OWEN

Moore, Carman (Leroy) (*b* Lorain, OH, 8 Oct 1936). Composer. At the Oberlin College Conservatory he studied with Martin Morris (horn), Peter Brown (cello), and Cecil Isaacs (conducting). He then attended Ohio State University (BM 1958) and played horn briefly with the Columbus SO (1958). In New York he studied composition with Overton from 1958 to 1963 and at the Juilliard School with Persichetti and Berio (MM 1966); in 1967 he was a pupil of Wolpe. In the following year, with Noel DaCosta, Kermit and Dorothy Rudd Moore, and Stephen Chambers (Talib Rasul Hakim), he founded the Society of Black Composers. Moore taught at a number of institutions, including the Dalton School (1964–8), Manhattanville College (1969–71), Yale University (1969–71), and Queens College (1970–71) and Brooklyn College (1972–4), CUNY. While still at Juilliard he wrote reviews for the *Village Voice*, and during the late 1960s and early 1970s he wrote several regular *Voice* columns, including "New Times," on contemporary music, and "Riffs," on pop and rock topics. He also became a regular contributor to the *New York Times* and in 1970–71 wrote the column "Spotlights on Music" for *Vogue*. During this time he produced a major biography of Bessie Smith, *Somebody's Angel Child* (1970). His other writings include a textbook for teaching popular music (1980) and *The Growth of Black Sound in America* (unpublished). During the mid-1970s he was lyricist for Felix Cavaliere and the rock group Foghat, and from 1978 served as an adjudicator for the NEA. He has received a number of awards, including grants from the Creative Artists Public Service (1970, 1976), NEA (1977), American Music Center (1974, 1978), and the Gracie Mansion Commission (1980–81), given by the mayor of New York.

An eclectic, Moore blends elements of jazz, gospel, rock, and avant-garde idioms in his music. His first major commissions were from the San Francisco SO (*Gospel Fuse*, 1974) and the New York PO (*Wildfires and Field Songs*, 1974). These two works, which received almost simultaneous premières in January 1975, firmly established his reputation as a composer; after 1975 he received an increasing number of commissions, and in 1978 a festival of his music was held at LaGuardia College, CUNY. Among recent works *Fixed Do, Movable Sol* (1980) and the Concerto for Blues Piano and Orchestra (1982) have been especially well received by critics.

WORKS

Orch: Sinfonia, 1964; Catwalk, 1966; Wildfires and Field Songs, 1974; 4 Movts for a Fashionable Five-Toed Dragon, Chin. insts, jazz qnt, chamber orch, 1976; Saratoga Festival Variations, 1976; Hit, perc, orch, 1978; Conc. for Blues Pf, 1982

Inst: Movt, str qt, 1961; Pf Sonata, 1962; Crossfire, pf, tape, 1965; Youth in a Merciful House, 6 insts, 1965; Drum Major: to the Memory of M. L. King, 2 tpt, trbn, tuba, 2 perc, tape, 1969; Flight Piece, fl, pf, 1969; Museum Piece, fl, vc, tape, 1975; Dawn of the Solar Age, brass, perc, synth, 1978; Qt for Saxophones with Echo Device, 1978; American Themes and Variations, nar, handbells, insts, 1980; Blue Drone and Canon, wind, 1981; Skydance, 2 synth, 7 insts, tape, 1984; several other works

Choral: Wedding Cantata (Moore, after Joyce, Herrick), SATB, fl, cl, trbn, vc, 1963; Gospel Fuse (Moore), S, 4vv, sax, pf, elec org, orch, 1974; Great American Nebula (Moore), cantata, nar, lv, SATB, concert band, jazz trio, str orch, 1976; Follow Light (Moore), SATB, perc, db, 1977; several other works

Mixed media: Broken Suite, actor-dancers, tape, insts, 1969; African Tears (Moore after K. Awooner), jazz ens, 7 perc, 3 actors, dancer, vv, 1971; Images and Body Music, collab. E. Summers Dance and Film, 1972; The Illuminated Working Man, wind, perc, 4 vc, synth, elec, dancers, film, 1975; Fixed Do, Movable Sol, 8 insts, dancers, tape, slides, 1980; The Masque of Saxophone's Voice, insts, vv, dancers, nar, 1981; many other works

Other: 4 songs, 1962–6; incidental music for 5 plays, incl. Jo Anne! (E. Bullins), 1978, and Wild Gardens of the Loup Garou (I. Reed, C. McElroy), 1983; 5 dance scores, incl. Memories (A. Sokolow), 1968; music for 2 video films

BIBLIOGRAPHY

D. Henahan: "This Week's Most Wanted Composer: Carman Moore," *New York Times* (19 Jan 1975)

NED QUIST

Moore, Dorothy Rudd (*b* New Castle, DE, 4 June 1940). Composer. She studied composition with Mark Fax at Howard University, Washington, DC (BMus 1963), with Boulanger at the American Conservatory at Fontainebleau, France (summer 1963), and with Chou Wen-chung in New York (1965). She taught theory and piano at the Harlem School of the Arts (1965–6) and music history and appreciation at New York University (1969) and Bronx Community College, CUNY (1971). She has also published poetry, some of which she has set, and has worked as a singer in New York. In 1968 she helped to found the Society of Black Composers. Her works are predominantly contrapuntal, sometimes with block harmonies, clusters, and chords built in 2nds and 4ths. Her husband Kermit Moore, a cellist, is among those who have given premières of her works.

WORKS

Orch: Reflections, sym. wind, 1962; Sym. no.1, 1963

Inst: Baroque Suite, vc, 1965; Adagio, va, vc, 1965; 3 Pieces, vn, pf, 1967; Modes, str qt, 1968; Moods, va, vc, 1969; Pf Trio, 1970; Dirge and Deliverance, vc, pf, 1971; Dream and Variations (Theme and Variations), pf, 1974; Night Fantasy, cl, pf, 1978; A Little Whimsy, pf, 1982

Vocal: Songs (O. Khayyam: The Rubaiyat), cycle of 12 songs, S, ob, 1962; From the Dark Tower (J. W. Johnson, A. Bontemps, H. C. Johnson, G. D. Johnson, W. Cuney, L. Hughes, C. Cullen), cycle of 8 songs, Mez, vc, pf, 1970, nos.1, 3, 6, and 8 arr. Mez, chamber ens, 1972; The Weary Blues (Hughes), Bar, vc, pf, 1972, arr. Bar, chamber orch, 1979; Sonnets on Love, Rosebuds, and Death (A. D. Nelson, C. S. Delaney, G. B. Bennett, Hughes, Bontemps, Cullen, H. Johnson), cycle of 8 songs, S, vn, pf, 1976; In Celebration (Hughes), Bar, SATB, pf, 1977; Frederick Douglass (opera, 3, D. R. Moore), 1979–85

Other works, unperf.

MSS in *DHU*

Principal publishers: ACA, Belwin-Mills

BIBLIOGRAPHY

SouthernB

A. Tischler: *Fifteen Black American Composers: a Bibliography of their Works* (Detroit, 1981)

DORIS EVANS McGINTY

Moore, Douglas S(tuart) (*b* Cutchogue, NY, 10 Aug 1893; *d* Greenport, NY, 25 July 1969). Composer and teacher. His ancestors were among the first to settle in the north fork of Long Island (in 1640), and it was there that Moore spent most of his free time. His music studies began conventionally in Brooklyn; his first composition, characteristically a song (though without words), was probably written when he was 13. At Hotchkiss School, collaboration with his classmate Archibald MacLeish quickened his desire to become a composer, and at Yale University (BA 1915, BM 1917) he continued to write college and popular songs, such as *Goodnight, Harvard* and *Naomi, my Restaurant Queen*, while pursuing serious studies chiefly with Horatio Parker. Moore then served in the US Navy, writing further popular songs, several of which were later included in his set of *Songs my Mother never Taught me*. In later years Moore sometimes regretted that he had not emulated the career of another Yale graduate, Cole Porter, but the commitment to serious music prevailed.

Leaving the Navy in 1919 he remained in Paris to study organ with Charles Tournemire and composition with Vincent d'Indy and Boulanger. The harmonic and tonal influence of d'Indy is present in Moore's later work, but the relationship with Boulanger was less rewarding. In 1921 Moore accepted a position with the Cleveland Museum of Art, where he initiated a concert series and played the organ; in Cleveland he also studied with Bloch and acted at the Playhouse. After another year of study in Paris on a Pulitzer Scholarship he was appointed in 1926 to teach at Barnard College. He taught at Barnard and at Columbia University until his retirement in 1962, serving as chairman of Columbia's music department from 1940 and holding the MacDowell Chair from 1943; in these positions he reinvigorated the music department, and his administrative abilities, together with his bright urbane manner and catholic taste, made him an effective leader of many American composers' organizations, several of which he helped to found. Moore was elected to the National Institute (1941) and the American Academy (1951) of Arts and Letters and later served as president of both. Awards made to him include a Guggenheim Fellowship (1934), the Pulitzer Prize (1951) for the opera *Giants in the Earth*, and a New York Music Critics' Circle Award for *The Ballad of Baby Doe* (1958). He wrote two books, *Listening to Music* (1932, enlarged 2/1937) and *From Madrigal to Modern Music: a Guide to Musical Styles* (1942), and several articles.

Although Moore's purely instrumental music is unpretentious, it is far from trivial. Moore's most distinctive music, however, is to be found in his vocal works, particularly the seven major operas. They are generally concerned with rural or pioneer American life; his numerous songs and instrumental pieces often draw on folk or popular genres. *The Devil and Daniel Webster* and *The Ballad of Baby Doe* have become staples in the modern American repertory. Moore's dramatic sense is evident in his choice of subject, keen timing and musical characterization, accurate colloquial prosody, and dominating vocal line. Though clearly and pointedly American in character, the operas owe something to 19th-century French and Italian models; there is virtually no Germanic flavor in them. In the later operas the instrumental

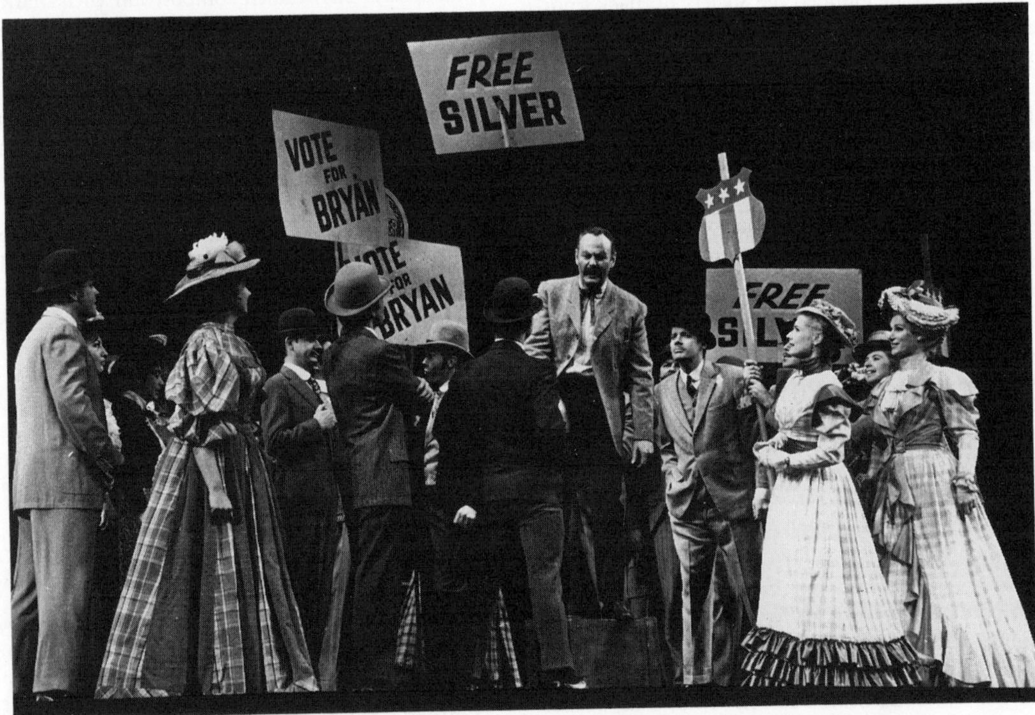

Scene from Moore's "The Ballad of Baby Doe" in the New York City Opera's production of 1966, with Walter Cassel (right of center) as Horace Tabor

accompaniments are more discriminating, effective, and individual.

The Ballad of Baby Doe (1956) is characteristic of Moore's approach. The story is authentically American, that of a Vermont stonecutter, Horace Tabor, who went West hoping to strike it rich as a silver miner (and initially did); divorced his wife Augusta in favor of marriage to the younger, prettier, and more pliant Baby Doe; supported William Jennings Bryan and the silver standard; was ruined when the nation went to a gold standard; and died and was mourned by the widowed Baby Doe, who kept a picturesque and lonely vigil at Tabor's Matchless Mine until her own death. Moore's music contrives to emphasize this period-piece atmosphere. Though it includes no actual folk or traditional music, its style is close to those of the 19th-century sentimental ballad, peppy dance-hall tunes, and the popular waltz song. The set pieces – the dialogued waltz during the first meeting of Tabor and Baby Doe, her first big solo (a "willow song" rendered at a piano in the parlor), her letter aria ("Dearest Mama, I am writing, For I'm lonely and distressed"), and others – all seem familiar, as if they had arisen from the attic pile of once popular sheet music. Details of plot, staging, and music are all mildly evocative of the American past. *Carry Nation* (1966) is similarly based on a historical figure of legendary proportions, the fierce, axe-wielding temperance advocate (and women's suffragist), and is similarly suffused with the homespun American atmosphere of an earlier era.

WORKS

(all published unless otherwise stated)

DRAMATIC

(operas)

Jesse James (J. M. Brown), 1928, inc. unpubd

White Wings (chamber opera, 2, P. Barry), 1935, unpubd; Hartford, 9 Feb 1949

The Headless Horseman (high-school opera, 1, S. V. Benét, after W. Irving: The Legend of Sleepy Hollow), 1936; Bronxville, NY 4 March 1937

The Devil and Daniel Webster (folk opera, 1, S. V. Benét), 1938; New York, 18 May 1939

The Emperor's New Clothes (children's opera, 1, R. Abrashkin, after H. C. Andersen), 1948; New York, 19 Feb 1949, rev. 1956

Giants in the Earth (3, A. Sundgaard, after O. E. Rölvaag), 1949; New York, 28 March 1951, rev. 1963

Puss in Boots (children's operetta, Abrashkin, after C. Perrault), 1949; New York, 18 Nov 1950

The Ballad of Baby Doe (folk opera, 2, J. Latouche), 1956; Central City, CO, 7 July 1958

Gallantry ("soap opera," 1, Sundgaard), 1957; New York, 19 March 1958

The Wings of the Dove (2, E. Ayer, after H. James), 1961; New York, 12 Oct 1961

The Greenfield Christmas Tree (Christmas entertainment, Sundgaard), 1962; Baltimore, 8 Dec 1962

Carry Nation (2, W. N. Jayme), 1966; Lawrence, KS, 28 April 1966

(other dramatic works)

Oh, Oh, Tennessee (musical comedy), 1925, unpubd; Twelfth Night (incidental music, Shakespeare), 1925, unpubd; Much Ado about Nothing (incidental music, Shakespeare), 1927, unpubd; The Road to Rome (incidental music, R. E. Sherwood), 1927; Greek Games (ballet), 1930; Friends, Elis, Countrymen (private entertainment, W. Griswold), unpubd; The Cruise (private entertainment, R. Loveman), unpubd; 3 film scores: Power in the Land, 1940, Youth Gets a Break, 1940, Bip Goes to Town, 1941

INSTRUMENTAL

Orch: 4 Museum Pieces, 1923 [arr. of org work]; The Pageant of P. T. Barnum, suite, 1924; Moby Dick, sym. poem, 1928, unpubd; A Sym. of Autumn, 1930; Ov. on an American Tune, 1932; Village Music, suite, 1941; In memoriam, sym. poem, 1943; Sym. no.2, A, 1945; Farm Journal, suite, chamber orch, 1947; Cotillion, suite, str, 1952; 2 student works

Chamber: Vn Sonata, 1929, unpubd; Str Qt, 1933; Wind Qnt, 1942, rev. 1948; Down East Suite, vn, pf/orch, 1944; Cl Qnt, 1946; Pf Trio, 1953; *c*8 student works

KEYBOARD

Prelude and Fugue, org, 1919–22, unpubd; 4 Museum Pieces, org, 1922, unpubd; March, org, 1922, unpubd; Scherzo, org, 1923, unpubd; 3 Contemporaries: Careful Etta, Grievin' Annie, Fiddlin' Joe, pf, *c*1935–40; Museum Piece, pf, 1939; Passacaglia, org, 1939 [arr. band by K. Wilson as Dirge]; Pf Suite, 1948; 4 Pieces, pf, 1955, unpubd; Dance for a Holiday, pf, 1957; Prelude, pf, 1957; Summer Holiday, pf, 1961; Summer Evening, pf; *c*13 student works

CHORAL

Perhaps to Dream (S. V. Benét), SSA, 1937; Simon Legree (V. Lindsay), TTBB, pf, 1937; Dedication (A. MacLeish), SSATBB, 1938; Prayer for England (W. R. Benét), TTBB, 1940; Prayer for the United Nations (S. V. Benét), A/Bar, chorus, pf/orch, 1943; Westren Winde, canon, 2 vv, *c*1946; Vayechulu (Heb.), cantor, chorus, org, 1947–8; Birds' Courting Song, T, chorus, pf, *c*1953; The Mysterious Cat (Lindsay), 1960; Mary's Prayer, S, SSA, 1962; a few arrs. of hymns and carols

SONGS

(all for 1v, pf, unless otherwise stated)

The Cuckoo, unpubd; Haying Johnnie, unpubd; Ballad of William Sycamore, Bar, fl, trbn, pf, 1926; The Apple Boughs Bend, ?1926–7, unpubd; The Cupboard (W. de la Mare), 1928; Fingers and Toes (Guiterman), 1928; Suite from Shakespearean Music, A, fl, hpd, 1928 [arr. from incidental music]: 1 Overture [from Much Ado], 2 Sigh no more, Ladies, 3 Come away, Death, 4 O Mistress Mine [no.2 arr. lv, pf, pubd, no.3 arr. B-Bar, pubd]; Songs my Mother never Taught me, collection, collab. J. J. Niles, A. A. Wallgren, 1929; Adam was my Grandfather (S. V. Benét), 1942

3 Sonnets of John Donne, 1942: 1 Thou hast Made me, 2 Batter my Heart, 3 Death, be not Proud; The Token (Donne), ?1942; Blow, blow thou winter wind (Shakespeare), 1943, unpubd; Brown Penny (W. B. Yeats), 1943, unpubd; The Cat Sat, 1943, unpubd; Not this Alone (P. Underwood), 1943; Spring and Winter, 1943, unpubd; Under the Greenwood Tree (Shakespeare), 1944; Old Song (T. Roethke), 1947; When the Drive goes Down (P. Malloch), 1951; Dear Dark Head (S. Ferguson), 1958; over 30 student songs, 3 children's songs

MSS in *DLC*; *NNC* (Butler Library) [incl. sketches and correspondence]

Principal publishers: Boosey & Hawkes, C. Fischer, Galaxy, G. Schirmer

BIBLIOGRAPHY

EwenD

W. Rhodes: "Douglas Moore's Music," *Columbia University Quarterly* (Oct 1940), 223

O. Luening: "Douglas Moore," *MM*, xx/4 (1942), 248

J. Edmunds and G. Boelzner: *Some Twentieth Century American Composers* (New York, 1959–60) [incl. bibliography]

J. Beeson: "In Memoriam: Douglas Moore (1893–1969): an Appreciation," *PNM*, viii/1 (1969), 158

H. Weitzel: *A Melodic Analysis of Selected Vocal Solos in the Operas of Douglas Moore* (diss., New York U., 1971)

D. J. Reagan: *Douglas Moore and his Orchestral Works* (diss., Catholic U. of America, 1972)

L. J. Hardee: "The Published Songs and Arias," *Notes*, xxix (1973–4), 28

H. Gleason and W. Becker: "Douglas Moore," *20th-century American Composers*, Music Literature Outlines, ser. iv (Bloomington, IN, rev. 2/1981), 129 [incl. further bibliography]

JACK BEESON/H. WILEY HITCHCOCK

Moore, Earl Vincent (*b* Lansing, MI, 27 Sept 1890). Music educator and administrator. He attended the University of Michigan (BA 1912, MA 1915). His training in composition, conducting, organ, and music theory was continued in Europe with several teachers, including Charles-Marie Widor (1913) and Gustav Holst (1925). At the University of Michigan he served as organist and theory teacher (1914–23), director of the school of music (1923–46), and its dean (1946–60). From 1960 to 1970 he was chairman of the music department at the University of Houston. Moore was national director and consultant for the WPA Music Project and its successor, the WPA Music Program (1939–43). He was one of the founder-members of the National Association of Schools of Music (1924) and also served as president of the Music Teachers National Association (1936–8) and Pi Kappa Lambda (1946–50). He was considered one of the most important figures in college and university music education.

WILLIAM McCLELLAN

Moore, Glen (*b* 1941). Jazz double bass player, co-founder of the jazz chamber ensemble OREGON.

Moore, Grace (*b* Nough, TN, 5 Dec 1898; *d* nr Copenhagen, Denmark, 26 Jan 1947). Soprano. She studied singing with Marafioti in New York, and then appeared in revue and operetta. She sailed for Europe in 1926 and worked with Richard Berthélemy in Antibes; she made her Opéra-Comique début in 1928. In the same year she made her début at the Metropolitan Opera as Mimì (7 February); she remained with the Metropolitan until 1946 (excepting 1933–4 and 1936–7), singing such roles as Lauretta (*Gianni Schicchi*), Tosca, Manon, Fiora (*L'amore dei tre re*), and Louise. She appeared at Covent Garden in 1935 as Mimì, and continued to give concerts internationally until her death in an airplane accident. The most important of her several films was *One Night of Love* (1934). Moore's voice was sensuous and substantial, though it lacked technical finish. A glamorous personality, she earned the American accolade "star of stage, screen, and radio."

BIBLIOGRAPHY

O. Thompson: *The American Singer* (New York, 1937/*R*1969), 382
G. Moore: *You're only Human once* (Garden City, NY, 1944/*R*1977)
R. Celletti: "Moore, Grace," *Le grandi voci* (Rome, 1964) [with discography by S. Smolian]
J. W. James: "Moore, Grace," *NAW*
W. E. Boswell: "Moore, Grace," *DAB*
L. Rasponi: "The Money-makers," *The Last Prima Donnas* (New York, 1982), 416

MAX DE SCHAUENSEE/R

Moore, Henrietta. Pseudonym of HENRY FILLMORE.

Moore, John W(eeks) (*b* Andover, NH, 11 April 1807; *d* Manchester, NH, 23 March 1889). Lexicographer and editor. He was the brother of Henry Eaton Moore (1803–41), a composer and teacher highly regarded in New England. After learning the printer's trade as an apprentice, he moved in 1828 to Brunswick, where he published the first weekly newspaper in Maine. He returned to New Hampshire, 1831–8, before settling in Vermont, where he became editor of the *Bellows Falls Gazette*. Here Moore compiled and published the first comprehensive encyclopedia of music in English, the *Complete Encyclopedia of Music* (1852/*R*1972). During this period he also published three collections of instrumental and vocal music and the *World of Music* (1843–9), then the longest-running American music periodical. After moving to Manchester in 1863, he edited additional installments of *World of Music* (1867–70), issued a supplement (1875/*R*1972) to his encyclopedia, and published *A Dictionary of Musical Information* (1876), an abridged version of the encyclopedia that includes a useful list of several thousand works published in the USA from 1640 to 1875.

Moore gathered much of the material for his encyclopedia from the writings of European scholars and historians such as Charles Burney and François-Joseph Fétis. This in part explains the curious lack of information on American music and composers; Moore's own views ("We are . . . too much a nation made up of others to possess a music of our own") probably also account for this. In spite of its bias and some inaccuracies, his work is a pioneering effort in the study of music in the USA.

See also DICTIONARIES, §2.

BIBLIOGRAPHY

S. P. Cheney: *The American Singing Book* (Boston, 1879/*R*1980), 201
F. O. Jones, ed.: *A Handbook of American Music and Musicians* (Canaseraga, NY, 1886/*R*1971), 102
F. H. Martens: "Moore, John Weeks," *DAB*

DALE COCKRELL

Moore, Mary (Louise) Carr (*b* Memphis, TN, 6 Aug 1873; *d* Inglewood, CA, 9 Jan 1957). Composer and teacher. She studied in San Francisco under J. H. Pratt (composition) and H. B. Pasmore (singing). By 1889 she had begun teaching and composing; a song from that year was later published. She sang the leading role in the première of her first operetta *The Oracle* (1894), but in 1895 she abandoned her singing career. For the rest of her life she taught and composed in Lemoore, California (from 1895), Seattle (1901), San Francisco (1915), and Los Angeles (1926). In Seattle in 1909 she established the American Music Center in association with Farwell's National Wa-Wan Society of America. In Los Angeles she taught at the Olga Steeb Piano School (1926–43) and was concurrently professor of theory and composition at Chapman College (1928–47). She organized a manuscript club, which has survived her, to secure readings for her students' music. In 1936, with Cadman and Grunn, she founded the California Society of Composers, which gave festivals of American music in Los Angeles in 1937 and 1938, and in 1938 she helped form its successor, the Society of Native American Composers, which was active until 1944. She was awarded an honorary DMus by Chapman College in 1936.

Farwell's American music movement inspired Moore greatly, and 19th-century German and French models studied in the populist context of the American West formed her style and esthetic approach. Her songs lie well for the voice and range from those in the style of parlor and dancehall music to evocative whole-tone experiments. Moore was at her best in opera, where she frequently challenged the limitations of the genteel culture to which she remained bound by inclination and family obligations. Mixed groups of amateurs and professionals assembled through her own efforts produced eight of her stage works. She herself conducted all three productions of *Narcissa* (Seattle, 1912; San Francisco, 1925; and Los Angeles, 1945), which in 1930 won a David Bispham Memorial Medal. The naive but often persuasive expressionism of *Narcissa* evolved into the post-romantic idioms of later works such as *David Rizzio* and *Legende provençale*, each of which contains reflections of Debussy and Puccini; she would not permit an ad hoc performance of the latter work, which is delicate and demanding. Both regional prejudice and sex discrimination prevented Moore from receiving the recognition that the achievement of *Narcissa* warranted and probably slowed her artistic development. Several of her works, including operas, songs, and chamber works, deserve revival; her published works include 65 songs, 15 choral works, some piano pieces, and vocal scores of *Narcissa* and *David Rizzio*.

WORKS

OPERAS

The Oracle (2, rev. 3, Moore), 1893–4; San Francisco 19 March 1894
Narcissa, or The Cost of Empire (4, S. P. Carr), 1909–11; Seattle, 22 April 1912
The Leper (1, D. Burrows), 1912
Memories (1, C. E. Banks), 1914; Seattle, 31 Oct 1914

Harmony (1, various students), 1917; San Francisco, 25 May 1917
The Flaming Arrow, or The Shaft of Ku'pish-ta-ya (1), 1919–20; San Francisco, 27 March 1922
David Rizzio (2, E. M. Browne), 1927–8; Los Angeles, 26 May 1932
Los rubios (3, N. Marquis), 1931; Los Angeles, 10 Sept 1931
Flutes of Jade Happiness (3, L. S. Moore), 1932–3; Los Angeles, 2 March 1934
Legende provençale (3, E. Flaig), 1929–35

OTHER WORKS

Orch: Ka-mi-a-kin, 1930; Pf Conc., 1933–4; Kidnap, 1937–8
Chamber: 3 pf trios, 1895, 1906, 1941; Saul (R. Browning), 1916; Vn Sonata, c, 1918–19; Str Qt, g, 1926; Str Qt, f, 1930; Str Trio, g, 1936; Brief Furlough, qnt, 1942; 57 piano pieces; 20 other pieces for various insts and pf
Vocal: Beyond These Hills (G. Moyle), song cycle, S, A, T, B, pf, 1923–4; 250 songs, 1889–1952; 57 choral pieces

MSS in *CLU-MUS*
Principal publishers: C. Fischer, G. Schirmer, Webster, Witmark

BIBLIOGRAPHY

"Mary Carr Moore – American Composer," *Christian Science Monitor* (16 April 1929), 11
E. E. Hipsher: *American Opera and its Composers* (Philadelphia, *c*1927, 2/1934)
R. Curtis: "A Club Comes of Age," *Life with Music*, ii/4 (1949), 28
M. Couche: "Mary Carr Moore: American Composer," *Music of the West*, ix/6 (1954), 13, 18
C. P. Smith: Introduction in M. C. Moore: *David Rizzio* (San Bruno, CA, *c*1937/*R*1981)
——: Liner notes, *The Songs of Mary Carr Moore* (Cambria 1022, 1985)
——: Introduction in M. C. Moore: *Songs* (in preparation)
C. P. Smith and C. S. Richardson: *Mary Carr Moore* (in preparation) [biography]

CATHERINE PARSONS SMITH

Moore, Undine Smith (*b* Jarratt, VA, 25 Aug 1905). Composer and educator. She studied piano and organ with Alice M. Grass at Fisk University, Nashville (BA, BMus), and continued her education at the Juilliard School, the Manhattan School, Columbia University Teachers College (MA, professional diploma), and the Eastman School. After teaching in the public schools of Goldsboro, North Carolina, she taught at Virginia State College, Petersburg, from 1927 to her retirement in 1972; there she cofounded and codirected the Black Music Center (1969–72). She also lectured extensively and served as a visiting professor at several colleges including Virginia Union University in Richmond.

WORKS

(selective list; for a fuller list see Baker, Belt, and Hudson, 1978)

Inst: Scherzo, pf, 1930; Valse Caprice, pf, 1930; Fugue, str trio, 1952; Reflections, pf, organ, 1952; Romance, 2 pf, 1952; Romantic Young Clown, pf, 1952; Introduction, March, and Allegro, cl, pf, 1958; 3 Pieces, fl, pf, 1958; Afro-American Suite, 2 fl, vc, pf, 1969; Org Variations on "Nettleton," 1976
Choral: Sir Olaf and the Erl King's Daughter, cantata, SSA, pf, 1925; Into my Heart's Treasury, 1950; Thou has made us for thyself, 1952; Teach me to hear mermaids singing, SSA, 1953; Mother to Son, 1955; When Susanna Jones Wears Red, *c*1958; Let us make man in our image, 1960; O spirit who dost prefer before all temples, chorus, pf/org, 1966; Lord, we give thanks to thee, 1971; Tambourines to Glory, 1973; Glory to God, cantata, nar, TTBB, fl, org/pf, 1974; A Time for Remembering, chorus, pf, 1976; Scenes from the Life of a Martyr, oratorio, nar, chorus, orch, 1982; many spiritual arrs.
1v, pf: Uphill, 1926; Heart, have you heard the news?, 1926; Set Down!, 1951; Love, let the wind cry how I adore thee, 1961; To be Baptized, 1973; Watch and Pray, 1973; Lyric for True Love, 1975; I want to die while you love me, 1975; I am in doubt, 1975

BIBLIOGRAPHY

SouthernB
H. Roach: *Black American Music: Past and Present* (Boston, 1973)
S. Stern: *Women Composers: a Handbook* (Metuchen, NJ, 1978)
D. N. Baker, L. M. Belt, and H. C. Hudson, eds.: *The Black Composer Speaks* (Metuchen, NJ, 1978) [incl. list of works]
R. D. Jones: *The Choral Works of Undine Smith Moore: a Study of her Life and Work* (diss., New York U., 1980)
A. Cohen: *International Encyclopedia of Women Composers* (New York, 1981)

DORIS EVANS McGINTY

Moorman, (Madeline) Charlotte (*b* Little Rock, AR, 18 Nov 1933). Cellist and performance artist. She studied music at Centenary College, Shreveport, Louisiana (BM 1955), and was a pupil in cello with Horace Britt at the University of Texas, Austin, 1956–7. In 1957–8 she began studying with Rose at the Juilliard School. She was a member of Jacob Glick's Boccherini Players (1958–63) and of the American SO (until 1967). In 1960 she heard a concert of works by Cage, Toshi Ichiyanagi, and Ono, in 1963 founded the Annual New York Avant Garde Festival, and in 1964, for the second festival's performances, she collaborated for the first time with the composer, video artist and performance artist Nam June Paik; Moorman has been closely associated with Paik, and has interpreted and collaborated with him on a large number of works diverse in aim, from *Cello Sonata no.1 for Adults Only* (1965), which associates music with sex and violence, to *Global Grove* (1973). Some of them use nontraditional instruments, as in *TV Cello* (1971), while others juxtapose the human and the technological (*TV Bra for Living Sculpture*, 1969). Moorman's cello performance in Paik's *Opéra sextronique* on 9 February 1967 resulted in arrest and conviction for indecent exposure, an event commemorated by their work *The People of the State of New York against Charlotte Moorman* (1977). On other occasions she has played her cello underwater, in a gondola, or wrapped only in cellophane. Her repertory includes, in addition to works by Paik, music by Cage, Ono, Joseph Beuys, Takehisa Kosugi, and Jim McWilliams.

BIBLIOGRAPHY

C. Barnes: "Don't Move! The Case of the Topless Cellist," *Financial Times* (17 May 1967); repr. in *Music and Musicians*, xv/12 (1967), 25
C. Moore: "Miss Moorman's Music," *Village Voice* (16 Feb 1967), 16
M. T. Kaufman: "Can a Girl from a Small Town in Arkansas Find Fame and Happiness by Floating over Central Park on Balloons, Playing her Cello?," *In their Own Good Time* (New York, 1973), 186
C. Tomkins: "Video Visionary," *New Yorker*, li (5 May 1975), 52
N. J. Paik and C. Moorman: "Videa, Vidiot, Videology," *New Artists Video: a Critical Anthology*, ed. G. Battcock (New York, 1978), 121
J. G. Hanhardt, ed.: *Nam June Paik* (New York, 1982)
"From Jail to Jungle, 1967–1977: the Work of Charlotte Moorman and Nam June Paik," *The Art of Performance: a Critical Anthology*, ed. G. Battcock and R. Nickas (New York, 1984), 278

SEVERINE NEFF

Moran, Peter K. (*b* Ireland; *d* New York, 10 Feb 1831). Composer, organist, violinist, cellist, and music dealer. He immigrated to the USA with his wife, a singer, in 1817, and announced their arrival "from Dublin" in a New York newspaper in December of that year. Both were active in New York's concert life (70 performances have been verified), and their daughter made her début as a singer and pianist in 1820 at the age of five. Moran was organist at Grace Episcopal Church (*c*1823–7), and St. John's Chapel (1828–31), as well as for the Handel and Haydn Society in 1820 and for the New York Choral Society's first concert in 1824. He played cello for the García Opera Company's appearance in New York in 1825, performed with the Philharmonic Society, and was concertmaster of the Musical Fund Society. From 1822 to 1823 he ran a piano and music store and published about 25 pieces, including 16 of his own compositions and arrangements.

At least 21 works composed or arranged by Moran were published in Dublin before his emigration. Many of these were reissued in New York, where he was second only to James Hewitt as the city's most prolific composer of piano music. He wrote both easy and technically demanding works, the most popular of which included the song *The Carrier Pigeon* (n.d. [1822]), which he arranged as a rondo for piano (*c*1825), and his variations on *Kinlock of Kinlock* (n.d. [1825]), *Stantz Waltz* (n.d. [?1817]), *Suabian Air* (n.d. [?1817]), and *Swiss Waltz* (n.d. [*c*1810]). He also arranged many traditional airs, and religious works by Handel and others.

WORKS

Selective list. Published in New York, n.d., unless otherwise indicated; estimated dates of publication are given in brackets.

SONGS

(for 1v, pf, unless otherwise stated)

The Carrier Pigeon (Percival) ([1822]); The Hebrew Mourner (J. W. Eastburn) ([1822]): Weep not for those (T. Moore) ([1822]); What the bee is to the flow'ret (Moore), 2vv, pf (1828); O say can this be love (1830)

PIANO

* – *also arr. harp*

Variations: *Swiss Waltz (London and Dublin, [*c*1810]); *Stantz Waltz (Dublin, [?1817]); *Suabian Air (Ach du lieber Augustin) ([?1817]), ed. in RRAM, ii (1977); Fantasia . . . Thine am I my Faithful Fair ([1818–21]), ed. in RRAM, ii (1977); Kinlock of Kinlock ([1825]); Ah beauteous maid if thou'lt be mine, pf 4 hands ([1825–6]); The Bonny Boat (1826); Whistle and I will come to thee my lad (1827); Coal Black Rose (1835)

Rondos: Come buy my cherries ([1819]); The Carrier Pigeon ([1825]); Barney Brallaghan (1830); National Guards March and Rondo ([1830]); Mi pizzica mi stimola (after D. Auber: La muette de Portici (Masaniello)) ([*c*1830])

Others, incl. Petit sonata, with fl ad lib ([1820]), waltzes, marches

PEDAGOGICAL

Moran's New Instructions for the Piano Forte (1828)

EDITIONS

S. Chapple: *Chapple's Anthems in Score* (New York, 1822)

A Collection of Psalm, Hymn, and Chant Tunes Adapted to the Service of the Protestant Episcopal Church in the United States of America (New York, 1823)

J. M. Wainwright: *Music of the Church* (New York, 1828)

BIBLIOGRAPHY

G. C. D. Odell: *Annals of the New York Stage*, ii-iii (New York, 1927–8/*R*1970)

R. J. Wolfe: *Secular Music in America, 1801–1825: a Bibliography* (New York, 1964)

B. A. Wolverton: *Keyboard Music and Musicians in the Colonies and United States of America before 1830* (diss., Indiana U., 1966)

J. BUNKER CLARK, EVE R. MEYER

Moran, Robert (Leonard) (*b* Denver, CO, 8 Jan 1937). Composer. He studied 12-tone composition privately with Hans-Erich Apostel in Vienna (1957–8) and composition at Mills College with Berio and Milhaud (MA 1963); in 1963 he returned to Vienna for private study with Roman Haubenstock-Ramati, who had a strong influence on his early works. At various times between 1959 and 1972 he lived in San Francisco, where he founded and codirected with Howard Hersh the New Music Ensemble at the San Francisco Conservatory. He was composer-in-residence at Portland (Oregon) State University from 1972 to 1974, and at Northwestern University (1977–8), where he also directed the New Music Ensemble. Moran has performed in Europe and throughout the USA as a pianist, and is a well-known lecturer on contemporary and avant-garde music. Among his awards are one from the Deutscher Akademischer Austauschdienst for study in Berlin (1974) and two NEA grants (1977, 1979); he has also received many commissions. He collaborated with Helps to produce *Waltzes*, a collection of 25 waltzes for piano, each by a different contemporary composer (1978; first performed with the New Music Ensemble, Chicago, May 1978). In 1984–5 he shared with Glass a residency at the Third Street Music School Settlement in New York, to collaborate on children's works.

Many of Moran's compositions are mixed-media pieces, and even in his other works the musicians often have an added theatrical function. His large-scale "city pieces" allow the audiences to participate in their realization under his guidance. *39 Minutes for 39 Autos* (San Francisco, 1969) employed a "potential of 100,000 performers, using auto horns, auto lights, skyscrapers, a TV station, dancers, theater groups, spotlights, and airplanes, besides a small synthesizer ensemble." *Hallelujah* (1971) required many varied musical forces and the entire city of Bethlehem, Pennsylvania. Two similar works in this series are *Pachelbel Promenade* (Graz, Austria, 1975, commissioned by the Austrian Radio) and *From the Market to Asylum* (Hartford, 1982).

Moran has also composed graphic works for a variety of instruments, specified and unspecified, in which he integrates the roles of composer and performer through improvisation and aleatory techniques; multi-orchestral works (*Emblems of Passage* and *The Eternal Hour*, both 1974, and *Enantiodromia*, 1977); and children's theater works (*Marktmenagerie*, 1975, and *Es war einmal*, 1976, a mixed-media work for the US Bicentennial). His later mixed-media operas are large-scale performance works that explore controversial subjects: *Erlösung dem Erlöser* is based on the death of Wagner; *Hitler: Geschichten aus der Zukunft* was banned in West Germany. His work blends elements of the style of "found art" of the 1960s and 1970s with aleatory techniques.

WORKS

STAGE AND MIXED-MEDIA

(all texts by Moran unless otherwise stated)

Let's Build a Nut House (chamber opera), 1969; Divertissement no.3: a Lunchbag Opera, paper bags, insts, 1971; Metamenagerie (department store window opera), 1974; Durch Wüsten und Wolken, shadow puppets, insts, 1975; Marktmenagerie, children, musique concrète, 1975; Es war einmal (children's show), film, slides, musique concrète, 1976; Musik für Haustiere, tape, 1977; Music for Gamelan (incidental music), 1978; Am 29.11.1780, tape, dancers, 1979; Spin Again (ballet, P. Lamhut), amp hpd(s), elec kbds, 1980; Hitler: Geschichten aus der Zukunft (opera), 1981; Erlösung dem Erlöser (music-drama), tape loops, pfmrs, 1982; Chorale Variations: 10 Miles High over Albania (ballet, Lamhut), 8 harps, 1983; The Juniper Tree (children's opera, 2, A. Yorinks, after Grimm), 1985, collab. P. Glass

City pieces: 39 Minutes for 39 Autos, pfmrs, amp auto horns, visuals, 1969, San Francisco, 1969; Hallelujah, 20 bands, 40 choruses, org, carillon, others, 1971, Bethlehem, PA, 1971; Pachelbel Promenade, gui ens, folk insts, str ens, jazz ens, 1975, Graz, Austria, 1975; From the Market to Asylum, pfmrs, 1982, Hartford, 1982; Music for a Fair, 1984, Yellow Springs, PA, 1984

INSTRUMENTAL

Orch: Interiors, orch/chamber orch/perc ens, 1964; Bombardments no.2, 1–5 perc, 1964; L'après-midi du Dracoula, any insts, 1966; Elegant Journey with Stopping-points, any ens, 1967; Bank of America Chandelier, 4 perc, 1968; Jewel-encrusted Butterfly Wing Explosions, orch, 1968; Silver and the Circle of Messages, chamber orch, 1970; Emblems of Passage, 2 orch, 1974; Angels of Silence, va, chamber orch, 1975; Enantiodromia, 8 orch, dancers, 1977

1–8 insts: 4 Visions, fl, harp, str qt, 1964; For Org, org, 1967; Waltz in memoriam Maurice Ravel, pf, 1976; The Last Station of the Albatross, 1–8 insts, 1978; Hour Sonata, pf, 1978; Salagrama, org, 1979; BASHA, 4 amp clvd, 1983; Survivor from Darmstadt, b oboes, 1984

With chorus (texts by Moran): The Eternal Hour, orchs, choruses, 1974; Landhausmusik, gui ens, orchs, alphorns, xyl ens, boys' chorus, 1975

Arr. J. Cage: Traveling through the Sonatas and Interludes, chamber orch

Principal publishers: Broude, Hansen, Peer, Peters, Schott, Source, Universal

BIBLIOGRAPHY

R. Moran: "Seven Essays Concerning a Concert," *Ear Magazine*, ii/4 (1976)

STEPHEN RUPPENTHAL

Morath, Max (Edward) (*b* Colorado Springs, CO, 1 Oct 1926). Ragtime pianist and entertainer. He studied piano with his mother (who had been an accompanist for silent films) and took private lessons in composition, but majored in English at Colorado College (BA 1948). He began his professional career in 1944 as a radio announcer for station KVOR in Colorado Springs, later moving into television as a producer and actor. He also worked as a pianist with a summer stock company performing American popular music of the early 1900s, and came to appreciate how the music reflected the society from which it emerged. With this realization he developed, in 1959–61, two multipart series for National Educational Television, *The Ragtime Era* and *Turn of the Century*; these were one-man shows that presented social history through a mélange of piano ragtime, songs, humorous commentary, and anecdotes. Morath's concept of "social history through music" became the basis of his professional life, and he elaborated this theme in such popular and highly acclaimed one-man shows as *Ragtime Revisited* (1964–7), *Max Morath at the Turn of the Century* (1969–73), *The Ragtime Years* (1973–8), and *Living a Ragtime Life* (1977–81). With *Pop Goes the Music* (1983–) he replaced his usual solo format with a quintet and expanded his programs to include all prerock popular music. Morath also made many guest appearances on television (with the Boston Pops, among others), compiled and edited popular music of the early 20th century (his *One Hundred Ragtime Classics*, 1963, was the first important ragtime anthology), composed piano rags and songs, and wrote articles for magazines and liner notes for recordings. His own recordings (mostly on Vanguard) include many solo and ensemble ragtime performances, songs by Irving Berlin and Bert Williams, show tunes from 1917 to 1936, and ethnic Irish show tunes of the late 19th century.

BIBLIOGRAPHY

"Morath, Max (Edward)," *CBY 1963*

EDWARD A. BERLIN

Moravian Church, music of the. The Moravians, a religious sect that established communities in America during the mid-18th century in Pennsylvania and North Carolina, produced a highly developed musical culture for over 100 years.

1. History. 2. Musical structure and sources.

1. History. The origins of the Moravian Church in the USA (or Unitas Fratrum) can be traced back more than five centuries to the Bohemian Brethren, followers of the Czech martyr Jan Hus. The Unitas Fratrum was organized in Bohemia in 1457 and for almost two centuries led a precarious existence in Bohemia, Moravia, and Poland. Never a large denomination, and without official recognition or support, the brethren nevertheless contributed much to Bohemian culture and education. The Thirty Years War destroyed much of their work and drove them into hiding, and the Peace of Westphalia (1648) left their lands under the control of the Roman Catholic Church, which continued the persecution begun more than three decades earlier.

In 1722 some remnants of the Bohemian Brethren took refuge on the estate of Count Nikolaus Ludwig von Zinzendorf in Saxony. They built the town of Herrnhut and over the next several years revitalized and renewed their church. Many of the customs and services unique to the Moravian Church date from these years: the love feast (*Liebesmahl*), the song hour (*Singstunde*), the choir system, and the book of *Daily Texts*. The role and influence of Zinzendorf in the renewed Moravian Church was central to its development.

Within ten years of its renewal at Herrnhut, the Moravian Church began sending missionaries to various lands to preach to the "heathen." The first group of Moravians to reach North America arrived in 1735 at Savannah, Georgia. Because of an imminent war with Spain over disputed territory and the Moravians' conscientious objection to bearing arms, they abandoned the Georgia settlement in 1740 and in 1741 established the town of Bethlehem in eastern Pennsylvania. From here other communities were founded: Nazareth (1748) and Lititz (1756), Pennsylvania, and Salem (1766, now in Winston-Salem), North Carolina; smaller communities and "preaching stations" were also established (Graceham, Maryland; Hope, New Jersey; Dover, Ohio), but music reached its highest development in the church communities.

From its renewal in 1722 the Moravian Church placed strong emphasis on music, both congregational and concerted. Music played a part in all its services and was almost continuous in the love feast (a simple, nonsacramental meal shared by the congregation) and song hour (a less formal musical service). The Moravians who colonized Pennsylvania and North Carolina carried on this musical tradition as much as they were able in the wilderness. At first their music consisted largely of hymns accompanied by a few instruments such as horns, trumpets, flutes, and violins. As the communities became more settled, organs were built for the churches, and orchestras (collegia musica) were organized among the men of the congregation. These not only accompanied the concerted anthems sung by the choir but often met several times during the week to rehearse and perform orchestral and chamber music imported from Europe.

This intense musical activity required a large amount of music, most of which was provided by composers within the Moravian Church itself. German Moravian composers such as Christian Gregor (1723–1801), Johann Christian Geisler (1729–1815), Johann Ludwig Freydt (1748–1807), and others wrote hundreds of anthems with orchestral accompaniment. Appropriate choruses by non-Moravian composers were also widely used. Many of the American Moravian communities had members who wrote hymns, songs, anthems, and liturgical music for the specific needs of the congregations.

The first Moravians in America known to have composed music were Johann Christoph Pyrlaeus (1713–85) and Christian Friedrich Oerter (1716–93), who wrote liturgical music as early as 1747. Pyrlaeus was also the leader of a collegium musicum organized in Bethlehem in 1744. The first composer to write concerted anthems in America was Jeremiah Dencke (1725–95), who arrived in Bethlehem in 1761. Dencke's earliest surviving anthem, dated 1766, is a doxology for a provincial synod held in Bethlehem that year. In 1765 he wrote two groups of songs for love feasts, on 29 August and 7 September (his earliest surviving compositions), and in 1767 and 1768 he wrote special music for Christmas love feasts.

The arrival in 1770 of Johann Friedrich Peter (1746–1813) and his brother Simon Peter (1743–1819) began a period of musical excellence in American Moravian communities that lasted well into the 19th century. J. F. Peter, who worked in all the major American Moravian communities, was the most important Moravian musician and composer of his time, and his anthems are among the best in the Moravian repertory. His brother, who was more important as a minister and teacher than as a composer, came to Salem in 1782 and spent the rest of his life there. He wrote only four known works, but each displays a remarkable talent.

The Moravian Bishop Jacob Van Vleck performing music with a group of girls, probably from the Pennsylvania School for Young Ladies, Bethlehem, of which he was principal: birthday greeting in watercolor and ink by an unknown artist (1795) in the Moravian Historical Society, Nazareth, Pennsylvania

Following the Peter brothers to America were Georg Gottfried Müller (1762–1821), a talented violinist who arrived in 1784, and JOHANNES HERBST (1735–1812), an excellent organist who came in 1786. Müller was a minister and congregational leader at Lititz and at Beersheba, Ohio. He is known to have composed nine anthems; the eight that survive are of high quality. Herbst's more than 100 anthems were widely used in Moravian communities during the late 18th and early 19th centuries.

In 1795 DAVID MORITZ MICHAEL (1751–1827) came to the USA for 20 years' service. He worked mostly in Nazareth and Bethlehem, and was a versatile musician: he could play many instruments and was a capable orchestra leader. His compositions include over a dozen anthems, 16 suites (*Parthien*) for woodwind sextet, and a monumental setting of Psalm ciii for soloists, chorus, and orchestra. Johann Christian Bechler (1784–1857) arrived in the USA in 1806 to teach at the newly founded theological seminary at Nazareth. From 1829 he was the pastor of the Salem congregation and after his consecration as a bishop (1835) went to Sarepta, Russia. An enthusiastic lover of music, Bechler composed hymns, anthems, liturgies, and a few pieces for wind instruments.

In addition to these European musicians there was also a group of composers born and trained in America who began contributing to American Moravian music during the 1790s. Jacob Van Vleck (1751–1831; see illustration) and Johann Christian Till (1762–1844) were the earliest; both wrote anthems, hymns, and liturgies. Peter Wolle (1792–1871), a student of Michael and Bechler, edited the first Moravian tunebook published in the USA, *Hymn Tunes Used in the Church of the United Brethren* (Boston, 1836); he wrote about 16 anthems and sacred songs, several of which were published (an unusual occurrence for Moravian music of that time).

About 1840 the musical life in American Moravian communities began to decline because of changes in musical taste, the opening of previously closed communities to secularizing influences (the communities of Bethlehem, Nazareth, Lititz, and Salem were owned by the Moravian Church, and residence there had been restricted to its members), and perhaps a decreasing need for new music, as much useful music was easily available. The love feasts, song hours, and other services had become more recreative than creative. Two composers active during this time deserve mention, however: Francis Florentine Hagen (1815–1907) and Edward W. Leinbach (1823–1901), both born in Salem. Leinbach stayed there, serving as organist, violinist, and general town musician. He is known primarily for his remarkable setting of the *Hosanna*, but also wrote hymn tunes. Hagen entered the ministry and served in Pennsylvania, North Carolina, New York, and Iowa. He wrote about a dozen anthems, some of which are harmonically daring, and a delightful overture for orchestra.

Moravian composers adopted the stylistic principles of the Classical era: balanced melodic phrases, straightforward rhythms, and clear homophonic textures. Among earlier composers, including Gregor, Geisler, Herbst, and J. F. Peter, the influence of C. P. E. Bach and the German song composers J. A. P. Schulz, J. F. Reichardt, Anton Neumann, and Johann Adam Hiller is to be noted. Later composers, such as JOHN ANTES, Bechler, and Michael, were strongly influenced by Haydn; Weber and Mendelssohn are evident as influences on the works of Wolle and Hagen. With few exceptions, the music composed by Moravian composers was written for performance on specific occasions by amateur performers, with little or no thought of wide distribution or financial gain; only a small quantity was published before 1950. The music of the 18th- and 19th-century American Moravians was not widely known beyond the limits of their towns. Although such men as Benjamin Franklin and the Marquis of Chastellux (quoted in Rau, 1927) and the Rev. John C. Ogden wrote enthusiastically of the musical life in Bethlehem, this music had little or no direct influence on the main stream of contemporary American sacred music.

2. MUSICAL STRUCTURE AND SOURCES. The musical life of the American Moravian communities revolved around the musical needs of the church. The choir system divided the congregation administratively by age, sex, and marital status: there were separate choirs of young boys, young girls, older boys, older girls, single men, single women, married people, widows, and widowers; each choir had a member designated as its spiritual leader; there were often special residences for each choir, particularly the older unmarried men and women, and each had its own devotionals and festivals. The principal musical service was the love feast, which had a particular theme, expressed in a continuous succession of anthems, hymns, sacred duets, and solo songs compiled for the occasion. Love feasts were frequently held on church and choir festival days, for various celebrations (e.g., of welcome or farewell), and for personal anniversaries of important or beloved members of the congregation. The song hour, consisting entirely of hymns, was organized around a single thought or subject; the music was sung by the congregation with organ accompaniment. Song hours were held several evenings a week to learn new music and share in the joy of singing.

The principal musical form was the anthem or "Coro," scored for mixed chorus (usually SSAB) and a small instrumental ensemble (usually strings and organ, occasionally with wind instruments). Some composers, principally Herbst and Bechler, also wrote solo songs (or "ariettas") with keyboard accompaniment. The anthem was used mostly in the love feast; its text was compiled from biblical sources and the Moravian hymnal, and until about 1850 was usually in German. Hymns were sung at all the Sunday services: the German preaching service, the English preaching service, the individual choirs' devotionals, etc. The hymns were selected from the *Gesangbuch, zum Gebrauch der Evangelischen Brüdergemeinen* (Barby, 1778), and sung to chorale melodies (many dating from the Bohemian Brethren) collected in the *Choral-Buch enthaltend alle zu dem Gesangbuch der Evangelischen Brüder-Gemeinen von Jahre 1778 gehörige Melodien* (Leipzig, 1784).

The American Moravian musical manuscripts are held in the Archives of the Moravian Church at Bethlehem, and the Moravian Music Foundation at Winston-Salem; both are under the administration of the Moravian Music Foundation. The congregational music collections of Bethlehem, Nazareth, and Lititz, and Dover, Ohio, as well as the Bethlehem and Lititz collegia musica collections, are virtually intact in the Bethlehem archives. The Salem congregation, Salem collegium musicum, and Bethania congregation collections are in the Winston-Salem archive. The Moravian archives consist of approximately 10,000 manuscripts including some 7000 individual works; about two-thirds of these were written by composers connected with the Moravian Church, and about 30% of the total are by American Moravian composers. Several recordings of Moravian music have been made, notable among which are those directed by Thor Johnson in the 1950s and 1960s (*Vocal Music in Colonial America: the Moravians*, New Records 2017; *The Unknown Century of American Classical Music*, i–ii, Col. ML5427, MS6288; *Music of the American Moravians*, Odyssey 32160340).

See also EUROPEAN-AMERICAN MUSIC, §III, 5(ii).

BIBLIOGRAPHY

* – *reprinted by the Moravian Music Foundation*

J. Ogden: *An Excursion into Bethlehem and Nazareth in Pennsylvania in the Year 1799* (Philadelphia, 1800)

J. Henry: "Music at Bethlehem and Nazareth," *Sketches of Moravian Life and Character* (Philadelphia, 1859)

R. A. Grider: *Historical Notes on Music in Bethlehem, Pa. from 1741 to 1871* (Philadelphia, 1873/*R1957)

[A. G. Rau]: "The Moravian Contribution to Pennsylvania Music," *Church Music and Musical Life in Pennsylvania in the Eighteenth Century*, ii (Philadelphia, 1927)

T. M. Finney: "The Collegium Musicum at Lititz, Pennsylvania, during the Eighteenth Century," *PAMS 1937*, 45

A. G. Rau and H. T. David: *A Catalogue of Music by American Moravians, 1742–1842* (Bethlehem, PA, 1938/*R*1970)

H. T. David: "Musical Life in the Pennsylvania Settlements of the Unitas Fratrum," *Transactions of the Moravian Historical Society*, xiii (1942), 19; *repr. (1956)

D. M. McCorkle: "The Moravian Contribution to American Music," *Notes*, xiii (1955–6), 597; *repr. (1956)

——: "The Collegium Musicum Salem: its Music, Musicians and Importance," *North Carolina Historical Review*, xxxiii (1956), 483; *repr. (1956)

——: *Moravian Music in Salem* (diss., Indiana U., 1958)

W. H. Armstrong: *Organs for America* (Philadelphia, 1967)

H. H. Hall: *The Moravian Wind Ensemble: a Distinctive Chapter in America's Music* (diss., George Peabody College for Teachers, 1967)

J. T. Hamilton and K. G. Hamilton: *History of the Moravian Church* (Bethlehem, PA, 1967)

M. P. Gombosi: *Catalog of the Johannes Herbst Collection* (Chapel Hill, 1970)

E. V. Nolte: "Sacred Music in the Early American Moravian Communities," *Church Music* (St. Louis, 1971), no.2, p.16; *repr. (1971)

K. Kroeger: "Moravian Music in 19th-century American Tunebooks," *Moravian Music Foundation Bulletin*, xviii/1 (1973), 1

C. F. Rierson, Jr.: *The Collegium Musicum Salem* (diss., U. of Georgia, 1973)

K. Kroeger: "Moravian Music in America: a Survey," *Unitas Fratrum* (Utrecht, Netherlands, 1975), 387

E. W. Pressley: *Musical Wind Instruments in the Moravian Musical Archives, Salem, NC* (diss., U. of Kentucky, 1975)

D. C. Runner: *Music in the Moravian Community of Lititz* (diss., U. of Rochester, 1976)

M. P. Gombosi: *A Day of Solemn Thanksgiving* (Chapel Hill, 1977)

J. S. Ingram: "Moravians and Music in America," *Southern Humanities Conference: Winston Salem, 1977*, ed. W. E. Ray (Winston-Salem, NC, 1977), 54

F. A. Cumnock: "The Lovefeast Psalm: Questions and a Few Answers," *Moravian Music Foundation Bulletin*, xxiii/1 (1978), 2

D. P. Keehn: *The Trombone Choir of the Moravian Church in America* (thesis, West Chester State College, 1978)

K. Kroeger: "On the Early Performance of Moravian Chorales," *Moravian Music Foundation Bulletin*, xxiv/2 (1979), 2

F. A. Cumnock: *Catalog of the Salem Congregation Music* (Chapel Hill, 1980)

H. H. Hall: "Moravian Music Education in America, *c*1750 to *c*1830," *JRME*, xxix (1981), 225

R. F. Steelman: *Catalog of the Lititz Congregation Collection* (Chapel Hill, 1981)

J. D. Jueckstock: *The Complete Works of Jeremias Dencke (1725–1795)* (diss., Southwestern Baptist U., 1984)

KARL KROEGER

Moreira, Airto (Guimorva) (*b* Itaiópolis, Brazil, 5 Aug 1941). Jazz percussionist. Until 1968, when he went to Los Angeles, he played with his own groups in Brazil. After moving to New York in 1970 he made the first of several recordings with Miles Davis; he also appeared on the original Weather Report album, and was the first percussionist and drummer for Chick Corea's group Return to Forever. During the 1970s he became one of the best-known percussionists in jazz. He skillfully manipulated such small instruments as the tambourine and bongos, and introduced many exotic percussion instruments to jazz, including the cuíca and berimbau; his brilliantly effective playing raised the prestige of these instruments in the USA. Since 1973 Moreira has led his own bands and has appeared with his wife, the singer Flora Purim, for whom he also writes arrangements.

RECORDINGS

(selective list)

As leader: *Seeds on the Ground* (1970, Buddah 5085); *Free* (1972, CTI 6020); *Fingers* (1973, CTI 6028); *Identity* (1975, Ari. 4068); *Touching You, Touching Me* (1979, WB 3279)

As sideman: M. Davis: *Miles Davis at Fillmore* (1970, Col. KG30038); *Weather Report* (1971, Col. KC30661); *Return to Forever* (1973, ECM 1022); F. Purim: *Five Hundred Miles High at Montreux* (1974, Mlst. 9070)

BIBLIOGRAPHY

D. Morgenstern: "Music is a Beautiful Game," *Down Beat*, xl/5 (1973), 18

L. Underwood: "Airto and his Incredible Gong Show," *Down Beat*, xlv/8 (1978), 15

MICHAEL ULLMAN

Morel, Jean (*b* Abbeville, France, 10 Jan 1903; *d* New York, 14 April 1975). Teacher and conductor. In Paris he studied piano with Isidore Philipp, theory with Noël Gallon, music history with Maurice Emmanuel, composition with Gabriel Pierné, and the lyric repertory with Reynaldo Hahn. From 1921 to 1936 he taught at the American Conservatory in Fontainebleau, near Paris, and also conducted a variety of French orchestras. His teaching affected a generation of American students: from 1940 to 1943, having moved to New York, he taught at Brooklyn College, CUNY, but it was from 1949 to 1971 in his dual capacity as a teacher at the Juilliard School and as conductor of the Juilliard Orchestra that he wielded his strongest influence. Among his protégés were James Levine, Jorge Mester, and Leonard Slatkin. He conducted opera in Rio de Janeiro and Mexico and at the New York City Center Opera Company, and also, from 1956, at the Metropolitan Opera.

BIBLIOGRAPHY

Obituary, *New York Times* (16 April 1975)

BERNARD JACOBSON

Morel Campos, Juan (*b* Ponce, Puerto Rico, 16 May 1857; *d* Ponce, 12 May 1896). Composer. He studied harmony, counterpoint, composition, and piano with Tavárez, and was regarded as the latter's protégé. In 1877 he served as principal baritone player in Cazadores de Madrid, a battalion band in San Juan; after returning to Ponce he organized in 1882 a fireman's band which he continued to conduct until his death. He appeared throughout Puerto Rico as a conductor of dance music, was organist of a local church, and founded La Lira Ponceña, a small municipal orchestra. For visiting troupes he arranged operas and *zarzuelas*, and he himself toured South America as music director and conductor of the Compañia de Zarzuela Española Bernard y Arabella.

Although influenced in his compositions by Italian musicians who performed in Puerto Rico, Morel Campos achieved a significant national expression in his *danzas*, of which he wrote nearly 300. While most are for the piano, some are scored for ensembles. Some, such as *La lila* and *Alma sublime*, are stylized and highly Romantic, with full harmonies and virtuoso passages, while others are simpler and more popular in character, with incisive rhythms (*No me toques* and *La bulliciosa*). Concomitantly, Morel Campos contributed to the emergence of a recognizably Puerto Rican dance-music ensemble in which the clarinet and baritone horn are leading instruments. In addition to *danzas*, he wrote three *zarzuelas* (*Un viaje por América*, *Amor es triunfo*, and *Un día de elecciones*), 60 sacred works, and accomplished symphonic works including the overture *La lira* (1882) and *Puerto Rico* (1893), a full-scale symphony based on popular airs. His music is still widely performed in Latin America.

BIBLIOGRAPHY

F. Callejo Ferrer: *Música y músicos puertorriqueños* (San Juan, PR, 1915, 2/1971)

J. A. Balseiro: *Juan Morel Campos, el hombre y el músico* (San Juan, PR, 1922); repr. as "Juan Morel Campos y la danza puertorriqueña," *El vigía: ensayos*, i (Madrid, 1925–8), 253

A. Mirabel: *Próceres de arte: Juan Morel Campos, ensayo biografico* (Ponce, PR, 1956)

C. Pardo de Casablanca: "La producción musical de Morel Campos," *Ensayos y otros artículos* (San Juan, PR, 1968), 169

GUSTAVO BATISTA

Moret, Neil. Pseudonym of CHARLES NEIL DANIELS.

Morgan, Justin (*b* West Springfield, MA, 28 Feb 1747; *d* Randolph, VT, 22 March 1798). Composer and singing master. He probably received no more than rudimentary musical training in a singing-school, but his natural genius was great. In 1788 he settled in Vermont, but his duties as a teacher led him to travel, probably as far south as Pennsylvania. Although a skilled composer, Morgan never published a tunebook of his own, and no manuscripts of his music have come to light. Of his nine known compositions – two plain tunes, five fuging-tunes, an anthem, and a moving lament, *Despair*, on the death of his wife (all ed. in Bandel) – all but the lament were first published in Asahel Benham's *Federal Harmony* (1790). His fuging-tune "Montgomery" was reprinted more than 50 times before 1811; his lengthy *Judgment Anthem* is particularly striking, with its vividly pictorial text, insistent rhythms, athletic vocal lines, and startling shifts between E minor and E♭ major. The power and pathos of his text settings, the strength of his melodies, and the sensitivity of his harmony make Morgan one of the most eloquent composers of the period.

BIBLIOGRAPHY

F. J. Metcalf: *American Writers and Compilers of Sacred Music* (New York, 1925/*R*1967)

B. Bandel: *Sing the Lord's Song in a Strange Land: the Life of Justin Morgan* (Rutherford, NJ, 1981)

NYM COOKE

Morganfield, McKinley. *See* MUDDY WATERS.

Morgenstern, Dan (Michael) (*b* Munich, Germany, 24 Oct 1929). Writer on jazz. After coming to the USA in 1947, he studied at Brandeis University (1953–6). He was New York correspondent for *Jazz Journal* (of London) from 1958 to 1961 and served in various editorial capacities for *Metronome*, *Jazz*, and *Down Beat* from 1961 to 1973. He has produced jazz concerts in New York City and on television. In 1976 he became director of the Institute of Jazz Studies at Rutgers University and in 1978 lecturer in jazz history at the Peabody Conservatory. Morgenstern is the author or editor of several pamphlets on jazz issued by the New York Jazz Museum, including *Bird and Diz: a Bibliography* (1973), and has translated and edited Joachim Berendt's *The New Jazz Book* (1962).

PAULA MORGAN

Morini (Siracusano), Erica [Erika] (*b* Vienna, Austria, 5 Jan 1904). Violinist. She studied with her father, and from the age of seven with Otakar Ševčik at the Vienna Conservatory. Her successful Viennese début in 1916 led to performances with the Leipzig Gewandhaus Orchestra and the Berlin PO. On 26 January 1921 she made her American début in a concert at Carnegie Hall at which she played three concertos with the Metropolitan Opera Orchestra under Bodansky; this was followed by several highly praised recitals in which her large, sympathetic tone and reliable technique were especially noted. On her return to Europe after three years she was admired as one of the finest string players of a particularly brilliant generation. She left Austria during the Anschluss and settled in New York, taking American citizenship in 1943. She played with major American orchestras, and toured South America, Australia, and the Far East. Her playing was characterized by its generous emotional response to the music, and at her best she also displayed a degree of interpretive adaptability to an extremely wide repertory. Among her honors are doctorates from the New England Conservatory and Smith College.

BIBLIOGRAPHY

B. Schwarz: *Great Masters of the Violin* (New York, 1983)

RICHARD BERNAS/RUTH B. HILTON

Mormon Church, music of the. *See* CHURCH OF JESUS CHRIST OF LATTER-DAY SAINTS, MUSIC OF THE.

Mormon Tabernacle Choir. Popular name for the Salt Lake Mormon Tabernacle Choir, a well-known sectarian ensemble in SALT LAKE CITY.

Moross, Jerome (*b* Brooklyn, NY, 1 Aug 1913; *d* Miami, FL, 25 July 1983). Composer. He held a Juilliard Fellowship (1931–2) and graduated from New York University in 1932. Initially he supported himself by writing ballets and music for the theater, although his first complete show, the revue *Parade* (1935), was not a great success. George Gershwin engaged him as assistant conductor and pianist for a West Coast production of *Porgy and Bess*, and Moross began training the principals during the summer following Gershwin's death in July 1937. During this period he went to Chicago for a production of his ballet *American Pattern* and began work on one of his most successful scores, the ballet *Frankie and Johnny*. Other works which established Moross's early reputation include the orchestral pieces *Biguine, Paeans, A Tall Story*, and *Those Everlasting Blues*. When he went to Hollywood in 1940, however, he found that this very reputation effectively prevented him from finding work; his American vernacular idiom was not understood by Hollywood producers, who preferred the romanticized Americana epitomized by such works as Grofé's *Grand Canyon Suite*. So for nearly ten years Moross earned a living as an orchestrator of film scores, collaborating with Copland (*Our Town*), Waxman, Adolph Deutsch, Frederick Hollander, and Friedhofer (*The Best Years of our Lives*).

During this period Moross produced a substantial number of works, notably the First Symphony (which received its première in Seattle under Sir Thomas Beecham in 1943) and *Ballet Ballads*, a series of four one-act ballet-operas. Much of Moross's most interesting theater music has been cast in hybrid or experimental forms, such as ballet-opera, or for the semipopular musical stage; he has been especially concerned to reconcile elements derived from popular and art genres. The two-act opera *The Golden Apple* (including the song "Lazy Afternoon") and *Gentlemen, Be Seated!*, a portrait of the Civil War in the form of a minstrel show, belong to this category.

In 1948 Moross composed his first original film score (*Close-up*), and after the success of *When I Grow Up* (1950) he found himself able to give up commercial orchestration more or less permanently. Other effective scores include *The Proud Rebel*, *The Adventures of Huckleberry Finn*, *The Cardinal*, *The War Lord*, and *The Big Country*; the last-named is one of the finest scores written for a western, and was nominated for an Academy Award. Moross assembled the highlights of his film career from 1952 to 1965 in the suite *Music for the Flicks*. He composed less music in other genres during this period, but his ballet *The Last Judgement* (1953) must be ranked among his best works.

Among his last compositions, the Concerto for flute and string quartet and the Sonata for piano duet and string quartet epitomize Moross's facility for writing music which has both spontaneous popular appeal and strength of musical purpose. American folk and popular idioms form the basis of his style, which is plain and vigorous, diatonically simple, and full of lyrical warmth and expressiveness. Reminiscences of rags, blues, and stomps abound (e.g., in *Frankie and Johnny*), but these are informed both with formal discipline and personal impress. The tone is unfailingly positive, the aggressive, spotlit scoring uses instruments at the upper extremes of their ranges (as when a D trumpet crowns the climax of the First Symphony's fugal finale), and the counterpoint is clean and sharp.

WORKS

(selective list)

STAGE

Parade (revue), 1935
American Pattern (ballet), 1936
Frankie and Johnny (ballet), 1937–8; arr. as orch suite
Ballet Ballads (4 ballet-operas, each 1, J. Latouche): Susanna and the Elders, 1940–41; Willie the Weeper, 1945; The Eccentricities of Davy Crockett, 1945; Riding Hood Revisited, 1946
The Golden Apple (opera, 2, Latouche), 1948–50
The Last Judgement (ballet), 1953; arr. as orch suite
Gentlemen, Be Seated! (opera, E. Eager), 1955–6
Sorry, Wrong Number! (opera, after L. Fletcher), 1977

FILM AND TELEVISION MUSIC

Film scores: Close-up, 1948; When I Grow Up, 1950; The Sharkfighters, 1952; Captive City, 1952; Hans Christian Andersen, 1952 [incl. The Little Mermaid (ballet), based on themes by F. Liszt]; The Seven Wonders of the World, 1955 [only part by Moross]; The Proud Rebel, 1957; The Big Country, 1958, arr. as orch suite; The Adventures of Huckleberry Finn, 1959; The Jayhawkers, 1959; The Mountain Road, 1960; Five Finger Exercise, 1961; The Cardinal, 1963; The War Lord, 1965; Rachel, Rachel, 1967; The Valley of Gwangi, 1968; Hail, Hero, 1969
Music for television: Wagon Train, Lancer

OTHER WORKS

Orch: Paeans, 1931; Those Everlasting Blues (A. Kreymborg), v, small orch, 1932; Biguine, 1934; A Tall Story, 1938; Sym. no. 1, 1941–2; Variations on a Waltz, 1946–66; Music for the Flicks, suite, 1965 [based on film scores, 1952–65]
Chamber: Recitative and Aria, vn, pf, 1944; [4] Sonatinas for Divers Instruments,

cl choir, 1966, db, pf, 1966, brass qnt, 1969, ww qnt, 1970; Sonata, pf 4 hands, str qt, 1975; Conc., fl, str qt/str orch, 1978

BIBLIOGRAPHY

EwenD

A. Copland: "Our Younger Generation: Ten Years Later," *MM*, xiii/4 (1936), 3

C. Palmer: "Popular Appeal Plus Musical Purpose: the Film Music of Jerome Moross," *Crescendo International*, xi/11 (1973), 25

CHRISTOPHER PALMER

Morris, George P(ope) (*b* Philadelphia, PA, 10 Oct 1802; *d* New York, 6 July 1864). Poet and librettist. He was one of the best-known poets and most important editors of his time. The *New York Mirror and Ladies' Literary Gazette* and *New York Home Journal*, both of which Morris had a hand in founding and editing, were highly influential literary magazines. Among the composers who set his sentimental verse were Stephen Foster (*Open thy Lattice Love*), members of the Hutchinson family (*My Mother's Bible* and other poems), Henry Russell (*Woodman, Spare that Tree*, which became enormously popular; for illustration *see* PUBLISHING, fig.2), and C. E. Horn (*Near the Lake, where Droop'd the Willow*). With Horn, Morris wrote the opera, *The Maid of Saxony*, which was produced at the Park Theatre in New York in 1842.

BIBLIOGRAPHY

H. B. Wallace: "Memoir of George P. Morris," in G. P. Morris: *Poems* (New York, 3/1860)

N. F. Adkins: "Morris, George Pope," *DAB*

DALE COCKRELL

Morris, Harold (*b* San Antonio, TX, 17 March 1890; *d* New York, 6 May 1964). Composer and pianist. He studied at the University of Texas (BA) and the Cincinnati Conservatory (MM 1922), where his teachers included Kelley, Rothwell, Scalero, and Godowsky. For a time he toured the USA and Canada as a solo pianist. He taught at the Juilliard School (1922–39) and the Columbia University Teachers College (1935–46), and was guest professor at several universities, including Rice Institute, where he gave the lectures published as *Contemporary American Music* (1934). In addition, he was active in associations promoting modern music and served on the ISCM directorate. His music won many awards and was often performed in the 1940s. Its style shows neoromantic traits: much of it is programmatic or impressionistic, and the influence of Scriabin can be detected in the harmonic and tonal thinking. Some of the thematic material, as well as the use of Afro-American rhythms, draws on both black and white Southern folk music. Morris's form, though skillful, sometimes appears contrived.

WORKS

Orch: Poem [after Tagore: Gitanjali], 1915; Dum-a-lum, variations on a Negro spiritual, chamber orch, 1925; 3 syms., no.1 [after Browning: Prospice], 1925, no.2 "Victory," 1943, no.3 "Amaranth," 1946; Pf Conc. on 2 Negro Themes, 1927; Suite, chamber orch, 1927; Vn Conc., 1938; Passacaglia and Fugue, 1939; American Epic, 1942; Heroic Ov., 1943; Passacaglia, Adagio, and Finale, 1955; *c*10 other orch works, incl. Pf Conc. no.2, Joy of Youth, Lone Star (A Texas Saga), Sam Houston Suite

Chamber: 2 pf trios, 1917, 1933; Vn Sonata, 1919; 2 str qts, 1928, 1937; 2 pf qnts, 1929, 1937; Suite, pf, str, 1943; *c*5 other chamber works

Pf: 4 Sonatas, no.1, no.2, 1915, no.3, 1920, no.4, 1939; Ballade, 1938; many other pieces

BARBARA H. RENTON

Morris, Joan (Clair) (*b* Portland, OR, 10 Feb 1943). Mezzo-soprano. She studied singing at Gonzaga University, received a diploma in speech and acting from the American Academy of Dramatic Arts in 1968, and later studied voice privately with Federica Schmitz-Svevo. Her début recital, at Brooklyn College, CUNY, in 1973, included songs by Berlin, Kern, George Gershwin, Cole Porter, Rodgers and Hart, and other Americans. She later established herself as a leading interpreter of American song, with a repertory encompassing art songs and popular works ranging in time from the Colonial period to the modern era. A consummate singing actress, Morris displays a keen sensitivity to nuances of text and musical phrasing. She appears most often in concert with her husband, the composer and pianist WILLIAM BOLCOM, with whom she has recorded several albums of songs by Henry Russell, Henry Clay Work, and other American composers, especially of popular songs. She joined the faculty of the University of Michigan in 1981.

MICHAEL FLEMING

Morris, Kenneth (*b* New York, 28 Aug 1917). Gospel composer, pianist, and publisher. He studied classical piano in New York as a youth but soon gravitated towards jazz, playing with a jazz combo at the Century of Progress Exposition in Chicago in 1934. There ill-health forced him to take up a less strenuous life, and in 1935 he became a staff arranger for the gospel songwriter and publisher Lillian E. Bowles, replacing Charles Pace. In 1940, with Sallie Martin, he opened the Martin and Morris Music Company in Chicago, which he continued to direct in the 1980s. Morris has composed more than 300 gospel songs, the most popular being *Just a closer walk with thee* (1940), *My life will be sweeter someday* (1940), *Yes, God is real* (1944), and *Christ is all* (1946). His company has published music by all the major gospel composers, including James Cleveland, Alex Bradford, Dorothy Love Coates, W. Herbert Brewster, and Willie Mae Ford Smith, and it was one of the first publishers to transcribe works by untrained composers.

BIBLIOGRAPHY

H. C. Boyer: *The Gospel Song: a Historical and Analytical Study* (thesis, Eastman School of Music, 1964)

I. V. Jackson: *Afro-American Religious Music: a Bibliography and Catalogue of Gospel Music* (Westport, CT, 1979)

W. T. Walker: *Somebody's Calling My Name* (Valley Forge, PA, 1979)

HORACE CLARENCE BOYER

Morris, Robert (Daniel) (*b* Cheltenham, England, 19 Oct 1943). Composer and theorist. He studied with La Montaine at the Eastman School (BM 1965) and with Finney and Bassett at the University of Michigan (MM 1967, DMA 1969). He has received awards from BMI (1969), the American Music Center (1975), and the NEA (1978) and was Crofts Fellow at the Berkshire Music Center in 1967 and a MacDowell Fellow in 1976. He has taught at Yale University (1972–7), where he was chairman of the composition department, the University of Pittsburgh (1977–80), and the Eastman School (from 1980); he was director of the electronic music studios at Yale and Pittsburgh. He also performs as a pianist and with live electronics. As a theorist Morris specializes in 12-tone set theory, on which he has published a group of seminal papers including "A General Theory of Combinatoriality and the Aggregate" (with D. Starr, *PNM*, xvi/1, 1977, pp.3–35; xvi/2, 1978, pp. 50–84). For his research he has created several computer programs in Fortran. In his music Morris combines 12-tone procedures with technical processes from other musics: *Motet on Doo-Dah* (Stephen Foster's *Camptown Races*) links 12-tone techniques with 14th-century isorhythmic motet style and ornamentation derived from Korean court music. By such catholic mingling of compositional devices, he achieves polyphonic and timbral textures that reinforce the structural and temporal design of his music. A number of his works have been recorded.

WORKS

Dramatic: Hagoromo (Zeami), S, B, male vv, 2 fl, 3 vn, db, bells, 1977; incidental music

Orch: Syzygy, 1966; Continua, 1969; Streams and Willows, conc., fl, orch, 1972; In Different Voices, band, 1975; Tapestries, chamber orch, 1976; Interiors, 1977

Chamber: Varnam, 5 insts, perc, 1972; Motet on Doo-Dah, a fl, db, pf, 1973; Not Lilacs, a sax, tpt, pf, perc, 1974; Strata, 12 insts, 1974; Variations on the Variations on the Quadran Pavan and the Quadran Pavan by Bull and Byrd, 2 pf, 1974; Either Ether, pf, 1978; Plexus, ww qt, 1978; Allies, pf 4 hands, 1979; Tigers and Lilies, 12 sax, 1979; Inter alia, fl, ob, vc, 1980; Variations on a Theme of Steve Reich, pf, 1980; In Variations, vn, pf, 1981; Passim, 8 insts, 1981; Tournament, 12/24 trbn, 1981; *c*20 other chamber works; pf pieces

Vocal: Versus, 5 A, db, chamber ens, jazz ens, 1968; Reservoir, chorus, 1971; other choral works, songs

Elec: Entelechy, 1v, vc, pf, elec, 1969; Phases, 2 pf, elec, 1970; Rapport, synth, tape, 1971, rev. 1972; Thunders of Spring over Distant Mountains, tape, 1973; Bob's Palin Bobs, perc, tape, 1975; Entelechy '77, pf, elec, 1977; Flux Mandala, tape, 1978; Ghost Dances, fl, tape, 1980; Aubade, tape, 1981; several other elec pieces

Principal publishers: Asterisk, Walton

BIBLIOGRAPHY

G. E. Clarke: *Essays on American Music* (Westport, CT, 1978), 201

RICHARD SWIFT

Morrison, Van (*b* Belfast, Northern Ireland, 31 Aug 1945). Rock singer, songwriter, guitarist, and saxophonist. He learned to sing, and to play guitar, harmonica, and saxophone, from listening to his father's collection of blues records. He left high school in 1961 at the age of 16 and with his rhythm-and-blues group, the Monarchs, went to Germany. He returned to Belfast in 1963 and formed a group called Them, which in London in 1965 made a series of recordings that became hits, including *Gloria* and *Mystic Eyes* (which Morrison wrote), and *Here comes the night*, written by the producer Bert Berns. The group disbanded in 1966 and Berns brought Morrison to the USA. In 1967 *Brown Eyed Girl* reached the Top Ten and Morrison's first solo album, *Blowin' your Mind*, was issued on Berns's Bang label. In 1968 Morrison recorded *Astral Weeks*, an ambitious album of moody, poetic folk-jazz, which introduced his inimitable vocal style, with its stammering, scat-sung vocalises, and lyrics built on dreamlike, autobiographical imagery. It also featured an outstanding rhythm section made up of the jazz double-bass player Richard Davis and the drummer of the Modern Jazz Quartet, Connie Kay. The basic tracks were first loosely improvised, and arrangements for wind and strings were later added. Many critics consider *Astral Weeks* a masterpiece, though Morrison's next album, *Moondance* (1970), was much more popular; this took the same jazz and rhythm-and-blues elements as *Astral Weeks* but structured them into shorter pop songs.

Morrison has continually oscillated between the mystical, literary, folk-jazz style of *Astral Weeks* and the earthy, white-soul style of *Moondance*. *His Band and Street Choir* (1970) yielded the hit single *Domino* (no.9), and *Tupelo Honey* (1971) included *Wild Night* (no.28); on both albums the sound introduced on *Moondance* was softened with an infusion of country-rock elements. The breakup of Morrison's marriage led to a more brooding, eclectic recording, *Saint Dominic's Preview* (1972), which included hard-edged rhythm-and-blues, softer country-influenced tunes, and two long, ethereal pieces reminiscent of *Astral Weeks*. *Hard Nose the Highway* (1973) again attempted an approach based on several styles, but the songs were lightweight and uninspired; the Caledonian Soul Orchestra, which Morrison assembled to make this recording, toured with him as a 12-piece band, and the double album made during the tour, *It's too Late to Stop Now* (1974), including a number of cover versions of blues songs, is one of the best concert albums recorded by a rock performer.

In 1974, inspired by a trip to Ireland, Morrison recorded *Veedon Fleece*, a haunting album that contains some of his most cryptic lyrics. For the next three years, in a state of depression and drinking heavily, Morrison played with local bands in the San Francisco Bay area. With the collaboration of Dr. John as bandleader, he returned to recording with *Period of Transition* (1977), an album of uneven quality. *Wavelength* (1978) was much sharper and the captivating title song made an effective single, but the lyrics on the album as a whole were undistinguished. He finally regained his earlier strength, variety, and energy with *Into the Music* (1979), which combined urban and country blues in the faster numbers with the Irish folk-jazz and poetic lyrics of his earlier extended pieces. *Common One* (1980), his most effusively romantic work, quotes English poetry, contains two songs lasting more than 15 minutes, and is marked by lush string arrangements that seem to take the indulgence of *Astral Weeks* to an extreme. Just as he had followed that album with the more tightly programmed *Moondance*, Morrison turned from the overflowing moods of *Common One* to dazzling, sophisticated pop arrangements in *Beautiful Vision* (1982), a celebration of religious joy with touches of gospel singing and instrumental textures influenced by cool jazz. *The Inarticulate Speech of the Heart* (1983) continued in this manner, but with its unprecedented number of instrumental compositions, its quiet mood, and subtle coloration, it tends towards background music. His long association with Warner Bros. terminated after this recording. He released the album *Sense of Wonder* on Mercury in 1984.

Morrison's music is eccentric and personal, yet in spite of this accessible to a wide audience. A brilliantly original artist, he has pursued the romantic aim of expressing the inexpressible through his improvisatory singing style, visionary lyrics, and imaginative arrangements, producing music that variously explores, contrasts, and combines stylistic elements drawn from rhythm-and-blues, folk, pop, and jazz.

RECORDINGS

(selective list; recorded for Warner Bros. unless otherwise stated)

Them (Parrot 71005, 1965); *Blowin' your Mind* (Bang 21, 1967); Brown Eyed Girl (Bang 545, 1967); *Astral Weeks* (1768, 1968); *Moondance* (1835, 1970); *His Band and Street Choir* (1884, 1970); *Tupelo Honey* (1950, 1971); *Saint Dominic's Preview* (2633, 1972); *Hard Nose the Highway* (2712, 1973); *It's too Late to Stop Now* (2760, 1974); *Veedon Fleece* (2805, 1974); *Period of Transition* (2987, 1977); *Wavelength* (3212, 1978); *Into the Music* (3390, 1979); *Common One* (3462, 1980); *Beautiful Vision* (3652, 1982); *The Inarticulate Speech of the Heart* (23802, 1983); *Sense of Wonder* (Mer. 822895-1, 1984)

BIBLIOGRAPHY

G. Marcus and H. Traum: "Van Morrison," *Rolling Stone*, no.62 (9 July 1970), 30

G. Cannon: "What's so Special about Van Morrison?," *Melody Maker*, xlvi (20 March 1971), 23

——: "Van – Them and Now," *Melody Maker*, xlvi (27 March 1971), 23

Van Morrison: Them and Now: being a Complete History of his U.S. Recordings from 1963 to the Present Day (Kingston, England, 1976)

J. Cott: "Van Morrison," *Rolling Stone*, no.279 (30 Nov 1978), 50
H. A. DeWitt: *Van Morrison: the Mystic's Music* (Fremont, CA, 1983)
J. Rogan: *Van Morrison: a Portrait of the Artist* (London, 1984)

JOHN PICCARELLA

Morrow, Charlie [Charles Geoffrey] (*b* Newark, NJ, 9 Feb 1942). Composer. He was educated at Columbia University (BA 1962) and the Mannes College of Music (diploma in composition, 1965), where he was a pupil of Sydeman. In 1968 he founded Charles Morrow Associates to produce commercial music, a field in which he has remained active. With La Barbara and others he began in 1973 a cooperative improvisational group, the New Wilderness Preservation Band; the same year he became artistic director of the New Wilderness Foundation, which produces concerts and sponsors *Ear* magazine. For his music Morrow has received two Creative Artists Public Service grants (1973, 1975) and an NEA grant (1978); he has won CLIO awards for his commercial music.

Morrow blends spontaneous sounds and movements with organized, pre-planned music and gesture, drawing on diverse instruments among which horns, whistles, and trumpets are prominent. For many works he has borrowed elements from other cultures, notably American Indian rattles and the extended chanting used in their ceremonies, as in *66 Songs for a Blackfoot Bundle* (1971). His outdoor "events" make use of their surroundings, both aural and visual, and often require very large performing forces; for example, *Toot 'n Blink Chicago*, performed as part of the New Music America festival of 1982, is for boat horns and lights, conducted by radio announcers. The events are usually planned to coincide with intrinsically significant moments in nature such as the summer solstice.

WORKS

Events: Triangulation Pieces, ens, radio transmitter, 2 repeater pickups, 1970; Blessingway – A Celebration, 1973; Sunrise Event, 1973; New Wilderness Riff Off – Open Jam in Central Park, 1974; Chanting Workshop, 1976; Cross Currents, 2 rock bands, American Indian and South Indian musicians, 2 composers, dancer, 1977; New Wilderness Country Fair, 100 artists, 1978; Inauguration Event, 1981; An Event for Art on the Beach, conch shells, cymbals, perc, 1981; Heavyweight Sound Fight, 1981; Toot 'n Blink Chicago, marine radios, horns, lights, 1982; Explosion at Penn Station, 1984; Citywave, 4000 pfmrs, 1985; other works, incl. Summer Solstice series and media (broadcast) events

Performance pieces: Toccata for Musicians and Audience, 1961; Dance Music for the Blind, dancers, contact mics, blind/blindfolded audience, 1962; A Little Brigati Music, 1969, collab. J. Rothenberg; 66 Songs for a Blackfoot Bundle, play, 9 musicians, 1971; A Healing Piece – A Non-verbal Piece, actors, 1972; Apsis, chanting weavers, audience, 1972; Fish and Frog Languages, 1974; Chanting in 6 Voices, 1975; The Light Opera, singers, actors, lights, sound system, 1983; many other works, 1957–84

Other: orch works, incl. Conc. for Bandoneon, 1968, and Variations on a Persian Theme, 1973; band works, incl. Two Charlie Event, 1973, and New Wilderness Preservation Band Pieces, 1973–4; many chamber ens works, incl. 3 str qts, 1964–7, and Bach Reconstructions, 4 pieces, 1970; many choral works; songs; kbd pieces; many film scores; incidental music for plays; dance scores; tape works, incl. Marilyn Monroe Collage, 1967; jingles and other commercial music

BIBLIOGRAPHY

W. Zimmermann: *Desert Plants: Conversations with 23 American Musicians* (Vancouver, BC, 1976), 269
T. Johnson: "And in this Corner," *Village Voice* (31 March 1981), 87
J. Rockwell: "'Druids' Mark Solstice Euphoniously," *New York Times* (22 June 1982)
T. Page: "'Light Opera' Composer is Also Writer of Jingles," *New York Times* (17 June 1983)
——: "Music: 30 Harpists Fill a Cathedral," *New York Times* (25 Sept 1984)

JOAN LA BARBARA

Morse, Theodore (*b* Washington, DC, 13 April 1873; *d* New York, 25 May 1924). Composer and publisher. He came to New York at the age of 14 and was employed as a clerk in various publishing houses. He also performed incidental music, and by 1898 was composing. In the same year he founded his own publishing house, but sold it in 1900 and joined the firm of Howley, Haviland & Dresser. During the next eight years Morse wrote several successful songs. After Dresser's death and the collapse of his firm, in 1905, Morse and Haviland formed their own company. About five years later Morse left Haviland and organized the Morse Music Company, but in 1915 he sold his holdings to Leo Feist, with whom he was associated until his death. Morse was also a performer; he appeared in a vaudeville trio with two other songwriters and was pianist for Henry Burr's Record Makers from 1916 to 1918.

As a composer Morse's earliest successes were sentimental ballads with lyrics by Raymond A. Browne, but his most characteristic works are lively love songs and novelty pieces (jungles and monkeys were favorite topics) with lyrics by Edward Madden and Jack Drislane. These are in brisk duple meter with energetic but conventional melodies; Morse's stylistic strengths were his lively rhythms and occasional spicy harmonies. His most famous song, *M-O-T-H-E-R* (1915, lyrics by Howard Johnson), was atypically maudlin. He also set texts by Richard Henry Buck, Vincent Bryan, and his wife, Alfreda Theodora Strandberg Morse (*b* Brooklyn, NY, 11 July 1890; *d* White Plains, NY, 10 Nov 1953). In collaborations with her husband, she used the names D. A. Esrom, Dorothy Terriss, and Dolly Morse; her most famous texts ("Three o'clock in the morning" and "My wonderful one") were set by other composers. She has been credited with the words to *Hail, hail, the gang's all here*, but her authorship of this is disputed.

WORKS

(selective list; all for 1v, pf, most published in New York)

In the Moonlight (1902); Dear Old Girl (1903); Hurray for Baffin's Bay (1903); Up in the Coconut Tree (1903); Blue Bell (1904); I've got a feelin' for you (1904); Woodchuck Song (1904); Keep a little cozy corner in your heart for me (1905); Starlight (1905); Arrah Wanna (1906); Keep on the sunny side (1906); In Monkey Land (1907); Down in Jungle Town (1908); I've taken quite a fancy to you (1908); Another Rag (1911); When Uncle Joe plays a rag on his old banjo (1912); M-O-T-H-E-R (1915); Sing me love's lullaby (1917)

BIBLIOGRAPHY

Obituary: *Clipper*, lxxii (31 May 1924), 17
J. Walsh: "Theodore Morse: a Centenary Tribute," *Hobbies*, lxxviii (1973), no.2, p.37; no.3, p.37
W. Craig: *Sweet and Lowdown* (Metuchen, NJ, 1978)

WILLIAM BROOKS

Morton, Benny [Henry Sterling] (*b* New York, 31 Jan 1907). Jazz trombonist. He first attracted attention as a member of Fletcher Henderson's orchestra in 1926 when he displayed his precocious talents on a recording of *Jackass Blues*. After distinguished periods in big bands led by Don Redman (1931–7) and Count Basie (1937–40), Morton concentrated on playing in small groups, where his unfailing reliability and thoughtful musicianship were always apparent. From 1940 to 1943 he worked with the Teddy Wilson Sextet, then joined Ed Hall's Sextet until he formed his own band in September 1944. After disbanding this group in January 1946 he worked for several years in Broadway theater orchestras and also played freelance with Red Allen, the Saints and Sinners, and Wild Bill Davison, among others. He toured with the World's Greatest Jazz Band in 1973–4 and resumed playing in the late 1970s after a period of illness. A disciple of Jimmy Harrison's playing, Morton was by nature a sideman rather than a leader; he did, however, organize his own recording bands with considerable success, notably on *The Gold Digger's Song* and *Conversing in Blue*. Although not an outstanding innovator, he was always capable of improvising interesting solos, and every performance was graced with feeling and an exquisite tone.

RECORDINGS
(selective list)

As leader: The Gold Digger's Song (1934, Col. 2924D); Conversing in Blue (1945, BN 46)

As sideman: F. Henderson: Jackass Blues (1926, Col. 654D); D. Redman: I Got Rhythm (1932, Bruns. 6354); E. Hall: Big City Blues (1944, BN 36); B. Clayton: Kandee, on *Buck Meets Ruby* (1954, Van. 8008)

BIBLIOGRAPHY

SouthernB

R. Bolton: "A Study in Excellence," *Jazz Journal*, xxvii/2 (1974), 4

JOHN CHILTON

Morton, Jelly Roll [LaMothe; Lemott, Ferdinand Joseph] (*b* New Orleans, LA, 20 Oct 1890; *d* Los Angeles, CA, 10 July 1941). Jazz composer and pianist.

1. Life. 2. Achievement.

1. LIFE. He grew up in New Orleans, starting to learn piano at the age of 10. By 1902 he was working in the bordellos of Storyville, playing ragtime, French quadrilles, and other popular dances and songs as well as a few light (mostly operatic) classics. Nothing is known of his formal musical training, but his major youthful influence appears to have been the early New Orleans ragtime pianist and entertainer Tony Jackson. Around 1904 Morton became an itinerant pianist, working in many cities in Louisiana, Mississippi, Alabama, and Florida. He was also apparently quite active as a gambler, pool player, and procurer, though music remained his first "line of business." Retaining New Orleans as his base, he later extended his travels to Memphis, St. Louis, and Kansas City, frequently working for prolonged periods in minstrel shows; eventually he traveled as far east as New York (where the pianist James P. Johnson heard Morton play his *Jelly Roll Blues* in 1911), and as far west as Los Angeles, where he arrived in 1917. During these dozen years of travel Morton apparently fused a variety of black musical idioms – ragtime, vocal and instrumental blues, items from the minstrel show repertory, field and levee hollers, religious hymns, and spirituals – with hispanic music from the Caribbean and white popular songs, creating a musical amalgam that bore a very close resemblance to the music then beginning to be called "jazz."

Morton enjoyed such success in Los Angeles that he remained there for five years. In 1922, however, he moved to Chicago, the new center of jazz activity. His first recordings were made there in 1923: two performances with a sextet (*Big Foot Ham* and *Muddy Water Blues*) and a series of solo piano renditions of his own works. The compositional maturity and the advanced conception of the ensemble and solo writing revealed in these recordings suggest that Morton's style must have crystallized many years previously. By 1926–7 Morton was recording with his Red Hot Peppers, a seven- or eight-piece band organized for recording purposes and comprising colleagues well-versed in the New Orleans style and familiar with Morton's music. The resultant recordings were a triumphant fusion of composition and improvisation. Pieces like *Grandpa's Spells*, *Black Bottom Stomp*, and *The Pearls* are masterly examples of Morton's creative talents, not only as composer–arranger but also as pianist. These works were ingeniously conceived so as to yield a maximum variety of texture and timbre without sacrificing clarity of form (see ex. 1); furthermore, unlike most jazz performances in those days, they were carefully rehearsed. Particularly noteworthy is the manner in which Morton provides opportunities for all seven performers to contribute significant solos (usually climaxing in exultant two-

Ex.1 From *Grandpa's Spells*, recorded by the Red Hot Peppers (1926, Vic. 20221), transcr. G. Schuller

continued on p.280

bar breaks) without losing sight of overall structural unity and a balance between solo and ensemble. As pianist Morton contributed not only some of his most inspired solos, such as those on *Smokehouse Blues* and *Black Bottom Stomp* (see ex.2), but also sensitive counter-melodies that were without precedent in 1920s jazz; no similar ideas were taken up until the arrival of Earl Hines and Art Tatum some years later.

In 1928 Morton moved to New York. There he continued to record such pieces (not necessarily his own) as *Kansas City Stomp*, *Tank Town Bump*, *Low Gravy*, and *Blue Blood Blues*. He gradually made use of such "modern" devices as homophonically harmonized ensembles and laid a greater emphasis on solo improvisation. However, he remained at heart true to the New Orleans spirit of collective improvisation and was never able to assimilate the new orchestral styles advanced in the late 1920s by Don Redman, Fletcher Henderson, and John Nesbitt. By 1930 Morton's style, both as arranger and pianist, came to be regarded as antiquated. Ironically, some of his compositions, such as *Wolverine Blues*, *Milenberg Joys*, and especially *King Porter Stomp*, continued to be performed regularly, remaining as influential pieces in the repertory throughout the 1930s. Indeed, it was Benny Goodman's performance of the last-named title, in Fletcher Henderson's updated arrangement (1935), that was largely responsible for ushering in the swing era.

In the early 1930s Morton drifted into obscurity. He settled in Washington, DC, where he managed a jazz club and also played intermittently. In 1938 the folklorist Alan Lomax, later Morton's biographer, recorded him in an extensive series of interviews held at the Library of Congress (issued on disc in 1948 and reissued in 1957). In this invaluable oral history Morton recalled in words and performances his early days in New Orleans, recreating the styles of many of his turn-of-the-century contemporaries. His accounts, both verbal and pianistic, have the ring of authenticity, and revealed Morton as jazz's earliest musician-historian and a perceptive theorist and analyst of the music. The Library of Congress recordings rekindled public interest in Morton, eventually leading to further recording sessions in 1939–40 and, in tandem with the New Orleans revival, a renewed career; this was cut short in 1940, however, owing to his ill health.

2. Achievement. Morton was the first important jazz composer. His compositions, many written long before he began recording, represent a rich synthesis of Afro-American musical elements, particularly as embodied in the pure New Orleans collective style which he helped to develop to its finest expression. Paradoxically, his emphasis on composition and well-rehearsed, coordinated performances was unique and antithetical to the primarily extemporized, polyphonic New Orleans style. In his best ensemble work, especially with the Red Hot Peppers, Morton showed that composition and meticulously rehearsed arrangements were not incompatible with the spontaneity of improvised jazz but could in fact retain and enhance it. In this respect Morton's achievement can be ranked with that of Duke Ellington, Thelonious Monk, Charles Mingus, and Gil Evans.

Morton's sophisticated conception of jazz is all the more remarkable since the origins of his style lie primarily in classic midwestern ragtime and simple instrumental blues. His piano pieces (such as *Grandpa's Spells* and *Kansas City Stomp*) strongly resemble ragtime in their form, but by elaborating these works with composed and improvised variation Morton was able to

Ex.2 Morton's solo chorus from *Black Bottom Stomp* (1926), transcr. G. Schuller

Jelly Roll Morton, c1926

transcend ragtime's formal conventions. Ultimately he freed ragtime from its narrow strictures by developing within it an ensemble style embracing homophony, improvised polyphony, solo improvisations, breaks, and a constant variation of texture and timbre.

WORKS

(selective list; dates of composition are mostly conjectural)

* – date of first solo piano recording; † – date of first ensemble recording
© – date of copyright

Edition: *The Collected Piano Music of Ferdinand "Jelly Roll" Morton*, ed. J. Dapogny (Washington, DC, 1982)

New Orleans Blues, 1902, © 1925, *1923 (Gennett 5486); Jelly Roll Blues, 1905, © 1915, *1924 (Gennett 5552), †1926 (Bluebird 10255); King Porter Stomp, 1906, © 1924, *1923 (Gennett 5289), †1924 (Autograph 617); Buffalo Blues, 1907, © 1928, *1939 (General 4004), †1928 (Col. 14358); Georgia Swing, 1907, © 1928, †1928 (Vic. 38024); Frog-i-more Rag (Sweetheart o' Mine), 1908, © 1918, *1924 (Para. 14032); The Crave, 1910–11, © 1939, *1938 (Circle 31); Bert Williams, 1911, © 1948, *1938 (Circle 45–71); Grandpa's Spells, 1911, © 1923, *1923 (Gennett 5218), †1926 (Bluebird 10254)

Wolverine Blues, 1915–16, © 1923, *1923 (Gennett 5289), †1925 (Autograph 623); Mamanita, 1917–22, © 1949, *1924 (Para. 12216); Kansas City Stomp, 1919, © 1923, *1923 (Gennett 5218), †1928 (Vic. 38010); The Pearls, 1919, © 1923, *1923 (Gennett 5323), †1927 (Vic. 20948); Big Foot Ham, 1923, © 1923, *1924 (Gennett 5552), †1923 (Para. 12050); London Blues (Shoe Shiner's Drag), 1923, © 1923, *1924 (Rialto, unnumbered), †1923 (OK 8105); Mr. Jelly Lord, 1923, © 1923, *1924 (Vocal Style Song Roll 12973), †1923 (Para. 20332); Milenberg Joys, 1924, © 1925, *1924 (unissued), †1926 (unissued)

Perfect Rag (Sporting House Rag), 1924, © 1939, *1924 (Gennett 5486); Shreveport Stomp, 1924, © 1925, *1924 (Gennett 5590), †1928 (Vic. 21658); Black Bottom Stomp (Queen of Spades), 1925, © 1925, †1926 (Vic. 20221); Dead Man Blues, 1926, © 1926, *1926 (QRS 3674), †1926 (Vic. 20252); Fickle Fay Creep, 1926, © 1930, *1938 (Circle 32–46), †1926 (OK 8404); Hyena Stomp, 1927, © 1927, *1938 (Circle 8–55), †1927 (Vic. 20772); Jungle Blues, 1927, © 1927, *1938 (Circle 32–46), †1927 (Bluebird 10256); Sweet Peter, 1929, © 1933, *1938 (Circle 73–69), †1929 (Vic. 23402)

BIBLIOGRAPHY

J. R. Morton: "I Created Jazz in 1902," *Down Beat*, v (Aug 1938), 3
C. E. Smith: "Oh, Mr. Jelly!," *Jazz Record*, no.17 (1944), 8
J. R. Morton: "Fragment of an Autobiography," *Record Changer*, iv (1944), March, p.15; April, p.27
O. Simeon: "Mostly about Morton," *Jazz Record*, no.37 (1945), 5
P. E. Miller, ed.: *Esquire's 1946 Jazz Book* (New York, 1946)
R. Blesh and H. Janis: *They All Played Ragtime* (New York, 1950, rev. 4/1971)
A. Lomax: *Mister Jelly Roll* (New York, 1950, 2/1973)
M. Williams: Liner notes, *Jelly Roll Morton: the Library of Congress Recordings* (Riv. 9001–9012, 1957)
S. B. Charters: *Jazz: New Orleans: 1885–1957* (Belleville, NJ, 1958, rev. 2/1963)
W. Russell: "Morton and *Frog-i-more Rag*," *The Art of Jazz*, ed. M. Williams (New York, 1959/*R*1979)
R. Hadlock: "Morton's Library of Congress Albums," *Jazz*, i (1959), 133
K. Hulsizer: "Jelly Roll Morton in Washington," *This Is Jazz*, ed. K. Williamson (London, 1960), 202
D. Locke: "Jelly Roll Morton: the Library of Congress Recordings," *Jazz Journal*, xiii/1 (1960), 15
G. Waterman: "Jelly Roll Morton," *Jazz Panorama*, ed. M. Williams (New York, 1962/*R*1965), 31
M. Williams: *Jelly Roll Morton* (London, 1962)
C. E. Smith: Liner notes, *Stomps and Joys* (Vic. LPV508, 1964)
K. Kramer: "Jelly Roll in Chicago: the Missing Chapter," *The Ragtimer*, vi/1 (1967), 15
M. Williams: *Jazz Masters of New Orleans* (New York 1967/*R*1979)
J. R. T. Davis and L. Wright: *Morton's Music* (London, 1968)
G. Schuller: *Early Jazz: its Roots and Musical Development* (New York, 1968)
M. Williams: *The Jazz Tradition* (New York, 1970, rev. 2/1983)
M. A. Hood and H. N. Flint, eds.: *"Jelly Roll" Morton: the Original Mr. Jazz* (New York, 1975)
L. Wright: *Mr. Jelly Lord* (Chigwell, England, 1980)
L. Gushee: "Would you Believe Ferman Morton?," *Storyville*, no.95 (1981), 164; no.98 (1981–2), 56
W. Balliett: *Jelly Roll, Jabbo and Fats* (New York, 1983), 16
J. Dapogny: "Jelly Roll Morton and Ragtime," *Ragtime: its History, Composers, and Music*, ed. J. E. Hasse (New York, 1985), 257
L. Gushee: "A Preliminary Chronology of the Early Career of Ferd "Jelly Roll" Morton," *American Music*, iii (1985), 389

GUNTHER SCHULLER

Moryl, Richard (*b* Newark, NJ, 23 Feb 1929). Composer and conductor. His early professional experience included arranging popular music, performing in touring bands, and conducting for the US Army. Subsequently he attended Montclair State College, Montclair, New Jersey (BA 1957), and Columbia University (MA 1959). He also studied with Boris Blacher at the Berlin Hochschule für Musik, on a Fulbright grant (1963–4), and with Arthur Berger at Brandeis University (1970). He has received numerous awards, including grants from the Ford Foundation (1973), the NEA (1973, 1975), and the Martha Baird Rockefeller Fund for Music (1977). From 1960 to 1970 and from 1973 he has taught at Western Connecticut State College; he also spent two years at Smith College (1970–72). He founded the New England Contemporary Music Ensemble in 1970 and has been its director for many years; with his wife, the pianist Joanne Moryl, he founded and then directed (from 1979) the Charles Ives Center for American Music, presenting each summer a week-long composers' conference and concert series devoted to a particular aspect of American music.

Moryl's own compositions are an eclectic fusion of elements from both past and present: *Das Lied* (1975) has obvious and literal connections with Mahler's *Das Lied von der Erde*, and *Atlantis* (1976) quotes from Lassus and Varèse. While rigorously controlling certain elements, Moryl reveals a sense of fantasy and humor, creating colorful, evocative sounds and combining "precise *notation* and spontaneous *manner*" (Whittenberg). Moryl has used an acute aural imagination to develop his appealing, abstract lyrical style.

WORKS

Orch: Serenade, vn, orch, 1967; Multiples, amp chamber orch, 1968; Total, 1969; Balloons, solo perc, orch, radios, audience, 1971; Volumes, pf, org, large orch, 1971; Chroma, 1972; Loops, large orch, tape, 1973; Meta, large orch, lights, 1973; Optima, band, 1973; Particles, low/high ens, 1974; Strobe, large orch (any insts), 1974; The Untuning of the Skies, 1981; The Pond, fl, chamber orch, 1984

Inst: over 20 works incl. Improvisations, fl, cl, vn, vc, mic, 1967; Systems, db, 1968; Contacts, pf/amp pf, perc, 1968; Modules, pf, ob, trbn, perc, 1969; Salvos, tpt, 1969; Soundings, ww qnt, opt. tape, 1970; Corners, 4 tpt, 1970; Strobe, hpd, vc, mar, 1972; Particles, pf, 1973; Summer's Music, fl, ob, gui, 1977; Rainbows, tpt, 1980; Rainbows II, db + perc, b fl + perc, 1982; Rainbows III, tape, any insts/vv, 1983; The Golden Pheonix, str qt + perc, 1983–4

Vocal: Many Moons (chamber opera, 2, J. Thurber), 1963; Flourescents, 2 choruses SATB, 2 perc, org, 1970; Illuminations, S, 4 choruses SATB, chamber orch, 1970; Aria, 6 solo vv, 8vv, db, tuba, perc, 1972; De morte cantoris (Joyce, Requiem text), S, Mez, ob, pf/cel, harp, 2 perc, 1973; Das Lied (H. Bethge), S, ob, amp db, amp pf, perc, 1975; Stabat Mater (In memoriam Horace Grenell), solo vv, SATB + perc, pf, 1982; Come, Sweet Death, SATB, pf, 1983; 3 other choral works

Mixed media: Passio avium (Yeats), nar, S, T, mime, dancer, ob, vc, amp pf/hpd, perc, 1974; Atlantis, mime, eng hn, amp pf, perc, tape, 1976; Visiones mortis, amp fl, amp vc, amp pf, slides, tape, 1977; Music of the Spheres, ob, cb cl, amp pf, lights, slides, tape, 1977; An Island in the Moon (Blake), S, pf, slides, 1978; A Sunflower for Maggie, cb cl/slide whistle, perc, pf, slides, 1979

Tape: 14 works incl. 8 for tape, inst

Principal publishers: ACA, Joshua

BIBLIOGRAPHY

C. Whittenberg: "Younger American Composers: Richard Moryl, *Multiples*," *PNM*, viii/1 (1969), 126

BARBARA A. PETERSEN

Moseley, Carlos (Du Pré) (*b* Laurens, SC, 21 Sept 1914). Administrator and pianist. After graduating from Duke University (1935) he did graduate work at the University of Michigan and the Philadelphia Conservatory. He later studied piano under Harold Morris and Olga Samaroff and appeared in recitals and as a soloist, winning the MacDowell Young Artists Competition in 1939. During and after the war he held various government positions, and then became director of the school of music and professor of music (piano) at the University of Oklahoma, Norman (1950–55). He was director of press and public relations (1955–9), associate managing director (1959–61), and managing director (1961–70) of the New York PO, and president of the New York Philharmonic-Symphony Society in 1970–78; this was the first time a major American symphony orchestra had appointed a professional, salaried president. Since his retirement he has continued his performing career as well as administrative duties; in 1984 he became chairman of the board of the Philharmonic.

Moseley made a lasting impression on the New York PO. Besides working as an administrator he helped to shape its artistic policies in the later years of Leonard Bernstein's tenure as music director and, especially, from 1969 in the years under Pierre Boulez. Certain innovations, such as the Promenade Concerts (begun in 1963), the concerts in New York's parks (begun in 1965), and the "Rug Concerts" (1974–8), were largely or wholly due to Moseley. His working relationship with Boulez was a model of how artistic and administrative activities can unite to achieve a result that is both artistically fruitful and appropriate to the needs of the time.

PATRICK J. SMITH

Moses(-Tobani), Theodore. *See* TOBANI, THEODORE MOSES.

Moss, Lawrence K(enneth) (*b* Los Angeles, CA, 18 Nov 1927). Composer and teacher. He attended UCLA (BA 1949), the Eastman School (MA 1950), and the University of Southern California (PhD 1957), where he studied with Dahl and Kirchner. After teaching at Mills College (1956–9) and Yale University (1960–68), he joined the faculty of the University of Maryland in 1969. His honors include Fulbright (1953–4), Guggenheim (1959–60, 1968–9), and Maryland Artist (1980) fellowships, and grants and commissions from the Fromm Foundation (1961), New Haven SO (1967), NEA (1975, 1977, 1980, 1981), University of Maryland International Piano Festival (1979), and the Kindler Foundation (1981). Moss's music is characterized by a concern for the shapes of linear events, which are often presented in transparent polyphony. Timbral relationships play a large part in shaping global structures. He has used electronic sounds in conjunction with conventional instruments, as in *Auditions*, to extend sonorities and structures; works from the early 1980s involve dancers, actors, and various light arrangements (*Dreamscape* and *Images*). His recorded works include the Violin Sonata, *Timepiece*, *Evocation and Song*, Fantasy for piano, and *Flight*.

WORKS

Stage: The Brute (comic opera, Chekhov), 1960; The Queen and the Rebels (opera, U. Betti), 1965, rev. 1981; Unseen Leaves (theater piece, Whitman), S, ob, tapes, slides, lights, 1975; Nightscape (theater piece, J. G. Brown), S, fl, cl, vn, perc, dancer, tape, slides, 1978; Dreamscape (A. Lusby-Pinchot), dancer, tape, lights, 1980; Images, dancer, cl, tape, 1981; Rites, dancer, slides, tape, 1983; Song to the Floor, dancer, tape, 1984

Orch: Suite, 1950; Scenes, chamber orch, 1961; Paths, 1970; Syms., brass qnt, chamber orch, 1977

4–8 insts: 3 Str Qts, 1958, 1975, 1980; Music for 5, brass qnt, 1963; Remembrances, 8 insts, 1964; Patterns, fl, cl, va, pf, 1967; Exchanges, 2 fl, ob, 2 tpt, trbn, perc, 1968; Auditions, ww qnt, tape, 1971; Flight, brass qnt, 1979; Chanson (Omaggio III), 8 fl, 1979

2–3 insts: Trio, fl, vn, vc, 1953; Vn Sonata, 1959; Windows, fl, b cl, db, 1966; Elegy, 2 vn, va, 1969; Timepiece, vn, pf, perc, 1970; Evocation and Song, a sax, tape, 1972; B. P.: a Melodrama, trbn, pf, tape, 1976; Toot-sweet, ob, 2 perc, 1976; Omaggio II, pf 4 hands, tape, 1977; Little Suite, ob, hpd, 1978; Hands across the C, pf, tape, 1979; Aprèsludes, fl, perc, 1983; V/Aria, va, tape, 1984

Solo inst: Fantasia, pf, 1952; 4 Scenes, pf, 1961; Omaggio, pf 4 hands, 1966; Fantasy, pf, 1973; Ballad, pf, 1979; Espressivo, vc, 1981; A Musical Trip, pf 4 hands, 1984

Vocal: A Song of Solomon (Bible), SSA, pf, 1956; Song of Myself (Whitman), Bar, chamber ens, 1957; 3 Rilke Songs, S, pf, 1963; Ariel (S. Plath), S, orch, 1969; Exercise (J. Harrison), chorus, tape, 1973; Hear this Touch (Harrison), S, tape, 1976; Tubaria (Requiem), B-Bar, tuba, 1979; Loves (Catullus: Catulli carmina nos. 11, 87, 85, 38, 101, trans. Moss), S, fl, cl, va, harp, pf, 1982; Dark Harbor (N. Bond), S, tape, 1983; Portals (Whitman: Songs of Parting, Portals, A Clear Midnight), T, fl, cl, perc, vn, va, vc, 1983, arr. T, pf, 1984

Principal publishers: C. Fisher, Presser, Seesaw

BIBLIOGRAPHY

EwenD

E. Barkin: "Lawrence Moss's *Three Rilke Songs*," *PNM*, vi/1 (1967), 144

RICHARD SWIFT

Moten, Bennie [Benjamin] (*b* Kansas City, MO, 13 Nov 1894; *d* Kansas City, 2 April 1935). Jazz pianist and bandleader. He studied piano with two of Scott Joplin's pupils and by 1918 was working professionally as leader of the ragtime trio B. B. & D. By 1922 his group had expanded to six members, and in the next year they issued their first recordings, playing mostly blues with a heavy, stomping beat. Within ten years Moten's ensemble included among its members such outstanding performers as Walter Page, Hot Lips Page, Eddie Durham, Ben Webster,

Buster Smith, Count Basie, and the blues singer Jimmy Rushing, and had largely established the southwest or Kansas City style of orchestral jazz. This style was based on a four-beat rhythmic pattern that emphasized horizontal "flow," on a flexible and texturally well-integrated rhythm section, and on frequent use of instrumental riffs and blues chord sequences. The arrangements (by Durham, Eddie Barefield, and Basie) were, except for Ellington's, the most advanced of their time, offering highly virtuoso performances, often at breakneck tempos, which effectively blended soloists and ensembles into organic compositions. These characteristics are well represented in a series of ten performances from the group's final recording session in 1932. On Moten's death his group was led briefly by Basie and Buster (Ira) Moten (who was Moten's brother or perhaps his nephew). From 1936 its personnel and style went on, through the Count Basie Orchestra, to become an important force in big-band swing, and a formative influence on bop and modern jazz.

RECORDINGS

(selective list)

Elephant's Wobble/Crawdad Blues (1923, OK 8100); The New Tulsa Blues (1927, Vic. 21584); Moten Stomp (1927, Vic. 20955); Kansas City Breakdown (1928, Vic. 21693); When I'm Alone (1930, Vic. 22734); Toby/Moten Swing (1932, Vic. 23384); Lafayette (1932, Vic. 24216); Prince of Wales (1932, Vic. 23393)

BIBLIOGRAPHY

SouthernB

F. Driggs: "Kansas City and the South West," *Jazz*, ed. N. Hentoff and A. J. McCarthy (New York, 1959/*R*1974), 189–230

G. Schuller: *Early Jazz: its Roots and Musical Development* (New York, 1968), 283ff

R. Russell: *Jazz Style in Kansas City and the Southwest* (Berkeley, 1971, 2/1973)

D. Bakker: "Bennie Moten, 1923–1932," *Micrography*, no.24 (1973), 2 [discography; addns in no.26 (1973), 1]

A. McCarthy: *Big Band Jazz* (London, 1974), 33ff

GUNTHER SCHULLER/R

Mother Earth. Rock group formed in 1966 by TRACY NELSON.

Mother Mallard's Portable Masterpiece Co. Electronic music ensemble formed in 1969 by DAVID BORDEN.

Mothers of Invention. Rock group led by FRANK ZAPPA.

Motown. (1) Recording and music publishing company specializing in black popular music. The company was formed in Detroit (from whose nickname, "Motortown," its name presumably derives) in 1960 by Berry Gordy, Jr. (*b* 28 Nov 1929), a producer and songwriter; during the 1960s it became the most successful American corporation owned and controlled by Blacks, and one of the most influential recording companies in the history of pop music. Motown's songwriters, arrangers, and producers (notably Smokey Robinson, Norman Whitfield, and the Holland–Dozier–Holland team) forged a distinctive pop-soul style (see (2)) that made black popular music acceptable for the first time to white audiences, not only in the USA but also in Europe. In 1971 the company moved to Hollywood, where Gordy developed its film interests. Among the musicians who achieved success through their association with Motown are Mary Wells, the Temptations, Diana Ross and the Supremes, Martha and the Vandellas, Smokey Robinson and the Miracles, the Four Tops, Tammi Terrell, Jr. Walker, Marvin Gaye, Stevie Wonder, and the Jackson Five; several white performers, Frankie Valli and the Four Seasons for example, also recorded on the label. Although by the early 1980s a number of singers who wanted greater artistic freedom (including Ross, Gaye, and the Jacksons) had left Motown for other labels, the company continues to represent a vital force in black popular music, with such performers as the Commodores, Lionel Richie, Rick James, and Jimmy Ruffin. (For illustration *see* DETROIT.)

(2) The style of music developed by the house writers and producers employed by Motown in the 1960s; the term is used specifically to refer to the distinctive type of pop-soul recorded by artists in the first years of the company's existence. The Motown sound drew on elements of blues, rhythm-and-blues, gospel music, and rock; it differed from the music of other regional centers of black popular music (e.g., Chicago, Memphis, and New York) in its greater reliance on conventions of mainstream Anglo-American urban popular music (such as sophisticated arrangements, with large studio orchestras, usually including strings) and a muting of the more vigorous characteristics of Afro-American music and performance practices. Set to lyrics that were also of broader appeal and couched in less esoteric imagery than those of other black styles, Motown soul music was sufficiently eclectic to find widespread acceptance among Whites. (*See also* SOUL MUSIC.)

BIBLIOGRAPHY

D. Morse: *Motown and the Arrival of Black American Music* (New York, 1972)

I. Hoare and others: *The Soul Book* (London, 1975)

J. McEwen and J. Miller: "Motown," *The Rolling Stone Illustrated History of Rock & Roll*, ed. J. Miller (New York, 1976, rev. 2/1980)

J. Futrell and others: *The Illustrated Encyclopedia of Black Music* (New York, 1982)

D. Waller: *The Motown Story* (New York, 1984)

MIKAL GILMORE, ROBERT WITMER

Mount, William Sidney (*b* Setauket, NY, 26 Nov 1807; *d* Setauket, 18 Nov 1868). Painter and violinist. He invented an "improved" model of the violin, which was patented in 1852. The patent model, a $\frac{7}{8}$ instrument (Smithsonian Institution), was patterned after a design which required fewer constituent parts than usual; it incorporated a boutless, almond-shaped body, a "hollow" (i.e. concave) back, a "spring-beam" bass-bar, and rectangular soundholes. In its final form, as exemplified by a full-sized violin of 1857 (Museums at Stony Brook, NY), it possessed a boutless, guitar-shaped body, a concave back, a conventional bass-bar, and soundholes in reversed position. Under the trade name "The Cradle of Harmony" various models were displayed during the Exhibition of Industry of All Nations, New York (1853). Later that year favorable testimonials on behalf of the design were obtained from Ureli Corelli Hill and other professional musicians. In spite of these efforts, which were renewed after the Civil War, investors willing to underwrite the cost of its mass production could not be found.

BIBLIOGRAPHY

A. Frankenstein: *William Sidney Mount* (New York, 1975) [with disc]

A. Buechner: "William Sidney Mount's 'Cradle of Harmony': a Unique 19th Century American Violin," *Journal of the Violin Society of America*, iii/2 (1977), 35–71

J. G. Armstrong, ed.: *Catching the Tune: Music and William Sidney Mount* (Stony Brook, NY, 1984)

ALAN BUECHNER

Mountain dulcimer. *See* APPALACHIAN DULCIMER.

Mountain Fern. *See* O'DAY, MOLLY.

Mu Beta Psi. Music honor society for men and women, founded in 1925; *see* GREEK-LETTER SOCIETIES, §2.

Muck, Carl [Karl] (*b* Darmstadt, Germany, 22 Oct 1859; *d* Stuttgart, Germany, 3 March 1940). German conductor. He did not undertake any formal training as a conductor, but studied classical philology in Heidelberg and Leipzig. He made his conducting début in 1880 and after various engagements was appointed principal Kapellmeister at the Deutsches Landestheater in Prague (1886). In 1892 he became principal Kapellmeister, and in 1908 general music director, of the Berlin Opera, where he gained a reputation for his performances of Wagner's works. From 1906 to 1908 and from 1912 to 1918 he directed the Boston SO. His second stay in Boston ended abruptly, during the height of anti-German hysteria in 1917. A newspaper editor in Providence demanded, on the morning of the appearance of the Boston SO in that city, that Muck should affirm his allegiance by opening the evening's concert with a performance of *The Star-Spangled Banner*. The orchestra's founder (Henry Lee Higginson) and its manager decided that the demand was not worthy of notice and did not even mention it to the conductor. After the concert the newspaper made much of the supposed fact that Muck had "refused" to play the patriotic song, and despite Higginson's efforts to set the matter straight, Muck was arrested on 25 March 1918 and interned for the remainder of the war.

Muck has been regarded as the finest conductor of the Boston SO. His programs emphasized stylistic consistency within a single concert (he did not like to mix Classical and Romantic works) and thus tended to alternate between the styles from one week to the next. He was considered by his contemporaries to be the greatest living conductor of Wagner's works and performed the symphonies of Bruckner and Mahler frequently; he also introduced new works, including the first (and for some years the only) performances in Boston of Schoenberg's Five Orchestral Pieces op.16. He continued the orchestra's traditional support of American composers, especially Bostonians, with performances of works by Chadwick, Clapp, Converse, Hadley, E. B. Hill, Kelley, Loeffler, MacDowell, John Knowles Paine, and Strube.

BIBLIOGRAPHY

N. Stucker: *Karl Muck* (Graz, Austria, 1939)
I. Lowens: "L'affaire Muck," *Musicology*, i (1945–7), 265
H. Schonberg: *The Great Conductors* (New York, 1967)
J. J. Badel: "The Strange Case of Dr. Karl Muck, who was Torpedoed by *The Star-Spangled Banner* during World War I," *HiFi/MusAm*, xx/10 (1970), 55

STEVEN LEDBETTER

Muczynski, Robert (*b* Chicago, IL, 19 March 1929). Composer, pianist, and teacher. He studied piano with Walter Knupfer and composition with Alexander Tcherepnin at DePaul University (BM 1950, MM 1952). In 1954 he was commissioned to write a piano concerto for the Louisville Orchestra, with which he recorded the work soon after. He made his New York début in 1958 in a recital of his own works. Muczynski's compositions for piano and his chamber works demonstrate superb craftsmanship and represent his most significant efforts. Influenced by such composers as Bartók, Piston, and Barber, his style is earnest, economical, and unostentatious, characterized by spare, neoclassical textures, a gently restrained lyricism, and, in fast movements, strongly accented, irregular meters, which create a vigorous rhythmic drive. His honors include two fellowships from the Ford Foundation's Young Composers Project (1959–62). In addition to composing and performing, Muczynski directed the piano department at Loras (Iowa) College from 1956 to 1959 and has taught at the University of Arizona since 1965. He has recorded most of his piano music for Laurel Records.

WORKS

Orch: Divertimento, pf, orch, op.2, 1952; Sym., op.5, 1953; Pf Conc., op.7, 1954; Dovetail Ov., op.12, 1960; Dance Movts, op.17, 1963; Sym. Dialogues, op.20, 1965; Charade, op.28, 1971; Serenade for Summer, op.38, 1976; Cavalcade, op.39, 1978; Sax Conc., op.41, 1981

Pf: Sonatina, op.1, 1950; 5 Sketches, op.3, 1952; 6 Preludes, op.6, 1954; Variations on a Theme of Tcherepnin, op.8, 1955; 3 pf sonatas, op.9, 1957, op.22, 1966, op.35, 1974; Suite, op.13, 1960; Toccata, op.15, 1962; A Summer Journal, op.19, 1964; Seven, op.30, 1971; Maverick Pieces, op.37, 1976; Masks, op.40, 1980; Profiles, hpd, op.42, 1982; Dream Cycle, op.44, 1983; several pedagogical pieces

Chamber: Fl Sonata, op.14, 1961; Movts, ww qnt, op.16, 1962; 2 pf trios, op.24, 1967, op.36, 1975; Vc Sonata, op.25, 1968; Fantasy Trio, cl, vc, pf, op.26, 1969; Voyage, tpt, hn, trbn, op.27, 1969; Sax Sonata, op.29, 1970; Str Trio, op.31, 1972; Impromptus, tuba, op.32, 1972; Duos, 2 fl, op.34, 1973; Time Pieces, cl, pf, op.43, 1983; Ww Qnt, op.45, 1985; several other short pieces

Several documentary filmscores

Choral works

Principal publishers: G. Schirmer, Presser

BIBLIOGRAPHY

J. A. Hawkins: *The Piano Music of Robert Muczynski* (diss., U. of Maryland, 1980)

WALTER G. SIMMONS

Muddy Waters [Morganfield, McKinley] (*b* Rolling Fork, MS, 4 April 1915; *d* Downers Grove, IL, 30 April 1983). Blues singer and guitarist. He first learned the harmonica and changed to the guitar when he was 17. In 1941–2 he was recorded in Mississippi for the Library of Congress; his *I be's troubled* and *Country Blues* (both 1941, AAFS 18) from these sessions show the influence of Son House, whom he knew personally, and the recordings of Robert Johnson. In 1943 he moved to Chicago, where in 1947 he began to record commercially under the name Muddy Waters. By this time he had taken up the electric guitar, which he played with a vibrant slide technique, singing with a louder and harder voice. His *Walkin' Blues* (1950, Chess 1426), based on *Country Blues*, was the last title he made with just a bass to support him.

Muddy Waters

From 1950 he recorded regularly with the harmonica player Little Walter, with whom he made the splendidly integrated *Louisiana Blues* (1950, Chess 1441); they were soon joined by Muddy Waters's half-brother Otis Spann (pianist) and Jimmy Rogers (second guitarist) to form the nucleus of a long-lived blues band based in Chicago. By 1953 Muddy Waters was performing such dramatically phrased songs as *I'm your Hoochie Coochie Man* (1953, Chess 1560) and *Manish Boy* (1955, Chess 1602); these established him among the most important postwar blues singers, and set the model for later performances such as *Got my Mojo Working* (1956, Chess 1620) and *Tiger in your Tank* (1960, Chess 1765), which in their declamatory style and loud amplification express the militant spirit of the ghetto at that time. In the 1960s Muddy Waters toured extensively in the USA and Europe, but lost much of his black audience and frequently re-recorded his songs of the 1950s without meeting their standards. A serious automobile accident in 1970 obliged him to sing from a chair from then onwards.

BIBLIOGRAPHY

SouthernB ("Morganfield, McKinley")

P. Oliver: *Muddy Waters* (Bexhill-on-Sea, England, 1964)

P. Welding: "Interview with Muddy Waters," *American Folk Music Occasional*, no.2 (New York, 1970), 2

P. Guralnick: *Feel Like Going Home* (New York, 1971)

J. Rooney: *Bossmen: Bill Monroe and Muddy Waters* (New York, 1971)

R. Palmer: *Deep Blues* (New York, 1981)

PAUL OLIVER

Mueller [Müller], Johann Christoph (*b* Württemberg, Germany, 1777; *d* Bridgewater, PA, 1845). Flutist, violinist, and pianist. After completing university training in botany and medicine, he came under the influence of the separatist preacher Johann Georg (George) Rapp, with whom he came to the USA in 1803. Rapp's congregation followed in 1804 and they formed a religious commune, the Harmony Society, in Butler County, Pennsylvania, in 1805. Mueller served until 1831 as the society's physician, schoolteacher, and music director, both in Pennsylvania and at the settlement of New Harmony in Indiana. As music director he was responsible for music in the school and church, and on social occasions. He supervised the printing of several collections of Harmonist hymn texts, and copied and arranged hundreds of marches, waltzes, overtures, sinfonias, and vocal works by European and American composers for Harmonist instrumentalists and singers. Under Mueller's direction the Harmonist orchestra grew to classical proportions, and between 1827 and 1831 concerts were given fortnightly at Economy, Pennsylvania. These were open to the public, and attracted tourists, political figures, and musicians. Mueller's own works include German strophic songs, odes with sectarian texts, and instrumental pieces.

BIBLIOGRAPHY

K. J. R. Arndt: *George Rapp's Harmony Society: 1785–1847* (Philadelphia, 1965)

R. D. Wetzel: *The Music of George Rapp's Harmony Society, 1805–1906* (diss., U. of Pittsburgh, 1970)

K. J. R. Arndt and R. D. Wetzel: "Harmonist Music and Pittsburgh Musicians in Early Economy," *Western Pennsylvania Historical Magazine*, liv (1971), no.2, pp.125–57; no.3, p.284; no.4, p.391

RICHARD D. WETZEL

Mulder, Richard (*b* Amsterdam, the Netherlands, 31 Dec 1822; *d* San Francisco, CA, 22 Dec 1874). Impresario who married the soprano INEZ FABBRI.

Mulligan, Gerry [Gerald Joseph] (*b* New York, 6 April 1927). Jazz baritone saxophonist and arranger. He grew up in Philadelphia, and first learned piano, which he still plays in public occasionally. While in his teens he wrote arrangements for Johnny Warrington's radio band (1944) and played reed instruments professionally. After moving to New York in 1946 he joined Gene Krupa's big band as reed player and staff arranger, attracting attention with his *Disc Jockey Jump* (1947). He then became involved with the nascent cool-jazz movement in New York, taking part in the performances (1948) and recording sessions (1949–50) of Miles Davis's nonet and contributing scores to the Elliot Lawrence and Claude Thornhill big bands. By this time he was specializing in baritone saxophone, on which he was heard in combos with Kai Winding and others. He also wrote scores for Stan Kenton's band and recorded with his own tentet, modeled on Davis's combo (1951).

In 1952 Mulligan, then based in Los Angeles, formed his first "pianoless" quartet, with Chet Baker on trumpet. The group was instantaneously successful, and brought Baker and Mulligan international acclaim. Mulligan led a new tentet and various versions of the quartet throughout the mid-1950s, making a sensational appearance at the Salle Pleyel, Paris, in 1954 and dominating jazz opinion polls for his instrument, as he has done ever since. In 1960 he organized his own concert jazz band with which he toured Europe in that year and Japan in 1964. After it disbanded he became an active sideman, working often with Dave Brubeck from 1968 to 1972, and a freelance arranger for other jazz groups. He formed a new big band, the Age of Steam, in 1972, and was artist-in-residence at Miami University in 1974. Since the mid-1970s he has also played soprano saxophone. He remains an active figure on the international jazz scene.

Mulligan is among the most versatile figures in modern jazz. Although slow to develop as an instrumentalist, he has long been recognized as the most important baritone saxophonist in jazz since Harry Carney. Besides the cool idiom which he helped to create, he is equally at home in a big-band, bop, or even dixieland context (playing clarinet in the last), and his excellent recordings with musicians as varied as Johnny Hodges and Thelonious Monk show an unusual musical adaptability. Initially, however, Mulligan made his reputation as an arranger of band scores with intricate inner parts, careful balancing of timbres, low dynamics, and light swing, all of which features are present in his settings of *Jeru*, *Godchild*, and *Venus de Milo* for the Davis nonet. Later he abstracted these qualities in his pianoless combos, where the low volume and absence of chordal underpinnings freed the wind players to improvise in delicate two-part counterpoint. Some of Mulligan's best playing can be heard in his recordings with Chet Baker, Bob Brookmeyer, and most notably Paul Desmond, with whom he shares an unusual talent for improvised countermelody.

RECORDINGS

(selective list)

As leader: Line for Lyons/Carioca (1952, Fan. 522); My Funny Valentine/Bark for Barksdale (1952, Fan. 525); Walkin' Shoes/Rocker (1953, Cap. EAP 1-439); *Paris Concert* (1954, Vogue 7381, 7383); *Presenting the Gerry Mulligan Sextet* (1955, EmArcy 36056); *Desmond Meets Mulligan* (1957, Verve 8246); *Concert Jazz Band* (1960, Verve 68388); *Jeru* (1962, Col. CS8732); *Two of a Mind* (1962, RCA LSP2624); *Idle Gossip* (1976, Chiaroscuro 155)

As sideman: G. Krupa: Disc Jockey Jump (1947, Col. 37589); M. Davis: Jeru/Godchild (1949, Cap.60005), Boplicity/Israel (1949, Cap. 60011); Venus de Milo/Darn that Dream (1949–50, Cap. 1221)

BIBLIOGRAPHY

G. Mulligan: *Sketch-Orks* (Hollywood, CA, 1957–64)

A. Morgan and R. Horricks: *Gerry Mulligan: a Biography, Appreciation, Record Survey and Discography* (London, 1958)
M. Harrison: "An Ensemble Style for Jazz," *These Jazzmen of our Times*, ed. R. Horricks (London, 1959), 68
——: "Gerry Mulligan," *Jazz Review*, iii/7 (1960), 23
M. James: *Ten Modern Jazzmen* (London, 1960), 93ff
W. Mellers: *Music in a New Found Land* (London, 1964), 357f
J. Goldberg: *Jazz Masters of the Fifties* (New York, 1965/R1980), 9ff
A. Smith: "Jeru's Views," *Down Beat*, xliii/13 (1976), 13
A. Tercinet: "Discographie de Gerry Mulligan," *Jazz hot*, no.335 (1977), 25; no.336 (1977), 21
R. Brown: "Gerry Mulligan: Cool Charts, Bearish Tone," *Down Beat*, xlvi/11 (1979), 12

J. BRADFORD ROBINSON

Mulvihill, Martin (*b* Ballygoughlin, Co. Limerick, Ireland, 18 July 1919). Fiddler. He studied first with his mother, a traditional fiddler, and learned tunes and instrumental techniques from local musicians; he later learned to play piano and button accordion. He moved to New York in 1971 and began teaching Irish music to local children. In performance he is sometimes joined by his children: Dawn, a fiddler and tin whistle player; Gail, a tenor banjo player; Brian, a drummer; and Brenden, a fiddler. Mulvihill uses the long bowing technique of southern Ireland; he plays rolls rather than triplets for embellishment. He often travels to Ireland in search of new repertory. In 1984 he received a National Heritage Fellowship Award from the NEA.

Mumma, Gordon (*b* Framingham, MA, 30 March 1935). Composer and performer of electronic music. He attended the University of Michigan (1952–3) and studied composition, piano, and horn privately. As a composer and performer he worked in Ann Arbor with Milton Cohen's Space Theater (1957–64) and with the ONCE festivals and ONCE Group (1960–68), and in New York with the Merce Cunningham Dance Company (1966–74) and the Sonic Arts Union (from 1966), which specialized in the presentation of live electronic music. With these ensembles and as a soloist, he has toured widely in the Americas, Europe, and Japan. Beginning in 1973 he taught at the University of California, Santa Cruz; he was also a visiting faculty member at the University of Illinois (1969–70), Darius Milhaud Professor at Mills College (1981), and on the faculty of the Cursos Latinoamericanos de Música Contemporánea (1975, 1977, 1981). Mumma received commissions from the Venice Biennale (1964), the New York State Council on the Arts (1973), the Merce Cunningham Dance Company (1974), and the Portland Dance Theater (1977, 1979), among others. He has written a number of articles on electronic music and other aspects of 20th century music.

A wide-ranging innovator, Mumma is best known for his contributions to electroacoustic music, particularly for his pioneering of "cybersonic music," in which sounds, by means of feedback, control the production and modification both of themselves and of subsequent sounds. His earliest work in the medium stemmed from mixed-media collaborations at the Space Theater, where, with Ashley, he wrote electroacoustic scores and invented elaborate electronic devices for live generation, manipulation, and deployment of sound. He has incorporated cybersonic procedures, primarily as an aspect of live electroacoustic music, into numerous works, beginning with *Medium Size Mograph 1963* (for illustration *see* ELECTROACOUSTIC MUSIC, fig.2). In experimenting with circuits, Mumma discovered certain phase- and time-shifting effects that he has used to create the impression of rapid changes in the size and shape of the performance space, as in *Passenger Pigeon 1776–1976* (1976) and *Pontpoint* (1980). He has also made increasing use of digital-control circuitry and computers. His electronic music has influenced his pieces for conventional sound-sources chiefly in their nonmetricality, in the fluid unfolding of events, and the manipulation of the listener's sense of time.

Collaboration with other artists has been central to Mumma's career from the 1950s on, especially his work with Cunningham and the composer-performers Tudor, Cage, and Behrman. He joined with the writer Tom Robbins, choreographer Jann McCauley, and sculptor David Cotter to create *Earheart* (1977); *Fwyynghn* (1979) was composed with Oliveros.

WORKS

(selective list)

Dramatic: 5 Short Films, film score, 1963, collab. G. Manupelli, R. Ashley; Greys, film score, 1963, collab. D. Scavarda; Megaton for Wm. Burroughs, pfmrs, elec, lights, 1963; Telepos, dancers, elec, 1971, collab. M. Cunningham; Some Voltage Drop, variable duration theater piece, elec, 1974; Earheart, dancers, elec, 1977, collab. T. Robbins, J. McCauley, D. Cotter; Echo-BCD, dancers, elec, 1978, collab. J. McCauley; Fwyynghn (B. Manley), incidental music, 1979, collab. Oliveros

Inst: Pf Suite, 1959; A Quarter of Fourpiece, 4 insts, 1962; Gestures II, 2 pf, 1962; Large Size Mograph 1962, pf, 1962; Medium Size Mograph 1962, pf, 1962; Very Small Size Mograph 1962, pf, 1962; Small Size Mograph 1964, pf, 1964; Very Small Size Mograph 1964, pf, 1964; Schoolwork, crosscut saw, psaltery, piano-melodica, 1970; Equale: Zero Crossings, vn, fl, cl, t sax, bn, vc, bandoneon, 1976; 11-note Pieces and Decimal Passacaglia, hpd, 1978; Los desaparacidos, elec clvd, 1980; Faisandage et galimafree, insts, 1983

Inst and tape/cptr: Sinfonia, 12 insts, tape, 1960; Meanwhile, a Twopiece, perc, tape, 1961; Le Corbusier, orch, org, tape, cybersonic vn, cybersonic db, 1965; Conspiracy 8, digital cptr, 1–8 pfmrs, 1970, collab. S. Smoliar

Tape: Epoxy (Sequence I), 1962; Music for the Venezia Space Theatre, 1964; The Dresden Interleaf 13 February 1945, 1965; Pontpoint, 1980

Live elec: Medium Size Mograph 1963, cybersonic pf, 1963; Temps for Space Theater, 1963; Horn, cybersonic console, hn, 1965; Hornpipe, cybersonic hn, 1967; Beam, vn, va, cybersonics, 1969; Ambivex, cybersonic cornet, 1971; Cybersonic Cantilevers, audience, cybersonics, 1973; Passenger Pigeon 1776–1976, synth, 1976

Principal publisher: Berandol

BIBLIOGRAPHY

EwenD
H. W. Hitchcock: "Current Chronicle," *MQ*, xlviii (1962), 245
U. Kasemets: "Current Chronicle," *MQ*, l (1964), 515
C. Tomkins: *The Bride and the Bachelors* (New York, 1968)
"Mixture Space," *Space Design: Journal of Art and Architecture*, lxxx (1969), 62
D. Cope: *New Directions in Music* (Dubuque, IA, 1971, rev. 4/1984)
M. Nyman: *Experimental Music* (London, 1974)
R. Reynolds: *Mind Models – New Forms of Musical Experience* (New York, 1975)
P. Griffiths: *Modern Music: the Avant Garde since 1948* (New York, 1981)
B. Schrader: *Introduction to Electro-acoustic Music* (Englewood Cliffs, NJ, 1981)

RICHARD S. JAMES

Munch [Münch], **Charles** (*b* Strasbourg, France, 26 Sept 1891; *d* Richmond, VA, 6 Nov 1968). French conductor and violinist. He studied violin at the Strasbourg Conservatory, with Carl Flesch in Berlin, and with Lucien Capet in Paris. After serving in the German army (1914–18), he taught violin at Strasbourg (in 1919) and then at Leipzig, where he was concertmaster of the Gewandhaus orchestra under Wilhelm Furtwängler (1926–33). On his return to Paris in 1933, he made a successful conducting début, and for the next 15 years introduced new works into the programs of several orchestras there while also teaching at the Ecole Normale de Musique. Munch toured widely as a conductor in Europe before making his American début with the Boston SO in 1946; he became its chief conductor in 1949 and remained until 1962, resuming the policy initiated there by Pierre Monteux in the 1920s of making the Boston SO the chief agent for the introduction of new French music to the American public, as well as of new works by Barber, Foss, Piston, Schuman, Sessions, and others (for illustration, showing Munch with Monteux, *see* BOSTON (i), fig.2). He was welcomed in Boston for the feeling of spontaneity he brought to his performances, and under his direction the Boston SO maintained a high standard of brilliance and discipline that reflected his own dynamic personality. He was responsible for organizing the first tours to Europe by the Boston SO, in 1952 and 1956; these were conducted by Monteux. Munch returned to France after leaving Boston and in 1967 shared in the formation of the Orchestre de Paris, with which he was on an American tour when he died. He wrote *Je suis chef d'orchestre* (1954, Eng. trans., 1955/*R*1978).

BIBLIOGRAPHY

"There will be Joy," *Time* (19 Dec 1949), 26
R. Gelatt: *Music-makers* (New York, 1953), 43
H. Stoddard: "Charles Munch," *Symphony Conductors of the U.S.A.* (New York, 1957), 136
G. Collard: "Charles Münch," *Audio and Record Review*, ii/9 (1963) [with discography by F. F. Clough and G. J. Cuming]
D. Wooldridge: *Conductor's World* (New York, 1970), 284

MARTIN COOPER/R

Munsel, Patrice (Beverly) (*b* Spokane, WA, 14 May 1925). Soprano. A student of William Herman and Renato Bellini in New York, she made her début as Philine in Thomas' *Mignon* at the Metropolitan Opera on 4 December 1943; at that time she was the youngest singer ever to be engaged by that company. Because Lily Pons frequently left the Metropolitan to contribute to the war effort, Munsel appeared, perhaps too soon and too often, in the major roles of the coloratura repertory – Lucia, Rosina, Gilda, and the Queen in *The Golden Cockerel*. A youthful pluck and the appeal of her timbre and natural agility carried her through, though the early exposure in this repertory harmed her vocally. Rudolf Bing rehabilitated her career by presenting her as a soubrette and comedienne in roles such as Zerlina, Despina, Strauss's Adele, and particularly Offenbach's Périchole; in the early 1950s – aided by adroit publicity, a delightful appearance, and her considerable personal charm – she was enormously popular. In 1953 she starred in *Melba*, a British film biography of the Australian diva; in 1957–8 she had her own weekly national television show. By the end of the decade, she had virtually retired from opera. She appeared for the next 20 years only in musical comedy (mostly in summer stock and regional theater), with diminishing vocal resources, but audiences always respected her complete professionalism and undimmed zest.

BIBLIOGRAPHY

J. Hines: "Patrice Munsel," *Great Singers on Great Singing* (Garden City, NY, 1982), 189

RICHARD DYER

Mu Phi Epsilon. Honorary music society for women founded in 1903; *see* GREEK-LETTER SOCIETIES, §2.

Murphy, Turk [Melvin E.] (*b* Palermo, CA, 16 Dec 1915). Jazz trombonist. A stalwart of traditional jazz in California, he first came to fame in the band led by the trumpeter Lu Watters in the early 1940s. Murphy formed his own band in 1947 and continued to lead it into the 1980s. The band was based in San Francisco, where they had a permanent booking for many years at a club called Earthquake McGoon's. They also worked occasionally on the East Coast, and toured Australia and Europe during the 1970s. Murphy's trombone style was robust and full of good humor; the repertory of his band blended jazz classics of the 1920s with well-known ballads and original compositions. The consistency of Murphy's style is clearly apparent on the huge number of recordings that his band, with various changes of personnel, made from 1950 to 1980.

RECORDINGS

(selective list)

Sidewalk Blues (1953, Col. CL6324); Maryland, my Maryland (1955, Col. 40586); *Music for Losers* (1957, Verve 1013), incl. The Yama Yama Man; *Turk Murphy at the Newport Jazz Festival 1957* (1957, Verve 8232), incl. Weary Blues; *Turk Murphy*, iii (1974, GHB 93), incl. Wild Man Blues

BIBLIOGRAPHY

E. Condon and R. Gehman, eds.: *Eddie Condon's Treasury of Jazz* (New York, 1956/*R*1975), 176
R. Gleason, ed.: *Jam Session* (New York, 1958), 116
J. Goggin: *Turk Murphy: Just for the Record* (San Francisco, 1982)

JOHN CHILTON

Murray, Sunny [James Marcellus Arthur] (*b* Idabel, OK, 21 Sept 1937). Jazz drummer. He grew up in Philadelphia, and in 1956 moved to New York, where he played with various traditional jazz musicians, including Henry "Red" Allen and Willie "the Lion" Smith. In 1959 he met the avant-garde pianist Cecil Taylor, under whose influence he began to play more freely; but it was only after hearing and playing informally with the John Coltrane Quartet in 1963 that he developed his own aggressive and freely floating style, with its characteristic waves of cymbal sound and heavy punctuations on bass drum and tom-toms. He performed with Albert Ayler in 1964–5, and issued recordings for ESP (1966) and BYG (1969). Although Murray was an innovator with considerable influence among younger musicians, he was never able to work full-time as a percussionist. In the 1980s he modified his style somewhat in an attempt to adapt to more traditional jazz styles.

RECORDINGS

As leader: *Sunny Murray* (1966, ESP 1032); *Homage to Africa* (1969, BYG 529.303); *Sunshine* (1969, BYG 529.348); *Never Give a Sucker an Even Break* (1969, BYG 529.332); *Apple Cores* (1978, Philly Jazz 1004)
As sideman: C. Taylor: *Live at the Cafe Montmartre* (1962, Fan. 86014); A. Ayler: *Bells* (1965, ESP 1010); A. Shepp: *Yasmina, A Black Woman* (1969, BYG 529.304); D. Eyges: *Crossroads* (1981, Music Unlimited 7432)

BIBLIOGRAPHY

L. Jones: *Black Music* (New York, 1970)
R. Levin: "Sunny Murray: the Continuous Crackling of Glass," *Black Giants*, ed. P. Rivelli and R. Levin (New York, 1970), 56
V. Wilmer: *As Serious as your Life* (London, 1977, rev. 2/1980)
S. Weston: "Interview with Sunny Murray," *Cadence*, v/6 (1979), 14
M. Hames: *Albert Ayler, Sunny Murray . . . on Disc and Tape* (Chigwell, England, 1983)

MICHAEL ULLMAN

Murray, Thomas (Mantle) (*b* Los Angeles, CA, 6 Oct 1943). Organist. He attended Occidental College (BA 1965) where he studied organ with Clarence Mader and choral conducting with Howard Swan. In 1966 he won the National Competition of the American Guild of Organists. He was organist of Immanuel Presbyterian Church, Los Angeles (1965–73), and organist and choirmaster at St. Paul's Episcopal Cathedral, Boston (1973–80). In 1981 he joined the faculty of the Yale University School of Music. A technically gifted and musically inspired performer, Murray has specialized in organ literature of the Romantic period and has a scholarly knowledge of the organ works of Elgar, Franck, Mendelssohn, and Saint-Saëns, as well as of the 19th- and 20th-century American instruments best suited to this repertory. His periodical articles and recordings are a contribution to the documentation of the Romantic era. Murray is a commanding performer and a fine choral conductor.

VERNON GOTWALS

Murray, William (*b* Schenectady, NY, 13 March 1935). Baritone. Educated at Adelphi University, he won a Fulbright scholarship to Rome in 1956 and made his début at Spoleto the following year as Count Gil (*Il segreto di Susanna*). He sang at Detmold, Brunswick, Munich, Frankfurt, Amsterdam, Salzburg, and Berlin, where he became a member of the Deutsche Oper in 1969 and was made a *Kammersänger*. He sang the title role of Dallapiccola's *Ulisse* at La Scala (1970), took part in the world première of Nabokov's *Love's Labours Lost* in Brussels (1973), and sang the General in the first German performance of Henze's *We Come to the River* in Berlin (1976). His wide repertory also includes the roles of Don Giovanni, Paisiello's King Teodoro, Wolfram, Rigoletto, Germont, Di Luna (*Il trovatore*), Macbeth, Paolo (*Simon Boccanegra*), Don Carlo (*La forza del destino*), Yeletsky (*The Queen of Spades*), Scarpia, Lescaut, and Creon (Orff's *Antigonae*). A stylish singer and a fine actor, he excels in dramatic and character roles.

ELIZABETH FORBES

Mursell, James L(ockhart) (*b* Derby, England, 1 June 1893; *d* Jackson, NH, 1 Feb 1963). Music educator. He was educated in Britain, at the University of Queensland, Brisbane, Australia (BA 1915), and at Harvard, where he studied philosophy with Josiah Royce (PhD 1918). He then studied for the ministry at Union Theological Seminary (1918–20) and took a staff position with the Interchurch World Movement in New York City. He taught psychology and education at Lake Erie College, Painesville, Ohio (1921–3), and philosophy, psychology, and education at Lawrence College, Appleton, Wisconsin (1923–35). He also studied at the Lawrence Conservatory with Gladys Brainard. In 1935, he became professor of education at Teachers College, Columbia University, and later succeeded Peter W. Dykema as chairman of the music education department there (1939–57).

Although something of a novice as a musician and almost without experience in teaching public school music, Mursell made remarkable contributions to the profession. He was a profound thinker and a prolific writer: in accessible language he urged a generalized and humanistic approach to music education against formidable advocates of specialization; as an administrator he applied intellectual rigor in setting objectives and defended freedom in teaching methods. Mursell contributed to two school music series, *New Horizons* (1944–54) and *Music for Living* (1956–62). Besides a number of books on music education, he wrote more than 100 articles on music, the psychology of education, and philosophy (listed in Simutis, Metz, and O'Keefe).

See also EDUCATION, §I, 3, and PSYCHOLOGY OF MUSIC.

WRITINGS

Principles of Musical Education (New York, 1927)
with M. Glenn: *The Psychology of School Music Teaching* (New York, 1931, 2/1938)
Human Values in Music Education (New York, 1934)
The Psychology of Music (New York, 1937)
Music in American Schools (New York, 1943)
Education for Musical Growth (Boston, 1948)
Music and the Classroom Teacher (New York, 1951)
Music Education: Principles and Programs (Morristown, NJ, 1956)

BIBLIOGRAPHY

L. J. Simutis: *James Lockhart Mursell as Music Educator* (diss., U. of Ottawa, 1961)
H. R. Wilson: "James L. Mursell," *MEJ*, xlix/5 (1963), 116
D. E. Metz: *A Critical Analysis of the Thought of James L. Mursell in Music Education* (diss., Case Western Reserve U., 1968)
——: "Inconsistencies in the Writings of James L. Mursell," *Council for Research in Music Education Bulletin*, no.23 (1971), 6
V. C. O'Keefe: *James Lockhart Mursell: his Life and Contributions to Music Education* (EdD diss., Teachers College, Columbia U., 1970)

GEORGE N. HELLER

Musgrave, Thea (*b* Barnton, Midlothian, Scotland, 27 May 1928). Scottish composer. She studied in Scotland (with Hans Gál and Mary Grierson) and graduated from the University of Edinburgh (BMus 1950), where she won the Donald Tovey Prize. She went to Paris and studied privately and at the Paris Conservatoire with Boulanger. Afterwards she returned to Great Britain and worked as a coach and pianist, and in 1959 came to the USA on a scholarship to the Berkshire Music Center. There she studied with Copland, met Babbitt, and became more familiar with the music of Ives – whose influence is noticeable in several later works. She served as a lecturer at London University (1958–65) and in 1970 returned to the USA, where she was visiting professor of composition at the University of California, Santa Barbara (1970). She married the American violinist Peter Mark in 1971; for a time she commuted between London and Santa Barbara, but from 1975, when her husband was appointed artistic director (later general director) and conductor of the Virginia Opera Association in Norfolk, she has lived in Norfolk during the opera season and in Santa Barbara for the remainder of the year. She spends most of her time composing but has lectured at many universities in the USA, England, and Scotland.

Musgrave has won international renown not only as a composer but also as a conductor of opera and concert music. In 1976 she became the first woman to conduct her own composition with the Philadelphia Orchestra (Concerto for Orchestra); the next year she made her New York conducting début in a performance of *The Voice of Ariadne* (1972–3) with the New York City Opera (30 Sept 1977), which also produced *Mary, Queen of Scots* in 1981. She has conducted her own compositions in performances by numerous other British and American ensembles, including the English Opera Group, the Scottish and San Francisco spring opera companies, the Scottish Ballet, the BBC, London, San Diego, and San Francisco symphony orchestras, the Scottish National Orchestra, the English, Los Angeles, and St. Paul chamber orchestras, and the Royal PO (London).

A remarkably successful composer, Musgrave has had her works performed throughout the USA and in Great Britain. Among her earlier works that are most frequently performed in the USA are the concertos for clarinet (1967), horn (1971), and viola (1973), and the orchestral works *Night Music* (1969) and the concerto-like *Memento vitae* (1970). Since the mid-1960s most of her works have been written to commission. Her personal and idiomatic style cannot be pigeon-holed; she has at various times utilized most of the compositional techniques of the 20th century, including serialism and free chromaticism, as well as abstract instrumental forms and prerecorded electronic tapes, although she has avoided the more advanced avant-garde idioms. In her opera *Harriet, the Woman Called Moses*, her first on an American subject (the life of Harriet Tubman), she quotes numerous American melodies, including folksongs and spirituals; it was commissioned jointly by the Royal Opera House, Covent Garden, and the Virginia Opera Association and was first performed in Norfolk on 1 March 1985. Among her many other commissions are those from the BBC (for *An Occurrence at Owl Creek Bridge*), the Royal PO (*Peripeteia*), the City of Norfolk Tricentennial Commission (Fanfare for Brass Quintet), and the American Guild of Organists (*The Lord's Prayer*). Musgrave's honors include an award from the Koussevitzky Foundation (1974) and two Guggenheim fellowships (1974–5, 1982).

WORKS

(only those composed after 1974)

Dramatic: Mary, Queen of Scots (opera, 2, Musgrave, after A. Elguera: Moray), 1975–7; A Christmas Carol (opera, Musgrave, after Dickens), 1978–9; The Last Twilight (theater piece), chorus, insts, 1980; An Occurrence at Owl Creek Bridge (radio opera, 1, Musgrave, after A. Bierce), 1981; Harriet, the Woman Called Moses (opera, 2, Musgrave), 1982–4

Inst: Orfeo I, fl, tape, 1975; Orfeo II, fl, str, 1975; From One to Another, va, str, 1980; Soliloquy III, gui, fl, ob, cl, bn, str qnt, 1980, arr. from Soliloquy, gui, tape, 1969; Peripeteia, orch, 1981; Fanfare, brass qnt, 1982; Moving into Aquarius, orch, 1985, collab. R. R. Bennett

Vocal: O caro m'è il sonno, SATB, 1978; The Lord's Prayer, SATB, org, 1983

Principal publishers: Chester, Novello

BIBLIOGRAPHY

N. Kay: "Thea Musgrave," *Music and Musicians*, xviii/4 (1969), 34

J. W. LePage: "Thea Musgrave," *Women Composers, Conductors, and Musicians of the Twentieth Century: Selected Biographies* (Metuchen, NJ, 1980), 145

D. L. Hixon: *Thea Musgrave: a Bio-bibliography* (Westport, CT, 1984)

H. Kupferberg: "Thea Musgrave," *HiFi/MusAm*, xxxv/3 (1985), 14

KATHERINE K. PRESTON

Musica Elettronica Viva. Ensemble for the production and performance of live electronic music, formed in Rome in 1966 by ALVIN CURRAN, FREDERIC RZEWSKI, RICHARD TEITELBAUM, and others.

Musical. A form of popular musical theater consisting of musical numbers (songs, ensembles, and dances) integrated into a dramatic framework. It evolved as a recognizably distinct genre in the early years of the 20th century and became the chief form of popular musical theater in the USA. Its main antecedents were comic opera, vaudeville, and burlesque. In due course the American musical superseded European operetta in popularity not only in the USA but around the world. As a source of popular song it reached its peak in the 1920s and 1930s in the works of such composers as Jerome Kern, George Gershwin, and Richard Rodgers; but the period since World War II has seen considerable development in the genre as a musico-dramatic form, notably in the works of Stephen Sondheim. The term "musical comedy" generally denotes a lighthearted piece with song-and-dance numbers linked by a flimsy and often contrived story, while the term "musical play" indicates a work where the musical score is more closely integrated with a more substantial (sometimes serious) plot. There is, however, no clear or consistent distinction between the two, and both are now commonly covered by the noun "musical." This article deals with "book" musicals for the theater (i.e., works with a connected story); parallel developments have taken place in REVUE and the MUSICAL FILM; *see also* MUSICAL THEATER.

1. MUSICAL STRUCTURE AND DEVELOPMENT. The prime purpose of the musical has always been to provide lighthearted entertainment, although increasingly adventurous themes and treatment have also made it a source of intellectual stimulation. Of particular importance up to and for some time after World War II was a quota of songs to catch the audience's imagination, which could be hummed as people went home and easily recognized when heard outside the context of the production. In later years, however, a concentration on closer integration of all elements of the production – story, words, music, choreography, direction – reduced the significance of individual numbers in favor of a more through-composed, declamatory style. With the evolution of rock music, the musical has largely lost its former close relationship with popular trends.

The structure of the American musical play or musical comedy as produced around the turn of the century by composers of European origin, such as Victor Herbert, was basically that of comic opera. A typical two-act score comprising about 20 numbers included opening choruses for both acts, an extended first-act finale, songs and duets with choral refrains or danced repeats, and concerted pieces. As a native style developed, the more extended items were discarded in favor of musically simpler and more immediately effective pieces that were often reprised later in the show. With a specifically American style of song came a move away from the employment of trained singers with operatic voices, and this in turn meant that songs rarely required a vocal range greater than an octave. The shape and rhythms of the pieces also changed; where earlier composers had written fluent melodies and regular rhythms (often those of the Viennese waltz and march), American composers of the interwar years made use of shifting rhythms more closely molded to lyrics that expressed genuine human emotions. Songs consisting of a lengthy verse followed by a straightforward, catchy refrain, in what might be characterized as an *AA* or *AA′* form (for example, Herbert's "The Streets of New York" in *The Red Mill*, 1906), were supplanted in the works of Kern and others by melodies where the refrain was the significant and distinctive portion, and the verse little more than a preamble. These refrains were usually in 32-bar *AABA* form (for example, "Ol' man river" and "Can't help lovin' dat man" in *Show Boat*, 1927), though part of the appeal of the genre lies in variations from this conventional pattern.

The change from comic opera to musical comedy introduced other modifications in techniques. Whereas fully trained theater musicians such as Herbert had been capable of harmonizing and orchestrating their scores, the specialist songwriter was usually less thoroughly qualified; even if he had the ability to harmonize and orchestrate his scores, the rewards for doing so were small by comparison with those for creating further successful songs. Moreover, changes in vocal technique and theater instrumentation, and the resulting problems of balance, confirmed orchestration of theater works as a specialist art; even a thoroughly trained composer such as Leonard Bernstein used the services of specialist orchestrators for his theater scores.

The works written in the early 20th century made use of the classical string-based orchestra of up to 30 players that had served in the popular musical theater for many years; Herbert's *Mlle. Modiste* (1905), for instance, used strings, flute, oboe, two clarinets, bassoon, two trumpets, trombone, and percussion. Although the size of orchestra naturally varied for individual shows (especially in times of financial stringency), the full theater orchestra remained broadly stable in numbers over the years; its composition, however, changed significantly in favor of the louder reeds, brass, and percussion, and during the interwar years saxophones (first used in Kern's *Oh, I Say!* in 1913) became standard, along with one or two pianos. A typical postwar work, Cole Porter's *Kiss me, Kate* (1948), calls for a small body of strings to be supplemented by five reed players (each playing saxophone and one or two other instruments), two horns, three trumpets, trombone, percussion, harp, piano, and guitar. In more recent years the quest for originality has led to more varied combinations, including electric guitars and synthesizers. Electronic amplification, introduced in 1939, has enabled singers with untrained voices to be heard over these increasingly loud orchestras.

2. 19TH-CENTURY PREDECESSORS. Until the third quarter of the 19th century the American musical theater was heavily dependent on works imported from Europe, for instance the *opéras bouffes* of Jacques Offenbach. The first significant form of American stage entertainment to make use of popular song was the minstrel show, which found success abroad as well as in the USA. It was not until 1866, however, and the production of the extravaganza *The Black Crook*, that a native musical show boasting a unified plot or theme emerged. *The Black Crook*, an important precursor of the American musical, was a lavish spectacle incorporating melodrama, "magic" transformations and supernatural elements, song, and dance; the score was put together from various sources by William Wheatley, the music director at Niblo's Garden, where the work was presented. A unified score by a single composer appeared shortly afterwards in *Evangeline* (1874), a burlesque based on Longfellow's poem, with music, consisting of topical songs, comedy numbers, ballads, a waltz, a march, and various ensemble and choral pieces, by Edward E. Rice. Rice was also successful with *Adonis* (1884), a parody on the theme of Pygmalion and Galatea, which ran in New York for over 600 performances.

Other important precursors of musical comedy were found in the variety or vaudeville theaters. Edward Harrigan and Tony Hart first sang David Braham's *The Mulligan Guard* in a variety sketch in Chicago in 1873 (fig. 1). The song was a sardonic comment on various organizations of a military cast that sprang up in the aftermath of the Civil War; it became so successful that Braham and Harrigan produced a whole series of shows for New York built around the character of Dan Mulligan, beginning with *The Mulligan Guard's Picnic* (1878).

Many of these shows, however, were considered to be frivolous, risqué, or otherwise unsuitable for respectable family theatergoing. American musical theater was thus reinvigorated by the production in 1878 of Gilbert and Sullivan's *H.M.S. Pinafore*, a witty and melodious show that was at once entertaining and inoffensive. As many as 40 different (unauthorized) productions were mounted around the country, and the success of the work not only encouraged the importation of further works by Gilbert and Sullivan but also persuaded Americans to try their hands at pieces in the same vein. At first such efforts made little headway. Max Maretzek, whose *Sleepy Hollow, or The Headless Horseman* achieved little when produced in New York in 1879, remarked ruefully (if immodestly) in his memoirs that if it and other comic operas "had been first brought out in Paris or London, they would have become popular there, and would have been imported to this country with a flourish of trumpets." Virtually the only American comic opera of the 1880s to achieve a long and profitable run was Willard Spenser's *The Little Tycoon* (1886); it included a pleasant though unremarkable waltz-song, "Love comes like a summer sigh," that achieved national popularity.

1. Sheet-music cover of the march-song "The Mulligan Guard" (lyrics by Edward Harrigan, music by David Braham), first performed by Harrigan and Tony Hart in a variety sketch in 1873 and published that year in New York by William A. Pond

The first American comic opera to achieve success not only in the USA but also in Europe was Reginald De Koven's *Robin Hood* (1891), which was followed by further significant successes, including his *Rob Roy* (1894) and *The Highwayman* (1897), John Philip Sousa's *El capitan* (1896) and *The Charlatan* (1898), and Herbert's *The Wizard of the Nile* (1895), *The Serenade* (1897), and *The Fortune Teller* (1898). Elsewhere undercurrents were gaining strength that led in due course to a more truly American style of musical theater. The extravaganza reached its zenith in Percy Gaunt's *A Trip to Chinatown*, a topical satire set in San Francisco, which toured the USA for a full year before reaching New York in 1891 for a run of 657 performances. And at such establishments as Tony Pastor's Music Hall the public were able to see first-rate and respectable vaudeville entertainment presented by such performers as Joe Weber and Lew Fields and the Four Cohans.

3. EARLY MUSICAL COMEDIES. Although late 19th-century works can conveniently be classified in such categories as "extravaganza," "burlesque," and "comic opera," there was certainly no consistency of classification at the time. Thus *Evangeline* was variously described as a "burlesque," an "extravaganza," an "opéra bouffe," and also as a "musical comedy," to indicate a work that was literally a comedy with music. The term "musical comedy" was used in this sense on both sides of the Atlantic; the London impresario George Edwardes applied it in the early 1890s to an experimental style of musical show, which utilized much of the basic structure of comic opera and burlesque but rejected their

old-fashioned humor and plots in favor of contemporary social relevance, and added the attraction of a chorus line of beautiful girls. When such works, including Sidney Jones's *A Gaiety Girl* (1893), proved a great success, the description "musical comedy" came to mean something more specific, as did the variant "musical play," which Edwardes attached to works with a stronger, more romantic story and fewer of the characteristics of the variety show. Chief among the early British musical plays was Jones's *The Geisha* (1896) which, like *A Gaiety Girl*, achieved great success in the USA; it gave rise to a number of native imitations, including Gustave Kerker's *The Belle of New York* (1897), which though only modestly successful in New York was welcomed in London and throughout the British Empire, and also (in translation) in Berlin, Vienna, Paris, and Brussels.

During the first years of the 20th century British importations continued to flourish in the USA alongside similar works by composers such as Herbert (*Mlle. Modiste*, 1905; *The Red Mill*, 1906), Gustav Luders (*The Prince of Pilsen*, 1903), and Ludwig Englander (*The Rich Mr. Hoggenheimer*, 1906). Yet whether styled "musical comedy" or "musical play" (rather than "comic opera" or "opéra bouffe"), all these were still essentially part of the European operetta tradition. At the same time, however, the successors to *The Black Crook*, *Evangeline*, and *A Trip to Chinatown* were emerging in extravaganzas such as *Fiddle-dee-dee* (1900), *Hoity-toity* (1901), *Twirly-whirly* (1902), and *Whoop-dee-doo* (1903) at the Weber and Fields Music Hall. Elsewhere the Four Cohans were extending their vaudeville sketches, culminating in what has come to be recognized as the first essentially American musical comedy, George M. Cohan's *Little Johnny Jones* (1904). By contrast with the romanticized subjects, idealized characters, and extended musical writing of European works, this was a show with patriotic American characters and everyday sentiment, its story line linking down-to-earth dances and songs such as "Yankee Doodle Boy" (fig.2) and "Give my regards to Broadway."

Cohan continued with works in a similar vein, notably *Forty-five Minutes from Broadway* (1906, including "Mary's a grand old name") and *George Washington, Jr.* (1906, with "You're a grand old flag"). However, they had limited success in comparison with a new generation of Viennese operettas, such as Franz Lehár's *Die lustige Witwe*, which had supplanted British musical plays and musical comedies in the American public's favor. Yet in this area too steps were being taken towards a native school of musical comedy through the songs by American composers, notably Jerome Kern, that were interpolated increasingly often in European works when they were performed in the USA. Kern enjoyed his first real success with "How'd you like to spoon with me?" (1905) in Ivan Caryll's *The Earl and the Girl*, and produced one of the first great standard songs of the American musical theater, "They didn't believe me" (1914), for another British import, Paul Rubens and Sidney Jones's *The Girl from Utah*. By that time, moreover, Kern was also writing complete musical comedy scores.

4. 1915–30. Beginning in 1915, with the librettist Guy Bolton (and later P. G. Wodehouse), Kern composed a series of intimate shows, using functionally simple sets and costumes and an 11-piece orchestra, for the 299-seat Princess Theatre in New York. They were light situation comedies involving everyday characters, and the simple, catchy songs, with witty lyrics and clever rhymes, contrasted with the high-flown concerted writing of many European works; *Very Good, Eddie* (1915) and *Oh Boy!* (1917) in particular were outstanding. These shows finally established, not only in the USA but also across the Atlantic, a taste for American musical comedy that was furthered by other works such as Louis A. Hirsch's *Going Up!* (1917), which was set partly on an airplane, and Harry Tierney's *Irene* (1919).

Kern's subsequent works, such as *Sally* (1920), with such elegantly spun melodies as "Look for the silver lining," helped to confirm the appeal of the American musical comedy. A simple variant of the Cinderella story written for the glamorous singer and dancer Marilyn Miller, *Sally* helped to set the trend for the escapist plots that audiences sought during the 1920s. Indeed, although songwriting in musical comedy continued to become more sophisticated, the plot was often sacrificed in the interest of providing a varied bill of performers. Kern's *Sunny* (1925), for example, has songs of the quality of "Who?" and "D'ye love me?"; but because Marilyn Miller, various song-and-dance comedians, and a band whose contract required them to appear on stage all had to be accommodated, the plot is a far-fetched story about a circus bareback rider who is forced into marriage with a fellow stowaway on a transatlantic liner.

Similarly inconsequential and unlikely "boy-meets-girl" stories provided the setting for other works in which teams of songwriters made the transition from revue to musical comedy. Prominent among these songwriters were George and Ira Gershwin; their *Lady, be Good!* (1924, including "Fascinating Rhythm"), with Fred and Adele Astaire in the leading roles, helped to make tap dancing a popular feature of musical comedies of the 1920s. The Gershwins had further successes with *Tip Toes* (1925), *Oh, Kay!* (1926), and *Funny Face* (1927). Another composer who made a significant contribution to popular song in the 1920s was Vincent Youmans; his *No, No, Nanette* (1924) and *Hit the Deck* (1927) contained such songs as "Tea for Two," "I want to be happy," "Sometimes I'm happy," and "Hallelujah!," which were notable for their simple economy of phrasing and insistent

2. Sheet-music cover of George M. Cohan's song "Yankee Doodle Boy" from his "Little Johnny Jones" (1904), published in New York by F. A. Mills

rhythms. The lyricists B. G. DeSylva and Lew Brown and the composer Ray Henderson made baseball the subject of their *Good News!* (1927), which included the song "The best things in life are free." From Richard Rodgers and Lorenz Hart, meanwhile, came the first of a series of works that presaged a more innovative approach to musical comedy subjects: *Dearest Enemy* (1925), which had a historical setting, and *Peggy-Ann* (1926), which concerned itself with dream psychology. Neither show, however, endeared itself to the public as much as their less pretentious *The Girl Friend* (1926), with its bright, up-to-date spirit, and sophisticated fusion of lyrics and music in such songs as "The Blue Room," which has an ingenious internal rhyme scheme.

It was during the 1920s that the American musical theater achieved its most brilliant flowering on a range of fronts. Black musicals, for instance, had enjoyed some temporary success in the early years of the century. In 1921 *Shuffle Along*, with songs by Eubie Blake and Noble Sissle which included the hit "I'm just wild about Harry," set a new fashion for black shows that finally established black artists on Broadway and brought about an enduring taste for jazz rhythms in dance music. Yet exactly contemporary with these developments, romantic musical plays that harked back to Ruritanian, romanticized European operetta were also enjoying enormous success; the American musical theater could now offer not only its own native type of musical but also works in other national styles that were more distinguished than the original models. Rudolf Friml's *Rose-Marie* (composed with Herbert Stothart, 1924) was a considerable success in Europe; scarcely less successful in the English-speaking world were Friml's *The Vagabond King* (1925), and Sigmund Romberg's *The Student Prince* (1924), *The Desert Song* (1926), and *The New Moon* (1928).

Show Boat (1927), with book and lyrics by Oscar Hammerstein II and music by Kern, ingeniously combined elements from all these traditions, and raised the musical to a new height of attainment. Unlike the usual musical comedy, in which an inconsequential story was written around songs, performers, and production ideas, *Show Boat* boasted a cohesive story into which were woven songs that were not only remarkable in themselves ("Ol' man river," "Make-believe," "Can't help lovin' dat man," and "Why do I love you?") but were unusually well integrated into the action in that they created mood, revealed character, and advanced the plot. The work firmly pointed the way to further advances in the 1930s and ultimately to the American musical play of the 1940s.

5. THE 1930S. With the demise of the spectacular revue, the 1930s saw the Broadway musical consolidate its position as the predominant stage musical form, while spreading its influence to, and competing with, the emerging Hollywood film musical. The background of economic depression against which the decade opened was captured in such songs as Rodgers and Hart's "Ten Cents a Dance" (in *Simple Simon*, 1930), the lament of a girl condemned to earn her living as a hostess in a cheap ballroom; it also provided the setting for the story of police and political corruption in Irving Berlin's *Face the Music* (1932), though the lighthearted nature of this work epitomized the role of musical comedy as an antidote to the prevailing mood.

Prominent among the writers to emerge at this time was Cole Porter, who had already given Broadway audiences a taste for his sophisticated, witty, sometimes risqué style of songwriting in such numbers as "Let's do it" (in *Paris*, 1928) and "Love for Sale" (in *The New Yorkers*, 1930). He continued the song-and-dance tradition of the 1920s with *Gay Divorce* (1932), in which Fred Astaire introduced "Night and Day," *Anything Goes* (1934), with the songs "I get a kick out of you" and "You're the top," and *Jubilee* (1935), in which his talent is seen at its most individual in "Begin the Beguine." Another composer previously prominent in revue who now turned his attention to musical comedy was Arthur Schwartz; with his regular lyricist, Howard Dietz, he wrote *Revenge with Music* (1934), an adaptation of Pedro de Alarcón's *El sombrero de tres picos*.

In general the 1930s saw the expansion of the genre as it attracted new writers who created tighter plots and sought more ambitious subjects. Kern and Hammerstein's *The Cat and the Fiddle* (1931) and *Music in the Air* (1932) both had European subjects. Like *Show Boat*, the former used the "show within a show" device, whereby a big production number could be made integral to the story by being performed in a show that formed part of the plot. The Gershwins' *Girl Crazy* (1930) created two new stars – Ethel Merman, who sang "I got rhythm," and Ginger Rogers, who sang "Embraceable you" – and included the distinguished jazz musicians Benny Goodman, Glenn Miller, Red Nichols, Gene Krupa, Jack Teagarden, and Jimmy Dorsey in its pit orchestra. The Gershwins also produced works with a more serious message, such as *Strike up the Band* (1930), which took a satirical look at war and big business, and *Of Thee I Sing* (1931), which lampooned the American presidential system and became the first musical to win a Pulitzer Prize for drama. Their final Broadway collaboration, *Porgy and Bess* (1935), succeeded in raising the musical to the status of opera in a work that combined black folk music, jazz, and popular song with powerful lyrical writing and big choral scenes in an integrated structure.

Other important songwriters of the decade included Harold Arlen, whose *Hooray for What?* (1938) was a warning about the dangers of the armaments race, presented within the old musical comedy format, and Vernon Duke, whose black folk musical *Cabin in the Sky* (1940) was commercially unsuccessful but critically respected. Another composer with origins in European serious music was Kurt Weill. He began his American career with *Johnny Johnson* (1936), a bitter yet amusing antiwar piece devoid of the female glamor that would have been an essential component of any musical a few years earlier; *Knickerbocker Holiday* (1938) drew analogies with fascist oppression and contained Weill's most celebrated American number, "September Song," while *Lady in the Dark* (1941) incorporated elements of psychoanalysis and dream sequences. Weill drew extensively on his experience of European musical theater to further the ideal of the integration of book and music. At a time when the use of specialist arrangers and orchestrators was standard practice, he was exceptional in completing his own scores.

Weill's concept of musical theater, however, was more remarkable for its anticipation of trends in the 1960s than for its immediate influence. A greater impact was made in the 1930s by the widening range of subjects and the development of song-and-dance forms in the works of Rodgers and Hart. *On your Toes* (1936) included the hit song "There's a small hotel" and a quasi-jazz ballet sequence "Slaughter on Tenth Avenue" choreographed by George Balanchine; *I'd Rather be Right* (1937) was a political satire, in which George M. Cohan portrayed an American president who bore a striking resemblance to Franklin D. Roosevelt; *I Married an Angel* (1938) was a satirical fantasy; *The Boys from Syracuse* (1938), a racy musical comedy adaptation of Shakespeare's *The Comedy of Errors*, contained the major hits "Falling in love with love" and "This can't be love"; and *Pal Joey* (1940) was notable not only for songs such as "Bewitched, bothered and bewildered" but for its cast of thoroughly disreputable characters, and its story of blackmail, illicit love affairs, and various types of skulduggery.

6. THE POSTWAR PERIOD. After his partnership with Hart ended in 1943 Rodgers collaborated with Oscar Hammerstein II on a series of works that consolidated the developments of the 1930s and marked a new era for the musical. *Oklahoma!* (1943; fig.3) was based on a proven play (Lynn Riggs's *Green Grow the Lilacs*) and had a well-constructed plot with credible characters and dialogue. Such musical comedy conventions as the female chorus line and the opening chorus were set aside in the interests of the play's development, the melodies were written to fit the lyrics rather than the reverse, and there were extended musical scenes and ballets. *Oklahoma!* confirmed the vogue for a more logically constructed musical play and initiated a period of great national and international acclaim for the musical, helped by soundtrack recordings by original casts and film versions. Increasing importance was ascribed to book authors, such as Hammerstein, Betty Comden and Adolph Green, Howard Lindsay and Russell Crouse, Abe Burrows, and Joseph, Herbert, and Dorothy Fields; directors, such as George Abbott and Joshua Logan; choreographers, such as Agnes De Mille, George Balanchine, and Jerome Robbins; and orchestrators, such as Robert Russell Bennett.

Rodgers and Hammerstein continued their success with *Carousel* (1945), an adaptation of Ferenc Molnár's Hungarian classic *Liliom* that moves the setting to a 19th-century New England fishing village and further departs from musical comedy convention in that the leading man is killed; *Allegro* (1947), which has a chorus in the style of ancient Greek drama; *South Pacific* (1949); *The King and I* (1951); *Flower Drum Song* (1958); and *The Sound of Music* (1959). Rodgers and Hammerstein also acted as producers for Berlin's *Annie Get your Gun* (1946), which had an unusually large number of hit songs, including "Anything you can do," "Doin' what comes naturally," and "There's no business like show business." Arlen produced *Bloomer Girl* (1944), a Civil War musical introducing themes of women's and civil rights; Cole Porter had his greatest stage success with *Kiss me, Kate* (1948), which, based on Shakespeare's *The Taming of the Shrew*, developed the idea of the play within a play and had lyrics that appropriated some of Shakespeare's lines.

3. *St. James Theater, Broadway, where the fifth anniversary of the first production of "Oklahoma!" by Richard Rodgers and Oscar Hammerstein II was celebrated in 1948*

Whereas most of the musicals of the interwar years had contemporary American settings, the settings of postwar musicals ranged far wider in both period and location. *The King and I* was set in 19th-century Siam and *The Sound of Music* in prewar Austria. Porter's *Can-can* (1953) was set in Paris during the 1890s, Harold Rome's *Fanny* (1954) in modern Marseilles, and Berlin's *Call me Madam* (1950) in an imaginary central European state. Of two fantasy musicals produced in 1947, *Finian's Rainbow*, with a score by Burton Lane, concerned Irishmen in a southern American state, and *Brigadoon*, with lyrics by Alan Jay Lerner and music by Frederick Loewe, American tourists in Scotland.

In their treatment of these varied subjects composers were increasingly concerned not simply with writing appealing songs but also with capturing the flavor of the setting and the viewpoints of the characters. In *The King and I* the consciously "nice," ladylike vocal style and phrasing of the English governess ("Whenever I feel afraid") contrasts with the pentatonic scale and clipped rhythms of the songs for the oriental characters; the orchestration contains oriental effects (just as that of *Brigadoon* incorporates bagpipe effects). In Lerner and Loewe's *My Fair Lady* (1956), based on George Bernard Shaw's *Pygmalion* and set in Edwardian London, the music captures the stately dignity of the English aristocracy ("The Ascot Gavotte") and also the robustness of the English music hall ("I'm getting married in the morning"). *My Fair Lady* became the most successful musical of the 1950s, highlighting the changes in the genre since the 1930s; whereas the European-born composers Vernon Duke and Kurt Weill had consciously sought to assimilate American life and musical styles in their works, Loewe produced a European setting and a score that was consciously European in style.

The American song-and-dance musical comedy tradition was kept up to date, most notably by Jule Styne in works involving star performers and big, brassy production numbers: *High Button Shoes* (1947) with Phil Silvers, *Gentlemen Prefer Blondes* (1949) with Carol Channing singing "Diamonds are a girl's best friend," and *Bells are Ringing* (1956) with Judy Holliday singing "Just in time." These were followed by two musical biographies: *Gypsy* (1959), based on the life of Gypsy Rose Lee, with Ethel Merman and the songs "Let me entertain you" and "Everything's coming up roses," and *Funny Girl* (1964), the story of Fanny Brice, with Barbra Streisand singing "People." Other works on thoroughly American subjects were *The Pajama Game* (1954), concerning American trade unionism, and *Damn Yankees* (1955), about a baseball championship, both works from the short-lived partnership of Richard Adler and Jerry Ross. Meredith Willson's *The Music Man* (1957) was another show that owed much of its success to a big production number ("76 Trombones").

Weill's ambitious and innovative attempts to elevate the

Broadway musical by using a more highly developed musical language culminated in the Broadway opera *Street Scene* (1947) and the tragic *Lost in the Stars* (1949), but his contribution to the American musical remained an individual one. The most significant contributions in terms of their immediate influence were the works of Frank Loesser and Leonard Bernstein, which offered sharp contrasts to the increasingly sentimental style of Rodgers and Hammerstein. Loesser's eclectic use of melodies and musical sequences to echo the vernacular phraseology of his lyrics produced varied and compelling works: the period musical comedy *Where's Charley?* (1948, after Brandon Thomas's *Charley's Aunt*), the gangster fable *Guys and Dolls* (1950, based on characters from Damon Runyon), the quasi-operatic *The Most Happy Fella* (1956), and the satire *How to Succeed in Business without Really Trying* (1961). Bernstein's highly developed and dynamic musical language combined classical and jazz elements with equally dynamic books, lyrics, choreography, and direction in *On the Town* (1944), *Wonderful Town* (1953), *Candide* (1956, after Voltaire), and *West Side Story* (1957); the last brilliantly transformed Shakespeare's *Romeo and Juliet* into a story of gang warfare on the upper West Side of New York City, presented through a remarkable fusion of dancing, singing, and acting (fig.4).

7. THE MODERN MUSICAL. The 1960s introduced a new generation of contributors to the musical, working in a very different artistic and financial environment. Earlier musical shows had made their profits largely from provincial tours, but the decline of regional theaters and the ever increasing costs of production and touring made a long Broadway run a matter of crucial importance. With the advent of rock music, too, the musical was losing its traditional links with popular music, so that a star name and a big production number that could be taken up outside the theater by prominent vocalists were important in attracting the public to a show. Theatrical conventions and stage techniques had also changed. For instance, the old musical comedy convention of a subplot for a secondary couple who performed in front of a backcloth while the main set was being changed was no longer valid; thus when *Annie Get your Gun* was revived in 1966 the secondary couple and their songs were omitted in the interests of strengthening the main story.

An alternative solution to the financial problems was to produce works less expensively in "off-Broadway" theaters; Harvey Schmidt's *The Fantasticks* (1960) ran throughout the 1960s and 1970s and was still playing in 1985 at the 149-seat Sullivan Street Playhouse in Greenwich Village. The main activity, however, continued to be on Broadway itself. Among composers who came to the fore was Charles Strouse, who, working mostly with the lyricist Lee Adams, produced *Bye Bye Birdie* (1960), a parody of the rock-and-roll cult with the songs "A lot of livin' to do" and "Put on a happy face," *Applause* (1970), and *Annie* (1977), with a child lead based on a comic-strip character. Jerry Herman composed a number of successful song-and-dance musical comedies, including *Milk and Honey* (1961), *Hello, Dolly!* (1964), *Mame* (1966), and *Mack and Mabel* (1974). Cy Coleman wrote the brash, lively *Wildcat* (1960, with the song "Hey, look me over"), *Little Me* (1962, with "Real Live Girl"), *Sweet Charity* (1966, with "Big Spender" and "If my friends could see me now"), which highlighted the talents of the dancer and singer Gwen Verdon and the choreographer and director Bob Fosse, *I Love my Wife* (1977), and *Barnum* (1980).

More thought-provoking in nature were two shows by the composer John Kander and the lyricist Fred Ebb: *Cabaret* (1966), with a skillful score evoking Berlin between the wars, and *Chicago* (1975), concerning American gang warfare in the 1920s. Mitch Leigh's *Man of La Mancha* (1965), built around the characters of Don Quixote and Sancho Panza, was a considerable international

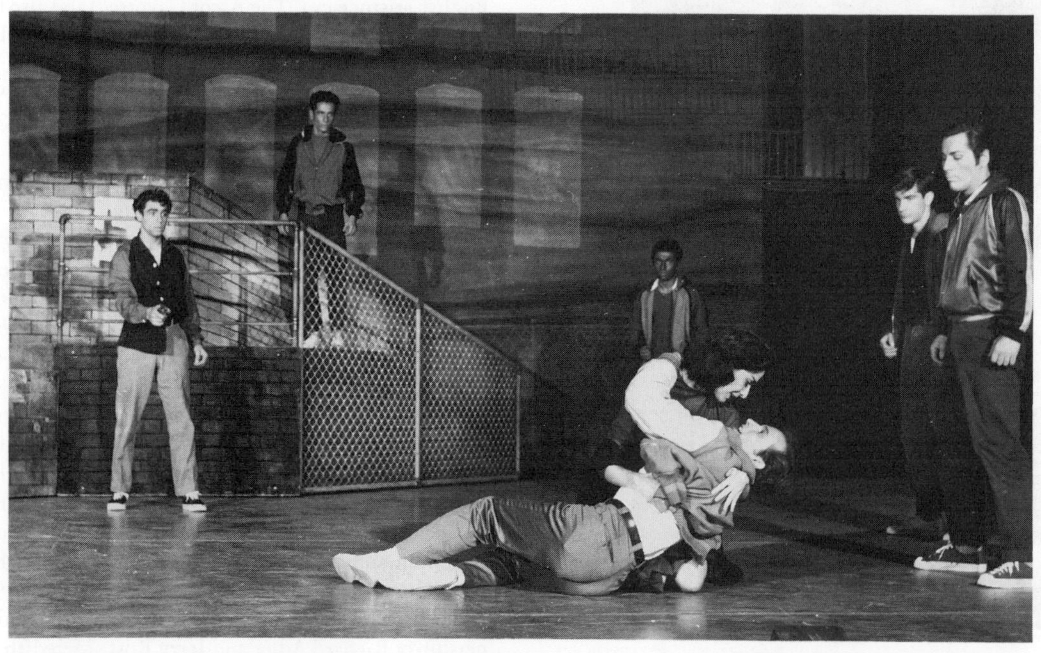

4. Carol Lawrence as Maria and Larry Kert as Tony (foreground) in the final scene of "West Side Story" in the first production (1957) at the Winter Garden, Broadway

success. But the most successful musical of the 1960s was the work of the composer Jerry Bock and the lyricist Sheldon Harnick, who, after the political *Fiorello!* (1959) and the gently intimate *She Loves Me* (1963), produced the long-running *Fiddler on the Roof* (1964); concerned with the persecution of Jews in czarist Russia and incorporating elements of Yiddish folklore, it epitomizes a trend towards the conceptualized musical in which stories and characters tend to be generated by attitudes and perceptions rather than the reverse.

A later example of the conceptualized musical is Marvin Hamlisch's *A Chorus Line* (1975), a vigorous exposé of the selection process among aspiring performers for a Broadway musical comedy. It was a product of Joseph Papp's experimental Public Theater, which had earlier been responsible for the rock musical *Hair* (1967). *Hair* dealt with hippies and dropouts, its first act ended with the cast totally nude, and its score, by Galt MacDermot, used heavily amplified electronic sounds in an effort to incorporate developments in popular music in the musical. Further experiments with rock included *Grease* (1972), with music and lyrics by Jim Jacobs and Warren Casey, but the inability of this style of music to express a wide range of moods has meant that its use has been limited. Efforts have been made to integrate rock numbers in more conventional works, notably in *Jesus Christ Superstar* (1971) by the English composer Andrew Lloyd Webber; though commercially successful, the result was an uneasy juxtaposition of styles. It nonetheless showed how a non-American could come to terms with the developments in the American musical, and Lloyd Webber confirmed this point with *Evita* (1978), about the Argentinian national heroine Eva Perón, and *Cats* (1981; after T. S. Eliot), a superbly original fusion of singing, dancing, costumes, and staging. These works also emphasize the continuing importance of outstanding hit numbers, for example, "Don't cry for me, Argentina" in *Evita*, "Memory" in *Cats*.

The acknowledged outstanding writer of the 1960s and 1970s, Stephen Sondheim, made his name as a lyricist for Bernstein (*West Side Story*), Styne (*Gypsy*), and Rodgers (*Do I Hear a Waltz?*, 1965), and revealed his ability as both lyricist and composer in *A Funny Thing Happened on the Way to the Forum* (1961) and *Anyone can Whistle* (1964). His is a highly intellectual style, marked by lyrics that are brilliantly witty but colored with cynicism, and music that conveys the fleeting mood of the action; set numbers are of comparatively little importance. *Company* (1970) takes marriage as its theme; *Follies* (1971) is about former showgirls reflecting on their lives; *A Little Night Music* (1972) is based on a screenplay by Ingmar Bergman and is composed entirely in waltz time or derivatives thereof; *Pacific Overtures* (1976) relates the westernization of Japan to the commercialized present; *Sweeney Todd* (1979) is a gruesome tale of throat-cutting; and *Merrily we Roll Along* (1980) deals with the experiences of college graduates in a novel form in which the action unfolds in reverse. All these works were directed by Harold Prince, whose bold ideas and methods of stagecraft have made him one of the most creative and influential forces in the modern musical.

Yet for all the conceptual brilliance of Sondheim's works, they have not consistently achieved commercial success. Complex structures, bloodthirstiness, and a persistently cynical attitude to conventional sexuality (notably in *Company*) are not the safe material that attracts audiences seeking lighthearted entertainment. Nor is Sondheim's avoidance of the type of song likely to become an independent hit unconnected with his mixed success: it is scarcely a coincidence that his greatest commercial triumph, *A Little Night Music*, is the only one of his works to contain a widely sung and recognized hit number ("Send in the clowns"). Theatergoers, then, have continued to welcome works in more glamorous, less demanding musical comedy style, such as Henry Krieger's *Dreamgirls* (1981) and Jerry Herman's *La cage aux folles* (1983). Moreover, producers have been successful in reviving earlier shows, whether in authentic recreations (*Oklahoma!*, 1979; *On your Toes*, 1983) or in revisions incorporating fresh compilations of songs (*Very Good, Eddie*, 1975), modernized staging and scoring (*No, No, Nanette*, 1971), or extensive reconstruction (*Irene*, 1973). In other cases material has been reworked in different forms, as in the stage version (1980) of Harry Warren's film musical *42nd Street* (1933) and the compilation of Gershwin's songs *My One and Only* (1983).

Like opera and European operetta before it, the American stage musical has reached a point at which artistic development no longer walks comfortably hand in hand with popular taste. But the genre continues to exercise a magnetic attraction for producers, writers, investors, performers, and audiences alike, notwithstanding the rival attractions of radio, film, television, and video.

See also DANCE, §§II, 3, III, 3.

BIBLIOGRAPHY

C. M. Smith: *Musical Comedy in America* (New York, 1950, rev. 2/1981 with G. Litton)
J. Burton: *The Blue Book of Broadway Musicals* (New York, 1952, rev. 2/1969)
J. Mattfeld: *Variety Music Cavalcade* (Englewood Cliffs, NJ, 1952, rev. 3/1971)
D. Ewen: *Complete Book of the American Musical Theater* (New York, 1958, rev. 3/1970 as *New Complete Book of the American Musical Theater*)
D. C. Blum: *A Pictorial History of the American Theatre, 1860–1960* (Philadelphia, 1960)
S. Green: *The World of Musical Comedy* (New York, 1960, rev. 4/1980)
D. Ewen: *The Story of America's Musical Theater* (Philadelphia, 1961, rev. 2/1968)
R. Lewine and A. Simon: *Encyclopedia of Theatre Music* (New York, 1961)
A. Churchill: *The Great White Way* (New York, 1962)
H. H. Taubman: *The Making of the American Theatre* (New York, 1965, rev. 2/1967)
L. Engel: *The American Musical Theater: a Consideration* (New York, 1967, rev. 2/1975)
D. Ewen: *Composers for the American Musical Theatre* (New York, 1968)
A. Laufe: *Broadway's Greatest Musicals* (New York, 1969, rev. 2/1973)
B. Atkinson: *Broadway* (New York, 1970)
T. Vallance: *The American Musical* (New York, 1970)
S. Green: *Ring Bells! Sing Songs! Broadway Musicals from the 1930s* (New York, 1971)
L. Engel: *Words with Music* (New York, 1972/R1981 as *Words with Music: the Broadway Musical Libretto*)
A. Wilder: *American Popular Song: the Great Innovators, 1900–1950* (New York, 1972)
R. Lewine and A. Simon: *Songs of the American Theater* (New York, 1973)
M. Wilk: *They're Playing our Song: from Jerome Kern to Stephen Sondheim* (New York, 1973)
L. Engel: *Their Words are Music* (New York, 1975)
S. Green: *Encyclopaedia of the Musical* (New York, 1976)
E. Mordden: *Better Foot Forward: the History of American Musical Theater* (New York, 1976)
D. Ewen: *All the Years of American Popular Music* (Englewood Cliffs, NJ, 1977)
A. Jackson: *The Book of Musicals from Show Boat to A Chorus Line* (London, 1977, rev. 2/1979)
G. Bordman: *The American Musical Theatre: a Chronicle* (New York, 1978)
M. Gottfried: *Broadway Musicals* (New York, 1979)
G. W. Hodgkins: *The Broadway Musical: a Complete LP Discography* (New York, 1980)
G. Bordman: *American Operetta from H.M.S. Pinafore to Sweeney Todd* (New York, 1981)
D. L. Root: *American Popular Stage Music, 1860–1880* (Ann Arbor, MI, 1981)
G. Bordman: *American Musical Comedy* (New York, 1982)

E. Mordden: *Broadway Babies: the People who Made the American Musical* (New York, 1983)
K. Bloom: *American Song: the Complete Musical Theatre Companion* (New York, 1985)
R. A. Simas: *The Musicals No One Came to See: Musical-comedy Casualties on Broadway, Off-Broadway, and in Out-of-town Try-out* (New York, 1985)

ANDREW LAMB

Musical Brownies. Western swing string band, formed by MILTON BROWN after 1932.

Musical comedy. A form of popular musical theater in which song-and-dance numbers are strung together within an often insubstantial plot; *see* MUSICAL.

Musical film. A film that includes musical numbers (songs, ensembles, dances) that are usually integrated (though not always closely) with the plot. A musical film is most commonly a film version of a musical comedy or MUSICAL originally written for the theater, or a work of the same type written for the screen (often by songwriters who established their reputations in the theater); this genre is sometimes called the "film musical," and although it reflects the stage history of the musical it has evolved its own distinctive settings and subjects, such as the rock-and-roll extravaganza and the backstage view of theater life. "Musical film" is also used of any film with occasional songs or other musical numbers. The distinction between such a film and a musical is sometimes difficult to draw: many films of the interwar period had two or three songs as a matter of course and others that were not advertised as musicals might contain as much music as films that were. Westerns, mysteries, and cartoons, for example, often include musical numbers but are not film musicals, and the full-length animated films made in the 1940s and 1950s by Walt Disney, though cast in the same format as the film musical, are not usually referred to as such. Since a generic definition is difficult to establish, the distinction between a film musical and a film with music may perhaps be drawn according to whether the actors are chiefly known for their musical talent. (The same confusion does not arise between the musical film – of either sort – and FILM MUSIC, which is normally understood to be music written to accompany or "underscore" film images.)

1. Introduction. 2. To the early 1930s. 3. 1933–40. 4. 1940–60. 5. After 1960.

1. INTRODUCTION. The musical film enjoyed an international vogue in the 1930s and early 1940s. Its development coincided with the Depression, a time at which film makers believed that opulent escapism was wanted by audiences; in fact the early musical films, no matter how spectacular, were stilted and hampered by cumbersome recording techniques and were very soon ignored by audiences; only the intimate, sophisticated, European "boudoir" operettas of the early 1930s had a lasting quality and style. *42nd Street*, made by Warner Bros. in 1933, was a landmark in the history of musical films: an assured, coherent, swift-moving comic drama, with lavish revue numbers. Once this assurance in musical films was attained, Hollywood went on to prove it could make a musical film on any subject incomparably and established the American film industry as the world leader in one of the most popular film genres. After World War II only American studios continued to make outstanding musicals, reaching a creative, if at times pretentious, zenith in the decade from 1945. Hollywood enjoyed great advantages over other centers of film making: it had a constant supply of writing and performing talent from Broadway (and an intense desire to rival or better Broadway productions in popularity and creative flair), and the investment capital required to make musical films that were more extravagant and lavish than anything that could be mounted in the theater.

2. TO THE EARLY 1930S. Short "musical" films were first made around the turn of the century, though since the synchronization of film images with sound had not yet been perfected they were silent films that had to be projected with phonograph recordings to supply the music. Silent versions of stage musical comedies and operettas were also made and were accompanied in the cinema by an orchestra often playing a score adapted from the original. Among the most notable of these were versions of Franz Lehár's *Die lustige Witwe*, directed by Erich von Stroheim as *The Merry Widow* (1925), and Sigmund Romberg's *The Student Prince*, directed by Ernst Lubitsch as *The Student Prince in Old Heidelberg* (1927); both were made by MGM. In 1927 Warner Bros. astonished audiences with *The Jazz Singer*, the first feature-length film with talking and singing sequences, in which Al Jolson played the leading role; besides its importance as a landmark in film technology, it demonstrated the appeal of the brash Broadway style of such performers and cemented the already existing relationship between Broadway and Hollywood.

During 1929 the Hollywood studios produced crude prototypes of every kind of musical that was to appear in the next decade. MGM, which became arguably the greatest maker of musical films, devised the genre of the backstage revue for *The Broadway Melody*; this was also the first sound film with an original score – the songs were by Arthur Freed (a lyricist who became the most creative producer of musicals) and Nacio Herb Brown – and it won the first Academy Award for the best picture of the year given to a "talkie." Operettas proved as popular as revues: Universal's first effort was a partial conversion of a silent film of Kern's *Show Boat*; Warner Bros. filmed Romberg's *The Desert Song*; RKO transferred Tierney's *Rio Rita* to the screen with Technicolor sequences; and 20th Century-Fox made the first sound film of a Viennese operetta, *Married in Hollywood*, with a score by Oscar Straus. Paramount eclipsed all its rivals by engaging Lubitsch to direct an original film operetta, Victor Schertzinger's *The Love Parade* (starring Maurice Chevalier and Jeanette MacDonald), and also produced the Marx Brothers' first film, a version of their Broadway hit *The Cocoanuts* (with songs by Berlin).

Noted Broadway songwriters were commissioned to write in California: Romberg and Oscar Hammerstein II (*Viennese Nights*, 1930), B. G. DeSylva, Lew Brown, and Ray Henderson (the "science fiction" musical *Just Imagine*, 1930), George and Ira Gershwin (*Delicious*, 1931), and Richard Rodgers and Lorenz Hart (*Hallelujah, I'm a Bum*, 1933). Studios experimented with melodramatic musicals such as *Applause* (1929; directed by Rouben Mamoulian, songs by various writers), the black musical pageant *Hallelujah* (1929; King Vidor, Berlin), *King of Jazz* (1930), stylishly staged in color by the Broadway revue director John Murray Anderson and featuring the big-band jazz of Paul Whiteman, and the first important film dealing with the world of radio, *The Big Broadcast* (1932; various writers). Bing Crosby, one of the most popular of all cinema singers, appeared in *King of Jazz* and *The Big Broadcast*. There were also collegiate and juvenile-

1. Production number, choreographed by Busby Berkeley, from the film "Gold Diggers of 1933"

romantic musicals such as Henderson's *Sunny Side Up* (1929) and *Good News* (1930).

Developments in Europe were especially noteworthy in this period and proved influential on American films. René Clair cleverly used sound and song with enviable charm in *Sous les toits de Paris* (1930) and *Le million* (1931). Parallel advances were made in Germany, with Wilhelm Thiele's engaging *Die Drei von der Tankstelle* (1930) and Erik Charell's *Der Kongress tanzt* (1931), a period re-creation that sumptuously retold history with touches of operetta. Both films consolidated the partnership of Lilian Harvey and Willy Fritsch, Europe's most popular musical stars. Such was the popularity of these and other, similar films that the film industry in Berlin often made versions in German, French, and English simultaneously. In Europe musical pot-pourris constructed around the talents of opera singers such as Jan Kiepura and Richard Tauber were also very popular, and this type of film was adopted in Hollywood to show off stars such as Grace Moore, Lawrence Tibbett, and the young Deanna Durbin. Josef von Sternberg directed Marlene Dietrich in *Der blaue Engel* (1930), a serious drama about romantic infatuation that included potently decadent musical numbers by Friedrich Holländer; the film enjoyed international success and all three artists later worked in Hollywood. The European influence was most clearly seen in two outstanding film operettas of 1932, Mamoulian's *Love me Tonight* with a score by Rodgers and Hart, and Lubitsch's *One Hour with You*, which had music by Oscar Straus and Richard Whiting.

3. 1933–40. *42nd Street* (1933; music by Harry Warren), which dealt with the backstage life of the modern Broadway theater, triumphantly established the genre of the musical within a musical. More than any earlier musical film it took full advantage of the technical possibilities of the medium and, in sumptuous production numbers, exploited the type of mass choreography devised by Busby Berkeley. Warner Bros. went on to issue a succession of highly elaborate musicals with Berkeley as choreographer and director, some less effective as films than as pure spectacle, such as *Gold Diggers of 1933* (and subsequent years; fig.1), *Footlight Parade* (1933), *Dames* (1934), and *Fashions of 1934*. These provided a showcase for the songs of Al Dubin and Warren and provided stereotyped roles for James Cagney, Dick Powell, Joan Blondell, and Ruby Keeler, among others. Other studios were quick to imitate Berkeley's mannerisms, and in 1933 RKO inadvertently caused a sensation by teaming Fred Astaire and Ginger Rogers in *Flying Down to Rio*, an otherwise pallid musical with an uneven score by Vincent Youmans. Their dancing was the highlight of a series of frivolous, enchanting films that attracted some of the greatest Broadway songwriters: Berlin (*Top Hat*, 1935), Kern and Dorothy Fields (*Swing Time*, 1936), and the Gershwins (*Shall we Dance*, 1937). It is likely that Astaire introduced more musical-film standards than any other performer, and his distinctive voice and phrasing were as memorable as his dancing.

During the 1930s and 1940s film makers rarely treated the original scores of Broadway musicals with much fidelity, even when they were the work of such masters of the genre as Cole Porter, the Gershwins, or Rodgers and Hart. For example, *The Gay Divorcee* (1934), an adaptation of Porter's stage musical *Gay Divorce*, retained only one song from the original score – "Night and Day," sung by Astaire. The decision to omit parts of the original show in this way was fundamentally the producer's, though the film's stars, writers, and music staff (whose motives were not always disinterested) often influenced his opinions.

The romantic operetta, following a decline on Broadway in the early 1930s, was revived in Hollywood in 1935 with MGM's version of Victor Herbert's *Naughty Marietta*, starring Jeanette MacDonald and Nelson Eddy. The pair became an enormously popular institution and MGM set its arrangers to work to adapt the scores of several operettas, generally by excising large portions and replacing them with operatic arias, light classical favorites, and reworked popular songs from the public domain, in order to display the vocal prowess of the two stars. MacDonald, who had perfected a saucy comic style under Lubitsch in film operettas, was obliged to abandon it for more direct sentiment in the films she made with Eddy, which included Friml's *Rose-Marie* (1936), Romberg's *Maytime* (1937), Herbert's *Sweethearts* (1938), Romberg's *The New Moon* (1940), and Noël Coward's *Bitter Sweet* (1940), all based to some degree on stage originals. Few other film operettas were as popular as these, though Universal tried to rival MGM by producing two films with attractive American themes starring Irene Dunne: a remake of Kern's *Show Boat* (1936), directed by James Whale, and an original screen musical by Kern, *High, Wide and Handsome* (1937), directed by Mamoulian. Studios in Nazi Germany also tried to emulate MGM by manufacturing lighthearted and glossy operettas, but the creators of many of their earlier musical films were no longer permitted to work there, and many found employment in Hollywood.

4. 1940–60. The 1940s and 1950s saw the development of several important musical film genres, the first examples of which were released late in the 1930s. In 1937 Walt Disney created the first feature-length cartoon, *Snow White and the Seven Dwarfs*, an awesome achievement in animation with an enchanting score by Frank Churchill and Larry Morey; it was followed by *Pinocchio* (1940, with music by Leigh Harline), *Bambi* (1942, Churchill), *Alice in Wonderland* (1951, Sammy Fain), and *Peter Pan* (1953, Fain). All were carefully composed to contain at least one exceptionally catchy song, usually either comic or romantic, that was intended to become a hit: "Heigh-ho" from *Snow White*, "I'm late" from *Alice*, and "When you wish upon a star" (which won an Academy Award) from *Pinocchio* continue to be remembered independently of the films. Later Disney also mixed animated figures with actors in an attempt to make such songs more memorable; this formula was adopted for "Supercalifragilisticexpialidocious" by Richard and Robert Sherman, sung by Julie Andrews in *Mary Poppins* (1964). The fantasy musical *The Wizard of Oz*, an extravagant expansion of the story by L. Frank Baum, filmed in Technicolor, was released by MGM in 1939 (fig.2); it had a brilliant cast that included Judy Garland, Ray Bolger, Margaret Hamilton, Bert Lahr, and Frank Morgan, and memorable songs by Harold Arlen and E. Y. Harburg, among them "Somewhere over the rainbow." Several biographical musicals loosely based on the lives of famous composers and with scores fabricated from their works were issued in the late 1930s and 1940s, including *The Great Victor Herbert* (1939), *Words and Music* (Rodgers and Hart, 1948), *Rhapsody in Blue* (George Gershwin, 1945), *Night and Day* (Cole Porter, 1946), and at least five films with songs by Berlin, beginning with *Alexander's Ragtime Band* (1937). Similar "biographies," with no greater claim to authenticity, were made about classical composers, from *A Song to Remember* (Chopin, 1945) to *Song of Norway* (Grieg, 1970).

In the mainstream of musical films the 1940s saw three of the

2. *Judy Garland as Dorothy in the film "The Wizard of Oz" (1939), with Jack Haley as the Tin Man, Ray Bolger as the Scarecrow, and Bert Lahr as the Cowardly Lion*

principal companies initiate popular and lucrative series. In 1939 MGM released *Babes in Arms* (songs by Rodgers and Hart), the first of several films in which the juvenile team of Mickey Rooney and Judy Garland played a pair of kids who put on improbably professional amateur shows. Paramount's comedy musical *The Road to Singapore* (1940, music by James Monaco and Victor Schertzinger), with Bob Hope, Bing Crosby, and Dorothy Lamour, led to a phenomenally successful series set in places all over the world. And *Down Argentine Way* (1940, music by Warren) inspired several more lighthearted Latin American stories in which 20th Century-Fox took advantage of the success of the "Brazilian bombshell" Carmen Miranda. The entry of the USA into World War II sent Hollywood back into the American past in search of story lines that had a patriotic slant. *For me and my Gal* (1942, George W. Meyer) revolved around World War I, as did the jingoistic *Yankee Doodle Dandy* (also 1942), which was remarkable for a superb performance by James Cagney in admirable re-creations of scenes from George M. Cohan's stage musicals. The folksy, reassuring Americana of the Broadway musical *Oklahoma!* (1943) by Rodgers and Hammerstein was reflected in Vincente Minnelli's meticulous evocation of middle America in the early 1900s, *Meet me in St. Louis* (1944, songs by Hugh Martin and Ralph Blane), and in George Sidney's western saga *The Harvey Girls* (1946, songs by Warren and Mercer). Most of the other nostalgic re-creations, often made by 20th Century-Fox for Betty Grable, were not memorable.

The musicals Minnelli made for MGM after the war were some of the best to come out of Hollywood: *Yolanda and the Thief* (1945, with music by Warren), *The Pirate* (1948, Porter), *An American in Paris* (1951, Gershwin), *The Band Wagon* (1953, Arthur Schwartz), and *Gigi* (1958, Frederick Loewe); among the stars who appeared in these were Fred Astaire, Gene Kelly, Judy Garland, and Maurice Chevalier. Minnelli's training as a theater designer and the technical improvement of color photography gave his films a pictorial magnificence attained by few other directors, and his fluid handling of musical movement and dance was difficult to rival. The last two films are unquestionably his masterpieces: *The Band Wagon* gave new life to the backstage revue, chiefly owing to a witty screenplay by Betty Comden and Adolph Green, and *Gigi*, a luxurious portrayal of fin-de-siècle Paris based on the novella by Colette, was impeccably composed (the songs were by Lerner and Loewe) and costumed (by Cecil Beaton).

After a period in which big bands and their singers dominated musical films – *Second Chorus* (1940, Artie Shaw), *The Fleet's In* (1942, Jimmy Dorsey), *No Leave, No Love* (1946, Xavier Cugat and Guy Lombardo), *Beat the Band* (1947, Gene Krupa) – dance came to the fore once again. Several dancers became choreographers and directors, among them Gene Kelly, who collaborated on a number of films with Stanley Donen. Their major achievement, *Singin' in the Rain* (1952), a clever comedy about the beginning of sound films with pastiche songs by Arthur Freed (who also produced the film) and Nacio Herb Brown, captured the period flavor of the late 1920s but was choreographed by Kelly and Donen in modern style. Their *On the Town* (1949, Leonard Bernstein), is regarded as having set the trend for filming dances on location; it made effective use of the streets and scenes of New York for its exuberant, balletic dance numbers. It also pioneered the use of the so-called dream ballet in musical films (where it was often performed by professional dancers substituting for the actors playing the characters concerned); created on Broadway in the 1940s, the dream ballet found favor in Hollywood, though its extreme artificiality was sometimes jarring in the more realistic context of the film. Donen, who specialized in developing the dance element of Broadway musicals in the setting of film, is regarded as having set the trend for filming dances on location. He was most at ease with the muscular vigor of the period comedy *Seven Brides for Seven Brothers* (1954, Gene de Paul) and the vibrant working-class spirit (notably in the factory and picnic scenes) of *The Pajama Game* (1957, Richard Adler), the best of Doris Day's films. He was also enormously successful in conveying the glossy world of New York fashion in *Funny Face* (1957), by means of artfully rearranged songs of the 1920s by the Gershwins and the ageless grace of Fred Astaire. Another dancer who took up directing was Charles Walters, who worked especially well with Judy Garland in *Easter Parade* (1948, Berlin) and *Summer Stock* (1950, Warren); his *High Society* (1956) was a smooth retelling of George Cukor's *The Philadelphia Story*, with new songs by Cole Porter and a cast that included Bing Crosby, Frank Sinatra, and Louis Armstrong.

In the 1950s the nostalgia prevalent during the war still provided material for some studios, including 20th Century-Fox, while others depended on popular crooners such as Frank Sinatra to make minor films successful. The biographical musical remained popular and examples were made based on the careers of Sigmund Romberg (*Deep in my Heart*, 1954), Glenn Miller (*The Glenn Miller Story*, 1953), and Enrico Caruso (*The Great Caruso*, 1951), the last starring Mario Lanza. Whereas it had earlier been the case that Broadway musicals were often butchered in film versions (a fate that befell, among others, the attractive score by Bernstein for *On the Town*), the 1950s saw a more faithful treatment of stage originals, and in some instances not only the scores but even the casts were adopted almost unchanged by film directors. The most notable of the film musicals of the 1950s were those of works by Rodgers and Hammerstein, beginning with *Oklahoma!* (1955), and Mamoulian's *Silk Stockings* (1957), based on both the stage musical by Cole Porter and its source, Lubitsch's film *Ninotchka* (1939).

5. AFTER 1960. By the 1960s film versions of Broadway musicals had become tremendously profitable for the Hollywood studios; the films of Bernstein's *West Side Story* (1961), Loewe's *My Fair Lady* (1964), and Rodgers's *The Sound of Music* (1965) all won Academy awards for best picture. Other notably successful film musicals were those directed by Bob Fosse, whose slick, expansive Broadway dances lent vigor to his film adaptation of *Sweet Charity* (1969, Cy Coleman) and were appropriately modified to depict the seedy Berlin nightlife of the early 1930s in *Cabaret* (1972, John Kander); these films were respectively the vehicles for the talents of Shirley MacLaine and Liza Minnelli, neither of whom recaptured the same magnetism in their later work. The enormous popularity of the musical films of the 1960s led to an increase in production, but no results that could match the commercial and artistic successes of earlier periods. In the area of original works for the screen *Lost Horizon* (1973, Burt Bacharach), based on James Hilton's oriental romance, was one of several works that failed to justify an extravagant budget. The performances of Barbra Streisand were the highlight of the last era of film musicals based on Broadway shows (Jule Styne's *Funny Girl*, 1968; Jerry Herman's *Hello, Dolly!*, 1969, fig.3, p.300), which came to a conclusive end with some expensive failures, including *On a Clear Day you can See Forever* (1970, Burton Lane),

3. Barbra Streisand with Louis Armstrong in the film "Hello Dolly!" (1969)

1776 (1972, Sherman Edwards), and *Man of La Mancha* (1972, Mitch Leigh). The death knell of the film musical was effectively sounded by MGM, the studio that had made some of the most memorable examples of the genre, with *That's Entertainment* (1974), a compilation of scenes from its past triumphs.

The ascendancy of rock-and-roll resulted in a few innovative feature films, beginning with Columbia's *Rock Around the Clock* (1956), with Bill Haley and the Comets. *A Hard Day's Night* (1964) and the animated *Yellow Submarine* (1968), both British films starring the Beatles, and the film version of the rock musical *Hair* (1979, music by Galt MacDermot) were further isolated examples of the type to achieve a measure of popularity. Also successful were several documentaries of rock events, such as *Monterey Pop* (1968) and *Woodstock* (1970), and a film about the rock group Talking Heads, *Stop Making Sense* (1984). Once dance was again given a dominant position the public was enthusiastic for films such as *Saturday Night Fever* (1977) and *Flashdance* (1983). But the area in which a new creativity in musical film began to emerge in the 1980s was the short music video, usually made to promote a recording, which, lacking a plot, often combines surreal images with the drive and verve of a television commercial.

See also DANCE, §III, 3.

BIBLIOGRAPHY

D. McVay: *The Musical Film* (London, 1967)

J. Kobal: *Gotta Sing Gotta Dance: a Pictorial History of Film Musicals* (London, 1970)

J. Springer: *All Talking! All Singing! All Dancing!* (New York, 1970)

T. Vallance: *The American Musical* (London, 1970)

M. Kreuger, ed.: *The Movie Musical from Vitaphone to 42nd Street* (New York, 1975)

R. Altman, ed.: *Genre: the Musical* (Boston, 1981)

S. Green: *Encyclopaedia of the Musical Film* (New York, 1981)

C. Hirschhorn: *The Hollywood Musical* (New York, 1981)

E. Mordden: *The Hollywood Musical* (New York, 1981)

T. Sennett: *Hollywood Musicals* (New York, 1981)

RICHARD TRAUBNER

Musical Fund Society. Benevolent organization for musicians, founded in 1820; *see* PHILADELPHIA, §§4, 6, and UNIONS, MUSICIANS', §1.

Musical Mutual Protective Union. Musicians' protective organization founded in New York in 1863; *see* UNIONS, MUSICIANS', §1.

Musical play. A term applied generally to any drama in which musical numbers (songs, ensemble pieces, dances, etc.) are inserted; it is commonly used more specifically of a form of popular musical theater in which such numbers are integrated with a plot of some substance (not always a comedy). *See* MUSICAL; *see also* MUSICAL THEATER.

Musical theater. A type of stage entertainment that combines drama and music, but does not necessarily have a unifying plot. This article makes a general survey of the development in the USA of those theatrical forms in which words and music are combined; further information may be found in articles on individual genres. For the history of nonverbal forms of musical theater *see* DANCE, §§II, 3, III, 3, and PANTOMIME.

American musical theater, like other forms, at first relied on music and musicians from the British Isles and Europe, but in the 19th and 20th centuries it took on a distinctively American form and substance, and at some stages in its development enjoyed almost worldwide dissemination.

I. European origins. II. Indigenous musical theater in the 19th century. III. The Tin Pan Alley era. IV. The rock era.

I. European origins

1. The 18th century. 2. The early 19th century.

1. THE 18TH CENTURY. The first theater in the colonies was built in Williamsburg, Virginia, in 1716, though there is evi-

dence of theatrical events' taking place in New York and Charleston even earlier. The New Theatre in New York offered its first season in 1732, while Charleston gave its first subscription series in 1735. A "Company of Comedians" from England offered entertainments in Maryland, Virginia, and New York around the middle of the century, and in 1752 the London Company of Comedians performed in Williamsburg, New York, Philadelphia, and Charleston. This troupe was revived in 1758 as the American Company, and remained active until it was forced into exile in Jamaica in the 1770s; as the Old American Company, it performed in 1784 in the larger cities of the Atlantic seaboard. A competing company, headed by Thomas Wignell and Alexander Reinagle, opened at the New Theatre, Philadelphia, in 1794, with singers and musicians recruited from England. Boston's first legal theatrical season was launched during the same year and the decade saw similar activity in Richmond, Baltimore, Providence, Hartford, Worcester, and many other cities and towns. By the first decade of the 19th century virtually every American community of any size boasted a theater or opera house, which served both resident groups and touring companies.

The chief musical offerings in these theaters were ballad operas and comic operas by British writers. Colley Cibber's *Flora, or Hob in the Well* was performed in Charleston in 1735; John Gay's *The Beggar's Opera*, Charles Coffey's *The Devil to Pay*, and Thomas Arne's *Thomas and Sally* and *Love in a Village* were also popular. After the Revolution a new British repertory dominated the American stage; most widely performed were Charles Dibdin's *The Padlock*, William Shield's *The Poor Soldier* and *Rosina*, Stephen Storace's *No Song, No Supper*, and works by Thomas Linley, William Reeve, and Samuel Arnold. There were only scattered attempts by Americans to write similar pieces. *The Fashionable Lady* (1762) was the work of the American-born James Ralph, who lived in London, but it was never produced in America; Andrew Barton's *The Disappointment, or The Force of Credulity* was announced for performance in Philadelphia by the American Company in 1767, but was withdrawn before reaching the stage. The only pieces written in America and performed during this era were the products of immigrant musicians: James Hewitt's *Tammany, or The Indian Chief* (1794); Victor Pelissier's *Edwin and Angelina, or The Banditti* (1796); and Benjamin Carr's *The Patriots, or Liberty Obtained* (1796) and *The Archers, or Mountaineers of Switzerland* in the same year. (*See* BALLAD OPERA.)

There was no distinction during the 18th century between musical theater and the legitimate stage. Operas were performed by companies offering spoken tragedy and comedy, often on the same program; short operas, or acts from longer ones, were often interspersed with the acts of a spoken drama, and the major offerings of a theatrical evening might alternate with short interludes of songs, dramatic monologues, comic skits, or dancing. Furthermore, English opera at the time consisted of spoken dialogue and songs, duets, dances, and ensemble numbers; spoken drama often included interpolated songs. It is thus impossible to separate the history of the musical theater of this period from a general consideration of theater in America.

2. THE EARLY 19TH CENTURY. A critical development during the 19th century was the gradual but eventually decisive split between "grand opera" and the popular musical stage. Although some French operas had been produced in New Orleans in the late 18th century and early 19th, grand opera – sung throughout, designed for performance by the best professional singers and instrumentalists, patronized by the aristocracy and the ruling classes, with plots based on history or mythology – remained unknown on the American stage until the introduction of "Englished" versions of Italian operas after 1810. Henry Bishop's reworking of Mozart's *Don Giovanni* as *The Libertine* was given at the Park Theatre, New York, in 1817, and was followed by his version of Rossini's *Il barbiere di Siviglia*. The most popular piece of this sort was Rophino Lacy's *Cinderella* (after Rossini), which was a staple of the American stage for more than two decades. Although such works substituted spoken dialogue for sung recitative and offered simplified versions of complex arias and ensemble scenes, they nevertheless served to acquaint American audiences with some of the elements of opera. At the same time Bishop and other English composers began to write works that were structurally more complex than the earlier ballad operas and incorporated elaborate vocal writing, ensemble pieces, an integrated chorus, and flexible treatment of the orchestra. Several pieces of this sort were written in the USA, including *The Indian Princess, or La belle sauvage* (1808) by J. N. Barker and John Bray (for illustration of title page *see* OPERA, fig. 1), and *The Aethiop* (1814), which had a book by William Dimond and music by Rayner Taylor.

Italian opera first reached New York in 1825, when Manuel García's opera troupe offered a season of some 80 performances at the Park Theatre. Other traveling troupes brought Italian and French opera to New York as well as other major American cities. In 1833 the Italian Opera House opened in New York, specifically for the performance of Italian opera; another opera house was established in 1844 by Ferdinand Palmo, the Astor Place Opera House opened in 1847, and the Academy of Music (with an excellent hall for opera) was finished in 1854 and remained the chief center of opera in New York until the opening of the Metropolitan Opera House in 1883. The construction of these houses underlined the fact that a growing segment of the population had the means to support opera in isolation from the popular musical stage, and that their taste was for European works rather than pieces by American composers. William Henry Fry's *Leonora*, which received its première in Philadelphia in 1845 and was performed at the Academy of Music in New York in 1858, was solidly in the style of Bellini and Donizetti; George Frederick Bristow's *Rip Van Winkle* (1855), despite its American subject matter, was likewise grounded in the European tradition.

II. Indigenous musical theater in the 19th century

1. The minstrel show. 2. After the Civil War.

1. THE MINSTREL SHOW. The portrayal in comic sketches, often involving music, of one or more characters representing an ethnic or racial group was a constantly recurring element of the popular stage in the early 19th century. Rayner Taylor composed songs depicting rustic English types, sometimes stringing a number of them together in what was called an "olio." In 1846 the Irish composer Samuel Lover toured the USA offering an entertainment that he called an "Irish Evening," a mixture of songs and sketches in dialect. Such portrayals were sometimes affectionate and sometimes satirically comic, as in the work of the English actor Charles Mathews who, having observed the speech patterns and physical movements of American Blacks while on a visit to the USA in 1822, used the material to create the character of Agamemnon in his entertainment *All Well at Natchitoches*.

American entertainers such as George Washington Dixon, Joel Walker Sweeney, Bob Farrell, and George Nichols began offering comic sketches of Blacks in Albany, New York City, and elsewhere in the 1820s. The most successful act of this sort was Thomas Dartmouth ("Daddy") Rice's impersonation of an old crippled black man, Jim Crow; Rice enjoyed great success in the Midwest, along the eastern seaboard, and later in England, and his grotesque dance-song *Jim Crow* became "the first great international song hit of American popular music" (Chase, 1955).

By the 1840s single "Negro impersonators" had been replaced by small groups of blackface performers, and their presentations, consisting of a succession of songs, dances, and comic sketches, developed from interludes between other acts into a chief attraction in the popular theater. Soon the new minstrel show became a full evening's entertainment. The minstrel show was firmly rooted in the traditions of the British stage, most importantly the comic or sentimental portrayal of racial and ethnic stereotypes. In time a satisfying format evolved, based on a standardized sequence of individual acts and events, performed by essentially the same cast throughout. But the notion of even a semblance of a plot remained alien to the genre.

It was minstrelsy that brought together for the first time dramatic and musical material that was recognized both in the USA and abroad as distinctively American. It is no accident that the first genre of musical theater to be so regarded, and the first to achieve international popularity, was the product of an amalgamation of the musical dialects of two of the country's largest subcultures, Afro-Americans and descendants of illiterate immigrants from the British Isles: it was only in the USA that these two groups, each with a rich musical heritage, had significant contact at this point in history. Recent research has established that many of the first "Negro impersonators" were acquainted with the life of the Blacks, and that many of the musical and textual elements of minstrel songs reflect contemporary black culture. The most characteristic instrument of minstrelsy, the banjo, is descended from African prototypes, and its early playing style drew on the ostinato patterns associated with African and Afro-American chordophones; some (but by no means all) song texts are more accurate representations of the English dialect spoken by slaves than had previously been thought; and the most characteristic type of minstrel song, a lengthy, strophic piece without narrative content but incorporating improvised stanzas making reference to contemporary and localized events, has many important precedents in African oral poetry. (*See* MINSTRELSY.)

2. AFTER THE CIVIL WAR. The two decades following the end of the Civil War brought about some significant advances in the Americanization of the musical theater. Shows fell into one of two large groupings: those including collections of unrelated songs, dances, and skits; and productions with at least the thread of a plot, where musical numbers were interspersed with spoken dialogue.

The popularity of the minstrel show continued to the end of the century and even beyond. Each decade brought change: casts became larger, and productions more lavish and polished; songs became closer in style to sentimental parlor songs, losing virtually all trace of African elements; black minstrel troupes appeared, without, however, changing the dramatic or musical content of the genre; and concert performances of arrangements of black spirituals by the Fisk Jubilee Singers and other groups from black colleges resulted in a new kind of minstrel song, the minstrel-spiritual. But the basic format, content, and spirit of the minstrel show remained the same, and its unity continued to depend not on dramatic content but on stereotyped characters and a predictable sequence of events.

The variety show, or VAUDEVILLE, was also extremely popular in the last third of the 19th century. The establishment of vaudeville, which is closely related to English music-hall entertainment but owes much of its character to the minstrel show, is usually traced back to the opening of Tony Pastor's Opera House in the Bowery area of New York in 1865. Pastor's background was that of a minstrel and circus performer, but in his new theater he largely abandoned blackface skits and the format of the minstrel show in favor of a succession of a larger and looser variety of acts, involving singing, comedy, acrobatics, pantomime, and dancing. His success prompted the opening of similar houses, and by the end of the century the vaudeville show was popular throughout the USA. The variety hall was an invaluable testing ground for most of the performers and writers who became prominent in musical theater, and individual acts and sketches were often miniature pieces of musical drama. But vaudeville never pretended to develop extended dramatic sequences, and like the minstrel show it remained peripheral to the history of the later musical comedy.

However, there were many shows during this time that combined music, dance, spectacle, and drama into an extended, satisfying whole. Laura Keene, from London, mounted several "grand burlesque spectacles" in New York in the 1860s; shows such as *The Seven Sisters* and *The Seven Sons*, with music by Thomas Baker and others, were direct precursors of one of the central stage works of the century. *The Black Crook* opened at Niblo's Garden on 12 September 1866, ran for 475 consecutive performances, was taken on tour, and was revived in New York in 1871. Advertised as "the most Resplendent, Grand and Costly Production ever presented on this continent," it attracted attention first through elaborate spectacle, involving the most expensive and dazzling scenery, stage machinery, and costumes seen in the USA, a complete European ballet troupe augmented by 50 additional dancers, and a large cast of principal singers and actors (fig. 1). But the success and longevity of the show also depended on its story, an amusing and skillful reworking of the Faust legend by Charles M. Barras, and songs, choruses, and dances by Thomas Baker among others.

A show cast in the same mold was *Evangeline* (1874), a burlesque by J. Cheever Goodwin of Longfellow's poem, which had a score by Edward E. Rice. More successful commercially, though less innovative, was Rice's *Adonis* (1884), which ran for 603 performances. The book, by William F. Gills, described as a "Delightful Perversion" of several well-known dramas, was little more than an excuse for stringing together various episodes of music, dance, and comedy; the music was attributed to "Beethoven, Audran, Suppé, Sir Arthur Sullivan, Planquette, Offenbach, Mozart, Hayden, Dave Braham, Eller – and many more too vastly numerous to individualize, particularize or plagiarize." This statement epitomizes the nature of most works for the musical stage at this time: their books parodied serious works of literature, while their music either borrowed from or imitated European models. (*See* BURLESQUE.)

Opera continued to represent a cultural oasis: only European works were offered, and they were performed almost exclusively by expatriate or visiting Europeans, for a small audience content to remain sheltered from the most distinctive products of an

1. Scene from "The Black Crook" (1866) by Charles M. Barras, showing the troupe of dancing girls marching in formation: woodcut from an advertising poster

emerging American culture. Light opera, however, was an important middle ground. Many urban theaters offered Michael Balfe's *The Bohemian Girl*, Vincent Wallace's *Maritana*, and other mid-19th-century British works which, because they were in English and written in a more accessible style, attracted large, heterogeneous audiences. The operettas of Jacques Offenbach and Charles Lecocq were also performed in English translation. John Hill Hewitt's several operettas enjoyed some regional success, and light operas by the immigrant Julius Eichberg, such as *The Doctor of Alcantara* (1862) and *The Two Cadis* (1868), had successful runs in New York and elsewhere. Modest works designed for performance by children or at female seminaries, by such Americans as George F. Root, Harrison Millard, and George W. Stratton, helped to cultivate a taste for operetta in several generations of educated Americans. To some extent light opera appealed to the educated middle classes, who tended to shun "grand opera" on the one hand and the most popular musical stage (the minstrel show and vaudeville) on the other. But the repertory of a group such as the Richings Grand Opera Company, which drew both on British works and "Englished" versions of Italian, French, and German comic operas, was attractive to a much broader range of the American public.

It was this same audience that responded with such enthusiasm to Gilbert and Sullivan's *H.M.S. Pinafore* on its first American production in 1878. Within a matter of weeks the piece was being performed all over the country, from New York (where five different stage productions were running simultaneously by early 1879) to San Francisco. The authors were prompted to stage the world première of *The Pirates of Penzance* in the USA at the end of 1879, and for the next decade the American musical stage appeared to be dominated by their works, in legitimate performances as well as in versions for minstrel and burlesque troupes, church choirs, and children's "operatic" companies. This had no immediate or obvious impact on indigenous musical theater, however, and no American composers emerged to take advantage of the mass enthusiasm for this type of operetta.

The most distinctive (and eventually most influential) genre of American musical theater had its modest beginnings in the variety show. Edward Harrigan and Tony Hart began to perform vaudeville sketches in Chicago and from 1872 in New York. Harrigan wrote their material, which consisted of comic dialogue followed by a song or two; the characters they portrayed were urban New Yorkers, of Irish descent like the performers themselves. *The Mulligan Guard* (1873) was followed by a series of increasingly long sketches; *The Mulligan Guard's Picnic* (1878) was a 40-minute comedy with a number of interpolated songs and other music, and *The Mulligan Guard's Ball* (1879) was virtually a full evening's entertainment, and ran for 100 consecutive performances at the Theatre Comique, New York. The music for these shows was by the immigrant English composer David Braham, whose musical taste and talents had been formed in the music hall. Perhaps their best work was *Cordelia's Aspirations*, which had a run of some 200 performances following its opening in 1883.

Although they were categorized as plays (or farces) with music, the shows by Harrigan and Braham contained the various elements essential to 20th-century musical comedy: introductory instrumental music and interspersed songs and dances by a single composer, and a unified plot concerning a group of characters involved in a conflict that is resolved at the end. Sets and costumes were not as lavish as those of earlier spectacles and burlesques, but the plots were tighter and the music much more consistent stylistically. In setting, characters, and spirit, these shows reflected the distinctive urban life of New York at the end of the century, and they drew audiences chiefly from that milieu.

See also MELODRAMA.

III. The Tin Pan Alley era

1. The turn of the century. 2. The golden age of musical comedy. 3. The changing character of musical theater.

1. THE TURN OF THE CENTURY. It is no coincidence that the most productive, memorable, and innovative era of the American musical theater began to emerge in the same decade that initiated one of the great ages of American popular song. Successful musical theater must combine many elements – drama, music, dance, stage decoration, costumes, lighting, direction – but the most dynamic change that came about in the American musical stage in the 1890s and the first two decades of the 20th century was in the character of its music. The historic success of *A Trip to Chinatown* (657 performances following its opening on 9 November 1891) cannot be explained by its book, the work of Charles H. Hoyt, or the production, which was neither particularly innovative nor unusually spectacular. What set it aside from previous farce-comedies and burlesques was its setting (like the Harrigan and Hart shows) in contemporary New York, and the astonishing popularity of its music, both on and off stage. Percy Gaunt contributed two memorable songs to the original production, "The Bowery" and "Reuben and Cynthia," and Charles K. Harris's "After the Ball" became inseparably linked with the show after being interpolated in a performance in Milwaukee in 1892.

George M. Cohan's *Little Johnny Jones* (1904) was also a landmark in the history of indigenous American musical theater. It owed much to the shows of Harrigan and Braham. It was called a "musical play," and had a tightly crafted book, aggressively American in setting and spirit, that was entertaining but also touched on themes deeply grounded in American life. But whereas Harrigan's plays were specifically concerned with New York and consequently enjoyed little popularity outside that city and Braham's music was often so British as to inhibit its appeal elsewhere, Cohan's story was more universally American and his music, with its sentimental Irish waltzes and its perky syncopated march and ragtime rhythms, reflected the Tin Pan Alley style that was sweeping the USA. *Forty-five Minutes from Broadway* (1906) and *George Washington, Jr.* (1906) were in the same mold. Cohan's works were the first to have skillful, if not profound, books and unified music in a style recognized as distinctively American, and to integrate the two convincingly.

Other varieties of musical theater coexisted with Cohan's pieces, however, and the success of the latter by no means brought about a narrowing of genres on the American stage. There was still a taste for British works, often coupled with a lingering distrust of American cultural products. Sidney Jones's *A Gaiety Girl* (1894), a "musical comedy" imported from London, was thought by critics to be better crafted and more substantial than contemporary American shows, and was one of the models for Gustave Kerker's extremely successful *The Belle of New York* (1897). Kerker was an immigrant from Westphalia and his stage works were in the style of European operetta, which reached a peak of popularity in the USA during the first two decades of the 20th century. Works by Johann Strauss the younger (most importantly *Die Fledermaus* and *Der Zigeunerbaron*) and Franz von Suppé were performed alongside the newer "romantic" Viennese operettas by composers such as Franz Lehár (*Die lustige Witwe*, 1905) and Oscar Straus. American composers, both native and immigrant, also made important contributions. Several operettas by Sousa, including *El capitan* (1896) and *The Charlatan* (1898), enjoyed some currency, although a number of pieces by Victor Herbert were far more successful commercially. From *The Wizard of the Nile* (1895) to *The Dream Girl* (1924) Herbert exhibited a genius for combining lovely and memorable songs (many of which became popular hits) and effective ensemble and instrumental writing. Other immigrants nourished in the tradition of Viennese operetta whose careers peaked in the 1920s were Friml (*Rose-Marie*, 1924; *The Vagabond King*, 1925) and Romberg (*Blossom Time*, 1921; *The Student Prince*, 1924).

Whether imported or composed in the USA, operetta of this period was European in style and content. The stories were usually set in 19th-century Europe and involved characters drawn from the upper classes or romanticized caricatures of the peasantry; the music was solidly based in late-19th-century harmonic and melodic practice, and reflected almost nothing of the developing Tin Pan Alley song style. The immense popularity of European operetta resulted from its appeal to a number of different groups: recent immigrants from Europe and first- or second-generation Americans enjoying a fairytale view of their ancestral culture; the upwardly mobile, who wished to associate themselves with a more sophisticated form of musical theater than the minstrel show or vaudeville, but were unwilling or unable to derive pleasure from opera in foreign languages; and the urban middle class, who responded to effective and well-crafted stage pieces produced by talented writers and composers.

Yet another genre, the REVUE, became popular in the 1890s. *The Passing Show* (1894) was like a vaudeville show in that it consisted of a series of unrelated acts, but a small cast made repeated appearances and came together in ensembles, and the textual and musical material was the work of a small group of writers working together, George Lederer, Sydney Rosenfeld, and Ludwig Englander. Ziegfeld's annual *Follies*, beginning in 1907, were built on the same model, as was a competing series entitled *The Passing Show*, produced from 1912 by the Shubert brothers.

Vaudeville and the minstrel show maintained their popularity in the new century and continued to engage the talents of many of the best songwriters and performers of the day. At the other end of the musical scale "serious" composers turned increasingly to opera. Herbert's *Natoma* was given its première in Philadelphia in 1911; the Metropolitan Opera Company produced a series of American works in New York, beginning with Frederick Converse's *The Pipe of Desire* in 1910 and including Horatio Parker's *Mona* in 1912; similar operas reached the stage in Chicago, Boston, San Francisco, and elsewhere. Despite the fact that some of these pieces had American settings and a few drew on indigenous musical material, their style was still so firmly grounded in 19th-century European music and its aesthetic that none had the desired effect of reaching out to a more general audience.

2. THE GOLDEN AGE OF MUSICAL COMEDY. The history of modern American musical comedy (*see* MUSICAL) may be said to have begun at the Princess Theatre in New York, where a show entitled *Nobody Home*, with a book by Guy Bolton and songs by Jerome Kern, opened in the spring of 1915. Though it ran for 135 performances its success was overshadowed by that of *Very Good,*

Eddie (1915), for which P. G. Wodehouse joined the team as lyricist. The series continued with *Have a Heart* (1916), *Oh Boy!* and *Leave it to Jane* (1917), and *Oh, Lady! Lady!* (1918). In broad outline these shows were not remarkably different from Cohan's "musical plays"; the key distinction was a matter of quality. Guy Bolton's books were fast-paced comedies set in the contemporary world, thoroughly amusing yet touching on a range of situations and emotions extending beyond Cohan's two chief moods of patriotism and sentimentality; and Kern was a superb melodic craftsman, whose best tunes were memorable on musical grounds alone, but who also captured appropriate nuances in the lyrics.

Kern continued to produce music of the same high quality for several shows each year, including *Sally* (1920), *Sunny* (1925), and *Show Boat* (1927; fig.2); written in collaboration with Oscar Hammerstein II, the last was hailed as a historic work, not only surpassing all earlier pieces of American musical theater in the quality of its music, text, and production, but also demonstrating that American subject matter of some seriousness could be dealt with on the musical stage. Kern's chief contribution to musical theater was his ability to bring a more complex musical vocabulary, derived in large measure from European music of the turn of the century, to popular American song and to make it acceptable to a larger audience than had responded to the music of Herbert, Friml, and Romberg.

Inspired at least in part by Kern's success, almost all the best songwriters of the era involved themselves with the musical stage. Irving Berlin contributed to the *Ziegfeld Follies of 1911* and a succession of revues during and after World War I before opening his own theater in 1921 specifically for the production of the *Music Box Revue* series. His first musical comedies, written in collaboration with Moss Hart, were *Face the Music* (1932) and *As Thousands Cheer* (1933). George Gershwin wrote songs for the *George White Scandals* from 1920 to 1924, and composed his first musical comedy, *Lady, be Good!*, in 1924; he then collaborated with his brother Ira on a series of sophisticated and satirical shows in the late 1920s and early 1930s. Richard Rodgers and Lorenz Hart wrote their first songs for *Poor Little Ritz Girl* (1920), which was followed by a series of shows including *A Connecticut Yankee* (1927). After a long apprenticeship Cole Porter had his first unqualified successes with *Fifty Million Frenchmen* (1929) and *The New Yorkers* (1930). Vincent Youmans, Arthur Schwartz, and Ray Henderson also made their first contributions to musical comedy in the 1920s.

Two stylistic threads came together in the songs of the 1920s and 1930s: the melodic style of European operetta and musical comedy, as popularized on the American stage by Kern, that had made itself felt in slow, lyrical ballads; and the ragtime, dance, and jazz styles, owing much to black-American music, that had given rise to lively, syncopated pieces. Another consensus was developing in the writing of books for the musical stage: the variety show and the revue rapidly declined in favor of the musical comedy, with its coherent plot. Almost all musical shows now had contemporary American settings matching the up-to-date, distinctively American flavor of their songs and dances, and although they were comedies concerned mostly with romantic involvements and intrigues, they often touched on topical issues. New York remained the artistic and commercial center of musical comedy, and shows established their success with initial runs at one of the theaters on Broadway (the term "Broadway musical" acknowledges the geographical origin and home of the genre). Many of the leading songwriters and lyricists reflected the unique cultural mix of the city in their style. Among the most successful musical comedies during the period of the genre's greatest popularity were Kern's *Roberta* (1933), Porter's *Anything Goes* (1934), Rodgers's *Pal Joey* (1940) and *Oklahoma!* (1943), Loesser's *Guys and Dolls* (1950), and Willson's *The Music Man* (1957).

2. Sketch for a set design by Joseph Urban for the first production (1927) of Jerome Kern's "Show Boat"

The spectacular stylistic maturation and commercial success of musical comedy from the 1930s to the 1950s tended to overshadow other forms of American musical theater, yet other important works were produced during this period. Sound film became a reality in the late 1920s, opening up new possibilities for the use of music (*see* FILM MUSIC). The first attempts at musical films drew on established stage works, including revues, operettas, and musical comedies. The first musical plays written especially for the screen, such as *The Broadway Melody* (1929) with songs by Nacio Herb Brown and Arthur Freed, and *Sunny Side Up* (1929) with songs by Ray Henderson, were closely based on contemporary musical comedies. With *42nd Street* (1933; songs by Harry Warren and Al Dubin), which included spectacular choreography by Busby Berkeley, the film musical began to develop its own techniques, and soon many of the best composers of musical comedy, including Gershwin, Kern, and Berlin, were writing for the screen. As moving pictures became widely disseminated, reaching every part of the USA and cutting across class and geographical barriers more effectively than any previous form of entertainment, the musical style of Tin Pan Alley song became familiar to an even wider audience. Musical films of the 1930s, whether original works or adaptations of stage pieces, were largely responsible for the nationwide popularity of Rodgers and Hammerstein's *Oklahoma!* and similar shows from the 1940s to the 1960s. (*See* MUSICAL FILM.)

Black musical theater was also flourishing during the Tin Pan Alley era. Musical shows written, produced, and acted by Blacks, such as Will Marion Cook's *Clorindy, or The Origin of the Cake Walk* (1898) and *In Dahomey* (1902), were presented at the turn of the century. *Shuffle Along* (1921), with music by Eubie Blake and Noble Sissle, was a successful revue, while *Green Pastures* (1930) offered a black cast in a stage musical with a continuous plot, though the book (by Marc Connelly) offered a simplistic white view of black religion, and the 95 black performers were involved in almost as stereotyped an image of their race as had been offered in the minstrel show. Hall Johnson directed his own "folk play" *Run Little Chillun'* (1933). *Cabin in the Sky* (1940), though an effective vehicle for Ethel Waters, Todd Duncan, and many other talented Blacks, actually reflected the Russian heritage of its composer Vernon Duke and choreographer George Balanchine. White audiences, who continued to dominate the theater, became increasingly receptive to black performers, but still expected to see them in the context of the musical and theatrical styles long associated with them. If there was a developing tradition of black theater – as opposed to Blacks performing in shows modeled after those for the white stage – it remained invisible to mainstream American culture.

Professional opera houses in the USA continued to introduce works by native and immigrant composers, though with little critical or commercial success. Some pieces, such as Deems Taylor's *The King's Henchman* (1927), Hanson's *Merry Mount* (1934), and Menotti's *The Island God* (1942) (all given their premières at the Metropolitan Opera), were criticized for being too derivative of European models, and also because they lacked the melodic inventiveness, spirit, and distinctively American character of the best musical comedies. But when Louis Gruenberg's *The Emperor Jones*, which was based on a play by Eugene O'Neill and deliberately introduced indigenous musical styles, was produced at the Metropolitan Opera in 1933, it was a failure; the audience found it too different in style from the classic operas of the 19th century and early 20th.

3. THE CHANGING CHARACTER OF MUSICAL THEATER. Although the period from the 1930s to the 1950s was one of stylistic stability, particularly for musical comedy, there existed a strong innovative undercurrent. Many composers for the stage had an extensive background in classical music. Kurt Weill, born and trained in Germany, came to New York in 1935 and became thoroughly and enthusiastically acclimatized to American culture. He produced the music for three important and popular musical shows: *Knickerbocker Holiday* (1938), *Lady in the Dark* (1941), and *One Touch of Venus* (1943), which had a first run of 567 performances. Leonard Bernstein had established himself as a conductor and pianist and had composed a number of important classical works by the time his *On the Town* opened on Broadway in 1944; he was appointed music director and chief conductor of the New York PO shortly after *West Side Story* began its two-year run in 1957.

While these composers adopted the general Tin Pan Alley style of the popular musical stage, their classical training prompted them to introduce more sophisticated and subtle melodic and harmonic variations into their music. Critics who had dismissed the popular style as unworthy of serious consideration gradually began to accept this newer style as a valid contemporary musical language. The books and lyrics of Hammerstein, Ira Gershwin, and other writers likewise came to be taken seriously. This was not solely a result of their literary quality; it also had to do with the new subject material that was being introduced to the popular stage. Gershwin's musical comedies of the early 1930s, for example, made effective use of political satire; Weill's *Knickerbocker Holiday* concerned the historical figure of Peter Stuyvesant, whose political tyrannies presented a telling parallel with the contemporary situation in Europe; Rodgers and Hammerstein's *Carousel* (1945) broke with an important tradition of musical comedy by ending with the death of the male principal; Porter's *Kiss me, Kate* (1948) was based on Shakespeare's *The Taming of the Shrew*; and Bernstein's *West Side Story* was not only derived from Shakespeare's tragedy *Romeo and Juliet*, but also confronted some of the realities of life in contemporary New York.

There seemed for some composers to be too wide a disparity between what was acceptable on the commercial musical stage, as epitomized by musical comedy, and the conventions of serious opera. Some of the most innovative and successful pieces of musical theater were produced as a result of attempts to bridge this gap. Gershwin's *Porgy and Bess* (1935), concerned with the lives of impoverished Blacks in Charleston, South Carolina, is one of the great American musical shows of all time (fig. 3). Its melodic, rhythmic, and harmonic vocabulary is essentially that of Tin Pan Alley song and musical comedy, though some of the orchestral and ensemble writing is more complex; virtually the entire text, including recitative, is sung; and extended ensembles bring together soloists, chorus, and orchestra in the style of operatic finales. Although Gershwin considered the work an opera, no opera house would stage a piece with such links to the popular stage, so it opened at the Alvin Theatre, billed as "An American Folk-Opera." Blitzstein's *The Cradle will Rock* (1937), which has a libretto concerning steelworkers fighting for union recognition and a score drawing on various popular styles for satirical effect, likewise resists categorization in terms of earlier types of musical theater. The same is true of Thomson's two large stage works of the period, *Four Saints in Three Acts* (1934) and *The Mother of us All* (1947). Menotti drew his musical vocabulary from Italian opera, but his librettos deal with contemporary situations and his stage direction strove for the fluid, fast-paced, directly dramatic impact of the legitimate theater. His double bill *The Medium* and *The Telephone* had a run of 211 performances in 1947–8; *The Consul* (1950) was an even greater commercial success, being awarded both the Pulitzer Prize and the Drama Critics Award; *The Saint of Bleecker Street* (1955) won these same awards, ran for some time on Broadway, and was televised to a nationwide audience. While Menotti's musical style was radically different from that of Gershwin, it achieved the same effect of being accessible to a much wider audience than was able to respond to the neoclassical, serial, or avant-garde music being produced by classical composers in the USA.

These pieces by Gershwin, Thomson, Blitzstein, and Menotti, though disparate in style, all resulted from the attempt to create works for the musical stage of more substance and complexity than would have been acceptable in musical comedy, yet more accessible than most opera. Performed in commercial theaters (as opposed to opera houses), and increasingly on college campuses, they helped to create the climate for an almost new genre of musical theater in the 1950s and 1960s, the American chamber opera. This was most commonly a one-act work for performance by amateurs or student singers, scored for keyboard or a small instrumental ensemble, and employing a musical vocabulary based on the practices of the late 19th century and early 20th (though sometimes spiced with more contemporary or popular coloring); such pieces soon formed the core repertory of countless community opera companies and college opera workshops. The most popular included Douglas Moore's *The Devil and Daniel Webster* (1939), Foss's *The Jumping Frog of Calaveras County* (1950), Bernstein's *Trouble in Tahiti* (1952), Menotti's *The Telephone*, Copland's *The Second Hurricane* (1937), and Floyd's *Slow Dusk* (1949).

IV. The rock era

1. Broadway shows. 2. Other developments.

1. BROADWAY SHOWS. The revolution in popular music prompted by the first great commercial success of rock-and-roll in 1955 had little impact on the American musical theater. Broadway continued to sustain musical comedies in the traditional mold with such works as Meredith Willson's *The Music Man* (1957), Frank Loesser's *How to Succeed in Business without Really Trying* (1961), Jerry Herman's *Hello, Dolly!* (1964), Hamlisch's *A Chorus Line* (1975), Strouse's *Annie* (1977), and Henry Krieger's *Dreamgirls* (1981). Even the critically acclaimed and successful musicals by the gifted Stephen Sondheim, such as *Company* (1970), *A Little Night Music* (1972), and *Pacific Overtures* (1976), did nothing to close the gap between the Tin Pan Alley style of Broadway and the various pop and rock dialects of the era.

As if to emphasize their distance from American mass culture, some of the most successful musical comedies of the period had European settings: *My Fair Lady* (1956) by Lerner and Loewe, *The Sound of Music* (1959) by Rodgers and Hammerstein, Jerry Bock's *Fiddler on the Roof* (1964), Mitch Leigh's *Man of La Mancha* (1965), and John Kander's *Cabaret* (1966). Even though some successful shows, such as Strouse's *Bye Bye Birdie* (1960) and *Grease* (1972) by Jim Jacobs and Warren Casey, dealt with the phenomenon of rock music in their plots, their scores had little to do with the rock idiom.

A handful of pieces did bring more contemporary popular styles to the stage. Galt MacDermot's *Hair* (1967) included songs suggestive of Motown soul music, psychedelic rock, and the urban folk revival. *Tommy* (1969) was performed by its creators, the British rock group The Who, at the Metropolitan Opera

3. George Gershwin's "Porgy and Bess": Act 1 scene i from the first production (1935) at the Alvin Theatre on Broadway

4. *Scene from the first Broadway production (1978) of "Ain't Misbehavin'," with music by Fats Waller: (left to right) Armelia McQueen, Ken Page, Charlaine Woodward, Andre de Shields, Nell Carter, and Luther Henderson (piano)*

House. And Andrew Lloyd Webber's *Jesus Christ Superstar* (1971) and Stephen Schwartz's *Godspell* (1971), both with music on the fringe of popular styles, enjoyed considerable success in the USA. But the vision of a bold new American musical stage based on rock music faded, perhaps in reflection of the fact that rock is itself a kind of musical theater. Like the earlier popular genres, the minstrel and vaudeville shows, rock concerts are presented on stage, with costumes, stage action, lighting, props, and direct dramatic communication with the audience. A good rock concert offers a sequence of pieces, often interspersed with dialogue, organized to form patterns of varying tension that supply satisfying contrasts and continuity; it culminates in an extended finale or familiar song to bring the evening to a climax.

Shows written, performed, and sometimes produced by Blacks proliferated in the 1960s and 1970s. Ossie Davis's book for *Purlie* (1970) concerned the struggles of a group of Blacks on a cotton plantation in Georgia. Melvin Van Peebles wrote the book, lyrics, and music for several shows about life in black ghettoes, including *Ain't Supposed to Die a Natural Death* (1971) and *Don't Play us Cheap* (1972), which were moderately successful. Judd Woldin's *Raisin* (1973), based on a novel by Lorraine Hansberry, was performed by a mostly black cast and choreographed by a Black, Donald McKayle. Charlie Smalls's *The Wiz* (1975), which ran for 1672 performances in New York and was equally successful on tour, was a reworking of *The Wizard of Oz*. *Bubbling Brown Sugar* (1976) and *Ain't Misbehavin'* (1978; fig.4) were revues with black casts performing music by black songwriters and jazz composers. Yet despite the invigorating impact of the singing and dancing of so many black performers, almost all shows with black casts were directed by Whites and were cast in molds established when the American musical stage was dominated by Whites.

2. OTHER DEVELOPMENTS. Opera has flourished since the 1950s. The radio and phonograph have brought the standard European repertory of the 19th century and early 20th to a wider audience, and most major cities now maintain professional opera companies. Generous grants from private foundations and federal endowments have funded performances and the commissioning of operas by distinguished composers. Several composers have made notable contributions to the operatic literature: Sessions wrote two large-scale pieces, *The Trial of Lucullus* (1947) and *Montezuma* (1941–63), Barber's *Vanessa* received its première at the Metropolitan Opera in 1958, and Schuller's *The Visitation* was first performed in Hamburg in 1966. Despite all this and the continuing attempts of many composers to create an American dialect of opera through the incorporation of indigenous musical elements and local settings into their stage pieces – as in Floyd's *Susannah* (1955) and *Of Mice and Men* (1970), and Moore's *The Ballad of Baby Doe* (1956) – no American opera has as yet become established in the repertory of a professional company. This is partly because, owing to the lack of a solid operatic tradition, American works are often theatrically ineffectual, and partly because audiences continue to reject most contemporary harmonic and melodic idioms, responding most readily to more conservative pieces, such as Pasatieri's *The Trial of Mary Lincoln* (1972) and *The Seagull* (1974).

Two very different composers overcame these problems in the 1970s. Glass's minimalist work *Einstein on the Beach* (1975) enjoyed a certain amount of critical and popular acceptance when it was first offered at the Metropolitan Opera and later at the Brooklyn Academy of Music; this positive reaction came not from connoisseurs of opera, however, but from those in art and theater circles. Sondheim's *Sweeney Todd* (1979), which draws on many of the forms and techniques of opera (though it has spoken dialogue rather than recitative), is a theatrically effective work, and its musical vocabulary, though expanded, is still grounded in the familiar style of the Broadway stage.

There have been occasional indications that musical theater might develop in radically different directions in the late 20th century. Cage and other members of the American avant-garde, most notably Oliveros, Reynolds, the Fluxus group, Ashley, and other composers associated with the ONCE festivals in Ann Arbor, have created mixed-media works combining music, action, visual materials, and sometimes dialogue; often abstract or aleatory in nature, these pieces appear fresh and promising, although they have had little impact outside academic or avant-garde circles and seem seriously limited in range of artistic expression. In a different sphere, various recording companies in the early 1980s began to issue short video presentations of their leading rock performers for promotional purposes. One enterprising television cable company, Music Television (MTV), began in 1981 to use these as the basis for its round-the-clock programming, and some were hailed by critics as a new musical-theatrical form. A few, including Michael Jackson's *Beat it* and *Thriller*, were elaborate and highly professional products using techniques learned from film and Broadway musicals; their chief disadvantage was that their brevity (each lasts no longer than the few minutes required to perform the song) allowed for only limited dramatic development.

The most viable products of the American musical stage continue in the 1980s to be retrospective in style and content. It seems likely that new peaks of achievement will be reached only when musical theater is again in phase with the best and most popular music of the day, as was the case with the minstrel show, vaudeville, and the Broadway musical comedy.

See also OPERA; POPULAR MUSIC, §§II, 3, III, 1–2; and ORCHESTRAS, §2(ii).

BIBLIOGRAPHY

H. C. Lahee: *Grand Opera in America* (Boston, 1902)
O. G. T. Sonneck: *Early Opera in America* (New York, 1915/*R*1963)
G. M. Cohan: *Twenty Years on Broadway* (New York, 1924)
J. Mattfeld: *A Hundred Years of Grand Opera in New York, 1825–1925* (New York, 1927)
G. C. D. Odell: *Annals of the New York Stage* (New York, 1927–49/*R*1970)
E. B. Marks: *They All Sang: from Tony Pastor to Rudy Vallée* (New York, 1934)
D. Gilbert: *American Vaudeville: its Life and Times* (New York, 1940)
E. B. Marks: *They All Had Glamour: from the Swedish Nightingale to the Naked Lady* (New York, 1944/*R*1972)
J. W. McSpadden: *Operas and Musical Comedies* (New York, 1946, rev. 2/1951)
E. Short: *Fifty Years of Vaudeville* (London, 1946)
C. M. Smith: *Musical Comedy in America* (New York, 1950, rev. 2/1981 with G. Litton)
H. Graf: *Opera for the People* (Minneapolis, 1951)
J. Burton: *The Blue Book of Broadway Musicals* (New York, 1952, rev. 2/1969)
G. Chase: *America's Music* (New York, 1955, rev. 2/1966/*R*1981)
E. J. Kahn, Jr.: *The Merry Partners: the Age and Stage of Harrigan and Hart* (New York, 1955)
D. Ewen: *Complete Book of the American Musical Theater* (New York, 1958, rev. 3/1976 as *New Complete Book of the American Musical Theater*)
E. Jablonski and L. D. Stewart: *The Gershwin Years* (Garden City, NY, 1958, 2/1973)
D. C. Blum: *A Pictorial History of the American Theater, 1860–1960* (Philadelphia, 1960)
S. Green: *The World of Musical Comedy* (New York, 1960, rev. 4/1980)
D. Ewen: *The Story of America's Musical Theater* (Philadelphia, 1961, rev. 2/1968)
R. Baral: *Revue: the Great Broadway Period* (New York, 1962)
M. Lubbock and D. Ewen: *The Complete Book of Light Opera* (New York, 1962)
J. Mates: *The American Musical Stage before 1800* (New Brunswick, NJ, 1962)
H. H. Taubman: *The Making of the American Theater* (New York, 1965, rev. 2/1967)
L. Engel: *The American Musical Theater: a Consideration* (New York, 1967, rev. 2/1975)
I. Kolodin: *The Metropolitan Opera, 1883–1966* (New York, 1967)
E. J. R. Isaacs: *The Negro in the American Theater* (New York, 1968)
A. Laufe: *Broadway's Greatest Musicals* (New York, 1969, rev. 2/1973)
B. Atkinson: *Broadway* (New York, 1970)
T. Vallance: *The American Musical* (New York, 1970)
S. Green: *Ring Bells! Sing Songs! Broadway Musicals from the 1930s* (New York, 1971)
J. V. Hatch: *Black Image on the American Stage: a Bibliography of Plays and Musicals, 1770–1970* (New York, 1971)
R. Kimball and W. Bolcom: *Reminiscing with Sissle and Blake* (New York, 1973)
S. Appelbaum, ed.: *Show Songs from the Black Crook to the Red Mill* (New York, 1974)
R. C. Toll: *Blacking up: the Minstrel Show in 19th-century America* (New York, 1974)
R. Rodgers: *Musical Stages: an Autobiography* (New York, 1975)
S. Green: *Encyclopaedia of the Musical* (New York, 1976)
E. Mordden: *Better Foot Forward: the History of American Musical Theater* (New York, 1976)
A. Jackson: *The Book of Musicals from Show Boat to A Chorus Line* (London, 1977, rev. 2/1979)
G. Bordman: *The American Musical Theatre: a Chronicle* (New York, 1978)
G. W. Hodgkins: *The Broadway Musical: a Complete LP Discography* (Metuchen, NJ, 1980)
H. T. Sampson: *Blacks in Blackface: a Source Book on Early Black Musical Shows* (Metuchen, NJ, 1980)
G. Bordman: *American Operetta from H.M.S. Pinafore to Sweeney Todd* (New York, 1981)
D. L. Root: *American Popular Stage Music, 1860–1880* (Ann Arbor, MI, 1981)
G. Bordman: *American Musical Comedy* (New York, 1982)
J. Mates: "The First Hundred Years of the American Lyric Theater," *American Music*, i/2 (1983), 22
D. Hummel: *The Collector's Guide to the American Musical Theatre* (Metuchen, NJ, 1984)
G. Loney, ed.: *Musical Theatre in America: Greenvale, NY, 1981* (Westport, CT, 1984)
J. Mates: *America's Musical Stage: Two Hundred Years of Musical Theatre* (Westport, CT, 1985)

CHARLES HAMM

Music Critics Association (MCA). Organization for music critics in the USA and Canada who review for newspapers, magazines, and the broadcast media. An outgrowth of discussions between critics and conductors during an American Symphony Orchestra League symposium in 1952, the association was inaugurated by a three-year series of workshops funded by the Rockefeller Foundation and sponsored by the league itself, as well as by the New York Music Critics Circle and the New York PO. Since its incorporation in 1958, the MCA has sponsored annual courses for younger professionals and senior critics in an effort to promote high standards of music criticism and to encourage educational opportunities and general interest in music. Its quarterly newsletter is published from the association's headquarters in Rockville, Maryland. Past presidents Miles Kastendieck, Irving Lowens, and Boris E. Nelson as well as Paul Henry Lang, Virgil Thomson, and Harold C. Schonberg have been elected to life membership. Robert Commanday was president from 1981 to 1985, when he was succeeded by Robert Finn. *See also* CRITICISM, §5.

RITA H. MEAD

Music Educators National Conference (MENC). Organization of school music teachers with members engaged in teaching at all educational levels. In 1907 a meeting was called in Keokuk, Iowa, by Phillip C. Hayden for supervisors who could not attend the convention of the National Education Association (NEA) in Los Angeles. Francis F. Clark, vice-president of the NEA's Department of Education, presided, and Hayden became the first elected president. A constitution for the new organization (which was called the Music Supervisors National Conference until 1934) was adopted in 1910. The popularity of instrumental music following World War I served to swell the membership, and MENC became one of the first professional education associations to develop a structure of state, divisional, and national units; membership was later extended to college students and numbered around 55,000 by the mid-1980s. By 1940 the organization had become such an influential force in music education that the NEA invited it to replace its own 56-year-old Department of Music Education. The office, in Chicago from 1930, moved to Washington, DC, in 1956, where it remained until relations with the NEA were severed in 1975. The organization's headquarters then moved to Reston, Virginia.

The many special interests of the members led to the formation of eight associated organizations (the American Choral Directors Association, the AMERICAN STRING TEACHERS ASSOCIATION, the COLLEGE BAND DIRECTORS NATIONAL ASSOCIATION, the NATIONAL ASSOCIATION OF COLLEGE WIND AND PERCUSSION INSTRUCTORS, the NATIONAL ASSOCIATION OF JAZZ EDUCATORS, the NATIONAL BAND ASSOCIATION, the National Black Music Caucus, and the National School Orchestra Association) and a Society of Research in Music Education. An auxiliary Music Industry Council develops educational exhibits for the biennial conferences and the alternating regional meetings. Much of MENC's work has been carried on by volunteer or appointed ad hoc committees and commissions. There has been close cooperation with other educational organizations, the Organization of the American States, the American Red Cross, the Kennedy Center, music publishing and recording associations, and various branches of the federal government.

The MENC cooperated in morale efforts during both world wars and played an important role in the preparation and adoption of the Service Version and the Code for the National Anthem. Cooperative efforts with the American Association of School Administrators on several occasions led to expansion of the music curriculum in schools as well as the establishment of credit for the study of music. With the National Association of Secondary School Principals, its members developed educational standards for interscholastic music events. Conference leaders assisted in the creation and growth of the International Society for Music Education and the development of organizations modeled after the MENC in other nations. The organization has created and/or conducted projects for the Ford Foundation, the Presser Foundation, music publishers, and the US Department of Education. Its publications have influenced curricula throughout the USA. A Historical Research Center, with an archive covering all aspects of music education from the colonial days to the present, was established at the University of Maryland in 1965. The official magazine of the MENC, the monthly *Music Educators Journal* (published from 1914 to 1934 as the *Music Supervisors Journal*, with Peter Dykema as its first editor), has long been one of the most widely circulated music periodicals. Allen P. Britton was the first editor of another of its publications, the quarterly *Journal of Research in Music Education* (1953–), which holds a similar place among scholarly magazines.

See also EDUCATION IN MUSIC, §I, 3.

BIBLIOGRAPHY

E. B. Birge: *History of Public School Music in the United States* (New York, 1928/*R*1966; Philadelphia, rev. and enlarged 2/1937)

H. M. Kauffman: *A History of the Music Educators National Conference* (diss., George Peabody College, 1942)

J. W. Molnar: "The Origin and Development of the Sectional Conference," *JRME*, i (1953), 127

——: "The Establishment of the Music Supervisors National Conference, 1907–1910," *JRME*, iii (1955), 40

J. E. Houlihan, Jr.: *The Music Educators National Conference in American Education* (diss., Boston U., 1961)

K. W. Gehrkens: "MENC: Remembering the Early Years," *MEJ*, liv/2 (1967), 59

"The MENC Historical Center," *MEJ*, lv/6 (1969), 60

"The First National Assembly," *MEJ*, lvi/3 (1969), 81

D. Willoughby: "MENC Historical Center Acquires CMP Library and Files," *JRME*, xxi (1973), 195

C. B. Fowler: "The Music Educators National Conference: David Faces New Goliaths," *HiFi/MusAm*, xxvi/4 (1976), 8

R. W. Kidd: *The Music Educators National Conference in the 1960's: an Analysis of Curricular Philosophy* (diss., Boston U., 1984)

CHARLES L. GARY

Music from Marlboro. Touring program created in 1965 as an extension of the MARLBORO MUSIC FESTIVAL.

Musicians Guild of America. Musicians' union founded in 1956; *see* UNIONS, MUSICIANS', §2.

Musicians' unions. *See* UNIONS, MUSICIANS'.

Music in our Time. Concert series for performance of contemporary chamber music, founded in 1954 by MAX POLLIKOFF.

Music Library Association (MLA). Association founded in 1931 by 19 members of the American Library Association to promote the establishment, growth, and use of music libraries in the USA. With Otto Kinkeldey as president, the MLA set out "to organize cooperative effort among the music libraries of the United States, and to foster the general aims of musical research." Kinkeldey's successors have included Oliver Strunk, Carleton Sprague Smith, Edward N. Waters, Harold Spivacke, and Vincent Duckles. In the first decade of its activities, a preference among the members for shared cataloguing led to the preparation of uniform codes (published in 1941–2). With a view towards increasing library service and administration, committees were also established to develop methods of indexing for periodical literature, create the regional structure of the organization nationwide, determine the level of training required for music librarians, and begin the publication of a journal (*Notes for the Members of Music Library Association*, published between 1934 and 1942).

The association was incorporated as a nonprofit organization in Washington, DC, in 1945 and had the benefit of a closely knit management group within the Music Division at the Library of Congress. Under the editorship of Richard S. Hill, a new series of the journal was initiated in 1943 as *Notes*; published quarterly, it contains reviews of books and music, and bibliographical and discographical contributions, as well as scholarly articles. Other MLA publications include, in addition to a quarterly *Newsletter*, *A Check-list of Thematic Catalogues* (1954), a *Manual of Music Librarianship* (1966), *Rules for the Brief Cataloging of Music in the Library of Congress* (1970), and *A Survey of Musical Instrument Collections in the United States and Canada* (1974), as well as two series: the *MLA Index Series* (1963–) and *Technical Reports for Music Media Specialists* (1973–). Music Library Association Publication Prizes are awarded for books, articles, and reviews. The association's headquarters are in Canton, Massachusetts.

BIBLIOGRAPHY

C. J. Bradley: "The Music Library Association: the Founding Generation and its Work," *Notes*, xxxvii (1980–81), 763–822 [see also *Notes*, xxxix (1982–3), 490]

W. Lichtenwanger: "When *Notes* was Young/1945–1960," *Notes*, xxxix (1982–3), 7

D. W. Krummel: "The Second Twenty Volumes of *Notes*: a Retrospective Re-Cast," *Notes*, xli (1984–5), 7

RITA H. MEAD

Musicology. The term "musicology" has been defined in various ways, each usually reflecting one of two different viewpoints; one emphasizes the methods of musicologists, the other the subject matter that they study. The approach through method identifies musicology as a form of scholarship characterized by the procedures of research; a simple definition in these terms would be: "the scholarly study of music." The approach through subject matter identifies musicology as "a field of knowledge having as its object the investigation of the art of music as a physical, psychological, aesthetic, and cultural phenomenon" (*JAMS*, viii, 1955, p.153). Yet a third view has claimed the attention of musicologists in recent years. This is the belief that the advanced study of music should be centered on Man, the musician, acting within a social and cultural environment. Harrison (in Harrison, Hood, and Palisca, 1963) expressed this view as follows: "It is the function of all musicology to be in fact ethnomusicology; that is, to take its range of research to include material that is termed 'sociological'." (*See also* ETHNOMUSICOLOGY.)

1. Historical background. 2. The birth of American musicology. 3. Learned societies. 4. Universities. 5. New directions.

1. HISTORICAL BACKGROUND. Musicology is a relatively recent phenomenon: its principles of investigation hardly extend back beyond the beginnings of the Enlightenment in the late 17th century, when the philosophical innovations of Descartes had made their impact on European thought, and when the methods of empiricism had replaced an uncritical reliance on the authority of the Church or myth. As an academic discipline musicology dates back no more than a century: a commonly accepted reference point is the publication by the Viennese scholar Guido Adler, in the first issue of the *Vierteljahrsschrift für Musikwissenschaft* (1885), of his "Umfang, Methode und Ziel der Musikwissenschaft." This paper codified the division between the historical and systematic areas of music study and tabulated their substance and method. In his tabulation Adler listed the auxiliary sciences of musicology. These are, for the historical field: paleography, chronology, diplomatic study (i.e., the form of manuscript documents), bibliography (i.e., the form of printed books), library and archive science; general history; literary history and languages; liturgical history; history of mime and dance; biography; and statistics of associations, institutions, and performances. For the systematic field, these are: acoustics and mathematics, physiology (aural sensations), psychology (aural perception, judgment, feeling), logic (musical thought), grammar, metrics and poetics, education, aesthetics, etc.

Germany led the rest of Europe in establishing the academic discipline of musicology, and the German university system provided the institutional framework within which the new study could evolve. Besides German pioneers, there was also in the 19th century a group of Viennese scholars who exerted considerable influence on the development of musicology. Carl Breidenstein at the University of Bonn was the first musician to occupy a professorial chair in music (1826), but it was not until 1870 that the Viennese music critic Eduard Hanslick became the first to bear the title "Professor ordinarius" in music history and aesthetics, at the University of Vienna. (Adler was his successor there.)

2. THE BIRTH OF AMERICAN MUSICOLOGY. In the USA, musicological scholarship began in the later 19th century with distinctive though inevitably isolated achievements by scholars who lacked the institutional bases that were later created by the development of the field as an intellectual enterprise. To its earliest phase belong such efforts as J. S. Dwight's *Journal of Music* (1852–81), which included material on music history, especially many valuable articles by A. W. Thayer (1812–97), the great pioneer of scholarly Beethoven biography, who was, however, geographically isolated from his homeland during all his later life as US consul at Trieste, Italy. The first important scholar to be based in the USA was Oscar Sonneck (1873–1928), an American by birth, who trained in Germany and for 15 years was chief of the Music Division of the Library of Congress (1902–17). Sonneck was not only instrumental in building the great music collection of the Library of Congress, he was the author of still-unmatched documentary studies of early American music – *A Bibliography of Early Secular American Music* (1905), *Early Concert-life in America* (1907), and *Early Opera in America* (1915) – and a richly annotated *Catalogue of Opera Librettos Printed before 1800* (1914). He was also the founding editor of the *Musical Quarterly* (published by G. Schirmer), which began publication in 1915 and remains one of the most widely circulated American periodicals containing the fruits of musicological research. In its very first issue the *Musical Quarterly* issued a program for musicology in an article by Waldo Selden Pratt entitled "On Behalf of Musicology." Although the term "musicology" at first rang strangely in American ears, by the early 1930s the field was fast acquiring in academic circles the status accorded to any other branch of humanistic scholarship.

A seminal figure in the establishment of musicology in American universities was Otto Kinkeldey (1878–1966). He was trained in Germany, where he was not only awarded the PhD but was also in 1910 named Royal Prussian Professor of Musicology at the University of Breslau. On returning to the USA in 1914 he became head of the Music Division of the New York Public Library, and in 1930 professor of musicology at Cornell University, the first such chair to be established in an American university.

3. LEARNED SOCIETIES. Kinkeldey was also the first president of the American Musicological Society (AMS), which was founded on 3 June 1934 by a group of nine scholars meeting in a private house at 25 Washington Square North, New York. In the early 1980s the society, which has issued a *Journal* regularly since 1950, had a national membership of more than 3500, and it has long been accepted as the central professional association for music scholarship in the USA. In addition to the annual meeting of the entire society, its 15 constituent regional chapters hold their own regular meetings during the year, at which scholarly papers are read. In 1961 the society was host to the eighth congress of the International Musicological Society in New York, and in 1977 to the twelfth congress at Berkeley, California. Although members of the AMS are active in every field of study, the main line of its activities – as reflected in papers presented at the annual meetings, articles published in the *Journal*, and musical editions and publications supported by the society – has so far been undeniably directed towards the Western historical tradition, and indeed primarily the European branch of that

tradition. Its early history was well summed up by Richard Crawford (1984).

In 1954 the Society for Ethnomusicology (SEM) was founded, reflecting an increased interest in that field, in the years after World War II, on the part of people trained in anthropology or musicology, or both. Like the AMS, the SEM was accepted (in 1955) by the American Council of Learned Societies as a constituent member. By the early 1980s, its membership had grown to about 2000 individuals and institutions.

4. UNIVERSITIES. Since the first American PhD in musicology was awarded at Cornell University in 1932 (to J. Murray Barbour), the discipline has spread widely in universities. Music in any form was relatively late in entering American university curricula (American professorships in music were established only in the late 19th century – one of the first being that at Harvard University set up in 1875 for John Knowles Paine); but curricular instruction in music has undergone enormous growth in the past 80 years. Today few universities or colleges in the USA fail to offer, in addition to practical vocal and instrumental music making, at least elementary courses devoted to music history and music theory. Many offer much more, including courses in more advanced theory, analysis, and related fields, and a full range of courses in the history and literature of music, often including offerings in one area or more of non-Western music.

The large number of PhDs awarded in musicology since 1945 is primarily indicative of the increase in university positions in music, themselves reflecting the great upsurge in college-student admissions in the postwar years. In part, the significant role of American musicology in every field of study now being pursued in the discipline is attributable to its substantial number of practitioners, to the location of its research bases in universities, and to the research support available to American scholars through such private organizations as the Guggenheim Foundation and the American Council of Learned Societies, and the federally supported National Endowment for the Humanities. Even more, it is attributable to the contributions of a score of eminent scholars who, in the generation after Kinkeldey, actually created the discipline in its modern forms in the USA. Among these seminal teacher–scholars were three of the founding members of the AMS: Gustave Reese, Charles Seeger, and Oliver Strunk. The first and last of these trained generations of scholars at, respectively, New York University and Princeton University; Seeger had perhaps a more general influence through his writings and lectures. To these names must be added those of such important figures as Paul Henry Lang (at Columbia University), Glen Haydon (University of North Carolina), Donald J. Grout (Cornell University), Charles Warren Fox (Eastman School of Music), and Arthur Mendel (Princeton University).

The Nazi period in Germany brought about the immigration to the USA of a large number of significant scholars in music, including Willi Apel, Manfred Bukofzer, Hans T. David, Alfred Einstein, Karl Geiringer, Otto Gombosi, Erich Hertzmann, Edward Lowinsky, Paul Nettl, Curt Sachs, Leo Schrade, and Emanuel Winternitz. All these men taught at major institutions and had vital roles in the training of younger American scholars. With the recovery of Europe after World War II, the increasing internationalization of the discipline was felt in many ways: in the resumption of European travel and research by American scholars, in their contacts with foreign scholars and some scholarly enterprises, and in the presence of other important foreign scholars in American teaching posts; among the latter was Nino Pirrotta, who taught at Princeton, Columbia, and then for many years at Harvard, before returning to his native Italy. Such teachers as these laid the foundations for a postwar generation of American scholars, among them Barry S. Brook, Howard Mayer Brown, James Haar, Daniel Heartz, Joseph Kerman, Jan LaRue, Lewis Lockwood, and Claude V. Palisca.

5. NEW DIRECTIONS. After the student disruptions of the 1960s and a rather more settled period in the 1970s, some of the trends in American musicology that one of these scholars, Palisca (1978), thought to be promising were the application of ethnomusicological method to historical studies of Western music; new theories of musical structure, such as those proposed by Milton Babbitt and Allen Forte; the use of computers to aid analysis, bibliography, and thematic indexing; and the diffusion of musicological knowledge at the elementary- and secondary-school levels and through the public media. In a later study, Palisca admitted his failure at divination; hardly any of these trends had flowered in a significant way (Holoman and Palisca, 1982). On the other hand, surveying the actual work of the 1970s, he was impressed by detailed studies of regional archives; efforts to establish links with the history of thought or particular strains of it, such as rhetoric and symbolism; renewed interest in musical sketches and autographs for what they reveal of the process of musical creation; a search for "historically valid, multilateral, and contextual approaches" to music analysis; and an increase in musical iconography as a source of musicological information.

Palisca might also have pointed to the increasingly promising but still complex relationship between musicology and performance, between the musical scholar and the practicing musician; the flourishing and growth of the whole field of ethnomusicology, and its impact on general education in music; and the broadening of American musicology to include new or formerly less emphasized areas of the field, among them speculative and descriptive theory and analysis (the work not only of Babbitt and Forte but of LaRue, Wallace Berry, Robert Cogan, and Charles Rosen), contemporary music, historiography, and – too long neglected by American musicologists – the music history of the American continent (to which such scholars as Gilbert Chase, Irving Lowens, Robert Stevenson, H. Wiley Hitchcock, Charles Hamm, and Richard Crawford have contributed substantially). Hazardous as it may be to speculate on the future, it appears that pluralistic definitions of musicology are the only realistic ones, and that the spectrum is likely to widen still more: one might, for example, mention the lag in scholarly attention to American popular music (including musical comedy) and jazz, which by the early 1980s a number of the youngest scholars seemed eager to make up for.

Perhaps the greatest challenge facing American musicology, now that its place among the academic disciplines is a settled matter, is to make its impact felt outside its own domains, especially in the world of performance – in commercial concert life, in conservatories, and even in the music industries. At present American musicology has barely breached the long-established barriers that divide the forces of serious intellectual life from the vast media that produce and disseminate music (especially as published, broadcast, and recorded). One result is the continued isolation of scholarship from practical musical life, the perpetuation of much traditional misinformation, and the persistence of long-held and deeply entrenched attitudes about music, largely inherited from the 19th century. Yet it may not be too optimistic to speculate whether, if the universities are indeed advance guards of the forms of knowledge that will eventually be assimilated by the public at large, the importance of disciplined knowledge of and about music will be more strongly felt in American society in the future than it has been in the past.

See also EARLY-MUSIC REVIVAL, §3, and THEORY.

BIBLIOGRAPHY

W. S. Pratt: "On Behalf of Musicology," *MQ*, i (1915), 1

O. Strunk: *State and Resources of Musicology in the United States* (Washington, DC, 1932)

O. Kinkeldey: "Changing Relations within the Field of Musicology," *PAMS 1936*, 42

C. Seeger: "Music and Musicology in the New World," *MTNAP*, xl (1946), 35; rev. in *HMYB*, vi (1949–50), 36, repr. in *Studies in Musicology, 1935–1975* (Berkeley, CA, 1977), 211

O. Kinkeldey: "Musical Scholarship and the University," *JRBM*, i (1946–7), 10

G. Haydon: "Musicology in the United States: a Survey of Recent Trends," *MTNAP*, xli (1947), 321

P. H. Lang: Editorial, *MQ*, xxxiii (1947), 557

M. Bukofzer: *The Place of Musicology in American Institutions of Higher Learning* (New York, 1957/*R*1977)

S. Goldthwaite: "The Growth and Influence of Musicology in the United States," *AcM*, xxxiii (1961), 72

F. Ll. Harrison, M. Hood, and C. V. Palisca: *Musicology* (Englewood Cliffs, NJ, 1963) [incl. Harrison: "American Musicology and the European Tradition," 3–85; Hood: "Music, the Unknown," 217–326; Palisca: "The Scope of American Musicology," 89–213]

J. Kerman: "A Profile for American Musicology," *JAMS*, xviii (1965), 61

E. Lowinsky: "The Character and Purpose of American Musicology: a Reply to Joseph Kerman," *JAMS*, xviii (1965), 222

M. M. Gallagher: "The State of Musicology in American Universities," *Student Musicologists at Minnesota*, ii (1967), 1–51

M. Griffel: "Musicological Method in American Graduate Schools," *CMc*, no.6 (1968), 7–50

G. S. McPeek: "Musicology in the United States: a Survey of Recent Trends," *Studies in Musicology: Essays . . . in Memory of Glen Haydon*, ed. J. Pruett (Chapel Hill, 1969), 260

L. Treitler: "The Present as History," *PNM*, viii/1 (1969), 1–58

B. S. Brook, ed.: *Musicology and the Computer. Musicology 1966–2000: a Practical Program* (New York, 1970) [incl. "Bibliography: Computer Applications to Music and Musicology," 229–70; papers by L. Dittmer, J. LaRue, E. Lippman, L. Lockwood, C. V. Palisca, F. Zimmerman, A. Mendel]

H. B. Lincoln: "The Current State of Music Research and the Computer," *Computers and the Humanities*, v (1970), 29

B. S. Brook, E. O. D. Downes, and S. Van Solkema, eds.: *Perspectives in Musicology* (New York, 1972) [incl. G. Chase: "American Musicology and the Social Sciences," 202]

J. H. K. Nketia: "The Study of African and Afro-American Music," *BPiM*, i (1973), 7

R. Crawford: *American Studies and American Musicology: a Point of View and a Case in Point*, ISAMm, iii (Brooklyn, NY, 1975)

W. S. Newman: "Musicology in the United States in 1975," *AcM*, xlviii (1976), 284

——: "Musicology in the United States in 1976," *AcM*, xlix (1977), 269

R. Stevenson: "American Musical Scholarship: Parker to Thayer," *19th Century Music*, i (1977–8), 191

W. S. Newman: "Musicology in the United States in 1977," *AcM*, l (1978), 275

C. V. Palisca: "Music," *Anthropological and Historical Sciences, Aesthetics and the Sciences of Art*, i, ed. J. Havet (New York, 1978), 791; repr. as "Reflections on Musical Scholarship in the 1960s," in Holoman and Palisca (1982)

J. Haar: "Musicology in the United States in 1978," *AcM*, li (1979), 279

R. Steiner: "Musicology in the United States in 1980," *AcM*, liii (1981), 216

G. Chase: "American Music and American Musicology," *Journal of Musicology*, i (1982), 59

D. K. Holoman and C. V. Palisca, eds.: *Musicology in the 1980s: Methods, Goals, Opportunities* (New York, 1982) [incl. A. V. Hallmark: "Teaching Music History in Different Environments," 131; D. K. Holoman: "Publishing and/or Perishing," 119; J. Kerman: "Sketch Studies," 53; M. R. Maniates: "Applications of the History of Ideas," 39; J. McKinnon: "Iconography," 79; J. Noble: "Archival Research," 31; repr. of Palisca (1978), 15; R. R. Subotnick: "Musicology and Criticism," 145; R. Taruskin: "The Musicologist and the Performer," 101; L. Treitler: "Structural and Critical Analysis," 67]

R. P. Morgan: "Theory, Analysis, and Criticism," *Journal of Musicology*, i (1982), 15

The American Musicological Society 1934–1984 (Philadelphia, 1984) [incl. R. Crawford: "American Musicology Comes of Age: the Founding of the AMS"]

R. Crawford: *Studying American Music*, ISAM special pubn no.3 (1985)

J. Kerman: *Contemplating Music: Challenges to Musicology* (Cambridge, MA, 1985)

VINCENT DUCKLES with LEWIS LOCKWOOD/
H. WILEY HITCHCOCK

Music Publishers' Association of the United States. Organization founded in New York in 1895 (incorporated 1907) to foster the trade, commerce, and interests of music publishers, to eliminate abuses in the industry, to protect musical works from piracy, and to promote uniformity in the customs and uses of the trade. The association has among its 60 members standardized the procedures for copyright clearance and the rental of performance materials. It has worked with the Music Educators National Conference (MENC) to put an end to sales and copyright abuses associated with school music and tries to inform the public about copyright infringement; it has also lobbied in Congress to secure book-rate postal charges for music. The association gives the annual Paul Revere Award for "excellence in music engraving and graphic design," and with the MENC published the pamphlet *Standard Music Engraving Practice* (1966). Among the association's other publications are the annual *Music Publishers Sales Agency List* (prepared in conjunction with the National Music Publishers Association), *the MPA Bulletin* (1949–), and the *MPA Newsletter* (1980–).

JOHN SHEPARD

Music Teachers National Association. Organization founded in 1876 by the musician and publisher Theodore Presser; its aims are to aid teachers, raise standards of music education, and gain recognition for the profession. Its members have included teachers, performers, composers, and conductors. In 1883 it helped to promote an international copyright law. In 1967 it approved a national certification plan for qualified teachers, and to support talent and promote achievement it holds auditions at local, state, and national levels. The association now comprises 51 autonomous groups in seven geographical divisions, each with its own constitution and officers. In 1972 it established the Independent Music Teachers Forum, a permanent committee and constituent part of the association, to care for the interests and professional growth of members not affiliated with a school or college. The association has the longest continuous history of any musical organization of its type in the USA and is the only professional music body to hold membership (since 1973) in the US Commission of UNESCO. Its official publication is the *American Music Teacher* (published since 1951, now bimonthly), and a microfiche edition of the proceedings of its annual meetings from 1876 to 1950 is in preparation. The association's headquarters are in Cincinnati.

RITA H. MEAD

Music therapy. The purposeful use of musical stimuli and activity for evaluation, remediation, maintenance, and development of mental and physical health. It has applications in three principal areas: developmental music therapy helps individuals to cope with or overcome genetic and developmental disadvantages;

rehabilitative music therapy aids the recovery of those who have suffered mental or physical ills; and preventive music therapy helps avert the onset of disability. Music has long been used therapeutically in cases of emotional and psychiatric disorder, and to provide a means of communication for those with visual, auditory, or other sensory disabilities. The work of therapists with handicapped children focuses on the development of basic cognitive skills and knowledge, as well as appropriate psychological, social, and physical functioning. Others specialize in helping those who have motor and psychomotor disabilities. A growing area of practice is work with geriatric clients.

Although the means by which music achieves therapeutic ends are not yet fully understood, clinical and laboratory research has investigated the characteristics that apparently contribute to its success. There are few for whom music of some sort does not have a strong attraction; preferred music provides a locus for therapeutic activity and can motivate and reinforce extended participation in therapeutic relationships. Music helps to fill basic needs for sensory stimulation and elaboration, and for pattern and form. It provides a way to control the auditory environment and the self, and it may be used to stimulate or sedate. Especially important for music therapy is the use of music for nonverbal and verbal communication. Musical stimuli may elicit responses ranging between basic physiological reactions to elements such as vibration or rhythm, and the profound affective communication labeled as "aesthetic." Music provides a means of expressing feelings in a healthy and socially acceptable way, allowing individuals to vent emotions that they would otherwise suppress. In some cases it permits and encourages psychological and physical contact.

In the initial stages of treatment of severely handicapped or withdrawn subjects, music therapy is usually practiced on a one-to-one basis; in this context music is used to stimulate and structure individual behavior, integrating cognitive, affective, and psychomotor functioning. The complexity of the structure can be adjusted as therapeutically appropriate. Properly selected stimuli and activities can help to reduce feelings of isolation, divert attention, and encourage imagination. Music can also serve the purposes of group therapy, and the music therapist uses this adaptability to organize constructive interaction among the participants. The sense of achievement in making music can lead to the development of self-esteem, and musical achievement can help to win the esteem of others. Participation in group music activity requires the individual to take part in a larger pattern of structured interaction. Thus music provides a favorable context in which both individually and socially integrated behavior may be practiced.

Long established in many cultures as an element in health practice, music has been used in American institutions for the disabled in speech and hearing since the 19th century. But it was not until World War II that music therapy developed as a profession in the USA. Music programs were organized for servicemen in psychiatric hospitals, and by 1944 over 200 such programs existed; although they were designed primarily for recreation and diversion, therapeutic effects were noted. At the same time industrial psychologists, seeking ways to improve productivity, were studying the effects on workers of background music and music as a recreational activity. Information from both these sources added to the profession's data base.

University curricula designed specifically to prepare professional music therapists were initiated in the late 1940s: at the University of Kansas E. Thayer Gaston organized a master's degree program with a strong emphasis on research, which was designed for those with a first degree in music education; and at Michigan State College (now Michigan State University) Roy Underwood set up a baccalaureate degree program in music therapy. Other pioneers in the field who developed degree programs (mostly at the undergraduate level) included Wilhemina K. Harbart at the College of the Pacific and Arthur Flagler Fultz at the New England Conservatory of Music. These early curricula were taught by musicians, educationists, and psychologists, but schools sought professional music therapists to teach in their programs as soon as they became available. Particularly influential among this group were Robert F. Unkefer (at Michigan State University), Donald E. Michel (Florida State University), William W. Sears (universities of Ohio, Indiana, and Kansas), and Charles Braswell (Loyola University, New Orleans).

In 1950 a group of practicing music therapists and college teachers began the National Association for Music Therapy (NAMT), which in 1954 recommended a specific curriculum for preparation of music therapists. After its affiliation with the National Association of Schools of Music it began approving music therapy curricula in member schools that met the specified standards; it later started a register of qualified music therapists, and in 1985 there were over 2000 Registered Music Therapists (RMT). A second professional music therapy organization was founded in the East during the 1960s. Known first as the Urban Federation of Music Therapists and later as the American Association for Music Therapy (AAMT), this group offers the professional qualification of Certified Music Therapist (CMT). In the early 1980s an organization was formed to develop the National Board Certification Examination (first administered in 1985).

In 1985 about 80 American colleges and universities offered music therapy curricula at the undergraduate level; over 60 were associated with the NAMT, and many of the others with the AAMT. Many music therapy positions require applicants to hold either RMT or CMT certification. Graduate study in music therapy has grown less rapidly than undergraduate programs. The master's degree can be earned in several institutions, and those that offer doctoral programs include Florida State University (director of music therapy Jayne Alley), University of Georgia (Richard Graham), University of Iowa (Erwin Schneider), University of Kansas (Alicia Gibbons), Michigan State University (Robert Unkefer), New York University (Jerrold Ross), and Temple University (Kenneth Bruscia).

The bulk of the profession's research is done in the universities that offer graduate study. A psychology of music laboratory was established at Kansas when the music therapy curriculum began, and it has supported many studies of the dynamics of human musical behavior, particularly of physiological and affective responses to musical stimuli; in the mid-1960s E. Thayer Gaston received funding from the US Office of Education for research into clinical techniques in music therapy, the results of which were later published in *Music in Therapy* (1968). In the late 1970s G. L. Duerksen, also at Kansas, mounted two projects (similarly funded) to prepare in-service training materials and techniques to help music educators and music therapists meet the intent of Public Law 94-142, the "Education of all Handicapped Children Act." Under the leadership of Donald Michel, Florida State University became a center for research into uses of music in speech therapy; the work of Clifford Madsen and others there has focused on the uses of music as a reinforcer for therapeutic and educational processes. Charles Braswell's program at Loyola University has produced important studies in the roles, tasks, and preparation of music therapists.

The professional associations have contributed significantly to the development of literature on music therapy. The NAMT published the proceedings of its annual conference, together with research reports, as the *Music Therapy Yearbook* until 1963, when the quarterly *Journal of Music Therapy* took its place; in 1981 it launched another journal, *Music Therapy Perspectives*. During the late 1970s, the NAMT carried out an extensive project on personnel preparation (sponsored by the Office of Education and directed by Wanda Lathom), which resulted in numerous workshop materials including the book *Role of Music Therapy in the Education of Handicapped Children and Youth*. In 1981 the AAMT published the first issue of its journal *Music Therapy*.

See also PSYCHOLOGY OF MUSIC.

BIBLIOGRAPHY

C. Diserens: *The Influence of Music on Behavior* (Princeton, NJ, 1926)
W. Van de Wall: *Music in Hospitals* (New York, 1946)
D. M. Schullian and M. Schoen, eds.: *Music and Medicine* (New York, 1948)
D. Soibelman: *Therapeutic and Industrial Uses of Music: a Review of the Literature* (New York, 1948)
Music Therapy Yearbook (1951–63)
Journal of Music Therapy (1964–)
E. T. Gaston, ed.: *Music in Therapy* (New York, 1968)
H. L. Bonny and L. M. Savary: *Music and your Mind* (New York, 1973)
R. M. Graham, ed.: *Music for the Exceptional Child* (Reston, VA, 1975)
D. E. Michel: *Music Therapy* (Springfield, IL, 1976)
Music Therapy Index (1976–)
A. L. Solomon: "Music in Special Education before 1930: Hearing and Speech Development," *Journal of Research in Music Education*, xxviii (1980), 237
W. Lathom: *Role of Music Therapy in the Education of Handicapped Children and Youth* (Lawrence, KS, 1981)
Music Therapy (1981–)
Music Therapy Perspectives (1981–)

GEORGE L. DUERKSEN

Music trades. The terms "music trade" and "music trades," slightly different in meaning but often used interchangeably, came into general use in the USA in the mid-19th century. Piano manufacture and music publishing were the giants of the music trades, but the area covers practically every kind of commercial activity in the manufacture, importation, and sale of printed music, musical instruments, and accessories.

1. History to *c*1800. 2. *c*1800 to *c*1900. 3. Music publishers' associations. 4. Music retailing since 1900. 5. Trade journals.

1. HISTORY TO *c*1800. As Oscar Sonneck showed in articles and books written early in the 20th century, music in the British colonies before 1800 was by no means limited to psalm singing, as 19th-century writers sometimes assumed. There were public concerts during the 1730s in Boston, and Charleston, South Carolina, and ballad operas were also performed in Charleston. The earliest known performance of a ballad opera with orchestral accompaniment was of *The Beggar's Opera* in the little tobacco town that is now Upper Marlboro, Maryland, in 1752. New York and Philadelphia also enjoyed a secular musical life before the Revolution. All this activity required musical merchandise, but it would be anachronistic to speak of American music trades in this early period; the necessary supplies were imported from England and Germany and sold usually by booksellers or by musicians who were also teachers.

Some notable names were, however, associated with these early music-supply activities. The earliest known music shop in the colonies was opened in 1759 by Michael Hillegas of Philadelphia, who advertised in the *Pennsylvania Magazine*. He did not keep his shop for more than a few years because he became active in pre-Revolutionary political affairs and in 1789 was sworn in as the first Treasurer of the United States. Paul Revere, a coppersmith, is said to have engraved the plates for Josiah Flagg's *Collection of the Best Psalm Tunes* (1764), and after the Revolution he became known as a bellfounder. Benjamin Franklin, also a Philadelphian, and a friend of Hillegas, did not allow his Revolutionary and other activities to interfere with his inventive proclivities in many fields, including music. As a consequence, during the Sesquicentennial celebrations of 1926 he was honored by the Music Industries Chamber of Commerce for his several achievements in music and adopted as "Patron Saint of the music industries of the United States."

2. *c*1800 TO *c*1900. Little has been written about sources of musical necessities during the Revolution, although the numerous military bands and drummer-boys of the Continental Army managed somehow to obtain instruments and accessories. Once the war was over there began an influx of musicians from Europe, including some notable figures in the music trades. One of the earliest of these, and without doubt the most commercially successful, was John Jacob Astor. He was apprenticed in 1779 to his elder brother George, of the London firm of Astor and Broadwood, makers of various musical instruments including flutes and pianos. John Jacob had had his mind on North America since his childhood in Waldorf, Germany, and in 1783 he left for the USA, carrying with him his capital in the form of seven flutes (which he may have had a hand in making). These he sold at a profit, and he then sent for more instruments from his brother and set up shop in New York. He soon entered the fur trade and then dealt in real estate, but as late as 1789 his shop front in Maiden Lane, New York, read "John Jacob Astor, Furs and Pianos."

With the arrival of musicians during and after the 1790s, still largely from Britain and Germany, the incipient music trades entered on a period of transition that lasted through the 1830s. Music, instruments, and accessories continued to be imported from Europe, but gradually the East Coast acquired a degree of self-sufficiency in musical products. The indexes of publishers, engravers, and printers in Sonneck (2/1945) and Wolfe, together with the editions they list, give a good idea of the infant music-publishing trade in that period. No equivalent sources exist for instrument making and allied crafts, but Loesser gives a good idea of the social importance of the piano during the transitional period.

By 1840 the USA was no longer confined to the land between the Appalachians and the Atlantic. The 1840s were a time of great change. The Erie and the Chesapeake and Ohio canals, followed closely by the railroads, took immigrants through what had once been a mountain barrier. The Mexican War, the California gold rush, the potato famine in Ireland, and the 1848 uprisings in Europe all affected what now came to be called the "music trades," as did new developments in instrument making – the application of valves and pistons to brass instruments, indigenous improvements in piano design, and the introduction into the USA of the reed organ (with alterations in the bellows action and a preference for the more mobile "melodeon" type). This rapid expansion, which was to continue throughout the century and was accompanied by increasing self-sufficiency, resulted in greater specialization and a new mechanism, called "jobbing" or "wholesaling," to get the merchandise from maker to seller, and from seller to user. These patterns are described with a certain gusto by Bill, whose *General History of the Music Trades in America* is devoted entirely to the making and selling of pianos and reed organs. Its four sections cover manufacturers; the supply trades (furnishing the felt, ivory keys, strings, and sometimes the whole action); wholesalers; and managers, travelers, and salesmen.

3. MUSIC PUBLISHERS' ASSOCIATIONS. During the second half of the 19th century there existed the BOARD OF MUSIC TRADE concerned largely with the other main area of the music trades, music publishing. (In those days most music publishers owned retail shops which sold not only their own publications but other products as well.) The Board of Music Trade, founded in 1855, operated apparently on a national basis from the beginning, and both its name and its general character may have been suggested by the Board of Trade that had been a department of the British government since 1786. (The National Board of Trade in the USA was based on the British model, but this did not come into existence until 1868, when the Board of Music Trade had been functioning more than a decade.)

In 1870 the Board of Music Trade issued a *Complete Catalogue of Sheet Music and Musical Works*; but it took no part in drafting the Copyright Act of 1891 (which, for the first time, gave protection in the USA to works published elsewhere), and it was by then in decline. By 1895 its membership had fallen to three firms. As early as 1880 it was occasionally referred to as the Music Publishers' Association, and in June 1895 it was reorganized as the Music Publishers' Association (MPA) of the United States. Still in existence, that organization works in cooperation with the National Music Publishers' Association (the publishers of popular music, who formed their own group in 1917) and the Church Music Publishers' Association (founded about the same time). The combined roster of the three groups for 1981 numbered 379 American agents or parent companies; in addition, about 1800 American and foreign music publishers are connected with the parent or agent companies. This catalogue, prepared by the Trade Relations Committee of the MPA, no longer refers to the "music trades" but to the "music industry."

4. MUSIC RETAILING SINCE 1900. Changes also took place in the other music trades. In 1902 the National Piano Manufacturers' Association met with more than 200 dealers from 37 states, who joined them to form the National Association of Piano Dealers of America. As the population grew, musical products continued to proliferate, and by the end of World War I there were booming markets for phonograph records and player pianos, and public schools were beginning to prepare their pupils for the orchestras and bands that in a few decades would constitute whole industries in themselves. Pianos and record players were often sold in furniture stores. Some of these developments are reflected in a further reorganization in 1919, by which the National Association of Piano Dealers of America became the National Association of Music Merchants (NAMM): the retail trade had finally come into its own. NAMM has a membership numbered in the thousands, including some manufacturers and wholesalers (who have also their own separate associations). Twice a year NAMM puts on trade shows: a Winter Market and, in summer, an International Music and Sound Expo. The *Musical Merchandise Review* is published monthly, and at intervals NAMM issues a *Retail Music Products Report*.

After World War II (during which all music-instrument manufacturing ceased by executive order, except for military contracts) a burst of technological advances resulted in the marketing of many new instruments, most of them electric or electronic; by the 1980s "chip" technology had brought into being a host of new gadgets in which music plays a part. The home use of audio tape has made serious inroads into the record business (just as 50 years earlier the record business eroded the sale of pianos for domestic use), and videotapes and discs have become a new area in the music trades.

5. TRADE JOURNALS. *Music Trades*, a monthly journal for the entire music industry, was started in 1890 by a British immigrant, John C. Freund, to help the music trades to keep pace with an expanding population and proliferating technology. In the first issue Freund wrote that *Music Trades* would be "devoted exclusively to all such matters that are of interest to music publishers, to piano and organ and musical instrument dealers and makers." The journal is still devoted to the concerns of those who make and sell instruments and accessories; it reports on NAMM's trade shows and on other events, covering music as an art, an entertainment, a profession, and a business.

While *Music Trades* and the *Musical Merchandise Review* (see §4, above) look at music products from the viewpoints of the maker, wholesaler, and retailer, the interests of performers and listeners are covered by *The Purchaser's Guide to the Music Industries*, published annually since 1897 by the Music Trades Corporation. The guide includes details of instrument makers, importers, suppliers, and repairers, as well as publishers and wholesalers of sheet music, with a paragraph of comment on each firm.

BIBLIOGRAPHY

Complete Catalogue of Sheet Music and Musical Works Published by the Board of Music Trade (New York, 1870/*R*1973 with an introduction by D. J. Epstein)
E. L. Bill: *General History of the Music Trades in America* (New York, 1891)
O. G. T. Sonneck: *A Bibliography of Early Secular American Music* (Washington, DC, 1905; rev. and enlarged by W. T. Upton, 2/1945/*R*1964)
D. Dixon: "Benjamin Franklin and Music," *The Amazing Benjamin Franklin*, ed. J. H. Smythe (New York, 1929), 185
W. A. Fisher: *One Hundred and Fifty Years of Music Publishing in the United States* (Boston, 1933/*R*1977)
P. S. Carpenter: *Music, an Art and a Business* (Norman, OK, 1950)
A. Loesser: *Men, Women and Pianos: a Social History* (New York, 1954)
S. Shemel and M. W. Krasilovsky: *This Business of Music* (New York, 1964, rev. and enlarged 5/1985)
R. J. Wolfe: *Secular Music in America, 1801–1825: a Bibliography* (New York, 1964)
S. Shemel and M. W. Krasilovsky: *More about this Business of Music* (New York, 1967, rev. and enlarged 3/1982)

WILLIAM LICHTENWANGER

Musin, Ovide (*b* Nandrin, Belgium, 22 Sept 1854; *d* Brooklyn, NY, 24 Nov 1929). Belgian violinist. He studied at the Liège Conservatory where his teachers included Hubert Léonard; at the age of 13 he shared first prize for violin with Ysaÿe and in 1869 won the gold medal for solo and quartet playing. In 1872 he moved to Paris where he continued study with Léonard, learned viola, and was coached by Henry Vieuxtemps. Between 1873 and 1882 he toured Europe, and in November 1883 made his first appearance in the USA as soloist with the New York SO under Walter Damrosch. He later played with the Philharmonic under Theodore Thomas, but the two did not agree: Musin accused Thomas of encouraging German musicians in the USA to look down on his style of playing. Musin then formed his own concert troupe and made many American tours. His 1892 tour to the West Coast included 164 concerts, and from California he went on to Honolulu, Australia, New Zealand, and Mexico. On his return he maintained a busy concert and tour schedule, and in 1896 traveled to Japan, China, and the Philippines. In 1898 he succeeded César Thomson as violin professor at Liège and conducted the Société Royal des Amateurs there, while spending half his time in New York. In 1908 he resigned the Liège post and established the Belgian School of Violin in New York.

Musin was known for his effortless and sensational playing; in the late 1880s he was regarded by some as perhaps the best popular violinist since Ole Bull. He composed works for violin and orchestra or piano, and made transcriptions or arrangements of music by Baroque composers. His publications include *System for Daily Practise* (1899), *The Belgian School of the Violin* (1916), articles for American and Belgian newspapers and journals, and his autobiography (1920). He married the soprano Annie Louise Hodges-Tanner in 1891, and she often joined him on tour.

BIBLIOGRAPHY

GroveAS
W. S. B. Mathews, ed.: *A Hundred Years of Music in America* (Chicago, 1889/*R*1970)
A. Bachmann: *An Encyclopedia of the Violin* (New York, 1925/*R*1975)
Obituary, *New York Times* (25 Nov 1929)
F. H. Martens: "Musin, Ovide," *DAB*
M. Campbell: *The Great Violinists* (Garden City, NY, 1981)

JEFFREY R. REHBACH

Muskogean. American Indian language family; *see* CHOCTAW, CREEK, and SEMINOLE.

Muslim music. For a discussion of Muslim music in the USA, *see* ISLAMIC MUSIC, AMERICAN.

Muti, Riccardo (*b* Naples, Italy, 28 July 1941). Italian conductor. He graduated from the Naples Conservatory as a piano student and later continued musical studies at the Milan Conservatory with Bruno Bettinelli (composition) and Antonino Votto (conducting). He won the 1967 Guido Cantelli International Conductors' Competition and made his début the next year with the orchestra of Italian Radio. After serving as principal conductor of the Florence Maggio Musicale (from 1969), he made his American début in 1972 with the Philadelphia Orchestra, of which he became principal guest conductor in 1975 and music director in 1980; in 1978 he also became music director of the New Philharmonia Orchestra (later the Philharmonia Orchestra), London. He has appeared with the leading orchestras in Europe and the USA and has toured internationally with the Philadelphia Orchestra and the Philharmonia Orchestra. He has been equally active in opera, conducting regularly at the Salzburg Festival since 1971 and frequently in Vienna, Paris, and Munich, and at La Scala and Covent Garden. Gifted with deep musical intuition and an efficient technique, he has conducted much 20th-century music by, among others, Britten, Dallapiccola, Hindemith, Ligeti, Petrassi, and Shostakovich. His recordings of works by Mendelssohn, Verdi, Mussorgsky, Orff, Stravinsky, Vivaldi, and Cherubini won awards in the 1970s.

BIBLIOGRAPHY

F. Granville Barker: "Riccardo Muti," *Records and Recording*, xviii/7 (1975), 12
S. Gould: "Riccardo Muti," *HiFi/MusAm*, xxvi/2 (1976), 28
D. Webster: "Riccardo Muti," *HiFi/MusAm*, xxviii/3 (1978), 6
P. Hart: *Conductors: a New Generation* (New York, 1979), 105
R. Baxter: "Pure Fire," *Opera News*, xlv/4 (1980), 18
"Muti, Riccardo," *CBY 1980*
H. Matheopoulos: "Riccardo Muti: a Normal Person Living a far-from-normal Life," *Maestro: Encounters with Conductors of Today* (London, 1982), 360
J. Rockwell: "Muti Changes Philadelphia's Tempo," *New York Times* (21 April 1985)

LEONARDO PINZAUTI/R

Muzak. The name of the first company in the USA to transmit background music; by extension the word has come to be applied to commercially produced ENVIRONMENTAL MUSIC of all types.

Muzio, Claudia [Muzzio, Claudina] (*b* Pavia, Italy, 7 Feb 1889; *d* Rome, Italy, 24 May 1936). Italian soprano. Among her teachers was Annetta Casaloni. She made her début on 15 January 1910 in Arezzo and subsequently appeared at La Scala, and at Covent Garden, where she performed some of her best roles, including Desdemona, Margherita (in Boito's *Mefistofele*), Tosca, and Mimì. After making her début at the Metropolitan Opera on 4 December 1916 as Tosca, she became a much valued member of the company for seven consecutive seasons, creating the role of Giorgetta there in Puccini's *Il tabarro* (December 1918). She also sang for all but one season between 1922 and 1930 with the Chicago Civic Opera and was much in demand in South American houses during the same period. At La Scala she gave notable performances under Toscanini as Violetta, Leonora (*Il trovatore*), and Tosca in 1926–7; thereafter she sang mostly in Rome, though she returned briefly to the Metropolitan in 1934.

Muzio's repertory embraced all the leading Verdi and Puccini roles, as well as those of the *verismo* school, which she interpreted in a more subtle and refined manner than was usual. Nobility and sweetness of voice and aspect, together with intense drama and pathos, were marked features of her style. Few of her many recordings do her full justice, although there are some unforgettable achievements, notably her infinitely pathetic reading of Germont's letter in the last act of *La traviata*.

BIBLIOGRAPHY

C. A. Jahant: "Muzio Onstage and Off," *Saturday Review*, xl (28 Dec 1957), 31
M. J. Matz: "First Ladies of the Puccini Premieres, 4: Claudia Muzio," *Opera News*, xxiv/24 (1960), 10
R. Celletti: "Muzio, Claudia," *Le grandi voci* (Rome, 1964) [with discography by R. Vegeto]
J. B. Richards: "Claudia Muzio," *Record Collector*, xvii (1967–8), 197–237, 256 [with discography by H. M. Barnes]

DESMOND SHAWE-TAYLOR/R

My country 'tis of thee. The first line of the national song entitled *America*; *see* PATRIOTIC MUSIC, §1.

Myers, Kurtz (*b* Columbus Grove, OH, 16 Feb 1913). Music librarian. He studied at Hillsdale (Michigan) College (BA 1934), the University of Michigan (ABLS 1936, MA 1936), and at Columbia University. After serving first as head of the Audio Visual Division (1946–54) and then as chief of the music and performing arts department at the Detroit Public Library, he was appointed head of the music department at the Buffalo and Erie County Library (1969–71) and of the arts and recreation department at the Denver Public Library (1971–6). Since 1948 Myers has compiled and edited the quarterly index to record reviews in *Notes*, the journal of the Music Library Association, on which were based his *Record Ratings* (1956) and *Index to Record Reviews* (1978–80).

PAULA MORGAN

NAACC. National Association for American Composers and Conductors; *see* NATIONAL ASSOCIATION OF COMPOSERS, USA.

Nabokov, Nicolas [Nikolay] (*b* Lyubcha, Novogrudok, nr Minsk, Belorussia, 17 April 1903; *d* New York, 6 April 1978). Composer of Russian origin, cousin of the writer Vladimir Nabokov. He first studied composition privately with Vladimir Ivanovich Rebikov in Yalta and St. Petersburg (1913–20), then at the Stuttgart Conservatory (1920–22) and the Berlin Hochschule für Musik with Paul Juon and Ferruccio Busoni (1922–3). He studied at the Sorbonne in 1923–6, and was awarded the degree of Licence ès lettres. From 1926 to 1933 he divided his time between Paris and Germany, privately teaching languages, composition, and literature. In 1933 Nabokov immigrated to the USA where, at the invitation of the Barnes Foundation (Merion, Pennsylvania), he gave a lecture series on the traditions of European music. He became an American citizen in 1939.

Nabokov taught at Wells College, Aurora, New York (1936–41), St. John's College, Annapolis (1941–4), and the Peabody Conservatory (1947–52). In 1944–7 he worked for the American government in Berlin, as an assistant in charge of film, theater, and music, and served as cultural adviser to the American ambassador. From 1946 to 1948 he was editor-in-chief of the USSR division of "Voice of America." From the 1950s he lived chiefly in Paris, although he was active as a composer and a promoter of music festivals all over the world. He became secretary-general of the Congress for Cultural Freedom in 1951, and organized the Paris festival "Masterpieces of the 20th Century" (1952), the "Music in our Time" festival (Rome, 1954), and the "East-West Music Encounter" in Tokyo (1961). He served as director of the Berlin Festival and acted as cultural adviser to the West German chancellor Willy Brandt (1963–6). In 1968 Nabokov taught at CUNY as a visiting professor of humanities, and in 1970–73 served as composer-in-residence at the Aspen Institute for Humanistic Studies. He was elected to the National Institute of Arts and Letters in 1970.

As a composer Nabokov is closely identified with music for dance. His first important work, the ballet-oratorio *Ode* (1927), was commissioned by Diaghilev, who produced it in London, Paris, and Berlin. Another ballet, *Union Pacific*, commemorates the completion of the transcontinental railroad and makes use of popular 19th-century American tunes. Nabokov's inspiration is basically lyrical, but his music shows strong dramatic powers and unusual orchestral eloquence. He wrote an entertaining volume of essays, *Old Friends and New Music* (1951), the books *Igor Stravinsky* (1964) and *Bagázh: Memoirs of a Russian Cosmopolitan* (1975), and articles – mainly on Russian music and musicians – for numerous periodicals including *Atlantic*, *Harper's*, *Musical America*, *New Republic*, and *Partisan Review*.

WORKS

(only those composed in the USA)

The Holy Devil (opera, 2, Spender), 1954–8, Louisville, 16 April 1958; rev. as Der Tod des Grigorij Rasputin (3), Cologne, Germany, 27 Nov 1959 [Eng. version, Rasputin's End]

Love's Labour's Lost (opera, Auden, Kallman, after Shakespeare), 1970–?73; Brussels, 7 Feb 1973

Ballets: La vie de Polichinelle, Paris, 1934; Union Pacific, Philadelphia, 6 April 1934; The Last Flower (after Thurber), 1941; Don Quixote (3, Nabokov, Balanchine), Aug 1965; The Wanderer, 1966

Samson Agonistes (incidental music, Milton), Aurora, NY, 14 May 1938

Vocal: Job (J. Maritain), oratorio, male vv, orch, 1933, unpubd; America was Promises (A. MacLeish), cantata, A, Bar, male vv, perf. 1940; The Return of Pushkin (V. Nabokov, after Pushkin), elegy, S/T, orch, perf, 1948; Vita nuova (after Dante), S, T, orch, perf. 1951; Symboli chrestiani, Bar, orch, perf. 1956; 4 poèmes de Boris Pasternak, 1v, pf (1961), arr. 1v, str, 1969; 6 Lyric Songs (Akhmatova: Requiem), 1966

Orch: Le fiancé, ov., after Pushkin, 1934; Vie de Polichinelle, suite, 1934; Sinfonia biblica, perf. 1941; Fl Conc., 1948; Concerto corale, fl, str, pf, 1950; Les hommages, conc., vc, orch, perf. 1953; The Last Flower, sym. suite, 1957; [4] Studies in Solitude, perf. 1961; Sym. no.3 "A Prayer," perf. 1968; Sym. Variations, 1967; Variations on a Theme by Tchaikovsky, vc, orch, ?1968; The Hunter's Picnic, sym. suite [from ballet Don Quixote] (1973)

Other works: Serenata estiva, str qt, 1937; Pf Sonata (1940); Bn Sonata, 1941; 3 Sym. Marches, band, 1945; Canzone, Introduzione e Allegro, vn, pf (1950)

Principal publishers: Editions Russes, Senart

BIBLIOGRAPHY

EwenD

A. Hughes: "Nicolas Nabokov, 75," *New York Times* (7 April 1978)

BRUCE CARR/KATHERINE K. PRESTON

NACUSA. *See* NATIONAL ASSOCIATION OF COMPOSERS, USA.

Nagano, Kent (George) (*b* Morro Bay, CA, 22 Nov 1951). Conductor. The son of Japanese-American parents, he was taught both Asian and Western music; although he began studying piano with his mother at the age of four, by his high school years he was specializing in the koto. Nagano was educated at Oxford University (1969), the University of California, Santa Cruz (BA 1974), where he studied with Grosvenor Cooper, San Francisco State University (MM 1976), and the University of Toronto. In San Francisco, he studied conducting with Laszlo Varga and piano with Goodwin Sammel. In 1976 his performance of Cavalli's *Ormindo* in San Francisco was heard by John Reeves White of the New York Pro Musica, which led to Nagano's appointment as a guest conductor representing the USA at the Curso Internacional de Musica do Parana in Brazil in 1977. Between 1977 and 1979, he worked as an apprentice, assistant conductor, and associate artistic director for Caldwell's Opera Company of Boston. In 1978 he became music director of the Berkeley (California) SO, where he became known as an adventurous musician with an innovative repertory. Among the works he has conducted are Janáček's *The Excursions of Mr. Brouček* and Busoni's *Turandot*. He is most closely associated with the compositions of Messiaen, having performed a number of the orchestral works in Berkeley, some under the composer's direction. In December 1983 he was Ozawa's assistant for the première of Messiaen's first opera, *Saint François d'Assise*, at the Paris Opéra; he conducted a subsequent performance there. In 1984 he became music director of the Ojai Music Festival, made his début with the Boston SO, and joined the faculty at the Tanglewood Music Center. The following year he was appointed chief guest conductor of Pierre Boulez's Ensemble Intercontemporain and, with Hugh Wolff, was a winner of the first Affiliate Artists' Seaver Conducting Award. Nagano's ability with complex scores, his confidence before large orchestral forces, and his remarkably inquisitive musical sense suggest he is destined for a major international career.

MICHAEL WALSH

NAJE. *See* NATIONAL ASSOCIATION OF JAZZ EDUCATORS.

Nakota [Yankton]. American Plains Indian group belonging to the SIOUX.

Nambe. American Indians belonging to the TEWA subgroup of the EASTERN PUEBLO.

NAMM. National Association of Music Merchants; *see* MUSIC TRADES, §4.

NAMT. National Association for Music Therapy; *see* MUSIC THERAPY.

Nancarrow, Conlon (*b* Texarkana, AR, 27 Oct 1912). Composer. As a young man he played both jazz and classical trumpet. He attended the Cincinnati College-Conservatory of Music (1929–32) and later studied composition and counterpoint in Boston with Slonimsky, Piston, and Sessions (1933–6). In 1937 he went to Spain to fight with the Abraham Lincoln Brigade against Franco. On his return to the USA in 1939, he became involved in New York's new-music scene and contributed several reviews to *Modern Music*, but the American government's hostility towards him because of his socialist views (he could not obtain a passport) prompted him to move to Mexico City in 1940, and he has lived there ever since, becoming a Mexican citizen in 1956.

From the late 1940s Nancarrow has composed exclusively for player piano, to which he turned mainly because of his frustration with the inability of performers to execute even moderately difficult rhythms. He returned briefly to New York in 1947 and had a machine built for him on which to punch piano rolls; he plots his music directly on the paper and then punches it note by note, achieving remarkable rhythmic accuracy. His two upright pianos, both fitted with Ampico reproducing mechanisms, have hammers modified to produce more incisive attacks; on one they are of wood covered with steel straps, and on the other standard felt hammers have been covered with leather to which metal tacks have been affixed. Nancarrow also experimented for a time, unsuccessfully, with a mechanically controlled percussion orchestra and a prepared grand player piano.

Nancarrow's primary interest is tempo, in particular the "temporal dissonance" of several different rates occuring simultaneously. In this he was influenced by the writings of Cowell, who in *New Musical Resources* (1930) not only discussed the concept of temporal dissonance but also suggested using the player piano to explore polyrhythms. Some of Cowell's proposals for relating rhythm to pitch are brilliantly realized in Nancarrow's music; in Study no.23, for example, each pitch corresponds to a rhythmic value whose duration is determined by the pitch's frequency. In some passages (as in Studies nos.23 and 35) Nancarrow has evidently organized pitch and rhythm graphically, by punching holes at the intersections of variously inclined straight lines drawn on the piano roll.

Nancarrow's abiding concern with formal structure is evident in his frequent use of melodic motifs (particularly the minor 3rd), sequence, isorhythm, arithmetic and geometric progressions, and various symmetrical relationships. The predominant structural device in Nancarrow's music is canon; most of the studies after no.12 are strictly canonic throughout. With rare exceptions, each voice moves at its own rate, producing shifting relationships as the faster voices catch up with, or move away from, the slower ones. Tempo ratios between voices range from the relative "temporal consonance" of 3 : 4 in Study no.18 to the "dissonance" of 17 : 18 : 19 : 20 in Study no.36 and $2 : \sqrt{2}$ in Study no.33. In some cases, Studies nos.22 and 27 for example, each voice is assigned its own rate of acceleration or deceleration; the imitation aids the listener in hearing the subtle tempo relationships.

Many of the canons involve a symmetrical partitioning of the piano's total range (*B″* to *a″″* on Nancarrow's instruments) into overlapping segments, one for each voice. Extremely high and low registers are usually treated equally, regardless of differences in tone quality. His harmonic and melodic vocabulary derives to a large extent from traditional tonality, especially in the earlier studies. But even within the free atonality of the later studies, tonal centers are often implied and diatonic materials are common; closely spaced major triads are a recurrent sonority, and the studies usually end with a rising V–I cadence. Jazz materials are present explicitly (no.3) and implicitly in both early and late studies. Two of the studies (nos.6 and 12) are based on Spanish music.

Nancarrow's studies fully exploit the player piano's potential for rhythmic complexity and textural variety; they are showpieces of virtuosity far beyond the capabilities of human performers, with extremely fast arpeggios, trills, and glissandos, effortless leaps, widely spaced block chords, and complex contrapuntal activity involving the entire keyboard. For the most part his music testifies to his great skill at breathing life into the instru-

Conlon Nancarrow at his punching machine, preparing a piano roll

ment, and many of the studies have an elegance and spontaneity that belie their mechanical origins.

The *New Music Quarterly* published three of Nancarrow's early works for conventional instruments in 1938 and his Rhythm Study no. 1 for player piano in 1952. In the late 1950s John Edmunds, then head of the Americana Division of the New York Public Library, brought tapes of Nancarrow's player piano music to the attention of John Cage, who then used several of the studies in Merce Cunningham's dance work *Crises*. Despite this, and a recording of 12 studies issued in the 1960s, Nancarrow's work first received serious attention only in the 1970s, when Peter Garland of Soundings Press began publishing the complete studies. Further recognition came in the form of a commission from the European Broadcasting System (for Study no. 39), a Letter of Distinction from the American Music Center, and a $300,000 fellowship from the Chicago-based MacArthur Foundation (1982). Complete recordings of the Studies are being made available by 1750 Arch Records.

WORKS

Sarabande and Scherzo, ob, bn, pf, 1930; Blues for Pf, 1935; Prelude for Pf, 1935; Toccata, vn, pf, 1935; Septet, 1940; Pf Sonatina, 1941; Trio, cl, bn, pf, 1942; Suite for Orch, 1943; Str Qt, 1945

Studies for Player Piano, nos. 1–29, 31–8, 42, n.d.: subtitles incl. no. 21 "Canon – X," no. 27 "Canon – 5%/6%/8%/11%," no. 37 "Canon – 150/160$\frac{5}{7}$/168$\frac{3}{4}$/180/187$\frac{1}{2}$/200/210/225/240/250/262$\frac{1}{2}$/281$\frac{1}{4}$"; Study no. 30 for Prepared Player Piano, n.d.; Studies for Two Player Pianos, nos. 39–41, 43–4, n.d.: subtitles incl. no. 40a "Canon e/pi"

Principal publisher: Soundings

BIBLIOGRAPHY

P. Garland, ed.: *Conlon Nancarrow: Selected Studies for Player Piano* (Berkeley, CA, 1977) [incl. writings on Nancarrow and his music by Amirkhanian, Cage, Mumma, Reynolds, and Tenney]

C. Gagne and T. Caras: "Conlon Nancarrow," *Soundpieces: Interviews with American Composers* (Metuchen, NJ, 1982), 281 [incl. list of works]

P. Garland: "Conlon Nancarrow: Chronicle of a Friendship," *Americas: Essays in American Music and Culture (1973–80)* (Santa Fe, 1982), 157

R. Reynolds: "Conlon Nancarrow: Interviews in Mexico City and San Francisco," *American Music*, ii/2 (1984), 1

P. Carlsen: *The Player Piano Music of Conlon Nancarrow* (diss., CUNY, 1985)

PHILIP CARLSEN

NANM. *See* NATIONAL ASSOCIATION OF NEGRO MUSICIANS.

Nanton, Tricky Sam [Irish, Joseph N.; Joe] (*b* New York, 1 Feb 1904; *d* San Francisco, CA, 20 July 1946). Jazz trombonist. After playing in the early 1920s with Cliff Jordan and Elmer Snowden, he joined Duke Ellington's orchestra in mid-1926, replacing Charlie Irvis (for illustration *see* JAZZ, fig. 5). He soon mastered the novel growl and plunger-mute technique pioneered by Ellington's trumpeter Bubber Miley, thus earning his unusual nickname and becoming a key figure in producing the familiar "jungle" sound of Ellington's early recordings. Nanton remained with Ellington for the whole of his career, contributing numerous excellent "talking" solos to Ellington's recorded output. Though limited in dexterity and range (his solos seldom span more than an octave and often merely elaborate two or three pitches), Nanton's performances have an earthy, poignant sincerity, which is heightened by the complexity of their musical surroundings.

RECORDINGS

(selective list)

As sideman with Duke Ellington: East St. Louis Toodle-Oo (1926, Voc. 1064); Black and Tan Fantasy (1927, OK 40955); Yellow Dog Blues (1928, Bruns. 3987); Harlem Flat Blues (1929, Bruns. 4309); Saddest Tale (1934, Bruns. 7310); Ko-Ko (1940, Vic. 26577); Bojangles/A Portrait of Bert Williams (1940, Vic. 26644); Blue Serge (1941, Vic. 27356)

As sideman with others: C. Williams: I can't believe that you're in love with me/Diga Diga Doo (1937, Variety 555); R. Stewart: San Juan Hill (1939, Voc./OK 5510)

BIBLIOGRAPHY

SouthernB

R. Stewart: "Tribute to Tricky Sam (Joe Nanton)," *Jazz Masters of the Thirties* (New York, 1972/*R*1980), 103

J. BRADFORD ROBINSON

Nash, (Frederic) Ogden (*b* Rye, NY, 19 Aug 1902; *d* Baltimore, MD, 19 May 1971). Poet and lyricist. He studied at Harvard University and worked in New York before settling in Baltimore as a full-time writer. He produced several volumes of light and satiric verse, a few screenplays, and lyrics for Broadway and television shows. More than 65 of his published poems have been set to music, the majority from his many verses about animals. The earliest known setting, *Quartet for Prosperous Love Children* (1933) by Robert Armbruster, is included in Nash's *Happy Days* (also 1933). Most of the settings are found in a few choral and song cycles, the earliest of which was *Ogden Nash's Musical Zoo* by Vernon Duke. Other cycles include *Who's Who in the Zoo* by Jean Berger, *Ogden Nash Suite* by Jerry Bilik, *Essays on Women* by Arthur Frackenpohl, and *A Musical Menu* and *A Musical Menagerie* by Philip Hagemann.

Nash was a skilled and prolific lyricist. He and S. J. Perelman collaborated with Kurt Weill on the popular Broadway musical *One Touch of Venus*. With Vernon Duke and others he wrote the musical comedy *Sweet Bye and Bye* and the musical revues *Two's Company* and *The Littlest Revue*. He also wrote verses to accompany Saint-Saëns' *Carnival of the Animals* and lyrics for two television programs, "Art Carney Meets 'Peter and the Wolf'" and "Art Carney Meets 'The Sorcerer's Apprentice'," which featured the Baird Marionettes with music adapted from Prokofiev and Dukas and composed by Paul Weston.

BIBLIOGRAPHY

D. Ewen: *New Complete Book of the American Musical Theater* (New York, 1970)

R. Lewine and A. Simon: *Songs of the American Theater* (New York, 1973)

C. D. Kinsman, ed.: *Contemporary Authors*, permanent ser., i (Detroit, 1975), 475

G. Bordman: *American Musical Theatre: a Chronicle* (New York, 1978)

M. A. Hovland: *Musical Settings of American Poetry: a Bibliography* (Westport, CT, in preparation) [incl. list of settings]

MICHAEL HOVLAND

Nashville. Capital city of Tennessee (pop. 455,651; metropolitan area 850,505). On the banks of the Cumberland River in the north central part of the state, the city was founded in 1779 by settlers of Irish and Scottish descent, and incorporated in 1806. In the mid-20th century it became known as the home of country music.

1. Art music. 2. Popular music.

1. ART MUSIC. A college was chartered within five years of the city's founding. The early settlers placed a strong emphasis on education, and by 1824 Nashville was referred to as the "Athens of the South." Despite the presence of several universities music did not figure prominently in higher education until 1871, when Fisk University sent its Jubilee Singers on tour to raise money for the school. As in many cities in the 19th century music instruction was offered principally in women's seminaries and black schools. Churches did not proliferate as rapidly as schools in Nashville; by 1833, however, First Presbyterian had an organ and a choir in its second building. Opera was introduced as early as 1854, when a performance of Donizetti's *Lucia di Lammermoor* was given at the Adelphi Theatre by Luigi Arditi's Italian Opera Company. By the 1860s operas by Verdi and other Italian composers were a regular feature of Nashville's concert life. Jenny Lind (who performed in 1851 as part of her tour managed by Barnum), Ole Bull, Henry Vieuxtemps, and Sigismond Thalberg were among the 19th-century concert artists who visited the city. Dancing schools flourished in spite of some moral and religious dissent expressed in newspaper editorials. Amateur organizations, especially those made up of children, were active in benefit concerts, and amateur musical groups on European models were often formed. The Schiller Music Festival was held in 1859, at which oratorios by Handel and Haydn were performed. There was little artistic activity during the Civil War; Nashville was occupied by Union armies, and many churches were badly damaged. In 1865 St. Mary's Catholic Church was the site of a concert given to celebrate its rebuilding; it prospered after the war, as did other churches in the city.

In the 1880s the impressive Vendôme theater opened with a gala performance of *Il trovatore* in which Abbott appeared. Later the theater was the site of concerts by Paderewski, Caruso, and the New York SO under Walter Damrosch (1904), and of a performance of Wagner's *Parsifal* given by members of the Metropolitan Opera (1905). Between 1890 and 1930 Nashville was an important city on the vaudeville circuit; Lillian Russell and Kitty Cheatham, a local resident, were among the most popular performers in this genre. Music stores sold sheet music and pianos from at least 1890. In 1892 the Union Gospel Tabernacle was opened; this building, the construction of which had been financed by Thomas Ryman, a wealthy steamboat captain, is notable for its fine acoustics. It was used first for revival meetings and, after Ryman's death, for secular entertainments ranging from Gilbert and Sullivan to the "Grand Ole Opry" (see §2 below), which appeared there for well over 30 years.

There were several early attempts to form a symphony orchestra in Nashville; an orchestra performed under the name Nashville SO in 1904, as did an ensemble of 62 players, founded and led by F. Arthur Henkel, from 1920 to 1927. A permanent organization was formed in 1946 by Walter Sharp; its conductors have been William Strickland (1946–51), Guy Taylor (1951–9), Willis Page (1959–67), Thor Johnson (1967–75), Michael Charry (1976–82), and Kenneth Schermerhorn (from 1983). In 1980 the orchestra moved to Andrew Jackson Hall, a handsome structure with an acoustically well-designed auditorium seating 2440; the hall is one of three buildings in the Tennessee Center for the Performing Arts.

Music instruction is offered at a number of colleges and universities. Belmont College grants BA and BM degrees in music, church music, commercial music, music education, theory and composition, and piano pedagogy; the school has about 200 students and 35 faculty members (20 full-time). The music department at Fisk University was founded in 1885; it offers BA, BM, and BS degrees in music and music education, and has five faculty members and about 20 students. Tennessee State University offers BA, BS, MA, and MS degrees in music and music education; the school has about 50 students and eight full-time faculty members.

2. POPULAR MUSIC. Vernacular musical traditions date back to early times; in 1820 Cary Harris published a tunebook, *Western Harmony for Singers*. By 1823 riverboat traffic with New Orleans had been initiated, and Nashville began to reap the advantages of its geographical position. In the 1850s several minstrel groups visited Nashville, of which the most renowned was Mat Peel's

Campbell Minstrels. In the 1890s W. D. Scanlon and his Irish Singing Comedians were immensely popular. The Fairfield Four, from Nashville's Fairfield Baptist Church, was perhaps the most influential male gospel quartet before World War II; they were heard extensively on radio and recordings. Nashboro Records, established in the early 1950s, built an important catalogue of black gospel music, and its subsidiary Excello Records recorded several rhythm-and-blues artists in the 1950s. Although Nashville's music industry remains dominated by country music, contemporary black styles are also performed and recorded by many musicians.

COUNTRY MUSIC began to evolve and become commercially successful in the 1920s. George D. Hay, an announcer for radio station WSM, elicited a strongly favorable response from his audience when he programmed music by a string band and an old-time fiddler. He became the host of an hour-long radio show, "WSM Barn Dance," modeled after that of Chicago's station WLS; among the musicians who performed was Uncle Dave Macon, a banjo player and singer with a repertory of vaudeville material and black and white gospel music. The program was expanded to three hours, and in 1927 was renamed the GRAND OLE OPRY; Hay helped to popularize the new name and also encouraged the (admittedly exaggerated) "hayseed" image of country music. The "Grand Ole Opry" was broadcast, before live audiences, from successively larger venues (see illustration). Local, amateur musicians were replaced gradually from the 1930s by nationally known professionals, and NBC broadcast half an hour of the program each week to a national audience. Hank Williams joined the "Grand Ole Opry" in 1949; his great popularity was an important factor in the growth of Nashville's country-music industry.

Despite the popularity of the "Grand Ole Opry," the focus of much country-music activity was eastward, in Knoxville and Bristol, Tennessee, for instance. Nashville did not have a significant recording or music-publishing industry until the 1950s, when the advent of rock-and-roll led rival cities (especially Chicago and Los Angeles) to abandon country music, leaving Nashville as its undisputed center. Bullet Records, a small, independent recording company formed during World War II, gave Nashville its first recording studio. The company recorded a mixture of country and popular music, and prepared the way for RCA (1946) and other important labels to establish operations in the city. Fred Rose and Roy and Mildred Acuff founded Acuff–Rose Publications in 1942; Hill & Range (1945), Tree, and other music publishers were formed in the 1940s and 1950s. The increasing popularity of country music abetted the growth of BMI, which opened an office in Nashville and acquired the catalogues of Acuff–Rose, Hill & Range, and several other publishers. The increasing number and quality of recording studios brought many musicians to Nashville, and Chet Atkins and Owen Bradley, who owned studios, helped broaden the appeal of the "Nashville sound." The Country Music Association (founded 1958) promotes and publicizes country music in Nashville, as do the Country Music Hall of Fame and Museum (founded 1961; museum opened 1967) and the Country Music Foundation Library and Media Center (opened 1972). Opryland USA, a music-oriented amusement center, which also opened in 1972, became the home of the "Grand Ole Opry" in 1974. The recording industry continues to flourish: in 1981 more than half of all recordings made in the USA were produced in Nashville.

See also LIBRARIES AND COLLECTIONS, §3.

BIBLIOGRAPHY

F. Davenport: *Cultural Life in Nashville on the Eve of the Civil War* (Chapel Hill, 1941)
J. Burt: *Nashville: its Life and Times* (Nashville, 1959)
A. Crabb: *Nashville, Personality of a City* (Indianapolis, 1960)
W. Waller: *Nashville in the 1890's* (Nashville, 1970)
——: *Nashville, 1900–1910* (Nashville, 1972)
C. Crain: *Music Performance and Pedagogy in Nashville: 1818–1900* (diss., George Peabody College for Teachers, 1975)
P. Carr, ed.: *The Illustrated History of Country Music* (New York, 1979)
J. Egerton: *Nashville: the Faces of Two Centuries 1780–1980* (Nashville, 1979)

STEPHEN E. YOUNG

Nashville Grass. Bluegrass band led by Lester Flatt from 1969 to 1979; *see* FLATT AND SCRUGGS.

Nashville sound. A term used in the late 1950s and early 1960s to describe the rock- and pop-influenced COUNTRY MUSIC being recorded in Nashville. The emergence of this style was the result of an attempt by the country-music industry to preserve and

Cast of the "Grand Ole Opry" on the stage of the Ryman Auditorium, Nashville, c1953, under the banner of one of the program's sponsors

expand its audience in the face of the threat posed by the enormous popularity of rock-and-roll. Chet Atkins, the guitarist and country-music director for RCA in Nashville, supported by Ken Nelson of Capitol, Owen Bradley of MCA, Billy Sherrill and Glen Sutton of Columbia, and other leaders of the industry, sought to create a musical sound that would preserve a rural flavor within an urban style, and thus broaden the appeal of country music to urban, middle-class listeners. Some critics, however, felt that such a compromise with popular taste destroyed the character of country music. Banjos, steel guitars, and the honky-tonk sound were replaced by string sections, brass instruments, and vocal choruses, and the studios built up a group of backing musicians who performed with a variety of soloists. The repertory emphasized melodic ballads and novelty songs over more traditional country material. Among the earliest performers influenced by this trend were Eddy Arnold, Patsy Cline, and Jim Reeves. Since the 1970s the term has gained broader usage, describing any kind of popular or traditional music produced in Nashville.

BIBLIOGRAPHY

B. C. Malone: *Country Music U.S.A.: a Fifty-year History* (Austin, 1968, 2/1985)
P. Hemphill: *The Nashville Sound: Bright Lights and Country Music* (New York, 1970)

BILL C. MALONE/R

NASM. *See* NATIONAL ASSOCIATION OF SCHOOLS OF MUSIC.

Nath, Pran. *See* PRAN NATH.

Nathan, Hans (*b* Berlin, Germany, 5 Aug 1910). Musicologist. In 1934 he received the doctorate in musicology from Berlin University, where he also studied art history and philosophy. From 1932 to 1936 he was a music critic in Berlin. After immigrating to the USA he studied for two years at Harvard University, then joined the faculty of Michigan State University (1946), where he taught until his retirement in 1981. Nathan's broad scholarly background has led to an equally broad range of musicological interests. His writings cover music from the 13th to the 20th centuries; in all of his work he attempts to place the composition or composer in question within the context of the artistic trends of his time. American blackface minstrel music and the works of Dallapiccola have been two of his particular interests, and he has both written about and edited music by William Billings. His publications include *Dan Emmett and the Rise of Early Negro Minstrelsy* (1962) and *William Billings: Data and Documents* (1976).

PAULA MORGAN

National Association for American Composers and Conductors (NAACC). The original name of the NATIONAL ASSOCIATION OF COMPOSERS, USA.

National Association for Music Therapy. Organization founded in 1950 by a group of practicing music therapists and college teachers; *see* MUSIC THERAPY.

National Association of College Wind and Percussion Instructors. Organization for teachers of wind and percussion instruments in American institutions of higher education, founded at the University of Michigan in 1951. The aims of the organization are to encourage and develop more effective ways of teaching wind and percussion instruments at the college level; to provide for an efficient interchange of information, ideas, and materials among members; to encourage the publication, recording, composition, and distribution of good music for wind and percussion instruments; to coordinate the activities of the membership with other groups having common interests; and to encourage the performance of solos and chamber music in which wind and percussion instruments have significant roles. The association publishes the quarterly *NACWPI Journal* (founded in 1952), maintains a job-vacancy announcement service for its members, and supports a composition project devoted to the commissioning and publishing of works for wind and percussion instruments. It sponsored *The Catalog of Chamber Music for Wind Instruments* by Sanford Helm (1952/*R*1969) and *Original Manuscript Music for Wind and Percussion Instruments* by Richard Weerts (1964/*R*1973). The association's headquarters are at Western Illinois University, Macomb.

RAOUL CAMUS

National Association of Composers, USA (NACUSA). Organization founded in 1933 as the National Association for American Composers and Conductors under the guidance of the composer and conductor Henry Hadley "to arrange and encourage performances of works by American composers and to help develop understanding and friendly cooperation between composers and conductors." To this end, regular seasons of concerts devoted to American music were for many years its major activity. The 5000 works presented during its first 40 years included 2000 premières and many performances of early works, some from the pre-Revolutionary period. In later years, under its president Leon Barzin, the final concert of each season was given by a full orchestra in Carnegie Hall as part of the American Music Festival mounted by the radio station WNYC. Other presidents over the years have included Lawrence Tibbett, Sigmund Spaeth, and Robert Russell Bennett. The organization established an archive of American music at the New York Public Library and held an annual concert and reception at which the Henry Hadley Medal was awarded to individuals or institutions for "distinguished services to American music." It also cosponsored the Lado Composition Competition and, in the 1950s, arranged orchestral "reading concerts" for trial performances of works by member composers. At the height of its activities, the association had 1200 members in 48 states. It became considerably less active after the death in 1971 of Inez Barbour (Mrs. Henry) Hadley, who had been the guiding spirit and benefactor since her husband's death in 1937. In 1975 the association was reorganized by John Vincent, professor of composition at UCLA, and changed its name to National Association of Composers, USA (NACUSA); it had about 350 members in 1984. It sponsors annual competitions for young composers and performers, as well as concerts in New York. The *Annual Bulletin* published by the earlier association between 1933 and 1970 was superseded by the quarterly journal *Composer/USA* in 1976.

JOHN SHEPARD

National Association of Jazz Educators (NAJE). An associate organization of the Music Educators National Conference (MENC) with the purpose of furthering the teaching of jazz at schools and fostering jazz appreciation. It was founded in 1968 as a result of the MENC's Tanglewood Symposium of 1967, one of its founders being the jazz bandleader Stan Kenton. Besides holding an annual convention, NAJE publishes various anthologies and works in book and booklet form as well as a quarterly *Jazz Educators Journal* (formerly *NAJE Educator*) and the *Proceedings of Jazz Research*, an annual periodical derived from papers presented at its research sessions.

BIBLIOGRAPHY

D. A. Herfort: *A History of the National Association of Jazz Educators and a Description of its Role in American Music Education, 1968–1978* (diss., U. of Houston, 1979)

LEE BASH

National Association of Music Merchants (NAMM). Organization for the retail music trade founded in 1919; *see* MUSIC TRADES, §4.

National Association of Negro Musicians (NANM). Organization founded in 1919 in Chicago to promote interest in Afro-American music. Earlier efforts to found such an organization had been made by Clarence Cameron White in 1916 and R. Nathaniel Dett in 1918, both of whom participated in the first convention of the association and served as president during the 1920s. Governed by a board of directors and elected officers, the organization meets annually in various cities during the summer for workshops, concerts, recitals, panel discussions, business meetings, and youth concerts, and its numerous regional branches sponsor other activities throughout the year. National scholarships are awarded annually following regional competitions, and among the recipients of these awards early in their careers were Hazel Harrison, Marian Anderson, N. Clark Smith, Arthur Cunningham, Coleridge-Taylor Perkinson, and John Young.

BIBLIOGRAPHY

SouthernB

L. H. White: "The NANM," *American Musician*, ii/2 (1921), 18

J. A. Mills: "The National Association of Negro Musicians," *HiFi/MusAm*, xxix/8 (1979), 14

DOMINIQUE-RENÉ DE LERMA

National Association of Schools of Music (NASM). Accrediting body for music in postsecondary education in the USA. Its membership includes more than 500 institutions, most of which are colleges, universities, and conservatories of music, and some of which are music schools that do not grant degrees but offer preprofessional programs or general music training; membership implies accreditation and is voluntary. The association was founded in 1924 by a group of leading conservatories and university schools of music to secure a better understanding among institutions; to establish a more uniform method of granting credit for music studies; and to set minimum standards for the granting of degrees and other credentials. Its accrediting activities began in 1928 with the establishment of standards for the bachelor's degree in music. In addition to its accrediting activities, it provides a national forum for the discussion of issues related to music in American life, especially in higher education. The association is governed by a board of directors and an executive committee elected by representatives of the member schools. Accrediting functions are conducted by elected commissions, one each for undergraduate studies, graduate studies, community and junior colleges, and non-degree-granting institutions. The executive director and staff occupy offices in Reston, Virginia.

BIBLIOGRAPHY

C. M. Neumeyer: *A History of the National Association of Schools of Music* (EdD diss., Indiana U., 1954)

B. C. Tuthill: *NASM: the First Forty Years* (Washington, DC, 1973)

R. Glidden: "An Introduction to NASM: Purpose and Philosophy," *Proceedings of the 59th Annual Meeting* (Reston, VA, 1984)

ROBERT GLIDDEN

National Association of Teachers of Singing (NATS). Organization founded in Cincinnati, Ohio, in 1944. Its aims are to establish and maintain the highest standards of ethics, practice, and competence in the teaching of singing, to conduct and encourage research, to disseminate information about the profession, and to encourage effective cooperation among vocal teachers for their welfare and advancement. The association's 4000 members are American or Canadian citizens who teach in private schools, colleges, and universities and who adhere to the NATS "Code of Ethics." Membership is limited in that each applicant must be sponsored by two current members and approved by an admissions committee and the association's executive committee; to be considered for membership a teacher must be trained professionally, must devote half of his or her time to the teaching of singing, and must have taught for five consecutive years. In addition to chapter meetings and summer workshops held in the 13 regions, a national convention is organized every 18 months. NATS supports the fellowship program of the American Institute of Vocal Pedagogy, which accredits teachers and school curricula for the association, and since 1955 has held the Singer of the Year Scholarship Auditions. A journal, the *NATS Bulletin* (now with five numbers each year), has been published since 1944.

JOHN SHEPARD

National Band Association (NBA). Professional organization founded in 1960 and affiliated with the Music Educators National Conference. Its purpose as stated in its constitution is "to provide a national voice fostering the continuous development of bands and band music and to promote the musical and educational significance of bands." Membership includes a subscription to *The Instrumentalist* magazine (founded in 1946 and now published monthly) and the quarterly *NBA Journal*. In addition to biennial conventions and other activities, the NBA sponsors the National High School Honors Band; the NBA Citations of Excellence, awarded to outstanding band directors; the Academy of Wind and Percussion Arts and the NBA Hall of Fame of Distinguished Band Conductors (in recognition of those who have made outstanding contributions to bands and band music); and the NBA – DeMoulin Band Composition Contest for new band works.

RAOUL CAMUS

National Barn Dance. Country-music radio program broadcast from Chicago between 1924 and 1970. On 19 April 1924, a week after the radio station WLS opened, its director Edgar L. Bill, anxious to attract audiences among the farming population (the principal customers of the station's sponsor, Sears Roebuck), allowed the fiddlers Tommy Dandurand and Rube Tronson to present a program of their music. This led to a regular Saturday night program, which, within a year, under the direction of George D. Hay, had become the first nationally known country-music program. George Biggar became the program's director in 1930 and presided over its greatest years, during which it played a major role in popularizing country music outside the South and pioneered important promotional and management techniques; its large audience (WLS transmitted a powerful signal that could be received over a wide area), the promotion of recordings and instruments through the Sears catalogue, and a series of publications connected with the program, such as *Stand By!*, combined to launch the careers of a new generation of entertainers. In the late 1920s these included Bradley Kincaid, Chubby Parker, Mac and Bob, and Gene Autry, and in the 1930s Lulu Belle and Scotty, Red Foley, Karl and Harty, John Lair, Doc Hopkins, Arkie the Arkansas Woodhopper (Luther Ossinbrink), and the Three Little Maids. Promoters seldom used the term "country music" to describe the WLS repertory, emphasizing instead its rural or "old-time" quality; the "National Barn Dance" style soon denoted a preference for vocal music, much of it in close harmony, a preponderance of sentimental songs, and a liking for refined vocal styles that contrasted with the harsher mountain sounds of the southern stations. The show was performed before huge audiences in the Eighth Street Theater in Chicago; beginning in 1936 it was carried over the NBC network. By the war many of its stars had defected to other stations; later, regular performers such as Bob Atcher, the Hoosier Hot Shots, and Rex Allen kept the program popular for a time, but the innate conservatism of the style it promoted gradually lost ground to the newer country styles of Hank Williams and Ernest Tubb. The "National Barn Dance" left WLS in 1960, when the station changed the format of its broadcasts, and was transmitted for another ten years on the rival station WGN.

BIBLIOGRAPHY

G. C. Biggar: "The Early Days of WLS & the National Barn Dance," *Old Time Music*, no.1 (1971), 11

——: "The WLS National Barn Dance Story: the Early Years," *JEMF Quarterly*, vii (1971), 105

T. A. Patterson: "Hillbilly Music among the Flatlanders: Early Midwestern Radio Barn Dances," *Journal of Country Music*, vi (1975), 12

W. W. Daniel: "The National Barn Dance on Network Radio: the 1930s," *Journal of Country Music*, ix/3 (1983), 47

CHARLES K. WOLFE

National Conservatory of Music of America. Conservatory founded in 1885 in New York, chiefly by Jeannette Thurber. *See* NEW YORK, §12.

National Endowment for the Arts. Independent grant-making agency established in 1965. *See* NATIONAL FOUNDATION ON THE ARTS AND THE HUMANITIES.

National Endowment for the Humanities. Independent grant-making agency established in 1965. *See* NATIONAL FOUNDATION ON THE ARTS AND THE HUMANITIES.

National Federation of Music Clubs (NFMC). World's largest music organization, with 600,000 members representing 5000 organizations in the USA and Puerto Rico. The NFMC was founded in Springfield, Illinois, in 1898 to foster cooperation among people and organizations in the furthering of musical education; to integrate music into civic, educational, and social life; to stimulate American composition; and to promote American performers. There are several categories of membership: group (Senior, Student, and Junior), individual (Special, Contributor, Life Subscriber, Donor, Patron, and Cradle Roll for infants enrolled by their parents), and national affiliate (for such organizations as the American Symphony Orchestra League and the Music Teachers National Association).

During its National Music Week in May, the NFMC has since 1924 marshaled its local organizations in nationwide community festivities celebrating the role of music in American life. Since 1955, it has also encouraged the performance of American works through a sponsorship program called the Parade of American Music, which takes place in February. The NFMC dispenses many awards to performers, young composers, veterans, dancers, music therapists, and blind musicians; some of these awards are in the form of scholarships to attend particular institutions and enroll in apprentice programs. Its biennial Young Artists Auditions have launched over 150 performers in professional careers since 1915, including Rosalyn Tureck, Nan Merriman, and Israel Baker. Immediately after World War II, the federation gave instruments and repair kits to European orchestras that had suffered losses or damage to their instruments. Today the NFMC presents packages of music to foreign organizations and gives an annual award of $1000 to encourage the performance of American music abroad. Its first journal, the *Musical Monitor* (published monthly 1912–34), was virtually superseded by a bulletin that was later renamed the *Music Clubs Magazine* (1922–). Other NFMC publications include directories, handbooks, and monographs.

JOHN SHEPARD

National Foundation on the Arts and the Humanities. Organization established in 1965 by Congressional statute "to promote progress and scholarship in the humanities and the arts in the United States." Under the same statute, two independent grant-making agencies – the National Endowment for the Arts (NEA) and the National Endowment for the Humanities (NEH) – were established to carry out the objectives of the foundation. Each of these agencies is headed by a chairman and 26 distinguished private citizens widely recognized in the appropriate disciplines, who form the National Council for the Arts and the National Council for the Humanities; both the chairman and the council for each agency is appointed by the President of the USA subject to Senate confirmation.

The stated aim of the NEA is to "foster the excellence, diversity and vitality" of the arts. Funding is provided through several sources: National Program Funds, which are authorized by Congress and granted to talented persons and nonprofit organizations in the categories of architecture and the environmental arts, dance, education, expansion arts (community centers, etc.), literature, museums, music, public media (radio, television, film), and the visual arts: Federal-State Partnership Funds, which are appropriated to arts councils in the states; and the Treasury Fund, a combination of private donations and matched federal funds. Many NEA grants, such as those to symphony orchestras and opera companies, require additional matching funds from local sources. The NEA has devoted a considerable amount of its funding to avant-garde repertory and to individuals. Its programs relating to music include fellowships, and finance for professional training for musicians, music festivals, and recordings, as well as solo recitals and other concerts (jazz, contemporary, choral, chamber, and orchestral). Its journal, the *Cultural Post* (founded in 1975), was superseded by the quarterly *Arts Review* in 1983.

Grant policies of the NEH are executed through six divisions (Education Programs, Fellowships and Seminars, Public Programs, Research Programs, Special Programs, and State Programs) and two offices (Planning and Assessment, and Challenge Grants). Some of these grants require matching funds from other sources. Areas funded by the NEH include the study of language; linguistics; literature; history; jurisprudence; philosophy; archaeology; comparative religion and ethics; the history, criticism, and theory of the arts; aspects of the social sciences; and the human environment, with particular emphasis on the relevance of the humanities to the current conditions of national life. In 1984 grants were awarded for independent study, summer research seminars, humanities projects in libraries and museums, youth activities in the humanities, scholarly publications, educational materials, and many other projects. The agency has published the journal *Humanities* since 1969, and annual reports and overviews for both organizations are available.

See also AWARDS, §2, and EDUCATION IN MUSIC, §II, 6.

BIBLIOGRAPHY

M. Straight: *Twigs for an Eagle's Nest: Government and the Arts: 1965–1978* (New York, 1979)

RITA H. MEAD

National Guild of Piano Teachers. Organization founded in 1929 to provide incentive for piano students and to promote education in music through examinations, auditions, and competitions. A division of the American College of Musicians and affiliated with the National Fraternity of Student Musicians, the guild has over 10,000 members in 700 local chapters; its headquarters are in Austin, Texas. Since 1959 it has dispensed $120,000 a year in $100 scholarships, and it sponsors the National Piano Playing Auditions, the International Piano Recording Competition, and the Van Cliburn International Competition, which in the early 1980s was televised nationally over the Public Broadcasting System. It has published the bimonthly journal *Piano Guild Notes* since 1945.

JOHN SHEPARD

National Institute for Music Theater. An organization founded in 1969 as the National Opera Institute by the theater producer Roger L. Stevens at the John F. Kennedy Center for the Performing Arts. Partly funded by the NEA, the institute encourages the evolution of music theater and the development of outstanding talent through various programs, including the Music Theater Workshop for the development of new works; apprenticeships in production, administration, and composition; grants for singers; and national colloquia. It is directed by a board of trustees (Beverly Sills was chairman, 1978–82) and a national artistic advisory committee (K. H. Adler, chairman, 1982–).

RITA H. MEAD

National League of Musicians. Musicians' union founded in 1886; *see* UNIONS, MUSICIANS', §1.

National Music Council. Organization whose members are national music organizations. Founded in 1940 by Julia Ober, Harold Spivacke, Franklin Dunham, and Edwin Hughes, it aims to provide a forum for the discussion of issues and problems concerning music in the USA, to act as a liaison among member organizations, and to serve as spokesman for them. It advises Congress on proposed legislation pertaining to music and in 1956 was granted a congressional charter. The National Music Council encouraged the formation of the American String Teachers Association, and both the National Association for Music Therapy and the National Opera Association were founded under its auspices. In 1959, with funds from the Ford Foundation, it established one of the first programs placing composers in residence in public schools. More recently the Council sponsored the concert series "Bicentennial Parade of American Music" (1976) and the National Black Music Colloquium and Competition at the John F. Kennedy Center for the Performing Arts (1980). The activities of the Council and its members have been reported in the *National Music Council Bulletin* (1940–82) and the *National Music Council News* (1984–). Gunther Schuller and Victor Fuentealba have served as chairman; past presidents include Howard Hanson, who served as president from 1944 to 1967, continuing as chairman until 1971.

BIBLIOGRAPHY

E. Hughes: "The National Music Council, 1940–1960," *National Music Council Bulletin*, xx/3 (1960), 1

J. Browning: "National Music Council – 25 Years of Service," *MJ*, xxiv/1 (1966), 77

Contemporary Music for Schools: a Catalog . . . sponsored by the Ford Foundation and the National Music Council, ed. MENC (Washington, DC, 1966)

EMILY GOOD

National Music Publishers' Association (NMPA). Trade association for firms that publish popular music. Founded in 1917 as the Music Publishers' Protective Association, the NMPA communicates with agencies of the federal government on legislation that affects its members, and studies technological developments (such as home video) that have implications for the publishing industry. The association set up and continues to operate the Harry Fox Agency (*see* PERFORMING RIGHTS SOCIETIES, §2 (iv)), which acts as its members' agent in administering mechanical rights licenses and represents their interests before the Copyright Royalty Tribunal of the federal government. Since 1980 the NMPA has given awards to its members for the best-selling songs in various categories (general popular, rhythm-and-blues, country, easy-listening, film, Broadway, Latin, and gospel). Membership in the NMPA is open to firms which have published music for one year, including compositions that have been used commercially. The association's headquarters are in New York and the president in the early 1980s was Leonard Feist. In conjunction with the Music Publishers' Association, the NMPA issues the *Music Publishers Sales Agency List*.

JOHN SHEPARD

National Opera Association (NOA) (i). Organization founded under the auspices of the National Music Council in 1955 to support all phases of opera production, composition, promotion, and appreciation in the USA and Canada. Its 700 members are composers, conductors, directors, managers, producers, publishers, librettists, teachers, translators, and organizations (opera companies, colleges and universities, schools, and opera workshops). NOA awards are given annually through its Professional Voice Auditions and (from 1984) the New Opera Competition for composers and the Opera Production Competition for institutions. Publications include a monograph series (of which Boris Goldovsky's *Touring Opera*, 1975, is vol.iii), an annual directory of members by profession or vocal category, the *Opera Journal* (founded in 1968, now quarterly), and the cumulative *NOA Catalogue of Contemporary American Operas* (since 1976).

JOHN SHEPARD

National Opera Association (ii). Opera company founded in 1948, based in Raleigh, North Carolina; *see* CHAPEL HILL, RALEIGH, DURHAM.

National Opera Company. Opera company founded in 1885 as the AMERICAN OPERA COMPANY.

National Opera Institute. Original name of the NATIONAL INSTITUTE FOR MUSIC THEATER.

National Orchestral Association. Organization founded in 1930 to maintain an orchestra for the training of young musicians in orchestral technique and routine, to prepare them for regular positions with symphony orchestras. The first concert was given at Carnegie Hall on 28 October 1930 under Leon Barzin, who held the position of music director until 1958 and again in 1970–76. (John Barnett was music director in 1958–70.) The orchestra has not only explored the standard repertory, but has given more than 60 world premières, 25 American premières, and 60 New York premières. It has rehearsed and performed under such renowned guest conductors as Aaron Copland and Bernard Haitink, and has accompanied eminent soloists, such as Elman, Feuermann, Myra Hess, Philippe Entremont, and Itzhak Perlman (the last two in their first concerts at Carnegie Hall). During World War II, the orchestra played at army camps and hospitals and gave 25 war-bond concerts over the New York radio station WQXR. It was the official orchestra of the Festival of Two Worlds in Spoleto in 1973, and it represented New York state at the Kennedy Center Bicentennial Celebration. In 1984 the association became affiliated with the School of Arts of Columbia University in an Institute for Orchestral Studies, a one-year fellowship program for graduate students. Its headquarters are in New York.

JOHN SHEPARD

National School Band Association. An organization founded in 1926 to administer contests for school wind bands; *see* BANDS, §4 (ii).

Naumburg, Walter W(ehle) (*b* New York, 25 Dec 1867; *d* New York, 17 Oct 1959). Patron. He was born into a musical family; his father Elkan Naumburg was the son of a cantor and a passionate amateur musician. As a child he studied cello, which he continued to play until he was nearly 90. He attended Harvard University, graduating in 1889, and in 1890 joined the family mercantile business. In 1905 Elkan Naumburg established a series of free concerts in Central Park, which Walter and his brother George continued after their father's death in 1924. The following year he established a series of auditions to select young musicians for Town Hall débuts and in 1926 he created the Walter W. Naumburg Foundation, which has carried out the same work since. Awards have been given in alternate years to instrumentalists and vocalists. In 1965 the first award to a chamber group was made (in 1972 the chamber awards became annual). The foundation has also given grants since 1949 to underwrite recordings. *See* AWARDS.

MICHAEL FLEMING

Navajo. The largest American Indian tribe of the USA. The Navajo are descended from Athapaskan-speaking hunters, gatherers, and raiders who entered the American Southwest from Canada between AD 900 and 1200. The Navajo were much influenced by the town-dwelling Pueblo, from whom they adopted a sedentary lifestyle. In the early 1980s the Navajo numbered some 180,000 and lived on a reservation extending across northern Arizona, northwestern New Mexico, and southern Utah (*see* INDIANS, AMERICAN, fig. 1). The other main group of southern, Athapaskan-speaking Indians are the Apache.

The Navajo genius for adapting new elements to their traditional cultural forms and ideas is evident in much of their daily life and music. Traditional music is based on the ritual drama

Navajo Indians performing the Yeibichai Dance

of 25 to 30 ceremonies, or "chants," which re-enact the creation story in a complex web of interrelated episodes. They are performed to restore harmony between the universe and individuals who have become ill; a Navajo might, for example, be treated for pneumonia at a hospital, and on recovering conduct a Windway ceremony at home to resolve the disharmony with the Wind People that led to the illness. The ceremonies tell of the creation in thousands of lines of ritual poetry recited in prayers and sung in song cycles. The songs are performed in powerful unison by a ceremonial practitioner and a group of male helpers, often to the accompaniment of rattles or a basket drum. Only the Enemyway ceremony uses a water-drum, a small, earthen pot half filled with water and covered with a buckskin membrane.

Ceremonial songs have a chorus–verse–chorus structure. The chorus is often highly melodic, with a scale based on the open triad, while the verses are chanted on a figure of only three or four notes. The alternation of verses describing male, then female, deities or attributes reflects the duality that shapes much of Navajo thought.

The Blessingway ceremony is central to traditional Navajo religion and philosophy. Its purpose is to create and maintain conditions of harmony, through rituals originating in myth, with the principal deity, Changing Woman. An important form of Blessingway is the girls' puberty rite, which initiates the girl to adulthood and brings blessing to the community; the marriage ritual and the House Blessing are other forms of Blessingway. All three re-enact the story of Changing Woman's birth, growth, and maturity. Parts of Blessingway are often included in other ceremonies to protect the participants from dangerous powers invoked in the course of the ritual. Enemyway, a ceremony for coping with dangers from outside Navajo culture, is based on the story of Changing Woman's warrior son, Enemy Slayer.

No recordings of sacred Navajo ceremonies are readily available, but such traditional popular music as songs for the Skip Dance, Circle Dance, and Yeibichai Dance (see illustration, p.327) have been recorded on many occasions. These songs are buoyantly melodic, and encompass a wide range of styles; new songs continue to be written. Traditional popular music either consists entirely of vocables, or incorporates brief lexical sections, often humorous. Navajo music is almost entirely vocal, sometimes with percussion accompaniment.

New Navajo music reflects the changes in Navajo culture. Abbreviated forms of some ceremonies have been developed for public events; a shortened House Blessing that can be incorporated into the dedication of a new school or chapter house is one such example. The pan-tribal Native American Church (Peyote religion) has thousands of Navajo adherents (*see* INDIANS, AMERICAN, §I, 6(ii)). On the reservation there are many Christian sects that sing hymns with English or Navajo words, and gospel music, often with electric instruments, is also heard. There are many Navajo country and rock bands; the Fenders and the Navajo Sundowners are two of the better-known country groups, and Mr. Indian in Time, a rock group from Kayenta, Arizona, performs songs that often stress traditional Navajo values. Arliene Nofchissey, a composer who works in a style reminiscent of Broadway musicals, incorporates Navajo melody, rhythm, and texts into her compositions. In its adherence to traditional values and styles and its lively exploration of new ones, Navajo music shows considerable adaptability and imagination.

Recordings of Navajo music are held at the Wesleyan University Archive of World Music, Wesleyan University, Middletown, Connecticut (Shootingway and Blessingway ceremonies, traditional and new popular music); the Indiana University Archives of Traditional Music, Bloomington, Indiana; the Library of Congress, Washington, DC (Wheelwright Collection); and the University of New Mexico, Albuquerque.

See also INDIANS, AMERICAN, esp. §I, 3, 4(ii)(c).

DISCOGRAPHY

Music of the American Indian: Navaho, recorded by W. Rhodes (AAFS L41, 1952) [reissued 1985 with descriptive notes]
Night and Daylight Yeibichai, recorded by T. Isaacs (IH 1502, 1968)
Navajo Skip Dance and Two-step Songs, recorded by T. Isaacs (IH 1503, 1969)
Proud Earth (Salt City 60, 1975)

BIBLIOGRAPHY

W. Matthews: "Navajo Gambling Songs," *American Anthropologist*, ii (1889), 1
G. A. Reichard: *Navaho Religion* (New York, 1950)
D. P. McAllester: *Enemy Way Music: a Study of Social and Esthetic Values as Seen in Navaho Music* (Cambridge, MA, 1954)
L. C. Wyman: *The Windways of the Navaho* (Colorado Springs, CO, 1962)
C. J. Frisbie: *Kinaaldá: a Study of the Navaho Girls' Puberty Ceremony* (Middletown, CT, 1967)
L. C. Wyman: *Blessingway* (Tucson, 1970)
G. Witherspoon: *Language and Art in the Navajo Universe* (Ann Arbor, MI, 1977)
F. Mitchell: *Navajo Blessingway Singer: the Autobiography of Frank Mitchell, 1881–1967*, ed. C. J. Frisbie and D. P. McAllester (Tucson, 1978)
D. P. and S. W. McAllester: *Hogans, Navajo Houses and House Songs* (Middletown, CT, 1980)

DAVID P. McALLESTER

Navarro, Fats [Theodore] (*b* Key West, FL, 24 Sept 1923; *d* New York, 7 July 1950). Jazz trumpeter. As a youth he played piano and tenor saxophone, but by the age of 17 he was touring with dance bands as a trumpeter. Three years later, in 1943, he joined Andy Kirk's nationally known jazz band, which then included the trumpeter Howard McGhee. In January 1945 Navarro replaced Dizzy Gillespie in Billy Eckstine's band. As the principal trumpet soloist in this important group he was among the foremost players in the new bop idiom. In autumn 1946, physically unequal to the heavy touring schedule and restricted musically by the big-band format, he left Eckstine. He spent the remainder of his brief career working mostly in small bop groups in New York, where he died of tuberculosis exacerbated by an addiction to heroin.

Although Navarro recorded a few solos with the Eckstine band, his main legacy is the approximately 150 small-group recordings he made between 1946 and 1950, mostly as a sideman in groups led by Kenny Clarke, Coleman Hawkins, Bud Powell, Charlie Parker, and especially Tadd Dameron. These recordings, of which one-third originated as radio broadcasts, reveal Navarro to be the rival of Dizzy Gillespie as the leading bop trumpeter of the 1940s. Gillespie was clearly one of his models, for Navarro used many of the older player's favorite phrases. Compared with that of Gillespie, however, Navarro's tone was sweeter; his style was also less dramatic, employing fewer passages of fast notes and fewer notes played in the upper register of the instrument. At times Navarro seemed to be more heavily influenced by the acknowledged leader of the bop school, the alto saxophonist Charlie Parker. Certain motifs in *Wail* (ex.1, marked *s–z*) were frequently used by Parker as building blocks for solo improvisations; the nearly continuous flow of 8th-notes with an unpredictable sprinkling of accents between the beats was also typical of Parker. The effective recurrence of motif *s*, however, which connects by chromatic descent the 13th and raised 11th of each chord, is a characteristic Navarro touch, as is the scale passage that ends the phrase. Navarro's recordings are of a consistently

Ex.1 Navarro's solo on B. Powell, *Wail* [take 3] (1949, BN 1567), transcr. T. Owens

high quality. *The Street Beat* and *Ornithology*, made with Charlie Parker in 1950, are particularly intriguing: if discographers have dated these pieces accurately, Navarro, emaciated and gravely ill, made these fine recordings just one week before he died.

RECORDINGS
(selective list)

As leader: Nostalgia (1947, Savoy 955); Barry's Bop (1947, Savoy 959); Nostalgia, Barry's Bop [alternative takes], on *Fat Girl* (1947, Savoy 2216)

As sideman: B. Eckstine: Air Mail Special, on *Together!* (1945, Spotlite 100); T. Dameron: Our Delight (1947, BN 540), Our Delight [alternative take], on F. Navarro: *Fabulous Fats Navarro* (1947, 1949, BN 1531); B. Ulanov: Fats' Flats, Koko, on *Anthropology* (1947, Spotlite 108); T. Dameron: Good Bait, on *The Tadd Dameron Band 1948* (1948, Jazzland 68); B. Powell: Wail [take 2], on F. Navarro: *Fabulous Fats Navarro* (1947, 1949, BN 1531); B. Powell: Wail [take 3] (1949, BN 1567); C. Parker: Ornithology (1950, Le Jazz Cool 101), The Street Beat (1950, Le Jazz Cool 102)

BIBLIOGRAPHY

SouthernB

I. Gitler: *Jazz Masters of the Forties* (New York, 1966/*R*1982), 97ff

R. Russell: "Fat Girl: the Legacy of Fats Navarro," *Down Beat*, xxxvii/4 (1970), 14

W. Balliett: "Jazz: Fat Girl," *New Yorker*, liv (12 June 1978), 116

J. L. Collier: *The Making of Jazz: a Comprehensive History* (New York, 1978), 398ff

M. Ruppli: "Fats Navarro Discography," *Discographical Forum*, nos.42–5 (1979–82)

THOMAS OWENS

Nazz. Rock group active in the Philadelphia area in the 1960s and led from 1967 to 1970 by TODD RUNDGREN.

NBA. *See* NATIONAL BAND ASSOCIATION.

NEA. National Endowment for the Arts; *see* NATIONAL FOUNDATION ON THE ARTS AND THE HUMANITIES.

Neblett, Carol (*b* Modesto, CA, 1 Feb 1946). Soprano. Her father was an accomplished pianist and her grandmother a renowned violinist. After early training in both of these instruments, Neblett studied singing privately with William Vennard, and at the University of Southern California with Lotte Lehmann and Pierre Bernac. She left without graduating in 1965 and became a soloist for a short time with the Roger Wagner Chorale. Encouraged by the impresario Sol Hurok, she embarked on a career in opera and made her début with the New York City Opera in 1969 as Musetta. Her subsequent débuts included Chrysothemis in Strauss's *Elektra* at the Chicago Lyric Opera (1975), Antonia in Offenbach's *Les contes d'Hoffmann* at the Dallas Civic Opera (1975), Minni in Puccini's *La fanciulla del West* at the Vienna Staatsoper (1976) and Covent Garden (1977), and Senta in Wagner's *Der fliegende Holländer* (1979). Among her other roles are Margherita and Elena (in Boito's *Mefistofele*), Monteverdi's Poppaea, Marietta-Marie (in Korngold's *Die tote Stadt*), Catalani's Wally, and Yaroslavna (in Borodin's *Prince Igor*). She has appeared with many of the leading American orchestras, including the Los Angeles PO in Beethoven's Ninth Symphony under Giulini, and performed the role of Vitellia in Jean-Pierre Ponnelle's film version of *La clemenza di Tito*. In 1973 the statuesque Neblett gained considerable notoriety in a production of Massenet's *Thaïs* in New Orleans by removing her costume at the end of the first act. Her singing and acting continue to be demonstrative and occasionally overtly sensual.

JAMES WIERZBICKI

Nee, Thomas (Bacus) (*b* Evanston, IL, 25 Oct 1920). Conductor. After graduating from the University of Minnesota (BS 1943) and Hamline University (MA 1947), where he was a pupil of Krenek, he studied with William Loibner and Hans Swarowsky in Vienna; he made his début at the Konzerthaus there in 1951. He later studied with Robert Shaw at the Berkshire Music Center, Hermann Scherchen in Zurich (where he went as a Fulbright scholar in 1951–2), and Stefan Wolpe at Black Mountain College (1953). He has taught at Hamline University (1947–56), Macalester College (1957–67), and at the University of California, San Diego, where he was appointed professor in 1967. In 1949–50 Nee was assistant conductor of the Minneapolis SO; he served as music director of the Civic Orchestra of Minneapolis (1953–67), the New Hampshire Music Festival (from 1960), the Minnesota Opera (1963–7), and the La Jolla Civic Orchestra (from 1967). He has a particular interest in contemporary music and has conducted the premières of works by Robert Erickson, Pauline Oliveros, and Eric Stokes, notably Stokes's opera *Horspfal* (1969).

GENE BIRINGER

NEH. National Endowment for the Humanities; *see* NATIONAL FOUNDATION ON THE ARTS AND THE HUMANITIES.

Neikrug, Marc (Edward) (*b* New York, 24 Sept 1946). Composer and pianist. The son of the cellist George Neikrug and the composer and painter Olga Zundel, he grew up in Los Angeles and then from 1964 to 1968 studied with the opera composer Giselher Klebe at the Nordwestliche Musikakademie, Detmold, Germany. Subsequently he attended SUNY, Stony Brook (MM in composition, 1971). He has received two awards from the NEA (1972, 1974) and commissions from, among others, the Houston SO (1983) and the St. Paul Chamber Orchestra (1984). In 1978 he was named special consultant on contemporary music to the latter organization.

Whether writing in an atonal or a chromatically tonal idiom, Neikrug is above all a harmonist. His orchestral works, which move in long, carefully orchestrated chordal blocks punctuated by virtuoso, repetitive fragments of melody, reveal the influence of the Danish composer Per Nørgård. Attacks of acoustically based harmonies and chord clusters lend his duo sonatas their rhythmic drive. Neikrug's best-known work is the theater piece

Through Roses (1979–80), which dramatizes the nightmares of a Jewish violinist who survived in a concentration camp by playing for members of the SS; the film version received prizes at both the Besançon Film Festival (1981) and the International Film and Television Festival, New York (1982).

As a pianist, Neikrug has appeared in a duo with the violinist Pinchas Zukerman.

WORKS

Dramatic: Through Roses (theater piece, Neikrug), actor, 8 insts, 1979–80

Orch: Pf Conc., 1966; Cl Conc., 1967; Va Conc., 1974; Eternity's Sunrise, 1979–80; Mobile, 1981; Vn Conc., 1982

Inst: Solo Vc Sonata, 1967; 2 str qts, 1969, 1972; Suite, vc, pf, 1974; Rituals, fl, harp, 1976; Concertino, fl, ob, cl, vn, va, vc, pf, 1977; 3 Fantasies, vn, pf, 1977; Continuum, vc, pf, 1978; Cycle of 7 for Pf, 1978; Kaleidoscope, fl, pf, 1979; Duo, vn, pf, 1983

Some early works withdrawn

Principal publishers: Bärenreiter, Chester, Hansen, Salabert

SEVERINE NEFF

Nelhybel, Vaclav (*b* Polanka nad Odrou, Czechoslovakia, 24 Sept 1919). Composer and conductor. After studying classics and musicology at Prague University and conducting and composition at the Prague Conservatory, he went in 1942 to Fribourg University, Switzerland, where he studied musicology and, from 1947, taught music theory. He held conducting positions with Radio Prague and the City Theater (1939–42), the Czech PO (1945–6), Swiss Radio (1946–50), and Radio Free Europe (1950–57), and appeared as guest conductor with several leading European orchestras. In 1957 he came to the USA, becoming an American citizen in 1962. He built a successful career as a freelance composer, guest conductor, and lecturer at schools and colleges throughout the USA and Canada, including the University of Lowell, Massachusetts (1978–9). A versatile composer, Nelhybel has written more than 300 compositions; he is best known for his wind and band works, and for his many compositions for children. Some 29 of his works have been recorded, in addition to his contribution to the Folkways *Music Theory Series*.

WORKS

Operas: Legend, 1954; Everyman, 1974; Station, 1978

Ballets: Morality de feux, 1942; In the Shadow of a Lime Tree, 1946; Cock and the Hangman, 1946

Orch: Sym., 1942; Etude symphonique, 1949; Sinfonietta concertante, 1960; Va Conc., 1962; Houston Conc., 1967; Polyphonies, 1972; Polyphonic Variations, tpt, str, 1976; Slavonic Triptych, 1976

Sym. band/wind ens: Caucasian Passacaglia, 1963; Conc. antiphonale, brass, 1964; Sym. Requiem, with Bar, 1965; Yamaha Conc., 1971; Concertino da camera, vc, wind, pf, 1972; Toccata, hpd, wind, perc, 1972; Cantus and Ludus, pf, wind, perc, 1973; Dialogues, with pf, 1976; Sinfonia resurrectionis, 1980; Music, 12 tpt, wind, 1980; Psalm xii, wind, perc, 1981; Conc. grosso, 1981; Cl Conc., 1982

Vocal: Cantata pacis, 6 solo vv, chorus, wind, perc, org, 1965; Epitaph for a Soldier, solo vv, chorus, 1966; Dies ultima, 3 solo vv, chorus, jazz band, orch, 1967; Sine nomine, 4 solo vv, chorus, orch, tape, 1968; America Sings, Bar, chorus, band, 1974; Estampie natalis, chorus, ens, 1975; Adoratio, chorus, 1979; Fables for All Time, nar, chorus, orch, 1980; Let there be Music, Bar, chorus, orch, 1982; songs, anthems

Chamber: 2 str qt, 1949, 1962; 3 wind qnt, 1948, 1958, 1960; 2 brass qnt, 1961, 1965; Quintetto concertante, vn, trbn, tpt, xyl, pf, 1965; Conc., perc, 1972; Conc. spirituoso nos. 1–4, 1974–7; Music, 6 tpt, 1975; Ludus, 3 tubas, 1975; Variations, harp, 1977; Praeambulum, org, timp, 1977; Oratio no. 2, ob, str trio, 1979; Sonate da chiesa and many other small chamber works; many pf and org pieces

Many works also for alternative forces; many more for children

Principal publishers: Barta, Belwin-Mills, Christopher, General, Kirby

RUTH B. HILTON

Nelson, John (*b* San José, Costa Rica, 6 Dec 1941). Conductor. He received his early musical training in Costa Rica (where his parents were Protestant missionaries), then studied piano and composition in Orlando, Florida, and at Wheaton (Illinois) College (BA 1963). At the Juilliard School he studied with Jean Morel (MM 1965), won the Irving Berlin Award in conducting, and received teaching assistantships in the opera, choral, and orchestral departments. Among his first professional posts were the directorships of the Pro Arte Chorale in New Jersey (1965–75) and the Greenwich (Connecticut) Philharmonia (1966–74). From 1968 to 1972 he taught at Juilliard.

Nelson first gained prominence in 1972, when he organized a full-length concert performance of Berlioz's *Les troyens* at Carnegie Hall; a year later, he conducted the same work at his Metropolitan Opera début. From 1976 he was music director of the Indianapolis SO (retirement announced for 1987); while maintaining this position he served as music director of the Caramoor Festival from 1983. His operatic repertory ranges from Monteverdi to Janáček, and as a symphonic conductor he has championed the works of Shostakovich, particularly the Suite on verses by Michelangelo Buonarotti (op. 145a) and the Symphony no. 15. His strengths include an undeniable flair for the dramatic, evident in his handling of the major operatic, choral, and orchestral repertory, and a fluent sense of musical architecture, which gives his interpretations, for all their surface color, both power and weight.

BIBLIOGRAPHY

R. Hemming: "John Nelson: Music is his Mission," *Opera News*, xxxix/11 (1975), 24

J. Boyd: "An Interview with John Nelson," *Choral Journal*, xix/6 (1979), 5

MICHAEL WALSH

Nelson [née Manes], **Judith (Anne)** (*b* Chicago, IL, 10 Sept 1939). Soprano. After studies at St. Olaf College, Minnesota, she sang with the Berkeley Chamber Singers, Musica Mundana (Berkeley), and the early music ensembles of the University of Chicago (under Howard Mayer Brown) and the University of California, Berkeley (under Alan Curtis); recordings that she made with all these groups showed particular distinction in 15th-century music. Her European début at the Concerts de la Société de Musique d'Autrefois in 1973 led to solo recitals and performances with many European and American ensembles, including the Academy of Ancient Music, the London Sinfonietta, the Concerto Vocale and Les Arts Florissants (with William Christie), and the American Bach Ensemble (under Joshua Rifkin). Her operatic début was in Brussels as Drusilla in *L'incoronazione di Poppea* (1979). She has sung at many festivals, including the Bruges Early Music Festival and Aston Magna, and has recorded for radio and television throughout Europe and the USA. She is noted for her stylish performances of early music and for the re-creation of vocal techniques appropriate to Baroque works. Her pure but spirited singing may be heard on more than 50 recordings of works by Bach, Charpentier, Handel (including *Messiah* with the Academy of Ancient Music), Haydn, Monteverdi, and Purcell. She has also recorded Schubert songs (with Jörg Demus) and given premières of British and American works.

Nelson, Rick(y) [Eric Hilliard] (*b* Teaneck, NJ, 8 May 1940; *d* nr De Kalb, TX, 31 Dec 1985). Rock-and-roll singer. He made his début as a singer on his parents' television program, "The Adventures of Ozzie and Harriet," in 1957. In the same year he had his first hit record, consisting of two songs: a version of Fats Domino's *I'm Walking* (no.17), and *A Teenager's Romance* (no.2). His songs became a regular feature of pop radio in the late 1950s and early 1960s; they included the rockabilly tune *Be-bop Baby* (no.3, 1957), *Stood Up* (no.2, 1957), the lovely *Poor Little Fool* (no.1, 1958), *Travelin' Man* (no.1, 1961), and *Hello Mary Lou* (no.9, 1961). With the advent of the Beatles in 1964 his career declined; he performed in supper clubs, and turned first to folk, then country music. With *Garden Party* (no.6, 1972), a brittle autobiographical tale of hard times at a rock-and-roll revival show, he recaptured some of his former success; the recording sold more than a million copies. In 1981 Capitol issued his album *Playin' to Win*. Though Nelson's success as a musician owed much to the exposure he received on television, his songs were often first-rate; his accounts of white, middle-class, teenage life, of which he was himself a typical product, were evocative and memorable. He had a fine sense of rhythm, and was a good judge of his material and his backup musicians; James Burton, his regular guitarist, was a celebrated performer. Between 1957 and 1972 Nelson made 18 recordings that reached the Top Ten on the chart; at the time of his death this figure had been exceeded by only six other recording artists.

BIBLIOGRAPHY

E. Ward: Liner notes, *Ricky Nelson: Legendary Masters* (UA 9960)

R. Christgau: "Rick(y) Nelson: How to Change your Name," *Any Old Way you Choose it: Rock and Other Pop Music, 1967–1973* (Baltimore, 1973), 262

GREIL MARCUS

Nelson, Ron (*b* Joliet, IL, 14 Dec 1929). Composer and conductor. He studied with Hanson, Rogers, Mennini, and Wayne Barlow at the Eastman School (1948–56), where he received the BMus, MMus, and DMA degrees, and with Tony Aubin in Paris at the Ecole Normale de Musique (1954–5). In 1956 he joined the faculty of Brown University, where he served as chairman of the music department (1963–73) and became professor in 1968. His numerous honors include a Fulbright award (1954–5), a Ford Foundation fellowship (1963), a Howard Foundation grant (1965–6), NEA grants (1973, 1976, 1979), and commissions from many orchestras and universities. His recorded works include *Savannah River Holiday*, *Sarabande: for Katharine in April*, and *Rocky Point Holiday*.

Nelson's music from early on reveals fine craftsmanship, particularly in its subtle control of rich and varied textures, and a keen sense of instrumental and vocal color. It has explored a wide range of styles while remaining accessible in its tonal focus, melodic inventiveness, and formal clarity. Nelson's exposure in the mid-1960s to non-Western cultures, particularly those of the Far East, and his growing fascination with meditation and music that would induce states of meditative calm have been the strongest influences on his mature style. His skilled and sympathetic writing for the voice, and his concern for rich and sonorous harmony, give his choral works a consistency that transcends stylistic shifts. In a number of later works, gamelan-like percussion textures, often created through a controlled aleatorism that can also affect the length of the work, provide kaleidoscopic canvases upon which lyrical melodies are drawn. The textures of Psalm xcv grew out of experiments with meditation and biofeedback devices; in Mass of St. La Salle, Nelson drew on the music of medieval and Renaissance composers, using specific traits, such as the relentless modal rhythms of Pérotin, to serve as a point of departure for his own musical imagination. Among his instrumental scores the *Five Pieces after Paintings by Andrew Wyeth* explore a number of styles, from sophisticated chromatic counterpoint to rock and jazz rhythms to Ivesian collage and layering, resulting in a vivid programmatic tapestry characteristic of his instrumental palette.

Nelson should not be confused with Ronald A. Nelson (*b* Rockford, IL, 29 April 1927), a church musician, arranger, and composer active in Minneapolis.

WORKS

Operas: The Birthday of the Infanta (Nelson), 1955–6; Hamaguchi (M. Miller), 1981

Choral: The Christmas Story (Bible), cantata, Bar, nar, SATB, brass, perc, org, 1958, arr. SATB, orch; 5 Anthems for Young Choirs (Heb. Book of Prayer), SA, pf, 1961; 3 Ancient Prayers (Heb. Book of Prayer), SATB, org, 1962; Triumphal Te Deum, SSAATTBB, org, brass, perc, 1963; What is Man? (S. Miller), oratorio, Bar, S, nar, SATB, orch/(org, brass, perc), 1967; Prayer of Emperor of China on the Altar of Heaven, December 21, 1539 (Emperor of China), SATB, wind, perc, 1972; Psalm xcv, SATB, insts ad lib, 1971; 4 Pieces after the Seasons (T. Ahlburn), SATB, insts ad lib, 1977; 3 Autumnal Sketches (Ahlburn), S, SATB, insts, 1980; Mass of St. La Salle, SATB, inst ens, 1981; 3 Nocturnal Pieces (Ahlburn), SATB, insts, 1982; 3 Seasonal Reflections (Ahlburn), 1982; *c*30 other choral pieces, incl. several on Biblical texts

Orch: Savannah River Holiday, 1953, arr. band 1973; Sarabande: for Katharine in April, 1954; Jubilee, 1960; Rocky Point Holiday, orch/band, 1969; 5 Pieces after Paintings by Andrew Wyeth, 1976; Medieval Suite, band, 1983; several other orch and band works

Film scores

Songs

Principal publisher: Boosey & Hawkes

LANCE W. BRUNNER

Nelson, Tracy (*b* Madison, WI, 27 Dec 1944). Popular singer and songwriter. She grew up in Wisconsin and attended the University of Wisconsin in Madison, where she formed her first, ephemeral bands. Her first solo album, the bluesy *Deep are the Roots*, was released in 1965, and early the next year she moved to the San Francisco area. In July 1966 she formed the band Mother Earth, which recorded for Mercury and Reprise and lasted, with constantly changing personnel, until 1973. Nelson moved to a farm near Nashville in 1969; at this time elements of country music began to infuse her style. She continued to compose, and her songs – notably *Down so low*, recorded by Linda Ronstadt in 1976 – attained a popular success that still eluded her as a performer. She recorded a solo album for Atlantic in 1974, *Tracy Nelson*, which included a duet with Willie Nelson, *After the fire is gone*. Later in the 1970s she recorded albums for the MCA, Flying Fish, and Adelphi labels. Although she possesses one of the most commanding contralto voices in folk, rock, and popular music, ranging from a confidential croon to impassioned utterances and soulful shouts, Nelson has never achieved either the artistic coherence or the commercial success which her talents might seem to have promised.

RECORDINGS

Deep are the Roots (Prst. 7393, 1965); *Living with the Animals* (Mer. 61194, 1968); *Make a Joyful Noise* (Mer. 61226, 1969); *Bring me Home* (Rep. 6431, 1971); *Tracy Nelson* (Atl. 7310, 1974); *Sweet Soul Music* (MCA 494, 1975); *Homemade Songs* (Flying Fish 052, 1978); *Doin' it my Way* (Adelphi 4119, 1980)

JOHN ROCKWELL

Nelson, Willie (Hugh) (*b* Abbott, TX, 30 April 1933). Country-music singer, songwriter, and guitarist. During his childhood he was exposed to a variety of musical styles, among them gospel, traditional country, popular, Czech-American, Mexican, black, and western swing. He was a disc jockey for seven years in Texas,

Willie Nelson

Oregon, and California, and served a long apprenticeship as a singer in the honky tonks of Texas. He moved to Nashville in 1960, where he became a highly regarded songwriter, composing hit songs for Patsy Cline (*Crazy*, 1961), Faron Young (*Hello Walls*, 1961), and Ray Price (*Night Life*, 1963); he also played double bass in Price's Cherokee Cowboys, but he was unsuccessful as a singer. For three years, beginning in 1965, he toured with western-swing fiddler Wade Ray, and in 1967 organized a band he called the Record Men. In 1971 Nelson moved to Austin, where a thriving music community already existed, and there he began to cultivate an image designed to appeal to a younger, rock-oriented audience; he abandoned his formerly conservative style of dress and grew his hair long. With Waylon Jennings, a colleague of long standing, he became a leader of the "outlaws," the loose group of musicians who rebelled against the Nashville country-music establishment. In the mid-1970s he was widely known for his catholic tastes in music and for his giant outdoor country-music festivals, which began with the Dripping Springs Reunion and continued with a series of annual Fourth of July Picnics. Nelson recorded his first album, *Shotgun Willie*, in 1973, and finally achieved wide success as a singer two years later with his album *Red-headed Stranger*, which included the best-selling country-music song of the year, *Blue Eyes Crying in the Rain*. Ironically, however, as he became increasingly identified with "progressive country music," his repertory became more traditional. In 1975 Nelson began a career as a film actor; he appeared in *Electric Horseman* (1979), with Robert Redford and Jane Fonda, and in *Honeysuckle Rose* (1980). He was elected to the Nashville Songwriters Hall of Fame in 1973.

RECORDINGS

(selective list)

Crazy/Hello Walls (Liberty 3239, 1962); Touch me (Liberty 55439, 1962); *Shotgun Willie* (Atl. 7262, 1973); *Phases and Stages* (Atl. 7291, 1974); Blue Eyes Crying in the Rain (Col. 3-10176, 1975); *Red-headed Stranger* (Col. KC33482, 1975); Remember me (Col. 3-10275, 1976); Uncloudy Day (Col. KC34112, 1976); Georgia on my Mind (Col. 3-10704, 1978); *Stardust* (Col. JC35305, 1978); *Willie and Family Live* (Col. KC2-35642, 1978); On the Road Again (Col. 11351, 1980); *Honeysuckle Rose* (Col. S2-36752, 1980) [soundtrack to the film]; *Always on my Mind* (Col. FC37951, 1982); *Angel Eyes* (Col. FC39363, 1984)

BIBLIOGRAPHY

"Nelson, Willie," *CBY 1979*

T. S. Johnson: *Willie Nelson: a Comprehensive Discographic Listing* (Danbury, CT, 1981, rev. 2/1982)

D. Breskin: "Willie Nelson," *Musician*, no.45 (1982), 40

R. Kienzle: Liner notes, *Willie Nelson* (TL CW11, 1983)

BILL C. MALONE/R

Nelsova [Katznelson], **Zara** (*b* Winnipeg, Man., 23 Dec 1918). Cellist. She began lessons in early childhood and accompanied her family to London, where she studied at the London Violoncello School and privately with its principal, Herbert Walenn. She was heard by Barbirolli and introduced by him to Casals, from whom she received some additional lessons. In 1932 she gave a London début recital and appeared as a soloist with Sargent and the London SO, playing Lalo's Concerto. Later she joined her two older sisters, who played violin and piano, and they toured extensively together as the Canadian Trio in Britain, Australia, and South Africa. She made her American début in 1942 at New York's Town Hall, and from 1949 was again based in Britain, where she presented new works by Barber, Hindemith, Shostakovich, and Bloch, who dedicated to her his three suites for unaccompanied cello. In 1955 she took American citizenship and in 1963 married the pianist Grant Johannesen, with whom she has given numerous duo recitals. In 1966 she became the first American cellist to tour the USSR. She has taken a continued interest in contemporary music but also excels in Romantic works, compensating for some lack of force with a sensitive feeling for melodic phrase and formal development. In 1960 she was bequeathed a Stradivari cello, the "Marquis de Corberon," dated 1726. She was awarded Canada's Centennial Medal of the Confederation in 1967.

NOËL GOODWIN

Nettl, Bruno (*b* Prague, Czechoslovakia, 14 March 1930). Ethnomusicologist. He was educated at Indiana University (BA 1950, PhD 1953) and trained in librarianship at the University of Michigan (MA 1960). After teaching at Wayne State University (1953–64) he joined the faculty of the University of Illinois; he was chairman of the musicology department there from 1966 to 1972 and again in 1975.

Nettl has written widely on North American Indian music, music of the Middle East, particularly Iran, and European and American folk music. His more general interests include acculturation and modernization in traditional music. Several of his works have become basic to the study of ethnomusicology, particularly *Music in Primitive Culture* (1956), one of the first introductions to the field published in the USA. *An Introduction to Folk Music in the United States* (1960, rev. and enlarged 3/1976) is one of the first studies of the subject by an ethnomusicologist.

See also ETHNOMUSICOLOGY, §§2, 3.

WRITINGS

American Indian Music North of Mexico: its Styles and Areas (diss., Indiana U., 1953; Philadelphia, 1954, as *North American Indian Musical Styles*)

Music in Primitive Culture (Cambridge, MA, 1956)

An Introduction to Folk Music in the United States (Detroit, 1960, rev. and enlarged 3/1976)

Cheremis Musical Styles (Bloomington, IN, 1960)

Reference Materials in Ethnomusicology (Detroit, 1961, 2/1967)

Theory and Method in Ethnomusicology (New York, 1964)

Folk and Traditional Music of the Western Continents (Englewood Cliffs, NJ, 1965, 2/1973)
ed.: *Tradition and Change in Urban Musical Cultures: Eight Ethnomusicological Essays* (Urbana, 1978)

PAULA MORGAN

Nettl, Paul (*b* Hohenelbe [now Vrchlabi, Czechoslovakia], 10 Jan 1889; *d* Bloomington, IN, 8 Jan 1972). Musicologist, father of Bruno Nettl. He was educated at the German University in Prague, where he studied law (JD 1913), musicology (PhD 1915), and theory. After military service in World War I, he returned to Prague in 1920, where he taught at the German University. In 1930, when it became clear that his Jewish origins would prevent permanent academic advancement, he became active in journalism. After the German occupation in 1939 he made his way to the USA, where he taught at the Westminster Choir College and in New York and Philadelphia. He was professor of musicology at Indiana University (1946–59), and after his retirement continued to write and to teach part-time there until 1963. Nettl's research subjects were 17th- and 18th-century music, Austrian and Bohemian music history, dance history, Mozart, and Beethoven. His earliest and most important scholarly works were published in German in the 1920s and early 1930s; he also wrote widely for the general reader.

WRITINGS

The Story of Dance Music (New York, 1947/*R*1969)
The Book of Musical Documents (New York, 1948/*R*1969)
Luther and Music (New York, 1948/*R*1969)
The Other Casanova (New York, 1950/*R*1970)
Forgotten Musicians (New York, 1951/*R*1970)
National Anthems (New York, 1952, enlarged 2/1967)
ed.: *Beethoven Encyclopedia* (New York, 1956; rev. 2/1967 as *Beethoven Handbook*)
Mozart and Masonry (New York, 1957/*R*1970)
The Dance in Classical Music (New York, 1963)

RAMONA H. MATTHEWS/R

Nettleton, Asahel (*b* North Killingworth, CT, 21 April 1783; *d* East Windsor, CT, 6 May 1844). Evangelist and hymnbook compiler. He was one of the earliest itinerant New England evangelists, and began preaching and conducting revival meetings throughout New England and New York in 1811. In response to the demand for a broader selection of hymns appropriate to evangelistic use, he compiled *Village Hymns for Social Worship* (Hartford, 1824), a landmark in American hymnody in that it moved away from the dominance of Isaac Watts and his school. The collection of 600 hymns was drawn partly from earlier American compilations, including Nathan Strong's *Hartford Selection* (1799), Samuel Worcester's *Select Hymns* (1819), and Leonard Bacon's missionary *Hymns and Sacred Songs* (1823), but also contained new hymns and some published for the first time in the USA. It was widely used as a source by later American and British compilers and went through numerous editions up to 1858. Nettleton approved the publication of a small tunebook, *Zion's Harp* (1824), to accompany his collection; of its 60 tunes, all but one, Jacob French's "Pilgrim's Farewell," were British.

BIBLIOGRAPHY

B. Tyler: *Memoir of the Life and Character of Rev. A. Nettleton* (Hartford, 1844, rev. 2/1854)
H. E. Starr: "Nettleton, Asahel," *DAB*
F. J. Metcalf: *American Writers and Compilers of Sacred Music* (New York, 1925/*R*1967), 65, 142
P. G. Hammond: *Music in Urban Revivalism in the Northern United States, 1800–1835* (diss., Southern Baptist Theological Seminary, 1974)

PAUL C. ECHOLS

Neuendorff, Adolph (Heinrich Anton Magnus) (*b* Hamburg, Germany, 13 June 1843; *d* New York, 4 Dec 1897). Conductor, impresario, and composer. He came to New York in 1854, and studied violin with George Matzka and Joseph Weinlich, and piano with Gustav Schilling. At the age of 16 he became concertmaster of the Stadt Theater orchestra in New York, and at 17 made his début as a pianist. After touring in Brazil as a violinist he studied theory and composition with Karl Anschütz. He spent the season of 1864–5 as conductor at the German theater in Milwaukee and then returned to New York as chorus master at the Stadt Theater, where Anschütz was trying to establish a German opera. In 1867 he took over from Anschütz as director for four seasons, during the last of which he brought a troupe from Europe to perform several German works, including the first American production of *Lohengrin* (3 April 1871). In 1872 he and Carl Rosa and the tenor Theodor Wachtel presented a season of Italian opera at the Academy of Music, and from 1872 to 1874 he was manager of the Germania Theatre. Wachtel returned to the Academy in 1875 with the soprano Eugenie Pappenheim for Neuendorff's season of German opera. Neuendorff attended the opening of the Bayreuth Festspielhaus in 1876 as correspondent for the *New Yorker Staats-Zeitung*, and in the next year directed a Wagner Festival at the Academy, which included the first American performance of *Die Walküre* (2 April 1877). He conducted the New York Philharmonic Society for a season after Theodore Thomas resigned in 1878.

Neuendorff transferred the Germania Theatre company (of which he had been manager from 1872 to 1874) to a new building in 1881, but the venture failed after two seasons and ruined him financially. He then moved to Boston, where he conducted the Music Hall Promenade Concerts (1884–9) and the Emma Juch Grand Opera Company (1889–91). In 1892 he conducted English opera in New York, then for the next three years conducted at the Vienna Hofoper where his wife, Georgine von Januschowsky, was a leading singer. He returned to New York in 1896 and became director of music at Temple Emanu-El. He succeeded Seidl the following year as conductor of the Metropolitan Opera.

Neuendorff's works include the comic operas *Der Rattenfänger von Hameln* (1880), *Don Quixote* (1882), *Prince Waldmeister* (1887), and *The Minstrel* (1892), two symphonies (1878, 1880), smaller orchestral works, quartets for male voices, and solo songs.

BIBLIOGRAPHY

"Neuendorff, Adolph," *Cyclopedia of Music and Musicians*, ed. J. D. Champlin and W. F. Apthorp (New York, 1888–90) [autobiographical article]
F. H. Martens: "Neuendorff, Adolph Heinrich Anton Magnus," *DAB*

BRUCE CARR

Neuhaus, Max (*b* Beaumont, TX, 9 Aug 1939). Composer. Following lessons in jazz drumming from Krupa, Neuhaus received BA and MA degrees from the Manhattan School (1961, 1962) and pursued a notable career as a solo percussionist specializing in avant-garde music. During 1962–3 he performed with the Contemporary Chamber Ensemble, conducted by Boulez, and in 1963–4 was soloist with Stockhausen. In 1968 he gave up performing to devote himself to composing electronic music. He has served as artist-in-residence at the University of Chicago, Bell Telephone Laboratories (Murray Hill, New Jersey), the Walker Art Center in Minneapolis, and Artpark in Lewiston, New York. In 1973 he received an NEA music fellowship, and in 1977 an NEA fellowship in the visual arts as well as a stipend from the Deutscher Akademischer Austauschdienst to work in Berlin.

Site of Max Neuhaus's sound environment in Times Square, New York, 1977; the sound drifts up through the sidewalk grate from an installation under ground

From the early 1970s he concentrated on two types of work: sound installations that listeners come upon in unexpected environments, and participatory radio pieces. The sound environments, aural equivalents of the work of such visual artists as Robert Smithson and Christo, offer gentle, sustained, overlapping, electronically generated sound textures and have been installed in such spaces as an underground subway chamber in Times Square, New York (the rich, low sound could be heard at ground level, drifting up through a sidewalk grate; see illustration), the Como Park Conservatory in St. Paul, and many museums. A related group of works, installations in swimming pools, explore the acoustic properties that affect the perception of sound made and heard in water (e.g., *Water Whistle* series, 1970–75). Radio pieces, for example *Radio Net* (1974–7), involve a network of stations, with listeners calling in bits of sonic material that are then combined in a fluctuating aural collage. After he devoted himself to electronic music, Neuhaus refused to countenance recordings of his work, believing that the interaction between music and listener in the intended environment is integral to the piece.

In recent years the sketches and renderings of Neuhaus's installations have been exhibited by several museums in Europe and the USA.

WORKS

Installations: Drive-in Music, 1967 [Lincoln Parkway, between the Albright-Knox Museum and Soldier's Circle, Buffalo; extant 1967–8]; Southwest Stairwell, 1968 [Ryerson University, Toronto; extant 1968]; Walkthrough, 1973 [subway entrance, Jay Street, Brooklyn; extant 1973–7]; Times Square, 1973–7 [traffic island between 45th and 46th streets, New York, extant 1977–]; Drive-in Music, 1974–5 [Artpark parking lot, Lewiston, New York; extant 1975]; Untitled, 1977 [Dokumenta 6, Kassel, Germany; extant 1977]; Untitled, 1978 [Sculpture Garden, Museum of Modern Art, New York; extant 1978]; Untitled, 1978–9 [stairwell, Museum of Contemporary Art, Chicago; extant 1979–]; Untitled, 1980 [Como Park Conservatory, Minneapolis; extant 1980–83]; Time Piece, 1983 [Sculpture Garden, Whitney Museum, New York; extant 1983]; Untitled, 1983 [wooded hillside, Villa Celle, Santomato di Pistoia, Italy; extant 1983–]; other works

Underwater works: Water Whistle I–XVII, 1970–75 [13 North American cities; extant 1971–5]; Underwater Musics I–IV, 1975–8 [I, Bremen; II, New York; III, Berlin; IV, Amsterdam; extant 1976–8]

Sound objects: Maxfeed, 1967–8 [edn of 50, private colls.]; Bluebox, 1970–74 [edn of 10, private colls.]; Untitled, 1974–5 [unicum, Christophe de Menil]; Time Piece, 1979–81 [edn of 31, private colls.]

Broadcast works: Public Supply I–IV, 1966–73 [I, WBAI, New York; II, CJRT, Toronto; III, WBAI; IV, WFMT, Chicago]; Radio Net, 1974–7 [NPR, 2 Jan 1977]; Audium, 1977– [international broadcast and television project]

Sound events: American Can [in 2 realizations: Central Park, 1966, and Lincoln Center Plaza, 1967, New York]; By-product [in 2 realizations: Town Hall, 1966, and Park Place Gallery, 1967, New York]

Telephone Access, 1968 [New York; individual interaction by telephone, with sound-responsive elec]

BIBLIOGRAPHY

"A Max Sampler," *Source*, no.5 (1969), 48

T. Johnson: "New Music," *HiFi/MusAm*, xxv/2 (1975), 14

M. Neuhaus and others: *Sound Installation* (Basel, 1983) [exhibition catalogue, Kunsthalle Basel]

J. Rockwell: "Environmental Composers & Ambient Music: Max Neuhaus," *All American Music: Composition in the Late Twentieth Century* (New York, 1983), 145

JOHN ROCKWELL

Nevada [Wixom], **Emma** (*b* Alpha, nr Nevada City, CA, 7 Feb 1859; *d* Liverpool, England, 20 June 1940). Soprano. A pupil of Mathilde Marchesi, she made her opera début in 1880 at Her Majesty's Theatre, London, in *La sonnambula*, an opera that brought some of her greatest successes (her medallion was later placed with those of Pasta and Malibran on Bellini's statue at Naples). She appeared with great success in Italy and Paris, where her roles included Lucia and Mignon. Returning to the USA in 1884 she appeared at the Academy of Music, New York, and, the following year, on alternate nights with Patti. She made several further tours of the USA and Europe, and sang at Covent Garden in 1887 in *La sonnambula* and *Mireille*, her intonation and flexibility being admired but not her free treatment of Gounod's score. In England she frequently sang in oratorio, including the first performance of Alexander Mackenzie's *Rose of Sharon* (1885), in which she sang the soprano part; the composer wrote that her "girlish simplicity . . . and unaffected interpretation of the part were admirably suited to it." Among her pupils was her daughter Mignon.

BIBLIOGRAPHY

W. Armstrong, ed.: "Reminiscences of Emma Nevada," *New York Tribune Sunday Magazine* (28 Oct 1906), 7

O. Thompson: *The American Singer* (New York, 1937/R1969), 190

G. Jellinek: "Nevada, Emma," *DAB*

T. Wilkins: "Nevada, Emma," *NAW*

J. B. STEANE/R

Nevin, Arthur (Finlay) (*b* Edgeworth, PA, 27 April 1871; *d* Sewickley, PA, 10 July 1943). Composer, educator, and conductor, younger brother of Ethelbert Nevin. He studied at the New England Conservatory from 1889 to 1893, and then for four years in Berlin, where his teachers included Karl Klindworth for the piano, and O. B. Boise and Engelbert Humperdinck for composition. The family seat outside Pittsburgh thereafter served as the base for a life of travel, research and composition, residence in artistic colonies, and private and public teaching. During the summers of 1903 and 1904 he lived among the Blackfoot Indians in Montana, studying their folklore and music. As a result of these studies he lectured and published an article "Two Summers with Blackfeet Indians of Montana" (*MQ*, ii, 1916, p.257); he also wrote the opera *Poia* in collaboration with the poet Randolph Hartley, and together they managed to secure its production (conducted by Muck) in Berlin in 1910. In 1911–14 he lived in Charlottesville, Virginia, devoting himself wholly to composition, but for the next five seasons he conducted the orchestra of the MacDowell Colony at Peterborough, New Hampshire. In 1915 he became head of the choral and extension departments of the University of Kansas, Lawrence, and in 1920–22 he directed the municipal music department and conducted the orchestra of Memphis, Tennessee. He left Memphis because of ill health and traveled in France, then in 1926 returned to the USA to teach privately in Sewickley. Nevin's musical training and output were typical of late 19th-century American composers, with an emphasis on large forms in the Germanic style. His operas *Poia* and *A Daughter of the Forest* are strongly influenced by naturalist philosophies.

WORKS

DRAMATIC

A Night in Yaddo Land (masque, E. Stebbins and W. Chance), vs (New York, 1900)

Poia (opera, 3, E. von Huhn, after R. Hartley), Berlin, Royal Opera, 23 April 1910 (Berlin, 1909)

A Daughter of the Forest (opera, 1, Hartley), Chicago, Auditorium, 5 Jan 1918, vs (Cincinnati, 1917)

OTHER WORKS

Vocal: The Djinns (cantata, after V. Hugo), 4vv, 2 pf (New York, 1913); Roland (cantata); 3 Songs (Boston, 1914); other songs, partsongs

Inst: Bakawali Dances, orch; 3 orch suites, incl. Lorna Doone, Love Dreams; At the Spring, str; Str Qt, d; Pf Trio, C; 3 pf suites; other works, pf

BIBLIOGRAPHY

MusAm, xii/2 (1910), 25 [interview with Nevin about Berlin production of *Poia*]

E. E. Hipsher: *American Opera and its Composers* (Philadelphia, 1934), 337ff

ERIC BLOM/BRUCE CARR

Nevin, Ethelbert (Woodbridge) (*b* Edgeworth, PA, 25 Nov 1862; *d* New Haven, CT, 17 Feb 1901). Composer, brother of Arthur Nevin. He took lessons in singing and piano with Franz Böhme in Dresden, 1877–8, then studied in Boston (1881–3), where his principal teachers were B. J. Lang (piano) and Stephen A. Emery (composition). During the years 1884–6 he was in Berlin, where he received instruction from Karl Klindworth. He returned to the USA, gave concerts, lectured, and taught for some years in Boston; then, from 1891, in Paris, Berlin, Boston (1893–5), Florence, and Venice, he spent his time in teaching, performing, studying, and composing. In 1892 he applied unsuccessfully to Richard Strauss for composition lessons. He returned to the USA finally in 1897, his health broken.

Nevin's work as a composer was confined almost entirely to songs and short piano pieces; these have a graceful lyric vein and a feeling for melody that appealed directly to the large audience of "nice" musicians whom Charles Ives found so offensive. Nevin's daintily chromatic harmony never moves outside comfortably predictable phrase-structures. The enormous popularity of his song *The Rosary* – which sold well over a million copies in the decade following its publication in 1898 – had as much to do with its text as with its tune, and almost the same is true of *Mighty Lak' a Rose* (whose persona, be it noted, is not black but Irish). The easy and attractive pianism of pieces like *Narcissus* further recommended them to domestic recitalists.

Ethelbert Nevin's other compositions include three pieces for piano and violin, several choruses, two cantatas, and the music to *Floriane's Dream*, a pantomime performed in 1898 by a small company including the relatively unknown Isadora Duncan, who later made *Narcissus*, *Ophelia*, and *Water Nymph* staples of her dance recitals. Nevin became a member of the National Institute of Arts and Letters in 1898.

WORKS

Vocal: A Book of [10] Songs (E. Field, Stevenson, C. Kingsley, and others), op.20 (Boston, 1893); Captive Memories (J. T. White), song cycle, Bar, 4vv, pf, op.29 (Cincinnati, 1899); The Quest (R. Hartley), cantata, Mez, Bar, 4vv, pf, vs (Cincinnati, 1902) [orchd H. Parker]; over 60 other songs, incl. The Rosary (R. C. Rogers) (Boston, 1898), Mighty Lak' a Rose (F. L. Stanton) (Cincinnati, 1901); *c*18 choruses

Pf: 3 Duets, op.6 (Boston, 1890); Water Scenes, suite, op.13 (Boston, 1891) [incl. Narcissus]; Maggio in Toscana, suite, op.21 (Boston, 1896); A Day in Venice, suite, op.25 (Cincinnati, 1898); over 25 other pieces

Other: Floriane's Dream (V. Thompson), pantomime, New York, 24 March 1898 [partly re-used in op.25]; Marche nuptiale, org, 1892; 3 vn, pf pieces

MSS at *PPiU*

Principal publishers: Boston Music, Church, Ditson, G. Schirmer

BIBLIOGRAPHY

V. Thompson: *The Life of Ethelbert Nevin* (Boston, 1913)

R. G. Cole: "Nevin, Ethelbert Woodbridge," *DAB*

J. T. Howard: *Ethelbert Nevin* (New York, 1935) [incl. full list of pubd works]

RICHARD ALDRICH/BRUCE CARR

Newark. City in New Jersey (pop. 329,248; metropolitan area 1,965,969). On the Passaic River, about 12 km west of Manhattan, it was founded by Puritan settlers from Connecticut in 1666 and incorporated in 1836.

1. Art music. 2. Popular music, jazz, and gospel music.

1. ART MUSIC. Early musical life centered around the church, which by 1720 was predominately Presbyterian. James Lyon (1735–94), the compiler of *Urania* (1761/*R*1973), an important early American tunebook, was born and educated in Newark. By the late 18th century private teachers were offering musical instruction, and in 1797 the first musical band of Newark citizens participated in the Independence Day celebration. Trinity Church (Episcopal) installed the first church organ in Newark in 1819. By 1830 Newark had three church organs, and the formation of three choral organizations, the Harmonic Society (1830), the Newark Handel and Haydn Society (1831), and the Mozart Sacred Society (1834), furthered the performance of sacred music. Henry Pilcher built his first organ in Newark in 1834. The composer William Batchelder Bradbury taught singing to children at the Presbyterian churches. The first oratorio heard in Newark, Handel's *Judas Maccabaeus*, was presented by the Newark Handel and Haydn Society in 1837. Between 1832 and 1841 there were 92 public concerts by well-known musicians, including violinists, pianists, opera singers, and the English singers Henry Russell and John Braham. The *New York Musical Review and Gazette* included reviews of concerts given by musicians resident in Newark.

The first secular music group, the Newark Amateur Glee Company, was organized in 1837, but concerts consisting principally of secular music were not tolerated by the churches and had to be held in hotels and the meeting halls of private clubs. Newark's Concert Hall, which was renamed many times after its inauguration in 1847, was the first public hall in the city to be lit by gas. Library Hall (capacity 600), which opened in 1848, and Oraton Hall (opened 1856) were also used for concerts.

By 1850 Newark had become the wealthiest and most populated city in New Jersey, and the wave of German immigrants who settled there in the middle of the century initiated a new era in the city's musical life. The first German singing-society, the Eintracht, was organized in 1846, followed by the Aurora (1852), the Concordia (1857), the Arion Men's Chorus (1859), the Germania (1865), and the Harmonie (1883) societies. An auditorium to house these groups was built in 1884 by Gottfried Krueger, after whom it was named. Among the many other choral groups that were formed around this time was the Newark Harmonic Society, which had its own orchestra and started sponsoring concerts in 1860.

The Orpheus Club, among the earliest glee clubs in the USA, was organized in 1889 by Samuel Augustus Ward, the organist and choirmaster at Newark's Grace Church who is remembered for his hymn tune *Materna* (1882, now sung as *America the Beautiful* with lyrics by Katherine Lee Bates). Newark's choral tradition has been continued with the formation in 1966 of the renowned Newark Boys Chorus (and School), a chiefly black group that has toured in Europe, Japan, and the USA and performs a wide range of music from all periods, and in 1967 of the New Jersey Symphony Chorus.

The first opera performed in Newark was Weber's *Der Freischütz*, presented in German on 2 June 1855 at the Concert Hall; in 1860 a season of Italian opera was given in English translation. Opera began to flourish in the city in the 1890s with performances at Miner's Newark Theater. Interest continued into the 1920s with the Newark Music Festivals and into the 1930s with performances sponsored by the Griffith Music Foundation (see below), the Newark Opera House, and the Grand Opera Company of New Jersey, which gave its first performance in Newark in 1937. The Opera Theatre of New Jersey moved to Newark and gave its first performance at Symphony Hall in November 1968; it was renamed the New Jersey State Opera in 1974.

The city's first permanent orchestra, the Newark SO, was formed in 1914 as the Eintracht Orchestra. It was followed by the Symphony Orchestra of Newark, the Newark Chamber Orchestra (1956), and the Little Symphony of Newark (1966). The New Jersey SO, founded in 1928, tours throughout the state and since 1964 has been based at Symphony Hall (capacity 3365) in Newark. The hall was built in 1925 as the Mosque Theatre and is the city's leading concert facility. Concerts are also presented by the Newark Museum (where free programs have been given since 1933) and the Sacred Heart Cathedral.

In 1938 Mrs. Parker O. Griffith established the Griffith Music Foundation, which for more than 20 years sponsored a variety of musical activities at the Mosque Theatre, including a piano master-class series, concerts by renowned conductors, instrumental virtuosos, and singers (e.g., Toscanini, Horowitz, Rubinstein, Feuermann, Marian Anderson, and Tagliavini) and orchestras (e.g., the Boston SO, the Cleveland Orchestra, and the New York PO), as well as ballet, opera, and children's programs. The foundation was closed in 1959, but similar events were sponsored first by Garden State Concerts, Inc., and later by Moe Septee, who brought to Newark such organizations as the Moscow and Leningrad symphony orchestras and the Royal Ballet from London; Septee became manager of the Mosque Theatre after it was refurbished.

A number of significant festivals and outdoor musical events have taken place in Newark, the first of which were the concerts given by the Newark Philharmonic Concert Band and guest bands at Branch Brook Park for more than 50 years from 1904. In 1915 C. Mortimer Wiske organized the Newark Music Festival, which was held annually until 1930, usually in the First Regiment Armory. It boasted choruses of 500–3000 voices and audiences of up to 40,000. The second festival (in 1916) was a historical pageant lasting four days, involving 4000 actors, 300 singers, and 90 instrumentalists in the celebration of the 250th anniversary of the founding of Newark. In 1936 the Essex County Music Society, under the leadership of Mrs. Griffith, began to sponsor a music series called "Symphonies under the Stars." The concerts, attended by up to 25,000 people, were held at the Newark Schools Stadium until 1942, when war restrictions required them to be moved indoors. Among the soloists who participated in the series were Heifetz, Menuhin, Kreisler, Pinza, Björling, and Robeson.

2. POPULAR MUSIC, JAZZ, AND GOSPEL MUSIC. Vaudeville shows were produced in Newark during the 1870s, but it was not until 1902, when Proctor's Park Palace was built specifically as a music hall, that vaudeville could be considered to have been well established. The first burlesque shows were offered in Newark during the 1880s at Waldman's Opera House (the renamed Concert Hall), and performances of this kind took place until 1956, when an anti-burlesque amendment was added to the city's theatrical ordinance. In 1872 one theater and three music halls were in use; by 1922 there were 62 such venues, two of them for theater, two for burlesque, and five for vaudeville. Musical productions were in their heyday in Newark in the 1920s and early 1930s, and the Shubert Theater accommodated a great many of them.

Newark provided a congenial atmosphere for jazz, which by the 1930s had several small clubs, including the Piccadilly and the Alcazar, and such larger halls as the Adams, Orpheum, and Paramount theaters, where, among others, Louis Armstrong, Duke Ellington, and Jimmy Lunceford performed. The Kinney Club, Skateland, and the Savoy Ballroom offered big-band music. During the late 1930s two local bands were established, the Savoy Dictators and Gil Fuller's Barons of Rhythm. Ellington, Art Tatum, Woody Herman, and Stan Kenton played at the Mosque and the Adams theaters in the 1940s, followed by Miles Davis, Art Blakey, and John Coltrane at various jazz clubs (Powell's Lounge, the Front Room, Sugar Hill, and the Key Club) in the 1950s. By the mid-1960s, however, when George Benson was becoming known, only the Key Club remained. Jazz in Newark was revived in the 1970s, with jazz services at Memorial West Church, weekly jam sessions at Pere's East, and activities at the Key Club and Sparky J's.

The INSTITUTE OF JAZZ STUDIES, founded in 1952 by Marshall Stearns of Hunter College, CUNY, and housed on the Newark campus of Rutgers, the State University of New Jersey, since 1967, is a leading archival collection of jazz and jazz-related material (*see* LIBRARIES AND COLLECTIONS, §3). The institute produces a computerized catalogue of its record collection, which serves as a model for cataloguing jazz music, and publishes the *Annual Review of Jazz Studies*, the only scholarly jazz periodical in English. The music department at Rutgers offers a BA in music and music education.

Gospel music became culturally more significant in Newark in the 1920s and 1930s with the growth in the black population and the number of black churches established at that time. Sarah Vaughan and Dionne Warwick both sang in Newark church choirs before they made their careers in jazz and popular music. Savoy Records, which has been particularly successful in black gospel music, started as a Newark-based company, issuing its first recording, a bop session, in 1944. Savoy's jazz recordings include the work of Charlie Parker, Miles Davis, Stan Getz, and Cannonball Adderley; its rhythm-and-blues repertory is represented by Johnny Otis and Big Jay McNeely, and its gospel music by James L. Cleveland. In 1978 the company moved to Elizabeth, New Jersey, where it was bought by Prelude Records five years later.

BIBLIOGRAPHY

W. H. Shaw: *History of Essex and Hudson Counties, New Jersey* (Philadelphia, 1884)

D. E. Hervey: "Music in Newark," in F. J. Urquhart: *A History of the City of Newark, New Jersey . . . 1666–1913* (New York, 1913)

C. H. Kaufman: *Music in New Jersey, 1655–1860: a Study of Musical Activity and Musicians in New Jersey from its First Settlement to the Civil War* (East Brunswick, NJ, 1981)

G. Bishop: "Gems of New Jersey Music," *Sunday Star-Ledger* (Newark, 2, 9, and 16 Oct 1983)

LYNNE M. SCHMELZ-KEIL

Neway, Patricia (*b* Brooklyn, NY, 30 Sept 1919). Soprano. She studied at Notre Dame College for women and developed her voice with Morris Gesell, whom she later married. Her stage début was as Fiordiligi (*Così fan tutte*) at the Chautauqua Festival in 1946. Two years later she joined the New York City Opera singing the Female Chorus in Britten's *The Rape of Lucretia*. She achieved a tremendous success in 1950 when she created the role of Magda Sorel in Menotti's *The Consul*, which she sang for nearly a year on Broadway and subsequently with many companies in Europe and America. In 1952 she was engaged by the Opéra-Comique for two years, and in 1958 she created another Menotti role, the Mother in *Maria Golovin*, at the Brussels World's Fair. Her voice, a steely dramatic instrument used with unstinting intensity, declined in the late 1950s, doubtless owing to the strain of repeatedly singing such a physically exhausting opera as *The Consul*. Her later career was devoted to concerts and guest opera appearances with numerous American companies, primarily in contemporary works by Britten, Berg, Poulenc, Hoiby, and Weisgall.

PETER G. DAVIS

New Christy Minstrels. Folk group. It was formed in 1961 by Randy Sparks (*b* Leavenworth, KS, 29 July 1933) and took its name from the minstrel troupe headed by E. P. Christy in the mid-19th century. The group generally consisted of ten members (there were numerous personnel changes over the years), who sang in close harmony and accompanied themselves with guitars and banjos. They performed some traditional songs but most of their hits were original works that were commercially oriented, such as *Today* (by Sparks) and *Green, green* (by Sparks and Barry McGuire). The lyrics usually embraced folk imagery. Unlike many other popular folk groups, the New Christy Minstrels eschewed the protest posture of the period, stressing instead a wholesome image; by 1964, when Sparks sold the rights to the name, they had become one of the most successful folk groups. They continued to perform with great success throughout the 1960s, touring Europe and forming a nightclub act towards the end of the decade. By the mid-1970s, when the group broke up, they had sold over 13 million albums.

BIBLIOGRAPHY

I. Dove: "Christy Minstrels Sing out Clear in No-protest Form," *Billboard*, lxxx (16 Dec 1966), 16

R. Shelton: "Smiling Minstrels," *New York Times* (2 Aug 1964)

"Take a Boy Like me," *Time*, lxxxi (29 March 1963), 40

TERENCE J. O'GRADY

New England composers, schools of. Two groups of composers. The members of each are considered by historians to be unified on account of the area of their activity (New England), their Anglo-Saxon ethnic background, and the similarity of their musical training, style, and career. Writers have used different terms to categorize them; the most neutral of these – First and Second New England schools – were introduced by Hitchcock (1969).

The First New England School, which has also been referred to as one of "native pioneers" (Chase) and "Yankee tunesmiths" (Hitchcock, 1966) includes the late 18th- and early 19th-century composers of music for singing-schools. Most of them were singing-school teachers themselves and composed or compiled at least one tunebook; they worked in the New England states, especially Massachusetts and Connecticut (*see* PSALMODY; HYMNODY, §§1, 2(i); SINGING-SCHOOL).

The Second New England School, termed also the "Academics" (Hughes), the "Boston Group" (Howard), and the "Boston classicists" (Chase), comprehends a group of late 19th-century composers, among them John Knowles Paine, Arthur Foote, Chadwick, Horatio Parker, Arthur Whiting, Amy Beach, and Daniel Gregory Mason. Almost all completed their musical training in Germany, pursued a career in the Boston area as organist or teacher (or both), and wrote songs, cantatas, oratorios, and instrumental works in the larger abstract forms of the Classic-Romantic European tradition.

BIBLIOGRAPHY

R. Hughes: *Contemporary American Composers* (Boston, 1900), chap.3

J. T. Howard: *Our American Music* (New York, 1931, rev. 4/1965)

G. Chase: *America's Music* (New York, 1955, rev. 2/1966/*R*1981)

H. W. Hitchcock: "William Billings and the Yankee Tunesmiths," *HiFi/Stereo Review*, xvi (1966), 55

——: *Music in the United States: a Historical Introduction* (Englewood Cliffs, NJ, 1969, rev. 2/1974)

New England Conservatory. School of music founded by EBEN TOURJÉE in 1867; *see* BOSTON (i), §9(i), and LIBRARIES AND COLLECTIONS, §3.

New Haven. City in Connecticut on Long Island Sound (pop. 126,109; metropolitan area 417,592) founded by English Puritans in 1638, and site of Yale University from 1716.

New Haven first came to musical prominence late in the 18th century as the home of Daniel Read, a composer and compiler of tunebooks, and Amos Doolittle, an engraver and publisher. Read and Doolittle together produced the first American periodical music publication, the *American Musical Magazine* (1786–7), consisting of American and English musical scores. About half of the tunebooks published in Connecticut from 1778 to 1810 originated in New Haven, but the number quickly declined when printing from type became more popular than engraving.

Although a New Haven Musical Society met in 1832, public musical entertainment in the city did not become important until the mid-century. It blossomed then largely due to the efforts of Gustave J. Stoeckel, who founded the Mendelssohn Society in 1858 and taught music at his conservatory and at Yale University, and through Morris Steinert, who organized a short-lived orchestra in 1867. In 1894 Steinert founded the New Haven SO, one of the oldest American professional orchestras in continuous existence; it gave its first performance in January 1895. Its conductors have been Horatio Parker (1895–1919), David Stanley Smith (1920–46), Hugo Kortschak (associate conductor, 1936–52), Richard Donovan (associate conductor, 1936–51), Frank Brieff (1952–74), Erich Kunzel (1974–7), and Murry Sidlin (1977–). In April 1968 the New Haven SO gave the modern première of the five-movement version of Mahler's First Symphony. Parker also founded a New Haven Oratorio Society (1903–14), and the Horatio Parker Choir was founded by Smith in 1920.

Yale University was founded in 1701 as a private institution in Saybrook and moved to New Haven in 1716. A musical society was established at the university by 1812, and in 1853 a book of Yale songs was published, supposedly the first college songbook in the USA. Stoeckel became the first music instructor and conductor at the school in 1855, and was appointed professor of music in 1890 when music was added to the formal curriculum. By 1894 a music school had been created and degrees in music were awarded. Parker served as the first dean of the school from 1904 to his death in 1919.

Yale University has two administrative units for the study of music, the School of Music and the Department of Music. The School of Music awarded its first MM in 1932. In 1958 it became exclusively a graduate professional school, and in 1968 it began a DMA program, in which performers and composers must prove themselves as professionals before receiving the degree (see Samuel, 1978). The Institute of Sacred Music was established in 1973 in affiliation with both the School of Music and the School of Divinity. In the early 1980s the School of Music enrolled about 150 students and had 60 faculty members. Concerts have been given in Woolsey Hall since 1902 (capacity 2695 seats). Chamber music is stressed in the regular programs and at the Yale Summer School for Music and Art on the Battell Estate in Norfolk, Connecticut, first sponsored by Yale in 1941.

During the 1930s an MA program in music history was introduced in the Graduate School. This led to the creation in 1940 of the Department of Music, headed by Leo Schrade, serving both Yale College (undergraduates) and the Graduate School. This department currently enrolls about 45 graduate students and 75 undergraduate music majors; it has 16 faculty members, administering a BA program in music, and MPhil and PhD degrees in music history and theory.

The John Herrick Jackson Music Library contains 110,000 volumes and serves both the department and school. The core of its rare-book collection came with the donation of Lowell Mason's library in 1873. In 1955 the library acquired Ives's manuscripts and papers (Ives graduated from Yale in 1898) and it has since become a center for archival materials of American composers, including Parker, Ruggles, and Thomson, as well as those of Weill. The school also administers the American branch of the archives of Hindemith, who taught at Yale from 1940 to 1953. Other musical resources of the university include the internationally known Yale Collection of Musical Instruments (over 800 instruments, including the Steinert Collection), a Historical Sound Recordings collection (about 100,000 items), an American Musical Theatre collection (including the papers of Cole Porter), and the archives of the Oral History American Music project (founded in 1972 by Vivian Perlis and including materials on Ives, Ellington, and many others). (For a fuller discussion of Yale's archival holdings, *see* LIBRARIES AND COLLECTIONS, §3, "Connecticut.")

Several of Yale's performing groups are well known. The Whiffenpoofs (founded 1909) were the first small, informal singing group on campus. The Glee Club was founded in 1861 and made its first European tour in 1928. The Yale Philharmonia Orchestra (made up of students from the School of Music) is said to be one of the best student orchestras in the country and gives concerts in New York and abroad.

The Neighborhood Music School in New Haven was formed in 1915 as part of a settlement house.

BIBLIOGRAPHY

E. E. Atwater, ed.: *History of the City of New Haven to the Present Time* (New York, 1887)
R. G. Osterweis: *Three Centuries of New Haven, 1638–1938* (New Haven, 1953)
C. A. Grimes: *They who Speak in Music: the History of the Neighborhood Music School, New Haven, Conn.* (New Haven, 1957)
H. H. Roberts and D. Cousins: *A History of the New Haven Symphony Orchestra Celebrating its Seventy-fifth Season 1894–1969* (New Haven, 1969)
R. Crawford: "Connecticut Sacred Music Imprints, 1778–1810," *Notes*, xxvii (1970–71), 445, 671
B. M. Kelley: *Yale: a History* (New Haven, 1974)
H. E. Samuel: "Yale's DMA: a Progress Report," *College Music Symposium*, xviii (1978), 97
L. Noss: *A History of the Yale School of Music, 1848–1970* (New Haven, 1984)
——: "Music Comes to Yale," *American Music*, iii (1985), 337

PEGGY DAUB (with VICTOR T. CARDELL)

New Jersey SO. Orchestra founded in Newark in 1928; *see* NEWARK, §1.

Newlin, Dika (*b* Portland, OR, 22 Nov 1923). Musicologist and composer. She was educated at Michigan State University (BA 1939), UCLA (MA 1941), and Columbia University, receiving that institution's first PhD in musicology (1945). At the same time she studied composition with Farwell, Schoenberg, and Sessions. She taught at Western Maryland College (1945–9), Syracuse University (1949–51), Drew University (1952–65), and North Texas State University (1965–73), and in 1978 was appointed to the faculty of Virginia Commonwealth University. Newlin's research has centered on Austrian composers of the late 19th and 20th centuries. Her book *Bruckner, Mahler, Schoenberg* (1947, rev. 2/1978) demonstrates the relationship between the three composers as heirs of the Romantic tradition. She has edited and translated some of the major writings by and about Schoenberg, and she is the author of *Schoenberg Remembered: Diaries and Recollections, 1938–1976* (1980), a collection of reminiscences that provides a fascinating picture of the man and teacher. Her interests include electronic and computer music, mixed-media works, and experimental musical theater, and she is active in all these areas as a composer, teacher, and performer. She has written songs, piano and chamber works, three operas, a piano concerto, and a symphony for chorus and orchestra.

BIBLIOGRAPHY

K. Wolff: "Dika Newlin," *ACAB*, x/4 (1962), 1

PAULA MORGAN

Newman, Alfred (*b* New Haven, CT, 17 March 1900; *d* Los Angeles, CA, 17 Feb 1970). Composer and conductor. At the age of 14 he was offered a piano scholarship by Stojowski and studied in New York with Goldmark and George Wedge and later in Hollywood with Schoenberg. Family poverty compelled him to abandon a concert career while still young, and he played in Broadway theaters and on vaudeville circuits. He studied conducting with William Daly, and was the youngest conductor ever to appear on Broadway; he was music director for the 1920 *George White Scandals* and for the *Greenwich Village Follies* of 1922 and 1923. In 1930 Newman went to Hollywood where he was soon appointed music director at United Artists. He worked primarily in film musicals but gradually became more interested in original composition, especially after the success of his score for *Street Scene* (1931). From 1940 to 1960 he was head of the 20th Century-Fox music department and divided his time between composing and the supervision and conducting of film musicals; he also aided and furthered the careers of such composers as Bernard Herrmann and Alex North, whose music was often regarded as unconventional. He recorded with the Hollywood Bowl orchestra and appeared as a guest conductor with various American orchestras. Newman worked on more than 230 films, winning nine Academy awards and 45 nominations; his last score (for *Airport*) was completed just before his death. His brothers Emil and Lionel also composed and conducted film scores in Hollywood; their nephew is the popular musician Randy Newman.

Newman was one of the key figures in the history of American film music, and was among the first screen composers to establish the romantic symphonic style of Hollywood music, which was prevalent from the early 1930s to the mid-1950s. His music was well wrought and full-textured, and sometimes (especially in his string writing) attained a high degree of lyrical and dramatic expressiveness. His scores for *Wuthering Heights*, *The Prisoner of Zenda*, *The Hunchback of Notre Dame*, *Captain from Castile*, and *The Robe* represent Hollywood film music at its best. As a conductor he had a great flair for molding music to the texture and rhythm of a picture and for coordinating the elements involved in the preparation and recording of a film musical. In his capacity as studio music director he encouraged the development of new ideas for improving the quality and technique of recording; the so-called Newman System for music synchronization, devised at United Artists during the 1930s, is still in wide use today.

See also FILM MUSIC, §3.

WORKS

(selective list; all film scores)

Street Scene, 1931; We Live Again, 1934; The Dark Angel, 1935; Beloved Enemy, 1936; The Prisoner of Zenda, 1937; Beau Geste, 1939; Gunga Din, 1939; The Hunchback of Notre Dame, 1939; Wuthering Heights, 1939; Young Mr. Lincoln, 1939; Brigham Young, 1940; The Song of Bernadette, 1943; Wilson, 1944; Captain from Castile, 1947; The Snake Pit, 1948; Prince of Foxes, 1949; Twelve O'clock High, 1949; The Robe, 1953; The Egyptian, collab. B. Herrmann, 1954; A Man Called Peter, 1955; Anastasia, 1956; The Counterfeit Traitor, 1961; How the West Was Won, 1963; The Greatest Story Ever Told, 1965; Nevada Smith, 1966; Airport, 1969

BIBLIOGRAPHY

F. Steiner: *The Making of an American Film Composer: a Study of Alfred Newman's Music in the First Decade of the Sound Era* (diss., U. of Southern California, Los Angeles, 1981) [incl. complete list of film scores]

CHRISTOPHER PALMER/FRED STEINER

Newman, Anthony (*b* Los Angeles, CA, 12 May 1941). Organist, harpsichordist, and composer. In 1959–60 he studied in Paris with Pierre Cochereau and Nadia Boulanger at the Ecole Normale de Musique. He received the BS degree in organ from the Mannes College in 1962, an MA in composition from Harvard University in 1963 after study with Kirchner and Berio, and the DMA in organ at Boston University in 1966. He served on the faculties of the Juilliard School (1968–73) and of SUNY, Purchase (1968–75). From 1978 to 1981 he was professor of music at Indiana University. In 1967 Newman made his début in Carnegie Recital Hall, New York, playing works by J. S. Bach on the pedal harpsichord. He is active as a recitalist, recording artist, and composer. His keyboard virtuosity has been demonstrated not only at the organ, but also at the harpsichord (with and without pedals) and the fortepiano. His compositions include works for organ, piano, guitar, flute, chamber combinations, and orchestra. Newman's scholarly interest is in the Baroque era, especially in the keyboard works of J. S. Bach about which he has written several articles. He is a compelling performer whose high tempos are balanced by brilliant and innovative insights.

BIBLIOGRAPHY

A. Satz: "Musician of the Month: Anthony Newman," *HiFi/MusAm*, xxii/4 (1972), 4

VERNON GOTWALS

Newman, Randy (*b* Los Angeles, CA, 28 Nov 1943). Popular singer, songwriter, and pianist. He was born into a musical family: three of his uncles – Emil, Alfred, and Lionel Newman – composed and conducted film scores in Hollywood. His family lived in various southern cities, then, when he was seven, settled in Los Angeles, where he began to take piano lessons. He started to write songs when he was 16 and became a staff songwriter for the Metric Music Company in California at a salary of $50 a week. He studied music at UCLA but left during his senior year. Some of his early songs were performed by the Fleetwoods, Gene McDaniels, and the O'Jays; the first of his mature songs to be widely recognized was *I think it's going to rain today*, which Judy Collins recorded in 1966. Other singers continued to record and perform his material: Peggy Lee sang *Love Story* in 1969, with Newman's arrangement for orchestra, and in 1970 Three Dog

Randy Newman

Night's recording of a truncated version of *Mama told me not to come* reached no. 1 on the chart; also in 1970 Harry Nilsson recorded an album of songs by Newman.

Newman began to record his own songs in 1968. He wrote and arranged all those on *Randy Newman*, often using full orchestra and working in an extravagantly chromatic idiom reminiscent of the music of Weill, Gershwin, and the film composer Elmer Bernstein. The contrast between the lush orchestrations and Newman's drawling, deadpan vocal style heightened the irony of his lyrics. His concise songs – many of the early ones are less than two minutes long – generally narrate stories; in *Davy the Fat Boy*, for example (the music of which is influenced by Chopin), the narrator has turned his orphaned childhood friend into a carnival attraction. Formally Newman's songs range from the standard pop structure of verse and chorus to through-composed pieces. *12 Songs* (1970), and all his later albums, use more conventional rock instrumentation than *Randy Newman*, and draw not only on rock styles but also blues, jazz, and show tunes, as well as classical sources. An album recorded at a concert performance in 1971 documents Newman's usual concert style: he accompanies himself on piano with little or no improvisation. On *Sail Away* (1972) Newman's humor is straightforwardly cynical; the lyric of *Political Science*, for example, contains the line "Let's drop the big one, there'll be no one left to blame us." A cover version of the title song of the album – a slave buyer's recruiting pitch – was later recorded by Linda Ronstadt.

Newman is a slow songwriter and has established a pattern of completing enough songs to fill an album every two or three years, recording the album, and then making a tour. *Good Old Boys* (1974), a "concept" album about the South, was followed by a tour on which the orchestra was conducted by Emil Newman. In 1978 Newman's *Short People*, a wry, sardonic novelty song about prejudice, reached no. 2 on the pop chart. *Born Again* (1979) and *Trouble in Paradise* (1983) reveal a familiarity with current pop styles, and the latter includes parodies of the styles of Paul Simon (who sings on *The Blues*) and Billy Joel. Besides his songwriting activities Newman composed and arranged the scores to the films *Ragtime* (1981), directed by Miloš Forman, and *The Natural* (1984), directed by Barry Levinson. He is widely respected in the rock community, and Ronstadt, Rickie Lee Jones, Bob Seger, and members of Fleetwood Mac and the Eagles (all of whom are commercially more successful than Newman) have recorded with him.

RECORDINGS

(selective list; recorded for Reprise unless otherwise stated)

Randy Newman (6286, 1968), incl. Davy the Fat Boy; *12 Songs* (6373, 1970); *Randy Newman Live* (6459, 1971); *Sail Away* (2064, 1972), incl. Political Science; *Good Old Boys* (2193, 1974); *Little Criminals* (3079, 1977), incl. Baltimore, Short People; *Born Again* (WB 3346, 1979); *Ragtime* (Elek. 565, 1981); *Trouble in Paradise* (WB 23755, 1983), incl. The Blues

BIBLIOGRAPHY

"Newman, Randy," *CBY 1982*

JON PARELES

Newman, William S(tein) (*b* Cleveland, OH, 6 April 1912). Musicologist and pianist. He studied composition and music history at Western Reserve University (BS 1933, MA 1935, PhD 1939), then enrolled as a postdoctoral student at Columbia University. He taught at the University of North Carolina from 1945; in 1962 he was appointed Alumni Distinguished Professor of Music and he was named emeritus professor on his retirement in 1970. Newman's interests center on performance practice in music of the 17th–19th centuries and the development of the sonata. His exhaustive *History of the Sonata Idea* (1959–69, rev. 2/1983) examines the uses of the term "sonata," the social function, dissemination, instrumentation, and structure of sonatas, and the works of many individual composers. His other writings include *Performance Practices in Beethoven's Piano Sonatas* (1971) and numerous articles.

Newman has performed throughout the USA as a pianist, both in solo appearances and with chamber groups and orchestras. He was president of the American Musicological Society in 1969–70.

PAULA MORGAN

New Mexico Symphony Orchestra. Orchestra based in ALBUQUERQUE, New Mexico.

New Music. Publishing and recording venture founded by Henry Cowell. The quarterly *New Music*, which first appeared in 1927, was the only journal of its day dedicated solely to the publication of new scores. These pieces, described by Cowell as "non-commercial works of artistic value," embraced advanced and innovative compositional techniques for which publishing houses had little sympathy. The first issue was devoted to Ruggles's *Men and Mountains*; subsequent issues included Ives's Fourth Symphony (the second movement), Ruth Crawford's String Quartet, Chávez's Sonatina, Schoenberg's *Klavierstück*, op.33b, Strang's *Mirrorrorrim*, and Slonimsky's *Studies in Black and White*. The New Music "Orchestra Series" was inaugurated in 1932 and the "Special Editions" in 1936. Although Cowell published music by European composers from time to time, works by Americans predominated. Many of these pieces were also heard in San Francisco at concerts of the New Music Society (1925–36; founded by Cowell).

In 1934 Cowell established New Music Quarterly Recordings to promote further the works of American composers. The discs, all first recordings, were more widely distributed than the scores, which were available only by subscription. Cowell served as head of all New Music projects until 1936. The recordings continued to be issued until 1942 under the direction of Otto Luening, while the New Music publications (*New Music Edition* from 1947) were edited by Strang, again by Cowell from 1941 to 1945, and later by Harrison, Wigglesworth, and Ussachevsky. In 1954 *New Music Edition* experienced financial difficulties after the death of Charles Ives, who had for many years been its patron, and in 1958 it was transferred to Theodore Presser.

BIBLIOGRAPHY

R. H. Mead: "Cowell, Ives, and *New Music*," *MQ*, lxvi (1980), 538

——: *Henry Cowell's New Music, 1925–1936: the Society, the Music Editions, and the Recordings* (Ann Arbor, MI, 1981)

——: "Henry Cowell's New Music Society," *Journal of Musicology*, i (1982), 449

——: "Latin American Accents in *New Music*," *Latin American Music Review*, iii (1982), 207

——: "The Amazing Mr. Cowell," *American Music*, i/4 (1983), 63

D. Hall: "New Music Quarterly Recordings – A Discography," *Journal* [Association of Recorded Sound Collections], xvi/1–2 (1984), 10

EMILY GOOD

New Orleans. City in Louisiana (pop. 557,515; metropolitan area 1,187,073). Few towns in the USA have preserved the musical taste of their first settlers as strikingly as New Orleans. One of the reasons for this is its position at the mouth of an extensive network of rivers; for long it could be reached only by water, and was the principal harbor serving the great land mass to the north from which raw materials were exported and to which manufacturing goods were imported. It is not surprising, therefore, that the city's musical relationships with Europe and in particular with France, from where many early settlers came, have always been extremely important. Furthermore, there were rich and noble families among the first settlers, who had not only a taste for culture but also the financial means to enjoy it. Children – even those of English, Spanish, and German descent – were sent to France to complete their education. In the late 19th century and the early 20th the city's musical importance shifted from opera to jazz, which had its roots in the popular music of the city's brass bands.

1. Opera. 2. Concert life. 3. Brass bands. 4. Jazz. 5. Publishing and recording. 6. Educational institutions.

1. Opera. Culturally New Orleans became the Paris of America, and the early opera repertory shows a marked preference for Italian and French works. The town was the first in the North American continent to have a permanent opera company and from 1859 to 1919 owned one of the biggest and most expensive opera houses in the West. Opera in New Orleans was initiated in 1792 with the building of the Spectacle de la Rue St. Pierre (by Louis Alexandre Henry), where the city's first known performance of opera, Grétry's *Silvain*, was given in 1796. Although documentation is scant before 1800, there are written references to two later performances, Dezède's *Blaise et Babet* (1796) and Dalayrac's *Renaud d'Ast* (1799). After a period of eclipse during which it was closed, the theater was restored and reopened by Jean Baptiste Fournier in 1804. The first documented opera production under Fournier was François Devienne's *Les visitandines* (June 1805), and at least 23 operas were staged during his tenure until March 1806, when Louis Tabary, a recent émigré from France, assumed charge of the theater. The ousted Fournier set up a rival theater and opera company in a dance hall called the Salle Chinoise (later renamed the Théâtre de la Rue St. Philippe), and a brisk competition between these two theaters resulted in a number of performances remarkable for a provincial city of 12,000 inhabitants. The general dearth of opera houses in North America and the cultivated tastes of the city's residents meant that most of these performances were American premières, among which the best known were Grétry's *Le jugement de Midas* (1806), Méhul's *Une folie* (1807), and Boieldieu's *Le calife de Bagdad* (1805) and *Ma tante Aurore* (1807). The Spectacle de la Rue St. Pierre closed permanently in 1810, while the St. Philippe theater continued as an active opera house until it was sold in 1832.

The most important opera house in New Orleans in the first half of the 19th century was the Théâtre d'Orléans. The original edifice, begun in 1806 by Tabary, opened belatedly in October 1815, only to burn down the next summer. It was rebuilt in 1819 by a French émigré, John Davis, under whose management it thrived as an opera center. In his first five years Davis mounted 464 performances of 140 operas, 52 of which were American premières. The composers best represented were once again French (e.g., Boieldieu, Isouard, and Dalayrac), and the quality of the performances steadily improved, owing to Davis's policy of engaging professional French singers, dancers, and instrumentalists. The Théâtre d'Orléans achieved national prominence when, between 1827 and 1833, Davis led the company on six acclaimed tours of the northeastern USA. For each of the cities visited, including Boston, New York, Philadelphia, and Baltimore, many of the company's touring productions were first performances. John Davis was succeeded after his retirement in 1837 by his son Pierre, and in 1853, by Charles Boudousquié, an American-born impresario who sustained the theater's reputation until his resignation in 1859. Many American premières were given under these two directors, including Thomas' *La double échelle* (1841), Donizetti's *Lucia di Lammermoor* (1841), Halévy's *La juive* (1844), Auber's *La sirène* (1845), and Meyerbeer's *Le prophète* (1850). The theater went into decline in the 1850s and closed permanently in 1866.

During the heyday of the Théâtre d'Orléans (1825–40) a rival impresario, James Caldwell, produced a significant number of ballad operas and Italian and French operas in English translation with an American company he brought from Virginia. He built the first two theaters in the city's new American sector, the Camp Street Theater (1824) and St. Charles Theater (1835). Between 1827 and 1833 Caldwell was responsible for over 100 productions at the former, including John Gay's *The Beggar's Opera*, Rossini's *The Barber of Seville* and *Cinderella* (*La Cenerentola*), and Boieldieu's *Jean de Paris*. In 1836 Caldwell introduced Italian opera to New Orleans with the Montresor troupe from Havana. In two successive seasons at the St. Charles Theater the company performed such staples as Bellini's *Norma* and *I Capuleti e i Montecchi* and Rossini's *Otello*, *Semiramide*, and *Il barbiere di Siviglia*.

The city's musical importance was increased further by the founding of the French Opera Company and the opening of the French Opera House in 1859 (fig. 1, p.342). Built by Charles Boudousquié, the theater was one of the largest and most expensive in the West and one of the finest in the USA. The opera ensemble Boudousquié established was by no means a provincial company: many fine singers worked there at all stages of their careers, including Julie Calvé, Adelina Patti, Mme. St. Urban, the tenors Lecourt, Mathieu, and Escarlate, the baritones Victor and Melchisadels, and the bass Genibrel. The theater's brilliance gradually waned, although its excellent organization continued. 17 operas had American premières there, among them Meyerbeer's *Dinorah* (1861, with Patti in the title role), Gounod's *Le tribut de Zamova* (1888), Lalo's *Le roi d'Ys* (1890), Massenet's *Le Cid* (1890), and Saint-Saëns' *Samson et Dalila* (1893). The French Opera House closed in 1913; in 1919 the theater was purchased by William R. Irby, who presented it to Tulane University with funds for its restoration. Its planned reopening in December 1919 was preempted by a fire on the night of 2 December. Most of its archives were destroyed, along with its valuable collection of operatic properties, costumes, scores and parts, and innumerable books and documents relating to opera.

New Orleans remained without a permanent opera organization until 1943, when Walter Loubart founded the New Orleans Opera Association. He was succeeded as music director by Walter Herbert (1944–54), Renato Cellini (1954–64), and Knud Andersson (1964–83), with guest conductors under the general directorship of Arthur Cosenza. Performances were given in the city's Municipal Auditorium until 1973, when the New Orleans Theater of the Performing Arts was opened. The seasons last from November to May and generally include ten operas from the standard Italian, French, and German repertory. There has been a return to the city's earlier tradition of French opera, with revivals of Halévy's *La juive*, Meyerbeer's *Les Huguenots*, Massenet's *Thaïs*, Gounod's *Roméo et Juliette*, and Bizet's *Les pêcheurs de perles*.

1. *The French Opera House, New Orleans: wood engraving by Fichot and Gaildrau from "L'illustration" (10 December 1859)*

2. CONCERT LIFE. In 18th-century New Orleans concerts were regularly given as preludes to the numerous balls for which the early French city was famous. A mixed group of amateur and professional instrumentalists known as the Philharmonic Society was founded in 1824 and gave frequent concerts until 1829, performing thereafter only sporadically until 1848. By the second quarter of the 19th century, a considerable number of freed black musicians trained in art music were resident in New Orleans, a few of them having studied in France. In the late 1830s a Negro Philharmonic Society of over 100 performing and nonperforming members was organized to provide opportunities to hear music for those who objected to sitting in segregated sections in the public theaters. The society gave concerts and arranged for performances by visiting artists. For scores requiring larger forces the orchestra was augmented by white musicians. A small string orchestra, the Philharmonic Society of the Friends of Art, was formed in 1853 but survived less than a year because of a yellow fever epidemic. It was replaced by the Classical Musical Society, founded in 1855 and reorganized with a larger orchestra in 1858. Throughout the 19th century orchestral concerts were also given by the various theater ensembles. Although, in contrast to the opera, the repertory was conservative and consisted mainly of well-established works, these concerts were of a high standard, judging by the critical reaction to them in New Orleans, New York, Boston, and Philadelphia. The custom of engaging an outstanding soloist for a whole series of concerts began in the 1830s. Such artists as Ole Bull, Henri Vieuxtemps, Julie Calvé, and Jenny Lind included New Orleans in their tours, and singers often remained there to join one of the theater ensembles.

Many attempts to found an independent professional symphony orchestra between 1917 and 1934 failed because of financial difficulties. The present New Orleans Philharmonic SO was founded in 1936; its conductors have been Arthur Zack (1936–40), Ole Windingstad (1940–44), Massimo Freccia (1944–52), Alexander Hilsberg (1952–60), James Yestadt (1960–63), Werner Torkanowsky (1963–77), Leonard Slatkin (1977–9), Philippe Entremont (1979–86), and Maxim Shostakovich (from 1986). The season runs from October to May and consists of two weekly subscription concerts in which leading artists appear as soloists or as guest conductors.

After World War II the Community Concerts Association (now defunct) and the New Orleans Opera Guild regularly presented concerts by leading American and European orchestras. Another organization, the New Orleans Friends of Music, arranges performances of chamber music at Dixon Hall, an excellent small theater on the campus of Tulane University. Professional and semiprofessional concerts and recitals are regularly given by the city's five universities and colleges (see §6 below).

3. BRASS BANDS. The brass (or military) band, frequently augmented by woodwind and percussion, has long been important to the musical life of New Orleans, a southern Catholic city with a penchant for open-air festivities. Parades and parade music became the focal point of social life in the 19th century: in 1838 the *Daily Picayune* remarked that the city's love of brass bands amounted to a "real mania." On Sundays parades began early, their number and fervor increasing as the day wore on. One visitor concluded that "the Sabbath in New Orleans exists only in its almanacs." Marching to bury the dead was customary as early as 1819, when the architect Benjamin Henry Latrobe went to New Orleans and described the burial parades as "peculiar to New Orleans alone among American cities." By the 1830s notices of such parades often appeared in the newspapers. Members of militia companies, veterans of the Revolution and the War of 1812, freemasons, fire companies, benevolent societies, mechanics' societies, and others all marched at any time of day to bury their dead. The death of a hero anywhere was sufficient reason in New Orleans to hold a parade, or even two, as when General Lafayette died. Only during epidemics did the city experience a surfeit of the "mournful notes of the death march customarily played by full brass bands en route to the grave." However, the bands did strike up a "gay and lightsome air as they returned

from the grave," a practice imitated later in such jazz numbers as Jelly Roll Morton's *Dead Man Blues*.

Military music flourished in New Orleans during the Civil War; in 1864 the famous bandleader Patrick S. Gilmore gave a concert there with 500 musicians.

A black marching-band tradition, which was of seminal importance in the genesis of jazz around 1900, was originated in New Orleans after the Civil War (see §4 below). The presence of numerous concert-trained teachers and a plethora of military wind instruments at this time spawned a new generation of freed black bandsmen. A decade after the war there were several black wind bands fully competitive with the best white marching bands. By 1878 Kelly's Band and the St. Bernard Brass Band were recognized as "splendid corps of musicians, excelled by none," and in 1885 the Excelsior Brass Band, considered the finest black band in the city, played for the formal opening of the Colored People's Exhibit at the New Orleans Cotton States Exhibition. An important early impetus for the proliferation of black street bands was the dynamic social change of Reconstruction itself. The stimulus of emancipation, the prolonged presence of federal troops and military bands in the city, and the promise of social and political equality for black people contributed to the style and content of the music. A particular catalyst was the establishment of numerous benevolent societies at the instigation of the black Reconstruction governor P. B. S. Pinchback. These black socio-political groups sponsored marching clubs and drill teams to perform at political rallies and outdoor social events with parades, including funerals.

While it is evident that the earliest black marching bands were musically trained and polished ensembles, a trend towards extempore performances with ad libitum embellishments developed among the New Orleans bands of the 1880s and 1890s, leading eventually to the fully improvisational smaller jazz bands. Documentation is extremely scant, but it appears that this approach to playing was influenced by the gradual infiltration into the best black bands of self-taught instrumentalists, some of whom came from the rough country bands of the surrounding region. The repertory was thus extended to include, in addition to military compositions, music based on song: religious spirituals and gospel songs, as well as secular ballads, reels, rags, and blues. By 1900 such spontaneous performances by black bands, notably the Excelsior, Onward, Alliance, Tuxedo (fig.2), and Eureka, were in great demand for all kinds of social occasion, including picnics, commercial publicity, boat excursions, and dancing. Concurrently, this style of band music was emulated by a number of white brass bands, notably that of Papa Jack Laine, a mentor to many early white jazz musicians.

4. JAZZ. Although elements of a jazz style developed in several urban centers of the USA, the earliest consistent such style arose in New Orleans; hence the city is generally regarded as the birthplace of jazz, with NEW ORLEANS JAZZ its first manifestation as an independent genre. The appearance of this style is difficult to document, owing to the absence of recordings until 1917 and the often inconsistent testimony of contemporary musicians. It is, however, evident that the character of this early jazz greatly depended on the social circumstances of its performance; blues intonations and timbre might be appropriate for lower-class black establishments, but certainly not for Creole or white ones, nor even for those of the aspiring black middle class, to whom they would merely be embarrassing crudities. These social differences ensured many separate strands of musical development which were probably made consistent only in the 1920s, in the work of jazz musicians who, however, had long before left New Orleans.

A more important element of early New Orleans jazz than rural blues was the music of the various black brass bands which performed at numerous outdoor occasions in the 19th century (see §3 above). Many black jazz musicians received their early musical training in these groups, and some of the marches permanently entered the jazz repertory. Equally important were the "string bands," small dance ensembles with violins and double bass which played at various social functions. It was in one such string band that the legendary cornetist Buddy Bolden, the earliest generally recognized jazz musician, developed his music, incorporating the clipped syncopations of ragtime and, judging from later accounts, playing a freely embellished heterophony with the other instruments of his group. Bolden was the first of a series of New Orleans cornet "kings," establishing his supremacy in "cutting contests," in which early jazz bands toured the city on open wagons, challenging each other to musical duels judged by the assembled onlookers. Other cornet kings included Kid Rena, Buddy Petit, Chris Kelly, Freddie Keppard, Mutt Carey, Bunk Johnson, and King Oliver, who as leaders of their respective groups dominated New Orleans jazz up to the 1920s.

As segregation laws in New Orleans intensified following a Supreme Court decision in 1896, certain basically independent strands of early jazz, particularly that of the better-trained Creole musicians, were brought together, and it was probably through them that many elements of French social dance music entered jazz. White jazz at that time remained largely independent, and in subsequent jazz literature has borne the name DIXIELAND JAZZ to distinguish it from its black counterparts. The earliest known

2. *The Tuxedo Brass Band on parade in New Orleans, 1973*

figure in this genre was the percussionist Papa Jack Laine, who led various brass and ragtime bands from 1888. The music probably reached its fullest expression in the Original Dixieland Jazz Band, a group of white New Orleans musicians formed in Chicago and led by Nick LaRocca, formerly a cornetist with Laine. The worldwide success of the group and its recordings (from 1917) established this brand of jazz, with its driving tempos and attenuated black instrumental effects, as a potent force in American popular music; their success, however, was largely outside New Orleans.

The decline of the city's pleasure district, Storyville, and its eventual closure in 1917 led to an exodus of black jazz musicians from New Orleans, and from then on the New Orleans style developed in the northern cities, albeit mainly in the work of former New Orleans musicians. Foremost among these was Louis Armstrong, who left in 1923, but there was also a notable "New Orleans" school of clarinetists (Jimmie Noone, Barney Bigard, Johnny Dodds, Edmond Hall, and especially Sidney Bechet), trombonists (Kid Ory and Honore Dutrey), and percussionists (Baby Dodds and Zutty Singleton), as well as the independent achievements of the Creole composer–pianist Jelly Roll Morton. The popular success of jazz in the 1920s brought several recording companies to New Orleans in the hope of exploiting those musicians who remained, and in this way the further development of indigenous New Orleans jazz was documented in the work of bands such as Sam Morgan's. But the New Orleans style itself was soon made obsolete by the developments of northern jazz.

The Depression forced a great many New Orleans jazz musicians, who lacked the commercial opportunities of their northern counterparts, into retirement or better-paid occupations such as farm labor, and virtually no jazz was recorded in the city in the early 1930s. Later in the decade, however, a historical interest in New Orleans jazz led a number of researchers to seek out these older musicians, many of whom (particularly Bunk Johnson and George Lewis) were then able to return to musical careers playing more or less authentic versions of their earlier music. The unexpected success of this New Orleans "revival" (*see* JAZZ, §IV, 7) and the formation of new, primarily white groups playing TRADITIONAL JAZZ once again made New Orleans an active jazz center (see Stagg and Crump, 1973); yet the essentially backward-looking nature of "revival" jazz has prevented New Orleans from reclaiming its former significance in this music, and later jazz musicians born in New Orleans, including Ed Blackwell and Wynton Marsalis, have generally taken up more modern styles. On the other hand, in the 1950s an indigenous style of rhythm-and-blues developed in the work of such musicians as Professor Longhair and Fats Domino. Furthermore, the historical interest in jazz led to the founding of the William Ransom Hogan Jazz Archive at Tulane University (see §6 below) in 1958 and continues to attract visitors to the city. Since 1969 New Orleans has celebrated its jazz heritage with an annual spring music festival entitled the New Orleans Jazz and Heritage Festival, which features, in addition to traditional New Orleans jazz, various styles of modern jazz and the whole spectrum of allied genres.

5. PUBLISHING AND RECORDING. The thriving musical life of New Orleans enabled several music publishers to become established there. Among the earliest was Paul Emile Johns, a Polish-born immigrant from Vienna who established a retail shop in 1830. In 1846 Johns sold his firm to William T. Mayo, who continued to print sheet music until he in turn sold the company in 1854 to Philip P. Werlein, a Bavarian immigrant known chiefly as the first southern publisher of Dan Emmett's *Dixie* (as *I wish I was in Dixie*, actually a pirated version preceding the authorized version of 1860). Werlein issued two sheet-music anthologies as serials, the *Song Journal* (1870s) and *Werlein's Journal of Music* (1880s).

The firm of Armand Blackmar was active primarily during the Civil War years and was responsible for publishing some of the best-known music of the Confederacy, including *The Bonnie Blue Flag*, *Maryland! My Maryland!*, and an 1861 edition of *Dixie*. Louis Grunewald, a German immigrant who started a business in 1858, was the most prolific and versatile of all the New Orleans music publishers, extending his output in the 1880s to include religious and French Creole songs and piano compositions in the then popular "Mexican" style. Both the Werlein and Grunewald firms continued into the early 20th century, but by the 1920s music publishing in New Orleans had declined.

Commercial recording was not established in New Orleans until well after the early jazz era. The earliest jazz recorded in the city was done for northern companies between 1924 and 1928; the first significant locally produced recordings were made during the New Orleans jazz revival of the late 1930s and 1940s. Professional studio recordings in New Orleans began in the late 1940s; Cosimo Recording, one of the leading recording studios for the national rhythm-and-blues industry by the mid-1950s, cut records for such artists as Fats Domino, Bobby "Blue" Bland, Big Joe Turner, Lloyd Price, and Ray Charles. When the Cosimo studio closed in 1966, New Orleans lost its status as a national recording center, although commercial recordings continue to be made by independent producers, notably Allen Toussaint.

6. EDUCATIONAL INSTITUTIONS. The music department in Newcomb College of Tulane University was founded in 1909 by Leon Maxwell, who served as chairman until 1952. The department offers BA and MA degrees in history, theory, and composition and BFA and MFA degrees in piano and other instruments and in singing. Distinguished teachers have included Giuseppe Ferrata, Gilbert Chase, Howard E. Smither, and Charles Hamm. Among the university's libraries, the William Ransom Hogan Jazz Archive is important as a repository of early American jazz (prints, recordings, and taped interviews), and the Louisiana Division of the Howard-Tilton Memorial Library includes American sheet music and documents pertaining to the southern states. The Latin American Library is the second largest archive of its kind in the USA and contains many musical items.

The Loyola University College of Music, founded in 1931 as a music conservatory, retains its emphasis on performance, which is reflected in its most distinguished alumni, the singers Norman Treigle, Marguerite Piazza, Harry Theyard, Charles Anthony, and Anthony Laciura. It offers BM, BME, MM, and MME degrees in performance and music therapy. The music department at Dillard University, one of three black collegiate institutions in New Orleans, was established in 1936 with Frederick Douglass Hall as its first chairman; Hall established the department's policy of emphasizing black music, especially spirituals, in its program. Among its most distinguished alumni are the composer Roger Donald Dickerson and the jazz pianist and composer Ellis Marsalis. The music department of the New Orleans Baptist Theological Seminary was founded in 1919, and its degree programs (for MA and DMA degrees in church music) are designed primarily for the training of church organists and choirmasters.

Undergraduate programs are also offered at Xavier University (music department founded 1934), for black Catholics, and at the University of New Orleans (music department founded 1963). There are substantial musical holdings in the libraries of Tulane University, the Theological Seminary, and at LOUISIANA STATE UNIVERSITY.

See also LIBRARIES AND COLLECTIONS, §3.

BIBLIOGRAPHY

G. King: *New Orleans: the Place and the People* (New York, 1895)

J. G. Baroncelli: *Le théâtre français a la Nouvelle Orléans* (New Orleans, 1906)

——: *L'opéra français de la Nouvelle Orléans* (New Orleans, 1914)

D. B. Fischer: "The Story of New Orleans's Rise as a Music Center," *MusAm*, xix/19 (1914), 3

O. G. T. Sonneck: *Early Opera in America* (New York, 1915/*R*1963)

J. S. Kendall: *History of New Orleans* (Chicago and New York, 1922)

G. P. Bumstead and L. Panzeri: *Louisiana Composers* (New Orleans, 1935)

L. Gafford: *History of the St. Charles Theater in New Orleans* (diss., U. of Chicago, 1938)

J. E. Winston: "The Free Negro in New Orleans, 1803–1860," *Louisiana Historical Quarterly*, xxi (1938), 1075

A. L. W. Stahl: "The Free Negro in Ante-bellum Louisiana," *Louisiana Historical Quarterly*, xxv (1942), 301–96

J. S. Kendall: "New Orleans' Negro Minstrels," *Louisiana Historical Quarterly*, xxx (1947), 128

——: "New Orleans Musicians of Long Ago," *Louisiana Historical Quarterly*, xxxi (1948), 130

——: *The Golden Age of the New Orleans Theater* (Baton Rouge, LA, 1952)

G. S. McPeek: "New Orleans as an Opera Center," *MusAm*, lxxiv/4 (1954), 25

O. Keepnews and W. Grauer: *Pictorial History of Jazz: People and Places from New Orleans to Modern Jazz* (New York, 1955)

W. Russell and S. W. Smith: "New Orleans Music," *Jazzmen*, ed. F. Ramsey, Jr., and C. E. Smith (London, 1957)

G. H. Yerbury: "Concert Music in Early New Orleans," *Louisiana Historical Quarterly*, xl (1957), 95

S. B. Charters: *Jazz: New Orleans, 1885–1957* (Belleville, NJ, 1958, rev. 1963)

G. S. McPeek: "New Orleans," *MGG*

R. J. LeGardeur, Jr.: *The First New Orleans Theater, 1792–1803* (New Orleans, 1963)

H. A. Kmen: *Music in New Orleans: the Formative Years, 1791–1841* (Baton Rouge, LA, 1966)

M. T. Williams: *Jazz Masters of New Orleans* (New York, 1967)

A. Rose and E. Souchon: *New Orleans Jazz: a Family Album* (Baton Rouge, LA, 1967, rev. and enlarged 3/1984)

G. Schuller: *Early Jazz: its Roots and Musical Development* (New York, 1968)

E. Borneman: "Jazz and the Creole Tradition," *Jazz Forschung*, i (1970), 99

R. J. Martinez: *Portraits of New Orleans Jazz: its Peoples and Places* (New Orleans, 1971)

J. Buerkle and D. Barker: *Bourbon Street Black* (New York, 1973)

T. Stagg and C. Crump, eds.: *New Orleans, the Revival: a Tape and Discography of Traditional Jazz Recorded in New Orleans by New Orleans Bands, 1937–72* (Dublin, 1973)

J. Broven: *Walking to New Orleans: the Story of New Orleans Rhythm-and-Blues* (Bexhill-on-Sea, England, 1974)

J. Joyce: "New Orleans Jazz: a Matter of Tradition," *New Orleans Review*, iv/1 (1974), 27

A. Rose: *Storyville, New Orleans* (University, AL, 1974)

L. H. Levy: *The Formalization of New Orleans Jazz Musicians: a Case Study of Organizational Change* (diss., Virginia Polytechnic Institute and State U., 1976)

P. C. Boudreaux: *Music Publishing in New Orleans in the Nineteenth Century* (thesis, Louisiana State U., 1977)

W. J. Schafer: *Brass Bands and New Orleans Jazz* (Baton Rouge, LA, 1977)

D. M. Marquis: *In Search of Buddy Bolden* (Baton Rouge, LA, 1978)

L. Ostransky: *Jazz City: the Impact of our Cities on the Development of Jazz* (Englewood Cliffs, NJ, 1978)

R. Palmer: *A Tale of Two Cities: Memphis Rock and New Orleans Roll*, ISAMm, xii (Brooklyn, NY, 1979)

K. Demetz: "Minstrel Dancing in New Orleans' Nineteenth Century Theaters," *Southern Quarterly*, xx/2 (1982), 28

F. Turner: *Remembering Song: Encounters with the New Orleans Jazz Tradition* (New York, 1982)

JOHN JOYCE (1–3, 5–6: 1, 2, with GWYNN SPENCER McPEEK; 3 with HENRY A. KMEN; 6 with JOHN H. BARON), J. BRADFORD ROBINSON (4)

New Orleans jazz. A style of small-ensemble jazz that originated shortly before World War I, became internationally known through recordings in the 1920s, and underwent a revival in the 1940s (*see* TRADITIONAL JAZZ, and JAZZ, §IV, 7). It now exists as an interrelated group of performance styles with fixed instrumentation and a relatively restricted repertory. Some writers distinguish it from DIXIELAND JAZZ, a label that they reserve for white musicians and orchestras.

The earliest New Orleans "hot" players in the first two decades of the century thought of their music as ragtime, albeit with a local accent. This music was for the most part learned and played by ear by amateurs or semiprofessionals, though some players were musically literate; it usually used a rhythm section of drums, guitar, and double bass (often bowed rather than plucked) and an unusually wide variety of timbres, and emphasized a continuous ensemble polyphony, in which the wind players rarely rested. The early repertory consisted of old-fashioned schottische, mazurka, and quadrille dance tunes as well as a number of local specialties, such as *Tiger Rag* and *Don't go way nobody*; other tunes were probably taken from a general southern repertory (*Make me a pallet on the floor*, *Easy Rider*, *Bucket got a hole in it*), while certain pieces that have become "New Orleans standards" (e.g., *High Society*, *Panama*, and *Moose March*) were nationwide hits which simply remained current in New Orleans.

The large dance bands before 1920 comprised violin, cornet, clarinet, trombone, drums, double bass, guitar, and sometimes piano. Many musicians gained their first experience in smaller, so-called string bands: violin, guitar, double bass, and one or two wind instruments. New Orleans bands followed a national fashion in dropping the violin and exchanging guitar and double bass for banjo and tuba; they also adopted the saxophone family, contrary to a longstanding jazz myth. The use of two cornets – which was thought on the evidence of King Oliver's recordings of 1923 to be essential to the authentic New Orleans style – was virtually never a feature of the older orchestras. Furthermore, though often imitated during the 1920s, the instrumentation of the Original Dixieland Jazz Band (cornet, trombone, clarinet, piano, and drums) was not common in New Orleans itself, and was perhaps fostered by the Chicago cabarets that used jazz bands between 1915 and 1918.

In early New Orleans groups, the melody often shifted from instrument to instrument. By the early 1920s, however, it was generally assigned to the cornetist, who most often functioned as leader, a role previously taken by the violinist. New Orleans cornetists born before about 1895 played the lead with relatively little variation, unlike later jazz trumpeters; they made use of clipped articulation with relatively precise binary subdivisions of the beat, cultivating the middle register to *f''* and employing a forceful tone, often with a "whinnying" rapid vibrato. The clarinet supplied a florid countermelody in eighth-notes over a wide range, and characteristically used a more limpid timbre than other jazz clarinet styles, perhaps because of a French bias in the training of early New Orleans clarinetists. (Some timbral differences resulted from an ingrained preference, persisting to the present day, for "Albert system" clarinets with wide bores.) While clarinets and their idiom were underemployed in American dance orchestras at this time, trombones were ubiquitous from 1910 on; hence the so-called TAILGATE style, with its many glissandos and its flexible mixture of tenor countermelody and doubling of the bass line, was perhaps the least local feature of New Orleans jazz. In general, the earliest recordings by King

Oliver, Sidney Bechet, and others show New Orleans players as the first to integrate blue notes as well as portamento and strong vibrato into an expressive melodic instrumental style.

New Orleans drummers used very large and resonant bass drums and employed the press roll on the snare drum, probably with comparatively little reliance on other percussion accessories. The much-discussed question of two-beat versus four-beat rhythm is related to the transition from ragtime to jazz (*see* JAZZ, §II, 5): the first New Orleans jazz drummer to be recorded, Tony Sbarbaro of the Original Dixieland Jazz Band in 1917–18, freely shifted from one to the other. Some early recordings indicate a predilection in New Orleans for somewhat slower tempos and a less assertive and heavily accented manner than elsewhere in the USA. Perhaps the most distinctive rhythmic feature was a pervasive but relaxed syncopation, particularly at the slower foxtrot or slow drag tempo.

The repertory and instrumentation of the white dixieland tradition became fixed to a far greater degree than in the black tradition. Particularly with the onset of the "revival" in the late 1930s, many hymn tunes and various Creole folk or popular songs entered the repertory of black New Orleans jazz, often at the behest of recording directors and jazz historians. The harmony of New Orleans jazz is often simpler than the ragtime progressions that underlie it: chords more complex than the dominant seventh and diminished seventh are seldom used; there is little modulation, except between the strains of march tunes; and keys with more than one sharp or four flats are avoided. Solo playing is generally confined to the frequent two-bar breaks or to brief moments when one player dominates the ensemble, but there are frequent duets for winds.

The classic bands of the early 1920s New Orleans style were King Oliver's Creole Jazz Band and the New Orleans Rhythm Kings, though some critics claim to find Chicago fashions in their recordings; later recordings of bands led by Jelly Roll Morton, Armstrong, and Johnny Dodds are also prized as early examples of New Orleans jazz. These were all recorded in Chicago for the so-called race record market. However, recordings made in the 1920s in New Orleans itself, especially by Sam Morgan's band and the Jones–Collins Astoria Hot Eight, are somewhat different in character from the groups recorded in the North.

The strong association in the public's mind between New Orleans jazz and the marching-band tradition is somewhat exaggerated: the custom is a picturesque survival of one widespread in the USA during the 19th century. Many musicians and historians also hold that certain features of New Orleans jazz derive from, or are common to, other musics of the West Indies. However, despite New Orleans's long history of close contact with the West Indies, this "Spanish tinge" (the term is Jelly Roll Morton's) has yet to be historically traced, even in the music of the colored Creoles, who played an important role in the emergence of New Orleans jazz.

See also JAZZ, §§II, 6; III, 2; IV, 7.

BIBLIOGRAPHY

S. B. Charters: *Jazz: New Orleans, 1885–1957* (Belleville, NJ, 1958, rev. 2/1963)

L. A. Pyke: *Jazz, 1920 to 1927: an Analytical Study* (diss., U. of Iowa, 1962)

M. Williams: *Jazz Masters of New Orleans* (New York, 1967)

M. Dorigné: *Les origines du jazz: le style Nouvelle Orléans et ses prolongements* (Paris, 1968)

G. Schuller: *Early Jazz: its Roots and Musical Development* (New York, 1968)

R. J. Martinez: *Portraits of New Orleans Jazz: its People and Places* (New Orleans, 1971)

C. G. Herzog zu Mecklenberg: *Stilformen des Jazz*, i (Vienna, 1973)

W. Schafer and R. B. Allen: *Brass Bands and New Orleans Jazz* (Baton Rouge, LA, 1977)

LAWRENCE GUSHEE

New Orleans Rhythm Kings (NORK). Jazz ensemble. Its three principal members, trumpeter Paul Mares (1900–49), trombonist Georg Brunis (1902–74), and clarinetist Leon Roppolo (1902–43), were boyhood friends from New Orleans who had played together in various bands during their adolescence. After moving separately to the North, these three musicians reunited in Chicago in the early 1920s to form a band for a 17-month residency at the Friar's Inn nightclub. Originally their colleagues in the band were Jack Pettis (tenor saxophone), Elmer Schoebel (piano), Arnold Loyocano (double bass), Louis Black (banjo), and Frank Snyder (drums). The group's first recordings (for Gennett in August 1922) were issued under the name of the Friar's Society Orchestra, but by 1923 they were known as the New Orleans Rhythm Kings. Loyocano's place on bass was taken by Theodore "Steve" Brown, who was in turn replaced by "Chink" Martin Abraham. Ben Pollack replaced Snyder as drummer, and Schoebel's place at the piano was taken by Mel Stitzel.

The instantaneous success of the New Orleans Rhythm Kings' recordings and live performances made them the most important white New Orleans group after the Original Dixieland Jazz Band. Though they never achieved the same widespread fame, and despite the fact that they partly based their style and repertory on those of the earlier band, on several counts they were superior to it. Their originality lay in blending the influences of the Original Dixieland Jazz Band with inspiration derived from the black New Orleans music of King Oliver's Creole Jazz Band. The New Orleans Rhythm Kings exuded a sense of relaxation that was rare among their contemporaries; they avoided the nearly ubiquitous jerky phrasing, and with no loss of expression concentrated on legato playing. The final choruses of their performances are stirring without seeming frantic.

Mares, the group's leader, was heavily influenced by King Oliver's cornet playing. He usually remained in the middle register and established an emphatic lead part; during his solos he seldom departed from the melody, relying on subtle rhythmic and tonal inflections for variation. The group's foremost improviser was Roppolo (whose name is often misspelled Rappolo), a highly original clarinetist whose solos on *Panama*, *Tiger Rag*, and *She's Crying for me Blues* are superb. His playing on the ingeniously arranged *Wolverine Blues* was much copied. Georg Brunis also played confident, adept solos, but his strength lay in creating clever "tailgate" patterns, many of which were rigorously imitated by other trombonists for decades afterwards. The band's front line inspired a school of young white Chicago jazz musicians, and it is regrettable that so few of their recordings are satisfactorily balanced.

After leaving the Friar's Inn, the group enjoyed brief residencies at two Chicago dance halls before disbanding altogether. In 1924 Mares moved back to New Orleans, as did Roppolo and Abraham; these three formed the nucleus of a revived New Orleans Rhythm Kings, which included the trombonist Santo Pecora. The new band made a series of recordings in January 1925 which show that Mares was ever improving and that Roppolo was still a consummate improviser; but there are few signs that the band was attempting to broaden or develop its musical style. The same can be said of the titles recorded two months later when Roppolo's place on clarinet was taken by Charlie Cordilla. The group disbanded permanently soon afterwards, Mares leaving music for a decade and Roppolo beginning the first of several long stays in a Louisiana asylum. Brunis, who remained in the North, later became a key figure in the New Orleans revival movement from the late 1930s, particularly with Muggsy Spanier and Eddie Condon.

RECORDINGS

(selective list)

Eccentric (1922, Gennett 5009); Bugle Call Blues (1922, Gennett 4967); Panama/Tiger Rag (1922, Gennett 4968); Weary Blues/Wolverine Blues (1923, Gennett 5102); Maple Leaf Rag (1923, Gennett 5104); Tin Roof Blues (1923, Gennett 5105); She's Crying for me Blues (1925, OK 40327)

BIBLIOGRAPHY

D. Dexter: "Immortals of Jazz – Leon Rappolo," *Down Beat*, vii/20 (1940), 10
A. Lee: "Brunies Faked Magnificently," *Metronome*, lvii/2 (1941), 19
D. Gayer: "There is a Chicago Style, Mares," *Down Beat*, x/4 (1943), 4
P. Mares: "Leon Rappolo as I Knew him," *Jazz Quarterly*, ii (1944), 3
G. Erskine: "Last of the New Orleans Rhythm Kings," *Down Beat*, xxix/10 (1962), 22
W. Balliett: "Lou Black – a Burning Desire," *Such Sweet Thunder* (New York, 1966), 90
M. Williams: "N.O.R.K.," *Jazz Masters of New Orleans* (New York, 1967/*R*1979), 121
D. Bakker: "N.O.R.K. 1922–1925," *Microgroove*, no.19 (1972), 4
D. Coller: "Frank Snyder," *Mississippi Rag*, x/6 (1983), 7

JOHN CHILTON

New Orleans Serenaders. Minstrel troupe formed (as the Congo Melodists) in 1843 by the BUCKLEY family.

Newport Jazz Festival. Summer music festival, held in Newport, Rhode Island, from 1954 to 1971, and in New York from 1972. It became the Kool Newport Jazz Festival in 1980 and the KOOL JAZZ FESTIVAL in 1981.

New River Shasta. American Indian group of California, belonging to the SHASTA.

New Thing. A term applied to the avant-garde jazz of the 1960s more commonly known as FREE JAZZ.

Newton-John, Olivia (*b* Cambridge, England, 26 Sept 1948). English popular singer. She began her career in 1965 while living in Melbourne, Australia, then moved to London, where she was a member of the rock group Toomorrow. Her first solo hit, a version of Bob Dylan's *If not for you* (1971), was a success in Europe, North America, and Australia. She then adopted a country-music idiom and became more widely known in the USA through *Let me be there* (1973), which resulted in her first American tour (1974) and earned her the first of many awards. A stream of recordings, concerts, and television appearances confirmed her international celebrity status. After starring in the film of the rock musical *Grease* (1978), she added to her repertory songs closer in style to contemporary rock-and-roll. Her voice is a clear crisp soprano, and her style is capable of accommodating folk, country, or rock settings. Her popularity is unusual: no other non-American singer has been so honored in the USA for singing country music or so supported by the public. Critical appreciation, however, has never matched her unqualified commercial success.

BIBLIOGRAPHY

"Newton-John, Olivia," *CBY 1978*

MICHAEL J. BUDDS

New wave. A type of rock music developed in the late 1970s. The term was originally used in the mid-1970s as a milder synonym for punk rock, but soon took on a meaning of its own: it came to refer to a clearcut, lean style of pop-rock that offered an alternative to the grandiosity and bombast of arena-rock groups; new wave was essentially a cleaner, more commercially viable version of punk. The groups who played new wave fell into one of two categories: those with overt commercial aspirations (such as the Cars) and those of a more marginally commercial, artistic orientation (such as Talking Heads, Love Tractor, and various so-called "no wave" groups of the early 1980s).

See also POPULAR MUSIC, §IV, 5, PUNK ROCK, and ROCK, §III.

BIBLIOGRAPHY

I. A. Robbins, ed.: *The Trouser Press Guide to New Wave Records* (New York, 1983)

JOHN ROCKWELL

New York. City in the state of New York (pop. 7,071,639, ranked largest in the USA; metropolitan area 9,120,346); it is the cultural center of the country. The fine natural harbor and waterways and the opening of the Erie Canal in 1825 quickly made New York the nation's principal commercial center. As the most important port, the city has been the gateway for both visitors and immigrants to the USA, bringing a density and variety of cultural influences that have created a dynamic and varied musical life. The heart of the nation's music industry is in New York, and the city is a showcase for individuals and organizations from other parts of the continent and from abroad. For the American musician a New York recital is the prerequisite of professional status.

1. Before 1800. 2. Concert life. 3. Concert halls and other performance venues. 4. Opera and musical theater. 5. Orchestras and bands. 6. Chamber music. 7. Choral societies. 8. Church music. 9. Avant-garde music. 10. Ragtime and jazz. 11. Ethnic and popular music. 12. Education. 13. Associations and organizations. 14. Publishing, instrument making, broadcasting, and recording. 15. Criticism and periodicals. 16. Libraries.

1. BEFORE 1800. The first documented concert in New York was given on 21 January 1736 by the German-born organist and harpsichordist C. T. Pachelbel, son of the renowned Johann, at the house of Robert Todd, a vintner, next to Fraunces' Tavern. An announcement of the event refers to songs and instrumental music with harpsichord, flute, and violin. Apparently the first organ was installed in the Dutch Reformed Church in 1724, followed in 1741 by an organ built by J. G. Klemm for Trinity Church. 46 concerts were advertised in New York between 1736 and 1775, more than in any other American city; they included a charity concert at City Hall after the installation of an organ in 1756 and, about 1766, the performance of a march from Handel's *Judas Maccabaeus* "accompanied with a side drum" at the City Tavern.

Visiting musicians, usually from London, rarely remained long in New York; W. C. Hulett, who taught violin and dancing in 1759 and was still in the city directory in 1799, was an exception. The arrival of William Tuckey in 1752 to become clerk of Trinity Church from 1 January 1753 marked a turning point in New York's musical life. Tuckey promptly took over the Trinity choir and became a champion of Handel's works. He organized subscription concerts and balls in the 1760s, and on 16 January 1770 sponsored a benefit at "Mr. Burns' New Room" with the first New York performance of the overture and 16 numbers from *Messiah*. Works by Haydn appeared on programs after 27 April 1782.

Various groups of New York musicians sporadically announced series of subscription concerts. Series of "City Concerts" begun in 1793 by Henri Capron, James Hewitt, and G. E. Saliment lasted until 1797, and included music by Haydn, Hewitt, Ignace Joseph Pleyel, André-Ernest-Modeste Grétry, Adalbert Gyrowetz, and Benjamin Carr; outdoor summer concerts initiated in 1765 by James Jones in the Ranelagh Gardens continued to be popular. Vocal and instrumental music by Haydn, Thomas Arne, and Carl Stamitz as well as popular ballads could be heard at Ranelagh and at Joseph Delacroix's Vauxhall Gardens (at Fourth Avenue and Astor Place) in the late 1790s.

New York music organizations in the 18th century combining social and choral activities included the Harmonic (1773–4), Musical (1788–94), St. Cecilia (1791–9), Harmonical (1796–9), Columbian Anacreontic (1795–?), Uranian (1793–8), and Philharmonic (1799–*c*1816) societies. The repertory usually consisted of hymns and, occasionally, anthems. Few societies survived their good intentions.

Theater flourished and ballad opera was popular. Opera could be heard at the Nassau Street Theatre from 1750; *The Beggar's Opera* was one of the first performed there. In 1753–4 a troupe from London directed by Lewis Hallam performed operas and plays; David Douglass reorganized it under the name of the American Company (later Old American Company), and it performed at the John Street Theatre and in other coastal cities from 1767 to 1774. During the British military occupation (1776–83) plays or ballad operas were occasionally performed, but it was not until 1785 that Lewis Hallam, Jr., and John Henry reopened the Old American Company, which they operated more or less regularly until the turn of the century. The musical repertory consisted largely of pasticcio arrangements of such popular works as *Thomas and Sally*, *Rosina*, *Love in a Village*, *Lionel and Clarissa*, *The Adopted Child*, *The Duenna*, *No Song no Supper*, and *The Flitch of Bacon*. Operas by Grétry (*Zémire et Azor*) and Egidio Duni (*Les deux chasseurs*) also served as a basis for local adaptation. For a short time in the 1790s French immigrants performed such works as *Les deux chasseurs*, Nicolas-Médard Audinot's *Le tonnelier*, and Jean-Jacques Rousseau's *Le devin du village* in French.

Native musical theater came into its own in the last quarter of the 18th century. Among the earliest examples was *May Day in Town* (18 May 1788) with "music compiled from the most eminent masters." Hewitt's *Tammany, or The Indian Chief* (from which only one song survives), the first opera on an American Indian subject, was produced on 3 March 1794; the libretto, by Anna Hatton, succeeded in its intention to arouse Federalist opposition, and *Tammany* had only three performances. The pantomime *The Fourth of July, or Temple of American Independence*, with music by Victor Pelissier, had one performance (4 July 1799) as did his *Edwin and Angelina* (19 December 1796). More successful was Benjamin Carr's comic opera *The Archers, or The Mountaineers of Switzerland* (1796), from which only the introductory rondo and a single song survive.

John Jacob Astor opened New York's first music shop by 1786, before concentrating on the fur-trading business. Carr and Hewitt were both important figures in the growth of the music trades in the city. Carr arrived from England in 1793 and set up a music shop in Philadelphia in 1794 and in New York in 1795; he sold the latter to Hewitt in 1797. English popular music and American patriotic songs were the mainstay of their sheet music sales.

2. CONCERT LIFE. In the early 19th century concert life in New York centered on outdoor summer gardens, patterned after their London counterparts, and later on their attendant theaters. Popular establishments such as Castle Garden in the Battery and Niblo's Garden at Broadway and Prince Street (built in 1822, rebuilt after a fire in 1846, and demolished in 1895) presented ballad singers and mixed programs of instrumental music.

1. *Jenny Lind's first appearance in the USA, at Castle Garden, New York, 11 September 1850: lithograph by N. Currier*

Economic opportunities in the USA and political uncertainties in Europe spurred the arrival of talented young musicians. A number of European singers, composers, conductors, and impresarios arrived during the early 19th century, as well as popular virtuosos such as the violinist Camillo Sivori (1846–50) and the pianists Leopold de Meyer (1845–6, 1867–8) and Henri Herz (1846–8). Jenny Lind was on the stage of Castle Garden before a cheering audience of 7000 on the evening of 11 September 1850 (fig. 1) for the first of about 20 concerts in New York, the last of which was on 24 May 1852. The significance of her tour, at first under the aegis of P. T. Barnum, lay less in her superb singing than in her impact on the box office, and the demonstration that a European artist of the first rank could find responsive American audiences.

Virtuoso pianists such as Louis Moreau Gottschalk, who gave 90 concerts in New York in seven seasons beginning in February 1853, and Sigismond Thalberg, who played 56 concerts from November 1856 to April 1858, presented well-received programs. Both artists, playing American Chickering pianos, concentrated almost exclusively on their own compositions, although Beethoven and Chopin were occasionally represented. Four resident pianists were active in the second half of the 19th century: Henry C. Timm, Richard Hoffman, Sebastian Bach Mills, and William Mason. Each maintained a high standard of technical and interpretive excellence, and introduced to the American repertory works of a higher standard than the usual operatic potpourris, fantasies, and variations.

The impresario and conductor Louis Jullien arrived in New York in August 1853 to give light concerts, including works by William Henry Fry and George F. Bristow, in the Crystal Palace. Other popular performers included the violinists Ole Bull and Henry Vieuxtemps, both of whom visited for the first time in 1843, and the pianist Alfred Jaëll (1851–2). Typical programs were mixed, usually including several arias and duets, one or two piano solos, a violin solo, an ensemble work, and, if there was an orchestra, an overture. The solo recital was virtually unknown; even the most celebrated virtuosos appeared with other performers.

The quality of visiting artists steadily improved. The arrival of Anton Rubinstein and Henryk Wieniawski on 23 September 1872 brought a serious note to concert programs of the day; a bold solo recital surprisingly brought in more money than a troupe. Hans von Bülow visited in 1875–6 and again in 1889–90. Most Europeans arrived with their reputations already made at home, but Americans made their own evaluations; for example, free tickets were given for Paderewski's début on 17 November 1891, but it was four seasons before he became a popular success.

The development of concert halls and the founding of cultural institutions (see below) meant that after 1900 New York concert life differed little from that of a large European city. With a population of about three and a half million, improved transport, and an assured audience, the city's musical life became more predictable. Solo recitals became distinct from chamber concerts and orchestral programs, and European artists made repeated visits to New York. After 1914 both American and European musicians frequently established a New York base.

By mid-century programs had changed; there were fewer solo recitals and more group events, chamber music was more popular, choruses were numerous but smaller, and the concert repertory became both more varied and more specialized within individual programs. A revitalization of the solo recital and further growth in chamber music activities took place from the 1960s, led by the city's two largest performing arts centers, Carnegie Hall and Lincoln Center (see §3 below), notably with Lincoln Center's "Great Performers" series. Concert activities during the summer months grew rapidly after the founding of the Mostly Mozart Festival in 1966 at Lincoln Center under the supervision of William Lockwood, Jr. At the festival, which has become a model for several others elsewhere in the USA, performances of orchestral and choral works alternate with chamber music concerts and recitals. Various ensembles have participated in the event, including the American String Quartet, the Beaux Arts Trio, the Boston Symphony Chamber Players, and the Cleveland, Emerson, and Guarneri string quartets. Pinchas Zukerman and Jean-Pierre Rampal made their conducting débuts at the festival, and such established artists as Byron Janis, Jaime Laredo, Alexander Schneider, Peter Serkin, Michael Tilson Thomas, and Barry Tuckwell have appeared as conductors and soloists; the music director is Gerard Schwarz.

See also EARLY-MUSIC REVIVAL, esp. §2.

3. CONCERT HALLS AND OTHER PERFORMANCE VENUES. The center of New York's classical musical life has moved steadily uptown since it began in what is now the financial district (Wall Street, lower Broadway, and the Battery). For many years the principal musical activities were in the midtown area bounded by the Metropolitan Opera House on West 39th Street and Carnegie Hall at 57th Street and Seventh Avenue. Carnegie Hall (seating 2784), for nearly a century New York's most important concert hall, has played host to virtually every significant American or visiting musician since its opening on 5 May 1891, when Tchaikovsky was guest of honor (fig. 2, p. 350). Famous for its superb acoustics, the hall has been the site of a number of historic débuts, including Paderewski's in 1891, Yehudi Menuhin's in 1927, and Sviatoslav Richter's in 1960; it is also the performance venue of choice for major visiting orchestras and until the opening of Lincoln Center was the home of the New York PO. Leonard Bernstein gave his memorable New York PO début at the hall in 1943; his "Jeremiah" Symphony had its première there in 1944. Gershwin's *American in Paris* (1928) and Reich's Octet (1980) also had first performances in Carnegie Hall. The adjacent Carnegie Recital Hall (seating 283) is used for many début recitals and performances of chamber, modern, and ethnic music.

Above and behind the main auditorium are thoroughly soundproofed studios that have provided work and rehearsal space and, until the late 1970s, living quarters for musicians, dancers, and other artists. In 1925 a syndicate headed by the realtor Robert E. Simon purchased the property from the Carnegie estate; when plans for Lincoln Center were announced in the mid-1950s, Simon's son determined to demolish Carnegie Hall to make way for new construction, but after protests from the Citizens Committee for Carnegie Hall, organized by Isaac Stern in 1960, New York City purchased the hall for $5 million and leased it to the newly formed Carnegie Hall Corporation, which became responsible for programming as well (before 1960 all events were independently booked). Revitalizing a tradition from earlier in the century of jazz and popular music presentations, the corporation developed programs in jazz and ethnic music for Carnegie Hall and Carnegie Recital Hall; it also sought to promote contemporary and early music by means of special series. In the 1980s both halls underwent extensive renovations.

Town Hall (seating 1498), which opened in 1921 as a public

2. *Carnegie Hall at the time of its opening: the entrance on 57th Street (above left), the lobby (above right), and the auditorium; engravings from "Harper's Weekly" (May 1891)*

meeting house on West 43rd Street, is another important performance venue; it was particularly popular in the middle decades of the century and many musicians made their débuts there, including Gina Bachauer, Elisabeth Schwarzkopf (her first appearance in the USA), and Marian Anderson, Nelson Eddy, Maureen Forrester, Dorothy Maynor, Patrice Munsel, Jan Peerce, Andrés Segovia, Blanche Thebom, and Helen Traubel (their first appearances in New York). Jazz and popular performers at Town Hall have included Eubie Blake, Peter Duchin, Johnny Mercer, and Teddy Wilson. The New Friends of Music presented chamber music concerts on Sunday afternoons from 1936, and the American Opera Society, Little Orchestra Society, Clarion Concerts, and Performing Arts Repertory Theater all performed there regularly. The hall was acquired by New York University in 1958 and closed temporarily in 1978, but after attaining landmark status in 1980, the building underwent a $1.5 million restoration and reopened in 1984.

Radio City Music Hall, a privately run subsidiary of Rockefeller Center, opened on 27 December 1932. Attempts at presenting vaudeville proved unsuccessful, and the format of film with a live stage show was quickly adopted; the Music Hall maintained its own symphony orchestra, a ballet company (until 1974), and the dancing troupe the Rockettes. The famed art deco music hall seats 6200 and houses a Wurlitzer theater organ reputed to be the world's largest. In 1978 the hall was designated a landmark and its management was taken over by the New York State Urban Development Corporation. Following a $5 million renovation, activities at the hall expanded to include rock and popular music concerts, opera (notably a revival of *Porgy and Bess* in 1983), and spectacular stage shows, such as appearances by Liberace.

In the 1960s the axis of concert life moved further north with the establishment of Lincoln Center for the Performing Arts, a complex of buildings and organizations including almost a dozen theaters and concert and lecture halls between 62nd and 66th streets on Broadway (see fig.3). Philharmonic Hall opened on 24 September 1962 to a capacity audience of 2646; it was subsequently modified to improve its acoustics. In 1973 it was renamed Avery Fisher Hall and in 1976 was completely gutted and rebuilt to a new, successful acoustical design (seating 2742 after renovation). The openings of the New York State Theater (1964) and the Metropolitan Opera (1966) (see §4 below), which also flank the main plaza, were followed in 1969 by that of Alice Tully Hall (seating 1096), an ideal hall for solo and chamber concerts. The Vivian Beaumont Theater and the Library and Museum of the Performing Arts of the New York Public Library occupy a corner position at 65th Street and Amsterdam Avenue, while the Juilliard School and Alice Tully Hall are across 65th Street on Broadway. Free outdoor concerts are given each summer in the plaza of Lincoln Center and in the bandshell of Damrosch Park (adjacent to the opera house). The 457-seat Merkin Concert Hall in nearby Abraham Goodman House (on 67th Street), dedicated in 1981, has already proved to be a favorite for smaller-scale events. At the 92nd Street Young Men's–Young Women's Hebrew Association is the Kaufmann Auditorium (seating 916), another important hall for chamber music, chamber orchestras (it is the home of the "Y" Chamber SO), recitals, and contemporary music. Symphony Space, established in 1979 in a remod-

3. Aerial photograph of Lincoln Center showing (clockwise, from lower left) the New York State Theater, Damrosch Park, the Metropolitan Opera House, the Vivian Beaumont Theater and New York Public Library, the Juilliard School and Alice Tully Hall, and Avery Fisher Hall

eled movie theater at Broadway and 95th Street (seating 900), sponsors a variety of activities and is perhaps best known for its "Wall-to-Wall" marathons, which have featured the music of Bach, Ives, Cage, and others.

The most important locus for "downtown" experimental music is the Kitchen, founded by Steina and Woody Vasulka in 1971 as a space for video, music, dance, and performance art. Each season ten visual exhibitions, 2000 hours of video screening, and 150 evenings of music, dance, performance art, and film are given. The Kitchen has a touring program and a library of more than 400 music, video, and dance items. The music director in the early 1980s was Anne DeMarinis. The Experimental Intermedia Foundation (founded in the late 1970s) and Roulette also sponsor experimental music activities (see §9 below).

Many of the city's schools maintain halls used for public concerts. Most prominent among these have been Hunter College and branches of CUNY (notably Queens, Brooklyn, and Lehman colleges), which have substantial concert facilities and sponsor a full range of concert activities. Many concerts and lectures have taken place at Cooper Union, and in the 1950s its "Music in the Making" series presented many world premières of American orchestral music; the Brooklyn PO performs there regularly.

Other concerts take place at the city's museums, including the Museum of Modern Art (at one time the location of concerts by the Composers Showcase and the League of Composers, and from 1971 the sponsor of the successful Summergarden series), the Whitney Museum (which emphasizes contemporary music, jazz, and experimental works in its concerts), and the Metropolitan Museum of Art, where David Mannes inaugurated free concerts in 1918, and where a series of some 80 concerts annually now includes chamber, orchestral, and early music. The Musica Aeterna Orchestra has performed at the museum for many years, and among those who have made their New York débuts at the museum's Grace Rainey Rogers Auditorium (seating 700) are Peter Serkin, Heinz Holliger, and Trevor Pinnock. The Asia Society founded a performing arts program in 1961, which specializes in music and dance from the Orient and the Middle East; in the 1980s composers who have been influenced by Asian music began to perform in its concert series. The Alternative Museum (known until 1980 as the Alternative Center for International Arts) emphasized folk, classical, and popular music from around the world until 1985; it also offers new music and jazz composers series, and has presented concerts since 1976.

Outside Manhattan, the most important concert center is the Brooklyn Academy of Music (BAM), which was incorporated in 1859 and opened in 1861 at a site on Montague Street. After a fire in 1903 the present building was constructed on Lafayette Avenue and opened in 1908. From the 19th century it was a cultural community and civic center presenting opera, oratorios, and plays. The academy was run by the Brooklyn Institute of Arts and Sciences from 1936 until 1971, when it became a private corporation. Since 1967, when Harvey Lichtenstein became executive director, the academy has encouraged subscription audiences and community events, and has played a prominent role in sponsoring modern dance (Merce Cunningham, Alvin Ailey, Twyla Tharp, Trisha Brown) and theater (productions by Peter Brook, Robert Wilson, and the Chelsea Theater Center) as well as music. Since its first season in 1955, the Brooklyn Philharmonia (now PO) has performed at the academy. The "Next Wave" activities, inaugurated in 1981 to critical acclaim, have expanded to include an annual festival and touring program; BAM was the location for performances of Laurie Anderson's four-part *United States* and for the 1984 run of Philip Glass's *Einstein on the Beach*.

Outdoors, summer concerts were held at Lewisohn Stadium from 1918 to 1966. Concerts are now held in Central Park and in parks in the other boroughs, under the auspices of the Department of Cultural Affairs and the Department of Parks and Recreation. The New York PO first gave outdoor concerts in 1965, and the Metropolitan Opera has done so since 1967. Popular performers such as Elton John, Simon and Garfunkel, and Diana Ross have also performed in the city's parks.

See also §§4, 8, 9, and 10.

4. Opera and musical theater. Italian opera first reached New York on 29 November 1825 with a performance at the Park Theatre of Rossini's *Il barbiere di Siviglia* by an Italian company led by Manuel García, the famous Spanish singer and teacher, who took the part of Count Almaviva. The ensemble of eight singers, four of them Garcías (including the 17-year-old Maria Felicia, later Malibran), had been recruited in London by a New York vintner, Dominick Lynch. Encouraged by Lorenzo da Ponte, then a professor of Italian at Columbia College, Lynch took García's troupe to New York for a season of nearly 80 performances, accompanied by a local orchestra of 24; the repertory included *Don Giovanni*, Rossini's *Tancredi*, *Otello*, *Il turco in Italia*, and *La Cenerentola*, Niccolò Antonio Zingarelli's *Romeo e Giulietta*, and García's own *La figlia dell'aria*. Before García's appearance opera in New York had consisted of makeshift adaptations of comic pasticcios with spoken dialogue and popular airs inserted in place of difficult arias (see §1 above). After the Garcías' departure for Mexico late in 1826, a French company from New Orleans took a brief season of French opera to the Park Theatre, opening on 13 July 1827 with Nicolas Isouard's *Cendrillon*. The French repertory included at least ten operas, among them Cherubini's *Les deux journées*, Daniel-François-Esprit Auber's *La dame blanche*, and Adrien Boieldieu's *Le calife de Bagdad*. The next opera company to appear was led by the tenor Giovanni Montresor in 1832–3; it gave about 50 performances of such works as Bellini's *Il pirata* and Saverio Mercadante's *Elisa e Claudio*, in addition to works of Rossini. Another French troupe from New Orleans introduced Rossini's *Le comte Ory* (Park Theatre, 19 August 1833) and Ferdinand Hérold's *Zampa*.

New York's first venue for opera, the Italian Opera House at Church and Leonard Streets, opened on 18 November 1833 with Rossini's *La gazza ladra*; among its backers were Lynch and Da Ponte. The repertory of the long but not very successful season (80 performances) consisted chiefly of the ever-popular Rossini, but Domenico Cimarosa and Giovanni Pacini were also introduced. A second season was financially disastrous; Italian opera suffered an eclipse, and the house burned down in 1839. Performances of opera, always a hazardous undertaking, were infrequent until Ferdinand Palmo, a restaurateur, opened Palmo's Opera House on 3 February 1844 with the New York première of Bellini's *I puritani*. In four seasons Palmo introduced Bellini's *Beatrice di Tenda*, Donizetti's *Lucrezia Borgia* and *Linda di Chamounix*, and Verdi's *I lombardi*. At other theaters pasticcios of opera in English by Michael Balfe, William Michael Rooke, and Julius Benedict remained popular. While Palmo's held sway on Chambers Street, 150 wealthy men were raising money for another opera house further uptown, and the Astor Place Opera House opened on 22 November 1847 with Verdi's *Ernani*. The guaranteed support lasted only five years, financial returns were slight, and the house closed in 1852.

The period between 1847 and the founding of the Metropolitan Opera in 1883 was a turbulent one in New York's operatic history, dominated by colorful impresarios, competitive prima donnas, and constantly changing personnel, who appeared in operatic performances in many New York theaters. After the closure of the house at Astor Place the only theater devoted specifically to concert and opera was the Academy of Music at 14th Street and Irving Place, which opened on 2 October 1854 with a performance of Bellini's *Norma* starring Giulia Grisi and Giuseppe Mario; it continued to present regular operatic seasons until 1886. When it was built (at a cost of $335,000), the house contained the largest stage in the world (21.5 by 30 meters) and seated 4600. During the first 24 years the management changed every season.

Max Maretzek, who left London in 1848 to conduct at the Astor Place Opera, was among the more prominent impresarios. A frequent lessee and conductor at the Academy of Music, he was associated with the first New York performances of many operas there. Academy audiences heard *Rigoletto* (19 February 1855), *Il trovatore* (2 May 1855), *La traviata* (3 December 1856), Meyerbeer's *L'africaine* (1 December 1865), and Gounod's *Roméo et Juliette* (15 November 1867), the last two in Italian. The brothers Maurice and Max Strakosch were also among the operatic producers active in New York from 1857. Most important was J. H. Mapleson, who went to the Academy of Music in 1878 and directed operatic activities there and abroad until 1886. Many great singers appeared in New York; audiences in 1853, for example, heard the nine-year-old Adelina Patti, Mario, Lind, Henriette Sontag, Grisi, and Marietta Alboni. Later decades saw the appearance of such singers as Christine Nilsson, Lilli Lehmann, and Italo Campanini. 39 American singers, among them Lillian Nordica, Clara Kellogg, Minnie Hauk, and Annie Louise Cary, sang at the Academy of Music before 1884. Local composers were not so fortunate, although George F. Bristow's *Rip Van Winkle* ran for four weeks in 1855 at Niblo's Garden, and William Henry Fry's *Leonora* was heard in March 1858, 13 years after its première in Philadelphia. The first opera by Wagner heard in New York was *Tannhäuser*, given on 4 April 1859 at the Stadt Theater with choruses sung by the Arion Society.

The Metropolitan Opera House at Broadway and 39th Street opened with Gounod's *Faust* on 22 October 1883 (see fig.4). Originally conceived as a social gesture by a score of millionaires who could not obtain boxes at the Academy of Music, the Metropolitan transcended its initial purpose. The Metropolitan quickly achieved international eminence – virtually every celebrated singer of the last 100 years has sung there – and the Metropolitan Opera Association has the longest continuous existence of any organization of its kind in the USA. Henry Abbey, a well-known theatrical producer with little operatic experience, directed the first season and incurred a loss of $500,000. The artistic importance of the house dates from the following season when the board of directors accepted Leopold Damrosch's proposal that he should direct a season of German opera. In the seven years after Damrosch's death in 1885 all of Wagner's mature works except *Parsifal* were introduced by his successor, Anton Seidl. Celebrated European singers like Lehmann, Marianne Brandt, Amalie Materna, and Albert Niemann were members of the company, and in effect the Metropolitan became a German opera house; even *Il trovatore* and *Aida* were given there in German.

The sobriety of the programs eventually exhausted the patience of the boxholders, and in 1891 Abbey returned as lessee, placing the management in the hands of Maurice Grau, a shrewd student of public taste. He built his company around such admirable singers as Emma Eames, the De Reszkes, Emma Albani, and Jean Lassalle, at first presenting the repertory exclusively in French and Italian. It was Grau's conviction that audiences attended opera primarily to hear fine singing, a belief he substantiated with some of the most brilliant casts Americans had ever heard.

METROPOLITAN
OPERA HOUSE.

MR. HENRY E. ABBEY, - - - - - - - - Director.
Acting Manager, - - - - - - MR. MAURICE GRAU.

MONDAY EVENING, OCTOBER 22, 1883,
INAUGURAL NIGHT
AND
First Night of the Subscription,
WHEN GOUNOD'S OPERA OF
"FAUST."
Will be presented with the following Cast:

FAUST, - - - - - - - Sig. ITALO CAMPANINI
MEPHISTOPHELES, - - - - Sig. FRANCO NOVARA
VALENTINO, - - - - - Sig. GIUSEPPE DEL PUENTE
WAGNER, - - - - - - - - - - Sig. CONTINI
SIEBEL, - - - - - - - - Mme. SOFIA SCALCHI
MARTA, - - - - - - - - Mlle. LOUISE LABLACHE
(Who has kindly consented to assume the part at short notice. Her first appearance.)
AND
MARGHERITA, - - - - - Mme. CHRISTINE NILSSON

Musical Director and Conductor, - Sig. VIANESI

WEBER PIANO USED.

Mason & Hamlin's Organ Used.

All the above Operas performed at this House can be had in every form, Vocal and Instrumental at G. SCHIRMER, No. 35 Union Square, Importer and Publisher of Music.

The Scenery by Messrs. Fox, Schaefler, Maeder, and Thompson.
The Costumes are entirely new, and were manufactured at Venice by D. Ascoli
The Appointments by Mr. Bradwell.
Machinists, Messrs. Lundy & Gifford.

NIGHTLY PRICES OF ADMISSION:

Boxes, holding six (6) seats.......... $50
Orchestra Stalls.......... 6
Balcony Stalls.......... 3
Family Circle (reserved).......... 2
Admission to Family Circle.......... 1

Seats and Boxes can be secured at the Box Office of the Metropolitan Opera House, which will remain open daily from 8 A. M. to 5 P. M.

Doors open at 7.15. Performances at 8 precisely

Gunerius Gabrielson & Son, Florists to the Metropolitan Opera House.

Opera Glasses on Hire in the Lobby.

L. F. Mazzetti, Caterer.
Parties desiring Ices can be supplied by the Waiter, in Corridor.

Business Manager - - - - - - - - - - Mr. W. W. TILLOTSON.
Treasurer - - - - - - - - - - Mr. CHAS. H. MATHEWS.

4. *Program for the opening of the Metropolitan Opera House on 22 October 1883*

Among them were Nordica, Eames, Zélie de Lussan, Victor Maurel, Edouard De Reszke, and Giuseppe Russitano in *Don Giovanni*; Melba, Nordica, Sofia Scalchi, the De Reszkes, Maurel, and Pol Plançon in Meyerbeer's *Les Huguenots*; and Nordica, Brema, the De Reszkes, and Giuseppe Kaschmann in *Tristan und Isolde* when the performance of German opera in German was resumed in 1896. In many respects these paralleled performances at Covent Garden, where Grau was also the impresario during part of this period. However, there were no Metropolitan performances in 1892–3, because of a disastrous fire that necessitated extensive reconstruction of the auditorium, or in 1897–8, when Grau reorganized his company. Otherwise a resident company has presented opera continuously at the Metropolitan from 1883. Only 16 Americans sang leading roles there before 1900; these included Hauk, Nordica, Albani, Eames, Olive Fremstad, Emma Nevada, and David Bispham.

Grau retired in 1903 and a new producing group was organized, with Heinrich Conried as manager. His theatrical experience as a producer of plays in German improved that aspect of the Metropolitan's productions considerably. Highlights of Conried's tenure included Enrico Caruso's début (23 November 1903), a sensational *Salome* with Fremstad (22 January 1907), Feodor Chaliapin as an almost nude Mephistopheles (20 November 1907), and Mahler conducting *Tristan und Isolde* (1 January 1908).

Giulio Gatti-Casazza, the director of La Scala, was engaged as general manager in 1908, and Arturo Toscanini came to the Metropolitan with him, making his conducting début in a performance of *Aida* (16 November 1908). With the musical cooperation of Toscanini and the financial assistance of Otto Kahn, Gatti-Casazza established an operatic enterprise of imposing scope and efficiency. Under him the policy of presenting opera in the language of its composition became the rule of the house. Important conductors during his 27-year tenure included Mahler (1908–10), Toscanini (1908–15), Alfred Hertz (1902–15), Artur Bodanzky (1915–39), and Tullio Serafin (1924–34). The repertory was expanded to include as many as 48 different works in a 24-week season. Puccini's *La fanciulla del West* and Humperdinck's *Königskinder* had their world premières at the Metropolitan in 1910. Gatti-Casazza continued to keep abreast of operatic developments in Italy and elsewhere, at the same time initiating the production of American operas, including Frederick Shepherd Converse's *The Pipe of Desire* (18 March 1910), Horatio Parker's *Mona* (14 March 1912), and Deems Taylor's *Peter Ibbetson* (7 February 1931). Although the company prospered under Gatti-Casazza's astute management, the 1929 stock market collapse and ensuing Depression severely depleted a reserve fund, and the season was shortened to 16 and later to 14 weeks. In 1935 Gatti-Casazza retired and was succeeded briefly by the singer Herbert Witherspoon, who died while planning his first season. His successor was the Canadian-born tenor Edward Johnson, long a member of the company, who managed the Metropolitan until 1950.

An experiment with a low-priced spring season featuring young American singers sponsored by the Juilliard Foundation lasted only two years (1936–7), but American singers such as Lawrence Tibbett, Eleanor Steber, Rose Bampton, Richard Crooks, Dorothy Kirsten, Leonard Warren, and Risë Stevens played an increasingly important role during Johnson's regime. Helen Traubel, Lauritz Melchior, and Kirsten Flagstad led a strong Germanic wing with Wagner performances in the late 1930s and early 1940s that were outstanding. Italian opera continued to dominate the repertory, French works being in the minority. Few modern operas were produced during Johnson's tenure, although the Metropolitan did give Walter Damrosch's *The Man without a Country* (12 May 1937) and Britten's *Peter Grimes* in 1948.

For the first part of the Metropolitan's existence its main financial base was a private company, which delegated the production of opera to an independent company; members occupied the single tier of (socially significant) boxes. In 1940 the property was sold to the producing company, the Metropolitan Opera Association, which raised a million dollars in public appeals to help finance the transaction. Public support for the company has become increasingly important. The Metropolitan Opera Guild, a supporting organization founded in 1935 by Mrs. August Belmont, has a national membership of over 100,000 and sponsors an educational program and special performances for school children. The guild issues *Opera News*, a periodical that includes articles, news, and details of the Saturday afternoon radio broadcasts of matinée performances (inaugurated in 1931). The Metropolitan Opera Auditions, which began as a radio broadcast in 1936, were sponsored by the National Council of the Metropolitan from 1953. Metropolitan contract winners have included Martina Arroyo, Shirley Verrett, Richard Tucker, and Robert Merrill. From 1960 to 1976 the Metropolitan Opera Studio, founded by John Gutman, gave young professionals an opportunity to sing repertory and unfamiliar works before school audiences. A short-lived National Company employing young singers toured the country from 1965 to 1967, and currently the Young Artists' Development Program provides training for new singers.

In 1950 Rudolf Bing, a Viennese impresario who had managed the Glyndebourne and Edinburgh festivals, became general manager of the Metropolitan. His tenure, which lasted until 1972, was marked by modernization of stage techniques, an increasingly international cast, and the move of the company to new quarters in Lincoln Center. Although the repertory remained basically conservative, Bing introduced several American operas: Barber's *Vanessa* (15 January 1958), Menotti's *Le dernier sauvage* (23 January 1964), and Marvin David Levy's *Mourning Becomes Electra* (17 March 1967); light operas such as Strauss's *Die Fledermaus* and Offenbach's *La Périchole* were also added to the repertory. Owing to jet travel, audiences have enjoyed international singers of the caliber of Renata Tebaldi, Birgit Nilsson, Joan Sutherland, Franco Corelli, and Montserrat Caballé, as well as such American singers as Sherrill Milnes and Leontyne Price.

The new Metropolitan Opera House at Lincoln Center opened on 16 September 1966 with the world première of Barber's *Antony and Cleopatra*, in which Justino Díaz and Price sang the title roles. Despite, or perhaps because of, an extravagant production designed by Franco Zeffirelli, the work was a spectacular failure; the house, on the other hand, was a success. Although the seating capacity of the new auditorium (3788) is not much larger than that of the 39th Street building (3625), the inadequate staging facilities of the old house were replaced by a much larger stage and generous backstage quarters. The $46 million required for construction was raised in contributions by Lincoln Center and the Metropolitan Opera Association. In addition to accommodating the regular Metropolitan season of 26 weeks, the house is used by visiting opera and dance companies from the USA and abroad. After Bing's resignation in 1972 the Metropolitan Opera management underwent several reorganizations. The Swedish director Goeran Gentele died before his first season, and Schuyler Chapin was named general manager. In 1975 the management was assumed by executive director Anthony Bliss, who appointed the conductor James Levine music director; Levine was named the artistic director of the company from 1986 and Bruce Crawford replaced Bliss the same year. Levine's interests range from the early Mozart operas to the classics of the 20th-century repertory; notable new productions in the 1970s and 1980s included Handel's *Rinaldo*, Mozart's *Idomeneo*, Berg's *Lulu* and *Wozzeck*, Weill's *Mahagonny*, *Parade* (uniting works by Satie, Poulenc, and Ravel) and a "triple bill" consisting of Stravinsky's *The Rite of*

Spring, *Le rossignol*, and *Oedipus rex*. The centenary of the company was celebrated during the 1983–4 season with museum exhibitions, a postage stamp, and a marathon "gala" on 22 October 1983, which was televised and in which more than 100 singers participated.

The New York City Opera was founded as the City Center Opera Company in 1943 and has established itself over the years as a legitimate rival to the Metropolitan. Opening at the City Center Theater on West 55th Street on 21 February 1944 with Dusolina Giannini as Tosca, the company has consistently encouraged participation by younger singers, composers, and audiences. At first seasons were short, a few weeks before and after the Metropolitan, but the spring and autumn periods were later lengthened to 11 weeks each, with about 175 performances given annually. In 1983 the schedule was reorganized to a single season lasting from July to December. A succession of conductor-managers – Laszlo Halász (1944–51), Josef Rosenstock (1952–5), Erich Leinsdorf (1956–7), and Julius Rudel (1957–79) – produced an imaginative repertory ranging from Prokofiev's *The Love for Three Oranges* (1949), *Wozzeck* (1959), Handel's *Giulio Cesare* (1971), and Monteverdi's *L'incoronazione di Poppea* (1973), to Gilbert and Sullivan, without neglecting standard works. American opera fared particularly well at the City Opera; premières included Still's *The Troubled Island* (1949), Copland's *The Tender Land* (1954), Kurka's *The Good Soldier Schweik* (1958), Douglas S. Moore's *Wings of the Dove* (1961), Robert Ward's *The Crucible* (1961), Rorem's *Miss Julie* (1965), Weisgall's *Nine Rivers from Jordan* (1968), and Menotti's *La loca* (1979). On 22 February 1966 the New York City Opera opened its spring season at its new home, the New York State Theater in Lincoln Center, with a performance of Alberto Ginastera's *Don Rodrigo*. The house (seating 2800) was originally designed for Balanchine's New York City Ballet, and was criticized as acoustically unsuited to opera, but a renovation in 1981–2 (new capacity 2737) resulted in improved acoustics for opera performances.

The City Opera has always stressed ensemble production in contrast to the international star system, and has produced some fine native singers, among them Patricia Brooks, Ashley Putnam, Samuel Ramey, John Reardon, Gianna Rolandi, Beverly Sills, Norman Treigle, and Carol Vaness. Sills became director of the company in 1969, and Christopher Keene acted as music director (1983–6). Sills's goals for the company were consistent with those of her predecessors; in addition she encouraged American conductors and opera in English. In 1984 the company was the first in the USA to introduce "surtitles" – an English translation of the libretto projected on a screen above the proscenium arch during performances to make foreign-language opera more accessible. Productions of Bernstein's *Candide* (1982) and Sondheim's *Sweeney Todd* (1984) demonstrated Sills's interest in forging links between opera and musical theater, and in 1984 the company received a gift of $5 million to present a musical-comedy season each spring, commencing in 1986.

Occasional opera performances characterized by such departures from the norm as unconventional repertory, opera in English, and opportunities for new singers and composers have always been a feature of the city's musical activity. The Amato Opera Theatre, founded in 1948 by Anthony Amato, presents 70 fully staged performances each year in its own theater. Its six annual productions are drawn principally from the standard repertory of French, Italian, and English-language opera, but it has also presented the American premières of Boito's *Nerone* and Verdi's *Alzira*. Young American artists are also given exposure in the Bronx Opera Company, founded in 1967 by Michael Spierman. The company's two annual productions juxtapose well-known repertory with lesser-known works such as operas by Schubert and Vaughan Williams; fully staged performances are given in English. The Opera Orchestra of New York, directed by Eve Queler, carries on a tradition established by the American Opera Society (1951–70) of unusual works given in concert form. Popular staged performances of more familiar operas are given by Vincent La Selva's New York Grand Opera (founded 1973) in the style of the former impresarios Fortune Gallo and Alfredo Salmaggi. Conservatories and schools combine training and performance in contemporary and standard repertory; among the most important in the 1980s were the Juilliard School's American Opera Center (see § 12 below) and the Manhattan School of Music. Besides the ensembles already mentioned, over 40 organizations produce operas regularly.

The New York stage has also played host to more popular musical entertainment throughout its history. Following the success of ballad opera in the 18th century, parody burlesques, minstrel shows, and extravaganzas dominated the scene in the mid-19th century. The extravaganza *The Black Crook* (music by Thomas Baker and others, 1866), *Evangeline* (1874) by E. E. Rice, and Charles Hoyt's *A Trip to Chinatown* (1890) were particularly successful productions in a developing vernacular form that eventually fused song, dance, and plot into the American musical comedy. (*See also* BURLESQUE.)

Operettas by Offenbach were popular from the 1860s, but in the two decades after the New York première of *H.M.S. Pinafore* (January 1879), European light opera by Sullivan, Edmond Audran, Carl Millöcker, and others competed with local operetta by Caryll, Kerker, De Koven, and Victor Herbert. Gilbert and Sullivan, Franz Lehár, and Johann Strauss the younger still draw enthusiastic audiences to both opera houses and off-Broadway theaters, especially the Light Opera of Manhattan (founded 1968).

George M. Cohan's first success, *Little Johnny Jones* (1904), popularized the patriotic American musical; "Give my regards to Broadway" became a theme that summed up the importance of the New York stage in the vernacular musical theater for the next 80 years. A Broadway run is a requisite for a successful musical comedy, and Broadway theaters have fostered such composers as Kern, Berlin, Gershwin, Porter, and Rodgers. Blitzstein, Menotti, Bernstein, and Sondheim have attempted to bridge the gap between the Broadway musical and opera with such works as *Regina* (1949), *The Consul* (1950), *Candide* (1956), and *Sweeney Todd* (1979). (*See also* MUSICAL and MUSICAL THEATER.)

Dance plays a vital part in New York's musical–theatrical life. Among the most prominent of the almost 100 dance companies in the city are the New York City Ballet, the American Ballet Theatre, the American Joffrey Ballet, the Alvin Ailey Dance Theatre, the Martha Graham Dance Company, the Dance Theatre of Harlem, the Judson Dance Theater, and the companies of Merce Cunningham, Paul Taylor, Eliot Feld, Erick Hawkins, and Twyla Tharp. (*See also* DANCE, §III.)

5. ORCHESTRAS AND BANDS. Amateur orchestras first appeared late in the 18th century. In 1799 two of these organizations, the St. Cecilia and Harmonical societies, joined forces to form the Philharmonic Society, which in that year participated in the funeral service for George Washington. This first Philharmonic ceased activity after 1816, to be followed in 1824 by a second

Philharmonic Society, which played the finale of Beethoven's Second Symphony for the first time in New York on 16 December 1824 and continued in existence until 1827. In 1825 unidentified groups essayed Beethoven's *Die Geschöpfe des Prometheus* (20 May, for the "first time in New York") and the *Egmont* overture (2 April), both at City Hotel. The Euterpean Club, which gave one orchestral concert annually, existed from 1800 to 1847. The New York Musical Fund Society, an orchestra that appeared in 1828, attempted the first movement of Beethoven's Symphony no.1 under Ureli Corelli Hill at City Hotel on 27 April 1831, but "the orchestra was weak [and] the instruments were frequently out of tune and out of time."

The Steyermarkische, Lombardi, Gung'l, Saxonia, and Germania orchestras arrived from Europe in 1848–9, but most were notable more for their discipline and uniforms than for the quality of their programs. Of the five groups, the Germania Musical Society survived, giving exemplary performances of great works. At their first concert in New York (5 October 1848) the audience was "awed by a sublimity of sounds too sensitively expressed to admit of more rapture than those created by supernatural agency." The orchestra had greater success elsewhere but continued to visit New York until it disbanded in 1854.

The Philharmonic Symphony Society of New York dates from 1842 and is the oldest orchestra in continuous existence in the USA. The impetus for its foundation came in June 1839 when a "musical solemnity" brought together a nucleus of musicians intending to form a permanent orchestra. The occasion of the event was the premature death of Daniel Schlesinger, a German pianist who had achieved great success in New York in the last three years of his life and who envisioned creating an orchestra of European caliber in New York. The first organizational meeting of the Philharmonic Society was called by Hill on 2 April 1842; among those attending were H. C. Timm, Anthony Rief, Jr., Charles Edward Horn, Vincent Wallace, Alfred Boucher, Edward Hodges, William Scharfenberg, George Loder, and Denis-Germain Etienne.

The first concert was held in the Apollo Rooms on 7 December 1842; an orchestra of 63 players performed Beethoven's Fifth Symphony under Hill, who had introduced the work to an American audience on 11 February 1841; Weber's *Oberon* overture led by Etienne; and an overture in D by Johann Wenzel Kalliwoda conducted by Timm. J. N. Hummel's Piano Quintet in D minor and vocal selections from Beethoven's *Fidelio*, Mozart's *Die Entführung aus dem Serail*, and Rossini's *Armida*, sung by Horn and Mme. Otto and conducted by Timm, made up the rest of the program. The first season consisted of three concerts; the second (18 February 1843) included the American première of Beethoven's Third Symphony. During the next 16 seasons the orchestra gave four concerts annually, in 1859–60 they gave five, and a decade later six. During its first ten years the orchestra numbered between 50 and 67 players. Various conductors, usually members of the orchestra, shared the podium, often during the same concert; Loder was perhaps the most outstanding. Later one or two conductors assumed the responsibility, beginning with Theodore Eisfeld, who was elected director in 1852 and served until 1865. Other conductors included Carl Bergmann (1855–76), Theodore Thomas (1877–91), and Anton Seidl (1891–8). Under the presidency of R. O. Doremus the number of players increased to 100 in 1867, and the orchestra moved to larger quarters at the Academy of Music.

The repertory of the New York Philharmonic reflected the European training of its conductors, and there was heavy emphasis on the Germanic school. On 20 May 1846 Loder led the first American performance of Beethoven's Ninth Symphony at Castle Garden before an audience of 2000; the same year saw performances of Chopin's First Piano Concerto and several Berlioz overtures. Although the orchestra performed Bristow's *Concert Overture* in 1847, European works continued to fill programs throughout the century. Thomas in particular championed the works of Liszt, Wagner, Brahms, and Richard Strauss.

The age of the Philharmonic and its 20th-century significance assure the orchestra a predominant place in New York's musical history, but at times during the 19th century other orchestras partly eclipsed its importance. Lighter music and American works were emphasized by Jullien, who conducted an occasional orchestra at the Crystal Palace after 1853; his concerts included Fry's programmatic symphonies *A Day in the Country*, *The Breaking Heart*, and *Santa Claus*. Thomas, who made his conducting début at Irving Hall in 1862, formed his own 60- to 80-piece orchestra in 1867, which performed in New York and on national tours until 1891. Programs included music from Bach to Saint-Saëns; some concerts were devoted to Wagner, Beethoven, Mozart, or Mendelssohn. Often the least varied programs drew the largest audiences. The first Brooklyn Philharmonic (1857) was similar to its New York counterpart; among its conductors were Eisfeld, Bergmann, and Thomas.

The New York Symphony was founded in 1878 by Leopold Damrosch, who conducted the orchestra until his death in 1885, at which time his son Walter assumed the position. Orchestras under Damrosch and Thomas competed in repertory and in festivals, each performing Brahms's First Symphony within a week and Saint-Saëns' Second Piano Concerto on successive days. In 1881 Damrosch conducted 1500 performers in Berlioz's *Grande messe des morts* before an audience of 10,000, and in 1882 Thomas directed a mammoth festival with a chorus of 3200 assembled from other cities. The Symphony Society (which sponsored the orchestra) was eventually more successful in soliciting support from local patrons, notably Andrew Carnegie, and in 1891 Thomas left New York for Chicago. Although the society's performances were not as well received critically as those of the Philharmonic, Damrosch's programs were often more adventurous, tempering the usual Germanic fare with works by Debussy and Berlioz. On 5 May 1891 Walter Damrosch conducted the Symphony Society Orchestra at the opening of Carnegie Hall in a program including the "Old Hundredth" and *America* (in both of which the audience participated), followed by Beethoven's *Leonore* overture no.3; in his first American appearance Tchaikovsky conducted his *Marche solennelle*, and Damrosch directed the first New York performance of Berlioz's *Te Deum*. During its first 25 years the Symphony Society's concerts had occasional lapses, particularly in the 1890s when Damrosch traveled with his own opera company, in 1899 when he devoted a year to composition, and in 1902–3 when he was conductor of the Philharmonic Society.

Damrosch reconstituted the orchestra on a cooperative basis in autumn 1903 as the New York SO. The system of sharing profits and losses among members of the organization and a group of guarantors proved unsatisfactory, and the Symphony Society was reorganized in 1907 with regular salaries for the musicians, and a board of directors who assumed all financial responsibilities. H. H. Flagler, a supporter of the society for several years, undertook its financial backing in 1914 and in 1920 provided an estimated $250,000 for a concert tour of Europe, the first by an

American orchestra. Long before then, however, Damrosch and his orchestra had been noted for their pioneering activities, bringing symphonic music to many communities in the USA for the first time. Until 1928 Damrosch conducted the majority of the concerts, although Felix Weingartner shared the 1905–6 season with him as guest conductor. In the 1920s a number of guest conductors appeared with the Symphony Society, including Vladimir Golschmann, Bruno Walter, Ravel, Eugene Goossens, Ossip Gabrilowitsch, Enrique Arbos, Fritz Busch, Vincent d'Indy, and Albert Coates.

From 1887 New Yorkers could hear the Boston SO in as many concerts as were given by the local Philharmonic. Late in the 19th century Thomas returned with his Chicago SO, and the Philadelphia Orchestra made regular visits from 1903. The local Russian SO (1904–18) under Modest Altschuler introduced works by Rachmaninoff, Scriabin, Rimsky-Korsakov, and Anatol Liadov, and the American débuts of Josef Lhévinne (1906), Mischà Elman (1908), Rachmaninoff (1909), and Prokofiev (1918) were made with the orchestra. The People's Symphony Concerts at Cooper Union (from 1902) provided programs of quality at minimum prices for those living on the lower East Side. An Italian SO conducted by Pietro Floridia appeared in 1913.

Meanwhile the Philharmonic continued a wavering but sedate course under Paur (1898–1902), Walter Damrosch (1902–3), various guest conductors (1903–6), Vasily Safonov (1906–9), Mahler (1909–11), and Josef Stransky (1911–22). In 1909 the orchestra, which had also been operated on a cooperative basis, was reorganized as a full-time professional ensemble with a group of guarantors to ensure financial solvency. In 1921 it merged with the two-year-old New/National SO, which had been conducted by Edgard Varèse, Artur Bodanzky, and Willem Mengelberg. The concert schedule had increased considerably, and it was decided that the conductor's task was too great for one man, so the duties were shared by two or three principal conductors and various guests. Regular conductors included Stransky (1921–3), Mengelberg (1921–30), Willem van Hoogstraten (1923–5), Wilhelm Furtwängler (1925–7), Toscanini (1927–36), Bernardino Molinari (1929–31), Erich Kleiber (1930–32), and Bruno Walter (1931–3).

During this period the Philharmonic Society, under a board of directors led by C. H. Mackay, absorbed several other new orchestras, among them the City Symphony (1921–3), the American National Orchestra (1923), and the State SO (1923–6). The most important merger was that of the Philharmonic with Damrosch's Symphony Society in March 1928, the orchestra being renamed the Philharmonic-Symphony Society Orchestra.

The growth of the USA, the cosmopolitan nature of its social order, and a new prosperity demanded more consistent bases to its performing organizations than personal whim, private philanthropy, or musicians' profit-sharing. All aspects of the business of music in the USA were now centered in New York: concert management, publishing, broadcasting, recording, and musicians' unions. The merger of two competing orchestras under a single board of trustees was a logical development, but a subsequent plan to unite the orchestra and the Metropolitan Opera was discarded. The new season lasted 28 weeks and included 103 concerts. Toscanini became the principal conductor, sharing the 1928–9 season with Mengelberg and Molinari. A European tour in the spring of 1930 offered 23 concerts in five weeks. Toscanini's tenure has become legendary, and many accounts describe the glamor of the years 1929–36.

After Toscanini's retirement, regular conductors of the Philharmonic included John Barbirolli (1936–43), Artur Rodzinski (1943–7), Bruno Walter (1947–9), Dimitri Mitropoulos (1949–57), Leonard Bernstein (1958–69), George Szell (music adviser and senior guest conductor, 1969–71), Pierre Boulez (1971–8), and Zubin Mehta (from 1978). Guest conductors were particularly prominent in the 1940s: Enescu, Carlos Chávez, and Stravinsky appeared with Barbirolli, and the 100th anniversary season (1942) was led by 13 guest conductors. Busch, Goossens, Fritz Reiner, Serge Koussevitzky, Efrem Kurtz, Leopold Stokowski, George Szell, Max Rudolf, Charles Munch, Walter Hendl, Victor de Sabata, Pierre Monteux, and Guido Cantelli shared the podium with the principal conductors between then and 1958. Bernstein introduced a new dimension into the role of the conductor; as the first American-born conductor to direct the orchestra, he brought an eager showmanship that did not earn universal approval but that undeniably produced vital interpretations both of the standard repertory and of lesser-known works. Although his programs were generally conservative, he gave the world première of Ives's Second Symphony (1902) in 1951 and included works of living American composers from Randall Thompson to Copland and Schuman. He maintained his association with the Broadway theater and continued to compose during his tenure as conductor.

Succeeding Bernstein, Boulez in his tenure emphasized unfamiliar repertory both of 20th-century composers and such earlier composers as Liszt, Schumann, and Haydn. He instituted a series of informal "rug concerts" and presented programs in less important auditoriums, with the intention of drawing a wider public than the subscription audience. The personally reticent Boulez was succeeded by the more flamboyant Mehta (fig.5, p.358), who had previously led the Los Angeles PO. With Mehta, whose greatest musical affinity is with the Romantic literature, the Philharmonic returned to a more conventional repertory, although the orchestra has continued to offer premières and landmark works of contemporary composers. Under the direction of Mehta and composer-in-residence Jacob Druckman, the orchestra presented the Horizons festivals of contemporary music in 1983 and 1984.

The Philharmonic's season has lengthened over the years, and the musicians are now active throughout the year. In the 1980s the orchestra gave nearly 200 concerts each year. The principal season runs from late September to May with four subscription concerts weekly in Avery Fisher Hall. In late spring and summer there have been various festivals (devoted to Haydn, Beethoven, Romantic music, and contemporary music), tours, and parks concerts.

Orchestral concerts for children were presented by Thomas as early as 1883, but their continuous history begins with the establishment of the Young People's Symphony Concerts of New York by Frank Damrosch in 1898, with the Symphony Society's orchestra. Walter Damrosch, succeeding his brother, added a series for younger children. The Philharmonic Society launched its own children's concerts in January 1924 under the direction of Ernest Schelling, who continued to conduct the program until his death in 1939. The society has maintained the Young People's Concerts. Between 1958 and 1969 Bernstein conceived, wrote, narrated, and conducted 47 televised shows before audiences of children. Radio broadcasting of the orchestra's concerts began in 1922 and continued until 1967; it was resumed in 1975.

Throughout the 20th century New York has been rich in

5. *Zubin Mehta conducting the New York PO*

orchestras. From 1940 to 1943 a New York City Symphony supported by government funds was conducted by Otto Klemperer, Thomas Beecham, and others. In 1944 a new orchestra under Stokowski was formed with the same name; the final season was conducted by Bernstein in 1947. Radio broadcasting networks have often formed their own orchestras in the city. One sponsored by CBS and conducted by Bernard Herrmann and Howard Barlow was active from 1927 to 1950, and Alfred Wallenstein led an orchestra for the Mutual network from 1933 to 1943. Probably the most famous was the NBC SO, formed in 1937 specifically for Toscanini, who conducted it until 1954 when he retired; the ensemble disbanded soon after.

In 1983 over 40 symphony orchestras were active in New York and its environs, some of which were amateur or community ensembles, others fully professional; most offer between three and six concerts each season. The Brooklyn PO, organized as the Brooklyn Philharmonia in 1955 by Siegfried Landau and directed by Lukas Foss from 1971, has been notable for its adventurous programming, which has included five-hour multi-media marathons of avant-garde music as well as more standard fare. The Little Orchestra Society, conducted from 1947 to 1975 by Thomas Scherman, and Newell Jenkins's Clarion Music Society (founded 1958) have been active in reviving neglected repertory. Other orchestras include the American SO, an ensemble of young professionals founded in 1962 by Stokowski and reorganized in 1973 as a cooperative orchestra; the American Composers Orchestra, founded in 1976 to promote American orchestral music, with Dennis Russell Davies as principal conductor; and the "Y" Chamber SO, founded in 1977 with Gerard Schwarz as conductor. The National Orchestra of New York (formerly the National Orchestral Association), conducted by Leon Barzin from 1930 to 1976 and a training ground for young musicians seeking orchestral experience, has been affiliated with Columbia University since 1984. The Queens SO, under David Katz, specializes in school programs, and the Julius Grossman Symphony (formerly the Municipal Concerts Orchestra, founded 1957; renamed for its founder and conductor) gives regular free concerts in the summer. The Long Island PO, formerly known as the Huntington SO (1949–75) and the Long Island SO (1975–9) and conducted since 1979 by Christopher Keene, the County Symphony of Westchester, formerly the Westchester Orchestral Society and conducted since 1963 by Stephen Simon, and the Music for Westchester SO are among the orchestras active in suburban New York. (*See also* ORCHESTRAS, esp. §2.)

Bands in New York were frequently affiliated with military regiments, but played public concerts in the parks and at Manhattan and Brighton beaches. Among the most famous bandmasters in New York were the Dodworth family, Claudio S. Grafulla, Carlo Alberto Cappa, Patrick S. Gilmore, and, later, Edwin Franko Goldman and his son Richard. Thomas Dodworth, Sr., joined the Independent Band of New York on his arrival in 1828; after the band was renamed the City Band in 1834, his son Allen took some of its members and formed the National Brass Band, which in turn was renamed the Dodworth Band from 1836. The Dodworth Band was active through the 19th century and was under contract to various military regiments; after the Civil War, it was the first band to give public concerts in Central Park. Grafulla directed bands in New York in the 1840s and 1850s; in 1859 he organized the new 7th Regiment Band. Cappa played in the Shelton Band of New York, which was led by Grafulla in the 1860s, as well as in the 7th Regiment Band, which he took over in 1881. Goldman formed his own band in 1911, and it performed continuously from 1918 to 1979 (from 1956 it was directed by Richard Franko Goldman). Ainslee Cox became director in 1980 and reconstituted the band as the Guggenheim Concerts Band; it was renamed the Goldman Memorial Band in 1984. The Goldman Band commissioned American works and did much to revive band music of the 18th and 19th centuries. (*See also* BANDS.)

6. CHAMBER MUSIC. Few concerts devoted to chamber music were given publicly in New York before 1850. In 1851 Theodor Eisfeld initiated a series of quartet concerts including works by Haydn, Beethoven, and Mendelssohn; these were succeeded in

1855 by the renowned Mason and Thomas Chamber Music Soirées, which continued until 1868. Their fine programs included music by Schubert, Schumann, and Bach. On 27 November 1855 William Mason, Theodore Thomas, and Carl Bergmann gave the first performance of Brahms's Trio op.8. The New York Trio, founded about 1867 by Bernardus Boekelman, was active until 1888. The Kneisel Quartet (1885–1917) and the Flonzaley Quartet (1903–29), founded by the New Yorker Edward J. De Coppet, played frequently in private homes and at public concerts. The Peoples Symphony Concerts, a series of public chamber music concerts, were inaugurated in 1902. In 1914 the pianist Carolyn Beebe founded the New York Chamber Music Society, a group of about 12 musicians who gave regular concerts at the Plaza Hotel and elsewhere for about 25 years. The Society of the Friends of Music (1913–31) was chiefly a sponsoring organization that introduced many unfamiliar works to New York, among them Schoenberg's Chamber Symphony op.9 and Mahler's Eighth Symphony (April 1916); from 1920 choral music sung by the Friends of Music chorus became prominent. The Barrère Ensemble, a wind group organized in 1910 by the flutist Georges Barrère, expanded in 1914 to become the Little Symphony.

In 1936 the New Friends of Music, founded by Ira Hirschmann, began an annual series of 16 concerts with a repertory ranging from solo sonatas to works for chamber orchestra, carefully selected to review certain eras or specific composers; the series lasted until 1953. While groups like the New Friends of Music concentrated on 18th- and 19th-century music, contemporary music was presented in regular concerts sponsored by the League of Composers and the American section of the International Society for Contemporary Music (both founded in 1923; they merged in 1954) and the National Association for American Composers and Conductors (1937). The music of young composers was heard in the Composers' Forum, active in New York until 1940 from its foundation in 1935 by Ashley Pettis; it was revived and sponsored jointly by the New York Public Library and Columbia University from 1947 to 1980, when it was reorganized independently. Early music became popular in performances by the New York Pro Musica (1952–73), founded by the conductor Noah Greenberg; the 13th-century *Play of Daniel* was performed in costume in 1958, and aroused an interest in authentic performance.

In 1925 40 chamber groups were identified as resident or as annual visitors; 50 years later at least 70 were resident and the number of visitors had increased. The Chamber Music Society of Lincoln Center, founded in 1968 by Charles Wadsworth with the support of Alice Tully, gives a series of programs emphasizing unfamiliar repertory performed by a group of outstanding musicians. Other mixed professional ensembles include the New York Chamber Soloists, Tashi, the New York Philharmonia, and the Bronx Arts Ensemble. The Juilliard, Galimir, Guarneri, Composers, American, Concord, Emerson, and Primavera string quartets are based in New York, as are the American Brass Quintet and the New York and Dorian woodwind quintets. 20th-century music in the city is performed by the Contemporary Chamber Ensemble (founded in 1960 by Arthur Weisberg), the Group for Contemporary Music (founded in 1962 by Harvey Sollberger and Charles Wuorinen), Continuum (founded in 1967 by Cheryl Seltzer and Joel Sachs as the Performers' Committee for 20th-century Music), Speculum Musicae, Parnassus, the Da Capo Chamber Players, and the New York New Music Ensemble, as well as several professional associations (see §13 below). Professional ensembles specializing in early music include the Waverly Consort, the Ensemble for Early Music, the Western Wind, Music for a While, Pomerium Musices, the New York Renaissance Band, Calliope, Concert Royal, and the New York Cornet and Sackbut Ensemble (*see also* EARLY-MUSIC REVIVAL).

7. CHORAL SOCIETIES. The earliest choral societies included a Handel and Haydn Society, which sang the first part of *The Creation* on 10 June 1818 at St. Paul's (in Trinity Parish), and the New York Choral Society, under James Swindells, which sang there before Lafayette during his visit in July 1824. The first established group on record is the Sacred Music Society (1823–49), which sang *Messiah* (using Mozart's accompaniments) under U. C. Hill in November 1831; the society had a chorus of 73 and an orchestra of 38 at that time, and the receipts of $900 imply a large audience. In 1838 the society performed Mendelssohn's *St. Paul* and Mozart's Requiem. The first serious rival to the Sacred Music Society was the Musical Institute, founded in 1844 and directed by H. C. Timm. In 1849 the two groups merged to form the New York Harmonic Society, their first concert being a performance of Mendelssohn's *Elijah* (June 1851) in Tripler Hall (seating *c*5000). The society lasted until 1868 and its conductors included Timm, Eisfeld, Bristow, Bergmann, Frederick Louis Ritter, and James Peck. An ambitious splinter group, the Mendelssohn Society, formed in 1863, was short-lived. In 1869 Peck directed the socially oriented Church Music Association; in 1873 Thomas imported a Boston chorus for a festival concert, an action considered an insult to the vocal and choral forces of New York.

New York's German population had two prominent men's choruses: the Deutsche Liederkranz, which gave its first concert on 17 May 1847 in the Apollo Rooms; and the Männergesangverein Arion, an offshoot formed in 1854. The Liederkranz numbered Thomas, Bergmann, Van der Stucken, and Leopold Damrosch among its conductors before 1895, while the Arion rose to prominence after getting Damrosch from Breslau to be its director in 1871. The two societies united in 1918 and celebrated a centenary in 1947. In 1866 a professional men's chorus, the Mendelssohn Glee Club, was formed, which also survived for a century. Its first permanent conductor (from 1867) was the violinist Joseph Mosenthal, a pupil of Louis Spohr and one of the city's leading church musicians; he died in 1896 while conducting a rehearsal of the group. Edward MacDowell then led the club until 1898; his successors were Arthur Mees, Frank Damrosch, Clarence Dickinson, Nelson Coffin, Ralph Baldwin, Cesare Sodero, and Ladislas Helfenbein. During the 20th century the membership shifted from professional to amateur singers, mainly businessmen, who sang popular favorites at private entertainments. Other men's clubs cultivating light music included the Downtown and University glee clubs, both conducted for many years by Channing Lefebvre and George Mead.

The longest-lived serious choral organization is the Oratorio Society of New York, founded in 1873 by Leopold Damrosch. Its first concert (3 December 1873) included works by Bach, Mozart, Palestrina, and Handel sung by a choir of about 50. In May 1874 the society gave Handel's *Samson* with orchestra, inaugurating the tradition of oratorio and large choral works that has continued to characterize the society's repertory. An annual Christmastide performance of *Messiah* was inherited from the late Harmonic Society in 1874 and has continued to be a feature of the group's program. Late in the 19th century choruses of 400 to 600 sang Brahms's *Ein deutsches Requiem* (1877), Berlioz's *Grande messe des morts* (1881), Liszt's *Christus* (1887), and Saint-Saëns' *Samson et Dalila* (1892), and introduced *Parsifal* to the USA in concert form (1886). After Leopold Damrosch's death in 1885 conductors of the Oratorio Society included his sons Walter (1885–98 and 1917–21) and Frank (1898–1912), Albert Stoessel (1921–43), William Strickland (1955–9), T. Charles Lee (1960–73), and Lyndon Woodside (from 1974).

Two organizations encouraging popular participation in music were the People's Choral Union and Singing Classes, organized in the city's lower East Side by Frank Damrosch in 1892 and continuing into the 1930s; and the People's Chorus of New York, founded and from 1916 to 1954 conducted by Lorenzo Camilieri. Both groups sometimes assembled choirs of 1000 voices.

Musical life was enriched by the Musical Art Society, a professional mixed chorus conducted by Frank Damrosch for 26 years from 1894, which performed Palestrina, Bach, and the *a cappella* repertory. Contemporary choral music including Hans Pfitzner's *Von deutscher Seele* (1923) and Arthur Honegger's *Le roi David* (1925) was presented by the Society of the Friends of Music (1913–31).

The Schola Cantorum grew out of a women's chorus established by Kurt Schindler in 1909, which became a mixed ensemble in 1910 and adopted its later name in 1912. Schindler conducted the choir until 1926, when Hugh Ross began a long tenure ending only with the group's final concert in 1971. The Schola Cantorum's programs often included unfamiliar works; Schindler introduced folk and religious music from the Basque region and Catalonia, and Ross conducted the New York premières of such works as Bloch's *Sacred Service* (1934), William Walton's *Belshazzar's Feast* (1935), Stravinsky's *Perséphone* (1936), and Delius's *Mass of Life* (1938).

Baroque music performed in authentic style characterized the programs of the Cantata Singers, founded in 1934 by Paul Boepple; later conductors of the ensemble – Arthur Mendel (1936–53), Alfred Mann (1953–9), Thomas Dunn (1959–67), and Robert Hickok (1968–9) – were also noted for their scholarship. The Dessoff Choirs grew out of Margarete Dessoff's Adesdi Chorus of women's voices organized in 1924; a mixed choir was begun in 1928, and from 1930 the combined ensembles directed by Dessoff performed under the present name. Boepple conducted the groups (which merged in 1942) from 1937 to 1968; subsequent conductors have been Thomas Sokol (1969–72), Michael Hammond (1973–82), and Amy Kaiser (from 1983). The Dessoff Choirs have specialized in music from the 14th to 17th centuries, often giving programs devoted to a single composer, like Josquin Desprez or Lassus. The Collegiate Chorale was founded in 1941 by Robert Shaw and conducted by him until 1953 with assistance (1949–52) from Margaret Hillis and William Jonson; later conductors were Mark Orton (1953–4), Ralph Hunter (1954–60), Abraham Kaplan (1961–73), Richard Westenburg (1973–9), and Robert Bass (from 1979); this amateur ensemble has performed both large standard works and contemporary pieces.

The Bach Aria Group, directed by William Scheide from 1946 to 1980, performed with internationally renowned operatic soloists and instrumentalists. Musica Sacra, organized by Westenburg in 1970 at the Central Presbyterian Church, has become the most prominent professional choral ensemble in New York, praised in particular for its annual Basically Bach Festival begun in the summer of 1978. Other organizations employing professional choral singers are Musica Aeterna, conducted from 1969 by Frederic Waldman, and the National Chorale (founded in 1959), led by Martin Josman.

Amateur singers participate in a variety of large and small choral groups, among them the Canterbury Choral Society (formed 1952, founding conductor Charles Walker), the New York Choral Society (1959, music director since 1970 Robert de Cormier), the Sine Nomine Singers (1967, founding conductor Harry Saltzman), the Canticum Novum Singers (1972, conductor Harold Rosenbaum), the New Amsterdam Singers (1968, 1968–72 as the Master Institute Chorus, conductor Clara Longstreth), Cappella Nova (1975, conductor Richard Taruskin), the New Calliope Singers (1976, founding conductor Peter Schubert), and David Randolph's Masterwork Chorus (1955), a New Jersey group that performs frequently in New York.

8. CHURCH MUSIC. Trinity Church at the top of Wall Street (fig.6) became the first important center of music in New York through the activity of William Tuckey (see §1 above), and the church continued to exert a powerful influence over sacred music in the city for over two centuries. The first organist, John Clemm (1741–4), was probably the son of Johann Gottlob Klemm, the builder of the organ. After a fallow period, during which George K. Jackson's *Te Deum* in F was sung weekly for over two decades, Edward Hodges's arrival in 1846 revived Trinity's music with the introduction of a new repertory and a boys' choir. 18,000 people attended a two-day inauguration of a new organ built by Henry Erben, installed in 1846. Later organists there included H. S. Cutler, A. H. Messiter, Victor Baier, Channing Lefebvre, George Mead, and Larry King, the last four of whom maintained the popular tradition of midday concerts.

One of the first examples of psalmody published in New York was *Psalms of David for the Dutch Reformed Church* (1767); a later important collection of psalm settings was *A Selection of Psalm Tunes for Use of the Protestant Episcopal Church in New York* (1812), revised to include the works of five American composers in 1828. Thomas Hastings held various positions in New York from 1832 to 1872 and was an influential force in the city's musical development.

During the 19th century many churches developed extensive musical programs. Large mixed choirs, led by quartets of highly paid professional singers, and organs with several manuals became standard. Many distinguished organists, who often shared the duties of choir director, composer, and teacher, served in the city, among them Samuel Prowse Warren at Grace Episcopal (1867–94), George William Warren at St. Thomas (1870–1900), and Harry Rowe Shelley at the Church of the Pilgrims and Central Congregational in Brooklyn and at the Fifth Avenue Baptist Church (1878–1936). G. W. Warren's son Richard held positions in various city churches for 50 years from 1880. William Crane Carl was at the First Presbyterian from 1892 to 1936, and Walter Henry Hall was active in New York from 1896 to 1935 at several churches, among them the Cathedral of St. John the Divine. Charles Ives served at Central Presbyterian (1900–02), and in Brooklyn Raymond Huntington Woodman was at the First Presbyterian (1880–1941), John Hyatt Brewer in several positions from 1871 to 1930, and Dudley Buck at Holy Trinity (1877–1901).

Pietro Yon at St. Francis Xavier (1908–26) and St. Patrick (1926–43), Clarence Dickinson at Brick Presbyterian (1909–59), and T. Tertius Noble at St. Thomas (1913–47) had long, distinguished careers. Like many of their colleagues they pub-

6. *Trinity Church (at the top of Wall Street) after its rebuilding in 1788; lithograph*

lished anthems and larger choral works, the octavo editions of which sold millions of copies. Seth Bingham at Madison Avenue Presbyterian (1912–51), Samuel A. Baldwin (active 1895–1932), and W. Lynnwood Farnam at the Church of the Holy Communion (1920–30) were especially fine organists.

By the 1970s choirs had become smaller, but many churches maintained the practice of performing large-scale sacred works, often on Sunday afternoons or evenings. Among these musically active churches are St. Bartholomew, the Church of the Ascension, Riverside, St. Thomas, the Cathedral of St. John the Divine, the Church of our Saviour, Holy Trinity Lutheran, St. Patrick's Cathedral, St. Ignatius, First Presbyterian, the Fifth Avenue Presbyterian, St. Mary the Virgin, Corpus Christi, and St. Peter (noted for its jazz and choral programs).

9. Avant-garde music. The conscious cultivation of experimental musical activity in New York dates from the 1920s, and was the result of the convergence of several trends. One was the nascent self-awareness of American composers. Another was the rise of New York as the capital of American culture and its music business. A third was the sudden internationalism forced upon American artists and intellectuals by the country's involvement in World War I. The timing meant that avant-garde activities in New York had a distinctively French cast. Unlike the previous generation of American composers, trained largely in Germany, most of those who were active in New York between the world wars were men who had studied in Paris with Nadia Boulanger (above all Aaron Copland and Virgil Thomson) or were part of Edgard Varèse's circle. There were exceptions, as in Roger Sessions's participation in the Copland–Sessions concerts from 1928 to 1931 (but Copland was more the driving force behind these than Sessions).

Although the history of new music in New York can be traced through the composers who lived in the city or who made it their showcase, a better measure is the shifting constellation of organizations, new-music publications, and performance spaces. Between the wars, sponsoring organizations included the League of Composers (founded 1923), with which Copland was deeply involved (its journal *Modern Music*, 1924–46, was particularly influential), the American branch of the International Society for Contemporary Music, and two organizations founded by Varèse – the International Composers' Guild (1921–7) and the Pan American Association of Composers (1928–34). Henry Cowell's series of scores (*New Music*), begun in 1927, was also important.

The Depression led to a diminution of overt experimentation in the 1930s. In a sense, this retrenchment lasted to the mid-1940s although the Composers' Forum, founded in 1935, carried on the sponsorship of new-music concerts. The arrival in New York of many important European composers reinforced internationalist tendencies and fostered a younger generation of American composers who came to dominate new music after World War II. The most creative of the immigrant composers to settle in New York was Béla Bartók, who taught at Columbia University; the most important immigrant teacher in New York was Stefan Wolpe. Paul Hindemith also had some impact on the city from his position at Yale in New Haven.

Beginning in the 1950s, New York avant-gardism became marked by a division of sensibilities that was subsequently labeled "uptown" and "downtown." More visible at first was the "uptown" serialist school (and its nonserialist but equally rationalist allies), linked with the academy. This group not only controlled the concerts of the combined League of Composers and ISCM, but later founded new performance groups that specialized in dense, highly dissonant, chromatic music: the Group for Contemporary

Music, begun at Columbia in 1962 by Charles Wuorinen and Harvey Sollberger, Speculum Musicae (1971), and the New York New Music Ensemble (1975).

The rationalist sensibility was also active in the first American experiments in electronic music, which centered on New York. The key figure was Milton Babbitt, although his serialist practices were not strictly followed by other pioneers of electronic composition. Landmark events included the creation by John Cage of the tape work *Imaginary Landscape no.5* (1951–2) and the first American tape-music concert, which Otto Luening and Vladimir Ussachevsky produced on 28 October 1952 at the Museum of Modern Art. In 1959 the RCA Mark II synthesizer was installed at Columbia University and the Columbia–Princeton Electronic Music Center, directed by Babbitt, Luening, Ussachevsky, and Sessions, was founded.

Cage's work became the focus of "downtown" new-music activity in the 1950s, in part because of his music directorship of Merce Cunningham's dance company and his classes at the New School for Social Research. Cage's closest disciples were Christian Wolff, David Tudor, Morton Feldman, and Earle Brown; their work was paralleled by the New York activities of Fluxus, which prefigured the varied forms of mixed-media experimentation of the 1960s and beyond. Allan Kaprow, the inventor of "happenings," was a part of the Cage circle, as were Toshi Ichiyanagi, Jackson Mac Low, Nam June Paik, and La Monte Young. In the 1960s another focus of "downtown" activity was Experiments in Art and Technology (EAT), which fostered collaborations among artists and between artists and scientists, owing to its association with the Bell Telephone Laboratories in Murray Hill, New Jersey.

Experimental concerts were held at nightclubs (the Electric Circus) and at the major New York art museums (the Whitney, the Guggenheim, the Museum of Modern Art) long before they were accepted by the more conservative midtown musical organizations. But the bulk of experimental activity in the 1970s and 1980s has taken place under the auspices of new organizations located in the lofts of lower Manhattan. Chief among them is the Kitchen, founded in 1971 as a video and music space in the former kitchen of a hotel. Other important music facilities in the New York vanguard include the Experimental Intermedia Foundation (located in Phill Niblock's loft), Roulette, and the Alternative Museum (see also §3 above).

The multi-media activities of some downtown artists (notably Meredith Monk) have resulted in the presentation of music in spaces normally devoted to other arts: the Dance Theater Workshop, Franklin Furnace, the Clocktower, and P. S. 122. There are also summer series, notably "Creative Time," which sponsors events outdoors and in unusual locales around the city.

Some performers have succeeded in expanding their audiences by appearing in rock clubs, notably Glass, Reich, Laura Dean, and Laurie Anderson, who gave rock concerts after her commercial success in Great Britain and her contract with a major record label. By the early 1980s experimental music in New York had begun to overlap with avant-garde jazz and rock. Composers such as Glenn Branca, Rhys Chatham, and Peter Gordon, and bands including Sonic Youth moved freely between experimental performance spaces and rock clubs; avant-garde rock musicians, among them Arto Lindsay, Elliott Sharpe, and John Zorn, have attracted some attention from new-music circles, and jazz composers such as Henry Threadgill and Joseph Jarman play both at jazz clubs and in Carnegie Recital Hall.

Experimental music has long been a limited offering at the city's major halls, although in the 1970s Reich and Glass gave sold-out concerts of their music at Town Hall and Carnegie Hall. "Uptown" new-music groups have also appeared at Hunter College, Alice Tully Hall, and the 92nd Street "Y". Concert spaces that present a large proportion of new music evolved elsewhere, notably Symphony Space uptown and Cooper Union downtown. By the 1980s, however, signs were pointing to the acceptance

7. *"The Gospel at Colonus" by Lee Breuer and Bob Telson, given its première at the Brooklyn Academy of Music during the "Next Wave" festival in December 1983; performers include (right) Clarence Fountain and the Five Blind Boys of Alabama*

of experimental music in more traditional locations. The Brooklyn Academy of Music became an important sponsor of new-music activities with its "Next Wave" events and festivals (fig. 7) and in Lukas Foss's "Meet the Moderns" series with the Brooklyn PO. At Lincoln Center, Horizons festivals in 1983 and 1984, sponsored by the New York PO under the direction of composer-in-residence Jacob Druckman, offered a dramatic midtown showcase for a wide variety of new music. Other performing groups – the American Composers Orchestra, the Composers' Showcase, and Continuum – perform contemporary music while steering a course between the various new-music factions.

Other factors contributing to a favorable climate for new music in New York are wide coverage in the *New York Times*, the *Village Voice*, and other publications, and a proliferation of recording companies devoted to new music, among them CRI, Nonesuch, Chatham Square, and Lovely Music. The New Music Distribution Service in New York is the principal distribution organization for these and other labels. Another important organization for the dissemination of avant-garde music is Performing Artservices, an arts-management firm that has arranged European tours for its clients, among them Cage, Glass, and Robert Ashley.

The first national New Music America festival was held in New York in 1979. Called New Music/New York, it was sponsored by the Kitchen. During the festival, the New Music Alliance was formed to create a network of performance spaces around the country; the Alliance has sponsored the subsequent festivals.

See also EXPERIMENTAL MUSIC.

10. RAGTIME AND JAZZ. Although New York was not the birthplace of jazz, the city's role in jazz history has been significant, and from the late 1920s it was decisive. As the seat of most major recording companies and radio networks, it has attracted the best jazz musicians and provided the most favorable opportunities for performing, hearing, and preserving the music. Most of the important innovations in jazz originated in New York, and for decades young jazz musicians throughout the USA and abroad have regarded success in New York as the true test of their talent.

New York's importance to jazz began with ragtime. A syncopated, rag-like music was heard on the New York minstrel stages in the late 1880s, but the term "ragtime" first became popularly associated with this music when it was introduced at Tony Pastor's Music Hall on 14th Street by the singer and pianist Ben Harney in the mid-1890s. By 1899 New York music publishers had issued dozens of instrumental and vocal rags, and ragtime was soon a regular feature in theaters and dance halls throughout the city. Indicative of the music's popularity, and of the reaction in some circles against it, was the decision of a city commissioner in 1902 to ban ragtime from a series of free summer concerts. In its more jazz-like manifestations, ragtime flourished in saloons, gambling houses, and brothels of the Tenderloin district, which extended from 23rd to 42nd streets along Sixth Avenue and to its west. Among the more notable establishments was a plush, genteel club called Ike Hine's, which had a clientele consisting principally of black intellectuals and entertainment figures. "One-leg" Willie Nelson, a pianist much admired by Eubie Blake, played at Barron Wilkins's Little Savoy Club, the most famous of the ragtime clubs, on 32nd Street at Eighth Avenue. In the second decade of the century the Little Savoy Club was moved to Harlem, where Luckey Roberts became the house pianist and Jelly Roll Morton was a frequent guest. In an area called "the jungles" (from 59th to 65th streets, west of Ninth Avenue) were several ragtime clubs, including the Jungles Casino (on 65th Street, near Ninth Avenue), a dance hall where some of the greatest talents of the period – Roberts, James P. Johnson, Abba Labba, and Willie "the Lion" Smith – were heard. It was frequented by merchant seamen from Charleston, and it was there that the charleston dance is said to have originated, and that Johnson wrote his famous song of the same name.

Ragtime was also played by large ensembles, particularly Sousa's band and the bands of his rivals Arthur Pryor and Charles Prince, as well as later groups led by James Reese Europe, Fred Bryan, and Tim Brymn. These groups recorded widely, beginning as early as 1897, and in May 1912 the Clef Club, a hiring hall for black musicians on West 53rd Street, sponsored a Carnegie Hall concert by a 125-member "jazz orchestra." Although orchestral ragtime (or "syncopated music," as it was also known) bore only a faint resemblance to later jazz, it set the stage for the remarkable school of orchestral jazz that flourished in New York from the 1920s.

New York had its own indigenous school of commercialized ragtime, which was certainly the most active and widely published of the time, but it also attracted musicians of the Missouri or "classic" school, the principal exponent of which was Scott Joplin and the main publisher John Stark, both of whom had moved to New York by 1910. Many elements of piano ragtime were taken up by the Harlem or "stride" pianists, who performed at clubs and private social functions throughout the city. The leaders of this school – Johnson, Smith, Roberts, and Fats Waller – were frequently recorded in the 1920s, and their high technical standards and inventive improvisation established them as the earliest jazz pianists (in the full sense of the term).

The beginning of New York's jazz history might be set at January 1917, when the Original Dixieland Jazz Band made a phenomenally successful appearance at Reisenweber's nightclub on Eighth Avenue. Although other New Orleans jazz groups such as Freddie Keppard's had already appeared in New York by that time, none had the combination of showmanship and shrewd publicity that made the Original Dixieland Jazz Band instantaneously an international phenomenon. The band made its first jazz recording (for Columbia Records in New York) in January 1917 and had sold two million copies of its second one, made in February, by the end of the year. The success of this ensemble spawned hundreds of similarly named white jazz groups in the city, of which the much-recorded Original Memphis Five with Miff Mole and Red Nichols was the most important. Jazz features were also taken over by many of the city's dance bands, particularly that of Paul Whiteman, whose name became a byword for jazz in the 1920s. Although Whiteman's "symphonic jazz" was later discredited as a bowdlerized form of the music, he hired true jazz performers such as Bix Beiderbecke and Frankie Trumbauer, and his performances set standards of musicianship that were emulated by large jazz ensembles throughout the country.

Among the important black New York bands to profit from Whiteman's example were those of Fletcher Henderson and Duke Ellington. Each of these leaders hired first-rate jazz soloists as early as 1924, notably Louis Armstrong (with Henderson) and Sidney Bechet (with Ellington). Henderson's arranger Don Redman was among the first to transform Armstrong's "hot" style into an orchestral idiom, developing a repertory that determined much of the swing-band music of the following decade. Less influential, though of greater artistic merit, were the experiments of Ellington, who from the mid-1920s combined commercial dance music with ingenious idiomatic arrangements and later produced what are widely regarded as the most significant efforts in jazz composition.

By the end of the 1920s New York had become the center of the American jazz scene. Armstrong, Jelly Roll Morton, King Oliver, and Red Allen, the leading musicians in the late New Orleans style, all lived there, as did most of the important musicians of the Chicago school following the suppression of that city's underground "speakeasy" culture. Nichols and Mole had created an indigenous New York style of small-combo jazz characterized by well-integrated ensembles and comparatively advanced arrangements, while Beiderbecke, in a great many recordings with various ad hoc studio groups, was producing some of the greatest masterpieces of early jazz. Important sites of jazz activity included the original Roseland, which opened on Broadway at 51st Street in 1919, and such Harlem clubs as the Cotton Club, the Renaissance Casino and Ballroom, the Lenox Avenue Club, the Apollo Theater (fig.8), and the Alhambra Ballroom. Big bands on the Henderson model proliferated: bandleaders such as Henderson, Ellington, Luis Russell, Jimmie Lunceford, Cab Calloway, Chick Webb, Benny Goodman, and Charlie Barnet, all performed, broadcast, and recorded in New York in the 1930s, and Count Basie's group, the most important jazz orchestra of the competing Kansas City tradition, was based in New York from 1937. The recognition of jazz by the country's established musical institutions was marked in 1938 by Benny Goodman's concert at Carnegie Hall, and the country's historical interest in the genre was demonstrated there the same year by John Hammond's retrospective "Spirituals to Swing" concerts.

8. *The Apollo Theater, Harlem, 1947*

The repeal of Prohibition led in the 1930s to the establishment of numerous small clubs, some of which featured jazz ensembles. Several clubs on 52nd Street – the Onyx, the Three Deuces, the Spotlight, Jimmy Ryan's, the Famous Door, and Kelly's Stable – promoted advanced swing jazz in small combinations. Ryan's club later became a center for traditional jazz, as did Nick's and Eddie Condon's in Greenwich Village; other 52nd Street clubs became important venues for the bop style after its early development in informal sessions in Harlem at Minton's Playhouse and Monroe's Uptown House in the early 1940s. Later jazz clubs specializing in bop and its offshoots included Café Society, Birdland, the Royal Roost, the Half Note, the Five Spot, the Village Vanguard, and the Village Gate. The Five Spot in particular fostered avant-garde jazz; the origins of free jazz are often dated from the appearance there of Cecil Taylor in 1957 and Ornette Coleman in 1959. Although developments in this genre took place in Europe, New York shared with Chicago the leadership of the free-jazz scene and saw the origins in the 1960s of free-jazz groups like the New York Contemporary Five with John Tchicai and Don Cherry, the New York Art Quartet, the Jazz Composer's Orchestra, and the musicians associated with LeRoi Jones's Black Arts Repertory Theater. Among the most important of the city's later developments in jazz was the relocation of the Newport Jazz Festival to New York in 1972. The festival (renamed the Kool Jazz Festival in 1981) is held for two weeks at various inner-city locations (ranging from Carnegie Hall to Roseland) and elsewhere outside the city limits. It is a showcase for traditional jazz, as well as for avant-garde music and other forms of popular music.

New York's leadership in avant-garde jazz continued unabated through the 1960s and 1970s, bolstered by new influxes of musicians from regional jazz centers in Chicago (many of whom were associated with the Association for the Advancement of Creative Musicians and its offshoots), St. Louis, and Los Angeles. The performance spaces of lower Manhattan provided black jazz musicians with the opportunity to develop a sharpened sense of artistic self-awareness. The concentration on rock by recording companies after the late 1960s made it difficult for stylistically venturesome jazz players to record. In New York, some older clubs – notably the Village Vanguard and the Village Gate – continued to provide employment; but in the 1970s, in emulation of visual artists and experimental classical musicians, many jazz players organized and performed in "loft" concerts.

By the late 1970s, avant-garde musicians (among them the groups Air and the World Saxophone Quartet, and such individuals as David Murray, Henry Threadgill, and Julius Hemphill) had become sufficiently successful to win recording contracts (often from small European labels) and to be engaged at newly revived jazz clubs, leading to a decline in loft concerts. They were joined by older musicians (such as Gil Evans), who were stimulated by the vitality of New York jazz. Such organizations as Soundscape and the Public Theater emphasized newer styles.

11. Ethnic and popular music. New York has enjoyed a rich exposure to many varieties of ethnic music as each successive wave of immigrants brought new musical cultures to the city. Mention has been made of the importance of German singing societies to the city's choral life in the 19th century (see §7 above); in the last decades of the century many Irish and Italian immigrants brought their traditional music to New York, as did the Hungarians, Czechs, Russians, Ukrainians, Greeks, and others. In the early part of the 20th century especially, Jewish actors

and dramatists from Russia made downtown Second Avenue a center of the Yiddish stage; operettas and musical revues presented there had a further influence on popular songwriters, many of whom were of Jewish origin. The 1960s and 1970s saw a constant flux of folk and ethnic styles that enjoyed a commercial viability in New York, either in their local communities or in the larger pop-music market. These included a wide range of Latin styles, principally Puerto Rican but also Cuban, Dominican, and others. Reggae has enjoyed favor in the Jamaican enclaves of Queens and Brooklyn, and at such Manhattan nightclubs as Negril. Greek, Middle Eastern, and Asian music is performed live and on radio. Country music found a foothold at the Lone Star Cafe. In the early 1980s various types of third-world music have become popular; after the craze for Brazilian jazz and bossa nova in the 1960s, there has been renewed interest in Brazilian music at such clubs as Sounds of Brazil. (*See also* ASIAN-AMERICAN MUSIC, EUROPEAN-AMERICAN MUSIC, HISPANIC-AMERICAN MUSIC, and JEWISH-AMERICAN MUSIC, §3(ii).)

Of all the folk-based popular musical styles, rock-and-roll provided New York's most notable pop-music contributions after 1950. Although it developed out of a rebellion by rural Whites and Blacks against the dominant New York and Hollywood pop styles, rock soon became firmly established in New York, owing in part to the extension of Tin Pan Alley's institutional structures into the rock field. Songwriters, including Carole King, Ellie Greenwich, and Doc Pomus, many of whom worked in teams in the Brill Building on Broadway, turned out rock songs with the same facility as songwriters of the big-band era. New York was also a center of doo-wop, which was largely a product of black and Italian-American communities of the East Coast. During the early and mid-1960s, such groups as the Blues Project and the Young Rascals (later the Rascals) gained local and national popularity, but they brought little of their New York background to their variants of pop styles of the day.

In the early 1960s, musicians who played in such Greenwich Village clubs as the Bitter End and Folk City forged a creative union between rock and folk music. The product of self-consciously artistic, city-born composers, folk-rock differed from the anonymous, oral folk tradition; rather it was derived from the narrative folk and blues song traditions, and was at first usually accompanied by an acoustic guitar played by the singer. The inspiration for the folk revival was Woody Guthrie, and the most famous figure to emerge in the 1960s was Bob Dylan; others included Peter, Paul and Mary, the Lovin' Spoonful, and Simon and Garfunkel, who popularized extended folk elements among a broader audience. Folk music of this sort lost its commercial cachet in the late 1960s, after Dylan took up electric instruments in 1965, but it has continued to produce fresh, young talent into the 1980s; notable performers include the McGarrigle Sisters (who returned to their native Montreal in the late 1970s), the Roches, and Suzanne Vega.

A new indigenous brand of New York rock emerged in the late 1960s with the Velvet Underground. Their spare, self-aware, ominous music, and their connections with Andy Warhol and the pop-art school, proved enormously influential. The group inspired the worldwide punk rock and new-wave movements, encouraging a return to the basics of rock music after the romanticized inflation of rock of the late 1960s and early 1970s. The New York Dolls may be seen as transitional figures; in the mid-1970s there emerged a number of striking performers, among them Patti Smith, Blondie, Television, and Talking Heads, whose cool rock minimalism proved most enduring.

New York rock evolved in the late 1970s and early 1980s into an often deliberately primitive art rock, fostered by such musicians as Glenn Branca, Sonic Youth, Arto Lindsay, and Elliott Sharpe. The New York area was also the spawning ground of such popular heavy-metal groups as Blue Oyster Cult and Kiss. Related to art rock and free jazz was a school of "free improvisation" or "noise rock." Such musicians as John Zorn and Fred Frith produced highly animated, extremely loud improvisations full of exotic sound effects and propelled by an almost visceral energy.

In the early 1980s the most influential innovation in New York popular music was rap, the cadenced, rapid-fire chanting of lyrics, which often reflected social concerns, over a pounding funk beat. This new upsurge of musical energy from the black community has not only led to a revival of black music-making of all kinds in New York, but has had a significant effect on pop music nationally.

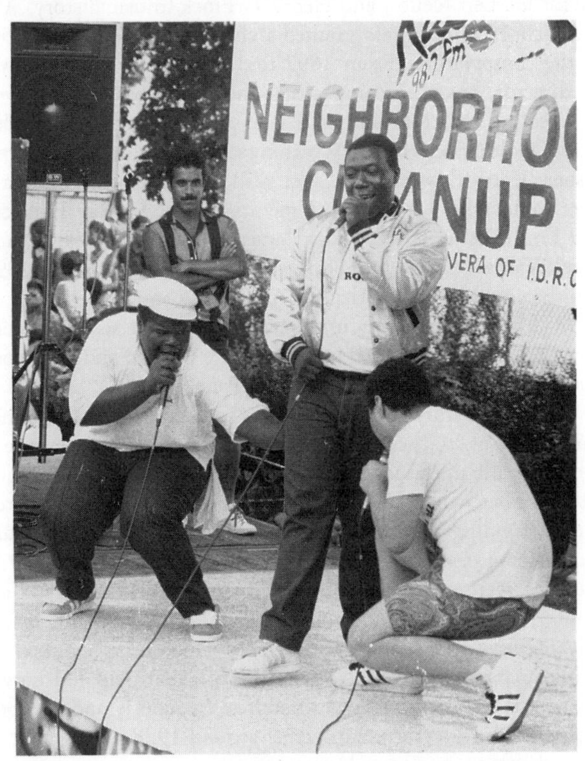

9. The Fatboys performing at a street concert in Staten Island, 1984, sponsored by the FM radio station WRKS-Kiss to promote the "Neighborhood Cleanup" campaign: (left to right) Darren "the Human Beat Box" Robinson, Damon "Kool Rocski" Wimbley, and Mark "Prince Markie Dee" Morales

See also POPULAR MUSIC, §§III and IV.

12. EDUCATION. Music schools offering professional training became important in New York in the second half of the 19th century. One of the longest-lived was the New York College of Music, founded in 1878. Having absorbed the German Conservatory in 1920 and the American Conservatory in 1923, it was itself incorporated into New York University in 1968. A Metropolitan Conservatory, begun as a school of singing in 1886,

became the Metropolitan College of Music in 1891 and the American Institute of Applied Music in 1900. It survived some 40 years but eventually succumbed to financial troubles.

The most ambitious of the schools during this period was the National Conservatory of Music in America, founded in 1885 by Jeannette Thurber and a group of financiers to encourage the growth of a viable, indigenous, national musical culture. Concentrating at first on a vocal curriculum, it opened at 128 East 17th Street with a small faculty under the direction of the Belgian baritone Jacques Bouhy; instruction followed the example of the Paris Conservatoire. In 1885 Thurber also established the American Opera Company, partly to give performance opportunities to the conservatory's students. From 1888 instrumentalists and theorists also joined the faculty: Rafael Joseffy and Adèle Margulies (piano), Leopold Lichtenberg (violin and chamber music), Victor Herbert (cello), and Henry T. Finck (music history). On 3 March 1891 Congress granted a charter (Public Act no. 159) to the conservatory. From 1892 to 1895 Antonín Dvořák was its director, teaching composition and instrumentation as well as directing the choir and orchestra, and his students included Rubin Goldmark, Harvey Worthington Loomis, William Arms Fisher, Harry Rowe Shelley, and Will Marion Cook. Goldmark later joined the faculty; other members were Gustav Hinrichs and Emil Fischer (opera class), James G. Huneker (piano), and Frank Van der Stucken (orchestra and chorus director). In 1894 Thurber established a prize for American composition, and in 1898–9 the conservatory orchestra gave its first season of concerts; these took place at Madison Square Garden and were conducted by the school's director Emil Paur.

The conservatory's initial plan was for a three-year full-time, paid course of study for students under 24; black, handicapped, and musically untrained students were to be among those admitted. Thurber, who gave $1 million to the conservatory, explored various funding proposals over the years and founded auxiliary fund-raising organizations in Eastern cities. Although by 1910 the conservatory's reputation rivaled that of the Peabody, Cincinnati, and New England conservatories, it fell far behind these private institutions in funding and ultimately succumbed to public apathy. It moved to West 79th Street around 1915; over the next ten years it changed its address frequently and dropped from musical directories altogether around 1928.

Settlement schools fared better than these early conservatories. Founded to provide musical training for underprivileged children and to provide service to the community, several schools of this kind are still active. The Henry Street Settlement was founded in 1893 by Lillian D. Wald. Music was offered as part of the curriculum from the beginning, but the music school opened only in 1927, with an enrollment of fewer than 100 students. Enrollment has reached 1000 pupils with a faculty of nearly 100; the preparatory and advanced departments offer courses in all instruments, theory, and performance by ensembles (including orchestra, opera, chorus, band, jazz group, and recorder ensemble). The Third Street Music School Settlement was founded in 1894 by Emilie Wagner and incorporated in 1903. Directors of the school have included David Mannes, Julius Rudel, and Robert Ward, and the school has been the training ground for many distinguished artists, among them Anthony di Bonaventura, Mario di Bonaventura, Samuel Dushkin, Joseph Gingold, and Sidney Harth. In the 1980s the school's concert series included "Music New to New York" (under the direction of Barbara Kolb) and "Music Downtown" (directed by Mimi Stern-Wolfe). The Turtle Bay Music School was founded by Eleanor Stanley White in 1925 and incorporated three years later. Regular students, whether their goals are professional or amateur, follow a program leading to a degree; lessons are offered in instrumental music, theory, and ensemble performance. The school also has a noteworthy program in music therapy. The Greenwich House Music School, founded in 1906, has been known for its opera department and its fine community orchestra.

State schools offered sporadic music education from 1856 but no clear course until 1898. In 1976 nearly 1700 music teachers served in elementary and secondary schools. The High School of Music and Art, from 1984 combined with the High School of the Performing Arts as the Fiorello LaGuardia High School, provides an opportunity for students to specialize in music theory, history, and performance, along with regular academic subjects. In addition to the settlement schools, instruction is available at such schools as the Harlem School of the Arts, the Dalcroze and Diller-Quaile schools, and the Bloomingdale House of Music.

The Juilliard School was founded in New York in 1905 by Frank Damrosch as the Institute of Musical Art. From the first, Damrosch recruited prominent European and American musicians for the faculty. In 1926 the institute was taken over by the Juilliard Musical Foundation, which had been established six years earlier through the legacy of Augustus D. Juilliard and had opened the Juilliard Graduate School in 1924. The institute and graduate school were amalgamated in 1946 under the new name of the Juilliard School of Music. A department of dance (later called the Dance Division) was added in 1951, and the Theater Center was founded in 1968. With the move to the present site at Lincoln Center in 1968, the name of the school was changed to the Juilliard School. The Juilliard's American Opera Center, begun in 1970 as a forum for young professional singers, presents at least three operas each year, and a program for the development of young American conductors was established in 1978.

Juilliard awards BM, MM, and DMA degrees in performance and composition and a BFA in drama and dance. Admission is based entirely on audition and enrollment is over 900. The school's facilities include Alice Tully Hall, two theaters, a recital hall, and the Lila Acheson Wallace Library, which houses some items of special interest, including the Edwards Collection of 19th-century chamber music, early and rare Liszt editions, opera scores and French opera librettos of the 19th and 20th centuries, the papers of the critic Ernest Newman, and 15 manuscripts of the composer Eugène Ysaÿe. Damrosch was succeeded as president by John Erskine (1928–37), Ernest Hutcheson (1937–45), William Schuman (1945–62), Peter Mennin (1962–83), and Joseph W. Polisi (from 1984). Among the school's most famous graduates are Leontyne Price, Leonard Rose, Itzhak Perlman, Pinchas Zukerman, Rosalyn Tureck, and Van Cliburn. Prominent among its teachers have been Milton Babbitt, Elliott Carter, Ivan Galamian, Dorothy DeLay, Josef Lhévinne, Rosina Lhévinne, and Olga Samaroff.

The Mannes College of Music was founded in 1916 by David Mannes and his wife Clara Damrosch; their son, Leopold Damrosch Mannes, was director from 1940 until his death in 1964. First known as the David Mannes School, the college became a degree-granting institution in 1953. It was the first school of music in the USA to offer a degree program in the performance of early music. Mannes awards a BS, BM, and an MM degree. Sidney Gelber was appointed president in 1964, Hubert Doris in 1970, and Risë Stevens in 1975. The college survived a financial crisis and reorganization in the mid-1970s, and under Charles Kaufman (appointed president in 1979) moved from East 74th Street to 150 West 85th Street in 1984.

The Manhattan School of Music, a conservatory founded by the philanthropist Janet D. Schenck in 1917 as the Neighborhood Music School, offers a BM degree and MM and DMA degrees in various subjects. John Brownlee, president from 1956 to 1969, expanded the school's opera department; in 1969 George Schick became president and the school moved to the Claremont Avenue building vacated by the Juilliard School. Schick was succeeded in 1976 by John Crosby. The school's facilities include the Martinson Electronic Music Laboratory, an auditorium (seating 1000), and two recital halls.

Two private universities in the city have strong academic courses in music. Columbia University (founded as King's College in 1754), the first institution of higher learning in New York state and the fifth in the country, received its first endowment for the study of music in 1896. The first professor of music to be appointed was Edward MacDowell; subsequent chairmen of the music department have included Daniel Gregory Mason and Douglas S. Moore. The first musicology chair at Columbia was endowed in 1931, and Paul Henry Lang was its first occupant. In 1944 Otto Luening became the chairman of the music department at Barnard College, Columbia's women's affiliate; he was one of the founders of the Columbia–Princeton Electronic Music Center. In addition to a BA degree and an MA in music theory, Columbia offers MA and PhD degrees in musicology, ethnomusicology, and composition. The university's Teachers College, devoted to graduate study in education, also maintains an active music department. New York University offers advanced degrees in musicology and education. The Union Theological Seminary's School of Sacred Music (1923–73) was absorbed by Yale University in 1974.

The City University of New York (CUNY) consists of a graduate center and many four- and two-year colleges, most of which offer academic and some both academic and practical instruction in music. Hunter, Queens, Brooklyn, and City colleges have strong music departments, and all offer opportunities for performance. In 1981 the Brooklyn and Queens departments were renamed respectively the Conservatory of Music and the Aaron Copland School of Music; the former is the seat of the Institute for Studies in American Music (founded 1971). A doctoral program was established at the University Graduate Center on 42nd Street in 1968; by 1983 it was ranked among the best in the country. The center is the home of two bibliographical projects, the Répertoire International de Littérature Musicale (RILM) and the Répertoire International d'Iconographie Musicale (RIdIM).

Cowell, Copland, and Cage all taught at the New School for Social Research, which offers courses in music appreciation, literature, theory, and chamber music. Frank Wigglesworth is the director of musical activities.

13. ASSOCIATIONS AND ORGANIZATIONS. One of the first associations organized to promote the works of local composers was the Manuscript Society, founded in August 1889 and reorganized in 1899 as the Society of American Musicians and Composers. In 1914 a group of men concerned principally with popular music, including Victor Herbert, formed the American Society of Composers, Authors and Publishers (ASCAP), later the foremost American association for the protection of copyright musical works. ASCAP is a nonprofit organization, representing both serious and popular music, that collects and distributes licensing fees for public performance. Broadcast Music, Inc. (BMI), an association formed in 1940, performs a similar function. The American Composers Alliance (ACA), founded in 1938 by Copland and others, was later affiliated with BMI. National in scope, these organizations have their headquarters in New York, ASCAP occupying a large building directly facing Lincoln Center. Organized labor is represented in New York by Local 802 of the American Federation of Musicians, which includes instrumental ensemble musicians in all spheres, and the American Guild of Musical Artists (AGMA), which has represented opera and concert artists since its formation in 1936.

Other nonprofit organizations in the city have been actively concerned with the promotion of music and the welfare of musicians. The Beethoven Association (1919–40) under its president Harold Bauer was an important force in sponsoring concerts, publications, and charitable works. The National Federation of Music Clubs (founded 1898) encourages young musicians throughout the country. The American Music Center (1939) has served as a reference and information center in New York, encouraging the performance of contemporary American music. The League of Composers, Composers Forum, ACA, and National Association for American Composers and Conductors (founded by Henry Hadley in 1933) have sponsored many concerts locally.

The principal musicians' club in New York is the Bohemians, a service and social organization founded in 1907 by Rafael Joseffy. More specialized societies have included the Composers Collective of New York; the New York Music Critics' Circle (1941–65), which offered citations, discussions, and professional encouragement; the American Guild of Organists, the headquarters of which have been in New York since its formation in 1896; and the Charles Ives Society, active from 1973.

New York is also the national center for concert management. In the 1980s over half the serious artists' representatives and concert managers, including the influential Columbia Artists Management, were in New York.

14. PUBLISHING, INSTRUMENT MAKING, BROADCASTING, AND RECORDING. Early music publishers were often also dealers. James Hewitt (active 1793–1819) and his son James L. Hewitt (1830–47) had a music store and published music, as did John Paff from 1798 to 1817 and Joseph Atwill from 1833 to 1850. William Dubois (1813–54) also dealt in pianos, and Edward Riley (1806–50) taught music. In 1815 Firth & Hall, joined in 1833 by William Pond, began an important association that lasted under various names until 1884. Sheet music in the form of patriotic songs, simple operatic selections, and piano pieces dominated the repertory. In the second part of the 19th century Harvey B. Dodworth (1845–87) and the Schuberth brothers, Julius and Edward (from 1858), became prominent. Of 27 firms belonging to the Board of Music Trade, however, only six were from New York. The introduction of the octavo anthem by Novello in 1870 infused new strength into serious music publishing, especially by the firms of G. Schirmer (set up as Beer & Schirmer in 1861 by Gustav Schirmer) and Carl Fischer (established in 1872). The 1880s saw the founding of two important popular publishers, Harms (in 1881) and M. Witmark (in 1885); both are now subsidiaries of larger organizations. From the 1890s a large part of the popular songwriting and music-publishing industry was in New York, its center moving gradually uptown on Broadway (fig. 10, p. 368; *see also* TIN PAN ALLEY). Leading

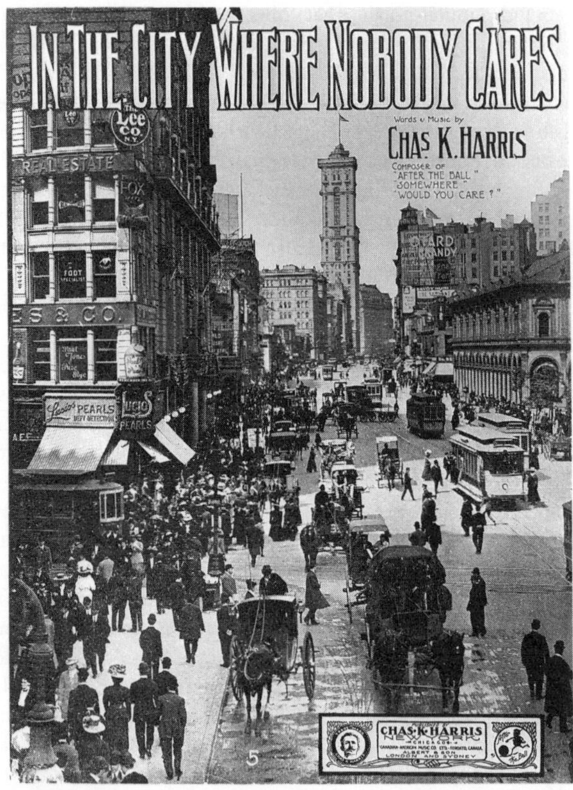

10. Sheet-music cover of "The City where Nobody Cares" (1908) by Charles K. Harris, showing Broadway to the north of 34th Street, the center of the popular-music industry

music publishers in New York in the 1980s included G. Schirmer, Carl Fischer, Boosey & Hawkes, Belwin-Mills, Associated Music Publishers (a division of Schirmer), C. F. Peters, Peer-Southern, and Chappell.

A recent development has been the acquisition of previously independent music publishers by large conglomerates, especially in the popular field; Warner Bros., Columbia Pictures, and Gulf & Western have absorbed many smaller firms. Beginning in the 1970s scholarly and reprint editions have been produced in quantity by such local firms as Broude, Garland, Da Capo, and Dover.

Instrument making in New York started around the beginning of the 19th century. John Geib, an organ builder from 1798, was joined by his brothers Adam and William in a firm that manufactured pianos until 1872. The firm of Dubois & Stodart made pianos from 1819 to the 1850s. Dominated by German-Americans, piano construction was one of the city's leading industries by the middle of the 19th century. Among the many piano-making firms active in the latter part of the century were Weber (founded 1852), Steck (1857), Hardman (1842), Bacon (1841), Haines (1851), Mathusek (1857), Behning (1861), Doll (1871), Sohmer (1872), and Behr (1881). The first three were absorbed by the Aeolian Corporation, which maintained its headquarters in New York into the 1970s. Most important among the city's piano makers, and outstanding in the country as a whole, is Steinway, founded by Heinrich E. Steinweg in 1853. As in the late 18th century and the early 19th, some later publishers also dealt in instruments. E. Riley made flutes, and Firth & Pond made woodwind instruments from 1848 to 1865. A. G. Badger was an important flute maker from 1845, the business being absorbed by the Penzel–Mueller Co. after the turn of the century. Among brass instrument makers the Schreiber Cornet Co. (from 1867) and Stratton (from 1859) were significant, the latter turning to guitar manufacture in 1890. August and George Gemunder and family arrived in the city from Germany before 1850 and made prizewinning violins for over 75 years. Rembert Wurlitzer, Inc., was noted for the restoration and sale of rare violins from 1949 to 1974.

New York became the national center of radio broadcasting with the founding of the first radio networks – NBC in 1926 and CBS in 1927. For a while, before the impact of populist aesthetics and, later, television was felt, the networks attempted to emulate state-supported European broadcasters by sponsoring their own studio orchestras. The best-known of these was the NBC SO, created in 1937 for Arturo Toscanini and led by him until 1954. NBC also commissioned and televised opera productions by its own opera company in the 1950s and 1960s. Ed Sullivan's Sunday evening television shows on CBS, which featured a variety of musical talent, originated from New York (1948–71).

Among New York's principal musical organizations, the New York PO has presented regular radio broadcasts since 1930 and more occasional telecasts and concerts for young people, these last under the aegis of Leonard Bernstein, who was music director from 1958 to 1969 and a charismatic media personality. The Saturday matinée performances of the Metropolitan Opera have been broadcast since 1931. The most influential broadcasts in the 1970s and 1980s were the "Live from Lincoln Center" television series and its related "Live from the Met" telecasts seen on the Public Broadcasting Service network. In 1984 Carnegie Hall began a weekly series of radio concerts carried nationwide on commercial radio and National Public Radio.

New York has several classical-music FM stations, notably WQXR (founded 1936) and WNCN (founded 1958). Both of these fell victim in the 1970s to conservative influences. More interesting were the city-owned outlet WNYC (a National Public Radio station) and WBAI, from 1960 part of the listener-supported Pacifica chain. These stations present a wide range of nonmusical programming as well. During the 1960s the WBAI Free Music Store under Eric Salzman gave innovative free concerts. Also of note are college radio stations, particularly Columbia's WKCR, which has presented day-long marathons of contemporary compositions and jazz.

Jazz has been less consistently represented on New York radio. Swing music, both recorded and live, was heard regularly on the radio in the 1930s and 1940s and was revived in the 1970s and 1980s by WNEW. In the mid-1940s "Symphony Sid" Torin was influential in broadcasting programs of bop. From 1962 to 1980 WRVR offered jazz regularly, but thereafter jazz listeners had to rely on the college stations, WBAI, and WBGO in nearby Newark. Oddly, country music found a secure outlet in WHN.

From Alan Freed's pioneering radio broadcasts on WINS and later WABC in the 1950s, rock has been amply represented on New York radio. For a long period, WABC was the leading Top 40 pop station in the city; more recently, WNEW-FM and many other stations have offered rock programming. In the 1970s and 1980s, black disco, funk, and rap stations such as WBLS and WKTU won a large audience. (*See also* BROADCASTING.)

New York was a center for the recording industry from its earliest days. Recordings of all musical genres were dominated by RCA Victor and Columbia, located in New York. After the rise of rock and the penetration of country music into the commercial mainstream, however, New York was successfully challenged by Los Angeles (for pop) and Nashville (for country) as a national recording center. But with the corporate headquarters of CBS, RCA, Polygram Classics, Warner Communications, CRI, New World, and other important labels in Manhattan, and with ample recording facilities and an active musical community, New York has retained its leading position in the recording industry, especially for classical music, contemporary music, and jazz.

15. CRITICISM AND PERIODICALS. Early reviews of public performances were unsigned. In the mid-19th century two literary figures, Walt Whitman in the *Brooklyn Eagle* (1841–5) and Margaret Fuller in Horace Greeley's *Tribune* (1844–6), included music in their critical writing. The city's first prominent music critic was William Henry Fry, who wrote for the *New York Tribune* from 1852 to 1863, but distinguished writing did not appear until the advent of H. E. Krehbiel's critical commentary in the *Tribune* in 1880. Krehbiel wrote until 1923, as did Henry Finck from 1881 in the *Evening Post*. J. G. Huneker's columns appeared in various publications from 1891 to 1921. William James Henderson in the *New York Times* (1887–1902) and *The Sun* (1902–37) and Richard Aldrich in the *Times* (1902–37) were particularly influential. These men were all cultivated university graduates with extensive musical training, as well as editors, lecturers, teachers, and authors; they were given free rein by their newspapers, and their judgments, standing the test of time, were accurate, vigorous, and constructive.

The tradition of fine critical writing was continued by Lawrence Gilman (active from 1901, with the *Tribune* 1923–37), Deems Taylor in *The World* (1921–5), and Olin Downes of the *Times* (1924–55). Virgil Thomson added his strongly individual voice to the *Herald Tribune* from 1940 to 1954, followed by Paul Henry Lang from 1954 to 1963. Harold Schonberg was chief music critic of the *Times* from 1960 to 1980, when he was succeeded by Donal Henahan. With ten regular music critics covering a broad range of music, the paper is the most influential reviewing medium in the city. Weekly periodicals also provide a forum for music critics, notably Leighton Kerner and Gregory Sandow in the *Village Voice* and, from 1972, Andrew Porter in the *New Yorker*. The number of reviewing media has declined in recent years, however, with the disappearance of most daily newspapers.

New York has long been a center of publishing activity of many kinds; 82 music periodicals appeared in the city between 1850 and 1900. Notable among them were the *Choral Advocate and Singing-class Journal* (1850–73), what was eventually called *Watson's Art Journal* (1864–1905), the *Music Trade Journal* (from 1879), and the *Music Trades* (from 1890); *Musical America* was founded by John Freund in 1898 and merged with *High Fidelity* in 1965. General periodicals such as *Scribner's Magazine* (1887–1900) and *Harpers* (from 1850) have also carried articles of musical interest. The *Musical Observer* (1907–31) and *Modern Music* (1924–46) were influential, and the *Musical Quarterly*, published from 1915 by G. Schirmer, is a leading scholarly journal, edited by Oscar G. T. Sonneck (1915–28), Carl Engel (1929–44), Paul Henry Lang (1945–73), Christopher Hatch (1973–7), Joan Peyser (1977–84), and Eric Salzman (from 1984). Two important journals for organists, the *Church Music Review* (1901–35) and the *American Organist* (1918–70), were published in New York, as was *Metronome*, a periodical devoted to bands and jazz (1885–1961). Several music periodicals for a more general readership have their editorial offices in New York, among them *Stereo Review*, *Opera News*, *Keynote*, and *Ovation*. *Ear*, devoted to new music, was founded in 1975, and *Rolling Stone* has been published in New York since 1977.

16. LIBRARIES. The New York Public Library, formed in 1895 by the amalgamation of the Astor (1849) and Lenox (1870) libraries with the Tilden Foundation (1887), includes one of the world's outstanding research collections. The Music Division (with nearly 700,000 titles as well as programs, clippings, photographs, and letters) is in the Library and Museum of the Performing Arts at Lincoln Center, and the Rodgers & Hammerstein Archives of Recorded Sound there include over 450,000 recordings of all kinds; in the same building the library maintains a circulating collection of over 150,000 scores, books, and recordings. Another division of the New York Public Library, the Schomburg Center for Research in Black Culture, collects materials on jazz and the music of black musicians. In other parts of the city the Queensborough and Brooklyn public libraries maintain large music collections, and there are additional centers for circulating recordings in Manhattan and the Bronx.

Each of the educational institutions offering advanced degrees has a good working collection to support its courses. Columbia, whose first music librarian, Richard Angell, was appointed in 1934, is one of the oldest. The Juilliard library has a collection of 50,000 books and scores. The Pierpont Morgan Library houses many valuable music manuscripts, and there are several distinguished private collectors living in New York, notably James Fuld. The collection of musical instruments at the Metropolitan Museum of Art is internationally famous; many of its 4000 Western and non-Western instruments are on display in the André Mertens Galleries, opened in 1971.

For a discussion of these and other important archives *see* LIBRARIES AND COLLECTIONS, §3.

BIBLIOGRAPHY

GENERAL

H. E. Krehbiel: *Review of the New York Musical Season, 1885–1890* (New York, 1886–90)

W. S. B. Mathews, ed.: *A Hundred Years of Music in America* (Chicago, 1889/*R*1970)

E. Clark: *History of the Seventh Regiment of New York, 1806–1889* (New York, 1890)

"The National Conservatory of Music in America," *Harper's Weekly*, xxiv (13 Dec 1890), 969

L. C. Elson: *The History of American Music* (New York, 1904, enlarged by A. Elson 3/1925/*R*1971)

O. G. T. Sonneck: *Early Concert-life in America (1731–1800)* (Leipzig, Germany, 1907/*R*1978)

C. Saerchinger: "Musical Landmarks in New York," *MQ*, vi (1920), 69

H. C. Lahee: *Annals of Music in America* (Boston, 1922)

J. T. Howard: *Our American Music* (New York, 1931, rev. 4/1965)

S. Salter: "Early Encouragements to American Composers," *MQ*, xviii (1932), 76

F. Damrosch: *Institute of Musical Art, 1905–1926* (New York, 1936)

E. R. Peyser: *The House that Music Built* (New York, 1936)

V. L. Redway: "A New York Concert in 1736," *MQ*, xxii (1936), 1970

N. Slonimsky: *Music since 1900* (London, 1938, rev. 4/1971)

R. Aldrich: *Concert Life in New York, 1902–1923* (New York, 1941)

V. L. Redway: *Music Directory of Early New York City* (New York, 1941)

A. C. Minor: *Pianoforte Concerts in New York 1849–1865* (thesis, U. of Michigan, 1947)

B. C. Landauer: *My Country 'tis of Thee* (New York, 1951) [sheet music covers illustrating New York]

V. Thomson: *Music Right and Left* (New York, 1951)
[R. F. Goldman]: *The Juilliard Report on Teaching the Literature and Materials of Music* (New York, 1953)
G. Chase: *America's Music* (New York, 1955, rev. 2/1966/*R*1981)
H. W. Schwartz: *Bands of America* (Garden City, NY, 1957/*R*1975)
R. Schickel: *The World of Carnegie Hall* (New York, 1960)
H. Cowell, ed.: *American Composers on American Music: a Symposium* (New York, 1962)
The New York Public Library: Dictionary Catalogue of the Music Collections (Boston, 1964–73)
R. J. Wolfe: *Secular Music in America, 1801–1825: a Bibliography* (New York, 1964)
R. M. Aborn: *The Influence on American Musical Culture of Dvořák's Sojourn in America* (diss., Indiana U., 1965)
D. D. Rogers: *Nineteenth Century Music in New York City as Reflected in the Career of Geo. Frederick Bristow* (diss., U. of Michigan, 1967)
M. Goldin: *The Music Merchants* (New York, 1969)
C. Gillett: *The Sound of the City* (New York, 1970, rev. 2/1983)
D. D. Rogers: "Public Music Performances in New York City from 1800 to 1850," *Yearbook for Inter-American Musical Research*, vi (1970), 5–50
M. M. Lowens: *The New York Years of Edward MacDowell* (diss., U. of Michigan, 1971)
R. G. Martin: *Lincoln Center for the Performing Arts* (Englewood Cliffs, NJ, 1971)
C. Pavlakis: *The American Music Handbook* (New York, 1974)
C. J. Oja: "The Copland-Sessions Concerts and their Reception in the Contemporary Press," *MQ*, lxv (1979), 212
M. C. McKnight: *Music Criticism in the New York Times and the New York Tribune, 1851–1876* (diss., Louisiana State U., 1980)
R. A. Moog: "The Columbia/Princeton Electronic Music Center: Thirty Years of Explorations in Sound," *Contemporary Keyboard*, vii/5 (1981), 22
N. Groce: *Musical Instrument Making in New York City during the Eighteenth and Nineteenth Centuries* (diss., U. of Michigan, 1982)
R. A. Lott: " 'New Music for New Ears': the International Composers' Guild," *JAMS*, xxxvi (1983), 266
J. Rockwell: *All American Music: Composition in the Late Twentieth Century* (New York, 1983)
J. W. Wagner: "New York City Concert Life, 1801–5," *American Music*, ii/2 (1984), 53
S. J. Freedman: "The Glory of Carnegie Hall," *New York Times Magazine* (19 May 1985), 44

OPERA AND VOCAL MUSIC

H. E. Krehbiel: *Notes on the Cultivation of Choral Music and the Oratorio Society in New York* (New York, 1884)
E. Singleton: "History of the Opera in New York from 1750 to 1898," *Musical Courier*, xxxvii/23 (1898)
G. von Skal: *History of the New York Arion, 1854–1904* (New York, 1904)
H. E. Krehbiel: *Chapters of Opera* (New York, 1908, rev. 2/1909/*R*1980, rev. 3/1911)
An Historical Sketch of 37 Seasons of the Oratorio Society of New York, 1873/74–1908/09 (New York, 1909)
F. Rogers: "America's First Grand Opera Season," *MQ*, i (1915), 93
O. G. T. Sonneck: *Early Opera in America* (New York, 1915/*R*1963)
J. Mattfeld: *A Hundred Years of Grand Opera in New York, 1825–1925* (New York, 1927/*R*1976)
G. C. D. Odell: *Annals of the New York Stage* (New York, 1927–49/*R*1970)
I. Kolodin: *The Metropolitan Opera* (New York, 1936, rev. and enlarged 4/1966)
W. H. Seltsam: *Metropolitan Opera Annals* (New York, 1947; suppls., 1957, 1968, 1978)
H. E. Johnson: *Operas on American Subjects* (Boston, 1964)
J. F. Cone: *Oscar Hammerstein's Manhattan Opera House* (Norman, OK, 1966)
M. Nelson: *The First Italian Opera Season in New York City: 1825–1826* (diss., U. of North Carolina, 1976)
M. L. Sokol: *The New York City Opera* (New York, 1981)
J. F. Cone: *First Rival of the Metropolitan Opera* (New York, 1983)
M. Mayer: *The Met: One Hundred Years of Grand Opera* (New York, 1983)
F. P. Fellers: *The Metropolitan Opera on Record: a Discography of the Commercial Recordings* (Westport, CT, 1984)

ORCHESTRAS

H. E. Krehbiel: *The Philharmonic Society of New York* (New York, 1892)
J. G. Huneker: *The Philharmonic Society of New York and its 75th Anniversary* (New York, ?1917)
J. Erskine: *The Philharmonic-Symphony Society of New York* (New York, 1943)
P. Hart: *Orpheus in the New World: the Symphony Orchestra as an American Cultural Institution* (New York, 1973)
H. Shanet: *Philharmonic: a History of New York's Orchestra* (Garden City, NY, 1975)
——, ed.: *Early Histories of the New York Philharmonic* (New York, 1979) [annotated edn of Krehbiel, 1892; Huneker, ?1917; Erskine, 1943]

SACRED MUSIC

A. H. Messiter: *A History of the Choir and Music of Trinity Church* (New York, 1906)
A. P. Alwardt: *Sacred Music in New York City, 1800–1850* (diss., Union Theological Seminary, 1950)
L. Ellinwood: *The History of American Church Music* (New York, 1953)

MUSICAL THEATER

C. Smith: *Musical Comedy in America* (New York, 1950)
G. Bordman: *American Musical Theatre: a Chronicle* (New York, 1978)
T. L. Riis: *Black Musical Theater in New York, 1890–1915* (diss., U. of Michigan, 1981)
D. L. Root: *American Popular Stage Music, 1860–1880* (Ann Arbor, MI, 1981)
R. A. Simas: *The Musicals No one Came to See* (New York, 1985) [New York shows with fewer than 300 perfs., 1948–81]

JAZZ AND POPULAR MUSIC

S. B. Charters and L. Kunstadt: *Jazz: a History of the New York Scene* (Garden City, NY, 1962)
M. Williams: "Jazz Clubs, Jazz Business, Jazz Styles in New York: a Brief History and a Cultural Lag," *Jazz Masters in Transition* (New York, 1970), 89
J. Schiffman: *Uptown: the Story of Harlem's Apollo Theatre* (New York, 1971)
A. Shaw: *The Street that Never Slept: New York's Fabled 52nd Street* (New York, 1971/*R*1977 as *52nd Street: the Street of Jazz*)
T. J. Hennessey: "New York Ballrooms, 1923–1929," *From Jazz to Swing: Black Jazz Musicians and their Music, 1917–1935* (diss., Northwestern U., 1973)
J. Haskins: *The Cotton Club* (New York, 1977)
B. A. MacLeod: *Music for All Occasions: the Club Date Business of Metropolitan New York City* (diss., Wesleyan U., 1979)
L. Ostransky: *Jazz City* (Englewood Cliffs, NJ, 1979), 179–230
E. A. Berlin: "Ragtime in Old New York," *NYC Jazz*, no.3 (2 June 1980), 22; repr. in *Ragtimer* (May–June 1980), 6
T. Fox: *Showtime at the Apollo* (New York, 1983)

MEMOIRS

M. Maretzek: *Crotchets and Quavers* (New York, 1855/*R*1968)
——: *Sharps and Flats* (New York, 1890/*R*1968)
C. Gottschalk, ed.: *Louis Moreau Gottschalk: Notes of a Pianist*, trans. R. E. Peterson (Philadelphia, 1881); ed. J. Behrend (New York, 1964/*R*1979) [incl. letters]
D. Mannes: *Music Is my Faith* (New York, 1938)
J. D. Schenk: *Adventure in Music: a Reminiscence* (New York, 1961)

1–8, 12–16: IRVING KOLODIN, FRANCIS D. PERKINS/
SUSAN THIEMANN SOMMER
(2 with JOHN SHEPARD and SARA VELEZ,
3 with JOHN SHEPARD,
12 with JOHN SHEPARD and NINA DAVIS-MILLIS,
14 with JOHN ROCKWELL)
9: JOHN ROCKWELL
10: EDWARD A. BERLIN, J. BRADFORD ROBINSON,
and JOHN ROCKWELL
11: SUSAN THIEMANN SOMMER and JOHN ROCKWELL

New York, State University of (SUNY). A public education system (headquarters in Albany) comprising in 1975 72 individual colleges of which four are major university centers, 14 are four-year liberal arts colleges, 38 are two-year community colleges, and the remainder are agricultural, technical, medical, and other specialized schools. The system was set up by Governor Thomas E. Dewey in 1948, and a number of the branches offer outstanding music programs, each with a different character and educational emphasis.

All of SUNY's university centers – Albany (founded in 1844), Buffalo (1846), Binghamton (1946), and Stony Brook (1957) – offer a BA degree in music. Binghamton in addition awards an MA in composition, performance, theory, ethnomusicology, and historical musicology, and Buffalo and Stony Brook grant undergraduate and graduate degrees in various areas of music, both academic and applied. Three colleges in the system that have undergraduate programs of particular interest are Fredonia (founded in 1867), which offers a degree in music education and excels in the field of public school music; Potsdam (1816), offering courses in a wide range of subjects at the Crane School of Music; and Purchase (1967), which offers a BFA degree in music and focuses on performance. Other four-year colleges that grant undergraduate music degrees are Brockport, Buffalo (not to be confused with the university at Buffalo mentioned above), Cortland, Geneseo, New Paltz, Oneonta, and Oswego. The campuses at Purchase, Albany, Binghamton, Stony Brook, Fredonia, and Potsdam have outstanding performing arts facilities that function as regional cultural centers; a theater and gallery complex is planned for the university center at Buffalo. In addition to the cultural activities sponsored by the individual campuses, SUNY administers several university-wide arts programs.

See also LIBRARIES AND COLLECTIONS, §3.

BIBLIOGRAPHY

W. D. Claudson: *The History of the Crane Department of Music, the State University of New York, College at Potsdam, 1884–1964* (diss., Northwestern U., 1965)

Architecture for the Arts: the State University of New York College at Purchase (New York, n.d. [*c*1971])

B. R. Bancroft: *The Historical Development of the Music Department of the State University College at Fredonia, New York* (diss., New York U., 1972)

A Most Unusual Place, ed. Office of University Affairs, SUNY (Albany, 1975)

This Is the State University of New York: 1984 Facts Book, ed. Office of University Affairs and Development (Albany, 1984)

NINA DAVIS-MILLIS

New York Dolls. Rock group. Its members were David Johansen (*b* New York, 9 Jan 1950), singer; Johnny Thunders (John Genzale; *b* New York), guitarist; Rick Rivets, guitarist, replaced in 1972 by Sylvain Sylvain (*b* Cairo, Egypt); Arthur Harold Kane (*b* New York), bass guitarist; and Billy Murcia (*b* New York, 1951; *d* London, England, 6 Nov 1972), drummer, replaced by Jerry Nolan (*b* New York). Formed in 1971, the group began playing the following year in the Mercer Arts Center in lower Manhattan, a focal point for art rock in New York at that time. They specialized in deliberately amateurish hard rock modeled after the music of the Rolling Stones, the MC5, the Stooges, and the Velvet Underground, and dressed in flamboyant, androgynous "glitter" costumes. After Murcia's death during a tour of England and his replacement by Nolan, the band recorded two albums, produced by Todd Rundgren and George "Shadow" Morton, that were critical successes but commercial failures. They lost their recording contract in 1975, and were managed briefly by Malcolm McLaren, who eventually returned to London to form the Sex Pistols in emulation of the New York Dolls. Nolan and Thunders left the band in the mid-1970s to form the Heartbreakers; Johansen and Sylvain continued to appear under the New York Dolls' name until 1977. Several members, notably Johansen, have since appeared as soloists or in new bands, and have recorded critically admired albums, but none has achieved mainstream success; Johansen's solo albums are in an idiom that recalls the work of the New York Dolls, with some concessions to commerciality.

The New York Dolls epitomized the New York glitter-rock movement of the early 1970s. Their strongest influence was on the nascent punk movement of the mid- to late 1970s, which adopted their defiant primitivism but slighted their warmth of spirit. Their aggressive, simple, passionate style purged rock of its affectations and led to a return to basics.

RECORDINGS

The New York Dolls (Mer. 1675, 1973); *Too Much Too Soon* (Mer. SRM 1001, 1974)

BIBLIOGRAPHY

R. Christgau: "New York Dolls," *Stranded: Rock and Roll for a Desert Island*, ed. G. Marcus (New York, 1979), 132

JOHN ROCKWELL

New York Pro Musica. Ensemble and educational organization founded as the Pro Musica Antiqua in 1952 by NOAH GREENBERG. Greenberg hoped to resurrect, by means of scholarship and convincing performances, the largely neglected music of the Middle Ages, Renaissance, and early Baroque. The core of his group was formed from members of the choir at St. Luke's Church in New York's Greenwich Village, augmented by instrumentalists, several of whom collaborated with instrument builders to produce facsimiles of period instruments (see illustration, p.372). The musicians often served as both singers and instrumentalists, and a motet choir was occasionally added. The Pro Musica developed a large repertory and achieved high standards of virtuosity. Among its artists were Shelley Gruskin (recorders), Judith Davidoff (viols), and the singers Bethany Beardslee, Charles Bressler, Jan DeGaetani, and Russell Oberlin. The ensemble created a sensation in the 1957–8 season with its production of the medieval liturgical drama *The Play of Daniel* and in 1963 with *The Play of Herod*, both of which opened at the Cloisters, New York. These works were recorded, televised, and performed on the group's tours, which included performances at various European cathedrals (1960), summer festivals (1963), and in the USSR (1964). The group's office served as a library, research center, rehearsal studio, and classroom for its courses in ensemble performance (chorus, viol consort, lute-song, and collegium musicum), which were supported by funding from the New York State Council on the Arts.

After Greenberg's death in 1966 the Pro Musica continued until 1974 under the direction of J. R. White (1966–70), Paul Maynard (1970–72), and George Houle (1972–4), its final performances including Marco da Gagliano's *La Dafne*. Many members of subsequent American early-music ensembles had trained with the Pro Musica, and the audiences for them had been created by Greenberg's pioneering efforts. The New York Pro Musica library went to SUNY, Purchase, its archives to the music division of the New York Public Library, and its collection of instruments to New York University.

See also EARLY-MUSIC REVIVAL, §4.

JOHN SHEPARD

New York Woodwind Quintet. Woodwind quintet formed in 1947; its present members are Samuel Baron, flute, David Glazer, clarinet, Ronald Roseman (replacing Jerome Roth), oboe, William Purvis (replacing John Barrows), horn, and Donald MacCourt (replacing Bernard Garfield), bassoon. The ensemble made its New York début in January 1954 and shortly thereafter began touring in the USA; tours followed under the auspices of the US State Department to Latin America (1956), Europe (1958), the Orient and the Pacific (1962), Central and South America (1969), and Russia (1972). It has given world premières of works by such composers as Quincy Porter, Carter, Schuller, Wilder, Laderman, and Riegger, and has also led the way in reviving

Noah Greenberg conducting the New York Pro Musica in the 1950s: Paul Maynard (keyboard), Martha Blackman and Paul Ehrlich (viols), Bernard Krainis (recorder), and Brayton Lewis, Arthur Squires, Russell Oberlin, Jean Hakes, and Betty Wilson (singers)

less-known works by Franz Danzi and Anton Reicha, among others. Through many school concerts given in 1953–5, it developed the format for the Young Audiences program. The quintet was in residence at the University of Wisconsin for 15 summers (1954–69) with the pianist Frank Glazer and the Fine Arts String Quartet, with whom it made a number of recordings.

JOANNE SHEEHY HOOVER

NFMC. *See* NATIONAL FEDERATION OF MUSIC CLUBS.

Niblock, Phill (*b* Anderson, IN, 2 Oct 1933). Composer. After studying economics at Indiana University, Bloomington (BA 1956), he moved to New York, where he has long been active as a filmmaker and composer of tape music. In both endeavors, he examines texture and process from a minimalist standpoint. From his early music of the late 1960s onward, Niblock has used long lines played on conventional instruments (cello, oboe, english horn, trombone) and sustained, closely juxtaposed pitches; the lines are spliced together to effect a dreamlike continuity, with the attacks and decays of each note removed. The closeness of the intervals frequently produces exotic acoustic "beats." Niblock has often presented his films and tape music together (although he attempts no direct correlation between the two) in his loft in lower Manhattan, which from 1973 was the site of concerts of experimental music by a wide range of composers. In 1976 he joined the faculty of the College of Staten Island, CUNY. Among his awards for music have been an NEA grant (1980) and several performance grants from the New York State Council on the Arts.

WORKS

(all for tape; sources of sounds given in brackets)

Tenor, 1970 [t sax]; Str Qt, 1972; Quarterbone, 1973 [trbn]; 3 to 7 – 196, for Vc, 1974; Cbn and B, 1975; Vc and Bn, 1975; First Performance, 1975 [eng hn]; Long Distance, 1976 [vc]; 261.63, – and –, 1976 [eng hn, vn, b fl, vc]; Descent, 1977 [vc]; Harm, 1977 [harmonica]; 12 Tones, 1977 [B]; Who Can Think of Good, Cute Titles for Every Tune, 1977 [cl]; E for Gibson, 1978 [vc]; 4 Arthurs, 1978 [bn]; Timps in E, 1978; 2 Octaves and a Fifth, 1978 [ob]; Winterbloom, 1978 [b fl]; A Third Trbn, 1979; V & V, 1979 [v, vn]; Fall and Winterbloom, 1980 [b fl]; Multimusti, 1980 [fl, trbn, B, ob]; P K, 1980 [a fl]; S L S, 1980 [fl]; 2nd 2 Octaves and a Fifth, 1980 [ob]; B Poore, 1981 [tuba]; Summing I, II, II, IV, 1981 [vc]; Unbridled, 1981 [vc]; other works

BIBLIOGRAPHY

T. Johnson: "Artists Meet at Niblock's Loft," *Village Voice* (9 May 1977)
——: "Sandow and Niblock at the End of the Spectrum," *Village Voice* (8 Jan 1979)
J. Rockwell: "Avant-garde: Niblock in Seven-hour Program," *New York Times* (24 Dec 1979)
R. Palmer: "Music: Phill Niblock in Concert," *New York Times* (25 Dec 1980)
T. Witham: "Composer's View," *EMAS Newsletter*, iii/1 (1981)

JOHN ROCKWELL

Nicholl, Horace (Wadham) (*b* Tipton, England, 17 March 1848; *d* New York, 10 March 1922). Composer and organist. He was taught to play the organ by his father, from whom he received lessons in theory and counterpoint, and in his teens also studied with the organist Samuel Prince in Birmingham. After serving as organist at Dudley (1867–70) and Stoke-on-Trent (1868–70), he immigrated to the USA and, at the urging of friends, went to Pittsburgh to take up a post as organist of St. Paul's Cathedral; later he served as organist of the Third Presbyterian Church. In 1878 he moved to New York, where he was organist at several important churches in Manhattan and Brooklyn, and also worked as an editor for the firms of Schuberth and G. Schirmer. As a regular contributor to the *Musical Courier* he wrote detailed analyses of new works by the major European composers of the day. He taught harmony and composition privately, and from 1888 to 1895 was on the faculty of Miss Porter's School in Farmington, Connecticut.

Nicholl's reputation as a composer grew during the 1880s and early 1890s largely through the efforts of the conductor Anton Seidl, who considered Nicholl the greatest composer in the USA. Seidl conducted the premières of several of Nicholl's most important scores, including the symphonic poem *Tartarus* and the

Heroic Overture (actually the first movement of his Second Symphony). Nicholl had another champion in the pianist William Sherwood, who gave two performances of the Piano Concerto in Pittsburgh in 1888. On the whole, however, his enthusiasm for the innovations of Wagner and Liszt alienated Nicholl from the conservative American musical establishment, and performances of his larger scores all but ceased in the mid-1890s. In 1900 he announced that he was taking up permanent residence in England, but the next year he was in Leipzig, where most of his organ works were published. By 1904, however, he had returned to New York, where he remained until his death.

Nicholl was one of the earliest American composers to anticipate trends in European music. The harmonic daring, elaborate contrapuntal textures, and inventive orchestration of his early works anticipate the tone poems of Richard Strauss. With the four oratorios *Adam*, *Abraham*, *Isaac*, and *Jacob*, Nicholl created the prototype for an "oratorio of the future"; unfortunately these ambitious pieces, originally intended as the first part of a cycle of 12 works, proved too technically and musically difficult for the American choral societies of the day and were never performed. Although Nicholl worked on them for almost 40 years, he left only *Adam* completely orchestrated at his death. Nicholl wrote numerous organ works (including *Life*, an ambitious "symphonic poem" in six movements) in which he achieved his most successful synthesis of traditional contrapuntal technique, post-Wagnerian chromaticism, and virtuoso instrumental writing.

WORKS

(selective list)

Vocal: Mass, E♭, 4 solo vv, chorus, org, op.1 (Boston, 1872); Elsie, or The Golden Legend (H. W. Longfellow), cantata, 3 solo vv, chorus, pf, op.4, portion perf. New York, 1888; A Cloister Scene, cantata, 3 solo vv, chorus, org, pf, op.6, vs (New York, 1888); First Cycle of Dramatic Oratorios: Adam, or The Fall of Man, 4 solo vv, 8vv, org, orch, op.16; Abraham, 4 solo vv, 8vv, pf, op.17; Isaac, 4 solo vv, 8vv, pf, op.18; Jacob, or Israel, 4 solo vv, 8vv, pf, op.19; anthems; songs

Orch: Suite, A, op.3, 1868–76; Sym. no.1 "The Nation's Mourning," g, op.8; Pf Conc., d, op.10, perf. Pittsburgh, 1888; Tartarus, sym. poem, op.11, 1877–8; Sym. no.2, C, op.12, *c*1878–89, 1st movt perf. 1889 as Heroic Ov.; Hamlet, psychic sketch, op.14, 1884–5 (New York, 1888); Scherzo-fugue (Humouresque), G, op.15, perf. New York, 1886

Inst: Vc Sonata, A, op.13, 1883 (New York, 1888); Sentiments poétiques, pf, op.21 (New York, 1888); 8 Character Pieces, pf 4 hands, op.23 (New York, 1889); 12 Etudes mélodiques, pf, op.26 (Boston, 1889); 12 Sym. Preludes and Fugues, org, op.30 (Leipzig, 1900); Pf Trio, b, op.34, 1901; Str Qt, C, op.39, 1901; 12 Concert Preludes and Fugues, pf, op.31 (New York, 1916–23); Life, sym. poem, org, op.50 (Leipzig, 1902)

DAVID KELLEHER

Nichols, Red [Ernest Loring] (*b* Ogden, UT, 8 May 1905; *d* Las Vegas, NV, 28 June 1965). Jazz cornetist and bandleader. He studied cornet with his father, a college music teacher, and acquired a sure technique. In 1923 he moved to New York, where he soon became a highly regarded sideman and the most prolifically recorded white jazz bandleader of the late 1920s. He toured the West Coast in 1928, and in the 1930s led a big band as well as working for radio; in the late 1930s he returned to small-group jazz. In 1959 he played for the soundtrack of *The Five Pennies*, a film based loosely on his life, as a result regaining much of his earlier popularity. He toured Europe in 1960 and 1964.

Nichols's playing has often been compared with that of Beiderbecke, with whom he shared a strong attack and clear tone, though his style was more rhythmically incisive, angular, and polished, and of a narrower emotional range. His many recordings of 1926–8 are the most progressive white jazz of the period in concept and execution, with wide-ranging harmonies and balanced ensemble; at this time his groups, most often known as Red Nichols and his Five Pennies, included such important musicians as Joe Venuti, Eddie Lang, Vic Berton, Jimmy Dorsey, Adrian Rollini, Fud Livingston, PeeWee Russell, and Miff Mole, later also featuring Benny Goodman, Jack Teagarden, Glenn Miller, and Artie Shaw at formative stages of their careers. The innovative style of these groups was almost entirely superseded by the swing style of the 1930s, to which Nichols turned as a bandleader and occasionally as a performer. His later small groups attempted to recapture the sound of his performances from the 1920s.

RECORDINGS

(selective list)

As leader or co-leader: That's no Bargain (1926, Bruns. 3407); with M. Mole: Delirium (1927, Vic. 20778); China Boy (1930, Bruns. 4877); *Syncopated Chamber Music* (1953, Audiophile 7–8)

As sideman: M. Mole: Imagination/Feelin' no Pain (1927, OK 40890)

BIBLIOGRAPHY

O. Ferguson: "The Five Pennies," *Jazzmen*, ed. F. Ramsey, Jr., and C. E. Smith (New York, 1939), 221

R. Venables and C. White: *A Complete Discography of Red Nichols and his Five Pennies* (Melbourne, Australia, 1946, 2/1947)

N. Shapiro and N. Hentoff, eds.: *Hear me Talkin' to ya* (New York, 1955), 248ff

H. H. Lange: *Loring "Red" Nichols: ein Porträt* (Wetzlar, Germany, 1960)

R. Hadlock: *Jazz Masters of the Twenties* (New York, 1965), 238ff

A. McCarthy: *Big Band Jazz* (London, 1974), 124ff

J. R. T. Davies: "Re-minting the Pennies," *Storyville*, nos.75–82 (1978–9)

JAMES DAPOGNY/R

Nickelodeon. A player piano or an early type of jukebox operated by the insertion of a nickel in a slot. The term was also used in the early 20th century for a motion-picture theater where the admission fee was five cents.

Nielsen, Alice (*b* Nashville, TN, 7 June 1868 or 1876; *d* New York, 8 March 1943). Singing actress. Her year of birth is ordinarily given as 1876, but according to her death record, she died at the age of 74. She began as a singer in church choirs, and made her professional début in 1893 with the Pike Opera Company in Oakland, California. She was then engaged to sing at the Tivoli Theatre in San Francisco, where she soon became a favorite. Henry Clay Barnabee heard her sing, and offered her a position with what was then America's leading light opera company, the Bostonians. She spent two years with the ensemble, singing such roles as Maid Marian in De Koven and H. B. Smith's *Robin Hood* and Yvonne in Victor Herbert's *The Serenade*. After she left the troupe (taking with her several of its leading players and precipitating its demise), she starred in two operettas which Herbert composed especially for her, *The Fortune Teller* (1898) and *The Singing Girl* (1899). In 1902 she abandoned the popular musical stage to study opera in Rome. The following year she made her European début in Naples as Marguerite in Gounod's *Faust*. For a time she was popular at Covent Garden, where among many other roles she sang Mimì to Caruso's Rodolfo and Gilda to Victor Maurel's Rigoletto. Later she sang with the San Carlo and Boston opera companies. By World War I her popularity had waned, and she attempted a return to Broadway in Rudolf Friml's *Kitty Darlin'* (1917). The critical consensus was that her small, pure voice and youthful appeal had faded; she later played small parts in a few non-musicals, then quietly retired.

BIBLIOGRAPHY
O. Thompson: *The American Singer* (New York, 1937/*R*1969), 347
M. N. Clinksdale: "Nielsen, Alice," *NAW*
E. N. Waters: "Nielsen, Alice," *DAB*

GERALD BORDMAN

Nightclub. An establishment, usually open only in the evening, in which music and other entertainment is provided, dancing is sometimes possible, and alcoholic beverages (and sometimes food) are served.

1. 1920–60. 2. After 1960.

1. 1920–60. Nightclubs became common after World War I, succeeding music halls, which were generally larger and less intimate. In the USA nightclubs evolved from cabarets, which in turn had developed, at the end of the 19th century, in imitation of European models, and were especially numerous in New York; by about 1910 large establishments such as Maxim's and Shanley's were presenting elaborate entertainments with music, and even the smaller cabarets appeared to pay as much attention to their stages as to their kitchens. The characteristic intimate atmosphere of the nightclub developed in the speakeasies that sprang up during Prohibition (1920–33). These were illegal saloons designed to be mobile so as to elude raids by law enforcement authorities; consequently they at first lacked the massive bars, decorated mirrors, spacious rooms, many tables, and large buffet boards that characterized other saloons. As speakeasies grew popular, however, food, entertainment, and dancing were added. The entertainment offered by these early nightclubs ranged from performances by a single pianist, singer, or four- or five-piece jazz group, to huge productions involving singers, dancers, comedians, fancy costumes, elaborate staging, and large jazz bands. Such clubs were usually run by bootleggers, who distilled or smuggled the liquor that was served. The Cotton Club in Harlem, New York, and the Grand Terrace in Chicago were typical of the establishments that could be found in most large American cities during Prohibition.

After the repeal of Prohibition the nightclub tradition begun in the 1920s continued. Small, intimate, relatively expensive establishments called supper clubs appeared; these offered performances by singers whose repertory was often specialized. A club might present a performer who sang songs by Cole Porter and other theatrical composers, or one whose material was considered risqué; the most celebrated effort of Dwight Fiske, for example, was a description of a Mrs. Pettibone's wedding night. Some supper clubs were located in hotels, among them the Persian Room in the Plaza Hotel in New York and the Pump Room in the Ambassador Hotel in Chicago. These had rooms large enough to accommodate a 14- or 15-piece dance band and vast dance floors. Hotel supper clubs became popular in the 1920s, after Vincent Lopez's orchestra made a series of live radio broadcasts (among the first "remote" broadcasts) from the Hotel Pennsylvania in New York. When such broadcasts became common, many bands and hotel rooms became identified with one another and bolstered each other's reputations; this was the case with the Coon–Sanders Kansas City Nighthawks and the Muehlbach Hotel in Kansas City, with Benny Goodman's ensembles and the Manhattan Room of the Hotel Pennsylvania, and, later, with Artie Shaw's band and the Hotel Pennsylvania's Café Rouge.

When bands left the hotels at which they had performed to travel, they played at nightclubs known as roadhouses; these were so named because they were located beyond the limits of large cities. Some of the best-known roadhouses were the Glen Island Casino in New Rochelle, New York, the Avalon Ballroom on Avalon Island, off the coast of Los Angeles, and Frank Dailey's Meadowbrook in Cedar Grove, New Jersey. There were also ballrooms within large cities, such as Roseland in New York, where Fletcher Henderson's orchestra appeared regularly for a decade, and the Aragon and Trianon ballrooms in Chicago, both owned by Andrew Karzas, where Wayne King performed.

Until the 1940s most nightclubs were devoted to popular music and jazz, while a few ethnic clubs presented Russian, Jewish, or Spanish acts in appropriate surroundings. In the 1940s folksingers began to play in clubs; Burl Ives, who had won large audiences through his recordings and radio broadcasts, became one of the first of these when he was engaged to play at the Persian Room of the Plaza Hotel in New York. Folk music was also heard in New York's Greenwich Village, in such clubs as Café Society (the first racially integrated nightclub in New York outside of Harlem) and the Village Vanguard, where Leadbelly and Richard Dyer-Bennett performed. Later Folk City, a nightclub devoted exclusively to folk music, opened in the same area.

Blues performers were heard in nightclubs in Kansas City from the 1920s; among these were the singers Joe Turner and Jimmy Rushing, and the bands led by Count Basie and Jay McShann. Kansas City blues flourished in an atmosphere of corruption, and blues clubs dwindled when the city's administration was reformed. Similarly, New Orleans jazz, a vital element in the city's nightlife until World War I, suffered a setback when the city's red-light district, Storyville, was closed in 1917; and Chicago's jazz clubs, which had brought Armstrong and Earl Hines to prominence in the 1920s, dwindled in number when the corrupt administration of Mayor William Hale Thompson ended. Chicago became a center of blues clubs after southern Blacks migrated to the city in large numbers around the time of World War II. At first the clubs catered specifically to the newly arrived residents, and presented blues singers, such as Big Bill Broonzy, with whom they were already familiar; later they specialized in electric blues, played by such performers as Muddy Waters and B. B. King.

Nightclubs on the West Coast were largely a reflection of their counterparts in New York until the early 1940s, when San Francisco became the center of a traditional-jazz revival. The Yerba Buena Jazz Band, led by Lu Watters, who was strongly influenced by the work of King Oliver and Jelly Roll Morton, performed at the Dawn Club near the Palace Hotel and played an important role in this movement.

Country music began to be heard in nightclubs in the 1940s. The music first became popular in Nashville and gradually built a following throughout the country. New York was the last large city to experience the trend towards country music; nightclubs devoted to the genre were established there in the 1970s.

2. After 1960. The advent of rock in the 1960s brought changes to the nightclub. The popularity of recordings enabled rock groups such as the Beatles to build large, international followings, and eventually to forsake nightclubs for concert halls and large arenas; as a result rock clubs became the favored performance venues of emerging rather than established musicians. Another effect of the growth of recordings was the appearance of discothèques, at which customers danced to recorded music; these had their origins in bars with dance floors, such as the Peppermint Lounge in New York, where free-style dances like the twist

were popularized in the early 1960s. In the mid-1960s psychedelic rock gave rise to a type of environmental concert hall in which live music was accompanied by elaborate "light shows"; the best-known of these establishments were the Avalon Ballroom in San Francisco and the Fillmore East and Electric Circus in New York. Folk music continued to flourish at Gerde's Folk City and the Bitter End in New York, the Troubadour in Los Angeles, the Matrix in San Francisco, the Main Line near Philadelphia, and Passim in Boston.

While comedy had always played a role in American nightclub repertory, clubs devoted entirely to comic acts did not emerge until the 1960s. Founded in 1965, the Improvisation in New York became the prototype of a new kind of club that fostered the talents of standup comedians for television and films. In the highly competitive atmosphere of the comedy club between ten and 15 acts were performed nightly, each lasting no longer than 20 minutes.

The 1970s saw the modest resurgence of a brand of nightclub pop music known as "cabaret" (after the film made by Bob Fosse in 1972), characterized by a quasi-theatrical delivery and a strong element of nostalgia. A number of nightclubs in New York, of which the best-known was Reno Sweeney, specialized in cabaret; the leading performers of the genre included Bette Midler, Peter Allen, Barbara Cook, and the members of the Manhattan Transfer. In 1976–7 the discothèque re-emerged as fashionable, in part owing to the film *Saturday Night Fever* (1977), which evoked a glamorous "disco" lifestyle. DISCO music, a mechanically propulsive offshoot of pop-soul, and other, emerging styles of electronic pop were played, often in specially mixed recordings sequenced into an uninterrupted soundtrack; the discothèques themselves became increasingly sleek and lavishly appointed; and the music was often enhanced by light shows. The Electric Circus, which became more of a club than a concert hall, was an early prototype for the dance halls of the disco period, and Studio 54, a semiprivate club in New York, the symbolic center of the movement. Live music continued to be heard at such clubs as the Bottom Line in New York and the Roxy in Los Angeles.

Rock clubs opened – and closed – in large numbers in the 1980s. Many had "video" installations and elaborate audio-visual displays; some specialized in a particular type of music, such as punk, salsa, or reggae. New York remained an important center for jazz and popular music. Some musicians became closely associated with the "piano bars" at which they performed: Bobby Short at the Café Carlyle, Steve Ross at the Algonquin Hotel, Dick Wellstood at Hanratty's. The city's jazz clubs included older establishments like the Village Vanguard, which celebrated its 50th anniversary in 1985, and such newer ones as Sweet Basil.

See also JAZZ, esp. §III, 1.

JOHN S. WILSON (1)
STEPHEN HOLDEN (2)

Nightingales. Gospel group formed in 1945, of which JULIUS CHEEKS was for a time a member.

Nikisch, Arthur (*b* Lébényi Szent Miklós [now in Hungary], 12 Oct 1855; *d* Leipzig, Germany, 23 Jan 1922). Austro-Hungarian conductor. In 1866 he became a student at the Vienna Conservatory, where he studied violin under Joseph Hellmesberger and composition under Felix Dessoff. He played in Beethoven's Ninth Symphony, conducted by Wagner at the laying of the Bayreuth Festspielhaus foundation stone, and in 1874 joined the Vienna Court Orchestra, where he played under Brahms, Liszt, Verdi, and Wagner, and also took part in the first performance of Bruckner's Second Symphony under the composer's direction.

In 1878 Nikisch became second conductor at the opera in Leipzig, and was named principal conductor the following year. In 1889 he accepted the conductorship of the Boston SO, making his début with it on 11 October. His programs emphasized the Romantic composers – from Beethoven and Weber to Liszt, Schumann, Brahms, Tchaikovsky, and Bruckner – but he also championed the works of American composers, particularly those in the Boston area. He presented premières of works by Chadwick, Foote, Loeffler, Louis Maas, and MacDowell. During his tenure the orchestra undertook several tours of the USA.

In 1893, Nikisch took over the Budapest Opera as music director; but two years later he was offered almost simultaneously the conductorship of the Leipzig Gewandhaus Orchestra (in succession to Reinecke) and of the Berlin PO (in succession to Bülow). He accepted both posts, retaining them to the end of his life, and in 1897 also succeeded Bülow as conductor of the Philharmonic concerts in Hamburg. As a guest conductor he led the Amsterdam Concertgebouw Orchestra, the Vienna PO, and the London SO, with which he toured the USA in April 1912. In addition to his many other duties he was director of the Leipzig Opera (1905–6) and the Leipzig Conservatory, where he was also in charge of the conductors' class.

Nikisch was the most impressive and influential conductor of his day. He was famous for the passionate yet controlled beauty of the string tone he elicited from his players, as well as for his broad and flexible sense of tempo. He influenced a generation of conductors who followed him, including in different ways Wilhelm Furtwängler, his successor in Leipzig and Berlin, and Adrian Boult. Among the contemporary composers whom he supported were Bruckner, Mahler, Reger, Strauss, and Tchaikovsky.

BIBLIOGRAPHY

A. M. Abell: "Arthur Nikisch: the World's Premier Conductor," *Musical Courier*, lxiv (3 April 1912), 5
"The Advent of Arthur Nikisch," *Musical Courier*, lxiv (10 April 1912), 21
E. S. Kelley: "The Art of Conducting as Exemplified in the Achievements of Arthur Nikisch," *Musical Courier*, lxix (16 Sept 1914), 5
M. A. D. Howe: *The Boston Symphony Orchestra: an Historical Sketch* (Boston, 1914, rev. and enlarged 2/1931/*R*1978), 153
A. C. Boult: "Arthur Nikisch," *ML*, iii (1922), 117
——: "Nikisch and Method in Rehearsal," *MR*, xi (1950), 122

HANS-HUBERT SCHÖNZELER/R

Nikolais, Alwin T(heodore) (*b* Southington, CT, 25 Nov 1912). Choreographer. He accompanied silent films and directed a marionette theater before he began to study dance. His teachers included Hanya Holm (whom he assisted at the Bennington School of the Dance and Colorado College), Martha Graham, Doris Humphrey, Charles Weidman, and Louis Horst. He choreographed his first major work, *Eight Column Line*, in 1939. In 1948 he became the director of the Henry Street Playhouse (New York); its affiliated dance company became the Alwin Nikolais Dance Theatre. In 1953, with *Masks, Props, and Mobiles*, Nikolais introduced a multi-media theatrical form in which the dancers, whose sexual identity he ignored, help create abstract patterns of shapes, colors, and lights. He composes the scores for many of his dances and often experiments with electronic music. In 1983 he and his longtime associate Murray Louis choreographed the musical *Lenny and the Heartbreakers* (music by Scott Killian and Kim D. Sherman).

See also DANCE, §III, 2.

BIBLIOGRAPHY

"Nikolais, Alwin," *CBY 1968*

M. B. Siegel, ed.: "Nik: a Documentary," *Dance Perspectives*, no.48 (1971) [whole issue]

SUSAN AU

Niles, John Jacob (*b* Louisville, KY, 28 April 1892; *d* nr Lexington, KY, 1 March 1980). Folksinger, folk-music collector, and composer. He began collecting and transcribing Appalachian songs at the age of 15, and over the next 20 years made regular trips through rural Kentucky and the adjoining states. He continued to collect while serving with the US Army Air Corps during World War I and in 1927 published the volume *Singing Soldiers*. He studied at the Cincinnati Conservatory in 1919 and later in France at the University of Lyon and the Schola Cantorum, Paris. He made his début as an opera singer in 1920, performing in Jules Massenet's *Manon* with the Cincinnati Opera, then taught briefly at various conservatories, including the Curtis Institute, the Eastman School, and the Juilliard School. Most of his career, however, was devoted to collecting, composing, and performing folk music. While the greatest portion of the more than 1000 tunes he collected are from the white Appalachian tradition (including *Songs of the Hill-folk*, 1934, and its sequel, 1935), his interest also extended to black music; he contended that it was the isolation of both groups that had preserved their distinctive forms of music. *The Ballad Book* (1961) contains anecdotes told by people from whom Niles gathered material as well as many fine ballads. Of his own compositions the best-known are *I wonder as I wander*, *Go 'way from my window*, and *Black is the color of my true love's hair*. His works were so frequently pirated or mistaken for folksongs in the public domain that he restricted their publication and recording shortly after 1940. Niles performed and toured until two years before his death. He had a high, light voice characterized by extraordinary control, and his enunciation was always clear; he accompanied himself with lutes and dulcimers of his own construction. He also contributed articles to the journal *Musical Quarterly*.

The John Jacob Niles Collection of manuscripts, field notebooks, photographs, instruments, and recordings, is at the University of Kentucky; the Library of Congress also holds some of Niles's manuscripts and correspondence. His principal publisher is G. Schirmer, and many of his original compositions are included in *The Songs of John Jacob Niles* (1975).

For illustration *see* APPALACHIAN DULCIMER.

BIBLIOGRAPHY

"Niles, John Jacob," *CBY 1959*

JEAN W. THOMAS

Nilsson [Svennsson], **(Märta) Birgit** (*b* Västra Karups, Sweden, 17 May 1918). Swedish soprano. From 1941 she studied at the Royal Academy of Music, Stockholm, where her teachers included the tenor Joseph Hislop. In 1946 she made her début at the Royal Opera, replacing an indisposed soprano as Agathe (Weber's *Der Freischütz*); her first significant success there was as Verdi's Lady Macbeth the next year. Nilsson's first important appearance outside Sweden was as Electra (*Idomeneo*) in the first Glyndebourne production (1951), but it was another four years before her international reputation was established. During the 1954–5 season she made her Munich début as Brünnhilde in the complete *Ring*, appeared in Vienna for the first time, and, as Elsa (*Lohengrin*), began her association with Bayreuth, where she sang regularly from 1959 to 1970 as Isolde, Sieglinde, and Brünnhilde.

Nilsson made her American début with the San Francisco Opera as Brünnhilde (*Die Walküre*) on 5 October 1956, and she first sang at the Metropolitan Opera on 18 December 1959 as Isolde, an occasion greeted with great enthusiasm. With the Metropolitan she has sung most of her important roles, including the three Brünnhildes, Elisabeth (*Tannhäuser*), Sieglinde, Beethoven's Leonore, Turandot, and Strauss's Salome. She made occasional appearances with the Chicago and San Francisco operas during the 1950s and 1960s. Her only new role in the 1970s was the Dyer's Wife (in Strauss's *Die Frau ohne Schatten*), first heard at Stockholm in December 1975.

Nilsson is generally considered the finest Wagnerian soprano of her day. Her voice in her prime years was even throughout its range, pure in sound, and perfect in intonation, with a free ringing top; in size it was as phenomenal as it was rare. The sheer power and opulence of her instrument, coupled with a certain Scandinavian coolness, made her an ideal Turandot, though her account of Strauss's Electra, which she did not choose to sing for a long time, remains possibly her finest achievement. Although she continued to sing such roles in the Italian repertory as Lady Macbeth, Amelia (*Un ballo in maschera*), and Aida, her performances of them were hardly idiomatic; but each appearance as Brünnhilde and Isolde showed artistic growth and development, and by the mid-1960s the dramatic tension and emotional power she was able to bring to these parts were considerable. She is the recipient of a number of awards, and the Birgit Nilsson Arts Center in Steubenville, Ohio, was named after her.

Birgit Nilsson as Isolde in Wagner's "Tristan und Isolde"

BIBLIOGRAPHY

W. Jefferies: "Birgit Nilsson," *Opera*, xi (1960), 607
"Nilsson, (Märta) Birgit," *CBY 1960*
A. Natan: "Birgit Nilsson," *Primadonna: Lob der Stimmen* (Basle, 1962), 106
G. Baldini: "Nilsson, Birgit," *Le grandi voci*, ed. R. Celletti (Rome, 1964) [with opera discography]
W. Weaver: "The Prima Donna at Work: Die Nilsson and La Nilsson," *HiFi/MusAm*, xv/2 (1965), 48
H. Rosenthal: "Birgit Nilsson," *Great Singers of Today* (London, 1966), 126
A. Blyth: "Birgit Nilsson Talks," *Gramophone*, xlvii (1969–70), 1123
J. B. Steane: *The Grand Tradition: Seventy Years of Singing on Record* (New York, 1974), 338
J. Young: "Skånska: Birgit Nilsson on Home Ground," *Opera News*, xxxix/15 (1975), 48
B. Nilsson: *Mina minnesbilder* (Stockholm, 1977; Eng. trans. as *My Memoirs in Pictures*, Garden City, NY, 1981/*R*1982)
S. Wadsworth: "And still Champ . . . Birgit Nilsson Revisited, on the Occasion of her Return to America," *Opera News*, xliv/13 (1980), 8

HAROLD ROSENTHAL/R

Nilsson, Harry [Nelson, Harry Edward, III] (*b* Brooklyn, NY, 15 June 1941). Rock singer and songwriter. He moved to California as a child, where he studied guitar and piano. He began writing songs in the mid-1960s, and recorded his first album, *The Pandemonium Shadow Show*, in 1967. In 1969 his song *Everybody's Talkin'* (no.6) was used as the theme for John Schlesinger's film *Midnight Cowboy*; he also wrote the soundtracks for Otto Preminger's *Skidoo* (1968) and for an animated television film called *The Point* (1971). His most successful recording was the album *Nilsson Schmilsson* (1971); this included the song *Without you* (no.1), a parody of romantic pop songs the irony of which apparently eluded many listeners. He continued to record throughout the 1970s; his most popular songs include *Me and my Arrow* (no.34, 1971), *Jump into the Fire* (no.27, 1972), *Coconut* (no.8, 1972), and *Spaceman* (no.23, 1972). He also collaborated with John Lennon on the album *Pussy Cats* (1974). His work is characterized by gentle pop melodies and lyrics that alternate between winsome gentility and coarse passion.

RECORDINGS

(selective list; all recorded for RCA)

The Pandemonium Shadow Show (LSP3874, 1967); *Aerial Ballet* (LSP 3956, 1968), incl. Everybody's Talkin'; *Nilsson Schmilsson* (ANL1-3464, 1971), incl. Coconut, Jump into the Fire, Without you; *The Point* (AYL1-3811, 1971), incl. Me and my Arrow; *Son of Schmilsson* (AYL1-3812, 1972), incl. Spaceman; *A Little Touch of Schmilsson in the Night* (AYL1-3761, 1973); *Son of Dracula* (ABL1-0220, 1974); *The World's Greatest Lover* (ABL1-2709, 1978)

KEN TUCKER

Nin-Culmell, Joaquín (María) (*b* Berlin, Germany, 5 Sept 1908). Composer and pianist of Cuban origin. His early training was in Paris, where he studied piano with Paul Braud, theory with Jean and Noël Gallon at the Schola Cantorum, and composition with Paul Dukas at the Conservatoire (1932–5). He was strongly attracted to Spanish music, and studied privately in Granada during the summers of 1930–34 with Manuel de Falla, his most influential teacher, while continuing his piano studies under Alfred Cortot and Ricardo Viñes. He made his début as a pianist in Madrid in 1931, and continued to perform mostly Spanish music (including his own) in later concerts. In 1938 he settled in the USA (though he maintained close ties with Spain), and his Piano Quintet received its première at the ISCM festival in London. His first teaching post at Williams College, Williamstown, Massachusetts (1940–50), was followed by one at the University of California, Berkeley (1950–74), from which he retired as professor emeritus.

In 1970 Nin-Culmell was commissioned to write a Mass for the consecration of the Cathedral of St. Mary in San Francisco. His most important stage work is the opera *La celestina* (1965–80), based on a famous Spanish play of the early 16th century. His ballet *Le rêve de Cyrano* was given its première by the San Francisco Ballet in 1979. The bulk of his music, such as the *Six Variations on a Theme by Luis de Milán* for guitar (1945) and his many traditional songs, exhibits strong Spanish elements. Highly characteristic are the *Tonadas* for piano, short pieces which combine folk elements with personal contours.

WORKS

Stage: Yerma (incidental music, Lorca), 1956; Don Juan (ballet), orch, 1958–9; El burlador de Sevilla (ballet), orch, 1965; La celestina (opera, 3, J. Nin-Culmell, after 16th-century Span.), 1965–80; Le rêve de Cyrano (ballet), 1978; Cymbeline (incidental music, Shakespeare), 1980

Orch: Homage to Falla (1933); Pf Conc., 1946; 3 piezas antiguas españolas, 1959–61; Diferencias, 1962; Vc Conc., 1962–3

Chamber and inst: Pf Trio, 1929; Sonata breve, pf, 1932; Pf Qnt, 1934–6; 6 Variations on a Theme by Luis de Milán, gui, 1945; Tonadas I–IV, pf, 1956–61; Vc Suite, 1964; Celebration for Julia, str qt, glock, 1981; Alexandro y Luis, pf, 1983; other gui and pf pieces

Vocal: 3 canciones místicas, lv, pf, 1929; 2 poemas de Jorge Manrique, S, str qt, 1934–6; 3 poemas de Gil Vicente, lv, pf, 1950; 3 canciones tradicionales cubanos, mixed chorus, 1952; 12 canciones populares de Cataluña, lv, pf, 1952–7; 4 canciones populares de Cataluña, lv, pf, 1960; Missa in honorem Sanctae Rosae, mixed chorus, brass, 1963; Cantata (J. Pradas), Mez, str, harp clvd, 1965–6; Dedication Mass, mixed chorus, org, 1970; 6 canciones populares sefardíes, lv, pf, 1982; other collections of Spanish songs, lv, pf

Ed.: *The Spanish Choral Tradition* (New York, 1975–)

Principal publishers: Broude, Eschig

BIBLIOGRAPHY

VintonD
G. Chase: *The Music of Spain* (New York, rev. 2/1959)

GILBERT CHASE

Nisenan. California Indian group belonging to the MAIDU.

Niska, Maralin (*b* San Pedro, CA, *c*1930). Soprano. She first trained as a librarian but her musical studies rapidly assumed greater importance – she studied singing with Louise Mansfield, and role preparation with Lotte Lehmann, among several others. After extensive workshop and concert activity from the mid-1950s, she sang Mimì for the inauguration of the San Diego Opera in May 1965. Later that year she became a principal with the Metropolitan Opera national company, appearing in its two years of touring as Floyd's Susannah, Violetta, Butterfly, Mozart's Countess, and Musetta. In 1967 she joined the New York City Opera, adding Donna Anna and Donna Elvira, Puccini's Manon, Gounod's Marguerite, Tosca, Turandot, Salome, Suor Angelica, the Governess (*The Turn of the Screw*), and Emilia Marty (*The Makropoulos Affair*) to her extensive repertory. Her official Metropolitan début as Musetta was in 1973, after a student matinée *La traviata* there. She has given concerts and recitals throughout the USA, and made her London début at a Promenade concert in 1972 (*Missa solemnis* under Boulez), her Italian début at the Maggio Musicale, Florence, in 1978 (Marie, in *Wozzeck*), and her South American début in Bogotá in 1981 (as Turandot). Her cool, sometimes steely lyric soprano and vivacious stage personality have been assets in a wide variety of roles, although some (notably Emilia Marty and Musetta) proved more congenial than others (Salome or Cherubini's Medea).

MARTIN BERNHEIMER/R

Nisqually. American Indian group of the northwest coast; *see* SALISH.

Nitty Gritty Dirt Band. Folk-rock group. It was formed in Long Beach, California, in 1966; during its heyday in the late 1960s and early 1970s the group included Jeff Hanna, lead singer and guitar; Jimmie Fadden, drums; Ralph Taylor Barr, bass guitar (replaced by Jim Ibbotson in 1971); and Leslie Steven Thompson, John McEuen, and Chris Darrow, guitarists and banjoists. The group, renamed the Dirt Band in 1976, has survived the many changes of fashion in American rock music since 1966, occasionally achieving a respectable hit (*Mr. Bojangles*, no.9, 1970; *An American Dream*, with Linda Ronstadt as guest singer, no.13, 1979) but never making a strong commercial impact. Its importance lies in its determined advocacy of a wide range of American vernacular idioms. The peak of its achievement was the three-disc album *Will the Circle be Unbroken?* (1972), recorded in Nashville and including performances by such country-music veterans as "Mother" Maybelle Carter, Earl Scruggs, Roy Acuff, and Merle Travis. By the early 1980s, the Dirt Band's members were sometimes appearing as backup musicians for other artists, but regrouped often enough to maintain their unpretentious and appealing shared identity.

RECORDINGS
(selective list)

Nitty Gritty Dirt Band (Liberty 7501, 1967); *Uncle Charlie and his Dog Teddy* (Liberty 7642, 1970), incl. Mr. Bojangles; *Will the Circle be Unbroken?* (UA 9801, 1972); *An American Dream* (UA 974, 1979); *Plain Dirt Fashion* (WB 251131, 1984)

JOHN ROCKWELL

Nixon, Marni [McEathron, Margaret Nixon] (*b* Altadena, CA, 22 Feb 1930). Soprano. After studying singing and opera at the University of Southern California (with Carl Ebert), Stanford University (with Jan Popper), and the Berkshire Music Center (with Goldovsky and Caldwell), she embarked on a remarkably varied career, involving film and musical comedy as well as opera and concert. She has appeared extensively on American television (notably as the star of the popular children's program "Boomerang," winner of 26 Emmy awards), dubbed the singing voices of film actresses in *The King and I*, *West Side Story*, and *My Fair Lady*, and acted in several commercial stage ventures. Her light, flexible, wide-ranging soprano and uncanny accuracy and musicianship have also made her valuable in more classical ventures. She has been particularly successful in works by Webern, Stravinsky, Ives, Hindemith, and Goehr, many of which she has recorded. Her opera repertory includes Zerbinetta (*Ariadne auf Naxos*), Mozart's Susanna, Blonde, and Constanze, Violetta, La Périchole, and Philine (*Mignon*), performed at Los Angeles, Seattle, San Francisco, and Tanglewood. In addition to giving recitals, she has appeared with orchestras in New York (under Bernstein), Los Angeles, Cleveland, Toronto, London, and Israel. She has taught at the California Institute of Arts (1969–71) and joined the faculty of the Music Academy of the West, Santa Barbara, in 1980.

MARTIN BERNHEIMER/R

Nixon, Roger (*b* Tulare, CA, 8 Aug 1921). Composer. He attended Modesto Junior College and the University of California, Berkeley (BA 1942, MA 1949, PhD 1952), and studied composition with Sessions, Schoenberg, Bliss, and Bloch; other teachers included Frank Mancini (clarinet), David Boyden, Manfred Bukofzer, and Beatrice Colton. After teaching at Modesto Junior College (1951–9), he joined the faculty of San Francisco State University in 1960. His honors include grants and commissions from the NEA, San Francisco Festival of the Masses, American Bandmasters Association, and the University of Redlands. Nixon is best known as a composer of serious works for concert band, though he has also composed extensively for orchestra, chamber ensembles, and voices. Essentially chromatic, his music emphasizes pitch and chord centers, creating harmonic progressions and cadences that articulate the musical structures; skillfully controlled contrapuntal textures and large thematic shapes abound. A feature of some of his band works is the inventive handling of fanfare-like materials. Several of Nixon's works have been recorded.

WORKS

Stage: The Bride Comes to Yellow Sky (opera, R. B. West, Jr.), 1967; incidental music

Orch: Air, str, 1953; Va Conc., 1969; San Joaquin Sketches, orch/band, 1982; several other works, withdrawn

Band: Elegy and Fanfare-March, 1958; Fiesta del Pacifico, 1959; Reflections, 1962; Nocturne, 1965; Prelude and Fugue, 1966; Centennial Fanfare-March, 1970; A Solemn Processional, 1970; Dialog, 1972; Festival Fanfare-March, 1972; Music for a Civic Celebration, 1975; Pacific Celebration Suite, 1976; Psalm, 1979; Chamarita!, 1980; Academic Tribute, 1982; California Jubilee, 1982

Chamber: Str Qt no.1, 1949; Nocturne, fl, pf, 1959; Duos, vn, va, 1960, fl/ob, cl, 1960, fl, a fl, 1978, pic, cl, 1978, fl, cl, 1978, pic, fl, 1978; Movt, cl, pf, 1975; Ceremonial Piece, brass, 1976; 12 Pf Preludes, 1977; Lament, solo vc, 6 vc, 1978; Variations, b cl, 1978, bn, 1978; Conversations, vn, cl, 1981

Vocal: Chinese Seasons (Chin.) song cycle, S, pf, 1942; 6 Moods of Love (15th-century anon., A. D. Ficke, P. Sidney, E. Dickinson, E. Tietjens, A. Lowell), song cycle, S, pf, 1950; Summer Rain (Nathan), SATB, 1958; Love's Secret (Blake), male vv, 1960; Swallows (Stevenson), SATB, 1964; Bye, Bye, Baby, Lullay! (15th-century anon.), SATB, 1965; 3 Transcendental Songs (Whitman), song cycle, S, pf, 1979; Christmas Perspectives (Shakespeare, Milton, Blake, various trad. folk), chorus, 1980; Festival Mass, chorus, 1980; Chaunticleer (Chaucer), TTBB, 1984; A Narrative of Tides (E. Barker), song cycle, S, fl, pf, 1984; other songs and choruses

Principal publishers: Boosey & Hawkes, C. Fisher, Galaxy, Kjos, Lawson-Gould, Presser, Southern

RICHARD SWIFT

Noack, Fritz (*b* Wolgast, Germany, 25 Sept 1935). Organ builder. In Germany he was apprenticed to Rudolph von Beckerath (1954–8) and worked later as a journeyman with Klaus Becker and Ahrend & Brunzema. He immigrated to the USA in 1959, working first for the Estey Organ Co., then for Charles Fisk, opening his own workshop in Lawrence, Massachusetts, in 1960. He then moved to Andover, Massachusetts, and in 1970 (as the Noack Organ Co.) to Georgetown, Massachusetts. Noack's work has been almost exclusively with mechanical-action organs and, although his background is German, he has assimilated aspects of the American tradition. Influenced initially by Bauhaus ideas, his case designs tend to be simple, balanced, and musically functional in accordance with the *Werkprinzip*. His more important organs include those in Unity Church, St. Paul, Minnesota (1965), Brandeis University (1967), Trinity Lutheran Church, Worcester, Massachusetts (1967), the Emma Willard School, Troy, New York (1970), Ardmore Methodist Church, Winston-Salem, North Carolina (1978), the Presbyterian Church, Beckley, West Virginia (1979), and the Wesley Memorial Methodist Church, Savannah, Georgia (1985). He has also built positive organs, regals, and compact practice organs. In 1983 he completed a substantial restoration of an organ by Hook (1864) at Mechanics Hall, Worcester.

BIBLIOGRAPHY

G. Bozeman: "The Noack Organ Co. of Georgetown, Mass.," *Art of the Organ*, i/2 (1971), 19

U. Pape: *The Tracker Organ Revival in America* (Berlin, 1978)

BARBARA OWEN

Noble, Ray(mond Stanley) (*b* Brighton, England, 17 Dec 1903; *d* London, England, 2 April 1978). Bandleader, arranger, and composer. He studied classical piano but became interested in dance music, serving as house conductor for HMV Records from 1929 and attracting attention with the recordings of his New Mayfair Dance Orchestra (1930–34), particularly those with the outstanding singer Al Bowlly. Among these were some of Noble's own song compositions, including *By the Fireside* (1932), *Love is the sweetest thing* (1932), and especially *Goodnight, sweetheart* (1931), which became an international hit. In 1934 he was invited to New York to direct a dance orchestra assembled by Glenn Miller (who provided many of its jazz-oriented arrangements) and featuring talented jazz musicians such as Pee Wee Erwin (trumpet), Bud Freeman (tenor saxophone), and Claude Thornhill (piano). Though successful, the orchestra disbanded in 1937, and Noble moved to Los Angeles, where he settled as a bandleader and radio personality. During his years in the USA Noble continued to write popular songs, notably *Why stars come out at night* (1935), *The touch of your lips* (1936), *If you love me* (1936), *I hadn't anyone till you* (1938), and *You're so desirable* (1938). His instrumental piece *Cherokee* (1938) became the theme tune of Charlie Barnet's band and a familiar test piece for jazz musicians in the early bop style. Though Noble's band music of these years maintained high standards of musicianship and shows his impeccable taste in arrangement, his popularity dwindled, and he finally retired in the mid-1950s to the Channel Islands, returning to Santa Barbara in 1970.

BIBLIOGRAPHY

G. T. Simon: *The Big Bands* (New York, 1967, rev. 2/1971)

A. McCarthy: *The Dance Band Era* (London, 1971, 2/1974)

A. Wilder: *American Popular Song: the Great Innovators, 1900–1950* (New York, 1972)

B. Rust: *The American Dance Band Discography, 1917–1942* (New Rochelle, NY, 1975)

S. Colin and T. Staveacre: *Al Bowlly* (London, 1979)

T. Staveacre: *The Songwriters* (London, 1980)

ANDREW LAMB

Noble, T(homas) Tertius (*b* Bath, England, 5 May 1867; *d* Rockport, MA, 4 May 1953). Organist and composer. He became organist of All Saints', Colchester, at the age of 14 and attended the Royal College of Music (1884–9), where he studied organ with Walter Parratt, theory with Frederick Bridge, and composition with Charles V. Stanford. He was assistant organist to Stanford at Trinity College, Cambridge (1890–92), and organist and choirmaster of Ely Cathedral (1892–8) and of York Minster (1898–1913). At York Noble became a prominent musician and made a substantial contribution to the musical life of the city. In 1913 he immigrated to the USA and was appointed organist and choirmaster at St. Thomas Church, New York, where he implanted and nurtured a traditional English cathedral practice. He became an influential church musician and teacher and received several academic honors. In 1943 he retired from St. Thomas and pursued a more active recital career. He wrote a wide variety of compositions (stage, instrumental, and choral) including at least 35 organ pieces, three complete services, many anthems, and other liturgical settings. (*See also* HYMNODY, ex.8.)

BIBLIOGRAPHY

"Dr. T. Tertius Noble," *American Organist*, xxvii (1944), 273 [incl. full list of works]

WILLIAM OSBORNE

Noehren, Robert (*b* Buffalo, NY, 16 Dec 1910). Organist, organ builder, and composer. He studied under Dethier at the Institute of Musical Art, New York, and under Farnam at the Curtis Institute (1930–31), and served as organist and choirmaster at churches in Buffalo and Grand Rapids, Michigan. He received the BM degree from the University of Michigan in 1948. After wartime service he taught from 1946 to 1949 at Davidson College and in 1949 moved to the University of Michigan, where he remained until his retirement in 1976. Well known as a recitalist, recording artist, and organ builder, he has played extensively at home and abroad and has studied many historic European instruments. He has designed and built a number of organs including those in St. John's Roman Catholic Cathedral in Milwaukee, the First Unitarian Church in San Francisco, and the First Presbyterian Church in Buffalo. He holds a patent for a combination action that controls all pistons by a punched data-processing card. Noehren has written numerous articles for professional journals, and among his compositions are two sonatas for organ. His scholarly pursuits, however, have not diminished his technical supremacy in which great ease and absolute accuracy serve the music played. In 1978 he won the first International Performer of the Year award from the New York chapter of the American Guild of Organists.

VERNON GOTWALS

Noir, A. Pseudonym of A. E. BLACKMAR.

Nolan, Bob (1908–80). Country-music songwriter and a founding member in 1933 of the group that later became the SONS OF THE PIONEERS.

Nollman, Jim [James Maurice] (*b* Boston, MA, 31 Jan 1947). Composer, guitarist, and animal communications researcher. He attended Tufts University (BA in English and music theater, 1969), and in 1970 became music consultant to the Children's Museum in Boston. After performing in nightclubs in New York and London for several years, he settled in the San Francisco Bay area and became music director of the Gallery Theater (1974–5). During this time he began experiments in communication with ocean mammals by means of amplified acoustic and electronic music. He founded and directed Interspecies Communication (Bodinas, California, 1978–82), and was the principal investigator for the Greenpeace Iki Island project (Japan, 1978–80) and John Lilly's Human/Dolphin Foundation (Careyes, Mexico, 1982–3). Other organizations to have sponsored his researches include the World Wildlife Fund, the California Arts Commission, and the Fund for Animals.

Nollman seeks to create improvised musical dialogues with the animals he investigates, which include dolphins, turkeys, and orcs. Among the instruments he employs are electric guitars, wooden drums, *shakuhachi* (traditional Japanese flute), and dolphin sticks; he also uses special animal communications equipment and an underwater simultaneous listening, recording, and playback system of his own design. His musical technique requires improvisation and the exact matching of frequency, timbre, sonic gesture, and phrasing. Two recordings of his work, *Interspecies Music* (1976) and *Playing Music with Animals* (1982), have been released commercially.

WORKS

Opera: Hoon I Kwak (1, Nollman), 1972, San Francisco, 1975

Performance works with animals: Turkey Song (Music to Eat Thanksgiving Dinner by), 300 turkeys, 3 fl, 1974; Interspecies Music, acoustic and elec insts, 300 turkeys, 12 wolves, 20 orcs, 1976; Orca Reggae, elec gui, 20 orcs, 1980; Smithsonian Monkeys, elec gui, shakuhachi, monkeys, 1983; Orca Shooting, elec gui, orcs, 1983; Human-Dolphin Reggae, elec gui, kbd, swimmers, dolphins, 1983–4

BIBLIOGRAPHY

T. Crail: *ApeTalk Whalespeak* (Los Angeles, 1981)
W. Doak: *Dolphin Dolphin* (White Plains, NY, 1981)
J. Obrecht: "Pro's Reply: Jim Nollman," *Guitar Player*, xv/1 (1981), 6

STEPHEN RUPPENTHAL

Nomlaki. American Indian group of California. Their music bore a resemblance to that of the WINTUN.

Nooksack. American Indian group of the northwest coast; *see* SALISH.

Noone, Jimmy [Jimmie] (*b* Cut Off, nr New Orleans, LA, 23 April 1895; *d* Los Angeles, CA, 19 April 1944). Jazz clarinetist and bandleader. After playing guitar as a youth he took up clarinet at the age of 15 and studied with the Creole clarinetist Lorenzo Tio, Jr., and possibly also with Sidney Bechet (who was two years his junior). In 1913–14 he substituted for and then replaced Bechet in Freddie Keppard's band; later, with Buddy Petit, he organized the Young Olympia Band (1916). Noone left New Orleans for Chicago in 1917 and toured the Midwest with Keppard's Creole Band until it broke up in spring 1918. After returning briefly to New Orleans he left the city permanently in autumn 1918, traveling with King Oliver to Chicago where they joined Bill Johnson's band at the Royal Gardens. Noone left the Royal Gardens in 1920 to join Doc Cook's (or Cooke's) Dreamland Orchestra, with whom he played until 1926. During this period he recorded 20 sides for Gennett, Okeh, and Columbia.

Noone's most important and influential period began after he left Cook in autumn 1926 to take up residence at the Apex Club in Chicago. Here he led his own group, Jimmie Noone's Apex Club Orchestra, which eventually included Joe Poston (alto saxophone), Earl Hines (piano), Bud Scott (banjo), and Johnny Wells (drums). With this group he made a classic series of recordings for Vocalion in spring and summer of 1928. During the 1930s, except for engagements in New York in 1931 and 1935, Noone remained in Chicago leading small groups at various clubs. In the early 1940s he was taken up by the New Orleans revival movement and joined Kid Ory, Zutty Singleton, Jack Teagarden, and others in club jobs and recording sessions in San Francisco and Los Angeles. Shortly before his death he joined an all-star revival band organized for an Orson Welles CBS variety show.

Noone, along with Sidney Bechet and Johnny Dodds, was one of the most significant New Orleans reed players, and a vital link between the older New Orleans style of clarinet playing and the Chicago swing manner. His musical style was influenced by his teachers and colleagues in New Orleans, especially Bechet. Later, in Chicago, his formal study with Franz Schoepp, a classically trained clarinetist, helped give him a secure command of all three clarinet registers. His expressive performance of blue notes and solo breaks is nowhere better illustrated than in his four recordings with King Oliver's band from October 1923. Later, his Apex Club recordings of *I Know that you Know*, *Four or Five Times*, and *Apex Blues* set a new standard for post-New Orleans ensemble playing. These recordings use the New Orleans ensemble style with a revised orchestration: alto saxophone as lead instrument, clarinet embellishments, and the support of a three-piece rhythm section, with Hines often supplying a third independent line with his "trumpet-style" right hand. Noone's manner influenced many of his contemporaries as well as subsequent generations of jazz musicians, including the clarinetists Buster Bailey, Barney Bigard, Joe Marsala, Omer Simeon, and, in particular, Benny Goodman; saxophonists as varied as Bud Freeman and Eric Dolphy also admitted to being influenced by Noone.

RECORDINGS

(selective list)

As leader: I Know that you Know (1928, Voc. 1184); Four or Five Times (1928, Voc. 1185); Apex Blues (1928, Voc. 1207); The Blues Jumped a Rabbit (1936, Parlophone 2303)

As sideman: O. Powers: Play that Thing (1923, Para. 12059); K. Oliver: Chattanooga Stomp/New Orleans Stomp (1923, Col. 13003D), Camp Meeting Blues (1923, Col. 14003D); Capitol Jazzmen: Clambake in B Flat (1943, Cap. 10009)

BIBLIOGRAPHY

SouthernB
J. G. Jepsen: "Discographie de Jimmie Noone," *Cahiers du jazz*, no.8 (1963), 93
M. Williams: *Jazz Masters of New Orleans* (New York, 1967)
G. Schuller: *Early Jazz: its Roots and Musical Development* (New York, 1968)

RICHARD WANG

Nootka. American Indian tribe of Cape Flattery (on the northwest tip of the Olympic Peninsula in the state of Washington), and of the southwest coast of Vancouver Island, British Columbia (*see* INDIANS, AMERICAN, fig. 1). The Nootka living in the USA are known as the Makah. They live in a lush rain-forest area that supports a wide variety of flora and fauna and provides abundant material for masks, drums, rattles, and totem poles. Their rich environment allowed them to devote relatively few of their energies to the acquisition of food, and consequently to develop complex cultural and social structures.

1. Ceremonial practices. 2. Instruments. 3. Style. 4. Song forms.

1. CEREMONIAL PRACTICES. The Makah tribe was organized according to a hierarchy of individuals and families, including chiefs and nobles, commoners, and slaves; music functioned principally to support this complex, hereditary sociopolitical structure. The chief, a wealthy, powerful man, possessed many rights and privileges, among them the ownership of specific songs, dances, masks, costumes, and ceremonies; he often lent these to relatives who performed at lavish ceremonials at which he acted as host. Commoners, who were collaterally related to the chief, had rights of ownership to less important songs. Slaves (prisoners of war and their children born in captivity) had no rights or privileges and owned no songs.

The rainy winter months signaled the beginning of the ceremonial season, which included much feasting, singing, and dancing in the Makah's cedar longhouses. During the *Klukwali* children were initiated into a secret society. The initiates were abducted by members of the tribe dressed as wolves and carried into the woods, where they spent four days learning tribal and familial songs and dances (which they performed on their return) and history. The *Tsayak*, an important healing ceremony, included many powerful songs. During the *Tla'iihl* ceremony individuals entered a trance and, to renew their power and strength, sang personal-guardian spirit songs. These ceremonies have ceased to be observed over the past 50 years, and much of the music that accompanied them has been lost.

One ceremony that survives is the potlatch. Its traditional purpose was to uphold the power, status, and prestige of the chief, who displayed his wealth and performed his music as he transmitted his family privileges, including songs and dances, to his eldest son, and gave lavish gifts to his guests. The modern potlatch, modified in part because the ceremony was outlawed by the US government in 1887, remains a vehicle for the display of wealth and songs. Rights and privileges are still transferred, but the ceremony generally is less elaborate and of shorter duration than in the past. The hosts of potlatches are members of chiefs' families (there are no longer any chiefs among the Makah); songs, dances, costumes, and masks, which are greatly treasured, continue to be passed on from one generation to the next.

The sociopolitical system to which Makah music is linked has ceased to function, an elected tribal council having replaced the hereditary chiefs. Song ownership remains important, however, because chiefs' songs symbolize power and prestige and thus are considered desirable property. In the past, tribal members knew the history of the ownership of each others' songs, and conflicts were infrequent. As a result of changes imposed by missionaries and the US government, however, and with the outlawing of native ceremonies, lines of ownership are now in dispute. Those who do not have traditional rights of ownership to particular songs, but who nevertheless sing them at potlatches, are said to have stolen them; this practice has led to serious feuding between factions. In the past, music served to support the sociopolitical system, renew myths, aid supernatural power, and foster enculturation. It also assured personal success in healing, hunting, fishing, whaling, and warfare, and provided a form of lighter entertainment during serious ceremonial events. Its use is now limited to entertainment, bone games, and potlatches.

2. INSTRUMENTS. Since vocal music has always been of primary importance among the Nootka, most instruments have been used to support the voice and provide percussive accompaniment. The hand-held frame drum is the most common instrument. Three idiophones, once most often used in the longhouse, are no longer played. These include a cedar box drum (*c*1.2 meters high, 1.8 to 2.4 meters long) that is pounded with the feet; and a drum made from a hollowed log (*c*75 cm long) and a plank drum (a long, wooden plank raised slightly above the ground), both played with wooden beaters.

Three types of rattle – a hoop on which scallop shells are strung; a piece of whalebone, folded in half, containing pebbles; and a pair of carved, bird-shaped pieces of wood, also containing pebbles – have similarly fallen into disuse. Carved wooden rattles in the shapes of wolves, grizzly bears, or thunderbirds have been used occasionally at potlatches in the early 1980s. Whistles, once important, are now seldom used. Of different lengths and sizes, all consisted of two hollowed pieces of wood, lashed together at the ends, and sometimes in the middle. Whistles were not used to accompany songs; rather they announced the presence of supernatural beings. Bullroarers, also connected with supernatural creatures, are no longer used.

3. STYLE. Although most Nootka music is monophonic, two-part singing in 4ths is not uncommon. It is not known whether this polyphonic phenomenon, rare in American Indian music generally, came from missionary influence or whether it was indigenous. The range of most songs is about an octave. Minor and major 2nds and minor and major 3rds are characteristic intervals; 4ths and 5ths occur less frequently. Three- and four-note scales are sometimes used, but five- and six-note scales are more common. Most melodies begin with a rising pattern, followed by undulation; there may be a descending phrase at the end. Prolongation of tones often occurs at the beginning or end of a phrase. Most songs are sung at the low end of the vocal register; when a song is begun too low, one or more half-step upward adjustments may be made in performance for the singer's comfort. Vocal ornaments, such as turns and grace notes, are fairly common. Rhythms are often highly complex, with a variety of drum patterns. The basic beat patterns, mostly in groups of two or three, may be used alternately within a song or may be played and sung simultaneously, creating cross-rhythms. It is proper for voices and drums to be out of synchronization in some songs.

4. SONG FORMS. Many songs are composed entirely of vocables; others contain some lexical text, but vocables often predominate. A story is connected with almost every song, and song and story are learned together; therefore most texts are brief, only a few key words being necessary to evoke the complete story. Non-Nootka words, altered linguistic structures, and altered pronunciation may appear in Nootka song texts.

Typically a Nootka song opens with a section that has a variable number of phrases and may or may not include meaningful text; normally this section is repeated one or more times during the song, and some songs consist solely of varied repeats of this section. This section is frequently followed by a verse that usually has meaningful text; this also has a variable number of phrases, and may be repeated one or more times. Repetition, with greater or lesser variation of a small number of musical motifs or short phrases, is frequently used, adding variety while maintaining the unity of a song. Formerly each song was sung four times through, but this practice has been largely abandoned.

Recordings of Nootka music are held at the Archive of Folk Culture, Library of Congress, Washington, DC; and the Archives of Ethnic Music and Dance, University of Washington School of Music, Seattle.

See also INDIANS, AMERICAN, esp. §I, 4(ii)(e).

DISCOGRAPHY

Northwest (Puget Sound), recorded 1950 by W. Rhodes (Library of Congress, AAFS L34, 1952) [reissued 1985 with descriptive notes]
Songs of the Nootka and Quileute, recorded 1923–6 by F. Densmore (Library of Congress AAFS L32, 1952)
Nootka Indian Music of the Pacific Northwest Coast (FW FE 4524, 1974)

BIBLIOGRAPHY

J. Swan: *The Indians of Cape Flattery* (Washington, DC, 1870)
F. Boas: "The Nootka," *British Association for the Advancement of Science*, lx (1890), 582, 668
E. Sapir: "Some Aspects of Nootka Language and Culture," *American Anthropologist*, xiii (1911), 15
E. S. Curtis: *The North American Indian* (Cambridge, MA, 1907–30)
F. Densmore: *Nootka and Quileute Music*, Bureau of American Ethnology Bulletin, no. 124 (Washington, DC, 1939)
E. Sapir and M. Swadesh: *Nootka Texts* (Philadelphia, 1939)
P. Drucker: *The Northern and Central Nootkan Tribes*, Bureau of American Ethnology Bulletin, no. 144 (Washington, DC, 1951)
A. Ernst: *The Wolf Ritual of the Northwest Coast* (Eugene, OR, 1952)

H. Roberts and M. Swadesh: *Songs of the Nootka Indians of Western Vancouver Island*, Transactions of the American Philosophical Society, xlv, part 3 (1955), 199–327
P. Drucker: *Indians of the Northwest Coast* (Garden City, NY, 1963)
L. J. Goodman: *Music and Dance in Northwest Coast Indian Life* (Tsaile, AZ, 1977)

LINDA J. GOODMAN

Nordica [Norton], **Lillian** (*b* Farmington, ME, 12 Dec 1857; *d* Batavia, Java, 10 May 1914). Soprano. She came from an established New England family and studied singing for four years with John O'Neill at the New England Conservatory in Boston, graduating in 1876. She made an impressive début with Patrick Gilmore's Grand Boston Band in Madison Square Garden, New York (30 September 1876), and toured with the band for nearly two years in the USA and Europe. Seeking further vocal training, she entered the Milan Conservatory, where she studied with Antonio Sangiovanni, who not only shaped her voice and stage personality but persuaded her to change her name to Nordica. In March 1879 she made her operatic début as Donna Elvira at the Teatro Manzoni, Milan, and over the next 15 years

Lillian Nordica as Cherubino in Mozart's "Le nozze di Figaro"

"the Lily of the North" performed in many of the greatest houses in Europe, while continuing to work on her vocal technique and acting (never her strong point). She made débuts at the Paris Opéra as Marguerite (22 July 1882), at Covent Garden as Violetta (12 March 1887), and at the Academy of Music, New York, once again as Marguerite, with Mapleson's company (26 November 1883). She made her début at the Metropolitan Opera as Valentine in Meyerbeer's *Les Huguenots* (18 December 1891); two years later she sang Elsa, a role in which she was then coached extensively by Cosima Wagner for the first performance of *Lohengrin* at Bayreuth a year later. To her Italian and French roles she added seven Wagnerian heroines, and it was for these that Nordica was best known during her years at the Metropolitan (1893–1909). Her voice was originally a clear mezzo-soprano, but through study with G. B. Sbriglia and hard work she was able to extend its range and sing the higher and more brilliant roles of the soprano repertory. She continued to sing past her prime and died of pneumonia following a shipwreck in the course of a world tour.

Gifted more with Yankee pluck and perseverance than with remarkable natural talents as a singer, and lacking great beauty, a strong dramatic flair, or the charm of temperament that distinguishes most prima donnas, she made her way by hard work, good humor, and shrewd common sense – qualities that appealed to her fellow countrymen and set her apart from her rivals. She was an ardent proponent of opera in English, and she died in the midst of plans for an "American Bayreuth" and an Institute for Girls, both to be located in Westchester County, north of New York City. Her second husband was the tenor Zoltan Doeme. The Nordica Homestead Museum in Farmington, Maine, holds the singer's personal library and considerable correspondence.

BIBLIOGRAPHY

F. H. Martens: "Nordica, Lillian," *DAB*
O. Thompson: *The American Singer* (New York, 1937/*R*1969), 159
I. Glackens: *Yankee Diva: Lillian Nordica and the Golden Days of Opera* (New York, 1963) [with discography; also incl. reprs. of Nordica: "How to Sing a Ballad," *Musical Digest*, xvi/3 (1931), 24f, 44, 50, and W. Armstrong, ed.: *Lillian Nordica's Hints to Singers* (New York, 1923)]
W. Lichtenwanger: "Nordica, Lillian," *NAW*

WILLIAM LICHTENWANGER

Nordoff, Paul (*b* Philadelphia, PA, 4 June 1909; *d* Herdecke, Germany, 18 Jan 1977). Composer and music therapist. He studied piano with Samaroff at the Philadelphia Conservatory (BM 1927, MM 1932) and composition with Goldmark at the Juilliard School. In 1960 he received the degree of Bachelor of Music Therapy from Combs College. He was head of composition at the Philadelphia Conservatory (1938–43), a teacher at Michigan State College (1945–9), and professor of music at Bard College (1948–59). Among the awards he received were two Guggenheim Fellowships (1933, 1935) and a Pulitzer Music Scholarship. Until 1959 he was a "conventional" composer; thereafter he devoted his attention to music therapy for handicapped children.

WORKS

Stage: Mr. Fortune (opera, after S. T. Warner), 1936–7, rev. 1956–7; Every Soul is a Circus (ballet), 1937; The Masterpiece (operetta, 1, F. Brewer), 1940, Philadelphia, 1941; Salem Shore (ballet), 1943; Tally Ho (ballet), 1943; The Sea Change (opera, Warner), 1951

Orch: Prelude and 3 Fugues, chamber orch, 1932–6; Pf Conc., 1935; Suite, 1938; Conc., vn, pf, orch, 1948; Vn Conc., 1949; The Frog Prince (H. Pusch, Nordoff), nar, orch, 1954; Winter Sym., 1954; Spring Sym., 1956; Gothic Conc., pf, orch, 1959

Vocal: Secular Mass (W. Prude), chorus, orch, 1934; 34 Songs (Cummings), 1942–57; Lost Summer (Warner), Mez, orch, 1949; Anthony's Song Book (Nordoff), 1950; other songs and song cycles, choral pieces

Inst: Pf Qnt, 1936; Qnt, wind, pf, 1948; Sonata, vn, pf, 1950; Sonata, fl, pf, 1953; pf pieces

Many works for handicapped children

MSS in private collection, Philadelphia

Principal publishers: Associated, C. Fischer, Presser, G. Schirmer

WRITINGS

(all in collaboration with C. Robbins)

Music Therapy for Handicapped Children; Investigations and Experience (New York, 1965)
Music Therapy in Special Education (New York, 1971)
Therapy in Music for Handicapped Children (New York, 1971)
Creative Music Therapy: Individualized Treatment for the Handicapped Child (New York, 1977)

BIBLIOGRAPHY

EwenD

RUTH C. FRIEDBERG

Norman, Jessye (*b* Augusta, GA, 15 Sept 1945). Soprano. She studied at Howard University (with Carolyn Grant), the Peabody Conservatory, and the University of Michigan (with, among others, Pierre Bernac and Elizabeth Mannion). After winning the Munich International Music Competition in 1968 she made her opera début the next year at the Deutsche Oper, Berlin, as Elisabeth in *Tannhäuser*, and later appeared there as Mozart's Countess. After further engagements in Europe, which included Aida at La Scala and Berlioz's Cassandra (*Les troyens*), both in 1972, she made her recital débuts in London and New York in 1973. For her American stage début she sang Jocasta in Stravinsky's *Oedipus rex* and Purcell's Dido in a double bill with the Opera Company of Philadelphia (22 November 1982; see illustration); she performed for the first time at the Metropolitan Opera on 26 September 1983, once again in the role of Cassandra (later she sang Dido in the same opera).

Norman's commanding stature and stage presence have made her a major operatic personality, but her special distinction lies in her ability to project drama through her voice as well as histrionically – a signal asset for concert and recital work. As a concert singer and recitalist she has been acclaimed internationally for her performances of a repertory that includes works by Schubert, Mahler, Berlioz, Wagner, Satie, Berg (*Der Wein* and the Altenberg songs op.4), Messiaen, and contemporary American composers. Her opulent and dark-hued soprano is not always under perfect control, and at times sounds smaller than her frame would attest, but at its finest it reveals uncommon refinement of nuance and dynamic variety. She has recorded lieder by Schubert and Mahler, Strauss's *Vier letzte Lieder* and Schoenberg's *Gurrelieder*, Mozart's Countess and *La finta giardiniera*, Haydn's Rosina (*La vera costanza*) and Armida, the title role in Weber's *Euryanthe*, and Verdi's Giulietta (*Un giorno di regno*) and Medora (*Il corsaro*).

Jessye Norman as Dido in Purcell's "Dido and Aeneas" during her American operatic début at the Academy of Music in Philadelphia (22 November 1982)

BIBLIOGRAPHY

SouthernB
"Norman, Jessye," *CBY 1976*
"Jessye Norman: la vérité du chant," *Harmonie*, no.132 (1977), 46
"Jessye Norman Talks to John Greenhalgh," *Music and Musicians*, xxvii/12 (1979), 14
M. Mayer: "Double Header: Jessye Norman in her Met Debut Season," *Opera News*, xlviii/11 (1984), 8

PATRICK J. SMITH

North, Alex (*b* Chester, PA, 4 Dec 1910). Composer and conductor. He attended the Curtis Institute, where he studied piano with George Boyle, then in 1929 won a scholarship to the Juilliard School. He went to the Moscow Conservatory on another scholarship in 1933 and became music director of the German Theater Group and the Latvian State Theater. He became the only American member of the Union of Soviet Composers, from which he received commissions for two choruses and a set of piano variations. In 1935 he returned to the USA and taught music for dance at Finch, Briarcliff, Sarah Lawrence, and Bennington colleges. In New York he studied composition with Copland and Toch, and composed ballet scores for Martha Graham, Hanya Holm, and Agnes de Mille. In 1939 he went to Mexico as music director for the Anna Sokolow dance troupe, and while there he studied with Silvestre Revueltas and conducted concerts at the National Palace of Fine Arts in Mexico City.

During World War II North served as a captain in the US Army, organizing therapeutic programs for veterans and scoring documentaries for the Office of War Information. In 1946 his *Revue* for clarinet and orchestra was performed by Benny Goodman with the New York PO under Leonard Bernstein. He continued to compose for the theater, particularly ballet scores, and after the success of his music for Elia Kazan's production of Arthur Miller's *Death of a Salesman*, Kazan invited him to write for the film version of Tennessee Williams's *A Streetcar Named Desire*. This, the first jazz-based score to be written for a film, brought North wide acclaim, and in the 1950s he became a leading Hollywood composer.

North's music encompasses violent dissonance and gentle lyricism. He makes frequent use of percussion and nonsymphonic instruments, for example, in *Viva Zapata!* (marimba, bongos, tuned timbales) and *Spartacus* (sarrusophone, kythara, dulcimer, recorder, lute, bagpipes, Ondioline). His sources include jazz (*The Long, Hot Summer*) and folk music (*Viva Zapata!*), or both (*The Rose Tattoo*). Although he has used the symphony orchestra to striking effect (notably in *Spartacus* and *Cleopatra*), his orchestration tends to be sparse; he often uses only small groups of instruments (as in *The Bachelor Party* and *Who's Afraid of Virginia Woolf?*).

WORKS

FILM SCORES

* – *documentaries*

*China Strikes Back, 1936; *Heart of Spain, 1937; *People of the Cumberland, 1937; *Mount Vernon, 1940; *A Better Tomorrow, 1944; *Library of Congress, 1945; *Venezuela, 1945; *City Pastorale, 1946; *Recreation, 1946;

*Rural Nurse, 1946; *Coney Island USA, 1950; Death of a Salesman, 1951; A Streetcar Named Desire, 1951; The 13th Letter, 1951; Viva Zapata!, 1952; Les misérables, 1952; Pony Soldier, 1952; *The American Road, 1953; *Decision for Chemistry, 1953; The Member of the Wedding, 1953

Desirée, 1954; Go, Man, Go!, 1954; Man with the Gun, 1955; The Racers, 1955; The Rose Tattoo, 1955; Unchained, 1955; The Bad Seed, 1956; I'll Cry Tomorrow, 1956; The King and Four Queens, 1956; The Rainmaker, 1956; The Bachelor Party, 1957; Hot Spell, 1958; South Seas Adventure, 1958; The Long, Hot Summer, 1958; Stage Struck, 1958; The Sound and the Fury, 1959; The Wonderful Country, 1959; Spartacus, 1960; The Children's Hour, 1961; The Misfits, 1961; Sanctuary, 1961

All Fall Down, 1962; Cleopatra, 1963; The Outrage, 1964; The Agony and the Ecstasy, 1965; Cheyenne Autumn, 1965; Who's Afraid of Virginia Woolf?, 1966; 2001: a Space Odyssey, 1967 [not used]; The Devil's Brigade, 1968; The Shoes of the Fisherman, 1968; A Dream of Kings, 1969; Hard Contract, 1969; Willard, 1971; Pocket Money, 1972; The Rebel Jesus, 1972; Once Upon a Scoundrel, 1973; Lost in the Stars (adaptation of work by Weill, 1949), 1974; Shanks, 1974; Bite the Bullet, 1975; Journey into Fear, 1975; The Passover Plot, 1976; Somebody Killed her Husband, 1978; Carny, 1980; Wise Blood, 1980; Dragonslayer, 1981; Under the Volcano, 1984; Prizzi's Honor, 1985; many other documentaries

TELEVISION MUSIC

The Billy Rose Show; Playhouse 90; Nero Wolfe; I'm a Lawyer; The FDR Story; Silent Night; Africa; The Man and the City; Rich Man, Poor Man; The Word; Sister-sister

DRAMATIC

Incidental music, revues: Dog Beneath the Skin (W. H. Auden, C. Isherwood), 1936; Life and Death of an American (G. Sklar), collab. E. Robinson, 1939; 'Tis of Thee (revue, A. Hayes), collab. A. Moss, 1940; Of V we Sing (revue), 1941; You Can't Sleep Here (revue), 1941; Blow your Top (revue), 1943; Song of our City (pageant), 1946; O'Daniel (G. Swarthout, J. Savacool), 1947; The Great Campaign (A. Sundgaard), 1947; Death of a Salesman (A. Miller), 1949; The Innocents (W. Archibald), 1950; Queen of Sheba (musical), 1950; Richard III (Shakespeare), 1953; Coriolanus (Shakespeare), 1954; The American Clock (A. Miller), 1984

Ballets, dance music: Ballad in a Popular Style, 1933; Case History, 1933; Into the Streets, 1934; Song of Affirmation, 1934; Façade, 1935; War is Beautiful, 1936; American Lyric, 1937; The Last Waltz, 1937; Slaughter of the Innocents, 1937; Inquisition, 1938; Lupe, 1940; Design for Five, 1941; Exile, 1941; Golden Fleece, 1941; Clay Ritual, 1942; Intersection, 1947; A Streetcar Named Desire, 1952 [based on film score]; Wall Street Ballet, for Show of Shows (television music), 1953; Dream Ballet, for Daddy Long Legs (film), 1955; Mal de siècle, 1958

Children's works: The City Sings for Michael, nar, orch, 1940; Hither and Thither of Danny Dither (opera, J. Gury), 1941; Waltzing Elephant, nar, orch, 1946; Little Indian Drum, nar, orch, 1947; Yank and Christopher Columbus, nar, orch, 1948

OTHER WORKS

Inst: Quest, chamber orch, 1938; Suite, fl, cl, bn, 1938; Rhapsody, pf, orch, 1939; Suite, str qt, 1939; Trio, ww, 1939; Qnt, ww, 1942; Window Cleaner, cl, 2 pf, 1945; Revue, cl, orch, 1946; Sym. no. 1, 1947; Dance Preludes, pf, 1948; Holiday Set, orch, 1948; A Streetcar Named Desire, suite, orch, 1951 [based on film score]; Death of a Salesman, suite, orch, 1951 [based on film score]; Viva Zapata!, suite, orch, 1952 [based on film score]; Rhapsody, tpt, pf, orch, 1956 [for film Four Girls in Town]; Sym. no.2, 1968 [based on television score Africa]

Vocal: Negro Mother (L. Hughes), cantata, A, chorus, orch, 1940; Ballad of Valley Forge (A. Kreymborg), Bar, chorus, orch, 1941; Rhapsody, USA (A. Hayes), S, A, T, B, chorus, orch, 1942; Morning Star (M. Lampell), cantata, chorus, orch, 1946; many songs

Principal publishers: Marks, Mills, North, Northern
MSS in *CLU-MUS*

BIBLIOGRAPHY

F. Lewin: "A Streetcar Named Desire," *Film Music*, xi/3 (1952), 13

L. Adomian: "Viva Zapata," *Film Music*, xi/4 (1952), 4

T. Thomas: *Music for the Movies* (South Brunswick, NJ, and New York, 1973), 179

K. Sutak: "The Return of *A Streetcar Named Desire*," *Pro Musica Sana*, iii/1 (1974), 4; iii/4 (1974–5), 9; iv/2 (1975), 18; iv/3 (1976), 13

I. Bazelon: *Knowing the Score* (New York, 1975), 214

M. Skiles: *Music Scoring for TV & Motion Pictures* (Blue Ridge Summit, PA, 1976), 248

F. Orowan: "A Look at Alex North's Use of Historical Source Music," *Film Music Notebook*, iii/1 (1976), 9

K. Sutak: "A *Dragonslayer* Inquiry," *Pro Musica Sana*, ix/4 (1982), 7

CHRISTOPHER PALMER/CLIFFORD McCARTY

North Carolina, University of. State-supported university at Chapel Hill chartered in 1789, whose department of music was formed in 1919; *see* CHAPEL HILL, RALEIGH, DURHAM, and LIBRARIES AND COLLECTIONS, §3.

North Carolina School of the Arts. A state-supported school for the performing arts in Winston-Salem, North Carolina. Founded in 1965, it provides education for careers in music, dance, drama, and design and production from grade 7 to college level. The School of Music, in the college and high-school division, has about 230 students and a faculty of 40; it offers the BM, college diploma in music, and high school diploma in music. The music library has nearly 60,000 items, including 24,000 scores and 26,000 recordings.

MARIE KROEGER

North Carolina Symphony Orchestra. Orchestra founded in 1932 by Lamar Stringfield and based in Raleigh, North Carolina; *see* CHAPEL HILL, RALEIGH, DURHAM.

Northeast Woodlands Indians. Group of American Indian tribes that share certain cultural traits, living in New England, New York, New Jersey, Pennsylvania, eastern Virginia and Kentucky, northern Ohio and Indiana, Illinois, Michigan, Wisconsin, and northern Minnesota, and adjacent areas of Canada. *See* IROQUOIS and WABANAKI; *see also* INDIANS, AMERICAN, §I, 4(ii)(b).

Northern Blackfoot. American Indian tribe of Montana, and Alberta, Canada; *see* BLACKFOOT (i).

Northern Marianas. *See* MARIANA ISLANDS.

Northrup, George. Pseudonym of WALLINGFORD RIEGGER.

North Texas State University. The state university at Denton, Texas, dates back to 1890 when the North Texas Normal College was founded; this became North Texas State College in 1899 and, in 1966, North Texas State University. The school of music was founded in 1890, and by 1980 it enrolled more than 1200 students and had a full-time faculty of 85 under Marceau Myers as dean. BM, MM, DMA, and PhD degrees are offered, in performance, music education, composition, musicology, theory, and jazz studies; the jazz studies program is outstanding and its One O'clock Lab Band has been nominated for several Grammy awards. Other performing groups sponsored by the school of music include an opera theater. The music library (established 1941) holds early manuscripts and letters of Schoenberg (catalogued in J. A. Kimmey, Jr.: *The Arnold Schoenberg–Hans Nachod Collection* (1979)). The library also houses material from the personal libraries of professors Lloyd Hibberd and Helen Hewitt (librarian from 1940 to 1965), and from those of Don Gillis, Duke Ellington, and Stan Kenton. The folklore archive in the media library also contains recordings of southwestern folk music. (For a further discussion, *see* LIBRARIES AND COLLECTIONS, §3.)

GRAYDON BEEKS

Northwest Coast Indians. Group of American Indian tribes that share certain cultural traits, living in a narrow band extending along the Pacific coast of North America from northern California, Oregon, and Washington, through Canada, and into Alaska. *See* NOOTKA and TLINGIT; *see also* INDIANS, AMERICAN, §I, 4(ii)(e).

Northwestern University. Privately endowed university in Evanston, Illinois, whose school of music was established in 1895. *See* CHICAGO (i), §4; *see also* LIBRARIES AND COLLECTIONS, §3, Illinois, Evanston.

Norton, Lillian. *See* NORDICA, LILLIAN.

Norvo, Red [Norville, Kenneth] (*b* Beardstown, IL, 31 March 1908). Jazz xylophonist and vibraphonist. He took up marimba at about the age of 14, and later xylophone. After touring with a marimba band in the late 1920s he joined the Paul Whiteman Orchestra, whose singer, Mildred Bailey, became his first wife. In New York from 1933 he worked as a freelance and, with Charlie Barnet, led a sextet on 52nd Street (1935–6), then formed a small orchestra with Bailey (1936–9). He continued to lead big bands and then combos before joining the Benny Goodman Sextet (1944–5), at which time he changed permanently to the vibraphone. Given carte blanche for a recording session in 1945, he organized an unusual swing and bop octet which included Charlie Parker, Dizzy Gillespie, and Teddy Wilson. He was a soloist with Woody Herman's First Herd (1946), and he toured with Billie Holiday. During the 1950s he led trios with guitar and double bass, one of which was an outstanding West Coast jazz ensemble with Tal Farlow and Charles Mingus (1950–51). In 1959 he toured Europe with Goodman. He rejoined Goodman briefly in 1961 and, after a serious ear operation, toured Europe as a soloist (1968) and with George Wein's Newport All Stars (1969), but through the 1960s and 1970s he worked mainly in Nevada and California. Several albums with famous swing musicians in the mid- to late 1970s announced his return to the international arena. In the 1980s he has toured Europe with regularity, re-formed a trio with Farlow, and joined Benny Carter, Louis Bellson, and others for an acclaimed swing concert in New York (1985).

In the early 1930s, with Whiteman and later with his own ensembles, Norvo proved himself an exceptional improviser on the xylophone, a previously neglected instrument in jazz. He has usually played the vibraphone without vibrato, almost like a xylophone. His improvising, strongly influenced by Teddy Wilson's piano style, suffers an occasional rhythmic stiffness at fast tempos, but is outstanding on jazz ballads such as *Ghost of a Chance* (1945), recorded during a concert at Town Hall in New York. As a bandleader Norvo prefers delicate sounds. In the 1930s he led a drummerless sextet (trumpet, tenor saxophone, clarinet, xylophone, guitar, double bass) and an orchestra noted for its subtle approach to swing. In 1936–7 this orchestra featured highly praised arrangements by Eddie Sauter, particularly *Remember*, which has an outstanding solo by Norvo. Subsequently bringing his concern for clarity and restraint to the trio with Farlow and Mingus, he was, among leading musicians of the swing era, unusually successful in making a transition to the bop style.

RECORDINGS

(*selective list*)

As leader: Knockin' on Wood/Hole in the Wall (1933, Bruns. 6562); Bughouse (1935, Col. 3079D); Remember (1937, Bruns. 7896); Hallelujah (1945, Dial 1045); Ghost of a Chance (1945, Baronet 47103); September Song (1950, Discovery 147); Move (1950, Discovery 145); *Red Norvo Trio* (1953, Fan. 3–12); *Vibes a la Red* (1974–5, Famous Door 105)

As co-leader with R. Tompkins: *Red and Ross* (1979, Concord 90)

As sideman: B. Goodman: Slipped Disc (1945, Col. 36817); W. Herman: Igor/Nero's Conception (1946, Col. 37228); G. Wein: *Newport All Stars* (1969, Atl. 1533)

BIBLIOGRAPHY

L. Feather: "The Vibraharp," *The Book of Jazz* (New York, 1957, rev. 2/1965)
G. T. Simon: *The Big Bands* (New York, 1967, rev. 4/1981)
A. Shaw: *The Street that Never Slept* (New York, 1971/*R*1983 as *52nd Street: the Street of Jazz*)
W. Balliett: "The Music is More Important," *Ecstasy at the Onion* (New York, 1972), 194; repr. in *Improvisiing* (New York, 1977)
R. Stewart: "Red Norvo: a Tale of a Pioneer," *Jazz Masters of the Thirties* (New York, 1972/*R*1980), 71
S. Woolley: "Red Norvo Interview," *Cadence*, ii/1 (1976), 3
J. McDonough: "Red Norvo: a Man for all Eras," *Down Beat*, xliv/18 (1977), 16
S. Klett: "Red Norvo: Interview," *Cadence*, v/7 (1979), 5
M. Williams: "Norvo, Red," *Grove 6*
L. Tomkins: "Happy Again with the Trio: Red Norvo," *Crescendo International*, xx/4 (1981–2), 22

BARRY KERNFELD

Norwegian-American music. The music of the Norwegian community in the USA is discussed as part of the Scandinavian tradition; *see* EUROPEAN-AMERICAN MUSIC, §II, 6.

Norworth, Jack [Knauff, John] (*b* Philadelphia, PA, 5 Jan 1879; *d* Laguna Beach, CA, 1 Sept 1959). Vaudeville performer and composer. After leaving home to join a minstrel show, he also tried his hand at vaudeville and straight drama. A man of small stature, he quickly became popular as a song-and-dance man, but he enjoyed his greatest success between 1907 and 1913, when he was partnered by his second wife, NORA BAYES; their celebrated billing read "Nora Bayes, Assisted and Admired by Jack Norworth." They played together in vaudeville and on Broadway and introduced Norworth's best-known song, *Shine on, Harvest Moon*, in Ziegfeld's *Follies of 1908*. Among the other songs for which Norworth is remembered are *Take me out to the ball game* and *Sister Susie's sewing shirts for soldiers*. He spent most of World War I performing in London, and during the early 1920s played important roles for companies in Chicago. Although he continued to be a favorite in vaudeville, his popularity gradually lessened, and one of his last appearances was in 1938 as the elderly stage doorman in *The Fabulous Invalid*.

GERALD BORDMAN

Notation. Any graphic means of representing musical sounds, either by symbolizing them, or by providing instructions for producing them physically. This article is concerned with notations unique to, or originating in, the USA; these systems have either developed from attempts to facilitate music reading or have been innovations resulting from compositional impulses. (The illustrations for this article appear on pp.388–95.)

1. Notations for ease of reading. 2. 20th-century notational innovations.

1. NOTATIONS FOR EASE OF READING. The first music printed in the English-speaking colonies of North America was a group of psalm tunes, with bass lines, added to the ninth edition of the Bay Psalm Book (1698). Their notation and the solmization system by which they were taught were the foundation of the first specifically American notational developments. Fig. 1 shows

the combination of staff notation and letters beneath the staves representing a four-syllable solmization system (*fa, sol, la, fa, sol, la, mi*); this was an adaptation of earlier English psalm notation (*see* FASOLA). In the early 18th century a movement to improve church music by encouraging congregations to sing in "regular" fashion (i.e., by note-reading) arose in New England; one of its first proponents, John Tufts, further adapted the earlier notation in *A Very Plain and Easy Introduction to the Singing of Psalm Tunes* (1721). He eliminated conventional note shapes but kept the staff, on which he placed letters representing the solmization syllables, adding dots to double their durations, and slurs between them to halve their durations (fig.2). This "plain and easy method" of literal notation had an explicit pedagogical aim: to enable the novice at reading music, "with a little practice, to sing all the tunes in this book in any of their parts, with ease and pleasure." Although the *Introduction* had appeared in 11 editions by 1744 (the earliest extant edition is the third, 1723), Tufts's method was not adopted by other New Englanders; they continued, as the singing-school movement grew during the 18th century, to use staff notation with conventional note shapes.

An important notational innovation was introduced by William Little and William Smith in their singing-school tunebook *The Easy Instructor* (1801), which used four differently shaped note heads to represent the four solmization syllables: ◸ (*fa*), ○ (*sol*), □ (*la*), and ◇ (*mi*) (fig.3). This "shape-note" system was used in many later tunebooks, especially in the South and West, among them the extremely popular and long-lived *Southern Harmony* (1835) of William Walker, and *The Sacred Harp* (1844) of B. F. White and E. J. King. The four-shape system was challenged, however, by the rising influence of European seven-syllable solmization: Jesse B. Aikin added three new shapes to the four of earlier shape-note tunebooks in *The Christian Minstrel* (1846; fig.4*a*); other tunebook compilers, under the impression that Aikin's new shapes were patented, invented other systems (figs.4*b–f*). (*See also* SHAPE-NOTE HYMNODY.)

Various other notations, mostly numerical and aiming similarly to simplify the task of learning to read music by combining some kind of staff notation with cues for solmization, were developed. In Thomas J. Harrison's *Sacred Harmonicon* (1839) the seven scale steps are represented by the numbers 1 to 7, which replace conventional note shapes; the staff is reduced to two lines, the space between them representing a "middle" octave (within which most vocal lines lie); and durations of notes and rests, as well as inflections of pitch, are represented by various signs and letters. Augustus D. Fillmore and his son James Henry Fillmore of Cincinnati both published tunebooks in which numbers (again, 1 to 7) either replaced note heads in an otherwise conventional staff notation, as in *The New Harp of Zion* (1866), or were placed in the note heads, as in *Songs of Gratitude* (1877; fig.5). 19th-century American pedagogical ardor, expressed in novel attempts to make music reading easier, knew no bounds; the immense variety of short-lived notational self-help systems reached a climax when an "animalistic" shape-note method was proposed (probably facetiously) in the *Musical Million* (xxi, 1890; fig.6).

Related to these kinds of notation, although not so explicitly pedagogical in their aim, were various methods developed in communities of Shakers (*see* SHAKER MUSIC) between about 1825 and 1870. Some Shaker manuscripts are written in adaptations of four-shape (fig.7*a*) and seven-shape systems; others display different kinds of literal notation (fig.7*b*) and numerical notation (fig.7*c*). Several Shaker scribes learned or invented shorthand systems (fig.7*d*), and one Shaker song – "learned by [the scribe] while sailin on de sea of de fate in de canoo. Nov. 6th 1842" – is uniquely notated in symbols apparently derived from American Indian pictographs.

In the first third of the 20th century certain practices arose in the notation of popular music which aimed at facilitating performance. In particular two ways of indicating the basic harmonies of a song were developed, either or both of which could supplement the conventional form of notation that had existed for decades (consisting of a voice part on one staff, and an accompaniment below it in two-staff keyboard notation). The first of these is tablature notation, in which a grid of four (for ukulele) or six (for guitar) vertical and four horizontal lines represents the fingerboard; dots represent the positions of the fingers on the strings that are to be stopped. The other system of harmonic indication (which can be combined with the grid; fig.8) is letter-based: a capital letter indicates the root of a triad; a minor triad is indicated by the suffix "m" or "mi"; and diminished and augmented triads are signified respectively by "dim" (or a superscript zero) and "aug" (or a plus sign). Numerals, with or without accidentals, are used for 3rd-based chords larger than triads (♭7, 9, ♯11, etc.). Similar harmonic indications are used in jazz musicians' "fake books," which include the melodic line and text (if any) of a composition; another convention represents "comping," or the playing of repeated chords on quarter-note beats, by slash marks. Some 20th-century popular guitar music uses another type of tablature notation, reminiscent of the lute tablatures of the Renaissance. A six-line "staff" corresponds to the strings of the instrument; time signatures, bar-lines, and rhythmic indications are as in staff notation; and the letters "TAB" often replace a clef (fig.9). In other respects different works observe different notational conventions and there is no standardization.

See also HISPANIC-AMERICAN MUSIC, §1.

2. 20TH-CENTURY NOTATIONAL INNOVATIONS. The traditional staff notation of Western music, originally designed for diatonic vocal genres, became increasingly inadequate as vocal music became more complex, as solo instrumental and ensemble music became more prevalent, and as chromaticism was introduced more and more broadly. By the early 20th century some composers had begun to supplement or replace traditional notation with new means more representative of the music they wrote. Especially after World War II, with a broadening of the range of musical styles, new notations proliferated from composer to composer and even from work to work. Only the most general account can be attempted here, since few of the new notational devices have achieved general acceptance, let alone universal adoption.

The pioneers in 20th-century American notation were Charles Ives and Henry Cowell. Ives was largely content with conventional notation but altered elements of it from time to time. In the song *Charlie Rutlage* (1920/21) he abandoned note heads briefly to encourage the singer into realistic unpitched declamation, but retained the note stems and flags to ensure precise rhythmic delivery (fig.10). In *The Cage* (1906) he achieved a meterless freedom of rhythm by omitting time signature and most bar-lines; in other works without time signature he changed bar lengths frequently to reflect accentual or phraseological patterns. In the "Hawthorne" movement (1911) of the Second ("Concord") Piano Sonata Ives enclosed in boxes high-pitched cluster chords, to be played by depressing the piano keys with a wooden board (fig.11); the massive clusters in the accompaniment of *Majority* (1921) are boxed to indicate that they are not to be played as arpeggios.

Cowell approached more systematically the notation of the new musical resources he envisioned. He devised several notations for tone clusters (fig. 12), some of which were taken up by later composers. For polyrhythms he developed an original shape-note notation that permitted a distinct, precise representation of complex rhythmic ratios (used in such works as *Fabric*, fig. 13), and, as he proceeded to explore rhythmic–harmonic relationships, he revealed them in similarly innovative notation in the Quartet Romantic (1917) and Quartet Euphometric (1919); his shape-note notation was not adopted by others, however. For the 12 different methods of producing sounds inside the body of the piano in *The Banshee* (1925) he employed a stop-gap notation using the letters A to L, each indicating a different kind of manipulation (fig. 14); in *Sinister Resonance* (?1930) a related system of numerals indicates different means of producing harmonics on the piano strings.

Another innovator between the wars was Harry Partch, who developed his own system of microtonal tuning and temperament and invented a battery of instruments; out of necessity he also developed idiosyncratic methods of notation, especially of pitch. These were not adopted by other composers, and indeed there has been no consensus on the notation of microtonal music, except that most composers have elaborated on conventional signs for accidentals and invented others; Ben Johnston's *Two Sonnets of Shakespeare* (1978), for example, uses ♯, ♭, ♯, ♯, ♭, ↑, ↓, +, and − (minus sign) to denote different degrees of microtonal inflection (fig. 15; *see also* TUNING SYSTEMS, esp. §3).

Most of the new notational techniques that appeared after World War II stemmed from one or the other of two opposed impulses: to render the composer's intentions ever more precisely and over a much broader range of musical elements and sound sources than before, or to be notationally ambiguous and non-prescriptive, with the aim of encouraging greater participation by the performer in the realization of the music. Most composers continued to rely on conventional notation, but their struggle to indicate with it the minute details of their increasingly complex music often strained it to the limits. The first six bars of the first of George Crumb's Five Pieces for Piano (1962; fig. 16), include a number of notational nuances developed in the postwar years: a time signature showing the unit of time (here an eighth-note) as a note shape rather than a number (not actually necessary in this instance but useful when the beat is not a conventional, simple unit of time, but rather, for example, a dotted eighth-note); instructions for plucking the piano strings in different ways (bars 1, 4, and 5); rubato-like changes of speed within a precise time span, with an unusual prime-number division of the time span (13 notes = ♩., with a beam calling for an accelerando followed by a decelerando, bar 4); and the most finicky indications of dynamics (*ppp, pppp, senza cresc.*), articulation (*poco fz*; *laissez vibrer* chords or tones at the end of each bar, indicated by slurs), pedaling, and expression (*Quasi improvvisando*). A passage from Elliott Carter's String Quartet no. 2 (1959; fig. 17) illustrates his attempt to realize in conventional notation the steady march of the second violin part in 4/4 at ♩ = 140 while the other instruments are proceeding in 5/4 at ♩ = 175 – for Carter a fairly simple bimetrical texture, but one that compels him to adopt both an inordinately complicated notation of the second violin part within the 5/4 context, and an extra cue line to clarify its true metrical and rhythmic shape.

The inability of conventional notation to convey clearly and simply to the performer the expanded vocabulary of imagined sounds and their articulation used by composers in the postwar years led inevitably to an extraordinary multiplication of signs and symbols, only a few of which came into general practice: Read (1964, 1978), Karkoschka (1966), Risatti (1975), and Stone (1980) attempted to analyze and codify them; and Cage (1969) put together a compendium of facsimiles of manuscript scores by more than 250 composers to document them.

Notational innovations understandably arose within the new field of electroacoustic music, partly because, until the late 1970s, protection under the US copyright laws required graphic representation of music (even when it existed only as invisible particles on tape), and partly because some composers of electroacoustic music used notation in their precompositional planning. The resulting notation is thus nonprescriptive (in that it does not consist of instructions for performance in the traditional way); rather it describes a composition already embodied on tape (Ussachevsky, 1960), or is a kind of blueprint of the technical processes involved in the making of a piece with a synthesizer (as in fig. 18, which shows the frequency, time, envelope, volume, and timbre characteristics of the synthetic materials on each of four channels at the beginning of Babbitt's *Correspondences* for string orchestra and tape, 1967).

The most extreme variety and range of notational innovations after World War II was introduced in connection with the aleatory and action music that developed in the 1950s. Cage was a leader notationally as well as conceptually; in a statement of 1962 outlining the various paths his musical thought had taken, his summary of postwar compositional methods is expressed largely in terms of his means of arriving at notation:

> composition using charts and moves thereon (1951); composition using templates made or found (1952–); composition using observation of imperfections in the paper upon which it is written (1952–); composition without a fixed relation of parts to score (1954–); composition indeterminate of its performance (1958–).

Many of Cage's works, regardless of the chance operations he used to substitute for his own will or taste in making compositional decisions, are notated in the most elegant, precise conventional notation. Others, however, led him into new notational territory (*see* CAGE, JOHN, fig. 3). Two among many varied examples that might be cited are *Imaginary Landscape no. 5* (1952), the score of which makes possible the creation of a recording on tape, using as source material any 42 phonograph records (fig. 19), or the notorious – and notationless – *4′33″* (1952), which has three score pages, each containing only a movement number and the word "Tacet."

Cage's musical associates in this period were equally inventive. Earle Brown made an important contribution, adopted by a number of other composers, with his "time notation" (later called more commonly "proportional notation") showing the durations of tones proportionally, independent of a strict pulse or metric system; in Music for Cello and Piano (1954–5) the lengths of the note heads suggest the relative durations of the tones within the time span represented by the score system; each system has the same duration, chosen within specified limits by the performers (fig. 20). Brown was also one of the first to write in wholly graphic notation, producing scores consisting only of squiggles, dots, lines, blocks, and other visual "events" that are to be translated, through the performers' imaginative interpretation of them, into sounds; the best-known of these is the one-page *December 1952* (*see* BROWN, EARLE, illustration). This offers

1. *Early American notation: staff and literal notation based on a four-syllable solmization system (Bay Psalm Book, supplement to the 9th edition; Boston, 1698)*

3. *Four-shape notation, in which distinctive note heads represent the four solmization syllables (William Little and William Smith, "The Easy Instructor"; Albany, NY, 1808 edition); though the excerpt is in E minor, the shapes are determined by the solmization of G major*

2. *Literal notation on staves (John Tufts, "An Introduction to the Singing of Psalm-tunes," 10th edition; Boston, 1738); the dots double and the slurs halve the notes' duration*

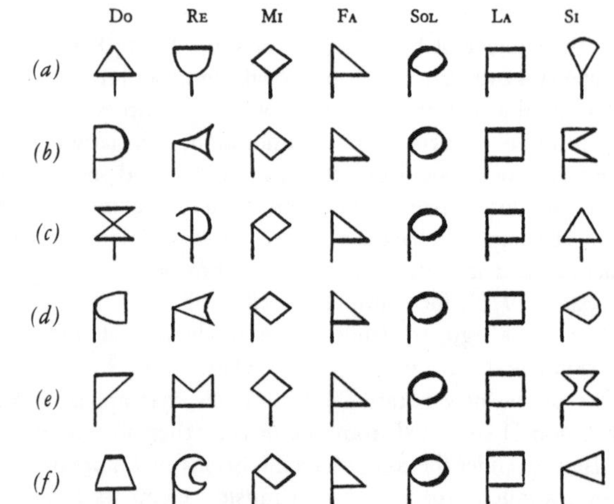

4. *Systems of seven-shape notation used by (a) Jesse B. Aikin in "The Christian Minstrel" (1846), (b) A. Auld in "The Ohio Harmonist" (1847), (c) W. H. Swan and Marcus Lafayette Swan in "The Harp of Columbia" (1848), (d) Joseph Funk in "Harmonia sacra, being a Compilation of Genuine Church Music" (5th edition, 1851), (e) A. W. Johnson in "The Western Psalmodist" (1853), and (f) William Walker in "Christian Harmony" (1867); each of the systems has conventional staff notation apart from the shape of the note heads (G. P. Jackson, "White Spirituals in the Southern Uplands," Chapel Hill, NC, 1933)*

5. *Numerical notation combined with conventional staff notation (James Henry Fillmore, "Songs of Gratitude"; Cincinnati, 1884 edition)*

6. *Shape notation using outlines of animals, the names of which supply mnemomics for the seven solmization syllables (Aldine S. Kieffer, "Musical Million," xxi; Dayton, VA, 1890)*

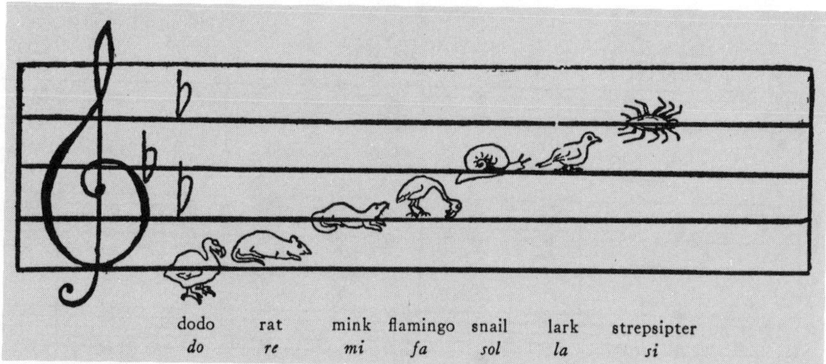

(a)

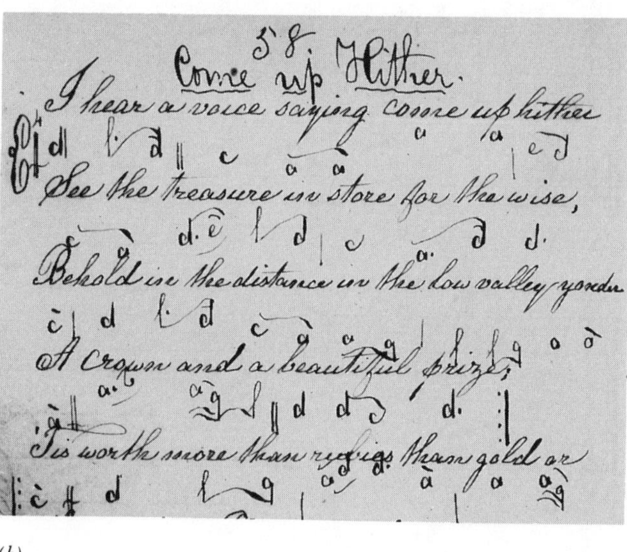

(b)

S. O. Watervliet – 1839

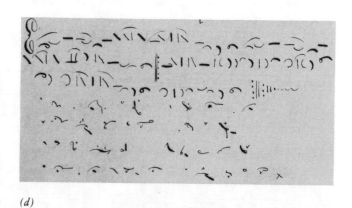

(c)

(d)

7. *Shaker notation systems in 19th-century manuscripts: (a) adaptation of four-shape notation ("That Beautiful City," 1830s; OClWHi); (b) small literal notation ("Come up Hither," 1855–63; private collection); (c) numerical notation ("S. O. Watervliet," 1838–42; OClWHi); (d) shorthand notation ("The Humble Heart," c1845–67; DeWint-M)*

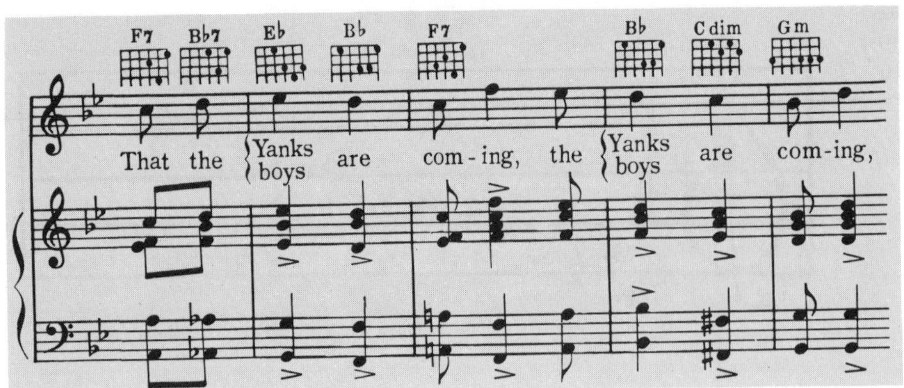

8. *Tablature for guitar, with chord indications, added above the staves (George M. Cohan, "Over there"; New York: Leo Feist, 1917)*

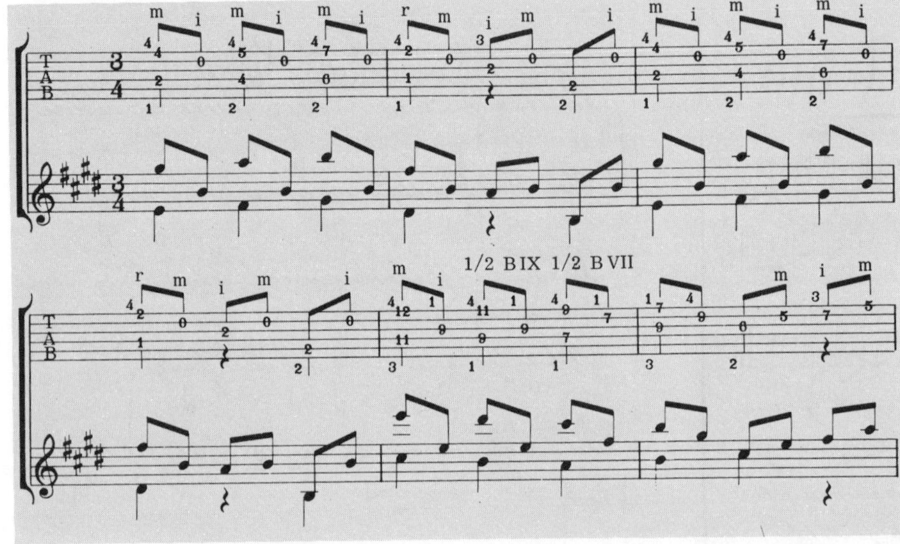

9. *Guitar tablature notating finger-picking figuration, with corresponding staff notation below: the six-lines represent the guitar strings, numerals on the lines indicate frets, and the other numerals and letters show fingering (H. Vinson, "A Folksinger's Guide to the Classical Guitar"; New York, 1971)*

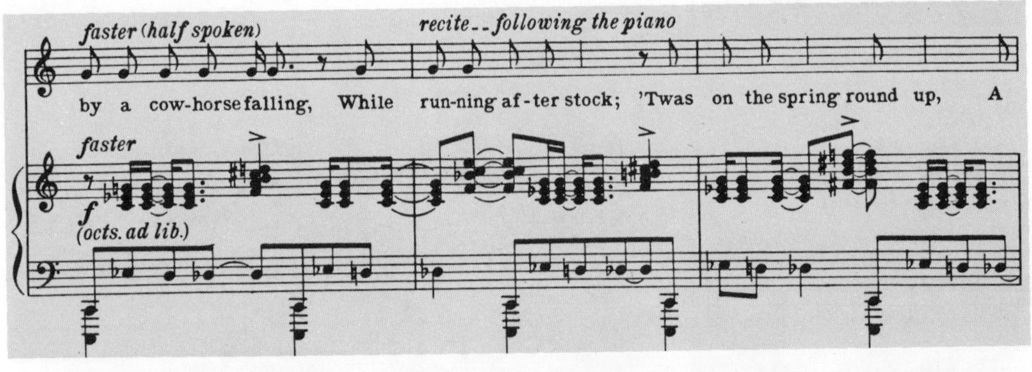

10. *Headless notes, indicating that the text should be recited rhythmically at no specific pitch (Charles Ives, "Charlie Rutlage," 1920/21, published in "114 Songs"; Redding, CT, 1922/R1975)*

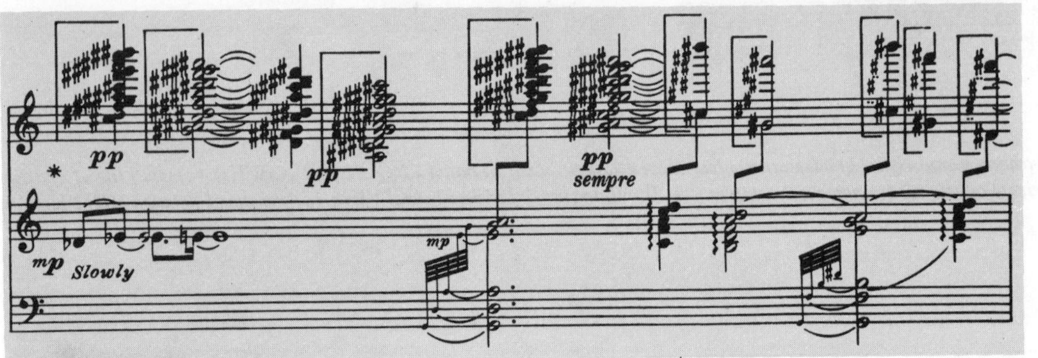

11. *Cluster chords enclosed in boxes (Charles Ives, "Hawthorne," Second Piano Sonata, first published 1920; revised edition, New York, 1947); the chords are played with a wooden board*

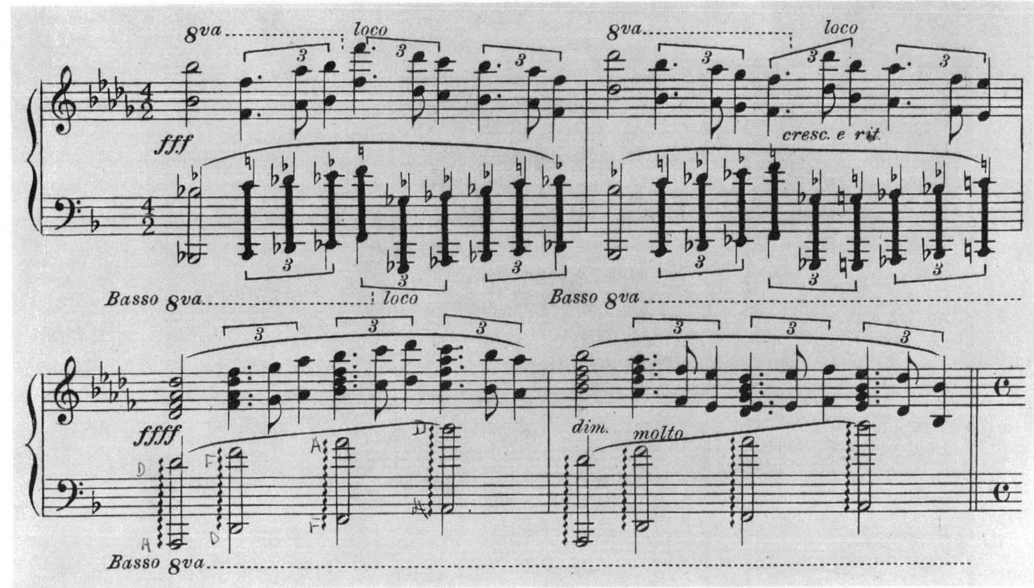

12. *Notation for tone clusters (lower staff), the superscript ♭ indicating black keys only and the ♮ white keys only (Henry Cowell, "The Tides of Manaunaun," ?1917; New York, 1922); the distinction between void and solid note heads is purely durational*

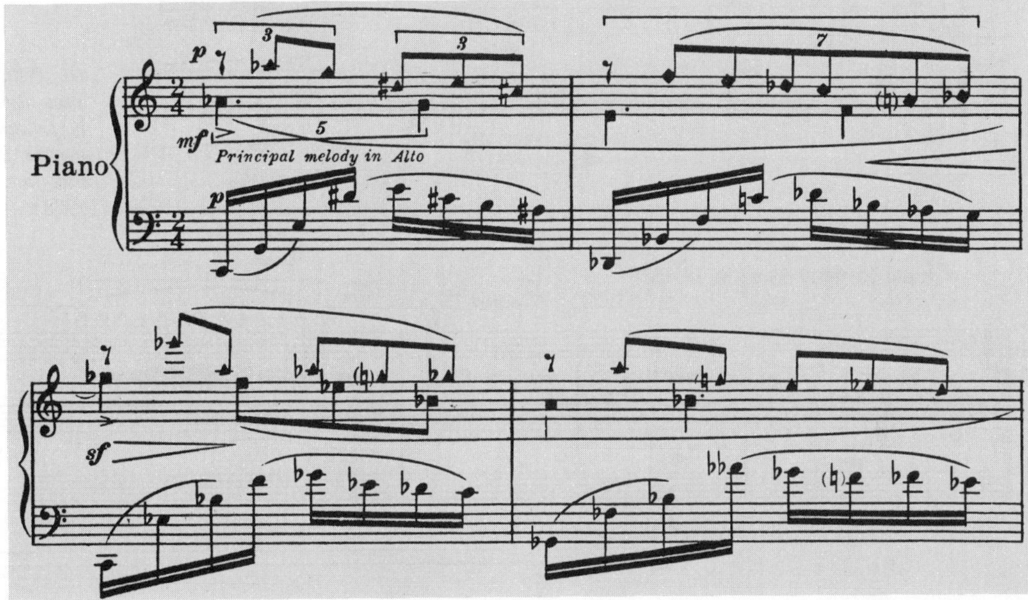

13. *Notation of polyrhythms (Henry Cowell, "Fabric," 1920; New York, 1922); the meaning of the note heads of different shapes (upper staff) for odd-numbered (non-duple) divisions of the beat is explained in the first two bars by the use of traditional numerals and braces*

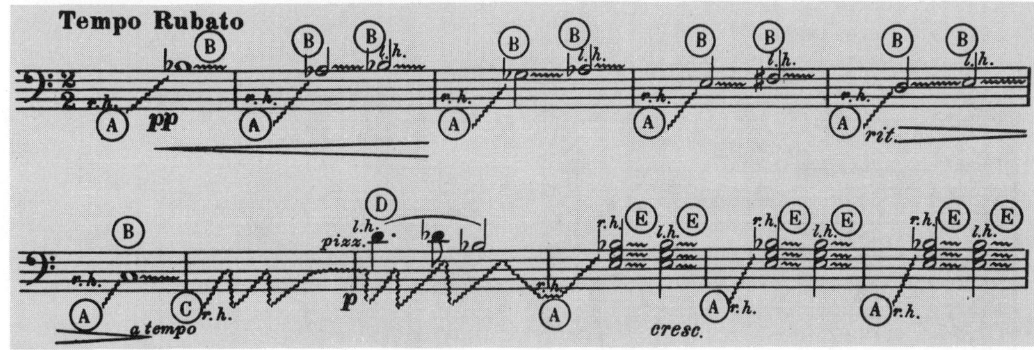

14. *Letters indicating methods of manipulating piano strings (Henry Cowell, "The Banshee," 1925; Los Angeles, 1930) (the work is played an octave lower than written pitch and the damper pedal is held down throughout): Ⓐ sweep with the flesh of the finger from the lowest string up to the note given; Ⓑ sweep with the flesh of the finger lengthwise along the string of the note given; Ⓒ sweep up and back from lowest A to the highest B♭ in the composition; Ⓓ pluck string with flesh of finger, where written, instead of octave lower; Ⓔ sweep along three notes together, in the same manner as Ⓑ*

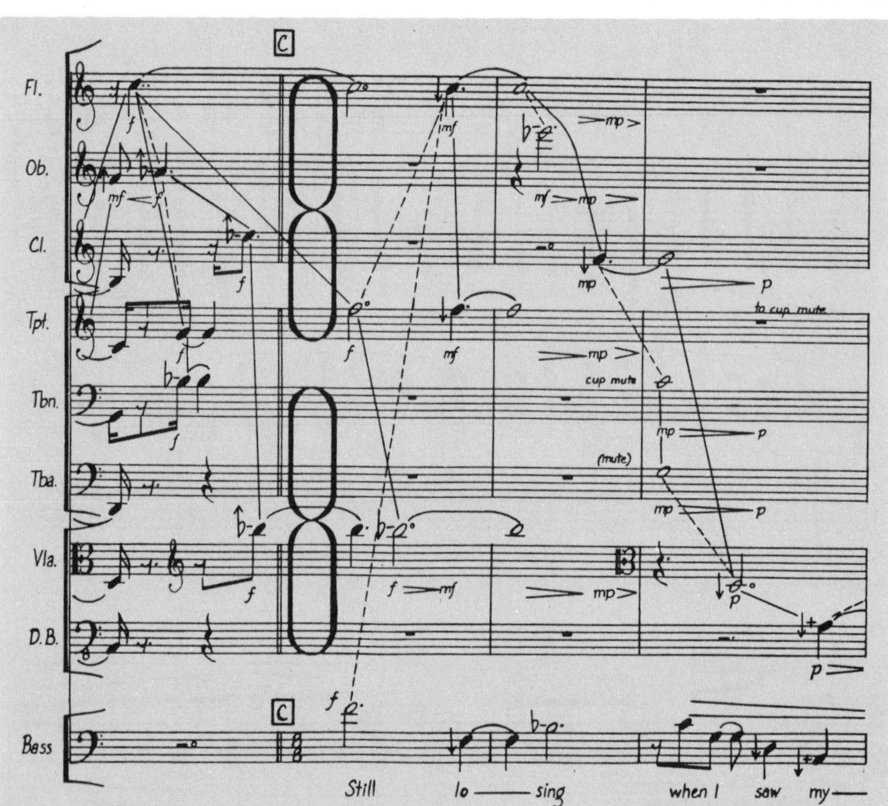

15. *Microtonal inflections, shown by arrows and plus and minus signs, sometimes in combination with accidentals (Ben Johnston, "Two Sonnets of Shakespeare," 1978; Baltimore, 1981)*

16. *Postwar notational innovations, including a note shape in the time signature, special beaming for accelerando followed by decelerando, and slurs for "laissez vibrer" chords (George Crumb, Five Pieces for Piano no.1, 1962; New York, 1973)*

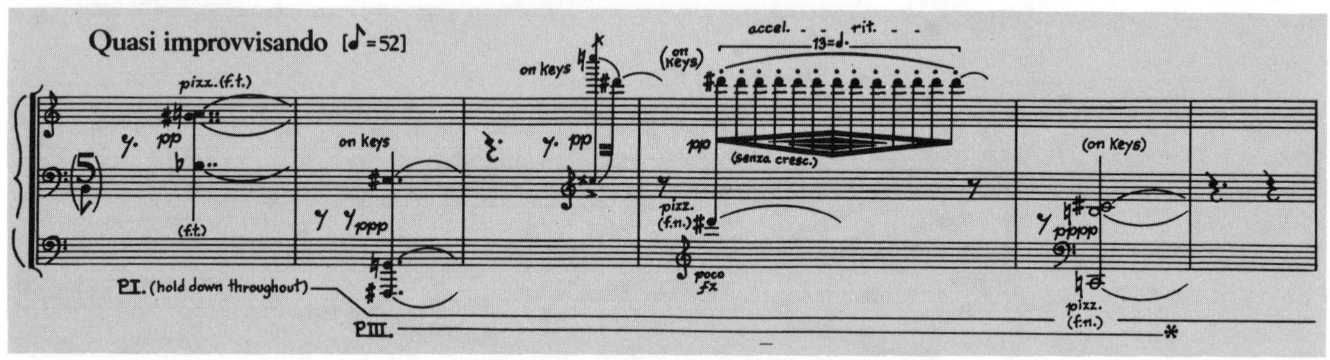

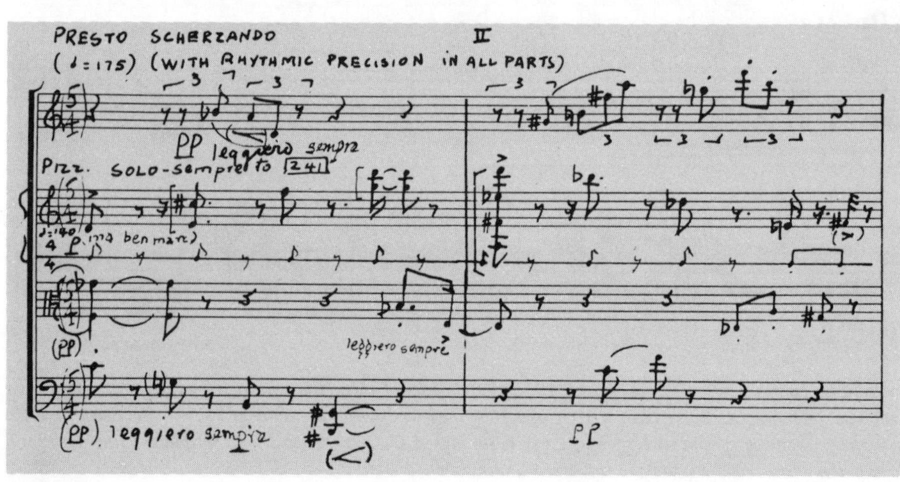

17. *Precise conventional notation, with an additional single line indicating the rhythms and true meter of the second violin part (Elliott Carter, String Quartet no.2, 1959, second movement; facs., New York, n.d.)*

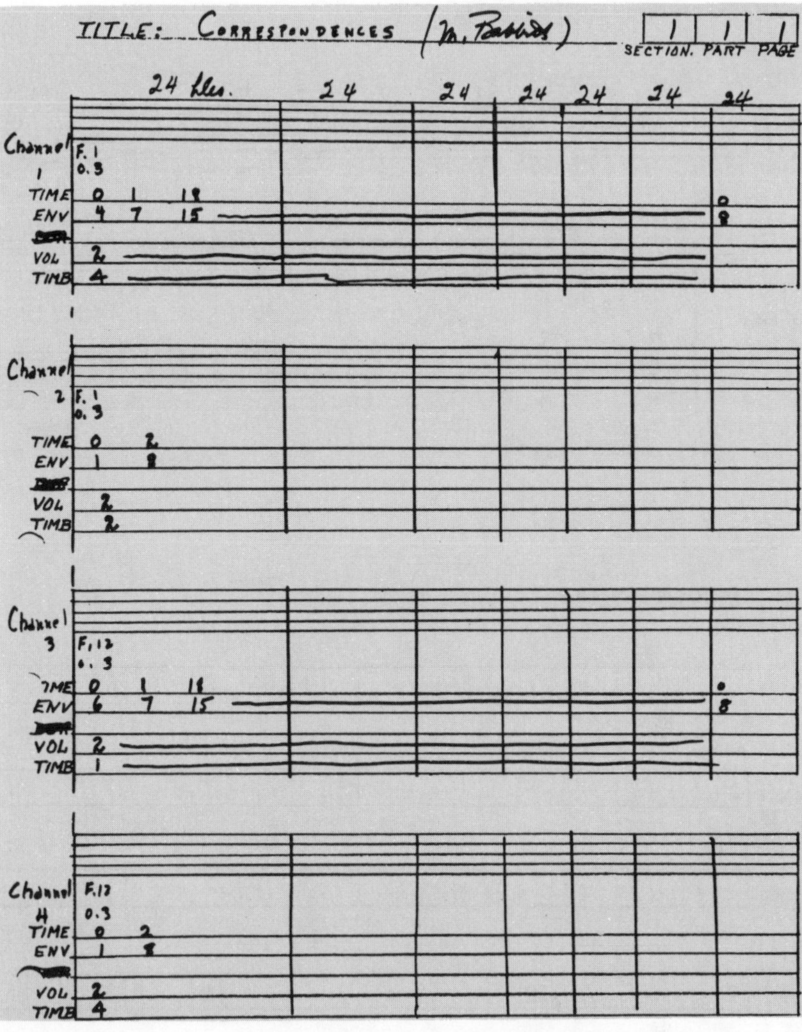

18. Specifications for synthesized sound, showing the settings for frequency, time, envelope, volume, and timbre controls on four channels (Milton Babbitt, "Correspondences"; New York, 1967)

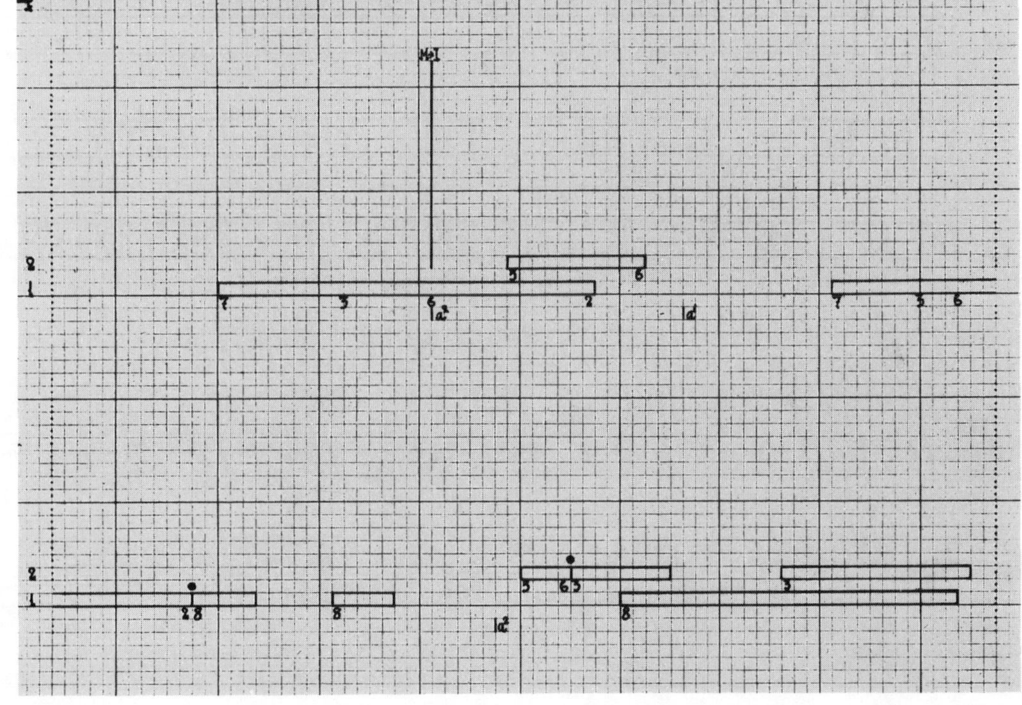

19. Graphic notation, conveying instructions for the creation of a recording on tape from phonograph records (John Cage, "Imaginary Landscape no. 5," 1952; New York, 1961); each graph unit represents three inches of tape (only two of the eight tracks are active at this point), dots indicate changes of record, and the numerals 1–8 show amplitude

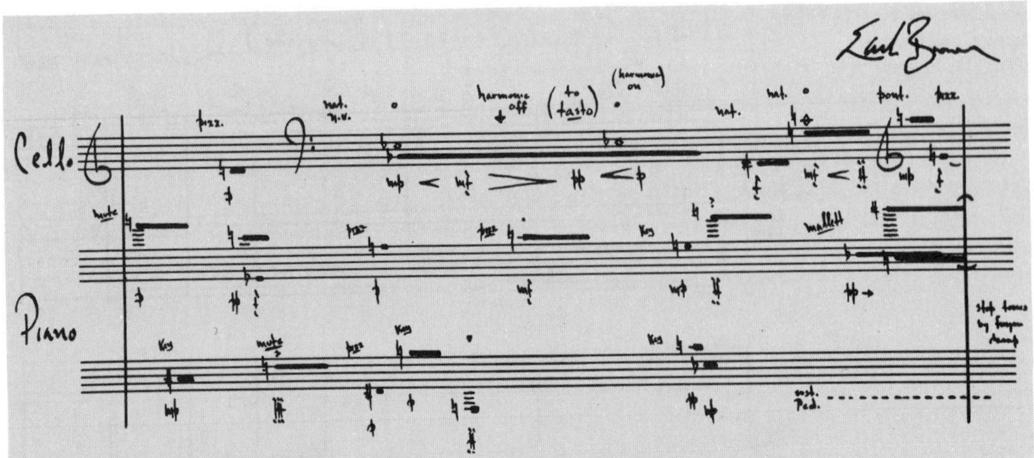

20. *Proportional (time) notation (Earle Brown, Music for Cello and Piano, 1954–5; New York, 1961); the lengths of the note heads suggest the relative durations of the tones*

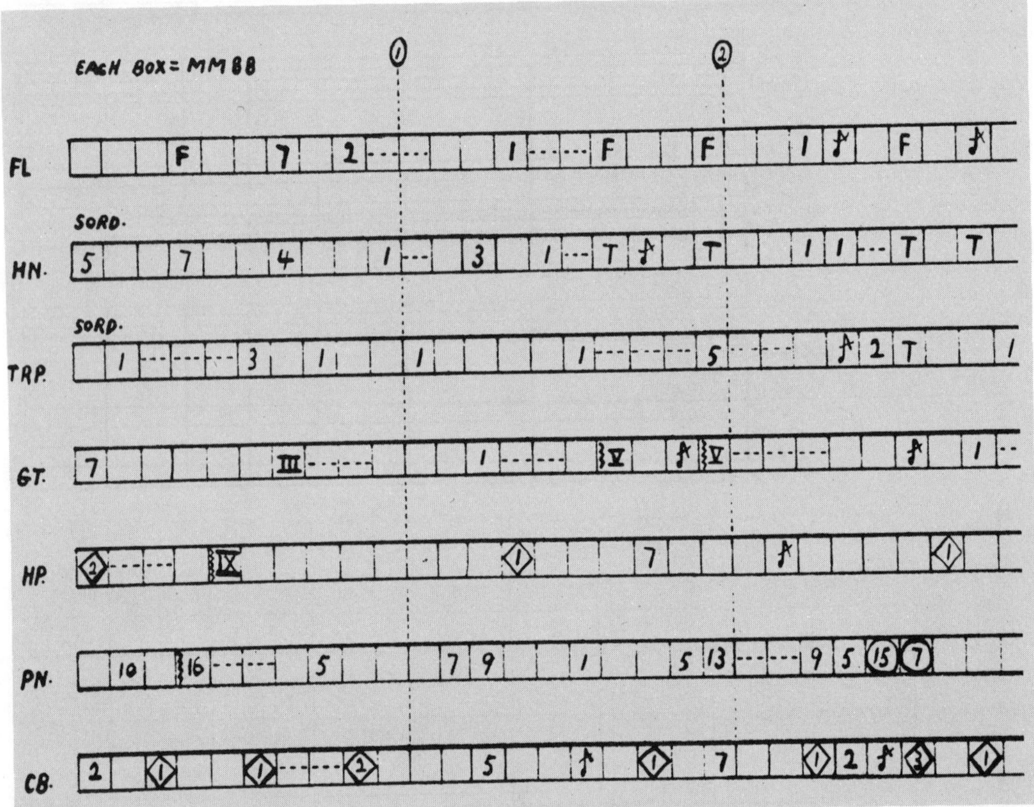

21. *Graphic notation, using a line of boxes for each instrumental part (Morton Feldman, "The Straits of Magellan," 1961; New York, 1962); each box denotes one beat, with arabic numerals indicating the number of notes to be played consecutively within the beat, roman numerals the number of notes to be played simultaneously*

22. *Black note heads without stems, flags, or beams, allowing the pianist to determine durations (Morton Feldman, "Last Pieces" no.2, 1959; New York, 1963)*

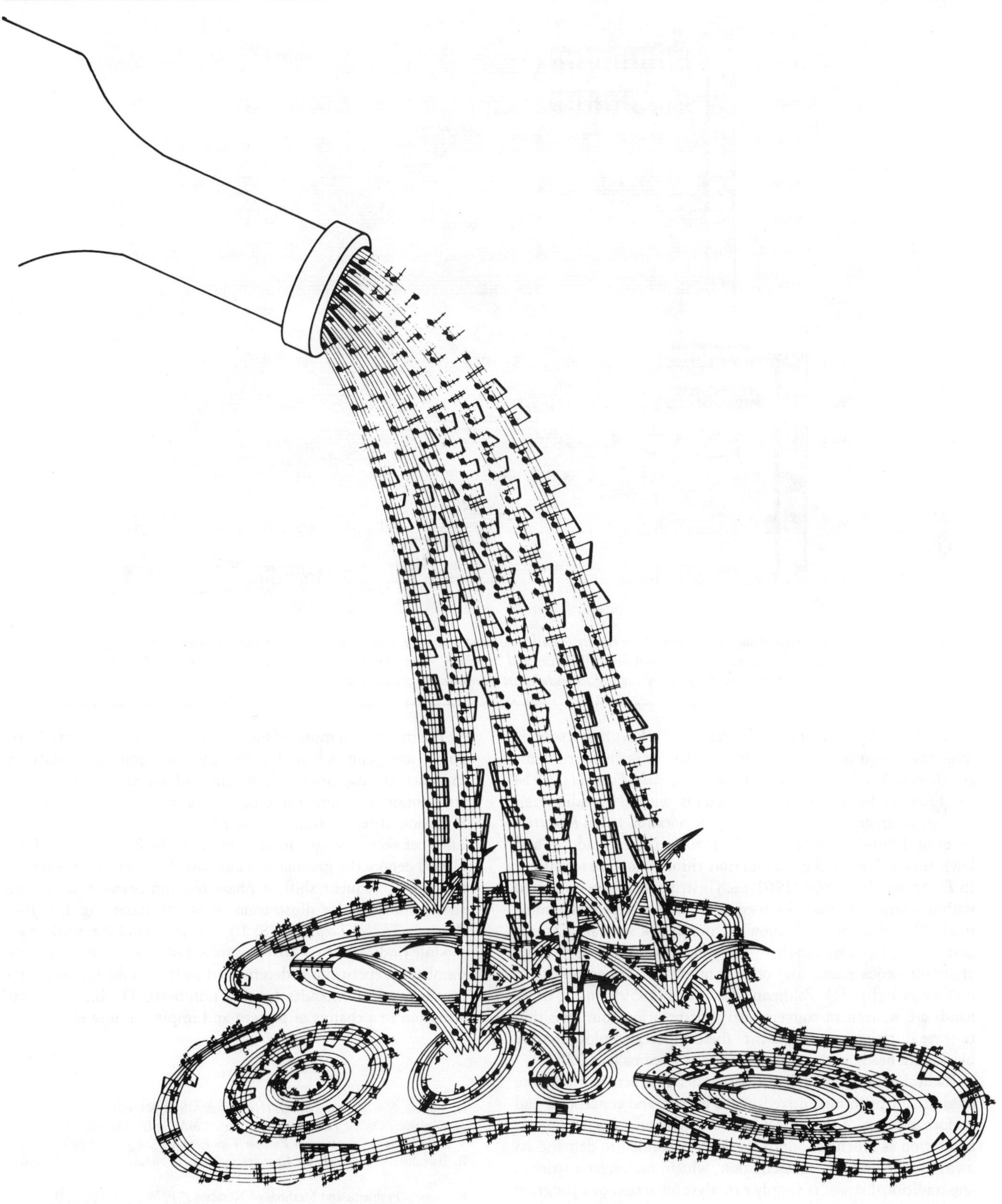

23. *Score designed for visual effect, using conventional notation (William Hellermann, "To the Last Drop," 1974)*

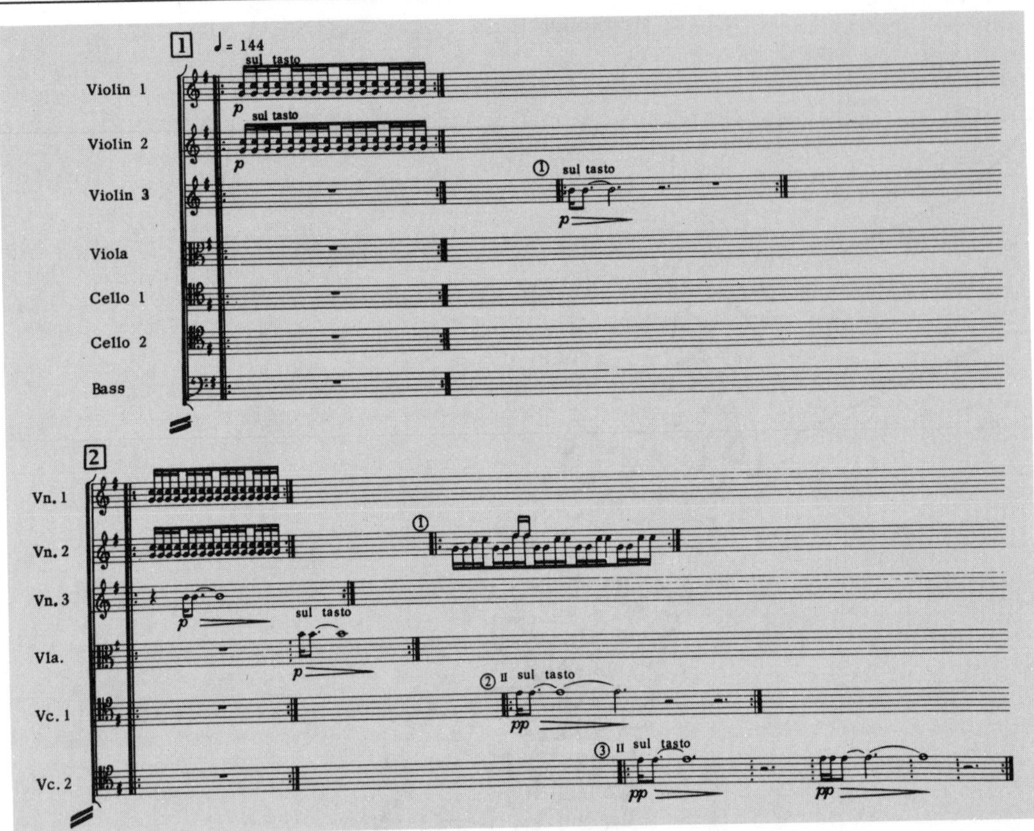

24. Conventional staff notation used for repetitive music consisting of modules (indicated by boxed numerals) and submodules (indicated by circled numerals) (John Adams, "Shaking and Trembling" from "Shaker Loops," 1978; New York, 1983); the number of repetitions and the points of entry of submodules are determined by the conductor

the performer a choice of musical events and allows him to determine their sequence, as do such modular, or open-form, compositions as *Available Forms I* (1961) and *Available Forms II* (1961–2) for large orchestra, "four hands" (that is, with two conductors). Morton Feldman also turned to graphic notation in his *Projection* series of 1950–51, in which only register (high, middle, and low), time values, and dynamics (soft throughout) are specified. In *The Straits of Magellan* (1961) each instrumental part is notated within a series of boxes, each equaling one beat at metronome mark 88; arabic numerals show the number of successive single notes to be played within that time, roman numerals the number of simultaneous notes, and other symbols still other aspects of performance (fig.21). Feldman's *Last Pieces* (1959), on the other hand, are written in conventional staff notation, but, wishing to leave durations to the pianist, the composer employs mainly black note heads without stems, flags, or beams (fig.22).

Radical notations of a diversity that defies generalization arose out of the happenings, mixed-media events, and conceptual and performance art of the 1960s (as did a view of music as process and action as much as sound). Each work seemed to demand its own, unique graphic representation, which, no longer a score in any traditional sense, is simply a catalyst for action or a program for activity. Some "notations" have been purely verbal, such as La Monte Young's *Composition 1960 #10* ("Draw a straight line and follow it") or Yoko Ono's *Beat Piece* of 1965 ("Listen to a heartbeat"); others are, or can be interpreted as being, wholly visual, such as *To the Last Drop* (1974) by William Hellermann (fig.23).

The minimalist music of such composers as Reich, Glass, Terry Riley, and John Adams has brought no significant notational innovations; adaptations of, or minor additions to, conventional staff notation or single-line percussion notation – often with a profusion of repeat signs – have proved serviceable. The dotted lines between passages in staff notation in Reich's *Piano Phase* (1967) denote the gradual acceleration of the second piano part, and the consequent shift of phase relation between it and the first piano part (for illustration *see* MINIMALISM, fig.1*a*). John Adams's *Shaker Loops* (1978; fig.24) is a modular work: each module (indicated by a boxed number) is to be repeated, but the number of repetitions is determined by the conductor, as are the entrances of submodules (circled numbers). Double stems call attention to a change of pattern and imply nothing else.

BIBLIOGRAPHY

STUDIES

VintonD

H. Cowell: *New Musical Resources* (New York, 1930/*R*1969)

A. Copland: "On the Notation of Rhythm," *MM*, xxi/4 (1944), 217

V. Ussachevsky: "Notes on *A Piece for Tape Recorder*," *MQ*, xlvi (1960), 202

B. Bartolozzi: "Proposals for Changes in Musical Notation," *JMT*, v (1961), 297

K. Stone: "Problems and Methods of Notation," *PNM*, i/2 (1963), 9

W. T. Marrocco: "The Notation in American Sacred Music Collections," *AcM*, xxxvi (1964), 136

D. Behrman: "What Indeterminate Notation Determines," *PNM*, iii/2 (1965), 58

K. Stone: "The Piano and the Avant-garde," *Piano Quarterly*, no.52 (1965), 14

E. Karkoschka: *Das Schriftbild der neuen Musik* (Celle, Germany, 1966; Eng. trans. as *Notation in New Music: a Critical Guide to Interpretation and Realization*,

New York, 1972) [see also K. Stone, *PNM*, v/2 (1967), 146]
D. Martino: "Notation in General – Articulation in Particular," *PNM*, iv/2 (1966), 47
"Percussive Arts Society: Project on Terminology and Notation of Percussion Instruments," *Percussionist*, iii/2–3 (1966), 47
J. Cage: *Notations* (New York, 1969)
S. Bauer-Mengelberg: "The Ford-Columbia Input Language," *Musicology and the Computer*, ed. B. S. Brook (New York, 1970), 48
T. Ross: *The Art of Music Engraving and Processing* (New York, 1970)
E. Borroff: "A New Notation: *Soliloquies* for Violin and Piano (1971) by Paul Cooper," *Notations and Editions: a Book in Honor of Louise Cuyler*, ed. E. Borroff (Dubuque, IA, 1974/*R*1977), 191
R. Kowal: "New Jazz and some Problems of its Notation: Exemplified in the Scores of Polish Jazz Composers," *Jazzforschung*, iii–iv (1971–2), 180
H. Cole: *Sounds and Signs: Aspects of Musical Notation* (London, 1974)
K. Stone: "New Music Notation: Why?" *HiFi/MusAm*, xxiv/7 (1974), 16
H. Risatti: *New Music Vocabulary: a Guide to Notational Signs for Contemporary Music* (Urbana, IL, 1975)
H. Sabbe, K. Stone, and G. Warfield, eds.: "International Conference on New Musical Notation: Proceedings," *Interface*, iv/1 (1975)
D. Cope: *New Music Notation* (Dubuque, IA, 1976)
K. Stone: "New Notation for New Music," *MEJ*, lxiii (1976), no.2, p.48; no.3, p.54
G. Warfield: *Writings on Contemporary Music Notation: an Annotated Bibliography* (Ann Arbor, MI, 1976) [452 titles cited and annotated]
V. Gaburo: *Notation* (La Jolla, CA, 1977)
J. R. McKay: *Notational Practices in Selected Piano Works of the Twentieth Century* (diss., U. of Rochester, 1977)
G. Read: *Modern Rhythmic Notation* (Bloomington, IN, 1978)
S. Smith and S. Smith: "Visual Music," *PNM*, xx (1981–2), 75
S. Smith: "Scribing Sound," *Percussive Notes*, xxiii/3 (1985), 34

MANUALS

H. M. Johnson: *How to Write Music Manuscript* (New York, 1956)
L. Boehm: *Modern Music Notation* (New York, 1961)
A. Donato: *Preparing Music Manuscript* (Englewood Cliffs, NJ, 1963)
B. S. Brook and M. Gould: "Notating Music with Ordinary Typewriter Characters (A Plaine and Easie Code System for Musicke)," *FAM*, xi (1964), 142; repr. in B. S. Brook, ed.: *Musicology and the Computer* (New York, 1970), 53
G. Read: *Music Notation: a Manual of Modern Practice* (Boston, 1964, rev. 3/1971)
Standard Music Engraving Practice (New York, 1966) [Music Publishers' Association pubn]
C. A. Rosenthal: *A Practical Guide to Music Notation for Composers, Arrangers, and Editors* (New York, 1967)
B. Fennelly: *A Descriptive Notation for Electronic Music* (diss., Yale U., 1968)
F. Pooler and B. Pierce: *New Choral Notation* (New York, 1971)
C. Roemer: *The Art of Music Copying* (Sherman Oaks, CA, 1973)
C. Brandt and C. Roemer: *Standardized Chord Symbol Notation* (Sherman Oaks, CA, 1975)
K. Stone: *Music Notation in the Twentieth Century: a Practical Guide* (New York, 1980)
W. Y. Elias: *Grapes: Practical Notation for Clusters and Special Effects for Piano and other Keyboards* (New York, 1984)

H. WILEY HITCHCOCK

Novelty piano. A term, used particularly in the 1920s, that was applied to a variety of piano music based on ragtime. A highly eclectic form, novelty piano music drew on sources as diverse as popular dance music, folk ragtime, and the music of the Impressionists (especially in its use of the whole-tone scale and the parallel 4th). Its most recognizable unifying feature was the "novelty break" – a stylized interruption of the melody and texture. This was often based on the motif of a tritone resolving onto a 3rd, although whole-tone passages and various figures used by dance orchestras and jazz bands of the 1920s were also employed. The novelty style was influenced by piano-roll arrangements, and many works demanded considerable pianistic skill; indeed, their composers were among the most adept pianists in the popular field.

The word "novelty" was used in association with various rags during the years of ragtime's popularity, including Scott Joplin's *Euphonic Sounds: a Syncopated Novelty* (1909), May Aufderheide's *Novelty Rag* (1911), and Clarence Wood's *Sleepy Hollow Rag* (*a Unique Rag Novelty*) (1918); but it was with the release on piano roll of Zez Confrey's *My Pet* in 1918 (published in 1921) that the identity of novelty piano was established. In Confrey's most ingenious creations elements of Impressionism and country ragtime combine to achieve a remarkable amalgamation without sacrificing the jagged dissimilarity of the components. In such works as *Kitten on the Keys* (published in 1921, though released earlier on piano roll), *You Tell 'em Ivories* (1921), *Greenwich Witch* (1921), *Poor Buttermilk* (1921), *Coaxing the Piano* (1922), and *Nickel in the Slot* (1923) Confrey explored familiar territory with an inventiveness that places him among America's most imaginative composers. Another exponent of novelty piano with a basis in Midwestern ragtime was Roy Bargy, whose *Sunshine Capers*, *Jim Jams*, and *Pianoflage* all appeared in 1922. The term "novelty ragtime" is sometimes applied to the music of these two composers. In New York Rube Bloom, Arthur Schutt, and Phil Ohman made contributions to the novelty genre. The Englishman Billy Mayerl adopted the style successfully and wrote novelties which are still played.

With the resurgence of ragtime in the 1950s the novelty style was revived to some degree. But the appearance in 1950 of the influential ragtime history *They All Played Ragtime* by Blesh and Janis initiated an attitude of dismissing novelty piano as frivolous and "inauthentic." The efforts of the pianist, editor, and record producer David Jasen, however, have been instrumental in fostering a more objective view of the novelty style. Contemporary appreciation of novelty piano has been furthered by such pianists as George Hicks, Robin Frost, Dick Wellstood, David Thomas Roberts, and Dick Hyman.

BIBLIOGRAPHY

R. Blesh and H. Janis: *They All Played Ragtime* (New York, 1950, rev. 4/1971)
D. A. Jasen: "Zez Confrey: Creator of the Novelty Rag," *Rag Times*, v (Sept 1971)
E. A. Berlin: *Ragtime: a Musical and Cultural History* (Berkeley, CA, 1980/*R*1984 with addenda)
D. A. Jasen: "Zez Confrey: Genius Supreme," *Zez Confrey Ragtime, Novelty and Jazz Piano Solos*, ed. R. S. Schiff (New York, 1982)
J. Hutton: "It's Time for a Fresh Look at Zez Confrey," *The Ragtimer* (sum. 1983)
M. Harrison: "Beyond Ragtime: the 'Novelty' Pianists," *The Wire*, no.11 (1985), 41
R. Riddle: "Novelty Piano Music," *Ragtime: its History, Composers, and Music*, ed. J. E. Hasse (New York, 1985), 285

DAVID THOMAS ROBERTS

Nowak, Lionel (*b* Cleveland, OH, 25 Sept 1911). Pianist and composer. He made his début as a pianist at the age of four and studied with Beryl Rubenstein and Edwin Fischer; as a teenager he was an organist and choirmaster. At the Cleveland Institute he studied composition with Elwell, Sessions, and Quincy Porter (diploma, 1936). He taught at Fenn College (1932–8) and in 1938 became the composer and music director for the Doris Humphrey-Charles Weidman Modern Dance Company, a position which he held until 1942. From 1942 to 1946 he taught at Converse College and conducted the Spartanburg (South Carolina) SO. He was professor of music at Syracuse University (1946–8) and then joined the faculty at Bennington College. He has toured as a pianist and lecturer for the Association of American Colleges (1945–63) and he helped to plan the 1963 Yale Conference on Music Education; he was also chief consultant to the

Manhattanville College (Purchase, New York) Music Curriculum Project. The style of his dance scores is accessible; since the mid-1950s he has made increasing use of serial techniques. The *Concert Piece* (1961) is among his recorded works. After suffering a stroke in 1980, Nowak paid special attention to composing piano pieces for the right hand alone and commissioned works from Otto Luening, Vivian Fine, and others.

WORKS

Dance scores: Square Dances (D. Humphrey), pf, 1938; Danzas mexicanas (J. Limón), pf, 1939; On my Mother's Side (C. Weidman), 1939; The Green Land (Humphrey), pf, 1941; Flickers (Weidman), 1942; House Divided (Weidman), 1944; Story of Mankind (Humphrey), orch, 1946

Orch and choral: Pf Concertino, 1944; Wisdom Exalteth her Children, double women's chorus, 1952; Concert Piece, timp, str, 1961

Chamber: Suite, 4 wind, 1945; 4 Pages from a Musical Diary, 1944; Ob Sonata, 1949; Orrea Pernel, sonata, vn, 1950; 3 vc sonatas, 1950, 1951, 1960; Diptych, str qt, 1951; Fantasia, 3 insts, 1951; Poems for Music (R. Hillyer), 5 songs, T, cl, 1951; Trio, cl, vn, vc, 1951; Quartet, ob, str, 1952; 4 Songs from Vermont, T, pf, 1953; Pf Trio, 1954; Duo, va, pf, 1960; Soundscape, pf, 1964; Soundscape, 3 ww; Soundscape, str qt; 4 Fancies for 5 Players, fl, cl, bn, va, vc, 1980; Suite, 2 vc, 1981; 4 Green Mountain Sketches, fl, vc, 1981; Games, suite, 4 fl, 1984

Songs: Cowboys and the Songs they Sang, collection of song settings, ed. S. J. Sackett (New York, 1967); 7 Songs from the Diary of Izumi Shikibu, 1v, pf, 1982

Principal publishers: ACA, New Music, Smith College Valley

BIBLIOGRAPHY

T. Strongin: "Composers on Main Street," *ACAB*, xii/1 (1964), 1

BARBARA L. TISCHLER

Nugent (Jerome), Maude (*b* Brooklyn, NY, 12 Jan 1874; *d* New York, 3 June 1958). Singer and composer. She began her career in vaudeville, achieving tremendous success in 1896 with her song *Sweet Rosie O'Grady*, which became the archetypal waltz ballad of the 1890s. Over the next few years Nugent's songs included *Mamie Reilly* (1897), *I can't forget you, honey* (1899), and *Somebody wants you* (1909), but none were more than minor successes. Nugent introduced many of her songs herself; for most she wrote both words and music, but the lyrics were occasionally supplied by her husband, William Jerome. At the age of 28 she retired from the stage to raise a family, although she made a brief return seven years later. After several decades in relative obscurity Nugent began appearing in "Gay Nineties" shows in the 1940s and, with her nostalgic appeal and lively presence, she enjoyed a brief vogue as a television personality in the 1950s.

BIBLIOGRAPHY

Obituary, *New York Times* (4 June 1958)

WILLIAM BROOKS

Nunns & Clark. Firm of piano manufacturers. It was active in New York from 1836 to 1860. The brothers Robert and William Nunns arrived in New York from London, England, around 1821 (William on 21 November 1821) and first worked for Kearsing & Sons, piano makers. In 1823 they started their own firm, R. & W. Nunns. They are reputed to have introduced a French-style "rocker" action to American pianos and manufactured some instruments for sale under other makers' names (e.g., Dubois & Stodart). In 1833 the English immigrant John Clark joined the firm, which became known as Nunns, Clark & Co. William withdrew in 1839 and the business was thereafter known as (R.) Nunns & Clark; it continued until 1860, though Clark is not listed in city directories after 1858. William was in partnership with Augustus Brumley as Nunns & Brumley from 1836, then in 1843 he joined John and Charles Fischer under the name Nunns & Fischer, and in 1848 he withdrew from that firm to found William Nunns & Co. This went bankrupt in 1853 (at a time when William Steinway was an apprentice) and William retired. Ironically, in 1853 Nunns & Clark exhibited to general acclaim at the Crystal Palace, New York.

An extraordinarily ornate Nunns & Clark square piano, dated 1853 (now in the Metropolitan Museum of Art), shows the heavily carved rosewood casework for which the firm was renowned; though highly decorative, the piano is of standard design internally. In 1855 Nunns & Clark employed 83 men and boys and produced 300 pianos worth $150,000 at a factory at Setauket, Long Island. Robert continued to be listed in New York directories as late as 1868. William Nunns, Jr., Robert Nunns, Jr., and John Francis Nunns were also active in the trade into the 1860s.

BIBLIOGRAPHY

N. Groce: *Musical Instrument Making in New York City during the Eighteenth and Nineteenth Centuries* (diss., U. of Michigan, 1982)

L. Libin: *American Musical Instruments in the Metropolitan Museum of Art* (New York, 1985)

LAURENCE LIBIN

Nygaard, Jens (*b* Stephens, AR, 26 Oct 1931). Conductor and pianist. As a child he took clarinet, cello, and piccolo lessons from his father (who had played under Sousa) and piano lessons from his mother. By the time he was 10 he was able to play all the orchestral instruments except harp. In 1948 he entered Louisiana State University on a clarinet scholarship, then worked in a dance band in Dallas, and in 1954 moved to New York to attend the Juilliard School as a piano student (BS 1956, MS 1957). About this time he met Mitropoulos, who, through informal discussion, exerted a lasting influence. On 26 January 1956 Nygaard began his conducting career with a concert commemorating Mozart's 200th birthday. He was conductor of "Music in our Time" at Columbia University (1964–7), and the founder of the Westchester (New York) Chamber Chorus and Orchestra (1965). In 1970 he participated in the Beethoven bicentenary in Vienna as conductor, performer, and teacher. During the 1970s he conducted programs that included seldom-heard compositions by Ethelbert Nevin, Kreisler, Mitropoulos, Szell, and Donald Francis Tovey. In 1974–5 he was soloist in all the Mozart piano concertos (conducting from the piano) at the Washington Heights (New York City) Young Men's Hebrew Association; there he also conducted Mozart's *Il rè pastore* and the first American performance of Pergolesi's *La contadina astuta*. He also led the fight to save George Gershwin's birthplace from demolition. In 1979, with the harpsichordist Mary Alderdice and the violist Sid Fried, he organized the Jupiter SO in New York, and in 1980 he was appointed music director of the Naumburg SO. In 1981–2 he taught at Columbia University Teachers College, and in 1982 he became conductor of the Rutgers University SO. Nygaard's unusual programs are characterized by attention to detail and clarity as well as intensity and drama.

BIBLIOGRAPHY

A. Kozinn: "Conductor Jens Nygaard: New York's Arkansas Maverick," *Symphony Magazine*, xxxiii/3 (1982), 34

DOUGLAS TOWNSEND

Nyiregyházi, Ervin (*b* Budapest, Hungary, 19 Jan 1903). Pianist. At the age of two he began to play the piano, and at four he started to compose; as a child prodigy, he was the subject of a detailed study (see Révész). He took piano lessons first with Frederick Lamond and later with Ernő Dohnányi. His early public appearances, including a performance of Liszt's Second Piano Concerto under Nikisch in Berlin (1918) and a New York début (1920), aroused highly favorable comment. His career, however, failed to develop, and though he performed occasionally in the 1920s and 1930s (Schoenberg was much impressed by his free, romantic style in 1935) he was reduced to working chiefly in film studios in the Los Angeles area. He continued to compose, and by 1978 was thought to have written 700 works. In 1973, in San Francisco, he was again heard in public, and made such an impression that he was taken up by those interested in the history of piano playing, notably the International Piano Archives, and made several recordings. In style he is influenced by Liszt, Busoni, and Paderewski; his slow tempos, textual freedoms, and individuality of interpretation have aroused particular comment.

BIBLIOGRAPHY

G. Révész: *Ervin Nyiregyházy: psychologische Analyse eins musikalisch hervorragenden Kindes* (Leipzig, 1916; Eng. trans., 1925/*R*1970 as *The Psychology of a Musical Prodigy (Ervin Nyiregyházy)*)

D. Smith: "Tribute to Ervin Nyiregyhazi: a Genius in Seclusion," *Los Angeles Times* (2 April 1978), Calendar, 50

C. Greenspan: "Nyiregyházi's Liszt," *19th Century Music*, iii (1979–80), 72 [review]

R. J. Silverman: "A Candid Talk with Erwin Nyiregyhazi," *Piano Quarterly*, no. 117 (1982), 18

Nyro, Laura (*b* New York, 18 Oct 1947). Songwriter and singer. She became known initially as the composer of songs popularized by other artists (for example, Barbra Streisand and the Fifth Dimension); but a comparison of their performances with Nyro's own, earlier, recordings of this material reveal her to have exercised an important influence on the sound of popular music in the late 1960s and early 1970s, and her own albums have won her an increasingly wide following. She is one of the only prominent singer-songwriters of her generation whose songs derive largely from Tin Pan Alley forms and styles and the more popular idioms of jazz, and rarely suggest any folk influence, either urban or rural (she accompanies herself on piano rather than guitar). Her lyrics almost invariably deal with romantic love, described, however, with an allusive imagery, forthright sexuality, and freedom of syntax that are thoroughly contemporary. The melodic, harmonic, rhythmic, and structural sophistication of her songs is allied in Nyro's performances with an extrovert, florid, intense singing style, suggesting antecedents in blues and rhythm-and-blues. The early results of this remarkable combination are well represented by *Eli & the 13th Confession* (1968) and *New York Tendaberry* (1969). Only on later albums does the sound and style of rock become a significant factor in her work; *Nested* (1978) reflects a mature synthesis of the varied aspects of her style.

RECORDINGS

(selective list; recorded for Columbia unless otherwise stated)

More than a New Discovery (Verve 3020, 1967); *Eli & the 13th Confession* (PC9626, 1968); *New York Tendaberry* (PC9737, 1969); *Christmas and the Beads of Sweat* (PC30259, 1970); *It's Gonna Take a Miracle* (PC30987, 1971); *Smile* (PC33912, 1976); *Season of Lights* (PC34331, 1977); *Nested* (PC35449, 1978); *Mother's Spiritual* (FC39215, 1984)

BIBLIOGRAPHY

B. Sarlin: "Laura Nyro: the City Songpoet," *Turn it Up! (I Can't Hear the Words): the Best of the New Singer/Songwriters* (New York, 1973), 122

LAWRENCE STARR

Oak Cliff T-Bone. *See* WALKER, T-BONE.

Oakland. City in California, part of the SAN FRANCISCO Bay area.

Oak Publications. Firm of music publishers. It was founded in New York in the late 1950s by Irwin Silber, who was associated with Folkways Records and was editor of the folk music journal *Sing Out!*, to publish songbooks that would be of interest to his readers. Oak's catalogue includes instruction manuals for guitar, dulcimer, banjo, pedal steel guitar, fiddle, and blues harp, and songbooks chiefly of blues, ragtime, bluegrass, folk, and country music. Its list includes such names as Alan Lomax, Woody Guthrie, Pete Seeger, Tom Paxton, Samuel Charters, and Jean Ritchie. The firm also publishes collections of folk music from other countries. In 1967 Oak was purchased by Music Sales Corporation.

BIBLIOGRAPHY

H. Traum: "The Story of Oak," *Sing Out!*, xxv/6 (1977), 26

FRANCES BARULICH

Oberhoffer, Emil (*b* Munich, Germany, 10 Aug 1867; *d* San Diego, CA, 22 May 1933). Conductor. He was taught first by his father, an organist, then studied piano and composition with Cyrill Kistler, and piano with Isidore Philipp in Paris. In 1885 he moved to New York, where he was musical director at Manhattan College for three years; he became an American citizen in 1893. In 1897 he was engaged as conductor of the Schubert Club chorus and orchestra and the Apollo Club of St. Paul, Minnesota. He was a professor of music at the University of Minnesota in 1902–5. In 1901 he became director of the Philharmonic Club of Minneapolis, and within two years secured an endowment for the establishment of a permanent symphony orchestra. The Minneapolis SO gave its first performance on 5 November 1903, and soon developed into one of the nation's leading orchestras. A tradition of extensive tours was begun in the summer of 1907, and the orchestra gave its first New York performance in 1912. Oberhoffer retired as director in 1923; the same year, and again in 1926, he conducted at the Hollywood Bowl. He also appeared as guest conductor of the Detroit, St. Louis, Cincinnati, and San Francisco symphony orchestras. On the death of W. H. Rothwell, conductor of the Los Angeles PO, in 1927, Oberhoffer conducted for the remainder of the season. Oberhoffer combined a practical knowledge of most of the instruments of the orchestra with a vital, enthusiastic manner.

Oberlin, Russell (Keys) (*b* Akron, OH, 11 Oct 1928). Countertenor and teacher. He was educated at the Juilliard School (diploma 1951). Oberlin was a founding member in 1952 of the New York Pro Musica with Noah Greenberg (for illustration *see* NEW YORK PRO MUSICA), and also appeared as a countertenor with numerous opera companies, orchestras, and ensembles, and in theatrical productions. Admired for his virile, sweet tone and subtle phrasing, he was a leading exponent of early music, and through his many recordings and appearances popularized not only music at that time unknown but also the repertory of the countertenor voice. In the mid-1960s he turned to teaching, and has appeared as lecturer and lecture-recitalist at colleges and universities throughout the USA and abroad. In 1971 he was appointed professor of music at Hunter College, CUNY, and director of the Hunter College Vocal Collegium.

BIBLIOGRAPHY

"Oberlin, Russell (Keys)," *CBY 1960*

PATRICK J. SMITH

Oberlin College Conservatory of Music. A conservatory affiliated with a private college in Oberlin, near Cleveland, Ohio. The college was founded by Congregationalists in 1833. In 1837 George N. Allen, a student, was designated instructor of sacred music; he later became a professor (1841–64), and in 1865 two of his students, John P. Morgan and George W. Steele, established a conservatory which was joined to the college in the following year. Under the directorship (1871–1901) of Fenelon B. Rice the conservatory attained a position of national prominence which it still holds. David S. Boe was appointed Dean in 1976. The conservatory had about 500 students and a faculty of 65 in the early 1980s. BA, BFA, BM, MME, and MMT degrees are awarded by the college, on recommendation from the conservatory, in music history, ethnomusicology, theory, composition, education, early music, and performance (all areas); it also offers an MM degree in conducting and opera theater, and a diploma in performance. The conservatory has 25 organs, about 12 harpsichords, a fortepiano, and facilities for electronic music and computer music. Its library has over 75,000 books and scores, and over 30,000 records and tapes (*see* LIBRARIES AND COLLECTIONS, §3).

BIBLIOGRAPHY

"Oberlin College," *GroveAS*
R. D. Skyrm: *Oberlin Conservatory* (diss., U. of Southern California, 1962)
W. Warch: *Our First 100 Years* (Oberlin, *c*1967)
E. B. Chamberlain: *The Music of Oberlin and Some who made it* (Oberlin, 1968)

BRUCE CARR

O'Brien, Daniel Webster. *See* BRYANT, DAN.

O'Brien, Eugene (*b* Paterson, NJ, 24 April 1945). Composer. He studied with Robert Beadell at the University of Nebraska (BM 1967, MM 1969), with Bernd Alois Zimmermann at the Staatliche Hochschule für Musik in Cologne on a Fulbright scholarship (1969), and with Eaton and Xenakis at Indiana University (1970–71). In 1971 he won the Rome Prize for the *Elegy for Bernd Alois Zimmermann*. He joined the faculty of the Cleveland Institute in 1973. O'Brien's music is frequently pictorial and suggestive, with titles that often reflect the emotions prompting his work (for example, *Embarking for Cythera*). His use of electronics is idiomatic rather than imitative, and a sparing use of aleatory procedures in such works as *Allures* lends an improvisatory dimension to his style.

WORKS

Orch: sym., 1969; 2 concs., vc, perc, 1967–71, 1983; Rites of Passage, 1978; 3 early works, withdrawn

Chamber: Ambages, pf 4 hands, 1972; Intessitura, vc, pf, 1975; Tristan's Lament, vc, 1977–9; Embarking for Cythera, chamber ens, 1978; Allures, perc, 1979; Fancies and Goodnights, chamber ens, 1981; Black Fugatos, chamber ens, 1983; Taking Measures, chamber ens, 1984; many early inst works, withdrawn

Vocal: Elegy for Bernd Alois Zimmermann (Pss.), S, chamber ens, 1970; Lingual, S, fl, vc, 1972; Dédales (Michelangelo, O. N. Yakamochi), S, orch, 1973; Dreams and Secrets of Origin (P. Neruda), S, chamber ens, 1982; *c*20 early vocal works, withdrawn

Principal publisher: Boosey & Hawkes

BIBLIOGRAPHY

"Eugene O'Brien: Winner of the Prix de Rome," *Your Musical Cue*, vii/7 (1971), 17
W. Salisbury: "Coup for Composer," *Cleveland Plain Dealer* (6 April 1980)
M. Evett: "Sounds of the City," *Live*, v/3 (1984), 63

MICHAEL MECKNA

Ochs, Phil(ip David) (*b* El Paso, TX, 19 Dec 1940; *d* Far Rockaway, NY, 8 April 1976). Folksinger and songwriter. His earliest musical influences were country and rock-and-roll singers, notably Faron Young, Johnny Cash, and Elvis Presley. He studied at Ohio State University, where he became familiar with the folk music of Woody Guthrie and Pete Seeger, then left college in order to play in coffeehouses in Greenwich Village. There he fell under the influence of Bob Gibson, with whom he wrote some songs. Ochs's first two albums, *All the News that's Fit to Sing* (1964) and *I ain't Marchin' Anymore* (1965), contained the songs *Draft Dodger Rag*, *Talking Vietnam*, and *The Power and the Glory*, which helped to establish his position as a protest singer and also demonstrated his colorful and often powerful imagery. Throughout the 1960s Ochs was a mainstay at rallies and benefits for liberal causes. Subsequent albums and singles showed a tendency towards songs with more personal themes (for example, *The Party* and *Changes*), and he sometimes exploited country and rock-and-roll idioms. Ochs's ironic and often expressionless vocal style placed emphasis on his lyrics, though the melodic and harmonic aspects of his songs became more original and distinctive in his later works. In 1971 he issued *The War is Over*, a volume containing interviews, articles, and songs.

RECORDINGS

(selective list)

All the News that's Fit to Sing (Elek. 7269, 1964), incl. Talking Vietnam, The Power and the Glory; *I ain't Marchin' Anymore* (Elek. 7287, 1965), incl. Draft Dodger Rag; *Pleasures of the Harbor* (A&M 4133, 1967), incl. The Party; *Tape from California* (A&M 4148, 1968), *Rehearsals for Retirement* (A&M 4133, 1969); *Chords of Fame* (A&M 4599, 1977), incl. Changes

BIBLIOGRAPHY

D. West: "Topical Songs and Folksinging, 1965," *Sing Out!*, xv/4 (1965), 10
G. Friesen: "I ain't Marching Anymore," *Sing Out!*, xvi/1 (1966), 13
V. Aletti: "Phil Ochs Thuds at Carnegie Hall," *Rolling Stone*, no.57 (30 April 1970), 9
M. Eliot: *Death of a Rebel* (New York, 1971)
T. Nolan: "God Help the Troubadour: Pissing Away the Memories with Phil Ochs," *Rolling Stone*, no.83 (27 May 1971), 22
B. Altman: "Phil Ochs Marches it all Back Home," *Crawdaddy*, no.35 (1974), 30

TERENCE J. O'GRADY

O'Connell, Charles (*b* Chicopee, MA, 22 April 1900; *d* New York, 1 Sept 1962). Recording executive and conductor. He was educated at the Catholic School and College of the Holy Cross, and then studied organ with Charles-Marie Widor in Paris. He was appointed head of the artist-and-repertoire department of the Victor Company (where he was responsible for all Red Seal records issued between 1930 and 1944), then became music director of the classical music (Masterworks) division of Columbia Records (1944–7). With both companies he conducted or rehearsed the studio orchestras for several recordings. He made substantial contributions in revising, updating, and providing new sections to editions of *The Victor Book of the Opera* and *The Victor Book of the Symphony*.

WILLIAM McCLELLAN

O'Day, Anita [Colton, Anita Belle] (*b* Kansas City, MO, 18 Oct 1919). Jazz singer. As a teenager she sang professionally in Chicago nightclubs. Later she joined Gene Krupa's big band (1941–3), with which she recorded her biggest hit, *Let me off Uptown*. After singing in Stan Kenton's band (1944–5) and again with Krupa (1945–6) she embarked on a solo career which was interrupted periodically by problems stemming from addiction to heroin. In the mid-1950s she recorded several albums for Verve which were well-received. She made a sensational appearance at the 1958 Newport Festival (captured in the film *Jazz on a Summer's Day*), and thereafter worked regularly in clubs both in the USA and abroad. In 1972 she established Anita O'Day (later Emily) Records. She gave a concert at Carnegie Hall in 1985 to celebrate her fiftieth year in jazz. O'Day excels at improvisation; whether scat singing or skillfully interpreting a song text she allows herself all the liberties of instrumental jazz performance in refashioning a popular song.

RECORDINGS

(selective list)

As leader: *Anita* (1955, Verve 2000); *Pick Yourself Up* (1956, Verve 2043); *Anita O'Day Sings the Winners* (1958, Verve 8283); *Cool Heat* (1959, Verve 8312); *All the Sad Young Men* (1961, Verve 68442); *Live at Mingos* (1976, Emily 11579); *Mello'Day* (1979, GNP 2126); *Live at the City* (1979, Emily 102479)

With G. Krupa: Let me off Uptown (1941, OK 6210)

BIBLIOGRAPHY

D. Cerulli: "Anita's Back," *Down Beat*, xxiii/18 (1956), 13
A. Surpin: "Dawn of a New O'Day," *Down Beat*, xxxvi/23 (1969), 16

H. Howard: "Anita O'Day," *Jazz Podium*, xxx/6 (1980), 4
A. O'Day and G. Eells: *High Times, Hard Times* (New York, 1981) [autobiography]
A. Duncan: "Anita O'Day Can Still Command a Band – and an Audience," *Christian Science Monitor* (18 June 1985), 29

BARRY KERNFELD

O'Day, Molly [Williamson, LaVerne] (*b* McVeigh, KY, 9 July 1923). Country-music singer, banjoist, and guitarist. She played in a family string band with her brothers, Skeets and Duke, and began her radio career in 1939; the banjoist Lily May Ledford, a member of the Coon Creek Girls, inspired her to learn the banjo. She used the stage names Mountain Fern, Dixie Lee, and then (from 1942) Molly O'Day. In 1941 she married the singer Lynn Davis, and for most of the 1940s the couple moved from one radio station to another. In 1945 the publisher Fred Rose heard O'Day sing the gospel song *Tramp on the Street* in Knoxville and arranged a contract for her with Columbia Records. She recorded the song as well as a new song by Hank Williams, *Six more miles to the graveyard*, at her first session (16 December 1946). Between 1946 and 1952 she made three dozen recordings, ranging from the traditional murder ballad *Poor Ellen Smith* to the apocalyptic gospel favorite *Matthew Twenty-four*. By 1950, though, the Davises had abandoned secular music in favor of preaching and gospel music; O'Day was forced into premature retirement when she contracted tuberculosis in 1952. In her prime (1946–50) O'Day was considered by many to be the greatest female singer in the traditional country style. At a time when country music was becoming increasingly pop-oriented, her short career reasserted the vitality of the distinctive mountain singing style and helped to show that women could perform serious lyrical and emotional material with conviction.

BIBLIOGRAPHY

I. M. Tribe and J. W. Morris: *Molly O'Day, Lynn Davis, and the Cumberland Mountain Folks* (Los Angeles, 1975)
C. K. Wolfe: *Kentucky Country* (Lexington, KY, 1982)

CHARLES K. WOLFE

Odell. Firm of organ builders. It was founded in 1859 in New York as J. H. & C. S. Odell by John Henry Odell (1830–99) and Caleb Sherwood Odell (1827–93). Before starting their own company, the Odell brothers had worked for Ferris & Stuart, and for William Robjohn, whom they succeeded. Although the firm's output was never great and was largely confined to the New York area, the Odells are credited with several important inventions, mostly patented during the 1860s and 1870s, including a reversible coupler action, an early combination action, and a crescendo pedal. They were also early experimenters with tubular-pneumatic action. Among their more notable instruments were those built for the Fort Street Presbyterian Church, Detroit (1876), and Fifth Avenue Presbyterian Church, New York (1893). After the deaths of the founders, the scope of the company's work gradually narrowed to small organs, rebuilding, and maintenance. The firm was run by William and J. F. Odell in the 1970s, and the business was closed in the early 1980s.

BIBLIOGRAPHY

O. Ochse: *The History of the Organ in the United States* (Bloomington, IN, 1975)
J. Ogasapian: *Organ Building in New York City, 1700–1900* (Braintree, MA, 1977)

BARBARA OWEN

Odetta [Gordon, Odetta Holmes Felious] (*b* Birmingham, AL, 31 Dec 1930). Singer and guitarist. She had singing lessons as a child and studied music at Los Angeles City College. Having taught herself to play the guitar, she established her reputation in San Francisco and New York in the early 1950s as a dynamic interpreter of Afro-American folk music – work songs, blues, ballads, and spirituals, with which she displayed a natural sympathy. She won the admiration of such noted popular singers as Harry Belafonte, who helped to promote her career, and the folk singer Pete Seeger. An important figure in the folksong revival of the 1950s and 1960s, her numerous recordings issued between 1956 and 1965, such as *Odetta Sings Ballads and Blues*, *Odetta at the Gate of Horn*, *My Eyes have Seen*, *One Grain of Sand*, and *Odetta Sings Dylan*, illustrate the versatility of her rich contralto voice, the emotionalism of her interpretations, and the diversity of her repertory. She has also earned great praise for her guitar playing. Odetta is one of the few folk singers of the time to have retained popularity after the heyday of the movement; she has pursued a diverse career, appearing in concert, as a club singer, on television, and in films and musical theater.

BIBLIOGRAPHY

"Odetta," *CBY 1960*
J. Vassal: *Folksong: une histoire de la musique populaire aux Etats-Unis* (Paris, 1971; Eng. trans. as *Electric Children: Roots and Branches of Modern Folk-rock*, New York, 1976)
K. Baggelaar and D. Milton: *Folk Music* (New York, 1976)

MICHAEL J. BUDDS

ODJB. *See* ORIGINAL DIXIELAND JAZZ BAND.

Ogdon, Will [Wilbur Lee] (*b* Redlands, CA, 19 April 1921). Composer. After attending the University of Wisconsin, Madison (BM 1942), he studied with Krenek at Hamline University, St. Paul (MA 1947), and with Sessions and Bukofzer at the University of California, Berkeley (1949–50). As a Fulbright scholar in 1952–3 he was a pupil of Honegger and René Leibowitz in Paris at the Ecole normale de Musique. In 1955 he received a PhD in music theory from Indiana University, Bloomington, where he also studied musicology with Apel and Paul Nettl. He was awarded an NEA grant in 1975. He taught at the University of Texas, Austin (1947–50), and Wesleyan University, Bloomington (1956–64); in 1966 he became professor at the University of California, San Diego, where he was founding chairman of the music department (1966–71). With Krenek and J. Stewart he wrote *Horizons Circled* (1974, on Krenek's music), and he has made important contributions to the study of early atonal music (published in the *Journal of the Arnold Schoenberg Institute*). Ogdon's music combines a liberal use of serial techniques with a refined sense of drama and comedy.

WORKS

Dramatic: The Awakening of Sappho (chamber opera, 4 episodes, Ogdon, after L. Durrell), 1976–80

Inst: Pf Sonatina, 1947; 3 Pieces, pf, 1951; Palindrome and Variations, str qt, 1961; 3 Pieces, cl, pf, 1964; 5 Comments and Capriccio, orch, 1979; 5 Pieces, vn, pf, 1982; 6 Small Trios, xyl/mar/cimb, pf, tpt, 1982

Vocal: 3 Songs, Bar, 1955; 3 Sea Choruses, SATB, 1962; Un tombeau de Jean Cocteau (Cocteau): I, S, pf, 1965, II, S, pf, cl, chamber ens, 1972, III, S, pf, ob, nar, 1976; By the Isar, S, a fl, db, 1969; Images, a Winter's Calendar, S, fl, cl, tpt, pf, 1980; Images of Spring and Summer, S, str qt, 1981

Principal publisher: Association for the Promotion of New Music

DAVID COPE

Oglala. American Plains Indian group belonging to the Teton division of the SIOUX.

Ohio Players. Funk septet. Formed in 1959 in Dayton, Ohio, it consisted of Leroy Bonner, guitar and voice; Clarence Satchell, saxophone; Ralph Middlebrooks, trumpet; Jimmy Williams, drums; Billy Beck, keyboards; Marvin Pierce, trumpet; and Marshall Jones, bass guitar. The group had its first success in 1962 as the backup band on the Falcons' hit *I found a love*. During the next 11 years they made many unsuccessful recordings, but in 1971 they signed a contract with Westbound and in 1973 their *Funky Worm* sold a million copies. After the group changed record labels again (it moved to Mercury in 1974) its next eight singles all reached the Top Ten on the soul chart; three of these (*Skin Tight*, 1974; *Fire*, 1974; and *Love Rollercoaster*, 1975) were awarded gold records. The Ohio Players' style of "street" funk – based more on hypnotic rhythms than melody – was distinctive for its lusty, overpowering rhythm section, and the jazzy, rapid vocal delivery of Bonner and others. Satchell described the group's sound as "progressive rock with a touch of jazz and blues"; the influence on its style of Sly and the Family Stone and James Brown was very clear. The Ohio Players' stage show was elaborate and glittery, featuring bizarre costumes, intricate lighting, and bubble and smoke machines; the group also gained attention for the mildly pornographic photographs that were used for its album covers. The Ohio Players' popularity faded in 1978, but they continued to record for Arista and Boardwalk before disbanding in the early 1980s.

RECORDINGS
(selective list)

Trespassin' (Compass 7015, 1968); Pain (Westbound 188, 1971); Funky Worm (Westbound 214, 1973); Skin Tight (Mer. 73609, 1974); Fire (Mer. 73643, 1974); Love Rollercoaster (Mer. 73734, 1975); Who'd she coo? (Mer. 73814, 1976); *Everybody up* (Ari. AB4226, 1979)

GARY THEROUX

Ohio State University. State-supported university (founded 1870; opened 1873) in Columbus. Its school of music, in the college of arts, was established in 1945, though music instruction was introduced shortly after the opening of the university. Its first director was Eugene J(ohn) Weigel (1894–1973), also leader of the university's renowned marching band (for illustration *see* EDUCATION IN MUSIC, fig.2). David L. Meeker, appointed director in 1979, has fostered the expansion of an analog and digital sound-synthesis laboratory and computer-based instruction in music theory. In 1971 the music library became one of the first research collections to be catalogued on computer (*see* LIBRARIES AND COLLECTIONS, §3). By the early 1980s the school had about 750 students and a faculty of about 80. BM, BMEd, and BA degrees are offered and also MA, MM, DMA, and PhD degrees in music history, theory, education, performance, and composition. The Weigel Hall (completed 1980) has a recital hall with a movable ceiling and other acoustical refinements.

BIBLIOGRAPHY

E. Aho, ed.: *Script Ohio: the Ohio State University Marching Band* (Columbus, OH, 1979)

BRUCE CARR

Ohlsson, Garrick (Olof) (*b* Bronxville, NY, 3 April 1948). Pianist. His first teacher was Thomas Lishman at the Westchester Conservatory, and at 13 he went to Sascha Gorodnitzki at the Juilliard School, where he also studied with Rosina Lhévinne. The most crucial influence, however, was Olga Barabini, a pupil of both Arrau and Hofmann. Ohlsson's career was established when he became the first American to win the Warsaw International Chopin Competition (1970); he had already attracted attention as the winner of competitions in Bolzano (1966) and Montreal (1968). Because of his Warsaw success he became known as a Chopin player, but his broad repertory includes even such early composers as Thomas Tomkins, and Scriabin is a special interest of his. Ohlsson is a large man with large hands who plays easily such works as Scriabin's Etude in 9ths. His technique is complete, his tone large and unpercussive, though hard-edged. He is a musician with a modest manner and exceptional intelligence, adept at projecting, for example, the subtle forms of late Chopin. He has made many recordings, including works by Chopin, and in 1984 was the soloist for the première of Wuorinen's Third Piano Concerto.

BIBLIOGRAPHY

"Ohlsson, Garrick (Olof)," *CBY 1975*
Great Pianists Speak with Adele Marcus (Neptune, NJ, 1979), 120
D. Dubal: "Garrick Ohlsson," *Reflections from the Keyboard: Conversations with Great Pianists* (New York, 1984)

MICHAEL STEINBERG/R

Ohman, Phil(more) (*b* New Britain, CT, 7 Oct 1896; *d* Santa Monica, CA, 8 Aug 1954). Popular pianist and composer. He began work in New York as a piano demonstrator and organist when in his late teens. In 1919 he arranged and composed for QRS piano rolls and toured as an accompanist. As a performer he is best remembered for his duo-piano work with Victor Arden (Lewis J. Fuiks); they played for Gershwin musicals throughout the 1920s, made recordings and piano rolls, and also appeared on radio. In later years Ohman worked primarily in the Los Angeles area and led his own orchestra there from 1934 to 1946. His broad repertory included popular songs, foxtrots, novelty pieces, and hymns. His own novelty-piano works, though not among the best in the genre, are of interest for being less affected by ragtime than those of other composers. Among his best pieces are *Try and Play It*, *Up and Down the Keys*, *Piano Pan*, and *Sparkles* (all 1922), as well as the unpublished *Dixie Kisses*.

BIBLIOGRAPHY

E. Jablonski and L. P. Stewart: *The Gershwin Years* (Garden City, NY, 1973)
D. A. Jasen: *Recorded Ragtime, 1897–1958* (Hamden, CT, 1973)
D. A. Jasen and T. J. Tichenor: *Rags and Ragtime: a Musical History* (New York, 1978)

DAVID THOMAS ROBERTS

Ohrlin, Glenn (*b* Minneapolis, MN, 26 Oct 1926). Folksinger. He traveled throughout the West as a working cowboy and rodeo rider, and absorbed an extensive repertory of songs; he also learned a number of popular, folk, and dialect pieces from his family, who were Scandinavian immigrants. He has occasionally written or parodied songs and poems, some of which he published in his *The Hell-bound Train: a Cowboy Songbook* (1974). From the 1960s he appeared in public and made recordings, including the albums *The Hell-bound Train* (1964, with liner notes by A. Green, J. McCulloh, and H. Daniel) and *Cowboy Songs* (1974). His performances, notable for the laconic and understated style of his singing, playing, and storytelling, have done much to introduce the cowboy repertory to audiences in an authentic form. In 1985 he was awarded a National Heritage Fellowship by the NEA.

JUDITH McCULLOH

Ojai Music Festival. A spring series of weekend concerts initiated in 1947 at Ojai, California, a small community near Los Angeles. The festivals began with a recital by the French baritone

Martial Singher. Most of the performers are Los Angeles musicians, including members of the Los Angeles PO, the New Wave Chamber Players, and amateur and professional choruses. The artistic director of the festival through the late 1960s was Lawrence Morton; the position of music director has been held for short terms by Thor Johnson, Bruno Walter, Pierre Boulez, and other leading conductors. In 1985 the position was held by Kent Nagano. The festival's programs range from music of the 13th century to the avant garde, with an emphasis on rediscovered or rare works of the past and on new compositions; Copland's *Elegies for Orchestra* and Wuorinen's *A Reliquary for Igor Stravinsky* received their world premières at the festival in 1973 and 1975 respectively. Although the repertory is broadly international, American composers, including many from southern California, have been generously represented. Participants have included Copland, Foss, Stravinsky, and Michael Tilson Thomas.

RITA H. MEAD

O'Jays. Soul vocal trio. After singing together as a gospel duo, Walter Williams (*b* 25 Aug 1942) and Eddie Levert (*b* 16 June 1942) formed a doo-wop quintet, the Mascots, in Canton, Ohio, in 1958. The other members were Bill Isles, Bobby Massey, and William Powell. They renamed their group after a Cleveland disc jockey, Eddie O'Jay, who had encouraged them. For ten years the O'Jays played concerts and recorded, with little success, for Wayco, Little Star, Apollo, King, Minit, Bell, and Imperial. Isles left the group in 1965. In 1968 the group signed a contract with the songwriting and production team of Kenny Gamble and Leon Huff for their Neptune label, but that company shortly went out of business. The group stayed together, despite Massey's departure in 1971. Later that year Gamble and Huff formed a new label, Philadelphia International, and organized an efficient distribution system through CBS Records. As a result of that arrangement, as well as fine songs and inspired production marked by powerful orchestral arrangements and a driving beat, the O'Jays, now a trio, began to have major hits: *Back Stabbers* (1972), *Love Train* and *Put your hands together* (1973), *For the love of money* (1974), *I love music (Part 1)* (1975), and *Livin' for the weekend* (1976). In 1976 the group lost its momentum when William Powell left (he died of cancer in 1977); his replacement, Sammy Strain (formerly of Little Anthony and the Imperials), participated in such later hits as *Used ta be my girl* (1978) and *Forever mine* (1979). The group also recorded eight albums that earned gold records during the 1970s. They owed their success to a sophisticated style of hard-edged soul music, skillfully orchestrated and joyfully performed.

RECORDINGS

(selective list; recorded for Philadelphia International unless otherwise stated)

I'll be sweeter tomorrow (Bell 691, 1967); Looky, looky, look at me girl (Neptune 31, 1970); *Back Stabbers* (31712, 1972), incl. Love Train; *Ship Ahoy* (32408, 1973), incl. For the love of money, Put your hands together; *Family Reunion* (33807, 1975), incl. I love music (Part 1), Livin' for the weekend; *So Full of Love* (35355, 1978), incl. Used ta be my girl; *Identify Yourself* (36027, 1979), incl. Forever mine; *My Favorite Person* (37999, 1982); *When Will I See you Again* (38518, 1983); *Love and More* (39367, 1984)

GARY THEROUX

Ojibwe [Chippewa, Ojibwa, Ojibway]. American Indian tribe living principally in the western woodlands area of the USA and Canada (*see* INDIANS, AMERICAN, fig. 1). They are a widely dispersed people; under pressures from the fur trade they originally migrated from the eastern shores of Lake Superior beginning in the 17th century. Culturally they belong to the central Algonquian family and speak a language related to Potawatomi and Cree, among others. They were one of the first North American tribes whose music received serious attention from ethnographers; Frederick Burton's *American Primitive Music* (1909) and Frances Densmore's *Chippewa Music* (1910, 1913) include transcriptions of 513 songs based on wax-cylinder recordings made by Burton at Desbarets, Ontario, and Densmore on reservations in Minnesota and Wisconsin.

The Ojibwe traditionally included song performance in a wide variety of contexts. In addition to the songs of the Grand Medicine lodge (*midewiwin*), an esoteric sodality with limited, purchased membership, there were songs for healing (dream songs), gambling (moccasin game songs), ritual solicitation (Begging Dance songs), gift exchange (Woman's Dance songs), general entertainment (Pipe Dance songs), story-telling, courtship, warfare, and hunting. With the exception of *mide* and love-songs, which had full texts, most songs contained only a brief text performed once during each strophe, with the remainder of the melody sung to vocables.

The songs of the medicine lodge are stylistically distinct from mainstream Ojibwe music and are characterized by deliberately unfocused intonation, unusually wide vibrato applied as an ornament to sustained tones, and the use of spoken exclamations between strophes. Texts, often archaic, had vocables inserted between syllables to disguise their occult meaning.

Love-songs, lullabies, and story songs, performed mostly by women, were the only songs lacking percussion. For almost all other singing the musician accompanied himself with a rattle or drum. The rattle was restricted to use by members of the medicine lodge. The cylinder was made from birch bark, thin wood, animal horn, or gourd; more recently baking-powder cans have been converted to this purpose. The cavity was filled with corn kernels, pebbles, or shot, and a handle was inserted through both ends of the container.

The drum was the principal instrument of the Ojibwe. Double-headed frame drums in a variety of sizes were used to accompany songs for war, healing, dancing, and gambling (see illustration). The large Grass Dance drum was used increasingly to accompany songs after its introduction in about 1880, the result of the Ojibwe's contact with tribes to their west. At first the drum was made from a wooden tub; when intended for ceremonial purpose in the Drum Dance it was elaborately decorated with cloth, ribbon, beads, fur, and eagle feathers, and its head was painted with symbolic designs, the colors of which were chosen for their ritual connotations. For secular events the Ojibwe later made greater use of store-bought bass drums, which they turned on their side; singers, each with his own beater, would surround the instrument.

Chordophones were unknown to the Ojibwe, and their only aerophone was the courting flute. A flageolet similar to flutes of other woodlands and Plains tribes, it was 37.5 to 50 cm long (somewhat shorter than those of other Indian tribes), usually had six holes, and was constructed of cedar; its tone was regulated by a carved, movable block. Flute melodies were usually love-songs; there is evidence that in performance, a young man would alternate singing with the playing of slow, rubato melodies.

Since the time of Densmore's field work there has been a gradual reduction in the number of song types in Ojibwe music. With the cessation of warfare, the settlement of the tribe on reservations, the incursion of nontraditional religions, and the

Ojibwe Indians playing a drum for the Dream Dance, Menominee County, Wisconsin

restriction of former economic pursuits, many of the traditional occasions for music ceased to exist, and the songs fell into disuse. Where once a great variety of genres existed, the textless, secular War Dance songs now constitute the greatest portion of the repertory, and the powwow has become the principal musical outlet. Because many songs are borrowed from tribes to the north and west of the Ojibwe, the continuing influence of Siouan on Ojibwe music should be noted. This process began long ago, when groups of the two tribes engaged in sporadic warfare as well as periods of peace, cultural exchange, and intermarriage; many of the songs collected by Densmore contained Siouan words in their texts or were otherwise acknowledged to have Siouan origins.

Recordings of Ojibwe music are held at the Archive of Folk Culture, Library of Congress, Washington, DC; and the Archives of Traditional Music, Indiana University.

See also INDIANS, AMERICAN, esp. §I, 4(ii)(b).

DISCOGRAPHY

Songs of the Chippewa, recorded 1907–10 by F. Densmore (Library of Congress AAFS L22, 1950)

Chippewa: War Dance Songs for Powwow (Can. C6082, 1971)

Chippewa Grass Dance Songs (Can. C6106, 1973)

BIBLIOGRAPHY

W. J. Hoffman: "The Midewiwin, or 'Grand Medicine Society' of the Ojibwa," *Bureau of American Ethnology, Seventh Annual Report, 1885–86* (Washington, DC, 1891), 113–300

F. R. Burton: *American Primitive Music, with Especial Attention to the Songs of the Ojibways* (New York, 1909)

F. Densmore: *Chippewa Music* (Washington, DC, 1910, 1913)

S. A. Barrett: "The Dream Dance of the Chippewa and Menominee Indians of Northern Wisconsin," *Bulletin of the Public Museum of the City of Milwaukee*, i (1911), 251–406

R. Landes: *Ojibwa Religion and the Midewiwin* (Madison, WI, 1968)

T. Vennum, Jr.: *Southwestern Ojibwa Music* (diss., Harvard U., 1975)

——: "Ojibwa Origin-migration Songs of the *Mitewiwin*," *Journal of American Folklore*, xci (1978), 753

——: *The Ojibwa Dance Drum: its History and Construction* (Washington, DC, 1982)

——: "The Ojibwa Begging Dance," *Music and Context: Essays for John M. Ward* (Cambridge, MA, 1985), 54

THOMAS VENNUM, JR.

Oklahoma, University of. State-supported university (founded 1890), with campuses at Norman, Oklahoma City, and Tulsa. Its school of music is in the college of fine arts at Norman. The music department was founded in 1893 and renamed the School of Music in 1899. Graduate degrees were granted from 1900 but a graduate school was not organized until 1909; the first PhD was awarded in 1929. In the 1980s the school of music had 400 students and a full-time faculty of about 40. The degrees offered include the BM and MM in performance, history, composition, and theory as well as an MM in choral conducting, the BMEd and MMEd with emphasis on choral, instrumental, or general music, the DMA in performance, composition, and choral conducting, and the PhD in music education. The school sponsors several performing groups, and the Stovall Museum of Science and History contains a collection of nearly 150 instruments, mostly ethnic.

See also LIBRARIES AND COLLECTIONS, §3.

GRAYDON BEEKS

Okwanachu. American Indian group of California belonging to the SHASTA.

Olcott, Chauncey [Chancellor John] (*b* Buffalo, NY, 21 July 1858; *d* Monte Carlo, Monaco, 18 March 1932). Singer, composer, and lyricist. He toured with several minstrel and opera companies, then went to London for two years, where he studied singing and appeared in comic opera. He achieved fame after his return to the USA when he joined forces with Augustus Pitou in 1893 and succeeded William J. Scanlan as the leading singer in Pitou's productions of sentimental operettas on Irish themes. His success, founded on his sweet tenor voice and his ingratiating acting and appearance, led to his concentrating on Irish roles for the remainder of his career. He contributed librettos, songs, and lyrics to many of the works in which he appeared, and wrote the complete scores of *Sweet Inniscarra* (1897), *A Romance of Athlone* (1899), *Garrett O'Magh* (1901), and *Old Limerick Town* (1902). His song *My Wild Irish Rose* (1899) and the lyrics *Mother Machree*

(1911) and *When Irish eyes are smiling* (1912), both with music by Ernest R. Ball, have attained lasting popularity. He made a few recordings of Irish-American ballads between 1913 and 1920, but his popularity waned after World War I and he retired in 1925. Olcott was considered neither a great singer nor actor, but at the height of his popularity commanded a large and loyal audience among the Irish-American community.

BIBLIOGRAPHY

"Olcott, Chancellor John (Chauncey Olcott)," *The National Cyclopedia of American Biography*, xi (New York, 1901/*R*1971)
W. P. Eaton: "Olcott, Chauncey," *DAB*
R. O. Olcott: *Song in his Heart* (New York, 1939)
J. Walsh: "Favorite Pioneer Recording Artists: Chauncey Olcott," *Hobbies*, lxxv (1970), no.6, p.37, no.7, p.37
D. Carroll: *The Matinee Idols* (New York, 1972)

MICHAEL J. BUDDS

Olcott, Ethel Lucretia. *See* BICKFORD, VAHDAH OLCOTT.

Old-folks concert. A type of entertainment, popular in the second half of the 19th century, which revived the music and performance practices of the 18th-century New England singing-schools. Accounts of early amateur old-folks concerts in New Haven, and Fall River, Massachusetts, suggest their rural origins. They began in the 1850s and peaked in the 1860s, but endured through the century in various forms, taking on aspects of broad caricature and minstrelsy after the Civil War. Although FATHER KEMP is credited with originating the genre, it is more likely that he professionalized amateur songfests which featured the "good old tunes" that had been superseded by 19th-century styles of church hymnody. Even before Kemp's first concert in 1855, there had been organized efforts to sustain the singing-school repertory. The Billings and Holden Society was established in Boston in the mid-1830s, and it soon published a collection called *Ancient Psalmody* (1836) in order that the music "might not only be rescued from oblivion, but again be presented to the public in its original form." Other anthologies were issued in conjunction with the old-folks concerts between 1857 and 1875, including *Father Kemp's Old Folks' Concert Tunes* (1860) and *The Continental Concert Tunes for ye Olde Folks' Concerts*, edited by John Church (1874). Among the most popular tunes were "Sherburne" by Daniel Read, "Northfield" by Jeremiah Ingalls, and "Anthem for Easter" and "Majesty" by William Billings. Kemp's Old Folks Concert Troupe added theatrical elements to the entertainment; performers impersonated Revolutionary War figures in costume and parodied old-time dialects.

BIBLIOGRAPHY

R. J. Kemp: *Father Kemp and his Old Folks* (Boston, 1868/*R*1982)
J. T. Steinberg: "Old Folks Concerts and the Revival of New England Psalmody," *MQ*, lix (1973), 602

JUDITH TICK

Oldmixon [née Sidus], **Mrs. (Georgina)** [Miss George]. (*b* Oxford, England, *c*1767; *d* Philadelphia, PA, 3 Feb 1835). Soprano. She made her début as Miss George at the Haymarket Theatre, London, on 2 June 1783. Later disputes with her associate Mrs. Billington probably contributed to her decision to move to the USA, where she joined Wignell's and Reinagle's company in Philadelphia and made her début on 14 May 1793. In the meantime she had married Sir John Oldmixon of Bath, who became an ardent democrat and gardener. In 1805 she moved to New York, but returned to Philadelphia for a farewell benefit on 19 February 1814, where she remained to manage her Female Academy. Parker (1825) mentions her wide vocal range, dramatic talents, and fine sense of the Italian style.

BIBLIOGRAPHY

J. R. Parker: *Musical Biography* (Boston, 1825)
W. Parke: *Musical Memoirs* (London, 1839)
C. Durang: "The Philadelphia Stage," *Philadelphia Sunday Dispatch* (1854) [series of articles, continued in 1856, 1860; compiled by T. Westcott as *History of the Philadelphia Stage, between the Years 1749 and 1855*, 1868, *PU*; similar compilations as *The Philadelphia Stage* in *PPL*, *History of the Philadelphia Stage* in *PHi*]
O. G. T. Sonneck: *Early Concert-life in America (1731–1800)* (Leipzig, 1907/*R*1978)
——: *Early Opera in America* (New York, 1915/*R*1963)
D. W. Krummel: "The Displaced Prima Donna: Mrs. Oldmixon in America," *MT*, cvii (1967), 25

D. W. KRUMMEL

Old Way of Singing. Term used from the 18th century for a slow, heterophonic style of unaccompanied congregational singing found in rural Protestant churches in Britain and the USA, also variously called the "Common Way" or the "Usual Way," to distinguish it from "Regular Singing." The practice is orally transmitted. Since the mid-17th century it has generally been associated with "LINING OUT." The essence of the "Old Way" is the manner in which the tunes are sung by the congregation. The tempo is extremely slow, lacking rhythmic drive and precision: singers may diverge on their way from one tune note to the next, some with what appears to be deliberate ornamentation, and their bearing is intense and unselfconscious, resembling that of folk ballad singers.

The origins of the "Old Way of Singing" are uncertain. Similar practices have been noted among German-speaking groups tracing their descent from the 16th-century Anabaptists (*see* AMISH AND MENNONITE MUSIC), and in several parts of Scandinavia. This gives rise to the possibility that the "Old Way" preserves an ancient, pre-Reformation mode of popular singing that was once prevalent in northern Europe. It may, on the other hand, have developed independently in various Protestant churches, where organs and choirs were outlawed for many generations. Lining out is peculiar to Anglo-Saxon communities.

The "Old Way of Singing" (which was prevalent in English and Scottish churches by the early 17th century) was evidently brought to America by the colonists, and flourished here, in the absence of professional guidance, for several generations. In Massachusetts lining out is mentioned with approval as early as 1647 by John Cotton. With no strong leadership of any kind, tunes were ornamented at will by individuals. The discordant heterophony that resulted was described by would-be reformers as "indecent," "like the braying of asses," and "tortured and twisted as every unskillful throat saw fit." Something of the chaos that prevailed may be gathered from entries in Judge Sewall's *Diary*, describing services at the South Meeting House, Boston:

1705, Dec. 28. Mr. Willard . . . spoke to me to set the tune; I intended Windsor and fell into High-Dutch, and then essaying to set another tune went into a key much too high. So I pray'd Mr. White to set it; which he did well, Litchf[ield] Tune.

1718, Feb. 2. In the Morning I set York Tune, and in the 2d going over, the Gallery carried irresistibly to St. David's which discouraged me very much.

"Regular Singing" in the American colonies began effectively in 1700 with the visit of Dr. Thomas Bray to the Anglican churches in Maryland, and thereafter leaders such as Cotton Mather, Thomas Symmes, and Nathaniel Chauncey spearheaded the reform movement in the Congregational churches of New England (*see* PSALMODY). By 1770 it seems unlikely that many Anglican or Congregational churches still harbored the "Old Way."

The influx of Scottish and Scots-Irish immigrants in the late 17th century and early 18th brought a distinctive brand of Presbyterianism, whose firmly held traditions included the Scottish psalter of 1650 sung in the "Old Way" with lining out. In urban centers there were schisms in the Presbyterian communities: "New Side" synods welcomed the influence of the Evangelical movement, but "Old Side" synods staunchly resisted all reforms. In 1774 John Adams, accustomed to the New England choir singing, reported in his diary that the Old Presbyterian Society of New York was still "in the *old way*, as we call it – all the drawing, quavering, discord in the world." In country places it probably continued into the 20th century.

The "Old Way" was never incorporated into the Methodist movement, being quite antithetical to John Wesley's ideas about singing. Baptists had been slow to accept congregational singing in worship at all, because it was a "set form" rather than a spontaneous act of praise: that issue was still alive late in the 18th century. But in the revival movement that swept the South and West in the 19th century, Baptist churches were strong among those that promoted camp-meeting, shape-note, and eventually gospel hymn singing.

The principal region in the USA where the "Old Way of Singing" still survives is southern Appalachia, where it is found in both black and white Baptist churches; these communities regard their musical practice as an essential part of their worship and resist any attempt to change it. Jackson describes the "surge songs" of the black churches. Tallmadge (1975) reports the use of "lined hymns" in several hundred white Primitive and Regular Baptist churches in Kentucky, North Carolina, and Virginia. The tune repertory is a mixture of gospel hymns, camp-meeting hymns, and older material.

BIBLIOGRAPHY

J. Cotton: *Singing of Psalms a Gospel Ordinance* (London, 1647)

T. Symmes: *Utiles dulci* (Boston, 1723)

N. Chauncey: *Regular Singing Defended* (New London, CT, 1728)

G. Hood: *A History of Music in New England* (Boston, 1846/*R*1970)

M. van Doren, ed.: *Samuel Sewall's Diary* (n.p. [New York], 1927)

G. P. Jackson: *Spiritual Folk-songs of Early America* (Locust Valley, NY, 1937, 3/1965)

G. Chase: *America's Music* (New York, 1955, rev. 2/1966/*R*1981), chap.2

A. C. Buechner: *Yankee Singing Schools and the Golden Age of Choral Music in New England* (diss., Harvard U., 1960)

L. H. Butterfield, ed.: *Diary and Autobiography of John Adams* (Cambridge, MA, 1961), ii, 104

W. H. Tallmadge: "Baptist Monophonic and Heterophonic Hymnody in Southern Appalachia," *Yearbook for Inter-American Musical Research*, xi (1975), 106

N. Temperley: "The Old Way of Singing: its Origins and Development," *JAMS*, xxxiv (1981), 512

W. H. Tallmadge: "Folk Organum: a Study of Origins," *American Music*, ii/3 (1984), 47

NICHOLAS TEMPERLEY

Olefsky, Paul (*b* Chicago, IL, 4 Jan 1926). Cellist. He attended the Curtis Institute, where he studied under Daniel Saidenberg (1941–3) and Piatigorsky (1943–7); later studies included cello work with Casals and conducting with Karajan and Monteux. In 1948 he won the Naumburg Award, and in 1953 the Michaels Memorial Award of the Young Concert Artists. He has been a member of several leading American orchestras, including the Philadelphia Orchestra and the Detroit SO, and has appeared and broadcast as a guest soloist with many others in the USA and abroad. As a recitalist, performing in North America and Europe, he has a diverse repertory, ranging from the Bach suites to Kodály's unaccompanied cello sonata, and he has given the premières of a number of contemporary compositions, including works by Kurt George Rogers, Virgil Thomson, Milhaud, Shapleigh, and Alexander Tcherepnin. In 1974 he was appointed professor of cello and chamber music at the University of Texas, Austin. Olefsky's playing is noted for energy, sensitivity, and the high level of artistry that he maintains throughout his performances. His recordings include the complete Beethoven and Brahms sonatas.

MARGARET DOUTT

Oliveira, Elmar (*b* Waterbury, CT, 28 June 1950). Violinist. His first teacher was his older brother John. At the age of 11, he received a scholarship to study at the Hartt School of Music with Ariana Bronne; he completed his studies at the Manhattan School with Raphael Bronstein. While still a student, he made his début in 1964 as soloist with the Hartford SO. Two years later he was chosen by Bernstein to perform at a New York PO Youth Concert which was televised nationally. Oliveira made his New York recital début at Town Hall on 18 March 1973. In 1975 he won the Naumburg Award, and in 1978 he became the first American violinist to win a gold medal at the Tchaikovsky Competition in Moscow. Since then his solo career has expanded rapidly; he has also played with the Chamber Music Society of Lincoln Center. In December 1980 he gave the world première of Laderman's Second Violin Concerto, composed for him, with the Philadelphia Orchestra under the composer's direction. He won the Avery Fisher Prize in 1983. He has taught at SUNY, Binghamton.

Oliveira's playing is distinguished by smooth elegance, taste, and impeccable technique. His temperament is warm but controlled in a wide-ranging repertory. Among his recordings is Tchaikovsky's Piano Trio, performed with Mikhail Pletnyov and Nathaniel Rosen, fellow prizewinners of the Tchaikovsky Competition. His violin is a Giuseppe Guadagnini "Il soldato," made in 1781.

BIBLIOGRAPHY

J. Hiemenz: "Elmar Oliveira," *HiFi/MusAm*, xxx/12 (1980), 4

B. Schwarz: "The American School: the Younger Generation," *Great Masters of the Violin* (New York, 1983), 558

BORIS SCHWARZ

Oliver, King [Joe] (*b* in or nr New Orleans, LA, 11 May 1885; *d* Savannah, GA, 8 April 1938). Jazz cornetist and bandleader. He is said to have begun to study music as a trombonist, and from about 1907 he played in brass bands, dance bands, and in various small groups in New Orleans bars and cabarets. Early in 1918 he moved to Chicago (at which time he may have acquired his nickname), and in 1920 he began to lead his own band. After taking it to California (chiefly San Francisco and Oakland) in 1921, he returned to Chicago and, with some of the same musicians, started an engagement at Lincoln Gardens as King Oliver's Creole Jazz Band (June 1922). This group was joined a month later by the 22-year-old Louis Armstrong as second cornetist. With two cornets (Oliver and Armstrong), clarinet (Johnny Dodds), trombone (Honore Dutrey), piano (Lil Hardin), drums (Baby Dodds), and double bass and banjo (Bill Johnson), Oliver began recording in April 1923 (see illustration, p.408). Many young white jazz musicians had the opportunity to hear him then, either on recordings or live at Lincoln Gardens.

King Oliver's Creole Jazz Band in 1923: (left to right) Baby Dodds, Honore Dutrey, Oliver, Louis Armstrong, Bill Johnson, Johnny Dodds, and Lil Hardin (later Armstrong)

By late 1924, after a tour of the Midwest and Pennsylvania, the completely reorganized band included two or three saxophones, and played in Chicago as the Dixie Syncopators (February 1925–March 1927); the most distinguished of the saxophonists who played with this band were Barney Bigard, Albert Nicholas, and Benny Waters. Soon after a brief but successful engagement at the Savoy Ballroom in Harlem (from May 1927), the band dispersed, but Oliver stayed in New York, recording frequently with ad hoc orchestras. From 1930 to 1936 he toured widely, chiefly in the Midwest and upper South, with various ten- to 12-piece bands; he himself seldom performed during this period, and he made no further recordings after April 1931. He spent the final months of his life in Savannah retired from music.

Oliver is generally considered one of the most important musicians in the New Orleans style. Like other early New Orleans cornetists, he played in a relatively foursquare rhythm and clipped melodic style (contrasting with the deliberate irregularity of Armstrong and his imitators) and had a repertory of expressive deviations of rhythm and pitch, some verging on theatrical novelty effects and others derived from blues vocal style. He frequently used timbre modifiers of various sorts, and was especially renowned for his "wa-wa" effects, as in his famous three-chorus solo on *Dipper Mouth Blues* (1923), which was learned by rote by many trumpeters of the 1920s and 1930s and which, as *Sugar Foot Stomp*, became a jazz standard. As a soloist he can be best heard in a number of blues accompaniments, notably with Sippie Wallace.

In contrast to his near-contemporaries Freddie Keppard and Bunk Johnson, Oliver integrated his playing superbly with his ensemble, and was an excellent leader; the Creole Jazz Band may have been successful largely because of the discipline he imposed on his musicians. Indeed, of the earlier New Orleans cornetists, only Oliver was extensively recorded in the 1920s with an outstanding ensemble, and the revival of New Orleans style, which began shortly after his death, owed much to the rediscovery of his early three dozen Creole Band recordings, which were internationally known by the 1940s. After 1924 the quality of his recordings declined, partly because of constant tooth and gum ailments and partly through his inability to assemble a rhythm section adequate to the requirements of his style; but with a good orchestra he was capable of coherent and energetic playing even as late as 1930. Almost all of his recorded performances have been reissued.

Oliver's influence is difficult to assess: his playing during his New Orleans period (his best years, according to Souchon) was not recorded, and by 1925 his style had largely been superseded by Armstrong's. He had an obvious formative impact on Ellington's sideman Bubber Miley, and perhaps on such white musicians as Muggsy Spanier; his mute tricks were copied by Johnny Dunn; and trumpeters such as Natty Dominique and Tommy Ladnier, who remained apart from Armstrong's influence, may have derived their styles from Oliver. The extent of Oliver's influence on Armstrong himself, though clearly audible and significant, has yet to be examined properly.

RECORDINGS

(selective list)

As leader with the Creole Jazz Band: Canal Street Blues (1923, Gennett 5133); Mandy Lee Blues/I'm going to wear you off my mind (1923, Gennett 5134); Chimes Blues (1923, Gennett 5135); Weather Bird Blues/Dipper Mouth Blues (1923, Gennett 5132); Snake Rag/High Society Rag (1923, OK 4933); Zulu's Ball/Working Man's Blues (1923, Gennett 5275); Chattanooga Stomp/New Orleans Stomp (1923, Col. 13003D); London Cafe Blues/Camp Meeting Blues (1923, Col. 14003D)

As leader with other groups: Deep Henderson/Jackass Blues (1926, Voc. 1014); Someday, Sweetheart/Dead Man Blues (1926, Voc. 1059); Call of the Freaks/

The Trumpet's Prayer (1929, Vic. 38039); St. James' Infirmary/When you're Smiling (1930, Vic. 22298)

As accompanist: S. Wallace: Morning Dove Blues/Every Dog has his Day (1925, OK 8205), Devil Dance Blues (1925, OK 8206); V. Spivey: My Handy Man/Organ Grinder Blues (1928, OK 8615); T. Alexander: 'Frisco Train Blues (1928, OK 8658)

BIBLIOGRAPHY

F. Ramsey, Jr.: "King Oliver," *Jazzmen*, ed. F. Ramsey, Jr., and C. E. Smith (New York, 1939)

R. Blesh: *Shining Trumpets* (New York, 1949/*R*1975)

W. Allen and B. Rust: *King Joe Oliver* (London, 1957)

S. B. Charters: *Jazz: New Orleans: 1885–1957* (New York, 1958, rev. 2/1963/*R*1983)

E. Souchon: "King Oliver: a Very Personal Memoir," *Jazz Review*, iii/4 (1960), 6; repr. in *Jazz Panorama*, ed. M. Williams (New York, 1962)

M. Williams: *King Oliver* (London, 1960); repr. in *Kings of Jazz*, ed. S. Green (New York, 1978)

L. Gushee: "King Oliver," *Jazz Panorama*, ed. M. Williams (New York, 1962)

G. Schuller: *Early Jazz: its Roots and Musical Development* (New York, 1968)

L. O. Koch: "Structural Aspects of King Oliver's 1923 Okeh Recordings," *Journal of Jazz Studies*, iii/2 (1976), 36

J. L. Collier: *Louis Armstrong* (New York, 1983)

LAWRENCE GUSHEE

Oliver, Sy [Melvin James] (*b* Battle Creek, MI, 17 Dec 1910). Arranger and composer. He studied piano and trumpet with his parents, both professional musicians, and was active while still in his teens, playing trumpet with Cliff Barnett's Club Royal Serenaders, Alphonso Trent, and, in 1927, Zach Whyte's Chocolate Beau Brummels. After teaching, performing, and arranging for three years in Columbus, Ohio, he joined the swing band of JIMMIE LUNCEFORD in 1933, playing trumpet and contributing many outstanding arrangements. Later he joined Tommy Dorsey as composer-arranger (1939–43). He led his own band at the Zanzibar Club in New York from 1946, and from 1954 served as music director for various recording companies for a decade. His band was revived in 1970 following a European tour, and in 1975 he began a residency at the Rainbow Room in New York. Among those for whom Oliver also arranged were Louis Armstrong, Frank Sinatra, Della Reese, Bing Crosby, Chubby Checker, and the Mills Brothers. In addition to his work for television (e.g., the "Tonight Show"), he prepared scores for *Ship Ahoy* (1942), *Dubarry was a Lady* and *Girl Crazy* (1943), *Go, Man, Go* (1954), and other films. In 1976 he won the National Urban League award for his musical work.

WORKS

(arrangements for jazz band; selective list)

For J. Lunceford: Swingin' Uptown, 1934; Black and Tan Fantasy, 1934; Dream of you, 1934; Stomp it off, 1934; Swanee River, 1935; The Melody Man, 1935; Organ Grinder's Swing, 1936; Runnin' a Temperature, 1936; Raggin' the Scale, 1937; Hell's Bells, 1937; For Dancers only, 1937; Margie, 1938; Shoemaker's Holiday, 1939; Blue Blazes, 1939; Dinah, 1940

For T. Dorsey: Quiet, Please, 1940; So What!, 1940; Swing High, 1940; Yes, Indeed!, 1941; Swingin' on Nothin', 1941; Well, Git it!, 1942; Opus no.1, 1944

BIBLIOGRAPHY

SouthernB

C. Carrière: "Welcome, Sy Oliver," *Jazz hot*, no.294 (1973), 16

S. Dance: *The World of Swing* (New York, 1974), 125

Z. Knauss: *Conversations with Jazz Musicians* (Detroit, 1977), 150

"Sy Oliver," *BMI: the Many Worlds of Music* (1981), no.3, p.35

D. Travis: *An Autobiography of Black Jazz* (Chicago, 1983), 435

DOMINIQUE-RENÉ DE LERMA

Oliveros, Pauline (*b* Houston, TX, 30 May 1932). Composer and performer. As a child she studied piano, violin, accordion, and french horn. She attended the University of Houston (1949–52), where she studied composition with Paul Koepke and accordion with William Palmer, and San Francisco State College (BA 1957); she also had private composition lessons with Robert Erickson (1954–60). She was codirector (1961–5) of the San Francisco Tape Music Center with Ramon Sender and Morton Subotnick and director (1966–7) when it became the Mills Tape Music Center. From 1967 to 1981 she taught at the University of California, San Diego. While in San Diego she organized a group of women musicians and dancers to perform mixed-media works; it toured extensively, performing primarily her music. She has been composer-in-residence at the University of Washington, Wesleyan University, the San Francisco Conservatory, Stanford University, the Cornish School, the Walker Art Center, the Cleveland Museum of Art, and the Cabrillo Festival. She has received a number of awards and commissions including the Pacifica Foundation Prize (1961, for the Variations for Sextet), a Gaudeamus Foundation Award (1962, for *Sound Patterns*), a Guggenheim Fellowship (1973–4), and a commission from the city of Bonn (1977, for *Bonn Feier*). In 1981 she became consulting director of the Creative Music Foundation at West Hurley, New York.

Oliveros's compositions range from music for acoustic instruments to mixed-media works that incorporate both electronically produced and live sounds, film, texts, theatrical events, and dance. Concerned with improvisation guided by meditation, which she uses to achieve a sense of communion among performers, her sonic meditations are characterized by drone effects and the prolongation of sounds. The resulting sound environments take the form of scenarios with directions for the performers' physical and musical activities, which interact with other performers and on occasion invite audience participation. Oliveros's music is recorded on Odyssey, Nonesuch, and 1750 Arch records. She has written a book, *Pauline's Proverbs* (1976), and articles for *Numus West* and other periodicals; her collected writings were published in 1984 as *Software for People: Collected Writings 1963–80*.

Pauline Oliveros, 1979

WORKS
(selective list)

DRAMATIC

George Washington Slept Here Too (theater piece), 4 pfmrs, 1965; Pieces of Eight (theater piece), wind octet, tape, 1965; Theater Piece for Trombone Player, garden hoses, tape, 1966; Aeolian Partitions (theater piece), fl, cl, vn, vc, pf, 1968; Sonic Meditations, vv, insts, pfmrs, 1971–2

Crow Two: a Ceremonial Opera, 1974; Theatre of Substitution, 1975; Theatre of Substitutions: Blind/Dumb/Director, 1977; Bonn Feier (theater piece), actors, dancers, pfmrs, 1977; The Yellow River Map (meditation), 50 or more pfmrs, 1977; Traveling Companions, dancers, perc ens, 1980

Many film scores

OTHER WORKS

Orch: To Valerie Solanas and Marilyn Monroe in Recognition of their Desperation, orch/chamber ens, 1970; Tashi gomang, 1981

Chamber: Variations for Sextet, fl, cl, tpt, hn, vc, pf, 1960; Trio, fl, pf, page turner, 1961; Outline, fl, perc, db, 1963; Double Basses at 20 Paces, 2 db, tape, slides, cond. + referee, 2 pfmrs, 1968; To those in Gray Northwestern Rainforests, unspecified insts, 1976; Double X, meditation, pairs of like insts with overlapping ranges, 1979; The Witness, 1979; The Wheel of Time, str qt, 1983; Spiral Mandala, 4 cl, 8 crystal glasses, b drum, finger cymbals, 1984

Vocal: Sound Patterns, chorus, 1961; The C(s) for Once, vv, fls, tpts, tape delay, 1966; SY*YdY = 1, 4 readers (4 solo vv), 4 vc, 4 bn, amp. heartbeat, shakuhachi, 1969; Meditations on the Points of a Compass, 12 solo vv, chorus, perc, 1970; Willow Brook Generations and Reflections, vv, wind, brass, 1976; Horse Sings from a Cloud (Rose Mountain), 1v, accordion, 1977; King Kong Sings Along, chorus, 1977; Rose Moon, chorus, perc, 1977; The Wheel of Life, vocal ens, 1978; El relicario de los animales, S, 20 insts, 1979

Tape: Big Mother is Watching You, 1966; I of IV, 2-track tape, 1966; Beautiful Soop, 1967; Jar Piece; Bye Bye, Butterfly

Principal publisher: Smith

BIBLIOGRAPHY

EwenD; *VintonD*
M. Subotnick: "Pauline Oliveros: *Trio*," *PNM*, ii/1 (1963), 77
E. Kefalas: "Pauline Oliveros," *HiFi/MusAm*, xxv/6 (1975), 24
J. Mac Low: "Being Pauline: Narrative of a Substitution," *Big Deal*, no.4 (1976), 168
W. Zimmermann: "Pauline Oliveros," *Desert Plants: Conversations with 23 American Musicians* (Vancouver, BC, 1976)
M. Roth: "An Interview with Pauline Oliveros," *New Performance*, i/2 (1977)
Z. Cleigh: "All Sounds are Music," *San Diego Magazine*, xxxi/9 (1979), 190
G. Von Gunden: *The Music of Pauline Oliveros* (Metuchen, NJ, 1983)

RICHARD SWIFT

Olmstead [Olmsted], **Timothy** (*b* Hartford, CT, 13 Nov 1759; *d* Phoenix, Oswego Co., NY, 15 Aug 1848). Composer, tunebook compiler, singing master, and fifer. His known career as a musician began during the War of Independence, when he played fife in a Connecticut regimental corps (1775), becoming a fife major in 1776. He played in a regimental band from 1777 to 1780. After the war he apparently settled in Connecticut and worked as a singing master, though the only school of his that can now be documented was held at Wethersfield in 1804. He served in the War of 1812, and in his later years lived in Whitestown, New York.

Olmstead compiled *The Musical Olio* (Northampton, MA, 1805, 2/1811), which was devoted mostly to European pieces and favored the Methodist style, but also contained 25 of his own compositions. Drawing on his experience as a bandsman he also compiled *Martial Music* (Albany, NY, 1807), a collection of instrumental marches and dances, including nearly a dozen of his own. Olmstead's range as a musician was unusual for Americans of his generation. As a psalmodist, he composed in both the indigenous New England idiom and a more Europeanized style, and he also wrote with some skill for instruments.

BIBLIOGRAPHY

H. K. Olmsted and G. K. Ward: *Genealogy of the Olmsted Family in America* (New York, 1912), 40
F. J. Metcalf: *American Writers and Compilers of Sacred Music* (New York, 1925/*R*1967)
F. H. Johnson: *Musical Memories of Hartford* (Hartford, 1931/*R*1970), 40
R. J. Wolfe: *Secular Music in America, 1801–1825: a Bibliography* (New York, 1964)
R. Crawford: *Andrew Law, American Psalmodist* (Evanston, IL, 1968/*R*1981), 65, 71, 178, 228
R. F. Camus: *Military Music of the American Revolution* (Chapel Hill, 1976), 77
P. R. Osterhout: *Music in Northampton, Massachusetts to 1820* (diss., U. of Michigan, 1978), 275
R. M. Wilson: *Connecticut's Music in the Revolutionary Era* (Hartford, 1979), 71, 76, 84

RICHARD CRAWFORD

Omaha (i). American Indian tribe of the north-central Plains, members of the Siouan language family. Before relocation to their present-day reservation in Nebraska (*see* INDIANS, AMERICAN, fig. 1), they ranged over the upper Missouri River Valley, leading a semisedentary life that combined horticulture and buffalo-hunting. Music was an integral part of traditional Omaha life, and the focus of religious rituals and secret societies. Songs had various sources; they could be composed by an individual, borrowed from a neighboring tribe, or, according to traditional belief, received from a supernatural being in a dream or vision. Since songs were considered property, they could also be purchased, though only personal songs were transferable in this manner. The right to sing songs that belonged to a society or tribal group came only through membership or hereditary privilege.

Like many other Plains tribes the Omaha lived in a state of continual conflict with their neighbors. War parties were organized to secure horses and property, and to avenge previous injuries. Before departure, a feast and dance were held in which members of the war party performed the Wolf Dance (the wolf was the patron of warriors), which, with trotting steps and sudden stops, was imitative of a wolf's movements. At this time a warrior also sang his personal medicine song, typically said to have been received from a guardian spirit in a vision. A successful return prompted a victory dance performed, by both men and women, around a central pole to which scalps of the enemy were tied. Men who had distinguished themselves in war usually belonged to one of several warrior societies; by the mid-19th century the *Haethu'shka* was the largest. Meetings included dances that pantomimed battle movements, a feast, and honorific songs. These were either new compositions or reworkings of existing songs, the texts of which were altered by the addition of another warrior's name and descriptions of his deeds. The use of one item of *Haethu'shka* regalia, a long bunch of grass (representing scalps), gave rise to the name "Grass Dance," as it was adopted by the Dakota Indians. On the northern Plains the war dance performed at contemporary powwows may still be called the Grass or Omaha Dance. The Omaha also performed the *Wa'wan*, a ceremony in which calumets were presented to unrelated groups or distant tribes as a peace offering. Songs, which accompanied the "waving of the pipes" by two dancers who simulated the flight of eagles, were an important feature. As the *Wa'wan* was not the exclusive privilege of any group, its songs were widely known and sung by both men and women.

The most important religious ceremony of the Omaha, involving two elaborate song cycles, occurred annually in July following the summer buffalo hunt. The first song cycle thanked the Creator for the buffalo; the second recounted the events of the hunt. In their narrative function the songs had repetitive and recitative-like qualities, and their sacred nature required performance in a rigidly prescribed sequence. After these rites the annual tribal dance, *He'dewachi*, was held. Originally associated with the cultivation of corn, by the mid-19th century this showed many similarities with the Sun Dance of nonagricultural Plains tribes. In the dance, which lasted one day, two concentric circles, one formed of men and the other of women, moved in opposite directions around a pole. The Omaha had several secret medicine societies, each with sacred songs and dances to be performed during a healing ceremony. Membership was open to men and women who reported having had a vision or dream in which a medicine song was received from the supernatural being that was the society's patron.

As music played a significant part in many Omaha ceremonies, singers who knew the repertory and had strong, reliable voices were sought after and paid to perform. Singing technique was typical of the Plains style, with a fair amount of tension in the voice, a high tessitura, high dynamic level, and pulsations on longer tones. Women often accompanied male singers, doubling the melody at the octave. Songs, which were fairly short, usually consisted of five to eight phrases that became longer towards the end of the piece. A common song form consisted of one long section of three to five phrases, all of which save the first were then repeated (e.g., *ABB'* or *ABCBC*). Others were through-composed, with no repetition of melodic material, but with repeated rhythmic motifs. The range of Omaha songs varied greatly; some, as was typical of the Plains style, had a range of an octave or more; others, especially older songs associated with the cultivation of corn, had a range of a 5th. Melodies were most often pentatonic with a descending contour. The most common intervals were major 2nds, minor 3rds, and to a lesser extent perfect 4ths. Drum accompaniment with a steady, regular pulse was the rule, the beats consistently falling either just ahead of or behind the pulse of the song. Most sacred songs had texts, but these consisted only of a few words that were liberally interspersed with vocables to suit the melodic phrase. Songs of the *Wa'wan* ceremony differed from other Omaha music, exhibiting characteristics of the eastern woodlands musical style: a more undulating melodic contour, stepwise descent, and a drumbeat synchronized with the voice.

The Omaha instrumentarium was fairly large. A water-drum, made from a hollowed section of a tree partially filled with water and covered with buffalo hide, was used to accompany most songs, both sacred and secular. Before playing the drum was tuned by wetting the hide and stretching it tightly over the frame. Frame drums with single heads were used by members of medicine societies during healing ceremonies. A sheet of rawhide was beaten by women as they sang songs intended to give strength to warriors away from home. For the *Haethu'shka* meetings, a large drum, suspended on four stakes and struck with padded beaters, was played by two to four singers. Three types of rattle provided rhythmic accompaniment: gourd rattles, used in the *Wa'wan* and by the medicine societies; and hide-container and cluster rattles, made of deer hooves tied to the end of a stick, which were part of the regalia of the warrior societies. The eagle-bone whistle was used only in the *Wa'wan*, and the cedar flute, with an external duct and six fingerholes, was played by young men during courtship.

By 1900 traditional Omaha culture had virtually disappeared. Nevertheless the Omaha continue to participate in the pan-Indian songs and dances of the northern Plains, and hold an annual powwow in August at Macy, Nebraska. Recordings of Omaha music are held at the Bureau of American Ethnology, Smithsonian Institution, Washington, DC; the Archive of Folk Culture, Library of Congress, Washington; and the Archives of Traditional Music, Indiana University, Bloomington, Indiana.

See also INDIANS, AMERICAN, esp. §I, 4(ii)(a).

BIBLIOGRAPHY

J. O. Dorsey: "Songs of the Hecucka Society," *Journal of American Folklore*, i (1888), 65

A. C. Fletcher: "A Study of Omaha Indian Music," *Archaeological and Ethnological Papers of the Peabody Museum*, i/5 (Cambridge, MA, 1893)

A. C. Fletcher and F. LaFlesche: *The Omaha Tribe*, 27th Annual Report of the Bureau of American Ethnology, 1905–06 (Washington, DC, 1911)

R. F. Fortune: *Omaha Secret Societies* (New York, 1932/*R*1969)

J. H. Howard: "Notes on the Dakota Grass Dance," *Southwestern Journal of Anthropology*, vii/1 (1951), 82

MARY RIEMER-WELLER

Omaha (ii). City in Nebraska (pop. 314,225; metropolitan area 569,614). It is situated at the confluence of the Platte and Missouri rivers on the Nebraska-Iowa border. The city was incorporated in 1857. In 1819 the regimental band at Fort Atkinson offered concerts and evenings of musical entertainment. 15 years later a Baptist missionary, Moses Merrill, taught music to the Otoe Indians and transcribed a book of hymns into their language. Shortly after the Nebraska Territory was opened for settlement in 1854, Peter Sarpy, a fur trader with the American Fur Company, shipped the first piano up the Missouri River from St. Louis, and the territory's musically inclined European settlers established the Germania Männerchor, a philharmonic society, and a singing society.

When Nebraska became a state in 1867, Omaha opened a music school. During the next two decades the citizens formed many musical organizations, including the Omaha City and Union Pacific bands, the Swedish Brass Band, the Arion Singing Club, the Omaha and Norden glee clubs, the Apollo Club, the Omaha Harmonic Society, the Schumann, Beethoven, and Orpheus quartets, the Haydn Trio, and a number of church choirs. Several theaters and opera houses were built, including Redick's Opera House, the Grand Opera House, the Farnam Street Theatre, and Boyd's Opera House. The Orpheum Theatre, a magnificent example of late 19th-century architecture that was completely restored in 1974, continues to be used for musical performances. By the end of the 19th century the Musical Mutual Protection Union (later the Musicians' Union) had been formed, the Apollo Club had received national recognition at the World's Columbian Exposition (1893), and Dvořák had visited Omaha, where he was entertained by the Czech Band and the Seventh Regiment Band. Music also played an important role at the city's Trans-Mississippi and International Exposition (1898).

In the 1920s several jazz bands became prominent, including the Dan Desdunes Band, Maceo Pinkard's Jazz Band, and the Ted Adams Orchestra. Musical activity was encouraged during the Depression by the federal government, which sponsored the Omaha Civic Orchestra. By 1958 two semiprofessional companies, the Omaha Lyric Theatre and the Civic Opera Society, had been established. In 1965 the Omaha Regional Ballet Company was founded, and in 1976 the Omaha Sinfonia began a series of "Bagels and Bach" concerts on Sunday mornings at the Joslyn

Art Museum. The Omaha Musicians Association arranges almost 250 concerts annually through such programs as Music in the Parks, the Summer Arts Festival, and the September-Fest, which was once attended by 500,000 people. The Jazz Society holds public jam sessions, and various rock, country music, and folk groups perform locally. Perhaps the most innovative group now active in Omaha is the Mannheim Steamroller, whose recordings combine classical music and jazz, and make use of electronic materials.

BIBLIOGRAPHY

A. Sorenson: *History of Omaha: from the Pioneer Days to the Present* (Omaha, 1889)
D. D. Dustin: *Omaha and Douglas County: a Panoramic History* (Woodland Hills, CA, 1980)

KAREN M. DYER

ONCE. Association of composers and avant-garde artists. The group evolved in the late 1950s in Ann Arbor, Michigan; its central figure was the composer Robert Ashley. Other composers who were members included Gordon Mumma, co-organizer with Ashley of the ONCE festivals, Roger Reynolds, who was active in the founding of the group and in the organization of the first festival, George Cacioppo, Donald Scavarda, Bruce Wise, and, in later festivals, Robert Nathan Sheff ("Blue" Gene Tyranny). Artists, filmmakers (notably George Manupelli), architects, poets, and performance artists were all involved in ONCE mixed-media activities, and many guest composers and musicians took part. ONCE festivals were given annually from 1961 to 1968, and the ONCE Group, a smaller performance art ensemble founded by Ashley, performed, recorded, and made tours from 1965 to 1969. After Ashley moved to California in 1969, ONCE activities declined in importance.

The most significant focus for avant-garde mixed-media activity in the Midwest during the 1960s, ONCE sponsored performances of works from the entire range of Cageian and post-Cageian experimental American music; its programs also included music by prominent European contemporaries and works of the classic modernist repertory. The emphasis that ONCE placed on mixed media had an influence on subsequent collaborative ventures in California and New York.

BIBLIOGRAPHY

R. N. Sheff and M. Slobin: "Music Beyond the Boundaries," *Generation*, no.17 (1965), 27
G. Mumma: "The ONCE Festival and How it Happened," *Arts in Society*, iv (1967), 381

JOHN ROCKWELL

Oneida. Indian tribe of the IROQUOIS confederacy.

One-step. One of the lively "animal" dances of the early 20th century associated with the music of ragtime. It consisted of a simple walking step for eight counts with a pivot on the first; a variant introduced by the dance team of Vernon and Irene Castle known as the "Castle walk" was danced on the toes with stiff knees. Any quickstep or ragtime tune in a brisk march tempo was suitable for the one-step. Examples of such compositions include *The Bon Ton One Step* (1915) by Luckey Roberts (a variant of his *Junk Man Rag* written two years earlier) and arrangements of Irving Berlin's *Alexander's Ragtime Band* (1911).

BIBLIOGRAPHY

V. Castle and I. Castle: *Modern Dancing* (New York, 1914/*R*1980)

For further bibliography *see* DANCE; for illustration *see* CASTLE, VERNON.

PAULINE NORTON

Ono, Yoko (*b* Tokyo, Japan, 18 Feb 1933). Rock singer and songwriter. She was born into a wealthy banking family and raised in Tokyo, and in 1953 moved to New York to attend Sarah Lawrence College. After her graduation she became active in Manhattan's conceptual-art circles, and in 1966 met JOHN LENNON of the Beatles at an exhibition of her work in London. With him she recorded an experimental album, *Unfinished Music no.1: Two Virgins* (1968). When Lennon and his wife were divorced in 1968 he and Ono became companions and collaborators; under Ono's influence he became interested in avant-garde art forms that contrasted starkly with his work with the Beatles. Their early recordings were free-form vocal and electronic collages; *Live Peace in Toronto 1969* included both rock standards and experimental improvisations. Lennon and Ono were married in 1969 and the following year the Beatles disbanded, partly owing to tensions between Ono and members of the group. She and Lennon continued to record jointly and separately, then in the mid-1970s they withdrew from professional life; they reemerged in 1980 to record a fine pop album, *Double Fantasy*. After Lennon's death Ono recorded *Season of Glass* (1981), a moving, musically straightforward account of her loss; her next album, *It's Alright* (1982), continued this move towards mainstream rock music and revealed Ono as a mature artist in her own right. Ono's and Lennon's final collaboration, *Milk and Honey*, was issued in 1984.

Much of the work recorded by Ono and Lennon seemed indulgent and self-absorbed at the time it was issued, and Ono's own music often failed to reach a sizable pop audience. In time, however, her high-pitched voice with its shrill tremolo influenced performers as diverse as Meredith Monk, Joan La Barbara, and the B-52s.

RECORDINGS

(selective list)

As soloist: *Yoko Ono/Plastic Ono Band* (Apple 3373, 1970); *Fly* (Apple 3380, 1971); *Approximately Infinite Universe* (Apple 3399, 1973); *Feeling the Space* (Apple 3413, 1973); *Season of Glass* (Geffen 2004, 1981); *It's Alright* (Pol. 16364, 1982)

With J. Lennon: *Unfinished Music no.1: Two Virgins* (Apple 5001, 1968); *Unfinished Music no.2: Life with the Lions* (Zapple 3357, 1969); *Wedding Album* (Apple 3361, 1969); *Live Peace in Toronto 1969* (Apple 3362, 1970); *Double Fantasy* (Geffen 2001, 1980); *Heart Play: Unfinished Dialogue* (Polygram 8172381, 1983); *Milk and Honey* (Polygram 8171601, 1984)

BIBLIOGRAPHY

"Ono, Yoko," *CBY 1972*
J. Cott and C. Doudna, eds.: *The Ballad of John and Yoko* (New York, 1982)

MIKAL GILMORE

Onondaga. Indian tribe of the IROQUOIS confederacy.

Oohenonpa [Two-kettle]. American Plains Indian group belonging to the Teton division of the SIOUX.

Opera. Generic term for a work combining music, drama, and spectacle, in which the onstage participants sing and act some or all of their roles. As a form of musical theater, in which music usually plays the dominant role, opera is perhaps the most elaborate of art forms; it may call on the united skills of composer, librettist, director, designer, choreographer, performers, and impresarios to attain realization. Opera has traditionally attracted an audience drawn from the élite of society, although recent changes have brought it a much wider public (see §§5, 7 and 8 below). In its generally understood sense, opera originated in Italy about 1600. The first operatic works heard in the USA were examples of the English type known as ballad opera, which originated in London in the 1720s and was quickly transplanted to America; by the 1790s Americans were composing their own operas. Foreign-language operas were introduced at about that time: first French opera, in New Orleans, in the 1790s; then Italian opera, in New York, in the 1820s; then, slightly later in New York, German opera. Not until much later were operas in other languages performed in the USA.

This article is concerned with both the native and imported (English-language and foreign-language) operatic traditions in the USA (they are sometimes differentiated as "American opera" and "opera in America") and with their synthesis in an American operatic culture of international outlook that has experienced remarkable growth since the mid-1960s. The lighter forms of American musical theater are considered in detail elsewhere (*see* BALLAD OPERA, BROADCASTING, BURLESQUE, FILM MUSIC, JEWISH-AMERICAN MUSIC, §3(ii), MELODRAMA, MINSTRELSY, MUSICAL, MUSICAL FILM, MUSICAL THEATER, PANTOMIME, and VAUDEVILLE). For a discussion of some of the most recent trends in music theater, *see* EXPERIMENTAL MUSIC, §3. Information on opera houses and their resident companies will be found in entries on the cities in which they are situated. Individuals involved with opera – composers, librettists, directors, stage designers, singers, administrators, patrons, and critics – are discussed in their own entries.

1. ENGLISH-LANGUAGE OPERA TO 1815. The first operatic music heard in America was that of English ballad opera, a genre that had originated in London in 1728 with John Gay's *The Beggar's Opera*. Ballad operas were essentially spoken dramas on topical subjects with interpolated songs and choruses. The first of these known to have been performed in America was Colley Cibber's *Flora, or Hob in the Well*, produced at Charleston in 1735 as part of that city's first theatrical season. Various troupes in the eastern seaboard cities mounted British ballad operas later in the 18th century. The work that may be considered the first American opera is *The Disappointment, or The Force of Credulity*; it is thought to have been written by Andrew Barton, and its libretto was published anonymously in Philadelphia in 1767 (though the work was not performed then). Based on ballad opera conventions, *The Disappointment* reveals its American origins by combining Pennsylvania-German dialect with the tune of *Yankee Doodle* to characterize a rascal named Raccoon.

Besides ballad operas, with music drawn from popular and traditional sources, comic operas with scores by 18th-century English composers were also played on American stages. Among the most popular were Thomas A. Arne's *Love in a Village*, Charles Dibdin's *The Padlock*, Thomas Linley's *The Duenna*, *The Poor Soldier* by John O'Keeffe and William Shield, and Stephen Storace's *No Song, No Supper*. Such works as these provided the basis for operas composed in the USA in the late 18th century.

Operatic activity was largely suspended during the Revolution, having already been inhibited by a congressional resolution of 1774 which discouraged "every species of extravagance and dissipation," and by religious objections to theatrical enterprises. Musical theater did, however, continue on a limited scale; the religious objections were overcome by the use of puppets or by the billing of theater productions as "moral dialogues" or concerts, and amateur companies were sponsored by the three leading generals of the British expeditionary forces, William Howe, Henry Clinton, and John Burgoyne.

When the hostilities ceased, a new period of American opera began, during which the foundations were laid for professional and aesthetically superior institutions that shaped operatic life until the mid-19th century. In most of the commercially active seaport cities, theaters with facilities for opera production were constructed by investors and leased to theatrical companies; the most significant of these were in Boston, Newport (where the original Brick Market Theatre still stands), New York, Philadelphia (its companies serving also Baltimore and Washington), Charleston, and New Orleans. Many well-trained and gifted musicians and singing actors were attracted by the musical opportunities in these thriving communities. Most of them came from England, but substantial numbers were also forced to immigrate as a result of the French Revolution and its aftermath; others had come from Germany as musicians in the bands of British mercenary units, or to enjoy religious freedom. Among the most significant of the immigrants who became active as entrepreneurs, music directors, composers, and teachers were Rayner Taylor, Alexander Reinagle, Benjamin Carr, James Hewitt, Victor Pelissier, and Gottlieb Graupner. Their main operatic work consisted in supplying orchestral accompaniments and arrangements for English comic operas. Occasionally, though, when scores were not available, or when new productions were planned, they wrote original music. Thus was an American operatic tradition founded, of which the most notable early works were Hewitt's *Tammany, or The Indian Chief* (New York, 1794), Carr's *The Archers, or The Mountaineers of Switzerland* (New York, 1796),

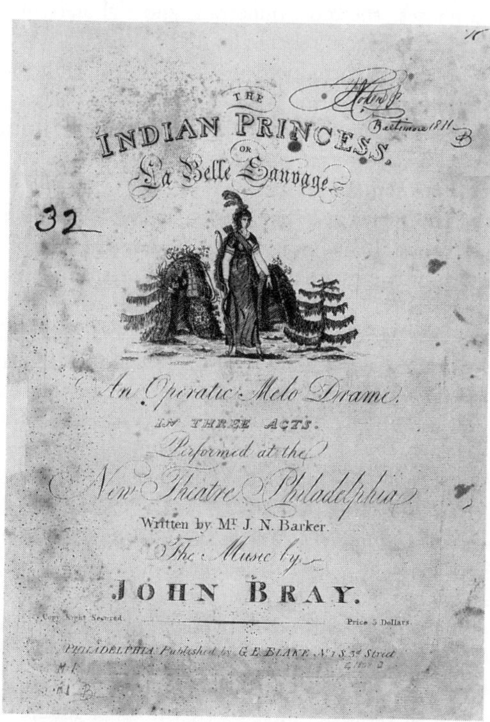

1. Title page of the vocal score of "The Indian Princess, or La belle sauvage" by James Nelson Barker, with music by John Bray, first performed in Philadelphia in 1808

Pelissier's *Edwin and Angelina* (New York, 1796), Reinagle's orchestral accompaniments for Samuel Arnold's *The Mountaineers* (Philadelphia, 1796), John Bray's *The Indian Princess* (Philadelphia, 1808; fig. 1), and Taylor's *The Aethiop* (Philadelphia, 1814). Much of this music is no longer extant.

In Philadelphia musical theater flourished from about 1794 to 1822, largely owing to the fact that the city was, initially, the seat of the national government. It was the home of the New Theatre in Chesnut Street, the dominating manager of which, Reinagle, was a musician of style and social influence. He assembled a cadre of singing actors of recognized quality, and an orchestra, unquestionably the best in the USA, that compared favorably with those in London. The high point of the period was reached with Taylor's score for the "Grand Romantick Drama" *The Aethiop*, originally written in 1812 for Covent Garden by William Dimond (with music by Henry R. Bishop). The overwhelming success of the work, with Taylor's sophisticated overture, choruses, songs, and musical scenes, seems to prove that Philadelphians appreciated a high level of musical and dramatic expertise in their theater.

2. European opera to the mid-19th century. Foreign-language operatic activity in the USA began in 1791 in New Orleans, with the arrival of a French theatrical troupe headed by Louis Tabery. In 1792 he opened the city's first theater, later called the Spectacle de la rue St. Pierre. In the 1805–6 season alone the St. Pierre theater produced 16 different operas by nine composers including Pierre-Alexandre Monsigny, André Grétry, Nicolas Dalayrac, François-Adrien Boieldieu, Etienne-Nicolas Méhul, and Giovanni Paisiello. A permanent opera company was established at the Orleans Theater in 1810, and French opera continued to flourish in New Orleans in a succession of theaters and opera houses, the most important and elaborate of which, the French Opera House, opened in 1859.

French opera was introduced in the North during the same period, initially by a touring company from New Orleans led by John Davis, which appeared in Philadelphia and Baltimore as well as New York, Boston, and other eastern cities as far north as Quebec in the summers of 1827–33. Better received, however, than French operas were Italian works, at first in English adaptations. Henry R. Bishop's version of Mozart's *Don Giovanni* (as *The Libertine*) was presented at the Park Theatre in New York on 7 November 1817; his version of Rossini's *Il barbiere di Siviglia* (as *The Barber of Seville*) was produced there on 3 May 1819 and repeated during every season until 1824. Such adaptations of Italian operas were the most popular works on American musical-theater stages into the 1840s. The most successful of all was Rossini's *La Cenerentola* in a version by Rophino Lacy called *Cinderella, or The Fairy-Queen and the Glass Slipper*, which received its American première at the Park Theatre on 24 January 1831 and was performed in New York and many other American cities for three decades; it was the first opera to be produced in St. Louis (9 October 1837), and it became so widely known that it spawned burlesque and parody versions in the minstrel shows of the 1840s and 1850s.

Italian opera in the original language was introduced in 1825, when a Spanish company directed by the tenor Manuel García presented *Il barbiere di Siviglia* on 29 November at the Park Theatre, New York. During the next nine months it gave almost 80 performances, including Rossini's *La Cenerentola*, *Semiramide*, *Tancredi*, and *Il turco in Italia*, Mozart's *Don Giovanni*, and two of García's own operas. Exposure to such an expressive and powerful style of singing as offered that season by García, his daughter Maria Malibran, and his troupe in works of universal appeal, was ultimately to divert one channel of American musical theater in a new direction. The older lyric-theater tradition – works in English with songs and choruses (written for singing actors) interspersed with spoken dialogue – continued; but the new European opera, with dialogue in recitative, arias and ensembles written for virtuoso singers trained in the bel canto manner, and orchestral accompaniment in the Romantic style, soon began to take hold. Other troupes, both visiting and resident, rode the wave of enthusiasm, particularly evident in New York and Philadelphia, for Italian operas by Rossini, Bellini, Donizetti, and later composers. This vogue was reflected concretely in 1832, when Lorenzo Da Ponte formed his own company and built the Italian Opera House in New York. It opened on 18 November 1833 with Rossini's *La gazza ladra*, but burned down two years later. The next opera house to be built in New York was the Astor Place Opera House (with 1500 seats the largest theater in the USA at that time); it opened on 22 November 1847 with Verdi's *Ernani*. The much larger Academy of Music (4600 seats) opened on 2 October 1854 with Bellini's *Norma*.

Although German opera, sung in German, did not gain a foothold in the USA until the 1850s, English-language "paraphrases" of Weber's *Der Freischütz* had been heard in 1825, his *Oberon* in 1827, Mozart's *Die Zauberflöte* in 1832, and Beethoven's *Fidelio* in 1839. In 1855 a series of German operas in the original language was presented at Niblo's Garden in New York; important American premières that followed were of the complete *Fidelio* (1856), Wagner's *Tannhäuser* (Stadt-Theater, New York, 4 April 1859), Mozart's *Die Entführung aus dem Serail* (Brooklyn Athenaeum, 16 February 1860), and Wagner's *Rienzi* (Academy of Music, 5 March 1878).

During the half century between 1825 and 1875 operatic activity increased significantly, with regular visits by operatic divas such as Jenny Lind, Maria Malibran, Adelina Patti, and Christine Nilsson and the arrival of large numbers of immigrant musicians, many from Germany. Just as English immigrant musicians had influenced the style and direction of American music during the Federal period, so in the mid-19th century the Germans led Americans into an appreciation of the passionate and sensitive aspects of European Romanticism – though not without some opposition. (For example, the opera manager and conductor Max Maretzek was accused not only of allowing immoral activities in his theater – the Academy of Music in New York – but of depicting them on stage in his production of Verdi's *Rigoletto*.) Among the better-educated and -informed in the USA, European opera was equated with elevated and progressive taste. Yet even though some populist writers such as Walt Whitman celebrated its expressive sensuality and reveled in its mellifluous foreign tongues, a combination of the unintelligibility of its texts, the complexity of its vocal style, and the unacceptability of its scenarios (which often dealt with illicit erotic love, diabolism, or mythology) conspired to isolate "grand opera" from mainstream American culture. As a result it came to be considered by many somewhat suspect as entertainment for the élite. The coexistence of popular musical plays in English and a more formal grand opera has continued to characterize American musical theater; the former ultimately developed into the Broadway and Hollywood musicals, the latter gave rise to such cosmopolitan institutions as the Metropolitan Opera.

3. English-language opera during the 19th century. In the mid-19th century, opera began to reach across the USA, chiefly owing to the activities of traveling companies which performed in almost every population center along the expanding network of railroads. This dissemination was also aided by the advent of inexpensive printed music and the easy availability of pianos (purchased on installment), on which the songs, choruses, and dance music of operas could be played as home entertainment.

As support for opera increased, so did the building of opera houses equipped with the latest theatrical technology; longer seasons were sustained, especially in New York. And, as larger orchestras and choruses, and more numerous soloists, were recruited, a number of American composers began seriously to consider writing for the operatic stage. Others, who did not, nonetheless infused their compositions with operatic expression. In 1845 William Henry Fry composed the first full-length American grand opera, the Italianate *Leonora*. A decade later George Frederick Bristow wrote the first grand opera on an American subject, *Rip Van Winkle*. Fry exhorted his musical friends not to oppose opera:

> To destroy dramatic music is to endanger all music [and] to bring back monkish formality and abused mathematics in the science. The chief interest of all instrumental music, of the passion displayed in the modern oratorio and the Mass, lies in the dramatic expression derived originally from the universal lyrical delineations of the stage.

Later in the 19th century a number of American composers followed the examples of Fry and Bristow in writing grand operas on English-language librettos, though with a marked lack of success; among them were Julius Eichberg (*The Doctor of Alcantara*, 1862), Charles Jerome Hopkins (*Samuel*, 1877), Max Maretzek (*Sleepy Hollow, or The Headless Horseman*, 1879), Dudley Buck (*Deseret, or A Saint's Affliction*, 1880), Silas G. Pratt (*Zenobia, Queen of Palmyra*, 1882), and Frederick G. Gleason (*Otho Visconti*, composed 1876–7, posthumously produced in 1907).

The impetus for other operatic activity was provided by the comic operas of the Britons W. S. Gilbert and Sir Arthur Sullivan; a craze for their works was initiated by the great success in the USA of *H.M.S. Pinafore* (1878) – so great, in fact, that it was decided to give the first run of performances of *The Pirates of Penzance* in New York (beginning 31 December 1879) rather than London. The production of operas by Gilbert and Sullivan became a ritual for amateur companies as well as a guarantee of box-office success for professionals. These works filled a need, unmet by American writers, for dramatic entertainment which the most fastidious might attend without fear of transgressing rules of modesty or morality, and they provided models of witty English texts – set impeccably to music – in easily accessible scenarios that emphasized the lot of ordinary people in extraordinary situations. Although the Gilbert and Sullivan "invasion" did not, like that of English operas in the Federal period, bring with it a number of English musicians, it did rekindle the flame of opera in English conforming to Anglo-American dramatic sensibilities, and thus revived an operatic tradition that went back to the mid-18th century.

A number of operatic enterprises capitalized on this new-found zeal for musical theater in English, though with varying success. The most ambitious was the American Opera Company, begun in New York in 1886 in order to provide "grand opera sung in our own language by the most competent artists." Accordingly, it engaged the conductor Theodore Thomas and his orchestra and assembled American singers to perform the standard foreign repertory in English and to encourage American works. It lasted only through the 1887–8 season. More successful was Henry W. Savage's Castle Square Opera Company in Boston, which opened in 1897 and achieved some notoriety by giving Wagner's *Parsifal* in English (1905). Less ambitious traveling troupes, dedicated to similar ideals of singing opera in English, abounded at the end of the century. The McCaull Opera Company, the New York Casino, the Augustin Daly Musical Comedy Company, Ford's Opera Company, the Wilbur Opera Company, the Templeton Opera Company, the Alcazar Opera Company, and the Boston Ideal Opera Company were some of them, the last-named attaining great popularity with Reginald De Koven's comic masterpiece *Robin Hood* (1890). As Henry Clay Barnabee, the leading light of the Bostonians, said, such companies were content "to give light opera with occasional grand opera effects [rather] than the reverse."

Nearly all the composers of the Second New England School wrote operas or other large-scale works in what Fry would have identified as a "dramatic" – that is, operatic – style. John Knowles Paine did not compose an opera until the end of his career (*Azara*, 1893–8, performed 1903), but his earlier Mass in D (1865), his oratorio *St. Peter* (1870–72), and even his orchestral works are suffused with operatic gestures. Younger than Paine, and quicker to follow his natural inclination towards dramatic music, was George Whitefield Chadwick, who wrote seven works for the stage. In these the influence of the Gilbert and Sullivan repertory can be seen clearly, especially in *The Peer and the Pauper*, *A Quiet Lodging* (première 1892), the burlesque opera *Tabasco* (1894), and the later Broadway extravaganza *Everywoman: her Pilgrimage in Quest of Love* (1910), composed for Savage's company. Chadwick's two major theater works, the "lyric drama" *Judith* (1901) and *The Padrone* (composed 1912–13) – which displays the influence of the Italian *verismo* school – both reconcile a concern for correct musical diction in English with the expressive aims of grand opera as found in such composers as Saint-Saëns, Massenet, and Puccini. *The Padrone*, which deals with a system of labor that exploited Italian immigrants for several generations, may be viewed as an operatic counterpart to the realist school of American literature, painting, and drama. Frederick Shepherd Converse's *The Pipe of Desire* (1906), the first American opera to be performed at the Metropolitan Opera, deals with the romantic perils of an Arcadian setting; he treated more topical subjects in *The Sacrifice* (1911), a Mexican-American romance set in 1846, and *The Immigrants* (1914), commissioned but not performed by the Boston Opera Company. Horatio Parker's *Mona* (1912), which won a $10,000 prize from the Metropolitan Opera, portrays the struggle of Druidic Britons against Roman invaders.

4. The development of operatic institutions. One of the most fascinating chapters in the history of American opera is that of the leading operatic institution since the late 19th century, the Metropolitan Opera. Built to rival the Academy of Music, the Metropolitan Opera House (3625 seats, at Broadway and 39th Street in New York) opened on 22 October 1883, presenting opera in Italian (Gounod's *Faust*, in translation). In its first season the company offered exclusively Italian-language productions, which proved to be a financial disaster. For the second season the company abandoned opera in Italian and, under a new director, Leopold Damrosch, offered only works sung in German. This was a success, and the same policy was adhered to through 1890–91; with it came the introduction,

on a large scale, of the music dramas of Wagner to the USA.

Until Giulio Gatti-Casazza became director of the Metropolitan Opera in 1908 (with Arturo Toscanini as conductor), no American opera was produced there. Under Gatti-Casazza (who remained with the company until 1935), 17 new American operas were presented, 11 of them full-length productions, as well as several ballets with scores by Americans. Beginning in 1910 with Converse's *The Pipe of Desire* (first performed on 18 March), almost every one of the first six seasons under Gatti-Casazza brought a new American work: Victor Herbert's *Natoma* (28 February 1911), Parker's *Mona* (14 March 1912), Walter Damrosch's *Cyrano de Bergerac* (27 February 1913), Herbert's *Madeleine* (24 January 1914), De Koven's *The Canterbury Pilgrims* (8 March 1917), and Charles Wakefield Cadman's *Shanewis* (fig.2) along with a mimed version of Henry F. Gilbert's symphonic poem *The Dance in Place Congo* (23 March 1918). In the years immediately after World War I, shorter works were offered: Henry Hadley's *Azora* (26 January 1919), Joseph Carl Breil's *The Legend* and John Adam Hugo's *The Temple Dancer* (12 March 1919), and Hadley's *Cleopatra's Night* (31 January 1920). After a lapse of a few years Gatti-Casazza produced the two most successful American operas of his regime, Deems Taylor's *The King's Henchman* (17 February 1927) and *Peter Ibbetson* (7 February 1931), and during his last seasons at the Metropolitan Louis Gruenberg's *The Emperor Jones* (7 January 1933), Howard Hanson's *Merry Mount* (10 February 1934), and John Laurence Seymour's *In the Pasha's Garden* (24 January 1935). The success of Taylor's operas was, however, relative: *The King's Henchman* received 14 performances, *Peter Ibbetson* 16; the latter was the first American opera to be honored with a performance on a Metropolitan Opera season's opening night (26 December 1933).

Once the Metropolitan Opera was on a firm financial footing, no other American company could rival it. Opera at the Academy of Music in New York was soon discontinued. Oscar Hammerstein organized the Manhattan Opera Company in 1906, and for four years it vied with the Metropolitan for star performers. Among other works, it presented the American premières of Massenet's *Thaïs* (25 November 1907), Gustave Charpentier's *Louise* (3 January 1908), Debussy's *Pelléas et Mélisande* (19 February 1908), and Richard Strauss's *Elektra* (1 February 1910); but lacking the financial support accorded the Metropolitan, it was unable to sustain so expensive an operation and went out of business.

Elsewhere in the USA opera companies were established, but were able to survive only for a limited time. The Boston Opera Company, for example, founded in 1909 by Eben D. Jordan, Jr., and Henry Russell (ii), was to be part of an ambitious scheme for a network to include companies in New York, Chicago, Philadelphia, and possibly San Francisco. The plan did not materialize owing to the disruptions of World War I, and after a costly tour to Paris in 1914 the Boston company declared bankruptcy the following year. Chicago's first complete opera production (of Bellini's *La sonnambula*) was in 1850, but for many decades opera was given in the city only by touring companies. The first resident company, the Chicago Grand Opera Company, was formed in 1910; headed by the former Metropolitan Opera tenor Andreas Dippel with Cleofonte Campanini as music director, it opened with Verdi's *Aida*. Financial difficulties led to frequent replacements of its management (Campanini took over as manager in 1913 and the soprano Mary Garden headed the organization in the 1921–2 season), and the company barely survived the stock market crash of 1929, closing in 1932. Perhaps its high point was reached on 30 December 1921, when Prokofiev conducted the première of his *The Love for Three Oranges*, which

2. Scene from the first performance (23 March 1918) of "Shanewis or The Robin Woman" by Charles Wakefield Cadman, at the Metropolitan Opera; it was staged there again the following year

the company had commissioned. The opera company established as the Lyric Theatre of Chicago in 1954, renamed the Lyric Opera in 1956, became the city's principal operatic organization and is one of the leading American opera companies. For several decades it was strongly oriented to the Italian repertory; it was the first American company to engage Maria Callas (1954). In only a few cities have companies established in the first half of the 20th century survived. Cincinnati's Summer Opera Association was set up in 1920, when summer seasons in an open-air pavilion at the municipal zoo were introduced. In 1972 the same company was renamed the Cincinnati Opera; it performs in the Music Hall. The San Francisco Opera Company was founded in 1923 by the Italian conductor Gaetano Merola, with a season of works drawn from the standard repertory and casts closely linked to the Metropolitan Opera's roster. It has enjoyed particular continuity of leadership; Merola was succeeded in 1953 by the conductor Kurt Herbert Adler, who in turn led the company until 1982, when Terence A. McEwen became general director. Especially under Adler's direction the company presented a number of operas in American and world premières, including Poulenc's *Dialogues des carmélites* (1957) and Strauss's *Die Frau ohne Schatten* (1959), and introduced several major artists in their American débuts, among them Boris Christoff, Birgit Nilsson, and Luciano Pavarotti, as well as Leontyne Price and Marilyn Horne in their operatic débuts. Until the mid-1960s the company gave a brief season in Los Angeles.

5. AMERICAN OPERA: 1900–65. At the turn of the century many American composers wrote operettas in the romantic style of European works that had been produced in the USA in the previous decades. Among the best-known new additions were *El capitán* (1896) by John Philip Sousa, *The Belle of New York* (1898) by Gustave Kerker, De Koven's *The Red Feather* (1903), and *Naughty Marietta* (1910) by Victor Herbert. Later examples by two European-born composers were Rudolf Friml's *Rose Marie* (1924) and *The Vagabond King* (1925) and Sigmund Romberg's *The Student Prince in Heidelberg* (1924), *The Desert Song* (1926), and *The New Moon* (1928).

In the years immediately before and after World War I, many operas with American Indian settings were essayed. Some composers exploited the theme of reconciliation between the races through love; others revived the Enlightenment image of the noble savage. All tried to find the path to a distinctive American style by using authentic or pseudo-authentic Indian or Hispanic music in combination with existing styles of vocal and orchestral expression – with varying degrees of success. Herbert's *Natoma* portrays an Indian girl (sung in the première at Philadelphia by Mary Garden) linked romantically with an American naval lieutenant who, in turn, is in love with her Mexican mistress. Arthur Nevin's *Poia* (Berlin, 1910), based on observation and collection of music of the Montana Blackfoot Indians, strives more for anthropological accuracy than exotic romance. Other "Indian" operas were William F. Hanson's *The Sun Dance* (1913), Hadley's *Azora*, Cadman's *Shanewis*, Mary Carr Moore's *The Flaming Arrow* (1922), and Paul Hastings Allen's *The Last of the Mohicans*, which in 1916 was performed in Florence in Italian. These works did not fulfill their composers' intention to develop a national school of American opera. They fell from notice for the most part because they could attract neither the interest of the American opera companies, dominated by a repertory of foreign operas, nor the support of American audiences.

In the years following World War I the very existence of opera in the USA was threatened. Its dramaturgical conventions and musical gestures seemed stale, and as the 1920s unfolded the developing Hollywood movie industry as well as two other new sources of entertainment – radio and recordings – undermined serious musical theater, especially opera productions that demanded immense amounts of money for their proper presentation. Even more problematic was the fact that almost no composer had effectively met the challenge of creating opera based on a truly American-English prosody. On a small scale such prosody had of course been developed in hymns and popular songs; and indeed, much of the popular musical theater exhibited a distinct American-English vocal style. But not until Virgil Thomson's *Four Saints in Three Acts* (1934), with a libretto by Gertrude Stein, were all the elements put together and extensively applied in a coherent manner (for illustration *see* THOMSON, VIRGIL, fig.2). Thomson's American-English recitative marked a turning-point for American opera in a number of ways. First, it created a usable musical speech, suitable for narrative dialogue as well as lyric excursions, in which every syllable is intelligible; the rhythms and melodic inflections of Thomson's vocal lines are constructed on the last of American speech. Second, Thomson freed the orchestral accompaniment from the weight of tired Romantic figuration and exaggerated sonority. Third, with the collaboration of Stein and Maurice Grosser, who created the scenario, Thomson dismissed the obligatory love triangle from the plot. Above all, not only in *Four Saints* but in *The Mother of us All* (1947) and to a lesser degree in *Lord Byron* (completed 1968, première 1972) Thomson reestablished poetry as the equal of music in his operas.

Thomson's operatic manner drew largely upon traditional Anglo-Celtic musical roots for its nourishment, not upon other sources which, especially since the great immigrations of the 19th and early 20th centuries, have broadened the definition of "American." Marc Blitzstein's works offer contrast by tapping these other sources. Coming from an urban, sophisticated, and liberal background, Blitzstein was deeply marked by the experience of the Great Depression. He wrote the libretto for his first well known work, *The Cradle will Rock* (1937), as well as for *No for an Answer* (1941; fig.3, p.418); both deal with the struggle for labor rights. In them the popular music of a commercialized American society is integrated with the mixed ethnic speech rhythms of the city, and these elements are bound together by the stage conventions of the Broadway musical (which they parody at the same time). *Regina* (1949), again to his own libretto (based on Lillian Hellman's *The Little Foxes*), transcends his earlier narrow ideological concerns to explore the nature of good and evil in advanced psychological terms. Drawing on such materials as black spirituals, jazz, Broadway and Second Avenue (Yiddish) musicals, and even the music of Louis Moreau Gottschalk (mentioned by name in the score), Blitzstein evolved a crisp musical diction that parallels Thomson's middle-American musical language. Douglas S. Moore treated pioneer American life as subject matter for his operas, among them *The Devil and Daniel Webster* (1939), *Giants in the Earth* (1951, rev. 1963), *The Ballad of Baby Doe* (1958), and *Carry Nation* (1966). His music evokes popular genres of the 19th century, while the overall structure of the works is similar to that of 19th-century French and Italian operas. Carlisle Floyd's *Susannah* (1954) and Robert Ward's *The Crucible* (1961), two consistently popular operas, also have American settings.

Although George Gershwin was not accepted as a member of

3. *Stage design, 1940, by Howard Bay for the first production of Marc Blitzstein's "No for an Answer" at the Metropolitan Opera in 1941 ("Modern Music," xviii/2, 1941)*

the art-music community, either by its older Yankee constituents or by the younger modernists, his *Porgy and Bess* (1935) stands as an example of authentic American opera. Yet it was many years before the work was performed by one of the major opera companies (it was produced by Houston Grand Opera in 1976). Highly successful are the works of the most prolific contemporary opera composer, Gian Carlo Menotti. His success began in 1937 with the Metropolitan Opera's production of his *Amelia al ballo*, and he went on to compose and receive performances of such staples of the American operatic scene as *The Medium* (1946), *The Telephone* (1946), and *The Consul* (1950), which had extended runs on Broadway, and *Amahl and the Night Visitors*, the first opera written expressly for television, on commission from NBC (1951).

The uncertainty of securing performances of newer American works, despite the development of many institutions committed to such repertory (see §§6 and 7 below), made many 20th-century American composers reluctant to turn to opera composition. Yet operas of merit have been written by a number of composers better known for their output in other genres, among them George Antheil (*Transatlantic*, première 1930), Albert Stoessel (*Garrick*, 1937), Randall Thompson (*Solomon and Balkis*, 1942), Normand Lockwood (*The Scarecrow*, 1945), Bernard Rogers (*The Warrior*, 1947), Lukas Foss (*The Jumping Frog of Calaveras County*, 1950) Bernard Herrmann (*Wuthering Heights*, composed 1943–51), Jan Meyerowitz (*Eastward in Eden* [*Emily Dickinson*], 1951), Lamar Stringfield (*Carolina Charcoal*, 1953), William Schuman (*The Mighty Casey*, 1953), Aaron Copland (*The Tender Land*, 1954), William Bergsma (*The Wife of Martin Guerre*, 1956), Ned Rorem (*The Robbers*, 1958, and *Miss Julie*, 1965), Samuel Barber (*Vanessa*, 1958, and *Antony and Cleopatra*, 1966), Roger Sessions (*Montezuma*, 1964), and Elie Siegmeister (*The Plough and the Stars*, 1969).

If such distinguished composers have been attracted to opera, so, too, have some popular tunesmiths, who have elevated musicals virtually to operatic status. Besides Gershwin's *Porgy and Bess*, there is the example of Richard Rodgers's *Oklahoma!* (1943), in which choreography by Agnes de Mille approaching balletic sophistication and symphonic orchestral arrangements by Robert Russell Bennett helped to integrate a racy Broadway style with operatic control and continuity. Another important work in this genre is Frank Loesser's *The Most Happy Fella* (1956). Kurt Weill's *Street Scene* (1947), Leonard Bernstein's *West Side Story* (1957), and, later, Stephen Sondheim's *Sweeney Todd* (1979) are all examples of works by academically trained composers who have attempted to reach out to an audience that consists of both theater-goers and opera-lovers. These composers have used an orchestra smaller than is usual for opera and, instead of operatic virtuosos, actors whose singing voices required amplification; and they have collaborated with directors who could create slick stagings. This development of an American opera on Broadway overlaps with the musical, not only in its style, content, and presentation, but also in the custom of the composers' assignment to specialists of creative tasks such as orchestrating, making choral arrangements, and composing dance sequences.

6. Opera in the academy. In the late 1930s a new wave of immigrants, fleeing Nazi persecution in Germany and Austria, included many professional musicians formerly active in opera. Owing to the paucity of American opera companies, many of them sought employment in universities, colleges, and conservatories, where they established opera workshops that decisively influenced operatic development in the USA. One result was a decentralization of opera, away from the major metropolitan centers. The academic institutions sponsoring these workshops became in effect opera producers, presenting works mainly with student casts and orchestras under the guidance of professional directors and conductors. The early workshop founders included Boris Goldovsky and Richard Rychtarik, who established an opera workshop at the Cleveland Institute of Music in 1936; Goldovsky then formed a workshop in 1942 at the New England Conservatory, where Sarah Caldwell joined him in 1949 as his assistant. In New York, an opera workshop was organized at Columbia University in 1943 by Herbert Graf and Nicholas

Goldschmidt, and at the Juilliard School in 1947 by Frederic Cohen (with Frederic Waldman as associate director). Carl Ebert founded a workshop in 1948 at the University of Southern California, where he was joined in 1953 by Walter Ducloux (Ducloux moved to a similar position at the University of Texas, Austin, in 1968). Hans Busch and Ernst Hoffman initiated an opera department at Indiana University (1948) as did Ludwig Zirner at the University of Illinois (1948), Jan Popper at UCLA (1950), and Josef Blatt at the University of Michigan (1952). Other important workshops were led by Peter Paul Fuchs at Louisiana State University and Elemer Nagy at the Hartt College.

The training provided in the opera workshops resulted in an abundance of talented young American opera singers. Emerging professional companies (see §7 below) presented only a few productions annually, and were not able to support all of these singers, but many found opportunities abroad, especially in Germany. In the years after World War II German opera houses began to reinstate their year-round seasons, and as the war had depleted the numbers of young, trained, native singers they welcomed Americans. During the 1950s an estimated 600–800 American singers performed on German opera stages; some of the most successful returned to the USA as stars.

In addition to training singers for professional careers, the academic workshops made other contributions to the expansion of opera in the USA. By offering performances on a regular basis they developed new audiences. They also contributed significantly to an expansion of the operatic repertory: whereas professional companies, dependent on box-office receipts and full houses, had to restrict their productions to the standard repertory, the academic workshops, with perhaps limited budgets but nevertheless guaranteed support from their sponsoring institutions, could be more adventurous.

Thus, opera workshops at colleges and universities assumed the leading position in the USA for producing rarely performed or unknown operas of the past and present. They were responsible for the American premières of a number of foreign operas, and for commissioning or giving the first performances of new operas by Americans; among the composers whose early operas they produced were Dominick Argento, Jack Beeson, Seymour Barab, Bernstein, Floyd, Menotti, and Ward. Several hundred such American and world premières occurred at academic institutions in the 1940s and 1950s.

7. Further development of operatic institutions. The Metropolitan Opera remained the dominant American opera company and the one that many other professional companies took as their model. For almost 83 years "the Met" presented annual seasons of opera in the same house, then in 1966 it moved to its new home in Lincoln Center (3788 seats). During most of those years it followed the regular season with a tour of other cities. Its presentation of so many leading international stars, its tours, and, from 1931, its regular Saturday afternoon broadcasts live from the stage, confirmed the national status of the Metropolitan company. In this light, some facts about it are striking, and contrast markedly with almost all European opera companies: no work by a native American has ever had lasting success at the Metropolitan; with few exceptions, its policy since the turn of the century has been to present operas in their original languages

4. Boris Goldovsky directing the New England Opera Theater in a rehearsal (1948) of the quintet from Act 2 of Bizet's "Carmen"; to promote the singers' self-reliance and dramatic integrity in the performance the company frequently rehearsed with the singers facing away from the conductor

(it was not until after World War II that this practice was adopted by most European companies); and, perhaps most important, until the establishment of the NEA in 1965, financial support for the Metropolitan came almost entirely from private sources (in addition to income from ticket sales, which never covers production costs), not from federal, state, or municipal funds. During the eight decades in the old house, the company presented (according to Kolodin, 4/1966) a total of 218 different operas in more than 11,000 performances. The operas that received more than 200 performances – all composed within the period 1816–1904 and more than half of them Italian, only two French, and none American – tell much about American operatic taste between the 1880s and the mid-1960s: Verdi's *Aida* (511 performances, in 74 seasons), Puccini's *La bohème* (444, 62), Bizet's *Carmen* (380, 59), Gounod's *Faust* (362, 63), Wagner's *Lohengrin* (341, 63), Verdi's *La traviata* (339, 65), Puccini's *Tosca* (326, 53) and *Madama Butterfly* (325, 52), Leoncavallo's *Pagliacci* (319, 59), Verdi's *Rigoletto* (312, 66), Wagner's *Tristan und Isolde* (299, 61) and *Die Walküre* (292, 63), Mascagni's *Cavalleria rusticana* (290, 59), Wagner's *Tannhäuser* (263, 54) and *Die Meistersinger* (243, 57), Verdi's *Il trovatore* (242, 59), Donizetti's *Lucia di Lammermoor* (234, 58), and Rossini's *Il barbiere di Siviglia* (200, 47). During this period a total of 20 American operas, including 16 premières, were presented. After its move to Lincoln Center, the Metropolitan expanded its season from 150 performances annually to nearly 300 (no other company in the USA has so extensive a season). Its repertory also expanded to include rarely performed Baroque, Classical, and contemporary works.

Given the dominance of the Metropolitan Opera, the second opera company in New York, the New York City Opera, whose first season was in 1944, made its aims complementary to those of the major company. The City Opera used younger singers, especially Americans, rather than established international stars; presented a larger proportion of rarely performed or new operas, as well as operas from the standard repertory in English translation; and maintained lower ticket prices. For a time it appeared that American operas would be especially favored among the new productions – indeed, with support from the Ford Foundation in 1958, 1959, and 1960, the spring seasons were all-American ones. Although economic problems prevented the City Opera from living up to that early promise, by the mid-1980s it had produced more than 50 new American operas, maintained its policy of keeping American works in the repertory, and helped bridge the gap between opera and musical theater. Initially, it was also more adventurous than the Metropolitan in presenting 20th-century works, reviving forgotten 19th-century ones, offering Baroque operas (notably Monteverdi's *Orfeo* and *L'incoronazione di Poppea* and Handel's *Giulio Cesare*).

A significant consequence of the new interest in opera aroused by the academic opera workshops was the proliferation of regional opera companies, such as the Kentucky Opera (1952), the Tulsa Opera (1953), the Houston Grand Opera (1955), Opera Memphis (1956), the Santa Fe Opera (1956), the Opera Company of Boston (1958), the Lyric Opera of Kansas City (1958), and the Seattle Opera (1962). Like the New York City Opera, most new companies differed from the older ones in philosophy and procedure. Instead of relying on a few internationally famous singers and concentrating on the standard operatic repertory, they engaged young American artists, shaped them into resident ensembles, and offered a varied fare of classical and contemporary or rarely performed works. Many adhered to a policy of performing only in English in order to attract an audience ordinarily oriented to theater. Companies devoted principally to operetta and musical theater were also established. Significant among these were the St. Louis Municipal Opera Association (MUNY), founded in 1919, the Civic Light Opera of Pittsburgh (1945), and the Long Beach (California) Civic Light Opera (1950).

8. Operatic activity after the mid-1960s. There has been an extraordinary development of operatic activity in the USA since the mid-1960s. Its principal features have been a sudden and substantial increase in the number of opera companies and the size of the audience for opera; the recognition by local as well as international audiences of young American singers as established professional artists; an expansion of the operatic repertory to include not only more new and early works and works by a larger number of European and American composers, but also more works related to the Broadway musical and more avant-garde music-theater works; a wider variety of sources of financial support, including funding by government at various levels; and broader community outreach by opera companies, with a greater role for opera in the broadcast media, especially television.

Between 1964 and 1984 the number of American opera companies with annual budgets exceeding $100,000 increased nearly sixfold (from 27 to 154), and annual attendance at operas presented by these companies tripled (from 4.5 million to 13.04 million), as did the number of performances of operas and musicals (from 4176 to 13,442). The 1983–4 repertory of American opera companies included almost as many works by American composers (261) as by foreign composers (315); these figures may be compared with those for 1970–71 (the earliest season for which they are available), when 99 American operas and 225 foreign operas were produced. In 1983–4 American opera companies presented 101 world premières (of which 98 were of operas by Americans), compared with 35 in 1970–71; to these might be added a number of revivals of operas predating those in the standard repertory – for example, Cavalli's *Ormindo* (1644), given by the Opera Society of Washington in 1969, and Vivaldi's *Orlando* (1727) by the Dallas Civic Opera in 1980 (*see* Early-music revival).

One important stimulus to opera composition and production since the 1960s has been the programs of grant assistance by the NEA after its establishment in 1965. A separate Opera-Music Theater program was set up at the NEA in 1978, thereby providing support for the first time for musicals performed by non-profit organizations. The NEA has also supported experimental music-theater works. State arts councils and municipal agencies, some predating the NEA, add support from other levels of government. Nevertheless, the principal sources of funding for American opera companies continue to be outside government: according to *Profile: 1984*, in the 1982–3 season earned income accounted for about half of their total income; federal, state, and local government contributions provided 9%; the remainder came from individual contributions (16%), corporations (6%), foundations (5%), and miscellaneous other sources. This contrasts markedly with European companies, which receive 65–90% of their budgets from governments. For American companies fund raising and marketing are essential components of administration.

Seeking to serve a wider public, to provide artists with more work, and to encourage support from these various sectors, the opera companies have extended their efforts in a number of ways.

5. Marie Angel as Tye and Christopher Robson in the title role (with moving figures, background) in a scene from Act 2 of "Akhnaten" by Philip Glass, during the first performance of the joint production by the Houston Grand Opera and the New York City Opera at Houston on 12 October 1984

Most have initiated special educational programs and performances in schools, community centers, senior citizens' residences, hospitals, and even prisons. A number have instituted regional tours by subsidiary ensembles: the first of these, begun by the San Francisco Opera in 1966, was the Western Opera Theater, which has toured throughout California, Arizona, Oregon, and Alaska; others include the Houston Grand Opera's Texas Opera Theater, the New York City Opera's National Company, the Boston Opera's Opera New England, the Fort Worth Opera's Southwestern Opera, the Charlotte Opera's North Carolina Opera, the Cincinnati Opera's ECCO!, and the Connecticut Opera's Opera Express. In 1983–4, 127 company-affiliated touring groups offered some 5500 performances. One of the most successful methods of making opera more accessible to a wider public has been the projection above the proscenium of English translations of operas performed in foreign languages. This system of "surtitles," "supertitles," or "supratitles," developed by the Canadian Opera Company in 1982 and introduced by the New York City Opera the following year, found quick acceptance by singers, opera directors, and audiences alike. Within two years over 50 companies had adopted some form of title projection.

The broadcasting media, especially television, have accorded opera a steadily increasing role in their programming. The Saturday afternoon radio broadcasts from the Metropolitan Opera during the regular season – a staple of the networks nationwide since 1931 – have been supplemented by shorter-range broadcasts by various other companies. The first live telecast of opera in the USA was of Verdi's *Otello* on the opening night of the Metropolitan Opera's 1948–9 season. NBC commissioned Menotti's *Amahl and the Night Visitors* and produced it in 1951; beginning in 1954 with Strauss's *Salome*, its Opera Theater staged some 30 opera productions. Since the late 1960s the Public Broadcasting System has relayed operas in the series "Live from the Met" and "Live from Lincoln Center" (with performances by the New York City Opera), and occasionally in the series "Great Performances"; PBS has also presented video recordings of operas performed in London, Salzburg, Milan, Bayreuth, and other European centers.

The surge in construction of performing-arts centers from the 1960s onwards contributed to the increase in opera presentations and to a flexible approach to their production by individual companies. At the John F. Kennedy Center for the Performing Arts the resident Washington Opera Company has utilized the large Opera House for grand operas and the Terrace Theater for chamber operas. In 1966 Lincoln Center became the new home of the Metropolitan Opera Company, performing in its own house, and, two years later, of the New York City Opera Company, which moved into the smaller New York State Theater. Special, more intimate opera productions – for example, of Thomson's *Four Saints in Three Acts* and Peter Brook's *La tragédie de Carmen* (1983), a chamber adaptation of Bizet's original – have been staged in Lincoln Center's smaller theaters. The season of the San Francisco Opera was lengthened in 1980, when a symphony hall was added to the performing arts center and it no longer had to share the facilities of the War Memorial Opera House with the San Francisco SO. In Louisville the Kentucky Opera plays in three different halls in the new municipal center – one with a capacity of 2400, another of 1450, and the third of 600. Opera "in the round" is a specialty of Opera Colorado in Boettcher Hall, Denver.

Other architectural and technological advances have worked to the advantage of opera in the USA. Air conditioning has made possible, or at least pleasanter and therefore financially more viable, such summertime events as the Verdi Festival produced by the San Diego Opera in the city's Civic Theatre (1980–84), the Pacific Northwest Wagner Festival, under the sponsorship of the Seattle Opera Association, which has presented Wagner's *Der Ring des Nibelungen* both in German and in English translation since 1974, and a four-week summer festival by the San Francisco Opera. Other notable summer-season opera companies are the Central City (Colorado) Opera House Association (founded 1932), and the Chautauqua Opera (1929), the Lake George Opera Festival (1962), and the Glimmerglass Opera Theater (1975), all in New York State. Open-air facilities have been built or adapted for opera; unique in design is the half-covered Opera House of the Santa Fe Opera. Opera is also often presented at such major festivals as the Aspen (Colorado) Music Festival, the Tanglewood Festival in Lenox, Massachusetts, and the summer festivals at Wolf Trap Farm Park (Vienna, Virginia) and Artpark (Lewiston, New York).

The current operatic scene shows all the signs of a vital movement. More and more opera administrators are native Americans, educated in the USA. American conductors, singers, orchestral musicians, and dancers not only dominate the American stage but are in demand in European opera establishments. Conversely, it is difficult for performers to make international operatic reputations without winning approval in American opera houses. Some of the major opera companies have mounted programs to bring in young singers and ease them through the transition between academic training and professional requirements. The Santa Fe Opera (founded 1956) was the first to develop such an apprentice program; other important ones include the San Francisco Opera's Merola Program (1962), which evolved into the San Francisco Opera Center in 1982, Chicago Lyric Opera's Center for American Artists (1974), the Cincinnati Opera's Young American Artists Program (1974), the Houston Grand Opera Studio (1977), the Metropolitan Opera's Young Artists Development Program (1980), and several programs organized jointly by universities and professional opera companies. In addition, many less formally structured cooperative arrangements have been organized between professional companies and academic workshops. During the 1983–4 season, 3916 (nearly 40%) of the 10,693 performances of operas in the USA were of American works, with 261 different operas presented.

Taking advantage of this new climate, an increasing number of American composers have turned to opera composition. Some have even made a specialty of it and have made notable contributions to the repertory since the 1960s: Argento (his many operas include *Postcard from Morocco*, 1971, *Miss Havisham's Fire*, 1979, *Casanova's Homecoming*, 1985), Robert Ashley (*That Morning Thing*, 1968, and the television operas *Atalanta*, 1982, and *Perfect Lives Private Parts*, 1984), Beeson (*Lizzie Borden*, 1965), John Eaton (*Myshkin*, 1971, *The Cry of Clytaemnestra*, 1980, *The Tempest*, 1985), Floyd (his numerous operas include *Of Mice and Men*, 1970, *Bilby's Doll*, 1976), Philip Glass (*Einstein on the Beach*, 1976, *Satyagraha*, 1980, *Akhnaten*, 1984, fig.5), the European-born Thea Musgrave (*Mary, Queen of Scots*, 1977, *A Christmas Carol*, 1978–9, *Harriet, the Woman Called Moses*, 1982–4), Thomas Pasatieri (*Calvary*, 1971, *The Trial of Mary Lincoln*, 1972, *Washington Square*, 1976, *Maria Elena*, 1983), Stephen Paulus (*The Village Singer*, 1979, *The Postman always Rings Twice*, 1982, *The Woodlanders*, 1985), Stanley Silverman (*Elephant Steps*, 1968, *Dr. Selavy's Magic Theatre*, 1972, *Madame Adare*, 1980), and Robert Ward (*The Crucible*, 1961, *Abelard and Heloise*, 1982). Other major composers, while not specializing in opera, have also written important operatic works: Bernstein (*Trouble in Tahiti*, 1952, *A Quiet Place*, 1983), John Harbison (*Winter's Tale* and *Full Moon in March*, 1979), Lee Hoiby (*Summer and Smoke*, 1971), Andrew Imbrie (*Angle of Repose*, 1976), Leon Kirchner (*Lily*, 1977), Libby Larsen (*Clair de lune*, 1985), George Rochberg (*The Confidence Man*, 1982), Peter Schickele [P. D. Q. Bach] (*The Abduction of Figaro*, 1984), Gunther Schuller (*The Visitation*, 1966), and Robert Starer (*Pantagleize*, 1974). Although it was not until 1978, when a program was established by the O'Neill Theater Center in Connecticut, that professional organizations created opportunities for composers and librettists to try out new operas, by the mid-1980s some 40 companies had such programs. They range from unpretentious showcase and workshop productions with piano accompaniment to actual commissions and fully staged productions by professional companies; they also include composer-in-residence programs, the first of which was established in 1984 by the Chicago Lyric Opera Center.

OPERA COMPANIES IN THE USA: SIZE AND SEASONS

The table below is based on the Central Opera Service national survey of the 1983–4 season. Not listed are music festivals that include opera performances, light opera companies, or musical theater companies. The numbers of productions and performances within parentheses indicate educational and touring activities by a subsidiary ensemble, operating under the same management as the principal company and within its budget. A comma between months indicates a break within a season; otherwise the season is continuous.

Company	*First Season*	*Productions/Performances*	*Season*
		Budgets over $10 million	
Metropolitan Opera	1883	25/263	Sept–June [incl. tour April–June]
San Francisco Opera	1923	14/95 (4/87)	Sept–Dec, May–June
New York City Opera	1944; founded 1943	17/138 (1/32)	June–Nov
Lyric Opera of Chicago	1954	7/55 (4/24)	Sept–Dec, May
		Budgets of $3–10 million	
Greater Miami Opera	1941	4/20 (2/109)	Jan, Feb, March, April
Houston Grand Opera	1956; founded 1955	9/57 (3/100)	Oct, Nov, Dec, Jan, March, April, May, June
Dallas [Civic] Opera	1957	5/24 (2/80)	Nov–Dec, April
Santa Fe Opera	1957; founded 1956	5/35 (1/2)	July–Aug
Washington Opera	1957; founded 1956	7/63	Nov–Jan
Seattle Opera	1962 (reorganized 1964)	9/29 (2/290)	Sept, Nov, Jan, March, May, July
San Diego Opera	1965	8/30 (4/104)	Sept–Oct, Feb–March, June
		Budgets of $1–3 million	
Cincinnati [Summer] Opera	1920	7/20 (4/192)	Nov, April, June–July
Central City Opera	1932	3/30 (2/9)	July–Aug
Pittsburgh Opera	1940	6/12 (1/20)	Oct, Nov, Dec, Jan, Feb, April
Connecticut Opera (Hartford)	1942	4/10 (6/183)	Oct, Dec, Feb, March
New Orleans Opera	1943	4/13	Oct, Nov, Dec
Fort Worth Civic Opera	1946	4/8 (3/65)	Nov, Jan, March, April
Baltimore Opera	1950; founded 1949	5/39 (1/40)	Nov, Jan, Feb, March, May

Company	First season	Productions/Performances	Season
Portland (Oregon) Opera	1951; founded 1950	4/12 (5/65)	Oct, Nov, March, April
Kentucky Opera (Louisville)	1953; founded 1952	4/11 (1/200)	Oct, Dec, Feb, April
Tulsa Opera	1953	3/9 (4/54)	Nov, March, May
Opera Company of Boston	1958	5/22 (3/30)	Nov, Dec, Feb, April, May, June
Lyric Opera of Kansas City	1958	5/26 (5/152)	Sept–Oct, April
Minnesota Opera Company (Minneapolis)	1964	4/13 (3/116)	Dec, Jan, March, April
Michigan Opera Theatre (Detroit)	1971	4/29 (3/93)	Oct–Nov, June
Texas Opera Theater (Houston) (touring company)	1974	3/72	Jan–May tour
Virginia Opera (Norfolk)	1974	4/24 (2/80)	Oct, Dec, Jan, March
Opera Company of Philadelphia	1975	5/10 (1/10)	Oct, Nov, Jan, Feb, April
Opera Theatre of St. Louis	1976	5/32 (2/102)	Dec, May–June
San Francisco Opera Center (subsumes Western Opera tour, founded 1967)	1982	3/72	May, July tour
Opera Colorado (Denver)	1983	2/10 (2/85)	May
	Budgets of $500,000–$1,000,000		
Florentine Opera of Milwaukee	1933 (reorganized 1950)	3/9 (2/18)	Nov, March, April
Charlotte Opera	1949	3/6 (3/98)	Nov, Jan, March
Opera Memphis	1957; founded 1956	4/8 (2/48)	Oct, Nov, Feb, April
Opera/Columbus	1958 (reorganized 1981)	3/6 (1/45)	Nov, Feb, March
Opera Omaha	1959	3/9 (2/263)	Nov, Feb, March
Dayton Opera	1961	4/9 (1/100)	Oct, Dec, Feb, March
Hawaii Opera Theatre (Honolulu)	1961; founded 1960	3/9 (2/88)	Jan–Feb
Lake George Opera Festival	1962	3/20 (2/30)	July–Aug
Palm Beach Opera	1962	3/6	Dec, Jan, March
Orlando Opera	1962 (reorganized 1974)	3/7	Nov, Feb, March
New Jersey State Opera	1964	3/3	Feb, March, April
Light Opera of Manhattan	1969	15/320	Sept–Aug
Arizona Opera (Tucson and Phoenix)	1972	3/11	Oct, Feb, April
Music Theatre of Wichita	1972	5/35 (2/135)	June–Aug
Chicago Opera Theatre	1973	3/18 (1/22)	Feb, April, May
Des Moines Metro Opera	1973	3/13 (2/7)	June–July
Sarasota Opera	1973	4/16 (3/18)	Jan–Feb
Syracuse Opera	1974	3/8 (2/77)	Nov, Feb, March
Anchorage Civic Opera	1975	2/13 (4/46)	March, April
Cleveland Opera	1976	3/12 (2/168)	Nov, Feb, April
Indianapolis Opera	1976; founded 1975	3/6 (1/50)	Dec, Feb, March
Utah Opera (Salt Lake City)	1977	4/14 (3/110)	Oct, Dec, Jan, May
Long Beach Opera	1979	4/26	Sept, Oct, Jan, March
Los Angeles Opera Theatre	1979	3/12	Oct, Nov, April
New York City National [touring] Company	1980	1/26	Jan–Feb tour

BIBLIOGRAPHY

GENERAL

W. Dunlap: *A History of the American Theatre* (New York, 1832/*R*1963)

G. O. Seilhamer: *History of the American Theatre: New Foundations* (Philadelphia, 1891/*R*1968)

H. C. Lahee: *Grand Opera in America* (Boston, 1902/*R*1973)

O. G. T. Sonneck: "Early American Operas," *SIMG*, vi (1904–5), 428–95

H. E. Krehbiel: *Chapters of Opera* (New York, 1908, rev. 2/1909/*R*1980, rev. 3/1911)

O. G. T. Sonneck: *Early Opera in America* (New York, 1915/*R*1963)

H. E. Krehbiel: *More Chapters of Opera* (New York, 1919/*R*1980)

H. C. Lahee: *Annals of Music in America* (Boston, 1922/*R*1969)

A. H. Quinn: *A History of the American Drama from the Beginning to the Civil War* (New York, 1923, 2/1943/*R*1951)

E. E. Hipsher: *American Opera and its Composers* (Philadelphia, 1927/*R*1978)

Opera News (1936–)

H. Graf: *The Opera and its Future in America* (New York, 1941)

Central Opera Service Bulletin (1959–)

J. Mates: *The American Musical Stage before 1800* (New Brunswick, NJ, 1962)

J. Mattfeld: *A Handbook of American Operatic Premieres, 1731–1962* (Detroit, 1963)

H. E. Johnson: *Operas on American Subjects* (New York, 1964)

C. Hamm: "Opera and the American Composer," *The American Composer Speaks*, ed. G. Chase (Baton Rouge, LA, 1966), 284

E. I. Zimmerman: *American Opera Librettos, 1767–1825* (diss., U. of Tennessee, 1972)

A. H. Drummond: *American Opera Librettos* (Metuchen, NJ, 1973)

C. Northouse: *Twentieth Century Opera in England and the United States* (Boston, 1976)

K. E. Gombert: *Leonora by William Henry Fry and Rip Van Winkle by George Frederick Bristow: Examples of Mid-nineteenth-century American Opera* (diss., Ball State U., 1977)

P. H. Virga: *The American Opera to 1790* (Ann Arbor, MI, 1982)

J. Mates: "The First Hundred Years of the American Lyric Theater," *American Music*, i/2 (1983), 22

Profile: 1984 – Opera America and the Professional Opera Companies (Washington, DC, 1984)

K. K. Preston: *Traveling Opera Troupes in the United States, 1830–1860* (diss., CUNY, in preparation)

OPERA IN AMERICAN CITIES

C. Durang: "The Philadelphia Stage," *Philadelphia Sunday Despatch* (1854, 1856, 1860) [series of articles; compiled by T. Westcott as *History of the Philadelphia Stage, between the Years 1749 and 1855*, 1868, *PU*; similar compilations as *The Philadelphia Stage* in *PPL*, and *History of the Philadelphia Stage* in *PHi*]

J. N. Ireland: *Records of the New York Stage* (New York, 1866–7/*R*1968)

W. G. Armstrong: *A Record of the Opera in Philadelphia* (Philadelphia, 1884/*R*1976)

J. C. Baroncelli: *L'Opéra français de la Nouvelle Orléans* (New Orleans, 1914)

J. Curtis: *One Hundred Years of Grand Opera in Philadelphia* (MS, 1920, *PP*, *PHi*)

J. Mattfeld: *A Hundred Years of Grand Opera in New York, 1825–1925* (New York, 1927/*R*1976)

G. C. D. Odell: *Annals of the New York Stage* (New York, 1927–49/*R*1970)

E. C. Moore: *Forty Years of Opera in Chicago* (New York, 1930)

R. D. James: *Old Drury of Philadelphia: a History of the Philadelphia Stage, 1800–1835* (Philadelphia, 1932/*R*1968)

I. Kolodin: *The Metropolitan Opera* (New York, 1936, rev. and enlarged 4/1966/*R*1967)

Works Progress Administration: *The History of Opera in San Francisco*, San Francisco Theatre Research, vii–viii (San Francisco, 1938)
W. H. Seltsam: *Metropolitan Opera Annals* (New York, 1947; suppls., 1957, 1968, 1978)
Q. Eaton: *Opera Caravan: Adventures of the Metropolitan on Tour, 1883–1956* (New York, 1957/*R*1978)
R. L. Davis: *A History of Opera in the American West* (Englewood Cliffs, NJ, 1965)
Q. Eaton: *The Boston Opera Company* (New York, 1965/*R*1980)
R. L. Davis: *Opera in Chicago: a Social and Cultural History, 1850–1965* (New York, 1966)
H. A. Kmen: *Music in New Orleans: the Formative Years, 1791–1841* (Baton Rouge, LA, 1966)
A. Stoutamire: *Music of the Old South: Colony to Confederacy* (Rutherford, NJ, 1972)
M. Nelson: *The First Italian Opera Season in New York City: 1825–1826* (diss., U. of North Carolina, Chapel Hill, 1976)
E. Scott: *The First Twenty Years of the Santa Fe Opera* (Santa Fe, NM, 1976)
A. Bloomfield: *The San Francisco Opera, 1922–1978* (Sausalito, CA, 1978)
H. F. Jennings: *Grand Opera in Kansas in the 1880s* (diss., U. of Cincinnati, 1978)
O. E. Albrecht: "Opera in Philadelphia, 1800–1830," *JAMS*, xxxii (1979), 499
C. Cassidy: *Lyric Opera of Chicago* (Chicago, 1979)
M. L. Sokol: *The New York City Opera* (New York, 1981)
J. F. Cone: *First Rival of the Metropolitan Opera* (New York, 1983)
M. Mayer: *The Met: One Hundred Years of Grand Opera* (New York, 1983)
L. R. Wolz: *Opera in Cincinnati: the Years before the Zoo, 1801–1920* (diss., U. of Cincinnati, 1983)
P. E. Eisler: *The Metropolitan Opera: the First Twenty-five Years* (Croton-on-Hudson, NY, 1984)
F. P. Fells, ed.: *The Metropolitan Opera on Record: a Discography of the Commercial Recordings* (Westport, CT, 1984)

IMPRESARIOS AND MANAGERS

M. Maretzek: *Crotchets and Quavers* (New York, 1855/*R*1968)
J. H. Mapleson: *The Mapleson Memoirs* (New York, 1888, rev. 2/1966, ed. H. Rosenthal)
M. Maretzek: *Sharps and Flats* (New York, 1890/*R*1968)
G. Gatti-Casazza: *Memories of the Opera* (New York, 1941/*R*1973)
J. F. Cone: *Oscar Hammerstein's Manhattan Opera Company* (Norman, OK, 1966)
L. M. Lerner: *The Rise of the Impresario: Bernard Ullman and the Transformation of Musical Culture in Nineteenth Century America* (diss., U. of Wisconsin, 1970)
R. Bing: *5000 Nights at the Opera* (Garden City, NY, 1972)
——: *A Knight at the Opera* (New York, 1981)
D. McKay: "Opera in Colonial Boston," *American Music*, iii (1985), 133

MARIA F. RICH, VICTOR FELL YELLIN/
H. WILEY HITCHCOCK (text)
R. ALLEN LOTT (bibliography)

Opera Colorado. Opera company organized in 1981 in DENVER.

Operetta. A light opera with spoken dialogue, songs, and dances. The form flourished in the USA during the second half of the 19th century and the early part of the 20th. *See* DANCE, §III, 3; MUSICAL, §§1–3; MUSICAL FILM, §2; MUSICAL THEATER, §II, 2, and §III, 1; OPERA, §5; and POPULAR MUSIC, §III, 1.

Oppens, Ursula (*b* New York, 2 Feb 1944). Pianist. She studied at Radcliffe College (BA 1965) before deciding to become a pianist and enrolling at the Juilliard School, where she was a pupil of Rosina Lhévinne, Leonard Shure, and Guido Agosti (1966–9). After graduating she won several international competitions, including the Busoni International Piano Competition (1969) and the Avery Fisher Prize (1976). She has performed with the New York PO, the Boston SO, and many other American orchestras; has given solo recitals in the USA, Europe, and Central America; and has participated in the Aspen, Berkshire, and Marlboro music festivals, among others.

Oppens was a founding member of Speculum Musicae, the highly praised contemporary music ensemble that won the Naumburg Chamber Music Award in 1972. She has also performed with the Chamber Music Society of Lincoln Center, the Group for Contemporary Music, and the Center for Creative and Performing Arts. Although she is known particularly for the intelligence, technical skill, and warmth she brings to her performances of contemporary music, she is equally at home with the standard repertory. Compositions written for her include Rzewski's *The People United will Never be Defeated* (1975) and Four Pieces, Christian Wolff's *Hay una mujer desaparecida* (1979), Carter's *Night Fantasies* (1980, also for Paul Jacobs, Gilbert Kalish, and Charles Rosen), and Wuorinen's *The Blue Bamboula* (1980). Oppens is on the faculty of Brooklyn College, CUNY.

ELLEN HIGHSTEIN

Orange Blossoms. Dance band formed in 1927, later known as the CASA LOMA ORCHESTRA.

Orbison, Roy (Kelton) (*b* Vernon, TX, 23 April 1936). Rock-and-roll singer, songwriter, and guitarist. He studied geology at North Texas College, and was inspired by the success of Pat Boone, also a student, to embark on a musical career. He sang and played with two local rockabilly bands, the Wink Westerners and the Teen Kings, then recorded (unsuccessfully) for Jewel. In 1956 he signed a contract with Sun Records; although he considered himself principally an exponent of ballads, the company chose instead to issue his nonsense "beat" songs, of which only one, *Ooby Dooby* (no.59, 1956), was successful. He moved to Nashville, where he became a staff songwriter for the Acuff–Rose publishing company. In 1958 his song *Claudette*, in a recording by the Everly Brothers, reached the Top 30. He began recording ballads for Monument and had a series of hit recordings, beginning with *Uptown* (no.72, 1960), that lasted until 1965. Most of these (such as *Running Scared*, *Only the Lonely*, and *It's Over*) had melancholy texts that dealt with unrequited love; their precise instrumental backings were characterized by a Latin beat, a full string section, and a strong percussion climax. Although a product of the timeworn Tin Pan Alley tradition, his songs were a welcome alternative to the blues-dominated clamor of most early rock-and-roll and the levity of pop-rock. In 1965, lured by the promise of film opportunities and greater artistic freedom, he signed a contract with MGM; from this point the quality of his work declined into formula and, in such songs as *Communication Breakdown* (no.60, 1966), pretentiousness. He continued to perform into the 1980s, however, and had some successful recordings in England, where he has consistently been more popular than in the USA. Orbison's songs are notable for their unusual bar lengths and key changes; his extraordinary vocal range includes a very high falsetto. In performance he affects a dramatic stage presence that is heightened by his dark clothing and sunglasses. Many of his songs have become pop standards; among those who have achieved success with his material are Linda Ronstadt (*Blue Bayou*) and Don McLean (*Crying*).

RECORDINGS

(selective list; recorded for Monument unless otherwise stated)

Ooby Dooby (Sun 242, 1956); Blue Angel (425, 1960); Only the Lonely (421, 1960); Uptown (412, 1960); Crying (447, 1961); Running Scared (438, 1961); Dream Baby (456, 1962); In Dreams (806, 1963); Mean Woman Blues/Blue Bayou (824, 1963); It's Over (837, 1964); Oh, Pretty Woman (851, 1964); Communication Breakdown (MGM 13634, 1966)

BIBLIOGRAPHY
I. Whitcomb: *After the Ball: Pop Music from Rag to Rock* (New York, 1973)
——: *Whole Lotta Shakin': a Rock and Roll Scrapbook* (London, 1982)
——: *Rock Odyssey: a Chronicle of the Sixties* (New York, 1983)

IAN WHITCOMB

Orbón (de Soto), Julián (*b* Avilés, Spain, 7 Aug 1925). Cuban composer. He studied at the Conservatory of Oviedo (1935) and then moved to Havana, where he began composing at an early age and had lessons from José Ardévol. In Cuba he was active as a critic and pianist at concerts of contemporary Cuban music. In 1946 he studied with Copland at the Berkshire Music Center; later he taught composition at the National Conservatory in Mexico City (1960–63). In 1964 he settled in New York where he composed the liturgical works *Introito* (1967–8) and *Liturgia de tres días* (1975), as well as the Partita no.3 for orchestra (1965–6). He has taught at SUNY, Purchase, and Washington University (1964, 1965), and has lectured at other academic institutions. He has received commissions from the Fromm Foundation (1955), the Koussevitzky Foundation (1958), and the Dallas SO (1983, for Partita no.4 for piano and orchestra). He received two Guggenheim Fellowships (1959, 1969) and an award from the American Academy of Arts and Letters (1967). Orbón's output includes orchestral works, of which *Tres versiones sinfónicas* (1953) is the most successful early example, secular and sacred choral music, and chamber music. His Spanish-Cuban music has been influenced by a wide range of musical and literary interests, including Catholic liturgy, Gregorian chant, the music of Falla and the Halffters, and contemporary poetry; moreover, his close friendships with Carlos Chávez and Heitor Villa-Lobos have had their effect. Whether in the formal neoclassicism of his early works or the more expansive, vigorous, and romantic traits of his later style, his music has always been marked by strict structural design. Occasionally he has used "white" Cuban and Afro-Cuban rhythms, as in the String Quartet (1951) and *Tres versiones sinfónicas*. His recorded works include *Himnus ad galli cantum* (1955) and *Tres cantigas del Rey* (1960), both for female voice and chamber ensemble, and Partitas no.1 for harpsichord (1963) and no.2 for keyboard instruments and string quartet (1964). Boosey & Hawkes and Southern Music are his principal publishers.

BIBLIOGRAPHY
R. Parmenter: "Find from Cuba: Julián Orbón Scores at Composer Forum," *New York Times* (7 March 1955)
Compositores de América/Composers of the Americas, ed. Pan American Union, vi (Washington, DC, 1960)
H. C. Schonberg: "Latin Composer," *New York Times* (9 Nov 1961)

AURELIO DE LA VEGA

Orchestral music. The music written for orchestra by American composers has followed the traditional European forms of symphony, concerto, overture, and symphonic poem. The foundations of American orchestral music were laid in the 18th century by immigrant musicians who established and manned small orchestras, usually associated with theater and opera companies, and composed music for them. From the mid-19th century on, independent orchestras were established, and, influenced primarily by the Classical and Romantic music of central Europe, American composers increasingly produced music to be played by them. In the early 20th century, and especially after World War I, the Austro-German influence on American orchestral music yielded to a French one and the influence of jazz and popular music also began to be felt; these new currents led to a transformation of American orchestral music, which culminated, in the 1930s and 1940s, in a "golden age." The far-reaching effects of World War II and, in the postwar years, a new diversity of ideals and expression (including serial and aleatory procedures and the development of electroacoustic music) resulted in a splintering of idiom and practice. Out of this diversity there emerged, by the 1970s, a "new romanticism," the proponents of which included conductors and instrumentalists as well as composers, so that the performance of orchestral music became a potent force in the dissemination of new American music. Detailed discussion of individual items of American orchestral music may be found in articles on composers; for information on orchestral music written for films *see* FILM MUSIC. The history of American orchestras is discussed in ORCHESTRAS, and to some extent in articles on conductors. The commissioning of orchestral compositions is dealt with in AWARDS and in articles on music patrons and organizations (*see* especially COOLIDGE, ELIZABETH SPRAGUE; FROMM, PAUL; KOUSSEVITZKY FOUNDATIONS; and LOUISVILLE ORCHESTRA COMMISSIONING PROJECT).

1. To 1850. 2. 1850–1920. 3. 1920–50. 4. 1950–70. 5. After 1970.

1. TO 1850. Lacking the powerful sources of patronage – church, state, and aristocracy – which in Europe had made possible the development of orchestras and the composition of music for them, musicians in colonial America produced no such music. Nevertheless, in the 18th century the cities of Boston, New York, Philadelphia, and Charleston attracted musicians in sufficient numbers to form small orchestras, and orchestral performances are reported from the 1770s on. A symphony by J. C. Bach was performed in Boston on 17 May 1771; one by Haydn was played in New York on 14 May 1774, and his Symphony no.85 ("La reine") was given in Philadelphia on 29 December 1792. The first American performance of a symphony by Beethoven seems to have been on 13 June 1813, in the Moravian community of Nazareth, Pennsylvania.

It is unclear exactly when orchestral music was first composed in the New World; 18th-century programs are ambiguous in their naming of composers and performers, and terminology is often confused. The earliest orchestral score published in the USA was Hans Gram's *The Death Song of an Indian Chief*, which appeared in the *Massachusetts Magazine* in March 1791; it calls for tenor voice and two clarinets, two horns, and strings. John Christopher Moller published a sinfonia in the first issue of *Moller and Capron's Musical Numbers* (1793), but it is in short score with only a few instrumental indications. Whether James Hewitt's potpourris, *New Medley Overture* (1799–1800) and *The New Medley Overture* (1801–2), published for piano, are reductions of orchestral scores is uncertain; probably such piano scores, of which a large number appeared during the Federal era, served as the basis for ad hoc orchestrations depending on the instrumental resources at hand.

Several scores from the first third of the 19th century survive in Pennsylvania, including a two-movement symphony in D (Andante and Rondo) composed in 1831 by W. C. Peters for George Rapp's Harmony Society (in the archives of the society in Old Economy Village at Ambridge; fig. 1, p.426), an overture in C and a four-movement symphony in E♭ by Charles Hommann (archives of the Bethlehem Philharmonic Society), and an overture in D by Hommann that won a prize in 1835 (library of the Musical Fund Society of Philadelphia). These are all well-crafted,

1. Autograph MS of the first violin part of the Symphony in D, 1831, by W. C. Peters (Old Economy Village, Ambridge, Pennsylvania)

pleasant works, close in style to Haydn and Ignace Joseph Pleyel (both of whom figured prominently on American concert programs in this period). Anthony Philip Heinrich, sometimes termed by his contemporaries "the Beethoven of America," left a much more impressive body of orchestral works. As a composer he was an autodidact and, though it is apparent that Haydn and Beethoven were his models, he brought to his music an individualistic penchant for wild fantasy and a fascination with American Indian lore (without, however, incorporating any Indian music in his works) and romantic natural phenomena. These are reflected in such orchestral extravaganzas as the fantasia *Pushmataha, a Venerable Chief of a Western Tribe of Indians* (1831), the concerto grosso *The Treaty of William Penn with the Indians* (1834, rev. 1847), and the symphony *The Ornithological Combat of Kings, or The Condor of the Andes and the Eagle of the Cordilleras* (1847, rev. 1856). Heinrich's works were performed in both the USA and Europe, and he was regarded with affection, though not universally with respect. John Sullivan Dwight took him to task (in *The Harbinger*, 4 July 1846) for his preoccupation with "mere outward scenes and histories [which] seem to have . . . disturbed the pure spontaneous inspiration of his melodies." Modern critics have noted that his music lacks development, but they find in it an interesting additive structure, if also a tendency to overembellish melodies. There is also a certain naiveté that sometimes results in incongruity – as when Heinrich writes a Minuetto as the second movement of the "gran sinfonia misteriosa-Indiana" *Manitou Mysteries, or The Voice of the Great Spirit* (before 1845).

2. 1850–1920. The period 1850–1920 saw the rise of stable, "permanent" symphony orchestras in the USA, the first of which, the Philharmonic Society of New York, had been founded in 1842. In 1864 the Theodore Thomas Orchestra was founded (also in New York), and in 1878 the New York Symphony Society was formed by Leopold Damrosch, the first of a family of conductors important in New York musical circles until the late 1920s. The Boston SO was founded in 1881. In 1891 a group of Chicago businessmen engaged Thomas to organize an orchestra there, which became the Chicago SO; and in 1900 a group of civic leaders organized the Philadelphia Orchestra. By 1920 most of the major American symphony orchestras were in operation.

Composers of American orchestral music continued to model their works on the European compositions that dominated concert programs. The first American-born composer whose works were performed by the New York Philharmonic Society was George F. Bristow, a violinist in the orchestra. His Overture in E♭ (1845) was played on 9 January 1847, and the next year his Sinfonia in E♭ received a performance in an open rehearsal. The Philharmonic also presented his Second Symphony (the "Jullien" Sinfonia) (1 March 1856) and Third Symphony in F♯ minor (26 March 1859). The latter's programmatic tendencies (its second movement is a nocturne and the scherzo is titled "Butterfly's Frolic") were confirmed in Bristow's Fourth Symphony ("The Pioneer," retitled "Arcadian"), first played by the Brooklyn PO on 8 February 1873, and in his grandiose Niagara Symphony for vocal soloists, chorus, and orchestra (1893), apparently modeled on Beethoven's Ninth Symphony and Mendelssohn's Second ("Lobgesang"). Bristow's music is more than a reflection of such models: it flows, the themes are apt, and the orchestration is colorful and effective. A solo trombone in the "Jullien" Sinfonia has elaborate passagework in the first movement, and is assigned the cantabile theme of the third, a usage Bristow must have learned from the brass bands of his time since it has no precedent in conventional European orchestral practice. Popular-music idioms often influenced the shape of Bristow's melodic material.

William Henry Fry also composed some ambitious orchestral works, including descriptive symphonies with such titles as *The Breaking Heart* (1852), *Santa Claus* (1853), *A Day in the Country* (*c*1853), *Childe Harold* (1854), *Niagara* (1854), and *Hagar in the Wilderness* (1854). All of these were performed in New York soon after their composition; half of them are lost. The style of Fry's orchestral music depends primarily on Italian models, especially Donizetti and Bellini; formally, it is programmatic, based on elaborate scenarios that are followed in minute detail, sometimes to the detriment of the musical continuity.

The orchestral music of John Knowles Paine is the first by an American to demonstrate a complete grasp of the symphonic idiom. Paine wrote two symphonic poems (*The Tempest*, *c*1876, and *An Island Fantasy*, *c*1888), an overture to *As you Like it* (1876), and a *Duo concertante* for violin, cello, and orchestra (*c*1877), as well as two symphonies. The Symphony no.1 (1875) is Beethovenian in its first and second movements (the latter a scherzo), but the slow movement, an outpouring of tranquil beauty, owes little to anyone; the finale, which stays close to convention, is Schumannesque. The Second Symphony ("In the Spring," 1879) is entirely different: in it Paine reveals a remarkable ability to build extensive formal structures and to integrate them with subtle cyclic procedures. The opening motif of the introduction to the first movement is interwoven, in many permutations, with the melodic material of every other movement save the Scherzo. Paine's use of such thematic procedures predates similar techniques in the symphonies of Brahms.

Paine was the mentor and patriarch of the Second New England School of American composers, which included Arthur Foote, George W. Chadwick, Horatio Parker, and Amy Marcy Beach. All composed orchestral music of distinction, though only Chadwick and Beach wrote symphonies. Beach's single symphony, the "Gaelic" in E minor (1894), has a fine sweep and sense of spontaneity; her Piano Concerto (1899) is notable for its brief but charming Scherzo. Chadwick produced a significantly larger body of orchestral works, from his early overture *Rip Van Winkle* (1879) – a success in Leipzig while he was still a conservatory student there – to the late "symphonic ballad" *Tam O'Shanter* (1914–15). The Celtic atmosphere of *Tam O'Shanter* appears in others of his works: the Symphony no.2 (1883–5) contains modal and rhythmic elements associated with Scottish folk music, and the Symphony no.3 (1893–4) is replete with them. Especially attractive are the four *Symphonic Sketches* (1895–1904), the first two of which – "Jubilee" and "Noel" – are the most often played of Chadwick's orchestral works. Foote favored writing for string orchestra: of his Serenade (1891) and two suites, one in D (1889) and the other in E (1907, rev. 1908), the last claims a niche in the standard repertory; and *A Night Piece* (1922), Foote's arrangement for flute and strings of his Nocturne (1918), is his most frequently performed large work. Parker, after some student efforts composed in Munich, left five major mature works for orchestra: the overture *Count Robert of Paris* (1890), the symphonic poem *A Northern Ballad* (1899), an organ concerto (1902), the symphonic poem *Vathek* (1903), and a suite arranged in 1915 from the opera *Fairyland*. The orchestral works may have influenced Parker's compositions in other genres: *A Northern Ballad* shares certain gestures and motifs with his oratorio *A Wanderer's Psalm* (1900), while *Vathek*, which shows some influence of Richard Strauss, is close to the idiom of the opera *Mona* (composed 1910).

Related aesthetically and stylistically to these Bostonians was Edward MacDowell, who completed eight orchestral works. The two piano concertos (1882 and 1884–6) are very different from each other: the first is quite conventional in shape and expression; the second is unusual in its design (it has a fleet scherzo as the second movement, flanked by a first movement marked "Larghetto calmato" and a fast finale with a slow introduction) and (in the view of some critics) its foreshadowing of Rachmaninoff's style. The three symphonic poems – *Hamlet and Ophelia* (1884–5), *Lancelot and Elaine* (1886), and *Lamia* (1887–8) – as well as the two completed movements ("Die Sarazenen," "Die schöne Alda") of an unfinished program symphony (1886–90) after *The Song of Roland* and the First Suite for orchestra (1888–93), are all characterized by a fertile melodic invention, chromatic harmony, and a rhythmic quality that often seems to suggest that the music was written to words. MacDowell's last and in some ways best orchestral work, the Suite no.2 ("Indian," 1891–5), is ironically the least characteristic, being based on American Indian melodies; of the five movements ("Legend," "Love Song," "In War Time," "Dirge," and "Village Festival") the "Dirge" is especially successful, and has been compared favorably with Wagner's funeral music for Siegfried.

A number of other composers wrote distinguished orchestral works during this period. Arthur Bird and George Templeton Strong both became expatriates and their music offers no hints of their American origins. Bird composed more than a dozen orchestral works beginning with his Symphony (1885). Strong was more prolific; his *Sintram* (Symphony no.2, 1887–8), based on the novel by the German writer Friedrich Heinrich Karl de la Motte Fouqué and Albrecht Dürer's print *Ritter, Tod und Teufel*, has among other virtues a gracefully lyrical slow movement. As an orchestral composer, Victor Herbert is best known for his Cello Concerto no.2 (1894), which inspired Dvořák to compose his Cello Concerto, but Herbert's greatest contribution is surely the sweep, skill, and imagination he brought to the orchestration of his operettas, suites from which appear regularly on the programs of "pops" orchestras. Arthur Farwell and Henry F. Gilbert turned for inspiration respectively to the music of American Indians and black Americans. Farwell looked also to Russia and France for models that might liberate his work from Austro-German hegemony, but periodically returned to Indian themes, as in the fantasia *Dawn* (1904) and the Indian Suite (1944). Gilbert's best-known orchestral works are the *Comedy Overture on Negro Themes* (*c*1906) and the symphonic poem *The Dance in Place Congo* (*c*1908, rev. 1916); his last piece for large orchestra, Nocturne (1925–6), based on a passage from Whitman (beginning "I am he that walks with the tender and growing night"), is attractive and skillfully orchestrated, and shows no ethnic influences. Charles Martin Loeffler, a long-time member of the Boston SO, developed a style heavily influenced by French music, but he also drew on other national styles (Russian, Spanish, and Irish) and on American popular music. Many of his orchestral works utilize chorus or solo singers; he also scored for unusual instruments, including viola d'amore and saxophone. Henry Hadley amalgamated elements of late German romanticism and early French impressionism in five symphonies, overtures, suites, and tone poems, bringing to them also, as a prominent conductor, a profound knowledge of orchestration.

The work of Charles Griffes reflects the stylistic reorientation of American orchestral music in the years around World War I. His first piece for orchestra was the *Symphonische Phantasie* (1907), a very Germanic, Romantic, sprawling – and lovely – work; at about the same time he began sketching the *Notturno* (completed ?1918), which is reminiscent of Richard Strauss. During the next years Griffes concentrated on songs and piano works, and the style of his music veered towards French impressionism and even oriental music. *The Pleasure-Dome of Kubla Khan* (1917), a recasting of a piano work of 1912, was his first orchestral piece in the new idiom; his only other major original composition for orchestra (as distinct from arrangements of earlier works) was the *Poem* for flute and orchestra of 1919, skillfully constructed, sensitively orchestrated, and, though recalling Griffes's interest in oriental melody, lacking any hint of "chinoiserie."

3. 1920–50. The impulse of American composers to turn away from central European, postromantic models, already in evidence in the first two decades of the 20th century, increased after World War I. One attractive source for a number of composers was the new ragtime- and jazz-influenced popular music. An early example was the "jazz pantomime" *Krazy Kat* (1921) by John Alden Carpenter (one of its most successful sections, the "Kat-nip Blues," was unfortunately omitted in the work's revision of 1939). Carpenter's ballet score *Skyscrapers* of 1923–4 has alternating sections of "work" and "play," both of which are informed by varied elements of popular music. In 1924 came the première of George Gershwin's *Rhapsody in Blue* for piano and jazz band; orchestrated by Ferde Grofé, it quickly entered the symphonic repertory, as did Gershwin's tone poem *An American in Paris* (1928) and, to a lesser extent, his Concerto in F for piano and orchestra (1925). Grofé himself explored SYMPHONIC JAZZ in more than a dozen works, of which only the *Grand Canyon Suite* (1931) has remained in the repertory. Aaron Copland also ventured into the field with his suite *Music for the Theatre* (1925) and Piano Concerto (1926) but soon abandoned it, having concluded that once one had done "the blues and the snappy number" there was little potential left in popular source materials.

Other composers differed. American popular and folk idioms were fundamental resources for Virgil Thomson's concert and film scores, beginning with his first symphony, the *Symphony on a Hymn Tune* (1928). William Grant Still, a prolific composer of orchestral music including five symphonies (1930–58), seven symphonic poems (1924–60), and a number of suites (1926–62), drew often on black popular styles, especially the blues, as in his Symphony no.1 (the "Afro-American") of 1930; Howard Swanson used the same sources for a number of orchestral works including the award-winning Short Symphony (1948). Howard Hanson, composer of seven symphonies and many other orchestral compositions, is rightly considered a neoromantic, but such a work as his Symphony no.2 (the "Romantic") of 1930 is in fact permeated with harmonic progressions typical of popular song; Randall Thompson's Second Symphony (1932) reveals the same influence, as does Douglas S. Moore's Symphony no.2 in A (1945) and other works.

Much other orchestral music in the three decades after 1920 was shaped under the combined influences of the teacher Nadia Boulanger and the conductor Serge Koussevitzky. Many promising American composers went to France for study with Boulanger (and through her were exposed to the works of Stravinsky and the younger French composers such as Les Six); once back in the USA, a number of them received commissions and performances from Koussevitzky, who had left Paris in 1924 to direct the Boston SO. Copland was the first to benefit from this support. After the early period in which his works show popular inspiration, his style turned more acerbic, with acrid harmonies, jagged melodies, and nervous rhythms; this manner reached a culmination in the Short Symphony (Symphony no.2) of 1932–3. Thereafter, influenced by the populism and socialist realism of the Depression era, Copland simplified his idiom and began to investigate American folksong and folklore. The first result of this new orientation was *El salón México* (1933–6); this was followed by the ballets *Billy the Kid* (1938) and *Rodeo* (1942), *Lincoln Portrait* for speaker and orchestra and *Fanfare for the Common Man* for brass and percussion (both 1942), and the "ballet for Martha [Graham]" *Appalachian Spring* (1943–4), along with the *Lincoln Portrait* Copland's most popular work. This phase of Copland's career as an orchestral composer culminated in the Third Symphony (1944–6); folksong quotation makes no appearance in it, but so deeply had this influence permeated Copland's subconscious that a folkish atmosphere pervades the work.

Another pupil of Boulanger, who was also supported strongly by Koussevitzky, was Roy Harris, who began composing for orchestra early in his career (Andante, 1926; *American Portrait 1929*, 1929) and for whom orchestral music remained the main focus (he composed 14 symphonies besides many smaller works). The *Symphony 1933*, his first symphony, was a response to Koussevitzky's call for "a great symphony from the West." The Symphony no.3 (1937), in one movement, became Harris's most frequently performed work; abandoning most elements of conventional structure, he here permitted the musical materials to develop and shape their own forms. Thereafter, he tended to alternate between multi-movement design (e.g., the Fifth Symphony, 1942) and single-movement form (Seventh Symphony, 1952). In some of his later symphonies Harris added solo vocal and choral parts, and in his last, written on the occasion of the US Bicentennial, he included (somewhat unsuccessful) passages of choral declamation.

Other major composers of orchestral music who were less influenced by the so-called "Boulangerie" included Walter Piston (though in fact he studied with Boulanger), Roger Sessions, and Wallingford Riegger. All three shared a lack of interest in "Americanism" as an aesthetic goal and wrote in a comparatively abstract, international style. Piston composed many orchestral works, including eight symphonies, in a manner that developed early and remained relatively constant; his style is characterized by classic clarity of form, with themes aptly conceived for such form, and a mixture of triadic and quartal harmony that emphasizes the linear integrity of the texture. Most of Sessions's nine symphonies and other orchestral works were composed after the mid-1950s, once he had turned to a personal version of serialism and a harmonic language of ambiguous tonality (see below). His First Symphony (1927) combines Stravinskian short motifs with the long lines that Sessions favored; the Violin Concerto (1935) and Second Symphony (1946) are increasingly chromatic. Riegger was another who developed his own brand of dodecaphony, which he employed with exemplary clarity of line and texture. After a long career of working in comparative obscurity, Riegger achieved significant recognition only with the Third Symphony (1946–7), first performed in 1948; commissions for other orchestral works followed.

It was not until after World War II that two of the most individualistic American composers of orchestral music – by then elderly men – came to national prominence: Charles Ives and Carl Ruggles. Ives's complex personality is reflected in his music, which ranges from the conventional, even banal, to the original, radical, and sometimes chaotic. Of his numbered symphonies the last, the Symphony no.4 (1909–16, but not heard in full until 1965), embodies all the Ivesian paradoxes: its tangled second movement is a "comedy," inspired by Hawthorne's short story *The Celestial Railroad*, full of multiple layers of simultaneous events, montages based on sacred and secular tunes, and harmonic aggregates sometimes involving microtones; the third movement is by contrast an almost academically conventional fugue (though its principal subject is derived from a hymn tune by Lowell Mason); and these movements are framed by brooding outer movements in which the orchestra is joined by a chorus. Ives's other symphonies are less challengingly complex, though parts of the four-movement quasi-symphony *Holidays* (1904–13) come close. Some of the smaller orchestral works are unprecedented in their originality, notably *The Unanswered Question* and its companion piece *Central Park in the Dark* (both 1906), as well as the three-part tone poem *Three Places in New England* (1908–?1914) and the similarly conceived and shaped *Second Orchestral Set* (1909–15). Ruggles's orchestral output was scanty: between the earliest, *Sun-treader* (?1920; rev. 1926–31), and the last, *Organum* (1944), he wrote only a handful of works originally conceived for the medium. Their idiom is rather limited in scope, with a certain grayness in the instrumental coloring and a static rhythmic quality, though melodic lines are jagged and gestures are monumental.

An ardent partisan of Ives and Ruggles, and like them identified with innovation and experiment, was Henry Cowell. His catalogue of orchestral works is enormous, including more than 20 symphonies, most of them bearing suggestive titles such as those of no.2 ("Anthropos," 1938–9), no.3 ("Gaelic," 1942), no.11 ("Seven Rituals of Music," 1953–4), no.13 ("Madras," 1957–8), and no.16 ("Icelandic," 1962). Almost all of these postdated Cowell's youthful avant-garde period; some reflect his absorption of the music of the many countries to which he traveled. He wrote two koto concertos (1962, 1964–5) after a trip to Japan, and used the Japanese word for "music," *ongaku*, as the title of a work in 1957. Cowell's Irish-American background is reflected in *Celtic Set* (1938–9), *Fiddler's Jig* (1952), a number of works titled *Hymn and Fuguing Tune*, and the Symphony no.4 (Short Symphony, 1946) with its movements "Hymn," "Ballad," "Dance" (an Irish jig), and "Introduction and Fuguing Tune."

Another prolific contributor to the orchestral repertory from the 1930s on was William Schuman, who wrote ten symphonies and many other works including ballet scores, symphonic poems, concertos, and suites. His first orchestral work to gain prominence was *American Festival Overture* (1939), based on a city boy's street cry and incorporating an elaborate fugue and a brassy bitonal canon. Similar textures and sonorities characterize the Symphony no.3 (1941) – the earliest one Schuman acknowledged – which also turns to neobaroque formal principles in its two double movements ("Passacaglia and Fugue," "Chorale and Toccata"). The Symphony no.6 (1948), perhaps Schuman's masterpiece, is a departure from earlier symphonies in form (being in one movement) and harmonic vocabulary (it eschews polychords). Schuman's later works show an increasing density of harmonic material but no basic change in idiom. Some are in a somewhat more popular vein, however, like the *New England Triptych* (1956) and *A Song of Orpheus* (1961), a fantasia for cello and orchestra based on an earlier song.

Like Schuman, Samuel Barber wrote music of powerful personal expression, but his is more aristocratic or at least less brash. Whether working in abstract orchestral forms (Symphony no.1, 1936; Violin Concerto, 1939), telling a story (*Medea*, 1946), or painting a scene (*Music for a Scene from Shelley*, 1933; *Fadograph of a Yestern Scene*, 1971), he wrote elegant music marked by great clarity of formal structure, lyrical melody, and neoromantic harmony. His ability to infuse elaborate contrapuntal technique with evocative expression is perhaps best displayed in the Adagio for Strings (1936), his best-known work. The First Symphony combines dramatic gesture, prickly wit, and effusive lyricism in a single, compact, four-part movement. The three works titled *Essay* (1937, 1942, 1978) are in an original form in which two themes are set in opposition to each other rather than being developed.

By the 1940s a number of European composers had immigrated to the USA, among them Ernest Bloch, Darius Milhaud, Paul Hindemith, Arnold Schoenberg, Béla Bartók, and Igor Stravinsky. Even though, for the most part, the styles of their orchestral music did not change appreciably after their arrival in the USA, their presence, established reputations, and occupancy of academic posts, and their consequent ability to attract performances of their works meant that much contemporary music was heard during this period. Bloch's best-known works, such as *Voice in the Wilderness* (1936) and *Suite hébraïque* for violin or viola and orchestra (1951), are based on Jewish themes, though he also wrote in a neoclassical vein (in the two concerti grossi, 1924–5, 1952) and occasionally in a self-consciously American manner (as in *America* (1926), an "epic rhapsody" for chorus and orchestra). Milhaud's compositional style was well established before he settled in the USA in 1940, and after World War II he spent equal time in France and at Mills College. But he paid homage to his adopted home in such works as *Kentuckiana* (1948), *Aspen Serenade* (1957), *A Frenchman in New York* (1962), *Meurtre d'un grand chef d'état* (1963), *Music for Boston* (1965), *Music for New Orleans* (1966), and *Music for San Francisco* (1971). Schoenberg's serial Violin Concerto (1935) and Piano Concerto (1942) date from his American years, but these isolated works were less important than his influence as the symbolic embodiment in the USA of serial thought. Hindemith asserted his concept of a functional harmony in the best-known orchestral works of his American years, the jaunty *Symphonic Metamorphosis on Themes of Carl Maria von Weber* (1943) and the Symphony "Die Harmonie der Welt" (1951); but in some of his late compositions he experimented with 12-tone and serial techniques – the finale of the Pittsburgh Symphony (1958) is based on an eight-note series. Bartók's four years in the USA were not sufficient for him to leave a legacy as a teacher, but they did see the composition of the Concerto for Orchestra (1943), to a commission from Koussevitzky, and the uncompleted Third Piano Concerto and Viola Concerto. Stravinsky settled in the USA in 1940, though he had been a frequent visitor for the preceding 15 years and his Symphony of Psalms (1930), which gives chorus and orchestra equal weight, was written to a commission from the Boston SO. His American works include the neoclassical Symphony in C (1939–40) and the lively Symphony in Three Movements (1942–5); then, in an extraordinary transformation, he adopted serial techniques in *Agon* (1953–7), *Movements* (1958–9), and Variations (1963–4).

Besides the leaders already cited, a number of other, younger composers came to prominence in the 1940s, making the period a "golden age." Robert Ward wrote the first of his five euphonious symphonies in 1941 (among his other orchestral pieces is one of 1954 titled *Euphony*). Peter Mennin's second and third symphonies (1944, 1946) brought him to public attention while he was still a student. In these, and the six others he wrote over the next 30 years, he forged an intense and energetic contrapuntal style. Vincent Persichetti had his Symphony no.3 (1946) performed by Ormandy and the Philadelphia Orchestra; his works for band are better known than his nine symphonies, but all are informed by a fluent craftsmanship covering a wide range of styles. David Diamond's rigorous pandiatonic style reached its climax in his Fourth Symphony (1945), though it is his *Rounds* (1944) for string orchestra that remains his most often played work. By the time of his Symphony no.5 (1951), Diamond's idiom had developed into an extremely chromatic one. He wrote his next three symphonies while based in Europe, where he was untouched by avant-garde movements, and revised the Fifth Symphony in 1964 before returning to the USA the following year. It took him 20 years to complete his next symphony (no.9), a two-part work scored for bass-baritone and orchestra, with texts by Michelangelo Buonarroti. Leroy Anderson composed a number of novelties, many for the Boston Pops Orchestra, with catchy rhythms, singable melodies, and creative use of instruments. Among these are *Jazz Legato* and *Jazz Pizzicato* (both 1938), *The Syncopated Clock* (1945), *Sleigh Ride* (1948), *A Trumpeter's Lullaby* (1949), and *The Typewriter* (1950).

4. 1950–70. One of the most remarkable developments in American orchestral music in the 1950s was the LOUISVILLE ORCHESTRA COMMISSIONING PROJECT. From 1948 to 1960 over 100 works, mostly by American composers, were commissioned for an orchestra of 50 players. The range of compositions and composers was staggering: from works by established composers such as Copland (Orchestral Variations, 1957), Harris (Piano Concerto no.2, 1953), Riegger (Variations for piano and orchestra, 1952–3, and Variations for violin and orchestra, 1958), and Schuman – whose choreographic poem *Judith* (1949), was danced to by Martha Graham – to compositions by younger composers such as Lukas Foss (*A Parable of Death*, 1954), Chou Wen-chung (*And the Fallen Petals*, 1953), and Ned Rorem (*Design for Orchestra*, 1953), and experimental works such as the Rhapsodic Variations, a collaborative piece for tape and orchestra by Otto Luening and Vladimir Ussachevsky (1953–4). The project, with funding from the Rockefeller Foundation, established a record label, which ensured the widespread distribution of classical American music through the relatively new medium of the LP.

Elliott Carter's Variations for Orchestra (1954–5), a Louisville commission, was the first of his orchestral works to embody the characteristics of form, texture, tempo, rhythm, and harmony found in his mature music. The Variations consist of a theme and two ritornellos, which have contrasting (and changing) tempos. Strings, winds, and brass have separate and distinct functions. The nine variations move with diminishing textural contrast from activity (variations 1–4) to stasis (5) and, with increasing contrast, back to activity (6–9); Carter's innovative "metric modulation" is found in variations 4 and 6 (for illustration *see* CARTER, ELLIOTT, fig.2). He explored similar terrain in his Double Concerto for harpsichord and piano (1961), which also moves to and from its midpoint in a symmetrical manner. The solo instruments are given contrasting rhythmic and melodic material and each is accompanied by an independent ensemble, which solves the problem of balancing instruments of such different volume and timbre; moreover the percussion and pitched instruments are assigned different functions, the keyboard instruments acting as intermediaries. Both the Piano Concerto (1964–5) and the Concerto for Orchestra (1969) utilize virtuoso concertino groups within the orchestra which have their own chordal harmonies; the latter piece is as glittering as the former is dark. *A Symphony of Three Orchestras* (1976) further extends Carter's awesome handling of textures, simultaneous events, and spatial relationships. Each orchestra plays four movements, which intersect and lash the others to create a complex collage. The 12 movements have distinct and unique tempos, characters, harmonies, and timbres.

If Carter's music presents a stringent complexity, necessitating virtuoso performances in order to be properly realized, John Cage's music is at the opposite extreme. Cage's studies of Zen Buddhism and the I Ching led him to experiment with a music of chance, in which sound in and of itself is more important than the composer's intentions. In the Concerto for prepared piano and chamber orchestra (1950–51) the orchestral material is derived from a number chart; the soloist has composed material of an improvisatory nature in the first movement but becomes dependent on the chart in the second and third movements. Even the concept of "musical" sound is extended, for lengthy silences are a fundamental component of the third movement. Indeterminacy was a key factor in Cage's work by the time of the *Concert for Piano and Orchestra* (1957–8), in which the solo part and the 13 other instrumental parts can be played in any order with any portion omitted, for any length of time, and (for the "orchestral" parts) by any number of players; the piece may also be performed simultaneously with other compositions by Cage from the same period. *Atlas eclipticalis* (1961), written with the aid of I Ching operations, calls for optional live electronics and 86 parts that need not all be used in full; the notation for these is based on patterns derived from an astronomical atlas. More recent orchestral works by Cage have utilized voices (*Renga*, 1976, and *Atlas borealis*, 1982), more than one orchestra (*Dance Four Orchestras* and *30 Pieces for 5 Orchestras*, both 1981), and no conductor (*A Collection of Rocks, 1984*).

Cage's associate, Morton Feldman, was principally interested in timbral relationships: his characteristic orchestral sound is soft and static, and consists of isolated events. Early in his career he adopted graphic notation, which functions as a blueprint for the production of sounds of indeterminate pitch and length. In *Marginal Intersection* (1951) Feldman determines relative pitches (high, middle, and low) for wind, brass, and strings, while allowing piano, guitar, and percussion to choose pitches from any register; within the confines of the graph structure, specific entrances and durations are chosen by the performer. By the 1960s he had moved back towards conventional notation, assigning pitches but not durations. *First Principles* for chamber orchestra (1966–7) contains notated changes from sound to sound, but the changes are so broadly spaced that they are difficult to discern. Feldman ultimately found that he wanted precise control over musical events – *The Viola in my Life IV* (1971) is a conventionally notated orchestral work; such procedures were, however, presaged in *Structures* (1960–62), where he did "'fix' (precisely note) what might occur if the work utilized indeterminate elements." Although such scores are meant to have a liberating effect on music, the absence of specific directions has for the most part discouraged orchestral musicians from attempting to perform such works.

Composer–conductors such as Leonard Bernstein and Lukas Foss enjoyed a degree of success with their orchestral works, which derived in part from their ability to conduct them. Bernstein's three symphonies ("Jeremiah," 1942, "Age of Anxiety," 1947, and "Kaddish," 1963), are intensely personal, post-Mahlerian *cris-de-coeur* about 20th-century crises of faith. In each, Bernstein goes beyond the boundaries of the standard symphony orchestra, using a mezzo-soprano soloist in the First Symphony, a pianist as "protagonist" in the Second, and speaker, mezzo-soprano, and chorus in the Third. The "Kaddish" Symphony represents Bernstein's attempt to come to grips with atonality and the ultimate confirmation of his faith in tonality. The most successful moments in these works come when Bernstein lets loose with breezy, jazzy music, as in the Masque in the "Age of Anxiety." He acknowledges the "theatricality" of his orchestral music, and in fact it has been the arrangements of his theater pieces, notably the overture to *Candide* and the Symphonic Dances from *West Side Story*, that have attained the most enduring place in the orchestral repertory. Foss's orchestral compositions are also eclectic, but more experimental than Bernstein's: he borrows chorale settings by Bach for his Symphony of Chorales (1956–8) and themes by Scarlatti, Handel, and Bach for his Baroque Variations (1967). Early works, such as the two piano concertos, Symphony in G, and *Recordare*, are neoclassical, while his suite from the cantata *The Prairie* (1944) contains hints of Americana. *Concert for Cello and Orchestra* (1966) pits a cellist against a prerecorded tape; here again a piece by Bach is used, and is gradually distorted by cellist and tape. *Time Cycle* for soprano and orchestra (1959–60), one of Foss's most important works, explores the nature of time; it originally included improvisatory sections. The wit and humor that mark many of these works are completely absent from *Exeunt* (1982), a serial composition concerned with the vision of human annihilation.

In the 1960s, scores of great complexity proliferated, especially by composers who studied with Milton Babbitt and Sessions at Princeton University or at the Juilliard School (where Carter also taught). Even Copland, in his late orchestral scores, *Connotations* (1962) and *Inscape* (1967), made use of serial methods, although in the former piece only as "building blocks" for a succession of variations based on the opening four-note chords and their implied melodic intervals. Babbitt's early orchestral scores have been withdrawn; *Relata I* (1965) divides the orchestra into separate timbral groups, each correlated with set structure, while *Correspondences* (1966–7), for string orchestra and tape, gives both media similar pitch and durational material without attempting to simulate the characteristic sounds of the other. The technical difficulties of these and his other orchestral works have meant they receive only occasional performances, in contrast to Babbitt's chamber music, which is played regularly. Charles Wuorinen, who studied at Columbia University and performs many of his own pieces as pianist or conductor, was drawn to the music of Babbitt, Schoenberg, Stravinsky, and Varèse, and early assimilated a wide variety of techniques into his own clear, uncompromising sound. Before he was 25 he had written three symphonies and four concertante works, marked by rhythmic buoyancy and striking timbres. Serial techniques appear in *Orchestral and Electronic Exchanges* (1965), but Wuorinen found them less binding than many of his contemporaries. *A Reliquary for Igor Stravinsky* (1975) incorporates the master's last sketches, while the Two-part Symphony (1978) is a Stravinskian homage of another kind (to the Symphony in C) in its clear rhythms, concertante writing, and wit. Both the Violin Concerto no.2 (1972) and the Piano Concerto no.2 (1973) use amplified solo instruments, while *Bamboula Squared* (1984) effectively combines orchestra and quadraphonic tape in a driving, suspenseful manner. In the Short Suite for conventional orchestra (1981), Wuorinen creates a noteworthy variety of tempo, rhythm, and timbre. Sessions's densely contrapuntal, elegantly arched symphonies of the 1950s and 1960s range from the serial Third Symphony (1957) to the exuberant Sixth Symphony (1966) and the fluid and expressive Eighth Symphony (1968). He was tied to no specific structure: the symphonies vary in number of movements; some contain prologues and epilogues; several are played through without pause. After completing his opera *Montezuma* (1963), Sessions orchestrated his works with a new brilliance. He celebrated the virtuosity of the Boston SO (especially woodwind and brass players) in his last completed work, the epigrammatic Concerto for Orchestra (1981). Sessions's student Andrew Imbrie has adopted the long lines favored by his teacher and energized them, while keeping the overall texture clear; this is evident in his three symphonies (1965, 1970, 1970), concertos for violin (1954), piano (1973, 1974), and flute (1977), and *Prometheus Bound* for soloists, chorus, and orchestra (1980; fig.2).

Exposure to Asian culture influenced a number of composers in the 1950s and 1960s, as it had Colin McPhee and others in the 1920s. Notable among them were Lou Harrison and Henry Cowell (see §3 above). Harrison, like Cowell a champion of Ives and his radical experimentation, had long been interested in integrating nonwestern sounds and just intonation into his musical language (as in his Suite for violin, piano, and small orchestra, 1951; Four Strict Songs for eight baritones and orchestra, 1955; and Suite for Symphonic Strings, 1936–60); after traveling to the Far East in 1961–2 he wrote *Pacifika Rondo* (1963) for a chamber orchestra of Eastern and Western instruments. Since the early 1970s the majority of Harrison's compositions have been for gamelan; they include a double concerto for violin and cello with Javanese gamelan. Henry Cowell's travels were increasingly reflected in his late orchestral works. Henry Brant's *Meteor Farm* (1982) is a large work involving traditional music of Java, India, and West Africa performed by two choruses, symphony orchestra, and jazz orchestras. Like many of his works since *Antiphony I* (1953, rev. 1968), it is "spatial music," in which separated groups of musicians are assigned contrasting music; the procedure owes much to Ives. Alan Hovhaness heard Indian music in Boston in the 1930s, but it was not until after extensive travels in the 1950s that he began to incorporate elements of Asian music – instruments, modes, rhythms – into his many orchestral pieces, which were further affected by his intense involvement with meditation and mysticism. Asian music was also of significance for the early minimalist composers.

On the West Coast a number of composers followed the lead of Luening and Ussachevsky and experimented with combining orchestra with tape or computer. Morton Subotnick, director of the San Francisco Tape Music Center in the 1960s, wrote for tape and orchestra in *Play! no.2* (1964), *Laminations* (1968), and *Before the Butterfly* (1975). After completing *Two Butterflies* (1975) for amplified orchestra, he began a series of "ghost pieces" in which a digital program (the ghost) modifies the pitch, timbre, attack, volume, and direction of instrumental sounds; among the "ghost" orchestral scores are *Axolotl* and *Liquid Strata* (both 1982). Roger Reynolds's scores use live performers, electronically altered tape of conventional instruments, and computer-generated sound, which are combined in predetermined temporal relationships logarithmically derived; the results, as in *Transfigured Wind II* (1984), are complex but expressive. Robert Erickson, a colleague of Reynolds at the University of California, San Diego, made use of tape in some works of the 1960s and 1970s, but for his recent orchestral works has derived unusual sonorities from the use of homemade instruments such as stroked rods (in *Aurora*, 1982). The university orchestra's conductor, Thomas Nee, has been responsible for commissioning several of Erickson's scores since the early 1970s, as part of a sympathetic collaboration between campus performers and composers that has produced rich results.

5. After 1970. The explosion of orchestral activity since 1970 – year-round orchestras, national and international tours, commissions, recordings – owes much to the creation of the NEA in 1965. The existence of nationally supported funding for programs that hitherto had existed through the vision and generosity of individual patrons, private foundations, or local institutions (many of whom now teamed up with the NEA to create grander programs), provided new-found stability for composers, performers, and orchestras alike.

One manifestation of this activity has been the proliferation of professional chamber orchestras, the most prominent of which are the St. Paul Chamber Orchestra (founded 1959), the Concerto Soloists of Philadelphia (1965), the Los Angeles Chamber Orchestra (1968), and the 92nd Street "Y" Chamber Orchestra (1977). Each of these has presented new works, often their own commissions; among the scores are William Bolcom's *Commedia* (1971), *Open House* (1975), and Symphony for chamber orchestra (1979); Sydney Hodkinson's *Valence* (1970) and Sinfonia concertante (Symphony no.5, 1980); Henri Lazarof's Chamber Symphony (1976) and Sinfonietta (1981); Robert Starer's *Concerto a quattro* (1983); Joseph Schwantner's *Distant Runes and Incantations* (1983); and Eric Stokes's *On the Badlands-Parable* (1972) and *Five Verbs of Earth Encircled* (1973).

A combination of commissions from orchestras and relationships developed between individual composers and performers has accounted for the composition of many new concertos since 1970. The principal players of the New York PO have been the beneficiaries of a continuing series of commissions, which includes Colgrass's *Déjà vu* (1977) for percussion quartet and orchestra (which won the Pulitzer Prize), John Corigliano's Clarinet Concerto (1977), Imbrie's Flute Concerto (1977), Persichetti's Concerto for english horn and string orchestra (1977), Schuman's *Three Colloquies* for horn (1979), and Jacob Druckman's Viola Concerto (1979). Gunther Schuller has contributed to the concerto repertory with works for instruments that are seldom used in a soloistic capacity – double bass (1968), contrabassoon (1978), trumpet (1979), and alto saxophone (1983) – as well as concertos for orchestra, piano, violin, and horn. (Schuller earlier wrote most inventively for orchestra in his "third stream" works, such as the Concertino for jazz quartet and orchestra, 1959, and *Journey into Jazz*, 1962, which synthesize classical forms with the improvisatory elements of jazz.) George Rochberg's five-movement Violin Concerto (1975), written for Isaac Stern, is perhaps his best-known orchestral score since his celebrated "conversion" from serialism to tonality in the 1960s. The flutist Paula Robison commissioned Leon Kirchner's Music for Flute and Orchestra (1978), while John Harbison wrote his three-movement, clas-

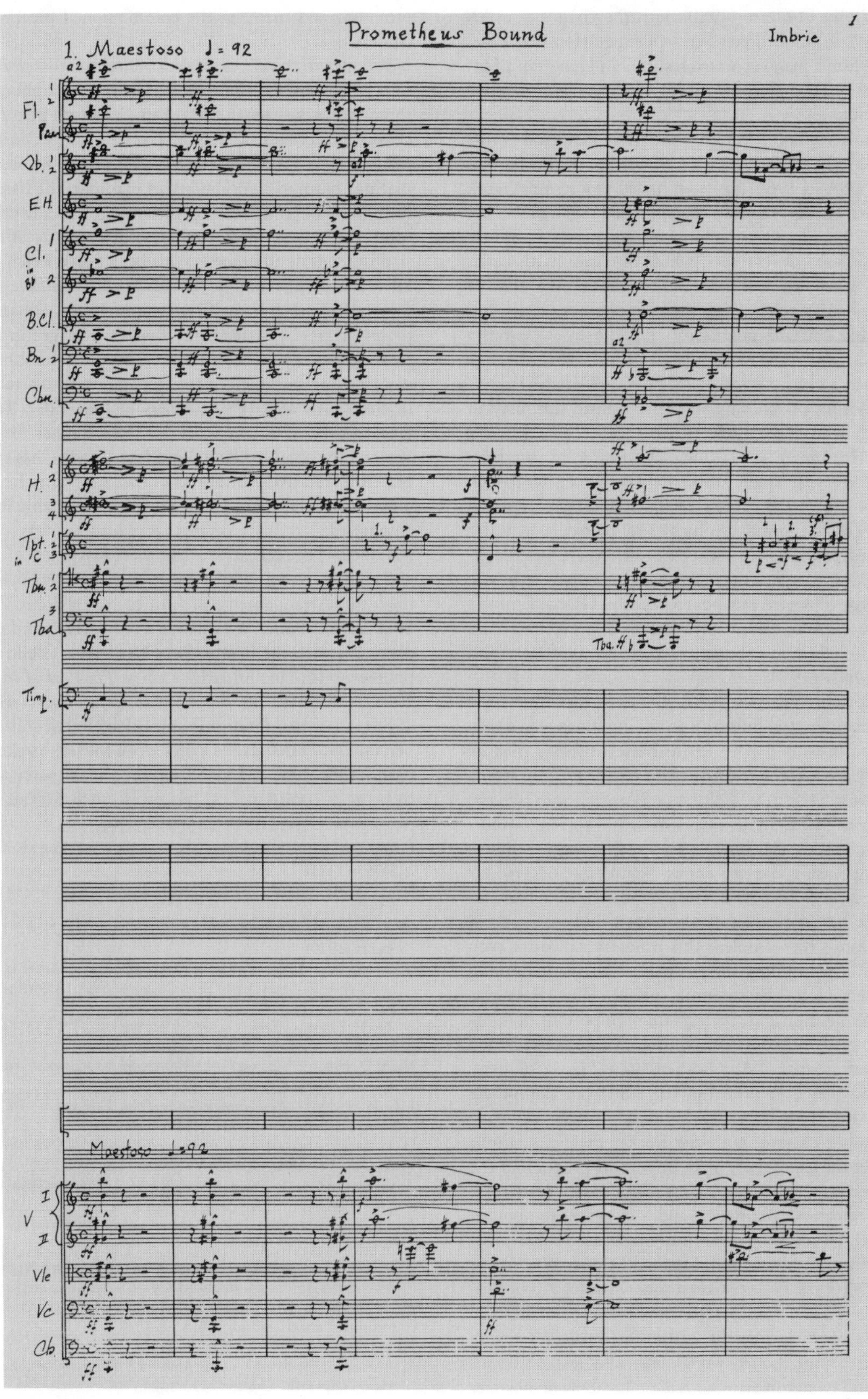

2. *Autograph MS of the opening of Andrew Imbrie's "Prometheus Bound," 1980, for soloists, chorus, and orchestra*

sically drawn Violin Concerto (1980) with the virtuosity of his wife, Rose Mary, in mind; Peter Serkin's suggestion that Peter Lieberson write him a piano concerto resulted in Lieberson's first orchestral work (1983), a piece of striking vitality, commissioned by the Boston SO.

Luciano Berio's *Sinfonia* – topical, political, historical (in its homage to Mahler), and provocative – written while he was resident in the USA in 1968, has been hailed as a seminal work of the "new romanticism" that has characterized much orchestral music of the 1970s and 1980s. Its most fervent American adherent is, perhaps, David Del Tredici, whose obsession with Lewis Carroll's *Alice's Adventures in Wonderland* has produced a number of grandiose Straussian tone poems and symphonies (1968–84) that have enjoyed extreme popularity. Druckman (who ran a New York PO festival of the new romanticism in 1983) has, like Rochberg, turned away from serialism; he writes dramatic, colorful scores, quoting or alluding to earlier music (Debussy in *Windows*, which won the Pulitzer Prize in 1972, Bernstein's "Kaddish tune" in *Aureole* of 1979) without losing his own brilliant voice. Alive with color, also, are the scores of Joseph Schwantner; his use of the more ethereal-sounding percussion instruments – gongs, bowed cymbals, and particularly water goblets – permeates his works, but compositions such as *Magabunda* for soprano and orchestra (1983) have enormous dramatic impact because the colors are used so masterfully. George Crumb's wondrous explorations of timbre have found their way into *Starchild* (for soprano, children's chorus, and orchestra) of 1977 and *A Haunted Landscape* (1984).

For the US Bicentennial the NEA helped to document the state of American orchestral music by providing funds for a dozen orchestras to commission works: Leslie Bassett's *Echoes from an Invisible World*, Cage's *Renga* and *Apartment House, 1776*, Carter's *A Symphony of Three Orchestras*, Colgrass's *Theater of the Universe*, Del Tredici's *Final Alice*, Druckman's *Mirage*, Morton Gould's Symphony of Spirituals, Rochberg's Violin Concerto, Rorem's *Air Music*, Loren Rush's *Song and Dance*, Schuller's Concerto for Orchestra no.2, and Subotnick's *Before the Butterfly*. American orchestral music has at times suffered from a lack of repeated hearings. To address that problem this program called for each orchestra to perform not only the composition it had commissioned but others of the Bicentennial pieces. The result was widespread dissemination and, perhaps more important, a number of interpretations of works containing an impressive range of styles. The performance of American orchestral music of many styles and periods has been a goal of the American Composers Orchestra, founded in 1977.

The NEA was also active, with the Rockefeller Foundation, Exxon, and Meet the Composer, in an important program of the early 1980s that appointed John Adams, Druckman, Harbison, William Kraft, Robert X. Rodriguez, and Schwantner composers-in-residence with five leading American orchestras; subsequent participants included Libby Larsen, Stephen Paulus, Wuorinen, Stephen Albert, Tobias Picker, Christopher Rouse, Alvin Singleton, and Joan Tower. Composers, chosen by the orchestras' music directors, worked with the orchestral musicians before composing their commissioned works, and also learned about administrative and economic structures of professional orchestras. Conductors have often repeated the commissioned pieces on their orchestra's tours as well as when they have conducted other orchestras. New-music festivals sponsored by the orchestras have exposed audiences to works by other composers than those in the residency program, and many of the commissioned pieces have been recorded.

Adams effectively extended the minimalist style of composition to encompass the forces of a large symphony orchestra in three scores written for the San Francisco SO: *Harmonium* for chorus and orchestra (1980), *Grand Pianola Music* (1982), and *Harmonielehre* (1984–5; see fig.3). In these he uses a rich, modulating, harmonic vocabulary to maintain the listener's involvement over the length of a composition. (The only other minimalist composer to have made so successful a transfer of this style from small ensemble to orchestra has been Steve Reich, in Variations for wind, strings, and keyboards, 1980; *Tehillim*, 1982; and *The Desert Music*, 1984; the first two, however, are arrangements of pieces originally written for Reich's own group and the latter two rely heavily on their texts for overall structure.) Larsen, one of a growing number of women composers to attain prominence in the 1970s and 1980s (others include Ellen Taaffe Zwilich, who won the Pulitzer Prize in 1983 for her First Symphony, Vivian Fine, Barbara Kolb, and Joan Tower), has striven to write practical, relatively brief works that can easily be learned by an orchestra in the short rehearsal periods available for professional ensembles.

Concepts of orchestral music were expanded in the late 1970s and 1980s by composers not traditionally associated with the medium. Arrangements of film scores by John Williams, Max Steiner, and Franz Waxman are regularly found on Williams's programs with the Boston Pops Orchestra. Glenn Branca's symphonies, with fanciful titles such as *The Peak of the Sacred* (no.2, 1982) and *Describing Planes of an Expanding Hypersphere* (no.5, 1984), are scored for highly amplified electric guitars, brass, and percussion. Frank Zappa's orchestral music, marked by frequent changes of timbre and mood and prominent percussion, is related to his rock compositions, but owes much to Varèse as well.

BIBLIOGRAPHY

F. O. Jones, ed.: *A Handbook of American Music and Musicians* (Canaseraga, NY, 1886/*R*1971)

W. S. B. Mathews, ed.: *A Hundred Years of Music in America* (Chicago, 1889/*R*1970)

H. E. Krehbiel: *The Philharmonic Society of New York* (New York, 1892); ed. in Shanet (1979)

L. C. Madeira: *Annals of Music in Philadelphia and History of the Musical Fund Society from its Organization in 1820 to the Year 1858* (Philadelphia, 1896/*R*1973)

O. G. T. Sonneck: *Early Concert-life in America (1731–1800)* (Leipzig, 1907/*R*1978)

M. A. D. Howe: *The Boston Symphony Orchestra: an Historical Sketch* (Boston, 1914, rev. and enlarged 2/1931/*R*1978)

J. G. Huneker: *The Philharmonic Society of New York and its 75th Anniversary* (New York, ?1917); ed. in Shanet (1979)

H. C. Lahee: *Annals of Music in America* (Boston, 1922/*R*1969)

P. A. Otis: *The Chicago Symphony Orchestra* (Chicago, 1925/*R*1972)

A. G. Rau and H. T. David: *A Catalogue of Music by American Moravians, 1742–1842* (Bethlehem, PA, 1938/*R*1970)

List of American Orchestral Works Recommended by WPA Music Project Conductors (Washington, DC, 1941)

J. Erskine: *The Philharmonic-Symphony Society of New York: its First Hundred Years* (New York, 1943); ed. in Shanet (1979)

H. Leichtentritt: *Serge Koussevitzky, the Boston Symphony Orchestra and the New American Music* (Cambridge, MA, 1946/*R*1978)

M. Smith: *Koussevitzky* (New York, 1947)

P. J. Korn: "The Symphony in America," *The Symphony*, ii, ed. R. Simpson (Harmondsworth, England, 1967), 243

R. C. Marsh: *The Cleveland Orchestra* (Cleveland, 1967)

R. S. Hines, ed.: *The Orchestral Composer's Point of View: Essays on Twentieth-century Music by Those who Wrote it* (Norman, OK, 1970)

American Composers' Concerts, and Festivals of American Music, 1925–1971: Cumulative Repertoire (Rochester, 1972)

3. *Page from the autograph score of John Adams's "Harmonielehre," completed in 1985*

K. Krueger, ed.: *The Musical Heritage of the United States: the Unknown Portion* (New York, 1973)
H. Shanet: *Philharmonic: a History of New York's Orchestra* (Garden City, NY, 1975)
H. E. Johnson: *First Performances in America to 1900: Works with Orchestra* (Detroit, 1979)
H. Shanet, ed.: *Early Histories of the New York Philharmonic* (New York, 1979) [annotated edn of Krehbiel, 1892; Huneker, ?1917; Erskine, 1943]
K. M. Famera: *Catalog of the American Music Center Library*, iii: *Music for Orchestra, Band and Large Ensemble* (New York, 1982)
J. Rockwell: *All American Music: Composition in the Late Twentieth Century* (New York, 1983)

RODNEY H. MILL (1–3, 3 with SUSAN FEDER)
SUSAN FEDER (4–5)

Orchestras. The word "orchestra" is used here to denote an organized ensemble of bowed strings with more than one player to a part, combined with any number of wind, brass, and percussion instruments. This article is concerned with the development of orchestras in the USA; detailed information about specific orchestras and related societies and instrumental groups can be found in the articles on the cities in which they are based.

1. To 1800. 2. 19th century. 3. 20th century. 4. List of orchestras.

1. To 1800. The American colonists derived their cultural institutions from European models, but being preoccupied in their early years with the material problems of establishing their economy and society, and lacking the aristocratic establishments of the Old World, they did not produce in the 17th century any large and permanent instrumental ensembles of the kind that flourished at the royal courts of France and England. Some of the settlers, moreover, particularly in parts of Massachusetts and Pennsylvania, had purposefully chosen, for religious and moral reasons, to leave behind the rich social and musical life of Europe in order to set up an austere society in the New World. Considering these conditions, the young cities of America may be regarded as having progressed rapidly in the development of orchestras. The semipublic concerts presented in London before 1700 could hardly have been organized successfully in New York, Boston, and Philadelphia at the same date, because the populations of these new towns were still small; a century later, however, when their populations had grown to tens of thousands, these cities could profitably adapt the musical institutions of Europe to American circumstances.

From the early 1730s press announcements of concerts of instrumental and vocal music appeared in such cities as Boston, New York, and Charleston. When the number of available professional musicians (often singers and instrumentalists from resident or traveling theater companies) was insufficient to make up a large ensemble, talented amateurs were recruited to join them. Although there were no opera houses, theater in colonial America was essentially musical theater from the start – even ordinary plays were expected to have overtures and incidental music – and by the 1760s the small pit orchestras that played in all theaters constituted a pool of talent for concert performances. After the Revolution, as the economy of the new country stabilized, professional musicians from Europe were attracted by the opportunities it offered; many settled here and helped in the training of native musicians and the establishment of musical institutions. The French Revolution and upheavals in Haiti caused another wave of immigration, which brought more professional musicians and gentlemen amateurs to the USA (including the great gastronomist Brillat-Savarin, who played in the orchestra of the John Street Theatre in New York in the 1790s).

Long before 1800 many American cities had formed musical societies for the reading and performing of vocal and instrumental music, and the resulting ensembles of professionals and amateurs were often of orchestral size. Philadelphia had an Orpheus Club in 1759, Charleston's St. Cecilia Society was founded in 1762, and in Boston the Music Society was active by 1786 and the Philharmonic Society by 1799. As for New York, its roster of organizations was astonishing for a city that, even at the end of the century, had fewer than 60,000 inhabitants: as early as 1744 there is mention of a concert by the Musick Club, in 1773 a concert was given by the Harmonic Society, and between 1789 and 1799 frequent reports appeared of presentations by the Musical Society of the City of New York, the Haydn Society, the Columbian Anacreontic Society, the Uranian Musical Society, the Calliopean Society, the Polyhymnian Society, the Euterpean Society, the Harmonical Society (distinct from the earlier Harmonic Society), and the St. Cecilia Society. In 1799 the last two named combined to form New York's first Philharmonic Society.

2. 19th century.

(i) To 1830. The Philharmonic Society of New York, which began its operations only a few days before the beginning of the 19th century, can serve to illustrate the stage of development American orchestras reached in the early years of the century. The society was democratic in its government, with a constitution and bylaws that provided for elected officers. It engaged a professional "leader" (principal violinist) on an annual salary, and certain other professionals as needed, but its members were required to pay dues. It gave three kinds of performance: the so-called "weekly concerts," which were restricted to the members themselves and were apparently more like readings than like concerts in the modern sense; the last of these in every month, called the "monthly concert," which was semipublic in that each member received three or more tickets to admit the ladies of his family; and the "annual concert," which was public in that some tickets were sold to outsiders, the proceeds being sometimes given to charity. The society had the honor of participating in the New York funeral ceremonies for George Washington on 31 December 1799, and for as long as it was active (until about 1816) claimed to offer "Vocal and Instrumental Music by the most celebrated performers in the City." Its programs were very much like those heard in London at that time and not very different from what was played in Paris or Vienna. There were concertos, overtures, minuets, and sinfonias by such composers as Haydn, Ignace Pleyel, Adalbert Gyrowetz, Paul Wranitzky, Daniel Steibelt, and Rodolphe Kreutzer, as well as vocal pieces, usually by English or local American composers. Annual and monthly concerts were sometimes followed by a ball.

A second New York Philharmonic Society was founded in 1824 and illustrates the social and artistic changes that had taken place in a quarter of a century in what had become the most dynamic city in the USA. Nurtured by wealthy and socially prominent laymen, who as governors of the society ran all of its affairs with a benevolent paternalism towards the musicians, it had several forward-looking projects. In order to induce professional musicians to commit themselves to the society's work, the constitution and bylaws provided an insurance system that guaranteed substantial payments to a musician's widow and heirs on his death. To encourage American composers, of whom the young country now had hopes, cash prizes were awarded for works in categories ranging from songs and glees to concertos and symphonies, and monthly meetings were established for reading the pieces submitted and giving amateurs experience in performance. Before most other musical societies of its time, the Philharmonic appointed a permanent professional conductor for the whole season (the London Philharmonic, by contrast, named a leader and a conductor for each concert until 1846). Programs favored music of the preceding 25 years by such composers as Rossini, E.-N. Méhul, Adrien Boieldieu, and Beethoven, and they were modeled on the contemporary European style of program construction in which orchestral and operatic selections alternated with solo and chamber pieces. When the Italian opera company of Manuel García, with his sensationally successful young daughter Maria (later Malibran), took New York by storm, the Philharmonic Society several times presented them under its patronage. The excellent 25-piece orchestra of New York musicians employed for the García opera performances was directed by D.-G. Etienne, the conductor of the Philharmonic, and many of the other players were subscribing members of the society.

Despite its excellent organization and ambitious plans, however, the second New York Philharmonic Society lasted only three years, for it could not compete with such glamorous importations as García's company or the French opera and ballet, all of which attracted the fashionable public from 1825 onwards.

(ii) Theater and concert orchestras. In the second quarter of the century the taste of the wealthy and well-educated classes of the older cities shifted increasingly towards foreign art, while English and American vocal music and theater retained favor with the broad popular audience, especially in the newer communities of what was then considered the West. At the same time New York and other large cities were beginning to develop the corps of experienced players required for the 19th-century orchestral repertory, and the musical theater, which had contributed to the demise of the second New York Philharmonic Society, became an ally of orchestral societies in that it schooled musicians who then staffed symphony orchestras.

During the first half of the century, in fact, there was no sharp distinction between theater and concert performers: theater orchestras and companies provided musicians with employment and thereby maintained a supply of performers for the city's concert life; concert activities gave the instrumentalists and singers of the theater staffs additional income and performing experience. The pit orchestras, though fairly permanent, tended to be small, not because of a shortage of musicians but because space and money were seldom available for a larger ensemble, which might anyway cause problems of acoustics and balance with the singers. From the 1790s to the 1830s a group of 18 or 20 players was considered a reasonable size for a theater orchestra. They were required to play not only appropriate supporting music for the dramatic action in every play, but often overtures and other instrumental pieces between the two or more plays presented. Certain overtures of Rossini, Mozart, and Weber were so often played in New York around 1830 that the press complained of the repetition; the players, meanwhile, were gaining experience in such concert literature.

For concerts involving orchestra, one of the recurrent formulae used in advertising was that the orchestra would "embrace all the talent in the city." Musical societies and enterprising individuals assembled ad hoc orchestras, comprising freelance professionals and accomplished amateurs. In the 1830s an orchestra of 35 players was considered a sizable one in both Europe and the USA (Mendelssohn used about that number in his world-famous Gewandhaus Orchestra in Leipzig after 1835), yet larger ones were not uncommon in New York (as at a Musical Fund concert using 38 professionals and a Sacred Music Society performance of Handel's *Messiah* with an orchestra of 42 and a chorus of 135, both in 1834, and the 40th anniversary concert of the Euterpean Society in 1839, played by a well-balanced orchestra of at least 40 musicians).

New York, followed closely by several other American cities, compared favorably with all but the greatest of the old European centers, not only in the size and balance of its orchestras but in their artistic quality and the general healthiness of the musical milieu. When U. C. Hill, later one of the principal founders of the third New York Philharmonic Society, visited Germany in 1835, he noted in his diary that some of the players in Spohr's orchestra in Kassel were not up to New York standards. Similarly, when the Bohemian-American composer A. P. Heinrich had a composition performed in Graz in 1836 by the orchestra of the Styrian Music Society under a distinguished conductor, he reported not only that the number of players in some sections was disappointingly small, but that many who played in the rehearsals were different from those who performed at the concert. Yet only three years later it was possible in New York for Heinrich's colleagues to assemble a skillful and balanced orchestra of 60 musicians for powerful performances of music by Weber and Beethoven, and in 1842 Heinrich himself could present there an orchestra of about 80, a full chorus, and vocal and instrumental soloists in a music festival centering on his own compositions.

(iii) The permanent establishment of the New York Philharmonic Society. By this time, New York was economically, socially, and

1. Interior of the Park Theatre, New York, November 1822, showing the pit orchestra: watercolor by John Searle in the New-York Historical Society

artistically ready to support a permanent and professional symphony orchestra. The community was large and wealthy enough to provide an audience to fill concert rooms of considerable size, and there were finally enough professional musicians with the practical and political experience to staff and run a full and balanced orchestra. The subscription system guaranteed the orchestra a broad and stable financial base and assured the subscribers a degree of respectability that was lacking in the theaters (where, as in England, space was usually set aside for prostitutes). By the 1840s the concert-going public was thoroughly familiar with many of the great works of European musical culture, and could appreciate the difference a large and efficient orchestra could make in presenting them.

New York was ahead of other American cities, and of all but a few European ones, in the convergence of the conditions necessary for the establishment of a permanent orchestra. That New York launched its Philharmonic concerts in the same year as Vienna – 1842 – shows that the social, economic, and cultural requirements for the presentation of symphonic music had reached equal readiness in both places. Indeed conditions in New York were apparently more favorable since the Viennese orchestra collapsed twice between 1850 and 1860, while the young New York orchestra continued to grow. Boston, like Berlin, did not succeed in establishing its permanent professional orchestra until amost 40 years later, and Philadelphia, like Warsaw, Copenhagen, Prague, and Stockholm, could not do so until almost 20 years after that.

In the middle of the century the New York Philharmonic stood as a model for other city orchestras, although none achieved the same degree of permanency. It was founded as a cooperative society, whose members shared in the profits of each season. The constitution specified the size of the orchestra (at least 53 players) and even the proportions of the sections. In the first year there were three concerts, then four each year until 1858, and by the end of the century eight pairs of concerts were given every season (at a transitional stage each pair consisted of a "public rehearsal" followed next day by an official concert). As the repertory expanded to include large-scale Romantic works, the size of the orchestra was increased to about 100 players. The conductors were elected democratically; at first several were chosen from the society's members for each concert, then one conductor for one or more concerts in a season, and eventually a conductor for one or more whole seasons. Under Theodor Eisfeld and Carl Bergmann the Philharmonic became a disciplined professional orchestra in the best German tradition, and under Theodore Thomas and Anton Seidl it became one of the great orchestras of the world, an orchestra that Ysaÿe and Busoni were glad to play with and one for which Dvořák was glad to write. In the last quarter of the 19th century, however, despite the successful operations of Thomas and Seidl, it began to appear that changing economic and social conditions were causing strains in the Philharmonic's structure as a cooperative, and by the end of the century it was clear that a reorganization was required. In 1878, when Leopold Damrosch founded the New York Symphony Society, a rival to the Philharmonic, he tried to finance it by means of guarantees from a number of wealthy men; his son Walter succeeded in making such a plan work at a later date.

(iv) Foreign influences and touring orchestras. The association in the USA of "cultivated" musical taste with European art music was reinforced by continuing waves of immigration, first in the 1830s because of hard times in Europe and again after 1848 as a consequence of the political revolutions there. The new immigrants brought their cultural heritage with them, and the Germans and Austrians in particular arrived at a time when their orchestral and operatic music was aesthetically and artistically dominant. Unlike the visiting virtuoso performers from abroad, who dazzled provincial American audiences briefly and then moved on, German immigrants came to constitute entire segments of the population and settled in their new homes with their own materials and methods of music education, repertory, performance practice, social and cultural institutions, and artistic ideals.

Within the sphere of German influence, a special contribution was made by the Germania Musical Society, a touring orchestra of 25 well-trained young German musicians, dedicated to the propagation of the German and Austrian repertory from Haydn to Mendelssohn and early Wagner; the group came to the USA in 1848 and gave hundreds of efficiently played concerts over the next six years. Many of its members continued to be active as performers, conductors, and teachers for years afterwards in the American cities where they settled. Outside the German tradition, a strong impression was made by the visit of the French conductor and showman Louis Jullien, who came here in 1853–4 with 40 brilliant European players, to whom he added 60 of the best American musicians to form the largest and most dazzling professional orchestra that had ever been heard in the USA. Fashionable musical tastes had already become so refined by this time that Jullien's inclusion of Stephen Foster's *Old Folks at Home* in a concert program was likened by one journalist to "picking up an applecore in the street."

A somewhat later stimulus came from Theodore Thomas, who, with his touring orchestra, did much to prepare the ground for the cultivation of symphonic music in this country. Beginning in 1869, Thomas and his orchestra traveled indefatigably for two decades throughout the USA, presenting thousands upon thousands of performances and creating interest in the establishment of local symphony orchestras in many of the cities they visited. A man of musical talent, high standards, persistence, missionary zeal, and tactical acumen, Thomas may sometimes have provided more competition than the local musicians could meet, but in the long run – and in any case, when the Thomas Orchestra stopped touring after 1888 – many American communities found that he had defined orchestral music for them and left a clearly marked path for their own musicians to follow. For better or worse he had also trained audiences all over the USA to identify "good music" principally with the serious and elevated examples of the German and Austrian repertory (light or popular music he pronounced to have "more or less devil in it").

(v) Boston. The example of the New York Philharmonic and the visits of the Germania and Thomas orchestras all had their effects on the musical life of Boston, though the city already had a long history of orchestral experience. As early as 1799 there is mention of a Philharmonic Society of Boston, and when Gottlieb Graupner, who had played in Haydn's London concerts, settled in Boston, he led a Philo-Harmonic Society from about 1809 to 1826 in programs that were similar in some respects to those of New York's first Philharmonic Society; in 1815 he also helped to establish the Handel and Haydn Society. Before the Germania Musical Society came to Boston in 1849 the orchestras of the Boston Musical Fund Society and Lowell Mason's Academy of Music had introduced the first eight Beethoven symphonies to

the city. Carl Zerrahn, who had come to Boston as a flutist with the Germania, remained to lead the Handel and Haydn Society for 42 years, conducting as well another Boston Philharmonic Orchestra from 1855 to 1863 and the Harvard Music Association's semiprofessional orchestra from 1865 to 1882.

By 1881, however, when Boston was ready to establish its own permanent and fully professional symphony orchestra, the organizational models it had in the New York Philharmonic, with its failing cooperative structure, and the Thomas Orchestra, with its exhausting schedule of tours and concert enterprises, were both outmoded. Instead, in an age of wealthy American philanthropists, the Boston SO was created with the backing of a single benefactor, the banker Henry Lee Higginson, who undertook to defray most of the orchestra's costs so that it could give "the best music in the best way to all who could pay a small price"; at a time when the venerable New York Philharmonic was able to mount only six pairs of concerts per season, the subsidized Boston SO was able to offer 24 pairs. Although the German population of Boston was not as large as that of some other American cities, there were strong German leanings in the city's intellectual circles, and Higginson, who controlled his orchestra's musical policies, chose the many-talented German singer Georg Henschel (later Sir George Henschel) as the orchestra's first conductor, and engaged musicians mostly of German background for the 68 orchestra positions. For the rest of the century the orchestra's musical leadership remained in the hands of the well-known German and Austro-Hungarian conductors Wilhelm Gericke, Arthur Nikisch, and Emil Paur.

(vi) The Midwest. In a number of cities, particularly those in what is now the Midwest, which unlike Boston and New York had been settled so recently that they really had no 18th-century history, a typical pattern emerged. The German immigrants of the 1830s and 1840s generally established in a city one or more male choruses (frequently under the name "Liederkranz," or "Arion," or simply "Männerchor" or "Musikverein"); once a sufficient level of performance skill had been achieved, the choruses began to want to give public performances with orchestral accompaniment, and often with the addition of women's voices for the great works of the choral literature. Sometimes several cities combined their choruses in grand festivals (Sängerfests) for which they were able to hire either Thomas's traveling orchestra or an orchestra of freelance musicians. When such an orchestra was assembled the opportunity was created to perform works of the orchestral repertory in a grand style. At the same time local musicians, stimulated by the touring orchestras and guided by the examples of the orchestras in New York and Boston, tried to give a stable organization to their own orchestral activities, and in many cases it was at such a juncture that a city's symphony orchestra was born. Chicago, Cincinnati, St. Louis, and Cleveland shared some elements of this pattern of development in the 19th century, though each had its idiosyncratic features.

Chicago was incorporated as a village only in 1833, yet so rapidly did it develop that by 1850 the city had established a Philharmonic Society of its own. This orchestra lasted only a short time, as did several subsequent ones, but under the direction of Hans Balatka, a Moravian who had directed a Musikverein in Milwaukee and enjoyed much success in Chicago at the German Sängerfest, the reorganized Philharmonic became a fashionable attraction. It remained so until 1869, when Thomas's first concert in Chicago so outclassed any orchestral performance the city had known that support for the local orchestra fell away. Throughout the 1870s and 1880s, Thomas and his orchestra returned frequently for concerts and festivals, which attracted and consolidated a concert-going public in the city. When it became known around 1890 that Thomas, having already disbanded his private touring orchestra, was also ready to leave the New York Philharmonic for lack of the financial support that he regarded as essential for the maintenance of a "permanent" symphony orchestra of the highest quality, a group of wealthy and public-spirited citizens of Chicago came forward with exactly the kind of assurance he was looking for, and in 1891 offered him the post of conductor and music director of the new Chicago Orchestra.

Cincinnati, settled in 1788 and incorporated as a town in 1802, had a somewhat earlier start than Chicago: there is evidence of a Haydn Society in 1819 and of early orchestras performing

2. *Boston SO in 1915, before traveling to the International Exposition in San Francisco on its first transcontinental tour*

overtures by Handel and Mozart. The immigration of the 1840s, which raised the German population of the city to 30% of the whole, led to the holding in 1849 of a Cincinnati Sängerfest, involving a small orchestra and singing societies from three states, and to the formation of the German Sängerbund of North America. Of the annual Sängerfests that were held thereafter in various cities, those in Cincinnati were so warmly received by the community that in 1870 (when the chorus had reached 2000 members) the merchants of the city found it worthwhile to build a 5000-seat hall expressly for the festival. When Thomas brought his orchestra to Cincinnati on his first tour (1869–70) he found "excellent choral societies . . . and an orchestra superior to that of any city west of New York."

It was a natural development from the mutual sympathy between Thomas and the musical community of Cincinnati that he should be invited to establish a music festival on a regular basis; the first festival used choruses from all over the Midwest and an orchestra made up of the Thomas Orchestra augmented by good local players. In 1872 the local musicians he employed for the festivals were organized into the Cincinnati Orchestra. Six years later, when Thomas accepted an invitation to become music director of the new College of Music, it was expected that a permanent symphony orchestra of the highest quality would be formed for him, but the plan collapsed when Thomas resigned from the college in a dispute (1880); he nevertheless continued to direct the Cincinnati May Festival until the end of his life.

Here, as in Chicago, Thomas's awesome presence may have inhibited the establishment of a permanent orchestra by other conductors, and it was not until 1895 that moves were made to establish the Cincinnati SO by the formation of the Cincinnati Orchestra Association, with Mrs. William Howard Taft as president and the backing of wealthy guarantors. The first permanent conductor of the Cincinnati SO was the American-born but European-trained Frank Van der Stucken, who had already led the Arion Society chorus in New York and introduced American orchestral compositions in France and Germany. A versatile musician of great gifts, Van der Stucken was also the director of the Cincinnati College of Music.

The orchestral history of St. Louis is similar in some respects to that of Cincinnati. Although the city was settled by French Canadians in 1764, it did not become part of the USA until it was acquired in the Louisiana Purchase of 1803, about the same time that Cincinnati was incorporated. The resulting influx of Anglo-Americans led to the production of English ballad operas by 1817 and other operas in English in the 1830s and 1840s. A Philharmonic orchestra and Musical Fund Society were started in 1838, and the Polyhymnia Society consisting of 35 local musicians gave concerts from 1845 to 1852. As in other cities, the influx of German immigrants in the 1830s and 1840s led to the founding of male singing societies; German influence increased thanks to the visits in 1853–4 of the Germania orchestra. And when a new St. Louis Philharmonic Society was founded in 1860, it engaged a German musician of distinguished background, Eduard Sobolewski, as its salaried conductor. This organization lasted for ten years, and it is possible that here, too, the competition of the visiting Thomas Orchestra after 1869, while it elevated orchestral standards, paradoxically delayed the firm establishment of a local symphony orchestra in the city. Finally, in 1890 the St. Louis Choral Symphony Society was formed from the merging of two strong organizations, the Choral Society (founded in 1880 and aided subsequently in its financing by the philanthropist Robert S. Brookings) and the Musical Union (founded 1881). The society divided its performances between choral and orchestral concerts, providing a concert tradition in the city until a permanent symphony orchestra, the St. Louis Symphony Society, was founded in 1907, with Max Zach as its first conductor. (For purposes of historical record, the origins of the St. Louis orchestra can be dated from the Symphony Society in 1907, or the Choral Symphony Society in 1890, or the two parent societies in 1880–81; if the last dates are used, the orchestra becomes the second oldest in the USA.)

In Cleveland, too, it was the German immigrants arriving after 1848 who sparked the attempts to establish an orchestra: in 1852, when the city had only 20,000 inhabitants, a local Germania orchestra was formed, and in 1854 a Caecilian orchestra; two Sängerfests in the 1850s led to the formation of orchestras to play with the choruses; and of course the Thomas Orchestra had Cleveland also on its itinerary. But Cleveland was peculiar in that, more than other cities of its size and resources, it continued to rely heavily on outside orchestras. Although two Americans of German descent and education, George Lehmann and Johann H. Beck, led orchestras in the city in 1886 and 1900, Cleveland entered the 20th century without having a permanent orchestra of its own. A series of concerts using orchestras from other American cities was instituted and in 1902 the Musical Arts Association was incorporated to administer them. It was not until 1918 that, through the special efforts of Adella Prentiss Hughes and the support of the Musical Arts Association, the Cleveland Orchestra was founded and Nicolai Sokoloff appointed as its first conductor.

(vii) Philadelphia and Pittsburgh. Although in Philadelphia and Pittsburgh musical development began at least as early as in the cities of the Midwest, their orchestras did not achieve permanent status until the 20th century. Philadelphia, the largest city in the colonies at the time of the American Revolution, had enjoyed subscription concerts and English operas since the 1750s; around 1800, some excellent English musicians were active in the city's concerts and musical theater offerings, and there were summer garden concerts like those at London's Vauxhall. In the second quarter of the 19th century Philadelphia, like New York, experienced a wave of interest in French and Italian opera, which competed with orchestral concerts for the attention of the fashionable public; nevertheless the Musical Fund Society (founded in 1820) gave notable concerts until the middle of the century. German influence began to be felt in the 1830s (even earlier than in some of the western cities) and again in the 1850s, and a number of singing societies were formed. Carl Lenschow, who had come to the USA as leader of the Germania Musical Society in 1848, established another Germania orchestra in Philadelphia in 1856, which gave concerts until 1895 and was the nearest thing to a city orchestra that Philadelphia could claim up to that time. Thomas gave regular series of concerts in the city until his move to Chicago in 1891, and the opera conductor Gustav Hinrichs tried to found an orchestra just before the end of the century. But all of these efforts fragmented the support of the musicians, the public, and the civic leaders. In 1900, however, two concerts, conducted by the German musician Fritz Scheel, for the benefit of families of American soldiers killed in the Philippines, brought together the necessary supporters and spurred the Musical Fund Society into raising a guarantee fund for a "permanent Philadelphia Orchestra." As the first conductor of the orchestra, Scheel

recruited skilled players from Europe (mostly from Germany) despite the protests of the displaced Philadelphia musicians.

Pittsburgh – further west than Philadelphia – retained in the early 19th century some of its frontier roughness amid the bustle of its river trade, shipbuilding, and manufacturing. Nevertheless, in 1817 it had a theater for which A. P. Heinrich was engaged as music director. Welsh immigrants brought their tradition of singing festivals with them, followed by the Germans somewhat later; the first Sängerfest, with chorus and orchestra, was held in 1858. The Germania Musical Society introduced one of Beethoven's symphonies to Pittsburgh in 1853, a Pittsburgh Orchestral Society was organized not long after, and the Thomas Orchestra played in Pittsburgh on its tours. When the Pittsburgh Orchestra was founded in 1895, it avoided Cleveland's problems and quickly began to function in the modern style of the Boston and Chicago orchestras: adequate financial contributions were raised to engage an orchestra of 70 players, and after two years with a little-known conductor, the management engaged the widely admired composer and cellist Victor Herbert as its conductor. The orchestra gave about 1000 concerts before it suspended operations because of financial difficulties in 1910. Symphonic music was then supplied to Pittsburgh by visiting orchestras until 1926, when the present Pittsburgh SO was established.

3. 20TH CENTURY.

(i) Early decades: changes in organization. By 1900 it had become clear that to run an orchestra as a democratic cooperative (after the model of the New York Philharmonic) was no longer possible. Of the funding methods used by orchestras at the turn of the century, support by a single patron (Boston SO), and finance by public contributions and the fund-raising efforts of a group of guarantor directors (Chicago SO) were those most commonly adopted by the next generation of orchestras, many of which evolved their own variants of one or the other system.

The Minneapolis SO (now the Minnesota Orchestra), founded in 1903, was remarkably successful in adapting Chicago's plan to its local conditions. Although the city's population was only about 200,000, Emil Oberhoffer, conductor of one of the local choral societies, and Elbert L. Carpenter, a civic-minded businessman, obtained sufficient financial resources from the city's commercial and business sectors to establish a professional orchestra of 60 players. With inventive management, the Minneapolis SO between 1907 and 1923 added to its regular concerts such projects as Sunday "pops" concerts, extensive tours, children's concerts, and recordings. By 1914 the orchestra was playing 175 concerts each season, more than double the number being given by the New York Philharmonic.

The New York orchestra itself found that it had to adopt Chicago's method of funding in 1909. Demoralized by their inability to earn a living from the concerts given by the society, many of the Philharmonic members had resigned and others resorted to sending substitutes on occasions when they could secure more lucrative engagements elsewhere in the city. In the 1908–9 season, when there were only 37 true members out of a total of 100 players, a group of public-spirited guarantors led by Mary R. Sheldon assumed control of the Philharmonic Society and, in return for the players' committing their time to the orchestra for the season, assured them their salaries for at least 23 weeks a year (then considered a very satisfactory length for a season); they also engaged Gustav Mahler as the conductor and arranged for the orchestra's first tour outside the city.

San Francisco, too, in 1911, organized an orchestra based on the Chicago model of enlisting a large number of backers. In the reconstruction period after the earthquake of 1906 civic leaders had planned to found a symphony orchestra in conscious emulation of the cities further east. But in 1935 a novel element was added to the financial scheme: the voters of the city approved a special tax to enable the Art Commission to "buy" concerts from the symphony orchestra and then sell them to the public at affordable prices.

The Philharmonic Society
of New York

1910... SIXTY-NINTH SEASON ...1911

Gustav Mahler ... Conductor

MANAGEMENT LOUDON CHARLTON

Carnegie Hall

TUESDAY NIGHT, NOVEMBER FIRST
FRIDAY AFTERNOON, NOVEMBER FOURTH

... Programme ...

BACH (by request) Suite, arranged by Mr. Mahler from the 2nd and 3rd Suites B minor, D major
MR. MAHLER AT THE HARPSICHORD

SCHUBERT - - - Symphony, C major

MOZART - - (*a*) Ballet Music from "Idomeneo" (*b*) Deutsche Tänze

R. STRAUSS - - "Thus Spake Zarathustra"
MR. ARTHUR S. HYDE AT THE ORGAN

Steinway Piano Used

3. Program for a concert given by the New York Philharmonic Society under Gustav Mahler in November 1910

A different form of municipal aid was employed in Baltimore, where in 1914 the Baltimore SO was founded by an appropriation from the city; when the orchestra ran into difficulties in 1942 a plan was introduced along the lines of Mendelssohn's in Leipzig and not unlike Thomas's in Cincinnati, whereby principal players were appointed to the faculty of the local conservatory (the Peabody, in this case). The Baltimore SO continues to receive subsidies from both the city and the state of Maryland, and a large number of American orchestras similarly benefit from some form of municipal, state, or federal funding.

The risk of relying on a single patron for financial subsidy was illustrated in Boston when Higginson died in 1919 without leaving an expected bequest of $1 million. However, he had announced his retirement the previous year, and the transition to a trusteeship had already begun, with steps being taken to widen the basis of the orchestra's support. The Los Angeles PO suffered similar difficulties: when it was founded in 1919 it depended for its financial security on William Andrews Clark, Jr., who left no endowment for it on his death in 1934; fortunately, the necessity for broadening the orchestra's financial backing had in fact been recognized and acted on (by the organizing of the Southern California Symphony Association) before Clark's death.

(ii) Effects of the world wars. With the involvement of the USA in World War I in 1917–18, German and Austrian music, although still the largest component of the repertory of American symphony orchestras, received many fewer performances; conversely, the number of performances of music by Americans and composers of the allied nations increased. Even in the 1920s the prewar proportions of the repertory were not restored. Most American orchestras in the large cities, heavily staffed with German players at the turn of the century, had, even before the war, begun to hire more French, Italian, Russian, and central European musicians, and a modest number of native Americans; this process accelerated somewhat during the war years. As for German conductors, at least two of them were treated as enemy aliens: Ernst Kunwald of the Cincinnati SO and Carl Muck of the Boston SO were both arrested and interned, and Kunwald was eventually deported. The conductor's post in Boston, previously occupied by musicians of German background, was filled first by Frenchmen and then by the Russian émigré Serge Koussevitzky.

The overwhelmingly German aspect of American orchestral life had been considerably altered. In the late 1920s and early 1930s, when Koussevitzky reigned at the Boston SO, Stokowski in Philadelphia, and Toscanini in New York, the eastern cities of the USA had a constellation of orchestras that few countries could match in variety and brilliance. On a less glamorous level, in order to provide work for unemployed musicians during the Depression, the WPA sponsored ensembles that in some cases survived as community or professional orchestras in later years (e.g., the Huntington Chamber Orchestra and the Buffalo PO).

World War II affected the symphonic repertory in 1941–6 even more deeply than the first war had in 1917–18, the amount of German and Austrian music performed by most American orchestras falling to a new low and the proportion of American music climbing to a new high. After the war German and Austrian music recovered some but not all of its former importance, and it seemed unlikely that it would ever again dominate the symphonic repertory as it did before the two world wars.

(iii) After World War II. The musical world was much affected by the great economic, social, and political changes that followed World War II. The wartime economic boom and the considerable redistribution of the nation's wealth gave lower-income groups the means of enjoying some of the cultural commodities that had previously been reserved for the rich, as well as the sense that they were entitled to them. For symphony orchestras there were new publics and new markets, and these were further expanded by radio, television, and recordings.

In 1940 Grant and Hettinger listed 16 "major" orchestras (i.e., with annual budgets of $100,000 or more) and more than 220 lesser orchestras in the USA; in 1951 Mueller counted more than 20 major orchestras, about 60 minor ones with smaller budgets but predominantly professional players, and about 600 community ensembles. As the number and activity of orchestras increased the American Symphony Orchestra League (ASOL), founded in 1942, developed into a coordinating agency for orchestras at all levels. Its figures for its member organizations in 1984–5 showed that there were 800 orchestras in its seven categories (defined principally by annual operating income): 30 major (more than $3,400,000), 39 regional ($950,000–$3,400,000; this total excludes the Kansas City SO, which is not a member of ASOL, but which is listed in §4 below in the regional category), 88 metropolitan ($265,000–$950,000), 86 urban ($125,000–$265,000), 320 community (less than $125,000), 69 college (faculty and students only), and 168 youth (consisting of students not affiliated with a single institution). The league's estimated total of all orchestras in the USA is 1400. (For the names of major and regional orchestras, see §4 below.)

(iv) The modern orchestra. A major, regional, or metropolitan symphony orchestra in the USA is a fully professional body of musicians that provides its members with their major source of income. Unlike many European concert orchestras, it is independent of any opera or theater duties. A principal conductor is generally responsible for its artistic direction, and a lay board of directors determines its overall administrative policies, employing a manager and staff to execute them. In most American cities the symphony orchestra is the principal and most influential institution in the musical culture.

Characteristically, the activities of a major orchestra include subscription concerts (two to four performances of a program each week during the regular season, from about October to May); nonsubscription concerts; summer concerts (sometimes whole summer seasons in special locations; *see* FESTIVALS, §2); educational programs (school and young people's concerts); "pops" concerts; tours (domestic and international); radio and television performances; recordings; and official performances for national, state, or local occasions. The number of concerts given by such orchestras in each season ranges from 175 (Philadelphia Orchestra) to 260 (Boston SO).

Community, college, and youth orchestras provide a number of other services to local areas. Some bring live performances of the standard repertory to places that have no other access to live music. Others serve as a trial platform for talented local performers before they venture into larger centers. College and university orchestras often present new or unusual works that would otherwise be unlikely to be heard.

To finance their varied activities the large orchestras now rely on a combination of earned income (ticket sales and recording and broadcasting fees), endowments, contributions from individuals and businesses, and grants from foundations or from such agencies as the NEA, state arts councils, and municipal governments. In the early years of the century such municipal subsidies as those of Baltimore and San Francisco were exceptional, and orchestra boards feared that artistic independence might be compromised by government subsidy. But as American orchestras have striven, for ideological reasons, to broaden their relations with the public, they have found it appropriate and advisable to seek more of their financial support from government funding and from the contributions of the public rather than from the few members of a board of directors. In connection with financing and administration, it is a remarkable characteristic of many American orchestras that much of the work is done by volunteer women, either as individuals or as committee members; their diverse activities may include selling ticket subscriptions, raising funds, administering educational projects, carrying out promotional campaigns, and providing hospitality. These functions have become so typical that the ASOL has issued a handbook and other printed materials expressly for women's associations connected with symphony orchestras. A higher level of service has been rendered by a number of women who are usually given credit for the organizational leadership of the orchestras of their cities, notably Adella Prentiss Hughes in Cleveland and Leonora Wood Armsby in San Francisco.

Major orchestras mostly have a membership of between 104 and 106 players (some have rather fewer, and the Chicago SO more, with 110). The musicians' union, the American Federation of Musicians, has become increasingly important in defining the working conditions that are stipulated in the contracts of orchestral players (seating order, maximum number of hours of service per week, audition procedures, rest breaks, and the privilege of absences for outside engagements). Fringe benefits such as medical insurance and pensions are now regularly negotiated into contracts. In 1964 the New York PO became the first symphony orchestra in the country to offer its members a 52-week annual contract, and orchestras in the largest cities have since followed suit. Musicians in the major and some regional symphony orchestras are paid at about the level of university professors of comparable rank. The members of most other American orchestras, however, cannot earn from their symphony work an income commensurate with their education and professional standing, and most of them supplement their incomes from other sources. Since World War II ethnic minorities and women have become increasingly well represented in orchestras' memberships. There has also been a marked Americanization of the ranks of orchestral players: the European teachers who settled here just before and after World War II contributed to the training of skilled Americans who have been able to enter the increased number of orchestras. The important role of the thousands of school and college bands and of local jazz and rock bands in attracting young Americans to the study of wind and percussion instruments deserves recognition.

See also AMERICAN SYMPHONY ORCHESTRA LEAGUE; BANDS; EARLY-MUSIC REVIVAL; FESTIVALS; LOUISVILLE ORCHESTRA COMMISSIONING PROJECT; ORCHESTRAL MUSIC; UNIONS, MUSICIANS'; WOMEN IN MUSIC.

4. LIST OF ORCHESTRAS.

The following is a list, in chronological order by date of founding, of the major orchestras (annual operating income over $3,400,000) in the USA in 1984–5. Name, date of founding, first conductor, residence, and summer activities (including summer residence, festivals, or other summer affiliations) are listed. It should be noted that in some cases information given here (particularly dates) is based on data that are open to question or differences of interpretation; further details may be found in the articles on the cities in which the ensembles are resident.

New York PO, 1842, U. C. Hill (with D.-G. Etienne and H. C. Timm); Avery Fisher Hall at Lincoln Center for the Performing Arts; Free Parks Concerts

Boston SO, 1881, Georg(e) Henschel; Symphony Hall; Berkshire Music Festival (from 1985 Tanglewood) in Lenox, MA

Chicago SO, 1891, Theodore Thomas; Orchestra Hall; Ravinia Festival

Cincinnati SO, 1895, Frank Van der Stucken (from 1896); Music Hall; summer home at River Bend Music Center nr Cincinnati, and performances with the Cincinnati Opera

Oregon SO (formerly Portland SO), 1896, Carl Denton; Arlene Schnitzer Concert Hall at the Portland Center for the Performing Arts

Philadelphia Orchestra, 1900, Fritz Scheel; Academy of Music; Mann Music Center (formerly Robin Hood Dell Concerts) in Fairmount Park, and Saratoga Festival in Saratoga Springs, NY

San Diego SO, 1902, R. E. Tragnitz; Civic Theatre; San Diego Pops series

Minnesota Orchestra (formerly Minneapolis SO), 1903, Emil Oberhoffer; Orchestra Hall in Minneapolis and I. A. O'Shaughnessy Auditorium in St. Paul; Viennese Sommerfest, Symphony for the Cities, and (from 1985) Ordway Music Theatre in St. Paul

Seattle SO, 1903, Harry F. West; Seattle Center Opera House

St. Louis SO, 1907, Max Zach; Powell Symphony Hall; St. Louis County Pops at Queeny Park

Dallas SO, 1911, Carl Venth; Music Hall at Fair Park; Starfest "pops" concerts and classical series

San Francisco SO, 1911, Henry Hadley; Louise M. Davies Symphony Hall; Beethoven Festival, and Arts Commission–San Francisco Symphony Pops

Houston SO, 1913, Julian Paul Blitz; Jesse H. Jones Hall; Houston Symphony Summer Festival

Baltimore SO, 1914, Gustav Strube; Joseph Meyerhoff Symphony Hall; summer concert series at Symphony Hall and Oregon Ridge Park in Baltimore County

Detroit SO, 1914, Ossip Gabrilowitsch (from 1919); Ford Auditorium; Meadow Brook Music Festival in Rochester, MI

Cleveland Orchestra, 1918, Nicolai Sokoloff; Severance Hall; Blossom Music Center in Cuyahoga Falls, OH

Los Angeles PO, 1919, Walter Henry Rothwell; Dorothy Chandler Pavilion at the Los Angeles County Music Center; Hollywood Bowl Summer Festival

Rochester PO, 1923, Eugene Goossens; Eastman Theatre; Finger Lakes Music Festival in Canandaigua, NY

Syracuse SO, 1924; Crouse-Hinds Concert Theater in the Onondaga County Civic Center

Pittsburgh SO, 1926, Antonio Modarelli (from 1927); Heinz Hall for the Performing Arts; Junefest series, and Symphony at the Point free park concerts

Indianapolis SO, 1930, Ferdinand Schaeffer; Circle Theatre; Symphony on the Prairie at Conner Prairie Pioneer Settlement nr Noblesville, IN

National SO, 1931, Hans Kindler; Concert Hall at the John F. Kennedy Center for the Performing Arts in Washington, DC; concerts at the Kennedy Center and at Wolf Trap Farm Park

Denver SO, 1934, Horace E. Tureman; Boettcher Concert Hall; Rocky Mountain Music Festival at various locations

Buffalo PO, 1935, Franco Autori; Kleinhans Music Hall

New Orleans Philharmonic SO, 1936, Arthur Zack; Orpheum Theater

San Antonio SO, 1939, Max Reiter; Lila Cockrell Theatre for the Performing Arts and Laurie Auditorium at Trinity U.; Summer Concert Series (various quartets of orchestra members)

Utah SO, 1946, Maurice Abravanel (from 1947); Symphony Hall in Salt Lake City; Summer Pops Series in Symphony Hall and at Snowbird Ski Resort nr Salt Lake

Atlanta SO, 1947, Henry Sopkin; Symphony Hall at Robert W. Woodruff Arts Center; Summer Pops Series

Milwaukee SO, 1958, Harry John Brown; Uihlein Hall at the Milwaukee County Performing Arts Center; summer concerts at Milwaukee County Zoo, and free park concerts

St. Paul Chamber Orchestra, 1959, Leopold Sipe; I. A. O'Shaughnessy Auditorium

The following is a list of regional orchestras (annual operating income $950,000–$3,400,000) in the USA in 1984–5.

Alabama SO (Birmingham), American SO (New York), Austin SO, Charlotte (NC) SO, Colorado Springs SO, Columbus (OH) SO, Dayton (OH) PO, Florida Orchestra (formerly Florida Gulf Coast SO) (Tampa), Florida SO (Orlando), Florida PO (Fort Lauderdale), Fort Worth SO, Grand Rapids (MI) SO, Hartford SO, Honolulu SO, Jacksonville SO, Kansas City SO, Long Beach (CA) SO, Long Island PO, Los Angeles Chamber Orchestra, Louisville Orchestra, Memphis SO, Nashville SO, New Haven SO, New Jersey SO (Newark), New Mexico SO (formerly Albuquerque SO) (Albuquerque), North Carolina SO (Raleigh), Oakland (CA) SO, Oklahoma SO (formerly Oklahoma City SO) (Oklahoma City), Omaha SO, Phoenix SO, Puerto Rico SO (San Juan), Richmond (VA) SO, Sacramento (CA) SO, San Jose (CA) SO, Spokane (WA) SO, Springfield (MA) SO, Toledo (OH) SO, Tulsa (OK) PO, Virginia Symphony (formerly Virginia Orchestra Group) (Norfolk), Wichita SO

BIBLIOGRAPHY

Constitution and Bye-laws of the Philharmonic Society, as Amended 3d December, 1801, ed. Philharmonic Society of New-York (New York, 1801)

"German Music," *The Euterpeiad: an Album of Music, Poetry & Prose*, i (1830), 25

Charter and By-laws, ed. New-York Sacred Music Society (New York, 1833)

"On the Evidences of Musical Taste," *American Musical Journal*, i (1834–5), 16

M. Maretzek: *Crotchets and Quavers* (New York, 1855/*R*1968)

Constitution and By-laws of the Philadelphia Philharmonic Society, ed. Philadelphia Philharmonic Society (Philadelphia, 1869)

J. Offenbach: *Offenbach en Amérique: notes d'un musicien en voyage* (Paris, 1877, 2/1877; Eng. trans. as *Orpheus in America*, Bloomington, IN, 1957)

M. Goldstein: "Der Stand der öffentlichen Musikpflege in den Vereinigten Staaten von Nord-Amerika," *Sammlung musikalischer Vorträge*, ii (Leipzig, 1880), 107–38
H. E. Krehbiel: *The Philharmonic Society of New York: a Memorial Published on the Occasion of the Fiftieth Anniversary of the Founding of the Philharmonic Society* (New York, 1892) [in Shanet, 1979]
L. C. Madeira: *Annals of Music in Philadelphia and History of the Musical Fund Society from its Organization in 1820 to the Year 1858* (Philadelphia, 1896/*R*1973)
T. Ryan: *Recollections of an Old Musician* (New York, 1899/*R*1979)
A. Laser: "Die Geschichte der Philharmonischen Gesellschaft von New-York," *Die Musik*, ii/19 (1903), 19
Arion, New York, von 1854 bis 1904, ed. Arion Society, New York (New York, 1904) [incl. G. von Skal: "Historical Sketch," 5–35]
T. Thomas: *Theodore Thomas: a Musical Autobiography*, ed. G. P. Upton (Chicago, 1905/*R*1964)
O. G. T. Sonneck: *Early Concert-life in America (1731–1800)* (Leipzig, 1907/*R*1978)
The Musical Fund Society of Philadelphia, ed. Musical Fund Society of Philadelphia (Philadelphia, 1910)
R. F. Thomas: *Memoirs of Theodore Thomas* (New York, 1911/*R*1971)
O. G. T. Sonneck: *A Survey of Music in America, Read before the "Schola Cantorum," at New York City, April 11, 1913* (Washington, DC, 1913)
M. A. D. Howe: *The Boston Symphony Orchestra: an Historical Sketch* (Boston, 1914, rev. and enlarged 2/1931/*R*1978)
H. B. Baerman: "American Symphony Orchestras," *Musical Courier*, lxx/6 (1915), 23
J. G. Huneker: *The Philharmonic Society of New York* (New York, ?1917) [in Shanet, 1979]
W. Damrosch: *My Musical Life* (New York, 1923/*R*1972, rev. 2/1930)
P. I. Tchaikovsky: Dnevniki [Diaries] (Moscow, 1923; Eng. trans. by W. Lakond, New York, 1945)
G. C. D. Odell: *Annals of the New York Stage* (New York, 1927–49/*R*1970)
C. E. Russell: *The American Orchestra and Theodore Thomas* (New York, 1927/*R*1971)
J. T. Howard: *Our American Music: Three Hundred Years of It* (New York, 1931, rev. 4/1965)
A. Lourié: *Sergei Koussevitzky and his Epoch*, trans. S. W. Pring (New York, 1931/*R*1979) [orig. version in Russian]
Repertoire 1878–1928 (MS, 1934, *NN-L* 32A) [works performed by the New York Symphony Society]
"Symphony Finance," *Fortune*, xi/3 (1935), 78
R. F. Eyer: "America's Notable Orchestras," *MusAm*, lvi–lviii (1936–8) [series of articles: New York PO, Boston SO, Philadelphia Orchestra, Chicago SO, Cleveland Orchestra, St. Louis SO, Detroit SO, National SO, San Francisco SO, Rochester PO, Los Angeles PO, Minneapolis SO]
W. T. Upton: *Anthony Philip Heinrich: a Nineteenth-century Composer in America* (New York, 1939/*R*1967)
M. Grant and H. S. Hettinger: *America's Symphony Orchestras* (New York, 1940)
J. Erskine: *The Philharmonic-Symphony Society of New York: its First Hundred Years* (New York, 1943) [in Shanet, 1979]
H. E. Johnson: *Musical Interludes in Boston, 1795–1830* (New York, 1943/*R*1967)
H. Leichtentritt: *Serge Koussevitzky, the Boston Symphony Orchestra and the New American Music* (Cambrige, MA, 1946/*R*1978)
W. Sargeant: *Geniuses, Goddesses, and People* (New York, 1949)
A. Judson: "American Orchestras," *MusAm*, lxxi/3 (1951), 8
J. H. Mueller: *The American Symphony Orchestra: a Social History of Musical Taste* (Bloomington, IN, 1951)
A. Nevins and M. H. Thomas, eds.: *The Diary of George Templeton Strong* (New York, 1952/*R*1974)
H. E. Johnson: "The Germania Musical Society," *MQ*, xxxix (1953), 75
W. T. Upton: *William Henry Fry: American Journalist and Composer-Critic* (New York, 1954/*R*1974)
G. Chase: *America's Music* (New York, 1955, rev. 2/1966/*R*1981)
BMI Orchestral Program Surveys [1959–60 to 1969–70] (New York, 1960–71)
H. M. Thompson: "The American Symphony Orchestra," *One Hundred Years of Music in America*, ed. P. H. Lang (New York, 1961), 36
——: *Economic Conditions of Symphony Orchestras and their Musicians* (Charleston, WV, 1961)
J. Mates: *The American Musical Stage before 1800* (New Brunswick, NJ, 1962)
H. M. Thompson: *Handbook for Symphony Orchestra Women's Associations* (Vienna, VA, 1963)
I. Lowens: *Music and Musicians in Early America* (New York, 1964)
W. J. Baumol and W. G. Bowen: *Performing Arts – the Economic Dilemma: a Study of Problems Common to Theater, Opera, Music, and Dance* (New York, 1966)
H. A. Kmen: *Music in New Orleans: the Formative Years, 1791–1841* (Baton Rouge, LA, 1966)
R. C. Marsh: *The Cleveland Orchestra* (Cleveland, 1967)
H. W. Hitchcock: *Music in the United States: a Historical Introduction* (Englewood Cliffs, NJ, 1969, rev. 2/1974)
H. Kupferberg: *Those Fabulous Philadelphians: the Life and Times of a Great Orchestra* (New York, 1969)
McKinsey and Company: *The Need for Concerted Action: Memorandum to the Presidents of the Boston Symphony Orchestra, the Chicago Symphony Orchestra, the Cleveland Orchestra, the New York Philharmonic, the Philadelphia Orchestra* (Cleveland, 1969)
A. Ames: "The Silent Spring of our Symphonies," *Saturday Review*, liii (28 Feb 1970), 81
N. Hanks: "Music and Money," *International Musician*, lxviii/12 (1970), 6
H. Taubman: *The Symphony Orchestra Abroad* (Vienna, VA, 1970)
Symphony News is Good News: a Publicity Handbook for Symphony Orchestras and Symphony Women's Associations, ed. American Symphony Orchestra League (Vienna, VA, 1971)
P. Hart: *Orpheus in the New World: the Symphony Orchestra as an American Cultural Institution* (New York, 1973)
K. H. Mueller: *Twenty-seven Major Symphony Orchestras: a History and Analysis of their Repertoires* [1842–3 to 1969–70] (Bloomington, IN, 1973)
H. Shanet: *Philharmonic: a History of New York's Orchestra* (Garden City, NY, 1975)
O. E. Albrecht: "Opera in Philadelphia, 1800–1830," *JAMS*, xxxii (1979), 499
H. Shanet, ed.: *Early Histories of the New York Philharmonic* (New York, 1979) [annotated edn of Krehbiel, 1892; Huneker, ?1917; Erskine, 1943]
O. Daniel: *Stokowski: a Counterpoint of View* (New York, 1982)
H. Shanet: "New York Philharmonic: the Tradition of Greatness Continues," *New York Philharmonic 10,000th Concert* (New York, 1982) [program]
J. Mates: "The First Hundred Years of the American Lyric Theater," *American Music*, i/2 (1983), 22
D. Schneider: *The San Francisco Symphony: Music, Maestros, and Musicians* (Novato, CA, 1983)

HOWARD SHANET (1–3, bibliography)

Oregon. Jazz chamber ensemble. Its original members, Paul McCandless (*b* Indiana, PA, 24 March 1947) (oboe, english horn, bass clarinet), Glen Moore (*b* Portland, OR, 28 Oct 1941) (double bass, violin, piano, flute), Ralph Towner (*b* Chehalis, WA, 1 March 1940) (acoustic guitar, piano, french horn, trumpet, flugelhorn), and Collin Walcott (*b* New York, 24 April 1945; *d* Magdeburg, Germany, 8 Nov 1984) (tablā, sitar, clarinet, percussion), all played in the Paul Winter Consort before forming their own group in 1970; Walcott was replaced by Trilok Gurtu. Oregon's eclectic but integrated style combines elements of classical music, modern jazz, and ethnic music, and reveals the influence of composers and musicians as diverse as Dowland, Bach, Stravinsky, Bartók, the serialists, John Coltrane, Bill Evans, and Scott LaFaro. Their sensitive interaction in performance allows them to improvise collectively without assuming rigidly defined roles. Their recordings include pieces based upon complex harmonies, such as *Yellow Bell*, and others based on a drone or totally free improvisation. While the soaring oboe in *Icarus* is characteristic, the fact that the musicians play 60 to 80 different instruments gives the group a wide palette of sounds. Each member of Oregon has also pursued an independent career: Towner has recorded solo albums and continues a fruitful association with the guitarist John Abercrombie; McCandless has produced albums of jazz-influenced performances and woodwind octets; Moore has recorded as a soloist and performs with the saxophonist Jim Pepper; and Walcott played in a "world music" trio, Codona, with Don Cherry and Nana Vasconcelos.

RECORDINGS
(selective list)

Our First Record (1970, Van. 79432); *Together* (1976, Van. 79377); *Friends* (1977,

Van. 79370); *Violin* (1978, Van. 79397); *Out of the Woods* (1978, Elek. 154), incl. Yellow Bell; *Oregon in Performance* (1979, Elek. 304), incl. Icarus; *Oregon* (1983, ECM 1258)

BIBLIOGRAPHY

M. Bourne: "The Natural Timbre of Oregon," *Down Beat*, xli/16 (1974), 14
C. Mitchell: "Ralph Towner: a Chorus of Inner Voices," *Down Beat*, xlii/12 (1975), 16
R. Henschen: "The Musical Worlds Meet in Oregon," *MJ*, xxxvii/2 (1979), 5
M. Zipkin: "Oregon: Out of the Woods, Into the World," *Down Beat*, xlvi/5 (1979), 13
L. Lyons: "Goodbye Oregon," *Musician*, no.29 (1981), 56
S. Larson: *Some Aspects of the Album "Out of the Woods" by the Chamber Ensemble "Oregon"* (thesis, U. of Oregon, 1981)
——: "Yellow Bell and a Jazz Paradigm," *ITO*, vi/2 (1982), 31

STEVE LARSON

Oregon, University of. State university, founded in 1876 in Eugene. It is the oldest of the eight state institutions of higher education. Music was accorded academic status by the regents of the university in 1886 as a professional school; the music program was independent and self-supporting until 1915. The school of music offers courses leading to the degrees of BA and BS in music, BMus, MMus, and DMA; its curricular strengths are in music performance, music education, and composition. In the early 1980s it enrolled about 300 undergraduate majors and 100 graduate students. The present facilities of the school of music were constructed in 1921 and enlarged in 1950 and 1978. They include a 550-seat concert hall (site of an annual summer Bach festival since 1970) that houses one of the largest instruments of the German organ builder Jürgen Ahrend. The main library of the university houses the substantial holdings in music (about 30,000 books and scores), collections of music manuscripts, musical Oregoniana, and 200,000 items of sheet music of the period 1896–1956 (*see also* LIBRARIES AND COLLECTIONS, §3).

DOUGLAS LEEDY

Oregon SO. Orchestra founded (as the Portland SO) in Portland, Oregon, in 1896 (renamed 1967); *see* PORTLAND (ii).

Organ (from Gk. *organon* via Lat. *organum*). A keyboard instrument having one or more manuals and usually a pedal-board, the keys of which operate valves that admit air under pressure (supplied by a wind-raising device) to pipes arranged in one or more scale-like rows. The earliest, simplest organs consisted of one set of pipes, each pipe corresponding to one key of the keyboard. Beginning in the Middle Ages organs could include many sets of pipes of different pitches and tone-colors, and several keyboards. Modern organs are found in all sizes, from one-manual instruments with two or three sets of pipes, to ones with four or more manuals and several thousand pipes.

The first organs in the Americas were brought from Spain to Central America by Franciscan and Dominican missionaries in the mid-16th century. During the 17th century the use of organs – both imported and locally built – was widespread throughout Spanish colonial America; 17 small organs are reported as being in use in 1630 in what is now New Mexico. By the early 18th century many Mexican cathedrals had organs equal to any on the Iberian peninsula, among them the two instruments of 1688 and 1735 extant in Mexico City Cathedral. By the early 19th century small organs were used in most mission outposts, including some in present-day California. In the northern French colonies, there was a church organ at Quebec City as early as 1657, and between 1698 and 1705 a two-manual organ was imported for the Notre Dame Parish Church in Montreal.

1. Up to 1800. 2. The 19th century. 3. The 20th century.

1. UP TO 1800. The first documented use of an organ in a church in the British or German colonies of the eastern seaboard dates from 1703. A small German religious colony had settled near Philadelphia in 1694, apparently bringing with it a small positive organ, and this was lent in 1703 for use at a Lutheran ordination ceremony in the "Old Swede's" Church, Philadelphia. In 1713 a four-stop chamber organ, possibly built by "Father" Smith, active in London from 1667, was placed in King's Chapel, Boston (for illustration *see* BOSTON (i), fig.3); it was mentioned as early as 1708 in connection with its original owner, Thomas Brattle, by the diarist Samuel Sewall, and it may have been imported before 1700.

English organs, including some significant examples of the work of Bridge, Jordan, Green, England, and Snetzler, continued to be imported in increasing numbers to the eastern coastal colonies during the rest of the 18th century. The first person known to have built an organ in the colonies was Johann Gottlob Klemm, a Saxon who immigrated in 1733, and who built several organs, the largest of them a three-manual instrument installed in Trinity Church, New York, in 1739. His work was carried on by his apprentice, DAVID TANNENBERG, who built more than 40 organs between 1758 and his death in 1804, mostly for Moravian churches in a small area of Pennsylvania (see fig. 1). He built his largest instrument, however, for Zion Lutheran Church in Philadelphia. Other German-born builders, notably Philip Feyring, were active around Philadelphia in the late 18th century.

Tannenberg's work reflected the influence of the Silbermann school, as transmitted by Klemm, but he also kept pace with newer European developments and was familiar with the writings

1. One-manual organ by David Tannenberg (1797), now in the Single Brothers' House, Old Salem, North Carolina

of the theorist Georg Andreas Sorge. Following in his footsteps were Conrad Doll and several generations of the Krauss and Dieffenbach families, who, culturally removed from the urban mainstream of East Coast organ building, continued to produce small organs in the "Pennsylvania Dutch" tradition for rural churches well past 1850.

Puritan (Calvinist) objections to the use of instruments in worship prevailed throughout the northern colonies until the last decade of the 18th century, so that most of the early church organs were built for the Anglicans, Lutherans, and Moravians. There is also evidence for a number of domestic chamber organs in this period. Most organs (of all types) were still imported, but after the mid-18th century American builders began to appear in the colonies north of Pennsylvania.

The first true organ builder in Boston was Thomas Johnston, who, beginning about 1753, built a small number of church and chamber organs modeled after imported English instruments. Among his followers were Josiah Leavitt and Henry Pratt, both of whom built several small church and chamber organs, primarily for rural churches west and north of Boston. The prejudice against instruments began to break down in churches of the Puritan tradition by the 1790s, creating a new demand for church organs that was largely met by American builders.

These early New England builders were essentially self-taught and supported themselves only partly through organ building. New York and Philadelphia, however, attracted some English-trained builders during the final years of the 18th century. One of the earliest to arrive was Charles Tawse, who in 1786 advertised himself as a builder of "finger and barrel organs" in New York. He later moved to Philadelphia, where he was joined in 1795 by John Lowe, trained in the workshop of Gray of London. The most notable immigrant, however, was John Geib, who shortly after his arrival in New York around 1798 built several substantial church organs, most of them for New York, although some went to other cities.

2. The 19th century. None of the late 18th-century builders, whether foreign-trained or self-taught, seemed able to found a true "school" in their respective areas. None but Geib had successors (though even Geib's sons soon abandoned organ building for the burgeoning piano trade). Yet in the first decades of the 19th century foundations were laid for two very important and influential centers of organ building in New York and Boston. The founder of the New York school was Thomas Hall, who worked briefly for Lowe in Philadelphia before moving to New York in 1817. He soon secured substantial contracts in both New York and the coastal cities of the South; one of his largest instruments was built in 1820 for the Catholic cathedral of Baltimore. An early apprentice of Hall was his brother-in-law Henry Erben, later briefly his partner, who in 1824 founded the firm that virtually dominated organ building in New York for 60 years.

The founder of the Boston school was William Marcellus Goodrich. Like other early New England builders, he was largely self-taught but had been briefly associated with Leavitt and Pratt as well as the piano maker Crehore. He learned tuning from a French organist, metalworking from a pewterer, and virtually everything else from the study of English organs in Boston and a copy of Bédos de Celles' *L'art du facteur d'orgues* (1766–78). Goodrich began making chamber organs and claviorgana in 1804, and by his death in 1833 had built significant instruments for many churches in Boston and elsewhere as far south as Savannah. His largest instrument was a three-manual organ completed in 1827 for St. Paul's Church, Boston. The next generation of Boston organ builders – Goodrich's brother Ebenezer, Thomas Appleton, George and William Stevens, Josiah H. Ware, and Elias and George Hook (*see* Hook & Hastings) – were all trained in his workshop. Appleton, known for his handsome casework, at first replaced Goodrich as the leading Boston organ builder, but was eventually overtaken by the Hook brothers and his own apprentice, William Benjamin Dearborn Simmons.

For the first half of the 19th century organ building in both New York and Boston was strongly influenced by late 18th- and early 19th-century English work. Specifications were conservative, manual compasses usually began at G''', pedals were of short compass or nonexistent, and until nearly 1850 variants of meantone tuning were in common use. Metal pipework was usually 25% tin; zinc for basses and spotted metal (50% tin) did not come into general use until after 1850. Around the mid-century New York once more saw an influx of immigrant builders. A few, such as George Jardine, remained; others, such as Henry Pilcher and George Kilgen, worked there briefly before seeking their fortunes to the west, but their influence was felt in the New York workshops.

Fewer immigrants settled in Boston, but several influential Boston organists returned from European study in the 1850s and 1860s, bringing new ideas. Boston builders, particularly Simmons and the Hook brothers, studied European publications and experimented with new ideas from abroad. Pedal compasses increased, such stops as the Gamba and Harmonic Flute began to appear in specifications, and in 1859 Simmons experimented with the use of cone-valve wind-chests. Although this sensitive type of action was defeated by the New England climate, another recent European invention, the pneumatic-lever (Barker) action, was found useful in larger organs, and both the Hook firm and Simmons had employed it by 1860. Developments in Boston soon spread to western Massachusetts, where they were adopted by such builders as William Allen Johnson and John W. Steere; their trade was expanding into the northwestern states and included substantial contracts in Buffalo, Chicago, and elsewhere. Organ production increased steadily throughout the second half of the 19th century. Beginning with an instrument by Hook for Tremont Temple, Boston (1853; four manuals, 70 stops), organs began to be installed in concert halls throughout the USA, and organ recitals (in both halls and churches) became popular. The importation of an organ from Walcker of Germany for Boston Music Hall in 1863 was in many ways anticlimactic, yet it introduced novelties such as free reeds and the crescendo mechanism, and brought workmen such as Sturm and Baumgarten to Boston.

Organ building in Philadelphia had stagnated; Standbridge and Corrie were the only builders of any consequence there. In New York, however, Erben, Jardine, J. H. & C. S. Odell, and Hall & Labagh were making important contributions, and in 1869 Hilborne Lewis Roosevelt, a 19-year-old former apprentice of Hall & Labagh, drew attention by exhibiting an organ with a primitive electrically operated action at an industrial fair. With his brother Frank he visited Europe to study the latest developments there, and founded his own company in 1872. Until his death in 1893 he was an uncontested pioneer among the New York builders.

August Pomplitz and Henry Niemann of Baltimore were the only builders of any importance in the South, but during the second half of the 19th century organs were built in new settlements as the frontier advanced. Nearly all the inland builders were immigrants, including M. P. MÖLLER in Hagerstown, Maryland; John Gale Marklove in Utica, New York; and Garrett House in Buffalo. German organ builders were active throughout the USA, beginning with Matthias Schwab and J. H. Koehnken, who were well established in Cincinnati before 1850. Later builders included A. B. Felgemaker in Buffalo, J. G. Pfeffer in St. Louis, William Schuelke in Milwaukee, John Hinners in Pekin, Illinois, G. F. Votteler, Carl Barckhoff, and Philip Wirsching in Ohio, and Joseph Mayer and Felix Schoenstein in California, the last an orchestrion maker who settled in San Francisco in 1877.

New tonal and technical resources continued to be developed in the large eastern factories, and their work reached all parts of the country. Simmons died in 1876 and was followed as one of the leaders of the Boston trade by George S. Hutchings, who had been trained at the firm of Hook (known as HOOK & HASTINGS after 1871). Hutchings and Hook, as well as Roosevelt in New York, were responsible for many of the developments that would shape the 20th-century organ. Farrand & Votey bought the Roosevelt firm in 1893 and merged with Aeolian of Garwood, New Jersey, in 1897; having patented many improvements in organ mechanism, Votey turned increasingly to automatic instruments. Ernest M. Skinner, who had worked in Hutchings's factory, invented the "pitman" type of electro-pneumatic windchest and was a strong proponent of orchestral tonal design. At the turn of the century two influential builders arrived in the USA from England: JOHN TURNELL AUSTIN, who founded an organ company in Hartford on the strength of his unique "universal air chest" designs, and ROBERT HOPE-JONES, who became known as "the father of the theater organ."

3. THE 20TH CENTURY. The early 20th century was a period of great change and much tonal and mechanical experimentation. Electrically controlled key and stop actions superseded all earlier forms, including mechanical and pneumatic-lever ones, and the intermediate types of tubular-pneumatic action successfully developed by Steere, ESTEY, and Kimball. Transcriptions of orchestral works and compositions in the orchestral style assumed great prominence in the repertory, and for a few decades the organ was regarded more as an imitator of the orchestra than an instrument with its own characteristic sound and literature. Secular use of the organ was widespread – in concert halls and ballrooms, at trade fairs and expositions, and perhaps most significantly in theaters and residences (*see* THEATER ORGAN). Hope-Jones devised means for making a few sets of pipes do service at several pitches on different manuals and named his creation the "unit orchestra"; his patents ultimately were assigned to the WURLITZER firm, which, along with Robert Morton and others, built thousands of organs of this type (usually with elaborate sound-effects) for movie theaters during the silent film era. The Aeolian Co. was the leading maker of domestic player organs, often sizable and placed behind elaborate case fronts. Kimball, Skinner, Möller, Kilgen, and Austin built a number of important concert-hall organs which differed little from those built for large churches. Size became an end in itself, resulting in monstrous organs such as that in the grand court of the department store John Wanamaker & Co. in Philadelphia.

2. Organ by the Holtkamp Organ Co. (inaugurated 1967) at the University of New Mexico, Albuquerque

The theater organ era ended around 1930 with the introduction of the film soundtrack, and the reversal of fortunes caused by the Depression coupled with the technical progress of the phonograph and radio virtually eliminated the market for domestic player organs. In this same period a younger generation of organists – among them E. Power Biggs, Carl Weinrich, Melville Smith, and Ernest White – began to be concerned with the loss of the organ's historical repertory, particularly the music of Bach, for which the orchestral organ was a poor vehicle. Influenced by Albert Schweitzer's writings and the growing European "organ reform" movement, they actively advocated a return to a more eclectic organ design, eschewing uniformity and incorporating a completely developed principal chorus along with reeds and flutes consciously based on historical models.

Certain prominent organ builders and voicers, including Walter Holtkamp, Sr. (*see* HOLTKAMP ORGAN CO.), G. Donald Harrison of the Aeolian-Skinner firm, and Richard Whitelegg of the Möller firm, received encouragement for experimentation along "reformed" tonal lines in the 1930s. Holtkamp went even further, becoming an early and influential advocate of slider chests and the open, unencumbered placement of pipes (fig. 2). Between 1937 and 1940 Harrison built several small unenclosed organs of severely classical tonal design, one of which, in the Germanic (now Busch-Reisinger) Museum at Harvard University, achieved widespread popularity and acceptance through its use for many years in E. Power Biggs's Sunday morning radio broadcasts. Biggs, an outspoken advocate of organ reform, also made recordings on this organ and encouraged composers to write for it.

Progress was suspended during World War II because the necessary materials were not available; organ factories restricted themselves to rebuilding, converted to production of war material, or closed. In the late 1940s and early 1950s, however, the reform movement received new impetus from organists and builders who had visited the historic organs of Europe while on duty with the occupation forces, as well as from a younger generation of organists who studied abroad under Fulbright grants. Several of these organists, along with some of the younger organ builders such as Charles Brenton Fisk, felt that tonal reform was not enough, and that classic principles of mechanical action, wind systems, and casework were also important musically. Significant organs by leading European "reform" builders such as Dirk Flentrop and Rudolf von Beckerath earned additional converts to the reform cause. Flentrop's first major organ in the USA was built for the Busch-Reisinger Museum at Harvard University in 1958 (for illustration *see* BIGGS, E. POWER), and other notable instruments by him include organs for St. Mark's Cathedral, Seattle (1965); Salem College, Winston-Salem, North Carolina (1965); Warner Hall, Oberlin Conservatory, Oberlin, Ohio (1974); and Duke University Chapel, Durham, North Carolina (1976). Beckerath's work includes organs for Trinity Lutheran Church, Cleveland, Ohio; St. Paul's Cathedral, Pittsburgh; and Dwight Chapel, Yale University.

The challenge of the reform cause was first taken up in the USA by less-established and younger builders. Otto Hofmann's all-mechanical encased organ of 1956 in Matthews Memorial Church, Albany, Texas, and Fisk's similar though even larger instrument of 1961 in Mt. Calvary Church, Baltimore, Maryland, were early landmarks that attracted much attention. Such builders were shortly followed by FRITZ NOACK and John Brombaugh, both of whom had European training. By the mid-1960s the larger companies, less flexible in their production methods, began to heed the trend, and certain of them – notably Schlicker (*see* HERMAN LEONHARD SCHLICKER), Casavant, and later Holtkamp – began to produce a few classically conceived mechanical-action organs. With few exceptions (notably Fisk's eclectic instrument (1967) for Memorial Church, Harvard University), these American "reform" instruments tended to emulate the modern "neo-Baroque" style of contemporary European examples. During the 1970s organists and organ builders alike became aware of a greater need to study the historic instruments of all countries and periods. Brombaugh and Fisk were among the first to do so, along with younger builders such as Taylor and Boody, Gene R. Bedient, Manuel Rosales, A. David Moore, Helmuth Wolff, and George Bozeman (for illustration *see* BROMBAUGH, JOHN). This study resulted in both the conscious copying of historic examples (primarily for colleges) and a new kind of eclecticism, particularly evident in some of Fisk's larger instruments, in which Renaissance, German Baroque, French classic, and even Romantic elements are harmoniously combined.

One particular avenue opened to exploration in the late 1970s had to do with temperament. Interest in pre-19th-century music and its authentic performance has initiated a growing concern with various historical unequal temperaments. Werckmeister and Kirnberger tunings are gaining acceptance in church organs and are extensively used by some builders along with their own "shop" temperaments; builders such as Fisk, Noack, Brombaugh, Taylor and Boody, and Flentrop are now routinely tuning even large instruments in unequal temperaments. A four-manual Flentrop at Duke University, Durham, North Carolina (1976), is tuned in Chaumont, and Fisk's large four-manual at House of Hope Church in St. Paul, Minnesota (1978), is tuned to a special shop temperament, as are the Fisk organ at Stanford University Chapel (1984), and the Taylor and Boody organ at Holy Cross College (1985). Split-key mean-tone instruments have been built by Brombaugh (Oberlin College, Ohio, 1981) and Fisk (Wellesley College, Massachusetts, 1981; for illustration *see* FISK, CHARLES BRENTON).

Among the larger firms still working mostly with electro-pneumatic action – Schantz, Möller, Holtkamp, Austin, Reuter, Casavant, and others – a similar eclecticism of design is evident, but one more strongly rooted in the "American classic" style of the 1950s and 1960s and more influenced by the "Romantic revival" of the early 1980s.

BIBLIOGRAPHY

The Great Organ in Boston Music Hall (Boston, 1865)
G. L. Miller: *The Recent Revolution in Organ Building* (New York, 1909/*R*1969)
R. Hope-Jones: *Recent Developments of Organ Building* (North Tonawanda, NY, 1910)
E. M. Skinner: *The Modern Organ* (New York, 1917)
G. A. Audsley: *The Organ of the Twentieth Century* (New York, 1919/*R*1970)
W. H. Barnes: *The Contemporary American Organ* (Glen Rock, NJ, 1930)
C. G. Vardell: *Organs in the Wilderness* (Winston-Salem, NC, 1944)
V. A. Bradley: *Music for the Millions: the Kimball Piano and Organ Story* (Chicago, 1957)
T. W. Dean: *The Organ in Eighteenth Century English Colonial America* (diss., U. of Southern California, 1960)
J. E. Blanton: *The Revival of the Organ Case* (Albany, TX, 1965)
B. Owen: *The Organs and Music of King's Chapel* (Boston, 1966)
W. H. Armstrong: *Organs for America: the Life and Work of David Tannenberg* (Philadelphia, 1967)
J. Johnson: *Henry Erben, American Organ Builder: a Survey of his Life and Works* (thesis, Yale U., 1968)
W. H. Barnes and E. B. Gammons: *Two Centuries of American Organ Building* (Glen Rock, NJ, 1970)
W. J. Beasley: *The Organ in America, as Portrayed in Dwight's Journal of Music* (diss., U. of Southern California, 1971)
J. T. Fesperman: *Two Essays on Organ Design* (Raleigh, NC, 1975)
O. Ochse: *The History of the Organ in the United States* (Bloomington, IN, 1975)
B. W. Downward: *G. Donald Harrison and the American Classic Organ* (diss., Eastman School of Music, 1976)
A. F. Robinson, ed.: *The Bicentennial Tracker* (Wilmington, OH, 1976)
J. Ogasapian: *Organ Building in New York City, 1700–1900* (Braintree, MA, 1977)
L. J. Schoenstein: *Memoirs of a San Francisco Organ Builder* (San Francisco, 1977)
U. Pape: *The Tracker Organ Revival in America* (Berlin, 1978)
J. A. Ferguson: *Walter Holtkamp: American Organ Builder* (Kent, OH, 1979)
B. Owen: *The Organ in New England* (Raleigh, NC, 1979)
J. T. Fesperman: *Organs in Mexico* (Raleigh, NC, 1980)
J. Ogasapian: *Henry Erben: Portrait of a 19th Century American Organ Builder* (Braintree, MA, 1980)
U. Pape: *Organs in America*, i (Berlin, 1980)
J. T. Fesperman: *Flentrop in America* (Raleigh, NC, 1982)
M. D. Coffey: *Charles Fisk: Organ Builder* (diss., Eastman School of Music, 1984)
U. Pape: *Organs in America*, ii (Berlin, 1984)
D. J. Holden: *The Life & Work of Ernest M. Skinner* (Richmond, VA, 1985)
B. Owen: "Eighteenth-century Organs and Organ Building in New England," *Music in Colonial Massachusetts, 1630–1820*, ed. B. Lambert, ii (Boston, 1985), 655

BARBARA OWEN

Organ music. Before the end of the 18th century, almost no organ music was written in America: an initial lack of instruments and Calvinist proscriptions of instrumental music in their churches led to a void. From then on, however, organists, nearly all of them European immigrants, began to preside at increasingly imposing instruments in the more important churches of the Eastern seaboard cities. Although a few of them wrote modest voluntaries on the English model, variation sets, and pedagogical works, apparently most did not compose, and little that survives is worthy of resurrection. A roster of such individuals would include William Selby, Benjamin Carr, Rayner Taylor, Francis Linley, Henry C. Timm, Edward Hodges, Samuel P. Jackson, A. W. Haytor, Charles Zeuner, and John Zundel.

After 1860 the situation changed radically. John Knowles

Paine, a representative figure, was a practicing organist who received advanced training in Germany and then, having returned home, promoted the works of Bach, Mendelssohn, and Louis Thiele. Paine was one of the first Americans successfully to cultivate the classical Germanic forms (symphonies, sonatas, etc.); he also wrote other kinds of large-scale organ work, primarily variation sets, and one-movement character-pieces intended either for use in church or in recital programs. Paine's teacher in Berlin, Karl-August Haupt, and others such as Joseph Rheinberger in Munich served as mentors to several generations of American organists; their more prominent pupils included Thayer, Buck, Whiting, Chadwick, and Parker (Foote remained at home but received similar training in Boston under Paine). The German-trained organists, while not exclusively organ composers, produced a considerable body of sonatas, suites, and variation sets, as well as preludes and postludes, canzonettas, impromptus, romanzas, and concert pieces. Mendelssohn was their implicit model, but hints of Wagnerian chromaticism gradually intruded into their music, and some of this group even came to an awareness of what they referred to as "the modern French school." The more long-lived never managed, however, to reconcile themselves to the innovations of the 20th century, and maintained a retrospective stance to the end.

After 1890 the Germanic orientation was supplanted by a fascination with the French symphonic style of César Franck and his followers. Prominent recitalists competed to play the first American performances of the new symphonies of Charles Widor; Alexandre Guilmant was invited by Clarence Eddy to head the group of organists engaged to give a series of 62 recitals at the 1893 World's Columbian Exposition in Chicago; and increasing numbers of Americans went to Paris to study with Widor, Guilmant, and Joseph Bonnet. In New York in 1899 Guilmant's disciples even established an organ school named after him for those unable to travel abroad. French influence is also mirrored in the grand organ symphonies, splashy toccatas, and evocative program works of composers such as Clarence Dickinson, Eric De Lamarter, Seth Bingham, and Garth Edmundson.

The fashion for explicitly programmatic music coincided with the development of instruments capable of simulating orchestral sounds. Especially popular as a recital item was Alexander Russell's suite-like set *St. Lawrence Sketches* (1921–37). The trend reached its peak in the works of Ray Spalding Stoughton, whose Persian and Egyptian suites are almost outrageously vivid in their descriptiveness. The impulse to explore the organ's coloristic resources resulted in many transcriptions of orchestral, choral, and piano works, a category that decorated, and sometimes dominated, recital programs into the 1930s. Certain virtuosos specialized in rousing versions of the overture to Rossini's *Guillaume Tell*, or in storm pieces so realistic that listeners instinctively reached for their umbrellas. The work of European arrangers such as W. T. Best predominated at first, but soon Americans such as Samuel P. Warren, Samuel A. Baldwin, and Edwin Lemare acquired a reputation for their skillful and often dazzling borrowings, particularly from Wagner. The evolution of the "orchestral" organ reached its culmination in the theater organ, which had its heyday in the USA in the late 1920s. With the great advantage over an orchestra of being able to extemporize, theater organists could provide individualized accompaniment to any film; in a comedy the audiences often found as much to laugh at in the musical comments of an accomplished player as in the film.

Even while French and German organ music held general sway, British influence remained strong in the realm of church music. The larger Episcopal churches called on Englishmen like T. Tertius Noble to introduce musical practices associated with the English cathedral tradition. The hymn-tune preludes of Joseph Clokey, Everett Titcomb, and others satisfied a widespread need. Leo Sowerby was undoubtedly the most important composer to work within this tradition, cultivating an entirely personal idiom in his diverse preludes and meditations on hymn melodies; he also made a significant contribution to the concert literature with one-movement display pieces, an imposing organ suite and symphony, chamber music with organ, and several concerted pieces for organ and orchestra.

A number of prominent 20th-century composers, though not themselves organists, have composed works for the instrument. The important Contemporary Organ Series of the H. W. Gray firm includes works by Copland, Piston, Sessions, Cowell, Quincy Porter, and Douglas S. Moore, none of whom has written more than a handful of organ pieces; to these may be added Roy Harris, Luening, Finney, Barber, and Bassett. His experience as a church organist notwithstanding, Ives wrote little organ music, and his quirky *Variations on America* (?1891) has achieved wider circulation in Schuman's orchestral transcription than in the original version for organ. Others have created a more considerable repertory, however. Thomson, an organist early in his career and usually mentioned only for his irreverent *Variations on Sunday-school Tunes* (1926–7), wrote more sober pieces, in his lean, transparent idiom, during the same decade and afterwards. Pinkham, a successor of Thomson's at King's Chapel in Boston, has composed organ works ranging from utilitarian service music to impressive recital pieces in several movements, which often have a programmatic overlay; they employ an austere neo-classical style and the later of them show the influence of serialism. His *Toccatas for the Vault of Heaven* and Felciano's *Ekāgrata*, both written in 1972, combine prerecorded sounds with the organ. A substantial body of chamber music for conventional instruments with organ has been produced by these composers and Piston, Hovhaness, Rayner Brown, and Samuel Adler, among others. Americans over the years seem to have developed a special predilection for the solo organ with orchestral accompaniment (Parker, De Lamarter, Bingham, Sowerby, Hanson, Harris, Copland, and Barber). Other mainstream figures who have contributed many works to the organ repertory are Persichetti (Organ Sonata, 1960; *Shimah B'kohli*, 1962) and Rorem (*A Quaker Reader*, 1976). In the last several decades composers have begun to exploit the organ as a sound source, sometimes achieving effects similar to those that may be produced by a synthesizer. Although much recent organ music remains bound to convention and isolated from contemporary trends, some composers, notably Bolcom and Albright, write in advanced styles and use spatial notation, tone clusters, aleatory techniques, and antimetrical rhythms, combining their often witty language with an awareness of more traditional modes of expression. Comprehensive editions of American organ music include J. Beck and D. D. Woomer's *19th-century American Organ Music* (1975), J. S. Hart's *American Organ Music: a Glance at the Past 100 Years* (1975), and B. Owen's *A Century of American Organ Music (1776–1876)* (1975–83).

BIBLIOGRAPHY

H. Westerby: *The Complete Organ Recitalist, British and American: Historical, Editorial, and Descriptive* (New York, 1927)

B. Owen: "American Organ Music and Playing, from 1700," *Organ Institute Quarterly*, x/3 (1963), 7
W. Osborne: "Five New England Gentlemen," *Music: the A.G.O. and R.C.C.O. Magazine*, iii/8 (1969), 27
C. R. Arnold: *Organ Literature: a Comprehensive Survey* (Metuchen, NJ, 1973)
M. S. Anderson: *"The Organ without a Master" – a Survey of Nineteenth-century Organ Instruction Books in the United States* (diss., U. of Minnesota, 1977)
M. Kratzenstein: *Survey of Organ Literature and Editions* (Ames, IA, 1980)
J. B. Clark: "American Organ Music before 1830," *The Diapason*, lxxii/11 (1981), 1
P. B. Curtis: *American Organ Music North of Philadelphia before 1860: Selected Problems and an Annotated Bibliography* (diss., Manhattan School of Music, 1981)

WILLIAM OSBORNE

Original Dixieland Jazz [Jass] **Band** (ODJB). Jazz ensemble. Its original members, all from New Orleans, were Nick LaRocca (1889–1961), leader and cornet; Larry Shields (1893–1953), clarinet; Eddie Edwards (1891–1963), trombone; Tony Spargo or Sbarbaro (1897–1969), drums; and Henry Ragas (1891–1919), replaced by J. Russel Robinson (1891–1963), piano. After playing in Chicago in 1916, the five musicians moved to New York where they enjoyed sensational receptions during their residency at Reisenweber's Restaurant from January 1917. During the same year, the group became the first jazz band to make phonograph recordings, and in doing so they achieved a degree of eminence that was out of proportion to their musical skills. During the mid-1920s, when the vogue for jazz dancing temporarily subsided, the group disbanded; they re-formed again in 1936, but the reunion was brief and only moderately successful.

No member of the Original Dixieland Jazz Band was particularly talented as an improviser, and the group's phrasing was rhythmically stilted; but even so, their collective vigor had an infectious spirit. When black jazz bands began to record regularly it soon became apparent that others were more adept at jazz improvising and phrasing than was the Original Dixieland Jazz Band. Detractors of the band maintain that it merely simplified the music of black New Orleans groups, and cite specific antecedents for the band's compositions *Tiger Rag* and *Sensation Rag*. Casual listeners were intrigued by their repertory, which was unlike anything else then on record. They presented a new sound rather than a new music; this sound, and the rhythms it was couched in, appealed to young dancers, who were eager to break away from the rigidly formal dance steps of the era.

The most passionate advocate of the Original Dixieland Jazz Band's importance to jazz history was LaRocca himself, who never ceased claiming that his band had played a vital role in the "invention" of jazz in New Orleans during the early years of the 20th century. The fact that there is no evidence to support LaRocca's contention has caused many jazz devotees to ignore the merits of the band's music. But it is indisputable that the group played a major part in popularizing the dixieland style of jazz throughout the USA and Europe.

See also NEW YORK, §10.

RECORDINGS
(selective list)

Livery Stable Blues (1917, Vic. 18255); Tiger Rag (1918, Vic. 18472); Sensation Rag (1918, Vic. 18483); Clarinet Marmalade Blues (1918, Vic. 18513); Jazz me Blues (1921, Vic. 18722); Royal Garden Blues (1921, Vic. 18798); Skeleton Jangle/Tiger Rag (1936, Vic. 25524)

BIBLIOGRAPHY

Second Line, vi/9–10 (1955) [issue devoted to Original Dixieland Jazz Band]
H. H. Lange: *Nick LaRocca: ein Porträt* (Wetzlar, Germany, 1960)
H. O. Brunn: *The Story of the Original Dixieland Jazz Band* (Baton Rouge, LA, 1960/*R*1977)

The Original Dixieland Jazz Band: (left to right) Tony Spargo (Sbarbaro), Eddie Edwards, Nick LaRocca, Larry Shields, and Henry Ragas

M. Williams: *Jazz Masters of New Orleans* (New York, 1967), 26
G. Schuller: *Early Jazz: its Roots and Musical Development* (New York, 1968), 175
T. D. Brown: "Tony Sbarbaro and the Original Dixieland Jazz Band," *A History and Analysis of Jazz Drumming to 1942* (diss., U. of Michigan, 1976), 169
H. Lyttelton: *The Best of Jazz* (New York, 1979), 12

JOHN CHILTON

Orioles. Rhythm-and-blues vocal group. Formed in Baltimore, the group originally called itself the Vibra-Naires; it was led by Sonny Til (Earlington Carl Tilghman; *b* Baltimore, MD, 18 Aug 1925; *d* Washington, DC, 9 Dec 1981), and also included George Nelson, Alexander Sharp, Johnny Reed, and Tommy Gaither. Because doo-wop vocal harmony was the first rock-and-roll genre to take shape, the Orioles may be regarded as the earliest rock-and-roll group and their first hit, the ghostly, ethereal *It's too soon to know* (1948), as the first recording in the style. This was written by Deborah Chessler, an admirer of the group and later its manager. Unlike earlier black harmony groups, such as the Ink Spots and the Ravens, who had performed mostly in conventional nightclubs, the Orioles stood outside the American mainstream; motivated by a desire not only for success but also for self-expression, they sang a type of individualistic urban folk music, which was received by a young, multi-racial audience as yet unaffected by the values later purveyed by the entertainment industry. Led by Til's preternaturally delicate tenor and accompanied only by guitar, the Orioles made many more hit recordings: *Tell me so* (1949) reached no. 1 on the rhythm-and-blues chart, as did *Crying in the Chapel* (1953), which reached no. 11 on the pop chart. They appeared with Duke Ellington, Billie Holiday, Sarah Vaughan, and Dinah Washington at the Apollo Theater in Harlem, where their performances – slow, quiet, and lacking any indulgence in emotional display – provoked the audience to frenzy. They were widely imitated by doo-wop groups of the 1950s. The Orioles disbanded in 1954, but Til continued to perform; his last album was issued the year of his death.

RECORDINGS

(selective list; recorded for Jubilee unless otherwise stated)

It's too soon to know (Natural 5000, 1948); Forgive and Forget (5016, 1949); Tell me so (5005, 1949); What are you doing New Year's Eve?/It's gonna be a lonely Christmas (5017, 1949); Moonlight (5026, 1950); I Miss you So (5051, 1951); Crying in the Chapel (5122, 1953); In the Chapel in the Moonlight (5154, 1954)

BIBLIOGRAPHY

M. Goldberg: "Biography: the Orioles," *Record Exchanger*, ii/3 (1971), 4
——: "The Orioles," *Whiskey, Women, and . . .*, nos. 12–13 (1983) [incl. discography 1948–81]
P. Groia: *They All Sang on the Corner: a Second Look at New York City's Rhythm and Blues Vocal Groups* (West Hempstead, NY, 1983)
J. McGowan: *Hear Today! Here to Stay!: a Personal History of Rhythm and Blues* (St. Petersburg, FL, 1983)
G. Marcus: "Never Too Late," *Artforum*, xxii/7 (1984), 86

GREIL MARCUS

Ormandy, Eugene [Blau, Jenő] (*b* Budapest, Hungary, 18 Nov 1899; *d* Philadelphia, PA, 12 March 1985). Conductor. Having been admitted to the Budapest Royal Academy at the age of five as a violin pupil, he began giving concerts two years later. He studied further with Jenő Hubay, graduated at 14, and was appointed professor of violin at 17. By then he had begun touring in central Europe, and in 1921 was attracted to New York by the offer of a lucrative concert tour. The tour failed to materialize, and Ormandy was forced to seek work at the Capitol Theatre, New York, where a large orchestra accompanied silent films and provided musical interludes. He swiftly advanced from the back of the section to concertmaster, and his conducting début took place there in 1924, when the regular conductor fell ill.

Eugene Ormandy

Ormandy became an American citizen in 1927. He obtained alternative work conducting programs of lighter classics for the new medium of radio, as well as occasional summer orchestral concerts. He was engaged in the latter capacity by the Philadelphia Orchestra in 1930, and the following year he substituted for Toscanini in three programs of the orchestra's major concert series at Philadelphia (début, 30 October 1931). These led directly to a contract with the Minneapolis SO as successor to Henri Verbrugghen. Ormandy remained at Minneapolis for five years (1931–6), becoming nationally known through his first recordings made with the Minneapolis SO.

In 1936 he went to the Philadelphia Orchestra under regular contract, sharing the conductorship with Stokowski for two seasons, becoming sole music director in 1938 – an appointment he held for over 40 years – and continuing as Conductor Laureate from 1980. He initiated no revolution at Philadelphia, but gradually brought about the more voluptuous orchestral sound associated with his performances, which mainly concentrated on a repertory of late-Romantic and early 20th-century works demanding a wealth of saturated orchestral tone, presented with a high degree of technical proficiency and polish.

These qualities to some extent governed his choice of new music: he conducted the premières of Rachmaninoff's *Symphonic Dances*, Bartók's Piano Concerto no. 3, and Britten's *Diversions* for left hand, in addition to many works by Barber, Creston, Sessions, and others (and the American premières of several Shostakovich symphonies). His recordings include the first of Shostakovich's Cello Concerto no. 1 and Symphony no. 4, and Mahler's Tenth Symphony in the performing version by Deryck Cooke.

In 1948 Ormandy conducted the first symphony concert shown on American television (beating Toscanini on a rival network by one and a half hours), and in 1949 he made his British début during the Philadelphia Orchestra's first overseas tour. He toured internationally as a guest conductor of many orchestras, and in 1973 he led the Philadelphia Orchestra on the first tour by an American orchestra of the People's Republic of China. He conducted little opera apart from his début at the Metropolitan in 1950 in *Die Fledermaus*. He was made an honorary KBE in 1976 as part of the American Bicentennial celebrations.

BIBLIOGRAPHY

R. Gelatt: *Music-makers* (New York, 1953/*R*1972), 155

H. Stoddard: "Eugene Ormandy," *Symphony Conductors of the U.S.A.* (New York, 1957), 147

H. C. Schonberg: *The Great Conductors* (New York, 1967)

H. Kupferberg: *Those Fabulous Philadelphians* (New York, 1969)[with discography of Philadelphia records]

P. Hart: *Orpheus in the New World* (New York, 1973), 140

J. L. Holmes: *Conductors on Record* (London, 1982)

NOËL GOODWIN

Ornstein, Leo (*b* Kremenchug, Ukraine, 2 Dec 1892). Composer and pianist. A musical prodigy, he studied with his father, a cantor, in Kiev and St. Petersburg until he entered the Petrograd Conservatory. In 1907 he immigrated to the USA, where he studied at the Institute of Musical Art in New York with Bertha Fiering Tapper, the strongest single influence on his life and music. He made his début recital in 1911 in New York and, after European tours in 1913 and 1914, he was recognized as an outstanding concert pianist. In 1913 he wrote his first "modern" music, *Dwarf Suite*, followed by the notorious *Wild Men's Dance*, *Impressions de Notre Dame*, and others. His spectacular performances of these experimental pieces made him the center of a violent controversy between conservative and radical musicians and critics. After his 1914 London recital he became known as the leading futurist composer. He abruptly ended his concert career at its height in 1920, appearing only occasionally thereafter: with the Philadelphia Orchestra under Stokowski in 1925 in his Piano Concerto; later with the Pro Arte and Stradivarius quartets in his Piano Quintet. In 1920 he became head of the piano department at the Philadelphia Musical Academy, and a few years later he established the Ornstein School of Music (Philadelphia). Ornstein continued to compose during his teaching years and after his retirement in 1953.

Ornstein's works composed before 1920 are considered his most interesting, with their early use of dissonance, polyrhythm, polytonality, and unusual color effects; his later works seem more conservative. But he has always worked in a wide range of musical styles, sometimes simultaneously, his choice dependent on the demands of each composition. A renewed interest in his music and a steady increase in performances and recordings began in the 1970s. In 1975 he received the Marjorie Peabody Waite Award from the National Institute of Arts and Letters.

WORKS

(selective list)

ORCHESTRAL

Evening Song of the Cossack, chamber orch, op.14 no.1, 1923, arr. Nicolaj Hanson

Piano Concerto, 1923

Lysistrata Suite, 1930

Nocturne and Dance of the Fates, *c*1937

CHAMBER

2 vn sonatas, op.31, *c*1915, op.26, *c*1918; 3 Russian Impressions, vn, pf, 1916; 2 vc sonatas, op.52, *c*1918, *c*1920; Pf Qnt, 1927; 3 str qts, op.28, op.99, *c*1929, no.3, 1976; 6 Preludes, vc, pf, 1931; Allegro (Intermezzo), fl, pf, 1959; Fantasy Pieces, va, pf, 1972; Hebraic Fantasy, vn, pf, 1975; Poem, fl, pf, 1979

Undated: Ballade, sax/cl/va, pf; Minuet in Ancient Style, fl, cl; Prelude in Ancient Style, fl, cl; Prelude, fl, pf; Nocturne, cl, pf; Waltz, vn, pf; Composition no.36, vc, pf; [untitled], op.33 nos.1–2, vc, pf; [untitled], chamber ens

PIANO

(for pf solo unless otherwise stated)

6 Lyric Fancies, op.10, 1911; A Paris Street Scene at Night, op.4 no.3, 1912; Suicide in an Airplane, *c*1913; Pièce, pf 4 hands, op.19 no.1, 1913; 3 Preludes, op.20, *c*1914; Suite russe, op.12, *c*1914; 3 Moods, 1914; Cossack Impressions, op.14, *c*1914; Impressions de Notre Dame, op.16 nos.1–2, 1914; Wild Men's Dance, op.13 no.2, *c*1915; Dwarf Suite, op.11, *c*1915; A la Chinoise, op.39, *c*1918; Poems of 1917 (W. Frank), op.41, 1918; Serenade, op.5 nos.1–2, 1918

A la Mexicana, op.35, *c*1920; Impressions de la Tamise, op.13 no.1, *c*1920; Arabesques, op.42, *c*1920; 6 Watercolors, op.80, *c*1921; 2 Improvisations, pf 4 hands, op.95, 1921; Nocturnes nos. 1–2, *c*1922; Sonata no.4, *c*1924; 2 Lyric Pieces, *c*1924; 15 Waltzes and 42 numbered pieces, 1950–72; Tarantelle diabolique, 1960; 5 Intermezzi, 1965–8; 3 Landscapes, 1968; A Morning in the Woods, 1971; Some New York Scenes, 1971; Biography in Sonata Form, 1974; 4[untitled], 1976; Burlesca, 1976

Impromptu no.1 (Epitaph), no.2 (A Bit of Nostalgia), 1976; A Dream almost Forgotten, 1978; An Autumn Fantasy, 1978; Barbaro, 1978; 5 pieces, 1978; Just a Fun Piece, 1978; The Recruit and the Bugler, 1978; A Small Carnival, 1978; Valse diabolique, 1978; A Reverie, 1979; Chromatic Dance, 1980; Sonata no.6, *c*1981; The Deserted Garden, 1981; 2 Legends, 1982

Undated: [untitled], op.17 nos.1–5; Bagatelle no.1; Barcarolle, op.6 no.4; 4 Fantasy Pieces; 9 Miniatures; Prélude tragique; Sonata, 2 pf, op.89; Tarantelle; To a Grecian Urn

For children: In the Country, *c*1924; Seeing Russia with Teacher, 10 duets, *c*1925; Memories from Childhood, 8 pieces, *c*1925; Piano Sketch Book, 2 vols., *c*1939; Musings of a Piano, 4 pieces, 1960; Mindy's Piece; Mindy's Piece no.2, 1967

Juvenilia

VOCAL

Songs, 1v, pf: 3 Songs, op.33, *c*1915; Mother o'mine (Kipling), *c*1916; There was a Jolly Miller Once, *c*1916; The Corpse, 1917; Two Oriental Songs (F. Martens), *c*1918; 5 songs [untitled] (W. Frank), op.17, *c*1928, arr. 1v, orch, *c*1929; 4 songs without words [untitled], 1928; Lullaby

Choral: 3 Russian Choruses, SATB, op.61, 1918; America [various arrs.]

MSS in *CtY-Mus*

Principal publisher: Joshua (General)

BIBLIOGRAPHY

EwenD

F. Martens: *Leo Ornstein: the Man, his Ideas, his Work* (New York, 1918/*R*1975)

P. Rosenfeld: "Ornstein," *Musical Portraits* (London, 1922)

——: *An Hour with American Music* (New York, 1929)

V. Perlis: "The Futurist Music of Leo Ornstein," *Notes*, xxxi (1974–5), 735

T. E. Darter, Jr.: *The Futurist Piano Music of Leo Ornstein* (diss., Cornell U., 1979)

VIVIAN PERLIS

Orpheus (Chamber Orchestra). Chamber orchestra, formed in 1972 by the cellist Julian Fifer. The group now consists of 26 members, who perform without a conductor. The Orpheus Chamber Orchestra made its début at Alice Tully Hall in 1974; it is based in New York and presents an annual series at Carnegie Hall (début 1978 with Peter Serkin as guest soloist). It tours annually throughout the USA and in Europe, Israel, India, and South America, performing both the chamber and chamber-orchestral repertories for varying combinations of wind instruments and strings. It is completely self-governed, the members themselves being responsible for interpretive decisions as well as for programming, repertory, and soloists; they rotate seating so that each player eventually assumes the position of section leader. The artistic cooperation and commitment that result from this arrangement have brought the ensemble general acclaim from both critics and audiences.

ELLEN HIGHSTEIN

Orrego-Salas, Juan (Antonio) (*b* Santiago, Chile, 18 Jan 1919). Chilean composer and musicologist. In 1943 he completed his composition studies with Pedro Allende and Domingo Santa-Cruz, and also received a diploma in architecture. He taught history at the Santiago Conservatory and conducted the Catholic University Choir, which he had founded in 1938. From 1944 to 1946 Rockefeller and Guggenheim grants enabled him to come to the USA, where he studied composition with Thompson and Copland and musicology with Lang and Herzog. He was then appointed professor of composition at the University of Chile (1947), editor of the *Revista musical chilena* (1949), and music critic for *El mercurio* (1950). After completing the degree of Profesor Extraordinario at the University of Chile (1953) he returned to the USA under a second Guggenheim Fellowship. Back in Chile he was for two years director of the Instituto de Extensión Musical and dean of the music department of the Catholic University. He moved again to the USA to found and direct the Latin American Music Center at Indiana University (from 1961), where he has been involved in promoting Latin American music through festivals, concerts, broadcasts, and the compiling of the largest existing library of scores and recordings of 20th-century Latin American works. In 1971 he received an honorary doctorate from the Catholic University, Santiago, and was accorded corresponding membership in the Chilean Academy of Fine Arts. He has won the Olga Cohen Prize twice (1956 and 1958) and a Biennial Chilean Music Festival Award three times. Works have been commissioned by leading institutions and ensembles, including the National SO and the Beaux Arts Trio, and his music has been widely performed.

A neoclassical craftsmanship, tempered by free invention, is characteristic of Orrego-Salas's music, and he freely uses formal procedures taken from all historical periods. Something of the variety in his output is demonstrated in the modal linearity of the *Canciones castellanas* op.20, the colorful instrumentation and energetic rhythm of the Sonata a 4 op.55, and the declamatory monody and concertante writing of the cantata *América, no en vano invocamos tu nombre* op.57. He created a unique blend of "nationalism" and "realism" through his use of texts by Chilean poets, including himself, in works from the late 1970s and early 1980s. Orrego-Salas has written extensively on aesthetics and poetics. He edited *Music of the Americas* (1967; with G. List) and *Music from Latin America Available at Indiana University: Scores, Tapes and Records* (1971).

WORKS

(only those composed after 1960)

INSTRUMENTAL

(orchestral)

Sym. no.3, op.50, 1961; Conc. a 3, pf trio, orch, op.52, 1962; Conc., wind, op.53, 1964; Sym. no.4 "Of the Distant Answer," op.59, 1966; Variaciones serenas, str, op.69, 1971; Ob Conc., op.77, 1980; Vn Conc., op.86, 1983–4; Pf Conc. no.2, op.93, 1985

(chamber)

Concertino, brass qt, op.54, 1963; Sonata a 4 (Edgewood Sonata), fl, ob, hpd, db, op.55, 1964; Pf Trio, op.58, 1966; Pf Sonata, op.60, 1967; 4 liriche brevi, sax, pf, op.61, 1967; Mobili, va, pf, op.63, 1967; A Greeting Cadenza for William Primrose, va, pf, op.65, 1970; Volte, pf, 15 wind, harp, perc, op.67, 1971; Esquinas, gui, op.68, 1971; Serenata, fl, vc, op.70, 1972

Sonata de estio, fl, pf, op.71, 1972; Presencias, fl, ob, cl, hpd, str trio, op.72, 1972; Pf Trio no.2, op.75, 1977; De profundis, tuba, vc qt, op.76, 1979; Variations for a Quiet Man, cl, pf, op.79, 1980; Tangos, 11 players, op.82, 1982; Balada, vc, pf, op.84, 1982–3; Dialogues in Waltz, pf 4 hands, op.89, 1984; Rondo Fantasia, pf, op.90, 1984; Glosas, vn, gui, op.91, 1984; Variations on a Chant, harp, op.92, 1984–5

VOCAL

Psalms, reciter, wind orch, op.51, 1962; Alboradas (De Vega), SSA, harp, pf, perc, op.56, 1965; América, no en vano invocamos tu nombre (Neruda), S, Bar, male chorus, op.57, 1966; 3 Madrigals (15th-century Sp.), chorus, op.62, 1967; Missa in tempore discordiae, T, SATB, orch, op.64, 1969; Words of Don Quixote, Bar, ens, op.66, 1970; The Days of God (after Genesis), oratorio, S, A, T, B, chorus, orch, op.73, 1974–6; Psalms, Bar, pf, op.74, 1977

Un canto a Bolivar, TTB, folk insts, op.78, 1980–81; Canciones en el estilo popular (Neruda), lv, gui, op.80, 1981; Bolivar, nar, SATB, orch, 1981–2; Lo que digo (Orrego-Salas), solo male vv, folk insts, op.83, 1982; Biografia minima (D. Valjalo), lv, tpt, gui, perc, op.85, 1983; 5 Songs in 6 (20th-century Sp. poets), Mez, 2 vn, cl, vc, pf, op.87, 1984; Ash Wednesday (T. S. Eliot), cantata, Mez, str orch, op.88, 1984

Principal publishers: Barry, Chester, Hargail, Instituto de Extensión Musical, Pan-American Union, Peer-Southern, Peters

BIBLIOGRAPHY

VintonD

V. Salas Viú: *La creación musical en Chile (1900–1951)* (Santiago, 1951)

D. Santa-Cruz: "El concierto para piano en la obra de Orrego-Salas," *Revista musical chilena*, no.39 (1959)

S. Claro and J. Urrutia-Blondel: *Historia de la música en Chile* (Santiago, 1973)

L. Merino: "Visión del compositor Juan Orrego-Salas," *Revista musical chilena*, nos.142–4 (1978), 5–105

GERALD R. BENJAMIN

Ortmann, Otto Rudolph (*b* Baltimore, MD, 25 Jan 1889; *d* Baltimore, 22 Oct 1979). Music educator and administrator. He received his formal education at Baltimore City College and then at the Peabody Conservatory, where he gained a teacher's certificate in piano (1913) and an artist's diploma in composition (1917). From 1917 to 1941 he served on the faculty of Peabody (1928–41 as its director), and from 1942 to 1957 taught in the music department at Goucher College (1948–57 as its chairman). He also taught courses in the psychology of music at Johns Hopkins University (1921–4). He combined research on acoustics, anatomy, physics, and physiology with an investigation of musical talent and problems of music pedagogy, making a valuable contribution by synthesizing various conflicting historical principles and schools of technical thought; his articles and books in the area of piano pedagogy, in particular, gained for him national and international recognition.

WILLIAM McCLELLAN

Ory, Kid [Edward] (*b* La Place, LA, 25 Dec 1886; *d* Honolulu, HI, 23 Jan 1973). Jazz trombonist and bandleader. He led one of the most prominent bands in New Orleans between 1912 and 1919, and in Los Angeles in 1922 made one of the first jazz discs in the New Orleans style to be recorded by black artists, *Ory's Creole Trombone/Society Blues*. In the 1920s he participated in some of the period's most important jazz recordings, with Louis Armstrong's Hot Five, Jelly Roll Morton's Red Hot Peppers, the New Orleans Bootblacks, the New Orleans Wanderers, and King Oliver's Dixie Syncopators. He abandoned music in 1933 to work on a poultry farm and in a railroad office, but resumed playing in 1942, regaining prominence through Orson Welles's radio broadcasts of 1944. He then toured extensively with his band until 1966, when he retired to Hawaii. Ory's playing was highly rhythmic; he made full use of slurs and glissandos in the early jazz "tailgate" trombone style, of which he was the most famous exponent. He composed the well-known *Muskrat Ramble.*

RECORDINGS
(selective list)

As leader: Spikes' Seven Pods of Pepper: Ory's Creole Trombone/Society Blues (1922, Nordskog 3009); *Kid Ory's Creole Jazz Band – 1954* (1954, Good Time Jazz 12004)

As sideman: L. Armstrong: Muskrat Ramble (1926, OK 8300); New Orleans Wanderers: Gate Mouth (1926, Col. 698D); J. R. Morton: Doctor Jazz (1926, Vic. 20415); L. Armstrong: Ory's Creole Trombone (1927, Col. 35838)

BIBLIOGRAPHY

SouthernB

R. Blesh: "Listen to what Ory says," *Jazz Record*, no.37 (1945), 8

K. Ory: "What did Ory say?," *Record Changer*, vi/9 (1947), 5

J. G. Jepsen: *Kid Ory* (Copenhagen, 1957) [discography]

R. M. W. Dixon: *Kid Ory: a Biography, Appreciation, Record Survey and Discography* (London, 1958)

M. Williams: "The Kid," *Jazz Masters of New Orleans* (New York, 1967), 205

JOSÉ HOSIASSON/R

Osborne, Conrad L(eon) (*b* Lincoln, NE, 22 July 1934). Music critic and vocal coach. He was educated at Columbia University and studied singing with Cornelius Reid and acting with Frank Corsaro. He has acted in the theater and on television and has sung operatic baritone roles with several musical organizations in the New York area. As a writer, he was chief critic of vocal music and contributing editor of *High Fidelity* (1959–69), New York music critic for the London *Financial Times* (1962–9), and advisory editor of the *Musical Newsletter* (1970–77). Osborne has contributed numerous articles to publications in the USA and Britain, including detailed critical discographies of the operas of Verdi (1963), Mozart (1965), Wagner (1966–7), and Russian composers (1974–5) for *High Fidelity* and articles and reviews for *Opus* (1984–). His chief interest is opera, and his background as a performer has strongly influenced his critical writing on the subject. Since the early 1970s he has devoted more of his time and interest to private teaching of singing and to consulting in arts management than to journalism. He is widely regarded as one of the most discriminating vocal critics in the USA.

PATRICK J. SMITH

Osborne [Osborn], **John** (*b* New England, *c*1792; *d* New York, 27 May 1835). Piano maker. He was one of several outstanding apprentices who learned their craft under Crehore of Milton, Massachusetts, often called the founder of the New England piano industry. According to Oliver, he served this apprenticeship during the years (*c*1808–14) when Crehore was associated with the Boston shop of Lewis and Alpheus Babcock and Thomas Appleton. By 1815 Osborne had set up his own firm on Newbury Street, Boston, and by 1819 had moved to Orange Street, where he trained such apprentices as Jonas Chickering (from 1819 to 1823), Lemanuel and Timothy Gilbert, and John Dwight.

Osborne described himself as a builder of upright, grand, square, and cabinet pianos, and soon became known for his fine craftsmanship. He entered into a short-lived partnership with James Stewart in 1822, remained in Boston until 1829, then moved to Albany, New York, to work first for Meacham & Pond, then, from 1831 to 1833, as a partner of Peter King; he moved to New York in 1833. His pianos won several awards, including the first premium at the American Institute. According to Spillane, in October 1834 Osborne moved into a large factory that he had built on Third Avenue at 14th Street. The firm of Stodart, Worcester & Dunham occupied the building by 1836, and was followed by a succession of piano manufacturers until 1880.

Osborne's pianos can be seen in American museums and private collections. His square instruments are similar to those of his contemporaries, with mahogany veneer, fretted nameboards, and a range of *F'* to *c''''*. An Osborne upright (*c*1820) at the Smithsonian Institution is one of the earliest extant uprights built in New England; it has a range of *F'* to *f''''*, damper and una corda pedals, and a handsome case that includes a radially pleated drapery drawn together at its center with a brass medallion.

BIBLIOGRAPHY

R. G. Parker: *A Tribute to the Life and Character of Jonas Chickering by one who Knew him Well* (Boston, 1854), 40ff

H. K. Oliver: *Reports and Awards of the International Exhibition, 1876* (Philadelphia, 1878), 28f

D. Spillane: *History of the American Pianoforte* (New York, 1890/*R*1969), 54ff, 87ff, 139, 156f

CYNTHIA ADAMS HOOVER

Osborne Brothers. Country-music duo. It consists of Bobby (Robert, Jr.) Osborne (*b* Hyden, KY, 7 Dec 1931) and Sonny Osborne (*b* Hyden, 29 Oct 1937). As children they were exposed to a variety of religious music and to that of Jimmie Rodgers and the Carter Family. Bobby made his professional début in Dayton, Ohio, playing guitar with Junior Collett and Dick Potter. He later played with the Lonesome Pine Fiddlers and the Stanley Brothers, switching from guitar to mandolin in 1951. Sonny played banjo in Bill Monroe's Blue Grass Boys (1952–3). The Osborne Brothers were first billed as such in 1953 on radio station WROL in Knoxville, Tennessee, where their backup band, the Sunny Mountain Boys, consisted of Enos Johnson and L. E. White. In 1954 the Osbornes worked in Detroit with the singer and guitarist Jimmy Martin, who had just left Monroe, and also recorded for RCA Victor. In 1955 they went to work for Charlie Bailey at station WWVA, Wheeling, West Virginia, but left by mid-1956 and signed with MGM Records. They made their first guest appearances on the "Grand Ole Opry" in 1959 and in 1964 became regular cast members. In 1963 they began a long association with Decca (later MCA) Records. Their choice of songs was considerably more eclectic than the usual bluegrass repertory, encompassing both folk (*Take this hammer*, 1963) and mainstream country (*Making plans*, 1965) styles. By the mid-1960s, aiming their music at the basic country audience, they were attaining modest chart successes. Their most memorable release was *Rocky Top* (1968), a composition by Boudleaux and Felice Bryant that became a Tennessee state song. The Osborne Brothers performed at several Newport Folk Festivals during the 1960s, and in the mid-1970s signed with the CMH label and returned to a traditional bluegrass sound.

Noted for their high, intricate harmonies as well as for their virtuoso mandolin and banjo picking, the Osborne Brothers have been a progressive force in bluegrass music. Their recordings have used the finest studio musicians – including Buddy Spicher (fiddle), Grady Martin (guitar), and Willie Ackerman (drums) – many of them performing on atypical bluegrass instruments, such as electric guitar, steel guitar, drums, and piano.

BIBLIOGRAPHY

N. Rosenberg: "Osborne Brothers Discography," *Bluegrass Unlimited*, i/12 (1967), 2; ii/1 (1967), 6; ii/3 (1967), 2

——: "The Osborne Brothers," *Bluegrass Unlimited*, vi/3 (1971), 5; vi/8 (1972), 5

P. Kuykendall: "The Osborne Brothers – from Rocky Top to Muddy Bottom," *Bluegrass Unlimited*, xii/6 (1977), 10

RONNIE PUGH

Osborn-Hannah, Jane (*b* Wilmington, OH, 8 July 1873; *d* New York, 13 Aug 1943). Soprano. She studied with Mathilde Marchesi in Paris and with Rosa Sucher in Berlin and made her début in 1904 at Leipzig as Elisabeth in *Tannhäuser*. After appearances in Dresden, Munich, and Berlin, she sang Eva in *Die Meistersinger* at Covent Garden (1908). Two years later she made her début at the Metropolitan Opera, again as Elisabeth (5 January 1910), and sang with the Chicago Grand Opera Company for the first time, as Nedda in *Pagliacci*. Her other roles there included Wagner's Elsa, Sieglinde, and Gutrune, Verdi's Desdemona, Puccini's Butterfly, and Barbara in Herbert's *Natoma*; she retired in 1914. Her voice was a lyric soprano, not large, but pure in tone and technically secure.

ELIZABETH FORBES

Ossman, Vess L. [Sylvester Louis] (*b* Hudson, NY, 21 Aug 1868; *d* Fairmount, MN, 7 Dec 1923). Ragtime banjoist. He began studying banjo at the age of 12, and by 1896 was recording ragtime for Victor, Columbia, Berliner, and Edison. He extended his popularity by accompanying Arthur Collins, a leading popular singer. He made concert tours of England in 1900 and 1903, when he played for Edward VII; he also performed for President Theodore Roosevelt. Ossman formed various recording groups, usually consisting of banjo, mandolin, and harp-guitar. The most popular of these was the Ossman–Dudley Trio (with Audley Dudley, mandolin, and Roy Butin, harp-guitar); its recording of *St. Louis Tickle* (1906) was particularly successful. After 1910 Ossman preferred to travel with his groups away from the eastern recording centers, and made extended stays in both Indianapolis and Dayton, Ohio. He consequently recorded less frequently – his last disc was made in 1917 – and his position in the recording world passed to the banjoist Fred Van Eps. Ossman, however, was the leading ragtime banjoist at a time when the five-string banjo was preferred to the piano for recording purposes. He had an especially clean technique and a flair for syncopation, emphasizing strong two-step rhythms in his playing. One of his last and best recordings, his arrangement of Tom Turpin's *Buffalo Rag*, remained in the Victor catalogue until 1925.

RECORDINGS
(selective list)

Ragtime Medley (1897, Berliner 467); Smoky Mokes (1900, Berliner 6311); Whistling Rufus (1900, Vic. 149); Rusty Rags (1901, Vic. 811); St. Louis Rag (1904, Edison 8726) [cylinder]; Buffalo Rag (1906, Vic. 16779); Dixie Girl (1906, Vic. 4679); St. Louis Tickle (1906, Vic. 4624); Chicken Chowder (1907, Col. 3591); Maple Leaf Rag (1907, Col. 3626); Persian Lamb Rag (1908, Vic. 16127); Bunch of Rags (n.d., Edison 7305) [cylinder]; Creole Belles (n.d., Edison 7971) [cylinder]; Yankee Land (n.d., Col. 3155)

BIBLIOGRAPHY

U. Walsh: "Sylvester Louis Ossman: the Banjo King," *Hobbies Magazine* (Sept 1948–Feb 1949)

D. A. Jasen: Liner notes, *Kings of the Ragtime Banjo* (Yazoo 1044)

——: *Recorded Ragtime, 1897–1958* (Hamden, CT, 1973)

TREBOR JAY TICHENOR

Ostinelli, Sophia Henrietta Hewitt. *See* HEWITT, (3).

Ovation. Firm of guitar manufacturers. It was founded in Bloomfield, Connecticut, in the 1960s by Charles Huron Kaman (*b* 1919) as a subsidiary of the Kaman Corp., which makes aerospace products. Kaman became interested in guitars and guitar production, and began to test for this purpose materials that the company had developed in experiments on the vibrational and acoustical properties of helicopter rotor blades. The result was the first series of Ovation acoustic guitars, introduced in 1966 and 1967, which included the Balladeer six-string and the Pacemaker 12-string models. Both had Ovation's now famous rounded back, made from a synthetic material resembling fiberglass (patented by Ovation as "Lyrachord"), which enhances reflection, and thereby projection, of the sound.

Three years later Kaman unveiled another innovation in the form of a pickup built into the bridge saddles of the instrument; this senses vibrations in both the strings and the top of the guitar, and is connected to a small preamplifier inside the body, which is controlled by a volume potentiometer mounted on the heel of the instrument. This device effectively creates a hybrid "electric-acoustic" guitar, which has become the first choice of many pop guitarists who want to achieve the sound quality of a good acoustic instrument at relatively high amplification levels on stage. Ovation has also produced some less successful solid-bodied electric guitars, including the Breadwinner (1972), and the UK II (1979), the body of which is made of another plastic developed by Ovation (patented as "Urelite") over an aluminum frame.

The most expensive and distinguished of Ovation's guitars are the Adamas models, launched in the mid-1970s. The top is made from a sandwich of ultrastiff graphite fiber and wood, and has multiple soundholes, positioned at the upper end, for extra projection.

BIBLIOGRAPHY

T. Bacon, ed.: *Rock Hardware: the Instruments, Equipment and Technology of Rock* (Poole, England, 1981)

T. Wheeler: *American Guitars: an Illustrated History* (New York, 1982)

TONY BACON

Ovcharov, Jascha. *See* DELANO, JACK.

Overton, Hall (*b* Bangor, MI, 23 Feb 1920; *d* New York, 24 Nov 1972). Composer. He began his music studies in Grand Rapids, Michigan, composing an overture and a polytonal orchestral piece while still in high school. He pursued studies in counterpoint with Gustav Dunkelberger (1940–42) and in composition with Persichetti at the Juilliard School (1947–51); later he took private lessons with Riegger and Milhaud. Serving overseas in the US Army (1942–5), he developed remarkable skill in jazz improvisation and later appeared with such jazz musicians as Getz, Pettiford, Teddy Charles, and Jimmy Rainey; he also made arrangements for the Thelonious Monk Orchestra and contributed to *Down Beat* and *Jazz Today*. His own music was deeply influenced by jazz, but without his trying to make jazz "respectable" through the unnatural imposition of classical forms or materials. He taught at Juilliard (1960–71), the New School, New York (1962–6), and the Yale School of Music (1970–71). Among his many honors were two Guggenheim Fellowships (1955, 1957), a BMI award (1962), and the combined award of the American Academy of Arts and Letters and the National Institute of Arts and Letters (1964). The text of his opera *Huckleberry Finn* abandons the simple nature of the character and treats him as one concerned with issues of conscience.

WORKS

Dramatic: The Enchanted Pear Tree (opera buffa, 4 scenes, J. Thompson, after Boccaccio: Decameron), 1950; Nonage (ballet), 1951; The New Look is the Anxious Look (film score), 1960; Pietro's Petard (chamber opera, 1, R. DeMaria), 1963; Huckleberry Finn (opera, 2, Overton, J. Stampfer, after Twain), perf. New York, May 1971

Orch: Sym. Movt, 1950; Sym. no. 1, str, 1955; Concertino, vn, str, 1958; Sym.

no.2, 1962; Dialogues, chamber orch, 1963; Interplay, 1964; Sonorities, 1964; Rhythms, vn, orch, 1965; Pulsations, chamber orch, 1972

Other inst: 3 str qts, 1950, 1954, 1967; Sonatina, vn, hpd, 1956; Fantasy, brass qnt, pf, perc, 1957; Str Trio, 1957; Polarities no.1, pf, 1959; Va Sonata, 1960; Vc Sonata, 1960; Pf Sonata, 1963; Processional, brass qt, perc, 1965; Polarities no.2, pf, 1971; other pf and chamber pieces

Vocal: Captivity (Chaucer), male vv; 3 Elizabethan Songs (B. Jonson), S, pf, 1953; other songs

Principal publishers: ACA, Peters

BIBLIOGRAPHY

J. T. Howard: *Our American Music* (New York, 1931, rev. 4/1965)
D. Cohen: "The Music of Hall Overton," *ACAB*, x/4 (1962), 8
W. Mellers: *Music in a New Found Land* (London, 1964)
G. Green: "Current Chronicle," *MQ*, lvii (1971), 659 [analysis of Va Sonata]

OLIVER DANIEL

Owens, Buck [Alvis Edgar, Jr.] (*b* Sherman, TX, 12 Aug 1929). Country-music singer, guitarist, and songwriter. As a teenager he played mandolin and guitar on radio station KTYL in Mesa, Arizona. In 1951 he moved to Bakersfield, California, where he joined the Bill Woods band as a guitarist. He later played as a sideman on numerous recordings for Capitol in Hollywood, and was lead guitarist for Tommy Collins. He began recording as a soloist in 1956 for the Pep label and transferred to Capitol in the following year. His most successful period was 1963–9, when 17 of his recordings reached no.1 on the country chart. His pleading tenor voice, the harmony achieved with his guitarist, Don Rich, and the electrified instrumental accompaniment of his band, the Buckaroos, proved to be a commercially successful mixture; it soon became known as the "Bakersfield sound." Owens's popularity was enhanced by his nationally syndicated television program, the "Buck Owens Ranch Show." He built a minor commercial empire, including a music publishing house, Bluebook Music, and recording studios in Bakersfield, as well as radio stations in Arizona and California. After about 1970 he did not enjoy the success as a singer that he had in the mid-1960s, but he remained in the public eye as host (with Roy Clark) of the very popular "Hee Haw" television program (from 1969).

RECORDINGS
(selective list)

Above and Beyond (Cap. 4337, 1960); Excuse me (I think I've got a heartache) (Cap. 4412, 1960); Foolin' Around (Cap. 4496, 1961); Under the Influence of Love (Cap. 4602, 1961); Love's gonna live here (Cap. 5025, 1963); I've got a tiger by the tail (Cap. 5336, 1965); Buckaroo (Cap. 5517, 1965); Waitin' in your welfare line (Cap. 5566, 1966); Think of me (Cap. 5647, 1966); Tall Dark Stranger (Cap. 2570, 1969); Great Expectations (Cap. 3976, 1974)

With E. Harris: Play together again, again (WB 8830, 1979)

BILL C. MALONE

Oxford University Press (OUP). Firm of publishers. The English parent company dates back to 1478, but its first music publication did not appear until 1659; a separate music department was established under Hubert J. Foss in London in 1924–5. The New York music department was established in 1929 and handled by the firm of Carl Fischer. In 1959 it was consolidated into the New York branch of Oxford University Press in America. Although it is principally the sole selling agent in the USA for Oxford (which publishes music by English composers, educational series, and scholarly texts), the New York firm supports its own publication program, issuing works by American composers including Laderman, Beeson, and Adler, as well as editions by American performers and scholars, notably Greenberg's edition of *The Play of Daniel*. Susan Brailove became head of the department in 1973, succeeding Duncan Mackenzie (1929–49), Lyle Dowling (1949–57), and John Owen Ward (1957–72).

FRANCES BARULICH

Ozawa, Seiji (*b* Fenytien [now Shenyang, Liaoning, China], 1 Sept 1935). Conductor of Japanese descent. At seven, more interested in Western music than in oriental, he began piano lessons. At 16 he entered the Toho School, Tokyo, intending to be a pianist, but he broke both index fingers playing rugby and had to turn to composing and conducting, with Hideo Saito as his principal teacher. Hearings of the Symphony of the Air and particularly the Boston SO under Munch on their Japanese tours were crucial experiences. He began to conduct in Tokyo, including some concerts with the NHK Orchestra and the Japan Philharmonic SO, and in 1959 he left for Europe. Seeing a notice of the Besançon International Conductors' Competition, he entered and won. Munch, one of the judges, arranged for him to study at the Berkshire Music Center the following summer (1960), and there he won the Koussevitzky Prize. Next, he won a scholarship to work with Karajan in Berlin, where he was noticed by Bernstein and invited to accompany the New York PO to Japan in spring 1961 and to be an assistant conductor for 1961–2. He was sole assistant conductor during the 1964–5 season.

Seiji Ozawa, 1984

Ozawa's career expanded rapidly. He was music director of the Ravinia Festival (1964–8; principal guest conductor, 1969) and of the Toronto SO (1965–9). In 1965 he made his British début with the London SO. In 1968 he was appointed music adviser to the Japan PO. In 1970 he assumed the music directorship of the San Francisco SO (the first American orchestra he had conducted professionally, in January 1962), a position he held until 1976, when he became music adviser for the following season. In 1970 he also became artistic director of the Berkshire Music Festival (at the same time that Schuller became director of the Berkshire Music Center), with responsibility for most of the Boston SO concerts at Tanglewood. It was a most important homecoming, given the roles in his life of that orchestra, of Munch, and of Tanglewood. The Tanglewood appointment led to his becoming music adviser in 1972 and music director in 1973 of the Boston SO (concurrently with his San Francisco appointment); in 1973 he became sole artistic director of the Berkshire Music Center. In 1976 he toured Europe with the Boston SO, and then took it to Japan in 1978. After working for a week in 1978 with the Peking Central PO, Ozawa was invited to bring the Boston SO on an official cultural visit to China in March 1979; later that year the orchestra performed at the major European music festivals. To celebrate the orchestra's 100th anniversary in 1981, Ozawa led tours in the USA and Europe, embarked on a series of centenary commissions, and gave new performances of earlier Boston SO commissions. He has an extensive discography with the orchestra.

Ozawa maintains an active international career. He made his opera début at Salzburg with *Così fan tutte* in 1969, and in 1974 first appeared at Covent Garden in a revival of *Eugene Onegin*, winning praise for his warmth and acute sense of pace. He has appeared at La Scala and the Paris Opéra, where he conducted the première of Messiaen's *Saint François d'Assise* in November 1983. Ozawa has shown a special affinity for big 19th- and early 20th-century pieces with a certain element of display; but some of his failures (Verdi's Requiem, for example, and much of Berlioz) have been as surprising as some of his successes (*Così fan tutte*, much of Schoenberg, Bartók, and Stravinsky). He has a good ear, a ready and clear technique, abundant vitality, and charm. Orchestras enjoy working with him and tend to play beautifully; audiences respond to him. He learns quickly when necessary (but dislikes doing so), and his fast rise has sometimes led to his conducting works for which, interpretively, he was not fully ready; but his musical gift is not in question. Ozawa holds honorary doctorates from the University of Massachusetts, the New England Conservatory, and Wheaton College (Norton, Massachusetts).

BIBLIOGRAPHY

"Ozawa, Seiji," *CBY 1968*

P. Hart: "Seiji Ozawa," *Conductors: a New Generation* (New York, 1979), 165

H. Matheopoulos: "Seiji Ozawa," *Maestro: Encounters with Conductors of Today* (London, 1982), 384

MICHAEL STEINBERG/DENNIS K. McINTIRE

P

Pace, Charles Henry (*b* Atlanta, GA, 4 Aug 1886; *d* Pittsburgh, PA, 16 Dec 1963). Gospel composer and publisher. When he was 13 he settled with his family in Chicago, where he continued to study piano and began to write gospel songs and arrange black spirituals for the Beth Eden and Liberty Baptist churches. In 1925 he formed the Pace Jubilee Singers, an early conservative gospel group which recorded songs by Pace, Tindley, and others for Victor and Brunswick (1926–9). For a short time the group was accompanied by Thomas A. Dorsey, for whom Pace published several songs through his Pace Music House (established in Chicago in 1910). Pace moved to Pittsburgh in 1936 and shortly afterwards organized the Pace Gospel Choral Union, a 25-member ensemble that was enlarged to as many as 300 singers for special celebrations; its repertory consisted of gospel songs and spirituals. Pace also founded two highly successful music publishing houses in Pittsburgh – the Old Ship of Zion Music Company (1936–51) and Charles H. Pace Music Publishers (1952–63) – from which he published most of his 104 sacred compositions and arrangements and 26 secular songs. Pace's gospel songs, the best known of which are *Bread of Heaven*, *Hide my soul*, and *Nobody but you, Lord*, are in the style of Tindley's songs, with a verse–chorus structure, memorable melodies, and simple, effective harmonies.

BIBLIOGRAPHY

M. A. L. Tyler: *The Music of Charles Henry Pace and its Relationship to the Afro-American Church Experience* (diss., U. of Pittsburgh, 1980)

HORACE CLARENCE BOYER

Pacheco, Johnny [John] (*b* Dominican Republic, 25 March 1935). Flutist, percussionist, and bandleader. He moved to the USA when he was 17, and began his musical career as a bongo player. He appeared on several jazz and salsa albums before taking up flute, and it was as a flutist that, in 1960, he first made his mark. This was in a band led by Charlie Palmieri, which specialized in the Latin *charanga* style involving flute and violin. The following year Pacheco formed his own group and almost immediately became one of the most popular salsa bandleaders in New York, a position he retained in the early 1980s. During the 1970s he recorded a highly popular series of albums with the Cuban singer Celia Cruz. Since that time he has concentrated less on playing, although he has continued to record with his band. In the 1970s he also became more involved in his business as a record producer (he was a founding partner of Fania Records, the largest producer of salsa recordings).

BIBLIOGRAPHY

J. S. Roberts: *The Latin Tinge* (New York, 1979)

JOHN STORM ROBERTS

Pachelbel [Pachelbell], **Charles Theodore** [Carl Theodor] (baptized Stuttgart, Germany, 24 Nov 1690; buried Charleston, SC, 15 Sept 1750). Organist, harpsichordist, teacher, and composer. He was the son of Johann Pachelbel, and immigrated to Boston in about 1732. He was organist of Trinity Church, Newport, Rhode Island in 1734–5, and in 1736 he played harpsichord at concerts in New York. From 1737 to his death he was organist of St. Philip's Church, Charleston. He gave his first public concert in South Carolina on 22 November 1737. Peter Pelham was among his pupils. On 29 March 1749 he opened a singing-school at Charleston, though later the same year increasing lameness in his hands caused him to consider leaving South Carolina. At his death he left an estate valued at £579.14.9 which included "Sundry books English and German, Sundry books on Musick," a spinet, and a clavichord. Pachelbel's sole extant composition is a *Magnificat* for eight voices and continuo composed before he immigrated to America.

Johann [John] Michael Pachelbel (*b* Nuremberg, 15 Oct 1692), a younger brother of Charles Theodore, was an instrument maker. He played at festivities in Kingston, Jamaica, in 1728.

BIBLIOGRAPHY

V. L. Redway: "A New York Concert in 1736," *MQ*, xx (1936), 170

——: "Charles Theodore Pachelbell, Musical Emigrant," *JAMS*, v (1952), 32

G. W. Williams: "Early Organists at St. Philip's, Charleston," *South Carolina Historical Magazine*, liv/2 (1953), 84

R. Stevenson: "Caribbean Music History," *Inter-American Music Review*, iv/1 (1981), 82

ROBERT STEVENSON

Packard. Firm of reed organ and piano manufacturers. It was founded by Isaac T. Packard of Campello [now in Brockton], Massachusetts, who patented an exhaust bellows for reed organs in 1852. In 1871, with local backing, he established a sizable reed organ factory in Fort Wayne, Indiana, which produced instruments highly regarded for their superior construction. While Packard continued as designer and superviser of the business, its president and guiding force was S. B. Bond (1833–1907), a Fort Wayne banker. His son, Albert S. Bond, entered the firm as an apprentice in 1879, became general manager in 1886, and in 1893 expanded the firm's operations to include piano making. When reed organ sales declined after 1900, piano making became the firm's predominant concern, and this trend intensified after Packard introduced a highly successful player piano a few years later. The Packard Piano and Organ Co. was noted for its deluxe cabinet work, and some of its more elaborate reed organs, notably the Humanola models of the 1890s, have become collector's items.

BIBLIOGRAPHY
A. Dolge: *Pianos and their Makers*, i (Covina, CA, 1911/*R*1972)
R. F. Gellerman: *The American Reed Organ* (New York, 1973)

BARBARA OWEN

Paderewski, Ignacy Jan (*b* Kuryłówka, Podolia, 12 Nov 1860; *d* New York, 29 June 1941). Polish pianist, composer, and statesman. He attended the Music Institute in Warsaw from 1872, and on his graduation in 1878 was immediately engaged as a piano teacher. He studied composition under Friedrich Kiel and Heinrich Urban in Berlin (1881–3), then went to Vienna in 1884 to continue his piano studies with Theodor Leschetizky. Although Paderewski had given his first recital in Paris on 3 March 1883, he regarded a performance in Vienna in 1888 as his début. He gave concerts in France, the Netherlands, Germany, Poland, and Britain before making his American début at the Music Hall (Carnegie Hall), New York, on 17 November 1891. He completed 20 tours of the USA, giving over 1500 concerts and performing in every state; these were mostly solo recitals, but he also appeared with orchestras, usually performing two concertos as well as solo pieces in a single evening. He also toured in South America, Australia, New Zealand, and South Africa.

In his memoirs Paderewski stated that he did not consider himself a typical representative of Leschetizky's school, and criticized his teacher's playing as "sometimes brilliant, not always in the best of style, too exaggerated and decorative." His talent, musicality, intuition, and hard work enabled him to evolve his own style of playing, in which his contemporaries emphasized his individual treatment of rubato. His repertory consisted mainly of Romantic works, particularly those of Chopin and Liszt; early in his career he also played his own compositions. His opera *Manru* was given at the Metropolitan Opera in New York in 1902.

Paderewski gave the proceeds of many of his concerts to charity, including war relief and musicians' funds. In 1896 he established the Paderewski Foundation to award prizes to young American composers; among its winners were Parker, Bird, Hadley, Shepherd, and Riegger. He received honorary doctorates from Yale (1917), Columbia (1922), and the University of Southern California (1923).

Paderewski's musical career was interrupted in 1919 when he served in independent Poland as prime minister and minister of foreign affairs, and as the country's representative he signed the Versailles Treaty. He died in New York while conducting a campaign for assistance to Poland after the Nazi invasion, and was given a state burial in the Arlington National Cemetery.

BIBLIOGRAPHY
H. T. Finck: *Paderewski and his Art* (New York, 1895)
C. Phillips: *Paderewski: the Story of a Modern Immortal* (New York, 1934/*R*1978)
R. Landau: *Ignace Paderewski: Musician and Statesman* (New York, 1934/*R*1976)
I. J. Paderewski and M. Lawton: *The Paderewski Memoirs* (New York, 1938/*R*1980)

MAŁGORZATA PERKOWSKA/R

Padilla, Juan de (*b* Andalusia, Spain, *c*1500; *d* nr Quivira, Kansas plains [now Lyons, KS], Dec 1542). Missionary and music educator. He was probably the first European to teach music in America. He was trained and ordained by the Franciscans in Spain and in 1528 or 1529 traveled to Mexico, where he served in various missions. On 17 November 1532 he and nine other Franciscans wrote from the convent at Guatitlán to the King of Spain describing their missionary work, which included teaching Indian children to sing plainchant and organum. In 1540 he went with Francisco Vásquez de Coronado to colonize New Mexico, and worked there among the Moqui Pueblo and Zuni Indians. He traveled north as far as Kansas with Coronado the following year, then returned to New Mexico, and set out again with three companions in 1542. The four missionaries reached a large settlement of Pawnee near present-day Junction City, Kansas, where they spent four months successfully teaching. Padilla's expedition at the end of the year to preach to a nearby camp of Kansa Indians led to hostilities between the two tribes, however, and Padilla was killed by the Pawnee.

BIBLIOGRAPHY
A. F. Bandelier: "Fray Juan de Padilla, the First Catholic Missionary and Martyr in Eastern Kansas, 1542," *American Catholic Quarterly Review*, xv (1890), 551
J. B. Dunbar: "The White Man's Foot in Kansas," *Collections of the Kansas State Historical Society*, x (1907–8), 68
G. P. Morehouse: "Padilla and the Old Monument near Council Grove," *Collections of the Kansas State Historical Society*, x (1907–8), 472
L. M. Spell: *Musical Education in North America during the Sixteenth and Seventeenth Centuries* (diss., U. of Texas, 1923)
G. N. Heller: "Fray Juan de Padilla: the First Euro-American Music Educator," *Kansas Music Review*, xliv/4 (1982), 6

GEORGE N. HELLER

Page, Hot Lips [Oran Thaddeus] (*b* Dallas, TX, 27 Jan 1908; *d* New York, 5 Nov 1954). Jazz trumpeter and singer. He worked as a professional musician in his home state of Texas during the 1920s, and maintained that he learned to play authentic blues by listening to the local performers there. During the early 1930s he was a stalwart of Bennie Moten's band in Kansas City. In 1936 he briefly joined Count Basie's band as a principal soloist, then left to become a solo artist at the behest of Louis Armstrong's manager Joe Glaser (a move generally regarded as having crippled a potentially illustrious career). Page gained much publicity during his brief stay with Artie Shaw's band (1941–2). He also made many fine recordings under his own name (1938–54), often leading bands made up of some of the finest swing musicians, including Earl Bostic, Don Byas, J. C. Higginbotham, and Ben Webster. His purposeful, exciting trumpet playing and his deeply felt blues singing were probably too rugged to gain widespread favor. Throughout his career he thrived on the atmosphere of impromptu jam sessions, in which his searing tone, dramatic phrasing, and improvised blues lyrics were a source of considerable inspiration to fellow musicians.

RECORDINGS
(selective list)
As leader: Skull Duggery (1938, Bluebird B7583); Pagin' Mr. Page (1944, Savoy

520); The Sheik of Araby (1944, V-Disc 418); St. James Infirmary (1947, Harmony 1069)

As sideman: B. Moten: Milenberg Joys (1932, Vic. 24381); A. Shaw: St. James Infirmary, pts i–ii (1941, Vic. 27895); E. Condon: Uncle Sam Blues (1944, V-Disc 191)

BIBLIOGRAPHY

SouthernB

E. Anderson: "Lips the Hard-Luck Man," *Melody Maker*, xxx (20 Nov 1954), 7

J. G. Jepsen and K. Mohr: *Hot Lips Page* (Basle, 1961) [discography]

JOHN CHILTON

Page, Patti [Fowler, Clara Ann] (*b* Tulsa, OK, 8 Nov 1927). Popular singer. She began her career singing on a local radio show sponsored by the Page dairy company, from which she took her name. This led to an engagement with a local band whose manager secured her a place on the nationally broadcast "Breakfast Club" and also a recording contract. Like Les Paul and Mary Ford, Page became a pioneer of multiple voice overdubbing, a procedure initially followed for reasons of economy on her first hit, *Confess* (1948). The huge popularity and sales of *Tennessee Waltz* (1950) laid the basis for the song's adoption as the offical State song. Although Page's forte was the popularization of such country-styled songs as *Mocking Bird Hill* (1951) and *I went to your wedding* (1952), she was equally effective on a pretty number like *How much is that doggie in the window?* (1953) or the evocative mood songs *Allegheny Moon* and *Old Cape Cod* (both 1956).

BIBLIOGRAPHY

"Page, Patti," *CBY 1965*

A. Pavletich: *Rock-a-bye, Baby* (New York, 1980)

ARNOLD SHAW

Page, Walter (Sylvester) (*b* Gallatin, MO, 9 Feb 1900; *d* New York, 20 Dec 1957). Jazz double bass player and bandleader. He played occasionally with Bennie Moten's band in the early 1920s, and in 1925 founded his own band, the Blue Devils, in Oklahoma City. At various times this group included Hot Lips Page, Buster Smith, Count Basie, Jimmy Rushing, Lester Young, and other leading figures in the southwest style, making the Blue Devils, along with Moten's group, the most influential jazz band in the area. In 1931 Page was forced for financial reasons to give up leadership of the Blue Devils, and he joined Moten until 1934. After playing briefly with Count Basie and then with the Jeter–Pillars band in St. Louis, he began a fruitful association with the Count Basie Orchestra (1936–42, 1946–9). He was a mainstay of Basie's celebrated rhythm section, where the solidity and swing of his playing enabled Basie to dispense with stride left-hand patterns and Jo Jones to transfer the pulse to the hi-hat cymbals. *Pagin' the Devil*, recorded with the Kansas City Six, a unit from the Basie band, includes one of the earliest jazz solos on double bass. These and other performances established Page as the leading jazz bass player of the late 1930s, and a creator of the "walking" bass style. Page returned to Basie from 1946 to 1949, but otherwise played mainly on a freelance basis with various swing and dixieland groups in New York.

RECORDINGS

(selective list)

As leader: Blue Devil Blues/Squabblin' (1929, Voc. 1463)

As sideman: Kansas City Six: Pagin' the Devil (1938, Com. 512); Count Basie: Oh! Red/Fare thee Honey, Fare thee Well (1939, Decca 2780)

BIBLIOGRAPHY

SouthernB

W. Page: "About my Life in Music," *Jazz Review*, i/1 (1958), 12

G. Schuller: *Early Jazz: its Roots and Musical Development* (New York, 1968), 293ff

R. Russell: *Jazz Style in Kansas City and the Southwest* (Berkeley, CA, 1971, 2/1973)

J. BRADFORD ROBINSON

Paine, John Knowles (*b* Portland, ME, 9 Jan 1839; *d* Cambridge, MA, 25 April 1906). Composer and teacher. He was the first native American to win acceptance as a composer of large-scale concert music, and one of the first to be named professor of music in an American university (Harvard).

As a youth, Paine studied organ, piano, harmony, and counterpoint with Hermann Kotzschmar, a musician who had fled from Germany in 1848 and settled in Maine. After a thorough musical grounding, Paine sailed for Europe in September 1858. In Berlin he studied organ with Karl-August Haupt (who was apparently his principal mentor), and orchestration and composition with Wilhelm Friedrich Wieprecht, among others. He remained abroad for three years, traveling during vacations, playing the organ, and giving piano recitals in Germany and England; he met and played for Clara Schumann; and he was affected by the rediscovery of the music of Bach then current in Berlin. During this visit and also during a second, lengthy one to Germany at the end of the 1860s, Paine absorbed the style, manner, and taste of the German musical world, and put it to immediate use upon his return to the USA.

When he settled in Boston in 1861, Paine started a series of organ recitals and public lectures on musical style, forms, and history; these ultimately won him an appointment to the faculty of Harvard, which he retained until towards the end of his life. The department of music that he organized was to be a model for many others in American universities. Paine became the idol of the arbiter of the Boston genteel tradition in the arts, John Sullivan Dwight, whose Boston-based *Journal of Music* was always flattering when reporting Paine's concerts and lectures and, more important, when lobbying for more attention to music at Harvard.

Paine was a charter member of the American Guild of Organists, and played at Harvard's Appleton Chapel for several decades before his energies were directed towards composition and teaching. His early organ recitals were models of catholicity and included major works of Bach, not often heard in the USA at that time. Paine also lectured at the New England Conservatory, on whose board he sat as a friendly adviser; he taught at Boston University; and he appears to have had a large circle of musical friends, notably the conductor Theodore Thomas, the pianist Amy Fay, and the singer Emma Eames. Paine's Harvard composition students included John Alden Carpenter, Frederick S. Converse, Arthur Foote, Edward B. Hill, Daniel Gregory Mason, and Walter Spalding; his students in music history and style included Richard Aldrich, Archibald Davison, Olin Downes, Henry Finck, M. A. D. Howe, Hugo Leichtentritt, Owen Wister, and Henry Lee Higginson. Paine advised the last-named in the founding and early development of the Boston SO. In 1898 he became a member of the National Institute of Arts and Letters.

Paine served the Harvard community for 43 years. By his presence and by his serious concern with music in a liberal arts college he awakened a regard for music among many generations of Harvard men. His writings testify to his insistence upon the place of music within the liberal arts. Performances of his compositions were treated as major cultural events in American public life, to judge from the reviews they attracted in the major literary journals. He was commissioned to write a major commemorative composition for each of America's expositions during his lifetime. His compositions formed a major part of the musical activities in Cambridge, most notably his music for the performance in Greek of Sophocles' *Oedipus tyrannus* (at Harvard's Sanders Theatre in 1881). Paine nourished the Harvard community with over 100 original musical compositions for use in campus plays, concerts, and other diversions; with numerous lectures and prose articles; and by his presence as college organist, teacher, and companion. He made Cambridge a center of musical America and attracted such members of the Cambridge and Boston intelligentsia as H. W. Longfellow, R. W. Emerson, O. W. Holmes, J. R. Lowell, J. G. Whittier, C. W. Eliot, J. Fiske, W. D. Howells, the James brothers, F. J. Turner, C. E. Norton, and G. Santayana. He pioneered not only in the setting up of a collegiate department of music, but in being a "composer-in-residence," in contrast to the nature of appointments in contemporary European universities.

Paine modeled his early works upon the style of the masters he had studied, especially Bach and the Viennese classicists. The early keyboard music, the Mass in D, the First Symphony, the oratorio *St. Peter*, and the early cantatas are all in the accepted academic style prevalent before 1860 in German and German-American circles. Some of them, notably the Mass in D, go beyond mere competence to genuine inspiration and grandeur. Then, in a desire to align himself with musical progress (even after having written scathingly against the corruption of chromaticism), Paine altered his musical style by infusing it with greater chromatic activity. Finally, a decline in health, bitterness at the lack of acceptance of his opera *Azara* (never staged), and the wear upon him of the academic *ennui* built into such a long teaching career contributed to a lessening of quality in his compositions in the last two decades of his life.

Title page of John Knowles Paine's Symphony no.1 op.23, first published by Breitkopf & Härtel in Leipzig (1908)

The change in style may be seen by comparing his two symphonies. The first (see illustration), while not of uniformly superior quality, states its classical case with force and eloquence. A masterly handling of the sonata idea is notable in the opening movement and a lovely, mid-19th-century melodic slow movement, with no unnecessarily cloying chromaticisms present. The second attempts to be programmatic, and rambles into mere derivation of more current European models. A similar change may be seen in the choral and keyboard music, the latter shifting from a clear-textured style to one in which elaborate Chopin-like figurations predominate at the expense of musical intelligibility. Perhaps the finest work from his later years is the Prelude to *Oedipus tyrannus*. Paine's music is characterized by a strong sense of tonality, by regular metric organization, by sensitive orchestration and textural devices, and by harmony marked by an increasing chromaticism (*see also* ORCHESTRAL MUSIC, §2).

Paine was rewarded in his lifetime by massive attention to his large works: the Mass in D, the oratorio *St. Peter*, the two symphonies, some of the cantatas, and music for plays. His music was performed frequently by the Boston SO and the Theodore Thomas orchestra. In 1883 George Henschel, then the conductor of the Boston SO, was sent the following Valentine greeting:

> Oh, Henschel, cease thy higher flight!
> And give the public something light;
> Let no more Wagner themes thy bill enhance
> And give the native workers just one chance.
> Don't give the Dvořák symphony again;
> If you would give us joy, oh give us Paine!

WORKS

Editions: *The Complete Organ Works of J. K. Paine*, ed. W. Leupold (Dayton, OH, 1975) [L]
J. K. Paine: Complete Piano Music, ed. J. C. Schmidt (New York, 1984) [S]

op.

STAGE

— Il pesceballo (comic opera, F. J. Child, J. R. Lowell), 1862, lib. (Cambridge, MA, 1862), music (mostly arrs. of pieces by Mozart, Rossini, Bellini, Donizetti) lost

35 Oedipus tyrannus (incidental music, Sophocles), T, male chorus, orch, 1880–81 (Boston, 1881), Cambridge, 17 May 1881; rev. 1895; version for large orch (Boston, 1908); Prelude pubd separately (Leipzig, 1903)

— Azara (grand opera, 3, Paine), 1883–98 (Leipzig, 1901), concert perf., Boston, 7 May 1903

— The Birds (incidental music, Aristophanes), T, male chorus, orch, 1900 (Boston, 1902), Cambridge, 10 May 1901

CHORAL

— Agnus Dei, 1861, lost

— Benedictus, 1861, lost

— Hymn for Harvard Commencement (J. B. Greenough), 1862, rev. 1883 (Boston, 1883)

8 Domine salvum fac, inauguration hymn for Harvard president, male chorus, orch, 1863 (Cambridge, 1915)

10 Mass, D, S, A, T, B, chorus, org, orch, 1865 (New York, 1866); Berlin, 16 Feb 1867

14/1 Funeral Hymn for a Soldier, male chorus, *c*1863

14/3 Minstrel's Song, male chorus, *c*1863

— Peace, peace to him that's gone, male chorus, *c*1863

— The Summer Webs, male chorus, c1863
— Radway's Ready Relief (advertisement text), male chorus, c1863 (Boston, 1883)
— Soldier's Oath (C. T. Brooks), male chorus, 1865
— O bless the Lord, my soul (I. Watts), male chorus (Boston, 1911)
20 St. Peter (oratorio), S, A, T, B, chorus, org, orch, 1870–72 (Boston, 1872); Portland, ME, 3 June 1873
27 Centennial Hymn (J. G. Whittier), chorus, org, orch, 1876 (Boston, 1876), for Centennial Exposition, Philadelphia, 1876
36 The Realm of Fancy (after J. Keats), cantata, S, A, T, B, chorus, orch, 1882 (Boston, 1882)
37 Phoebus, Arise! (W. Drummond), cantata, T, male chorus, orch, 1882 (Boston, 1882)
38 The Nativity (after J. Milton), cantata, S, A, T, B, chorus, orch, 1883 (Boston, 1883), for Handel and Haydn Society, Boston; rev. 1903 as op.39 (Boston, 1903)
— Divine Love (C. Wesley), 1883, lost
43 Song of Promise (after G. E. Woodberry), cantata, S, chorus, org, orch, 1888 (Cincinnati, 1888), for Cincinnati May Festival
— Columbus March and Hymn (Paine), chorus, org, orch, 1892 (Boston, 1892), for World's Columbian Exposition, Chicago, 1893
— Freedom, our Queen (O. W. Holmes), children's chorus, 1893, for World's Columbian Exposition, Chicago, 1893 (London, 1893); arr. SATB (New York, 1902)
— Hymn of the West (E. C. Stedman), chorus, orch, 1903 (St. Louis, 1904/R), for Louisiana Purchase Exposition, St. Louis, 1904

Other occasional works, chorus, kbd

SONGS

(all for 1v, pf)

29 Four Songs, c1866–c1878 (Boston, 1879): Matin Song (B. Taylor), ed. R. Hughes, Songs by Thirty Americans (Boston, 1904/R1977); I wore your roses yesterday (C. Thaxter); Early Springtime (T. Hill); Moonlight (J. von Eichendorff)
— Spring, 1869
— The Fountain (G. P. Lathrop), c1878
— The clover blossoms kiss her feet (O. Laighton), 1882
40/1 A bird upon a rosy bough (C. Thaxter) (Boston, 1884)
40/2 A Farewell (C. Kingsley) (Boston, 1885)
40/3 Beneath the starry arch (H. Martineau) (Boston, 1885)
40/4 Music when soft voices die (P. B. Shelley), lost

Other songs

ORCHESTRAL

23 Symphony no.1, c, 1875 (Leipzig, 1908); repr. in H. W. Hitchcock, ed., Earlier American Music, i (New York, 1972)
28 As you Like it, ov., c1876, pubd as Was ihr wollt (Leipzig, 1907)
31 The Tempest, sym. poem after Shakespeare, c1876 (Leipzig, 1907)
33 Duo concertante, vn, vc, orch, c1877
34 Symphony no.2 "In the Spring," A, 1879 (Boston, 1880)
44 An Island Fantasy, sym. poem, c1888, pubd as Poseidon and Amphitrite: an Ocean Fantasy (Leipzig, 1907)
— Lincoln: a Tragic Tone Poem, c1904–6, inc.

CHAMBER

5 String Quartet, D, c1855 (New York, 1940)
22 Piano Trio, d, c1874
24 Violin Sonata, b, 1875, rev. c1905
30 Romanza and Scherzo, vc, pf, c1875
32 Larghetto and Scherzo, vn, vc, pf, c1877

ORGAN

— Prelude and Fugue, g, 1859
— Prelude, c
2/1 Fantasia and Fugue, e, 1860
2/2 Double Fugue on God Save the Queen or Heil dir im Siegeskranz, D, 1860; L
3/1 Concert Variations on the Austrian Hymn, F, 1860 (Boston, 1876); L
3/2 Concert Variations on The Star-Spangled Banner, c1861 (Boston, 1865); L [as op.4]
— Concert Variations upon Old Hundred, c1861 (Cambridge, 1916)
6 Fantasia, F, 1865, lost
— Reverie, after Longfellow's Song of the Silent Land, c1862, lost
17 Andante con variazioni, from lost Fantasia Sonata, c1863
— Caprice, c1863, lost
19 Two Preludes, D♭, b, c1864 (Boston, 1892); L
— Fantasia on the Portuguese Hymn, c1864, lost
— Pastorale, c1865, lost
13 Fantasie on Ein' feste Burg, c1869 (Cambridge, 1916); L

Many preludes, fugues, other pieces

PIANO

1 Sonata no.1, a, 1859
4 Sonata no.2, f♯, before 1861, lost
7 Christmas Gift, 1862 (Boston, 1864); ed. M. Hinson, Piano Music in 19th-century America, ii (Chapel Hill, 1975); S
9 Funeral March in Memory of President Lincoln, 1865 (New York, 1865); S
— Valse Caprice
11 Four Character Pieces, c1868 (Leipzig and Boston, 1872), incl. Welcome Home to my Darling Lizzie! From John
12 Romance, c, c1868 (Boston, 1869); S
15/1 Prelude and Fugue, b, before 1865
15/2 Prelude, f♯, before 1865
15/3 Fugue, A, before 1865
25 Four Characteristic Pieces, 1876 (Boston, 1876); S
26 Ten Sketches: In the Country, c1873 (Boston, 1876); S
39 Romance, E♭, c1882 (Boston, 1883); S
41 Three Piano Pieces, c1882–4 (Boston, 1884), no.2 previously pubd (Boston, 1882); S; nos.2–3 ed. J. Gillespie, Nineteenth Century American Piano Music (New York, 1978)
45 Nocturne, B♭, c1889 (Boston, 1889); S

MSS of most unpubd works in *MH*
Principal publishers: Ditson, Schmidt, Breitkopf & Härtel

WRITINGS

with T. Thomas and K. Klauser: *Famous Composers and their Works* (Boston, 1891, rev. 2/1894, rev. 3/1901) [incl. "Beethoven as Composer" and "Music in Germany" by Paine]
The History of Music to the Death of Schubert (Boston, 1907/R1971)

BIBLIOGRAPHY

EwenD
Letters, scrapbooks, programs, etc. in *MB*, *MH*
G. L. Osgood: "St. Peter, an Oratorio," *North American Review*, cxvii (1873), 247
W. F. Apthorp: Reviews of Paine's music, *Atlantic Monthly*, xxxi (1873), 506; xxxvii (1876), 633; xxxviii (1876), 124
J. Fiske: Reviews of Paine's music, *Atlantic Monthly*, xxxii (1873), 248; xxxvii (1876), 763
L. C. Elson: "Native Music and Musicians," *Musical Herald*, iii (1882)
W. S. B. Mathews, ed.: *A Hundred Years of Music in America* (Chicago, 1889/R1970), 675
C. Thaxter: *Letters* (Cambridge, MA, 1895)
J. L. Mathews: "Music in American Universities – in Harvard University – an Interview with J. K. Paine," *Music*, ix (1896), 644
T. Thomas: *A Musical Autobiography*, ed. G. P. Upton (Chicago, 1905/R1964)
L. C. Elson: "John Knowles Paine," *The Etude*, xxiv (1906), 104
W. S. B. Mathews: "German Influence upon American Music as Noted in the Work of Dudley Buck, J. K. Paine, . . . ," *The Musician*, xv (1910), 160
R. F. Thomas: *Memoirs of Theodore Thomas* (New York, 1911)
E. Eames: *Some Memories and Reflections* (New York, 1927)
G. T. Edwards: *Music and Musicians of Maine* (Portland, ME, 1928)
W. R. Spalding: *Music at Harvard* (New York, 1935)
R. Aldrich: "Paine, John Knowles," *DAB*
A. Foote: "A Bostonian Remembers," *MQ*, xxiii (1937), 37
M. A. D. Howe: "John Knowles Paine," *MQ*, xxv (1939), 257
E. Fisk, ed.: *The Letters of John Fiske* (New York, 1940)
K. C. Roberts: *John Knowles Paine* (thesis, U. of Michigan, 1962)
R. Stevenson: *Protestant Church Music in America* (New York, 1966)
J. C. Huxford: *John Knowles Paine: Life and Works* (diss., Florida State U., 1968)
J. W. Barker: "A Report on the Society for the Preservation of the American Musical Heritage," *American Record Guide*, xxxiv (1968–9), 766
J. A. Mussulman: *Music in the Cultured Generation: a Social History of Music in America, 1870–1900* (Evanston, IL, 1971)
R. Smith: "American Organ Composers: John Knowles Paine," *Music: the AGO and RCCO Magazine*, x/2 (1976), 31

P. E. Stone: Liner notes, *John Knowles Paine Mass in D* (NW 262-3, 1978)
B. Owen: *The Organ in New England* (New York, 1979)
J. C. Schmidt: *The Life and Works of John Knowles Paine* (Ann Arbor, MI, 1980)
K. C. Roberts, Jr.: *John Knowles Paine* (Detroit, in preparation)

KENNETH C. ROBERTS, JR.
(work-list with JOHN C. SCHMIDT)

Paine, Thomas D(udley) (*b* Foster, RI, 1813; *d* Woonsocket, RI, 1 June 1895). Instrument maker and inventor. In 1848 he patented a rotary valve with three passages through the rotor instead of the usual two. His instruments are also the earliest known to use string linkage to turn rotary valves. A set of Paine brasses won a first prize at the 1852 Exhibition of American Manufacturers of the Franklin Institute in Philadelphia.

Paine first appears as a musical instrument maker in the Boston city directory of 1841. He exhibited a key trumpet at the Massachusetts Charitable Mechanic Association fair in that year. From 1844 to about 1880 he worked in Woonsocket, Rhode Island, supplying valve brasses of all sizes to many amateur bands. He was evidently assisted in the business by a younger brother, Emery A. Paine, and by his father, John O. Paine. Several examples of Paine's instruments are found at the Rhode Island Historical Society in Providence. He is also known to have made over 130 violins.

BIBLIOGRAPHY

R. E. Eliason: "Early American Valves for Brass Instruments," *GSJ*, xxiii (1970), 86
——: *Early American Brass Makers* (Nashville, 1979)

ROBERT E. ELIASON

Paiute. American Indians of the Great Basin area of Nevada, southern Idaho, Oregon, Utah, and eastern California (*see* INDIANS, AMERICAN, fig. 1). They comprise many small bands or groups, each of which has political autonomy and its own informal social organization, and all of which share a common language, culture, and territory. Many groups, such as the Bannock, Snake, Piavosoto, and Kaibab, are known by their band names, though all are Paiute.

The most important Paiute instrument is the split-stick clapper, used to accompany most social and ceremonial songs; the most unusual instrument is the shaman's rattle, made from a cocoon filled with rattling pieces and suspended from a forked stick. The flute, bone whistle, small double-headed drum, and bullroarer are also used. The musical bow, once prominent among many Paiute bands, was made from a piece of elderberry or maple wood 1.2 to 1.5 meters long; it was plucked with the finger, using the mouth as a resonating chamber.

The unique Paiute song form has greatly influenced the music of Plains tribes and other cultures, chiefly through the Ghost-Dance songs of the late 19th-century as sung by Wovoka (Jack Wilson) after 1889 and to a lesser extent by his father around 1870 (*see* INDIANS, AMERICAN, §I, 6(iii)). This form, called the "paired-phrase" pattern, is typical of the Great Basin area and is nearly always present in Paiute song. It is characterized by symmetrical sections with each phrase repeated (*AA BB CC*, etc.); phrases may be established by textural or accentual qualities or by melodic or rhythmic movement, and are frequently of unequal length. A second Paiute musical genre is "song recitative," in which narrative portions of Paiute myths are recited in a musical style unique to the animal character who is believed to be speaking. For example, "Badger-chief" recitations sound the same in any myth, and badger recitations sound different from "wolf" recitations. The recitation of "Badger-chief" (ex. 1) consists of a single measure of five beats with an anticipation of the second beat and a staccato final note. Textural phrases with fewer than eight syllables are lengthened by adding nonlexical vowels, while longer phrases of text are split between musical repetitions. This type of recitative occurs in a less developed state in other American Indian cultures.

Ex.1 Paiute "Badger-chief" recitation (from Sapir, 1910, p.461)

An interesting type of borrowing, the use of the Yuman rise, may be observed in a few Paiute songs. This may have entered the Paiute repertory through the so-called southern Paiute (Chemehuevi or Kawaiisu), who live along the Colorado River and have borrowed complete song cycles from the Yuma, including funeral songs, and salt, deer, and mountain-sheep cycles. Most songs have a comparatively narrow range, and their phrase endings tend to cluster around the final pitch (usually the lowest pitch of the song). They employ three to five tones and intervals of major 2nds and minor 3rds. Paiute music is representative of simpler Indian musical styles; it has profoundly influenced other North American Indian cultures from the 19th-century Ghost Dance to the pan-Indian songs of the modern era.

Collections of Paiute music are held at the Archives of Traditional Music, Indiana University, Bloomington, Indiana.

See also INDIANS, AMERICAN, esp. §I, 4(ii)(a), (c), (d).

DISCOGRAPHY

Great Basin: Paiute, Washo, Ute, Bannock, Shoshone (AAFS 38, 1954)
Chants of the Native American Church of North America, iii (Can. 6050, 1971)
Songs of the Warm Springs Indian Reservation (Can. 6123, 1974)

BIBLIOGRAPHY

E. Sapir: "Song Recitative in Paiute Mythology," *Journal of American Folklore*, xxiii (1910), 455
F. Densmore: *Northern Ute Music*, Bureau of American Ethnology Bulletin, no.75 (Washington, DC, 1922)
E. Sapir: "Texts of the Kaibab Paiutes and Unitah Utes," *Proceedings of the American Academy of Sciences*, lxv (1930), 297
I. Kelly: "Ethnography of the Surprise Valley Paiutes," *University of California Publications in American Archaeology and Ethnology*, xxxi (1932), 67–210
J. H. Steward: "Ethnology of the Owens Valley Paiute," *University of California Publications in American Archaeology and Ethnology*, xxxiii (1933), 233–350
G. Herzog: "Plains Ghost Dance and Great Basin Music," *American Anthropologist*, xxxvii (1935), 403
A. Pietroforte: *Songs of the Yokuts and Paiutes* (Healdsburg, CA, 1965)

J. RICHARD HAEFER

Palange, Louis S(alvador) (*b* Oakland, CA, 17 Dec 1917; *d* Burbank, CA, 8 June 1979). Conductor, composer, and arranger. His early musical training included clarinet and bassoon lessons as well as composition studies with his father and with Domenico Brecia at Mills College, Oakland. He settled in Los Angeles in 1936 and became assistant conductor, composer, and arranger for the Los Angeles County Band and arranger for the United Artists Studio and the Werner Janssen SO. He also studied composition privately with La Violette. During World War II Palange served in the US Navy, conducting and composing much music for the Naval Training School Orchestra in San Diego (1942–3) and documentary film scores for the Photographic Science Laboratory in Washington, DC (1943–6). From 1946 until 1962 he worked as an arranger and instrumentalist for various television studios in the Los Angeles area. Palange conducted numerous amateur and semiprofessional orchestras during the years 1953–79 and was music director of the Los Angeles Philharmonic Band (1953–79); the West Coast Opera Company, which he founded (1962–79); the Downey SO (1967–79); and the Los Angeles County Concert Orchestra (1972–9).

WORKS

Stage: Handsome Harpy (operetta, F. Smithee), 1965

Orch: Evangeline, tone poem, 1943; The Plagues of Egypt, tone poem, 1945; Sym. no.1 "Invasion," 1946; Pictures, fl, orch, 1948; Poker Deck Ballet Suite, 1949; Romantic Conc., pf, orch, 1949; Sym. no.2, 1950; 2 vn concs., 1950, n.d.; *c*30 shorter works

Sym. band: Sym. in Steel, 1940; Hollywood Panorama, tone poem, 1950; Campus Bells, ov.; Jazz Rhumba; Brass Woodwind Clique; Navy Forever March; Intrigue; Driftwood; Beginning of Time, suite; over 20 shorter works, many arrs. of orch works

Chamber: Classical Trio, fl, vn, va, 1942; 4 Generations, str qt, 1950

Film scores: 8 full-length scores, incl. Dark Venture, Juvenile Delinquent, and 6 US Navy documentaries; over 50 scores for short clips

Numerous arrs. of popular songs, opera excerpts, and inst works, for orch/band

Principal publishers: Boosey & Hawkes, Highland, Presser

GENE BIRINGER

Palestine, Charlemagne [Martin, Charles] (*b* Brooklyn, NY, 15 Aug 1945). Composer, pianist, and video artist. Although chiefly self-taught, he had early training at the Mannes College (1967–9) and studied electronic music at New York University with Subotnick (1969). From 1962 to 1970 he was a bellringer at St. Thomas Church, New York; this experience has had a pronounced effect on his music, which has a relentless and sustained quality. He was graduate assistant to Subotnick at the California Institute of the Arts (1970–71), where he developed a style of music based on drones using both electronic and instrumental sources, mainly the organ. His vocal improvisations, loosely derived from Indian music, emerged from working with the dancer Simone Forti and have become a focal point in his performances. Most notable, however, are his piano works, which are long, quasi-improvisational pieces using an incessant "strumming" technique for which Palestine has developed a unique virtuosity; his work is considered as much performance art as concert music. In New York (from 1973), he has become known as a video artist and sculptor as well as a composer and performer. His work in various media constitutes an artistic continuity unnoticed by those who see him only as either a musician or as an artist. He has received many commissions from European radio stations and festivals and has performed widely in North America; with few exceptions, his music is self-performed.

WORKS

Pf: Strumming Music, 1972–3, arr. hpd; Lower Depths, 1974–5; Wallenda, 1979; Timbral Assault, 1980; Musashi, 1981

Other: Diverse Etudes, carillon, 1964–82; L'avventura, elec series, 1966–70; Birth of a Sonority, elec, 1966–81, arr. str ens as Evolution of a Sonority, 1975–80; Spectral Continuum, org, 1970–81

BIBLIOGRAPHY

T. Johnson: "Meditating and On the Run," *Village Voice*, xix/5 (31 Jan 1974), 44

——: "Experimental Music Takes a Trip to the Arts World," *New York Times* (5 Dec 1976)

W. Zimmermann: *Desert Plants: Conversations with 23 American Musicians* (Vancouver, BC, 1976)

T. Johnson: "Charlemagne Palestine Ascends," *Village Voice*, xxii/16 (18 April 1977), 74

R. Mortifoglio: "Charlemagne Palestine's Badass Formalism," *Village Voice*, xxiv/26 (25 June 1979), 55

INGRAM D. MARSHALL

Palisca, Claude V(ictor) (*b* Fiume [now Rijeka, Yugoslavia], 24 Nov 1921). Musicologist. He studied at Queens College, CUNY (BA 1943), and Harvard University (MA 1948, PhD 1954). After teaching at the University of Illinois (1953–9) he joined the faculty of Yale University in 1959. Palisca's main interests are late Renaissance and Baroque music and the history of music theory. In *Baroque Music* (1968, rev. 2/1981) he emphasizes stylistic development, supporting his discussion of the music with citations from writers of the period and showing how Baroque practices grew from those of the Renaissance. His more specialized writings on late Renaissance and Baroque theory include a study and annotated edition of Girolamo Mei's letters on music (1960) and a large number of authoritative articles; as co-translator (with G. Marco) of Zarlino's *Istitutioni harmoniche*, he has been praised for an accurate and idiomatic text. Palisca has also pursued an interest in musicology as a discipline and its relation to music education in the USA. As director of a much-discussed seminar on music education sponsored by the American Office of Education and Yale University, he was responsible for the preparation of its report (1964); he was also director of research for the Yale Music Curriculum Project. His educational concerns include the music education syllabus of state schools, undergraduate training for musicological research, and the direction that research might most profitably take at graduate and postgraduate levels. He has served as president of the American Musicological Society (1970–72) and the National Council of the Arts in Education (1967–9), and as a director of the International Musicological Society (1972–7). (*See also* MUSICOLOGY, §5.)

PAULA MORGAN

Palmer, Ada. Pseudonym of SIBYL SANDERSON.

Palmer, Horatio R(ichmond) (*b* Sherburne, NY, 26 April 1834; *d* Yonkers, NY, 15 Nov 1907). Music educator and composer. He was educated by his father and at Rushford Academy, New York, where he taught from 1855 to 1865 as well as giving singing classes in the surrounding area. After the Civil War he moved to Chicago, where he directed the music in the Second Baptist Church, published the monthly magazine *Concordia*, and taught at assemblies throughout the Midwest and Canada. The success of his compilation *The Song Queen* (1867) encouraged Palmer to issue other collections, including *The Song Monarch* (1874) and *The Choral Union* (1884), and pedagogical works, such as *Palmer's Theory of Music* (1876) and *The Common Sense Music Reader* (1883). In the 1870s and 1880s his publications were among the most popular of their type in the USA. In 1874 Palmer returned to New York, where he organized the Church Choral Union in 1881. Since this proved successful, he was called upon to organize similar groups in other eastern cities. He was active at the Chautauqua assemblies as early as 1879 and was director of music there from 1888 to 1901; under his guidance performances of secular music at Chautauqua were expanded significantly. Although Palmer composed much music, only the hymn tunes "Yield not to temptation" (1868) and "Vincent" (1887) achieved wide popularity. As a pedagogue, however, his impact was substantial; widely traveled and widely read, he was an engaging lecturer and a forceful conductor and teacher.

BIBLIOGRAPHY

W. S. B. Mathews, ed.: *A Hundred Years of Music in America* (Chicago, 1889/*R*1970)

G. H. Jones: "Dr. Palmer," *The Musician*, iv (1899), 427
F. J. Metcalf: "Palmer, Horatio Richmond," *DAB*

WILLIAM BROOKS

Palmer, Larry (*b* Warren, OH, 13 Nov 1938). Harpsichordist and organist. He received undergraduate training at the Oberlin College Conservatory and completed his DMA at the Eastman School in 1963. His organ teachers included Fenner Douglass and David Craighead, and he studied harpsichord in Austria with Isolde Ahlgrimm at the Salzburg Mozarteum, and in Holland with Gustav Leonhardt at the Haarlem Summer Academies. From 1969 he has been harpsichord editor of *The Diapason*. An authority on the German composer and organist Hugo Distler (1908–42), Palmer has published English-language editions of Distler's choral works and written *Hugo Distler and his Church Music* (1967); his recordings include organ works of Distler, as well as harpsichord music of the 17th, 18th, and 20th centuries. He has performed as a recitalist throughout the USA and Europe, and has commissioned and given premières of numerous works for harpsichord by such composers as Bruce, Shackelford, Ross Lee Finney and Persichetti. In 1970 he was appointed professor of harpsichord and organ at Southern Methodist University in Dallas.

CHARLES M. JOSEPH

Palmer, Robert (Moffat) (i) (*b* Syracuse, NY, 2 June 1915). Composer and teacher. He won a scholarship to the Eastman School as a pianist, but gradually shifted his emphasis to composition, studying with Bernard Rogers (BM 1938, MM 1940). He also studied composition with Roy Harris, Aaron Copland, and, most important, Quincy Porter. He taught at the University of Kansas from 1940 to 1943, and at Cornell University from 1943 to 1980, when he retired from full-time teaching. He won an American Academy of Arts and Letters award in 1946 and has been a Guggenheim Fellow (1952–3, 1960–61) and a Fulbright Senior Fellow (1960–61). He has received commissions from the Koussevitzky Foundation (1942, for the String Quartet no.2), the Elizabeth Sprague Coolidge Foundation (1950, for the Piano Quintet), the National Association of Educational Broadcasters (1959, for the *Memorial Music*), Lincoln Center (1965, for the *Centennial Overture*), and Cornell University.

Palmer found his distinctive style early and developed it steadily. It can be seen as an outgrowth of the styles of his teachers, though it is connected equally with the work of Milhaud, Hindemith, Tippett, Petrassi, and, above all, Bartók; its vigor, lyricism, and depth (though not its full range) are represented by the First Piano Quartet (1947). Palmer's best-known piece, the *Toccata ostinato* for piano (1945), is an exciting treatment in 13/8 time of a boogie-woogie inspiration, familiar to Palmer from his experience playing jazz duets with the playwright William Gibson. The Piano Concerto (1971) is noteworthy for its culmination in a swinging long-breathed tune that incorporates motifs from the first movement, which have meanwhile been developed fugally and combined with contrasting motifs. These works together illustrate his stylistic consistency, his individual blend of diverse elements, and his hopes for the growth of what he has called a "structural organic music."

WORKS

Orch: Poem, vn, chamber orch, 1938; Conc., small orch, 1940; K 19, sym. elegy for Thomas Wolfe, 1945; Variations, Chorale and Fugue, 1947, rev. 1954; Chamber Conc., vn, ob, str, 1949; 2 syms., 1953, 1966; Memorial Music, 1960; Centennial Ov., 1965; Choric Song and Toccata, band, 1968; Pf Conc., 1971; Symphonia concertante, 9 insts, 1972; Ov. on a Southern Hymn, sym. band, 1979; Conc., 2 pf, 2 perc, str, brass, 1984; incidental music

Vocal: 2 Songs (Whitman), 1v, pf, 1940; Abraham Lincoln Walks at Midnight (V. Lindsay), chorus, orch, 1948; Carmina amoris (Sappho, others), S, cl, vn, pf, 1951, arr. with chamber orch; Slow, slow, fresh Fount (B. Jonson), SATB, 1953, rev. 1959; Of Night and the Sea (Whitman, Dickinson, others), chamber cantata, S, B, orch, 1956; And in that Day (Isaiah), anthem, chorus, 1963; Nabuchodonosor (Daniel), T, B, TTBB, wind, perc, 2 pf, 1964; Portents of Aquarius, nar, SATB, org, 1975

Chamber and inst: 4 str qts, 1939, 1943, rev. 1947, 1954, 1960; Conc., 5 insts, 1943; 2 pf qts, 1947, 1974; Pf Qnt, 1950; Va Sonata, 1951; Qnt, cl, str trio, pf, 1952, rev. 1953; Vn Sonata, 1956; Pf Trio, 1958; Organon I, fl, cl, 1962; Epithalamium, org, 1968; Tpt Sonata, 1972; Organon II, vn, va, 1975; 2 Vc Sonatas, 1978, 1983

Pf: 3 sonatas, 1938, rev. 1946, 1942, rev. 1948, 1979; 3 Preludes, 1941; Sonata, 2 pf, 1944; Toccata ostinato, 1945; Sonata, pf 4 hands, 1952; Evening Music, 1956; 7 Epigrams, 1957–9; Morning Music, 1973

MSS and scores in *NIC*

Principal publishers: Elkan-Vogel, Peer, Peters, G. Schirmer, Valley

BIBLIOGRAPHY

EwenD
E. Carter: "New Compositions," *Saturday Review*, xxvii (22 Jan 1944), 33
H. Livingston: "Current Chronicle," *MQ*, xli (1955), 511 [on String Quartet no.3]
W. W. Austin: "The Music of Robert Palmer," *MQ*, xlii (1956), 35
W. Holmes: "Current Chronicle," *MQ*, l (1964), 367 [on *Nabuchodonosor*]
P. Chihara: *Studies of Melody* (diss., Cornell U., 1965)

WILLIAM W. AUSTIN

Palmer, Robert (ii) (*b* Little Rock, AR, 19 June 1945). Rock and jazz critic. As a youth he played reed instruments with rock, country, and soul bands and later with an eclectic, psychedelically tinged group called the Insect Trust, with which he recorded two albums. He was a co-founder of the Memphis Blues Festival in 1966, and reviewed books and music for the *Arkansas Gazette* before graduating from the University of Arkansas (BA 1967). In New York thereafter he became a widely published freelance writer; from 1975 he was a regular reviewer for the *New York Times* and in 1981 he was appointed to its staff of jazz and pop critics. He has written four books, the most important being his study of the Delta blues (*Deep Blues*, 1981), and has held teaching positions at Bowdoin College, Memphis State University, Brooklyn College, CUNY, and Yale University. He has also collaborated musically on informal projects with Ornette Coleman, Sid Selvidge, and CeDell Davis, among others. Palmer's writing reflects his interest in all forms of pop, jazz, and avant-garde music and an encyclopedic knowledge of the blues and early rock; his prose style is direct and unmannered. More a celebrator than a critic, he brings a musician's understanding and sympathy to his subjects.

WRITINGS

Baby, That was Rock and Roll: the Legendary Leiber and Stoller (New York, 1980)
Deep Blues (New York, 1981)
Jerry Lee Lewis Rocks! (New York, 1981)
The Rolling Stones (New York, 1983)

JOHN ROCKWELL

Palmieri, Eddie [Eduardo] (*b* New York, ?1936). Pianist and bandleader. From the beginning of his recording career, when on his album *Eddie Palmieri and his Conjunto "La Perfecta"* (1962) he made use of a highly unconventional front line of flute and two trombones, he has been regarded as a creative and influential salsa bandleader. After the breakup of La Perfecta in 1968 he began to experiment with free-form piano solos that were strongly influenced by the modal approach of the jazz pianist McCoy Tyner. An excellent example of Palmieri's ability to inspire his sidemen in a performance owing some allegiance to free jazz may be found on the album *Sun of Latin Music* (1975), where on *Dia bonito* the conventional salsa percussion and brass instruments are combined with synthesizers. Palmieri also has an interest in Afro-Cuban religious drumming, heard on the album *Lucumi Macumba Voodoo* (1978).

BIBLIOGRAPHY

R. F. Thompson: "New Voice from the Barrios," *Saturday Review*, l (28 Oct 1967), 53

J. S. Roberts: "Salsa's Prodigal Son: Eddie Palmieri," *Down Beat*, xliii/8 (1976), 21 [interview]

J. McDonough: "Eddie Palmieri, King of Salsa Piano," *Contemporary Keyboard*, iii/12 (1977), 18

J. Rockwell: "Latin Music, Folk Music and the Artist as Craftsman: Eddie Palmieri," *All American Music: Composition in the Late Twentieth Century* (New York, 1983), 198

JOHN STORM ROBERTS

Palo Alto. City in California, site of Stanford University. *See* SAN FRANCISCO, §II, 7.

Palombo, Paul (Martin) (*b* Pittsburgh, PA, 10 Sept 1937). Composer. He attended Indiana University of Pennsylvania (BME 1962), where he studied composition with Charles Hoag; his other teachers were Robert Hall Lewis, at the Peabody Conservatory, 1963–6, and Barlow and Rogers, at the Eastman School (PhD 1969). While at Eastman he was awarded the Howard Hanson Prize for composition. In 1981 he was named composer of the year for the state of Washington. From 1969 to 1978 he taught at the Cincinnati College-Conservatory and developed and then directed the conservatory's electronic music studio, where he produced most of his music dating from this period. In 1978 he was appointed director of the music school at the University of Washington, Seattle; he became composer-in-residence there in 1981. He was then appointed dean of the College of Fine Arts at the University of Wisconsin, Stevens Point. Palombo's early works exemplify a strongly motivic and pointillistic approach, but since 1981 he has adopted a lyrical, even popular idiom in works that rely more on intuitive energy than on methodical structures. With Lucas Drew he edited Barry Green's *Advanced Techniques of Double Bass Playing*, an important two-volume compendium of bass techniques.

WORKS

Large ens: Serenade, str orch, 1964; Sinfonietta, chamber orch, 1965; Movt for Orch, 1967; Variations, orch, 1968; The Dance, dance band, 1980; Moody, Moody Blues, vv, dance band, 1981

Inst: Pf Sonata, 1965; Vc Sonata, 1966; Miniature, fl, 1966; Composition for 3 Insts, fl, cl, bn, 1967; Str Qt, 1967; 3 Manners of Chance, ob, cl, bn, 1967; Metatheses, fl, ob, hpd, db, 1970; Montage, vn, pf, 1971; Ritratti anticamente, va, pf, 1972; Variants, hpd, 1975; Music for Triceratops Americus, elec, 1977; Variatione da camera, fl, cl, va, vc, pf, 2 perc, 1980

Tape: Proteus (C. Geerling), orch, tape, 1969; Miniature, org, tape, 1970; Morphosis, ballet, 1970; Crystals, 1971; Sonos I–III, 1 inst, tape, 1972–3; Et cetera, ballet, 1973–4; Sonos IV, str trio, tape, 1974; Music for Stegowagenvolkssaurus, 1974; Theme: Horizons of the Air, 1974; Theme: We the Women, 1974; Laser Music, 1975; Laser Images, film score, 1975

1v, pf: Morning Memories (C. Henry), 1981; It's Over, 1981

Works composed 1978–9, withdrawn

DAVID COPE

Pan American Association of Composers. Organization dedicated to the promotion of experimental contemporary music and its performance in the USA, Latin America, and Europe, founded by Edgard Varèse in New York in 1928 after the discontinuation of the INTERNATIONAL COMPOSERS' GUILD (1921–7). The association was one of the first to encourage cooperation among composers throughout the Americas and to stimulate performances of American music outside the USA. Henry Cowell was acting president from 1929 to 1933; other composer-members were Antheil, Carlos Chávez, Ives (who gave considerable financial support), Riegger, and Salzedo. Membership was small, and concerts were managed by the composers themselves. Slonimsky, the regular conductor for the association from 1931, directed the premières of several significant American works, and in 1933 the association sponsored a series of weekly concerts on radio station WEVD, New York. Although it achieved greater success and recognition than the International Composers' Guild, the Pan American Association fell victim to the Depression and was disbanded in 1934.

BIBLIOGRAPHY

D. L. Root: "The Pan American Association of Composers (1928–1934)," *Yearbook for Inter-American Musical Research*, viii (1972), 49

VIVIAN PERLIS

Pan-Indianism. An intertribal movement of the American Indians which evolved in the 20th century; *see* INDIANS, AMERICAN, §I, 6 (iv).

Pantomime (from Gk. *pantomimos*: "one who does everything by imitation"). A theatrical genre in which mimed action is accompanied by music, sometimes combined with dialogue and sung text. In colonial America pantomime was an offshoot of the English tradition and in the 1790s French pantomime and *ballet d'action* were influential. After 1810 indigenous pantomime declined in popularity, but was incorporated into circus acts, where vestiges still remain in the mimed antics of the clowns and some of the equestrian routines. The influence of the mimed action, stage machinery, and action music of pantomime are also found in 19th-century genres such as melodrama and vaudeville.

1. The colonial period. 2. The post-Revolutionary period. 3. The 19th century.

1. THE COLONIAL PERIOD. The first documented performance of musical theater in America was *The Adventures of Harlequin and Scaramouch*, a pantomime performed as an afterpiece to Thomas Otway's play *The Orphan* as seen in Charleston on 4 February 1735, two weeks before the production there of the first ballad opera to be heard in America, *Flora*, by the English dramatist Colley Cibber. Like the dozen other pantomimes known to have been presented in the 1750s and 1760s, it was based on an English model, probably the comic portion of *Perseus and Andromeda* (1730) by Lewis Theobald with music by John Ernest Galliard. However, just as its title differs from that of the English version, so too must the music, stage design, and choreography have been reworked for the more modest theatrical capabilities of the colonies. In English pantomimes, besides an overture, there were often songs similar to those of BALLAD OPERA and "comic tunes" – short binary instrumental pieces to accompany the grotesque and stylized dances that formed an important part of the entertainment.

Besides *The Adventures of Harlequin*, at least a dozen more pantomimes (most of them also based on the characters of the traditional harlequinade) were presented in the colonies (in New York, Philadelphia, and Annapolis) between 1750 and the Revolution. A few of these are known to have been English works,

John Durang as Harlequin: watercolor from "John Durang's Memoir of his Life and Travels," c1821 (Historical Society of York County, Pennsylvania)

and it is probable that most were. The American composers (if any) of music for these productions remain unidentified and no music or librettos for pantomimes of the colonial period are extant; some indication of performance practices may be obtained, however, from playbills and from descriptions of differences between American and English productions.

2. THE POST-REVOLUTIONARY PERIOD. There are 14 extant pieces of pantomime music (dances, songs, and overtures) written by American composers between the years 1784 and 1812, including five by Pelissier and four by Reinagle. There is evidence from reviews, playbills, and librettos that a great deal more was composed; Pelissier, for example, is known from advertisements to have composed or arranged music for 14 pantomimes, Reinagle for more than half a dozen, Rayner Taylor for five, and Benjamin Carr for two. Overtures were frequently advertised as having been composed by local musicians; extant examples by Reinagle (*Harlequin's Invasion*, 1795) and James Hewitt (two overtures for unknown works) are of the medley type, characterized by the ingenious combination of fragments of popular tunes. Most of the surviving pieces, however, are single songs or dances that were published in anthologies of piano and vocal music; Reinagle's "Hunting Song" (published *c*1804) from *Harlequin's Almanac* (*c*1800) is a typical example.

Certain performers became particularly well known for their pantomime roles: John Durang (see illustration) and Lewis Hallam, director of the Old American Company, were famous as Harlequin, and Alexander Placide, a theater manager in Charleston, as a clown. French actors such as M. Francisquy, M. Quesnet, and Mme. Gardie, unable to perform English-language roles, appeared almost exclusively in pantomime, and they brought with them from France a new style of ballet-pantomime influenced by the *ballet d'action* of J. G. Noverre. This was grander, more spectacular, and more serious than the works based on the antics of the harlequin characters; the short, comic tunes expressive of specific actions were mostly replaced by more extended and abstract music characteristic of late 18th-century English and French ballet.

3. THE 19TH CENTURY. While pantomime did not flourish in the USA in the 19th century, English pantomime continued to be imported, among the most popular works being *Cinderella* (1804), *Mother Goose* (1805), and *Dick Whittington* (1814). Several imports were devised by James Byrne, the Harlequin and ballet-master at Drury Lane and Covent Garden, London, who was born in Philadelphia and had worked at the Chesnut Street Theatre before emigrating to England. According to Charles Durang, pantomime ceased to be attractive to audiences after about 1810 and, except in Philadelphia, where a pantomime was presented during the Christmas season well into the 1850s, performances were rare. The shift in performance style was also recorded by Durang; writing in 1856 of Lewis Hallam as a Ground Harlequin in the 1780s he states, "The modes of then executing that agile parti-colored cavalier's movements are now entirely obsolete and unpracticed by the modern representatives of his antics." At Niblo's Garden in New York, however, the French ballet-pantomime (with the addition of acrobatics and rope-dancing), as perfected by the Ravel family in the 1830s and 1840s, was more successful. A return to slapstick antics within a fairytale plot, characteristic of earlier pantomime, was offered by George Fox at the Bowery Theatre in 1865; his show *Humpty Dumpty*, a highly successful pastiche of existing songs and dances, outlasted even *The Black Crook* (1866) in number of performances, being frequently revived over the next two decades. Very little of the musical accompaniment for these later pantomimes, apart from patriotic songs, is known; it is quite likely that, as in England, the music was borrowed from other genres.

Although pantomime as a separate type of theater died out in the 19th century (with the exception of the occasional imported English production), elements survived in other genres. By the end of Fox's career in the 1870s his pantomime had become mixed with other specialty acts to form the VAUDEVILLE show. Patriotic and spectacular pantomime found a permanent home in the circus: John Durang and others performed such works as *The Independence of America, or The Ever Memorable 4th of July, 1776*, with music by Reinagle, for Ricketts' Circus in the 1790s. The true legacy of American pantomime music, however, is probably to be found in the machinery and scenic effects of 19th-century MELODRAMA, where music, often cued using the same titles as those used for 18th-century pantomime – for example, "hurry," "fright," "battle" – is used to underline the most dramatic scenes.

BIBLIOGRAPHY

W. Dunlap: *A History of the American Theatre* (New York, 1832)

W. W. Clapp: *A Record of the Boston Stage* (Boston, 1853/*R*1960)

C. Durang: "The Philadelphia Stage," *Philadelphia Sunday Dispatch* (1854, 1856, 1860) [series of articles; compiled by T. Westcott as *History of the Philadelphia Stage, between the Years 1749 and 1855*, 1868; *PU*; similar compilations as *The Philadelphia Stage* in *PPL*, *History of the Philadelphia Stage* in *PHi*]

O. G. T. Sonneck: *A Bibliography of Early Secular American Music* (Washington, DC, 1905, rev. and enlarged by W. T. Upton 2/1945/*R*1964)

——: *Early Opera in America* (New York, 1915/*R*1963)

E. Willis: *The Charleston Stage in the 18th Century* (Columbia, SC, 1924)

G. C. D. Odell: *Annals of the New York Stage* (New York, 1927–49/*R*1970)

T. Pollock: *The Philadelphia Theatre in the 18th Century* (Philadelphia, 1933)

L. Moore: "John Durang: the First American Dancer," *Dance Index*, i (1942), 120

R. J. Wolfe: *Secular Music in America, 1801–1825: a Bibliography* (New York, 1964)
D. Mayer: "The Pantomime Olio and Other Pantomime Variants," *Theatre Notebook*, xix (1965), 22
H. F. Rankin: *The Theater in Colonial America* (Chapel Hill, 1965)
A. S. Downer, ed.: *The Memoirs of John Durang, American Actor, 1785–1816* (Pittsburgh, 1966)
D. Mayer: *Harlequin in his Element, 1806–1836* (Cambridge, MA, 1969)
R. Fiske: *English Theatre Music in the 18th Century* (London, 1973)
J. Moy: *John B. Ricketts' Circus, 1793–1800* (diss., U. of Illinois, 1977)
L. Senelick: "George L. Fox and American Pantomime," *Nineteenth Century Theatre Research*, vii (1979), 1
A. D. Shapiro: "Action Music in American Pantomime and Melodrama 1730–1913," *American Music*, ii/4 (1984), 49

ANNE DHU SHAPIRO

Paoli, Antonio [Bascaran, Ermogene Imleghi] (*b* Ponce, Puerto Rico, 14 April 1871; *d* San Juan, Puerto Rico, 24 Aug 1946). Puerto Rican tenor. He studied in Spain and at the Milan Conservatory, making his début at the Paris Opéra in 1899, as Arnold in Rossini's *Guillaume Tell.* He returned to Puerto Rico and in 1901 traveled to Caracas, Havana, and New York. He was back in Italy in 1902 and then toured with the Mascagni Opera Company, visiting New York, Boston, and Philadelphia. He sang regularly in Central and South America, Europe, and Russia; his roles included Verdi's Otello and Manrico (*Il trovatore*), Saint-Saëns's Samson, and Vasco da Gama (Meyerbeer's *L'africaine*). In 1908 he sang at the opening of the new Teatro Colón, Buenos Aires; his La Scala début was during the 1909–10 season as Samson. His career declined after World War I, but he continued to sing until 1928, when he retired to a teaching position at the University of Puerto Rico. During his prime he was praised for his powerful, dramatically intense tenor. Among his recordings was a performance of *Pagliacci*, with Leoncavallo conducting (1907).

BIBLIOGRAPHY

C. N. Carreras: *Hombres y mujeres de Puerto Rico* (México, 1957), 185
F. Franco Oppenheimer: "Antonio Paoli, el tenor de la voz incomparable," *Contornos, ensayos* (San Juan, Puerto Rico, 1960), 127
H. V. Tooker: "Puerto Rico's Tenor," *San Juan Review*, iii/3 (1966), 4
M. de Schauensee: "The Lion of Ponce," *Opera News*, xxxvi/20 (1972), 6
C. Dower: *Puerto Rican Music Following the Spanish American War (to) 1898: the Aftermath of the Spanish American War and its Influence on the Musical Culture of Puerto Rico* (Lanham, MD, 1983), 12

GUSTAVO BATISTA

Papago. American Indian tribe inhabiting the harsh, barren desert land of southern Arizona (*see* INDIANS, AMERICAN, fig. 1). Extremely high summer temperatures and little rainfall make life in this environment quite unpredictable. The Papago have for years sought ways to propitiate the forces of nature in their daily and ceremonial life. Music and dance have played important roles for many centuries, as prehistoric iconographic representations indicate. Papago music includes both traditional ceremonial and social songs, and adaptations of nontraditional music in a form called CHICKEN SCRATCH by outsiders and *waile* by the Papago. Traditional musical instruments include the gourd rattle (*ṣawikuḍ*), rasping stick (*hiwçulidakuḍ*), cane flute, bullroarer, inverted basket drum, and a rattle made from a cocoon which is suspended from a leg band. The flute and bullroarer are seldom encountered today, and the rasp is used only in healing or other ceremonial songs, but the rattle is ubiquitous. The basket drum is frequently played with the rattle, and seldom on its own. The modern Papago instrumentarium also includes various European string and wind instruments. Papago singers use little vocal tension and a modest vibrato, and their music lacks the pulsations of many other Indian styles. A leader usually begins the song, and the rest of the singers join in after the first phrase. Almost all Papago songs have the same structure: each stanza, which contains three to five phrases, is repeated four or more times (if more, the number of repetitions is a multiple of four). Pairs of complete repetitions alternate with incomplete ones; in ex. 1 a complete repetition consists of *ABCD*, and an incomplete repetition of *BCD*. In many songs the second phrase is either an exact repetition or a variant of the first, both musically and textually. Examples of typical Papago song form include *AA′BC AA′BC A′BC A′BC* and *ABCD ABCD BCD BCD*. The drummer usually changes from a rubbing to a striking sound, and the rattle player from a continuous sound to a pulsating rhythm, to signal incomplete repetition. Rhythmic characteristics show a degree of complexity, with accent divisions occasionally shifting freely between three, four, five, or more beats per unit based on the text; the accents of the voice and accompaniment normally coincide on the beat. Each piece has as many as four rhythmic values, and rhythmic motifs often unify each song. The pulse is set by the accompanying instrument before the voices enter, and the song concludes with several sharp drum beats, a continuous rattle tremolo, or both. The melody typically descends, most songs ending a 5th to an octave below the highest song pitch. The compass is usually confined to an octave. The Papago tonal system resembles that of equal temperament, but it incorporates the neutral 3rd, and certain notes may be unstable, especially during the first strophe. Papago melodies have five to eight notes and use all combinations of internal intervals, though pentatonic scales are most common. Polyphony is rare (though historically found in the south-central reservation area); the usual vertical arrangement is an octave displacement between the male and female voices. Papago songs are, with very few exceptions, set to indigenous texts, which exemplify an old style of "song language."

Ex.1 Papago song, transcr. J. R. Haefer

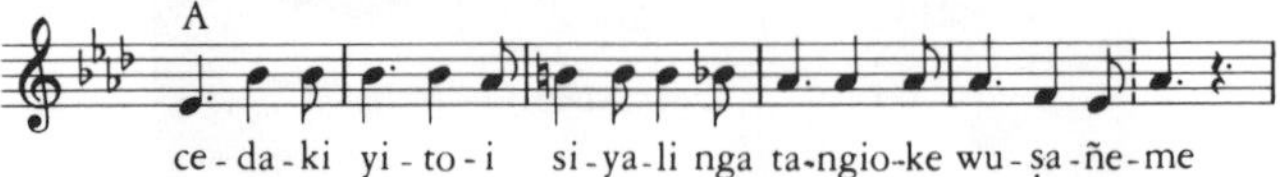
A
ce - da - ki yi - to - i si - ya - li nga ta-ngio-ke wu - ṣa - ñe - me

B
ce - da-kiya - li - toi si-ya-li-nga ta-ngio-ke wu-ṣa-nge-me ku-ñe

C
da - me ke - ki-wua k nei - na

D
je - we-ne ka - ci-me koi - de - he ki-ya-me ce - do-ngi-me

trans.: Green *I'itoi* came from the East.
Little green *I'itoi* came from the East.
And there he stood up and saw
The land apparently getting green.

Contemporary song types include both social and ceremonial genres, of which the social repertory is larger. The most common genre is the Round Dance (*keihina*), for which many songs that once had a ritual function are now used (see illustration). Other dances are still performed occasionally for entertainment, and the Skipping Dance (*celkona*) has been revived. Although once a part of intervillage games practiced in the 19th century, the *celkona* is now performed for entertainment and to foster cultural awareness; its songs are usually part of a cycle of eight or 16 songs. One of the most popular types of social dance is chicken scratch, found throughout southern Arizona, which has replaced the Round Dance as the predominant social event. A few Papago *pascola* (clown) dancers are still active in the southern parts of the reservation. The *pascola* dance was borrowed from the Yaqui (probably in the late 19th century), and the Papago version is now accompanied by guitar and fiddle, though the harp was used as recently as the 1940s. The types of ceremonial music most frequently performed are healing and wine songs. Each village has at least one healer who uses songs called *doajida n̄eñ'ei* to determine the cause of an illness; proper treatment requires the use of songs called *wusota n̄eñ'ei*, usually sung by a group. The *gohimeli*, or saguaro wine ceremony, the most important communal ceremony of the Papago, is celebrated in late July or August during the summer rains; elaborate preparations include several days spent in a foothill camp gathering the fruit of the saguaro cactus. Each family participates, and gives fruit to the elders to be fermented into *nawait* (cactus wine). An elaborate ceremony of recitations, songs, and dances surrounds the process of fermentation and consumption, which lasts four days.

Recently several new musical activities have been introduced among the Papago. Powwow dancing was taught to some Papago children through recordings, and around 1980 the first Papago Plains-style Drum was organized, although several members were not Papago. Powwow contests have been held during the annual tribal rodeo, and the first powwow based on Papago rules (such as a prohibition against songs dedicated to those deceased less than a year, and dancing in Papago rather than Plains direction), called the *Wa:k* powwow, began at San Xavier in 1983. This annual event, which includes such typical powwow activities as the grand entry Gourd Dance and contest dancing, also has tribal dances (Creek Stomp Dances, Yaqui deer and *pascola* dances, the Pima *matachini*, the Apache Mountain Spirit), traditional Papago games (women's field hockey, stick and foot-racing gambling games), and (from 1984) the Papago Old Time Fiddle Contest. The contest, with rules devised entirely by Papago musicians, is a fiddle-band, rather than a solo, competition. Many musical styles are now actively practiced among the Papago, all of which, secular and ceremonial, function as controlling forces in Papago life.

See also INDIANS, AMERICAN, esp. §I, 4(ii)(c).

DISCOGRAPHY

Songs of the Papago, collected by F. Densmore (AAFS 31, 1952)

An Anthology of Traditional Papago Music, collected by J. R. Haefer (Can. 6084, 1972)

"Chicken Scratch": Popular Dance Music of the Indians of Southern Arizona, collected by R. Nuss (Can. 6085, 1972)

An Anthology of Traditional Papago Music, ii: *Papago Dance Songs*, collected by J. R. Haefer (Can. 6098, 1973)

BIBLIOGRAPHY

F. Densmore: *Papago Music*, Bureau of American Ethnology Bulletin, no.90 (Washington, DC, 1929)

G. Herzog: "A Comparison of Pueblo and Pima Musical Styles," *Journal of American Folklore*, xlix (1936), 283

J. P. Shinham: *Die Musik der Papago und Yurok* (diss., U. of Vienna, 1937)

J. Chesky: *The Nature and Function of Papago Music* (thesis, U. of Arizona, 1943)

R. Underhill: *Singing for Power* (Berkeley, CA, 1946)

J. R. Haefer: *Papago Music and Dance* (Tsaile, AZ, 1977)

D. M. Bahr and J. R. Haefer: "Songs of Piman Curing," *EM*, xxii (1978), 89–122

D. M. Bahr, J. Giff, and M. Havier: "Piman Songs on Hunting," *EM*, xxiii (1979), 245–96

D. M. Bahr: "Four Papago Rattlesnake Songs," *Speaking, Singing and Teaching*, ed. F. Barkin and E. Brandt (Tempe, AZ, 1980)

J. R. Haefer: "O'odham celkona Papago Skipping Dance," *Southwestern Indian Ritual Drama*, ed. C. J. Frisbie (Albuquerque, 1980)

——: "Songs of a Papago Celkona," *Speaking, Singing and Teaching*, ed. F. Barkin and E. Brandt (Tempe, AZ, 1980)

——: *Musical Thought in Papago Culture* (diss., U. of Illinois, 1981)

J. RICHARD HAEFER

Papas [Papadopoulos], **Sophocles** (*b* Sopiki, Greece, 18 Dec 1893; *d* Alexandria, VA, 26 Feb 1986). Guitar teacher and

Papago Indians performing the Round Dance during Tucson Rodeo Week, February 1974

publisher. At the age of 14 he moved from Greece to Cairo, Egypt, where he learned to play the mandolin. In 1912 he returned to Greece, but in 1914 he immigrated to the USA. After serving in the US Army, he settled in 1920 in Washington, DC, where he began performing on radio shows in addition to teaching banjo, mandolin, and classical guitar. As a publisher he established the Columbia Music Company in Washington, and in the late 1920s he was one of very few Americans (others were Bickford, Krick, and Foden) promoting serious guitar literature, especially solo works by European masters. Papas befriended the guitarist Andrés Segovia soon after the latter's début in the USA in 1928, and later published his *Segovia Scales* (1953), a book on technique for aspiring classical guitarists, often reprinted. Papas himself is the author of the popular *Method for the Classic Guitar* (rev. and enlarged 1963). He was also the proprietor of a number of music schools in Washington, DC: Papas Studios (1938–47), the Columbia School of Music (1947–56), the Guitar Shop (1956–68), and a private studio in the Dupont Circle Building (1968–82). Notable among his students are Aaron Shearer, John Marlow, Clare Callahan, Sharon Isbin, Charlie Byrd, Dorothy DeGoede, Alvino Rey, and Joe Breznikar.

BIBLIOGRAPHY

J. Dallman: *Guitar Teaching in the United States: the Life and Work of Sophocles Papas* (Washington, DC, 1978) [interviews]

THOMAS F. HECK

Papi, Gennaro (*b* Naples, Italy, 11 Dec 1886; *d* New York, 29 Nov 1941). Conductor. A child prodigy, he studied piano, organ, violin, and theory at the Naples Conservatory. He was engaged as a chorus master at S. Severo (1906), Warsaw (1909–10), Turin, and Covent Garden, London (1911), and conducted his first opera, *La traviata*, at Milan in 1910. He was Toscanini's assistant first on a tour of Argentina (1912), then at the Metropolitan Opera (1913–15). He conducted *Rigoletto* on tour in Atlanta in 1915. Between 1916 and 1931 he appeared regularly at the Ravinia Park festivals in Chicago. After leaving the Metropolitan in 1932, he conducted in St. Louis, San Francisco, and Mexico, with the touring Scotti Opera, and with the reorganized Chicago Opera in 1934. The Metropolitan again engaged him in 1935. He was sometimes criticized as a lethargic leader; like Toscanini he always conducted from memory.

CHARLES JAHANT

Paranov, Moshe (*b* Hartford, CT, 28 Oct 1895). Conductor, pianist, and educator. He studied piano with Julius Hartt and Harold Bauer, and composition with Ernest Bloch and Rubin Goldmark. He made his New York début as a pianist in 1920, subsequently appearing as a soloist with the New York Philharmonic Society and with other East Coast ensembles. In the early to mid-1920s he appeared with Irene Kahn in two-piano recitals, and with Bauer and Gabrilowitsch in three-piano recitals. In 1920 he was the co-founder of the Hartt School of Music in Hartford, serving as its director (1938–57) and, after its merger with the University of Hartford, as president (1957–71). He was also music director of the Hartford radio station WTIC (1938–49), the Hartford SO (1947–53), and the Brockton (Massachusetts) Orchestral Society (1954–64). From 1942 until his retirement in 1971, he conducted the Hartford Opera Guild and the Hartt SO, and was music director of the Hartt Opera Theater, with which his name is most closely associated. After retiring, he remained active with this group, conducting every year.

GENE BIRINGER

Paray, Paul (M. A. Charles) (*b* Le Tréport, France, 24 May 1886; *d* Monte Carlo, Monaco, 10 Oct 1979). French conductor and composer. He studied organ in Rouen and became an organist at the cathedral there when he was 17; a year later he entered the Paris Conservatoire. After success as conductor of the Lamoureux Orchestra (1923–28), the Monte Carlo Orchestra (1928–33), and the Concerts Colonne in Paris (from 1933), he became principal conductor of the Detroit SO (1951–63). At Detroit he inaugurated the Ford Auditorium in 1956 with his *Mass of Joan of Arc* (1931). Paray acquired a reputation as a reliable conductor in a wide range of the classical repertory. As a composer he tended towards academic propriety.

BIBLIOGRAPHY

W. L. Landowski: *Paul Paray* (Lyons, 1956)
H. Stoddard: "Paul Paray," *Symphony Conductors of the USA* (New York, 1957), 160

NOËL GOODWIN/R

Parepa-Rosa [née Parepa de Boyescu], **Euphrosyne** (*b* Edinburgh, Scotland, 7 May 1836; *d* London, England, 21 Jan 1874). Scottish soprano. Daughter of Georgiades de Boyescu, a Wallachian baron from Bucharest, and the singer Elizabeth Seguin, she received her vocal training from her mother. After making her début in 1855 as Amina in *La sonnambula* in Malta, she sang in many European cities from 1857 to 1865. She was then brought to the USA by H. L. Bateman to undertake a lengthy concert tour with Theodore Thomas's orchestra. In February 1867 she married her second husband, Carl Rosa, a violinist who had accompanied her on the tour. With a two-and-a-half octave range, Parepa-Rosa was one of the best and most popular singers of her era in opera, concert, and oratorio. She appeared in Patrick S. Gilmore's Peace Jubilee in Boston in 1869 and gave concerts with her husband, with whom in 1869 she formed the Parepa-Rosa English Opera Company, a 100-member group generally regarded as the finest of its kind in America. It toured the USA extensively, presenting operas in English translation, and was successful both artistically and financially. Parepa-Rosa suspended the activities of her troupe in 1871, and with her husband formed a new group that featured the German tenor Theodor Wachtel and the English baritone Charles Santley. She returned to Europe in 1872. Her husband endowed the Parepa-Rosa Scholarship in her memory at the Royal Academy of Music.

BIBLIOGRAPHY

Obituary, *New York Times* (23 Jan 1874)
R. H. Legge: "Parepa-Rosa, Euphrosyne," *DNB*
G. P. Upton: *Musical Memories* (Chicago, 1908)
E. B. Marks: *They All had Glamour* (New York, 1944), 153

DEE BAILY

Parisot, Aldo (Simoes) (*b* Natal, Brazil, 30 Sept 1920). Cellist. He made his début at the age of 12 and studied first with his stepfather Thomazzo Babini and then for five years with Ibere Gomes Grosso in Rio de Janeiro. He also studied architectural engineering. He came to the USA in 1946 to study at Yale University (MA), and the next year made his début as soloist with the Boston SO at the Berkshire Music Center; he served as principal cellist of the Pittsburgh SO, 1949–50. Since 1948 tours have taken him throughout the USA and to Europe, Asia,

Africa, and South America. Although he favors suites by Bach and sonatas by Beethoven and Brahms, he is also a champion of contemporary music and his many recordings cover a wide repertory. He has given premières of works composed for him by Quincy Porter (Fantasia and Dance, 1950), Villa-Lobos (Cello Concerto no.2, 1955), Camargo Guarnieri (*Choro*, 1962), Claudio Santoro (Cello Concerto, 1963; Sonata no.3, 1964), Alvin Etler (Cello Concerto, 1971), Yehudi Wyner (*De novo*, 1971), and Donald Martino (*Parisonatina al'dodecafonia*, 1976), among others. Parisot taught at the Peabody Conservatory (1956–8) before joining the faculty at Yale in 1958; he has also held positions at the Mannes College (1962–6) and the New England Conservatory (1966–70), and was artist-in-residence at the Banff Center for the Arts, Canada (1981–3). Since 1977 he has been music director of the Aldo Parisot International Cello Course and Competition in Brazil. He has received many awards, among them the United Nations Peace Medal (1982). He plays the "Swan" Stradivari of 1731, formerly owned by Emanuel Feuermann.

BIBLIOGRAPHY

M. Fellowes: "Mastering the Cello – from an Interview with Aldo Parisot," *Etude*, lxxi (1953), 17, 61

A. Parisot: "Parisot on Parisot," *MusAm*, lxxxii/12 (1962), 64

S. Fleming: "The Aldo Parisot International Cello Competition," *HiFi/MusAm*, xxxii/6 (1982), 34

MINA F. MILLER

Parker, Charlie [Charles, Jr.; Bird; Yardbird] (*b* Kansas City, KS, 29 Aug 1920; *d* New York, 12 March 1955). Jazz alto saxophonist. He was one of the most important and influential improvising soloists in jazz, and a central figure in the development of bop in the 1940s. A legendary figure in his own lifetime, he was idolized by those who worked with him, and he inspired a generation of jazz performers and composers.

1. Life. 2. Style. 3. Influence.

1. LIFE. He was the only child of Charles and Addie Parker. In 1927 the family moved to Kansas City, Missouri, an important center of black-American music in the 1920s and 1930s. Parker had his first music lessons in the local public schools; he began playing alto saxophone in 1933 and worked occasionally in semiprofessional groups before leaving school in 1935 to become a full-time musician. From 1935 to 1939 he worked mainly in Kansas City with a wide variety of local blues and jazz groups. Like most jazz musicians of his time, he developed his craft largely through practical experience: listening to older local jazz masters, acquiring a traditional repertory, and learning through the process of trial and error in the competitive Kansas City bands and jam sessions.

In 1939 Parker first visited New York (then the principal center of jazz musical and business activity), staying for nearly a year. Although he worked only sporadically as a professional musician, he often participated in jam sessions. By his own later account (see Levin and Wilson), his individual style emerged at the end of this period:

> I'd been getting bored with the stereotyped changes that were being used . . . and I kept thinking there's bound to be something else. I could hear it sometimes, but I couldn't play it . . . . I was working over *Cherokee*, and, as I did, I found that by using the higher intervals of a chord as a melody line and backing them with appropriately related changes, I could play the things I'd been hearing.

Yet it was not until 1944–5 that his conceptions of rhythm and phrasing had evolved sufficiently to form his mature style.

Parker's name first appeared in the music press in 1940; from this date his career is more fully documented. From 1937 to 1944 he played in Jay McShann's band, with which he toured the Southwest, Chicago, and New York, and took part in his first recording sessions in Dallas (1941). These recordings, and several made for broadcasting from the same period, document his early, swing-based style, and at the same time reveal his extraordinary gift for improvisation. In December 1942 he joined Earl Hines's big band, which then included several other young modernists such as Dizzy Gillespie. By May 1944 they, with Parker, formed the nucleus of the Billy Eckstine band.

During these years Parker regularly participated in after-hours jam sessions at Minton's Playhouse and Monroe's Uptown House in New York, where the informal atmosphere and small groups favored the development of his personal style, and of the new bop music generally. Unfortunately a strike by the American Federation of Musicians silenced most of the recording industry from August 1942, causing this crucial stage in Parker's musical evolution to remain virtually undocumented (there are some obscure acetate recordings of him playing tenor saxophone dating from early 1943). When the recording ban ended Parker recorded as sideman (from 15 September 1944) and as leader (from 26 November 1945), which introduced his music to a wider public and to other musicians.

The year 1945 marked a turning-point in Parker's career: in New York he led his own group for the first time and worked extensively with Gillespie in small ensembles. In December 1945 he and Gillespie took the new jazz style to Hollywood, where they fulfilled a six-week nightclub engagement. Parker continued to work in Los Angeles, recording and performing in concerts and nightclubs, until 29 June 1946, when a nervous breakdown and addiction to heroin and alcohol caused his confinement at the Camarillo State Hospital. He was released in January 1947 and resumed work in Los Angeles.

Parker returned to New York in April 1947. He formed a quintet (including Miles Davis on trumpet, Duke Jordan on piano, Tommy Potter on double bass, and Max Roach on drums), which recorded many of Parker's most famous pieces. The years from 1947 to 1951 were Parker's most fertile period. He worked in a wide variety of settings (nightclubs, concerts, radio broadcasts, and recording studios) with his own small ensembles, a string group, Afro-Cuban bands, and as a guest soloist with local musicians when traveling without his own group. He visited Europe (1949 and 1950) and recorded slightly over half his surviving work. Though still beset by problems associated with drugs and alcohol, he attracted a very large following in the jazz world, and enjoyed a measure of financial success.

In July 1951 Parker's New York cabaret licence was revoked at the request of the narcotics squad: this banned him from nightclub employment in the city and forced him to adopt a more peripatetic life until the licence was reinstated (probably in autumn 1953). Sporadically employed, badly in debt, and in failing physical and mental health, he twice attempted suicide in 1954 and voluntarily committed himself to Bellevue Hospital, New York. His last public engagement was on 5 March 1955 at Birdland, a New York nightclub named in his honor. He died seven days later in the Manhattan apartment of his friend the Baroness Pannonica de Koenigswarter, sister of Lord Rothschild.

2. STYLE. Parker was among the supremely creative improvisers in jazz, one whose performances, like Armstrong's before him,

changed the nature of the music. The force and originality of his style was such that many listeners rejected his music as no longer part of the jazz tradition, and as other jazz musicians took up and elaborated his innovations the music sank to what was then its lowest ebb in popular acceptance. Only decades after his death did Parker shed the élite aura attached to him by fellow musicians and admiring jazz fans and begin to assume a classical status in the popular imagination.

Although Parker was an innovator, his music is rooted firmly in tradition. Like the Kansas City music he heard when young, Parker's repertory was built on a very limited number of models: the 12-bar blues, a number of popular songs, several jazz standards, and newly invented jazz melodies using the underlying harmonies of popular songs. This last-named category and blues account for about half of the pieces he recorded. Although the device of composing new melodic themes to borrowed chord progressions was not new to jazz, bop musicians of the 1940s employed this technique much more extensively, partly for financial reasons (to avoid paying copyright royalties) and partly to frighten the uninitiated (who could not always recognize the underlying chord patterns), but also to invent themes that were more consistent with the new jazz style than the original melodies. Thus, by restricting himself to a few harmonic sources, Parker was able to improvise over a few familiar patterns, against which he constantly tested his ingenuity and powers of imagination. A number of Parker's newly composed melodic themes (based on existing harmonic and metric structures) themselves became jazz standards, among them *Anthropology* (based on the chord progressions of George Gershwin's *I got rhythm*, and written in collaboration with Gillespie), *Now's the Time* (blues), *Ornithology* (based on Morgan Lewis's *How High the Moon*, and incorporating a melodic phrase improvised by Parker on Jay McShann's *Jumpin' the Blues* in 1942), and *Scrapple from the Apple* (the A section from *I got rhythm* and the bridge from Fats Waller's *Honeysuckle Rose*).

Parker's outstanding achievement was not his composition but his brilliant improvisation. His improvised line combined drive and a complex organization of pitch and rhythm with a clarity rarely achieved by earlier soloists. In contrast to the rich timbres of Johnny Hodges and Benny Carter, the two most important predecessors on his instrument, Parker developed a penetrating tone with a slow, narrow vibrato. This suited the aggressive nature of the new music, and allowed him to concentrate on line and rhythm. Parker's improvisations usually ignore the original

Ex.1 Parker's opening thematic statement on *Out of Nowhere* (1948, Le Jazz Cool 102), transcr. J. Patrick

Ex.2 Parker's improvisation on D. Gillespie, *Groovin' High* (1945, Guild 1001), transcr. J. Patrick

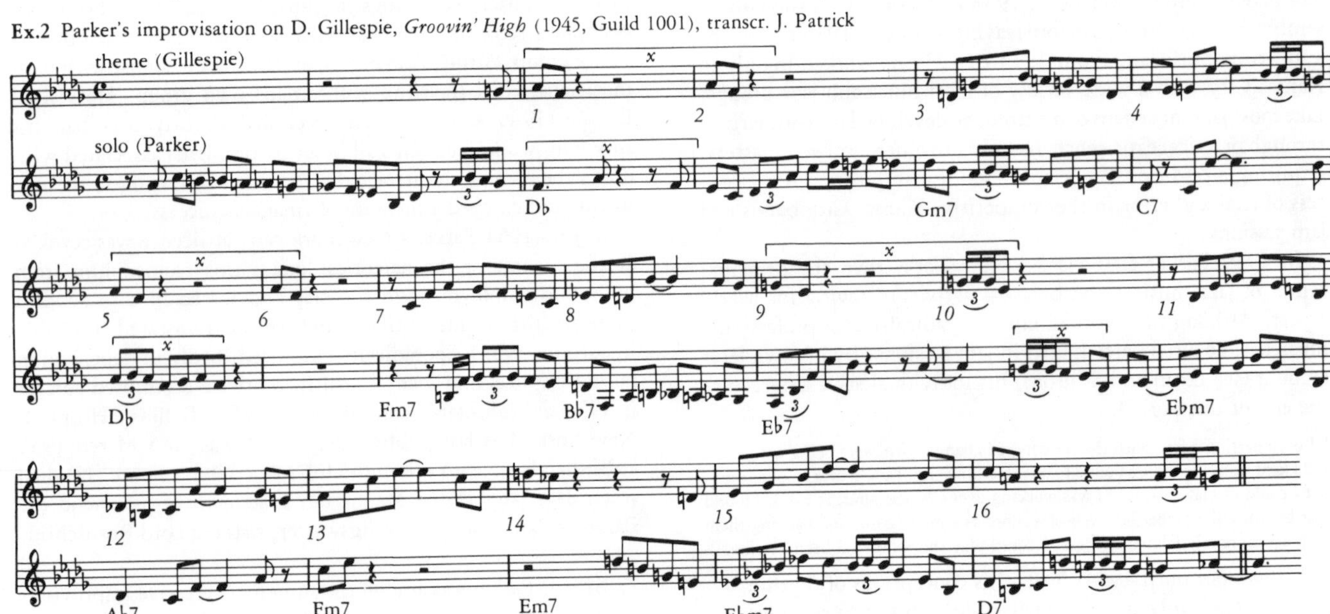

melody, being based instead on its harmonic structure. Melodic ornamentation or paraphrase occasionally occur, but characteristically these are reserved for thematic statements of popular melodies in the opening or closing choruses (ex. 1). However, his use of rhythm and pitch is sometimes subtly linked to the pulse and the chord progressions of the original. In *Groovin' High* (ex. 2) Parker maintained the prominent descending 3rds of Dizzy Gillespie's theme, but distorted them by inversion and elision (bar 1), compression (bar 5), and displacement (bar 10), the last two being ornamented as well. Other portions of the solo (bars 4, 7–8, 11–15) likewise follow the theme in pitch and contour, with bar 12 reducing the corresponding bar of the theme at the same time that it foreshadows the broken chords of the succeeding bar. In contrast to Gillespie's theme, Parker's solo breaks the quarter-note pulse, steadfastly maintained by the accompanying double bass, into a succession of varied and discontinuous subdivisions; this rhythmic variety is one of the foremost features of his style. The pulse, meter, and harmonic rhythm are further obscured by syncopation and the persistently contrasting accents and phrase lengths.

Parker's line typically includes pitches outside the given harmony: in addition to those produced by passing notes, suspensions, and other familiar devices, these result from free use of chord extensions beyond the 7th (particularly the flatted 9th and raised 11th), chromatic interpolations suggesting passing chords, the interchange of triads with others on the same root, and the anticipation or prolongation of chords within the given progression. Despite this harmonic complexity, Parker's best work has a clear and coherent line. Sometimes this is achieved by motivic development, as in the first ten bars of his solo on *Klactoveedsedstene* (ex. 3), based on the chord progressions of Juan Tizol's *Perdido*. This passage is constructed almost entirely of three very short ideas, developed and combined (bars 4 and 8), with silences of subtly varied length throughout.

Ex.3 *Klactoveedsedstene* (1947, Dial 1040), transcr. J. Patrick

Parker most often used a technique of improvisation known in musicology as the *cento* (or patchwork) method, where the performer draws from a corpus of formulae and arranges them into ever-new patterns. This aspect of Parker's art has been exhaustively investigated by Owens (*Charlie Parker*, 1974), who codified Parker's improvisational work according to about 100 formulae. Many of these are specific to certain keys (where they may be easier to finger) or to particular pieces. Some occur in earlier swing music, particularly in the work of Lester Young, but others originated with Parker himself, and later became common property among musicians working in the bop style. Ex. 4 shows a few of Parker's favorite and most characteristic formulae. Although it is based on a limited number of such formulae, Parker's work is neither haphazard nor "formulaic" in a restricted sense: the arrangement of the formulae was subject to constant variation and redisposition, and his performances of a piece were never identical. The overriding criterion was always the coherence and expressiveness of the musical line.

Ex.4 Some characteristic Parker formulae

Closely related to this "formulaic" approach is Parker's use of musical quotations. Probably no jazz musician before him was as fond of this device, or as wide-ranging in his choice of material, as Parker, particularly in private performances in a relaxed atmosphere. His improvisations contain snatches of melody from Wagner, Bizet, and Stravinsky; from popular songs and light classics; from earlier jazz performances such as Armstrong's *West End Blues*; and even self-quotations from his own jazz compositions. He retained this device throughout his career, and it is another measure of his authority in jazz that witty quotations became characteristic of the bop style as a whole.

3. Influence. Although Parker was not solely responsible for the development of the bop style, he was its most important representative and a source of inspiration to all musicians who took part in its early development. His influence was not limited to performers on his own instrument: his lines, rhythmic devices, and favorite motifs were transferred to instruments other than reeds, such as the trombone, vibraphone, piano, and guitar, and many innovations of bop drummers were made in response to the increased rhythmic complexity of his music.

Parker's influence was immediate and intense. His most famous early solos were learned note-for-note by thousands of aspiring young bop musicians on all instruments; as early as 1948 published transcriptions of them were available for study purposes. Some were even given texts by bop singers and performed as independent pieces. Parker's impact was naturally strongest on alto saxophonists such as Sonny Stitt, Cannonball Adderley, Phil Woods, and many others; only Lee Konitz and West Coast musicians such as Paul Desmond managed to create viable independent styles on alto saxophone. Despite the differences in timbre and mobility of the lower-pitched, bulkier instrument, many tenor saxophonists also came under Parker's sway, most notably Sonny Rollins and John Coltrane. Only in the early 1960s did Parker's influence gradually wane as the modal style led to the abandonment of bop's formulaic approach and the smoothing out of its erratic rhythms, and the free jazz style dispensed with preset harmonic patterns; nor did Parker's music play a role in the emergence of jazz-rock in the early 1970s. Nevertheless, his work remained available on disc in more or less "complete" reissue series, and recordings of his performances were discovered on private tapes, matrices, or radio recordings, and issued posthumously.

Charlie Parker (right) with Thelonious Monk (piano), Charles Mingus (double bass), and Roy Haynes (drums) in the 1950s

With the revival of bop in the mid-1970s Parker's music once again became a vital force in the evolution and teaching of jazz. Hundreds of his solos are now available to the student in published transcriptions. The group Supersax, based in Los Angeles, achieved some popular success playing Parker's solos in harmonized arrangements for saxophone chorus. His work has been the subject of several university dissertations. Although the evanescent, hieratic, and emotionally disturbing nature of Parker's music precludes popularity on a par with Armstrong's or Ellington's, his place alongside them as a creative force in jazz history is assured.

See also JAZZ, §V, 2, 3.

RECORDINGS
(selective list)

EARLY STYLE

As sideman with J. McShann: Lady be Good (1940, Onyx 221); Swingmatism (1941, Decca 8570); The Jumpin' Blues (1942, Decca 4418); Sepian Bounce (1942, Decca 4387)

Others: Cherokee (?1942–3, Onyx 221) [jam session]

MATURE STYLE

As sideman: T. Grimes: Tiny's Tempo (1944, Savoy 526), Red Cross (1944, Savoy 532); D. Gillespie: Groovin' High (1945, Guild 1001), Dizzy Atmosphere (1945, Musicraft 488), Shaw 'Nuff (1945, Guild 1002), Salt Peanuts/Hot House (1945, Guild 1003); R. Norvo: Slam Slam Blues (1945, Dial 1045); C. Thompson: 20th-century Blues/The Street Beat (1945, Apollo 759)

As leader, all recorded for Savoy: Billie's Bounce/Now's the Time (1945, 573); Thriving from a Riff (1945, 903); Koko (1945, 597); Donna Lee (1947, 652); Chasin' the Bird (1947, 977); Cheryl (1947, 952); Bluebird (1948, 961); Klaunstance (1948, 967); Barbados (1948, 936); Ah-leu-cha (1948, 939); Parker's Mood (1948, 936); Perhaps (1948, 938)

As leader, all recorded for Dial: Moose the Mooche/Yardbird Suite (1946, 1003); Ornithology/A Night in Tunisia (1946, 1002); Lover Man (1946, 1007); Cool Blues (1947, 1015); Relaxin' at Camarillo (1947, 1030); Carvin' the Bird (1947, 1013); Dexterity (1947, 1032); Embraceable you (1947, 1024); Klactoveedsedstene (1947, 1040); Scrapple from the Apple (1947, 1021); Crazeology (1947, 1034)

As leader, all recorded for Mercury/Clef: The Closer (1949, Mer. 35013); Bloomdido (1950, Mer./Clef 11058); An Oscar for Treadwell (1950, Mer./Clef 10082); Relaxin' with Lee (1950, Mer./Clef 11076); Au Privave (1951, Mer./Clef 11087); Blues for Alice (1951, Clef 337); Swedish Schnapps (1951, Mer./Clef 11103); Chi Chi (1953, Clef 89138)

Others: Out of Nowhere (1948, Le Jazz Cool 102); Anthropology, on *Charlie Parker and the Swedish All Stars* (1950, Sonet 27); Quintet of the Year: Perdido/Salt Peanuts/All the Things You Are (1953, Debut 2)

BIBLIOGRAPHY

DOCUMENTS AND SOURCES

N. Hentoff and R. Sanjek: *Charlie Parker* (New York, 1960) [list of compositions]

R. Reisner: *Bird: the Legend of Charlie Parker* (New York, 1961, 2/1962)

J. G. Jepsen: *A Discography of Charlie Parker* (Copenhagen, 1968)

T. Williams: "Charlie Parker Discography," *Discographical Forum* (Sept 1968–Sept 1970)

G. R. Davies: "Charlie Parker Chronology," *Discographical Forum*, nos. 17–26 (1970–71)

D. Morgenstern and others: *Bird and Diz: a Bibliography* (New York, 1973)

P. Koster and D. M. Bakker: *Charlie Parker*, i: *1940–1947* (Alphen aan den Rijn, Netherlands, 1974); ii: *1948–1950* (Alphen aan den Rijn, 1975); iii: *1951–1954* (Alphen aan den Rijn, 1975); iv: *1940–1955* (Alphen aan der Rijn, 1976)

C. Parker and F. Paudras: *To Bird with Love* (Poitiers, France, 1981) [photographs]

TRANSCRIPTIONS

[M. Feldman, ed.:] *Charles Parker's Bebop for Alto Sax: 4 Solos* (New York, 1948)

P. Pinkerton, ed.: *Charlie Parker: Nine Solos Transcribed from Historic Recordings* (New York, 1961)

W. D. Stuart: *Famous Transcribed Recorded Jazz Solos: Charlie "Bird" Parker* (New York, 1961)

Charlie Parker: Sketch Orks, Designed for Small Groups (New York, 1967)

T. Owens: *Charlie Parker: Techniques of Improvisation*, ii (diss., UCLA, 1974) [190 pieces]
S. Watanabe, ed.: *Jazz Improvisation: Transcriptions of Charlie Parker's Great Alto Solos* (Tokyo, *c*1975) [25 pieces]
J. Aebersbold and K. Slone, eds.: *Charlie Parker Omnibook* (New York, 1978) [60 pieces]
A. White, ed.: *The Charlie Parker Collection: 308 Transcribed Alto Saxophone and Tenor Saxophone Solos* (Washington, DC, 1978–9)

BIOGRAPHICAL STUDIES

L. Feather: *Inside Bebop* (New York, 1949/*R*1972), 11ff
M. Levin and J. S. Wilson: " 'No Bop Roots in Jazz': Parker," *Down Beat*, xvi/17 (1949), 1; rev. as "The Chili Parlor Interview," *Down Beat*, xxxii/6 (1965), 13
N. Shapiro and N. Hentoff, eds.: *Hear me Talkin' to ya* (New York, 1955), esp. 312ff
M. Harrison: *Charlie Parker* (London, 1960); repr. in *Kings of Jazz*, ed. S. Green (New York, 1978)
I. Gitler: "Charlie Parker and the Alto and Baritone Saxophonists," *Jazz Masters of the Forties* (New York, 1966)
J. Burns: "Bird in California," *Jazz Journal*, xxii/7 (1969), 10
D. Amram: "Bird in Washington," *Jazz Journal*, xxiii/8 (1970), 4
R. Russell: *Jazz Style in Kansas City and the Southwest* (Berkeley, CA, 1971, 2/1973)
——: *Bird Lives: the High Life and Hard Times of Charlie (Yardbird) Parker* (New York, 1973)
——: "West Coast Bop," *Jazz and Blues*, iii/2 (1973), 9
J. Patrick: "Al Tinney, Monroe's Uptown House, and the Emergence of Modern Jazz in Harlem," *Annual Review of Jazz Studies*, ii (1983), 150
B. Priestley: *Charlie Parker* (New York, 1984)

ANALYTICAL STUDIES

A. Morgun: "Charlie Parker: The Dial Recordings," *Jazz Monthly*, i/7 (1955), 7
A. Hodeir: *Jazz: its Evolution and Essence* (New York, 1956/*R*1975), 99
L. Feather: *The Book of Jazz* (New York, 1957, rev. 2/1965), 231
R. Russell: "The Evolutionary Position of Bop," *The Art of Jazz*, ed. M. Williams (New York, 1959), 195ff
J. Mehegan: *Jazz Improvisation*, ii (New York, 1962), 101ff
D. Heckman: "Bird in Flight: Parker the Improviser," *Down Beat*, xxxii/6 (1965), 22
J. Siddons: "Parker's Mood," *Down Beat*, xxxii/6 (1965), 25
F. Tirro: "The Silent Theme Tradition in Jazz," *MQ*, lii (1967), 313
D. Baker: "Charlie Parker's 'Now's the Time' Solo," *Down Beat*, xxxviii/19 (1971), 32
O. Peterson: "Early Bird," *Jazz Journal*, xxiv/4 (1971), 34
R. Wang: "Jazz Circa 1945: a Confluence of Styles," *MQ*, lix (1973), 531
T. Owens: "Applying the Melograph to 'Parker's Mood'," *Selected Reports in Ethnomusicology*, ii/1 (1974), 167
——: *Charlie Parker: Techniques of Improvisation* (diss., UCLA, 1974)
L. Koch: "Ornithology: a Study of Charlie Parker's Music," *Journal of Jazz Studies*, ii/1 (1974), 61; ii/12 (1975), 61
J. Patrick: "Charlie Parker and Harmonic Sources of Bebop Composition: Thoughts on the Repertory of New Jazz in the 1940's," *Journal of Jazz Studies*, ii/12 (1975), 3
——: Liner notes, *Charlie Parker: the Complete Savoy Studio Recordings* (Savoy 5501, 1978)
T. Hirschmann: *Untersuchungen zu den Kompositionen von Charlie Parker* (diss., U. of Mainz, 1982)

OTHER STUDIES

Down Beat, xxxii/6 (1965) [Parker issue]
J. Patrick: "The Uses of Jazz Discography," *Notes*, xxix (1972–3), 17
——: "Discography as a Tool for Musical Research and Vice Versa," *Journal of Jazz Studies*, i/1 (1973), 65
——: "Musical Sources for the History of Jazz," *BPiM*, iv (1976), 46
Coda, no.181 (1981) [Parker issue]
B. Priestley and others: "Charlie Parker: Thirty 'Bird' Years Away," *The Wire*, no.13 (1985), 25

JAMES PATRICK

Parker, Horatio (William) (*b* Auburndale, MA, 15 Sept 1863; *d* Cedarhurst, NY, 18 Dec 1919). Composer, music educator, and church musician. He began the study of music at the age of 14 with piano and organ lessons from his mother. He later studied composition with Chadwick, piano with John Orth, and theory with Emery in Boston. From 1880 to 1882 he served as church organist in Dedham, Massachusetts. His first compositions were 50 songs on poems by Kate Greenaway, written shortly after his first year of musical study; within the next few years he composed keyboard, chamber, and some short orchestral pieces. From 1882 to 1885 he studied at the Hochschule für Musik in Munich, including composition under Josef Rheinberger. During this time he wrote his first extensive compositions, including *The Ballad of a Knight and his Daughter*, the cantata *King Trojan*, and the Symphony in C.

On returning to the USA, Parker spent the years 1886–93 in New York, where he taught at the cathedral schools of St. Paul and St. Mary from 1886 to 1890, at the General Theological Seminary in 1892, and at the National Conservatory of Music from 1892 to 1893. He was organist and choirmaster at St. Luke's in Brooklyn from 1885 to 1887, St. Andrew's in Harlem from 1887 to 1888, and at the church of the Holy Trinity in Manhattan from 1888 to 1893.

Parker's reputation as a composer was established during the early 1890s with performances of his student works, the publication of a considerable amount of church music, and major works including the overture *Count Robert of Paris*, heard at the first public concert of the New York Manuscript Society in 1890; the cantata *Dream-king and his Love*, which won the National Conservatory prize in 1893; and the oratorio *Hora novissima*, written for the Church Choral Society of New York in 1893. There followed a series of major vocal and choral compositions, including *Cáhal Mór of the Wine-red Hand*, a rhapsody for baritone and orchestra first performed by the Boston SO (1895); the dramatic oratorio *The Legend of St. Christopher*, a commission from the Oratorio Society of New York (1897); and the motet *Adstant angelorum chori*, which received a prize and performance by the Musical Art Society of New York (1899).

Frequent performances of *Hora novissima* during the 1890s brought Parker to national prominence. In autumn 1893 he left New York to become organist and choirmaster at the fashionable Trinity Church in Boston. The following year he received an honorary Master of Music degree from Yale University and accepted the Battell Professorship of the Theory of Music there, a position he retained until his death. In 1904 he was made dean of the School of Music, and under his guidance Yale gained a national reputation for training composers; his pupils included Bingham, Walter Ruel Cowles, Ives, Quincy Porter, Sessions, and David Stanley Smith. Parker was elected to the National Institute of Arts and Letters in 1898 and to the American Academy of Arts and Letters in 1905. He also became an important musical figure in the New Haven community by organizing and conducting the New Haven SO (from 1895 to 1918) and the Oratorio Society (from 1903 to 1914). He conducted various choral societies and glee clubs both in the vicinity of New Haven and as far away as Philadelphia. He continued in his post at Boston's Trinity Church until 1902, when he left to take up a similar post at the collegiate church of St. Nicholas in New York; he served this Dutch Reformed church until 1910.

A performance of *Hora novissima* at the Three Choirs Festival in Worcester in 1899 was the first of a series of activities in England which included the commission of *A Wanderer's Psalm* for the Hereford Festival and the performance of *Hora novissima* in Chester (both in 1900) and of part iii of *St. Christopher* at

Worcester and *A Star Song* at Norwich (both in 1902). England's recognition of Parker culminated in an honorary MusD from Cambridge University in 1902.

Significant vocal and choral compositions from his later years include *Crépuscule*, a prizewinning concert aria performed by the Philadelphia Orchestra in 1912; the cantata *King Gorm the Grim* (1908) and the morality *The Dream of Mary* (1918), both for the Norfolk (Connecticut) Festival; and the oratorio *Morven and the Grail* (1915), commissioned for the centennial celebration of the founding of the Handel and Haydn Society of Boston.

Parker's second area of composition was theater music. After writing incidental music for two plays, *The Eternal Feminine* (1904) and *The Prince of India* (1906), he composed music for two grand operas: *Mona*, which won a prize offered by the Metropolitan Opera Company and received four performances in that house (1912; see illustration); and *Fairyland*, which won a prize offered by the National Federation of Music Clubs and six performances in Los Angeles (1915).

Parker composed numerous songs, anthems, and hymns. Apart from some character-pieces for organ and piano, his instrumental composition was infrequent after the early years; however, two pieces – the symphonic poem *A Northern Ballad* (1899) and the Concerto for Organ and Orchestra – were performed by major American orchestras. Parker performed his Concerto with the Boston SO (1902) and the Chicago SO (1903).

Parker's health, which had been uncertain since his youth, deteriorated rapidly during World War I, and he died of pneumonia while on the first part of a recuperative trip to the West Indies during the winter of 1919. His last compositions, *The Red Cross Spirit Speaks* (1918) and *A.D. 1919*, are marked more by emotional fervor than by his creativity.

Parker composed steadily throughout his life, although his church, educational, and conducting duties were extensive. He was capable of intense concentration and frequently used the time while commuting from New Haven to Boston or New York for composing. After 1907 many of his largest works were written

METROPOLITAN OPERA HOUSE

GRAND OPERA SEASON 1911~1912
GIULIO GATTI-CASAZZA, General Manager

THURSDAY EVENING, MARCH 14TH, AT 8 O'CLOCK

MONA

OPERA IN THREE ACTS
(IN ENGLISH)
LIBRETTO BY BRIAN HOOKER
MUSIC BY HORATIO PARKER
(FIRST PERFORMANCE ON ANY STAGE)

MONA, Princess of Britain . . . LOUISE HOMER
ENYA, Her Foster-Mother . . . RITA FORNIA
ARTH, Husband of Enya . . . HERBERT WITHERSPOON
GLOOM, Their Son, A Druid . . . WILLIAM HINSHAW
NIAL, A Changeling . . . ALBERT REISS
CARADOC, Chief Bard of Britain . . . LAMBERT MURPHY
THE ROMAN GOVERNOR OF BRITAIN . . . PUTNAM GRISWOLD
QUINTUS, His Son . . . RICCARDO MARTIN
AN OLD MAN . . . BASIL RUYSDAEL

CONDUCTOR . . . ALFRED HERTZ

STAGE MANAGER, LOOMIS H. TAYLOR
TECHNICAL DIRECTOR, EDWARD SIEDLE
CHORUS MASTERS: GIULIO SETTI, HANS STEINER

Programme Continued on Next Page
Correct Librettos For Sale in the Lobby
HARDMAN PIANOS USED EXCLUSIVELY

Page from the program for the first performance of Parker's "Mona" at the Metropolitan Opera, 14 March 1912

during summers at his family's vacation home in Blue Hill, Maine.

Parker's career as a composer can be divided into three periods. The first was strongly eclectic and included the student and New York cantatas as well as the oratorio *Hora novissima*. The latter contains flowing, balanced melodic lines, moderately chromatic harmony, colorful orchestration, and stirring polyphonic effects.

The second period was marked by an increasing concern for dramatic expression in several of the larger choral works, and the fulfilment, with *Mona*, of a desire to write an opera. The contrasting, sectional structures of the first period gave way to an increasingly unified, highly expressive style. The key works are *Cáhal Mór of the Wine-red Hand*, with its integration of solo voice and orchestra; *The Legend of St. Christopher*, with its well-developed leitmotif technique; *A Star Song*, with its long-phrased melodies, tonally evasive harmony, and unified structure; and finally *Crépuscule* and *Mona*, with their pervading chromaticism, vacillating tonalities, and sometimes angular, disjunctive melodies.

During this same period Parker wrote a number of cantatas and ceremonial pieces which had a more conservative cast. These sustained his reputation as a traditionalist. They include *Adstant angelorum chori*, with its allusions to Renaissance polyphony; *A Wanderer's Psalm*, with its contrasting sections and unifying *tonus peregrinus*; *Hymnos Andron*, with its application of the rhythm and structure of Greek poetry; and the occasional pieces *Union and Liberty* and *Spirit of Beauty*, with their balanced sections.

The third period, following *Mona*, was stylistically regressive: for example, *An Allegory of War and Peace*, *The Dream of Mary*, *The Red Cross Spirit Speaks*, and *A.D. 1919* are marked by a return to diatonic harmony, more traditional key relationships, balanced structures, and clearly defined melody. Parts of *Morven and the Grail* and *Fairyland* also show these tendencies. These works reflect Parker's concern, avowed during the last few years of his life, to communicate more directly with the large American public.

After his death the number of performances of Parker's major works declined steadily. Even his more imaginative works, in which he attempted to follow such composers as Wagner, d'Indy, Strauss, Debussy, and Elgar, are received no better than the more conservative pieces, which show the influence of Brahms, Dvořák, and Gounod. Parker's inability to achieve a strongly individualistic style, and his reliance on chromatic formulae which came to be considered too sentimental, undoubtedly contributed to the neglect of his music. His hymns and anthems continue to be performed in some American churches, and several of his songs have a beauty which should rescue them from obscurity. During his lifetime Parker was considered a craftsman without equal and was one of America's most highly respected composers. Most of his music was published during his lifetime. The manuscripts of many of his works are in the Yale University Library.

See also ORCHESTRAL MUSIC, §2.

WORKS

(all printed works published in New York unless otherwise stated)

CHORAL

op.

2 5 Part Songs, 1882; listed in Strunk

— 2 Gesänge für Gemischten Chor, 1882; listed in 9. *Jahresbericht der Königlichen Musikhochschule in München* (1882–3), 37

1 Mountain Shepherd's Song (Uhland), TTBB, pf, 1883 (Boston, 1884)

3 Psalm, S, women's chorus, org, harp, 1884; Munich, Königliche Musikhochschule, 23 Dec 1884 (pubd as The Lord is my Shepherd, 1904)

6 Ballade, f, chorus, orch (F. L. Stolberg), 1884; Munich, Königliche

Musikhochschule, 7 July 1884 (pubd as The Ballad of a Knight and his Daughter, 1891)

8 König Trojan (A. Muth), ballad, T, Bar, SATB, orch, 1885; Munich, Königliche Musikhochschule, 15 July 1885 (pubd as King Trojan, Boston, 1886)

15 Idylle (Goethe), cantata, T, B, SATB, orch, 1886 (1891)

14 Blow, Blow thou Winter Wind (Shakespeare), TTBB, pf, 1888 (1892)

16 Normannenzug (H. Lingg), cantata, TTBB, orch, 1888 (pubd as The Norsemen's Raid, Cincinnati, 1911)

— Ecclesia, 4vv, org, 1889, *CtY-Mus*

21 The Kobolds (A. Bates), cantata, SATB, orch, 1890; Springfield, MA, Choral Festival, 7 May 1891 (London, 1891)

26 Harold Harfager, partsong, SATB, orch, 1891 (1891)

31 Dream-king and his Love (Geibel, trans. E. Whitney), cantata, T, SATB, orch, 1891; New York, 30 March 1893 (1893)

27 2 Part Songs: The Fisher (Goethe), SA, pf, The Water Fay (Heine), SSAA, pf (1892)

30 Hora novissima (B. de Morlaix), oratorio, S,A,T,B, SATB, orch, 1893; New York, Church Choral Society, 3 May 1893 (London, 1893)

33 3 Choruses, male vv: My Love (L. E. Mitchell), Three Words (W. B. Dunham), Valentine (C. G. Blanden) (1893)

37 The Holy Child (I. Parker), Christmas cantata, S,T,B, SATB, pf/org, 1893 (1893)

39 4 Choruses, male vv: Behold, how Good and Joyful; Blest art the Departed; Lord Dismiss us with thy Blessing; Softly now the Light of Day, 1893 (1894)

42 Ode for Commencement Day at Yale University (E. C. Stedman), 1895 (1895)

— In May, partsong, female chorus, harp, orch, 1897 (1897)

— Grant, we Beseech thee, partsong, SATB (Boston, 1898)

— Laus Artium, cantata, solo v, SATB, orch, 1898, *CtY-Mus*

43 The Legend of St. Christopher (I. Parker), dramatic oratorio, solo vv, chorus, orch, 1897; New York, Oratorio Society, 15 April 1898 (London and New York, 1898)

45 Adstant angelorum chori (Thomas à Kempis), motet, 8vv, 1899; New York, Musical Art Society, 16 March 1899 (1899)

50 A Wanderer's Psalm (after Ps. cvii), cantata, solo vv, chorus, orch, 1900; Hereford, Three Choirs Festival, 13 Sept 1900 (London, 1900)

48 3 Part Songs, TTBB: Awake, my Lady Sweetlips (E. Higginson), The Lamp in the West (Higginson), The Night has a Thousand Eyes (F. W. Bourdillon) (Cincinnati, 1901)

53 Hymnos Andron (T. D. Goodell), solo vv, TTBB, orch, 1901; Yale U., 23 Oct 1901 (pubd as Greek Festival Hymn, 1901)

54 A Star Song (H. B. Carpenter), lyric rhapsody, solo vv, chorus, orch, 1901; Norwich (England) Festival, 23 Oct 1902 (Cincinnati, 1902)

54b Come Away! (Dowland), SATB (London, 1901)

— The Robbers (J. Baillie), SATB, pf; in W. L. Tomlin: *The Laurel Song Book* (Boston, 1901)

— An Even Song (C. Thaxter), SA, pf (London, 1901)

— Come, Gentles, Rise! (D. Evans), Christmas carol, unison chorus, pf (1905)

60 Union and Liberty (O. W. Holmes), chorus, band/orch, 1905; commissioned for and perf. at inauguration of President T. Roosevelt (1905)

61 Spirit of Beauty (A. Detmers), ode, male chorus, band/orch, 1905; Buffalo, NY, ded. of Albright Art Gallery, 31 May 1905 (1905)

63 The Shepherds' Vision (F. Van der Stucken, trans. A. Jennings), Christmas cantata, solo vv, chorus, org, (ob, str, harp ad lib), 1906 (1906)

64 King Gorm the Grim (T. Fontane, trans. M. P. Whitney), ballad, chorus, orch, 1907; Norfolk Festival, 4 June 1908 (1908)

— Piscatrix, TTBB (1908)

— Songs for Parker daughters, trios, female vv, 1911: I Remember the Black Wharfs and Ships (Longfellow), September Gale (C. H. Crandall), Rollicking Robin (L. Larcom), no.4 unidentified, *CtY-Mus*

66 School Songs, SATB, pf: no.1 unidentified, Springtime Revelries (N. Waterman), The Storm (Waterman), Freedom Our Queen (O. W. Holmes); nos.2–4 (Boston, 1912, 1919, 1911)

— The Song of the Swords (from opera, Mona), SATB, pf (New York and Boston, 1911)

73 A Song of Times (J. L. Long), cantata, S, chorus, bugle corps, band/orch, org, 1911; Philadelphia, Wanamaker Dept. Store, 1 Dec 1911 (1911)

— A Song of a Pilgrim Soul (H. Van Dyke), partsong, vv, pf (1912)

74 7 Greek Pastoral Scenes (Meleager, Argentarius), SA, female chorus, ob, harp, str, 1912 (1913)

75 The Leap of Roushan Beg (Longfellow), ballad, T, TTBB, orch; Philadelphia, Orpheus Club, 1913–14 season (1913)

76 Alice Brand (Scott), cantata, solo vv, SSA, pf (1913)

— It was a Lover and his Lass, SS, vn, pf, 1915, *CtY-Mus*

— Gloriosa patria, patriotic hymn (1915)

79 Morven and the Grail (B. Hooker), oratorio, solo vv, chorus, orch, 1915; Boston, 13 April 1915 (Boston, 1915)

— Ave virgo gloriosa (from opera, Fairyland), female chorus, pf, 1915 (1915)

82 The Dream of Mary (J. J. Chapman), morality, solo vv, children's chorus, chorus, congregation, org, orch, 1918; Norfolk Festival, 4 June 1918 (1918)

— Triumphal March (D. K. Stevens), SATB, pf; in G. Parsons: *High School Song Book* (Boston, 1919)

84 A.D. 1919 (B. Hooker), cantata, S, chorus, orch, 1919; Yale U., 15 June 1919 (New Haven, 1919)

— I Remember (Longfellow), female vv, pf; in *A Book of Choruses for High Schools and Choral Societies* (Boston, 1923)

STAGE

— The Eternal Feminine (incidental music, F. Nathan), chorus, orch, 1903–4; New Haven, 7 Nov 1904; lost

— The Prince of India (incidental music, J. I. C. Clarke, after L. Wallace), lv, chorus, orch, 1905; New York, Broadway Theatre, 24 Sept 1906, *CtY-Mus*

71 Mona, opera, 3 (Hooker), 1910; New York, Metropolitan, 14 March 1912 (1911)

77 Fairyland, opera, 3 (Hooker), 1914; Los Angeles, 1 July 1915 (1915)

80 Cupid and Psyche, masque, 3 (J. J. Chapman), 1916; New Haven, 16 June 1916, *CtY-Mus*

81 An Allegory of War and Peace (F. H. Markoe), chorus, band, 1916; New Haven, 21 Oct 1916, *CtY-Mus*

SONGS

(lv, pf unless otherwise stated)

— Kate Greenaway Songs, 50 settings, 1878; see Kearns for individual listing, *CtY-Mus*

— It is the Sabbath Morn, *c*1880, *CtY-Mus*

— 3 Songs: Goldilocks, Slumber Song, Wedding Song, 1881 (Boston, 1882)

10 3 Love Songs: Love's Chase (T. L. Beddoes), Night Piece to Julia (R. Heink [Herrick]), Orsame's Song (Suckling), 1886 (Boston, 1886)

— Devotion (F. L. Humphreys) (1886)

— 2 Sacred Songs: Rest, There is a Land of Pure Delight, 1890 (Boston, 1890)

— 12 Christmas Carols for Children, unison chorus, pf (1891)

22 3 Sacred Songs: Evening, Heaven's Hope, Morning (1891)

23 3 Songs: My Love, O Waving Trees, Violet, 1891 (1891)

24 6 Songs: Cavalry Song (E. C. Stedman), Egyptian Serenade (G. W. Curtis), O Ask me Not (H. Hopfen), Pack, clouds, away! (T. Heywood), Spring Song (Curtis), The Light is Fading (E. A. Allen) (1891)

29 6 Songs, 1892, listed in Strunk

— Come see the Place (1893), also arr. as anthem

34 3 Songs: I know a Little Rose, My Lady Love, On the Lake (1893)

— In Glad Weather (C. B. Going) (1893)

— A Rose Song, unison chorus, pf (London, 1893)

— 2 Songs: Fickle Love (L. C. Moulton), Uncertainty (C. Swain) (Boston, 1893)

— 2 Songs: A Song of Three Little Birds, Love is a Rover (S. M. Peck), 1893 (Cincinnati, 1893)

— Divine Care (A. Jennings) (Boston, 1894)

— 2 Shakespeare Songs: A Poor Soul Sat Sighing, It was a Lover and his Lass (Boston, 1894)

40 Cáhal Mór of the Wine-red Hand (J. C. Mangan), rhapsody, Bar, orch, 1893; Boston, 29 March 1895 (1910)

— Salve regina (1895)

— Spanish Cavalier's Song (I. Parker) (Boston, 1896)

47 6 Old English Songs: Come, O Come, My Life's Delight (T. Campion), Love is a Sickness (S. Daniel), He that Loves a Rosy Cheek (T. Carew), Once I Loved a Maiden Fair (Old English), The Complacent Lover (C. Selby), The Lark (W. Davenant), 1897–9 (Cincinnati, 1899)

— The Green is on the Grass Again, 1900, *CtY-Mus*

51 4 songs: A Spinning Song (I. Parker), At Twilight (E. A. Baker), June Night (E. Higginson), Love in May (Higginson), 1901 (Cincinnati, 1901)

52 3 Songs, 1900, listed in Strunk

— Hapless doom of woman; Shame upon you, Robin; 1903, *CtY-Mus*

— The Toedt Songs, S, vn, pf, 14 songs as Christmas gifts for children of

close friends, 1903–16, microfilm of MS, *CtY-Mus* (for individual listing see Nesnow)
59 4 Songs: Good-bye (C. Rossetti), Serenade (N. H. Dole), Songs (R. L. Stevenson), The Blackbird (W. E. Henley) (1904)
— My Heart Was Winterbound until I Heard You Sing, 1904, *CtY-Mus*
— 2 songs from Tennyson's Queen Mary: Lute Song, Milkmaid's Song (1904)
58 3 Sacred Songs, org acc.: Come, Holy Ghost (St. Ambrose), Declining now, the sun's bright wheel (C. Coffin), Lo, now the shades of night (St. Gregory) (London, 1905)
— Come, Gentles, Rise! (D. Evans), 1v, org (1905)
— Springtime of Love (F. D. Sherman), 1905 (1905)
— Last Night the Nightingale (T. Marzials); The Garden Pirate (G. Rogers); 1906, *CtY-Mus*
62 Crépuscule (J. de Beaufort, trans. E. Whitney), concert aria, Mez, orch, 1907; Philadelphia, 27 March 1911 (1912)
— The Wandering Knight's Song (Cincinnati, 1908)
— Oh, I will Walk with you, 1909, *CtY-Mus*
— On the Hillside; The Presence Dwells among the Starlit Places; The Sun has Gone from the Shining Skies; Thy kiss, beloved (trans, G. Morris); 1909, *CtY-Mus*
70 7 Songs (B. Hooker): A Man's Song, A Robin's Egg, A Woman's Song, I Shall Come Back, Offerings, Only a Little While, Together, 1910 (Cincinnati, 1910)
— A Christmas Song (J. G. Holland), 1911; in *Century Illustrated Monthly Magazine* (Dec 1911)
— The Swallows, 1911, *CtY-Mus*
— 2 Songs: A Perfect Love (A. H. Hyatt), 1913, Her Cheek is Like a Tinted Rose (F. E. Coates), 1912 (Boston, 1914)
— 3 Songs: Across the Fields (W. Crane), Morning Song (M. Schütze), Nightfall (Schütze), 1914 (Boston, 1914)
76 3 Songs, listed in Strunk
78 The Progressive Music Series for Basal Use in Primary, Intermediate and Grammar Grades, 61 songs, 1914–19 (Boston and New York, 1914–19); for individual listings see Kearns
— Tomorrow (F. E. Coates), 1915; The Pearl (A. Hyatt), 1916; *CtY-Mus*
83 The Red Cross Spirit Speaks (J. Finley), 1v, orch, 1918 (1918)
— Hymn for the Victorious Dead (H. Hagedorn); in *The Outlook* (18 Dec 1918)

ANTHEMS, SERVICES

(for SATB, org; solo vv as indicated)

— Bow down thine Ear; Christ Our Passover, 1890; Deus misereatur, E, 1890; Magnificat, E♭, with solo v; Nunc dimittis, E♭; The Lord is my Light; There is a Land of Pure Delight, with solo v (all pubd in 1890)
— Give unto the Lord; I will Set his Dominion in the Sea (both pubd London, 1891)
— The Riven Tomb, in *New York Herald* (29 March 1891); Te Deum, A (1891); Who shall Roll us away the Stone?, with S solo (1891)
18 The Morning and Evening Service, E, together with the Office for The Holy Communion, 1890 (London, 1892)
— Let us Rise up and Build, 1892, *CtY-Mus*
— Before the Heavens were Spread Abroad, with T solo (London, 1893)
— Come See the Place, arr. as anthem, 1v, chorus/qt, org (1893)
34b Magnificat and Nunc Dimittis, E♭, 1893 (London, 1893)
— Te Deum, B♭ (1893)
— Light's Glittering Morn, with B solo, 1894 (1894)
— Far from the World, with S/T solo (1896)
— O Lord, I will Exalt thee, 1897 (1897)
— Calm on the Listening Ear of Night, with S/T solo, 1898; in *The Churchman* (10 Dec 1898)
— Grant, we Beseech Thee (Boston, 1898)
— Behold, ye Despisers, with B solo (London, 1899)
— Rejoice in the Lord (Boston, 1898)
— Jubilee Hymn, 1899, *DLC*
— Now Sinks the Sun (from The Legend of St. Christopher), a cappella, 1897 (London, 1900)
— In Heavenly Love Abiding, with S solo; While we have Time; 1900 (both pubd London, 1900)
— Thou Shalt Remember, with Bar solo, 1901 (London, 1901)
— Brightest and Best, with S solo, 1904 (1904)
57 The Office for the Holy Communion, B♭, 1904 (New York and London, 1904)
— It Came upon the Midnight Clear, solo vv, chorus, org, (vn, harp ad lib), 1904 (Boston, 1904)
— I Shall not Die but Live, with Bar solo, 1905 (Boston, 1905)
— To Whom then Will ye Liken God, with T solo, 1909 (1909)
— He Faileth Not, with S/T solo, 1919 (1919)
— He who Hath Led Will Lead, *CtY-Mus*
— God, that Makest Earth and Heaven, *DLC*
— O 'twas a Joyful Sound (Boston, n.d.)

The following hymnals contain the majority of Parker's hymn settings (for individual listings see Kearns):
H. Parker, ed: *The Hymnal, Revised and Enlarged . . . of the Protestant Episcopal Church in the USA* (1903)
H. Parker and H. B. Jepson, eds: *University Hymns for Use in the Battell Chapel at Yale with Tunes Arranged for Male Voices* (1907)
The Hymnal . . . of the Protestant Episcopal Church in the USA (1918)
The Hymnal of the Protestant Episcopal Church in the USA (1943)

KEYBOARD

(all published within one year of composition)

9 5 morceaux caractéristiques, pf (Boston, 1886)
19 4 Sketches, pf (Boston, 1890)
17 4 Compositions, org (1890)
25 6 Lyrics, pf (1891)
20 4 Compositions, org (1891)
28 4 Compositions, org (1891)
32 5 Sketches, org (1893)
36 4 Compositions, org (1893)
— 2 Compositions, pf (Boston, 1895)
— 3 Compositions, org; in D. Buck: *Vox organi* (Boston, 1896)
49 3 morceaux caractéristiques, pf (Cincinnati, 1899)
65 Organ Sonata, E♭ (1908)
67 4 Compositions, org (pubd as op.66, 1910)
68 5 Short Pieces, org (1908)
— Introduction and Fugue, e, org, 1916, *CtY-Mus*

ORCHESTRAL AND CHAMBER

4 Concert Ov., E♭, orch, 1884; Munich, Königliche Musikhochschule, 7 July 1884, *CtY-Mus*
5 Regulus, ov. héroïque, orch, 1884, *CtY-Mus*
12 Venetian Ov., B♭, orch, 1884, *CtY-Mus*
13 Scherzo, g, orch, 1884, *CtY-Mus*
7 Symphony, C, orch, 1885; Munich, Königliche Musikhochschule, 11 May 1885, *CtY-Mus*
11 Str Quartet, F, 1885; Detroit, MI, 29 Nov 1887, *NPV*
24b Count Robert of Paris, ov., orch, 1890; New York, 10 Dec 1890, *CtY-Mus*
35 Suite, pf, vn, vc, 1893 (1904)
38 Str Quintet, d, 1894; Boston, 21 Jan 1895, New England Conservatory, Boston (parts only)
41 Suite, e, pf, vn, 1894; Boston, 15 Jan 1895, *CtY-Mus*
46 A Northern Ballad, sym. poem, 1899; Boston SO, 29 Dec 1899, *CtY-Mus*
55 Organ Concerto, 1902; Boston SO, 26 Dec 1902 (London, 1903)
56 Vathek, sym, poem, 1903, *CtY-Mus*
72 Collegiate Ov., with male chorus, 1911; Norfolk Festival, 7 June 1911, *CtY-Mus*
77d Fairyland Suite (prelude, intermezzo, ballet from opera, Fairyland), 1915, *CtY-Mus*

BIBLIOGRAPHY

EwenD
R. Hughes: *Contemporary American Composers* (Boston, 1900)
"Horatio Parker," *MT*, xliii (1902), 586
L. C. Elson: *The History of American Music* (New York, 1904, enlarged by A. Elson 3/1925/*R*1971)
J. van Broekhoven: "*Mona*: a Thematic Analysis," *Musical Observer*, vi/4 (1912), 22
G. W. Chadwick: *Horatio Parker* (New Haven, 1921/*R*1972)
E. E. Hipsher: *American Opera and its Composers* (Philadelphia, 1927)
P. Rosenfeld: *An Hour with American Music* (Philadelphia, 1929)
D. S. Smith: "A Study of Horatio Parker," *MQ*, xvi (1930), 153
W. O. Strunk: "Works of Horatio W. Parker," *MQ*, xvi (1930), 164
W. T. Upton: *Art-song in America* (Boston, 1930/*R*1969 with suppl. 1938)
J. T. Howard: *Our American Music* (New York, 1931, rev. 4/1965)
I. Parker Semler: *Horatio Parker: a Memoir for his Grandchildren* (New York, 1942/*R*1975)
G. Chase: *America's Music* (New York, 1955, rev. 2/1966/*R*1981)
W. K. Kearns: *Horatio Parker 1863–1919: a Study of his Life and Music* (diss., U. of Illinois, 1965)

W. Mellers: *Music in a New Found Land* (New York, 1965)
R. Stevenson: *Protestant Church Music in America* (New York, 1966)
H. W. Hitchcock: *Music in the United States: a Historical Introduction* (Englewood Cliffs, NJ, 1969, rev.2/1974)
H. Dart: "An Introduction to Selected New England Composers of the Late Nineteenth Century," *MEJ*, lx/3 (1973), 47
W. C. Rorick: "The Horatio Parker Archives in the Yale University Music Library," *FAM*, xxvi (1979), 298
A. Nesnow: *Horatio Parker Papers* (MS 32, 1981, *CtY-Mus*)

WILLIAM KEARNS

Parker, J(ames) C(utler) D(unn) (*b* Boston, MA, 2 June 1828; *d* Brookline, MA, 27 Nov 1916). Composer, organist, and teacher. A graduate of both the Boston Latin School and Harvard College (1848), he decided to abandon law (after reading it 1848–51) in favor of music. From 1851 to 1854 he studied with Moritz Hauptmann, Ignaz Moscheles, Louis Plaidy, E. F. Richter, and Julius Rietz in Leipzig. When he returned to Boston he began teaching the piano, organ, and harmony at the New England Conservatory (1871–97) and was organist at the fashionable Trinity Church (1864–91). His compositions, always thoroughly conservative, included a cantata, *St. John*, written for the 75th anniversary of the Handel and Haydn Society (of which he was organist), and an Easter oratorio, *The Life of Man*, sung by that society in 1895. He published a *Manual of Harmony* (Boston, 1855), edited a large anthology called *Sacred Choruses: Selected, Translated, and Arranged from the Works of Celebrated Composers* (Boston, 1861), and translated theoretical works by Plaidy (*Technical Studies for the Piano Forte*, 1855), Vaccai (*Practical Method of Italian Singing*, 1865), and Richter (*Manual of Harmony*, 1873, with many later editions), among others, as well as the texts of some of Mendelssohn's part-songs (1856) and Niels Gade's *Comala* (1875).

WORKS

(selective list; all published in Boston)

7 Part Songs (1875)
Redemption Hymn, A, 4vv, vs (1877)
The Blind King (after L. Uhland), ballad, Bar, male vv, orch, vs (1883)
St. John, cantata, solo vv, 4 vv, orch, vs (1890)
The Life of Man, oratorio, solo vv, 4vv, orch, vs (1894)

BIBLIOGRAPHY

C. C. Perkins, J. S. Dwight, W. F. Bradbury, and C. Guild: *History of the Handel and Haydn Society of Boston, Massachusetts* (Boston and Cambridge, MA, 1883–1934/*R*1977–9), i, 511, 515; ii, 50
W. S. B. Mathews, ed.: *A Hundred Years of Music in America* (Chicago, 1889/*R*1970), 700
L. C. Elson and others: "Passing of J. C. D. Parker," *New England Conservatory Magazine-Review*, vii (1916–17), 45
J. T. Howard: *Our American Music* (New York, 1931, rev. 4/1965), 296
F. W. Coburn: "Parker, James Cutler Dunn," *DAB*

ROBERT STEVENSON

Parker, John Rowe (*b* Boston, MA, 24 Oct 1777; *d* Boston, 29 Dec 1844). Music dealer, and publisher. After a brief career as a merchant and importer he opened a music store, the Franklin Music Warehouse, at 6 Milk Street, Boston, in 1817. According to an announcement of 1819 he sold pianofortes and church and chamber organs, all built on the premises; in 1820 he published a 55-page catalogue (see illustration), one of the earliest extant music trade catalogues in America. The same year he began publication of a weekly musical periodical, *The Euterpeiad: or Musical Intelligencer, Devoted to the Diffusion of Musical Information and Belles Lettres* (1820–23/*R*1977). Each issue contained some historical narrative and a musical biography or "scientific" report, drawn mostly from English sources; short musical anecdotes alternated with serious commentary on music publications and performances, mainly in the Boston area. A musical supplement, in the form of a sheet of piano or vocal music, was included; the works were often by contemporary European masters, but such Americans as Lowell Mason and Heinrich were also represented. The bias towards European music, criticized by one subscriber, Benjamin Carr, was typical of the period.

The Franklin Music Warehouse stamp from the title page of John Rowe Parker's "Catalogue of Music and Musical Instruments" (Boston, 1820)

The Euterpeiad ceased publication in March 1823; a year later Parker brought out a compilation of reprints from it under the title *A Musical Biography*. Parker left the Franklin Warehouse in 1824 to become an import agent. His last contribution to the musical life of Boston was his participation with Mason, George Webb, and John S. Dwight on the editorial board of the *Boston Musical Gazette*, founded in 1838. Although he was not active as a musician, Parker played an important role in the dissemination of American and European music and musical opinion in the early 19th century. Some of his correspondence, dating from 1802 to 1840, is at the University of Pennsylvania, and a manuscript daybook is in the Reynolds Collection at Brown University.

BIBLIOGRAPHY

H. E. Johnson: "Early New England Periodicals Devoted to Music," *MQ*, xxvi (1940), 153
——: *Musical Interludes in Boston, 1795–1830* (New York, 1943)
J. C. Haskins: "John Rowe Parker and *The Euterpeiad*," *Notes*, viii (1950–51), 447
C. E. Wunderlich: *A History and Bibliography of Early American Music Periodicals, 1782–1852* (diss., U. of Michigan, 1962)
H. E. Johnson: "The John Rowe Parker Letters," *MQ*, lxii (1976), 72
R. J. Wolfe: *Early American Music Engraving and Printing* (Urbana, IL, 1980)
J. A. Cuthbert: "John Rowe Parker and *A Musical Biography*," *American Music*, i/2 (1983), 39

ANNE DHU SHAPIRO

Parker, William (*b* Butler, PA, 5 Aug 1943). Baritone. He studied Germanic languages and literature at Princeton between 1961 and 1965 and later took up singing. His teachers included Rosa Ponselle, Pierre Bernac, Erik Werba, and John Bullock, and by 1971 he had won competitions in Paris, Toulouse, and Baltimore. In 1979 he won the International American Music Competition sponsored by the Rockefeller Foundation and the Kennedy Center. This led to débuts with the principal regional opera companies of the USA and to recitals in New York and, in 1982, throughout Europe. He has recorded American songs for New World Records, and joined Elly Ameling, Nicolai Gedda, and Gérard Souzay in EMI's recording of the complete songs of Poulenc. He has often appeared in recital with Rorem, and gave the première of his *Santa Fe Songs*. Parker possesses a lyric baritone voice of great natural beauty and a most assured technique. His sunny personality immediately brings an audience into his confidence, and he is an ideal interpreter of Mozart's Papageno; but his emotional range is broad enough to encompass a raptly spiritual account of the music of Jesus in the Bach Passions.

RICHARD DYER

Parliament/Funkadelic. The name by which the loose agglomeration of musicians led by GEORGE CLINTON in the 1970s is commonly known; they formed the constantly changing membership of groups known as Parliament and Funkadelic.

Parly, Ticho (*b* Copenhagen, Denmark, 16 July 1928). Tenor. He began his vocal training while in Paris at the Sorbonne. In 1953 he went to the USA, where he studied at Indiana University, appearing there in 1955 in the première of Dello Joio's *The Ruby*. After further studies at the Mannes College of Music, he made his professional début as Pong in *Turandot* with the New Orleans Opera Association in 1957 and was a leading tenor with the Wuppertal Opera (1961–2) and at the Staatstheater, Kassel (1962–5). He achieved international prominence in the mid-1960s as guest artist at most of the major opera houses in Europe, including Bayreuth (Siegmund and Siegfried), Covent Garden (Siegfried), and the Royal Opera, Copenhagen (Florestan, Erik, and Tannhäuser over several seasons). He sang Tristan at the Metropolitan Opera in 1967, and has performed in various television and radio productions of complete operas.

ALAN BLYTH/R

Parnas, Leslie (*b* St. Louis, MO, 11 Nov 1931). Cellist. He studied under Piatigorsky at the Curtis Institute (1948–53) and then served as principal cellist of the St. Louis SO (1954–62). He has won several coveted awards and competitions: he came second in the Geneva International Music Competition (1957), won the Prix Pablo Casals at the International Cello Competition in Paris (1957), gained top honors at the Trofeo Primavera (1959), and was awarded joint second prize in the Tchaikovsky International Competition in 1962 (no first prize was awarded that year). Since then he has appeared as a soloist with the New York PO, the Boston PO, the Philadelphia Orchestra, the National SO, and the St. Louis SO, with which he performed the première of Dmitry Kabalevsky's Cello Concerto no.2 op.77 in 1964; he also gives recitals, performs regularly with the Chamber Music Society of Lincoln Center (which he helped to found in 1968; for illustration *see* CHAMBER MUSIC SOCIETY OF LINCOLN CENTER), and has participated in the Marlboro, Berkshire, Casals, and Spoleto (USA) music festivals. He has taught at Boston University since 1962 and the St. Louis Conservatory of Music since 1982. Parnas's playing is characterized by sure technique and an aggressive approach to phrasing. His instrument is the "Rosette" cello made by Matteo Groffriller in 1698, which he acquired in 1955.

JAMES WIERZBICKI

Parnell, Paul. Stage name of PAUL PRATT.

Parris, Robert (*b* Philadelphia, PA, 21 May 1924). Composer. After receiving degrees in music education at the University of Pennsylvania (BS 1945, MS 1946), he studied composition at the Juilliard School (BS 1948), where he was a pupil of Mennin and Bergsma. He took further lessons in composition from Ibert and Copland at the Berkshire Music Center in 1950 and 1951 and with Honegger at the Ecole Normale de Musique while in Paris on a Fulbright Fellowship (1952–3). He held an instructorship at Washington State College, Pullman (1948–9), and taught at the University of Maryland (1961–2); in 1963 he joined the faculty of George Washington University, Washington, DC, where he became head of the theory department the following year and from 1976 was a full professor. He also taught composition and keyboard privately and has been on the faculty of the Holton-Arms School and the Washington Jewish Community Center. In addition to contributing music criticism to both the *Washington Post* and *Washington Star* (intermittently, 1958–78), he has written articles on contemporary music for the *Kenyon Review* and *Juilliard Review*. His awards include two NEA grants (1974, 1976); he has received commissions from the Detroit SO (1969, *The Phoenix*) and the Contemporary Music Forum (1983, *The Book of Imaginary Beings II*).

Parris began by writing primarily chamber music and later added significantly to the contemporary concerto literature. He first received wide recognition in 1958 after the National SO gave the première of the Concerto for Five Kettledrums. Whether for small ensemble or large orchestra, his instrumental writing is colorful and idiomatic. The solo parts in his concertos and several of his chamber works make great demands on virtuoso performers. Within a clear formal structure, Parris stresses thematic invention while exercising considerable harmonic and rhythmic freedom. Although works such as his Piano Concerto are somewhat tonal, and others incorporate serial techniques, the majority employ an expressionistic, highly chromatic style.

WORKS

Orch: Sym. Movt no.1, 1948; Harlequin's Carnival, 1949; Sym. Movt no.2, 1951; Sym., 1952; 7 concs., pf, 1954, 5 timp, 1955, va, 1956, vn, 1958, fl, 1960, trbn, chamber orch, 1964, timp (The Phoenix), 1969; The Messengers, orch, 1974, retitled Angels; Rite of Passage, cl, elec gui, chamber orch, 1978; The Unquiet Heart, vn, orch, 1981; Chamber Music for Orch, 1984

Inst: 2 str trios, 1948, 1951; 2 str qts, 1951, 1952; Fantasy and Fugue, vc, 1955; 3 Sonatas, vn, 1956, va, 1957, solo vn, 1965; Lamentations and Praises, 9 brass, opt. perc, 1962; Conc., vn, vc, pf, perc, 1967; St. Winifred's Well, fl, vn, 2 vc, pf, 2 perc, 1967; Book of Imaginary Beings I, fl, vn, vc, pf, 2 perc, 1972, II, cl, vn, va, vc, 2 perc, 1983; 3 Duets, elec gui, amp hpd, 1984; *c*20 other works, 1948–84

Choral: Hymn for the Nativity (Peter the Venerable), SATB, 8 brass, 3 timp, perc, 1962; Walking Around (Neruda), SATB, cl, vn, pf, perc, 1973; 7 other works, 1949–73

Vocal: Night (R. Jeffers), Bar, cl, str qt, 1951; 3 Passacaglias (W. J. Smith, Hopkins), S, vn, vc, hpd, 1957; The Leaden Echo and the Golden Echo (Hopkins), Bar, orch, 1960; Mad Scene (S. Cammarano: Il trovatore), S, 2 Bar, chamber orch/pf, 1960; The Raids: 1940 (E. Sitwell), S, vn, pf, 1960; Dreams (D. Parker, L. Bogan, W. Cather), S, 7 insts, perc, 1976; Cynthia's Revells (B. Jonson), Bar, pf, opt. gui, 1979; songs

Principal publishers: ACA, C. F. Peters

BIBLIOGRAPHY

EwenD

BARBARA A. PETERSEN

Parrish, Carl (*b* Plymouth, PA, 9 Oct 1904; *d* Valhalla, NY, 27 Nov 1965). Musicologist and composer. He studied at the American Conservatory in Fontainebleau (1932), the MacPhail School of Music (BM 1933), Cornell University (MA 1936), and Harvard University (PhD 1939). After teaching at Wells College

(1929–43), he held positions at Fisk University (1943–6), Westminster Choir College (1946–9), Pomona College (1949–53), and Vassar College (1953–65), and during summer sessions at Stanford University and at the universities of Minnesota, North Carolina, and Southern California. Parrish's compositions include partsongs for chorus, choral arrangements of folksongs, pieces for piano and for orchestra, a set of organ preludes, a song cycle, a string quartet, and a *Magnificat* for soprano solo, women's voices, and organ. He is best known for his writings, of which the most important are *Masterpieces of Music before 1750* (with J. F. Ohl, 1951) and *A Treasury of Early Music* (1958), showing the styles of composition at different periods, and *The Notation of Medieval Music* (1957/*R*1978).

RAMONA H. MATTHEWS/R

Parsons, Albert Ross (*b* Sandusky, OH, 16 Sept 1847; *d* Mount Kisco, NY, 14 June 1933). Pianist, teacher, composer, and writer. He studied with Frédéric Ritter in New York (1863–6), with Ignaz Moscheles, Carl Reinecke, Benjamin Papperitz, E. F. Wenzel, and E. F. Richter at the Leipzig Conservatory (1867–9) and with Carl Tausig, Theodor Kullak, and Carl Friedrich Weitzmann in Berlin (1870–72). Having settled permanently in New York, he was organist at Holy Trinity Church (1872–6) and at the Fifth Avenue Presbyterian Church (1876–85), but he attained greater prominence as a piano teacher. He maintained a private teaching studio in the city for more than 50 years and also taught from 1886 at the Metropolitan Conservatory of Music (from 1891 the Metropolitan College of Music, and reorganized in 1900 as the American Institute of Applied Music). Parsons composed mostly songs and piano arrangements (transcriptions and paraphrases). A man of many interests, he wrote a book on Egyptology, studied philosophy and genealogy, and published poetry. He was an early promoter of Wagner in America, and made an English translation of Wagner's *Beethoven* (1872); he also wrote *Parsifal, or The Finding of Christ through Art* (1893). His pedagogical works include *The Science of Pianoforte Practice* (1886) and *The Virtuoso Handling of the Pianoforte* (1917). He translated O. Lessmann's *Franz Liszt*, and revised Kullak's edition of Chopin and Alexis Holländer's edition of Schumann, translating the commentaries into English.

BIBLIOGRAPHY

Obituary, *New York Times* (15 June 1933)
J. T. Howard: "Parsons, Albert Ross," *DAB*

JOHN GILLESPIE

Parsons, Bill. Pseudonym of BOBBY BARE.

Parsons, Gram [Connor, Cecil] (*b* Winter Haven, FL, 5 Nov 1946; *d* Joshua Tree National Monument, CA, 19 Sept 1973). Country-rock singer, songwriter, and guitarist. He played guitar in a rockabilly group while at high school in Waycross, Georgia. In 1963 he formed the Shilohs, a bluegrass group, which played at folk-music venues in the Northeast until 1965, when Parsons went to Harvard. There he put together the first country-rock group, the International Submarine Band, whose album *Safe at Home* (1967) included cover versions of songs by Merle Haggard and Johnny Cash and made distinctive use of pedal steel guitar in a rock style. In 1968 Parsons and three other members of the International Submarine Band joined Roger McGuinn and Chris Hillman of the Byrds to make the influential *Sweetheart of the Rodeo* (1968); Parsons left a few months later after refusing to tour South Africa. With Hillman he formed the Flying Burrito Brothers, whose *Gilded Palace of Sin* (1969) is perhaps the most powerful of all country-rock albums. Parsons left the group in 1970 (it continued under Hillman and Rick Roberts) and two years later embarked on a solo career in which Emmylou Harris joined him as a backup singer.

Parsons's country-rock style is distinguished from that of other performers by its strain of authentic country-music feeling; he combined the lyrical dolor of hillbilly harmonies with the classic sound of honky tonk to create a compelling music that seems to capture the pain and sense of loss that is fundamental to the country style. He left a substantial body of music which has exercised an influence on a number of other performers in surprisingly disparate styles, including the English new-wave artist Elvis Costello, Keith Richards of the Rolling Stones, and the country-music singer John Anderson.

RECORDINGS
(selective list)

With International Submarine Band: *Safe at Home* (LHI 12001, 1967)
With Byrds: *Sweetheart of the Rodeo* (Col. 9670, 1968)
With Flying Burrito Brothers: *The Gilded Palace of Sin* (A&M 4175, 1969); *Burrito Deluxe* (A&M 4528, 1970)
As soloist: *G. P.* (WB 2123, 1973); *Grievous Angel* (WB 2171, 1974)

BIBLIOGRAPHY

S. Griffin: *Grievous Angel* (Los Angeles, n.d.)

JOHN PICCARELLA

Partch, Harry (*b* Oakland, CA, 24 June 1901; *d* San Diego, CA, 3 Sept 1974). Composer, instrument maker, and performer. Largely self-taught, he pursued independent research into natural tuning systems of the past and traditional skills of instrument construction. These, together with a predominant concern with the physical, "corporeal" aspects of musical performance, led him to reject equal temperament and to invent his own tuning system; this necessitated the design and construction of new instruments and the composition of new music, as well as the training of his own performing groups, including the Gate 5 ensemble.

Partch began his work in the early 1930s, when he lengthened the fingerboard of his own instrument, a viola, and that of a guitar (the Adapted Viola and Adapted Guitar), and retuned a bellows reed organ to his 43-note scale based on just intonation (the Ptolemy). The first music he composed and performed in this new system was for voice and either one of the string instruments. During the next 40 years he created many other original instruments, primarily idiophones and chordophones, for his own use, and a body of compositions, mostly theatrical, for his own ensembles. His 43-note scale is constructed so that the intervals of the second half are a retrograde of those of the first half. The starting-point is G, and the frequency ratios of the scale members within a rising just major 2nd (9 : 8) from this are 1 : 1, 81 : 80, 33 : 32, 21 : 20, 16 : 15, 12 : 11, 11 : 10, 10 : 9 and 9 : 8. The system is fully expounded in Partch's *Genesis of a Music* (1949, rev. and enlarged, 1974), together with theories of consonance and dissonance vital to his instrument designs, and, in the second edition, detailed photographs and descriptions of most of his instruments.

Spending his life in the Midwest and on the West Coast, Partch held no teaching appointments, but had research posts at the universities of Wisconsin, Illinois, and California. His primary means of support were receipts from performances and from the private marketing of his recorded music (on the Gate 5 label),

Harry Partch with his gourd tree and cone gongs

supplemented by grants from the Carnegie, Guggenheim, and Fromm foundations and from BMI. His compositions combine American folklore (he spent the Depression years traveling around the USA, and later used the material he collected for scenarios and texts), African and Oriental literature, and mystical and pre-Christian magical thought, laced with parody, satire, studied naivety, and irony. His works received wide attention only late in his life, largely as a result of a performance of *Delusion of the Fury* in 1969.

Partch was highly skilled in realizing the musical potential of wood (particularly spruce) and other found materials. His instruments are of superior timbre and able to withstand the demands of vigorous performance; indeed, since his death, Partch's long-time assistant and colleague Danlee Mitchell has continued to direct performances of his music on the original instruments under the auspices of the Harry Partch Foundation of San Diego, California. All the instruments have sculptural integrity and they form the stage set of his theatrical works. The writing for large ensembles is often designed so that the separate parts, normally paired, are musically self-sufficient; various subgroups, sometimes with different meters and accent patterns with strong motor rhythms, may be formed, or all of the parts may be played together. Partch seldom wrote for conventional forces other than the human voice (though a band including piccolos, trumpets, trombones, tuba, and snare and bass drums was used in *Revelation in the Courthouse Park*, 1960).

In constructing his instruments Partch made extensive use of strings (usually guitar strings), glass, metal, bamboo, and gourds. Many of his early instruments were influenced by the scale experimentation of Greek and medieval theorists, for example the Harmonic Canon and Kithara; others were modifications of contemporary instruments (the Koto, Chromelodeon, Adapted Guitar, and Adapted Viola). He also created a complete family of marimbas (Marimba Eroica, Bass Marimba, Quadrangularis Reversum, and Diamond Marimba). All his instruments are featured in *And on the Seventh Day Petals Fell in Petaluma* (1963–6). The original instruments he created and employed, excluding hand instruments used in stage productions, are as follows:

chordophones (plucked or struck with mallets unless otherwise noted): Adapted Guitars I and II, Adapted Viola (bowed), Kitharas I and II, Surrogate Kithara, Harmonic Canons I, II (Castor and Pollux), and III (Blue Rainbow), Koto, Crychord

idiophones (all tuned): Diamond Marimba (wood), Quadrangularis Reversum (wood), Bass Marimba (wood), Marimba Eroica (wood), Boos I and II (bamboo), Mbira Bass Dyad (wood), Eucal Blossom (bamboo), Gourd Tree and Cone Gongs (metal), Cloud-Chamber Bowls (glass), Spoils of War (metal and wood), Zymo-Xyl (glass and wood), Mazda Marimba (glass)

aerophones: Chromelodeons I and II (modified reed organs), Bloboy (pipes and bellows)

As Johnston (1975) suggests, the problems posed by a music tied almost exclusively to its creator and his instruments (a fragile and unique set) seem nearly insurmountable; transcriptions of the tablatures, recordings, and films may have to suffice to preserve Partch's actual music, which is ironical in light of his belief in an ancient "corporeal" ideal. Partch's effect on other composers, however, has been profound and unabating, as is evident in the works of composers experimenting with just intonation, in mixed-media works since the 1960s, and in the percussive motor-rhythmic music of the minimalists.

See also THEORY, §4(i), and TUNING SYSTEMS.

WORKS

Early works, destroyed: Pf Conc., sym. poem, str qt, *c*50 songs

17 Lyrics by Li Po, 1v, adapted va, 1930–33; San Francisco, 9 Feb 1932

2 Psalms: The Lord is my Shepherd, By the Rivers of Babylon (Ps. cxxxvii), 1v, adapted va, 1931, rev. 1941, with chromelodeon and kithara; San Francisco, 9 Feb 1932

The Potion Scene from Romeo and Juliet (Shakespeare), 1v, adapted va, 1931; rev. 1955, with chromelodeon, kithara, b mar, mar eroica, 2 S; San Francisco, 9 Feb 1932

The Wayward: Barstow: Eight Hitchhiker Inscriptions from a Highway Railing at Barstow, California, 1v, adapted gui, 1941, rev. 1954, with 1v, surrogate kithara, chromelodeon, diamond mar, boo; US Highball: a Musical Account of a Transcontinental Hobo Trip (Partch), vv, gui I, kithara, chromelodeon, 1943, rev. 1955 for "subjective v," "several objective vv," ens of original insts; San Francisco: a Setting of the Cries of Two Newsboys on a Foggy Night in the Twenties, 2 Bar, adapted va, kithara, chromelodeon, 1943; The Letter: a Depression Message from a Hobo Friend, intoning v, orig. insts, 1943; New York, 22 April 1944

Dark Brother (T. Wolfe), 1v, chromelodeon, adapted va, kithara, b mar, 1942–3

Two Settings from Joyce's Finnegans Wake: Isobel, Annah the Allmaziful, S, kithara, 2 fl, 1944

Yankee Doodle Fantasy (Partch), S, tin fls, tin ob, flex-a-tones, chromelodeon, 1944; New York, 22 April 1944

I'm very happy to be able to tell you about this (W. Ward), S, Bar, kithara, drum, lost

11 Intrusions, large ens [orig. insts], 1946–50, incl. 2 Studies on Ancient Greek Scales

Plectra and Percussion Dances: Castor and Pollux: a Dance for the Twin Rhythms of Gemini, Ring around the Moon: a Dance Fantasm for Here and Now (Partch), Even Wild Horses: Dance Music for an Absent Drama (Rimbaud), vv, orig. insts, 1949–52; Berkeley, CA, 19 Nov 1953

Oedipus (dance music after Sophocles), 10 solo vv, orig. insts, 1951, rev. 1952–4; Oakland, CA, 14 March 1952

2 Settings from Lewis Carroll: The Mock Turtle Song, O Frabjous Day!, 1v, orig. insts, 1954; Mill Valley, CA, 13 Feb 1954

Ulysses at the Edge, a sax/tpt, bar sax, orig. insts, 1955 [added to The Wayward]

The Bewitched (dance satire, Partch), S, ens [orig. and trad. insts], 1955; Urbana, IL, 26 March 1957

Windsong (film score, dir. M. Tourtelot), 1958, rev. 1967 as Daphne of the Dunes, ballet

Revelation in the Courthouse Park (after Euripides: Bacchae), 16 solo vv, 4 speakers, dancers, large inst ens, 1960; Urbana, 11 April 1961

Rotate the Body in all its Planes (film score), 1961; Urbana, 8 April 1961

Bless this Home (V. Prockelo), 1v, ob, orig. insts, 1961
Water! Water! (farcical "intermission," Partch), 1961; Urbana, 9 March 1962
And on the Seventh Day Petals Fell in Petaluma, large ens [orig. insts], 1963–6; Los Angeles, 8 May 1966
Delusion of the Fury: a Ritual of Dream and Delusion (dramatic work, Partch, after Jap. and African trad.), large ens, 1965–6; Los Angeles, 9 Jan 1969
The Dreamer that Remains: a Study in Loving (film score, dir. S. Pouliot), 1972

BIBLIOGRAPHY

EwenD
C. W. Fox: Review of *Genesis of a Music, Notes*, vi (1948–9), 621
P. Yates: "Music," *Arts and Architecture*, lxx/7 (1953), 32; lxxi/12 (1954), 30
O. Daniel: "Harry Partch," *Music at Home*, i/6 (1955), 30, 46
J. Barzun: "Genesis of a Music by Harry Partch," *American Panorama*, ed. E. Larrabee (New York, 1957), 262
M. Schafer: "New Records," *Canadian Music Journal*, iii/2 (1959), 55 [on *US Highball*]
P. Earls: "Harry Partch: *Verses* in Preparation for *Delusion of the Fury*," *Yearbook, Inter-American Institute for Musical Research*, iii (1967), 1
A. Woodbury: "Harry Partch: Corporeality and Monophony," *Source*, i/2 (1967), 91
M. Bowen: "Harry Partch," *Music and Musicians*, xvi/5 (1968), 20
E. Paul: "Delusion of the Fury," *Delusion of the Fury, a Ritual of Dream and Decision* (Col. M2 30576, 1971) [liner notes]
J. Cott: "The Forgotten Visionary," *Rolling Stone*, no.158 (1974), 19
B. Johnston: "The Corporealism of Harry Partch," *PNM*, xiii/2 (1975), 85
W. Zimmermann: *Desert Plants: Conversations with 23 American Musicians* (Vancouver, BC, 1976), 347
D. S. Augustine: *Four Theories of Music in the United States, 1900–1950* (Ann Arbor, 1979)
G. A. Hackbarth: *An Analysis of Harry Partch's "Daphne of the Dunes"* (Ann Arbor, 1979)
J. Smith: "The Partch Reverberations: Notes on a Musical Rebel," *San Diego Weekly Reader* (25 Sept 1980); repr. in *Interval*, iii/1 (1981), 7; iii/2 (1981), 6
P. Garland: *Americas: Essays on American Musicians and Culture, 1973–80* (Santa Fe, 1982), 56, 267

PAUL EARLS (with RICHARD KASSEL)

Parton, Dolly (*b* Locust Ridge, TN, 19 Jan 1946). Country-music and popular singer, guitarist, and songwriter. As a child she sang in the church where her grandfather was minister, and also with her uncles on the "Farm and Home" television program in Knoxville; she made her first recordings at the age of 13. On graduating from high school she moved at once to Nashville to further her singing career. She was introduced to a national audience through Porter Wagoner's popular television series, in which she appeared regularly from 1967 to 1974. Since 1968 she has recorded many kinds of music, from traditional mountain ballads to rock-influenced popular songs; she writes much of her own material and is considered one of the most able songwriters in country music, her most famous songs being *Coat of Many Colors* (1971), based on a bittersweet childhood experience, *Jolene* (1973), and *9 to 5* (1980), which is best known as the title song of the film of the same name. Parton represents an important aspect of American popular culture, and has been active in films and on television as well as in concert; part of her appeal undoubtedly depends on her stage appearance, which exploits a buxom figure and flamboyant attire and hairstyles. Although she continues to be identified with country music, she has branched out into the performance of mainstream popular music.

RECORDINGS
(selective list)

Dumb Blonde (Monument 982, 1967); Just because I'm a woman (RCA 9548, 1968); Joshua (RCA 9928, 1970); Mule Skinner Blues (RCA 9863, 1970); Coat of Many Colors (RCA 0538, 1971); Jolene (RCA 0145, 1973); I will always love you (RCA 0234, 1974); Love is like a butterfly (RCA 10031, 1974); The Bargain Store (RCA 10164, 1975); The Seeker (RCA 10310, 1975); All I can do (RCA 10730, 1976); Here you come again (RCA 11123, 1977); Heartbreaker (RCA 11296, 1978); You're the only one (RCA 11577, 1979); 9 to 5 (RCA 12133, 1980)

BIBLIOGRAPHY

L. Scobey: *Dolly: Daughter of the South* (New York, 1977)
"Parton, Dolly," *CBY 1977*
G. Buchalter: "Dolly," *Country Music*, ix/3 (1980), 32

BILL C. MALONE

Pasatieri, Thomas (*b* New York, 20 Oct 1945). Composer. He was educated on Long Island near New York City, and at the age of 16 won a scholarship to the Juilliard School, where he studied with Giannini and Persichetti, obtaining the first doctorate awarded by the school in composition (1969). He also studied with Milhaud at Aspen Music School. A prolific composer from his student years, he has written piano, chamber, and orchestral works, but his chief output is vocal music – songs and, in particular, operas. His earliest dramatic pieces were produced in college workshops; then in 1971 he scored a success with *Calvary*, a setting of the play by W. B. Yeats, which has been performed in churches throughout the USA. Many of his operas were commissioned: *The Trial of Mary Lincoln* (for National Educational Television, transmitted 1972); *The Seagull* (by the Houston Grand Opera); *Inez de Castro* (Baltimore Opera); *Washington Square* (Michigan Opera Theater, Detroit); and *Maria Elena* (University of Arizona).

The style of Pasatieri's music is frankly conservative, a neoromantic idiom derived mainly from Puccini and Richard Strauss; his avowed operatic aim is to entertain. The vocal line is always written rewardingly for the singer and consequently his operas not only attract excellent casts and are frequently performed, but artists of the caliber of Evelyn Lear and Thomas Stewart have commissioned works from him.

Dolly Parton, late 1970s

WORKS

OPERAS

The Women (1, Pasatieri), Aspen, CO, 20 Aug 1965
La Divina (1, Pasatieri), New York, 16 March 1966
Padrevia (1, Pasatieri, after Boccaccio), Brooklyn, NY, 18 Nov 1967
Calvary (1, W. B. Yeats), Bellevue, WA, April 1971
The Trial of Mary Lincoln (A. H. Bailey), National Educational Television, 14 Feb 1972
Black Widow (3, Pasatieri, after M. de Unamuno: Dos madres), Seattle, WA, 2 March 1972
The Seagull (3, K. Elmslie, after Chekhov), Houston, TX, 5 March 1974
Signor Deluso (1, Pasatieri, after Molière: Sganarelle), Vienna, VA, 27 July 1974
The Penitentes (3, Bailey), Aspen, CO, 3 Aug 1974
Inez de Castro (3, B. Stambler), Baltimore, MD, 1 April 1976
Washington Square (2, Elmslie, after H. James), Detroit, MI, 1 Oct 1976
Three Sisters (1, Elmslie, after Chekhov), 1979
Before Breakfast (1, Corsaro, after O'Neill), New York, 9 Oct 1980
The Goose Girl (children's opera, 1, Pasatieri, after brothers Grimm), Fort Worth, TX, 15 Feb 1981
Maria Elena (1, Pasatieri), Tucson, AZ, 6 April 1983

OTHER WORKS

Invocations, orch, 1968
Vocal works, incl. Heloise and Abelard (L. Phillips), S, Bar, pf, 1971; Rites de passage (Phillips), 1v, chamber orch/str qt, 1974; Three Poems of James Agee, 1v, pf, New York, 1974; Far from Love (Dickinson), S, cl, pf, 1976; Permit me Voyage, cantata, S, chorus, orch, 1976; Mass, 4 solo vv, chorus, orch, 1983; over 400 songs
Pf works, incl. Cameos; 2 sonatas, 1976

Principal publisher: Belwin-Mills

BIBLIOGRAPHY

EwenD
A. Sperber: "Let me Entertain you," *Opera News*, xxxvi/15 (1972), 26
R. Jackson: "Finding the Seagull," *Opera News*, xxxviii/17 (1974), 14

ELIZABETH FORBES

Pasmore, Harriet Horn. *See* PAZMOR, RADIANA.

Pass, Joe [Passalaqua, Joseph Anthony Jacobi] (*b* New Brunswick, NJ, 13 Jan 1929). Jazz guitarist. Soon after beginning his career he began to take drugs and spent many years in prisons, hospitals, and halfway houses. In 1961, together with other jazz musicians in Synanon, a self-help organization for drug addicts, he issued a collective album which attracted some critical attention to his easy-going manner and astounding technical prowess. He then worked for several years in Los Angeles studios, but remained more or less in obscurity until 1973, when he was retained for the Pablo label and recorded his first solo album, *Virtuoso*. The success of this album catapulted him to fame and he immediately began to dominate jazz popularity polls for his instrument. From that time on he was greatly in demand for concerts, festivals, and recording sessions, notably as an accompanist to Ella Fitzgerald and Sarah Vaughan, and as a member of Oscar Peterson's groups.

Pass is one of the few jazz guitarists to have mastered the technique of finger picking, which allows him to give fully satisfying performances as an unaccompanied soloist. Like Art Tatum, with whom he is often compared because of his comprehensive grasp of jazz guitar technique, Pass is heard to best advantage in his elaborate solo paraphrases of popular songs, where he reveals a refined sense of harmony and an uncommonly wide array of accompaniment textures.

RECORDINGS

(selective list)

As soloist: *Virtuoso* (1973, Pablo 2310708); *At the Montreux Jazz Festival* (1975, Pablo 2310752); *Virtuoso*, ii (1976, Pablo 2310788); *Virtuoso*, iii (1977, Pablo 2310805); *I Remember Charlie Parker* (1979, Pablo Today 2312109)

As sideman: A. Ross: *Sounds of Synanon* (1961, Pacific Jazz 48); E. Fitzgerald and J. Pass: *Take Love Easy* (1973, Pablo 2310702)

BIBLIOGRAPHY

"Joe Pass Discography," *Swing Journal*, xxix/6 (1975), 238
B. James: "Joe Pass Interview," *Jazz Journal*, xxix/5 (1976), 12; xxix/6 (1976), 24
J. Sievert: "Joe Pass," *The Guitar Player Book* (New York, 1978), 181
L. Underwood: "Joe Pass: Virtuoso Revisited," *Down Beat*, xlv/7 (1978), 16
J. Pass: *Intercontinental* (Brookline, MA, 1979) [10 transcrs.]
——: *Portraits of Duke Ellington* (Brookline, 1981) [9 transcrs.]
——: *Virtuoso* (Brookline, 1981) [12 transcrs.]

J. BRADFORD ROBINSON

Passamaquoddy. American Indian tribe of the WABANAKI confederacy.

Pasticcio (It.: "mess," "hodge-podge"; Fr. *pastiche*). A dramatic vocal work, the music for which is wholly or partly borrowed from existing works by various composers; the term originated in Italian operatic practices of the 18th century. For a discussion of the pasticcio in the USA *see* BALLAD OPERA.

Pastor, Tony [Antonio] **(i)** (*b* New York, 28 May 1837; *d* Elmhurst, NY, 26 Aug 1908). Impresario and singer. As a boy he performed in minstrel shows and circuses, and in the 1860s he began writing and singing topical songs, drawing upon Civil War events for his subjects. He opened his first "theater" (actually a bar with live entertainment) in 1861. Over the next two decades he ran theaters in various locations in New York, including Tony Pastor's Opera House (1865). In 1881 he opened a new theater, Tony Pastor's Music Hall, on East 14th Street, where he offered the public a more wholesome brand of variety show, or vaudeville. Pastor's Music Hall was one of New York's leading theaters until the early years of the 20th century; many rising stars as well as established performers appeared there, including Ben Harney, May Irwin, Weber and Fields, Lillian Russell, and Sophie Tucker.

BIBLIOGRAPHY

P. Zellers: *Tony Pastor: Dean of the Vaudeville Stage* (Ypsilanti, MI, 1971)
D. Ewen: *All the Years of American Popular Music* (Englewood Cliffs, NJ, 1977)

MARK TUCKER

Pastor, Tony [Pestritto, Antonio] **(ii)** (*b* Middletown, CT, 26 Oct 1907; *d* Old Lyme, CT, 31 Oct 1969). Bandleader, singer, and saxophonist. He began playing as a sideman in the orchestras of John Cavallaro, Irving Aaronson, and Vincent Lopez, before joining Artie Shaw's band in 1936, where he was tenor saxophone soloist and singer (*Indian Love Call*, 1938, offers a good example of his throaty, somewhat gruff vocal style). After Shaw dissolved his band Pastor formed his own in 1940, taking some of Shaw's players with him. Many of Pastor's arrangements were written by the guitarist Al Avola, though Budd Johnson, Walter Fuller, and Ralph Flanagan also made contributions. Pastor's singing (greatly influenced, he acknowledged, by Louis Armstrong) was always an important part of his shows; in the late 1940s he also performed with Betty and Rosemary Clooney. He broke up his big band in 1959 and formed a smaller group with his two sons, appearing with them in nightclubs until his retirement in 1968.

BIBLIOGRAPHY

G. Simon: *The Big Bands* (New York, 1967, 4/1981), 391
C. Garrod: *Tony Pastor and his Orchestra* (Zephyrhills, FL, 1973) [discography]
L. Walker: *The Big Band Almanac* (Pasadena, CA, 1978), 335

MARK TUCKER

Pastorius, Jaco [John Francis] (*b* Norristown, PA, 1 Dec 1951). Jazz-rock bass guitarist. He grew up in Fort Lauderdale, Florida, where he accompanied visiting rhythm-and-blues and pop musicians while still a teenager. By 1975 he had come to the attention of jazz musicians such as Pat Metheny, and in the following year he attracted widespread notice with his performances on the album *Heavy Weather* by Weather Report, with whom he had a long association. From that time he has been much in demand as a bass player and producer in a wide variety of settings. Unlike many jazz and rock bass guitarists, Pastorius uses a fretless instrument, with immaculate intonation. Though sometimes faulted for his flamboyant stage personality and eclecticism, he has won the admiration of jazz and rock bass players for his fleet technique and the imaginative fusion of styles in his solos. From 1980 he toured with his own group, Word of Mouth.

RECORDINGS

(selective list)

As leader: *Jaco Pastorius* (*c*1975, Epic 33949); *Word of Mouth* (1980, WB 3535)

As sideman: P. Metheny: *Bright Size Life* (1975, ECM 1073); Weather Report: *Heavy Weather* (1976, Col. PC34418); A. Mangelsdorff: *Trilogue* (1976, Pausa 7055); J. Mitchell: *Hejira* (1976, Asy. 7E1087); Weather Report: *Night Passage* (*c*1980, Col. JC36793)

BIBLIOGRAPHY

J. E. Berendt: "Jaco Pastorius: the Human Sound on the Bass Guitar," *Jazz Forum*, no.48 (1977), 35

D. Roerich: "Jaco Pastorius: the Musician Interviewed," *Musician*, no.26 (1980), 38

C. Silvert: "Jaco Pastorius: the Word is Out," *Down Beat*, xlviii/12 (1981), 17

J. BRADFORD ROBINSON

Patent notes. Notes used in shape-note notation; *see* SHAPE-NOTE HYMNODY.

Paton, Mary Anne (1802–64). Scottish soprano, wife of JOSEPH WOOD.

Patriotic music. The democratic and self-expressive spirit of the USA has encouraged the writing of much excellent patriotic music, especially songs. Through them it is possible to trace aspects of the nation's history and development.

1. Up to the Civil War. 2. After 1865.

1. UP TO THE CIVIL WAR. The resistance of the American colonists to the British Stamp Act (1765) led to the country's first patriotic music, and the music and words of the *Liberty Song* were published in 1768, declaring that "In freedom we're born, and in freedom we'll live." John Dickinson, an ardent colonial statesman, wrote the words to an English tune, and this song, together with similar ones published in newspapers, magazines, almanacs, and sheet music, stimulated the revolutionary spirit.

Yankee Doodle, the best-known patriotic music during the Revolutionary period, is of American origin but of unknown authorship. The earliest written reference to it is in the libretto (published in New York in 1767) of *The Disappointment*, an American comic opera; in 1768 a newspaper reported that when the British warships arrived in Boston "the Yankee Doodle song was the Capital Piece in their Band of Music." During the Revolutionary War the British used the tune derisively, but the Americans made it their patriotic song and are believed to have played it at Cornwallis's surrender at Yorktown in 1781. The word "Yankee" refers to a New Englander; "doodle" remains a puzzle. The texts were varied, simple, humorous, and jaunty (the verse containing the rhyme "pony" and "macaroni" did not appear until 1842).

The words of *The Star-Spangled Banner* were written in 1814 by a Washington lawyer, Francis Scott Key, in patriotic circumstances. Securing the release of a friend under a truce, Key was aboard ship during the night of 13–14 September, watching the British bombardment of Fort McHenry, which protected the entrance to Baltimore. Suddenly the bombardment ceased. Wondering whether the fort had surrendered or the attack had been abandoned, Key paced the deck in suspense during the remainder of the night. When dawn came he saw that "our flag was still there," and wrote the poem while aboard the ship. On Key's return to Baltimore he requested Thomas Carr to adapt the poem to the melody of the *Anacreontic Song* (*To Anacreon in Heaven*) by the English composer John Stafford Smith; in this form it was promptly published in broadsides, sheet music (fig. 1, p.486), newspapers, magazines, and songsters. *The Star-Spangled Banner* was repeatedly sung in theaters by a traveling troupe. *To Anacreon in Heaven* had been sung in the 1780s at the Anacreontic Society, a convivial music society in London, and was well known also in North America. Key's manuscript had no title; the original broadside and most early prints bore the title *Defence of Fort M'Henry*. The words "the star-spangled banner" occur only once (near the end) in each stanza, and the present title was probably suggested either by the first sheet music publisher or by a member of the traveling theatrical troupe. *The Star-Spangled Banner* has been criticized as a national anthem because the melody was composed by a foreigner and because its wide range makes it difficult to sing; yet, because of its patriotic associations and the quality of the poem, it has continued as the American anthem ever since its official adoption in 1931.

During the undeclared naval war with France in 1798 *Hail Columbia!* was written by Joseph Hopkinson to the melody of *The President's March* by Philip Phile, and became a popular national song, but it is rarely played today. The words of *America* or *My country, 'tis of thee* were written in 1831 by a young clergyman, Samuel Francis Smith (1808–95), who had been asked to write English texts to certain German music. He chose one German hymn, not recognizing that its melody was that of the British *God Save the King*, and promptly wrote the words of *America* at one sitting. Smith's words were sung on 4 July 1831 under the title "Celebration of American Independence" in Boston. The poem originally had five stanzas; the third, calling the British "tyrants," is not sung today. *America* is now also considered a hymn, partly because of the final stanza which begins "Our fathers' God! to Thee" and ends "Great God, our King!"

Hail to the chief has been played for many years to announce the arrival, or to acknowledge the presence, of the President of the USA; the first presidential inauguration at which the march was played was President Van Buren's on 4 March 1837. The words are by Sir Walter Scott and first appeared in his *The Lady of the Lake* (1810); the poem is in honor of a favorite chief of the highlanders of Scotland. The music is usually ascribed to "Mr. Sanderson," apparently the English songwriter James Sanderson; however, the earliest printings (about 1812) are American. No English printing has been found, and it is believed that the melody was not known in England.

There has been controversy as to whether *Columbia, the Gem of the Ocean* is an American song or an adaptation of the British *Britannia, the Pride of the Ocean*. However, the American song was copyrighted in the USA in 1843 under the title *Columbia*

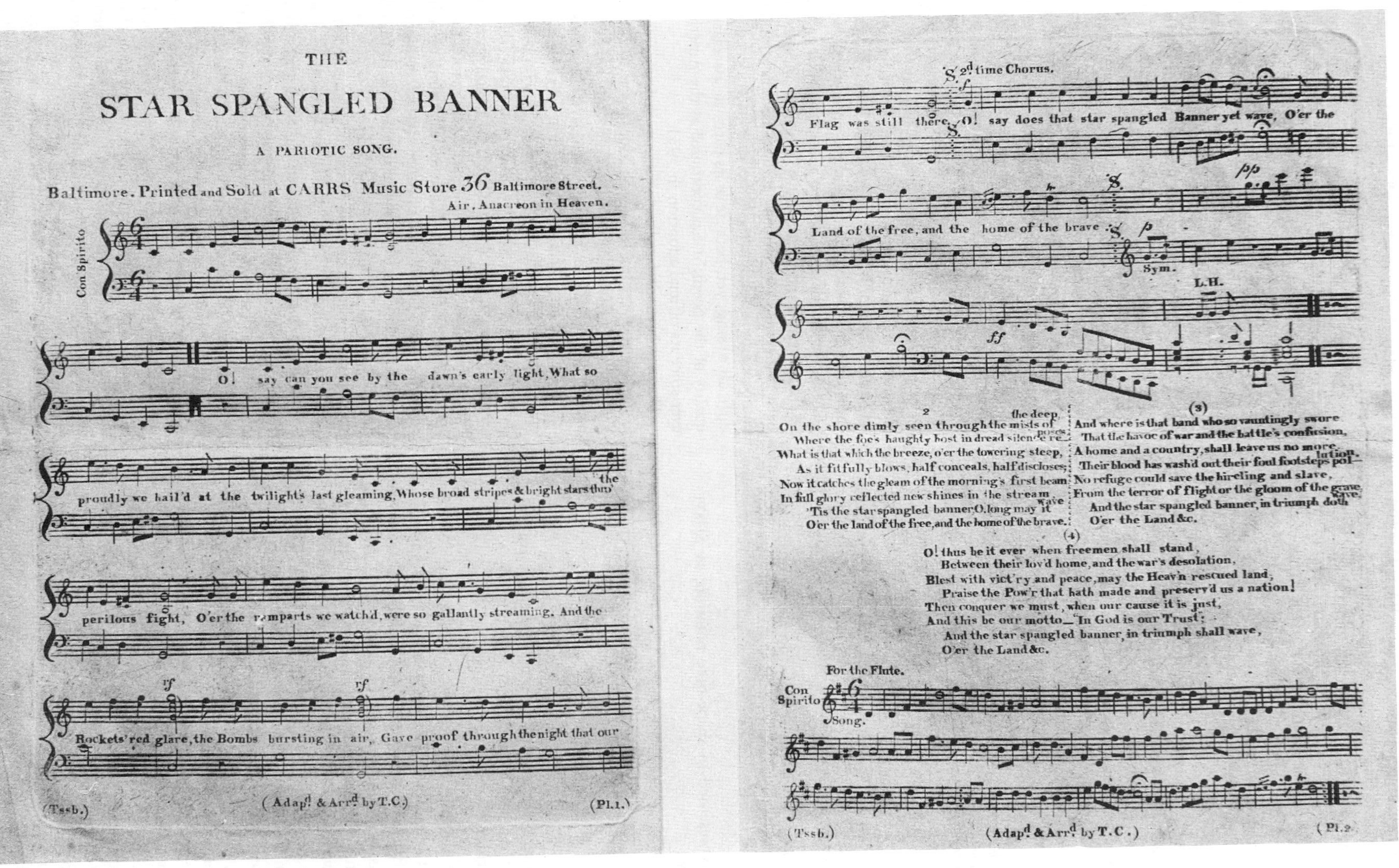

1. *The first sheet-music publication of "The Star-Spangled Banner" with words by Francis Scott Key and music by John Stafford Smith (Baltimore, 1814)*

the Land of the Brave, "Columbia" being a frequently used name for the USA during its early history. No British printing is known until 1852, and this bears the legend "Melody collected . . . abroad." The song is also known in both the USA and England as *The Red, White and Blue*, after the colors of the flags of both countries. David T. Shaw, a singer, and Thomas à Beckett, a musician and actor, separately claimed authorship of the American version.

Many strongly patriotic songs were composed and sung during the American Civil War. After Fort Sumter had been fired on in April 1861, *Glory hallelujah* was played publicly in May at a flag-raising ceremony for the training of Northern recruits near Boston, and contemporary newspapers reported that troops sang the song as they marched in Boston in July. One magazine that month claimed that *Glory hallelujah* was a "people's tune" and that "one can hardly walk on the streets for five minutes without hearing it whistled or hummed." Yet the origins of *Glory hallelujah* are baffling. There is no real substantiation for the various claims that have been made, and the earliest evidence is that the music and words of the chorus were printed in 1858 in the hymn *Say, brothers, will you meet me (us)*. Julia Ward Howe's poem *Battle Hymn of the Republic* was written to this music in or near Washington in November 1861. Howe had heard soldiers singing the song and was asked to provide a worthier text. A pioneer for women's rights, she said "My poem did some service in the Civil War. I wish very much that it may do good service in the peace."

Dixie originated in 1859 as a minstrel number, but the nature of its popularity afterwards changed. Dan Emmett wrote it in New York City for Bryant's Minstrels, in which he was a blackface performer. The song was introduced in New York City in April 1859, but it was performed only intermittently and without success until it was sung without authorization in New Orleans in April 1860; it created such excitement that it was repeated 13 times that month, and unauthorized sheet music editions were published in New Orleans without reference to Emmett or to Bryant's Minstrels. The North never conceded that *Dixie* belonged exclusively to the South. Emmett was born and died in Ohio, the song was written and introduced in New York City, many Northern publishers printed it before, during, and after the Civil War, and only a few days before his assassination President Lincoln proclaimed *Dixie* a national song by asking a serenading band at the White House to play it. A contemporary explanation of the word "Dixie" is given in a program of Bryant's Minstrels dated February 1861: "As many inquiries have been made in regard to the meaning of 'Dixie Land,' and as to its location, it may be well to remark that, with the Southern Negroes, Dixie Land is but another name for home."

The words of *Maryland, my Maryland* were inspired by the tragedy in Maryland, where sometimes brother fought against brother. The author of the words was James Ryder Randall, a native of Baltimore and professor in Louisiana, who had read of a riot in Baltimore between pro-Northerners and pro-Southerners. Randall wrote the poem in Louisiana in April 1861 and mailed a copy to a friend in Baltimore, where it was published with the music of the German folksong *O Tannenbaum, o Tannenbaum!*

Two other patriotic songs of the Civil War are George F. Root's *The Battle Cry of Freedom* and *Tramp! Tramp! Tramp!* (for illustration *see* ROOT, GEORGE FREDERICK). President Lincoln wrote to Root: "You have done more than a hundred generals and a thousand orators." Another Civil War song is the rousing *When Johnny comes marching home*, usually credited to Patrick Gilmore, though the melody may be of Irish origin. Stephen Foster also wrote several patriotic songs during the Civil War, with titles like *We are coming Father Abraam 300,000 more*, but none of these became popular.

See also POPULAR MUSIC, §II, 7.

2. AFTER 1865. The lofty words of *America the Beautiful*, or *O beautiful for spacious skies*, were inspired by Katherine Lee Bates's view from Pike's Peak in Colorado in summer 1893 and describe the splendors of the possessions given to the American people. The poem by Bates, an English professor at Wellesley College, was published on 4 July 1895, but it is not known who set it to the music of *Materna* by Samuel Augustus Ward; *Materna* had been composed in 1882 and was published a few years later. The first known printing of poem and music together was in 1910, after Ward's death.

2. Sheet-music cover of John Philip Sousa's march "The Stars and Stripes Forever!," first published by the John Church Co. (Cincinnati, 1897)

John Philip Sousa composed his stirring march *The Stars and Stripes Forever!* (fig.2) on a ship from England to the USA in 1896; "I paced the deck with a mental brass band playing the march fully a hundred times during the week I was on the steamer." Sousa said "A march should make a man with a wooden leg step out," and *The Stars and Stripes Forever!* epitomized the enthusiastic optimism of a country then beginning to come into its own.

The most famous patriotic song from World War I, George M. Cohan's *Over there*, was written in 1917, after the USA had entered the war, and was introduced by Nora Bayes at a Red Cross benefit performance. Largely for this song Cohan was awarded the Congressional Medal; as one observer commented, "there is the whole arrogance of the strength of the New World in its lines."

Irving Berlin wrote *God bless America* in 1918 as a finale for the soldier show *Yip, Yip, Yaphank*, but he did not consider it appropriate, and the song was not performed until Kate Smith asked him for a patriotic song to introduce on the radio on Armistice Day (the earlier name for Veterans Day) 1938. Berlin altered the words slightly to change it into a peace song, and as an expression of gratitude to the country he assigned all his royalties from it to the Boy Scouts of America and Girl Scouts of America. Largely in recognition of *God bless America*, Berlin received a gold medal from President Eisenhower by act of Congress. The composer stated that he never expected *God bless America* to be a great national song, as it is a prayer and lacks the nobility of an anthem; and yet some have argued that this sincere, simple, and effective song should replace *The Star-Spangled Banner* as the national anthem.

The words "Praise the Lord and pass the ammunition!" were spoken by Chaplain William Maguire on board a US Navy warship during the Japanese attack on Pearl Harbor in December 1941; they inspired the best-known American patriotic song of World War II, written shortly afterwards by Frank Loesser. No noteworthy patriotic music has survived from the Mexican, Spanish-American, Korean, or Vietnam wars.

A number of patriotic songs have strong associations with the military services. The army's *The caissons go rolling along* was written in 1907 by Edmund L. Gruber, an officer in the Philippine Islands; it was occasioned by the reunion of two portions of his regiment which had been separated. The navy's *Anchors aweigh* was written for the army–navy football game in 1906 by Alfred H. Miles and Charles A. Zimmerman, the former an undergraduate at the Naval Academy and the latter the academy bandmaster. The music of *The Marines' Hymn* is by the French composer Jacques Offenbach; it was written for the 1867 revision of his *Geneviève de Brabant*. The author of the words is unknown, and no printing of them is known until 1918. The air force's *The Army Air Corps Song* was written in 1939 by Robert Crawford, a member of the music faculty at Princeton University.

Some of the most gifted American composers have contributed in various ways to the repertory of patriotic music. Charles Ives composed orchestral works with patriotic titles: *Washington's Birthday* (1909) and *The Fourth of July* (1911–13). In 1931 George and Ira Gershwin wrote a patriotic lovesong, "Of thee I sing" ("thee" referring to the USA), and a satirical patriotic piece, "Wintergreen for president," for the musical comedy *Of thee I Sing*, the title of which was derived from the first stanza of *America*. More recently Richard Rodgers composed music for *Victory at Sea* (1952), a television series tracing the USA's naval history during World War II.

See also BATTLE MUSIC and CONFEDERATE MUSIC.

BIBLIOGRAPHY

O. G. T. Sonneck: *Report on "The Star-Spangled Banner," "Hail Columbia," "America," "Yankee Doodle"* (Washington, DC, 1909/R1972, rev. and enlarged 2/1914/R1969)

American War Songs (Philadelphia, 1925/R1974)

J. T. Howard: *Our American Music* (New York, 1931, rev. 3/1946/R1954 with suppl. by J. Lyons, rev. 4/1965)

H. Dichter and E. Shapiro: *Early American Sheet Music: its Lure and its Lore, 1768–1889* (New York, 1941/R1977)

S. Spaeth: *A History of Popular Music in America* (New York, 1948)

G. Chase: *America's Music: from the Pilgrims to the Present* (New York, 1955, rev. 2/1966/R1981)

H. Nathan: *Dan Emmett and the Rise of Early Negro Minstrelsy* (Norman, OK, 1962/R1977)

J. J. Fuld: *The Book of World-famous Music: Classical, Popular and Folk* (New York, 1966, rev. 2/1971)

P. W. Filby and E. G. Howard: *Star-spangled Books* (Baltimore, 1972)

V. B. Lawrence: *Music for Patriots, Politicians and Presidents* (New York, 1975)

W. Lichtenwanger: "The Music of 'The Star-Spangled Banner'," *College Music Symposium*, xviii (1978), 34–81

JAMES J. FULD

Pattern music. A term applied to one of the compositional practices generally referred to as MINIMALISM.

Patti, Adelina [Adela Juana Maria] (*b* Madrid, Spain, 19 Feb 1843; *d* Craig-y-Nos Castle, nr Brecon, Wales, 27 Sept 1919). Soprano. She was the youngest daughter of the tenor Salvatore Patti (*b* Catania, Italy, *c*1800; *d* Paris, France, 21 Aug 1869) and the soprano Caterina Chiesa Barrilli-Patti (*b* Rome, Italy; *d* Rome, 6 Sept 1870). She had two older sisters, both sopranos: Amalia (*b* Paris, 1831; *d* Paris, 1915) appeared in opera and concerts in the USA from 1850 until her marriage with the pianist and impresario Maurice Strakosch; Carlotta (*b* Florence, Italy, 30 Oct 1835; *d* Paris, 27 June 1889), after making her début in 1861 at a concert in New York, sang for one season in opera at the Academy of Music and then devoted the rest of her career to concert performances in Europe and the USA.

In 1844, a year after Adelina was born, the Patti family left Europe for New York, where Caterina sang for a few years before retiring. Salvatore managed Italian opera at Palmo's Opera House and later at the Astor Place Opera House for several seasons, but neither venture was successful and he eventually returned to Europe. Adelina first sang in public at the age of seven in a charity concert at Tripler Hall, New York. Accompanied by Strakosch and the violinist Ole Bull, she toured the USA for three years as a child prodigy, and from the start it was on her earnings that the family lived. In 1857 she embarked on another tour, this time through the southern states and to the West Indies with the pianist and composer Gottschalk. She made her stage début on 24 November 1859 at the Academy of Music, New York, as Donizetti's Lucia, having studied the role with Emanuele Muzio. The following winter, after a tour of eastern cities, she returned to the Academy for a second season.

On 14 May 1861 Patti made a spectacular European début at Covent Garden as Amina in Bellini's *La sonnambula*, and for the next two decades sang exclusively in Europe with great success. During the winter of 1881–2 she returned to New York for concerts, and for the next three winters was engaged by J. H. Mapleson for his opera tours of the USA, appearing in New York at the Academy (where as Martha she celebrated the 25th anniversary of her operatic début) and in Chicago, Cincinnati, and elsewhere. Her fee during these tours was as high as $5000 per performance; she also endorsed many commercial products (see illustration). Another tour, this time managed by H. E. Abbey and announced as her farewell to the stage, ended in the spring of 1887 with six performances at the Metropolitan Opera. She was back with Abbey's company at the Metropolitan in 1890 and again in 1892, and her final American tour opened in New York at Carnegie Hall on 4 November 1903.

In the early years of her long career, the roles that formed the staples of her repertory included Lucia, Amina, Rosina, Elvira (*I puritani*), Norina, Adina, Martha, Zerlina, Violetta, and Gilda (all of which she had sung during her first season at the Academy of Music). She later added a number of heavier parts, including

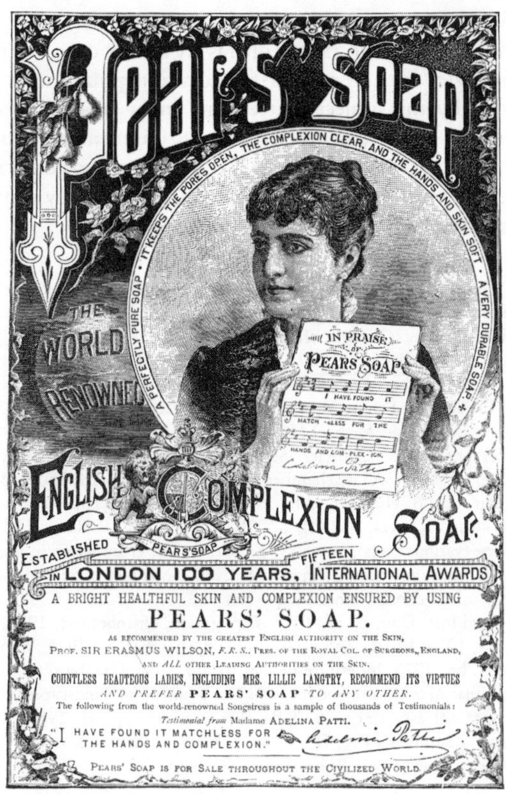

Adelina Patti portrayed in an advertisement for Pears' Soap

Valentine (*Les Huguenots*), Gounod's Marguerite and Juliet, Aida, and even Carmen (one of the very few mistakes that she made). She never attempted Norma, which lay emotionally, if not vocally, well outside her range. She was a very competent actress, particularly in comedy, while the amazing purity of tone and flexibility of voice that she retained for well over half a century were proof of the exemplary way in which she used and nurtured her extraordinary gifts.

BIBLIOGRAPHY

T. de Grave: *Le biographie d'Adelina Patti* (Paris, 1865)
M. Strakosch: *Souvenirs d'un impresario* (Paris, 1866, 2/1887)
L. Lauw: *Fourteen Years with Adelina Patti* (New York, 1884/*R*1977)
J. H. Mapleson: *The Mapleson Memoirs* (London, 1888; ed. H. Rosenthal, 1966)
M. Maretzek: *Sharps and Flats* (New York, 1890/*R*1968)
L. Arditi: *My Reminiscences* (New York, 1896/*R*1977)
H. Klein: *The Reign of Patti* (New York, 1920/*R*1978)
H. Pleasants: *The Great Singers* (New York, 1966), 204
E. Tribble: "Patti, Adelina," *NAW*

ELIZABETH FORBES

Pattison, Lee (*b* Centralia [now Wisconsin Rapids], WI, 22 July 1890; *d* Claremont, CA, 22 Dec 1966). Pianist. He studied piano with Baermann and composition with Chadwick at the New England Conservatory, graduating in 1910, and then studied with Schnabel in Berlin. In 1916 he formed a two-piano team with GUY MAIER, and the two performed together regularly from 1919 to 1931. A number of composers, including John Alden Carpenter, Edward Burlingame Hill, and Leo Sowerby, dedicated works to them. From 1932 until 1937 he was head of the piano department at Sarah Lawrence College; he was also on the summer school faculty of the Juilliard School and the New England Conservatory. He composed several pieces for piano, including *Florentine Sketches* and *Told in the Hills*.

R. ALLEN LOTT

Patton, Charley (*b* ?Bolton, MS, *c*1887; *d* Indianola, MS, 28 April 1934). Blues singer and guitarist. In 1912 he moved to the Dockery plantation near Drew, where he worked with Tommy Johnson, Willie Brown, and other Mississippi blues singers who exchanged songs and techniques. Patton was noted for his clowning and entertaining, but his recordings, made from 1929 until his death, present a more serious musician. Generally regarded as the archetypal Mississippi blues singer, he had a rasping voice of the "heavy" kind admired by many other singers. *Pony Blues* (1929, Para. 12792), included in his first recording session, was his most celebrated blues item, though *Down the Dirt Road* (1929, Para. 12854) and *Moon Going Down* (1930, Para. 13014), the latter with Willie Brown playing the flat-pick guitar in accompaniment, are perhaps his best recorded blues. The themes of his blues were often autobiographical, though sometimes the stanzas were confused; *High Sheriff Blues* (1934, Voc. 02680) is more consistent as a narrative. Patton's recordings are sombre, often with percussive accompaniment on a guitar in open G tuning. He also performed ballads, including *Elder Greene Blues* (1929, Para. 12972) and *Frankie and Albert* (1929, Para. 13110), ragtime or dance-songs, such as the spirited *A Spoonful Blues* (1929, Para. 12869), and spirituals from the songster repertory. His blues influenced Bukka White, Howlin' Wolf, and many later singers.

BIBLIOGRAPHY

SouthernB
P. Oliver: *The Story of the Blues* (London, 1969)
J. Fahey: *Charley Patton* (London, 1970)
G. Oakley: *The Devil's Music: a History of the Blues* (London, 1976)
J. T. Titon: *Early Downhome Blues* (Urbana, IL, 1977)

PAUL OLIVER

Patwin. American Indian group in California. Their music bears a resemblance to that of the WINTUN.

Paul, Les [Polfus, Lester] (*b* Waukesha, WI, 9 June 1915). Guitarist and inventor. He was largely self-taught on the guitar and played with country-music groups before performing on his own radio show in Chicago during the 1930s. A growing interest in jazz led to the formation of the Les Paul Trio (with singer Jimmy Atkins and bass player Ernie Newton), with which he went to New York in the late 1930s; the trio appeared with Fred Waring and his Pennsylvanians for five years, and later performed with Bing Crosby and the Andrews Sisters. After years of experimenting with methods of guitar amplification, Paul developed a prototype for the solid-body electric guitar in 1941. Further refinements led to the production by Gibson of the Les Paul Standard model in 1952; it became a favorite instrument for many guitarists, especially rock musicians. Paul explored techniques of multitrack recording, and is often referred to as the inventor of the first eight-track tape recorder. He also invented "sound-on-sound" recording (overdubbing), the floating bridge pickup, the electrodynamic pickup, and various types of electronic transducer, innovations that made a great impact on the recording industry in general and guitarists in particular. He applied them with some success in recordings, such as *How High the Moon* and *Vaya con Dios*, made during the 1950s with his wife, singer Mary Ford (Colleen Summers; *b* Pasadena, CA, 7 July 1924; *d* Los Angeles, CA, 30 Sept 1977). Paul's technical wizardry gave the music novelty value and also pointed the way for future recording processes. He ceased to perform in the early 1960s in order to devote his time to his inventions.

BIBLIOGRAPHY

C. Flippo: "I Sing the Solid Body Electric," *Rolling Stone*, no. 180 (13 Feb 1975), 44

MARK TUCKER

Paul, Thomas (Warburton) (*b* Chicago, IL, 22 Feb 1934). Bass. He studied violin and viola as a child. After graduating from Occidental College, Los Angeles (BA 1956), he immediately began studies at the Juilliard School in violin, viola, and conducting. During military service (1957–60) he joined the US Army Chorus in Washington, DC, and this encouraged him to embark on a career as a singer. In 1961 he made his début at Carnegie Hall in Handel's *Belshazzar*, and that same year won first prize in the New York Liederkranz Foundation contest, and was awarded a Ford Foundation grant. From 1962 to 1971 he was with the New York City Opera, making his début as Sparafucile in *Rigoletto*. He then joined the faculty of the Eastman School of Music as visiting professor, becoming professor there in 1974.

Paul's diverse roles with American opera companies include Pimen in Mussorgsky's *Boris Godunov*, Tiresias in Stravinsky's *Oedipus Rex*, Ramfis in Verdi's *Aida*, Seneca in Monteverdi's *L'incoronazione di Poppea*, and the title role in Boito's *Mefistofele*. His oratorio roles have also been numerous. His European début, with the Gächinger Kantorei Stuttgart in Bach's *St. Matthew Passion*, was in 1976. In 1978 he performed with DeGaetani and the group Speculum Musicae in the world première of Carter's *Syringa*, a work which he recorded (1983). His recital début was in 1980 at Alice Tully Hall. He has also appeared with orchestras throughout North America, and at the Aspen Music Festival, and frequently tours with the Bach Aria Group.

BIBLIOGRAPHY

R. Ericson: "About Two Basses," *New York Times* (7 Dec 1980), §II, p.21

P. G. Davis: "Bass: Thomas Paul, Solo," *New York Times* (10 Dec 1980), §III, p.24

MARY A. WISCHUSEN

Paulus, Stephen (Harrison) (*b* Summit, NJ, 24 Aug 1949). Composer. He attended the University of Minnesota where he was awarded the BM (1971), the MM (1974), and the PhD (1978) in theory and composition; his principal composition teachers were Paul Fetler and Dominick Argento. In 1973 he cofounded with Larsen the Minnesota Composers Forum, which he continued to serve as one of its managing composers; in 1983 he and Larsen were appointed composers-in-residence of the Minnesota Orchestra. Paulus was awarded a NEA grant in 1978 and a Guggenheim Fellowship in 1982. He came to national attention in 1979 when his one-act opera *The Village Singer* was first performed by the Opera Theater of St. Louis. The Opera Theater then commissioned a second opera, *The Postman always Rings Twice*, for its 1982 season, and performed it at the Edinburgh International Festival (1983), where it was the first opera by an American composer to be presented.

Though Paulus's instrumental works employ a variety of idioms and coloristic effects, the operas are solidly conservative and tonal in style, with frequent references to popular music genres suggested by the subject matter, and many repetitions of and variations on easily remembered melodic fragments that function as leitmotifs. *The Postman always Rings Twice* is a powerful music-drama with clearly defined characters and a carefully controlled emotional range.

WORKS

Operas: The Village Singer (1, M. D. Browne, after M. W. Freeman), 1979; The Postman always Rings Twice (2, C. Graham, after J. M. Cain), 1982; The Woodlanders (Graham, after T. Hardy), 1985

Orch: Spectra, small orch, 1980; Divertimento, harp, chamber orch, 1982; Conc., 1983; 7 Short Pieces, 1983

Vocal: 3 Elizabethan Songs, S, pf, 1973; 3 Chinese Poems, SATB, 1973; Mad Book, Shadow Book: Michael Morley's Songs (Browne), T, pf, 1976, arr. T, chamber ens, 1978; Canticles: Songs and Rituals for Easter and the May (Browne), S, Mez, SATB, chamber orch, org, 1977; North Shore (Browne), Mez, Bar, SATB, chamber orch, 1977; Letters for the Times (17th-century American newspapers, diaries), SATB, chamber ens, 1980; So Hallow'd is the Time (various texts), boy S, S, T, Bar, SATB, chamber orch, org, 1980; Artsongs (Rilke and others), T, pf, 1983; *c*10 choral pieces; folksong and carol arrs. for mixed chorus; other song cycles

Chamber and inst: Duo, cl, pf, 1974; Exploration, chamber ens, 1974; Colors, brass qnt, 1974; Village Tales: a Tree of Life, chamber ens, 1975; Wind Suite, fl, ob, cl, bn, 1975; Indefinite Images, cl, bn, 1976; Graphics, chamber ens, 1977; Lunar Maria, chamber ens, 1977; 5 Translucent Landscapes, pf, 1978; Music for Contrasts, str qt, 1980; Banchetto musicale, pf, vc, 1981; Courtship Songs for a Summer's Eve, fl, ob, vc, pf, 1981; other works

Tape: Dance a Line, 1976; Prison Songs, 1976

Principal publishers: European American, C. Fischer, Jenson, Shawnee

BIBLIOGRAPHY

M. A. Feldman: "Triple Header," *Opera News*, xlix/17 (1985), 24

JAMES WIERZBICKI

Paur, Emil (*b* Czernowitz [now Chernovtsy, Ukraine], 29 Aug 1855; *d* Mistek [now in Czechoslovakia], 7 June 1932). Austrian conductor, violinist, and composer. He was at first a pupil of his father, the director of the Vienna Musikverein. In 1866 he entered the Vienna Conservatory, studying composition with Dessoff and violin with Hellmesberger. He became a member of the court orchestra in 1870, and from 1876 held conducting appointments in Kassel, Königsberg, Mannheim, and Leipzig. In 1893 he came to the USA, succeeding Nikisch as conductor of the Boston SO.

In 1898 Paur was elected conductor of the New York Philharmonic Society in succession to Seidl, and in 1899 he succeeded Dvořák as director of the National Conservatory in New York. Both positions terminated in 1902. In 1900 he visited London, conducting German opera at Covent Garden, and in 1903 he returned to Europe, where he conducted concerts in Madrid as well as in Berlin. From 1904 to 1910 (when the orchestra disbanded), he was conductor of the Pittsburgh Orchestra, where his Symphony "In der Natur" was played (1909). Again returning to Europe, he succeeded Muck as director of the Berlin Opera (1912), but resigned after a few months, remaining however in Berlin as a concert conductor. His other compositions include a piano concerto, a violin concerto, and some chamber music.

BIBLIOGRAPHY

M. A. D. Howe: *The Boston Symphony Orchestra: an Historical Sketch* (Boston, 1914, rev. and enlarged 2/1931/*R*1978), 99

J. G. Huneker: *The Philharmonic Society of New York and its 75th Anniversary: a Retrospect* (New York, ?1917), 18

Obituary, *ZfM*, xcix (1932), 642

W. Stark: *Emil Paur and the Pittsburgh Symphony, 1904–1910* (MS, 1935, *PPi*)

E. Kenny: "Some Letters to Emil Paur," *Notes*, viii (1950–51), 631
R. Wolfe: *A Short History of the Pittsburgh Orchestra* (diss., Carnegie Library School, Carnegie Institute of Technology, 1954)

J. A. FULLER MAITLAND/R

Pavarotti, Luciano (*b* Modena, Italy, 12 Oct 1935). Italian tenor. He studied with Arrigo Pola and Ettore Campogalliani, won the international competition at the Teatro Reggio Emilia in 1961, and made his début there as Rodolfo that year. He established himself internationally in the 1960s, making his débuts at Covent Garden as Rodolfo (1963) and at La Scala, Milan, as the Duke in *Rigoletto* (1965); at La Scala he also sang in a performance of Verdi's Requiem to mark the centenary of Toscanini's birth (1967). He first appeared in the USA as Edgardo to Sutherland's Lucia (Miami, February 1965); he made both his San Francisco and his Metropolitan Opera débuts once again as Rodolfo, respectively on 11 November 1967 and 23 November 1968, and has appeared in "Live from the Met" telecasts many times since the first broadcast in the series in March 1977. He was the first singer to give a recital at the new opera house (13 February 1978). Among his finest performances on disc are his Rodolfo for Karajan, his Calef for Mehta, and his Arturo (*I puritani*) with Sutherland. He is also a master of lighter Italian songs to which he brings irresistible panache.

Pavarotti has a bright, incisive voice with a typically open, Italianate production, full and vibrant throughout its range, with penetrating high notes; his performing style attractively combines energy and musicianship. During the early 1980s, his popularity was such that he became known far beyond operatic circles; his extraordinary fame has occasionally led him to inartistic gestures of voice and a coarsening of style, and at times it seemed as if his career might be wholly taken over by an enthusiastic publicity machine.

BIBLIOGRAPHY

"Pavarotti, Luciano," *CBY 1973*
H. Saal: "The Great Pavarotti," *Newsweek*, lxxxvii (15 March 1976), 56
"Opera's Golden Tenor," *Time*, cxiv (24 Sept 1979), 60
L. Pavarotti, with W. Wright: *My Own Story* (Garden City, NY, 1981)
J. Hines: *Great Singers on Great Singing* (Garden City, NY, 1982), 212
W. Crutchfield: "Those Superstar Tenors," *New York Times* (11 Nov 1984), §II, p.1

ALAN BLYTH

Pawnee. American Indian tribe of the south-central Plains; formerly a confederacy of the Skiri, Chawi, Pithawirata, and Kitkahahki Indians. Prior to the mid-19th century the Pawnee lived in permanent earth-lodge villages along the rivers of Nebraska and northern Kansas. They subsisted by cultivating corn, beans, and squash, and by taking part in buffalo hunts twice a year. During the 19th century the traditional life of the Pawnee was threatened by a severe population decline and by their relocation to Oklahoma, directed by the US government, in 1875–6 (*see* INDIANS, AMERICAN, fig. 1). This article is principally a description of Pawnee culture before its disruption.

1. Music and ceremonial life. 2. Instruments. 3. Composition. 4. Style.

1. MUSIC AND CEREMONIAL LIFE. The Pawnee are noted for their elaborate religious system and mythology based on cosmological powers, and for the beauty of the songs and rituals related to their ceremonial life. Almost all important ceremonies were associated with sacred bundles believed to have derived from supernatural powers. Bundles attributed to celestial powers were owned by each village and used by priests to perform ceremonies necessary for the welfare of the community; those attributed to animal supernatural powers belonged to doctors' and warriors' societies and were used for the benefit of the individual.

The ceremonial season, which lasted from early spring through the autumn harvest, was prescribed by stellar observation, the occurrence of natural phenomena, and the yearly agricultural cycle. A ceremony might consist of several ritual acts such as a smoke offering, food offerings of corn and meat, and gift giving, but sacred songs were its essential feature. The season began with the Thunder, or Creation, Ceremony, in which the priests sang for the revitalization of the earth. The songs, the meanings of which were generally obscure to the listeners, were long and formulaic. They were based, as were many of the priests' ritual songs, on a series of word substitutions called "steps"; there were 26 steps for women and 30 for men. Women's steps used words associated with the fields and home life, men's with animal powers and warfare. The first song of the Thunder Ceremony used the complete series of women's and men's steps. Its basic form (a four-line stanza sung twice) was extended in performance to 448 lines as each of the steps was substituted during 56 repetitions of the eight lines. Subsequent songs were rendered in abbreviated form, using only four women's and six men's steps. The descending melodic line of the songs and the priests' manner of singing were intended to imitate the descent from heaven to earth of rolls of thunder.

The agricultural cycle continued with rituals to ensure the growth and abundant harvest of corn. At planting time the women danced with hoes and baskets, in imitation of the motions of ground-breaking and planting. After the corn sprouted the priests led a procession to the fields while singing songs to Mother Corn. A final ceremony, after the harvest, replenished the sacred bundles with new corn. Beyond the agricultural ceremonies, the priests were responsible for rituals to purify the sacred bundles, rituals associated with the buffalo hunt, and others not part of the yearly cycle. The Calumet Ceremony (also called *Hako*, from the Wichita word for "pipe") could be initiated in any season except winter to maintain peace and trade between the Pawnee and neighboring tribes. During this elaborate, four-day ceremony the priests sang for the welfare of the people.

Traditional Pawnee society was hierarchical and had, beyond its hereditary classes of chiefs and priests, a group of doctors organized into several secret medicine societies. Each society centered around an animal guardian (e.g., bear, buffalo, otter, beaver, owl) that was its source of power. Membership, although sometimes obtained by means of a vision (common among other Plains tribes), was more often achieved through long apprenticeship. Among the Skiri, the societies met in combination after the harvest for the grand Thirty Day, or Medicine Lodge, Ceremony. Here each doctor was required to demonstrate his powers to his fellows and the public. Performances were elaborate and dramatic, involving sleight-of-hand, hypnotism, and trance-induction. Each doctor dressed as his animal benefactor to reaffirm kinship with it, and sang and danced the story of the original vision experience. Although these songs were the individual creations of each doctor, they generally followed a standard pattern, consisting of four to eight stanzas (usually six), each with two lines (*AB*) alternating with a refrain and a longer, repetitive chorus. Dances were mimetic, and their rhythmic accompaniment suggested a particular animal's movements. Buffalo Society songs, for example, had a steady, unchanging accompaniment that imitated the sound of a running herd. For "bear" singing the beat was slow and heavy. Each class of songs also had a particular formulaic ending (such as *o ho o* or *ha wa wa*) that further distinguished the type of song.

In pre-reservation days most young men could belong to a number of warrior societies, each of which had its own songs, dances, and costume. Although most were disbanded after the Pawnee were relocated to Oklahoma, a few societies were revived around 1900 under the impetus of the Ghost Dance movement (*see* INDIANS, AMERICAN, §I, 6(iii)). After the demise of the movement the Pawnee continued the dance in a syncretic form called the Ghost Dance Hand Game, in which the songs of the Ghost Dance were combined with the old hand game (a guessing game very widely distributed among Indian tribes) and elements of Pawnee ritualism. In intervals between games the Pawnee danced slowly in a large circle, moving clockwise, to Ghost Dance songs. Songs of the old warrior societies were also part of the ceremony.

2. INSTRUMENTS. The Pawnee instrumentarium was large and varied, with many instruments having particular ritual significance. Gourd rattles were shaken during priests' rituals and ceremonies of the medicine societies. Rawhide rattles, either spherical or ring-shaped, were part of the regalia of several warriors' societies. Buffalo dancers carried cluster rattles made of small pieces of buffalo hoof that were strung on leather thongs attached to the end of a stick covered with buckskin; similar rattles were also made of deer hoof. Several types of drum were known. A WATER-DRUM, used in doctors' ceremonies, was made of a hollowed cottonwood log half-filled with water; it was covered with a water-soaked hide and struck with an unpadded beater. During preparation of the drum doctors breathed into its cavity; thus they intended both to give the instrument life and inhale its healing power. The drum's "voice" was believed capable of driving away disease. Doctors' apprentices, who sang at certain medicine society meetings, accompanied themselves by beating on a large, dry cowhide without a resonating chamber; a single-headed frame drum was used by some warrior societies. With the development of the Ghost Dance Hand Game a large double-headed drum, suspended from forked sticks, came into use. Wind instruments included small reed and eagle-bone whistles used by the doctors' and warriors' societies, and a flute used for courting.

3. COMPOSITION. Songs were actively sought by all young men and were essential to members of warriors' and doctors' societies; the sounds of nature often provided inspiration. Commonly a song would come to an individual while he wandered over the prairie; a person who received a song in this way was said to have been in an uncommon state of heightened awareness. Songs received during the day were dance songs, or songs that could only be sung in the daytime; those dreamed were sung only at night. An individual's songs were his personal property and were usually passed on through inheritance. Songs of the sacred bundle ceremonies and of the medicine societies were said to have been received in visions; these were passed on to new priests and doctors during their apprenticeship. Occasionally entire ceremonies and their songs were borrowed from neighboring tribes (e.g., the Deer Dance from the Wichita).

4. STYLE. Pawnee singing style was characterized by a moderately high degree of vocal tension, with pulsation on long notes and downward glides at phrase endings. Songs related to the sacred bundles and those of the medicine societies usually had meaningful texts, set syllabically, while songs of the warrior societies more often contained vocables. The average range was an octave to a 10th; larger ranges of up to two octaves occurred occasionally in warrior songs. Pentatonic scales without half-steps predominated. A song generally began on its highest note, descended in terrace fashion, and ended on its lowest note, which usually was also the tonic. Intervals of the melodic line were mostly major 2nds and minor 3rds, with 4ths common in songs of the warrior societies. Often several phrases of a song shared the same rhythmic pattern. Rhythmic accompaniment varied according to song type, but a regular steady beat that coincided with the melodic pulse was most common. Drum beats occurring regularly just before or after the pulse were usually found in warriors' songs. Pawnee songs exhibited a wide variety of forms. Commonly a song consisted of repetitions of several short phrases in various orders; their reiterations were often a 5th or octave lower than their initial statement. Incomplete repetition (i.e., *AA′ BC A′ BC*) was found principally in warriors' songs. Ghost Dance song form was typically *AABB* or *AABBCC*.

Both traditional and modern elements are present in contemporary Pawnee music and dance. At hand games, Ghost Dance songs are still occasionally performed, and two dances from old warriors' societies, the Young Dog Dance and the Iruska, are current. The Pawnee also hold an annual Homecoming on Independence Day at which the popular powwow dances of the southern Plains, such as the War, Round, Forty-niner, Two-step, Buffalo, and Gourd dances, can be heard.

Recordings of Pawnee music are held at the Archive of Folk Culture, Library of Congress, Washington, DC (including recordings by James R. Murie); the Indiana University Archives of Traditional Music, Bloomington (recordings by Murie, George Dorsey, Alexander Lesser, and Gene Weltfish); the Bureau of American Ethnology, Smithsonian Institution, Washington, DC (recordings by Alice C. Fletcher); the Nebraska State Historical Society, Lincoln; and the Columbia University Department of Anthropology, New York (recordings by Weltfish).

See also INDIANS, AMERICAN, esp. §I, 4(ii)(a).

DISCOGRAPHY

Songs of the Pawnee and Northern Ute, recorded 1919 by F. Densmore (AAFS 25, 1951)

Plains: Comanche, Cheyenne, Kiowa, Caddo, Wichita, Pawnee, recorded in 1951 by W. Rhodes (AAFS 39, 1954)

Music of the Pawnee: Sung by Mark Evarts, recorded in 1936 by G. Weltfish (FW 4334, 1965)

BIBLIOGRAPHY

G. B. Grinnell: "The Young Dog's Dance," *Journal of American Folklore*, iv (1891), 307

A. C. Fletcher: *The Hako: a Pawnee Ceremony*, Bureau of American Ethnology Annual Report, xxii/2 (Washington, DC, 1904)

N. Curtis: *The Indians' Book* (New York, 1907, 2/1923/*R*1968)

J. R. Murie: "Pawnee Indian Societies," *American Museum of Natural History Anthropological Papers*, xi (1914), 543–644

H. H. Roberts: *Ceremonial Songs of the Pawnee: Transcriptions of Music and Musical Analysis* (MS, 1922, *DSI* 1788)

R. Linton: "Annual Ceremony of the Pawnee Medicine Men," *Field Museum of Natural History, Department of Anthropology, Leaflet*, no.8 (1923), 1

F. Densmore: *Pawnee Music*, Bureau of American Ethnology Bulletin, no.93 (Washington, DC, 1929)

A. Lesser: *The Pawnee Ghost Dance Hand Game: a Study of Cultural Change* (New York, 1933)

J. R. Murie: *Ceremonies of the Pawnee*, Smithsonian Contributions to Anthropology, no.27 (Washington, DC, 1981)

MARY RIEMER-WELLER

Paxton, Tom [Thomas Richard] (*b* Chicago, IL, 31 Oct 1937). Folksinger and songwriter. He taught himself to play guitar as a teenager, and first became interested in folk music while studying drama at the University of Oklahoma. In 1960 he moved to New York, where he met other young folk musicians such as Bob Dylan and Phil Ochs. In 1961–2 Paxton sang in coffeehouses in Greenwich Village, and his songs began to attract the attention of other folk musicians, notably the Weavers, who performed his *Ramblin' Boy* at their Carnegie Hall concert in 1963. Paxton's first album, *Ramblin' Boy*, recorded in 1964, was not a commercial success, but it contained a number of sensitive songs such as *I can't help but wonder where I'm bound* and *The last thing on my mind*. Five more albums were released in the 1960s, containing topical protest songs such as *The willing conscript*, *A thousand years*, and *Lyndon Johnson told the nation*. In this period he performed frequently in the USA, England, and Europe. In the early 1970s he recorded three more albums and settled for a number of years in England. He returned to the USA in 1977 and released a much heralded new album, *New Songs from the Briar Patch*, which demonstrated his continuing penchant for political material in such songs as *Talking Watergate* and *The white bones of Allende*. Paxton has written over 500 songs and made successful tours in the USA, Europe, and Australia. His songs range from gentle, nostalgic love-songs to political commentary that can be forceful and passionate or keenly ironic; his work is often seen as an extension of the tradition of socially conscious folk music exemplified by Woody Guthrie and Pete Seeger.

RECORDINGS

(selective list)

Ramblin' Boy (Elek. 7277, 1964), incl. I can't help but wonder where I'm bound, The last thing on my mind; *Ain't that News* (Elek. 7289, 1965); *Outward Bound* (Elek. 7317, 1966); *Morning Again* (Elek. 74019, 1968), incl. A thousand years, Talking Vietnam pot luck blues; *Peace will Come* (Rep. 2069, 1972); *New Songs from the Briar Patch* (Van. 79395, 1977), incl. Talking Watergate, The white bones of Allende

BIBLIOGRAPHY

G. Friesen: "Something New has been Added," *Sing Out!*, no.13 (1963), 12
A. Means: "The Politics of Paxton," *Melody Maker*, xlvi (20 Feb 1971), 13
M. Jones: "The Complete Tom Paxton," *Melody Maker*, xlvii (22 April 1972), 28
A. Edelstein: "The Last Thing on Tom Paxton's Mind is Writing Safe Songs," *Songwriter*, v (1980), 52
"Paxton, Tom," *CBY 1982*

TERENCE J. O'GRADY

Paycheck, Johnny [Lytle, Donald] (*b* Greenfield, OH, 31 May 1941). Country-music singer, guitarist, and songwriter. He began his career as a bass guitarist for Porter Wagoner, Faron Young, Ray Price, and George Jones, changing to steel guitar while he was with Jones's group. Also a powerful vocalist, he was a backup singer on recordings by Price, Young, Roger Miller, Sheb Wooley, and Webb Pierce. Under the name Donny Young he recorded rockabilly songs for Decca; he then moved to the Mercury and Hilltop labels and made his first successful singles, *A-11* (1965) and *Heartbreak, Tennessee* (1966). In 1966 Paycheck and his manager, Aubrey Mayhew, formed Little Darlin' Records, for which he recorded several hits, including *The Lovin' Machine* (1966). During this period he also began to gain recognition as a songwriter through such songs as *Apartment no.9* (for Tammy Wynette) and *Touch my heart* (for Ray Price). After a period during which he suffered from alcoholism, Paycheck signed a recording contract with Epic in 1971; working with the producer Billy Sherrill, he made a number of hits, such as *She's all I got* (1971), *11 months and 29 days* (1976), and (most successful of all) *Take this job and shove it* (1977). In the early 1980s his career was again interrupted by personal problems. Heavily influenced by George Jones, Paycheck's singing style is in the classic country tradition, marked by a strong delivery but lacking Jones's vocal smoothness.

RECORDINGS

(selective list)

A-11 (Hilltop 3007, 1965); Heartbreak, Tennessee (Hilltop 3009, 1966); The Lovin' Machine (Little Darlin' 008, 1966); She's all I got (Epic 10783, 1971); *Someone to Give my Love to* (Epic 31449, 1972); Mr. Lovemaker (Epic 10999, 1973); *Song and Dance Man* (Epic 32570, 1974); 11 months and 29 days (Epic 50249, 1976); Take this job and shove it (Epic 50469, 1977); *Armed and Crazy* (Epic 35444, 1978)

DON CUSIC

Payne, Maggi (*b* Temple, TX, 23 Dec 1945). Composer, flutist, and video artist. She studied flute with Walfrid Kujala and composition with Theodore Ashford, Karlins, and Stout at Northwestern University (BM 1968). After a brief stay at Yale University (1968) she attended the University of Illinois (MM in flute, 1970), studying with the composers Martirano and Johnston, and began to compose electronic music. After studies in electronic music (with Ashley) and sound recording at Mills College (MFA 1972) she remained there, working as a recording engineer (1972–81) with Ashley and other composers, including Lucier, Mumma, Behrman, and Christian Wolff, and teaching sound recording techniques for film, audio, and video (1980–81). In 1982–3 she taught sound design at the San Francisco Art Institute. As a flutist she has performed throughout the USA and in Europe and lectured on contemporary flute techniques. She has also worked as a recording engineer for Lovely Music Records, producing works of Behrman, "Blue" Gene Tyranny, and Peter Gordon. The Mills Crothers Award (1972) and a grant from the NEA (1979–80) are among the honors she has received.

Payne composes mostly electronic music using synthesized material and extensive multi-tracking. Spatial location of sound, an acute attention to gradual alterations of timbre and rhythm, and visual elements – usually abstract imagery produced on video, film, or 35mm slides – are vital concerns in her work. She is the author of a monograph on Gordon Mumma, published in 1983.

WORKS

(tape works with 4-track tape)

Ametropia, fl, 1970; Hum, taped fl, opt. fl, 1973; Allusions, tape, dancers, lights, film, 1973; House Party (dance music, C. Brown), 1974; Synergy 2 (dance music, Brown), 1974; Voices (radio play, S. Griffins), 1974; A Winter's Tale (incidental music, Shakespeare), 1975; Farewell, taped fl, slides, 1975; Orion, elec film score, 1975; Transparencies, tape, slides, 1977; Spirals, tape, slides, 1977; Spheres, tape, slides, 1977

Lunar Earthrise, tape, slides, 1979; Lunar Dusk, tape, slides, 1979; Voyages, tape, slides, 1979; Rising, tape, slides and/or dancers, 1980; Blue Metallics, tape, slides, 1980; Ling, tape, slides, 1981; Circular Motions, tape, video, 1981; Io, tape, video, 1982; Crystal, tape, video/slides, 1982; Solar Wind, tape, video/slides, 1983; Scirocco, taped fl, opt. fl, 1983; Noms de plume, tape, 1984

STEPHEN RUPPENTHAL

Pazmor, Radiana [Pasmore, Harriet Horn] (*b* San Francisco, CA, 12 May 1892). Contralto and teacher. She studied singing with her father Henry Bickford Pasmore (1857–1944), a prominent local musician, and piano with Arthur Fickénscher and her sister Suzanne Pasmore. After attending the University of California, Berkeley (BA in French, 1914), she taught first piano and then singing at Pomona College (1914–20). After study and concert performances in Europe (1920–25) she returned to the USA and performed and taught privately, first in New York (1925–35) and then in Hollywood, California (1936–40), where she sang often in the "Concerts on the Roof" series and at the Hollywood Bowl. In 1941 she accepted a teaching post at Converse College (Spartanburg, South Carolina), where she remained until 1960; during this time she also studied music therapy (MM, Boston University, 1955). From 1960 to 1969 she worked in that field, rehabilitating patients with vocal disorders; she was also visiting professor at St. Andrew's Presbyterian College, Laurinburg, North Carolina (1963–9). Later she settled in Sonoma, California.

During the 1930s Pazmor was noted especially for her performances of contemporary American art songs. Her programs regularly included works by Ives (whose *General William Booth Enters into Heaven* she recorded), Cowell, Ruggles, Cage, Bacon, Ruth Crawford, Sessions, Harrison, Copland, Still, and her father. She gave recitals for organizations such as the League of Composers and the Pan American Association, and at academic institutions including the New School for Social Research, Columbia University, Princeton University, and Harvard University. Throughout her concert career Pazmor was lauded for her exceptional dramatic sense, her articulation, diction, and tone quality, her ability to sing difficult music with apparent ease, and her gift of ironic humor. Tall and striking in appearance, she was known for her magnetic personality and her poise on stage.

Pazmor's papers are held by the Gwathmey Library, Converse College; the Bancroft Library, University of California, Berkeley; the Music Library, Yale University; and the Music Division, New York Public Library.

BIBLIOGRAPHY

Early Master Teachers, History of Music in San Francisco, vi (San Francisco, 1940), 65

J. Rodriguez, ed.: *Music and Dance in California* (Hollywood, CA, 1940), 411

San Francisco Examiner (14 July 1963), §2, p.8

R. Warren, Jr.: *Charles E. Ives: Discography* (New Haven, CT, 1972), 114

L. Kibler: *The History of Converse College* (Spartanburg, SC, 1973), 381

R. Mead: *Henry Cowell's New Music, 1925–1936*, Studies in Musicology, xl (Ann Arbor, MI, 1981), 127

JOHN A. EMERSON

Peabody, George (*b* South Danvers [now in Peabody], MA, 18 Feb 1795; *d* London, England, 4 Nov 1869). Philanthropist. From 1806 he worked in retail stores and dry-goods businesses in New England, Baltimore (with branches in New York and Philadelphia), and England. He settled in London in 1837, having already established the firm of George Peabody & Co., which specialized in foreign exchange and American securities. His business prospered and he spent most of his fortune in philanthropy; his gifts enabled several institutes, libraries, lyceums, and museums to be established in the USA during the 1850s and 1860s, and he was also a major benefactor of the poor by financing housing in London. On visits to the USA he promoted public education in the southern states, made substantial gifts to museums at Harvard and Yale universities, and founded the Peabody Institute (Peabody, Massachusetts) and the Peabody Academy of Science (Salem, Massachusetts). In Baltimore, he gave $1,500,000 to establish the Peabody Institute in 1857; it included a free library, an endowment for lectures, an academy of music (now known as the Peabody Conservatory), and an art gallery. In England he came to be regarded as an unofficial Anglo-American ambassador; his honors included a doctorate from Oxford University (1867).

BIBLIOGRAPHY

J. R. MacDonald: "Peabody, George," *DNB*

S. H. Paradise: "Peabody, George," *DAB*

WILLIAM McCLELLAN

Peabody Conservatory of Music. Music conservatory, part of the Peabody Institute, founded by George Peabody in Baltimore in 1857. *See* BALTIMORE, §1; *see also* LIBRARIES AND COLLECTIONS, §3.

Peacock, Gary (*b* Burley, ID, 12 May 1935). Jazz double bass player. He played piano and drums from the age of 13, and took up the bass in the mid-1950s while stationed in Germany with the US Army. After his discharge he remained in Germany, playing with musicians such as Bud Shank and Bob Cooper. He returned to Los Angeles in 1958, then moved in the early 1960s to New York, where he played with the Bill Evans Trio (1962–3). In 1964 he toured with Miles Davis and the avant-garde saxophonist Albert Ayler, and made the first of a series of adventurous recordings with Ayler, as well as several others with the pianist Paul Bley. These performances established him as one of the most important and accomplished bass players of the period. In the mid-1960s Peacock gave up music temporarily to study Eastern philosophy and medicine, eventually moving to Japan. He returned to the USA in 1972, and in 1977 began to record for ECM Records as a composer and leader.

RECORDINGS

(selective list)

As leader: *Tales of Another* (1977, ECM 1101); *Shift in the Wind* (1980, ECM 1165); *Voice from the Past* (1981, ECM 1210)

As sideman: B. Evans: *Trio '64* (1963, Verve 68578); A. Ayler: *New York Eye and Ear Control* (1964, ESP 1016); P. Bley: *Ballads* (1967, ECM 1010), *Paul Bley with Gary Peacock* (1970, ECM 1003); K. Jarrett: *Standards*, i (1983, ECM 1255), *Changes* (1983, ECM 1276), *Standards*, ii (1983, ECM 1289)

BIBLIOGRAPHY

M. Williams: "Gary Peacock: the Beauties of Intuition," *Down Beat*, xxx/13 (1963), 16

M. Solomon: "Bassist Peacock into Zen, Est and ECM," *Down Beat*, xlvi/10 (1979), 9

G. Endress: *Jazz Podium: Musiker über sich selbst* (Stuttgart, Germany, 1980), 196

MICHAEL ULLMAN

Pearce, S(tephen) Austen (*b* Brompton, Kent, England, 7 Nov 1836; *d* Jersey City, NJ, 9 April 1900). Organist. As a child he was a cathedral chorister before studying at Oxford University (BM 1859, DM 1864). He played at various London churches and gave recitals at the Hanover Square Rooms and elsewhere; in 1872 he immigrated to the USA. In New York he played successively at St. Andrew's, St. George's, St. Stephen's, Zion Church, the Church of the Ascension, and the Fifth Avenue Collegiate Church. He ended his career at the Jersey Heights Presbyterian Church in Jersey City. Pearce was also active as a teacher and a writer: in New York he taught and lectured at Columbia College, the New York College of Music, and the General Theological Seminary, and in Baltimore at the Peabody Conservatory and Johns Hopkins University. He was appointed music editor of the *Evening Post* in 1874, and contributed to both the *Musical Courier* and the *Encyclopedia Americana*. His major literary effort was a *Pocket Dictionary of Musical Terms* in 21 languages that was issued in 1889. In 1877 he published the collection *Columbia College Chapel Music*. His compositions, all unpublished, include a three-act children's opera, an oratorio *Celestial Visions*, a cantata *Psalm of Praise*, some orchestral music, songs, and music for piano and organ.

WILLIAM OSBORNE

Pearl, Minnie [Cannon [née Colley], Sarah Ophelia] (*b* Centerville, TN, 25 Oct 1912). Country-music singer and comedienne. After studying theater at Ward-Belmont College, Nashville, Colley joined the Sewall Production Company, working in minstrel and musical shows in small southern towns, and eventually became a dramatic coach, teacher, and director. In 1936, while staging a play in Alabama, she met the prototype for the character that eventually became Minnie Pearl; after a few months she began to portray this character, using rural anecdotes and jokes she had collected in her travels, to promote her plays and to interest her colleagues in the Sewall organization in new ideas. She added to the act burlesque versions of country songs, sung in a cracked, out-of-tune voice, and by 1939 she was making appearances in the guise of the spinster Minnie Pearl, recounting family happenings at Grinder's Switch, a fictional hamlet based on a settlement near Centerville. She worked briefly on a WPA project, then joined the cast of the "Grand Ole Opry" in November 1940.

Tours with Roy Acuff, Pee Wee King, and Eddy Arnold followed, and in 1946 she began a 12-year association with Rod ("Boob") Brasfield, a native of Mississippi, who had worked for many years in rural vaudeville. Unlike most earlier country humor, which had depended heavily on visual jokes, slapstick, and exaggerated accents, the Pearl–Brasfield routines in the "Grand Ole Opry" were tailored to radio, and were based on verbal humor and quick repartee. In later years Pearl was better able to exploit her visual image (including her famous hat with a price tag) on a series of television shows, notably the long-running "Hee Haw"; at the end of her routine she often sang a traditional country song, such as *Careless Love* or *Jealous-hearted me*. She recorded parts of her comedy act for Everest, Starday, and RCA Victor, but her recorded work is uneven. She was elected to the Country Music Hall of Fame in 1975.

BIBLIOGRAPHY

M. Pearl and J. Dew: *Minnie Pearl: an Autobiography* (New York, 1980)

CHARLES K. WOLFE

Pease, Alfred H(umphreys) (*b* Cleveland, OH, 6 May 1838; *d* St. Louis, MO, 12/13 July 1882). Composer and pianist. According to family genealogies, his mother, Marianne Humphreys Pease, was a descendant of the English composer Pelham Humfrey. Although Pease showed early musical talent, his parents were opposed to his becoming a professional musician. From 1855 to 1857 he studied classics at Kenyon College, Gambier, Ohio; he then went to Germany, where he studied the piano with Theodor Kullak, composition with R. F. Wüerst, and orchestration with W. F. Wieprecht until about 1860. After a brief return to the USA he spent another three years in Germany as a pupil of Bülow. He made his début as a pianist on 8 February 1864 at Dodworth's Hall, New York, and continued to perform both as a soloist and as an assisting artist until his death.

Pease wrote about 100 songs noteworthy for their sensitive text settings and for harmonies that are more striking than those of his contemporaries. He also wrote a Piano Concerto in E♭, performed at Philadelphia on 19 July 1876 in an all-American concert conducted by Theodore Thomas.

BIBLIOGRAPHY

W. T. Upton: *Art-song in America* (Boston, 1930/*R*1969 with suppl. 1938)
F. L. G. Cole: "Pease, Alfred Humphreys," *DAB*

CARL S. ROGERS

Pease, James (*b* Indianapolis, IN, 9 Jan 1916; *d* New York, 26 April 1967). Bass-baritone. He studied at the Curtis Institute and first appeared with the Philadelphia Opera Company as Mephistopheles in Gounod's *Faust* in 1941. He sang with the New York City Opera between 1946 and 1953, and at the Berkshire Music Festival between 1946 and 1949, where he took part in the first American performances of Britten's *Peter Grimes* (as Balstrode) and *Albert Herring* (as the Vicar). He was engaged by the Hamburg Staatsoper from 1953 to 1958, sang at Covent Garden for six years, and in Zurich for three years. He performed the baritone roles in *Don Giovanni*, *Die Walküre*, *Die Meistersinger von Nürnberg*, Tchaikovsky's *The Queen of Spades*, and Strauss's *Elektra*. He also sang the roles of King Marke in *Tristan und Isolde*, Baron Ochs in Strauss's *Der Rosenkavalier*, and the Inquisitor in Verdi's *Don Carlos*. Pease's performances were not profound, but they were pleasing and well-conceived.

CHARLES JAHANT

Pedreira, José Enrique (*b* San Juan, Puerto Rico, 2 Feb 1904; *d* San Juan, 6 Jan 1959). Music educator and composer. He took piano lessons in San Juan with Ana and Rosa Sicardó before studying piano and composition in New York with Zygmunt Stojowski for five years. In 1928 he returned to Puerto Rico, where he established himself as a teacher of piano, founding his own academy in Santurce in 1931. Among his pupils were Alba Rosa Castro, Irma Isern, and Jose Raul Ramírez. Although he was primarily a teacher, Pedreira is acknowledged as the most significant Puerto Rican composer of his generation. His stylistic evolution was gradual, from a late Romanticism through an identifiably Puerto Rican impressionism to a more personal idiom that is especially evident in his eloquent *danzas*. He represents the transition between Quintón (1881–1925) and the nationalist composers of the 1950s.

WORKS

Inst: Pf Conc., d, 1936; vn, pf duos, incl. Elegía India; numerous pf works, incl. mazurkas, waltzes, danzas, opera fantasias, nocturnes, études, caprices, and 1 sonata

Vocal: 3 Diálogos con el silencio, song cycle, 1956; many songs, 1934–54
1 ballet, El jardín de piedra, 1957

Principal publisher: E. B. Marks

BIBLIOGRAPHY

R. Sacarello: "José Enrique Pedreira y la escuela de Stojowsky," *Puerto Rico ilustrado* (15 June 1940), 9
H. Campos-Parsi: "El fin del Modernismo: Pedreira," *Le gran enciclopedia de Puerto Rico*, vii (San Juan, PR, 1981), 266

GUSTAVO BATISTA

Peerce, Jan [Perelmuth, Jacob Pincus] (*b* New York, 3 June 1904; *d* New York, 15 Dec 1984). Tenor. Before turning to opera, he played violin in dance bands, sang at Radio City Music Hall (1932), and became a broadcasting favorite throughout the USA. He studied with Giuseppe Boghetti and in 1938 sang in Beethoven's Ninth Symphony under Toscanini, the conductor who later chose Peerce for broadcasts and recordings of *La bohème*, *La traviata*, *Fidelio*, *Un ballo in maschera*, and the last act of

Rigoletto. He made his stage début in Philadelphia as the Duke of Mantua on 14 May 1938 and joined the Metropolitan Opera in 1941, making his first appearance as Alfredo on 29 November; he stayed with that company until 1968. He sang with every leading American ensemble, including the Bach Aria Group (1951–64), and in the USSR, Austria, Germany, and the Netherlands, specializing in the Italian and French *spinto* repertories. In 1956 he became the first American to sing with the Bolshoi Opera since the war. He made numerous worldwide concert tours, appeared in films (*Carnegie Hall*, *Tonight we Sing*, and *Goodbye, Columbus*) as well as on television, and recorded popular songs in addition to Jewish liturgical music. In 1971 he made his Broadway début as Tevye in *Fiddler on the Roof*. Although plagued in later years by physical infirmities and failing eyesight, he continued to be active in concerts. In 1980 he celebrated his 50th anniversary as a performer in a recital at Carnegie Hall. He joined the faculty of the Mannes College of Music in 1981. In his prime Peerce was most admired for a remarkably even scale, a strong technique, and a tenor that had dark vibrance in the middle register and a metallic ring at the top. Though his diminutive size precluded an ideal romantic illusion, he was an actor of restraint and dignity.

BIBLIOGRAPHY

G. Gualerzi: "Peerce, Jan," *Le grandi voci*, ed. R. Celletti (Rome, 1964) [with inc. discography by S. Smolian]

A. Levy: *The Bluebird of Happiness: the Memoirs of Jan Peerce* (New York, 1976)

J. Hines: "Jan Peerce," *Great Singers on Great Singing* (Garden City, NY, 1982), 224

Obituary, *New York Times* (17 Dec 1984)

MARTIN BERNHEIMER/R

Peer-Southern. Firm of music publishers. It was founded as Southern Music Publishing Company in 1928 by Ralph S. Peer, who had spent several years in the South recording jazz and country music for the Victor Talking Machine Company; Southern became a major publisher and distributor of this music. Peer remained president and sole owner of the firm until his death in 1960. In 1940 he established the Peer International Corporation. This, together with Southern, became known as the Peer-Southern Organization, which also includes the American Performing Rights Society (from 1940); Editorial America (1941, from 1944 Brazilian Music, Inc.); La Salle Music Publishers, Inc. (1941); Melody Lane Publications, Inc. (1941); Chas. K. Harris Music Publishing Co., Inc. (1943); R. F. D. Music Publishing Co., Inc. (1946); Panther Music Corp. (1955); Pera Music Corp. (1955); Iver Recording Corp. (1961, from 1966 Peer Southern Productions, Inc.); and PSO Ltd. (1984). Monique I. Peer became president of the organization in 1960 and was succeeded in 1981 by Ralph Peer, II.

The Concert Music Division was formed in 1948 to publish educational and serious contemporary music. With the advice and editorial guidance of Henry Cowell, the division rapidly expanded in the 1950s, and Peer-Southern became a principal publisher of Ives, David Diamond, Fuleihan, Lou Harrison, Orrego-Salas, Manuel M. Ponce, Silvestre Revueltas, Serebrier, and Wolpe. A strong emphasis has also been placed on the publication of works by 20th-century Latin American composers; the firm represents the catalogues of Ediciones Mexicanas de Musica (Mexico City), the Pan American Union (Washington, DC), A. Cranz (Brussels), Editorial Argentina de Musica (Buenos Aires), Editorial Cooperativa Interamericana de Compositores (Montevideo), Enoch & Cie. (Paris), C. Gehrman (Stockholm), and Liber-Southern Ltd. (London).

W. THOMAS MARROCCO, MARK JACOBS/PAUL C. ECHOLS

Pelham, Peter, III (*b* London, England, 9 Dec 1721; *d* Richmond, VA, 28 April 1805). Organist, harpsichordist, teacher, and composer. He was the eldest son of Peter Pelham, a noted mezzotint engraver who immigrated to Boston in 1726. From 1732 to 1741 he studied with Pachelbel – first in Boston, then in Newport, Rhode Island (1734–5), and finally in Charleston. After earning his livelihood as a harpsichord teacher in Charleston from 1740 to 1742, Pelham returned to Boston in 1743, becoming, in the following year, the first organist to be engaged by Trinity Church. In 1750 he moved to Hampton, Virginia.

From 1755 to 1802 he served as organist of Bruton Church, Williamsburg, where he also supervised the printing of currency (1758–75), acted as town jailer (1770–80), made an inventory of the music collection of the harpsichordist Cuthbert Ogle, and kept a music store where he sold all the fashionable London publications. His organ concerts in 1769 included works by Handel, Vivaldi, and William Felton. In 1771 he "furnished the musical accompaniments" for the theater season of Lewis Hallam's American Company of Comedians. An original minuet (in J. S. Darling, ed.: *A Little Keyboard Book*, Williamsburg, 1972) probably typifies the repertory Pelham taught his many aristocratic pupils in Charleston and Williamsburg; the dirge he played at a Masonic funeral in August 1773 is lost.

BIBLIOGRAPHY

J. S. Darling and M. M. Wiggins: "A Constant Tuting: the Music at Williamsburg," *MEJ*, lxi/3 (1974), 60

R. Stevenson: "The Music that George Washington Knew: Neglected Phases," *Inter-American Music Review*, v/1 (1982), 19–77

ROBERT STEVENSON

Pelissier [Pelesier, Pelliser, Pellisier], **Victor** (*b* ?Paris, France, *c*1740–50; *d* ?New Jersey, *c*1820). French composer, arranger, and horn virtuoso active in the USA from 1792. He was first mentioned in an advertisement for a concert in Philadelphia (1792) as "first French horn of the theatre in Cape François." In 1793 he joined the orchestra of the old American Company in New York, and became one of its principal composers and arrangers. From 1811 to 1814 he was back in Philadelphia, where he published *Pelissier's Columbian Melodies* (1811–12), 12 volumes of songs, dances, and instrumental pieces arranged for piano, many of them originally for New York and Philadelphia theaters. He may also have composed the Symphony in G but probably not the *Amusements variés* mentioned by Eitner.

Pelissier's American career extended through a change in theatrical music from an emphasis on historical spectacle, pantomime, and comic opera to an age of sentimental melodrama. His *Ariadne Abandoned by Theseus in the Isle of Naxos* (1797) was one of the earliest and most influential melodramas composed in America, though a more complete idea of his style is shown in the incidental music to William Dunlap's play *The Voice of Nature* (1803) and in the *Ode on the Passions . . . every stanza expressing a different passion*, included in the *Columbian Melodies*. Pelissier was a prolific composer who displayed "variety of thought and readiness of invention, with the full knowledge of all the powers of an orchestra" (Parker). He was honored in 1814 and 1817 with benefit concerts given by New York musicians.

See also MELODRAMA, §2.

WORKS

Collection: *Pelissier's Columbian Melodies*, i–xii (Philadelphia, 1811–12) [PCM]; ed. K. Kroeger, RRAM, xiii–xiv (1984)

STAGE

Operas: Edwin and Angelina, or The Banditti (3, E. H. Smith, after O. Goldsmith), New York, 19 Dec 1796, 2 songs in PCM, i, vi; Sterne's Maria, or The Vintage (2, W. Dunlap), New York, 14 Jan 1799, 3 songs in PCM, xi

Pantomimes: The Death of Captain Cook, New York, 1793, lost; Sophia of Brabant, Philadelphia, 1 Nov 1794, lost; Harlequin Pastry Cook, Philadelphia, 21 Nov 1794, lost; La forêt noire, New York, 30 March 1795, lost; Danaides, or Vice Punished, Philadelphia, 1795, lost; Robinson Crusoe, New York, 15 June 1796, lost; The Fourth of July, or Temple of American Independence, New York, 4 July 1799, lost; Obi, or Three-fingered Jack, Boston, 1801, dances in PCM, vii, ix; Gil Blas, New York, 1802, fandango in PCM, xi; La fille hussar, New York, 1803, lost; Raymond and Agnes, or The Bleeding Nun, New York, 1804, lost; Mother Goose, Philadelphia, 1810, lost; The Milleners, allemande in PCM, xi; The Archers, Philadelphia, air in PCM, xi

Melodramas: Ariadne Abandoned by Theseus in the Isle of Naxos, New York, 1797, lost; A Tale of Mystery (3, T. Holcroft), New York, 16 March 1803, collab. J. Hewitt, 2 dances in PCM, i; The Bridal Ring, Philadelphia, ov., dances, 2 marches in PCM, iii–vii; Valentine and Orson, New York, 1805, song in PCM, xii; The Lady of the Lake, Philadelphia, songs in PCM, iii, iv

Incidental music: The Mysterious Monk (tragedy, Dunlap), New York, 31 Oct 1796, ode and choruses, lost; Virgin of the Sun (5, A. von Kotzebue, trans. Dunlap), 12 March 1800, Chorus of Priests, lost; The Voice of Nature (3, Dunlap), New York, 1803, 2 choruses, processional music, score and parts *NN-L*

Arrs. of orch accs. to stage works by other composers, perf. New York, Philadelphia, most lost

OTHER

Vocal: Ode on the Passions, speaker, pf, PCM, v; 24 songs, some in PCM, others also pubd

Inst: Sym., G, *c*1780, Berne, Stadt- und Universitätsbibliothek, ?by Pelissier; 3 ovs., arr. pf, PCM, i–iii, v, ix; dances, marches, variations, arr. pf, PCM; March to Canada, pf (Philadelphia, 1813); 22 other pieces, arr. pf, PCM

BIBLIOGRAPHY

EitnerQ

J. R. Parker: "Musical Reminiscences: Pelliser," *The Euterpeiad*, iii/3 (1822), 18

W. Dunlap: *History of the American Theatre* (New York, 1832)

C. Durang: "The Philadelphia Stage," *Philadelphia Sunday Dispatch* (1854, 1856, 1860) [series of articles; compiled by T. Westcott as *History of the Philadelphia Stage, between the Years 1749 and 1855*, 1868, *PU*; similar compilations as *The Philadelphia Stage* in *PPL*, and *History of the Philadelphia Stage* in *PHi*]

O. G. T. Sonneck: *A Bibliography of Early Secular American Music* (Washington, DC, 1905; rev. and enlarged by W. T. Upton, 2/1945/*R*1964)

——: *Early Concert-life in America (1731–1800)* (Leipzig, 1907/*R*1978)

——: *Early Opera in America* (New York, 1915/*R*1963)

W. T. Upton: *Art-song in America* (Boston, 1930/*R*1969 with suppl. 1938)

J. T. Howard: *Our American Music* (New York, 1931, rev. 4/1965) [incl. list of works]

J. Mates: *The American Musical Stage before 1800* (New Brunswick, NJ, 1962)

R. J. Wolfe: *Secular Music in America, 1801–1825: a Bibliography* (New York, 1964)

ANNE DHU SHAPIRO

Pellegrino, Ron(ald Anthony) (*b* Kenosha, WI, 11 May 1940). Composer and performer. After early training as a clarinetist, he studied theory, composition, and philosophy at Lawrence University (BM 1962) and later studied with Rudolph Kolisch, René Leibowitz, and Robert Crane at the University of Wisconsin (MM 1965, PhD 1968). He began working in electronic music in 1967 at the University of Wisconsin and in 1969 published *An Electronic Music Studio Manual*, which became the standard text on the Moog synthesizer. He directed the electronic music studios at Ohio State University (1968–70) and the Oberlin Conservatory (1970–73), and was associate professor at Texas Tech University, Lubbock (1978–81). He has received two Ford Foundation awards (1967, 1969), and grants from the NEA and NEH for establishing the Leading Edge music series (a forum for contemporary music performance and scholarship), and for research on his book, *The Electronic Arts of Sound and Light* (1983). Pellegrino's works reflect his interest in psychoacoustics and psycho-optics. His main concerns are the composition of sound and light structures derived from common electronic sources, the process of improvisation, and the creation, using electronic instruments, of works whose sonic and visual aspects are fully integrated. He has further explored these areas by founding two electronic music performance ensembles, the Real Electric Symphony (R*ES) and the Sonoma Electro-Acoustic Music Society (SEAMS), and has developed a theory of music based on the structure and behavior of waves and vibrations, which he calls "cymatic music." He has written articles on topics including synthesizers and laser composition.

WORKS

Elec and mixed media: S & H Explorations, cl, elec, 1972; Metabiosis IV, mixed media, 1972; Figured, film, perc, tape, 1972; Cries, film, perc, tape, 1973; Kaleidoscopic Electric Rags, 1974; Video Slices, film, perc, tape, 1975; Ephemeral Forms, mixed media, 1976; Metabiosis VI, mixed media, 1977; Setting Suns and Spinning Daughters, mixed media, 1978; Words and Phrases, 1v, perc, elec, 1980; Siberian News Release, perc, elec, 1981; Spring Suite, elec, 1982; Laser Seraphim and Cymatic Music, mixed media, 1982; a few other works

Tape and inst: The End of an Affair, perc, tape, 1967; Dance Drama, S, timp, 1967; Passage, tape, 1968; Markings, S, timp, tape, 1969; ETT/Y, 4-track tape, 1970; Leda and the Swan, S, synth, 1970; Phil's Float, cl, tape, 1974; Wavesong, pf, tape, 1975; Issue of the Silver Hatch, perc, 1979

Principal publishers: American Society of University Composers, Electronic Arts

STEPHEN RUPPENTHAL

Pelletier, Wilfrid (*b* Montreal, Que., 20 June 1896; *d* New York, 9 April 1982). Canadian conductor and music educator. After elementary training in Canada, he was sent by the government of Quebec Province to Paris in 1915 where he studied with Isidore Philipp (piano), Marcel Samuel-Rousseau (harmony), Camille Bellaigue (opera repertory), and Charles-Marie Widor (composition). In New York in 1917 Pierre Monteux heard Pelletier accompanying a singer and, on his recommendation, the young pianist was engaged by Gatti-Casazza as a rehearsal pianist and assistant conductor at the Metropolitan Opera. In 1932 he was made conductor of the Metropolitan's Sunday Night Opera Concerts, and under Edward Johnson's administration he became director of the company's French repertory, a post he filled until the arrival of Bing. Pelletier initiated the Metropolitan Opera Auditions of the Air, a radio competition for young singers, and was a conductor of the children's concerts of the New York PO.

From 1935 he became increasingly involved in music in Montreal, founding the Société des Concerts Symphoniques de Montréal, Les Festivals de Montréal, and the Conservatoire de Musique et d'Art Dramatique (1943). He was music director in the Ministry of Cultural Affairs of the Quebec government (1961–70). He was married to the sopranos Mario (1926–36) and Bampton (from 1937).

BIBLIOGRAPHY

W. Pelletier: *Une symphonie inachevée* (Quebec, 1972) [autobiography]

ERIC McLEAN/R

Pelliser [Pellisier], **Victor.** *See* PELISSIER, VICTOR.

Peloubet, (Louis Michel François) Chabrier (de) (*b* Philadelphia, PA, 22 Feb 1806; *d* Bloomfield, NJ, 30 Oct 1885). Maker of woodwind instruments and reed organs. His father, Louis Alexander de Peloubet, was a French royalist who escaped from a death sentence during the Revolution and fled to Germany, where he learned to make flutes, fifes, and clarinets. In October 1803 he immigrated to New York, where he married in 1805; he advertised in the *Albany Argus* as "musical instrument maker" from 26 November 1810 to 28 May 1811. The family resided in Athens, Hudson, and Catskill, New York. Chabrier Peloubet, who undoubtedly learned the woodwind maker's trade from his father, was in business in New York from 1829 until 1836, when he transferred his family to Bloomfield, New Jersey. His first factory was in "Pierson's Mill," 3 Myrtle Court; in 1842 it moved to 86 Orange Street. After these premises were destroyed by fire in 1869, he built two new factory buildings on Orange Street.

In 1849 the Peloubet firm began production of melodeons (the first in the USA) and reed organs; advertisements for them appeared in newspapers in Newark, New Jersey, during the 1850s and 1860s. George Duncklee, a dealer of musical instruments in Newark, sold an assortment of "Peloubet's melodeons, with the Improved Tone that everyone admires who hears them" (1854). Peloubet's instruments were also available in New York in the showrooms of H. Warren and in the Chickering establishment, and in Boston through J. C. Bates, of 129 Washington Street. The firm grew appreciably during the 1850s. Peloubet's son Jarvis (1833–1902) joined him in the family business and in 1860 they produced 90 melodeons to the value of $8000, most of them apparently small instruments for home use.

Although Peloubet manufactured melodeons and reed organs for 31 years, only three of these survive: two in the museum of the Bloomfield Historical Society and one in a private collection. The Bloomfield instruments display evidence of careful workmanship and good intonation and tone. Only four of Peloubet's clarinets have been traced, but 20 flutes survive, including two in the Smithsonian Institution, six in the Dayton C. Miller collection of flutes at the Library of Congress, and seven in private collections. They range in complexity from the boxwood, one-keyed instrument in E♭ with brass and ivory fittings (Miller no.79) to the eight-keyed cocuswood instrument in C with silver fittings and an ivory head (Miller no.1556).

It is difficult to date Peloubet's flutes and clarinets. None of the clarinets is dated; of the flutes, 12 have Peloubet's numbers, which may be serial, but none is dated. All are stamped (usually on the foot-joint) "C. Peloubet New York (City)," and all but five say "Factory Bloomfield NJ."

CHARLES H. KAUFMAN

Pendergrass, Teddy (*b* Philadelphia, PA, 26 March 1950). Soul singer and songwriter. He was ordained a minister at an early age and was introduced to secular music by his mother. He taught himself to play drums and several other instruments, and sang with a local group in Philadelphia while in his teens. When he was 19 he became the drummer for the Cadillacs; a year later he joined HAROLD MELVIN AND THE BLUE NOTES and soon replaced John Atkins as the group's lead singer. Melvin remained its nominal leader, however, and Pendergrass's dissatisfaction with this arrangement led him to leave the ensemble in 1976 and begin a career as a soloist. In the late 1970s and early 1980s he made several hit recordings, including *I don't love you anymore* (no.41, 1977), *Close the Door* (no.25, 1978), and *Love TKO* (no.44, 1980); these were lavishly produced soul ballads notable for their rich vocal textures, elaborate instrumental arrangements, and overt sensuality. Pendergrass's career was interrupted in 1982 by an automobile accident that left him partially paralyzed; it resumed in 1984 when he recorded an album of new material, *Love Language*, that strongly recalled his earlier style.

RECORDINGS

(selective list; recorded for Philadelphia International unless otherwise stated)

Teddy Pendergrass (34390, 1977), incl. I don't love you anymore; *Life Is a Song Worth Singing* (35095, 1978), incl. Close the Door; *Teddy* (36003, 1979); *TP* (36745, 1980), incl. Love TKO; *It's Time for Love* (37491, 1981); *Love Language* (Asy. 60317, 1984)

Penn, William (Albert) (*b* Long Branch, NJ, 11 Jan 1943). Composer. He studied with Pousseur and Kagel at SUNY, Buffalo (BFA 1964, MA 1967), and received the PhD from Michigan State University, East Lansing (1971). At the Eastman School, where he was a faculty member from 1971 to 1978, he pursued further studies in composition with Wayne Barlow. He was staff composer for the New York Shakespeare Festival (1974–6) and from 1975 was associated with the Folger Shakespeare Theatre and Sounds Reasonable Records in Washington, DC. He has received a number of awards, including several from ASCAP and three NEA fellowships (1974–6). His output covers a wide range of genres including jazz and mixed media works. Penn's intensely dramatic music draws on a general poetic inspiration to which melody, harmony, texture, and instrumentation all correspond. He has also explored experimental sound sources.

WORKS

Str Qt, 1968; At Last Olympus! (musical), 1969; Spectrums, Confusions, and Sometime – Moments beyond the Order of Destiny, orch, 1969; The Pied Piper of Hamlin (musical), 1969; Chamber Music no.1, vn, pf, 1971, no.2, vc, pf, 1972; Sym., 1971; The Boy Who Cried "Wolf" is Dead (musical), 1971; Ultra mensuram, 3 brass qnts, 1971; And Among the Leaves we were Passing, synth, 1972; Designs, wind, jazz qnt, perc, 1972; The Canticle (musical), 1972; Inner Loop, band, 1973; Niagara 1678, band, 1973; Night Music, fl choir, 1973; Miroirs sur le Rubaiyat, pf, nar, 1974; incidental music, mixed media works, songs, other inst pieces

DAVID COPE

Pennario, Leonard (*b* Buffalo, NY, 9 July 1924). Pianist. His earliest teachers included the pianists Guy Maier, Isabelle Vengerova, and Olga Steeb, and the composer Ernst Toch. At the age of 12 he made his début, playing Grieg's Concerto with the Dallas SO. His New York début came on 17 November 1943, in Liszt's E♭ Concerto with the New York PO under Rodzinski in Carnegie Hall. In 1952 he gave his first European performances, including his London début, and then toured extensively, winning praise for the power and brilliance of his playing. As a chamber musician he has worked and recorded with Heifetz and Piatigorsky, among others. He gave the first performance of Miklós Rózsa's Piano Concerto (1966), composed for him, with the Los Angeles PO under Mehta, although in the 1970s his repertory became lighter and more popular.

BIBLIOGRAPHY

"Pennario, Leonard," *CBY 1959*

GEORGE GELLES

Pennington, John. Pseudonym of LOUIS GRUENBERG.

Pennsylvania, University of. Privately endowed university founded in Philadelphia in 1740 and offering music courses from

1875; *see* PHILADELPHIA, §6, *see also* LIBRARIES AND COLLECTIONS, §3.

Penobscot. American Indian tribe of the WABANAKI confederacy.

Pepper, Art(hur Edward, Jr.) (*b* Gardena, CA, 1 Sept 1925; *d* Panorama, CA, 15 June 1982). Jazz alto saxophonist. In 1943 he played in the big bands of Benny Carter and Stan Kenton. After serving in the US Army he toured with Kenton as the band's outstanding soloist (1946–51) and also performed freelance in Los Angeles. Thereafter his career was hampered by a series of jail terms for drug abuse. He attempted several times to resume playing, joining a quintet with Jack Montrose (1956), issuing several acclaimed recordings for Contemporary (1957–60), and performing with Howard Rumsey's Lighthouse All-Stars (1960). In 1964 he adopted the tenor saxophone and began to play free jazz, then in 1968 returned to mainstream jazz by joining Buddy Rich's band; serious ailments forced his departure in the following year, however. He spent three years in a rehabilitation center and worked as a bookkeeper before returning to music as a demonstrator for Buffet instruments (1973) and as a saxophonist in Don Ellis's orchestra (1975). From 1977 until his sudden death he gave a series of sensational bop performances in Japan and Newport, and at the Village Vanguard in New York, which brought him increasing recognition and popularity.

Pepper was a leading figure in West Coast jazz, a movement with which he was associated not only because of his choice of location and musical colleagues but also because of his light, clear, precise sound on the alto saxophone. He took part in the earliest recordings in this style under Shorty Rogers's leadership in 1951. However, Pepper was a stronger, more fiery improviser than his fellow West Coast musicians, as amply demonstrated by his recordings in 1957 and 1960 with Miles Davis's rhythm section. His *Art Pepper + Eleven* album (1959), with its harmonized recastings of Charlie Parker solos, anticipated by 15 years the popular recordings of the Los Angeles group Supersax. In the mid-1960s, under the overwhelming influence of John Coltrane, his playing stressed intense and expressive noise elements. Eventually he combined the two approaches in performances such as *Cherokee* (1977), in which traditional bop lines erupt at explosive moments into squeals, growls, and flurries of notes.

RECORDINGS
(selective list)

As leader: *The Early Show* (1952, Xanadu 108); *Art Pepper Meets the Rhythm Section* (1957, Cont. 3532); *Art Pepper + Eleven* (1959, Cont. 3568); *Gettin' Together* (1960, Cont. 3573); *Smack Up* (1960, Cont. 3602); *Living Legend* (1975, Cont. 7633); *Saturday Night at the Village Vanguard* (1977, Cont. 7644), incl. Cherokee; *Straight Life* (1979, Gal. 5127); *Roadgame* (1981, Gal. 5142)

As sideman: S. Kenton: Art Pepper (1950, Cap. 28008), Jump for Joe (1951, Cap. 1704), Street of Dreams (1951, Cap. 1823); S. Rogers: Over the Rainbow (1951, Cap. 15764); B. Rich: *Mercy, Mercy* (1968, Pacific Jazz 20133)

BIBLIOGRAPHY

J. McKinney: "Art Pepper: Profile of a Comeback," *Metronome*, lxxvii (Sept 1960), 26

J. Tynan: "Art Pepper's not the Same," *Down Beat*, xxxi/22 (1964), 18

L. Underwood: "Pepper's Painful Road to Pure Art," *Down Beat*, xlii/11 (1975), 16

A. Pepper and L. Pepper: *Straight Life: the Story of Art Pepper* (New York, 1979)

"Art Pepper," *Swing Journal*, xxxiv/1 (1980), 162 [discography]

BARRY KERNFELD

Pepper, J(ames) W(elsh) (*b* Philadelphia, PA, 1853; *d* Philadelphia, 28 July 1919). Instrument maker and publisher. He worked as an engraver in his father's printing business, gave music lessons, and in 1876 founded a publishing house at 9th and Filbert streets in Philadelphia. From copper plates and a manually operated press he issued instrumental tutors, quicksteps, and from 1877 to 1912 a monthly periodical entitled *J. W. Pepper's Musical Times and Band Journal* (later the *Musical Times*). Around 1887 he acquired a structure at 8th and Locust streets, which came to be known as the J. W. Pepper Building, that accommodated a large salesroom, an instrument factory, and a printing plant, equipped with steam-powered presses that produced sheet music on a large scale. During the next four decades the firm published nearly 200 new titles a year; except for a small group of sacred songs issued by Pepper Publishing Co. in 1901–4, these were all orchestral and band works intended for civic, commerical, and school ensembles. Many compositions and arrangements appeared in journals – *Quickstep*, *Brass and Reed Band*, *Ballroom*, *Theatre and Dance*, and *Opera House*. The *J. W. Pepper Piano Music Magazine* was begun in 1900, and a separate 20th-century series was also established. Among the composers whose works were published by Pepper were Sousa, Pryor, Grafulla, William Southwell, William Paris Chambers, Nick Brown, Thomas H. Rollinson, William Henry Dana, and Fred Luscomb. Publication of new works ceased in 1924.

Pepper's first involvement with musical instruments was as a dealer; for a decade he sold imported instruments, some of which were procured with Henry Distin. Pepper maintained a branch in New York at 294 Bowery from 1881 to 1885; he opened a branch in Chicago in 1884 to replace the New York facility. In 1882 Distin moved to Philadelphia from New York, apparently to help Pepper organize an instrument factory, but their association was short-lived, and in 1886 Distin established his own business in Williamsport, Pennsylvania. Distin's presence in Philadelphia had evidently induced Walter Barnes and Alexandre LeForestier, who had worked in Europe with the firms of Higham, Besson, and Courtois, to immigrate, for they were superintendents in Pepper's factory. Pepper was an aggressive businessman who made considerable use of advertising; he sold, under such trade names as Premier, Perfected, Excelsior, American Favorite, Surprise, and Specialty, more than 70,000 brass instruments and a similar number of drums, woodwinds, and string instruments. His instruments were moderately priced and, like his sheet music, were intended for a mass audience. The manufacture of Pepper instruments continued until J. W. Pepper & Son was formed in 1910, after which most instruments sold by the firm were imported. Many instruments were made for Pepper by Thibouville-Lamy, C. A. Mouchel, M. Brisson, and Buffet-Crampon in Paris, by W. Hillyard in London, and by Bohland and Fuchs in Kraslice (now in Czechoslovakia). Pepper's brass instruments had Périnet valves and were of French design (LeForestier was responsible for Pepper's important developments in this field); clarinets and flutes used only simple key mechanisms. Pepper held five patents for accessories, and shared or used the drum patents of Augustus L. Fayaux (1880), Adolphe S. Soistman (1892, 1900), and William J. Rappold (1894). He exhibited and received awards at the World's Columbian Exposition, Chicago (1893).

On Pepper's death the direction of J. W. Pepper & Son was assumed by Howard E. Pepper (1882–1930), who was in turn succeeded by his widow, Maude E. Pepper. The firm was sold in 1942 and was moved to Valley Forge, Pennsylvania, in 1973.

Guided by Harold K. Burtch and his son Dean C. Burtch, who became president on his father's death in 1963, the firm grew by the mid-1980s to be the largest retailer of sheet music for instrumental ensembles in the USA.

BIBLIOGRAPHY

J. W. Pepper's Musical Times and Band Journal (Philadelphia and Chicago, 1877–1912)
W. H. Dana: *J. W. Pepper's Guide . . . Arranging Band Music* (Philadelphia, 1878)
——: *J. W. Pepper's Guide . . . Orchestra Music* (Philadelphia, 1879)
J. W. Pepper: *How to Tune Valve Instruments* (Philadelphia, 1903)

LLOYD P. FARRAR

Perabo, (Johann) Ernst (*b* Wiesbaden, Germany, 14 Nov 1845; *d* Boston, MA, 29 Oct 1920). Pianist, teacher, and composer. He began piano lessons with his father at the age of five, and was able to play all of Bach's *Das wohltemperirte Clavier* from memory by the time he was 12. His family moved to New York in 1852, but he went back to Germany to complete his musical education. Between 1858 and 1865 he studied with Johann Andersen in Eimsbüttel, near Hamburg, then attended the Leipzig Conservatory, where his teachers were Ignaz Moscheles and E. F. Wenzel (piano), Alfred Richter, Moritz Hauptmann, and Benjamin Papperitz (harmony), and Carl Reinecke (composition). He returned to the USA in 1865, and gave a number of concerts in the West before settling in Boston, where he made his first appearance with the Harvard Musical Association on 19 April 1866. He became well known as a pianist and as a composer and arranger of piano music. He gave a notable series of concerts where he performed the complete solo piano works of Schubert. Perabo was also renowned as a teacher: among his many pupils was Amy Beach. His works for the piano include *Moment musical* op.1, Scherzo op.2, Prelude op.3, Waltz op.4, Three Studies op.9, *Pensées* op.11, *Circumstance, or Fate of a Human Life* op.13 (after Tennyson), and Prelude, Romance, and Toccatina op.19. His arrangements include ten transcriptions from Sullivan's *Iolanthe* op.14, concert fantasies on themes from Beethoven's *Fidelio* opp.16 and 17, and transcriptions of Schubert's "Unfinished" Symphony and Anton Rubinstein's "Ocean" Symphony.

JOSEPH REZITS

Perahia, Murray (*b* New York, 19 April 1947). Pianist. He began piano lessons in 1953 with Jeanette Haien, then in 1966 entered Mannes College, where he learned composition and conducting (BS 1969) while continuing piano studies with Balsam. In 1968 he was a private pupil of Horszowski, and, after winning the Young Concert Artists Award and the Kosciuszko Chopin Prize, made his Carnegie Hall début. He first appeared with the New York PO in 1972, and in the same year achieved international fame as the winner of the Leeds International Pianoforte Competition, the first American to capture that prize. A memorable first London recital (Queen Elizabeth Hall, 1973) confirmed the impression of rich gifts. He won the first Avery Fisher Prize jointly with the cellist Lynn Harrell in 1975, and the Edison Prize in 1978 and 1981. He was appointed associate artistic director of the Aldeburgh Festival in England in 1982.

Perahia, acknowledged as one of the foremost pianists of his generation, eschews virtuosity for its own sake; it is particularly for the translucent, many-shaded delicacy of his *piano* tones, and the effortlessly natural lyrical impulse of his phrasing, that he has been acclaimed as a musician of rare sensitivity. His interpretations of Mozart, Chopin, Mendelssohn, and Schumann are exemplary; in 1977 he began recording all the Mozart piano concertos, directing the English Chamber Orchestra from the keyboard. Other recordings include solo music by Chopin, Mendelssohn, Schumann, and Bartók, as well as Chopin's First Concerto (with Mehta and the New York PO) and both Mendelssohn concertos (with Marriner and the Academy of St. Martin-in-the-Fields). He is also a chamber pianist and an accompanist.

Murray Perahia

BIBLIOGRAPHY

"Perahia, Murray," *CBY 1982*

MAX LOPPERT/DENNIS K. McINTIRE

Percussion music. Music written for groups of percussion instruments. The percussion ensemble (a 20th-century phenomenon in the West) has no fixed instrumentation and is of variable size; this article discusses the specific repertory for such groups (primarily by American composers or composers who have worked in the USA) as well as works for more diverse ensembles which rely heavily on percussion.

Highly original experiments in the use of percussion were carried out in Europe by the Italian futurists before World War I and by the American composer George Antheil (*Ballet mécanique*, 1923–5). In the USA Cowell was a major innovator as early as 1914 by virtue of both his unorthodox treatment of the piano as a percussive instrument in many works, and his experiments with exotic percussion instruments: the original version of *Ensembles* (1924) was scored for string quintet and three American Indian bullroarers. Varèse's *Ionisation* (1929–31), which requires 13 percussionists to play some 40 instruments, was the earliest piece exclusively for percussion to be written in the USA. It was followed in the 1930s by a wave of works for percussion ensembles of varying size and composition, many written by Cowell and the West Coast composers associated with him. As a group these early composers of percussion music were remarkably open to non-Western and popular influences, drawing on sources as diverse as the music of Eastern traditions, jazz, and Latin American dances. They experimented with changes of meter and uneven rhythmic patterns, explored microtonal and other, newly contrived, scales, and made use of instruments (such as sirens) to create noise rather than melody. Cowell's works in particular had a strong oriental flavor with their use of gongs, rice bowls, and tom-toms (*Ostinato pianissimo*, 1934; *Pulse*, 1939). The complex interplay between performers in the music of William Russell (*Three Dance Movements*, 1933) and Gerald Strang (*Percussion Music*, 1935) took full advantage of the linear possibilities inherent in percussion writing. A programmatic aspect is prominent in works by Johanna Beyer (*Auto Accident*, 1935) and Ray Green (*Three Inventories of Casey Jones*, 1939).

Slightly later two of Cowell's pupils made particularly important contributions to the repertory of experimental percussion music. Harrison extended his teacher's explorations of exotic percussion in *Simfony in Free Style* (1939), *Canticle no.3* (1941), *Labyrinth* (1941), and other works, while Cage developed the PREPARED PIANO (first used in *Bacchanale*, 1940) and took a radically eclectic approach in scoring other percussion compositions; *First Construction (in Metal)* (1939), for example, calls for six performers to play Japanese temple gongs and other non-Western traditional instruments, sleigh bells, oxen bells, cowbells, and thundersheets and brake drums, as well as several conventional percussion instruments. Written the same year, the even more daring *Imaginary Landscape no.1* employs two variable-speed turntables, frequency recordings, a muted piano, and cymbals. Cage and Harrison collaborated on the influential *Double Music* (1941). Among the works of this period for more conventional percussion, Alan Hovhaness's *October Mountain* (1942) achieved particular popularity.

During and just after World War II there seemed to be a hiatus in the production of adventurous works for percussion ensemble. Those written during the preceding years, however, influenced the treatment of percussion within a broad range of symphonic music, which began to make use of more instruments, require more percussion players, and include extensive passages for percussion ensembles. (This trend has continued, so that recent works often demand that each player be responsible for a large assembly of instruments.) On the other hand there was a new interest in music for a percussion ensemble of a different sort: a rudimentary marching band consisting of snare drums, bass drums, and cymbals – in short, a drum corps of the kind popular in schools.

There was a revived interest in writing for more diverse ensembles in the 1950s. A traditionalist impulse has found expression in works by, among others, Gardner Read (*Los dioses aztecas*, 1959), Robert Kelly (Toccata for marimba and percussion, 1960), and Charles Wuorinen (*Ringing Changes*, 1971); these are compositions that use well-wrought, extended forms in the service of direct emotional expression. Aleatory techniques, including scores in graphic notation, were early associated with percussion music – notably in Earle Brown's *Synergy* (1952). Significant explorations of new sound sources were continued by Henry Brant (*Origins*, a percussion symphony, 1950) and Harry Partch, who used a large array of tuned idiophones of his own invention in works such as *The Bewitched* (1955). Serial procedures were successfully applied in Krenek's *Marginal Sounds* (1957) and Donald Erb's *Four* (1963), as well as in Davidovsky's *Synchronism no.5* for tape and percussion (1969). From the late 1960s onwards percussion ensembles assumed prominence in many theater pieces and performance works, e.g., Tom Johnson's *Nine Bells* (1979), where the player is required to walk rhythmically through bells suspended from the ceiling. At the same time Barbara Benary, Philip Corner, Harrison, Steve Reich, and a number of other American composers began writing for GAMELAN (either traditional or modified "American" gamelan that incorporate new materials and instruments); the music ranges from re-creations of the Indonesian practices to avant-garde experimentation using serial techniques, mathematical patterning, or indeterminacy.

Few composers have specialized in writing music for percussion, but many have added individual works to its permanent repertory. Some of the more outstanding compositions are Michael Colgrass's virtuoso *Three Brothers* (1951), Malloy Miller's orchestral Prelude for Percussion (1956), and Warren Benson's *Streams* (1961), notable for its sustained soft timbres. John Beck's *Jazz Variants* (1969) is representative of a large number of works that have absorbed the influences of later jazz and of rock, while Thomas Gauger's *Gainsborough* (1974) is remarkable for its melodic treatment of percussion. Programmatic concepts continue to find expression in works by Stanley Leonard (*Fanfare, Meditation, and Dance*, 1982) and others. Rhythmic complexity is a leading characteristic of many recent percussion works, for example, Richard Trythall's *Bolero* (1979).

Several American publishing companies dealing exclusively in percussion music have been formed; the earliest was Music for Percussion, founded by Paul Price in 1952. Other houses, such as Belwin-Mills and Carl Fischer, have devoted an increasing proportion of their lists to the percussion repertory, and a number of percussionists (including William Cahn, Arnold Lang, Al Payson, and Mike Udow) set up companies to issue primarily their own percussion music. Another indication that percussion music has established a firm position in American musical life is seen in the increasing number of schools that have begun to offer training in percussion-ensemble performance; Price initiated the first curriculum of this kind at the University of Illinois in 1950.

BIBLIOGRAPHY

Percussive Notes (1962–83), *Percussionist* (1963–82) [journals of the Percussive Arts Society, amalgamated as *Percussive Notes/Percussionist Research Edition* (1983–)]

E. B. Gangware: *The History and Use of Percussion Instruments in Orchestration* (diss., Northwestern U., 1962)

G. B. Peters: *Treatise on Percussion* (Rochester, NY, 1962, rev. 2/1975 as *The Drummer Man: a Treatise on Percussion*)

P. Price: "Percussion up-to-date," *MJ*, xxii/12 (1964)

J. Blades: *Percussion Instruments and their History* (London, 1970, rev. 3/1984)

L. D. Vanlandingham: *The Percussion Ensemble: 1930–1945* (diss., Florida State U., 1971)

J. Holland: *Percussion* (London, 1978)

JOHN H. BECK

Perera, Ronald (Christopher) (*b* Boston, MA, 25 Dec 1941). Composer. He studied with Kirchner at Harvard (BA 1963, MA 1967), then with Gottfried Michael Koenig at the Studio voor Elektronische Muziek, University of Utrecht (1968). An extended study of electronic and computer music culminated in his editing with Appleton of *Development and Practice of Electronic Music* (1975), a major text. He has been a MacDowell Colony Fellow three times (1974, 1978, 1981) and in 1976 received a fellowship award from the National Institute for the Arts. Both the Paderewski Fund (1972) and the Goethe Institute (1974) have commissioned works from him. From 1968 to 1970 he taught at Syracuse University, and, in 1970, at Dartmouth College; in 1971 he joined the faculty of Smith College, Northampton, Massachusetts, where he became a full professor. In *Alternate Routes* (1971), a score for the Dartmouth Dance Company, Perera conceived of all sounds as having kinetic properties: either wild runs and spins or delicate, subtle departures from complete stillness. In contrast to this physical orientation, his settings of three poems by Günther Grass (1974) use quotations of jazz, march music, and a Strauss waltz to evoke the nostalgic or even bizarre inner experiences of the personae. Some of Perera's works, which are mostly for instruments and tape, are available from Opus One and CRI Records.

WORKS

Orch: Chanteys, 1976

Inst: Suite, pf, 1966; Improvisation for Loudspeakers, tape, 1969; Reverberations, org, tape, 1970; Alternate Routes, dance score, elec, 1971; Reflex, va, tape, 1973; Fantasy Variations, pf, elec, 1976; Bright Angels, org, perc, tape, 1977; Tolling, 2 pf, tape, 1979

Choral: Mass, solo vv, chorus, orch, 1967; Did You Hear the Angels Sing? (S. Miller), S, SATB, org, 1968; 3 Night Pieces, S, A, SSAA, vc, perc, pf, 1974; Everything That Has Breath (Pss. cxlviii, cl), male/female/mixed 2vv, tape, 1976; other works

Songs: Dove sta amore (L. Ferlinghetti), S, tape, 1969; 5 Summer Songs (Dickinson), S, pf, 1972; Apollo Circling (J. Dickey), S, pf, 1972; 3 Poems of Günther Grass, Mez, chamber ens, tape, 1974; Children of the Sun (Stevenson), S, hn, pf, 1979; The White Whale (Melville), Bar, orch, 1981

Principal publisher: E. C. Shirmer

DAVID COPE

Peress, Maurice (*b* New York, 18 March 1930). Conductor and trumpeter. He attended New York University and the Mannes College, studying trumpet with Harry Freistadt and Jerome Cnudde and conducting with Philip James and Carl Bamberger. At the outset of his career he made appearances as a trumpet player before turning to conducting. In 1961 Bernstein appointed him assistant conductor of the New York PO; later, in association with Bernstein, he conducted revivals of *Candide* (Los Angeles, 1966) and *West Side Story* (New York, 1968). He was music director of the Corpus Christi (Texas) SO (1962–75), the Austin SO (1970–73), and the Kansas City PO (1974–80); he was also a conductor for the Joffrey Ballet in 1964.

Peress has appeared as a guest conductor in Mexico City, Jerusalem, Brussels, Hong Kong, and Vienna, as well as in the USA. He conducted the première of Bernstein's Mass at the opening of the Kennedy Center in 1971 (as well as the first professional European performance at the Vienna Staatsoper in 1981); he has also appeared with the San Francisco Opera, conducting the American première of Gottfried von Einem's *Der Besuch der alten Dame* in 1972. He has made recordings both as a conductor and trumpet soloist. Peress's considerable experience in jazz includes the orchestration of Ellington's *Black, Brown and Beige* in 1970 for the Chicago SO; in 1984 he was named editor of Ellington's symphonic works (for G. Schirmer). He was writer, conductor, and narrator of the program "12th Street Rag," on the music of Virgil Thomson and Eubie Blake, which was televised nationally in 1981. To commemorate the 60th anniversary of Paul Whiteman's Aeolian Hall concert of 12 February 1924 (which included the première of Gershwin's *Rhapsody in Blue*) Peress reconstructed the program and conducted it at Town Hall, New York. Peress has taught at New York University, the University of Texas, Austin, and Queens College, CUNY (where he became a professor in 1982). In 1981 he assumed the presidency of the Conductors' Guild of the American Symphony Orchestra League.

MARTIN BERNHEIMER/DENNIS K. McINTIRE

Peresson, Sergio (*b* Udine, Italy, 29 March 1913). Violin maker. He initially learned to make violins as a hobby in Udine. After World War II he immigrated to Venezuela, where he took up violin making professionally. In 1963 he became associated with Moennig & Son, Philadelphia, and about the same time established his own workshop in New Jersey. His instruments are modeled on an amalgamation of the Stradivari and Guarneri "del Gesù" patterns; his choice of wood is invariably excellent and the varnish a golden orange brown. The tone quality is strong and even, although the resonance of some of his instruments is inconsistent. Peresson has been particularly successful with his violas, which are used by many distinguished musicians; his violins are also greatly sought after. He is considered to be the leading North American luthier.

JAAK LIIVOJA-LORIUS

Performance art. A form of theatrical art popular in the 1970s and 1980s. It traces its origins to the solo and small-group theatrics staged by visual artists and poets of the Dada, Futurist, and Constructivist movements in Europe during the first decades of the 20th century, and to the "happenings" and other art events of the 1960s. In the early 1970s performances by visual artists, often intended as protests against the commercialization of painting and sculpture, inspired similar efforts by poets, dancers, and musicians; this led to an entire movement of solo performance centered in New York in the mid- to late 1970s. Performance art shared much with conceptual art (in which the concept supplanted the artifact as the art work's essence), minimalism, and non-narrative theater. Performance artists frequently made use of rock music; some, like Patti Smith and Laurie Anderson, even became rock stars. In the 1980s performance art both influenced, and was popularized by, videotape art and commercial "rock video." Although most performance art was staged before small audiences, some of its exponents worked on a larger scale: Robert Wilson devised elaborate performance-art spectacles from the late 1960s (such as *The Life and Times of Joseph Stalin*, 1973), and the composer Philip Glass, who had collaborated with Wilson on *Einstein on the Beach* in 1976, translated performance art into quasi-conventional opera in *Satyagraha* and *Akhnaten*.

BIBLIOGRAPHY

R. Goldberg: *Performance: Live Art 1909 to the Present* (New York, 1979)

J. G. Hanhardt, ed.: *Nam June Paik* (New York, 1982)

JOHN ROCKWELL

Performing rights [copyright collecting] **societies.** Organizations that protect musical works registered by their members and collect fees payable in respect of the performance of such works.

1. Definition. 2. American societies.

1. DEFINITION. The legal provisions described in the article COPYRIGHT give rise to certain economic rights, which are enjoyed by the owner of the copyright. In music, the most important is the right of public performance, known as the "performing right." Others include the right to reproduce musical works in sound recordings (such as phonograph records and audio tapes), known as the "mechanical right," and the right to reproduce musical works in the soundtracks of audio-visual recordings (such as films or videotapes for the cinema and television), known as the "synchronization right." In some countries a right exists in the public use or transmission of sound recordings, so that performers in particular recordings receive royalties for the use of their music. The civil right in the recorded performance as such (not to be confused with the performing and broadcasting right in the works

performed) is not widely established internationally, and does not exist in the USA.

Once these rights are established, the problem of collecting license fees arises. It is almost always impossible for an individual copyright holder to recover royalties on more than a very small number of the performances on which they are due. Even if he could locate a few of the performances, he would not always have the means or the expertise to negotiate appropriate royalties and issue licenses. Collection for performances nationwide or overseas would be out of the question for the individual or small publishing company. Societies have therefore been set up in most countries to collect royalties for the use of copyrighted music and to distribute the revenue among the parties entitled to it. It is, equally, an immense advantage to the music user to have a central body that can be approached for licenses and will clear the rights automatically with each copyright owner, not only in his own country, but also in virtually every other country in the world. Performing rights societies offer a blanket license to the music user who would otherwise be put to considerable administrative expense in acquiring these rights and would also have to pay the individual copyright owners in respect of each use.

Performing rights societies typically license only the right of nondramatic public performance (the "small right"). They do not license the "grand right," i.e., the right of dramatic public performance, which attaches to all forms of musical theater, such as operas, ballets, and musicals. Works such as these can be staged only in a limited number of places and can therefore be traced comparatively simply. It is much more difficult to collect in respect of the small right, and it is in the administering of this right that the collecting societies have performed a needed function for creators and copyright owners of music. Collection of mechanical-right fees is usually the province of the copyright owner; in the USA many publishers use the services of the Harry Fox Agency, Inc., for this purpose (see §2 (iv) below).

The members of the two international organizations of copyright collecting societies, the Confédération Internationale de Sociétés d'Auteurs et Compositeurs (CISAC), founded in 1928, and the Bureau International de l'Edition Mécanique (BIEM), are linked by international contracts of affiliation, whereby each society collects on its own territory for the works of its own members and the members of the other societies with which it is affiliated. By the same contract, each national society is empowered to grant licenses on its own territory in respect of the repertories of each society with which it is affiliated, so that the society is able to offer its licensees access to a virtually worldwide range of copyright music. Thus, a licensee in New York, for example, has available to him almost the whole catalogue of music that he is likely to need, both serious and popular.

2. AMERICAN SOCIETIES. Copyright owners may not concurrently be members of more than one American performing rights organization. However, it is possible to resign from one organization and join another after contracts have been fulfilled. Publishers, following carefully established procedures and regulations of the various societies, may set up different companies in each. In this way they can handle the works of writers they wish to represent without restrictions incurred from societal affiliation.

(i) American Society of Composers, Authors and Publishers (ASCAP). Until 1897 Congress had not included in the copyright law a performing right in musical works, and it was not until 1914 that the first performing rights society, ASCAP, was founded. A performing right offered a collecting society in the USA enormous scope, for although the territory was large, communications were good and the population was spread much more evenly than in other large countries, such as Canada, making it practical to collect in cities and large towns. As various types of popular music spread across the country, there were countless performances in dance halls, nightclubs, restaurants, and cafés, which had previously been beyond the control of an individual copyright owner but which a central agency such as ASCAP could effectively monitor. A further enormous increase in the performance of popular music came with the introduction of radio broadcasting in the 1920s and the establishment in a single year of more than 500 radio stations. Naturally, not all music users immediately accepted the claims of the new society, and ASCAP was obliged to establish its position by court actions against users of music, such as restaurants, dance halls, background-music operators, concert promoters, and broadcasters.

ASCAP is an unincorporated membership association managed by a board of 24 directors (12 writers and 12 publishers); three writers and three publishers represent serious music. ASCAP's writer members elect the writer-directors, and its publisher members elect the publisher-directors; as such, ASCAP is the only performing rights society in the USA that is owned, controlled, and run by the creators and copyright owners of music. The directors hold office for two years. A two-thirds majority vote is necessary to carry a motion, with at least nine directors present.

Any writer or publisher meeting minimal requirements may become an ASCAP member; the estates of deceased writers may also become members. Members (who pay annual dues to the society) are elected by a majority of the board, and upon election, must sign an agreement by which they assign to the society the nonexclusive right to license the nondramatic public performance of their works for the period of the agreement. ASCAP itself is not a "copyright owner." However, because earlier American copyright law did not acknowledge divisibility of ownership, and lawsuits had to be brought in the name of the copyright owner, the society sought and acquired the right to sue in the member's name. Under the 1976 law, the ownership of copyright may be transferred in part or subdivided. Members assign rights in all compositions then or thereafter written, composed, published, acquired, or owned by the member, whether alone, jointly, or in collaboration with others.

ASCAP distributes all the revenues it collects after deducting its expenses and payments to foreign societies, operating in this sense on a nonprofit basis. Half of all royalties are distributed to writer-members and half to publisher-members. Distribution is accomplished by means of a scientifically designed survey that represents all licensed performances. Thus, for example, radio performances are objectively determined by sampling approximately 60,000 hours of radio broadcasts annually. Performances are given objective values relative to each other through a complex weighting formula; by way of illustration, television performances are weighted in such a way that feature performances are worth more than background performances, which in turn are worth more than theme-music performances, which in turn receive higher credits than advertising jingles. Domestic royalties are distributed quarterly and foreign royalties semiannually; a writer member may not irrevocably assign his royalties to another. Two relief committees, one for publishers and one for writers, give financial assistance to needy members or their dependants.

ASCAP typically negotiates license agreements with trade associations or groups representing user industries. The licenses granted are termed "blanket" licenses because, in return for payment of a specified (usually an annual) fee, the music user is entitled to perform any works in the ASCAP repertory. The rate for each license is structured for the particular user industry involved. For example, hotels pay fees dependent on their annual expenditures on live entertainment and their use of recorded music; colleges and universities pay a fee dependent on the number of full-time students. Radio and television broadcasting organizations choose one of two kinds of license, either of which gives them the right to perform any work in the ASCAP repertory: under one type, also called a "blanket" license, an organization pays a percentage of its total advertising revenue, and a fixed sum for music used on unsponsored programs; under the "per program" license, a relatively higher percentage of advertising receipts is paid, but only on income from programs making use of ASCAP music. Virtually all broadcasters choose the "blanket" license.

The federal government has attempted through antitrust litigation to promote competition in the area of musical performing rights. In 1941, after the Department of Justice took action against ASCAP under the Sherman Act, the society agreed to a consent decree (i.e., it was deemed not to have broken any law, nor was evidence taken or judgment given). The decree, which has been amended from time to time and regulates virtually all aspects of ASCAP's operations, established membership requirements, the principles of the distribution system, and licensing procedures (the "per program" license for broadcasters was one result of the decree). The decree made two provisions of particular significance for music users. First, if ASCAP and a potential licensee fail to agree on a royalty, the user may apply for a determination of a reasonable license fee by the US District Court for the Southern District of New York, which supervises the decree; pending judgment, the licensee may have access to works in the society's repertory, and ASCAP may ask the court to fix an interim license fee. Second, ASCAP may not discriminate in the license fees, terms, or conditions between "similarly situated users."

After a case in 1948 that deemed ASCAP to be in violation of the antitrust laws (and eventually made it impossible for the society to license the public performance of music in the theatrical exhibition of motion pictures), the consent decree of 1941 was completely altered: in the words of one court, the resulting amended decree (1950) "disinfected" ASCAP of any antitrust taint. In subsequent court decisions, the blanket license ASCAP offered was repeatedly, but unsuccessfully, attacked on antitrust grounds, on behalf of users such as local radio broadcasters, television networks, "general" establishments (such as taverns, restaurants, and nightclubs), and local television stations. The legality of the blanket license is now well established.

In terms of the number of works in its repertory and amount of revenue it collects, ASCAP is the largest performing rights society in the USA. It is a member of CISAC. For the society's activities outside the area of performing rights *see* AMERICAN SOCIETY OF COMPOSERS, AUTHORS AND PUBLISHERS.

(ii) Broadcast Music, Inc. (BMI). A number of broadcasting organizations opposed ASCAP's attempts to license them in the early days of radio, but ASCAP succeeded in setting up a procedure for licensing them for a fixed lump sum, which persisted until 1932, when the concept of a percentage of the broadcaster's revenue was introduced. Such a fee was unwelcome to the National Association of Broadcasters, but the association had to accept the society's terms. In 1940 ASCAP again sought to introduce new license terms, but this time the members of the National Association of Broadcasters decided to boycott ASCAP music by using material in the public domain (some of it in versions updated to suit the popular styles of the time) and to arrange for new music to be composed that would not pass into ASCAP's net.

ASCAP's repertory was very extensive, and up to 1940 the society had an effective monopoly. It was at this time that some 600 enterprises, most of them engaged in broadcasting, formed Broadcast Music, Inc. (BMI), for the sole purpose of creating a competitive source of music licensing in the USA. At the time, ASCAP was also involved in antitrust proceedings and was obliged to settle its dispute with the broadcasters. Few at ASCAP expected BMI to survive, but by the mid-1960s its share of the market (the amount of music played by American broadcasting organizations) had become greater than ASCAP's, although its repertory was and still is smaller. BMI is the world's largest performing rights organization in terms of the number of affiliated writers and publishers (respectively 46,000 and 28,000 active members). BMI's initial success was largely attributable to its open-door policy. For the first time, writers of country music, jazz, gospel, rhythm-and-blues, and other types of music that had not previously been eligible to earn performing money could share in performing rights income.

The prospectus under which stock in BMI was originally offered stated that no dividends were to be expected from the company, and no dividends have been paid. Stock in the company continues to be held by members of the broadcasting industry, and the board of directors is drawn from this area. Except for operating expenses all the collected revenue from the works that it has logged in broadcast and live performances is redistributed to its writer and publisher affiliates. Like ASCAP, BMI is subject to a consent decree under antitrust legislation, and disputes between BMI and licensees are settled according to the rules of the American Arbitration Association. BMI has reciprocal agreements with 37 foreign societies, and it is a member of CISAC. For the company's activities outside the area of performing rights *see* BROADCAST MUSIC, INC.

(iii) SESAC Inc. Founded in 1931 as the Society of European Stage Authors and Composers, SESAC Inc. (now the official name of this organization) is a private licensing company owned by the Heinicke family; it represents approximately 500 music publishers that have put their catalogues under its control, and just under 2000 authors and composers. Unlike ASCAP and BMI, SESAC collects in respect of mechanical and synchronization rights (covering commercial recordings for private use, and films) as well as in respect of the performing right. Royalty distributions (made quarterly) are based on such external factors as the number of recordings released, placement and movement on popularity charts, and local surveys. Both ASCAP and BMI levy their royalties as a percentage of the licensee's revenue, but SESAC's charges are based on fixed, lump-sum payments according to a broadcasting user's advertising rates and the population of the market it serves. (Assessment according to the number of hours of broadcasting was dropped in favor of charges based on advertising rates.) A SESAC license is taken out by virtually all broad-

casting organizations in the country. The society has no printed catalogue of its works, but a computer listing is available for review in its three offices (New York, Nashville, and Los Angeles). At one time SESAC maintained what was known as the "transcribed library," a program service it made available to broadcasters. For the society's activities outside the area of performing rights *see* SESAC INC.

The scale of the activities of the three American organizations can be compared by looking at their receipts from performing rights licenses in particular years. In 1952 ASCAP received over $17 million, BMI over $5 million, and SESAC about $1 million. By 1957 ASCAP's receipts were about $27 million and BMI's about $9.5 million, while SESAC's remained at $1 million. In 1963 ASCAP's income had risen to $38 million and BMI's to about $15 million, while SESAC's income was still $1 million. In 1982 ASCAP's total receipts came to about $187 million, BMI's to nearly $120 million, and SESAC's to approximately $5 million.

(iv) Harry Fox Agency, Inc. In 1927 the Music Publishers' Protective Association (later the National Music Publishers' Association) set up the Harry Fox Agency to license musical copyrights other than the performing right on behalf of its members and other, nonmember publishing firms. The rights in respect of which it collects are the mechanical and synchronization rights, the right in broadcast commercials (for which the royalties for each use, as in the case of films, are negotiated by the agency), and the right to transmission of recorded music by radio and in public places such as restaurants, stores, and airplanes. The agency grants licenses to recording companies and others availing themselves of the mechanical right and collects the royalties from them. The revision of the copyright act that came into effect on 1 January 1978 stipulated the royalty in respect of each work on a phonograph recording or tape to be $2\frac{3}{4}$¢ per composition or $\frac{1}{2}$¢ per minute of playing time, whichever is the greater; a commission of $4\frac{1}{2}$% for discs and tapes is charged by the agency on the royalties it collects. The Fox agency has an effective collection system in Japan through the Japanese Society for Rights of Authors, Composers and Publishers, and works through various other foreign societies as well.

BIBLIOGRAPHY

T. Solberg: *Copyright Enactments 1783–1900* (Washington, DC, 1900, rev. 5/1973 as *Copyright Enactments: Laws Passed in the United States since 1783 Relating to Copyright*)
R. Hubbell: *The Story of ASCAP by a Founder* (MS, *c*1937, *NN*)
The ABC of BMI (New York, 1940)
D. MacDougald, Jr.: "The Popular Music Industry," *Radio Research, 1941*, ed. P. F. Lazarsfeld and F. Stanton (New York, 1941), 65–109
A. Green and J. Laurie, Jr.: *Show Biz, from Vaude to Video* (New York, 1951)
H. Finkelstein: "The Composer and the Public Interest – Regulation of Performing Right Societies," *Law and Contemporary Problems*, xix (1954), 275
E. N. Waters: "ASCAP," *Victor Herbert: a Life in Music* (New York, 1955/*R*1978), 431
A. D. Neale: *The Antitrust Laws of the United States of America: a Study of Competition Enforced by Law* (Cambridge, England, 1960)
S. Shemel and M. W. Krasilovsky: *This Business of Music* (New York, 1964, rev. and enlarged 5/1985)
——: *More about this Business of Music* (New York, 1967, rev. and enlarged 3/1982)
D. D. Braun: *The Sociology and History of American Music and Dance* (Ann Arbor, MI, 1969)
M. Goldin: *The Music Merchants* (New York, 1969)
I. Tarr: "Tape Systems – Cartridge and Cassette: Current Impact in the United States – and Prospects," *The Complete Report of the First International Music Industry Conference, April 1969* (New York, 1969)
B. Ringer: *Two Hundred Years of Copyright in America* (Washington, DC, 1976)
B. L. DeWhitt: *The American Society of Composers, Authors, and Publishers 1914–1938* (diss., Emory U., 1977)
L. S. Schultz: "Performing-Rights Societies in the United States," *Notes*, xxxv (1978–9), 511
L. Feist: *An Introduction to Popular Music Publishing in America* (New York, 1980)
G. W. M. McFarlane: *Copyright: the Development and Exercise of the Performing Right* (London, 1980)
——: *A Practical Introduction to Copyright* (London, 1982)
R. Sanjek: *From Print to Plastic: Publishing and Promoting America's Popular Music (1900–1980)*, ISAMm, xx (Brooklyn, NY, 1984)
G. W. M. McFarlane: *Copyright through the Cases* (London, 1985)
For further bibliography, *see* COPYRIGHT.

GAVIN MCFARLANE/R

Periodicals. Periodicals are publications appearing at regular (or sometimes irregular) intervals and, normally, furnished with serial numbers indicating volumes (usually annual) and/or issue numbers. They primarily contain such material as essays, reports, critiques, and news items. In addition to their periodical mode of publication they have in common with newspapers an intention of continuance, an approach determined by publisher or editor, and an objective of variety of content and, to some extent, contemporary relevance. In music, the concept of the periodical also includes yearbooks, annual reports, and the proceedings of institutions, almanacs on music, and similarly oriented publications. Works published in fascicles (part-works, serials, etc.) are to be distinguished from periodicals proper. The essential criterion is that of periodical appearance, be it regular (daily, weekly, fortnightly, monthly, bimonthly, quarterly, half-yearly, or annually) or occasional.

This article provides a general account and history of music periodicals in the USA. Dates given normally represent first and last volumes or, in certain cases, issues; dates given with an oblique stroke (e.g., 1971/2) refer to a volume beginning in one year and ending in another. Fuller information on title changes and on breaks in a periodical's run will be found in the comprehensive list of music periodicals (which has an alphabetical index) at the end of the discussion.

I. History. II. List and Index.

I. History

1. To 1915. 2. 1915–65. 3. After 1965.

1. TO 1915. The forerunners of true music periodicals in the USA were periodical music publications, obviously influenced by earlier, English publications. The first, edited by Amos Doolittle and Daniel Read, was *The American Musical Magazine* (1786–7), which consisted of compositions by American and English composers. But a successor, *The Musical Magazine* (1792–1801), edited by Andrew Law, offered, in addition to "Psalm and Hymn Tunes," an essay – an exception to the general trend in early American music periodicals, and one that cannot be seen as a first step, historically, towards a true musical journal. The *Ladies' Literary Museum, or Weekly Repository* (1817–20) was a literary journal that included music supplements from 1818 and from 1819 turned occasionally to musical topics.

The Euterpeiad, or Musical Intelligencer (1820/21–1822/3), edited by J. R. Parker, may be seen as the first true music periodical in the USA. In addition to a serial conspectus of music history, it offered mainly news and reviews of Boston musical life, which was becoming increasingly lively in the 1820s. Among other early, short-lived periodicals were a New York *Euterpeiad* (1830/31–1831), containing essays on musical and stylistic

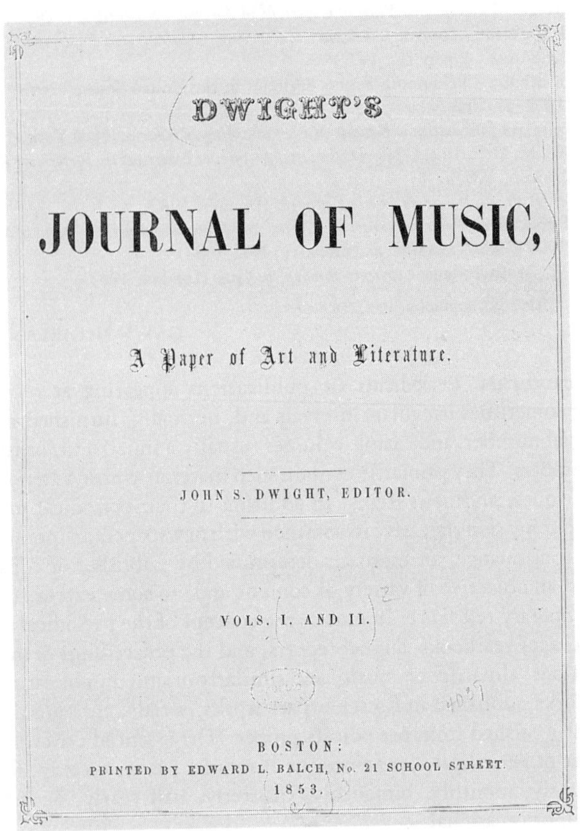
DWIGHT'S
JOURNAL OF MUSIC,
A Paper of Art and Literature.
JOHN S. DWIGHT, EDITOR.
VOLS. I. AND II.
BOSTON:
PRINTED BY EDWARD L. BALCH, No. 21 SCHOOL STREET.
1853.

1. Title page of the first cumulative index to "Dwight's Journal of Music" (Boston, 1853)

questions, biographical sketches, and anecdotes about well-known musicians as well as discussion of printed music and concert reviews, and *The Musical Magazine* (1839–1841/2), which strove to familiarize its readers with the European musical scene. The first really ambitious music journal was *Dwight's Journal of Music* (1852–81), published in Boston. In a circular of 1852 its editor, John Sullivan Dwight, stressed the independence of his publication: "The tone to be impartial, independent, catholic, conciliatory, aloof from musical clique and controversy, cordial to all good things, but not eager to chime in with any powerful private interest of publisher, professor, concert-giver, manager, society, or party." The journal offered essays on such composers as Handel, Haydn, Mozart, and Beethoven and on music history, theory, education, and style, together with critical reports on the musical scene and announcements of new compositions.

As musical culture spread in the 1870s, numerous publications appeared dealing with particular interests. The movement, European in origin, towards the revival of church music and sung services led in the USA to the publication of several church music magazines, including *Caecilia*, which began in Germany in 1874 and was continued in New York in 1877 as the journal of the American Cecilia Society, incorporating *The Catholic Choirmaster* (the journal of the Society of St. Gregory of America) in 1965. *The Church Music Review* (1901/2–1934/5) of the American Guild of Organists was another such publication. With the growing commercialization of musical life, these were joined by periodicals devoted to the music trade (e.g., *The Music Trades*, 1890–), the sale of musical instruments (e.g., *Music Industry*, ?1906–), light music (e.g., *Metronome*, 1885–1961), and the various branches of music entertainment (e.g., *Billboard Advertising*, 1894/5–). Interest in music education reform led to the foundation of journals dealing generally with the subject, such as *The Etude* (1883–1957), which circulated widely, and *The Musician* (1896–1948), or with new methods of notation, such as the *Tonic Sol-fa Advocate* (1881/2–1885/6), the organ of the Tonic Sol-fa Movement.

Around the turn of the century, more comprehensive music periodicals of extra-regional significance included the New York publication *Musical America* (1898–1964). Other general music periodicals focused on individual centers, for example, *The Musical Leader and Concert-goer* (1895–1967), published in Chicago, and the *Pacific Coast Musician* (1911–48), published in Los Angeles and the oldest important Californian music periodical.

2. 1915–65. The first comprehensive musicological periodical, *The Musical Quarterly* (1915–), was founded by the pioneer of American musicology, Oscar G. T. Sonneck; successive editors have followed his declared policy of securing contributions from the best scholars regardless of nationality. As well as essays on various aspects of musicology, there later followed selective book, music, and record reviews, and "Current Chronicle" (reports on performances of new music), as well as quarterly book and recording lists. The 1940s saw the inauguration of the *Journal of Renaissance and Baroque Music* (1946–, from 1948 *Musica disciplina*) and the *Journal of the American Musicological Society* (1948–), edited in its early years by Oliver Strunk. Mention should also be made of *Notes*, the organ of the American Music Library Association (second series, 1943/4–), with its comprehensive bibliographical contributions and useful conspectuses of new music, books, and records. *The Music Index* (1949–), published in monthly parts and collected in annual volumes, offers a continuous guide, in the form of an author and contents index, to over 100 musical periodicals mainly in English. The *Ethno-musicology Newsletter* (later *Ethnomusicology*) was founded in 1953 by the Society for Ethno-musicology and soon became a leading publication in this field.

Many special interests began to be reflected in music publications in the 20th century. In a deliberate campaign on behalf of progressive European music and the works of the incipient American avant garde, the magazine *Modern Music* (at first *The League of Composers' Review*) was founded in 1924. More traditional in scope were such publications as *Chord and Discord* (1932/9–), the magazine of the Bruckner Society of America, which has been devoted to the works of Bruckner and Mahler. In the 1936–7 season the Metropolitan Opera Guild began publishing *Opera News*, still a leading magazine in this genre. Sheets dealing with recordings, jazz, and film music followed at the beginning of the 1940s (e.g., *Cash Box*, 1942–; *The Record Changer*, 1942/3–1957). The 1940s and 1950s also saw the inception of many Music Educators Association state chapters' journals and music club magazines. The *Journal of Music Theory* (1957–) was the first of a number of important periodicals in this field; it includes scholarly articles on such topics as analytic technique, the history of theory and aesthetics, and pedagogy.

3. After 1965. Musicological periodicals of diverse kinds and genres have been established since 1965. The music department of Columbia University started to publish *Current Musicology* in 1965, and other periodicals published by students began to appear in the late 1960s. *The Journal of Musicology* (1982–) aims to unify

"the disparate branches of the discipline by providing a forum for communication among the various groups," treating critical analysis, performance practice, and source studies, as well as historical musicology. There have been scholarly periodicals concerned with specific periods. *19th Century Music* (1977/8–) contains analysis and criticism and also deals with interdisciplinary topics. *Divisions* (1978–) is concerned with such matters as Baroque improvisational techniques, guidelines for performance, and English translations of theoretical works. Other research periodicals are devoted to music education, such as *Update* (1982–), and psychology, such as *Psychomusicology* (1981–) and *Music Perception* (1983/4–).

The emphasis of many periodicals founded after 1965 has been on the music of the USA and the North American continent. *The Sonneck Society Newsletter* (1975–) gives important information on the music of this country; the same society together with the University of Illinois Press founded the quarterly *American Music* (1983–). Afro-American music has been represented by *The Black Perspective in Music* (1973–) and the periodical publications (beginning in 1977 and 1980) of the Institute for Research in Black American Music of Fisk University. General ethnomusicological studies are published in *Ethnomusicology at UCLA* (1983–), and the music of particular ethnic populations is discussed in *Asian Music* (1968/9–) and *Chinese Music* (1978–).

THE MUSICAL QUARTERLY

VOL. I JANUARY, 1915 NO. I

ON BEHALF OF MUSICOLOGY

By WALDO S. PRATT

PERHAPS the first question is, Do we really need the *word* "musicology?" It is a word not instantly grateful to the ear or to the mind. The eye may confuse it with the botanist's "muscology," and the humorous fancy may even connect it with the ubiquitous *musca* of entomology. Even when we see what it is and that it is etymologically correct, we have to confess that it seems almost as hybrid as "sexology." At all events, it is more ingenious than euphonious, more curious than alluring.

One trouble is that it is extremely recent. It is so new and rare that it is not yet listed in any general English dictionary or in any catalogue of English musical terms. I doubt whether it even occurs in Grove's big "Dictionary of Music and Musicians." Yet it has been creeping in as a twentieth-century innovation. We may guess that it was suggested by the French *musicologie*, or perhaps coined to match the German *Musikwissenschaft*. Like them, it plainly means "the science of music"—a phrase, however, which has often been loosely used, in America at least, for the theory of composition, and which, therefore, does not at all express the proper sense of "musicology," if the latter corresponds to its French and German analogues. Assuming that there is a more general "science of music," for which a single technical term is required, "musicology" offers points of practical convenience. It resembles many other words ending in "-ology" or "-logy." It yields several handy derivatives, such as "musicologist" (or "musicologue"), "musicological," and the like. And, being new, it is free from entangling associations.

We may conclude, then, that the word will take its place in usage if its proper meaning justifies it. We need it if it represents

1

2. *Page one of the first issue of "The Musical Quarterly" (New York, 1915)*

Somewhat broader in scope are the *Newsletter* of the Institute for Studies in American Music (1971/2–), which deals with art music as well as folk and urban music of North America; the *Inter-American Music Review* (1978/9–), edited by Robert Stevenson, in which emphasis is laid on the history of art music in the Americas, especially events before 1900; and the *Revista de música latino americana/Latin American Music Review* (1980–), edited by Gerard Béhague, which contains articles on the musical traditions of Latin America and of Mexican Americans, Puerto Ricans, Cubans, and Portuguese in the USA and Canada.

Music theory has been the focus of a number of recent periodicals. *In Theory Only* (1975–), the journal of the Michigan Music Theory Society, treats a variety of theory-related topics. *Music Theory Spectrum* (1979–), the journal of the Society for Music Theory, is intended to assume a central position within this discipline. In addition to the periodicals devoted to composers and composition in general, such as *The Composer* (1969/70–1981), which represented "a completely free forum for the composer to express his thoughts without reservation," there are those that deal with special techniques of composition, such as *Interval: a Microtonal Newsletter* (1978/9–). Many are dedicated to individual composers of the past and present and are published by societies devoted to the music of these composers or the archives that preserve their works. The journal *Bach* (1970–), the organ of the Riemenschneider Bach Institute, offers analyses and essays on the forms, styles, and performances of the music of Bach and other Baroque composers, and there are publications concerning the works of, among others, Liszt (1977–) and Brahms (1983–). *The International Alban Berg Society Newsletter* (1968–) and the *Journal of the Arnold Schoenberg Institute* (1976/7–), which succeeded the *Arnold Schoenberg Institute Bulletin* (1975–6), are among the periodicals that deal with the music of later composers.

A large number of periodicals are devoted to particular genres of music. Choral music in general is represented by *The Choral Journal* (1959/60–), sponsored by the American Choral Directors Association; denominational publications include *Musica judaica* (1975/6–), the organ of the American Society for Jewish Music. Another periodical in this field, *Modern Liturgy*, founded in 1973 as the *Folk Mass and Modern Liturgy Magazine*, fosters the liturgical use of folk and new music. Several journals deal exclusively with opera (e.g., the *Opera Journal*, 1968–, sponsored by the National Opera Association; *The Opera Quarterly*, 1983–); some of these ceased publication after short runs. Vocal music is treated in a general way in *Voice* (1980–), as well as pedagogically in the *Journal of Research in Singing* (1977/8–) and analytically in *Ars lyrica* (1981–). The *Chamber Music Quarterly* (1982–) is another important genre periodical, as are *Chamber Music Magazine* (1984–, the journal of Chamber Music America), and *Keyboard Classics* (1981–). An increasing number of periodicals have been entirely devoted to popular music. The *JEMF Quarterly* (1965–) of the John Edwards Memorial Foundation, originally a newsletter, covers commercial recordings of American traditional music, including the various folk, ethnic, and popular music genres. Sociological aspects are discussed in *Popular Music and Society* (1971/2–), and information for sheet-music collectors and dealers is published in *The Sheet Music Exchange* (1982–) and in *RPM* (1983–). Periodicals dealing with jazz include the *Annual Review of Jazz Studies* (founded 1973 as the *Journal of Jazz Studies* by the Institute of Jazz Studies at Rutgers, State University of New Jersey), which contains scholarly articles on the theory, analysis, sociology, history, politics, and psychology of jazz, and

Jazz Line (1981–), devoted to activities in the field. *New Music* (1982–) is one of a number of periodicals devoted to rock topics.

Musical instruments and instrumental groups have been the special interest of a number of journals. The *Newsletter of the American Musical Instrument Society* (founded in 1971 as the *Newsletter of the Historical Musical Society*) presents scholarly articles on the history, design, and use of musical instruments; others include *Guitar and Lute* (1974–), the *Winds Quarterly* (1980–), the *Flute Journal* (1982–), and *ClariNetwork* (1982–). Other specialist music periodicals deal with sound reproduction and technology (e.g., *The Antique Phonograph Monthly*, 1973–), record reviews (e.g., *Fanfare: the Magazine for Serious Record Collectors* and the *Record Review*, both begun in 1977), and computer music (e.g., the *Computer Music Journal*, 1977–). Mention should also be made of the *Journal* of the Association for Recorded Sound Collections (1967/8–), which contains articles on the recording industry, recording artists, and recording history.

Among the most recently founded journals of American music libraries and sound archives are *Cum notis variorum* (1976–), the newsletter of the music library of the University of California, Berkeley; *Impromptu* (1982–), which notifies librarians, scholars, and musicians about the activities of the Music Division of the Library of Congress; *The Full Score* (1984–), published by the music library of the University of California, Los Angeles; and *Resound* (1982–), the journal of the Archives of Traditional Music at Indiana University, Bloomington. In addition to these important publications devoted to documentation and research, attention has been given to the cataloguing and classification of sources to increase their accessibility and usefulness to scholarship, as in the *Music Cataloging Bulletin* (1970–) of the Music Library Association.

BIBLIOGRAPHY

GENERAL

E. von Lannoy: "Was ist die Aufgabe einer musikalischen Zeitung?," *Neue Wiener Musik-Zeitung*, i (1852), 1

G. W. Cooke: *John Sullivan Dwight: Brook-farmer, Editor, and Critic of Music* (Boston, 1898/*R*1969)

O. G. T. Sonneck: "Die musikalische Zeitschriften-Literatur," *ZIMG*, i (1899–1900), 388

L. N. Richardson: *A History of Early American Magazines, 1741–1789* (New York, 1931)

E. N. Waters: "John Sullivan Dwight, First American Critic of Music," *MQ*, xxi (1935), 69

F. L. Mott: *A History of American Magazines* (Cambridge, MA, 1936–68)

H. E. Johnson: "Early New England Periodicals devoted to Music," *MQ*, xxvi (1940), 153

J. C. Haskins: "John Rowe Parker and The Euterpeiad," *Notes*, viii (1950–51), 447

A. H. King: "Periodicals," §IV, *Grove 5*

D. W. Krummel: "Twenty Years of 'Notes' – a Retrospect," *Notes*, xxi (1963–4), 56

P. L. Miller: "Twenty Years After," *Notes*, xxi (1963–4), 55

E. Salzman: "*Modern Music* in Retrospect," *PNM*, ii/2 (1964), 2

J. R. Holmes: *"The Musical Quarterly": its History and Influence on the Development of American Musicology* (diss., U. of North Carolina, 1967)

I. Fellinger: *Verzeichnis der Musikzeitschriften des 19. Jahrhunderts*, i: *Historischer Überblick* (Regensburg, Germany, 1968)

——: "Zeitschriften," §§I, II, V, *MGG*

N. Zaslaw: "Free Music Periodicals," *CMc*, no.10 (1970), 140

R. Ceely: "Communications," *PNM*, xi/1 (1972), 258

H. E. Karjala: *A Critical Analysis of "School Music Magazine" 1900–1936* (diss., U. of Minnesota, 1973)

J. F. Schoof: *A Study of Didactic Attitudes on the Fine Arts in America as expressed in Popular Magazines during the Period 1786–1800* (Ann Arbor, MI, 1977)

C. E. Wunderlich: *A History and Bibliography of Early American Musical Periodicals, 1782–1852* (Ann Arbor, MI, 1977)

C. B. Grimes: *American Musical Periodicals, 1819–1852: Music Theory and Musical Thought in the United States* (Ann Arbor, MI, 1978)

J. H. Alexander: "Brainard's (Western) Musical World," *Notes*, xxxvi (1979–80), 601

I. Fellinger: "Periodicals," §§I–III, *Grove 6*

M. V. Davison: *American Music Periodicals, 1853–1899* (Ann Arbor, MI, 1981)

M. Lederman: *The Life and Death of a Small Magazine (Modern Music 1924–1946)*, ISAMm, xviii (Brooklyn, NY, 1983)

I. Fellinger: *Periodica musicalia 1789–1830*, i: *Historischer Überblick* (Regensburg, Germany, 1985)

LISTS OF PERIODICALS

(dates in brackets indicate period of coverage)

RiemannL 12 ("Zeitschriften")

"Periodische Schriften," *JbMP 1894–1938*

Union List of Serials in the Libraries of the United States and Canada, ed. W. Gregory (New York, 1927, 2/1943, rev. E. B. Titus 3/1965; suppls., Washington, DC, 1973– as *New Serial Titles*, from 1982 in 3-month cumulations)

D. H. Daugherty, L. Ellinwood, and R. S. Hill: *Bibliography of Periodical Literature in Musicology and Allied Fields and a Record of Graduate Theses* (Washington, DC, 1940–43/*R*1973)

L. Fairley: "A Check-list of Recent Latin-American Music Periodicals," *Notes*, ii (1944–5), 5, 120 [lists 23 periodicals established 1940–45, in *DLC, DOAS*]

"Periodicals," *Harvard Dictionary of Music*, ed. W. Apel (Cambridge, MA, 1947, rev. and enlarged 2/1969)

F. Campbell, G. Eppink, and J. Fredericks: "Music Magazines of Great Britain and the United States," *Notes*, vi (1948–9), 239, 547; vii (1949–50), 372 [lists periodicals of the 1940s, but without years or vol. nos.]

Bibliographie des Musikschrifttums 1950/1951 [–1977] (Frankfurt am Main, Germany, 1954–64; Hofheim am Taunus, Germany, 1968; Mainz, Germany, 1969–85)

A. H. King: "Periodicals," §II, *Grove 5* and suppl.

I. Lowens: "Writings about Music in the Periodicals of American Transcendentalism (1835–1850)," *JAMS*, x (1957), 71 [discusses 7 periodicals established 1835–50]

Early American Periodicals Index to 1850 (New York, 1964) [microprint of O. Cargill's card index completed in 1934 and maintained at New York U. by N. F. Adkins]

C. R. Nicewonger and others, eds.: *A Union List of Music Periodicals in the Libraries of Northern California* (Berkeley, CA, 1965, rev. A. Basart and others 6/1979)

F. Blum: "Music Serials in Microfilm and Reprint Editions," *Notes*, xxiv (1967–8), 670

I. Fellinger: *Verzeichnis der Musikzeitschriften des 19. Jahrhunderts* (Regensburg, Germany, 1968; suppls. in *FAM*, xvii (1970), 7; xviii (1971), 59; xix (1972), 41; xx (1973), 108; xxi (1974), 36; xxiii (1976), 62) [lists 2305 international periodicals established 1798–1918, plus additions]

——: "Zeitschriften," §IV, *MGG*

W. J. Weichlein: *A Checklist of American Music Periodicals, 1850–1900* (Detroit, 1970) [lists 309 titles]

American Periodicals, 1741–1900 (Ann Arbor, MI, 1972–?; index, ed. J. Hoornstra and T. Heath, 1979) [microfilm reproductions of periodicals in 3 pts: 1741–99, 1800–50, 1850–1900]

C. E. Lindahl: "Music Periodicals: New Music and the Composer," *Notes*, xxxii (1975–6), 784

——: "Music Periodicals: Woodwind and Brass," *Notes*, xxxii (1975–6), 558

——: "Music Periodicals," *Notes*, xxxiii (1976–7), 308, 851

——: "Music Periodicals: Early (and Later) Musical Instrument Journals," *Notes*, xxxiii (1976–7), 86

Ulrich's International Periodicals Directory (New York, 16/1976 [1975–6]; 17/1978 [1977–8]; 18/1980 [1979–80]; from 19/1980 [1980] yearly)

C. Lawrence Mekkawi: "Music Periodicals: Popular and Classical Reviews and Indexes," *Notes*, xxxiv (1977–8), 92

C. E. Lindahl: "Music Periodicals," *Notes*, xxxiv (1977–8), 883

C. Wunderlich: *A History and Bibliography of Early American Musical Periodicals, 1782–1852* (Ann Arbor, 1977), 304–655 [list]

C. E. Lindahl: "Music Periodicals," *Notes*, xxxv (1978–9), 323, 895; xxxvi (1979–80), 662; xxxix (1982–3), 106

J. M. Meggett: *Music Periodical Literature: an Annotated Bibliography of Indexes and Bibliographies* (Metuchen, NJ, 1978)

I. Fellinger: "Periodicals," §IV, *Grove 6*

C. E. Lindahl: "Music Periodicals in U.S. Research Libraries in 1931: a Retrospective Survey, Part iii: The United States," *Notes*, xxxviii (1981–2), 320

S. M. Fry: "New Periodicals," *Notes*, xxxix (1982–3), 833

L. I. Solow: "Index to 'Music Periodicals' reviewed in Notes (1976–1982)," *Notes*, xxxix (1982–3)
S. M. Fry: "New Music Periodicals," *Notes*, xl (1983–4), 275

II. List and Index

1. Preface. 2. List. 3. Index.

1. PREFACE. The list that follows provides information on music periodicals from the earliest (1820) to 1984. It includes yearbooks and almanacs on music and the annual reports of musical institutions. Though intended as comprehensive, the list is not claimed as complete. Art, theater, and other general cultural periodicals containing musical sections, as well as journals in other fields closely related to music such as acoustics and liturgy, are included selectively according to their musical significance; so are periodicals on recording, dance, jazz, rock, and pop. Music periodicals published as supplements to newspapers or nonmusical periodicals are named only when they are of special importance. Excluded are publicity and sale sheets from music publishers, concert guides and programs, and periodical publications consisting solely of music, as well as congress reports, periodical Festschriften, monograph series, and series containing collections of essays. Journals are numbered chronologically according to the date of their first issue, and alphabetically within each year. An alphabetical index of titles (with variations) and organizations follows the chronological list.

Each entry is based on the following scheme:

1. *Title.* Each periodical is given under its full original title, normally according to the title-page of the first volume. Subsequent title changes, as well as details of incorporations, combinations, etc., with other periodicals are given in chronological order after the first title when the numbering system is continuous. Title variations are shown, with their dates, in parentheses; the word or words within the parentheses replace the single word immediately preceding (e.g., "*American* (from April 1898 *Conkey's*) *Home Journal*" indicates that the *American Home Journal* was published as *Conkey's Home Journal* after March 1898). Abbreviations used for the periodical throughout this dictionary are noted in brackets. Subtitles are given only when the main title is of a nonmusical or a general musical nature (e.g., *At Home and Abroad: a Monthly Review devoted to Music and the Kindred Arts*). If the journal's contents are not sufficiently clear from the title information, an annotation is supplied in brackets. Titles in less familiar languages are translated.

2. *Sponsoring organization.* Any sponsoring organization is named. Later name variations are given in parentheses.

3. *Editors, publishers.* Founding editors' names are given where they are particularly significant. Publishers are named if of special importance and if not identical with the sponsoring organization or founding editor.

4. *Places and dates of publication.* Places of publication and their significant changes are noted, with the dates of the publication, in parentheses; ellipses indicate the omission of one or more places of publication. Actual places of publication are named; these may not necessarily correspond with title-page imprints. Dates given with an oblique stroke (e.g., 1931/2) indicate that the journal's publication year, or volume arrangement, does not correspond with a single calendar year; lacunae in publication are normally indicated. Dates of yearbooks, etc., if different from publication years, are given in angled brackets (e.g., Boston, later Chicago, ⟨1883/4–1892/3⟩ 1884–93) and are used in preference to publication dates as the basis for chronology. Information that is partly conjectural or dependent upon secondary sources is preceded by a question mark. "1950–" indicates that a journal is still being published, "1950–?" that it ceased publication at an unknown date; "?1950– . . ." or ". . . –?1970" indicates that the first or last volume available belongs to the date given. Reprint information is given (without dates): *R* – photographic reprint; *Rp* – partial photographic reprint; *Rm* – microfilm or microfiche; and *Rmp* – partial microfilm or microfiche.

5. *Volume arrangement.* When a journal is defunct, the number of volumes and/or issues it comprised is indicated if available. When a journal is untraceable after a certain date the number of volumes and/or issues published to that date is given if available. Continuous numeration as a coordinating system to the volume numbering is shown as "1051 nos. in 41 vols."

6. *Frequency of publication.* The periodicity is indicated as follows: D – daily, W – weekly, F – fortnightly, S – semimonthly, M – monthly, B – bimonthly, Q – quarterly, H – half-yearly, Y – yearly, O – occasionally or irregularly. A formula such as "4 nos. Y" signifies the publication of four numbers at irregular intervals over a publishing year.

7. *Additional information.* Other features of a journal are indicated as follows: music – regular single music supplements; music suppl. – music supplements under a separate title, with dates and frequency if different from the periodical itself; bibl. – regular bibliographical material, including booklists, but not lists of publications received; Fs – Festschrift issues, with the name of the person honored and the year; yb – yearbooks, with title and dates if different from the periodical itself; c.i. – cumulative indices, with dates of coverage if less than the complete run; suppl. – general supplements, with title, dates, and frequency if different from the periodical itself. Other special features are noted in brackets: for example, "[in 2 pts: text and music]" indicates that a periodical consists of distinct textual and musical parts.

8. *Language.* The language of a journal, if not English, is noted. Languages are also cited for bilingual and multilingual journals where the contents are in more than one language (e.g., "[in Eng., Fr.]").

9. *Relationships between periodicals.* Relationships between periodicals with their own numbering systems – continuation, incorporation, and combination – are shown by reference to the numbers of the periodicals concerned (e.g., "550 *Bulletin of the American Musicological Society* . . . [contd as 633]" and "633 *Journal of the American Musicological Society* . . . [contd from 550]"; "210 *Ziarno* . . . [incorp. into 315]" and "315 *Harmonia* . . . [incorp. 210; contd as 361]").

The alphabetical index that follows the list contains titles, title changes, versions in other languages, supplement titles, and the names of organizations; some are given in shortened form. When the title of a periodical varies or when the title of a periodical and that of the organization that publishes it largely coincide the entries are conflated and the variation shown in parentheses (e.g., American Organ Monthly (Quarterly), American Harp Journal (Soc.)). The definite article is omitted. All numbers are assumed to refer to the United States section of the list unless prefaced by the abbreviation "Intl" – International (in this case further numbers in the same entry referring to periodicals in the United States section are prefaced by "US").

2. List.

SPECIAL ABBREVIATIONS

AFM	American Federation of Musicians
Amer.	American
approx.	approximately
Assn	Association
bibl.	bibliography
c.i.	cumulative index
Coll.	College
Conf.	Confederation
contd	continued
educ.	education
Fdn	Foundation
Fed.	Federation
Fs	Festschrift
incorp.	incorporated
Inst.	Institute
MEA	Music Educators Association
MENC	Music Educators National Conference
MTA	Music Teachers Association
Natl	National
Soc.	Society
yb	yearbook

INTERNATIONAL (Intl)

1 *American* (from 1901/2 *International*) *Musician*, from 1919/20 subtitle *Official Journal of the American Federation of Musicians of the United States & Canada* (St. Louis, 1898/9–1922; Newark, . . . 1922–75; New York, 1975–) M

2 *The Diapason*, 1918–27 Organ Builders Assn of America, 1919–34 Natl Assn of Organists, 1934–68 (from Oct 1967 Royal Canadian) Coll. of Organists, 1935–67 Amer. Guild of Organists, 1936–55 Hymn Soc. of America, 1967–72 Unión Nacional de Organistas, Mexico, from 1976 Amer. Inst. of Organbuilders (Chicago, 1909/10–/*Rmp*) M

3 *International Folk Music Council: Bulletin*, from 1957 (no.11) *Bulletin of the International Folk Music Council*, from 1981 *Bulletin of the International Council for Traditional Music* (London, 1948–67; Copenhagen, 1967–9; Kingston, Ont., 1969–80; New York, 1981–) approx. Y, from 1957 2 nos. Y

4 *Boletín de música y artes visuales*, Unión Panamericana, Departamento de Asuntos Culturales (Washington, DC, 1950–56) 76 nos., M [in Sp.; contd as 5]

5 *Boletín interamericano de música*, Unión Panamericana, Departamento de Asuntos Culturales, from 1970 (no.75/6) Organización de los Estados Americanos (Washington, DC, 1957–73) 87 nos., B, from 1970 (no.78) 3 nos. Y [in Sp., parallel Eng. edn; contd from 4]

6 *Musik aus Amerika*, US Information Service (Vienna, Austria, 1958/9–62) 5 vols. [in Ger.; see also A285 in *Grove 6*]

7 *The Haydn Yearbook/Das Haydn Jahrbuch*, from 1975 Verein Internationale Joseph Haydn Stiftung, Eisenstadt, Austria, ed. H. Singer, K. H. Füssl, and H. C. Robbins Landon, pubd Presser and Universal (Bryn Mawr, PA, and Vienna, Austria, 1962–5, 1968–71; Vienna, 1975–8; Cardiff, 1980–) O, 1969–71 Y, from 1975 O [in Eng., Ger.]

8 *Music: the A.G.O.* (from 1968 (no.10) *A.G.O. and R.C.C.O.*) *Magazine*, from 1979 *The American Organist*, Amer. Guild of Organists and Royal Canadian Coll. of Organists (New York, 1967–) M

9 *RILM Abstracts of Music Literature: répertoire international de la littérature musicale/International Repertory of Music Literature*, Intl Musicological Soc., Intl Assn of Music Libraries, and Amer. Council of Learned Socs., at the Graduate School, CUNY, ed. B. S. Brook (New York, 1967–) 3 nos., index, Y; c.i. 1967–71, 1972–6

10 *IAJRC Record* (from Jan 1969 *Journal* [*IAJRCJ*]), Intl Assn of Jazz Record Collectors (Staten Island, NY, later Indianapolis, 1968–) Q except 1982–3; c.i.

11 *Yearbook of the International Folk Music Council* [*YIFMC*], from 1981 *Yearbook for Traditional Music*, ed. A. L. Ringer (Urbana, IL, 1969–80; New York, 1981–) Y

12 *The World Saxophone Congress Newsletter* (Evanston, IL, 1970–74) 4 vols., Q; c.i. in 17 [contd as 17]

13 *Swinging Newsletter*, from 1973 *Jazz Forum*, from June 1979 *Jazz Echo* (from 1982 *World Index*), European (later Intl) Jazz Fed. (Vienna, 1972–7; New York, 1977–) M, later B

14 *Senza sordino*, Intl Conference of Symphony & Opera Musicians (Chicago, 1973–) 2–6 nos. Y

15 *ILWC Newsletter*, Intl League of Women Composers (Knoxville, 1975–) B, later Q

16 *RIdIM Newsletter: répertoire international d'iconographie musicale/International Repertory of Musical Iconography*, Research Center for Musical Iconography, Graduate School, CUNY, ed. B. S. Brook (New York, 1975/6–) O [in Eng.]

17 *Saxophone Symposion: a Newsletter*, N. Amer. Saxophone Alliance of the World Saxophone Congress, Northwestern U., School of Music (Evanston, IL, 1975–) Q [contd from 12]

18 *World Jazz Calendar of Festivals & Events*, Intl Jazz Fed. (New York, 1980–) H

19 *The International Congress on Women in Music Newsletter* (Los Angeles, 1983–) Q

UNITED STATES (US)

1 *The Euterpeiad, or Musical Intelligencer*, ed. J. R. Parker (Boston, 1820/21–1822/3; new ser. 1823/*R*, *Rm*) 3 vols., new ser. 2 nos., W, from 1821/2 (no.1) F, from 1822/3 (no.14) M; music

2 *The Lyre, or The New York Musical Journal* (New York, 1824/5/*Rm*) 1 vol., M; music

3 *Theatrical Censor and Musical Review* (Philadelphia, 1828) 28 nos., D, from no.4 3 nos. W

4 *The Euterpeiad: an Album of Music, Poetry, and Prose*, ed. C. Dingley (New York, 1830/31–1831/*Rm*) 2 vols., S; music

5 *American Musical Journal* (New York, 1834/5/*Rm*) 1 vol., B, from Feb 1835 M; music

6 *Boston Musical Gazette* (Boston, 1838–9/*Rm*) 2 vols., F; music

7 *Musical Review and Record of Music Science, Literature, and Intelligence* (New York, 1838/9–1839) 2 vols., W, from 1838/9 (no.14) F

8 *Parlour Review and Journal of Music, Literature, and the Fine Arts* (Philadelphia, 1838) 10 nos., W; music [also Fr. edn]

9 *Proceedings of the Musical* (later *American Musical*) *Convention* (Boston, etc., 1838–?) Y

10 *The Musical Magazine, or Repository of Musical Science, Literature, and Intelligence* (Boston, 1839–1841/2 except 4–18 Sept 1841 and 4 Dec 1841 to 10 April 1842) 78 nos. in 3 vols., F, from 1841/2 (no.71) O

11 *Boston Eoliad: devoted Exclusively to the Science of Music* (Boston, 1840/41) 2 nos., H

12 *Musical* (from 1842/4 *Boston Musical*) *Visitor*, from 1844/6 *American Journal of Music and Musical Visitor* (Boston, 1840/41–1846/*Rm*) 5 vols., S; music

13 *Musical Cabinet: a Monthly Collection of Vocal and Instrumental Music and Musical Literature* (Boston, 1841/2/*Rm*) 1 vol., M [in 2 pts: text and music]

14 *Musical Reporter* (Boston, 1841) 9 nos. in 1 vol., M; music

15 *World of Music* (Bellows Falls, VT, 1843/4–1848) 5 vols., S; music [contd as 19]

16 *Boston Musical Review* (Boston, 1845/*Rm*) 4 nos., S; music

17 *The Boston Musical Gazette* (Boston, MA, and Bellows Falls, VT, 1846/7–1850) 5 vols., F, from 1848/9 S; music [contd as 21]

18 *The American Musical Times* [also literature, fine arts, drama] (New York, 1847/8–?1849) 3 vols., W; music

19 *Philharmonic Journal* (Claremont, NH, 1848/9) 24 nos. in 1 vol., F; music [contd from 15]

20 *Saroni's* (from 8 Nov 1851 *The*) *Musical Times* (New York, 1849/50–1852/*Rm*) 5 vols., W; music [incorp. into 21]

21 *The Message Bird: a Literary and Musical Journal*, from 1 May 1851 *The Journal of the Fine Arts* (from 16 June 1851 *Arts and Musical World*), from 2 Feb 1852 *The Musical World and Journal of the Fine Arts*, incorp. 20 on 15 July 1852 to form *The Musical World and New York Musical Times*, from 9 Sept 1854 *Musical* (from 2 Jan 1856 *New York Musical*, from 5 Jan 1858 *The Musical*) *World* (New York, 1849–60) 25 vols., S, from 4 Sept 1852 W; music [contd from 17; incorp. into 25]

22 *American Musical Fund Society: Annual Report* (New York, 1850–?60) 10 vols., Y

23 *The American Musical* (from 1850 (no.3) *Monthly Musical*) *Review and Choir Singers' Companion* [church music], pubd Huntington & Savage, from 1851 Huntington (New York, 1850–51/*Rm*) 2 vols., Q, from 1850 (no.2) M; music [incorp. into 25]

24 *The Baltimore Olio and American Musical Gazette* (Baltimore, 1850) 1 vol., M; music

25 *The Choral Advocate and Singing-class Journal*, incorp. 23 in Jan 1852 to form *Musical Review and Choral Advocate*, wrapper title *American Musical Review and Choral Advocate*, from 1854 *New-York Musical Review and Choral Advocate*, incorp. 31 1855 (no.11) to form *New-York Musical Review and Gazette*, incorp. 21 1860 (no.16) to form *The Musical Review and Musical World*, from 1865 *New York Weekly Review of Music, Literature, Fine Arts, and Society*, from 1867 *New York Weekly Review*, pubd Mason & Law, from 1854 Mason (New York, 1850–73) 766 nos. in 24 vols., M, from 1854 S, from 1865 W; music

26 *The Lorgnette, or Studies of the Town, by an Opera Goer* (New York, 1850) 24 nos.
27 *The North-western Musical Herald* [also educ., literature, fine arts] (Detroit, 1851) 2 nos., M
28 *Dwight's Journal of Music*, ed. J. S. Dwight, pubd Balch, from 1858 Ditson, from 1879 Houghton, Mifflin (Boston, 1852–81/*R, Rm*) 1051 nos. in 41 vols., W, from April 1863 F; c.i. every 2 vols.
29 *Boston* (from 18 April 1854 *The Boston*) *Musical Journal* (Boston, 1853/4) 19 nos., S; music
30 *Monthly Musical Gazette* (New York, 1853) 10 nos. in 1 vol., M
31 *The Musical Gazette*, pubd Mason (New York, 1854/5/*Rmp*) 26 nos. in 1 vol., W [incorp. into 25]
32 *Massachusetts* (from 1856 *Boston*) *Musical Journal* (*Journal and Literary Gazette*) (Boston, 1855/6–1856/7) 2 vols., S; music
33 *New York Musical Pioneer and Choristers' Budget*, from Oct 1859 *New York* (from Oct 1863 *The*) *Musical Pioneer*, from ?Jan 1865 *Musical Pioneer*, pubd Huntington (New York, 1855/6–?1870/71 except Oct–Dec 1868) 16 vols., M; music
34 *Deutsche Musikzeitung für die Vereinigten Staaten* (*Staaten von Nordamerika*) (Philadelphia, 1856/7–1860/61) 5 vols., S, later M, W, F; music; suppl.: *Die Wespe*, 1859/60–1860/61, O [in Ger.]
35 *Philadelphia Musical Journal and Review* (Philadelphia, 1856/7) 26 nos. in 1 vol., F; music
36 *Western Journal of Music* (Chicago, 1856–?) 1 no., F
37 *Educational Herald and Musical Monthly* (New York, 1857–64) 8 vols., M
38 *Kleine Musik-Zeitung: Musical Gazette*, Oct/Dec 1867 to Dec 1868 *Little Musical Gazette: kleine Musik-Zeitung* (New York, 1858/9–1870) 13 vols., Q, from 1868 4, in 1870 2 nos. M [in Eng., Ger.; contd from D85 in *Grove* 6]
39 *Southern Musical Advocate and Singers' Friend*, from 1866 *Musical Advocate and Singers' Friend* (Mountain Valley, VA, and Singer's Glen, VA, 1859; Singer's Glen, 1860, 1867–9) 5 vols., M [contd as 84]
40 *The Chorister* (from 1861 *Chorister and Musical Advisor*) (New York, 1859–?65 except Oct 1861 to May 1862, July–Sept 1862, and Jan–April 1864) 5 vols., M
41 *The Boston Musical Times*, from Feb 1869 *Musical Times* [also art, literature] (Boston and New York, 1860–71) 13 vols., F
42 *Bühnen-Almanach des St. Louis-Opern Hauses* (St. Louis, 1861) 1 vol., Y [in Ger.]
43 *The Monthly Choir and Organ Journal* (New York, 1862/3) 1 vol., M
44 *The Song Messenger of the Northwest*, from 1870 *The Song Messenger* (from ?1874 *Messenger Monthly*), pubd Root & Cady (Chicago, 1863–75 except Dec 1872 to Feb 1873) 13 vols., M; music [incorp. into 87]
45 *The Orpheonist and Philharmonic Journal*, from Nov 1873 *Philharmonic Journal and Orpheonist* (from Nov 1873 *Advertiser*) (New York, 1864/5–1879/80) 108 nos. in 16 vols., M Nov–April, from 1875/6 S Nov–April, from 1876/7 M
46 *Watson's Weekly Art Journal*, from 1866 *American* (1867 (no.9) to 1874/5 (no.10) *Watson's*) *Art Journal*, ed. H. C. Watson (New York, 1864–1905) 87 vols., W [incorp. into 186]
47 *Western* (from Jan 1869 *Brainard's*) *Musical World*, running title *The Musical World* (Cleveland, later Chicago, 1864–95) 32 vols., M; music [incorp. into 183]
48 *Music-class Journal and Organist's Companion* (Dubuque, 1865–?6) 2 vols., M
49 *New-Yorker Musik-Zeitung*, from 1877 *New-Yorker Musik- und Unterhaltungs-blätter*, from 1878 *New-York Musik-Zeitung* (New York, 1865–?79) 22 vols., F, from 1866 W [in Ger.]
50 *The* (from March 1867 *Butterfield's*) *Musical Visitor* (Indianapolis, 1865–7) 3 vols., M [contd as 85]
51 *The Orpheus: a Repository of Music, Art, and Literature*, subtitle varies (New York and Boston, 1865–80) 16 vols., M; music
52 *The Seven Sounds: a Musical Magazine devoted to the Youth* (Chicago, 1865–?) 3 nos. in 1 vol., Q
53 *Chicago* (from no.3 *Higgins'*) *Musical Review* (Chicago, 1866/7) 9 nos. in 1 vol., M
54 *Neue New-Yorker Musik-Zeitung*, wrapper title *New Yorker Musik-Zeitung* (New York, 1866/7–?1870/71) 5 vols., W [in Ger.]
55 *The Concordia* (Chicago, 1866–?7) 2 vols., M
56 *The New York Musical Gazette*, pubd Mason, from 1869 Biglow & Main (New York, 1866/7–1874) 8 vols., M; music
57 *Vermont* (from Jan 1868 *American*) *Musical Journal* (Burlington, VT, 1866/7–?1867/8) 2 vols., M
58 *Western* (from Jan 1870 *Benham's*, from July 1879 *Baldwin's*) *Musical Review* (Indianapolis and Cincinnati, 1866–?83) M
59 *Albany Musical Bulletin* (Albany, NY, 1867–?8) 2 vols., M
60 *Compton's St. Louis Musical Journal* (St. Louis, 1867/8–?) ?5 nos., M
61 *Loomis Musical* (from 1870 *Musical and Masonic*) *Journal* (New Haven, 1867–1900) 34 vols., M
62 *Moore's Musical Record* [also science, literature, news] (Manchester, NH, 1867–70) 5 vols., M
63 *Musical Bulletin-extra*, from no.2 *The Musical Bulletin* (Troy, NY, later also New York, 1867–?73) 7 vols., M
64 *Musical Journal* (Philadelphia, 1867) 1 vol., M
65 *The Pacific Musical Gazette* (San Francisco, 1867/8–?) M
66 *The Southern Journal of Music* (Louisville, 1867/8–?) 14 nos. in 1 vol., S, later M
67 *United States* (from 1869 *Peters' Musical Monthly and United States*) *Musical Review* (New York, 1867–?74) 14 vols., M; music
68 *Walter S. Pierce's Musical Circular* (San Francisco, 1867/8–?) F
69 *Whitney's Musical Guest* (from Jan 1873 *Guest and Literary Journal*) (Toledo, OH, 1867/8–1880/81) 14 vols., M
70 *Figaro: devoted to Music and Drama* (New York, 1868–?72) M
71 *Green Mountain Musical Journal* (Fair Haven, VT, 1868–?) M
72 *Mellor's Musical Mirror* (Pittsburgh, 1868/9) 1 vol., M
73 *The Musical Independent* [news, music literature, musicology] (Chicago, 1868/9–1872/3 except Nov 1871 to Nov 1872) 4 vols., M; music [contd as 101]
74 *The New York Journal of Music* (New York, 1868–?) 7 nos., M
75 *Folio* (from 1886 *The Folio*): *a Journal of Music, Art, and Literature*, subtitle varies (Boston, 1869–95) 42 vols., M; music
76 *Hitchcock's New Monthly Magazine: Choice Music, Art Notes, and Select Reading for the Family Circle* (New York, 1869–70) 2 vols., M
77 *Rochester Musical Times*, from 1871 *Musical Times* [also art, literature] (Rochester, NY, 1869–72) 4 vols., M
78 *The National Peace Jubilee and Music Festival Reporter* (Boston, 1869) Q, later W
79 *The Silver Tongue and Organists' Repertory* (New York, 1869–?71) 3 vols., M
80 *The Singing People: an Advocate for Congregational Singing* (New York, 1869/70–1870/71) 2 vols., Q, from Jan 1871 M
81 *Musical Monthly* [music and musicians of the West] (?Chicago, 1870–77) M [probably contd as 126]
82 *The Amateur: a Repository of Music, Literature, and Art*, subtitle varies (Philadelphia, 1870–74; new ser. 1875) 5 vols., new ser. 11 nos., M; music
83 *The Chicago Magazine of Fashion, Music, and Home Reading* (Chicago, 1870–76) 7 vols.
84 *The Musical Million* [also literature] (Dayton, VA, and Singer's Glen, VA, 1870–1913) 44 vols., M [contd from 39]
85 *Willard's Musical Visitor* [also art, literature] (Indianapolis, 1870/71) 1 vol., M [contd from 50]
86 *Zundel's Organ and Choir Monthly*, pubd Zundel and Zundel & Brand (Brooklyn, NY, and Toledo, OH, 1870–?) 1 no., M
87 *Church's* (from Feb 1883 *The*) *Musical Visitor* (Cincinnati, 1871–97) 26 vols., M [incorp. 44 in Nov 1875]
88 *Metronome: a Monthly Review of Music* (Boston, 1871/2–1873/4) 3 vols., M; music, 1873/4
89 *Newburgh Musical Bulletin* (Newburgh, NY, 1871–?2) 2 vols., M
90 *Southern Musical Journal* [news, literature, musicology] (Savannah, GA, 1871–82) 11 vols., M; music [combined with 100 to form 179]
91 *The Song Journal* [music, music literature] (Detroit and New York, 1871–97) 18 vols., M; music [contd as 292]
92 *Winner's Musical Trumpet* (Philadelphia, 1871/2–?) 2 nos., Q
93 *American Musical Gazette* [educ., news] (New York, 1872–?3) 2 vols., M
94 *Dexter Smith's Musical, Literary, Dramatic, and Art Paper*, from July 1873 *Dexter Smith's* (from March 1876 *Smith's Pictorial*,) *Musical, Dramatic, Literary, Humorous, Art, Household, and Fashion Magazine* (Boston, 1872–8) 14 vols., M; music [incorp. into 129]
95 *Musical Visitor and Lesson Manual for the Sunday-school and Home Circle* (Lebanon, PA, 1872–6) 5 vols., M
96 *New Hampshire Journal of Music*, from 1874 *Whitney's New Hampshire Journal of Music* (Manchester, NH, 1872–82) 11 vols., M
97 *The Vox humana: a Journal of Music and Musical Information* (Cambridgeport [now in Cambridge], MA, and Chicago, 1872–9) 8 vols., M
98 *Zundel and Brand's Quarterly*, pubd Zundel & Brand (Toledo, OH, 1872–?) 1 no., Q
99 *Echo: devoted to Music, Literature, Art, and Drama* (Providence, 1873–4) 2 vols., M
100 *Georgia Music Eclectic* (Atlanta, 1873–?4) 2 vols. [combined with 90 to form 179]
101 *Goldbeck's Monthly Journal of Music* [also art, literature, drama] (Chicago, 1873) 2 nos., M [contd from 73]
102 *Musical Bouquet* [also art, literature, drama] (New York, 1873–?) 1 no., M

103 *Musical Echo* [music, music literature] (Milwaukee, 1873–5) 6 vols., M
104 *The Globe: Music, Drama, Literature, and Art*, from 1876 *Musical Globe and Ladies Fashion Bazaar* (New York, 1873–?6) 5 vols., M
105 *The Kansas Folio: a Monthly Journal of Music, Art, and Literature* (Leavenworth, KS, 1873–?) 2 nos., M
106 *Caecilia: Vereinsorgan des Amerikanischen Caecilien-Vereins*, incorp. 449 in 1965 to form *Sacred Music*, Church Music Assn of America, pubd Pustet (Regensburg, Germany, 1874–6; New York, . . . 1877–) M, later Q [in Eng. and Ger., from 1925 in Eng.; *Caecilia* = D204 in *Grove* 6]
107 *Organist's Quarterly Journal and Review* (Boston, 1874/5–1876/7) 3 vols., Q; music
108 *Sherman and Hyde's Musical Review* (San Francisco, 1874–9) 6 vols., M
109 *The Amphion* [music, music literature] (Detroit, 1874–?85 except Oct–Nov 1877) 11 vols., M
110 *The Leader: devoted to Music and General Literature* (Boston, 1875–1904) 30 vols., M
111 *The Musical Casket* [also literature] (Singer's Glen, VA, 1875/6) M
112 *The Musical Gazette* (Chicago, 1875–?) 1 no., M
113 *The Music Trade Review*, from Nov 1878 *The Review*, from Dec 1878 *The Music* (from Sept 1879 *Musical Times and*, from 1879 *Musical and Dramatic Times and Music*) *Trade Review* (New York, 1875/6–1879/80) 11 vols., S, from Nov 1878 W; bibl.
114 *Trumpet Notes: a Monthly Paper devoted to the Interests of Amateur Bands* (Elkhart, IN, 1875–?81) 10 vols., M
115 *Daniel F. Beatty's Illustrated Piano and Organ Advertiser* (Washington, DC, and Warren County, NJ, 1876–?7) 7 nos., M
116 *Knake's Monthly Journal of Music and General Miscellany* (Pittsburgh, 1876/7–?1882/3) 5 vols., M
117 *Lauter's Monthly Journal of Music and General Miscellany* (Newark, 1876–?8) 3 vols., M; music
118 *Musician and Artist* (Boston, 1876) 5 nos., M
119 *Music Teachers National Association: Proceedings of the Annual Meeting*, from 1880 *Official* (also *Annual*) *Report* [*MTNAP*] (n.p., 1876–8, 1880–90, 1892–1905) 27 vols., Y; c.i. 1876–87, 1888–1902 [contd as 370]
120 *New England Monthly Journal of Music and General Miscellany* (Boston, 1876–?) 1 no., M
121 *The Footlight: devoted to Art Industries of California – Music and the Drama* (San Francisco, 1876–?80) D
122 *Utah Musical Times* (Salt Lake City, 1876/7–1877/8) 2 vols., M
123 *J. W. Pepper's Musical Times and Band Journal*, masthead title *Musical Times and Band Journal*, later title *Musical Times* (Philadelphia and Chicago, 1877–1912) M
124 *Seltzer and Ammel's Monthly Journal of Music and General Miscellany* (Columbus, OH, 1877–?) 1 no., M
125 *The Musical Advocate* (Altoona, PA, 1877/8–?1881/2) 5 vols., M
126 *The Musical Review* (Chicago, 1877) 1 no., M [probably contd from 81]
127 *The Score* [also drama, literature] (Boston, 1877–82) 10 vols., M; music
128 *Brainard's Sunday-school Singer* (Cleveland, 1878–?) 1 no., M
129 *Ditson and Co.'s Musical Record*, from 1879 (no.17) *Musical Record* (from 1900 (no.468) *Record and Review*), pubd Ditson (Boston, 1878–1903) 504 nos., Sept 1878 2 nos. in 1 vol., from Oct 1878 F, from Oct 1878 W, from Oct 1883 M [incorp. 94; incorp. into 288]
130 *Kunkel's Musical Review* (St. Louis, 1878–1909) 32 vols., M; music
131 *The Baton*, Richmond Mozart Assn (Richmond, VA, 1878–?88) 11 vols., W, from 1886 S
132 *The* (from 2 Oct 1915 *Music Trade*) *Indicator* (Chicago, 1878–1929/30) 52 vols., W [incorp. into 369]
133 *The Musician's Journal* (Somerset, PA, 1878–?) 1 no., M
134 *Thomas Brothers' Musical Journal* (Catskill, NY, 1878–85) 6 vols.
135 *Art Critic: devoted to Music, Art, and Literature* (Jersey City, NJ, and New York, 1879–80) 3 vols., M
136 *Figaro: Wochenschrift für Theater, Kunst, und Literatur*, from 1879 (no.12) *New York Figaro: belletristische Wochenschrift für Theater, Musik, Kunst, Literatur, und Unterhaltung* (New York, 1879–81) 3 vols., W [in Ger.; contd as 161]
137 *Foster's Musical Journal* (Geneva, OH, 1879–?84) 5 vols., M
138 *J. W. Smith, Jr., & Bro's Musical Journal*, sometimes *Smith's Monthly Journal of Music and General Miscellany* (Brooklyn, NY, 1879–?) M
139 *Musical Bulletin*, Hershey School of Musical Art (Chicago, 1879/80–1882/3) 4 vols., M
140 *Musical Review* (New York, 1879–81) 3 vols., W [contd as 162]
141 *Music Trade Journal*, later *Musical Critic and Trade Review*, from 20 Aug 1885 *The Music Trade Review*, from March 1956 *Piano and Organ Review*, incorp. 494 in Jan 1958 to form *Musical Merchandise Review* (New York, 1879–) S, from 20 Aug 1892 W, from July 1929 M [incorp. 184 in 1898; incorp. as a section into 365 March–May 1933, into *Radio-journal* April 1942 to Jan 1943, into 494 Feb 1943 to Jan 1945]
142 *Song Friend* (Chicago, 1879–94) M
143 *The Musical Bulletin* (Washington, DC, 1879–80) 2 vols., M
144 *The Musician* [also art, literature] (Philadelphia, 1879–80) 2 vols., M
145 *The Princeton Musical Journal* (Princeton, NJ, 1879/80–?) 10 nos., M
146 *The Voice: an International Review of the Speaking and Singing Voice*, from 1889 *Werner's Voice Magazine*, from 1893 *Werner's Magazine* (New York, 1879–1902) 30 vols., M [incorp. into 342]
147 *The Zitherplayer* (Washington, DC, 1879–?81) O
148 *Young Folks' Musical Monthly* (Strongsville, OH, 1879–?80) 2 vols., M
149 *Molineux' Organists' and Conductors' Monthly* (Brooklyn, NY, 1880–?) 1 no., M
150 *Monthly Musical Review* (Indianapolis, IN, and Warren, OH, 1880–82) 11 nos., M
151 *Musical Banner* (Mondamin, IA, 1880–?) 1 no., M
152 *Musical Harp* (Berea, OH, 1880–97)
153 *Musical News* (New York, 1880/81) 26 nos. in 1 vol., W, from 15 April 1881 S
154 *Orchestra* [also drama, military and brass bands] (Boston, 1880) 5 nos., M
155 *The Musical and Sewing Machine Gazette* (from 1880 (no.4) *Courier*), from 1880 (no.9) *The Musical* (from no.41 *Musical and Dramatic*) *Courier*, from 1884 (no.24) *The Musical Courier* (from Feb 1961 *Courier and Review of Recorded Music*), incorp. 763 in Oct 1961 to form *The Music Magazine and Musical Courier* (Philadelphia, 1880–84; New York, 1884–1961; Evanston, IL, 1961–2/*Rmp*) 164 vols., W, from 15 June 1937 S, from June 1941 S Oct–May and M June–Sept, from Oct 1954 S Nov–Feb and M March–Oct, from March 1958 M; directory issue, 1957–61, Y [incorp. 382 in Dec 1931; incorp. 562 in June 1958]
156 *The* (from 1889 *Boston*) *Musical Herald*, from Nov 1892 *The Musical Herald of the United States* (Boston and Chicago, 1880–93) 14 vols., M; music
157 *The Musical People* (Cincinnati, 1880–84) 8 vols., M except 1882 to April 1883 W
158 *Chicago Musical Times* (Chicago, 1881–1926) 51 vols., M, from Nov 1887 S, from April 1891 W [incorp. into 193]
159 *Hovey's Musical Review* (Three Rivers, MI, 1881–?) 1 no., M
160 *Musical Messenger* [also literature] (Battle Creek, MI, 1881–2) 2 vols., M
161 *New York Figaro: belletristische Wochenschrift für Theater, Musik, Kunst, Literatur, und Unterhaltung*, new ser. (New York, 1881–1900) 20 vols., W; suppl.: *New York Phonograph* [in Ger.; contd from 136]
162 *Studio and Musical Review* [also painting, sculpture, architecture, engraving] (New York, 1881) 13 nos., W [2 pts: *Art Department* and *Musical Department*; contd from 140]
163 *Tonic Sol-fa Advocate*, Tonic Sol-fa Movement in the US and Canada (New York, 1881/2–1885/6) 5 vols., M, from Jan 1886 Q [contd as 203]
164 *American Musical Journal* (Chicago, 1882–?) 4 nos. in 1 vol., M
165 *Echo* [reformation of Catholic church music], Amer. St. Cecilia Soc., ed. J. Singenberger, pubd Pustet (New York and Cincinnati, 1882/3–1884/5) 3 vols., M; music
166 *Freund's Daily Music and Drama* (New York, 1882–?3) 78 nos., D
167 *Goldbeck's* (running title *The*) *Musical Instructor*, from April 1883 *Goldbeck's Musical Art, or Practical Exposition of the Art of Music* (St. Louis, 1882/3–1884/5) 3 vols., M; music; bibl.; suppl.: *Goldbeck's Art Critic or Musical and General Observer*, from Oct 1884, F
168 *La América musical* (New York, 1882–4) 36 nos., M [in Sp.]
169 *Music* (later *San Francisco Music*) *and Drama* (San Francisco, 1882/3–1901)
170 *Music: a Review*, from 29 April 1882 *Music & Drama*, from 13 Jan 1883 *Weekly Music and Drama*, from 2 June *Music and Drama* (New York, 1882–3) 7 vols., W; bibl.; suppl.: *The Music Trade* [contd as 175]
171 *Songster and Fireside Friend* (Springfield, OH, 1882–?) 6 nos., M
172 *S. S. Stewart's Banjo and Guitar Journal*, later *Stewart's Banjo, Guitar, and Mandolin Journal* (Philadelphia, 1882–?1902) 19 vols., B, from Dec 1900 M; bibl.
173 *The Apollo: a Journal of Music, Literature, and Art* (Boston, 1882/3) 5 nos., M
174 *The Courier: a Monthly Review devoted to Music and Literature* (Cincinnati, 1882–6) 5 vols., M [contd as 215]
175 *Freund's Weekly* (from 1884/5 (no.8) *Music and Drama*) (New York, 1883/4–1891/2) 17 vols., W; suppl.: *The Music Trade Review*, from 15 Aug 1885 *The Music Trade*, 1885–1892, W [contd from 170]
176 *Musical Items* (New York, 1883/4–1886/7) 4 vols., M
177 *Musical Observer* [also art, drama] (Boston, 1883/4) 2 vols., mainly W
178 *New England Conservatory of Music: Alumni Annual* (Boston, 1883–93) 11 vols., Y [contd as 265]

179 *Southern Musical Journal and Educational Eclectic* (Macon, GA, 1883–?) 10 nos., M; music [contd from 90 and 100]

180 *The Boston Musical Year-book* (from 1885/6 *Year-book and Musical Year of the United States*), from 1886/7 *The Musical Yearbook of the United States* (Boston, later Chicago, ⟨1883/4–1892/3⟩ 1884–93) 10 vols., Y

181 *The Concert Quarterly* [musical services for Easter and other feasts] (Buffalo, NY, 1883–?4) 2 vols., Q

182 *The Echo: a Music Journal* (Lafayette, IN, in 1894 also Chicago, 1883–1901) 17 vols., M; music

183 *The Etude* (1896 to Dec 1897 *Etude and Musical World*), from Feb 1922 *Etude Music Magazine*, from Dec 1948 *Etude: the Music Magazine*, ed. T. Presser (Lynchburg, VA, 1883–4; Philadelphia, 1884–1957/*Rm*) 75 vols., M, from May 1956 B, later M, B; music [incorp. 47 in Nov 1895]

184 *The Keynote: a Weekly Review devoted to Music and the Drama*, subtitle varies (New York, 1883/4–1896/7) 19 vols., W, from Oct 1886 M [incorp. into 141]

185 *The Keynote: Topics of Musical and Literary Interest* (Harrisburg, PA, 1883–?) 1 no., M

186 *American* (from 1886 (no. 16) *American Musician and American*) *Music Journal*, from 1888 *The American Musician*, incorp. 46 in 1906 to form *The American Musician and Art Journal*, from 1914 (no.8) *American Musician*, 1915 (no.4) *Music Publisher and Dealer*, 1884–8 Musical Mutual Protective Union, 1886–7 Natl League of Musicians (New York, 1884/5–1915) 31 vols., M, from 1885 S, later W, S, M; bibl.

187 *Galop: devoted to Dancing, Music, Etiquette, and Dress* (Boston, 1884–1900) 17 vols., M

188 *La propaganda musical*, from Nov 1884 *Musical Propaganda* (New York, 1884–?5) 2 vols., M; music [in Eng.]

189 *Musical and Home Journal* (Brooklyn, NY, 1884–?91) M; music

190 *Musical Visitor*, from 1885 *The Music Teacher* (Dalton, GA, later Dallas, 1884–?1915) M

191 *Music and Drama* (Chicago, 1884–?) W

192 *Parmelee's Musical Monthly* (New London, CT, 1884–?5) M; music; bibl.

193 *Presto*, incorp. 158 in April 1926 to form *Presto-Times*, from 1938 *Presto Music Times* (Chicago, 1884–?1941) M, from Nov 1887 S, from 9 April 1891 W, from 1 March 1929 S, later M, B, from Feb 1939 mainly M; yb, 1887–9 [see also F224 in *Grove 6*]

194 *Schleicher and Sons' Musical Monthly* (Mount Vernon, NY, and Stamford, CT, ?1884–?96) 113 nos., M; music; bibl.

195 *Shoninger Musical Monthly* (Chicago, . . . South Norwalk, CT, 1884–?94) 115 nos., M; music; bibl.

196 *American Tonic Sol-fa Normal* (Rocky Hill, OH, 1885–?) 3 nos., M

197 *Chicago Music and Drama* (Chicago, 1885–?) 1 no., W

198 *Metronome*, Jan 1959 to April 1960 *Music U.S.A.* (New York, 1885–1961/*Rmp*) 78 vols., mainly M; music suppl., 1914, M [Oct 1914 to Dec 1924 in 2 edns: *Metronome Orchestra Monthly* and *Metronome Band Monthly*, Jan 1925 to Jan 1932 either *Orchestra Edition* or *Band Edition*; incorp. 259 in Jan 1925]

199 *School Music Journal* (Boston, 1885–?7) 3 vols., M in school year

200 *Tway's Musical Guest* [also drama, literature, society] (New York, 1885–?92) 10 vols., M, later Q

201 *Brooklyn Musical Monthly* (Brooklyn, NY, 1886/7–?1898) M; music; bibl.

202 *Musical Advocate* (Cleveland, 1886–90), 5 vols., M

203 *Musical Reform* (New York, 1886/7–1887/8) 2 vols., M [contd from 163]

204 *North's Philadelphia Musical Journal*, from April 1889 *Philadelphia Musical Journal*, Pennsylvania State MTA (Philadelphia, 1886–?90) 5 vols., M, also W edn

205 *Opera Glass* (New York, 1886–?) 8 nos. in 1 vol., W

206 *Reading Musical Monthly* (Reading, PA, 1886–?) 1 no., M

207 *The Gleaner* (Pittsburgh, ?1886–?1900) M

208 *The People's Educational Quarterly* (Dayton, VA, 1886/7–?) 1 vol., Q

209 *Worch's Musical Monthly* (Washington, DC, 1886–?97) 131 nos., M

210 *Ziarno: wydawnictwo poświecone miłośnikom muzyki i śpiewu narodowego oraz życiu społeczno-towarzyskiemu Polaków w Ameryce* [The seed: pubn dedicated to lovers of music, folksong, and the community life of Poles in America], from 1890 Soc. of Pol. Singers (Chicago, 1886–1903) M [in Pol.; incorp. into 315]

211 *Gatcomb's Banjo and Guitar Gazette*, from 1892 *Gatcomb's Musical Gazette* (Boston, 1887–?99) 12 vols., M, later B

212 *Illinois Music Teachers Association: Proceedings* (Lincoln, IL, 1887–?1920) 32 vols.

213 *Preacher and Chorister* (Tipton, MO, 1887–?9) 3 vols., M

214 *The Clef: published in the Interests of Organists, Choir Leaders, Vocal Societies, and the Music Public Generally* (New York, 1887–?9) 3 vols., M

215 *The Courier*, later also *Cincinnati College of Music Courier*, new ser. (Cincinnati, 1887–93) 11 vols., M [contd from 174]

216 *Concert-goer* (Denver, 1888–97) 218 nos.

217 *Lights of Music and the Stage* (New York, 1888) 1 no., M

218 *Musical Enterprise* [brass bands, orchs, news of the AFM] (Camden, NJ, and Atlantic City, NJ, 1888/9–1930/31) 43 vols., M

219 *Tam-tam: Almanach* (Chicago, 1888–97) 10 vols., Y

220 *The Muse: Music, Drama, Literature, Social Science* (Minneapolis, 1888/9–1889/90) 2 vols., M

221 *The Musical Messenger* (Washington, DC, 1888–?9) 2 vols., M

222 *Voice Quarterly*, from Jan 1892 *Vocalist* [science and art in music] (New York, 1888/9–1897) 13 vols., Q, from Jan 1892 M; bibl.

223 *Musical Advance* [also art, literature, drama] (Minneapolis, 1889) 6 nos., M

224 *The Violin* (Boston, 1889–?90) 2 vols., M

225 *Universal Song*, Amer. Tonic Sol-fa Assn and Coll. of Music (New York, 1889–?92) 2 vols., mainly Q

226 *J. E. Henning's Elite Banjoist and Guitar and Mandolin News* (Chicago, 1890/91) 2 nos., Q; music

227 *Musical Gazette* (from May 1891 *Magazine*) (Brooklyn, NY, 1890/91–1892) 2 vols., M, later Q; music

228 *New York Musical Era* (New York, 1890–?91) 2 vols.

229 *Organ* (New York, 1890–1914) 150 nos. in 25 vols., B

230 *Organist's Journal* (Arlington, NJ, and New York, 1890–1903) 14 vols., M

231 *Philadelphia Music and Drama* (Philadelphia, 1890–?92) 3 vols., W; music

232 *The Music Trades*, Feb–July 1929 *Music Trades*, ed. J. C. Freund (New York, 1890–1971; Englewood, NJ, 1972–/*Rmp*) W, from Feb 1929 M [incorp. 486 in 1933]

233 *At Home and Abroad: a Monthly Review devoted to Music and the Kindred Arts* (New York, 1891–?5) 8 vols., M; music

234 *Denver Music and Drama* (Denver, 1891–?) 36 nos., W

235 *Deutsch-amerikanische Chor-Zeitung* [music in church, school, home] (Chicago, 1891/2–1893/4) 3 vols., M [in Ger.]

236 *Home* (from Aug 1898 *Choir*) *Music Journal* (Logansport, IN, 1891/2–1899/1900) 9 vols., M

237 *Musical Advocate* (Oxford, GA, 1891/2) 9 nos. in 1 vol.

238 *Music: a Monthly Magazine* (Chicago, 1891/2–1902 except May–Aug 1902) 22 vols., M [incorp. into 342]

239 *Salmisten: kirkelig sång og musiktidende för kirker, skoler, hjem, og foreninger* (Chicago, 1891/2–?) 5 nos., M [in Swed.]

240 *The American Musical Times* (Youngstown, OH, 1891–?5) 5 vols., M

241 *The Musical Age: a Monthly Magazine devoted to Music and Kindred Arts* (Jersey City, NJ, 1891–?) 1 no., M

242 *The Musical Messenger: a Monthly Magazine* (Cincinnati, from 1895 also New York, 1891–1917) 13 vols., M

243 *The Music Review* (Chicago, 1891/2–1894) 4 vols., M [contd as 330]

244 *Utah Musical Journal* [also art, literature, drama] (Salt Lake City, 1891–?) 1 no., M

245 *American Musical Journal: a Literary Monthly devoted to the Mutual Advancement of the Interests of the Musical Producer and Consumer* (Chicago, 1892–?) 4 nos., M

246 *Gittit: manadtlig sangtidning för hemmet, söndagsskolan, och församlingen* (Minneapolis, 1892–?1903) 17 vols., M; music [originally only music, later incl. news, reviews; in Swed.]

247 *M.T.N.A. Messenger*, from March 1898 *The Messenger*, Music Teachers Natl Assn (Wellesley Hills, MA, 1892–1905) 6 vols., Q, later B, from April 1903 W

248 *School Record*, Michigan MTA (Detroit, 1892–?9) 7 vols., M

249 *The Cabinet: a Journal of Music, Education, Art*, Michigan MTA (Detroit, 1892–3) 10 nos., M, B in sum.

250 *The Organ* (Boston, 1892/3–1893/4) 2 vols., M

251 *The Violin World* [strings] (New York, 1892–1927/8) 35 vols., M, later B

252 *Amusement Globe: devoted to the Dramatic, Theatrical, Musical, Vaudeville, and Circus Professions* (New York, 1893/4–?) 23 nos. in 1 vol., W

253 *Choir Herald* (Chicago, 1893–7) 5 vols., M; music [contd as 291]

254 *Freund's Weekly* (from 2 Dec 1893 *Musical Weekly*), from 15 Jan 1896 *The Musical Age* (New York, 1893–1914) 85 vols., W

255 *Musical Notes: a Monthly Journal for the Studio and Home* (New York, 1893–?) 2 nos., M

256 *Musical Recorder* (Brooklyn, NY, 1893–?) 1 no., M

257 *National Home and Music Journal* (Chicago, 1893–?5) 3 vols., M

258 *Opera* (New York, 1893–?5) 68 nos. in 2 vols., B

259 *The Dominant* (Philadelphia and New York, 1893–1925 except Dec 1914) 32 vols., M; music [incorp. into 198]

260 *Wing's Musical Journal* (Lynn, MA, 1893–?) 2 nos., M

261 *Ashmall's* (running title *The*) *Monthly Vocalist* (Arlington, NJ, 1894) 2 nos., M
262 *Billboard Advertising*, from 1 Nov 1896 *The Billboard*, from 9 Jan 1961 *Billboard Music Week*, from 5 Jan 1963 *Billboard: the International Music-record* (from 7 June 1969 *Music-record-tape*) *Newsweekly* (Cincinnati, later New York, 1894/5–1971; Los Angeles, 1971–/*Rmp*) W; song charts; c.i. 1972–3; suppls.: *Billboard: Index of the New York Legitimate Stage*, 1931/2–1938/9, Y; *Band Yearbook*, 1939–42, Y; *Talent and Tunes on Music Machines*, 1939–41, Y, which later became a separate pubn: *Who's Who in the World of Music*, 1961–, Y
263 *Harmony*, People's Choral Union and Singing Classes (New York, 1894/5–1899/1900, 1903) 5 vols., M [contd as 349]
264 *Musical News* (New York, 1894/5) 4 nos. in 1 vol., M
265 *New England Conservatory Quarterly* (from Aug 1898 *Magazine*) (Boston, 1894/5–1903/4) 10 vols., Q, from 1898/9 5 nos. Y in school term; music; bibl. [contd from 178; contd as 407]
266 *Opera* (Chicago, 1894–5) 2 vols., W, 1895 F
267 *Opera Glass: a Musical and Dramatic Magazine* (Boston, 1894–8) 5 vols., M
268 *Pacific Coast Musical Journal*, from May 1895 *California Musical Journal* (San Francisco, 1894/5–?1896) 3 vols., M
269 *The Cadenza*, Amer. Guild of Banjoists, Mandolinists, and Guitarists (Kansas City, 1894/5–1899/1900; New York, 1900/01–1907/8; Boston, 1908/9–1924) 31 vols., B, from Sept 1900 M; music [incorp. *The Concerto* in 1901; incorp. into 399]
270 *The Choir Leader* (Dayton, OH, 1894/5–?) M; music
271 *The Two-step*, after 1900 *Dancing Master* (Buffalo, NY, and Chicago, 1894–1935) 44 vols., M except July–Aug
272 *American Federation of Musicians: Official Proceedings* (St. Louis, 1895–)
273 *Baton: a Monthly Journal devoted to Western Music Matters* (Kansas City, 1895–?7) 4 vols., M, later B
274 *Ev'ry Month: an Illustrated Magazine of Literature and Popular Music*, incorp. 329 in Oct 1902 to form *Ev'ry Month and Piano Music Magazine* (New York, 1895–1903) 15 vols., M
275 *Levassor's Musical Review* (Cincinnati, 1895–?) M
276 *Musical Clipper* (Philadelphia, 1895) 6 nos. in 1 vol., M
277 *Pianist*, from July 1896 *Pianist and Organist*, Amer. Guild of Organists (New York, 1895–8) 5 vols., M; music
278 *The Looker-on: Musical, Dramatic, Literary* (New York, 1895–7) 4 vols., M
279 *The Musical Leader and Concert-goer*, from 1907 (no.14) *The Musical Leader: with which is incorporated the Concert-goer of New York*, from 1910 (no.14) *The Musical Leader: a Weekly Record of Musical Events, Dramatic, and Society Topics*, from 1933 (no.24) *Musical Leader* (Chicago, 1895–1967) 99 vols., W, from 1934 F, later M, S, from Oct 1942 M [incorp. 292 in 1903]
280 *The Phonograph Record* (Chicago, 1895–?6) 2 vols., M
281 *The Song Writer* (New York, 1895–?6) 16 nos., M
282 *American Choir* (New York, 1896–9) 78 nos.
283 *Jennings Musical Tidings* (Cincinnati, 1896–?) M
284 *Missouri Music Teachers Association: Official Report of the Annual Convention* (Kansas City, 1896–?1918) Y
285 *Musical Trio* (Waco, TX, 1896–1917) 21 vols., M
286 *Musical Worker: a Journal of Music, Musical Literature, and Social Ethics* (Atlanta, 1896–?) 2 nos., M
287 *The Allegretto* [bands, orchs], Natl League of Musicians of the US (Minneapolis, 1896/7–?1897/8) 2 vols., M, sometimes B
288 *The Musician* [educ.] (Philadelphia, 1896–1903; Boston, 1903–18; New York, 1919–48) 53 vols., M; music [incorp. 129 in Dec 1903, incorp. 336 in 1904]
289 *American* (from April 1898 *Conkey's*) *Home Journal*, Amer. Musical Assn (Chicago, 1897–1903) 11 vols., M
290 *American Musician*, AFM (Cincinnati, 1897–?1903) 7 vols., M
291 *Choir Herald*, new ser. (Dayton, OH, 1897/8–1915/16) 19 vols., M; music [contd from 253]
292 *Concert-goer*, NY State MTA (New York, 1897–1903) 220 nos., M, from May 1899 W; suppl.: *Report of the Annual Meeting*, 1899–1902, Y [contd from 91; incorp. into 279]
293 *Der Kirchenchor* (Dayton, OH, 1897/8–1929/30) 33 vols., M [in Eng., Ger.]
294 *Musical Critic* (Chicago, 1897/8–1899/1900) 3 vols., M
295 *Musical News* (St. Louis, 1897/8–?) 11 nos. in 1 vol., M
296 *School Music: a Journal devoted to Music Education* (New York, 1897) 2 nos., M
297 *The Aeolian Quarterly* (New York, 1897/8–1899) 3 vols., Q
298 *The Chicago Trio: a Banjo, Guitar, and Mandolin Journal devoted to the Interests of Teachers, Players, and Makers* (Chicago, 1897/8–?) 4 nos., B
299 *The Herald of Music* (St. Louis, 1897–?) 3 nos., M
300 *The Musical Herald*, W. W. Kimball Company (Chicago, 1897–1916) mainly M
301 *The Musical Temple: a Monthly devoted to the Interests of Mandolin, Guitar, and Banjo Players* (Philadelphia, 1897) ?1 no.
302 *Musical America* [*MusAm*] ed. J. C. Freund (New York, 1898–9, 1905–64/*Rm*) 84 vols., W, from 1929 varies between S and M, from Feb 1960 M [suspended June 1899–Oct 1905]; directory issue, 1930–/*Rmp*, Y [incorp. into 681]
303 *Musical Mirror*, Indiana MTA (Lafayette, IN, 1898–?1901) 4 vols., M except Aug
304 *Music and Literature* (Frederick, MD, 1898–?9) 2 vols., M
305 *Music Review*, pubd Ditson (Boston, 1898–1900) 3 vols., M
306 *Music, Song, and Story* (New York, 1898/?9 except April 1898 to March 1899) 4 nos. in 1 vol., M
307 *Symphony: a Magazine devoted Entirely to Music in Every Form* (Cleveland, 1898–?) 1 no., M
308 *The Musical Gem* (San Francisco, 1898–?) 1 no., M
309 *American Phonographic and Literary Journal* (Allentown, PA, 1899–?1900) 2 vols.
310 *Brainard's Musical* (New York and Chicago, 1899–?1909) Q
311 *Choir: a Monthly Journal of Church Music* (Cincinnati, 1899–1922) 23 vols., M
312 *Choral Society Bulletin* (Washington, DC, 1899–)
313 *Edgewood* (from 1900/01 *Columbia*) *Music and Home Journal* (Cincinnati, 1899/1900–1902/3) 4 vols., M
314 *Gleanings from the World of Music* (Cleveland, 1899–?) 1 vol., B
315 *Harmonia* (Buffalo, NY, from 1903 Bay City, MI, 1899/1900–1905) 6 vols., M [in Pol.; incorp. 210; contd as 361]
316 *Music and Childhood* (Chicago, 1899/1900) 11 nos. in 1 vol., M
317 *Music Life* (New York, 1899/1900–1904/5) 6 vols., M except July–Aug
318 *Music Lover* (Worcester, MA, 1899–?) 6 nos. in 1 vol., M
319 *Piano, Organ, and Musical Instrument Workers' Official Journal*, Piano, Organ, and Musical Instrument Workers of America (Chicago, 1899–1911) 13 vols., M
320 *The Choir Journal* (Boston, 1899–1908) 240 nos., S; music
321 *Western Music Trades Journal* (Los Angeles, 190?–1910) [contd as 413]
322 *American Music Journal*, Natl Qualified Music Teachers League (Cleveland, 1900–07) 7 vols.
323 *Chicago Music Journal* (Chicago, 1900–01) 2 vols., M
324 *F.O.G. Mandolin, Banjo, and Guitar Journal*, Qualified Teachers League (Cleveland, 1900–?04) 4 vols.
325 *Key Note: a Magazine of Music, Society, and the Stage* (Elmira, NY, 1900/01–1903/04) 4 vols.
326 *Lyra: populäre Monatsschrift für Musik, Kunst, Wissenschaft, und Leben*, Verband Deutscher Chordirigenten Amerikas (New York, 1900/01) 1 vol., M [in Ger., sometimes in Eng.]
327 *School Music* (Indianapolis, 1900–02) 3 vols. [incorp. into 328]
328 *School Music Monthly*, from 1908 *School Music* (Quincy, IL, 1900; Keokuk, IA, 1901–33; Mount Morris, IL, 1934; Chicago, 1935–6) 36 vols., M; c.i. 1927–31, 1932–4, 1935–6; music, Jan 1905 [incorp. 327 Feb 1902]
329 *The J. W. Pepper Piano Music Magazine* (Philadelphia, 1900–02) 24 nos. in 4 vols. [incorp. into 274]
330 *The Music Review*, new ser. (Chicago, 1900/01) 1 vol., M except July–Aug [contd from 243]
331 *The Violinist* (Chicago, 1900–37 except Jan–Sept 1930 and 1932 to Sept 1935) 50 vols., M, from 1929 3–5 nos. Y, from 1935 Y, 1937 2 nos. Y; music, 1914 [incorp. into 364 from Sept 1905 to Sept 1908]
332 *Western Musician* [also drama] (Dixon, IL, 1900/01–?1906/7) 7 vols., M
333 *Bohémienne*, from 1903 *Musical* (from 1907 *Pacific Musical*, from 1931/3 (no.3) *Pacific Coast Music*) *Review* (San Francisco, 1901–1931/3 except Oct 1928 to July 1930) 57 vols.
334 *Musical Century* (Springdale, PA, 1901–?) 2 nos., M
335 *Musical Life* (New York, 1901/2–1903/4) 3 vols., M
336 *Musical World* (Boston, 1901–4/*Rm*) 4 vols., M; music [incorp. into 288]
337 *Music and Stage: New York, London, Paris* (New York, 1901/2) 2 nos.
338 *Music of the Future and of the Present*, from 1901/7 (no.4) *Das Musizieren der Zukunft*, ed. F. H. Clark (Chicago, from 1901/7 (no.4) Berlin and Chicago, 1901/7–1912) 2 vols. [in Eng., from 1901/7 (no.4) in Ger.]
339 *National Federation of Music Clubs: Biennial Proceedings* (Chicago, 1901–34) 18 vols., biennially [contd as 547]
340 *School Music Success* (Paterson, NJ, 1901–?2) 3 vols.
341 *The Church* (from Nov 1904 *New Music Review and Church*) *Music Review*, Amer. Guild of Organists (New York, 1901/2–1934/5/*Rm*) 404 nos., M; music; bibl.
342 *The Philharmonic: a Magazine devoted to Music, Art, Drama*, from April 1903

The Muse [contemporary arts] (Chicago, 1901–3) 3 vols., Q, in 1902 6, in 1903 5 nos. Y [incorp. 146 in Jan 1903; incorp. 238 in Feb 1903]

343 *Philharmonic Review: a Monthly Magazine devoted to Musical Subjects and the Official Program of the Great Philharmonic Course*, from 1939 *Magazine of Celebrities* (Los Angeles, 1902–) M

344 *Profession*, from 1904 *Musical Profession: a Magazine for Teachers and Students of Music* (New York, 1902–4) 3 vols.

345 *The Negro Music Journal* [educ.], Washington Conservatory of Music (Washington, DC, 1902–3/*R*) 2 vols., M

346 *Calendar of the University School of Music*, U. of Michigan (Ann Arbor, ⟨1903/4–1904/5⟩ 1904–5) 2 vols., Y

347 *Exchange Journal of Music*, from May 1904 *Journal of Music* (New York, 1903/4–?1904/5) 2 vols.

348 *Focus: a Weekly devoted to the Musical and Theatrical World* (New York, 1903–?4) 3 vols., W

349 *Harmony: a Bulletin of the P.S.M.* [People's Singing Movement], from March 1904 *Harmony: devoted to the Interests of the People's Choral Union and People's Singing Classes*, new ser. (New York, ?1903/4–1904/5) 2 vols., M, later O [contd from 263]

350 *Masters in Music: a Monthly Magazine*, ed. D. G. Mason (ii) (Boston, 1903–5/*R*) 36 pts in 6 vols., M; music

351 *Mirth and Music* (New York, 1903–?)

352 *University School of Music Record*, U. of Michigan (Ann Arbor, MI, 1903–?) M

353 *Conservatory: a Journal devoted to Music and the Kindred Arts* (New York, 1904–9) 6 vols.

354 *Knocker: a Humorous Musical Monthly* (New York, 1904–?) 1 no., M

355 *Musical Messenger* (Chicago and Cincinnati, 1904–24) 20 vols., M [incorp. into 399 and 455]

356 *Music and Story* (Florence, CO, 1904–?) 1 no., M

357 *Music Land Messenger* [children's music educ.] (Chicago, 1904–?) 2 nos., B

358 *Music Student* (Springfield, MO, 1904/6–?) 7 nos. in 1 vol., O

359 *Southern Music Teachers Association: Quarterly Bulletin* (Washington, DC, 1904–?) Q

360 *Church Music* (Philadelphia, 1905/6–1908/9) 4 vols., Q, from 1906/7 B; music; bibl.

361 *Harmonia*, Choral Soc. of Milwaukee (Milwaukee, 1905–10) [in Pol.; contd from 315]

362 *Institute: a Periodical devoted to Singers and the Voice* (Chicago, 1905/6–1906/7) 2 vols.

363 *Monthly Music Folio* (Memphis, 1905–?) M

364 *Musical Standard: incorporating The Violinist* (Chicago, 1905–8) 9 vols., M; music [incorp. 331 from Sept 1905 to Sept 1908; contd as 391]

365 *Talking Machine World*, from Aug 1930 *Radio Music Merchant*, from May 1932 *Radio-merchant* (New York, 1905–34/*Rmp*) 30 vols. [incorp. 141 as a section March–May 1933]

366 *The Neume*, New England Conservatory of Music (Boston, 1905–13) 9 vols.

367 *Triangle of Mu Phi Epsilon* (1905–) Q

368 *Aus der musikalischen Welt* (New York, 1906/7–1908/9) 3 vols., Q; music [in Ger., sometimes in Eng.]

369 *Music* (from 1910 (no.4) *The Piano Magazine and Music*) *Industry*, incorp. *Piano Trade* in Oct 1915 to form *Piano Trade Magazine*, from 1929 (no.5) *Piano Trade and Radio Magazine*, from 1932 (no.8) *Piano Trade Magazine*, from 1953 (no.4) *PTM: Piano Trade Magazine*, from 1965 *PTM Magazine*, from 1971 *World of Music* (New York, ?1906–) M, from 1967 F, from May 1968 M [incorp. 132 in March 1930]

370 *Studies in Musical Education, History, and Aesthetics: Papers and Proceedings of the Music Teachers National Association*, 1927 *Papers and Proceedings of the Music Teachers National Association*, from 1928 *Volume of Proceedings of the Music Teachers National Association* [*MTNAP*] (Hartford, CT, 1906–28; Oberlin, OH, 1929–38; Pittsburgh, 1939–50/*Rm*) 44 vols., Y; c.i. 1906–15, 1918–29, 1930–36, 1937–46 [contd from 119]

371 *Symphony*, Southern MTA and Georgia MTA (Atlanta, 1906–?) 1 no., M

372 *The Green-room-book, or Who's Who on the Stage* (New York and London, from 1907 London, 1906–9) 4 vols., Y

373 *Western Musical Herald* (Des Moines and Chicago, 1906–?16) 9 vols.

374 *Edward MacDowell Memorial Association* (from 1920 *Association, Inc.*): *Report* (later *Annual Report*) (New York, 1907–) Y

375 *Fortnightly: a Journal of Music, Letters, Painting, and General Civic Interest* (Philadelphia, 1907/8) 7 nos., F

376 *Musical Medium* (New York, 1907–?8) 17 nos. in 2 vols., M

377 *Musician's Chronicle* (New York, 1907–?) 4 nos. in 1 vol., O

378 *Musician's Monthly Magazine* (Cleveland, 1907–?9) 3 vols., M

379 *Music Supervisors' National Conference: Journal of Proceedings*, from 1931 *Yearbook of the Music Supervisors'* (from 1934 *Educators*) *National Conference* (Madison, WI, 1907–26; Chapel Hill, NC, 1927–8; Ithaca, NY, 1929–30; Chicago, 1931–1939/40) 31 vols. to 1938, 1939/40 pubd as vol.xxx, Y; c.i. 1925–38

380 *Music World* (Philadelphia, 1907–?8) 3 vols.

381 *Steinway Bulletin* (New York, 1907) 8 nos. except no.6, M

382 *The Musical Observer* (New York, 1907–31) 30 vols., M; music [incorp. into 155]

383 *American Music Society: Bulletin* (New York, 1908) 2 nos.

384 *Der Barde: devoted to Art, Music, Literature* (New York, 1908–9) 2 vols. [in Ger.]

385 *L'allegro: a Magazine of Music and Literature* (Aurora, NY, and Washington, DC, 1908–?) 4 nos. in 1 vol., M

386 *Musical Light* [also poetry] (Fort Worth, TX, 1908–15) 8 vols.

387 *Saugerties Musical Review* (Saugerties, NY, 1908/9) 1 vol., M

388 *The American Bandsman* (New York, 1908/9–?) 5 nos. in 1 vol.

389 *The Crescendo*, Amer. Guild of Banjoists, Mandolinists, and Guitarists (Boston, 1908/9–1928; Hartford, CT, 1929–33) 25 vols., M; music

390 *The Journal of School Music* (Chicago, 1908/9) 9 nos. in 1 vol., M

391 *The Music News*, from 1912 (no.35) *Music News* (Chicago, 1908/9–1952) 44 vols., W, from 1933 (no.25) M, later W, B, from 1935 B Oct–June and M July–Sept, from 1945 M [contd from 364]

392 *Tone: the Only Musical Magazine* (New York, 1908–?) 1 no., M

393 *C. G. Conn. Ltd. Musical Truth*, from 1928 (no.45) *Musical Truth* (Elkhart, IN, 1909–41) 30 vols., O

394 *Musical Messenger* [opera, concerts] (New York, 1909) 2 nos. in 1 vol., M

395 *Musical Register: America's Leading Musical Journal* (Chicago, 1909–10) 2 vols.

396 *Musical Squibs* (New York, 1909–?) 2 nos., W

397 *Opera News* (Philadelphia and New York, 1909/10–1920) 11 vols., W aut.–spr. [contd as 478]

398 *Pan Pipes of Sigma Alpha Iota*, Sigma Alpha Iota Intl Music Fraternity for Women (Menosha, WI, later Sarasota, FL, 1909–) 4 nos. Y

399 *Jacobs' Orchestra Monthly*, incorp. 355 in March 1924 to form *Jacobs' Orchestra Monthly: with which is combined the Musical Messenger*, incorp. 269 in April 1924 to form *Jacobs' Orchestra Monthly and The Cadenza*, from Nov 1927 *Jacobs' Orchestra Monthly* (Boston, 1910–41) 32 vols., M; music

400 *Kronika muzyczna* (New York, 1910–?) [in Pol.]

401 *Music Era* [bands, orchs] (Boston, 1910–16) 7 vols., M

402 *Psycho-vowel Herald and Voice Building* (New York, 1910–?) 1 no.

403 *Studio: a Monthly Magazine devoted to the Interests of Music Teachers, Music Students, and all Music Lovers*, Michigan MTA (Detroit, 1910–14) 5 vols., M

404 *Music* [news, criticism] (Boston, 1911/12) 18 nos. in 1 vol.

405 *Musical Advocate: a Journal of Music, Poetry, and Chaste Literature* (Little Rock, 1911–?14) 4 vols.

406 *Music Teachers Association of California: Official Bulletin* (San Francisco, 1911–?35) 25 vols.

407 *New England Conservatory Review* (from Sept 1913 *Magazine and Alumni Review*, from Dec 1914 *Magazine–Review*), Alumni Assn (Boston, 1911–18) 8 vols., Y, from 1913 2 nos. Y, from Sept 1913 Q [contd from 265; contd as 470]

408 *Pacific Coast Musician* (Los Angeles, 1911–48) 37 vols., M, from Sept 1923 W, from Feb 1935 S; music; yb: *Year Book*, 1925–46

409 *Player Piano*, from March 1913 *Player Piano Journal*, from 1917 *Piano Journal* (New York, 1911/12–1918/19) 8 vols., M [incorp. into 456]

410 *Scherzo: a Quarterly Bulletin of New Music* (New York, Boston, and Chicago, 1911–?) 1 vol., Q

411 *Thoth-Apollo Magazine: devoted to Speech, Art, and Music* (Columbus, OH, 1911–?) 1 no., M

412 *True Tone Musical Journal*, 1940 (no.4) *The Buescher: True Tone Musical Journal* (Elkhart, IN, 1911–?41) 30 vols., Q

413 *Western Music* (from ?1927 *Music and Radio Trades Journal*, from Nov 1931 *Radio and Refrigeration Journal*) (Los Angeles, 1911–?33) 14 vols. [contd from 321]

414 *Art and Music* (Cleveland, 1912/17) 17 nos. in 1 vol.

415 *Harvard Musical Review* (Cambridge, MA, 1912/13–1915/16) 4 vols., M except Aug–Sept; music

416 *Institute of Music Pedagogy: Monthly News Letter* (Northampton, MA, ?1912–15; Yonkers, NY, 1916–18; Flint, MI, 1919; Hartford, CT, 1920–28) 17 vols., M, from 1921 Q

417 *Manager and Musician* (Chicago, 1912–13) 6 nos. in 1 vol., O

418 *Musical Progress* (Washington, DC, 1912–?14) 3 vols.

419 *The Musical World* (1912 (nos.7–8) *Monitor*, from 1912 (no.9) *World*, from 1913 (no.7) *Monitor and World*, from 1915 (no.5) *Monitor*), 1912 to June 1913 Natl Assn of Organists, 1913–14 Natl Assn of Teachers of Singing, from Sept 1913 Natl Fed. of Music Clubs (Chicago, 1912–17; New York, 1917–24) 14 vols., O, from 1913 M; music

420 *Wisconsin Music Teacher*, Wisconsin MTA (Madison, WI, 1912/13–1918/19) 7 vols.
421 *Century Opera Weekly*, from no.8 *Opera* (New York, 1913) 13 nos. in 1 vol., W
422 *Foyer: Music and Drama* (Philadelphia, 1913/14–?1915/16) 3 vols.
423 *Music and Health* [music therapy] (Croton-on-Hudson, NY, 1913) 3 nos., Q
424 *Musicians' Journal*, MTA of California (San Francisco, 1913–15; new ser. 1929/30) 3 vols., new ser. 4 nos., W
425 *Music Magazine and Musical Stage Review* (Boston, 1913) 4 nos. in 1 vol., W
426 *The Musical Advance* (New York, 1913/14–1948 except June–Sept 1913) 36 vols., mainly M
427 *Tuner's Magazine* (Cincinnati, 1913–?16) 4 vols., M
428 *United States Service Musician* (Elkhart, IN, 1913) 3 nos. in 1 vol., M
429 *Volunteer Choir* (Dayton, OH, 1913–?39) 27 vols., M
430 *Christiansen's Ragtime Review*, from 1916 (no.6) *Ragtime Review* (Chicago, 1914/15–?1917/18) 4 vols.
431 *Console*, Natl Assn of Organists (New York, 1914–?19) 5 vols.
432 *International Music and Drama*, Bertrand De Berny's Opera and Oratorio Soc. (New York, 1914/15–1915/16) 4 vols., W
433 *Minnesota Music* (St. Paul, 1914–19) 6 vols.
434 *Music Bulletin* (New York, 1914/15–1931/2) 17 vols., M, from 1916/17 Q; music
435 *Music Supervisors'* (from 1934/5 *Educators*) *Journal* [from 1934/5 *MEJ*], Music Supervisors' Natl Conference, later MENC (Madison, WI, . . . 1914/15–/*Rp*) Q, from 1919/20 5, from 1934/5 6 nos. Y, from 1966/7 M except June–Aug; bibl. [incorp. 461 in 1926]
436 *Opera Magazine* (New York, 1914–16) 3 vols., M
437 *Gospel Choir* (Philadelphia, 1915–?) M
438 *Illinois Music Teachers Association: Bulletin* (Lincoln, IL, 1915; new ser. 1916–?18) 1 vol., new ser. 4 vols.
439 *Musical Art*, Inst. of Musical Art (Detroit, 1915/16–1916/17) 2 vols.
440 *Musical Messenger* (Pittsburgh, 1915/16) 6 nos. in 1 vol.
441 *Music and Musicians* (Brooklyn, NY, 1915–22 except July–Oct 1920 and early 1921) 8 vols., S, from 1916 (no.5) M, from 1918 W, later S, M; music
442 *Music and Musicians* [in the Northwest] (Seattle, 1915–37) 23 vols., M
443 *Music Lover* (Philadelphia, 1915–?) 4 nos. in 1 vol., M
444 *Music Merchant* (New York, 1915–?) 1 no.
445 *Music Student* (Los Angeles, later Chicago, 1915/16–1916/17) 4 vols., M
446 *Music Survey* (Jacksonville, IL, 1915–17) 2 vols. [in Amer. Braille]
447 *Sharps and Flats* (Chicago, 1915–?)
448 *Southern Musician*, Maryland Musical Assn (Baltimore, 1915–?)
449 *The Catholic Choirmaster*, Soc. of St. Gregory of America (Baltimore, 1915–17; Philadelphia, 1917–38; Arlington, VA, . . . Buffalo, 1938–64) 50 vols., 3 nos. Y, from 1916 Q; music [incorp. into 106]
450 *The Musicale* (from 1930 (no.10) *Southwestern Musicale*), Texas MTA (Dallas, TX, and Arlington, VA, 1915–33) 19 vols., M [contd as 541]
451 *The Musical Quarterly* [*MQ*], ed. O. G. T. Sonneck, pubd Schirmer (New York, 1915–/*Rp*) Q; bibl.; c.i. 1915–59, 1960–64 [Americana index to *MQ* 1915–57 in 693, 1958 (no.2)]
452 *The Wheel of Delta Omicron*, Delta Omicron Intl Music Fraternity (Columbus, OH, 1915–) Q
453 *United Musician* [bands, orchs, publishers] (New York, 1915–?) M
454 *Art and Artists*, from 1920/21 *All the Arts* (from 1921/2 *Arts, Commerce, and Government*), Detroit Orchestral Assn (Detroit, 1916–22) 4 vols., Q
455 *Jacobs' Band Monthly: a Music Magazine* (Boston, 1916–41) 26 vols., M; music [incorp. 355 in 1924]
456 *Mist*, from April 1920 *MIST: Musical Instrument Sales Tips* (New York, ?1916–22) 13 vols., M [incorp. 409 in Feb 1919]
457 *Selmer's Modern Musician* (New York, 1916–?)
458 *Standard Player Monthly* [player piano industry] (New York, 1916–29) 15 vols., M
459 *The Phonograph*, from July 1919 *The Phonograph and Talking Machine Weekly*, from Sept 1928 *The Talking Machine and Radio Weekly*, from Dec 1933 *The Radio* (from May 1939 *Radio and Television*) *Weekly*, from Jan 1978 *Electronic Industry Weekly* (New York, 1916–) W
460 *Washington Musician*, Musicians' Protective Union (Washington, DC, 1916; new ser. 1929/30–?1931/2) 9 nos., new ser. 3 vols.
461 *Eastern School Music Herald*, Eastern Music Supervisors' Conference (Yonkers, NY, and Ithaca, NY, 1917/18–1925/6) 9 vols., 9 nos. Y [incorp. into 435]
462 *Teachers' Music Sentinel* (Hudson, NC, 1917/18–1918/19) 2 vols.
463 *The Tuneful Yankee*, from 1918 *Melody* (Boston, 1917–30) 14 vols., M
464 *The American Organist*, Amer. Guild of Organists (New York, 1918–70) 53 vols., M; bibl.
465 *Community Music Service Weekly*, from Sept 1919 *Community Music Service*, from Nov 1920 *Music Service*, Community Music League (New York, 1919–20) 2 vols., W
466 *Marley* (from May 1920 *Southern*, from Nov 1920 *Whittle*) *Musical Review* (Dallas, 1919–28) 7 vols., M
467 *Master Musician*, from Sept 1920 *American Musician and Sportsman Magazine* (Philadelphia, 1919–22) 2 vols.
468 *Musical Field* (New York, 1919–23) 5 vols.
469 *Music Lover: devoted to the Interests of Earnest Music Students* (Denver, 1919–?) 3 nos., B
470 *New England Conservatory News and Alumni Bulletin* (Boston, 1919–37) 18 vols., M [contd from 407; contd as 556]
471 *The American Organ Monthly* (from 1922 *Quarterly*) (Boston, 1920–34) 15 vols., M except July–Aug, from April 1922 Q [vols.i–viii mainly music]
472 *The Flutist* (Asheville, NC, 1920–29/*Rm*) 10 vols., M
473 *The Musical Digest* (New York, 1920/21–1948) 30 vols., W, from 1927 (no.8) M, from 1941 B, later Q, B, M [incorp. 518]
474 *Educational Music Magazine* (Chicago, 1921–57/*Rmp*) B [incorp. into 592]
475 *Eolian Review*, from 1925 *Eolus*, Natl Assn of Harpists (New York, 1921/2–1932) 11 vols., 3 nos. Y, from 1925 H, from 1927 Y
476 *Musical Forecast*, Musicians' Club of Pittsburgh (Pittsburgh, 1921–48) 45 vols., M
477 *Music and Poetry* (Chicago, 1921–?) 10 nos.
478 *Music Record and Opera News* (New York, 1921–) [contd from 397]
479 *Overture*, Musicians' Mutual Protective Assn, later Local 47 of the AFM (Los Angeles, ?1921–) M
480 *Baton*, Inst. of Musical Art (New York, 1922–32) 11 vols., M except sum.
481 *Baton: a Monthly Journal published in the Interests of Professional and Amateur Musicians* (Los Angeles, 1922–?3) 2 vols., M
482 *Music Box* (New York, 1922–34) 13 vols.
483 *Music Education* (Washington, DC, 1922–5) 4 vols.
484 *Music Lover's Magazine* (Portland, OR, 1922–?3) 2 vols.
485 *National Federation of Music Clubs: Official Bulletin*, from 1928/9 *The Music Club Magazine*, from 1931/2 *Music* (1960/63 *Showcase: Music*) *Clubs Magazine* (Peoria, IL, . . . 1922–/*Rm*) M except July–Aug, from 1925/6 8, from 1930/31 7 nos. Y, from 1931/2 B except July–Aug [in 2 issues: *Music U.S.A. Issue* and *International Issue*; incorp. 504 and 509 in 1931 and 762 in 1962]
486 *Sheet Music Trade News*, from April 1924 *Music Trade News* (New York, 1922–33) 11 vols. [incorp. into 232]
487 *Northwest* (from 1925 *Musical West and Northwest*) *Musician*, from 1927 *Musical West: Music and the Dance* (San Francisco, 1923–37) 14 vols., M
488 *Echo muzyczne* (Chicago, 1924–37) 14 vols., M [in Pol.]
489 *Music* (New York, 1924) 1 no., M
490 *Musical Booster* [bands, orchs] (Kansas City, 1924–?6) 2 vols.
491 *Music Hour* [bands, orchs, school and community music] (Chicago, 1924) 3 nos., M
492 *Music Journal for Music Lovers*, from Feb 1926 *Youth's Musical Companion* (Sharon, PA, 1924–?6) 3 vols.
493 *The League of Composers' Review*, from Nov 1925 *Modern Music* [*MM*] (New York, 1924–46/*R*) 23 vols., H, from 1925/6 4 nos. Y, 1946 Q; c.i. 1924–35; suppls., 1930, 1931
494 *Musical Merchandise* (from Feb 1953 *Merchandise Magazine*) (New York, 1925/6–1957) 65 vols., M [incorp. into 141]
495 *Music and Youth*, 1930 (no.7) *Music* (Boston, 1925/6–1929/30) M
496 *Pierre Key's* (1928–1929/30 *Key's International*) *Music Year Book* (New York, 1925/6–1938) 6 vols., O
497 *Sänger-Zeitung*, Fed. of Workers' Singing Socs. of the USA (New York, 1925–?48) M [in Eng., Ger.]
498 *Musical Washington* (Washington, DC, 1926) 3 nos.
499 *Musicians' Service Magazine*, from 18 June 1926 *Musicians'* (from Aug 1927 *Music*) *Magazine* (Chicago, 1926–9) 4 vols., W [contd as 517]
500 *Northwest Musical Herald* (St. Paul, 1926–34) 9 vols., 5 nos. Y
501 *Pianist Pedagogue*, from 1926 (no.5) *American Musician* (Chicago, 1926–?7) 2 vols.
502 *The* (from July 1927 *Music Lovers'*) *Phonograph Monthly Review* (Boston, 1926/7–1931/2) 6 vols., M [contd as 530]
503 *Woodwind* (1927 *Ensemble*) *News* (New York, 1926–7) 2 vols., Q
504 *Church Music Bulletin*, from 1929 *Music in Religious Education*, Natl Fed. of Music Clubs (Los Angeles, 1927–31) [incorp. into 485]
505 *Keynote*, Associated Glee Clubs of America (New York, 1927–65) 40 vols., 2, from 1946 3, from 1960 2 nos. Y
506 *Matthay News*, Amer. Matthay Assn (Springfield, OH, later Gettysburg,

PA, 1927–) 3 nos. Y
507 *Musical Philadelphia* (Philadelphia, 1927–8) 2 vols.
508 *Musical Record*, Natl Acad. of Music (New York, 1927–?) 2 nos., Q
509 *National Federation of Music Clubs: Junior Bulletin* (Merchantville, NJ, 1927–31) 5 vols., 9 nos. Y [incorp. into 485]
510 *Harmony: a Liberal Education in Music* (Chicago, 1928–?) 4 nos.
511 *Musical Re-education*, Soc. for Musical Re-education (New York, 1928) 1 no.
512 *The Fortnightly Musical Review* (New York, 1928) F
513 *Triad*, Ohio MEA (Fairfield, OH, later Elyria, OH, 1928–) 6 nos. Y
514 *Western Musical Times* (San Francisco, 1928–9) 9 nos., S
515 *Blues: Magazine of the New Rhythms* (Columbus, MS, 1929–30) 9 nos.
516 *The Baton: Magazine for School Music Supervisors* (Elkhart, IN, 1929–) O
517 *The School Band and Orchestra Musician*, from Sept 1930 *The School Musician* (from 1963 *Musician/Director & Teacher*), Natl School Band and Orchestral Assn, later Amer. School Band Directors' Assn (Chicago, 1929/30–1953/4; Joliet, IL, 1954/5–) M except July–Aug [contd from 499]
518 *Top Notes* (East Stroudsburg, PA, 1929–30) [incorp. into 473]
519 *Bulletin of the Folk-song Society of the Northeast* (Cambridge, MA, 1930–37/*R*) 12 nos., O; c.i.
520 *Disques* (Philadelphia, 1930/31–1932/3) 3 vols., M
521 *Musical Instrument Merchandiser* (Elkhart, IN, 1930/31–1931/2) 2 vols.
522 *Musical Review for the Blind* (New York, 1930–33) 42 nos. in 4 vols.
523 *Music World* (Los Angeles, 1930–?32) M
524 *Wisconsin School Musician*, Wisconsin School Music Assn (Madison, WI, 1930–) 4 nos. Y
525 *Lilly-Foster Bulletin*, from 1931 (no.3) *Foster Hall Bulletin* (Indianapolis, 1931–5, 1940) 12 nos., O
526 *New York Musicological Society Bulletin* (New York, 1931–4)
527 *The Collaborator* (New York, 1931) 2 nos., M
528 *Brooklyn and Long Island Musical Review*, from Feb 1934 *Musical* (from Sept 1936 *Music Teachers'*) *Review* (from sum. 1942 *Quarterly*) (New York, 1932–?48 except Feb–Sept 1932 and June 1942 to Nov 1943) 14 vols.
529 *Chord and Discord*, Bruckner Soc. of America (New York, 1932/9–1940/63, 1969, ?1979–) O; c.i. 1932/9–1940?, 1940/63
530 *The Music Lovers' Guide* [recordings, broadcasts] (New York, 1932/3–1934/5) 3 vols., M [contd from 502; contd as 548]
531 *The Sacred Musician* (South Pasadena, CA, 1932–)
532 *Hawaiian Guitarist*, from Feb 1935 *Guitarist*, from Nov/Dec 1942 *Music Today*, from 1945 *Music* (Cleveland, 1933–) M
533 *Musical Record* (Baltimore and Philadelphia, 1933/4) 1 vol., M
534 *National Association for American Composers and Conductors: Annual Bulletin* (New York, 1933/4–1969/70) 37 vols., Y
535 *Tempo*, United Hot Clubs of America (Los Angeles, 1933–40) 8 vols.
536 *Down Beat* [popular music, jazz, blues, rock] (Chicago, 1934–/*Rm*) M, from 1940 S, from 1946 F except July–Sept M; music O
537 *Musical Mercury* (New York, 1934–49) 17 vols., 5, from 1935 4 nos. Y; music [vols.vii–xvii only music]
538 *National Association of Schools of Music: Bulletin* (Cincinnati, 1934–?) 38 nos. to 1954, O; bibl.
539 *Notes for the Members of the Music Library Association*, from 1940 (no.7) *Notes for the Music Library Association* (Rochester, NY, later Buffalo, NY, 1934–8, 1940–42/*R*) 15 nos., O; bibl.; c.i. in 594 1943/4 (no.2) [contd as 594]
540 *Opera, Concert, and Symphony*, later *Counterpoint* (San Francisco, 1934–53) 18 vols.
541 *Southwestern Musician*, incorp. 543 in Sept 1954 to form *Southwestern Musician/Texas Music Educator*, Texas MEA, Texas MTA, etc. (Lubbock, TX, 1934–) [contd from 450]
542 *Tempo*, Music Educ. League (New York, 1934–5) 2 vols.
543 *Texas Music Educator*, Texas MEA (Borger, TX, 1934–54) [incorp. into 541]
544 *The Jewish Music Journal* (New York, 1934/5) 1 vol., B
545 *Music Front*, Pierre Degeyter Music Club of New York City (New York, 1935–?6) 2 vols.
546 *Music Vanguard: a Critical Review* (New York, 1935) 2 nos.
547 *National Federation of Music Clubs: Book of Proceedings* (Chicago, 1935–) [contd from 339]
548 *The American Music Lover*, Sept 1944 *The Listener's* (from Oct 1944 *American*) *Record Guide* (New York, 1935/6–1940/41; Pelham, NY, 1941/2–1956/7; New York, 1957–72; Melville, NY, 1976–) M; c.i. 1935–53 [contd from 530]
548*a* *Women in Music*, Orchestrette Classique, ed. F. Petrides (1935/6–1940) M
549 *Accordion World*, from 1958 *Accordion and Guitar World* (also *Magazine*) (Mount Kisco, NY, 1936–?71) M, later B
550 *Bulletin of the American Musicological Society* [*BAMS*] (New York, 1936–48) 13 nos., Y, during World War II O [contd as 633]
551 *Music Teachers National Association: Advisory Council Bulletin*, from 1938 *Bulletin* (Lincoln, NE, . . . 1936–50) 15 vols., O [contd as 679]
552 *Opera News*, Metropolitan Opera Guild (New York, 1936/7–) W in opera season, from 1939/40 also F in aut. and spr., from 1972/3 M except W in opera broadcast season
553 *Papers read* (from 1937 *read by Members of the American Musicological Society*) *at the Annual Meeting*, from 1940 *Papers of the American Musicological Society* [*PAMS*] (Oberlin, NY, . . . 1936–8, 1940–41) 5 vols., Y [contd as 860]
554 *The School Music News*, New York State School Music Assn (Little Falls, later Schenectady, NY, 1936/7–) M Sept–May
555 *Fretted Instrument News*, Amer. Guild of Banjoists, Mandolinists, and Guitarists (Providence, 1937–57) B
556 *New England Conservatory of Music, Boston: Alumni Quarterly* (Boston, 1937–) Q [contd from 470]
557 *ACA Bulletin*, from 1952 (no.1) *Bulletin of* (from 1959 (no.2) *of the*) *American Composers Alliance*, from 1961 (no.4) *American Composers Alliance Bulletin* [*ACAB*] (New York, 1938, 1952–65) 13 vols., mainly Q
558 *The Gramophone Shop, Inc., Record Supplement* (New York, 1938–54) 17 vols., M
559 *Violins*, from 1938 *Violins and Violinists*, from Feb 1942 *Violins' and Violinists' Magazine* (Evanston, IL, and Chicago, 1938–60) 168 nos. in 21 vols., O, from 1953 B
560 *Jazz Information* (New York, 1939–41) 2 vols.
561 *Keyboard* (New Haven, 1939–42) 4 vols., M except June–Sept
562 *Steinway Review of Permanent Music*, from Feb 1942 *Review of Permanent* (from 1950 *Recorded*) *Music* (New York, 1939–58 except June–July 1941 and Nov 1943) 21 vols. [incorp. into 155]
563 *The Journal of Musicology* (Greenfield, OH, 1939/40–1947) 5 vols., Q
564 *Composers and Authors of America*, Composers' and Authors' Assn of America (Cleveland and San Antonio, 1940–) Q
565 *Guild of Carillonneurs in North America: Bulletin* (Darien, CT, 1940–) O
566 *Listen: the Guide to Good Music* (New York, 1940–51) 12 vols., M
567 *Musical Facts* (Chicago, 1940–41) 2 vols.
568 *Musical Record* (New York, 1940–41) 2 vols., M
569 *Music and Rhythm* (Chicago, 1940–) O
570 *Music Makers of Stage, Screen, Radio* (Dunellen, NJ, 1940) 3 nos.
571 *Nebraska Music Educator*, Nebraska MEA (Lincoln, NE, 1940–) 4 nos. Y
572 *National Music Council Bulletin* (New York, 1940/41–) 3 nos. Y, from 1975/6 H
573 *The Jewish Music Forum: Bulletin*, Soc. for the Advancement of Jewish Musical Culture (New York, 1940–59) O
574 *Film Music Notes*, from 1951 *Film* (from 1956 *Film and TV*) *Music*, Natl Film Music Council (New York, 1941–) B
575 *Journal of Aesthetics and Art Criticism*, Amer. Soc. for Aesthetics (Baltimore, later Cleveland, 1941/2–) Q
576 *Recorder Review*, Amer. Recorder Soc. (New York, 1941–?3)
577 *The Musician* [Salvation Army] (Chicago, 1941–?) M
578 *Cadenza*, Montana MEA (Bozeman, MT, 1942–) 4 nos. Y
579 *Cash Box: the International Music-record Weekly* (New York, 1942–) W
580 *Illinois Music Educator*, Illinois MEA (Mendota, IL, later Urbana, IL, 1942–?72) 5 nos. Y, later Q
581 *International Records Agency: Bulletin* (Richmond Hill, NY, 1942–?) O
582 *Leschetizky Association of America: News Bulletin* (New York, 1942–) O
583 *Piano Technician*, Amer. Soc. of Piano Technicians (Delavan, WI, ?1942–57) 16 vols. [contd as 732]
584 *SESAC Music*, SESAC Inc. (New York, 1942–) M, later O
585 *Song Hits* (Derby, CT, 1942–) M; texts
586 *The Record Changer* [jazz] (Fairfax, VA, . . . 1942/3–1957) 15 vols., M
587 *Army and Navy Musician*, from March 1951 *Musicana*, US Army, Navy, and Air Force Bandsmen's Assn (New Haven, 1943–?)
588 *Classical Recordaid* (Philadelphia, 1943–?71) M
589 *Keyboard, Jr.: the Magazine for Young Musicians* (New Haven, 1943)
590 *Mississippi Notes* (later *Music Educator*), Mississippi MEA (Hattiesburg, MS, 1943–51) 9 vols., 4 nos. Y
591 *Music Dial: a Musician's Magazine* (New York, 1943–?)
592 *Music Publishers' Journal*, from 1946 (no.5) *The Music Journal*, from 1950 (no.4) *Music Journal* [*MJ*] (New York, etc., 1943–/*Rp*) 7, from 1951 8–10 nos. Y; c.i. 1943–8; suppl.: *MPJ New Music List*, from 1947 *Index to New Music*, 1946–9, 4 vols.; incl. *Music Journal* (from 1958 *Journal Annual*, from 1962 *Journal Anthology*, 1970–71 *Journal Annual Anthology*), 1957– [incorp. 474 in April 1957; incorp. 849 in Feb 1973]

593 *Northwest Music Review*, Washington State MTA and Washington MEA (Seattle, ?1943–9) 5 vols.
594 *Notes*, 2nd ser., Music Library Assn, ed. R. S. Hill to 1960 (Washington, DC, . . . 1943/4–/*Rp*) Q; bibl.; c.i. every 2 years 1943/4–1965/6; suppl.: *Notes for Members*, 1947–64, 36 nos. [contd from 539]
595 *Notes from Purdue University Musical Organizations*, later *P.M.O. Notes* (Lafayette, IN, 1943–) mainly M
596 *The Braille Musician*, Library of Congress, Division for the Blind and Physically Handicapped (Washington, DC, 1943–69) 27 vols., B [in Braille; contd as 873]
597 *Washington Music Review* (Seattle, 1943–?4) 10 nos., M
598 *American Musicological Society News Letter* (New York, 1944–)
599 *Gopher Music Notes*, Minnesota MEA (Alexandria, MN, 1944–) Q
600 *Music* (New York, 1944) 1 no.
601 *The* (from 1962/3 *The NATS*) *Bulletin*, Natl Assn of Teachers of Singing (New York, . . . 1944/5–1965/6/*Rp*) 22 vols., 5 nos. Y, from 1953/4 Q [contd as 915]
602 *The Score*, Amer. Soc. of Music Arrangers (Beverly Hills, CA, . . . 1944–?53 except Nov 1946 to Dec 1949 and April 1950 to 1952) 5 vols., B
603 *Tune-dex Digest*, from 1946 *Music Business*, Amer. Soc. of Disc Jockeys (New York, 1944–65) M [incorp. into 611]
604 *Music of the West*, Music Trades Assn of Southern California (Pasadena, CA, 1945–?50) M
605 *Musicology* (Middlebury, VT, 1945/7; New York, 1948/9) 2 vols., O; music, 1948/9
606 *A.T.G. Bulletin*, Accordion Teachers Guild (Minnetonka, MN, later Rochester, NY, 1946–) 10 nos. Y, later B
607 *Indiana Musicator*, Indiana MEA (Indianapolis, later Muncie, IN, 1946–) Q
608 *International Lyric Courier* [It. opera and musicians] (New York, 1946–) B [in Eng., It.]
609 *Journal of Renaissance and Baroque Music* [*JRBM*], from 1948 *Musica disciplina* [*MD*], Inst. of Renaissance and Baroque Music, from 1948 Amer. Inst. of Musicology in Rome, ed. A. Carapetyan and L. Schrade (Cambridge, MA, from no.2 New Haven, 1946/7; mainly Rome, 1948–) 4, from 1951 1–3 nos. Y, from 1953 Y; Fs Apel 1963, Fs Grout 1972; c.i. 1946–66; special section: *Renaissance News*, 1946/7, separately pubd as *Renaissance News* [*RN*] until aut. 1947
610 *Music Studio News* [culture and guitar music of Hawaii] (Oakland, CA, 1946–?) M
611 *Music Vendor*, from 1964 (no.881) *Record World* (New York, 1946/7–) W [incorp. 603 in 1965]
612 *The Guitar Review*, from 1961 (no.25) *Guitar Review*, Soc. of the Classic Guitar (New York, 1946/8–/*Rp*) O
613 *The Instrumentalist*, Assn for the Advancement of Instrumental Music (Glen Ellyn, IL, and Evanston, IL, 1946–1953/4; Evanston, 1954/5–/*Rm*) B Sept–May, from 1950/51 6 nos. Y Sept–May, from 1953/4 9–12 nos. Y, from 1963/4 M except July
614 *The Jewish Music News*, Jewish Music Council of Philadelphia (Philadelphia, 1946–?)
615 *The Jewish Music Notes*, Natl Jewish Music Council and Natl Jewish Welfare Board (New York, 1946–9) 4 vols., O [contd as section 3 of *Circle* from March 1950]
616 *The Songwriter's Review* (New York, 1946–) B
617 *The Year in American Music* (New York, 1946/7–1947/8) 2 vols., Y
618 *Western Music, Drama, and Art* (Phoenix, 1946–?8)
619 *Choir Guide, with Organ Guide*, from Feb 1952 *Choral and Organ Guide*, Intl Choir Directors' League (New York, 1947–?64) M
620 *Hymn Writers'* (from Nov/Dec 1948 *Lovers'*) *Magazine*, from July 1952 *Christian Etude*, Hymn Writers' (Lovers') Fellowship (Los Angeles, 1947–?) B
621 *Music Dealer* (from May 1955 *Industry*) (New York, 1947–55) 9 vols., M
622 *Pianist*, Intl Piano Teachers Assn (Erie, PA, 1947–)
623 *The Composer's News Record*, League of Composers (New York, 1947–9) 9 nos., O
624 *The School* (from 1959 *Music*, from 1969 *Florida Music*) *Director*, Florida MEA (Tampa, FL, 1947–) 11, from 1969 10, from 1982 5 nos. Y
625 *Woodwinds* (New York, 1947–8) 2 vols. [contd as 652]
626 *Allegro*, Associated Musicians of Greater New York (New York, ?1948–?) M
627 *Arpeggio Music Magazine* (Philadelphia, 1948/9) 7 nos., M
628 *ASSW News*, Amer. Soc. of Songwriters (Boston, 1948) 1 vol., O
629 *Bulletin* (April–Dec 1948 *Notes*) *for Northern California Music Libraries*, Music Library Assn (San Francisco, later San Jose, 1948–53; new ser. 1953) 6 vols., 8–10 nos. Y, new ser. 1 no.
630 *Catholic Music Educators Bulletin*, later *Musart*, Natl Catholic MEA (Hyattsville, MD, later Washington, DC, 1948–1975/6) 28 vols., 6, from 1971/2 3–5 nos. Y [contd as 1005]
631 *CMEA News*, California MEA (San Diego, CA, later Bakersfield, CA, 1948–?67) 20 vols., 6 nos. Y; c.i.
632 *Iowa Music Educator*, Iowa MEA (Des Moines, 1948–) Q
633 *Journal of the American Musicological Society* [*JAMS*], ed. O. Strunk, etc. (Boston, 1948; Richmond, VA, 1949–) 3 nos. Y; bibl.; Fs Kinkeldey 1960, Fs Beethoven 1970; c.i. 1948–66 [contd from 550]
634 *Just Records* (New York, 1948–50) 34 nos., M
635 *Life with Music*, Bureau of Musical Research (Hollywood, CA, 1948–?) M
636 *MTA California Keynotes*, MTA of California (Burbank, CA, ?1948–?) O
637 *Musical News*, AFM (San Francisco, ?1948–?) M
638 *Music and Art* (Fresno, CA, 1948–?)
639 *Music Magazine of Los Angeles* (Los Angeles, 1948–?)
640 *Music-Q* (Washington, DC, ?1948–?) M
641 *Music Reporter* [reprints of New York reviews] (New York, ?1948–?9) M
642 *News Letter of the American Symphony Orchestra League, Inc.*, from 1952 (no.5) *Newsletter*, from 1971 (no.5) *Symphony News* (from 1980 (no.3) *Magazine*) (Charleston, VA, 1948–61; Vienna, VA, 1962–82; Washington, DC, 1982–) B; directory issue, 1980–, Y
643 *Phonolog Reporter* (San Diego, CA, 1948–) W
644 *Plein jeu: the Quarterly Magazine devoted to the Electronic Organ* (Olympia, WA, 1948–?) Q
645 *Symphony* (New York, 1948–?) M except Aug
646 *Tennessee Musician* (Tampa, FL, 1948–) Q
647 *The Cantors Voice* [for Jewish cantors], Cantors Assembly of America (New York, 1948–66) B
648 *The Harmonizer*, Soc. for the Preservation and Encouragement of Barber Shop Quartet Singing in America (Detroit, MI, later Kenosha, WI, 1948–) Q, later 6 nos. Y
649 *The Hospital Music Newsletter*, Committee on Music in Hospitals, Natl Music Council (New York, 1948–51) 3 vols., O; bibl. [contd as 689]
650 *The Independent Songwriter*, Independent Song-writers Assn (Somerville, NJ, 1948–?) B
651 *The News Sheet*, Pennsylvania Fed. of Music Clubs (Pittsburgh, ?1948–?) 4 nos. Y
652 *Woodwind Magazine* (New York, 1948/9–1954/5) 7 vols., M except June–July, from 1953/4 7 nos. Y; music; bibl. [contd from 625]
653 *AGMAzine*, Amer. Guild of Musical Artists (New York, 1949–) Q
654 *CMC Journal*, Student Assn of the Chicago Musical Coll. (Chicago, ?1949–?) O
655 *Country Song Roundup* (Derby, CT, 1949–54) 33 nos., M; suppl.: *Country Song Roundup Annual*
656 *Georgia Music News*, Georgia MEA (Collegeboro, later Athens, GA, ?1949) Q
657 *Music Forum* (from 1949 (no.3) *Forum and Digest*) (New York, 1949–50) 2 vols., M
658 *Long Playing Record Catalog*, title varies, from Jan 1972 *Schwann-1 Record & Tape Guide*, from Dec 1983 *The New Schwann* (Cambridge, MA, 1949–53; Boston, 1953–) M; artist index, 1953–, O [incorp. 796 in 1983]
659 *Oregon Music Educators News*, from 1954 *Oregon Music Educator* (Salem, later Roseburg, OR, 1949–) 3 nos. Y
660 *Pittsburgh Musician*, Pittsburgh Musical Soc., Local 60 AFM of the (Pittsburgh, 1949–?) M, later B
661 *Soundings: a Monthly Sounding of the New Records* (New York, ?1949–?) M
662 *String News*, Division of U. Extension, U. of Illinois Music Section (Urbana, IL, ?1949–?) O
663 *Texas String News*, Amer. String Teachers Assn, Dept of Music, U. of Texas (Austin, ?1949–?) ?Q
664 *The Hymn*, Hymn Soc. of America (New York, 1949–76; Springfield, OH, 1976–) 3 nos. Y, from 1952 Q
665 *The Kansas Music Review*, Kansas MEA (Emporia, later Wichita, KS, 1949–) 6, later 5 nos. Y
666 *The MPA Bulletin*, Music Publishers' Assn of the US (New York, 1949–) O
667 *The M.S.V.A. Journal*, Michigan School Vocal Assn (Port Huron, MI, ?1949–?) 4 nos. Y
668 *The Music Index* (Detroit, 1949–) M, cumulations Y
669 *The Music News Directory*, Washington MTA (Washington, DC, 1949–) H
670 *V.M.E.A. Notes*, Virginia MEA (Richmond, VA, 1949–) 6 nos. Y

671 *Young Keyboard, Jr.: the Magazine for Music Appreciation* (New Haven, 1949–) M Oct–May; music

672 *American Recorder Society: Newsletter* (New York, from no.25 Stony Point, NY, 1950–59) 38 nos., O, from 1963 Q [contd as 755]

673 *Church Musician*, Sunday School Board, Southern Baptist Convention (Nashville, 1950–/*Rm*) M

674 *Harp News of the West*, from 1950 (no.2) *Harp News*, Northern California Harpists' Assn (Oakland, CA, . . . 1950/4–1965/6) 4 vols., H [contd as 823]

675 *Notes a tempo*, West Virginia MEA (West Liberty, WV, 1950–) M Sept–June

676 *Sing Out!: the Folk Song Magazine* (New York, 1950–/*Rmp*) B; music

677 *The Clarinet* (New York, 1950–57) 26 nos. [contd as 722]

678 *The Second Line*, New Orleans Jazz Club (New Orleans, 1950–) O

679 *American* (from 1963/4 *The American*) *Music Teacher*, Music Teachers Natl Assn (Pittsburgh, . . . 1951–1962/3; Cincinnati, 1963/4–/*Rm*) 5 nos. Y, from May 1961 B [contd from 551]

680 *American String Teacher*, Amer. String Teachers Assn (Urbana, IL, 1951–60; Mankato, MN, 1960–71; Trenton, NJ, 1972–) 3, from Nov 1960 4 nos. Y, from 1962 (no.4) Q

681 *High Fidelity* (1958 (no.12) to 1959 (no.3) *Fidelity and Audiocraft*) [*HiFi*], incorp. 302 in Feb 1965 to form *High Fidelity*/(from 1970 *Fidelity and*) *Musical America* [*HiFi/MusAm*], (Great Barrington, MA, 1951/2–) Q, from Sept 1952 B, from 1954 (no.1) M; directory issue: *High Fidelity/Musical America: Special Directory Issue*, from 1968/9 *Musical America: Annual Directory Issue*, 1965–, Y [incorp. 700]

682 *Music Box News Bulletin*, Musical Box Hobbyists (Pelham, NY, 1951–)

683 *Music News*, Florida U., Division of Music (Gainesville, FL, ?1951–)

684 *Music Therapy: Book of Proceedings*, Natl Assn for Music Therapy (Chicago, IL, later Lawrence, KS, ⟨1951–62⟩ 1952–63) 12 vols., Y [combined with 689 to form 790]

685 *Organ Institute Bulletin* (from 1951 (no.2) *Quarterly*) (Andover, MA, 1951–?) Q

686 *Piano Guild Notes*, Natl Guild of Piano Teachers (Austin, 1951–) B

687 *Musicana Newsletter* (Pomona, CA, 1952–?) O

688 *NACWPI Journal*, Natl Assn of Coll. Wind and Percussion Instructors, Northwest Missouri State U., Division of Fine Arts (Kirksville, MO, 1952–) Q

689 *National Association for Music Therapy: Bulletin* (Chicago, 1952–4; Lawrence, KS, 1955–63) 12 vols., 3 nos.Y, from 1961 Q [contd from 649; combined with 684 to form 790]

690 *Piano Quarterly Newsletter*, later *The Piano Quarterly*, Piano Teachers Information Service (New York, 1952/3–1972; Melville, NY, 1972–4; Wilmington, VA, 1975–) Q

691 *PMEA News*, Pennsylvania MEA (West Chester, PA, 1952–) 4 nos. Y

692 *Ethno-musicology* (from 1957 *Ethnomusicology*) *Newsletter*, from 1957 (no.9) *Ethnomusicology* [*EM*], Soc. for Ethno-musicology (from 1957 Ethnomusicology) (Middletown, CT, 1953/7–1958/72; Ann Arbor, MI, 1973–/*Rmp*) Y, from 1954 2, from 1956 3 nos. Y; bibl.; c.i. 1953–66, 1967–76

693 *Journal of Research in Music Education* [*JRME*], MENC (Chicago, 1953–6; Washington, 1956–65; Baltimore, 1965–72; Washington, 1972–3; Vienna, VA, 1974–5; Reston, VA, 1975–/*Rp*) H, from 1964 Q, from 1977 3 nos. Y

694 *Music Makers*, Cleveland Music School Settlement (Cleveland, 1953–)

695 *Music* (later *MMEA Music*, from 1973 *Massachusetts Music*) *News*, Massachusetts MEA (Brockton, MA, later West Springfield, MA, ?1953–) Q

696 *New Mexico Musician*, New Mexico MEA (Albuquerque, 1953–) 3 nos. Y

697 *Selmer Bandwagon* [wind insts, instrumentalists] (Elkhart, IN, 1953–) 4 nos. Y

698 *Hit Parader* (Jan–April 1974 *Parader & Stories*) (Derby, CT, 1954–) B

699 *Michigan Music Educator*, Michigan MEA (Lansing, later Ypsilanti, MI, 1954–) 3 nos. Y

700 *Music at Home*, from 1955 *Hi-fi Music at Home* (New York, 1954–9) 6 vols. [incorp. into 681]

701 *The Berlioz Society Newsletter* (Exeter, NY, later New York, 1954–1959/60) 6 vols., O; suppls.

702 *The Gregorian Review* (Toledo, OH, 1954–8) 5 vols. [Amer. edn of F423 in *Grove 6*]

703 *The Juilliard Review*, Juilliard School of Music (New York, 1954–62/*R*, *Rm*) [contd as 768]

704 *The Musician's Guide*, Music Information Service (New York, 1954–7, 1968–) Y

705 *Music and Recordings* (New York, 1955)

706 *Record Research: a Magazine of Record Statistics and Information* (New York, 1955–)

707 *Washington Music Educator*, from 1971 *Voice of Washington Music Educators*, Washington MEA (Ellensburg, WA, 1955–) Q

708 *American Guild of Organists Quarterly* (New York, 1956–) Q

709 *Down Beat* (sometimes *Beat's*) *Music* [*DBY*], title varies (Chicago, 1956–) Y

710 *Musical Americana Newsletter* (Philadelphia, 1956–)

711 *Music Business* (later *Reporter*) (Nashville, ?1956–?)

712 *Rock & Roll* (later *Soul*) *Songs*, from 1984 *Rock & Roll* (Derby, CT, 1956–) every 6 weeks, later M

713 *The Tracker: Unofficial Newsletter of the Unofficial "Organ Historical Society"* [organ construction] (Wilmington, OH, 1956–/*Rmp*) Q

714 *Brass Quarterly* (Durham, NH, 1957/8–1963/4) 7 vols., Q; bibl. [contd as 811]

715 *Journal of Church Music*, Lutheran Church in America (Philadelphia, 1957–) M; music

716 *Journal of Music Theory* [*JMT*], Yale U., School of Music (New Haven, 1957–/*Rp*) 2 nos. Y; bibl.; c.i. 1957–8, 1959–60, 1961–2, 1963–70, 1971–3, 1974–5

717 *Musical Box Society: Bulletin* (later *International Bulletin*) (Springfield, MA, . . . 1957–) 3 nos. Y

718 *Music Listener's Guide* (North Hollywood, CA, 1957–)

719 *Nevada Notes*, Nevada MEA (Reno, NV, 1957–) Q

720 *News and Notes*, from Sept 1959 *The Composer and Conductor*, Natl Assn for Amer. Composers and Conductors, Los Angeles Chapter (Los Angeles, 1957–75) O [contd as 993]

721 *News Bulletin of the Moravian Music Foundation*, from 1964 (no.2) *Bulletin*, from 1965 (no.2) *The Moravian Music Foundation Bulletin*, from 1981 *Moravian Music Journal* (Winston-Salem, NC, 1957–) H, from 1981 Q

722 *Woodwind World*, incorp. 923 in 1975 to form *Woodwind World, Brass & Percussion*, from Sept 1981 *Woodwind/Brass & Percussion* (Mount Kisco, later Bedford Hills, NY, 1957–70; Oneonta, NY, 1971–80; Deposit, NY, 1981–) 5 nos. Y, from 1976 B, from 1981 8 nos. Y [contd from 677]

723 *American Choral Review*, Assn of Choral Conductors, Amer. Choral Fdn (Columbia, MO, later New York, 1958–) O, from 1961 Q

724 *Arizona Association of Violin Makers and Musicians: Monthly Publication*, from 1958/9 (no.11) *Violin-guitar* (from 1959/60 (no.4) *Violin, Guitar*) *Makers and Musicians: Monthly Journal*, later *International Violin, Guitar Makers' and Musicians' Association: Monthly Journal* (Miami, AR, 1958/9–1965, 1980–) M, later Q

725 *Die Reihe: a Periodical devoted to Developments in Contemporary Music* (Bryn Mawr, PA, . . . 1958–68) 8 vols., O [Amer. edn of Austrian ser., Vienna, 1955–62]

726 *Hi Fi and Music Review*, from 1958 (no.11) *Hi Fi Review*, from 1960 (no.2) *Hi Fi Stereo Review*, from Nov 1968 *Stereo Review* (Chicago, 1958–70; New York, 1970–/*Rm*) M

727 *Musical Clarion* (New York, 1958–?)

728 *Musica liturgica* (Cincinnati, 1958–60) 2 vols.

729 *Music Today* (from 1962 *Today Newsletter*), from 1969 *American Music Center: Newsletter* (New York, 1958–) B, later Q

730 *New Hampshire Quarter Notes*, New Hampshire MEA (Laconia, later Concord, NH, 1958/9–) Q

731 *NSOA Bulletin*, Natl School Orchestra Assn (Terre Haute, IN, 1958–) Q

732 *Piano Technicians Journal*, Piano Technicians Guild (Seattle, 1958–) M; incorp. *Piano Technicians Directory*, 1961–, ?Y [contd from 583]

733 *The Cornell University Music Review*, Dept of Music, Cornell U. (Ithaca, NY, 1958–?67) Y

734 *The Folklore and Folk Music Archivist*, Indiana U. (Bloomington, IN, 1958–68/*Rm*) 10 vols., Q, from 1963 3 nos. Y

735 *The Jazz Review* (New York, 1958–61/*R*) 4 vols.

736 *American Choral Foundation: Research Memorandum*, Assn of Choral Conductors (New York, 1959–) 6 nos. Y

737 *Central Opera Service Bulletin*, Metropolitan Opera Natl Council, Central Opera Service (New York, 1959–) 5–7 nos. Y, from 1965/6 (no.3) B, from 1971/2 (no.4) Q; bibl.

738 *Close-up*, later *CMA Close-up*, Country Music Assn (Nashville, 1959–) M

739 *Country Dancer*, Country Dance and Song Soc. of America (New York, ?1959–)

740 *Music Ministry*, Methodist Church (Nashville, 1959–68) 9 vols. [contd as 850]

741 *One-spot Monthly Popular Guide* [index of pop music titles and artists] (Mount Prospect, IL, 1959–) M

742 *One-spot New Release Reporter* (Mount Prospect, IL, 1959–) W

743 *Quarterly Check-list of Musicology* (Darien, CT, 1959–/*Rp*) Q
744 *Response in Worship, Music, the Arts*, Lutheran Soc. for Worship, Music, and the Arts (St. Paul, 1959–)
745 *Theatre Organ*, combined with *Bombarde* in sum. 1966 to form *Theatre Organ/Bombarde*, Amer. Assn of Theatre Organ Enthusiasts (Vallejo, CA, later Middleburg, VA, 1959–) B
746 *The Choral Journal*, Amer. Choral Directors Assn (Tampa, FL, 1959/60–/*Rmp*) Q, from 1960 B, from 1969 9 nos. Y
747 *FIGA News*, title varies, Fretted Instrument Guild of America (Chicago, 1960–) B; music
748 *Jazz Report* (Ventura, CA, 1960/61–1962/3) 3 vols., B [incorp. into 761]
749 *Music in America*, Soc. for the Preservation of the Amer. Musical Heritage (New York, 1960)
750 *Music Products Evaluation Index* (Long Beach, NY, 1960–) 10 nos. Y
751 *Music Tempo* (Toledo, OH, 1960–) B
752 *NBA Journal of Proceedings*, later *NBA Journal*, Natl Band Assn (Lafayette, IN, from 1977 Muncie, IN, 1960–) Q
753 *North Carolina Music Teacher*, North Carolina MTA (Chapel Hill, 1960–) H
754 *WFLN Philadelphia Guide* (later *Guide to Events and Places*) (Philadelphia, 1960–) M
755 *The American Recorder*, Amer. Recorder Soc. (New York, 1960–/*Rmp*) Q; c.i. 1960–64, 1965–6, 1967–8, 1969–70, 1971–2 [contd from 672]
756 *ASCAP*, Amer. Soc. of Composers, Authors and Publishers (New York, 1961–6) [contd as 825]
757 *College Music Symposium*, Coll. Music Soc. (Winston-Salem, NC, later New Brunswick, NJ, 1961–9; Geneva, NY, 1970–74; Madison, WI, 1975–) Y, from 1977 H; Fs W. J. Mitchell 1971
758 *Drum Corps News* (Revere, MA, 1961–) W Sept–May and F June–Aug; directory issues 1962/3–?, Y [contd from *Drum Corps Directory*]
759 *Gregorian Institute of America: Quarterly* (Toledo, OH, 1961/2–1966/7) 6 vols., Q
760 *Music Guild: Newsletter* (New York, 1961–) O
761 *Music Memories*, incorp. 748 in 1963 (no.6) to form *Music Memories and Jazz Report* (Birmingham, 1961–)
762 *Show Case: American Music Clubs Magazine* (Chicago, 1961–2) [incorp. into 485]
763 *The Music Magazine* (Evanston, IL, 1961) [incorp. into 155]
764 *Clavier* (Evanston, IL, 1962–/*Rm*) 6, from 1966 (no.4) 9 nos. Y
765 *Crescendo* (New York, 1962–) 3 nos. Y
766 *Critics Criteria*, from 1974/5 *Music Critics Association: Newsletter* (Rockville, MD, 1962–) 3 nos. Y, from 1982/3 Q
767 *Jazz*, from 1967 (no.8) *Jazz and Pop* (New York, 1962–71) 10 vols., M
768 *Juilliard News Bulletin*, Juilliard School of Music (New York, 1962/3–/*Rm*) 8, from 1963/4 6 nos. Y [contd from 703]
769 *Missouri Journal of Research in Music Education*, Missouri MEA (St. Louis, 1962–)
770 *Percussive Notes*, Percussive Arts Soc. (Columbus, OH, later Urbana, IL, 1962–) 3 nos., from 1983 6 nos. Y [incorp. 782 in 1983]
771 *Perspectives of New Music* [*PNM*], to 1971 (ix/2–x/1) Fromm Music Fdn (Princeton, NJ, 1962/3–1972/3; Annandale-on-Hudson, NY, 1973/4–/*Rp*) H; bibl. 1972–; Fs Stravinsky 1971; c.i. every 2 years
772 *The Juilliard Review Annual*, Juilliard School of Music (New York, 1962/3–1967/8) Y
773 *The Stereophile* [sound equipment] (Philadelphia, 1962–6/*R*) 12 nos.
774 *A.S.C.A.P. Jazz Notes*, Amer. Soc. of Composers, Authors and Publishers (New York, 1963–?)
775 *BMI: News About Music & Writers*, from Nov 1964 *BMI: the Many Worlds of Music*, Broadcast Music, Inc. (New York, 1963–/*Rmp*) 10, from 1972 7, from 1973 3–4 nos. Y; suppl.: *Rhythm and Blues 1943–1968*
776 *Council for Research in Music Education Bulletin*, School of Music, Coll. of Educ., U. of Illinois, and Office of the Superintendent of Public Instruction (Champaign, IL, 1963–) Q; c.i. 1963–9
777 *Country Music Report* (from 1964 (no.5) *Review*) (Orange, CA, ?1963/4–)
778 *Junior Musician*, later *Young Musicians*, Sunday School Board, Southern Baptist Convention (Nashville, 1963–) Q
779 *Listen: a Music Monthly* (New York, 1963–5) 3 vols., M
780 *Musician's Voice* (New York, 1963–) 10 nos. Y
781 *Musigram*, Natl Sheet Music Soc. (Covina, CA, 1963–6) 3 vols.
782 *Percussionist*, from 1981 *Percussive Notes/Percussionist Research Edition*, Percussive Arts Soc. (Carbondale, IL, . . . Urbana, IL, 1963–82) 19 vols., 3 nos. Y [incorp. into 770]
783 *Viola da Gamba Society of America: News*, later *VDGSA News* (Edgewater, MD, . . . 1963/4–) O, from 1971 Q
784 *American Music Conference Report on Amateur Instrumental Music in the United States* (n.p., 1964–)
785 *American Old Time Fiddlers' News*, Amer. Old Time Fiddlers' Assn (Lincoln, NE, 1964–) M
786 *AMICA Bulletin*, Automatic Musical Instrument Collectors' Assn (Campbell, CA, 1964–) M
787 *Colorado Journal of Research in Music Education* (Boulder, CO, 1964–?8)
788 *Disc Collector Newsletter*, from 1972 *Disc Collector* (Cheswold, DE, 1964–) 6–9 nos. Y
789 *Journal of Band Research*, Amer. Bandmasters Assn, Coll. Band Directors Natl Assn, Natl Band Assn, and Amer. School Band Directors' Assn (College Park, MD, 1964/5–1968/9; Ames, IA, 1969/70–1976/7; Troy, AL, 1977/8–) Q, from 1966/7 H
790 *Journal of Music Therapy*, Natl Assn for Music Therapy (Lawrence, KS, 1964–) Q [contd from 684 and 689]
791 *Journal of the Viola da Gamba Society of America* [*JVdGSA*] (Edgewater, MD, 1964–71; Memphis, 1972–5, 1977–) Y; c.i. 1964–75
792 *Le grand baton: Journal of the Sir Thomas Beecham Society* (Cleveland, 1964–) Q
793 *Music Business* (New York, 1964–?) W
794 *Music City News* [country music, gospel] (Nashville, 1964–) M
795 *Notes of N.A.O.T.*, from 1974 (no.5) *The Organ Teacher*, Natl Assn of Organ Teachers (Hammond, IN, 1964/5–) B except July/Aug
796 *Schwann Catalog of Imported Records*, from 1972 *Schwann-2 Record & Tape Guide* (Boston, 1964–83) H [incorp. into 658]
797 *The Catgut Acoustical Society Newsletter* (Cincinnati, OH, later Montclair, NJ, 1964–84) H
798 *AMC of A: Newsletter*, Associated Male Choruses of America (Appleton, WI, 1965–) M
799 *Boosey and Hawkes Newsletter* (New York, 1965–) 3 nos. Y
800 *Current Musicology* [*CMc*], Dept of Music, Columbia U. (New York, 1965–) 2 nos. Y, 1967 Y; bibl.; Fs P. H. Lang 1969, Fs Ives 1974; c.i. 1965–70; incl. *Bibliography of Performance Practices*, 1969, and *The Spheres of Music: Harmony and Discord*, 1972–3
801 *Inter-American Institute for Musical Research: Yearbook/Instituto interamericano de investigación musical: Anuario*, from 1970 *Anuario interamericano de investigación musical/Yearbook for Inter-American Musical Research/Anuario interamericano de pesquisa musical*, Tulane U., from 1970 U. of Texas Inst. of Latin Amer. Studies and Dept of Music, ed. G. Chase (New Orleans, 1965–9; Austin, 1970–77) 11 vols., Y [in Eng., Fr., Port., Sp.; incorp. into 1061]
802 *JEMF Newsletter* (from 1969 *Quarterly*), John Edwards Memorial Fdn (Los Angeles, 1965–) Q
803 *MTAC News* (from 1971 *News and Views*), MTA of California (San Francisco, 1965–)
804 *Music Digest* (New York, 1965–) W
805 *Music Guide*, RCA Victor Record Club (Indianapolis, 1965–) Y
806 *Music Now*, Southeastern Composers' League (College Park, MD, later Athens, GA, 1965–) Q, from 1978/9 3 nos. Y
807 *Peters Notes*, pubd C. F. Peters (New York, 1965–) H
808 *The Brass World* (Des Moines, 1965/6–1973/4) 9 vols.
809 *American Society of University Composers: Proceedings* [*PASUC*] (New York, 1966–8; Lake Grove, OR, 1969–) Y, from 1972/3 biennially
810 *Bluegrass Unlimited* (Broad Run, VA, 1966–) M
811 *Brass and Woodwind Quarterly* [*BWQ*] (Durham, NH, 1966/8–1969) 2 vols., O; bibl. [contd from 714]
812 *Church Music*, Concordia Teachers' Coll. (River Forest, IL, 1966–) S; music
813 *Crawdaddy: Magazine of Rock* (New York, 1966–) M
814 *Institute of Ethnomusicology, University of California: Selected Reports* (from 1974 *Reports in Ethnomusicology*) (Los Angeles, 1966–) O; Fs Kunst 1966, Fs Luang Pradit Phairọ 1975
815 *Musical Box Society: International Directory* (Springfield, MA, . . . 1966–) biennially
816 *Music Article Guide* (Philadelphia, 1966/7–/*Rmp*) Q
817 *Music for Primaries*, Sunday School Board, Southern Baptist Convention (Nashville, 1966–) Q
818 *Music Journal Artists Directory*, title varies (New York, 1966/7–1973, 1975–) Y
819 *Notes from Eastman*, later *Eastman Notes*, Eastman School of Music (Rochester, NY, 1966–) mainly Q
820 *Student Musicologists at Minnesota* (Minneapolis, 1966–) O; c.i., 1966–71; Fs D. N. Ferguson 1972
821 *The Lute Society of America, Inc.: Newsletter* (Silver Spring, MD, later San Francisco, 1966–) 3, from 1967 mainly 4 nos. Y; music
822 *Who Put the Bomp*, later *Bomp* [rock-and-roll] (Burbank, CA, 1966–) Q,

later 6 nos. Y

823 *American Harp Journal*, Amer. Harp Soc. (New York, later Los Angeles, 1967/8–) H [contd from 674]

824 *American Society of University Composers: Newsletter* (New York, 1967–) 3 nos. Y

825 *ASCAP Today*, Amer. Soc. of Composers, Authors and Publishers (New York, 1967–72, 1974–9) H [contd from 756; contd as 1045]

826 *Association for Recorded Sound Collections: Journal* (Silver Spring, MD, 1967/8–) mainly 3 nos. Y

827 *Bass Sound Post*, 1972 (no.18) *Probas* (North Plainfield, NJ, 1967–72) 18 nos., O [incorp. into 953]

828 *Devil's Box*, Tennessee Valley Old Time Fiddlers Assn (Madison, AL, 1967/8–) Q

829 *Electronic Music Review*, Independent Electronic Music Center (Trumansburg, NY, 1967–8) 7 nos., Q; incl. *Répertoire international des musiques électro-acoustiques*, 1967

830 *Guitar Player: the Magazine for Professional and Amateur Guitarists* (San Jose, later Saratoga, CA, 1967–71; Los Gatos, CA, 1971–) 4, from 1968 6, from 1970 8 nos. Y, from 1974 M

831 *Journal of Synagogue Music*, Cantors Assembly of America (New York, 1967–) mainly Q; c.i. 1967 to Jan 1978

832 *Music at Georgia*, Music Dept, U. of Georgia (Athens, GA, 1967/8–) Q

833 *Music in Higher Education*, Natl Assn of Schools of Music (Washington, DC, 1967–)

834 *Music: the A.G.O.* (from Oct 1968 *A.G.O. and R.C.C.O.*) *Magazine*, from Jan 1979 *American Organist*, American Guild of Organists and, from Oct 1968, Royal Canadian Coll. of Organists (New York, 1967/8–) M

835 *Newsletter of the Group for Contemporary Music at Columbia University*, from 1968 (no.2) *Contemporary Music Newsletter*, Group for Contemporary Music at Columbia U., Dept of Music, New York U., and Dept of Music, Princeton U. (New York, 1967–75, 1977–) 5, from 1977 4 nos. Y

836 *Pick'n' & Sing'n' & Gather'n' Inc. Newsletter* (Voorheesville, NY, 1967–) M

837 *Rag Times*, Maple Leaf Club (Los Angeles, 1967–) B

838 *Rolling Stone* (San Francisco, 1967/8–1976/7; New York, 1977/8–/*Rmp*) F

839 *S.E.M. Newsletter*, Soc. for Ethnomusicology (Milwaukee, 1967–8; Hayward, CA, 1968–70; Ann Arbor, MI, 1970–) B

840 *Source: Music of the Avant Garde* (Davis, CA, 1967–9; Sacramento, CA, 1969–77) 6 vols., H; music

841 *The Bulletin of the Ernest Bloch Society*, from 1967 (no.3) *Ernest Bloch Society Bulletin* (Portland, OR, from 1967 (no.8) Gualala, CA, 1967–) mainly Y

842 *Asian Music*, Soc. for Asian Music (New York, 1968/9–) 1–2 nos. Y; Fs Picken 1975

843 *Association for Recorded Sound Collections: Bulletin* (New York, 1968–) Y

844 *Counterpoint* (Seattle, 1968–9) 2 vols.

845 *Country Dance and Song Society News* (New York, 1968–) Y

846 *Early Music Laboratory Bulletin* (Los Angeles, 1968–)

847 *Intermission*, New Orleans Jazz Club of Southern California (Buena Park, CA, 1968–) M

848 *Musical Electronics* (New York, 1968–) B

849 *Music and Artists* (New York, 1968–72) 5 vols. [incorp. into 592]

850 *Music Ministry*, United Methodist Church (Nashville, 1968–78) 10 vols., M [contd from 740]

851 *Music Notes*, Idaho MEA (Rupert, ID, 1968–)

852 *National Association of Jazz Educators: Newsletter*, from 1969/70 (no.2) *NAJE Educator*, from 1980/81 (no.2) *Jazz Educators Journal* (Manhattan, KS, 1968–) Q, 1969/70 (no.2) to 1980/81 (no.1) 5 nos. Y

853 *Opera Journal*, Natl Opera Assn (University, MS, later Columbia, MO, 1968–) Q

854 *Selective Music Lists*, MENC and Amer. Choral Directors Assn (Washington, DC, 1968–) Y

855 *The Harpsichord*, Intl Soc. of Harpsichord Builders, from 1969/70 Intl Harpsichord Soc. (Denver, 1968/9–) Q; c.i. 1968–70

856 *The International Alban Berg Society Newsletter*, from 1977 Graduate School, CUNY (Durham, NH, 1968–76; New York, 1977–) O

857 *The Lute Society of America, Inc.: Journal* (Silver Spring, MD, from 1979 Lexington, VA, 1968–) Y; c.i. 1968–75

858 *Violoncello Society, New York: Newsletter* (New York, 1968–)

859 *AAMOA Reports*, Afro-Amer. Music Opportunities Assn (Minneapolis, 1969–) B

860 *Abstracts of Papers read at the Annual Meeting of the American Musicological Society* (n.p., 1969–) Y [contd from 553]

861 *American Musical Digest*, Music Critics Assn (New York 1969/70) 6 nos., M

862 *Barba: the Rock Newspaper of Puerto Rico* (Rio Piedras, PR, 1969–) M [in Eng., Sp.]

863 *CMP Newsletter*, MENC, Contemporary Music Project for Creativity in Music Educ. (Washington, DC, 1969/70–1972/3) 4 vols., 3 nos. Y

864 *Creem* [rock music] (Pelham Manor, NY 1969–) M, from 1981/2 B

865 *Dissonance*, Dept of Music, Drew U. (Madison, NJ, 1969–1975/6) 7 vols., H, from 1974 Y

866 *Journal of the Graduate Music Students at the Ohio State University*, School of Music, Ohio State U. (Columbus, OH, 1969–) O

867 *Music Library Association: Newsletter*, School of Music, U. of Michigan (Ann Arbor, MI, 1969–) Q, from 1970 3, from 1973 4 nos. Y

868 *Orff Echo*, Amer. Orff Schulwerk Assn (Cleveland, 1969–) 3 nos. Y, from aut. 1976 Q

869 *Record Exchanger* (Orange, CA, 1969–) B; c.i. 1969–76

870 *Sabin's Radio Free Jazz!*, from June 1975 *Radio Free Jazz*, from June 1980 *Jazz Times* (Washington, DC, 1969–) M

871 *Singing News: the Printed Voice of Gospel Music* (Pensacola, FL, 1969–) M

872 *The Composer*, cover title frequently *The Composer Magazine* (Redondo Beach, CA, . . . 1969/70–1981) 12 vols., Q, from 1971/2 H, from 1974/5 Y; c.i. 1969–70

873 *The New Braille Musician*, Library of Congress, Division for the Blind and Physically Handicapped (Washington, DC, 1969/70–1976/7) 8 vols., B, later H; music [in Braille, parallel print edn; contd from 596; contd as 1029]

874 *To the World's Bassoonists*, Intl Double Reed Soc., School of Fine Arts, Texas Christian U. (Fort Worth, TX, 1969–77) 3 nos. Y [incorp. into 1042]

875 *Western Pennsylvania Bluegrass Committee: Newsletter* (Pittsburgh, 1969–) M

876 *Bach*, Riemenschneider Bach Inst., Baldwin-Wallace Coll. (Berea, OH, 1970–) Q

877 *Living Blues* (Chicago, 1970–/*Rmp*) B, from sum. 1979 Q

878 *Metropolitan Opera Association Annual Report*, Metropolitan Opera Guild (New York, 1970–)

879 *Musicast* (New York, 1970–) S

880 *Music Cataloging Bulletin*, Music Library Assn (Ann Arbor, MI, 1970–) M; c.i. 1970–74

881 *Music Indexes and Bibliographies* (Hackensack, NJ, 1970–)

882 *Music Leader*, Sunday School Board, Southern Baptist Convention (Nashville, 1970/71–) Q

883 *Music Makers*, Sunday School Board, Southern Baptist Convention (Nashville, 1970/71–) Q

884 *Performance: the International Talent Weekly* (Fort Worth, TX, 1970–) W

885 *The Country Music Foundation Newsletter*, from 1971 (no.4) *The Journal of Country Music* (Nashville, 1970/71–) Q

886 *The Horn Call*, Intl Horn Soc. (Elmhurst, IL, 1970–) H; incl. newsletter, O

887 *Willem Mengelberg Society: Newsletter* (Greendale, WI, 1970–) 3 nos. Y

888 *WPAS Museletter* (Washington, DC, 1970–) O

889 *AMS Newsletter*, Amer. Musicological Soc., ed. C. V. Palisca (New Haven, 1971–) 2 nos. Y; 3 unnumbered issues 1969–70

890 *Composium: a Quarterly Index of Contemporary Compositions: Directory of New Music*, later *Composium: Annual Index of Contemporary Compositions* (Los Angeles, CA, later Sedro Woolley, WA, 1971–) Q, from 1972 Y

891 *Institute for Studies in American Music: Newsletter* (Brooklyn, NY, 1971/2–) H

892 *Musical Newsletter* (New York, 1971–7) 7 vols., Q; c.i. 1971–3, 1974–6

893 *Music at Yale*, Yale U. (New Haven, 1971/2–) Q

894 *Music Teacher's Workshop* (West Nyack, NY, 1971–) 10 nos. Y

895 *Music World*, Chicago Musical Instrument Co. (Lincolnwood, IL, 1971/2–)

896 *Newsletter of the Historical Musical Society*, title varies, from 1971/2 (no.3) *Newsletter of the American Musical Instrument Society* (Massapequa Park, NY, . . . 1971/2–) Q, later 3 nos. Y

897 *Popular Music and Society*, Center for the Study of Popular Culture, Dept of Sociology, Bowling Green State U. (Bowling Green, OH, 1971/2–/*Rmp*) Q

898 *Synthesis and Electronic Music Quarterly* (Minneapolis, 1971) ?1 no., Q

899 *Up with People News* (Tucson, 1971–) Q

900 *Words & Music* (New York, 1971–) M; music

901 *Band Fan* (Grosse Pointe Woods, MI, 1972–) 3 nos. Y

902 *Country Music* (New York, 1972–) M

903 *Country Music World*, Country Music Soc. (Arlington, VA, 1972–) M

904 *Dead Relix*, later *Relix* [popular music] (New York, 1972–) B

905 *Electronotes: Newsletter*, later *Electronotes*, Musical Engineering Group (Ithaca, NY, 1972–) 16 nos. in 2 vols., Y, later M

906 *Gospel Music Directory* (sometimes *Association Annual Directory*) & *Yearbook*, later *Gospel Music Official Directory*, Gospel Music Assn (Nashville, ⟨1972/

3–) 1973–) Y
907 *Hurdy Gurdy*, Amateur Organists Assn Intl (Edina, MN, later Minneapolis, 1972–) B
908 *Keyboard Arts* (Princeton, NJ, 1972–7) 6 vols., 3 nos. Y
909 *Musical Analysis* (Denton, TX, 1972/3–1973/4) 2 vols., 2 nos. Y
910 *Musical Six-six Newsletter/Muzika ses-ses bulteno* [notation] (Kirkville, MO, 1972–) Q, from 1976 H [in Eng., Esperanto]
911 *Music World Magazine* (Los Angeles, 1972–) M
912 *NUMUS-West: North America's New Music Journal* (Mercer Island, WA, 1972–5) 8 nos., H
913 *Soundings*, ed. P. Garland (Los Angeles . . ., 1972–6; Santa Fe, 1981–) O; music
914 *Sunrise*, later *Prairie Sun* (Peoria, IL, 1972–/*Rm*) W
915 *The NATS Bulletin*, Natl Assn of Teachers of Singing (New York, 1972–) B except July/Aug [contd from 601]
916 *To the World's Oboists*, Intl Double Reed Soc., School of Fine Arts, Texas Christian U. (Fort Worth, TX, 1972/3–1977) 3 nos. Y [incorp. into 1042]
917 *Up-beat*, later *Music Power*, MENC (Reston, VA, 1972–7?) Q
918 *Absolute Sound* (Seacliff, NY, 1973–/*Rm*) Q
919 *American Suzuki Journal*, Suzuki Assn of the Americas (Muscatine, IA, 1973–) 6 nos. Y
920 *Banjo Newsletter* (Greensboro, MD, 1973–) M
921 *Bells* [improvisation] (Berkeley, CA, 1973–) B
922 *Boombah Herald: a Band History Newsletter* (Lancaster, NY, 1973–) H
923 *Brass and Percussion* (Laurens, NY, 1973–4) 2 vols. [incorp. into 722]
924 *Cashbox: the International Music-record Weekly* (New York, 1973–) W
925 *Computational Musicology Newsletter* (Piscataway, NJ, 1973; San Francisco, 1975) 2 nos., O
926 *Different Drummer: the Magazine for Jazz Listeners* (Rochester, NY, 1973–5) 15 nos., M
927 *Disc and That* [popular music, recording industry] (New York, 1973–) M
928 *Ear*, from vol.ix *Ear Magazine West* [new music] (San Francisco, 1973–?83) 4–6 nos. Y
929 *Folk Harp Journal* (Mount Laguna, CA, 1973–) Q
930 *Folk Mass and Modern Liturgy Magazine*, from 1976 (no.6) *Modern Liturgy* (San Jose, CA, 1973/4–) 8 nos. Y; music
931 *Guild of American Luthiers: Newsletter* (from 1976 (no.2) *Quarterly*) (Tacoma, WA, 1973–) 2, from 1974 6 nos. Y, from 1976 Q
932 *International Trombone Association Journal* (Normal, IL, 1973–) Y; incl. newsletter, H
933 *Journal of Jazz Studies: incorporating Studies in Jazz Discography*, from 1982 *Annual Review of Jazz Studies*, Inst. of Jazz Studies, Rutgers, State U. of New Jersey (New Brunswick, NJ, 1973/4–) H, from 1982 Y
934 *MABC Bluegrass Ramblin's*, Missouri Area Bluegrass Committee (Hamburg, IL, 1973–) M
935 *Mountain Newsreal*, later *Newsreal* (Tucson, 1973–/*Rmp*) M
936 *Music Library Association: Technical Reports* (Rochester, NY, 1973–)
937 *Rock Scene* (Bethany, CT, 1973–) 8 nos. Y
938 *RTS Music Gazette*, vols.iv–v *Music Gazette* [film music recordings] (Costa Mesa, CA, 1973–) M
939 *The Ancient Times*, Company of Fifers and Drummers (Deep River, CT, 1973–) Q
940 *The Antique Phonograph Monthly* [recording industry, 1877–1929] (New York, 1973–) M
941 *The Black Perspective in Music* [*BPiM*], Fdn for Research in the Afro-Amer. Creative Arts (New York, 1973–) 2 nos. Y; Fs W. G. Still 1975; c.i. 1973–82
942 *The Clarinet*, Intl Clarinet Soc., Kansas State Coll., School of Music (Pittsburg, KS, 1973–) Q
943 *The Journal of the International Double Reed Society*, School of Fine Arts, Texas Christian U. (Fort Worth, TX, 1973–) Y
944 *The Mississippi Rag* [jazz] (Minneapolis, 1973–) M
945 *T.U.B.A. Newsletter* (from 1976 *Journal*), North Amer. Region of Tubists Universal Brotherhood Assn (Cedar Falls, IA, later Denton, TX, 1973–) 3, from 1976 4 nos. Y
946 *Violone*, Ohio State U., School of Music (Columbus, OH, 1973–) Y
947 *Alternate Sounds Newsletter* (Winlock, WA, 1974–) Q
948 *Analog Sounds* [elec music] (New York, 1974–) Q
949 *And All That Jazz*, New Orleans Jazz Club of California (Kerrville, TX, 1974–) 4 nos. Y
950 **Asterisk: a Journal of New Music* (Ann Arbor, MI, 1974–) H
951 *Country Music News* (Turbotville, PA, later Pittsburgh, 1974/5–) M
952 *Guitar and Lute* (Honolulu, 1974–) Q
953 *International Society of Bassists: Newsletter*, each 4th issue *Bass World: Annual Journal*, from 1982 *International Society of Bassists: Journal*, Coll.-Conservatory of Music, U. of Cincinnati (Cincinnati, 1974–) Q, from 1982 3 nos. Y [incorp. 827]
954 *International Trumpet Guild Newsletter*, later *ITG Newsletter* (Bloomington, IN, 1974/5–1982) 8 vols., 3 nos. Y [incorp. into 1000]
955 *Jersey Jazz*, New Jersey Jazz Soc. (Pluckemin, NJ, . . . Verona, NJ, 1974–) M
956 *Mecca: the Magazine of Traditional Jazz* (New Orleans, 1974) 3 nos., M
957 *Music Researcher's Exchange*, School of Music, Indiana U. (Bloomington, IN, . . . 1974–) 5 nos. Y
958 *Paid my Dues: Journal of Women & Music* (Milwaukee, 1974–80) Q, from 1975 O
959 *Pickin': the Magazine of Bluegrass & Old-time Country Music* (Cedar Knolls, NJ, later Philadelphia, 1974–9) 6 vols., M [incorp. into 1048]
960 *Soundboard*, Guitar Fdn of America (Los Angeles, 1974–/*Rmp*) Q
961 *The American Society for the Advancement of Violin Making News Bulletin*, from 1976/7 *The Violin Society of American News Bulletin*, from 1976/7 (no.2) *Journal of the Violin Society of America* (Pasadena, CA, later New York, 1974/5–) Q
962 *The Dobro Nut*, from 1976 *Resophonic Echoes*, from 1982 (no.10) *Country Heritage* (Madill, OK, 1974–) B, from 1977 (no.6) M
963 *The New England Musician's Guide*, from 1975 (no.8) *Musician's Guide*, New England Musician's Guild (Boston, 1974–) M
964 *Trans-oceanic Trouser Press*, later *Trouser Press* [rock music] (New York, 1974–) B, from 1977 (no.3) M
965 *Westcoast Early Music*, Westcoast Early Music Soc. (El Cerrito, CA, 1974–5) 2 vols. [contd as 1006]
966 *Xenharmonikôn: an Informal Journal of Experimental Music* (Rahway, later Highland Park, NJ, 1974–5) 2 vols., 2 nos. Y
967 *Arnold Schoenberg Institute Bulletin*, U. of Southern California, ed. L. Stein (Los Angeles, 1975–6) 3 nos., O [contd as 1002]
968 *Ballroom Blitz*, from May 1978 *Blitz* [rock-and-roll] (Los Angeles, 1975–) B
969 *Contemporary Keyboard*, from July 1981 *Keyboard* (Saratoga, later Cupertino, CA, 1975–/*Rm*) B, later M
970 *Dulcimer Players News* (Front Royal, VA, 1975–) M, from 1975 (no.3) S, from 1976 (no.2) Q
971 *Ear Magazine – New York*, from 1975 (no.4) *Ear Magazine* (1980 (no.6) to 1983 *Magazine East*) [new music], from 1976 (no.3) New Wilderness Fdn (New York, 1975–) 5–8 nos. Y
972 *Fritz Reiner Society Newsletter*, from 1976 *The Podium* (Novelty, OH, 1975–) O, from 1976 H
973 *Ha'ilono mele* [News of Hawaiian music], Hawaiian Music Fdn, ed. M. Hood (Honolulu, 1975–) M; music [in Eng.]
974 *In Theory Only* [*ITO*], Michigan Music Theory Soc., School of Music, U. of Michigan (Ann Arbor, MI, 1975–/*Rmp*) M, from 1978 8 nos. Y
975 *Mean Mountain Music: Records of the 50's* (Milwaukee, 1975–) B
976 *Musica judaica: Journal of the American Society for Jewish Music* (New York, 1975/6–) Y [in Eng., Fr., Ger., Heb.]
977 *Oklahoma Bluegrass Gazette*, Oklahoma Bluegrass Club (Shawnee, OK, 1975–) M
978 *Northwest Arts* (Seattle, 1975–) F
979 *Polyphony: Electronic Music and Home Recording* (Oklahoma City, OK, 1975–) Q
980 *Quality Rock Reader* (New York, 1975–) Q
981 *Replay Magazine*, later *Replay* [music industry] (Woodland Hills, CA, 1975–) M
982 *Songwriter Magazine* (Hollywood, CA, 1975/6–1979/80) 5 vols., M
983 *The American Musical Instrument Society: Journal*, from 1978 *Journal of the American Musical Instrument Society* [*JAMIS*] (Shreveport, LA, 1975–) Y
984 *The International Trumpet Guild Newsletter*, School of Music, Indiana U. (Bloomington, IN, 1975–)
985 *Theory and Practice*, Music Theory Soc. of New York State (Ithaca, NY, 1975–) H
986 *The Sonneck Society Newsletter*, Sonneck Soc. (Brighton, MA, 1975–) Q, from aut. 1979 3 nos. Y
987 *Viol: a Magazine for the Stringed Instrument Musician* (Decatur, GA, 1975/6–) 4, from 1976/7 5 nos. Y
988 *Accent: a Magazine for Young Musicians* (Evanston, IL, 1976–) 5 nos. in school year
989 *AIVS Newsletter*, from 1977 (no.3) *Verdi Newsletter*, Amer. Inst. for Verdi Studies, Dept of Music, New York U., ed. A. Porter (New York, 1976–) O
990 *BAM: Bay Area Music*, later *BAM: the California Music Magazine* (Oakland, CA, 1976–) F
991 *Cadence: the American Review of Jazz & Blues* (Redwood, NY, 1976–) M
992 *Chelys: Monthly Journal of the New England Society for the Plucked String*, from 1977 *Chelys: a Journal for the Plucked String*, from 1978 (no.3) *The Electric*

Chelys: an Iconoclastic Journal for the Plucked String (Exeter, NH, 1976/7–) O
993 *Composer/USA*, Natl Assn of Composers, USA (Los Angeles, 1976–) Q [contd from 720]
994 *Country Style* (Franklin Park, IL, 1976–81) 6 vols., M
995 *Cum notis variorum: Newsletter*, U. of California Music Library (Berkeley, CA, 1976–) 10 nos. Y
996 *Disc-o-graph* (Baltimore, 1976–) M
997 *Drumworld* (New York, 1976–) Q, from 1977 6 nos. Y
998 *Euphonium: a Journal for Friends of the Euphonium* (Arlington, VA, 1976/7–) B
999 *International Castelnuovo-Tedesco Society Newsletter* (New York, 1976–) O
1000 *ITG Journal*, Intl Trumpet Guild (Potsdam, NY, later Nashville, 1976–) Y, from Sept 1982 Q [incorp. 954 after May 1982]
1001 *Jazz Magazine* (Northport, NY, 1976–) Q
1002 *Journal of the Arnold Schoenberg Institute*, U. of Southern California, ed. L. Stein (Los Angeles, 1976/7–) 3 nos. Y, from vol.iii H; bibl. [contd from 967]
1003 *Music America Magazine*, from 1977 (no.8) *Musician, Player, and Listener* (Boulder, CO, 1976–) 10, from 1977 8 nos. Y
1004 *New on the Charts: Music Reference Index* (New Rochelle, NY, 1976–) M; index Y
1005 *Pastoral Music*, Natl Assn of Pastoral Musicians (Washington, DC, 1976/7–) 6 nos. Y [contd from 630]
1006 *Pro musica* (El Cerrito, CA, 1976–) B [contd from 965]
1007 *The Grackle: Improvised Music in Transition* [jazz] (Brooklyn, NY, 1976–) O
1008 *The National Flute Association Newsletter*, from 1984 (no.2) *The Flutist Quarterly* (Denton, TX, 1976–) 2 nos. Y, from 1977 Q
1009 *ARSC Newsletter*, Assn for Recorded Sound Collections (Albuquerque, 1977–) Q
1010 *Black Music Research Newsletter*, ed. S. A. Floyd, Jr., from 1978 (ii/2) Inst. for Research in Black Amer. Music, Fisk U., and from 1983 (vi/1) Center for Black Music Research, Columbia Coll., Chicago, from 1985 (vii/2) Center for Black Music Research (Carbondale, IL, 1977/8; Nashville, 1978/9–1981/2; Nashville and Chicago, 1983/4–1984; Chicago, 1985–) Q, from 1980 H
1011 *Computer Music Journal*, People's Computer Co. (Menlo Park, CA, 1977–) Q
1012 *Dallas Jazz News* (from Dec 1977 *News Letter*), from Nov. 1978 *Texas Jazz* (from 1983 *Ragg*) (Dallas, 1977–) M
1013 *Dialogue in Instrumental Music Education* (also *DIME*) (Madison, WI, 1977–) H
1014 *Fanfare: the Magazine for Serious Record Collectors* (Tenafly, NJ, 1977–) B
1015 *Indiana Theory Review*, Graduate Theory Assn, School of Music, Indiana U. (Bloomington, IN, 1977–) 3–4 nos. Y
1016 *Journal of Research in Singing*, Intl Assn for Experimental Research in Singing (La Jolla, CA, from 1979 Denton, TX, 1977/8–) H
1017 *Journal of the American Liszt Society*, later *American Liszt Society Journal* (Louisville, 1977–/*Rm*) H
1018 *Keynote: a Magazine for the Musical Arts*, Radio Station WNCN (New York, 1977–) M
1019 *Listener's Review Finder* (New Orleans, 1977–) Q
1020 *Modern Drummer* (Clifton, NJ, 1977–) Q, later 6, later 9 nos. Y, later M
1021 *Musical Heritage Review Magazine*, from 1977 (no. 13) *Musical Heritage Review* (Neptune, NJ, 1977–) M
1022 *NARAS Institute Journal*, Natl Academy of Recording Arts and Sciences (Coral Gables, FL, later Atlanta, 1977–) H
1023 *National Association of Negro Musicians: Bulletin* (1977–) Y
1024 *19th Century Music*, ed. J. Kerman (Berkeley, CA, 1977/8–) 3 nos. Y
1025 *Opera Review* (Washington, DC, 1977) 2 nos., Q
1026 *Record Review* (Los Angeles, 1977–) B
1027 *Rockingchair: the Review Newsletter for Libraries who Buy Records* (Philadelphia, 1977–82) 6 vols., M
1028 *The Audio Critic* (Bronxville, NY, 1977–) B, later O
1029 *The Musical Mainstream*, Library of Congress, Natl Library Service for the Blind and Physically Handicapped (Washington, DC, 1977–) B [in Braille, parallel large-print and cassette edns; contd from 873]
1030 *The Stanza*, Hymn Soc. of America (Springfield, OH, 1977–) H
1031 *American Ensemble*, Chamber Music America (New York, 1978–83) Q [contd as 1107]
1032 *Chinese Music General Newsletter*, from June 1979 *Chinese Music*, Chin. Music Soc. of North America (Woodridge, IL, 1978–) 2 nos. Y, from 1979 Q
1033 *CMJ: College Media Journal*, later *CMJ: Progressive Media* (Roslyn, NY, 1978–) F
1034 *Contemporary Christian Music*, from 1984 *Contemporary Christian* (Laguna Hills, CA, 1978–) M
1035 *Divisions: a Journal for the Art and Practice of Early Musick* (Cleveland Heights, OH, 1978–) Q
1036 *Imagine Magazine* [rock music] (Waterbury, CT, 1978–) B
1037 *Inter-American Music Review*, ed. R. Stevenson (Los Angeles, 1978/9–) 2 nos. Y
1038 *Interval: a Microtonal Newsletter* (San Diego, 1978/9–) Q
1039 *Music Competition Circuit* (Washington, DC, 1978–) B
1040 *New Wave Rock* (New York, 1978–) B
1041 *OP: Independent Music*, Lost Music Network (Olympia, WA, 1978–) B
1042 *The Double Reed*, Intl Double Reed Soc. (East Lansing, MI, 1978–) 3 nos. Y [incorp. 874 and 916]
1043 *The Record Finder* (Newport News, VA, 1978/9–) 10 nos. Y
1044 *The World of Opera* (New York, 1978/9) 6 nos. in 1 vol., B
1045 *ASCAP in Action*, Amer. Soc. of Composers, Authors and Publishers (New York, 1979–) 3 nos. Y [contd from 825]
1046 *Bullet*, Amer. Record Producers Assn (New York, 1979–) Q
1047 *Composers' Forum New Music Calendar*, later *New Music News*, Composers' Forum (New York, 1979–80) 2 vols., M [contd as 1069]
1048 *Frets Magazine: the Magazine of Acoustic Stringed Instruments* (Cupertino, CA, 1979–/*Rm*) mainly M [incorp. 959 in 1979]
1049 *Music Theory Spectrum*, Soc. for Music Theory, School of Music, Indiana U. (Bloomington, IN, 1979–) Y
1049*a* *Recordings of Experimental Music*, ed. T. Holmes (Audubon, NJ, 1979–85) 3–6 nos. Y
1050 *Také-no-michi: a Newsletter of Shakuhachi and Related Arts*, from 1981 (no.3) Traditional Jap. Music Soc., Music Dept, Graduate Center, CUNY (New York, 1979/80–) 5, later 3 nos. Y, later Q
1051 *Black Music Research Journal*, ed. S. A. Floyd, Jr., Inst. for Research in Black Amer. Music, Fisk U., and from 1983 Center for Black Music Research, Columbia Coll., Chicago, from 1985 Center for Black Music Research (Nashville, 1980–82; Nashville and Chicago, 1983–4; Chicago, 1985–) Y; bibl.
1052 *International Banjo* (Kissimmee, FL, 1980–) B, from 1983 Q
1053 *Journal of Guitar Acoustics* (Michigan Center, MI, 1980–) Q
1054 *Journal of the Conductors' Guild* (Vienna, VA, later Washington, DC, 1980–) Q
1055 *MadAminA!: a Chronicle of Musical Catalogues*, Music Associates of America (Englewood, NJ, 1980–) H
1056 *Music Business Contacts* (New York, 1980–) 5 nos. Y
1057 *Music Circular*, Library of Congress, Natl Library Service for the Blind and Physically Handicapped (Washington, DC, 1980–)
1058 *Music, Sound, Output* (Carle Place, nr Mineola, NY, 1980/81–) B
1059 *Oak Report* (from spr. 1981 *Music Report*) (New York, later Chester, NY, 1980–/*Rm*) Q
1060 *Ovation: the Magazine for Classical Music Listeners* (New York, 1980–) M
1061 *Revista de música latino americana/Latin American Music Review*, U. of Texas, ed. G. Béhague (Austin, 1980–/*Rm*) H [in Eng., Port., Sp.; incorp. 801]
1062 *Song of Zion: a Journal of Mormon Music* (Orem, UT, 1980–) 5 nos. Y
1063 *SONUS: a Journal of Investigations into Global Musical Possibilites* (Cambridge, MA, 1980/81–) H
1064 *The Autoharpoholic* (Brisbane, CA, 1980–) Q
1065 *Virtuoso*, from 1981 *Virtuoso & Keyboard Classics* (Paramus, NJ, 1980–81) 2 vols., Q [incl. 1073 in 1981]
1066 *Voice: the Magazine of Vocal Music* (Honolulu, 1980–) B
1067 *Winds Quarterly* (Needham, MA, 1980–) Q
1068 *Ars lyrica: Newsletter of the Society for Word-music Relationships*, later Lyrica Soc. (New Haven, 1981, 1983–) O
1069 *Calendar for New Music*, Soundart Fdn (New York, 1981–) M [contd from 1047]
1070 *Ex tempore*, Dept of Music, U. of California at San Diego (La Jolla, CA, 1981–) 3 nos. Y
1071 *High Performance Review: the Magazine for Perceptive Listeners* (Stanford, CA, 1981/2–) Q
1072 *Jazz Line* (Mineola, NY, 1981–) M
1073 *Keyboard Classics* (Paramus, NJ, 1981–) B; music [first 3 nos. also issued in 1065]
1074 *Music Insider* (New York, 1981–) 10 nos. Y
1075 *Psychomusicology: a Journal of Research in Music Cognition* (Nacogdoches, TX, 1981–) H
1076 *Chamber Music Quarterly* (St. Cloud, MN, 1982–) Q
1077 *ClariNetwork* (Hilliard, OH, 1982–) 6 nos. Y
1078 *Flute Journal* (Needham, MA, 1982–) Q [sample issue Oct 1981]
1079 *Impromptu*, Library of Congress, Music Division (Washington, DC, 1982–) Q
1080 *Marching Bands & Corps* (Jacksonville, 1982–) M
1081 *Music Therapy Perspectives*, Natl Assn for Music Therapy (Washington, DC,

1982–)
1082 *New Music* [punk rock] (New York, 1982–) Q
1083 *On Key: the Magazine for Young Pianists* (Montclair, NJ, 1982–) 10 nos. Y
1084 *Resound: a Quarterly of the Archives of Traditional Music*, Indiana U. (Bloomington, IN, 1982–) Q
1085 *Suzuki World*, Ability Development Associates (Athens, OH, 1982–) B
1086 *The Black Sheep Review* [folk music of the Northeast] (Cambridge, MA, 1982–) B
1087 *The Journal of Musicology* (Louisville, 1982–) Q
1088 *The Sheet Music Exchange* (Winchester, VA, 1982–) B
1089 *Update: the Applications of Research in Music Education*, Dept of Music, U. of South Carolina (Columbia, SC, 1982–) 3 nos. Y
1090 *American Music*, Sonneck Soc. (Champaign, IL, 1983–) Q
1091 *Bhairavi: Journal of Studies in Indian Music*, Bhairavi, Indian Cultural Studies Program, Music Dept, Cleveland State U. (Cleveland, 1983–) H
1092 *Ethnomusicology at UCLA*, U. of California at Los Angeles (Los Angeles, 1983–) Q
1093 *Exchange*, Music Events, Inc. [Chicago area music industry] (Chicago, 1983–) 6 nos. Y
1094 *Kurt Weill Newsletter*, Kurt Weill Fdn for Music (New York, 1983–) 2 nos. Y
1095 *Living Music* (Desert Hot Springs, CA, 1983/4–) Q; c.i.
1096 *Music Explorer* (Evanston, IL, 1983/4–) 9 nos. Y
1097 *Music Perception: an Interdisciplinary Journal*, Dept of Psychology, U. of California at San Diego (Berkeley, CA, 1983/4–) Q
1098 *RPM* [Review of Popular Music], Intl Assn for the Study of Popular Music (1983–)
1099 *Serenade News*, Serenade Record Shop (Washington, DC, 1983–) M
1100 *String Explorer* [for students], Instrumentalist Co. (Evanston, IL, 1983–) 9 nos. Y
1101 *The American Brahms Society Newsletter* (Seattle, 1983–) H
1102 *The Courant*, Academy for the Study and Performance of Early Music, School of Music, U. of Michigan (Ann Arbor, MI, 1983–) Q
1103 *The Musical Woman: an International Perspective* (Westport, CT, ⟨1983–⟩ 1984–) Y; bibl.
1104 *The Opera Quarterly* (Chapel Hill, 1983–) Q; bibl.
1105 *ASCAP Click-track*, Amer. Soc. of Composers, Authors and Publishers (Hollywood, CA, 1984–)
1106 *Balungan*, Amer. Gamelan Inst. for Music and Educ. (Oakland, CA, 1984–) 3 nos. Y
1107 *Chamber Music Magazine*, Chamber Music America (New York, 1984–) Q [contd from 1031]
1108 *Church Music Digest* (Cincinnati, 1984–) B
1109 *College Band Directors National Association Journal*, cover title *CBDNA Journal* (Buffalo, NY, 1984–) Q
1109*a* *Essays on Modern Music*, League of Composers–ISCM, Boston Chapter (Boston, 1984–) Y
1110 *Opus: the Magazine of Recorded Classics* (Harrisburg, PA, 1984/5–) B
1111 *The Archer*, Intl Heinrich Schütz Soc., Amer. Section (Princeton, NJ, 1984–) H
1112 *The Cue-sheet*, Soc. for the Preservation of Film Music (Los Angeles, 1984–) O
1113 *The Full Score*, U. of California at Los Angeles, Music Library (Los Angeles, 1984–)

3. Index.

A

D

E

F

G

H

I

J

K

L

M

N

O

P

Q

R

S

T

U

V

W

X

Y

IMOGEN FELLINGER/JOHN SHEPARD

Perkins, Carl (*b* Lake City, TN, 9 April 1932). Rock-and-roll singer, songwriter, and guitarist. The son of an indigent farmer, his early musical influences were country blues and hillbilly music. He began his career performing with his brothers Jay and Clayton at country dances, and by 1955 he had signed a contract to record for Sam Phillips's Sun label, for which Elvis Presley had already recorded successful songs that blended blues and hillbilly music. (Perkins and Presley, with Jerry Lee Lewis and Johnny Cash, eventually took part together in the famous recording sessions for Sun that resulted in the *Million Dollar Quartet* album.) With his brothers, Perkins recorded his classic rockabilly song *Blue Suede Shoes* (1956), which was the first song to reach the top of the rhythm-and-blues, country, and pop charts simultaneously. This success quickly made Perkins a star, but in 1956 he was badly injured in an automobile accident, in which his brother Jay and manager, David Stewart, were killed. During the year Perkins spent in hospital as a result, Presley achieved phenomenal success with *Blue Suede Shoes* and the rockabilly style reached the peak of its popularity. Although Perkins went on to make other hit recordings, and is regarded as one of the finest writers of early rock-and-roll songs, his career never regained its earlier momentum. In the 1960s he performed with Johnny Cash, and the Beatles paid a tribute to him by recording several of his songs (*Matchbox*, *Honey don't*, and *Everybody's trying to be my baby*). In the 1970s and early 1980s he composed for and recorded with popular artists such as Bob Dylan, NRBQ (with whom he made the album *Boppin' the Blues*, 1970), Jeff Lynne, and Paul McCartney.

RECORDINGS

(selective list)

Blue Suede Shoes (Sun 234, 1956); Boppin' the Blues (Sun 243, 1956); Your true love (Sun 261, 1957); Pink Pedal Pushers (Col. 41131, 1958); *Whole Lotta Shakin'* (Col. 1234, 1959); *Blue Suede Shoes* (Sun 112, 1969)

BIBLIOGRAPHY

A. Shaw: *The Rockin' 50s* (New York, 1974), 164, 188
P. Guralnick: "Rockabilly," *The Rolling Stone Illustrated History of Rock & Roll*, ed. J. Miller (New York, 1976, rev. 2/1980)

MIKAL GILMORE

Perkins, Henry S(outhwick) (*b* Stockbridge, VT, 20 March 1833; *d* Chicago, IL, 20 Jan 1914). Music educator and composer. His father, Orson Perkins (1802–82), was well known as a singing-school teacher in Vermont. Henry Perkins was educated at the Boston Music School. From 1867 to 1872 he was director of the Normal Academy of Music at Iowa City, and from 1870 to 1874 director of the Kansas Normal Academy at Leavenworth. He devoted much of his career to directing music festivals and singing-school conventions, and teaching at normal schools in all parts of the country. In 1875 he went to Europe to observe teaching methods, and studied singing with Pierre Wartel in Paris and Luigi Vannuccini in Florence. He was one of the organizers and a charter member of the Music Teachers National Association (1876), and the leading organizer of the Illinois Music Teachers Association (1886), serving as its president for the first ten years. In 1891 he founded and became director of the Chicago National College of Music, with which he was associated for the remainder of his life. Perkins composed a considerable amount of music, sometimes in collaboration with others, which was published in sheet-music form and in about 40 collections; most of his works are songs and hymns typical of the time.

Three of Perkins's brothers were also musicians. William Perkins (1831–1902) was widely known as a conductor of conventions and compiler of tunebooks. Edwin Perkins (1840–1916) taught in the area of Taftsville, Vermont. Julius Perkins (1845–75) sang at La Scala and was principal bass at Her Majesty's Theatre, London, at the time of his early death.

BIBLIOGRAPHY

R. D. Comstock: *Contributions of the Orson Perkins Family to Nineteenth Century American Music Education* (diss., U. of Iowa, 1970)

RAYMOND D. COMSTOCK

Perkins, John MacIvor (*b* St. Louis, MO, 2 Aug 1935). Composer and teacher. He was educated at Harvard University (BA 1958) and the New England Conservatory (BMus 1958); he also studied with Boulanger in Paris, with Roberto Gerhard and Edmund Rubbra in London (1958–9), and with Arthur Berger, Harold Shapero, and Irving Fine at Brandeis University (MFA 1962). He has taught at the University of Chicago (1962–5), Harvard (1965–70), and Washington University, St. Louis (from 1970), where he is chairman of the Music Department. His honors include a Woodrow Wilson National Fellowship (1959–61), commissions from the Fromm Foundation, the St. Louis Bicentennial, and the Smithsonian Bicentennial, and an award from the National Institute of Arts and Letters (1966).

Perkins frequently uses serial procedures to generate pitch and interval successions. In the course of a work musical events, such as thematic structures or sections of textural density, often occur at different rates of speed, and textures are subjected to modifications of density (as in *Music for 13 Players*). Perkins's compositions are notable for virtuoso instrumental writing and for their sonorous integrity. His work with interwoven or contrasting tempo characteristics has resulted in such theoretical studies as "Note Values" (*PNM*, iii/1, 1965, p.47), and in articles on the music of Dallapiccola and Arthur Berger. Some of his compositions have been recorded by CRI.

WORKS

Stage: Divertimento (chamber opera), 1958; Andrea del Sarto, 1980
Inst: Canons, 9 insts, 1958; Fantasy, Intermezzo, Variations, pf, 1959–62, orchd 1961; 5 Miniatures, str qt, 1962; Qnt Variations, 1962; Caprice, pf, 1963; Music for Carillon, 1963; Music for Orch, 1964; Music for 13 Players, 1964–6; Music for Brass, 1965; Cadenza, 1978
Vocal: 8 songs, 1956–62; 3 Studies, chorus, 1958; Alleluia, 1971; After a Silence–Alpha, 1976

BIBLIOGRAPHY

C. Spies: "John M. Perkins, Quintet Variations," *PNM*, ii/1 (1963), 67

RICHARD SWIFT

Perkins, (David) Walton (*b* Rome, NY, 16 Nov 1847; *d* Chicago, IL, 8 Feb 1929). Pianist and educator. He studied with S. B. Mills and Alfred H. Pease, then with Theodor Kullak and Anton Rubinstein in Berlin. His début as a pianist was in New York in 1869; he remained active as a pianist until 1887, when he became a teacher. Having settled in Chicago, he helped William H. Sherwood found the Sherwood School of Music in 1897 and served as its associate director until 1901. From 1907 until his death he was president of the Chicago Conservatory of Music. He also composed piano pieces, songs, and choral works, and contributed to the journal *Music Magazine*.

R. ALLEN LOTT

Perkinson, Coleridge-Taylor (*b* New York, 14 June 1932). Composer and conductor. He studied composition with Vittorio Giannini and Charles Mills at the Manhattan School (BMus 1953, MMus 1954) and with Earl Kim at Princeton University, and learned conducting at the Berkshire Music Center (summer 1954), the Salzburg Mozarteum (summer 1960), and the Netherlands Radio Union in Hilversum, where he worked with Dean Dixon (summers of 1960, 1962, and 1963). Perkinson has held conducting positions with the Dessoff Choirs (1956–7), the Brooklyn Community SO (1959–62), and the Symphony of the New World (1965–75), of which he was co-founder; he has appeared as guest conductor with such orchestras as the Dallas SO, the Bogotá PO, the Albany SO, and the North Carolina SO. He also served as music director of the American Theatre Lab (1966–7, with Jerome Robbins) and the Alvin Ailey American Dance Theatre (1968, 1978). Perkinson's compositions are characterized by accessibility, energy, and a fusion of elements of serious and black-American music.

WORKS

Ballets: Ode to Otis (A. Mitchell), 1971; Carmen (after Bizet, Mitchell), 1972–3; Forces of Rhythm (Mitchell), 1972–3; Beber (A. Ailey), 1984; To Bird with Love (Ailey), 1984

Inst: Variations and Fugue on "The Ash Grove," vn, pf, early 1950s; Str Qt no.1 "Calvary," 1952; Scherzo, pf, 1953; Toccata, pf, 1953; Va Conc., 1953; Grass, pf, str, perc, 1956; Sinfonietta no.1, str, 1956; Commentary, vc, orch, 1964; Sonatina, perc, *c*1965; Pf Sonata, 1965; Blues Forms, vn, 1972; Lamentations: a Black Folk Song Suite, vc, 1973; Pf Sonata no.2 "Statements," 1975

Vocal: Psalm c, female vv, str, brass, 1949; 3 Songs (R. Hillyer), early 1950s; 9 Elizabethan Love Lyrics, 1v, pf, *c*1952; Attitudes (L. Ferlinghetti, E. E. Cummings, D. Thomas, J. Donne, and others), cantata, T, vn, vc, pf, 1962–3; Psalm xxiii, motet, 5 solo vv, late 1960s; Song to Spring (D. de Prima), 1v, pf, late 1960s; 13 Love Songs in Jazz Settings (De Prima), 1v, pf, late 1960s; Fredome-Freedom (J. Barbour, J. R. Lowell), chorus, chamber ens, 1970; The Legacy (Perkinson), nar, 1v, chorus, orch/rhythm section, 1982

Incidental music: To Damascus (Strindberg), 1960; Song of the Lusitanian Bogey (P. Weiss), 1967; God is a Guess What? (R. McIver), 1968; Malcachon (D. Walcott), 1969; Man Better Man (E. Hill), 1969; The Great MacDaddy (P. C. Harrison), 1974; The Emperor Jones (E. O'Neill), 1984

Film scores: Crossroads Africa, *c*1962; Montgomery to Memphis, 1969; The McMasters, 1969; Happy Birthday Mrs. Craig, 1971; A Warm December, 1972; Together for Days, 1972; Amazing Grace, 1974; The Education of Sonny Carson, 1974; Thomasine & Bushrod, 1974; Freedom Road, 1979; Boardwalk, late 1970s; Bearden on Bearden, *c*1980

10 television scores, incl. A Woman Called Moses, 1978

BIBLIOGRAPHY

SouthernB

D. N. Baker, L. M. Belt, and H. C. Hudson, eds.: *The Black Composer Speaks* (Metuchen, NJ, 1978) [incl. list of works, discography, and bibliography]

CARMAN MOORE

Perle, George (*b* Bayonne, NJ, 6 May 1915). Composer and theorist. He studied composition with Wesley LaViolette (1934–8) and Krenek (early 1940s), and was awarded the PhD at New York University (1956). A member of the faculty at the University of Louisville (1949–57), the University of California, Davis (1957–61), and Queens College, CUNY (1961–84), he has also held visiting professorships at Yale University (1965–6), the University of Southern California (summer 1965), SUNY, Buffalo (1971–2), the University of Pennsylvania (1976, 1980), and Columbia University (1979, 1983). He was elected to the Institute of the American Academy and Institute of Arts and Letters in 1978.

During the 1930s Perle was among the first American composers to be attracted by the music and thought of Schoenberg, Berg, and Webern. His interest, however, was not so much in the 12-tone system itself as in the idea of a generalized systematic approach to dodecaphonic composition. Using some of the fundamental concepts of the 12-tone system, such as set and inversion, he developed an approach to composition which attempts

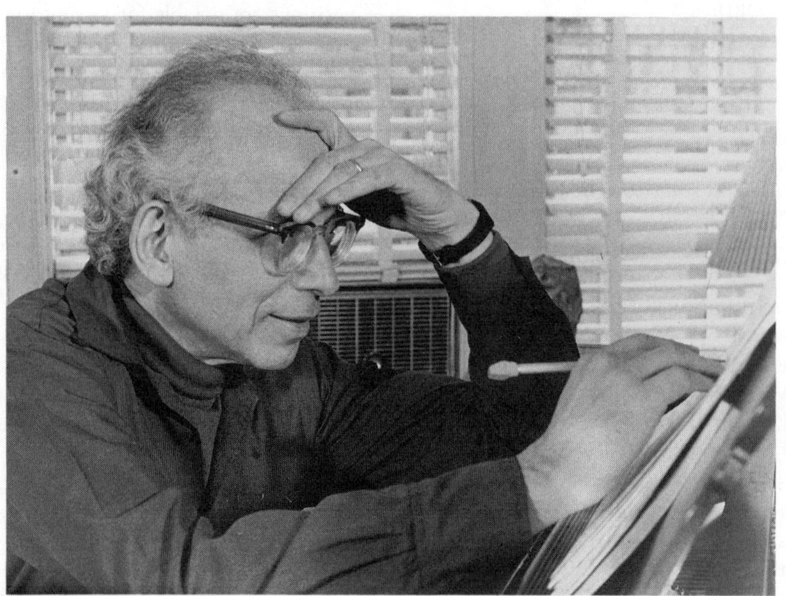

George Perle, 1984

to incorporate such 12-tone ideas with some of the basic kinds of hierarchical distinction found in tonal practice, such as the concept of a "key" as a primary point of reference. His "12-tone tonality," developed continuously from 1939 (and in collaboration with Paul Lansky from 1969), is, in simplest terms, an attempt to create useful distinctions and differentiations in a 12-tone context by defining functional characteristics of pitch-class collections, "chords," in terms of the intervals formed by component pairs of notes, on the one hand, and the properties of these same pairs with respect to an axis of symmetry, a point about which they are symmetrically disposed, on the other. (In an abstract sense these two concepts are roughly analogous to familiar notions of "mode" and "key" in tonal music.) In a composition these kinds of distinction are made useful and noticeable by a consistent use of only a few interval complexes and large-scale reference to only a few points of symmetry. Perle's approach does not define explicit procedures for composition but rather outlines a large and highly structured network of pitch-class and formal relations which can then serve as points of reference for compositional development. (In this sense, too, it is like tonal composition in that the composer's "system" is a general guide to a musical language and a given composition constructs a unique interpretation of that language.)

Perle has a large and varied compositional output; however, he has withdrawn many of his works, in some instances even after performance, publication, and recording. This is the result of uncompromising standards and the technical difficulties associated with developing his theory of 12-tone tonality and its progressively larger structural and integrative implications. If Perle deems one movement of a withdrawn work successful he may use it as part of a new setting. The *Solemn Procession* for band, for example, was taken from the String Quartet no.4 and later became part of a *Symphony for Band*, a work that was itself eventually withdrawn. The original Fourth Quartet was replaced by an entirely new work, but this was also subsequently withdrawn. In the early 1970s the codification of the advancements in 12-tone tonality enabled Perle to realize more fully his artistic vision; the number of withdrawn and revised works has therefore decreased dramatically.

Most of Perle's compositions written before 1967 are based on his theory of 12-tone tonality – notably Three Movements for Orchestra (1960), the String Quartet no.5 (1960, rev. 1967), the Cello Concerto (1966), and *Serenade no.1* (1962) – as are all of his works since 1967, but his earlier pieces include many that he has described as

> "freely" or "intuitively" conceived, combining various serial procedures with melodically generated tone centers, intervallic cells, symmetrical formations, etc. A rhythmic concept, or rather ideal, toward which I progressed in these and other works was that of a beat, variable in duration but at the same time as tangible and coherent as the beat in classical music, and of an integration between the larger rhythmic dimensions and the minimal metric units.

These works include the String Quintet (1958), three wind quintets (1959, 1960, 1967), and a series of works for solo instruments.

In comparison with much music of the time, the "sound" of Perle's music and the manner in which he unfolds his musical ideas are usually straightforward and relatively uncomplicated. His music eschews the veneer of the avant garde and what he considers the wrong-headed association of musical complexity with perceptual difficulty. The complexities that concern him are those arising from the many levels on which his pitch, pitch-class, and motivic relations interact and interrelate, and for him difficulties are only in making these relations as interesting and understandable as possible. In many of his compositions a few relatively simple musical ideas will appear in different ways and contexts so that the character and quality of these ideas become richer in the process.

Perle's writings on 20th-century music, particularly that of Schoenberg, Berg, and Webern, have contributed much to a wider and deeper understanding; his book *Serial Composition and Atonality* has become a standard text. His most extensive work has been on the music of Berg and has revealed in great depth and detail the richness and subtlety of Berg's work, dispelling popular notions that Berg's music, in contrast with that of Schoenberg and Webern, is arbitrary with respect to its use of 12-tone and serial procedures. In addition, extensive research and study of Berg's opera *Lulu* convinced him that its third act could be completed accurately with respect to Berg's intentions; his publications on the matter were highly influential in bringing this about. His discovery of an annotated score of Berg's *Lyric Suite*, revealing biographical aspects of the work's composition, has led to major changes in the accepted view of the composer's life. Perle's book *Twelve-tone Tonality* is a highly detailed text outlining his compositional theory, the system of 12-tone tonality briefly described above. In this book and in a number of articles he attempts to recharacterize procedures in some of the music of Bartók, Stravinsky, and Scriabin, and the early atonal works of Berg, in ways which consequently demonstrate historical bases for his theoretical assumptions.

See also THEORY, esp. §5(ii).

WORKS

(all published unless otherwise stated)

ORCHESTRAL

Solemn Procession, band, 1947

Symphony no.2, op.26, 1950, unpubd, withdrawn; Louisville, KY, 6 Dec 1950

Variations on a Welsh Melody, band, op.30, 1952, unpubd, withdrawn; Louisville, 5 May 1953

Symphony no.3, op.31, 1952, unpubd, withdrawn

Rhapsody, op.33, 1953, withdrawn; Louisville, 16 Jan 1954, cond. R. Whitney

Symphony for Band, op.38, 1959, unpubd, withdrawn

Three Movements for Orchestra, 1960; Amsterdam, Netherlands, 16 June 1963, cond. R. Krol

Serenade no.1, va, chamber orch, 1962; New York, 10 May 1962, W. Trampler, cond. A. Weisberg

Six Bagatelles, 1965; Riverhead, NY, 18 Nov 1977, cond. S. Lipkin

Cello Concerto, 1966

Serenade no.2, chamber orch, 1968; Washington, DC, 28 Feb 1969, cond. Weisberg

Concertino, pf, wind, timp, 1979; Chicago, IL, 20 April 1979, M. Ritt, cond. R. Shapey

A Short Symphony, 1980; Lenox, MA, 16 Aug 1980, cond. Ozawa

An Anniversary Rondo for Paul, chamber orch, ?1982, unpubd; Chicago, 17 Jan 1982, cond. Shapey

Serenade no.3, pf, chamber orch, 1983; New York, 14 Dec 1983, R. Goode, cond. G. Schwarz

CHAMBER

5 insts: Qnt, 2 vn, 2 va, vc, op.35, 1958; 4 Wind Qnts, no.1, op.37, 1959, no.2, op.41, 1959, no.3, 1967, no.4, 1984

4 insts: Molto adagio, str qt, 1938, unpubd, withdrawn; Triolet, str qt, op.2, 1938, unpubd, withdrawn; 3 Very Short Pieces, str qt, op.7, 1940, unpubd, withdrawn; 6 Str Qts, no.2, d, op.14, 1942, unpubd, withdrawn, no.3, op.21, 1947, withdrawn, no.4, op.24, 1948, unpubd, withdrawn, no.5, op.42, 1960, rev. 1967, no.6, 1969, unpubd, withdrawn, no.7, 1973; Scherzo, fl, cl, vn, vc, 1979, incl. in Sonata a quattro, fl, cl, vn, vc, 1982

2–3 insts: Trio, fl, va, pf, op.11, 1942, unpubd, withdrawn; Prelude, Invention and Ostinato, va, pf, op.15, 1943, unpubd, withdrawn; Slow Piece, vn, va, op.18, 1944, rev. cl, va, 1951, unpubd, withdrawn; Lyric Piece, vc, pf, op.21a, 1946, rev. 1949, unpubd; Va Sonata, op.25, 1949, unpubd, withdrawn; Invention, rec, pf, op.36, 1958, unpubd, withdrawn; Introduction and Rondo Capriccio, vn, pf, op.39, 1959, unpubd, withdrawn; Solo Partita, vn, va, 1965; Sonata quasi una fantasia, cl, pf, 1972; Vc Sonata, 1985, unpubd

1 inst: Sonata, va, 1942; 3 Sonatas, cl [orig. vn], op.16, 1943; Heb. Melodies, vc, op.19, 1945; Sonata, vc, op.22, 1947; 2 Inventions, fl, op.34, 1954, unpubd, withdrawn; Sonata no.1, vn, op.40, 1959; Monody I, fl, op.43, 1960; Monody II, db, 1962; 3 Inventions, bn, 1962; Sonata no.2, vn, 1963

PIANO

Pantomime, Interlude and Fugue, 1937; Classic Suite, op.3, 1938, unpubd, withdrawn; 2 Pieces, op.4, 1939, unpubd, withdrawn; Little Suite, op.5, 1939, unpubd; Suite, op.6, 1940; 2 Little Pieces, op.17, 1943, unpubd, withdrawn; Pf Piece, op.18b, 1945, rev. 1952, unpubd; 6 Preludes, op.20a, 1946, unpubd, withdrawn; 6 Preludes, op.20b, 1946; 6 Preludes, op.20c, 1947, unpubd, withdrawn

Pf Sonata, op.27, 1950; 3 Inventions, op.32, 1957, unpubd; Interrupted Story, 1956; Short Sonata, 1964; Toccata, 1969; Suite in C (Dodecatonal Suite), 1970, unpubd; Fantasy-Variations, 1971, unpubd; 6 Etudes, nos. 1–3, 1973, nos.4–6, 1976; Ballade, 1981; 6 New Etudes, pf, 1984

VOCAL

2 [R. M.] Rilke Songs: Du meine heilige Einsamkeit, Der Bach hat leise Melodien, S, pf, op.9, 1941, unpubd; Herbsttag (Rilke), Bar, pf, op.29, 1951, unpubd, withdrawn; With thee Conversing (J. Milton), medium v, pf, op.30a, 1952, unpubd, withdrawn; The Birds (incidental music, Aristophanes, trans. W. Arrowsmith), solo vv, chorus, 7 insts, 1961, unpubd; Sonnets of Praise and Lamentation: From the 18th Psalm (Heb.), SATB, orch, Sonnets to Orpheus (Rilke), SATB, unacc., In eius memoriam (J. Hollander), solo vv, SATB, orch, 1974

13 [E.] Dickinson Songs: From a Childhood (Perhaps you'd like to buy a flower, I like to see it lap the miles, I know some lonely houses off the road, There came a wind like a bugle), Autumn Day (Beauty, The wind, These are the days when birds come back, The heart asks pleasure), Grave Hour (What if I say I shall not wait, If I'm lost, The loneliness one dare not sound, Under the light, yet under), Closing Piece (She bore it till the simple veins), S, pf, 1979

Arrs.: 2 Fr. Christmas carols: Christ is Born Today, The Miracle of St. Nicholas, SATB, unacc., 1958

Principal publishers: Boelke-Bomart, Galaxy, Margun, Presser

WRITINGS

Serial Composition and Atonality: an Introduction to the Music of Schoenberg, Berg, and Webern (Berkeley, CA, 1962, 5/1981)

Twelve-tone Tonality (Berkeley, CA, 1977)

The Operas of Alban Berg, i: *Wozzeck* (Berkeley, CA, 1980), ii: *Lulu* (Berkeley, CA, 1985)

Numerous articles in *JAMS*, *MQ*, *MR*, *PNM*, and others

BIBLIOGRAPHY

EwenD

H. Weinberg: "The Music of George Perle," *ACAB*, x/3 (1962), 6

L. Kraft: "The Music of George Perle," *MQ*, lvii (1971), 444

P. Lansky: *Affine Music* (diss., Princeton U., 1973)

B. Saylor: "A New Work by George Perle," *MQ*, lxi (1975), 471

O. Knussen: "George Perle, Composer," *Tempo*, no.137 (1981), 38

R. Swift: "A Tonal Analog: the Tone-centered Music of George Perle," *PNM*, xxi/1–2 (1982–3), 257

PAUL LANSKY (text), T. PATRICK CARRABRE (work-list)

Perlis, Vivian (*b* Brooklyn, NY, 26 April 1928). Musicologist. She was educated at the University of Michigan (BM 1949, MM 1952), where she studied the history of music and also piano and harp. She continued studying harp at the Philadelphia Academy of Music (1953–4) and was harpist of the New Haven SO from 1960 to 1977. A graduate student in musicology at Columbia University (1962–4), she taught the history of music at several colleges in New England before becoming a reference librarian at Yale University in 1967; the following year she organized the Ives Oral History Project. For *Charles Ives Remembered* (1974), the informative study that resulted, she received the Kinkeldey Award of the American Musicological Society; her many other awards include four NEH grants (1970–83) and two Martha Baird Rockefeller Fund grants (1977–8, 1982). In 1972 Perlis founded Oral History, American Music, also based at Yale, and has continued as its director. The project is an extensive repository on tape and videotape of source material on composers and other major figures in American music. Perlis was also co-director of the Ives Centennial Festival-Conference (1974) and with Hitchcock edited its proceedings (*An Ives Celebration*, 1977). Her other activities have included lecturing and teaching for the American Studies program and the School of Music at Yale. She has collaborated on several recordings and television documentaries, the latter including *Memories of Eubie* (1980), on the jazz pianist Eubie Blake. She is co-author with Aaron Copland of his autobiography (*Copland: 1900 through 1942* (1984) is the first of two volumes) and has written articles on Copland, Ives, Cage, and Ornstein. Her work represents an imaginative and timely contribution to the investigation of the recent history of American music.

Perlman, Itzhak (*b* Tel-Aviv, Israel, 31 Aug 1945). Violinist. A victim of poliomyelitis at the age of four (which deprived him of the use of his legs), he began violin lessons shortly afterwards at the Shulamit High School in Tel-Aviv, and by the age of ten had given numerous public recitals and broadcast concerts with the Israel Broadcasting Orchestra. In 1958 he won a talent competition to appear on the Ed Sullivan television show in New York, and subsequent scholarship awards enabled him to remain there to continue studies at the Juilliard School with Galamian and DeLay. He made his professional début at Carnegie Hall on 5 March 1963, and the following year won the Leventritt Competition, which brought him immediate engagements with the New York PO and other major American orchestras, as well as important support from Stern. He returned to Israel in 1965 for a successful concert tour, and made his British début in 1968. An interest in all aspects of violin music led him to take a prominent part in chamber concerts during the London South Bank Summer Music series, 1968–9. He initiated his own master class at the Meadow Brook Music Festival (Rochester, Michigan) in 1970, has given master classes at the Aspen Music School, and in 1975 joined the faculty at Brooklyn College, CUNY.

Itzhak Perlman (left) with Samuel Sanders

Perlman's instinctive directness of musical expression, combined with brilliant technique and a concern for refinement of detail, has brought him international recognition as the outstanding American violinist of the 1980s. He has recorded most of the major repertory of the 19th and 20th centuries and has given the premières of several new works, among them concertos by Earl Kim (1979) and Robert Starer (1981). He has also played and recorded rags by Joplin and jazz compositions by Previn. A prominent spokesman for the interests of the disabled, he served as a committee member for the United Nations International Year of Disabled Persons (1981).

BIBLIOGRAPHY

S. Regan: "Itzhak Perlman," *Gramophone*, l (1972–3), 27
J. Creighton: *Discopaedia of the Violin, 1889–1971* (Toronto, 1974)
"Perlman, Itzhak," *CBY 1975*
S. Collins: "Itzhak Perlman," *The Strad*, lxxxvi (1975–6), 911
M. Bookspan: "A Conversation with Itzhak Perlman," *Journal of the Violin Society of America*, iii/2 (1977), 5
M. M. Kushick: "An Interview with Itzhak Perlman," *The Instrumentalist*, xxxi/8 (1977), 41
J. Hiemenz: "On Television: Itzhak Perlman, Superstar," *HiFi/MusAm*, xxix/8 (1979), 18
A. Swan: "Itzhak Perlman, Top Fiddle," *Newsweek*, xcv (14 April 1980), 62
H. Kupferberg: "Itzhak Perlman: the Year of his Big Breakthrough," *Ovation*, ii/1 (1981), 8
J. McLellan: "Perlman to the Defense," *Symphony Magazine*, xxxii/3 (1981), 33
B. Schwarz: *Great Masters of the Violin* (New York, 1983)

NOËL GOODWIN/R

Perry, Edward Baxter (*b* Haverhill, MA, 14 Feb 1855; *d* Camden, ME, 13 June 1924). Pianist. He lost his sight in an accident at the age of two. After studying the piano with J. W. Hill in Boston, he went in 1875 to Germany, where he studied with Theodor Kullak, Dionys Pruckner, Clara Schumann, and in 1878 with Liszt. He taught at Oberlin College (1881–3) and then devoted himself to his performing career. In his recitals he presented explanatory comments on the pieces being performed, thus originating the lecture-recital; he gave over 3300 such programs throughout the USA. He later taught at Woman's College, Montgomery, Alabama (1917–20), Hood College, Frederick, Maryland (1921–2), and Lebanon Valley College, Annville, Pennsylvania (1922–4). He also composed a number of piano pieces, contributed frequently to music magazines, principally *The Etude*, and wrote two books, *Descriptive Analyses of Piano Works* (1902) and *Stories of Standard Teaching Pieces* (1910). In his lectures and writings he attached more importance to literary ideas than to technical analysis.

BIBLIOGRAPHY

GroveAS
W. F. Gates: "Edward Baxter Perry," *Musical Courier*, xxxiv/22 (1897), 10

R. ALLEN LOTT

Perry, Julia (Amanda) (*b* Lexington, KY, 25 March 1924; *d* Akron, OH, 24 April 1979). Composer. She studied at Westminster Choir College (MMus 1948), the Juilliard School, and in Europe, her principal teachers being Henry Switten, Nadia Boulanger, and Luigi Dallapiccola (composition), and Emanuel Balaban and Aleco Galliera (conducting). Her honors included two Guggenheim Fellowships, an award from the National Institute of Arts and Letters, and a Boulanger Grand Prix. She was active as a lecturer in Europe and the USA and as a college teacher. Her eclectic music reflects wide cultural interests; her style is neoclassical, with richly dissonant harmonies, contrapuntal textures, and an intense lyricism. In her late works, such as *Soul Symphony* (1972), she employed black folk idioms. Several of her compositions, including *Short Piece for Orchestra*, *Stabat mater*, and *Homunculus C. F.*, have been recorded.

WORKS

Stage: The Bottle (opera, 1, J. Perry); The Cask of Amontillado (opera, 1, after E. A. Poe), New York, 1954; The Selfish Giant (opera-ballet, 3, after O. Wilde), 1964; 3 Warnings (opera)

Orch: Short Piece (1952); Study, 1952; Pastoral, fl, str, 1959; Requiem, 1959; 12 syms., 1959–72, incl. no.11 "Soul Symphony," 1972; 2 pf concs., 1964, (1965); Vn Conc., 1964; Episodes; Homage to Vivaldi; Module, 1975; works for band

Vocal: Chicago, cantata (after C. Sandburg), Bar, nar, chorus, orch, 1948; Ruth, cantata, chorus, org, 1950; Stabat mater (J. da Todi, trans. Perry), A, str, 1951; Quinary Quixotic Songs, B-Bar, 5 insts, 1976; Frammenti dalle lettere de Santa Caterina, 1v, chorus, orch; Missa brevis; 7 Contrasts, Bar, chamber ens; many songs, arrs. of spirituals, 1947–52

Chamber and inst: Homunculus C. F., harp, 10 perc, 1960; ww trio; str qt; 3 pf pieces for children

Principal publishers: C. Fischer, Galaxy, Peer-Southern, Southern

BIBLIOGRAPHY

SouthernB
E. Southern: *The Music of Black Americans: a History* (New York, 1971, rev. 2/1983)
M. Green: *Black Women Composers: a Genesis* (Boston, 1983)

EILEEN SOUTHERN

Persichetti, Vincent (*b* Philadelphia, PA, 6 June 1915). Composer, educator, theorist, pianist, and conductor. At the age of five he enrolled in the Combs Conservatory (Philadelphia), where he studied piano, organ, and double bass; there he also studied theory and composition under Russell King Miller, his most influential teacher. While in high school, he acquired professional experience performing on radio, in churches, and in recital. After graduating from Combs (BMus 1936), he served as head of its theory and composition departments while studying piano with Samaroff and composition with Nordoff at the Philadelphia Conservatory (MMus 1941, DMus 1945) and conducting with Reiner at the Curtis Institute. In 1941 Persichetti was appointed head of the theory and composition departments at the Philadelphia Conservatory, and in 1947 he joined the faculty of the Juilliard School, where he became chairman of the composition department in 1963 and of the literature and materials department in 1970. From 1952 he has also served as director of publications for Elkan-Vogel.

Persichetti's prodigious musical output exemplifies a principle that underlies his teaching and theoretical writing as well: the composer's challenge is to integrate into a fluent working vocabulary the wealth of materials placed at his disposal by the expansion of musical language over the course of this century. Drawing on a full range of expressive possibilities, from simple diatonicism to complex atonal polyphony, Persichetti has produced an array of works whose varied moods, styles, and levels of difficulty have bewildered those who search for a conventional chronological pattern of development. His mastery of compositional technique is perhaps unequaled by any American composer, but many have noted a cold detachment in his art and have questioned whether a musical personality emerges from the virtuoso craftsmanship. Viewed as a whole, however, Persichetti's work reveals a strong personal profile. The composer himself has cited two main currents within his creative disposition: one "graceful" and the other "gritty." Beyond this, his music has a propensity for lucid textures, a fondness for pandiatonic and polytonal harmony, a playful rhythmic vitality, and a pervasive geniality of spirit. Following the lineage of Mozart, Mendelssohn, and Ravel, Persichetti's music suggests the innocence and childlike joy of pure musical creativity. Hence many works for beginners stand, with neither condescension nor apology, alongside more difficult composi-

Vincent Persichetti, 1981

tions. Although Persichetti has often worked in large forms, he is inclined toward sparse gestures and epigrammatic forms – indeed, many large works are based on an integration of diminutive concepts.

A prolific composer, Persichetti has made substantial contributions to most musical genres; worthy of particular mention are his piano works, which provide a microcosmic representation of his entire compositional output while offering a comprehensive survey of contemporary piano techniques. Also important are his works for wind band, which reveal a natural affinity for the medium and have given many students an accessible yet sophisticated introduction to contemporary music.

Persichetti is one of America's most widely performed composers and many of his works appear on recordings. Most significant are a series produced by Arizona State University, including the four string quartets, the piano quintet, and *Harmonium*; two concerts of band works; and a recital of his piano music from the USSR. Among his many honors and awards are three Guggenheim Fellowships, two grants from the National Foundation on the Arts and Humanities, and one from the National Institute of Arts and Letters, of which he is a member (elected 1965). He has received commissions from several of the country's leading orchestras and institutions, and has appeared as guest lecturer and performer at many colleges and universities. Persichetti has written the monograph *William Schuman* (with F. R. Schreiber, 1954) and he is the author of the text *Twentieth Century Harmony* (1961).

WORKS

(all published unless otherwise stated)

OPERA

The Sibyl (Parable XX) (1, Persichetti, after fable, Chicken Little), op.135, 1976; Philadelphia, 13 April 1985, Pennsylvania Opera Theatre

ORCHESTRAL

Concertino, pf, orch, op.16, 1941; Rochester, NY, 23 Oct 1945, cond. Hanson
Symphony no.1, op.18, 1942, unpubd; Rochester, NY, 21 Oct 1947, cond. Hanson
Symphony no.2, op.19, 1942, unpubd
Dance Overture, op.20, 1942; Tokyo, 7 Feb 1948, cond. Konoye
Fables, nar, orch, op.23, 1943; Philadelphia, 20 April 1945, cond. Ormandy
The Hollow Men, tpt, str, op.25, 1944; Germantown, PA, 12 Dec 1946, cond. A. Lipkin
Symphony no.3, op.30, 1946; Philadelphia, 21 Nov 1947, cond. Ormandy
Serenade no.5, op.43, 1950; Louisville, 15 Nov 1950, cond. R. Whitney
Fairy Tale, op.48, 1950; Philadelphia, 31 March 1951, cond. Hilsberg
Symphony no.4, op.51, 1951; Philadelphia, 17 Dec 1954, cond. Ormandy
Symphony for Strings (Symphony no.5), op.61, 1953; Louisville, 28 Aug 1954, cond. Whitney
Symphony no.7 "Liturgical," op.80, 1958; St. Louis, 24 Oct 1959
Piano Concerto, op.90, 1962; Hanover, NH, 2 Aug 1964, cond. M. di Bonaventura
Introit, str, op.96, 1964; Kansas City, MO, 1 May 1965, cond. J. Herriman
Symphony no.8, op.106, 1967; Berea, OH, 29 Oct 1967, cond. G. Poinar
Symphony no.9 "Sinfonia Janiculum," op.113, 1970; Philadelphia, 5 March 1971, cond. Ormandy
Night Dances, op.114, 1970; Kiamesha Lake, NY, 9 Dec 1970, cond. Fennell
A Lincoln Address, nar, orch, op.124, 1972; St. Louis, 25 Jan 1973, cond. Susskind
Concerto, eng hn, str, op.137, 1977; New York, 17 Nov 1977, cond. Leinsdorf

BAND

(all first performances cond. Persichetti unless otherwise stated)

Divertimento, op.42, 1950; New York, 16 June 1950
Psalm, op.53, 1952; Louisville, 2 May 1952
Pageant, op.59, 1953; Miami, FL, 7 March 1953
Symphony for Band (Symphony no.6), op.69, 1956; St. Louis, 16 April 1956, cond. C. Mitze
Serenade no.11, op.85, 1960; Ithaca, NY, 19 April 1961
Bagatelles, op.87, 1961; Hanover, NH, 21 May 1961
So Pure the Star, chorale prelude, op.91, 1962; Durham, 11 Dec 1962
Masquerade, op.102, 1965; Berea, OH, 23 Jan 1966
Turn not thy Face, chorale prelude, op.105, 1966; Ithaca, NY, 17 May 1967, cond. F. Battisti
O Cool is the Valley (Poem for Band), op.118, 1971; Columbus, OH, 5 Feb 1972
Parable IX, op.121, 1972; Des Moines, 6 April 1973, cond. D. R. Marcouiller
A Lincoln Address, nar, band, op.124a, 1973; Russellville, AR, 1 Feb 1974, cond. G. Witherspoon
O God Unseen, chorale prelude, op.160, 1984; Winston-Salem, NC, 4 Nov 1984

KEYBOARD

Serenade no.2, op.2, pf, 1929; Pf Sonata no.1, op.3, 1939; Poems, vol.1, pf, op.4, 1939; Poems, vol.2, pf, op.5, 1939; Pf Sonata no.2, op.6, 1939; Sonatine, org pedals, op.11, 1940; Sonata, 2 pf, op.13, 1940; Poems, vol.3, pf, op.14, 1941; Pf Sonata no.3, op.22, 1943; Variations for an Album, pf, op.32, 1947; Pf Sonata no.4, op.36, 1949; Pf Sonata no.5, op.37, 1949; Pf Sonatina no.1, op.38, 1950; Pf Sonata no.6, op.39, 1950; Pf Sonata no.7, op.40, 1950; Pf Sonata no.8, op.41, 1950; Pf Sonatina no.2, op.45, 1950; Pf Sonatina no.3, op.47, 1950; Hpd Sonata no.1, op.52, 1951

Serenade no.7, op.55, pf, 1952; Conc., pf 4 hands, op.56, 1952; Parades, pf, op.57, 1952; Pf Sonata no.9, op.58, 1952; Little Piano Book, op.60, 1953; Serenade no.8, pf 4 hands, op.62, 1954; Pf Sonatina no.4, op.63, 1954; Pf Sonatina no.5, op.64, 1954; Pf Sonatina no.6, op.65, 1954; Pf Sonata no.10, op.67, 1955; Org Sonata, op.86, 1960; Shimah b'koli, org, op.89, 1962; Pf Sonata no.11, op.101, 1965; Drop, Drop Slow Tears, chorale prelude, org, op.104, 1966; Parable V, carillon, op.112, 1969; Parable VI, org, op.117, 1971; Do not Go Gentle, org pedals, op.132, 1974; Parable XIX, pf, op.134, 1975; Auden Variations, org, op.136, 1977

Reflective Studies, pf, op.138, 1978; Little Mirror Book, pf, op.139, 1978; 4 Arabesques, pf, op.141, 1978; 3 Toccatinas, pf, op.142, 1979; Mirror Etudes, pf, op.143, 1979; Dryden Liturgical Suite, org, op.144, 1980; Pf Sonata no.12, op.145, 1980; Hpd Sonata no.2, op.146, 1981; Song of David, org, op.148, 1981; Hpd Sonata no.3, op.149, 1981; Hpd Sonata no.4, op.151, 1982; Hpd Sonata no.5, op.152, 1982; Parable XXIV, hpd, op.153, 1982; Hpd Sonata no.6, op.154, 1982; Little Hpd Book, op.155, 1983; Hpd Sonata no.7, op.156, 1983; Hpd Sonata no.8, op.158, 1984; Serenade no.15, hpd, op.161, 1984

CHAMBER

Serenade no.1, 10 wind, op.1, 1929; Str Qt no.1, op.7, 1939; Suite, vn, vc, op.9, 1940, unpubd; Sonata, vn, op.10, 1940; Concertato, pf qnt, op.12, 1940, unpubd; Fantasy, vn, pf, op.15, 1941, unpubd; Serenade no.3, vn, vc, pf, op.17, 1941; Pastoral, ww qnt, op.21, 1943; Str Qt no.2, op.24,

1944; Vocalise, vc, pf, op.27, 1945; Serenade no.4, vn, pf, op.28, 1945; King Lear, ww qnt, timp, pf, op.35, 1948; Serenade no.6, trbn, va, vc, op.44, 1950; Sonata, vc, op.54, 1952; Pf Qnt, op.66, 1954

Little Recorder Book, op.70, 1956; Serenade no.9, 2 rec, op.71, 1956; Serenade no.10, fl, harp, op.79, 1957; Str Qt no.3, op.81, 1959; Infanta Marina, va, pf, op.83, 1960; Serenade no.12, tuba, op.88, 1961; Serenade no.13, 2 cl, op.95, 1963; Masques, vn, pf, op.99, 1965; Parable [I], fl, op.100, 1965; Parable II, brass qnt, op.108, 1968; Parable III, ob, op.109, 1968; Parable IV, bn, op.110, 1969; Parable VII, harp, op.119, 1971; Parable VIII, hn, op.120, 1972; Str Qt no.4 (Parable X), op.122, 1972

Parable XI, a sax, op.123, 1972; Parable XII, pic, op.125, 1973; Parable XIII, cl, op.126, 1973; Parable XIV, tpt, op.127, 1973; Parable XV, eng hn, op.128, 1973; Parable XVI, va, op.130, 1974; Parable XVII, db, op.131, 1974; Parable XVIII, trbn, op.133, 1975; Parable XXI, gui, op.140, 1978; Parable XXII, tuba, op.147, 1981; Parable XXIII, vn, vc, pf, op.150, 1981; Serenade no.14, ob, op.159, 1984

CHORAL

Magnificat and Nunc dimittis, SATB, pf, op.8, 1940; Canons, SSAA/TTBB/SATB, op.31, 1947; 2 Cummings Choruses, 2vv, pf, op.33, 1948; Proverb, SATB, op.34, 1948; 2 Cummings Choruses, SSAA, op.46, 1950; Hymns and Responses for the Church Year (Auden and others), op.68, 1955; Seek the Highest, SAB, pf, op.78, 1957; Song of Peace (anon.), TTBB/SATB, pf, op.82, 1959; Mass, SATB, op.84, 1960; Stabat Mater, SATB, orch, op.92, 1963; Te Deum, SATB, orch, op.93, 1963

Spring Cantata (Cummings), SSAA, pf, op.94, 1963; Winter Cantata (11 Haiku), SSAA, fl, mar, op.97, 1964; 4 Cummings Choruses, 2vv, pf, op.98. 1964; Celebrations (Whitman), SATB, wind ens, op.103, 1966; The Pleiades (Whitman), SATB, tpt, str, op.107, 1967; The Creation (Persichetti), S, A, T, Bar, SATB, orch, op.111, 1969; Love, SSAA, op.116, 1971; Glad and Very (Cummings), 2vv, op.129, 1974; Flower Songs (Cantata no.6), SATB, str, op.157, 1983

SOLO VOCAL

E. E. Cummings Songs, op.26, 1945, unpubd; 2 Chinese Songs, op.29, 1945; 3 English Songs (17th-century texts), op.49, 1951, unpubd; Harmonium (Stevens), song cycle, S, pf, op.51, 1951; Sara Teasdale Songs, op.72, 1957, unpubd; Carl Sandburg Songs, op.73, 1957, unpubd; James Joyce Songs, op.74, 1957; Hilaire Belloc Songs, op.75, 1957; Robert Frost Songs, op.76, 1957, unpubd; Emily Dickinson Songs, op.77, 1957; A Net of Fireflies (Jap., trans H. Steward), cycle of 17 songs, op.115, 1970

Principal publisher: Elkan-Vogel

BIBLIOGRAPHY

EwenD

R. Evett: "The Music of Vincent Persichetti," *Juilliard Review*, ii/2 (1955), 15

W. Schuman: "The Compleat Musician," *MQ*, xlvii (1961), 379

H. Weisgall: "Current Chronicle: New York," *MQ*, l (1964), 379 [on Stabat Mater]

W. Simmons: "A Persichetti Perspective," *American Record Guide*, xl/6 (1977), 6

D. M. Rubin: "Vincent Persichetti," *ASCAP in Action* (spr. 1980), 8

R. Shackelford: "Conversation with Vincent Persichetti," *PNM*, xx/1–2 (1981–2), 104–34

D. Webster: "Vincent Persichetti," *HiFi/MusAm*, xxxv/4 (1985), 4

WALTER G. SIMMONS

Persinger, Louis (*b* Rochester, IL, 11 Feb 1887; *d* New York, 31 Dec 1966). Violinist, pianist, and teacher. He had early lessons in Colorado, appearing in public at the age of 12. His main studies were at the Leipzig Conservatory (1900–04) under Hans Becker (violin), Carl Beving (piano), and Arthur Nikisch (conducting), who described him as "one of the most talented pupils the Leipzig Conservatory ever had." He then settled in Brussels for three years, combining studies under Ysaÿe with concerts in Belgium and Germany and two summers' coaching from Jacques Thibaud. Returning to the USA, he made his début on 1 November 1912 with the Philadelphia Orchestra under Stokowski, followed by many engagements with orchestras. In 1914 Nikisch invited him to become concertmaster of the Berlin PO and in 1915 he became concertmaster of the San Francisco SO. Two years later he resigned to form his own string quartet and to direct the Chamber Music Society of San Francisco (1916–28), where he began his teaching career. One of his earliest pupils was Yehudi Menuhin, who followed Persinger to New York in 1925. An accomplished pianist, he was the accompanist for Menuhin's first New York recital in 1926 and on his American tour in 1928–9. On his 75th birthday Persinger gave a recital at the Juilliard School, playing half the program on the piano and half on the violin.

Persinger taught at the Cleveland Institute of Music (1929–30), and in 1930 succeeded Auer at the Juilliard School, where he taught violin and chamber music until his death. Among his pupils were Stern, Ricci, Guila Bustabo, Arnold Eidus, Frances Magnes, Sonya Monosoff, and Camilla Wicks. He said that his unorthodox teaching method was "based on keeping a child's interest, in sensing what might be amusing or arresting to him, and in using as few pedantic words as possible. I teach through the sound of the instrument." Menuhin wrote that Persinger "has done perhaps more than anyone else to establish a genuine American school of violin playing." He served as a member of the jury in the Queen Elisabeth and Wieniawski competitions, and published transcriptions and editions of violin music.

BIBLIOGRAPHY

R. Magidoff: *Yehudi Menuhin* (Garden City, NY, 1955)

M. C. Hart: "Louis Persinger, a Tribute on his 75th," *Juilliard Review*, ix/1 (1961–2), 4

Y. Menuhin: "Louis Persinger," *Juilliard Review Annual* (New York, 1966–7), 15

Obituaries, *Juilliard News Bulletin*, v/3 (1967), 1; *New York Times* (1 Jan 1967)

J. Creighton: *Discopaedia of the Violin, 1889–1971* (Toronto, 1974), 578

Y. Menuhin: *Unfinished Journey* (New York, 1977)

B. Schwarz: *Great Masters of the Violin* (New York, 1983)

BORIS SCHWARZ

Persuasions. Vocal group. It was formed in Brooklyn, New York, in 1962 by Jerry Lawson (*b* Fort Lauderdale, FL, 23 Jan 1944), baritone; Jayotis Washington (*b* Detroit, MI, 12 May 1945), tenor; Joseph "Jesse" Russell (*b* Henderson, NC, 25 Sept 1939), tenor; Herbert "Tubo" Rhoad (*b* Bamberg Co., SC, 1 Oct 1944), baritone; and Jimmy Hayes (*b* Hopewell, VA, 12 Nov 1943), bass. All five men had had previous experience performing in vocal groups. Washington left the group briefly in the mid-1970s and was replaced by Willie Daniels. The Persuasions' first recording was *A capella* in 1968 on the Straight label, owned by Frank Zappa. Their music is a blend of soul, doo-wop, traditional rhythm-and-blues, gospel, and pop; except for a short-lived and unsuccessful experiment with instruments in the 1970s, they have always sung unaccompanied. They have never achieved commercial success through their recordings and at times have been unable to work as full-time musicians, but their live performances continue to be popular. They have also appeared as a backup group on recordings by Stevie Wonder, Phoebe Snow, Joni Mitchell, and other performers.

RECORDINGS

(selective list)

A capella (Straight 1062, 1968); *We Came to Play* (Cap. 791, 1971); *Spread the Word* (Cap. 11101, 1972); *Street Corner Symphony* (Cap. 872, 1972); I really got it bad for you (A&M 1531, 1974); One thing on my mind (A&M 1698, 1975); *Chirpin'* (Elek. 7E1099, 1977)

JOHN MORTHLAND

Peter, Johann Friedrich [John Frederick] (*b* Heerendijk, Netherlands, 19 May 1746; *d* Bethlehem, PA, 13 July 1813). Moravian composer, violinist, and organist, of German ancestry. He was educated at the Moravian schools in the Netherlands and Germany, finally entering the theological seminary of the church at Barby, Saxony. After his graduation in 1769, he was sent to America in 1770. From 1770 to 1780 he served the northern Moravian communities of Nazareth, Bethlehem, and Lititz, Pennsylvania. In 1780 he was transferred to the southern community of Salem, North Carolina, where he spent the next ten years in various church positions, including that of music director to the Salem congregation. In 1790 he was again transferred to the North, serving successively at Graceham (Maryland), Hope (New Jersey), and Bethlehem again. Although his official position was often that of schoolteacher, clerical assistant, or diarist, unofficially he was always concerned with music. While a student at the seminary he copied much of the music that came his way. When he came to America he brought with him an extensive library of instrumental works in manuscript, including several works by J. C. F. Bach which survive only in Peter's copies. Although he must have studied with such Moravian composers as Johann Daniel Grimm (1719–60) and Christian Gregor (1723–1801), it is thought that he gained more from his studies of the works he copied than from formal instruction.

Peter composed six quintets for two violins, two violas, and cello, and about 105 concerted anthems and solo songs. The musical style of the quintets is close to that of the early Classical masters, such as Carl Stamitz, J. B. Vanhal, and early Haydn. They were completed in Salem in 1789 and are the earliest known chamber music composed in America. Peter's anthems and solo songs feature grateful vocal writing and a considerable depth of musical expression. The orchestral accompaniment of these works, for strings and organ with occasional woodwind and brass, is always well worked out and often elaborate. His sacred vocal music is the finest body of concerted church music written in America at the time and compares well with that of European Moravian composers of his era. Manuscripts of his music are in the Archives of the Moravian Church in Bethlehem and the Moravian Foundation at Winston-Salem, North Carolina.

See also MORAVIAN CHURCH, MUSIC OF THE.

BIBLIOGRAPHY

A. G. Rau: "John Frederick Peter," *MQ*, xxiii (1937), 306

A. G. Rau and H. T. David: *A Catalogue of Music by American Moravians, 1742–1842* (Bethlehem, PA, 1938/*R*1970), 18–52

H. T. David: "Musical Life in the Pennsylvania Settlements of the Unitas Fratrum," *Transactions of the Moravian Historical Society*, xiii (1942), 19; separately pubd (Winston-Salem, NC, 1959)

D. M. McCorkle: *Moravian Music in Salem* (diss., Indiana U., 1958)

W. E. Schnell: *The Choral Music of Johann Friedrich Peter* (diss., U. of Illinois, 1973)

J. S. Ingram: "A Musical Pot-pourri: the Commonplace Book of Johann Friedrich Peter," *Moravian Music Foundation Bulletin*, xxiv/1 (1979), 2

KARL KROEGER

Peter, Paul and Mary. Folk group. Peter Yarrow (*b* New York, 31 May 1938), (Noel) Paul Stookey (*b* Baltimore, MD, 30 Nov 1937), and Mary (Ellin) Travers (*b* Louisville, KY, 9 Nov 1936) formed a trio in 1961 and began performing in the New York area the following year. Travers and Yarrow had previously been active in folk music while Stookey's experience was in rock-and-roll. They combined solo singing with simple, three-part harmony that was occasionally enlivened by contrapuntal independence. By the end of 1962 their highly successful album *Peter, Paul and Mary* had sold over a million copies; it incorporated original songs in a contemporary folk style (Yarrow's *Cruel War*) as well as songs by other contemporary folksingers (Pete Seeger's *Where have all the flowers gone?*). Subsequent successful albums and singles during the 1960s included further original works, such as the children's song *Puff, the magic dragon*, a number of pieces by the contemporary folksingers Bob Dylan and Gordon Lightfoot, and various traditional songs. In 1967 the trio had a hit single with *I dig rock and roll music*, a salute to such rock groups as the Beatles and the Mamas and the Papas. Although the sales of their recordings diminished in the late 1960s and they ceased to receive the same critical acclaim, they had another success in 1969 with John Denver's *Leaving on a jet plane*. Throughout their career, Peter, Paul and Mary supported various political causes, notably the civil rights and antiwar movements of the 1960s; *The Great Mandella* (1967) was one of the most eloquent and poignant antiwar songs of the period. The trio disbanded in 1970, and all three members recorded solo albums, with mixed commercial and critical success. They regrouped occasionally for benefit appearances and to record the album *Reunion* (1978), and in 1982 re-formed on a more permanent basis.

RECORDINGS

(selective list; all recorded for Warner Bros.)

Peter, Paul and Mary (1449, 1962), incl. Cruel War, Where have all the flowers gone?; *Moving* (1473, 1963), incl. Puff, the magic dragon; *See What Tomorrow Brings* (1615, 1965); *Album 1700* (1700, 1967), incl. I dig rock and roll music, Leaving on a jet plane, The Great Mandella; *Late Again* (1751, 1968); *Reunion* (3231, 1978)

BIBLIOGRAPHY

R. Coleman: "They're Sick of the Pseudo!," *Melody Maker*, xxxviii (5 Oct 1963), 10

R. Grevatt: "Folk Leader Asks of Material: Is it Honest, Does it Move?," *Billboard*, lxxv (2 March 1963), 18

I. Mothner: "Big Folk Singers on Campus: Peter, Paul & Mary," *Look*, xxvii (2 July 1963), 59

A. G. Arnowitz and M. Blonsky: "Three's Company: Peter, Paul and Mary," *Saturday Evening Post* (30 May 1964), 30

F. Kirby: "Peter, Paul & Mary: Still the Masters of Fine Art of Folk Singing," *Billboard*, lxxviii (29 Oct 1966), 26

"Peter, Paul and Mary: Time out," *Rolling Stone*, no.69 (29 Oct 1970), 22

R. Williams: "Our Battle for Peace Goes on Says Peter Yarrow," *Melody Maker*, xlv (13 June 1970), 5

TERENCE J. O'GRADY

Peters. Family of music publishers. The Peters family came to the USA from England around 1820. William Cumming Peters (*b* Woodbury, Devon, England, 10 March 1805; *d* Cincinnati, OH, 20 April 1866) was in Pittsburgh in the early 1820s, where he opened one of the city's first music stores. In 1830 his Musical Repository was located at 19 Market Street, and in 1831 he entered into partnership with W. C. Smith and John H. Mellor at 9 Fifth Avenue. Between 1827 and 1831 he also arranged and composed music, including a Symphony in D in two movements, for the Harmony Society at Economy, near Pittsburgh. He became known as a songwriter in the 1830s, and by 1845 his work had been issued by the leading publishers in New York, Philadelphia, and Baltimore, often under the pseudonym William Cumming. Early titles include *There's not a word thy lip hath breath'd* (1831) and *Wound not the heart that loves thee* (1835). In 1832 Peters sold his Pittsburgh business interests to his partners Smith and Mellor and moved to Louisville.

The Peters' publishing ventures may have begun as early as 1838, when *The Bloomington Waltz* was issued in Louisville, although early publications were probably borrowed from other publishers.

There followed a succession of partnerships, the principals of which are not always identifiable: Peters & Co. (W. C. Peters and his brother Henry J. Peters, 1842); Peters & Webster (W. C. Peters and F. J. Webster, 1845); Henry J. Peters & Co. (partners, if any, not known, *c*1846); Peters & Webb (Henry Peters and Benedict Webb, *c*1848); W. C. Peters & Co. (W. C. Peters and his son Alfred C. Peters, *c*1848); Peters, Webb & Co. (Henry Peters, Webb, F. M. Burkett, and R. S. Millar, *c*1849); and Peters, Cragg, & Co. (Henry Peters, Timothy Cragg, and Webb, *c*1851–2 and *c*1858–60). While these companies were in operation (not totally independent of one another, for some of their plate numbers interlock), W. C. Peters also issued music in Baltimore, and moved to the city in 1849. In 1850 he issued his *Baltimore Olio and Musical Gazette* (12 numbers), a magazine containing music, excerpts from pedagogical works, and topics of current musical interest. Several songs by Stephen Foster helped to establish the Peters name including *There's a good time coming* (1846), *Lou'siana Belle* (1847), *What must a fairy's dream be?* (1847), and *Summer Longings* (1849).

W. C. Peters moved to Cincinnati in 1851 or 1852, and with his sons William and Alfred formed W. C. Peters & Sons there in 1851. This was a very successful company and a charter member of the Board of Music Trade organized in New York in 1855. In 1857 William was replaced by his brother John L. Peters, and the company continued until 1862. It issued numerous pedagogical works, music for the Roman Catholic Church, and popular sheet music, for which the plate numbers exceeded 3000 by 1862. By 1860, however, Alfred and John had registered copyrights under the names A. C. Peters & Brother, A. C. & J. L. Peters, and J. L. Peters & Brother, suggesting the gradual retirement of their father, who appears to have devoted more time to composition and the compilation of sacred music, such as *Peters' Catholic Harp* (1863). On 22 March 1866 the company's entire stock was destroyed by fire; W. C. Peters died the following month, and A. C. Peters & Brother went out of business about a year later.

John Peters had also established a business with Alfred in St. Louis in 1851; John L. Peters & Brother issued largely the same music as the Cincinnati firm until 1866, when John opened a music store in New York. In 1869 the firm became J. L. Peters & Co. (John Peters and T. August Boyle). John sold his New York business to Oliver Ditson in 1877 and returned to St. Louis. He was the last of the Peters family to remain active in the music trade, and continued publishing until 1885; he appears to have gone out of business in 1892. Henry Peters dissolved his partnership with Benedict Webb in 1877 and moved to Texas, where he died the following year.

BIBLIOGRAPHY

S. V. Connor: *The Peters Colony of Texas* (Austin, TX, 1959)
E. C. Krohn: *Music Publishing in the Middle Western States before the Civil War* (Detroit, 1972)
——: *Music Publishing in St. Louis* (MS, *MoSW*)
R. D. Wetzel: *Frontier Musicians on the Connoquenessing, Wabash, and Ohio* (Athens, OH, 1976)

RICHARD D. WETZEL, ERNST C. KROHN

Peters, C. F. Firm of music publishers. It was founded in New York in 1948 by WALTER HINRICHSEN, who had worked for his father, Henri Hinrichsen (head of the Peters firm in Leipzig), for five years before coming to the USA in 1936. Although a separate business from Peters in Leipzig (later Frankfurt am Main) and Peters in London (founded by Walter's older brother Max in 1938 as Hinrichsen Edition), it shares the same ideals. One of its first priorities was to reissue the "Edition Peters" publications, a series known since its inception in 1867 for its superior quality of production and high editorial standards, and covering the standard repertory as well as including Urtext and scholarly editions. The Collection Litolff, the American Music Awards sponsored by Sigma Alpha Iota, the American Wind Symphony Editions, and the New York Public Library Music Publications are also published by the firm. Another major commitment is to the publication of contemporary music; since 1948 over 1700 works (of which 98% are contemporary) have been introduced. The Peters catalogue lists among its composers Babbitt, Cage, Cowell, Crumb, Morton Feldman, Ives, Penderecki, Schoenberg, Christian Wolff, and Wuorinen. The firm has also become the American agent for a number of European publishers. After Hinrichsen's death, his widow Evelyn continued to maintain the high standards of the firm as well as expanding the catalogue. His son Henry Hans Hinrichsen became president of the firm in 1978, and was succeeded by Stephen Fisher (a staff member since 1964) in 1983. On 19 December 1983 Evelyn Hinrichsen and C. F. Peters were awarded the American Music Center's Letter of Distinction for their continued commitment to the advancement of new music.

BIBLIOGRAPHY

"The C. F. Peters Company," *Music Journal Annual* (1973), 56, 96
H. W. Hitchcock: "C. F. Peters Corporation and Twentieth-century American Music," *An Introduction to Music Publishing*, ed. C. Sachs (New York, 1981), 15

FRANCES BARULICH

Peters, Roberta (*b* New York, 4 May 1930). Soprano. She began to study singing when she was 13 with William Hermann; encouraged by Jan Peerce and Sol Hurok, she was engaged by the Metropolitan Opera at 19, without previous stage experience. She made her début on 17 November 1950 as Zerlina, a last-minute replacement for Nadine Conner (her official début had been scheduled for two months later, as the Queen of Night). By her 25th anniversary with the company she had given 303 performances of 20 roles in 19 operas, the most notable being Despina (*Così fan tutte*), Rosina, Donizetti's Norina (*Don Pasquale*) and Lucia di Lammermoor, and Verdi's Gilda and Oscar (*Un ballo in maschera*); in 1964 she sang the role of Kitty in the American première of Menotti's *Le dernier sauvage*. In later years she attempted to broaden her repertory in lyric soprano parts, playing Violetta, Mimì, and Massenet's Manon outside New York. She also performed at Covent Garden (in Michael Balfe's *The Bohemian Girl* under Beecham, 1951) and in various other leading European companies in the 1960s and 1970s. She appeared frequently on television, in films, and in musical comedy. Her recordings include her most successful roles. A singer of considerable charm and flute-like accuracy, she maintained the Pons and Galli-Curci tradition of coloratura singing at a time when the more dramatic attitudes of Callas and, later, Sutherland were in vogue. She was married briefly, in the early 1950s, to the baritone Robert Merrill.

BIBLIOGRAPHY

"Peters, Roberta," *CBY 1954*
M. de Schauensee: "Coloratura," *Opera News*, xxix/9 (1965), 27
R. Peters and L. Biancolli: *A Debut at the Met* (New York, 1967)
J. Gruen: "Lucky Star: Roberta Peters," *Opera News*, xl/6 (1975), 16

J. Hines: "Roberta Peters," *Great Singers on Great Singing* (Garden City, NY, 1982), 231

MARTIN BERNHEIMER/R

Peterson, John Willard (*b* Lindsborg, KS, 1 Nov 1921). Composer and publisher. He studied at the Moody Bible Institute and the American Conservatory of Music in Chicago. In 1954 he joined Singspiration, Alfred B. Smith's gospel music publishing firm, in Montrose, Pennsylvania; with P. J. and B. D. Zondervan he purchased the company in 1963 and moved to Grand Rapids, Michigan. In 1971 he moved to Arizona, but continued to serve as executive editor for Singspiration. Peterson received the International Gospel Songwriting Award of the Society of European Stage Authors and Composers in 1975. He established another firm to publish contemporary gospel music in 1977; Good Life Publications, of Scottsdale, Arizona, became a division of Belwin-Mills in 1982. Peterson's cantatas for church use have sold over eight million copies. His most popular gospel songs include *It took a miracle*, *Heaven came down*, and *Surely goodness and mercy*. He wrote an autobiography, *The Miracle Goes On* (1976), and a film of the same title was made about his life.

BIBLIOGRAPHY

W. J. Reynolds: *Companion to Baptist Hymnal* (Nashville, 1976)

HARRY ESKEW

Peterson, Oscar (Emmanuel) (*b* Montreal, Que., 15 Aug 1925). Jazz pianist. He studied classical piano from the age of six and, at the age of 14, won a local talent contest. During his late teens he played on a weekly Montreal radio show and, throughout the mid-1940s, was heard with Canada's well-known Johnny Holmes Orchestra, playing in a style which blended elements from the styles of Teddy Wilson, Art Tatum, Nat "King" Cole, Erroll Garner, and others. Norman Granz invited him to appear at Carnegie Hall in 1949 in a Jazz at the Philharmonic concert, and has managed the pianist's career ever since.

Peterson toured regularly with Jazz at the Philharmonic during the early 1950s and formed his own trio using the combination of piano, guitar, and double bass popularized by Nat "King" Cole. His most popular trio, including Herb Ellis (guitar) and Ray Brown (double bass), remained together from 1953 until 1958, when the guitarist was eventually replaced by a drummer, Ed Thigpen. This latter group, considered by many to have been the ideal vehicle for Peterson's unique talents, remained intact from 1959 until 1965. During that year he also recorded the album *With Respect to Nat*, dedicated to Cole, on which Peterson sang for the first time since the mid-1950s.

In the early 1970s Peterson began concentrating on solo performances, proving incontestably to be one of the greatest solo pianists in the history of jazz. Since the mid-1970s he has played with symphony orchestras throughout North America and has joined established jazz musicians such as Dizzy Gillespie, Clark Terry, Joe Pass, and the double bass player Niels-Henning Ørsted-Pedersen for a number of memorable duo performances, many of them recorded by Granz for Pablo Records.

Peterson is a prolific recording artist, having issued as many as five or six albums a year. He has also been active as a jazz composer (his *Canadiana Suite* was nominated by the National Academy of Recording Arts and Sciences as one of the best jazz compositions of 1965). Because of his extraordinary technique and his comprehensive grasp of jazz piano history, Peterson is often compared to Art Tatum, with whom he shares a unique gift for inspiring awe from musicians, critics, and listeners alike.

RECORDINGS

(selective list)

Affinity (1962, Verve 68518); *The Oscar Peterson Trio Plus One – Clark Terry* (1964, Mer. 60975); *With Respect to Nat* (1965, Lml. 86029); *Oscar Peterson and Dizzy Gillespie* (1974, Pablo 2310740); *Oscar Peterson in Russia* (1974, Pablo 2625711); *The Way I Really Play* (1980, MPS 68075); *My Favorite Instrument* (1980, MPS 68076)

BIBLIOGRAPHY

SouthernB
B. James: "Oscar Peterson," *Essays on Jazz* (London, 1961), 134
L. Feather: *From Satchmo to Miles* (New York, 1972), 187ff
——: "Piano Giants of Jazz: Oscar Peterson," *Contemporary Keyboard*, iv/7 (1978), 53
L. Lyons: "Oscar Peterson," *Contemporary Keyboard*, iv/3 (1978), 30
J. Litchfield: *The Canadian Jazz Discography, 1916–1980* (Toronto, 1982), 552–640
"Peterson, Oscar," *CBY 1983*

BILL DOBBINS

Petit, Buddy [Crawford, Joseph] (*b* New Orleans, LA, *c*1897; *d* New Orleans, 4 July 1931). Jazz trumpeter and bandleader. He began attracting favorable attention with his trumpet playing in New Orleans while he was still a teenager. After working in the Young Olympia Band, he became joint leader of a group with the clarinetist Jimmie Noone (whose place was taken later by Albert Nicholas). In 1917 he played briefly in California with Jelly Roll Morton; he then returned to New Orleans and formed his own band which, for the next ten years, had long-term engagements in several Louisiana towns, including Mandeville and Covington. The band also worked in Florida occasionally, and in New Orleans regularly. Petit himself paid another short visit to California around 1922 as a member of Frankie Dusen's band. There are no recorded examples of Petit's playing, which over the years has taken on legendary qualities. There can be no doubt that he was an exceptional musician, remembered even more for his tone and expressive ideal than for his range. Several New Orleans trumpeters, including Punch Miller, Herb Morand, and Wingy Manone, cited Petit as an influence.

BIBLIOGRAPHY

J. D. Donder: "My Buddy," *Footnote*, xiv/3 (1983), 24; xiv/4 (1983), 4

JOHN CHILTON

Petri, Egon (*b* Hanover, Germany, 23 March 1881; *d* Berkeley, CA, 27 May 1962). Pianist of Dutch descent. He was the son of Henri Petri (1856–1914), a fine violinist, who was his first teacher. He studied piano with Richard Buchmayer and Teresa Carreño. Until 1901 he was an orchestral violinist, and also played in his father's string quartet. The composer and pianist Ferruccio Busoni recognized his specific talent as a pianist, and Petri became Busoni's most important pupil and interpreter; from 1914 he assisted with Busoni's edition of Bach. As a pianist he traveled widely through Europe and made tours of the USSR from 1923. He taught in England at the Royal Manchester College (1905–11) and in Germany at the Berlin Hochschule für Musik (1921–6), and then moved to Zakopane (Poland), chiefly to teach but also to give recitals. After making his New York début on 11 January 1932 and teaching at the Malkin Conservatory in Boston (1934–5), he settled in the USA in 1938 and later taught at Cornell University (1940–46), Mills College (1947–57), and the San Francisco Conservatory (1952–62).

Petri's style, like Busoni's, was characterized by flexible, independent hands, dignified movements, astonishing memory, analytical perception, and a personal, variegated touch, steely and always clear. In Berlin he was considered the most important pianist next to Fischer and Schnabel; in London he was admired for his profound, subtle, and masculine style. His playing of Bach and Liszt in particular was regarded as exemplary.

BIBLIOGRAPHY

E. Petri: "Reminiscences," *Musical Facts*, i/4 (1940), 15

A. Londonderry: Obituary, *MT*, ciii (1962), 489

"The Recordings of Egon Petri," *78 r.p.m.* (1969), no.7, p.21 [with partial discography]

REINHOLD SEITZ/R

Petrides, Frédérique Joanne [née Mayer, Frédérica Jeanne Elisabeth Petronille] (*b* Antwerp, Belgium, 1903; *d* New York, 12 Jan 1983). Conductor. She studied violin with Mathieu Crickboom, Gösta Andreasson, and Paul Stassevitch. In 1923 she came to the USA and worked in New York as a freelance violinist and teacher. She married Peter Petrides in 1931. In 1932–3 she attended John Lawrence Erb's summer conducting classes at New York University, but it was Mitropoulos, whose rehearsals with the New York PO she attended regularly from 1950 to 1956, who most strongly influenced her conducting. In 1933 she founded the Orchestrette of New York (known first as the Orchestrette Classique) for female instrumentalists; it gave concerts in Aeolian Hall and Carnegie Recital Hall from 1934 to 1943. The orchestra's newsletter, *Women in Music* (1935–40), edited by Petrides, was very effective in promoting the activities of women in professional music. In addition to the Orchestrette, Petrides conducted the Hudson Valley SO, the West Side Community Concerts, the Student Symphony Society of New York, and summer concerts in Washington Square and Carl Schurz parks. A pioneering woman conductor, she was one of the first to demonstrate that women could work successfully in the field of professional concert music.

BIBLIOGRAPHY

C. Neuls-Bates: *Women in Music* (New York, 1982), 230

JEAN BOWEN

Petrillo, James C(aesar) (*b* Chicago, IL, 16 March 1892; *d* Chicago, 23 Oct 1984). Labor leader. He played trumpet and at the age of 14 organized a dance band. He was soon attracted into union activity, and in 1914 he was elected president of the American Musicians Union (AMU) in Chicago. After being defeated for reelection three years later, he resigned from the AMU and joined the American Federation of Musicians (AFM). He became president of the Chicago local in 1922, was named to the parent union's executive board in 1932, and in 1940 was elected national president, a post he held until he retired in 1958 (although he retained the presidency of the Chicago local for another four years).

Petrillo was an aggressive, shrewd, and powerful fighter for the musicians in the AFM. He built the Chicago local into a disciplined force in municipal politics, and worked to expand the membership at the national level (by 1951 the 20 largest AFM locals had a total of nearly 98,000 members). He was particularly active in the matter of the threat to musicians' income and employment posed by recorded music, and in August 1942 called a strike banning AFM members from making recordings until the record manufacturers would agree to pay the union a fee for every disc produced. Decca Records signed such an agreement about a year later; RCA Victor and Columbia, the other major companies, held out until autumn 1944, when they too signed, and agreed to pay between .25¢ and 5¢ per disc. The gain to AFM was reported to be $4 million per year.

See also CHICAGO (i), §3, and UNIONS, MUSICIANS', §2.

BIBLIOGRAPHY

P. S. Carpenter: *Music, an Art and a Business* (Norman, OK, 1950), 137ff

R. D. Leiter: *The Musicians and Petrillo* (New York, 1953)

P. Hart: "James Caesar Petrillo and the Militant Musician," *Orpheus in the New World* (New York, 1973), 96

Obituary, *New York Times* (25 Oct 1984)

H. WILEY HITCHCOCK

Pettiford, Oscar (*b* Okmulgee, OK, 30 Sept 1922; *d* Copenhagen, Denmark, 8 Sept 1960). Jazz double bass player, cellist, and bandleader. Of mixed black and Indian extraction, he was born into a large, musical family and learned many instruments in the family's touring band, which was based in Minneapolis. In 1943 he was engaged as a bass player for Charlie Barnet's band, with which he traveled to New York in the same year. After working with a quintet led by Roy Eldridge (1943), he found a place in the emerging bop scene, as co-leader, with Dizzy Gillespie, of a combo at the Onyx (winter 1943–4). Personal differences caused this pioneering group to disband, but one year later he and Gillespie recorded together. From 1944 Pettiford played in numerous small bop combos and in various big bands, notably Duke Ellington's (1945–8) and Woody Herman's (1949). In the mid-1950s he led his own big band which, though highly regarded for its inventive arrangements and instrumentation, suffered from instability of personnel, owing in part to Pettiford's difficult temperament. He emigrated to Europe in 1958, and in his final years was based in Copenhagen.

Pettiford was the first jazz bass player to adapt and elaborate the innovations of Jimmy Blanton within a bop context, and his ideas and discoveries had a lasting influence on the bop style as a whole. His earliest recorded solos, such as *The Man I Love* (1943), were learned by rote by many aspiring bop bass players, though few could approach his penetrating tone and clear projection of ideas. Later, from about 1950, he transferred his solo style to amplified cello, which he played in a bouncy, dexterous style, reminiscent of Charlie Christian. Together with Ray Brown and Charles Mingus, who owed much to his influence, Pettiford was influential in establishing the double bass as a jazz solo instrument equal in importance to the winds.

RECORDINGS

(selective list)

As leader: *Basically Duke* (1954, Bethlehem 1019); *Oscar Pettiford Orchestra in Hi-Fi*, i–ii (1956–7, ABC-Para. 135, 227)

As sideman: C. Hawkins: The Man I Love (1943, Signature 9001); D. Ellington: Swamp Fire (1946, Vic. 201992); *Lucky Thompson Featuring Oscar Pettiford*, i–ii (1956, ABC-Para. 111, 171)

BIBLIOGRAPHY

SouthernB

P. Harris: "Oscar Pettiford Now on Cello Kick," *Down Beat*, xvii/26 (1950), 20

G. Hoefer: "Oscar Pettiford," *Down Beat*, xxxiii/11 (1966), 25

I. Gitler: *Jazz Masters of the Forties* (New York, 1966), 150ff

J.-E. Berendt: "Thank You, Oscar Pettiford," *Ein Fenster aus Jazz* (Frankfurt am Main, Germany, 1977), 141

J. BRADFORD ROBINSON

Petty, Tom [Thomas] (*b* Gainesville, FL, 1952). Rock singer, songwriter, and guitarist. He played with the guitarist Mike Campbell and keyboard player Benmont Tench in the group

Mudcrutch in north Florida. Around 1971 the group went to Los Angeles and recorded one single for Shelter Records; it then broke up, but was re-formed after Petty heard a demonstration tape that Campbell and Tench recorded with Stan Lynch (drums) and Ron Blair (bass guitar; replaced by Howie Epstein in 1982). These musicians, as the Heartbreakers, released a first album, *Tom Petty and the Heartbreakers*, in 1976; it was distinguished by the resemblance of Petty's voice to Bob Dylan's and, especially, that of Jim McGuinn of the Byrds, and by the Heartbreakers' style, which emphasized bluesy guitar and keyboard figures over sinuous rock rhythms. The group's first hit single was *Breakdown* (1977), a rather slower song than they usually sang, which evoked the Rolling Stones' early style. Petty spent much of the next three years in contractual litigation. The Heartbreakers' *Damn the Torpedoes* (1979) established him as an important rock songwriter and performer in the mainstream style characterized by Bruce Springsteen and Bob Seger; a single from the album *Refugee* is a definitive example of the genre. Petty's later albums have been less intense and the songwriting weaker, though they have shown the distinctive talents of members of the Heartbreakers, notably Tench. In 1981 Petty and some members of his group appeared on Stevie Nicks's album *Bella Donna*; this contained *Stop draggin' my heart around*, a duet by Petty and Nicks, which reached no.3 on the chart. *Southern Accents*, a poorly realized "concept" album about southern life and culture, was released in 1985.

RECORDINGS

(selective list; recorded for Backstreet unless otherwise stated)

Tom Petty and the Heartbreakers (Shelter 52006, 1976); Breakdown (Shelter 62008, 1977); *You're Gonna Get It!* (Shelter/ABC 52029, 1978); *Damn the Torpedoes* (5105, 1979), incl. Refugee; *Hard Promises* (5160, 1981); The Waiting (51100, 1981); *Long after Dark* (5360, 1982); You got lucky (52144, 1982); *Southern Accents* (MCA 5486, 1985)

DAVE MARSH

Peyote drum. A water-drum used in meetings of the Native American (or Peyote) Church of the American Indians. The standard drum consists of well-soaked buckskin stretched over an iron kettle about 25 cm high. The skin is attached by means of an intricate tying method that has symbolic import. The kettle is half-filled with water, which represents rain or the water of the earth; the sound of the drum represents thunder. Live coals, which are symbolic of lightning, are put in the water before the skin is attached. The drumhead is kept moist during meetings by vigorous shaking of the kettle between songs. The beater is an unpadded stick, about 30 cm long, which may be carved and decorated; it is used with force, producing a loud, resonant sound.

Drumheads of canvas or rubber have been used when buckskin was not available. Earthenware crocks and tin cans have been used for drum bodies, and in recent years aluminium copies of the standard iron kettle have been made specially for use as drums; they are light and easy to handle. The drum rests on the ground, tilted towards the drumming hand of the player, who kneels. The thumb of the hand holding the drum is pressed against the drumhead to govern tone and pitch. The songs are performed in sets of four; a fast, even drum-beat continues throughout each song but the tempo slows and the pitch drops between them. Women attend meetings but ordinarily do not drum or sing. The drum is played at the same time as the Peyote rattle.

BIBLIOGRAPHY

D. P. McAllester: *Peyote Music* (New York, 1949)

DAVID P. McALLESTER

Peyote music. The music of the official Native American Church, the beliefs and practices of which are a fusion of the American Indian "peyote cult" with Christian elements; *see* INDIANS, AMERICAN, §I, 6(ii).

Peyote rattle. Small vessel rattle used by American Indian singers during ceremonies of the Native American Church. It consists of a gourd of about 8 to 9 cm in diameter filled with small stones, and a straight wooden handle of about 25 to 30 cm. The handle passes through the gourd, from which it projects slightly. A tuft of dyed horsehair, representing the peyote cactus blossom, is fixed to the projecting end. During a Peyote ceremony the rattle, followed by the PEYOTE DRUM, is passed clockwise round the circle of participants. Each person is expected to sing (usually four songs) before passing it on. Often a song is introduced with a tremolo on the two instruments, which then maintain the same, rather quick, tempo of the song.

BIBLIOGRAPHY

D. P. McAllester: *Peyote Music* (New York, 1949)

MARY RIEMER-WELLER

Peyser, Ethel R(ose) (*b* New York, 6 March 1887; *d* New York, 12 Sept 1961). Writer. She was educated at Vassar College, Barnard College, and Columbia University Teachers College (BS 1908). From 1912 to 1914 she worked in the editorial department of the *New York Herald Tribune* and in 1914 for the *New York Evening Mail*. She was music critic for the *Musical Leader* from 1926 until 1934 and contributed to other music journals; she also worked on the staff of general magazines and wrote articles and books on hobbies and domestic topics. In conjunction with Marion Bauer she wrote two successful popular histories of music: *How Music Grew* (1925, rev. 2/1939) and *Music through the Ages* (1932, rev. 3/1967). Her other books include *How to Enjoy Music* (1933), *The Book of Culture: the Basis of a Liberal Education* (1934/*R*1941), *The House that Music Built: Carnegie Hall* (1936), and *How Opera Grew* (1956).

BIBLIOGRAPHY

J. T. Howard: *Our American Music* (New York, 1931, rev. 4/1965), 566

E. N. C. Barnes: *American Women in Creative Music* (Washington, DC, 1937), 19

Obituary, *New York Times* (14 Sept 1961), 31

MARY A. WISCHUSEN

Peyser [née Gilbert], **Joan** (*b* New York, 12 June 1931). Editor and writer on music. She studied at Smith College (1947–9), Barnard College (BA 1951), and Columbia University (MA 1956, further study until 1958). She has written numerous articles for such periodicals as *Commentary*, *Vogue*, *Hi-Fi Stereo Review*, and *Opera News*, and is the author of many pieces for the Sunday *New York Times* which were based on interviews with European and American musicians. Her books *The New Music: the Sense behind the Sound* (1971, rev. 2/1981 as *Twentieth Century Music: the Sense behind the Sound*) and *Boulez: Composer, Conductor, Enigma* (1976) are intended as a history of music from 1880 to the present; the first discusses Schoenberg, Stravinsky, Webern, and Varèse, and the second, Stockhausen, Cage, and Babbitt in addition to Boulez. From 1977 to 1984 she was editor of the *Musical Quarterly*. She also is the editor of *The Orchestra: Origins and Transformations* (1986) and the author of a biography of Leonard Bernstein (in preparation).

PAULA MORGAN

Pfatteicher, Carl F(riedrichs) (*b* Easton, PA, 22 Sept 1882; *d* Philadelphia, PA, 29 Sept 1957). Organist and teacher. He was trained in music and theology at Harvard (1912) and Freiburg University. From 1912 to 1947 he was professor of music at Phillips Academy in Andover, Massachusetts, where he established a tradition of playing the complete organ works of Bach each academic year in the college chapel. He then taught at Franklin and Marshall College, the University of Pennsylvania, and Trinity University in San Antonio. He edited a number of volumes of organ and choral music, including the organ works of John Redford, *The Christian Year in Part Songs* (1915), *The Christian Year in Chorals* (1917), *Thesaurus musicae sacrae* (1920), and *The Oxford American Hymnal* (1930). He was co-editor of *The Church Organist's Golden Treasury* (*c*1949) and *The Office Hymns of the Church in their Plainsong Settings* (1951).

MICHAEL FLEMING

Pfeil [Pfylo, Pheil], **Philip.** *See* PHILE, PHILIP.

Phase music. A term applied to one of the compositional practices generally referred to as MINIMALISM; it is associated particularly with the work of STEVE REICH.

Phelps, Lawrence Irving (*b* Somerville, MA, 10 May 1923). Organ builder. He studied conducting, organ, and various orchestral instruments at the New England Conservatory of Music, Boston. He sought to design an organ which would restore the fundamental principles of the so-called "classic" organ, typified by the German 17th-century school of the Schnitger family, yet which in its approach to technical problems and its greater versatility would be a genuinely modern instrument. At the Aeolian-Skinner Organ Co., Boston, he worked for five years with G. Donald Harrison, and for a further year with Walter Holtkamp. From 1949 Phelps worked as an independent consultant, his most important project being the large instrument he designed for the First Church of Christ, Scientist, Boston, in which he incorporated several technical and tonal innovations, among them dissonant mutations and modifications to the electrical and winding systems. In 1958 he became tonal director of the firm of Casavant Frères, Quebec, and in 1961 began making modern mechanical-action (tracker) organs, then largely unknown in North America; these instruments were not only of an advanced tonal design, successfully reconciling the two main schools of organ building and composition (German Baroque and French Classical), but also introduced sophisticated technical improvements in the action, notably special low-pressure reeds and electronic control of playing aids. During his 14 years at Casavant he produced some 650 organs, of which typical examples in the USA are at the State University of Colorado, Fort Collins, and at Lewis and Clark College, Portland, Oregon (a four-manual organ suspended from the roof). From 1972 to 1981 he operated his own company in Erie, Pennsylvania. In 1974 he built a mechanical-action instrument for the 1300th anniversary of Hexham Abbey, the only American-built organ in Britain to date. His four-manual, 70-stop mechanical-action organ at Oral Roberts University, Tulsa, Oklahoma, is the largest such organ yet built by an American firm.

Phelps's organs are noted chiefly for their musically functional qualities; their tonal design is based firmly on musical requirements of all periods, and their particularly subtle key action further assists the musician. Phelps was a board member of the International Society of Organbuilders and American editor of its journal, *ISO Information* (until 1980), and a visiting lecturer at Westminster Choir College, Princeton, New Jersey (1969–71). He has written many articles on the organ's history, design and acoustical problems, and related subjects, and his influence as a pioneer and reformer has been widespread. He now acts as a consultant and designer, specializing in electronic organs.

GILLIAN WEIR

Phi Beta. A professional society for men and women in the creative and performing arts, founded in 1912; *see* GREEK-LETTER SOCIETIES, §2.

Phi Beta Mu. Society for bandmasters, founded in 1937; *see* GREEK-LETTER SOCIETIES, §2.

Philadelphia. City in Pennsylvania (pop. 1,688,210, ranked fourth largest in the USA; metropolitan area 4,716,818). It is one of the country's main music centers. Philadelphia was founded in 1682 by William Penn as the chief town in the Pennsylvania colony, which had been granted to him by Charles II and designed as a refuge for victims of religious persecution. It soon became the largest city in the American colonies and their cultural capital, yielding that position to New York about 1820. (It was in fact the official capital of the new nation from 1776 to 1800.) Its orchestra and its largest conservatory, the Curtis Institute, are known throughout the world. Although the original settlers were English Quakers who had little interest in music, Penn's hospitality to other religious groups ensured the growth of musical activities. Indeed, as early as 1700 a group of German Pietists there had musical instruments, and one of them, Justus Falckner, wrote a number of hymns, the music to which survives.

1. CONCERTS. Subscription concerts were given from 1757 by a chamber orchestra, largely through the efforts of Francis Hopkinson, one of the first American-born composers, and the governor, John Penn. The programs included music by the best English, Italian, German, and Bohemian composers of the time. A few months before his graduation in 1757 from the College of Philadelphia (later the University of Pennsylvania), Hopkinson mounted an elaborate performance of Thomas Arne's masque *Alfred*. The British occupation of the city by Lord Howe's army in 1777 was marked by the splendid musical pageant *Mischianza*.

Three immigrant English musicians, Rayner Taylor, Alexander Reinagle, and Benjamin Carr, were the leading figures in the city's musical life at the turn of the century. Philadelphia had garden concerts in the summer in imitation of those at Ranelagh, Vauxhall, and other London pleasure gardens. However, it was not until the second half of the 19th century that the city had a resident orchestra of any importance. Taking its name from an earlier group that had come from Germany in 1848, the Germania Orchestra under the leadership of Carl Lenschow gave annual series of concerts from 1856 to 1895. During the celebration of the centenary of American independence in 1876, Theodore Thomas conducted a long series of concerts by his orchestra. The opening program included works by the American composers John Knowles Paine and Dudley Buck, as well as Wagner's *Grosser Festmarsch*. But Thomas's programs were too weighty and difficult for the visitors and were given in a hall too far from the center of the city to draw a large audience; consequently they could not compete with the lighter program offered by Jacques Offenbach at the exhibition grounds. It was 12 years before Thomas was able to pay off the heavy debts resulting from this undertaking. (*See also* CENTENNIAL EXHIBITION.)

Thomas settled permanently in Chicago in 1891. The loss of the annual concert series his orchestra had given in Philadelphia was only partly compensated for by concerts given by the Boston SO, the New York PO, and the New York SO from the 1890s to about 1926. In the late 1890s Gustav Hinrichs, the opera conductor, Henry Gordon Thunder, a choral director, and William Wallace Gilchrist, a composer, tried to form a local orchestra on a permanent basis. In the spring of 1900 two concerts, called the "Philippine concerts," for the benefit of the families of soldiers killed in the war with Spain and for men who had been wounded, provided the direct impetus for the founding of the Philadelphia Orchestra. The concerts were directed by Fritz Scheel, who had led American orchestral musicians in Chicago and San Francisco. A guarantee fund was raised, and Scheel conducted the first concert of the Philadelphia Orchestra, with 85 players, on 16 November 1900. The financial stability of the new group was ensured not only by the large guarantee fund, but also by the intensive efforts of a number of women's committees. Scheel quickly strengthened the orchestra by engaging players trained in Europe and perfecting the ensemble. He died in 1907 and Karl Pohlig, who had been a friend and pupil of Liszt and assistant to Mahler at the Vienna Opera, took over. Pohlig returned to Germany in 1912.

The appointment in 1912 of Leopold Stokowski as conductor helped seal the orchestra's eventual reputation as one of the world's finest ensembles. Until his retirement in 1941, his dynamic direction was constantly in evidence, both in the introduction of contemporary scores to a conservative audience (he gave American premières of works by Ferruccio Busoni, Mahler, Alexander Scriabin, Stravinsky, Schoenberg, and Varèse) and in experimentation with the seating of the players, orchestral sonorities, and broadcasting techniques. The orchestra gained national attention with the first American performance of Mahler's Eighth Symphony in 1916; musical forces of more than 1000 gave nine performances of the work. The number of players was increased to 104, and the orchestra became widely known through broadcast concerts and a series of recordings. In 1936 the Philadelphia Orchestra made the first of several tours of the USA, giving 36 concerts in 27 cities. In 1933, with the assistance of telephone engineers, Stokowski pioneered stereophonic recording. Perhaps his only unsuccessful experiment was the formation under the auspices of the Philadelphia Forum of a symphonic band known as the Philadelphia Band, popularly called the Band of Gold. It disbanded in 1929 after two concerts.

Stokowski kept the title of conductor until he retired. Ossip Gabrilowitsch was assistant conductor of the orchestra from 1929 to 1930 and Eugene Ormandy from 1936 to 1937. The latter was appointed music director in 1938, a post he held for an unparalleled 42 years, retiring in 1980 with the title of conductor laureate; he continued to conduct the orchestra occasionally until his death in 1985. Ormandy was succeeded by Riccardo Muti, who has stressed the importance of concert performances of operas. The orchestra continues to make extensive tours, not only in the USA but also in Europe, the USSR, and the Far East. For more than 50 years it has given outdoor summer concerts in Fairmount Park (the Robin Hood Dell Concerts, now held in the Mann Music Center, an outdoor auditorium built in 1976) and has made regular appearances over a long period at festivals in Worcester, Massachusetts, and Ann Arbor, Michigan; since the establishment in 1966 of the Saratoga Festival in New York state, the orchestra has played there each August. Nearly all the world's great conductors and performing artists have appeared with the Philadelphia Orchestra, beginning with Gabrilowitsch, who was soloist at the opening concert, and including Richard Strauss in 1904 and Felix Weingartner in 1905. Rachmaninoff, who lived for a period in Philadelphia, performed and recorded there, and dedicated several of his works to the orchestra. (*See also* ORCHESTRAS, §2.)

From 1896 to 1920 a series of concerts given in an amusement park at suburban Willow Grove attracted thousands of listeners to hear music-making of a high standard. During a three-month season, Frederick Stock with the Theodore Thomas Orchestra, Walter Damrosch with the New York SO, and Victor Herbert with his own group gave two concerts a day for periods of two to five weeks; band concerts were given under the direction of John Philip Sousa, Arthur Pryor, and Giuseppe Creatore. The Willow Grove concerts were the forerunners of a summer festival established by Temple University at Ambler, near Philadelphia, in 1967; for about ten years the Pittsburgh SO was the resident orchestra and concerts of orchestral and chamber music and performances of ballet were presented. The festival was discontinued in 1980.

Smaller instrumental ensembles were formed in Philadelphia as early as the 1750s. The Symphony Club, founded in 1909 by Edwin A. Fleisher, meets weekly, devoting half its time to sight-reading; at times it has maintained two string groups and one full orchestra. At the beginning of the 20th century the Kneisel Quartet made frequent visits to Philadelphia. After the quartet disbanded in 1917, the Chamber Music Association was founded, which gave eight subscription concerts a year until 1932, bringing most of the best international ensembles to the city. A somewhat similar group, the Coffee Concerts, has been active since 1959. In 1925 Fabien Sevitzky, a bass player in the Philadelphia Orchestra, established the Philadelphia Chamber String Sinfonietta, consisting of 18 string players from the orchestra; the organization disbanded after its leader became conductor of the Indianapolis SO in 1937. The Society for Contemporary Music, founded in 1927, introduced a large number of important new scores in the few years of its existence.

Ben Stad founded the American Society of Ancient Instruments in 1925. This small group devotes itself to the performance (on authentic instruments) of the music of the 16th century to the 18th; it resembles the Dolmetsch and Casadesus groups in its choice of music and in that it is largely a family ensemble (*see* EARLY-MUSIC REVIVAL, §2). The Curtis String Quartet, consisting of four graduates of the Curtis Institute, was active from 1932 to 1981; it traveled widely in the USA and gave concerts in Europe. The Philadelphia String Quartet, made up of members of the Philadelphia Orchestra, was formed in 1959 as successor to the Stringart Quartet. It toured in Europe in 1964 and 1965, and in 1967 became quartet-in-residence at the University of Washington. The Concerto Soloists, a chamber orchestra with 16 members led by Marc Mostovoy, was founded in 1965; it was the second professional chamber orchestra formed in the USA. Other local ensembles include the Composers' Forum, which performs contemporary works, Philomel, which

(*a*)

(*b*)

1. *(a) The American Academy of Music, Philadelphia, 1860; (b) the interior of the building in about 1875*

plays original instruments, the Amerita Strings, and 1807 and Friends. Among the festivals held in the city are the Mozart on the Square Festival, which takes place around Rittenhouse Square in May, and the Basically Bach Festival, held at Chestnut Hill in November.

2. Opera. The earliest recorded performance of a musical drama in Philadelphia was *Flora, or Hob in the Well*, a ballad opera given by an English company in 1754. For 75 years the resident theatrical troupes usually performed a musical piece (ballad opera, comic opera, or ballet) in addition to a play. The American Company of David Douglass opened the Southwark Theatre in 1766 with Arne's *Thomas and Sally*, and in the following years the comic operas of Thomas Attwood, Arne, Samuel Arnold, Charles Dibdin, William Shield, and Stephen Storace were frequently performed, often soon after their creation in London. In 1767 the first American ballad opera was announced: *The Disappointment*, by Andrew Barton; but it was canceled at the last moment "as it contained personal reflections . . . unfit for the stage" and was not performed until 1976, though two editions of the libretto were published in the 18th century. An exception to the English character of nearly all the operas presented were the performances of a troupe of French refugees from Santo Domingo in 1796–7. Manuel García's family group, the first European company to visit New York, could not be persuaded to go to Philadelphia, which had to be content with concerts by García's daughter, Maria Malibran. In 1827 the impresario John Davis brought his French company from New Orleans for several weeks; it enjoyed such success that the troupe made eight visits over a period of 16 years, introducing a wide variety of operas in French by both French and Italian composers. Nearly all these works – by D.-F.-E. Auber, Adrien Boieldieu, A.-E.-M. Grétry, Fromental Halévy, Ferdinand Hérold, E.-N. Méhul, and Giacomo Meyerbeer as well as lesser-known composers – and those of Donizetti, Rossini, and Gaspare Spontini were new to Philadelphia.

Lorenzo Da Ponte, a familiar figure in Philadelphia in his later years, was instrumental in bringing the first Italian companies to the city and in igniting an enthusiasm for Italian opera that has been maintained ever since by its large Italian population. Rossini and Vincenzo Bellini were the most frequently performed composers by both the Montressor troupe and the Rivafinoli company in 1833–4, which performed in the Chesnut Street Theatre, also known as the New Theatre and renamed the Italian Opera House. Bellini's *La sonnambula* was immensely popular (61 performances in three years) and dealt the death-blow to English opera,though a few of the more popular ones continued to have occasional performances. 1845 saw the première of the first American grand opera, *Leonora* by William Henry Fry, based on Edward Bulwer-Lytton's *The Lady of Lyons*. The Havana Opera Company brought Verdi's music to Philadelphia in 1847. The success of Michael Balfe's *The Enchantress*, performed 32 times in ten weeks in 1846, proved an exception to the long series of Italian operas.

With the erection of the American Academy of Music in 1857, the city acquired the finest opera house in the country (fig. 1). Built by Napoleon Le Brun on the model of La Scala, the house has three balconies and 2900 seats. The impressive interior and fine acoustics are still enjoyed by more than half a million people a year; the Academy (which never was a teaching institution) is also the home of the Philadelphia Orchestra.

Many first American performances were given in the Academy of Music (as it was later called), including Gounod's *Faust* (in German, 1863) and *Mireille* (1864), Otto Nicolai's *Die lustigen Weiber von Windsor* (1863), Louis Spohr's *Jessonda* (1864), and Wagner's *Der fliegende Holländer* (in Italian, 1876). In the second half of the 19th century many visiting companies brought famous European singers to Philadelphia, under the management of Max Maretzek, Maurice Strakosch, Maurice Grau, Gustav Hinrichs, and James Henry Mapleson. Two more theaters, the Chestnut Street Opera House (1885) and the Grand Opera House (1888), offered additional facilities for opera. Among the American premières given by Hinrichs were Pietro Mascagni's *Cavalleria rusticana* (1891) and *L'amico Fritz* (1892), Bizet's *Les pêcheurs de perles* (1893), Puccini's *Manon Lescaut* (1894), and the première of Hinrichs's own opera, *Onti-Ora* (1890).

The Metropolitan Opera of New York first appeared in Philadelphia in 1885, and in 1889 gave the first complete performance in the city of Wagner's *Ring* cycle, under Anton Seidl. From that time until 1968 (when production costs became prohibitive) the company presented an annual season in Philadelphia, ranging from six to 25 performances a year. Oscar Hammerstein, challenging the supremacy of the Metropolitan, built a new theater in Philadelphia to seat 4000; this was one of the largest opera houses in the world. It opened in 1908 as the Philadelphia Opera House but was sold to the Metropolitan in 1910, renamed the Metropolitan Opera House, and used for some years for the performances of that company. The new house was far from the center of the city and after 1931 was seldom used for opera; its impressive interior was destroyed by fire in 1948. Hammerstein, in his two seasons in Philadelphia, gave the first local performances of Debussy's *Pelléas et Mélisande* and Strauss's *Salome* and *Elektra*, and his reorganized company, the Philadelphia–Chicago Opera Company, gave the world première of Victor Herbert's *Natoma* in 1911.

Since the end of World War I there have been many local opera companies. The Philadelphia Civic Opera Company (1924–30) under the musical direction of Alexander Smallens announced "professional performances but not for profit" and was subsidized for a short time by the city. Among the operas given their first American performance by the company were Strauss's *Ariadne auf Naxos* and *Feuersnot* and E. W. Korngold's *Der Ring des Polykrates*. The Philadelphia Grand Opera Company (1926–43) gave the first American performance of Alban Berg's *Wozzeck* in 1931, conducted by Stokowski with the Philadelphia Orchestra, and of Eugene Goossens's *Judith* in 1929. The Pennsylvania Grand Opera Company, founded in 1927, presented the American première of Mussorgsky's *Khovanshchina* in 1928. This company was later re-formed as the Philadelphia–La Scala Company and in 1954 merged with the Civic Grand Opera Company; this and the Lyric Grand Opera Company were the major local companies. They performed the popular Italian repertory, with only an occasional sortie into French or German opera. In 1976 the two companies merged to form the Opera Company of Philadelphia. The principal singers are generally brought from France and Italy; the directors in recent years have included Frank Corsaro and Menotti. The Pennsylvania Opera Theatre, established in 1975 with Barbara Silverstein as conductor, has specialized in little-known works of the past and in contemporary music; in 1985 it gave the première of Persichetti's *The Sibyl*.

Stokowski's interest in contemporary opera continued with the American première of Schoenberg's *Die glückliche Hand* (1930) and the first staged performance of Stravinsky's *Oedipus rex* (1931). In 1934–5 the Philadelphia Orchestra gave a series of operatic performances under Smallens and Fritz Reiner, which included first American performances of Stravinsky's *Mavra* and Gluck's *Iphigénie en Aulide*, and a performance of Shostakovich's *Lady Macbeth of the Mtsensk District*. The season was an artistic success but a financial disaster. The world premières of Menotti's *Amelia al ballo* (1937) and *The Consul* (1950) were both given in Philadelphia, the first at the Curtis Institute. The première of *William Penn*, an opera by Romeo Cascarino, a local composer, was given in 1982 with the support of a private foundation to mark the 300th anniversity of the establishment of the city.

3. CHORAL SINGING. Choral singing has flourished in Philadelphia since the end of the 18th century. In 1784 Andrew Adgate organized the Institution for the Encouragement of Church Music, which in 1787 became the Uranian Academy. Although Adgate succumbed to yellow fever in 1793, his academy survived until about 1800. The city's large German population has supported four singing societies. The Männerchor (1835–1962) and the Arion (1854–1969) have gone, but the Junger Männerchor, founded in 1835, and the Harmonie, established in 1855, are still active. Other important choruses were the Abt Male Chorus, led successively by Michael Cross and H. A. Clarke; the Philadelphia Choral Society, conducted by Henry Gordon Thunder from 1897 to 1946; the Treble Clef Club (1884–1934) and the Eurydice Chorus (1886–1918), both for women; the Fortnightly Club (founded 1893); the Palestrina Choir (1915–48), which specialized in earlier Roman Catholic church music under the direction of Nicola Montani; the Accademia dei Dilettanti di Musica (1928–60); and the Choral Art Society (founded 1922). Still flourishing are the male-voice Orpheus Club (founded 1872), the Mendelssohn Club (1874), and the Singing City (1947). Groups formed later include the Philadelphia Singers (1971), the Pennsylvania Pro Musica (1972), and the Choral Arts Society (1982).

4. THE MUSICAL FUND SOCIETY. What is perhaps the oldest music society in the USA in continuous existence was founded on 3 February 1820 by a group of musicians, professional and amateur, who had been playing quartets for some years previously (*see also* UNIONS, MUSICIANS', §1). It was inspired by the Royal Society of Musicians of Great Britain, and it was dedicated to "the relief of decayed musicians and the cultivation of skill and diffusion of taste in music." Among the founders were Benjamin Carr, Rayner Taylor, J. George Schetky, Benjamin Cross, Charles Frederic Hupfeld, Charles Hommann, Joseph C. Taws, and the painter Thomas Sully, who made many portraits of his fellow members. In its early years the society ordered a vast collection of instrumental music from Germany, most of which is still preserved in the Free Library of Philadelphia. It also published an inventory of its manuscripts and prints from the period 1790–1840 as *Catalog of Orchestral & Choral Compositions* (1974), which lists many rare sets of parts of early symphonies.

The society's first concert, in which at least six conductors took part, included Beethoven's Symphony no.2; in 1822 Haydn's *The Creation* was given by more than 100 performers to an audience of nearly 2000. William Strickland, the distinguished architect and a member of the society, designed the Musical Fund Hall, which was completed in 1824 and used for the society's many concerts and for other musical and nonmusical events until the Academy of Music was built in 1857. The hall's remarkably fine acoustics made a favorable impression on the many famous musicians who appeared there in concert. These included Malibran, Jenny Lind, Henriette Sontag, the eight-year-old Adelina Patti, Elsie Hensler (later Queen of Portugal), Henri Herz, and Gottschalk. Mozart's *Die Zauberflöte* was given its first performance in the USA there (1841, in English), with an orchestra of 64 conducted by Benjamin Cross. By 1847 the hall had to be enlarged and the work was carried out under the direction of Le Brun (who later designed the Academy of Music). In 1982 the hall was scheduled for demolition, after repeated efforts to preserve it had failed; the façade remains but the hall itself has been replaced by a residential development. In the 20th century the society's chief activities have been the presentation of free public concerts, the granting of scholarships, and the sponsorship of occasional competitions. The first prize in the 1928 contest was shared by Béla Bartók, for his Third String Quartet, and Alfredo Casella, for the original version of his Serenata (1927).

5. Popular music and jazz. The first Quaker settlers in Philadelphia viewed music, theater, and dancing with distaste, not so much because they believed these pursuits to be sinful but because they saw them as unproductive. The Swedes, who founded Gloria Dei Church in 1700 on the banks of the Delaware River, and the Germans, who settled along Wissahickon Creek, enthusiastically embraced both religious and secular music of the folk tradition. As the nation's capital for a time, Philadelphia attracted a diversity of settlers, including Blacks who, as early as 1763, sang in the streets while playing guitars made from gourds. With the Revolution came a growing interest in martial music, parades, and theatrical productions. Tavern fiddlers and church organists alike played lilts and jigs; enthusiasm for the French after the victory at Yorktown was reflected in the French flavor of concerts and dances. But a conservative attitude still remained Philadelphia's dominant characteristic; as late as 1785 even the singing of new and unfamiliar hymns was deemed "disagreeable and inconvenient."

From 1792 until shortly before the opening of the American Academy of Music in 1857, the Chesnut Street Theatre was an important center for theatrical music; in 1860 a new theater of the same name (though by now spelled "Chestnut") was built on the same street and it continued the tradition of the old one through many changes of name and management until 1940. By the latter half of the 19th century more than 100 songwriters were publishing popular songs for theater and salon orchestras; hop waltzes, polkas, and ethnic dances enjoyed brief vogues. Music by black composers, such as John Clemens's *Coal Black Rose* (1829), which has been called the first widely popular American song, and John Sanford's *Lucy Neale* (1844), had great success. The band of Frank Johnson played for parades and balls, and made a European tour in 1837. Minstrel shows grew in popularity, and the first black minstrel theater (built as a Presbyterian church) opened as the 11th Street Opera House in March 1855 and became the New American Opera House the following month. James Bland, a local black minstrel performer, composed *Carry me back to old Virginny* (1878) and *Oh, dem golden slippers* (1879), which became associated with the Mummers parade, an annual celebration incorporating elements of English, Welsh, Swedish, Finnish, German, and black traditions that first took place in 1901. The New Year's Day Parade is accompanied by unique bands that include massed banjos, guitars, saxophones, and glockenspiels, mostly playing in unison. More conventional bands have also played for dancing at the Woodside and Willow Grove amusement parks, on college campuses, at ballrooms such as the Sunnybrook and Chez Vous, and in large hotels. In the first half of the 20th century movie theaters, such as the Stanley, Fox, and Mastbaum, varied their program of films with stage shows, and big bands and vocal soloists performed at the Earle.

Philadelphia played an important role in the development of popular music after World War II. Dick Clark's "American Bandstand" (fig.2), which began as a local television program, was broadcast nationally from 1957 and brought fame to many pop artists, including Frankie Avalon, Fabian, and James Darren. Bill Haley and the Comets (from nearby Chester) and Chubby Checker were early performers of rock-and-roll. The area's folk clubs include the Second Fret, the Gilded Cage, and the Main Point in Bryn Mawr, where early in their careers James Taylor, Todd Rundgren, and Bruce Springsteen achieved wide exposure. In 1962 the Philadelphia Folk Festival was first held (outdoors) in Tredyffrin Township; it was later moved to a site near Schwenksville, northwest of Philadelphia, and continued into the 1980s. Among those who have appeared at the festival are Pete Seeger, Emmylou Harris, Doc Watson, Bo Diddley, and

2. Dancers on "American Bandstand," Philadelphia, late 1950s, with Dick Clark (rear, on the podium)

the Roches. Electric Factory Concerts, a booking service for rock and pop events, scheduled concerts in many small clubs, arenas, and theaters in its early years of operation; it now uses the Spectrum sports stadium and Tower theater for most performances. The Spectrum, despite its shortcomings, has become the only location suitable for large rock concerts other than JFK Stadium (seating 100,000), where concerts by the Rolling Stones and the Jacksons, and the Live Aid benefit concert of 1985, were staged.

The city became known for a distinctive brand of black popular music, often referred to as Philadelphia soul, in the 1960s. The Sound of Philadelphia, an organization comprising soul and disco groups, was responsible for many artists who made hit recordings in the 1970s; the best-known local exponents of black popular music in the early 1980s were Patti LaBelle and Teddy Pendergrass. Philadelphia soul exerted an influence on the members of the rock duo Hall and Oates, who were brought up in the area. The expertise of the noted Sigma Sound Studios led such well-known artists as Stevie Wonder to record in Philadelphia. Live performances by important pop musicians, however, have been staged only at the suburban Valley Forge Music Fair and the Spectrum, though the casinos of Atlantic City, New Jersey, are close enough for audiences from Philadelphia to attend performances there. Small showcase clubs for performers in Philadelphia are few; the city remains to a large extent a point of departure for performers who achieve success elsewhere.

Philadelphia's gospel tradition, fostered by churches such as Charles Tindley's Temple, led to appearances in the city by important gospel performers from the South; singers such as Bessie Smith and Billie Holiday performed in black neighborhoods near the central city. By the 1940s nightclubs such as the Arcadia Restaurant and the Downtown Club were the scene of jam sessions in which band musicians from the Earle often participated after hours. Concerts in Norman Granz's Jazz at the Philharmonic series were given at the Academy of Music for several years beginning in 1946, and smaller groups give concerts in the academy's lobby.

The strict "blue laws" of Pennsylvania, which, among other things, prohibited liquor sales on Sundays until the late 1960s, did not prevent the spread of jazz clubs. The Blue Note, Click, Pep's, Show Boat, Cameo Room, Sahara, Cadillac, Aqua Lounge, Underground, Zanzibar, Cafe Society, and Latin Casino (the last of which continued to operate for 13 years after moving to New Jersey), and the Red Hill Inn and Charlie Ventura's Open House in Pennsauken, provided bandstands for many jazz groups in the 1950s and 1960s. A wealth of noted jazz musicians have had connections with Philadelphia, including the Barron and Bryant families, the saxophonists Stan Getz and Gerry Mulligan, the trumpeters Dizzy Gillespie and Rex Stewart, the guitarist Eddie Lang, and the singers Eddie Jefferson and Ethel Waters. The 1970s saw a decline in jazz, although neighborhood clubs and summer programs by big bands in the Robin Hood Dell Concerts helped keep it alive. From 1982 to 1984 the Kool Jazz Festival brought summer concerts to the Mann Music Center and the Academy of Music. The exodus of many local players to casinos in Atlantic City, however, and the lack of downtown jazz clubs have reduced the level of activity to a point inconsistent with the wealth of local talent.

6. Educational institutions. The Curtis Institute of Music is one of the foremost conservatories in the USA. It was founded in 1924 by Mary Louise Curtis Bok (fig.3), the daughter of Cyrus H. K. Curtis, the magazine and newspaper publisher, himself a patron of music. Bok was president of the school until her death in 1970. With an endowment of $12,500,000 it was possible to assure free tuition to gifted students from all over the world and to attract teachers of world fame. Its directors have been Johann Grolle, then William E. Walter (1924–6), Josef Hofmann (1926–38), Randall Thompson (1939–41), Efrem Zimbalist (1941–68), Rudolf Serkin (1968–76), and John de Lancie (from 1977). The institute's teaching staff has included Auer, Feuermann, Flesch, Goldovsky, Kincaid, Landowska, Bohuslav Martinů, Gregor Piatigorsky, Primrose, Reiner, Leonard Rose, Salzedo, Elisabeth Schumann, Sembrich, Stokowski, and Herbert Sumsion. Well-known alumni have included Barber, Leonard Bernstein, Foss, Moffo, Istomin, Jaime Laredo, and Menotti. Curtis offers a BM degree and a professional diploma, as well as a full-time program for high-school students. Among the important holdings in its library is the music collection of Leopold Stokowski.

3. Mary Louise Curtis Bok, founder and president of the Curtis Institute of Music

Apart from Adgate's singing-school already mentioned, the first institution for general musical instruction was the American Conservatorio, founded in 1822 by Filippo Trajetta; it did not survive the founder's death in 1854. The Musical Fund Society set up an academy of music in 1825 but found it financially unprofitable and abandoned it in 1832. The Philadelphia Musical Academy was founded in 1870 by John Himmelsbach and directed by Richard Zeckwer and his son Camille from 1876 to 1924. In 1917 this school absorbed the conservatory founded by Henry Hahn, and in 1963 merged with the Philadelphia Conservatory of Music, which had been established in 1870. The activities of the academy expanded greatly in the 1970s, and the name was changed in 1976 to the Philadelphia College of the Performing Arts.

In 1875 the University of Pennsylvania (founded in 1740)

appointed Hugh A. Clarke, the son of the Scottish organist James Paton Clarke, professor of the science of music. This was one of the earliest chairs of music in an American university and was held by Clarke for 50 years. He concerned himself only with theory and composition, and indeed performance has never been taught at the university. In the 1960s the music department gained an international reputation in the areas of composition and history under the chairmanship of George Rochberg. Besides a BA in music, an MA is awarded in composition, as are an MA and a PhD in history and theory. Its library, named after the musicologist Otto E. Albrecht, has become one of the best on the eastern seaboard. Gilbert R. Combs established a conservatory bearing his name in 1885; it exists today as the Combs School of Music. The Russian pianist Constantin Sternberg founded the Sternberg School of Music in 1890 and directed it until his death in 1924.

The 20th century has seen the establishment of several schools that are still active. The Settlement Music School dates from 1908; from a student body of 40 in its first year it has grown to a total of 3000, a figure that includes students enrolled at its branches. Temple University's school of music dates from 1913, although honorary degrees in music were granted as early as 1897; a department of music education was founded in 1923. Temple's present College of Music awards an MM degree in various fields of study, a BM, BME, and MM in choral conducting, and a DMA degree in composition and music education. The Presser Learning Center at Temple was designed for the training of music educators. The Academy of Vocal Arts, established in 1935, offers scholarships to most of its students, as does the Curtis Institute. The New School of Music was organized in 1943 by the members of the Curtis Quartet, but now gives instruction in all branches of music. The suburban colleges Haverford and Swarthmore both offer courses in music as well as opportunity for choral and orchestral experience. Bryn Mawr College offers a BA in music and an MA and PhD in historical musicology.

Public school music dates from the inclusion of music in the curriculum of the Normal School in 1848, but formal organization had to wait until 1897. The program is very extensive and offers many opportunities for both vocal and instrumental instruction and performance. An annual concert of the combined chorus and orchestra of the public schools and the schools of the city's archdiocese has been instituted. The public school program is supplemented by the activities of Young Audiences, the local counterpart of the Jeunesses Musicales. The private secondary schools in the Philadelphia area and two specialized institutions, the Pennsylvania School for the Blind and Girard College (for orphaned boys), also have active musical programs.

For description of the principal libraries in Philadelphia, *see* LIBRARIES AND COLLECTIONS, §3.

7. MUSIC PUBLISHING. The first music published in Philadelphia was included in the hymnbooks in English and German produced by the publishing firms of Benjamin Franklin and Christopher Sauer. The first published secular music in the city was printed by Thomas Dobson from 1787 to 1798. In 1793–4 J. C. Moller and Henri Capron brought out some important items (some in *Moller & Capron's Monthly Numbers*), and Filippo Trisobio, copies of whose publications are now very scarce, was active from 1796 to 1798. Benjamin Carr, with his family and his associate J. G. Schetky, published great quantities of music from his arrival at Philadelphia in 1793 until 1827. The firm of George Willig, established in 1794, was the leading publishing house in the first half of the 19th century and was sold to Lee & Walker in 1856. Willig's chief rival was the firm of George E. Blake, active from 1803 to 1871. Allyn Bacon, under various firm names, published from 1816 to 1880. G. André & Co., a branch of the well-known Offenbach house, was in business from 1850 to 1879, and Fiot, Meignen & Co., under various names, was in operation from 1835 to 1863. The W. H. Boner firm lasted from 1865 to 1900. In 1884 Theodore Presser came to Philadelphia and founded the publishing firm bearing his name. The Presser Home for Retired Music Teachers, modeled on Verdi's Casa di Riposo at Milan, was established in 1906 and is operated by the Presser Foundation; in 1980 the residents were moved to more modern premises. The foundation also offers scholarships and grants for the construction of music buildings in colleges.

8. INSTRUMENT MAKERS. From the earliest period in its history the city has had able instrument builders. The Swedish organ builder Gustavus Hesselius constructed spinets and virginals as early as 1742, and John Behrent produced the first piano in the colonies in 1775. James Juhan advertised himself in 1783 as the manufacturer of a mysterious "great North American fortepiano." Charles Albrecht began to manufacture pianos as early as 1789, and a similar business was carried on by C. F. L. Albrecht (to whom he may or may not have been related) until 1843. Charles Taws, who had immigrated from Scotland in 1786, was also producing pianos in Philadelphia a few years later; his sons carried on the business until the 1830s. John I. Hawkins appeared in Philadelphia in 1799 and the following year took out the first patent for an upright piano ("portable grand," as he called it). He cannot be traced after 1802. Thomas Loud, Jr., possibly the son of the English piano maker, came to Philadelphia in 1812 and began the manufacture of pianos in 1816; the business was continued by members of the family until 1854. From 1828 until 1878 Conrad Meyer was one of the country's leading piano makers, though his claim to have invented the solid metal plate has not been substantiated. The Prussian piano maker Johann Heinrich Schomacker settled in Philadelphia in 1837 and the firm he founded continued under his son until about 1935.

Violin makers also have a long history in Philadelphia. John Albert, like many other Germans, came to the USA in 1848, and his shop was continued by Charles Francis Albert, father and son, until about 1921. Carmen Primavera established his business in 1888, which was carried on by the House of Primavera. William Moennig's shop dates from 1909.

BIBLIOGRAPHY

C. Durang: "The Philadelphia Stage," *Philadelphia Sunday Despatch* (1854, 1856, 1860) [series of articles; compiled by T. Westcott as *History of the Philadelphia Stage, between the Years 1749 and 1855*, 1868, *PU*; similar compilations as *The Philadelphia Stage* in *PPL*, and *History of the Philadelphia Stage* in *PHi*]

W. G. Armstrong: *Record of the Opera at Philadelphia* (Philadelphia, 1884/*R*1976)

L. C. Madeira: *Annals of Music in Philadelphia and the History of the Musical Fund Society from its Organization in 1820 to the Year 1858* (Philadelphia, 1896/*R*1973)

O. G. T. Sonneck: *Early Concert-life in America (1731–1800)* (Leipzig, 1907/*R*1978), 65-157

R. R. Drummond: *Early German Music in Philadelphia* (New York, 1910)

H. M. Lippincott: *Early Philadelphia: its People, Life, and Progress* (Philadelphia, 1917)

J. Curtis: *One Hundred Years of Grand Opera in Philadelphia* (MS 1920, *PP*, *PHi*)

Pennsylvania Composers and their Compositions, ed. Pennsylvania Federation of Music Clubs (Philadelphia, 1923)

F. A. Wister: *25 Years of the Philadelphia Orchestra* (Philadelphia, 1925)

Church Music and Musical Life in Pennsylvania in the 18th Century, ed. Pennsylvania

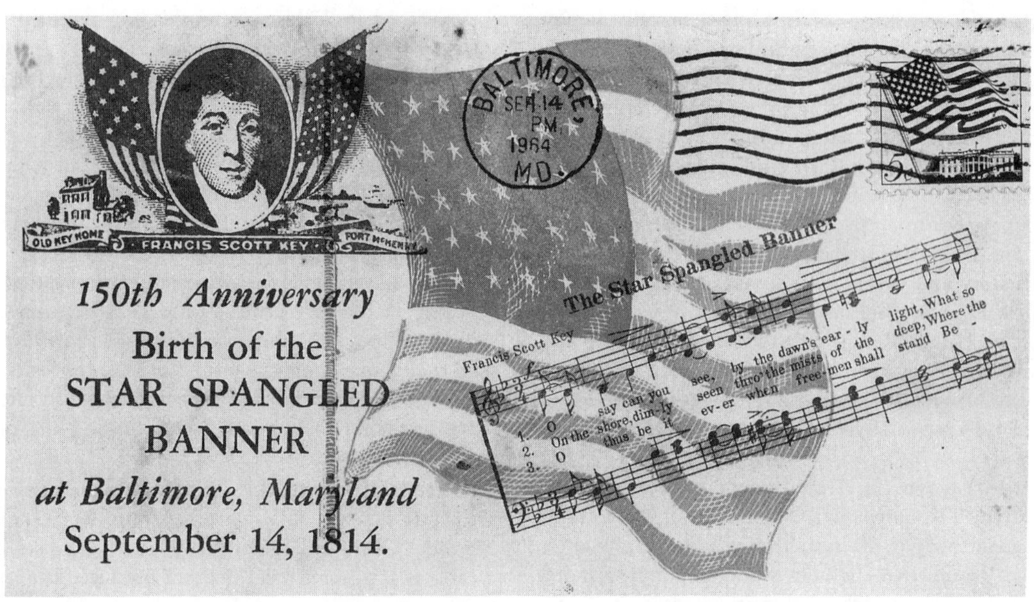

Commemorative cover (14 September 1964) to celebrate the 150th anniversary of the song "The Star-Spangled Banner"

Society of the Colonial Dames of America (Philadelphia, 1926–47)
Mrs. A. A. Parker: *Music and Musical Life in Pennsylvania in the Eighteenth Century* (Philadelphia, 1926–7)
R. D. James: *Old Drury of Philadelphia: a History of the Philadelphia Stage, 1800–1835* (Philadelphia, 1932)
T. C. Pollock: *The Philadelphia Theater in the 18th Century* (Philadelphia, 1933)
R. A. Gerson: *Music in Philadelphia: a History of Philadelphia Music, a Summary of its Current State and a Comprehensive Index Dictionary* (Philadelphia, 1940)
G. M. Rohrer: *Music and Musicians of Pennsylvania* (Philadelphia, 1940/*R*1970)
S. Spaeth: *Music and Dance in Pennsylvania, New Jersey, and Delaware* (New York, 1954)
D. W. Krummel: *Philadelphia Music Engraving and Publishing, 1800–1820: a Study in Bibliographical and Cultural History* (diss., U. of Michigan, 1958)
H. Kupferberg: *Those Fabulous Philadelphians: the Life and Times of a Great Orchestra* (New York, 1969)
The Musical Fund Society of Philadelphia (Philadelphia, 1970)
E. Arian: *Bach, Beethoven, and Bureaucracy: the Case of the Philadelphia Symphony Orchestra* (University, AL, 1971)
P. Hart: *Orpheus in the New World* (New York, 1973), 139
J. J. Kelley: *Life and Times in Colonial Philadelphia* (Harrisburg, PA, 1973)
T. Cummings: *The Sound of Philadelphia* (London, 1975)
J. Boswell and T. Gerber: "The Presser Learning Center: a Resource for Creativity in Teaching," *MEJ*, lxiii/9 (1977), 48
M. D. Hermann: *Chamber Music by Philadelphia Composers, 1750–1850* (diss., Bryn Mawr College, 1977)
M. Meyerson and D. P. Winegrad: *Gladly Learn and Gladly Teach: Franklin and his Heirs at the University of Pennsylvania, 1740–1976* (Philadelphia, 1978)
O. E. Albrecht: "Opera in Philadelphia, 1800–1830," *JAMS*, xxxii (1979), 499
J. A. Taricani: "Music in Colonial Philadelphia: Some New Documents," *MQ*, lxv (1979), 185
"American Conservatories," *Virtuoso*, i/3 (1980), 21
D. Webster: "The Curtis Institute: a Decade of Change," *HiFi/MusAm*, xxx/3 (1980), 20
S. Carrow: "Some Notes on the History of Music at Temple," *Libretto*, xii/1 (1983), 1
A. B. Ballard: *One More Day's Journey* (New York, 1984)

OTTO E. ALBRECHT (1–4, 6–8; 6 with NINA DAVIS-MILLIS)
TOM DI NARDO (5)

Philately, musical. The study of postage stamps and related items containing musical allusions. The most popular philatelic items produced by the US Postal Service are regular-issue stamps (including commemoratives, which honor individuals, organizations, activities, and historical events) issued individually or in series and printed in sets, booklets, sheets, or coils (continuous rolls); airmail stamps; prestamped postcards and envelopes; cancellation marks; first-day covers; and souvenir sheets. Christmas seals and similar materials not issued by the US Postal Service are also popular collectables but do not fall within the scope of this article.

Although philatelists have been intrigued with musical allusions on stamps since the turn of the century, the US Postal Service has only recently begun to commemorate individual composers and performers on stamps. In fact, many well-known American musicians who have been honored in this way by the postal services of other countries have yet to appear as subjects on American stamps. To the beginning of 1984 there were only 13 musicians commemorated on philatelic items, the earliest of which were the five stamps issued in the Composers subseries of the Famous Americans Issue of 1940, followed many years later by stamps honoring Paderewski (1960) and W. C. Handy (1969).

First-day covers (envelopes bearing new stamps, which are canceled on the first day of issue) are important to collectors as much for the musical cachet on the envelope as for the stamp itself, which does not necessarily contain a musical allusion. An example of a nonmusical stamp on a commemorative cover with a musical design is the common 5¢ stamp showing the American flag on an envelope celebrating the 150th anniversary of *The Star-Spangled Banner* (see illustration) imprinted with the first few bars of the song and a portrait of the author of the words, Francis Scott Key. Several souvenir sheets (sheets containing one or more stamps that often bear an inscription) for Christmas stamps also include music incipits.

The largest organization devoted to music topical collecting is the Philatelic Music Circle, founded in 1969 in Harrow, England, which has members in many countries, including the USA; the group publishes *The Baton*, a journal devoted to musical stamp collecting. The American Topical Association, based in Milwaukee, bonds several groups of music topical collectors, and in addition to its journal, *Topical Times*, publishes a number of booklets describing music topicals. The Fine Arts Philatelists in Chilton, Wisconsin, publish the *Fine Arts Philatelist*, in which such items are also discussed.

The first great American music topical collector was the piano manufacturer Theodore G. Steinway (1883–1957), whose collection contained musical stamps, postmarks, and first-day covers, as well as visiting cards, autographs, and a large variety of business envelopes imprinted with music advertisements. Another well-known American collector is F. C. Schang, who has published six books illustrating his collection of autographed visiting cards and musical stamps.

LIST

This list of regular-issue stamps, airmail stamps, and stamped envelopes and postcards is arranged chronologically in five categories: Composers and performers, Instruments, Music and American independence, Music and Christmas, and Miscellaneous. The name of the item, title of the series to which it belongs (if any), type of item (where necessary), Scott catalogue number, postage value, and date of issue are given for each item. Names are taken from *The Postal Service Guide to U. S. Stamps* and may differ from those in the Scott catalogue. Not included are stamps commemorating amateur musicians (e.g., Albert Einstein and Benjamin Franklin) and those that have only a peripheral connection with music (e.g., stamps commemorating Walt Disney and Joseph Pulitzer). All are regular issues unless otherwise stated.

COMPOSERS AND PERFORMERS

Stephen Collins Foster, Famous Americans Issue: Composers, 879, 1¢ (3 May 1940)
John Philip Sousa, Famous Americans Issue: Composers, 880, 2¢ (3 May 1940)
Victor Herbert, Famous Americans Issue: Composers, 881, 3¢ (13 May 1940)
Edward MacDowell, Famous Americans Issue: Composers, 882, 5¢ (13 May 1940)
Ethelbert Nevin, Famous Americans Issue: Composers, 883, 10¢ (10 June 1940)
I. J. Paderewski, Champion of Liberty, 1159, 4¢, and 1160, 8¢ (8 Oct 1960)
W. C. Handy, 1372, 6¢ (17 May 1969)
Sidney Lanier, 1446, 8¢ (3 Feb 1972)
George Gershwin, American Arts Issue, 1484, 8¢ (28 Feb 1973)
Jimmie Rodgers, Performing Arts Issue, 1755, 13¢ (24 May 1978)
George M. Cohan, Performing Arts Issue, 1756, 15¢ (3 July 1978)
Igor Stravinsky, Great Americans Issue, 1844, 2¢ (18 Nov 1982)
Scott Joplin, Black Heritage USA Issue, 2045, 20¢ (9 June 1983)
John McCormack, Performing Arts Issue, 460, 20¢ (1984)
Jerome Kern, Performing Arts Issue, 486, 22¢ (1985)

INSTRUMENTS

Troops Guarding Train [soldier with bugle], Trans-Mississippi Exposition Issue, 289, 8¢ (17 June 1898)
American Woman [violin in inset], 1152, 4¢ (2 June 1960)
William M. Harnett [bugle, violin, and bow in painting], 1386, 6¢ (3 Dec 1970)
Drum [with quote "Beat the drum for liberty and the spirit of '76"], coil, 1615, 7.9¢ (23 April 1976)
Guitar [with quote "Listen with love to the music of the land"], coil, 1613, 3.1¢ (25 Oct 1976)
Saxhorns [with quote "Marching in step to the music of the Union"], coil, 1614, 7.7¢ (20 Nov 1976)
Piano [with quote "Peace unites a nation like harmony in music"], coil, 1615C, 8.4¢ (13 July 1978)
Violins [with quote "The music of America is freedom's symphony"], coil, 1813, 3.5¢ (23 June 1980)
Violins [same as no. 1813, without the quote, but with the words "Authorized nonprofit org."], stamped envelope, U590, 3.5¢ (23 June 1980)

MUSIC AND AMERICAN INDEPENDENCE

Independence, 150th Anniversary, 627, 2¢ (10 May 1926)
Liberty Bell, stamped envelope, U522, 2¢ (27 July 1926)
George Rogers Clark [soldier with drum, commemorating the Battle of Vincennes], 651, 2¢ (25 Feb 1929)
Liberty Bell [with quote "Let freedom ring"], airmail, C57, 10¢ (10 June 1960)
Liberty Bell [with quote "Let freedom ring"], airmail, C62, 13¢ (28 June 1961)
Liberty Bell, stamped envelope, U547, 1.25¢ (6 Jan 1965)
Liberty Bell, stamped enveloped, U548, 1.4¢ (26 March 1968)
Drummer [with quote "Rise of the Spirit of Independence"], American Revolution Bicentennial Issue, Communications in Colonial America, 1479, 8¢ (28 Sept 1973)
Liberty Bell, stamped envelope, U567, 10¢ (5 Dec 1973)
Bells, coil, 1518, 6.3¢ (1 Oct 1974)
Liberty Bell [with quote "Proclaim liberty throughout all the land"], Americana Issue, 1595, and coil, 1618, 13¢ (31 Oct 1975)
Drummer Boy [with quote "Spirit of 76"], 1629, 13¢ (1 Jan 1976)
Old Drummer [with quote "Spirit of 76"], 1630, 13¢ (1 Jan 1976)
Fifer [with quote "Spirit of 76"], 1631, 13¢ (1 Jan 1976)
Spirit of 76, 1631a [1629–31 in set of 3]
Saxhorns: see "Instruments"
Drum: see "Instruments"

MUSIC AND CHRISTMAS

Christmas Issue [angel with straight trumpet], 1276, 5¢ (2 Nov 1965)
Partridge in a Pear Tree by Jamie Wyeth [with quote "On the first day of Christmas my true love sent to me"], Christmas Issue, 1445, 8¢ (10 Nov 1971)
Angel from "Mary, Queen of Heaven" [with trumpet and vielle in painting], Christmas Issue, 1471, 8¢ (9 Nov 1972)
Santa Claus [with toy trumpet; with quote " 'Twas the night before Christmas"], Christmas Issue, 1472, 8¢ (9 Nov 1972)
Christmas Tree in Needlepoint [toy trumpet tree decoration], Christmas Issue, 1508, 8¢ (7 Nov 1973)
Christmas Card by Louis Prang, 1878 [cherubim ringing bell], Christmas Issue, 1580, 10¢ (14 Oct 1975)
Christmas Antique Toys [toy trumpet and drum], 1843, 15¢ (16 Oct 1980)

MISCELLANEOUS

Mexican Independence [bell], 1157, 4¢ (16 Sept 1960) [issued simultaneously with an identical Mexican stamp with Spanish text]
American Music [instruments and music book, commemorating the 50th anniversary of ASCAP], 1252, 5¢ (15 Oct 1964)
California Settlement [Carmel Mission belfry, commemorating the bicentennial of the settlement of California], 1373, 6¢ (16 July 1969)
Wolf Trap Farm, National Parks 100th Anniversary Issue, 1452, 6¢ (26 June 1972)
Microphone, Speaker, Vacuum Tube, TV Camera, Electronics Progress Issue, 1502, 15¢ (10 July 1973)
Tin Foil Phonograph [with words "Centennial of Sound Recording"], American Bicentennial Issue, 1705, 13¢ (23 March 1977)
Ballet, American Dance Issue, 1749, 13¢ (26 April 1978)
Theater, American Dance Issue, 1750, 13¢ (26 April 1978)
Folk Dance, American Dance Issue, 1751, 13¢ (26 April 1978)
Modern Dance, American Dance Issue, 1752, 13¢ (26 April 1978)
American Dance Issue, 1752a [1749–52 in set of 4]
Cincinnati Music Hall, Historical Preservation Issue, postcard, UX73, 10¢ (12 May 1978)
Flag and Anthem [with quote ". . . for amber waves of grain"], Flag Issue, 1890, 18¢ (24 April 1981)
Flag and Anthem [with quote ". . . from sea to shining sea"], Flag Issue, 1891, 18¢ (24 April 1981)
Flag and Anthem [with quote ". . . for purple mountain majesties"], Flag Issue, 1893, and booklet, 1893a, 18¢ (24 April 1981)
Philadelphia Academy of Music, postcard, UX96, 13¢ (13 June 1982)
Wolf Trap Farm Park, 2018, 20¢ (1 Sept 1982) [different from 1452]
Metropolitan Opera, 2054, 20¢ (14 Sept 1983)

BIBLIOGRAPHY

S. Peat: *Music on Stamps* (Chippenham, England, 1972–5)
A. H. Grimsey: *Checklist of Postage Stamps about Music* (Harrow, England, 1974; suppl., 1975)
M. J. Whitehead: *Music World of Stamps* (Milwaukee, 1975)
G. K. Senior: *Music and Musicians on Postage Stamps* (Orrell, England, 1979)
The Postal Service Guide to U. S. Stamps (Washington, DC, 1982)
Scott Specialized Catalogue of United States Stamps, 1984 (New York, 62/1983)

STEPHEN M. FRY

Phile [Fyles, Pfeil, Phyles, etc.], **Philip** (*d* ?Philadelphia, PA, 1793). Violinist and composer. He was active in Philadelphia from 1784, becoming about that time leader of the orchestra of the Old American Company. He wrote a violin concerto which was performed in Philadelphia on 12 April 1787. His only extant composition is *The President's March*, said to have been written for the inauguration of George Washington in 1789, though the earliest printed editions date from 1793–4 (ed. V. B. Lawrence in *Music for Patriots, Politicians, and Presidents*, 1975). The tune was subsequently set to the text "Hail Columbia" by Joseph Hopkinson, and the song received its first performance on 25 April 1798.

BIBLIOGRAPHY

O. G. T. Sonneck: *A Bibliography of Early Secular American Music* (Washington, DC, 1905; rev. and enlarged by W. T. Upton, 2/1945/*R*1964)

R. R. Drummond: *Early German Music in Philadelphia* (New York, 1910/*R*1970)

R. J. Wolfe: *Secular Music in America, 1801–1825: a Bibliography* (New York, 1964)

J. BUNKER CLARK

Philidor Trio. Ensemble formed in 1965 by the flutist SHELLEY GRUSKIN, with Elizabeth Humes, soprano, and Edward Smith, harpsichord. It disbanded in 1980.

Philipp, Adolf (*b* Hamburg, Germany, 29 Jan 1864; *d* New York, 30 July 1936). Composer, librettist, singer, actor, and theater owner. He began a career as a tenor with operetta companies in Germany and Austria, and beginning in 1881 wrote the librettos for several German operettas. In 1890 Gustav Amberg brought Philipp to New York to sing operetta roles at his Amberg Theater (later the Irving Place Theatre), though he also sang in opera, most notably in the role of Turridu in Pietro Mascagni's *Cavalleria rusticana* (November 1891). In 1893 Philipp left Amberg's employ and opened the Germania Theater (formerly Aberle's Theatre), where he produced musical comedies modeled after Harrigan's stage works, until 1902. He composed, wrote the librettos for, and appeared in such portrayals of German-American immigrant life on New York's East Side as *Der Corner Grocer aus der Avenue A* (1893), *Arme Maedchen* (1893), *Ein New Yorker Brauer* (1894), and *New York bei Nacht* (1897). *Ein New Yorker Brauer* was performed more than 700 times in New York up to 1909. Revised as *Über'n grossen Teich*, it received more than 1300 performances in Germany – in Berlin (where at the Deutsch-Amerikanischer Theater it was directed by Philipp and his brother between 1903 and 1907), Hamburg, and elsewhere. It was given on Broadway as *From Across the Pond* (1907). Others of Philipp's German works were also adapted for the Broadway stage, the most successful being *Alma, wo wohnst du?* (*Alma, Where do you Live?*, 1909). *Adele* (1913), *Two Is Company* (1915), and *The Girl who Smiles* (1915) are apparently the only original English-language operettas that he composed, written under his pseudonyms Jean Briquet and Paul Hervé. Philipp's activities were greatly reduced because of World War I, though he wrote and appeared in an anti-German play, *Tell That to the Marines* (1918). He also produced and appeared in films, his Adolf Philipp Film Corporation issuing *The Midnight Girl*, *Oh! Louise*, and *My Girl Suzanne* in 1919. His last musical comedy was *Mimi* (1920). Philipp's compositions exhibit an assimilation of many musical styles, from Viennese waltz operettas and French comic opera to the American musical theater of Harrigan and David Braham.

WORKS

Selective list. Unless otherwise indicated, all are musicals and all librettos are by Philipp; all were first performed in New York.

Arme Maedchen, 1893, trans. as Poor Girls, 1894; Der Corner Grocer aus der Avenue A, 1893, trans. as About Town, 1894; Ein New Yorker Brauer (Über'n grossen Teich), 1894, trans. as From Across the Pond, 1907; Klein Deutschland, 1897; New York bei Nacht, 1897; Im Lande der Freiheit, 1901; Alma, wo wohnst du? (operetta), 1909, trans. as Alma, Where do you Live? (G. Hobart), 1910; Theresa sei nicht böse (operetta), trans. as Teresa be mine, 1910; Auction Pinochle (Une partie de cartes) (operetta), 1912, trans as Auction Pinochle (E. Paulton), 1914; Adele (operetta, Paulton), 1913; Das Mitternachtsmaedel (operetta), trans. as The Midnight Girl (Paulton), 1914; Two Lots in the Bronx, 1913; My Shadow and I, 1914; The Girl who Smiles (operetta, Paulton), 1915; Sadie from Riverside Drive, 1915; Two is Company (operetta, Paulton), 1915; Mimi (Paulton), 1920

Principal publisher: Remick

JOHN KOEGEL

Philipp, Isidore (*b* Budapest, Hungary, 2 Sept 1863; *d* Paris, France, 20 Feb 1958). French pianist, teacher, and composer of Hungarian origin. He studied with Stephen Heller and Camille Saint-Saëns. He was professor of piano at the Paris Conservatoire from 1893 to 1934 and was extraordinarily successful as a teacher. With the outbreak of World War II he came to the USA where, despite his age, he continued to teach; he also arranged works for two pianos and edited many well-known piano pieces. He gave his last public performance in New York in 1955. Philipp's ability to solve pianistic problems has remained legendary. No fewer than 13 of his collections of piano exercises and studies were published in the USA between 1898 and 1953, and they are still highly regarded. In 1977 the American Liszt Society established the Isidore Philipp Archive and Memorial Library at the University of Louisville School of Music.

BIBLIOGRAPHY

H. Bellamann: "Isidore Philipp," *MQ*, xxix (1943), 417

E. Fisher: "Busoni and Philipp," *Recorded Sound*, i/8 (1962), 242 [with discography by P. Saul]

M. Hinson: "Isidore Philipp – an Appreciation," *Piano Quarterly*, no.88 (1974–5), 20

MAURICE HINSON

Phillipps, Adelaide (*b* Stratford-on-Avon, England, 26 Oct 1833; *d* Karlsbad [now Karlovy Vary, Czechoslovakia], 3 Oct 1882). Singer. Her family moved to Canada and then to Boston, where from 1842 she appeared as an actress, singer, and dancer, principally at the Boston Museum. In 1851 she studied singing with Manuel García in London and in 1853 made her operatic début in Brescia, Italy. After two years of sporadic engagements in Italy as Signorina Fillippi, she returned to the USA and performed operatic roles under Max Maretzek in New York and Havana; her first important appearance in New York was as Azucena in Verdi's *Il trovatore* on 17 March 1856. In 1861–2 she made a European tour, then appeared regularly throughout the USA in opera, concert, and oratorio. After an unsuccessful season with her own Adelaide Phillipps Opera Company, she sang with the Boston Ideal Opera Company (1879–81).

BIBLIOGRAPHY

Mrs. R. C. Waterston: *Adelaide Phillipps: a Record* (Boston, 1883)

O. Thompson: *The American Singer* (New York, 1937/*R*1969), 42

C. McGlinchee: *The First Decade of the Boston Museum* (Boston, 1940)

V. F. Yellin: "Phillipps, Adelaide," *NAW*

Phillips, Burrill (*b* Omaha, NE, 9 Nov 1907). Composer, educator, and pianist. His theory and composition teachers were Edwin Stringham at the Denver College of Music (1928–31) and Howard Hanson and Bernard Rogers at the Eastman School (BM 1932, MM 1933). He has been a faculty member at Eastman (1933–49, 1965–6), the University of Illinois (professor, 1949–64), the Juilliard School (1968–9), and Cornell University (1972–3), as well as visiting composer at the universities of Texas, Kansas, Southern California, and Hawaii. Among his awards are two Guggenheim Fellowships (1942–3, 1961–2) and an award from the American Academy of Arts and Letters (1944). He was a Fulbright Lecturer at the University of Barcelona in 1960–61. He has received commissions from the League of Composers (Scherzo for orchestra, 1944), the Koussevitzky Foundation (*Tom Paine*, overture for orchestra, 1946), the Fromm Foundation (*The Return of Odysseus*, 1956), and the Elizabeth Sprague Coolidge Foundation (String Quartet no.2, 1958).

Phillips's first important orchestral work, *Selections from McGuffey's Reader* (1933), was an immediate success and established his reputation as a composer with a consciously American style – a reputation that has tended to overshadow the subsequent development of his musical language. The elements of his early style – an emphasis on melodic line, a rich harmonic texture, and rhythmic associations with jazz – had evolved by the late 1930s and early 1940s into a drier, more acerbic idiom, with asymmetrical rhythms and broadened expressiveness. Many of the works written in the 1940s and 1950s reveal a new intensity and compression; imitative counterpoint is characteristic of the piano writing. In the early 1960s Phillips began to work with free serial techniques, less sharply accented rhythms, and an increasing sense of fantasy. Although he can in no sense be considered an imitator of earlier models, his works show a clarity of line and texture that reflects his great admiration for the music of Domenico Scarlatti and Henry Purcell.

WORKS

STAGE

Katmanusha (ballet), 1932–3; Play Ball (ballet), 1937; Step into my Parlor (ballet), 1942; Don't We All (opera buffa, 1, A. Phillips), 1947; Dr. Faustus (incidental music, Marlowe), org, brass qt, timp, 1957; Nine from Little Rock (film score), 1964; La piñata (ballet, J. Limón), chamber orch, 1969; The Unforgiven (opera, 3, A. Phillips), 1981; other incidental music

ORCHESTRAL

Selections from McGuffey's Reader, 1933; Sym. concertante, chamber orch, 1935; Courthouse Square, 1935; Concert Piece, bn, str, 1942, arr. bn, sym. band/pf, 1953; Pf Conc., 1942; Scherzo, 1944; Tom Paine, ov., 1946; Scena, chamber orch, 1946; Conc. grosso, str qt, chamber orch, 1949; Triple Conc., cl, va, pf, orch, 1952; Perspectives in a Labyrinth, 3 str orchs, 1962; Soleriana concertante, 1965; Theatre Dances, 1967; Fantasia, sym. band, 1968; Yellowstone, Yates, and Yosemite, t sax, sym. band, 1972

VOCAL

Declaratives (T. Boggs, Cummings, B. Phillips), SSAA, chamber orch, 1943; What will Love do and The Hag (Herrick), SSAA, 1949; A Bucket of Water (A. Phillips), SATB, pf, 1952; The Age of Song (Raleigh, Campion, Donne, Shakespeare), SATB, 1954; The Return of Odysseus (A. Phillips), Bar, nar, chorus, orch, 1956; The First Day of the World (A. Phillips), TTBB, pf, 1958; 4 Latin Motets, SATB, 1959; Canzona III (A. Phillips), S, fl, pf, perc, 1964; Canzona IV (A. Phillips), S, fl, perc, 1967

That Time may Cease (Marlowe), TTBB, pf, 1967; Canzona V (A. Phillips), SATB, pf, 1971; Eve Learns a Little (A. Phillips), S, 4 ww , pf, 1974; The Recesses of my House (A. Phillips), S, cl, pf, perc, 1977; Hernán y Marina (A. Hurtado), S, pf, 1981; Song in a Winter Night (B. Noll), S, pf, 1981; Letters from Italy Hill (A. Phillips), S, fl, cl, str qt, pf, 1984

INSTRUMENTAL

Pf works incl. 4 sonatas, 1942–60; Toccata, 1944; Music, 1949–50; Serenade, pf duet, 1956; Commentaries, 1983

Qts incl. 2 str qts, 1939–40, 1958; Partita, pf qt, 1947; Conversations and Colloquies, 2 vn, 2 va, 1950; Ob Qt, 1967

Sonatas: vn, pf, 1941; vc, pf, 1948; org, 1964; vn, hpd, 1965

Other: Trio, 3 tpt, 1937; Piece, 6 trbn, 1940; 4 Figures in Time, fl, pf, 1952; A Rondo of Rondeaux, va, pf, 1954; Music for this Time of Year, wind qnt, 1954; Sinfonia brevis, org, 1959; 3 Nostalgic Songs, fl, pf, 1962; Intrada, wind ens, perc, pf, vn, vc, 1975; Huntingdon Twos and Threes, fl, ob, vc, 1975; Scena da camera, vn, vc, 1978; Canzona VI, wind qnt, 1985

MSS in *DLC*, *NRU-Mus*

Principal publishers: Elkan-Vogel, Fallen Leaf, C. Fischer, Hargail, Presser, Southern

BIBLIOGRAPHY

J. T. Howard: *Our American Music* (New York, 1931, rev. 4/1965)
C. Reis: *Composers in America* (New York, 1938, 4/1947)
J. T. Howard: *Our Contemporary Composers* (New York, 1941)
J. C. Paz: *La musica en los Estados Unidos* (Mexico, 1952)
B. Phillips: "Saluting the American Composer: Burrill Phillips," *Music Clubs Magazine*, 1 (1970–71), 6 [autobiographical statement]

ANN P. BASART

Phillips, Esther [Jones, Esther Mae] (*b* Galveston, TX, 23 Dec 1935; *d* Torrance, CA, 7 Aug 1984). Blues singer. She began singing in church as a child. In 1948 she won first prize in an amateur talent show in Los Angeles, and the following year joined the band of Johnny Otis, performing under the name Little Esther. With Otis she recorded *Double Crossing Blues* (1950), which reached no. 1 on the rhythm-and-blues chart, and toured with his group until it disbanded in the early 1950s. She then moved to Houston and, on account of illness, retired from public life until 1962, when her version of the country-music standard *Release Me* became her only recording to reach the Top Ten. In the mid-1960s she had some success with jazz and pop audiences, and in 1972 she recorded what is probably her finest album, *From a Whisper to a Scream*. An intense, passionate singer whose performances recalled those of Dinah Washington, Phillips was acknowledged by the Beatles as an important influence on their work. In 1975 she issued *What a Difference a Day Makes*, a disco single which reached no. 20 on the pop chart; this exhibited her strong voice and versatility.

BIBLIOGRAPHY

SouthernB

JIM MILLER

Phillips, Harvey (Gene) (*b* Aurora, MO, 2 Dec 1929). Tuba player and teacher. He learned the sousaphone from his high school music teacher, a former circus bandleader. After graduation (1947) he took a summer job playing the tuba in a local circus and then attended the University of Missouri. He left school in 1948 to join the band of the Ringling Bros. and Barnum & Bailey Circus. In 1950 he went to New York to study at the Juilliard School (1950–54) and the Manhattan School (1956–8); he has played with numerous ensembles and orchestras including the New York City Opera and Ballet orchestras, the Sauter-Finegan Orchestra, the NBC Opera Orchestra, the Goldman Band, the Symphony of the Air, and the New York Brass Quintet, of which he was a founding member. He has taught at the Hartt School of Music, Hartford (1962–4), and the Mannes College and the New York College of Music (both 1964–5). In 1971 he was made a professor in the Indiana University School of Music where in spring 1973 he financed the First International Tuba Symposium-Workshop, attended by 400 composers, performers, and students, and that autumn sponsored his first "Octubafest," five nights of student recitals. (In 1976 there were 80 "Octubafests" on as many American campuses.) In January 1975 at Carnegie Recital Hall in New York he gave a series of five recitals with various accompanists in which he played 39 pieces, including many composed for him, and jazz numbers. In addition to his teaching and performing career, which from 1977 has also included a position as visiting professor at Northwestern University, Phillips has been involved in arts management and publishing and co-founded several organizations, including Tubists

Universal Brotherhood Association (1972) and the International Brass Society (1975). He is regarded by many as one of the finest brass players of his day; his technique is prodigious and flexible, his tone smooth and perfectly focused, even in the lowest register. He has commissioned works from such composers as David Baker, Morton Gould, Wilder, Beversdorf, Heiden, and Schuller, many of which he has recorded.

BIBLIOGRAPHY

W. Balliett: "Profiles (Harvey Phillips)," *New Yorker*, li (15 Dec 1975), 46

DENNIS K. McINTIRE

Phillips, Liz [Elizabeth] (*b* Jersey City, NJ, 13 June 1951). Composer and artist. She graduated from Bennington College in 1973 with a degree in art and music. In her early career as an artist she created sculptures using light. Later she incorporated sound as a logical extension of her work: "What I wanted to do . . . was to change three dimensional space over time, and sound was the best way to do this," Phillips stated in an interview (1982). She has earned considerable recognition for her sound sculptures, created for indoor and outdoor installation (for illustration *see* ENVIRONMENTAL MUSIC, fig.2). They contain electronic circuitry that responds to elements of the environment in which they are positioned – in some cases the presence and movement of people (as in *Sunspots*) and in others a changing landscape (as in *Windspun* and *Come About*). From a visual standpoint *Windspun* is typical of many of Phillips's sculptures in that the "sensor" (in this case a windmill) serves both an artistic and practical purpose. Information about the speed and direction of the wind and the presence of nearby people is gathered by the sensor and then transformed into sound by means of a synthesizer, using the hollow shaft of the windmill as a resonator. Phillips's sculpures have been exhibited throughout Europe and the USA.

WORKS

Sound sculptures: T. V. Dinner, 1971; Electric Spaghetti, 1972; Sound Structure, 1972; Sumtime, collab. Y. Wada and A. Knowles, 1973; Broken/Unbroken Terracotta, 1975; Cityflow, 1977; Metrosonic Province, 1978; Sunspots, 1979; Windspun for Minneapolis, 1980; Come About, 1981; Windspun, 1981; Multiple Perspectives, 1982; Sound Syzygy, 1982; Sonar Eclipse, collab. M. Cunningham, 1983

BIBLIOGRAPHY

R. Cohen: "Sound articulates Space," *Synapse* (1977), Jan–Feb, 14
J. La Barbara: "New Music," *HiFi/MusAm*, xxix/5 (1979), 12
C. Drewes: "A Sculptor with Sound," *San Francisco Examiner* (21 June 1981)
D. Ahlstrom: "Liz Phillips: Sunspots," *Computer Music Journal*, vi/3 (1982), 5
R. Close: "Composer's Works lend New Meaning to Movement," *St. Paul Pioneer Press* (13 Dec 1982)

CHARLES PASSY

Phillips, Olga. Pseudonym of ERNEST GOLD.

Phillips, Philip (*b* Chautauqua Co., NY, 13 Aug 1834; *d* Delaware, OH, 25 June 1895). Evangelistic singer, composer of gospel hymns, and compiler of hymnbooks. He was largely self-taught in music, and began teaching singing-schools at the age of 19. In about 1863 he established Philip Phillips & Co. in Cincinnati to sell pianos and melodeons and publish Sunday-school songbooks. He later moved to New York, where he became the music editor for the Methodist Books Concern. He was known primarily as a singer of sacred songs, and his appearance before President Lincoln in 1865 brought him widespread fame. He gave his own services in which he accompanied himself at the reed organ, and was also associated with Moody and other evangelists. He became known as the "Singing Pilgrim," and entitled one of his collections *The Singing Pilgrim, or Pilgrim's Progress Illustrated in Song* (New York, 1866). His *Hallowed Songs* (with Theodore E. Perkins and Sylvester Main; Cincinnati, 1865) was used in meetings by Moody and Sankey before Sankey and Bliss began their gospel hymn collections. Two of Phillips's tunes, to the texts "Home of the soul" and "One sweetly solemn thought," are included in *The Broadman Hymnal* (1940). Phillips also made singing tours. In 1875 he began a tour of Australia, Ceylon, India, Japan, Palestine, Egypt, Italy, Switzerland, Germany, Austria, Holland, and England; it is described in his *Song Pilgrimage* (1882).

BIBLIOGRAPHY

P. Phillips: *Song Pilgrimage Around and Throughout the World* (New York, 1882)
A. Clark: *Philip Phillips: his Songs and Tours* (New York, n.d. [*c*1887])
J. H. Hall: *Biography of Gospel Song and Hymn Writers* (New York, 1914/*R*1971)
F. H. Martens: "Phillips, Philip," *DAB*

HARRY ESKEW

Phillips, Sam(uel Cornelius) (*b* Florence, AL, 5 Jan 1923). Record producer and record company president. He was brought up on a farm in Alabama and became a disc jockey in Muscle Shoals while he was still a teenager. After working as a radio engineer in Nashville he moved to Memphis in 1944, where he converted a disused workshop into a recording studio, which he called the Memphis Recording Service. Early contact with the blues had made him interested primarily in black popular music forms, and at first he recorded almost exclusively black singers. Jackie Brenston, the singer in a group led by Ike Turner, recorded *Rocket 88* at the studio in 1951; with its urgent vocal line, driving beat, and raucous saxophone parts, this became one of the first rock-and-roll hits. In the same year Phillips founded his own company, Sun Records, which enjoyed some localized commercial success with recordings of rhythm-and-blues artists, including Howlin' Wolf, Rufus Thomas, and Jr. Parker.

Phillips once said that he could "make a million dollars if [he] could find a white singer with the Negro sound and the Negro feeling." This he found in Elvis Presley, who used the studio in 1954 to make a demonstration recording. In the next two years Phillips and Presley made five singles which all became substantial hits. These perfected the style now known as rockabilly, a blend of country music with rhythm-and-blues, which was characterized by metallic lead guitar and percussive double bass treated with all-enveloping reverberation. In adopting this style, Phillips moved further away from the blues, which he had championed at the beginning of his career. After Presley, Phillips worked with Johnny Cash, Carl Perkins, Charlie Rich, Roy Orbison, and Jerry Lee Lewis early in their careers; though all of them were connected in some way with the country-music tradition, Phillips's recordings remained faithful to the rhythm-and-blues style, and are distinguished by a clear sound, exciting arrangements, and considerable emotional depth. He retired from the recording business in 1969, selling Sun Records to Shelby Singleton.

See also MEMPHIS, §2.

BIBLIOGRAPHY

G. Marcus: *Mystery Train: Images of America in Rock 'n' Roll Music* (New York, 1975, rev. and enlarged 2/1982)
P. Guralnick: "Epilogue: Sam Phillips Talking," *Lost Highway: Journeys and Arrivals of American Musicians* (New York, 1979)
C. Escott and M. Hawkins: *Sun Records: the Brief History of the Legendary Record Label* (London, 1980)

CHRIS WALTERS

Phi Mu Alpha Sinfonia Fraternity. Music society for men, founded in 1898; *see* GREEK-LETTER SOCIETIES, §2.

Phi Mu Gamma. The oldest national professional fine arts sorority in the USA, founded in 1898; *see* GREEK-LETTER SOCIETIES, §2.

Phoenix. Capital city of Arizona (pop. 789,704, ranked ninth largest in the USA; metropolitan area 1,509,052). It was founded in 1870. Newspaper accounts dating from 1880 mention concerts and benefits performed by the Phoenix Brass Band and similar groups, but it was not until 1902, ten years before Arizona became a state, that a community orchestra was first formed. It existed under various names until 1947 when the Phoenix SO was organized under the direction of John Barnett; he was succeeded by Robert Lawrence (1949–52), Leslie Hodge (1952–9), Guy Taylor (1959–69), Phillip Spurgeon (1969–71), Eduardo Mata (1971–8), and Theo Alcanta (from 1978). The orchestra has commissioned works from the composers Robert Ward, Carlos Surinach, Paul Creston, Leroy Robertson, and John Vincent, and performs in Symphony Hall (capacity 2500), which opened in 1972. Four community orchestras also offer concert seasons. Opera enthusiasts have choices of performances by the Arizona Opera Company, a professional company that began in 1971 as the Tucson Opera, and the Lyric Opera Theatre (founded in 1963), which is affiliated with Arizona State University, Tempe. Community musical theater is represented by the Phoenix Little Theatre and Mesa Music Theatre.

The Orpheus Male Chorus was founded in 1929 and the Phoenix Boys Choir in 1949; both groups have toured the USA and Europe. The Bach and Madrigal Society (founded 1958) and various chamber music groups, including Bach West and Musica Dolce Early Music Ensemble, contribute much to the concert life of the city. The Phoenix Chamber Music Society, the Phoenix Symphony Guild, and the Arizona Commission on the Arts encourage and support interest in local music activities. Jazz in AZ, a nonprofit organization, sponsors concerts and festivals and funds scholarships for jazz students. Numerous folk music and dance groups, including several culturally indigenous to the Southwest, are also active in the metropolitan area. Musical events are reviewed in the *Phoenix Gazette* and the *Arizona Republic*, both founded in the 1880s.

Concerts and musical events are held in Symphony Hall, and in nearby Scottsdale at the Kerr Cultural Center (capacity 320) and the Scottsdale Center for the Arts (capacity 822; built 1976). The Gammage Center for the Performing Arts (originally Grady Gammage Memorial Auditorium; capacity 3029), which was designed by Frank Lloyd Wright and completed in 1964, is on the campus of ARIZONA STATE UNIVERSITY, the major center for music education in the area. Music education is also offered at the nearby Grand Canyon College.

BIBLIOGRAPHY

Arizona: its People and its Resources (Tucson, 1960, rev. 2/1972)

D. Scoular: *The First Decade: a History of Events at Grady Gammage Memorial Auditorium, 1964–1974* (Tempe, 1976)

B. C. Stoneburner: *The Phoenix Symphony Orchestra, 1947–1978: Leadership, Criticism and Selective Commentary* (thesis, Arizona State U., 1981)

ARLYS L. McDONALD

Phyles [Phyla], **Philip.** *See* PHILE, PHILIP.

Piano(forte). A keyboard instrument, the strings of which are struck by rebounding hammers. It was originally called pianoforte (It.: "soft-loud") or fortepiano, because the loudness of its sound could be varied by the player's touch. The piano has played an important role in American life since the late 18th century, when learning the instrument was considered a genteel occupation for young ladies; by the late 19th century it had become an essential item in many homes. American piano builders, seeking to satisfy the taste of American musicians and to meet the challenges of the American climate, developed manufacturing and sales techniques and new features, such as the one-piece metal frame, which by the 1870s enabled them to dominate the world piano trade.

Pianos were used and made in America by the 1770s. On 31 January 1771, the Englishman David Propert, organist of Trinity Church, Boston, advertised that he taught fortepiano (as well as harpsichord, guitar, and German flute), and he played the fortepiano in a concert in early March. In Virginia, Thomas Jefferson ordered a fortepiano from London for his Monticello home in June 1771. In New York, John Sheiuble (Sheybli) announced in March 1772 that he made and repaired pianos, among other instruments, and in the *New-York Gazette* (10 October 1774) he advertised for sale "one hammer spinnet," which he may have made himself. Another German craftsman, John Behrent, who is usually credited with making the first piano in America, advertised in Philadelphia (*Pennsylvania Packet*, 13 March 1775) that he had "just finished for sale, an extraordinary fine instrument by the name of Piano Forte, of Mahogany, in the manner of an harpsichord, with hammers and several changes." The piano must have attracted some interest, for six months later John Adams mentioned in his diary (28 September 1775) that Michael Hillegas, a Philadelphia music dealer and treasurer of the Continental Congress, talked "perpetually of the Forte and Piano" during a trip on the Delaware River to inspect war boats.

The type of piano most often played and owned by 18th-century Americans was the square piano, a rectangular horizontal instrument similar in shape to the clavichord; this style remained in favor until the 1890s. The early square pianos were built with wooden framing in handsome cases veneered with mahogany and other exotic woods. The range was usually five to five and a half octaves (*F'*-*c''''*), the action was English, and changes in registration were activated by handstops. After a hiatus caused by the Revolution, in the mid-1780s many builders and performers began to immigrate to the USA, among them the builders Thomas Dodds (New York, 1785), Charles Taws (New York, 1786; Philadelphia, 1787), Charles Albrecht (Philadelphia, 1788), and John Geib (New York, 1797), and the performers Alexander Reinagle (New York and Philadelphia, 1786), Benjamin Carr (Philadelphia, 1793), and Peter and Elizabeth von Hagen (Charleston, South Carolina, 1774; New York, 1792; Boston, 1796). In Milton, Massachusetts, the American-born Benjamin Crehore was building pianos by the 1790s. Many diaries and accounts by European visitors comment upon the piano playing of the daughters of their American hosts.

As early as 1792 Dodds & Claus noted the need to "prepare their wood to stand the effect of our climate," a prime concern of American builders throughout most of the 19th century. JOHN ISAAC HAWKINS, an English civil engineer working in Philadelphia, included an iron frame and iron bracing rods in his ingenious 1800 patent for an upright piano, an example of which is in the Smithsonian Institution. Although his invention (one

1. Square piano with a one-piece metal frame made by Alpheus Babcock in Philadelphia, c1835 (Smithsonian Institution)

of the earliest examples of an upright) did not succeed musically, it represented one of the earliest attempts to use iron to withstand climatic changes.

In 1825, ALPHEUS BABCOCK, a Boston maker who had worked with Crehore, was the first to be issued a patent (17 December 1825) for a one-piece metal frame, which he claimed would create a piano frame "stronger and more durable than a wooden frame or case" and, because the strings and metal frame would expand or contract equally, an instrument that "would not be put out of tune by any alteration in the temperature of the air." He fitted this frame in a piano typical of the late 1820s: a mahogany square with decorative stenciling, two pedals, and a compass of six octaves (F'-f''''); that only one Babcock square with an iron frame is extant (fig.1) suggests that very few were actually manufactured. Many builders, especially those in New York, Philadelphia, and Baltimore, opposed the iron frame, claiming that it resulted in a thin and nasal tone quality. Instead, many used heavy wooden bracing and a solid five-inch (12.7 cm) wooden bottom for stability in tuning. But by the 1840s, wooden framing alone was not strong enough to withstand the enormous string tension of the piano's expanded compass (seven octaves, A''–a'''') and the rigors of American climatic extremes and heating.

The Boston piano maker Jonas CHICKERING, a New Englander with whom Babcock worked from 1837 to 1842, considered the one-piece metal frame to be an element essential to the developing American piano. In 1840 he patented a metal frame with a cast-iron bridge for a square piano (US patent no.1802) and in 1843 patented a one-piece metal frame for grands (US patent no.3238). He was the first to devise a successful method of manufacturing and selling pianos with metal frames and was the first major American builder to make grand pianos, for which he won special notice at the Crystal Palace Exhibition, London (1851). The Chickering factory manufactured about 10% of the 9000 pianos produced in the USA in 1851. After a fire destroyed his factory in late 1852, Chickering and his three sons built a new factory, on Tremont Street, which they claimed was "the most perfect and extensive piano forte establishment in the world" (fig.2) and the largest building in the USA except for the US Capitol. The Chickering firm set the standard for the American piano industry: production of quality pianos with metal frames, an extensive steam-powered factory operation with workers who developed a high degree of skill specialization, an energetic sales program, and support for musical events and performers.

In 1853, the year of Jonas Chickering's death, the firm of Steinway & Sons was established in New York (*see* STEINWAY). Within a decade the Steinway brothers and their father Henry, who had immigrated from Germany in 1850, had equaled the Chickering firm in production and prestige. Soon after the 1867 Paris Exhibition, at which both the Steinways and Chickerings won gold medals, Steinway pianos dominated the world piano trade. Like Chickering, the firm designed pianos with metal frames. In 1859 Steinway patented a new arrangement for the grand piano called overstringing (US patent no.26,532): the bass notes were strung over the middle and upper register strings, which permitted the use of longer strings (for an extended lower range and a richer sound) and the location of bridges in the middle of the soundboard (for better vibration). At the 1873 Vienna Exhibition, more than two thirds of the pianos displayed were overstrung. Between 1857 and 1885, the Steinways were granted 54 patents, 41 of them to C. F. Theodore Steinway, who concentrated upon greater strength and stability (by 1875 he claimed a metal plate that would sustain string pressure up to 35 short tons), more responsive action, and bigger, purer sound. Coming from Europe in 1865 where the square had lost favor in the 1840s, he improved and promoted the upright which the firm began making in 1862 (they made their last square in 1889). The combination of technical excellence, aggressive promotion through concerts and advertisements (especially by William Steinway), efficient quality production, and a shrewd business sense made possible the company's rise to world prominence.

The Steinways, Chickerings, and numerous other piano builders (among them the English immigrants Thomas Loud and Robert and William Nunns, and the Germans William Knabe, Albert Weber, Frederick Mathusek, and Hugo Sohmer) supplied pianos primarily for the amateur musician. But they achieved world prominence by obtaining endorsements from performing artists, whose concerts were often organized and financed by major manufacturers. The earliest virtuosos to come to the USA, such as Leopold de Meyer (1845) and Henri Herz (1846) brought their own European pianos (Erard and Herz, respectively). The American-born Louis Moreau Gottschalk, who started his 1853 American tour with a Pleyel piano he had used during his period of training in Europe, soon became an advocate of Chickering pianos, the tone quality of which was compatible with his compositions and his playing style. After the 1866 opening of Steinway Hall in New York and the favorable notice at the 1867 Paris Exhibition, Steinways won the favor of Anton Rubinstein (1872), Ignace Paderewski (1891), and many others; the Chickerings arranged for Hans von Bülow to open Chickering Hall in New York in 1875. American performers went to Europe to study, among them William Mason with Liszt and Ignaz Moscheles, and Amy Fay with Liszt and Rubinstein. The excitement created by touring artists led thousands of Americans, mostly young ladies, to study piano and play it in homes, schools, and churches, if not concert halls. The piano also became a staple of public entertainment, spawned the development of new musical styles (ragtime and jazz), and promoted the burgeoning popular song business.

Even though the piano industry was dominated by the Steinways and Chickerings in the 19th century, many smaller firms flourished – first in the East and later in Cincinnati (e.g., Baldwin) and Chicago (Kimball). Most obtained their parts from suppliers such as Alfred Dolge (felts for hammers, soundboards), Pratt, Read & Co. (keys and actions), and Wessell, Nickel & Gross (actions). After various financial depressions (late 1870s, 1884, 1893, 1907, 1921, 1930s) many firms went out of business; others consolidated into larger piano trusts such as the American Piano Company (1908) and the Aeolian Company; these combined in 1932 to form the Aeolian American Corporation.

The demand for pianos was great. According to statistics gathered by Loesser, Ehrlich, and Dolge, one of every 4800 Americans bought a new piano in 1829, in 1851 one of 2777, in 1870 one of 1540, in 1890 one of 874, and in 1910, a peak year when 350,000 pianos were produced, one of 252. By 1919 the more than 333,000 pianos that were made included 177,000 regular pianos and 156,000 player pianos, a trend that had begun with the introduction of mechanically operated pianos at the end of the 19th century (1923 was the peak year for player pianos, which were much more popular in the USA than in Europe). The competition from radio and recordings (and the automobile, which had begun to replace the piano as a status symbol) is reflected in the 1929 statistics: only 130,000 pianos were produced (a decrease of 183,000 in ten years). In 1932, three years into the Depression, only 25,000 pianos were made. Since that time the piano has never regained the prominence it held, especially on the amateur level where high fidelity audio systems, films, television, and instruments such as the electric guitar became more popular. New piano models such as the baby grand and the small "spinet" upright were introduced in the 1930s in an attempt to encourage sales. Since the late 1960s, American piano manufacturers have ranked second to the Japanese in world output and sales. Piano sales did not cease in the 1930s, however: one of every 1354 Americans bought a piano in 1983; 155,000 of those sold were produced in the USA (of which 6,500 were grands) and 37,000 were imported (15,000 grands).

BIBLIOGRAPHY

"Felix": "Piano Fortes," *The Euterpeiad*, iii (1823), 179

R. G. Parker: *A Tribute to the Life and Character of Jonas Chickering* (Boston, 1854)

J. L. Bishop: *A History of American Manufacturers from 1608 to 1860* (Philadelphia, 1866)

J. Parton: "The Piano in the United States," *Atlantic Monthly*, xx (July 1867), 82

H. K. Oliver: "Musical Instruments," *International Exhibition 1876: Reports and Awards, Group XXV* (Philadelphia, 1878)

T. Appleton and others: "The American Pianoforte Manufacture," *Musical and Sewing Machine Gazette* (21 Feb 1880), 35

D. Spillane: *History of the American Pianoforte* (New York, 1890/R1969)

W. Steinway: "American Musical Instruments," *One Hundred Years of American Commerce 1795–1895*, ed. C. M. Depew (New York, 1895), 509

2. View of the Action Room in the Chickering Pianoforte Manufactory, Tremont Street, Boston, in 1887

A. Dolge: *Pianos and their Makers* (Covina, CA, 1911/R1972)
C. M. Ayars: *Contributions to the Art of Music in America by the Music Industries of Boston, 1640 to 1936* (New York, 1937/R1969)
T. E. Steinway: *People and Pianos: a Century of Service to Music* (New York, 1953)
A. Loesser: *Men, Women and Pianos: a Social History* (New York, 1954)
K. Grafing: *Alpheus Babcock: American Pianoforte Maker (1785–1842): his Life, Instruments, and Patents* (diss., U. of Missouri, Kansas City, 1972)
C. Ehrlich: *The Piano: a History* (London, 1976)
C. A. Hoover: "The Steinways and Their Pianos in the Nineteenth Century," *JAMIS*, vii (1981), 47–89
E. M. Good: *Giraffes, Black Dragons, and Other Pianos: a Technological History from Cristofori to the Modern Concert Grand* (Stanford, CA, 1982)
N. J. Groce: *Musical Instrument Making in New York City during the Eighteenth and Nineteenth Centuries* (diss., U. of Michigan, 1982)
A. W. J. G. Ord-Hume: *Pianola: the History of the Self-playing Piano* (London, 1984)

CYNTHIA ADAMS HOOVER

Pianola. Term for a PLAYER PIANO, a trademark of the AEOLIAN CORPORATION; *see also* AEOLIAN CO.

Piano music. The USA was established as an independent nation at about the time that the piano superseded the harpsichord in general use, and piano music and its composition have flourished here since the colonial period. In the 19th century the piano was a standard item of drawing-room furniture in all but the meanest homes; the manufacture and sale of pianos flourished, and American piano builders such as Alpheus Babcock, Jonas Chickering, and Henry Steinway were among the best in the world. Even in the 20th century, when radio, recordings, and television, and an increased popularity of other instruments for domestic use have threatened its dominance, the piano has remained in wide use in all kinds of music-making, amateur and professional. Accordingly, American music publishing has always tended to center on piano music: almost from the beginning of the printing of music in the USA, music for piano was rivaled in quantity of publication only by songs (most of which, of course, included a piano accompaniment), and an immense amount of piano music, by American as well as foreign composers, was issued. This article surveys the main lines of development of American piano music and the most important contributions of its chief composers.

1. To 1865. 2. 1865 to 1920. 3. After 1920.

1. To 1865. The transition from harpsichord to piano as the principal keyboard instrument in use is reflected in the title of the first keyboard work to be published in the USA, William Brown's *Three Rondos for the Piano Forte or Harpsichord* (1787), and in that of Benjamin Carr's collection, including a set of six tiny sonatas, *A New Assistant for the Piano-forte or Harpsichord* (1796). Similarly titled is the group of eight songs for voice and keyboard that Francis Hopkinson had printed as *Seven Songs for the Harpsichord or Forte Piano* (1788). Such titles avoided designating a single instrument, undoubtedly to maximize sales. Another feature of the transitional period until about 1820 was the laying out of music in manuscripts and imprints in "keyboard score" (i.e., on treble and bass clefs) but without any instrumental designation; these may be simply skeletal cue sheets, to have been fleshed out by improvisation on whatever instruments were at hand, and this is almost certainly the case with the numerous anthologies of dance music, such as the anonymous *A Collection of the Most Favorite Cotillions* (n.d. [?1804]) and James Hewitt's compilation *A Collection of the Most Favorite Country Dances* (n.d. [?1802]). Hewitt similarly published in keyboard score *The Battle of Trenton* (1797), as did Carr his patriotic potpourri *The Federal Overture* (1794), though there is evidence that both were performed by ensembles. More clearly conceived for keyboard instrument (probably the piano) are some sets of variations by Carr and Hewitt, divertimentos and rondos by Rayner Taylor, and sonatas and rondos by J. C. Moller.

All these works are in the early Classical style: thin-textured, short-breathed, foursquare in phrase structure, and formally and harmonically simple. Much more sophisticated and with a broader stylistic and expressive range, approaching that of C. P. E. Bach's keyboard sonatas and rondos, are the four three-movement "Philadelphia sonatas" (1786–94), left in manuscript, by Alexander Reinagle; they are certainly the finest American keyboard music before 1820.

Between 1820 and the Civil War, American piano music, especially that intended for amateur performers and domestic use, developed rapidly. Publishers could hardly satisfy the demand, and a legion of minor figures, many of them amateurs themselves, appeared as composers of the airy trifles that were the principal products of the burgeoning sheet-music industry. The repertory consisted mainly of three kinds of pieces: sets of variations, usually based on popular songs, hymn tunes, or (from the 1830s on) opera arias; dances (waltzes, polkas, schottisches, galops, cotillions and quadrilles, and marches and quicksteps); and – distinctly in the minority – abstract genres (rondos are the most numerous). In time Romantic ideals of fantasy, irregularity, and individuality began to be reflected in American piano music – partly under the influence, from the 1840s, of touring European virtuosos (Leopold de Meyer, Henri Herz, and Sigismond Thalberg, among others); sets of variations took on the character of rhapsodic fantasies, simple dances became stylized – a tendency expressed in the appending of the phrase "de concert" to the dance title – and most piano works became programmatic or pictorial.

The first, and possibly the most extravagant, composer of piano music reflecting the new ideals was Anthony Philip Heinrich: as Dwight put it (in *The Harbinger*, 4 July 1846), "Mr. Heinrich belongs to the romantic class, who wish to attach a story to everything they do." In about 100 compositions for piano, beginning with those in his op. 1, *The Dawning of Music in Kentucky* (1820), Heinrich ranged from the naive to the prophetic, from the primitively simple to the elaborately grandiloquent. An ardent lover of the American wilderness, he celebrated it in such amazing works as *A Sylvan Scene in Kentucky, or the Barbecue Divertimento*, in which nearly 30 musical ideas appear without any repetitions, and *A Chromatic Ramble, of the Peregrine Harmonist*, a tour de force of harmonic and enharmonic complexity. Only slightly less extravagant is much of the piano music by Louis Moreau Gottschalk, who triumphed in Paris in the 1840s as a young pianist and composer, then returned to the USA in 1853 to take up a nomadic life as a touring virtuoso, succeeding so dramatically that he has been called "our first matinee idol." His early pieces were the first to borrow from Afro-Caribbean and Creole sources; his later ones often draw on other folk, popular, and patriotic materials, as in *The Union* (1852–62), a grand "paraphrase de concert" on national airs (*Yankee Doodle*, *The Star-Spangled Banner*, *Hail Columbia!*, and some trumpet calls), or *Columbia, caprice américain* (1859), based on Stephen Foster's *My Old Kentucky Home*. Gottschalk seems also to have been the first American to write piano duets, for both one instrument (an arrangement of Rossini's overture to *Guillaume Tell*, 1850–54) and two, and concerto-like works (*Grande tarantelle*, 1858–64, for piano and orchestra); he also organized grand concert extravaganzas at which such works as his arrangements of Gounod (*Grande marche de Faust*) and Wagner (*Grande marche de Tannhäuser*), both for 16 pianos (31 pianists) and orchestra, were performed.

A much more restrained Romantic pianism is found in the music of Richard Hoffman (almost 100 pieces) and William Mason (like Hoffman a pupil of Liszt in Weimar).

2. 1865 TO 1920. Piano music from the end of the Civil War to the early 20th century was dominated, as was other music of the increasingly assured "cultivated tradition" of American concert music, by central European models. Most members of the preeminent Second New England School studied in Germany and returned to the USA committed to the tradition of "the three Bs" (Bach, Beethoven, Brahms). Among the works of such composers as John Knowles Paine, George W. Chadwick, Arthur Whiting, Horatio Parker, Amy Beach, D. G. Mason, and Arthur Foote (all of them keyboard players), there is a liberal sprinkling of abstract piano music in the form of suites and sonatas, fugues, and sets of small pieces. Related to these Boston academics in his German training, but more strongly influenced by the New German School of Liszt and Wagner, was Edward MacDowell, himself a virtuoso pianist. MacDowell's large body of piano music – four sonatas, two concertos, some suites, and 16 collections of character-pieces – is stylistically the most individual of any American's after Gottschalk. Moreover, his occasional allusions in titles to American subject matter, as in "From an Indian Lodge" and "From Uncle Remus" in *Woodland Sketches* and several compositions among the *Sea Pieces* and *New England Idyls*, are echoed musically (if only faintly) with evocations of American Indian and Afro-American idioms.

More purposeful and consistent attempts to find a national identity in ethnic sources were made by others. An important influence was Dvořák, who during his years (1892–5) at the National Conservatory in New York urged the development of a national school; among those who responded were Harvey Worthington Loomis (*Lyrics of the Red Man*, 1903–4) and Harry T. Burleigh (*From the Southland*, 1907). Arthur Farwell, having founded the Wa-Wan Press in 1901 partly in "definite acceptance of Dvořák's challenge to go after our folk music," published several hundred works, many of them for piano, by 37 composers. Farwell himself left an important body of piano music, from his tiny, ingenious *What's in an Octave?* (1930) to the craggy Sonata (1949), as well as some overtly Indian works such as *From Mesa and Plain* (1905). Henry F. B. Gilbert turned not only to Indian sources (*Indian Scenes*, 1912) but to black-American ones (*Negro Dances*, 1914), as did John Powell, a concert pianist (*Rhapsodie nègre*, for piano and orchestra, 1918; individual movements in several suites for piano).

Of the various attempts made by American composers of the early 20th century to break away from the musical domination of an Austro-Germanic vocabulary and aesthetic, Charles Griffes's was notably successful – in piano music as in songs and orchestral pieces. Having assimilated the idioms of French impressionism (as is shown by the original version, for piano, of *The Pleasure-dome of Kubla Khan*, 1912, and "The White Peacock" and others of the *Roman Sketches*, 1915–16) and some aspects of oriental music (though these are not evident in solo piano works), Griffes completed before his early death a single sonata (1917–18), which, while owing something to Scriabin's sonatas, is his most original and powerful composition. Even more remarkably individual was the achievement of Charles Ives: although his music remained virtually unknown until many years later, by 1920 he had virtually completed his oeuvre, which includes two piano sonatas (Ives had the second, "Concord, Mass., 1840–1860," 1910–15, printed privately in 1920), an eight-minute *Three-page Sonata* (1905), *Varied Air and Variations* (?1923; it has been suggested that the title is a pun on "Very Darin' Variations"), and a large number of briefer pieces and studies, many with provocative titles such as *The Anti-abolitionist Riots in Boston in the 1850s* (1908) and *Some South-paw Pitching* (?1909).

3. AFTER 1920. To summarize the piano music written by Americans in the middle decades of the 20th century is a formidable task: it is not only extremely diverse in style but vast in quantity, and a remarkable amount is of high quality.

(i) The mainstream concert tradition. Most of the piano works written between the wars, and many written since World War II, may be seen as products of the serious, craftsmanlike tradition of abstract music established first in the USA by the composers of the Second New England School. Like them, the 20th-century composers in this tradition have been thoroughly grounded in European music, many having studied either in Europe (with teachers such as Nadia Boulanger and Luigi Dallapiccola) or at home with immigrant or resident European masters (Schoenberg, Hindemith, Milhaud, Berio, and others). As with their 19th-century forebears, "Americanism" in a stylistic sense has been of no particular concern to these composers; theirs has been, predominantly, a competent, well-crafted, but neutral music of individual expression, cast in traditional forms. The number of piano sonatas, alone, composed by Americans in this tradition is staggering: some 800 between 1920 and 1980.

Although the works that have been written in the mainstream tradition are numerous, only a few have entered the permanent repertory. Perhaps at the head of the list are Aaron Copland's Piano Variations (1930), Piano Sonata (1939–41), Piano Fantasy (1952), and *Night Thoughts* (1972). Roger Sessions is known for his three sonatas (1928–65) and the serial set of Five Pieces (1974–5), but more especially for the four intense character-pieces originally entitled *From my Diary* (1937–9), retitled *Pages from a Diary*. Ross Lee Finney's five sonatas (1933–61), smaller sets of pieces (including the attractive serial teaching pieces *Inventions*, 1956), and *Variations on a Theme by Alban Berg* (1952; Finney studied with Berg) are notable contributions, as are the many compositions for piano by the prolific Vincent Persichetti. Samuel Barber, with his single sonata (1949), added music of quality to the repertory but wrote little else for solo piano; the same has been true of Elliott Carter, who produced an early sonata (1946) and much later wrote *Night Fantasies* (1980).

Among composers of 12-tone music must be cited Milton Babbitt, whose Three Compositions for Piano (1947) were among the first examples of total serialism; George Rochberg, whose first 12-tone work was the 12 Bagatelles (1952); and Charles Wuorinen, whose Piano Variations (1963) and other pieces reflect his virtuosity as a pianist. Rochberg's 12-tone phase culminated (at least among his piano works) in the Sonata-fantasia (1956); he later moved in other directions, and by the early 1980s had made important neotonal statements (Partita-variations, 1976).

Some of the most unusual piano music in this tradition – on the edge of the avant-garde in its explorations of piano sonorities – is that by George Crumb. *Makrokosmos I* (1972) and *Makrokosmos*

Henry Cowell demonstrating one of his techniques of sound modification: while a chord is depressed silently on the keyboard with the left hand the strings inside the piano are strummed or plucked with the right hand

II (1973) for amplified piano comprise 24 fantasies inspired partly by Debussy's 24 *Préludes* and Bartók's *Mikrokosmos*. Diverse in style, they call not only for traditional keyboard and pedal techniques but for operations within the body of the instrument and a variety of sounds from the pianist (such as singing, speaking, and groaning). Collage also plays a part: in "Nightfall I" the pianist is to whistle phrases of the revival hymn *Will there be any stars in my crown?* and in "Dream Images" there are fragments of Chopin's *Fantaisie-impromptu*.

(ii) Music of popular inspiration. The syncopated music of ragtime and early jazz, both of them created by black Americans, spread in modified form to mainstream white culture early in the century, transforming the nature of American social dancing and popular music. From the 1920s there were attempts to adapt the new idioms to concert music, including music for piano. The best-known examples are those of George Gershwin, especially *Rhapsody in Blue* (1924), for piano and dance band, and the Concerto in F (1925); among his solo piano music are the lapidary Three Preludes (1926) and the 18 too-brief song transcriptions in *The Gershwin Song Book* (1932). Many minor composers, especially during the Depression years when populist feeling was strong and the war years when the prevailing sentiment was nationalistic, dabbled briefly in popular-music idioms, as did some major ones, among them Copland (Four Piano Blues, 1926–47), Virgil Thomson ("Ragtime Bass" in the Ten Etudes, 1943), Barber (*Excursions*, 1944), Roy Harris (*American Ballads*, 1942–5), and William Schuman (*Three-score Set*, 1943). Such borrowings were infrequent after World War II; however, with the revival in the 1970s of ragtime, some composers saw its pianistic possibilities and enlarged the repertory of piano rags (William Bolcom, with *Ghost Rags*, 1970–71, and other compositions), or composed larger works influenced by ragtime (William Albright, with *Grand Sonata in Rag*, 1968). Jazz too had some influence, both direct (as in Lalo Shifrin's *Jazz Sonata*, *c*1963) and indirect (as in Frederic Rzewski's *Four North American Ballads*, 1978–9, and, in their underlying idea if not their idiom, aleatory works by various composers).

Jazz pianists themselves produced some of the most brilliant, inventive, and artful piano music of the era (although until transcriptions from recordings were made the music was not available for performance by other pianists unless they learned it by ear). Some were noteworthy for their originality (Duke Ellington, Lennie Tristano, Thelonious Monk, Cecil Taylor); others offered music full of surprises and shifts of style and idea (Jelly Roll Morton, Dave Brubeck, Bill Evans, John Lewis, Dave McKenna); still others produced pieces of coruscating virtuosity (Earl Hines, Erroll Garner, and especially Art Tatum).

(iii) The avant garde. A strong current in American music of the 20th century has been the continuing presence of avant-garde composers with private visions and unique voices; among them are a few who have expressed their ideas significantly, even predominantly, in piano music. The patriarchs were Ives and Henry Cowell. Ives not only wrote music for two pianos tuned a quarter-tone apart (Three Pieces, 1923–4) but called for the performer of the "Concord" Sonata to strike the keyboard with a board (of a specific length) to produce massive cluster chords; in the accompaniment to the song *Charlie Rutlage* (1920/21) he requires the pianist to play with his fists (noting that the pitches are not important). Cowell arrived independently at the idea of tone clusters, produced by fists or forearms, first in *The Tides of Manaunaun* (?1917); he also, in *Fabric* (1920), wrote music of unprecedented poly-rhythmic complexity. Then in the following decade he wrote a whole series of pieces (including *Aeolian Harp*, *c*1923, *Sinister Resonance*, 1925, and *The Banshee*, 1930) that explored a previously untapped reservoir of sonorities produced by playing directly on the strings (see illustration) – plucking, stroking, or striking them, muting or stopping them, and producing harmonics on them.

Cowell's freethinking was passed on to his pupil John Cage. Cage's main contribution to avant-garde pianism was to turn the instrument into a kind of delicate-sounding one-man percussion band by "preparing" it – placing on and between the strings various objects and bits of material, to transform the sound quality (*see* PREPARED PIANO). His works for prepared piano culminated in the 70-minute *Sonatas and Interludes* (1946–8), which became his most frequently performed piece. His efforts in the 1950s to reduce his role as composer – to let the music "happen" – were realized in the lengthy *Music of Changes* (1951), *4'33"* (1952; the notorious "silent" composition, most often performed as a piano solo), and *Music for Piano 4-19* (1953). Cage also wrote (and surely was the first to do so) for a child's miniature piano (Suite for Toy Piano, 1948).

Cage in turn inspired numbers of younger composers, some of whom produced remarkable piano music. Morton Feldman's *Last Pieces* (1959) consist of nothing but soft, complicated chords, their duration and that of the silences between them being left to the performer; Christian Wolff's *For Piano I* (1952) is even more spare and silence-dominated. The instructions for Robert Moran's *Composition for Piano with Pianist* (*c*1965) read: "A pianist comes onto the stage and goes directly to the concert grand piano. He climbs into the piano and sits on the strings. The piano plays him." Larry Austin calls for the performer of his *Accidents* (1967) to make not sounds but very rapid gestures; the player must repeat any gesture within which an unintended, accidental sound occurs, until it is free of "error."

Perhaps influenced by Cowell, Conlon Nancarrow has pushed back even further the frontiers of rhythmic complexity, and also velocity, in his music, almost all of which is exclusively for player piano. Envisioning a literally superhuman music, Nancarrow learned how to punch his works onto player-piano rolls and, beginning with *Study for Player Piano I* (late 1940s), produced a long series of fantastic etudes, rich in canons and almost unfathomable polyrhythms, for one and two player pianos. Rhythmic complexity of a different nature has preoccupied Steve Reich, one of whose first "live" instrumental works (most of his early works are for tape) of pulse music (or phase music) was *Piano Phase* (1967) for two pianists or marimba players, in which the same material is played by the two performers at slightly different speeds, creating constantly changing relationships (*see* MINIMALISM, fig. 1*a*). The title of Reich's *Six Pianos* (1933) is self-explanatory.

Yet another area in which music for piano has broken new ground is that of the musical scale itself: inspired by the work of Harry Partch (who wrote not for piano or other conventional instruments but for inventions of his own), composers such as Ben Johnston (Sonata for Microtonal Piano, 1965) have sought, in music based on just intonation (giving untempered intervals), to "reopen doors closed by the acceptance of the twelve-tone equal-tempered scale as the norm of pitch usage" (Hamm, 1976, quoting Johnston).

See also EXPERIMENTAL MUSIC; JAZZ, §§III, 6; V, 4, 8; POPULAR MUSIC, esp. §II, 6. For the role of the piano in song and chamber works *see*, respectively, ART SONG and CHAMBER MUSIC.

BIBLIOGRAPHY

A. Loesser: *Men, Women and Pianos* (New York, 1954)
M. L. McKeon: *Stylistic Tendencies in Mid-twentieth-century American Piano Music* (diss., Eastman School of Music, 1957)
B. A. Wolverton: *Keyboard Music and Musicians in the Colonies and United States of America before 1830* (diss., Indiana U., 1966)
M. Williams: *The Jazz Tradition* (New York, 1970, 2/1983)
M. Hinson: *Guide to the Pianist's Repertoire* (Bloomington, IN, 1973; suppl., 1979)
J. B. Clark: "The Renaissance of Early American Keyboard Music: a Bibliographic Review," *CMc*, no.18 (1974), 127
C. Hamm: Liner notes, *Sound Forms for Piano* (NW 203, 1976)
R. Offergeld: "Gottschalk and Company: the Music of Democratic Sociability," *The Wind Demon* (NW 257, 1976) [liner notes]
J. B. Clark: Preface, *Anthology of Early American Keyboard Music, 1787–1830*, RRAM, i–ii (1977)
R. Hopkins: Preface, *Alexander Reinagle: The Philadelphia Sonatas*, RRAM, v (1978)
K. R. Gartner: *The Expansion of Pianism since 1945* (diss., New York U., 1979)
E. A. Berlin: *Ragtime: a Musical and Cultural History* (Berkeley, 1980/*R*1984 with additions)
W. Brooks: "The American Piano," *The Book of the Piano*, ed. D. Gill (Ithaca, NY, 1981), 172
J. Gillespie and A. Gillespie, eds.: *A Bibliography of Nineteenth-century American Piano Music* (Westport, CT, 1984)

MAURICE HINSON, H. WILEY HITCHCOCK

Piano Technicians Guild. Organization formed in 1958 by the merger of the National Association of Piano Tuners (founded 1908) and the American Society of Piano Technicians (founded 1940) as an international nonprofit association of piano-tuning and -servicing craftsmen; its aim is "to achieve the highest possible service standards and to most effectively promote the technical, economic, and social interests of piano technicians." Its 3000 members are classified either as Registered Technicians, who adhere to the guild's code of ethics, or as Apprentices, Students, or Allied Tradesmen. Among its publications are several manuals including *Piano Parts and their Functions* (1981), a *Classified Index to Published Piano Technology* (1982), the monthly *Piano Technicians Journal* (founded in 1958), and an annual *Official Directory* (since 1961). The guild's headquarters are in Seattle.

JOHN SHEPARD

Piantadosi, Al (*b* New York, 18 July 1884; *d* Encino, CA, 8 April 1955). Songwriter. He worked as a pianist in Callahan's saloon and other nightclubs in the Chinatown district of New York, and wrote his first song, *My Mariuccia take a steamboat*, in 1906. He published several commercially successful songs before 1920, including the ethnic *I'm a Yiddish cowboy* (1908), *I'm awfully glad I'm Irish* (words by E. Leslie, 1910), and *That Italian Rag* (Leslie, 1910), and two sentimental ballads which sold over a million copies each, *That's how I need you* (J. McCarthy, J. Goodwin, 1912) and *The Curse of an Aching Heart* (H. Fink, 1913). He also wrote the controversial *I didn't raise my boy to be a soldier* (A. Bryan, 1915), which reflected the sentiments of those Americans who wanted no part in World War I. As an accompanist for vaudeville performers such as Anna Chandler, Piantadosi toured widely in the USA and also traveled to Europe and Australia, where he was a pioneer performer of ragtime. On his return he worked for music publishers in New York and retired in 1930 to California.

RONALD RIDDLE

Piastro, Mishel [Michel] (*b* Kerch, Crimea, Russia, 19 June 1891; *d* New York, 10 April 1970). Violinist. He attended the St. Petersburg Conservatory from 1903 to 1910, where he was a violin pupil of Leopold Auer. He was active as a concert violinist before immigrating to the USA in 1920; that same year he made his début in New York and then toured the country. In 1925 he was appointed concertmaster and assistant conductor of the San Francisco SO; from 1931 to 1943 he was concertmaster of the New York PO, under Toscanini and then Barbirolli, and while with the orchestra appeared frequently as a soloist. He was also first violinist of the New York Philharmonic-Symphony String Quartet, and in the 1930s and 1940s often appeared as a recitalist and chamber-music performer in New York. For over 25 years beginning in 1941 he conducted radio station WOR's "Longines Symphonette." Piastro was also active as a teacher for most of his professional life.

Piatigorsky, Gregor (*b* Ekaterinoslav [now in Dnepropetrovsk], 17 April 1903; *d* Los Angeles, CA, 6 Aug 1976). Cellist and composer. He began to play cello when he was seven and two years later was admitted to the Moscow Conservatory as a scholarship student of Alfred von Glehn; later he had some private lessons with Anatoly Brandukov. In 1919 he joined the Lenin Quartet, and the same year he was appointed principal cellist of the Bolshoi Theater orchestra. He left the USSR surreptitiously in 1921, going first to Warsaw, then to Leipzig where he studied with Julius Klengel. In 1924 Furtwängler engaged him as principal cellist of the Berlin PO, a post he left in 1928 to devote himself to a solo career. In Berlin he formed a distinguished sonata partnership with Schnabel, and a trio with Schnabel and Flesch. He came to the USA in 1929 and made his American début in Oberlin, Ohio, on 5 November; his début with the New York PO on 29 December 1929 was the triumphant beginning of an international career. In 1930 he was heard in trios with two eminent Russian colleagues, Horowitz and Milstein, and he formed another famous trio in 1949 with Heifetz and Rubinstein. He taught at the Curtis Institute from 1942 (the year he became an American citizen) until 1951. Having settled in California, in 1961 Piatigorsky joined Heifetz in establishing a chamber music series in Los Angeles, known as the Heifetz-Piatigorsky Concerts; some of their programs were heard in New York in 1964 and 1966 and were also recorded. For a number of years he was director of chamber music at the Berkshire Music Center, and from 1962 until his death was a professor at the University of Southern California, where his cello classes were renowned; in 1975 a Piatigorsky chair of music was established there. Piatigorsky performed until late in his life, playing at several concerts given for his 70th birthday in 1973, and in London in 1974.

At the height of his career Piatigorsky was acclaimed as a leading cellist of his generation, combining a flair for virtuosity with an exquisite taste in style and phrasing; technical perfection was never a goal in itself. His vibrant tone had infinite shadings and his sweeping eloquence and aristocratic grandeur created an instant rapport with his audience. He was at his best in emotional Romantic music, and Strauss commented after hearing him play *Don Quixote*: "I have heard the 'Don' as I thought him to be." He gave the premières of concertos by Castelnuovo-Tedesco, Hindemith, Dukelsky, and Walton, as well as Foss's *Capriccio* and Webern's early Cello Sonata and Three Little Pieces; he also gave the first American performance of Prokofiev's Concerto op.58 (1940). Besides original works for cello (including *Pliaska*, Scherzo, Variations on a Theme of Paganini for cello and piano or orchestra), he published some skillful transcriptions and collaborated with Stravinsky on the cello version of the "Suite italienne" from *Pulcinella*. There is a rich legacy of Piatigorsky recordings in the solo and chamber repertory. His autobiography *Cellist* (1965) has been translated into several languages. Among his numerous awards were seven honorary doctorates and membership in the Légion d'honneur. Piatigorsky owned two magnificent Stradivari cellos, the "Batta" (1714) and the "Baudiot" (1725).

Gregor Piatigorsky (left) with Alexander Hilsberg and Efrem Zimbalist at a rehearsal of Brahms's Double Concerto, Curtis Hall, Philadelphia, January 1949

BIBLIOGRAPHY

P. Yates: "Visit to an Untyped Cellist . . . /Gregor Piatigorsky," *HiFi*, xi/2 (1961), 45

G. Piatigorsky: "A Cellist's View of Conducting," *Saturday Review*, xlviii (30 Jan 1965), 47

Obituary, *New York Times* (7 Aug 1976)

I. Marinel: "The Last Word," *MJ*, xxxv/6 (1977), 62

D. and B. Rosenberg: *The Music Makers* (New York, 1979), 205

BORIS SCHWARZ

Piavosoto. American Indian group of the Great Basin area, belonging to the PAIUTE.

Picker, Tobias (*b* New York, 18 July 1954). Composer and pianist. He gained experience as a pianist for the Martha Graham School of Contemporary Dance while in his teens and studied with Wuorinen at the Manhattan School (BM 1976) and with Carter at the Juilliard School (MM 1978). His early works for chamber ensembles and solo instruments enjoyed successful performances in New York; Andrew Porter, in the *New Yorker*, praised him as "a genuine creator with a fertile, unforced vein of invention . . . one of the most gifted, individual, and unschematic of our young composers." Picker's music shows detailed knowledge of the technical and expressive possibilities of instruments, particularly the piano, and a finely conceived sense of form. The Piano Concerto and Violin Concerto have shown that he can revitalize formal devices such as orchestral introductions and cadenzas, and technical devices such as trills, scales, and arpeggios, with cunning originality. In addition, there is an emotional involvement that, while at times offset by wit and zest of expression, is nonetheless praiseworthy for its drama and deep sense of personal communication. Picker's awards include a Bearns Prize (1977), a Charles Ives Scholarship (1978), NEA grants (1979, 1981), a Rockefeller Foundation award (1979), and a Guggenheim Fellowship (1981). In 1985 he was appointed composer-in-residence for the Houston SO. He has received commissions from Speculum Musicae, Parnassus, the New Hampshire SO, the American Composers Orchestra, the San Francisco SO, the Honolulu SO, the St. Paul Chamber Orchestra, the Boehm Quintet, and the pianist Ursula Oppens. His works have been recorded on the CRI label.

WORKS

4 Sextets, mixed insts, no.1, 1973, no.2, 1976, no.3, 1977, no.4 "The Blue Hula," 1981; When Soft Voices Die, pf, 1977; Rhapsody, vn, pf, 1978; Octet, vn, vc, db, b cl, hn, harp, mar + vib, 1978; Nova, vn, va, vc, db, pf, 1979; Romance, vn, pf, 1979; Pf Conc., 1980; Vn Conc., 1981; Sym., 1982; Encantadas (Melville), nar, orch, 1983; Keys to the City (Pf Conc. no.2), pf, orch, 1983; Serenade, pf, wind qnt, 1983; Dedication Anthem, band, 1984; Pian-o-rama, 2 pf, 1984; *c*13 other works, incl. vocal pieces, early pf pieces, other chamber works

Principal publisher: Helicon

BIBLIOGRAPHY

A. Porter: "Musical Events," *New Yorker* (20 Nov 1978), 10; (15 Jan 1979), 94

JAMES G. ROY, JR.

Pickett, Wilson (*b* Prattville, AL, 18 March 1941). Soul singer and songwriter. His family moved in the 1950s to Detroit, where he formed a gospel group, the Violinaires. In 1959 he joined a rhythm-and-blues group, the Falcons, but he continued to emulate the shouting gospel style of Julius Cheeks. In 1962 he made a hit recording, *I found a love*, with the Falcons, and the following year he made two, *If you need me* and *It's too late*, as a soloist. All were ballads in 3/4 time; formally they resembled Sam Cooke's *Bring it on home to me*, but the ferocity of Pickett's singing, nearly unprecedented in secular music, made the recordings exemplars of the emerging genre of soul. His greatest hits were recorded for Atlantic Records. The first of these was *In the Midnight Hour* (no.21, 1965), which was recorded in Memphis with Booker T. and the MGs, and was written by Pickett and Steve Cropper. This was followed by several hits, including *Land of 1000 Dances* (no.6, 1966) and *Funky Broadway* (no.8, 1967). These were strutting dance recordings on which his hotblooded vocal style was to some extent tempered by the cool authority of the instrumental backing supplied by experienced studio musicians. Pickett's rhythmic use of baritone grunts and falsetto squeals, which drive these songs along, shows the way in which elements of the gospel tradition were converted by soul singers into an irresistible dance music. In 1971 Pickett toured Ghana with American and African musicians. Pickett's voice was too gruff and his rhythms too harsh and pounding to allow him to adapt to the smoother disco style of the 1970s; his later albums contained some striking material, but none had the impact of his work from the 1960s.

RECORDINGS

(selective list; all recorded for Atlantic)

In the Midnight Hour (2289, 1965); 634-5789 (2320, 1966); Land of 1000 Dances (2348, 1966); Funky Broadway (2430, 1967); I'm a Midnight Mover (2528, 1968); Don't let the green grass fool you (2781, 1971); Don't knock my love, part 1 (2797, 1971)

BIBLIOGRAPHY

SouthernB

P. Guralnick: "Soul," *The Rolling Stone Illustrated History of Rock and Roll*, ed. J. Miller (New York, 1976, 2/1980)

G. Hirshey: *Nowhere to Run: the Story of Soul Music* (New York, 1984)

KEN EMERSON

Picon, Molly (*b* New York, 28 Feb 1898). Singer and actress. The date of birth commonly given for Picon, 1 June 1898, is incorrect though she herself long thought it to be true. In Philadelphia, where she grew up, she performed with vaudeville acts (from 1904) and Yiddish repertory companies. After a nationwide tour with a vaudeville act in 1918–19, she married Jacob (Yonkel) Kalich (1981–1975), the manager of the Grand Opera House in Boston; he subsequently wrote over 40 musicals for her, beginning with *Yonkele* (1921). Their first tour to Europe, in 1921, marked a change of style in European Yiddish theater from music dramas to musical comedy and also enhanced Picon's reputation in the USA. On her return she became the leading performer at the Second Avenue Theatre in New York. She first sang on Broadway in 1929, and from 1940 performed in dramatic productions starting with *Morning Star*; she also performed on radio and in films and continued to appear in vaudeville. The works by Kalich in which she was most successful included *Shmendrick* (1924), *The Little Devil* (1926), *Hello Molly* (1929), the biographical *Oy is dus a Leben*, which opened at the newly named Molly Picon Theater in 1942, *Abi gezunt* (1949), *Mazel tov, Molly* (1950), and *Farblondjete Honeymoon* (1955); she also created the role of Clara Weiss in Jerry Herman's *Milk and Honey* (1961). Kalich occasionally performed with her – they were the first entertainers to visit surviving Jews in Europe after World War II – and their best-known appearances together were in the play *The World of Sholem Aleichem* (1957) and the film of *Fiddler on the Roof* (1970). In collaboration with Joseph Rumshinsky, Picon wrote songs and lyrics for Kalich's works; the most famous were *East Side Symphony*, *Song of the Tenement*, *The Story of Grandma's Shawl*, *Working Goil*, and *Hands*. An exuberant actress whose performances often included acrobatics and tap dances, the diminutive Picon coupled a natural comic flair with ingratiating warmth that made her a much-loved performer with both English- and Yiddish-speaking audiences. She wrote two memoirs, *So Laugh a Little* (1962, with E. C. Rosenberg) and *Molly!* (1980, with J. B. Grillo).

BIBLIOGRAPHY

"Picon, Molly," *CBY 1951*

SUSAN FEDER

Picou, Alphonse (Floristan) (*b* New Orleans, LA, 19 Oct 1878; *d* New Orleans, 4 Feb 1961). Jazz clarinetist. He regularly played with "reading" bands and orchestras in New Orleans, but his improvising skills also allowed him to work successfully with smaller jazz groups. He often played in the Tuxedo Brass Band, on B♭ and E♭ clarinets, and while with this ensemble is said to have developed a solo on *High Society* which has since become a traditional part of the tune's performance. In 1932 Picou reduced his musical activities and devoted more time to his occupation as a tinsmith; but, with the revival of interest in traditional jazz, he reemerged to record with Kid Rena in 1940. He worked with Papa Celestin in the late 1940s, and led his own small group at The Paddock in the early 1950s. Picou became a doyen of New Orleans music, playing fairly regularly until just before his death. His recorded work lacks the fire and the passionate flow of the great New Orleans clarinetists, but his tone and graceful articulation won him admirers.

RECORDINGS

(selective list)

As sideman: K. Rena: Low Down Blues (1940, Delta 803), High Society Rag

(1940, Delta 804), Weary Blues (1940, Delta 806); R. Alexis: Clarinet Marmalade (1951, Palm 30 20); Paddock Jazz Band: *Paddock Jazz Band – 1953* (1953, Center 10), incl. Eh la bas

BIBLIOGRAPHY

SouthernB

G. Hoefer: "The Hot Box," *Down Beat*, xvii/19 (1950), 6

K. G. Mills: "Discography of Alphonse Picou," *Jazz Report*, i/8 (1961), 3

P. Haby: "Alphonse Picou: New Orleans Creole," *Footnote*, xi/5 (1980), 4

JOHN CHILTON

Picuris. American Indians of Taos County, New Mexico, belonging to the Tiwa subgroup of the EASTERN PUEBLO. Their culture and music bear a strong resemblance to those of the TAOS Indians. The Picuris, who numbered about 125 in 1980, live in relative isolation; they speak a dialect of the Tiwa language.

The music of the Picuris reflects both traditional Pueblo culture and a number of foreign influences. It is largely functional and, except for the Matachina Dance music, vocal. Among the instruments used for accompaniment are gourd rattles; notched-stick rasps; metal bells; large, double-headed drums; rolled hides struck with sticks; and arrows, which are struck together to accompany ceremonial picnic songs. The violin and guitar, played by Spanish-American musicians, accompany the Matachina Dance. The songs of the Picuris are, with the exception of lullabies, written and performed by men. The Picuris song repertory also includes dance songs, and gambling, corn-grinding, ditch-cleaning, and story-telling songs. The structure of Picuris music is simple; it conforms in general to the style of that of the Eastern Pueblo. Its chief characteristics include descending melody, and elaboration through repetition of short phrases, often incomplete or modified.

The diminishing population of the Picuris since the arrival of Europeans in the 16th century has been accompanied by a loss of traditional musical forms; in recent years, however, there has been a renewal of interest in their music.

See also INDIANS, AMERICAN, esp. §I, 4(ii)(c) and fig. 1.

DISCOGRAPHY

Picuris Indian Songs (Taos Recordings and Publications 5, 1964); *So these won't Be Forgotten: Music of Picuris Pueblo, New Mexico*, recorded 1966 (Taos Recordings and Publications 121, 1968); *Ditch-Cleaning and Picnic Songs of Picuris Pueblo*, recorded 1966, 1970 (IH 1051, 1971)

BIBLIOGRAPHY

H. H. Roberts: "Analysis of Picuris Songs" and "Picuris Children's Stories with Texts and Songs," in J. P. Harrington and H. H. Roberts: *43rd Annual Report, Bureau of American Ethnology* (Washington, DC, 1928), 399–447

A. Ortiz: Review of *So these won't Be Forgotten: Music of Picuris Pueblo, New Mexico*, *EM*, xiii (1969), 586

For further bibliography, *see* TAOS.

DONALD N. BROWN

Piegan. American Indian tribe of Montana, and Alberta, Canada; *see* BLACKFOOT (i).

Pierce, Webb (*b* nr West Monroe, LA, 8 Aug 1926). Country-music singer, guitarist, songwriter, and publisher. He performed as a guitarist on radio station KMLB (Monroe, Louisiana) before 1950, when he joined the "Louisiana Hayride" on KWKH (Shreveport, Louisiana). Recording contracts with the local Pacemaker label (about 1950), 4-Star, and Decca (1951) allowed him to resign his part-time job as a clerk at Sears, Roebuck and concentrate on music. After his initial hit, *Wondering* (1952), he gained national attention with *Back Street Affair* (1952), one of the first country songs to deal forthrightly with adultery. An equally important landmark was *There stands the glass* (1953), a classic drinking song and the first country hit to use the pedal steel guitar, played by Bud Isaacs. It became the favorite backup instrument in country music for the next two decades, and Pierce was the first of many country singers whose slurs, octave jumps, and use of dynamics complemented its sound. During his peak years (1951–71), Pierce had eight no. 1 hits, and 81 sides on the country chart; among the most influential were *Slowly* (1954); *In the jailhouse now* (1955), a remake of the old Jimmie Rodgers tune; and *Why, baby, why* (1955), a duet with Red Sovine. In 1952 he joined the cast of the "Grand Ole Opry," where he inherited Hank Williams's mantle as the show's leading honky-tonk singer. With "Opry" manager Jim Denny he founded Cedarwood Music in 1953; it became a leading Nashville publishing firm whose writers included Danny Dill, John D. Loudermilk, Carl Perkins, and Mel Tillis. One of the most commercially successful of modern country singers, Pierce had a nasal tenor voice that was influential in defining the honky-tonk vocal style in the 1950s.

RECORDINGS

(selective list; all recorded for Decca)

As soloist: Back Street Affair (28369, 1952); Wondering (46364, 1952); There stands the glass (28834, 1953); Slowly (28991, 1954); In the jailhouse now (29391, 1955); Holiday for Love (30419, 1957); A thousand miles ago (30858, 1959); Sweet Lips (31249, 1961); Memory #1 (31617, 1964); Fool, fool, fool (32167, 1967)

With R. Sovine: Why, baby, why? (29755, 1955)

CHARLES K. WOLFE

Pi Kappa Lambda. Music honor society for men and women, founded in 1918; *see* GREEK-LETTER SOCIETIES, §2.

Pikuni. American Indian tribe of Montana, and Alberta, Canada; *see* BLACKFOOT (i).

Pilcher. Firm of organ builders. It was founded by Henry Pilcher (1798–1880), a native of Dover, England, who immigrated to the USA about 1832. He set up a business in Newark in 1833, moved to New Haven in 1839, and returned to Newark in 1844. In 1856 his sons Henry Pilcher, Jr. (1828–90), and William (*b* 1830) joined the firm, which became known as Henry Pilcher & Sons; it moved to St. Louis about 1858, where it built some notable organs, including a large instrument for St. Paul's Church (1859). In 1863 the firm moved to Chicago, where it remained until its factory was destroyed in the great fire of 1871. The elder Henry Pilcher retired in the following year and under the directorship of Henry, Jr., and his sons R. E., William E., Paul B., and J. V. Pilcher, the firm opened a new factory in Louisville, where it prospered. In 1904 one of its largest organs was built for the Louisiana Purchase Exposition, St. Louis. The firm carried on the English tonal tradition and was noted for its complex but reliable wind-chest design, patented early in the 20th century by William E. Pilcher. His sons Gerard W. and William E., Jr., continued to run the firm until shortly after Gerard's death in 1941; in 1944 the company was sold to the M. P. Möller Co.

BIBLIOGRAPHY

M. Lippincott: "Henry Pilcher, Organ Builder," *Quarterly Bulletin* [New York Historical Society], xxvii/4 (1943), 87

O. Ochse: *The History of the Organ in the United States* (Bloomington, IN, 1975)

BARBARA OWEN

Pilgrim, Neva (Stevens) (*b* Cottonwood County, MN, 21 Nov 1938). Soprano. After studying music and English at Hamline University (BA 1960), she attended Yale University (MMus 1962) and the Vienna Academy of Music (1963–4); while there she sang Gilda with the Vienna Volksoper. Shortly after her return to the USA she made her first appearance at Carnegie Recital Hall (March 1965); her first solo recital in New York was given there on 9 March 1970. During the late 1960s, she worked with Shapey's Contemporary Chamber Ensemble in Chicago and spent several summers at the Berkshire and Marlboro music festivals. She has taught at Hamilton College (1971–6), Colgate University (from 1976), and Syracuse University (from 1977). Pilgrim is especially active in the performance of contemporary music, and many composers, including Ralph Shapey, George Rochberg, Richard Wernick, Easley Blackwood, Ann Silsbee, and Dexter Morrill have written works for her.

ELLEN HIGHSTEIN

Pima. American Indians of central Arizona. They inhabit a stark desert along the dry river beds of the Salt and Gila rivers; as recently as the early 20th century these flowed year round, and the Pima practiced irrigation agriculture and ate fish. Owing to their central location on two important waterways the Pima had regular contact with many other cultures. The Apache, to the northeast, and the Yuma, to the west, were dreaded enemies. The Maricopa, fleeing from the Yuma, eventually settled in central Arizona near the Pima, who learned from them much about Yuman lifestyle, including songs. The Pima maintained friendly relations with the Papago, who live just to their south (they speak mutually intelligible dialects of the Piman language). In the last half of the 19th century, the Pima provided food and assistance to many English-speaking travelers (including missionaries) in Arizona; as a result of these friendly contacts many settled in the area. A majority of the Pima were Christianized by the early 20th century; Protestant missionaries forbade the celebration of traditional ceremonies, dancing, and singing, resulting in a loss of many traditional song genres. Frank Russell, who visited the Pima in 1901–2, reported that no traditional songs were heard in the Pima villages, although he elicited over 200 song texts with the help of José Lewis, a Papago.

Pima musical style is nearly identical to that of the PAPAGO, though more individual singing styles may be noted now, possibly because a strong performance continuum was lacking from the 1890s to the 1960s. The main accompanying instrument is the gourd rattle, used by some singers as a drumstick with which they strike an inverted cardboard box. The rasp (for healing songs), the inverted basket drum, and a three-hole cane flute were played and may still be encountered. Eight categories of song existed: myth, game, Round Dance, hunting, medicine, girl's puberty, rain, and war. Only social and Round Dance songs remain widely known; these are often named for birds or other animals (such as the swallow, bluebird, oriole, or butterfly). Specific songs open and close the singing and dancing that take place during a night's ceremonies; the bulk of the songs are chosen, from a corpus of about 200, at the discretion of the lead singer. Each song cycle is said to have been dreamed by a Pima (*see* INDIANS, AMERICAN, §I, 3), and is normally named for the being who taught the songs. The cycles often tell of a journey in which the singer and teacher are transported to important landmarks in Pima land. The songs describe various creatures and nocturnal objects made by Earth Medicine Man and are intended to help the Pima better understand their relation to the universe. The opening songs of a cycle usually speak of the sun setting in the west and the sound of songs in the distance, while the closing songs tell of the sky in the east becoming light and the animals waking.

In the 1960s and 1970s several traditional song and dance genres were reintroduced, to teach Pima traditions to younger members. At the Salt River community Basket Dance songs were relearned, and young girls were taught how to make traditional dance dresses and yucca baskets, and how to dance with the baskets. One of the Gila River communities now performs the *Matachina*, a dance of Spanish origin found throughout the Southwest. Another modern genre, developed in the early 20th century, is the Heaven song. Heaven songs describe Jesus and Mary and tell of the salvation offered the Pima through Christian beliefs. They are not translations of Christian hymns, but rather indigenous expressions of Christian doctrine in traditional Pima musical style. These songs also are dreamed, often in association with a ritual event such as baptism or first communion.

Nontraditional musical groups of the Pima include the Salt River Indian Band (an amateur community ensemble), and various rock and acculturated popular groups with varying organization and membership (for example, *see* CHICKEN SCRATCH). Since the mid-1970s a pan-Indian style drum has developed in the town of Sacaton, Arizona, and powwow music can be heard at community events, such as annual rodeos.

See also INDIANS, AMERICAN, esp. §I, 2, 3, 4(ii)(c) and fig.1.

DISCOGRAPHY

Songs from the Pima (Can. ARP 6066, 1970)
Traditional Pima Dance Songs (Can. 8011, 1978)

BIBLIOGRAPHY

F. Russell: "The Pima Indian," *Bureau of American Ethnology, 26th Annual Report* (Washington, DC, 1904–5/*R*1975)
G. Herzog: "A Comparison of Pueblo and Pima Musical Styles," *Journal of American Folklore*, xlix (1936), 284–427
N. Ware: "Survival and Change in Pima Indian Music," *EM*, xiv (1970), 100
D. Bahr, J. Giff, and M. Havier: "Piman Songs on Hunting," *EM*, xxiii (1979), 245–96
J. Giff: "Pima Blue Swallow Songs of Gratitude," *Speaking, Singing and Teaching*, ed. F. Barkon and E. Brandt (Tempe, AZ, 1980)

J. RICHARD HAEFER

Pimsleur, Solomon (*b* Paris, France, 19 Sept 1900; *d* New York, 22 April 1962). Composer. His family immigrated to New York in 1903. He received an MA in literature at Columbia University (1923), where he studied composition with Daniel Gregory Mason. After receiving a fellowship in 1926, he studied with Goldmark at the Juilliard School, and then at the Mozarteum in Salzburg. With his sister, Susan Pimsleur Puma, he ran an artists' agency and production company; he was also known as a pianist and lecturer. Pimsleur wrote over 120 works for a range of ensembles. He frequently combined musical with literary interests, setting to music poetry of Shakespeare, the English Romantics, and 20th-century authors (including Kathleen Raine, Wilfred Owen, and himself). His romantic neoclassicism was often the vehicle for emotional indulgence (*Symphony to Terror and Despair* op.55, *Melancholy Sonata* op.56, *Heart Rending Sonata for String-Sextet* op.77), though he achieved a greater universality of expression in, for example, the *Symphonic Ballade* op.18 no.5. At the time of his death he had finished two acts of an opera based on the *Diary of Anne Frank*. His music manuscripts are at Columbia University and the Moldenhauer Archives, Spokane, Washington.

BIBLIOGRAPHY

Compositores de América/Composers of the Americas, ed. Pan American Union, xiii (Washington, DC, 1967), 94 [incl. list of works]

DAVID HUNTER

Pinewood Tom. Pseudonym of JOSH WHITE.

Pinkham, Daniel (Rogers, Jr.) (*b* Lynn, MA, 5 June 1923). Composer. He studied at Harvard University with Merritt, Piston, Archibald Davison, and Copland (BA 1943, MA 1944), at the Berkshire Music Center with Honegger and Barber, and privately with Boulanger. He studied the harpsichord with Putnam Aldrich and Landowska, and the organ with Biggs. Previously on the faculty at Simmons College, Boston University, and Harvard, in 1959 he joined the faculty of the New England Conservatory as a lecturer on composition and chairman of the department of performance of early music; he is also music director of King's Chapel, Boston. His many awards include a Fulbright scholarship (1950) and a Ford Foundation fellowship (1962), and he is a fellow of the American Academy of Arts and Sciences. A prolific, widely performed composer, he has received many commissions. His earlier music is neoclassical; soon after 1950 he began to use serial techniques, at first with 12-tone melodies in tonal settings. In 1970, after some help from his conservatory colleague Ceely, Pinkham started to explore electronic music, which he has used in conjunction with instruments or voices more frequently than alone. His music has remained sturdy in architecture and energetically polyphonic and his harmony has become more chromatic. He composed a sequence of chords for orchestra, *Catacoustical Measures*, commissioned by the acousticians Bolt Beranek & Newman to test the acoustics of Philharmonic Hall, New York.

WORKS

VOCAL

Chorus, orch, unless otherwise stated: Wedding Cantata, 1956; Easter Cantata, 1957; Christmas Cantata, 1957; Requiem, 1963; Stabat mater, 1964; St. Mark Passion, 1965; Jonah, Mez, T, B-Bar, chorus, orch, 1966; Ascension Cantata, chorus, wind, perc, 1970; To Troubled Friends (J. Wright), 1972; Daniel in the Lions' Den (Bible), 1973; Fanfares (Bible), 1975; 4 Elegies (Herrick, R. Crashaw, Vaughan, Donne), 1975; The Passion of Judas (Bible), 1976; The Descent into Hell (Pinkham, after Gk.), 1979; Hezekiah (Bible), 1979; When God Arose (Bible), 1979; Before the Dust Returns (Bible), 1981; The Conversion of Saul (Bible), 1981; Lauds, 2vv, 2 hn, db, org, perc, 1984; *c*50 other choral works incl. many religious settings

Solo vocal: The Song of Jephtha's Daughter, S, pf, 1963; 8 Poems of Gerard Manley Hopkins, Bar, va, 1964; Letters from St. Paul, S/T, org, 1965; Safe in their alabaster chambers (E. Dickinson), Mez, tape, 1972; Charm me Asleep, Bar/Mez, gui, 1977; Transitions, Mez, bn/pf, 1979; Manger Scenes (N. Farber), S, pf, 1980; The Death of the Witch of Endor, A, hpd, perc, 1981; Music in the Manger (Farber), S, hpd/pf, 1981; The Wellesley Hills Psalm Book, medium v, org, 1983; many others

INSTRUMENTAL

Orch: Vn Conc., 1956; 3 syms., 1961, 1963, 1985; Catacoustical Measures, 1962; Signs of the Zodiac, orch, opt. nar, 1965; Org Conc., 1970; Serenades, tpt, wind orch, 1979; *c*20 film scores

Chamber: Pf Concertino, 1950; Partita, hpd, 1962; Concertante, org, cel, perc, 1963; Lessons, hpd, 1971; Toccatas for the Vault of Heaven, org, tape, 1972; Blessings, org, 1977; Epiphanies, org, 1978; Masks, hpd, chamber ens, 1978; Miracles, fl, org, 1978; Diversions, org, harp, 1980; Proverbs, org, 1980; Holland Waltzes, 2 pf, 1982; Vigils, harp, 1982; Brass Qnt, 1983; Psalms, org, tpt, 1983; A Proclamation, org, 1984; *c*20 others, incl. tape pieces with vv and/or insts

OTHER

Stage: The Dreadful Dining Car (Pinkham, after Twain), Mez, actors, soloists, chorus, 7 insts, 1982; 2 others

Arrs., most vocal, of works by Handel, Purcell, Schubert, Selby

Principal publishers: Peters, E. C. Schirmer

BIBLIOGRAPHY

EwenD

W. S. Smith: "Daniel Pinkham," *ACAB*, x/1 (1961), 9

M. Johnson: *The Choral Works of Daniel Pinkham* (diss., U. of Iowa, 1966)

M. L. Corzine: *The Organ Works of Daniel Pinkham* (diss., U. of Rochester, Eastman School, 1979)

R. Dyer: "A Natural Musical Resource," *Boston Globe* (4 Oct 1981)

L. Raver: "The Solo Organ Music of Daniel Pinkham," *American Organist*, xvii/6 (1983), 35

M. E. Stallings: *Representative Works for Mixed Chorus by Daniel Pinkham: 1968–1983* (diss., U. of Miami, 1984)

MICHAEL STEINBERG/R

Pinza, Ezio (Fortunato) (*b* Rome, Italy, 18 May 1892; *d* Stamford, CT, 9 May 1957). Italian bass. Having studied at the Bologna Conservatory, he made his début in 1914 as Oroveso (*Norma*) in Soncino, near Cremona. After World War I he began to sing in the principal Italian houses, notably at Rome (1920) as King Marke (*Tristan und Isolde*), and at La Scala, Milan (1922–4), in various roles, including Tigellino in the première of Arrigo Boito's *Nerone* (May 1924). His appearance at the Metropolitan Opera on 1 November 1926 as the Pontifex Maximus in Spontini's *La vestale* began a period of 22 consecutive seasons as one of the company's leading basses. His repertory there of 50 roles included, in addition to all the important parts for bass in Italian operas, an outstanding Don Giovanni (he sang in more than 150 performances in Europe and the USA) and Figaro, many French parts (notably Gounod's Mephistopheles), Boris Godunov (in Italian), and occasionally Wagnerian roles. He also sang during the same period with other American companies, in Europe, and elsewhere; in the 1930s, he was at Covent Garden for five seasons and sang frequently at the Salzburg Festival. After leaving the Metropolitan, he began a second career in musical comedy and films, scoring an enormous success on Broadway in *South Pacific*

Ezio Pinza in the title role of Mozart's "Don Giovanni"

in 1949. Pinza's beautiful and cultivated *basso cantante*, his handsome presence, engaging personality, and spirited acting made him the most richly gifted and accomplished Italian bass of his day, as is clearly demonstrated by his numerous recordings.

BIBLIOGRAPHY

L. Rasponi: "Ezio Pinza Discusses his Roles," *Opera News*, x/22 (1946), 9
M. de Schauensee: "A Don among Men," *Opera News*, xxii/6 (1957), 14
P. Verducci: *The First Pinza Discography* (New York, 1957)
E. Pinza and R. Magidoff: *Ezio Pinza: an Autobiography* (New York, 1958/*R* 1977)
J. B. Richards: "Pinza, Ezio," *Le grandi voci*, ed. R. Celletti (Rome, 1964) [with discography]
J. B. Richards and J. P. Kenyon: "Ezio Pinza," *Record Collector*, xxvi (1980), 51, 101 [with discography]
R. Tuggle: "Ezio Pinza," *The Golden Age of Opera* (New York, 1983), 214

DESMOND SHAWE TAYLOR/R

Pips. Soul vocal group, backup singers for GLADYS KNIGHT.

Pirrotta, Nino [Antonino] (*b* Palermo, Sicily, 13 June 1908). Italian musicologist. He studied music at the conservatories in Palermo and Florence (diploma 1930), and art history at the University of Florence, graduating in 1931. He taught music history and worked as librarian at the Palermo Conservatory (1936–48), later becoming chief librarian of the Accademia di S. Cecilia in Rome (1948–56). He was one of the founders in 1951 of the International Association of Music Libraries and served as its vice-president in 1951–4. In 1954–5 he taught at Princeton University and also lectured at UCLA and Columbia University; he was professor at Harvard University from 1956 until 1972, and also served as chairman of the music department (1965–8). He returned to Italy in 1972 to take up an appointment as professor of music history at Rome University.

Pirrotta's earliest writings dealt with the 14th-century madrigal and caccia and French influences on Italian music of that period; one of his most important publications is his edition *The Music of Fourteenth-century Italy* (CMM, viii, 1954–64; to be continued). His broad inter-disciplinary background is reflected in his later studies, including *Li due Orfei: da Poliziano a Monteverdi* (1969, enlarged 2/1975, Eng. trans. 1981) and *Music and Culture in Italy from the Middle Ages to the Baroque* (1984). Pirrotta's thorough knowledge of many historical periods made him highly influential in the forming of several prominent American musicologists, and in Italy his careful, methodical approach has greatly benefited young scholars.

CAROLYN M. GIANTURCO/R

Pisk, Paul A(madeus) (*b* Vienna, Austria, 16 May 1893). Composer, musicologist, and pianist. He studied composition with Franz Schreker and Arnold Schoenberg and musicology at the University of Vienna (doctorate in 1916), later graduating from the Vienna Conservatory (1919). While still in Vienna he helped to found the ISCM, worked as a periodicals editor and theory teacher (1920–34), and directed the music department of the Volkshochschule (1922–34). In 1936 he immigrated to the USA, taking citizenship in 1941. He taught at the University of Redlands, California, from 1937 to 1951 (chairman of the music department from 1948), at the University of Texas, Austin (1951–63), at Washington University, St. Louis (1963–72), and briefly elsewhere. In California, during the early 1940s, he was the regional director of the League of Composers. He then settled in Los Angeles and continued to teach, compose, lecture, and write, his chief topics being Schoenberg and the Second Viennese School. He also edited the fourth edition of *Baker's Biographical Dictionary*. Pisk's compositions are atonal, but he did not adopt 12-tone techniques. His String Quartet won the City of Vienna composition prize in 1925, and he has received a number of commissions and honors in the USA, among them the 1944 Texas Composers Prize.

BIBLIOGRAPHY

K. Kennan: "Paul A. Pisk," *ACAB*, ix/1 (1959), 7
J. Glowacki, ed.: *Paul A. Pisk: Essays in his Honor* (Austin, 1966) [incl. bibliography of his writings and compositions by L. P. Farrar, p.279]
T. W. Collins: *The Instrumental Music of Paul A. Pisk* (diss., U. of Missouri, 1972)

RAMONA H. MATTHEWS/RUTH B. HILTON

Piston, Walter (Hamor, Jr.) (*b* Rockland, ME, 20 Jan 1894; *d* Belmont, MA, 12 Nov 1976). Composer and teacher. Almost exclusively a composer of instrumental music, he was much respected during his lifetime for his carefully crafted, rational, and tasteful works. His influence as a teacher was considerable, thanks in part to several widely adopted textbooks he wrote.

1. Life and teaching. 2. Works.

1. LIFE AND TEACHING. His paternal grandfather, Antonio Pistone, came to New England from Italy. Walter Piston taught himself violin and piano after the family moved to Boston in 1905. After graduating from the Mechanic Arts High School he worked briefly as a draughtsman for the Boston Elevated Railway Co. and played violin in theater orchestras and dance bands. In 1912 he entered the Massachusetts Normal Art School, where he studied architectural drawing and received his diploma in 1916. Piston's draughtsmanship can be seen in his published scores, most of which are facsimiles of his manuscripts and have the clarity of engraved music. All but one of the precise and detailed drawings of instruments in his book *Orchestration* are his own.

During World War I he volunteered to play saxophone in the navy band, learning the instrument within several days. After the war, music-making became his livelihood: he played in dance halls, hotels, and restaurants and at social events. He studied piano and violin and considered making a career as an orchestral violinist, but broader intellectual interests and the reputation of Archibald T. Davison's counterpoint class led him to enroll as a special student at Harvard University in 1919. On completing certain courses required before matriculation, he entered Harvard in 1920 and on 14 September of the same year he married Kathryn Nason, a classmate from art school. While an undergraduate he became an assistant to Davison and other professors and conducted the Harvard student orchestra (the Pierian Sodality). He graduated in 1924, and a John Knowles Paine Traveling Fellowship enabled him to go to Paris for study with Boulanger and at the Ecole Normale de Musique with Dukas. Rigorous study of species counterpoint, encounters with new music, and the communication with his fellow students, established composers, and an inspiring teacher completed his formal education. But, as he said: "Training in the technical branches of the art of composition is never completed. It is a lifetime's continuing pursuit."

Piston enjoyed academic life, and when he returned from France in 1926 he accepted a position at Harvard. Edward Burlingame Hill brought him to the attention of Koussevitzky, conductor of the Boston SO. Thus began a continuing relationship between Piston and the orchestra, which gave the premières of 11 works composed between 1927 and 1971. Piston continued to teach at Harvard until 1960. For a time he was chairman of the music department; in 1944 he became a full professor and in 1951 was appointed to a newly endowed chair, the Walter W. Naumburg Professorship of Music. As a teacher of music theory Piston encouraged a broad interest in music of all periods. One product of Piston's fresh approach was his textbook *Harmony* (1941), which became one of the most widely used; it has since been translated into many languages. One of the most important and original contributions of the book is its study of relationships between harmonic and rhythmic structure. *Harmony* had been preceded by *Principles of Harmonic Analysis* (1933) and was followed by *Counterpoint* (1947) and *Orchestration* (1955). The title of the earliest book is indicative of Piston's educational approach: he did not teach rules, but guided the student to a recognition of basic principles. Piston had many noted composers as students, among them Elliott Carter, Leonard Bernstein, Arthur Berger, Irving Fine, Harold Shapero, Robert Moevs, Daniel Pinkham, Jr., and Billy Jim Layton. (*See also* THEORY, §4(ii).)

Many prizes and honors were bestowed upon him: a Guggenheim Fellowship and the Coolidge Medal in 1935; the New York Music Critics' Circle Award in 1944 (Symphony no.2), 1959 (Viola Concerto), and 1964 (String Quartet no.5); the Pulitzer Prize in 1948 (Symphony no.3) and 1961 (Symphony no.7); and eight honorary doctorates. He was elected to the National Institute of Arts and Letters in 1938, the American Academy of Arts and Sciences in 1940, and the American Academy of Arts and Letters in 1955. In 1969 the French government bestowed the decoration Officier dans l'Ordre des Arts et des Lettres and in 1971 the Governor of Vermont presented him with an award "for Excellence in the Arts."

2. WORKS. The majority of Piston's works were written on commission; five chamber works were commissioned by the Elizabeth Sprague Coolidge Foundation. Piston had a sure sense of instruments and the capabilities of players, and his music often shows a concern for specific performers, as he described in the program notes for the première of his Symphony no.6: "I was writing for one designated orchestra, one that I had grown up with and that I knew intimately. Each note set down sounded in the mind with extraordinary clarity, as played immediately by those who were to perform the work." For his Symphony no.7 he had in mind not only the rich string sound of the Philadelphia Orchestra but also the acoustics of its hall, the Academy of Music.

Walter Piston

Piston composed a large amount of instrumental music. His early works were influenced in part by Stravinsky but more deeply by the French neoclassicism of the later works of Fauré and Roussel. Gallic qualities of clarity and proportion are found throughout his work; the neobaroque element which developed in the 1920s can be found in much of it. The first movement of the Concerto for Orchestra (1933) suggests a gritty Brandenburg in its melody, rhythm, and counterpoint, and the finale combines elements of passacaglia and fugue. The Suite for oboe and piano (1931) consists of a Prelude, Sarabande, Minuetto, Nocturne, and Gigue. The Second Suite for Orchestra (1948) opens with a French Overture (entitled Prelude), contains a Sarabande and an Intermezzo, and closes with a Passacaglia and Fugue.

The openings of most of his symphonies are characterized by a great melodic breadth as are all of his slow movements. Motifs built from 2nds and 3rds expand into larger intervals to form long arch-shaped phrases; vigorous dance-like melodies have the same breadth of phrase as lines in slower tempos. Melody is propelled by rhythms that make refined use of syncopation; this is often highly complex but always convincing in its bending and extension of meters of 6/4, 5/4 or 8/8. In rapid tempos changing meters often interact with syncopations; on occasion there are melodic and rhythmic hints of jazz. Traditional contrapuntal devices are frequently found in the early works: canon, fugue, and the use of retrogrades and inversions. More common, particularly in Piston's later music, is a subtle interplay of lines that are related but without obvious imitative connections.

Most of Piston's works are in three or four movements whose forms can be related to traditional patterns. The Cello Variations (1966), written for Rostropovich, show greater formal originality in what the composer described as "six or seven ways to regard a musical idea, different aspects or facets, each growing out of another." In general, Piston's sense of form is well balanced and concise.

An emphasis on perfect 4ths and 5ths gives a solidity to Piston's harmony. His tonality frequently reveals its heritage of triadic functions, but more commonly it is of a linear or modal kind. Within a single phrase, such as the opening of the slow movement of the Symphony no.3, all 12 pitch classes may appear, but there is a strong and individual tonal direction, here leading to the tonic G. 12-note series and other dodecaphonic elements occur throughout his music but always in a personal tonal context. Piston's compositions after the early 1960s show a new interest in complex chords of six, nine, and even twelve notes (Symphony no.8, Violin Fantasia, Cello Variations) and further uses of dodecaphonic techniques. At the other extreme of his harmonic language are the more consonant middle period works like the Symphony no.4, about which he wrote "my music is becoming more relaxed . . . more flowing, less angular and nervous." His most popular work is the suite from the ballet *The Incredible Flutist* (one of only two instrumental departures from absolute music, the other being the *Three New England Sketches*). Piston's music covers a wide range of moods from energetic, witty scherzos and furiously driving finales to the serious introspection of many slow movements.

WORKS

(all published unless otherwise stated)

ORCHESTRAL

Orchestra Piece, 1925, unpubd
Symphonic Piece, 1927, unpubd; Boston, 23 March 1928, cond. Piston
Suite no.1 for Orchestra, 1929; Boston, 28 March 1930, cond. Piston
Concerto for Orchestra, 1933; Boston, 6 March 1934, cond. Piston
Prelude and Fugue, 1934; Cleveland, 12 March 1936, cond. R. Ringwall
Concertino, pf, chamber orch, 1937; New York, CBS radio, 20 June 1937, J. M. Sanromá, cond. Piston
Symphony no.1, 1937; Boston, 8 April 1938, cond. Piston
The Incredible Flutist, ballet, 1938, Boston, 30 May 1938; suite, 1938, Pittsburgh, 22 Nov 1940, cond. Reiner
Violin Concerto no.1, 1939; New York, 18 March 1940, Posselt, cond. Barzin
Sinfonietta, chamber orch, 1941; Boston, 10 March 1941, cond. Zighera
Prelude and Allegro, org, str, 1943; Cambridge, MA, 8 Aug 1943, Biggs, cond. Fiedler
Symphony no.2, 1943; New York, 5 March 1944, cond. H. Kindler
Fugue on a Victory Tune, 1944, unpubd; New York, 22 Oct 1944, cond. Rodzinski
Variation on a Theme by Eugene Goossens, 1 of 10 variations [each by a different composer], 1944, unpubd; Cincinnati, 23 March 1945, cond. Goossens
Symphony no.3, 1947; Boston, 9 Jan 1948, cond. Koussevitzky
Suite no.2 for Orchestra, 1948; Dallas, 28 Feb 1948, cond. Dorati
Toccata, 1948; Bridgeport, CT, 14 Oct 1948, cond. Munch
Symphony no.4, 1950; Minneapolis, 30 March 1951, cond. Dorati
Fantasy, eng hn, harp, str, 1952; Boston, 1 Jan 1954, L. Speyer, Zighera, cond. Munch
Symphony no.5, 1954; New York, 24 Feb 1956, cond. Morel
Symphony no.6, 1955; Boston, 25 Nov 1955, cond. Munch
Serenata, 1956; Louisville, 25 Oct 1956, cond. R. Whitney
Viola Concerto, 1957; Boston, 7 March 1958, J. de Pasquale, cond. Munch
Concerto for Two Pianos and Orchestra, 1959; Hanover, NH, 4 July 1964, N. Horowitz, M. Stecher, cond. M. di Bonaventura
Three New England Sketches, 1959; Worcester, MA, 23 Oct 1959, cond. Paray
Symphony no.7, 1960; Philadelphia, 10 Feb 1961, cond. Ormandy
Violin Concerto no.2, 1960; Pittsburgh, 28 Oct 1960, J. Fuchs, cond. Steinberg
Symphonic Prelude, 1961; Cleveland, 20 April 1961, cond. Szell
Lincoln Center Festival Overture, 1962; New York, 25 Sept 1962, cond. Ormandy
Capriccio, harp, str orch, 1963; Madrid, Spain, 19 Oct 1964, N. Zabaleta
Variations on a Theme by Edward Burlingame Hill, 1963; Boston, 30 April 1963, cond. K. Novak
Pine Tree Fantasy, 1965; Portland, ME, 16 Nov 1965, cond. A. Lipkin
Symphony no.8, 1965; Boston, 5 March 1965, cond. Leinsdorf
Variations, vc, orch, 1966; New York, 2 March 1967, Rostropovich, cond. G. Rozhdestvensky
Clarinet Concerto, 1967; Hanover, NH, 6 Aug 1967, D. Wendlandt, cond. Di Bonaventura
Ricercare, 1967; New York, 7 March 1968, cond. Bernstein
Fantasia, vn, orch, 1970; Hanover, NH, 11 March 1973, S. Accardo, cond. Di Bonaventura
Flute Concerto, 1971; Boston, 22 Sept 1972, D. A. Dwyer, cond. M. T. Thomas
Bicentennial Fanfare, 1975, unpubd; Cincinnati, 14 Nov 1975, cond. Schippers
String Quartet Concerto, str qt, wind, perc, 1976; Portland, ME, 26 Oct 1976, Portland Str Qt, cond. B. Hangen
Salute, 4 tpt, perc, n.d., unpubd
Arrs., all unpubd: Debussy: Clair de lune, 1936; Fauré: Prométhée, Act 2 scene i, 1945; Beethoven: Pf Sonata op.14 no.2 ("Moonlight"), 1st movt, n.d.

FOR 4–9 INSTRUMENTS

Minuetto in Stile vecchio, str qt, 1927, unpubd
String Quartet no.1, 1933
String Quartet no.2, 1935
Quintet, fl, str qt, 1942
Divertimento, fl, ob, cl, bn, str qt, db, 1946
String Quartet no.3, 1947
Piano Quintet, 1949
String Quartet no.4, 1951
Wind Quintet, 1956
String Quartet no.5, 1962
Piano Quartet, 1964
String Sextet, 2 vn, 2 va, 2 vc, 1964
Fugue . . . sur un sujet de Fenaroli, str qt, n.d., unpubd

FOR 1–3 INSTRUMENTS

Piano Sonata, 1926, unpubd, withdrawn
Three Pieces, fl, cl, bn, 1926
Flute Sonata, 1930
Suite, ob, pf, 1931
Piano Trio no.1, 1935
Violin Sonata, 1939
Chromatic Study on the Name of Bach, org, 1940
Interlude, va, pf, 1942
Passacaglia, pf, 1943
Partita, vn, va, org, 1944
Improvisation, pf, 1945
Sonatina, vn, hpd, 1945
Duo, va, vc, 1949
Piano Trio no.2, 1966
Souvenirs, fl, va, harp, 1967, unpubd
Variation on Happy Birthday, pf, 1970, unpubd
Duo, vc, pf, 1972, unpubd
Three Counterpoints, vn, va, vc, 1973

BAND AND OTHER WORKS

Carnival Song (L. De' Medici), male vv, 4 hn, 3 tpt, 3 trbn, tuba, 1938; Boston, 7 March 1940
Fanfare for the Fighting French, brass, perc, 1942; Cincinnati, 23 Oct 1942
Tunbridge Fair, intermezzo, band, 1950
Psalm and Prayer of David: O Sing unto the Lord a New Song (Ps. xcvi), Bow Down thine Ear, O Lord (Ps. xxcvi), chorus, fl, cl, bn, vn, va, vc, db, 1958
Ceremonial Fanfare, brass, perc, 1969; New York, 10 Feb 1970, cond. W. Stein
Intermezzo, band, n.d., unpubd

Most MSS in *MB*
Principal publishers: Associated, Boosey & Hawkes, E. C. Schirmer, G. Schirmer

BIBLIOGRAPHY

EwenD
R. L. Finney: "Piston's Violin Sonata," *MM*, xvii (1939–40), 210
E. Carter: "Walter Piston," *MQ*, xxxii (1946), 354
W. W. Austin: "Piston's Fourth Symphony: an Analysis," *MR*, xvi (1955), 120
M. J. Colucci: *A Comparative Study of Contemporary Musical Theories in Selected Writings of Piston, Krenek and Hindemith* (diss., U. of Pennsylvania, 1957)
"Piston, Walter (Hamor, Jr.)," *CBY 1961*
O. Daniel and others: *Walter Piston* (New York, 1964)
R. L. Donahue: *A Comparative Analysis of Phrase Structure in Selected Movements of the String Quartets of Béla Bartók and Walter Piston* (diss., Cornell U., 1964)
C. Taylor: "Walter Piston: for his Seventieth Birthday," *PNM*, iii/1 (1964), 102
D. Ewen: *The World of Twentieth-century Music* (New York, 1968), chap. "Walter Piston"
P. Westergaard: "Conversation with Walter Piston," *PNM*, vii/1 (1968), 3
K. G. Roy: "Walter Piston," *Stereo Review*, xxiv/4 (1970), 57
C. E. Hamm, R. Byrnside, and B. Nettl: *Contemporary Music and Music Cultures* (Englewood Cliffs, NJ, 1975)
H. N. Lindenfeld: *Three Symphonies of Walter Piston: an Analysis* (diss., Cornell U., 1975)
H. Gleason and W. Becker: "Walter Piston," *20th-century American Composers*, Music Literature Outlines, ser. iv (Bloomington, IN, rev. 2/1981), 138 [incl. further bibliography]
H. Pollack: *Walter Piston* (Ann Arbor, MI, 1981) [incl. catalogue, further bibliography, and discography]

BRUCE ARCHIBALD

Pitahawirata. American Indian tribe of the PAWNEE confederacy.

Pitney, Gene (*b* Hartford, CT, 17 Feb 1941). Popular singer and songwriter. He wrote his first songs while still in high school, studied piano, guitar, and drums, and attended the University of Connecticut. He began performing as part of a duo called

Jamie and Jane, then worked as a singer and songwriter under the name Billy Brian. His first hit was *I wanna love my life away* (no.39, 1961). *Every breath I take* (no.42, 1961), an effective pop song, was one of the first successes of the producer Phil Spector; sung with Pitney's characteristic, telling glottal stops and hysterical hesitations, it is perhaps his finest recording. He wrote *He's a rebel* for Spector's girl group the Crystals and *Hello Mary Lou* for Ricky Nelson; he also composed *Mecca* (no.12, 1963) and, with Burt Bacharach and Hal David, *The Man who Shot Liberty Valance* (no.4, 1962), both of which he sang himself. His last hit song in the USA was the formulaic *She's a heartbreaker* (no.16, 1968), but he remained popular in Britain until the mid-1970s. An accomplished songwriter and versatile instrumentalist, he is remembered for his crying voice and passionate singing style, which transformed each of his recordings into a virtual melodrama.

RECORDINGS

(selective list; all recorded for Musicor)

Every breath I take (1011, 1961); I wanna love my life away (1002, 1961); The Man who Shot Liberty Valance (1020, 1962); Mecca (1028, 1963); Twenty-four hours from Tulsa (1034, 1963); Looking through the eyes of love (1103, 1965); She's a heartbreaker (1306, 1968)

BIBLIOGRAPHY

N. Cohn: *Rock from the Beginning* (New York, 1969, rev. 2/1972), 82

Pittel, Harvey (*b* Great Falls, MT, 22 June 1943). Saxophonist. He studied with Kalman Bloch and Franklyn Stokes and from 1961 to 1965 attended the University of Southern California, where he obtained his doctorate in music education. Further studies were with Frederick Hemke at Northwestern University (1965–6) and with Joseph Allard (1966–9) while he was in the US Military Academy Band. In 1970 he won a silver medal at the Concours International in Geneva. He made his solo début with the Boston SO in Dahl's Saxophone Concerto (1971); his recital début was in 1973 at Carnegie Recital Hall. He has performed with major orchestras in the USA and Europe. In 1972 he formed a saxophone quartet; he has also performed in a trio consisting of saxophone, piano, and cello. Among the premières he has presented are those of Berio's *Chemins II b/c*, Babbitt's *Images*, and Chihara's Saxophone Concerto. Pittel has taught at the University of Southern California, California State University (Fullerton and Long Beach campuses), Boston University, the Mannes College, and, from 1980, the University of Texas, Austin. He has also held workshops at the Aspen Music School and the Berkshire Music Center.

SORAB MODI

Pitts, Lilla Belle (*b* Aberdeen, MS, 26 Sept 1884; *d* Nashville, TN, 24 Jan 1970). Music educator. She studied piano, voice, and violin at Ward Seminary in Nashville (diploma 1904) and piano at the North Texas Female College in Sherman, Texas (1904–5). She was a private piano teacher in Louisiana and later taught in the public schools of Amarillo, Texas (1910–14), Dallas (1915–21), and Elizabeth, New Jersey (1924–38). Meanwhile she had studied with Charles H. Farnsworth and Peter W. Dykema at Teachers College, Columbia University (BA 1935). She was a faculty member at Teachers College (1938–54) and ended her career at Florida State University (1957–8). Pitts served as president of the Music Educators National Conference (1942–4). She edited a school music textbook series and wrote four books and many articles, most of them on school music, music appreciation, and related subjects.

BIBLIOGRAPHY

G. L. Blanchard: *Lilla Belle Pitts: her Life and Contribution to Music Education* (EdD diss., Brigham Young U., 1966)

Obituary, *MEJ*, lvi/7 (1970), 105

GEORGE N. HELLER

Pittsburgh. City in western Pennsylvania (pop. 423,938; metropolitan area 2,263,894). It was founded in 1758 as a military settlement, and until the turn of the century had little of the cultivated musical environment found in the towns along the East Coast. The earliest musical heritage was English, although many important contributions to the cultural life of the city in the 19th century were made by Welsh and German immigrants. The first piano in Pittsburgh of which notice survives was made by Charles Fans of Philadelphia and given by General Richard Butler to his daughter in 1791; it is now in the Historical Society of Western Pennsylvania. The first establishment to offer popular music and refreshment was the Eagle Ice Cream Saloon, which opened in 1846 and in 1847 was the site of the first performance of *Oh, Susanna!* by Stephen C. Foster, who was born in Pittsburgh. Music was, however, not found in every aspect of the city's life; in Presbyterian churches the presence of choirs and instruments remained matters of great controversy throughout much of the 19th century.

1. Orchestras. 2. Organs and the choral tradition. 3. Opera. 4. Music education. 5. Broadcasting and other musical activities.

1. Orchestras. Pittsburgh's first music organization, the Apollian Society, was founded in 1807 by the American artist Samuel H. Dearborn. The society performed the popular songs and marches of the day as well as the music of J. C. Bach, Mozart, and I. J. Pleyel. The first ensemble in Pittsburgh that endured for more than a couple of concerts was the Pittsburgh Orchestral Society (1854–6), under the direction of Gottlieb A. Anton. Many orchestras were subsequently organized to perform in the city's various choral festivals, including the May Music Festival, celebrated five times between 1879 and 1889, but these were ad hoc groups. Much of the effort that went into organizing the festivals, which were never financially successful, was transferred to the establishment of the city's first permanent professional orchestra, the Pittsburgh Orchestra, in 1895.

Backed by such prominent Pittsburgh residents as H. C. Frick and George Westinghouse, Jr., the Pittsburgh Orchestra had a brief but distinguished career under its music directors Frederick Archer (1896–8), Victor Herbert (1898–1904), and Emil Paur (1904–10). It performed in Carnegie Music Hall (capacity 1972), part of the arts complex built in Oakland in 1895 and funded by Andrew Carnegie. The founding manager of the orchestra was George H. Wilson, a Bostonian who had been the music manager of the World's Columbian Exposition (Chicago, 1893) and manager of the Theodore Thomas Orchestra, which had played in Pittsburgh on its tours. Wilson's responsibilities included running the Art Society (which financed the orchestra), managing the hall, and preparing the program notes for the concerts. Under the sponsorship of Carnegie, the orchestra also performed annually at Carnegie Hall in New York. Although it made extensive tours (performing in as many as 23 states in a single season) and was reported to rank third of the nation's orchestras in artistic importance, it was forced to disband in 1910 because of financial difficulties. The void was filled by the Pittsburgh Orchestra Association, which was formed by members of the Art Society and which between 1910 and 1950 sponsored concerts by visiting orchestras from Philadelphia, Cleveland, New York, Boston, Chicago, Minneapolis, and Detroit. The association also arranged for children's concerts as early as 1916.

The present Pittsburgh SO was founded in 1926 and had its first season the following year amid a storm of controversy: the necessity of scheduling concerts on Sundays (because most of the players held weekday jobs) put the orchestra in conflict with Pennsylvania's Sunday Blue Laws of 1794, which forbade selling anything (including tickets) on the Sabbath. After the first concert (24 April 1927), nine of the board members were brought before a magistrate. The orchestra's ultimate victory in this case made it possible for other Pennsylvanian orchestras to perform on Sundays.

The orchestra's permanent conductors have been Antonio Modarelli (1927–37), Fritz Reiner (1938–48, following reorganization in 1937 by Otto Klemperer), William Steinberg (1952–76), and André Previn (1976–84); Lorin Maazel, who was educated in Pittsburgh, was appointed music consultant in 1984. The orchestra gave its first performances at the 3750-seat Syria Mosque, which was built in 1916; it now owns and gives its 24-week season in the 2847-seat Heinz Hall for the Performing Arts (formerly the Penn Theater). Its summer activities have included concerts at the Ambler Festival at Temple University in Philadelphia (until 1981) and free concerts in parks. *See also* ORCHESTRAS, §2 (vii).

The Pittsburgh Youth Symphony (founded 1945) is managed by Marie Maazel (mother of Lorin Maazel) and has been conducted by a succession of associate and assistant conductors of the Pittsburgh SO. The New Pittsburgh Chamber Orchestra (1978) was founded by its conductor Grover Wilkins III. The American Wind SO (1960), conducted by Robert Boudreau, performs in the *Point Counterpoint* (see illustration), a custom-designed concert barge, and offers a mixture of traditional and new music; the latter is often commissioned and subsequently published in a series by C. F. Peters. The orchestra tours the rivers of the eastern USA giving riverbank concerts. The Pittsburgh New Music Ensemble, founded by D. F. Stock in 1977, performs the music of local composers both in the city and on tour.

2. ORGANS AND THE CHORAL TRADITION. Religious communities provided many opportunities for public musical performances in early Pittsburgh. While the conservative Presbyterians kept both choirs and instruments out of their churches before 1820, music was still an important part of the service. Some branches continued such restrictions until the 1880s, and then lifted them only reluctantly. One of the reasons given for the establishment of the Second Presbyterian Church in 1804 was that it was the custom at the First Presbyterian Church for the precentor to line out two lines of a psalm at a time, making it difficult for the congregation to follow the words and tune.

The Episcopal and Roman Catholic churches eventually had organs installed in 1820. The organist of Trinity Episcopal Church from 1831 was John H. Mellor, a partner in a musical instrument store that supplied the Chickering piano for Jenny Lind's concert in Masonic Hall in 1851; his firm also published the city's first known music magazine, *Mellor's Musical Mirror* (one volume only, 1868–9), and in the hands of his son and grandson remained a force in Pittsburgh's musical life into the next century.

In 1890 Andrew Carnegie, who saw the organ as an economical means of bringing great music to the general public, presented the city of Allegheny (which became part of Pittsburgh in 1906) with a library, a music hall, and a large Roosevelt organ selected by Charles C. Mellor. Leonard Wales was appointed city organist and, supported by public funds, gave the first known series of free organ recitals in the USA at the Allegheny Carnegie Hall. Wales was succeeded by Henry P. Ecker, Casper P. Koch, and, in 1951, Koch's son Paul W. Koch. The position was discontinued in 1974 and the organ eventually removed. The hall has been remodeled, renamed the Hazlett Theater, and is no longer used for musical performances.

Another organ selected by Mellor was installed in 1895 at the

The American Wind SO performing from the floating arts center "Point Counterpoint" on the Mississippi River

Oakland Carnegie Music Hall. The first organist at this hall was Frederick Archer, who was succeeded by Edwin Lemare, Charles Heinroth, and Marshall Bidwell, and free concerts were also given there each week. The programs of these early organ concerts consisted of symphonic and operatic transcriptions interspersed with vocal works. Among the most important modern organs in Pittsburgh are those in St. Paul's Cathedral (built by the German firm Beckerath in 1962) and Calvary Episcopal Church (by the Canadian firm Casavant Frères in 1964).

The German choral society tradition was brought to Pittsburgh in 1854 through the formation of the Teutonia Männerchor, thought to be the earliest musical organization in the area; a number of other singing-societies were soon founded. After the Civil War, Pierre Louis Clement Tetedoux, a singing teacher and former pupil of Rossini, organized the Cantata Society, which in the 1870s gave elaborate performances of sacred music. The Mozart Club (1879–1919), founded and directed by James Knox Polk McCollum, presented many oratorios and other large-scale works and engaged many famous singers. The Mendelssohn Choir, established in 1909, was until 1950 directed by its founder, Ernest Lunt, who was succeeded by Russell G. Wichmann, Henry Mazer, Hugh B. Johnson, and Robert Page. Often serving as the choir of the Pittsburgh SO, it specializes in oratorio.

The Bach Choir, founded in 1934 and directed by Max Peterson, has introduced many of Bach's choral works to Pittsburgh audiences. Other groups include the Pittsburgh Oratorio Society, founded in 1960 by Donald G. Wilkins and specializing in a sacred repertory that includes many works by Bach, and two smaller ensembles, the Pittsburgh Madrigal Singers (founded in 1963) and the Pittsburgh Camerata, an *a cappella* chamber choir founded in 1974 by Arthur Wenk.

3. Opera. The first opera given in Pittsburgh was an English version of Rossini's *Il barbiere di Siviglia* by the visiting Francis Courtney Wemyss Troupe on 16 April 1838. The prevailing mores did not provide an encouraging climate for local productions until 1873, when the Frohsinn Society gave Flotow's *Stradella* (in German) to much acclaim. In 1874 the Gounod Club performed another of Flotow's operas, *Martha*, in its first operatic series. While famous opera companies visited the city on their tours, its first permanent company, the Pittsburgh Opera Society, was not established until 1939. Richard Karp directed it from 1942 to 1975, when he resigned in favor of his daughter Barbara; she was succeeded by James de Blasis and Tito Capobianco. The company gives two performances of six works each year; it played in the Syria Mosque until Heinz Hall was opened.

The Pittsburgh Chamber Opera, directed by Mildred Miller Posvar, gives young professional singers opportunities to perform in the city and in the surrounding communities. The Pittsburgh Savoyards company became a member of the Gilbert and Sullivan Society of London, which provided production assistance for its first operetta, *The Pirates of Penzance*, in 1939; based at the Pittsburgh Center for the Arts (which does not have a concert hall), the group gives two or three productions each year. The Civic Light Opera Association engages local musicians and actors (except for the leading characters) for a six-week season of musical comedy. It began in 1945 with open-air performances and moved in 1962 to the Civic Arena (which has a retractable roof) and to Heinz Hall in 1974.

4. Music education. The earliest music teachers and performers in Pittsburgh were trained in England. The first known teacher of music was Peter Declary, who arrived in Pittsburgh in 1799; the first to have a broad influence on the city's musical education, however, was William Evens, born in Sussex, England. Evens arrived from Philadelphia in 1811 and opened a singing-school soon thereafter, the first of many he organized in Pittsburgh and the surrounding communities during the next 30 years. He had a special love of Handel's choral music and in 1820 introduced the "Hallelujah Chorus" from *Messiah* to the city. He also amassed Pittsburgh's first music archive, which included scores, histories, theory books, and biographies, but had the reputation of being a reluctant lender and allowed few people access to his collection. Some of these volumes, along with the best of his scrapbooks on music, were purchased after his death by the Mellor family and given to the Carnegie Library of Pittsburgh when it opened in 1895. They are now housed in the library's music collection, established by Irene Millen in 1938 and the richest music archive in the city.

Pittsburgh was one of the first American cities to introduce music into the public schools (in 1844). The music educator Will Earhart, who became director of music for the city's public schools in 1912, gave new impetus to the development of school orchestras. His report "Music in the Public Schools" (*United States Bureau of Education Bulletin*, 1914, no.33, pp. 1–81) was widely read and marked the beginning of a new era in music education at the public-school level.

Three institutions in Pittsburgh offer graduate programs in music. The Carnegie Institution of Technology (now Carnegie-Mellon University) was founded in 1900 by Andrew Carnegie. General classes began in 1908, and the first head of the music department, James Vick O'Brien, was appointed in 1912. It currently awards BFA and MFA degrees in music. The University of Pittsburgh, a state institution, had developed an understanding with the Carnegie school and had no music classes of its own until 1936, when Theodore M. Finney was appointed chairman of its department of music. It awards BA, MA, and (from 1960) PhD degrees. Duquesne University, affiliated with the Roman Catholic Church, started a music program in 1926 and offers BM, BS (in music education), MM, and MME degrees. (*See also* Libraries and collections, §3.)

5. Broadcasting and other musical activities. Pittsburgh was an early center in the development of radio and the home of KDKA (founded 1920), one of the first commercial radio stations in the USA (*see* Broadcasting, §1). KDKA is thought to have been the first to broadcast religious services (from the Calvary Episcopal and Shadyside Presbyterian churches), the first to produce a choral broadcast (1922, a performance by the Westinghouse Community Chorus), and the first to have its own radio orchestra. This group, conducted by Victor Saudek, was drawn from employees of the Westinghouse Electric and Manufacturing Company in 1912 and became known as the KDKA Orchestra on its first broadcast (November 1922); it was renamed the KDKA Little Symphony in 1933. Pittsburgh's fine arts radio station, WQED-FM, was founded in 1973 and has become an important part of the city's cultural life. It broadcasts local events and sponsors the Three Rivers Piano Competition. Its associated television station, WQED-TV, has produced a wide range of programs for national distribution.

A large number of song and dance societies featuring musical traditions of groups that have settled in Pittsburgh – German, Swiss, Italian, Irish, Scottish, Welsh, Latvian, Lithuanian,

Ukrainian, Israeli, Filipino, Vietnamese, Chinese, and numerous others – perform in national costumes in the Pittsburgh Folk Festival, an annual event initiated in 1960. Duquesne University sponsors the Pittsburgh Tamburitzans (organized in 1936), a group that performs the songs and dances of eastern Europe accompanied by folk instruments.

BIBLIOGRAPHY

G. M. Rohrer: *Music and Musicians of Pennsylvania* (Philadelphia, 1940)
J. Evanson: "Folk Music in an Industrial City," *Pennsylvania Songs and Legends*, ed. G. Korson (Philadelphia, 1949)
E. G. Baynham: *A History of Pittsburgh Music 1758–1958* (MS, 1970)
Carnegie Magazine, xlix (1975) [whole issue]

IDA REED

Plains Indians. Group of American Indian tribes that share certain cultural traits. They live between the Mississippi River and the Rocky Mountains, including parts of Montana, North Dakota, South Dakota, Minnesota, Wyoming, Nebraska, Iowa, Colorado, Kansas, Missouri, Oklahoma, Arkansas, and Texas, as well as eastern Alberta, southern Saskatchewan, and southwestern Manitoba. *See* ARAPAHO, BLACKFOOT (i), CROW, KIOWA, OMAHA (i), PAWNEE, and SIOUX; *see also* INDIANS, AMERICAN, §I, 4(ii)(a).

Plamenac, Dragan (*b* Zagreb [now in Yugoslavia], 8 Feb 1895; *d* Ede, Netherlands, 15 March 1983). Musicologist. He developed an interest in music at an early age but took a degree in law at Zagreb before studying composition in Vienna and Prague and musicology at the Sorbonne and in Vienna, where he received the doctorate in 1925. He first worked at the Städtische Oper in Berlin (1926–7), then taught musicology at the University of Zagreb (1928). In 1939 he came to the USA as Yugoslav representative to the International Musicological Society Congress and remained here after the outbreak of war, becoming an American citizen in 1946. He was professor of music at the University of Illinois from 1954 to 1963. Plamenac's research and publications centered on music of the 14th to 16th centuries and of the Adriatic coastal areas in the Renaissance and early Baroque periods; his edition of the works of Ockeghem made possible for the first time a serious evaluation of this composer's position in the development of musical style in the second half of the 15th century, and his articles on and edition of the Faenza Codex provided important insights into the practice of early 15th-century instrumental music. His research into the Burgundian chanson repertory was marked by an understanding both of the sources and of the music itself. A Festschrift in his honor, edited by Gustave Reese and R. J. Snow, was published in 1969.

TOM R. WARD/R

Plançon, Pol (Henri) (*b* Fumay, France, 12 June 1851; *d* Paris, France, 11 Aug 1914). French bass. He studied with Gilbert Duprez and Giovanni Sbriglia and made his début in Lyons in 1877. He first appeared at the Paris Opéra on 23 June 1883 as Gounod's Mephistopheles, and remained there for ten seasons, taking part in the premières of Massenet's *Le Cid* and Saint-Saëns' *Ascanio* among other operas in the French repertory. On 29 November 1893 he appeared for the first time at the Metropolitan Opera as Jupiter in Gounod's *Philémon et Baucis*. His first Mephistopheles for the Metropolitan was a month later, while the company was on tour. For the next 15 years he was a leading bass at the Metropolitan, where he participated in a number of American premières, notably of Berlioz's *La damnation de Faust* (1906). Among the parts with which he was most closely associated were Capulet and Friar Laurence (Gounod's *Roméo et Juliette*), Hermann (*Tannhäuser*), Ramfis (*Aida*), and St. Bris (Meyerbeer's *Les Huguenots*), as well as Mephistopheles. He was also well known in the USA as a recitalist.

Plançon was the most polished singer of whose work there are satisfactory recordings. His voice, a *basse chantante* of singularly pure and beautiful quality, had been schooled to a rare pitch of perfection, and his style was elegant in the extreme. His many recordings (1902–8) are therefore of peculiar value, since they offer some impression of a standard of execution and distinction of manner that are otherwise outside one's experience. At a first encounter with them the listener is most struck by the singer's flexibility and agility, his flawless trills and rapid scales, in Vulcan's song from *Philémon et Baucis* or in the arias from Thomas' *Le Caïd* and Adam's *Le châlet*; but no less remarkable are his cantabile and impeccable legato (comparable with the phrasing of a fine cellist) in "Voici des roses" (*La damnation de Faust*), "Elle ne m'aime pas" (*Don Carlos*) and "Vi ravviso" (*La sonnambula*).

BIBLIOGRAPHY

J. Dennis: "Paul Henri Plançon," *Record Collector*, viii (1953), 148–91 [with discography and commentary by L. Hevingham-Root]
R. D. Daniels: "The Odor of Sanctity," *Opera News*, xxx/15 (1966), 26

DESMOND SHAWE-TAYLOR/R

Plantation song. A type of 19th-century popular song originating in the minstrel show and current from the 1840s, generally with a text in pseudo-black dialect. Plantation songs, especially those of STEPHEN C. FOSTER, had musical and poetic ties to sentimental balladry, generally portrayed Blacks more sympathetically than had earlier blackface-minstrel songs, and were often portraits of southern slave women (as in James Sanford's *Miss Lucy Neal*, 1844; Foster's *Nelly was a Lady*, 1849; or B. R. Hanby's *Darling Nelly Gray*, 1856). Such songs became extremely popular as domestic music. *See* POPULAR MUSIC, §II, 5; *see also* JAZZ, §II, 2, and MINSTRELSY.

Plantinga, Leon B(rooks) (*b* Ann Arbor, MI, 25 March 1935). Musicologist. He studied at Michigan State University (MM), then continued his graduate education at Yale (PhD 1964), where he joined the faculty in 1963. In 1971–2 he was a Fellow of University College, Oxford.

Plantinga has been primarily concerned with musical style and music criticism in the late 18th and early 19th centuries. His book *Schumann as Critic* (1967/*R*1977) has been praised as a careful study of this aspect of the composer. In *Muzio Clementi* (1974), which has been greeted as the new standard work on that composer, Plantinga combines a critical biography and the first comprehensive study of the music. He contributed the volume *Romantic Music* (1984) to the W. W. Norton history of music series.

PAULA MORGAN

Plateau Indians. Group of American Indian tribes that share certain cultural traits, living in northern Oregon and Idaho, western Montana, eastern Washington, and British Columbia. *See* FLATHEAD and SALISH.

Platters. Rock-and-roll vocal group. Formed in Los Angeles in 1953, the original members were Tony Williams (*b* Roselle, NJ,

15 April 1928), David Lynch (*b* St. Louis, MO, 1929; *d* 2 Jan 1981), Herbert Reed (*b* Kansas City, MO), and Alex Hodge; later Paul Robi, Zola Taylor, and others were members. The Platters modeled their singing style after that of the Ink Spots. They had little commercial success until Buck Ram, a former pupil of Joseph Schillinger who had been a big-band arranger in the 1940s, became their manager. They were signed to the Federal label and recorded a version of Ram's *Only You*, but it was slackly played and sung out of pitch, and failed to capture the public's attention. They rerecorded the song for Mercury in 1955. This version, marked by Williams's falsetto voice and precise, if eccentric, diction, the group's harmonious backup singing, and the efficient rhythmic accompaniment provided by the Ernie Freeman Combo and Ram's piano playing, reached no.5 on the pop chart. The Platters' next recording, *The Great Pretender* (1956), a song in a country-music style also written by Ram, reached no.1. Their revival of *My Prayer* (1956), which had been a hit in Europe in 1939, became their best-selling single, and they subsequently recorded a number of standards (including *Smoke gets in your eyes*, 1959, and *Harbor Lights*, 1960) while continuing to perform material by Ram (such as *Twilight Time*, 1944). Between 1955 and 1967 they made 39 hit recordings and sang in nightclubs in Las Vegas and New York (including the Copacabana), where their performances were noted for their careful pacing and choreography. They appeared in the film *Rock around the Clock* in 1956. In 1961 Williams embarked on a career as a soloist and left the group, which continued as a "nostalgia" act, with many changes in personnel, into the 1980s. The Platters' sound, distinguished by a high solo voice with smooth vocal backup and light rhythmic underpinnings, helped bring the musical tradition of groups like the Ink Spots into the rock-and-roll era.

BIBLIOGRAPHY

I. Whitcomb: *After the Ball: Pop Music from Rag to Rock* (New York, 1973)

——: *Whole Lotta Shakin': a Rock and Roll Scrapbook* (London, 1982)

——: *Rock Odyssey: a Chronicle of the Sixties* (New York, 1983)

IAN WHITCOMB

Player piano. A piano which automatically plays music recorded by means, usually, of perforations in a paper roll. From the 1880s various patents were taken out in the USA for pneumatic pianos, notably by Merritt Gally, Mason J. Matthews, and Harry B. Tremaine, but the invention of the player piano is usually attributed to the organ builder Edwin Scott Votey (1856–1931), who patented it in 1897. In its heyday in the early 1920s when nearly half a million player pianos were manufactured in two years, the instrument was a focal point for music-making in the home, where families would gather round to sing popular songs to its accompaniment. The most sophisticated form of the instrument – the reproducing player piano – re-created the nuances in performance of artists such as Paderewski and Rachmaninoff. Under contract with the Aeolian Co., Stravinsky composed his Etude for the pianola op.7 no.1; Hindemith also wrote for the player piano. Unique use of the player piano as a compositional medium has been made by CONLON NANCARROW, all of whose works (except for a few early pieces) have been written for the instrument. Production of player pianos reached its peak in 1923, but their popularity declined thereafter, largely as a result of the increased use of the radio and phonograph and the Depression. Firms which now produce player pianos include the Universal Piano Company of Los Angeles.

In the first stage of its technical development, in the 1890s, the player piano consisted of a cabinet called a "piano player" pushed in front of an ordinary piano and having a row of felt-lined wooden "fingers" projecting over the keyboard. Inside the cabinet a music roll or note-sheet would pass over a "tracker bar," usually of brass, with some 65 (later 88) slots or ports, one for each note. When a perforation in the moving notesheet uncovered a port in the tracker bar, suction (generated by pedals) would draw air through the port to operate a pneumatic valve and lever, forcing the wooden finger down. Levers in the front of the cabinet controlled tempo, the relative loudness of treble and bass, and the operation of the sustaining pedal of the piano, which could also be depressed by the automatic "foot" that was a feature of many cabinets.

Around the turn of the century this apparatus was built into the piano itself, and the control knobs were placed along the front of the keyboard, the pumping pedals underneath. This became the standard form of the player piano. Important manufacturers included such companies as Aeolian (its trademark "pianola" was frequently misapplied to denote any player piano; for illustration *see* AEOLIAN CO.), American Piano, Auto-Pneumatic Action, Melville Clark Piano, Standard Player Action, and Wilcox & White; it was also made in Germany, and in England by the Aeolian Co. Ltd (a branch of the American firm, also known as the Orchestrelle Co.). Many other piano manufacturers purchased player mechanisms for installation in their own pianos. In addition to player pianos for the home, coin-operated machines were produced for use in cafés, restaurants, hotels, and other public places.

The player piano reached its fullest development with the incorporation of devices to reproduce the performing nuances of an artist. By 1913 two American reproducing player mechanisms had been developed – the "Duo-Art," made by the Aeolian Co., and the "Ampico," made by the American Piano Co. (which became the Ampico Corporation in 1915). The method of reproducing a performance usually involved making two "recordings" – one of the notes and pedaling, a separate one of the dynamics – as the artist played the piece on a recording piano. To record the dynamics the Duo-Art used a delicate mechanical device to register the rebound of the hammer from the string. The Ampico employed a spark chronograph to record the speed of the hammer during its last quarter inch of travel before it struck the string, with a trace on a revolving cylinder to record the power applied. Reproducing player mechanisms, which were usually powered by electricity, were installed in pianos of many makes, including Knabe, Chickering, Steinway, and Weber. At their best, reproducing player pianos could re-create the style of the original artist to a remarkably fine degree. Among the pianists who made recordings were Carreño, Rachmaninoff, and Artur Rubinstein (for Ampico); Victor Herbert (for Ampico and Duo-Art); and Harold Bauer, George Gershwin, and Paderewski (for Duo-Art). An interest in the performing styles of such artists led to performances and recordings of their rolls in the 1960s and 1970s.

BIBLIOGRAPHY

W. B. White: *The Player Piano, up to Date* (New York, 1914)

J. McTammany: *The History of the Player* (New York, 1913)

——: *The Technical History of the Player* (New York, 1915/*R*1971)

E. Newman: *The Piano-player and its Music* (London, 1920)

S. Grew: *The Art of the Player Piano* (London, 1922)

W. B. White: *Piano Playing Mechanisms* (New York, 1925)

H. N. Roehl: *Player Piano Treasury* (New York, 1961, rev. and enlarged 2/1973)

L. Givens: *Re-enacting the Artist: a Story of the Ampico Reproducing Piano* (New York, 1970)
A. W. J. G. Ord-Hume: *Player Piano: the History of the Mechanical Piano and how to Repair it* (London, 1970)
Q. D. Bowers: *Encyclopedia of Automatic Instruments* (Vestal, NY, 1972)
A. A. Reblitz and Q. D. Bowers: *Treasures of Mechanical Music* (New York, 1981)
A. W. J. G. Ord-Hume: *Pianola: the History of the Self-Playing Piano* (London, 1984)

FRANK W. HOLLAND

Pleasants, Henry (*b* Wayne, PA, 12 May 1910). Writer on music. He studied at the Philadelphia Musical Academy and the Curtis Institute. From 1930 to 1942 he was music critic for the *Philadelphia Evening Bulletin*; after World War II he was central European music correspondent for the *New York Times* (1945–55), also holding positions with the US Foreign Service in Munich, Berne, and Bonn from 1950 to 1964. In 1967 he was appointed London music critic for the *International Herald Tribune* and London editor of *Stereo Review*. Pleasants is the author of numerous articles and has translated and edited writings by Hanslick, Hugo Wolf, and Schumann.

WRITINGS

The Agony of Modern Music (New York, 1955)
Death of a Music? (New York, 1961)
The Great Singers (New York, 1966, rev. and enlarged 3/1985)
Serious Music, and all that Jazz (New York, 1969)
The Great American Popular Singers (New York, 1974)

NOËL GOODWIN/R

Pleskow, Raoul (*b* Vienna, Austria, 12 Oct 1931). Composer. He immigrated to the USA in 1939 and was naturalized in 1945. From 1950 to 1952 he attended the Juilliard School; at Queens College, New York (BM 1956), he studied composition with Karol Rathaus, and at Columbia University (MM 1958) he was a pupil of Luening. In 1959 he joined the faculty of C. W. Post College, Long Island University (from 1970 he was a full professor), where he was a colleague of Wolpe. He has received awards from, among others, the Ford Foundation (1972), the Martha Baird Rockefeller Fund for Music (1972), the NEA (1974, 1975, 1978), the National Institute of Arts and Letters (1974), and the Guggenheim Foundation (1977).

Pleskow has acknowledged the importance of his "apprenticeship" with Wolpe in learning a "manner of covering musical space" and speaks of his "admiration for the coolness and serenity of 'classicism'." Earlier pieces such as *Movement for Nine Players* (1966) and Three Bagatelles for solo piano (1969) are in an atonal, or loose 12-tone idiom; their motifs and melodies, disjunct in register and rhythmically asymmetrical, are punctuated by chordal attacks or silences. More recent pieces combine tonal and atonal elements. The Four Bagatelles for Orchestra (1981), the best-known of his works in this style, are distinguished by their long Romantic melodies in *tempo rubato*, treated contrapuntally.

WORKS

Orch: 2 Movts, 1968; 3 Pieces, 1974; Music for Orch, 1980; 4 Bagatelles, 1981

Insts: Movt, fl, vc, pf, 1962; Music for 2 Pf, 1965; Movt, ob, vn, pf, 1966; Movt for 9 Players, 1966; 3 Short Pieces, pf 4 hands, 1968; Duo, vc, pf, 1969; Per vege viene, vn, pf, 1970; 3 Movts for Qnt, fl, cl, vn, vc, pf, 1971; 2 canzoni, vn, vc, pf, 1973; Fantasia sopra Ave regina coelorum, pf, chamber orch, 1976; Bagatelles, pf, 6 insts, 1977; Str Qt, 1979; Variations on a Lyric Fragment, vc, pf, 1980; Suite of Bagatelles, vn, pf, 1981; Intrada, fl, cl, vn, vc, 1984

Solo inst: Bagatelles, vn, 1967; 3 Bagatelles, pf, 1969; 2 Bagatelles, ob, 1973

Vocal: For 5 Players and Bar (postcard texts), 1969; 2 Songs on Latin Fragments, S, pf, 1972; 3 Songs (anon. Lat.), T, 6 insts, 1972; Motet and Madrigal (Good Friday Service), S, T, 5 insts, 1973; Due bicinia (Lat. Pss.), 2 S, fl, cl, vn, vc, 1974; Cantata no.1 (Bible), 2 S, T, small orch, 1975; On 2 Ancient Texts (trouvère song, Ave regina coelorum), S, fl, cl, vc, pf, 1975; On 3 Old English Rhymes, S, fl, cl, vc, pf, 1976; 4 Songs (Liber usualis), S, chorus, org, 1976; Cantata no.2 (Bible), solo vv, chorus, orch, 1978; Villanelle, Dirge (O. Wilde, J. Webster), S, orch, 1982; 6 Brief Verses (Liber usualis), female vv, str orch, pf, 1983; Of Rome, Parting and Spring (goliard song, Leopardi, Petrarch), S, fl, cl, vc, pf, 1985

Principal publishers: ACA, McGinnis & Marx

SEVERINE NEFF

Plimpton, Job (*b* Medway, MA, 27 Feb 1784; *d* Brookline, MA, 1864). Composer, compiler, teacher, and organ builder. He worked from 1806 to 1820 as a music teacher in New York City, though he spent some time in Albany in 1819. In September 1820 he performed at Boston's Columbian Museum on the Apollino, a panharmonicon that he claimed to have invented (announced in *The Euterpeiad*, i/23 (1820), 91). He later built reed organs and in 1836 exhibited an eight-stop instrument of his own design at Boston's Mechanic's Fair. He compiled *The Washington Choir* (Boston, 1843), a collection of temperance music that identifies him on its title-page as "pupil of Dr. G. K. Jackson," who was active in New York between 1802 and 1812. Plimpton's few surviving compositions include eight marches, an air, a waltz, and a minuet in *The Universal Repository of Music* (a collection now in the New York Public Library, which he copyrighted on 10 December 1808 but apparently never published), *Behold the lovely vernal rose*, a song for voice and keyboard (New York, 1816), and a few songs in *The Washington Choir*.

BIBLIOGRAPHY

R. J. Wolfe: *Secular Music in America, 1801–1825: a Bibliography* (New York, 1964)
B. Owen: *The Organ in New England* (Raleigh, 1979), 410

RICHARD CRAWFORD

Plishka, Paul (Peter) (*b* Old Forge, PA, 28 Aug 1941). Bass. He began singing lessons at the age of 18 at Montclair State College, and two years later became a pupil of Armen Boyajian, director of the Paterson Lyric Opera, New Jersey, receiving his initial stage experience with this company. In 1965 he joined the Metropolitan Opera National Company, singing Mozart's Bartolo and Puccini's Colline. When the touring company was disbanded, he was invited to join the parent company. He made his début as the Uncle-Priest in a concert performance of *Madama Butterfly* (at the Botanical Gardens in the Bronx on 27 June 1967), followed by his first appearance on the stage of the Metropolitan at Lincoln Center as the Monk in *La Gioconda* on 21 September 1967. Gradually he took on leading roles in both the serious and *buffo* repertories, among them Leporello, Oroveso (*Norma*), King Marke, Procida (*Les vêpres siciliennes*), and both Varlaam and Pimen in *Boris Godunov*. He has sung at many of the other leading American opera houses and from time to time abroad (he made his La Scala début in Berlioz's *La damnation de Faust* in 1974); he has also appeared frequently with the major American orchestras. His mellow, voluminous bass can be heard in recordings of Bellini's *I puritani* and *Norma*, Donizetti's *Anna Bolena* and *Gemma di Vergy*, Massenet's *Le Cid*, Gounod's *Faust*, and Puccini's *Turandot*.

BIBLIOGRAPHY

J. Hines: "Paul Plishka," *Great Singers on Great Singing* (Garden City, NY, 1982), 240

MARTIN BERNHEIMER/R

Poe, Edgar Allan (*b* Boston, MA, 19 Jan 1809; *d* Baltimore, MD, 7 Oct 1849). Writer. He attended the University of Virginia, Charlottesville (1826), and after serving in the US Army (1827–9) became a journalist and editor for various magazines in Philadelphia and New York.

Beyond its bizarre and macabre surface, Poe's writing consistently reveals a concern with neurotic states, with frequent hints of interpretation in Freudian terms. This, and his technique of symbol and suggestion, recommended his work to many composers at the turn of the century. Debussy, who was fascinated by the tales in Baudelaire's translation, planned a work based on *The Fall of the House of Usher* at least as early as 1890; 18 years later he was projecting this (with *The Devil in the Belfry*) as a double bill for the Metropolitan Opera. Poe's view of music as "suggestive and indefinite" – "sensations which bewilder while they enthral" – bears comparison with that of the Symbolists. The sympathy he found between musical sounds and mental states is most fully expounded in *The Bells*, which inspired Rachmaninoff's choral symphony of the same name; a similar link is found between the portrayal of the sensitive and troubled Roderick Usher and the vibrating strings of a guitar. Besides Debussy's sketches, operas based on this story include Avery Claflin's version of 1920–21.

Over 150 composers have been attracted to Poe's tales and poems in such diverse genres as opera, ballet, choral works, and songs and as inspirations for orchestral pieces and chamber music. Among notable settings by American composers are E. S. Kelley's orchestral suite drawn from *The Pit and the Pendulum*, Bertram Shapleigh's and Leonard Slatkin's settings of *The Raven*, and Charles Sanford Skilton's cantata *Lenore*.

BIBLIOGRAPHY

G. W. Peck: "Mere Music," *Literary World*, vi (1850), 225

A. Coeuroy: "Poe and Music," *Sackbut*, ii (1922), 6

A. W. Kelley: *Music and Literature in the American Romantic Movement: a Study of the Knowledge of, Use of, and Ideas relating to the Art of Music in Emerson, Hawthorne, Longfellow, Poe, Thoreau, Lowell, Whitman, and Lanier* (diss., U. of North Carolina, 1929)

Anon.: "Finding the Harmonic Equivalent of Edgar Allan Poe," *Newsweek*, vii (15 Feb 1936), 30

M. G. Evans: *Music and Edgar Allan Poe* (Baltimore and Oxford, 1939)

R. C. Archibald: "Music and Edgar Allan Poe," *Notes and Queries*, clxxix (1940), 170

B. M. Cadman: "Poe Music," *The Etude*, lviii (1940), 159

C. McGlinchee: "American Literature in American Music," *MQ*, xxxi (1945), 101

I. B. Cauthen, Jr.: "Music and Edgar Allan Poe," *Notes and Queries*, cxciv (1949), 103

C. S. Lenhart: *Musical Influence on American Poetry* (Athens, GA, 1956)

E. Schoettle: "A Musician's Commentary on Poe's 'The Philosophy of Composition'," *Forum*, iv (Houston, 1964), 14

M. H. Frank: *Music in American Literary History: a Survey of the Significance of Music in the Writings of Eight American Literary Figures* (diss., New York U., 1968)

H. E. Johnson: "Musical Interests of certain American Literary and Political Figures," *JRME*, xix (1971), 272

B. R. Pollin: "More Music to Poe," *ML*, liv (1973), 391

R. Wallace: " 'The Murders in the Rue Morgue' and Sonata Allegro Form," *Journal of Aesthetics and Art Criticism*, xxxv (1977), 457

C. Abbate: " 'The Heart Laid Bare': in Search of Debussy's Second Opera, inspired by a Short Story by Edgar Allan Poe," *Opera News*, xlii (1978), 30

R. C. Friedberg: *American Art Song and American Poetry*, i: *America Comes of Age* (Metuchen, NJ, 1981)

M. A. Hovland: *Musical Settings of American Poetry: a Bibliography* (in preparation) [incl. list of settings]

PAUL GRIFFITHS/R

Pointer Sisters. Popular vocal group. The four Pointer sisters Ruth (*b* 19 March 1946), Anita (*b* 23 Jan 1949), Bonnie [Patricia] (*b* 11 July 1950), and June (*b* 20 Nov 1953), were born in Oakland, California, where their father was a minister in the West Oakland Church of God; they were brought up in a strict environment and heard little music other than gospel until they were adults. Bonnie and June first worked as a duo, then as a trio with Anita. During the early 1970s they were backup singers for Elvin Bishop, Esther Phillips, Boz Scaggs, and others, and recorded two unsuccessful singles for Atlantic Records. In 1972 they were joined by Ruth and signed a contract with Blue Thumb, a subsidiary of ABC Records, which released the single *Yes we can can* (no. 11, 1973). This was written by Allen Toussaint and was a rhythm-and-blues song, but the group was equally adept at singing in other styles – in 1974 they received a Grammy Award for best country single with *Fairy Tale*, which reached no. 13 on the pop chart. By 1977, however, their success had diminished, possibly because the variety of styles they employed led to them being classed as a novelty act. In 1978, the year in which Bonnie left the group to pursue a career as a soloist, they began working with the producer Richard Perry, who emphasized their affinities with soul music. Their first hit on his label, Planet Records, a cover of Bruce Springsteen's song *Fire*, reached no. 2 on the chart in 1978; since then they have enjoyed consistent commercial success performing an appealing blend of pop and soul music. The album *Break Out* (1984) contained several hit singles, including *Automatic*, which displayed Ruth's extraordinarily powerful low voice, and *Neutron Dance*, which was included in the soundtrack for the film *Beverly Hills Cop*.

BIBLIOGRAPHY

L. Feather: "Pointers to the Future," *Melody Maker*, xlviii (4 Aug 1973), 26

J. L. Wasserman: "Yes They Could Could," *Rolling Stone*, no. 163 (20 June 1974), 36

K. McKenna: "Richard Perry Fires up the Pointer Sisters," *Rolling Stone*, no. 288 (5 April 1979), 28

BARRY KERNFELD

Poister, Arthur William (*b* Galion, OH, 13 June 1898; *d* Durham, NC, 25 Feb 1980). Organist. He studied at the American Conservatory, Chicago (BM 1925, MM 1931). After teaching at Central High School in Sioux City, Poister studied abroad with Marcel Dupré (Paris, 1925–6, 1927–8) and with Karl Straube (Leipzig, 1933–4). He taught organ and theory at the University of Redlands, California (1928–37), and was professor of organ at the University of Minnesota (1937–8), Oberlin Conservatory (1938–48), and Syracuse University (1948–67), where he was also university organist and director of music for Hendricks Chapel. After his retirement from Syracuse, he taught at Hollins College, Oberlin, the University of Colorado, Longwood College (Farmville, Virginia), and Meredith College (Raleigh, North Carolina). In his younger years Poister was a successful touring recitalist, but he is better known as a teacher. Among his many students were Will Headlee, Wayne Leupold, Leonard Raver, Roger Nyquist, Donald Sutherland, and Marianne Webb. Poister also had a close working relationship with the Cleveland organ builder Walter Holtkamp, Sr.

VERNON GOTWALS

Pojoaque. American Indians of the TEWA subgroup of the EASTERN PUEBLO.

Polacco, Giorgio (*b* Venice, Italy, 12 April 1873; *d* New York, 30 April 1960). Italian conductor. After studies in Venice, Milan, and St. Petersburg, he made his début in London with Gluck's *Orfeo ed Euridice* (1891), then conducted opera in Europe, Russia, and South America, and for Tetrazzini's American débuts in Mexico (1905) and San Francisco (1906). In 1911 he toured the USA with Henry Savage's company, directing the first English production in America of Puccini's *La fanciulla del West*. The next year he made his Metropolitan Opera début with another of Puccini's operas, *Manon Lescaut* (11 November); he stayed with the Metropolitan until 1917, succeeding Toscanini as director of Italian repertory (1915–17). He then conducted in Chicago (1918–19, 1921) and Boston (1927) and was principal conductor of the Chicago Civic Opera from its foundation in 1922 until 1930, when he retired and settled in New York. Polacco's performances were noted for their precision and vigor, and under the influence of Mary Garden at Chicago he became a leading conductor of French opera.

RICHARD D. FLETCHER/R

Poleri, David S(amuel) (*b* Philadelphia, PA, 10 Jan 1921; *d* Hanalei, HI, 13 Dec 1967). Tenor. He studied at the Philadelphia Academy of Vocal Arts and appeared with the Philadelphia Orchestra in 1945. He moved to New York, twice attended the Berkshire Music Center, and became a pupil of Alberto Sciarretti. In 1949 he made his operatic début in Chicago with Fortune Gallo's touring San Carlo Opera, singing the title role in Gounod's *Faust*. He sang with the New York City Opera (in *La traviata* and Massenet's *Manon*, 1951), with the opera companies of New Orleans, Cincinnati, Philadelphia, Pittsburgh, and Houston, and with the Lyric Opera of Chicago and the Cosmopolitan Opera of San Francisco. Abroad he appeared at the Edinburgh Festival (1951 and 1955) and Covent Garden (1956), in Italy (La Scala, Florence, Perugia, and Genoa), and in Havana. In 1954 he created the role of Michele in Menotti's *The Saint of Bleecker Street* in New York. He was a pioneer in televised opera, and in 1955 sang the role of Cavaradossi in an NBC television production of *Tosca*. Among his orchestral performances were appearances with the Chicago SO under Bruno Walter (in Verdi's Requiem), with the Philadelphia Orchestra under Ormandy, with the Minneapolis SO under Dorati, and with the Boston SO under Munch (in Berlioz's *La damnation de Faust*). His career suffered after he left the stage during a performance of *Carmen* given by the New York City Opera in Chicago in 1953. He died in a helicopter crash in Hawaii, where he was to begin teaching.

CHARLES JAHANT

Polish-American music. *See* EUROPEAN-AMERICAN MUSIC, §III, 8.

Political music. While much American political music has roots in traditional song and balladry, the category includes also many other kinds of music, from electoral songs of the 1730s to punk-rock protests of the 1980s. Political music belongs to no one form nor does it fall entirely into any one of the categories of popular, traditional, or art music. Music may be said to be political when its lyrics or melody evoke or reflect a political judgment in the listener. Thus in some cases, depending on the period, performer, and audience, a single piece may or may not qualify as political music: *Who killed Cock Robin?*, for example, and many other pieces now regarded as nursery rhymes, began as political allegories and have themselves been parodied. Among the most common types of political music are campaign songs and music of political protest, including labor, populist, suffragist, and abolitionist songs. Any comprehensive definition of political music must also take into account the context in which it is performed.

1. To the Civil War. 2. From 1861 to World War I. 3. Since 1919.

1. TO THE CIVIL WAR. The history of political music in the USA predates the founding of the Union. From Europe, Britain, West Africa, and the Caribbean settlers brought distinct musical traditions; and with these traditions came a socio-political context. The first Colonial broadsides were probably those sold on the streets of Boston complaining of injustices by colonial governors. In New York in the early 18th century, during a period when the laboring classes were disenfranchised, election day inspired many class-conscious songs and verses, and in the 1760s campaign songs dealing with the struggles between American Whigs and Tories appeared in penny broadsides and the columns of colonial papers. Songs circulated against the Stamp and Game Acts and against the British presence in North America. In the 1780s songs such as *God Save George Washington* (sung to the tune of *God Save the King*) helped to elect the first president, and others aided the campaign to ratify the constitution. According to Silber (1971) American campaign songs had their most sweeping effect in the election of 1840, when supporters of W. H. Harrison assembled collections such as *The Tippecanoe Songbook*. The result was not only electoral victory but, during the next 75 years, a stream of odes, songs, waltzes, marches, and polkas for presidential candidates. (*See also* GLEE.)

Campaign music circulated initially in political journals, but there is little evidence to show how widely such songs were sung in the 18th century. By the mid-19th century the campaign songster (a collection of lyrics without printed music) had become standard equipment in electoral campaigns, aided by the many sheet-music publishers who looked for commercial success in a song about a popular candidate. The melodies were mostly popular or patriotic tunes, such as *The Star-Spangled Banner*.

From its birth the labor movement was rich in music, and with the formation of the first unions, in the early 19th century, came the first union songs, which opposed the outlawing of organized labor and protested against economic and social injustice. Foner (1975) summarizes the themes of 19th-century labor song as "the organizations and struggles of working people, their hatred for the oppressors, their affirmation of the dignity and worth of labor, their determination to endure hardships together and to fight together for a better life." These early songs rarely found their way into songsters or hymnals such as the *Pocket Hymn Book* (a model for later political chapbooks), but they circulated in print as broadsides and orally at processions and parades. Their tunes came from popular songs and hymns, reflecting the exhortative tradition of Puritan and Methodist religious music.

Songs of class protest made a regular appearance in the first labor newspapers, such as the Philadelphia *Mechanics' Free Press* and the New York *Working Man's Advocate*. Editors seldom published melodies but they frequently printed columns of songs and doggerel contributed by readers and union members. When hard times hit industrial and self-employed craftsmen, as in the depression of 1819–22, songs were a convenient means of voicing discontent, and the labor press became a principal forum for sentiments which before had been expressed only orally.

In the period of Jacksonian democracy in the 1820s and 1830s, labor song flourished alongside workers' political parties. The following lines, published in 1829 (in the *Mechanics' Free Press* of 5 December), predate the *Communist Manifesto* by almost 20 years:

> The poor could live without the rich
> As every man may know
> But none that labour for their bread
> Could by the rich be spared . . .
> A truth it is both clear and plain
> Which every one may know
> That always in the richest earth
> The rankest weeds do grow.

Political songs in the Jacksonian era were not, however, limited to labor issues; among other topics were the limited term for officials (elected and otherwise), imprisonment for debt, indentured servitude, public health, and landlords.

With the widespread industrialization of New England in the early 19th century came child labor and some of the most famous factory protest ballads; *The Factory Girl* was a title given to half a dozen songs that circulated widely. Each wave of industrial and social change was reflected in song: the great depression of 1837, as well as the utopian movements of the 1840s and 1850s. There were songs for political meetings and rallies, and, as support for the abolitionist movement grew in the North, this also produced a large repertory of song. The Hutchinsons, a family of singers and entertainers, performed traditional and topical songs for the abolitionist cause, using tunes such as that of *Old Dan Tucker* for their new text "Get off the track!".

Abolitionist songs represented the culmination of a tradition of anti-slavery songs that dated back for two centuries. Living in isolation and denied literacy by their masters, black slaves preserved many elements of their distinctive oral culture, at least through the 19th century. For Afro-Americans, more than for most other groups, political sentiments surfaced in folklore and folksongs, particularly in the music of black protest: the FIELD HOLLER (as a means of communication beyond the hearing of the field boss), the spiritual (with its veiled references to a "great getting-up morning"), work songs (allowing a degree of control over the pace of labor), and folksongs encoded with directions to the "Underground Railway" (such as *Follow the drinking gourd*, in which slaves were encouraged to follow the Big Dipper northwards to freedom). Slaves also made up ballads about outlaws, tricksters, and "bad" slaves such as High John the Conqueror. This music fed political protests and more defiant acts of sabotage, escape, and revolt. For disenfranchised and illiterate Afro-Americans music was a principal means of expressing sentiments which could otherwise be uttered only on pain of death. Throughout the 19th century Afro-American spirituals expressed hopes of release from bondage on earth. The symbolic content of this music ranged from the fairly explicit *We shall be free* to more coded interpretations of Biblical narratives, such as *Didn't my Lord deliver Daniel (and why not you or I)*.

2. FROM 1861 TO WORLD WAR I. About the time of the Civil War the American trade union movement began to solidify its base in urban centers, and a specialized labor culture emerged which brought with it occupational songs protesting about wages, working conditions, and industrial accidents. The trend combined with music of European immigrants to revitalize political song in the USA. The depression songs of 1873, like those of 1819, 1837, and 1857, pointed the contrast between the American dream offered to new immigrants and workers and the actual conditions of labor. The Knights of Labor, a national labor organization founded in Philadelphia in 1869, produced popular political songbooks, believing that songs and ballads educated workers on political issues; they opened local assemblies with songs of labor unity.

Two other movements generated political music in the 19th century: the suffragists and the farmer–labor alliances. Agitation for female suffrage began soon after the Civil War, with a referendum in Kansas. When Wyoming became the first state with women's suffrage, on its admittance to the Union in 1890, a body of songs developed which advocated suffrage as a means of increasing democracy and keeping society "pure" by introducing a body of voters that could outnumber immigrants and Blacks. Suffrage songs continued to be sung (and parodied) until the passing of the 19th Amendment in 1920. Along with the suffragists should be mentioned the temperance movement, whose fiery songs helped to pass Prohibition into law, also in 1920.

Another movement contemporary with the suffragists after the Civil War was that known as "Populism." As the army had cleared the frontier of American Indian settlements earlier in the century, farming had spread through the Midwestern and Western states. Unfortunately for the farmers, working conditions were determined by large trusts made up of landholders, banks, and railroads. In the 1830s and 1840s agrarian reform movements, such as Dorr's Rebellion in Rhode Island and the Antirent Wars in upstate New York, had given birth to humorous and biting songs about landholders. After the Civil War, with rising costs for rail transportation and mortgage foreclosures, farm tenancy increased considerably, and these developments led to the founding of the Farmers' Alliance in 1877. This populist political movement parodied many popular tunes, such as *When Johnny comes marching home* and *John Brown's body*. In the 1890s the Alliance merged with the Knights of Labor and published two popular political songsters, *The Alliance and Labor Songster* and *The Labor Reform Songster*. The simple, familiar tunes and direct, exhortative lyrics were sung in many farmhouses and at grange meetings. In 1892 the Alliance and Knights of Labor coalition formed the Populist (or People's) Party, which used traditional tunes such as *Rosin the Bow* for campaign songs.

Towards the end of the 19th century several bitter strikes and labor battles produced memorable political songs. The Coal Creek rebellion of 1892 is remembered in *Payday at Coal Creek*, and both the Homestead steel strike of 1892 and the Pullman strike of 1894 (watersheds in the development of American unionism) gave rise to a wealth of protest songs, some written to popular tunes such as *After the Ball* (*After the Strike*) and *Old Black Joe* (*The Poor White Slave*). Mines and mills were well represented in this upsurge of political music. The feudal conditions under which many miners labored produced numerous protest songs, one of which, *Miner's Lifeguard*, was written during the first national strike of the United Mineworkers in 1897. Songs of the New England textile industry, like others, expressed feelings about occupational safety, wages, and working hours. A classic political song, *Bread and Roses*, originated in a mill strike at Lowell, Massachusetts, in 1912.

Among the most vigorous political songs of the 20th century were those of the Industrial Workers of the World (IWW), which was formed in 1905 from the remains of the Socialist Labor Party, the Western Federation of Miners, and other socialist groups.

The IWW's practice of combining singing and rousing speeches may have originated in Spokane early in the century in competition with the Salvation Army's street bands, whose hymns they parodied with verses pleading the IWW cause. The IWW opened its meetings with songs, and its songbook (*Songs of the Workers*, 1934, 34/1974) included the first printing of *Solidarity forever*, *The Preacher and the Slave* (or *Pie in the Sky*), *Hallelujah, I'm a bum*, and *The Red Flag*. The tunes were taken largely from popular songs of the period 1909–15, or from familiar gospel revival songs.

3. SINCE 1919. Following the example of the IWW (which lost much of its membership after taking an anti-war stance during World War I), a number of socialist and communist movements fashioned music for their causes in the 1930s and 1940s. In the COMPOSERS COLLECTIVE OF NEW YORK (1931–7) classically trained musicians collaborated to produce music that would serve on picket lines while simultaneously improving the supposedly poor taste of the proletariat. They believed that music itself, and not merely the lyrics, could stir a revolutionary impulse, but the 12-tone political music some of them composed under the influence of Schoenberg, Webern, and Berg was wholly unsuited to the New York ethnic laborers who were expected to sing it. Some members of the group went on to use musical theater for their political aims in works such as Marc Blitzstein's *The Cradle will Rock* (1936–7).

The Almanac Singers (1941–4) were a group of about 12 young musicians who provided support for political and labor campaigns sponsored by the Congress of Industrial Organizations. They adapted Appalachian folksongs to topical issues and sang them mainly to east European immigrants in New York unions. People's Songs (1945–9) was a national organization of radical songwriters and performers who set out to disseminate labor and political protest songs. The association, whose magazine, at its most successful, attracted as many as 2000 subscribers, employed various types of music (cabaret, jazz, ethnic, and folk music) for its political message.

Following the dissolution of these groups, songs urging political change were adopted by various mass movements, a development aided by radio and television. From 1954 civil rights campaigns in the South made effective use of spirituals and gospel songs such as *We are soldiers in the army*. In a second phase this movement adapted traditional songs and melodies, much as union organizers had done in radical labor schools in the 1930s. Perhaps the most famous example was the traditional hymn *I'll overcome*, the words, tempo, and meter of which were revised for mass singing over a period of 15 years, ultimately becoming *We shall overcome*. The musical and religious roots of songs such as this were so deeply embedded in the culture of the southern Blacks that they succeeded where previous political song campaigns did not. By 1965, however, songs began to disappear from civil rights marches as their novelty, along with that of the non-violent tactics associated with them, began to fade.

Music for presidential campaigns has declined in importance since World War I. Two candidates who used song effectively were Franklin Roosevelt, whose *Happy days are here again* and *We've got Franklin D. Roosevelt back again* came to symbolize his era, and Henry Wallace, for whose ill-fated 1948 campaign Woody Guthrie and Pete Seeger contributed music. Eubie Blake's *I'm just wild about Harry* was revived for Harry Truman's campaign that year, but songs such as *Happy landin' with Landon*, *We're madly for Adlai*, and *Go with Goldwater* were soon forgotten.

In the 1960s the songs of the nuclear disarmament movement, sung by a few in the late 1950s, found new life in the rising dissatisfaction with American involvement in Vietnam. Although rarely broadcast, anti-war songs such as *Feel like I'm fixing to die* by Country Joe McDonald achieved wide popularity. During the same period several of Bob Dylan's songs, including *Blowin' in the Wind* (1962), were adopted as anthems for protest and civil rights movements. Dylan had been greatly influenced by Woody Guthrie and Pete Seeger, both formerly with the Almanac Singers. Joan Baez, with whom Dylan toured the USA and Britain in 1965, was another performer whose songs expressed a strong social and political concern. At the Monterey Pop Festival in 1967 black rock star Jimi Hendrix voiced his political disaffection by savaging the tune of the national anthem in a psychedelic frenzy. Since then many insurgent groups – feminists, environmentalists, and even fantasists – have increasingly turned to music for political expression, drawing on most contemporary styles, including folk, rock, country and western, and punk rock. Experimental jazz has been interpreted by some as conveying a dissident message without the need for lyrics.

Although most 20th-century political musical campaigns have come from the left wing of the political spectrum, groups such as the Ku Klux Klan have sponsored barbershop quartets to put across their views about racial supremacy. Politically oriented musicians of all kinds have tried to elevate the role of music in their activities, but its effects have seemed ephemeral when compared with those of votes and bullets.

See also CONFEDERATE MUSIC; PATRIOTIC MUSIC.

BIBLIOGRAPHY

M. Larkin: "Revolutionary Music," *New Masses*, viii/7 (1933), 27
E. Siegmeister: *Music and Society* (New York, 1938)
W. Alderson: "On the Wobbly 'Casey Jones' and Other Songs," *California Folklore Quarterly*, i (1942), 373
J. Greenway: *American Folksongs of Protest* (Philadelphia, 1953)
T. P. Coffin: "Folksongs of Social Protest: a Musical Mirage," *New York Folklore Quarterly*, xiv/1 (1958), 3
A. Green: "A Discography of American Coal Miners' Songs," *Labor History*, ii (1961), 101
——: "A Discography of American Labor Union Songs," *New York Folklore Quarterly*, xi/3 (1961), 1
C. Keil: *Urban Blues* (Chicago, 1966)
M. Orth: "The Crack in the Consensus: Political Propaganda in American Popular Music," *New Mexico Quarterly*, xxxvi (1966), 62
J. A. Scott: "Ballads and Broadsides of the American Revolution," *Sing Out!*, xvi/2 (1966), 18
D. A. DeTurk and A. Poulin, Jr., eds.: *The American Folk Scene* (New York, 1967)
R. Brazier: "The Story of IWW's Little Red Songbook," *Labor History*, ix (1968), 91
R. S. Denisoff: "Protest Movements: Class Consciousness and the Propaganda Song," *Sociological Quarterly*, ix (1968), 228
L. Miller and J. K. Skipper, Jr.: "Sounds of Protest: Jazz and the Militant Avant-garde," *Approaches to Deviance: Theories, Concepts and Research Findings*, ed. M. Letton, J. K. Skipper, Jr., and C. McCaghy (New York, 1968), 129
J. Boskin and R. A. Rosenstone, eds.: "Protest in the Sixties," *Annals of the American Academy of Political and Social Science*, ccclxxxii (1969)
J. L. Rodnitzky: "The Evolution of the American Protest Song," *Journal of Popular Culture*, iii/1 (1969), 35
M. Truzzi: "The 100% American Songbag: Conservative Folksongs in America," *Western Folklore*, xxviii (1969), 27
R. S. Denisoff: "The Almanac Singers: 'Take it Easy, but Take it'," *Journal of American Folklore*, lxxxiii (1970), 21
F. Kofsky: *Black Nationalism and the Revolution in Music* (New York, 1970)
B. D. Collins: "Music in the Labor Movement," *Industrial and Labor Relations Forum*, vii/4 (1971), 41

R. A. Reuss: *American Folklore and Left-wing Politics, 1927–1957* (diss., Indiana U., 1971)
I. Silber: *Songs Americans Voted by: the Words and Music that Won and Lost Elections and Influenced the Democratic Process* (Harrisburg, PA, 1971)
J. Sinclair and R. Levin: *Music and Politics* (New York, 1971)
R. S. Denisoff: *Sing a Song of Social Significance* (Bowling Green, OH, 1972)
A. Green: *Only a Miner* (Urbana, IL, 1972)
P. Seeger: "Some Folk Roots and Protest Traditions," *Incompleat Folksinger* (New York, 1972), 62–151
G. H. Lewis: "Social Protest and Self Awareness in Black Popular Music," *Popular Music and Society*, ii (1973), 327
P. Foner: *American Labor Songs of the Nineteenth Century* (Urbana, IL, 1975)
B. Reagon: *Songs of the Civil Rights Movement 1955–1965: a Study in Cultural History* (diss., Howard U., 1975)
R. A. Reuss: "American Folksongs and Left-wing Politics, 1935–1956," *Journal of the Folklore Institute*, xii (1975), 89
A. Paredes: "Songs of Border Conflict," *A Texas-Mexican Cancionero* (Urbana, IL, 1976), 59–109
D. K. Dunaway: "A Selected Bibliography: Protest Song in the United States," *Folklore Forum*, x/2 (1977), 8
L. W. Levine: *Black Culture and Black Consciousness* (New York, 1977)
D. K. Dunaway: "Songs of Subversion: the Weavers," *Village Voice*, xxv (21 Jan 1980), 39
E. Lewis: *Songs of the Abolitionist Movement* (Urbana, IL, in preparation)

DAVID K. DUNAWAY

Polka. A lively couple dance thought to be of Bohemian origin. It appeared in the USA for the first time in 1844 and was the first of several eastern European dances to become popular in this country in the middle of the 19th century. It consists of a walking step, a hop, and a pivot; although it was one of the more energetic of the turning dances performed in 19th-century ballrooms, it was considered graceful and elegant. Music for the polka is in a moderately fast 2/4 meter (about 104 beats to the minute); there is an accent on the second of the two beats in each bar (ex. 1).

Ex.1 Polka rhythms

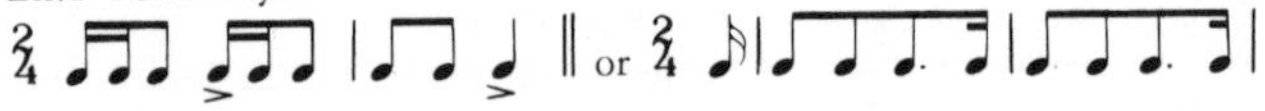

or

The strong duple rhythm made the polka a frequent choice for parade music, giving rise to the MARCH genre known as the "polka quickstep" or "military polka." Examples of the polka in early collections include the *Cally Polka* by Allen Dodworth and the *Serious Family Polka* (1851), arranged by Johann Munck. (For the cultivation of the polka by ethnic communities *see* EUROPEAN-AMERICAN MUSIC, §III, 8, and 12(ii).)

BIBLIOGRAPHY

E. Howe: *American Dancing Master and Ball-room Prompter* (Boston, 1862)
W. B. DeGarmo: *The Dance of Society* (New York, 1875, rev. and enlarged 5/1892)
C. Sachs: *Eine Weltgeschichte des Tanzes* (Berlin, 1933; Eng. trans. 1937/*R*1963)
P. Buckman: *Let's Dance: Social, Ballroom & Folk Dancing* (New York, 1978)
J. E. Kleeman: *The Origins and Stylistic Development of Polish-American Polka Music* (diss., U. of California, Berkeley, 1982)

For further bibliography *see* DANCE.

PAULINE NORTON

Pollack, Ben (*b* Chicago, IL, 22 June 1903; *d* Palm Springs, CA, 7 June 1971). Jazz drummer and bandleader. By 1923 he was playing with the NEW ORLEANS RHYTHM KINGS, where he established himself as the leading drummer in the early Chicago style of white jazz. He had a particularly innovative cymbal technique. In 1926 he founded the first of several jazz-oriented dance bands for which he is largely remembered today. Though commercially only moderately successful, these bands were highly regarded by contemporary jazz musicians, and provided valuable exposure early in their careers for such important players as Benny Goodman, Glenn Miller, Bud Freeman, Jack Teagarden, Harry James, and Muggsy Spanier. In 1934 his band broke up in California, and most of its members subsequently formed the nucleus of the Bob Crosby Band. From the 1940s Pollack occasionally organized groups in California in the dixieland revival style, but was chiefly active as a restaurateur.

RECORDINGS

(*selective list*)

As sideman with the New Orleans Rhythm Kings: Sweet Lovin' Man (1923, Gennett 5104); Shimmeshawabble (1923, Gennett 5106); Tin Roof Blues (1923, Gennett 5105)
As leader: 'Deed I Do (1926, Vic. 20408); My Kinda Love (1929, Vic. 21944); Two Tickets to Georgia (1933, Vic. 24284); Song of the Islands (1937, Decca 1424)

BIBLIOGRAPHY

S. B. Charters and L. Kunstadt: *Jazz: a History of the New York Scene* (Garden City, NY, 1962/*R*1981), chap. 13
A. Napoleon and J. R. T. Davies: "A Discography," *Storyville*, no. 36 (1971), 222
A. McCarthy: *Big Band Jazz* (London, 1974), 182ff
T. D. Brown: *A History and Analysis of Jazz Drumming to 1942* (diss., U. of Michigan, 1976), 282ff, 560f

J. BRADFORD ROBINSON

Pollikoff, Max (*b* Newark, NJ, 30 March 1904; *d* New York, 13 May 1984). Violinist and promoter of contemporary music. After showing early promise as a violinist he was awarded a scholarship in 1917 by the MacDowell Club of New York to study violin (with Auer), composition, and piano, and another scholarship the following year to continue his work with Auer. Pollikoff made his New York début on 30 October 1923 at Aeolian Hall in a program which included his own *Légende* for violin, and pursued a successful career as a concert artist, often introducing works by relatively unknown composers. In 1950 he gave the first public performance of Ives's Violin Sonata no. 1 (1908). From 1953 to 1973 he was associated with the Bennington Composers and Chamber Music conferences, and in 1956 he instituted a series at Columbia University devoted to reading new compositions. His most important achievement, however, was the establishment in 1954 of "Music in Our Time," a series of chamber music concerts presented at the 92nd Street Y and later at Town Hall, New York. At first the series presented mainly works by well-known composers such as Gershwin, Copland, Hindemith, and Rorem; later several younger composers including Chou Wen-chung, Da Costa, Kupferman, and Wuorinen received commissions from the series. Altogether it presented more than 250 contemporary works by such composers as Babbitt, Brant, Luigi Dallapiccola, Davidovsky, Luening, Rochberg, Saburo Takata, Trimble, and Wolpe. Often several pieces would be performed concurrently in different rooms and repeated, while the audience would wander about at will. The series ended in 1974, although a few individual concerts were given in later years under its title. After 1974 Pollikoff performed as soloist, made recordings, assisted in television commercials, and continued to promote contemporary music.

BIBLIOGRAPHY

R. Parmenter: "Violinist Offers First of Eight Concerts," *New York Times* (6 Feb 1956), 27
——: "World of Music: Under the Door," *New York Times* (6 Dec 1959), §X, p. 13
D. Henahan: "5 Musical Works Echo New Theory," *New York Times* (2 March 1970), 45
C. Moore: "New Concert Procedures, 'the Walk-Around'," *Vogue*, clvi/3 (1970), 38

J. Rockwell: "Music: 20th for Pollikoff," *New York Times* (19 April 1974), 26
——: "Max Pollikoff Plays New Compositions for Violin," *New York Times* (22 April 1978), 10
C. G. Fraser: "Max Pollikoff, Violinist, Dies; Created 'Music in Our Time'," *New York Times* (14 May 1984), §D, p.18
O. Luening: [letter] "An Invaluable Champion," *Keynote*, viii/5 (1984), 4

MARY A. WISCHUSEN

Pomeroy, Jim [James Calwell, Jr.] (*b* Reading, PA, 21 March 1945). Performance artist, composer, writer, and arts administrator. He studied sculpture at the University of Texas, Austin (BFA 1968), and at the University of California, Berkeley (MFA 1972). As an administrator, he co-founded and was vice-president and curator of the performance space 80 Langton Street (San Francisco, 1975–6) and was a trustee of the San Francisco Art Institute (1975–8). As artist-in-residence at the Exploratorium in San Francisco (1976–7), he created the visual installation *Light Weight Phantoms*; and in 1977 he joined the sculpture department of San Francisco State University. He has acted as consultant to museums and galleries and to the NEA, and his performances and sound sculptures have been presented in the San Francisco Museum of Modern Art (1979), the Los Angeles Institute of Contemporary Art (1979), and the CEPA Gallery, Buffalo (1981), and elsewhere.

Though Pomeroy is primarily a multi-media performance artist, his work also encompasses sound sculptures, handmade instruments, experimental music, and comic, ironic, and political vocal music. He performs under various names such as B. lind Nake, blind snake, and Rod Staph 'n' th' cumforts. Musicians and performers with whom he has collaborated include Paul DeMarinis, Jock Reynolds, Tom Marioni, Suzanne Hellmuth, and Jim Melchert. *A Byte at the Opera* (1974), one of his best-known works, employs sound generated by a computer which is suspended from the ceiling on a panel (measuring about 120 × 180 cm), 150 cm above a powder-covered plane (485 × 485 cm) whose underside is displayed on a large video screen. The patterns of movement of small objects described on the plane are reflected on the screen; and, with the aid of the accompanying sounds, the image eventually revealed is of a mechanic using a magnet to manipulate ball bearings. This image alters in the course of the work. *Double Read for Doubled Reeds* (1980), commissioned by the oboist Joseph Celli, is the only work of Pomeroy's which he created for another performer. A recording of his work, *Sound*, was produced by the Los Angeles Institute of Contemporary Art in 1979.

WORKS

(all texts by Pomeroy)

Sound sculptures: 3 Music Boxes, watches, clocks, metronomes, 1974–5; Fear Elites, music boxes, 1975; Mozart's Moog, 49 amp music boxes, 1978; Hat Dance, amp hard hat, slides, 1979; Mechanical Music, combination wrenches, 1979; Back on the Ladder . . ., vacuum cleaners, pipes, 1979–83; Whillikers in G, 5-gallon cans, 1980

Others: A Byte at the Opera (collab. P. DeMarinis), cptr, visual effects, 1974; Light Weight Phantoms, 1976–7; Fluteloops, with North Beach Memoranda, fl, tape, 1979; Double Read for Doubled Reeds, sloboe [mechanical inst], 5 tape recorders, 1980; Fl Trio, solo fl, 1981; Magnetic Music, amp fl, toys, 1981; Muzak of the Spheres, battery gramophone, 1982; performance and improvisational works for insts, tape, mechanical insts, hardware

BIBLIOGRAPHY

S. Foley: *Space Time Sound, Conceptual Art in the San Francisco Bay Area: the 1970s* (Seattle, 1981)
K. Norklun: "View from Within," *Artweek* (San Francisco, 7 Nov 1981)
Soundings, no.12 (1982) [incl. discussion by Pomeroy of his works]

STEPHEN RUPPENTHAL

Pomo. American Indians of northern California. They inhabited an area along the Pacific Coast extending from the mouth of the Russian River to what is now Fort Bragg, and inland slightly further east than Clear Lake.

Like other tribes of the area (such as the Maidu and Wintun), the Pomo embraced the Kuksu cult, a religious complex centering around impersonation of supernatural beings in rituals that aimed to ensure communal welfare. The Ghost Dance movement of 1870 had a great impact among the Pomo and led to the origin of the Bole Maru (Dream Dance) cult (*see also* INDIANS, AMERICAN, §I, 6 (iii)). Music was a central feature of all Pomo ritual; it was principally vocal and bound to religion in purpose and conception. Lole Kilak dances and songs were performed to ensure the availability of food and other natural resources. These were performed at ceremonies that were mainly the province of women, who also presided over celebrations for each year's first issue of acorns, clover, manzanita, and wild strawberries. The Pomo also had songs for institutions that were virtually universal among California Indians: shamanistic songs, war dance songs, girls' puberty dance songs, gambling songs, and songs for ritual mourning. The Pomo instrumentarium included the clapstick, footdrum, cocoon rattle, deer-hoof rattle, whistle, flute, and musical bow (for descriptions *see* YOKUTS and MAIDU). Only the flute and musical bow were used independently of singing; these were played only as solo instruments.

White settlers in Pomo territory during the latter 19th century brought disease and environmental destruction, both of which threatened the survival of Pomo culture. Nevertheless some traditional ceremonies are still observed at the Kashia Rancheria and elsewhere, and Pomo musical practices have been comparatively well documented in early and recent recordings of Pomo songs.

The structure of Pomo song is similar to that of the songs of other northern and central California tribes in many respects: melodic form is generally based on rather steady repetition of short, litany-like phrases of a descending or undulating nature, and the ambitus of most songs is restricted to an octave or less; tonal material is based on pentatonic scales or fragments; and vocables are more common than lexically meaningful texts. Pomo songs show a number of distinctive performance characteristics, however. Besides solo and choral unison singing, some examples exhibit alternation between soloists, responsorial singing between soloist and chorus, or accompaniment of a soloist by another singer who sustains what may be called an ostinato or drone. This practice recalls the multi-part styles of northwestern California groups (such as the YUROK).

The Pomo Dance Song (ex. 1) was repeated as often as wanted

Ex.1 Pomo dance-song, transcr. R. Keeling

in performance, with variation and alternating soloists. Since all parts save that of the soloist were of fixed or indistinct pitch, there was no intervallic coordination, and the main organizing principle was rhythmic. The assymetric meter (7/8) of this example is another feature that distinguishes Pomo music from that of the Maidu, Yokuts, or Wintun, but it is not an element of all Pomo singing.

Pomo singing is distinguished from that of other Indians of northern and central California in its vocal quality. It does not have the extreme raspiness, nasality, pulsation, and glottalization that gives northwestern California (e.g., Yurok) singing its dramatic character, nor is the voice so smooth and relaxed as among the central California tribes (e.g., Yokuts). Rather, the preferred vocal quality falls somewhere between these extremes, and songs are generally sung in the lower register of the singer's range.

Resources for the study of California Indian musical traditions are limited; serious archival research has only recently begun, although early collectors did record Pomo music (usually that of solo performers rather than ensembles) on wax cylinders. Were there more evidence regarding early performance practice, it might show that the music of other California tribes closely approximated the multi-part textures found among the Pomo and the Yurok. Recordings of Pomo music are held at the Lowie Museum of Anthropology, University of California, Berkeley.

See also INDIANS, AMERICAN, esp. §I, 4(ii)(c) and fig. 1.

BIBLIOGRAPHY

E. Loeb: Pomo Folkways, *University of California Publications in American Archeology and Ethnography*, xvix/2 (1926), 149–405

J. de Angulo and B. d'Harcourt: "La musique des Indiens de la Californie du Nord," *Journal de la Société des Américanistes de Paris*, xxiii/1 (1931), 189–228

W. Wallace: "Music," *Handbook of the Indians of North America*, viii (Washington, DC, 1978)

RICHARD KEELING

Pond, Sylvanus Billings (1792–1871). Music seller, publisher, and composer. He was a partner in the firm of FIRTH, HALL & POND. On its division in 1863 his son established the firm of William A. Pond & Co.

Poné, Gundaris (*b* Riga, Latvia, 17 Oct 1932). Composer and conductor. He studied violin in Latvia, lived with his family in Germany for several years after World War II, and came to the USA in 1950. Shifting his emphasis from violin performance to composition, he received a PhD in composition from the University of Minnesota in 1962. He made his New York début as a conductor in 1966 at a concert that included some of his own compositions. From 1963 he taught at SUNY, New Paltz, where he conducts the Poné Ensemble for New Music (founded in 1974). Poné has composed for a wide range of forces, especially orchestra and large, mixed chamber ensemble. Many of his works refer – through title, choice of text, or quoted thematic material – to radical political movements of the past. Examples include his use of the "Internationale" in *Vivos voco, mortuos plango* (1972) and of a text by Rosa Luxemburg in *Junius Broschüre* (1970). The political element in his music had largely disappeared by the end of the 1970s, though *Avanti!* (1975) does quote a Latvian revolutionary song.

Poné came to broader public attention in the 1980s when his works began to win prizes and receive performances by important orchestras. *Diletti dialettici* (1973) for nine virtuosos, one of whom is the conductor, was performed at the Fromm Festival of Contemporary Music at the Berkshire Music Center in 1980. The following year *La serenissima* (1979–81) received first prize in the City of Trieste International Competition for Symphonic Composition, and in 1984 the same work received the Whitney Prize of the Louisville Orchestra. In 1982 the Kennedy Center Friedheim Award competition selected *Avanti!*, a work of flamboyant gesture and bravura ranging between extremes of energetic activity and utter stasis, as the best new American orchestral work. Many of Poné's scores, beginning with *Diletti dialettici*, present special challenges to the performers and, in particular, the conductor, who must sometimes control complex polyrhythmic textures. At the same time his music often has a vivid directness of expression, as at the end of *Avanti!*, where a vertiginous waltz passage gives way to a hushed, premonitory cuckoo call that in turn introduces a quotation from a Bach funeral chorale.

WORKS

(selective list)

Orch: Concerto, vn, orch, 1959; Composizione, 4 orch, 1967–9; Vivos voco, mortuos plango, exegesis on "Internationale," large orch, 1972; Avanti!, 1975; Concerto, hn, orch, 1976; La serenissima, 7 Venetian portraits, 1979–81; American Portraits, 1984

Vocal: Quattro temperamenti d'amore (Petrarch), Bar, orch, 1960; Daniel propheta, oratorio, 3 vv, chorus, orch, 1962; Mit Trommeln und Pfeiffen (Goethe, Schiller, others), high v, pf, 1963; Junius Broschüre (R. Luxemburg), 4 speakers, 18 female vv, inst ens, 1970; American Songs, medium v, small orch, 1975

Chamber, inst: Sonata, va, 1959; Klavierwerk I, pf, 1963; Str Qt, "Hetaera Esmerelda," 1964; Serie – Alea, fl, ob, cl, bn, pf, 1965; Reaktionen, pf, 1966; Sonata, vc, 1966; Klavierwerk II, "Montage – Demontage," pf, assistant, 1967; Oltre questa porta geme la terra, 3 pf, 1969; San Michele della laguna, cl, vn, pf, 1969; De mundo magistri joanni, 2 cl, 2 vn, pf, marimba, 2 perc, sound effects, 1972; Diletti dialettici (Concerto for 9 Virtuosos), fl, cl, hn, perc, pf, vn, va, vc, cond., 1973; Eisleriana, conc., fl + a fl, cl, bn, tpt, pf, 2 perc, vn, va, vc, db, 1978; Ely (7 Studies in Nature), fl + a fl, perc, vn, vc, pf + cel, 1978; On Black Holes, pf trio, 1979; 5 Woodland Elegies, cl + b cl, vib + marimba, db, 1980; Di gran maniera, vn, 1981; 3 Farewell Pieces, pf, 1984

STEVEN LEDBETTER

Pons, Lily [Alice Joséphine] (*b* Draguignan, nr Cannes, France, 12 April 1898; *d* Dallas, TX, 13 Feb 1976). Soprano. After studying piano at the Paris Conservatoire, she decided upon a career as a singer and began extensive vocal training with Alberti de Gorostiaga. She made her opera début in 1928 at Mulhouse as Lakmé (Delibes), then sang in provincial French opera houses. On the recommendation of Zenatello, Gatti-Casazza invited her to join the Metropolitan Opera, where she made her début on 3 January 1931 as Lucia. She caused a sensation and remained with the company for 27 seasons (1944–5 excepted), becoming one of its most famous members. She had much success as Gilda, Amina (*La sonnambula*), Marie (*La fille du régiment*), Philine (*Mignon*), Olympia (*Les contes d'Hoffmann*), and, above all, Lakmé. She sang in South America and London (Covent Garden, 1935, as Rosina), and made some films. In 1938 she married Kostelanetz, with whom she appeared in numerous concerts. She made her farewell appearance at the Metropolitan on 12 April 1958, as Lucia, but returned in 1960 for a concert performance; her retirement followed shortly after. In 1972 she made her last public appearance as a singer at a New York PO Promenade Concert. A singer of international standing, Pons possessed an agile, fragile, and extremely high coloratura voice; it suited her to sing the Mad Scene from *Lucia* a whole tone higher than written. Her intonation was not always accurate, but her technique was otherwise exceptionally secure.

BIBLIOGRAPHY

B. Park: "Lily Pons," *Record Collector*, xiii (1960–61), 245 [with discography]

L. Rasponi: "The Money-makers," *The Last Prima Donnas* (New York, 1982)

MAX DE SCHAUENSEE/DENNIS K. McINTIRE

Ponselle [Ponzillo], **Rosa (Melba)** (*b* Meriden, CT, 22 Jan 1897; *d* Green Spring Valley, MD, 25 May 1981). Soprano. She studied singing with her mother and then with Anna Ryan. After some experience in church singing, she began to appear in movie theaters and vaudeville, often in duet with her elder sister Carmela (*b* Schenectady, NY, 7 June 1892; *d* New York, 13 June 1977), a mezzo-soprano who was to sing at the Metropolitan Opera from 1925 to 1935. In 1918 her coach William Thorner brought her to the attention of Caruso and Gatti-Casazza. In the first Metropolitan production of *La forza del destino*, she gave the first operatic performance of her life as Leonora (15 November 1918), opposite Caruso and De Luca; she had prepared the role with Romano Romani, who remained her principal operatic and vocal tutor throughout her career. She sang at the Metropolitan for 19 seasons, undertaking 22 roles in the dramatic and dramatic-coloratura repertories. Perhaps most celebrated as Norma (see illustration), she also enjoyed extraordinary successes in *Oberon*, *Ernani*, *Don Carlos*, *La Gioconda*, *Andrea Chenier*, *Guillaume Tell*, Italo Montemezzi's *L'amore dei tre re*, *Don Giovanni* (Donna Anna), *Cavalleria rusticana*, *La traviata*, *La vestale*, and *L'africaine*. She also participated in such little-known operas as Breil's *The Legend*, Montemezzi's *La notte di Zoraïma*, and Romani's *Fedra*. In 1935 she attempted Carmen, perhaps unwisely, and experienced her only notable failure. Two years later she retired from opera, reportedly after her request for a revival of *Adriana Lecouvreur* was rejected, and vowed never again to set foot in the Metropolitan after her final performance (as Carmen, 15 February 1937). She made her Covent Garden début as Norma on 28 May 1929, returning as Violetta, Leonora (*La forza del destino*), and the heroine of Romani's *Fedra*; at the Florence Maggio Musicale in 1933 she sang Julia (*La vestale*). Although her repertory was broad, she never sang Puccini or Wagner, about which she confessed regret in later years.

Rosa Ponselle in the title role of Bellini's "Norma"

Ponselle's voice is generally regarded as one of the most beautiful of the century. She was universally lauded for opulence of tone, evenness of scale, breadth of range, perfection of technique, and communicative warmth. Many of these attributes are convincingly documented on recordings. She sang briefly in concerts and at public ceremonials after her premature operatic retirement, then moved to a mansion in Green Spring Valley outside Baltimore, where she concentrated on teaching. In 1954 she made a few private song recordings, later released commercially, revealing a still opulent voice of darkened timbre and more limited range. She was artistic director of the Baltimore Civic Opera, which (belatedly) commemorated her 70th birthday with a new production of *La forza del destino* on 10 March 1969. Her 80th birthday was marked by tributes from her many admirers, friends, and former students.

BIBLIOGRAPHY

O. Thompson: *The American Singer* (New York, 1937/*R*1969), 335

I. Cook: "Rosa Ponselle," *Opera*, iii (1952), 75

L. Riemens: "Ponselle, Rosa," *Le grandi voci*, ed. R. Celletti (Rome, 1964) [with opera discography by S. Smolian and R. Vegeto]

T. Villella and B. Park: "Rosa Ponselle Discography," *Grand baton*, vii/1–2 (1970), 5

J. B. Steane: *The Grand Tradition* (New York, 1974)

J. Ardoin: "A Footnote to Ponselle's Norma," *Opera*, xxvii (1976), 225

A. Hughes: Obituary, *New York Times* (26 May 1981)

J. Hines: "Rosa Ponselle," *Great Singers on Great Singing* (Garden City, NY, 1982), 250

MARTIN BERNHEIMER/R

Poole, Charlie (Cleveland) (*b* Randolph Co., NC, 22 March 1892; *d* Spray, NC, 21 May 1931). Country-music singer, banjoist, and songwriter. He was brought up in the textile towns of North Carolina, where he learned many old songs while working in the mills; studies of his repertory have shown that most of his compositions were in fact arrangements of traditional songs or popular material from the turn of the century. In 1925 he began to record and tour with his string band, the North Carolina Ramblers, the members of which included the guitarist and singer Norman Woodleiff, the guitarist Roy Harvey, and the fiddlers Posey Rorer, Lonnie Austin, and Odell Smith. Poole's banjo playing was precise, restrained, and melodic; he used a picking technique (employing the thumb and two fingers) that he had learned from Daner Johnson (another North Carolina banjoist), who had adapted to traditional southern tunes the classical banjo styles of the 1890s. Poole's playing was matched by that of the band, which cultivated a cool, "polite" sound in contrast to the rough, driving style of other early country-music bands, such as the Skillet Lickers. Poole recorded some 84 titles on the Columbia, Paramount, and Brunswick labels, many of which became bluegrass, folk, and country standards.

In the late 1920s Poole tried to broaden his style, but was frustrated by record executives, who insisted that he follow his older, proven formulae; this frustration, combined with the Depression's effect on the recording industry and growing personal problems, led Poole to alcoholism and premature death.

He was the first commercially successful country singer to perform in a folk-derived style to string-band accompaniment. Unlike those of most of his contemporaries, Poole's recordings have enjoyed substantial popularity with modern listeners, and as late as 1982 six albums compiled from his early recordings (comprising about 75% of his output) were available.

RECORDINGS

(selective list)

Can I sleep in your barn tonight, mister/Don't Let your Deal Go Down Blues (Col. 15038-D, 1925); I'm the man who rode the mule around the world (Col. 15043-D, 1925); There'll come a time (Col. 15116-D, 1926); White House Blues (Col. 15099-D, 1926); Sunset March (Col. 15184-D, 1927); Tennessee Blues (Para. 3200, 1929)

BIBLIOGRAPHY

N. Cohen: "Early Pioneers," *Stars of Country Music*, ed. B. C. Malone and J. McCulloh (Urbana, IL, 1975), 3–39

K. Rorrer: *Rambling Blues: the Life and Songs of Charlie Poole* (London, 1982)

CHARLES K. WOLFE

Pop, Iggy [Osterberg, James Newell] (*b* Ann Arbor, MI, 21 April 1947). Rock singer and songwriter. He played drums and sang in a group called the Iguanas, from which he gained his nickname. In the mid-1960s he went to Chicago, where he met Sam Lay, the drummer in the Paul Butterfield Blues Band, and played drums for visiting blues musicians. He then formed the Prime Movers (later the Psychedelic Stooges) with Ron Ashton, guitarist, Dave Alexander, bass guitarist, and Scott Ashton, drummer. The group played loud, droning, repetitive psychedelic music, to which Pop improvised lyrics (he did not write structured songs until the group had a recording contract) and performed violent theatrical antics, involving physical contortions, leaping from the stage into the audience, cutting himself with broken glass, and smashing his microphone against his teeth.

In 1969 he recorded *The Stooges*, an album produced by John Cale that includes songs expressing pessimistic, anti-hippie sentiments, such as *No Fun* and *I wanna be your dog*. *Funhouse* (1970) added saxophone solos in a free-jazz style to the band's hard psychedelic sound, with its pervasive use of fuzz box and wah-wah pedal; it is one of the most powerful hard-rock albums ever recorded. These albums sold poorly, and for several years Pop and the Stooges were without a recording contract. In 1973, however, David Bowie produced *Raw Power*, on which James Williamson played guitar; this included such brutally effective songs as *Search and Destroy*, but their impact was somewhat dampened by Bowie's poorly balanced sound mix. A recording of the group's final performance, in 1974, which ended with a brawl in which Pop was badly beaten, was issued as *Metallic K.O.* in 1976. Some interesting demonstration tapes, recorded with Williamson, were released as *Kill City* in 1978.

After a hiatus of several years Iggy Pop's career was again revived by David Bowie. He began performing and recording as a soloist; on *The Idiot* (1977) he sang in a deep monotone to the accompaniment of Bowie's grinding electronic settings (*China Girl*, a moving ballad from that album, was a hit for Bowie in 1983 on his *Let's Dance*). *Lust for Life* (1977) is a more conventional hard-rock album, and *TV Eye* (1978) was recorded on a tour during which Bowie played piano in Pop's backup group. Pursuing a moderately successful solo career, Pop has continued to record albums of strong but uninspired hard rock with various collaborators; the best of these is *New Values* (1979), in which he was joined by Williamson.

RECORDINGS

(selective list)

With the Stooges: *The Stooges* (Elek. 74051, 1969); *Funhouse* (Elek. 74071, 1970); *Raw Power* (Col. KC32111, 1973); *Metallic K.O.* (Skydog 1015, 1976); *Kill City* (Bomp 4001, 1978)

As soloist: *Lust for Life* (RCA AFL12488, 1977); *The Idiot* (RCA APL12275, 1977); *TV Eye* (RCA APL12796, 1978); *New Values* (Ari. 4237, 1979); *Party* (Ari. 9572, 1981); *Zombie Birdhouse* (Animal FV-41399, 1982)

BIBLIOGRAPHY

I. Pop and A. Wehrer: *I Need More: the Stooges and Other Stories* (New York, 1982)

JOHN PICCARELLA

Pope, W(ilfred) Stuart (George) (*b* Folkestone, England, 9 Aug 1921). English music publisher. Educated at the Royal College of Organists, he joined the publishing firm of Boosey & Hawkes in 1937, and after wartime service filled several managerial posts before becoming managing director of the company's affiliate in South Africa (1958). He was also active as an organist, serving at the Crown Court Church, London (1946–58), and St. Mary's Cathedral, Johannesburg (1960–64). He came to the USA to assume the managing directorship of Boosey & Hawkes in 1964, and was appointed president in 1974. In 1984 he retired from Boosey & Hawkes and became president of BTG Management, a division of Birch Tree Group, Ltd, of which he is vice-president. He serves on the boards of directors of ASCAP, the American Music Center, and the Music Publishers Association and is a member of the Century Association.

ELLEN HIGHSTEIN

Popovich, Adam (*b* Denver, CO, 24 Dec 1909). Instrumentalist, singer, and composer. He began studying Serbian music with his father as a child. In 1924 he took up the tambura, a Serbian long-necked lute, and soon became an accomplished performer on the celo (a type of tambura) and the violin. In 1925 he formed the Popovich Brothers Yugoslav Tamburitza Orchestra with his brothers Eli, Ted, and Marko (for illustration *see* EUROPEAN-AMERICAN MUSIC, fig.7); they toured extensively in the West, and in 1928 settled in the large Serbian community of South Chicago, where they became well known. They performed at the Smithsonian Institution's 1973 Festival of American Folklife; in 1978 they were portrayed in a film, *The Popovich Brothers of South Chicago*. Popovich directed the Sloboda choir of the Serbian Orthodox Church from 1936; for it he made many arrangements of traditional folk melodies. He also composed several original works for chorus and for tamburitza ensemble. He received a National Heritage Fellowship from the NEA in 1982.

DANIEL SHEEHY

Pops. *See* ARMSTRONG, LOUIS.

Pops [Pop, Promenade] **concerts.** Orchestral programs modeled after European promenade concerts of the 19th century, in which light classical music is played while the audience is served refreshments. The Boston SO, in 1885, was the first institution to establish such orchestral concerts in the USA; its pops orchestra has served as the model for many other "pops" orchestras (*see* BOSTON (i), §3). "Pops" concerts are traditionally structured in three parts, in which lively pieces – overtures, marches, and galops – are played in the outer sections while the middle section often contains more serious pieces; encores are a regular feature. During the two intermissions, the audience promenades. Initially, works by European composers such as Rossini, Grieg, Liszt, and Strauss dominated the programs of "pops" concerts, but excerpts from musicals and operettas by De Koven and Herbert, among others, soon became a significant component. A number of works have been written especially for the Boston Pops Orchestra, notably by LEROY ANDERSON. Selections of patriotic music, especially *The Star-Spangled Banner* and Sousa's *The Stars and Stripes Forever!* (as well as others of his many marches), are regularly included on "pops" programs, particularly on Independence Day, when outdoor concerts often conclude with a display of fireworks. The conductor ARTHUR FIEDLER became inextricably identified with "pops" concerts through his leadership of the Boston Pops Orchestra (1930–79) and the San Francisco Pops Orchestra (1951–78), as well as his many recordings, television broadcasts, tours, and guest appearances. Other conductors associated with "pops" concerts include John Williams, who succeeded Fiedler in Boston, John Covelli, Erich Kunzel, who founded the Cincinnati Pops Orchestra in 1977, Richard Hayman (who has held the title "principal pops conductor" for concerts presented by the Detroit SO and the St. Louis SO), and Skitch Henderson (whose New York Pops Orchestra made its début in 1983). A professional "pops" orchestra was formed in Houston in 1971 (*see* HOUSTON, §2(i)).

BIBLIOGRAPHY

S. Ledbetter: *100 Years of the Boston Pops*, ed. J. C. Marksbury (Boston, 1985)

SUSAN FEDER

Popular music. A genre of music, encompassing several styles, that is readily comprehensible to a large proportion of the population; its appreciation requires little or no knowledge of musical theory or techniques. It differs in important ways from classical and FOLK MUSIC, and from much jazz. Popular pieces are usually of modest length, have a prominent melodic line (often vocal), and a simple, restricted harmonic language. In the USA the emergence of popular music coincided with the rise of a large, literate middle class in the 18th and 19th centuries (and of an even larger literate working class in the late 19th and early 20th centuries), with a gradual shift of population and cultural life from rural areas to urban centers, and with the development of a national consciousness. The growing middle and working classes acquired the leisure time and financial means to enjoy music, but they generally lacked the cultural heritage and musical training that would have helped them to appreciate classical music. Unlike folk music, which is a product of the oral tradition and is often confined to a particular region, popular music has been widely disseminated, first by printed sheet music and lyrics, then by phonograph recordings; from the 1930s radio broadcasting played an important role in its propagation.

I. European origins. II. Early American song and piano music. III. The Tin Pan Alley era. IV. The rock era.

I. European origins

1. English traditions. 2. Scottish and Irish melodies. 3. Bel canto. 4. Continuing European influences.

1. ENGLISH TRADITIONS. The first secular music printed in North America was associated with the broadside ballad. Some broadsides were printed in England and brought to the colonies; others were printed in such American cities as Boston, Philadelphia, and New York. They usually consisted only of a text, which was intended to be sung to a tune already familiar to the purchaser through oral tradition; even when a melody was printed on a broadside, it served only as a reminder, and was never newly composed. Many of these tunes have been preserved in oral tradition, in notated instrumental music as airs for variation, or in tutors and such contemporary sources as *The English Dancing Master* (1651), published by John Playford, *A Choice Collection of 180 Loyal Songs* (1685), and *Wit and Mirth, or Pills to Purge Melancholy* (1699), published by Henry Playford; the last is an anthology of several volumes, which contains the words and music to almost 1000 songs, some by known composers of the 16th to 18th centuries, some by unknown and probably earlier composers. Popular ballads can be reconstructed by matching their lyrics, as printed in broadsides, with tunes from these and other sources. The printing of secular music in North America began in earnest only after the Revolution. A few items were published in the 1780s, but it was not until the 1790s that such music appeared in great quantity. Early printers and publishers included Benjamin Carr (Philadelphia and New York), James Hewitt (New York), P. A. von Hagen (Boston), and George Willig (Philadelphia); most of their issues were songs, for voice and keyboard, that had been popularized on the stages of the theaters and pleasure gardens of the day.

Musical life in the new nation was closely linked with that of England. Ballad operas had been performed in America since 1735, when *Flora, or Hob in the Well* was staged in Charleston, South Carolina. John Gay's *The Beggar's Opera* was staged in New York in 1750, and in 1752 an English theatrical troupe landed in Virginia at Yorktown, and gave its first performances in Williamsburg. It soon began calling itself the American Company, and traveled throughout the colonies, performing ballad and comic operas. It was inactive during the Revolution, but resumed its operation afterwards and remained in existence for almost 50 years. Among the works most often performed by this troupe and others were *Love in a Camp*, *Rosina*, and *The Poor Soldier* by William Shield, *The Children in the Wood* and *Zorinski* by Samuel Arnold, Charles Dibdin's *The Deserter*, Stephen Storace's *No Song, No Supper*, and Thomas Arne's *Love in a Village*. Songs from all these operas were issued by early American music publishers.

Solo songs with instrumental accompaniment, either taken from stage works or written for concert performances, were sung at benefit and subscription concerts in various cities, as part of the programs of musical societies in Charleston, New York, Boston, and Philadelphia, and at the outdoor performances at many pleasure gardens. Almost all of these were written by English composers in the "London" style fashionable at the time, which combined elements of English airs with stylistic traits from the works of Handel, J. C. Bach, and other European composers. They are strophic songs, the melodies of which are mostly diatonic, with scale passages and melodic skips outlining basic triads, and accompaniments that are confined to simple figuration and repeated chords; their texts are mostly pastoral, comic, or moralizing. James Hook's annual collections of songs written for Vauxhall Gardens in London (1774–*c*1820) furnished American publishers with several hundred items.

Many musicians who had been active in London immigrated to the USA soon after the Revolution, and helped shape the musical life of the new country by playing, singing, and conducting, and organizing musical events. Most of them also composed music, though none had outstanding talent; many of their compositions were songs in the London style. Benjamin Carr, who had been associated with the London Ancient Concerts, went to Philadelphia in 1793 and was active there and in New York as a pianist, singer, composer, and music publisher; among the most successful of his several dozen published songs were Four Ballads (1794), to texts by Shakespeare, and *The Little Sailor Boy* (1798). Reinagle arrived in the USA in 1786 and worked as a conductor, performer, and impresario in several cities; most of his published songs, which number more than 50, are arrangements of pieces by Arnold, Kelly, Dibdin, and Shield. James Hewitt came to the USA in 1792; he composed and conducted ballad and comic operas. Other song composers from England were George K. Jackson (*One Kind Kiss*) and Rayner Taylor. All these men lacked a distinctive style of composition, but their songs enjoyed considerable success and were an important part of the first body of popular song printed in the USA.

Among the most popular songs in the first decades of the 19th century were those of John Braham, including the duet "All's well" from his opera *The English Fleet in 1342*, and the ballad *Is there a heart that never lov'd?*. When Braham toured the USA with his son Charles in 1840–42 he was warmly received because of his fame as a songwriter, though he was well past his prime as a singer. The songs of Henry R. Bishop were even more popular in the USA at this time: *Home, Sweet Home* (1823) was almost immediately successful and became the most universally known song of the 19th century; others of his songs, such as "Love has eyes" from the comic opera *The Farmer's Wife* and *The bloom is on the rye*, enjoyed almost equal, though less enduring, popularity. Bishop's songs, like the best work of other English songwriters of the era, have an easy melodic charm, express emotions directly, and use simple accompaniments that do not draw attention from the singer and the text. The style of American popular music to the mid-19th century was decidedly English, though it often drew on other national styles heard in the British Isles at the time; this reflected the close cultural ties that still existed between the USA and Britain.

2. SCOTTISH AND IRISH MELODIES. Hook and his contemporaries sometimes wrote songs derived from, or imitative of, Scottish and Irish tunes. Hook's *Within a Mile of Edinboro' Town* and several arrangements of the anonymous *The Blue Bells of Scotland* were among the most popular sheet-music publications in the USA at the turn of the century, as were a number of songs by Robert Burns (*John Anderson my Jo*, *Auld Lang Syne*, and *Comin' thro the Rye*), which were set to traditional Scottish tunes; first published in *The Scots Musical Museum* beginning in 1787, these songs were distributed in the USA in the form of separate sheet-music issues.

By far the most successful of the many collections of Irish songs that appeared in the late 18th and early 19th centuries was the ten-volume *A Selection of Irish Melodies*, with texts by Thomas Moore and accompaniments by John Stevenson (i–vii, 1808–18) and Bishop (viii–x, 1821–34). Like Burns, Moore added his own poetry to tunes taken from traditional music; though arrangements in the original editions of the collection were for one to four voices, the pieces were most popular as solo songs with keyboard accompaniment. They were enthusiastically received in the USA, as they had been in England; the first volume was printed, from new plates, by G. E. Blake in Philadelphia as early as 1808, and succeeding volumes were published in the USA soon after their first appearance in London and Dublin. Individual songs were published separately, and many of these (*Believe me if all those endearing young charms*, *The Last Rose of Summer*, *The Minstrel Boy*, *The harp that once thro Tara's halls*) became enduring parts of the American musical heritage, remaining in print throughout the 19th century and in some cases passing into oral tradition (whence their melodies had come in the first place). Their immense popularity, cutting across social and economic divisions, was due both to their texts, which were more concerned with the direct expression of universal human sentiments than had been those of the earlier song repertory, and to their melodies, which were drawn from a musical style already familiar to the musically educated and uneducated alike.

3. BEL CANTO. The music of Italian opera of the early 19th century had a profound impact on popular song in the USA. Simplified arrangements, for voice and keyboard, of excerpts from operas by Mozart enjoyed some currency in the first decades of the century, and in 1818 G. E. Blake brought out the first music by Rossini to be printed in the USA, an arrangement of an aria from *Tancredi*. Productions of Italian operas in English at the Park Theatre in New York and in other cities became popular; an "Englished" version, by Bishop, of *Il barbiere di Siviglia* was first staged at the Park in 1819, and frequently repeated in the next years. Many other reworkings of Italian operas, by Bishop and Rophino Lacey, followed. Lacey's *Cinderella, or The Fairy-queen and the Glass Slipper*, based loosely on Rossini's *La Cenerentola*, was first performed at the Park in 1831 and was given some 50 times in its first season alone; it remained in the repertory for decades. Vincenzo Bellini's *La sonnambula* was first performed in the USA in an English version in 1835, and his *Norma* came to the USA in 1840; the latter became the most popular opera of the decade. At the same time European companies were touring the USA and performing Italian opera in the original language. Manuel García brought a troupe to New York in 1825; it gave about 70 performances of nine Italian works, then moved on to other American cities, offering the same repertory. In 1832 the Montresor Company, brought to the USA through the efforts of Lorenzo da Ponte (then a professor of Italian literature at Columbia College), gave 30 performances in New York. Local residents subsequently raised $150,000 to construct the Italian Opera House and assemble a company of professional European musicians; the grand opening of the opera house took place on 18 November 1833 with a performance of Rossini's *La gazza ladra*, and 80 performances of various operas were given in its first season.

The influence of Italian melody on American culture was felt outside the opera house as well. For several decades after 1820 the melodies of arias, ensembles, and choruses by Rossini, Bellini, Donizetti, and their contemporaries were arranged as simple, strophic songs for voice and keyboard, given English texts, and published as sheet music; their sales approached, and sometimes surpassed, those of English and Irish songs. With the increasing popularity of the Italian style, English composers began emulating its most obvious characteristics; this is evident in the songs of Henry Russell, who enjoyed enormous success as a singer and songwriter after arriving in the USA in 1835. Schooled in Italian opera, he wrote and performed songs that had an easy, Italianate, melodic charm, and texts expressing nostalgia for lost youth (the principal theme of Moore's *Irish Melodies*) or addressing issues relevant to American life, such as the treatment of the American Indian and the black slave. Most of his songs were unadorned, strophic ballads, but some (*The Maniac* and *The Ship on Fire*) were more extended, complex pieces resembling the scena of contemporary Italian opera. Russell's appealing, dramatic voice, and the intensity of his delivery, inspired by the oratorical style of Henry Clay, made him the most popular singer in the USA to that date; the widespread appeal of his songs, some of which remained in the repertory for more than half a century, brought further currency to the Italian style. For more than 50 years American songwriters absorbed elements of Italian melody into their music. This influence remained strong even though Italian immigrants comprised only a tiny fraction of the population of the USA, and lived outside the mainstream of American life.

4. Continuing European influences. Even after American songwriters began to write in a distinctive, indigenous style, the flow of music from Europe continued. Samuel Lover, the most important Irish songwriter after Moore, toured the USA as a singer and poet in 1846–8; he tapped the rich strain of Irish folk music, and the increasingly sentimental style of 19th-century parlor song, in the songs *Rory O'More* and *The Low-backed Car*, and in dozens of other pieces that were widely popular. In 1827 Charles Edward Horn came to the USA, preceded by the popularity of his *Cherry ripe*, *I've been roaming*, and many other songs in styles forged by Bishop. Charlotte Alington Barnard, who published songs and poetry under the pen name "Claribel," was popular in the USA just after the mid-century for several dozen exquisite miniatures, including *I cannot sing the old songs*, *Come back to Erin*, and *Take back the heart*. Many German songs in English translation were widely disseminated and were sung in the concert hall and the parlor: Schubert's *Serenade* and *Ave Maria*, Beethoven's *Adelaide*, Franz Wilhelm Abt's *When the swallows homeward fly* (*Wenn die Schwalben heimwärts ziehn*), and Friedrich Wilhelm Kücken's *Good night, farewell* were particular favorites. The appeal of these songs, however, was limited to the classical-music audience; American songwriters paid the music little heed, and indigenous popular song had by this time developed such a lively, distinctive character that most Americans preferred it to its European counterpart.

II. Early American song and piano music

1. The expanding market. 2. The first American songwriters. 3. Songs of the minstrel stage. 4. Singing families. 5. Stephen Foster. 6. Popular piano music. 7. The Civil War period. 8. The postwar years.

1. The expanding market. During the Revolutionary period few Americans were musically literate, and the sale of sheet music was consequently a small business confined mostly to larger cities, and to the most affluent, best-educated members of society, who were also those most likely to have some acquaintance with classical music. The style of popular vocal and keyboard music offered for sale was not markedly different from that of the classical music of the era, merely simpler in structure and less technically demanding. The rise of American music education soon contributed to a sharp increase in the market for sheet music for home use, and eventually to a much clearer distinction between the styles of art and popular music.

The first singing-schools, led in New England by William Billings and his contemporaries, brought basic musical literacy to great numbers of people who had formerly had no musical instruction; in the early 19th century singing-schools spread to large areas of the South and West. At the same time instruction in music became common in private schools for women; musical literacy was seen as a desirable social attribute, and as a symbol of culture and refinement. Many academies and "female seminaries" helped the American woman to "attain a moderate execution of music, with correct time and pure taste, so as to please others and amuse herself" (*Thoughts on Domestic Education*, 1829).

In the second and third decades of the 19th century, a group of New Englanders led by Hastings and Lowell Mason set out to "elevate the taste" of the public and develop more effective methods of "scientific" instruction in music. The Boston Academy of Music (established 1833) was dedicated to offering musical instruction to as many citizens as possible, and became a model for similar institutions elsewhere. In 1837 the Boston School Committee authorized music instruction in the city's public-school system, and sought guidance from Mason and the Boston Academy. Within a few years Mason could remark that "A multitude of young persons have been raised up who are much better able to appreciate and to perform music than were their fathers." Most musical instruction was in sacred and secular vocal ensemble music, and the first public evidence of the USA's growing musical sophistication came in performances of large choral works by Boston's Handel and Haydn Society and similar organizations in other cities. At the same time singing and playing from sheet music in the home became widespread, thanks to the increase in the numbers of people who had learned basic musical skills.

The early 19th century saw a sharp increase in the quality and quantity of pianos constructed in the USA; at the same time changes in the economic life of the country made it possible for more people to own such instruments. By 1830 2500 pianos were being manufactured every year; a significant proportion of the population owned or had access to a piano, and sheet music sold in ever larger quantities for use in the home.

2. The first American songwriters. Francis Hopkinson wrote songs as early as 1759, and his *Seven Songs for the Harpsichord* (1788) was one of the first publications of secular music in the new republic. In the last decade of the 18th century about 50 secular songs by musicians living in New England were published in *The American Musical Miscellany* (1798) and in such periodicals as the *Massachusetts Magazine*. Oliver Shaw of Providence composed dozens of songs in the first decades of the 19th century, several of which (for example, *Mary's Tears* and *There's nothing true but heav'n*, both settings of sacred poems by Thomas Moore) were published, sold, and sung throughout the country. These were solidly in the mold of the English songs of the day, as were the early songs of John Hill Hewitt, including his remarkably successful *The Minstrel's Return'd from the War* (?1828), strongly reminiscent of *The Wounded Hussar* by James Hewitt, his father.

3. Songs of the minstrel stage. In ballad and comic operas the black slave sometimes appeared as a minor character, singing songs considered appropriate, in their music and texts, to his role; two examples are Stephen Storace's "Poor Black Boy" (from *The Prize*, 1793) and Charles Dibdin's *Yanko Dear*, which have deliberately simplistic music (though they have nothing to do with authentic African styles) and lyrics in heavy dialect. Charles Mathews, an English stage comedian who came to the USA in 1822, was fascinated by the speech patterns and physical characteristics of American Blacks; his subsequent incorporation into his popular stage acts of skits, mock lectures, and songs drawing on black material was largely responsible for the increasing trend towards stage impersonation of black characters. By the late 1820s several American entertainers – George Nichols, Bob Farrell, and George Washington Dixon – were making use of comic "negro" songs, many of them published as sheet music. *The Coal*

Black Rose and *Long Tail Blue* were popularized by Dixon; others were *De Boatman's Dance*, *Clare de Kitchen*, and *Zip Coon* (*c*1834), which became popular as *Turkey in the Straw*.

In 1828 Thomas Dartmouth ("Daddy") Rice introduced the song *Jim Crow* to audiences in the Midwest as part of his impersonation of an old black man performing a comic shuffling dance; this piece enjoyed immediate success on the stage and, from 1829, as sheet music. Rice was acclaimed in Cincinnati, Pittsburgh, Baltimore, Washington, New York, and, eventually, London. Other white entertainers impersonated Blacks in the popular theater and, beginning with the Virginia Minstrels in 1843, entire troupes did so as well, the performers appearing with blackened faces. Christy's Minstrels, the Kentucky Minstrels, the Ethiopian Serenaders, and the Sable Harmonists were a few of the groups offering shows made up of comic dialogues and skits interspersed with dance and song, all supposedly reflecting the culture and character of American Blacks. By mid-century these minstrel shows had become the most popular and distinctive product of the American stage; they reached a new peak of popularity after the Civil War, were widely admired and imitated abroad, and persisted well into the 20th century (*see* MINSTRELSY).

1. *Title page of "Music of the Ethiopian Serenaders," published in New York in 1847*

The English, when introduced to the minstrelsy of Rice (1836) and the Virginia Minstrels (1843), viewed these entertainments as a purely American form of musical theater, and regarded minstrel songs as the first characteristically American music of any sort. In fact most minstrel songs were derived from music brought to the USA from the British Isles. *Jim Crow*, which Chase called the "first great international song hit of American music," has melodic similarities to English folksong, as do many other early minstrel songs. A handful of them, however (among them *Old Dan Tucker* and *De Boatman's Dance*), are based on repetitive melodic figures possibly taken from slave songs of African origin. Moreover, the central instrument of the minstrel stage, the banjo, had its origins in Africa, and recent research has suggested that its playing style during the first decades of minstrelsy – a style continued into the 20th century in culturally isolated pockets of the South – grew out of the nonharmonic, ostinato patterns played on African chordophones. Thus minstrel song brought together the traditional music of two of the USA's large subcultures: the African slaves and the descendants of English peasantry (*see also* AFRO-AMERICAN MUSIC, §§1 and 2).

The process of preparing minstrel songs for mass distribution in the form of sheet music, which required their transcription into musical notation and a degree of adaptation to the musical tastes of the intended consumers, necessarily obscured much of their distinctive character. Minstrel songs as performed on the stage therefore differed somewhat in style from those sung to piano accompaniment in the American parlor – an early instance of the market shaping the product.

4. SINGING FAMILIES. In 1839–43 the Rainers, an Austrian singing family, performed with great success in the USA; they wore Tyrolean costumes, were influential in popularizing the yodel, and introduced a new song literature to American audiences. Other Tyrolean and Swiss family groups toured the USA in the same period. They were a model for similar American family groups, the most successful of which, the HUTCHINSON family, had a great impact on American popular music. There were 13 Hutchinson children, most of whom sang in church and social gatherings in Milford, New Hampshire. Four of them began performing in villages in New Hampshire and Vermont, then moved on to more important communities such as Saratoga Springs and Albany in New York. In September 1842 they sang in Boston, then gave concerts in Philadelphia, Baltimore, and Washington, where they appeared before President John Tyler in 1844. By then they were the most successful popular entertainers in the country, with dozens of songs in print (mostly brought out by Ditson of Boston), and when they went to England in 1845 they were accepted as further evidence of the USA's growing indigenous popular culture.

At the core of the Hutchinsons' early repertory were sentimental and melodramatic ballads popular in the 1840s, such as *The Snow Storm*, a tale of a young couple freezing to death in a blizzard, and Russell's *The Maniac* and *The Old Sexton*. They were also concerned with social and political issues, and performed such temperance songs as *King Alcohol* and *Cold Water*, and abolitionist songs like *The Bereaved Slave Mother* and *Gone, Sold and Gone*. In 1851 they sang for the first Women's Rights Convention, in Akron, Ohio. In 1855 they performed in Kansas, during the violent, bloody struggle surrounding that territory's admission to the Union, and later they helped to popularize the abolitionist song *John Brown's Body*, and *The Indian's Lament*, which denounced the persecution of American Indians. They campaigned for Lincoln, and performed and published songs on his behalf. After the Civil War a trip to the South brought them into contact with former slaves, whose music so excited them that they began including versions of spirituals, such as *My Jesus says there's room enough*, on their programs. Perhaps their chief contribution to the emerging character of American popular music was their demonstration that song could be as potent a force for arousing public sentiment on controversial issues as political oratory or crusading journalism.

5. STEPHEN FOSTER. Born into an educated and well-to-do family in Pittsburgh in 1826, Foster wrote some of the best-loved songs of the 19th century, and, more than any other songwriter, was responsible for forging a uniquely American style. His first song to be printed was *Open thy lattice, love* (1844); by the time of his death 20 years later he had written about 200 songs. Much has been made of the "folk nature" of his songs, and many did pass into oral tradition; but all were newly composed, and there is no evidence that he had significant contact with any body of folk music. He did have an intimate knowledge of the various sorts of popular music of the day, including minstrel songs; his own first songs in this genre, written in 1847 and 1848 (*Lou'siana Belle*, *Away down South*, *Old Uncle Ned*, and *Oh! Susanna*), have melodic similarities to the standard repertory. Other early songs, such as *Molly! Do you Love me?* and *Stay, summer breath*, reveal his familiarity with the English style of Henry Bishop and his peers. Foster's *The Social Orchestra*, a set of instrumental arrangements for home use, contains pieces by Bellini, Mozart, Michael William Balfe, and Vincent Wallace. He knew the songs of Henry Russell, whom he heard in Pittsburgh, and is known to have been fond of attending the opera. His familiarity with melodies in the Italian style prompted him to imitate them in *The voice of bygone days*, the duet *Wilt thou be gone love?*, and a number of other songs. He was of Irish ancestry, and knew and admired Moore's *A Selection of Irish Melodies*; unmistakable traces of these tunes may be found in a number of his own songs, among them *Sweetly she sleeps, my Alice fair*, *Gentle Annie*, and *Jeanie with the light brown hair* (fig.2).

Foster's songs are astonishingly simple. The melodies are wholly diatonic, built on conjunct motion, and their phrase structure and larger forms are completely symmetrical. They are always in a major key. Harmonies are diatonic, relieved only occasionally by a secondary dominant; many songs, including some of the most familiar ones (*Oh! Susanna* and *Old Folks at Home*), use only tonic, dominant, and subdominant chords. This simplicity does not result from ignorance or poverty of invention: Foster had some knowledge of classical music, and in his early songs, such as *Wilt thou be gone love?*, he sometimes devised more complex melodies and harmonies than he used later. He simply understood, as had no American songwriter before him, that to be universally popular music must be grasped and remembered after only a few hearings, and must be easily performed by those with only rudimentary musical skills. His texts, most of which he wrote himself, are rarely topical, and usually nostalgic. They reflect the events of his own, unhappy life, as well as the longing for a return to a simpler era that was the dominant mood of the period before the Civil War.

Around 1850 Foster began writing a new type of song, the "plantation melody," which synthesized several earlier styles into one that served several generations of American songwriters and came to be widely imitated in Europe. Examples of this new style are *Old Folks at Home*, *My old Kentucky home, good night*, and *Old Dog Tray*. The melodic lines integrate elements of the Irish, Italian, and English styles so successfully that they have a character of their own; the harmonic and melodic language is still completely diatonic, and the accompaniment is further simplified; the verses, for a single voice, are followed by a refrain arranged in three- or four-part harmony. The texts are mostly nostalgic and lamenting, rarely refer specifically to black subjects, and contain no black dialect.

Foster's extreme simplicity of means reflected his decision to write songs that would appeal to the widest possible audience. By the early 1850s several of his songs had sold more than 100,000 copies, and though his share of the profit was small, he decided to give up other employment to devote himself completely to writing music; he was the first American composer to do so.

2. Sheet-music cover of Stephen Foster's "Jeanie with the light brown hair," published in New York in 1854

6. POPULAR PIANO MUSIC. Some of the sheet music published during the early 19th century consisted of pieces for keyboard; publication of marches and dances (mostly waltzes) had begun in the last decade of the 18th century. Some of this repertory was originally composed for keyboard, some was arranged from classical compositions or from pieces written for band or small dance orchestra. Many early waltzes were anonymous, identified only by such labels as "German Waltz" or "Hungarian Waltz." Others were simple arrangements of pieces by European composers such as Beethoven, Mozart, Muzio Clementi, and Johann Nepomuk Hummel; not all of these were waltzes in their original form. Still others were new pieces written in the USA by such composers as Charles Gilfert, who was active in Charleston and New York after his arrival from Europe, Peter K. Moran, who came to New York from Dublin in 1813, and Peter Weldon, the most prolific composer of waltzes in the USA in the first quarter of the century. Whatever their origin, all these waltzes resemble one another in that they are simple pieces with several strains, capable of being played by amateur musicians of modest technique.

Other social dances also appeared in sheet-music form: first minuets, then reels and country dances used for the widely popular cotillion, and, in the early 1840s, polkas, brought to the USA from central Europe. The schottische, mazurka, and polka redowa soon followed. The keyboard repertory also included descriptive BATTLE MUSIC (František Kočzwara's *The Battle of Prague* was a favorite, and was imitated by James Hewitt in *The Battle of Trenton*), variations on favorite airs, and various types of program piece and character-piece. As with vocal music in the decades following the Revolution, there was not always a clear distinction between classical and popular piano music; the latter, in fact, often consisted of simplified arrangements of the former. Selections from the classical repertory continued to be performed in the parlor well into the 19th century, just as some singers of popular songs had sufficient technique to sing operatic arias and lieder in their homes. Later in the 19th century there came to be a growing market for short piano works requiring modest technique and little musical sophistication on the part of performers and listeners. Eventually this repertory shifted from European pieces, and native works written in imitation of them, to compositions with a distinctively American character.

7. THE CIVIL WAR PERIOD. The Civil War occurred just as popular music began to reach large numbers of Americans, and as popular songs began to deal with contemporary events and issues. As a result popular music just before and during the war not only concerned itself with political and military events, it also contributed to and affected them. There were great patriotic rallying songs that reflected the political sympathies of millions of people and sought to influence others; these included the *Battle Hymn of the Republic*, *Dixie*, *The Battle Cry of Freedom*, and *The Bonnie Blue Flag*. Other songs narrated military events and individual acts of heroism (*The Drummer Boy of Shiloh*, *Stonewall's Requiem*, *Marching through Georgia*), or treated serious and humorous aspects of life in the army (*Tenting on the Old Camp Ground*, *Goober Peas*). Among the best songs were those that expressed the loneliness, fear, and sorrow of soldiers, their families, and their friends (*When this cruel war is over*, *The Vacant Chair*, and *When Johnny comes marching home*).

All Civil War songs were written or arranged by Americans. Musically, most were cast in the verse–chorus patterns that had been popularized by Foster and widely imitated by his peers and successors, with their choruses set in four-part harmony. Foster's many war songs, however, are not among his best efforts. The most successful songwriters in the North were George Frederick Root, who wrote such popular songs as *The Battle Cry of Freedom* and *Just before the battle, mother*, and Henry Clay Work, who wrote *Wake Nicodemus* and *Marching through Georgia*. John Hill Hewitt was the leading Southern songwriter; his *All Quiet along the Potomac Tonight* is a poignant antiwar song, and like many pieces of the time was equally popular in the South and the North.

In many respects popular music and the traditional oral repertory were closely linked during the war years. A large proportion of Civil War songs consisted of arrangements of traditional Irish, Scottish, and English tunes with new, topical lyrics: *The Bonnie Blue Flag*, the anthem of the Confederacy, uses the tune of *The Irish Jaunting Car*; Gilmore's *We are coming, Father Abraam* is based on *The Wearing of the Green*, and his still popular *When Johnny comes marching home* is a clever reworking of *John Anderson my Jo*, itself an arrangement by Robert Burns of an older traditional tune.

Many songs originated in popular minstrel shows, and a significant number of newly composed songs resembled traditional music in their melodic style; moreover, a number of songs composed during the war years passed quickly into the oral tradition. The Civil War was a "people's war," and it gave rise to a body of popular music that cut across class and ethnic divisions to an unprecedented extent.

See also CONFEDERATE MUSIC, PATRIOTIC MUSIC, and POLITICAL MUSIC.

8. THE POSTWAR YEARS. Many songwriters who first became successful during the war continued to write in the same style in the following years. Work's temperance song *Come home, Father* and his *Grandfather's Clock* (1875) are examples of this tendency, as are *Write me a letter from home* and *We parted by the river side* by Will Hays, whose first successful song had been *The Drummer Boy of Shiloh* (1862). With the exception of a number of songs concerned with temperance and women's rights, the texts of postwar songs were once again devoted to personal rather than public subjects, and musically the period saw little stylistic innovation. Among the most popular songs were H. P. Danks's *Silver threads among the gold* (1872), Thomas Westendorf's *I'll take you home again, Kathleen* (1875), Henry Tucker's *Sweet Genevieve* (1869), Charles A. White's *Put me in my little bed* (1869), Frank Howard's *When the robins nest again* (1883), Banks Winter's *White Wings* (1884), James A. Bland's *Carry me back to old Virginny* (1878), and David Braham's *Over the Hills to the Poor House* (1874).

The minstrel show continued to be the most popular form of American stage entertainment, and for the first time black performers took part, not as members of a racially mixed cast but, beginning with the Georgia Minstrels in 1865, in separate black troupes. Kersands, Lucas, Bland, and Charles B. Hicks were among the successful black minstrel performers. Bland's *Oh, dem golden slippers* and *In the evening by the moonlight* were among the first pieces by a black composer to become widely known in the form of commercial sheet music; stylistically they were virtually indistinguishable from the work of white songwriters. A new type of piece for the minstrel stage, the "minstrel spiritual," developed when vocal groups from black schools, among them the Fisk Jubilee Singers, became popular for their performances of arrangements of prewar spirituals or "shouts"; *Angels, meet me at the cross road* (1875) by Hays and *Oh, dem golden slippers* are examples of this genre (*see* SPIRITUAL, §II). At the same time the popular piano repertory began to reflect certain rhythmic aspects of black music (or, more accurately, white perceptions of them) in a number of character-pieces and "patrols," with their characteristic crescendo and decrescendo plan of dynamics.

The opening of Tony Pastor's Opera House in 1865, in the Bowery area of New York, was the first important step in the development of VAUDEVILLE, a stage genre that eventually eclipsed the minstrel show. The two forms were similar in that both consisted of songs, dances, comic acts, ensemble numbers, and other entertainments unencumbered by a plot. But while the minstrel show ostensibly referred constantly to the culture of the American South, and its music pretended to derive from that of the American Black, vaudeville was an urban, northern product that reflected the new ethnic mix of American cities. Initially most songs of the vaudeville stage were interchangeable with those of the minstrel show, and the minstrel song remained a staple of vaudeville well into the 20th century. Nevertheless vaudeville began developing characteristic song styles almost from its beginnings. David Braham, an English-born composer, was the most successful early vaudeville songwriter; he wrote hundreds of pieces for individual vaudeville entertainers, and for a succession of shows performed by the team of Ned Harrigan and Tony Hart during the 1870s and 1880s.

American popular song of the late 19th century had a wide, varied audience. Songwriters lived and worked in the East, the Midwest, and the South; important music publishers were situated in various regions of the USA; minstrel and variety shows carried the latest repertory to almost every part of the country; musical style was similar to that of a cherished body of song familiar to most of the population; and song texts continued to mine the popular sentiments of nostalgia, faded love, lost youth, and the simple pleasures of pastoral life. The level of musical literacy continued to rise, and revenue from the sale of sheet music accounted for a growing share of the income of music publishers and songwriters.

III. The Tin Pan Alley era

1. The early years. 2. Mainstream developments between the world wars. 3. Traditional and ethnic music. 4. Synthesis with jazz. 5. The end of the era.

1. THE EARLY YEARS. New York became the focus of the popular music industry in the last decade of the 19th century. The city began to play a more important role in musical and theatrical life in general, and a new generation of music publishers brought great energy, ambition, and foresight to their business in the 1880s and 1890s. The most successful publishers were Thomas B. Harms, who brought out his first songs in 1881, Willis Woodward, who formed a business in 1883, and Isidore Witmark, who established M. Witmark & Sons in 1885. They specialized in popular songs, unlike such earlier publishers as Ditson of Boston, who had published a wide range of music, including classical, popular, and religious works, and instructional material. The key to their remarkable commercial success was their sophistication in identifying and appealing to their market; they conducted simple but effective surveys to determine the types of song that sold well, and tested new songs on prospective performers and listeners. "House" songwriters, who worked under contract, adapted their styles to the dictates of the publishers. By the turn of the century most of the successful publishers had offices on West 28th Street; this became known as Tin Pan Alley, supposedly from the sound of the inexpensive upright pianos on which song-pluggers accompanied themselves as they sang their compositions to potential buyers. The term "Tin Pan Alley" was eventually used to refer to the period of American popular music history from the late 19th century to the 1920s, and the style then prevailing.

The first great songwriter of the era was Paul Dresser; his songs are mostly sentimental ballads in the style of the years after the Civil War. *The Pardon that Came too Late* (1891), *Just tell them that you saw me* (1895), *On the Banks of the Wabash* (1899), and *My Gal Sal* (1905) have simple melodies and nostalgic texts like the best songs of Foster, though they employ slightly more complex harmonies, with characteristic chromatic passages (often including a string of secondary dominants) at the approach to cadences.

More typical of the newer style is Charles K. Harris's *After the Ball*, which sold more than five million copies following its publication in 1892. In its first decades Tin Pan Alley produced dozens of such songs, remarkable for their commercial success and their enduring quality: *Daisy Bell* (Harry Dacre, 1892), *The Sidewalks of New York* (Charles Lawlor and James Blake, 1894), *The band played on* (Charles Ward, 1895), *Sweet Rosie O'Grady* (Maude Nugent, 1896), *My wild Irish rose* (Chauncey Olcott, 1899), *A Bird in a Gilded Cage* (Harry Von Tilzer, 1900), *In the good old summertime* (George Evans, 1902), *Sweet Adeline* (Harry Armstrong, 1903), *Give my regards to Broadway* (George M. Cohan, 1904), *In the shade of the old apple tree* (Egbert Van Alstyne, 1905), *Shine on, harvest moon* (Nora Bayes and Jack Norworth, 1908), *Down by the old Millstream* (Tell Taylor, 1910), *Let me call you sweetheart* (Beth Slater Whitson and Leo Friedman, 1910), and *When Irish eyes are smiling* (Ernest R. Ball, 1912). The texts refer mostly to urban life, picture the city as a lively, happy environment, and suggest that the USA was making an easy transition from rural to urban life. The popular image of the "gay nineties" as a carefree, untroubled time was formed in part by this music; Tin Pan Alley's publishers and songwriters were interested in selling songs rather than solving social problems, and found that this could best be accomplished by entertaining people with a product divorced from the unpleasant realities of day-to-day life.

Stylistically most early Tin Pan Alley songs are waltz-songs. A few, based on march rhythms, also bear a relationship to dance music in that the popular two-step dance used music indistinguishable from the march. The songs are strophic, with a succession of verses each followed by a chorus usually of 16 or 32 bars. Throughout the 19th century strophic forms had typically been used for popular songs with both narrative and contemplative texts; some had a brief refrain or chorus at the end of each verse (which often repeated or extended the musical material of the verse), but it was for its verses, not its chorus, that a song was usually known and remembered. In the Tin Pan Alley style, however, the principal melodic material was reserved for the chorus, and as the era progressed this gradually grew longer. The verse began to assume the role of an introduction, and its function became more narrative, establishing a dramatic situation that was treated lyrically in the chorus.

During its early history, the melodic and harmonic vocabulary of popular music was closely linked with that of classical music. Hook, Shield, and Braham had written music in the same style, albeit simplified, as that of contemporary classical composers. The melodies, harmonic progressions, and accompaniments of Bishop, Russell, and John Hill Hewitt are similar to those of Rossini, Bellini, and Mendelssohn. But by the middle of the 19th century the situation had changed: the songs of Foster, Root, and Work in no way approach the harmonic richness or the melodic complexity of Verdi, Chopin, or early Wagner. By the early 20th century the contrast between classical and popular styles was even greater; the songs mentioned above have no affinity with the music of Debussy, the early works of Stravinsky and Schoenberg, or the "Concord" Sonata and Second String Quartet of Ives.

It was precisely the simplicity and accessibility of Tin Pan Alley songs that accounted for their extraordinary popularity. While art music became increasingly complex in its harmony, melody, form, and instrumentation, popular composers continued to work in a common-practice style that was also the vernacular of church, dance, and band music. This style was closer to European music of an earlier time than to any body of folk music; but although it did not derive from traditional music, Tin Pan Alley song became folk music in that, owing to its great popularity, it passed into the oral tradition. Students of folklore have noted that certain elements of the Tin Pan Alley style were absorbed by inhabitants of the rural South and other regions who were musically uneducated immigrants from the British Isles. The same process occurred among Blacks, as can be seen from the role played by popular song in the early stages of jazz.

The early Tin Pan Alley era was also the age of RAGTIME. This was largely an improvised form of music, but some ragtime pieces did become popular as sheet music. The first published rags date from early 1897; Scott Joplin's *Maple Leaf Rag*, the first ragtime piece to enjoy wide commercial success, was published in 1899. For more than a decade the sales of some published piano rags by Joplin, Tom Turpin, and others approached those of Tin Pan Alley songs.

Ragtime's rhythms had a strong influence on American popular song. Its characteristic syncopations were quickly adopted, in simplified form, by songwriters to give their work spice and topical appeal. Coon songs, which used black dialect in their texts and evoked syncopated dances in the accompaniments (*see* COON SONG), were published in large numbers in the 1880s and 1890s, but later gave way to ragtime songs in the Tin Pan Alley style. These included Ben R. Harney's *You've been a good old wagon* (1895), Joe Howard's *Hello my baby* (1899), Hugh Cannon's *Bill Bailey* (1902), *Under the Bamboo Tree* (1902) by Bob Cole, J. Rosamond Johnson, and James Weldon Johnson, and the early songs of Irving Berlin, including *Alexander's Ragtime Band* (1911; fig.3), the most commercially successful example of the genre. By this time the ragtime song was the most popular type of vaudeville music, and sales of sheet music reflected its appeal.

Ragtime played a role in the early days of mechanical sound reproduction. Thomas A. Edison invented the phonograph in 1877, and by 1888 the "talking machine" was sophisticated enough for a recording of music to be attempted. Commercial phonographs and recordings were manufactured in Germany the following year, and in the 1890s, as the Tin Pan Alley era was beginning, the "nickel-in-the-slot" machine, the forerunner of the JUKEBOX of the 20th century, became popular. As recording and playback equipment was not yet sophisticated enough to permit accurate reproduction of the human voice, the first mechanically reproduced popular pieces were instrumental; rags and other syncopated dance tunes, often played by woodwind or brass instruments, were most common. At the same time the player piano was enjoying its first vogue; ragtime pianists made numerous piano rolls, and these became the second medium, after sheet music, through which popular pieces became known.

The first decades of Tin Pan Alley also saw the development of a relatively sophisticated type of popular song, with melodies and harmonies reminiscent of European art music. A leading exponent of the genre was Victor Herbert, whose songs, such as *Ah! Sweet mystery of life*, were often as successful as those of commercial songwriters. The songs of Reginald De Koven ("Oh promise me" from the opera *Robin Hood*, 1890), Ethelbert Nevin (*The Rosary*, 1898), Carrie Jacobs-Bond (*I love you truly*, 1901), and Ernest R. Ball (*Love me and the world is mine*, 1906) are notable for their structural complexity, chromaticism, and elaborate accompaniments; they foreshadow the advanced style of a second generation of Tin Pan Alley songwriters.

A number of important works for the musical stage were written during the Tin Pan Alley era. Unlike earlier shows, which were sequences of unrelated musical numbers, these were based on coherent plots; as such they prefigured the American musical. Among the most important were Cohan's "musical plays," including *Little Johnny Jones* (1904) and *Forty-five Minutes from Broadway* (1906), and a number of stage works with music by Jerome Kern, including *The Red Petticoat* (1912) and *Very Good, Eddie* (1915), one of several shows written for the Princess Theatre.

3. *Sheet-music cover of Irving Berlin's "Alexander's Ragtime Band," first published in 1911*

2. MAINSTREAM DEVELOPMENTS BETWEEN THE WORLD WARS. The period after World War I was marked by innovations that deeply affected the dissemination of popular music. At the turn of the century songs were introduced and popularized principally in musical stage productions (vaudeville, revue, operetta, and musical comedy), and the sale of sheet music was the music industry's main source of revenue. More than 100 American companies manufactured pianos, and most families with some degree of education owned a piano and played popular songs and piano pieces in their homes. As electric sound reproduction became more sophisticated, however, the phonograph disc began challenging the primacy of printed sheet music. In 1919 the song *Mary* by George Stoddard, issued by the Victor firm, sold 300,000 copies without having been performed on the vaudeville stage. Later that year Selvin's Novelty Orchestra recorded for Victor *Dardanella*, with words by Fred Fisher and music by Felix Barnard and Johnny S. Black; more than a million copies of the recording were sold. Whiteman's recording of *Whispering* (1920) more than doubled that figure, and by the mid-1920s it was common for sales of a recording of a song to surpass those of the sheet music. The implications of this trend were not fully grasped by the music industry for some time.

Experiments in the radio transmission of recorded music made by Frank Conrad of the Westinghouse Electric Company led to the establishment of one of the first commercial radio stations, KDKA, in Pittsburgh, in 1920. Within a decade more than 600 commercial stations were in operation, and the number of radio sets in American homes soon reached the millions. From the inception of broadcasting, radio programming emphasized popular music. Many performers whose reputations had been made on the stage moved successfully to the new medium; a new generation of singers adapted their vocal techniques to the new technology, and achieved a more intimate delivery through the use of the microphone (*see* CROONING). "Whispering" Jack Smith, Frank Parker, and Kate Smith were among the most successful radio performers. In 1935 "Your Hit Parade" began offering the most popular songs of the week to a nationwide radio audience of several million, and became a potent force in the popular music industry. (*See also* BROADCASTING.)

Popular music was closely linked with the film industry from 1927, when Al Jolson appeared in *The Jazz Singer*, the first commercial motion picture with continuous sound. *Broadway Melody* (1929) was the first successful MUSICAL FILM; early examples of the genre were little more than filmed versions of Broadway shows, but in the early 1930s Busby Berkeley's *Footlight Parade*, *42nd Street*, and *Gold Diggers of 1933*, with their extravagant production numbers, gave the musical film new dimensions and a distinct character. Songs were also interpolated into many other films. By the mid-1930s motion pictures had become the chief form of American entertainment; some 60 million tickets were sold each week. Film companies engaged hundreds of songwriters, arrangers, and other musicians, for the most part recruited from Broadway and Tin Pan Alley.

The sale of sheet music continued to be the economic mainstay of the popular music industry in the 1920s and 1930s, but phonograph recordings, radio, and film brought popular songs to millions of Americans who could not read music. Increasingly the enjoyment of music took the passive form of listening rather than the active one of performing; a new type of consumer, one with no training in music, emerged and eventually predominated.

The style of popular song remained relatively constant during this period of technological revolution; while composers continually modified the musical means established in the first decades of Tin Pan Alley, they never broke away from them. Songs were cast in common structures and used a common harmonic and melodic vocabulary, which grew progressively closer to the style of such early 20th-century composers as Debussy, Grieg, Fauré, Puccini, and Rachmaninoff. The narrative character of many songs of the 1890s and early 1900s gave way to a lyric or reflective quality. Most songwriters of the second generation of Tin Pan Alley were schooled in European music, or were at least well acquainted with it. Almost all songs consisted of one or two verses, followed by a 32-bar "chorus" cast in four phrases and set in such patterns as *AABA*, *ABAB*, *ABCA*, or *AABC*. The verse was increasingly often omitted in performance and on recordings, and by the 1930s songwriters often did not write verses at all. Harmonically the music was basically triadic, diatonic, and tonal, but individual chords were often more complex, and included seventh and ninth chords, triads with added sixths and seconds, and a wide range of chromatically altered chords. Modulations to remote keys could occur in the second or third section of a song, or even within a phrase. The principal rhythmic characteristic continued to be the syncopations borrowed from American dances; the instrumental backings evoked the scoring of contemporary dance-band music, from the mixed wind and strings of the early 1920s, and the instrumentation of smaller jazz ensembles, to the big bands of the 1930s and 1940s. (*See also* GERSHWIN, GEORGE, §4.)

In the early 1900s, for the first time in almost a century, many stylistic features of American popular song resembled those of art music – not that of Stravinsky, Schoenberg, or Bartók, but that written by composers of the previous generation. Indeed, melodies from the classical repertory were, with some alteration of length, shape, and lyrics, made into successful popular songs, much as melodies by Mozart and Bellini had been adapted a century earlier. As early as 1918 Joseph McCarthy and Harry Carroll transformed a theme from Chopin's Fantaisie-impromptu op.66 into *I'm always chasing rainbows*; in 1920 Puccini's publisher successfully brought a suit against the American publisher of the song *Avalon* by Al Jolson and Vincent Rose, on the grounds that its tune was taken from *Tosca*. In 1939 *The Lamp is Low* was adapted from Ravel's *Pavane pour une infante défunte*, and many songs were reworkings of music by Tchaikovsky, including *Our Love* (1939, taken from *Romeo and Juliet*), and *Tonight we love* (1941, taken from his First Piano Concerto). As Tin Pan Alley strengthened its stylistic ties with European music in general, and the classical repertory in particular, its songs became more closely identified with middle- and upper-class American life, and few of them passed into oral tradition.

Tin Pan Alley's tendency to offer the public a familiar product led to a long period of stylistic equilibrium in American song. The American Society of Composers, Authors and Publishers (ASCAP), organized in 1914 to protect songwriters and publishers from unauthorized public performance of their music, contributed to the climate of stability and orthodoxy. After a number of court actions, a ruling by the US Supreme Court in 1917 allowed ASCAP to collect fees from restaurants, theaters, and other establishments offering live music to their customers. These fees, supplemented by those demanded of recording companies and broadcasters, came to represent a considerable sum. In 1921 $80,000 accrued to the society from performing rights; by the mid-1920s the figure exceeded $10 million. At that time membership of ASCAP was limited to 1000 composers and lyricists and 150 music publishers; new members were selected by the society itself, which insured a certain conformity of attitudes and musical styles.

Of the individual songwriters of the period, Irving Berlin must be considered first. His songs span almost the entire age of Tin Pan Alley, from 1907 to the 1950s; stylistically they range from rags and waltzes early in his career to more sophisticated ballads in his mature period. He is regarded by many as the most talented songwriter and lyricist of his age. Among his most famous songs, most of which were written for inclusion in stage revues and films, are, besides *Alexander's Ragtime Band*, *God bless America* (1918), *Always* (1925), *How deep is the ocean?* (1932), and *White Christmas* (1942), which is perhaps the most commercially successful American popular song of all time. His stage musicals, which include the *Ziegfeld Follies of 1919*, *1920*, and *1927*, the *Music Box Revues* (1921–4), *Face the Music* (1932), *Louisiana Purchase* (1940), and *Annie Get your Gun* (1946), contain many more, such as "Oh! how I hate to get up in the morning" (*Yip, Yip, Yaphank*, 1918) and "Easter Parade" (*As Thousands Cheer*, 1933). These and many other songs by Berlin were performed on the

4. Bing Crosby, 1935

stage, on the radio, and in films, by such leading entertainers as Irene and Vernon Castle, Eddie Cantor, Fanny Brice, W. C. Fields, Grace Moore, Ethel Waters, Ethel Merman, Al Jolson, Ginger Rogers and Fred Astaire, Rudy Vallee, Bing Crosby, Bob Hope, and Judy Garland.

Jerome Kern wrote many songs, mostly for musicals and films, that achieved great critical and popular success. They include "Look for the silver lining" (from *Sally*, 1920), "Ol' man river" (*Show Boat*, 1927), "Smoke gets in your eyes" (*Roberta*, 1933) and "The last time I saw Paris" (*Lady be Good*, 1941). George Gershwin was one of the most talented, successful composers of the era; most of his songs, also, were written for revues, musicals, or films, among them "Somebody loves me" (1924), "Embraceable you" (1930), and "The man I love" (1924). Cole Porter's best songs, written for stage musicals and films from the late 1920s, include "What is this thing called love?" (*Wake Up and Dream*, 1929), "Night and Day" (*Gay Divorce*, 1932), "Begin the Beguine" (*Jubilee*, 1935), and "So in love am I" (*Kiss me, Kate*, 1948). Richard Rodgers collaborated with the lyricist Lorenz Hart on a number of musicals, which included many successful songs; after Hart's death, he wrote three of the most popular musicals of the century with Oscar Hammerstein II: *Oklahoma!* (1943), *Carousel* (1945), and *South Pacific* (1949). Each contained songs that became standards, including "O what a beautiful mornin'," "If I loved you," and "Some enchanted evening." Among the other successful songs of the era were Harold Arlen's *Over the Rainbow* (1939) and *That old black magic* (1942), Vincent Youmans's *Tea for two* (1924), Jimmy McHugh's *I can't give you anything but love* (1928), Hoagy Carmichael's *Stardust* (1929), Arthur Schwartz's *You and the night and the music* (1934), and Harry Warren's *Lullaby of Broadway* (1935) and *You'll never know* (1943).

In the first two decades of the 20th century the majority of Tin Pan Alley's successful songwriters were Jewish, and many of them were immigrants or first-generation Americans. A significant number of black songwriters also figured prominently in Tin Pan Alley. Gussie Lord Davis (1863–99) wrote a number of successful songs, notably *In the Baggage Coach Ahead* (1896), of which more than a million copies were sold. A succession of musical comedies written and performed by Blacks yielded many songs that enjoyed commercial success, including *Who dat say chicken* (1898) by Paul Laurence Dunbar and Will Marion Cook, *My Castle on the Nile* (1901) by James Weldon Johnson and Bob Cole, *Under the Bamboo Tree* (1902) by Cole, Johnson, and J. Rosamond Johnson, and "In Honeysuckle Time" and "I'm just wild about Harry" from the revue *Shuffle Along* (1921) by Noble Sissle and Eubie Blake. Black composers continued to write enduring songs in the latter decades of Tin Pan Alley; some typical examples are *Honeysuckle Rose* (1929) by Fats Waller and a number of songs by Duke Ellington (often with lyrics by white writers), such as *Mood Indigo* (1931), *Solitude* (1934), and *Don't get around much anymore* (1942). Stylistically these songs resemble those of white Tin Pan Alley writers, even when they borrow rhythmic devices from ragtime and jazz.

Tin Pan Alley exemplified the conviction, developed as far back as the 1890s, that popular music was intended to entertain and must therefore avoid all difficult, painful, and controversial subjects. The USA's involvement in World War I produced a scattering of war songs – patriotic (Cohan's *Over there!*, 1917), humorous (Berlin's *Oh! how I hate to get up in the morning*, 1918), or sentimental (Richard A. Whiting's *Till we meet again*, 1918) – but in general popular songs were concerned with personal, not public, matters. The cataclysmic events of the 1920s and 1930s – the Depression, the rise of totalitarian governments in Europe, the outbreak of World War II – were largely ignored by American songwriters, who continued to write love-songs the tone of which was governed by the customs and mores of the mainstream of white American society. Even the USA's entry into the war inspired only a few topical songs, such as *Praise the Lord and pass the ammunition* (1942) by Frank Loesser, *I left my heart at the stage door canteen* (1942) by Berlin, and *They're either too young or too old* (1943) by Loesser and Schwartz. Popular songs about World War II were either patriotic or humorous; one would not know, from even a careful reading of song lyrics written between 1941 and 1945, that a single American had been killed or wounded in battle.

The work of Berlin, Kern, Gershwin, and their peers was popular throughout the world: in western Europe, in central Europe and the Balkans among the upper classes, and in the Third World among citizens of the colonizing nations. But, as in the USA, the popularity of their songs rarely extended to the lower classes. A number of European songwriters wrote songs in the Tin Pan Alley style, but with only a few exceptions, such as *Red sails in the sunset* (1935) by the Britons Jimmy Kennedy and Hugh Williams, they enjoyed little success in the USA.

The years between the two world wars were a transitional period, during which the established music industry, still dominated by large publishers of sheet music, defined "popular music" in terms not only of sales but also of musical style; a Tin Pan Alley song was "popular" because of its musical idiom, whether or not it was financially successful. Technology brought popular music to a wider audience than ever before, but the style and content of the music remained essentially unchanged from before 1920. The important songwriters of the period were white, urban, and oriented towards the European style. At the same time a number of ethnic musical styles, derived from the oral tradition, reached new audiences through recordings and broadcasts.

3. Traditional and ethnic music. Wide areas of the rural South and West, particularly the mountainous regions, were populated largely by descendants of English, Irish, and Scottish immigrants, who remained relatively isolated from the mainstream of American life until well into the 20th century, and retained a close connection with their native traditions. The narrative ballad, an important type of secular music among these people, was often concerned with historical or mythical characters and events. Many ballads were variants of those brought over from the British Isles; others were written in the USA in the same general style. They were strophic pieces, often modal or pentatonic, and were originally sung by a single unaccompanied voice; by the 20th century they were often accompanied by banjo, fiddle, or guitar. Dance music, such as reels and hornpipes, was at first played by fiddle or pipe alone, but later banjo and guitar were used as well; many of these tunes, too, had been brought over from the British Isles. A number of composed songs of the 19th century had also passed into the oral tradition, including minstrel songs, many pieces by Foster, and some of the sentimental verse–chorus songs of the decades following the Civil War.

In the early 1920s the music of the rural USA, previously transmitted only through oral tradition, began to be disseminated by the mass media (*see* Country music). Victor, Okeh, and other recording companies issued phonograph discs of "old-time music" that were distributed regionally, and radio stations in the South, Midwest, and Southwest offered live programs devoted to the music. Individual performers and groups began to command wide audiences and sell significant numbers of recordings; among the most important were Fiddlin' John Carson, Charlie Poole, Uncle Dave Macon, Riley Puckett, and Ernest V. Stoneman. The Carter Family became the most successful early performers of Hillbilly music. This consisted of solo singing, alternating with two- or three-part vocal harmony, accompanied by guitar, autoharp, and sometimes steel or Hawaiian guitar. Their repertory drew on traditional songs and ballads, composed songs of the 19th century, and new pieces in traditional styles. Jimmie Rodgers developed a more urban style; he sang mostly newly composed songs that combined traditional elements with traces of mainstream popular music and even blues. The next generation of performers, which included Roy Acuff, Gene Autry, Bob Wills, Ernest Tubb, and Hank Williams, followed Rodgers's lead in forging a distinctive country-music style that retained some of the vocal timbre and instrumental sound of older music but made use of modern resources; among these were chord-playing instruments, which soon included the electric guitar; a rhythm section, which was unusual in traditional Anglo-American music; and a firm, sometimes sophisticated harmonic language. The distinctive sound of the music of the rural South was, for the most part, unacceptable to listeners accustomed to Tin Pin Alley songs. It can be considered as popular music, however, because of its wide currency and because most of its performers sought a national style that transcended regional differences.

The recording and broadcasting industries discovered another type of ethnic music in the early 1920s, that of black Americans. In 1920 the Blues singer Mamie Smith recorded a historic disc consisting of *That thing called love* and *You can't keep a good man down*; this was followed by a large number of blues, jazz, and religious recordings, released by both large and small companies. The music was extremely varied: it encompassed blues singing accompanied by a single chord-playing instrument; rhythmic blues, or boogie-woogie, played on the piano (*see* Boogie-woogie (i)); Jazz played by small and large ensembles; and religious pieces, inspired by 19th-century spirituals, sung either by male quartets and quintets, or – in the form that became known as gospel music (*see* Gospel music, §II) – by solo singers backed by a chorus and instruments. The recording industry classified all this black music as "race" music, and distinguished it from the popular music of Tin Pan Alley by listing it in separate catalogues (fig.5). Yet its wide distribution and large audience (soon numbering millions) brought it into the body of popular music.

Other types of regional and ethnic music disseminated by recording companies and radio stations included the distinctive music of the French-speaking Cajuns of Louisiana, and the songs and instrumental music of Slavic, Mediterranean, and Scandinavian immigrants in American cities (*see* European-American music).

4. Synthesis with jazz. Many Tin Pan Alley composers (particularly Gershwin, Arlen, and Berlin) listened with interest to the syncopated dance music and early jazz of black Americans, and incorporated rhythmic and melodic elements of these repertories into their own pieces. Conversely, many black composers and performers, especially those active in New York, drew on

5. *Advertisement for the Okeh company's race record catalogue*

the musical style and repertory of Tin Pan Alley. Some of the songs in Sissle's and Blake's black revue *Shuffle Along* are indistinguishable in general style from some of those by Berlin and other white composers, though their spirit and vitality owe much to earlier Afro-American music. The songs of Waller and Ellington (see §2 above) are among the many by black composers of the period that use the formal patterns and harmonic vocabulary of Tin Pan Alley. Billie Holiday was often labeled a blues singer, yet most of her repertory consisted of songs by such white songwriters as Gershwin, Kern, Porter, Johnny Green, and Johnny Mercer; many other black singers also specialized in Tin Pan Alley, rather than Afro-American, songs.

Throughout the second quarter of the 20th century jazz and Tin Pan Alley were linked by a common repertory. The syncopated dance music of the 1910–20 period and the earliest styles of jazz used sectional, two- or three-strain dance forms and the 12-bar blues. By the mid-1920s, as jazz ensembles increased in size, with many (including those of Ellington, Fletcher Henderson, Chick Webb, and Charles L. Johnson) depending on written arrangements, the repertory began to draw heavily on 32-bar, four-phrase songs. Some of these were written by members of the bands, but many were from the Tin Pan Alley song repertory. In performance the first and last statements of a song were usually played by the entire band; between them, other statements amounted to a succession of improvised solos backed by the rhythm section, and sometimes by repetitive riffs from the band. By the 1930s jazz musicians were expected to know the harmonic design (the "changes") of a core repertory of Tin Pan Alley songs by Gershwin, Green, Waller, Mercer, and others, and virtually every black jazz band (the best-known being those of Count Basie, Jimmie Lunceford, Cab Calloway, Louis Armstrong, Benny Carter, and Lionel Hampton) played versions of them.

White jazz bands with instrumentation and repertory similar to those of black bands were active in the 1920s and into the 1930s. Paul Whiteman was called the "King of Jazz" by New York writers; though recent jazz historians have tended to denigrate his accomplishments, he employed a number of the best white jazz performers of the 1920s, and his black contemporaries admired and emulated his best work. His band sold more recordings than any other group of the decade. Other excellent white bands of the 1920s were led by Jean Goldkette, Ben Pollack, Vincent Lopez, Ben Selvin, Sam Lanin, and Roger Wolfe Kahn, who based their repertory on Tin Pan Alley songs. The Casa Loma Orchestra (fig.6) enjoyed a vogue in the early 1930s; its arranger, Gene Gifford, had learned his art largely from listening to black ensembles. The orchestra's recordings, including *Black Jazz*, *Smoke Rings*, and *White Jazz*, introduced jazz to many white listeners, particularly those of college age, many of whom had never heard a black band. Benny Goodman, with a band of four reed and five brass instruments, and four rhythm players, used arrangements by Benny Carter and Fletcher Henderson, and became the new leader of white jazz in 1934 following a series of nationwide broadcasts. He made such best-selling recordings as *Blue Skies*, *King Porter Stomp*, and *Goody-goody*; the term SWING was coined for this music, probably by a BBC announcer in the early 1930s. The bands of Jimmy and Tommy Dorsey, Artie Shaw, Woody Herman, Harry James, Glenn Miller, and many others soon contributed to the growing popularity of "big-band" music; for almost a decade, beginning in 1935, most best-selling recordings were of this sort of music, including such classics as Goodman's *One O'Clock Jump*, Shaw's *Begin the Beguine*, and Miller's *In the Mood* and *A String of Pearls*.

Stylistically, swing stood between Tin Pan Alley and jazz. Bands often employed one or more singers; among the more notable were Frank Sinatra, Jo Stafford, Doris Day, Perry Como, Billie Holiday, Dick Haymes, Bob Eberle, Helen Ward, Helen Forrest, and Bing Crosby, who all sang mostly slow Tin Pan Alley ballads. Instrumental pieces were usually fast, with the rhythm section maintaining a steady beat, the brass and reeds playing syncopated patterns, and various soloists improvising full or half choruses. The music was of the same sort as that

6. *The Casa Loma Orchestra, 1930*

played by the bands of Ellington, Basie, Lunceford, and Carter, sometimes even using the same arrangements, and the popularity of big-band music brought at least some recognition among white audiences of black jazz bands.

Of all the genres of popular music in the prewar era, big-band swing came closest to representing a successful blend of white and black musical styles. But, with rare exceptions, bands were either white or black, as were their audiences. With the demise of swing after the end of World War II, the stylistic differences between white and black music were again sharpened.

5. THE END OF THE ERA. By 1945 the Tin Pan Alley song had dominated American popular music for more than half a century without undergoing significant changes in style; and although the demand for music had increased owing to the growth of the recording, broadcasting, and motion-picture industries, marketing techniques had essentially changed little since the turn of the century. During World War II, however, a number of forces were set in motion that threatened the prevailing equilibrium.

In 1940 ASCAP attempted to negotiate a new contract with the country's radio networks, to ensure that its control over broadcast music would continue. Radio executives objected to the proposed fee structure, which would have doubled the amount paid to the society. During the stalemate no music protected by ASCAP could be broadcast, and a new organization of songwriters, lyricists, music publishers, and radio stations – Broadcast Music Incorporated (BMI) – was formed. ASCAP settled its differences with its licensees within a year, but by this time it had a competitor in BMI. While some of BMI's songwriters remained faithful to the Tin Pan Alley style, many, some of whom were younger than most ASCAP members, and some of whom had a background in country music, sensed that the country was in a mood for change and explored new idioms. Large numbers of songs were produced that, although not written in an authentic country-music style, evoked the American West; among them were *Deep in the Heart of Texas* (1941) by Don Swander and June Hershey, *Pistol Packin' Mama* (1942) by Al Dexter, and such adaptations of Latin pieces as *Tico-Tico* (1943), a reworking of a song by the Brazilian songwriter Zequinha Abreu. Half a century of stylistic consistency in mainstream popular song soon gave way to variety; the popular repertory became a miscellany of comic songs (Charles Grean's *The Thing*, popularized in 1950 by Phil Harris; *Come on a my House*, written by William Saroyan and Ross Bagdasarian, and sung by Rosemary Clooney, 1951; and Bob Merrill's *That Doggie in the Window*, 1953), cover versions of country songs (Tony Bennett's recording of Hank Williams's *Cold, Cold Heart*, 1951), songs in a cowboy vein (Frankie Laine's *Mule Train*, 1949), instrumental pieces (Anton Karas's theme from the film *The Third Man*, 1949), arrangements of traditional Anglo-American songs (the Weavers' *On top of old Smokey*, 1951), and versions by white performers of pieces first performed by blacks for black audiences (the Crew-Cuts' hit of 1954, *Sh-boom*, which had been recorded by the Chords).

IV. The rock era

1. Rock-and-roll: the background. 2. Rock-and-roll: the music. 3. The folk-music revival. 4. Rock: the background. 5. Rock: the music. 6. Other music of the period. 7. Stylistic pluralism.

1. ROCK-AND-ROLL: THE BACKGROUND. When rock-and-roll emerged in the mid-1950s it met with a good deal of resistance from the established music industry, and from many elements of American society. Notwithstanding their opposition rock-and-roll became the most commercially successful musical genre of the day, and in the early years it cut across cultural lines of demarcation that had never before been breached by a single type of popular music. The advent of rock-and-roll and its impact on American life can best be understood in light of certain cultural currents running through the first half of the 20th century in the USA.

For most of the 19th century immigration to the USA had been dominated by arrivals from the British Isles and northern Europe. This began to change in the early 1880s: millions of immigrants arrived from Italy, Greece, Portugal, and Turkey, central and eastern Europe, and the Far East (the last group settled particularly along the West Coast). In addition internal migration accelerated, chiefly among black Americans who left the South in search of jobs and better social conditions. As a result of these changes many parts of the USA, especially its cities, became more diverse racially and ethnically. Despite this diversity, as late as the mid-1950s the country's institutions continued to be controlled, as they had been for two centuries, by white Anglo-Americans. The tensions caused by these conditions were brought to the fore by the civil rights movement. In 1954 the US Supreme Court prepared the way for the integration of Blacks and Whites in schools by ruling, in *Brown v. Board of Education*, that "separate but equal" schooling was unconstitutional; at the same time black Americans fought for equal voting rights and access to public facilities. Other racial and ethnic minorities, prompted by the Blacks' success, engaged in similar struggles for equality. It was against this background that, in the 1950s, the most radical change in American popular music in more than half a century took place. Significantly, the new style emerged from the music of the country's minority groups, notably its black population.

2. ROCK-AND-ROLL: THE MUSIC. In May 1955 *Rock around the clock* by Bill Haley and the Comets was certified by *Billboard* magazine as the best-selling recording in the country. This confirmed what the music industry and many young Americans had known for some time: that rock-and-roll, a dynamic popular style that was little indebted to the music of Tin Pan Alley, appealed to a large, diverse audience.

The musical characteristics of rock-and-roll were not new in the mid-1950s. Its most distinctive features were its propulsive, dance-like rhythms, articulated chiefly by prominent bass and percussion, which marked heavily the first beat of each 4/4 bar and distinguished the backbeats (the second and fourth) by a different timbre; formal patterns generally based on the 12-bar blues structure; the use of electric guitar and amplification of the other instruments; suggestive lyrics, delivered by a solo vocalist in a rough, jerky, highly embellished style indebted to the tradition of blues singing; and the alternation of vocal lines with instrumental choruses consisting of saxophone, electric guitar, or keyboard improvisations. These features had antecedents in the black popular music (particularly RHYTHM-AND-BLUES) and the country music of the two preceding decades. In fact, many early rock-and-roll hits were merely COVER versions, often by white performers, of rhythm-and-blues songs first recorded by Blacks for black audiences. *Shake, rattle and roll*, Haley's most successful disc before *Rock around the clock*, had been first recorded by Joe Turner. *Hound Dog* had been recorded by Big Mama

7. *Bill Haley and the Comets, c1955*

Thornton in 1953, and had been a rhythm-and-blues hit, but it became known to most white listeners only in 1956, in the version by Elvis Presley. Country musicians, similarly, recorded versions of black songs in the 1940s and 1950s (e.g., Hank Williams, *Mind your own business*, 1949).

Most pieces called "rock-and-roll" in 1955–7 were cover versions of this sort, but from early on the term was applied to a variety of styles. Since rock-and-roll was perceived to have evolved from the music of Blacks and the rural South, other pieces of similar origins that found favor with a mainstream audience, including the work of black vocal ensembles, were also referred to as rock-and-roll whether they shared the vitality of rhythm-and-blues (*Get a Job* by the Silhouettes) or not (*The Great Pretender* and *My Prayer* by the Platters). The jazz-inspired songs of Fats Domino and new versions of Tin Pan Alley songs by black performers were also considered to be rock-and-roll, as was music performed by white singers from the rural South (*I walk the line* by Johnny Cash, and a number of songs by the Everly Brothers), and songs in an older, more conservative style promoted by some elements of the music industry, including those of Pat Boone, Paul Anka, Frankie Avalon, and other "teen idols."

Just as racial integration was challenged and delayed even after the legal changes needed to effect it had been made, so too the interracial character of early rock-and-roll was soon mitigated by conscious design as well as by cultural resistance. From 1956 to 1958 a number of rock-and-roll songs by such white performers as Presley and the Everly Brothers, and by black performers like the Platters, Sam Cooke, and Chuck Berry, did appeal to both black and white listeners, but by the end of the 1950s popular music had largely reverted to the condition that had obtained before 1955, with clear boundaries that were seldom breached between types of music, performers, and audiences. By 1960, five years after the music had been accepted by the industry, few rock-and-roll recordings were being made. Instead the mainstream market was largely dominated by music that took superficial elements of the early rock-and-roll style and incorporated them into songs otherwise reminiscent of the late Tin Pan Alley era. Examples of the genre are *Everybody's somebody's fool* (1960) by Connie Francis, *Moody River* (1961) by Pat Boone, and *Come softly to me* (1959) by the Fleetwoods; all were major successes on the *Billboard* chart. Similarly, country-music audiences seemed to back away from the heavily rhythmic, raucous, black-influenced brand of early rock-and-roll known as ROCKABILLY, in favor of music in a more traditional country style by Ray Price, Don Gibson, Marty Robbins, and Webb Pierce, and songs by Jim Reeves and Eddy Arnold that epitomized the new NASHVILLE SOUND. Rhythm-and-blues remained an important part of black popular music, but performers such as Ray Charles, James Brown, and Jackie Wilson began to introduce new elements into their songs, which in a few years culminated in a type of music known as "soul" (see §6 below).

The shift away from the musical language of early rock-and-roll was apparent in the work of many performers. Presley first became known as a dynamic, provocative interpreter of such seminal rock-and-roll songs as *Heartbreak Hotel* (1956), *All Shook Up* (1957), and *Jailhouse Rock* (1957), but by the end of the 1950s his greatest successes were much more lyrical songs, often suggestive in musical and poetic style of the late Tin Pan Alley years; among these were *A fool such as I* (1959), *It's now or never* (1960), and *Are you lonesome tonight?* (1960). Jerry Lee Lewis often abandoned rock-and-roll altogether for country songs appealing to a specialized audience. Some black performers who had enjoyed success with white listeners during the first breakthrough of rock-and-roll began to redirect their efforts principally towards Blacks.

By the early 1960s the dynamic, cross-cultural language of early rock-and-roll had virtually disappeared in the USA. There were, however, occasional reminders of its potential appeal. A new dance, the twist, spread through both the black and white communities, sparked by Chubby Checker's *The Twist* (1960), a rhythmic, 12-bar blues that contained all the basic elements of rock-and-roll. The Beach Boys, a group from California, developed a style known as SURF MUSIC, based on a combination of rock-and-roll and the vocal ensemble singing of black DOO-WOP groups. They performed their own songs, as well as older ones by Chuck Berry, and by 1963 were one of the most popular groups in the country, with three successful albums and a number of hit singles to their credit. Still the music industry clung to its notion that interest in rock-and-roll had been contained and that the music it was offering in its stead (and often in its name) was preferred by American audiences.

The falseness of this assumption was laid bare, however, when in 1964 the Beatles and then other British groups burst onto the American musical scene with such force that American performers had to struggle for their survival. After their first single recording, *I want to hold your hand*, was released in the USA in early 1964, the Beatles dominated record sales and radio play in an unprecedented way. At the peak of their first success their recordings accounted for 60% of all sales; in April 1964 the top five songs on the *Billboard* chart were all by the Beatles, as were the two best-selling albums. The Dave Clark Five, Herman's Hermits, the Rolling Stones, The Who, and other British groups soon enjoyed almost as great a success in the USA, and for several years it appeared that American performers' long-standing dominance of rock-and-roll had come to an end, even in their own country.

Ironically, the music of the "British invasion" was firmly based on American rock-and-roll and its antecedents. The Beatles had begun by playing mostly cover versions of rock-and-roll, rhythm-and-blues, and country music of the 1950s. Although their repertory gradually shifted to their own songs, written by John Lennon and Paul McCartney, their style retained all the elements of early rock-and-roll, from the obsessive "big beat" of drums and electric bass guitar to the clean, amplified sound of a small instrumental ensemble dominated by drum and guitars. British groups of the early 1960s developed some characteristics of their own, but still their music was essentially rhythm-and-blues or rock-and-roll. The Beatles' success was due above all to their talent as songwriters and performers, but they were popular also because they played in a style that had widespread appeal but had been largely suppressed by the American music industry.

3. THE FOLK-MUSIC REVIVAL. In the 1930s and 1940s a handful of American musicians sang contemporary versions of Anglo-American folk songs to small but loyal audiences in college communities and urban areas; among the most successful performers were Burl Ives, John Jacob Niles, and, somewhat later, Pete Seeger. At the same time a politically oriented movement led by Woody Guthrie, Will Geer, Alan Lomax, and Seeger (and sometimes including Aunt Molly Jackson, Leadbelly, and other traditional performers as well) used folk music to publicize the deprived conditions under which many Americans lived, and to rally support for political activity aimed at attacking these problems. Guthrie, whose recording *Dust Bowl Ballads* (1940) is an early and outstanding example of the genre, and the Weavers fashioned new pieces by adding political texts to traditional tunes; they used guitars and banjos for accompaniment, and performed at labor rallies and other gatherings.

The political folksong movement crumbled in the early 1950s, as the Cold War led to attacks on leftist activity by reactionary political forces. But the commercial potential of refined arrangements of traditional tunes had been demonstrated by the Weavers in a series of discs made with Gordon Jenkins and his Orchestra. One of these, *Goodnight Irene*, had become a best-selling recording in the summer of 1950, just before the Weavers were blacklisted by the music industry for their earlier political stance. Later, passions cooled to some extent and folk music was no longer necessarily regarded with suspicion; other singers began to perform and record smoothly arranged, apolitical versions of traditional songs and ballads. The Kingston Trio, three well-groomed college students who had no direct connection with traditional Anglo-American music, caused a sensation with their version of *Tom Dooley* in 1958, and for some years their recordings outsold even those of the most popular rock-and-roll performers. Another vocal group, Peter, Paul and Mary, enjoyed similar success. Harry Belafonte drew on a more international folk repertory, including that of the Caribbean. Other urban performers contributed to the popularity of the folk movement, which coexisted with rock-and-roll well into the 1960s. This strain of popular music appealed to a slightly older, more affluent audience, and was disseminated principally in the form of LP discs, which became more affordable as the USA's economy expanded.

The arrival in New York of Bob Dylan, a young singer from Minnesota, brought a change of direction to the urban folk movement. He idolized Woody Guthrie, and had gone east to seek

8. Bob Dylan, 1965

him out. After only a few performances at folk clubs, Dylan was granted a recording contract, and made his first recording, an album entitled *Bob Dylan*, in 1962. He made highly acclaimed appearances at the Monterey and Newport folk festivals; in 1963 two more albums, *Freewheelin' Bob Dylan* and *The Times they are a-Changin'*, established him as an important, innovative figure in American popular music. He sang in a rasping, declamatory voice, in contrast with the smooth, trained voices of earlier urban folksingers, and provided his own instrumental backing on guitar and harmonica. His songs combined elements of country music, blues, and rock-and-roll; their texts were biting, satirical, intensely personal commentaries on his own life and the world around him. Their language was idiosyncratic and often obscure, but filled with such vivid images that he was often taken seriously as a poet. Although Dylan was rejected by many members of the older generation of politically oriented folk musicians, he accomplished what they had failed to, by introducing millions of listeners to a song style with legitimate roots in traditional American music. He claimed to be apolitical, but his attitudes and the bitterness and cynicism of his song lyrics colored the views of a generation of young people, whose political activism greatly influenced American life in the later 1960s. His success helped to prepare the way for Joan Baez, Phil Ochs, Tom Paxton, Gordon Lightfoot, Judy Collins, and many other folk performers.

Although many of Dylan's early songs were adaptations of traditional songs and ballads, as early as 1963 his repertory was almost wholly original. He rarely had recourse to folk materials after this time, but his vocal style and accompaniments continued to draw on traditional music, and his compositions – including such strikingly original pieces as *Don't think twice, it's all right*, *Masters of War*, *Only a pawn in their game*, *Blowin' in the wind*, *One too many mornings*, and *Mr. Tambourine Man* – were still referred to as "folksongs." Other performers of the era, including Paul Simon and the group Peter, Paul and Mary, followed his lead in writing their own songs rather than adapting older ones. The term "folksong" acquired a new meaning: a newly composed piece, usually in strophic, narrative form, sung by one or more solo voices accompanied by acoustic guitar and, sometimes, other instruments associated with traditional music. Throughout the 1960s and into the 1970s folksongs of this sort, written and performed by Paul Simon, Joni Mitchell, Kris Kristofferson, John Prine, Steve Goodman, Randy Newman, and many others, challenged the supremacy of other types of popular music in terms of record sales and radio play; they seemed to many critics to be as distinctively American, and of as high a quality, as the best of rock-and-roll. Folk-music audiences were predominantly white, urban, and somewhat older than other popular-music audiences; folksinging appealed to many adults who had rejected rock-and-roll. Although this folk repertory had at least an indirect link with traditional Anglo-American music, country-music performers and their audiences had no interest in it, and black Americans were, by and large, indifferent to it as well. Thus the emergence of urban folksong contributed to the factionalism that had prevailed among popular-music listeners from the early days of rock-and-roll.

4. ROCK: THE BACKGROUND. ROCK, as opposed to rock-and-roll, eludes definition as a single musical style; rather it is a conglomeration of styles, unified by a common spirit, a common environment, and a common audience. There could be no single musical definition for a repertory encompassing, for example, Joni Mitchell, Sly and the Family Stone, Jefferson Airplane, Jimi Hendrix, Paul Simon, Creedence Clearwater Revival, and Janis Joplin. The music of these and many other performers, however, came to be understood by its listeners as forming a single repertory.

The rise of rock in the 1960s cannot be viewed apart from socio-political events of the time. This was a period when many small countries sought to escape domination by larger or stronger nations, when various racial and ethnic groups fought to overcome historical patterns of repression and persecution, and when individuals in many parts of the world began to liberate themselves from social, cultural, political, and sexual constraints. Instantaneous, worldwide communication led groups that were widely separated geographically and ideologically to identify with one another; student demonstrations in Paris, Berkeley, Warsaw, New York, and Berlin were part of a global movement, and were in turn linked to a large, loosely formed network of politically repressed ethnic groups, small countries, and individuals throughout the world. Almost without exception, rock musicians allied themselves with this curious coalition, and their music became an integral part of the many public acts of defiance and rebellion that characterized the 1960s.

Despite this global, idealistic view held by rock performers and their audiences, rock music was dominated from the beginning by white Americans and western Europeans. Within the USA, despite the involvement of a handful of black performers in the formative years of rock, the new style failed to achieve the cross-cultural appeal of early rock-and-roll, and quickly became identified with the white mainstream. This pattern was repeated worldwide: the global dissemination of rock resembled that of Tin Pan Alley music; it was most popular in western Europe and other parts of the world closely identified with the West, much less so in the Third World.

5. ROCK: THE MUSIC. One of the first important American rock groups was the Byrds. In the mid-1960s they acquired a considerable following with such successful recordings as *Mr. Tambourine Man* (1965, their version of Dylan's song), *Turn! Turn! Turn!* (1965, by Pete Seeger), and their own *Eight Miles High* (1966). The group was to some extent oriented towards traditional American styles, but also used electronic technology to amplify and alter instrumental and vocal sounds. At about the same time a number of bands with similar backgrounds began to flourish in the San Francisco area. They played at community dances and other events involving members of the area's rapidly evolving "alternative" communities; these consisted mostly of young people seeking alternatives to mainstream American life through experimentation with communal living, drugs, Eastern philosophy, rejection of the work ethic, and freer attitudes to politics, sex, and language. Important early groups in the area included the Charlatans, Big Brother and the Holding Company, Country Joe and the Fish, the Great Society, Quicksilver Messenger Service, and Moby Grape.

At first the style of San Francisco rock varied from one group to another and even from one song to the next; some groups were strongly indebted to country and urban folk music, others were influenced by country blues, and still others engaged in free group improvisations. In time, however, certain common elements took shape. Instrumentation became more or less standard: one or more electric guitars (usually divided between lead and rhythm guitar parts when several were used) were supplemented by an electronic keyboard instrument, an electric bass guitar, and drums. The wind instruments sometimes heard in earlier rock-and-roll were almost never used, and the acoustic piano also had virtually no role. Ensemble singing was used to support or augment the voice of the lead singer, or to replace it altogether. Each singer and instrumentalist had a separate microphone and amplification system, but soon the output of each performer was fed into a central mixing board and through increasingly powerful and sensitive amplifiers and loudspeakers. The lead electric guitar took on the role of chief melodic instrument, using new technology that allowed it to play sustained notes and lines with considerable flexibility of timbre, pitch, and volume.

Jefferson Airplane was the first group from the Bay area to bring PSYCHEDELIC ROCK, or "acid" rock, to the rest of the country. The group recorded its first album in 1966, had two hit singles in early 1967 (*Somebody to Love* and *White Rabbit*), and first performed in New York in 1967. The principal recording companies, which had yielded much of their dominance over the music industry by refusing to record early rock-and-roll performers in the mid-1950s, now hastened to sign up and promote rock groups. Within a year many of the best British groups were incorporating elements of San Franciso rock into their music. The Beatles had moved away from their early rock-and-roll style with the albums *Rubber Soul* (1965) and *Revolver* (1966); *Sgt. Pepper's Lonely Hearts Club Band* (1967), their most sophisticated psychedelic recording, was an extremely influential "concept" album that altered the style of rock music for some years. The Rolling Stones were also influenced by the California style, as were the Animals. Eric Clapton, in his recordings with the group Cream, became one of the most influential exponents of a new style of electric guitar playing. The Who likewise abandoned their early rhythm-and-blues style in favor of rock. Rock may therefore be seen as a fusion of British and American popular-music elements, developed by both British and American performers.

Rock lacked the interracial character of early rock-and-roll, and black audiences by and large had little interest in it. But some black musicians were involved in the early stages of rock. Jimi Hendrix established himself as the most innovative and talented guitarist of the era with his first album, *Are you Experienced?* (1967); this and his later albums profoundly influenced other guitarists. The group Sly and the Family Stone often participated in rock concerts and festivals, and made recordings that were important in the early rock repertory. Billy Preston performed with the Beatles just before they disbanded in 1970. In general, however, rock became closely identified with white, Anglo-American culture in the 1970s, and Blacks were little concerned with the music, either as performers or consumers.

Almost from its inception, rock was combined with other genres – jazz, classical music, urban folk music, and country music – to form new hybrids. The singer who wrote his own material became an important force in rock. Dylan incorporated rock elements into his style in the mid-1960s. His *Bringing it All Back Home* (1965) narrowed the distance between rock and urban folksong, and such songs as *Subterranean Homesick Blues* combined the strophic forms and intensely personal lyrics of his earlier work with the instrumentation and rhythmic drive of rock. Paul Simon and many other songwriters followed suit. By the 1970s few people distinguished between rock groups and singer–songwriters, and the urban folk movement had run its course. James Taylor, Bruce Springsteen, and Harry Chapin were accepted as "rock" performers, though their songs were usually dominated by their solo voices, with instruments functioning chiefly as accompaniment and coming to the fore only in breaks between the verses.

There was remarkable continuity in the style of mainstream rock from its inception in the 1960s into the 1980s. This can most clearly be seen by examining the output of two groups that retained their popularity throughout the period: the Grateful Dead and Jefferson Airplane (later Jefferson Starship). Although there were changes in the groups' personnel, and some changes in style (often brought about by innovations in electronic tech-

9. *Jefferson Airplane, c1969*

nology), the entire output of each (spanning about 20 years) stands as a single, coherent repertory. This continuity of style is also apparent in the music of many other groups. The basic rock style did allow for regional variants (notably in California, New York, and the South), and certain performers and groups modified the rock vocabulary to suit their individual tastes and talents. Most rock music, however, is characterized by an instrumental base of electric guitars, bass guitar, keyboard, and drums; a prominent rhythm section; electronic mixing and alteration of sound; sectional song forms, with instrumental breaks (typically played by lead electric guitar) interspersed throughout a song and often bringing it to its musical climax; and vocal lines that are part of the general sound mix rather than the predominant element in it (often with the result that lyrics are difficult to follow).

In the late 1970s PUNK ROCK emerged as a subgenre of rock. Its songs were characterized by brevity, simplicity of means, extremely high levels of amplification, a deliberately crude, amateurish style of playing, and defiant, frequently obscene lyrics. In general punk was less popular in the USA than it was in Britain, where it had originated in certain class conflicts that had no real counterpart in the USA; moreover, a number of American performers, including the Ramones, Iggy Pop, Lou Reed, and Patti Smith, were already playing music that resembled it. Among the best-known American punk groups were X, the Plasmatics, Black Flag, and the Dead Kennedys.

Within a few years punk was largely superseded by NEW WAVE. The distinction between the two genres was not always clear, but in general new wave was less angry and raucous than punk, and somewhat more sophisticated in its music and lyrics. Its performers projected a less threatening image than did punk musicians, and most worked comfortably with the established music industry; many of their songs were accepted by a wide audience. At first new wave was characterized by great simplicity, but by the early 1980s many new-wave groups were making use of synthesized sound and African and Caribbean rhythms. The term "new wave" has been applied to such diverse bands as the Cars, Devo, Blondie, Talking Heads, and the B-52s.

Despite its having its roots in the so-called counterculture of the 1960s, rock music has coexisted comfortably and profitably with the music industry. Recording companies sensed correctly that rock appealed chiefly to affluent, white youth who had the means and inclination to purchase phonographic equipment and discs. From the late 1960s the recording industry channeled a large proportion of its capital and promotion into rock and was rewarded by a decade of steadily increasing sales and profits. Notwithstanding rock music's having grown out of a community with avowedly anti-capitalist views and its continuing to purvey those attitudes, it has become one of the mainstays of the capitalist economy. Far from posing a threat to free enterprise, rock helped to make the manufacture and sale of discs, cassettes, and related products the seventh largest industry in the country.

At its peak in the 1970s, the American music industry produced two-thirds of the discs and cassettes sold worldwide, and Anglo-American rock accounted for a majority of these sales. In less than a decade, however, the American share of the world market dropped, for a number of reasons, to only a third. Advances in recording technology made it possible to produce discs and cassettes of the highest quality virtually anywhere in the world, rather than in only a handful of complex, costly recording studios. Moreover, the stylistic consistency of American rock had led to a period of inertia; more dynamic, innovative music from other parts of the world – REGGAE from Jamaica, punk rock from Britain, and "African pop" from Nigeria – came to be increasingly favored in many countries.

6. OTHER MUSIC OF THE PERIOD. American popular music from 1955 has been dominated, as in earlier times, by music aimed at and listened to by white, middle-class audiences. At the same time other genres and styles associated with smaller, less powerful segments of the population have gained a large audience across much of the country, and thus should also be classified as popular music; although many of these types of popular music are closely identified with certain racial and ethnic groups, the distinctions between musical styles have become increasingly imprecise and the audiences that enjoy them increasingly mixed.

Black Americans have produced a wide variety of popular music, written and performed by a seemingly endless succession of talented musicians. The Motown Record Corporation, established in Detroit and managed by Berry Gordy, Jr., produced a greater number of best-selling recordings in the 1960s than did the Beatles. Gordy was instrumental in advancing the careers of such performers as Smokey Robinson and the Miracles, Marvin Gaye, Mary Wells, the Marvelettes, the Supremes, Martha and the Vandellas, the Temptations, the Four Tops, Stevie Wonder, Gladys Knight and the Pips, the Jackson Five, and Jr. Walker and the All Stars. At first producing the recordings himself, Gordy built his company into one of the most consistently successful operations in the history of the industry; at one point it had the largest gross income of any black enterprise in the USA. Motown recordings were a successful blend of rhythm-and-blues, gospel, and white popular styles. Although the company was at first a regional operation that distributed discs to radio stations and retail outlets in the urban Midwest, Blacks all over the country responded to the MOTOWN style, and soon Whites did so as well. In late 1961 the Marvelettes' version of *Please Mr. Postman* became the best-selling single disc on both the rhythm-and-blues and the pop charts, and even the arrival of the Beatles in 1964 did nothing to check the popularity of Motown artists. Success brought changes of style to many later Motown recordings; they had larger, lusher instrumental backings, including strings (from the Detroit SO) and harps, song forms resembling those of Tin Pan Alley, elaborate studio production, and a less prominent rhythm section than on early issues. When a number of Motown singers gained entry into the white nightclub circuit, it was not so much a result of diminishing racial tensions in the USA as a consequence of their music's appeal to the same audiences that appreciated Frank Sinatra and Tom Jones.

At the same time a number of black performers gained a wide audience while performing in a style that owed less to that of white popular music. Ray Charles and Sam Cooke were instrumental in introducing music influenced by gospel to a secular audience. James Brown's LP recording *The James Brown Show Live at the Apollo* (1963) is considered to have been the first widely successful soul recording, and was the first album to achieve popularity with Blacks, who had previously bought mostly single recordings. The sparser, more controlled style of Stax Records in Memphis created a type of soul music quite different from the lush, exuberant Motown sound, with such artists as Wilson Pickett, Otis Redding, and Booker T. and the MGs. The Stax label was distributed by Atlantic Records, which was also responsible for launching the career of Aretha Franklin. In 1969 *Bill-*

10. *James Brown, c1962*

board changed its designation of music by black performers from "rhythm-and-blues" (a term that had been used for 20 years) to "soul"; eventually this term was used to describe most black popular music. (From 1982 *Billboard* used the label "Black" to describe this music.)

Much SOUL MUSIC of the 1960s was closely associated with the black-power and black-consciousness movements of the period; this was often reflected in the texts of songs performed by soul musicians. The music appealed at first largely to Blacks; the early hit recordings of James Brown (such as *Try me*, 1958, and *Baby, you're right*, 1961), for example, were seldom played by radio stations catering to white audiences. By the mid-1960s, however, as many young, liberal, white listeners began to identify with black concerns, soul often enjoyed equal popularity with both audiences; this trend was epitomized by the success among Whites of Brown's *Say it loud, I'm black and I'm proud*. As soul began to be assimilated by white listeners, many soul singers absorbed elements of white popular styles, and their music in turn gradually lost some of its distinctiveness.

Philadelphia first rivaled, then surpassed, Detroit as the center of elaborately produced pop-soul; such writers and arrangers as Thom Bell and Gamble and Huff furnished material for Jerry Butler, the O'Jays, Harold Melvin and the Blue Notes, the Delfonics, and the Spinners. Other black groups, such as the Ohio Players and Edwin Starr, stressed a more rhythmic style, with insistent, repetitive patterns given out most prominently by the electric bass. The term FUNK began to be used for this style, which had its origins in the harsh, percussive recordings of James Brown in the mid-1960s. It began to dominate the sound of Earth, Wind and Fire, the Trammps, Parliament/ Funkadelic, and Tavares, and spread to such white and mixed groups as K.C. and the Sunshine Band, which in 1975 made two successful recordings, *Get down tonight* and *That's the way I like it*. Both songs reached no.1 on the *Billboard* pop chart and on its soul chart; many other funk songs had similar widespread appeal.

In the mid-1970s DISCO established itself as the most thoroughly interracial music since early rock-and-roll. Disco grew out of the hard rhythms of pop-soul but differed from it in the greater slickness of its performance, and in its increasingly pervasive use of electronic sound modification and electronic instruments. These factors were derived in part from the production techniques of the Philadelphia soul style. At the height of the popularity of disco music white performers gained prominence in a genre that was essentially black; some groups were racially mixed, and the same disco songs frequently appeared on both the pop and soul charts. The album *Saturday Night Fever* (1977), which featured the Bee Gees, was the first by white performers to become a best-selling recording among Blacks (there were several songs by black groups on it).

The appeal of disco, stemming from its insistent, almost hypnotic beat, its appropriateness for dancing, and its use of contemporary electronic techniques in performance and recording, was quickly felt by a wide audience in the USA, Europe, and the Third World. By 1978 it had the largest worldwide audience of any type of American music since the first wave of rock-and-roll just after 1955. Advances in technology and communications facilitated its dissemination and acceptance, but the very factors that contributed to its universal popularity – specifically its directness and extreme simplicity of means – led most listeners to tire of disco after only a few years. As an antidote to the slickness of disco, musicians began to experiment with funk styles once again: Tom Browne's *Funkin' for Jamaica* (1980) stands midway between funk and disco with a more relaxed tempo and a more aggressive beat than authentic disco. Increased use of synthesizers and electronic percussion led to a sharp, cracking beat which came to be known as electro or hip-hop. This new style became the foundation for a genre known as RAP, which, as the 1980s began, emerged from the black street culture of New York. It began as a largely improvised form in which disc jockeys rapidly recited "street poetry" against a background of one or more prerecorded instrumental and rhythm tracks. The earliest recordings were made by the Sugar Hill Gang, Kurtis Blow, and Grandmaster Flash and the Furious Five; the popularity of rap spread quickly across the USA, and elements of the style were soon absorbed by white American and European musicians. In turn, some rap groups began to incorporate aspects of rock into their music in the early 1980s: Run-DMC, for example, made use of heavy metal electric guitar on recordings such as *Rock Box* (see illustration, p.608).

Country music has developed from a group of regional styles transmitted orally in the 19th and early 20th centuries, to a more homogeneous style with wide appeal in the later 20th century; in the process it has lost some of its stylistic and cultural distinctiveness. Early recordings occasionally reconciled the differences between traditional rural styles and urban popular song (Vernon Dahlhart's *The Prisoner's Song*, 1924, was one of the first to do so), but this fusion of styles was only fully accomplished in the 1950s when Nashville emerged as the commercial center of country music; a number of recording companies established studios there, the Country Music Association was formed there in 1958 for the purpose of "improving, marketing, and publicizing" country music, and the "Grand Ole Opry" radio program, broadcast from Nashville since 1925, became the most popular country-music program in the USA.

A succession of commercially successful country-music recordings were made in the 1960s. Under the direction of Chet Atkins, RCA Victor began to issue songs by Jim Reeves (*Four Walls*, 1957; *He'll have to go*, 1959), Eddy Arnold (*A Little Heartache*, 1962; *Make the world go away*, 1965), and Skeeter Davis (*The End*

11. Run-DMC at the Beacon Theatre, New York

of the World, 1963) that incorporated many of the traits of mainstream urban popular music. These were nonnarrative songs concerned mostly with romantic love; the traditional high, nasal vocal quality of country music was replaced by a smoother, more legato line, and accompaniments used strings and humming voices. The new style was popular both with audiences accustomed to traditional country music and listeners who had previously rejected country music as a culturally inferior product. Many older, more conservative listeners found the "country-pop" style a welcome alternative to rock-and-roll and rock music.

Other recording companies followed RCA Victor's lead; Decca had considerable success with Patsy Cline, who sang songs in the same country-pop style. By the late 1960s the stylistic differences between country music and mainstream popular styles had become so indistinct that Glen Campbell could release a series of discs, including *By the time I get to Phoenix* (1967) and *Wichita Lineman* (1968), that resisted classification as one genre or the other. The 1970s brought even further blurring of earlier musical and cultural distinctions; a number of country-music performers, including Johnny Cash, Kenny Rogers, Dolly Parton, Willie Nelson, Crystal Gayle, and Eddie Rabbit, successfully modified their styles to appeal to an urban audience. At the same time listeners accustomed to traditional country music accepted singers whose cultural backgrounds had little to do with their own, but whose discs were produced and promoted as country music; among these were Olivia Newton-John and Linda Ronstadt.

Another section of the audience for popular music, defined largely by age, political orientation, and conservative taste, has been catered for by various kinds of pop and light music widely disseminated by the media and referred to as "easy listening." Though Tin Pan Alley was superseded by a new and more vital body of music from the mid-1950s, the characteristics of these new songs are essentially those of the older style. A number of singers of the Tin Pan Alley era, notably Frank Sinatra, continued to perform and record a repertory of Tin Pan Alley standards, and newer songs in the same vein, for large, enthusiastic audiences. Barbra Streisand, whose first album in 1963 was followed by a series of even more successful ones, further popularized her singing through roles in films and on the musical stage. Barry Manilow made a string of best-selling recordings, beginning in 1974 with *Mandy*, and quickly became one of the most commercially successful musical performers in the USA. By the mid-1970s the audience for this traditional brand of American popular music extended beyond New York and other major cities, and elements of its style began to be found in the music of such rock performers as Billy Joel.

By the mid-1980s ethnic minorities, particularly the Hispanic Americans, were present in sufficient numbers in certain urban centers to make the broadcasting of music suited to their taste profitable for the media. Popular music of Latin origin was therefore beginning to be cultivated commercially in much the same way that black styles had been two decades before.

7. Stylistic pluralism. By the mid-1980s it was both possible and profitable for the popular music industry and the media to cater to the tastes of a number of different groups within the population and to make these different styles available in all parts

of the country. This pluralistic structure is in marked contrast to the earlier patterns of development of popular music in the USA. In the 18th and 19th centuries one style of popular music was disseminated through the medium of print to one class of Americans, while a variety of musically uneducated groups enjoyed a range of orally transmitted repertories. Similarly in the 20th century, from the 1920s to the 1950s, a single mainstream style reached the whole country through sheet music, the phonograph, radio, and film; at the same time regional and ethnic styles became more widely available as they began to exploit recordings and radio as extensions of oral dissemination.

BIBLIOGRAPHY

GENERAL

J. T. Howard: *Our American Music* (New York, 1931, rev. 4/1965)
S. Spaeth: *A History of Popular Music in America* (New York, 1948)
G. Chase: *America's Music* (New York, 1955, rev. 2/1966/*R*1981)
D. Ewen: *Popular American Composers, from Revolutionary Times to the Present* (New York, 1962; suppl. 1972)
W. Mellers: *Music in a New Found Land* (New York, 1964/*R*1975)
J. Rublowsky: *Popular Music* (New York, 1967)
H. W. Hitchcock: *Music in the United States* (Englewood Cliffs, NJ, 1969, rev. 2/1974)
D. Ewen: *All the Years of American Popular Music* (Englewood Cliffs, 1977)
C. Hamm: *Yesterdays: Popular Song in America* (New York, 1979)
R. Middleton and D. Horn, eds.: *Popular Music: a Yearbook* (Cambridge, England, 1981–)
D. Horn and P. Tagg, eds.: *Popular Music Perspectives* (Göteborg, Sweden, and Exeter, England, 1982)
M. W. Booth: *American Popular Music: a Reference Guide* (Westport, CT, 1983)
C. Hamm: *Music in the New World* (New York, 1983)

EARLY AMERICAN SONG AND PIANO MUSIC

T. Williams: *A Discourse on the Life and Death of Oliver Shaw* (Boston, 1851)
W. Chappell: *Popular Music of the Olden Time* (London, 2/1859/*R*1965 in *The Ballad Literature and Popular Music of the Olden Time*)
J. H. Hewitt: *Shadows on the Wall* (Baltimore, 1877)
G. F. Root: *The Story of a Musical Life* (Cincinnati, 1891)
H. Russell: *Cheer Boys, Cheer! Memories of Men and Music* (London, 1895)
J. W. Hutchinson: *Story of the Hutchinsons (Tribe of Jesse)* (Boston, 1896/*R*1977)
O. G. T. Sonneck: *A Bibliography of Early Secular American Music* (Washington, DC, 1905, rev. and enlarged by W. T. Upton 2/1945/*R*1964)
J. M. Chapple: *Heart Songs* (Boston, 1909/*R*1983)
H. V. Milligan: *Stephens Collins Foster* (New York, 1920)
G. C. D. Odell: *Annals of the New York Stage* (New York, 1927–49/*R*1970)
C. Wittke: *Tambo and Bones: a History of the American Minstrel Stage* (Durham, 1930)
S. F. Damon: *Series of Old American Songs, Reproduced in Facsimile* (Providence, RI, 1936)
D. Gilbert: *American Vaudeville: its Life and Times* (New York, 1940)
H. Dichter and E. Shapiro: *Early American Sheet Music: its Lure and its Lore, 1768–1889* (New York, 1941/*R*1977)
E. F. Morneweck: *Chronicles of Stephen Foster's Family* (Pittsburgh, 1944)
E. J. Kahn, Jr.: *The Merry Partners: the Age and Stage of Harrigan and Hart* (New York, 1955)
W. A. Heaps and W. Porter: *The Singing Sixties: the Spirit of Civil War Days Drawn from the Music of the Times* (Norman, OK, 1960)
H. Nathan: *Dan Emmett and the Rise of Early Negro Minstrelsy* (Norman, 1962/*R*1977)
P. Glass and L. C. Singer: *Singing Soldiers: a History of the Civil War in Song* (New York, 1964)
R. J. Wolfe: *Secular Music in America, 1801–1825: a Bibliography* (New York, 1964)
L. S. Levy: *Grace Notes in American History: Popular Sheet Music from 1820 to 1900* (Norman, OK, 1967)
S. Applebaum, ed.: *Show Songs from "The Black Crook" to "The Red Mill": Original Sheet Music for 60 Songs from 50 Shows, 1866–1906* (New York, 1974)
R. C. Toll: *Blacking Up: the Minstrel Show in Nineteenth-century America* (New York, 1974)
W. W. Austin: *"Susanna," "Jeanie," and "The Old Folks at Home": the Songs of Stephen C. Foster from his Time to Ours* (New York, 1975)
J. A. Stephens: *Henry Russell in America: Chutzpah and Huzzah* (diss., U. of Illinois, 1975)
R. Jackson: *Popular Songs of Nineteenth-century America* (New York, 1976)
L. S. Levy: *Picture the Song: Lithographs from the Sheet Music of Nineteenth-century America* (Baltimore, 1976)
R. Crawford, ed.: *The Civil War Songbook: Complete Original Sheet Music for 37 Songs* (New York, 1977)
G. Bordman: *American Operetta* (London, 1980)
H. T. Sampson: *Blacks in Blackface: a Source Book on Early Black Musical Shows* (Metuchen, NJ, 1980)
N. E. Tawa: *Sweet Songs for Gentle Americans: the Parlor Song in America, 1790–1860* (Bowling Green, OH, 1980)
D. L. Root: *American Popular Stage Music, 1860–1880* (Ann Arbor, MI, 1981)
S. Dennison: *Scandalize my Name: Black Imagery in American Popular Music* (New York, 1982)
C. Moseley: "The Maids of Dear Columbia: Images of Young Women in Victorian American Popular Song," *Journal of American Culture*, vi/1 (1983), 18

THE TIN PAN ALLEY ERA

G. M. Cohan: *Twenty Years on Broadway* (New York, 1924)
C. K. Harris: *After the Ball: Forty Years of Melody* (New York, 1926)
P. Dresser: *The Songs of Paul Dresser: with an Introduction by his Brother Theodore Dreiser* (New York, 1927)
J. W. Johnson: *Black Manhattan* (New York, 1930)
E. B. Marks: *They All Sang: from Tony Pastor to Rudy Vallée* (New York, 1934)
I. Witmark: *The Story of the House of Witmark: from Ragtime to Swingtime* (New York, 1939/*R*1976)
E. B. Marks: *They All Had Glamor: from the Swedish Nightingale to the Naked Lady* (New York, 1944/*R*1972)
R. Blesh and H. Janis: *They All Played Ragtime* (New York, 1950, rev. 4/1971)
A. Shaw: *Lingo of Tin Pan Alley* (New York, 1950)
J. Burton: *The Blue Book of Tin Pan Alley* (Watkins Glen, NY, 1951, enlarged 2/1965)
R. Gelatt: *The Fabulous Phonograph: from Edison to Stereo* (Philadelphia, 1954, rev. 2/1965)
H. Meyer: *The Gold in Tin Pan Alley* (Philadelphia and New York, 1958)
H. Pleasants: *Death of a Music?: the Decline of the European Tradition and the Rise of Jazz* (London, 1961)
D. Ewen: *The Life and Death of Tin Pan Alley* (New York, 1964)
N. Shapiro: *Popular Music: an Annotated Index of American Popular Songs* (New York, 1964)
B. C. Malone: *Country Music, U.S.A.: a Fifty-year History* (Austin, 1968)
H. F. Mooney: "Popular Music since the 1920s: the Significance of Shifting Taste," *American Quarterly*, xx (1968), 67
A. Schoener, ed.: *Harlem on my Mind: Cultural Capital of Black America, 1900–1968* (New York, 1968)
M. Williams: *The Jazz Tradition* (New York, 1970, rev. 2/1983)
N. I. Huggins: *Harlem Renaissance* (New York, 1971)
I. Whitcomb: *After the Ball* (London, 1972)
A. Wilder: *American Popular Song: the Great Innovators, 1900–1950* (New York, 1972)
J. R. Williams: *This Was "Your Hit Parade"* (Rockland, ME, 1973)
B. W. Anderson: *Popular American Music: Changes in the Consumption of Sound Recordings, 1940–1955* (thesis, U. of Pennsylvania, 1974)
R. D. Kinkle and N. McCaffrey: *The Complete Encyclopedia of Popular Music and Jazz, 1900–1950* (New Rochelle, NY, 1974)
A. McCarthy: *Big Band Jazz* (London, 1974)
H. Pleasants: *The Great American Popular Singers* (New York, 1974, 2/1985)
B. C. Malone and J. McCulloh, eds.: *Stars of Country Music* (Urbana, IL, 1975)
B. Rust: *The American Dance Band Discography, 1917–1942* (New Rochelle, NY, 1975)
I. Whitcomb: *Tin Pan Alley: a Pictorial History (1919–1939)* (New York, 1975)
I. Howe: *World of our Fathers* (New York, 1976)
R. Pearsall: *Popular Music of the Twenties* (London, 1976)
E. A. Berlin: *Ragtime: a Musical and Cultural History* (Berkeley, CA, 1980/*R*1984 with addns)
L. A. Erenberg: *Steppin' Out: New York Nightlife and the Transformation of American Culture, 1890–1930* (Westport, CT, 1981)
P. Fryer: "Can you Blame the Colored Man: the Topical Song in Black American Popular Music," *Popular Music and Society*, viii/1 (1981), 19
J. Shepherd: *Tin Pan Alley* (London, 1982)

THE ROCK ERA

B. Rosenberg and D. M. White, eds.: *Mass Culture: the Popular Arts in America* (New York, 1957)

J. S. Patterson: *The Folksong Revival and Some Sources of the Popular Image of the Folksinger* (diss., Indiana U., 1963)
A. Beckett: "Popular Music," *New Left Review*, xxxix (1966), 87
D. A. De Turk and A. Poulin, eds.: *The American Folk Scene: Dimensions of the Folksong Revival* (New York, 1967)
C. Belz: *The Story of Rock* (New York, 1969, 2/1972)
D. D. Braun: *Toward a Theory of Popular Culture: the Sociology and History of American Music and Dance* (Ann Arbor, MI, 1969)
R. J. Gleason: *The Jefferson Airplane and the San Francisco Sound* (New York, 1969)
H. Pleasants: *Serious Music and all that Jazz* (London, 1969)
C. Gillett: *The Sound of the City: the Rise of Rock and Roll* (New York, 1970, 2/1972)
R. S. Denisoff: *Great Day Coming: Folk Music and the American Left* (Urbana, IL, 1971)
R. Middleton: *Pop Music and the Blues* (London, 1972)
I. Stambler: *Encyclopedia of Popular Music and Rock* (New York, 1973)
I. Hoare and others: *The Soul Book* (New York, 1975)
G. Marcus: *Mystery Train: Images of America in Rock 'n' Roll Music* (New York, 1975, rev. and enlarged 2/1982)
I. Stambler: *Encyclopedia of Pop, Rock & Soul* (New York, 1975)
T. W. Adorno: *Introduction to the Sociology of Music* (New York, 1976)
P. Hardy and D. Laing: *The Encyclopedia of Rock* (London, 1976)
J. Miller, ed.: *The Rolling Stone Illustrated History of Rock & Roll* (New York, 1976, rev. 2/1980)
S. Chapple and R. Garofalo: *Rock 'n' Roll is Here to Pay: the History and Politics of the Music Industry* (Chicago, 1977)
J. Shepherd, P. Virden, G. Vulliamy, and T. Wishart: *Whose Music?: a Sociology of Musical Languages* (London, 1977)
G. Bordman: *American Musical Theatre: a Chronicle* (New York, 1978)
P. Willis: *Profane Culture* (London, 1978)
B. C. Malone: *Southern Music, American Music* (Lexington, KY, 1979)
J. S. Roberts: *The Latin Tinge: the Impact of Latin American Music on the United States* (New York, 1979)
P. Tagg: *Kojak: 50 Seconds of Television Music* (Göteborg, Sweden, 1979)
D. Harker: *One for the Money: Politics and Popular Song* (London, 1980)
S. Denisoff and J. Bridges: "The Battered and Neglected Orphan: Popular-music Research and Books," *Popular Music and Society*, viii/1 (1981), 43
D. Marsh and J. Swenson: *The New Rolling Stone Record Guide* (New York, 1983)
J. Rockwell: *All American Music: Composition in the Late Twentieth Century* (New York, 1983)
N. Tosches: *Unsung Heroes of Rock 'n' Roll* (New York, 1984)

CHARLES HAMM

Porter, Andrew (*b* Cape Town, South Africa, 26 Aug 1928). British writer on music. From 1947 to 1950 he was organ scholar at University College, Oxford, where he read English. He then embarked on a career in music criticism in London, contributing to several newspapers before joining the *Financial Times* in 1952. There he built up a distinctive tradition of criticism, based on his elegant, spacious, and imaginative literary style – which is always informed by a detailed knowledge of music history and the findings of textual scholarship. He wrote regularly for *Opera* and the *Gramophone*. He was editor of the *Musical Times*, 1960–67. In 1972–3 he spent a concert season in New York as critic of the *New Yorker*; after a year in England, he returned for a longer-term appointment. His *New Yorker* articles, which often discuss new or rarely performed works, have established a standard in readable, scholarly music criticism rarely aspired to by American journalists. Several anthologies of his reviews have appeared in book form. In the USA he undertook some teaching (notably at CUNY and the University of California, Berkeley, where he was Ernest Bloch lecturer, 1980–81) and broadcasting; he also became editor of the newsletter of the American Institute for Verdi Studies and a member of the editorial board of *19th Century Music*. Porter has prepared singing translations of many operas, including Wagner's *Ring*, several works by Verdi, and all Mozart's mature operas, and has supplied librettos for operas by Roger Sessions (*The Emperor's New Clothes*, unfinished at the composer's death) and John Eaton (*The Tempest*, 1985). He has also been involved in directing operas in authentic staging style. As a scholar his work has centered on Verdi, particularly *Don Carlos*, the full original version of which he was principally responsible for rediscovering in the Paris Opéra library, and *Macbeth*, on which he has published a book.

See also CRITICISM, §5.

BIBLIOGRAPHY

P. J. Smith: "American Criticism: the Porter Experience," *19th Century Music*, ii (1978–9), 254

STANLEY SADIE

Porter, Cole (Albert) (*b* Peru, IN, 9 June 1891; *d* Santa Monica, CA, 15 Oct 1964). Songwriter. His parents were wealthy, and his mother, Kate, an accomplished amateur pianist, arranged for him to learn violin from the age of six and piano from the age of eight at the Marion Conservatory, Indiana. Porter began writing melodies – *The Bobolink Waltz* (1902) for piano was his first published work – and contributed words and music for amateur shows at the Worcester (Massachusetts) Academy (1905–9) and for the Dramatic Club at Yale University (1909–13). He sang with and conducted the university glee club and wrote two songs, *Bingo Eli Yale* and *Bulldog*, which remained popular as Yale football songs. For a time he studied law, but in 1915–16 studied harmony and counterpoint at Harvard University. In 1915 two of his songs were performed on Broadway ("Esmerelda" in *Hands Up*, and "Two Big Eyes" in *Miss Information*) and in 1916 he had his first Broadway show, *See America First*, a "patriotic comic opera" modeled on Gilbert and Sullivan; all these shows were failures.

Cole Porter

Porter moved to Paris in 1917 and, in a capricious act (not out of despondency), joined the French Foreign Legion. For almost three years he served in Paris and Fontainebleau and after his discharge in 1919 remained in Paris, married a socialite, and gained a reputation for giving fashionable parties in Paris, Venice, and on the Riviera, attended by the young, wealthy social élite. Meanwhile in 1919 he briefly studied counterpoint, composition, orchestration, and harmony with Vincent d'Indy at the Schola Cantorum. He frequently performed his own songs at his parties; they matched the chic, esoteric mood of his social circle, but were slow to find acceptance in the theater despite performances of *Hitchy-koo of 1919*, *Greenwich Village Follies of 1924*, and *Paris* (1928). In 1923 he wrote music for a ballet, *Within the Quota*, which was introduced in Paris and New York by the Swedish Ballet (revised as *Times Past*, 1970) and is one of the earliest examples of symphonic jazz. Porter first achieved popular success in 1929 with *Wake Up and Dream* in London, and *Fifty Million Frenchmen* in New York. There followed *Gay Divorce* (1932) with Fred Astaire, and *Anything Goes* (1934) and *Panama Hattie* (1940) with Ethel Merman; for these and other song-and-dance musicals (some of which were later filmed) he wrote songs combining witty, often cynical words with what were to become some of his best-known melodies, for example "Let's do it," "Night and Day," "I get a kick out of you," "Begin the Beguine," "Just one of those things," "You're the Top," and "It's De-lovely." He also wrote songs for several films, notably *Born to Dance* (1936) and *Rosalie* (1937), and for revues.

In 1937 Porter was injured in a riding accident on Long Island, which cost him the use of his legs and required the eventual amputation of one, and caused him constant pain for the rest of his life. The demoralizing effect of this and the lack of any success with his songs for the next ten years gave rise to self-doubts and public speculation about his abilities as a songwriter. In 1948, however, he produced his masterpiece, *Kiss Me, Kate*; this musical play, based on Shakespeare's *The Taming of the Shrew*, was a departure from the song-and-dance musical comedies he had written, but it included some eight songs that became immensely popular. Of his later musicals only *Can-can* (1953) was successful. He also wrote songs for films in Hollywood, notably *High Society* (1956), in which Bing Crosby and Grace Kelly sang "True Love"; a film biography with 14 of his songs, called *Night and Day*, was made in 1946. Porter's wife died in 1954 and he became a semirecluse in New York for the last years of his life. Several of his shows were revived in the 1960s, and there have been revues based on his life and work.

Porter was musically one of the most thoroughly trained popular songwriters of the 20th century, though he was perhaps better known as a lyricist; his texts were in the height of fashion, seldom sentimental, and filled with *doubles-entendres* and witty rhymes, even referring directly to sex and drugs. At first his songs were too shocking for the theater (he never wrote for Tin Pan Alley) and they retain much of their freshness. Many of his melodies have chromatic descending lines (e.g., "Let's do it"), or are slow with long lines spun from repetitions, sequences, and variations of single motifs (e.g., "What is this thing called love?"). Many have sections of repeated notes, chromatic figures, or narrow ranges suggesting monotony (e.g., "Ev'rytime we say goodbye"). Porter sometimes wrote for particular performers, first with "Night and Day" for Fred Astaire. He experimented with harmony, used triplet figures within duple meters, and wrote in extended forms unusual in popular song ("Begin the Beguine" is 108 bars long). Wilder (1972) observed that after the mid-1950s the quality of Porter's songs deteriorated, but that until then he had created perhaps the most theatrically elegant, sophisticated, and musically complex songs of American 20th-century popular music.

WORKS

Editions: *The Cole Porter Song Book* (New York, 1959)
The Complete Lyrics of Cole Porter, ed. R. Kimball (New York, 1984)

* – *score not wholly by Porter*

STAGE

Only professional productions are listed. Unless otherwise stated, all works are musicals and dates are those of first New York performance. Vocal scores or selections were published for most works. Book authors are shown in parentheses; lyrics are mostly by Porter. Lists of works are given in Eells, and Kimball and Gill.

*Hands Up, 22 July 1915
*Miss Information, 15 Oct 1915
See America First (T. L. Riggs, Porter), 28 March 1916 [incl. I've a shooting box in Scotland]
*Telling the Tale, London, 1918
*Very Good Eddie, London, 18 May 1918
Hitchy-koo of 1919 (revue, G. V. Hobart), 6 Oct 1919 [incl. Old-fashioned garden]
*Buddies, 27 Oct 1919
*The Eclipse, London, 12 Nov 1919
*As You Were, 27 Jan 1920
*A Night Out, London, 18 Sept 1920
Hitchy-koo of 1922 (revue, H. Atteridge), Philadelphia, 19 Oct 1922
*Mayfair and Montmartre, London, 9 March 1922
*Phi-phi, London, 16 Aug 1922
Within the Quota (ballet), Paris, 25 Oct 1923
Greenwich Village Follies of 1924 (revue), 16 Sept 1924 [incl. I'm in love again]
La revue des ambassadeurs, Paris, 10 May 1928
Paris (M. Brown), 8 Oct 1928 [incl. Let's do it]
Wake up and Dream (revue, J. H. Turner), London, 27 March 1929 [incl. What is this thing called love?]
Fifty Million Frenchmen (H. Fields), 27 Nov 1929 [incl. You do something to me, You've got that thing]
The New Yorkers (Fields, after E. R. Goetz and P. Arno), orchd H. Spialek, 8 Dec 1930 [incl. Love for sale]
Gay Divorce (D. Taylor), orchd Spialek, R. R. Bennett, 29 Nov 1932 [incl. Night and Day]; film as The Gay Divorcee, 1934
Nymph Errant (R. Brent, after J. Laver), orchd Bennett, London, 6 Oct 1933
Anything Goes (G. Bolton, Wodehouse, H. Lindsay, R. Crouse), orchd Bennett, Spialek, 21 Nov 1934 [incl. All through the night; Anything goes; Blow, Gabriel, blow; I get a kick out of you; You're the top]; film, 1936
Jubilee (M. Hart), orchd Bennett, 12 Oct 1935 [incl. Begin the Beguine, Just one of those things]
Red, Hot and Blue (Lindsay, Crouse), orchd Bennett, 29 Oct 1936 [incl. Down in the depths, It's De-lovely, Ridin' high]; film, 1949
*The Sun Never Sets, London, 9 June 1938
You Never Know (R. Leigh), orchd Spialek, 21 Sept 1938 [incl. At long last love]
Leave it to Me (B. and S. Spewack), orchd D. Walker, 9 Nov 1938 [incl. My heart belongs to daddy]
Du Barry was a Lady (Fields, B. DeSylva), orchd Spialek, Bennett, T. Royal, 6 Dec 1939 [incl. Do I love you?, Friendship]; film, 1943
Panama Hattie (Fields, DeSylva), orchd Bennett, Spialek, Walker, 30 Oct 1940 [incl. Let's be buddies, Make it another old fashioned, please]; film, 1942
Let's Face it (H. Fields, D. Fields), orchd Spialek, Walker, Royal, 29 Oct 1941; film, 1944
Something for the Boys (H. Fields, D. Fields), orchd Spialek, Walker, Bennett, Royal, 7 Jan 1943; film, 1944
Mexican Hayride (H. Fields, D. Fields), orchd Bennett, Royal, 28 Jan 1944 [incl. I love you]; film, 1948
Seven Lively Arts (revue), orchd Bennett, Royal, Spialek, 7 Dec 1944 [incl. Ev'ry time we say goodbye]
Around the World in Eighty Days (O. Welles, after J. Verne), orchd Bennett, Royal, 31 May 1946
Kiss Me, Kate (B. and S. Spewack, after Shakespeare: The Taming of the Shrew), orchd Bennett, 30 Dec 1948 [incl. Another op'nin', another show; So in love; Wunderbar]; film, 1953
Out of this World (Taylor, R. Lawrence), orchd Bennett, 21 Dec 1950 [incl. Use your imagination]
Can-can (A. Burrows), orchd P. J. Lang, R. Noeltner, 7 May 1953 [incl. Allez-vous-en, Can-can, C'est magnifique, I love Paris, It's all right with me]; film, 1960
Silk Stockings (G. S. Kaufman, L. McGrath, Burrows), orchd Walker, 24 Feb 1955 [incl. All of you]; film, 1957

FILMS

*The Battle of Paris, 1929
Born to Dance, 1936 [incl. I've got you under my skin]
Rosalie, 1937 [incl. In the still of the night; Rosalie]
*Break the News, 1938
Broadway Melody of 1940, 1940 [incl. I concentrate on you]
You'll Never Get Rich, 1941
Something to Shout About, 1942 [incl. You'd be so nice to come home to]
*Hollywood Canteen, 1944 [incl. Don't fence me in]
Night and Day, 1946
The Pirate, 1948 [incl. Be a clown]
*Adam's Rib, 1949
High Society, 1956 [incl. True Love]
Les Girls, 1957
Aladdin (for television), 1958

OTHER SONGS

Bingo Eli Yale, 1910; Bridget, 1910; Bulldog, 1911; Esmerelda, 1915; Two Big Eyes, 1915; Let's misbehave, *c*1925; The Laziest Gal in Town, 1927; Miss Otis Regrets, 1934; Thank you so much, Mrs. Lowsborough-Goodby, *c*1935; From this moment on, 1950

Principal publishers: Chappell, Harms

BIBLIOGRAPHY

D. Ewen: *The Cole Porter Story* (New York, 1965)
C. Porter and R. Hubler: *The Cole Porter Story* (Cleveland, 1965)
G. Eells: *The Life that Late he Led* (New York, 1967)
R. Kimball and B. Gill: *Cole* (New York, 1971)
L. Smit: "The Classic Cole Porter," *Saturday Review*, l (25 Dec 1971), 48
A. Wilder: *American Popular Song: the Great Innovators, 1900–1950* (New York, 1972)
C. Schwartz: *Cole Porter* (New York, 1977)
J. Johnson: "Cole Porter, 1944–1948: *Don't fence me in*," *Musical Theatre in America: Greenvale, NY 1981*, ed. G. Loney (Westport, CT, 1984), 257

DEANE L. ROOT/GERALD BORDMAN

Porter, Hugh (*b* Heron Lake, MN, 18 Sept 1897; *d* New York, 22 Sept 1960). Organist and educator. The son of a Methodist minister, he received the BM degree from the American Conservatory in Chicago in 1920 and the BA from Northwestern University in 1924. He also studied with Wilhelm Middelschulte, Lynnwood Farnam, T. Tertius Noble, and Nadia Boulanger, and at Union Theological Seminary (MSM 1930, DSM 1944). He taught at Northwestern, the Juilliard School, New York University, the Mannes College, and, from 1931, the School of Sacred Music of Union Theological Seminary. In 1945 he became director there, following Clarence Dickinson, and was Clarence and Helen Dickinson Professor from 1947 until his death. Porter toured as a recitalist, served in many churches (including the Collegiate Church of St. Nicholas in New York), and was organist for several years at the Chautauqua Institution. He and his wife, Ethel K. Porter, were the music editors of the *Pilgrim Hymnal* (1958) of the United Church of Christ. Writing of his special talents, Bingham noted "a keen artistic sense, technical proficiency and mastery of style," and a "thorough knowledge of hymnody and liturgy." Porter died from a heart attack while he was inside the chamber of the new organ at James Memorial Chapel, repairing a cipher.

BIBLIOGRAPHY

S. Bingham: "An Appreciation of Hugh Porter," *The Diapason*, li/12 (1960), 5

VERNON GOTWALS

Porter, (William) Quincy (*b* New Haven, CT, 7 Feb 1897; *d* Bethany, CT, 12 Nov 1966). Composer, violist, and educationist. He studied violin as a child, and began to compose at an early age. At Yale University (BA 1919, BMus 1921) he studied composition with Parker and David Stanley Smith. In 1920 he took lessons in composition with Vincent d'Indy and violin with Lucien Capet in Paris. On returning to the USA in 1921, he studied with Bloch in New York, and later in Cleveland, where he joined the De Ribaupierre Quartet as violist in 1922, and the faculty of the Cleveland Institute as a teacher of music theory in 1923. With the aid of a fellowship from the Guggenheim Foundation, Porter returned to Paris in 1928 for a three-year stay, this time not to study but to compose. During these years in Paris, Porter developed his personal style, and produced the works which first established his reputation – in particular, the Violin Sonata no.2 and the String Quartet no.3, both of which won awards of the Society for the Publication of American Music. In 1932 Porter was appointed professor of music at Vassar College, where he remained until called in 1938 to become dean of the faculty of the New England Conservatory. He succeeded Wallace Goodrich as director of the conservatory in 1942. Porter returned to Yale in 1946 as professor of music, and in 1958 he also became master of Pierson College, a post he held until his retirement in 1965. Among the larger works written at Yale were the Viola Concerto, first performed by Paul Doktor in New York in 1948, and the Concerto concertante, which won the Pulitzer Prize in 1954. In 1943, Porter was awarded the Elizabeth Sprague Coolidge Medal, and the following year he was elected to the National Institute of Arts and Letters.

Porter's personal style was characterized by smooth, scalic melodic movement in a sometimes highly chromatic, polyphonic texture. Although he wrote colorfully for the orchestra, his compositional technique was best adapted to chamber music, a medium in which he remained active as a player all his life. His nine string quartets, together one of the most substantial contributions to that literature made by any American composer, reflect by their fluency and sensitivity the composer's intimate involvement with the genre.

WORKS

(juvenilia, composition exercises, incomplete works, and sketches not listed)

INCIDENTAL MUSIC

A Midsummer Night's Dream (Shakespeare), 1926; The Sunken Bell (Hauptmann), 1926; Sweeney Agonistes (T. S. Eliot), 1933; Antony and Cleopatra (Shakespeare), 1934; Song for a Broken Horn (H. M. Hill), 1952; The Merry Wives of Windsor (Shakespeare), 1954; Music for a Film on Yale Library, 1956; The Mad Woman of Chaillot (Giraudoux), 1957; Music for the Elizabethan Club, 1959, incl. 3 Elizabethan Songs

ORCHESTRAL

Ukrainian Suite, str, 1925; Suite in c, 1926, arr. pf/pf 4 hands/2 pf; Poem and Dance, 1932, arr. 2 pf; Sym. no. 1, 1934, arr. 2 pf; Dance in 3-Time, chamber orch, 1937, arr. 2 pf; 2 Dances for Radio, in 4- and 5-Time, 1938; Music for Str, 1941; Fantasy on a Pastoral Theme, org, str, 1943; The Moving Tide, 1944; Va Conc., 1948, arr. va, pf

The Desolate City (Arabian, trans. W. S. Blunt), Bar, orch, 1950; Fantasy, vc, orch, 1950; Conc. concertante, 2 pf, orch, 1953; New England Episodes, 1958 [based on Music for a Film on Yale Library]; Conc. for Wind Orch (Concertino), 1959; Hpd Conc., 1959; Sym. no.2, 1962; Ohio, ov., 1963

Arrs.: Beethoven: Pf Sonata, op.49 no.2, str; Monteverdi: Orfeo, excerpts, brass, str; J. S. Smith: The Star-Spangled Banner, str

CHAMBER AND INSTRUMENTAL

9 str qts, 1922–3, 1925, 1930, 1931, 1935, 1937, 1943, 1950, 1958

Boutade, pf, 1923; The Cloisters, pf, 1923; Nocturne, pf, 1923; Our Lady of Potchaiv, Ukrainian folksong, str qt, 1923; 2 preludes, str qt, 1923; Scherzo, str qt, 1923; Ukrainian Folk Songs, vn, pf, n.d.; Vn Sonata no.1, 1925–6; In monasterio, str qt, 1927, arr. small orch; Pf Qnt, 1927; Blues lointains, fl, pf, 1928; Counterpoint, str qt, 1928; Little Trio (Suite in E), fl, vn, va, 1928; Berceuse for Little Helen, vn/fl, pf, n.d.; Cl Qnt, 1929; Vn Sonata no.2, 1929; Toccata, Andante & Finale, org, 1929–32; Pf Sonata, 1930; Suite, va, 1930; Fl Qnt on a Childhood Theme, 1937

Lonesome, pf, 1940; Canon and Fugue, org, 1941; Fugue, str qt/ob qt, 1941;

Pony Ride, 2 pf, ?1941; 8 Pieces for Bill, pf, 1941–2, nos.2 and 8 lost; 4 Pieces, vn, pf, 1944–7; Hn Sonata, 1946; Str Sextet on Slavic Folk Songs, 1947; Juilliard Pieces for Str, 1948–9; Divertimento, (2 vn, va)/(ob, vn, va), 1949; Fugue in d, pf/org, 1949; Promenade, pf, 1953; Duo, vn, va, 1954; Nocturne, pf, 1956; Duo, va, harp, 1957; Day Dreams, pf, 1957 [based on 8 Pieces for Bill]; Divertimento, ww qnt, 1960; Hpd Qnt, 1961; Chorale, org, 1963; Variations, vn, pf, 1963; Ob Qnt, 1966

8 other vn, pf, and org pieces; occasional pieces

VOCAL

(1v, pf, unless otherwise stated)

To the Moon (Shelley), 1922; And, like a dying lady (Shelley), 1923, orchd; Go to sleep (Negro song), 1923, arr. Bar, str orch; Music, when soft voices die (Shelley), 1924; The Silent Voices (Tennyson), 1924; 12 Songs for Helen on Nursery Rhymes, 1931, arr. 1v, 4 ww, str orch, 1955; This is the house that Jack built, 1937/8, orchd 1955; Cantata for the Composers' Guild, ?chorus, 1949; Introspections on The Banks o' Doon, 1v, fl, pf, 1955; 2 Songs (A. Porter), 1956; 7 Songs of Love (R. Graves), 1961; Jubilate Deo, men's chorus, org, 1965; [6] Songs for Rose Jackson (P. Colum, Shakespeare), 1966

MSS (incl. juvenilia and composition exercises), tape recordings, and memorabilia in *CtY-Mus*

Principal publishers: ACA, Music Press, Peters, G. Schirmer, Valley Music

BIBLIOGRAPHY

EwenD
H. Elwell: "Quincy Porter," *MM*, xxiii (1946), 20
H. Boatwright: "Quincy Porter," *ACAB*, vi/3 (1957), 2
——: "Quincy Porter (1897–1966)," *PNM*, v/2 (1967), 162

HOWARD BOATWRIGHT/R

Portland (i). City in Maine (pop. 61,572; metropolitan area 183,625). Formal interest in music is first evidenced in 1756, when the First Parish Church voted to raise £25 to purchase an edition of Tate and Brady's psalm book (with tunes annexed); the Second Parish Church installed the city's first church organ in 1798. A short-lived Handel Society of Maine, founded in Portland in 1814, was the first of several musical organizations formed in the first half of the 19th century: the Beethoven Musical Society of Portland, Maine (1819–26), the Handel and Haydn Society (1828–31), the Mozart Musical Society (1832–4), and the Portland Sacred Music Society (1836–54). The last had among its members the music retailer Jacob S. Paine and his brother David, an organist and teacher who compiled the *Portland Sacred Music Society's Collection of Church Music* (1839).

Jacob Paine's son, John Knowles Paine, born in Portland in 1839, was one of the first American composers to write large-scale musical works and the first full professor of music at Harvard University. In 1873 he oversaw the first performance of his oratorio *St. Peter* in Portland; it is thought to be the first such work by an American composer to be performed in the USA. The conductor of the Haydn Association at that event and through much of the organization's existence (1857–96) was Hermann Kotzschmar, who taught Paine and who was himself a composer and organist for the First Parish Church (1851–98). The magnificent organ presented to the city in 1912 by Cyrus H. K. Curtis was installed at the City Hall and named in Kotzschmar's honor. The Kotzschmar Club (formed in 1900) and the Marston Club for women (1887), named after the Portland composer and teacher George Marston, merged in 1965 to form the Marston–Kotzschmar Club. Among other early musical organizations that have remained active are the Portland Rossini Club (founded 1869), which is probably the first musical organization for women in the USA, and the MacDowell Club for women (1908).

The Maine Music Festival, promoted by William R. Chapman, was held annually in Portland and Bangor from 1897 to 1926, with performances by renowned soloists, a large orchestra, and a chorus of over 1000 participants. The Portland Choral Arts Society (formed in 1972) and the Community Chorus (1979) of about 90 members continue the city's strong choral tradition. The Portland Band, organized in 1827 by Jacob Paine, was led from 1843 to 1860 by Daniel Hiram Chandler, who formed his own band in 1876; a group known as Chandler's Band continues to give free summer concerts.

The Portland SO was organized in 1923–4 and incorporated in 1932; it became fully professional in 1953 and engaged its first resident conductor, Arthur Bennett Lipkin, in 1962; Paul Vermel conducted from 1967 to 1975 and Bruce Hangen became director in 1976. The orchestra presents annual series of classical, popular, and children's concerts in the City Hall Auditorium (capacity 2340), which was refurbished in 1968. The Portland SO also sponsors the Community Orchestra of the Portland SO (founded 1967), the Portland Youth Symphony, which was led from 1942 to 1978 by Clinton W. Graffam, and the Portland SO Chamber Orchestra (1977). The Portland Symphony String Quartet (formed in 1969), originally affiliated with the orchestra and in residence at the University of Southern Maine from 1978, was renamed the Portland String Quartet in 1980. Further concert life is provided by the Portland Chamber Music Society, which presented its first series in 1982–3 at the State Street Church, and the Portland Concert Association (founded 1931), which sponsors an annual series of concerts by musicians of international reputation at City Hall. The Cumberland County Civic Center (capacity 8800–9500) opened in 1977 and is used for pop and rock concerts and other musical events.

Although amateur productions of operetta have been given in Portland since the Revolutionary period, it was not until 1974, when Sarah Caldwell's Opera New England of Maine (one of eight regional branches that sponsor productions from the Opera Company of Boston) began presenting fully staged operas in the city, that a professional company could be heard on a regular basis. Co-Opera, a community group designed to foster an interest in the genre, was established in 1976; another community organization, the Portland Lyric Theater, was formed in 1953 to present musicals.

The University of Southern Maine, with campuses in Portland and nearby Gorham, has an active undergraduate music program; a variety of student and faculty ensembles and guest performers bring additional concerts to the area. Westbrook College also sponsors musical programs, as does the Portland Museum of Art. Early local musical groups are documented in the library of the Maine Historical Society and in the Portland Public Library, which also has a special collection of sheet music by Maine composers, as well as a substantial lending collection of sheet and choral music, general music literature, and 5000 recordings.

BIBLIOGRAPHY

S. Freeman, ed.: *Extracts from the Journals kept by the Rev. Thomas Smith* [1720–88] (Portland, ME, 1821, rev. and enlarged W. Willis 2/1849 as *Journals of the Rev. Thomas Smith, and the Rev. Samuel Deane*)
W. Willis: *The History of Portland, from its First Settlement* (Portland, ME, 1831–3, rev. and enlarged 2/1865/*R*1972)
I. Berry: *Sketch of the History of the Beethoven Musical Society of Portland, Maine, 1819–1825* (Portland, ME, 1888)
G. T. Edwards: *Music and Musicians of Maine* (Portland, ME, 1928/*R*1970)
C. P. Small: *Handbook of First Parish Church of Portland* (Portland, ME, 1942)
F. T. Wiggin: *Maine Composers and their Music: a Biographical Dictionary*, i (Rockland, ME, 1959), ii (Portland, ME, 1976)
D. A. Sears: "Music in Early Portland," *Maine Historical Society Quarterly*, xvi/3 (1977), 131

PRISCILLA HUBON McCARTY

Portland (ii). City in Oregon (pop. 366,383; metropolitan area 1,242,594). It was chartered in 1851. Music instruction was provided to settlers in the Oregon Territory by missionaries, among them Narcissa Whitman, a singer who settled across the Columbia River from present-day Portland in 1836. Music was also taught at the city's first school, St. Mary's Academy, founded in 1859. The Pillow and Drew Music Store, Portland's first music retail shop, opened in 1850 and specialized in "pianos of the most celebrated makers," accordions, and sheet music. Many of the city's early musical performances were provided by visiting groups, such as the Oregon City Chorus, which gave a concert in Portland in 1856, and the Bianca Opera Company, which presented Verdi's *Il trovatore* in 1867. Music for weddings and ceremonial occasions was supplied by the Fort Vancouver Post Band until 1898 (the fort itself had been founded across the river in 1848). The band of the Aurora Colony (see illustration), a nearby commune of German immigrants, performed frequently in Portland in the 1860s and 1870s; its instruments and repertory have recently been revived by John Keil Richards.

Among the city's own performing ensembles, the Portland Mechanics Band was founded in 1864, and on 15 June 1866 the Philharmonic Music Society gave its first concert in Oro Fino Hall, the site of musical performances until 1878. An Apollo Club, which existed as early as 1883, continued to give choral concerts until it disbanded around 1960. The Portland SO, the sixth major orchestra to be estabished in the USA and the first in the western USA, was formed in 1896 and renamed the Oregon SO in 1967. Carl Denton was resident conductor from 1918 to 1925, followed by Willem van Hoogstraten (1925–38), Werner Janssen (1947–9), James Sample (1949–53), Theodore Bloomfield (1955–9), Piero Bellugi (1959–61), Jacques Singer (1962–72), Lawrence Leighton Smith (1973–80), and James DePreist (from 1980). In 1924 an informal group of young musicians was organized under the guidance of Mary Dodge as the Portland Junior SO, the first youth orchestra in the USA. It was conducted by the Russian immigrant Jacques Gershkovich until his death in 1953 and from 1954 by Jacob Avshalomov. Renamed the Portland Youth PO in 1979, the orchestra has commissioned and given the world premières of works by Roy Harris, David Diamond, Benjamin Lees, William Bergsma, and others.

Portland had a local opera company from 1917 to 1923. The Opera Association was founded in 1950 and has been under the musical direction of Ariel Rubstein, Eugene Fuerst, Henry Holt, Herbert Weiskopf, and, from 1970 to 1984, Stefan Minde, after which a series of guest conductors was announced. Choral music is provided by the Portland Symphonic Choir (founded 1946) and the Oregon Repertory Singers (1974), and music programs of local importance are offered by the Apostolic Faith Church (which formed its own orchestra in 1921), Trinity Episcopal, the First Presbyterian, and Temple Beth Israel. The Friends of Chamber Music began an annual concert series in 1948, and in 1971 Portland became host of the Chamber Music Northwest summer festival. In 1949 the Portland Park Bureau began sponsoring free summer concerts ranging from opera to folk music in the Washington Park Amphitheater.

The splendid Marquam Grand Theater, opened in 1890 but eventually demolished for reasons of safety, gave impetus to Portland's musical life. It was succeeded by a civic auditorium inaugurated in 1917 and modernized to seat 3000 in 1968. Popular music concerts are held at the Memorial Coliseum (capacity 11,500; opened 1960) and at the Paramount Theater (capacity 2800). The Paramount, rebuilt and renamed the Arlene Schnitzer Concert Hall (after its principal private benefactor), became the home of the Oregon SO in 1984 and is the largest of three performance areas at the Portland Center for the Performing Arts. Other halls include the Old Church (capacity 350; built in 1883 and renovated in 1968), which has a restored organ of 1883 by Hook & Hastings, and the Berg Swann Auditorium (capacity

The band of the Aurora Colony assembled for a performance in Portland, July 1876

480; opened 1970) at the Portland Art Museum.

Among the city's relatively few resident composers are Jacob Avshalomov, Tomáš Svoboda, Douglas Leedy, and Vincent McDermott. In jazz circles Portland is known for such artists as Jeannie Hoffman, John Stowell, David Friesen, Jeff Lorber Fusion, Tom Grant, and the Ron Steen Trio. Folk music thrives, and performances by traditional Irish bands and fiddlers have become particularly popular. A large community of instrument makers, notably Jess Wells (viols) and Robert Lundberg (lutes), has become established in the area, largely because of the climate and the availability of raw materials.

The public-school system offered an excellent program in music performance, especially from 1947 to 1954 under the direction of Karl Ernst. A subsequent reduction of public-school music has been partly offset by the activities of the Community Music Center (founded 1955), operated by the Portland Park Bureau. Private music schools included the Oregon Conservatory (1898–1932, 1945–54) and the Ellison-White Conservatory (later the Portland School of Music; 1918–59), but the city no longer has an independent music conservatory.

The music department of Lewis and Clark College (founded in 1867 as Albany College) was established in 1892; the name of the college was changed when it moved from Albany, Oregon, to Portland in 1942. It became a School of Music in 1972 in recognition of its professional orientation, acquired largely under the chairmanship of John Stark Evans (1944–57), but reverted to being a music department in 1984. The Fenwick Javanese gamelan "Venerable Showers of Beauty" is among its resources, and degrees are offered in music, music education, composition, and performance. Programs in music are also offered by the University of Portland (founded 1901), Concordia College (1905), Marylhurst College (1930), Portland State University (1946), and Mount Hood Community College (1966), which has a nationally recognized jazz curriculum.

The music collection of the Multnomah County public library (founded in 1864 as the Library Association of Portland) contains 33,000 books and scores, and is especially rich in early sheet music.

BIBLIOGRAPHY

J. MacQueen: *Pioneer Music of the Oregon Country* (MS, *OrP*, 1935)

"Music in Portland," *Oregon, End of the Trail*, ed. Federal Writers Project (Portland, OR, 1940), 116

S. A. Smith: "Portland: the Musical Capital of the Northwest," *University of Portland Bookman*, vii/1 (1955) [extract]

D. M. Olsen and C. M. Will: "Musical Heritage of the Aurora Colony," *Oregon Historical Quarterly*, lxxix/3 (1978), 233–67

J. Avshalomov: *Music is Where you Make it*, ii (Portland, OR, 1979)

M. J. Harold: *Music in the Oregon Province, 1859 to 1981* (Marylhurst, OR, 1982)

DOUGLAS LEEDY

Porto Rico. *See* PUERTO RICO.

Portuguese-American music. *See* HISPANIC-AMERICAN MUSIC, §2(iii).

Posselt, Ruth (*b* Medford, MA, 6 Sept 1914). Violinist. She studied with Emanuel Ondříček (1922–9) and made her first appearances at Carnegie Hall and in Boston's Symphony Hall at the age of ten; she continued to play frequently in Boston and made an appearance with Walter Damrosch and the New York PO when she was 14. She made her European début in Paris in 1929, then spent two summers there working through the French repertory with Jacques Thibaud. In 1935 she became the first female American violinist to tour the USSR, playing in Moscow, Leningrad, and Kiev. She first appeared with the Boston SO in 1935, in a performance of Tchaikovsky's Concerto under Koussevitzky, and it was at that time that she met the orchestra's concertmaster, RICHARD BURGIN, whom she married in 1940. For the next 25 years Posselt was a regular soloist with the orchestra, with which she played the world premières of concertos by Piston, Barber, Vladimir Dukelsky, and Edward Burlingame Hill; she also gave the first American performances of works by Hindemith, Bloch, Khachaturian, and Dallapiccola (*Tartiniana*, which she recorded with Bernstein and the Columbia SO), as well as the world premières of Copland's Violin Sonata and Martinů's Duo. She continued to tour nationally and internationally as a soloist and chamber music player, founding the Bell'Arte Trio (with Joseph di Pasquale and Samuel Mayes), and participating in the revival of early music that began in Boston in the early 1950s. In 1962 she took up a teaching appointment at Florida State University, where she was also artist-in-residence and a member of the Florestan Quartet. She was in her 70s when she made her first appearance in the pit, joining the orchestra of the Opera Company of Boston for the American première of Michael Tippett's *The Ice Break* (18 May 1979). Nearly 30 recordings document her powerful tone, solid technique, authoritative style, and ability to realize demanding new works.

RICHARD DYER

Post-bop. *See* HARD BOP.

Pound, Ezra (Loomis) (*b* Hailey, ID, 30 Oct 1885; *d* Venice, Italy, 1 Nov 1972). Poet and amateur composer. His musical achievements include an unorthodox *Treatise on Harmony*, a body of criticism, a role in the revival of older music, and, most notably, music for two "operas," *The Testament of François Villon* (1923) and *Cavalcanti* (1932). As a student Pound formed his taste on the Provençal troubadours, with their ideal union of composer and poet. Acquaintance with Arnold Dolmetsch deepened his love for early music, while other friendships broadened his experience. In 1913 the pianist Walter Rummel and Pound published arrangements of nine troubadour songs. From this unorthodox base, Pound, as "William Atheling," reviewed London concerts from 1917 to 1920 in the *New Age*, attacking current repertory and performance practice. In the 1930s local concerts sponsored by Pound in Rapallo formed a model for the 1939 Settimana Vivaldiana at Siena, which helped to establish Vivaldi's modern reputation.

Villon, composed with help from George Antheil, illustrates Pound's theories of song, combining troubadour monody with rhythmic notation intended to reproduce asymmetrical word rhythms with scientific precision. Such complex meters as 7/16 or 19/32 are frequent. Harmony is minimal, instrumentation pointillist, dialogue perfunctory, staging stylized, the performer's personality effaced – all operatic resources are subordinated to the rhythmic-melodic verse line. Pound's style is possibly the most original devised by an amateur. *Villon*, first performed in 1926, has been produced twice by the BBC, staged by Robert Hughes at the Western Opera Theatre (1971), and recorded by Fantasy Records of Berkeley, California (1972). *Cavalcanti*, a similar work, was first performed by Hughes in 1983.

Pound's *Treatise on Harmony*, in his *Antheil and the Treatise on Harmony* (Paris, 1924, 2/1927/*R*1968), is a somewhat obscure attempt to substitute rhythmic organization for textbook harmony or the vertical sonorities of impressionism. Best understood against the background of Antheil's *Ballet mécanique*, Stravinsky's music of the 1920s, and the general revolt against tonality, it is one of the earliest attempts to theorize about music purely as an arrangement of *objets sonores*.

Settings of Pound's poetry are not numerous. Among the early works are some songs by Rummel and male choruses by Granville Bantock. Jacob Avshalomov, Gordon Binkerd, and Copland have also composed choral settings. More recent compositions include those by Luciano Berio (*Laborintus II*), Elisabeth Lutyens, and David Wooldridge.

BIBLIOGRAPHY

V. Thomson: "Antheil, Joyce, and Pound," *Virgil Thomson* (New York, 1966), 73

M. H. Frank: *Music in American Literary History: a Survey of the Significance of Music in the Writings of Eight American Literary Figures* (diss., New York U., 1968)

N. Rorem: "Ezra Pound as Musician," *Music and People* (New York, 1968), 167

W. W. Hoffa: "Ezra Pound and George Antheil: Vorticist Music and the *Cantos*," *American Literature*, xliv (1972–3), 52

Paideuma: a Journal devoted to Ezra Pound Scholarship, ii/1 (1973) [special music issue]

S. J. Adams: *Ezra Pound and Music* (diss., U. of Toronto, 1974)

——: "Are the *Cantos* a Fugue?," *University of Toronto Quarterly*, xlv (1975), 67

——: "Pound, Olga Rudge, and the 'Risveglio Vivaldiano'," *Paideuma*, iv (1975), 111

R. M. Schafer, ed.: *Ezra Pound and Music* (New York, 1977)

S. Lippmann: *Music after Modernism* (New York, 1979)

S. J. Adams: "Musical Neofism: Pound's Theory of Harmony in Context," *Mosaic: a Journal for the Interdisciplinary Study of Literature*, xiii/2 (1980), 49

D. C. Gillespie: "John Becker's Correspondence with Ezra Pound: the Origins of a Musical Crusader," *Bulletin of Research in the Humanities*, lxxxiii (1980), 163

N. A. Cluck, ed.: *Literature and Music: Essays on Form* (Provo, UT, 1981)

A. Henderson: "Ezra Pound: Composer," *Paideuma*, xii (1983), 499

M. A. Hovland: *Musical Settings of American Poetry: a Bibliography* (in preparation) [incl. list of settings]

STEPHEN J. ADAMS

Powell, Bud [Earl] (*b* New York, 27 Sept 1924; *d* New York, 1 Aug 1966). Jazz pianist. From 1940, while still a teenager, he took part in informal jam sessions at Minton's Playhouse, New York, where he came under the tutelage and protection of Thelonious Monk and contributed to the emerging bop style. By 1942–4, when he played in the band of his guardian Cootie Williams, he had already developed his individual style in most of its essentials. After sustaining a head injury during a racist incident in 1945, he suffered the first of many nervous collapses, which were to confine him to sanatoriums for much of his adult life. Thereafter, in the late 1940s and early 1950s, he appeared intermittently in New York clubs with leading bop musicians or in his own trio. From the mid-1950s, as his mental health and musical powers deteriorated, he gradually restricted his public appearances. He moved in 1959 to Paris, where he led a trio (1959–62) with Kenny Clarke, the third member of which was usually Pierre Michelot, and enjoyed a certain celebrity status. After returning to the USA in August 1964, he made a disastrous appearance at Carnegie Hall (1965), and soon was obliged to abandon music altogether.

Powell was the most important pianist in the early bop style, and his innovations transformed the jazz pianism of his time. A prodigious technician, he was able at will to reproduce the demanding styles of Art Tatum and Teddy Wilson, echoes of which can sometimes be heard in his ballad performances. At fast and medium tempos, however, he preferred the spare manner that he devised in the early 1940s: rapid melodic lines in the right hand punctuated by irregularly spaced, dissonant chords in the left. This almost antipianistic style (which was adopted by most bop pianists of the time) left him free to pursue linear melody in the manner of bop wind players, and it was as a melodist that Powell stood apart from his many imitators. At its best, Powell's playing was sustained by a free unfolding of rapid and unpredictable melodic invention, to which he brought a brittle, precise touch and great creative intensity. Except in his later years, when his virtuosity flagged and he selfconsciously adopted a primitivism resembling Monk's, Powell never altered this basic approach, but worked ceaselessly within it to devise new melodic ideas, harmonies, and ways of coupling the hands. He greatly extended the range of jazz harmony by reducing his chordal underpinning to compounds of 2nds and 7ths, and achieved an extraordinary variety in his phrase lengths, which range from brief flurries to seemingly inexhaustible lines that ignore the structure of the original.

Although most at ease in a trio setting, Powell was stimulated to his best work in competition with other leading bop soloists such as Charlie Parker, Dizzy Gillespie, J. J. Johnson, Sonny Stitt, and especially Fats Navarro. Powell also composed a number of excellent jazz tunes, among them *Hallucinations* (recorded by Miles Davis as *Budo*), *Dance of the Infidels*, *Tempus Fugue-it*, and *Bouncing with Bud*, as well as the remarkable *The Glass Enclosure*, a musical impression of his experiences in mental asylums, which points to a talent for composition that was unfortunately left undeveloped.

See also JAZZ, §V, 4 and fig.8.

RECORDINGS

(selective list)

As leader: Bud's Bubble (1947, Roost 509); Tempus Fugue-it (1949, Clef 11045); All God's Chillun got Rhythm (1949, Clef 11046); Bouncing with Bud (1949, BN 1567); Dance of the Infidels (1949, BN 1568); Hallucinations (1950, Clef 610); Un poco loco (1951, BN 1577); The Glass Enclosure (1953, BN 1628)

As sideman: C. Williams: Floogie Boo (1944, Hit 8089); J. J. Johnson: Jay Bird (1946, Savoy 975); Bebop Boys: Webb City, pts. i–ii (1946, Savoy 585); S. Stitt: Fine and Dandy (1950, Prst. 706); Quintet of the Year: Perdido/Salt Peanuts/All the Things You Are (1953, Debut 2)

BIBLIOGRAPHY

SouthernB

S. Pease: "Bud Powell's Style," *Down Beat*, xviii/12 (1951), 16

L. Feather: *The Book of Jazz* (New York, 1957, rev. 2/1965), 238f

M. James: *Ten Modern Jazzmen* (London, 1960), 125ff

M. Harrison: "Bud Powell," *Jazz Era: the 'Forties*, ed. S. Dance (London, 1961), 200f

I. Gitler: *Jazz Masters of the Forties* (New York, 1966), 110ff

J. G. Jepsen: *A Discography of Thelonious Monk and Bud Powell* (Copenhagen, 1969)

R. Johnson: "Bud Powell on Blue Note," *Jazz Monthly*, no. 188 (1970), 8

"Bud Powell," *Swing Journal*, xxxi/13 (1977), 298 [discography]

C. J. Safane: *Bud Powell* (New York, *c*1979) [6 transcrs.]

J. Réda: "La force de Bud Powell," *L'improviste* (Paris, 1980), 158

J. BRADFORD ROBINSON

Powell, John (*b* Richmond, VA, 6 Sept 1882; *d* Richmond, 15 Aug 1963). Pianist and composer. After graduating from the University of Virginia in 1901, he studied in Vienna with Theodor Leschetizky (piano, 1902–7) and Karel Navrátil (composition, 1906–7). He made his début as a pianist in Berlin in December 1907, and he performed widely in Europe before World War I. In 1912 he was in the USA, and gave recitals in New

York and Richmond. He returned to Europe for a few years and then settled in Richmond and toured throughout the USA. In 1924 he was elected to the National Institute of Arts and Letters. From the late 1920s until World War II he was prominent in Virginian musical life, and was particularly active in the White Top folk music festivals and the Virginia state choral festivals. He was also closely identified with the Virginia Federation of Music Clubs. His early works are in a late-Romantic style; the later pieces use Anglo-American folk idioms and many quote Negro melodies. Powell bequeathed his manuscripts, extensive music library, and various memorabilia to the University of Virginia, where they form a major portion of the John Powell Collection.

WORKS

Orch: Vn Conc., op.23, 1910, 2nd movt arr. vn, pf as From a Loved Past, op.23a; Rhapsodie nègre, pf, orch, op.27, 1918, arr. 2 pf, 1922; In Old Virginia, op.28, 1921; 2 Interludes, 1921; Natchez-on-the-Hill (3 Virginian Country-dances), op.30, 1932, arr. vn, pf, op.30a, arr. 2 pf, op.30b; A Set of 3, op.33, 1935; Sym., A, 1945

Vocal: Phantoms, 1v, pf, op.15 no.1, 1906; Chorale Finale, SATB, band, arr. SATB, pf, as The Landing of the Pilgrims (1922); The Babe of Bethlehem, SATB, op.32, 1934; Soldier, Soldier, S, Bar, SATB, op.35 no.2, 1934; The Deaf Woman's Courtship, Mez, T, SATB, op.34 no.4a, 1934, arr. Mez, T, male vv, op.35 no.1 (1950); 5 Virginian Folk Songs, Bar, pf, op.34, 1938; 15 other songs, 6 hymns, 3 other choral works

Inst: Sonata Virginianesque, vn, pf, op.7, 1906; 2 str qts, 1907, 1922; Vn Sonata, op.26, 1918; Larry O'Gaff, carillon, 1941; Patriotic Interlude, org

Pf: In the South, suite, op.16, 1906; Variations and Double-fugue on a Theme of F. C. Hahr, op.20, 1906; At the Fair, suite, 1907, orchd A. Schmid (1925); 3 sonatas, incl. Sonate noble, op.21, 1907; In the Hammock, 2 pf, 8 hands, op.19, 1915; Dirge, 2 pf 12 hands, op.26 (1928); 14 others, all unpubd

MSS in *ViU*

Principal publishers: J. Fischer, G. Schirmer

BIBLIOGRAPHY

EwenD

P. L. Williams: *Music by John Powell in the John Powell Music Collection at the University of Virginia: a Descriptive Bibliography* (thesis, U. of Virginia, 1968)

L. M. Simms, Jr.: "Folk Music in America: John Powell and the 'National Music Idiom,' " *Journal of Popular Culture*, vii (1973–4), 510

R. D. WARD

Powell, Maud (*b* Peru, IL, 22 Aug 1867; *d* Uniontown, PA, 8 Jan 1920). Violinist. She began violin and piano lessons in Aurora, Illinois, then studied violin for four years with William Lewis in Chicago. She was a pupil at the Leipzig Conservatory under Henry Schradieck (1881–2) and at the Paris Conservatoire under Charles Dancla (1882–3), then in 1883 made a tour of England. The following year she studied with Joachim at the Berlin Hochschule für Musik. She made her European début with the Berlin PO under Joachim in 1885, and her American début with the New York PO under Theodore Thomas in the same year. She toured Europe with the New York Arion Society in 1892, and performed twice under Thomas at the World's Columbian Exposition (1893), at which she delivered a paper "Women and the Violin" to the Women's Musical Congress. Her mission was to advance America's cultural growth by bringing the best in classical music to Americans in remote areas as well as the large cultural centers. She promoted works by American composers and introduced concertos by Tchaikovsky, Dvořák, Saint-Saëns, Lalo, Sibelius, Coleridge-Taylor, and Arensky. She also toured widely in Europe, and was particularly popular with audiences in England. Maud Powell became the first American woman to form and lead a string quartet (1894). The Maud Powell Concert Company, a group of six musicians, visited South Africa in 1905; in 1908 she formed the Maud Powell Trio with the company's cellist May Mukle and her sister Ann Mukle Ford and toured the USA with them in 1908–9. In 1904 she became the first violinist to record for the Victor Talking Machine Co. She made transcriptions for violin and piano, and composed an original cadenza for Brahms's Violin Concerto; she also contributed articles to music journals and wrote her own program notes. The brilliancy, power and finish of her playing combined with an unusual interpretative gift led her to be recognized as one of America's greatest violinists; contemporary reviewers ranked her alongside Kreisler and Ysaÿe.

BIBLIOGRAPHY

GroveAS

F. H. Martens: "Maud Powell," *Violin Mastery* (New York, 1919), 183

E. L. Winn: "Maud Powell as I know her: a Tribute," *Musical Observer*, xix/3 (1920), 58

F. H. Martens: "Powell, Maud," *DAB*

A. R. Coolidge: "Powell, Maud," *NAW*

N. G. Greenwood: "Maud Powell," *The Strad*, xci (1980–81), 237

B. Schwarz: *Great Masters of the Violin* (New York, 1983), 494

NEVA GARNER GREENWOOD, KAREN A. SHAFFER

Powell, Mel (*b* New York, 12 Feb 1923). Composer and teacher. He studied piano with Reisenberg and was for some years noted as a jazz pianist, composer, and arranger (for Benny Goodman and Glenn Miller). After service in the US Army Air Force, he attended Yale University, where he studied composition with Hindemith (BM 1952). He taught at the Mannes College and at Queens College, CUNY, before returning to Yale (1957–69), where he became chairman of the composition faculty and director of the electronic music studio, one of the first in the USA. In 1969 he went to the California Institute of the Arts as dean of the school of music; he was provost there from 1972 to 1976 and was appointed to the school's first endowed chair in 1978. Among his many awards and commissions are those from Sigma Alpha Iota (1956), the Guggenheim Foundation (1960), the American Academy of Arts and Letters (1963), and the NEA (1982). He has served as president of the American Music Center (1961–3) and on the editorial boards of *Perspectives of New Music* and *Journal of Music Theory*. In 1972 he was guest composer at the University of Wisconsin, River Falls, and at the Holland Festival, by invitation of the Dutch government.

Powell's use of 12-tone techniques makes possible the density of interval relationships and of durations, registers, and phrases that is characteristic of his music. In some works, such as *Filigree Setting* (1959), he uses quasi-improvisational techniques to extend durations and to permit the performer some choice of pitch succession or contour within an otherwise rigorously controlled context. In other compositions interval relations derived from pitch sets take precedence over ordered pitch succession, as in *Haiku Setting* (1960), to frame ordered elements. There is a similar use of pitch sets in his electronically synthesized music, which also takes into account the non-tempered nature of the electronic medium. He has also modified live sounds electronically in some of his music.

WORKS

Orch: Stanzas, 1957; Setting, vc, orch, 1961; Immobiles 1–4, tape and/or orch, 1967; Modules, chamber orch, 1985

Inst: Beethoven Analogs, str qt, 1948; Pf Sonatina, 1953; Recitative and Toccata Percossa, hpd, 1953; Capriccio, sym. band, 1954; Pf Trio, 1954; Divertimento, vn, harp, 1954; Divertimento, wind qnt, 1957; Miniatures, fl, ob, vn, va, vc, hpd, 1957; Pf Qnt, 1957; Etude, pf, 1957; Filigree Setting, str qt, 1959; Improvisation, cl, va, pf, 1962; Str Qt, 1982; Intermezzo, pf, 1984;

Madrigal, 2 pf, 1985; Nocturne, vn, 1985, rev. of Cantilena, 1970 [see "Tape"]; Wind Qnt, 1985

Vocal: 6 Love Songs, chorus, 1950; Sweet Lovers Love the Spring (Shakespeare), female chorus, pf, 1953; Haiku Setting, S, pf, 1960; 2 Prayer Settings (Goodman, Gregory), T, ob, vn, va, vc, 1962; Settings (Joyce, Milton, Euripides, trad.), S, chamber ens, 1979; Little Companion Pieces (Baudelaire, W. C. Williams, Joyce, Asian and African trad.), S, str qt, 1980; Strand Settings: "Darker" (M. Strand), song cycle, Mez, elec, 1983

Tape: Elec Setting, 1961; Elec Setting no.2, 1962; Events (H. Crane), 1963; Analogs 1–4, 1966; Immobile 5, tape, chamber ens, 1967; Cantilena (anon. Heb., Chin., Sanskrit), S, vn, tape, 1970, rev. as Nocturne, vn, 1985; Setting, wind insts, vn, tape, 1972; 3 Synth Settings, 1981; Cantilena, trbn, tape, 1982

Principal publishers: MKS Music, G. Schirmer

BIBLIOGRAPHY

VintonD
J. Machlis: *Introduction to Contemporary Music* (New York, 1961)
H. Sollberger: "Mel Powell's *Haiku Setting*," *PNM*, iii/1 (1964), 147
L. Thimmig: "The Music of Mel Powell," *MQ*, lv (1969), 31 [with list of works]

RICHARD SWIFT

Powell, Verne Q. (*b* Danville, IN, 7 April 1879; *d* Boston, MA, 3 Feb 1968). Woodwind instrument maker. He grew up in Kansas, and was largely self-taught. At an early age he learned to play flute and piccolo, and he made a fife when only seven. He performed regularly with bands in Fort Scott, Kansas, where he was being trained with his brothers as a jeweler. By the time he was 16 he had become an expert engraver and in 1904 he started his own jewelry business in Fort Scott.

In 1910 Powell heard Georges Barrère in Chicago playing on a silver flute; this inspired him to make a silver flute by melting down old spoons, watch cases, etc. William S. Haynes, who had been making wooden flutes, heard about this and asked Powell to join his firm in Boston. Powell worked with Haynes, mainly supervising the production of silver flutes, until 1926, in which year he started his own business, specializing in Boehm flutes and piccolos. In 1927 he set up his shop at 295 Huntington Avenue, Boston, opposite the New England Conservatory of Music.

Besides silver flutes, Powell made piccolos in wood and silver, alto flutes in silver, and concert flutes in gold and platinum. One platinum flute was made for the New York World's Fair (1939–40) and is engraved with the trylon and perisphere, the symbol of the fair. This instrument was later purchased by William Kincaid, who bequeathed it to Elaine Shaffer.

Powell, while foreman at the Haynes factory, was responsible for introducing French-model silver flute making to the USA. Later, as an independent maker, he changed the scale of his flutes, which were formerly patterned after the then famous Louis Lot flutes, thereby perfecting the design of his own instruments. He gained the respect and friendship of many internationally known flutists, and he made Boston a leading center of flute making.

In 1961 Powell sold his business to four of his employees, Edward Almeida, Richard Jerome, Edmund Machon, and Elmer Waterhouse; under their management the firm expanded and moved to Arlington, Massachusetts. In 1984 the foreman Robert Viola and the general manager James Phelan bought the firm from the two remaining partners, Jerome and Waterhouse. Verne Q. Powell Flutes Inc. was then employing 20 craftsmen with an annual production of about 240 flutes and 40 piccolos.

BIBLIOGRAPHY

L. R. Gallese: "Music Makers: Serious Flute Players Insist Two Companies are Most Noteworthy," *Wall Street Journal* (1 Feb 1977), 1
N. Toff: *The Development of the Modern Flute* (New York, 1979)
E. T. Livezey: "Makers of the Magic Flute," *Christian Science Monitor* (2 Jan 1980), B4
M. Goodman: *Haynes and Powell: the Facts and Figures, a Guide to their Production and Prices* (Santa Monica, CA, 1984)
M. Silk: "Boston's flutemakers found excellence just wasn't enough," *Boston Globe* (11 Sept 1984), 39

FRIEDRICH VON HUENE/R

Powers, Harold S(tone) (*b* New York, 5 Aug 1928). Musicologist. He attended Stanford and Syracuse universities (BMus 1950), then studied at Princeton (MFA 1952) and was awarded the PhD in 1959 with a dissertation on the South Indian raga system. He taught at Princeton (1955–8), Harvard (1958–60), and the University of Pennsylvania (1960–73). In 1973 he became professor of music at Princeton.

Powers's interests include theory, Italian opera, and Indian music. His operatic studies are centered on later 17th-century Italian compositions and the development within them of formal organization for dramatic purposes; his comparative examinations of different settings of the same libretto reveal both progressive and conservative techniques employed by composers of the time. Powers, who has received several grants to study music in India (1952–4, 1960–61, 1967–8), is aware of the problems encountered by a Westerner in approaching non-Western music; in his writings he cautions the reader against making comparisons between Western mode and Indian raga, or attempting to account for present-day Indian practice in the light of early Indian theory. His historical and analytical study of raga classifications (*Selected Reports*, i/3, 1970, pp. 1–78) is a lucid exposition, and its musical and historical methods should be applicable to any body of music, Eastern or Western.

Pownall, Mary Ann (*b* London, England, Feb 1751; *d* Charleston, SC, 11 Aug 1796). Actress, singer, and composer. She made her performing début at Drury Lane in 1770 under the name Mrs. James Wrighton, and was praised by the English critics for her role as Lucy in John Gay's *The Beggar's Opera*. In 1792 she came to the USA with Mr. Pownall, her second husband, and became a member of the Old American Company. Before her death in 1796 she appeared in concerts in Charleston, Philadelphia, New York, and Boston. Her repertory ranged from popular songs to opera, oratorio, and dramatic readings. One of her most successful appearances was at a "Grand Concert Spirituel" given in Charleston on 24 March 1796, consisting of songs, duets, and instrumental music from oratorios by Handel; such was the public interest that she gave an additional concert of spiritual music two days later. Pownall's songs *Jenny of the Glen*, *Lavinia*, and *The Straw Bonnet* (all included in the volume *Six Songs for the Harpsichord*, 1794, written in collaboration with James Hewitt), and *Kisses Sued For* (1795) were among the first by a woman to be published in the USA. Her vocal writing is characterized by strong leaps in the melody and a variety of rhythmic patterns; her harmonic language, however, is straightforward.

BIBLIOGRAPHY

O. G. T. Sonneck: *A Bibliography of Early Secular American Music* (Washington, DC, 1905, rev. and enlarged by W. T. Upton, 2/1945/*R*1964)
——: *Early Concert-life in America (1731–1800)* (Leipzig, 1907/*R*1978)
J. Tick: *American Women Composers before 1870* (Ann Arbor, MI, 1979)

LORETTA GOLDBERG

Pozo, Chano [Pozo y Gonzales, Luciano] (*b* Havana, Cuba, 7 Jan 1915; *d* New York, 2 Dec 1948). Drummer, singer, and dancer. His drumming and singing were rooted in the Cuban *lucumí* faith, derived from West African rituals. On 29 September 1947 he and the bongo player Chiquitico performed in a concert at Carnegie Hall with the bop trumpeter Dizzy Gillespie – the first time a serious attempt had been made to fuse elements of jazz and Latin music. Pozo was murdered before he could fully develop his ideas with Gillespie, but during his brief career in the USA he provided the starting point for much popular music of the late 1940s and the 1950s. The collaboration between the two men supplied the initiative for American musicians, and some of the listening public, to appreciate fully the tradition of Latin music.

BIBLIOGRAPHY

D. Gillespie: *To Be or not to Bop: Memoirs* (Garden City, NY, 1979)
J. S. Roberts: *The Latin Tinge* (New York, 1979)

JOHN STORM ROBERTS

Pozzi Escot, (Olga) (*b* Lima, Peru, 1 Oct 1933). Composer and theorist. Of French-Moroccan background, she studied in Lima at San Marcos University (mathematics, 1950–52) and received musical training at the Sás–Rosay Academy of Music, Peru (1949–53), before immigrating to the USA in 1953 (she became a naturalized American citizen in 1963). She attended the Juilliard School (MS 1957) and the Hamburg Hochschule für Musik (1957–61). Her principal teachers were Andréas Sás, William Bergsma, and Philipp Jarnach. She has lectured widely in Europe and the Americas and has held faculty positions at the New England Conservatory (1964–7, 1980–81) and Wheaton College, Norton, Massachusetts (from 1972), where she is director of the electronic music studio. Her awards include grants from the West German government (1957–9), MacDowell Colony Fellowships (1962–5), a Ford Foundation grant (1966), Radcliffe Institute Fellowships (1968–70), and an invitation to the Camargo Foundation Residence in Cassis, France (1982). She has received many commissions.

Pozzi Escot writes chiefly for chamber ensembles and solo instruments. Her rigorous precompositional mathematical planning, which is sometimes computer-assisted, yields a highly structured music that is clear, meticulous, timbrally striking, and often dramatic. A discerning commentator on contemporary music, she has contributed articles to several theory journals and is editor of *Sonus, Journal of Investigation into Global Musical Possibilities*. With her husband, Robert Cogan, she has written two books on sonic design (1976, 1981), in which they propose analytical concepts and principles applicable to the understanding of music from diverse cultures and historical periods.

WORKS

Orch: Sands . . ., 5 sax, amp gui, 17 vn, 9 db, perc, 1965

Inst: 3 Poems of Rilke, reciter, str qt, 1959; 3 Movts, vn, pf, 1959–60; Differences Group I, II, pf, 1960–61, 1963; Lamentus (Trilogy no. 1) (Pozzi Escot), S, 2 vn, 2 vc, pf, 3 perc, 1962; Cristhos (Trilogy no. 2), a fl, cbn, 3 vn, perc, 1963; Visione (Trilogy no. 3) (Pozzi Escot, after Rimbaud, Kandinsky, G. Stein, G. Grass), S, speaker, fl/pic, a fl, a sax, db, perc, 1964; Neyrac lux, 2 gui, amp gui, 1978; Eure pax, vn, 1980

Tape: Interra, pf, tape, lights, film, 1968; Fergus Are, org, tape, 1975; Interra II, pf (left hand), tape, 1980; Pluies, a sax, tape, 1981

Vocal: Ainu (Pozzi Escot), 4 ens of 5 vv, 1970, arr. 1v, 1978; Missa triste (Pozzi Escot), 3 female choruses, 3 opt. tr insts, 1981

Many early works incl. 3 str qts, 3 syms., 3 pf sonatinas, songs, 1942–58, withdrawn

Principal publisher: Publication Contact International

WRITINGS

with R. Cogan: *Sonic Design: the Nature of Sound and Music* (Englewood Cliffs, NJ, 1976)

with R. Cogan: *Sonic Design: Practice and Problems* (Englewood Cliffs, NJ, 1981)

BIBLIOGRAPHY

W. Thomson: "*Sonic Design* by Robert Cogan and Pozzi Escot," *JMT*, xxiii (1979), 125
J. W. LePage, ed.: "Pozzi Escot," *Women Composers, Conductors and Musicians of the Twentieth Century: Selected Biographies*, ii (1983), 58

RICHARD S. JAMES

Prado, Perez (*b* Matanzas, Cuba, 1922). Pianist and bandleader. He first came to attention in Cuba as the pianist of the Orquesta Casino de la Playa. In 1948 he moved to Mexico, where he made a series of (mostly instrumental) mambo recordings. Partly on account of a ban on the broadcast of recorded American music by the musicians' union, several of these were played in the USA; Prado subsequently toured the country (1951) and capitalized on his success. He attempted to make his music more accessible to the American public by decreasing the emphasis on brass and percussion instruments, and became a highly influential exponent of this style. He was never popular with the large Cuban and Puerto Rican population on the East Coast, however, and the musical quality of his recordings gradually deteriorated as he tried to maintain contact with a mass Anglo-American audience for whom Latin music was an amusing novelty rather than a tradition of considerable depth.

JOHN STORM ROBERTS

Pran Nath (*b* Lahore, India [now Pakistan], 3 Nov 1918). Indian vocalist and composer. From the age of 13 he studied for 20 years as a disciple of Ustad Abdul Waheed Khan, the foremost master of the Kirana *gharāna*. In performances on All India Radio (from 1937) and at music conferences throughout India Pran Nath established his reputation as a leading interpreter of Kirana style with an exceptional knowledge of traditional compositions and the delineation of raga. From 1960 to 1970 he taught at Delhi University. His first appearances in the West in 1970 introduced the vocal tradition of Hindustani classical music to the USA; subsequently he became the most widely influential exponent of the Kirana style, performing extensively in Europe, the USA, and elsewhere. He became a permanent resident of the USA and in 1971 established a school in New York, the Kirana Center for Indian Classical Music; in 1973 he was artist-in-residence at the University of California, San Diego, and from 1973 was on the faculty of Mills College, Oakland, California. His awards in composition include a Guggenheim Fellowship (1975) and an NEA award (1978). In 1976 he was commissioned by the Pellizzi Foundation to perform and record a repertory in the Kirana style, and the following year the Dia Art Foundation appointed him to oversee a new facility established in New York to preserve and promote the Kirana tradition.

Pran Nath's majestic expositions of the slow *ālāp* sections of ragas, together with his emphasis on perfect intonation and the clear evocation of mood, profoundly influenced Western composers and performers; La Monte Young, Terry Riley, and the artist-performer Marian Zazeela became his disciples, while Jon Hassell, Rhys Chatham, Don Cherry, Jon Gibson, Lee Konitz, Charlemagne Palestine, and Douglas Leedy all studied with him. Also known as a designer of instruments, Pran Nath after coming to the USA contributed innovations to the design of the *tambūrā*, and his unvarnished "Pandit Pran Nath style" *tambūrā* achieved a worldwide recognition. Another of his instruments, a continuous drone called the *prānda nāda*, is based on the tuning fork.

For illustration *see* YOUNG, LA MONTE.

WORKS

(only those composed in the USA)

Raga: Ānant bhairavī, 1973–4

Vocal, all texts by Pran Nath: Hārī terō nām [Lord, thy name], khayāl in raga *ānant bhairavī*, 1973–4; Hey dekhō [O, Look], khayāl in raga *bhairavī*, 1974; Hey Gīradhāra Gōpāla Lāl [O, Supporter of Mountains, Lord Krishna], khayāl in raga *āsāvarī-tōdī*, 1976; Jaga maga jyōtā jārey mandīr meṅ [Flickering candle burning in the temple], khayāl in raga *dīpak*, 1976; Dira dira tānā dere nā [vocalise], tarānā in raga *bhairavī*, 1979

BIBLIOGRAPHY

L. Young: "Singing of Pran Nath: the Sound is God," *Village Voice* (30 April 1970)

R. Palmer: "India's Master of Breath," *Rolling Stone*, no.92 (30 Sept 1971)

S. de Nussac: "Musique: la paix des indes," *L'express*, no.1089 (28 May 1972)

J. Rockwell: "What's New?," *HiFi/MusAm*, xxiii/12 (1973), 12

R. Palmer: "Ragas for a Sunday Morning," *New York Times* (24 Sept 1976)

P. Wdowczak: "Raga a Hinduskie myślenie muzyczne próba jednostkowej charakterystyki muzycznej," *Muzyka*, xxvi/1 (Warsaw, 1981), 3

J. M. Reusser: "Musique: Pandit Pran Nath," *L'autre monde* (Paris, March 1983), 62

LA MONTE YOUNG

Pratt, Carroll C(ornelius) (*b* North Brookfield, MA, 27 April 1894). Psychologist and musicologist. He studied at Clark College (BA 1915), Clark University (PhD 1921), the University of Cambridge (1919), and the University of Berlin (1931). After serving as instructor and assistant professor of psychology at Harvard University (1923–37) he moved to Rutgers University, where he was professor and chairman of the department of psychology. He directed the Institute of Psychology and Philosophy at Ankara University (1945–7) before being appointed chairman and professor of psychology at Princeton University (1947–62) and then at Rider College (1962–71). He has served as editor of the *Psychological Review*, and as president of the American Society for Aesthetics (1950–52).

Pratt has studied and written about various aspects of aesthetics and of the psychology of music. Examining objective and subjective musical experience, he concluded that the hearer responds primarily to the inherent tonal design of the music rather than to its symbolic references, and that therefore some important aspects of musical response are not culturally determined. His writings include *The Meaning of Music* (1931/*R*1968) and *Music as the Language of Emotion* (1952).

RAMONA H. MATTHEWS/R

Pratt, Paul (Charles) (*b* New Salem, IN, 1 Nov 1890; *d* Indianapolis, IN, 7 July 1948). Ragtime composer and pianist. In 1909 he became the manager for the recently established popular-music publisher J. H. Aufderheide & Co. in Indianapolis. That same year Aufderheide issued Pratt's first piano rag, *Vanity*, and in 1911 Pratt moved to Chicago to open a short-lived branch office for the firm, and began collaborating on popular songs with the lyricist J. Will Callahan (1874–1946). In 1914 John Stark issued Pratt's *Hot House Rag*, a virtuoso showpiece and his finest work. From 1917, as a piano-roll artist for the United States Music Company, he recorded several of his own rags which were never published in sheet-music form. With the demise of ragtime Pratt began traveling as a piano accompanist in vaudeville, playing under the stage name of Paul Parnell. In 1924 he conducted Paul Whiteman's band the James Boys on a tour of the USA, and later conducted the orchestras in several Broadway musicals, including Rodgers and Hart's *Peggy-Ann* (1926) and *A Connecticut Yankee* (1927). The Depression ended his musical career, and from 1934 he lived in relative obscurity in Indianapolis. Pratt was a gifted pianist and composed several enduring rags noteworthy for their relative difficulty and their use of unconventional harmonic progressions.

WORKS

(selective list)

Pf rags: Vanity Rag (Indianapolis, 1909); Colonial Glide (Indianapolis, 1910); Walhalla Rag (Indianapolis, 1910); Teasing Rag (Chicago, 1912); Hot House Rag (St. Louis, 1914); Spring-time Rag (St. Louis, 1916); On the Rural Route (St. Louis, 1917)

Songs: Gee, but I'm crazy for rag (A. Warren) (Chicago, 1912); That gosh ding hiram tune (J. W. Callahan) (St. Louis, 1912); Gasoline (Callahan) (New York, 1914); Beneath your window (Callahan) (New York, 1925)

Orch: Siren of the Nile (Chicago, 1921)

Principal publishers: Aufderheide, Stark

BIBLIOGRAPHY

Obituary, *Indianapolis Star* (8 July 1948)

D. A. Jasen and T. J. Tichenor: *Rags and Ragtime: a Musical History* (New York, 1978), 180ff

J. E. Hasse: *The Creation and Dissemination of Indianapolis Ragtime, 1897–1930* (diss., Indiana U., 1981), 152ff

J. E. Hasse and F. J. Gillis: Liner notes, *Indiana Ragtime: a Documentary Album* (Indiana Historical Society, 1981)

T. Parrish: "The Paul Pratt Story," *Rag Times*, xvii (1984), no.5, p.2; no.6, p.3

JOHN EDWARD HASSE

Pratt, Silas G(amaliel) (*b* Addison, VT, 4 Aug 1846; *d* Pittsburgh, PA, 30 Oct 1916). Composer and author. He left school at the age of 12, and while working in three Chicago music stores he saved enough money to spend the years 1868–71 in Germany studying with Franz Bendel, Theodor Kullak, and others. A wrist injury caused by too-strenuous practice precluded a career as concert pianist. On returning to Chicago, he became organist of the Church of the Messiah, and with George P. Upton organized the Apollo Club. During his next trip to Germany (1875–7) Liszt gave him some lessons, and he conducted his own *Centennial Overture* in Berlin (4 July 1876). From 1877 to 1888 he again lived in Chicago, where in June 1882 his second opera, *Zenobia, Queen of Palmyra*, was produced in concert form at Central Music Hall and staged the following March at McVicker's Theater. His first opera, titled *Antonio* when begun in 1870 but retitled *Lucille*, had a three-week run at the Columbia Theater in Chicago during March 1887. His third opera *Ollanta*, on an Inca subject, was never produced. In 1888 Pratt moved to New York, where in 1895 he became principal of the West End School of Music. In 1906 he founded the Pratt Institute of Music and Art in Pittsburgh, and was its president until his death. He wrote *Lincoln in Story* (1901) and *The Pianist's Mental Velocity* (1905).

WORKS

OPERAS

Antonio, 1870–71, selections perf. Chicago, Farwell Hall, 1874; rev. as Lucille, Chicago, Columbia Theater, 14 March 1887

Zenobia, Queen of Palmyra (4, Pratt), concert perf. Chicago, Central Music Hall, 15 June 1882, staged Chicago, McVicker's Theater, 26 March 1883, vs (Boston, 1882)

The Musical Metempsychosis (musical entertainment), 1888

Ollanta (Pratt), not produced

OTHER WORKS

A Columbian Festival Allegory: the Triumph of Columbus, New York, Metropolitan Opera, 10 Oct 1892, vs (New York, 1892)

The Inca's Farewell, cantata, Bar, chorus, vs (Boston, 1891)
?3 syms., incl. no. 1, perf. Chicago, 1871; "Prodigal Son," 1875; Lincoln Sym.
3 sym. poems: Magdalene's Lament, *c*1870; Sandalphon; A Tragedy of the Deep [on the sinking of the Titanic], *c*1912
Centennial Ov., perf. Berlin, 4 July 1876
*c*50 pf pieces
Choruses, songs, incl. The [Civil] War in Song: a Military and Musical Allegory (New York, 1891)

BIBLIOGRAPHY

W. S. B. Mathews, ed.: *A Hundred Years of Music in America* (Chicago, 1889/ *R*1970), 688
The National Cyclopedia of American Biography, x (New York, 1900/*R*1967)
E. E. Hipsher: *American Opera* (Philadelphia, 1927), 361
F. L. G. Cole: "Pratt, Silas Gamaliel," *DAB*

ROBERT STEVENSON

Pratt, Waldo Selden (*b* Philadelphia, PA, 10 Nov 1857; *d* Hartford, CT, 29 July 1939). Musical scholar. He was educated at Williams College (BA 1878, MA 1881) and at Johns Hopkins University, where he studied Greek, archaeology, and aesthetics. In music he was largely self-taught. After two years with the Metropolitan Museum of Art in New York, he went to the Hartford Theological Seminary in 1882 as professor of ecclesiastical music and hymnology, a position he retained until his retirement in 1925. Concurrently he taught at several other colleges, including the Institute of Musical Art (now the Juilliard School) and served as a church organist and choral conductor. He was president of the Music Teachers National Association (1906–8), an editor of its *Proceedings*, and president of the American section of the International Musical Association (1911–16). He wrote a standard history of music (1907, enlarged by A. Mendel 3/1935) and several books on the use of music in the church, and edited the American supplement to *Grove 2*, a book of children's songs, and a Sunday-school hymnbook.

WRITINGS

The History of English Hymnody (Hartford, 1895)
Musical Ministries in the Church (New York, 1901, rev. 4/1915)
The History of Music (New York, 1907, repr. 1919, enlarged 3/1935)
Class Notes in Music History (New York, 1908, rev. 5/1938)
ed.: *Grove's Dictionary of Music and Musicians: American Supplement* (New York, 1920, rev. 2/1928)
The Music of the Pilgrims (Boston, 1921/*R*1971)
ed.: *The New Encyclopedia of Music and Musicians* (New York, 1924, rev. 2/1929/ *R*1960)
The Problem of Music in the Church (Chicago, 1930)
The Music of the French Psalter of 1562 (New York, 1939)

BIBLIOGRAPHY

F. H. Johnson: *Musical Memories of Hartford* (Hartford, 1931), 71
O. Kinkeldey: "Waldo Selden Pratt," *MQ*, xxvi (1940), 162

RAMONA H. MATTHEWS/R

Prausnitz, Frederik [Frederick] **(William)** (*b* Cologne, Germany, 26 Aug 1920). Conductor. After immigration to the USA as a youth, he was trained at the Juilliard School, where he stayed on as a member of the conducting staff and faculty. He conducted the New England Conservatory SO (1961–9) and was music director of the Syracuse (New York) SO (1971–4). The education of young professionals has been one of his particular interests, and he joined the faculty of the Peabody Conservatory as music director of its symphony orchestra and opera in 1976; he became music director emeritus in 1980, continuing as director of the conducting studies program and the Contemporary Music Ensemble. He has also been a visiting lecturer or consultant at Harvard, the University of Michigan, and Sussex University (England).

Prausnitz, a champion of contemporary music, has appeared widely as a guest conductor in the USA, Central America, and Europe. He has given the first American performances of works by, among others, Dallapiccola, Gerhard, Goehr, Lutyens, Petrassi, Schoenberg, Stockhausen, Varèse, and Webern; conversely, he has introduced American composers such as Carter, Schuman, Sessions, and Wolpe to European audiences. He has made a number of recordings of 20th-century music, ranging from the first complete recording of Walton's *Façade*, with Edith Sitwell, to Sessions's Symphony no.8; Sessions dedicated his Ninth Symphony to Prausnitz. He conducts the music of late 19th- and early 20th-century composers – Mahler, for example, early Schoenberg, and, notably, Elgar – with a special sense of identification and communicative power. By virtue both of technique and temperament, Prausnitz is most effective in music whose expressive gestures are sweeping and grand, but all his work is marked by the imprint of a probing and original mind. In 1974 he was awarded the Gustav Mahler Medal of Honor of the Bruckner Society of America. He has written *Score and Podium: a Complete Guide to Conducting* (1983) and *Roger Sessions: a Critical Biography* (1983). For the unusual spelling of his first name, he is indebted to an Italian poster printer, who omitted the penultimate "c" on the occasion of his Rome début.

MICHAEL STEINBERG/R

Prepared piano. A piano in which the pitches, timbres, and dynamic responses of individual notes have been altered by means of bolts, screws, mutes, rubber erasers, and/or other objects inserted at particular points between the strings. The technique of altering the tone of a piano in this way was developed by Cage for his *Bacchanale* (1940; *see* CAGE, JOHN, fig. 2), and the prepared piano is used in a number of his subsequent compositions, as well as in works by Lou Harrison, Toshiro Mayuzumi, and Christian Wolff. Since the tonal alteration desired varies from one piece to another and depends on the nature and placement of the objects used to effect it, these have to be indicated in the score, as shown in the illustration (p.622), which reproduces the table of preparations for Cage's *Sonatas and Interludes* (1946–8).

BIBLIOGRAPHY

R. Bunger: *The Well-prepared Piano* (Colorado Springs, CO, 1973); with foreword by John Cage, "How the Piano Came to be Prepared," rev. in J. Cage: *Empty Words* (Boston, 1980), 7

EDWIN M. RIPIN

Presbyterian Church, music of the. The Presbyterian Church is a Protestant denomination based on the ideas of John Calvin (1509–64) concerning theology and church government. In the USA it has about 3,250,000 members in approximately 13,000 congregations. The earliest congregations of Presbyterians in the American colonies were established in the 17th century by New England Puritans; in the same period, English, Scots-Irish, Welsh, and other settlers founded Presbyterian churches in Pennsylvania, Maryland, and Delaware.

Music has been an integral part of Presbyterian worship and life. The Presbyterian Church offers official support and guidance for its music through the Office of Worship, established in 1970; in the same year the Presbyterian Association of Musicians was founded. These agencies publish a quarterly, *Reformed Liturgy & Music*. The Association also sponsors music workshops and conferences, the largest of which is held each summer at the Montreat, North Carolina, Presbyterian conference center.

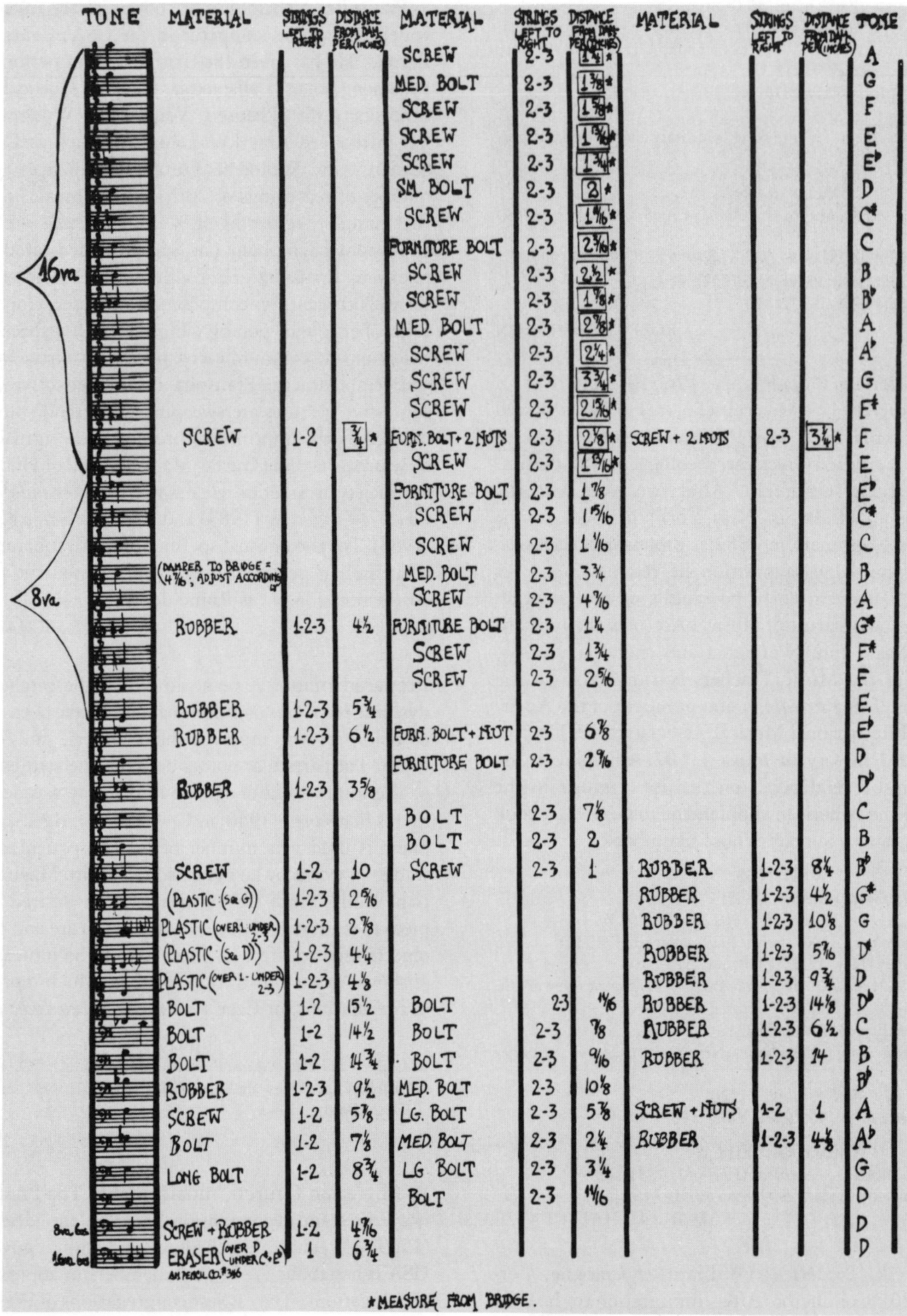

TONE	MATERIAL	STRINGS LEFT TO RIGHT	DISTANCE FROM DAMPER (INCHES)	MATERIAL	STRINGS LEFT TO RIGHT	DISTANCE FROM DAMPER (INCHES)	MATERIAL	STRINGS LEFT TO RIGHT	DISTANCE FROM DAMPER (INCHES)
A				SCREW	2-3	1 1/4*			
G				MED. BOLT	2-3	1 3/8*			
F				SCREW	2-3	1 5/8*			
E				SCREW	2-3	1 13/16*			
E♭				SCREW	2-3	1 3/4*			
D				SM. BOLT	2-3	2*			
C♯				SCREW	2-3	1 9/16*			
C				FURNITURE BOLT	2-3	2 3/16*			
B				SCREW	2-3	2 1/2*			
B♭				SCREW	2-3	1 7/8*			
A				MED. BOLT	2-3	2 7/8*			
A♭				SCREW	2-3	2 1/4*			
G				SCREW	2-3	3 3/4*			
F♯				SCREW	2-3	2 15/16*			
F	SCREW	1-2	3/4*	FURN. BOLT + 2 NUTS	2-3	2 1/8*	SCREW + 2 NUTS	2-3	3 1/4*
E				SCREW	2-3	1 13/16*			
E♭				FURNITURE BOLT	2-3	1 7/8			
C♯				SCREW	2-3	1 15/16			
C				SCREW	2-3	1 1/16			
B	(DAMPER TO BRIDGE = 4 7/16"; ADJUST ACCORDINGLY)			MED. BOLT	2-3	3 3/4			
A				SCREW	2-3	4 7/16			
G♯	RUBBER	1-2-3	4 1/2	FURNITURE BOLT	2-3	1 1/4			
F♯				SCREW	2-3	1 3/4			
F				SCREW	2-3	2 5/16			
E	RUBBER	1-2-3	5 3/4						
E♭	RUBBER	1-2-3	6 1/2	FURN. BOLT + NUT	2-3	6 7/8			
D				FURNITURE BOLT	2-3	2 9/16			
D♭	RUBBER	1-2-3	3 5/8						
C				BOLT	2-3	7 1/8			
B				BOLT	2-3	2			
B♭	SCREW	1-2	10	SCREW	2-3	1	RUBBER	1-2-3	8 1/4
G♯	(PLASTIC (see G))	1-2-3	2 5/16				RUBBER	1-2-3	4 1/2
G	PLASTIC (OVER 1 UNDER 2-3)	1-2-3	2 7/8				RUBBER	1-2-3	10 1/8
D♯	(PLASTIC (see D))	1-2-3	4 1/4				RUBBER	1-2-3	5 7/16
D	PLASTIC (OVER 1 - UNDER 2-3)	1-2-3	4 1/8				RUBBER	1-2-3	9 3/4
D♭	BOLT	1-2	15 1/2	BOLT	2-3	11/16	RUBBER	1-2-3	14 1/8
C	BOLT	1-2	14 1/2	BOLT	2-3	7/8	RUBBER	1-2-3	6 1/2
B	BOLT	1-2	14 3/4	BOLT	2-3	9/16	RUBBER	1-2-3	14
B♭	RUBBER	1-2-3	9 1/2	MED. BOLT	2-3	10 1/8			
A	SCREW	1-2	5 7/8	LG. BOLT	2-3	5 7/8	SCREW + NUTS	1-2	1
A♭	BOLT	1-2	7 1/8	MED. BOLT	2-3	2 1/4	RUBBER	1-2-3	4 1/8
G	LONG BOLT	1-2	8 3/4	LG BOLT	2-3	3 1/4			
D				BOLT	2-3	1 11/16			
D	SCREW + RUBBER	1-2	4 7/16						
D	ERASER (OVER D UNDER C♯+E♭) AM. PENCIL CO. #346	1	6 3/4						

*MEASURE FROM BRIDGE.

Prepared piano: table of preparations from Cage's "Sonatas and Interludes" (1946–8)

1. Congregational singing. 2. Choral music. 3. Instrumental music.

1. Congregational singing. The Presbyterian Church in the American colonies followed the custom of metrical psalm-singing favored by the Presbyterian and Puritan sects of Europe, notably of Calvin in Geneva. The Bay Psalm Book (1640) supplied colonial Presbyterians with materials for congregational song. In addition, the Scots and Scots-Irish colonists brought with them the Scottish psalter (*Psalms of David in Meeter*, 1650). This psalter drew on Francis Rous's version (1641), the revision of Rous's version by the Westminster Assembly of Divines, 1643–7, as the *Psalms of David in English Meeter* (1646), and the Bay Psalm Book, among others.

Because of illiteracy and the scarcity of psalters, the psalms were "lined out" in Presbyterian public worship. Contemporary accounts describe the cacophony that frequently resulted. The first American Presbyterian General Assembly recommended in 1788 that the custom of lining out be laid aside, partly because of the successful establishment, since about 1720, of singing-

the release of *Pretenders II* (1981). At the end of the tour, however, Farndon left the group, and shortly afterwards Honeyman-Scott died. Hynde re-formed the Pretenders with Chambers, Rob McIntosh (guitar), and Malcolm Foster (bass guitar). This group's first album, *Learning to Crawl* (1983), was marked by a new maturity in its sound and in Hynde's approach, which, though still tough and defiant, was deepened by a more compassionate intelligence. The Pretenders' instrumental framework is basic hard rock leavened by considerable verve and freshness in the compositions and arrangements. But the band's real distinction lies in Hynde's rough, bruised-sounding voice and in the multi-layered, ironic, yet deeply impassioned sentiments of her songs.

RECORDINGS
(all recorded for Sire)

Pretenders (6083, 1980), incl. Brass in Pocket; *Pretenders II* (3572, 1981), incl. Pack it up; *Learning to crawl* (23980-1, 1983)

JOHN ROCKWELL

Previn, André (George) [Priwin, Andreas Ludwig] (*b* Berlin, Germany, 6 April 1929). Conductor, pianist, and composer, of Russian-Jewish descent. He studied piano as a child at the Berlin Hochschule für Musik, until the Nazi regime's antisemitic policies caused his expulsion in 1938. His family moved to Paris, where Previn continued his studies at the Conservatoire with Marcel Dupré (1938–9). In 1939 they immigrated to the USA, where Previn's second cousin, Charles Previn, was music director for Universal studios in Hollywood. The family settled in Los Angeles, and Previn studied piano there with Max Rabinowitsch, theory with Joseph Achron and Ernst Toch, and composition with Mario Castelnuovo-Tedesco. He became an American citizen in 1943. He was a professional jazz pianist and an orchestrator for MGM studios before leaving high school and was soon appointed one of MGM's music directors. He composed his first film score in 1948 for *The Sun Comes Up*, and his recordings as a jazz pianist were notably successful. In 1951, during army service, he began to study conducting with Pierre Monteux in San Francisco. He left MGM but continued freelance film work (winning Oscar awards for *Gigi* in 1958, *Porgy and Bess* in 1959, *Irma la Douce* in 1963, and *My Fair Lady* in 1964), and began to develop a career as a concert pianist and conductor. He made his conducting début with the St. Louis SO in 1962, and after various guest conducting appearances succeeded Barbirolli as conductor-in-chief of the Houston SO (1967–9). In 1965 he began, in the recording studio, an association with the London SO that led to his appointment as its principal conductor (1968–79; thereafter he was Conductor Emeritus).

Previn has continued to make occasional appearances as a pianist (sometimes combining the role with that of conductor in a Mozart concerto), and as a composer, and also established a reputation as an engaging and fluent talker about music on the television screen in both Britain and the USA. Conversations with another verbal expositor, Antony Hopkins, resulted in an anecdotal book, *Music Face to Face* (1971). His musical versatility and his winning public manner gave him a following (even among non-concertgoers) comparable to Leonard Bernstein's in the USA, unparalleled in Britain since Sir Malcolm Sargent. Musically his acclimatization to the British scene was confirmed by his success as a conductor of Vaughan Williams (he recorded all nine symphonies with the London SO) and Walton. From his earliest professional years he became a master of the problems of timing and tact in the recording studio, and under his direction the London SO fulfilled an extensive and profitable recording program, including much music by Tchaikovsky, Rachmaninoff, and Prokofiev.

Previn has a declared predilection for nationalistic or otherwise strongly colored orchestral music. His repertory has generally not gone further back than Mozart, nor much forward from Bernstein and Britten, and in his early years in London there was an impression that, precipitated from a brilliant career in a different field, he was not wholly familiar with the symphonic repertory. He successfully toured with the London SO in western Europe and the USA on numerous occasions, and in 1971 and 1975 to the Far East. In London, as pianist and chamber musician rather than conductor, he was the artistic director for South Bank Summer Music, 1972–4, and he has been guest conductor with leading orchestras in Berlin, Vienna, Amsterdam, New York, Chicago, Boston, and elsewhere. From 1976 to 1984 he was music director of the Pittsburgh SO, with which he made several outstanding recordings and toured Europe (1978, 1982); he has also conducted an annual series with the Vienna PO (from 1977), taught at the Berkshire Music Center (from 1979), and served as director of the British Music Festival in Pittsburgh, New York, and Washington, DC (1981). In 1985 he was appointed principal conductor of the Royal PO, London, and music director of the Los Angeles PO.

Previn has been bold enough not to repress his flair for popular music, composing the scores for the musicals *Coco* (1969) and *The Good Companions* (1974). Among his other compositions are such orchestral works as a Symphony for strings (1962), concertos for cello (1968) and guitar (1971), *Principals* (1980), *Reflections* (1981) and *Divertimento* (1982), as well as chamber and piano works including *Four Outings* for brass quintet (1974), and a piece for actors and orchestra, *Every Good Boy Deserves Favour* (to words

André Previn

by Tom Stoppard). He prepared the volume *Orchestra* (1979) and edited *André Previn's Guide to the Orchestra* (1983).

BIBLIOGRAPHY

"Previn, André (George)," *CBY 1972*
E. Greenfield: *André Previn* (London, 1973) [with discography by M. Walker]
M. Bookspan and R. Yockey: *André Previn: a Biography* (Garden City, NY, 1981)
H. D. Ruttencutter: "Profiles: André Previn," *New Yorker*, lviii (10 Jan 1983), 36; (17 Jan 1983), 44
——: *Previn* (New York, 1985)

ARTHUR JACOBS/DENNIS K. McINTIRE

Prévost, Eugène-Prosper (*b* Paris, France, 23 April 1809; *d* New Orleans, LA, 19 Aug 1872). Conductor and composer. He studied with Jean-François Le Sueur at the Paris Conservatoire, and immigrated to the USA in 1838, settling in New Orleans, where he was the principal conductor of the Théâtre d'Orléans until 1859. He then became conductor of the new French Opera House, but the onset of the Civil War forced him to return to France in 1862. He spent five years in Paris, where he collaborated with Offenbach. Prévost returned to New Orleans in 1868 as a teacher of music and was to have resumed his conducting in the 1872–3 season, but died in summer 1872.

While in New Orleans Prévost conducted American premières of many well-known European operas and also world premières of his own *Esmeralda* (1842), *La chaste Suzanne* (1845), *Adolphe et Clari* (1846), and *Blanche et Renée* (1871). He also composed a Requiem (1857) for his son, who was accidentally shot, an oratorio, the *Patriotic Overture*, several cantatas, other religious pieces, and many parlor works. His songs demonstrate his dual national interests: some are topical American songs and others typical French ballads (ten of the latter were published in *Album musical*, n.d.). Collections of his works are in the Boston Public Library, the Library of Congress, Louisiana State University Library, the Historic New Orleans Collection, and the Tulane University libraries.

BIBLIOGRAPHY

Obituary, *Bee* (New Orleans, 20 Aug 1872)
E. L. Jewell: *Jewell's Crescent City Illustrated* (New Orleans, 1873)
L. Panzeri: *Louisiana Composers* (New Orleans, 1972)
J. Mongrédien: "Prévost, Eugène-Prosper," *Grove 6*
J. Belsom: "Prévost," *Dictionary of Louisiana Biography* (Lafayette, LA, in preparation)

JOHN H. BARON

Price [née Smith], **Florence Bea(trice)** (*b* Little Rock, AR, 9 April 1888; *d* Chicago, IL, 3 June 1953). Composer and teacher. She was the first black woman to win widespread recognition as a symphonic composer, rising to prominence (with William Grant Still and William Dawson) in the 1930s. After receiving early training from her mother, she attended the New England Conservatory, where her teachers included Chadwick, Converse, and Benjamin Cutter. She graduated with diplomas in organ and piano in 1906 and the same year returned to the South to teach at Shorter College, North Little Rock. In 1910 she moved to Atlanta to become head of the music department at Clark University, and afterwards returned to Little Rock, where she married Thomas J. Price in 1912. The Price family moved to Chicago in 1927, presumably to escape the increasing racial oppression in the South at that time. In Chicago Florence Price entered a period of compositional creativity and study under Leo Sowerby, Carl Busch, and others. In 1932 she achieved her first major success by winning first prize in the Wanamaker Competition for her Symphony in E minor, and several other prizes as well. This led to a performance of the symphony by the Chicago SO (1933) and to further performances of her works throughout the USA and in Europe. She received additional recognition after Marian Anderson's performances of her spiritual arrangement *My soul's been anchored in de Lord* and *Songs to the Dark Virgin*. The latter, a setting of a text by Langston Hughes, is one of her most powerful works and was hailed by the *Chicago Daily News* as "one of the greatest immediate successes ever won by an American song." Price remained active as a composer and teacher until her death.

Price is best known for her songs; she has been credited with elevating the Negro folk song to a level comparable to that of art song. With the exception of a handful of songs, her output, which comprises close to 300 compositions, remains largely unpublished and unknown. Her style is conservative; she was uninfluenced, for the most part, by 20th-century techniques. She combined elements of her Negro heritage with traditional Western European forms and a distinctive individual voice to produce a wide variety of works. Unlike Dawson, Price did not use actual Negro melodies in her own works; rather, she drew on characteristic musical elements such as folk and spiritual melodic types, simple harmonic structures, and Juba dance rhythms. To these she brought a thorough knowledge of instrumental writing and orchestral sonorities, colorful harmonies and exotic modulations, skill in handling both miniature and large-scale forms and, above all, a personal warmth and directness of expression.

WORKS

(selective list)

Orch: Sym. no.1, e, 1931–2; Ethiopia's Shadow in America, 1932; Mississippi River, sym., 1934; Pf Conc., f, perf. 1934; Sym., d; Sym. no.3, c, 1940; Sym. [no.4], g; 2 vn concs., no.1, n.d., no.2, D, 1952; Chicago Suite; Colonial Dance, sym.; Dances in the Canebrakes [arr. of pf piece]; 2 concert ovs, based on spirituals; Pf Conc. in 1 Movt, d; Rhapsody, pf, orch; Songs of the Oak, tone poem; Suite of Dances

Chamber: Moods, fl, cl, pf, 1953; Negro Folksongs in Counterpoint, str qt; 2 pf qnts; other str qt works, pieces for vn, pf; arrs. of orch works

Choral: The Moon Bridge (anon.), SSA, 1930; Witch of the Meadow (M. R. Gamble), SSA (1947); Nature's Magic (Gamble), SSA (1953); Song for Snow (E. Coatsworth), SATB (1957); Sea Gulls, female chorus, by 1951; Abraham Lincoln walks at Midnight (V. Lindsay), mixed vv, orch, org; After the 1st and 6th Commandments, SATB; Communion Service, F, SATB, org; Nod (W. de la Mare), TTBB; The Wind and the Sea, mixed vv, orch, org; *c*10 or more works for female/mixed vv, all with pf

Songs, 1v, pf: Dreamin' Town (P. L. Dunbar), 1934; Songs to the Dark Virgin (L. Hughes) (1941); Night (L. C. Wallace) (1946); Out of the South Blew a Wind (F. C. Woods) (1946); An April Day (J. F. Cotter) (1949); Dawn's Awakening (J. J. Burke); The Envious Wren (A. Carey, P. Carey); Fantasy in Purple (Hughes); Forever (Dunbar); Love-in-a-Mist (Gamble); Nightfall (Dunbar); Resignation (Price), arr. chorus; Song of the Open Road; Sympathy (I know why the caged bird sings) (Dunbar); To my Little Son (J. J. Davis); Travel's End (M. F. Hoisington)

Pf: At the Cotton Gin (1928); Sonata, e (1932); 2 fantasies on folk tunes; Fantasy no.4, 1932; 3 Little Negro Dances (1939), arr. 2 pf (1949); Bayou Dance, 1938; Dance of the Cotton Blossoms, 1938; Dances in the Canebrakes (1953); numerous educational pieces

Org: Impromptu, 1941; Adoration (1951); Evening Song, 1951; In Quiet Mood; Passacaglia and Fugue; Retrospection (An Elf on a Moonbeam); Sonata no.1; Suite no.1; Variations on a Folksong

Spiritual arrs: My soul's been anchored in de Lord, 1v, pf (1937), also arr. chorus; Nobody knows the trouble I see, pf (1938); Were you there when they crucified my Lord, pf (1942); I am bound for the kingdom, 1v, pf (1948); I'm workin' on my building, 1v, pf (1948); Heav'n Bound Soldier (1949); I couldn't hear nobody pray, SSAATTBB

MS of Sym. no.3 in *CtY-Mus*; MSS of 40 songs in *PU-Music*; other MSS in private collections; papers and copy MSS in *ArU*

Principal publishers: C. Fischer, Gamble-Hinged, Handy, Lorenz, Marks, Oxford, Presser, G. Schirmer, Summy

BIBLIOGRAPHY

SouthernB

M. C. Hare: *Negro Musicians and their Music* (Washington, DC, 1936/*R*1974)

M. Bonds: "A Reminiscence," *The Negro in Music and Art*, International Library of Negro Life and History, ed. L. Patterson (New York, 1967)

M. D. Hudgins: "Chicago School Named for Composer," *Arkansas Gazette* (30 June 1968), §E, p.5

E. Southern: *The Music of Black Americans: a History* (New York, 1971)

H. E. Roach: *Black American Music: Past and Present* (Boston, 1973)

M. D. Green: *A Study of the Lives and Works of Five Black Women Composers in America* (diss., U. of Oklahoma, 1975)

R. Abdul: *Blacks in Classical Music: a Personal History* (New York, 1977)

B. G. Jackson: "Florence Price, Composer," *BPiM*, v (1977), 30

O. Williams: *American Black Women in the Arts and Social Sciences* (Metuchen, NJ, rev. 2/1978)

C. Ammer: *Unsung: a History of Women in American Music* (Westport, CT, 1980)

B. G. Jackson: "Price, Florence Beatrice Smith," *NAW*

M. D. Green: "Florence Price," *Black Women Composers: a Genesis* (Boston, 1983), 31

R. L. Brown: *The Orchestral Music of Florence B. Price (1888–1953): a Stylistic Analysis* (diss., Yale U., in preparation)

MYRNA S. NACHMAN (work-list with BARBARA GARVEY JACKSON)

Price, (Mary Violet) Leontyne (*b* Laurel, MS, 10 Feb 1927). Soprano. While training as a teacher, she sang with her college glee club. In 1949 she won a scholarship to the Juilliard School, where she sang Alice Ford in *Falstaff*. In 1952 Thomson chose her for a Broadway revival of his opera *Four Saints in Three Acts*; thereafter she was immediately engaged as Bess in a new production of Gershwin's opera, which later made a world tour, and in which she remained for two years. A concert career (including first performances of works by Barber and Henri Sauguet) was interrupted by a highly successful television appearance as Tosca (1955). This, and appearances at San Francisco in 1957 (as Madame Lidoine in the American première of Poulenc's *Dialogues des Carmélites* and as Aida), decided the course of her career. At her débuts at the Verona Arena, Vienna, and Covent Garden (all 1958) and La Scala (1960), she had further triumphs as Aida. In 1960 she first appeared at the Salzburg Festival as Donna Anna, returning there in 1962–3 as Leonora in *Il trovatore*; in the latter role she had made an acclaimed Metropolitan début (27 January 1961). A notable appearance among many in New York was as Cleopatra in Barber's *Antony and Cleopatra*, commissioned for the opening of the new Metropolitan Opera House (1966); in 1975 she played Puccini's Manon there. She retired from the stage in January 1985 after a televised performace of *Aida* at the Metropolitan Opera, but continued to give recitals. Though her repertory embraced Poppaea, Handel's Cleopatra, Tchaikovsky's Tatyana, and Mozart and Puccini roles, it was principally in Verdi that she achieved fame as one of the world's foremost sopranos. Her voice was a true *lirico spinto*, able to fill Verdi's phrases with clean, full, dusky tone. Musically she was a subtle interpreter, though her acting did not always show great dramatic involvement. Many recordings, of Mozart, Puccini, and especially Verdi operas, have faithfully documented her career.

Leontyne Price in the title role of Verdi's "Aida"

She was married, 1952–72, to the bass-baritone William Warfield. She has been awarded a Presidential Medal of Freedom (1965), a Kennedy Center Honor (1980), a National Medal of Arts (1985), the Handel Medallion (1985), and a number of honorary doctorates.

BIBLIOGRAPHY

SouthernB

A. Blyth: "Leontyne Price Talks," *Gramophone*, xlix (1971–2), 303

H. L. Lyon: *Leontyne Price: Highlights of a Prima Donna* (New York, 1973)

W. Sargeant: "Leontyne Price," *Divas* (New York, 1973), 135–67

J. B. Steane: *The Grand Tradition* (New York, 1974), 407

S. E. Rubin: "Price on Price," *Opera News*, xl/17 (1976), 16

"Price, Leontyne," *CBY 1978*

R. Jacobson: " 'Collard Greens and Caviar'," *Opera News*, l/1 (1985), 18

ALAN BLYTH

Price, Lloyd (*b* New Orleans, LA, 9 March, 1933). Rhythm-and-blues and rock-and-roll singer. In the late 1940s he formed a rhythm-and-blues quintet in New Orleans, and composed and recorded for a local radio station. His first recording, *Lawdy, Miss Clawdy* (with the pianist Fats Domino), reached no.1 on the rhythm-and-blues charts in 1952. He had three more Top Ten hits before being drafted into the armed forces in 1954. After entertaining troops in the Far East until 1956, he moved to Washington, DC. There he formed his own company, KRC, to record his composition *Just because*, which was the first in a succession of his songs in the late 1950s to reach the Top Five on the rhythm-and-blues charts and to appear as well on the rock-and-roll charts; foremost among them were *Stagger Lee* (based on the traditional blues song *Stack-o-lee*), *Personality*, and *I'm gonna get married*, which were all composed by Price and his manager Harold Logan, and which display Price's round, deep, booming voice. In the 1960s Price founded the record labels Double L (for which Wilson Pickett first recorded) and Turntable, and continued to compose, record, and perform; he also established his own nightclub, the Turntable, in New York. Later he moved to Philadelphia, where he appeared in rock-and-roll revival concerts.

RECORDINGS

(selective list)

Lawdy, Miss Clawdy (Specialty 428, 1952); Oooh, oooh, oooh/Restless Heart (Specialty 440, 1952); Just because (ABC-Para. 9792, 1957); Stagger Lee

(ABC-Para. 9972, 1958); Personality (ABC-Para. 10018, 1959); I'm gonna get married (ABC-Para. 10032, 1959); Lady Luck (ABC-Para. 10075, 1960); Misty (Double L 722, 1963)

BIBLIOGRAPHY

A. Shaw: *Honkers and Shouters: the Golden Years of Rhythm and Blues* (New York, 1978), 188

BARRY KERNFELD

Price, Ray (Noble) (*b* nr Perryville, TX 12 Jan 1928). Country-music singer and guitarist. He grew up in Dallas, where in the 1940s he worked at the Jim Beck studio, then the foremost country-music recording studio. There he came under the influence of Lefty Frizzell, who wrote *If you're ever lonely, darling*, the first song that Price recorded (for Columbia, in 1951). Radio work followed, first on the "Big D Jamboree" on the Dallas station, and then, starting in January 1952, on the "Grand Ole Opry," and Price continued to have modest success with his recordings. He became a close friend of Hank Williams, and after Williams's death, he took over his band, renamed it the Cherokee Cowboys, and continued performing in the Williams style. By 1956, however, he had forged his own style, characterized by two or three fiddles and steel and electric guitar played in jazz style, supporting Price's high-pitched, unadorned vocal line. His first recording to sell a million copies was *Crazy Arms* (1956), and his second was *City Lights* (1958), composed by Willie Nelson. Price's use of drums and a strong electric bass played in "walking" rhythm helped him withstand the challenge of rock music in the late 1950s, and such band members as Buddy Emmons (steel guitar), Jimmy Day (electric guitar), Willie Nelson (acoustic guitar), and Johnny Bush (guitar) made the Cherokee Cowboys the best back-up band in country music at that time. In the mid-1960s Price successfully anticipated the pop crooning style that was shortly to infiltrate country singing: *For the good times* (1970), a version of Kristofferson's *I won't mention it again* (1971) with lush orchestration, and *You're the best thing that ever happened to me* (1973) are his best-known creations from this period. His long association with Columbia, which had brought him 62 hit records, ended in 1975; he later recorded, with less commercial success, for the gospel label Myrrh and for ABC/Dot. His resonant, mellow voice influenced many younger singers, including Mel Tillis, Johnny Bush, and Willie Nelson.

BIBLIOGRAPHY

B. C. Malone: "A Shower of Country Stars: Country Music since World War II," *Stars of Country Music*, ed. B. C. Malone and J. McCulloh (Urbana, IL, 1975), 397

——: Liner notes, *Honky-Tonkin'* (TL CW12, 1983)

CHARLES K. WOLFE

Pride, Charley (*b* Sledge, MS, 18 March 1938). Country-music singer and guitarist. As a child, he responded more enthusiastically to the country music of the "Grand Ole Opry" than to the blues styles of the Mississippi Delta region where he grew up. He was self-taught as a guitarist. Pride had a brief career as a minor-league baseball player and as a zinc smelter in Helena, Montana. In 1963, after an informal backstage audition for Red Sovine and Red Foley in Montana, he moved to Nashville, and the following year Chet Atkins signed him to RCA Records. He thus became the first black country-music performer to record for an important company. At the beginning of this affiliation, RCA suppressed the fact that he was black, an omission made possible by his rich, smooth, but slightly nasal baritone voice, which did not sound typically black. Later, however, RCA capitalized on Pride's unique status. He had his first hit record, *Just between you and me*, in 1966, and went on to have many songs in the no. 1 position, including *All I have to offer you (is me)* (1969), *Is anybody goin' to San Antone* (1970), and *Honky Tonk Blues* (1980). In January 1967 Ernest Tubb introduced him to the "Grand Ole Opry," and he subsequently won virtually every award available to a male performer in country music. In the 1970s and 1980s he toured and appeared on television with his band, the Pridesmen.

BIBLIOGRAPHY

A. Malone: "Charley Pride," *Stars of Country Music*, ed. B. C. Malone and J. McCulloh (Urbana, IL, 1975), 340

"Pride, Charley," *CBY 1975*

BILL C. MALONE

Priestman, Brian (*b* Birmingham, England, 10 Feb 1927). English conductor. He studied at the University of Birmingham (MA 1952) and at the Brussels Conservatory. He was music director of the Edmonton SO, Canada, 1964–8, and resident conductor of the Baltimore SO, 1968–9. In 1970 he became music director of the Denver SO, a post he retained until 1978, when he was appointed music director of the Florida PO. He was appointed professor at the University of Cape Town College of Music in 1981.

Priestman combines a sound classical style with a strong interest in contemporary music and a scholarly grasp of Baroque performance. He has given the premières of works by Gerhard, Joubert, and others. His recordings include three major Handel works – *Hercules*, *Rodelinda*, and *Serse* – and he has published useful performing editions of *Messiah* and the *Water Music*.

BERNARD JACOBSON

Charley Pride, 1970s

Primavera String Quartet. String quartet. It was formed in New York in 1975 and, until it disbanded in the spring of 1983, it attracted much attention as one of the few all-female chamber music ensembles performing in the USA. The original members were first violinist Martha Caplin, second violinist Kathryn Caswell, the violist Diann Jezurski, and the cellist Melissa Meell (Deborah Berlin replaced Caswell in 1977; later second violinists were Mitsuru Tsubota and Catherine Metz). The ensemble won the Naumburg Award in 1977; their subsequent concert at Alice Tully Hall in April 1978 included the world première of Chihara's string quartet, written especially for the group. Perhaps due to frequent personnel changes, the Primavera String Quartet seldom achieved an extremely high level of ensemble refinement, but its interpretations were characteristically intelligent and sensitive.

JAMES WIERZBICKI

Primrose, William (*b* Glasgow, Scotland, 23 Aug 1904; *d* Provo, UT, 1 May 1982). Violist. He studied violin in Glasgow with Camillo Ritter, then at the Guildhall School of Music, London, and in Belgium under Ysaÿe (1925–7), who advised him to change to the viola. He toured as a soloist and in the London String Quartet (1930–35). Toscanini chose him as principal viola in the NBC SO (1937–42). He appeared as a soloist with orchestras in Europe and the USA, becoming the foremost viola virtuoso. In 1939 he formed the Primrose Quartet. In 1944 he commissioned Bartók to write a viola concerto, and five years later gave the first performance of the work, which was completed by Tibor Serly after Bartók's death. Among other composers inspired to write for him were Britten, Milhaud, Rochberg, Edmund Rubbra, and P. R. Fricker. He formed the Festival Quartet (1954–62) from the faculty of the Aspen Music School. In 1962 the University of Southern California, Los Angeles, invited Heifetz, Piatigorsky, and Primrose to teach their respective instruments and chamber music. The three also made various recordings together.

In 1963 Primrose suffered a heart attack, and from that year onwards, though still making an occasional concert appearance, he devoted most of his time to teaching, first at Indiana University (1965–72), and later at the Tokyo University of Fine Arts and Music (1972). In Japan he was also associated with Tōhō Gakuen School in Tokyo and Suzuki's institute in Mutsumoto. He gave master classes in the USA and Europe, judged many international music competitons, then taught at Brigham Young University from 1979 until his death. He wrote *Technique is Memory* (1963) and collaborated with Menuhin on another technique book; he also edited works from the viola repertory and made numerous arrangements for viola. His memoirs, *Walk on the North Side*, were published in 1978. He was made a CBE in 1953 and received an honorary doctorate from Eastern Michigan University.

Generally Primrose played on a viola of moderate size, producing a tone of rare sweetness and beauty. His first viola was an Amati of 1600, but he also played on a viola by Andrea Guarneri (1697) and two Stradivari instruments, the "Gibson" (1734) and the "MacDonald" (1700); he also favored instruments by modern makers, including William Moening, Yu Iada, and Pierre Vidoudez. He was concerned with and learned in American history and was an engaging raconteur.

WATSON FORBES

Prince (i). Firm of melodeon manufacturers. About 1840 George A. Prince (*b* Boston, MA, 17 Feb 1818; *d* Buffalo, NY, 3 March 1890) established the firm of George A. Prince & Co. in Buffalo. This was one of the first firms to attempt large-scale production of reed organs in the USA; by 1846 it had 150 employees and was producing 75 instruments a week. Prince took out several patents in 1846 for improvements to melodeons. In 1847 Emmons Hamlin, then working for Prince, discovered a method of improving the tone of reeds by slightly bending and twisting their tongues; in the early 1850s he also introduced the double bellows. In 1854 Hamlin left Prince, and with Henry Mason, son of Lowell Mason, founded the Mason & Hamlin Organ & Piano Co., which dominated reed organ manufacturing in the USA in the late 19th century. In the 1860s Prince began making larger reed organs, including the New Organ Melodeon, which had two manuals, four sets of reeds, and one and a half octaves of pedals. The firm went into bankruptcy in 1875.

BIBLIOGRAPHY

R. F. Gellerman: *The American Reed Organ* (Vestal, NY, 1973)

BARBARA OWEN

Prince (ii) [Nelson, Prince Rogers] (*b* Minneapolis, MN, 7 June 1960). Rock singer and songwriter. He began his career with two albums (*For You*, 1978, and *Prince*, 1979) of unremarkable romantic ballads sung in a feathery falsetto voice. In *Dirty Mind* (1980), however, the style of both lyrics and music changed notably: texts containing explicit sexual references, often couched in jokes and puns, are set to music that ranges from gentle ballads to inventive disco variations and curt, hard-rock melodies; the songs are sung in a mixture of soft growls and moans and with a playfulness that underlines the ribaldry of the lyrics. *Controversy* (1981) and *1999* (1982, which includes the hit song *Little red Corvette*), show a more refined style of sensuous dance music and add a new theme of imminent apocalypse. In 1984 the film *Purple Rain*, in which Prince took the leading role, was released, and the album of the same name yielded the phenomenally successful single *When doves cry*. Prince received three Grammy Awards at the 1985 ceremonies. After an arduous but well-received North American tour (1984–5) he announced his retirement from live performances in order to devote himself exclusively to recordings.

RECORDINGS

(all recorded for Warner Bros.)

For You (3158, 1978); *Prince* (3366, 1979); *Dirty Mind* (3478, 1980); *Controversy* (3601, 1981); *1999* (23720, 1982), incl. Little red Corvette; *Purple Rain* (25110, 1984), incl. When doves cry; *Around the World in a Day* (25286, 1985)

KEN TUCKER

Princeton University. Private university in Princeton, New Jersey, chartered in 1746 and opened the following year. Musical activity was informal until 1917, when the donation of a new organ prompted a series of recitals and lectures on music; these led to the offering of undergraduate courses. From 1934 Roy Dickinson Welch was influential in shaping the department, which he led until his death in 1951. Subsequent chairmen have been Arthur Mendel, Kenneth J. Levy, Lewis Lockwood, Peter Westergaard, and Harold S. Powers; faculty members have included Sessions, Strunk, Babbitt, Cone, and Spies. The university offers a BA in music, and MFA and PhD degrees in theory, composition, and historical musicology. The Harvey S. Firestone Library houses an outstanding research collection; its strongest areas include

Roman and Byzantine chant, medieval and Renaissance music theory, and the works of Bach, Beethoven, Handel, and Wagner (*see also* LIBRARIES AND COLLECTIONS, §3).

BIBLIOGRAPHY

M. R. Bryan and P. Morgan, eds.: "Music Exhibition" and "Checklist of the Exhibition," *Princeton University Library Chronicle*, xxviii/2 (1967), 113

A. Leitch, ed.: *A Princeton Companion* (Princeton, NJ, 1978)

NINA DAVIS-MILLIS

Prine, John (*b* Maywood, IL, 10 Oct 1946). Folksinger and songwriter. He began performing in the Chicago area in the 1960s. In 1971 he went to Memphis, where he recorded his first album, *John Prine*; this included two protest songs, "Sam Stone," about the plight of Vietnam veterans, and "Hello in there," which dealt with the insensitive treatment of elderly people; the recording brought him critical acclaim but little commercial success, a pattern that has repeated itself throughout his career. His later albums include *Common Sense* (1975), on which he used electric instruments and rock rhythms, *Bruised Orange* (1978), a more conventional folk recording, and *Pink Cadillac* (1979), recorded at Sun Studios in Memphis; the last album was made during the period of Prine's most intense interest in rock music, which he has continued to explore intermittently. Early in his career Prine was often compared with Bob Dylan, with whom he shares a scratchy, unconventional singing style and a penchant for topical lyrics that can veer suddenly into humor or surreality. He has attracted an enthusiastic cult following that appreciates the twists he applies to folk and pop forms, particularly the odd rhyme schemes and fatalistic message of his lyrics, and the hoarse, cracked vocal effects that characterize his singing. Some of his songs have been recorded by other performers, including the Everly Brothers, Joan Baez, and Bette Midler.

RECORDINGS

(selective list)

John Prine (Atl. 8296, 1971); *Diamonds in the Rough* (Atl. 7240, 1972); *Sweet Revenge* (Atl. 7274, 1973); *Common Sense* (Atl. 18127, 1975); *Bruised Orange* (Asy. 6E139, 1978); *Pink Cadillac* (Asy. 6E222, 1979); *Storm Windows* (Asy. 280, 1980)

KEN TUCKER

Printing of music. *See* PUBLISHING AND PRINTING OF MUSIC.

Pro Arte Quartet. Belgian string quartet. Formed in 1912 by Alphonse Onnou (1893–1940), Laurent Halleux (*b* 1897), Germain Prévost (*b* 1891), and Robert Maas (1901–48), the quartet became known as an exponent of modern music and achieved greatest recognition in the 1920s and 1930s, performing new works by Bartók, Casella, Honegger, Martinů, Milhaud, and Rieti, among others. The ensemble toured Europe, Canada, and the USA, where in 1925 it played at the inauguration of the Coolidge Auditorium in the Library of Congress. From 1940 to 1947 the group was quartet-in-residence at the University of Wisconsin, led first by Antonio Brosa and from 1944 by Rudolph Kolisch. Since 1947 the title Pro Arte Quartet has been taken by the faculty quartet of the university, led from 1967 by Norman Paulu.

At first less successful with the Classical repertory than with modern works to which it brought exceptional polish and ease, the quartet in time came to be equally highly regarded for its performances of music by Mozart, Haydn, and Schubert. Its style concentrated on finesse, lucidity of texture, and rhythmic buoyancy. The ensemble recorded many of Haydn's quartets, as well as works by Mozart, Schubert, Brahms, Dvořák, Debussy, and Ravel. An Austrian quartet of the same name was founded in Salzburg in 1973.

ROBERT PHILIP/R

Process music. A term applied to one of the compositional practices generally referred to as MINIMALISM; it is associated particularly with the work of STEVE REICH.

Professor Longhair [Byrd, Henry Roeland; Byrd, Roy] (*b* Bogalusa, LA, 19 Dec 1918; *d* New Orleans, 30 Jan 1980). Rhythm-and-blues pianist and singer. He grew up in New Orleans, where he lived most of his life. He was a street tap dancer in his youth, and in his teens mastered the rough-hewn blues piano style played in the brothels and nightclubs of New Orleans. Among his influences were Isidore "Tuts" Washington, Robert Bertrand, and Sullivan Rock. He was drafted into the army in World War II, but returned to New Orleans in the mid-1940s and became a prominent figure in that city's rapidly evolving rhythm-and-blues scene. In 1949 he made his first recordings, playing the piano and singing, and accompanied by a small combo. *Bald Head* (1950) was his first and only rhythm-and-blues hit.

Longhair's energetic piano playing, characterized by a rolling boogie-woogie bass, rumba rhythms, and good-humored syncopation, inspired New Orleans rock-and-roll musicians of the 1950s and 1960s. As a performer and piano teacher he helped shape the music of Fats Domino, Huey "Piano" Smith, Ernie-K-Doe, Allen Toussaint, James Booker, Mac ("Dr. John") Rebennack, and countless others; expressing a debt that many acknowledged, Toussaint dubbed him the "Bach of Rock-and-Roll." In the late 1970s Longhair was discovered by rock critics and audiences, enabling him to tour again and record several fine albums. His songs *Tipitina* and *Mardi Gras in New Orleans* are frequently performed during Mardi Gras celebrations.

RECORDINGS

(selective list)

Bald Head (1950, Mer. 8175); *New Orleans Piano* (1970, Atl. 7225); *Rock and Roll Gumbo* (1980, Mardi Gras 1003); *Mardi Gras in New Orleans* (1981, Nighthawk 108)

BIBLIOGRAPHY

J. Broven: *Walking to New Orleans: the Story of New Orleans Rhythm and Blues* (Bexhill-on-Sea, England, 1974)

R. Palmer: *A Tale of Two Cities: Memphis Rock and New Orleans Roll*, ISAMm, xii (Brooklyn, NY, 1979)

LANGDON WINNER

Proffitt, Frank (*b* Laurel Bloomery, TN, 1913; *d* Reese, NC, 24 Nov 1965). Banjo maker and singer. He learned to make banjos and dulcimers from his father and as an instrument maker became most famous for his banjos, which were typical of those made in the mountains of northwestern North Carolina where he lived. A fine traditional singer (who was also a tobacco farmer and part-time carpenter), he was important in the folk music revival of the late 1950s and early 1960s. He was the source of the song "Tom Dooley." The song collector and performer Frank Warner recorded this song from Proffitt in 1939, reshaped it over years of performing it himself, and taught his version to Alan Lomax, who published it in 1947 in *Folksong USA*, giving credit only to Warner. "Tom Dooley" became a commercial hit when the Kingston Trio recorded this version in 1957, giving credit to no one. This recording was largely responsible for initiating the urban folk music boom. Through Warner's efforts,

Proffitt finally became known as the source of the song, which created a demand both for his appearance at folk festivals and for his handmade banjos. These are made out of native hardwoods, and are characterized by a long, fretless neck, a small body (about 25 cm in diameter) with a wide wooden rim into which is set a small skin head (15 cm), and a wooden back with a small sound-hole (8–10 cm). Although this style has been taken to be the authentic mountain folk banjo, it is only one of the many varieties of homemade mountain banjos. Proffitt made recordings for Folk Legacy Records and Folkways Records.

BIBLIOGRAPHY

F. Warner: "Frank Proffitt," *Sing Out!*, xiii/4 (1963), 6

C. P. Heaton: "The 5-String Banjo in North Carolina," *Southern Folklore Quarterly*, xxxv (1971), 62

F. and A. Warner: "Frank Proffitt," *Appalachian Journal*, i/3 (1973)

ROBERT B. WINANS

Progressive country music [redneck rock]. A term used to describe a style of COUNTRY MUSIC combining country and rock techniques, developed during the 1970s. It is particularly associated with Austin, Texas, where an eclectic musical community experimented with such styles as folk, rock, jazz, western swing, Tex-Mex, and mainstream country; the resulting amalgam was aimed at a young audience and widely publicized as an alternative to the NASHVILLE SOUND, which was regarded as too homogenized. Progressive country music's instrumentation is similar to that of mainstream country music. Its name came to imply an open cultural attitude, defined as much by the dress and lifestyle of the musicians as by their music: those who sported "hippie" hairstyles and clothes as well as traditional cowboy costumes were seen to have forged an alliance between two highly diverging communities – the student population of Austin and the local "redneck" culture. Exponents of the style included Marcia Ball, Doug Sahm, Michael Murphey, and Willie Nelson. The Austin radio station KOKE extended the use of the term by applying it to the contents of its broadcasts, which reflected a flexible programming policy that avoided the usual emphasis on the Top 40; its format was copied by other stations. By the mid-1980s progressive country music had been absorbed into the mainstream of country music as exemplified by the careers of such performers as Nelson and Waylon Jennings.

BIBLIOGRAPHY

J. Reid: *The Improbable Rise of Redneck Rock* (Austin, 1974/*R*1977)

BILL C. MALONE

Progressive jazz. A term applied, mainly in the 1940s and 1950s, to continuations and extensions of the jazz orchestral tradition. It is associated chiefly with the more ambitious parts of the output of Stan Kenton's large band, though it is also applied to shorter-lived ensembles of Boyd Raeburn and, less importantly, Earle Spencer; it is used, too, in connection with a few bands whose main activity lay elsewhere, for example, the group with which Charlie Barnet recorded some excellent pieces for Capitol in 1949, such as *Cu-Ba* (Cap. 15417).

The music of these bands grew directly out of that of the big swing groups of the 1930s and early 1940s – Kenton's *Intermission Riff* (1946, Cap. 298), for instance, using the same theme as Jimmy Lunceford's *Yard Dog Mazurka* (1941, Decca 4032). In pieces such as *Chorale for Brass, Piano and Bongos* (1947, Cap. 10183) and *Fugue for Rhythm Section* (1947, Cap. 10127), however, Kenton and, more particularly, Pete Rugolo (Kenton's chief composer and arranger during this period) arrived at a significant further development of orchestral jazz. This was consolidated by later recordings by Kenton, such as Bill Holman's *Invention for Guitar and Trumpet* (1952, Cap. EAP2-383). In partial contrast, Robert Graettinger's music for the Kenton band made additional use of a medium-sized string section and a considerably more dissonant harmonic vocabulary, and conveyed a dark emotional turbulence that almost invoked the Second Viennese School. An example is the four-movement *City of Glass* (1951, Cap. 28062-3).

Boyd Raeburn's output during the same period was also self-consciously modernistic, as is suggested by titles such as *Boyd meets Stravinsky* (1946, Jewell 10002). Yet the scores, by George Handy (a pupil of Aaron Copland), Ed Finckel and others, retain their interest; their characteristically complex textures and dissonant harmony were qualified by the exhilaratingly full-throated power of the band's performance. Raeburn also performed works in a quieter, pastel-toned vein, exemplified by Handy's and Hal McKusick's *Yerxa* (1945, Jewell 10001).

For a while "progressive" was also used as a generic term for postwar jazz styles (including bop and its offshoots) now known collectively as "modern jazz."

See also JAZZ, §V, 6.

BIBLIOGRAPHY

A. Jackson: "Boyd Raeburn," *Jazz Monthly*, xii/11 (1966), 5

M. Sparke: *Kenton on Capitol* (Hounslow, England, 1966)

A. Morgan: "The Progressives," *Jazz on Record*, ed. A. McCarthy (London, 1968), 361

M. Harrison: "Stan Kenton: the 'Innovations' Band," *Jazz Journal*, xxxii (1979), no.4, p.4; no.5, p.18

W. F. Lee: *Stan Kenton: Artistry in Rhythm* (Los Angeles, 1980)

MAX HARRISON

Pro Musica Antiqua. Name under which the NEW YORK PRO MUSICA ensemble was founded by NOAH GREENBERG in 1952.

Pro-Musica Society. Society founded in New York in 1920 as the Franco-American Musical Society by the French pianist E. Robert Schmitz, who also directed its activities. It was one of several bodies formed in the 1920s to promote new and unfamiliar music. After a few years the aims of the society broadened and its name was changed to Pro-Musica Inc.; chapters were established in the West and Midwest, as well as in Canada, Europe, and the Far East. It was Schmitz's talents as a concert pianist, educator, and entrepreneur that made Pro-Musica a thriving organization for 12 years. He established more than 40 chapters in major cities and sought support from socially and financially prominent patrons for the advisory boards in each city. Schmitz's European education, reputation, and contacts abroad made possible the first American appearances of some of the most prominent composers of the century, including Ravel, Bartók, and Ottorino Respighi; these three (independently) gave lecture-recitals in 30 chapters in the USA and Canada in 1928. American composers were sent to the Paris chapter, and the tenor Roland Hayes sang in Moscow and Leningrad under the society's auspices. Among the many artists and composers to appear under Pro-Musica sponsorship were Hindemith, Schoenberg, Arthur Honegger, Milhaud, Albert Roussel, Alexandre Tansman, Prokofiev, Alfredo Casella, Arthur Bliss, Germaine Tailleferre, Florent Schmitt, Kodály, Stravinsky, Webern, Alexander Tcherepnin, and Ernst Toch. From 1923 the society sponsored a series of International Referendum Concerts with programs suggested by its international advisory board. Several important premières were given, such as two of Ives's *Three Quarter-tone Pieces* in 1925. The society published the *Pro-Musica Quarterly*, edited by Germaine Schmitz (Robert Schmitz's wife) under the pseudonym Ely Jade.

BIBLIOGRAPHY

V. Perlis: *Two Men for Modern Music*, ISAMm, ix (Brooklyn, NY, 1978)

VIVIAN PERLIS

Protestant Episcopal Church in the USA, music of the. *See* EPISCOPAL CHURCH, MUSIC OF THE.

Providence. Capital city of Rhode Island (pop. 156,804; metropolitan area 919,216). A concert of instrumental music was announced for 2 August 1768 in the large assembly room in the home of Joshua Hacker, a wealthy shipowner, and a reading of *The Beggar's Opera* took place there a year later, in spite of the general censure of opera and other forms of dramatic entertainment in colonial Providence. In 1772 the well-known tunebook compiler Andrew Law led a chorus at Rhode Island College (now Brown University), from which he graduated in 1775; at around the same time organs were installed at the Congregational Church (where William Billings conducted a singing-school in 1774) and at King's Church. *The Poor Soldier*, a ballad opera, was performed in Providence in 1795, and Oliver Shaw, a blind organist and composer, was active in the city after 1807. He founded the Psallonian Society, a large choral organization incorporated by legislature in 1816.

Providence profited by its proximity to Boston in the 19th century, and Henry Russell, Jenny Lind, Louis Gottschalk, Anton Rubinstein, Hans von Bülow, Ole Bull (15 performances), and Clara Louise Kellogg (34 performances) were among those who included Providence on their tours. The pianist, composer, and teacher Francis H. Brown (not related to the family connected with Brown University) left Boston for Providence in 1849 and remained as organist at the First Baptist Church until 1856. Musical activity increased with the formation of such organizations as the Beethoven Society, which performed the Fifth Symphony for the first time in Providence in January 1847, and the Mendelssohn Choral Union, which gave the first hearings of the composer's *Lobgesang* (Symphony no.2) (in 1868) and Psalm xcv (1884), conducted by Carl Zerrahn. The Arion Club, founded in 1881 by the tenor and composer Jules Jordan, presented large-scale choral works and concert versions of operas with such soloists as Nellie Melba, Lillian Nordica, Italo Campanini, and Myron Whitney. Jordan had sung the title role in the first American performance of Berlioz's *La damnation de Faust* in a New York production conducted by Leopold Damrosch in 1880, and one of his own operas, *Rip Van Winkle*, was performed in the Providence Opera House in 1897. This theater (built in 1871; capacity 1000) was a favorite venue for the 40 opera companies (chiefly visiting troupes) that performed in Providence during the late 19th century; minstrel shows were still more popular.

Orchestral concerts were also presented in Providence by the touring Germania Musical Society and the Theodore Thomas Orchestra. The Boston SO has made regular visits since 1881. Fairman's Orchestra, an ad hoc ensemble occasionally referred to as the Providence Symphony, gave concerts during the 1920s. The Providence SO was founded by Wassili Leps in 1932. The Rhode Island PO was established in 1945 and directed by Francis Madeira until he resigned in 1979; he was succeeded by Alvaro Cassuto, whose resignation in 1985 was followed by a season of guest conductors.

One of the city's earliest ensembles in continuous existence is the American Band, which was founded in the 1830s and directed from 1866 to 1900 by the composer and cornetist David Wallis Reeves; it continued with fewer activities under other conductors but has recently been revived by Francis Marciniak for local concerts and tours outside the state. Important concert series in the 20th century have been organized by the Community Concerts Association, the Steinert family (which owned music stores in a number of cities and began to sponsor concerts at the Majestic Theater around 1920), and Temple Beth-el. The Rhode Island Chamber Music Concerts, inaugurated at the Museum of Art of the Rhode Island School of Design in the 1930s, have been sponsored by Brown University since 1954. Rhode Island College and Providence College also have concert series.

Choral music is offered by the Rhode Island Civic Chorale (founded in 1956 by Louis Pichierri), which performs at the Veterans Memorial Auditorium, the Providence Singers, and by the Peloquin Chorale, founded by the composer Alexander Peloquin, who has directed choral festivals at the Cathedral of Saints Peter and Paul, where he is director of music. Music for male chorus has been presented regularly by the University Glee Club of Providence (founded 1911).

The main venue for the Boston SO, the Rhode Island PO, the Providence Opera Theater (founded in 1978), the Rhode Island Festival Ballet, and various ensembles from Brown University and Rhode Island College is the 3200-seat Providence Performing Arts Center (known as the Loewe State Theater until its renovation). Concerts and other musical activities are also given in the Mary K. Hail Music Mansion (built 1928), endowed by a well-known local patron. Mrs. Hail, who had been a delegate to the board of the National Federation of Music Clubs, stipulated before her death (in 1948) that students and club members who used the building could continue to do so without cost; the Rhode Island Federation of Music Clubs, including such groups as the Chopin Club (founded 1879) and Chaminade Club (1905), meet there regularly. The City's Civic Center (capacity 20,000) hosts rock concerts and other musical events.

Brown University was founded as Rhode Island College in 1764 and took its present name in 1804; women were first admitted in 1891, and in 1928 the Women's College became Pembroke College, which merged with Brown in 1971. In addition to a BA degree, the university offers an MA in music and composition and both an MA and a PhD in ethnomusicology. The ethnomusicology program, created in 1968 to complement the university's Asian Language and Area Center, is one of the few available to undergraduate as well as graduate students in the USA. The university's library contains the Hamilton C. MacDougall Collection of psalters and hymnals, the John Carter Brown Library of publications dating from the colonial period, and the McLellan Lincoln Collection of materials related to Abraham Lincoln. The John D. Rockefeller, Jr., Library, the main university library, houses extensive general holdings in music, and the John Hay Library contains several special collections. (*See also* LIBRARIES AND COLLECTIONS, §3.)

BIBLIOGRAPHY

H. C. Thrasher: *Two Hundred and Fifty Years of Music in Providence, Rhode Island, 1636–1886* (MS, *RP*, 1937)

J. E. Mangler and W. Dinneen: "Early Music in Rhode Island Churches," *Rhode Island History*, xvii/1–4 (1958), 1, 33, 73, 108

F. Lieberman: "An Undergraduate Curriculum in Ethnomusicology at Brown University," *College Music Symposium*, xi (1971), 55
F. Marciniak and J. Lemons: *Strike up the Band* (Providence, 1979)

ARLAN R. COOLIDGE

Pruett, James W(orrell) (*b* Mount Airy, NC, 23 Dec 1932). Music librarian and musicologist. He attended the University of North Carolina (BA 1955, MA 1957, PhD 1962) and from 1955 was on the staff of the library there, first as a reference assistant and later (1961–76) as music librarian. In 1963 he joined the faculty of the music department, where he became professor of music and chairman in 1976. Pruett has been active in the American Musicological Society and the Music Library Association (president, 1973–5), and was editor of *Notes* from 1974 to 1977. He has written numerous journal and encyclopedia articles in addition to book and music reviews, and edited *Studies in Musicology* (1969), a memorial volume for Glen Haydon. He is preparing an edition and study of the Laborde Chansonnier.

PAULA MORGAN

Pruslin, Stephen (Lawrence) (*b* Brooklyn, NY, 16 April 1940). Pianist, composer, and writer. He studied music at Brandeis University (BA 1961) and Princeton University (MFA 1963), teaching at Princeton until 1964. His piano teachers were Luise Vosgerchian and Eduard Steuermann. In 1964, under the auspices of a Hertz Memorial Scholarship from the University of California, he went to Europe and settled in London, where he has remained. He established an international career as a pianist, making his recital début at the Purcell Room, London (1970), and appearing as a soloist with the BBC SO and the Royal PO and in recital with Elisabeth Söderstrom, Bethany Beardslee, and Jan DeGaetani. He is a member of both the London Sinfonietta and the Fires of London, which he founded (and named) with Peter Maxwell Davies as successor to the Pierrot Players in 1970. A leading interpreter of contemporary keyboard music, he has given the European premières of many of Elliott Carter's compositions as well as Davies's Piano Sonata (written for him in 1981). Among his other specialties are the late Beethoven piano works and keyboard works of Bach and John Bull, which he performs on a modern piano. In 1985 he was a soloist at the Bach-Tagen, Berlin. A number of his solo and ensemble recordings have won international awards.

Pruslin has composed or arranged music for film and theater, including Ken Russell's *The Devils* and *The Boy Friend*, Derek Jarman's *The Tempest*, and Peter Ustinov's *Beethoven's Tenth*, as well as scores for British television series. In 1965 he wrote the libretto to Harrison Birtwistle's *Punch and Judy*. He has also made a translation of Schoenberg's *Pierrot lunaire*, written articles on contemporary music in a number of journals, and lectured on music for the BBC. As the editor of *Peter Maxwell Davies: Studies from Two Decades* (1979), he is as passionate and articulate a spokesman for Davies's music in words as he is at the keyboard.

SUSAN FEDER

Pryor, Arthur (Willard) (*b* St. Joseph, MO, 22 Sept 1870; *d* West Long Branch, NJ, 18 June 1942). Trombonist, conductor, and composer. He began to study piano and cornet with his father at the age of six, changing to valve trombone when he was 11. By the age of 15 he was playing slide trombone in his father's band. He joined the Liberati Band in 1888, where he became known as "the boy wonder trombonist from Missouri." He served as conductor of the Stanley Opera Company from 1890 to 1892, when he was offered a position as trombone soloist with the Sousa Band. His solos, in a popular idiom, which incorporated trombone glissandos or "smears," complemented Herbert L. Clarke's sophisticated cornet solos, and by 1900 Pryor was a star attraction of the band, second only to Sousa himself. He was also assistant conductor of the band from 1895 to 1902. Pryor left Sousa in 1903 to form his own band, which gave its first concert in New York on 15 November. It made six nationwide tours (1903–9), but thereafter its engagements were limited to Asbury Park, New Jersey (over 20 summers); Willow Park Grove, New Jersey (10 summers); and Royal Palm Park, Miami, Florida (10 winters); it also made recordings. Pryor retired in 1933, but his band continued to reassemble occasionally to give concerts.

Pryor was one of the greatest trombone virtuosos in the band tradition, and during his career played about 10,000 solos, earning the title "the Paganini of the trombone." He was also an eminent bandmaster – a charter member of ASCAP (1914) and of the American Bandmasters Association (1929). He conducted what may have been the first commercial recording made by an American band, and directed the Sousa Band in many of its recordings, even after he had left the group; his own band made some 1000 recordings before 1930.

Pryor wrote over 300 compositions, including three operettas (apparently lost), *Jingaboo*, *On the Eve of her Wedding Day*, and *Uncle Tom's Cabin*. Most of his works are for band, including marches (e.g., *Will Rogers March*), rags (*Razzazza Mazzazza*), waltzes (*The Love Kiss Waltz*), and novelties (*The Whistler and his Dog*); he also wrote piano pieces and songs. Much of his music was designed to display his own virtuosity. He limited himself to four forms of predictable format – theme and variations, "valse caprice," "valse de concert," and polka caprice – resulting in a certain similarity of style and repetition of musical ideas. These works were written at a time when the trombone had little solo repertory of consequence; they are technically demanding, and are still widely played. Among the most popular are *Blue Bells of Scotland*, *Love's Enchantment*, *The Patriot*, and *Thoughts of Love*. The principal publisher of his works was Carl Fischer.

BIBLIOGRAPHY

C. H. Larkin: "Memories of Arthur Pryor and his Band," *School Musician*, xiv (1943), no.6, p.8; no.7, p.14
N. H. Quayle: "Arthur Pryor: Some Reminiscences," *MJ*, xii/3 (1954), 37
H. W. Schwartz: *Bands of America* (Garden City, NY, 1957/*R*1975), 198
G. Bridges: *Pioneers in Brass* (Detroit, 1965), 101
P. E. Bierley: "Pryor, Arthur W.," *DAB*
J. R. Smart: Liner notes, *The Sousa and Pryor Bands* (New World 282, 1976)
S. Wolfinbarger: "The Solo Trombone Music of Arthur Pryor," *International Trombone Association Journal*, xi (1983), no.1, p.13; no.2, p.27; no.3, p.20
D. E. Frizane: *Arthur Pryor (1870–1942): American Trombonist, Bandmaster, Composer* (diss., U. of Kansas, 1984)

JAMES M. BURK

Psalmody. A general term for music sung in Protestant churches in England and America from the 17th century to the early 19th. The term was first associated with the chanting of psalms (following traditional practices of the Roman Church), and later with the singing of metrical psalms, but as these were gradually replaced by hymns the term was retained to cover all kinds of sacred music sung by amateur choirs.

1. Early psalm books, congregations, and singing-schools. 2. The rise of choirs and elaborate psalmody. 3. Musical style. 4. Reform.

1. Early psalm books, congregations, and singing-

SCHOOLS. When the Pilgrims landed at Plymouth in 1620 they carried with them Henry Ainsworth's *Book of Psalmes: Englished both in Prose and Metre* (Amsterdam, 1612), which included 39 unharmonized tunes. Sternhold's and Hopkins's *Whole Booke of Psalmes* (London, 1562), later called the "Old Version," also circulated in America during the 17th and 18th centuries, as well as Thomas Ravenscroft's *Whole Booke of Psalmes* (London, 1621), containing four-part settings of the British psalm-tune repertory for recreational use. The tunes in Ainsworth's psalter, many of them traceable to French and Dutch folk sources, were generally rather long (eight lines is typical) and often enlivened by syncopation. Ravenscroft's harmonizations, set mostly in block chords, still contained elements of the contrapuntal tradition. The earliest American psalmody was thus rooted in a European tradition of considerable musical power.

To these English publications 17th-century New Englanders added one of their own that attests to the importance they attached to psalmody. It was no accident that the first full-length book printed in the English-speaking colonies was a metrical psalter, *The Whole Booke of Psalmes* (Cambridge, MA, 1640; rev. 3/1651; pubd thereafter as *The Psalms, Hymns, and Spiritual Songs of the Old and New Testament*), known as the Bay Psalm Book. The clergymen who assembled it sought fidelity to the original scriptures. They also discarded some of the more complex textual meters of Ainsworth and Sternhold and Hopkins, setting almost all of the psalms in four-line stanzas in common meter (alternating lines of eight and six syllables, 8:6:8:6), long meter (8:8:8:8), and short meter (6:6:8:6). Before the ninth edition (1698) all editions of the Bay Psalm Book were printed without music. (*See* PSALMS, METRICAL, §§1(iv) and 2(ii).)

For most New Englanders during the first century of English settlement, psalm singing was partly or entirely an oral practice. Calvinist theology, mistrustful of musical elaboration, encouraged congregations to make their own music, without instrumental accompaniment or professional leadership, and according to the wishes and skills of a majority of the congregation's members. As time passed, moreover, contact with Old World musical traditions lessened, the level of the settlers' musical skill declined, and the ability to read music grew rarer. Furthermore, literacy was by no means universal, and not all worshipers could afford to own psalm books. Each of these factors helped to introduce oral elements into the practice of psalmody. By the 18th century, most New England congregations sang their psalms in a slow, parlando–rubato tempo, with much sliding and ornamental embellishment, usually under the leadership of a clerk or "precentor" who may or may not have been an accomplished singer. The technique of lining out, in which the leader intoned or read the text line-by-line and the congregation sang back the lines in alternation with the leader, was widespread. Its appeal was at least partly practical, as a proponent in the 1780s explained: "It is impossible for all to gėt books; and if all had books, they could not be benefitted by them, some being old and dim-sighted, others young and not versed enough in reading to keep pace while singing." It may be noted, incidentally, that the encroachment of oral practice into what had first been a written tradition was paralleled in the parishes of the Church of England, where music-making was also entrusted to congregations who sang without organs to lead them.

Early in the 18th century, New England clergymen, among them Cotton Mather and Thomas Symmes, began to express dissatisfaction with the way congregations sang. Some had come to believe that however satisfying to participants the OLD WAY OF SINGING might be, it was not contributing to a proper atmosphere in worship. From 1720 polemical tracts began to appear in Boston deploring the state of psalmody and recommending improvements. The agency for reform was the SINGING-SCHOOL, a series of instructional sessions led by an accomplished musician. Scholars in the school would learn the rudiments of psalm singing: the basic elements of vocal technique, pronunciation, and the ability to sing the psalm tunes as they were written down in the books. Then, when they returned to sing in their congregations, their mode of singing (i.e., "singing by rule") would presumably be followed by others, and the congregation would abandon the Old Way in favor of "Regular Singing."

That was the theory. In fact, the process did not work out quite so neatly, for the reformers encountered strong resistance. Many colonial Protestants did not share the belief that the Old Way was a corruption of correct psalmody. Sanctioned by use, and gratifying in the relaxed freedom it allowed the singer, it was set aside only very reluctantly and continued in many congregations, throughout the century and later, as an indigenous folk tradition that grew from a written practice.

Nevertheless, the singing-school, introduced to New England by the 1720s and flourishing there and elsewhere through the rest of the century and into the next, began a process of disseminating musical learning that during the course of the century was to have a powerful effect on psalmody. One of the first results was the publication of tunebooks: collections of psalm tunes, each with an instructional preface, designed for use in the singing-schools. The first compilers of these works were themselves clergymen: John Tufts, whose *A Very Plain and Easy Introduction to the Singing of Psalm Tunes* went through 11 editions between 1721 and 1744 (see illustration); and Thomas Walter, whose *Grounds and Rules of Musick* (1721) was still in print nearly half a century later as part of Daniel Bayley's *A New and Complete Introduction to the Grounds and Rules of Musick* (Newburyport, MA, 5/1768). A sizable majority of the sacred tunebooks brought out later in the century – and by the end of 1810 some 350 such works had been published in America – were designed for singing-school use. As well as stimulating the publication of tunebooks and, eventually, the composition of music to fill them, the singing-school served a second important function. It provided institutional support, however fragile, for musical professionalism. For most of the 18th century, and in some places well into the 19th, the only way a native American was likely to earn even a part of his living in music was as a singing-master, a teacher of singing-schools. A third effect of the singing-school was that, by teaching Americans to sing with greater attention to the niceties of voice production and choral blend, and introducing them to musical notation as well, it inspired a wish for a more elaborate kind of music-making than congregational singing could provide. In this impulse lies the beginning of the New England church choir, an institution that began to take shape shortly after the mid-century.

2. THE RISE OF CHOIRS AND ELABORATE PSALMODY. As long as tunebooks were geared to the needs of beginning singing-school and congregational singing, there was no reason for them to contain more than a limited repertory. Before 1760 more than 30 separate publications containing sacred music appeared in the American colonies, including various editions of the Bay Psalm Book and the many issues of Tufts's and Walter's collections.

Together these made available a repertory of no more than 75 different tunes, almost all of British origin, which typically moved in uniform note values and were harmonized in block chords.

Urania (Philadelphia, 1761), compiled by James Lyon, is the earliest sign of the increase in the size and stylistic range of the printed repertory of psalmody in the 1760s. With its 198 pages it dwarfed all earlier American musical publications, and its inclusion of elaborate, modern British music (more than a dozen anthems and set-pieces, and several hymn tunes, as well as a selection of psalm tunes), most of it never before published in America, make it a landmark in American psalmody. Two publications by Josiah Flagg, *A Collection of the Best Psalm Tunes* (Boston, 1764) and *Sixteen Anthems* (Boston, 1766), further established the American tunebook as a forum for the publication of "modern" music. Finally, the American editions of William Tans'ur's *Royal Melody Complete* (Boston, 1767, with many later editions) and Aaron Williams's *Universal Psalmodist* (Newburyport, MA, 1769, published by Daniel Bayley with Tans'ur's work as *The American Harmony*) were another step towards broadening the stylistic framework of American psalmody. Between 1760 and 1770 the printed repertory burgeoned beyond oral command.

The tunebooks of the 1760s, both in number and in content, signal a new energy in American sacred music-making. Whereas in the two preceding decades only 12 tunebooks had been printed, roughly twice that many were published between 1760 and 1769. Moreover, more than 300 new compositions were added to the published repertory. Among them were many pieces incorporating texture changes, melismas, and – especially in fuging-tunes – brief contrapuntal sections. This new, more elaborate style was being developed around the mid-century by the psalmodists working in English parish churches. Tunebooks by Tans'ur, William Knapp, John Arnold, and other provincial English psalmodists circulated in America during the 1750s and 1760s; moreover, music by these men began to appear in tunebooks printed in the colonies during the 1760s. The presence of so much new elaborate music in this decade signifies that a new branch of psalmody had been established, one in which singers were more accomplished and some degree of musical literacy was required.

AN
INTRODUCTION
To the Singing
OF
Psalm-Tunes,
In a plain & easy Method.
With
A COLLECTION of Tunes
In Three Parts.

By the Rev. Mr. *TUFTS.*

The FIFTH EDITION.
Printed from *Copper-Plates,*
Neatly Engraven.

BOSTON, in N. E.
Printed for *Samuel Gerrish*,
at the Lower End of Corn-
hill. 1726.

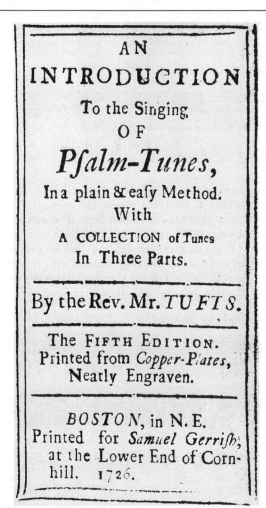

Title page of the fifth edition of John Tufts's tunebook: "An Introduction to the Singing of Psalm-tunes" (Boston, 1726)

The origins of the 18th-century New England Protestant church choir appear to lie in two impulses: a desire to improve and regularize congregational singing, and the singers' wish to perform. The former appears to have originated with the clergy, or church leaders, or perhaps the wishes of the congregation as a whole; the latter originated with the singers themselves. Although no systematic study of the 18th-century New England choir has been undertaken, evidence suggests that more often than not it was the singers' insistence that led to the formation of a choir. No Congregational church choirs are known to have existed before 1750, but a number were formed during the 1750s and 1760s, and by the 1780s and 1790s choirs were common.

Typically, choir members were singing-school alumni. When a school was held in a town, the more accomplished scholars sometimes expressed a wish after it was over to continue singing as a group. In many towns, "the singers" petitioned to sit together during public worship, a request that was not always granted. That arrangement might be recommended, however, as in Boston's First Church (1758), because "skilful Singers, sitting together in some convenient place, would greatly tend to rectify our singing on the Lord's Day, and would render that part of Divine Worship more agreeable." It also gave the choir a chance to perform its own special music, including elaborate pieces of the kind that began to appear in American tunebooks of the 1760s – surely not by coincidence precisely the time when church choirs were beginning to spring up in New England.

Singing-schools and church choirs lie behind the sharp increase in the printed repertory in the 1760s, which testifies that the ability to read music was no longer a rare skill. Though slowed down by the war (1775–81), the repertory continued to grow during the rest of the century. By 1800 more than 1000 different compositions had been printed in American tunebooks. (By 1811 the figure had reached 7500.) When that figure is compared with the few tunes used by colonial Christians earlier in the century (75 tunes available in American tunebooks by 1760; 400 tunes printed before 1770), it is clear that the tradition was transformed by the appearance of new institutions and the impact of musical literacy, and that the 1760s were a crucial time in that transformation.

From 1770 the contributions of native composers increased. Much of the music in American tunebooks was still taken from British sources, but more was composed by Americans who over the next several decades formed what some historians have called "the first school of New England composers" (*see* NEW ENGLAND

COMPOSERS, SCHOOLS OF). Most of these men were Anglo-Celtic by lineage and Protestant (probably Congregational) by religion, born and brought up in the towns and villages of Massachusetts and Connecticut. Most were not full-time musicians but tradesmen who practiced music in their spare time. Few had training beyond what they had picked up in singing-schools and from British treatises. Few were tutored in orthodox European musical grammar. Nevertheless, they composed and published, and saw their music eagerly taken up by their countrymen. As a group they embodied the quality of self-reliance that Americans often associate with the beginnings of their history as a nation.

The most prominent of them and the first American psalmodist–composer of real consequence was William Billings, whose *New-England Psalm-singer* (Boston, 1770) is another landmark. Published at a time when only a dozen or so American tunes had appeared in print, Billings's work, made up entirely of his own compositions, increased the figure tenfold. Moreover, the patriotic overtones of his prefatory remarks (and of some of the texts he set) and his unabashed confession of his own inexperience and unwillingness to follow established compositional rules provided musical Americans with a bold example of a native composer.

Billings's example was not ignored. By the end of 1782, compositions by at least 19 different Americans had appeared in print. The sudden increase can be traced to two Connecticut collections, *Select Harmony* (Cheshire, 1779) by Andrew Law and *The Chorister's Companion* (New Haven, 1782) by Simeon Jocelyn and Amos Doolittle. Like Lyon, Flagg, and Bayley before them, Law and Jocelyn were primarily compilers rather than composers. Many of the tunes introduced into print in their books soon became American favorites. The two works also provided a new model for American tunebooks. Earlier collections had generally been either assortments of British music, or entirely original, such as Billings's publications. *Select Harmony* and *The Chorister's Companion* were eclectic compilations in which both British tunes, many of them established favorites, and newly composed American tunes appeared. It is noteworthy that later tunebooks that went through many editions displayed a similar combination of European and American music, among them *The Worcester Collection* (Worcester, MA, 1786, 8/1803), Andrew Adgate's *Philadelphia Harmony* (Philadelphia, 1789, 9/1807), and *Village Harmony* (Exeter, NH, 1795, 17/1821).

The years between the end of the War of Independence and the beginning of the War of 1812 – the so-called Federal era of American history – brought conspicuously increased activity in all areas of psalmody. Tunebook production grew from some 60 issues in the 1780s and more than 100 in the 1790s to more than 220 in the 1800s. New Englanders traveled southward and westward, teaching singing-schools and establishing their books in New York state, Pennsylvania, Maryland, and the Carolinas, and making their regional music into a national music. Younger composers and compilers appeared – not only from Massachusetts and Connecticut but from New Hampshire, Vermont, and Maine – setting their printed works before the singing public. (A reliable estimate is that by 1810 nearly 300 natives or residents of America had published sacred music.) And although institutions like singing-schools and church choirs continued to flourish, more and more singers were forming "musical societies" – groups of citizens devoted to sacred music-making but existing independently of any structure of formal worship. Evidence of the existence of American musical societies can be found as early as the 1760s; but it was in the postwar period that the impulse to form groups such as the Stoughton Musical Society (Massachusetts, 1786; still in existence), the Uranian Musical Society (New York, 1793–8), the Hampshire Musical Society (Hampshire Co., Massachusetts, *c*1800–1802), or the Handel Society at Dartmouth College (Hanover, New Hampshire, *c*1810) really took hold. Like the church choir, the existence of musical societies demonstrates the desire of Americans to sing the most challenging and artistic music available to them, and to perform at a high level of proficiency.

3. MUSICAL STYLE. Written for worship and recreational and instructional use – for singing-schools, choirs, and musical societies – the choral music of 18th-century Americans answered specific needs and is best understood as a community practice. American psalmodists usually composed for four-part chorus, with the melody in the tenor voice. Set in open score, the music seldom calls for instrumental accompaniment, although by around 1800 and after, "gallery orchestras" of treble instruments (flute, violin, clarinet) with bass support (most often cello or "church bass," but sometimes bassoon) often accompanied the singers by doubling voice parts. Since most American composers of the time lacked keyboard skill or knowledge of 18th-century European harmonic practice, their music often lacks harmonic direction and gives the impression of crudeness. That quality can be a strength, as in Daniel Read's "Sherburne," where instead of following the expected path to a cadence on the tonic, the first phrase discovers its destination as the submediant (ex. 1). Such

Ex.1 Daniel Read: "Sherburne" (1785), bars 1–3

tonal freedom, and the sacred texts they set, could inspire the New Englanders to bold and memorable melodies. Timothy Swan's "China," celebrated in Harriet Beecher Stowe's novel *The Minister's Wooing* (1859; chap. 38) as "one of those wild, pleading tunes, dear to the heart of New England" and long admired by both singers and scholars, skillfully balances leaps and stepwise motion, creating the effect of a good singer's spontaneous embellishment of a slow-moving triple-time dirge (ex. 2).

Ex.2 Timothy Swan: "China" (1801)

Most American tunes of the time set only one stanza of metrical text. Plain tunes (settings in block-chord texture in which the phrase structure reflects the textual meter exactly) are in the majority. Sometimes, however, the composer transcends the meter by repeating or extending certain words. Fuging-tunes make particular demands on the composer's ability to extend his material. Set-pieces (through-composed settings of metrical texts) constitute only a small proportion of the repertory composed by Americans. Limited compositional training is most apt to show up as a defect rather than an asset in these larger-scale works; many founder for lack of tonal variety. Billings's comments on composition emphasize the importance he attached to the independence of voice parts. "The grand difficulty in composition," he wrote in *The Continental Harmony* (Boston, 1794), "is to preserve the air through each part separately, and yet cause them to harmonize with each other at the same time" (p.xxxi). Billings's own custom was to compose the tenor part, the "air" or melody, first, and then to add the bass part, the treble (soprano), and the counter (alto) in turn. Such an approach helps to explain how the New Englanders arrived at the kind of harmony found, for example, in the first part of Lewis Edson's "Lenox" (ex.3).

Ex.3 Lewis Edson: "Lenox" (1782), bars 1–10

Each phrase begins and ends with a consonance; but within each, a harmonic collision or unexpected chord occurs: an *f/f'*♯ clash, generated contrapuntally (bar 2, beat 4); a submediant chord where the bass movement seems to promise tonic (bar 4, beat 3); a second-inversion dominant and submediant, both in the same measure (bar 7, beats 2 and 4); and a free-floating seventh (bar 9, beat 2).

Once thought by some to be a unique New World practice, American psalmody can now be seen to have been modeled upon British prototypes, and several styles of English Protestant psalmody influential in America can be distinguished. Perhaps the clearest way of differentiating between them is to notice how each approaches the declamation of the text. A brief survey using well-known American pieces as examples will illustrate this.

The basic style of Anglo-American psalmody, the "common" tune style, gives each syllable of text the same weight by moving in equal note values in slow duple time. English psalmody was given over almost exclusively to this kind of tune (e.g., "Old

Ex.4 William Billings: "Lebanon" (1770, in the revised version of 1778), bars 1–7, with text quoted from *The Village Harmony* (1796)

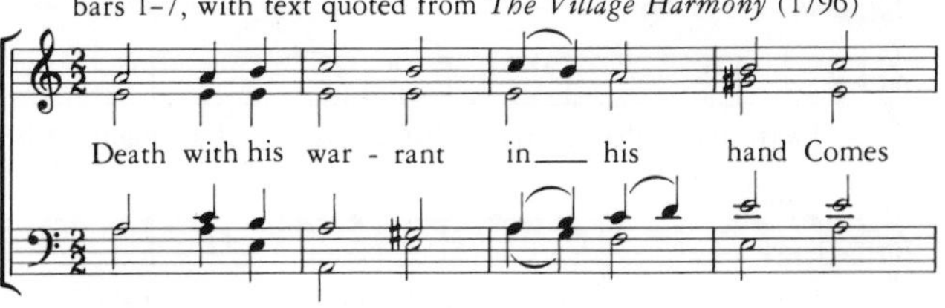

Hundredth," "St Anne") until the beginning of the 18th century; and Billings's "Lebanon," which is only lightly decorated, shows that as late as 1770 a compositional approach more than two centuries old could still serve a New World psalmodist (ex.4). Early in the 18th century, two variations on the "common" tune style appeared in England, both animating its stolid tread. One retained duple meter but enlivened it with dactyls. Read's "Windham" (1785) shows an especially skillful use of dactylic motion; its first three phrases hammer home the text's grim message through a series of dactyls broken only in the fourth phrase (ex.5). The other approach introduced iambic declamation in triple meter, assigning longer notes to accented syllables and

Ex.5 Daniel Read: "Windham" (1785)

Ex.6 William Billings: "Brookfield" (1770), quoted from *The Worcester Collection* (1786)

'Twas on that dark, that_ dole - ful night, When
pow'rs_ of earth_ and hell_ a - rose, A -
- gainst_ the Son_ of God's_ de - light, And
friends_ be - tray'd_ him to_ his foes.

opening the door to melodic embellishment. Billings's "Brookfield," by far the most widely circulated American triple-time sacred piece of its era, avoids any hint of the limping gait that such tunes sometimes assumed. It does so chiefly by a varying motion from phrase to phrase (ex.6).

Each of the three styles noted so far arose within Anglican parish psalmody – the first at its beginning, the second apparently during the second decade of the 18th century, and the third perhaps slightly earlier. A fourth style, introduced by and associated with a dissenting sect that began within the Church of England but soon broke away, appeared around 1740: the so-called "Methodist" style of hymnody, described by Temperley (1979) as "popular and strongly secular in style." Its hallmarks include a brisker tempo (usually notated as 4/4, 2/4, or 3/4 instead of the traditional 2/2 or 3/2); trochaic declamation, often with feminine phrase-endings; melodic ornamentation, sometimes written as grace notes; and repetition of either text or music or both. "Middletown" by Amos Bull, first published in 1778, was one of the most widely accepted American attempts to seize the "modern," cosmopolitan spirit of the Methodists' emphasis on catchy melodies (ex.7).

One other approach to declamation introduced by mid-century English psalmodists had an especially strong impact on New England composers; it might be called "declamatory duple" style: the basic half-note beat is enlivened by bursts of quarter-notes, often sung on repeated pitches and tending to appear towards the end of a piece. The clearest and by far the most famous example of the declamatory duple style is the FUGING-TUNE, a piece of strophic music containing at least one section involving contrapuntal vocal entries with overlapping text. Appearing in England before 1750, the fuging-tune first circulated in the colonies in English tunebooks. Beginning with Lyon's *Urania*, English fuging-tunes were also printed in American collections. By the 1780s, rural American psalmodists had taken up the form, and choral singers had embraced it with enthusiasm, both because each voice-part had its own chance to strike in with the subject and because the piling up of declamatory entries generated a momentum that inspired spirited performances. Edson's "Lenox," the most widely printed American fuging-tune of its time, demonstrates the appeal of the declamatory duple style especially well. Beginning with four short, distinct phrases, separated by definite pauses, it then unleashes a "fuge" that, with 26 consecutive quarter-note articulations, proceeds like a relentless rhythmic engine (ex.8).

The fuging-tune, though a form in which the declamatory duple style flourished conspicuously, is by no means the only form in which it appeared. Oliver Holden's "Coronation," the American hymn tune whose popularity has lasted the longest, is

Ex.7 Amos Bull: "Middletown" (1778), bars 1–8

Hail the_ day that_ sees_ him rise, Rav - ish'd
from our wish - ful_ eyes;

Ex.8 Lewis Edson: "Lenox" (1782), bars 10–18

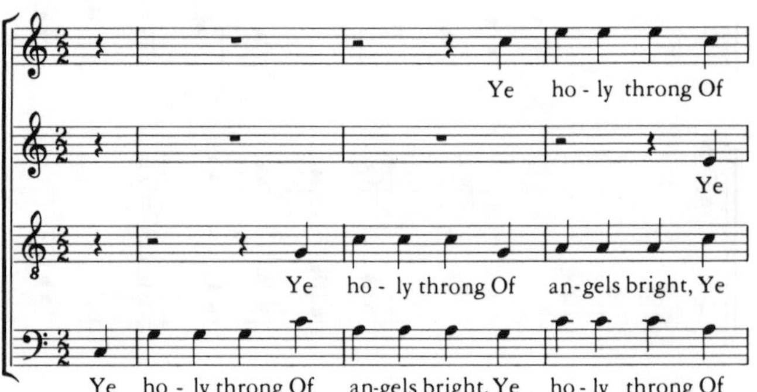
Ye ho - ly throng Of
Ye
Ye ho - ly throng Of an-gels bright, Ye
Ye ho - ly throng Of an-gels bright, Ye ho - ly throng Of

15
an - gels bright, In worlds of light Be -
ho - ly throng Of an - gels bright, In worlds of light Be -
ho - ly throng Of an - gels bright, In worlds of light Be -
an - gels bright, In worlds of light, Be -

-gin the song.
-gin the song.
-gin the song.
-gin the song.

Ex.9 Oliver Holden: "Coronation" (1793), bars 1–9

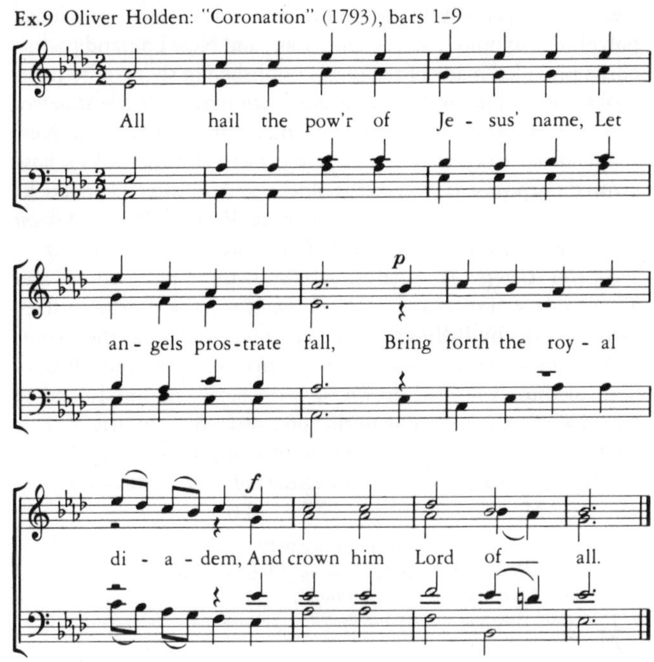

a fine example of a declamatory duple piece (ex.9). And nowhere was it used to more dramatic effect than in Billings's *Anthem for Easter*, where the triumph of the Resurrection is dramatized in a burst of choral recitative with the force of a lightning bolt (ex.10).

Ex.10 William Billings: *Anthem for Easter* (1787), bars 77–84

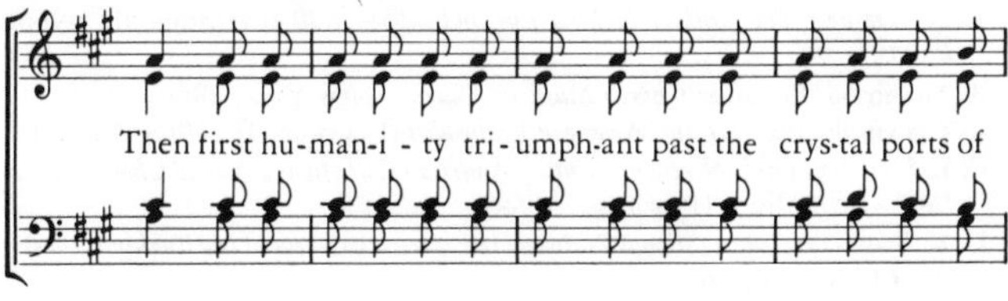

With all of these styles of declamation at hand, American psalmodists of the period were equipped to set the available repertory of texts (chiefly metrical psalms and hymns, and especially those versified by Isaac Watts) either in a single style or by mixing them, as Swan skillfully did in "Bristol" (ex.11).

A stylistic gamut, with those American composers who were in close contact with cosmopolitan urban music-making at one end and those without such contact at the other, would reveal sharp differences in melodic–harmonic practice. Men such as Holden, Samuel Holyoke, and Jacob Kimball all knew, and perhaps studied with, the learned immigrant organist–composer Hans Gram. Their music tends to favor full triads and to move according to the formulae of 18th-century textbook harmony. Moreover, Holyoke and Timothy Olmstead explored the elaborately ornamented melodic style of Methodist music, an idiom seldom essayed successfully by Americans of their generation. If the melodic–harmonic idiom of these men closely resembles that favored in the cities, it diverges strongly from that of Edson, Oliver Brownson, Justin Morgan, Stephen Jenks, and Abraham Wood, at the other end of the gamut. These men were self-taught, spending their lives mostly in New England villages and the countryside, unexposed to more cosmopolitan musical learning. The folklike melody, harmonic exploration, and fondness for dissonant clashes that can be found in their music show that they worked more by trial and error than by precept. Beyond setting textual accents faithfully to music, placing consonances on most strong beats, and giving each vocal part some melodic independence, they were bound by few conventions, which created differences in style one from another make it awkward to consider them as a group. Somewhere closer to the center of the gamut might be placed the music of Billings, Read, and Swan, whose work is less polished and more clearly provincial in melody and harmony than that of the first group, but all of whom were more strongly affected than the second group by precepts derived from Europe. Each of these men produced enough music over a long enough period to have arrived at a distinctive melodic–harmonic style of his own. Of the three, Billings was perhaps the least pungent in his harmony and the most given to writing melodies with sweep and aggressive momentum, which he often did by sequentially repeating small units of text and music. The potent resource of Read's harmony and the craftsmanship of his melodies helped to make him especially skilled at plain tunes and short fuging-tunes, in which he wrote some of the most

Ex.11 Timothy Swan: "Bristol" (1785), bars 1–15

tersely concentrated music of his time. Swan was blessed with an exceptionally free imagination, capable of strikingly expressive responses to images in the text and unexpected melodic and harmonic twists. The widely varied melodic–harmonic idiom of these three and their contemporaries suggests that, when a close study of the sacred style of 18th-century New England is undertaken, stylistic diversity is likely to be one of its chief topics.

4. Reform. From the 1760s, American psalmody had evolved without reference to any stylistic standard or ideal. Towards the end of the century American collections frequently contained, printed side by side, "common" tunes almost as old as Protestantism itself, recent pieces by Yankee psalmodists, and the often florid Methodist tunes from mid-18th-century Britain – many of them drawn from Thomas Butts's *Harmonia sacra* (London, *c*1760) and Martin Madan's *Lock Hospital Collection* (London, 1769) – which in style resembled the Italianate solo songs favored in drawing rooms and theaters. Andrew Law, apparently the first to see any incongruity in this kind of musical mixture, attacked native composers in the preface of his *Musical Primer* (Cheshire, CT, 1793). His attack, and similar comments by others, expressed dissatisfaction with the absence of a standard in American psalmody. It signaled that a process of musical reform was under way that would set up a standard of musical style modeled on that of late 18th-century British psalmody.

Reform assumed a variety of guises. Some American composers began in the 1790s to follow British or European models more closely. Samuel Holyoke and Oliver Holden joined with Hans Gram to produce *The Massachusetts Compiler* (Boston, 1795), a reform landmark which introduced an assortment of European or Europeanized compositions with a lengthy digest from prominent European thoroughbass manuals and instructional treatises. European music occupied an increasingly large proportion of the repertory in tunebooks published after the turn of the century, and especially after 1805. The American tunes that did survive were often purged of at least some of their supposed crudities, as in William Cooper's *Beauties of Church Music* (Boston, 1804). Denunciations of the native idiom became increasingly frequent, and fuging-tunes came in for special attack for their obfuscation of the text – for example by John Hubbard in his *Essay on Music* (Boston, 1808). Some reformers sought to encourage the cultivation of increasingly elaborate music by European masters; others, viewing psalmody as a liturgical practice in which solemnity and decorum should outweigh all other qualities, advocated a return to the ancient "common" tunes in use before the War of Independence. The former impulse led to the establishment of more musical societies; the latter led to a rejection of musical elaboration and eventually to the formulation of a kind of latterday "common" tune devotional style by Thomas Hastings and Lowell Mason and their followers. However divergent these two approaches may have been, they shared a rejection of the native composer and of the American idiom developed around the time of the War of Independence.

The success of the reform movement in the cities of the Atlantic seaboard and New England marked the end, by 1820, of the indigenous New England compositional style as a creative force. It did not, however, end the circulation of its repertory. New England tunes survived in collections published in upstate New York, western Pennsylvania, Ohio, and the Shenandoah Valley of Virginia, as well as in the shape-note collections published farther south (*see* SHAPE-NOTE HYMNODY). In these outlying areas, and especially in the South, new traditions of provincial polyphonic hymnody were taking root, and New England psalmodists provided many of the pieces published in shape-note tunebooks. Meanwhile, in New England, beginning with *The Stoughton Collection* (Boston, 1829), favorite pieces from the earlier New England repertory were regularly reprinted in tunebooks whose avowed purpose was to keep the older repertory alive. Tunebooks such as *The Billings and Holden Collection* (Boston, 1836), *Ancient Harmony Revived* (Boston, 1847; five more edns), *Father Kemp's Old Folks' Concert Tunes* (Boston, 1860; three more edns), and *The Stoughton Musical Society's Centennial Collection* (Boston, 1878) carried works by Billings, Read, Holden, Swan, and their compatriots in something like their original form, giving pleasure both to those who had grown up with native psalmody and to others who could see value in the long-discredited music of their forefathers. (For a modern edition of many items of psalmody see R. Crawford, ed.: *The Core Repertory of Early American Psalmody*, RRAM, xi–xii (Madison, WI, 1984).)

BIBLIOGRAPHY

G. Hood: *A History of Music in New England* (Boston, 1846/*R*1970)
N. Gould: *Church Music in America* (Boston, 1853)
F. J. Metcalf: *American Writers and Compilers of Sacred Music* (New York, 1925/*R*1967)
A. P. Britton: *Theoretical Introductions in American Tune-books to 1800* (diss., U. of Michigan, 1949)
G. Chase: *America's Music: from the Pilgrims to the Present* (New York, 1955, rev. 2/1966/*R*1981)
A. C. Buechner: *Yankee Singing Schools and the Golden Age of Choral Music in New England, 1760–1800* (diss., Harvard U., 1960)
M. Frost, ed.: *Historical Companion to Hymns Ancient & Modern* (London, 1962)
J. W. Thompson: *Music and Musical Activities in New England, 1800–1838* (diss., George Peabody College for Teachers, 1962)
I. Lowens: *Music and Musicians in Early America* (New York, 1964)
R. T. Daniel: *The Anthem in New England before 1800* (Evanston, IL, 1966/*R*1979)
R. Stevenson: *Protestant Church Music in America* (New York, 1966)
R. Crawford: *Andrew Law, American Psalmodist* (Evanston, IL, 1968/*R*1981)
C. E. Lindsley: *Early Nineteenth-century American Collections of Sacred Choral Music, 1800–1810* (diss., U. of Iowa, 1968)
D. K. Stigberg: *Congregational Psalmody in Eighteenth Century New England* (thesis, U. of Illinois, 1970)
R. Crawford: "Connecticut Sacred Music Imprints, 1778–1810, Part II," *Notes*, xxvii (1970–71), 671
J. W. Worst: *New England Psalmody 1760–1810: Analysis of an American Idiom* (diss., U. of Michigan, 1974)
R. G. Appel: *The Music of the Bay Psalm Book, 9th Edition (1698)*, ISAMm, v (Brooklyn, NY, 1975)
D. P. McKay and R. Crawford: *William Billings of Boston: Eighteenth Century Composer* (Princeton, NJ, 1975)
K. D. Kroeger: *The Worcester Collection of Sacred Harmony and Sacred Music in America, 1786–1803* (diss., Brown U., 1976)
P. R. Osterhout: *Music in Northampton, Massachusetts to 1820* (diss., U. of Michigan, 1978)
R. Crawford: "A Historian's Introduction to Early American Music," *Proceedings* [of the American Antiquarian Society], lxxxix (1979), 261–98
N. Temperley: *The Music of the English Parish Church* (Cambridge, England, 1979)
R. M. Wilson and K. V. Keller: *Connecticut's Music in the Revolutionary Era* (Hartford, 1979)
L. Inserra and H. W. Hitchcock: *The Music of Henry Ainsworth's Psalter*, ISAMm, xv (Brooklyn, NY, 1981)
K. D. Kroeger: Introduction, *The Complete Works of William Billings*, i (Charlottesville, VA, 1981), pp.xiii–xxviii
N. Temperley: "The Old Way of Singing: its Origins and Development," *JAMS*, xxxiv (1981), 511–44
D. W. Steel: *Stephen Jenks (1772–1856): American Composer and Tunebook Compiler* (diss., U. of Michigan, 1982)
R. Crawford and D. W. Krummel: "Early American Music Printing and Publishing," *Printing and Society in Early America*, ed. W. Joyce and others (Worcester, MA, 1983), 186, 215

R. Crawford: "Massachusetts Musicians and the Core Repertory of Early American Psalmody," *Music in Colonial Massachusetts, 1630–1820*, ed. B. Lambert, ii (Boston, 1985), 583

RICHARD CRAWFORD

Psalms, metrical. Paraphrases of the biblical psalms in verse, often designed for singing to tunes of a simple, popular type (known today as hymn tunes). In the early years of the Protestant settlements of North America, metrical psalm singing was often the only form of organized music. It occupied a most important place in the cultural life of the people, and was invested with the strong feelings of a struggling community far from home. The Puritans, in particular, treated the psalms and their tunes with veneration, and sang them in everyday situations as well as at church on Sundays. The tradition naturally followed very similar patterns to those of the parent countries in Europe. By the time a more assertively American school of psalmody had arisen in the late 18th century, metrical psalms were rapidly giving way to hymns in many churches. (A number of metrical psalms are included in R. Crawford, ed.: *The Core Repertory of Early American Psalmody*, RRAM, xi–xii (Madison, WI, 1984).)

1. History of psalm singing: (i) Episcopal churches (ii) Pilgrims (iii) Dutch Reformed Church (iv) Puritans (v) Presbyterian churches (vi) German Reformed Church. 2. Psalm books: (i) Function and character (ii) The Bay Psalm Book.

1. History of psalm singing.

(i) Episcopal churches. The psalms of Calvin's French psalter were sung in America as early as 1564–5 during the Huguenot expeditions to Florida and South Carolina, just as Sir Francis Drake's men sang psalms, to the delight of the Indians, while camping on the coast of California in 1579. However, the first Protestant church to establish itself permanently on the American continent was the Church of England: at Jamestown, Virginia, a church was built in 1607, the year that the colony was founded. Commercial enterprise rather than religious fervor was dominant in the minds of the early Virginian colonists. They were content to continue the traditions of the Anglican church, which was established there by law, as it was later in Maryland, North and South Carolina, and Georgia. In the northern colonies Anglican churches were organized by the early 18th century.

The bibles and prayer books imported from England had the usual metrical psalms bound in the back – *The Whole Booke of Psalmes, Collected into Englishe Meter* by Thomas Sternhold and John Hopkins (first published 1562) or, later, *A New Version of the Psalms of David, fitted to the Tunes used in Churches* (1696) by Nahum Tate and Nicholas Brady. The singing was very much as it was in English parish churches. In the larger town churches organs were gradually acquired: at King's Chapel, Boston, in 1714; at Trinity Church, Newport, Rhode Island, in 1733; at Trinity Church, New York, in 1737; at five Virginia churches between 1737 and 1767; at two Connecticut churches by 1756; at all three Anglican churches in Philadelphia in 1762–6. In smaller churches, parish clerks led the people in unaccompanied singing. Tate and Brady's *New Version of the Psalms*, which was first published in America in New York in 1710, was very widely used by the mid-18th century. In some country churches, societies of singers were organized, first in Maryland during Thomas Bray's visitation of 1700.

After the Revolution authority over the congregations passed to the Protestant Episcopal Church, and for the first time, in 1789, a selection of psalms and hymns for use in the churches was laid down by authority, and annexed to the Book of Common

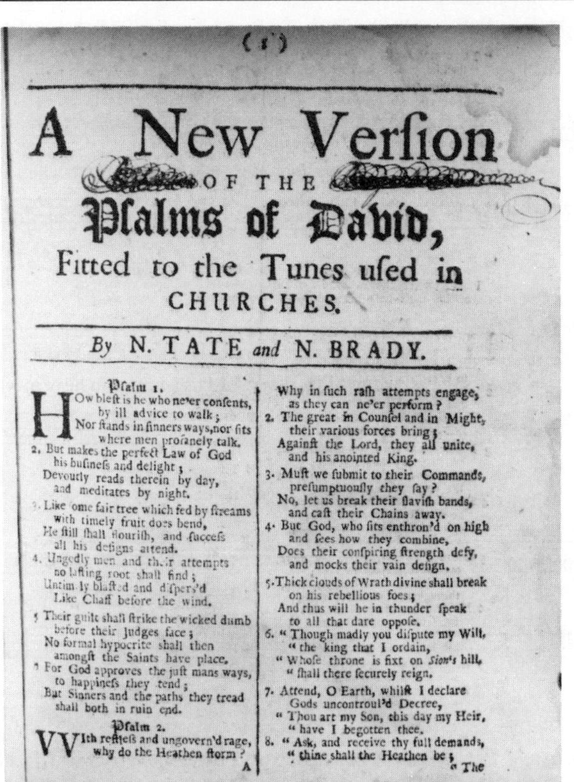
(1)

A New Verſion OF THE Pſalms of David, Fitted to the Tunes uſed in CHURCHES.

By N. TATE *and* N. BRADY.

Pſalm 1.

How bleſt is he who ne'er conſents,
by ill advice to walk;
Nor ſtands in ſinners ways, nor ſits
where men profanely talk.
2. But makes the perfect Law of God
his buſineſs and delight;
Devoutly reads therein by day,
and meditates by night.
3. Like ſome fair tree which fed by ſtreams
with timely fruit does bend,
He ſtill ſhall flouriſh, and ſucceſs
all his deſigns attend.
4. Ungodly men and their attempts
no laſting root ſhall find;
Untimely blaſted and diſpers'd
Like Chaff before the wind.
5 Their guilt ſhall ſtrike the wicked dumb
before their Judges face;
No formal hypocrite ſhall then
amongſt the Saints have place.
6 For God approves the juſt mans ways,
to happineſs they tend;
But Sinners and the paths they tread
ſhall both in ruin end.

Pſalm 2.

With reſtleſs and ungovern'd rage,
why do the Heathen ſtorm?
Why in ſuch raſh attempts engage,
as they can ne'er perform?
2. The great in Counſel and in Might,
their various forces bring;
Againſt the Lord, they all unite,
and his anointed King.
3. Muſt we ſubmit to their Commands,
preſumptuouſly they ſay?
No, let us break their ſlaviſh bands,
and caſt their Chains away.
4. But God, who ſits enthron'd on high
and ſees how they combine,
Does their conſpiring ſtrength defy,
and mocks their vain deſign.
5. Thick clouds of Wrath divine ſhall break
on his rebellious foes;
And thus will he in thunder ſpeak
to all that dare oppoſe.
6. "Though madly you diſpute my Will,
"the king that I ordain,
"Whoſe throne is fixt on *Sion's* hill,
"ſhall there ſecurely reign.
7. Attend, O Earth, whilſt I declare
Gods uncontroul'd Decree,
"Thou art my Son, this day my Heir,
"have I begotten thee.
8. "Ask, and receive thy full demands,
"thine ſhall the Heathen be;

A

"The

1. Title page of the first American edition of "A New Version of the Psalms of David, fitted to the Tunes used in Churches" by Nahum Tate and Nicholas Brady, printed by William Bradford (New York, 1710)

Prayer. It consisted of the entire *New Version* of Tate and Brady, with 27 hymns. A revised selection was made in 1833, still including a large number of Tate and Brady's psalms, and continued in use until 1866. Thus the Episcopal Church was one of the last to sing metrical psalms as a regular part of its services.

The tunes sung with these psalms were at first the same as those used in England, as can be seen from a tune supplement bound in with a Boston edition of Tate and Brady in 1720; they were also the same as those used by the Puritan churches. A later tune supplement to Tate and Brady was engraved and probably compiled by Thomas Johnston, who was also one of the first American organ builders; Daniel Bayley's collections indicate a more florid taste. On the whole, however, Episcopal churches were musically more conservative than Congregational ones, avoiding the excesses of fuging-tunes and elaborate "set-pieces." A most influential Anglican musician was Francis Hopkinson. His *Collection of Psalm Tunes . . . for the Use of the United Churches of Christ Church and St. Peter's Church in Philadelphia* (Philadelphia, 1763) contains some fairly ornate tunes, including some of Hopkinson's own, but they are in the *galant* taste of the time, resembling the music of town rather than country churches in England. The prevalence of organs and the stronger links with the mother country tended to keep Anglican church music closer to the European art music of the time. The same tendency is shown in the tunes of *The Book of Common Prayer . . . Proposed to the Use of the Protestant Episcopal Church* (Philadelphia, 1786) and in Jacob Eckhard's Choirmaster's Book of 1809, used at St. Michael, Charleston, South Carolina, together with a special

Ex.1 Peter Valton (*c*1740–1748): "St. Peters," in Eckhard's book of 1809, where it is allocated to "Psalm 46" – i.e., Psalm cl *(New Version)*, v.1 of which is underlaid here.

O praise the Lord in that blest place From whence his
good - ness large - ly flows; Praise him in heav'n, where
he his face Un - veil'd in per - fect glo - ry shows.

Selection of Psalms and Hymns prepared by the rectors of the two principal Charleston churches in 1792 (see ex. 1).

See also EPISCOPAL CHURCH, MUSIC OF THE.

(ii) Pilgrims. The band of about 100 English Pilgrims who founded the colony at Plymouth, Massachusetts, in 1620 were members of a group of "Separatists" who had gone into exile at Leiden, Holland, in 1609. They had rejected the worship of the Church of England, and so instead of Sternhold and Hopkins's psalms they adopted the version of Henry Ainsworth, pastor of a neighboring Separatist community at Amsterdam. Ainsworth was one of the most cultivated biblical scholars of his day, and in *The Book of Psalmes: Englished both in Prose and Metre* (Amsterdam, 1612) he offered not only a complete new prose translation of the psalms accompanied by a pithy commentary but also a new metrical version and an excellent selection of tunes. In variety of meters and in his choice of tunes, Ainsworth was as much influenced by the Franco-Dutch psalter as by Sternhold and Hopkins:

> Tunes for the Psalms I find none set of God; so that each people is to use the most grave, decent and comfortable manner of singing that they know. . . . The singing-notes, therefore, I have most taken from our former Englished Psalms, when they will fit the measure of the verse. And for the other long verses I have also taken (for the most part) the gravest and easiest tunes of the French and Dutch Psalms.

Details of Ainsworth's tunes and their origins are provided by Pratt and Frost. The tunes, like the rest of the book, are learned rather than popular, and are not all easy to sing. However, Edward Winslow recalled that there were "many of our congregation very expert in music" at Leiden; some of these must have been on the momentous voyage of the *Mayflower*, for Ainsworth's *Psalmes* were used for many years in the Plymouth colony, in the total absence of instrumental or professional aid. Later generations lost their forefathers' skill. In 1681 Plymouth church decided to institute lining out, and in 1691, on the amalgamation of the Plymouth colony with the much larger and more successful settlement to the north, the church formally recognized the "difficulties" of many of the Ainsworth tunes and allowed the substitution of easier ones used with the Bay Psalm Book. So Ainsworth's book was never to be widely popular in America, though it was used at Ipswich and Salem, both outside the Plymouth colony, until 1667. It was reprinted several times, but never in America.

(iii) Dutch Reformed Church. Dutch settlers first landed in what is now New York in 1613, but the first church was not organized until 1628, when the Dutch and French Protestant settlers combined; the two parts of the congregation knew identical tunes, and sang them in their own languages. The Dutch psalter, prescribed by the Synod of Dort (1618), was used with strict invariance for a full 100 years after the English conquest of the colony in 1664. An organ was erected in the New York church in 1727. The first English psalm book for the Dutch Reformed Church was *The Psalms of David . . . for the Use of the Reformed Dutch Church of the City of New York* (New York, 1767). Francis Hopkinson was the translator, and his job was the singular one of adapting the psalm versions of Tate and Brady to fit the tunes of varying meters in the old Dutch psalter. The music still remained unaltered.

The new book did not long satisfy the English-speaking congregations; many of the tunes in peculiar meters were unfamiliar through long disuse, and there was a demand to relax the strict confinement to psalms and to introduce some of the hymns popular in other American churches. The central Synod continued to maintain a strict control over the worship of individual congregations, but after the Revolution it authorized a new book (1789) that included 135 hymns selected by Dr. John Livingston. The psalms in this book were selected largely from Tate and Brady's and Watts's versions, with only a few of Hopkinson's remaining; and the great majority were in common, short, or long meter. No music was provided and no tunes suggested. Later editions increased the proportion of hymns, until in *Hymns of the Church* (New York, 1869) the remaining metrical psalms were mixed in with hymns.

Despite these updating procedures, congregational singing remained at a low ebb. In the parochial school system sponsored by the Church, the leader of the church psalmody was also the schoolmaster; but he did not generally use his position to teach the school children how to sing. As a result congregations were generally unable to take part in the psalm singing. Until the mid-19th century the schoolmaster and the organist often performed the music alone.

See also DUTCH REFORMED CHURCH, MUSIC OF THE.

(iv) Puritans. The Massachusetts Bay colony was founded in 1629 by puritan members of the Church of England, who had at first no idea of seceding from the church, though they rejected its ritual. They brought with them Sternhold and Hopkins's psalms, and we may suppose that they sang them mainly to the handful of four-line tunes then in common use. They were not of a temper to concern themselves with artistic improvements in the singing. But they were unhappy with Sternhold and Hopkins because "their variations of the sense, and alterations of the sacred text too frequently, may justly minister matter of offence." Accordingly, a group of 30 divines assembled to prepare a still more literal translation, "that as wee doe injoye other, soe (if it were the Lord's will) we might injoye this ordinance also in its native purity." They published, in 1640, *The Whole Booke of Psalmes Faithfully Translated into English Metre* (see §2(ii) below).

The Bay Psalm Book, or New England Psalm Book, as this collection became known, was at once adopted by almost every church in the colony. By means of lining out, which was in use in 1647 and perhaps earlier, the people could easily be taught to fit the new words to the old tunes. The compilers referred at the end of the book to 48 tunes to which the psalms might be sung, including 39 common-meter tunes "as they are collected, out of our chief musicians, by Tho. Ravenscroft." But it is highly unlikely that more than a handful of these were used in church. Copies of Ravenscroft's and Alison's harmonized settings are known to have been in the possession of early New England settlers, but, as in the old country, they would have been used domestically.

The Bay Psalm Book was used for over a century, and spread to other American colonies and even to many dissenting churches in Britain. There is no doubt that the new psalms continued to be sung to the old tunes. When for the first time a musical supplement appeared, with the ninth edition of 1698, the 13 tunes in it were all standard ones from English sources (see illustration below). They were set for tenor and bass, with fasola letters below the staves, suggesting that the basses were sung, not played, though they are angularly instrumental in character (see ex.2). In later editions the tunes were printed without basses.

Ex.2 "Low Dutch Tune," from the Bay Psalm Book (9/1698)

Psalm xxiii, as sung to the above tune (v.1)

The Lord to me a shepherd is,
Want therefore shall not I:
He in the folds of tender grass
Doth make me down to lie.

As in English country churches, the speed of singing had slowed to a drawl by this date. A type of melismatic heterophony, known to would-be reformers as the "Old" or "Common Way," prevailed in Congregational churches everywhere until about 1720 (*see* OLD WAY OF SINGING). The long absence of professional musicians led to an almost primitive practice which many deplored. Something of the chaos that often prevailed may be gathered from entries in Samuel Sewall's *Diary*, describing services at the South Meeting House, Boston:

1705, Dec. 28. Mr. Willard . . . spoke to me to set the Tune, I intended Windsor and fell into High-Dutch, and then essaying to set another Tune went into a key much too high. So I pray'd Mr. White to set it, which he did well, Litchf[ield] Tune

1718, Feb. 2. In the Morning I set York Tune, and in the 2d going over, the Gallery carried irresistibly to St. David's which discouraged me very much.

But the people liked this way of singing, and in some churches persisted with it despite efforts at reform. In the strongly individualistic, Congregational tradition of New England, every church was at liberty to govern its own practice.

Reform got under way in 1720, with the appearance of the Reverend Thomas Symmes's anonymous pamphlet, *The Reasonableness of Regular Singing, or Singing by Note*. In the following year two important singing methods were published by John Tufts and Thomas Walter. Each carried an appendix of psalm tunes, and Tufts introduced a new musical notation based on fasola letters. Walter's appendix presented the tunes in three-part harmony. (For discussion of the new era of American singing that resulted from these publications and from the formation of singing-schools, *see* PSALMODY.) It is sufficient to point out here that the teaching of singing from notes naturally generated church choirs, which tended, as in Anglican churches, to take the singing out of the hands of the people – if the people would let them. The attention which was thus focused on singing led in turn to a desire for better literary and musical materials to sing. The Bay Psalm Book soon gave way in popularity to more elegant if less literal translations – the *New Version* of Tate and Brady, and (particularly among Congregationalists) Isaac Watts's *Psalms of David Imitated in the Language of the New Testament* (first American publication, Philadelphia, 1729). More conservative congregations stuck to the old book (revised in 1758), but the supplements attached to later editions show that the traditional psalms, as well as the newer ones, were sung to increasingly elaborate tunes.

Ex.3 "Southwel New Tune," from Walter (1721) [originally on three staves]

Two tunes of this time appear to be the first printed compositions of American origin: "Southwel New" (ex.3) from Walter (1721), and "100 Psalm New" from Tufts (1723). Some of the earliest tunes containing florid melismas ("Northampton," "Isle of Wight," "24 Psalm") were drawn from English sources. But at the mid-century two tune supplements from New England, engraved (and possibly compiled) by James Turner and Thomas Johnston respectively, include some ornate tunes probably of American origin. One of them in the Johnston supplement (1755), called "Psalm 136," comes near to being a fuging-tune, though for tenor and bass only (ex.4, p.646). In the latter part of the century, especially after the Revolution, there was a burgeoning of elaborate psalmody in which the Congregational churches (descendants of the old Puritan bodies) were often in the vanguard (*see* PSALMODY, §2). It was perhaps partly for the purpose of countering this trend that organs were gradually introduced in Congregational churches towards the end of the 18th century. The first was at Providence, Rhode Island, in 1770; in 1798 Bentley had heard of only four Congregational churches with organs in America – three in Boston and one in Newburyport.

Under the influence of the Great Awakening and subsequent evangelical movements, metrical psalms tended to be replaced

Ex.4 "136 Psalm Tune," from Johnston's tune supplement to Tate and Brady's *New Version* (1755), here underlaid with the first verse of Psalm cxxxvi

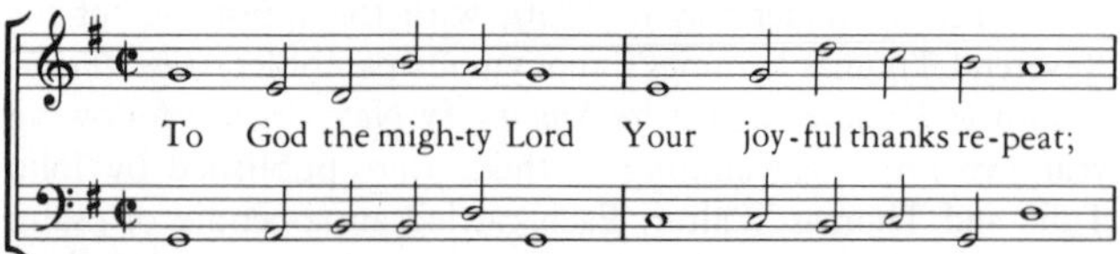
To God the migh-ty Lord Your joy-ful thanks re-peat;

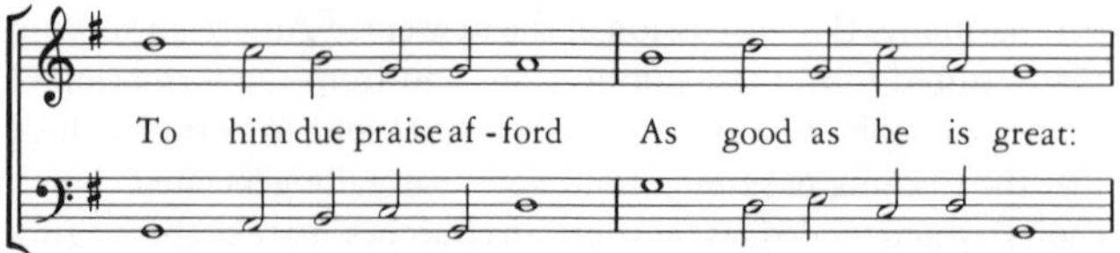
To him due praise af-ford As good as he is great:

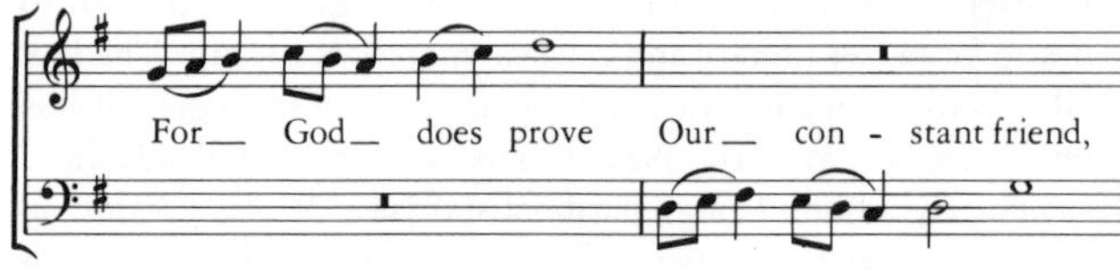
For— God— does prove Our— con - stant friend,

His
bound-less love

Shall
ne - ver end.

by hymns, and by 1830 formed a small proportion of the verses in most Congregational hymnbooks (*see* HYMNODY, §2).

See also UNITED CHURCH OF CHRIST, MUSIC OF THE.

(v) Presbyterian churches. The Presbyterians also claimed descent from the Puritans, but retained a more authoritarian and centralized form of church government by Synod. From 1668, and especially in the 18th century, both in what is now the USA and in Canada, a constant influx of Scots and Scots–Irish produced a distinctive brand of Presbyterianism – one that was strongly resistant to liberal trends. *The Psalms of David in Meeter*, in the Scottish version of 1650, was to Presbyterian minds almost a part of the Bible with which it was usually bound. The success of the Scots in colonizing the frontier outposts of the American and Canadian interiors left them often remote from acculturating influences, and they continued to use the Old Way of Singing long after it had been forgotten elsewhere. The 12 common tunes were lined out by a precentor, and sung by the people in the Old Way, which survived well into the 20th century in remote places. In urban centers such as Boston, Philadelphia, and New York, there were schisms in the 18th century: "New Side" synods welcomed the influence of the evangelical movement; "Old Side" synods preferred to continue in the old traditions. The psalm singing was, indeed, often the central issue in the fierce disputes that raged in Presbyterian circles at this date. James Lyon's *Urania* (Philadelphia, 1761) was subscribed to by a number of prominent Presbyterian clergymen; it must have represented the avant garde of Presbyterian singing. In 1774 John Adams, accustomed to the elaborate choir singing of New England, reported that the Old Presbyterian Society of New York was still "in the *old way*, as we call it – all the drawling, quavering, discord in the world." A revision of Watts's *Psalms* in a conservative direction, restoring those portions that Watts had deliberately omitted, was prepared by Joel Barlow in 1785, and the synods of Philadelphia and New York left individual parishes to decide whether to use it or to continue to sing the old psalms in the old way. The *Directory for the Worship of God* (1788) at last substituted "singing psalms or hymns" for the 1644 Westminster directory's "singing of psalms," paving the way for the authorization of Watts's hymns in 1802. In town churches the sterner kind of Presbyterianism faded gradually; organs were purchased, choirs took over the psalms and hymns. Congregational singing survived only in the wild country places.

See also PRESBYTERIAN CHURCH, MUSIC OF THE.

(vi) German Reformed Church. Of the various sects that flourished among the German communities in Pennsylvania during the 18th century, only the Reformed Church, with its Calvinist ancestry, sang metrical psalms. The first settlements were founded by Dutch Reformed ministers early in the century. They used the Marburg Collection of psalms in Lobwasser's version, and in 1753 this book was reprinted by Christopher Sauer at Germantown, Pennsylvania, as *Neu-vermehrt und vollständiges Gesang-Buch*, with all the traditional tunes. But the knowledge of the old chorale melodies was disappearing among the people; lining out had to be introduced, and by the end of the century it often happened that the minister and the organist were the only audible singers. At a synod held in Reading in 1794, it was resolved "that a new hymn-book be prepared, of which the Psalms shall be taken from Lobwasser and Spreng's improved version, and the Palatine hymn-book shall form the basis of the hymns." This, the first officially authorized book, was published in 1797. The psalm tunes had been greatly reduced in number, by the omission of little-used tunes. Between 1800 and 1850 there was a gradual change to the English language in many churches, and the first English collection, *Psalms and Hymns for the Use of the German Reformed Church in the United States of America*, appeared in 1830: all 150 psalms were still included, but they were largely in Watts's version and drew on Anglo-American sources for their tunes. A newly compiled German book appeared in 1842, and another, *Deutsches Gesangbuch* (edited by Philip Schaff), in 1861. By this time such metrical psalms as survived were embedded in a large collection of hymns, arranged by the church year. Tunes were no longer printed with the words; suggestions for tunes showed, however, an interest in reviving the traditional German chorale melodies.

2. PSALM BOOKS.

(i) Function and character. Of the psalm books printed in America only those for the Dutch and German Reformed Churches contained tunes printed with the psalms. In the Dutch version the tune was reprinted over each verse of the psalm; in the German, the first verse was underlaid and the rest printed beneath. These formats were modeled on European books that had been used with a tradition of accompanied singing. When an organ could not be obtained the congregation was at a loss and the knowledge of the tunes quickly faded. With the introduction of English

psalms and hymns the older type of underlaid psalm book disappeared.

The great majority of psalm books in the English American tradition had no music at all (perhaps 80% of the surviving editions up to 1800). Before the era of the singing-schools, there were so few tunes that they were known from memory, having been sung unaccompanied for generations. After choirs were well established, they generally sang from their own books containing special selections of psalm and hymn tunes and through-composed set-pieces and anthems. Most of the tune supplements date from the intermediate period (about 1720–75).

In the early days, when psalms were lined out, the congregation did not really need books at all in church. They knew the tunes, and they took the words from the parish clerk, elder, or minister. No doubt the Bay Psalm Book was designed, as much as anything, for domestic singing and private reading – as the title of the third edition suggests (see §ii below). In the same way the early tune supplements were for the benefit of devout singers at home rather than for the church; bass parts were soon found unnecessary. With the singing-school movement came the possibility of learning new music in parts, and for this Walter and Tufts prepared their instructional books. When the music was sung in church it was convenient for the singers to have it in the psalm book. The tune appendix of Tufts was itself used as a supplement for editions of psalm books; others had supplements of similar scope, usually (from 1737 onwards) in three parts. Tune supplements were only loosely attached to psalm books. The same supplement was used for different psalm books and vice versa, while most psalm books had no tunes at all. Evidently it was up to the purchaser to order whatever tunes he liked. Very probably the books with tunes were used by the members of the "choir" – those who had rehearsed them in the singing-school or psalmody society. The tunes attached to the 1774 Tate and Brady are entitled *A New Collection of Psalm Tunes Adapted to Congregational Worship*, which might seem to indicate an effort to prevent choirs from monopolizing the singing. But all the tunes in it are in four-part harmony, many are elaborate, and some are of the fully fuging variety. It seems that in some churches tunes of this sort were actually sung by congregations at large. With the disappearance of tune supplements and the flowering of psalmody books after the Revolution, choirs took over an increasing share of the music, singing anthems and set-pieces in which nobody could take part without rehearsal. When evangelical hymn singing made its way into churches congregations could once more take their full part (*see* HYMNODY). However, psalm books (without tunes) continued to appear until after the middle of the 19th century.

(ii) The Bay Psalm Book. The Bay Psalm Book (1640; fig.2) was the first English book ever printed in America: 1700 copies were run off on a small press belonging to Harvard College. The compilers, like Barton and Rous in England, eliminated some of the more unusual meters found in Sternhold and Hopkins, thus allowing all 150 psalms to be sung to the few tunes that were at the command of congregations. The collection was thoroughly revised for the third edition of 1651, chiefly by Henry Dunster and Richard Lyon. They polished the versification somewhat and added alternative translations. They further reduced unusual meters, so that 125 (instead of 112) out of 150 psalms were now in common meter; and they added 36 other "scripture-songs," still maintaining the Calvinistic principle that only inspired words were suitable for singing in worship. The new title was *The Psalms Hymns and Spiritual Songs of the Old and New Testament Faithfully Translated into English Metre for the Use, Edification, and Comfort of the Saints in Publick and Private, especially in New England.* This proved to be the definitive edition. It was reprinted under this title, with scarcely any alterations in the verbal text, for over a century.

When for the first time a tune supplement, printed from woodblocks, was bound in with the ninth edition (1698), the 13 tunes in it, and their basses, were drawn from the 1679 edition of John Playford's *Breefe Introduction to the Skill of Musick*, though the preface and the idea of using fasola letters probably came from the 1672 edition of the same book (see illustration). Lowens conjectured that the supplement was printed in England as part of a lost London edition of the Bay Psalm Book, but it does not resemble other English music printing of the time. The tunes are as set out in Table 1. It is a curious fact that the allocation of "Lichfield" to Psalm lxix, like the rest, is copied from Playford, where it is actually a misprint for xcvi (through printing 69 for 96): the first verse of Psalm xcvi is printed under the tune in Playford. In New England, however, the tune (as a result of this misprint) came to be associated with Psalm lxix, the first verse of which is printed with it in editions from 1705 to 1730. Other misprints closely follow Playford, proving the provenance of the tunes beyond doubt.

For the 1705 edition the music was completely reset in a different style, without basses or fasola letters but with the first verse of the allocated psalm underlaid. Many of the tunes are

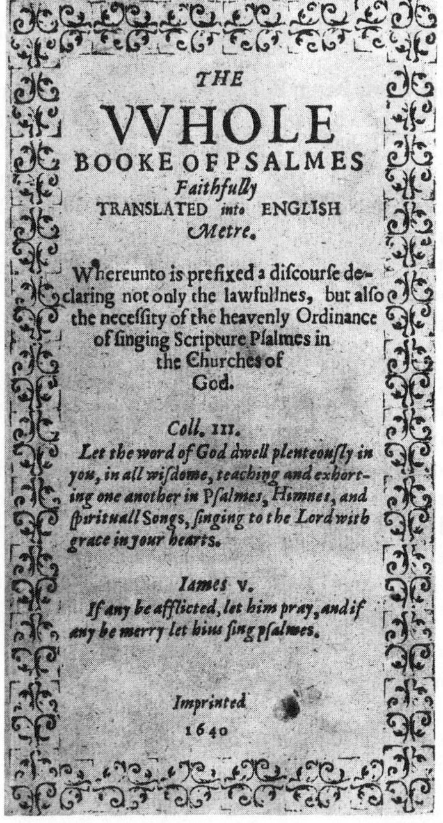
THE
VVHOLE
BOOKE OF PSALMES
Faithfully
TRANSLATED into ENGLISH
Metre.
Whereunto is prefixed a discourse declaring not only the lawfullnes, but also the necessity of the heavenly Ordinance of singing Scripture Psalmes in the Churches of God.
Coll. III.
Let the word of God dwell plenteously in you, in all wisdome, teaching and exhorting one another in Psalmes, Himnes, and spirituall Songs, singing to the Lord with grace in your hearts.
Iames v.
If any be afflicted, let him pray, and if any be merry let him sing psalmes.
Imprinted
1640

2. *Title page of "The Bay Psalm Book" (1640)*

TABLE 1

C.M. – *common meter*; S.M. – *short meter*; L.M. – *long meter*; D.C.M. – *double common meter*

Frost no.	*Tune name*	*Meter*	*Key*	*Psalm*
121	Oxford	C.M.	g	iv
25	Lichfield	C.M.	g	lxix
19	Low Dutch	C.M.	G	xxiii
205	York	C.M.	F	lxxiii
129	Windsor	C.M.	g	cxvi
154*a*	Cambridge Short	S.M.	g	lxx
234	St. David's	C.M.	F	xcv
209	Martyrs	C.M.	g	xxxix
333*a*	Hackney	C.M.	d	lxi
132	Psalm cxix Second Meeter	D.C.M.	e	cxix
114	Psalm c First Meeter	L.M.	G	c
125	Psalm cxv [sic] First Meeter	8:8:8:8:8:8:8:8: 8:8:8:8	G	(cxiii)
174	Psalm cxlviii First Meeter	6:6:6:6:4:4:4:4	C	cxlviii

transposed up a tone ("Martyrs" down a 3rd), a somewhat pointless maneuver for unaccompanied singing. The reason appears to have been that the 1705 tunes were copied from the 1694 or 1697 edition of Playford, where the same transpositions had been made to bring the tunes into line with Playford's *Whole Book of Psalms* (1677). The 13 tunes were reduced to 11 by omitting "Hackney" and "Psalm 115." The printer evidently had little competence in music: there are no clefs, several misprints, and "Oxford" has a key signature of one flat despite transposition to A minor. These mistakes were not corrected until 1726. The next few editions were very similar to that of 1705, with one other tune, "Ten Commandments" (Frost no. 178), appearing in some editions and not others. The tune selection was a standard one in New England, for the 1720 Boston edition of Tate and Brady had the very same 11 tunes in a different order. One British edition of the Bay Psalm Book (Glasgow, 1720) contains a similar selection, printed by James Duncan, printer to the city of Glasgow.

The 1737 edition carries an entirely different tune supplement of a much more ambitious kind, along the lines of Tufts's and Walter's books. It has 34 tunes in three-part harmony, with fasola letters underlaid. The selection of tunes owes far more to Tufts and Walter than to the previous supplements, reprinting some of their most "advanced" and ornate tunes and such novelties as "100 Psalm New."

Two copies of the 1744 edition are bound up with the Tufts supplement itself, printed from the plates of the 1738 edition. The 1758 edition has Turner's supplement, first printed with a psalm book of local use only, made by John Barnard, minister of a church in Marblehead, Massachusetts. This edition has also a revised text, by Thomas Prince. But the days of the Bay Psalm Book were numbered. A few more editions were still to come, without music, but between 1761 and 1780 the *New Version* and Watts's *Psalms* each appeared in more than ten times as many editions.

See also PUBLISHING AND PRINTING OF MUSIC, §1.

BIBLIOGRAPHY

The Whole Booke of Psalms Faithfully Translated into English Metre (Cambridge, MA, 1640/*R*1956) [the Bay Psalm Book]

J. Cotton: *Singing of Psalms a Gospel Ordinance* (London, 1647)

T. Symmes: *The Reasonableness of Regular Singing, or Singing by Note* (Boston, 1720)

J. Tufts: *An Introduction to the Singing of Psalm-tunes* (Boston, 3/1723)

Das neue und verbesserte Gesang-Buch (Philadelphia, 1797)

G. Hood: *A History of Music in New England* (Boston, 1846/*R*1970)

D. D. Demarest: *History and Characteristics of the Reformed Protestant Dutch Church* (New York, 1856, rev. and enlarged 4/1889 as *The Reformed Church in America*)

J. S. Curwen: *Studies in Worship Music* (London, 1880–85), 57ff

C. W. Baird: *History of the Huguenot Emigration to America*, i (New York, 1885), 65ff

J. Sabin: *Bibliotheca americana*, xvi (New York, 1886), 27ff

O. Seidensticker: *The First Century of German Printing in America, 1728–1830* (Philadelphia, 1893)

S. L. Thorndike: "The Psalmodies of Plymouth and Massachusetts Bay," *Colonial Society of Massachusetts Publications*, i (1895), 228

J. H. Dubbs: "History of the Reformed Church, German," *American Church History*, viii (1902), 213–423

L. F. Benson: "The American Revisions of Watts's Psalms," *Journal of the Presbyterian Historical Society*, ii (1903–4), 18

O. G. T. Sonneck: *Francis Hopkinson, the First American Poet-Composer (1737–1791) and James Lyon, Patriot, Preacher, Psalmodist (1735–1794)* (Washington, DC, 1905/*R*1967)

A. H. Messiter: *A History of the Choir and Music of Trinity Church, New York* (New York, 1906/*R*1970)

W. Bentley: *Diary*, ii: *1793–1802* (Salem, MA, 1907), 259

L. F. Benson: *The English Hymn* (New York, 1915/*R*1962)

W. S. Pratt: *The Music of the Pilgrims* (Boston, 1921/*R*1971)

M. van Doren, ed.: *Samuel Sewall: Diary* (New York, 1927)

W. S. Pratt: *The Music of the French Psalter of 1562* (New York, 1939)

H. C. Macdougall: *Early New England Psalmody: an Historical Appreciation, 1620–1820* (Brattleboro, VT, 1940/*R*1969)

W. W. Sweet: *Religion in Colonial America* (New York, 1942)

D. Wing: *A Short-title Catalogue of Books Printed in England, Scotland and Ireland . . . 1641–1700* (New York, 1945–51, rev. 2/1972)

A. P. Britton: *Theoretical Introductions in American Tune-books to 1800* (diss., U. of Michigan, 1949)

H. B. Satcher: "Music of the Episcopal Church in Pennsylvania in the Eighteenth Century," *Historical Magazine of the Protestant Episcopal Church*, xviii (1949), 372–413

M. Frost: *English and Scottish Psalm and Hymn Tunes c.1543–1677* (London, 1953)

G. Chase: *America's Music: from the Pilgrims to the Present* (New York, 1955, rev. 2/1966/*R*1981)

L. Ellinwood, ed.: *The Charleston Hymnal of 1792* (Charleston, 1956)

T. W. Dean: *The Organ in Eighteenth Century English Colonial America* (diss., U. of Southern California, 1960)

I. Lowens: *Music and Musicians in Early America* (New York, 1964), 25ff

T. M. Finney: "The Third Edition of Tufts' *Introduction* . . . ," *JRME*, xiv (1966), 163

C. K. Shipton and J. E. Mooney: *National Index of American Imprints through 1800* (n.p., 1969)

D. K. Stigberg: *Congregational Psalmody in Eighteenth Century New England* (thesis, U. of Illinois, 1970)

G. W. Williams, ed.: *Jacob Eckhard's Choirmaster's Book of 1809* (Columbia, SC, 1971)

N. Temperley: "John Playford and the Metrical Psalms," *JAMS*, xxv (1972), 331–78

R. G. Appel: *The Music of the Bay Psalm Book, 9th Edition (1698)*, ISAMm, v (Brooklyn, NY, 1975)

N. Temperley: *The Music of the English Parish Church* (Cambridge, England, 1979)

R. M. Wilson and K. V. Keller: *Connecticut's Music in the Revolutionary Era* (Hartford, 1979)

L. Inserra and H. W. Hitchcock: *The Music of Henry Ainsworth's Psalter*, ISAMm, xv (Brooklyn, NY, 1981)

N. Temperley: "The Old Way of Singing: its Origins and Development," *JAMS*, xxxiv (1981), 511–44

N. Temperley and C. G. Manns: *Fuging Tunes in the Eighteenth Century* (Detroit, 1983)

NICHOLAS TEMPERLEY

Psychedelic rock [acid rock]. A style of rock, played chiefly by bands in the San Francisco area in the 1960s. It is characterized by extended, blues-inspired improvisations and surrealistic lyrics, and sometimes uses exotic (especially Indian) instruments; the music is intended to evoke or accompany a drug-induced state. Among the most important psychedelic rock bands were the Grateful Dead, Jefferson Airplane, Quicksilver Messenger Service, and Country Joe and the Fish; their performances characteristically took place in large "rock palaces" and were accompanied by lavish light shows. Other bands incorporated elements of psychedelic rock into short pop songs that contained little or no improvisation; among these were the Electric Prunes, Moby Grape, and Strawberry Alarm Clock. Psychedelic rock did not die out entirely after the 1960s; the Grateful Dead sustained its popularity, and there were periodic revivals of the style, notably by various British bands in the 1980s and by Prince, in his album *Around the World in a Day* (1985).

See also POPULAR MUSIC, §IV, 5; ROCK, §2.

BIBLIOGRAPHY

C. Perry: "The Sound of San Francisco," *The Rolling Stone Illustrated History of Rock & Roll*, ed. J. Miller (New York, 1976, rev. 2/1980), 265

G. Sculatti and D. Seay: *San Francisco Nights: the Psychedelic Music Trip 1965–1968* (New York, 1985)

JOHN ROCKWELL

Psychology of music. The scientific investigation of cognitive, affective, and psychomotor aspects of music, and the knowledge resulting from this investigation. The areas of interest in the study of human musical behavior may be conveniently grouped as follows: sensation and perception; musical ability and aptitude; music learning and teaching; musical memory; responses to music; performance; and therapeutic and industrial uses of music (*see* MUSIC THERAPY).

The interpretation of data resulting from research in the psychology of music varies in tune with prevailing ideas in other areas of psychology. In music perception and learning, associationist and operant views contrast with interpretations based on cognitive studies and field theory. In the area of the nature and development of musical ability various views exist concerning the influences of heredity and environment. Among the theories in the main body of psychological research that have proved influential are the "homeostatic/cybernetic" interpretation, which integrates Walter Cannon's idea of the way systems operate to maintain a "steady state" or balance and Norbert Weiner's ideas in cybernetics; the "humanistic" view of psychology, developed around concepts such as Carl R. Rogers's "client-centered therapy," G. W. Allport's "becoming," and A. H. Maslow's "self-actualization"; several variants of B. F. Skinner's "operant behavior" theories and earlier "stimulus–response" theories represented by Thorndike; linguistic and communicative interpretations; and information theory. Psychoanalytic explanations have not been widely accepted.

Since its recognition in the early 1900s as a field of interest, the psychology of music has been a lively area of research in the USA. Scientific methodology, ranging from case studies and single-sample designs to large-sample parametric examinations of data, has been employed; research techniques have advanced with the improvement of technology for producing, controlling, and measuring musical stimuli, and with the development of equipment and methods for measuring human responses to music. The diverse, eclectic, and empirical approaches adopted by American scientists have given rise to a number of opposing theories of musical behavior, represented in a wealth of published material. Among the earliest and best-known of all figures in the psychology of music was Carl E. Seashore, whose books (1919, 1938) expound the view (later adopted by his student Schoen) that musical ability is composed of specific talents, which can be measured separately and independently of a musical context; he regarded these talents as hereditary and insusceptible to improvement through environmental influences. Mursell presented a substantially different view, interpreting "musicality" as an integrated whole, and arguing that musical ability can be developed through environment. Lundin adopted the orientation of "objective" psychology, criticizing the "mentalism" of earlier writings on the psychology of music, while Farnsworth's work reflects the view of social psychology and takes account of data from sociology and anthropology. Radocy and Boyle presented traditional topics such as psychoacoustics and music learning in a behavioral context that integrates individual and cultural aspects of human musical behavior.

Standardized tests have played an important part in research, providing a means of measuring musical perception, practical skills, and knowledge. They focus on four main areas (the first of which has received greater emphasis than the others): musical ability or aptitude, musical achievement, musical performance, and musical taste. Seashore developed the first standardized test of musical ability, which has been revised several times since it was first published in 1919 and is still widely used. Reflecting Seashore's view that musical ability consists of individual talents each of which can be measured alone, it consists of six tests, for pitch, loudness, rhythm, time, timbre, and tonal memory; the subject is asked to discriminate between electronically generated recorded sounds, presented in isolated, nonmusical contexts. The Kwalwasser and Dykema *Music Tests* resemble Seashore's, except that the recorded sounds are created by musical instruments instead of an electronic oscillator. Seashore's critic Mursell developed no tests based on his "integrated" view of musical ability, but the tests published by Gaston (1944) and Gordon (1965) reflect a similar concept of "musicality."

Tests of musical achievement measure a variety of perceptual skills and musical knowledge; those most widely used are by Kwalwasser and Ruch, Aliferis, Colwell, and Gordon (1970). Only a few standardized tests of musical performance have been published, and the leading test in this area is that of Watkins and Farnum. Hevner and Lansbury developed a test of musical taste, asking listeners to discriminate between more or less desirable versions in pairs of recorded musical excerpts. The *I.P.A.T. Music Preference Test of Personality* uses the preferences indicated by listeners to a series of recorded musical excerpts to suggest their personality characteristics.

Major research on the psychology of music has been carried out at the University of Iowa, where Seashore did his work in the psychology laboratories and where later Gordon, in the school of music, developed his tests of musical aptitude and literacy. The psychology of music laboratory in the department of music education at the University of Kansas supported the development of the Gaston test, the investigation of physiological and mood responses to music, and a variety of studies in music perception, learning, and taste; since 1977 Kansas has sponsored a series of symposia under the title "Research in Psychology and Acoustics of Music." The Center for Music Research in Florida State University's School of Music has produced extensive research into operant music learning, music as a reinforcer, music perception, and applications of computer music.

Researchers who specialize in music education, music therapy, psychology, speech and hearing science, and acoustics have all contributed to the literature on the psychology of music, which is scattered through the journals of these and related disciplines; the only American specialist journals in the area are *Psychomusicology* and *Music Perception*. A useful forum for informal communication is provided by the *Music Researcher's Exchange* (1974–), edited by Harold Abeles at Indiana University. Many of those who share particular research concerns participate in the special interest groups of the Music Educators National Conference (MENC) Research Council, the American Educational Research Association, and the American Psychological Association, and in the professional music therapy organizations and the Acoustical Society of America. In 1978 and 1979 the MENC sponsored two symposia on applications of psychology to the teaching and learning of music; they provided the opportunity for psychologists and music educators to assess the state of knowledge about auditory perception, motor learning, child development, cognitive skills, memory and information processing, and affect and motivation. A further conference, on motivation and creativity, was held in 1982.

Although most work on the psychology of music is done in universities, other agencies contribute. Commercial enterprises such as Muzak report that their provision of background music to business, industry, shops, and offices is based on their corporate research into the influence of music on behavior; although the results of much of this research are protected as corporate property, the companies publish occasional research reports. Practicing music therapists sometimes carry out clinical research and report the results in the literature. A conference on the biology of musical behavior, held in Denver in 1984, marked a growing interaction among music psychologists, neurologists, physicians, musicians, and others with interests focused on musical behavior.

Recent research shows increasing emphasis on the examination of complex musical behavior, and in particular the musical aspects of experimental aesthetics. This emphasis is reflected in studies of the relationship between the complexity of a stimulus and the subject's like or dislike of the music, studies of musical memory, research into child development in music following the pattern set by Piaget, and studies of the neuroanatomy and neurophysiology of musical functioning.

PUBLISHED TESTS

C. E. Seashore: *Measures of Musical Talent* (New York, 1919; rev. 2/1939 by C. E. Seashore, D. Lewis, and J. G. Saetviet, as *Seashore Measures of Musical Talents*)
J. Kwalwasser and G. M. Ruch: *Kwalwasser–Ruch Test of Musical Accomplishment* (Iowa City, 1924)
J. Kwalwasser and P. W. Dykema: *Kwalwasser–Dykema Music Tests* (New York, 1930)
K. Hevner and J. Lansbury: *Oregon Musical Discrimination Test* (Chicago, 1935); rev. N. H. Long, as *A Revision of the University of Oregon Music Discrimination Test* (diss., Indiana U., 1965)
E. T. Gaston: *A Test of Musicality* (Lawrence, KS, 2/1944)
R. B. Cattell and J. C. Anderson: *The I.P.A.T. Music Preference Test of Personality* (Champaign, IL, 1953)
J. Aliferis: *Music Achievement Test Manual, College Entrance Level* (Minneapolis, 1954)
J. G. Watkins and S. E. Farnum: *The Watkins–Farnum Performance Scale* (Winona, MN, 1954)
E. Gordon: *Musical Aptitude Profile* (Boston, 1965)
R. Colwell: *Music Achievement Tests* (Chicago, 1969–70)
E. Gordon: *Iowa Tests of Music Literacy* (Iowa City, 1970)

BIBLIOGRAPHY

C. E. Seashore: *The Psychology of Musical Talent* (Boston, 1919)
M. Schoen, ed.: *The Effects of Music* (New York, 1927)
C. Diserens and H. Fine: *A Psychology of Music* (Cincinnati, 1937)
J. L. Mursell: *The Psychology of Music* (New York, 1937)
C. E. Seashore: *Psychology of Music* (New York, 1938/*R*1967)
R. W. Lundin: *An Objective Psychology of Music* (New York, 1953, 2/1967)
P. R. Farnsworth: *The Social Psychology of Music* (New York, 1958, 2/1969)
A. P. Merriam: *The Anthropology of Music* (Evanston, IL, 1964)
E. Gordon: *The Psychology of Music Teaching* (Englewood Cliffs, NJ, 1971)
J. Roederer: *Introduction to the Physics and Psychophysics of Music* (New York, 1973, 2/1975)
M. Critchley and R. A. Hensen, eds.: *Music and the Brain: Studies in the Neurology of Music* (Springfield, IL, 1977)
J. B. Davies: *The Psychology of Music* (Stanford, CA, 1978)
Music Psychology Index (1978–)
R. E. Radocy and J. D. Boyle: *Psychological Foundations of Musical Behavior* (Springfield, IL, 1979)
D. A. Hodges, ed.: *Handbook of Music Psychology* (Lawrence, KS, 1980)
Psychomusicology (1981–)
D. Deutsch: *Psychology of Music* (New York, 1982)

GEORGE L. DUERKSEN

Ptaszyńska, Marta (*b* Warsaw, Poland, 29 July 1943). Polish composer and percussionist. Having earned three diplomas with distinction (composition, theory, and percussion) from the Warsaw Conservatory, she won a grant from the French government to study with Boulanger (1969–70). A Kosciuszko Foundation grant then brought her to the Cleveland Institute of Music (1972–4), where she studied with Cloyd Duff (to whom she dedicated *Space Model*, 1970), Richard Weiner, and Donald Erb. While living in Cleveland, she lectured frequently on Polish music and made concert appearances throughout the USA, performing a wide repertory that included her own works. She taught intermittently at Bennington College, Vermont (1974–7), and since 1977, when not in Europe, she has been composer-in-residence at the University of California campuses in Berkeley and Santa Barbara. She remains active as a recitalist, holds performance clinics, and serves as a director of the Percussive Arts Society.

Ranging widely from pointillism to a *cantabile* idiom, Ptaszyńska's music is colorful and often delicate, with a keen sense of architecture and an occasional use of aleatory procedures. Her scores make prominent use of percussion instruments and frequently specify an exact spatial arrangement of performers. In 1974 the Cleveland Orchestra gave the première of her *Spectri sonori*; *Siderals* and *Classical Variations* won prizes in Percussive Arts Society competitions (1974, 1976).

WORKS

Stage: Oscar from Alva (opera, Ptaszyńska, after Byron), 1972; Helio, centricum musicum (spectacle), dancers, vv, insts, 1978
Orch: Improvisations, 1968; Spectri sonori, 1973; Conc., 4 perc, 1974; Chimes, Bells, Wood, Stones, ww, str, perc, 1977; other works
Inst: Preludes, vib, pf, 1965; Scherzo, xyl, pf, 1967; A Tale of Nightingales, Bar, 6 insts, 1968; Space Model, solo perc, 1970; Madrigals, large ens, 1971; Sonospheres I–III, chamber ens, 1971–2; Siderals, 2 perc qnts, lights, 1974; 2 Poems, solo tuba, 1973–5; Touracou, hpd, 1974; Mobile, perc, 1975; Classical Variations, 4 timp, str qt, 1976; Quodlibet, solo db, 1976; Linear Construction in Space, perc qt, 1977; Dream Lands, Magic Spaces, vn, pf, perc, 1979; other works
Vocal: Chant for All the People on Earth, oratorio, 1969; Epigrams, women's chorus, fl, harp, perc, pf, 1976–7; Ave Maria, 4 male vv, brass, perc, 1982; other choruses

Principal publisher: E. B. Marks

BIBLIOGRAPHY

T. Marek: "Composer's Workshop: Marta Ptaszyńska's *Siderals*," *Polish Music*, x/2 (1975), 20
B. Murray: "The Influence of Polish Music on American Culture," *Polish Music*, xi, (1976), no. 1, p. 6; no. 2, p. 10

MICHAEL MECKNA

Publishing and printing of music. This article focuses on the history of music publishing in the USA, although the technology of printing is necessarily a part of the picture. The publishers cited in this text are given in the form most frequently encountered on title pages of editions, though minor modifications have been made in the interest of clarity (e.g., in company names "&" is used for "and" throughout, and, because of the many changes of title, such abbreviations as "Co." and "Inc." are omitted). For a full discussion of printing techniques, see H. E. Poole and D. W. Krummel: "Printing and Publishing of Music," *Grove* 6. *See also* MUSIC TRADES.

1. Early sacred music publishing. 2. Sheet music to 1865. 3. Commercial activity, 1865–1945. 4. Developments since 1945.

1. EARLY SACRED MUSIC PUBLISHING. Music printing in the New World dates from the 1540s, when several plainchant books were issued in Mexico by immigrant printers from Spain, but the earliest musical publication from the English colonies dates from a century later. The earliest surviving book printed in the English-speaking New World was a psalter, the Bay Psalm Book, issued in 1640 by Stephen Day at Cambridge in the Massachusetts Bay Colony. Containing no musical notation, it names the tunes to which the texts were to be sung, and the many editions that appeared during the next few decades showed a strong English influence in both content and method of production. The book was produced by letterpress, a process that involved fixing type or block cuts on a flat bed and inking them so as to transfer the text to the paper. Musical notation appeared for the first time only in the ninth edition ("printed by B. Green and J. Allen for Michael Perry" in Boston, 1698; fig. 1), and the crude woodcuts used to produce the eight-page tune supplement were re-used in several of the later editions as well.

1. The "York" tune for Psalm lxxiii, with fasola letters, from the supplement to the ninth edition (1698) of the Bay Psalm Book

Freehand music engraving was introduced during the period when the New England reform movement of congregational singing flourished. It involved the incision of a text into a flat plate (at first usually of copper, but later of pewter); the plate was then inked and wiped clean so that the ink remaining in the incisions was transferred to the paper during pressing. The process was used in two celebrated instruction books published in Boston in 1721, one by John Tufts entitled *A Very Plain and Easy Introduction to the Singing of Psalm Tunes* (the first extant edition is the third, 1723, "printed from copper-plates, neatly engraven . . . for Samuel Gerrish"), and the other by Thomas Walter entitled *Grounds and Rules of Musick*, printed by James Franklin, also for the bookseller Gerrish.

Freehand engraving continued to be used in the early Yankee tunebooks, which bear the names of America's prominent copperplate engravers: Thomas Johnston, who engraved his own booklet of rules for singing (1755) as well as several editions of Walter's *The Grounds and Rules of Musick* around 1760; Henry Dawkins (James Lyon's *Urania*, 1761); Paul Revere (Josiah Flagg's *A Collection of the Best and Most Approved Tunes*, 1764, and *The New-England Psalm-singer* by William Billings, 1770); John Ward Gilman, who engraved several books around 1770, including American editions of works by the English psalmodist William Tans'ur; and Amos Doolittle, who prepared most of Daniel Read's compilations.

Movable type was introduced in the English colonies by Christopher Saur in Germantown, Pennsylvania; his sacred collection *Kern alter und neuer . . . geistreicher Lieder* (1752) was the first of several German religious books with music issued from his press in subsequent decades. Although Saur is thought to have cast the type himself, his matrices came from Europe, probably Frankfurt am Main. The music typeface used in William Dawson's *The Youth's Entertaining Amusement* (Philadelphia, 1754) appears to be unique; Wolfe (1980) identified the printer as Anton Armbrüster, who also issued a collection of *Tunes in Three Parts* in 1763. The last of the early American music typefaces (which was acquired from the Dutch firm of Johannes Enschedé) is seen in two books printed for the Reformed Protestant Dutch Church in New York, Francis Hopkinson's translation of *The Psalms of David* (1767) and *A Collection of the Psalm and Hymn Tunes* (1774).

Movable type began to be used more frequently in the 1780s, when the fonts were first imported from the Caslon foundry in London. This also marks the rise of specialty publishing (exemplified by a broadside songsheet printed by William Norman in Boston, 1783) and of religious music publishing. In 1785 Isaiah Thomas in Worcester and William M'Culloch in Philadelphia also imported fonts, and the adoption of this practice eventually led to the decline of freehand engraving, as well as to the establishment of a formal repertory of religious music and the tunebook as a distinct physical object. Set in movable type, such tunebooks were oblong in format and bound in heavy boards; a theoretical introduction generally preceded the music. The several hundred different tunebooks that appeared around the turn of the century were printed in the Caslon typeface, in the special music type without staff lines developed by Andrew Law for his solfège system, or in a new and tidier face (which also had a special solfège version) introduced soon after 1800 by the Binney & Ronaldson foundry in Philadelphia. Centered at first in the cities of the East Coast, interest in religious music publishing eventually spread to the West and South and resulted in the publication of collections of sacred music (especially hymns) by Lowell Mason and his contemporaries, as well as the shape-note tunebooks (*see* SHAPE-NOTE HYMNODY).

2. SHEET MUSIC TO 1865. As early as 1768 John Mein and John Fleming prepared a broadside engraving of *The New and Favourite Liberty Song*, the plates for which were used in *Bickerstaff's Boston Almanack* for 1769. In 1786 Chauncey Langdon's *The Select Songster* was engraved in New Haven by Amos Doolittle, and during the course of the next few years, a group of prominent Philadelphians – Reinagle (composer), Aitken (engraver), Thomas Dobson (pressman), Henry Rice (bookseller), and Hopkinson (composer and patron) – assembled their talents to produce several major anthologies: vocal and instrumental collections by Reinagle (notably a set of keyboard variations thought to be the first solely secular musical publication in the USA), Hopkinson's famous *Seven Songs* (1788), and a Roman Catholic service book. The introduction of music engraving punches in America can probably be traced to these books. Each instance of a particular sign was identical, having been produced from the same punch; with freehand engraving, by contrast, each sign was drawn separately and therefore differed, albeit minutely, from all others of its kind.

Sheet-music publishing was firmly established in America by the mid-1790s. In 1793 J. C. Moller and Henri Capron established a music store in Philadelphia and published four issues of *Moller and Capron's Monthly Numbers*, a periodical collection of vocal and instrumental music (their business was taken over by George Willig the following year). Benjamin Carr settled in Philadelphia in 1793 and soon became established as a publisher; that year J. H. Smith and James Harrison founded their companies in New York. In 1794 Carr's father Joseph immigrated from London and opened a shop in Baltimore and Frederick Rausch established another in New York. Peter Albrecht von Hagen started his own firm in Boston in the late 1790s. These firms were located in major urban centers and had close ties with the theatrical companies that were being founded at the time. Many of the publishers themselves had been theater musicians, and their catalogues consisted largely of theater songs. At the turn of the century two more major publishers were established, Gottlieb Graupner in Boston and George E. Blake in Philadelphia. While Philadelphia maintained its leadership through the shops of Willig and Blake, New York grew in importance through the work of smaller firms, including those of John Paff, Joseph Willson, the Geib family, and William Dubois.

Three interrelated events date from the late 1820s. The new printing method of lithography, involving a flat printing surface marked, dampened, and then inked so as to leave ink on only the marked areas for transfer to the paper, was first used in the USA by Henry Stone in Washington, DC, around 1822, but was taken up more extensively in New York five years later by Edward S. Mesier, Anthony Fleetword, and G. Melkham Bourne. The introduction of lithography coincided with the rise of blackface minstrelsy, and notable early examples of the process can be found in editions of *Jim Crow* and other works in this repertory (*see* MINSTRELSY). These events may be seen in another context, as a reflection of the rise of "Jacksonian democracy," with its emphasis on the new values of the western frontier rather than the more traditional values cultivated in the eastern cities. Clearly, early music lithographs, with their imperfectly drawn musical figures but better prospects for music illustration, interested a different public from the one that purchased engraved music editions, which had become largely devoted to the fashionable repertories of Italian opera and guitar songs. Lithographic sheet music virtually disappeared in the 1830s, perhaps because the engraved editions looked so much less amateurish. The process re-emerged, however, in the 1840s with the development of chromolithography for cover illustrations; notable among the specialty shops using this technique, by which several colors could be printed, were John H. Bufford, W. S. and J. B. Pendleton, and B. W. Thayer in Boston; Peter S. Duval and Thomas Sinclair in Philadelphia; and Nathaniel Currier (famous through his later partnership with J. Merritt Ives), George Endicott, and Napoleon Sarony of Sarony, Major & Knapp in New York.

2. Title page of Henry Russell's "Woodman! Spare that Tree!," published by Firth & Hall (New York, 1837)

The publishers John Cole and the younger George Willig were particularly active in Baltimore around 1830. The 1840s saw the emergence of Charles Keith and George P. Reed in Boston; James G. Osbourn, Augustus Fiot, Leopold Meignen, and Lee & Walker in Philadelphia; and Frederick Benteen in Baltimore. It was during this decade that the family of William Cumming Peters became active, at first in Baltimore, and later in Pittsburgh, Cincinnati, and Louisville. Music publishing in San Francisco flourished for the first time during the Gold Rush years, the firm of Sherman & Hyde being particularly important. In the 1850s several new firms were established on the East Coast, notably S. T. Gordon in New York and Miller & Beacham in Baltimore, but more significant was the continuing activity in the West, involving such major firms as Balmer & Weber in St. Louis, Root & Cady in Chicago, and Silas Brainard in Cleveland. Confederate firms included A. E. Blackmar (in Vicksburg, Mississippi; Augusta, Georgia; and New Orleans) and W. T. Mayo, Philip P. Werlein, and Louis Grunewald in New Orleans. Foremost among America's music publishers by the middle of the century were the various partnerships of John Firth, William Hall, and William A. Pond in New York (who were responsible for publishing much of the music of Stephen Foster) and Oliver Ditson in Boston.

3. COMMERCIAL ACTIVITY, 1865–1945. The period from the end of the Civil War to the end of World War II saw a vast expansion in publishing activity and an increase in specialization. An unprecedented amount of music for domestic use was published in what has been described as the "age of parlor music." The consolidation of over 50 firms under the control of Oliver Ditson during the second half of the 19th century was an event of crucial importance. Other significant firms publishing serious music emerged, many of them founded by German immigrants. The largest was probably G. Schirmer in New York (formally established in 1861 but active earlier), which began to publish the extensive Schirmer Library of Musical Classics in 1892 and achieved great success with its highly regarded catalogue of art songs. Other firms established by German immigrants included Carl Fischer, founded in New York in 1872, specializing at first in band music, then in choral and orchestral works; Arthur P. Schmidt in Boston, founded in 1876, noted for its sponsorship of American composers, among them MacDowell and the Second New England School; and the smaller firm of J. Fischer in Dayton, founded in 1864 and specializing in Roman Catholic choral music. Theodore Presser, founded in 1883 in Lynchburg, Virginia, but soon moved to Philadelphia, enhanced its catalogue by publishing what came to be the major music journal of the time, *The Etude*.

For the best editions of art music, however, purchasers in the USA (as elsewhere) looked mostly to Germany. Among those who attempted to promote American-born composers in the first part of the 20th century were Arthur Farwell, active from 1901 to 1912 at the Wa-Wan Press in Newton Centre, Massachusetts, and specializing in music derived from American Indian traditions; the members of the SOCIETY FOR THE PUBLICATION OF AMERICAN MUSIC, founded in 1919; and Henry Cowell, whose *New Music* series (1927–58) was substantially underwritten by Charles Ives.

Popular-music publishing emerged as a specialty in its own right after the Civil War as publishers began to look for "hit tunes." By the end of the century, the center for this kind of music publishing was midtown Manhattan, an area that came to be known as TIN PAN ALLEY. Among the major popular-music firms were Belwin-Mills, Leo Feist, Charles Foley, Sam Fox, T. B. Harms, Edward B. Marks, J. J. Robbins, Shapiro & Bernstein, and M. Witmark. Chicago also enjoyed a bustling activity in this area, its practitioners including Sol Bloom, later a prominent member of the US Congress. Detroit was known for its musical-comedy firms (among them Henry Whittemore, Clark J. Whitney, and Jerome H. Remick). Even Sedalia, Missouri, could claim John Stark, who issued the early rags of Scott Joplin. As Hollywood became the home of the film industry, Los Angeles developed a music publishing community of its own, one that in later years, however, degenerated into the center for "song shark" practices, whereby dealers with questionable reputations charged exorbitant fees to print and copyright a song and ostensibly to promote it into a lucrative hit.

Other sources of popular music were the Sunday newspapers which featured special music supplements printed in color (if on poor-quality paper). The Bromo Seltzer Company issued music with covers advertising its product, and countless local music shops offered printing, publishing, and retail services to local composers anxious to establish a reputation. Only as the recording industry began to flourish in the 1920s did the great age of popular-music publishing show the first signs of decline and redirection.

Other kinds of music publisher emerged to accommodate the particular needs of various types of performance. Educational firms provided materials for public-school use, continuing a tradition that had roots in the pedagogically oriented collections published by Lowell Mason. The "basic series" (i.e., sets of graded materials for use at the elementary school level) proved to be particularly valuable for general textbook publishers such as the American Book Company, Allyn & Bacon, Follett, Ginn, and Silver Burdett, as well as for such music firms as C. C. Birchard, Neil A. Kjos, and E. C. Schirmer. Band music continued to be issued nationally by Carl Fischer and another general music firm, John Church; it was also provided by such specialist publishers as E. F. Ellis in Washington, DC, J. W. Pepper in Philadelphia, Vandersloot in Williamsport, Pennsylvania, and C. L. Barnhouse in Oskaloosa, Iowa. Choral music was a specialty of E. C. Schirmer in Boston and H. W. Gray in New York, though amateur choirs requiring a simpler repertory turned to E. S. Lorenz in Dayton, Ohio. Hymnals were produced mostly under official denominational auspices or by individual evangelists, for instance Homer Rodeheaver of Winona Lake, Indiana, while topical songbooks were issued by or for innumerable political, ethnic, social, fraternal, and occupational groups. An important publisher of opera librettos was Fred J. Rullman, who was associated with the Metropolitan Opera in New York.

Common concerns of music publishers came to be addressed through special organizations, beginning with the BOARD OF MUSIC TRADE, founded in 1855 but moribund by the end of the century. In the 20th century, a growing concern for performance rights led to the establishment of the American Society of Composers, Authors and Publishers (ASCAP) in 1914 and Broadcast Music, Inc. (BMI) in 1940 (*see also* PERFORMING RIGHTS SOCIETIES). Music publishers now generally affiliate themselves with either the MUSIC PUBLISHERS' ASSOCIATION OF THE UNITED STATES founded in 1895 and serving chiefly the publishers of serious music, or the NATIONAL MUSIC PUBLISHERS' ASSOCIATION, founded in 1917 as the Music Publishers' Protective Association and serving mostly the publishers of popular music.

4. DEVELOPMENTS SINCE 1945. The common view of postwar American music publishing is that after a quarter-century of continued happy expansion, from about 1945 to about 1970, the industry has been going through an unsettling time of economic uncertainty and volatility. The arrival in the USA of experienced music publishers escaping the Holocaust had proved highly beneficial in serving the increasingly sophisticated tastes of performers and listeners during the 1950s, yet, in the 1960s, many of the stable giants of music publishing found themselves, for better or worse, absorbed into the great financial conglomerates. G. Schirmer and Associated Music Publishers, for instance, became subsidiaries of Macmillan, Inc. Although new firms have continued to appear, many of them are small and serve only specialty audiences. Serious music has begun to be issued by academic presses, Smith College in the 1950s being a particularly notable example. Popular-music firms, which in more recent times have found a home in Nashville, have in many instances

become extremely successful. Experimentation has characterized methods of production (as reflected in the passing use of "black-line" prints and of the ozalid process, which involves special photocopying techniques applied to manuscript copies made on special papers); distribution, especially of music published for a limited audience, exemplified by the activities of the AMERICAN COMPOSERS ALLIANCE; and music rental. There has also been, on the other hand, a disturbing decline in local music retailing, with outlets being closed or forced to provide a more limited range of services to their customers. The inconvenience has perhaps been offset by the rise of national retailing activities and by the expanded services of public and academic music libraries.

The two overriding changes in music publishing since World War II – the burgeoning impact of the sound recording as a musical document and the demands made on publishers as a result of the copyright act of 1976 to collect and distribute royalties – have both served to direct the music publisher's attention increasingly towards legal and proprietary activities and away from printing, and often distribution as well. Photo-lithography (the copying of a page of music with a camera for reproduction by the lithographic process) has clearly come to be the dominant printing process, whether (as in the 1950s) for reprinting pre-war editions of the standard repertory for use in performance, or (in the 1960s) for reprinting scholarly editions for use in the new and expanding libraries, or (in the 1980s) to replace music engraving through, for example, computerized layout of musical texts (the method used by A-R Editions). Meanwhile, the rise of the quick photocopying machine has severely diminished the sale of copies for music publishers, forcing increases in price and causing the publishers to look even more to performance rights for their income. Such circumstances, influenced variously by the different kinds of repertory, documentation, and audience, have no doubt served to diminish even further the commonalities shared by music publishers. In any event, the availability of music can always be expected to fluctuate, reflecting as it does the industry's sensitivity to changing musical, social, technological, and commercial developments.

BIBLIOGRAPHY

W. A. Fisher: *One Hundred and Fifty Years of Music Publishing in the United States* (Boston, 1933/*R*1977)

H. Dichter and E. Shapiro: *Early American Sheet Music: its Lure and its Lore* (New York, 1941/*R*1970 as *Handbook of Early American Sheet Music*)

V. L. Redway: *Music Directory of Early New York City: a File of Musicians, Music Publishers and Music Instrument-Makers Listed in New York Directories from 1786 to 1835, together with the Most Important Music Publishers from 1836 through 1875* (New York, 1941)

W. T. Upton: "Early American Publications in the Field of Music," *Music and Libraries*, ed. R. S. Hill (Washington, DC, 1943), 60

J. H. Stone: "The Merchant and the Muse: Commercial Influences on American Popular Music before the Civil War," *Business History Review*, xxx (1956), 1

P. H. Lang, ed.: *One Hundred Years of Music in America* (New York, 1961) [incl. R. F. French: "The Dilemma of the Music Publishing Industry," p.171]

D. J. Epstein: *Music Publishing in Chicago before 1871: the Firm of Root & Cady, 1858–1871* (Detroit, 1969)

G. T. Tanselle: *Guide to the Study of United States Imprints* (Cambridge, MA, 1971) [see also Krummel, 1972]

E. C. Krohn: *Music Publishing in the Middle Western States before the Civil War* (Detroit, 1972)

D. W. Krummel: "American Music Bibliography: Four Titles in Three Acts," *Yearbook for Inter-American Musical Research*, viii (1972), 137 [analysis of and addenda to Tanselle, 1971]

J. L. Fleming: *James D. Vaughan, Music Publisher, Lawrenceburg, Tennessee, 1912–1964* (diss., Union Theological Seminary, New York, 1972)

D. J. Epstein: "Introduction," *Complete Catalogue of Sheet Music and Musical Works*, ed. Board of Trade (New York, 1973) [original catalogue, 1870]

D. W. Krummel: "Counting Every Star: or, Historical Statistics on Music Publishing in the United States," *Yearbook for Inter-American Musical Research*, x (1974), 175

C. Pavlakis: "Music Publishers," *The American Music Handbook* (New York, 1974), 625

D. P. McKay and R. Crawford: *William Billings of Boston* (Princeton, NJ, 1975)

K. Kroeger: "Isaiah Thomas as a Music Publisher," *Proceedings of the American Antiquarian Society*, lxxxvi (1976), 321

P. Dranov: *Inside the Music Publishing Industry* (White Plains, NY, 1980)

L. Feist: *An Introduction to Popular Music Publishing in America* (New York, 1980)

J. Taubman: *In Tune with the Music Business* (New York, 1980)

R. J. Wolfe: *Early American Music Engraving and Printing* (Urbana, IL, 1980)

C. Sachs, ed.: *An Introduction to Music Publishing* (New York, 1981)

"Small Music Presses," *Notes*, xxxviii/4 (1982) [complete issue, incl. articles by S. Smith, J. McKelvey, A. Seay]

R. Crawford and D. W. Krummel: "Early American Music Printing and Publishing," *Printing and Society in Early America*, ed. W. L. Joyce and others (Worcester, MA, 1983), 186–227

M. K. Duggan: "A Provisional Directory of Music Publishers, Music Printers, and Sheet-music Cover Artists in San Francisco, 1850–1906," *Kemble Occasional*, no.30 (1983), 1

"Music Publishing in America," *American Music*, i/4 (1983) [whole issue, incl. articles by P. R. Osterhout, R. D. Wetzel, D. P. Walker, R. H. Mead, and L. S. Levy]

R. Sanjek: *From Print to Plastic: Publishing and Promoting America's Popular Music (1900–1980)*, ISAMm, xx (Brooklyn, NY, 1984)

D. W. KRUMMEL

Pueblo, eastern. American Indians of New Mexico who live along the Rio Grande and its tributaries (*see* INDIANS, AMERICAN, fig. 1). The ancestors of the current Pueblo residents settled this region in about 1300, almost three centuries before the first Europeans colonized the area and gave the name *pueblo* (Sp.: village) to settlements of sedentary Indians. Members of the 16 eastern Pueblo groups, who now number 20,000, share many characteristics and are grouped by language. The Keresan-speaking eastern Pueblo – Cochiti, San Felipe, Santa Ana, Santo Domingo, and Zia – are known for their conservatism and unique language. The Pueblo belonging to the Kiowa-Tanoan linguistic family are divided into three subgroups: TEWA (Nambe, Pojoaque, San Ildefonso, San Juan, Santa Clara, and Tesuque); Tiwa (Isleta, PICURIS, TAOS, and Sandia); and Towa (Jemez Pueblo).

The semiarid environment of the eastern Pueblo strongly influences their cultural patterns and religious practices. Complex ceremonial activities are focused on weather control (especially precipitation), fertility, hunting, and the change of seasons. Traditional rituals persist as a vital element of Pueblo life. In the Colonial period severe religious persecution by European clergy forced the eastern Pueblo to perform their ceremonies privately, and many rituals are still closed to nonresidents. The secrecy surrounding religious practices has helped preserve each Pueblo's identity, integrity, and conservatism, while making study by outsiders very difficult. Eastern Pueblo music is part of an oral tradition performed principally in a ceremonial context. Structurally it is among the most complex of all North American Indian music. Songs are deemed to possess power and so must be used only in appropriate situations – unless their sacredness has been nullified by changes in structure, text, or both.

The principal function of eastern Pueblo music is to accompany ceremonial dances. Singers, usually male, can be either self-accompanying dancers or a separate, well-trained chorus (see illustration). The number of singers ranges from a soloist to 200; dances may be performed by a single dancer or a group of any size up to several hundred. Pueblo songs are monophonic and use pentatonic, hexatonic, and heptatonic scales. Melodic move-

Chorus of San Ildefonso Pueblo

ment commences with a phrase centered on the ground tone, leaps to the upper range of the song (usually a 5th to a 10th above the base pitch), and cascades down to the ground tone. The leap and descent will be repeated several times, often using only the lower half to two-thirds of the melodic range. The standard metric pattern is duple; triple pulsations, which are occasionally found, often represent borrowings from non-Pueblo music. A characteristic of eastern Pueblo music is the disruption of the steady duple beat by a brief, different rhythmic pattern, which, although it provides a distinct change, often seems completely natural. The singing style is marked by pulsations, accents, vocal tension, and, except among the northern Tiwa, where higher-pitched melodies show Plains influences, a low tessitura. That singers are expected to blend their voices with those of their fellow performers illustrates the Pueblo norms of moderation and lack of individual display.

Musical form reflects the Pueblo characteristics of correct order, repetition, and duality. The most common sacred song forms are *AA′BB′A* and forms using paired phrases (such as *AABBCC*). A brief, introductory melodic pattern identifies the song's function. Much use is made of repeated subsections; a song that lasts ten minutes typically contains only 60 to 90 seconds of thematic material. The structure of a representative *AA′BB′A* song is:

A	Introduction	||: a b c :||	||: d b c :||	||: e f :||
A′	Repeat of A with altered text			
B	Altered introduction	||: g c :||	||: d b c :||	||: e f :||
B′	Repeat of B with altered text			
A	Repeat of A			

The melody ascends to a higher range in the initial part of subsection *d*. New songs, which are constantly composed, must fit the proper mold for a specific song type; anyone can submit a new song, but most are created by recognized composers. If a song does not have a proper structure or correct rhythmic, textual, and melodic relationships, it will be refined by the main singers until it is acceptable. New songs often contain phrases from earlier compositions, or melodies borrowed from other cultures transformed into a Pueblo style.

The predominant eastern Pueblo instruments are percussive; these include double-headed wooden drums crafted from logs and animal skins, and rattles made from gourds, turtle shells, seashells, hooves, and metal bells. Notched sticks with gourd resonators are used in a few ceremonies; wooden flutes and bull-roarers are rare. The fiddle and guitar, borrowed from European colonizers, accompany the nonindigenous *matachines* pageant.

Music is sung by individuals for enjoyment, personal religious experiences, and healing, but most songs are performed in a group ceremonial context. Some rituals occur on specific dates, others are seasonal, and a few are enacted throughout the year. There are six general categories of eastern Pueblo dance: kachina (with masked representations of specific deities), "maskless kachina," animal, corn, borrowed, and social. Kachina and maskless kachina songs are in *AA′BB′A* form. Animal dance songs consist of paired phrases; for each dance appearance there is an entrance song, a slow dance-song, and a fast dance-song. Corn dances use two songs, the second of which is in *AA′BB′A* form.

Although the eastern Pueblo have been subjected to outside influences for centuries and, though newly composed songs continue to enter the repertory, there is little evidence of substantial change in their music; it is a vital art and an integral part of their continuing ceremonial activity. Recordings of eastern Pueblo music are held at the John Donald Robb Archive of Southwestern Music, University of New Mexico Fine Arts Library, Albuquerque.

See also INDIANS, AMERICAN, esp. §I, 4(ii)(c) and figs.6 and 7.

DISCOGRAPHY

Pueblo: Taos, San Ildefonso, Zuni, Hopi (Library of Congress AAFS L43, 1954)
Pueblo Indian Songs from San Juan (Canyon 6065, 1969)
Cloud Dance Songs of San Juan Pueblo, recorded 1972 (IH 1102, 1972)

Pueblo Songs of the Southwest, recorded 1969 (IH 9502, 1972)
Turtle Dance Songs of San Juan Pueblo, recorded 1972 (IH 1101, 1972)
Oku Shareh: Turtle Dance Songs of San Juan Pueblo (NW 301, 1979)

BIBLIOGRAPHY

G. Herzog: "A Comparison of Pueblo and Pima Musical Styles," *Journal of American Folklore*, xlix (1936), 283–417
G. P. Kurath: "The Origin of the Pueblo Indian Matachines," *El Palacio*, lxiv (1957), 259
——: "Cochiti Choreographies and Songs," in C. H. Lange: *Cochiti: a New Mexico Pueblo, Past and Present* (Austin, 1959/*R*1968), 539
D. N. Brown: "The Distribution of Sound Instruments in the Prehistoric Southwestern United States," *EM*, xi (1967), 71
G. P. Kurath and A. Garcia: *Music and Dance of the Tewa Pueblos* (Santa Fe, 1970)
D. N. Brown: "Ethnomusicology and the Prehistoric Southwest," *EM*, xv (1971), 363
D. L. Roberts: "The Ethnomusicology of the Eastern Pueblos," *New Perspectives on the Pueblos*, ed. A. Ortiz (Albuquerque, 1972), 243
C. J. Frisbie: *Music and Dance Research of Southwestern United States Indians* (Detroit, 1977)
D. N. Brown: "Dance as Experience: the Deer Dance of Picuris Pueblo," *Southwestern Indian Ritual Drama*, ed. C. Frisbie (Albuquerque, 1980), 71
M. La Vigna: "Okushare, Music for a Winter Ceremony: the Turtle Dance Songs of San Juan Pueblo," *Selected Reports in Ethnomusicology*, iii/2 (1980), 77
D. L. Roberts: "A Calendar of Eastern Pueblo Indian Ritual Dramas," *Southwestern Indian Ritual Drama*, ed. C. Frisbie (Albuquerque, 1980), 103
N. Yeh: "The Pogonshare Ceremony of the Tewa: San Juan, New Mexico," *Selected Reports in Ethnomusicology*, iii/2 (1980), 101–45
P. Humphreys: "The Tradition of Song Renewal Among the Pueblo Indians of North America," *American Indian Culture and Research Journal*, vi (1982), 9
F. W. Champe: *The Matachines Dance of the Upper Rio Grande: History, Music, and Choreography* (Lincoln, NE, 1983)

DON L. ROBERTS

Pueblo, western. American Indians of the southwestern USA. Western Pueblo Indians include the Acoma and Laguna, who speak Keresan; the Hano; the HOPI; and the ZUNI.

Puente, Tito [Ernest Anthony] (*b* New York, 20 April 1923). Vibraphonist, percussionist, and bandleader. Of Puerto Rican extraction, at the age of 16 he joined the Noro Morales Orchestra as a drummer. He studied composition, orchestration, and piano at the Juilliard School and later at the New York School of Music. In 1947 he formed a nine-piece band, the Piccadilly Boys, then expanded it into a full orchestra two years later. As a vibraphonist he also led a successful Latin-jazz quintet in his early years. With his stirring rhythmic compositions and arrangements he gained a reputation during the 1950s as the "King of the Mambo." Since that time he has recorded more than 120 albums with his orchestra, as well as several others accompanying singers or as a member of another group; such hits as *Cuban Mambo*, *Babarabatiri*, and *Mambo la roca* have become standards. In 1979 his recording *Homenaje a Beny More* won a Grammy Award. Puente has always been a flamboyant timbales player, and by the 1970s his solo performances had become a regular part of major salsa concerts. In March 1980 he formed a quintet along the lines of his earlier successful small group.

BIBLIOGRAPHY

"Puente, Tito," *CBY 1977*
J. S. Roberts: *The Latin Tinge* (New York, 1979)

JOHN STORM ROBERTS

Puerto Rico [Porto Rico, 1898–1932]. Island in the West Indies (pop. 3,196,520; 8958 sq. km) associated with the USA since 1898, with commonwealth status from 1952. The first contact of Europeans with the Caribbean island was in 1493 during Christopher Columbus's second voyage to America. Colonization by Spain began in 1508, and the seat of government became established at San Juan, now the island's largest city and the center of commercial and cultural life.

I. Art music. II. Folk music.

I. Art music. During the first three centuries of Puerto Rican history, musical life centered on the church and the military garrison. Early documentation is scarce because many ecclesiastical archives and other sources of information were destroyed in fires, hurricanes, sackings, and sieges. Early in the 16th century an organist and a *chantre* were requested for the cathedral, of which construction had begun in 1511. At the end of the 16th century the cathedral, described as being as beautiful as any in England, possessed a fine organ. The Capitulary Acts of 1660 indicate that the permanent musical staff of the cathedral consisted of an organist and a *sochantre*, but in 1672 two new posts were created, *maestro de capilla* and cantor. There is no account

Panoramic view of San Juan (lithograph, c1860); the Municipal Theater is shown on the far left

of specific nominations to posts in cathedral music from 1698 to 1756, but organists, *maestros de capilla*, and other musicians attached to the church are documented thereafter. These musicians, including both clerics and laymen, provided the first regular music instruction in Puerto Rico.

Secular music before the 19th century was connected mainly with public celebrations. Among these were also events of religious significance, but mounted at the expense of secular authority: Corpus Christi and the celebration of the patron saints of Spain, of the Spanish West Indies, and of Puerto Rico. In addition, *fiestas reales* were organized on occasions connected with accessions of Spanish monarchs. Military musicians provided the nucleus of orchestras for opera and concerts and were among the first teachers of wind instruments in Puerto Rico.

Construction of the island's first permanent theater began in 1824; the building, still in use as the San Juan Municipal Theater, was inaugurated in 1832. A philharmonic society was formed and established a music academy, organized an orchestra, and presented operas and zarzuelas.

One of Puerto Rico's first native composers was Felipe Gutiérrez (1825–99). He wrote the first opera on a Puerto Rican subject, *Guarionex* (?1856), as well as two other operas, a zarzuela, and a large quantity of religious music. Concerts by visiting artists began in 1827 with a series of three recitals by the pianist Eduard Edelman and the cellist Henry Femy. The British tenor William Pearman visited Puerto Rico in 1832, giving performances in the Municipal Theater. Louis Moreau Gottschalk and Adelina Patti spent a year touring Puerto Rico in 1857–8, during the period when San Juan and Ponce, the island's second-largest city, were becoming regular stops in the itineraries of touring Italian opera companies. Short works of light lyric theater, including *tonadillas* and *sainetes*, were regularly presented by theatrical companies, and the first complete opera (Rossini's *Il barbiere di Siviglia*) was given by a visiting Italian company in 1835.

Puerto Rican composers of the late 19th and early 20th centuries include Manuel Gregorio Tavárez (1843–83), Juan Morel Campos (1857–96), and Braulio Dueño Colón (1854–1934), noted for adopting the *danza* (originally a social figure dance) into a highly stylized form of concert music, particularly for the piano. Traditional Spanish modes of musical patronage declined or disappeared during the early 20th century. Composers active at this time include José I. Quintón (1881–1925), José Enrique Pedreira (1904–59), and Augusto Rodríguez (*b* 1904), whose output was limited almost entirely to chamber music, piano music, and songs.

During the 1940s and 1950s the insular government created new educational and cultural agencies, and as a result music began to regain its traditional importance. The Division of Community Education was created in 1946 and soon began to commission film scores from young Puerto Rican composers. A government-owned radio station began operation in 1949, expanding into television in 1958. In 1955 the Institute of Puerto Rican Culture was created, and a newly organized Puerto Rico SO was established in 1958. These government branches engage performers and commission new works either directly or through grants to such groups as ballet and theater companies. The Festival Casals of Puerto Rico, established in 1957, is held each summer at San Juan.

Most of the art music composed during the 1950s displays the deliberate use of folk elements in a conscious attempt to create a distinctive Puerto Rican music. Since 1960, however, composers have taken a much more eclectic view, embracing styles and techniques ranging from post-Romantic to serial, aleatory, and mixed-media expression. Composers active in Puerto Rico include Jack Delano (*b* 1914), Héctor Campos-Parsi (*b* 1922), Amaury Veray (*b* 1922), Luis A. Ramírez (*b* 1923), Rafael Aponte Ledée (*b* 1938), Luis M. Alvarez (*b* 1939), Francis Schwartz (*b* 1940), Ernesto Cordero (*b* 1946), and Roberto Sierra (*b* 1953).

Music education in Puerto Rico is administered through two governmental programs and by numerous private academies. One government program was created in 1947 to provide every elementary school child with an understanding of the basic elements of music. The second program is a network of junior conservatories, the Free Schools of Music, which offer specialized instruction for children aiming to become professional musicians. Further technical instruction is given at the Puerto Rico Conservatory of Music, established in 1960. University studies in music are conducted, and academic degrees granted in recognition of higher musical studies, at the Inter-American University of Puerto Rico, San Germán, and at the University of Puerto Rico, Río Piedras. (*See also* LIBRARIES AND COLLECTIONS, §3.)

BIBLIOGRAPHY

P. Callejo: *Música y músicos portorriqueños* (San Juan, 1915, 2/1971)

E. Pasarell: *Orígenes y desarrollo de la afición teatral en Puerto Rico* (Río Piedras, 1951–67, 2/1970)

M. L. Muñoz: *La música en Puerto Rico: panorama histórico-cultural* (Sharon, CT, 1966)

R. Fitzmaurice: *Music Education in Puerto Rico: a Historical Survey with Guidelines for an Exemplary Curriculum* (diss., Florida State U., 1971)

F. Caso: *Héctor Campos Parsi in the History of Twentieth-century Music of Puerto Rico* (thesis, Indiana U., 1972)

A. F. Thompson: *An Annotated Bibliography of Writings about Music in Puerto Rico* (Ann Arbor, MI, 1975)

R. Stevenson: "Music in the San Juan, Puerto Rico, Cathedral to 1900," *Inter-American Music Review*, i (1978–9), 73

A. Villarini: *A Study of Selected Puerto Rican Danzas for the Piano* (diss., New York U., 1979)

A. F. Thompson: *Puerto Rican Newspapers and Journals of the Spanish Colonial Period as Source Materials for Musicological Research* (diss., Florida State U., 1980)

D. Thompson: "Puerto Rico," *Grove 6*

R. Stevenson: "Caribbean Music History: a Selective Annotated Bibliography with Musical Supplement," *Inter-American Music Review*, iv (1981–2), 36

D. Thompson: "Nineteenth Century Musical Life in Puerto Rico," *Die Musikkulturen Lateinamerikas im 19. Jahrhundert*, ed. R. Günther (Regensburg, 1982), 327

C. Dower: *Puerto Rican Music following the Spanish American War: 1898: the Aftermath of the Spanish American War and its Influence on the Musical Culture of Puerto Rico* (Lanham, MD, 1983)

D. Thompson: "Music Research in Puerto Rico," *College Music Symposium*, xx (1983), 81

II. Folk music

1. Introduction. 2. African-derived genres. 3. Hispanic genres. 4. Instruments.

1. INTRODUCTION. Until the 20th century interest in Puerto Rican folklore and customs was expressed principally through travelers' descriptions and the introduction of folk themes in 19th-century Puerto Rican *costumbrista* literature; precise knowledge of the island's folk music from the 16th to 19th centuries is therefore slender.

The predominant elements in the folk and traditional music of Puerto Rico have been traced to Spain and West Africa; Spanish settlement and colonization began in 1508, while West African influence is due to the direct importation of African slave laborers until the 19th century and the introduction of American-born Blacks at various periods. The indigenous Arawak Indian contribution is minimal; so rapid was the Spanish domination of the island's indigenous population that within a few generations of the Conquest scarcely a trace of Arawak influence could be noted.

Early descriptions of the musical and ceremonial use of Arawak instruments are limited to gourd rattles and to the *bastón*, an ornamented stick struck heavily against the ground. The *areito* (a ceremonial dance) was practiced throughout the Greater Antilles by pre-Columbian inhabitants and performed on a wide variety of occasions involving instruments and antiphonal chanting.

2. AFRICAN-DERIVED GENRES. African influences have been strong, particularly in the coastal regions. Several Puerto Rican folk-music customs clearly show indebtedness to African antecedents, although by no means unaffected by contact with Spanish music and the Spanish language. Among the most important of these forms are the *bomba*, the *plena*, and the *baquiné*.

The *bomba*, which some writers have associated with the Cuban *conga* and with the more generalized Antillean *bamboula*, is practiced in the coastal lowlands; it is characterized by the use of drums as accompanying instruments, by responsorial singing, and by individuals or couples spontaneously dancing within a circle of participants (for illustration *see* HISPANIC-AMERICAN MUSIC, fig.2). Song texts may be improvised by a leader and repeated by the chorus, or may consist of traditional texts in which leader and chorus sing alternating stanzas. Many other names of dances associated with the *bomba* and presumably of African origin have been noted.

Another form showing marked African influence is the *plena*. The Puerto Rican *plena* is a short narrative song that describes, often with sharply satirical intent, an individual or an event. The earliest documented performances of the *plena* date from the first decade of the 20th century, though the style (if not the name) may have been current in Puerto Rico half a century before. The first known performances are attributed to English-speaking black immigrants from the Virgin Islands and St. Christopher who had settled in Ponce on the southern coast. The earliest accompanying instruments appear to have been the tambourine and *güiro* (scraper) with guitar or concertina. The heavy striking of the tambourine, on the beat in binary meter, is believed to have been extremely important in establishing the definitive style of the *plena* developing in the 1920s. The characteristic form of the *plena* consists of the alternation of stanzas and refrains (either improvised or composed) by soloist and chorus; many have become classics of popular folk music and are well-known not only in Puerto Rico but abroad.

Baquiné is the communal vigil over the body of a dead child during the night preceding Christian burial. As the child is presumed to have died without sin, the occasion is more one of rejoicing than one of grief. However, songs of consolation are sung to the bereaved parents, and occasionally African deities are invoked in order to repel an evil spirit.

3. HISPANIC GENRES. In contrast to the African-related folk music of the coastal lowlands, many of the songs and dances from the interior mountains display relatively pure derivation from Spanish sources. As cultivated by *jibaros*, rural descendants of early Spanish and other white settlers, many folksong species use the Spanish *décima*, a ten-line stanza of octosyllabic or hexasyllabic structure.

The most important form of folk music in the interior is the *seis*. As dance music, the *seis* is in simple binary meter, richly syncopated, and frequently overlaid with triplet figurations in melody or accompaniment; more than 80 types have been identified, distinguishable by tempo, rhythmic figuration, melody type, or choreography. As accompaniment to song, the *seis* is closely associated with *décima* texts. The improvisation of *décimas* at social occasions and community festivities is basic to Puerto Rican folk custom. In a *seis de controversia* two singers may engage in a contest, improvising *décimas* according to a subject and rhyme established by the contest judge.

The repertory of Puerto Rican *bailes de garabato*, or popular folkdances, also includes the *vals criollo*, the *mazurca*, and the *polca*, all modifications of the corresponding 19th-century European social dances.

Folk and popular religious music in Puerto Rico centers on the *aguinaldo* and the villancico, descendants of the 16th-century Spanish villancico. In popular usage the names are almost interchangeable and refer to a repertory of well-known songs whose texts deal with the Christmas cycle. The melodies are usually in simple or compound binary meter; the rhythmic syncopation of *aguinaldos* or villancicos may be the result of African influence.

The *Cruz de mayo* or Fiesta de Cruz is a popular religious festivity of early May; it enjoyed a revival during the 1960s and early 1970s after several decades of decline. Dedicated to the Virgin Mary, the *Cruz de mayo* consists of nine consecutive evenings of fiesta, involving a great deal of music, and is similar to the traditional Roman Catholic Novena. Rhythms, tempos, and forms are based on such traditional genres as the waltz and march. The traditional group of accompanying instruments (*conjunto típico*) consists of guitar, *cuatro*, and *güiro*, although in some areas flutes and violins or instruments associated with popular commercial music may also be used. The cycle ends with social dancing.

Another religious folk activity, the *rosario cantao* (sung rosary), also involves music of Spanish derivation. It is a family or neighborhood observance arranged for the purpose of redeeming a vow made to a saint. The event, which lasts all night, is divided into periods of singing (*tercios*) and relaxation; after the final *tercio*, at daybreak, a dance begins which may last until noon. Such urban folk-music genres as the *salsa* originally arose in the poorer parts of the cities but have also been developed commercially to appeal to many sections of the population.

4. INSTRUMENTS. Puerto Rican folk instruments include drums of various types, the modern representatives of a continuous tradition of African music in the Caribbean. The use of musical bows has also been observed. The *marimbula*, an Antillean modification of the African lamellaphone (a plucked idiophone whose sound is produced by the vibration of thin tongues), serves as a bass instrument during many popular festivities. Maracas and *güiros*, descendants of pre-Columbian Arawak instruments, appear in most folk and popular music.

The construction and playing of plucked fretted chordophones have been skillfully cultivated. Guitar construction, tuning, and playing technique follow Spanish usage, but a number of other instruments, some of them unique to Puerto Rico, have evolved. Among these is the *cuatro*, descended from the Spanish vihuela. The modern *cuatro* is made of indigenous woods and exists in a wide variety of shapes while retaining the plectrum technique of the ancestral *vihuela de peñola*. Formerly, the *cuatro* had four double courses of strings tuned in 4ths (*e–a–d′–g′*); at the end of the 19th century a fifth single or double course was added below, giving the pitch *B*.

The *tiple* and *tres* are smaller instruments of the same general type as the *cuatro*. The four or five single-string courses of the *tiple* have had no standardized tuning. The *tres* has three single strings, tuned *b–g′–d″*. Other plucked instruments are the flat-backed *laúd español* and the *bordonúa*; the latter, which is rare, has five courses of strings, tuned *A–d–f♯–b–e′*.

See also HISPANIC-AMERICAN MUSIC, §2 (ii).

BIBLIOGRAPHY

M. Alonso: *El gíbaro* (Barcelona, 1849, 5/1971)

J. A. Mason: "Porto Rican Folklore: Decimas, Christmas Carols, Nursery Rhymes, and Other Songs," *Journal of American Folklore*, xxxi (1918), 289–450

M. Cadilla de Martínez: "La música popular de Puerto Rico," *Puerto Rico ilustrado* (4 June 1938), no.1473, pp.22, 117

G. Durán: "Romance, corrido y plena," *Boletín de la Unión Panamericana* (1942), no.76, p.630

M. Cadilla de Martínez: "La conga," *Estudios afrocubanos*, v (1945–6), 176

F. López Cruz: *El aguinaldo y el villancico en el folklore puertorriqueño* (San Juan, 1956)

M. Alvarez Nazario: "Historia de las denominaciones de los bailes de bomba," *Revista de ciencias sociales*, iv (1960), 59

E. Figueroa Berríos: "Los sones de la bomba en la tradición popular de la costa sur de Puerto Rico," *Revista del Instituto de Cultura Puertorriqueña*, vi (1963), 46

C. Rosa Nieves: *Voz folklorica de Puerto Rico* (Sharon, CT, 1967)

F. López Cruz: *La música folklorica de Puerto Rico* (Sharon, CT, 1967)

C. Marrero de Figueroa: *Tierra y folklore* (San Juan, 1967)

M. Canino Salgado: *La copla y el romance populares en la tradición oral de Puerto Rico* (San Juan, 1968)

J. McCoy: *The Bomba and Aguinaldo of Puerto Rico as they have Evolved from Indigenous, African and European Cultures* (diss., Florida State U., 1968)

H. Vega Drouet: *Some Musical Forms of African Descendants in Puerto Rico: Bomba, Plena and Rosario Francés* (thesis, Hunter College, CUNY, 1969)

P. Escabí, ed.: *Estudio etnográfico de la cultura popular de Puerto Rico: Morovis: vista parcial del folklore de Puerto Rico* (Río Piedras, 1971)

D. Thompson: "The Marímbula, an Afro-Caribbean Sanza," *Yearbook for Inter-American Musical Research*, vii (1971), 103

M. E. Davis: "The Social Organization of a Musical Event," *EM*, xvi (1972), 38

J. V. Montalvo: *Estudio psico-etnográfico de la música "salsa" en Puerto Rico* (thesis, U. of Puerto Rico, 1978)

H. Vega Drouet: *Historical and Ethnological Survey on the Probable African Origin of the Bomba, including the Festivities of Loíza Aldea* (diss., Wesleyan U., 1979)

D. Thompson: "Puerto Rico," *Grove 6*

J. E. Dufrasne-Gonzalez: *La homogeneidad de la música caribeña: sobre la música comercial y popular de Puerto Rico* (diss., UCLA, 1985)

DONALD THOMPSON

Pulitzer Prize. Prize given annually by Columbia University for achievements in American journalism, letters, and music. A prize for musical composition was first awarded in 1943; for further information and a list of recipients, *see* AWARDS, §1.

Punk rock. A genre of rock that evolved in the mid-1970s. "Punk" dates from the earliest days of rock-and-roll, when nearly all rock musicians were perceived as alienated from the mainstream. In the 1960s, a selfconsciously nonconformist American rock style developed in response to the more genteel groups that epitomized the "British invasion." The term "punk rock" began to take on its currently accepted meaning in the mid-1970s, at the height of the commercialization of American rock, when a number of outrageous and eccentric musicians emerged who played in a deliberately raw, amateurish style and espoused nihilistic or politically radical sentiments; this trend, set in motion by the Velvet Underground, the New York Dolls, and the Ramones in New York, developed fully in London in the late 1970s, where the characteristic and elaborate dress code and hairstyles associated with punk were invented. The movement spread throughout the USA (it was particularly strong in Los Angeles) in the next few years, some well-known groups being Black Flag, X, and the Dead Kennedys. By that time punk had mutated into a brutal, monochromatic "hard-core" style, played fast and at high volume, while NEW WAVE, a gentler, more accessible, and more commercially oriented type of rock, had developed out of it.

See also ROCK, §3.

JOHN ROCKWELL

Putnam, Ashley (Elizabeth) (*b* New York, 10 Aug 1952). Soprano. Her early musical training was as a flutist; she entered the University of Michigan in 1970 and became an accomplished professional flutist before studying voice there with Elizabeth Mosher and Willis Patterson (MM in voice, 1975). She joined the Santa Fe Opera Company as an apprentice and made her début in January 1976 in the title role of Donizetti's *Lucia di Lammermoor* with the Virginia Opera. The same year she won first prize in the Metropolitan Opera Auditions and as a result received the Weyerhauser Award. Her European début, as Musetta in Puccini's *La bohème*, took place in 1978 at Glyndebourne, England, and her début at Lincoln Center, as Violetta in the New York City Opera's production of Verdi's *La traviata*, was the same year. Her recorded performances include the title role in Thea Musgrave's *Mary, Queen of Scots*, Angel More in Thomson's *The Mother of us All*, and Musetta. During the 1983–4 season she toured the USA as a recitalist. Putnam is a dramatic soprano; she has established herself as a singer who displays considerable acting talent and has acknowledged a preference for roles offering wide dramatic scope.

BIBLIOGRAPHY

R. Jacobson: "Achiever: Ashley Putnam at Twenty-six, one of America's Heralded Young Singers, is in a Quandary Facing New-found Fame," *Opera News*, xliv/1 (1979), 8

"Putnam, Ashley," *CBY 1982*

SORAB MODI

Puyallup. American Indian group of the northwest coast; *see* SALISH.

Q

Quadrille. Social dance of the 19th century. First danced in England in 1815, the "plain" (or "first") quadrille became the model for the American quadrille, a geometric dance performed by four couples in a square. The basic walking step was executed in a graceful, sliding manner slowly enough to allow the dancers to converse as they moved. The practice of performing several cotillions in succession formed the basis of the plain quadrille, which consisted of five "grand" figures, each of which comprised a number of smaller figures (the *chassez*, *balancé*, ladies chain, etc.) and concluded with a pause in the music before the start of the next grand figure; the small figures corresponded to phrases of four, eight, 12, or 16 bars of music. In the USA it was common to end the quadrille with a round dance, such as a waltz, galop, or schottische. In the middle of the century, round-dance movements were occasionally substituted for the small figures; these dances became known as waltz quadrilles, galop quadrilles, polka quadrilles, and the like.

The tempo of the quadrille was lively (about 120 beats to the minute), and the rhythmic pattern complete in a single bar of 2/4 or 6/8 meter. Unlike European quadrille music, in which each grand figure is traditionally assigned a specific meter, American quadrille music uses either meter for any figure. The quadrille rhythm has a characteristically strong downbeat and light upbeat, which impart a certain spring that propels the dance movement forward. As in the cotillion, the music was generally arranged from existing melodies. Minstrel tunes were often used in the middle of the century; John C. Scherpf's popular *African Quadrilles* (1844) were arranged from such melodies as the *Boatman Dance*, *Lucy Neal*, and *Ole Dan Tucker*. Quicksteps were also frequent choices, but melodies from current operas, especially those of Rossini, were the most commonly used sources. Some original music for the quadrille was written by dance-band leaders such as Frank Johnson, who published his *Voice Quadrilles* in 1840. L. DeGarmo Brookes, a New York composer and dancing-master, was especially known for his quadrilles, which included the *Quadrille russe* (1860) and the *Waltz Quadrilles* (1875). (*See also* DANCE, §II, 1.)

The French conductors Louis Jullien and Philippe Musard stimulated much of the interest in the USA for the concert quadrille. Jullien's *American Quadrille* and its companion piece, the *Fireman's Quadrille*, which he wrote for his American tour in 1854, were very popular with American audiences. Jullien created a dramatic scene out of each of the five sections. In the *Fireman's Quadrille*, for example, he used marching bands in parade on the stage and had a fire engine and company simulate a fire being extinguished, an event that caused near panic in the audience.

Variants of the quadrille included the caledonian, the imperial, and the lancers, which was the most popular variant in the USA.

Cover of "Original Polka Quadrilles" published by Louis Jullien in London around 1845: lithograph

Although some dance historians claim that the lancers was first danced in England in 1819 as *Les lanciers*, the American version seems instead to have originated in France in 1856 with specific music of its own. Its appeal has been attributed to the complexity of its figures and the placement of the dancers in diagonal rows. It frequently concluded with a march figure performed with a graceful *chassez*.

BIBLIOGRAPHY

Saltator: *A Treatise on Dancing* (Boston, 1802)
E. Ferrero: *The Art of Dancing* (New York, 1859)
E. Howe: *American Dancing Master and Ball-room Prompter* (Boston, 1862)
T. Hillgrove: *A Complete Practical Guide to the Art of Dancing* (New York, 1863)
S. F. Damon: "The History of Square Dancing," *Proceedings of the American Antiquarian Society*, lxii/1 (1952)

For further bibliography *see* DANCE.

PAULINE NORTON

Queler, Eve (*b* New York, 1 Jan 1936). Conductor. She studied piano and conducting at the Mannes College and, on a Martha Baird Rockefeller Fund grant, conducting with Joseph Rosenstock and accompaniment with Paul Ulanowsky and Paul Berl; her later teachers were Walter Susskind and Leonard Slatkin in St. Louis and Igor Markevitch and Herbert Blomstedt in Europe. After working as music assistant to the New York City Opera and the Metropolitan Opera, she formed in 1968 the Opera Orchestra of New York, with herself as music director. A professional training group, based from 1971 at Carnegie Hall, it has presented concert performances of over 30 rarely performed operas, most of which have been American premières, including *Parisina* (Donizetti, 1973 season), *Edgar* (Puccini, 1977), *Aroldo* (Verdi, 1978), *Nerone* (Boito, 1982), and *Guntram* (Strauss, 1983).

As associate conductor of the Fort Wayne PO (1970–71), Queler became the first American woman to hold a full-time conducting appointment; she was also the first woman to conduct the symphony orchestras of Philadelphia, San Antonio, Montreal (Canada), Hartford, Cleveland, Toledo, Jacksonville, and Edmonton (Canada), and she has given master classes at the Peabody Conservatory. Abroad she has staged opera performances for the Orchestre Lyrique of Paris, the Prague National Theater, the Puerto Rico SO, the New Philharmonia of London, and the Gran Teatro del Liceo of Barcelona, Spain. Authoritative and dynamic as a conductor, she is known for her enthusiasm in introducing new operas to new audiences, for reviving many long-neglected works, and for developing the careers of young singers and instrumentalists. She has made recordings with some of the world's leading singers.

BIBLIOGRAPHY

"Queler, Eve," *CBY 1972*

ELIZABETH WOOD

Quicksilver Messenger Service. Rock group. It was formed in San Francisco in 1965; the original members were John Cipollina (lead guitarist), Gary Duncan (guitarist and singer), David Freiberg (bass guitarist and singer), Greg Elmore (drummer), and Jim Murray (harmonica player and singer). After Murray's departure in 1967 the group recorded two albums, *Quicksilver Messenger Service* (1968) and *Happy Trails* (1969). Unfortunately even the most successful songs failed to capture the fiery, blues-based, intertwining guitar improvisations that made the group one of the finest concert attractions of the psychedelic movement in San Francisco. The group's sound became less exciting when pianist Nicky Hopkins replaced Duncan in 1969, and in turn more romantic in 1970 when Duncan returned and the singer and songwriter Dino Valenti joined. Dominating the group, Valenti wrote several mildly commercial songs, including *Just for Love* and *What about me?*. Hopkins, Cipollina, and Freiberg left in rapid succession between 1971 and 1972, but Valenti's music and the group's past reputation propelled every new album onto the charts. After continuing as a quintet (to 1973) and then a septet, Valenti, Elmore, and Duncan disbanded the Quicksilver Messenger Service in 1974; in 1975 they re-formed briefly with Cipollina and Freiberg, but had little success.

RECORDINGS

(selective list; all recorded for Capitol)

Quicksilver Messenger Service (2904, 1968); *Happy Trails* (120, 1969); *Shady Grove* (391, 1969); *Just for Love* (498, 1970); *What about me?* (630, 1971); *Solid Silver* (11492, 1975)

BARRY KERNFELD

Quickstep. A type of MARCH.

Quinby, Benjamin F(ranklin) (*b* Minot, ME, 3 July 1830; *d* Boston, MA, 9 July 1890). Brass instrument maker and inventor. He produced large quantities of brass instruments from 1861 to 1884 while associated with several instrument-making firms. He came to Boston as a machinist in 1853 accompanied by his twin brother, George. In 1861 he began a long association with the bandleader and instrument maker D. C. Hall, working first for a year for the firm Allen & Hall, then with Hall's own firm; in 1867 Hall & Quinby was founded. It was very successful and the business continued as Quinby Brothers in 1876 after Hall had withdrawn. Most of the instruments made by these firms were equipped with flat-windway Allen valves. In 1872 Quinby patented a valve system for brass instruments featuring very simple construction and clear windways, but these "box valves" (as they were called) were not very successful. Quinby Brothers ceased making brass instruments in 1884 and began the manufacture of rotary machine shoe-brushes.

BIBLIOGRAPHY

H. C. Quinby: *Genealogical History of the Quinby Family* (New York, 1915)
R. E. Eliason: "Early American Valves for Brass Instruments," *GSJ*, xxiii (1970), 86

ROBERT E. ELIASON

Quintón, José I(gnacio) (*b* Caguas, Puerto Rico, 1 Feb 1881; *d* Coamo, Puerto Rico, 19 Dec 1925). Composer and pianist. From his father, a graduate of the Paris Conservatoire, and a church organist, he received lessons in harmony, counterpoint, composition, and piano. He was also influenced by the Spanish pianist Ernesto del Castillo and the Puerto Rican composer Angel Mislán, but was to some extent self-educated. From the age of 12 until his death he lived in Coamo; he became a teacher of instrumental music at the Coamo Municipal Academy of Music and also organized several musical groups as well as the municipal band. As a composer Quintón appropriated Classical forms and a Romantic idiom, while searching constantly for sonorities that he called "music of the future" (as a pianist he was one of the first to perform Debussy, Ravel, and Schoenberg in Puerto Rico). He took a historic step in elevating the *danza* to the level of concert music. His several chamber works, including the String Quartet in D (1913), are well written and somewhat Brahmsian in style.

WORKS

Orch: Marcha triunfal, 1911; Conc. Ov., 1913

Insts: Str Qt, D, 1913; Pf Trio; trio, fl, pf, vn; several other ens works; pf works, incl. Variaciones sobre un tema de Hummel, 1913, Una página de mi vida, rhapsody, 1920, many danzas, waltzes; other character pieces

Vocal: Requiem, orch, SATB, 1903; 10 Salve Reginas, orch, SATB

BIBLIOGRAPHY

F. Ferrer Callojo: *Música y músicos puertorriqueños* (San Juan, PR, 1915, 2/1971)

J. E. Astol: "José Ignacio Quintón músico," *Puerto Rico ilustrado*, xxviii (17 July 1937), 26

R. Montañez: "Un homenaje a José Ignacio Quintón," *Puerto Rico ilustrado*, xlii (2 Feb 1952), 4

C. Dower: "Quintón Bridges Centuries," *Dateline Puerto Rico, U.S.A.*, iii/3 (1981), 38

R. Rivera Bermúdez: *Biografía de José Quintón* [MS in *NN*]

GUSTAVO BATISTA

Illustration Acknowledgments

We are grateful to those listed below, who have supplied illustrative material, or given permission for it to be reproduced, or both: where two or more names are given, separated by a spaced slash (/), the name given first is usually that of the supplier of the illustration, who may or may not be the copyright holder; names of photographers are given wherever possible, preceded by "photo." Every effort has been made to contact copyright holders and we apologize to anyone whose name may have been omitted from this list. Where an illustration is taken from a book or article out of copyright, the title and place and date of publication are given here unless they appear in the caption to the illustration. The names of contributors (though they are not necessarily the contributors of the articles for which they have supplied illustrations) are preceded by a double dagger sign; their last known places of work or residence are given in the List of Contributors at the end of Volume 4.

La Barbara, Joan Wizard Music, Los Angeles, CA
Laderman, Ezra photo Aimlee D. Laderman, Teaneck, NJ
Lamb, Joseph F. John Edward Hasse Collection, Alexandria, VA
Lang, Margaret Ruthven Boston Public Library, Boston, MA
Leadbelly David Redfern Photography, London, England / photo William Gottlieb
Leinsdorf, Erich RCA Ltd., Record Division, London, England / photo Marvin Lichtner
Lennon, John Pop Record Research, Ossining, NY
Lenya, Lotte National Portrait Gallery, Smithsonian Institution, Washington, DC
Levine, James Metropolitan Opera Archives, New York / photo Lauterwasser
Lewis, Jerry Lee Michael Ochs Archive, Venice, CA
Lhévinne, Josef G. D. Hackett, New York
Liberace Syndication International 1986 Ltd., London, England
Libraries and collections Popperfoto, London, England
Lind, Jenny Prints and Photographs Division, Library of Congress, Washington, DC
Little Richard Richard Wootton, London, England
Little Walter Val Wilmer/Format, London, England
Loeffler, Charles Martin *1* Isabella Stewart Gardner Museum, Boston, MA; *2* Music Division, Library of Congress, Washington, DC
Loewe, Frederick Theatre Archives, Museum of the City of New York, New York
Los Angeles *1* Los Angeles Public Library (Security Pacific National Bank Collection), Los Angeles, CA; *2, 3* Popperfoto, London, England
Lucier, Alvin Arnolfini Gallery, Bristol, England / photo Damian Gillie
Ludwig Ludwig Drum Co., Chicago, IL
Luening, Otto ‡Otto Luening / photo Esther Brown, New York
Lunceford, Jimmie Frank Driggs, Brooklyn, NY
Lynn, Loretta Richard Wootton, London, England

Maazel, Lorin copyright First Agricultural Bank, Pittsfield, MA, as Trustee under will Olga Koussevitzky (© 1986)
MacDowell, Edward *1* Music Division, New York Public Library at Lincoln Center (Astor, Lenox and Tilden Foundations), New York; *2* Music Division, Library of Congress, Washington, DC
MacDowell, Colony Music Division, Library of Congress (MacDowell Collection), Washington, DC
Macon, Uncle Dave Country Music Foundation, Inc., Nashville, TN
Marable, Fate Max Jones, Middleton-on-Sea, West Sussex, England
Martinelli, Giovanni Metropolitan Opera Archives, New York
Mason Music Division, New York Public Library at Lincoln Center (Astor, Lenox and Tilden Foundations), New York
Meat Loaf Arista, London, England / photo Simon Fowler
Mehta, Zubin New York Philharmonic Public Relations Department, New York / photo David Rentas
Memphis Handy Brothers Music Co., Inc., New York
Mennin, Peter ‡Walter G. Simmons / photo Christian Steiner
Menotti, Gian Carlo Curtis Institute of Music, Philadelphia, PA
Menuhin, Yehudi photo Clive Barda, London, England
Merman, Ethel National Portrait Gallery, Smithsonian Institution, Washington, DC
Midler, Bette Academy of Motion Picture Arts and Sciences, Beverly Hills, CA / copyright 1979 20th Century-Fox Film Corporation, Beverly Hills
Military music *1* National Archives, Washington, DC; *2* photo MSgt LeRoy E. Sundberg, Fort Myor, VA
Miller, Glenn Academy of Motion Picture Arts and Sciences, Beverly Hills, CA / copyright 1942 20th Century-Fox Film Corporation, Beverly Hills
Milnes, Sherrill Metropolitan Opera Archives, New York
Milwaukee Milwaukee County Historical Society, Milwaukee, WI
Mingus, Charles Rare Pic, London, England
Minimalism *1a, 1b* Universal Edition (London) Ltd., London, England (*1a* Steve Reich, New York)
Minneapolis and St. Paul ‡Mary Ann Feldman / Minnesota Orches-

tra, Minneapolis, MN / photo *Minneapolis Star and Tribune*

Minstrelsy Harvard Theatre Collection, Houghton Library, Harvard University, Cambridge, MA

Mitchell, Joni London Features International Ltd., London, England, and New York / photo Michael Putland, London

Mitropoulos, Dimitri Minnesota Orchestra, Minneapolis, MN

Modern Jazz Quartet photo David Redfern, London, England

Monk, Meredith House Foundation for the Arts, New York / photo Bob Shamis, New York

Monk, Thelonious David Redfern Photography, London, England / photo William Gottlieb

Moog, Robert A. Thomas L. Rhea, Buffalo, NY

Moore, Douglas S. Music Division, New York Public Library at Lincoln Center (Astor, Lenox and Tilden Foundations), New York / photo Fred Fehl, New York

Moravian Church, music of the Moravian Music Foundation, Winston-Salem, NC

Morton, Jelly Roll William Ransom Hogan Jazz Archive, Tulane University, New Orleans, LA

Muddy Waters *Jazz Journal*, London, England

Musical *2* Music Division, Library of Congress, Washington, DC; *3* Billy Rose Theatre Collection, New York Public Library at Lincoln Center (Astor, Lenox and Tilden Foundations), New York / Eileen Darby, Point Lookout, NY; *4* Billy Rose Theatre Collection, New York Public Library at Lincoln Center (Astor, Lenox and Tilden Foundations), New York / photo Fred Fehl, New York

Musical film *1* Stills Collection, National Film Archive, London, England / copyright 1933 Warner Bros., renewed 1960; *2* Academy of Motion Picture Arts and Sciences, Beverly Hills, CA / copyright 1939 Loew's, Inc., renewed 1966 Metro-Goldwyn-Mayer Inc., Culver City, CA; *3* Academy of Motion Picture Arts and Sciences, Beverly Hills / copyright 1969 Chenault Productions, Inc., and 20th Century-Fox Film Corporation, Beverly Hills

Musical theater *1* Peter Newark's Western Americana, Bath, England; *2* Music Division, Library of Congress (Hammerstein Collection), Washington, DC; *3* Mander and Mitchenson, London, England; *4* Billy Rose Theatre Collection, New York Public Library at Lincoln Center (Astor, Lenox and Tilden Foundations), New York / photo Martha Swope

Nancarrow, Conlon 1750 Arch Records, Berkeley, CA / photo Philip Makanna

Nashville Country Music Foundation, Inc., Nashville, TN

Navajo Museum of New Mexico (negative no.47917), Santa Fe, NM

Nelson, Willie Country Music Foundation, Inc., Nashville, TN

Neuhaus, Max Max Neuhaus, New York

Newman, Randy Music Division, New York Public Library at Lincoln Center (Astor, Lenox and Tilden Foundations), New York

New Orleans *1* Historic New Orleans Collection, New Orleans, LA; *2* Val Wilmer/Format, London, England

New York *1, 2, 10* Theatre Archives, Museum of the City of New York (*1*, J. Clarence Davies Collection), New York; *3* Lincoln Center for the Performing Arts, Inc., New York/photo William Dietz Associates; *5* New York Philharmonic Public Relations Department, New York / photo Marianne Barcellona; *6* New-York Historical Society, New York; *7* Brooklyn Academy of Music, Brooklyn, NY / photo Tom Caravaglia; *8* Buck Clayton, New York; *9* photo Chris Ross, New York

New York Pro Musica Music Division (New York Pro Musica Archive), New York Public Library at Lincoln Center (Astor, Lenox and Tilden Foundations), New York

Nilsson, Birgit ‡Harold Rosenthal / photo Louis Melancon

Nordica, Lillian Stuart-Liff Collection, Port Erin, Isle of Man

Norman, Jessye photo Johan Elbers, New York

Notation *2, 3, 12, 13* Music Division, Library of Congress, Washington, DC; *4* G. P. Jackson / Dover Publications, Inc., New York, from G. P. Jackson: *White Spirituals in the Southern Uplands* (*R*1965); *6* Dover Publications, Inc., New York, from G. P. Jackson: *White Spirituals in the Southern Uplands* (*R*1965); *7a, 7c* Western Reserve Historical Society, Cleveland, OH; *7b* Raymond Adams, Chapel Hill, NC; *7d* Joseph Downs Manuscript and Microfilm Collection, Winterthur Museum Library (Edward Deming Andrews Memorial Shaker Collection, no.SA1128), Winterthur, DE; *9* Oak Publications (Embassy Music Corporation), New York; *10, 11, 14, 17, 20, 24* Associated Music Publishers, Inc., New York; *15* Smith Publications, Baltimore, MD (1981); *16, 21, 22* C. F. Peters Corporation, New York, reproduced by permission of Peters Edition, London, England, and New York; *18* ‡Milton Babbitt, from J. Cage: *Notations* (New York: Something Else Press, Inc., 1969) / Associated Music Publishers, Inc., New York (© 1968); *19* Henmar Press, Inc., New York, reproduced by permission of Peters Edition, London and New York; *23* William Hellermann, New York (1976)

Ojibwe Milwaukee Public Museum of Milwaukee County, Milwaukee, WI

Oliver, King Jazz Music Books, Middleton-on-Sea, West Sussex, England

Oliveros, Pauline Pauline Oliveros / photo Becky Cohen, Leucadia, CA

Opera *1* Music Division, Library of Congress, Washington, DC; *2* Metropolitan Opera Archives, New York; *3* Music Division, Library of Congress (*Modern Music* Archive), Washington, DC; *4* Music Division, New York Public Library at Lincoln Center (Astor, Lenox and Tilden Foundations), New York; *5* Houston Grand Opera, Houston, TX / photo Jim Caldwell, Houston

Orchestral music *1* Music Archives Collection, Pennsylvania Historical and Museum Commission, Old Economy Village, Ambridge, PA; *2* Andrew Imbrie, Berkeley, CA; *3* ‡John Adams / Associated Music Publishers, Inc., New York (© 1985)

Orchestras *1* New-York Historical Society, New York; *2* Boston Symphony Orchestra, Inc., Boston, MA; *3* Sigrid Wiesmann, Bayreuth, Germany (BRD)

Organ *1* photo ‡Barbara Owen; *2* University of New Mexico Photo Service, Albuquerque, NM

Original Dixieland Jazz Band Culver Pictures, Inc., New York

Ormandy, Eugene Philadelphia Orchestra, Philadelphia, PA / photo Adrian Siegel

Ozawa, Seiji Boston Symphony Orchestra, Inc., Boston, MA

Paine, John Knowles University of Michigan Music Library, Ann Arbor, MI

Pantomime Historical Society of York County, York, PA

Papago Arizona State Museum, University of Arizona, Tucson, AZ / photo Helga Teiwes

Parker, Charlie Max Jones, Middleton-on-Sea, West Sussex, England

Parker, Horatio Metropolitan Opera Archives, New York

Parker, John Rowe Houghton Library, Harvard University, Cambridge, MA

Parton, Dolly Richard Wootton, London, England

Patriotic music *1* James J. Fuld Collection, New York; *2* Music Division, Library of Congress, Washington, DC

Patti, Adelina BBC Hulton Picture Library, London, England / Bettmann Archive, Inc., New York

Perahia, Murray New York Philharmonic Public Relations Department, New York / photo Frank Salomon Associates, New York

Periodicals *1* Trustees of the Boston Public Library, Boston, MA

Perle, George photo Johanna I. Sturm, Englewood, NJ

Perlman, Itzhak New York Philharmonic Public Relations Department, New York / photo Julian Kreeger, ICM Artists, New York

Persichetti, Vincent ‡Walter G. Simmons / photo Michael Ahearn

Philadelphia *1* Philadelphia Orchestra, Philadelphia, PA; *2* Dick Clark Productions, Burbank, CA; *3* Curtis Institute of Music, Philadelphia

Philately, musical ‡Stephen M. Fry / US Postal Service, Washington, DC

Piano *1* Smithsonian Institution (photo no.56445A), Washington, DC; *2* Culver Pictures, Inc., New York
Piano music G. D. Hackett, New York
Piatigorsky, Gregor Curtis Institute of Music, Philadelphia, PA
Pinza, Ezio ‡Harold Rosenthal
Piston, Walter Associated Music Publishers, Inc., New York
Pittsburgh American Wind Symphony Orchestra, Pittsburgh, PA / photo Herb Ferguson
Ponselle, Rosa *Opera News*, New York
Popular music *2* Bodleian Library (Harding Collection), Oxford, England; *3* Theatre and Music Collection, Museum of the City of New York, New York; *4* Culver Pictures, Inc., New York; *5* Paul Oliver Collection, Woodstock, England; *6* Duncan Schiedt, Pittsboro, IN; *8* Val Wilmer/Format, London, England; *10* Cliff White, London; *11* photo Chris Ross, New York
Porter, Cole Music Division, New York Public Library at Lincoln Center (Astor, Lenox and Tilden Foundations), New York
Portland (ii) Oregon Historical Society (negative no.55129), Portland, OR
Prepared piano Henmar Press, Inc., New York (© 1960), reproduced by permission of Peters Edition, London, England, and New York
Presley, Elvis David Redfern Photography, London, England / photo Stephen Morley
Previn, André Pittsburgh Symphony Orchestra, Pittsburgh, PA / photo Ben Spiegel
Price, Leontyne San Francisco Opera, San Francisco, CA / photo Pete Peters
Pride, Charley Richard Wootton, London, England
Psalmody American Antiquarian Society, Worcester, MA
Psalms, metrical *1* Historical Society of Pennsylvania, Philadelphia, PA; *2* Bodleian Library (Arch.G.e.40.), Oxford, England
Publishing and printing of music *1* Tracy W. McGregor Library, University of Virginia, Charlottesville, VA
Pueblo, Eastern Museum of New Mexico (negative no. 10865), Santa Fe, NM
Puerto Rico Arts, Prints, and Photographs Division, New York Public Library at Lincoln Center (Astor, Lenox and Tilden Foundations), New York

Music Example Acknowledgments

We are grateful to music publishers, and others, as listed below, for permission to reproduce copyrighted material. Every effort has been made to trace copyright holders and we apologize to anyone whose name may have been omitted from this list.

Martino, Donald E. C. Schirmer, Inc., Boston, MA

Melodrama *3* © 1909 The Oliver Ditson Company, by permission of the Theodore Presser Co., Bryn Mawr, PA; *4* Boosey & Hawkes Music Publishers Ltd., London, England

Monk, Thelonious *1, 2* © Bocu Music Ltd., London, England, transcriptions by permission of GPI Publications, from R. Blake: "The Monk Piano Style," *Keyboard*, viii/7 (1982)

Paiute American Folklore Society, Washington, DC, from E. Sapir: "Song Recitative in Paiute Mythology," *Journal of American Folklore*, xxiii (1910)

Pomo Robert H. Lowie Museum of Anthropology, University of California, Berkeley, CA